# The
# Encyclopedia
## of the
# Irish in America

# The

# *Encyclopedia*

## of the IRISH in
## AMERICA

MICHAEL GLAZIER,
*General Editor*

UNIVERSITY OF NOTRE DAME PRESS
Notre Dame, Indiana

*Library of Congress Cataloging-in-Publication Data*
The encyclopedia of the Irish in America / Michael Glazier,
editor.
p.    cm.
Includes bibliographical references.
ISBN 0-268-02755-2 (cl.  :  alk. paper)
1. Irish Americans Encyclopedias.   I. Glazier, Michael.
E184.I6E53   1999
973'.049162'003—dc21        99-22389

∞ *The paper used in this publication meets the minimum requirements*
*of the American National Standard for Information Sciences—*
*Permanence of Paper for Printed Library Materials, ANSI Z39.48-1984.*

# CONTENTS

*for*

## JOAN WALSH GLAZIER

For what books had never told me, dear,
and what I never knew
was that, when the great day came, dear,
love would be merely . . . you!

From *In Retrospect* by Christy Brown

# ACKNOWLEDGMENTS

The publisher and editor wish to express their deep gratitude to Lawrence McCaffrey, the scholarly pioneer of Irish studies in America. He supported the *Encyclopedia* from its inception and it benefited from his good counsel and suggestions. A special word of thanks to J. G. E. Hopkins whose long experience as an author and as a former editor at Charles Scribner's Sons of New York made his advice most helpful. Patrick Blessing, author and research scholar, John Deedy, author and journalist, and Charles Fanning, literary expert, were generous with their time and suggestions. Marianna McLoughlin was always most helpful with her most perceptive opinions; and James S. Rogers of the Center for Irish Studies and Rev. Vincent Lapomarda, S.J., of Holy Cross College provided invaluable assistance on many occasions.

The editor is thankful to friends in Ireland especially Padraig Kennelly, founder and publisher of *Kerry's Eye*, Tralee, and to publisher Michael Gill of Gill & Macmillan, Dublin. Special thanks to four New Yorkers: Angela Carter of the Irish Book Shop, Darina Malloy of *Irish America*, John Concannon and Rev. Thomas J. Shelly of Fordham University; and a particular word of gratitude to Rory O'Loughlin whose computer expertise was most helpful.

Finally, much gratitude to James Langford and Jeffrey Gainey, the managing executives of the University of Notre Dame Press, who undertook publication of the *Encyclopedia* without foundation grants or subventions. The editor also expresses appreciation to the staff at the Press but especially to Jeannette Morgenroth and Zan Ceeley, whose professionalism, courtesy and patience aided every aspect of the project. And to Ann Charles, who labored with good cheer and great organization on the photo research for the *Encyclopedia*. Many thanks also to Wendy McMillen and her staff at The Book Page in Acworth, Georgia, for their typesetting skills, countless suggestions, and dedication to quality.

# INTRODUCTION

As the twentieth century was closing and the door to a new century was opening, the exilic feeling of loss and clouded expectation drifted back to memory. I recalled a cold winter afternoon years ago when I stood on the deck of the *Saxonia* and watched Ireland recede into the horizon while the big ship plowed relentlessly on to the shores of America. Over the years I have read and thought much about the centuries of Irish emigrants who made that same Atlantic journey. America was good to them and their descendants and they were good for America. *The Encyclopedia of the Irish in America* attempts to recall their colorful saga.

The *Encyclopedia* is the first work of its kind and hopefully students and everyday readers will explore and enjoy its pages. It benefits from the many excellent studies on Irish America whose insights are reflected in the pages of this work. The entries were written by scholars in America, Ireland, Canada and Britain who were free to express their opinions without any constraint. A one-volume encyclopedia has limited space and an editor has to be selective in choosing the subjects to be included. Winnowing down a list of possible entries was an unwelcome task and the editor takes responsibility for omissions. The work is alphabetically, rather than thematically, arranged to facilitate access to the contents, which are intended to be a springboard for further reading or research.

A background knowledge of Ireland's history is an entrée to a better understanding of the Irish in America. Here are three examples of how the *Encyclopedia* meets that need. First, the 15,000-word entry "Ireland: 1798–1998," together with a cluster of other historical articles, will give the reader insights into the vicissitudes of Ireland's story. Second, the latest research on Irish emigration, from colonial times down to our era, is expertly and lucidly handled in a series of informative essays. Emigration was a focal social and economic factor in Irish life for centuries. But its painful human dimensions are often fogged in a maze of necessary statistics, and only become humanized when, for instance, one considers that most Irish parents between 1850–1950 accepted the reality that some of their children would have to emigrate and often more than half of them did. Third, the Great Famine of the 1840s is Day One of modern Irish history for many Americans—its enormity beclouds most of what preceded it. The entry "The Great Famine" and a few complementary articles analyze and elucidate that bewildering human tragedy which had a transforming impact on the course of Irish and American history.

The *Encyclopedia* takes a new departure by having individual entries on each of the fifty states and major cities. Writers usually treat the Irish in America on a regional basis; but too often they give scant notice to states like West Virginia, Mississippi, New Mexico, Oregon, the Dakotas or New Hampshire. Surprisingly, individual articles on the Irish in most of the states had not been written before now, and the entries illustrate the great diversity of the Irish-American experience. The *Encyclopedia* also gives special attention to neglected topics, including the Scotch-Irish, that large and important body of Protestant immigrants who contributed so much to the making of America. And such entries carry longer bibliographies. Also, entries on special subjects such as education and ethnic relations are grouped together. At a time when Irish studies are in academic vogue, one is tempted to hope that more time will be devoted to overlooked areas of Irish-Americana.

It is a happy coincidence that *The Encyclopedia of the Irish in America* is published when emigration is no longer taken for granted in a culturally vibrant and economically prosperous Ireland. "America's First Irish Visitor" relates that in 1584 Richard Butler from Tipperary was the first Irishman to step on American soil—at least he was the first whose arrival is documented. Over the following centuries millions of Irish came and labored and sometimes prospered in this promised land. Times have changed, and today the small island of Ireland says to her scattered children: "Come back to Erin." The tide of history has turned. *Buíochas le Dia.*

Michael Glazier
*General Editor*

# Descriptive List
# of Entries

# THE
# ENCYCLOPEDIA
## OF THE
# IRISH IN AMERICA

# A

## ACHIEVEMENT OF THE IRISH IN AMERICA

There were in fact two major Irish immigrations to America, the first for the most part completed before the Civil War and disproportionately to the South and the second completed for the most part before the First World War. The descendents of the first immigration are at the present time mostly Protestant and tend to live in the rural and southern regions of the country. The second are mostly Catholic and tend to live in the northern and urban regions of the country. The descendents of the second immigration are the most successful gentile ethnic group in America while the descendents of the first immigration are the least successful. These complexities of Irish immigration make it impossible to estimate the story of Irish immigration from census data and force historians to consider evidence from survey data, the collectors of which are not barred by (a blatantly unjust) law from asking a religious question.

More than 5% of all Americans are Irish Protestant, and a little less than 5% of all Americans are Irish Catholic. Many Americans are astonished that there are more Irish Protestants in the country than there are Irish Catholics. Indeed one scholar—unaware that it is fashionable to be Irish—refused to believe that a Protestant would admit to being Irish (Presidents Nixon, Carter, and Clinton to the contrary notwithstanding). Indeed it is commonly assumed that most Irish are Catholic because in the big cities and the cultural centers of this country one can reasonably assume that someone with an Irish name is Catholic. Rural and southern, Irish Protestants tend to be invisible. Moreover, while they still participate in St. Patrick's Day parades in Savannah, they do not seem inclined to emphasize their ethnic identity, much less to be ethnic activists. Irish Protestants are the invisible ethnic group.

The Protestant Irish come from different streams of immigration. The first stream is the so-called Scotch-Irish, most of whom came to America before the beginning of the 19th century (and who claim more presidents than any other American group) and settled especially in the South. They were lowland Scots who had first settled in Ulster and moved on to America to escape the tax they (as Presbyterians) were forced to pay to the Church of Ireland (Anglican). They described themselves simply as Irish and proudly so. The "Irish" regiments which fought in the Revolutionary War were mostly if not entirely Protestant. They did not use the term "Scotch-Irish" (a pejorative label) until the beginning of the 19th century and then to distinguish themselves from the "mere" Irish who were beginning to migrate to America and whom Americans despised even more than they did the Scotch-Irish.

A second group of Irish immigrants who are (and probably were) Protestants are the descendents of those Irish townsfolk who converted to Protestantism in penal times and migrated to America before 1850 because they saw better chances for financial success in the United States, particularly in the time of the Famine. Many Southern Irish Protestants have names that are clearly Celtic, not Saxon. Either they are from this second group or from yet another group of immigrants, rural Irish Catholics who had only a thin connection to the Church and lost that connection shortly after their immigration to the southern United States before the Famine.

There has been considerable debate about this third immigration. Gerald Shaughnessey argued in the 1920s that as many as two million Irish Catholics may have left Catholicism because there were neither priests nor an organized church waiting for them in the rural South. Later authors questioned this scenario. Now, however, there is agreement among writers on both sides of the Atlantic that a large number of the so-called "bog Irish"—Irish-speaking, illiterate, rural day laborers—left Ireland for America even before the Great Famine. These men and women were on the fringes of the Church before immigration and easily left it in the rural South. However, they continued to be Irish in their customs and culture and exercised considerable influence on antebellum rural culture in the South, so much so that Grady McWhiney in his book *Cracker Culture* could argue that the South was Irish at the time of the Civil War. Indeed he reports that there were counties in rural Mississippi where the Irish language was spoken in the 1820s.

In Ireland the repeated famines took a terrible toll on the rural proletarians, who for the most part either migrated or died (and many of course died in the migration). Descendents of tenant farmers constitute most of the population of modern Ireland as well as the descendents of post-Famine immigration to the cities in the northern United States.

Yet another stream of Irish immigration, this one necessarily small, is that of the Huguenot Irish (especially into Delaware, before the Revolutionary War), who became the first Methodists in the United States.

Irish Protestants in this country therefore seem to be a disparate group composed of peoples with different histories and different motives for leaving Ireland. One simply cannot estimate what proportion of them are descendents of the Scotch-Irish, of the Celtic townsfolk, and of the rural day laborers. One lumps them together in analysis merely because one has no choice.

If one speaks of the success or failure of the Irish in the United States, one must distinguish between Irish Catholics and Irish Protestants. The former have been extremely successful, the latter have not. The difference is correlated with religion but not caused by it. For the most part Irish Protestants settled in the rural South in their search for land and were caught in a mobility trap from which there were few opportunities for escape. Irish Catholics (and those pre-Famine immigrants who remained Catholic) for the most part settled in the urban north where in the last half of the 19th century there were extraordinary opportunities for mobility. One must keep in mind that data in the United States Census about the Irish lump Catholics and Protestants together and thus the statistics are a balance between a very successful group and one much less successful. Many authors, who are not aware of this fact and believe that most of the Irish in the census data are Catholic, have written about the relative failure of Irish Catholics in the United States. They could not be more wrong.

The major Irish Catholic immigration to this country occurred in the latter half of the 19th century. Irish Catholics are disproportionately (46%) third generation, the grandchildren of immigrants; 41% are fourth (or higher order) generation (as opposed to 60% of the total population and 83% of the Irish Protestants). Thus the model Irish Catholic is someone for whom the memory of immigration may be alive in the stories told by a grandparent or a parent who is relating a grandparent's story. However, the actual immigrant experience itself is someone else's memory.

Data sets like the General Social Survey of the National Opinion Research Center of the University of Chicago, which has interviewed Americans for the last quarter century, can recreate birth cohorts and ask questions about educational and social progress. Thus the cohort born in the first decade of this century made its educational and occupational decisions during the 1920s. One can thus recreate the history of the social "climate" of an immigrant group by such cohort analysis.

The Irish Catholic cohort born in the first decade of this century had already higher odds of college attendance, college graduation, white-collar career and professional status than the national average of white Americans. Since then they have surged even higher and have in fact caught up with the Episcopalians. Fifty-three percent of Irish Catholics have attended college and 24% have graduated from college as opposed to 38% and 16%, respectively, for the white national average. Thirty-eight percent have professional careers as compared to 27% of white Americans.

Among the Irish Protestants, who had been in the country much longer, the lines have been relatively flat in both education and occupation among this century's birth cohorts. While the odds of college attendance have increased for average white Americans across cohorts, they have not increased nearly so sharply for Irish Protestants who, from the 1930 cohort on, have fallen beneath the national average in their likelihood of college attendance. On measures of education, income, and occupation, Irish Protestants are now the poorest white ethnic group in the country. Only 31% of fourth-generation Irish Protestants have attended college and only 13% have graduated. Only 20% have professional careers.

Much of the explanation of this difference is geographic. Forty-six percent of Irish Catholics live in New England and the Mid-Atlantic states as opposed to 7% of the Irish Protestants. Eleven percent of the latter live in the twelve largest Standard Metropolitan Statistical Areas while 29% of Irish Catholics live in these urban regions. Fifty-eight percent of Irish Catholics live in the next one hundred largest cities as opposed to 34% of Irish Protestants. On the other hand 14% of Irish Catholics live in the South while more than half of the Irish Protestants are southern.

When Irish Protestants and Irish Catholics who live in the large cities in the North are compared there is no difference on the economic and social measures. Region and urbanity account for the differences, not religious faith.

The children of the Irish Catholic immigrants "made it" in the early decades of this century. Despite the setback of the Great Depression, they have continued to expand their success ever since. Moreover this success has not diminished their affiliation with the Democratic Party, despite the stereotypes to the con-

trary. Finally, the cohorts maturing during the last two decades are also notably more likely to describe themselves as politically "liberal" in comparison both with other Americans and with their own predecessor cohorts. At the same time, their Irish Protestant counterparts lost the rough parity they had with the rest of the country in education and won the unenviable position of being the least successful major white ethnic group in the country.

How can one explain this difference in outcome between two groups who at least to some extent share a common ancestry?

The success of immigrants may depend to a considerable extent on the time of immigration, the nature of the immigrants themselves, the occupations at which they worked when they arrived, and the region of the country into which they moved. One must ask what was the "push" in the native land which caused the immigrants to leave, the "pull" in the host country which attracted them, and what was the social class of those who chose to migrate.

The Irish immigrants in the South during the late 18th and early 19th century to some extent were members of a rural proletariat, landless workers without literacy or extended social structure and perhaps even without a mastery of English. The dangers of ocean travel cut them off from the community they had left behind, a community of which they had been at best marginal members. They became corn and hog farmers in the rural South, and drifted away from the mainstream of American life, especially after the Civil War in which they fought on the losing side.

The immigrants of the years after the Famine were tenant farmers; they were able to read and write and speak English (in some cases as a second language). They settled in the expanding industrial cities of the North and became an important part of the economic and political life of the cities. The Catholic Church in Ireland (rejuvenated after emancipation and the founding of the seminary in Maynooth) was able to provide a clergy and social structure for them. They quickly became members in and then leaders of the urban political machines. With the advent of safer sailing ships and then steamers, they were able to maintain closer connection with the community they left behind, a community of which to some extent they were still a part. From a different social class, they migrated with different skills to a different place and at a different time than the cousins of their ancestors who had migrated to the rural South a half century and more before them.

Not only were the immigrants of the two movements different, they also were drawn by different opportunity structures. The earlier group were landless farmers searching for land of their own. They found it in the rural South and were able to develop their farms in an environment of personal liberty free from exploitation by government and landlord. They were content, one suspects, with their corn and their hogs, and their music, and their homemade whiskey, all enjoyed with greater freedom and greater abundance than was possible in the old country. Small wonder that they were willing to fight for it during the Civil War, although few of them owned slaves. The industrial (and English) North was perceived as a threat to their life style to which they had migrated to protect themselves from English oppression.

The opportunity road down which they walked eventually became a dead end; but it was a road which provided them with the life they wanted. It would not have occurred to them that their opportunity structure would prove a limitation for their descendants. Even if they had thought of such a possibility, there was no alternative for them.

Thus it seems reasonable to believe that the culture we today call Appalachian ("Mountain") is in fact descended from the culture of the agricultural working class of eighteenth-century Ireland (and Wales and the Scotch Highlands too). This culture—described by John Fetterman in his classic study of Appalachian culture *Stinking Creek*—certainly seems similar to the life of the Irish countryside as described by visitors for centuries. One might add that it looks much more "Celtic" than the less-laid-back culture of urban Irish-American Catholics who came in the years after the Famine.

The opportunity road available for this latter group was provided by the nation's need for unskilled or semi-skilled labor in the factories and mines of the industrial North. They came not seeking land but jobs. Perhaps their predecessors in the mountains had an easier time of it at first. Life was probably healthier and more pleasant on farms in Mississippi or Alabama than it was in the coal fields of Pennsylvania and the factories of New England.

Nonetheless the post-Famine immigrants became part of the enormous economic expansion of industrial America and were able to profit from it, turn it to their own purposes, and become enormously successful. On the other hand this expansion and the resultant prosperity passed by the rural South and the earlier immigrants.

There is a nice irony: the first immigration was from peasant field to peasant field, in the latter case your own field, and was—once the Atlantic had been crossed—probably an easier migration; but the descendants of the immigrants ended up in a backwater of the changing nation. The second immigration was from field to factory; but the descendants of this immigration were to ride the mainstream of American expansion to great success.

The Irish Catholics, in other words, lucked out in both time and place of emigration and immigration (though many of the first generation would hardly have thought so). Good fortune was a major cause of their success.

The luck of the Irish! But they're not Irish any more, are they?

That question raises the fascinating issue of the survival of cultural traits after immigration and the equally fascinating question of what it means to be Irish. Consider four characteristics from the General Social Survey whose Irishness not even the most stuffy Dublin (or Cork) academic will deny: gregariousness, gathering in a public house, religious intensity, and activity in religious organizations.

Thirty-eight percent of all Americans socialize with friends at least several times a month, as opposed to 49% of Irish Catholics; 16% of Irish Catholics socialize in a bar several times a week (twice the national average) and 28% socialize in a bar at least several times a month (again twice the national average). Eighty-eight percent of Irish Catholics drink, twenty-one percentage points above the national average (and four percentage points above other Catholics)—a statistically significant difference. Thirty-five per cent of Irish Catholics as opposed to 30% of other Catholics belong to a church-related organization. Fifty-one percent say that they are "strong Catholics" as opposed to 41% of other Catholic ethnics. Thus on four characteristics which might

well distinguish the real Irish from their counterparts in the European Union, Irish-American Catholics are also distinguished from their fellow Americans.

One hears frequently when Irish and Irish-American sociologists gather together that something has been lost in the transition to American success. In the old country, it is argued, our ancestors were poor but happy. In this country they are affluent but not so happy. It is impossible to compare the happiness of those alive today with that of their ancestors. But one can at least compare the happiness of Irish-Americans with that of other Americans.

Thirty-six percent of Irish Catholics say they're "very happy," as opposed to 31% of other Catholics; 37% of the Irish Protestants make the same claim compared with 33% of their fellow Protestants. The Irish, whatever their religion, are more likely to claim happiness than other Americans (and at levels of statistical significance). They are also significantly more likely than their co-religionists to claim satisfaction with job and family and happiness in marriage, and to say that their health is excellent and that life is exciting. Perhaps these similarities in life satisfaction between Irish Catholics and Protestants, despite considerable economic differences, offer some confirmation for Professor McWhiney's suggestion that the "crackers" are Irish Celts. In any case, immigration does not seem to have depressed the good spirits of either group. (Only 5% of Irish Protestants were raised Catholic—the same proportion of Irish Catholics who were raised Protestant.)

Moreover in international studies, the Irish, whether in Northern Ireland or the Republic, are the most likely to claim that they are "very happy." Not only are the proportions not statistically different from their Irish-American counterparts, they are not even numerically different. The Irish, whatever their religion and wherever they live, like to claim that they are happy. Maybe they are.

After at least three generations of immigration and success, Irish cultural traits have not been eliminated from Irish-American Catholics. Nor made them unhappy. Their distant cousins in the South, Protestant now, Americans much longer, and not nearly so affluent, are not unhappy either. There are then still a few Irish around.

Indeed more than a few. There are in fact more than there ought to be. Michael Hout and Joshua Goldstein report that approximately 4.5 million Irish immigrants became forty million Irish-Americans by the 1980 census, though natural increase should have raised the number to only twenty-two million. Intermarriage certainly played a part in this phenomenon, creating a large population of part-Irish, part-something-else Americans. When the census asked about their ethnicty, a very high proportion of part something-else said "Irish." Despite anti-Irish sentiment in the media and the academy, it is fashionable to be Irish.

What are the future prospects for the American Irish, in this case meaning Irish Catholics? Will they become progressively more successful and less Irish? Surely this would be the suggestion of those assimilationist social scientists who are offended by diversity, unless it is a politically correct diversity—and the Irish have never been a group thought to be politically correct.

Yet if after four generations in America and with success beyond their ancestors' wildest dreams—success which they are often unwilling to admit themselves, Irish-Americans are still recognizably Irish, and predictions of their demise as an identifiable American sub-culture seem premature.

*See* Irish in America; Scots Irish; Emigration (5 entries)

S. J. Connolly, *Priests and People in Pre-Famine Ireland* (Dublin, 1982).

Leroy Eld, "The Colonial Scotch Irish," *Erie/Ireland* (1986).

John Fetterman, *Stinking Creek* (New York, 1967).

Andrew Greeley, "The Success and Assimilation of Irish Protestants and Irish Catholics in the United States," *Sociology and Social Research* (1988).

Michael Hout and Joshua Goldstein, "How 4.5 Million Immigrants became 40 Million Irish Americans," *American Sociological Review* (1994).

Gerald Shaughnessy, *Has the Immigrant Kept the Faith* (New York, 1925).

Grady McWhiney, *Crackers* (Shreveport, 1987).

ANDREW GREELEY

## ALABAMA

In an early book on Irish immigration in America (*The Irish in America,* 1868) John Francis Maguire records and analyzes his interviews and conversations with Irish people throughout Canada and the United States. When his inquiries reached the South he discovered that numbers were few, and he concluded that there was a reluctance on the part of the Irish to venture into that territory. "There is a prejudice, and a somewhat ignorant prejudice, against the South; the prevalent idea being that no one but a negro can venture to brave its climate—that open-air labor is death to the white man." He encouraged those from rural areas of Ireland to consider farming in the South, quoting Bishop Lynch of Charleston as saying, "I do not know any part of the country where industry and sobriety would ensure to the immigrant who engages in agriculture an ampler compensation." Maguire's conclusion is that, if an organization were formed to advise and direct the Irishmen, "the South could offer a better field for emigration than any other part of the country."

Maguire's proposal had little effect, at least in Alabama, for the flood of Irish immigrants into the United States in the last half of the nineteenth century reached Alabama only as a minor stream. The U.S. Census reports that by 1900 there were over a million and a half people in the United States whose parents had been born in Ireland, with New York state having over four hundred thousand and Massachusetts over two hundred and fifty thousand. Yet Alabama had fewer than two thousand, and few of these were in rural areas. Most were in counties that contained urban centers: Mobile County, seven hundred and eleven; Jefferson County (Birmingham) four hundred and sixty-six; and Montgomery, one hundred and sixteen. Thus only about seven hundred were distributed among the sixty-three remaining counties. Of those centers which attracted the Irish, Mobile was the southernmost and the oldest (founded in 1702). That it was urban and Catholic no doubt contributed to its attractiveness.

### IRISH BISHOPS OF MOBILE

The first bishop of the Diocese of Mobile (it extended over all of Alabama and the Floridas) was a Frenchman from the Diocese of Lyons, Michael Portier. Appointed to the See as Vicar-Apostolic in 1826 and as bishop in 1829, he served his massive area with dedication, productivity, and a widely celebrated good nature until his death in 1859.

He was succeeded by an Irishman, Bishop John Quinlan, a native of Cloyne in County Cork. Following his death in 1883, he was succeeded briefly by Bishop Dominic Manuci, who because of ill health remained in office for less than a year. Another Irishman, Bishop Jeremiah O'Sullivan, also from County Cork, succeeded him, and supervised the diocese ably from 1885 to 1897. Thus it can be said that the Diocese of Mobile, which is to say all of Alabama, remained under Irish-born bishops for the better part of the last half of the century. The tradition continued well into this century, with two bishops of Irish descent: Bishop Edward Patrick Allen (1897–1926) and Bishop Thomas Toolen (1927–1969). The Catholic Church in Alabama was in Irish hands for over a century.

### IRISH COMMUNITIES OF MOBILE

Mobile's second bishop, John Quinlan, may himself have been one of the reasons why the Irish chose Mobile immediately before and after the Civil War. That Mobile was urban and also a port city may have been other good reasons. Then, too, there was the development of railroads, such as the Gulf, Mobile, and Ohio, with their promise of work. In any event the Irish who settled in and near Mobile seem to have prospered, and it was not only laboring jobs that they filled. Herbert Weaver, in an article on foreigners in the ante-bellum towns of the lower South (*Journal of Southern History,* 13, 1947), reports that the Battle House Hotel in Mobile employed seventy-two Irish in 1860, many of them women working as chambermaids. Men were porters and runners. Weaver says that employees "in larger hotels were overwhelmingly of Irish birth."

The Irish communities in the Mobile area were thriving in the years following the Civil War, to the extent that Bishop Quinlan founded, within five years, three new parishes which served largely Irish parishioners: St. Patrick's (1866), in an area close to the GM&O terminal known as The Orange Grove; St. Bridget's (1868) in a railroad area known as Whistler, north of the city; and St. Francis Xavier, roughly between the two, in Toulminville. The latter two are still in existence, while St. Patrick's closed in 1971, after the movement of most of the Irish to western Mobile.

### SPRING HILL COLLEGE

Spring Hill College was founded in what is now western Mobile by Bishop Portier in 1830. Devoted to the education of young men, it operated on several levels. Today's terminology would label them middle school, high school, college, graduate studies and a seminary. Finding himself unable to staff the college with its many levels, Bishop Portier invited the Jesuits of the Lyons Province of France to take over. The first Jesuit President, Francis Gautrelet, S.J., arrived with a small group of Jesuits in 1847, and the institution has operated under Jesuit supervision ever since.

Thus in its origins Spring Hill College was, like the diocese, French. And, like the diocese when it relinquished French leadership, it turned to the Irish.

John A. Downey, S.J., born in London of Irish parents, became the first Irish president in 1880, and was the first of five successive Irish presidents, the four successors all born in Ireland: Fathers David McKinery, S.J. (1883–1887); James Lonergan, S.J. (1887–1896); Michael S. Moynihan, S.J. (1896–1899); and William J. Tyrrell, S.J. (1899–1907). The names of a half-dozen of the twentieth-century presidents suggest Irish parentage, and

Richard Dalton
Williams

the current president, Gregory F. Lucey, S.J., boasts jovially of his Irish bloodlines.

## Two Poets and a Chess Master

Three Irishmen, one a priest and the other two laymen, all of whom are associated with Spring Hill College and Mobile, achieved a considerable degree of fame.

The first, Richard Dalton Williams, was born in Dublin in 1822. He attended medical school as a young man and eventually completed his degree, but not without delay. Under the pen name of "Shamrock" he was publishing poems which the British thought incendiary. He was charged with treason and felony and imprisoned. The jury returned a "Not Guilty" verdict, and Williams went to Edinburgh to complete his medical studies, but after practicing medicine in Dublin for a short time he decided he would do well to leave the country.

He came to Mobile and Spring Hill under the sponsorship of a Jesuit, George Blackney, S.J. He continued to write poetry while he taught in the college for five years. His decision to resume medical practice eventually took him to Thibodaux, Louisiana. There he died from a lung disease at the age of forty. Some Federal soldiers, Irishmen from New Hampshire, noticed his name on a simple grave marker and recognized it as the name of their revolutionary poet. They erected a marble monument as a "testimonial of their esteem for his unsullied patriotism and his exalted devotion to the cause of Irish freedom."

The second man of fame was not of Irish birth but of partial Irish descent. His name was Paul Morphy (a variant of Murphy). He attended Spring Hill from 1850 to 1855 (and thus may well have studied under Dalton Williams) and earned both a bachelor's and a master's degree. Shortly after graduation he gained an international reputation as a chess master. Celebrated and honored throughout Europe and this country, he is still considered in the first rank of chess masters. He refused to take money for playing and in that respect refused to become a professional, but he was a true world celebrity. (See *The World of Hibernia,* Spring, 1997, for a recent, brief account.)

The third man of Irish descent who gained considerable fame was Father Abram Ryan. He was a parish priest in Mobile for many years, and he wrote and published, to considerable acclaim, Civil War poems, celebrating, of course, the Confederate cause. He became known as "The Poet-Priest of the South" and as "The Poet of the Confederacy." His best known poems are "The Conquered Banner" and "The Sword of Robert Lee." (Again, see *The World of Hibernia,* Winter, 1997.)

## North Alabama

If south Alabama, being largely Catholic, proved hospitable to the Irish, the northern parts of the state were not always so. True, there was a small Irish community in Moulton, the county seat of Lawrence County in northwestern Alabama, which was flourishing sufficiently as early as 1829 to invite Bishop Portier to establish his proposed college in Moulton, but he chose the Spring Hill area near Mobile instead.

The first major Irish community in north Alabama was considerably later in its establishment. The industrial city of Birmingham was officially established in 1871, located in an area of coal and iron mines. It quickly developed as a center of industry and attracted Irish people, many of whom were interested in work in the mines and mills. Early Irish settlers found the area congenial. In fact they established themselves fully enough to contribute significantly to the political and economic development of the young city.

A well-researched master's thesis by Kay J. Blalock (University of Alabama at Birmingham, 1989) supplies information about the Irish in the north of Alabama. It is entitled "The Irish Catholic Experience in Birmingham, Alabama, 1871–1921." Blalock notes that "Catholicism and Irish nationalism did not hinder Birmingham's Irish in their desire to become active participants in the growth and development of the new city in their adopted homeland." As one of her examples she cites Dublin-born Frank P. O'Brien, whose list of accomplishments includes his being mayor, alderman, and representative to the state legislature. His major business was that of a building contractor, and he played a large part in the construction of some of the rolling mills. He made cultural contributions as well, including O'Brien's Opera House. He was also instrumental in bringing a Catholic mission to the city and later in establishing the first parish, St. Paul's. His daughter, Bossie O'Brien Hudley was also politically active, promoting, after her father's death, the cause of women's suffrage.

There were other Irish settlers whose careers and accomplishments paralleled those of O'Brien, Patrick Byrne and Hugh McGeever among them.

But the peaceful acceptance that the first Irish settlers of Birmingham enjoyed was not to last into the new century. Unlike Catholic Mobile, Birmingham and the northern parts of the state were largely Protestant. In the early decades of the new century, a kind of xenophobia spread over the South, with Catholicism one of its major fears. Irish Catholics became the targets of many an attack in newspapers and from pulpits. Blalock provides an alarming example written in 1916 by Rev. R.L. Durant. One point of dissent had to do with a movement to show movies on Sunday afternoons. Catholics apparently offered no objections. Some even defended the idea. Durant wrote that Catholics "have destroyed the Christian Sabbath, by law if possible, and if not by law, then by every kind of desecration conceivable to the mind of the devil and his Dago pontiff."

The Irish pastor of St. Paul's, James E. Coyle, V.F., who had been made Dean of North Alabama in 1913, became engaged in this conflict, but it was not this matter which brought national fame to his name in 1921.

On August 11 of that year he was sitting on the porch of the rectory reading his breviary, when Edwin R. Stephenson, an itinerant Methodist minister, not in good standing with his own church, stepped onto the porch and fired three shots, one of which killed Father Coyle. Stephenson was arrested and brought to trial. The case became a major news item in newspapers across the country, including the *New York Times.* The theme of many of the reports was the intolerance of Birmingham. In addition to religious intolerance, the matter of race also intruded itself. Father Coyle had officiated at the marriage of Stephenson's daughter, a recent convert to Catholicism, to a man named Pedro Gussman, who insisted that he was of Spanish descent but whom Stephenson insisted was black.

It was this that he blurted out before he shot Father Coyle. Some of the national news attention focused on the anti-Catholicism, branding Birmingham a hotbed of religious intolerance. Others emphasized the racial dimension, and Birmingham was labeled with a different, but hardly more flattering, prejudice. National disapproval of the city was by no means improved when the jury returned a "Not Guilty" verdict, and Stephenson was freed. Father Coyle was widely seen as a victim of religious prejudice, so that Rose Gibbons Lovett, in her 1980 book, *The Catholic Church in the Deep South,* calls him "a martyr for his faith."

Father Coyle's tragic experience, however, did not lessen the flow of Irish priests to Alabama. The state was long considered by the Church to be mission territory. (It met the major criterion: less than five percent of the population were Catholic.) Bishop Toolen, during the 1930s and continuing through the 1950s, used this as the basis for active recruitment of Irish clergy to his diocese. Toward the end of his term of office more than fifty percent of the priests in Alabama were Irishborn. Raymond Boland, presently bishop of Birmingham, is Irish-born and a product of All Hallows Seminary, County Dublin.

## The Current Situation

If the 1900 Census showed that fewer than two thousand people in the state reported Irish parentage, the 1990 Census shows a remarkable increase of those who claim Irish ancestry: over three hundred and fifty thousand. Jefferson County (that is to say, Birmingham) has the highest concentration, over eighty-five thousand, while Mobile County shows almost fifty-four thousand, and Montgomery over twenty-two thousand. A truly remarkable increase, especially in Birmingham. Labeled a city of extreme prejudices in the early part of the century, a reputation that continued in part well into the 1960s, the religious prejudice, at least, seems to have been laid to rest.

A 1997 candidate for the office of President of Ireland, singer Rosemary Scallon ("Dana") was a resident of Birmingham. In a television interview prior to the elections, she told of her surprise on first seeing the fine city. She had had, she said, preconceptions of Alabama as dirt roads and cotton fields. She took delight in the reality of a beautiful modern metropolis. Apparently the misconceptions that John Francis Maguire wrote of in 1860 still have some currency. However, the realities of modern Alabama have appealed to over three hundred and fifty

thousand of those who think of themselves as loyal sons and daughters of St. Patrick.

*See* Birmingham, Alabama

Kay J. Blalock, *The Irish Catholic Experience in Birmingham, Alabama,* unpublished master's thesis, 1989, The University of Alabama, Birmingham.

Oscar H. Lipscomb, *The Administration of John Quinlan, Second Bishop of Mobile,* 1859–1883, unpublished master's thesis, 1959, The Catholic University of America, Washington, D.C.

John Francis Maguire, *The Irish in America* (New York, 1868).

Herbert Weaver, "Foreigners in the Ante-Bellum Towns of the Lower South," *The Journal of Southern History,* XIII, 62–73, 1947.

*The World of Hibernia,* The Magazine for the Irish Diaspora, Spring, 1997, and Winter, 1997.

CHARLES J. BOYLE

# ALASKA

In search of a better way of life, the Irish have wandered across the length and breadth of America. Most of those who emigrated from Ireland since the 1840s stayed in industrial cities east of the Mississippi River. But the Irish, along with many other nationalities, joined the Westward Movement, and many came to Alaska. Irish immigrants have lived in America's "Last Frontier" since the earliest days of American rule. Alaska has been enriched by the contributions of many immigrant groups—Norwegian, Swedish, Canadian, and German among them—but the Irish are one of the state's most vibrant, admired, and well-known ethnic groups.

## The Lure of Alaska

The first group of Europeans to visit Alaska was headed by Vitus Bering, a Danish navigator in the employ of Russian czar Peter the Great. Bering's voyage was largely unsuccessful—it never reached the Alaska mainland—but in the years that followed, Russian trading vessels returned in search of sea otters. In 1783, Russian officials established Alaska's first permanent settlement, on Kodiak Island. Shortly after 1800, the seat of Russian America's government moved to Sitka.

Although the Russians ruled Alaska for more than 125 years, relatively few Europeans ever lived there. Most, predictably, were ethnic Russians, but Finns, Swedes, and Ukrainians were also scattered across the colony. During this period, seamen representing competing powers—France, Britain, and Spain—sailed up and down Russian America's coastline. Few if any Irishborn individuals, however, either lived in or visited present-day Alaska during the Russian period.

In March 1867, the United States government purchased Russian America for $7.2 million, and in October of that year it assumed possession of the far-flung province. Most of the Russians, both military and civilian, departed quickly; taking their place was a ragamuffin outfit, based almost entirely in Sitka, which consisted of U.S. Army personnel and commercial entrepreneurs. Three years later, an informal census among Sitka's civilian population showed an Irish presence: of a total population of 391, ten natives of Ireland were represented. Only Russia and the various German states claimed a larger share of the foreign-born population.

Alaska's non-Native population remained tiny until 1880, when gold was discovered along Gold Creek and the Juneau camp sprang to life. The following year additional gold was found at nearby Douglas, and by 1890, thousands of non-Native men and women, many of them prospectors, lived in Alaska, primarily along the coast. The 1890 U.S. census tallied 4,298 "white" males aged 10 or more; among that group were found many Irish, who were outnumbered only by Swedes, Norwegians, Germans, and English, in that order.

## THE KLONDIKE GOLD RUSH

During the early to mid-1890s, Alaska's population grew slowly, fueled by gold discoveries in scattered areas and also by growth in the fishing industry. But by far the most dramatic growth took place beginning in mid-1897, when news reached the outside world of the huge Klondike gold strike which had occurred in the remote, isolated Yukon River valley, in northwestern Canada, almost a year earlier. Almost overnight, "gold fever" swept the U.S., Canada, and much of the rest of the world, and by the summer of 1898, an estimated 100,000 people had pulled up stakes and headed north toward the gold fields. Of this number, perhaps 60 to 70 percent of these were U.S. residents, while another 20 to 25 percent hailed from Canada.

The Irish, along with many other groups, were swept up in the excitement; perhaps 1 to 2 percent of the "stampeders" headed straight from Ireland toward the gold fields, along with a far larger number of Irish-born Americans and Canadians. Included in the frenzy were Finley Peter Dunne's famous fictional Irishmen, Mr. Dooley and Mr. Hennessy. Mr. Hennessy, feeling hopeful, said "Well, sir, that Alaska's th' gr-reat place . . . [T]hey tell me 'tis fairly smothered in goold. A man stubs his toe on th' ground, an lifts th' top off iv a goold mine. Ye go to bed at night, an' wake up with goold fillin' in ye'er teeth."

Mr. Dooley, however, was more cautious. Back in the Old Country, he had been told that the streets of America were paved with gold. But when he arrived in New York, he found nothing but mud under the pavement, and as he headed west, the only mine he ever fell into was a sewer hole in Pittsburgh. "Me experyence with goold minin'," Mr. Dooley said, "is it's always in th' nex' county. If I was to go to Alaska, they'd tell me iv th' finds in Seeberya."

Although neither Dooley nor Hennessy succumbed to "gold fever," hundreds of Irishmen did. It is likely that a majority of them, like the majority of all the other "stampeders," never made it to Dawson; they were beaten back by the expense, the tremendous physical efforts required, or the miserable weather encountered along the way. Even so, an estimated 30,000 to 40,000 completed the trek.

The Irish comprised a small but identifiable group in the Yukon gold fields; as the *Klondike Nugget* reported, "Here in Dawson the Irish are as numerous, or more so, than any other race," even though "the only resemblance between Ireland and the Yukon is that there are no snakes or reptiles in either. . . ." Michael MacGowan, a recent immigrant from Donegal, wrote that the hundreds of Irishmen in the area hailed "from every corner of the country from Cork to Donegal . . . at nighttime, we'd go visiting each other just as if we were at home [and] in the twinkling of an eye, the talk would turn to home and you'd soon think that you were in some remote part of Ireland." MacGowan recalled that one March 17, he headed outside to get a bucket of snow to melt for water when he imagined he heard the tune of a bagpiper in the distance. The tune was "St. Patrick's Day," and as he remembered it, "in the time it would take you to clap your hands, I fancied I was back again among my own people in Cloghaneely."

## AFTER THE GOLD RUSH

Although some remained in the Dawson area, most stayed only a short time because the gold fields, rich as they were, were limited in their geographical scope. Thus when gold discoveries were made near Eagle in 1898 and near Nome in 1899, many headed downriver and moved across the border to Alaska. The 1900 census, taken at the height of the Nome gold stampede, showed that 8,784 of Alaska's 63,592 people were classified as "foreign-born whites." Immigrants born in Ireland comprised 1.1% of all Alaskans that year; they were outnumbered only by those who were native to Canada, Sweden, Norway, and Germany.

For the next four decades, Alaska's total population remained fairly static. It rose only about one percent from 1900 to 1910, fell more than ten percent during the 'teens, rose by a few percentage points during the 1920s, and enjoyed a more robust growth rate during the 1930s. Between 1900 and 1939, the total population of Alaska rose by fewer than 9,000 people—a 14.0% gain. But because many of those who had rushed north during the Klondike and later gold rushes were foreign-born whites who later left Alaska, the number of foreign-born whites steadily dwindled after 1910. Census figures note that the population of foreign-born whites in Alaska more than doubled (to almost 18,000) from 1900 to 1910. In 1910, foreign-born whites comprised more than a quarter (27.9%) of all Alaskans. But by 1920 there were only about 11,500 Alaskans in this category, and by 1939 the number of foreign-born whites—8,786—was almost identical to the 1900 total in that category.

During the first four decades, the number of Irish-born Alaskans roughly followed the pattern of other foreign-born white ethnic groups. Between 1900 and 1910, the number of Irish rose from 1.1% to 1.8% of Alaska's population. But in later decades, the proportion of Irish-born people in the population steadily fell—back down to 1.1% in 1920, to 0.5% in 1929, and to 0.3% in 1939.

During the decades which have followed World War II, the number of foreign-born white Alaskans has stabilized; in 1980, for instance, the census counted 9,741 foreign-born whites, only 10.8% more than in 1939. But Alaska's total population exploded during that period, so as a result, the proportion of foreign-born whites in Alaska's population dropped from 12.1% to 2.4% of the population. The number of Irish-born Alaskans has followed suit; although 0.3% of all Alaskans were born in Ireland when the 1939 census was taken, by 1980 fewer than one of every one thousand Alaskans was Irish born. Throughout this period, Irish immigrants were never the dominant immigrant group—Norwegians consistently held that niche—but the Irish usually ranked in the top five among the foreign-born white ethnicities.

## THE IRISH IN ALASKA'S MINES

Between 1880 and 1920, mining was the most important industry in Alaska. The Juneau-Douglas area boomed in the early 1880s; the Nome area witnessed a gold rush beginning in 1899;

and thousands of hopeful miners descended on the Fairbanks area shortly after 1900. In these and scores of other camps, the early boom town excitement was quickly superseded by corporate interests which bought large blocks of claims. Soon afterward, large-scale methods of mining—underground, hydraulic, and dredge mining—replaced the crude methods used during the boom days. The Irish, who had been carrying on a centuries-old mining tradition before they ever emigrated to North America, were commonly seen in mineral extraction areas, both in the boom-town camps and as part of large, corporate mining operations.

No one knows how many of the Juneau-area miners were Irish, but their numbers were apparently considerable. In 1881, miners unearthed a major gold lode on nearby Douglas Island. As historians David and Brenda Stone have noted in *Hard Rock Gold*, a history of Juneau-area mines, Irish and German miners responded to the news by rushing to the site and making additional discoveries. These nationalities doubtless remained common in the Juneau and Douglas areas for the remainder of the 19th century if not longer.

By 1900, mining was a more widespread activity in Alaska, and wherever mining strikes took place, the Irish were sure to be there. A 1983 study by James Ducker, based on the admittedly sketchy data provided in the 1900 U.S. Census, notes that of 2,889 people in nine Alaskan towns who listed their occupations as "miners," 4.9 percent of them were born in Ireland. (Other occupations in those towns also showed a sprinkling of Irishmen, although not in as high a proportion.) In most of the nine towns, Canadians were the primary immigrant group, but in Ruby, located along the Yukon River in Alaska's interior, the Irish were the predominant foreign group.

Mining towns during this era were national "melting pots," where people born in the U.S. and Canada mingled with those from Ireland, England, Germany, Norway, Sweden, Italy, Yugoslavia and Poland. Available records from Alaska's largest mines show that Irish workers were well represented there, too. At the Alaska-Gastineau mine in Thane, just south of Juneau, company personnel records dating from 1913 show that 70.2 percent of the workers were foreign born; Austrians constituted the largest single foreign nationality, although sizable numbers came from Ireland as well. Two years later, sizable numbers of Irish miners remained at the mine.

RAILROAD WORKERS

Alaska is not now well served by railroads, nor has it ever been. Just three trunk line railroads, along with numerous shorter lines that connect a mine with a nearby port, have been built. The trunk line railroads include the White Pass and Yukon Route, built from Skagway, Alaska, to Whitehorse, Yukon Territory, between 1898 and 1900; the Copper River and Northwestern, built from Cordova to the Kennecott Copper Mine between 1907 and 1911; and the Alaska Railroad, constructed from Seward to Fairbanks between 1915 and 1923. The Alaska Railroad was financed and built by the U.S. government; portions of its trackage, however, had been previously built by two private entities: the Tanana Valley Railroad in the Fairbanks area and the Alaska Central Railroad on the Kenai Peninsula near Seward.

To a large extent, each of Alaska's railroads was built by foreign laborers, and the Irish were almost certainly the most well-represented foreign group. Statistics detailing the ethnic composition of the railroad labor force are few and far between, but the 1900 U.S. Census, which was tallied when the White Pass and Yukon Route were still under construction, indicated that of Alaska's 192 known railroaders, 22.4 percent of them were born in Ireland. They were more than twice as numerous as any other ethnic group in that occupational classification. Essentially all of Alaska's railroad workers in 1900 lived in or near Skagway. Skagway, however, had such a large, diverse population that the Irish comprised just 4.7 percent of Skagway's 3,117 residents. Ten years later, Skagway had lost more than two-thirds of its population, and the number of Irish-born residents had dropped to such an extent that they comprised just 3.9 percent of the town's population.

Irish celebrations in early Alaska were relatively rare, but when they became public events, they were bound to have unintended consequences. The Irish in Skagway, for example, held a parade, banquet and ball for St. Patrick's Day in 1899. A celebration was repeated in 1900. Skagway's U.S. Census taker, A. A. Richards, worked his regular shift on March 17, 1900; perhaps unaware of the day's significance, he was forced to redo his work when he belatedly discovered that scores of residents—of all nationalities—claimed to be Irish.

FAMOUS IRISH ALASKANS

Because of the preponderance of Irishmen in Alaska's mining industry, it is perhaps unsurprising that some of the better-known Irish Alaskans worked as miners or in mining camps.

Two of Alaska's most famous early prospectors were Arthur Harper and Fred Hart. These two men, both from County Antrim, began prospecting in the Yukon River basin back in 1873, a quarter century before the Klondike gold rush. Harper and Hart, along with Leroy "Jack" McQuesten and Alfred H. Mayo, were the first to penetrate the vast Alaskan interior in their search for gold. Although both men made herculean efforts to find gold, neither ever became wealthy, and both died during the heyday of the Klondike rush.

A well-known Irish woman connected with the Klondike rush was Mollie Walsh. When she heard about the rich gold fields, she left Butte, Montana and soon afterwards set up a tent restaurant on the White Pass Trail outside of Skagway. She became the object of affection for many of the trail's commercial packing fraternity. She eventually married packer Mike Bartlett and moved with him to Dawson. But "Packer Jack" Newman, one of her spurned suitors, never forgot her; and when, in 1902, Mollie was killed by her husband, he vowed to perpetuate her memory. Finally, in 1930, Newman had a monument erected to honor Mollie, the "Angel of the White Pass." The statue was installed in a Skagway park and has been a local point of interest ever since.

Irish-born Alaskans have become distinguished in a wide variety of fields. One of the most colorful was Captain James Carroll, perhaps the best-known steamboat pilot to sail Alaska's "Inside Passage" route during the 1880s and 1890s. Carroll, a pilot for the Pacific Coast Steamship Company, became an icon to early "excursionists" [cruise ship passengers], earning a reputation for being both rugged and courtly.

Alaska has not yet had an Irish-born governor or congressman, but state house representatives born in Ireland include Thomas Gaffney, a Nome resident (who served from 1913–15 and 1927–29), Charles J. Murray from Valdez (1935–37), and Michael Walsh from Nome (1945–47). (A fourth man, James J.

Mike Heney

*See* Harper, Arthur; Heney, Michael;
Alaska-Yukon Gold Rush

Evangeline Atwood and Robert DeArmond, comps., *Who's Who in Alaskan Politics; A Biographical Dictionary of Alaskan Political Personalities, 1884–1974* (Anchorage, Alaska, 1985).

Terrence M. Cole, "The Hard Road to Klondike: Irish Pioneers in the Alaska-Yukon Gold Rush," in Timothy J. Sarbaugh and James P. Walsh, eds., *The Irish in the West* (Manhattan, Kansas, 1993).

Robert N. DeArmond, *The Founding of Juneau* (Juneau, 1967).

Merrill Denison, *Klondike Mike, An Alaskan Odyssey* (New York, 1943).

James H. Ducker, "Carmack's Alaskans; A Census Study of Alaskans in 1900," *Alaska Historical Commission Studies in History*, No. 97 (Anchorage, 1983).

Frank Norris, "North to Alaska: An Overview of Immigrants to Alaska, 1867–1945," *Alaska Historical Commission Studies in History*, No. 121 (Anchorage, 1985).

David and Brenda Stone, *Hard Rock Gold: The Story of the Great Mines That Were the Heartbeat of Juneau* (Juneau, 1980).

Elizabeth A. Tower, *Big Mike Heney, Irish Prince of the Iron Rails* (Anchorage, Alaska, 1988).

FRANK NORRIS

## ALASKA-YUKON GOLD RUSH

The Right Honorable Augustine Birrell, the Chief Secretary of Ireland from 1907–1916, never had a stranger request than the letter he received in June 1908 postmarked Fairbanks, Alaska. Martin Gately, an Irish gold miner living in Fairbanks, had an unusual proposition for the crown from himself and several other miners. Distressed about Ireland's lack of progress in achieving Home Rule, they wanted to know "if England would feel disposed to sell Ireland, and at what price?"

Gately's modest proposal was that his consortium of Alaskan miners buy Ireland for a "moderate" sum, because the "present expensive method of holding her down" was so costly to the United Kingdom. Moreover he reasoned that since England ruled "Ireland without her consent, you may dispose of her as you desire, without consulting her wishes."

From his distant vantage point, Martin Gately may not have grasped all of the realities of international politics, or perhaps he had an extreme sense of ironic humor. Yet his proposal to buy Ireland in order to set it free demonstrated that English misrule and Irish misery were known in far-off Alaska, as well as New York and Boston.

In search of a better way of life, Irish people have wandered everywhere on earth, and have settled in some of the most isolated places on the globe, such as the Alaska-Yukon frontier in the late 19th and early 20th centuries. Though the vast majority of the approximately 4.5 million Irish men and women who emigrated overseas in the 70 years from 1851 to 1921 settled in the United States east of the Mississippi, Irish names could be found throughout the American frontier. As David Emmons' study of Butte demonstrates, the copper mining capital of Montana was "one of the most overwhelmingly Irish cities in the Unites States" (*The Butte Irish,* p. 13).

When news of the discovery of gold on the Klondike reached the outside world in 1897, American Alaska and the Canadian Yukon became the "land at the end of the rainbow," and a sizable minority of Irish and Irish-Americans were among the thousands who rushed north.

Mullaley from Fairbanks, was elected to the state house in 1912 but refused to serve due to ill health.) Each of these leaders, plus others who served as attorneys, labor negotiators, marshals or in other prominent positions, immigrated to the U.S. as children or young adults and spent most or all of their adult lives in Alaska.

Three of the best-known Irish Alaskans are of Irish stock but were born in North America. Richard Harris and his partner Joe Juneau are widely acclaimed as the founders of Juneau, Alaska. At least one source has noted that Harris was born in County Down, but he was actually born in Cleveland, Ohio.

One gold rush personality, Michael "Klondike Mike" Mahoney, was the subject of a full-length biography and became known throughout the north country for reputedly hauling a piano over Chilkoot Pass. Mahoney is also widely thought to have been born in Ireland; however, he was a second-generation Irishman and was born in Buckingham, Quebec.

Finally, perhaps the most famous person in the history of Alaska railroading was Mike Heney. An engineer and construction supervisor, he was the driving force behind the building of the 110-mile White Pass and Yukon Route railway, which was laid from Skagway, Alaska, to Whitehorse, Yukon Territory, from May 1898 to July 1900. Not one to rest on his laurels, he was called back to service in 1907 to construct a railroad from the port of Cordova, Alaska, 200 miles inland to the copper-mill town of Kennecott, high in the Wrangell Mountains. Both lines were built through rugged, tortuous country, and both routes required innovative engineering solutions. Heney, however, was an equal to both tasks; he was praised by the owners for his obvious talents, and admired by his workers. Because of his background, he was known far and wide as "the Irish Prince." Heney, however, was actually a second-generation Irishman, born and raised in the town of Pembroke, Ontario.

During the 1898 gold rush the two most famous fictional Irishmen in the United States, Finley Peter Dunne's Chicago barroom characters, Mr. Dooley and Mr. Hennessy, talked of the riches that were attracting thousands of people to the north that year. "Well sir," said Mr. Hennessy, "that Alaska's th' gr-reat place. . . . (T)hey tell me 'tis fairly smothered in goold. A man stubs his toe on th' ground, an lifts th' top off iv a goold mine. Ye go to bed at night, an' wake up with goold fillin' in ye'er teeth."

Mr. Dooley was somewhat more cautious. He claimed the stories of the Klondike reminded him of the tales he used to hear in the old country about the streets of America being paved with gold. When he got to New York he found nothing but mud under the pavement, and on his travels west the only mine he ever fell into was a sewer hole in Pittsburgh. "Me experyence with goold minin'," Mr. Dooley said, "is it's always in th' nex' county. If I was to go to Alaska, they'd tell me iv th' finds in Seeberya" (*Mr. Dooley in Peace and in War*, 100–104).

Precise statistics about the number of Irish goldstampeders are impossible to determine, because Irish were sometimes counted as British, and Irish-Americans were of course not enumerated separately. However, as a Yukon newspaper columnist noted in 1900, "Here in Dawson the Irish are as numerous, or more so, than any other race." In the 1900 Alaska census one out of every 20 foreign-born immigrants had been born in Ireland, and overall the Irish-born comprised about 1.1 percent of the total population. By the 1910 U.S. census residents born in Ireland constituted nearly 2 percent of the population; in comparison Scandinavians were the largest foreign-born group in Alaska, with Norwegians and Swedes amounting to 8.2 percent of the total population.

Despite the relatively small numbers of Irish-born residents compared to the Scandinavians, they played an important role. In fact it was an Irishman who started it all. The first prospector to systematically hunt for gold in Alaska was a refugee from the Famine named Arthur Francis Sean Harper. Born in County Antrim near Belfast in 1835, Arthur Harper emigrated to New York in 1847 at age 12. Harper lived with an uncle in Brooklyn, who found him a job as a clean-up boy in a factory. According to family tradition he did not take well to orders from either the factory boss or his uncle. "He and his uncle had a stubborn trait in their temperaments," Harper's grandson wrote many years later, "which led, naturally, to a deadlock in all of their arguments."

Harper left his uncle's house while still a teenager to become a muleskinner, and worked his way west towards the gold mines of California. Saving money was hard for a footloose adventurer, whose code of life—according to his son—was to "'live high' when money was plentiful, and 'sleep in the streets' when it was not." Harper eventually decided to try a region where no prospector had ever gone before. Studying Arrowsmith's map of British North America, Harper thought the large blank space on the map near the top of the world was potentially rich in gold deposits. From his study of the map he became convinced that the golden belt which prospectors believed encircled the globe, a belt which ran up the continent along the backbone of the Rocky mountains through Colorado, Idaho, Montana, and British Columbia, would logically continue northwest into the Yukon basin. In September 1872 Harper and four other men, including Frederick Hart, a fellow native of County Antrim, started northwards into the unknown terrain of the Northern Rockies, en route to the Mackenzie and the Yukon Valleys.

The United States had purchased Alaska from the Czar of Russia only half-a-dozen years earlier, and Harper was one of the first U.S. traders in America's vast new empire. At the time it was estimated that throughout all of Interior Alaska—an area of several hundred thousand square miles—about the size of France—there were only 32 white men. For 24 years Harper concentrated on the search for gold, and used his profits from fur trading with the Indians to fund his remarkable prospecting trips in the north country. Only sketchy details survive about his specific expeditions, but on rivers such as the Fortymile, the Sixtymile, the Stewart, and the Tanana, gold was eventually found in paying quantities, and in every case Harper had been there first. Though he never found a lucrative mine himself, his backbreaking expeditions across hundreds of miles demonstrated single-handedly the extent of gold-bearing gravel in the Yukon basin. He blazed the trails which were followed by all the prospectors who came after him.

Alfred H. Brooks of the U.S. Geological Survey credited Harper as the "discoverer of gold in the Yukon" and the "pioneer prospector whose efforts directly led to the discovery of Fortymile, the Klondike, and Fairbanks. These in turn led to the finding of gold at many other Yukon camps, and also at Nome." According to Brooks, Harper was not only "the first to appreciate the latent mineral wealth of the Yukon," but he was "also the first to make this wealth known through his letters to his friends in the Cassiar and other placer camps of British Columbia." Furthermore in 1897 Harper took part in the founding of Dawson City, the community which became the center of the Klondike gold fields (*Blazing Alaska Trails*, 317–318).

Yet Arthur Harper never lived to profit from the Klondike gold rush of 1898. Sick with tuberculosis Harper went down to San Francisco in September 1897, and two months later he died at age 62 in Yuma, Arizona, where he had gone to take the cure in the dry desert air. Harper's obituary noted that his death was due to the rigors of the northern climate and "the dread disease, consumption, which had been pursuing him for years and had been his incessant though unwelcome companion in the hunt for gold." William Ogilvie, the Commissioner of the Yukon Territory, who interviewed Harper on several occasions and recorded a few of the details of his life, wrote that he could not help feeling that fate was unkind to the old gentleman he admired so much (*Early Days on the Yukon Trail*, p. 13).

Within less than a year of the death of Arthur Harper, Dawson City had become a cosmopolitan city with a temporary population of perhaps as many as 25,000 people. One of those gold seekers swept up in the Klondike excitement was 33-year-old Michael MacGowan. MacGowan not only participated in the gold rush, but he left an enduring legacy in Alaskan and Irish literature with a remarkable memoir of his adventures, originally published in Irish as *Rotha Mor an tSaoil,* and translated into English as *The Hard Road to Klondike.*

Micky MacGowan was born in a small thatched cottage in the northwest of Ireland on November 22, 1865. One of 12 children, he was raised in the parish of Cloghaneely, where his family farmed "little bits of soil between the rocks" on a poverty-stricken piece of land on the coast of Donegal. MacGowan and two friends—including Jimmy Anthony, his next-door neighbor—decided in 1885 to try their luck in the United States. Following a year in the mills at Bethlehem, Pennsylvania, MacGowan moved west to Montana, where he mined for silver and gold until he first heard of the discoveries in the Klondike in 1897.

MacGowan and a party of several other Irishmen traveled to the Klondike together in 1898. Eventually he acquired a claim on All Gold Creek about twenty-five miles out of town, where MacGowan said he found a "crowd of men from Donegal" working nearby. Digging in the frozen ground was backbreaking work. "The ground was frozen so hard that you couldn't lift a spadeful," he said, "even if you were chipping away with a pick-axe the live-long day." The ground had to be thawed a foot at a time with bonfires all the way to bedrock. Though the ground was not spectacularly rich, he made good money. Still the work was hard and slow. "If anyone, at the beginning of my life," Mac-Gowan said, "had told me that you get tired shoveling gold, I wouldn't have believed it but . . . many is the time I was fed up with it."

What helped make the work more tolerable to MacGowan was that there were so many Irishmen in the gold fields that it sometimes felt like home. MacGowan said there were hundreds of Irishmen in the Yukon who came "from every corner of the country from Cork and Donegal. The little cabins we lived in were all more or less together and at nighttime, we'd go visiting each other just as if we were at home. Plenty of our own country-men were among them as well as men from further south and from Connaught but our men could hold their own no matter what company they found themselves in." In the long winter nights the Irish would gather in a cabin and, "in the twinkling of an eye, the talk would turn to home and you'd soon think that you were in some remote part of Ireland." He remembered one notable evening when about 20 men were swapping stories in Irish, and debating what part of Ireland the best milk cows came from.

St. Patrick's Day was as honored in the northern goldfields as it was throughout America. Early one March 17 MacGowan was getting a bucket of snow to melt for water, when he imagined he heard in the distance the tune of a bagpiper. "At first I thought it was a dream but in a short while I heard it again . . . and wasn't the tune he was playing 'St. Patrick's Day'!" Though half-way around the world from home, "in the time it would take you to clap your hands, I fancied I was back again among my own people in Cloghaneely." Eventually MacGowan did re-turn home to Donegal. After about four years in the Klondike he said his mining claim was nearly exhausted, and he was tired of spending his life digging a hole in the ground. With the money he had accumulated from mining, he was able to return home to Ireland—this time sailing first class—and to buy an estate of about 150 acres near his old family homestead, where he lived for the rest of his life and raised a family of 11 children. He died in November 1948.

Neither Michael MacGowan nor his Klondike adventures have ever been forgotten. The house where he was born still stands at Gortahork in County Donegal, where it has been restored—thatched roof and all—in memory of his efforts to preserve the Irish language. In fact MacGowan's adventure in the Yukon gold fields is well known today among many young people in Ireland, because for years the original Irish lan-guage version of his memoirs—which noted Irish folklorist Sean O hEochaidh first recorded and Proinsias O Conluain subse-quently edited into a book—was a standard exam text for stu-dents of Gaelic.

Many an Irish emigrant dreamed of striking it rich in the States and one day making a triumphant return home like Michael MacGowan. The vast majority of course did neither, but never-theless the dream lived on. To generations of immigrants, Amer-ica was a land of promise, where anyone might find their fortune across the next bend in the river. Prospectors on the Alaska-Yukon frontier and immigrants to America had much in com-mon, especially a strong faith in a better future and a willingness to risk everything for it. Those who had gambled all they owned on coming to America, who had forever left behind their family and friends, knew the struggle of life in a strange land. Arthur Harper's fruitless quest for gold that lasted nearly a quarter of a century, and Michael MacGowan's diligent four-year effort to save enough treasure to pay his way back home, represent two extremes of the Irish experience in America, the hard road to Klondike.

*See* Alaska

Pierre Berton, *The Klondike Fever* (New York, 1974).
Alfred H. Brooks, *Blazing Alaska's Trails* (Fairbanks, 1973).
Terrence Cole, "The Hard Road to Klondike: Irish Pioneers in the Alaska-Yukon Gold Rush," in *The Irish in the West,* Tim Sabaugh and James Walsh, eds. (Kansas, 1993).
James H. Ducker, *Carmack's Alaskans: A Census Study of Alaskans in 1900* (Anchorage, 1985).
Finley Peter Dunne, "On Gold-Seeking," in *Mr. Dooley in Peace and in War* (Boston, 1898).
David Emmons, *The Butte Irish: Class and Ethnicity in an American Mining Town, 1875–1925* (Urbana, 1989).
Michael MacGowan, *The Hard Road to Klondike* (London, 1962).
Melody Webb, *The Last Frontier: A History of the Yukon Basin of Canada and Alaska* (Albuquerque, 1985).

TERRENCE M. COLE

## ALISON, FRANCIS (1705–1779)

Leading Presbyterian clergyman, educator, and champion of American rights in pre-revolutionary Pennsylvania, Alison was born in the parish of Leck, Co. Donegal, the son of a poor weaver, but through charity was able to train for the ministry at the universities of Edinburgh (M.A., 1732) and of Glasgow, where he studied moral philosophy under the Ulster-born Fran-cis Hutcheson (1694–1746), the "father of the Scottish Enlight-enment." After immigrating to Pennsylvania in 1735, Alison—through his sermons, teaching, and political writings—became the principal disseminator in the colonies of Hutcheson's ideas concerning human nature, liberty of conscience, and the citi-zen's right to resist oppression, thus shaping the radical ideology that led to the American Revolution. In 1737 Alison became minister at New London, Chester Co., Pennsylvania, as well as the ablest leader of the anti-evangelical, Old Side Presbyterians in the controversy over the Great Awakening that temporarily split the American church between 1741 and 1758. In 1743 Ali-son established the New London Academy to train ministerial candidates for the Old Side, but in 1752 he moved to Philadel-phia and became co-pastor of the First Presbyterian Church and, in 1755, vice-provost and professor of moral philosophy at the new College of Philadelphia. Alison's students at New London and Philadelphia included future revolutionary leaders Charles Thomson (1729–1824), Thomas McKean (1734–1817), Thomas Mifflin (1744–1800), and George Read (1733–1798), all but Mif-flin of Irish birth or descent. Most important, in the mid and late 1760s, Alison played a major role—along with Thomson, John Dickinson (1732–1808), and George Bryan (1731–1791)—

in mobilizing Presbyterians in the Middle Colonies against the Stamp Act (1765), the Townshend Acts (1767), and the threat of an Anglican bishopric. In 1768 Alison was principal author (with Dickinson and Bryan) of *The Centinel,* essays warning of an "episcopal plot" to subvert American religious liberty, and in 1767–75 he forged and led an intercolonial General Convention of Presbyterian and Congregational clergy to resist British measures. According to John Adams, Alison's writings were instrumental in arousing "the common people" to question parliamentary authority and preparing them for revolution, but Alison regarded his greatest achievement as the creation, for Presbyterian clergy, of America's first life insurance program.

*Dictionary of American Biography.*

E. A. Ingersoll [Nybakken], "Francis Alison: American *Philosophe,* 1705–1779" (Ph.D. diss., Univ. of Delaware, 1974).

J. L. McAllister, Jr., "Francis Alison and John Witherspoon: Political Philosophers and Revolutionaries," *Journal of Presbyterian History* 54 (1976): 33–60.

E. I. Nybakken, ed., *The Centinel: Warnings of a Revolution* (Newark, Del., 1980).

T. C. Pears, "Francis Alison," *Journal of Presbyterian History* 30 (1952): 213–25.

W. B. Sprague, *Annals of the American Pulpit,* III (New York, 1861).

R. A. Webster, *A History of the Presbyterian Church in America* (Philadelphia, 1858).

KERBY MILLER

## ALLEN, FRED (1894–1956)

Comedian and entertainer. He was born John Florence Sullivan on 31 May 1894 in Cambridge, Massachusetts. The son of parents of Irish heritage, John Henry Sullivan and Cecilia (Herlihy) Sullivan, he was baptized a Roman Catholic. With the death of his mother in his third year, young John came under the care of an aunt, his deceased mother's sister. Years later, when a student at the Boston High School of Commerce, he worked nights at the public library. There he discovered a book on comedy which fascinated him and turned his life in the direction of pursuing a career in comedy entertainment (Weeks, 12).

Initially billing himself as a juggler, he built his stage act on a repertoire of juggling padded with comedic glib and rapid chatter poking fun at himself. At that time in his life, Sullivan discarded his Irish surname and his given name as well, performing in vaudeville and other shows using several stage names: Paul Huckle and Freddie St. James being the most prominent among them. Returning to the United States from a 1916 tour of Australia and New Zealand, he then permanently assumed the name Fred Allen.

From that point on, Fred Allen the Irish-American moved up in his profession, eventually, as one biographer reminds, attaining "top billing in the prestigious Palace Theatre in New York City"(Liselle Drake, *The Encyclopedia of American Catholic History,* 19). In October 1932, Fred Allen made his debut on radio with "The Linit Bath Club Revue"(Weeks, 13). Meanwhile, in May 1927, he married fellow performer Portland Hoffa, who became his partner in comedy as well as in life.

In 1934 Fred Allen inaugerated the program that has gone down in history as his classic, the one-hour "Town Hall Tonight." In 1939 its title was changed to "The Fred Allen Show." Three years later Allen added to the script a segment known as

Fred Allen

"Allen's Alley." But then, in 1949, he retired from radio. Not long thereafter, in 1952, as he was about to prepare for a television series, Fred Allen suffered a heart attack. Four years later, on St. Patrick's Day, 17 March 1956, Allen, the Irishman, died in New York City.

Steve Allen, *The Funny Men* (New York, 1956).

Liselle Drake, "Allen, Fred (1894–1956)," *The Encyclopedia of American Catholic History* (Collegeville, 1997).

John Dunning, *Tune in Yesterday* (New York, 1976).

Edward Weeks, "Allen, Fred," *Dictionary of American Biography, 1956–1960* Supplement Six: (New York, 1973).

Maurice Zolotow, "Fred Allen: Strictly From Misery," *These Were The Years,* ed. Frank Brookhouser (New York, 1959).

PATRICK FOLEY

## AMERICAN CONFERENCE FOR IRISH STUDIES: A CO-FOUNDER'S MEMOIR

In September 1957, when I was researching in the National Library of Ireland, Professor R. Dudley Edwards invited me to dinner at his Clontarf home. On that occasion, Dudley, professor of history at University College, Dublin, and coeditor of *Irish Historical Studies,* suggested that I should organize a North American version of the Irish Historical Society. When I returned to my teaching duties at the College of St. Catherine in St. Paul, Minnesota, I wrote to my close friends, Emmet Larkin at Brooklyn College, and Gilbert Cahill, a member of the history faculty at the State University of New York, concerning my interest in Dudley's idea and asked their advice on the subject. In December 1958, during the American Historical Association meeting in Washington, Emmet, Gil, and I got together with Thomas N. Brown, who at the time was with the State Department; Helen Mulvey, Connecticut College; and Arnold Schrier, University of Cincinnati. We agreed on the feasibility of initiating a North American Irish Historical Society, and decided that we would work out details at the 1959 AHA meeting in Chicago.

By the time we met in Chicago, Emmet, Gil, and I already had decided to expand the concept of a North American Committee for Irish Historical Studies into an interdisciplinary American

Committee for Irish Studies. This strategic change was dictated by both idealistic and pragmatic evaluations of the situation. As the 1950s came to a close, few Americans or Canadians were engaged in Irish historical research and hardly any colleges or universities had offerings in Irish history. But Irish literature attracted a large number of publishing scholars and many institutions of higher learning had courses on Joyce, Yeats, and/or the Literary Revival. In addition to realizing the practical necessity of enlisting the cooperation and support of literary scholars, we also believed that like other academic areas, Irish studies suffered from excessive specialization. Anthropologists, Celtic studies scholars, folklorists, historians, literary scholars, political scientists, and sociologists researching and writing on Irish topics functioned in isolation, seldom aware of important discoveries in other disciplines or how they could illuminate their own work.

After four days of intense conversations in Chicago, Emmet, Gil, and I went to work on converting our vision into reality. Emmet quickly contacted two friends in Irish literature, David Greene, New York University and John Kelleher, Harvard University, explained what we were trying to do, and requested and got their assistance. In the spring of 1960, ACIS began its official existence with the following panel of officers: Gilbert Cahill, president; David H. Greene, John Kelleher, and Thomas N. Brown, vice-presidents; Emmet Larkin, treasurer, and myself as secretary.

I sent out notices to scholarly journals informing their readers of ACIS's existence and invited them to join. In reply to the many inquiries I received, I sent a letter with the following information:

> The American Committee for Irish Studies has been formed to stimulate and encourage significant research and writing in Irish studies by establishing means of communication between scholars interested in Irish folklore, history, language, and literature. We hope to achieve our objectives through annual conferences, information bulletins, and, if possible, a journal. Our committee will make it possible for those Americans and Canadians widely scattered over the continent who are pursuing research in Irish studies to communicate with others sharing their interests.

This letter also emphasized that non-academic friends of Irish studies were more than welcome to join ACIS. When a surprising number of people enrolled in ACIS, James McCrimmon, Head of DGS, kindly provided me with a small budget and a student secretary, Danute Gudaetis, so that I was able to compose and mail a *Newsletter*.

Shortly after ACIS was off the ground, Harold Orel, a Hardy and Yeats scholar in the English Department at the University of Kansas, visited me in my Champaign, Illinois home to learn more about it. Because of his eagerness to further Irish studies, we added him to the panel of vice-presidents. Other scholars who would become important in the development of ACIS also were early members, namely Thomas Flanagan, a literary scholar and later a distinguished novelist, Alan Ward, a political scientist who first wrote me from Australia (later at William and Mary), and John Messenger, anthropologist and sociologist at Indiana University, and later Ohio State University. Alan, John, and John's wife, Betty, provided us with a valuable social science nucleus.

In late December 1961, ACIS held its premier joint sessions with the Modern Language Association in Chicago and the

T. K. Whitaker, Chancellor of the National University of Ireland, with Lawrence McCaffrey and Emmet Larkin, both of whom received honorary degrees in 1987.

American Historical Association in Washington, D.C. While we were in Washington, Ireland's ambassador to the United States, Thomas J. Kiernan, hosted a luncheon for Emmet, Gil, and myself at the Cosmos Club, and assured us of his and his government's interest in and friendship for ACIS.

Purdue University in Lafayette, Indiana hosted the first annual conference in the spring of 1963. Since then colleges and universities throughout the United States have brought ACIS to their campuses. Ireland was the setting for three well-attended conferences. In 1987, University College, Dublin was the setting with the School of Irish Studies and Trinity College providing hospitality for a reception and a dinner. In 1992, University College, Galway was our gracious host. Three years later, Queens University of Belfast offered ACIS its cordiality and impressive facilities, and our members were able to experience Northern Ireland during a cessation in the violence of its sectarian troubles. Many of the over five hundred present at each of the Irish meetings were from the Republic and Northern Ireland, and there were representatives from Britain, the Continent, Australia, and Latin America, but most came from Canada and the United States.

In 1976, on the recommendation of Emmet and myself, the executive committee decided to establish regional branches with autumn meetings. That year the Midwest held the first regional meeting at Loyola University of Chicago where I was on the history faculty. In 1978, a previously existing New England Irish studies group decided to affiliate with ACIS. At present, there are thriving Midwest, Mid-Atlantic, New England, Western, and Southern regionals.

In addition to sponsoring national and regional conferences, ACIS has been involved in a number of Irish studies projects. In the late 1960s, Emmet Larkin received financial support from the American Council of Learned Societies and Chicago's Newberry Library in filming Irish and British materials in the Vatican's Propaganda archives. The Newberry, National Library of Ireland, and the British Museum are repositories for this valuable collection.

In 1966 an anonymous donor in Ireland made a financial contribution to ACIS. It provided the seed money for a Reprint

Series that republished eleven significant essays in Celtic studies, Irish history, and Anglo-Irish literature. Emmet was responsible for most of the decisions and editorial work. He persuaded the Massachusetts Institute of Technology Press to publish the first three reprints. After Emmet became a member of the University of Chicago's history faculty in 1968, its press turned out the final eight.

At its beginning, ACIS included Canadians as well as Americans, but in 1967 the former organized the Canadian Association for Irish Studies. The parting was friendly. A number of people belong to both organizations. ACIS and the CAIS have held joint conferences at the University of Vermont (1982) and in Dublin (1987), Galway (1992), and Belfast (1995).

From the early 1960s to the present, ACIS continually has increased its numbers. By 1966, there were close to three hundred members, six years later over five hundred, by 1979 more than seven hundred, and in 1997 about 1,500. From the start, non-academics accepted our invitation to join. ACIS has been most fortunate in obtaining the allegiance of many elementary and secondary school teachers and members from Ireland, Britain, the Continent, Australia, and Latin America. Much of the credit for a rapid 1980s membership increase belongs to James S. Donnelly, Jr., University of Wisconsin-Madison history professor, who as secretary conducted a productive recruiting campaign.

An expanding membership has necessitated changes in the governance of ACIS. In 1972, at the request of the executive committee, Larkin and I wrote a constitution that provided a more flexible executive committee. Eight years later, Alan Ward revised the constitution, giving it an even more democratic flavor. At present the executive committee includes the president, vice-president, secretary, treasurer, and representatives from history, literature, Celtic studies, social sciences, the Irish language, the arts and from each of the regional branches. The retiring president remains on the executive committee in an ex-officio capacity. All terms of elected offices are for two years, and the president, with the approval of the executive committee, appoints the secretary and treasurer.

Women have played an important role in the ACIS story. Some have served as discipline and regional representatives on the executive committee and as officers of the organization. From 1987 to 1989, Maureen Murphy, dean of students, Hofstra University, was the first woman president of ACIS. Since then Mary Helen Thuente, professor of English, Indiana University-Purdue University at Fort Wayne; Blanche Touhill, provost and professor of history, University of Missouri-St. Louis; and Lucy McDiarmid, professor of English, Villanova University, have held that office. Nancy Curtin, professor of history, Fordham University, succeeded McDiarmid as vice president.

For many years it was argued that Committee was an inadequate definition for an organization with as many members as ACIS. After repeated discussions, and a referendum on the issue, in 1987 the executive committee, with the consent of a general meeting, changed the name of the American Committee for Irish Studies to the American Conference for Irish Studies.

Because of the tremendous expense involved, and after a divisive debate within the organization, ACIS decided against starting a journal, but in 1997 it published the first of its annual book of essays. The initial volume, edited by Maryann Gialanella Valiulis, director of women's studies, Indiana State University, and Anthony Bradley, professor of Irish literature, University of Vermont, featured Irish women as its subject.

Although ACIS is an undoubted success, the impressive growth of the organization and trends in academia have challenged its original interdisciplinary purpose. So many members want to read papers at national and regional conferences that organizers of these events have had to schedule two, sometimes three sessions at the same time. Unfortunately, few are interdisciplinary. Consequently scholars in history, literature, social sciences, and Celtic Studies have fewer opportunities to learn from each other. But even in infrequent favorable settings, communications within and between disciplines have become difficult. Theoretical approaches, expressed in vocabularies and rhetoric incomprehensible to non-specialists, have obstructed dialogue between scholars. These barriers afflict all aspects of academic life.

Although ACIS has failed to fully satisfy all of its original expectations, it certainly deserves the major credit for advancing Irish studies in the United States, Canada, Britain, and Ireland itself. In American colleges and universities, Irish studies enjoys a prestige unimaginable forty-five years ago. Irish literature courses are even more popular than they were then. Irish history has established an identity related to but independent of British history, is flourishing as a research area, and has attracted large student interest on both the undergraduate and graduate level. With the exceptions of Britain, France, Germany, and Russia, Ireland has inspired more historical research and writing from Americans than other European countries.

*See* Irish Studies in the U.S.

LAWRENCE J. McCAFFREY

## AMERICAN IRELAND FUND, THE

The mission of The American Ireland Fund is to be the largest worldwide network of people of Irish ancestry and friends of Ireland dedicated to raising funds to support programs of peace and reconciliation, arts and culture, education and community development in Ireland, North and South.

In 1976, Dr. Anthony J. F. O'Reilly, former president, chairman and chief executive officer of H.J. Heinz Co., created what was then called the Ireland Fund with fellow Pittsburgh businessman Dan Rooney, owner of the Pittsburgh Steelers football team. With a trinity of goals—Peace, Culture and Charity—the Ireland Fund appealed for support for Ireland and its people from all Americans, but especially those of Irish descent.

Over the following decade, the Ireland Fund formed a thriving fundraising network of chapters in cities across the U.S. including Boston, Chicago, Palm Beach, New York, Houston, Los Angeles, Pittsburgh, San Francisco, San Diego, Phoenix, Denver, Dallas and Washington, D.C.

On St. Patrick's Day 1987, the Ireland Fund and the American Irish Foundation merged at a White House ceremony to form The American Ireland Fund and became the nation's and the world's largest private organization funding constructive change throughout Ireland, North and South.

Today, The American Ireland Fund is part of an international Confederation of Concern. Ireland Funds in Australia, Canada, France, Germany, Great Britain, New Zealand, Japan, South Africa, Monaco and Mexico are uniting the aspirations of the Irish diaspora, a global community of more than 70 million people. With 60 events in 39 cities around the world attended by 30,000 people, The Ireland Funds are poised for further growth in the United States and elsewhere. Thus far, the AIF has raised $100 million to support its growing grants program. The Fund also has begun to build a permanent endowment through a series of "named" funds established by prominent American business people as well as by bequests and other large gifts. The total of the Endowment Fund exceeds $20 million.

The American Ireland Fund's grant-making guidelines currently focus on several specific areas. These are peace and reconciliation between the communities in Northern Ireland, culture and the arts, education and community development. The need in Ireland is great. There are virtually no private foundations that people and organizations can turn to for support. Today, through The American Ireland Fund, support has been given to over 1,000 worthy projects.

BRIDGET SIMMONS

## AMERICAN IRISH HISTORICAL SOCIETY

The American Irish Historical Society was founded in Boston in 1897 to document and celebrate the contributions of the Irish in America. Founded in part to counteract anti-Irish prejudice and discrimination, the AIHS has, for over one hundred years, adhered to its original mission: "To make better known the Irish chapter in American History."

Under the early leadership of Teddy Roosevelt, Augustus Saint Gaudens, Joseph I. C. Clarke, and Daniel Cohalan, the AIHS discovered immediate success—by 1898 over 820 men had enrolled, at a yearly membership fee of $3.

These early years were marked by a nomadic existence, with meetings up and down the East Coast. Finally, in 1919 Dr. John T. Nagle provided the first permanent Society headquarters by donating his home in New York City. The new headquarters became a meeting place for Society events and a home for the Society's growing collections, including the donated libraries of Dr. Thomas Addis Emmet and John Crimmins. Building on these donations, the Society created one of the largest and most extensive collections of Irish material in the United States.

Having outgrown the original home by 1940, the AIHS, with assistance from the Irish Palace Building Association, purchased its current home on Fifth Avenue. Built in 1901, this landmark townhouse provided a fitting location for the growing aspirations of the Society. By 1941, the membership rolls boasted 2,200 men and women and included vice presidents for every state, Ireland, Mexico, Canada, Australia, and the Philippines.

In addition to maintaining the library, the Society continues to honor men and women of Irish descent who have contributed to life in America. Past recipients of the Gold Medal include Anne O'Hare McCormick, George Meany and John Sweeney, Padraic Colum, Mary Higgins Clark and Thomas Flanagan, and Cardinals Cooke, Cushing and O'Connor.

The Society also publishes the *Recorder,* a semi-annual historical, cultural, and literary journal.

Through the years, the Society has remained at the center of American Irish affairs and continues to offer a full program of lectures, readings and concerts. The library remains one of the most extensive in the United States, containing monographs, periodicals, photographs and archival material that record the history of the American Irish from the colonial era to the present.

PAUL W. RUPPERT

## AMERICAN REVOLUTION, THE

Writing in 1778, Sir Henry Clinton, Commander-in-Chief of the British forces in America, declared that "the Emigrants from Ireland were in general to be looked upon as our most serious antagonists. They had fled from the real or fancied oppression of their landlords. . . . They had transplanted themselves into a country where they can live without apprehension and had estranged themselves from all solicitude for the welfare of Britain." Immediately after the successful outcome of the revolution, George Grieve noted that "whilst the Irish emigrant was fighting the battles in America by sea and by land, the Irish merchants, particularly at Charleston, Baltimore and Philadelphia, labored with indefatigable zeal, and at all harzards, to . . . maintain the credit of the country; their purses were always open, and their persons devoted to the common cause. On more than one occasion, Congress owed their existence, and America possibly her preservation to the fidelity and firmness of the Irish" (Introduction, Marquis de Chastellux, *Travels in North America in the Years 1780, 1781 and 1782).*

There was, indeed, a marked Irish presence in that famous struggle. Irishmen were to be found on all sides of the conflict—in the ranks of both the Continental Army and the British Army, as Loyalists and as French legionaries. They served as seamen and as soldiers, financiers and politicians. Certainly they were an important force in the achievement of American independence.

The immigrant or ethnic aspect of the Revolution has been given little attention by historians. This is due, in part, to the fact that this matter often was overlooked during the course of the conflict. The first national census, in 1790, greatly underestimated the non-English element in the European population and this assessment remained unchallenged for a century. Also, American historians generally have treated their country's history as if it was the story of a homogenous people (barring the African slaves) advancing towards world greatness. This approach suited the needs of a country that during the nineteenth century was attempting to mold a national consciousness out of people from many European countries. As a result, the contributions of various ethnic groups were largely ignored. Although as many as half the people in the thirteen colonies in 1770 had been born in Europe, histories of the colonial period almost invariably do not present a picture of ethnic diversity. In recent years there has been an upsurge in the study of the settlement and development of these peoples in the United States. It is appropriate that attention should be focused on one of the most important European nationalities in the formation of the American state.

As recently as 1969 a widely-used textbook co-authored by three leading American historians, S. E. Morison, H. S. Commager and W. E. Leuchtenburg, declared: "Although the spokesmen of Irish-Americans, German-Americans and other racial minorities like to claim that the American army was largely composed of themselves, there is no evidence of racial groups favoring either side" (*Growth of the American Republic,* vol. 1).

There is very considerable evidence that Irish people strongly supported the Patriot side, but this has not been brought together in a single scholarly study. Some of the evidence is to be found in the memoirs of participants and contemporaries. In what is generally considered to be the best contemporary treatment of the subject, David Ramsay declared in his history of the revolution, "The Irish in America, with a few exceptions, were attached to independence. They had fled from oppression in their native country, and could not brook the idea that it should follow them" (*History of the American Revolution*, 1793, vol. II). This view is supported by the writings of Alexander Garden and Alexander Graydon. In his memoirs, published in 1811, Graydon wrote: "As to the genuine sons of Hibernia, it was enough for them to know that England was the antagonist. Stimulants here were wholly superfluous, and the sequel has constantly shown that in a contest with Englishmen, Irishmen, like the mettlesome coursers of Phaethon, only required reining in."

Were Irish people and those of Irish descent a sizeable part of the population of the thirteen colonies at the time of the revolution? People from Ireland were the largest group of Europeans to arrive there in the seventy-five years leading up to the war. The Irish proportion of the population was underestimated by the first national census, but a committee of scholars in 1931 determined that those of Irish origins had comprised about ten percent (9.5%) of the white population, thus making them the second largest European group, coming far behind those of English stock (60.1%), but ahead of the Germans (8.6%), the Scots (8.1%), the Dutch (3.1%) and the French (2.3%) (*Report of the Committee on Linguistic and National Stocks in the Population of the United States, A.H.A., Annual Report, 1931*).

There was a noticeable Irish population in all of the thirteen colonies, but it was most prominent in the South. The 1931 study estimated that among the white population in 1790 those of Irish stock were 15% of the population of Georgia, 14% of South Carolina, 12% of Kentucky and Tennessee, and 11% of Virginia and North Carolina. The largest number of Irish settlers, as opposed to percentage of population, was to be found in Pennsylvania, an area vital to the success of the Patriot cause in the war.

For long historians made the assumption that the vast majority of those who came from Ireland were of "Scotch-Irish" stock, and, therefore, not really Irish at all. This label was popularized only in the middle of the nineteenth century, in an attempt to distinguish those Ulstermen of Protestant and Scottish background from the flood of Catholic Irish of the time.

The same committee of scholars declared that this picture was also inaccurate. They concluded that only three-fifths (190,000) of those of Irish stock were of Ulster origin (and some of these would not fit the "Scotch-Irish" category), while two-fifths (116,000) had roots in the other three provinces. At least some of the immigrants from Leinster, Munster and Connaught were of English and Scottish backgrounds, but port records provide abundant evidence of boatload followed by boatload of arrivals with distinctively ancient Irish names.

Although the term "Scotch-Irish" sometimes is a convenient one, it was rarely used by the people to whom it was later applied. These people sometimes referred to themselves as Ulstermen or as being from the north of Ireland but they generally called themselves simply Irishmen. Of course, they were well aware of their political and religious differences from the majority population in Ireland. But these differences seemed to be largely muted in the New World: the Irish organizations formed at the time of the revolution, in Philadelphia, Charleston and New York, for example, included both Catholics and Protestants in apparent harmony.

Why did they come? Both Irish groups were motivated to emigrate as a result of religious and political discrimination as well as economic restrictions. Another factor was a series of devastating crop failures. There was also the lure of a new country and abundant land.

The Ulster Protestants were the first to leave in large numbers. They did not have deep roots in Ireland and English restrictions on Irish exports effectively stifled the many enterprises they established. Most of them were Presbyterians, and only Anglicans could participate in the government. The full weight of religious and political discrimination fell upon the Irish Catholics. Although not directly affected by English economic restrictions, which undermined mercantile and industrial activity, their peasant status left them in the hands of English and Anglo-Irish landlords. This group followed in the wake of the Ulster Protestant exodus.

Most of the Irish who emigrated left as indentured servants; this was the status of most eighteenth-century immigrants. In the eyes of many colonists of English stock, Irish people were viewed generally as being all alike. They were noted as being poor, turbulent, courageous, clannish and adventuresome. There was a strong anti-Catholic feeling in colonial America, so Irish Papists were not welcomed. Due in part to this hostility, but much more to the lack of a Catholic church organization, most Irish Catholics did not and could not continue to practice this religion. In New England Irish Presbyterians were also objectionable because they set up their own chapels rather than join the dominant Congregational Church.

What is striking is how much alike both of the Irish groups seemed to be in colonial America. Upon entering an Irish Presbyterian settlement along the Virginia frontier, one traveller reported that he was met with "full-mouthed, blubbering Irish compliments."

The tide of Irish immigration for both groups was governed by crop failures at home. In the last few years before the outbreak of the revolution, the inflow from Ireland was particularly heavy. So there was a sizeable Irish population in the thirteen colonies and many of those from Ireland had suffered under English rule at home.

Could it not be argued that the bulk of the Irish supported the Revolution, not because of their experiences with British rule in their native land, but because they were almost entirely in the lower social and economic ranks in the colonies and expected independence to benefit them? According to an eminent American historian, the lower social and economic groups did not back the Patriot cause *en masse*, but were divided in their allegiances. Richard B. Morris has stated that the struggle "while containing elements of both a social and political revolution, failed to align social classes in a clear-cut manner for or against independence. Instead, the divided allegiance of the lower classes converts the American Revolution into a classic example of a civil war."

If the lower classes were divided, then the bulk of the Irish did not support the Patriot cause because of their lower class status. One is forced to the conclusion that they gave this support after their experiences with British rule in Ireland because they were Irish.

Professor Morris also has declared "save in cases of bound servants gaining their freedom by enlistment, often over the vehement protests of their masters, the Revolution did nothing to end and little to ameliorate the practice of white bondage." This advantage of enlistment for indentured servants surely accounts, in part at least, for the large number of Irishmen in the Continental Army. But Morris adds: "Loyalists were heavily recruited from the ranks of the more recent emigrants, regardless of social position . . ." (*The American Revolution Reconsidered*).

There was a fresh wave of immigration from Ireland in the last few years before 1775 and very few Irish joined the Loyalist forces. Thus, one is again driven to the conclusion that most of the Irish opposed the continuation of royal rule because they were Irish. Irish involvement with the struggle for American independence extends from the Boston Massacre of 1770 to the surrender of the British forces at Yorktown in 1781.

Irishmen figured largely in the first major battle of the conflict—Bunker Hill, on 17 June 1775. The casualty figures are revealing: sixty-three of the Patriot companies suffered casualties; of these forty-one contained Irish-born members or sons of Irish immigrants, including seven deserters from the British Army. Seven of the officers were Irish-born, while five were sons of Irish descent. One of the participants in the battle was the Reverend John Martin, an Irish-born clergyman who wrote an account of the famous encounter. Sir Henry Clinton, who took part on the other side, declared that the Irish were the chief Patriot defenders of the hill, "thinking the vengeance of their landlords was still pursuing them." John Daly Burk, a refugee from Ireland, wrote an enormously popular play about the battle, which was first produced in 1797.

Five days before Bunker Hill a minor but encouraging Patriot victory occurred at Machias, Maine, where the O'Brien clan launched a family-led attack on the British Navy. Five sons of a Dublin immigrant, led by the eldest, Jeremiah (1744–1818), organized about forty men, armed with guns, swords, axes and pitch forks, who attacked and captured the British cutter, *Margaretta*. As the first naval hero of the revolution, Jeremiah O'Brien was appointed commander of the infant Massachusetts navy (and is commemorated by a plaque in the State House in Boston).

In the weeks that followed Bunker Hill an American army formed for the siege of Boston. Groups of riflemen from Maryland, Virginia and western Pennsylvania, led by Daniel Morgan, arrived in July. According to Benson Lossing, "A large portion of them were Irishmen, and were not very agreeable to the New Englanders." Michael J. O'Brien has estimated that 3,000 Irishmen served in the polyglot siege army (*Irish at Bunker Hill*). Whether they were drawn from New England or elsewhere, the presence of a significant number of Irishmen in the infant army can be seen in George Washington's orders for 17 March 1776 when he appointed John Sullivan as officer of the day and made the words "Saint Patrick" the counter-sign for sentries. To add to the honor, this was the day the British forces evacuated Boston. At this time Washington denounced the anti-Catholic spectacle of "Pope's Day."

Of the many generals in the Continental Army, at least sixteen were from Ireland. This figure stands in marked contrast to the number born in other countries. Three were from Germany, two from Scotland, two from Poland, two from France, one from Denmark, one from the Netherlands and one from England.

The Irish-born generals included John Armstrong, Andrew Browne, Richard Butler, Richard Butte, Thomas Conway, John Clarke, Edward Hand, James Hogun, William Irvine, Andrew Lewis, William Maxwell, Richard Montgomery, Stephen Moylan, John Shee, Walter Stewart and William Thompson. As was true of the Irish population as a whole, most of these military leaders were from Ulster. Many of them reached their senior rank at the end of the war, but these retirement promotions were rewards for long and dedicated service. There were also several outstanding Irish naval leaders including Captains John Barry, Gustavus Conyngham and Hector McNeill.

One of the most prominent Irishmen in the revolution was Stephen Moylan (1737–1811), who came from Cork. Emigrating to Philadelphia in 1768, he became a wealthy merchant and ship-per by the time of the Revolution. His character and ability made a strong impression on John Adams, who for long had a very negative view of Roman Catholics. During the war, Moylan became the army's first muster-master general, then secretary to Washington, quarter-master general and finally the army's senior cavalry officer. Three of his brothers also served the cause of American independence. One was clothier-general to the Continental Army, another was a lawyer in Philadelphia. His third brother, James, acted as business agent for the Continental Congress at the port of Lorient in France. He was instrumental in securing a ship for John Paul Jones; in 1778 this vessel gained naval fame as the *Bonhomme Richard*. His youngest brother, Francis, rose to be bishop of Kerry and then of Cork. Moylan remained a friend of Washington after the war and, as president, Washington appointed him commissioner of loans in Philadelphia.

The Butlers of Pennsylvania were another notable military family in the Revolution. The two eldest brothers, William and Richard, were born in Dublin and emigrated with their father around 1754; Thomas and Percival were born in Lancaster, Pennsylvania. The brothers served in a large number of campaigns in the north. Richard attained the highest rank, rising to be a brigadier general. After the war he was appointed major general of U.S. Levies and died in battle against Indians in 1791.

A famous American general in the war was Richard Montgomery, who was born in Donegal, attended Trinity College, Dublin, and joined the British Army. He resigned his commission, settled in New York in 1773 and quickly became involved in politics. He lost his life leading the Patriot attack on Quebec on 1 January 1776. Then there was Edward Hand, who also served in both the British and American armies. Born in the County Laois in 1774, he resigned his commission and established a surgeon's practice in Lancaster, Pennsylvania. Upon the outbreak of the revolution he joined the Continental Army, rising to the position of Adjutant General.

Andrew Browne was another of many Irishmen who came to America as a British soldier. Born in the mid-18th century, he was educated at Trinity College, Dublin, and arrived in the colonies in 1773. On the eve of the Revolution he deserted the British Army and led a company at Bunker Hill. In 1777 he became Muster-master General of the Continental Army. After the war he became a journalist in Philadelphia, founded the *Federal Gazette* and was active in Irish organizations.

The date and place of General James Hogan's birth in Ireland is not known. He settled in Halifax, North Carolina, about 1751. After service on the local Patriot committees and the provincial congress, he was appointed the first major of the Halifax militia in April 1776; the following November he became colonel of the 7th North Carolina Continentals. During the next four years he divided his time between service in Washington's army (he fought at Brandywine and Germantown) and raising troops in his state. Promoted to Brigadier General in 1779, he became a prisoner when the Patriot army at Charlestown, South Carolina, was forced to surrender in May 1780. Refusing parole in order to remain with his troops, then under British pressure to serve in Jamaica as royal militia, he died in captivity in January 1781.

Other generals of Irish birth were John Clarke, from Antrim, John Shee, from Westmeath, William Irvine, from Enniskillen, Co. Tyrone, Walter Stewart, from Derry, Andrew Lewis, from Donegal, William Thompson, William Maxwell, Thomas Conway, and Richard Butte, who was born in Dublin in 1743 and was killed fighting Indians in 1791. The fathers of three other generals, John Sullivan, "Mad" Anthony Wayne, and Henry Knox, were from Ireland.

Sullivan probably is the most important of the latter group. His mother Margery was from Cork and his father Owen emigrated around 1723 from Limerick to Maine where he became one of a group of itinerant Irish school masters in New England and lived to the age of 105. John Sullivan has been described as contentious, courageous and unlucky. Washington spent an inordinate amount of time trying to placate him. The leader of the New Hampshire volunteers, Sullivan took the initiative in capturing the fort at Portsmouth in December 1774 and then joined the Patriot forces at the beginning of the struggle in Boston. As a military commander, he suffered a series of reverses in the campaigns at Newport and Long Island; his principal victory was against the Indians in up-state New York. The pugnacious Sullivan resigned from the army in 1779 and began a political career. As a delegate to the Continental Congress in 1781, he rejected a British offer brought to him by his brother Daniel that he join the loyalist side. He later served as attorney general and president (governor) of New Hampshire. His anti-Catholic diatribes can be viewed as his politically inspired effort to distinguish his religious views from those of his forebears.

Another of the Sullivan brothers, James, also achieved political prominence. During the war he served as Commissary General in Massachusetts. He then settled down to a career as a lawyer, journalist and politician. In the 1790s he wrote several anonymous articles praising the role of Irishmen in the revolution and defending Ireland's right to self-government. He eventually attained his long sought political goal, serving as Governor of the Bay State in 1807–8. Among his minor achievements was the founding of the town of Limerick in Maine, named in honor of the birthplace of his father.

There were many noteworthy Irishmen who served in lesser ranks. One of these was Major Patrick Carr of the Georgia Continental Line. The Georgia colonial records show a large number of Irish arrivals in 1767 and 1768; Carr may have been one of these. He learned about guerilla warfare from the Indians. During the revolution he led a unit known as Carr's Independent Corps. He played a leading part in the battle of Kettle River, Georgia, which resulted in the destruction of a Loyalist force in that state.

Another Continental Army officer was Patrick O'Flynn, who became a personal friend of Washington during the long independence struggle. After the war he became a tavern keeper in Wilmington, Delaware, where he was host to the general on several occasions when Washington visited the city. Then there was Colonel John Fitzgerald, an *aide de camp* to Washington, who has been described as "an agreeable and broad-shouldered Irishman."

John Haslet was born around 1745 in Ireland, where he studied theology and then medicine. He immigrated to Delaware, where he practiced medicine and was active in political affairs. At the beginning of 1776 he became colonel of the Delaware Regiment, which became one of the best units in the Patriot army. Just a year later, in January 1777 he was killed at the battle of Princeton. Another Irishman who was an officer in this regiment was Major Thomas McDonough, who led the force in the battle of Long Island and who was father of Commodore Oliver McDonough, the American naval hero in the War of 1812.

The term "Lynch law" has its origins, at least in America, in the war-time activities of Charles Lynch (1736–1796). The son of

John Barry, "Father of the American Navy"

an Irish indentured servant, Lynch was born near the modern Lynchburg, Virginia, a city named after his youngest brother, John. As a justice of the peace and leader of a band of Virginia militiamen, Lynch established his "law" by providing extra-legal punishment to local Tories, but this punishment was limited to whippings, not execution. There also was the Lynch family of South Carolina: Thomas, Senior, signed the Declaration of Independence while Thomas, Junior, signed the Constitution of 1789.

Jeremiah O'Brien may have been the revolution's first naval hero, but the title of "Father of the American Navy" belongs to John Barry. Born in Rosslare, County Wexford, in 1745, he went to Philadelphia in 1760, to be followed by several brothers and sisters. After years of experience as a merchant sailor, he became an officer in the infant Patriot navy. In May 1776, while commanding the brig *Lexington,* he captured the first British ship taken by the American Navy, which had been specially constituted by the Continental Congress eight months before. Thomas D'Arcy Magee claimed that on one occasion when British ships challenged him to identify his vessel and its captain, Barry replied, "The United States ship *Alliance;* saucy Jack Barry, half-Irishman, half-Yankee, captain." In a force riven by rivalry and bickering, he was, according to Samuel Eliot Morison, the most popular captain in the navy. Second only to John Paul Jones in fighting fame, he earned the title of founder of the United States Navy by his devoted efforts in shaping the first effective American naval force and then sustaining it. Named the navy's senior officer in 1794, he died in 1803. He is memorialized by statues in his native Wexford, his adopted city of Philadelphia and the Naval Academy at Annapolis.

Jones, of course, was a Scot. It is interesting to note that the crew of his famous ship, the *Bonhomme Richard,* included 21 Irishmen (along with 79 Americans, 59 Englishmen, 29 Portuguese and a smattering of sailors from other countries). What is more noteworthy is the fact that the only non-American officers were three Irishmen, Lieutenant Eugene McCarthy and Sub-lieutenants James Gerald O'Kelly and Edward Stack, all of whom were volunteers from the Walsh Regiment of Marine Artillery in the French Army.

Surely the equal of Jones in combat achievement was Gustavus Conyngham, "The Dunkirk Pirate." Born in County Donegal of a landed gentry family in 1747, he emigrated to Philadelphia at the age of sixteen, where his cousin Redmond Conyngham had established a shipping business. At the beginning of the Revolution Conyngham sailed to Europe, but his first venture as a raider on British commerce was unsuccessful. Then the Continental Congress gave him command of the *Revenge* in 1777 and that July he set out from Dunkirk on a remarkable cruise. During the next two months he raided the North Sea, the Baltic, circumnavigated Britain and Ireland and safely sailed to Spain.

From there he continued his raids on British shipping until the Spanish forced him to shift his operations to the West Indies in 1778. At the end of this eighteen month onslaught, he had captured sixty prizes. Later he was twice captured and suffered severely in prison. When the war was over he was not given a permanent commission in the American Navy, but returned to the merchant marine. Why was he not afforded proper recognition in his own time or later? In part this is due to his turbulent personality. Other factors in his lack of acclaim were his inarticulate and modest manner and the fact that he worked in a period of secrecy. Morison has termed Conyngham "the most successful commerce-destroyer in the United States Navy and the most unfortunate."

Another outstanding Irish seaman in the Continental Navy was Captain Hector McNeill, who was born at Ballycastle, Country Antrim, in 1728. According to McNeill's own account, his grandfather was from Kintyre in the West Highlands of Scotland. A follower of the Stuarts, he lived in exile in France for a time. He later settled in Antrim and married a woman named O'Neil. His grandson emigrated to Boston when he was nine years old; his family was given a most unfriendly reception. McNeill embarked on a career as a merchant sailor and in 1776 was given the command of the twenty-four gun frigate, *Boston,* one of the first major ships in the revolutionary navy. After a dispute with Captain John Manley, he resigned his command in 1778 and later was a captain of privateers. He was lost at sea in 1785.

The large number of men with obviously Irish names who served under McNeill on the *Boston* is further evidence of Irish prominence in the Continental Navy. They include Patrick Burns, Patrick Connor, John Costelloe, Philip Connell, John Carrel, Henry Connell, Patrick Connell, Dennis Connell, John Fitzgerald, Lawrence Furlong, James Griffin, John Irish, John Keef, Matthew Kelly, Michael Murphy, Jeremiah Meahney, Michael Mullcahey, Lawrence McLaughlin, Richard Nowland, William O'Brien, Joseph O'Brien, Michael Ryan and Patrick Tobine. These men totalled twenty-three of the crew of 237 listed for the year 1777.

How many Irishmen fought in the Patriot forces? What percentage were they? These questions cannot be given definitive answers until a scholarly study of the national origins of the participants has been undertaken. But there is abundant evidence that various British observers considered the Irish their most adamant opponents in America.

The *Hibernian Magazine* of Dublin in 1776 printed a letter of a British officer who declared that the Patriot militiamen who "kept up the spirit and life of the rebellion were totally Scotch and Irish," many of the latter being tenants forced by eviction to emigrate. The American loyalist, Joseph Galloway, told a House of Commons committee in March 1779 that one-half of the rebel force was Irish, while a quarter was American born and the other quarter was English and Scotch. On another occasion he declared, "the rebels are not one in ten of their whole army who are not either English, Scotch or Irish, but by far the greater number of Irish." Galloway had been in a good position to know about the composition of the rebel army. Appointed Superintendent of Philadelphia by General Howe, he submitted reports of deserters from the Continental Army who appeared in that city.

Parliament also heard testimony from Major General James Robertson, who reported the statement of Charles Lee, a discredited American general, that half of the Continental Army was from Ireland. It was the view of Joshua Pell, a British Army officer in America, that "the rebels consist chiefly of Irish Redemptioners and Convicts. . . ." Ambrose Serle, Admiral Richard Howe's secretary, shared the same belief: "Vast numbers of Irish are in the Rebel Army." Major Patrick Ferguson, the Scottish-born leader of loyalist militiamen in South Carolina, said of the Patriot forces that "rebels, the common Irish and other Europeans . . . make up the strength of their armys." The historian John Shy comments, "Many British observers thought that the real American Revolutionaries were the religious Dissenters, Congregationalists and Presbyterians who had always been secretly disloyal to the Crown because they rejected the whole Anglican Establishment, whose head was the king; and that these Revolutionaries persuaded poor Irishmen, who poured into the American colonies in great numbers during the middle third of the eigtheenth century, to do most of the dirty business of actual fighting" (*A People Numerous and Armed; Reflections on their Military Struggle for American Independence*).

After lengthy study of revolutionary muster-rolls, the Irish-born historian Michael J. O'Brien concluded that thirty-eight *percent* of the Patriot army was Irish (*A Hidden Phase of American History*). This calculation certainly overstated the case and, thus, seriously undercut the acceptance of his research. However, no other historian has attempted to establish a different figure. Suffice it to say that the Irish were an important component in the Patriot forces and that Irishmen played significant roles at crucial points in the revolutionary struggle.

Irish involvement in four developments are especially noteworthy—the Patriot seizure of control of the middle colonies in 1775–76, the British invasion of upstate New York in 1777, the near-mutiny of Washington's army at the beginning of 1781 and the conflict in the Carolinas in 1780–81.

In a wide-ranging article on the interaction of culture, ethnicity and political development, Robert Kelley in 1977 declared, "It was the Scotch-Irish who in the 1770s took control of the Middle Colonies and pulled them out of the empire. New York, after all, was strongly Anglicized, Church of England and loyal. In Philadelphia the Quaker oligarchy would have nothing to do with the patriot cause" ("Ideology and Political Culture from Jefferson to Nixon," *American Historical Review,* v. 82, no. 3 [June 1977] pp. 531–82). It was not just the Ulster Irish from the hills of Pennsylvania that forced this result; the effort equally was supported by the other kind of Irish people, who in Philadelphia constituted the largest urban concentration of this group in the colonies.

Following their expulsion from New England in 1776, the British military launched a campaign to cut off that region the next year. Under the leadership of General John "Gentleman Johnny" Burgoyne, a force from Canada invaded New York in June 1777. It expected to join forces with the army of General William Howe which was to have marched up the Hudson River from New York City. Unfortunately for Burgoyne, Howe's army sailed off to occupy Philadelphia.

As he pushed on, Burgoyne was faced with declining food and supplies. In hopes of replenishment, as well as striking at his foes, he sent an expedition to Bennington, Vermont. He believed that area abounded in the most active and most rebellious race on the continent. His raiding party was met by a determined and largely "Scotch-Irish" force, led by John Stark of Londonderry, New Hampshire. The British force was routed. A veteran of the French wars, Stark was, at the age of forty-nine, one of the oldest of the Continental generals.

After the defeat at Bennington, Burgoyne was faced with the difficult choice of advancing or withdrawing. He decided to go forward, but at Saratoga he met final defeat. The famous conflict at that site, which had an Irish aspect, began with the prospect of British victory. The British battle commander, General Simon Fraser, was successfully directing his men when he was shot and killed by a sniper. This act traditionally has been credited to Timothy Healy of Daniel Morgan's Rangers, a unit with a large Irish component. Healy, whose parents came from Ireland, was born in New Jersey in 1751 and grew up along the frontier. A master scout and marksman, he served in the Patriot army throughout the war and afterwards became a farmer and extensive landowner in New York. A monument to his memory is to be found on the Saratoga battlefield.

Another Patriot soldier at Bennington was Matthew Lyon (1750–1822) who was born in County Wicklow, Ireland. He came to America as an indentured servant in 1765. After the war he served in Congress as a Representative from three states and achieved fame as a result of a bitter conflict with President Adams over the Sedition Act.

Irishmen also played an important part in maintaining the struggle in Pennsylvania. The Pennsylvania Line, as the troops from that state were called, included a large number of soldiers of northern Irish stock. General Henry Lee commented that "they might have been, with more propriety, called the Line of Ireland."

The strength of the Irish in the Pennsylvania Line is also seen in the figures of its first regiment (from the Cumberland Valley) upon disbandment. Of the 1,057 men on its rolls, 731 had countries of nativity listed; of these 361 were from Ireland; 215 from America; 71 from England; 51 from Germany and 18 from Scotland. Of the remaining 370, 171 had Irish names.

The men of the Pennsylvania Line took part in one of the most dangerous threats to the existence of the Continental Army—the mutiny of 1781. As early as April 1778 Washington warned his troops against the inducements to desert offered by the British Army. At that time he addressed a statement to his foreign-born soldiers. He warned them not to be "deluded by the treacherous promises of the enemy, that under pretense of sending deserters from this army passage free to Great Britain or Ireland, there to be set at large," the British intended to confine them on ship-board with a view either to force them into their service as seamen, or transport them as recruits to some garrison.

The British commander, Sir Henry Clinton, persisted in wooing the foreign soldiers. Not only did he create two regiments for them, but, in early 1780, he also attempted to lure soldiers from Washington's army as well as win back deserters from his own army. In January 1781, with their pay a year in arrears and left without proper food and clothing, a group of men in the Pennsylvania Line, stationed at Morristown, New Jersey, rebelled. Clinton sent confidential messengers to them, with offers of amnesty and pay if they would come over to the loyalist side. Commenting on this situation, the nineteenth-century historian

W. E. H. Lecky said: "In the weak condition of the American forces such a body, if it had gone over to the English, might have turned the fortunes of the war."

Generals Butler, Stewart and Moylan, all Irish-born, joined General Anthony Wayne in placating the soldiers. John Sullivan was appointed chairman of a Congressional Committee which provided assistance. In the aftermath of the affair, two persons were hanged: "Macaroni Jack," a leading mutineer whose real name probably was John Maloney, and John Mason, a British agent, who used the alias Murphy. Washington said of the mutineers: "It is extraordinary that these men, however lost to a sense of duty, had so far retained that of honor, as to reject the most advantageous propositions from the enemy."

Another important area of the war with a significant Irish dimension was the struggle in the South. After the capture of Charleston in May 1780, a British force in October headed west across South Carolina, hoping to meet with loyalist Scottish Highlanders. A formation composed largely of Scotch-Irish back countrymen, drawn from areas later named Burke County, Tennessee, and Sullivan County, Georgia, among other places, met and mastered the British body. The battle of King's Mountain, together with the struggle at Cowpens, was instrumental in defeating the British in the Carolinas.

One of the areas of greatest Patriot support in South Carolina, the area around Chester, also had a large Irish population. The leading rebel in the area was General Edward Lacey. His biographer, Maurice Moore, has declared: "In the Chester District of South Carolina, Lacey organized companies and battalions as the fortunes of war demanded and after the manner of partisan leaders, with which he annoyed the Tories greatly, taking many of them prisoners. Of these there were a few in his neighborhood, but not among the Irish. To their eternal honor let it be spoken, none of these York or Chester Irish were Tories, and but few of them took British protection."

The foreign agents of the Continental Congress—Benjamin Franklin, John Adams, John Jay and Silas Deane—received many offers from Irish soldiers in the French forces to serve in the rebel army. One of the Irish officers who came to America was General Thomas Conway, a veteran of thirty years service in France who was born in County Kerry in 1733 and had risen to the rank of colonel by 1772. Apparently an intriguing and ambitious person, he became the center of the "Conway cabal," the only serious threat to Washington's military leadership. In the Autumn of 1777 there was criticism both in the army and Congress of Washington's generalship. One of the congressmen who was in contact with the Irishman was James Duane of New York, the son of an Irish immigrant. Congress appointed Conway Inspector General of the army, but when Washington challenged his critics, they ceased their attacks, and Conway was forced to leave the country.

There was another group of Irishmen who fought on the Patriot side, soldiers of the Irish regiments in the French Army. From the Treaty of Limerick in 1690 to the Revolution of 1789, the French Army included such units (similar regiments in the Spanish Army originated a hundred years before). Following the signing of the Franco-American treaty on 6 February 1778, three Irish regiments (along with a Scottish unit) were among the French forces shipped to the New World. One of these, the O'Brien Regiment, remained in the West Indies, but the other two, the Dillon Regiment, led by Count Arthur Dillon, and the Walsh Regiment of Marine Artillery, arrived on the continent.

This Irish brigade represented about 1,000 troops in the French force of 40,000.

The principal activity of the Irish troops was to serve in the ill-fated siege of Savannah of September–October 1779. An account of that struggle declares that "the Irish Brigade and . . . the Second South Carolina regiment particularly distinguished themselves and suffered most." The latter unit, led by Francis Marion, was drawn from an area of high Irish settlement. Another account declares that Lieutenant Colonel O'Dune of the Irish unit "was drunk. . . . His natural courage and the excitement caused by the wine carried him beyond the proper limits which had been prescribed." His impulsive attack on the enemy resulted in forty fatalities among his men. Two years later, however, the Dillon regiment took part in the final and victorious campaign of the American war of independence—at Yorktown.

Irishmen also took an active part in the political events of the revolution. Eleven of the fifty-six delegates to the first Continental Congress, which met in 1774, were born in Ireland: Thomas Fitzsimmons and Pierce Long in Limerick, Matthew Thornton in Wicklow, Thomas Burke in Galway, Edward Hand in Laois, Pierce Bulter in Carlow, James Smith in Dublin, John Armstrong in Donegal, William Irvine in Fermanagh, James McHenry in Antrim and George Taylor in an unknown location there. Nine of the signatories of the Declaration of Independence were of Irish birth or stock. Three of these were born in Ireland: Matthew Thornton of New Hampshire, James Smith of Pennsylvania and George Taylor, also of Pennsylvania. Those of Irish background were Charles Carroll, whose forebears came from County Laois, Thomas Lynch, Senior of South Carolina, whose grandfather came from Connaught, Thomas McKean, from Ulster, Edward Rutledge, also from Ulster and George Read, from Dublin. The Secretary of the Congress, Charles Thomson, who also signed the document, was born in County Derry in 1730. John Dunlop, a native of Strabane, County Fermanagh, was the printer of the declaration and he also produced the first daily newspaper in the colonies.

The English philosopher John Locke is usually acknowledged as the inspirer of this famous statement of human rights. But some credit might possibly be given to William Molyneux (1656–98), an Irish parliamentarian and friend of Locke. In a book published in 1698 Molyneux declared: "All men are by nature in a State of equality, in respect of Jurisdiction or Dominion: this I take to be a principle in itself so evident that it stands in need of little proof. . . . On this equality in Nature is founded that Right which all men claim, of being free from all subjection to positive laws, till by their own consent they give up that freedom by entering into civil societies for the common benefit of all members thereof." Thomas Jefferson was, perhaps, aware of Molyneux's work, but this is not noted in studies of Jefferson or the document.

Two state governors who were born in Ireland were Thomas Burke and John McKinly. Burke was born in Galway in 1747 and attended Trinity College, Dublin. He settled in North Carolina in 1771, where he named his estate "Tyaquin" after the family seat in Ireland. A combative member of Congress from 1777 to 1781, he was a champion of civil rights and civilian control of the military. In 1781 he became governor of his adopted state where he rallied opposition to the British invasion. Captured, he managed to escape. He declined to seek re-election in 1782 and died the next year.

Doctor John McKinly was born in the north of Ireland in 1721. After qualifying as a physician, he emigrated to Delaware. He had a long political career, first holding public office in 1757. He became President and Commander-in-Chief of Delaware early in 1777 but later that year was captured by the British. He was released a year later and returned to his medical practice in Wilmington.

A notable figure in revolutionary South Carolina was Aedanus Burke. Born in Galway in 1743, Burke was a grandson of an officer in the Irish army of James II in 1689–90. He immigrated to the New World some time before 1769 and studied law. With the outbreak of the independence struggle he became a lieutenant in the 2nd South Carolina regiment. He resigned his commission in 1778 to become a judge in the revolutionary judicial system; his charge to a grand jury set forth the democratic basis of the new state government. When the British occupied Charleston two years later, Burke again took up the sword as a captain of the militia. After the war he served in the state legislature, where he was a strong opponent of the creation of any form of nobility; his study of the subject, *Considerations on the Order of the Cincinnati*, was translated into French by Mirabeau. As a representative of a back country district, Burke opposed the adoption of the Federal Constitution in the state convention on the grounds that it did not securely safeguard the liberties of the people, but he served as a congressman when the new constitution went into effect.

Irishmen made other than military and political contributions to the success of the American cause. In 1780 the Friendly Sons of Saint Patrick of Philadelphia, led by Thomas Fitzsimmons, contributed nearly half a million dollars to a fund to keep the Continental Army in being. The printer John Dunlap alone gave $4,000. Oliver Pollock, a native of Coleraine, County Derry, has been called "the financier of the American Revolution in the West." As the commercial agent for Congress in New Orleans, Pollock was in charge of organizing supplies for Patriot forces up the Mississippi. He spent his own money freely to keep alive the western Patriot efforts while waiting for a negligent Congress to provide funds.

George Washington was supplied a wealth of intelligence about British activities in New York City by an undercover agent with the remarkable name of Hercules Mulligan. Another native of Coleraine, Mulligan was six years old when he immigrated with his family in 1746 to New York. He later became a clothier and was active in opposing British colonial policies. When the revolution broke out, he dropped his Patriot activities and became a valuable agent in the "Culper Ring." When Washington occupied the city at the end of the war, he met with his long-time correspondent.

The Patriot side also had Irish traitors and rascals; none of them, however, were of major importance. In June 1776 the Patriot Army was in New York anxiously anticipating the arrival of the British Army. One soldier who was particularly concerned was Sergeant Thomas Hickey, a member of Washington's bodyguard. As a native of Ireland, he probably had a better understanding than most Americans concerning what would be the consequences of unsuccessful revolt against the British Government. He told other Irishmen that the British would make a victorious descent on the city and "it was best for us Old Countrymen to make our peace before they came or they will kill us all." Hickey was arrested with Private Michael Lynch, also of Washington's bodyguard, and two others, but was the only one put on trial. Convicted of mutiny and sedition, he was sentenced to death and was hanged before a crowd of about 20,000 on Bowery Lane, New York. Arising from this affair there was a movement to exclude the foreign-born from Washington's entourage, but the general dismissed the idea.

Another Irish turncoat was Daniel Hammil, a farmer in Duchess County, New York, who was serving as a brigade major when he was captured by the British along the Hudson. He thereupon proposed to Sir Henry Clinton a plan to get Irishmen to desert the Continental Army. Caught in this activity in 1779, he managed to escape and went to England. There was also John Connolly, a nephew of George Croghan, the Irish-born Indian trader. Connolly was born in Pennsylvania and served as a captain in the Virginia militia. In exchange for a land grant, he offered the royal governor of Virginia a plan to attack the Patriot stronghold of Pittsburgh. He too was captured, and after a long spell in prison was allowed to leave the country.

At the very beginning of the conflict, on 7 December 1775, a group of Irish merchants in Boston formed the Loyal Irish Volunteers. Their leader was James Forrest, the "Irish Infant" who was involved in the aftermath of the Boston Massacre. Forrest emigrated from Ireland in 1761 and was a wealthy man by the eve of the Revolution. The Volunteers, composed of five officers and ninety-seven men, served on guard duty during the siege of Boston and left with the British in 1776, to be heard of no more. Forrest lost all his property and was later captured and imprisoned by the Patriots.

The man in charge of supervising the removal of British property and stores during the evacuation of Boston was Crean Brush. Born in Dublin in 1725, he came to New York in 1761 where he practiced law and served in the colonial assembly. His stripping activities in Boston made him a hated man in Patriot ranks. He failed to get all his shipment away in time and was himself captured on the way to Nova Scotia. Managing to escape, he returned to New York and died there two years later. He was the model for the title character in John Trumbull's *McFingal*, a satirical work of great fame in the post-revolutionary period.

There also was "Bloody Bill" Cunningham, who arrived from Ireland in 1774 and served as provost marshal in Boston, Philadelphia and New York. During his period of authority, several thousand Patriot prisoners died in captivity. Benson Lossing refers to him as "that infamously cruel scoundrel, Captain Cunningham, a burly, ill-natured Irishman of sixty years, whose conduct as provost marshal . . . has connected his name with all that is detestable" (*Pictorial Field Book of the Revolution*, II).

When Sir Henry Clinton became Commander-in-Chief of British forces in America in May 1778, he was of the opinion that one of the things wrong with his army was that it contained too high a proportion of Irishmen, among both officers and men. As a former governor of Limerick, he could claim to know Ireland, and he believed that "education as it stands at present in Ireland is inimical to all subordination." Within a few months of assuming command, however, Clinton decided he wanted more, not fewer, Irish soldiers. He did this by establishing in June 1778 two new regiments, the Roman Catholic Volunteers and the Volunteers of Ireland, with both regiments to be stocked by deserters. The Roman Catholic regiment was commanded by Lieutenant Colonel Alfred Clifton and had officers with names of Lynch, Hanley, O'Neil, Kane, McKinnon and McAvoy. The unit gained only about 180 troops and in October 1778 was merged with the Volunteers of Ireland.

To command the Volunteers of Ireland Clinton appointed a favorite of his, Lord Francis Rawdon, a twenty-five-year-old Anglo-Irish nobleman. As in the case of the Roman Catholic regiment, the British sought recruits, first in Philadelphia and then in New York. The unit reached a peak strength of about 300 men, apparently all deserters from the Continental Army.

In May 1780 the Volunteers were sent to South Carolina to join Cornwallis. The British general dispatched Rawdon's regiment to the settlement of Waxhaw in the belief that "as it was an Irish corps it would be received with a better temper by the settlers of that district who were universally Irish and universally disaffected." Instead of gaining recruits, Rawdon found he was losing soldiers. In response, he issued the following offer: "I will give the inhabitants ten guineas for the head of any deserter belonging to The Volunteers of Ireland and five guineas only if they bring him in alive." The Volunteers took part in the British victory at Camden, South Carolina, on 16 August 1780. What remained of the regiment was shipped to Ireland when the war ended in 1782 and was disbanded two years later.

There were many Irishmen serving in the British Army at the time of the revolution, and they were among the 50,000 troops sent to quell the rebellion. There were two Irish regiments in Boston in 1770, at the time of the massacre. Seven regiments were sent from Ireland in 1775–76. One of these was the 5th Regiment of Foot, known as the Irish regiment and led by Colonel Daniel O'Brien, Viscount of Clare. This unit fought in eleven battles, including Lexington, Concord and Bunker Hill. The Queen's Rangers served in America from 1777 to 1781; of its 484 soldiers, 121 were Irish-born or of Irish descent. Seven Irish regiments took part in the defense of Quebec in December 1776. The same month the Patriot leader Joseph Warren informed the Council of Massachusetts that a body of seventy Irish prisoners being held at Plymouth were very troublesome and, further, were a potential danger, should they join forces with the local Tories.

The presence of many Irishmen in the British Army can also be seen by the large number of them who deserted that force. Once the revolution had begun, British attempts to recruit soldiers in Ireland met with little success. Among those already in the army there was strong opposition to fighting the Americans. Arthur Lee, one of the American diplomatic agents in Europe, wrote to Washington on 15 June 1777: "Every man of a regiment raised in Ireland last year obliged them to ship him off tied and bound, and most certainly they will desert more than any troops whatsoever."

On the other hand, Irish people also figured among the exiled loyalists who sought compensation from the British Government. Of those claiming losses, there were 280 Irishmen, 470 Scots, 120 Americans and only 290 Englishmen. Almost all of the Irish involved were persons of considerable wealth, which undoubtedly was the reason they opposed the sweeping change of government.

A figure of obvious Irish extraction played a prominent part in the last major scene of the Revolution. With General Cornwallis claiming illness, Brigadier General Charles O'Hara was given the task of surrendering the British force at Yorktown to Washington in October 1781. Of illegitimate birth, O'Hara was born in England in 1740. His grandfather had been born in County Mayo, Ireland, about 1640, rose to be a general and was made Baron Tirawley (after an area of his home county). O'Hara's father was also a soldier as well as a governor and diplomat. At the capitulation ceremony a band played *The World Turned Upside Down*. Standing in the ranks of the victorious Franco-American army, members of the Dillon Regiment observed the surrender.

In his study, *Ireland, Irishmen and Revolutionary America, 1760–1820*, David N. Doyle has noted that as a result of the successful independence struggle, Irish people gained for themselves and others civil equality, religious freedom and representative government. This enhanced status was earned, not given.

William B. Clark, *Gallant Jack Barry, 1745–1803* (New York, 1938).

David N. Doyle, *Ireland, Irishmen and Revolutionary America, 1760–1820* (Dublin, 1981).

Leroy V. Eid, "The Colonial Scotch-Irish: A View Accepted Too Readily," *Éire-Ireland* (Winter 1986).

Arthur Mitchell, ed., *Ireland and Irishmen in the American War of Independence: Some Historical Documents* (Dublin, 1976).

———, "Irishmen and the American Revolution," *Capuchin Annual* (Dublin, 1977).

Frank Monaghan, "Stephan Moylan in the American Revolution," *Studies; An Irish Quarterly Review* (Dublin, 1930): xxiv.

W. S. Murphy, "The Irish Brigade of France at the Siege of Savannah, 1779," *Irish Sword: The Journal of the Military History Society of Ireland* (Summer 1955 and Winter 1957).

Michael J. O'Brien, *A Hidden Phase of American History; Ireland's Part in America's Struggle for Liberty* (New York, 1919; reprinted by Genealogical Publishing, Baltimore, 1973).

———, *The Irish at Bunker Hill* (New York, 1968).

David Ramsay, *History of the American Revolution*, 2 vols. (London, 1793).

Oliver Snoddy, "The Volunteers of Ireland," *Irish Sword: The Journal of the Military History Society of Ireland* (Winter 1965).

ARTHUR MITCHELL

## AMERICAN WEST AND IRISH SOLDIERS

By the mid-nineteenth century the American West stretched from the Mississippi River to the Pacific Ocean. The final link securing the political perimeter of the United States was the Gadsden Purchase acquired from Mexico in 1853. However, while these national borders were becoming finalized the vast interior was fragmenting—into battle zones—each the object of a deadly struggle. Throughout the West, Native inhabitants defended their lands, resources, and peoples against the ambitions of various intruders including settlers, miners, traders, and corporations (railroads). Although the intruders battled Indians for control of the West, the United States Army handled the fighting. Most of the warfare occurred between 1850 and 1890 and involved a considerable number of Irish participating as U.S. Army regulars.

While the Irish presence within the Army reflects the limited economic choices available to Irish immigrants, it also reveals the widespread reluctance of native-born Americans to enlist both before and after the Civil War. Irish immigrants presented recruiters with abundant numbers of prospects whose cultural fabric ascribed considerable status to military service, a respect not especially prevalent among nineteenth-century Americans, excepting the Civil War years. Furthermore, the realization that a recruit would be among his own people as a soldier was comforting to many immigrants especially those not interested in farming and disdainful of an urban existence. The army provided food, clothing, and shelter while offering Irish "exiles" an opportunity to achieve personal dignity via military service. One Irish soldier serving in Wyoming Territory in 1869 enthusiastically explained: "A man (in the) United States Army can learn a good deal in his turn and will see all sorts of work done, more especially in the western country (for) he must be a carpenter, mason, painter, clerk, and glazier and a good soldier to boot."

This observation reflects the responsibilities placed on frontier soldiers who often constructed the very forts they garrisoned. However, these words also suggest the investment many Irish made in the West. Military service was only the first step that transformed western landscapes from loosely defined aboriginal homelands into territories and states. Many Irish veterans remained or returned to the West after their enlistments where they invited or welcomed new Irish immigrants to the towns and settlements their military service made possible.

Published studies on the nineteenth-century U.S. Army generally estimate that Irish-born recruits constituted between twenty and twenty-five percent of personnel from the 1850s until the 1880s. Furthermore, these studies find Irish to be a significant presence among non-commissioned officers serving military units as corporals and sergeants. Only among the commissioned ranks are Irish a conspicuous minority. Nearly all lieutenants, captains, majors, colonels and generals in the nineteenth-century army began their careers as Military Academy appointees and few Irish attended West Point. However, nearly two hundred Irish officers served in the post-Civil War Army, almost all receiving their commissions before or during the Civil War.

### THE PRE–CIVIL WAR WEST

The discovery of gold in California greatly accelerated the Army's mission to establish federal authority in the West. Posts were situated so as to afford protection to settlers and travelers. Edward Coffman explains that recruiters in the nineteenth century "depended on cities of the Northeast" to fill the ranks and this insured that unemployed immigrants became soldiers. After a brief training period the Army assigned recruits to areas where Indian resistance was greatest. By 1850 the American West was home to over sixty military posts and thousands of Irish soldiers became their occupants. Although the regular Army never assigned soldiers according to ethnicity, the sheer numbers of Irish recruits insured that garrisons in Arizona, New Mexico, Oregon, Minnesota, and Texas accumulated high concentrations of Irish soldiers.

Nebraska Territory, organized in 1854, encompassed over 350,000 square miles and was home to garrisons located at Fort Larmie (WY), Fort Randall (SD), and Fort Kearny (NB). Statistics from the 1860 census show that 45 percent of the nearly 700 men spread among these three forts were born in Ireland. Furthermore, Irish stationed in this territory were nearly equally distributed among companies of cavalry, infantry, and artillery. For example 42 percent of dragoons (cavalry) stationed at Fort Kearny and Fort Larmie were Irish. The infantry was similarly staffed. At these same forts there was a total of 284 infantry of which 45 percent were Irish-born. A report prepared by Paul Riley based on the 1860 census discovered that all of the sergeants, three of the nine corporals, and fifty-seven percent of the infantry stationed at Fort Kearny were Irish-born. He also found that quite often the non-military personnel working at these forts reflected the diversity of the command especially at "Fort Randall where almost all of the workers were Irish or foreign-born." Not all Western posts enjoyed such high percentages of Irish, but the military played a significant role in delivering Irish to Western territories where many remained after their enlistments.

### THE CIVIL WAR WEST

The Civil War brought dramatic changes to the Western command as the Army reassigned most units to the East. Taking their places were numerous volunteer armies drawn from the western civilian population. Except for units formed in California, Oregon, and Nevada, native-born Americans staffed these armies. An infantry column formed in California in late 1861 recruited soldiers from mining regions in Tuolumne and Calaveras counties, each home to a considerable Irish population. This troop became the Third Infantry California Volunteers filled by some 750 soldiers under the able command of Kerry-born Patrick Edward Connor. Hoping to engage rebels in the East, General Connor's Infantry never advanced farther then Salt Lake City. His troops did battle Shoshoni and Utes during the Civil War years and also expended considerable energy establishing mining districts in Utah and Idaho. Remembered as the "Father of Utah Mining" Connor's influence helped establish settlements like Park City, Utah, that became heavily populated by Irish in the post-Civil War years.

In 1865, General Connor led a military expedition into Wyoming's Powder River country. His command included several regiments of U.S. Volunteers or "Galvanized Yankees." The Army recruited these Volunteers from Civil War prison camps and these included many Irish ex-Confederates who exchanged their confinement for service in the West. These U.S. Volunteers also fought Cheyennes at the Battle of Platte Bridge and protected surveying parties of the Union Pacific Railroad. Irish-born officers in the U.S. Volunteers included Patrick Caraher who commanded the Second Regiment and Washington Matthews, an assistant surgeon in the Forth Regiment. Matthews gained notoriety after his Army service as a celebrated ethnologist working with Indians in the American Southwest.

## Post–Civil War West

Irish soldiers joining or remaining in the regular Army after the Civil War either found themselves serving in the South or reassigned to the West. As the Army downsized in the postwar period the percentage of Irish soldiers increased and reached its highest totals by the mid-1870s. Although Irish immigrants continued to enlist for the remainder of the century they competed with Germans, English, and Swedes for positions. Irish troops served in all of the cavalry, infantry, and artillery units except those reserved for African-American soldiers. However, the Ninth and Tenth Cavalry or "Buffalo Soldiers" were staffed with Irish-born officers. Irish also served as surgeons, musicians, in the quartermaster department, as clerks, and in the Signal Corps. On those occasions when the Federal Government ordered the Army to intervene in labor disputes, Irish soldiers sometimes faced Irish workers as adversaries. Although the total number of Irish soldiers in the post-Civil War Army is unknown, thousands made the Army their career and either died as soldiers or as veterans spending their declining years at government Soldier and Sailor homes. Many Irish soldiers regarded the Army as a vehicle that transported them to the American West. Although some deserted their units, the majority who served a five-year enlistment were honorably discharged and eventually settled in Western towns and cities.

## Social, Cultural, and Spiritual Life on Post

Although there were more then two-hundred engagements between the U.S. Army and Indian adversaries from 1865 to 1890, a soldier spent most of his enlistment in garrison. Since the men followed the same basic routines each day, Irish soldiers expressed their cultural identity during free time or holidays. Be-

cause most forts were both small and isolated, the men relied upon themselves for entertainment. Irish fiddle players and others with musical abilities played informally or at post dances helping to convey Irish folk music to the American West. Most posts also had choral groups who performed Irish songs and ballads on important occasions like St. Patrick's Day. Theatrical troupes joined the singers each spring and staged plays commemorating the Irish patron or the life of Robert Emmett whose birthday falls in early March. Horse races in early summer reminded one soldier of the "Limerick Races" back home.

The lack of religious services was a sore point with many Irish-Catholic soldiers and some complained about being marched to Protestant services by their commanders. Earl Stover's study of Army Chaplains explains that although Catholics were a majority in the post-bellum Army, "no Catholic Priest was appointed until 1872, and only seven were appointed between then and the Spanish-American War." In lieu of Easter Mass in 1868, the officers at one Dakota fort provided eggs to their troops, "the majority of whom are Irish . . . (so they could) keep up the time honored (sic) custom, of eating eggs on Easter Sunday Morning." Catholic soldiers receiving sacraments between 1870 and 1890 obtained them from traveling missionaries or at a Catholic parish located in a larger settlement. Irish-Protestant soldiers found services familiar to them in the Army and sometimes enjoyed the guidance of Irish-born Protestant chaplains. Chaplain James Laverty was born in Ireland and served the Twenty-Fourth Infantry at Fort Supply, Oklahoma, between 1876 and 1886. William Larkin and Robert McWatty were also Irish-born Protestant chaplains who served in the American West.

The principal links between soldiers and the homeland were letters and newspapers. Soldiers stationed at the larger posts or near the railroads were blessed with fairly regular and dependable postal service and enjoyed access to a variety of newspapers. Irish papers like *The Nation* (Dublin), *Flag of Ireland* (Ireland), and *Cork Telegraph* (Ireland) could be found in the West along with Irish-American issues of the *Boston Pilot* (Boston), *Western Celt* (St. Louis), *Freemans Journal* (New York), *Western Watchman* (St. Louis), *Northwestern Chronicle* (St. Paul), and American mainstream papers like the *Chicago Times*. Galway-born journalist John Finerty accompanied several military expeditions in the northern plains during the 1870s for the *Chicago Times*. Not only was the large Irish readership in Chicago able to follow the exploits of Irish soldiers, but the men themselves often received an issue shortly after it was published. Finerty's stories became immensely popular among the Irish in Chicago and even served to attract Irish there into the Army.

## Distinguished Service

Much like their brethren in the Civil War, Irish soldiers in the West garnered numerous commendations for bravery and service. Awards such as the *Distinguished Service Medal, Certificate of Merit, Indian Wars Campaign Medal,* and *Legislative Resolutions* were widely distributed among Irish soldiers. However, the list of the *Congressional Medal of Honor Winners* (MOH) is especially impressive. John M. Carroll located seventy-three Irish-born soldiers who received this award for service during the Indian Wars. Two Army units contained especially large numbers of MOH winners. Nine of the forty-six MOH winners in the Fifth U.S. Infantry were Irish. One member, Henry Hogan of County Clare, won the award twice. He received one medal for his bravery at Bear Paw Mountain, Montana, where under heavy fire he carried an injured lieutenant from the battlefield. Hogan's other award was for gallantry at Cedar Creek, Montana. The Indians encountered at Cedar Creek were present when Custer's command, including over forty Irish, was destroyed the previous summer. Irish soldiers fighting at Cedar Creek were especially courageous and eleven received the Medal of Honor for gallantry. Another group harboring an unusually high number of Irish MOH winners was the Eighth Cavalry who served principally in the Southwest. This unit had seventeen Irish MOH winners, most gaining the honor battling Apaches in Arizona Territory.

Alexander D. Brown, *The Galvanized Yankees* (Urbana, 1963).

John M. Carroll, ed., *The Medal of Honor: Its History and Recipients for the Indian Wars* (Bryan, TX, 1979).

Edward M.Coffman, *The Old Army: A Portrait of the American Army in Peacetime, 1784–1898* (New York, 1986).

Francis B. Heitman, *Historical Register and Dictionary of the United States Army, from its Organization, September 29, 1789, to March 1903* (Washington, D.C., 1903).

John F. Finerty, *War-Path and Bivouac* (Norman, Ok., 1961).

Jack D. Foner, *The United States Soldiers Between Two Wars: Army Life and Reforms, 1865–1898* (Humanities Press, 1970).

Brigham D. Madsen, *Glory Hunter: A Biography of Patrick Edward Connor* (Salt Lake City, 1990).

Don Rickey, *Forty Miles a Day on Beans and Hay: The Enlisted Soldier Fighting the Indian Wars* (Norman Ok., 1963).

Earl F. Stover, *Up From Handymen: The United States Army Chaplaincy, 1865–1920* (Washington, D.C., 1977).

Robert Utley, *Frontier Regulars: The United States Army and the Indian, 1866–1891*. The Wars of the United States (New York, 1973).

KEVIN STANTON

## AMERICA'S FIRST IRISH VISITOR

From the early years of the 16th century, Irishmen in the service of Spain could be found in the Caribbean and in South America. And Irish ships worked the Newfoundland fishing grounds as early as the 1530s. But it was not until 1584, when a visiting seaman named Richard Butler landed in what is now North Carolina, that the first historically documented person of Irish birth set foot on the soil of the present-day United States.

Richard Butler was born in Clonmel, Co. Tipperary, during the 1560s. About the age of ten, he sailed from the port of Waterford for London, where he entered the service of Walter Raleigh as a page. Raleigh, who would eventually own a 42,000-acre Irish estate in Waterford and Cork and receive a knighthood from his patron Queen Elizabeth I, was then an ambitious but impoverished young gentleman at the Elizabethan Court. By 1578, he was busy planning English colonies in North America under the guidance of his elder half-brother, Sir Humphrey Gilbert, a ruthless veteran of Elizabeth's Irish wars.

Gilbert was lost at sea in 1583 while returning from a voyage to Newfoundland. In April 1584, Raleigh dispatched his own expedition, under Captains Philip Amadas and Arthur Barlowe, to explore the North American coast. Among the crewmen under Amadas was Richard Butler, who held the rank of corporal during the voyage. On July 4, 1584, Barlowe and Amadas sighted the barrier islands now known as North Carolina's Outer Banks. Later, in a deposition given in Spain around 1593, Butler recalled that they disembarked first "at a place called Ococa" and then

A late sixteenth-century ship

farther to the north at a place "known to the English as Puerto Fernando, and to the savages as Ataurras." Although time and tides have altered the coastal geography, historian David B. Quinn estimates that Butler's landing places fall respectively in the area of modern Ocracoke Island and near the modern Oregon Inlet, at the northern end of Hatteras Island. Beyond the inlet, in the sheltered waters of Pamlico Sound, Raleigh's explorers found Roanoke Island. They made friendly contact with the local Indians and took two of them, Manteo and Wanchese, back to England in September 1584.

In April 1585, Butler embarked on a second American voyage under Raleigh's cousin Sir Richard Grenville. Raleigh, Butler recalled, had requested his presence "in view of his experience in those parts." In Virginia, as Raleigh named the newly discovered American territory, Butler spent a week exploring the mainland in the company of Indians. The Irishman also said he understood some of their language, having learned Algonquian words from Manteo and Wanchese. In August 1585, Butler returned to England with Grenville, leaving a colony of 108 men at Roanoke under Ralph Lane as governor.

There is no evidence that Butler ever returned to America. By 1587, he was captain of a privateer owned by Raleigh, preying on Portuguese and Spanish shipping. In 1592, Butler secretly landed on the Portuguese coast. He was arrested and imprisoned, first in Lisbon and later in Madrid, as a suspected English spy and possible Protestant heretic. But the prisoner convinced his interrogators that he was Catholic by reciting the Creed in Latin, and made his confession to Fr. James Archer, an Irish Jesuit from Kilkenny. And Butler confused the authorities by claiming to be a defector, bearing valuable information about an English spy in the Spanish administration then ruling Portugal. After four years of legal arguments, a commission of judges in Madrid, nevertheless, recommended that Butler be hanged. But the Irishman's luck had not yet run out. In December 1596, King Philip II of Spain personally commuted Butler's death sentence to an unspecified term as a galley slave. Having survived this horrific ordeal for twelve years, Butler was released in 1608 during a thaw in Anglo-Spanish hostilities. His later history is unknown.

*See* Roanoke Island

Martin A.S. Hume, ed., *Calendar of Letters and State Papers Relating to English Affairs, preserved in, or originally belonging to, the Archives of Simancas,* Volume IV, *Elizabeth, 1587–1603* (London, 1899).

David B. Quinn, ed., *New American World: A Documentary History of North America to 1612,* Vol. III, *English Plans for North America. The Roanoke Voyages. New England Ventures* (New York, 1979).

David B. Quinn, *England and the Discovery of America, 1481–1620* (New York, 1974).

Michael E. Williams, "Alarms and Excursions in Lisbon under Castilian Domination: The Case of Captain Richard Butler," in *Portuguese Studies,* Vol. 6 (London, 1990).

BRIAN McGINN

## ANCIENT ORDER OF HIBERNIANS

The Ancient Order of Hibernians is the largest fraternal order in the United States composed of individuals of Irish descent. Membership is limited to individuals who can trace their ancestry to Ireland and who are practicing Roman Catholics. Branches, called divisions, are located in more than thirty states as well as Canada.

The earliest origins of the Ancient Order of Hibernians are traced to Ireland in the year 1565 when Roman Catholics first combined to actively defend the rights of their religion in the face of increasing repression and persecution by the English monarchy. Owing to frequent military and political setbacks of the Irish Catholic cause, a largely secret movement developed in Ireland, a movement which became increasingly active after the collapse of the efforts of Rory O'More and the Catholic Confederation of 1641. Under various names such as the Defenders, the Terry Alts, the Ribbonmen or the Whiteboys, these largely rural secret societies acted to defend the interests of the Catholic cause and Irish nationality for more than two centuries thereafter. Ireland by the 18th-century was a country under the total control of the occupying British military and the common people of Ireland were almost powerless to combat the many excesses directed against them. During the penal times when the sacrifice of the Mass was forbidden, the members acted as watchmen and guardians for the priests who were often forced to perform their duties in the open countryside. Resistance by the Irish secret societies was most often relegated to local actions, often under the cover of night, which were carried out against the largely alien class of land owners who controlled virtually all real property in the country.

The exact nature of the secret societies and their relationship with one another will probably never be known. Because of the inherent dangers involved, the branches were kept small and knowledge of their activities confined to a small number. It was only after Irish emigrants had settled in various parts of England and Scotland early in the 19th century that a hint of a hidden national organization became apparent for the first time. A governing body headquartered in Britain, which called itself the St. Patrick's Fraternal Society, surfaced in public for the first time about 1825. It was this group which issued a charter in 1836 to a group of Irishmen in New York, but there was no universal name for the order at this time in Ireland and Britain. It was not until 1903 that the name Ancient Order of Hibernians was universally adapted. The charter issued to the New Yorkers was signed by fourteen representatives of the order in England, Scotland and Ireland. The Irish signers were all located in the Ulster counties and the northern half of the country where land agitation was then at its height.

The New York group met at St. James Church on the Lower East Side of the city and shortly afterward another branch was organized in the Pennsylvania coal country, but a cloak of secrecy surrounded the early American years. It is apparent that like the organization in Ireland and Britain, the society existed under different names and it makes it difficult to trace the organization's descent. Tradition links it with the defense of Old St. Patrick's Cathedral from nativist mobs in 1844, but the name Ancient Order of Hibernians does not seem to have been used before 1851. Prior to this in 1850, the organization used the name "Friendly Sons of Erin" or "Ancient Friendly Sons of Erin," but there were probably other titles for the society used during the secret years.

The A.O.H. suffered the attacks of the anti-Catholic elements which in the 1850s were contending for power and influence in American government. On several occasions, including the infamous attack on the Hibernians while they participated in the Fourth of July parade in New York in 1853, the society came to physical confrontation with their enemies. Again in 1854 members of the Ancient Order of Hibernians helped defend Old St. Patrick's Cathedral from surging mobs of Know-Nothings.

The main focus of the Order, however, at this time was beneficial. The monthly dues established a rudimentary insurance fund which provided for sick and death benefits for members (typically one dollar per work day) and a death benefit (commonly one hundred dollars) for their spouses. This beneficial role was one which they proudly advertised by banners in 19th-century parades which bore the slogan "We Bury our Dead and Visit Our Sick." The benefit provisions remained important up to World War I when the cut-off in emigration from Ireland, the aging of its membership, the loss of young members to the military and the disastrous influenza epidemic of 1918–19 combined to wreck many of the small division treasuries and cause many individual branches to fail. The benefits provisions up to this time also kept the eligibility for membership confined to those under forty. Consequently, the public displays of young marching men created a very favorable appearance up to the turn of the century.

It was the St. Patrick's Day Parade in New York and in hundreds of other cities and small towns that put the A.O.H. in the public mind. It was an obligation of membership to celebrate the day by participating in March 17th processions and consequently by the 1870s the A.O.H. was the dominant or sole organizer of the St. Patrick's Day parade in most localities across the United States. The occasion became as much a demonstration of Irish ethnic and political strength as the commemoration of a feast day since the 19th-century parade route almost invariably included a formal review of the neat and martial ranks at the local city hall by the mayor and city leaders.

Before the civil war the A.O.H. was largely confined to the eastern seaboard states with the bulk of its membership in the Northeast. Thousands of members, including Captain James Saunders, its first National Director ( the original name for national president), who served bravely with the New York Irish 69th Regiment, loyally entered the Union ranks. Entire A.O.H.

divisions in Pennsylvania and New York were absorbed into the military. Officers of the order conducted an active campaign to recruit new immigrants directly from the arriving immigrant ships. Hibernians in the south, although in far fewer numbers, went into the Confederate armies.

By the 1870s the organization was well represented from coast to coast. The bulk of its membership came from laborers who were engaged in occupations like railroading or mining. Their work often made them live in the most remote locations. Irish farming communities in the mid-west and west also formed divisions, but organizing in rural areas sometimes became difficult due to the distances involved. A network of Hibernian divisions composed of miners stretched from the coal mines of Pennsylvania, West Virginia and southern Ohio to the iron mines of the upper peninsula of Michigan and across the country to the copper mines of Montana and the gold mines of Colorado, Nevada and California. Most mining communities in hundreds of locations in between usually had at least one division of the A.O.H. The cities, however, contained the bulk of A.O.H. membership and it was here that the goal became the organization of at least one branch in each Catholic parish. Hundreds of divisions soon flourished in each of the metropolitan regions of New York, Philadelphia, Boston and Chicago alone.

Although membership remained heavily Irish-born until World War I, the earliest surviving constitution of 1871 allowed membership to anyone who was of Irish descent and Roman Catholic parentage. This provision was liberalized to include anyone of Irish descent to an unspecified degree in 1884. This change and a number of other jurisdictional controversies resulted in the defection of a faction called the Board of Erin A.O.H., which was centered mainly in New York and several of the larger cities. The Hibernians were not reunited until 1898.

Support for efforts aimed at the liberation of Ireland gained support from the A.O.H. at an early date. The Fenians, the organization aiming to free Ireland by military force, received financial and moral backing from the order and most of the leaders like Michael Doheny, John O'Mahony, Michael Corcoran and Joseph Denieffe were both Fenians and Hibernians. At one point in 1865 the New York A.O.H. pledged to supply a battery of artillery for the Fenian army for what many believed to be only a question of time when well-armed and veteran Irish-American soldiers returned to the old country to free it by force of arms. All the efforts of the Irish-American militants came to little, and for most of the period from the rise of Parnell up to World War I, the majority of the leaders of the A.O.H. backed the more moderate figures in Irish nationalism who stressed the issues of land reform and home rule for Ireland. Irish members sitting in the House of Parliament in London were consequently frequent visitors to A.O.H. gatherings and meetings throughout the 19th and early 20th centuries.

But militancy was never completely out of sight and various plans to win Irish freedom by force received financial and moral backing from time to time. A long line of exiled ex-prisoner Irish revolutionaries were accorded a similarly warm reception as had the members of parliament. The funding in 1900 of an "Irish Ambulance Fund" by the A.O.H. during the Boer War, a fundraising effort which sent volunteer members to aid the resistance to the British in South Africa, was typical of the readiness to adopt a physical force solution to the Irish question should the opportunity present itself. Several members traveled to South Africa and took up arms against the British during that struggle.

The Hibernians maintained their own military wing called the Hibernian Rifles for many years. Just before World War I, these trained soldiers numbered at their highest strength about 5,000 men. It was hoped that the occasion might arise when an insurrection might take place in Ireland and volunteers from America could be sent to the old country. The Easter Rising of 1916 was over before anything could be done, but a small unit called the Irish-American Alliance, composed of Dublin Irishmen affiliated with the American A.O.H., participated in the rebellion.

A show-down between the militants and moderates took place at the A.O.H. National Convention in 1906 when Matthew Cummings of Boston, a member of the secret Irish revolutionary society Clan na Gael, was elected national president for the first of two one-year terms. He represented the viewpoint that Ireland's problems could only be solved by complete independence from Britain which would in all probability be gained by force of arms. The seemingly impending implementation of Home Rule for Ireland strengthened the moderate wing for a time after Cummings, but by 1916 and the Easter Rising the militant pro-independence for Ireland faction had finally won complete control of the order.

The relationship of the A.O.H. in its early years with the Roman Catholic hierarchy and some clergymen of the church was often a stormy one. The campaign of the mine bosses and many newspapers to link the crimes of the so-called "Molly Maguires" in the Pennsylvania coal fields to the Ancient Order of Hibernians resulted in the placement of the Order under a ban in many dioceses in the late 1870s. The council of bishops which conferred in Baltimore in 1884 helped relieve some of the pressure on the A.O.H. after the organization was assured by Archbishop Feehan of Chicago that he could find nothing objectionable in the rules and practices of the Order. Two years later Cardinal Gibbons of Baltimore gave his endorsement of the Hibernians by noting that he could see a great deal in the society which was "meritorious and commendable."

In 1886 the A.O.H. numbered just 53,000 members, but in the following twenty years it grew steadily. By 1894 it had reached almost 94,000 members and by 1908 it reached its all time high of 132,173. The Ladies Auxiliary of the A.O.H., formally chartered in 1894, counted 55,000 members in 1908. Combined with juvenile divisions and the military wing, the grand total reached 195,173 members.

Conditions for growth rapidly changed however. After years of falling Irish immigration, the passing of thousands of older immigrants who had made up the "famine" generation, a world war, an economic depression and changing social patterns, the membership of the men's Hibernian divisions fell to less than 30,000 by 1933. Since that time the membership stabilized as the organization drew from the large pool of eligible Irish-Americans in lieu of immigrants. The old immigrant neighborhoods of the cities declined and with them many of the older divisions of the Ancient Order of Hibernians, but the suburbs became the most fertile ground for membership as thousands of new members were added and new Hibernian halls were dedicated in these areas. Thanks to the continuing diaspora of Irish across the country, a re-birth of the A.O.H. has again taken place in several communities in the South and West where divisions have not existed in over seventy-five years. The modern organization is now composed overwhelmingly of the descendants of Irish-born immigrants many of whom can trace their ancestry back over many generations.

The Ancient Order of Hibernians strongly continues a tradition of charity in times of need, not only for its members and their families, but in periods of local or national disaster for all who need help regardless of ethnic origin. Frequently, the various units of the organization are involved in holding benefit functions for individuals and families who have suffered serious medical or financial hardship and have resulted in millions being raised by methods as simple as the neighborhood social or dance. Consistently, the Order has maintained a long history of donations to Catholic charities and causes ranging from donations for the up-keep of individual parishes and schools in both the U.S. and Ireland, and has helped to support missionary and charity programs around the world.

Ireland is still the object of many of the charitable endeavors of the A.O.H., but unlike the response to the harsh conditions in the old country of a generation or two ago, most of the donations and fund-raising efforts are made in the spirit of simple good will between the millions of Irish in the new world and those in the old. Northern Ireland, however, occupies a separate place in the minds of many Hibernians. Fund-raising has followed the long pattern of support for Irish nationalism which stretches back to the foundation of the Order in America. One of the most active committees of the Order, the Freedom for All Ireland Committee, functions at division, county board, state board and national board levels providing information to the membership on developments in Ireland and the progress of its various fund-raising drives.

The program of the modern A.O.H. surprisingly resembles the activities of a century ago. It still struggles to maintain a balance of religious and ethnic themes, neither exclusively Catholic nor exclusively Irish. As direct links to Ireland become somewhat more remote, it has had to assume a more educative role to familiarize many of the newer members with the social and cultural traditions of Ireland. The well-established structure of the order and the regular neighborhood meetings provide not only a place to socialize with people of common interest and background, but to connect to the larger community of Americans of Irish descent and its myriad of activities.

James J. Bergin, *History of the Ancient Order of Hibernians* (Dublin, 1910).

John O'Dea, *History of the Ancient Order of Hibernians and Ladies Auxiliary,* vols. I, II, III (National Board, Philadelphia, 1923).

John O'Dea, "History of the A.O.H. of New York City," *Irish World* (July 10, 1915).

George R. Reilly, *Hibernians on the March* (San Francisco, 1948).

John T. Ridge, *Erin's Sons in America: The Ancient Order of Hibernians* (Ancient Order of Hibernians 150th Anniversary Committee, New York, 1986).

JOHN RIDGE

## ANTHRACITE MINING

### Background

Anthracite (hard coal) is found in the northeastern corner of Pennsylvania. There, an area of roughly 484 square miles contains most of the known deposits of anthracite coal. It is located in three fields running northeasterly. Anthracite should not be confused with bituminous (soft coal) which, in Pennsylvania, is located in the central and western parts of the state. It is also found in a number of other states unlike anthracite. Where bituminous coal is usually found in veins which are relatively flat and conducive to mechanized mining, anthracite veins undulate deep below the surface and are normally more costly to mine.

Anthracite was recognized for its economic potential in the 1830s by Philadelphian Henry Charles Carey, son of a (very literate) Irish immigrant, Matthew Carey of Dublin, who escaped to America in 1784 and prospered as a book publisher in Philadelphia. Henry Carey took over the publishing business when his father retired in 1822 and became not only wealthy, but also one of the leading American economists of the nineteenth century. Retiring from the publishing business in 1835, and aware of the possibilities of anthracite, he invested heavily in land where that mineral is to be found. He foresaw an industrial revolution in the United States in which anthracite coal would play a key role. In the 1830s, when it was discovered that anthracite coal could be used in smelting iron ore more efficiently and cheaply than the charcoal method which uses wood, he was further convinced of Pennsylvania's future as the leader of industrial development in America.

Through the influence of Carey and his associates coal operators began to come to the anthracite region. They were drawn by what they thought would be a highly profitable business. Native Americans, English mining engineers, miners from Britain, Wales and Scotland came with the same optimistic hopes. A few Irish miners, who had learned the trade in Wales or Scotland, also arrived. The industry grew, towns expanded and coal patches were established near outlying collieries.

### Irish Arrive

At the time of the Great Famine in the second half of the 1840s, substantial numbers of Irish refugees found their way to the anthracite region for work. Because there are very few mines in Ireland, nearly all of them had no previous experience in mining. As greenhorns, Catholics, and very poor, they were subjected to pronounced prejudice by earlier entrants to these communities.

The work of mining was done by two main groups, contract miners and mine laborers or helpers. Contact miners learned the skills needed to do the highly dangerous work of underground coal extraction. While the contract miner performed the skilled work, drilling, blasting, and so forth, the laborer loaded the coal onto wooden rail cars for transport to the mine entrance or shaft. It was heavy physical work and usually took the entire working day. The pay of the laborer was normally about one third that of a contract miner. Irishmen tended to be laborers with few exceptions, and to remain in that category well beyond when they had learned the skills of a contract miner. The reason for this may be found in the prejudice of miners and mine operators against their "papist" religion, alleged propensity for liquor and rebellious attitude.

In the anthracite region the Irish learned that justice was available to them neither from courts nor local government and usually not from state government. They found the environment not all that different from that which they had left in the old country. Government officials, more often than not, were of British, Welsh, or Scottish descent and Protestant. Owners of the collieries tended to be of that background as well. As mine laborers, the Irish rarely owned their own homes, but rented cabins from their employer. In the small mine patches on the outskirts of towns, laborers were ordinarily dependent on company-owned "pluck me" stores for provisions they could not cultivate in their own yards. Payment of wages was frequently in

Boys from Irish families working in a coal mine

the form of scrip, honored only in the company store, where prices tended to be higher.

During the Civil War resistance to the draft of 1863 was common in anthracite communities. The Irish, predominantly Democrats, were suspicious of the draft to serve in a war about which they had reservations. Although a significant number had volunteered for the Union Army, nevertheless, the draft imposed by a Republican administration was opposed. Furthermore, wartime inflation fell heavily on workers in a competitively low wage industry. Strikes for wage increases by incipient unions erupted. Federally-appointed provost marshals sent to enroll conscripts viewed draft resistance and strikes in the same way—interruptions of the war effort and one step from treason. Mine operators held the same attitude and condemned Irish militants and unions generally.

### ECONOMIC ORGANIZATION

The lure of great wealth from mining anthracite proved illusory. After surface deposits were exhausted, deep mining was necessary and very expensive. The cost of hoisting coal, ventilation of mine shafts, pumping out water and breaking coal into marketable sizes proved to be very high. To accomplish it steam power was required. As more operators entered anthracite mining it became highly competitive. Pressure to hold down costs tempted them to skimp on measures for safety. Explosions, fires, cave-ins, and gassy mines became all too frequent. The response of operators was to blame careless miners. The Irish especially were scapegoats for such problems. The worst example of the hazard of underground mining occurred in Avondale on 5 September 1869, where 110 men were killed in a mine fire.

### ORGANIZATION OF LABOR

In 1863 John Siney settled in St. Clair, Schuykill County and began work in the mines. He was thirty-two and a native of Bornos, County Queens in Ireland. Earlier his family had moved to Wigan in Lancashire in England where he worked as a bricklayer, organized a union in that craft and presided over it for a number of years. In 1868, with others, he founded the Workingmens' Benevolent Association of St. Clair and later that year orchestrated a county-wide Miners' and Laborers' Benevolent

Association. From 1868 to 1875 this association effectively resisted wage cuts, handled employee grievances, provided sickness, accident and death benefits. It successfully lobbied for a state mine safety law that was passed in 1869. Unfortunately, a senator from Luzerne County (north of Schuykill County) objected and was able to exempt that county (where Avondale was located), from the coverage of the law. Siney came to Avondale and gave a moving speech as the dead miners were brought from the mine, urging that the safety law be changed to apply statewide and that it be made more effective. This was done in 1870. One provision, requiring a second or escape shaft, was inspired by the Avondale situation where there was but a single shaft.

### LONG STRIKE AND SECRET SOCIETIES

While labor organizations directed by Siney were functioning, activity by secret societies, allegedly composed of Irishmen, were quiet for the most part. But in 1875 Franklin Gowen, president of the Reading Railroad, which had invested heavily in coal properties, determined to break the union. During a strike in 1875 he accomplished his purpose by intransigent refusal to negotiate. Through shrewd publicity he persuaded the public that the union was part and parcel of the Molly Maguires. Labor conditions at the mines deteriorated thereafter and violence by secret societies reappeared.

*See* Coal Miners; Labor Movement

Alfred D. Chandler, Jr., "Anthracite Coal and the Beginnings of the Industrial Revolution in the United States," *Business History Review*, vol. 46 (1972): 141–81.
Edward Pinkowski, *John Siney: The Miners' Martyr* (Philadelphia, 1963).
Anthony F. C. Wallace, *St. Clair* (New York, 1987).

L. A. O'DONNELL

## ARIZONA

### INTRODUCTION

Although Irish-born immigrants made up the largest foreign-born segment of the population during the early Territorial period, the number of Irish-born immigrants in Arizona has been relatively small. After 1880, other foreign-born groups, especially Hispanics, began coming into Arizona in increasing numbers, replacing the Irish as the dominant foreign-born group. Therefore the impact of the Irish on Arizona history has been, for the most part, as individuals rather than as a group. While Irish-Americans came to Arizona in larger numbers, it was not until after World War II that their numbers became large enough to make an impact as a group. The following is an overview of Irish and Irish-American contribution to the history and development of Arizona.

### SPANISH AND MEXICAN PERIOD

For a variety of reasons, the foreign-born population in the Spanish missions and the presidios at Tubac and Tucson never grew very large. Mainly made up of native Pima and Papago Indians and mestizos from other parts of the Spanish empire, the settlements included few foreigners other than Spanish soldiers. The frequency of Indian attacks and raids against the missions and settlers was one reason for the small population. In addition, the lack of water made most of the land in Arizona unfavorable for farming and settlement, and the area was considered too remote and uninviting for settlement. Finally, the Spanish government actively discouraged foreigners from coming to their territories although they made exceptions if the foreigners were Catholic, or could claim Spanish citizenship. The Irish could claim an exemption on both counts. Quite a few Irish expatriates fled to Spain because of the Irish conflict with England. They became Spanish citizens, were involved in the Spanish government and fought in the Spanish military. The most notable of the Irish expatriates in Arizona under the Spanish was Hugh (Hugo) O'Conor. As commander of the presidios in the Spanish Southwest, O'Conor established the presidio at Tucson in 1775 near the mission of San Xavier de Bac, moving the troops stationed at Tubac to do so (Kessell 1976).

After it achieved its independence from Spain in 1821, the Mexican government at first encouraged foreign settlers to come to their territories. However, foreigners did not come to Arizona during the Mexican period for the same reasons they did not come during the Spanish period. In addition, after Mexico opened Arizona for colonization, settlers often found the most desirable land already taken; they could find land cheaper and easier elsewhere. Finally, after their experiences with foreign settlers in Texas, Mexican officials were wary of letting foreigners into their other territories. They allowed few land grants to foreign settlers in Arizona after the mid-1830s. However, a few Irish and Irish-Americans were able to buy land in the Mexican territory. William Henry Harrison (H. H.) Burke, born in Boston, Massachusetts in 1825, the son of Irish emigrant Patrick Burke, bought land on Sonoita Creek near Tucson in 1852. Burke was one of only about thirty Anglo settlers living in or near Tucson when the Americans took command of the settlement in 1856 (Hayden Files).

Some foreigners came to Arizona during the Mexican period to trap and trade with the Indians. Irish-born trader James Kirker was born in Belfast, Ireland in 1793, and came to Mexico in 1824 on a trapping expedition. However, since he did not have a license, Sonoran Governor Narbone had his furs and possessions seized. In 1835, Kirker obtained a license from Governor Don Alvino Perez to trap and trade with the Apaches for a year. The Mexican government, however, confiscated his property and ordered his arrest on the grounds that Perez did not have the authority to grant a license to an alien and heretic. In 1836, the new Governor, Manuel Armijo, invited him back to the territory. After he successfully led a party in pursuit of a band of Apaches which had broken up a friend's mining operation, the Governor of Chihuahua asked Kirker to head a party of fifty men on other raids against the Apaches. Kirker remained in the service of the Mexican government until the outbreak of the Mexican War with the United States (Hayden Files).

## THE TERRITORIAL PERIOD (1848–1912)

The history of the Irish in Arizona really began with the arrival of American troops to the area during and after the Mexican War. During this period, the Irish were involved in three areas of employment: as soldiers, as miners and in building roads and railroads.

### Soldiers

The first group of Irish to come to Arizona came as soldiers with American forces during and after the Mexican War. While most of the action during the war took place elsewhere, troops under Colonel Stephen Watts Kearny passed through Arizona on their way to California in 1846. James Kirker left the service of the Mexican government and joined Colonel Doniphan's command at Val Verde, serving as a guide and interpreter. Among other Irish immigrants who served in the Mexican War who became involved in Arizona's development was William H. H. Burke. Burke enlisted as Second Class boy on February 5, 1845 on the *U.S.S. Raritan,* commanded by Commodore F. H. Gregory, at Rio de Janeiro, Brazil. The *Raritan* became part of the United States gulf squadron during the Mexican War, seeing action at Vera Cruz, Yampico, Tobasco and Fort Yeabel. Burke was honorably discharged at Norfolk, Virginia on November 30, 1846, emigrated to California in 1850 and then to Tucson, Arizona in 1854.

The Treaty of Guadalupe Hidalgo, which ended the Mexican War in 1848, brought the area north of the Gila River in Arizona into the United States as part of the Territory of New Mexico. Tucson and Tubac, which were south of the river, remained under Mexican control. After gold was discovered in California, the United States government realized that a good year-round route to the goldfields was needed. The best southern route turned out to be in Arizona. However, most of the Arizona routes lay south of the Gila River, which was still part of Mexico. The United States, therefore acquired the area in the Gadsden Purchase in 1854, adding it to the New Mexico Territory. John Costello, born in County Clare, Ireland about 1838, was among those involved in the survey to establish the Arizona/Mexico border under the terms of the purchase. William H. H. Burke helped raise the American flag at Tucson when Mexican troops left on March 10, 1856 (Hayden Files).

The first consideration of the United States government in Arizona was to protect the trade routes and the settlers and miners going to California from Indian attacks. Therefore, the first American settlements in Arizona were military forts, placed at strategic points to block the Indian's traditional raiding routes. By 1860, Federal troops were located at Fort Arivaypa, Fort Buchanan, Fort Defiance, Fort Lowell near Tucson, Fort Yuma and Fort Mohave. The majority of the soldiers in these forts were Irish-born immigrants. For example, 47 percent of the soldiers at Fort Arivaypa and 45 percent of the soldiers at Fort Defiance were Irish immigrants (U.S. Census 1860; Hayden Files).

The outbreak of the Civil War led to the closure of military posts in Arizona as Federal troops were withdrawn to fight the Confederates in the east. Some troops deserted to fight for the south. Jefferson Davis, the Confederate President, recognized the importance of Arizona to the Confederate cause, both for its mineral resources, and for its importance as a link between Texas and California. Davis also knew that many of the settlers in Arizona were unhappy about being part of the New Mexico Territory. The government's failure to keep the Indians in check, and their isolation due to the distance involved in traveling to the Territorial capital in Mesilla, caused the settlers to feel that their needs were being ignored by the Territorial government. On April 2, 1860, some Arizona settlers, including William H. H. Burke, held a convention in Tucson to form a separate Arizona Territory, but were not able to get sufficient support for their proposal (Hayden Files; O'Leary 1996).

In July of 1861, Colonel John R. Baylor and a Confederate army organized in Texas, occupied Mesilla. On August 1, 1861, Baylor issued a proclamation annexing the area south of the thirty-fourth parallel to the Confederacy as the independent territory of Arizona, with himself as the first governor. On February 14, 1862, President Davis and the Confederate Congress offi-

William Owen
"Bucky"
O'Neill

cially recognized Arizona as a Confederate territory. Baylor sent a force of men under Captain Sherod Hunter to occupy Tucson, which arrived on February 28, 1862. In response to the Confederate occupation of Arizona and New Mexico, Federal officials in California raised a force of 2,300 men, known as the California Column, which was placed under the command of Colonel James Carleton. Many of the officers and troops in the Column were Irish-born immigrants (O'Leary 1996) and they helped to oust the Confederates.

After the Civil War, the United States government established additional forts in Arizona to deal with the Indians. In 1870, 42 percent of the Irishmen in Arizona were still serving as soldiers. However, by 1880, while the 226 Irish soldiers in Arizona still made up 17 percent of the Irish-born population, most of the Irish settlers were now involved in other occupations, notably mining. The Irish soldiers in Arizona faced dangers not only from Indians, but also from sickness, disease and accidents.

Despite the bad conditions and remote locations, some of the soldiers brought their wives and families with them to the forts. The women served as army laundresses, servants for the officers, and as midwives and nurses and were often the only women in the more remote outposts. Eliza Flynn Campbell met and married Daniel Campbell, the son of Scottish immigrants, in Kansas when she worked as a maid for his commanding officer there. Jane Meehan Tiernan, wife of Farrell Tiernan, was one of three women at Fort Mohave, Arizona and was the only woman at Fort Valdez, Alaska when he was stationed there (AHS; Hayden Files).

While the number of Irish soldiers declined after 1880, Irish immigrants and Irish-Americans continued to serve as soldiers during the Territorial period. William Owen "Bucky" O'Neill, born in St. Louis, Missouri of Irish immigrant parents, came to Prescott, Arizona in 1881. The first person in Arizona to offer his services in the Spanish American War, he formed a cavalry regiment of cowboys, former Indian fighters and frontiersmen which was given the name "Rough Riders" by Teddy Roosevelt. Only six weeks after leaving Prescott, the Rough Riders saw their first action at La Guasimas, losing 16 men killed and 52 wounded. A week later, on July 2, 1898, while deploying his men on Kettle Hill before the battle of San Juan Hill, O'Neill was killed by sniper fire. O'Neill had refused to get under cover, saying "The Spanish bullet isn't moulded (*sic*) that will kill me!" A moment later a bullet struck him in the head. On May 1, 1899, he was buried in Arlington National Cemetery. In 1907, a bronze statue of a horseman on a rearing mount, designed by Solon Borglum, was dedicated to his memory in the City Hall plaza in Prescott (Phoenix Public Library).

### Mining

While some mining occurred in Arizona during the Spanish and Mexican period, extensive mining activity did not develop until the American period because of Indian raids and attacks on miners, the lack of water and adequate transportation systems. However, a number of Irish miners and prospectors were active in Arizona from the beginning. William H. H. Burke went to La Paz during the gold rush between 1862 and 1864, where he located mining claims in the Flemosa District, the La Paz District, and the Castle Dome District. Daniel O'Leary, acting as a scout for some miners, discovered gold along Yampa Creek in 1864. In 1877, Dan and Charles Spencer found a silver mine about sixty miles from Roger's camp, north of San Francisco Mountain. One account of the naming of the town, which grew up near the mine found by Edward Scheiffelin in the San Pedro Valley, credits Dan with being the one to tell Scheiffelin he would only "find your tombstone" in the Valley. In 1888, Dan made a rich strike on the Old Hardy mine on Silver Creek and he had an interest in the Old Michigan mine in 1894. James Lee invested in mining in the Amole District, and he patented the Naguila silver and lead mine in 1869, the first mine to be patented in the Territory. Andrew Curtin, born in County Clare, Ireland in 1845, discovered a lode of silver near the Peck mine in 1875, including a chunk weighing fifty pounds. He also was the first to discover valuable ore in the Bradshaw mountains and was one of five partners in the Black Warrior mine, which was sold in 1880 for about $60,000 to a New York syndicate. Thomas Farrell, born in County Longford, Ireland owned the Blue Bird mine and found the Martinez silver mine north of Florence, the Lone Hand and the Golden Queen in Black Canyon district. He was also involved in placer mining along Lynx Creek. In 1876, a group of Irish-born prospectors including John Kelly, John Boyd, Josiah Riley, George Kell and Edward, John and A.B. O'Daugherty, located ten copper claims and a mill site near present day Jerome. Jack Dunn, an Irish army scout at Fort Huachuca, found silver and copper ore in Mule Pass near Bisbee while searching for water for the Fort (Hayden Files; Malach 1982; Young n.d.).

After 1880, the solitary, individual Irish miners and prospectors gave way to the large mining companies such as Phelps Dodge. The majority of the Irish settlers and Irish-Americans in Arizona worked for these companies, reflecting their importance in Arizona's economy. Although copper mining was developed last, it became the most important mining industry in Arizona by the turn of the century. By the time of statehood, Arizona was the number one copper-producing state in the nation.

While most of the Irish mine workers never progressed past the back-breaking labor involved both above and below ground, others became successful in mine management or in other fields. William "Billie" H. Brophy, born in Ireland in 1863, came to Arizona at the age of nineteen to stay with his brother James at his ranch in the Sulphur Springs Valley. In 1884, Billie obtained a position with the Copper Queen Consolidated Mining Company

William
"Billie" H.
Brophy

Nellie
Cashman

in Bisbee as a clerk. Taken under the wing of the owner, Dr. James Douglas, he rose to the position of General Manager of the Company Stores in 1886. As General Manager, he oversaw all the stores operated by the Mercantile Company, including those in Bisbee, Lowell, Naco, Douglas, Clifton, Morenci and Dawson, New Mexico. Brophy used his position to purchase extensive mining interests of his own. This in turn led him to found and become president of the Bank of Bisbee and the Bank of Douglas which later became the Arizona Bank. He also had an interest in the Douglas Investment Company, which played a role in establishing the town of Douglas, Arizona and in the Bisbee Improvement Company, a utility company providing power and ice in Cochise County.

### Transportation

Like their compatriots nationally, Irish immigrants were involved in building roads and local and transcontinental railroads across and through Arizona. Transportation systems in Arizona developed slowly because of the difficult terrain, Indian raids, and the disruption of the Civil War. However, once construction began, many of the laborers building the roads and railroads were Irish. In addition, Irishmen such as John Welsh were prominent as freighters, wagon drivers and teamsters along the wagon roads. After the arrival of the stage lines, Irish immigrants worked as stage drivers, station keepers, and stage agents. James Lee came to Arizona with the Overland Mail Company, while Frank Cosgrove came to Arizona with the Great Overland Stage and Express Company as drivers. William H. H. Burke operated a stage station on the Colorado desert, forty miles west of Yuma and Burke's station on the south bank of the Gila River west of Oatman Flat. Michael O'Reilly, a mail carrier between Tucson and Fort Bowie after 1865, also kept a stage station at Point of Mountains, eighteen miles northwest of Tucson, between 1866 and 1871. O'Reilly set up Crittendon Station in 1871 at the junction of the Bowie and Crittendon roads, and set up Kennedy's Wells, or O'Reilly's Station, thirteen miles from Camp Grant, on the main road to San Carlos and Camp Apache in 1873. In 1875, he dug twelve wells between the San Pedro River and Camp Grant, built sixteen miles of road from Three Oaks to Dos Cabezas and built a station two miles south of Croton Springs.

O'Reilly also built a station on Turkey Creek, eighteen miles from Camp Rucker and built eighteen miles of road to the same place in 1878. Joseph Sexton Hopley carried mail between Pantano and Greaterville and operated a mail stage and express line (Hayden Files).

Irish-born workers associated with building the railroads in Arizona included surveyors, rail layers, engineers, tie contractors, wood choppers, conductors and firemen. Daniel O'Leary served as a guide for the W. J. Palmer party which surveyed a route for the railroad across northern Arizona.

### Other Employment

The building of new towns and communities because of mining operations and the railroad also provided economic opportunities for Irish-born immigrants and their descendants. Irishmen in Arizona became landlords, merchants, tradesmen, hotel owners, restaurant owners or saloon keepers. Irish women worked as domestic servants, nurses, seamstresses, milliners, cooks and teachers. Julia Bushford worked as a hospital matron at Fort Mohave; Mary McGraff was a servant for John Fremont, Arizona's Territorial Governor in 1880. The most famous Irish woman in Arizona during the Territorial period was Nellie Cashman. Nellie, born in Queenstown, County Cork, Ireland in 1845, emigrated to Boston as a young girl where she worked as a hotel bellhop and messenger. She operated a restaurant in Virginia City, Nevada in 1872 and prospected and ran a boarding house for miners in upper British Columbia in 1874. In 1879, she opened the Delmonico Restaurant, the first business owned by a woman in Tucson. The following year, Nellie went to Tombstone, where she operated the Nevada Boot and Shoe Store and opened the Russ House, a boarding house for miners. She became a landmark in the town. Known for her charitable work, she acquired the nicknames "Angel of Tombstone," "Frontier Angel," and "Saint of the Sourdoughs." In all, Nellie spent fifty years prospecting in Arizona, Nevada, Alaska, Canada and Mexico (*Desert Shamrock* 1992; U.S. Census 1870; 1880).

Unlike other areas of the United States, the Irish found traces of a Catholic church in Arizona. The first Catholic missions in Arizona had been established under the Spanish by the Jesuits. Father Eusebio Francisco Kino established missions in the San

Pedro and Santa Cruz Valleys in 1692. In 1700, Kino opened the mission San Xavier at the Papago village of Bac. However, by the time the Jesuits were expelled and the Franciscans took over the missions in 1767, the Spanish missions had been reduced by Indian attacks to the mission of Guevavi, its *visitas,* Calabazas, Sonoita and Tumacacori, and San Xavier del Bac and its visita at Tucson, "the farthest Christian pueblo." By 1774, Guevavi and Sonoita were also abandoned. Hugo O'Conor established the presidio at Tucson in 1775 in an effort to better protect the missions from Indian attacks (Kessel 1976).

After the secularization of the missions in 1827 by the Mexican government, priests from Magdalena rarely visited the Arizona missions. The San Xavier de Bac and Tumacacori missions were in ruins when the Americans arrived.

Most of the priests and nuns who came to Arizona during the early Territorial period were from Spain, England and France. However, a few Irish priests and nuns came during this period. The 1870 U.S. Census listed one Irish-born nun Nellie Peters, a Sister of Saint Joseph, in Tucson and no Irish priests. Father Michael Murphy arrived in Prescott in October of 1877 to establish the first church there. However, he died of consumption two months later. The Sisters of St. Joseph, including Mary Dunne and Mary Rose Doran, established a small hospital in Prescott in 1878. In 1880, the U.S. Census listed two Irish-born Sisters of Mercy, Sister Frances and Sister Mary Martha, serving in Yuma (U.S. Census 1870; 1880; Salpointe 1898; Sharlot Hall Churches).

Since parish records do not show the nationality of parishioners, it is not possible to determine how many Irish belonged to the various Catholic churches in Arizona. However, because of their numbers, they must have dominated some parishes. Individual Irish immigrants certainly became involved in their local churches. Eliza Flynn Campbell and Nellie Cashman helped build the first churches in Prescott and Tombstone in the 1880s. In 1903, Frank Murphy donated ten acres of land for a Catholic school in Prescott (Sharlot Hall Obit Books; Sharlot Hall Churches).

William O'Neill was elected mayor of Prescott in 1898, resigning to form the Rough Riders during the Spanish-American War (Goff 1975; Hayden Files; Phoenix Public Library).

## Statehood-Present

On February 14, 1912, fifty years after it was designated a Confederate territory, Arizona became the forty-eighth state of the United States. Irish-born Thomas Molloy was a leader in the drive for statehood and was in Washington for the signing of the Statehood Bill along with Bill McBridge and Timothy Riordan. The Irish and their descendants in the newly formed state built on the gains and opportunities they made during the Territorial period (Hayden Files; *Desert Shamrock* 1992).

Mining continued to be the major employment for the Irish and their descendants for five decades after Statehood. Again, most worked as laborers in the mines and smelters. Michael Curley came to Arizona in 1913 and served as manager of the Calumet and Arizona Mining Company at Ajo. In 1925, he became executive manager of the New Cornelia branch of the Phelps Dodge Copper Company in Ajo, which he operated until his retirement in 1939. He was instrumental in the development of the mine and town of Ajo. With the decline of the copper industry in the 1970s and 1980s, the Irish and Irish-American mine workers, like the rest of the mine workers, had to find other

employment in high-tech companies such as Motorola and Dial (AHS).

Irish priests and nuns served in Arizona before and after statehood. The growth of the Catholic population justified the establishment of the diocese of Phoenix in 1968. (The other diocese, Tuscon, was established in 1897.) Irish and Irish-American nuns were deeply involved in education and charitable activities.

The Irish and Irish-Americans have been active in politics proportionate to their numbers. Most served on a local and state level. Some achieved wider recognition. Thomas Edward Campbell, of Scotch-Irish decent, after years in politics, was elected governor of Arizona, on the Republican ticket, in 1918, and was re-elected in 1920. In 1930 President Hoover appointed him chairman of the United States Civil Service Commission. On the Democratic side, President Kennedy appointed William P. Maloney, Jr., U.S. ambassador to Ghana in 1962 and he held the post until 1968.

After World War II, an increasing number of Irish-Americans moved to Arizona from the east and mid-west to take advantage of military, high-tech and other employment opportunities. By 1990, more than 530,000 Irish-Americans lived in Arizona, most of them in Maricopa County and the Phoenix area. Their increasing numbers led to the organization of Irish-American associations and businesses specifically designed to appeal to their Irish-American consciousness. The Irish American Social Club, founded in Phoenix in 1947, is still active in the Phoenix area. The Phoenix St. Patrick's Day Parade, first held in 1984, has developed into a two-day event featuring the parade and an Irish Fair with Irish music, dancing and crafts. Two Irish American newspapers, *Desert Shamrock* and *Irish Eyes,* feature articles on Irish music, art, films, news from Ireland, Irish-American organizations and events in Arizona, and advertisements for Irish and Irish-American businesses while an Irish radio show is featured on KXEG (1010 AM). Robert Emmit Field, an Irish-American from Chicago who came to Phoenix in 1960 to work for Motorola, founded the Executive Resources for Irish Networking (E.R.I.N.) in 1987 to provide a forum for the exchange of business information between Arizona and Ireland. Ties between Arizona and Ireland have been recognized by the selection of Ennis, Ireland as Phoenix's sister city and of Roscommon, Ireland as Tucson's sister city.

## Conclusion

Most Irish and Irish-Americans quickly passed through Arizona and left no records or achieved fame elsewhere. Others were born, lived, worked and died in Arizona quietly. However, as can be seen, the Irish and their descendants have been instrumental in the history, settlement and development of Arizona. Their contribution is reflected in place names, businesses and buildings throughout the state. O'Leary Peak, twenty miles north of Flagstaff, and O'Leary Pass in Mohave County were named for army scout and guide Daniel O'Leary. Geeson, Arizona was named for the son of Irish-born John Geeson, the first white male child born in the settlement. Duffy School in Tucson was named in honor of the five daughters of Martin J. Duffy, who all served as school teachers in the Tucson school system over a thirty-year period. McClelland Hall, the University of Arizona College of Business and Public Administration building, was named after Norman McClelland, President of Shamrock Foods, who donated a major portion of the funds for the building in 1987. Only the future will reveal what other contributions the Irish will make to Arizona's history and development (AHS; Hayden Papers; Malach 1982, *Arizona Republic* 1987).

Arizona Historical Society, Biographical Clipping Books, Tucson, Arizona.

John S. Goff, *Arizona Territorial Officials,* vol. 1: *The Supreme Court Justices, 1863–1912* (Cave Creek, AZ, 1975): 68–71.

Carl Hayden, Biographical Files. Tempe: Arizona State University, Hayden Library.

John L. Kessell, *Friars, Soldiers and Reformers: Hispanic Arizona and the Sonora Mission Frontier, 1767–1856* (Tucson, AZ, 1976).

Roman Malach, *Mohave County Pioneer: Daniel O'Leary* (Kingman, AZ, 1982).

John L. Myers, ed., *The Arizona Governor's, 1912–1990* (Phoenix, AZ, 1989): 19–27.

Jennie L. O'Leary, "Picacho Pass: Arizona's Civil War Battlefield," *Family Connections* (Phoenix, AZ, January–March 1996): 15–16.

Phoenix Public Library, Arizona Collection. "William O'Neal" Biography File (Phoenix, AZ).

J. B. Salpoint, *Soldiers of the Cross: Notes on the Ecclesiastical History of New Mexico, Arizona and Colorado* (Banning, CA, 1898).

JENNIE L. O'LEARY

## ARKANSAS

The first official Irishman to visit Arkansas would also be the last Catholic missionary of the Spanish era. Fr. Juan Brady, a member of the Order of Our Lady of Mt. Carmel or Carmelites, was working at a parish in east central Louisiana. He traveled up the Mississippi River to the Arkansas Post during the summer of 1802, staying the week of July 12–16th, and for two days in early August. While in Arkansas, Brady baptized forty-nine persons and witnessed three marriages. He would be the last Catholic priest to serve in Arkansas before the United States acquired the territory the following year. The Louisiana Purchase was signed and ratified in 1803, yet not until March 23, 1804 did an American military officer assume control of the Post from its last commander, ending the European era of Arkansas history.

As a new American acquisition on the southwestern frontier, Arkansas filled up rapidly. In 1802, a Frenchman estimated that the population at the Post at 450; the first American census in 1810 at over a thousand, 924 whites, 136 African slaves, and two free persons of color. In 1820, just one year after the creation of the Arkansas Territory, the U.S. census had the Arkansas white population at 12,579, slaves at 1,617, and fifty-nine free blacks. Within twenty years, four years after Arkansas became the twenty-fifth state in 1836, the white population had jumped to 77,174, the slave population at 19,935, and free blacks now numbered 475. In just three decades the Arkansas population had gone from just over one thousand to almost one hundred thousand. These new settlers were primarily English, but they did contain some sizable number of Scotch-Irish as this group was the largest white minority in the south during the ante-bellum era. Yet, as historian Grady McWhiney has maintained, the Scotch-Irish were generally blended into the majority Anglo-American population by the time of the Civil War.

By the time of the Civil War, Arkansas was a major cotton producing state with an ever-expanding slave population. The trans-Mississippi states were really now the last frontier of the Old South. The state was increasingly tied in economically, demographically, socially, and culturally with the South and so, after some hesitancy, followed that region into secession after the outbreak of hostilities in 1861.

Ironically, it would be the Civil War which produced the first Arkansas governors of Irish descent. Harris Flanagin was Arkansas's second and last Confederate war governor; yet he was the first state chief executive of Irish ancestry. His grandfather had immigrated to America from Ireland in 1765 and young Harris was born in New Jersey on November 3, 1817. He migrated first to Pennsylvania at the age of eighteen, then to Illinois where he was admitted to the bar. He moved to Arkadelphia, Arkansas in 1839 where he soon distinguished himself both in law and politics. He married Martha E. Nash on July 3, 1851, and the couple produced two sons and a daughter. Raised as a Baptist, he never formally joined the Baptist church in Arkansas, yet he did attend Presbyterian churches with his wife although he did not become a member of that denomination either. A slaveowner, his biographer claims that most slaves stayed with the family even after the war.

A political Whig until the collapse of that party, Harris Flanagin won election of the Arkansas secession convention of 1861 and he supported disunion. With the outbreak of war, he served in the Confederate army until he won election as Arkansas's second Confederate governor. Inaugurated on November 12, 1862, in Little Rock, he had to move the Arkansas Confederate government to Washington in the southwestern part of the state after the Federals overran Arkansas's capital on September 10, 1863. Governor Flanagin really faced an impossible task of trying to keep some political order as the cause of the Confederacy collapsed during his tenure. After Appomattox, Flanagin attempted to negotiate with the Federals for surrender, but they would only allow the Confederate governor to bring the state archives with him as a condition of surrender. Flanagin surrendered on behalf of Confederate Arkansas in Little Rock on May 27, 1865. During Reconstruction he joined with others to oppose the state's Republican rule. He died on October 23, 1874, just a few days after Conservative Democrats won the election reestablishing their power in Arkansas.

The other Arkansas governor of Irish descent was on the opposite side of Flanagin during the war. This "Pennsylvania Irishman," as his biographer referred to him, was born on a farm near Pittsburgh on October 16, 1799. His family had come from Dublin around 1740 and settled the Pennsylvania backcountry where they were active in both the late colonial wars and the Revolution. After some education, he was admitted to the bar in western Pennsylvania in 1825, yet he moved to Clarksville, Tennessee, five years later. While in Clarksville, he met and eventually married Angelina Lockhart, and the couple produced six daughters. This quiet lawyer, who was also a teacher, would have a reputation throughout his life for honesty and independence. He never joined any particular church yet Murphy was a quiet, simple man of faith. He lived in a slaveholding society, yet refused to inherit slaves with his bride's dowry because he believed the peculiar institution was immoral.

Murphy soon joined the swelling western migration from the mountains of eastern Tennessee to the Arkansas Ozarks, settling in Fayetteville by 1834. He went out to California at the age of fifty to participate in the Gold Rush, but he returned all the poorer. He moved to nearby Huntsville in Madison County in 1854 where he went back to his usual job of being an attorney-teacher. He soon got involved in politics, serving as a Democratic state senator between 1856 and 1860, representing two Ozark counties. In 1861, Madison county voters sent him to the secession convention where he adamantly refused to support disunion even after the firing on Ft. Sumter. The initial vote on

May 6, 1861, was sixty-five to five for secession, and the minority were given a chance to make it unanimous for disunion. All changed their vote that day except Murphy who said, "I have cast my vote after mature reflection, and have duly considered the consequences, and I cannot conscientiously change it. I therefore vote no!"

Murphy returned to Huntsville that summer, yet he was continually held suspect by Confederate authorities. After the appearance of a Federal army under General Samuel R. Curtis in northwestern Arkansas the following spring, Murphy sought the protection of the Union army. After April, 1862, he served as a civilian advisor on the staff of General Curtis, a position he held for the next year and a half.

President Lincoln in late 1863 launched his own version of Reconstruction in states like Tennessee, Louisiana, and Arkansas. His administration sponsored the establishment of Unionist civilian government. An assembly met in Union-controlled Little Rock on January 4, 1864. While it represented only twenty-four of the fifty-seven existing counties (primarily those in the northern and northwestern part of the state), this body wrote a new state constitution and elected Isaac Murphy provisional governor, swearing him in on January 20th. Two months later, another election was held only in the northern and northwestern parts of the state and the voters approved the new state constitution and elected Murphy as governor with no opposition. On April 14, 1864, Murphy was inaugurated as Arkansas's first popularly elected Unionist governor.

Over the next three years, Governor Murphy would be the Arkansas leader recognized and supported by the Lincoln and Johnson administrations. Almost sixty-five when he assumed office, he faced an empty treasury with a war-torn state afflicted by lawless men working for both sides of the conflict. The new governor was almost totally dependent on Federal troops to maintain his power. The Unionist legislature, with Murphy's support, ratified the thirteenth amendment on April 13, 1865, ending slavery in the United States. Once the Arkansas Supreme Court nullified a state law which prohibited ex-Confederates from office, another state election brought many Democrats, especially ex-Confederates, back into a legislative majority by November, 1866. Murphy was generally quite fair and even-handed with ex-Confederates, yet this new legislature generally ignored the governor. This General Assembly rejected the fourteenth amendment to the U.S. Constitution, and passed laws forbidding blacks from voting, marrying whites, or attending public schools. Arkansas's Unionist governor opposed these measures and correctly warned the legislature that such policies would bring down the wrath of the national government. That was not long in coming. In March 1867, Arkansas's civilian government was abolished and the state, along with much of the old southern Confederacy, was placed under military rule. Over the course of the next fifteen months, his role was just as titular governor; he oversaw some fiscal matters, yet he never challenged the military operations of this new Reconstruction government.

New elections were held in 1868, but under the guidelines established by Congress, most of the ex-Confederates and Democrats were barred from participation. The main people elected were radicals, carpetbaggers and freedmen. Murphy did not even attempt to be reelected and he handed power over to the new Radical governor on July 2, 1868. He then returned to his mountain home in the Ozarks where he died at the age of eighty-two in 1882. Interestingly enough, there would not be another Arkansan with an Irish surname to serve as governor for the rest of the nineteenth-century. It took a civil war, it seems, to bring these men of Irish ancestry to serve as Arkansas's chief executive.

The Great Famine in Ireland drove millions of Irish from their homes and many migrated to America. Only a few made it to Arkansas by 1850. Out of the white population of 162,189, only 1,642 were foreign-born or about one percent. The number from Ireland was only 514 or about 31.3% of that total. (But those from German-speaking states were 540.)

By far the most significant Irish immigrant arrived in Arkansas in 1850 and his name was Patrick Ronayne Cleburne. The son of a well-to-do Irish Protestant doctor, Cleburne was born in County Cork, March 16, 1828. After failing to get into medical school in 1846, he joined the British army and served until September, 1849. Three months after his release he entered the United States at New Orleans and soon traveled to Cincinnati where he worked as an apprentice to an apothecary. By the summer of 1850, he migrated to Helena, Arkansas, to open his own drugstore. He soon became an active member of this river-town community.

He so identified with his adopted state and region that he enthusiastically volunteered for the local Arkansas militia in May, 1861. On July 23, 1861 he entered Confederate service where he saw action in Tennessee and Kentucky, and participated in the battle of Shiloh, about a month after he had been promoted to the rank of brigadier general on March 4, 1862. Later that year, on November 23, 1862, Cleburne was promoted to the rank of major general, making him the highest ranking Confederate military officer of foreign birth. At Chickamauga the following year, he earned the title "Stonewall of the West" from President Jefferson Davis for his distinguished action. By early 1864, Cleburne authored a plea for slaves used in the Confederate army to help supplement the dwindling numbers, and in return the slaves would be given their freedom. While his idea was suppressed at the time, it was belatedly proposed by General Robert E. Lee and President Davis a year later as the confederacy was faltering. Continuing to serve valiantly with both Generals Joseph E. Johnston and John B. Hood in the defense of Atlanta in 1864, Cleburne was killed during the battle of Franklin, Tennessee, on November 30, 1864. First buried near Franklin, his body was removed to Helena in 1870. Though an Irish immigrant, General Patrick R. Cleburne was the most distinguished military figure Arkansas has ever produced.

Overwhelmingly, most of the Irish immigrants who came in the two decades just prior to the Civil War were Catholic. Probably the most prominent Irish Catholic immigrant in antebellum Arkansas was Andrew Byrne, the first bishop for the Diocese of Little Rock. Byrne was born in 1802 in the small town of Navan, about forty miles northwest of Dublin. While at a diocesan seminary in Navan, the young man heard the plea of American Catholic Bishop John England for missionaries for his South Carolina diocese. Responding to the call, he came to Charleston, S.C., where Bishop England ordained him for the priesthood on November 11, 1827. Nine years later, for reasons not really clear, Byrne transferred to the Diocese of New York where he served in the metropolitan area of the city. His strong connection with New York's Bishop John Hughes, and his past association with the South may have made him a natural for a newly created diocese in Arkansas. After Pope Gregory XVI erected the Arkansas see on November 28, 1843, Bishop John Hughes consecrated Andrew Byrne as the Bishop of Little Rock in New York City's old St. Patrick's Cathedral on March 11, 1844.

Once in Arkansas with only two other Irish Catholic priests to work in a diocese which encompassed the whole state, Byrne quickly realized that he had a daunting task. He complained to Rome in 1847 that he had pastored churches in New York City which had more Catholics than the whole state of Arkansas. Byrne hoped to rectify his small Catholic population with additional immigration from his famine stricken homeland. With the help of a wealthy relative and of Catholic mission societies in France and Austria, Byrne purchased a large amount of land just south of Ft. Smith, an Arkansas River town on the western edge of the state. Some Irish families had already settled in Sevier County in southwestern Arkansas, and most of these would move to the Ft. Smith area. Bishop Byrne recruited the Irish Religious Sisters of Mercy to come to Arkansas in 1851 and they opened St. Mary's Academy that fall; it is the state's oldest educational institution.

Yet Byrne's major contribution to the Irish story in Arkansas was his attempt to bring in about one thousand immigrants to Arkansas to save them from the famine stricken homeland and bolster the Arkansas Catholic population. Led by Irish priest Fr. Thomas Hore (spelled Hoare in some accounts), these poor migrants left their homeland for Liverpool in the summer of 1850. By October, they boarded ships for New Orleans and various groups landed in New Orleans in December and January. By February 1851 the first groups arrived, yet their initial warm welcome quickly turned sour when the first groups contracted cholera, and an old church was turned into a hospital. One contemporary described the plight of these poor Irish as having only "withered leaves for their bed, ragged garments for their covering, and the winter sunlight as it streamed through shattered windows, the only fire to warm them, and death entering every pew." About twenty died in Little Rock, yet about eight families did stay in the Arkansas capital. Most moved on to Ft. Smith, while others settled in Iowa, Texas, or St. Louis. The 1860 census found 158 Irish families still living close to Ft. Smith in Sebastian County.

Bishop Byrne's efforts were not all for naught. By 1860, the number of foreign-born in Arkansas had increased to 3,740 or 1.1% of the white population. Irish-born amounted to 1,315, or 35% of the foreign-born. Only in the 1860 census would the Irish in Arkansas make up such a high percentage of the state's foreign-born. In the eleven states of the Southern Confederacy, the number of Irish immigrants amounted to 79,857, out of a foreign-born population of 233,124. This was when the total white population of these eleven future states of the Confederacy amounted to 5,451,220. Six states had a greater percentage of Irish among the foreign-born, and in two states, Tennessee and Georgia, that percentage equaled 58.9% and 56.5% respectively. Nationally, the Irish-born population was 1,611,304 out of a foreign-born population of 4,038,884 or 39.2%.

The Irish plurality within the state's foreign-born did not survive the Civil War, and neither did Bishop Byrne who died in Helena, Arkansas, on June 10, 1862. In the post-bellum era, Arkansas's foreign-born population never equaled more than one percent of the existing white population. Between 1870 and 1890, the state drew its European immigration primarily from the German-speaking areas of Europe.

By 1890, the number of foreign-born in Arkansas was 14,464 out of a total white population of 818,752 or 1.7%. The number of Irish-born immigrants rose in number to 2,021, yet the percentage of Irish among the state's foreign-born slipped to 14.1%.

This was just above the South's regional average of 12.3%, as the number of Irish in the eleven former Confederate states equaled 40,067 out of a regional foreign-born population of 323,140. As fewer Irish immigrants traveled to the United States after 1870, the numbers of Irish in the southern region and nation reflected this change. In no southern state did the percentage of Irish immigrants go over thirty percent, whereas thirty years earlier the regional average had been over that number. Nationally, the number of Irish-born immigrants was 1,871,509 out of a total foreign-born population of 9,249,547 or 20.2%. Interestingly enough, four southern states, Georgia, South Carolina, Tennessee, and Virginia had higher percentages of Irish among the foreign-born than the national average.

Without a doubt the most historically significant Catholic figure from Arkansas was the Irish immigrant Bishop Edward Mary Fitzgerald. With Byrne's death, the diocese was administered for five years by Fr. Patrick Reilly, one of the priests Byrne had brought back with him from Ireland in 1851. Bishop Fitzgerald was born in the city of Limerick on the Shannon River on the west coast of Ireland. Like Bishop Byrne, the exact date of his birth has not been pinpointed; no doubt he was born sometime during the month of October, 1833, and was baptized on October 26, 1833. His father was Irish to be sure, but his mother, though living in Ireland, was of German descent. He came to America with his family in 1849 and entered a Catholic seminary in Missouri the following year. After further seminary work at Mount St. Mary's in Cincinnati, he graduated from St. Mary's College in Emmitsburg, Maryland. On August 22, 1857, Archbishop John B. Purcell ordained the young man just short of his twenty-fourth birthday. His first and only assignment as a priest was at St. Patrick's Church in Columbus, Ohio, the place he was still pastoring when word came of his appointment as Arkansas's second Catholic prelate on June 22, 1866. At first he declined the position, but later changed his mind, which was fortunate for by the time he had reconsidered the offer, the Vatican issued him a *mandamus* (literally meaning "we command"), a direct order for him to take the Arkansas diocese under holy obedience. Consecrated as bishop at St. Patrick's Church on February 3, 1867, by the same bishop who ordained him, Fitzgerald left for Arkansas. At the age of thirty-four, he was the youngest Catholic bishop in the United States. He arrived in his city on the Feast of St. Patrick.

Bishop Fitzgerald spent forty distinguished years as Arkansas's Catholic bishop. A more complete treatment of his life and career are covered in another article, yet some of the highlights are mentioned here. His most famous action was his decision to vote *non placet* (meaning "it does not please") on the issue of papal infallibility during the First Vatican Council in Rome. During his career in Arkansas, he oversaw some real progress and growth of the diocese by the turn of the century. Like Byrne before him, Bishop Fitzgerald tried to augment the Catholic population through foreign migration, especially those of fellow religionists fleeing from Bismarck's *Kulturkampf*. Bishop Fitzgerald made real efforts also to convert Blacks to Catholicism, establishing schools and parishes for them in the late nineteenth century. At the third Plenary Council of American Catholic bishops, he once again dissented from the majority of fellow prelates by opposing the mandating of Catholic schools for every parish. Like Archbishop James Gibbons, he supported the rights of workers to organize and form unions. With the aid of the Sisters of Charity from Kentucky, Fitzgerald opened St.

Vincent's Infirmary, Arkansas's first Catholic hospital in 1888; it is still the state's oldest medical facility.

Furthermore, he was not punished for his *non placet* vote at the First Vatican Council. The record shows that he turned down two Archbishoprics at Cincinnati and New Orleans and numerous other dioceses in the 1880s. His great courtesy won him admirers inside and outside his denomination. After his death in Hot Springs after a long illness on February 21, 1907, over five thousand people met the funeral train at the station in Little Rock three days later. For two days, his body lay in state in the Cathedral of St. Andrew. After his funeral Mass on February 27th, his remains were buried in St. Andrew's, the ecclesiastical edifice he had erected in 1881.

A year after Fitzgerald's death, Arkansas elected its last governor of Irish descent. George Washington Donaghey's father was of Irish descent while his mother was of Scottish ancestry. Born on July 1, 1856, in Union Parish, Louisiana, just below the Arkansas-Louisiana line, his father later moved just across the border into Union County, Arkansas. His father served in the Confederate army and was taken prisoner. Young Donaghey was the oldest of five children and worked for a time in west Texas as a cowboy. He eventually settled in Conway in Faulkner County, about thirty miles northwest of Little Rock. Donaghey first became known in Conway as a skilled carpenter, and later branched out into cabinet making, furniture making and repair, and eventually became a building contractor. Although married, he and his wife produced no children and so Donaghey concentrated his energies and skills in his building industry. Appointment to a state commission to study building a new state capital eventually lured this "Carpenter from Conway" into state politics. On a promise to finally build the new state capital, Donaghey won the Democratic nomination for governor and then easily defeated his Republican and Socialist opponents to win the election as governor in November, 1908.

As governor for four years (two, two-year terms) Governor Donaghey had a very successful career as a progressive political leader, especially in the area of public education, public health, and ending the notorious convict lease system in the state. He did see the new state capital well on its way to completion by the time he left office in 1913. The capital officially did not open until the following year. Under his leadership, Arkansas became the first southern state to allow the people to enact referendums. The Conway carpenter was not as successful in his efforts to support statewide prohibition, a cause he passionately believed in as a lifelong member of the Southern Methodist church. Donaghey failed to win a third Democratic nomination for governor, defeated in 1912 by future Arkansas power broker, Joseph T. Robinson. Donaghey continued to work for the people of Arkansas in various capacities, especially on boards dealing with charities and education. He never again returned to Conway to live, but had a major contracting and building firm in Little Rock where he oversaw construction of several downtown buildings during the 1920s. He died in Little Rock on December 15, 1937, the last Arkansas governor whose surname and ancestry can be traced back to the Emerald Isle.

While it may be true that a few Irish immigrants and some of Irish ancestry made some significant contributions to the state at this time, most of the Irish immigrants in Arkansas remained poor. Dan Hogan, an Arkansas-born son of an Irish immigrant in Fort Smith, became one of the founders and leaders of the Arkansas Socialist Party. Initially trained as a lawyer, he went into politics and publishing. At first a Democrat, Hogan was attracted to the farmers reform movement and began editing a populist newspaper in Mansfield in western Arkansas in 1891. Hogan also began representing the miners in the coal mines of western Arkansas. With the collapse of the Populist Party in the late nineteenth century, this lawyer-turned-journalist embraced socialism and the Socialist party in 1900. In 1901, he published the first socialist newspaper in Arkansas in Huntingdon, the *Southern Worker*. By 1910, about 120 small Socialist weeklies had been published throughout the state, yet most were short-lived. In 1903, Hogan met with others of like mind to organize the Socialist Party in Arkansas. Hogan soon rose in the ranks of the national Socialist Party, serving on its national council where he became a close friend and associate with its national party leader Eugene V. Debs. Hogan also ran twice for governor on the Socialist ticket in 1906 and 1910 and continued to work in the state party until 1917. After that date he moved to Oklahoma where he continued to work for the Socialist movement until his death in 1935. By 1920, however, the Arkansas Socialist Party was dead. As one historian has put it, "Because Arkansas Socialism owed much to immediate conditions and little to theoretical Marxism, it may be considered as a continuation of agrarian radicalism."

The 1920 census has been considered significant by American historians for two reasons. For the first time, more people lived in the cities than in the rural areas; and the great wave of European migration to the United States stopped after almost eighty years. By that year, the number of foreign-born in Arkansas amounted to 14,137 out of a white population of 1,279,757, or 1.1%. At this time nationally the ratio of foreign-born to the overall white population of the nation was at 14.8%. The number of Irish-born immigrants in Arkansas had now fallen to 679, and the number of Irish in the former Confederate states equaled 14,421 out of a total foreign-born population in the South of 587,466. It must also be pointed out that by 1920, the foreign-born in Texas alone equaled 363,832, which means that the Lone Star State had 61.9% of all the foreign-born in the former Confederate states. When you add in the states of Louisiana and Florida, these three southern states contained 79.8% of all the foreign-born, leaving the remaining eight former Confederate states with just over one fifth of all the foreign-born immigrants. Immigration, whether Irish or other, would really have a profound impact on only a few states of the old Southern Confederacy, and Arkansas was not one of them.

It really then is no mystery as to why Arkansas had so few major leaders who came from Ireland or were Irish-Americans. Only in the Arkansas Catholic Church can one see strong Irish continuity in leadership. In more than 150 years as a diocese, Arkansas has had only five bishops, and four of the five have been either Irish immigrants or second or third generation Irish. Bishop John B. Morris, bishop from 1906–1946, was born in Tennessee of parents who were Irish immigrants. Bishop Andrew J. McDonald, consecrated bishop in 1972, was born in Georgia of two Irish parents, who were both first generation Americans.

The Irish made a small but distinctive contribution to the life of Arkansas and are today an integral part of Arkansas history.

*See* Irish Heritage of the South

Population statistics are taken directly from the Census records of 1850, 1860, 1890, 1920.

Morris S. Arnold, *Unequal Laws Unto a Savage Race: European Legal Traditions in Arkansas, 1636–1836* (Fayetteville, AR, 1985).

————, *Colonial Arkansas, 1686–1804: A Social and Cultural History* (Fayetteville, AR, 1991).

Timothy P. Donovan, et. al., *The Governors of Arkansas: Essays in Political Biography,* 2nd ed. (Fayetteville, AR, 1995).

Michael B. Dougan, *Arkansas Odyssey: The Saga of Arkansas from Prehistoric Times to the Present* (Little Rock, AR, 1994).

————, *Confederate Arkansas: The People and Policies of a Frontier State in Wartime* (Tuscaloosa, AL, 1976).

James R. Green, *Grassroots Socialism, Radical Movements in the Southwest, 1895–1943* (Baton Rouge, LA, 1978).

C. Gregory Kiser, "The Socialist Party in Arkansas, 1900–1912," *Arkansas Historical Quarterly,* 40 (Summer 1981): 119–153.

Calvin R. Ledbetter, Jr., *Carpenter from Conway: George Washington Donaghey as Governor of Arkansas, 1909–1913* (Fayetteville, AR, 1993).

Grady McWhiney, *Cracker Culture: Celtic Ways in the Old South* (Tuscaloosa, AL, 1988).

John I. Smith, *The Courage of a Southern Unionist: A Biography of Isaac Murphy, Governor of Arkansas, 1864–1868* (Little Rock, AR, 1979).

Craig L. Symonds, *Stonewall of the West: Pat Cleburne and the Civil War* (Lawrence, KS, 1997).

————, *Mission and Memory: A History of the Catholic Church in Arkansas* (Little Rock, AR, 1993).

James M. Woods, *Rebellion and Realignment: Arkansas's Road to Secession* (Fayetteville, AR, 1987).

JAMES M. WOODS

## ARTHUR, WILLIAM (1797–1875)

Clergyman, antiquarian, father of President Chester A. Arthur. William Arthur came to America from County Antrim, Ireland, settling first in New York then moving to Vermont. He acquired an excellent education in Ireland and briefly taught school and studied law after emigrating to America. He married Malvina Stone in 1821. The union produced seven children, the fifth of which, Chester, grew up to become the twenty-first president of the United States. In 1827, he experienced a religious conversion while attending a Free Will Baptist revival in Waterville, Vermont. He joined the Baptist clergy and received his ordination in 1828. William Arthur first preached in Fairfield, Vermont. His confrontational preaching style and abolitionist leanings irritated many of his parishioners, forcing the Arthurs to move often. After many years in Vermont, William Arthur moved his family to New York in 1835. He spent the next twenty years moving from church to church in cities and towns across the state. Finally, in 1855, he settled somewhat permanently in Albany, where he remained until his retirement in 1864. Arthur also possessed a keen interest in history and the classics, becoming a local antiquarian of some little note. While residing in Schenectady, Arthur briefly published and edited his own magazine, *The Antiquarian and General Review,* often printing his own writings on Irish antiquity, a subject in which he had a particular interest. He died in retirement at Newtonville, New York, in 1875.

*Dictionary of American Biography*, Vol. I, part 1: 379.

George Frederick Howe, *Chester A. Arthur, A Quarter-Century of Machine Politics* (New York, 1935; reprint 1957).

Thomas C. Reeves, *Gentleman Boss: The Life of Chester Alan Arthur* (New York, 1975).

TOM DOWNEY

# B

## BAILEY, JOHN MORAN (1904–1975)

Lawyer and political party official. Born into Irish ancestry to Dr. Michael and Louise (Moran) Bailey, he entered St. Peter's Parochial School and then Hartford Public High School in Hartford, Connecticut. Bailey attended the Catholic University of America in Washington, D.C., where he earned a B.A. degree in science in 1926. He then enrolled in Harvard Law School where he earned the LL.B. degree in 1929. Later the same year he opened a law office in Hartford and launched his political career under the auspices of Thomas J. Spellacy, a well-known and powerful persona in Democratic state affairs.

Bailey was elected judge of the Hartford Police Court in 1933 and again in 1939. His rising ambition in politics gained him recognition and from 1941–1946 he served as a member of the Connecticut Statute Revision Commission; prior to this appointment he was treasurer of the National Young Democrats from 1937–1941. In 1946 Bailey became executive secretary to Governor Wilbert Snow and later the same year won the post of chairman of the Democratic State Commission. In the variety of political experiences, Bailey became one of the most effective politicians in the United States.

Bailey took up advocacy for the John F. Kennedy cause in 1956, especially at the Democratic National Convention where he and Governor Ribicoff proposed Senator Kennedy for the vice presidency. Because of this initiative, Bailey was summoned for full-time service in the Kennedy campaign for Democratic nomination. At the 1960 convention Bailey played a crucial role in serving as a personal liaison between Senator Kennedy and both local and national political leaders. On January 21, 1961, the day after the presidential inauguration of Kennedy, Bailey was elected by 100 party leaders in Washington to act as chairman of the Democratic National Committee.

Bailey married Barbara Leary on August 1, 1933, and was the father of four children.

*See* Connecticut

*Democratic Digest* (January 1961): 47.
*Who's Who in America* (1962–1963).
*Who's Who in United States Politics* (1952).
*CAB* (1962).

JOY HARRELL

## BALTIMORE

Baltimore town was established in 1729 on land bought from the Carroll family who had themselves come from Ireland. It was one of more than a dozen settlements in Maryland named for an Irish town or city. The Irish Baltimore is on the coast of Cork.

Many of the most prominent Irish in early Baltimore were Presbyterian. In 1761 nine or ten Scots-Irish families formed Baltimore's First Presbyterian Church, calling the Rev. Patrick Allison as their parson. From this church would emerge a number of Baltimore's leaders. One was James Calhoun. A recent immigrant from Ireland, he served as Baltimore's first mayor in 1797. Oxford-educated Drs. John and Henry Stevenson were powerful figures in the Baltimore community. Another was William Patterson, wealthy Scots-Irish merchant. His daughter Betsy outstripped him in notoriety when Bishop John Carroll presided at the nuptials of Betsy Patterson and Jerome Bonaparte, younger brother of Napoleon at Christmas, 1803. The union was short-lived but Betsy Patterson Bonaparte lived to the ripe old age of 94.

In 1801 Robert Garrett arrived in Baltimore. Born in County Down he founded a dynasty of merchants and financiers. The Garretts were very influential in the early years of the Baltimore and Ohio Railroad and Johns Hopkins University.

The year 1803 marks the foundation of the Hibernian Society of Baltimore. Irish-born John Campbell White was the founding president. He had been involved in the Rising of 1798. Other prominent members of the Hibernian Society were John O'Donnell, shipping magnate, Robert Oliver, one of the wealthiest men in the Union, Cumberland Dugan, importer, and William Patterson. Their projects included a free school, relief for Famine ships, and job placement for the immigrants from Ireland. From its foundation this Hibernian Society was non-denominational. Its membership was consistently drawn from the mercantile and professional community. Not many of the "Ward Irishmen" were involved. This latter group would support the Friendly Sons of St. Patrick in the later decades of the century.

Baltimore did not know many Nativist outbursts. Perhaps the most outstanding was the Carmelite Riot in the summer of 1839. It followed the standard motif of the "escaped nun" tale. Sister Isabella (Olivia Neale) departed from her cloister in East Baltimore, rallying the support of the Nativist segment of the population. The rioting went on for three days.

The Know-Nothing phenomenon of the 1850s was a much more grave problem for the Irish. It seriously divided their ranks along religious lines.

Dublin-born Francis Patrick Kenrick was the first native Irishman to serve as Archbishop of Baltimore. His tenure, 1851–1863, was a difficult one, especially the Civil War days. His widely read moral theology was unfortunate in that it seemed to link Catholicism with a toleration of slavery. Michael J. Kelly, a publisher of the *Catholic Mirror* in Baltimore during the Civil War, was twice arrested for his Southern sympathies. Eventually he was imprisoned in Fort McHenry.

Loyola College was established in 1852 by the Jesuits. The founding president was Fr. John Early, S.J., who had emigrated from County Fermanagh. Loyola moved from Holliday Street to Calvert Street to North Charles Street. At the Calvert Street site it was located near the Tenth Ward. From this "Little Limerick" Loyola drew many students.

The strictly Catholic Ancient Order of Hibernians came to Baltimore in 1886 and soon a number of local divisions were set up. Robert Emmet Guerin and Jere O. Hamil were effective leaders of the A.O.H.

One of the staunchest allies of the interdenominational Hibernian society was Father James Dolan from Cashel, pastor of St. Patrick Church, Falls Point. In 1817 a prominent member of the Hibernian Society, Hugh Jenkins, financed the first of three orphanages Fr. Dolan organized. He became known as "the Apostle of the Point" and was described as one of the most spectacular pastors in the history of the Baltimore Archdiocese. On the west end of the city a contemporary of Fr. Dolan was Fr. Edward McColgan, a Donegal man. He built St. Peter the Apostle Church which he shepherded for over a half century. He was a prime mover in the founding of St. Mary's Industrial School after the Civil War. Other notable nineteenth-century Irish Catholic parishes in Baltimore City would be St. Ann, St. Brigid, St. John, Old St. Joseph, St. Lawrence O'Toole, St. Martin, and St. Mary Star of the Sea.

James Cardinal Gibbons stands as the premier figure among Irish-Americans in Baltimore for the four decades before his death in 1921. Though he was born in Baltimore, his family moved back to Ireland where he received much of his education in County Mayo. But he did not emphasize his Irish heritage. Cardinal Gibbons may well have been as one newspaper described him, "the most influential private citizen in the nation." He was clearly the head of the American Catholic Church. Gibbons forged the alliance between the Catholic Church and the labor movement in the United States. The Cardinal called his own style of leadership "a masterly inactivity with a watchful eye."

Cardinal Gibbons' successor was Athlone-born Michael J. Curley. He had come to the United States to work in the mission diocese of St. Augustine, Florida, where he was named bishop in 1914. His appointment to Baltimore was a surprise to many. Archbishop Curley was then the youngest archbishop in the United States. His oratory was very powerful but he was betrayed by his health in the last decade before his death in 1947.

Numerous Irish-Americans from Baltimore were named bishops in the Catholic Church particularly in the South. They include William Hafey (Raleigh), Peter Ireton (Richmond), John Keane (Richmond), Jeremiah O'Sullivan (Mobile), John Russell (Charleston and Richmond), William Russell (Charleston), Thomas Toolen (Mobile), and J. Francis Stafford (Memphis), who was named a Cardinal in 1998.

Irish women religious served in the works of education and health care in Baltimore City. As early as 1855 Irish Sisters of Mercy from Pittsburgh arrived in West Baltimore. About twenty of them headed South to serve as nurses during the Civil War. Among their early members was Sister M. Camillus Byrne, godchild of Mother Catherine McAuley. Sister M. Veronica Daily guided Mercy Hospital as administrator. With a strong hand, Mother M. Philemon Doyle directed the Baltimore Province of the School Sisters of Notre Dame to its status as the largest community of women religious in the city. Sister M. Pierre O'Regan gave tremendous leadership to St. Joseph Hospital as it moved from an urban to a suburban setting. Two Irish Sisters have found their way into the standard lore of Baltimore. Bon Secours Sister Malachy McAtee was a dynamo in bringing aid to the poor and sickly. Her methodology was said to be somewhat reminiscent of that of Robin Hood. She met her death in 1954 when hit by a street car while making her rounds of West Baltimore. Sister Nativity Maguire served Saint Agnes Hospital as night supervisor and in many other capacities for almost five decades. This Daughter of Charity was famous for her very direct methods in getting patients back to the practice of their faith. She would note that she was not born in Ireland but in the "annex": Boston.

Patients would long remember her after having forgotten the names of the doctors, the nurses, and the chaplains who had attended them. She lived 97 years.

City politics has long been the bailiwick of the Irish-American. Herbert Romulus O'Conor was a great force in local politics. He came from the most Irish of neighborhoods, the Tenth Ward. In 1923 he was elected State's Attorney for Baltimore City. At age 27 he was the youngest man ever to be elected to that office. His rise in the political realms was meteoric. By 1939 he was governor. He resigned in 1947 to serve in the United States Senate. His biography is aptly called *The Inevitable Success*. Other Irish-American politicians of varying influence in the city include Willy Curran, Frank Gallagher, Harry "Soft-shoes" McGuirk, T. Barton Harrington, John "Frank" Kelly, Ambrose Kennedy, A. Leo Knott, Dan Loden, Sonny Mahon, and Sugar McElgunn. Less given to the rough and tumble was J. Harold Grady who served as mayor of Baltimore from 1959 to 1962.

The Baltimore Orioles baseball team began in 1885. The mid-1890s were the championship days for the team. Making the difference were "Foxy Ned" Hanlon and John McGraw. After the turn of the century Jack Dunn led the team for several decades.

For much of their history, the Baltimore Irish lived in the southern precincts of the city: Canton, Fells Point, Locust Point, and the neighborhoods around the B&O Railroad yards in Southwest Baltimore. At the end of the nineteenth century there was a migration northward, especially along the York Road. In the twentieth century this movement would continue though in diverse directions until today when there are no thoroughly Irish neighborhoods in Baltimore City.

The philanthropy of the Irish-American community has always been noteworthy in Baltimore. The Caton Sisters, the granddaughters of Charles Carroll of Carrollton, set the standard by continuing and expanding the generosity of their venerable grandfather by countless benefactions of land and revenue to the Catholic Church. Isabella McLanahan Brown established Bolton Hill's Brown Memorial Presbyterian Church. Ardent Scots-Irishman John McDonogh left a goodly portion of his fortune to the city of his youth to establish a farm school just northwest of Baltimore in 1873. The Blake family provided for the new Loyola High School while the Misses Bogue were consistent benefactors of Loyola College. Charles Dougherty endowed both St. Agnes Hospital and Mt. St. Agnes College in memory of his wife. Theatrical impresario James Lawrence Kernan used his fortune to establish a noted orthopedic hospital in his name. A legacy of Thomas O'Neill built the Cathedral of Mary Our Queen. James Keelty, Henry Knott, William and Catherine Lanahan, and George McManus were notable for their philanthropy.

The annual St. Patrick's Day parade was revived in 1956. It had not been held since 1910 but now continues to be a major spring event. In addition to the major Irish societies mentioned, supporting groups include The Emerald Isle Club, The Emerald Society of The Baltimore Fire Department, The Emerald Society of the Baltimore Police Department, The Ladies Ancient Order of Hibernians, St. John's Old Timers, and St. Peter's Cemetery Restoration Foundation. A very successful Irish Festival is held in the late summer each year.

*See* Carrolls of Maryland; Scots Irish

Jean H. Baker, *Ambivalent Americans, The Know-Nothing Party in Maryland* (Baltimore, Maryland, 1977).

Francis F. Beirne, *The Amiable Baltimoreans* (Baltimore, Maryland, 1951).

Nicholas W. J. Dohony, *Souvenir Book, Sesquicentennial Saint Patrick's Parish, 1792–1942* (Baltimore, Maryland, 1942).

James F. Schneider, *A Baker's Dozen of Historical Minutes from the 225th Anniversary of the First and Franklin Street Presbyterian Church* (Baltimore, Maryland, 1988).

Thomas W. Spalding, *The Premier See: A History of the Archdiocese of Baltimore, 1798–1989* (Baltimore, Maryland, 1989).

Harold A. Williams, *A History of the Hibernian Society of Baltimore, 1803–1957* (Baltimore, Maryland, 1957).

———, *Robert Garrett & Sons Incorporated, Origin and Development 1840–1965* (Baltimore, Maryland, 1965).

MICHAEL ROACH

## BARRY, PATRICK (1816–1890)

Horticulturist. Born the son of a farmer in Belfast, Ireland, Barry received a liberal education and became a teacher in the Ireland national schools. In 1836 he emigrated to the United States where he began working in a nursery; during this time he gained an extensive knowledge of horticulture practice. Later, he moved to Rochester, New York, where he befriended George Ellwanger. Together he and Ellwanger founded the Mt. Hope Nursery which eventually became the leading U.S. nursery. In 1847, he married Harriet Huestis and they had six sons and two daughters.

The Mt. Hope Nursery began with a variety of imports from France and Germany which were tested for durability in the New York environment. Barry began to make use of his prior experience and his willingness to expand the business led him to various fruit-growing techniques which he developed and introduced into the region for the first time. In 1848 he was named secretary of the national convention of fruit growers. In 1851 he published *The Fruit Garden* in which he provided illustrations of his work on the physiology of fruit trees, the techniques associated with growing, preserving, and preventing damage to the trees. In this significant work Barry outlined various methods of growing which he extracted from his own experience on various farms in surrounding villages and towns. He also contributed to other publications such as the *Genesee Farmer,* the *Horticulturist* and the *American Agriculturalist.*

In 1872, after several revisions, the name of Barry's book was changed from *The Fruit Garden* to *Barry's Fruit Garden.* Due to his influence and inspiration, the national convention of fruit growers expanded and became the American Pomological Society which began in 1852. Barry was elected to serve as chairman of this committee and he served to initiate the society's classified *Catalogue of Fruits* in 1862; this classification system was formulated by Barry and his precision succeeded in making the system the standard code of authority on this subject within the field at large. He continued to exert his influence and talent and was a significant contributor to the organization of the Fruit Growers Society of Western New York from 1855 until he was elected to serve as chairman of the executive committee. He remained on this board until 1870 when the society was changed in name to the Western New York Horticultural Society. In 1877 he continued his work and became president of the New York State Agricultural Society. From 1882 to 1889 Barry served as a member of the first board of control of the New York State Agricultural Experiment Station at Geneva.

Barry's contribution to the field of horticulture was monumental. He made a lucrative living in publishing and other activities such as banking and the promotion of civic activities. He died on June 23, 1890, and was succeeded by his son William C. Barry in the nursery business.

*Western New York Horticultural Society* (1891).

L. R. Doty, *History of Genesee County* (1925).

*American Agriculturalist* (August, 1890).

*Dictionary of American Biography,* 1.

JOY HARRELL

## BARRY, PHILIP JAMES QUINN (1896–1949)

Playwright. Philip Barry was born in Rochester, N.Y., to James Corbett Barry and Mary Agnes (Quinn) Barry. James Barry came to the United States when he was ten years old and eventually became a well-to-do marble and tile contractor. His wife was of Irish descent and the daughter of the owner of a lumber business in Philadelphia.

After studying in parochial schools, Barry attended Yale, where he contributed to the "Daily News" and the "Literary Magazine." When World War I broke out, he served in the State Department and the American embassy in London.

In 1919 he enrolled at Harvard and studied dramatic writing under George Baker. His first play, *A Punch for Judy,* was performed in New York in 1921. To finance his studies, Barry worked for a year in a New York advertising firm. He then returned to Baker's workshop and turned out two plays, *You and I* and *The Youngest,* that launched a Broadway career that lasted through three decades.

Although critics saw romantic comedy as his strength, Barry ventured into serious, ambitious plays that earned praise from the critics but weren't as successful with audiences. In the 1920s he illustrated that contrast with two highly successful sophisticated comedies, *Paris Bound* (1927) and *Holiday* (1928), and also wrote *White Wings* (1926), a fantasy about a street cleaner, *John* (1927), a tragedy concerning John the Baptist, and a murder mystery, *Cock Robin* (1928).

The Great Depression of the 1930s did not provide a favorable background for the romantic comedies on which Barry had earned his reputation. However, *Tomorrow and Tomorrow* (1931), a serious drama that concerned marriage and illicit love, was a surprise hit, possibly due to the leading actor, Leslie Howard. In his serious plays, Barry was interested in making a statement about humankind's religious dilemma, deliberating on the ancient questions of evil, free will and human nature.

His play *Here Come the Clowns* was adapted from his only novel, *War in Heaven* (1938), and was a study of good and evil in the world. Although *Here Come the Clowns* wasn't a box-office hit, it was the most discussed play of the 1938–1939 season.

In 1939, the play for which Barry is best remembered, *The Philadelphia Story,* was produced. The play starred Katherine Hepburn, Joseph Cotten, Van Heflin and Shirley Booth. True to Barry comedy, the rich Main Line girl doesn't marry the successful young businessman or the reporter, but after heartwrenching confrontations, she returns to her former husband.

In the 1940s Barry wrote three plays reflecting his concern with the war: *Liberty Jones* (1941), *Without Love* (1942) and *Foolish Nation* (1945). Barry also dealt with Irish material, *The Joyous Season* (1934), in which he reminded his fellow Irish that they shouldn't lose sight of all the good qualities they possessed, especially a sense of humor and independence.

On July 15, 1922, Barry married Ellen Marshall Semple of Mount Kisco, N.Y. They had two sons, Philip Semple and Jonathan Peter; a daughter died in infancy. He established a home in Cannes, France, where he did most of his writing. From September to January he lived in Mount Kisco in order to travel to New York City when his plays were in production.

Barry was working on *Second Threshold* when he died in New York City on Dec. 3, 1949. The play was completed by Robert Sherwood and produced in 1951.

Barry was a playwright of substantial achievement. He used versatility in experimenting with writing, acting and stagecraft. He was a prolific writer who turned out every form of drama, whose work reflected that he was a romantic, moralist, and observer of the human condition.

*See* Theater, Irish in

*Dictionary of American Biography* (New York, 1974).
William V. Shannon, *The American Irish* (New York, rev. ed., 1966).

MARIANNA McLOUGHLIN

## BARTON, THOMAS (c. 1728–1780)

Anglican missionary, political pamphleteer, and scientist in eighteenth-century Pennsylvania. Barton was born in Carrickmacross, Co. Monaghan, into a prominent family of Cromwellian settlers. His father's apparent illegitimacy doomed Barton's branch of the family to genteel poverty, and, after studying at Trinity College, Dublin, he emigrated to Pennsylvania, where he established a school at Norriton and tutored his future brother-in-law, David Rittenhouse (1732–96), later a celebrated astonomer and one of revolutionary Philadelphia's most radical leaders. In 1752 Barton moved to Philadelphia and taught in the Academy (later, the College) of Philadelphia, where he gained the patronage of Rev. William Smith (1727–1803), a Scottish-born Anglican who encouraged Barton to seek ordination in the Church of England. In 1754, after a hasty marriage to Esther Rittenhouse, Barton journeyed to London where he was ordained and, through the friendship of Thomas Penn (1702–75), Pennsylvania's chief proprietor, appointed a missionary by the Society for the Propagation of the Gospel (S.P.G.). Barton's intimacy with Penn and Smith linked him to Pennsylvania's "proprietary party," a pragmatic alliance of normally-antagonistic Anglican gentry and Scots-Irish farmers, joined in hostility to the "Quaker party," led by Benjamin Franklin, that dominated the colonial Assembly and feuded with the Penn family's administration. In 1755 Barton became minister of three frontier churches, largely composed of Irish-born parishioners, at Huntingdon, York, and Carlisle. When the French and Indian War began in 1755, Barton rallied western settlers with a rousing, anti-Catholic sermon that Smith published before learning that Barton had plagiarized it. Embarrassed, Barton secured appointment as military chaplain in the British army that captured Fort Duquesne (Nov. 25, 1758); his journal remains the best description of that expedition. At Penn's urging, in 1759 the S.P.G. appointed Barton to the richer ministry of St. James' Church in Lancaster, but in May 1763 Pontiac's Rebellion convulsed the frontier, and on December 14 and 27 the "Paxton Boys," largely Scots-Irish frontiersmen, took revenge by massacring twenty Christianized Indians on their reservation at Conestoga Manor and in the Lancaster workhouse. Although personally horrified by the slaughter of apparent innocents, as a service to proprietary interests Barton published an anonymous pamphlet, *The Conduct of the Paxton Men, Impartially Represented* (1764), which vilified the victims and blamed Pontiac's Rebellion on Quaker pacifism; in return, Penn's agents gave him Conestoga Manor. An effective pastor, Barton started Lancaster's fire company and public library, conducted missionary work among the Indians, aided Rittenhouse's scientific experiments, and accumulated large botanical and minerological collections, all of which—joined to proprietary favor—won him election to the American Philosophical Society and honorary degrees from the College of Philadelphia and King's College in New York. However, in the late 1760s and early 1770s, colonial agitation against Britain split the proprietary party, isolating Anglican loyalists like Barton from their former allies. An ardent Tory, in 1776–80 Barton took refuge in British-controlled New York City, where he died just five days before his ship was scheduled to sail for Ireland. Ironically, three of Barton's sons held political or military office under the revolutionary régime, and William (1754–1817) was primarily responsible for designing the great seal of the American republic. His youngest son, Benjamin (1766–1815), became one of Philadelphia's leading physicians and scientists, as well as a member of the city's Hibernian Society.

Barton's correspondence with the S.P.G. is in W. S. Perry, ed., *Historical Collections Relating to the American Colonial Church,* II and V (New York, 1969 ed.).
W. F. Diller, *The History of St. James' Church (Protestant Episcopal), 1744–1944* (Lancaster, Pa., 1944).
W. A. Hunter, "Thomas Barton and the Forbes Expedition," *Pennsylvania Magazine of History & Biography,* 95 (1971): 431–83.
T. W. Jeffries, "Thomas Barton (1730–1780): Victim of the Revolution," *Journal of the Lancaster County Historical Society,* 81 (1977): 39–64.
J. P. Meyers, Jr.: "Preparations for the Forbes Expedition . . .," *Adams County History,* 1 (1995): 4–26.
———, "Rev. Thomas Barton's Authorship of *The Conduct of the Paxton Men . . .,*" *Pennsylvania History,* 61 (1994): 155–84.
———, "Rev. Thomas Barton's Conflict with Col. John Armstrong, ca. 1758," *Cumberland County History,* 10 (1993): 3–14.
———, "Thomas Barton's *Unanimity and Public Spirit* (1775): Controversy and Plagiarism on the Pennsylvania Frontier," *Pennsylvania Magazine of History & Biography,* 119 (1995): 225–48.
M. F. Russell, "Thomas Barton and Pennsylvania's Colonial Frontier," *Pennsylvania History,* 46 (1979): 313–34.
A. H. Young, "Thomas Barton: A Pennsylvania Loyalist," *Ontario Historical Society Journal,* 30 (1934): 33–42.

KERBY MILLER

## BASEBALL: THE EARLY YEARS

Who build[t] our jails? The Irish. Who fill our jails? The Irish, and it might also be said the Irish do their share towards building up the national game [baseball]. (*Sporting News,* 3 March 1894)

It can be argued that baseball, our "national pastime," owes more to Irish-Americans than to any other ethnic community. For many generations of American youth, baseball was a sort of "melting pot" reflection of our society. One writer suggested that baseball is "one of the nation's most effective bubbling cauldrons" (Bjarkman, 46). Historically, many first-generation Americans, and foreign-born Hispanics, have impacted the "national game" and were acculturated in the process. Each group promoted its own litany of heroes and heralded the feats and contributions associated with its ethnicity. Although only about a dozen players have been identified as native-born Irish, no group pervaded any era of baseball like nineteenth-century Irish-Americans. Their dominance went beyond actual numbers and percentages to seasonal statistics and league championships. They also changed how the game of baseball was played and their mastery represented a kind of "Emerald Age" of American baseball.

Baseball has a controversial and disputed genesis. Nineteenth-century nativists claimed the game as their own and scoured the countryside for baseball's home-grown antecedents. In a post-Civil War campaign of national pride, foreign sports, particularly the English game of rounders, were given little credibility when compared to rural Yankee-American prototypes. In 1907, former player and sporting goods manufacturer, Albert Spalding and his Special Baseball Commission officially disowned foreign influences and concocted an origin myth around Civil War hero Abner Doubleday and his boyhood memories of Cooperstown, New York. But five years before the Commission's alleged findings, *The Gael* magazine entered the debate with an article celebrating the contributions of Ireland and Irish-American players. The author, James Mitchell, lauded Irish influences on the American pastime and declared that "all outdoor games played with a stick and ball have their origin in the ancient [Irish] game of hurling." He asserted that wherever the Celtic "race flourished the original game and its various offspring can be found in use." For him rounders and all Yankee games could be traced back to the Tailten Games and the sport of *iomain* (Mitchell, 151). This ethnic pride neither discounted English-Yankee influences nor did it plant Irish roots on the evolutionary tree of baseball. The role of the Irish on baseball was more subtle. It was based on Ireland's popular bat-ball traditions and the peculiar circumstances that greeted Irish immigrants in America.

Much of the Irish bat-ball experiences are linked to varieties of hurling that have been played in Ireland for more than a millennium. Irish boys, long adept at handling a long crooked stick-bat, called a hurley, were accustomed to the hand-eye coordination of striking a spherical object. Trying to explain an Irishman's affinity to baseball, the popular press of the nineteenth century exaggerated and confused the art of wielding a shillelagh, with the skills of handling a hurley stick. This popular mythology did not make all Irish kids natural baseball players. It only explained their attraction to American bat-ball games. This relationship, though nurtured by their comfort with bat-ball sports, had more to do with their peculiar immigration experiences.

The collapse of Ireland's agricultural economy that drove more than two million people to North America coincided with the transformation of Protestant-Yankee versions of rounders, like townball, into a recognizable form of modern day baseball. Termed the "New York" or the "Knickerbocker" game, the sport rooted itself in the northeastern cities of the United States that became havens for Irish famine refugees. With forty-five percent of these immigrants being males between the ages of 14 and 24, a new potential sporting base was introduced into American society. Initially, the immigrants were driven by survival and no thought was given to the games or sporting interests of their adopted homeland. But the growth and popularity of recreational activities were part of the evolving urban culture that greeted Ireland's dispossessed. In this setting the offspring of these desperate famine refugees associated themselves closely with a game they were destined to transform.

In less than a decade after the American Civil War, baseball permeated all aspects of urban culture. Mark Twain said baseball became the "very symbol, the outward and visible expression of the drive and push and rush and struggle of . . . [our] raging, teeming [and] booming society" (*Spalding Scrapbook,* Vol. I, 1889, 117). The sport also went from a leisure game played by young businessmen and artisans to an intensely competitive game between specific clubs and identifiable urban teams. This mutation led to bidding for the services of specialized position-skilled athletes. By 1869, baseball at its highest levels became a game played by professionals. Fueled by waves of immigrant labor, post-war industrial cities like Chicago, New York, Philadelphia, Boston, St. Louis and Cleveland prospered and stood as major baseball foci. On the undeveloped and vacant lots of these swelling cities, the baseball craze and the children of Irish immigrants came together.

Most of the economic refugees from the Irish famine were unskilled Catholic agricultural laborers, unsuited for America's urban economic opportunities. The typical rural immigrant was generally employable as a casual or seasonal worker in low-paying manual jobs. In 1870, urban America sheltered 44% of over a million Irish-born immigrants and their children. (Ibson, 10; Doyle, 53). The stunted mobility of these manual workers was reinforced by unflattering traditional religious and cultural images of the childlike and brutish "Paddy." But alternatives to "pick and shovel" jobs were not plentiful. The success of some enterprising contractors, well-connected politicans and dutiful municipal workers did not change the Irish forecast. America's grand promise still eluded them. For sons of immigrants the swiftest path to acceptance, and perhaps the wealth and fame of their parents' dreams, came from the expansion of urban professional sports.

For many young Irish-Americans, baseball was an early totem of the new culture. Historians Dennis Clark and Steven Reiss agreed that baseball was a high profile urban sport with acculturating facets. Already identified as the national pastime, baseball was appreciated for its democratic flavor and non-elite pretentions. Defiant of time restrictions and strict cricket-style playing codes, baseball possessed societal conventions attractive to Irish-American youths (Clark, "Sports Cults," an unpublished paper; Reiss, 65–66, 103–4). Less dangerous than boxing and physically less restrictive than horse-racing, baseball was a sporting crucible for Irish boys raised in ancestral bat-ball customs.

To identify Irish athletic ambitions as a conscious medium for social mobility is to exaggerate the intentions of young boys whose expectations were personal and immediate. Baseball for Irish kids was a short-cut to self-indulgent glory and fortune. Each successful athlete, regardless of their ethnicity, inspired and modeled the emulation of their community. Promoting these associations was another conduit to baseball, the neighborhood bachelor sub-culture.

The local saloon, barbershop and firehouse became congregating spots for immigrant male-centered working-class communities. These masculine enclaves provided men with a much needed sense of identity, status and security. Drawing on old world social gathering patterns, these havens segregated the sexes and became a kind of surrogate family where the male rites of passage and bonding were consummated. Less formal than the tradition-laden Gaelic Athletic Association and the *Clan-na Gael* clubs, neighborhood working class "bhoys" found sponsorship to play competitive baseball that "upheld a vision of masculinity that valorized camaraderie, loyalty to peers, prowess, bravado and courage" (Gorn, 28).

Mike "King" Kelly

Charlie Comiskey

The popular crest of nineteenth-century baseball was first ridden by English and German players. The Irish first made their pre-war mark on the Washington Club of Hoboken and the Columbia team of Orange, New Jersey. As the sport's popularity grew, first generation Irish-American boys took baseball over in unheard of numbers. By the 1880s, examination of surnames on team rosters, competing at the top levels of baseball in the National League and the American Association, showed one third of the ballplayers were Irish. For the next two decades these percentages sometimes ranged as high as 50%. These numbers were not surprising given the large number of Irish-American boys growing up in cities with long traditions of baseball franchises. Drawn to local ball parks by the exploits of a succession of popular sporting models, the Irish "crank," or fan, sat in the inexpensive bleacher sections that were termed "Kerry Patches." Pitchers like "Old Horse" Radbourne, Jim Devlin, Frank Larkin, "Pud" Garvin, Larry Corcoran, Tony Mullane, "Smiling Mickey" Welsh, Tim Keefe and Charlie Ferguson shaped the ambitions of "Sadie" MacMahon, "Kid" Carsey, "Brickyard" Kennedy, Frank Killen, James Callahan, "Iron Man" McGinnity, "Red" Donahue and Rube Waddell. Offensively, Irish batters such as James "The Orator" O'Rourke, Roger Connors, "Big Dan" Brouthers, Mike "King" Kelly, Charlie Comiskey, Tommy McCarthy and "Long John" Reilly inspired youngsters like Ed Delahanty, "Wee Willie" Keeler, John McGraw, Hugh Jennings, Mike Tiernan, Joe Kelley and Jimmy Collins.

Irish kids were also impressed with their hero's successful demeanor. But the newly acquired affluence of ballplayers, evidenced by their fashion and lifestyles, were shallow success models. This reality made no difference to young Irish adolescent athletes who saw "King" Kelly as the embodiment of the American dream. It was an adulation that rivaled today's adoration of contemporary basketball players.

Irish dominance of the national pastime also affected the popular image of late nineteenth-century baseball. Observers took the rowdy and brash play of Irish ballplayers at face value and associated it with their off-field lifestyles. Their hard work and injury-shortened careers were ignored and only the self-indulgent activities of high-profile Irish players, who lived in the headlines, got attention. Even the famous poem "Casey at the Bat" was intended to satirize the bravado and arrogance of a popular Irish slugger, like "King" Kelly. "Cap" Anson, the great player and manager of the Whitestockings of Chicago, who played such a prominent role in excluding "colored" ballplayers from baseball, held the Irish player in low regard. He did not like working with the Irish and never lost an opportunity to demean players of "Irish blood" (*Cleveland Plain Dealer,* 4 January 1890). But contrary to popular perceptions many Irish ballplayers saved their money, invested wisely, got an education and to make ends meet held rather pedestrian jobs in the off-season. These positive traits were overlooked, as were the drinking, carousing, and gambling habits associated with players of other nationalities. These negative stereotypes also ignored the impact the Irish-Americans had on the national game of baseball.

By the mid-1880s a style of play, described as heady, daring and spontaneous, was successfully applied to major league baseball. Until the turn of the century four teams with Irish ballplayers and managers dominated championship play. This tradition extended into the new century as former Irish players became innovative winning managers. The formula for this success was astute Hibernian managers, a core of crafty Irish ballplayers and active on-field leadership from players "of the Shamrock persuasion" (*Sporting Life,* 19 Sept. 1896).

Identifying the pedigree of this kind of baseball is not straightforward. Smart and team-oriented ball playing had always been a prescription for a winning franchise and Mike "King" Kelly had already popularized conniving ball playing. The problem is that no recognizable or singular source has been credited with this Irish playing style. The closest point of origin appears to be a hybrid form of scheming baseball perfected by the Chicago-born son of an Irish alderman, Charlie Comiskey. The "old Roman," or more precisely Celt, played first base and managed the American Association St. Louis Brownstockings to four consecutive championships in the mid-1880s. Comiskey was driven to win and resorted to any trick or device that brought him victory. He competed by upsetting his opponents, believing if players were disturbed and distracted their play fell off. He asserted that all was fair "in war and baseball" and nothing should stand in the way of winning a ball game (*Ibid.,* 10 May 1897; *Sporting News,* 13 Feb. 1897; 20 Oct. 1900). Comiskey baited umpires and rel-

Willie Keeler

John McGraw

ished the challenge of molding difficult players into a cohesive group of wily winners. Comiskey worked closely with his quick-witted catcher, William "Yank" Robinson, whose "cute Irish way" of flattering and scheming helped his manager gain the upper hand (*Phila. Evening Item,* 18 July 1897; *Sporting News,* 23 Dec. 1899). Charles Comiskey's success immediately became a formula for a new group of successful managers—Ned Hanlon in Baltimore and Brooklyn, Frank Selee in Boston, and Patsy Tebeau in Cleveland.

The non-Irish Selee, without any major league experience, was the first to follow Comiskey's tactics. He put together a smart and winning combination of Irish players and from 1891 to 1893 won three straight pennants with a style of play that Hanlon admired and Comiskey recognized. With alert and crafty players centered around the "heavenly-twins," Tommy McCarthy and Hugh Duffy, the Beaneaters of Boston played intelligent, aggressive and intimidating baseball. At the extreme was Patsy Tebeau, who represented a cruder and more abusive style of play. His Cleveland teams played a physical and in-your-face kind of baseball. His old adversary, Connie Mack, once characterized Tebeau's rough side by saying that "Patsy . . . came over [to America] in a potato sack from County Armagh" (*Ibid.,* 4 Dec. 1895). But it was Hanlon's Orioles from Baltimore who set the standard for the Emerald Age of baseball. Without a dominant pitching staff, the Orioles won the league championship from 1894 to 1896. But after two second-place finishes, the franchise was dismantled and the players taken by Hanlon to Brooklyn captured the league title in 1899 and 1900. Called "Foxy Ned" and the "Napoleon of baseball," Hanlon did not have the temperament of Comiskey or Tebeau. He was described as "stoical as a sphinx" and immune to criticism (*Sporting Life,* 29 June 1895). He understood what it took to win and sought out imaginative players who would follow his lead.

Beyond their shared style of play these managers were linked by common influences. Charlie Comiskey was brought to St. Louis by his mentor, Ted Sullivan, a native of Ireland and a successful enterprising schemer and promotional wizard. Patsy Tebeau, born and raised in St. Louis, was a devoted follower of Comiskey's Brownstockings and their winning tactics. Comiskey and Selee were bonded by players like Tommy McCarthy, who

learned the game from Comiskey and brought this style of play to Boston. American Association players said that next to "Long John" Reilly of Cincinnati, McCarthy was "the dirtiest player in the country" (*Ibid.,* 6 June 1888). Years later, playing under Selee, he was described as "brainy, clever and audacious" (*Ibid.,* 5 May 1894). Selee in Boston also managed the irrepressible Mike Kelly in 1891. As for Hanlon, he learned the game from his manager in Detroit, the venerable Scotch Irishman Jack Chapman, and honed his craft by studying the successes of Comiskey and Selee. Hanlon also managed the old Brownstockings' strategist "Yank" Robinson in the 1890 Players League. Two of Hanlon's leading Orioles shared a familar background. Hugh Jennings was taught by Jack Chapman, and Wilbert Robinson's first minor league manager was Frank Selee.

Another factor shared by these managers was the hard-nose play of their largely Irish ball clubs. Despite the high percentage of Irish players on their rosters, being Irish did not guarantee a winner. To play for Hanlon a ballplayer had to be unwilling to settle for anything less than winning. But there were two Irish playing traditions in vogue. The first type of player took the form of the "Casey at the Bat" Irishman, the powerful Irish slugger like James O'Rourke, Roger Connors, Dan Brouthers and Ed Delahanty. Each was a great hitter with many batting honors, but by the 1890s a second kind of Irish batter emerged, the scientific hitter who selectively went with a pitch and was content to move a runner along or get on base with skilled place-hitting. Leading the way was Willie Keeler, Mike Tiernan, John McGraw, and Hugh Jennings.

But having great hitters did not ensure winning baseball. Hanlon and Comiskey would say that when a ballplayer was not playing well he had to know how to scrounge about looking for ways to take a ball game away from an opponent. From the Orioles coaching box and the players' bench the cry went out—"Get at 'em." This attacking expression and style of play was associated with Hanlon's Irish players, particularly third baseman John McGraw. When the President of the New York ball club turned his back on two exciting prospects, he justified his actions by saying he was looking for "Irishmen" in his infield (Murphy, 14), a clever, take-charge field captain, like McGraw of Baltimore. In 1896, *Sporting Life,* evaluating the ethnicity of baseball, gave the nod to the descendents of the Emerald Isle. Quoting New York Manager Bill Joyce, the Irishman declared:

> Give me a good Irish infield and I will show you a good team. I don't mean that it is necessary to have them all Irish, but you want two or three quick-thinking sons of Celt to keep the Germans and others moving.

Joyce apologized for any ethnic slight and remarked,

> Now you take a German, you can tell him what to do and he will do it. Take an Irishman and tell him what to do, and he is liable to give you an argument. He has his own ideas. So I have figured it out this way. Get an Irishman to do the scheming. Let him tell the Germans what to do and then you will have a great combination.

The example he gave was the Orioles' infield of "Dirty Jack" Doyle, Hugh Jennings, John "Muggsy" McGraw and Jimmy Donnelly (*Sporting Life,* 19 Sept. 1896).

This was the "smart and inside" baseball that teams were trying to emulate. It was the alert and unrelenting ballplaying taught by Hanlon, Selee and Tebeau. But Irish or Orioles baseball combined both intelligent and coercive playing which meant smart and aggressive base-running, bunting and sacrifice hitting. It was characterized by Comiskey's getting men on base by any means, unnerving opponents and umpires and capitalizing on game situations. This kind of baseball brought with it a full array of tactics that transformed the national pastime. The "Baltimore chop," hit and run plays, double steals, bunting for a hit, pitchers covering first base, playing off the corner bases, foul-ball hitting, cutting off throws, the trap play, hidden-ball tricks and slap and "hit them where they ain't" batting were part of their daily repertoire. Many of these stratagems were encouraged by the handicapped on-field authority of a single umpire trying to cover the entire playing field. His limited vista moved players to cut corners when they ran the bases, trip runners, obstruct the base paths, and in the case of John McGraw, slowing up runners by grabbing their belts and pants. Even the gentlemanly Cornelius McGuillicuddy, Connie Mack, perfected the art of interfering with a batter's swing when he played for Hanlon's Pittsburgh club in 1891. This caper was not as bad as "Irish Jack" Corcoran's spitting birdshot at a batter's neck. Other ploys had players leave equipment on the base paths and hide baseballs in unkept parts of the outfield grass. What bothered most critics about this style of play was its unsavory side that bordered on rowdyism. Players and umpires were spiked and collisions at first base were commonplace. These antics were directed at upsetting players and intimidating overworked umpires. It was a kind of psychological warfare. What the "pugnacious" Hanlon called "disorganizing baseball" (*Ibid.,* 9 Apr. 1892; *Sporting News,* 4 Apr. 1896). For the Oriole manager, "artful kicking" or disputing calls, was a message given to umpires that players "would not slink away like whipped schoolboys" (*Sporting Life,* 10 Apr. 1897). McGraw declared these confrontations were part of the "never say die spirit" of the Orioles and were done "to impress the umpire that the players are not going to let anything slip by them." In this tactic he was following a Charlie Comiskey tenet that "kicking" would not reverse a call, but could affect an umpire's judgment about the next close decision. To McGraw's way of thinking this contention could gain fifty runs a years (McGraw, 78; Burk, *Never Just a Game,* 134; *Phila. Inquirer,* 5 June 1897; *Sporting News,* 15 Aug. 1896).

Fans appreciated these antics and found them very entertaining. This was especially true with the bleacher "cranks" who sat in the cheap planked seats. Owners, wary of fights and the threat of riots, frequently spoke about curtailing this behavior. But this intimidating play was exciting and brought fans out to the ball park. In many ways this form of baseball provided entertainment that bordered on stage-acting. Players dramatically reacted to umpire's calls, preened themselves in the batter's box and bowed to admiring fans after a good play. It was mindful of an open-air vaudeville show played before thousands of spectators.

The popular press contributed to the Hibernian image of the sport. Newspapers wrote that baseball played with "brain, pluck and skill" was an Irish trait. One columnist said that "Teams need an infusion of Irish blood to make it [sic] win and that crafty Irishmen provided the sport with its generals and diplomats" (*Ibid.,* 27 June 1896). The catalogue of Irish names at the top of every seasonal category testified to the dominance. By the end of the century Hanlon, Tebeau and Selee were joined by a growing list of Irish managers. For most of the 1890s, 50% of all National League managers were of Irish descent. Greater percentages persisted for on-field Irish captains (*Ibid.,* 27 June 1896; *The Gael,* May 1902). The Irish character of the national pastime also spilled over into the umpires, groundkeepers and trainers. In contrast, only Ned Hanlon in Baltimore and Brooklyn, Charlie Byrne in Brooklyn and J. Palmer O'Neill in Pittsburgh held front office positions during the decade. In later years they were joined by John McGraw in New York, Connie Mack in Philadelphia and Charlie Comiskey in Chicago. Explaining the Irish competitive nature was another matter.

If Irish ballplayers were skilled, fleet-footed and crafty, they could also be "strong-headed" and slow like a "weary elephant." The problem is to determine whether there was a "peculiar trait" that distinguished Irish athletes (*Sporting Life,* 1 Oct. 1892). In comparing the two dominant ethnic groups in baseball, German and Irish players, the *Sporting News* asserted the latter were more "active and possess better heads for quick action—think more quickly and devise plans and schemes better" (*Sporting News,* 17 Aug. 1895). *Sporting Life* said the Germans were known for their "solidity and persistence" and the Irish for their "alertness and aggressiveness" (*Sporting Life,* 6 Oct. 1894). Harry Chadwick, who had been following sports for almost forty years, spoke of young Irishmen's "pluck, courage, endurance and physical activity" that were required for vigorous outdoor athletics (*Ibid.,* 23 Jan. 1889). The American Press Association said Irish domination on the ball field was due to their "love of a scrap or his [sic] proficiency in the use of a club" (*Sporting Life,* Quoted by 1 May 1897). Another tactic was tried by Ted Sullivan, the manager who brought Comiskey to St. Louis. He remarked how the sons of Erin were natural leaders and responded well to crises. He believed the Irish pass the test when you consider the character and success of the Irish soldier; fighting men known world-wide "for their dash, valor and impetuosity." He cited officers and political leaders as his examples. Returning to sports, Sullivan said the tradition of "shinny" or hurling and the love of the outdoors were inherent in the Irish race (*Sporting News,* 20 Jan. 1894; 11 Feb. 1899; 21 Dec. 1901). But these popularizing pundits never fully appreciated what in the Irish character made the Celt better ballplayers. Talent and physical dexterity were only part of the recipe.

The hard-nose, clever and passionate play that distinguished them on the ball field also reflected the Irish struggle for survival. Free from the constraints of their ancestral homeland, the Irish immigrant strove and worked hard at finding ways or angles to beat the system and succeed in their new homeland. Without the fetters of landlordism and centuries of alien domination, the

Irish recognized America as a true land of opportunity, a country where success or failure was theirs to be earned or lost. Baseball, like the competition of life, was akin to the Social Darwinism of the era. This drive was also apparent in the labor-union movement that disrupted baseball for almost two decades. In 1884, 1890 and 1900 Irish ballplayers were in the forefront trying to unfetter themselves from the constraints of the "reserve clause." The leverage they sought at the bargaining table and the way they played the sport demonstrated that the fittest and best prepared would survive. This attitude when applied to playing is what Comiskey called "beating the rule." Rules were meant to be bent and authority was there to be challenged. Baseball was a microcosm of Irish endurance. The sport became the alluring prize for young men blessed with the right skills who shaped the game to their overbearing drive to succeed.

Hugh Jennings summarized it best when he explained that the Orioles needed to stay ahead of the league by having something "new up our sleeves" to maximize favorable game conditions (*Ibid.,* 11 Jan. 1902). Hanlon said his teams played the "unexpected game." They never lost track of where they were in a contest and competed with their heads rather than just their hands. Hanlon wanted fast pace and unpredictable playing. He detested loafing, quitting and players who were unwilling to learn. One writer said, "it was like going through college to watch them [Orioles] work" (*Sporting Life,* 5 July 1902; 23 May 1903).

Hanlon and Comiskey always stressed team play. For the Baltimore Irishmen, the ball club was an extended family. The players were close-knit and singular in their purpose. No Oriole ever rebuked a teammate in public. Players were always taken aside for instruction or a scolding. Off the field it was hard to believe the Orioles were the same driven ball club. They had no real abusive drinkers or high-livers. McGraw and his buddies did, however, enjoy the racetrack. One writer said Hanlon's team were "regular Jekyl and Hyde beings." On the field they were artful about manipulating decisons. "Uncle Robbie" Robinson, the Orioles' catcher, would sweet-talk and chat politely with the umpires while McGraw was "barking and snapping" at their heels as if he had eaten "gunpowder . . . for breakfast and washed it down with warm blood" (*Ibid.,* 7 Oct. 1899). Ned Hanlon often let his three Irish leaders, McGraw, Jennings and Joe Kelley, handle game situations. It surprised no one that the trio and Wilbert Robinson went on to be successful managers.

Oriole "hoodlumism" or what Hanlon called "inside" baseball should not be misconstrued. Irish players often outnumbered and out-hustled their peers, but the Irish on Philadelphia or the Germans on Cincinnati, both non-champion clubs, could have practiced Comiskey-Hanlon baseball. Success came to teams playing heads-up all-out baseball, who were willing to extend the rules and practices of the sport to their limits. These tactics and their ultimate success determined how the national pastime was played. It was not until foul balls were called strikes, the pitching mound was raised and the livelier cork-centered baseball came into use that the style of baseball began to change. But by that time the Irish had already modified and extended the game and given it character and vitality. By the end of the first decade of the new century, the two umpire system and the standards of the upstart American League curbed on-field rowdyism of in-your-face baseball. The new league also recruited beyond the northern cities a different class of ballplayers which provided opportunities to a wider range of ethnic groups. Not to be overlooked was the expectation by second-generation Irish-American youngsters of better career and educational advantages. The

backgrounds and very names of Wagner, Cobb, Mathewson, Speaker and Johnson testified to these changes. However, the Irish persisted to play a key role in baseball, but never again approached the degree or magnitude of previous seasons. The tradition of the Emerald Age was perpetuated by managers who had once performed so well as quick-witted and scheming players. The list is an impressive one—John McGraw, Connie Mack, Hugh Jennings, Bill Joyce, Jimmy Collins, Joe Kelley, Hugh Duffy, Roger Bresnahan, Pat Moran, "Kid" Gleason, Jimmy McAleer, and Irish-born Patsy O'Donovan. From 1900 to 1922, including non-World Series years, fourteen out of twenty-five champions had Irish managers. The lustre of the Emerald Age was eclipsed, but the Irish legacy still illuminated the baseball diamond and the game it helped to shape.

C. Alexander, *John McGraw* (New York, 1988).

M. Appel, *Slide Kelly Slide: The Wild Life and Times of Mike "King" Kelly* (Lanham, Md., 1996).

P. Bjarkman, "Forgotten Americans and the National Pastime: Literature on Baseball's Ethnic, Racial and Religious Diversity," *Multicultural Review,* Vol. 1 (Apr. 1992): 46–48.

J. Bowman and J. Zoss, *Diamonds in the Rough: The Untold History of Baseball* (New York, 1987).

R. Burk, *Never Just a Game: Players, Owners and American Baseball to 1920* (New York, 1995).

J. Casway, *Ed Delahanty and the Emerald Age of Baseball.* An unpublished manuscript.

S. Gelber, "Working at Playing: The Culture of the Workplace and the Rise of Baseball," *Journal of Social History,* 16 (1983): 3–20.

M. Isenberg, *John L. Sullivan and His America* (Urbana, 1988).

J. McGraw, *My Thirty Years in Baseball* (Lincoln, Nebr., 1995, ed.)

J. Mitchell, "The Celt as a Baseball Player," *The Gael* (May 1902): 150–55.

J. Moore and N. Vermilyea, *Ernest Thayer's "Casey at the Bat," Background and Characters of Baseball's Famous Poem* (Jefferson, N.C., 1994).

J. Murphy, "Napoleon Lajoie," *National Pastime* (1988).

"Race and Ethnicity in American Baseball, 1900–1919," *The Journal of Ethnic Studies,* Vol. 44: 39–43.

S. Reiss, *City Games: Evolution of American Society and the Rise of Sports* (Chicago, 1989).

J. Rossi, "Glimpses of the Irish Contributions to Early Baseball," *Éire-Ireland* (Summer 1988): 116–21.

H. Seymour, *Baseball: The Early Years* (New York, 1989, ed.)

D. Voigt, *American Baseball,* Vol. I (Norman, Okla., 1968).

K. Whelan, "The Geography of Hurling," *History, Ireland,* Vol. 1 (1993): 27–31.

R. Wilcox, "Shamrock and the Eagle: Irish Americans and Sports in the Nineteenth Century," *Ethnicity and Sport in North American History and Culture* (Westport, CT, 1994): 55–71.

JERROLD CASWAY

## BEERY, WALLACE FITZGERALD (1885–1949)

Stage and screen actor. Born to Noah and Margaret (Fitzgerald) Beery April 1, 1885, Wallace grew up a large boy in Kansas City, Missouri. He was often teased for this at school and after running away from home as a teenager, he refused to continue his education. He instead worked for the railroad and later as a circus elephant handler which led him to a job with Ringling Brothers as head elephant trainer.

By 1904, Beery left the circus for the New York city stage where he sang in musical comedies like *Babes in Toyland, The Prince of Pilsen,* and *The Student King.* In 1907 Beery stood in for Raymond Hitchcock in *A Yankee Tourist* which exposed him to a much larger audience and led to a contract with the Chicago Essanay film company six years later. Beery's gruff character and husky frame made his Swedish housemaid role hilariously funny at Essanay and led to a string of "Sweedie" films.

Essanay next sent Beery to California to manage a new film studio. The project failed, so Beery moved to Universal Studios where his career appeared to stagnate. After drifting from one job to another, Beery's career was rescued with the role of a German villain in a World War I film, *The Unpardonable Sin* (1919). Beery's sinister character led to similar roles for films like *The Four Horsemen of the Apocalypse* (1921) and *Robin Hood* (1922).

From 1925 to 1929, Beery was back in comedy, but this time at Paramount Pictures. Here he attracted large audiences until Paramount dropped him with the advent of sound pictures. Metro-Goldwyn-Mayer picked him up, however, where he became a major attraction in roles like the master-mind behind a prison uprising in *The Big House* (1930) and the down-and-out prizefighter in *The Champ* (1931), for which he won an Academy Award. After his last film, *Big Jack*, the actor died in Beverly Hills on April 15, 1949, worth more than $2 million.

Earlin Anderson, *Films in Review* (June–July 1973).

Wallace Beery, "It's Funny about My Face," *American Magazine* (June 1934).

Bosley Crowther, *The Lion's Share: The Story of an Entertainment Empire* (New York, 1957).

———, *Hollywood Rajah Hollywood Rajah: The Life and Times of Louis B. Mayer* (New York, 1960).

John A. Gallagher, "Beery, Wallace," *International Dictionary of Films and Filmmakers—3 Actors and Actresses*. Amy L. Unterburger, ed. (New York, 1997).

Richard Griffith and Arthur Mayer, *The Movies: The Sixty-Year Story of the World of Hollywood and Its Effect on America; from Pre-Nickelodeon Days to the Present* (New York, 1957).

Leonard Maltin, *Film Fan Monthly* (July–August 1967).

DANIEL J. KUNTZ

## BEGLEY, EDWARD JAMES (1901–1970)

Actor. Ed Begley was born of Irish heritage to Michael Joseph and Hannah (Clifford); very early on he became fascinated with stage productions and befriended the leading organizer of the Poli Stock Company at the Poli Theater. By the age of eleven, he was participating in walk-on parts at the Poli Theater and at the age of fifteen he had won an amateur acting contest. However, his shyness kept him from fully capitalizing on his talent early on and in later years he regretted his initial lack of confidence.

In 1910, Begley joined the U.S. Navy and eventually was transferred to the U.S. Naval Radio Station in Tuckerton, New Jersey. After having been discharged, Begley moved to Philadelphia and then later New York where he found employment at WNBC from 1940–1942. Begley was featured in several programs: *Amanda of Honeymoon Hill, Mr. Keen, Tracer of Lost Persons,* the *Kate Smith Show* and the *Phillip Morris Playhouse.* He also took on roles in two detective shows, *Charlie Chan* and *Official Detective* and likewise created his own role in such productions as the *Aldrich Family* and *The Fat Man.*

Begley's professional stage career began in 1943 with his role as a Nazi general in the film *Land of Fame* and later in the drama *Get Away, Old Man* and in *Pretty Little Parlor.* Begley's career advanced further with his role in the 1947 acclaimed play *All My Sons.* His career continued in the following productions: *Boomerang, Deep Waters, Sitting Pretty, Sorry Wrong Number, Stars in My Crown,* and *Lone Star.* Begley also appeared in several television shows such as: *Lights Out, Cameo Theatre, Big Town, Martin Kane, Danger, The Web, Leave It to Larry, The Guiding Light,* and the *Aldrich Family.*

In 1954, Begley appeared in the Broadway production *All Summer Long.* However, the focal point of his career revolved around his portrayal of a character fashioned after William Jennings Bryan in *Inherit the Wind.* Begley acted alongside Paul Muni during the season of April 1955, and his performance brought him overdue recognition. In time, Begley received the Donaldson Award for best supporting actor of the New York City theatre season in 1954–55. He also won the Sylvania Award for his portrayal of Andy Sloane in the famed teleplay "Patterns" aired by *Kraft Television Theatre.* In April 1956, Begley won the Antoinette Perry (Tony) award for his performance in *Inherit the Wind.*

Begley's career was immensely successful. In addition to his early radio career, he acted in over twenty films and sixty dramatic parts. He was married in 1922 to Amanda Hoff and was an active member of the Lambs Club in New York. Begley died in 1970.

*See* Cinema, Irish in

*New York Herald Tribune,* V (April 1947): 3.

*New York Post* (June 12, 1955): 16.

*Motion Picture and Television Almanac* (1955).

*CAB* (1956).

JOY HARRELL

## BENNETT, ROBERT S. (1939–    )

Attorney. Robert Stephen Bennett was born in Brooklyn, New York, August 2, 1939, son of F. Robert and Nancy (Walsh) Bennett. He was graduated from Georgetown University in 1961, and did postgraduate work at the University of Virginia. He originally planned a career in medicine, but switched from pre-med to law and went on to receive degrees from both Georgetown and Harvard Law Schools. He said of his dalliance with medicine, "Thank God for the human race I didn't stick with it."

Bennett clerked at the United States District Court in Washington, D.C. from 1965–1967 and was assistant United States attorney for the District of Columbia from 1967–1970, thereupon entering private practice of law. He was an adjunct professor of law at George Washington University from 1975–1979, and has lectured and conducted law seminars across the country, many dealing with so-called "white-collar" crime. In 1980 he served as legal counsel to the Senate Foreign Relations Committee, and in 1981–1982 he was special counsel to the Senate's Select Committee on Ethics. He is now a partner in the Washington law firm of Skadden, Arps, Slate, Meagher & Flom.

Over the years Bennett has represented a number of high-profile Washington personalities, including presidential advisors and high government officials, including President Bill Clinton himself. Clinton selected Bennett to defend him in the sexual harassment lawsuit brought by Paula Jones stemming from an alleged incident in an Arkansas hotel room. He is still retained by the president. His skills have won him designation as the city's number-one lawyer by *Washingtonian* magazine.

Nine Burleigh, "The Man to See," *ABA Journal* (September, 1994).

*Who's Who in America, 1997* (New Providence, N.J., 1996).

JOHN DEEDY

## BENNETT, WILLIAM J. (1943–   )

Educator, cabinet member, author. A native of Brooklyn, New York, William John Bennett is the son of F. Robert and Nancy (Walsh) Bennett. The family moved to Washington, D.C., while he was a teenager, and there he graduated from Gonzaga High School. He went on to Williams College, graduating in 1965. He received a doctoral degree in philosophy from the University of Texas in 1970 and a law degree from Harvard in 1971.

Bennett taught religion and philosophy at the University of Southern Mississippi in 1967–1968, was a social-science tutor at Harvard in 1970–1971, and from 1972–1976 was assistant to the president and a professor at Boston University. He helped found the National Humanities Center in Triangle Park, North Carolina, in 1976, and became its president and director in 1979. Meanwhile, he continued to teach, conducting classes in philosophy at North Carolina State University in Raleigh and the University of North Carolina in Chapel Hill. He also wrote articles for leading opinion journals, many stressing the importance of a strong moral content in education.

In 1981 President Ronald Reagan named Bennett as head of the National Endowment for the Humanities, and over three years he moved the agency in markedly conservative directions. In 1985 he was Reagan's choice as Secretary of Education. Though some educators expressed misgivings over the appointment, the nomination won unanimous approval from the ninety-three senators present on voting day. During the Bush administration, Bennett was director of the Office of National Drug Control Policy.

Looking back in 1992 on his years in government, Bennett wrote that he "came away from public life as I went in— encouraged and hopeful, reassured in my belief that it is possible to make a positive difference. In that sense, I remain an unreconstructed advocate of the possible."

Bennett has written several books, including two surprise bestsellers, *The Book of Virtues: A Treasury of Great Moral Stories* and *The Moral Compass: Stories for a Life's Journey.* The volumes, heavily stocked with inspirational writings from Aesop and Plato to Longfellow and Frost, complement his philosophical and moral concern for a return to family values and for an improved educational system.

William J. Bennett, *The De-Valuing of America: The Fight for Our Culture and Our Children* (New York, 1992).

Terri M. Rooney and Jennifer Gariepy, eds., *Contemporary Authors,* Vol. 153 (Detroit, 1997).

Charles Moritz, ed., *Current Biography Yearbook 1985* (New York, 1985).

JOHN DEEDY

## BERKELEY, SARA (1967–   )

Poet and short story writer. Sara Berkeley was born in Dublin and educated at Trinity College, Dublin and at the University of California-Berkeley. She lived in Ireland until she was 22 and since then has lived in London and she "emigrated to America several times" before finally settling in Inverness, California. In addition to being a writer, Sara Berkeley works as a technical editor and writer for a San Francisco computer company.

Sara Berkeley burst on the Irish literary scene when *Penn,* her first volume of poetry, was published in 1986 when she was a nineteen-year-old undergraduate at Trinity College. *Penn* was shortlisted for the *Sunday Tribune* Arts Award and the Irish Book

Award. In a poem entitled "Fall," from *Facts About Water* (1994), her most recent collection, Berkeley provides some indication of the themes and states of mind she explores in her work. She reminds us that "confusion/is all part of what is meant to be," that "such bewilderment/is part of what is meant to be," and that it is difficult for the poet to locate a deep language which will approximate to deep experience. The world Berkeley evokes is, like Emily Dickinson's, deeply personal, fractured by death and violence, but held in place by the four elements of fire, air, earth, and water, by love or the possibility of love, and by the imagination. The women and men at the center of Berkeley's poems are often lost and seeking a language so they can communicate their feelings and fears to others, whether distant from them or next to them on a street, a beach, or in an airplane. If the ice between humans can be broken, then love and healing will be possible. An important medium in this process is nature: "I am asking green to heal me/or in some gesture/mutely to acknowledge me" ("Everything Green"). Berkeley's brilliant images juxtapose the concrete and the surreal, with the former generally representing the external world and the latter the individual's tenuous connection to it. Berkeley's language, to capture the internal world, is rich, sensual, and associative, and she is peerless in contemporary poetry for her dexterity with both word and image. Coming to live in California, at the edge of the American West, has produced a subtle, but marked, change in Berkeley's work. Her recent work takes a much stronger interest in the external world which is now more likely to be explored for its own sake than as a mere entry way to the unconscious. It is clear that in the great emptiness of the American West Berkeley has located the object correlative of the unconscious. Furthermore, although her work remains raw with emotion, her vision has brightened. As a poet, Berkeley is a unique voice who goes from strength to strength with each volume.

*See* Poetry, Irish-American

Sara Berkeley, *Facts About Water: New & Selected Poems* (Dublin, Ireland, 1994).

———, *Home Movie Nights* (Dublin, Ireland, 1989).

———, *Penn* (Dublin, Ireland, 1986).

———, *The Swimmer in the Deep Blue Dream* (Dublin, Ireland, 1991).

EAMONN WALL

## BERRIGAN, DANIEL (1921–   ) and PHILIP (1923–   )

Peace activists, writers, priests. No two names more personify the Catholic peace movement of the latter decades of twentieth-century America than those of Daniel and Philip Berrigan. They were born in Virginia, Minnesota—Dan on May 9, 1921; Phil on October 5, 1923. They were the last of Thomas and Freda (Fromhart) Berrigan's six sons. Soon after Phil's birth, the father relocated the family to the town of Livingston near Syracuse in up-state New York in order to be near a colony of Irish farmers. Tom Berrigan, a descendant of Tipperary parents, felt perfectly at home. It is less certain about Freda, an emigrant from Germany as a youngster. In Dan's words, "she being German was an outsider . . . We [brothers] didn't like that."

In 1939, at age 18, Dan Berrigan entered the Society of Jesus (Jesuits). Brother Phil, after heroic service in World War II (that as a pacifist he now is equivocal about), enrolled under the G.I.

Daniel Berrigan

Philip Berrigan

Bill at the College of the Holy Cross, graduated in 1950, and after a year of casting about joined the Society of St. Joseph (Josephites). Dan was ordained in 1952; Phil, in 1955.

The priest-brothers came to their social activism through the inspiration of their mother and the civil-rights struggle of the late 1950s, early 1960s. The rights issue quickened in both a conflict between conscience and authority, and put their vocations to their first test—as in 1963 when the two were barred by their respective religious superiors from taking part in a Freedom Ride to protest the segregation of bus terminals in Jackson, Mississippi. Though both Berrigans respected the orders of authority in that instance, conscience would eventually triumph and lead them to courageous displays of witness and of protest, particularly when the civil-rights struggle spilled over into opposition to the war in Vietnam.

It was Phil who initiated the Berrigan family's protest against the war, when on October 27, 1967, he and three others poured blood into the draft files of Selective Services offices at the Customs House in Baltimore. Dan joined in a kindred protest on May 17 of the year following, when with eight others he entered Selective Service offices in Catonsville, Maryland, helped empty 1-A files from several cabinets into wire trash baskets and hurry them to the parking lot, where, as cameras rolled and reporters took notes, the files were incinerated with napalm.

The Catonsville raiding party comprised seven men and two women, but it was the Berrigan brothers, Dan and Phil, who captured the most media attention. Impact was widespread. The deep religious foundations of their protest (on the Eucharist and Gospel values) combined with the imaginativeness of their example to inspire large numbers of young people to take up the challenge for peace. Within days "communities of resistance," largely Catholic in composition, were springing up across the country. Located in Milwaukee, Camden, Washington, New York, Chicago, and Rochester, among other cites, they would spawn many more Berrigan-type actions.

Dan and Phil Berrigan served stiff Federal jail sentences for the Catonsville action, but they did not go quietly into lock-up. While free on appeal, they went underground as "fugitives for peace." Phil's escapade ended fairly quickly, when after ten days he was plucked from hiding in a closet of St. Gregory the Great

rectory in Manhattan. Dan's underground trip, on the other hand, extended for five months and involved J. Edgar Hoover and the Federal Bureau of Investigation (FBI) in a spectacular, sometimes comic chase up and down the East Coast, before he was caught August 11, 1970 on Block Island, off Rhode Island, by agents posing as bird watchers.

The post-Vietnam years had seen no diminishment of commitment on the part of the Berrigans.

Phil, now married (to Elizabeth [Liz] McAlister, a former Religious of the Sacred Heart of Mary) and no longer a Josephite (though ever convinced of the validity of his priestly orders), lives at Jonah House, a resistance-community center he co-founded with his wife in Baltimore. Today, through a program called Ploughshares, his activism is directed against nuclear weaponry and the military-industrial complex, and this activism seems to have him in jail as often as not. He and Liz are parents of three children.

Dan resides with a Jesuit community in New York City. He travels much, giving lectures, poetry readings and conducting retreats. Health permitting, there are demonstrations at weapons plants and abortion facilities, but for the last decade his defining work has been working with AIDS patients at St. Vincent's Hospital, New York. The previous five years it was with terminally ill patients at St. Rose's Cancer Home.

The Berrigans have left a detailed record of thoughts and opinions in many books and articles. Dan's books include several volumes of poetry, one of which *Time Without Number* (1957), won the Lamont Prize. In 1971 the Unitarian Universalist Association awarded him its Melcher Book Award for *No Bars to Manhood, The Trial of the Catonsville Nine* (a stage drama) and *Trial Poems*. The Melcher Award honored the year's most significant contribution to religious liberalism.

John Deedy, *'Apologies, Good Friends,' An Interim Biography of Daniel Berrigan, S.J.* (Chicago, 1981).

Francine du Plessix Gray, *Divine Disobedience: Profiles in Catholic Radicalism* (New York, 1970).

Murray Polner and Jim O'Grady, *Disarmed and Dangerous: The Radical Lives and Times of Daniel and Philip Berrigan* (New York, 1997).

**JOHN DEEDY**

## BIGOTRY: NO IRISH NEED APPLY

Colonial legislatures placed a number of restrictions on Irish Catholics to prevent their mass emigration to the New World. In 1704, for example, the Maryland legislature imposed a head tax on indentured servants from Ireland. The purpose of the act was "to prevent the importing of too great a number of Irish Papists." Although wealthy families, such as the Carrolls of Maryland, were accepted during the colonial and post-revolutionary periods, the majority, who were not wealthy, were viewed as "different" by Americans.

In 1845, the "potato blight" destroyed the basic food crop of Ireland's rural population. This event marked the beginning of a new phase in the history of Irish immigration to the United States; between 1840 and 1860 around 1.7 million Irish people would leave their homeland for America. As they struggled to survive in America's growing cities, these newcomers found themselves unwelcome and unwanted by the Anglo-Saxon power structure.

### EMPLOYMENT AND ECONOMIC DIFFICULTIES

Nineteenth-century Irish immigrants were faced with seemingly insurmountable obstacles. Most of the men, women, and children who left Ireland for America during the famine arrived penniless. Many of them were peasants who found themselves in an urban, commercial environment, with neither the training to become merchants or clerks nor the capital to become shopkeepers. The great majority of men found work as unskilled laborers, employed on the docks or on public works projects. Women, however, were often hired as domestic servants. In New England, for example, there had been a shortage of domestic help for a number of years prior to the arrival of the poverty-stricken Irish. The Irish, who needed to send women out to work to help support the family, were able to fill this gap handily.

The lowest paying and most menial jobs were left for the Irish. Although the law would not allow an employer to ban someone from a profession based on nationality, it was not uncommon to see job advertisements reading, "None need apply but Americans." The ability of the Irish to enter any trade in significant numbers varied inversely with the "desirability" of the profession. The new arrivals, men and women, were sometimes able to find work in a service industry; most Americans thought these jobs were demeaning and refused to accept positions in this sector. Many Irish men cared for the horses used in public transportation, either as blacksmiths or hostlers. Others worked as waiters, gardeners, or chauffeurs. Those that chose to work in industry were usually hired to be sweepers and janitors in a mill or factory—the jobs paying the least and requiring the least skill, the jobs Americans would not accept.

The labor contractor served as a source of employment when no other was available. Newspapers advertised jobs on the railroad promising steady work and good wages. Most who accepted employment under these circumstances found themselves in an even worse situation than before. It was not unusual for a man to travel several hundred miles only to find that the pay was not that originally promised.

### LIVING CONDITIONS

The home was one of the centers of life in Irish culture. Irish newcomers often were without a home, however, and forced to live with friends and relatives in one and two room "apartments." In many cities, real estate agents attempted to solve the housing shortage for poor families by converting old mansions (and sometimes unused warehouses) into tenements. The conditions of these tenements were substandard at best. Rents were high and people often could not afford to furnish their "homes." Those immigrants living in tenements that had formerly been basements were in an even worse situation. Their homes were subject to floods, and some routinely held two to three feet of water.

These living conditions led to other problems associated with urban poverty. Raw sewage flowed through streets and alleys, and any sort of sanitation was completely lacking. Many apartments did not have access to a street, making it difficult for people to dispose of their trash properly. Residents were responsible for their own heat, and since coal and wood were both expensive, they frequently had no heat. The result was the frequent outbreak of diseases such as smallpox, cholera, and tuberculosis in the slums where the Irish lived.

### NATIVISM

The Irish immigrants were overwhelmingly Catholic in a Protestant world. Non-Catholic Americans, particularly those already threatened by the immigrants' invasion of the job market, saw the Irish as part of a larger plot to convert the United States and bring it under the control of the Pope. During the nineteenth century, the Catholic Church in America was the church of the poor. As Protestants watched large Catholic churches being built with the pennies of those poor, their anti-Catholic sentiments deepened.

Americans observing the dramatic increase in Irish immigration could foresee nothing but problems ahead. The Irish were crowding the cities, forcing the wealthier residents to take care of them. They drank too much and did not work hard enough to pull themselves out of poverty. A prominent Bostonian, Joseph Brickingham, blamed the Yankee "plentitude of generosity which has induced us to feed the hungry [and] clothe the naked." Coming to the aid of the poor immigrants would be disastrous for those settled Americans and their leaders who would be forced out of power by the very people they had saved. According to Brickingham, "Irishmen fresh from the bogs of Ireland are led up to vote like dumb brutes . . . to vote down intelligent, honest, native Americans." Others who spoke out against the Irish equated them with the dangers inherent in Catholicism. Lyman Beecher responded to the dramatic numbers of Irish immigrants by claiming, "The Catholic Church holds now in darkness and bondage nearly half the civilized world. . . . It is the most skillful, powerful, dreadful system of corruption to those who wield it, and of slavery and debasement to those who live under it."

The response to this situation, on the part of some, was violence. In 1831, an angry mob burned a convent in Charlestown, Massachusetts; a church in Philadelphia was destroyed in 1846. Others issued a political response. In 1854, members of the Know-Nothing Party pledged to do all they could to combat the Pope and those who followed him in America.

### CIVIL WAR YEARS

The Civil War years created a special obstacle for Irish men. In 1863, the first conscription act was signed by Abraham Lincoln. All men between the ages of twenty and forty-five were eligible to serve in the union forces. One could be exempt from the law, however, by either paying $300 or finding a replacement who would serve for three years. The act clearly hurt poor whites; in most cities poor whites were synonomous with Irish. In addition, the Irish were unpopular in the north because many of them opposed abolitionism. They believed freed Blacks would move into the lower paying jobs (their jobs) after emancipation. *Tribune* editor Horace Greeley claimed the Irish "have been and are today foremost in the degradation and abuse of this persecuted [black] race." The controversy resulted in the New York draft riots in July, 1863.

### ACCEPTANCE

The bigotry leveled against the Irish immigrants began to lessen in the decades following the Civil War. Many were still members of the working class and did not earn much above a subsistence level, but they were gaining a place in the political system. Not everyone, however, was willing to accept their voting power. During the election of 1884, a supporter of James G. Blaine, the Republican candidate for president, referred to the Democrats as the party of "rum, Romanism, and rebellion," a slur clearly aimed at Irish Catholic voters.

By 1900, the Irish image was no longer dominated by the "poor immigrant." They were not living in urban slums; they were employed as school teachers, civil servants, and police and fire officials. Andrew Greeley once noted that the Irish were probably on the verge of achieving success within the American context when the Great Depression began. The end of World War II and the benefits of the G.I. Bill allowed many Irish-Americans to move into the upper-middle class. Despite their growing political power, however, they were still not accepted by the elite of American society. Several historians of the Irish experience argue that the Irish were not fully accepted until John F. Kennedy was elected to the presidency in 1960. Overall, it appears that the anti-Irish bigotry prevalent in the United States has disappeared. Traces of this bigotry may be present in some individuals living at the end of the twentieth century, but not enough to be noticeable on any measurable scale.

*See* Nativism

Jay P. Dolan, *The American Catholic Experience: A History from Colonial Times to the Present* (Garden City, New York, 1985).
Andrew M. Greeley, *That Most Distressful Nation: The Taming of the American Irish* (Chicago, 1972).
Oscar Handlin, *Boston's Immigrants: A Study in Acculturation* (New York, 1972).
James Hennesey, S.J., *American Catholics: A History of the Roman Catholic Community in the United States* (New York, 1981).
James K. Kenneally, *The History of American Catholic Women* (New York, 1990).
William V. Shannon, *The American Irish* (New York, 1963).

MARGARET M. McGUINNESS

### BINNS, JOHN (1772–1860)

Journalist, politician. Born in Dublin on December 22, 1772, Binns was in London consorting with dissidents such as William Godwin by 1794. Joining the London Corresponding Society, Binns became president of this organization which officially promoted reform of Parliament based on universal suffrage but purportedly stood for the formation of a British republic. After being identified as espousing revolutionary ideals, Binns was imprisoned several times before a general release of English political prisoners restored his freedom.

Binns arrived in America in September 1801, settling at Northumberland, Pennsylvania. Soon thereafter, he survived a duel

and later married Mary Anne Boyseter, with whom he would have ten children. From 1802–07, Binns published the *Northumberland Republican Argus* before relocating to Philadelphia to print the *Democratic Press* from 1807–29. Known for having a direct, personal style, it was among the prominent partisan organs in Pennsylvania.

In publishing an engraving of the Declaration of Independence in 1819, charges of plagiarism and nativist sentiments led some to criticize Binns as unworthy of public trust. Further trouble came when Binns, believing Andrew Jackson to be tyrannical, opposed his 1828 bid for the presidency. During the campaign, Binns distributed depictions of eight coffins bearing the names of soldiers executed at Jackson's command for leaving the service at the end of their enlistment but prior to the passing of the emergency. This act brought a mob's vengeance upon Binns' home and financial difficulties led him to cease printing his paper.

From 1822–44, Binns served as a Philadelphia alderman and was famed for his Irish eloquence, boasting that not until he was nearly sixty did he compose a speech in advance. In 1840, he published a book on Pennsylvania law entitled *Binns' Justice*. He died on June 16, 1860.

*See* Philadelphia

H. C. Bell, ed., *History of Northumberland County, Pa.* (1891).
John Binns, *Recollections of the Life of John Binns Written by Himself* (Philadelphia, 1854).
———, *Binns' Justice* (Philadelphia, 1840).
———, *Monumental Inscriptions* (1828).
———, *The Trial of John Binns; Deputy of the London Corresponding Society, for Sedition . . . August 12, 1797* (Birmingham, 1797).
John T. Scharf and Thompson Westcott, *History of Philadelphia*, 3 vols. (Philadelphia, 1884).

CHRISTIAN G. SAMITO

### BIRMINGHAM, ALABAMA (1870–1990s)

In 1891, twenty years after Birmingham's incorporation, Frank O'Brien, one of the city's Irish-born pioneers and future mayor, noted, "many of the details of her [Birmingham] history are interwoven with my own personal recollections." Like O'Brien, other Irish-born and their descendants contributed to the economic, political, and cultural development of Birmingham more than their numbers might suggest. Census records indicate that in 1880, the percentage of Irish-born to total population in Birmingham [Jefferson County] yielded less than 1 percent (0.6). Despite the low figure, however, the Irish comprised the highest percentage, 27 percent, of foreign-born in the county. These figures fail to take into account the number of Irish descendants, who neither claimed nor took notice of their Irish heritage. With the creation of the Irish Free State and the end of the civil war in the early 1920s, a majority of Irish-Americans' interest in the political situation in Ireland waned. For the next forty years, they joined the rest of white America in urban flight, making a "decent" living, and sending their children to college, in other words, being American. Since the 1960s, the heated political climate in Northern Ireland caught the attention of some, and over the past couple of decades there has been a renewed interest, at least among the area's Irish Catholics, to manifest their heritage. For nearly 130 years, since the emergence of an industrial-based town in the Deep South, the Irish, Catholic and Protestant, have left their mark on Birmingham's history.

The year in which plans for Birmingham began to take shape, the county's 1870 census enumerated twenty-three Irish-born: seven railroad workers (all single men), four stonemasons, two farmers, one ditcher, one carpenter, one physician, and one domestic. The remaining six included one widow, wives, and daughters. Fourteen months later, December 19, 1871, the city of Birmingham, Alabama, incorporated. Colonel Daniel Shipman Troy, a third-generation Irishman and Confederate veteran, arrived in the new city as the legal advisor of the Elyton Land Company, formed by capitalists to develop Birmingham. In addition to his duties as attorney and stockholder, he invested in other endeavors. He helped to reorganize a defunct iron and coal company, renamed it Oxmoor after his father's residence in North Carolina, and placed it under the direction and control of local investors. One of the investors was Colonel James W. Sloss. A son of Irish immigrants, who settled in the state in the early years of the nineteenth century, he came to the city and began his long-time involvement in Birmingham's iron and steel industry.

While many Irish-Americans, such as Sloss, could be found among the members of local Protestant churches, the city's Irish-born and other first- and second-generation Irish who settled in Birmingham adhered to the Catholic faith. Confederate veterans such as Frank P. O'Brien, self-proclaimed capitalist and future mayor, Michael Murray Cahalan, railroad contractor, and James O'Connor, businessman, provided the impetus for establishing the first Catholic church in the new community. On October 18, 1871, two months before the incorporation of the city of Birmingham, the first Catholic Mass ever performed in Jefferson County was heard at the Cahalan home. As Birmingham's industrial future seemed assured, more Irish Catholics migrated to the area to take advantage of the religious tolerance, job opportunities, and business ventures the new city offered in its early years of development.

Patrick McCrossin arrived in the 1890s to take advantage of the business opportunities available in the iron and steel industry. With property holdings in Philadelphia and Virginia, he had money to invest; his name became tied to the Ivy Coal and Coke Company in Birmingham. Having spent a considerable time in America, since his arrival from Ireland as a boy, McCrossin knew the importance of new industries to America's future and his own. He and his family took advantage of what another newcomer, Englishman James Bowron, Jr., described as an unprecedented opportunity in this new city of the South. In his autobiography Bowron wrote, "I found on coming to Birmingham that to be in the iron trade was to be respectable. To be an officer of an iron-making corporation was to have an entry to the best society." McCrossin's daughters married into the circle of industrialists investing in Birmingham's future. His sons and grandsons entered the legal and medical professions, becoming important figures in Birmingham society.

Like Patrick McCrossin, Hugh McGeever arrived in America as a young boy and eventually made his way with his family to Birmingham. Like the McCrossins, the McGeevers belonged to St. Paul's Cathedral, the first Catholic Church founded in Birmingham. Like McCrossin and his sons, McGeever and his progeny belonged to local Irish-American organizations such as the Ancient Order of Hibernians, which by the turn of the century boasted four branches. Unlike McCrossin, McGeever's business ventures, that often included his brothers, did not revolve around the city's iron and steel industries. In 1898, the governor of Alabama appointed McGeever to the city's first Board of Revenue, to which the citizens of Birmingham reelected him for three successive four-year terms, indicative of the importance of his business investments to the city's future. In addition to his participation in the church, local Irish organizations, and St. Patrick's Day celebrations, Hugh McGeever and his Irish-born wife, Mary O'Byrne, named their children in true Irish fashion. Sons Parnell and Emmet, as well as daughter Kathleen, like the offspring of other Irish immigrants who settled in Birmingham, moved into "white-collar" careers.

Like the McGeevers, the Irish who migrated to Birmingham and the Pratt Mines, a community that would be annexed by the larger city in 1910, hailed mainly from Donegal, Cork, Mayo, Limerick, and Sligo. A few came from County Tipperary, which differed little in social and economic terms from its neighboring counties of Limerick and Cork. They gained labor skills and became acclimated to American culture in other urban centers before they arrived in Alabama. Chain migration contributed most to the increased numbers who migrated to Birmingham during the early twentieth century. Relatives or friends provided a place to stay and entry to a job. They retained a connection to Ireland through their participation in local Land League organizations during the nineteenth century and chapters of the Friends of Irish Freedom in the twentieth.

Birmingham city directories and naturalization records list a variety of occupations for the Irish and Irish-American laborers who migrated to Birmingham: lumberman, railroader, foundryman, coppersmith, stonemason, carpenter, miner, and roller and puddler (both to be found in steel and iron mills). Others listed occupations such as traveling salesman, secretary or bookkeeper, baker, farmer, and merchant. Attorneys, physicians, teachers, as well as other professionals, could be found particularly among the second and later generations, though a few Irish-born could be counted in this category. Some, like Sylvester Daly, born in Middlesborough District, England, of Irish parents, began as laborers, saved their earnings, and started their own businesses. Daly, who came to Birmingham as a skilled laborer, having gained experience in Pennsylvania's steel mills, eventually opened a saloon near the Birmingham Rolling Mill, where he had worked. From this location he established himself in the late nineteenth century as a political boss of Birmingham's Ninth Ward, heavily populated by first- and second-generation Irish. When Daly died at age thirty-nine, his daughters came under the guardianship of his brother-in-law, Patrick Walsh, who also held membership in local political and Irish nationalist organizations, such as the Irish Democratic Society and the Ancient Order of Hibernians (A.O.H.). Even in Birmingham, Alabama, the Irish more often than not married other Irish.

In an interview conducted by Sister Rose Sevenich, Sister Dorothy Flynn, who grew up near the Pratt mines, vividly remembered Grandmother Sullivan's stories of leprechauns and banshees as well as the exclusiveness of the Irish community. "It was quite a gathering of the Irish [who] settled on Hibernian Hill [and] we were prejudiced against anybody not Irish. Another woman who grew up near Irish Hill recalled, "We didn't go out with any sagers, meaning anyone not our kind. It was just accepted that Irish boys would date Irish girls," a custom not limited to the mining community or the laboring class. Local attorney Frederick Monks, a native of Ireland and naturalized as an American citizen in 1906, returned to Dublin in February of 1915, to marry. He returned to Birmingham with his Irish wife four months later.

While most of Birmingham's Irish-American women married, more often than not choosing men of like religion and ethnic identity, others remained single, taking religious vows or joining the growing ranks of women in nursing and teaching. A statue representing the likeness of Miss Mary Cahalan, who taught and administered in the public school system for over twenty years, stands in Linn Park in downtown Birmingham, outside the main entrance to the Linn-Henley Research Library. Dedicated by the citizens of Birmingham in 1908, and accepted by Mayor George B. Ward, a former pupil, it is believed to be the first public memorial to a woman educator in the United States. On March, 17, 1993, eighty-five years after the statue's unveiling, the Birmingham St. Patrick's Day Committee organized and held a rededication ceremony, in which Miss Cahalan's descendants added a commemorative plaque to the base of the memorial. The Wards and the Henleys, whose names and the city's history are hard to separate, also belong to the story of the Irish in Birmingham, though their connection may not be as recognizable as that of others.

In a quiet room on the second floor of the Mervyn H. Sterne Library on the campus of the University of Alabama at Birmingham (UAB) hangs the portrait of John Charles Henley, Captain, Confederate States Army. The room, among other things, serves as a repository for some of his father's books, sent sometime near the end of the Civil War to Alabama from the library of the family home in Ireland. Captain Henley's father, described as an "Irish cotton broker," operating out of Montgomery, sent his sons to the University of Alabama. When war broke out, the father returned to Ireland; the sons joined the Confederate Army. Over the years, the descendants of that Irish cotton broker have enhanced the city's educational and cultural endeavors. According to material supplied by UAB's library staff, the Linn-Henley Charitable Trust has supported public television specials and the production of videos on Alabama history and Indians of the Southeast. It has helped to restore the research library that bears its name in downtown Birmingham and fund the park in which Mary Cahalan's statue can be found. Trust donations and materials funded and supplied the Henley Room on UAB's campus, as well as many other philanthropic projects. John Charles Henley, Jr., grandson of the Irish cotton broker, authored *This Is Birmingham: The Story of the Founding and Growth of an American City* (Southern University Press, 1960), an early history of the city. Like the Henleys, the Ward family also made their mark on Birmingham.

George B. Ward's father ran the Relay House, the first building to accommodate travelers who journeyed to the emerging city of Birmingham in the 1870s. Though biographic sketches of the Birmingham mayor and his ancestors do not indicate an Irish connection, other families bearing the Ward surname, who claim their Irish roots, can be found in the city. There exists, however, a well-known story about city politics during the early years of the twentieth century that may be quite telling regarding Mayor Ward's background.

According to his biographer, local historians, and city newspapers, George B. Ward, considered a prohibitionist by his opponents, was elected mayor in 1904. The board of aldermen, which included the Irish-Catholic businessman John W. O'Neill, opposed tighter controls of liquor licensing. The aldermen blocked the mayor's attempts to regulate saloons during his first term in office. In the 1907 reelection, Frank P. O'Brien was to oppose Ward. Campaigning quickly became a contest between Protestant and Catholic. The local priest, an ardent Irish nationalist, even got into the fray, denouncing all that focused on the candidates' religious affiliations instead of the issues. Before the elec-

tion, while Mayor Ward vacationed in Ireland, an O'Neill-led faction took over city government. When the mayor returned to Birmingham and found he had lost control, he fought back. Wearing an Irish green hat and armed with a large shillelagh, Ward took charge of the new city council and, supported by a few loyal police officers, denied entrance to the faction that had ousted him. Additionally, he brought charges of graft against O'Neill. Both the state legislature and the Alabama Supreme Court ruled against Ward, who did not seek reelection in the upcoming primary. Frank P. O'Brien became the next mayor of Birmingham.

During his term of office, O'Brien served the city well, as he had done since arriving in the city over thirty years earlier. O'Brien built an opera house for the citizens' entertainment in the 1880s. He served in the state legislature and as the city's sheriff. During his tenure as mayor, he supported a citywide playground movement, as well as other progressive reforms. His daughter, "Bossie" O'Brien Hundley, joined other women in calling for their right to vote. She acted as chairman of the Legislative Committee of the Alabama Equal Suffrage Association during the reemergence of the women's movement in the state between 1914 and 1916. As an Irish Catholic and Democrat, her father, had he lived, might not have approved of his Republican daughter's progressive efforts. The Hundleys, like other well-off Irish-Americans in Birmingham at the turn of the twentieth century, supported several philanthropic endeavors.

Religious institutions as well, supported by their members, offered community services. Under the direction of Father Patrick O'Reilly, Irish-born pastor of St. Paul's Cathedral, St. Vincent's Hospital, established for the care of Birmingham's indigent citizens and the first teaching hospital in the state, came into being, as did the East Lake Atheneum Orphans Home, later called St. Thomas-on-the-Hill. The Ladies' Auxiliary of the Ancient Order of Hibernians sponsored annual picnics to benefit the orphanage. Although St. Thomas-on-the-Hill is no longer an orphanage, St. Vincent's Hospital still commands a central place on a hill overlooking downtown Birmingham.

Since the 1920s, recognizable manifestations of Irish identity began to disappear as Birmingham's Irish were replaced numerically by Italians after the turn of the twentieth century. During the same period, local events led to a changed atmosphere; the tolerance of earlier times gave way to the prejudices that would haunt Birmingham for the next fifty years. The decade of the twenties produced some of the most violent verbal and physical abuses against Catholics, whatever ethnic affiliation, that the city had ever known. These abuses occurred during the reemergence and visible presence of the Ku Klux Klan in Alabama and other states across the nation. In Birmingham, religious hatred merged with racial prejudices. Results included, but were not limited to, the death of the city's most outspoken Irish-Catholic priest, the acquittal of his accused murderer, and the emerging career of a young Alabama lawyer who would become one of the most recognizable members of the United States Supreme Court.

In the early evening of August 11, 1921, Edwin R. Stephenson, an itinerant Methodist minister, shot the Reverend James Edwin Coyle. The Irish-born priest died at St. Vincent's Hospital within the hour. Two eyewitnesses said Stephenson approached the priest as he sat on the front porch of the rectory. Shortly after he fired the shots, Stephenson turned himself in to the police claiming he fired in self-defense. During the trial, and under oath, Stephenson claimed "no ill-will against the Catholic Church." He did, however, admit his anger when he discovered that Father Coyle had officiated at the ceremony uniting his daughter and a local Puerto Rican. He told the court he yelled at the priest, "You have married her to that nigger! You have treated me dirtier than a dog," to which, according to Stephenson, the priest replied by calling him a foul name, striking him three times, and reaching toward his hip pocket. Feeling threatened, the Methodist minister fired his weapon.

On cross-examination, Stephenson reiterated he regarded Pedro Gussman a "Negro." In Stephenson's case and that of the majority of Birmingham's citizens, the term encompassed more of the local populace than former slaves and their descendants. Any darker-skinned ethnic—Italian, Greek, or Puerto Rican—was considered inferior and treated by custom and by law as such. During the trial, Gussman's color rather than his religion became a major issue. Defense Attorney Hugo Black summoned Gussman to the courtroom after arranging the lights to accentuate the darkness of the man's complexion. During his summation, Attorney Black told the jury that with twenty mulattos to every Negro in Puerto Rico, if Gussman was "of proud Castilian descent [as he claimed]," he had descended a long way. After five days of testimony and less than two hours of deliberation during which the jury foreman stated they "carefully and prayerfully" reviewed all the evidence, the jury unanimously found Stephenson not guilty. The court discharged Stephenson, who remained in Birmingham until his death thirty-five years later. Hugo Black's successful defense of Stephenson and subsequent membership in the local chapter of the Ku Klux Klan represents the level of racial intolerance that existed in Birmingham by the 1920s as well as the importance of Klan membership for assuring one's political future. On the other hand, Birmingham's Irish Catholics felt the ramifications of this racial distrust merely because they shared the same religion with the growing numbers of darker-skinned Catholics in the community, such as Gussman and Italians.

In 1925 the convent and church on Irish Hill was destroyed by fire of unknown, yet suspicious, origins. The A.O.H. hall across the road met the same fate. A year later, Birmingham directories no longer contained a listing for the A.O.H. or any other distinctively Irish organizations. Although St. Paul's Cathedral remains in downtown Birmingham, surnames of those who attend reflect the changed ethnic character of the city. Near the old Pratt mines, African-Americans live in the homes once occupied by the Irish. St. Catherine of Siena Church closed its doors in the early 1970s and followed its members to outlying communities. They built a new church on Shamrock Trail in Adamsville, a few miles northwest of Birmingham, and called it St. Patrick's to remind them of the Irish heritage of its earliest members. They continued to hold an annual St. Patrick's Day festival, but today, as it has been for several years now, the "spring fest" takes place on either the last Sunday of April or the first in May, according to the church's secretary.

Like the members of St. Catherine's, evidence of migration to outlying areas of the city by others of Irish ancestry can be found in a report generated in 1980. Titled, "Bureau of Census Neighborhood Statistics Program Narrative Profiles of Neighborhoods in Birmingham (including recent annexations and vicinity)," the figures suggest that the number of citizens claiming Irish ancestry has increased since the early decades of the century. In 1980, the largest segment of Birmingham's Irish-American population resided east of Birmingham's center. East Lake, an area considered the working-class suburb during the 1940s and 1950s, had begun by the 1980s to show the effects of continued migration east into newer neighborhoods. Over the past decade, with the establishment of promotional groups such as Operation New

Birmingham, there has been a renewed interest in the city's ethnic diversity. An annual St. Patrick's Day parade, held in downtown Birmingham, is once more a March event.

Additionally, the library at Samford University in Birmingham boasts among its holdings the Albert E. Casey Collection. According to the library's literature, "it is the most extensive collection in the South of books, manuscripts, microfilm, and maps relating to Irish history and genealogy. [It is] particularly rich in materials on counties Cork and Kerry. In addition, the library has some 500 other volumes dealing with Ireland, and complete or extensive runs of nine Irish genealogical periodicals."

The Irish who came to Birmingham during the city's infancy built a legacy of which their descendants and those who came after them could be proud. There is more to Birmingham's history than the story of the Civil Rights Movement. At least for a time during the late nineteenth and the early years of the twentieth centuries, Birmingham's Irish, Catholic and Protestant, contributed to the growth and development of one of the South's future metropolises.

*See* Alabama; Irish Heritage of the South

Kay J. Blalock, *Shades of Green: Ethnic Diversity and Gender Considerations Among the Irish in a Southern Industrial Community, 1871–1921* (Ph.D. diss., University of Toledo, 1998).
John Witherspoon DuBose, *Jefferson County and Birmingham, Alabama: Historical and Biographical* (Birmingham: F. W. Teeple and A. Davis Smith Publishers, 1887; reprinted, Easley, S.C.: Southern Historical Press, 1976).
Albert Burton Moore, *History of Alabama and Her People,* 3 vols. (Chicago: The American Historical Society, Inc., 1927).

KAY J. BLALOCK

## BLAIR, SAMUEL (1712–1751)

Presbyterian clergyman and educator in early eighteenth-century Pennsylvania. Blair was born in Ulster and in early youth emigrated with his parents who settled on a farm in Chester County, Pennsylvania. After a childhood conversion experience, Blair studied for the ministry in the famous "Log College" founded in 1726 by the Ulster-born William Tennent, Sr. (1673–1746), at Neshaminy, in Bucks County. In 1733 Blair was licensed to preach by the Philadelphia Presbytery. His first pastorates in Middletown and Shrewsbury, New Jersey, were less than successful, but in 1739–40 he became minister of the Scots-Irish congregation at Fagg's Manor, in Chester County's New Londonderry township. There he achieved spectacular success as a revivalist and became a controversial spokesman for the evangelical New Side faction, led by Tennent's son, Gilbert (1703–1764), in the colonial Presbyterian church. Blair also founded his own academy, Fagg's Manor Classical School, modeled after the Log College, to train New Side ministerial candidates. By 1741 Blair's attacks on the Old Side clergy, as "dry, sapless, unconverted ministers" who opposed the Great Awakening, helped precipitate a split in the Philadelphia Synod and the expulsion of the New Side ministers by the Old Side majority. Blair and his allies formed the schismatic Conjunct Presbyteries of New Brunswick and Londonderry, later the Synod of New York, and in 1746 he led the effort to establish the New Side's College of New Jersey (Princeton University), of which his student at Fagg's Manor, Rev. Samuel Davies (1723–1761), colonial Virginia's greatest Presbyterian revivalist, would subsequently be president. Exhausted by travelling and preaching, Blair died before the 1758 reunion of the Old and New Sides, leaving behind a wife and ten children and a younger brother, Rev. John Blair (1720–1771), who succeeded him at Fagg's Manor and later became professor of divinity at Princeton.

*Dictionary of American Biography.*

Rev. A. Alexander, *Biographical Sketches of the Founder and Principal Alumni of the Log College* (Philadelphia, 1851).

Rev. W. B. Noble, *History of the Presbyterian Church of Fagg's Manor, Chester Co., Pa., 1730–1876* (Parkesburg, Pa., 1876).

Rev. W. B. Sprague, *Annals of the American Pulpit,* III (New York, 1868).

KERBY MILLER

## BLARNEY

Blarney is a multilayered linguistic gift attributed to the Irish. Sometimes it is hyperbolic praise lavished smoothly and affluently. This is also covered by the simple Irish word *plamás;* or it can be the elusive lie colorfully clothed in a wonderful effusion of verbiage and double-talk; or it may be the exaggerated claim, boastfully made with a rich flow of words and gestures. Practitioners of the art must have "the gift of the gab" laced with a mischievous sense of subtle humor.

Tradition claims that Queen Elizabeth I (1533–1603) coined the word when she futilely tried to persuade Cormac McCarthy, Lord of Blarney, Co. Cork, to surrender title to his lands in exchange for the status of tenant under protection of the crown. Cormac sidestepped her repeated requests with plentiful flattery, wordy and bewildering evasions, and perplexing promises. The vexed Elizabeth snapped: "This is all Blarney. What he says he never means." So we should appreciate that the good queen gave more than Trinity College to Ireland.

Leslie C. Corola, *The Irish: A Treasury of Art and Literature* (New York, 1993).

William V. Shannon, *The American Irish* (New York, 1966).

MICHAEL GLAZIER

Queen Elizabeth I

Patrick Blessing

## BLESSING, PATRICK (1937–  )

Historian. Patrick Blessing was born in Dublin. After a stint in James' Street Christian Brothers Schools, he worked as a laborer for Bord Na Mona and as a bicycle messenger in Kimmage before departing for America in December 1957. Following a bicycle trip across the American continent, one of the few activities for which his background in Ireland fully prepared him, he was drafted into the military in Los Angeles in January 1960 and served in the United States Marine Corps for a decade, which included two tours in the infantry in Vietnam.

He earned a Ph.D. in American History from the University of California at Los Angeles in 1977 and won a Warren Fellowship at Harvard University in 1980 followed by an appointment as a visiting professor over the 1984–85 academic year. In 1990 he volunteered for military service during the Gulf War and was appointed to the Marine Corps Battle Assessment Team for the duration of the crisis. Presently on a leave of absence from the University of Tulsa, he is completing an extensive study on the Gulf War and modern America. He has also lectured at universities in Dublin and Moscow. Among his publications are *The British and Irish in Oklahoma* (1980); "The Irish," in *Harvard Encyclopedia of American Ethnic Groups* (1980); and *The Irish in America: A Guide to the Literature and the Manuscript Collections* (1992).

## BOSTON

Few cities in the United States have been more clearly identified as centers of the Irish and Irish-Americans than Boston, Massachusetts. Though the Irish population there was minimal throughout the colonial, Revolutionary, and early national periods, Boston became perhaps the foremost Irish-American city in the nineteenth and early twentieth centuries; allowing for the admixture of other ethnic and racial groups since, it remains so today. Facing initial hostility and discrimination from the established population, largely of English stock, the Irish in Boston came to dominate the political life of the city and its environs, and they also exerted a broad influence in local society.

## EARLY IMMIGRATION AND SETTLEMENT

Given its origins, Boston would seem to be the least likely American city to become the informal capital of Irish America. The first settlers of the Shawmut peninsula and the surrounding lands along Massachusetts Bay in the 1630s were of overwhelmingly English stock, and some of their motivations for settlement in the New World could be interpreted as more or less overtly anti-Irish. Adherents of the Puritan party within the Church of England, these first settlers, led by such figures as John Winthrop, John Cotton, and Thomas Shepard, believed that the English church retained too many of the "popish" elements of Roman Catholicism, beliefs and practices which they thought the Reformation should have fully purged from Christianity but had not. For the Massachusetts Puritans, the Irish were exemplars of the superstition, underdevelopment, and even barbarism which resulted from failure to break the thrall of the Catholic religion, and their own "errand into the wilderness" was intended to provide both a refuge for the purity of religion and a model for England to emulate. Coming mainly from the counties of East Anglia, this original population in and around Boston was probably the most homogeneous of any American colony for two hundred years.

Such Irish as did come to the Boston area in the seventeenth and eighteenth centuries were largely from the northern counties of Ulster and are generally identified as members of that vaguely defined category, "Scots-Irish." Many came as servants or workers indentured to more prosperous colonists, while others brought skills (in the woolen trades, for example) which helped establish them in America. Until after the American Revolution, however, few of these earliest Irish immigrants remained in Boston proper, most of them settling instead in New Hampshire and along the rivers inland from the Maine coast. The first federal census of 1790 identified a total population in the new republic of about 4 million, of whom an estimated 400,000 (10 percent) were of Irish stock. The same census listed Boston's population at slightly more than 18,000, of which fewer than 5 percent could be described as either Irish-born or of relatively proximate Irish extraction. Those Irish who managed to succeed in Massachusetts did so by assimilating into the dominant Yankee society. James Sullivan (1744–1808), for example, descended from a leader of the Catholic "wild geese" who fled Ireland in the 1690s, was elected to the first of two terms as governor of Massachusetts in 1807, but only long after his family had converted to Protestantism.

Boston seemed destined to remain a stronghold of English-stock Yankees, but the failure of the potato crop in Ireland in the 1840s changed all that. Immigration to Boston from all over Ireland, especially the counties of the south and west, exploded in the twenty years before the American Civil War, and it resumed at only a slightly slower pace after the conflict. Whereas the total number of immigrants to Boston in 1820 had been only about 4,000, in 1850 new arrivals numbered more than 117,000, of whom close to half had come directly from famine-starved Ireland. Another significant number of Irish took a more circuitous route, emigrating first to Maritime Canada and then making their way overland or by coastal ship to their intended destination. By 1850, approximately one in every four Bostonians had been born in Ireland, and the Irish became the city's most significant "alien" population practically overnight. German immigrants and African Americans, by contrast, each made up barely 1 percent of the city's inhabitants.

Economic opportunities in the Boston area were hardly extensive, but they still compared favorably with those in Ireland itself. Many immigrants were able to find work in manual labor, including the massive land reclamation projects in antebellum Boston which more than doubled the city's geographic area; others, both men and women, went to work in the burgeoning cotton mills of nearby Lowell, Lawrence, and Waltham. Still, living conditions for Irish immigrants and their families were frequently harsh. Crowded into unhealthy tenements, especially in the city's North End, the Irish experienced unusually high rates of infant mortality and other social pathologies. One analyst noted in 1845 that almost two-thirds of the Irish who died in Boston were under the age of five. Less sympathetic observers fretted over rapid increases in expenditures for poor relief and an even steeper crime rate. In 1864, for instance, the Boston police reported that more than 75 percent of those arrested and detained on a variety of offenses had been born in Ireland. Even later historians sometimes viewed the Irish in largely unflattering terms; as late as the 1940s one scholar was describing Boston's immigrants as "a massive lump in the community, undigested and undigestible."

In spite of the pressures created by such a substantial movement of population, the Irish in Boston were able in their earliest years to establish the basic institutions of community. A Charitable Irish Society, made up largely of old stock Northern Irish settlers and devoted to promoting the social welfare of immigrants, had been founded as early as 1737, and it was now joined by newer groups in meeting the needs of the immigrants and their families. Foremost of these was the Roman Catholic Church, of which the vast majority of famine immigrants were members. Though the Puritan founders had been overtly hostile to the Roman church and had even, in 1647, passed a law (never enforced) making it a capital offense for any Catholic priest to enter Massachusetts, Catholicism had managed to plant itself and to survive in the Boston area. The first public Mass was celebrated in 1788, and a formal Catholic parish was organized a year later. A diocese with a resident bishop had been established in 1808, and it was led for a century after 1845 by a succession of bishops who were the American-born sons of Irish immigrants. These leaders oversaw not only a multiplication of the number of local parish churches but also, equally significant, an expansion of the network of educational and charitable institutions operated under church auspices. These included hospitals, such as Carney Hospital (1863); orphanages, such as Saint Vincent's Orphan Asylum (1832), the House of the Angel Guardian (1851), and the Home for Destitute Catholic Children (1864); and schools at all levels, including the College of the Holy Cross in Worcester, Massachusetts (1843).

At the same time, other social and cultural institutions began to serve the growing population. Most important for maintenance of the Irish sense of community was a newspaper, *The Pilot,* which began publication in 1829. Devoted to addressing the interests of the Irish population in Boston and around the country, *The Pilot* remained "the Irishman's Bible" for the rest of the nineteenth century, featuring "county news" from Ireland itself and other features designed to promote connections within the Irish diaspora in America. The paper had a series of distinguished editors, including Patrick Donahoe (1811–1901), John Boyle O'Reilly (1844–1890), James Jeffrey Roche (1847–1908), and Katherine Conway (1852–1927), all of whom were important early figures in the development of Irish-American letters. More practically,

John Boyle O'Reilly

for nearly a century the newspaper also published weekly lists of "missing friends"—classified advertisements in which individuals sought information about relatives and acquaintances with whom they had lost touch during the emigration to America. Purchased as the official organ of the Boston diocese in 1908, *The Pilot* today remains the oldest, continuously published ethnic and religious newspaper in the United States.

### Nativist Opposition and the Boston Irish Response

The large-scale and rapid change in the character of the city's population naturally led to social tensions of various kinds, and the Irish in Boston faced successive waves of anti-immigrant hostility throughout the nineteenth century and into the twentieth. Though these periods of nativist reassertion were usually short-lived, they had an enduring effect on the outlook of the Boston Irish. An oppositional mindset was fixed in the consciousness of the city's Irish immigrants, their children and grandchildren, a view of themselves as outsiders which managed to endure even after they had made substantial political, economic, and social progress. The Irish never lost the collective memory of the animus they encountered from the more established portions of the community. In the colonial period, for instance, Boston's streets had been the scene for annual commemorations of "Pope's Day," anti-Catholic parading and brawling when gangs of roving toughs would randomly attack Irish neighborhoods and individuals. Even after 1775, when George Washington, upon taking command of the nascent American army in Massachusetts, banned the practice for the sake of solidarity at the beginning of the Revolution, informal repetitions continued. The most serious of these occurred in 1837 in what came to be called the Broad Street Riot. A company of local firemen returning from a blaze encountered an Irish-Catholic funeral procession, and for two hours a pitched battle between them raged in the streets, until the mayor called out the local militia to restore order.

As opposition continued to build to the increasing numbers of immigrants in the city, it was often difficult to disentangle the intertwined motives of the nativists. How much of their anger was aimed at immigrants in general, how much at the newcomers because they were Irish, and how much because they were Catholics is difficult at this point to specify. "Immigrant," "Irish," and "Catholic" had become sufficiently synonymous that haters of one were haters of all. The long-standing suspicions of the Irish

and their church resurfaced with particular violence in August 1834, when a native working-class mob destroyed the convent and school of a community of Ursuline sisters in Charlestown, Massachusetts, located directly across the harbor from downtown Boston. Convinced that young women were being held there against their will, the mob attacked and burned the convent in the middle of the night, and the impact of this event was a lasting one. Though the respectable members of the Boston establishment quickly condemned the action, the Irish had reason to think that they never received full satisfaction in its aftermath. Several rioters were tried, but all were acquitted in spite of the testimony of eyewitnesses, and efforts by Bishop Benedict Fenwick (1782–1846) to recover financial damages for the destruction of the property were repeatedly unsuccessful. Memories of what "they" had done to "us" were seared into Irish-Catholic consciousness for generations, and such recollections were perpetuated in countless ways. For forty years, church officials left standing the burnt-out shell of the convent building, a silent rebuke along the skyline of the city even as the monument commemorating the Revolutionary Battle of Bunker Hill rose nearby. When, during the same period, newspaper advertisements for domestic help regularly began to include the explicit warning "No Irish Need Apply"—sometimes abbreviated simply as "NINA"—Irish stories of exclusion were formed that would be passed down through the years.

Anti-Irish sentiment returned in the 1850s, and this time it found expression largely in state and local politics. A political party, known officially as the American Party but whose members were popularly called "Know-Nothings" (ostensibly because they replied "I know nothing" when queried about its mostly secret activities), had been organized in several places around the country. The party was nowhere more popular than it was in Boston and Massachusetts. In the state elections of 1854, the Know-Nothings swept to power on the heels of the rapidly collapsing Whig Party; the governor and other statewide officers were all Know-Nothings, and there was but a single member of the state legislature who was not affiliated with the new party. Know-Nothings embarked on a series of "reforms" designed to control the impact of immigrants in the state and to restrict the growing political power of those already there. They sought to put severe limits on the number of immigrants who could enter the country, and they passed legislation requiring that newcomers live in the state for twenty-one years before they could vote, even if they had long since become citizens. The Know-Nothings also directed a number of measures specifically against Catholic institutions serving the Irish community, seeking greater state control over church-related schools and prohibiting the expenditure of public funds on any religious institution. Most notoriously, they authorized a "convent smelling committee," charged with sniffing out the nefarious and criminal activities which, they were certain, were taking place inside the houses of religious sisters. This last measure helped undo the Know-Nothings' power. When the committee descended on a convent of Notre Dame sisters in the Boston suburb of Roxbury in 1855, most of the investigators were apparently drunk, and they later adjourned to a hotel with women of questionable reputation. Public reaction was strong, driving the Know-Nothings from power by 1857 as the newly formed Republican Party focused local and national attention on the larger issue of slavery. Once again, however, Boston's Irish saw themselves as put-upon by the dominant forces in the community, and they resolved to seek political and social power on their own.

In spite of these reminders that the Irish were still outsiders in Boston even after long residence in the city, by the middle of the nineteenth century they showed many signs of stability and success. Like other immigrant groups, the Irish generally took advantage of the opportunity afforded by the Civil War to demonstrate their loyalty to their new homeland, thereby giving the lie to nativist accusations that they made unreliable citizens. A regiment of Irish volunteers (the Ninth Massachusetts Infantry) was organized immediately on the outbreak of the war, eventually distinguishing itself at Malvern Hill and the Wilderness campaign; other predominantly Irish regiments soon followed. Individual local heroes, including Generals Thomas Francis Meagher (1823–1867) from Waterford and Tipperary-born Patrick R. Guiney (1835–1877), came to symbolize Irish-American patriotism. Irish support for the war turned mainly on preservation of the Union; however, patriotic enthusiasm cooled after the Emancipation Proclamation of 1863 turned the struggle into a war to free the slaves, a cause with which the Irish had little sympathy. There had always been some competition in the labor market between African-Americans and Irish-Americans, thereby creating antipathy between the two groups. More important, Boston's generally Democratic Irish suspiciously observed that many local Republicans, now ardent defenders of black civil rights, had been anti-immigrant Know-Nothings only a few years before. Like their counterparts in other northern cities, the Boston Irish also objected to the start of a military draft in 1862. Draftees could avoid service through the payment of a fee of $300, a sum few recent immigrants could afford, and many Irish thus concluded that the burden of the draft fell disproportionately on them, rendering the conflict "a rich man's war, but a poor man's fight." Resistance to the draft was only episodic, however, and the destructive rioting seen in Irish neighborhoods elsewhere (especially New York City) in the summer of 1863 was largely absent in Boston.

The expansion of institutional life also contributed to the assimilation of the previously "undigested lump" of the Irish in Boston, especially after the Civil War. New charitable institutions serving and largely supported by the Irish community were established, including Saint Elizabeth's Hospital (1868), the first hospital exclusively for women in the city, and the House of the Good Shepherd (1869), which provided temporary shelter for "fallen women," a residence for their children, and training in skills they could take into the legitimate workforce. Educational institutions likewise grew, helping to create and sustain the possibility that the Irish might advance in America, as other groups had, through preparation for middle-class and professional jobs. Foremost of these was Boston College, established in 1863 in the heart of the city to serve as a secondary school and college for the sons of immigrants. An institution for the training of Catholic priests, Saint John's Seminary, was opened in 1884, and it, too, offered a means of advancement in this world as well as the next one. Far into the twentieth century, it was common for first- and second-generation Irish-American families to send some of their sons to Boston College and others to the seminary, advancing the family's fortunes and status through the careers of its children. Higher education for Irish and Catholic young women had to wait a few years longer, until the establishment of Emmanuel College in Boston (1919) and Regis College in nearby Weston (1927).

Like other Americans, the Irish in Boston were also "joiners," and they came together in all sorts of voluntary associations. In addition to county societies (social clubs organized on the basis of the county in Ireland from which its members came), there were also many groups dedicated to backing various political causes in the homeland of the immigrants. Earlier in the nineteenth century, there had been support for Daniel O'Connell's Catholic Emancipation and for Repeal associations, and after the war there was no diminution of interest in emerging Irish nationalism. Home Rule associations, affiliates of the Land League, the Clan na Gael, the Irish Republican Brotherhood, the Ancient Order of Hibernians, and other groups all found supporters among Boston's Irish, though not so many or so fanatic as in some other cities. Fenianism in particular, for example, was never as extensive in Boston as the size of the local Irish community might lead one to expect. By the twentieth century, most of these groups had died out or had been converted (like the Clan na Gael) into societies for the promotion of Irish culture generally; by then they were joined by other organizations, such as the Eire Society (founded 1937), which was devoted especially to literary and historical interests. In large numbers, the Irish also formed local temperance societies, especially those inspired by the Irish Capuchin priest Theobald Mathew, who had preached against liquor in Boston in 1849 and who was committed to battling a temptation to which many thought the Irish particularly susceptible.

By the middle of the nineteenth century, the Boston Irish had also produced some prominent and successful businessmen, individuals who could demonstrate to the dominant Yankee community and to their own people that the Irish would not always remain undigested in Boston. Andrew Carney (1794–1864) had been born in Cavan and came to Boston in 1816 as an apprentice tailor. By the 1830s he had established a successful business in the manufacture of ready-made clothing, and his ventures prospered even more when he won contracts to provide uniforms for the U.S. army. Retiring from active involvement in his business in 1845, he devoted the last years of his life to philanthropy, helping to endow a number of religious and other institutions, including Boston College and the Carney Hospital in South Boston, which was named for him. Patrick Donahoe (1811–1901), also from Cavan, used his long tenure as editor of *The Pilot* to become a leader of the Irish community to whom non-Irish citizens could point as an example of growing respectability; his investments in other businesses and in real estate had combined to make him a very wealthy man. George P. A. Healy (1813–1894) also rose from the Boston Irish working class to become a successful portrait painter. By the end of the century, however, surely the best known Boston Irishman in America was John Boyle O'Reilly (1844–1890), whose life had been colorful and whose literary accomplishments were many. After escaping from penal servitude in Australia for his Fenian activities at home, he made his way to Boston in 1870. In addition to editing *The Pilot* for fifteen years, he was renowned as a poet and essayist, one who could bridge otherwise seemingly unbridgeable social gaps. When he was chosen in 1889, over such more likely candidates as Oliver Wendell Holmes, to deliver the main address at the dedication of a new monument at Plymouth Rock, O'Reilly came to symbolize the prospect that the Irish had indeed begun to "arrive" in the land of the Pilgrims and Puritans.

## The Irish in Politics

It was through participation in elective politics, however, that the Irish left their deepest impression on Boston. The sheer force of their numbers was bound to make them a political force in the city and the state of which it was the capital, and by the 1880s these forces began to coalesce into sustained political power.

Boston had been the first town in Massachusetts to incorporate as a city in 1822, and it had been served by a succession of distinguished Yankee mayors and by a bicameral city council: a twelve-seat Board of Aldermen and a seventy-five member Common Council. The mayor's position was largely ceremonial, with most of the real authority for running the city vested in the council, thus making it the prize which the politically ambitious coveted. Because members of the council's lower house were elected from local wards, this proved a relatively easy starting point for any Irish-American to get a start in politics, especially in certain neighborhoods. As the century proceeded, the Irish had gradually moved out of the slums of the North End into more comfortable areas of the city, including South Boston (a peninsula jutting out into the harbor from downtown) and the "streetcar suburbs" of Roxbury, Dorchester, Jamaica Plain, and West Roxbury, all of them separate towns which were consolidated into the city proper in the last quarter of the century. Competition for nomination to office from these districts was usually stiff in ward caucus meetings, and ward leaders came to exercise real, if often temporary, power. For the most part, ward bosses remained influential in their own districts only. In contrast to Irish political organizations elsewhere (New York, Jersey City, and Chicago, for example), there was never one centralizing boss who managed to consolidate his influence over the entire city; even the most successful bosses in Boston retained resolutely local identifications which left them all-powerful in their own neighborhood but essentially impotent outside it.

Those who wanted to have a broader impact on the city's politics thus had to build coalitions carefully, not only within the Irish population but also with the better established Yankees. Boston's first successful Irish politicians in the 1880s did just this. Patrick A. Collins (1844–1905), a state legislator and congressman originally from Cork, was the first to forge an effective bond between Irish and Yankee Democrats. He was joined in this effort by his fellow immigrants and local political leaders, Thomas Gargan (1844–1908) and Patrick J. Maguire (1838–1896), who had established a popular newspaper, *The Republic,* in 1882 to promote his own and his fellows' political fortunes. Marshaling their own voters and drawing on the support of Yankee Democrats, who were badly outnumbered in overwhelmingly Republican Massachusetts, this group managed to elect Hugh O'Brien (1827–1895) as the city's first Irish-Catholic mayor in 1884. O'Brien was the perfect candidate to appeal to a broad spectrum of the electorate and to reassure doubting Yankees that the Irish really had the interests of "their" city at heart. An immigrant in childhood, he had become a printer's apprentice and, Horatio-Alger-like, had made a success of himself through study and hard work, first achieving prominence by publishing a newspaper devoted to the city's commercial and business establishment. O'Brien served two successive terms as mayor and was shortly afterward followed in that position by Collins himself, first elected in 1902 and dying in office in 1905. Both were praised for their ability to win support outside the Irish community, and their administrations were noted for efficiency and the absence of any kind of scandal.

With the passing of the O'Brien-Collins generation, however, a new kind of Irish political leader took center stage. The American-born sons of immigrants, these younger politicos found that, as the number of voters like themselves continued to grow, they needed non-Irish coalition partners less and less; moreover, they learned to galvanize their own supporters by openly playing

James Michael
Curley

on ethnic tensions and long-standing resentments. One of the most successful of these was Martin Lomasney (1859–1933). Seldom holding elected office himself, Lomasney (nicknamed "the Mahatma") was the widely feared boss of the West End, who could make or break the careers of the rising generation of Irish leaders. The mayoral election of 1910 proved the decisive turning point. Under a newly revised city charter which vested real power in the mayor's office and expanded the job to a four-year term, the contest pitted James Jackson Storrow (1864–1926), a dour Yankee banker, against John Francis Fitzgerald (1863–1950), a flamboyant ward boss from the North End whose sweet singing voice (which he never hesitated to show off on the campaign trail) had earned him the nickname "Honey Fitz." Storrow openly warned voters about "Fitzgeraldism," a code word for the prospect of rampant corruption, while Fitzgerald denounced his opponent as a puppet of sinister business interests. Fitzgerald's decisive victory over Storrow ushered in a succession of Irish-American mayors over the next half-century. Most famous of these was Fitzgerald's sometime rival, James Michael Curley (1874–1958), who served as mayor at least once in every decade from the 1910s to the 1940s and who was also elected to one term as governor of Massachusetts, in spite of the odor of corruption which always lingered about him.

For most of the remainder of the twentieth century, politics in Boston was dominated by Democrats who were second- and third-generation Irish-Americans. The traditional focus on local, ward-based politics persisted, and few of these leaders ever achieved success by promising voters a larger vision of public life. Patronage networks for delivering very particular needs to constituents (jobs, social services, housing, and so on) became the mainstay of politics, and elected officials at all levels devoted themselves to these tasks. Such a focus often left them open to charges of corruption, and there were just enough real cases of influence peddling and other illegal practices over the years to give substance to those accusations. Boston Irish politicians never apologized, however, for their attention to the immediate interests of their voters. One of them, Thomas P. O'Neill (1912–1994), who served as speaker of the Massachusetts House of Representatives (1949–1952) and later speaker of the United States House of Representatives (1977–1986), even enshrined this approach to public policy in a frequently quoted maxim: "all politics is local." The exception who proved this rule was John Fitzgerald Kennedy (1917–1963), grandson and namesake of Honey Fitz, whose political career was built on a deliberate turning away from the local issues and conflicts which absorbed his contemporaries. First elected to Congress in 1948, he advanced to the Senate in 1952, defeating a scion of the once-powerful Lodge family, and he became the first Irish-Catholic president of the United States in 1961. Though identified nationally as a quintessential Boston Irish politician, Kennedy had in fact always maintained a careful distance from the lower-level political factionalism of his home state. This approach was continued by his brother, Edward Moore Kennedy (1932– ), who succeeded him in the Senate in 1962.

On the local scene, after decades of Irish political dominance, new tensions became apparent after the Second World War. Though much of Boston was physically remade in the 1950s and 1960s as part of an ambitious urban renewal program, spearheaded by Mayors John B. Hynes (1897–1970) and John F. Collins (1919–1995), social change eventually brought to the fore issues which the city's political leadership found difficult to resolve. In particular, conflict between the city's white residents of all ethnic backgrounds and its rapidly growing population of African-Americans (16 percent by 1970) was often bitter. Especially troublesome were battles over the public school system. In a case brought by several black parents of school-age children, a federal court found in 1974 that the Boston School Committee, for generations dominated by Irish-Americans, had engaged in practices which resulted in the de facto racial segregation of the city's schools. As a remedy, the judge ordered crosstown "busing" of students, and this called forth massive and sometimes violent resistance from white parents, especially in the largely Irish-American working class neighborhoods of South Boston and Charlestown. Though other Irish Bostonians accepted the court's decision reluctantly, the turmoil resulted in little improvement in the schools themselves, while contributing to "white flight" to the suburbs. This trend was only partially reversed as upwardly mobile families began to return to the city with a generally rising economic and business tide in the 1980s and after. By then, politics in Boston may have been moving in a "post-ethnic"—or at least "post-Irish"—direction. In the election of 1993, an Italian-American, city councillor Thomas Menino, was decisively elected mayor over James Brett, the Boston-born son of Irish immigrants. If this was not enough to signal the end of Irish-American dominance in Boston politics, it at least indicated that the future of ethnic politics in Boston would be more complicated than it had been for most of the previous century.

## SOCIAL, CULTURAL, AND RELIGIOUS LIFE

Even as well-known political leaders came to represent and symbolize the Boston Irish, broader social forces affecting the community were also at work. As with other immigrants, the Irish experienced a degree of upward social mobility the longer their families remained in America. Though progress was slow at first in comparison with some other ethnic groups, by the twentieth century most Irish in Boston could confidently expect that life would be better for their children than it had been for them. The educational institutions which fueled such advancement elsewhere played similarly important roles in Boston, from the lower grades through university training. Boston College was particularly important in this, especially after moving from the center of the city to a spacious campus in suburban Chestnut Hill in 1913. Enrollments grew steadily thereafter, and the college was able to offer a wider range of programs, opening a school of education in 1919, a law school in 1929, a school of social work in 1936, a school of business administration in 1938, and a nursing school in 1947. Graduates used this increasingly specialized training to advance into professional careers, establishing themselves firmly in the middle and upper-middle class. This kind of progress also frequently entailed a move from the city itself to the suburbs, and shifts due to internal migration were readily apparent. The city's population hit its peak at just over 800,000 in 1950, steadily losing ground to its suburban ring thereafter. In 1950, the city accounted for 36 percent of the population living within the encircling highway known as Route 128; in 1970, the city counted for less than 24 percent of the residents of the same territory.

Irish professional development was particularly strong in several fields. A certain number of Irish Bostonians had found employment in the law throughout the nineteenth century, establishing small firms which catered to their own community. Many of those who took part in elective politics maintained legal offices to which they could return if unsuccessful at the polls. By the middle years of the twentieth century, their better educated sons—it would not be until the 1970s that their daughters had these opportunities—were achieving even greater success and cracking some previously impenetrable barriers. The old-line Yankee law firm Ropes and Gray hired its first Irish-American associate in 1932, and he eventually rose to the position of managing partner in the firm, an accomplishment that would have been impossible only a few years earlier. The Irish also came to outnumber all other groups in the ranks of teachers and administrators in the public school system, a dominance which resulted in the comparative underdevelopment of the Catholic school system in Boston. Since Irish Catholics seemed to be in charge of the public schools, many saw little reason to establish and maintain a competing parochial school system. Many second- and third-generation Irish Bostonians also found professional employment in such fields as insurance, banking, medicine, and general business management.

The Catholic Church in Boston also continued to be a predominantly Irish institution. In contrast to the structure of Catholicism elsewhere in the United States, where the Irish contended with nearly equal numbers of Germans and other ethnic groups for control of parishes and institutions, the church in Boston was always divided unevenly into the Irish on the one hand and everybody else on the other. Ironically, this meant that there were fewer interethnic tensions within the Catholic Church in Boston than in other parts of the country. Whenever a sufficient number of Italians, Poles, or other groups wanted to withdraw into their own distinct parishes, the Irish clergy and hierarchy were willing to let them do so, confident that the loss of these parishioners would constitute no threat to the continued flourishing of the church. Strong Irish-American bishops, including William H. O'Connell (1859–1944) and Richard J. Cushing (1895–1970), led the Boston church in the twentieth century, presiding over an impressive institutional expansion and creating a strong public presence for the church beyond matters of religion. In the same way, the ranks of Catholic sisterhoods in Boston were overwhelmingly Irish, affording the daughters of immigrant and second-generation families opportunities for careers as teachers, nurses, and social workers which were not

William Henry
Cardinal O'Connell

so widely available to women until later in the twentieth century.

Irish contributions to the broad cultural life of Boston similarly expanded as the community grew into its position as the new establishment which had supplanted the older Yankee aristocracy. Prominent individuals distinguished themselves in various fields, including some that were previously closed to the Irish because of a lack of opportunity or education. In architecture and design, for example, Louis H. Sullivan (1856–1924) became known for the construction of skyscrapers throughout the country, and Charles Donagh Maginnis (1867–1955) became one of the foremost designers of churches in America. Sportsmen were never numerous among the ranks of Boston's Irish, but when one was successful it was usually on a grand scale. John L. Sullivan (1858–1918), known as "the Boston strongboy," became the heavyweight boxing champion in 1882 and built his tumultuous career on the supposed boast that he could "lick any man in the house." Irish labor leaders, like their counterparts the political ward bosses, tended to focus on local rather than national organizing activities, and thus they were not so widely recognized as Irish union officials from other parts of the country. Women were unusually active in union efforts in Boston; however, Mary Kenney O'Sullivan (1864–1943) helped organize workers for the AFL in Boston, and Margaret Foley (1875–1957), another union organizer, became more prominent in the movement for women's suffrage, earning the nickname "the Great Heckler" for her willingness to take on public speakers who challenged her views. In the arts, some Boston Irish managed to achieve wider fame, including the poet Louise Imogen Guiney (1861–1920), as well known in England as she was in America; the radio personality Fred Allen (1894–1956), whose real name was John Florence Sullivan; and the novelist Edwin O'Connor (1918–1968), whose 1956 novel, *The Last Hurrah*, based loosely on the life of James M. Curley, captured for many the image of the Boston Irish politician.

In the nearly four centuries of European settlement, Boston has been transformed from what may have been the least to the most Irish city in America. Though the massive immigration of the mid-nineteenth century has long since ceased and the descendants of those migrants have risen to play a central role in the life of the city, new Irish immigrants continue to come to Boston every year, often in response to changing economic circumstances in Ireland itself. Throughout these centuries, the Boston Irish have overcome many obstacles and face now the challenges of incorporating the heritage of their ancestors with the opportunities they continue to make for themselves.

*See* Emigration (5 entries); Irish in America

Historical works on the Irish in Boston are numerous and varied. The earliest study is James Bernard Cullen's *The Story of the Irish in Boston* (1889). In the twentieth century, the seminal work is Oscar Handlin, *Boston's Immigrants: A Study in Acculturation* (first published 1941) which laid the groundwork for future research, even though it is occasionally marked by an anti-immigrant tone. More helpful recent studies include Thomas H. O'Connor, *The Boston Irish: A Political History* (1995), and Dennis P. Ryan, *Beyond the Ballot Box: A Social History of the Boston Irish* (1989). For biographies of some of the more colorful characters in Boston Irish history, see Doris Kearns Goodwin, *The Fitzgeralds and the Kennedys: An American Saga* (1987), James M. O'Toole, *Militant and Triumphant: William Henry O'Connell and the Catholic Church in Boston* (1992), and Jack Beatty, *The Rascal King: The Life and Times of James Michael Curley* (1992). For broadly based social studies, see Stephan Thernstrom, *The Other Bostonians: Poverty and Progress in the American Metropolis* (1973), Ronald P. Formisano, *Boston Against Busing: Race, Class, and Ethnicity in the 1960s and 1970s* (1991), and James J. Connolly, *The Triumph of Urban Progressivism: Urban Political Culture in Boston, 1900–1925* (1998).

JAMES M. O'TOOLE

## BOSTON, TWELVE IRISH-AMERICAN MAYORS OF

### The Mayors

In the history of Boston, Massachusetts, there have been twelve Irish mayors, namely, Hugh O'Brien (1885–88), Patrick A. Collins (1902–05), Daniel A. Whelton (1905), John F. Fitzgerald (1906–07, 1910–13), James M. Curley (1914–17, 1922–25, 1930–33, and 1946–49), Frederick W. Mansfield (1934–37), Maurice J. Tobin (1938–44), John E. Kerrigan (1945), John B. Hynes (1950–59), John F. Collins (1960–67), Kevin H. White (1968–83), and Raymond L. Flynn (1984–93).

### Hugh O'Brien (1818–95)

Although New York was the first major city in the country to elect an Irish Catholic as mayor, with William R. Grace (1832–1904) in 1880, Boston elected one five years later with Hugh O'Brien who was born in Maguiresbridge, County Fermanagh, Ireland, on July 13, 1818, and died in Somerville, Massachusetts, on August 1, 1895. Coming to Boston in August of 1828, O'Brien was educated in the grammar school on Fort Hill and became interested in printing at the age of twelve. So diligent was he in learning that trade and in studying at the public library that O'Brien had prepared himself to be a very effective editor and publisher after he had become a naturalized American citizen on September 18, 1840.

In fact, at age twenty-five, O'Brien had his own publication, *Shipping and Commercial List*, which brought him into contact with the city's leaders in commerce, industry, and politics. The newspaper brought recognition and advancement for O'Brien as a leader in organizations like the Charitable Irish Society, the Franklin Typographical Society, St. Vincent Orphan Asylum, and the Union Institution for Savings. Following his election as alderman in 1874, O'Brien served for six years before he was elected mayor with the support of *The Republic,* the newspaper of Patrick J. Maguire, the most powerful Democrat among the city's Irish whose foreign-born population had outnumbered all others by two to one in 1880. Thus, O'Brien defeated Augustus Martin, the incumbent mayor, in 1884 and, thereafter, won in the next three elections until Thomas Hart defeated the mayor in 1888.

As Mayor of Boston, O'Brien defended the workers, fought discrimination, slashed the high tax rate, and uprooted corruption. At the same time, the mayor encouraged the development of the city's streets, parks, and library. Though O'Brien dedicated the cornerstone of the new library, he used to close the old one to celebrate St. Patrick's Day. His businessman's approach to politics enabled O'Brien to get along well with the city's power structure. Though he helped to undermine Yankee fears of Irish Catholics in politics, there was enough bigotry around to help defeat O'Brien in 1888. When he died in 1895, he was buried in Holyhood Cemetery, Brookline, MA.

### Patrick Andrew Collins (1844–1905)

The second Irish Mayor of Boston was Patrick Andrew Collins who was born in Ballynafauna, a townsland in the Clondulane part of Fermoy in County Cork, Ireland, on March 12, 1844, and died while vacationing in Hot Springs, Virginia, on September 14, 1905. The son of Bartholomew and Mary (Leahy) Collins, Patrick left Ireland at the age of four and arrived in Boston with his widowed mother in 1848. They settled in Chelsea where young Collins broke an arm in confronting the Know-Nothings in an anti-Catholic demonstration.

Inspired by Robert Morris, a Catholic and the state's prominent Black lawyer, Collins studied hard and, eventually, began a career in politics by winning a seat in the state legislature (1868–69). Then Collins served as the youngest member of the state senate (1870–71) and acquired a law degree from Harvard (1871) before he was thirty. Through the practice of law, Collins became known in the Democratic Party outside of the city's Irish community and received a gubernatorial appointment as the state's advocate general in 1874.

With his election to the United States House of Representatives in 1882, Collins remained in this office until 1889. Having been involved in the 1884 presidential campaign, Collins chaired his party's national convention in 1888. For helping Grover Cleveland win the Irish vote, especially in Boston in 1888, the President appointed him consul general in London during his second term. In returning to Boston from his consular post in 1897, Collins found his party split over the Spanish War, which he supported, and the acquisition of territories like the Philippines and Puerto Rico, which he opposed.

Consequently, Collins decided to try to unite the Democrats in Boston. Although he was defeated in his first run for mayor during 1899, he won overwhelmingly against Republican Thomas N. Hart in 1901 when the Irish numbered more than 225,000 or half the city's population. The first American to be President of the Irish Land League, Collins was, at the time of his re-election in 1903, Boston's most prominent Irishman in public life.

If Collins was not an extraordinary mayor, he always defended civil rights and he was an honest and tough opponent of corruption in politics and of spending in government. A resident of South Boston and of Dorchester in his later years, Collins sought to strengthen the commercial and industrial base of the city by encouraging business expansion beyond its downtown center.

Dying in office, Collins was survived by Mary (Carey) Collins, his wife, a son and two daughters. After he was buried in Brookline's Holyhood Cemetery, he was honored by Boston Brahmin with a unique monument which stands today on the mall on Commonwealth Avenue not far from Charlesgate West, between Dartmouth and Clarendon Streets. And, recently, inspired by Michael Barry's sketch of Collins, "The Fermoy Born Farmer's Son Who Became Mayor of Boston," a plaque in his memory was erected in the Urban Council at Fermoy in Ireland.

### Daniel A. Whelton (1872–1953)

Daniel A. Whelton, whose paternal roots stem from County Cork, was the third Irish Mayor of Boston. Born in the West End of Boston on January 1, 1872, he died at Boston's Baker Memorial Hospital on November 27, 1953. Often overlooked among the city's mayors, this son of Daniel and Annie (Gorkey) Whelton was an 1886 graduate of St. Mary's School in Boston's North End. Employed in printing and in sales, Whelton, who was elected to Boston's common council in 1894 and in 1895, was appointed a gauger of revenues for the federal government (1895–1903).

Coming from the old Ward Eight, an Irish stronghold in the city's West End, Whelton was in Martin M. Lomasney's political camp and, as Chairman of the Boston Board of Alderman, he clashed with James Michael Curley. With the death of Collins in 1905, Whelton became the first Boston-born Irish Catholic to be Mayor of Boston. As one of the city's youngest mayors at age thirty-three, he served the remainder of his predecessor's term. In less than four months in office, Whelton's tenure was marked by an outpouring of patronage in new jobs and by increases in salaries which helped to consolidate the grip of the Irish and the Democrats on City Hall.

After his brief service as mayor, Whelton became one of Boston's deputy sheriffs before he faded into the background of the city's political life. When Whelton died, the Boston City Council passed a resolution saluting Whelton for his contributions to the city. At least two former mayors, Curley and Mansfield, and future Speaker of the House, U.S. Congressman John W. McCormack, served as honorary pallbearers at his funeral in the Cathedral of the Holy Cross in Boston. Whelton is buried in St. Joseph's Cemetery in West Roxbury.

### John Francis Fitzgerald (1863–1950)

Whelton's successor, John Francis Fitzgerald, was born in Boston's North End on February 11, 1863, and died in his native city, on October 2, 1950. The son of Thomas and Rose Mary (Murray) Fitzgerald, immigrants from County Wexford in Ireland, "Honey Fitz," as he was known, was the first of his nationality and religion to study at Boston Latin School where he had so excelled in studies and sports that he was able to enter Harvard and study medicine until his father's death forced him to leave school.

Initially attracted to insurance, Fitzgerald found politics more to his liking. He won a seat on the city's common council in 1892 and control of the Irish enclave of the North End just as Patrick J. Kennedy did in the East End, and James Michael Curley would do in the South End in a city with 750,000 people. With the backing of Lomasney from the West End, Fitzgerald was elected a state senator in 1892 and a representative to the United States Congress in 1894. Once the only Catholic and Democrat in the delegation from New England, he served three terms in Washington (1895–1901).

Returning to Boston, Fitzgerald defended the Irish and the Democrats in his weekly, *The Republic,* which he had purchased and thereby had broadened his influence prior to his run for mayor in 1905. Despite the opposition of the other Irish ward bosses, including Lomasney, Fitzgerald won by defeating Louis Frothingham, a Republican. However, in 1907, when all the ward bosses, except Lomasney, opposed Fitzgerald, they helped to elect George A. Hibbard, a Republican. Coming back in 1909, Fitzgerald defeated Republican James J. Storrow.

While Fitzgerald became the first mayor to serve a four-year term (1910–13), his confrontational style exacerbated the split between the Yankee and the Irish. Yet, Mayor Fitzgerald was known for his deep personal interest in the problems of voters, his provision of entertainment facilities for Bostonians, his generous exercise of patronage for his supporters, and his campaign for better harbor and waterfront facilities for the city's economy. Except for returning to Washington as a congressman for another term in 1919, Fitzgerald did not win any more elections even though he was a candidate for mayor again in 1914, for the United States Senate in 1916, and for governor in 1922 and 1930.

Having married Mary Josephine Hannon in 1889, Fitzgerald became linked to the Kennedys in 1914, when his oldest daughter, Rose, married into the family of his political rival. Years later, his grandson, John Fitzgerald Kennedy, ran for his old congressional seat and Fitzgerald had the consolation of witnessing a victory that would lead to the first Irish Catholic in the White House a decade after he died. Interred in St. Joseph's Cemetery in West Roxbury, Fitzgerald has been honored in his native city with an expressway named in his memory.

### James Michael Curley (1874–1958)

Of all the Irish Mayors of Boston, James Michael Curley, who was born in the Roxbury section of Boston on November 20, 1874, and died in his native city on November 12, 1958, was the most colorful. The son of Michael Curley of Galway and Sarah (Clancy) Curley of Connemara, immigrants from Ireland, James started his education in the public schools of his native city. When his father died, he was forced to go to work and to complete high school by going to night school. Gifted with a good mind, Curley enhanced his education by much reading on his own.

But it was politics that attracted Curley who, despite his involvement in the Ancient Order of Hibernians, continually ran into difficulties with the other Irish leaders in the various sections of Boston. In 1896, Curley unsuccessfully opposed his own ward boss, P. J. ("Pea Jacket") Maguire, as the candidate for mayor; and, in 1898, the young candidate failed to win a seat on the common council. However, success came to Curley when he became a state representative (1902–03), a Boston alderman (1904–09), and a city councilor (1910–11). Curley was elected to the United States House of Representative in 1910 and in 1912, the year when he decided that he would run for mayor.

With the help of Boston's poor Irish, Curley was elected mayor in 1913 and left his seat in Washington to care for their needs. While his building projects provided employment for them, his spending policies stirred up opposition in the business establishment. With his lack of support from Martin Lomasney, whose candidates split the Irish vote, Curley was defeated in 1917. However, by 1921, when he ran again, Curley was wiser and stronger with a political machine which defeated his three opponents, including two Irishmen. Thus, Curley opened the way to another

administration in which spending became the order of the day by creating jobs which decreased unemployment by thirty thousand.

After his third successful victory as mayor in 1929, Curley was on a fast track and later backed away from Alfred E. Smith to support Franklin D. Roosevelt for the Democratic nomination for the presidency. Hoping for a cabinet position from Roosevelt, Curley was disappointed when the President separated himself from the party bosses in the larger cities. Although Curley was elected Governor of Massachusetts in 1934, failure plagued him when he ran for the United States Senate in 1936, for mayor again in 1937 and once more in 1941, and a second time for governor in 1938. Then, after an absence for a generation from Washington, Curley won back his old seat in the elections of 1942 and 1944. But, still bent on the mayor's office, at Boston's City Hall, Curley was victorious again in 1945 before his final defeat for mayor in 1949.

Curley had lived a fascinating life as the standard bearer of Boston's Irish even though he had created many enemies along the way. His confrontational style within and without his own community led many of the players and shakers among the power elite of the city to avoid and oppose him. His rascality, which was epitomized in his own words ("Vote often and early for James Michael Curley"), led him to serve part of his last term as Mayor of Boston in prison until President Harry S Truman pardoned him in 1947.

His passing was mourned by the whole city. Curley was interred in Old Calvary Cemetery in Jamaica Plain. Statues and a park bench near City Hall indicate that Boston still cherishes his memory. And he is immortalized in Edwin O'Connor's great novel *The Last Hurrah.*

### Frederick W. Mansfield (1877–1958)

Frederick W. Mansfield, who was born in East Boston on March 26, 1877, and died at St. Elizabeth's Hospital in the Brighton section of Boston on November 6, 1958, was the sixth Irish-American Mayor of Boston. The son of Michael Read and Catherine (McDonough) Mansfield, immigrants from Ireland, Mansfield had served in the navy during the Spanish War in 1898 and earned a law degree from Boston University in 1902. Having pursued a career in law after passing the bar, he was the nominee of the Democratic Party for statewide office in a number of elections, including that of state treasurer in 1914, when he became the first Democrat to win that office. In his second attempt for mayor in 1933, Mansfield was elected by defeating District Attorney William J. Foley of South Boston.

Mansfield was a strong advocate of the rights of the working man and prominent among the Catholic lawyers of Boston. A friend of United States Senator David I. Walsh, Mansfield was the preferred candidate of William H. O'Connell, the Cardinal-Archbishop of Boston, for whom he later served as legal advisor. Though James Michael Curley, Mansfield's predecessor, derided his rival as "Ferocious Freddy," the new mayor, unlike Curley, pursued a stringent fiscal policy. With funds forthcoming from Washington for school construction, Mansfield restored the annual increment in the salaries of teachers. Thus, Mayor Mansfield was able to win the confidence of some twenty thousand employees on the city's payroll after Curley's spending policies had depleted the municipal coffers.

Despite help from the programs of the New Deal, Mansfield was not able to leave Boston with any monumental accomplish-

Maurice J. Tobin

ments from his administration as Curley had done with the Boston City Hospital and other projects. Though Mansfield might have done so with a new City Hall, the Great Depression prevented this. Yet, Mansfield's legacy was that he had proven himself at least adequate to the challenges that confronted him and, given his times, this was no small achievement. At his death at the age of eighty-one, Mansfield was buried in Holyhood Cemetery in Brookline and was survived by his wife, Helena Elizabeth (Roe) Mansfield, herself an Irish-American, and one son.

### MAURICE J. TOBIN (1901–53)

Maurice Joseph Tobin, who was born in Roxbury, Massachusetts, on May 22, 1901, and died in Scituate, Massachusetts, on July 19, 1953, was the seventh Irish-American Mayor of Boston. The son of Irish immigrants, James Tobin from Clogheen in County Tipperary, and Margaret Daly from Mitchelstown in County Cork, Tobin was a product of both parochial and public schools and had acquired his legal education at Boston College. His political career began when Tobin won a seat in the state legislature for one term in 1926. Then he was elected to a seat on the Boston School Committee in 1931 and in 1935 before he twice defeated James Michael Curley for mayor, once in 1937 and again in 1941.

Originally, Tobin had been an ally of Curley from whom he had received his early political education. However, Curley's confrontational style of politics did not appeal to Tobin whose approach was more in line with the policy of accommodation so evident in the early Irish Mayors of Boston. In this way, Tobin was able to win the confidence of the establishment and fuse together a coalition of Republicans and Democrats. In seven years as Mayor, Tobin pursued a fiscal policy of retrenchment that forced Boston to avoid the pitfalls of excessive spending. Apart from World War II, the worst tragedy of Tobin's years at City Hall was the Coconut Grove Fire, on November 28, 1942, in which close to 500 people at the nightclub perished, many of them Irish-American Catholics who had attended the traditional game between the two Jesuit rivals, Boston College and Holy Cross College.

For Tobin, City Hall became a springboard to higher office as he moved away from ward politics to a greater preoccupation

with city and state politics. Elected Governor of Massachusetts in 1944, Tobin continued his support of the social, political, and economic policies of the Democratic Party as proposed by Franklin D. Roosevelt's New Deal and Harry S. Truman's Fair Deal. Nominated as United States Secretary of Labor, on August 7, 1948, Tobin became one of Truman's most effective campaigners in the presidential election that year and, later, in explaining and defending his party's domestic and foreign policies.

Certainly, in the history of the Irish in politics, Tobin was a distinctive figure between the style of a James Michael Curley and that of a John F. Kennedy. Married to Helen Noonan in 1932, they were the parents of two daughters and a son. After he was interred in Holyhood Cemetery in Brookline, Tobin was memorialized in a regal bronze statue on Boston's Esplanade and in the bridge over the Charles River named for him.

### JOHN E. KERRIGAN (1907–87)

John E. Kerrigan, who was born in South Boston on October 1, 1907, died there on May 2, 1987. The third of four boys of Michael and Annie (Laffey) Kerrigan, immigrants from Ireland, John grew up in the Irish neighborhood of South Boston where he had received his elementary and grammar school education at St. Augustine's. Then, having graduated from its high school in 1926, Kerrigan's interests led him to the politics of Ward Seven which he represented on the city council after his successful bid in 1933. Subsequently, Kerrigan won a seat in the state senate for one term (1939–41), served in the army for a year (1942–43), and lost two bids for sheriff (early 1940s). Yet, with his quiet approach, he was able to establish himself on the city council where he became its president three times (1938, 1944, and 1945).

From that position, Kerrigan was catapulted into City Hall as Acting Mayor of Boston in early January of 1945 when Maurice J. Tobin became governor of the state and made it possible for his successor to enjoy full power as the city's mayor. But the new mayor, despite his constructive initiatives for improving the city, was not strong enough to win election in his own right on November 6 of that year when the nation was converting from war to peace. In a six-way contest, Kerrigan came in second as James Michael Curley captured 111,824 votes, compared to 60,413 for himself. In defeating Kerrigan, an ally of Governor Tobin, Curley had evened the score with the man who had defeated him in 1937 and 1941.

Subsequently, Kerrigan had the unique role of a former mayor serving the City of Boston as a member of the city council. As he had for almost a decade before he became mayor, Kerrigan was elected continuously to the city council where he was able to monitor the programs of mayors who undertook the renewal of Boston from 1951 to the end of 1973. Though not inclined to engage in confrontational politics, Kerrigan was not completely supportive at times of some of the ideas for the city's renewal. When, for example, such plans threatened South Boston, where he lived the life of a quiet bachelor, Kerrigan was very protective of his neighborhood. After leaving the council in 1974, Kerrigan served as a consultant on real estate before death overtook him at the age of eighty; he was buried in New Calvary Cemetery in the Mattapan section of the city.

### JOHN B. HYNES (1897–1970)

The ninth Irish Mayor of Boston was John Bernard Hynes who was born in the Dorchester section of Boston on September 22, 1897, and died there on January 6, 1970. The son of Irish immigrants, Bernard J. and Anna (Healy) Hynes, young Bernard, who was known for his family's Galway roots, was forced to leave high school to help his family as a breadwinner. Having served in the army during World War I, Hynes had developed his skills so effectively that he was hired as a civil servant in various municipal offices. By making good use of his evening and night hours, Hynes was able to acquire his high school diploma, and earned a law degree from Suffolk University in 1927 before passing the bar exam in 1928.

After serving in World War II, Hynes resumed his career in municipal government and became City Clerk in 1945. In 1947, he was designated by state legislature as Acting Mayor of Boston when James Michael Curley was imprisoned for fraud. This tenure of five months at City Hall evoked the wrath of Curley when the latter was released from federal prison. While Curley did not like what Hynes, his former ally, had done, a coalition of Democrats and Republicans backed the acting mayor in the 1949 mayoral election. Even though the campaign was Hynes' first run for public office, he defeated Curley, his strongest rival in a five-way contest, by at least ten thousand votes.

Bostonians liked Hynes once they saw him in office in 1950. Since they were impressed with his quiet style and sterling integrity, they helped him win in 1951, when the office was restored to a four-year term, and again in 1955. With their support, Hynes restructured city government to reduce the opportunities for graft and corruption. He also inaugurated a commercial and residential renewal in the Back Bay and in the West End to eliminate commercial and residential blight in a city of 800,000 people.

Having exercised leadership among the nation's mayors, Hynes retired from public life in 1960. In the subsequent years, he assumed a number of other responsibilities, including commissioner of banks and banking. At his death, survived by his wife, Marion H. (Barry) Hynes, and five children, Hynes was buried in St. Joseph's Cemetery in West Roxbury and Boston named the War Memorial Convention Center in his memory.

## JOHN F. COLLINS (1919–95)

John F. Collins, the tenth Irish Mayor of Boston, was born in Roxbury, Massachusetts, on July 20, 1919, and died in Boston on November 23, 1995. The son of Frederick B. and Margaret (Mellyn) Collins, John was a product of the schools in his native section of the city. Having obtained a law degree from Suffolk University in 1941, he served in army intelligence during World War II. Discharged as a captain, he began his rise in politics by winning a seat in the state legislature in 1946 and 1948 and by supporting John B. Hynes against James Michael Curley for Mayor of Boston in 1949. Then, Collins was elected a state senator in 1950 and in 1952 before he was defeated as the Democratic nominee for attorney general of the state in 1954.

Stricken, along with his four children, with poliomyelitis during his successful campaign for city council in 1955, Collins, unlike his children who recovered, was handicapped for the rest of his life. However, with the help of crutches and a wheelchair, not to mention Mary Patricia (Cunniff) Collins, his devoted wife, Collins continued his political career, becoming the register of probate, first by appointment in 1957 and, then, by election in 1958. In the next year, in a race against John E. Powers, one of the state's most influential politicians and one who had the backing of John F. Kennedy and the business community, Collins was

elected mayor by a wide margin of some twenty-five thousand votes reflecting widespread support in a city whose population had declined by 100,000. Although Collins won a second term as mayor in 1963, he failed to win the Democratic nomination to the United States Senate in 1966.

During his tenure, Collins brought down the real estate tax, had the state assume the costs for welfare, and obtained federal support for his urban renewal plans. Ably assisted by the urban plans of Edward J. Logue, Collins had reshaped a "New Boston" that became an example which other cities sought to imitate. Having written *Boston's Second Revolution* (1962), Collins had achieved such eminence in office that, in 1964, he became the first Mayor of Boston to receive an honorary doctor of laws from Harvard University. "Courageous rebuilder of an old Boston; his leadership has given the Hub a new spin," the citation read.

The transformation which Collins had achieved in Boston's landscape by the construction of the Prudential Center and Government Center led to a consulting professorship in 1967 at the Massachusetts Institute of Technology and to national recognition of his expertise in the redevelopment of America's cities. At his death, Collins was interred in St. Joseph's Cemetery in West Roxbury, and Boston later renamed City Hall Plaza in his memory.

## KEVIN H. WHITE (1929–   )

Kevin Hagan White was born into a political family in the West Roxbury section of Boston on September 25, 1929. The oldest child of Joseph C. and Patricia (Hagan) White, Kevin was educated at Tabor Academy, Williams College, and Boston College Law School before he passed the bar in 1955. The following year, he married Kathryn H. Galvin, daughter of Charlestown Boss William J. "Mother" Galvin, and they became the parents of five children. Serving in the district attorney's office in Boston, White was elected secretary of state in 1960 and continued to win re-election to that office until he ran for Mayor of Boston in 1967. Having won this office by defeating Louise Day Hicks, the favorite of the Irish from South Boston, White failed to win his statewide campaign for governor in 1970.

White, however, broke all records as Mayor of Boston by being elected to that office for four consecutive terms. In achieving this, White had the support of Boston's establishment, which found him, like his immediate predecessors, a mayor with whom it could cooperate. Having also won the backing of the city's Blacks (who had no confidence in Hicks) both in 1967 and 1971, White set up adjuncts to City Hall throughout the metropolitan area to provide for the concerns of the city's people. Consequently, in facing Joseph F. Timilty in 1975 and 1979, the mayor had already forged a coalition of forces that made him unbeatable even though White projected, as George V. Higgins pointed out in his study of the mayor, more style than substance.

To his credit, though, White gave Boston what it needed in those sixteen years. While he was not entirely successful in pushing for reforms in the city's charter, White kept in touch with the various neighborhoods of Boston where he was able to defuse crime and violence. However, he appeared more interested in continuing to renew the face of the city so as to make Boston more attractive to outsiders in a particularly trying period. When, on June 21, 1974, Federal Judge W. Arthur Garrity, Jr., ordered some of the city's schools in South Boston to be integrated through busing, White disagreed with the court order but said it should be peacefully obeyed. The mayor entered his most challenging period at City Hall.

Fortunately, the confidence which White had gained in his early years as Mayor of Boston enabled him to govern effectively in the following decade despite the problems which emerged. That Senator George McGovern had White on his list of possible vice presidential candidates for the 1972 presidential campaign can be taken as a measure of Kevin H. White's stature as a national figure.

## RAYMOND L. FLYNN (1939– )

White's successor was Raymond L. Flynn, who was born in South Boston on July 22, 1939. The son of Irish-American parents, Stephen and Lillian Flynn, young Raymond was educated in his native section of the city where he graduated from its high school before he earned his bachelor's degree (1963) at Providence College in Rhode Island. Flynn became interested in politics as a youth as he followed the career of John W. McCormack, United States Congressman from South Boston and future Speaker of the House, who was an inspiration to him. Although he had assumed the role of aide to Hubert H. Humphrey in the 1968 presidential campaign, Flynn had to win election to prove himself in politics.

Subsequently, running for the state legislature in 1970, Flynn won a seat after failing in his initial attempt. Then he was elected to the city council for the first of three terms in 1978. Widely recognized in Boston, especially during the fight over the 1974 federal court order to integrate the schools through busing in his own neighborhood, Flynn decided to run for the mayor's office. His knowledge and sincerity so attracted Boston voters that Flynn was elected mayor in 1983 over Mel King, a Black, whose candidacy was evidence of the change taking place in Boston's population. Four years later, despite his poor showing in South Boston, Flynn was re-elected and again in 1991 when he won seventy-five percent of the vote.

As Mayor of Boston Flynn proved himself to be very much up to the challenge. In trying to keep the city solvent, Flynn had to cope with decay in the city's neighborhoods and with its racial problems. In tune with the problems of the people, Flynn was very effective in relocating and helping Blacks in South Boston itself. His special contribution to solving urban problems was in nudging those reshaping the skyline of Boston's downtown to pour some of their wealth into improving its neighborhoods. Then, as a leader at the United States Conference of Mayors, Flynn was able to bring national attention to such problems.

Having backed William J. Clinton in the 1992 presidential campaign, Flynn was rewarded with an appointment as the American Ambassador to the Vatican (1993–1997). Out of this background, the last of the Irish Mayors of Boston, with a devoted wife, Catherine (Coyne) Flynn, and their six children, chose to campaign for congress in 1998. He lost the seat vacated by Joseph Kennedy. By this time, it was clear that the monopoly of the Irish-Americans on the mayor's office in Boston was at an end because the city's ethnic composition had changed dramatically and Boston watched the end of the Irish era.

## THEIR LEGACY

The mayors who had governed Boston for the greater part of the twentieth century were Irish Democrats. Among the mayors

have been some of the more colorful and exceptional Irish politicians in American history. Of these, three were congressmen, two were governors, one was an ambassador, and one was a cabinet officer.

*See* Boston; Curley, James Michael

Leslie G. Ainley, *Boston Mahatma* (Boston, 1949).

Jack Beatty, *The Rascal King: The Life and Times of James Michael Curley* (Reading, 1992).

Boston City Record, *Boston's 45 Mayors: From John Phillips to Kevin H. White* (1975).

James Bernard Cullen, *The Story of the Irish in Boston* (Boston, 1889).

Michael P. Curran, *Life of Patrick A. Collins* (Norwood, 1906).

John Henry Cutler, *"Honey Fitz": Three Steps to the White House* (Indianapolis, 1962).

Ronald P. Formisano and Constance K. Burns, eds., *Boston 1700–1980: The Evolution of Urban Politics* (Westport, 1984).

George V. Higgins, *Style Versus Substance: Boston, Kevin White & the Politics of Illusion* (New York, 1984).

Melvin G. Holli and Peter d'A. Jones, eds., *Biographical Dictionary of American Mayors, 1820–1980* (Westport, 1981).

Vincent A. Lapomarda, *The Boston Mayor Who Became Truman's Secretary of Labor* (New York, 1995).

Thomas H. O'Connor, *The Boston Irish: A Political History* (Boston, 1995).

VINCENT A. LAPOMARDA, S.J.

## BOSTON CHARITIES AND THE IRISH

Poverty and charity have long histories in Boston. Both have influenced—and have been influenced by—a variety of ethnic groups in the city, but one of the most notable in each case is the Irish. A review of Boston charities and the Irish sheds light on several important issues, including the unique plight of the Irish in the city; their individual and collective efforts to improve the social and economic standing of those of Irish descent; the role of the Catholic Church in local life; and the nature of the relationship between Yankee natives and Irish newcomers.

### EARLY EFFORTS

The Puritan inhabitants of seventeenth-century Boston viewed poverty as a "crime and disgrace" against society, and responded to the poor first by categorizing them. The "worthy poor" received provisions through direct aid and eventually by way of an almshouse; the "unworthy poor" were placed in a workhouse, and made to labor productively. By 1692 a Board of Overseers had been established to look over these early efforts.

In the early eighteenth century the Puritan orthodoxy felt especially threatened by foreigners in general and the Irish in particular. During the 1720s and 1730s local authorities voiced concern that immigrants from Ireland would become public charges. Even though at this time most of those sailing from Ireland were Ulster Protestants, the townspeople tried in various ways to prevent them from settling in Boston. Gradually, however, they established a certain presence.

In 1737 a number of Irishmen in town founded the Charitable Irish Society to assist "those of the Irish nation who might be reduced by sickness, age or other infirmities and accidents of distress." Members paid dues and distributed funds to the poor at quarterly meetings. They agreed that Catholics should be excluded from positions of authority in their organization, but this policy had changed by the 1760s. The society was incorporated in 1809, and social activities, particularly an annual dinner on St. Patrick's Day, assumed great importance.

The Charitable Irish Society developed alongside other Boston charities. By the early 1800s there existed in town a substantial number of social agencies, both public and private. Many of them provided assistance in one way or another to the Irish. Yet as the century progressed, specifically Catholic efforts to aid the Irish emerged. This development was almost inevitable, given the fact that more and more immigrants came to Boston from Ireland's southern counties. At first, Catholic efforts were modest. They consisted largely of the personal works of clergymen like John Cheverus, who maintained a Charity Fund at the Cathedral of the Holy Cross and made direct visitations to the poor. At times the Catholic clergy cooperated with Protestant ministers in this field. In the very early nineteenth century, Catholic laity were involved in charitable work, but not in any significant way.

### THE ADVANCE OF ORGANIZED CHARITY

Boston's Irish Catholic population began to swell even before the Great Famine of 1845, and many of the new arrivals faced economic difficulties. Organized efforts to deal with poverty grew accordingly. Reflecting a national trend, more formal organization of charity could be detected at first in the appearance of mutual relief societies. In 1832 the Boston Roman Catholic Mutual Relief Society was formed by members of the cathedral parish, and similar organizations arose at other parishes in succeeding years. Members paid various fees in return for support in times of sickness and death.

Other Catholic organizations—again operated largely by and for the Irish—focused on the special needs of children. In 1829 the Roman Catholic Poor Children Society was established in the Cathedral parish to assuage the material needs of children, particularly young girls. The Young Catholic's Friend Society, founded in 1835, devoted its attention to boys, and for many years served as the most prominent Catholic charitable organization in the city. It provided clothing to indigent children, and engaged in other activities, such as the sponsorship of a lecture series. Catholic attempts to deal with poverty exhibited a desire not only to help the needy, but also to solidify local Irish-Catholic identity and to gain a measure of respectability from the larger society.

These efforts did not fully meet the needs of the community, however, and outside assistance was needed. In 1832 the Sisters of Charity came to Boston and settled in the Fort Hill area, which was fast becoming an Irish ghetto. At first the women religious ran a school, but eventually their energies were directed toward the operation of an orphanage. St. Vincent's Orphan Asylum opened in 1843 to serve abandoned girls in Boston. The Board of Directors was mainly Irish, as were some of the Sisters who staffed the institution. Perhaps even more significant, though, was the fact that most of the girls enrolled in St. Vincent's had Irish names.

Bostonians forwarded aid to Ireland throughout much of the nineteenth century, but it was around mid-century that they expended most of their charitable energies in that direction. From 1845 famine spread in Ireland as a result of a blight in the potato crop, and by the end of the year, meetings, rallies, and other activities were being held within the Boston Catholic community to raise funds for those suffering abroad. The Boston Repeal

Association organized the Boston Friends of Ireland in 1845, and following a brief period of inactivity, the Relief Association for Ireland was established in 1847 with the help of Bishop John Fitzpatrick. Non-Catholic residents also rendered assistance through a body known as the Boston Relief Committee.

Yet Boston itself was greatly affected by the famine. Irish immigrants poured into the city to such an extent that by 1850 nearly a quarter of the population claimed Ireland as its birthplace. Although some immigrants were able to find work as laborers, a great number of them were poor, and many were either sick or infirm. As a result of these circumstances, a serious drain on public resources ensued. Until they were legal residents, the newcomers fell under the care of the state. Once settled, they usually went either to Deer Island for medical treatment, or the City Lands in South Boston, where stood houses of correction and reformation, the almshouse, and a lunatic asylum. After several abortive efforts, the Irish themselves were able to form an Irish Immigrant Society (later known as The Emigrant Society) in 1850. This organization established an office and hired an agent who gave advice to new arrivals, but support was lacking and by 1856 it had disappeared. Despite the efforts of the society— and other groups who encouraged the Irish to move west—a substantial portion of those landing in Boston decided to settle in the city, and many streets and neighborhoods became vastly overcrowded.

It was largely in response to these conditions that Irish Catholics renewed their efforts to offer charity to their countrymen, and developed during the second half of the nineteenth century an entire network of Church-sponsored institutions in Boston. Many of the new institutions served Irish children and were operated by religious orders with Irish members. The House of the Angel Guardian was an orphanage and reformatory for boys founded in 1851 and taken over by the Brothers of Charity in 1872; the House of the Good Shepherd, a similar institution for girls and young women, was administered by the Sisters of the Good Shepherd beginning in 1867. The Home for Destitute Catholic Children, which provided temporary assistance for boys and girls, was opened in 1864; from 1866 it was staffed by the Sisters of Charity. St. Mary's Infant and Lying-In Asylum was established in 1874 to care for infants and unmarried mothers. In addition, St. Vincent's Orphan Asylum continued to function and obtained new quarters in 1858.

Other kinds of institutions emerged to serve the needs of the community. In 1866 a home for Irish "working-out girls" was founded; this later expanded to become St. Joseph's Home. It eventually merged with the Working Girls Home, which had opened in 1888 under the direction of the Grey Nuns of Montreal. A "Miss Walsh's Home" operated from the 1870s, and in 1899, the Daly Industrial School was opened by the Sisters of St. Joseph to provide training for young girls. The Working Boys Home was founded in 1883, also to provide training for the youth of the city. What is more, a number of other Catholic institutions—boarding homes, shelters, hospitals—all operated for the sick and working poor during this period.

Despite the prominent role of religious in the operation of institutions, the Irish-Catholic laity were also active. They helped found homes, served on director's boards, and participated extensively in various charitable organizations. Some Bostonians joined in the work of the Irish Catholic Benevolent Union—a national organization—but mainly they focused their attention on local concerns. Of special note was the St. Vincent de Paul

Society, first established in 1861, and for many years directed by Thomas Ring. Ring's concern to serve the Irish was made plain when he stated that "we of the second and third generation . . . have a duty to perform to the children sprung of a common ancestry." Dominated by Irish members, the St. Vincent de Paul Society organized into local branches and specialized in direct contact with those in need.

Charity toward the Irish was also distributed through other private and public means. The Charitable Irish Society had continued to function, and even collaborated at times with organizations like the St. Vincent de Paul Society. At the same time another group, the Irish Protestant Mutual Relief Society, operated around mid-century. The work of these and other private societies was coordinated, beginning in 1879, by the Associated Charities of Boston. Equally important was the aid provided to the Irish during the late nineteenth century by various state and municipal agencies. A State Board of Charities, formed in 1863, had divisions for the "adult poor" and "minor wards," while the Overseers of the Poor and the Commissioners of Public Institutions directed public charity efforts in Boston. The majority of children in city institutions were Catholic, and many of these were Irish.

The disbursement of charity by Catholic, Protestant, and public charities during this period reflected larger issues in the urban landscape. Irish Catholics developed a system of charity to serve the poor, to guard against what they perceived as Protestant proselytizing, and to earn the respect of the larger society. Simultaneously the other private and public agencies in Boston, which had long been dominated by a Yankee presence, were both helpful to, and afraid of, foreign groups like the Irish. As a result, Catholic and other charity groups recognized and cooperated with the other, but at an appropriate distance.

### The Consolidation Movement and Beyond

Over the course of the nineteenth century, the Boston Irish began to advance themselves socially and economically. They influenced the larger society not only by their numerical presence but also by their political clout. Though of course some members of the Irish community continued to struggle to make ends meet, as a group it could be said that their situation had improved by the early 1900s and that future prospects were good.

In the early years of the new century, private and public institutions and organizations continued to play a large part in the provision of charity. Newer organizations, such as the Ancient Order of Hibernians, the Knights of Columbus, and the League of Catholic Women, took up benevolent work in the community even though they had not been formed originally for such purposes. In addition, the Irish contribution to public efforts expanded, as they became more involved in agencies like the Overseers of the Poor.

An especially important development was the creation of a Catholic Charitable Bureau in the Archdiocese of Boston, complete with an immigration office. The original intent of the bureau was to consolidate charitable activity within the Church in order to bring about a higher degree of efficiency. This philosophy reflected a national trend but also revealed a concern to develop further a distinct network of charity. Bureau staffers—many of whom, after 1936, were educated at Boston College's School of Social Work—worked among the Irish and other Catholic groups. During the 1960s the bureau shed much of its traditionalism and expanded into new areas.

Though many Irish-Americans moved to suburbia in the twentieth century, some stayed behind, and among these could be found a measure of economic difficulty. Some indication of this was provided by a 1972 independent study of city ethnic groups. The report indicated that among the Irish sample, many households lived on the edge of financial instability. The report also revealed that the Irish tended to have a high awareness of assistance programs available to them, and suggested that this may have been related to their long group residence in Boston.

During the 1970s and 1980s the Irish economy experienced a certain stagnation, and as a result many young people began again to look abroad for better material prospects. Naturally the United States emerged as a popular destination, and familiar places like Boston witnessed the arrival of the "new Irish." Though their needs could not compare with those of their nineteenth-century forebears, these immigrants did stand in need of certain kinds of assistance. The Irish Immigration Center and the Irish Pastoral Center were two private agencies—the latter an apostolate of the Catholic Church—founded in the late 1980s to help ease the transition to American life for immigrants from Ireland. The interaction between the Boston Irish and charity not only has a long and varied history, it continues into another century.

Peter C. Holloran, *Boston's Wayward Children: Social Services for Homeless Children, 1830–1930* (Rutherford, New Jersey, 1989).

Daniel McLellan, "A History of the Catholic Charitable Bureau of the Archdiocese of Boston" ( Ph.D. diss., University of Notre Dame, 1984).

Mary J. Oates, *The Catholic Philanthropic Tradition in America* (Bloomington, Ind., 1995).

Thomas H. O'Connor, "To Be Poor and Homeless in Old Boston," in *Massachusetts and the New Nation*, ed. Conrad Edick Wright (Boston, 1992).

Dennis P. Ryan, *Beyond the Ballot Box: A Social History of the Boston Irish, 1845–1917* (Amherst, Mass., 1989).

Susan S. Walton, "To Preserve the Faith: Catholic Charities in Boston, 1870–1930" (Ph.D. diss., Boston University, 1983).

RONALD D. PATKUS

## BOUCICAULT, DION (1820?–1890)

Actor, director, stage manager, and playwright. As to the exact day Dionysius Lardner Boucicault was born, no one can say for certain. Several conflicting dates have been recorded in various records. This ambiguity surrounding his early life also extends to his paternity. Officially, he is listed as the son of Samuel Smith Boursiquot, a Dublin wine merchant of Huguenot descent, and Anne Maria Darley Boursiquot, who came from Wicklow and was the sister of the poet and dramatist George Darley. It was, however, persistently rumored throughout Boucicault's lifetime that he was the illegitimate son of Dr. Dionysius Lardner, a celebrated author and university professor whom Boucicault was named after, and who served as Boucicault's guardian for a number of years.

Boucicault appears to have been an indifferent student, despite having attended a number of distinguished schools. However, while at school, he began to develop a fluency in French which would serve him when he began to "borrow" material from French plays.

Favorable experiences with student drama productions guided Boucicault towards the theater. Taking the stage name

"Lee Moreton," he began his professional career as an actor in England, working in a provincial repertory company.

### EARLY SUCCESS

While steady work came to Boucicault as an actor, his first real breakthrough success came with his play *London Assurance,* which premiered in 1841. (A theater favorite throughout the 19th century, it was performed as recently as 1970 by the Royal Shakespeare Company.) Thereafter, Boucicault wrote or adapted a large number of plays which contributed to his theatrical success. All in all, he would write over 200 plays in his lifetime.

Boucicault spent four years in France where, it seems, he took to calling himself "Viscount de Boucicault." (Apparently, this was the first time he took to spelling his name "Boucicault" instead of "Boursiquot.") He returned to England where he went to work as a literary advisor for the celebrated actor Edmund Kean. While working for Kean, Boucicault met a young Scottish actress named Agnes Robertson who would become his common law wife and bear him four children, all of whom would later become actors (their daughter Nina Boucicault would be the first actress to perform the title role of *Peter Pan* on stage).

### BOUCICAULT IN AMERICA

After a disagreement with Kean, Boucicault and his wife went to America in 1853. They enjoyed extensive success there, traveling to major cities like Boston (where Boucicault made his first American performance), New Orleans, and New York. During this period, Congress approved a copyright law which acknowledged the rights of dramatists, in part due to the efforts of Boucicault.

While in America, Boucicault debuted two of his best-remembered plays: *The Octaroon* (1859) and *The Colleen Bawn* (1860). *The Colleen Bawn* was the first of three plays by Boucicault—the other two being *Arrah-na-Pogue* (1864) and *The Shaughraun* (1874)—which are considered to be his most noteworthy Irish plays. The leading role of Conn the Shaughraun in the latter play became the signature role of Boucicault's final years.

After his first tour of America, Boucicault returned to England with his family and continued to enjoy considerable success as an actor and a playwright. In 1872 he returned to America where he formed a traveling company which played cities in from San Francisco to Virginia City (where the future theater impresario David Belasco worked briefly as his assistant).

In 1885 he abandoned his wife Agnes to marry a American actress named Louise Thorndyke who was forty-four years younger than himself. Boucicault died in 1890 and was buried in Mount Hope Cemetery.

### THE INFLUENCE OF BOUCICAULT

His celebrated career as a thespian, and a brief period when he served as the head of a school of acting associated with Madison Square Garden, put him in a position to affect the work of other actors. And, as a stage manager, he was credited with using such innovations as fire-proof scenery.

As a dramatist, he had both admirers and detractors. According to Christopher Fitz-Simon, Yeats and Lady Gregory disliked his work. Yet his plays were praised by such luminaries as George Bernard Shaw, J. M. Synge, and Sean O'Casey.

*See* Theater, Irish in

"Belasco, David," *The Oxford Companion to the Theatre.* Ed. Phyllis Hartnoll, 4th ed. (Oxford, 1983).

"Boucicault, Dion," *The Oxford Companion to the Theatre.* Ed. Phyllis Hartnoll, 4th ed. (Oxford, 1983).
"Boucicault, Dion," *The Cambridge Guide to the Theatre.* Ed. Martin Banham, new ed. (Cambridge, 1995).
Christopher Fitz-Simon, *The Irish Theatre* (Dublin, 1979).
Robert Hogan, *Dion Boucicault* (New York, 1969).

PETER G. SHEA

## BOURKE, JOHN GREGORY (1846–1896)

Soldier, ethnologist. John Bourke was born in Philadelphia on June 23, 1846, to Edward and Anna (Morton) Bourke, immigrants from Galway, Ireland. His parents insisted on beginning Bourke's training in Latin, Greek and Gaelic at the age of eight under a Jesuit priest. For the next eight years, he followed this course of study until at the age of sixteen he ran away from home, passed himself off as eighteen and joined the 15th Pennsylvania Cavalry. After serving with the 15th from 1862 until the end of the Civil War in 1865, Bourke won an appointment to the United States Military Academy and graduated in 1869. He was commissioned a second lieutenant and detailed to the 3rd United States Cavalry in the Southwest territories. There he developed a keen interest in Indian culture. Taking extensive notes about their customs, their habits, and varying levels of aggressiveness, Bourke catalogued them for use in diplomatic missions between the Army and the Indians of the Southwest. From these notes Bourke later produced several works on Native American culture. His first work, *The Snake Dance of the Moquis of Arizona,* appeared in 1884 and proved to be a pioneering work that led to his transfer back to Washington, D.C. There he produced ten more ethnological papers for the *American Anthropologist,* and in 1886, published *An Apache Campaign* for the Bureau of American Ethnology. Bourke's work matured, and with vivid history, colorful detail and lively wit, Bourke produced several more works like *Mackenzie's Last Fight with the Cheyennes* in 1890, *On the Border with Crook* in 1891, *The Medicine Men of the Apache* and *Scatalogic Rites of all Nations* in 1892. Bourke's husky build and agile mind further helped him to maintain remarkable endurance out in the field and a probing sense of culture in the lives of the Native Americans of the Southwest. Bourke died four years after his last work, on June 8, 1896.

F. W. Hodge, "John Gregory Bourke," *American Anthropologist,* IX: 245–48.
Joseph C. Porter, *Paper Medicine Man: John Gregory Bourke and his American West* (Norman: University of Oklahoma Press, 1986).

DANIEL J. KUNTZ

## BOURKE-WHITE, MARGARET (1904–1971)

Photographer. Born June 14, 1904, in the Bronx, New York, the second of three children, acclaimed commercial photographer and photojournalist Margaret Bourke-White grew up in Bound Brook, New Jersey. Her father, Joseph White, an engineer-designer in the printing industry, abandoned the Jewish orthodoxy of his Polish family and embraced Ethical Culture instead. Her mother, Minnie (Bourke), whose father was a successful carpenter and builder in Dublin, Ireland, was of an independent nature. The philosophy and attitudes of both parents influenced Margaret, and early attracted her to architecture, machines, and technology. She studied engineering and biological sciences at Columbia University, University of Michigan and Cornell, embarking on a photography career in 1927 in Cleveland. Two years later she joined the new *Fortune* magazine, and opened a studio in New York City's Chrysler Building, engaging in both commercial and freelance work on industrial and architectural subjects. Her first book, *Eyes on Russia* (1931), was a photographic survey of the Soviet Union. A growing reputation followed her cover photo and lead story for the first issue of *Life*, Nov. 23, 1936. She turned from photographing largely inanimate objects to the human drama, capturing the Dust Bowl tragedy of the thirties, and collaborating with Erskine Caldwell on *You Have Seen Their Faces* (1937). She also joined Caldwell (to whom she was married 1939–1942) in covering early Nazi power in Europe, and was the only foreign photographer in the USSR when Germans invaded Moscow in 1941. Bourke-White was the first woman permitted on Air Force bombing missions in Europe and North Africa, and she used her skill in classic recording of German concentration camps. *Life* sent her to India (1948) as it became an independent nation. She made studies of life in South Africa in 1949–1950, and later the human effects of the Korean War. She began to develop Parkinson's Disease in the early fifties. With John LaFarge, S.J. she produced *A Report on the American Jesuits* (1956) resulting from her *Life* story in October 1954. Margaret Bourke-White combined charm with an adventurous spirit and made work a religion. She died in Stamford, Connecticut, August 27, 1971.

Margaret Bourke-White, *Portrait of Myself* (New York, 1963).
Vicki Goldberg, *Margaret Bourke-White* (New York, 1986).
*Notable American Women: The Modern Period* (Cambridge, MA, 1980).

ANNA M. DONNELLY

## BOXING

Throughout history, boxing was the sport of the underdog and the underprivileged. Late eighteenth-century immigrants, beginning with the Irish, discovered that some could physically fight their way out of poverty. Beginning with the legendary John L. Sullivan (1858–1918), boxers became heroes of the Irish. And later immigrants—Germans, Italians and Jews—had their own boxing idols, some of whom assumed Irish names to attract boxing fans.

Those early immigrants were probably ashamed of what they were and who they were. Gradually, they began to realize that they could lay more tracks, dig more canals, lay more bricks and build more bridges than anyone else. The Irishman turned to sports, especially boxing, both as inexpensive entertainment and for the adulation which America gave great boxers in less sophisticated times. Then, as now, it was regarded as a brutal sport but the poor had few sporting options.

The Irish story in America is indeed a fascinating tale. It takes us from steerage to suburbia, from tenements, stables, boxing rings, slaughterhouses, coal pits and factory fires right up through Tammany Hall, state capitols and into the White House.

From hundreds of Irish pugilists whose names blazoned the sports pages of their times, a small selection gives an idea of the prominent role of boxers in the sporting and entertainment perimeters of the Irish-American saga.

### JOHN L. SULLIVAN (1858–1918)

Recognized as the first heavyweight champion of the world (1882–1892), Sullivan was born in Boston (Roxbury), Massa-

John L. Sullivan

chusetts to Irish immigrant parents. His father was a native of Tralee in County Kerry and his mother was a native of Athlone in County Westmeath. In 1882, John L. Sullivan fought Tipperary-born Paddy Ryan and knocked him out to capture the bare knuckle championship of the world. The stakes were $5,000 and the American champion title. With the crowning of John L. Sullivan as champion, a new era in boxing began. Later, he toured the country offering $100 and later $500 to any man who could last four rounds with him. On July 8, 1889, the Boston "strong boy" defeated Jake Kilrain in the last championship bare knuckles bout.

At the height of his career, the "Boston Strong Boy" stood 5 feet 10 1/2 inches tall and weighed a solid 195 pounds. He faced 35 opponents, won 16 by knockouts, was held to a draw three times and was knocked out but once, when he lost the crown to Jim Corbett on September 7, 1892.

John L's popularity on the stage, in plays, vaudeville, and personal appearances was tremendous. Wherever he appeared was a guaranteed sell-out. Sullivan's theatre earnings, ending in 1915, were over $900,000.

In later years, Sullivan became a teetotaler and toured the states giving lectures to the public on the "Evils of John Barleycorn." He died in Abingdon, Massachusetts, and was inducted into the Boxing Hall of Fame in 1990.

### JAMES J. CORBETT (1866–1933)

Heavyweight champion 1892–1897. Born to a large Irish Corkonian family with 12 children in San Francisco, California, he started his career as a bank teller and switched to boxing and became boxing's first scientific fighter and revolutionized the boxing game.

In 1892, James J. Corbett faced the champion John L. Sullivan in New Orleans as part of the Carnival of Champions, fought under the Queensberry Rules. The fighters wore five-ounce gloves. The powerful, steadfast Sullivan had little use for ring trickery or defense. Corbett was known for his peerless boxing ability and wore down John L., knocking him out in the 21st round.

He lost the title on March 17, 1897 in the first filmed fight to Englishman Bob Fitzsimmons.

The theatrical Corbett later enjoyed a career in movies, plays, and vaudeville. His autobiography was published in 1925 under the title *The Roar of the Crowd*. When he answered the bell for the last time, the list of "honorary pallbearers" at his funeral included Jack Dempsey, John McGraw, George M. Cohan, Gene Tunney, Damon Runyon, Al Smith, Dan Parker, James Farley, Ring Lardner and Grantland Rice. He was inducted into the Boxing Hall of Fame in 1990.

### JACK DEMPSEY (1893–1982)

Heavyweight champion 1919–1926. He was born in Manassa, Colorado to a poor Scotch and mainly Irish family, with a trace of American Indian ancestry. His parents, Hyrum Dempsey and Mary C., were natives of West Virginia. They were Mormons. He began his pugilistic career in 1914 under the sobriquet of Kid Blackie. On July 4, 1919, Dempsey took the heavyweight crown from Jess Willard who outweighed him by 58 pounds, but fell victim to Dempsey's crouching, weaving and fierce punching power. Willard failed to answer the bell in the fourth round.

In the first world championship to be broadcast on radio, on July 2, 1921, Jack Dempsey vs. Georges Carpentier at Boyle's Thirty Acres in Jersey City, New Jersey, 80,183 fans paid $1,789,238, to see the fight. It was the first of the five million-dollar gates Dempsey drew, the others being Luis Firpo, Gene Tunney (twice) and Jack Sharkey.

Dempsey's most famous fights were with Gene Tunney. On September 23, 1926, Tunney feinted Dempsey dizzy, stung him with rapier-like left jabs and easily outboxed him to a ten-round decision and the title. More than 100,000 people jammed Chicago's Soldier Field on September 22, 1927 for the rematch. In the seventh round, Dempsey rocked Tunney with a left hook to the jaw, followed by a fusillade of punches that dropped the champion. Eager to get to his prey, Dempsey stood over his fallen foe and refused to go to a neutral corner before the count could begin. Fourteen seconds ticked off, giving Tunney time to recover. Regaining his feet, Tunney went on to win and Jack Dempsey ended his career. Jack's pugilistic career stretched from 1914 to 1940, when he retired to referee boxing and wrestling. Inducted into the Boxing Hall of Fame in 1990, he became one of the great legends of boxing.

Jack Dempsey
with his manager,
Jack Kearns

Gene Tunney

### GENE TUNNEY (1898–1978)

Born James Joseph Tunney in Greenwich Village, New York City, he traced his Irish roots to Bohola in County Mayo, Ireland. Both his parents, John Joseph Tunney and Mary Lyndon Tunney, were natives of Bohola. He attended LaSalle Academy and was nicknamed "The Fighting Marine" when he served with the Leathernecks in World War One.

On May 23, 1922, Tunney's only loss came at the hands of Harry Greb, a defeat that he avenged that same year. His two fights with Jack Dempsey (09/23/26 and 09/22/27) were legendary. The 1927 bout was the scene of the famous "Long Count" when, in the seventh round, a barrage from Dempsey leveled Tunney. When Dempsey delayed going to a neutral corner, the fourteen seconds lost allowed Tunney time to recover and go on to win the decision.

He served in the U.S. Navy during World War Two, followed by a very successful business career. George Bernard Shaw was one of his closest friends; and one of his four children, John, became a United States Senator. In 1938, Tunney became Board Chairman of the American Distilling Company and later served as a Director for the Boy Scouts of America and the Catholic Youth Organization. He was inducted into the Boxing Hall of Fame in 1990. He had a career record of 61 wins, one loss and one draw and was the first heavyweight champ to retire undefeated and stay retired as the title holder.

### JAMES J. BRADDOCK (1906–1974)

Heavyweight champion 1935–1937. He was born in New York City. His late-career success earned him the Damon Runyon nickname "The Cinderella Man." Mediocre in his early career, he took the title from heavily favored (10 to 1) Max Baer on June 13, 1935 in Long Island City, New York.

In a fight on June 22, 1937 in Chicago, Illinois, Joe Louis knocked out Braddock in the eighth round, taking away his title. Braddock enjoys the distinction of being the last Irishman to wear the world heavyweight crown.

### JACK O'BRIEN (1878–1942)

Light-heavyweight champion 1905–1912. Born James Francis O'Hagen to an Irish family from County Derry in Philadelphia,

Pennsylvania. He changed his name to Philadelphia Jack O'Brien to capitalize on his Irish roots and birthplace. He launched his career in England, where he won all nineteen of his fights there, fifteen by knockout. By beating Bob Fitzsimmons in 1905, he took the light-heavyweight crown from the 44-year-old former heavyweight champion. He then embarked on a vaudeville tour to capitalize on his fame. O'Brien was an accomplished violinist. He won 100 fights in his 16-year career. He retired in 1912, never having defended his light-heavyweight title, and was inducted into the Boxing Hall of Fame in 1994.

### MIKE McTIGUE (1892–1966)

Light-heavyweight champion 1923–1925. He was born in County Clare, Ireland.

When Gene Tunney moved into the heavyweight class, Mike McTigue, one of the top Americans in the division, went to Dublin, Ireland, where on Saint Patrick's Day 1923, in the midst of a civil war insurrection, he whipped Battling Siki in 20 rounds to capture the world crown. He went on to have classic ring battles with Young Stribling and Paul Berlenbach, who took the crown from him.

### BILLY CONN (1917–1993)

Light-heavyweight champion 1939–1941. He was born William David Conn to Pittsburgh Irish parents.

He turned professional at 16, having never fought as an amateur. Conn's first pro fight earned him $2.50 and after his manager took his cut, Billy Conn wound up with 50 cents.

On July 13, 1939, he won a decision over Melio Bettina to take the light-heavyweight title. In 1941, he relinquished his title to fight Joe Louis for the world heavyweight championship. He gained his greatest fame in this 1941 fight becoming best known as the contender who could have knocked off Joe Louis' heavyweight crown if he hadn't been so eager to punch it out with Louis. In the thirteenth round, Louis knocked Conn out. He was inducted into the Boxing Hall of Fame in 1990.

### MICKEY WALKER (1901–1981)

Middleweight champion 1926–1931; welterweight champion 1922–1926. Born Edward Patrick Walker in the Irish section of Elizabeth, New Jersey, he attended Sacred Heart School.

He was a world champion for nine consecutive years. He ran through millions of dollars during his lucrative career, living the lifestyle of a playboy.

In July of 1931, he battled heavyweight Jack Sharkey (who became champion the next year) at Brooklyn's Ebbets Field and, despite being a 2 to 1 underdog, fought him to a draw. He was inducted into the Boxing Hall of Fame in 1990.

### JACK McAULIFFE (1866–1937)

Lightweight champion 1886–1894. He was born in County Cork, Ireland and raised in Bangor, Maine. When he was working in Williamsburg in Brooklyn, New York, he took lessons from Jack (The Nonpareil) Dempsey. He also laid claim to the title when the top contender Jimmy Mitchen refused to face him. The Corkonian was one of only a handful of fighters to have retired undefeated and was inducted into the Boxing Hall of Fame in 1995.

### JOHNNY KILBANE (1889–1957)

Featherweight champion 1912–1923. On February 22, 1912 in Vernon, California, Kilbane triumphed over the legendary Abe Attell, ending Attell's eleven-year grip on the featherweight division. He served in the U.S. Army in World War One and was a State Senator in the Ohio State Legislature and Clerk of the Cleveland Municipal Court while operating a boxing gym in Cleveland. He was inducted into the Boxing Hall of Fame in 1995.

### BECOMING IRISH

Because the Irish-American had reached the pinnacle of success in the boxing game, many aspiring fighters who were not Irish-Americans changed their names to Irish surnames for business reasons. Some of the more prominent ones included heavyweight champion (1906–1908) Tommy Burns; heavyweight champion (1932–1933) Jack Sharkey; light-heavyweight champion (1926–1927) Jack Delaney; middleweight champion (1897–1907) Tommy Ryan; welterweight champion (1896) Kid McCoy; and lightweight champion (1914–1917) Freddie Welsh.

Bert Blewett, *The A-Z of World Boxing* (Robson Books, 1996).

John Concannon and Frank Cull, *Irish American Who's Who* (Port City Press, 1984).

James B. Roberts and Alexander G. Skutt, *The Boxing Register* (McBooks Press, 1997).

Harry Mullan, *Encyclopedia of Boxing* (Chartwell Books, 1996).

FRANK CULL

## BOYLE, KAY (1903–1992)

Author. Born in St. Paul, Minnesota, of Irish ancestry to Howard and Katharine (Evans), Boyle spent most of her childhood in Europe. Her childhood was a rich exposure to the European milieu of art, writing and music. Boyle began writing stories at an early age with a socially conscientious thematic emphasis. By age seventeen she had written many poems and a novel which dealt with organized labor in Cincinnati, as well as a children's history book which emphasized pacifism.

Boyle also studied music at the Cincinnati, Ohio Mechanics' Institute. It was there that she met her first husband, Richard Brault, and they soon moved back to Europe where Boyle remained for almost twenty years. She continued writing and her stories appeared in the London *Calendar, Transition, This Quarter*

Kay Boyle

and a collection of her stories was published in 1929 under the title *Wedding Days and Other Stories*. Boyle divorced Brault and married an American author, Lawrence Vail. The couple returned to the United States and Boyle produced some riveting and provocative works including *Plagued by the Nightingale, Gentlemen, I Address You Privately, First Lover and Other Stories, My Next Bride, Death of a Man, White Horses of Vienna, Monday Night, Glad Day* and *The Youngest Camel*.

Boyle was awarded a Guggenheim scholarship in 1934 for research she conducted on aviation. She used the research to produce a poem about aviation which was published in *The Nation*. Her stories continued to appear in American magazines such as the *New Yorker, Harper's, Harper's Bazaar, Reader's Digest* and *The Saturday Evening Post*. In 1942 Boyle's novel *Primer for Combat* was published and the autobiographical themes and treatment of the French social and political scene drew praise from the critics.

Boyle's career was rewarded twice with the O. Henry Memorial Short Story Prize. Her thirteen books and many writings have been compared to that of other authors such as Ernest Hemingway and D. H. Lawrence.

Throughout her life Boyle was politically active. This activism reflects a general belief, fostered by her mother, that privilege demands social responsibility. In the 1950s her activism became reinvigorated as she worked toward furthering integration policies, civil rights, a ban on nuclear weapons, and America's withdrawal from Southeast Asia. She died on December 27, 1992.

H. H. Hatcher, *Creating the Modern American Novel* (1935).
S. J. Kunitz, *Authors Today and Yesterday* (1933).
*Time* 32:43 D 26 (1938).
*CAB* (1942).

JOY HARRELL

### BRADLEY, WILLIAM O'CONNELL (1847–1914)

Governor, United States Senator. Born in Garrard County, Kentucky, Bradley was the son of Robert McAfee Bradley, a noted criminal lawyer. The Bradley family moved to Somerset, where William enjoyed only a brief formal education. His first exposure to politics came while serving as a page in the Kentucky legislature at Frankfort in 1861. He twice joined the Union army during the Civil War, serving in largely administrative posts, but was returned home both times after his father protested on account of his age. In 1865, at the age of 18, Bradley was admitted to practice law under special arrangements made by his father. Two years later, he married Margaret R. Duncan. In 1870, Bradley won elected office, running as a Republican for prosecuting attorney for Garrard County. However, future political office remained elusive over the ensuing decades. Continuing to run as a Republican in a predominantly Democratic state, Bradley met multiple defeats in seeking election to the United States House and Senate, as well as governor. He did, however, gain growing prominence in the National Republican Party, attending six nominating conventions and serving as a national committeeman for 12 years. In 1888, he ran unsuccessfully for the party's vice-presidential nominee, receiving 106 votes. Success for higher office finally came in 1895, when Bradley was elected governor of Kentucky, taking advantage of a disorganized state Democratic Party. In 1908, the state legislature elected him to the United

States Senate over Democratic contender, J.C.W. Beckam. Bradley died in Washington D.C. in 1914.

*Dictionary of American Biography*, Vol. I, part 2: 576–577.
John E. Kleber, ed., *The Kentucky Encyclopedia* (Lexington, 1992): 112.
Maurice H. Thatcher, *Stories and Speeches of William O. Bradley* (Lexington, 1916).

TOM DOWNEY

### BRADY, ALICE (1892–1939)

Actress. Born in New York City to William A. (actor-producer) and Rose Marie (Rene) of Irish heritage, Brady showed an early interest for acting but was discouraged by her father. She attended the Convent of St. Elizabeth in New Jersey then went to the New England Conservatory of Music in Boston according to her father's wishes. The young Brady soon began appearing in theatre performances as early as 1909, her first being an open air production of *As You Like It*.

She won her father's support after she appeared in the role of one of the three little maids in *The Mikado* at the Casino, New York City, in 1910. Brady then went on to appear in *The Balkan Princess, Little Women* and her regular work in the Casino in Gilbert and Sullivan roles. She also starred in many silent films from 1914 to 1918 before landing her greatest hit in her father's production of Owen Davis' *Forever After*. Brady became known for her versatility and impersonating talents; performances such as the one she gave as Lavina Mannon in Eugene O'Neill's trilogy *Mourning Becomes Electra* furthered her recognition.

Brady's life was marked by both success and trial. She suffered from cancer but continued to work and appeared in her last film, *Young Mr. Lincoln,* in 1939 with Henry Fonda. One year before her death, she was given an award by the Academy of Motion Picture Arts and Sciences for her role of Mrs. O'Leary in *In Old Chicago* (1937). She died in 1939 and was buried in Sleepy Hollow Cemetery in Tarrytown, New York.

John Parker, *Who's Who in the Theatre* (9th ed., 1939).
W. A. Brady's "Showman," published in the *Saturday Evening Post* (April 4, 1936).
*Dictionary of American Biography*, supplement 2.

JOY HARRELL

### BRADY, JAMES ("Diamond Jim") (1856–1917)

Manufacturer. James Brady was born in New York City, August 12, 1856. After completing a public school education, Brady worked a series of jobs at the New York Central railroad where, over the next seventeen years, he acquired a broad knowledge of the transportation industry. He put this knowledge to effective use as a railroad equipment salesman for the Manning, Maxwell & Moore manufacturing company where his sales commissions became substantial enough for him to finance, produce and market his own metal-cutting saw which became widely used throughout the industry. The steel railroad car industry attracted him most where he managed the Standard Car Company as vice-president. His fortunes grew steadily as his reputation spread throughout the country. His wealth further enabled him to indulge in the buying of expensive jewelry which earned him the nickname "Diamond Jim" Brady. He was a generous man as well. In gratitude for his recovery from a serious digestive disorder at Johns Hopkins Hospital, Brady donated $200,000 for a Urological Institute and an additional $300,000 for its maintenance. James Brady never married, but left his considerable estate to the New York Hospital at his death in Atlantic City, N.J., on April 13, 1917.

Parker Morell, *Diamond Jim: The Life and Times of James Buchanan Brady* (New York, 1934).

DANIEL J. KUNTZ

## BRADY, MATHEW (c. 1823–1896)

Photographer. Mathew Brady, early developer of photographic technology and acclaimed Civil War photographer, stated he was born about 1823–24 in Warren County, New York. His parents were believed to have been Irish immigrants, but their names on Brady's death certificate are listed as Andrew and Julia and their birthplace as the United States. At sixteen he left home for Saratoga, New York. In the 1830s he became friends with portrait painter William Page, who in New York City introduced him to Samuel F. Morse. Morse, a professor of painting and design at New York University (founded 1831), invented the telegraph in 1838; Brady became his painting student. In Paris in 1839 Morse met Louis Daguerre, learned of his imaging process, and offered classes on it in New York which Brady took while working as a department store clerk. He advanced enough to open an elaborate "Daguerrean Miniature Gallery" in 1844 at Broadway and Fulton Streets, having also had a business manufacturing jewelry and surgical instrument cases. The gallery may have been financed in part by P. T. Barnum who had a museum of oddities nearby. Brady's work was an immediate success, outdoing competitors, and by 1845 he was exhibiting portraits of famous Americans. Using many studio technicians, he directed artistic settings, lighting, costuming, and camera techniques, generally leaving others to operate the camera itself, but often hand painting or tinting his portraits. Known as "Brady of Broadway," he gained international recognition, won awards, and in 1850 published the *Gallery of Illustrious Americans,* a collection of twenty-four prominent persons, which included U. S. presidents, Henry Clay, Daniel Webster, John J. Audubon, and James Fenimore Cooper. He had also opened a Washington, D.C., studio in 1849, and about 1850–51 married Julia Handy of Maryland.

By 1855 he had shifted from the daguerreotype to a wet plate (collodian) process, invented in England by Frederick Scott Archer, which permitted unlimited positive print images and enlargements. Brady, now at his peak, could make over 30,000 portraits a year. He produced photographs on canvas with oil paint coloring, and *Harper's Weekly* published engravings based on his portraits. He opened his National Photographic Art Gallery in Washington, D.C., in 1858, and a year later, another New York City studio on Bleecker St. In 1860 he photographed the Prince of Wales and Abraham Lincoln's presidential campaign portrait, and added a fourth studio in New York, calling it the National Portrait Gallery.

Ironically, he is remembered most for his images of the Civil War, taken with a team of about twenty assistants, but which finally led him to financial ruin as he brought home the horrors of war over its glories to a weary nation. Commercial distribution of his work declined and he filed for bankruptcy in 1873, a year of national economic panic. Two years later he received $25,000 for his negatives and prints from Congress which enabled him to

pay his debts but left nothing for new enterprises. Brady recognized that his artistic and technical work gave him a public trust as one of the nation's historians. Eventually he attempted to give photographs made by his employees the same prestige as those he directed personally. His wife died in 1887 adding to his decline in health as well as finance. Mathew Brady's life spanned a rapid technological revolution, while his work had a major cultural impact on national self-perception. Virtually penniless and obscure, the influential photographer died January 15, 1896, of nephritis in the alms ward of Presbyterian Hospital, New York City. Mathew Brady is buried in the Congressional Cemetery, Washington, D.C.

James David Horan, *Mathew Brady, Historian with a Camera* (New York, 1955).

Roy Meredith, *Mr. Lincoln's Camera Man, Mathew B. Brady* (New York, 1946).

Mary Panzer, *Mathew Brady and the Image of History* (Washington, D.C., 1997).

ANNA M. DONNELLY

## BREEN, PATRICK (179?–1868)

Pioneer, diarist. Patrick Breen, remembered as diarist of the tragic Donner Party in the history of the American westward migra-tion, was born in Ireland and came to the United States in 1828, becoming a citizen in 1844. He and his wife Margaret and their seven children set out from their farm in Keokuk, Iowa, on April 5, 1846, to meet with other California-bound persons at Independence, MO, and joined the party of George and Jacob Donner. The Breens traveled in three wagons with seven yoke of oxen, cows, and riding horses. Reaching Fort Bridger in late July, the party attempted a supposedly shorter route at Salt Lake, but the choice led to delays through the mountains followed by large loss of livestock. As winter drew on, Breen chronicled the disastrous events in his diary with entries made November 20, 1846, to March 1, 1847. The Donner party was trapped in the Sierra Nevada mountains at Truckee Lake until spring in an exceptionally harsh winter. Breen recorded events affecting the ordinary migrants, some of whom rose to heroic heights, with simple, brief descriptions of weather, deaths, illnesses, starvation and survival before relief parties arrived. In desperation the survivors kept a fire burning in a snowy pit, and for a week fed on those who had died. Only forty-five of the eighty-three people lived to reach California, including all of the Breens, one of whom was only an infant. A devout Catholic, Breen saw that prayers were read daily. After reaching California he befriended an Irish emigrant rancher, Martin Murphy, Jr., and later settled with his family on a ranch in San Juan Bautista. His daughter Isabella, who was one year old when rescued, died in 1935, the last survivor of the Donner Party. Breen himself died in California December 21, 1868.

George Keithley, *The Donner Party* (New York, 1972).

George Rippey Stewart, *Ordeal by Hunger: The Story of the Donner Party* (Boston, 1960).

ANNA M. DONNELLY

## BRENDAN THE NAVIGATOR, ST. (c. 500–578)

Monk and sailor. Brendan was born in Fenit, County Kerry at the beginning of the sixth century. As a boy he was tutored by

Bishop Erc who years later ordained him after Brendan had stayed at some of the most famous monasteries in Ireland.

Brendan was a wanderer and a builder, and along the banks of the Shannon River, he built several monasteries; and in Galway he founded the great monastery of Clonfert, which thrived until the Reformation. He also established a convent at Annaghdown, where he died in 578.

Brendan's fame as a navigator rests on the extraordinary imagination and the humor of a medieval monk who, in the tradition of Homer's *Ulysses,* wrote *Navigatio Sancti Brendani.* In it the monk happily invents the awesome and fantastic adventures of the Kerry boatman. Many versions of the work, in several languages, exist; and some recount more breathtaking episodes than the original did, and that in itself is an imaginative achievement. Tall tales about Brendan's seafaring to Greenland and Iceland are part of Irish mythology, and eventually his story-loving countrymen took the final step and nominated Brendan the Navigator as the discoverer of America.

Samuel Eliot Morrison, *The European Discoverers of America* (New York, 1971).
Martin Wallace, *The Celtic Saints* (Belfast, 1995).

MICHAEL GLAZIER

## BRENNAN, MAEVE M. (1917–1993)

Author. Born in Dublin, Ireland, January 6, 1917, daughter of Robert and Anastasia (Bolger) Brennan, Maeve Brennan came to the United States in 1934. She was seventeen and fresh out of convent school. Her father served as Ireland's first Envoy Extraordinary to the United States, and when he and others in the family returned to Ireland in 1947, Maeve Brennan stayed on and pursued a literary career. She worked as a copywriter at *Harper's Bazaar,* then joined the staff of *The New Yorker* in 1949 and made the magazine her career.

Brennan was hired by *The New Yorker* to write about women's fashions, but she was soon doing short stories, book reviews, essays and "The Talk of the Town" items, which the magazine billed as "communications from our friend the long-winded lady." Her short stories attracted wide attention and were collected into two volumes—*In and Out of Never-Never Land* (1969) and *Christmas Eve* (1974). Forty-seven of her "Talk of the Town" items were gathered into the book *The Long-Winded Lady* (1969).

A woman of wit and strong in her likes and dislikes, Brennan venerated William Butler Yeats, but refused to read the novels of Elizabeth Bowen, because Bowen was Anglo-Irish.

In the 1970s Brennan began to experience what a colleague, William Maxwell, termed "psychotic episodes," adding that as her condition deteriorated "she settled down in the ladies' room at *The New Yorker* as if it were her only home." Brennan ceased writing in 1973, her books went out of print, and she pretty much disappeared from sight. Except for hospitalizations, little is known of her life in the 1980s. By the time she died in New York City in 1993, she was virtually forgotten as a literary personality.

But not permanently so. Brennan's best stories drew on Ireland, "her imagination's home," and twenty-one of those stories were culled from her two published collections and reissued in 1997 under the title *The Springs of Affection: Stories of Dublin,* with an introduction by Maxwell. Many of the stories are set in Ranelagh, a neighborhood on Dublin's south side, and are presumably autobiographical. The narrator's name is Maeve, for one

Maeve M. Brennan

thing, and the siblings of the stories have the same given names as Brennan's own brother and sisters. Reviewing the book in *The New York Times,* critic Jay Parini lauded it as "full of small miracles presented in elegant but simple prose." J. F. Powers said of the stories that they are "funny, sad, true."

Brennan's marriage in 1954 to St. Clair McKelway, a *New Yorker* reporter, ended in divorce.

*See* Fiction, Irish-American

Maeve Brennan, *The Springs of Affection: Stories of Dublin,* introduction by William Maxwell (New York, 1997).
Frances Carol Locher, ed., *Contemporary Authors,* vols. 81–84 (Detroit, 1979).
Jay Parini, "Dubliners," *New York Times Sunday Book Review* (December 7, 1997).

JOHN DEEDY

## BRENNAN, WALTER (1894–1974)

Actor. Walter Brennan was born on July 25, 1894 in Lynn, Massachusetts of Irish parents, William John Brennan and Margaret Elizabeth Flanagan Brennan. He married Ruth Wells in 1920 and fathered three children. Brennan worked as a lumberjack, a ditchdigger and a bank messenger, before enlisting in the Army the day after World War I was declared. After the war, he returned to the bank as a financial reporter and then, moving to California to sell real estate, a colleague convinced him to try out for the movies as an extra. Thus began his Hollywood career.

One of the greatest character actors of his day, Brennan is identified with the part of the cranky old man, having played the role opposite major film stars in dozens of classic Westerns. Although he played in over one hundred films, most of them amazingly good, he is best known for his roles in the Howard Hawks and John Ford westerns. His first important character part was that of Old Atrocity in Hawks' *Barbary Coast.* He played Stumpy, the shotgun-toting old man guarding the jail for John Wayne in *Rio Bravo;* Old Man Clanton opposite Henry Fonda as Wyatt Earp *My Darling Clementine;* and as Humphrey Bogart's friend in *To Have and Have Not.*

He is the only man to have received the Academy Award for Best Supporting Actor three times for his roles in *Come and Get It* (1936); *Kentucky* (1938); and for one of his greatest roles, as Judge Roy Bean in *The Westerner* (1940), starring Gary Cooper.

Brennan brought his character into the homes of millions of Americans in the 224 episodes of the television series, *The Real McCoys,* during the 1950s.

*See* Cinema, Irish in

Joseph Curran, *Hibernian Green on the Silver Screen* (Westport, CT, 1990). *Hollywood Album, Lives and Deaths of Hollywood Stars from the Pages of The New York Times* (New York, 1977).

EILEEN DANEY CARZO

## BRENNAN, WILLIAM J., JR. (1906–1997)

Justice of the Supreme Court for nearly 34 years, William Joseph Brennan, Jr. was a towering figure in modern law whose liberal interpretation of the Constitution as an instrument of social and political change fueled the revolution in constitutional law that took place in the 1960s and 1970s. Named to the Supreme Court in 1956 by President Dwight D. Eisenhower, Brennan wrote over 1,250 published opinions, including landmark decisions expanding the rights of racial minorities and women; protecting freeedom of expression; and reapportioning voting districts to guarantee "one-person, one-vote." An intellectual leader and consensus-builder during his long tenure on the bench, Justice Brennan had a profound impact on American public policy.

Born April 25, 1906 in Newark, New Jersey, Justice Brennan was the second of eight children of Agnes (McDermott) and William Brennan, who had separately emigrated from County Roscommon, Ireland, at the turn of the century, and married in the United States in 1903. His father worked as a metal polisher and brewery laborer, and became active in local Democratic politics in New Jersey. A member of the Essex County Trades and Labor Council, the senior Brennan was elected four times Commissioner of Public Safety in Newark, serving from 1917 until 1930, when he died at the age of 57. Justice Brennan attributed his success to his father, saying, "Everything I am, I am because of my father."

A Roman Catholic, Justice Brennan attended both parochial and public elementary schools, graduating from Barringer High School in New Jersey. He graduated with honors from the Wharton School of Finance and Commerce at the University of Pennsylvania in 1928, and earned a law degree from Harvard Law School in 1931. Brennan married Marjorie Leonard on 1928; the couple had three children: William 3rd, Hugh, and Nancy.

Returning to New Jersey with his law degree, Brennan practiced law with the firm of Pitney, Hardin & Skinner (later Pitney, Hardin & Brennan). A successful trial lawyer, Brennan specialized in representing management in labor cases, and also became known for his involvement in New Jersey's court reform movement. His practice was interrupted in 1942 by service in the U.S. Army, in which he was assigned to the legal division of the Ordinance Department, and handled labor disputes on the staff of the undersecretary of war. Brennan received the Legion of Merit, and was discharged with the rank of colonel.

Although a Democrat, Brennan was named a judge of the State Supreme Court in 1949 by New Jersey's Republican governor, Albert E. Driscoll. The following year, Brennan was named to the Appellate Division, and in 1952 was elevated to the New Jersey Supreme Court, where he introduced changes to reduce delays and backlogs of cases. While giving the keynote address in May 1956 at a large Washington, D.C., conference on the problem of overburdened courts, Brennan reputedly came to the attention of President Eisenhower's attorney general, Herbert Brownwell. Brownwell then recommended Brennan to Eisenhower when a Supreme Court vacancy arose four months later with the retirement of Justice Sherman Minton. Brennan, a Roman Catholic Irish-American from the Northeast, was a particularly attractive candidate, given the upcoming presidential election, and was confirmed easily.

Only 50 years old when named to the Court, Brennan was its youngest member. He formed a close alliance with Chief Justice Earl Warren, whose activist judicial philosophy he came to share. While he himself never served as chief justice, Brennan is credited with developing many of the strategies and constitutional arguments that would underpin the revolutionary decisions of the Warren Court.

Central to Brennan's judicial philosophy was his belief that the courts had to interpret the Constitution for the time, and not according to a fixed original understanding of its authors. For Brennan, the genius of the Constitution rested "not in any static meaning it might have had in a world that is dead and gone, but in the adaptability of its great principles to cope with current problems and current needs" (1986 Speech at Georgetown University Law School). He insisted that current justices could only read the Constitution as twentieth-century Americans and could not accurately guage the intent of the framers of the Constitution on the application of principle to specific contemporary questions (*Ibid*). This constitutional theory demanded that justices, when deciding the constitutionality of a particular statute, consider the mores of the particular age, and not simply the purported intent of the original framers.

Brennan's view of the Constitution as a living document took expression in a series of decisions from 1961 to 1969 that formed the so-called "due process" revolution of the Warren Court. The Bill of Rights was intended to protect individual liberties against the abuses of the federal government. Decisions of the Warren Court, however, expanded this protection by making provisions of the Bill of Rights applicable to state governments as well, thereby limiting state authority and enhancing the rights of the individual. Brennan authored one such decision, *Malloy v. Hogan* (1964), which made the Fifth Amendment right against self-incrimination applicable to the states, and engineered most others.

Brennan is also credited with developing the constitutional theory that there exist fundamental rights not expressly named in the Bill of Rights that nonetheless are entitled to the highest level of protection from government regulation. In *Shapiro v. Thompson* (1969), Brennan wrote for the majority that a one-year residency requirement to qualify for local welfare benefits violated the right to travel, a fundamental right protected by the Constitution. Similarly, in *Goldberg v. Kelly* (1970), Brennan, writing for the Court, found that welfare benefits were a kind of property that could not be taken away or denied without due process. Most controversial, perhaps, was the development by Brennan and the Warren Court of a "right to privacy." Not enumerated in the Constitution, this right to privacy was judged fundamental and underpinned decisions protecting use of contraceptives (*Griswold v. Connecticut,* 1965); establishing right of unmarried people to receive information about contraceptives (*Eisenstadt v. Baird*, 1972); and upholding a right to an abortion (*Roe v. Wade*, 1973).

Also central to Brennan's jurisprudence was his belief that the law should be a living process; accessible, responsive to changing human needs, and mindful of the human dignity of each individual. He thought the law should emphasize and reflect justice, not abstract logic and rules, and protect substantive and procedural rights of individuals. Many of his opinions expanded the role of the federal courts in protecting individuals, including *Baker v. Carr* (1962), which held that cases challenging unequal legislative opportunities could be held in federal court; *Bivens v. Six Unknown Named Agents* (1971), which recognized for the first time a constitutional right to sue a government official directly; and *Monell v. New York City Department of Social Services* (1978), which allowed individuals to sue local governments for violation of civil rights.

Other significant Brennan opinions include *New York Times v. Sullivan* (1964) which reshaped the First Amendment law of libel, allowing "breathing space" for free expression. The Court ruled that the press is not liable for publishing false statements about public officials, unless the official can show that the statement was deliberately false or published in reckless disregard of the truth. In *Texas v. Johnson* (1989), Brennan wrote the opinion for the Court holding that the First Amendment protected the act of burning an American flag as a political protest. Brennan authored *Katzenbach v. Morgan* (1965), in which the Court provided a basis through the 14th Amendment for Congressional power involving civil rights, as well as many decisions establishing the constitutional legitimacy of affirmative action programs, and limiting racial and gender-based discrimination.

Although a Roman Catholic, Brennan believed in a strict separation of church and state, and concurred in Court decisions prohibiting prayer in public schools and state aid to parochial schools. Brennan strongly opposed the death penalty, and thought it unconstitutional in all circumstances, a view not shared by a majority of his Supreme Court colleagues. He dissented every time the Court turned down an appeal from a death-row inmate.

Throughout his three-plus decades on the bench, Justice Brennan did not escape criticism for his activist jurisprudence. Many thought that Brennan, by treating the law as a living process, was usurping the proper role of legislature. Some also thought that Brennan substituted his own preferences for the preferences of the founding fathers, or for the language of the Constitution and the law. Brennan wanted laws to reflect justice; however, it seemed that the decisions emerging from the Supreme Court reflected Brennan's ideas of justice more than any objective standard of justice. Certainly the American landscape changed radically during Brennan's tenure. Brennan was perceived as the standard-bearer for a judicial liberalism that permitted, in the name of the Constitution, abortion, contraception, and flag burning, while prohibiting prayer in schools and curtailing the authority of the state.

From a more scholarly perspective, Brennan's belief that the essential meaning of the Constitution was located in the contemporary age put him on one side of the national debate over constitutional interpretation that raged in the 1980s. On the other side were those who believed the Constitution's essential meaning was found legitimately only in the framers' original intentions. This latter vision became ascendant in the 1980s and 1990s under Chief Justices Warren E. Burger and William H. Rehnquist, and Brennan found himself most often in dissent.

Still, Justice Brennan's impact cannot be overestimated. He wrote opinions in so many areas of the law that his influence is felt everywhere. Also of importance were his tremendous personal characteristics. A man of compassion and charm, Brennan was unassuming and collegial, and well able to build consensus among his colleagues. His extrajudicial writings also commanded attention. An article he wrote in a 1977 issue of the Harvard Law Review, entitled "State Constitutions and the Protection of Individual Rights," urging state judges to look to their own state constitutions for protections not afforded by the federal government, became one of the most frequently cited law review articles in history.

Devoted to his family, Brennan spent much of his time caring for his wife, who after a long struggle with the disease, died of cancer in 1982. The following year, Brennan married Mary Fowler, who had worked at the Supreme Court for over 40 years, and had been his secretary for over 25 years. After suffering a stroke in 1990, Brennan retired from the Court, and was replaced by Justice David Souter, an appointee of President George Bush. In addition to numerous other awards, including the Presidential Medal of Freedom, Brennan was honored in 1995 by his former law clerks who endowed The Brennan Center for Justice at New York University School of Law, a litigation and research center.

Justice Brennan died on July 24, 1997, in Arlington, Virginia, at the age of 91, seven years after his retirement from the Court.

Kim Issac Eisler, *A Justice For All: William J. Brennan, Jr. and Decisions That Transformed America* (New York, 1993).

Stephen J. Freedman, ed., *An Affair With Freedom: Justice William J. Brennan, Jr.* (New York, 1967).

Roger Goldman, *Justice William J. Brennan, Jr.: Freedom First* (New York, 1994).

Jeffrey T. Leeds, "A Life on the Court: Justice Brennan Discusses His Life on and off the Court," *New York Times Magazine* (October 5, 1986).

David E. Manon, *The Jurisprudence of William J. Brennan, Jr.: The Law and Politics of Libertarian Dignity* (Maryland, 1997).

Stephen, J. Wermeil, "William J. Brennan, Jr.," in Urofsky, Melvin I., ed. *Supreme Court Justices: A Biographical Dictionary* (New York, 1994).

"The Jurisprudence of Justice William J. Brennan, Jr." 139 *University of Pennsylvania Law Review*, 1317 (1991).

"A Tribute to Justice William J. Brennan, Jr." 104 *Harvard Law Review*, 1 (November 1990): 1–39.

"Special Issue Dedicated to Justice William J. Brennan." *John Marshall Law Review*, 20 (Fall 1986): 1–199.

KATHLEEN N. McCARTHY

## BRESLIN, JIMMY (1933–   )

Journalist, author. One of the great newspaper columnists of his times, Breslin was born and reared in Queens, the borough that would later provide endless material for his columns and novels. His father abandoned the family when Breslin was a child; his mother kept it together. Breslin's crusty compassion was born of his mother's struggle to overcome her husband's flight.

Breslin got his start in journalism in the sports department of the now-defunct *Long Island Press*. It was a modest beginning—the *Press* proudly served as a paper of record for Long Island's scholastic sports community.

Breslin left the *Press* behind and found his way into Manhattan in what became the last great years of New York print

Jimmy Breslin

journalism. While there had been signs of slippage, New York in the late 1950s still was a glorious newspaper town. Breslin went to work for one of them, the *Journal-American*, and then became a columnist for the newspaper that defined the era, the *Herald-Tribune*. It was known as a writer's newspaper, and there the young Breslin flourished.

Breslin already had won fame and a citywide following by the time of John Kennedy's assassination on Nov. 22, 1963. But a column he wrote after the president's murder became an instant classic, a piece that has been reprinted in textbooks and anthologies. While his colleagues observed the mournful comings and goings of great leaders gathered for the presidential funeral, Breslin went to Arlington National Cemetery to interview the man who was digging the president's grave. Among the poignant details Breslin discovered was the gravedigger's salary: $3.01 an hour. From that day on, city editors throughout the country ordered their eager young reporters to "find the gravedigger"— in other words, to find a story far from the beaten path, to break away from the pack.

In later years, Breslin became a passionate advocate for civil rights, and he immediately understood the connection between blacks marching for their rights in America and Catholics doing the same in Northern Ireland. In his journalism and in his fiction (*World Without End, Amen*), Breslin explored the connection between these two oppressed people and the irony of Irish Catholics who supported the struggle in Northern Ireland but were less than enthusiastic about the civil rights movement at home.

By 1969, Breslin was established as one of American journalism's great voices, one of the founders of the New Journalism movement that borrowed from the storytelling techniques of novelists. That year, as something of a lark, Breslin ran for city council president in New York on a ticket headed by novelist Norman Mailer, who ran for mayor. They didn't come close to winning, but they did advocate a radical view that has since been advocated from time to time—creating a 51st state consisting of the five boroughs of New York City.

Not long after his venture into politics, Breslin returned to the newspaper world as a columnist for the *Daily News*. There, he continued to rage against the follies of the moment, but he also built on his larger-than-life persona and brought to life a collec-

tion of hilarious characters from his home borough of Queens. Tragedy struck when his wife, Rosemary, died, leaving him to finish rearing their children. Breslin delivered his wife's eulogy, concluding it with a line from Yeats: "Earth receive an honored guest."

Breslin later married a New York politician named Ronnie Eldridge and moved from Queens to the Upper West Side. His new family situation—his children were Irish Catholic, hers were Jewish—was fodder for several hilarious columns. And in a tradition established by none other than Charles Dickens, Breslin set out to write a novel on deadline serialized in the *Daily News*. It went on to become *Table Money,* a fascinating study of blue-collar Queens.

In 1986, Breslin discovered something about some of the lovable rogues he knew in Queens: They were part of a huge political racket that was stealing money from the city, some of it through the city's Parking Violations Bureau. His investigation of the scandal led to indictments and resignations; for his work in 1986, Jimmy Breslin won the Pulitzer Prize for commentary.

The award hardly was the capstone of a memorable career. He continued to write brilliant columns for the *News,* so brilliant that when an upstart daily, *New York Newsday,* sought to make its mark in New York, it signed up Breslin as the paper's marquee columnist. While the experiment failed—*New York Newsday* folded—Breslin continues to ply the columnist's trade for Long Island-based *Newsday.*

*See* Fiction, Irish-American

Jimmy Breslin, *World Without End, Amen* (New York, 1973).
———, *Table Money* (New York, 1986).
———, *The World According to Breslin* (New York, 1982).
———, *I Want to Thank My Brain for Remembering Me* (Boston, 1996).

TERRY GOLWAY

## BRODERICK, DAVID COLBRETH (1820–1859)

Entrepreneur, politician. David Colbreth Broderick was born in Washington, D.C., February 4, 1820, of Irish extraction. Little is known of his mother, except that her maiden name was Copway. His father, an immigrant most probably, worked as a stone mason on the national Capitol, but moved the family to New York City before David was fourteen. Orphaned early in life, David Broderick had little formal education. But he was an aggressive, enterprising person, and involved himself early in Tammany Hall politics. He was a member of the City Charter Commission in 1846, and that same year stood for Congress with Tammany backing, a bid that failed. At the same time he ran a saloon which, besides providing a living, served as a political power base.

The gold-rush of 1849 lured Broderick to California, where he joined in a partnership for the coining of gold smelts, a profitable enterprise due to the scarcity of metal currency. He left that business for real estate and further riches in the sales of water-front properties. He also engaged in politics, and gained a seat in the California State Senate, where he was considered the personification of "the Democratic Party of California." His reputation as a private citizen was exemplary (as a young man he swore off drink, smoke and the playing of cards), but he played a rough game of politics. On the issue of slavery he stood on the side of the angels.

Broderick aspired to the United States Senate, and according to one account won election in 1857, becoming the first Irish-Catholic in the Senate. According to another, he struck a deal whereby his opponent would go to Washington in exchange for Broderick's controlling federal patronage in the state, an arrangement that foundered under opposition from President James Buchanan.

In any case, Broderick was not to live long. He entered a duel with California's Chief Justice David S. Terry, a pro-slavery partisan, over a personal slur which carried racial connotations. The two met the morning of September 13, 1859, and Broderick, allegedly equipped with a faulty weapon, was felled with a bullet in his breast. He lingered for three days, and before dying exclaimed: "They have killed me because I was opposed to the extension of slavery and a corrupt administration." The date was September 16, 1859. Broderick was only thirty-nine. It was to be the last legal duel in the state, the practice being outlawed soon after.

*See* California

John A. Barnes, *Irish-American Landmarks: A Traveler's Guide* (New York, 1995).

W. J. Ghent, "Broderick, David Colbreth," *Dictionary of American Biography* (New York, 1929).

JOHN DEEDY

## BROPHY, JOHN (1883–1963)

Miner, labor organizer. John Brophy was born in St. Helens, Lancashire, England on November 6, 1883. His parents were Patrick Brophy and Mary (Dagnall) Brophy, both of whom were Roman Catholic. John Brophy's father was the son of a Dublin shoe-cobbler who immigrated to Liverpool during the Great Famine. He married Bessie Carroll, daughter of a couple who came from Dundalk, north of Dublin, when she was a child. Patrick Brophy entered the mines in St. Helens at age nine, stayed until seventeen, when he joined the British Army. His six years of service saw him posted to Ireland, South Africa, Egypt and various other locales in the empire. Upon discharge he returned to England, resumed mining in St. Helens and married. John Brophy, first of eleven children born to his parents, was one of five who survived to adulthood. Short and slender of build, and, although involved in struggles of mining unionism and later in campaigns in other industries, he always managed to avoid violence. He was an avid reader of serious works throughout his life and developed definite ideas about social justice. He was both an activist and an intellectual.

### EMIGRATION

In December of 1889 Patrick Brophy came to America, stayed with relatives in the bituminous mining town of Philipsburg in central Pennsylvania for one year, and weighed the relative advantages of moving his family there. Returning to St. Helens, he decided that, on balance, life would be more promising in Pennsylvania. Four years later the family emigrated to America. Unfortunately, their arrival came just in time for the mid-nineties depression. Years would pass before they realized living standards equal to those left behind in Lancashire. For fourteen years the family was forced to move from one mining community to another in order to eke out a living.

### UNION MINER

John Brophy began in the mines at age twelve in Urey, Pennsylvania—as his father's helper. Three years later he joined the United Mine Workers (UMW) at South Fork (near Johnstown), where he worked. After years of intermittent work in mines, Brophy contracted typhoid fever and was laid up for several months. In 1904, after serving as acting secretary of a UMW local, John Brophy was elected to that post. With his father's help, he was elected checkweighman at the Greenwich mine. This was an important position as it required him to see that each miner was paid correctly for all coal he had dug, since miners were paid on a tonnage basis. Only genuinely trustworthy and responsible individuals were chosen as checkweighmen. It was an important steppingstone for a career in the UMW.

### CLASH WITH LEWIS

By 1916, Brophy, after holding offices in several UMW local unions, was elected president of District 2 of the union covering central Pennsylvania. He was elevated to that position because of his unimpeachable honesty and his growing reputation as a source of ideas for union policy. In that office he first met John L. Lewis, future UMW president and founder of the CIO. Brophy's reaction was not favorable. He found Lewis excessively ambitious, manipulative and capable of ruthless acts.

Brophy had numerous differences with Lewis—especially after Lewis became UMW president in 1920. The issue of nationalization of the coal industry was one source of conflict. Brophy saw it as a solution to the terrible instability and excessive competition in the industry. Lewis opposed government involvement of this kind. Brophy insisted upon organization of southern coal fields (West Virginia and Kentucky) as essential to maintaining wage gains in the north. Lewis did not give it the same emphasis. Finally, in 1926 he contested Lewis for the presidency of the UMW. Brophy lost, charged fraud and was eventually drummed out of the union in 1928. In 1918 he had married Anita Anstead. The couple had two children. John Brophy found it extremely difficult to support his family outside the mining industry. From 1930 for three years he was employed as a salesman for the Columbia Conserve Company—owned by the Hapgood family, one of whose sons—an idealist—had worked in the mines and had supported Brophy in his contest with Lewis. This young man, Powers Hapgood, was also expelled from the UMW.

### EMERGENCE OF THE CIO

With the advent of the National Industrial Recovery Act of the New Deal in 1933, Lewis campaigned to rebuild the UMW and recruited Brophy to return as a troubleshooter. The campaign's success built up the UMW's treasury and emboldened Lewis to organize mass production industries. For that purpose he and a few likeminded individuals founded the Committee of Industrial Organizations (CIO). In 1938, after being ejected from the American Federation of Labor, it became the Congress of Industrial Organizations. Lewis appointed Brophy as director of CIO for administration—in which position Brophy participated in most of the dramatic and effective organizing campaigns of the late thirties. However, Lewis's isolationist position clashed with Brophy's worldview and fear of him as a potential rival caused Lewis to downgrade Brophy's status in the CIO. Lewis chose James Carey for secretary of the CIO instead of the more experienced Brophy.

In early 1940 Brophy was struck by a heart attack. His outlook was bleak indeed, but Lewis resigned as president of the CIO as promised when, in November of that year, Franklin Roosevelt defeated Wendell Willkie (whom Lewis supported and vowed to resign from the CIO presidency if his candidate lost). Philip Murray, successor to Lewis as CIO president, restored Brophy to importance in the organization. In June of 1941 President Roosevelt appointed Brophy a member of the Fair Employment Practices Commission which the president had created by executive order. During World War II Brophy served as a labor representative on the War Labor Board. John Brophy retained important positions in the CIO during and after the war. He vigorously affirmed purging Communist-dominated unions from the CIO in 1949. In CIO conventions he enthusiastically advocated a tripartite industry council plan modeled on one proposed by Pope Pius XI in the 1931 encyclical *Quadrogesimo Anno*. His valuable contributions persisted after the merger of the AFL and the CIO in 1955. He retired in 1961. John Brophy died on February 19, 1963 in Falls Church, Virginia.

*See* Labor Movement; Coal Miners

John Brophy, *A Miner's Life* (Madison, 1964).
Brophy Papers, Archives, Mullen Library, Catholic University of America, Washington, D.C.
Melvyn Dubofsky and Warren Van Tine, *John L. Lewis* (New York, 1977).

L. A. O'DONNELL

## BROSNAN, PIERCE (1952– )

Actor. Born on May 16, 1952 in County Meath, Ireland, Brosnan moved with his family to London at an early age. He worked as a commercial illustrator and a cab driver and studied acting at the London Drama Centre. His debut stage performance in *Wait Until Dark* in 1976 brought him to the attention of playwright Tennessee Williams who chose him for the role of McCabe in *Red Devil Battery Sign*.

The American public was introduced to Brosnan in the television miniseries *The Manions of America* in 1981. But it was his portrayal of the handsome, charming and often inept private investigator Remington Steele in the television series of the same name that won him wide popularity in this country. The series, where he starred opposite Stephanie Zimbalist, ran on NBC from 1982 through 1987, ninety-one episodes, and owed much to the talented Brosnan and his dashing good looks, his self-deprecating humor and comic timing (often likened to Cary Grant).

Brosnan was the popular favorite to replace Roger Moore in the James Bond movies, but contractual agreements with *Remington Steele* prevented this match in 1986. He finally took over the Bond part in *Golden Eye* in 1995 and again with *Tomorrow Never Dies* in 1997. In the meantime, Brosnan had roles in a variety of motion picture films, including the hit *Mrs. Doubtfire* (1993), *Mars Attacks!* (1996) and *Dante's Peak* (1997); TV movies, including *Murder 101* (1991), and miniseries, including *Noble House* (1988).

*See* Cinema, Irish in; California

*Esquire* (November 1995).
*Parade* (November 1995).
*People* (October 31, 1983; August 1, 1986).

EILEEN DANEY CARZO

## BROWN, ALEXANDER (1764–1834)

Merchant, banker, millionaire. Alexander Brown began life in humble circumstances at Ballymena, County Antrim, Ireland. He began his merchant career with a small linen store in Belfast. In 1800, Brown, his wife, and one of his sons, emigrated to Baltimore, Maryland, with a stock of linen, clocks, and chairs. He reestablished his linen business, but soon diversified into a number of other commercial lines. Gradually, the firm of Alexander Brown & Sons grew to be one of the leading merchant houses in Baltimore, as well as the entire United States. Surviving the upheavals of the War of 1812, Brown expanded into the import/export trade, particularly in staple commodities such as cotton and tobacco. His overseas connections served him well and Brown gradually expanded into shipping and merchant banking as well. One by one, he took his sons into the family business, placing them in New York, Philadelphia, and Liverpool to establish new branches of the firm. Brown's great wealth made him a leading citizen of Baltimore and he sponsored many projects of civic improvement, including the city's first water works and the Baltimore Washington monument. With one of his sons, Brown also played a key role in founding the Baltimore & Ohio Railroad. The firm of Alexander Brown & Co. survived many years after its founder's passing in 1834. At the time of his death, Brown's estate was estimated at two million dollars.

*Dictionary of American Biography,* Vol II, part 2: 101–103.
John Crosby Brown, *A Hundred Years of Merchant Banking* (New York, 1909).
Frank R. Kent, *The Story of Alexander Brown and Sons* (Baltimore, 1950).

TOM DOWNEY

## BROWN, EDMUND GERALD ("Pat") (1905–1996)

Governor of California. Born of Irish-German descent, Brown was born to Edmund Joseph and Ida (Schuckman) Brown. Brown attended Catholic parochial school before he entered Lowell High School in San Francisco where his political ambition blossomed in his involvement in student elective offices. It was during his high school years that he was given the nickname "Pat" as a tribute to his impressive oratory skills during a Liberty Bond drive in which he recited Patrick Henry's "Give me liberty or give me death" speech.

Brown began working for his father after high school but his mother encouraged him to take college courses at night. In 1927 he completed his study of law at the San Francisco Law School and earned the LL.B. degree. He was then admitted to the California bar and began his own private practice. His political career began with a few unsuccessful attempts at office, but Brown became a common feature on the political scene and held several important positions: he was member of the California Code Commission, member of the Golden Gate Bridge and Highway District, chairman of the speaker's bureau for President Roosevelt's campaigns in 1940 and 1944 and delegate for California to the Democratic National Convention in 1940.

In 1943 Brown was elected district attorney for the city and county of San Francisco and then attorney general in 1950. Among his memorable acts as attorney general are his investigation into the State Liquor Administration and special investigations of drug trafficking, interracial problems and juvenile delinquency. In 1958 Brown won the Democratic nomination for governor of California and his campaign focused on what he called the "bread and butter" issues, from jobs and industry to education and public utilities. Brown became the thirty-second governor of California on January 5, 1959.

*See* California

*Who's Who in America* (1958–59).
*Who's Who in United States Politics* (1952).
*CAB* (1960).

JOY HARRELL

## BROWN, JERRY (1938–    )

Politician and presidential candidate. Brown was born of Irish heritage in San Francisco, California, on April 7, 1938 to Bernice and Pat Brown, the third of four children. He was raised in San Francisco where he attended public schools until the fourth grade when he began a Catholic parochial school education. Brown was introduced rather early to the political world by way of his father's own involvement as district attorney, attorney general and governor. He graduated from St. Ignatius High School in June 1955 and then expressed his desire to enter the seminary. However, at age seventeen he needed parental consent to enter the seminary but he was denied such consent; his parents instead insisted that he go to college for one year before making the decision to enter the seminary and the path towards priesthood.

Brown was enrolled at Santa Clara University and spent a year waiting to enter the seminary. On August 15, 1956 Brown and a few comrades from Santa Clara began their journey towards the priesthood and he was immediately drawn to Jesuit spirituality and ideal for living. However, after three and a half years in the formation program, Brown discerned that his call and vocation may be other than the priesthood and informed his father of his decision to leave. Nevertheless, Brown carried with him the wisdom of the Jesuit order in his ambition and focus. He left the seminary in February of 1960 and went to live at International House at Berkeley and graduated in 1961 and went on to Yale Law School where he became interested in civil rights activities. After graduation from Yale in 1964, Brown worked as a law clerk to Justice Matthew Tobriner and then moved to Los Angeles to seek job possibilities and budding political interests.

During the late 1960s, Brown worked as an attorney at the Tuttle and Taylor law firm and was active in the antiwar movement in Los Angeles; in 1968 he helped to form a peace slate to back Eugene McCarthy against President Johnson for the Democratic nomination. In 1968 he went to the Democratic convention as an alternate delegate for McCarthy. Brown then began networking politically and won a two-year position on a junior college board where he gained skills that would later help him in his position as governor. In 1971, Brown became secretary of state in California and worked towards championing appropriate campaign monetary maneuvers, notably Proposition 9, the political reform act.

On January 28, 1974 Brown announced his candidacy for governor; he identified himself as a former leader of the antiwar movement and expressed his want for a new spirit of activism and hope within a pragmatic viewpoint and application. Brown's promises for the future included improving the state's educa-tional system, promoting environmental protection and also his continuing work for political reform. Specifically, in regards to political reform, Brown focused on the reorganization of the executive branch and his idea to simplify and downsize many of its agencies and bureaus into a more unified whole. On November 5, 1974 Brown won his campaign for governor by a very slim margin of 2.9 percentage points and in his inaugural address on January 6, 1975 he announced his fervor for gaining farm workers the rights and responsibilities in relation to union which eventually became a reality in the Agricultural Labor Relations Act (ALRA).

Brown continued his work and the farm labor act went into effect on August 28, 1975. He took many risks in his political position and his advocacy of the farm worker's cause had many repercussions in his later campaigns. As interest in his political maneuvers grew, so too did interest in Brown's personal life precisely because he kept it personal. Similarly, his lack of interest in amenities ranging from his living quarters to transportation, diet and dress attracted much speculation as well as his single status and interest in religion. Overall, Brown emerged from his governorship with a respectable personality, a personality which allowed him to announce his dislike for certain aspects of the traditional political process while accentuating authenticity. Many attribute part of his success to the way paved by his father as well as his father's continuing support of his son in campaigns and in his personal life.

Known for being socially liberal while fiscally responsible, Brown decided to run for the presidency late in 1975; he announced his intention while speaking with several reporters but the news did not solicit much attention. Brown's campaign was relatively successful and he made an impressive effort. However, Jimmy Carter had locked the nomination by the time the primaries ended on June 8. Brown remained in the race until the end, an action many criticized as having harmed rather than helped his political position. After he lost the nomination, Brown continued to travel and to campaign for Carter and continues his activities in the political arena. In 1998, he was elected mayor of Oakland.

*See* California

Robert Pack, *Jerry Brown: The Philosopher-Prince* (New York: Stein and Day, 1978).

JOY HARRELL

## BROWN, MARGARET ("Molly") TOBIN (1867–1932)

Heroine, philanthropist. Margaret's father, John Tobin, was born in Ireland in 1823. After spending time in Virginia he moved to Hannibal, Missouri, and married Johanna Collins, also an Irish immigrant. These newlyweds were both widowers and each had a daughter from the previous marriage. Together they produced four children: Daniel, Margaret, William, and Helen. Margaret was known as Maggie during her life and at the age of nineteen she followed her half-sister Mary Ann to Leadville, Colorado. Within a year of her arrival Maggie married a young mining foreman named James Joseph ( J. J.) Brown, also the child of an Irish immigrant. Brown and Tobin exchanged wedding vows in 1886 at Annunciation Church in Leadville and began their marriage living in a two-room cabin adjacent to the gold mines that made

Molly Brown

them fantastically wealthy by the mid-1890s. This union produced two children, Helen and Lawrence. After striking it rich in Leadville, the family moved to Denver's Capitol Hill district. This area was the center of affluent society and Maggie desired admission into *chic* urban culture. Although her Irish ethnicity and Catholic religion impeded her elite aspirations, Maggie nevertheless devoted considerable energy to her education. According to Christine Whitacre she even spent a "winter at New York's Carnegie Institute studying languages, literature and dramatics."

Although Maggie desired the company of fashionable friends and societal fame, she was an extremely caring individual and spread her wealth to charitable causes wherever she lived. Tom Noel writes that "both she and J. J. gave generously to Leadville's St. Vincent's Orphanage, and in Denver (she) raised money for St. Joseph Hospital and the Cathedral of the Immaculate Conception." Yet, despite her generous philanthropy, Maggie's fame results from a famous shipping accident. After traveling abroad in 1912 she booked return passage on the *Titanic*, a vessel described as "unsinkable." Many of the ship's passengers were wealthy like Maggie, but a large number were poor European immigrants "on their way to reap the rewards of the great American dream—of which Maggie's life was such an outstanding example." After the *Titanic* struck an iceberg, Maggie found herself in a lifeboat with 13 other people. She reportedly helped sustain the spirits of these passengers until they were plucked from the sea by the crew of the *Carpathia*. Afterward, she led efforts to raise money for the survivors, particularly those poor immigrants who had lost their mates in the disaster and arrived in America with only the clothes on their backs.

The *Titanic* catastrophe brought Maggie fame and she was now welcome in "fashionable society." She parlayed her fame politically and according to Leigh Grinstead, director of the "Molly Brown House" in Denver, Colorado, she even ran for the U.S. Senate three times. Although Maggie never served as a government official, she did lend her celebrity to issues important to women and children. Sadly, Maggie's charitable behavior, eccentric lifestyle, and extensive travels led to a separation from her husband, but she remained close to her children. Her declining years were spent traveling between Denver, New York, and New-

port, Rhode Island. Finally, at age 65 she suffered a stroke and died on October 26, 1932, at New York's Barbizon Hotel. Margaret is buried next to her husband at Long Island's Holy Rood Cemetery.

*See* Colorado; *Titanic* and Irish Passengers

Thomas J. Noel, *Colorado Catholicism and The Archdiocese of Denver 1957–1989* (Denver, 1989).

Don L. Griswold and Jean Harvey Griswold, *History of Leadville and Lake County, Colorado: From Mountain Solitude to Metropolis* (Denver, 1996).

Christine Whitacre, *Molly Brown, Denver's Unsinkable Lady* (Denver, 1984).

KEVIN STANTON

## BRYAN, GEORGE (1731–1791)

Revolutionary and Anti-Federalist statesman in late eighteenth-century Pennsylvania. Bryan was the son of Presbyterian merchant Samuel Bryan of Dublin, whose contemporary patriot agitator, Charles Lucas (1713–1771), may have inspired his political ideas and later career as American agitator. In 1752 Bryan emigrated to Philadelphia and formed a profitable mercantile partnership with Irish-born James Wallace, trading in dry goods, rum, and wine with the British Isles, Iberia, and the West Indies, until 1755 when the firm was dissolved and Bryan embarked alone on an initially successful career as merchant, ship-owner, army contractor, and land speculator. He also became a leading spokesman for Pennsylvania's "Presbyterian interest," in opposition to both British taxation and the Quaker-dominated colonial legislature, and in 1764 he was elected to the Assembly and was appointed judge of the orphan's court and court of common pleas. In 1765 he was a delegate to the Stamp Act Congress; in 1767–70 he played a leading role in Philadelphia's non-importation campaign against the Townshend Acts (1767); and in 1768 he co-authored (with Rev. Francis Alison and John Dickinson) *The Centinel* essays that mobilized popular opinion against the threatened appointment of an Anglican bishop in the colonies. However, in 1771 Bryan went bankrupt, perhaps because of his strict fidelity to the trade embargo, and lost all his property. In 1774–75 he returned to political activity as the champion of revolution and radical democracy, alienating wealthy former associates such as Dickinson and Robert Morris, who were reluctant revolutionaries and opponents of the ultra-democratic 1776 Pennsylvania constitution, which Bryan may have helped to write. In 1776 Bryan was elected to the state Supreme Executive Countil, and in 1777–79 he served as Pennsylvania's Vice-President and then as President, steering the state through an "internal revolution" that witnessed confiscation of the Penn estates, imposition of test acts on Tories and pacifists, price controls to curb speculators, radical reformation of the College of Philadelphia, and the abolition of slavery. In 1780 Bryan became a judge of the state Supreme Court and in 1784 a member of the Council of Censors. However, despite his efforts and those of his backcountry Scots-Irish allies, such as William Findley and John Smilie, during the 1780s Bryan's Constitutionalist party lost power to Morris's Federalists, who repealed the test acts, won control of the Assembly, secured the state's ratification of the Federal Constitution (1787), and finally replaced the 1776 state constitution (1789–90). In 1790 Bryan became a charter member of Mathew Carey's Hibernian Society, but died early the next year, defeated, scorned, and impoverished.

*Dictionary of American Biography.*

J. S. Foster, *In Pursuit of Equal Liberty: George Bryan and the Revolution in Pennsylvania* (University Park, Pa., 1994).

B. A. Konkle, *George Bryan and the Constitution of Pennsylvania, 1731–1791* (Philadelphia, 1922).

KERBY MILLER

## BUCHANAN, PATRICK J. (1938– )

Assistant to presidents, presidential candidate. Patrick J. (Pat) Buchanan is held by many to be the quintessential Irish-American. The genealogical facts, as Buchanan himself has pointed out, are somewhat more complex. Buchanan is Scotch-Irish on his father's side and German on his mother's. But, he said, "we never protested the honor" of being taken for "pure Irish."

Buchanan was born in Washington, D.C., on November 2, 1938, son of William B. and Catherine E. (Crum) Buchanan. He majored in English at Georgetown University, received a master's in journalism from Columbia, then in 1962 joined the St. Louis *Globe Democrat* as an editorial writer, moving two years later into the assistant editorial-editor's chair. His career veered toward politics in 1966, when he became executive assistant to former Vice President Richard M. Nixon, then a partner in a Wall Street law firm and eyeing a run for the White House in 1968. Buchanan accompanied Nixon on his study tours of Africa and the Middle East, and worked as a speechwriter during his presidential campaign. After Nixon's election, he entered the White House as a member of the research and writing staff.

Nixon was one of three Republican presidents whom Buchanan, a confirmed, often contentious conservative, would serve. He was an adviser briefly in the administration of President Gerald R. Ford, and from 1985–1987 he was President Ronald Reagan's communications director. In the White House he acquired a reputation as a quick-witted stylist and caustic polemicist. In the mid-1970s, for example, he criticized mainline Protestantism for an alleged readiness to "cast morality and theology aside . . . and set as its goal on earth the recognition of Red China and the preservation of the Florida alligator." The provocative law-and-order speeches of Vice President Spiro T. Agnew were from Buchanan's pen, as was Agnew's virulent attack of November 13, 1969, on the major television networks, which categorized them as "a tiny and closed fraternity of privileged men, elected by no one, and enjoying a monopoly sanctioned and licensed by government." Buchanan revealed subsequently that the speech was written with Nixon's "silent benediction and collaboration."

During the Watergate crisis, Buchanan was one of Nixon's staunchest defenders. He discounted the break into Democratic National Committee headquarters as a sample of the "hardball" tactics that were part and parcel of American political life, and when the tapes surfaced that threatened the Nixon presidency, he counseled a "bonfire" approach. Buchanan conceded, in the paraphrase of writers Bob Woodward and Carl Bernstein, that there would be a firestorm afterwards, but he predicted it would blow itself out. His counsel was not accepted, other advisers fearing that destruction of the tapes might constitute obstruction of justice. Buchanan denied before the Senate Watergate Committee that there was anything immoral or illegal in his involve-

ments, and he escaped the grief that befell many others around Nixon.

In the world beyond the White House, Buchanan has evolved into a major media personality as a syndicated newspaper columnist and regular on talk-television. He seems never far from controversy, being hostile towards feminism, a rabid isolationist and protectionist, and militant in his opposition to abortion and homosexual rights. His positions on Israel and to Jewish causes have raised the question of anti-Semitism, an accusation he strenuously denies.

In 1992 and 1996 Buchanan stood for the Republican presidential nomination. Both times he was a long-shot candidate, but his following among far-right conservatives resulted in strong showings in some primaries, which in turn created a certain leverage within the party. This led to Buchanan's addressing the 1992 Republican National Convention on opening night and a biting speech which excoriated the Democratic ticket of Bill Clinton and Al Gore as pro-lesbian and pro-gay, and labeled Mrs. Clinton a radical feminist. The speech shocked moderate Republicans and reverberated through the election itself, some say to the ultimate hurt of the Republican ticket.

Buchanan is unapologetic about his ideology. "My views, my values, my beliefs," he has said, "were shaped by being a member of an Irish-Catholic conservative family of nine children." In 1987 he was named a Knight of Malta. In 1971 he married Shelley Ann Scarney, once a White House receptionist. They have no children.

Patrick J. Buchanan, *Right From the Beginning* (Boston, 1988).

William F. Buckley, Jr., *In Search of Anti-Semitism* (New York, 1992).

*Collier's Year Book* (New York, 1993).

Bob Woodward and Carl Bernstein, *The Final Days* (New York, 1976).

JOHN DEEDY

## BUCKLEY, WILLIAM F., JR. (1925– )

Editor, television personality, journalist, novelist. The most respected and arresting voice of American conservatism in the second half of the twentieth century has belonged to William F. Buckley, Jr. He arrived on the scene in 1951 with the first of two score books, *God and Man at Yale: The Superstitions of 'Academic Freedom,'* a work critical of liberal and secular values that he felt were being fostered at his alma mater. In the decades since, he has remained in the spotlight as editor, writer, lecturer, debater and media personality, his concerns ranging the gamut of human affairs, including developments in the Catholic Church, of which he is an intense loyalist. For Buckley there have been no sacred cows. When Pope John XXIII issued his landmark social encyclical *Mater et magistra,* he dismissed it as a "venture in triviality." When Vatican Council II published its decrees, he accepted the reforms, though he questioned premises and deplored many of the results. To him the changes in the liturgy have especially been "vexing." He has cited by way of example the "random cacophony" that passes for music in parish churches of his acquaintance—though adding with feigned resignation that he supposed "the Christian martyrs endured worse exasperations."

Buckley was born in New York City on November 24, 1925, son of William Frank and Aloise (Steiner) Buckley. His was a wealthy family, due largely to Latin American oil interests, and he was schooled at home by tutors and, when the family was traveling, in private schools of Great Britain and France. He studied in

William F.
Buckley, Jr.

1943–1944 at the University of Mexico, served two years in the United States Army, then enrolled at Yale, graduating in 1950 with honors—and material for *God and Man at Yale*. That book was followed in 1954 by *McCarthy and His Enemies: The Record and Its Meaning*. Co-authored with brother-in-law L. Brent Bozell, the book expressed certain reservations about Republican Senator Joseph R. McCarthy, the anti-communist witch-hunter from Wisconsin, but it defended McCarthyism as a movement "around which men of good will and stern morality can close ranks."

Buckley, a young man yet in his twenties, was breathing new life into a conservatism that had been moribund in the United States since the New Deal era of President Franklin D. Roosevelt, almost a quarter-century before.

In 1955, with the support of some one hundred and twenty investors, Buckley founded *National Review,* a journal of conservative opinion, and began a thirty-five year stint as its editor-in-chief. With wit, panache and a high-powered intellect, he made *National Review* into one of the country's most influential periodicals. President Ronald Reagan, for one, said it was his favorite magazine. In 1962 Buckley branched out with a three-times-a-week syndicated column, "On the Right," to which some three hundred and fifty newspapers subscribed, and in 1966 he launched "Firing Line," a weekly television discussion program with guests of the finest minds from all over the world. The program built an audience of several million viewers.

Though Buckley's intellectual interests have focused strongly on politics, he himself has largely remained a bystander so far as formal political life is concerned. In 1965 he ran for mayor of New York City, but that foray into politics seemed more mischievous than serious. Asked what he would do if elected, he declared, "Demand a recount." In 1973 he was a public member of the United States Delegation to the twenty-eighth General Assembly of the United Nations, but when his friend Ronald Reagan, newly elected as president, asked in 1980 if there was any position he would like in his administration, Buckley irreverently responded, "Ventriloquist."

In 1976 Buckley wrote the first of several espionage novels featuring a character named Blackford Oakes. That first in the series, *Saving the Queen,* drew on Buckley's own affiliation with the

Central Intelligence Agency in Mexico in 1951–1952. Succeeding Blackford Oakes thrillers have been less directly autobiographical, but all have been rooted in recent East-West history—the Cuban missile crisis, the erection of the Berlin Wall, etc.—and are viewed by critics as the author's statements on the events, their causes and resolution. An avid yachtsman, Buckley has also written several books about sailing, and in 1997 he published an "autobiography of faith," *Nearer, My God*, which *Commonweal* termed his testament that orthodox Roman Catholicism is "an appropriate and blessed life for a serious, intellectually rigorous modern."

Buckley has received many honorary degrees and other honors, among them an Emmy for his television work and designation as best columnist of the year. In 1991 he received the Presidential Medal of Freedom. Buckley married the former Patricia Taylor July 6, 1950. They have one son, Christopher.

*See* Journalism, Irish-American

William F. Buckley, Jr., *On the Firing Line: The Public Lives of Our Public Figures* (New York, 1989).
———, *Nearer, My God: An Autobiography of Faith* (New York, 1997).
Jeff Chapman, *et al.,* eds., *Contemporary Authors,* New Revision Series, volume 53 (Detroit, 1997).

JOHN DEEDY

## BUFFALO, NEW YORK

### The Beginning

Although the Irish have been a part of the population of Buffalo since its founding as the village of New Amsterdam in 1804, they did not have a significant impact on the cultural make-up of the area until after the completion of the Erie Canal in 1825. The earliest settlers that entered the area were viewed as "Yankees" attracted by the inexpensive arable land, teeming forests, and the beginnings of water-borne commerce on the Great Lakes. These early settlers are often referred to as Scotch-Irish, or Ulster Irish, and there is ample evidence that points to that origin. But there is no evidence to suggest that these early arrivals identified themselves as Irish. Many of these migrants were single men, discouraged with their opportunities in New England and anxious for better opportunity on the frontier. Although many of the new arrivals were Presbyterian or Episcopalian, there is a growing body of evidence that some of the new arrivals were not necessarily of either religious background. The Catholic Diocese of New York had been created in 1808 essentially to serve Catholics living in the eastern part of New York State. Catholics living on the frontier had to do without the services of the Church. Western New York was heavily forested, wild and exceedingly difficult to travel to. The primitive roads of the early period were all but impassable except in the months of summer. Travel by water was little better, although it was the preferred method. The major route was up the Hudson River, then the Mohawk River to Lake Ontario. From there they traveled to the Niagara River and on to Buffalo. From 1804 until after the War of 1812, those of Irish descent were a very small part of the population.

### War of 1812

The events of the War of 1812 had a significant impact on the village of Buffalo and western New York. After the burning of the village of Buffalo in retaliation for American forces torching

Newark (later Niagara-on-the-Lake), large military units were assembled on the Niagara Frontier to prevent the British forces from controlling the water routes into the interior of the young country. Significant battles occurred at Old Fort Niagara on the U.S. side and at various sites in Canada including Ft. Erie, Chippewa River, Lundy's Lane, and Fort George. Thousands of young men died on both sides. What occurred after the hostilities was that many of the soldiers gained a great appreciation for the natural beauty of the Buffalo area, and they recognized the opportunities that abounded there. Although travel conditions were still very harsh, many of the young men began to move to western New York along with their families. Slowly the Irish population of Buffalo began to grow. For the most part they were an accepted part of the community and did not tend to congregate in any particular area of the city as did later arrivals.

## THE ERIE CANAL

By the early 1820s Buffalo had a well-established commercial waterfront. The first steamship had appeared on the upper Great Lakes along with the proliferation of commercial sailing vessels. Commercial activities were growing along the Buffalo waterfront creating opportunity for investors and for workers looking for employment. The limiting factor was the primitive overland or water commerce between Buffalo and the East Coast cities. The most monumental change came with the construction and opening of the Erie Canal. This new water route became the high-speed highway of commerce and immigration. Buffalo became the largest inland port in the young country and New York City became the principal gateway for trade and immigration on the Eastern Seaboard. The digging of the canal was accomplished, at first, by the farmers that lived along the proposed route. Some of the labor force was Irish, most were not. As construction progressed westward from Albany, word arrived in Ireland of the opportunity for and the need of a flood of young men. They came—many single, some married men without their families, and to a lesser extent, some families with children seeking employment. Cities and towns swelled with the new arrivals. By the time the canal was completed at Buffalo, the Irish population of the city had soared. The laborers settled in along the Buffalo waterfront in what was then the 8th Ward. The new arrivals were not welcomed by the residents of Buffalo. The majority of the new arrivals were Catholic. The existing Irish population that had mixed freely with the other residents disassociated themselves from the new immigrants. The newly created canal district, "anchored by its principal street, Canal Street anchored one of the toughest, bawdiest and most dangerous port districts in the world; a place where Great Lakes sailors and Erie Canal boatmen met to spend their money on whiskey and women, and to spill each other's blood in a rivalry that dimmed only when the 19th century faded into history."

The Canal District of Buffalo quickly became a tenement district. The poorly constructed buildings, with primitive sanitation and almost non-existent ventilation, were teeming with impoverished immigrants. And, amid the poverty and squalor, and the crime that feeds on both, decent people tried to carve out a new life in a new land. The newly arrived Irish lived a very precarious existence in what eventually would be called the "Infested District." With little or no education, virtually no money or resources to sustain them and alienated from the general populace, the Irish clung to whatever opportunity presented itself. Most of the available jobs were on the docks, loading and unloading ships and canal-boats. Unemployment was frequent

and competition for employment was fierce. Periodic economic depressions destroyed what little gains the immigrants made. Charitable resources were few and dispensed frugally, causing real hardship for the Irish. The presence of the Catholic Church was slight in this early period and not very sympathetic to the problems of the Irish immigrant since the churches were controlled by civilian boards principally of French and German Catholics who openly despised the new Irish immigrants. The Irish population swelled anyway as scores of new arrivals fled the worsening conditions in Ireland. Through the 1830s the Irish population grew. Conditions did not improve but commerce and industry grew fast enough to allow the Irish to survive. Some of the young Irishmen were inspired by the rebellion in Canada in 1837 to join forces with McKenzie in invading Canada from Navy Island in the Niagara River. The goal was to cause England enough concern that they would get out of Ireland. Their cause may have been noble but their organization was weak and many of these young Irishmen died in their attempt. Those that were captured were deported to Australia and Tasmania. Very few managed to return to their families.

## THE GREAT FAMINE

Life continued in the same vein throughout the early 1840s. Competition among the Irish laborers was encouraged by unscrupulous contractors who pitted immigrants from Cork, or Mayo or Galway, or the "Fardowners" from Longford to vie against each other by agreeing to accept lower wages. On the docks, former slaves who had made their way North on the Underground Railroad to Buffalo, were used to force wages even lower. These actions frequently led to strikes, the most dramatic of which occurred in January of 1849, the "Towpath Rebellion." Almost 600 Irish laborers had gone out on strike against contractors widening the canal in the City along the Buffalo River. While generally supported by the Democratic *Courier,* the other Buffalo newspapers, the *Express* and the *Commercial Advertiser,* were extremely harsh in their judgment of the Irish strikers. The suffering among the Irish families was horrible. Indeed, the *Sentinel,* a church newspaper, warned that violence would be inevitable if the suffering of the people was not immediately relieved. What transpired next was amazing. Galvanized by the plight of the starving families, large numbers of the Irish community along with some Germans and others of the local populace armed themselves with pitchforks and a few guns to stand alongside the strikers on the Canal Towpath to intimidate the contractors and their strikebreakers. Even some of the more fortunate wealthy Irish in the City sided with the strikers and organized a rally in support of the strike. The newly organized Diocese of Buffalo under the new Irish bishop, John Timon, while not openly speaking out, used whatever resources it could muster to relieve the distress of the Irish families. In the confrontation ordered by the political structure of the City, a young German Lieutenant, Solomon Scheu, commanding the militia, was ordered to fire on the strikers. He refused to do so and was later arrested for expressing sympathy for the strikers. Years later when he ran for mayor the Irish community supported him. Forced by the growing pressure, the City government put pressure on the contractors to end the strike and return the men to work. It was in this mileau that many of the Great Famine immigrants found themselves. In the period between 1847 and 1852 huge numbers of starving Irish flooded into the 8th Ward and spilled over into the 1st Ward. The latter would become the primary Irish community in the ensuing years.

It was largest in numbers but in terms of influence it was virtually powerless. The best example of the general attitude towards the poor Irish was that of the existing Catholic churches. In the case of St. Louis, the oldest Catholic congregation primarily composed of French and some German Catholics, there was blatant discrimination against the Irish. Bishop Timon complained bitterly to the church board about forcing the Irish to attend Mass on the church steps rather than with the congregation. Eventually the bishop was forced to threaten the church board with excommunication. In a year-long legal battle which was eventually arbitrated to a conclusion, the Irish were allowed in the church but only to the extent that the bishop had to find a way to create an Irish church closer to the areas of the city where they lived.

## The Catholic Church and the Irish

The arrival of Bishop John Timon in Buffalo in 1847 was a beacon of hope for the Irish community. Although small in stature, he was a man of tremendous ability. His task was enormous. He had to serve a huge geographical area with limited resources and a basically hostile congregation used to controlling their own decisions. Timon recognized the plight of his own countrymen and slowly began to wrest control from the civilian boards and to establish a strong church institution that could be more responsive to the needs of the people. Timon believed in education and went on a very ambitious building program of constructing schools and churches. The Irish community welcomed this activity even while recognizing that many of their children would not be able to attend school because the family needed the income the child could earn. The religious community fought relentlessly to change the attitude of the Irish by convincing them to sacrifice even more to enable their children to have more opportunity. The gains that the community made as a whole were substantial even though it would take much more for the Irish to take their place as rightful members of the community. Education alone did not bring about change for the Irish. In fact they became even less influential during the mid-1850s as Buffalo literally became a German city with a huge influx of German immigrants fleeing the chaos in their own German states. It would take a lot more sacrifice on the part of the Irish to achieve parity with the rest of the population.

## The Irish Organizations

The Irish were not overly fond of organization in the early years. Other than the job actions against injustices and their attachment to the church, little was done to organize the community. The earliest organization to form in the city was The Friendly Sons of St. Patrick in 1842. Primarily started to ensure decent burial for its members, the organization flourished and began to broaden its outlook becoming involved in promoting the welfare of the Irish community and fostering appreciation of Irish culture. One of the other organizations which had an influence was The Ancient Order of Hibernians. At the turn of the century the Knights of Equity would become a part of the Irish Community as would the Blackthorn Club and several others. The real test for the Irish community as a group came with the onset of the Civil War.

## The Civil War

With the commencement of hostilities, the Irish community came forward in significant numbers in supporting the war effort. The Irish in Buffalo had been a part of the military community for a considerable number of years, mostly driven by economic necessity. This was also true during the Civil War. Employment was spotty at best and beset with labor troubles and long periods of unemployment. Military wages were better than no wages and the Irish joined the newly formed regiments that went off to war. While many enlisted in the "regular" army, most of the Irish joined the volunteer infantry regiments raised by the state. Two of the more well known regiments were the 155th New York Volunteer Infantry led by Col. John Byrne and the 164th New York Volunteer Infantry which was part of Corcoran's Legion. In all there were about 16,000 men from Erie County that served in the war and about 25% of which were Irish.

Not all of the community agreed with the war effort. There were draft riots in Buffalo that turned vicious. There was frustration at the draft system that seemed to fall disproportionately on the poor Irish. They were not alone in this matter since the German community responded the same way. But it was the blood sacrifice on the battlefields that would have such a significant impact on the Irish community after the war.

## Post Civil War

After the war, immigration of the Irish continued swelling the population in the 1st and 8th Wards in Buffalo. The returning veterans began to take a more active role in the community around them. Opposition was strong and in many cases blatantly illegal. The editor of the *Express,* Almon Clapp, tried to use strong arm tactics, hiring thugs to keep Irish voters away from the polls. There was a strong Nativist element in Buffalo that was determined to prevent the Irish from voting. The Irish refused to be denied and in several violent confrontations at the polls succeeded in forcing their way in to vote.

One of the sadder chapters in Buffalo's Irish history occurred in 1866. The Fenian movement had grown strong nationally. In late May of 1866 veterans from both North and South began to gather at various spots along the border with Canada in anticipation of an invasion to seize critical waterways in an attempt to coerce England to get out of Ireland. Only one year after the Civil War, enemies united in the endeavor to relieve their mother country from its distress. While their intentions were noble, their movement was riddled with incompetent leaders and informers. The major thrust took place from Buffalo on June 1, 1866 when forces that had marshalled and drilled in the Irish neighborhoods crossed the Niagara River. Success was immediate as they caught the Canadian militia and British regulars off-guard. At the Battle of Ridgeway the Fenians routed the combined British forces. Success was short lived. Two days later the Fenian forces desperately tried to escape back across the river as their reinforcements had been stopped by U.S. Army troops augmented by the gunboat *USS Michigan* stationed in the river. A small number of men were captured by the Canadian forces. The rest were held in temporary custody on the *Michigan.* Although they had violated the U.S. Neutrality Act public sympathy won release for the prisoners within a month. Later actions by the Fenians were weak and disorganized.

## Irish in Politics

After the Civil War the Irish gained strength in the political process. Successive waves of immigrants who became educated and involved in the community, coupled to the strong showing in the Civil War, eventually led to success at the polls for the Irish. While it would be some years before an Irish person would serve as mayor of Buffalo, one political figure achieved national prominence, William "Blue Eyed Billy" Sheehan. Although his brother John, a hard-fisted ward boss, had achieved prominence, it was Billy who would achieve national success as an insider in Boss Croker's Tammany Hall in 1892. Elected to the New York State Assembly at the age of 25, he would eventually become Lt. Governor and a major force in national politics. Many more would join him as the years went by.

## IMMIGRATION IN THE LATE 19TH CENTURY THROUGH THE 1950s

Immigration remained strong in the Irish community until the turn of the century when restrictive laws, and improving conditions in Ireland and other factors combined to slow the influx of new Irish families to Buffalo. By the 1920s it was a mere trickle of mostly single people coming into the community. This situation held true until the 1950s when there was a slight upswing in Irish families coming once again into Buffalo. It was this new group that would have a decided impact on the fostering of Irish culture in the city. Although the Irish held on to some aspects of their cultural background, the slowdown of immigration had curtailed and dimmed the cultural memory of the Irish in Western New York. With the new influx Buffalonians turned to a renewal of Irish activities with the growth of Irish sports like football and hurling. Irish step and social dancing became popular. There was a big upturn in the number of Irish organizations in Buffalo culminating in the formation and acquisition of the Buffalo Irish Center in 1970. Irish language classes flourished along with genealogical societies and historical programs. The culmination of all these activities was the joining of twenty-six Irish organizations in a two-year effort to erect a Famine Commemoration monument on the Buffalo waterfront. Joining with the City of Cork, the group received a gift of thirty-two historic stones from famine-labor built Penrose Quay in Cork, along with a large dolman-like stone from Connemara and erected and dedicated the monument in 1997. It is a fitting reminder of the terrible struggle that the Irish immigrants faced as the monument was erected in the old "Infected District" that was the scene of many of the struggles and triumphs of their spirit.

David A. Gerber, *The Making of an American Pluralism—Buffalo, New York 1825–1960* (Chicago, 1989).
David Owen, *The Year of the Fenians* (Buffalo, 1990).
Edward J. Patton, Various articles for the *Buffalo News* and the *Buffalo Irish Times*
———, "The Barbary Coast of the East" (February 1994).
———, "Uniontown: Part of the Old First Ward," Part I (January 1993).
———, "Uniontown: Part of the Old First Ward," Part II (March 1993).
———, "Uniontown: Part of the Old First Ward," Part III (April 1993).
———, "In Defiance of Nature—The Beach" (August 1993).
———, "The Beach" (December 1994).
———, "John C. and Blue-Eyed Billy" (April 1995).
Marvin A. Rapp, *Canal Water and Whiskey* (Buffalo, 1992).
Michael N. Vogel, Edward J. Patton, Paul F. Redding, *America's Crossroads—Buffalo's Canal Street/Dante Place—The Making of a City* (Buffalo, 1993).

EDWARD J. PATTON

## BULGER, WILLIAM M. (1934–   )

State legislator, university president. Born in South Boston February 2, 1934, son of James J. and Jane V. (McCarthy) Bulger, William Michael (Billy) Bulger is what is known in Boston as a

triple Eagle—a graduate of Boston College High School, Boston College and Boston College Law School. (The eagle is the Boston College symbol.) He was elected to the Massachusetts Legislature in 1961 and then in 1971 to the State Senate, serving as its president from 1978–1996. He was responsible for legislation curbing child abuse and for advancing numerous environmental causes, including solar energy, marine sanctuaries off the Massachusetts coast, and the cleanup of the Boston Harbor. In the 1970s, he opposed court-ordered busing as a means to achieve racial balance in Boston public schools. He left elective office after thirty-four years to become president in 1996 of the University of Massachusetts, a system with five campuses and more than 50,000 students.

A Latin and Greek scholar, Bulger is a celebrated wit. For years he presided at a St. Patrick's Day breakfast in South Boston that included a good-natured roast of political friends and foes and other celebrities. The breakfast grew into a national media event, with presidents calling in their greetings from Washington. Typical of the exchanges was one teasing the late Republican United States Senator Leverett Saltonstall, a descendant of one of Massachusetts' first families, as being "Irish on the chauffeur's side." When President Bill Clinton called, Bulger joshed, "Mr. President, I knew you had a great sense of humor when you appointed Ray Flynn [former mayor of Boston] ambassador to the Vatican. Would you consider our parade marshal, 'Wacko' Hurley, for secretary of defense?"

Bulger married the former Mary Foley, and they have nine children.

By contrast, an older brother, James (Whitey) Bulger, achieved notoriety for criminal activity and as an alleged "powerful gang boss" who was simultaneously an informant for the FBI. When Billy Bulger published his political memoir, the brother was a fugitive from justice and the subject of many "dark rumors." Bulger alleged in the book that his political opponents were not above using his brother's problems with the law as the basis of "an oblique political attack" on him. Nonetheless, he wrote with loyalty and affection for his brother, a man his children called "Uncle Jim." "[H]e is my brother," he stated, "and I love him, and pray that he will not damage himself again."

*See* Boston

William M. Bulger, *While the Music Lasts: My Life in Politics* (Boston, 1996).

JOHN DEEDY

## BURK, JOHN DALY (1772?–1808)

Dramatist, journalist, historian. John Daly Burk was born in Ireland, probably in Cork, about 1772. Brought up a Protestant, he was admitted as a scholarship student to Trinity College, Dublin in 1792. A supporter of the French Revolution, John Burk, according to his own account, began writing articles for the *Dublin Evening Post,* which advocated government reform and Catholic emancipation. In 1794 the Board of Trinity College expelled him on the charge of disseminating atheistic principles among the student body.

Burk then became active in the United Irishmen where he proceeded to establish two societies, really front organizations, which would be cells for revolution. When this activity was revealed by an informer, Burk faced the real likelihood of being arrested for high treason. With the assistance of a young lady named Daly, who dressed him up as a woman, he fled the country on a ship for Boston in 1796. In grateful recognition of her assistance, he adopted Daly as his middle name.

While enduring a fifty-day crossing of the Atlantic, Burk wrote a play, *Bunker Hill,* which extolled the virtues of American republicanism. In a whirlwind of activity upon his arrival in Boston, Burk sold his play and it had its first production in February 1797. The first play to be written about the Revolution, this patriotic potboiler became a staple in the American theater for the next fifty years. He also became the co-owner of a new paper, the *Polar Star,* which first appeared in October 1796 and was the first daily newspaper in that city. As editor, he proclaimed the glories of Jeffersonian republicanism and condemned the Federalists, then the dominant political force in Boston. He also included theatre reviews and literary commentary. Not given to false modesty, he presented himself as a marytr to freedom and liberty in his short book, *The Trial of John Burk.*

Due to the fact that Boston had six newspapers and the effect of Federalist hostility, the paper expired after six months and Burk moved to New York. He once again got involved in journalism and his play was performed several times beginning in September 1797. His second play, *Female Patriotism,* about Joan of Arc, was first performed in April 1798. In June of that year he became co-owner and editor of the *Time Piece,* but the paper closed in August. As a result of his political views, he became a friend of Aaron Burr, the Republican leader in New York.

Burk was electrified by the outbreak of rebellion in Ireland in 1798 and, although the revolt failed, he proceeded to write a history of the event, which was published in 1799. He was now viewed as a dangerous alien by the Federalists and Secretary of State Timothy Pickering began proceedings to have him deported. When Burk agreed to leave the country, the case was dismissed.

Rather than leave, however, Burk went into hiding in Virginia in May or June 1799. When Jefferson and the Republicans took control of the national government at the beginning of 1801, the five-year waiting period for naturalization was restored and Burk became an American citizen in 1802. He made his new home in the small Virginia town of Petersburg. A noted orator, he became a lawyer. He married a local woman and had a son, John Junius, who became a lawyer and a judge. A new play of his, *Oberon, or the Seige of Mexico,* in which he condemned the Spanish Conquest, was first performed there in 1802. He also wrote articles for Virginia newspapers and in 1804 produced the first of three volumes of his history of Virginia, the first comprehensive history of the state. In it he opposed slavery and defended the Indians against settler encroachment. Nor did he neglect his native land: "Ireland, rich in every species of genius, gave generals and governors and armies to the revolution." With John McCreery, he began collecting Irish songs; the resulting book, for which he wrote a historical introduction, did not appear until 1824. When the U.S. government became entangled in controversy with Napoleon's France, Burk vigorously supported his adopted country. In 1808 this led to a duel with a Frenchman and Burk was killed. A meteoric Irishman came to an early death. He was thirty-six years old.

Charles Campbell, *Some Materials . . . For a Brief Memoir of John Daly Burke. . . . With a Sketch . . . [by] Judge John Junius Burk* (Albany, N.Y., 1868).

*Dictionary of American Biography,* vol. ii (1929 ed.): 279–280.

Joseph, I. Shulim, "John Daly Burk, Irish Revolutionist and American Patriot," *Transactions of the American Philosophical Society,* vol. 54, part 6 (1964, new ser).

Edward A. Wyatt, *John Daly Burk; Patriot, Playwright, Historian* (Charlottesville, VA, 1936).

ARTHUR MITCHELL

## BURKE, ÆDANUS (1743–1802)

A principal spokesman for the Irish-stock Anti-Federalists and Jeffersonian Republicans in late eighteenth-century South Carolina, Burke was born in Co. Galway, into a once-affluent Catholic family whose estates had been confiscated. After studying at the Jesuit College of St. Omer, France, about 1766 Burke emigrated to Virginia where he studied law under transplanted Irishmen, Thomas Burke and John Mercer. In 1770 Burke returned to Ireland, later sojourned in the West Indies, and in 1775 moved to Charleston, South Carolina, where he became "a volunteer for American liberty" and served as an officer in the Continental Army. In 1778 Burke was appointed a judge of the Court of Common Pleas, and in 1779 was elected to the state General Assembly. Although Burke resided in Charleston and usually represented low country parishes in the Assembly, his judicial circuit included much of the heavily Scots-Irish backcountry, where his ultra-democratic political opinions enjoyed their strongest support. In 1783 Burke's published attack on the new Order of the Cincinnati, as elitist and threatening to American liberties, won him national attention—and Federalist enmity that intensified in 1788, when Burke, as a delegate to the South Carolina ratifying convention, spoke for the great majority of the state's white farmers who strongly opposed the U.S. Constitution. In 1788 Burke was one of the few Anti-Federalists elected to the new Federal Congress, but served only a single, frustrating term. Unable to secure Constitutional amendments that would restore authority to the states, and intensely hostile to Alexander Hamilton's financial policies, Burke retired to South Carolina where he resumed his judgeship and, in the 1790s, supported the French Revolution, opposed Jay's Treaty (1794), and joined the Irish-born Pierce Butler, a wealthy low country planter, in organizing the state's Jeffersonian Republicans. Although a convert to Episcopalianism, the ethnic taunts of Burke's political opponents, his hatred of England, and his boast of descent from "the old Milesian race" marked him as distinctly Irish. Never married, at his death Burke left most of his estate to "aid . . . poor Irish immigrants"—a legacy that in 1818 became the trust of Charleston's interdenominational Hibernian Society.

*See* South Carolina

R. M. Calhoon, "Aedanus Burke and Thomas Burke: Revolutionary Conservatism in the Carolinas," in D. R. Chesnutt and C. N. Wilson, eds., *The Meaning of South Carolina History* (Columbia, S.C., 1991).

J. C. Meleney, *The Public Life of Aedanus Burke* (Columbia, S.C., 1989).

KERBY MILLER

## BURKE, JOHN (1859–1937)

Politician, Supreme Court Justice. John Burke, called the "Abe Lincoln of North Dakota," became a governor, then Secretary of the United States Treasury, and finally a North Dakota Supreme Court Justice. A Catholic in a sometimes discriminatory part of America, a Democrat in a Republican state, he is the sole occupant of North Dakota's place of honor in the U.S. Capitol's Statuary Hall.

The "Abe Lincoln" description had some justification. Burke, like Lincoln, came from meager rural circumstances. Tall, gaunt and homespun, a lawyer with only a basic elementary education and two years of law school, he possessed a lifelong habit of study, a love of drama and poetry and an engaging oratorical style.

Above all, however, was his integrity that captured the admiration of North Dakota citizens. He is remembered as the leader of a political revolt that wrested power from a "Robber Baron" regime which ruled North Dakota's first two decades of history. He became known as "Honest John" Burke, and as governor, gave North Dakota its first experience of "honor, justice, and self respect."

He was Irish and relished that fact. His father was John Burke, a man who fled famine-stricken County Tipperary, arrived in New York in 1848, and within the year married Mary Ryan, also from Tipperary. By 1856, the Burke family found itself on a farm in Keokuk County, Iowa. John Burke, the future governor, was born there in 1859. It was in Iowa that he received his basic education.

As a lawyer, Burke first went to Henning, Minnesota, and then, to supplement his income, worked as a harvest hand in Dakota Territory. The prairies appealed to him and in 1888 he moved to the frontier towns of St. John and Rolla, and finally to Devils Lake, all the while acquiring a reputation of being bright, approachable, and truthful.

At St. John and nearby Rolla, Burke practiced law, taught school and started a short-lived newspaper. By 1890 he was elected to the North Dakota legislature. A year later he married Elizabeth Kane, who was to be his lifelong friend and wife. By 1892 he was elected to the North Dakota Senate.

### Leader for Political Reform

Representing farm and small town constituents, Burke developed an aversion to the outside interests—railroads, banks, and grain companies—that controlled the state's economic and political life through Alexander McKenzie, the boss of the Republican party. In 1906 Burke won the Democratic nomination for governorship. He enlisted the support of disillusioned Republicans and almost single-handedly roamed the state, seeking the vote of thousands of distressed citizens. In an upset victory, he was elected governor, and in eight years of office was able to galvanize a number of reform-minded forces that set in place laws curbing political corruption, controlling public utilities, allowing initiative, referendum, and recall, introducing a state tax commission and a presidential primary, and enforcing seed and food standards.

History still remembers Burke's election as "The Revolution of 1906." Burke was North Dakota's first Catholic and first Democratic governor. He said later that the state's struggling Democratic party was a "sort of Irish association."

John Burke's popularity as a reform political leader led to his appointment as Treasurer of the United States (1913–1921). He returned to North Dakota and served as a State Supreme Court Justice until his death in 1937 at the age of 78.

A remarkable man, an Irishman, a statue of Burke stands today in Statuary Hall as a representative of a state whose citizens are overwhelmingly of Scandinavian or German backgrounds.

*See* North Dakota

Charles N. Glaab, "John Burke and the Progressive Revolts," *The North Dakota Political Tradition*, ed. Thomas Howard (Ames, 1981): 40–53.

WILLIAM SHERMAN

## BURKE, JOHN JOSEPH (1875–1936)

Paulist. Born to Irish immigrant parents in New York City on June 6, 1875, John Burke graduated from St. Francis Xavier College in 1896 and entered the Missionary Society of St. Paul the Apostle (Paulists), founded by Isaac Hecker. He was ordained on June 9, 1899, and earned his licentiate in theology at Catholic University two years later.

After a few years spent in giving parish missions, he was appointed assistant editor and a year later editor of the *Catholic World*, *The Leader* and the Catholic Publication Society (later called Paulist Press) by the Paulist community. Following Pope Pius X's condemnation of Modernism in 1907, he discontinued publishing the work of avante garde theologians like George Tyrrell, but promoted social reform through articles by moral theologians like John A. Ryan. He remained as editor of the *Catholic World* until 1922.

Soon after the nation declared war in 1917, Burke founded the Chaplain's Aid Association to provide priests with necessities for their ministry in the military. He also organized the National Catholic War Council to coordinate the Catholic war effort and represent Catholic views in Washington. For this and similar efforts on the ecumenical level, the War Department awarded him the Distinguished Service Medal.

In 1919 the National Catholic Welfare Conference was organized by the American hierarchy to promote Catholic activity, social welfare work, education and aid to immigrants. A secretariat was established in Washington, D.C., and Burke was appointed general secretary with supervision over all NCWC departments. He also acted as liaison of the Vatican in the effort to resolve the church-state conflict in Mexico. He died on October 30, 1936.

See Catholicism, Irish-American

John F. Piper, Jr., "Father John Burke, C.S.P., and the Turning Point in American Catholic History" (Philadelphia, 1981).

Douglas J. Sheerin, *The Foundation and First Decade of the National Catholic Welfare Council* (Washington, D.C., 1975).

John B. Sheerin, C.S.P., *Never Look Back: The Career and Concerns of John J. Burke* (New York, 1975).

JAMES J. HALEY

## BURKE, THOMAS (c. 1745–1783)

Revolutionary War governor of North Carolina and an early exponent of the South's "state sovereignty" doctrine, Burke was the son of Ulick Burke of Tyaquin, Co. Galway, and Janet Shaw of Galway city. The Tyaquin Burkes were much reduced by confiscations and penal laws, and Burke himself suffered a youthful case of smallpox that left him blind in one eye and terribly scarred. However, his family's conversion to the Church of Ireland, and financial aid from his uncle, Sir Fielding Ould, master of Dublin's maternity hospital, enabled Burke to attend Trinity College, Dublin, until ca. 1760 when some quarrel or youthful misadventure obliged him to emigrate, at age fifteen, to America. Highly intelligent and ambitious, albeit profoundly insecure, Burke first settled in Northampton County, on Virginia's Eastern Shore, practiced medicine, and during the Stamp Act crisis (1765–66) gained local applause and national attention for his patriotic poem celebrating the Act's repeal. Flushed with success, in 1769 Burke migrated to Norfolk, married, and became a prosperous lawyer, but in 1772 he moved his family to backcountry

North Carolina and settled on a 600-acre plantation he named Tyaquin, near Hillsborough, seat of Orange County. Burke became a political ally of North Carolina's oligarchy of tidewater planters and slave-owners, whose oppression had driven Orange County's farmers (many of them Scots-Irish) into the Regulator revolt of 1766–71, and who subsequently led their colony into the American Revolution. In 1775–76 Burke served in the provincial congresses that dismantled royal authority and declared independence, and he played a major role in drafting the new state's 1776 constitution, which preserved tidewater dominance. In 1776–81 he was a member of the North Carolina Assembly and a delegate to the Continental Congress in Philadelphia, where his obsessive, irrascible insistence on absolute state sovereignty shaped the Articles of Confederation, weakened the government's ability to conduct the war, and eventually earned him Congress's formal censure for "disorderly and contemptuous conduct." In June 1781 the North Carolina Assembly elected Burke chief executive of a state government under assault from British armies and local loyalists. Burke performed well, but in early September was captured by British forces, imprisoned, and then, after promising not to escape, paroled to James Island, South Carolina. In January 1782, Burke absconded to North Carolina and resumed his governorship, but his political enemies charged that he had forfeited his honor by violating parole, and he soon died, disgraced and embittered, on his Tyaquin plantation.

*See* North Carolina

R. M. Calhoon, "Aedanus Burke and Thomas Burke: Revolutionary Conservatism in the Carolinas," in Dr. R. Chesnutt and C. N. Wilson, eds., *The Meaning of South Carolina History* (Columbia, S.C., 1991).

E. P. Douglass, "Thomas Burke, Disillusioned Democrat," *North Carolina Historical Review,* 26 (1949): 150–86.

J. N. Rakove, "Thomas Burke and the Problem of Sovereignty," in his *The Beginnings of National Politics: An Interpretive History of the Continental Congress* (New York, 1976).

J. B. Sanders, "Thomas Burke in the Continental Congress," *North Carolina Historical Review,* 9 (1932): 22–37.

R. Walser, ed., *The Poems of Governor Thomas Burke of North Carolina* (Raleigh, 1961).

J. S. Watterson III, *Thomas Burke: Restless Revolutionary* (Washington, D.C., 1980).

KERBY MILLER

## BUTLER, MARY JOSETTA (1904–1995)

Educator, administrator, religious leader. Eldest child of Thomas J. Butler from Ballylongford, County Kerry, and Mary (Fitzpatrick) Butler (stepmother). Mary Butler entered the Sisters of Mercy in 1929. Her impressive presence, contagious enthusiasm, open mind, and disarming power of persuasion were complemented by an empathy and goodness of heart which expressed itself in acts of caring, words of comfort, and warm companionship. Mercy became her.

In 1960, Mary Josetta Butler was named president of Saint Xavier University, an educational institution sponsored by the Sisters of Mercy since 1846. She led that University, as Dean and Executive Vice President before becoming President, during one of its most progressive eras (1940–63). Change marked her tenure, including curriculum reform, addition of a collegiate theology program, innovative liberal education supported by the Ford Foundation, a certificate program for teachers of religion,

an annual Mercy Educational Conference, and the Overseas Education Program.

Mary Josetta facilitated the founding of the Sister Formation Conference, supported its degree completion policy for young sisters, and held national office in the Conference and the Conference of Major Superiors of Women, a national organization for leaders of religious congregations of women.

The church-international called her in 1963 to organize the United States ministry of the Movement for a Better World. Later, as elected governing member and manager of its Rome center, Mary Josetta joined the retreat team in India and Pakistan. Here her reputation drew former participants in Saint Xavier's Overseas Education Program to the Movement for a Better World.

A contributor to *The Quality of Mercy* observed: ". . . she saw everything as part of her world, and she accepted responsibility for all of it" (Dwyer, ed., p. 29).

*See* Sisters of Mercy

Mary Josetta Butler, R.S.M., *That in Our Work the Church May Grow: A Report on the Overseas Education Program, 1959–79* (Chicago, 1980).

Joy Clough, R.S.M., *First in Chicago: A History of Saint Xavier University* (Chicago, 1997).

Claudette Dwyer, ed., *The Quality of Mercy: A Festschrift in Honor of Sister Mary Josetta Butler* (Chicago, 1996).

CLAUDETTE DWYER

## BUTLER, PIERCE (1866–1939)

Associate Justice of the U.S. Supreme Court. Pierce Butler was born to Irish parents in a log farmhouse near Northfield, Minnesota, on March 17, 1866. He earned his B.S. degree in 1887 from Carleton College and was admitted to the Minnesota bar in 1888. In 1891 he married Annie Cronin and they had eight children. Appointed assistant county attorney in 1891, Butler was elected county attorney in 1893 and 1895, but was defeated for state senator in 1906. Leaving politics, he began his association with the firm which became Butler, Mitchell and Doherty, and was known for his work in federal cases testing the application of the Sherman Anti-Trust Act. He was also renowned for his expert representation of railway corporations, particularly in rate cases, like the *Minnesota Rate Cases.*

In 1922 he was nominated to the Supreme Court by President Warren Harding. Butler served for sixteen years, writing more than 300 majority opinions and 140 dissents. He regularly voted to strike down government regulations of business. Beginning in 1933 he became the leader of the Court's conservative bloc, which resisted New Deal legislation. Butler was a chief target of President Roosevelt's "court packing" scheme in 1937. He died in Washington, D.C., on November 16, 1939.

F. J. Brown, *The Social and Economic Philosophy of Pierce Butler.* CUA Studies in Sociology, 13 (Washington, D.C., 1945).

John T. Noonan, Jr., "The Catholic Justices of the United States Supreme Court," *Catholic Historical Review,* 67/3 (1981): 369-85.

KATHLEEN N. McCARTHY

## BYRNE, DONN (1889–1928)

Novelist, short story writer. Born in New York City to an itinerant architect, Donn Byrne spent his youth in south Armagh and Antrim, where his fluency in Irish won him accolades at festivals organized by, among others, Sir Roger Casement. Impoverished by the death of his father, Donn Byrne financed his education at University College-Dublin with a modern language scholarship. There he came to the attention of Douglas Hyde, who admired his knowledge of colloquial Irish; helped found a student journal, in which he published poetry; and excelled at boxing. His early intentions of joining the British Foreign Service were superseded by his decision in 1911 to return to New York and try his hand at poetry. There, at the suggestion of his friend Joyce Kilmer, he submitted a short story entitled "Battle" to *Smart Set.* The story was published in February 1914, earning him $50, and launching his career.

His modern and historical tales of romance and adventure were so successful in the lucrative American magazine market that by the time of the publication of his first novel, in 1919, he had retired to Connecticut to write fiction professionally. This first novel, *The Stranger's Banquet,* an inexpert treatment of a labor dispute in a Massachusetts shipyard, and his second, a domestic drama entitled *Foolish Matrons* (1920), received mixed reviews. But it was with his third novel, *Messer Marco Polo* (1921), that he established his reputation. Based on an Irish folktale, *Messer Marco Polo* recounts Polo's travels, but Donn Byrne's conceit was to put the tale into the mouth of a ninety-year-old Irish storyteller. Though the story itself is a trifle, critics and audiences were won over by the audacious charm of a Celtic Twilight romance, which hinted that everyone, including the Kubla Khan, was Irish.

In 1922, plagued by debts resulting from an extravagant lifestyle, Donn Byrne sold his Connecticut house and, with his wife and children, began a peripatetic existence in Europe. During the balance of his life he wrote seven additional novels, dozens of short stories, and a personal appreciation, published in *National Geographic Magazine,* of his beloved Ireland. His works inspired two stage plays, two radio plays, and eleven movies, making him one of the most popularly successful writers in Irish-American literature.

Despite this success, the middle and later 1920s were not altogether a happy time for him. The Great War, the Anglo-Irish War, and the Irish Civil War had piqued his audience's tastes for bitter, ironic realism. Donn Byrne found himself increasingly out of critical fashion. Nonetheless, he remained loyal to his American Celticist notion of fiction: that is, a ballad or lament, whose scope encompasses high romance and adventure; whose tone, though often humorous, is characterized by Victorian enthusiasm, earnestness, and morality; and whose purpose is to offer an emotional and sensual experience, rather than an intellectual one. In 1928, he decided to settle down permanently in Ireland, and purchased an estate called Coolmain Castle in Cork. On 18 June 1928, three days after he took possession, he was killed in an automobile accident.

*Messer Marco Polo* (New York, 1921).
*Changeling, and Other Stories* (New York, 1923).
*O'Malley of Shanganagh* (New York, 1925).
*Destiny Bay* (Boston, 1928).

RON EBEST

## BYRNE, JOHN (1825–1902)

Physician, pioneer in electric surgery. John Byrne was born October 13, 1825, to Stephen Byrne, a merchant, and Elizabeth Sloane in Kilkeel, County Down, Ireland. He began the study of medicine at the Royal Institute, Belfast, when he was seventeen. He continued his studies in Dublin and Glasgow and earned a medical degree in 1846 at Edinburgh.

Since the Famine was rampant in Ireland at that time, Byrne was appointed medical officer at a hospital in Kilkeel. Due to his exceptional abilities and the use of advanced sanitary methods, Byrne was able to reduce the mortality rate at the hospital.

In 1848 Byrne left Ireland and made his home in Brooklyn, New York. He decided to continue medical studies at New York Medical College and graduated with a medical degree from that institution in 1853.

He was influential in negotiating a merger between the German General Dispensary and Long Island College Hospital in 1857. Byrne was appointed a member of the executive board and taught uterine surgery for many years. He also served as surgeon-in-chief at St. Mary's Hospital from 1858 until his death.

Byrne used his knowledge of physics to adapt the electric cautery knife for use in surgery on malignancies in the uterus. His research on the instrument and the technique of its use was published in *Clinical Notes on the Electric Cautery in Uterine Surgery* in 1872. A description of his twenty years' experience in using this surgical method was published in an 1889 report in the "Transactions of the American Gynecological Society." The report showed that his method resulted in low mortality rates and good final results.

Byrne's attention to detail and his interest in the sciences was not fully appreciated in the United States at the time. He died October 1, 1902, at Montreux, Switzerland.

William B. Atkinson, *Physicians and Surgeons of the United States* (1919).
Allan Johnson and Dunmas Malone, eds., *Dictionary of American Biography,* vol. II (New York, 1929).
James J. Walsh, *History of Medicine in New York* (1910).

MARIANNA McLOUGHLIN

## BYRNES, JAMES FRANCIS (1882–1972)

Supreme Court Justice, Secretary of State. James Francis Byrnes was born in Charleston, South Carolina, in 1882. He was the son of James Francis Byrnes, a young municipal clerk whose parents were Famine immigrants. At the age of twenty-six the senior Byrnes died of tuberculosis shortly before his son's birth, leaving his widow, Elizabeth E. McSweeney, the daughter of an Irish immigrant and dressmaker, to raise a boy and a girl. Byrnes attended Catholic schools and served as an altar boy in St. Patrick's Church, but, after learning shorthand, he left school at fourteen to become a law clerk.

He moved to Aiken, S.C., at the age of eighteen when he was appointed court stenographer, his predecessor having been murdered by a Baptist minister. He studied law and was admitted to the bar after three years. He bought a local newspaper and edited it for four years. In 1906 he married Maude Busch in an Episcopal service; he was to remain a member of this denomination for the rest of his life.

He was first elected to public office in 1908, serving as area solicitor. Two years later, in what was considered to be a surprising achievement for a newcomer to the district, he was elected to Congress. During his fourteen years in the House of Representatives he was a supporter of Woodrow Wilson and the progressive movement. He also established his credentials as an opponent of civil rights for Blacks. In 1919 and 1920 he made several strongly racist statements and supported A. Mitchell Palmer, the Red-hunting Attorney General, for the 1920 Presidential nomination.

In 1924 he sought and lost the Democratic nomination for the U.S. Senate. At this point Byrnes again shifted his base, moving to the upstate mill city of Spartanburg, where he practised law and bided his time for a political comeback. Interestingly, in 1928 he campaigned vigorously for Governor Alfred E. Smith in several Southern states. One of his biographers, David Robertson, has noted that Byrnes identified with Smith, both of whom were self-made men of Irish Catholic background.

In 1930 Byrnes narrowly defeated his 1924 rival for a U.S. Senate seat and was re-elected in 1936. He was an early supporter of Franklin D. Roosevelt for the presidential nomination in 1932. Although he generally supported the New Deal program of Roosevelt, he remained a staunch segregationist; he opposed the Wages and Hours Act of 1938 because the same minimum wage "would have to be paid to every Negro working in any store as well as to white employees." Byrnes had urged Roosevelt not to undertake a purge of his political opponents that year. In a brief appearance in South Carolina at Greenville, Roosevelt criticized a statement made by the other senator from the state, "Cotton Ed" Smith, that implied a man could live on fifty cents a day in South Carolina.

Byrnes was a possible nominee for vice president in 1940, but in the middle of the nominating convention Roosevelt told him his opposition to civil rights for Blacks and his leaving the Catholic Church precluded his selection. Byrnes still had presidential ambitions and Roosevelt's appointment of him to the Supreme Court in April 1941 allowed him to escape from the limitations of Southern segregationist politics. During his brief tenure on the court he demonstrated a clear support for civil liberties. The next year Roosevelt appointed him Director of Economic Stabilization and the following year as Director of War Mobilization. In these posts, he served as "assistant president" until nearly the end of the war.

In 1944 the vice presidency became a real possibility. Democratic Party leaders knew that Roosevelt was in rapidly declining health. The incumbent, Henry Wallace, was seen by both Southern leaders and Northern urban "bosses" as very much left of center and they wanted him replaced. Roosevelt told Byrnes that he wanted him and Byrnes proceeded to the convention in Chicago expecting to be nominated, but that was not to be. Sidney Hillman of the C.I.O. opposed him because of his labor record. With northern Blacks now a key factor in industrial states, their leaders did not want Byrnes. The big city bosses did not want a former Catholic on the ticket. In the middle of the convention Roosevelt indicated that Senator Harry S Truman of Missouri, who had none of these disadvantages, was his choice.

When Truman became President upon the death of Roosevelt in April 1945, one of the first things he did was to bring Jimmy Byrnes back from Spartanburg, S.C., and, on the basis of Byrnes having attended the Yalta conference, appointed him Secretary of State. In the year and a half that Byrnes held this vital position he had to deal with the difficult relationship with the Soviet Union. He also demonstrated a strong element of arrogance. He failed to keep Truman informed about the proceedings of the international conferences he attended. These differences led to his resignation in January 1947.

He returned to South Carolina and remained silent during the 1948 campaign. In 1950 he was elected governor with a huge vote. As governor he drove the Ku Klux Klan off the streets by means of a public uniforms law. In order to head off intergration, he secured a large appropriation to improve Black schools. Although he remained a nominal Democrat, he endorsed Republican presidential nominees for the rest of his life. In 1960 he refused to support John F. Kennedy. Rather, he presided at a huge rally, with prayers provided by Billy Graham, in Columbia, S.C., for Richard Nixon. He died in 1972.

James F. Byrnes, *Speaking Frankly* (New York, 1947).

———, *All in One Lifetime* (New York, 1958).

Kendrick A.Clements, ed., *James F. Byrnes and the Origins of the Cold War* (Durham, N.C., 1982).

*Dictionary of American Biography*, supplement 9 (1971–75): 149–152.

Robert H. Ferrell, *Choosing Truman: the Democratic Convention of 1944* (Columbia, MO, 1994).

David Robertson, *Sly and Able: A Political Biography of James F. Byrnes* (New York, 1994).

ARTHUR MITCHELL

## CAGNEY, JAMES (1899–1986)

Actor. Born of Irish and Norwegian parentage in the lower East Side of New York City on July 11, 1899, James Cagney became one of the greatest gangsters of the movies and one of its most often mimicked characters. After holding a variety of odd jobs—office boy, department store clerk, ticket seller—Cagney began his career in show business in vaudeville, stock shows, and in legitimate theater work on Broadway which brought him to Hollywood.

His first film was *Sinner's Holiday* (1930), but it was the 1931 *Public Enemy* which made him a star. The scene in which he shoves half a grapefruit into the face of Mae Clarke is one of the most famous in film history, and that film launched his persona as the fast-talking tough guy in dozens of films between 1932 and 1961. One of his most popular roles was that of a gangster in *Angels With Dirty Faces* opposite Pat O'Brien; and he teamed with some of Hollywood's best gangsters including George Raft (*Each Dawn I Die*), Humphrey Bogart (*The Roaring Twenties*), and Edgar Robinson (*Smart Money*).

Filmgoers knew him as a bad boy with a crooked Irish grin, ill-treating women and machine-gunning his way through speakeasies. His staccato delivery and constant tension underneath the smug exterior kept audiences on the edge of their seats. He did get to play other roles, and his acting and energetic tap-dancing talents were finally recognized in the 1942 *Yankee Doodle Dandy* about the life of songwriter George M. Cohan, for which he received the Best Actor Oscar. He played a fast-talking theatre producer in *Footlight Parade,* a cocky racing driver in *The Crowd Roars,* and an airline pilot in *Ceiling Zero.* He retired from films in 1961 after Billy Wilder's *One, Two, Three,* only to return one more time in the 1980 film, *Ragtime.* He was awarded the American Film Institute's prestigious Life Achievement Award in 1974.

In real life, James Cagney was a gentle family man with a quick Irish grin, drawing and painting and raising prize cattle in retirement in New York State.

*See* Cinema, Irish in

---

*Newsweek,* 17 (February 24, 1941): 59.
*Time,* 37 (March 3, 1941): 82.
*International Motion Picture Almanac* (1941–42).
*Who's Who in Theatre* (1939).

EILEEN DANEY CARZO

## CAHILL, KEVIN MICHAEL (1936–   )

Physician, author, professor. Kevin M. Cahill, author and editor of more than twenty books on medicine, diplomacy, and Irish culture, is a leading tropical disease specialist. Dr. Cahill has traveled to third world countries to develop medicine and health programs and has taught at medical schools in the U.S. and Ireland.

Kevin Cahill was born in the Bronx, New York on May 6, 1936, one of eight children whose grandparents had emigrated from Kerry and Clare. He graduated from Fordham University in 1957 with a B.A. in English Literature. In 1961, he earned his M.D. from Cornell University's School of Medicine.

Following two years in the U.S. Navy stationed in Egypt, and a fellowship in London, Dr. Cahill began his private practice in New York in 1965. His patients have included President Lyndon B. Johnson, John Cardinal O'Connor, and Pope John Paul II following his assassination attempt in 1981. Along with his private practice, Dr. Cahill has served as director of Lenox Hill Hospital's Tropical Disease Center since 1965.

Since 1969, Dr. Cahill has been a professor and board member of the Royal College of Surgeons in Dublin, Ireland. He is also a faculty member of the New York University Medical School and the University of New Jersey College of Medicine and has taught at Seton Hall University Medical School.

An early advocate of banning landmines and treating the AIDS epidemic, Cahill has written extensively on the challenges of the third world and the relationship between medicine and diplomacy. In his book, *Preventive Diplomacy,* he argues that "social detection and early intervention should be as honored in international relations as crisis management and political negotiations." In 1992, he founded the Center for International Health and Cooperation, which provides health care in crisis situations such as the recent conflicts in Somalia and the former Yugoslavia.

For the past twenty-five years, Dr. Cahill has served as President-General of the American Irish Historical Society in New York. During his presidency, the Society has seen an increase in membership, numerous renovations to its Fifth Avenue home, and a renewed sense of interest in its library, lecture series, and journal.

For many years, Dr. Cahill has been listed among the top 100 Irish-Americans in *Irish America* magazine. In 1981, he was the first American to receive the Grand Cross Pro Merito Melitensi from the Vatican. He has also been honored by the governments of Sudan, Somalia, Nicaragua, and Cuba.

*See* American Irish Historical Society

---

Kevin M. Cahill, M.D., *The American-Irish Revival* (New York, 1984).
———, *A Bridge to Peace* (New York, 1988).
———, *Preventive Diplomacy* (New York, 1996).

ELIZABETH TOOMEY

## CAHILL, T. JOE (1877–1964)

Philanthropist. Born of Irish lineage in Camp Carlin, Wyoming Territory, on August 7, 1877, his experience of frontier life and a church community were important factors in his formative years. He was an altar boy in Cheyenne's first Catholic church, St. John the Baptist, in 1887, when the Diocese of Cheyenne was created. Later he became a horse wrangler and a sheriff, whose duties brought him face to face with Tom Horn, one of the West's most controversial bad men.

But his most important claim to fame came as promoter and spokesperson for Cheyenne Frontier Days throughout the world. Through the force of his personality and many business contacts he was able to enlist the help of others in supporting

St. Joseph's Orphanage in Torrington, Wyoming, his greatest philanthropic activity. In this work he and his wife, Susan Brady, whom he married in 1901, found the joy that comes from serving the needs of others.

The last years of his life were spent in daily visits to the patients at DePaul Hospital in Cheyenne. He died on August 18, 1964.

JAMES J. HALEY

## CAHILL, THOMAS (1940– )

Author, scholar. One of six children of first-generation Irish-American parents, Thomas Cahill was born and raised in New York City. He attended a Jesuit high school and later entered the seminary, where he became fluent in Greek and Latin and earned a pontifical degree.

At Fordham University, he studied Greek and Latin literature and medieval philosophy, graduating with a B.A. in classical literature and philosophy. He also attained an M.F.A. in film and dramatic literature from Columbia University.

Cahill has enjoyed a varied career, spending time as a teacher at Queens College and Seton Hall University in New Jersey. He was also North American education correspondent for *The Times* of London. Perhaps the one constant in Cahill's career has been books: He was once advertising director at the *New York Review of Books* and contributed regularly to the *Los Angeles Times Book Review*. Along with his wife, Susan, he founded Cahill and Company in 1976, a company which produced a mail-order book catalogue called the *Reader's Catalogue*.

As director of religious publishing at Doubleday, a position he held for six years, Cahill encountered publisher Nan Talese at a sales conference and discussed with her his idea for a seven-part series of historical books.

In 1995, his first book in *The Hinges of History* series was published under Talese's imprint. She has also contracted the author to write a book about his childhood. Within three years, *How the Irish Saved Civilization: The Untold Story of Ireland's Heroic Role From the Fall of Rome to the Rise of Medieval Europe* had over 700,000 copies in print and had been translated into seven languages. From the opening paragraph, the book was every bit as "charming and poetic" as it was described by the *New York Times*.

"The word Irish is seldom coupled with the word civilization," wrote Cahill, who went on to explain that while the French and the Egyptians were a civilized people, the Irish were more inclined to be "wild, feckless and charming, or morose, repressed and corrupt, but not especially civilized."

Cahill followed up what he refers to as his "Irish book" in 1998, with *The Gifts of the Jews: How a Tribe of Desert Nomads Changed the Way Everyone Thinks and Feels*. Like method actors who throw themselves into a part, Cahill researches his books intensely.

The idea for *How the Irish Saved Civilization* came to him in the early 1970s, when he and his wife spent a year in Ireland researching a book for Scribner called *A Literary Guide to Ireland*. When it came time to prepare for *The Gifts of the Jews*, Cahill spent two years learning Hebrew at New York City's Jewish Theological Seminary of America. A true linguist, he is also proficient in French, Italian, German and Gaelic.

Cahill is the founder of the Friends of St. Giles, an offshoot of the Italian Community of Sant'Egidio. The group holds weekly prayer meetings, befriends foster children and indigent adults who have AIDS, and organizes other assistance programs for the poor of New York City.

Thomas Cahill

He and his wife Susan have a daughter, Kristin, and a son, Joey. They live in New York's Bronx.

Thomas Cahill, *How the Irish Saved Civilization* (New York, 1998).
———, *The Gifts of the Jews* (New York, 1998).
*Irish America Magazine*, Vol. XIII/2 (Mar./Apr., 1997); Vol. XIV/2 (Mar./Apr., 1998).

DARINA MOLLOY

## CALDWELL, JOHN (1769–1850)

United Irish exile in early nineteenth-century New York. Caldwell was born at Harmony Hill, near Ballymoney, in north Co. Antrim, the son of a prosperous Presbyterian farmer, miller, and linen manufacturer who, in the 1770s–80s, supported the American Revolution and Irish political reform. Educated in Derry city and in Bromley, Middlesex, in 1784 Caldwell moved to Belfast and engaged in trade. Caldwell became an early and prominent member of the Ulster branch of the revolutionary Society of United Irishmen, formed in Belfast in 1791, while his brother Richard organized the rebel forces in north Antrim. In 1798, when the United Irish rebellion was surpressed, John Caldwell was imprisoned and Richard sentenced to death, but their father's intercession with Irish Lord Lieutenant Cornwallis secured their release on the condition that the family go into exile. In 1799–1800 Caldwell and his kinsmen settled in New York City, where they enjoyed the patronage of mayor De Witt Clinton (1769–1828)—of Co. Longford Presbyterian origins. John Caldwell joined Clinton's Masonic lodge, as well as the Friendly Sons of St. Patrick, and formed a mercantile partnership with brother Richard, while his father purchased Salisbury Mills, an estate near Newburgh in Orange Co. However, mismanagement and the American embargo on transatlantic trade (1807) ruined the Caldwells' fortunes: John Caldwell's firm went bankrupt in 1808, and nearly all of Salisbury Mills were lost. Caldwell struggled to pay creditors until 1834, when he secured appointment as collector of arrear taxes in New York City and County. In 1839 he retired to the remaining Orange Co. property, where he lived in genteel poverty until his death. Despite his tribulations—and although never as prominent as his fellow exiles in New York—Thomas Addis Emmet (1764–1827), William James MacNeven

(1763–1841), and William Sampson (1764–1837)—Caldwell remained active in Irish affairs: as master of New York City's Erin Masonic Lodge; treasurer and vice-president of the Friendly Sons of St. Patrick; and in 1843 as an honored guest at the second national convention of the Irish-American Repeal Association, held in Manhattan. A living link with the largely-Protestant Irish nationalism of the late eighteenth century, Caldwell survived to witness the rise of the predominantly Catholic Irish and Irish-American nationalism, as well as the Great Famine immigration, of the mid-nineteenth century.

*See* United Irishmen and America

The most useful source is Caldwell's memoir, "Particulars of a North County Irish Family," copies of which are in the New York Genealogical and Biographical Society and in the Public Record Office of Northern Ireland (T.3541/5/3).

M. Durey, *Transatlantic Radicals and the Early American Republic* (Lawrence, Ks., 1997).

A. T. Q. Stewart, *The Summer Soldiers: The 1798 Rebellion in Antrim and Down* (Belfast, 1995).

KERBY MILLER

## CALHOUN, JOHN CALDWELL (1782–1850)

Statesman, political theorist. John C. Calhoun was the son of Irish immigrant Patrick Calhoun, a native of County Donegal who came to America in 1733. As part of the great Scotch-Irish migration to the southern piedmont, the Calhouns settled in the South Carolina back country, where John was born in 1782. Patrick became a leading planter and politician in the region, instilling a passion for politics in his son at an early age. Calhoun graduated from Yale in 1804, then returned to South Carolina and gained admittance to the bar in 1807, but soon after abandoned his legal practice for public life. He served in the state legislature from 1807 until his election to Congress in 1810. His ambition and ability soon placed him among the leaders in Congress, where he became an outspoken advocate of national defense, internal improvements, and federal support of economic development. He served as Secretary of War from 1817 to 1825 and vice president from 1825 to 1833. His ardent nationalism cooled by the 1830s however, as he and many southerners came to believe the federal government promoted northern welfare at the expense of the South. Calhoun soon became the leading proponent of southern interests and states' rights in Congress, primarily as a senator from South Carolina from 1833 until his death. He advocated the theory of nullification as a means of protecting state sovereignty against federal power. The final two decades of his life were spent as the nation's most prominent defender of southern interests, particularly slavery, while working to keep his region in the Union. Besides his countless accolades and accomplishments, Calhoun also expressed a lifelong satisfaction in his Irish ancestry, declaring late in life, "I am proud of my descent from so generous and gallant a race" (*Papers,* XVII, 124).

*See* South Carolina

Margaret L. Coit, *John C. Calhoun: American Portrait* (Boston, 1950).

Robert L. Meriwether, *et al.,* eds., *The Papers of John C. Calhoun,* 23 vols. to date (Columbia, S.C., 1959– ).

Charles M. Wiltse, *John C. Calhoun,* 3 vols. (Indianapolis, 1944, 1951).

TOM DOWNEY

John Caldwell
Calhoun

## CALIFORNIA

To the surprise of many, the 1990 federal census revealed that California has more people of Irish extraction than any other state in the Union. Some 1,952,000 Californians consider themselves Irish, accounting for about 6.5% of the population. In total numbers the Irish rank fourth behind Mexicans, Germans, and English.

Irish have played a prominent role in California from the Spanish period forward. Wild Geese and their descendants led the way. Although Juan Rodriquez Cabrillo, a Portuguese in Spanish service, made the European discovery of Alta California in 1542 (Baja California had been discovered a decade earlier), Spain, for a number of reasons, waited until the 1760s to initiate plans to colonize the region. Those settlement plans were inspired by Count de Lacy, an Irishman who was serving Spain as ambassador to Russia. While in St. Petersburg, de Lacy learned of Russian plans to occupy Alaska and the Pacific Northwest. He immediately dispatched a secret report to Spain, urging that Alta California be colonized to thwart the proposed Russian expansion. Madrid reacted with uncharacteristic swiftness, perhaps prompted by de Lacy's frequent dispatches during the next several years, and in 1769 Spanish settlement in Alta California commenced.

To bind the far-flung province of California to the rest of New Spain, the Spanish had to consolidate control of the Southwest. Hugh O'Conor (Hugo Oconor in Spanish records), called "Capitan Colorado" because of his red hair, was ordered to do the job. He reorganized Spanish garrisons in Texas and New Mexico and led expeditions against Apache who were raiding Spanish settlements. Within six years O'Conor pacified the frontier, founded Tucson, Arizona, rose in rank from sergeant major to general, and was made Comandante Inspector of Presidios and the Provinces. O'Conor was also responsible for designing leather jackets for his soldiers to protect them from the arrows of the Indians. Troops so clothed became known as *soldados de cuera* (soldiers of leather). These leather-jacketed soldiers were the ones who rode into California with Gaspar de Portola in 1769 and who later manned the presidios at San Diego, Santa Barbara, Monterey, and San Francisco.

Advising and directing O'Conor's work was General Alexander (Alejandro) O'Reilly, who was the governor of the Louisiana Territory and Spain's leading military authority. O'Reilly was born in Ireland in 1725 and fought in Spain, Italy, Germany, and France before coming to America during the late 1760s. He was decorated on several occasions for bravery and once saved the life of the king of Spain. He rose through the ranks to become Count Commander of the Spanish Armies, Field-Marshal, and Captain-General. It was his publicly-stated dream to lead a Spanish army of Irish Wild Geese to free Ireland, but, like other Wild Geese, he spent his life fighting in every cause but Ireland's. The viceroy of New Spain, Antonio Maria Bucareli, regularly sought O'Reilly's advice, especially about military matters and the frontier. At O'Reilly's urging a plan was formulated to establish an overland trail between Sonora and California. O'Conor subsequently laid the groundwork for the project, and Juan Bautista de Anza pioneered the trail.

The Irish connection with Spanish California was strengthened still further when, in 1770, Philip Barry (Felipe de Barri) was made governor of the province, a post he held until 1775. Then, in 1821, in the Treaty of Cordoba, Spain recognized Mexico (which included California) as an independent nation. Negotiating and signing the treaty for Spain was Captain-General John O'Donoghue. O'Donoghue then served as a member of the five-man Mexican regency that governed during the transition period.

Meanwhile, Irishmen were making their way to California as *extranjeros* (foreigners). In 1795, Joseph O'Cain arrived in Santa Barbara. O'Cain was born in Ireland but immigrated with his parents to America. He shipped before the mast as a young man and was soon in command of his own ship. In 1795 he rounded Cape Horn and sailed to California, where he hunted sea otters along the central coast. He then sailed to China to exchange otter pelts for silks and spices. Then disaster struck. Somewhere in the western Pacific a typhoon struck and wrecked his ship. O'Cain survived and hitched a ride on a British ship that was en route from India to California. The ship put in at Santa Barbara in September 1795, and Joseph O'Cain himself stepped ashore. O'Cain was said to have been greatly impressed by the "beautiful country, the delicious climate, the kind hospitality of the people and the bewitching grace of the lovely senoritas" and he requested resident status. Even though the comandante of the presidio at Santa Barbara described O'Cain as "a very handsome fellow, a skillful pilot and carpenter, of good parentage" and recommended that he be allowed to become a resident, the governor denied the request. A few months later O'Cain sailed away on a Spanish ship bound for San Blas, Mexico.

In 1803, some eight years after his first appearance, O'Cain arrived in California again, sailing his ship, *O'Cain*. After stopping at San Francisco, known in those days as Yerba Buena, he sailed on to the Russian settlement at Sitka in southeastern Alaska. He sold the Russians some 10,000 rubles worth of supplies and struck a deal with Alexander Baranov, the commander of the Russian fur-trading outpost. In return for the use of Baranov's Aleuts to hunt sea otters along the California coast, O'Cain would supply the Russians with vegetables and grain from California. As a result, O'Cain spent the next three years in California waters, putting in at such settlements as Yerba Buena, San Quentin, San Luis Obispo, and San Diego.

If O'Cain was denied permission in 1795 to settle permanently in California, Irishman John Milligan in 1814 was not.

Milligan (or Mulligan as his name appeared originally) sailed into Monterey, the capital of California, aboard *Isaac Todd*. He and Scotsman John Gilroy were suffering from scurvy and were put ashore to recover. They both regained their health but never again shipped before the mast and remained in California the rest of their lives. The two Gaels became the first foreigners to settle in Spanish California.

During the 1820s and '30s dozens of Irishmen took up residence in California. One of these was Timothy Murphy. Born in County Wexford, Ireland, in 1800, he arrived in Monterey (after a stay in Peru) in 1828. A contemporary described him as "a fine looking man, tall, powerfully and well built, a good horseman and keen hunter." Being a crack shot, he turned to otter hunting after his attempt to pack and export California beef failed. In a typically small California revolution (revolutions occurred every two or three years during the Mexican period) he helped Juan Bautista Alvarado regain the governorship. As a reward he was made administrator of Mission San Rafael and in 1843 received a 22,000 acre rancho grant bordering San Francisco Bay in today's Marin County. Two years later he became alcalde (a mayor-like figure who also had judicial power) of San Rafael.

The first foreign physician to reside in California was Nicholas Den. Born in County Kilkenny, Ireland, in 1812, the good doctor landed at Monterey in 1836. He began practicing in Santa Barbara where several other Irishmen had already settled. After naturalization he was granted Rancho Dos Pueblos, a 16,000 acre tract of land halfway between Santa Barbara and Gaviota. Den took to rancho life with a passion and spent more time tending to his land and cattle than to medicine. By the time he died in 1862 he had increased his holdings to 70,000 acres. He was active in public and religious life, becoming the alcalde of Santa Barbara in 1845 and donating considerable time to preserving the Mission Santa Barbara and to developing a Catholic seminary.

Nicholas Den's younger brother, Richard, also a physician, arrived in Santa Barbara in 1843 after serving as a ship's surgeon on a voyage that took him around the world. While staying with his brother, a dispatch reached Santa Barbara saying that a doctor was needed in Los Angeles. Richard Den immediately rode south and did not return until he had performed several successful operations. A petition requesting that he make Los Angeles his home followed him back to Santa Barbara. By the summer of 1844 he had returned to Los Angeles where he spent most of the next fifty years practicing medicine. He ventured into the Mother Lode country during 1848 and '49, treating miners for fevers and injuries. The sourdoughs paid him in gold nuggets. A common expression among the Mexicans of Los Angeles was "*Despues de Dios, Doctor Don Ricardo*" (after God, Dr. Richard). For his half century of pioneering medical work in Los Angeles he has been termed "the Nestor of the medical fraternity of Los Angeles County."

By the early 1840s parties of pioneer settlers began trekking overland from the United States to California. The first of these parties, the 1841 Bartleson-Bidwell party, had the good fortune to be led most of the way by the legendary mountain man, Thomas Fitzpatrick. John Bidwell said that without Fitzpatrick "probably not one of us would ever have reached California." Fitzpatrick was a County Cavan-born Irishman who immigrated to the United States as a teenager and spent the rest of his life as fur trapper, scout, guide, and Indian agent.

The first party of pioneer settlers to drive wagons all the way to California was the Murphy-Miller party (also called the

Stevens-Murphy party), led by Martin Murphy and his son-in-law, James Miller, both of County Wexford, Ireland. Murphy and his wife, Mary (Foley), and their children immigrated to Canada in 1820. Miller immigrated with his parents to Canada and there met and married one of the Murphys' daughters, Mary. In 1828 the combined families moved south to the Missouri frontier. In 1844 Murphy decided to move again, this time to California. By then the clan had grown still larger with the addition of more sons- and daughters-in-law and the birth of numerous grandchildren. Late in the spring of 1844 they left Missouri and by November they stood looking up at the eastern face of the Sierra Nevada. They decided to cross the great range by following a river which they named Truckee. Daniel Murphy, one of Martin Murphy's sons, scouted ahead and stumbled upon the most beautiful body of water he had ever seen, Lake Tahoe. The main party came up and made camp at Truckee Lake (later renamed Donner Lake). Again the scouts went ahead and found a practical wagon route. Before winter set in, the Irish pioneers crossed the crest of the Sierra and built shelters on the headwaters of the Yuba River. When spring arrived they broke a trail down the western slope of the Sierra and reached the Sacramento Valley with their wagons and livestock intact, the first overland party to accomplish the feat. The Truckee trail that they named and blazed became the favored route not only for other pioneer settlers, but also for the forty-niners, the stagecoach, the railroad, and today's principal interstate route across the Sierra, Highway 80.

Had it not been for the outbreak of the Mexican War during the spring of 1846, California might have become predominately Irish. Early in 1846 Eugene McNamara, a young Catholic priest, applied for a grant of land in the San Joaquin Valley. He proposed settling some 10,000 Irish colonists there. Such a number would have doubled the non-Indian population of California. The provincial assembly at Los Angeles approved McNamara's request on July 6, and Governor Pio Pico made the grant a week later. The grant included most of the eastern half of the San Joaquin Valley, an area of nearly 10,000 square miles (which would have made the colony almost a third the size of Ireland). The project never went any further, however. On July 7 Commodore John Sloat, the commander of the American Pacific fleet—only seven ships in those days—accepted the surrender of Monterey.

Meanwhile, a party of pioneer settlers that included two Irish families, the Breens and the Reeds, was working its way to California. The party would meet with tragedy when trapped by heavy snowfalls in the Sierra during the winter of 1846–47 and its name become legendary, the Donner party. Patrick Breen and his wife Margaret, immigrants from County Carlow, had seven children, ranging in age from one to fifteen. The entire Breen family survived the ordeal and were largely responsible for the survival of the Reed family, whom they took into their crude cabin.

James Reed, a County Antrim-born Protestant, and his wife Margaret had four children, the youngest three years old and the oldest 13. James Reed was not with the Donner party when they were snowed-in. He had been banished from the party earlier for killing another member of the party in a fight and crossed the Sierra in advance of the main body. He would later lead one of the relief parties. His wife and children took refuge with the Breens during the entrapment. One of the children, Virginia Reed, was so impressed with the religious devotion of the Breens that she made a silent vow that should she survive the ordeal she would become a Catholic. She survived in fine fashion and later converted. In 1850 she married John Murphy and went on to

have nine children. Her younger sister Martha ("Patty") followed close behind. She was married in 1856 and went on to have eight children.

The Breens also became prolific and prosperous in California. They became the first American family to settle in San Juan Bautista. Patrick operated an inn and later served as a postmaster and school trustee. Several of his sons became cattle ranchers, another became an attorney, one served as a county supervisor. His only daughter, the red-haired Isabella, married Thomas McMahon, whose sister was married to one of the Breen boys. Isabella died in 1935 in San Francisco, the last survivor of the Donner party.

San Francisco not only became home to many Irish, it was laid out by an Irishman, Jasper O'Farrell. O'Farrell was a Dublin-born civil engineer who arrived in California in 1843 after participating in a survey of South America's Pacific coast. By 1844 O'Farrell was working for the Mexican government as engineer and surveyor of land grants in California. His maps were later used to authenticate rancho boundaries before the United States Lands Commission. In partial payment for his services the governor of California granted him a rancho in Marin County.

With the eruption of the Mexican War in 1846 and the arrival of American troops in California, the new military governor made O'Farrell one of the future state's three official surveyors. O'Farrell first surveyed Sonoma County and then began his greatest project, San Francisco. In the meantime, he married a daughter of Patrick McChristian, an Irish immigrant who had been one of the Bear Flag rebels. O'Farrell built a home for his bride on his rancho, located near modern Sebastopol. He named the estate Annaly, the title of the ancient Gaelic patrimony of the O'Farrells in County Longford. During the 1850s and '60s, O'Farrell served as a state senator and as a harbor commissioner for San Francisco. He was famous for his hospitality and generosity, and for his early prediction that San Francisco would become "the Empire City of the Pacific."

Like O'Farrell, fellow Irishman William Shannon made enormous contributions to California at the very beginning of the American period. Shannon was born in Ireland in 1822, and immigrated with his parents to New York when he was seven. In 1845, he was admitted to the New York bar and began practicing law. The very next year, when war with Mexico was declared, Shannon joined an infantry regiment and was commissioned as a captain. His unit was shipped to California and he served as commandant of the port of San Diego. The Mexican War brought dozens of Irishmen such as Shannon into California. Mustered out of service in 1848, he made his way to the gold fields. At Coloma, where John Marshall had discovered gold late in January of '48, Shannon was elected alcalde. A short time later he was elected as a delegate to the state constitutional convention at Monterey. At the convention Shannon was responsible for the introduction and the adoption of a section of the constitution that prohibited slavery. When California was admitted to the Union in 1850, the Golden State tipped the scale in favor of free states over slave states by one, 16-15. Shannon was also instrumental in defeating proposals that would have injected religious discrimination into the constitution.

Following the convention, "the silver-tongued, moody-eyed young Irishman" was elected to the state senate. Before he could serve, however, he fell victim to Asiatic cholera in the great epidemic of 1850.

Also serving a critical role at the constitutional convention was Philip A. Roach, a native of County Cork who had immigrated as a boy with his parents to New York during the 1820s. At the convention Roach, who was fluent in Spanish, was chosen to translate the various drafts of the constitution into the native tongue of the several Mexican-Californian delegates. Following the convention he was elected mayor of Monterey, the old Spanish and Mexican capital of California. In 1851 he was elected to the state senate. As a state senator he got a law enacted that allowed a married woman to conduct business on her own without being considered a ward of her husband. He later served as United States Appraiser for the district of San Francisco, as Public Administrator of San Francisco, and as President of the Society of California Pioneers.

If the Mexican War brought dozens of Irishmen into California, the Gold Rush brought thousands. About a third of those who arrived in the gold fields came from overseas. Of the foreigners who rushed in, Ireland supplied the greatest number, followed by China, Germany, and Britain. During the 1850s, '60s, and '70s most of the gold camps had populations that were 10–20% Irish-born. Grass Valley was 22% Irish-born during its boom years and Bodie was 16%. San Francisco, competed with the mining camps with 16% Irish-born in 1860. By 1870 the percentage had increased to 17.

Then, too, California had good numbers of American- and Canadian-born Irishmen. The federal census of 1890 reported that an astounding 25% of those whites reporting foreign parentage had one or both parents born in Ireland. Germany was second with 21% and England third with 11%. San Francisco reflected this. In 1880 the city had some 31,000 or 13% Irish-born residents. However, the city also had some 43,000 second-generation Irish residents and 4,700 third-generation. Altogether, the Irish comprised about a third of San Francisco's population. The large Irish presence caused some unrest during the 1850s, when American nativism was at its peak, and to a lesser degree during the 1860s.

There is some evidence that the Vigilance Committee of 1856 was partly inspired by an anti-Irish agenda. The committee was dominated by Protestants and Masons who supported the Know-Nothing party and clearly feared the growing Irish-Catholic political and economic power in the city. Nonetheless, the committee had little effect on decreasing Irish power. In the fall of 1856 the state legislature elected David Broderick, the son of Irish immigrants, to the United States Senate with the backing of San Francisco politicians.

Irish senators would be elected again on the strength of San Francisco's political clout. In 1862 County Galway-born John Conness won a U.S. Senate seat. He was succeeded by County Westmeath-born Eugene Casserly in 1868. San Francisco elected its first Irish mayor in 1867 in the person of Frank McCoppin. McCoppin's victory came 13 years before New York City elected an Irish mayor and 17 years before Boston did so.

California elected its first Irish-born governor in 1860 when young, ruddy-faced John G. Downey swept into office. Born in County Roscommon in 1827, Downey immigrated to the United States in 1842. After finishing school in Maryland and working as a pharmacist in the nation's capitol, he caught the gold fever and sailed for California in 1849. Downey spent only a brief period in the Mother Lode country before travelling south to Los Angeles and opening the town's first drugstore in partnership with James P. McFarland. Within three years Downey saved enough money to buy a large rancho. Over the years he added more land to the rancho until it spread over 75,000 acres. In 1856 Downey was elected to the state legislature. Four years later, at the age of

32, he became governor of California. For the state, as for the nation, 1860 was a critical year. Pro-southern factions nearly won control of California but Downey frustrated their designs and put the state firmly in the Union camp. Downey also managed to end the waste, mismanagement, and corruption that had characterized the state government during the years following the Gold Rush. When he took office there was an enormous deficit. When he left there was a large surplus.

Downey won the admiration of San Franciscans when he vetoed the "Bulkhead Bill," a scheme designed to give monopolistic control of the port to a private corporation. When he later visited San Francisco, a huge crowd turned out to cheer him. In September 1863 Downey again won the Democratic nomination for governor but lost the general election two months later to Republican Leland Stanford. President Lincoln's leadership and the Civil War had greatly strengthened the hand of the Republicans. Following his defeat Downey returned to southern California and quickly demonstrated an uncanny ability to recognize the needs of the people and the region. He began to subdivide his rancho and sold the parcels as fast as they went on the market to land-hungry farmers from the Midwest. At the same time, in partnership with J. A. Hayward, he established the first bank in Los Angeles. To accommodate the town's growing number of merchants, he built a two-story block-long building at Main and Temple. The Downey Block became southern California's first shopping mall. To meet the rapidly increasing demand for water in the arid southland, he helped organize the Los Angeles City Water Company. Throughout his life Downey was known for his generosity. He contributed heavily to charities and often donated land for good causes. Among his gifts was a tract of land to be used for the proposed southern campus of the University of California. The land was appraised at something equivalent to $25 million in today's dollars.

If Downey, as governor, helped to keep California in the Union so, too, did hundreds of Irishmen in California who enlisted to fight. Most saw service only in the West but those in the "California Battalion" fought in 31 engagements, many of them in the Shenandoah Valley, as part of the 2nd Massachusetts Cavalry. Meanwhile, Irish-born Col. Patrick Edward Connor was leading the 3rd Infantry, California Volunteers. Connor had served with distinction in the Mexican War and then settled in California where he was active in business, politics, and the state militia. When the Civil War erupted he took command of the 3rd Infantry and was ordered to protect travellers, freight wagons, and the U.S. Mail on the overland trail. Early in 1863 he conducted a successful winter campaign in Utah against Bear Hunter and his Shoshones who had taken advantage of the white man's preoccupation with the Civil War to turn his warriors loose on homesteaders and overland migrants. Connor's performance earned him a promotion to brigadier general.

While Connor was fighting in Utah, Maj. John M. O'Neill and Capt. Moses A. McLaughlin were leading the 2nd Cavalry, California Volunteers, against the Paiutes in the Owens Valley. The Paiutes, like the Shoshones, had taken advantage of the Civil War to attack prospectors, cowboys, and isolated homesteaders. They killed some 30 white men, women, and children before the 2nd Cavalry managed to subdue them.

More than a few of the California Irishmen who served in the Civil War returned to San Francisco or other towns in California and became lawmen. The transition seemed natural and carrying a gun and dealing with outlaws appealed to the tough veterans. Nonetheless, one of California's most famous Irish lawmen came not from the ranks of the California Volunteers but from the ranks of the volunteer firemen of Stockton. Born in County Longford in 1838, Tom Cunningham immigrated as a boy to New York and then to California. By 1860 he had his own harness-making shop in Stockton and was serving as a volunteer fireman. In 1865 he was made chief of the fire department and, in the same year, elected to the city council. Six years later he was elected, for the first of many times, Sheriff of San Joaquin County. For the next three decades he was a terror to the outlaws who roamed the San Joaquin Valley and the foothills of the Sierra Nevada. He led manhunts for several of California's most notorious outlaws, including Tiburcio Vasquez, Black Bart, and Bill Miner (the "Grey Fox"). Before his career was over Cunningham had earned the title "Thief Taker of San Joaquin."

While John Downey was helping to develop Los Angeles and Tom Cunningham was tracking outlaws, San Francisco was benefiting from the business enterprise and largess of dozens of Irishmen. James Donahue supplied the city with its first natural gas, laying the original mains in 1854. By 1860 he was servicing some 6,200 customers. In 1851 John Sullivan, Timothy Murphy, and Jasper O'Farrell donated a lot on Market Street for a Catholic orphanage. Sullivan later donated six lots off Larkin Street for St. Mary's College and thousands of dollars to convents and churches and Sacred Heart College. Cornelius D. O'Sullivan, John Sullivan, and Richard Tobin founded the Hibernia Bank in 1859. Daniel J. Murphy developed the largest dry goods firm west of Chicago. The Donahue brothers, James, Michael, and Peter, established the first ironworks and built the first printing press, steam engine, mining machinery, quartz mill, and street railway in the city.

Irish were also prominent early on in law enforcement, law, education, and civic projects. When the San Francisco Police Department was organized in August 1849, Irish-born Malachi Fallon was made the first chief of police. Of the 30 officers who composed the original force 8 were Irish. Shortly after Fallon left office Irish police chiefs Martin Burke and Patrick Crowley followed. The deputy sheriff of San Francisco county in the early 1850s was Thomas Hayes, from County Cork by way of New York. Among the finest attorneys were John T. Doyle, D. C. McGlynn, and John Kelley, Jr. During the 1860s a public night school, particularly useful to Irish immigrants, was developed by a recent arrival from Ireland, Joseph O'Connor. Frank McCoppin, the city's first Irish mayor, was largely responsible for creating what became Golden Gate Park.

Although the Irish were more concentrated in some wards of the city than in others, nothing like a "Little Ireland" developed. The closest to a predominantly Irish area was the neighborhood at the foot of Telegraph Hill and the neighborhood surrounding Old St. Patrick's Church, south of Market Street. In 1870 five of the twelve wards had Irish-born populations that exceeded 20%. Nearly 28% of the residents of the Seventh ward were Irish-born, followed by the First with 23%, the Tenth with 22%, the Ninth with 21%, and the Eleventh with 20%. Only in the Fourth and the Sixth wards did the Irish-born percentage of the population not reach the double digits.

Irish immigration into California was at first predominantly male but this changed rapidly. In 1852 in San Francisco 70% of the Irish-born in the city were male. By 1860 the percentage had dropped dramatically to 53. By 1870 males were only 49% of the Irish-born population and by 1880 only 48%. Obviously, Irish females had begun immigrating to California in large numbers to take advantage of the surplus of Irish males and the seemingly endless opportunities the new state offered.

Most of the females were young and usually quickly found work as domestics in the homes of the upper class. As in the rest of America during the second half of the nineteenth century, Irish servant girls became so common that maids were often called "Bridgets" or "Cathleens." In 1860 69% of employed Irish females in San Francisco worked as domestics. In 1870 it was 71% and in 1880 61%. Irish females also worked in the clothing industry, in nursing, and in restaurants. Some ran their own boarding houses or owned stores.

The Irish generally made steady, if unspectacular, economic progress in California during the nineteenth century. In 1852 in San Francisco 48% of employed Irish males were classified as unskilled laborers. By 1860 the percentage had fallen to 37, by 1870 to 32, and by 1880 to 26. Second-generation Irish did even better. In 1880 more than 25% of employed Irish males worked in white-collar occupations while only 10% worked as unskilled laborers.

The Irish were quick to form a number of benevolent, fraternal, athletic, military, and revolutionary organizations. The 1850s, '60s, and '70s saw the organization of the Hibernian Society, the Sons of the Emerald Isle, St. Mary's Ladies' Society, Irish-American Benevolent Society, Celtic Protective and Benevolent Society, St. Patrick's Mutual Alliance of California, Hibernia Green Baseball Club, McMahon Grenadier Guard, Montgomery Guard, Shields Guard, Wolfe Tone Guard, Meagher Guard, Emmet Life Guard, Hibernian Rifles, Sarsfield Rifle Guards, California Rifles, the Legion of St. Patrick, and the Knights of the Red Branch.

During the 1850s Fenians in San Francisco organized three chapters of the Irish Republican Brotherhood: Thomas F. Burke, Erin's Hope, and Emmet. San Francisco was clearly a stronghold of Fenian sentiment, something that the worried British consul regularly reported to London. Irish revolutionaries such as Terence MacManus, Patrick O'Donohue, and John Mitchell arrived at different times during the early 1850s and were feted at banquets attended by the governor of California, the mayor of San Francisco, and dozens of prominent politicians and businessmen.

Following the death of Terence MacManus in late 1860 in San Francisco, local Fenians organized the journey to take his body across the country to New York City. Of the six American Fenian representatives at the funeral of MacManus in Ireland two were from San Francisco, Col. M. D. Smith and Jeremiah Kavanagh. Before the demise of the Fenian movement in America, following the failure of the second invasion of Canada in May 1870, Irish Fenians in the San Francisco Bay area regularly staged rallies and held picnics attended by 10,000 or more people. California Fenians raised thousands of dollars each year for Ireland's cause and forwarded the money to American Fenian headquarters in New York.

The longest lived and most successful of the Irish organizations in San Francisco was the Ancient Order of Hibernians, founded in 1869. By 1880 the Hibernians had ten divisions and several thousand members. Their principal objectives were benevolent and social and they often took the lead in providing for widows, arranging funerals, and organizing celebrations on the Fourth of July and on St. Patrick's Day. They steered clear of radical labor organizations and Irish revolutionary activity.

Orangemen among the Irish in San Francisco were generally inconspicuous, although they eventually did form two lodges of the Loyal Orange Institution of the United States: California True

Blues, No. 118, and Harmony, No. 127. Their combined membership does not seem to have exceeded 100 and they took no part in the celebrations, picnics, and parades organized by other Irish societies. Being Irish in San Francisco was, for all intents and purposes, synonymous with being Catholic.

St. Patrick's Day was celebrated with a parade and other activities every year beginning in 1851. By the early 1870s the parade stretched for two miles with 6,000 people in the procession and 50,000 watching. It rivalled the Fourth of July as an event. With more than a half-dozen Irish military organizations regularly participating, the parade always had an air of militant Irish nationalism about it. Speeches and toasts denouncing the British and calling for Irish freedom were the order of the day. At night halls throughout the city were filled with Irish who "enjoy themselves by dancing reels and jigs . . . to their favourite tunes on the Bagpipes."

The Irish played the predominant role in organizing unions in San Francisco and in the Democratic party. They also played the predominant role in the Workingmen's party, the party of the unskilled and semi-skilled laborer, which rose to importance during the late 1870s under the leadership of Irish-born Denis Kearney. The party often held its meetings in the Irish-American Hall or in the Hibernia Hall. Ironically, Kearney began to fear that the party was becoming too identified with the Irish and attempted to put forth slates of candidates that were not overwhelmingly Irish. Thirty Workingmen, about one-third of the delegates, were elected to the state constitutional convention in 1878. Of those 30 only six had been born in Ireland and only another three were of Irish descent. Nonetheless, in the San Francisco city and county elections of 1879 most of the Workingmen's candidates were Irish and three of them won office: Thomas Desmond, Sheriff; John P. Dunn, Auditor; and J. D. Connelly, Justice of the Peace.

If most of the Irish who supported the Workingmen's Party fought for survival day by day, there were California Irishmen who had, by the time the party came to power, become among the richest men not only in California but in the nation. Four such men were John W. Mackay, James G. Fair, William S. O'Brien, and James C. Flood. Known as the Silver Kings, they were second in wealth and power in California only to the Big Four, Leland Stanford, Collis Huntington, Mark Hopkins, and Charles Crocker, of the Southern Pacific Railroad.

Mackay, Fair, and O'Brien were born in Ireland and Flood was born in New York shortly after his Irish immigrant parents arrived in the United States. Each had some success in the California diggings during the early 1850s but none struck it really big until they formed a partnership in 1869 and developed the Consolidated Virginia mine of the Comstock Lode beginning in 1872. One of the shafts they sunk hit the Comstock Lode dead center—the "Big Bonanza" as it was termed by Dan DeQuille of the *Territorial Enterprise*. From 1873 through 1882 the Consolidated Virginia yielded some $65 million in gold and silver and paid almost $43 million in dividends, equivalent to perhaps $2 billion in 1998 dollars.

California benefited greatly from all the activity on the Comstock. The Silver Kings themselves invested heavily in California enterprises. William O'Brien donated large sums to charities and supported all his relatives, especially the McDonough and Coleman families of San Francisco. He still managed to leave a personal estate valued at $12 million (some $500 million today) at his death in 1879.

James Flood erected numerous buildings in San Francisco, funded dozens of business ventures, and established the Nevada Bank which later merged with Wells Fargo. He contributed heavily to charities and orphan asylums and developed his own 35-acre country estate at Menlo Park. He built a great brownstone mansion on Nob Hill which survived the great earthquake and fire of 1906 and is today the home of the exclusive Pacific Union Club. Later in life, Flood and his son, James Leary Flood, built two mansions in Pacific Heights. Today one of the mansions houses the Hamlin School and the other the Convent of the Sacred Heart High School.

James Fair served a term as a United States Senator from Nevada, developed properties by the dozen in San Francisco, established two banks, Mutual Savings and Merchants' Trust, and built a railroad. He was San Francisco's largest taxpayer. By the time of his death he had accumulated an estate valued at some $40 million. His daughter Theresa used some of her inheritance to build Nob Hill's first hotel, which she named the Fairmont in honor of her father.

John Mackay created the Commercial Cable and Postal Telegraph Company, laid cables across the Atlantic, broke the Western Union monopoly, and made more millions. He endowed the school of mining (named in his honor) at the University of Nevada, Reno, and gave away millions to charities and millions more to friends in the form of loans that he never bothered to collect. An avid athlete himself, Mackay helped sponsor a young Irish-American from San Francisco in boxing. The young lad, James J. Corbett, defeated John L. Sullivan in 1892 to become heavyweight champion of the world. Mackay, who was reared in a one-room cottage in Ireland that the family shared with pigs and cows during winter storms, left an estate of $50 million at the time of his death in 1902.

That the Silver Kings were Irish was not surprising. Nearly every mining camp of the West had large numbers of Irish. Bodie, a small portion of which is preserved as a state park, was typical of camps in California. The census of 1880 recorded nearly 5,400 people in the town. Some 850 or 16% of them were Irish-born. Including American, Canadian, and Australian-born Irish means that well more than 20% of the population was Irish. Lawmen in Bodie had the surnames O'Malley, Kirgan, Brodigan, Markey, Monahan, Flynn, and Phelan. Similarly the town's most prominent attorneys carried the family names Ryan, McQuaid, and Reddy. Gunfighters included McTigue, O'Hara, Carroll, Deegan, Dugan, McCormick, O'Farrell, Keogh, McGrath, Bannon, Ryan, and Shea. The group of five prospectors who discovered Bodie's gold included Garrity, Brodigan, and Doyle. Restaurants and saloons were owned by Callahan, McMahan, Gallagher, McDermott, Fahey, Buckley, Scully, Hogan, and Shannon. Nixon and Shaughnessy served as presidents of the miners' union. McTarnahan carried the town's mail. McDonald was president of the local chapter of the Land League of Ireland. Bodie's company of National Guardsmen looked suspiciously like a front for the Fenians. The officers included Callahan, Kelly, and McPhee; the noncommissioned officers, Fahey, Kearney, Markey, and O'Brien; and the privates, Boyle, Carroll, Costello, Finnegan, Lyons, McGrath, Mullin, O'Donnell, O'Keeffe, Phelan, Shea, Thornton, Tobin, and Whelan.

Most of the Irish in the mining camps arrived in California by ship and first spent time in San Francisco before proceeding to the mines. When they struck it rich or when the mines failed, it was to San Francisco they returned. By the 1880s San Francisco was a very Irish city and Christopher "Blind Boss" Buckley and his machine ran the town. The son of Irish immigrants, Buckley arrived in San Francisco from New York with his family in 1862 as a 17-year-old. His father never made much money and died relatively young. Said Buckley: "My father left me nothing but the state of California to make a living in." When Buckley died in 1922 his estate was valued at almost $1 million. Chris Buckley began his working career as a conductor on one of the city's horse-drawn railway lines but soon was tending bar at the Snug Saloon. By the early 1870s he was operating his own saloon and had become a force in Democratic party politics. Then, suddenly, he went blind. Undeterred by the misfortune Buckley continued to rise in politics. He compensated for his lack of sight with a phenomenal memory. He never forgot anything read to him or said to him. He also had organizational skills second to none. Although he himself never held or sought elective office, from 1882 through 1891 he controlled the city. Some have argued that he introduced big city corruption to San Francisco. Actually, corruption had already become rife and Buckley simply organized it to his advantage like no one else had done before him.

If Buckley was typical of the big city boss, then James D. Phelan was typical of the big city reformer. Phelan was born in San Francisco in 1861, the son of an Irish immigrant who was well on his way to wealth and prominence in business. Irish, Catholic, and Democrat though he was, Phelan, wealthy and well educated, lived the life of the patrician in San Francisco. He often found himself at odds with the Irish working class of the city. He was instrumental in bringing about the downfall of Blind Boss Buckley and later aided the prosecution in the graft trials of Abe Ruef and Eugene Schmitz, acts which did not endear him to many blue-collar Irish. Nonetheless, Phelan served as mayor of San Francisco, 1897–1901, and then as United States Senator, 1914–1920.

Southern California lagged well behind the mining camps and the San Francisco Bay area in numbers of Irish. During the 1870s and 80s thousands of Midwesterners poured into the greater Los Angeles region, until the area was populated largely with Protestant, old-stock Americans. By the 1890s, Long Beach, for example, had become something of a western extension of Iowa. Meanwhile, San Francisco remained populated mainly with recent immigrants or their children and stayed, because of the large Irish and German populations, mostly Catholic. By 1900 San Francisco had a population of some 343,000 people and 95,000 of them were of Irish descent or birth.

Church attendance reveals the difference between San Francisco and Los Angeles. In 1900, of San Francisco's 143,000 churchgoers 116,000 of them were Catholics while only 22,000 were Protestant. By contrast in Los Angeles Protestant churchgoers outnumbered Catholics 70,000 to 52,000.

Despite their significantly smaller numbers in southern California, Irishmen were contributing mightily to the development of the region. Probably the three most important factors in the growth of Los Angeles were the building of a harbor at San Pedro, the discovery of oil, and the delivery of water to the city. By 1890 the population of the greater Los Angeles area was pushing 100,000, yet the region lacked a deep-water harbor. The powerful Southern Pacific Railroad Company wanted the federal government to develop such a harbor in Santa Monica Bay at the mouth of Potrero canyon in what is now Pacific Palisades. It was a poor choice for the harbor but the Southern Pacific controlled all the railroad lines to the site and stood to make enormous

profits from the monopoly. The general public, on the other hand, demanded a "free harbor" be built at San Pedro. The battle began in Congress, pitting Collis P. Huntington of the railroad against Senator Stephen Mallory White.

White was born in San Francisco in 1853, the son of Irish immigrants who had met and married in Savannah, Georgia, in 1848 before sailing around the Horn in the Gold Rush to California. White worked his way through Jesuit College of St. Ignatius in San Francisco before attending law school at Santa Clara University. After admission to the bar he moved to Los Angeles and opened a law office. His practice got a big boost when he was asked by the St. Patrick's Day Committee of Los Angeles to deliver an oration on March 17th in the old plaza downtown. His extraordinary oratorical and legal talent won him acclaim almost immediately. Said a contemporary: "He mastered all branches of the law. He could jump from a bitter contest over a complicated probate matter to the defense or prosecution of a desperate criminal, or into a litigation involving property rights or damages for personal injuries inflicted. Almost without sleep, and apparently without preparation, he could leave a case submitted to the court or to a jury and begin the trial of some other case in some other court, equally difficult and intricate, and upon some subject entirely foreign to the case just finished by him."

White was elected a city councilman and then district attorney before winning a U.S. Senate seat. Nonetheless, the fight for the harbor would be White's greatest legal and political effort and would consume six years of his life. His adversary, Collis P. Huntington, was the lobbyist of the Big Four and one of the wealthiest and most powerful men in America. Huntington's influence in Congress was near supreme. During the harbor battle the New York *World* asked: "Is this a government by the people, for the people, or a government by Mr. Huntington, for Mr. Huntington." White was an indefatigable fighter, a persuasive orator, and a master of political strategy. For every move Huntington made, White made a counter move and then some. Finally, in 1896, White seemed to have victory in his grasp when a board of engineers, which had been created in a bill introduced by White, reported that it unequivocally favored San Pedro as the harbor site. This should have ended the battle but Huntington was not quite ready to call it quits. He had the Secretary of War, a personal friend of his, delay the official release of the board's report to provide time for the introduction of a bill in Congress that would nullify the report. Once again White rose to the occasion and blocked Huntington's move. The battle was over this time. In 1899 construction of the breakwater at San Pedro was finally begun. Huntington died a year later, and White the year after Huntington. Friends of White claimed that the long battle gave him little time for sleep or rest and was ultimately responsible for his death. A statue of White was erected in front of Los Angeles City Hall, making White the only resident of the city to be so honored.

While White was fighting for a harbor at San Pedro, Edward Doheny was drilling for oil. Born of Irish parents in Wisconsin, Doheny had just begun working as a government surveyor when gold was discovered in the Black Hills. The pull of the goldfields proved irresistible and in 1876 the 20-year-old Doheny headed for Deadwood. When the yields began to ebb, he was off to new strikes in Arizona. At Tombstone he worked awhile for Irish-born Nellie Cashman, who was rapidly becoming a legend in the West as the "Saint of the Sourdoughs" and the "Frontier Angel."

Other strikes took Doheny to New Mexico, then Mexico, and finally the Mojave Desert of California.

In 1892 Doheny arrived in Los Angeles with a wealth of experience and not a lot of money. One day he happened to notice tar clinging to the wheels of a passing carriage. He tracked the tar to a small oil seepage just north of present-day MacArthur Park. Together with an old friend from his mining days, he took out a lease on the property and, with pick and shovel, began to dig. At fifty feet he hit gas and was almost asphyxiated. He came back with a drilling rig, went another 600-feet deeper, and hit a gusher. Oil mania suddenly gripped Los Angeles. During the next five years more than 2,000 wells were drilled, many of them Doheny's. Doheny expanded his operations throughout the state and to Tampico, Mexico. It seemed that wherever he drilled, he struck oil. By the early 1900s the former prospector had become a multimillionaire. He lived until 1935, known for his business acumen and philanthropy and the controversy surrounding his lease of the Elk Hills oil reserves.

If Stephen White provided Los Angeles with a harbor, and Edward Doheny oil, then it was William Mulholland who provided the city with water. By 1904 Los Angeles was running out of water. The Los Angeles River, the city's principal source of water, had always been an unreliable source at best. Now as the city grew by thousands every year the river was being drained dry. William Mulholland was born in Belfast in 1855 but reared in Dublin. At the age of 15 he shipped before the mast and spent the next four years sailing the high seas. In 1874 he landed in New York and began a two-year odyssey which took him through the northeast and the upper midwest. Then, after reading a book on California while working in his uncle's store in Pittsburgh, he headed for the Golden State. He worked his way from New York to Colon to Panama City to Acapulco and, finally, to San Francisco. From the bustling city by the bay he made his way on horseback southward. He was astounded by California's beauty and the mildness of the climate. When he reached the willow-lined Los Angeles River and gazed upon seemingly endless vineyards and citrus groves, he knew he had found a new home.

Mulholland began his long career in Los Angeles by digging wells in Compton. Then, in 1878, he went to work for the Los Angeles City Water Company. On his first day he was put to work digging a ditch. As Mulholland threw large shovelsful of dirt out of the ditch the president of the company, William Perry, happened by and wondered who was this powerfully built and energetic new worker. When Perry called to Mulholland in a "rather peremptory way," asking him his name and what he was doing, the big Irishman fired back: "It's none of your damned business." As Perry rode off other workers ran to Mulholland and told him he had been speaking to the company president. Mulholland gasped, threw down his shovel, and rode to company office in an effort to draw his pay and quit before be could be fired. Too late. Perry had got there first. However, instead of firing the tough new worker, Perry made Mulholland the foreman of a crew.

Mulholland rose rapidly through the ranks of the company and, when it was absorbed by the City of Los Angeles, he became Chief City Engineer. As such, he was responsible for designing and building the Los Angeles Aqueduct. It was the nation's first long-distance aqueduct and an engineering marvel. More surprising, though, Mulholland built the aqueduct in less time and for less money than had been estimated—certainly a rare achievement for a government project.

"The Chief," as Mulholland became known, was largely self-educated. Nonetheless, he was said to be well informed on a great variety of subjects and his memory was described as nothing less than phenomenal. He was also noted for his "keen Irish wit." One day a cross-examining attorney sought to embarrass him when he was testifying as an expert witness in court: "Will you please tell us what preparation you had when you started out in the world on your own account?" the attorney demanded. With "an Irish twinkle" in his eyes Mulholland responded: "I learned the Ten Commandments and had me mother's blessing."

If Irishmen were responsible for building up Los Angeles, they also seem to have been responsible for blowing up a portion of it. While San Francisco was heavily unionized, Los Angeles was very much non-union. Leading the opposition to the formation of unions in the city was the publisher of the *Los Angeles Times,* Harrison Gray Otis, the descendant of an old New England family. Otis argued that not only did a worker have the right not to join a union but that an employer had the right to fire him if he did. Otis formed an association of employers that was responsible for breaking one union after another, beginning with the printer's union in 1890. Strikes and boycotts were short lived and small scale until June 1, 1910, when 1,500 metal workers, with aid from San Francisco unions, struck for an 8-hour workday.

As usual Otis used his newspaper to rail against the strikers and the union, saying that by striking in Los Angeles they were attacking "the cradle of industrial freedom." Labor leaders throughout the country responded by attacking the *Los Angeles Times* as the nation's foremost opponent of the workingman. Otis, a general in the California National Guard, drove about town with a small cannon mounted on his car. Month after month the strike continued. Then, a little after 1 a.m. on the morning of October 1, 1910, an explosion rocked the *Times* building. The building was severely damaged and 20 men were killed. The *Times* called it the "crime of the century." There was some evidence that a leaking gas main had caused the explosion, something Otis had been cited for on several occasions.

However, William J. Burns, a private detective, arrested Ortie McManigal after several months of investigation. McManigal, under duress, confessed to being a dynamiter for the Iron Workers union in its labor struggles with big business. The union secretary John J. McNamara and his brother, James B. McNamara, were arrested for complicity in the *Times* explosion. Labor leaders thought the McNamara brothers were being framed by an employer conspiracy and retained Clarence Darrow for their defense. The McNamaras entered pleas of not guilty. The trial began in October 1911. Suddenly, on December 1, 1911, the McNamaras stunned the nation by changing their pleas to guilty. It seems that a deal was arranged in which the prosecution agreed to drop pursuit of others in the union should the McNamaras plead guilty. James received a life sentence and John 15 years. McManigal was freed because he had turned state's evidence.

The Irish gained more positive national attention by helping to develop Los Angeles's leading business—the motion picture industry. Winfield R. Sheehan was general manager of Fox Studios from 1916 to 1935. Eddie Mannix was general manager of MGM from 1925 to 1955. Joseph P. Kennedy, the father of President John F. Kennedy, was responsible for organizing RKO. Max Sennett founded Keystone production company and produced, among other serials, the "Keystone Kops." After acting in several silent movies Hal Roach organized his own film company and began producing comedies, including the best of Laurel and Hardy and the original "Our Gang" serial.

Willis O'Brien was the best of the special effects men of the early era, winning lasting acclaim for *King Kong* in 1933. Cedric Gibbons, the son of Irish immigrants, won 11 Academy Awards for art direction, a record unequalled in any category, and was responsible for designing the "Oscar." John Meehan won three Oscars for art direction. C. Gardner Sullivan was a prolific screenwriter during the 1920s and '30s and Dublin-born Rex Ingram was the director who made Rudolph Valentino a star with *The Four Horsemen of the Apocalypse* in 1921. Irish-born William Desmond Taylor was another prominent director of the early era. His unsolved murder in 1922 remains one of Hollywood's greatest mysteries. Mickey Neilan, whose drinking cut short a promising career, and Jack Dillon were two actors who became successful directors. John Ford and Raoul Walsh got their start in the silent era but would achieve their greatest success in the '30s, '40s, and '50s. The outstanding Irish director of the 1920s and early '30s was Robert J. Flaherty, best remembered for *Nanook of the North* (1922) and *Man of Aran* (1934).

The 1920s saw several Irishmen rise to stardom. Thomas Meighan and Charles Farrell were popular leading men. Meighan is best known for *Irish Luck* (1925) and Farrell for *Seventh Heaven* (1927). George O'Brien, the son of an Irish-born San Francisco police chief, gained overnight success when John Ford cast him in the lead in the Western, *Iron Horse* (1924). O'Brien continued working in Ford Westerns until the early 1950s.

However, Timothy John Fitzgerald McCoy, known simply as Tim McCoy, became the Western hero of the 1920s and '30s. The son of Irish immigrants from the counties Kilkenny and Limerick, he inherited a wild and woolly spirit from his father who served in the Civil War and then joined the Fenian invasion of Canada. Following his father's example, Tim McCoy served in World War I and then worked as an Indian agent in Wyoming. He first worked in Hollywood as a technical advisor for *The Covered Wagon* (1923) before going on to play the lead in dozens of Westerns.

Appearing in supporting roles were such men as Dublin-born William Desmond, "Skeets" Gallagher, Cork-born Creighton Hale (Patrick Fitzgerald), Jack Mulhall, Charlie Murray, and J. Farrell MacDonald.

Irish women rose to stardom as well. May McAvoy played the romantic lead in *Ben Hur* (1926), *The Jazz Singer* (1927), and *Irish Hearts* (1927). When she was only 20 years old, Dolores Costello played opposite John Barrymore in *The Sea Beast* (1926). She went on to marry Barrymore, star in several other films, and retire in 1931 to raise a family. Colleen Moore (Kathleen Morrison) starred in a half-dozen movies during the '20s, several of them with Irish themes. Although it was not widely known, Mary Pickford, "America's Sweetheart," was half Irish. Her mother's people were immigrants from County Kerry. Alice Brady began her career as the romantic lead in silent movies but her greatest success came later on as the Irish mother in *In Old Chicago* (1937), for which she won an Oscar, and as the mother in *Young Mr. Lincoln* (1939).

The 1930s and '40s brought dozens of new Irish stars to Hollywood. New York-born James Cagney, the son of an alcoholic Irish saloon keeper and an Irish-Norwegian mother, led the way. Moving to Hollywood in 1930, the taut and muscular, redhaired former dancer gained national fame the very next year as Tom Powers in *The Public Enemy*. Although much of his early work was playing the role of the tough, streetwise kid who becomes a gangster, such movies as *Yankee Doodle Dandy* (1942), which won him an Oscar, *Mr. Roberts* (1955), and *Man of a Thousand Faces* (1957) demonstrate his range as an actor.

Close on Cagney's heels came Spencer Tracy and Pat O'Brien. Ironically, they both took roles away from Cagney because their screen personas were wholesome. The producers of *Boys Town* (1938) wanted Cagney to play Father Flanagan but authorities at Boys Town were upset because Cagney was known for his roles as the antihero and gangster. Tracy, who played a priest in *San Francisco* (1936), got the part. In real life Cagney was a devoted family man and a very light drinker, while Tracy was an adulterer and an alcoholic. Likewise, Pat O'Brien, who often played priests and was a heavy drinker and carouser off the screen, got the lead in *Knute Rockne, All American* (1940) when Rockne's widow objected to Cagney, the choice of Warner Bros. studio executives.

John Ford called Spencer Tracy "a great actor—the greatest, I guess, in my time." Tracy won two Oscars, for *Boys Town* and for *Captains Courageous* (1937) and was nominated on seven other occasions, the last, posthumously, for *Guess Who's Coming to Dinner?* (1967). While Pat O'Brien did not achieve the critical acclaim of Tracy or the longevity, he did star in dozens of major films, including two that he made with Cagney, *Angels with Dirty Faces* (1938) in which he played Father Jerry Connolly and *The Fighting 69th* (1940) where he appeared as Father Francis Duffy. O'Brien played priests again in *Fighting Father Dunne* (1948) and *The Fireball* (1950).

Also achieving some of his fame playing the role of a priest was Bing Crosby. He won the Oscar for his role as Father Chuck O'Malley in *Going My Way* (1944) and repeated the character in *The Bells of St. Mary's* (1945) and in *One for Me* (1959). First gaining popularity for his mellifluous, lyrical voice, the Washington state-born Crosby made an easy transition to films while continuing to record hit songs. His handsome countenance and lean physique were naturals for the screen. He appeared in a wide variety of roles, including the clever, but lovable, manipulator of Bob Hope in the "road" films.

Errol Flynn was anything but a priest. The role of the handsome and dashing rogue was a natural for the Tasmanian-born son of an Irish zoology professor. Flynn was an instant box-office success with such movies as *Captain Blood* (1935), *The Charge of the Light Brigade* (1936), *The Prince and the Pauper* (1937), *The Adventures of Robin Hood* (1938), *The Dawn Patrol* (1938), *Dodge City* (1939), *The Sea Hawk* (1940), *Virginia City* (1940), *Santa Fe Trail* (1940), *They Died with Their Boots On* (1942), *Gentleman Jim* (1942) and a dozen others before alcoholism and allegations of sexual escapades with teenage girls damaged his career. Flynn was so well known for his sexual conquests of women that "In like Flynn" became an American colloquialism.

Competing with Errol Flynn as a matinee idol was Tyrone Power. Power's father had appeared in some 40 silent films and his grandfather was a famous Irish actor in the theater. Power followed in their footsteps, starring in such films as *Second Honeymoon* (1937), *In Old Chicago* (1937), *Alexander's Ragtime Band* (1938), *Marie Antoinette* (1938), *Jesse James* (1939), *The Rains Came* (1939), *Johnny Apollo* (1940), *Blood and Sand* (1941), *The Black Swan* (1942), and *Crash Dive* (1943). After serving as a pilot in the Marine Corps—Power was one of the first Marine aviators to land on Iwo Jima—he returned to Hollywood to do some of his finest work, including the classic, *Witness for the Prosecution* (1957).

Something less of a heartthrob for the women but clearly much more of an action hero for the men was John Wayne. Although it is generally known that his real name was Marion Morrison, few seem to know that John Wayne was of mostly Irish descent. His paternal great-great grandfather was Robert Morrison who fled to the United States from County Antrim after taking part in the Rising of '98 as a member of the United Irishmen. His maternal grandfather was Irish immigrant Robert Emmet Brown, named for the revolutionary hero of 1803 himself. His mother, Mary ("Molly") Brown, was said to have been the typically strong, independently minded Irishwoman. Wayne named his sons Michael and Patrick and he christened his yacht "The Wild Goose." He made some 40 "B" Westerns before John Ford introduced him to the big time as the Ringo Kid in *Stagecoach* (1939). Wayne's characters often had Irish names—Brannigan, McNally, Cahill, Dooley, McLain, Thornton, Breen, Donovan, Ryan, Madden, Hayden, Shannon, and Tobin were some of them. Unquestionably one of his best performances was as Sean Thornton in John Ford's Academy Award winning *The Quiet Man* (1952). Including his "B" Westerns, Wayne appeared in more than 130 films in a career that spanned nearly 50 years.

Irishmen who became fixtures in Hollywood during the '30s, '40s, and '50s as supporting actors and occasionally as leading men included Irish-born George Brent (George Brendan Nolan), Thomas Mitchell, Walter Brennan (the first actor to win three Oscars), Alan Hale (McKahan), J. Carrol Naish, Walter Connolly, Irish-born brothers Barry Fitzgerald and Arthur Shields, Sean McClory, Brian Donlevy, Frank McHugh, James Gleason, Tom Dugan, Ed Gargan, James Burke, Dick Foran, Harry Shannon, Edgar Kennedy, Robert Emmet O'Connor, Regis Toomey, Ed Brophy, Allen Jenkins (McConegal), Barton MacLane, Dennis O'Keefe, J. M. Kerrigan, Ronald Reagan, Robert Ryan, Arthur Kennedy, Stephan McNally, Michael O'Shea, James Dunn, William Frawley, Pat Flaherty, Jack Haley, Horace MacMahon, Broderick Crawford (Pendergast), Jack MacGowran, Edmond O'Brien, and brothers Scott Brady (Gerald Tierney) and Lawrence Tierney.

Probably no Irish-born actress made a bigger name for herself in Hollywood than Maureen O'Hara (FitzSimons). Born in Dublin and discovered by Charles Laughton, she began to attract

Film stars Martha O'Driscoll and Errol Flynn entertain the troops during World War II.

attention in her third film, *The Hunchback of Notre Dame* (1939). It was in her eighth film, *How Green Was My Valley* (1941), that she first worked with John Ford, a relationship that would continue for decades. Ford often cast her opposite John Wayne. Standing a bit over 5'8" and having been a top athlete as a girl in Ireland, the strong and well-proportioned O'Hara was a female match for the 6'4" Wayne and Ford's other big men such as Victor McLaglen and Ward Bond. Unlike many Irish actresses, O'Hara was frequently cast in the role of the Irish colleen, as in Ford's cavalry Western, *Rio Grande* (1950), and in his Oscar-winning *The Quiet Man* (1952). O'Hara played the female lead in more than 50 motion pictures before retiring in 1973. She then came out of retirement to make appearances in movies in 1991 and 1995.

Also making names for themselves as female leads were Irish-Americans Gene Tierney, Barbara Stanwyck (four nominations for Best Actress), Ann Sheridan, Irene Dunne (five nominations for Best Actress), Dorothy McGuire, and Rosalind Russell (four nominations for Best Actress), and County Roscommon-born Maureen O'Sullivan who first gained fame playing Johnny Weissmuller's beautiful and scantily-clad Jane in a half-dozen Tarzan movies during the 1930s and early '40s.

Supporting actresses included County Down-born Greer Garson, Alice Brady, Aline MacMahon, Barbara O'Neil, Rita Johnson (McSean), Gail Patrick (Margaret Fitzpatrick), Ruth Hussey (O'Rourke), Mary Boland, Billie Burke, Irene Ryan, Una O'Connor (Agnes McGlade), Glenda Farrell, Patsy Kelly, Helen Broderick, Ruth Donnelly, Dorothy McNulty, Martha Raye (Margaret O'Reed), Margaret O'Brien, Ann Blyth, Maggie Hayes, Martha O'Driscoll, Nancy Kelly, Sally Forrest (Feeney), Janet Blair (Lafferty), Peggy Ryan, Sheila Ryan (McLaughlin), and Barbara Hale.

No Irish actress was more beautiful nor reached greater heights in a shorter time than Grace Kelly, the granddaughter of Irish immigrants. Her father, John Brendan Kelly, was a handsome and muscular rowing champion who also developed a highly profitable construction business in Philadelphia. He always reminded Grace that he and his father began their working careers as bricklayers. In a film career that spanned only six years Grace Kelly starred in eleven major motion pictures, won an Oscar, and became director Alfred Hitchcock's favorite leading lady. Several of her movies remain classics, including *High Noon* (1952), *Rear Window* (1954), *Dial M for Murder* (1954), *The Bridges at Toko-Ri* (1954), and *To Catch a Thief* (1955). Her leading men included Gary Cooper, James Stewart, Ray Milland, William Holden, and Cary Grant, a virtual who's who of male actors of the era.

Another Kelly who found stardom in Hollywood was Gene Kelly. Born Eugene Curran Kelly to Irish parents in Pittsburgh in 1912, he was a star athlete in four sports—football, baseball, hockey, and gymnastics—while growing up. After graduating from college and then dropping out of law school, he opened a dance studio. By the 1930s he was appearing on the Broadway stage. In 1942 he signed with MGM and moved to Hollywood to make his screen debut opposite Judy Garland in *For Me and My Gal* (1942). During the next three years he made seven more films and earned an Oscar nomination for his role as a sailor in *Anchors Aweigh* (1945). Kelly went on to star in two dozen more films, including *An American in Paris* (1951), for which he won an Oscar, *Singin' in the Rain* (1952), and *Brigadoon* (1954). As a dancer Kelly was unrivalled during his era. More athletic than Fred Astair, Kelly brought an explosive energy and a youthful vitality to the screen despite the fact that he did his greatest on-screen dancing when he was in his late 30s and early 40s.

Occasionally working with Kelly and stars in their own right were two other Irish song and dance men, Dan Dailey and Donald O'Connor. Dailey starred in such films as *Give My Regards to Broadway* (1948) and *There's No Business Like Show Business* (1954) while O'Connor was featured in, among others, *The Merry Monahans* (1944) and *Patrick the Great* (1945). The handsome and popular George Murphy, later to be a U.S. Senator from California, starred in several musicals, including *Little Nellie Kelly* (1940) with Judy Garland, before turning to dramatic roles.

The post–World War II era saw the rise of a new generation of Irish in film and in a new medium, television. The actors included America's most decorated war hero, Audie Murphy, who starred in the story of his own war exploits, *To Hell and Back* (1955), Belfast-born Stephen Boyd (Billy Millar), Richard Egan, Charles McGraw, Mickey Shaughnessy, Bobby Driscoll, Arthur O'Connell, Kevin McCarthy, Dan O'Herlihy, and Richard Kiley and the actresses Mercedes McCambridge, Dorothy Malone (Maloney), Kathleen Crowley, Pat Crowley, Maggie McNamara, and Mary Murphy. Towering over the others both figuratively and literally were the half-Irish Robert Mitchum and the half-Irish Gregory Peck.

Big Bob Mitchum, the son of an Irish railroad worker and a Norwegian mother, was born in Bridgeport, Connecticut, in 1917. His father died in a railroad accident when Mitchum was a child. An adventurous youth, Mitchum was on the road by the time he was 16 years old. He worked at a variety of odd jobs, served a short sentence on a Georgia chain-gang for vagrancy, and climbed into the ring as a prizefighter before settling in Los Angeles and going to work for Lockheed Aircraft. In 1942 he joined a local theater group and the next year appeared in the first of several Hopalong Cassidy Westerns as well as a dozen other movies, including *Doughboys in Ireland*. The ruggedly handsome and powerfully built young actor hit it big in 1945 when he was nominated for best supporting actor for his portrayal of Lt. Walker in *The Story of G.I. Joe*. After spending the rest of 1945 in the army, he returned to filmmaking and became something of a cult figure as a "tough guy" detective in the film noir genre. A 60-day jail sentence for marijuana possession in 1948 only seemed to enhance his image as Hollywood's "bad boy." Nonetheless, some of Mitchum's best work came in movies of a different nature, *The Enemy Below* (1957) and *Heaven Knows, Mr. Allison* (1957), two classic war movies, and *The Sundowners* (1960), the story of an Irish-Australian sheep-shearer, Paddy Carmody. Altogether he appeared in more than 80 films. He was not impressed with his own acting skills, although others were: Charles Laughton, after directing him in *The Night of the Hunter* (1955), called him "one of the greatest actors in the world."

Tall, lean Gregory Peck was born in 1916 at La Jolla, California. His father was partly reared in County Kerry before immigrating to the U.S. and his grandmother, Katherine Ashe of Dingle, was related to Irish patriot Thomas Ashe who died in prison on a hunger strike. Peck grew to maturity hearing stories of his father's childhood and family. At the University of California, Berkeley, Peck was a member of the varsity crew before turning to acting full time. During the late 1940s and early 1950s he received four Oscar nominations and then won as Best Actor for his role in *To Kill a Mocking Bird* (1962). Several of his movies remain classics including, *Twelve O'Clock High* (1949), *The Gunfighter* (1950), *Captain Horatio Hornblower* (1951), *The Snows of Kilimanjaro* (1952), *Roman Holiday* (1953), *The Man in the Grey Flannel Suit* (1956), *The Big Country* (1958), *On the Beach* (1959), and *The Guns of Navarone* (1961).

Standing even taller than Gregory Peck, although never achieving the same level of success, was Chuck Connors. Born Kevin Joseph Connors in Brooklyn in 1921, he played professional basketball and baseball before turning to acting in 1953. Handsome, muscular, and lantern-jawed, Connors stood over 6'5" tall. He appeared in more than a dozen movies, including one of the best Westerns ever made, *The Big Country* (1958). His real success, however, came as Lucas McCain in the television series, *The Rifleman*, which ran from 1958–1963.

Also gaining fame on television and filling the screen in another way was Jackie Gleason. The "Great One" weighed nearly 300 pounds at one point. Born Herbert John Gleason to Herb and Mae Kelly Gleason in 1916 in Brooklyn, New York, Gleason signed with Warner Bros. in 1941 and appeared in several movies. However, he hit the big time with his television series *The Honeymooners,* beginning in 1951, followed by the *Jackie Gleason Show*. Gleason later made a number of memorable films, including *The Hustler* (1961) and *Requiem for a Heavyweight* (1962). He also teamed with Bert Reynolds to make *Smokey and the Bandit* (1977) and its two sequels. Gleason's sidekick in *The Honeymooners*, Art Carney, also successfully moved between the two mediums.

Ryan O'Neal, a local California boy who was christened Patrick Ryan, got his start in television and went on to star in several films, including *Love Story* (1970) with Ali (Alice) MacGraw, of a New York Irish family, and Barbra Streisand in the comedy *What's Up, Doc?* (1972). His work in *Love Story* brought him a nomination for Best Actor. Perhaps it is surprising that O'Neal should have gained fame for such a role. As a teenager in his home town of Pacific Palisades "Pat" (as he was called in those days) was known for his hot temper and his lightning-fast fists, both in the ring and on the streets. However, his parents, Charles ("Blackie") and Patricia (nee Callaghan) O'Neal, had both been actors and they guided him into their own profession.

Irish-born Peter O'Toole and Richard Harris came to Hollywood after working in the theater in London. After a few forgettable films, O'Toole had a streak of brilliant successes in *Lawrence of Arabia* (1962), *Becket* (1964), *What's New Pussycat?* (1965), *Lord Jim* (1965), *How to Steal a Million* (1966), *Night of the Generals* (1967), and *The Lion in Winter* (1968). Altogether he has appeared in nearly 50 films. Harris came to Hollywood about the same time as O'Toole, appearing in such movies as *The Guns of Navarone* (1961), *Mutiny on the Bounty* (1962), *Major Dundee* (1965), *Hawaii* (1966), *Camelot* (1967), *The Molly Maguires* (1970), and *A Man Called Horse* (1970), which led to several sequels. More recently Harris was cited for outstanding performances in *The Field* (1991) and in *Unforgiven* (1992). Like O'Toole, Harris never seems to be without a movie and has appeared in nearly 60 to date.

More recent imports to Hollywood from Ireland include Pierce Brosnan, Gabriel Byrne, and Liam Neeson. The strikingly handsome Brosnan, after a very successful television series, *Remington Steele,* is the most recent incarnation of British intelligence agent 007, first played by half-Irish Sean Connery. Byrne may be the finest actor of the three and has appeared in nearly 40 films since 1979, including *Into the West* (1992), a tale about Irish tinkers. Neeson, a large-framed 6'4", seems to dominate the screen and may be destined for greatness as his work in *Schindler's List*

(1993), *Nell* (1994), *Rob Roy* (1995), and *Michael Collins* (1996) would suggest.

Many others, both Irish and American born, have contributed mightily to the industry since the 1950s, including Patrick McGoohan, Jack Lord (Ryan), Patrick O'Neal, Fionnula Flanagan, Malachy McCourt, Gerald O'Laughlin, Eileen Brennan, Bill Murray, Kevin McCarthy, Mike Farrell, Siobhan McKenna, Peter Boyle, Ellen Burstyn (Edna Rae Gillooly), Charles Durning, Jennifer O'Neill, Milo O'Shea, Carroll O'Connor, Mickey Rourke, M. Emmett Walsh, Michael Moriarty, Patrick Duffy, Susanne Sommers, Liam Sullivan, Kelly McGillis, John Cusack, Matt Dillon, Elizabeth McGovern, Brian Dennehy, Meg Ryan, Aidan Quinn, Tom Cruise (Mapother), and Mel (Columcille Gerard) Gibson.

Although many think of Mel Gibson as Australian, he was actually born in New York and stayed there until his father, a brakeman on the New York Central Railroad, moved the family of eleven children to Sydney when Gibson was 12 years old. The Irish-American-Australian won an Academy Award for Best Director for *Braveheart* (1995) and the film, in which he starred, won Best Picture.

New actors coming on the scene include Peter Gallagher, Roma Downey, Howie Long, Matthew McConnaughey, Dylan McDermott, Robin Tunney, and Ed Burns.

Looming as a giant among the Irish in Hollywood was John Ford, whose stellar career spanned more than 50 years and included a record four Oscars for Best Director. He was born John Martin Feeney in 1894 in Portland, Maine, to Gaelic-speaking parents who had immigrated separately before marriage from County Galway. One of 13 children, Ford grew to 6'2" in high school and starred in track and in football, where he was known as "Bull" Feeney for his explosive ball-carrying. After flunking an exam for the U.S. Naval Academy, he headed to Hollywood to join his older brother Francis who was already an established actor and director. By the 1920s Ford was a successful director whose credits included the classic Western epic *The Iron Horse* (1924). Ford won his first Oscar for *The Informer* (1935) in which Victor McLaglen portrays Gypo Nolan who betrays a fellow volunteer in the IRA. He would win Oscars again for *The Grapes of Wrath* (1940), *How Green Was My Valley* (1941), and *The Quiet Man* (1952). Several of his other movies also rank among the best ever made: *Stagecoach* (1939), *The Long Voyage Home* (1940), *Mister Roberts* (1955), and *The Searchers* (1956). Not far behind are *Drums Along the Mohawk* (1939), *Fort Apache* (1948), *She Wore a Yellow Ribbon* (1949), *Rio Grande* (1950), *The Last Hurrah* (1958), and *The Man Who Shot Liberty Valance* (1962). His documentary, *The Battle of Midway* (1942), in which he shot all the footage himself and was wounded in the Japanese bombing of Midway, won the Academy Award.

In 1973 Ford was the first filmmaker to receive the American Film Institute's Life Achievement Award. The same year he was also presented the Presidential Medal of Freedom. When asked to name his favorite directors, Orson Welles responded: "The old masters . . . by which I mean John Ford, John Ford, John Ford."

Irish contemporaries of John Ford who achieved some fame as directors included Raoul Walsh and Leo McCarey. Walsh, who got his start as an assistant director to D.W. Griffith and played John Wilkes Booth in *The Birth of a Nation* (1915), is perhaps best remembered for *They Died With Their Boots On* (1941) and *Gentleman Jim* (1942), both starring Errol Flynn. Leo McCarey got his start working for fellow Irishman Hal Roach in the 1930s

directing comedies. In 1937 McCarey won Best Director for *The Awful Truth*, starring Irene Dunne. His finest work was probably *Going My Way* (1944), starring Bing Crosby, Barry Fitzgerald, and Frank McHugh. The film won seven Academy Awards including Best Picture, Best Actor (Crosby), Best Supporting Actor (Fitzgerald), and Best Director (McCarey).

Irish writers in Hollywood included William Riley Burnett, Philip Dunne, John Patrick (Goggan), John Meehan, Emmet Lavery, Richard Murphy, John Michael Hayes, Don McGuire, Frank Gilroy, and Richard Breen, who won an Oscar for *Titanic* (1953). James Kevin McGuinness and the half-Irish Frank S. Nugent each wrote several screenplays for John Ford, including such classics as *Rio Grande, She Wore a Yellow Ribbon, The Quiet Man,* and *The Searchers.* Irish were also writing songs and composing music for the movies. Jimmy McHugh, Johnny Burke, and Robert Emmett Dolan were three of the best.

Partly because the Irish were disproportionately represented in Hollywood, the westside of Los Angeles tended to have more than its share of green. One such westside community, Pacific Palisades, has been at one time or another home to President Ronald Reagan, Congressman and Los Angeles County Supervisor Leland Ford, broadcaster Vin Scully, composer and pianist Fulton McGrath, actors Ryan O'Neal, Bobby Driscoll, and Patrick McGoohan, and several large Irish families including the McNultys, Flahertys, Sheas, Butlers, O'Tooles, and McGonigles.

There is also a good number of Irish who today call Malibu, immediately to the west of the Palisades, their home. Among the actors who have settled there are Carroll O'Connor, Ali MacGraw, Dan O'Herlihy, Pierce Brosnan, and Mel Gibson. Perhaps their residency is appropriate. For most of the second half of the nineteenth century Malibu—Rancho Topanga, Malibu, Sequit as it was formally known then—was owned and operated by Irish-born Matthew Keller.

Nonetheless, for concentrations of Irish there is nothing in California like San Francisco and, to an ever greater degree, its suburbs. The distinctly Irish neighborhoods of the nineteenth century began to wane as early as the 1920s when younger generations moved to outlying communities. This trend accelerated rapidly after World War II. Despite this movement certain districts of San Francisco, such as the Noe Valley, were predominately Irish into the 1950s. Kevin Mullen, who grew up in the Noe Valley during the 1930s and '40s and went on to become the deputy chief of police for San Francisco, said that "it was difficult to find someone in the neighborhood who was not Irish."

San Francisco's Irish population meant that the city's police department took on an Irish character. As Irish were attracted to Hollywood and the silver screen in disproportionate numbers they were also attracted to the San Francisco Police Department in disproportionate numbers. By 1875 Irish accounted for more than a third of the officers on the force. By the turn of the century Irish officers composed nearly 40% of the force. They maintained such a percentage for the next half century. Moreover, in the 150-year history of the department more than half of the police chiefs have been Irish. Since the 1970s, however, the Irish complexion of the force has changed dramatically as preferential hiring has greatly increased the numbers of Blacks, Asians, and Hispanics at the expense of Irish and other whites. Despite the changing racial composition of the force, the department's roll of honor still tells the story. In the lobby of the San Francisco hall of justice is a plaque with the names of those who have died in the line of duty since 1849—every third surname is Irish.

Dying in the line of duty is not something confined to the San Francisco Police Department. Beginning with the Civil War, Irish Californians have been disproportionately represented in America's wars, both in decorations and in death. In World War II, for example, the highest ranking U.S. Naval officer to die was a California Irishman, Adm. Daniel J. Callaghan. In the Naval Battle of Guadalcanal, one of the greatest naval battles in history, Callaghan commanded the U.S. fleet. When a Japanese salvo slammed into his flagship, *San Francisco*, he was killed. For his leadership and heroism he was awarded the Medal of Honor posthumously.

Another California Irishman to win the Medal of Honor in W.W.II was Chief Aviation Ordnanceman John W. Finn. At Kaneohe Naval Air Station in Hawaii on December 7, 1941, he single-handedly set up a .50 caliber machine gun and hammered away at incoming Japanese fighters. All alone and in an exposed position alongside the runway, he was an inviting target. Again and again he was wounded by the strafing fighters but he stayed at his gun for two hours and shot down one Zero and damaged several others. The Zero he destroyed was the only Japanese plane shot down at Kaneohe that day.

That the Irish have been a significant factor in the population of California since the earliest days is also evidenced by the number of Irish placenames scattered throughout the state: Dublin, Murphys, McGurk Meadow, Quinn Peak, Mt. Conness, Daly City, McGann Springs, O'Shaughnessy Dam, Turlock (originally Turlough), Rafferty Peak, O'Neals Meadow, Heenan Lake, Murphy Creek, Donahue Peak, Branigan Lake, McGrath State Beach, Downey, Mt. Broderick, Mulligan Head, Corcoran, Delaney Creek, Tracy, McGee Lake, Cudahy, and dozens of others.

There has been something of an Irish renaissance in California since the 1970s. Whereas San Francisco and the Bay Area in general had always been a hotbed of Irish activity, now Irish elements in the populations of other cities and regions became active, especially in the greater Los Angeles area. The phenomenon is partly explained by a general rediscovery of ancestral origins that began sweeping the country about then and partly by the escalating conflict in Northern Ireland. Bloody Sunday in 1972 and then the IRA hunger strikes in the late '70s and early '80s seemed to galvanize sizable numbers of Irish in Los Angeles. The local chapter of Irish Northern Aid, led by Michael Fitzpatrick, suddenly became a rallying force for Irish, much to the dismay of the British consulate. Protests in front of the consulate and appearances on radio and television by members of INA, as well as interviews with them in the newspapers helped create an Irish consciousness that had lain dormant in many third- and fourth-generation Irish.

Expressions of Irishness found outlets in a proliferation of social and cultural organizations. St. Patrick's Day parades were held in a half-dozen communities, several radio shows, led by Tom McConville's "Irish Hour," found that the numbers of their listeners had doubled and tripled, the Irish American Bar Association was created, Irish dance schools grew and multiplied, a police Emerald Society was founded, the Celtic Arts Center was established, Irish music began to be featured in restaurants and pubs, several Irish newspapers and newsletters began publication, and an Irish fair outgrew several venues until it finally settled on the spacious grounds of the Santa Anita racetrack.

Although spread over a much greater area than that of San Francisco, Irish activities in Los Angeles now rival those of her northern neighbor. Irish bands, in particular, have been very prominent in southern California in recent years and can be found performing at numerous locations and events on any weekend of the year. Several, such as Irish Eyes (reincarnated in 1998 as The Wrath of McGrath), Innisfree, The Mulligans, and Des Regan's Irish American Showband have stood the test of time and have recorded and performed regularly since the 1970s. Several new bands, such as The Fenians and Gaelic Storm (featured in *Titanic*), have more recently developed popular followings.

California may not be as Irish as New York or Massachusetts but the California Irish, nearly two million strong, have played an important role in the state's history and they seem determined to maintain a degree of identity and to proudly express their Irishness well into the foreseeable future.

*See* Los Angeles; San Francisco; Cinema, Irish in

Hubert H. Bancroft, *History of California*, 7 vols. (San Francisco, 1886–1890).

John A. Barnes, *Irish-American Landmarks* (Detroit, 1995).

John Boessenecker, *Badge and Buckshot: Lawlessness in Old California* (Norman, Ok., 1988).

R. A. Burchell, *The San Francisco Irish 1848–1880* (Berkeley, 1980).

Joseph M. Curran, *Hibernian Green on the Silver Screen* (New York, 1989).

Patrick J. Dowling, *California: The Irish Dream* (San Francisco, 1989).

Margaret E. Fitzgerald and Joseph A. King, *The Uncounted Irish in Canada and the United States* (Toronto, 1990).

Joseph A. King, *Winter of Entrapment* (Lafayette, Cal., 1994).

Roger D. McGrath, *Gunfighters, Highwaymen, & Vigilantes* (Berkeley, 1984).

Kevin J. Mullen, *Let Justice Be Done: Crime and Politics in Early San Francisco* (Reno, 1989).

Edward F. Murphy, *Heroes of World War II* (Novato, Cal., 1990).

Thomas F. Prendergast, *Forgotten Pioneers: Irish Leaders in Early California* (San Francisco, 1942).

Hugh Quigley, *The Irish Race in California and on the Pacific Coast* (San Francisco, 1878).

Robert M. Senkewicz, *Vigilantes in Gold Rush San Francisco* (Stanford, 1985).

James P. Walsh, *The San Francisco Irish 1850–1976* (San Francisco, 1978).

ROGER D. McGRATH

## CALLAHAN, DANIEL J. (1930– )

Institute director, ethicist, writer. Daniel Callahan was born in Washington, D.C., July 19, 1930, son of Vincent F. and Anita (Hawkins) Callahan. He was educated at Yale (B.A., 1952), Georgetown (M.A., 1957) and Harvard (Ph.D., 1965). He joined the editorial staff of *Commonweal* in 1961 as associate editor, became executive editor, and established himself as one of the leading liberal voices of the newly evolved Catholic lay person with books such as *The Mind of the Catholic Layman* (1963), *Honesty in the Church* (1965), and *The New Church* (1966).

Callahan left *Commonweal* in 1968 to co-found and direct the Institute of Society, Ethics and the Life Sciences, now The Hastings Center, in Briarcliff Manor, New York. With that move his professional interests locked on questions spawned by the new biotechnologies affecting human life and the environment. Several of his books—for example, *Setting Limits: Medical Goals in an Aging Society* (1987) and *What Kind of Life: The Limits of Medical Progress* (1990)—sparked major public debates centering on medical ethics and the moral contexts of health care. In all Callahan is the author or editor of thirty-five books.

An elected member of the Institute of Medicine, National Academy of Science, Callahan served in 1970–1971 as special consultant to the Presidential Commission on Population Growth and the American Future, and in 1991–1992 on the Advisory Committee on Scientific Integrity of the U.S. Department of Health and Human Services. He has held visiting professorships at many college and universities, among them Brown, Temple, the University of Pennsylvania and Marymount, and has been awarded several honorary degrees, including from the University of Colorado and Williams College. He won the 1996 Freedom and Scientific Responsibility Award of the American Association for the Advancement of Science.

Currently Callahan is director of The Hastings Center's international programs and Senior Associate for Health Policy. He is married to Sidney (de Shazo) Callahan, a social psychologist, author of several books, and a *Commonweal* columnist. They have six children.

JOHN DEEDY

## CANADIAN IRISH/AMERICAN IRISH

### IMMIGRATION AND SETTLEMENT

Being Irish in Canada was hardly synonymous with being Catholic, for two rival Irish ethnic groups settled in the country, the Orange and the Green. In fact, Irish Protestants outnumbered Irish Catholics. Irish Protestants immigrated to North America earlier than did Irish Catholics, and most of Canada's Irish arrived in North America before the Great Famine. Famine and post-Famine immigration did not appreciably alter the religious composition and the regional distribution of Canada's Irish population, some two-thirds of whom resided in the province of Ontario. Irish Protestants and Catholics were much more rurally oriented in Canada than were Irish-Americans, and this was especially the case among Irish Protestants. And finally, not only were Irish Catholics a minority among those claiming Irish ancestry, they were also a minority among the country's Roman Catholics, the vast majority of whom were French speakers descended from the country's earliest European settlers.

Regional differences between the British North American colonies took hold early and persisted long after their Confederation in 1867. (Newfoundland remained a separate colony until 1949.) Settlement in what is now Atlantic Canada began in the late eighteenth century. Between 1770 and 1830, the expanding Newfoundland fishery drew about 30,000 settlers from Ireland, mainly from counties Waterford and Wexford. Migration to Newfoundland stopped much earlier than it did elsewhere, but while it lasted was highly localized in its origins. It was for this reason also almost entirely Roman Catholic, very much unlike early Irish migration to other parts of North America at the time, which was predominantly Protestant. Newfoundland was also unique in that local emigration resulted in the transfer of Irish folk culture to the New World whose characteristics were preserved thanks to Newfoundland's comparative isolation and the concentrated nature of Irish settlement in the Avalon peninsula. A few of Newfoundland's Irish Catholics subsequently migrated to the Cape Breton and Halifax regions of Nova Scotia. The first Irish settlers in Nova Scotia were, however, overwhelmingly Protestant. Beginning in the 1760s Irish Protestants from Ulster settled in and around the towns of Truro and Onslow. Two decades later Irish settlers started moving into New Brunswick's

Saint John River valley. Most of these settlers were Protestant, but Roman Catholics nonetheless comprised a significant minority.

These first arrivals to the mainland paled in comparison to the massive influx of Irish migrants that was to follow the end of the Napoleonic wars in 1815. The collapse of agricultural trade with Britain, the mainstay of Ireland's economy, triggered mass emigration from the island. The new British policy of importing timber from its North American colonies on preferred terms made available to prospective immigrants cheap passage from Ireland's seaports on ships picking up their loads of lumber in Quebec City and Saint John, New Brunswick. Between 1825 and 1845 about 450,000 Irish men, women, and children entered British North America, compared to the some 400,000 who travelled directly to the United States. Yet for many of these arrivals to the British colonies, the United States and not British North America was their final destination. No firm figures are available, but Cecil J. Houston and William J. Smyth estimate that two thirds of all Irish immigrants to the British North American colonies eventually moved on to the United States.

Irish immigration to British North America peaked in 1847, when 100,000 immigrants arrived hoping to flee famine and disease. Black '47 was a tragedy of unimaginable proportions. In that year alone over 5,000 were buried at Gross Isle, the quarantine station on the St. Lawrence River near Quebec City. Desperate and in need of any work they could find, the immigrants who survived the Atlantic passage were even less likely to stay in Canada than their predecessors. Canada's fledgling economy could employ relatively few such immigrants, and after that year the vast majority of famine migrants bypassed British North America entirely and made their way directly to the United States. As result, the number of arrivals from Ireland had by 1848 returned to their pre-famine levels at about 20,000 arrivals a year. This, however, was not to last. After 1855 Irish immigration to British North America fell dramatically to an average of about 2,000 arrivals a year. By 1890 immigration from Ireland had slid down to less than 1,000 immigrants a year.

The post-famine drop in Irish immigration to British North America meant that the contours of the country's Irish population were largely set by 1845. Except in the case of Quebec, immigrants from Ireland arrived during the British colonies' formative stages of settlement and so belonged to their charter peoples, even if they were not always recognized as such. In the thirty years following the Napoleonic wars, arrivals from Ireland far exceeded those from England and Wales combined. Only in the mid-1850s did immigration from England overtake that from Ireland. By 1871, when the first national census was taken, those of Irish ancestry accounted for nearly 25 percent of the population compared to 20 percent who were English and under 15 percent who were Scottish. As one might expect, some regions drew larger proportions of Irish inhabitants than others. In Ontario and New Brunswick, residents of Irish ancestry made up 35 percent of the population. By contrast, they had a much less significant presence in Nova Scotia (16.2%) and Quebec (10.4%). Moreover, the regional distribution of the Irish also had a distinctive profile. In all, 66.1 percent of the Irish lived in Ontario, another 19.3 percent in the Maritime provinces, with the remaining 14.6 percent in Quebec.

The religious make-up of the population of Irish ancestry also varied from region to region. In Ontario Irish Protestants outnumbered Roman Catholics two to one, but in Quebec the ratios were almost the exact inverse of those in Ontario. By contrast, in

New Brunswick Protestants held the lead, accounting for three-fifths of the Irish population. And in Nova Scotia Catholics and Protestants of Irish ancestry were more or less evenly divided: in this province religion appears not to have influenced Irish patterns of settlement, except in Halifax which had a large Irish-Catholic population. New Brunswick's pattern of settlement could hardly have been more different. There a strong connection existed between religious affiliation and place of settlement. Protestants settled in the Saint John River Valley and along the Bay of Fundy, while Catholics moved into the Miramichi interior on the Gulf of St. Lawrence side of the province. In the city of Saint John itself, Catholics came to dominate the Irish population during the 1840s.

Irish settlement was also localized in Quebec. Pockets of Irish settlement could be found in the Gaspé (mostly Catholic) on the mouth of the St. Lawrence River, in the hinterland of Quebec City (again mostly Catholic), in St-Sylvestre to the south of Quebec City (mostly Catholic, but with a significant Protestant minority who tended to live in separate settlements), and the Eastern Townships south of Montreal (where again Catholics and Protestants clustered in separate areas). By contrast, the Irish established more continuous settlement in the Ottawa Valley region, where again Protestants and Catholics settled with their co-religionists. Quebec's two leading urban areas also had large Irish populations. Just under a third of the province's Irish population settled in Quebec City and Montreal, each with a distinctive religious profile. In Quebec City Irish Catholics predominated, but in Montreal the ratio of Irish Catholics to Protestants was roughly even.

In Ontario the Irish were widely dispersed in the back counties, with large concentrations in the triangle between the Ottawa and St. Lawrence rivers, the Peterborough region, and Peel and Simcoe counties to the north and west of Toronto. In these regions Catholics of Irish ancestry tended to mix in with a much larger Protestant Irish population, though occasionally small pockets of Catholic settlements did exist. Protestants tended to be rural residents, approximating the provincial norm of 80 percent. By contrast, two-thirds of Catholics lived in rural areas. As one might expect, bigger cities, such as Hamilton and Toronto had large Irish populations. In Toronto, for example, two out of every five of the city's inhabitants claimed Irish ancestry, and these Irish were equally divided between Catholics and Protestants. With the opening up of the west after Confederation in 1867, Canadian-born Irish Protestants from Ontario joined the first waves of settlement to Manitoba, peaking at the turn of the century at just under a fifth of the population, after which immigration from Europe rapidly diminished their representation in proportion to the general population.

Occupation, Social Mobility, and Acculturation

The occupation profile of Canada's Irish, both among Protestants and Catholics, did not resemble that found in the United States mainly because the Canadian economy and the opportunities that it offered differed profoundly from the American economy. During the heyday of Irish immigration, the British North American economy was based primarily upon agriculture and resource industries such as timber. Urbanization gathered momentum in the 1840s, but industrialization only took off much later, in the 1860s and 1870s. Even so, only one in every five Canadians lived in an urban area in 1871. Not only was Canada's workforce much smaller than that of the United States, but unskilled industrial labour accounted for a smaller proportion of the overall workforce than was the case in America. Facing a dearth of unskilled jobs in a largely agricultural and artisanal economy, the vast majority of Irish migrants headed south to look for work in the plants and mills of the United States. Those Irish who remained in Canada were an exception to the rule, and they thus developed an occupational profile very different from that of their cousins in the United States.

A. Gordon Darroch's and Michael D. Ornstein's large-sample study of the 1871 census for Ontario and Quebec, which cross-tabulates ethnicity, religion, and occupation, offers the best snapshot of Canada's occupational structure in the nineteenth century. Their results reveal some significant differences in occupational pursuits between Protestants and Catholics of Irish ancestry. Not only did Irish Protestants tend to live in rural areas, they also sought to cash in on "the promise of Canadian life" by taking up farming. Rural dwellers accounted for 83.2 percent of the Irish Protestant population, and 58.3 percent of all employed Irish Protestants were farmers compared to 53.8 for the general population. By contrast, fewer Irish Catholics opted for rural life. Only 66.3 percent of them lived in the countryside, and 44.3 percent listed their occupation as farmer, well below the national norm. Moreover, Irish Catholics were twice as likely as Irish Protestants to be found engaged in unskilled labour, with one in five Catholics taking up such jobs. Irish Protestants and Catholics were more evenly matched in other occupational areas, such as manufacturers, merchants, white-collar workers, and artisans. To be sure, the Maritimes departed in some key respects from the central Canadian pattern. In that region, Protestants of Irish ancestry were no more likely to be farmers than the provincial norm, but less than a third of Irish Catholics farmed. And in Nova Scotia, Irish Catholics were vastly over-represented among the semi-skilled.

In general, then, Darroch and Ornstein's sample demonstrate that Catholics of Irish ancestry in central Canada were far from being an urban proletariat. Although Irish Catholics were less likely to farm compared to the general population, a substantial number of them did become farmers. They were, moreover, fully represented in the nation's middle class and its artisanal occupations. Unskilled Irish Catholics were, however, a highly visible urban minority, accounting for some 30 percent of the Irish-Catholic urban population. And social mobility among these unskilled Irish Catholics occurred more slowly than it did for other groups. Studies of social mobility between the immigrant and Canadian-born generations of Irish Catholics are few, but an in-depth study has been done in the case of Toronto by Mark McGowan, and his study reveals that intergenerational mobility had far-reaching social consequences.

In the case of Toronto, the descendants of the immigrant generation had moved out of the lower working class and many of them had entered the middle class during the opening years of the twentieth century. Such occupational integration was also accompanied by a significant increase in inter-faith and inter-ethnic marriages. For instance, in 1890 one in every twenty weddings performed in the city's parish churches was an inter-faith marriage. By 1920 that figure had risen to one in three. Earlier data on inter-faith and inter-ethnic marriages are hard to come by, but for the most part such marriages were relatively rare among Irish-Catholic immigrants. A computerized analysis of the original census returns for New Brunswick in 1851 revealed that over nine in every ten Irish-Catholic husbands had an Irish-Catholic wife. Protestant immigrants from Ireland were also highly likely to marry their own, though their rate of intra-ethnic marriage was not nearly as high as found among Roman Catholics. Three in four Irish Protestant men in New Brunswick married an Irish partner. Love, it would seem, was hardly blind. Inter-ethnic marriages occurred more easily for Irish Protestants in large part because they shared the same religious background as the English-speaking majority. Even in their case, however, acculturation expanded their options for marriage, as it did for Irish Catholics.

In Quebec, Irish-Catholic immigrants likewise preferred to marry their own. Marriages between second- and third-generation Irish Catholics and French Catholics were quite common, presumably because they shared the same religion. The old adage heard in many parts of Quebec that every French-speaking family has at least one Irish ancestor illustrated the extent and depth of Irish Catholic acculturation and integration in French Canada. Louis St. Laurent, Prime Minister of Canada from 1948–1957, and Georges-Phileas Vanier, Governor General between 1959 and 1967, traced their Irish ancestry through their maternal line. Moreover, many of those Irish Catholics who remained in the more predominantly French-speaking regions of the province became thoroughly assimilated, as the names of well-known French-speaking politicians such as Claude Ryan, leader of the Quebec Liberal Party from 1978 to 1982, and the late Daniel Johnson, premier from 1966 to 1968, demonstrate.

## RELIGIOUS, CULTURAL, AND SOCIAL LIFE

For Catholics arriving from Ireland, the Roman Catholic church was the most familiar old-world institution they encountered in the new land. Among those Catholics who settled in Canada the church continued to play a central social and cultural role, but it did so in circumstances that differed radically from their homeland. There they formed the religious and cultural majority, even though they lacked social power. By contrast, in Canada Irish Catholics had moved to a country characterized by cultural dualism, in which language and religion overlapped and reinforced one another, the legacy of conquest and settlement of the land by two European empires, the French and the British. Irish Catholics thus stood between two blocs: one English-speaking and overwhelmingly Protestant; the other, French-speaking and Catholic. In 1871, these two groups accounted for nearly 9 out of every 10 Canadians. French-speaking Catholics comprised just over 30 percent of the population; English-speaking Protestants nearly 60 percent. In this context both language and religion served to differentiate Irish Catholics, who accounted for less than a tenth of the population. Catholics of Irish ancestry thus constituted a double minority: among their co-linguists they formed a religious minority, and they constituted a linguistic minority among their co-religionists. Their status as a linguistic minority in the Catholic church was particularly evident in Quebec, where in larger population centres Irish Catholics typically worshipped in national parishes, apart from the French-speaking majority. In other provinces, where English speakers made up the vast majority of the population, parishes were also typically Irish ethnic institutions. To take central Canada as an example, when one sets aside French-speakers, the Irish accounted for over three-quarters of the Catholic population. Other

Catholics, such as the Scots and Germans, were not very numerous (the Scots accounted for one in ten of the region's non–French speaking Catholics), and they were also concentrated regionally.

Irish-Catholic immigrants to Canada shared a common religion. Nonetheless, cultural differences between them were profound, as each region in Ireland had its own distinct culture. In the new land, the church provided Irish men and women with a common cultural identity that transcended regional differences. The first parishes, especially in rural areas, frequently owed their origins to lay initiative: Catholics from various regions from Ireland came together and volunteered their time, labour, and funds to build a church for their community and, when possible, to establish a fund (usually consisting of both cash and arable land) to attract a resident priest. Such tenacity suggests not only the strength of Irish-Catholic cohesiveness but also the strong hold that Catholicism had upon the heartstrings of the Irish-Catholic immigrant. Indeed, the attraction of a parish church was so strong that in rural areas Irish Catholics would whenever possible settle as near to one another as they could so as to build up a viable community with its own church and priest.

As was the case in Ireland and in the United States, the movement for renewal and reform associated with the influence of Ultramontanism fundamentally transformed Catholicism in Canada. This movement first took hold in Atlantic Canada and Quebec during the 1840s and then moved into what is now Ontario in the 1850s. One of the most obvious effects of this religious renewal was the strengthening of the clergy's spiritual and social authority, and in the process the clergy took over control of parish affairs from lay trustees. The church also began to play a more active role in people's daily lives by building up a network of social institutions, such as schools, hospitals, and orphanages staffed by women's religious orders, which quickly expanded as a consequence of religious revival and reform. Finally, this movement also had a far-reaching impact upon lay religious practice, much as it did in both Ireland and the United States. Not only did attendance at Mass on Sundays become more regular but the range of lay piety expanded vastly to include a wide variety of devotions. The Canadian study of lay religion is still in its early stages, but the findings in the case of Toronto are suggestive. Women from all but the poorest social classes took up the practice of devotions, but men only began to approach that level of observance two to three generations later, around the turn of the century.

One of the reasons for this development is that later generations came of age when a Catholic subculture was well developed and was shaping the ethos of the vast majority of Catholic households. The religious renewal associated with Ultramontanism hardened the social boundaries between Catholics and Protestants. The previous conciliatory attitude to the Protestant majority—Irish Catholics, for example, commonly attended Protestant services—yielded to militancy. Perhaps the most notable expression of that militancy was their growing demand for state support of Catholic schools: in Ontario, for example, Catholics gained significant concessions for their schools. The parish church became part of a vast network of social institutions such as orphanages, hospitals, and the like that nurtured and sustained a distinct religious and ethnic identity.

Unlike Irish Catholics, Irish Protestants did not share a common denominational affiliation. Indeed, the common association of Irish Protestantism with Presbyterianism is highly misleading. In central Canada in 1871, well over a third of all Irish Protestants were Anglican; just under a quarter were Presbyterian; and nearly another third were Methodists, almost all of whom converted from either Anglicanism or Presbyterianism in the new land or descended from those who had. Naturally, Irish Protestants had a greater impact upon some denominations than others. Among the Anglicans, they were the second-largest group after the English, accounting for just under two fifths of the church's membership. Protestants of Irish ancestry were staunch evangelicals, and their presence ensured that evangelicalism was a considerable force in the Anglican church. Although Irish Protestants had a significant presence in both the Methodist and Presbyterian churches, their contribution to Canadian Methodism and Presbyterianism still awaits historical investigation.

While Irish Catholics contributed to the formation of Canadian social landscape by creating an ethnic and religious subculture distinct from the country's two linguistic and religious blocs, Irish Protestants had a profound impact upon the formation of the country's English-speaking mainstream. At the time of Confederation the outlook and identity of the English-speaking Protestant majority was still very much in the process of being formed, mainly because that majority was itself an amalgam of various ethnic groups, albeit of United Kingdom ancestry but nonetheless distinctive and different from one another. Like other English speakers, Irish Protestants belonged to a variety of denominations, but there was one organization that did embody their unique cultural identity, the Orange Order—an organization that would influence profoundly the development of English-speaking Canada's cultural identity.

First established at the beginning of the nineteenth century by troops serving in British North America, the local Orange hall soon became a fixed feature along with schools and churches in small towns and cities alike across British North America. Originating in Ireland as an oath-bound paramilitary organization, the Orange Order had become by the 1850s the largest fraternal organization in the country, recruiting Protestant men from across the English-speaking mainstream. Like most other fraternal organizations, the Orange Order provided men with a full social life, rich in opportunities for conviviality and camaraderie, but it offered them much more than a good time. Formed in the crucible of ethnic and religious conflict by Anglo-Irish settlers in Britain's first colony, the Orange Order provided English-speaking settlers in British North America with a ready-made colonial identity based upon loyalty to the British monarchy and Empire as well as a shared Protestant faith.

The Orange Order instilled an overarching Protestant identity that transcended denominational differences, but it did so by fostering an abiding suspicion of Catholicism rooted in British nativism. As Catholic immigration from Ireland picked up after 1830, tensions between Protestants and Catholics rapidly escalated. The rise in popular anti-Catholic sentiment swelled the Orange Order's ranks, and at the same time it added further fuel to the Order's militancy. From the 1830s through to the 1860s, riots involving Orangemen (many of them native born as well as Irish Protestant immigrants) and Catholics regularly erupted, especially on the main holidays of the Irish calendar, Saint Patrick's Day on March 17 and the celebration of William of Orange's victory over King James at the Battle of the Boyne on July 12. As the nineteenth century wore on, however, Orangemen increasingly directed their ire towards Canada's French-speaking Catholics.

During each of the country's major religious and linguistic conflicts—the North West Rebellions of 1870 and 1885, the New Brunswick School Question of the mid-1870s, the Manitoba School Question of the 1890s, and the conscription crises of both World Wars—the Orange Order fanned the flames of religious and linguistic animosity. Both on account of their religion and their language, French Canadians were in the view of Orangemen as not truly Canadian, a charge that the Orangemen claimed was fully borne out by their opposition to conscription during the world wars when all true patriots had a special duty to come to Britain's aid.

The Orange Order was a political force to be reckoned with. The Order's garrison mentality and hyper-loyalism to the British Crown and Empire struck a resonant chord among English-speaking Protestants and so shaped their collective identity. In many communities the order functioned as the local political machine for the Conservative party. As a consequence, on the national level Conservative governments included at least one Orange representative in the cabinet: Mackenzie Bowell held a variety of ministerial posts between 1878 and 1896, including a two-year stint as Prime Minister, and Sam Hughes was the minister of the militia from 1911 to 1916. Irish Catholics likewise were typically represented in the federal cabinet. Though there were few electoral ridings with large concentrations of Irish Catholics, they did comprise a significant bloc of voters that no political party could ignore. Talented Irish-Catholic politicians were in short supply, but there were some notable exceptions such as D'Arcy McGee, Minister of Agriculture between 1864–67, and Charles Fitzpatrick, Minister of Justice from 1896 to 1902.

Canada was part and parcel of the British empire. In emigrating to Canada Irish Catholics had gone from one part of the empire to another. By contrast those who went to the United States had moved to a different country and lived under a new flag. As one would expect, this meant that the identity and self-image of Irish Catholics in Canada followed a very different trajectory from that in the United States. During the 1850s, Irish nationalism on both sides of the Atlantic took on a republican and revolutionary cast under the influence of the Fenian Brotherhood. For the most part, the response of Irish Catholics in Canada to this form of nationalism was deeply ambivalent, and so D'Arcy McGee's vehement denunciations of Fenianism offended many Irish Catholics. Most Irish Catholics strictly compartmentalized their sentiments regarding Great Britain: for Canada, the imperial tie brought freedom, self-government, and prosperity; for Ireland it resulted in tyranny, foreign domination, and oppression. Only a few Irish Catholics joined the Brotherhood, but many deplored the situation that had given rise to Fenianism and sympathized with the movement's idealism though most certainly not with its methods. For these reasons they refused to condemn the Brotherhood outright, even after the Fenian invasions of Canada in 1866 and the 1868 assassination of Thomas D'Arcy McGee, the leading Irish-Catholic politician of the day, in what was widely assumed at the time to be a Fenian conspiracy. In time, however, Irish-Catholic ambivalence gave way to outright opposition to republican nationalism. By the eve of the First World War, Catholics of Irish ancestry redefined themselves as English-speaking Canadians and, like other English-speaking Canadians of the time, as ardent British imperialists. This shift in identity did not preclude support for Irish Home Rule. Far from it, but it did mean that they were completely bewildered by the growing dominance of republican nationalism in Ireland and the outbreak of civil war in the Irish Free State.

Irish Catholics had regarded themselves as charter members of Canadian society long before this shift in their identity. They believed that their early settlement in the country, their United Kingdom ancestry, and their use of the English language all so qualified them. This sense of entitlement had a much less attractive side to it, namely Francophobia. That French speakers constituted the vast majority of the country's Catholics and dominated the church's hierarchy rankled with Irish Catholics. Time and time again, Irish Catholics failed to support their co-religionists when state-supported Catholic schools came under Protestant attack, as they did in New Brunswick in the 1870s and in Manitoba in the 1890s, or when French-language schooling came under attack in Ontario from the 1890s to the 1920s. Indeed in that latter conflict, far from sitting out the controversy on the sidelines, Irish Catholics joined in the fray and demanded that education be anglicized. Such a belief in the evident superiority of the English language also informed the campaign waged by the Archdiocese of Ontario from the 1870s through to the 1910s against the French-speaking Archdiocese of Ottawa. Although the majority of Catholics on the Ontario side of the Ottawa valley and surrounding region were French-speaking, Toronto's archbishops repeatedly sought to bring them under its control. In the 1910s the English-speaking bishops shifted their attention to Western Canada, where they launched a campaign to wrest the dioceses of the west from the hands of French-speaking bishops, a task they successfully completed by 1930.

Catholics and Protestants of Irish ancestry fundamentally shaped the social landscape of Canada, but today they are largely invisible. The Orange Order is no longer a central community institution, and the Twelfth draws scarcely any notice, except in Newfoundland where it is a bank holiday. Its vision of the country has gone the way of the empire itself, and changes in immigration policy following the introduction of multiculturalism by the federal government in the early 1970s have changed both the ethnic composition of Canadian society and the ways in which English-speaking Canadians view themselves. As one top Orangeman admitted in the late 1970s, the ideals that animated the Orange Order were as "dead as dodos." By the 1960s and 1970s Catholics of Irish descent represented a minority of English-speaking Catholics, as the descendants of immigrants from eastern and southern Europe became anglicized. But if they now see themselves and are seen by others as part of the social mainstream, they did contribute to diversifying the country's social fabric, even though they often were not nearly as tolerant towards others as they would have others be towards them.

*See* McGee, Thomas D'Arcy; Fenians and Clan na Gael

Donald Harman Akenson's *The Irish in Ontario: A Study in Rural History* (Kingston and Montreal, 1984) is the defining work in the field. Also indispensable are Cecil J. Houston and William J. Smyth, *Irish Emigration and Canadian Settlement: Patterns, Links, and Letters* (Toronto, 1990), A. Gordon Darroch and Michael D. Ornstein, "Ethnicity and Occupational Structure in Canada in 1871: The Vertical Mosaic in Historical Perspective," *Canadian Historical Review* 61 (1980): 305–33, and John S. Moir, "The Problem of a Double Minority: Some Reflections of the Development of the English-speaking Catholic Church in Canada in the Nineteenth Century," *histoire sociale/Social History* 7 (1971): 53–67. For a concise overview and a helpful bibliography consult David A. Wilson, *The Irish in Canada* (Ottawa, 1989). Ter-

rence Murphy and Gerald Stortz, eds., *Creed and Culture: The Place of English-Speaking Catholics in Canadian Society, 1750–1930* (Montreal and Kingston, 1993) is a ground-breaking work as is the exemplary study by Cecil J. Houston and William J. Smyth, *The Sash Canada Wore: A Historical Geography of the Orange Order in Canada* (Toronto, 1980). Toronto's Irish Catholics have to date received the most extensive treatment. See my *Piety and Nationalism: Lay Voluntary Associations and the Creation of an Irish-Catholic Community in Toronto, 1850–1895* (Montreal and Kingston: McGill-Queen's University Press, 1993) and Mark G. McGowan, *The Waning of the Green: English-Speaking Catholics and Identity in Toronto, 1887–1922* (Montreal and Kingston: McGill-Queen's University Press, forthcoming).

BRIAN CLARKE

## CANALS AND THE IRISH INVOLVEMENT

The great canal era in the United States lasted from approximately 1820 through 1850. Sparked by the phenomenal success of New York's Erie Canal, canal mileage grew from a mere one hundred miles nationwide in 1816 to 3,326 miles by 1840. By 1860, the total reached 4,254. Concentrated mainly in the Northeast and Midwest, these massive projects not only required unprecedented sums of capital to construct, but also vast armies of laborers to do the work. Early canal projects sought to fill this need with native whites, as well as indentured servants and slaves. However, these sources proved inadequate to meet the demand for labor. As a result, canal contractors recruited an ever increasing number of European immigrants to serve as wage laborers. Although sizable numbers of Germans, English, Scots, and Welsh could be found on many projects, canal work in the United States soon came to be dominated by the Irish. As early as 1818, three thousand Irish labored on the Erie Canal. In 1834, the Chesapeake and Ohio Canal employed at least eighteen hundred Irish. The Irish also predominated on western canals, such as the Illinois and Michigan, as well as several canal projects in Upper Canada. Even in the South, where slaves provided the labor for most public works projects, significant numbers of Irish could be found working on canals during winter months before returning North in the spring. Indeed, it was not long before the Irish became virtually synonymous with canal work. Looking back on the era, one scribe went so far as to assert, "To dig a canal, at least four things are necessary—a shovel, a pick, a wheelbarrow, and an Irishman" (Orser, 123).

### FROM PEASANTS TO PROLETARIAT

The Irish came to canal work with the breakdown of their traditional peasant cultures at home. By the mid-18th century, Irish

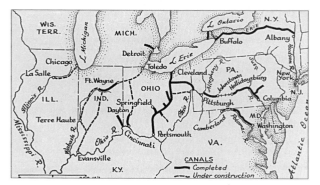

Canal system, 1840

landlords increasingly converted land to commercial production in order to meet the growing English demand for foodstuffs. This commercialization of Irish farmland led to a decline in subsistence farming, and forced a growing number of poor Irish to seek their livelihood by means of wage labor. Public works in Ireland and England, particularly road and canal projects, drew many displaced tenants. American canal companies, hoping to solve their own chronic labor shortages, sought to recruit workers from this swelling population of landless Irish. Company agents and newspaper advertisements enticed peasants to emigrate to canal projects in the United States with assurances of steady work, bountiful food, and generous wages. The president of the C&O promised prospective Irish émigrés "Meat, three times a day, a plenty of bread and vegetables, with a reasonable allowance of liquor, and light, ten, or twelve dollars a month for wages" (Way, *Common Labour,* 94). With little prospect of improved conditions in the countryside, thousands of poor Irish gave up the countryside and crossed the Atlantic to work on American canals. As labor historian Peter Way has noted, this process culminated the transformation of the Irish from peasants into laborers.

Arriving in America with few skills and little, if any, money, canal work became one of the few means by which Irish immigrants could eke out a subsistence. Canal work was plentiful during the era of the great construction boom, and the majority of the work required little expertise. The few tasks which did require skilled labor, mainly the masonry and stone cutting required for lock construction, generally fell to native-born workers or German and British immigrants. Irish dominated the ranks of the unskilled. In 1850, for example, Irish made up 380 of the 407 common laborers in one C&O camp. The jobs Irish canallers performed were hard, monotonous, and often dangerous, involving little skill and constant exertion. Once a canal route had been laid out, the first step in construction was grubbing, or clearing the path of all trees, brush, rocks, and other surface obstructions. Once completed, the route was ready for excavation, which required the removal of massive amounts of material ranging from the loosest soils to layers of the hardest rock. Gangs of Irish canallers worked their way through canal cuts with picks and shovels, carting away the refuse with wheelbarrows or horse-drawn carts to nearby tips. The final steps in canal construction involved ramming a layer of fine clay to the bed in order to waterproof the channel, damming streams to create reservoirs, and creating towpaths.

## The Life of an Irish Canaller

Labor conditions added to the difficulties Irish faced as canallers, or "navvies." The typical workday lasted from sunup to sundown, in full exposure to the elements. Irish canallers might work through pouring rain or searing heat, and occasionally in numbing cold. Where canal routes passed through swamps or bogs, diggers might find themselves working for days in water sometimes waist-deep, swelling the limbs of workers and subjecting them to plagues of disease carrying mosquitoes. A fellow Irishman visited a canal site near Louisiana in the 1830s and described hundreds of his countrymen at work in a swamp "wading amongst stumps of trees, mid-deep in black mud, clearing the spaces pumped out by powerful steam-engines; wheeling, digging, hewing, or bearing burdens it made one's shoulders ache to look upon" (Way, *Common Labour,* 132). At the opposite extreme, excavating through rock brought on the added dangers

inherent in blasting. Premature explosions and falling debris took a toll not only on Irish laborers, but sometimes nearby residents as well. This particularly dangerous labor forced contractors to offer higher wages to fill blasting positions, which in turn attracted eager, but often inexperienced, hands with tragic results. But most feared by canallers were the periodic epidemics which swept through worksites. Cholera, typhoid, malaria, dysentery, yellow fever, and other lethal diseases took a heavy toll on Irish laborers. One cholera outbreak on the C&O canal near Sheperdstown, Virginia in 1832 carried away 30 laborers in only a few days. In 1849, another cholera outbreak among the Irish workers on the Wabash & Erie canal killed hundreds.

Wages did little to compensate for the trials and travails of canal work. Few Irish shared the goals of antebellum artisans and farmers of obtaining a "competence" or rising to the level of independent small farmer or craftsman. Subsistence was the practical objective of most canallers, and even this modest aim often proved elusive. Until the late 1830s, wages were fairly good, particularly so when compared to the meager pay offered by European canal works. A general labor shortage on American canals kept pay favorable to workers, who could command anywhere from $8 to $10 per month on the C&O in 1828 to as much as $14 to $16 per month by the early 1830s. Pay was even higher on western canals, where labor was in even shorter supply. Also, many canallers received a part of their pay in kind from contractors, usually food and shelter, but at times included clothing and liquor as well. The practice of providing food and shelter, or "finding," supplied a significant portion of the earnings received by Irish laborers, but also made their state of dependence all the more apparent as they literally exchanged their labor for the basic necessities of life.

Living conditions for canallers were uniformly regarded by contemporary observers as wretched. Shelter generally consisted of crude shanties, either provided by contractors or constructed by the workers themselves. Often, little difference could be discerned between the housing provided for Irish canallers and animals. Indeed, laborers often shared accommodations with horses, oxen, pigs, or other livestock. One British traveler thought the shanties shared by Irish canallers near Troy, New York "more like dog-kennels than the habitations of men" (Way, *Common Labour,* 144). Almost any possible type of shelter was used to accommodate workers: tents, bunkhouses, cabins, converted canal barges and scows, etc. Some Irish diggers even burrowed into hillsides.

Work camps were the most common settlement pattern, generally collections of crude, temporary accommodation situated directly adjacent to the canal site. With populations numbering from a dozen to several hundred workers, these camps were generally male enclaves and communal living was the norm, with workers sharing sleeping, cooking, and cleaning arrangements. On occasion, Irish established more permanent settlements in urban shanty towns, with more substantial rented or self-constructed housing. In these "Corktowns," Irish diggers and their families managed a more recognizable family and community life, albeit still a shaky one. Some shantytowns even outlived the period of canal construction, becoming permanent Irish neighborhoods in established cities and towns, or even forming the basis of new towns, such as Akron, Ohio and Lockport, New York.

Few Irish were able to transform canal labor directly into a significantly better way of life. While pay rates compared favorably with unskilled labor in other parts of the country, a host of obstacles made even subsistence difficult for most canallers to attain. Unemployment and underemployment was a chronic problem for canal labor. Poor weather could halt work for days, during which idle canallers were not paid. The onset of winter forced almost a complete cessation of work for several months. At other times, laborers missed work due to injury or illness. Dishonest contractors occasionally absconded with payrolls, leaving their employees broke and irate. The Panic of 1837 took an even greater toll on Irish laborers. A general decrease in wage rates followed the depression, as many canal projects shut down altogether, throwing thousand of canallers out of work and increasing the competition for the jobs which remained. Contractors not only took advantage of the situation by cutting wage rates, but also phased out the practice of providing provisions and accommodations for employees.

Economic conditions and the transient nature of canal work made the establishment of any kind of lasting community difficult, if not impossible, for Irish on the canals. The overwhelmingly male and temporary populations of shantytowns bred a fiercely masculine worker culture along the canals. Most canallers were single, and even those Irish who managed to establish families found the setting difficult to maintain. Married men were often absent from spouses for weeks or months at a time, and even when together, married couples often had to share their accommodations with numbers of unmarried diggers. The rough-hewn masculine culture of canal life made worksites and shantytowns alike the site of constant contests of male prowess, both through sport and gaming as well as drinking and brawling. Alcohol was an omnipresent feature of canal life, and Irish navvies consumed amazing quantities of liquor both on the job and after hours. Religion only partially offset the rootlessness of canal life. Catholicism established a toehold in Irish labor camps, often due to exertions by the Irish themselves. But most religious organization was fleeting at best. Too few priests and the forced mobility of potential parishioners left the vast majority of the Irish on the canals without any regularized outlet for worship. A few churches were actually built, but more often than not, potential parishioners were no longer in the area once the church was completed.

PUBLIC ATTITUDES AND LABOR UNREST

The violent and foreign ways of the Irish on the canals led native inhabitants to view canallers with a mixture of fear, bigotry, and loathing. Emerging bourgeois mores and republican ideals in America looked with disdain upon wage labor of any kind, with canal work in particular perceived as the most degraded form of labor one could undertake. The willingness of so many Irish to accept such work, and the abject dependence and poverty it entailed, reduced their already low standing in the eyes of nearby residents. Their alien behavior and seemingly superstitious religious practices further set the Irish apart from much of the surrounding native population. Indeed, some native born citizens went so far as to see canallers as something almost subhuman, fearing the crowds of "wild Irish" who descended upon any local settlement through which a canal project passed. An observer on the Illinois & Michigan Canal echoed the opinion of most native residents in considering the Irish to be "not merely ignorant and poor . . . but they are drunken, dirty, indolent, and riotous, so as to be the objects of dislike and fear to all in whose neighborhood they congregate in large numbers" (Way, *Common Labour,* 165).

To combat the economic and social conditions they faced, Irish workers often turned to collective action to maintain, if not improve, their circumstances. Transferring the Irish tradition of banding into secret societies to America, canallers frequently mobilized their numbers and fought to protect their already tenuous hand-to-mouth existence. Violence and rioting often resulted. At first, gangs of Irish generally rioted over specific grievances, usually against contractors over nonpayment of wages or work and living conditions. Later, as economic circumstances worsened nationwide and canal projects scaled back or ceased construction altogether, canallers often found themselves in conflict with each other over the dwindling number of jobs available. As a result, strikes and riots became almost endemic to canal construction throughout North America, especially in the years between 1830 and 1850. Historian Peter Way counted at least 160 such incidents. Along the C&O Canal, for example, an almost constant series of riots disrupted construction in the 1830s, often requiring the use of state militia and even Federal troops to restore order.

Irish quite often fought Irish in these disturbances, as workers sought to reduce job competition by creating artificial labor shortages to keep wages high. In such cases, regional ties took precedence over shared ethnic heritage. A bitter and often murderous rivalry arose between workers from the South of Ireland ("Corkonians") and those from the North ("Fardowners" or "Connaughtmen"), frequently disrupting canal work throughout North America. While outside observers deemed such rioting as senseless and ethnically motivated, in reality riots represented a nascent class consciousness among canallers as they sought to stave off the worst aspects of economic exploitation arising from the transition to capitalism in America during the first half of the nineteenth century. But such tactics merely delayed the inevitable. The decrease in canal jobs in the 1840s coincided with an increase in the potential labor pool. As a result, canal companies and contractors reduced wages even further and abandoned the old practice of "finding." Day labor replaced monthly work contracts. Living conditions deteriorated rapidly for the Irish, who now comprised almost the entire labor pool for canal projects.

CONCLUSION

The Irish association with canals in America ended with the death of the industry by 1860. While a small handful of canallers managed to prosper after their time on the canal, most Irish went on to form yet another anonymous workforce elsewhere in industrial America. Some Irish drifted north to work on Canadian canal projects. Others became the common labor pool in new manifestations of industrialization, primarily railroads and mining. Still others migrated into the cities. Despite their omnipresence, the Irish seldom received recognition from contemporaries of their role in realizing the vision of canal backers and designers. But the Erie, C&O, Illinois & Michigan, and other canals remain an enduring reminder of the role of thousands of Irish navvies in the commercial and industrial development of America.

*See* Labor Movement

W. David Baird, "Violence Along the Chesapeake and Ohio Canal: 1839," *Maryland Historical Magazine,* 66 (1971): 121–134.
Ruth Bleasdale, "Class Conflict on the Canals of Upper Canada in the 1840s," *Labour/Le Travailleur,* 7 (1981): 9–39.

Richard B. Morris, "Andrew Jackson, Strikebreaker," *American Historical Review*, 55 (1949): 54–68.

Charles E. Orser, Jr., "The Illinois and Michigan Canal: Historical Archaeology and the Irish Experience in America," *Éire-Ireland*, 27 (Winter 1992): 122–134.

Carol Sheriff, *The Artificial River: The Erie Canal and the Paradox of Progress, 1817–1862* (N.Y., 1996).

Catherine Teresa Tobin, "The Lowly Muscular Digger: Irish Canal Workers in Nineteenth-Century America," (Ph.D. diss., University of Notre Dame, 1987).

Peter Way, "Shovel and Shamrock: Irish Workers and Labor Violence in the Digging of the Chesapeake and Ohio Canal," *Labor History*, 30 (1989): 489–517.

———, *Common Labour: Workers & the Digging of North American Canals, 1780–1860* (Cambridge, UK, 1993).

TOM DOWNEY

## CAREY, HUGH LEO (1919– )

United States Representative, governor of New York. Born in Brooklyn, New York, on April 11, 1919 into the Irish lineage of Dennis J. and Margret (Collins) Carey, the young Carey attended St. Augustine's High School and went on to college at St. John's College where his studies were interrupted by World War II. He enlisted in the 101st Cavalry, served in France, Belgium, Holland and Germany and rose to the rank of major. After the war, Carey entered St. John's Law School and received the LL.B. degree in 1951 and was admitted to the New York state bar.

In 1960 Carey replaced the Republican Francis E. Dorn in the House of Representatives and his first committee assignments were on the House Administration Committee and the Interior and Insular Affairs Committee. Carey's more memorable actions in the House include urging that a national park or patriotic shrine be built on Governor's Island in New York harbor; opposition to President's Kennedy's proposal to reduce income tax deductions for business entertainment expenses; advocating opposition to China becoming a part of the United Nations; the authorization of a communications satellite and purchase of United Nations bonds.

While Carey was often accused by his opponents of ultra-liberal leanings, he nonetheless prospered politically and retained his seat in the House through 1974. In 1974 he was elected 51st governor of New York and he served through 1982. As governor he was the architect of the financial plan that averted the bankruptcy of New York City and began a sweeping program of fiscal reform and economic development to restore the state's vitality. As governor, Carey also instituted the "I Love New York" program and began the Empire State Games. Since the end of his term and the election of Governor Pataki in New York, Carey has functioned as an advisor on matters such as trade and taxation.

*See* New York City; New York State

*Who's Who in America* (1964–65).
*Congressional Directory* (1965).
*CAB* (1965).

JOY HARRELL

## CAREY, MATTHEW (1760–1839)

Journalist, publisher. Known for both his Irish and American patriotism, Matthew Carey was a prolific author and one of the most influential American book publishers during the early decades of the American republic. He was born in Dublin on January 28, 1760, and by the age of seventeen he was working in his chosen profession.

The oppression of Irish Catholics by the English greatly offended Carey and in 1779 he published a pamphlet urging the repeal of the penal codes. For such a seditious act, Carey was forced to flee Ireland for France where he became acquainted with Benjamin Franklin and the Marquis de Lafayette.

Carey returned to Ireland in 1783 to establish himself as a printer and publisher of the *Volunteer's Journal*, a paper devoted to the defense of Ireland. Within a year, Carey was again forced to flee his native land, but this time he traveled to the United States.

Carey settled in Philadelphia late in 1784 and, with financial assistance from Lafayette, he established the *Pennsylvania Herald* in January 1785. Even though the paper was a success, Carey grew restless and in 1787 he began The American Museum, a digest of clippings from various periodicals and newspapers across the country. He expanded his publishing operations in 1790 to include books, pamphlets and during that decade he issued the first Roman Catholic Bible to be published in the United States. Over the next four decades Carey's firm would become one of the leading book publishers and distributors in the United States. Among the authors published by Carey were William Thackery, James Fenimore Cooper, and Charles Dickens.

Carey's love for Ireland never abated. Long after he had settled permanently in Philadelphia, Carey continued to work and write on behalf of Irish causes. In the early 1790s, he helped to establish the Hibernian Society for the Relief of Irish Immigrants and in 1795 he supported the efforts of Wolfe Tone and the United Irishmen in their ill-fated effort to establish an independent Ireland.

Carey's views on Irish independence and English injustice were recorded in a series of books published between 1819 and 1838. Carey spent several years writing his magnum opus, *Vindiciae Hibernicae or, Ireland Vindicated* (1819), a refutation of the English claim that the Irish had provoked the massacre of 1641. He later wrote *To the Friends of Ireland* (1828), *Vindication of the Early History of Ireland* (1829), and *Letter on Irish Immigrants* (1838).

Carey was also an American patriot and a loyal member of the Democratic-Republican party led by his friend Thomas Jefferson. Yet Carey had an independent streak that was reflected in his support for the "nationalist school" of economics and political affairs, a position normally associated with the Federalist Party.

Carey was elected a director of the Bank of Philadelphia in 1802 and 1810, and he was one of the few members of his party to support the charter renewal of the Bank of the United States. In fact, some have argued that his most important political role was as an intermediary between the Democratic-Republicans and the Federalists. His pamphlet, *The Olive Branch*, documents his efforts in this regard. Carey died in 1839 and was succeeded in his publishing enterprises by his son Henry. Matthew is chiefly remembered today for his many publications on economics and political affairs in the early Republic.

*See* American Revolution; Philadelphia

Earl L. Bradsher, *Matthew Carey: Editor, Author, and Publisher* (New York, 1912).

Matthew Carey, *The Autobiography of Matthew Carey* [1833] (New York, 1942).

Kenneth W. Rowe, *Matthew Carey: A Study in Economic Development* (Baltimore, 1933).

TIMOTHY WALCH

## CARNEY, ANDREW (1794–1864)

Merchant and benefactor. Andrew Carney was born on May 12, 1794, in Ballanagh, County Cavan, Ireland, and died in Boston, MA, on April 3, 1864. Having arrived in Boston as a poor immigrant in 1816, he became a very prosperous tailor and clothing merchant by 1845, especially after he had produced clothing that was ready for men to wear.

Following his success as a businessman, Carney invested his money in various ways. A devout layman who helped the Catholic Church in Boston under the episcopal leadership of both Benedict Joseph Fenwick and John Bernard Fitzpatrick, there was no one equal to Carney in philanthropy among the Catholics of New England in his era. When, for example, the Great Famine struck Ireland in 1845–49, Carney donated very generously to the fund which, on March 1, 1847, the Bishop of Boston sent to the Archbishop of Armagh to help the victims.

Though he is buried in Forest Hills Cemetery in Jamaica Plain, Carney's memory survives in two institutions for whose establishment in 1863 his benefactions were crucial. One is Carney Hospital, now located in Dorchester, and the other is Boston College, now in Chestnut Hill, which named Carney Hall in his memory a hundred years after his death.

John R. Betts, "Andrew Carney," *New Catholic Encyclopedia*, 3 (Washington, 1967): 128.

Andrew Carney, *The Will of Andrew Carney* (Boston, 1866).

Robert H. Lord, John E. Sexton, and Edward T. Harrington, *History of the Archdiocese of Boston in the Various Stages of Its Development*, 3 vols. (New York, 1944): vol. 2.

Gerald C. Treacy, "Andrew Carney, Philanthropist," *United States Catholic Historical Society Records*, 13 (1919): 101–105.

VINCENT A. LAPOMARDA, S.J.

## CARNEY, ARTHUR WILLIAM MATTHEW (1918– )

Actor and comedian. Born on November 4, 1918, in Mt. Vernon, New York, Art Carney was the youngest of six sons of Edward Michael and Helen (Farrell) Carney. Carney was a vivacious youngster and was a popular entertainer at A. B. Davis High School where he graduated in 1936. After graduating from high school, Carney traveled for three years with Horace Heidt who had a very popular orchestra and radio quiz show in the late 1930s. While with Heidt's group, he landed a bit part in his first movie, *Pot O'Gold*. Before serving in World War II, Carney worked during the 1930s as an entertainer at the local Elks Club and performed locally as an impressionist and tap dancer.

In 1942 he appeared in *Daytime Showcase* and *Man Behind the Gun* which won a Peabody Award. Carney's talent at mimicry soon impressed an important CBS executive and he was given his first break in 1947 on Morey Amsterdam's program. Carney's performances revealed a remarkable variety of dramatic talents which he developed over the radio in the 1940s, on daytime serials, mysteries, spot recordings, and children's shows, essentially in character and dialect parts. Carney reached the pinnacle in his career during the 1950s as the character Ed Norton. He is most remembered for his association with Jackie Gleason and

Art Carney

their work on *The Honeymooners* sitcom. Carney also appeared on *Suspense, Studio One, Kraft Theatre, Playhouse 90, Climax!* and *Best of Broadway*. Carney's Broadway performances include *The Odd Couple, The Rope Dancers, The Prisoners of Second Avenue, Take Her, She's Mine* and his movies include *A Guide for the Married Man, W. W. and the Dixie Dance Kings, Harry and Tonto,* and *The Late Show*. Carney won an Oscar in 1975 for his first starring movie role in *Harry and Tonto*.

*See* Cinema, Irish in

*Newsweek,* 43 (March 1954): 52.
*Colliers,* 129 (April 1952): 20.
*International Television Almanac* (1957).
Carlyle Wood, *TV Personalities,* vol. II (1956).
*CAB* (1958).

JOY HARRELL

## CARR, ANNE (1934– )

Theologian. Born in Chicago, Illinois, Anne Carr is the daughter of Frank Carr and Dorothy Graber. After graduating from Mundelein College, Chicago, she entered the Sisters of Charity, B.V.M., in Dubuque, Iowa, in 1958.

Upon earning a Ph.D. in theology from the Divinity School of the University of Chicago, she taught at Indiana University, Bloomington, Indiana. Carr is currently professor of theology at the Divinity School of the University of Chicago. She has also been visiting professor at Trinity College, Dublin, Ireland, at Boston College, and at Harvard Divinity School.

She is a major feminist theologian and her book *Transforming Grace: Christian Tradition and Women's Experience* is regarded as ground-breaking and has been translated into German, Italian, French and Portuguese. Carr describes theology and the spirituality that forms it as a struggle to recognize "the sin of human exploitation." Carr has written two other books, regularly publishes articles and reviews, has edited and co-edited six books, and has received honorary doctorates from the Jesuit School of Theology at Berkeley, California, and Loyola University, Chicago. She also serves on editorial boards of leading journals in religion and theology.

Anne Carr

In 1997 the Catholic Theological Society of America presented her with the John Courtney Murray Award for "practicing a dialogical style of thinking and writing, for careful study of the great masters and continual willingness to break new ground and for extensive reflection upon the nature of philosophical and theological methods."

Anne Carr, *The Theological Method of Karl Rahner* (Missoula, MT, 1977).
———. *The Search for Wisdom and Spirit: Thomas Merton's Theology of Self* (Notre Dame, IN, 1988).
———. *Transforming Grace: Christian Tradition and Women's Experience* (San Francisco, 1988).

KATHRYN LAWLOR, B.V.M.

## CARR, THOMAS MATTHEW (1750–1820)

Priest, founder of the Augustinian Order in the U.S. Carr was born in Dublin, Ireland to Michael and Mary (McDaniel) Carr and was baptized Matthew. In 1772, Carr joined the Augustinian Order in Dublin taking the name Thomas. He studied theology at the Augustinian house of studies in Toulouse and was ordained on June 13, 1778. After ordination, Carr held several positions, including that of prior, before being elected by his fellow friars for assignment to the U.S. Carr left Ireland with the blessing of Archbishop Troy of Dublin bearing papers and himself to Archbishop Carroll in response to the request for priests in America. In 1796, Carr was stationed at St. Mary's in Philadelphia where his work was twofold: mission work and the subsequent founding of the Augustinian Order in America. While Carr worked to establish the parish of St. Augustine, financial needs spurred contact and liaison with prominent figures such as President George Washington, whom he later commemorated in an address at St. Mary's in Philadelphia, February 1800.

In 1796, Carr was appointed superior of the American Augustinian missions by Rome with the title of vicar general. Three years later, during the last phases of construction of St. Augustine's, Archbishop Carroll also bestowed the power of vicar general on Carr, which allowed him to establish additional houses and a new novitiate. In 1804, Governor Thomas McKean of Pennsylvania granted legal recognition to the Order of Hermits of St. Augustine. In 1811, Carr opened St. Augustine's Academy, a secondary school for classical and religious studies. In 1812, he published a devotional book entitled *The Spiritual Mirror*. Before his death in Philadelphia on September 29, 1820, Carr willed all the properties in his name to the Order of St. Augustine, thereby ensuring continuation in the U.S.

*Dictionary of American Biography*, 3.
F. C. McGowan, *Historical Sketch of St. Augustine's Church* (Philadelphia, 1896).
T. C. Middleton, *Historical Sketch of Villanova College* (Philadelphia, 1893).

JOY HARRELL

## CARROLL, CHARLES (1737–1832)

Signer of the Declaration of Independence, statesman, financier. Born in Annapolis on September 19, 1737, Carroll was the only child of Charles Carroll II and Elizabeth Brooke. His paternal grandfather, also Charles, had left his native Ireland because of the continuing repression of Catholics and settled in Maryland in 1688. The third Lord Baltimore named him the colony's attorney general, and for this he received several large manor estates, eventually making him and his descendants extremely wealthy.

### EDUCATION

The young Carroll began his education at Bohemia Manor, a Jesuit school operated discreetly due to persistent anti-Catholic laws and sentiment. Since his religion precluded him from further education in Maryland, at the age of eleven he went to the Jesuit college at St. Omer in France. His cousin, John, the first American bishop, was also a student there. After further studies in Rheims and Paris, he studied law in Bourges and practiced this trade in Paris and London. In 1765 he returned to Maryland and his father gave him a ten-thousand acre estate in Frederick County, and it was here that he began to append "Carrollton" (the name of this manor) to his own name so as to distinguish himself from his father. In 1768 he married Mary (Molly) Darnell, a cousin, and the couple had seven children.

### PUBLIC LIFE

Beginning in 1773 Carroll took on a public role by arguing against Governor Robert Eden's unilateral increase of governmental fees which he levied without the approval of the Maryland colonial legislature. His fight was waged principally with Daniel Dulany, a well-connected political leader who supported Eden's actions in the pages of the *Maryland Gazette*. In his campaign against these fees, Carroll used the pen name "First Citizen" and eventually began also to criticize public support of the Anglican Church. The legislative elections later that year brought victory to Carroll and his supporters, and this band of like-minded men eventually went on to lead the colony during the Revolution.

Carroll and many other leaders in Maryland were at first hesitant when war with England seem imminent, and many still hoped for a reconciliation. Carroll's support of the patriot cause was not immediate but developed over time, possibly since it allowed him a more active participation in public life (something his religion had prevented in the past). As sentiment against England solidified across the other colonies, Carroll and the rest of the Maryland colony eventually agreed to join in the separation from Britain. Carroll attended the First Continental Congress in 1774 (though he had to attend as an observer rather than a representative since he was a Catholic). In March 1776 he traveled with Benjamin Franklin, Samuel Chase and his cousin, John Carroll, to Canada to enlist their support for the American

Charles Carroll
of Carrollton

rebellion, but ultimately their efforts proved unsuccessful. Also in 1776 he was elected as a regular delegate to the Second Continental Congress, and on August 2 he was the last man to sign his name to the Declaration of Independence.

From 1777 to 1800 Carroll served in the Maryland senate and in 1787 was invited to participate in the Constitutional Convention in Philadelphia (though he declined). In 1792 he was elected as a senator to the First Congress; however, since he already held a seat in the senate, he was prevented from holding both offices and thus withdrew from the federal body. It was also during this period that his wife died in 1782.

LATER LIFE

With the victory of Jeffersonian Republicans in 1800, Carroll, a Federalist in sympathies, lost his seat in the Maryland senate. After this defeat he largely withdrew from public life. He spent most of his later life managing his fortune, and he was involved in the foundation of the First Bank of the United States (1800) and was a principal stockholder in the Second Bank (1816). With the deaths of John Adams and Thomas Jefferson on July 4, 1826, Carroll was left as the last living signer of the Declaration of Independence. Carroll was a major investor in the Baltimore and Ohio Railroad and made his last public appearance when he laid the railroad's cornerstone on July 4, 1828. On November 14, 1832, a peaceful death came to Charles Carroll of Carrollton at the age of 95 at his home in Doughoregan Manor (near Baltimore). He left his heirs a massive legacy, and his will numbered 35 pages in small type. A fabulously wealthy man with a keen sense for finances and politics, Carroll forged a successful life despite early prejudices against his Catholic background.

*See* Carrolls of Maryland

Thomas O'Brien Hanley, *Charles Carroll of Carrollton: The Making of a Revolutionary Gentleman* (Washington, D.C., 1970).

———, *Revolutionary Gentleman: Charles Carroll and the War* (Chicago, 1983).

Kate Mason Rowland, *The Life of Charles Carroll of Carrollton, 1737–1832, With His Correspondence and Public Papers*, 2 vols. (New York and London, 1898).

Helen Hart Smith, *Charles Carroll of Carrollton* (Cambridge, 1942; repr. New York, 1971).

Ann C. Van Devanter, ed., *"Anywhere So Long As There Be Freedom": Charles Carroll of Carrollton, his Family & his Maryland* (Baltimore, 1975).

ANTHONY D. ANDREASSI

## CARROLL, CHARLES, "OF ANNAPOLIS" (1691–1755)

Prominent politician and planter in early eighteenth-century Maryland, Carroll was born in King's Co., the son of the last baron of Ely-O'Carroll whose family's vast holdings had been confiscated for rebellion, and grandson of the O'Conor Don of Co. Roscommon, descendant of Ireland's last high king. Avoiding official restrictions on Catholic education in Ireland, Carroll studied medicine in Europe and ca. 1715 emigrated to Maryland. By 1715 the Calvert family, Maryland's founders and proprietors, had abandoned Catholicism, and in 1718 the colonial Assembly stripped Catholics of the franchise and prohibited public worship. However, Carroll settled in Annapolis, married into the affluent Blake family, and prospered under the patronage of his distant Catholic kinsman, Charles Carroll "the Settler" (1660–1720), Maryland's wealthiest land- and slave-owner. Carroll soon abandoned medicine for a spectacularly successful career as tobacco planter, land speculator, merchant, shipbuilder, and manufacturer. In 1731 he founded the fabulously profitable Baltimore Iron Works, in partnership with the Settler's sons and with Irish-born Daniel Dulany (1685–1753), Maryland's most powerful politician. In 1738 Carroll converted to the Church of England and was elected to the colonial Assembly, where he served for the rest of his life—first representing Annapolis, later Anne Arundel Co.—and became a principal leader of the "country party," composed of wealthy planters, merchants, and land speculators who opposed the proprietary government. In 1750–51, provoked by charges from his Catholic kinsmen that he had cheated them in business, Carroll launched a political attack on Maryland's Catholic élite. Enflaming Protestant fears of "popery," Carroll urged the Assembly to apply England's penal code to Maryland, thus denying Catholics the right to own land, but proprietary opposition blocked anti-Catholic legislation until 1756, the year after Carroll's death. Carroll bequeathed to his children over 3,000 acres in Anne Arundel Co., patents on thousands more in western Maryland, and personal property worth at least £13,000. In 1776 his eldest son, Charles Carroll "Barrister" (1723–73), rejoined his Catholic relatives to declare Maryland's independence and to dismantle its penal laws.

*See* Carrolls of Maryland

Beatriz B. Hardy, "Papists in a Protestant Age: The Catholic Gentry and Community in Colonial Maryland, 1689–1776" (Ph.D. diss., Univ. of Maryland, 1993).

R. B. Harley, "Dr. Charles Carroll—Land Speculator," *Maryland Historical Magazine*, 46 (1951): 93–107.

E. C. Papenfuse, et al., eds., *A Biographical Dictionary of the Maryland Legislature, 1635–1789*, I (Baltimore, 1977).

Carroll's correspondence is in the *Maryland Historical Magazine*, 22 (1927) and *passim*.

KERBY MILLER

## CARROLL, DANIEL (1730–1796)

Statesman, signer of the Constitution. Daniel Carroll was born in Upper Marlboro, Maryland, on July 25, 1730, to Daniel Carroll and Eleanor Darnall. Several branches of the Carroll family had emigrated from Ireland, beginning in 1688 because of the harsh anti-Catholic penal laws. His father came to Maryland in 1720, and soon acquired extensive property in this colony in areas bordering on present-day Washington, D.C. In addition to Daniel, the Carrolls had six other children, including John Carroll (the first American bishop and first archbishop of Baltimore).

At the age of twelve Daniel was sent to the Jesuit college of St. Omer in Flanders. He spent six years studying in Europe, and after his return to Maryland, he married Eleanor Carroll, a distant cousin. He made his living through mercantile business, managing his plantation and tobacco farming, and soon went on to become quite wealthy. After the franchise was extended to Catholics in Maryland at the time of the American Revolution, Daniel Carroll ran for public office and served in the Maryland State Council, the state senate, and the first House of Representatives. He also served in the Second Continental Congress and signed the Articles of Confederation in 1781 as a delegate from Maryland.

In 1787 Carroll went to Philadelphia to serve as Maryland's delegate at the Constitutional Convention and was instrumental in getting his state to ratify it. In 1791 he was appointed as one of the three commissioners who surveyed the lands for the proposed District of Columbia and sold some of his own property that went on to comprise the new federal district. Also in this year he laid the cornerstone for the new Capitol.

Daniel Carroll is remembered best for his strong devotion to the Catholic Church and his unflagging support of the federal Constitution and the government it established. He died in Rock Creek, Maryland, at the age of sixty-one, but the site of his burial is unknown.

*See* Carrolls of Maryland

Virginia Geiger, *Daniel Carroll, A Framer of the Constitution* (Washington, D.C., 1943).
———, *Daniel Carroll: One Man and His Descendants* (Baltimore, 1979).
Joseph M. Ives, "Daniel Carroll" (unpublished manuscript in the Georgetown University Archives, LaFarge Papers).
Richard J. Purcell, "Daniel Carroll, Framer of the Constitution," *Records of the American Catholic Historical Society* 52/2 (June 1941): 67–87, 137–60.

ANTHONY D. ANDREASSI

## CARROLL, ELIZABETH (1913– )

Educator, author, feminist, religious leader. Elizabeth Carroll was born March 24, 1913, the eldest child of Edward J. and Stella (Bonner) Carroll. She grew up in Bloomfield, Pennsylvania, and spent much of a long life in the environs of Pittsburgh. She received her bachelor of arts degree from the University of Pittsburgh and, the following year, entered the Pittsburgh Sisters of Mercy. Her religious name was Thomas Aquinas. She made her final vows in that congregation on August 25, 1940.

Immediately she began a lengthy educational career. She received her master's and doctoral degrees from the University of Toronto and the Catholic University of America, the latter in medieval history. Thomas Aquinas taught at Marquette University, Catholic University and Carlow College (Pittsburgh), where she also served as Academic Dean and as President.

Thomas Aquinas Carroll offered leadership in the Vatican II renewal of religious life in the United States and, in the process, confronted matters of injustice within and without the church. As she remarked in a 1987 article in *The Journal* (Carlow College: Spring 1987, Vol. IX, No. 2): "There can be no 'after renewal.' Renewal continues as faith and freedom challenge us . . . to change the Church and the world." Feminist principles, astute social analysis and a forthright manner often placed her in the midst of controversy as well as change. Elizabeth Carroll's most recent publication is a work available in Peru—*Las Cadenas del Patriarcado* (The Chains of Patriarchy).

Works by Elizabeth Carroll include *Religious Life in the Seventies; Experience of Women Religious in the Ministry of the Church; Woman: New Dimensions;* and *The Wind Is Rising.*
Articles on Elizabeth Carroll can be found in *The World Who's Who of Women* (Cambridge, 1981); *Who's Who in the World* (Chicago, 1980); and "Sister Elizabeth Carroll," by Ginny Smith in *The Journal*, a publication of Carlow College, Pittsburgh, Vol. IX/2 (Spring 1987).

HELEN MARIE BURNS, R.S.M.

## CARROLL, JAMES P. (1943– )

Novelist, poet, playwright, and nonfiction writer.

### BACKGROUND

James P. Carroll was born January 22, 1943, in Chicago, the son of Joseph Carroll and Mary Morrissey Carroll. Carroll attended Georgetown University, and later St. Paul's College. In the mid-sixties, he studied poetry under writer Allan Tate at the University of Minnesota. At the time, Carroll was preparing to enter the Roman Catholic priesthood and, according to *Contemporary Authors*, Tate predicted that Carroll would not be able to be both a priest *and* a writer. Despite Tate's concerns, Carroll went ahead with his plans and was ordained a Paulist priest in 1969. He also began publishing a series of works on religious themes, such as *Tender of Wishes: The Prayers of a Young Priest* (1969), *Elements of Hope* (1971) and *A Terrible Beauty: Conversions in Prayer, Politics, and Imagination* (1973).

### FOLLOWING A DIFFERENT DRUMMER

Carroll worked at Boston University's campus ministry in the early 1970s where he frequently participated in anti-war activities such as sit-ins, and even appeared on the *Dick Cavett Show* to defend the activist-priest Daniel Berrigan, who was a fugitive at the time.

In 1973 Carroll suffered a crisis of faith which led him on a pilgrimage to the Holy Land. There he experienced both a renewal of his faith and an acceptance of his calling as a writer. In 1974 he made up his mind to leave the priesthood. That same year he published a collection of poetry, *Forbidden Disappointments*, which received a positive response from many critics. He also wrote a play that year *Oh Farrell! Oh Family!* that led to an appointment as a playwright-in-residence at the Berkshire Theater Festival.

*The Winter Name of God* (1975) chronicled his struggle with religious doubts and how he came to grips with them. Carroll followed this with *Madonna Red* (1976), a suspense novel which, aside from providing the reader adventure and intrigue, touches upon issues pertaining to change in the Catholic church.

### AN IRISHMAN'S ODYSSEY

*Mortal Friends* (1978) was Carroll's breakthrough work, "the book that gave me my career," (Szymczak). It tells the story of a young Irishman named Colman Brady who becomes involved in the Irish War of Independence, and the civil war that followed it. Brady, who is a friend and colleague of Michael Collins, leaves Ireland after Collins is killed and Brady's own family is massacred. He immigrates to Boston where he becomes an underling of Mayor James Michael Curley.

Brady's life in America follows a tragic path as he rises in the world by aiding corrupt men. In *Contemporary Literary Criticism*, critic Joseph Parisi wrote, "Carroll suggests [Brady's] lacks are the inevitable result of an incapacity to love truly, the corruption of power and a malignant destiny that is the peculiar curse of the Irish."

Carroll followed *Mortal Friends* with several other novels: *Fault Lines* (1980), *Family Trade* (1982), *Prince of Peace* (1984), *Supply of Heroes* (1986), *Firebird* (1989), *Memorial Bridge* (1991), and *The City Below* (1994).

### GOD AND THE FATHER

Much of Carroll's fiction deals with the theme of personal betrayal. In the foreword to the 1992 edition of *Mortal Friends*, the historian Doris Kearns Godwin wrote "Colman Brady . . . discovers to his horror that after a life full of enemies, his most mortal threat comes from his own son."

In 1996 Carroll published *American Requiem: God, My Father and the War That Came Between Us*, a memoir in which he looked at his early life, particularly his years in the priesthood, his decision to leave it, and how that choice, and others, affected his relationship with his father, a former seminarian who had abandoned his religious studies, and eventually became an air force general in charge of the Defense Intelligence Agency.

While the elder Carroll was actively helping to fight the Vietnam War, his son James was participating in peace rallies as an activist priest. A rift was inevitable, one that doubtlessly mirrored divisions between many men of Carroll's generation and their fathers. At the end of *American Requiem*, Carroll writes "My father was dead. A fallible man. A noble man. I loved him. And because I was so much like him, though appearing not to be, I had broken his heart. And the final truth was . . . he had broken mine." *American Requiem* won a National Book Award in 1996.

*See* Fiction, Irish-American

James P. Carroll, *Mortal Friends: A Novel*. Introduction by Doris Kearns Godwin (Beacon Press, 1992).

———, *An American Requiem: God, My Father, and the War That Came Between Us* (Houghton Mifflin, 1996)

"Carroll, James," *Current Biography, 1997* (H.W. Wilson, 1997).

"Carroll, James," *Who's Who in America 1998*, Vol. 1 (Marquis Who's Who, 1997): 52.

Alex Chisolm, "Daddy and Other Gods," *The Boston Book Review* (1998). http://www.bookwire.com/ BBR/Life-&-Letters/read.Review$2525 (19 May 1998).

Peter Gilmour, "Father, Son, and an Unholy War: Peter Gilmour Interviews James Carroll," *U.S. Catholic* (May 1, 1997) http://www.uscatholic.org (May 28, 1998).

"James P. Carroll," *Contemporary Authors* Gale Literary Databases (1998). http://galenet.gale.com/m/mcp/prodlist (Go to *Contemporary Authors* link) (24 May 1998).

"James P. Carroll," *Contemporary Literary Criticism*, Vol. 38 (Gale Research, 1986).

"James P. Carroll," *Contemporary Authors*, Vol. 81–84 (Gale Research, 1979).

Ralph Szymczak, "A Selective Bibliography on James Carroll." Brandeis University Library Collections & Reseach Online 1997. http://www.library.brandeis.edu/collections/carroll.html (May 19, 1998).

PETER G. SHEA

## CARROLL, JOHN (1736–1815)

First bishop and archbishop of Baltimore and founder of the American Catholic hierarchy. John Carroll was born at Upper Marlboro, Maryland, on January 8 (or 19), 1736, the son of Daniel Carroll, merchant and planter, and Eleanor Darnall, the daughter of Henry Darnall II, a descendant of some of the leading families of England. The father may have emigrated from Ireland to Maryland as early as 1718. He was the son of Kean Carroll, probably the Kean Carroll of Ahagurton attainted by the English in 1691, and grandson of John Carroll of Ballycrenode in County Tipperary. Though undoubtedly related to the older and more famous branch of the family, that of Charles Carroll of Carrollton, the exact degree of kinship on the father's side is unknown. On the mother's side, however, through the Darnalls, Archbishop John Carroll was the second cousin of Charles of Carrollton. The several branches of the Carroll family in Maryland, all related, intermarried with the leading Catholic families of English descent—the Darnalls, Digges, Brookes, Rozers, Blakes—with whom they came to be identified.

### THE EUROPEAN YEARS

In 1747 young John Carroll was sent to a school newly opened by the Jesuits at Bohemia Manor near the head of Chesapeake Bay to prepare him for entrance into St. Omer's College in French Flanders also conducted by the Jesuits. There many Marylanders, including John's older brother Daniel, had been and would

John Carroll

Tenth Congressional District of Pennsylvania, which includes several counties in the northeast section of the state.

*See* Pennsylvania

Michael Barone, et al., *The Almanac of American Politics, 1988* (New York and Washington, D.C., 1987).

Robert Patrick Casey, *Fighting for Life* (Dallas, 1996).

Michael Crowley, "Casey Closed," *The New Republic,* Vol. 215 (Sept. 16 and 23): 12–14.

Marie Marmo Mullaney, *Biographical Directory of the Governors of the United States 1983–1988* (Westport, Conn., 1989).

John Pekkanen, "Last Chance to Live," *Reader's Digest,* Vol. 47 (October, 1995): 115–22.

John Wouck, "Governor Casey vs. the Odds," *The Human Life Review,* Vol. 20/3: 15–27.

MARIANNA McLOUGHLIN

## CASEY, SOLANUS BERNARD (1870–1957)

Capuchin priest. Bernard Francis Casey was born on November 25, 1870 near the town of Prescott, Wisconsin. His father, Bernard James Casey, was born in Castleblaney, County Monaghan, in 1840, emigrated to the United States in 1857, and settled in Boston, Massachusetts. His mother, Ellen Elizabeth Murphy, was born in Camlough, County Armagh, in 1844 and emigrated to the United States in 1852. They were married in Salem, Massachusetts, in 1863, moved to Philadelphia and, in 1865, to an 80-acre farm near Prescott, Wisconsin. Bernard Francis, the sixth child in a family of ten boys and six girls, was born at Oak Grove, four miles south of Prescott, and baptized at St. Joseph's Church, Hudson, Wisconsin. Eight years later, two of his sisters, Mary-Ann and Martha, died of diphtheria, a disease which he also contracted but survived although his throat and voice were affected. He received his primary education in the rural schools of Trimbelle and Burkhardt, Wisconsin. When he turned 17, he moved to Stillwater, Minnesota, and worked in a lumber mill, as a part-time prison guard, and as one of Stillwater's first streetcar operators, a position he also held in Appleton and Superior, Wisconsin.

In 1891 Bernard entered Saint Francis de Sales Seminary in Milwaukee, Wisconsin, where he began his secondary education. As a young seminarian, he visited the Capuchins. On December 24, 1896, he arrived at St. Bonaventure Monastery in Detroit, and on January 14, 1897, he was invested as a novice. He was given the religious name, Francis Solanus. Solanus pronounced his simple vows on July 21, 1898, and returned to Milwaukee where at St. Francis Seminary he began his studies for the priesthood. Studies were extremely difficult for the young friar and questions arose among his professors and superiors as to his qualifications for ordination. His religious example eventually persuaded his superiors to permit his ordination and Solanus was ordained on July 24, 1904. However the young priest was not given faculties to preach or to administer the Sacrament of Penance.

His first assignment as a simple priest was to Sacred Heart Parish in Yonkers, New York, where he was given the responsibilities of sacristan and porter, as well as other non-sacramental positions, Director of the Young Ladies Sodality and of the Altar Boys. During the fourteen years in which he discharged these responsibilities in Yonkers, Solanus continued to be known for his deep life of prayer, his example of simplicity and humility, and especially for his charity toward the sick, non-Catholics and the

Solanus Casey

poor. His advice to those who came to him for help was simple. After encouraging them to make a sacrifice for the foreign missions, he would tell them to thank God ahead of time for granting the favor they requested.

Solanus was first sent to the Capuchin Friary of Saint Bonaventure in Detroit, Michigan, on August 1, 1924. He ministered there until April 25, 1946. Throughout those twenty-two years, Solanus became known for his charity to the poor whose numbers were daily increasing as the Great Depression of 1929 approached. The image of him in the Soup Kitchen offering to the poor food, clothing or simple advice was quite well known. During the war years, 1941–1945, much of his time was taken up consoling and strengthening the faith of those having a family member or loved one in service. Because his health was failing, Solanus was sent on July 23, 1945, to Saint Michael's Friary in Brooklyn, N.Y., and again on April 25, 1946, to the Capuchin novitiate in Huntington, Indiana, where he remained until his return to Detroit on May 10, 1956. Suffering from skin cancer and a chronic skin disease, much of the following year was spent in Detroit's St. John's Hospital. He died on July 31, 1957.

Shortly after Solanus's death, the process of gathering information about his life, work, and the favors granted through his intercession was begun. The data was presented to John Cardinal Dearden, Archbishop of Detroit, who presented it and four volumes of Solanus's writings to the Congregation for the Causes of Saints. On June 19, 1982, Pope John Paul II gave his official approval to introduce Solanus's cause in the Archdiocese of Detroit. On July 11, 1995, the Congregation, together with the Pope, promulgated the Decree of Heroic Virtue, a recognition of his great holiness.

Michael Crosy, *Thank God Ahead of Time* (Chicago, 1985).

James Patrick Derum, *The Porter of Saint Bonaventure* (1968).

Catherine Odell, *Father Solanus: The Story of Fr. Solanus Casey, O.F.M. Cap.* (Huntington, 1988).

REGIS J. ARMSTRONG, O.F.M. CAP.

## CASEY, WILLIAM (1913–1989)

Director of the C.I.A. and Chairman of the Securities and Exchange Commission. Casey was born in Elmhurst, Queens

County, on Long Island, New York. He was a very rambunctious youngster and learned early to channel his energy to the goals he set for himself. He went to Fordham University and obtained a B.A. and then went on to legal training at St. John's University Law School in 1934. Casey earned the LL.B. degree in 1937 and was admitted to the New York bar the following year.

At the outbreak of World War II Casey worked under David K. E. Bruce in helping to organize the Office of Strategic Services. From 1947–48 he worked in Washington, D.C. as special counsel to the Small Business Committee of the United States Senate where he became interested in international relations. Casey also taught at New York University, focusing on tax law from 1948 to 1962; he published several books on his research interests including *Tax Planning on Excess Profits* (1951), *Tax Sheltered Investments* (1952), *Executive Pay Plans* (1953) and *Tax Shelter for the Family* (1953). With his publishing connections Casey also became a member of the editorial board for the Institute for Business Planning while he practiced law as a partner of the New York firm of Hall, Casey, Dickler & Howley and the Washington, D.C. firm of Scribner, Hall, Casey, Thornburg & Thompson.

In 1966 Casey ran for office by seeking the Republican nomination for a seat in the United States House of Representatives. His opponent was Steven B. Derounian, a conservative Barry Goldwater supporter. Casey lost to Derounian in the primary election; however, later the same year he was elected chairman of the executive committee of the International Rescue Committee. In 1968 he participated in Richard Nixon's winning campaign for president. In 1969 Casey became the founder and chairman of the Citizens Committee for Peace with Security, a committee that supported the president's anti-ballistic missile program.

However, an advertisement that the committee bought in local newspapers for the promotion of the ABM proposal incited a controversy; it was discovered that many of the signers of the ad had connections with the defense industry. While in 1969 Nixon had named Casey to the Advisory Council of the United States Arms Control and Disarmament Agency, Casey also petitioned for a post on the Securities and Exchange Commission to which President Nixon conceded in 1971. Casey faced additional controversy in several lawsuits filed against him for various projects he headed but he maintained that they were only minor obstacles to his ambitious career. Casey assumed chairmanship of the SEC at a crucial time for the stock markets and he worked tirelessly on identifying critical areas for reform and reappraisal.

Casey's career came to a pinnacle with his position as director of the C.I.A from the years 1981–1987. With the prestigious position came many enduring trials, personally and professionally, particularly regarding the Iran-Contra affair. Casey weathered the many challenges presented during the mid-80s but finally was hindered by a brain tumor and died in 1989.

*Who's Who in America* (1972–73).
*Time* (98:99 N 22 1971).
*CAB* (1972).

JOY HARRELL

## CASHMAN, DENIS B. (1842–1897)

Journalist, poet, biographer. He was born in Dungarvan, near Waterford. Little is known of his early years, but by 1862, he was working as a law clerk for Dobyn and Tandy, a law firm

in Waterford, and in 1862 he was married. Between 1862 and 1867, Denis and Catherine Cashman had three children. In January of 1867, Cashman was arrested, tried and convicted of felony treason, and sentenced to seven years imprisonment (*Tracts* 155A).

In 1858, still a teenager, Cashman had joined the Irish Republican Brotherhood, the Fenians, and had been a very active member. He had helped Lawrence O'Brien hide in the Cashman home during O'Brien's escape "from a crown prison in Ireland . . . to freedom in America" (Ryan 1). By the time of his arrest, Cashman had become the "centre" (head) of the Waterford Fenian Circle and also had taken an increasing part in Fenian activities at the national level (*Tracts* 155A).

After his sentencing, in February of 1867, Cashman spent some time in Kilmainham Goal, Dublin, before being transferred to Millbank Prison, London, where he remained until September of that year. In September, along with several other Fenians and a larger number of nonpolitical prisoners, Cashman was placed aboard the *Hougoumont* and, after stops to pick up other convicts, including John Boyle O'Reilly, was transported to the penal colony at Fremantle, Western Australia. Aboard the ship, Cashman was one of the main forces, along with O'Reilly and John Flood, behind the publication of the ship-board newspaper, *The Wild Goose* (Cashman).

Cashman and a number of other civil Fenian convicts were pardoned in 1869, and Cashman made his way, via San Francisco, to Boston, where he was reunited with Catherine, his wife, and their children as well as with John Boyle O'Reilly, who had escaped from Australia earlier in 1869. O'Reilly helped Cashman find a job on *The Pilot*, of which he was then an editor. Cashman continued his Fenian activities in Boston, though, like O'Reilly, he did not become active within the established American branch of the organization (Evans 180–181).

In the early 1870s, Cashman and O'Reilly helped plan the *Catalpa* expedition which sent a whaling ship to Australia to rescue the remaining Fenian military prisoners sentenced, as O'Reilly had been, to life imprisonment there. Cashman then represented *The Pilot* in New York upon the *Catalpa's* successful return (Evans 203–206). In addition to writing poetry and pro-Irish articles for *The Pilot* and *The Boston Herald* (Ryan 5), at least, Cashman also wrote *The Life of Michael Davitt with a History of the Rise and Development of the Irish National Land League* (1881), still considered an important study of both Davitt and Land League.

Cashman left *The Pilot* "around 1876" and, according to Boston city records, held a number of positions, including one as "Storekeeper, with an office in the Post Office building" and "head of the Water Waste Department at City Hall" (Ryan 5). He may well have taken these jobs for their pensions.

Denis B. Cashman died in 1897, and an obituary noted that he was survived by his wife and his son, "now W. P. Cashman of the Probate Court in Boston" (5).

Denis B. Cashman, *Diary* (Manuscript Archives. East Carolina University, Greenville, N.C.).
A. G. Evans, *Fanatic Heart: A Life of John Boyle O'Reilly, 1844–1890* (Nedlands, WA, 1997).
*The Boston Transcript*, Obituary (11 January 1897): 5.
George Ryan, "Dennis [*sic*] B. Cashman: 'Warmly Devoted to His Native Land,'" *Bulletin of the Eire Society of Boston*, 41/3 (1983): 1–6.
*Tracts of Cases Under Habeas Corpus Suspension Act*. Volume I. *Ireland: Irish Crimes Records*. 1866 (National Archives, Dublin, IR).

C. W. SULLIVAN III

## CASS, THOMAS (1821–1862)

Merchant, soldier. Born in Farmsley, Queen's County (Offaly), Ireland in 1821, Cass' parents brought him to America as an infant. Educated in Boston, Cass married at the age of twenty and pursued a career in business. He became the owner of several ships trading in the Azore Islands and a stockholder in the Towboat Company operating in Boston Harbor.

Cass joined a Boston Irish militia company, the Columbian Artillery, and moved up the ranks to become its captain and commanding officer. In 1855, Nativist hostility against Irish Catholics led Massachusetts' Know-Nothing Governor Henry Gardner to disband militia companies composed of men of foreign birth, though the company survived under Cass' leadership as a civic organization. Having strong loyalty to the Democratic party, Cass also served as an officer of his Boston ward and was an influential member of the North End's Irish population.

With the outbreak of the Civil War, Governor John A. Andrew decided to put an Irish regiment in the field and Thomas Cass was to lead it. Many of Boston's Irish answered his call to service, and former members of the Columbian Artillery served as a nucleus for what would be designated the Ninth Massachusetts Volunteer Infantry.

Cass proved a strict disciplinarian who transformed his rough, Irish volunteers into trained soldiers. He led the regiment down to Washington, D.C., where the men helped defend the Federal capital. In the spring of 1862, the Ninth Massachusetts accompanied the Army of the Potomac on the Peninsula campaign to capture Richmond. Although ill, Cass led his Irishmen into battle at Hanover Court House on May 27, where the regiment's performance in recapturing two cannon earned it the sobriquet "Fighting Ninth."

At Gaines' Mill on June 27, Cass led his regiment until sickness forced him to relinquish command to Lieutenant Colonel Patrick Guiney. During that battle, the "Fighting Ninth" contested the Confederate advance across the mill creek and later served as rearguard for the retreating Federal column, suffering the most casualties of any unit on the field in the process. On July 1, Cass again took command of his regiment for the battle of Malvern Hill, despite his illness. The Ninth successfully defended a nearby battery but a bullet struck Cass' cheek, passing through the roof of his mouth and knocking out six teeth before exiting by his ear. Cass returned to Boston to recuperate, but succumbed to his wounds on July 12, 1862. His funeral services were marked with high honors as many mourned his loss.

*See* Boston; Civil War

Boston *Pilot* (July 27, 1861).
Daniel G. Macnamara, *The History of the Ninth Regiment Massachusetts Volunteer Infantry* (Boston, 1899).
Christian Samito, ed., *Commanding Boston's Irish Ninth: The Civil War Letters of Colonel Patrick R. Guiney Ninth Massachusetts Volunteer Infantry* (New York, 1998).
*The War of the Rebellion: A Compilation of the Official Records of the Union and Confederate Armies,* 128 vols. (Washington, D.C., 1880–1901).

CHRISTIAN G. SAMITO

## CASTLE GARDEN

Immigration station. From 1855 to 1890, New York City leased the building to a state-authorized Board of Commissioners of

Castle Garden

Emigration. Composed of government appointees and representatives of New York's Irish and German benevolent organizations, the commission oversaw collection of government-mandated statistics on migrants, customs inspection of migrants' luggage, and medical inspection of the migrants. It assisted migrants with exchanging money, delivering luggage, purchasing tickets for further transportation, and hunting jobs. *Henderson* v. *Mayor of New York* (1875) declared migration a federal responsibility, paving the way for federal takeover of commission work. In 1892, Ellis Island opened.

Fires at Castle Garden July 9, 1876, and at Ellis Island June 15, 1897, destroyed most Castle Garden records, but the building survives. In 1811, a fort named West Battery was erected 100 yards off Manhattan's southwest shore. Renamed Castle Clinton in honor of De Witt Clinton in 1815, it never fired a shot. The federal government ceded it to New York City in 1824. The city roofed it and, until 1855, leased it as an entertainment center. From 1896 to 1941, it housed New York's aquarium. Robert Moses moved the aquarium to build the Brooklyn-Battery Tunnel, but public outcry saved the building. In 1946 it became a national historic landmark. The National Park Service renovated it for tourism in 1976, began using it as a box office for tickets to the Statue of Liberty in 1986, and, since 1992, has used it for combination tickets to the Statue and Ellis Island (1992).

*See* Emigration: 1801–1921

George J. Svejda, *Castle Garden as an Immigration Depot, 1855–1890.* Washington, D.C.: National Park Service, Department of the Interior, 1968.

MARY ELIZABETH BROWN

## CATHOLICISM, IRISH-AMERICAN

RELIGION, CULTURE, AND ETHNICITY

About seventy-five percent of the close to five million Irish who arrived in the United States between 1820 and 1920 were Catholic, the first large group of their faith to enter the country. Although the vast majority had been tenant farmers or agricultural laborers in Ireland, they lacked skills and temperaments to be successful farmers in the vastness and loneliness of rural America. Against the advice and warnings of bishops and priests in

Ireland, and a few in the United States, who worried about the worldly temptations of urban life, most settled in cities and large towns. Men became unskilled laborers in the industrial and transportation revolutions. Women worked in textile mills and shoe factories or as domestic servants. As pioneers of the urban ghetto, the Irish played an important role in America's economic, political and social history. But their most important impact was on the character and personality of American Catholicism.

## THE PRE-IRISH AMERICAN CHURCH

Before the Irish, Catholicism was a tiny speck on America's religious and social landscapes. In the 1790s, about thirty thousand Catholics, one-tenth Black slaves, were heavily concentrated in Maryland and Pennsylvania. Only one bishop, John Carroll of Baltimore, and thirty priests, usually Anglo or Anglicized Americans and French Sulpicians, served them.

No-popery, the core of American nativism, inherited from English, Scotch, Welsh, and Irish Protestants who settled British North America, intimidated Catholics and made them shy and deferential. Their chapels and services were simple; their priests rejected clerical garb and preferred to be called mister rather than father or reverend. For a time, John Carroll, cousin of Charles, the only Catholic signatory to the *Declaration of Independence*, tried to navigate Catholicism into the cultural mainstream. He encouraged lay trustee control of parishes, an English language liturgy, and a theology more compatible with the rationalism of the American Enlightenment than with the devotionalism, emotionalism, and mysticism of European Catholicism.

Eventually, the conservatism of his Maryland gentry background, reactions to the excesses of the French Revolution, suspicions that Jeffersonian democracy had Jacobin colorations, and his duties and responsibilities as primate of the American church gave Carroll a more Roman perspective. However, many Catholics in the United States persisted in keeping their church American. Irish emigration turned the tide in the direction of Romanization.

## THE PERSONALITY OF IRISH CATHOLICISM

The Irish have felt and expressed their religion more intensely than most other Catholics. It has been their culture and identity, sustaining them through the dreary centuries of English conquest and Anglo-Irish Protestant domination. In the "Proem" of *King of the Beggars,* a biography of Daniel O'Connell, who in his 1820s agitation for Catholic Emancipation expanded a religious commitment into a nationality, Sean O'Faolain described Catholicism as a "not inconsiderable possession" for the impoverished and oppressed Irish masses: "They had in a word, with that one exception of their faith, nothing, neither a present, nor a past, nor a future" (p. 29). In *Ireland's English Question* (1971), Patrick O'Farrell perceptively analyzed Irish Catholicism as more "than the official pronouncements of the hierarchy: it is a set of values, a culture, a historical tradition, a view on the world, a disposition of mind and heart, a loyalty, an emotion, a psychology— and a nationalism" (p. 306).

## IRISH CATHOLICS AND AMERICAN NATIVISM

Inseparable links between Catholic and Irish led to clashes with Anglo-American Protestants who also associated their religion with culture and nationality. Secular features of American life also were hostile to Catholicism. Disciples of the Enlightenment considered authoritarian, superstitious popery the most obnox-

ious of all organized religions. They, along with traditional Protestants, were convinced that papists could never become assimilated and productive citizens of a nation dedicated to individual liberty.

As urban dwellers, Irish Catholics were unpleasantly conspicuous. According to the Jeffersonian ideal, the small, independent farmer was the perfect citizen. In this agrarian, populist vision, cities, industry, and commerce were at best necessary evils. Therefore, Irish Catholics for both religious and secular reasons represented a subversive threat to the nation's culture and institutions.

Determined to eliminate the alleged threat to American values, some nativists attacked Irish ghettoes, assaulting residents and burning their churches. In 1854, they launched the American (Know-Nothing) party that attracted voters in many states, especially Massachusetts where it controlled the executive and legislative branches of government. If sectionalism and slavery had not emerged as major issues, Know-Nothings might have won the presidential election of 1856, and then passed laws limiting immigration and denying newcomers to the United States first-class citizenship. As it was, the new Republican party embraced much of the nativist agenda.

Irish conduct as well as their religion provoked animosity. Psychologically traumatized by the transition from rural Ireland to urban America, they became its first massive social problem, filling jails, hospitals, orphanages, and mental hospitals. They crowded attics and basements or lived in tar-paper shacks. Pigs wandered and sewage flowed through ghetto streets. Anglo-Protestants despaired as many sections of their cities became bleak slums. As late as 1868, the *Chicago Evening Post,* commenting on the large Irish social burden, remarked: "Scratch a convict or pauper and the chances are that you tickle the skin of an Irish Catholic made a criminal or a pauper by the priest and politician who have deceived him and kept him in ignorance, in a word, a savage, as he was born." This editorial makes clear that nativists associated Irish behavior with a religion they said fostered ignorance and irresponsibility.

Rowdy Irish immigrants irritated American Catholics as well as Protestants. Franco-Americans in New Orleans despised them as much as Boston Protestants. And members of the American hierarchy, especially Ambrose Marechal, Carroll's successor as primate, worried, with considerable justification, that undisciplined and uneducated Irish immigrants would damage the image and tone of the church in the United States.

## THE "DEVOTIONAL REVOLUTION"

Many Irish immigrants, especially those who came during the late stages of the 1845–1849 Famine, knew little about their religion and were irregular in its practice. With a small number of priests, the American church found it difficult to provide for their spiritual comfort and education. And the Irish frequently objected to French pastors. Answering requests from bishops in the United States, those in Ireland sent priests on the American mission. Unfortunately, they often used it as a dumping ground for insubordinate, alcoholic, and womanizing clergy who became as troublesome in the New World as they were in the Old. Marechal complained that Irish priests, often as crude and ignorant as those they served, fueled anti-Catholicism.

Determined to remedy the situation, American bishops, such as Irish-born John England of Charleston and John Hughes of New York, pleaded with the Irish hierarchy to send them better men. What Emmet Larkin has described as a Devotional Revolution aided their cause. It began with the Great Famine that resulted in the death of at least a million and the emigration of another million-and-a-half. Most Famine victims were agricultural laborers and marginal tenant farmers, the most religiously ignorant and superstitious classes. Their absence from the Irish scene relieved serious priest and chapel shortages and provided Paul Cullen with an opportunity to bring Irish Catholicism into total conformity with Rome.

In 1849, Pius IX appointed Cullen, Rector of the Irish College in Rome, archbishop of Armagh, primate of the Irish church, and apostolic delegate. Three years later, he succeeded Daniel Murray as archbishop of Dublin, and in 1866 he became Ireland's first cardinal. Cullen ended open quarrels among the hierarchy; improved clerical education; encouraged and increased religious vocations; expanded the Catholic elementary and secondary educational systems; built churches and packed them with the most loyal, devout, and financially generous Catholics in the Roman fold. Although Cullen was hostile to nationalism, close associations between Irish and Catholics energized both. Religious enthusiasm became a visible sign of patriotism.

The Devotional Revolution also had an Irish-American dimension. Full of missionary zeal and encouraged by Cullen, Irish seminaries, especially All Hallows in Drumcondra, a Dublin suburb, sent priests to preserve the faith of the Irish Diaspora throughout the English-speaking world, and to search for converts in Britain's African and Asian colonies. Irish nuns and brothers also served the Irish spiritual empire as teachers, and, in the case of the former, as nurses and directors of Catholic institutions such as hospitals and orphanages. A reformed and energized post-Famine Catholicism certainly contributed to a better educated, more religious, and disciplined late nineteenth-century emigration. And in the United States, as in Ireland, close ties between religion and ethnicity did much to encourage Irish-Americans to devoutly and proudly practice Catholicism as their identity badge.

### Priests, Nuns, Brothers and Irish Religious Life

In addition to appealing to Ireland and other European countries to assist them in addressing the spiritual needs of a rapidly expanding Catholic population, American bishops opened local seminaries and vigorously encouraged religious vocations. Distinguished by talent and numbers, the Irish were most responsive to this appeal. Their eagerness expressed the prestige of the religious life in the Irish tradition. As symbols of resistance to English colonialism and Protestant ascendancy, and of the close ties between Catholicism and nationality, Ireland, more than other European Catholic countries, has honored priests (for similar patriotic reasons Poland is probably the only exception).

Beginning with O'Connell's campaign for Catholic Emancipation, nationalist leaders recruited priests as lieutenants to counter the influence of Protestant unionist landlords. Fenians in the 1860s, Parnellites in the 1890s, and post-1922 members of the Irish Republican Army have railed against the hierarchy and clergy for opposing their causes, but anti-clericalism has played a minor role in Irish history. Instead, for secular as well as religious considerations, Irish families offered their most gifted sons and daughters to the church. In a poor country, with few opportunities, a son in the priesthood elevated the social and sometimes economic status of his family. Nuns have been the most highly regarded Irish Catholic women. Usually, priests have been sons of strong farmers or shopkeepers. Brothers have tended to come from the small tenant farming or agricultural laboring classes. But they have had access to educational possibilities denied to others of their social level.

Secular motivations also have encouraged religious vocations in the United States. Priest families have had a special standing in parish communities. Nativist prejudices, limiting if not blocking the entry of Irish talent into business or the professions, forced it to seek fulfillment in religion, politics, or the labor movement. It takes the same kinds of personality and leadership skills to be successful in all three.

Until recently, both the Irish and Irish-American clergy, despite the intellectual limitations of seminary training, have been well educated compared to the laity. In Ireland and the United States, Irish priests have been conscientious pastors and curates. In addition to saying Mass, hearing confessions, and baptizing, marrying, and burying parishioners, they have had to build and maintain churches, rectories, convents, and schools. They also have had to attend meetings of a variety of parish organizations, counsel men and women of all ages. At a time when most Irish Catholics believed in clerical authority, the sometimes friendly and other times angry advice of the parish priest has had a tremendous influence on both the religious and secular conduct and opinions of the laity.

As Hasia Diner (*Erin's Daughters in America,* 1983) and other historians have noted, Irish-American women were the pillars of the immigrant church. While some men often spent their spare cash in saloons, domestic servants, waitresses, and women factory and mill workers dropped nickles, dimes, quarters, and dollars in the Sunday collection basket. In addition to their frequent presence at Mass and devotions, they cleaned and decorated churches and ran parish bazaars and socials. As wives and mothers, Irish-American women instilled a devotion to the church in their children, and, more than their husbands, fostered the religious vocations of sons and daughters.

Like priests, nuns have been the cream of their gender's talent pool. The Sisters of Mercy and the Presentation Sisters originated in Ireland and sent many recruits to serve the immigrant church. They and others with continental European beginnings, usually in France, enlisted large numbers of Irish and Irish-American women. Mary Francis Clarke and four of her friends from Ireland arrived in Philadelphia to teach the children of immigrants. In 1833, they founded the Sisters of Charity of the Blessed Virgin Mary (BVMs). During the American Civil War, Catholic sisters, many from Ireland, nursed and won the respect of wounded soldiers. In addition to operating hospitals, nuns opened schools for girls and young women and, on the hierarchy's insistence, expanded their teaching efforts to include boys.

Since today's Irish-American women have a multitude of opportunities in secular society, quite a few people, including Catholics, consider vocations restricted by convent walls and the vows of chastity, poverty, and obedience as confining and irrelevant. But not so long ago religious life was adventurous and liberating for women. As presidents of colleges, teachers in and principals of elementary and secondary schools, and hospital directors and nurses, nuns were pioneer professional women.

More than priests, nuns have shaped cultural and religious Catholicism. Some novelists, playwrights, and critics of Catholic background have accused them of propagating a narrow, cold, puritanical view of religion. But their secondary schools and colleges for women have fostered the arts and humanities more extensively than those that priests and brothers have operated for men. Mary McCarthy, the distinguished writer and critic, in her 1957 *Memoirs of a Catholic Girlhood,* credited nuns who taught her at St. Stephen's parochial school in Minneapolis and Sacred Heart Academy in Seattle for introducing her to a world of "mystery and wonder" that informed and inspired her literary imagination.

While not as conspicuous or respected as priests or nuns, Irish and Irish-American brothers have contributed to Catholic education in the United States. Differing from their colleagues in Ireland, they have come from the same social classes as other religious. Often better educated than priests, brothers have been content to serve the church in a less glamorous vocation.

Catholicism prepared the Irish for American nativist hostility, and enabled them to survive the ordeal. The church's devotions, liturgy, and sacraments were a bridge of familiarity connecting rural Ireland and urban America, providing spiritual and psychological comfort in strange, unfriendly surroundings. As a social as well as a religious community, the city parish functioned as a peasant village, sheltering immigrants from the competitive harshness of commercial and industrial America. In a number of essays and books, Ellen Skerrett, the leading historian on the role of the parish in Catholic ethnic life, has described churches with their stained glass windows, statues, incense, and candles as "sacred space" in a turbulent, insecure milieu, and how they brought beauty and a feeling of security to worshippers.

At a time when government shied away from alleviating social distress, and *laissez faire*–oriented Anglo-Protestants tended to blame poverty victims for their misfortunes, nuns, representing a more Christian view, provided hospitality and caring love to society's neglected. In "Charity, Poverty, and Child Welfare" (*Harvard Divinity Bulletin,* 25:4, 1996, pp. 12–17), Maureen Fitzgerald contrasts the cold-hearted, punitive Protestant response to individual and family destitution with the sheltering charity of nuns that radically transformed the welfare system in late nineteenth- and early twentieth-century New York. In "Walking Nuns: Chicago's Irish Sisters of Mercy" (*At the Crossroads: Old Saint Patrick's and the Chicago Irish,* ed. Ellen Skerrett, 1997, pp. 39–52), Suellen Hoy details how Mercy nuns provided social services to Chicago's indigent earlier and on a larger scale than Jane Addams and her Hull House staff.

## SECULAR AND RELIGIOUS VARIABLES IN IRISH AMERICA

Catholic moral teachings; the discipline and instruction of parochial schools; the guidance of priests, nuns, and brothers; and the social welfare provided by Catholic institutions were instrumental in the mobility of Irish-Americans. By the close of the nineteenth century, many had advanced from unskilled to skilled workers and a few penetrated the lower middle class. But progress exhibited regional and gender situations. Women as teachers and nurses, inspired by the nuns who instructed them in Catholic elementary and secondary schools, were more numerous as well-educated, middle-class professionals than Irish men. And, as Jo Ellen McNergney Vinyard's *The Irish on the Urban Frontier: Detroit, 1850–1880* (1976) has indicated, the Irish in midwestern and western cities achieved a higher degree of prosperity and respectability than those on the eastern seaboard, especially New England.

In urban centers such as Boston, Irish Catholics had settled in places with limited and fading economies and tight social structures, the preserves of a Yankee Brahmin ruling class that

In the 1950s nuns lead Catholic schoolchildren on a crusade to put the archdiocesan newspaper in every Catholic home. The religious life offered Irish-American women the opportunity for adventure, education, and leadership.

regarded them with contempt. They became victims of their own defeatism and paranoia as well as of nativism. Ghettos of place also became confining ghettos of mind.

Midwestern and western cities were relatively open societies where nativism was not deeply entrenched or well organized. They also had dynamic, multidimensional economies with unlimited potential. Because factories, mills, stockyards, slaughterhouses, and railroads needed workers, production and profit overcame prejudice. On the urban frontier, Buffalo and points west, the Irish were far more likely to advance into the upper-working and middle classes, and to have social contacts with non-Catholics than on the East coast.

Although religious expressions of Irish-American Catholicism and its subculture were consistent throughout the country, the response to things American reflected regional variations. During the 1880s and 1890s, some eastern bishops, particularly New York's Archbishop Michael Corrigan and Rochester's Bernard McQuade, rejected American culture and values as essentially anti-Catholic. Allied with Midwest German-American prelates, such as Sebastian Messmer of Green Bay, Wisconsin, they fostered ethnic isolation as a defensive measure to preserve the faith from American materialism and Protestant proselytism. Despite the desperate living conditions of many Catholics, they criticized social reform movements as either Protestant or secular in origin, and the labor movement as an agent of socialism. Corrigan, McQuade, and their allies preached acceptance of poverty as a Christian virtue and advised the laity to cheerfully bear the burdens of this world while waiting for God's mercy and justice in the next.

Most midwestern Irish bishops, led by St. Paul's Archbishop John Ireland, believed that American liberal democracy offered Catholicism an opportunity to grow and prosper. They refused to accept as irreconcilable the values and institutions of the United States and those of Roman Catholicism. Ireland and his colleagues encouraged contacts between Catholics and other Americans and voiced approval of public education. In two towns within Ireland's ecclesiastical jurisdiction, Faribault and

Stillwater, Minnesota, Catholic and public schools worked out a shared time experiment before Protestant opposition killed it.

In Baltimore, the Irish had achieved more economic and social mobility than in other eastern cities. Their spiritual leader, shrewd and pragmatic James Cardinal Gibbons, primate of the American church, was more in tune with liberal Americanizers than with Corrigan's conservative faction. He and Ireland strongly defended the labor movement, fearing that the church was in danger of losing the loyalty of the working class in the United States as it had in Europe. Against the pressures of bishops in Canada and the East, Gibbons in 1887 persuaded Leo XIII not to condemn the Knights of Labor, the first effort to organize North American laborers in one, large union.

Religious orders became embroiled in the controversy over an Americanized or culturally isolated church. Jesuits, teachers of the sons of the well-off and champions of papal authority, defended Catholic cultural separateness and criticized things American while the Paulists, founded by Isaac Hecker, a convert from Transcendentalism, and the Holy Cross fathers, an order in charge of a small Catholic college, Notre Dame, near South Bend, Indiana, insisted on Catholic and American accommodations. In 1899, Corrigan and his friends seemed to have won the conflict between pro- and anti-Americanists when Leo XIII informed Gibbons that such ideas that action was more important than contemplation, that natural were superior to supernatural virtues, and that private consciences took precedence over the teachings of the church were heretical. Gibbons and Ireland responded that the pope had condemned a distorted view of their opinions. They argued that their Americanism was cultural, economic, social, and political and not theological. Leo's attack on Americanism, followed by Pius X's crusade against modernism, put a damper on Catholic intellectual creativity throughout the world, but in the United States, attitudes on American values and institutions and on social questions continued to express regional distinctions.

Generally, Irish Catholic bishops and priests in the Midwest and West continued to feel more comfortable about the church in the United States, and more deeply concerned with the economic and social well-being of the laity than those in the East. Monsignor John Ryan was a good example of the midwestern frame of mind. A native of Minnesota and a protégé of Archbishop Ireland, in the 1920s, as head of the National Catholic Welfare Conference, he authored a social justice agenda that anticipated and influenced Franklin D. Roosevelt's New Deal.

Twentieth-century politicians who represented voters in urban, industrial states had to heed Catholic voices. Immigrants from Ireland, Germany, Italy, and eastern Europe had made the Catholic Church the largest and fastest growing religious denomination in the country. In 1900 it numbered twelve million. Thirty years later, over twenty thousand priests and five times that number of nuns ministered to twenty million, one-fifth the national population.

## Irish Features of American Catholicism

While a plurality, the Irish were far from a majority of Catholics in the United States, but they could claim over fifty percent of the clergy, and early in the twentieth century over seventy-five percent of the hierarchy. As religious, political, and labor leaders, the Irish shaped and defined Catholic America. Stereotypical images of priests, nuns, politicians, union bosses, policemen, and firemen in fiction, on the stage, and in films were Irish.

In the 1930s, except for Chicago's George Cardinal Mundelein, every important archbishop in the United States was Irish. And Mundelein appointed Irish auxiliary bishops, and surrounded himself with Irish diocesan administrators.

Irish-Americans have been as proud of their predominant position in the church as of their control of the urban wing of the Democratic party. But critics, frequently Irish, have lamented that such an economically and culturally impoverished people were the first Catholic immigrants to arrive in the United States and to take command of the church. They have said that if others, say Germans or Italians, would have preceded the Irish, American Catholicism would have been less puritanical, legalistic, aesthetically mediocre, and anti-intellectual.

Certainly, the Irish have been more preoccupied with sins of the flesh than most Catholics. Instead of Jansenism, as many have charged, Irish puritanism, a post-Famine phenomena, is an obedient acceptance of Rome's views on sex and marriage and not a Celtic heresy. Before the Great Hunger, Irish peasants were a raunchy lot. Priests complained about sex activities at wakes and holy well pilgrimages (patterns). As Eugene Hynes argues in "The Great Hunger and Irish Catholicism" (*Societas* 8, Spring 1978, pp. 137–56), to avoid a repeat of the Famine, a consequence of too many people on too little land, the Irish decided to postpone marriage until secure in the occupation of a farm. To emotionally and psychologically survive through long periods of, and sometimes permanent, celibacy, they relied on Catholic sexual morality to discipline their wills and console their longings. What began as economic necessity became a cultural characteristic that followed them wherever they journeyed.

The Devotional Revolution fostered a dour religious atmosphere in rural Ireland. Segregating men and women in Catholic chapels and in many aspects of social life, priests frequently broke up crossroad dances, and harrassed courting couples. But Irish puritanism had Anglicization as well as Romanization dimensions. Like other parts of the United Kingdom, Ireland accepted Victorian notions of respectability and its emphasis on rules and regulations.

Many young people left Ireland to seek economic opportunities and to escape a sexually oppressive religious and social climate. Unfortunately, puritanism emigrated with them. In the United States, its impact has been evident in a considerable amount of social gender isolation; late, often loveless marriages; large numbers of spinsters and bachelors; and the sublimation of sexual desires in heavy drinking. In *American Catholic: The Saints and Sinners Who Built America's Most Powerful Church* (1997), Charles R. Morris identifies a positive aspect of Irish puritanism: it assisted in providing the church with priests, nuns, and brothers. Until recently, Irish and Irish-Americans have found clerical celibacy much less of a challenge and sacrifice than other Catholics with more normal attitudes toward sex and marriage.

Critics have fairly complained that Irish Catholicism has focused on rules and regulations rather than the spirit of Christianity. Religious classes in Catholic schools and pulpit instructions used to emphasize the commandments, especially the sixth and ninth; the obligation to attend Mass on Sundays and Holy days of obligation; lenten fasting; and the importance of contributing financially to the church. Until recently not enough was said about the social and interracial justice implications of Christian charity. Novelists and playwrights, in analyzing the impact of the Irish influence on American Catholicism, have faulted it for emphasizing the negative rather than the positive, implanting guilt rather than joy. But for many, Catholic "dos and don'ts" have provided a sense of moral security in a rapidly changing secular society.

In 1956, Monsignor John Tracy Ellis's *American Catholics and the Intellectual Life* initiated a serious discussion of the failure of American Catholics to match their increasing material success with intellectual achievement. Much of the blame seemed to point to Irish leadership; a reluctance to move the church beyond its immigrant, defensive stage, and to strike out in a new, more confident, more culturally productive direction. Accusers also complained of the rote memory methods and respectability rather than creativity objectives of Irish administrators and teachers in Catholic educational institutions.

This evaluation of the intellectual defects of American Catholicism, and their Irish source, assumes that things were different in other parts of the Roman Catholic world. In some European countries, not Ireland, church art, architecture, music and the general ambience of Catholicism have been more sophisticated than in the United States. But intellectualism has not been a feature of Catholicism in any place. Starting with Pius IX, Rome had turned its back on the modern world, freezing Catholic philosophy and theology in a medieval mold. Backward-looking neo-Thomism had little to say to twentieth-century Europeans or Americans.

Commentators on Irish-American Catholicism have emphasized its insensitivity in relations with other ethnic and racial groups. Irish and Irish-American missionary priests and nuns have earned a reputation for racial tolerance. In Asia and Africa they have formed understanding ties with native populations and cultures. In the United States close connections between Irish and Catholic identities strengthened both, but they also contributed to an arrogance about Hibernian Catholicism that alienated other ethnics by suggesting that the Irish is a superior brand of Catholicism. Their record with African- and Hispanic-American racial minorities, particularly the former, has been sad and pervasive.

For a considerable period of time, anti-Black prejudice was a nasty feature of Irish America. As early as the 1840s, Daniel O'Connell verbally chastised the Irish in the United States for supporting slavery and hating Blacks, pleading with them to conform to the liberal, inclusive spirit of Irish nationalism and the American *Declaration of Independence*. But they angrily rejected his criticism and advice. Irish-American racial bigotry was rooted in competition for jobs in the unskilled labor market; employer use of Blacks as scabs during strikes; adoption of the attitudes of the host society; a massive Irish inferiority complex that achieved some ego lift by persecuting people even lower on the social ladder; and resentment that many abolitionists, especially New England Protestant clergymen, were anti-Irish Catholic nativists.

Before and during the Civil War, Irish Catholics opposed freeing the slaves. After it concluded they obstructed African-American efforts to achieve equality. Irish-American bishops and priests often shared and encouraged the prejudices of the laity. Following World Wars I and II, large numbers of Irish-Americans resisted African-American migrations from inner-city ghettos to Catholic ethnic neighborhoods. Frequently they segregated churches and Catholic elementary and secondary schools and colleges. Many Irish missionary priests in the South sided with regional white-supremacy attitudes and Jim Crow legislation.

Despite obvious limitations, the Irish influence on American Catholicism was more positive than negative. Irish bishops and priests adapted to American circumstances more easily than those from continental Europe. Coming from a peasant church, they had few aristocratic notions of class, and could adjust to American egalitarianism, at least for whites. Because of their long, often competitive and combative, associations with Anglo-Saxon and Anglo-Irish Protestants, and their skilled usage of English, they were equipped to deal with the ambience and the hostility of Anglo America.

During his 1830s travels in Ireland, Alexis de Tocqueville was surprised to learn that prominent members of the Catholic hierarchy and clergy were fervent champions of popular sovereignty. Obviously, the alliance between liberal and democratic Irish nationalism and Irish Catholicism had politically civilized the latter. Although the Irish church under Cullen's direction became increasingly authoritarian in religious matters, it never turned its back on the democratic values of Irish nationalism. This was in sharp contrast to the political, economic, and social conservatism of Rome and continental Catholicism. Since they had no quarrel with the principles and values of the American constitutional system, Irish Catholics, quickly and enthusiastically, adjusted to the American political consensus and led co-religionists into a similar adaptation.

In Ireland, until 1869, Protestantism was the state religion, leaving Catholicism to economically fend for itself. O'Connell's platform for Irish nationalism extolled separation of church and state. With the exception of demanding government money for religious schools, the hierarchy accepted this principle. Therefore, Irish Catholics felt more at home in the United States than Catholics who came from countries where the state had endowed their church. In the United States, as in Ireland, the Irish were quite magnanimous in building and maintaining churches, schools, rectories, and convents; in providing the funds for a massive Catholic institutional structure; in annual Peter's Pence donations to Rome; and in contributions to the foreign missions. In time, their example encouraged others to be almost as generous. By the late nineteenth century, the American church was the wealthiest branch of Roman Catholicism, and its leading financial resource.

## CATHOLIC POWER AND NATIVIST RESURGENCE

Early twentieth-century pockets of Irish social and economic failure, featuring unhealthy tenement slums, juvenile delinquency, dysfunctional families, alcoholism, and crime still existed. In general, however, most Irish-American Catholics were earning decent wages and living respectable lives. They had the satisfaction of knowing that they were in firm control of the American Catholic Church and most of the nation's large cities. With Jews, they shared leadership of the American labor movement. They could call on the services of lawyers and doctors from their own community. Irish women were teaching in and sometimes running parochial and public schools. In his 1996 *'Twas Only an Irishman's Dream: The Image of Ireland and the Irish in American Popular Song Lyrics, 1800–1920* (1996), William H. A. Williams indicates that the urban Irish profile had taken on pleasant features.

Despite advances on the road to acceptability and respectability, Irish Catholics continued to irritate nativists. Economic recessions and depressions combined with impressions that American opportunities were vanishing with the frontier, and fears of

politicians, bishops, and a host of Catholic newspapers warmly supported Senator Joseph McCarthy's spurious hunt for communist agents in the government and the armed forces that cost innocent people their jobs and seriously eroded American civil liberties. In 1949 when the junior senator from Wisconsin was desperately seeking a vote-grabbing issue, Reverend Edmund Walsh, S.J., founder and regent of Georgetown University's School of Foreign Service, suggested that he search for communist subversives in the inner circles of government. In fairness, it must be mentioned that there were Irish Catholic leaders who publicly denounced McCarthy and McCarthyism, including Senators Brien McMahon, Connecticut, and Joseph O'Mahoney, Wyoming; Congressman Eugene McCarthy, Minnesota; and Archbishop Bernard Sheil of Chicago. A most unfortunate aspect of Catholic anti-communism was its importance in propelling the United States into a nation-dividing catastrophe in Vietnam.

### THE TRIUMPH OF IRISH-AMERICAN CATHOLICISM

For the vast majority of Irish Catholics, John F. Kennedy's 1960 presidential election victory, followed by his national and international popularity, decisively ended their defensiveness and doubts about their American credentials. They agreed with famous movie director John Ford when he wrote a friend after Kennedy defeated Richard Nixon that for the first time he felt like a first-class citizen. But Kennedy's presidency was not a singular example of Irish-American Catholic political prominence. At that time, Mike Mansfield, Montana, was Senate majority leader; John W. McCormack, Massachusetts, was Speaker of the House; and John Bailey, Connecticut, chaired the Democratic National Committee.

Reflecting the new confidence and optimism of Irish America, and the idealism of Kennedy's New Frontier, nuns and priests marched in the streets of northern and southern cities for interracial justice. Later in the 1960s and early 1970s they demonstrated again, this time against the war in Vietnam. Some went to jail for their efforts. Irish-American idealism was also evident in the large numbers of college graduates enlisting in the Peace Corps or equivalent Catholic efforts to raise educational and living standards in the underdeveloped world and/or poverty stricken areas of the United States.

While Kennedy was in the White House, American Catholicism reached an apex of strength, prosperity, popularity, and self-assurance. Young men and women crowded seminaries, monasteries, and convents to save, not leave, the world. During Vatican II, Irish-American prelates contributed little to theological discussions, but were instrumental in the council's acceptance of separation of church and state, religious liberty and tolerance, and the priority of private conscience, a vindication of Archbishop John Ireland.

### THE END-OF-THE-CENTURY SITUATION

"A candle burns brightest just before it goes out" is an old cliche applicable to post-Kennedy American Catholicism. At the end of the twentieth century it suffers from a severe shortage of priests, nuns, and brothers. From 1966 to 1969, an estimated 3,413 priests resigned. Between 1964 and 1984 seminarians declined from 44,500 to 12,000, and 241 seminaries closed. At present sixty-two percent of American priests are past fifty-one years of age. In 1997, Chicago, the second largest archdiocese in the United States and once a producer of a priest surplus, ordained just six, only one with a clearly recognizable Irish name.

Recently, Francis Cardinal George announced that he was bringing in clergymen from Africa, Poland, and Latin America to serve the needs of Chicago's Black, Hispanic, and Polish parishes. Since 1965, the number of women religious has dropped from 181,421 to 87,644, seventy-seven percent of them over fifty-one. In a fifteen-year span, 1965–1980, the number of brothers teaching high school or college declined from 12,539 to 8,563. There are not nearly enough new priests, nuns, and brothers to replace those who die or retire.

Once full for Sunday Masses, some churches are no longer so. Lines outside of confessionals on Saturdays and before Christmas and Easter are either short or nonexistent. Financial contributions to the church have drastically diminished. With white Catholic ethnics fleeing city neighborhoods, bishops have closed churches and schools. Even in the suburbs there is a crisis in Catholic education. With the scarcity of nuns and brothers, parochial schools find it difficult to pay salaries for excellent lay teachers. Many have closed or consolidated with those in neighboring parishes, and a number of parents, who pay high taxes for the support of quality public schools, send children there rather than to expensive Catholic counterparts.

As previously mentioned, 1950s economic and social mobility, higher-education, often in secular universities, and suburbanization began to undermine the Catholic subculture. Disagreements with Rome, especially on contraception, evolved into a late 1960s revolt. Most Catholics in Western Europe, including Ireland, and the United States have rejected the church's position that the primary purpose of married sex is the production of children. They see it as essentially a binding act of love. Worried about overpopulation and determined to provide their children with the best in educational opportunities and health care, they have found it necessary to limit family size. And they have rejected the church's recommended means of birth control, the rhythm system, as unnatural and unreliable, referring to it as "Roman roulette." By Vatican II, most Catholics in the West expected that Rome would approve of the pill. Such hopes seemed justified when a papal commission approved such a step, but in his encyclical, *Humanae Vitae* (1968), Pope Paul VI reaffirmed papal opposition to any form of contraception except the rhythm system.

An overwhelming majority of American Catholics have rejected *Humanae Vitae,* and moved on to challenge Rome on such issues as clerical celibacy, an all-male priesthood, and divorce. While opposing abortion on demand, they do not want to outlaw the procedure, and have decided that in certain instances—incest, rape, danger to the physical or psychological health of the mother—it may be justified. The Irish, the most successful and best educated American Catholics, and once the most faithful, now tend to be the most critical and rebellious. In *Goodbye to Catholic Ireland* (1997), Mary Kenny has provided evidence to show that while Catholics in Ireland are more supportive of the church's stand on abortion than Irish-Americans, their positions on contraception, a married priesthood, women clergy, and divorce are similar.

Sexual scandals in the clergy also have damaged the church financially and lowered Catholic morale. A changing America has opened a vista of opportunities previously denied to American Catholics. Prospects in secular society, plus a considerable decline of religious enthusiasm among Irish Catholics, has meant that religious life no longer attracts their best and brightest. No doubt the quality as well as the quantity decline in the priesthood, plus the diminishing deference that the laity pays it, contributes to practicing homosexuality and pedophilia incidents among some clergy that has so shocked the laity. Without the power and respect of former times, and self-confidence in the worth of their vocation, it now is difficult for those in religious life to deal with the trials of loneliness and to sublimate temptations.

Some Catholic dissatisfaction results from post–Vatican II liturgical changes. Missing the days of Gregorian chant, some are displeased with Hallelujah, shake-hands-with-your-neighbor, guitar Masses often with mediocre homilies. Most of the criticism of the new comes from conservatives, but a number of liberals also resent a "low-church" Catholicism bereft of history and mystery. They had hoped for a more flexible liturgy not a serious break with liturgical tradition.

Pope John Paul II, explaining the troubles of the church in the United States, has complained that American Catholic spirituality has been compromised by materialism. Those who agree with him argue that too many members of the church, motivated by secular self-interests, have become "cafeteria Catholics," picking and choosing what to believe and practice.

Economic and social successes in the most affluent country in the world have lessened the discipline and obedience of American Catholics. But they have better reasons to distrust and question Roman authority. There is much more to being an American than the desire to attain comfort and wealth. More important is respect for individual liberty. There always have been contradictions between Irish commitments to the most liberal political and the most authoritarian religious systems in the West. Until recently they could not emotionally or psychologically afford to abandon either. Catholicism sustained them in the long struggle with British colonialism and Anglo-Irish Protestant ascendancy and later with American nativist bigotry. On both sides of the Atlantic, it has been their culture and nationality as well as their religion. America liberated them from poverty and oppression and provided them with dignity and opportunity. When the Irish achieved acceptability and respectability in the United States, they became even more enthusiastic about its liberal values, and less so about the absolutism of Rome. They now expect their church to have the same regard for individual rights and private consciences as their government.

Not everything is bleak in contemporary American Catholicism. While the hierarchy adheres to the Roman line, and appears unreasonable and insensitive on contraception and women's issues, atoning for the past and emancipated from the narrow confines of ethnic boundaries, it has displayed progressive attitudes on social and interracial justice, capital punishment, and peace. Unlike so many conservative anti-abortion Catholics among the laity, the bishops have insisted that the right to life includes a decent existence after birth. In wretched urban neighborhoods, where public schools are havens for drugs and gang violence, Catholic schools, that once taught mostly Irish-Americans, now provide African- and Hispanic-American children with the intellectual instruments of economic and social mobility. Catholics, not state or local governments, provide the funds to sustain these schools. In the case of African-Americans, the beneficiaries are not usually of their faith.

Despite the shortage of priests and nuns, many Catholic parishes are working quite well under the direction of strong lay leadership. And the ethnic tribalism of the old parishes has been replaced by a cosmopolitan religious perspective that embraces all ethnic groups and races. Once noted for anti-Black bigotry, Rev. Andrew Greeley's research demonstrates that Irish Catholics, especially those educated in Catholic schools, are now among the most racially tolerant Americans.

In 1999 the Irish are only about fifteen percent of American Catholics, in second place to Hispanics, but they still contribute a third of the priests and about half of the bishops. As Mary Kenny's *Goodbye to Catholic Ireland* makes clear, even in Ireland the identifying characteristics of what was Irish Catholicism have disappeared. In the United States, the church is American, no longer a segment of an Irish spiritual empire. Even less than Irish politicians, Irish bishops and priests do not have the same persuasive influence with Hispanic- and African-American Catholics that they once enjoyed with white ethnics.

Although the Celtic tapestry of American Catholicism has melded into a complex ethnic and racial mosaic, the church in the United States owes a debt of gratitude to the Irish who successfully shaped and guided it for over a century. While far from perfect leaders, they confronted and defeated the forces of nativism, and adjusted immigrants from politically and socially reactionary European climates to the American democratic consensus. In time they evolved from a conservative force into a constructive influence on American social, economic, and racial policies.

While Catholicism fades as the pivotal force in their ethnicity, many Irish-Americans have turned to history, literature, and other aspects of culture to sustain their identity. But failure to appreciate and pay tribute to the important religious dimension of Irish and Irish-American history and culture will leave a tremendous gap in the understanding of who they are and where they came from.

*See* Irish in America; Emigration (5 entries)

Joseph M. Curran, *Hibernian Green on the Silver Screen: The Irish and American Movies* (Westport, Conn., 1989).

Jay P. Dolan, *The American Catholic Experience: A History from Colonial Times to the Present* (New York, N.Y., 1985).

Charles Fanning, *The Irish Voice in America: Irish-American Fiction from the 1760s to the 1980s* (Lexington, Ky., 1990).

James Hennesey, S.J., *American Catholics: A History of the American Catholic Community in the United States* (New York, N.Y., 1981).

Emmet Larkin, *The Historical Dimensions of Irish Catholicism* (Washington, D.C., 1997).

Lawrence J. McCaffrey, *Textures of Irish America* (Syracuse, (N.Y., 1992); *The Irish Catholic Diaspora in America* (Washington, D.C., 1997).

John T. McCreevey, *Parish Boundaries: The Catholic Encounter with Race in the Twentieth-Century Urban North* (Chicago, Ill., 1996).

Charles R. Morris, *American Catholic: The Saints and Sinners Who Built America's Most Powerful Church* (New York, N.Y., 1997).

Ellen Skerrett, editor, *At the Crossroads: Old Saint Patrick's and the Chicago Irish* (Chicago, Ill., 1997).

LAWRENCE J. McCAFFREY

## CENTER FOR IRISH STUDIES, THE

The Center for Irish Studies (Lárionad an Léinn Éireannaigh) at the University of St. Thomas in St. Paul, Minnesota, was established in March 1996. The center advances teaching and scholarship in Irish Studies through publications, instruction and public programs. It provides a regional focus for the scholarly consideration of Irish culture. Established after the Irish

American Cultural Institute—which had been based at St. Thomas from 1962 to 1995—moved its offices off campus, the center continues the university's long-standing association with Irish matters. St. Paul philanthropist Lawrence M. O'Shaughnessy, a former trustee of the university, endowed the center with a lead gift of $1,000,000.

Chief among the center's activities is the publication of *New Hibernia Review,* a quarterly journal of Irish Studies. *New Hibernia Review* publishes annotated articles on Irish writing and history of all periods, memoirs and new poems by Irish authors, book reviews, and commentary on trends in Irish life. Thomas Dillon Redshaw of the St. Thomas English faculty edits the journal, aided by a board of scholars from American and Irish universities.

The center presents the annual Lawrence O'Shaughnessy Award for Poetry, which honors Irish poets. Eavan Boland received the first award in 1997; John F. Deane was the 1998 honoree. Other international speakers who have come to Minnesota under center auspices include Michael D. Higgins, then minister for arts, culture and the Gaeltacht, and poet Micheal O'Siadhail of Dublin. In 1998, the Center presented "Basil Blackshaw: Painter" a major retrospective exhibition developed by the Arts Council of Northern Ireland, and the first exhibition of Irish fine arts ever presented in the upper Midwest.

The center frequently collaborates with other Midwestern educational and arts organizations in presenting Irish cultural programming. It also participates in such national and international groups as the American Conference for Irish Studies, for which it publishes a newsletter and has been a regional conference host, and the North American Association of Celtic Language Teachers.

Additionally, the Center for Irish Studies has expanded the Irish-interest curriculum at the University of St. Thomas and in cooperating colleges, including the introduction of for-credit courses in the Irish language. The university's significant library holdings in Irish literature complement its work. The rarest of the materials are held in the 9,000 volume "Celtic Collection" in O'Shaughnessy-Frey Library Center.

JAMES SILAS ROGERS

## CHAMBERS, JOHN (1754–1837)

United Irish exile and publisher in New York City, Chambers was born into a Church of Ireland family, the son of a Dublin wine merchant. After completing his apprenticeship, Chambers eventually became Dublin's finest and wealthiest printer, with premises at 5 Abbet St. From 1793 he was master of the city's stationers' guild (St. Luke's), from 1789–98, a member of Dublin's city council, and in 1797 a director of the Bank of Ireland. Married to a Catholic Christian, Mary FitzSimon, Chambers was also a close friend of Dublin printer, Mathew Carey (1760–1839), whose radical journalism forced him into exile in Philadelphia in 1784. In 1791 Chambers was a founding member of the Dublin branch of the revolutionary Society of United Irishmen, and a member of the Society's Leinster Directory in March, 1798, when he was arrested for treason. Imprisoned in 1798–1802 at Fort George, Scotland, at his release Chambers first settled in France, but in 1805 emigrated to New York City where he prospered on Wall Street as a printer and stationer. Closely associated in New York with the celebrated United Irish exiles Thomas Addis

Emmet (1764–1827), William James MacNeven (1763–1841), and William Sampson (1764–1837), Chambers was active in Republican Party and Irish-American politics. In 1816 Chambers vainly petitioned Congress, on behalf of the New York Association for the Relief of Emigrant Irishmen, for a large land grant in Illinois to provide farms for poor Irish immigrants. In 1828–33 he was president of New York City's Friendly Sons of St. Patrick. Chambers's second wife was Catherine Caldwell Parks, widowed sister of fellow exile John Caldwell (1769–1850).

*See* United Irishmen and America

Chambers' correspondence can be found in the Mathew Carey Letterbooks, Pennsylvania Historical Society; and in D.1759/3B/6, Public Record Office of Northern Ireland, Belfast.
M. Pollard, *Dublin's Trade in Books, 1500–1800* (Oxford, 1989).
———, "John Chambers, Printer and United Irishman," *Irish Book,* 3 (1964): 1–22.

KERBY MILLER

## CHANDLER, RAYMOND THORNTON (1888–1959)

Author. Raymond Chandler was born July 23, 1888, in Chicago, Ill., to Maurice Benjamin and Florence Dart (Thornton) Chandler, who had emigrated to the United States from County Waterford, Ireland.

When his father left them, Chandler and his mother returned to Ireland. Eventually, they went to London where they lived with her family. Chandler attended English schools and toured Europe instead of going on to university. He joined the Civil Service for a time but after finding it boring, began writing for newspapers, the *Daily Express,* London, and *Western Gazette,* Bristol, England, from 1908–1912.

He set sail for America in 1912 and worked at various jobs while heading for the West Coast. Among the jobs he took in California between 1912 and 1932 were positions in a sporting goods store; a creamery in Los Angeles, as accountant and bookkeeper; a bank in San Francisco; a reporter for the *Daily Express,* Los Angeles; and a bookkeeper and auditor at Dabney Oil Syndicate, Los Angeles.

Although he was a United States citizen, Chandler went to Canada, joined the Gordon Highlanders and served in France during World War I. While serving in France, he was knocked unconscious by a German shell.

When Chandler met the stepmother of his army friend, Gordon Pascal, he fell in love with her. Although she was married and eighteen years older than Chandler, Pearl Cecily Hurlburt and Chandler were married in 1924. The marriage lasted almost thirty-one years (Cissy died in 1954).

Chandler had always been interested in writing, so in 1933 he began writing short stories for the pulp magazine *Black Mask.* Chandler studied the styles of American authors, especially Dashiell Hammett and Erle Stanley Gardner, adopting and remodeling elements. His stories and novels centered on the wealth and power of Los Angeles as a backdrop for the corruption also found there.

The first of his novels, *The Big Sleep,* in 1939 introduced the private detective Philip Marlowe. That was followed by six more novels, all with Marlowe as the hero: *Farewell, My Lovely* (1940), *The High Window* (1942), *The Lady in the Lake* (1943), *The Little Sister* (1949), *The Long Goodbye* (1953), and *Playback* (1958).

Among collections of his numerous short stories are *Five Murderers* (1944) and *The Midnight Raymond Chandler* (1971).

Chandler also was a successful screen writer. In 1943 he collaborated with Billy Wilder on *Double Indemnity,* which earned Chandler an Academy Award nomination. *The Blue Dahlia* was written in 1946 for Alan Ladd, for which Chandler again was nominated for an Academy Award. His final screen play was *Strangers on a Train* in 1951.

Almost all of Chandler's novels were adapted for the screen, including *Murder, My Sweet* with Dick Powell in 1945 and under its original title, *Farewell, My Lovely,* in 1975 with Robert Mitchum; *The Big Sleep* in 1946 with Lauren Bacall and Humphrey Bogart, and with Robert Mitchum in 1978; *The Lady in the Lake* in 1946 with Robert Montgomery.

Following his wife's death in 1954, Chandler returned to London. However, increasing dependence on alcohol cut him off from society, so he returned to California. He died March 26, 1959, in La Jolla, Calif. Seventeen people attended his burial in Mount Hope Cemetery, San Diego.

Philip Durham, *Down These Mean Streets a Man Must Go; Raymond Chandler's Knight* (Chapel Hill, N.C., 1963).

Miriam Gross, *The World of Raymond Chandler* (London, 1977).

Tom Hiney, *Raymond Chandler: A Biography* (London, 1979).

William Luhr, *Raymond Chandler and Film* (New York, 1982).

Frank MacShane, *The Life of Raymond Chandler* (New York, 1976).

William Marling, *Raymond Chandler* (Boston, 1986).

MARIANNA McLOUGHLIN

## CHARLESTON

### THE COLONIAL ERA

The Irish were in Charleston from its founding. The fleet of three English ships that landed on the south bank of the Ashley River in 1670 had stopped earlier at Kinsale, Ireland, to recruit colonists, and Captain Florence O'Sullivan, whose family came from Cork and Kerry, commanded one of the ships, the *Carolina.* The sea island which guards the north shore of Charleston's harbor—Sullivan's Island—now bears his name (Michael O'Brien, 134). In 1671 the ship *Blessing* brought more Irish emigrants to the fledgling colony. In 1680, the community moved to a larger peninsula between the Ashley and Cooper rivers, and in the first decade of this new settlement the Proprietors of the colony advertized in Dublin for emigrants. As the parish registery of St. Philip's Church in Charleston suggests, there was no lack of Anglican immigrants from Ireland, but throughout the eighteenth century and especially in the decades before the Revolution, most Irish immigrants were Presbyterian Scotch-Irish emigrating from Ulster. Many of these funnelled through Charleston to settle the Carolina upcountry, but some stayed in or near Charleston, where the wealthiest and the poorest Carolinians lived. The Irish thought of themselves as distinct from their English neighbors, at least to the degree of forming an Irish Society in 1749 and the Friendly Brothers of St. Patrick in 1773. Rugged, clannish, lovers of liberty and haters of the English crown, the Irish gave Charleston some of its most effective statesmen and soldiers, like the Rutledges, Burkes, Cosgroves and Barnwells; and they crowded the ranks of the Charleston Volunteers, the first unit organized in South Carolina to fight the British in 1775. Among whites in Charleston, the Irish were second only to the English in numbers, and clearly they suffered no disabilities on account of their country of origin. They were also a major labor force, as Ulster's poor were bound over to the Carolinas as indentured servants.

### EARLY REPUBLIC

Because Charleston was the southernmost English stronghold on the frontier of Spanish Florida, the city was particularly suspicious of "papists." In 1775, for example, two "Catholic Irishmen were tarred and feathered, charged with the doubtful crime of tampering with negroes" (O'Connell, 140), and such welcomes assured that virtually no Catholics immigrated in the colonial era. Despite its deserved reputation as a city friendly to political and religious refugees, the city's tolerance did not extend to Catholics until 1790, when in the spirit of the new republic religious disqualifications were abolished. Three years later, Father Simon Gallagher of Dublin was sent to Charleston by John Carroll, Bishop of Baltimore, and he assumed pastorship of the flimsy St. Mary's Church, a dilapidated, wooden Methodist meeting house bought by the few Catholics in the city. Within six months of arriving, Gallagher was teaching math, logic, and natural philosophy, or science, at the College of Charleston (Mitchell, 18). His willingness to scorn orthodoxy no doubt contributed to the city's regard for him. St. Mary's reflected not only the competition between the Irish and French churches for dominance in America, but it also often found itself in schism with Bishop Carroll. Father Gallagher joined the Hibernian Society of Charleston, which was informally organized in 1799 and chartered in 1801, when members elected Gallagher as their first president. The Hibernian Society was established to aid the refugees of the failed 1798 republican rebellion in Ireland, to which Charleston's Irish were naturally sympathetic. Simultaneously, the Irish Volunteers, a state militia unit, organized. Eventually it would fight in the Seminole and Mexican Wars, and take a leading role in the Confederate assault on Fort Sumter.

### CATHOLIC IMMIGRATION

Even as late as the turn of the nineteenth century, emigrants—refugees or not—sailed directly to Charleston from Belfast, and most of these were Presbyterians. The Irish population of the city in the early decades of the nineteenth century was sizeable and largely Protestant. As late as 1820, when Bishop John England arrived from Cork to take his seat as the first Bishop of Charleston, Catholics in his diocese (which included South Carolina, North Carolina, and Georgia) numbered about 3,600 out of a population of nearly one and a half million people; and while the white population of Charleston was about 15,000, only 1,000 were Catholic, and some of these were French who had fled the Haitian revolution (Joseph O'Brien, 12). Despite Gallagher's earlier status, none of the Catholics "were of high social standing" in the city (O'Connell, 42).

John England was born in Cork in 1786 to a middle-class family and grew up as devoted to the cause of Irish republicanism as he was to the Church. He angered the hierarchy and the crown authorities alike by openly decrying the repressive practices of the English colonial administration. The Irish Church disposed of the thorny, brilliant priest by elevating him to bishop and exiling him to the frontier diocese of Charleston.

Through his *U.S. Catholic Miscellany,* England carved out a space for the Irish Catholics in Charleston and in the nation. He argued that Catholicism posed no threat to democracy and explained to Catholics how to separate their loyalties. This role brought him before a joint session of the U. S. Congress in 1826, when he responded to John Quincy Adams's anti-Catholic slurs. When his old friend in Ireland, Daniel O'Connell, the Catholic Liberator, condemned American slavery, England became an apologist for the South. He lashed back that the treatment of the native Irish in Ireland was typically worse than the treatment of African slaves in America. His "Slave Letters," occasioned by Pope Gregory XVI's attack on the slave trade, argued that nothing in Catholic doctrine condemned the practice of slavery. Though his arguments were learned and technically accurate, and though he stated that he personally opposed the peculiar institution, history must judge England harshly for buying Southern acceptence of Irish Catholics with such equivocations.

As England tried to improve the situation of the Catholic Irish, Charlestonians of Protestant-Irish stock continued to lead the city. The rolls of the Hibernian Society include many of Charleston's most influential citizens, like Simon Magwood, who served as president of the Society from 1805 until 1836, as colonel in the Charleston Volunteers, city councilman, and state legislator. But the pattern of Irish immigration had changed by the 1840s and 1850s. Charleston itself, whose shipping once connected it to international ports like Dublin and Belfast, had become provincial. Irish immigration to the city largely consisted of New York Catholics who had escaped the famine in Ireland. As early as 1836 Bishop England established a new parish, St. Patrick's, in the soggy slums north of Calhoun Street to accommodate these workers, many of them migrants coming and going to New York as jobs waxed and waned. These Irish, largely unskilled, found themselves in competition with free blacks for stevedore and teamster and canal-digging jobs. Though both O'Connell and England had seen the similarities between the Irish and the African-American laborers, the Irish themselves, unfortunately, succumbed to a racial rather than a class consciousness. They fought their fellows at every opportunity and, by the eve of the Civil War, their own viciousness and the native white population's rising anxiety about free blacks secured Charleston's docks and wagons for the Irish.

According to the Confederate census of 1861, 3,662 white Charlestonians had been *born* in Ireland—13.6% of the white population—which constituted the largest white minority in the city; and the number of whites of Irish ancestry, though unrecorded by the census, must have been considerably higher. With the influx of these immigrants, Charleston was nearly as Irish as it was English.

TWENTIETH CENTURY

After the Civil War the city grew even more insular. The port decayed, European immigration ended, and the city's population was merely stable in good years and declined in bad. The unassimilated poor Irish Catholics still congregated in the low-lying, wet ghettos near the Cooper River—wards 3, 5, and 7—a disenfranchised population waiting for the new politics of the early twentieth century to muster them into a force in municipal elections.

Their organizer was John Patrick Grace, grandson of a rice mill foreman who immigrated from Tipperary in 1833, and who, as a Confederate officer, died in defense of Charleston harbor in 1863. The family achieved moderate wealth before the war and retained it and their respectable Society Street house in a prosperous section of ward 3. Grace built a political machine able to wrest the mayor's office from the clique of Charleston's South-of-Broad Street businessmen and shabby aristocrats in 1911. In the next two decades Grace led one of the Democratic party's two powerful and belligerent factions in elections that led often to bloodshed and always to cheating. He lost the 1915 election and spent the next four years advocating pro-Irish and anti-English politics. He joined the newly established Friends of Irish Freedom, supported the Easter Rebellion, advocated American neutrality during the First World War, and advised Woodrow Wilson to include Irish independence in the Treaty of Versailles. This advocacy of Ireland cost him his newspaper, the *Charleston American,* and nearly sent him to prison for sedition, but in later years it also brought Eamon de Valera to Charleston as his guest. Grace won back the mayoralty in 1919 and initiated a reform program modeled on the democratic policies he'd learned from Irish politicians in the North, like Al Smith. He supported women's suffrage, championed equal treatment of blacks (though he opposed integration), and winked at Charleston's illegal bars, gambling, and prostitution. He launched a number of public works projects based on deficit spending, paving the streets, bringing the railroad back to Charleston's docks, leading the city's purchase of the docks themselves, supporting public ownership of utilities, and building a spectacular bridge across the Cooper River.

Grace's bitter defeats in the 1923 and 1927 elections, which coincided with the resurgence of the Ku Klux Klan and anti-Catholic sentiment, tolled the end of Irish ward politics in Charleston. By the 1930s, his machine was obsolete, though Irishness was enough of a factor in local politics that Broad Street patricians called Senator James Byrnes a "ward 5 Irish mick" (Boggs, 256). But after World War II, the Irish ghetto dissolved under the gentle flow of prosperity, and the acid of racial animosity during the civil rights era finally dissolved any ethnic differences from other whites. In the 1980 Census, only 10,646 people in Charleston County bothered to claim Irish ancestry; the true number was almost certainly far higher. The Hibernian Society has taken its place among the other exclusive, patrician city clubs. Another Irish-American, Joseph P. Riley, has occupied the mayor's office since 1975, but anything resembling a distinctive Irish community has long since disappeared.

*See* South Carolina

Doyle Willard Boggs, *John Patrick Grace and the Politics of Reform in South Carolina, 1900–1931,* Doctoral dissertation, University of South Carolina (Ann Arbor, Michigan, 1977).

Peter Guilday, *The Life and Times of John England of Charleston,* 2 vols. (New York, 1927, repub. 1969).

Arthur Mitchell, *The History of the Hibernian Society of Charleston, South Carolina 1799–1981* (Charleston, 1980).

Joseph L. O'Brien, *John England—Bishop of Charleston, The Apostle to Democracy* (New York, 1934).

Michael J. O'Brien, "The Irish in Charleston, South Carolina," *The Journal of the American-Irish Historical Society* 25 (1926): 134–146.

Rev. J. J. O'Connell, O.S.B., *Catholicity in the Carolinas and Georgia: Leaves of its History* (New York, 1879).

Christopher Silver, "A New Look at Old South Urbanization: The Irish Worker in Charleston, South Carolina, 1840–1860," *South Atlantic Urban Studies,* 3 (1979): 141–172.

JOSEPH KELLY

# CHICAGO, ASPECTS OF

Although outnumbered by their countrymen in New York, Boston, and Philadelphia by 1850, the Chicago Irish nevertheless enjoyed the distinction of growing up with their city and exerting influence all out of proportion to their numbers. Their accomplishment is all the more remarkable considering that Chicago became one of the most ethnically and racially diverse metropolises in America by 1900. Equally important, although the Irish early on joined native-born Protestants in moving to middle-class residential districts, they established Catholic parishes and schools that insured the continuity of distinct cultural patterns.

In 1803, thirty years before the city was officially incorporated, Irish-born Captain John Whistler directed the construction of Fort Dearborn on the south bank of the Chicago River. When the War of 1812 broke out, the garrison at Chicago was ordered to evacuate. Among the civilians and soldiers killed by Indians as they marched along the lakefront was Ensign George Ronan, the first West Point graduate to die defending the United States. Survivors of the "Fort Dearborn Massacre," as it was popularly known, credited the intervention of Billy Caldwell, an Indian agent from Detroit whose father was an Irish officer in the British army and his mother a Potawatomie. Although "Sauganash" became one of Chicago's earliest settlers and voters, after the Treaty of Prairie du Chien in 1829, he sold his land along the river and eventually relocated with members of his tribe in Council Bluffs, Iowa, where he died in 1841. Ironically, the neighborhood named for Sauganash on Chicago's Northwest Side now includes many Irish-Americans who trace their roots in the city back to early settlements such as Bridgeport and Goose Island.

## A New City

By all accounts, it was the Illinois & Michigan Canal (1836–1848) that really put Chicago on the map. This public works project, designed to join Lake Michigan with the Mississippi River, attracted Irish immigrants who moved West with engineer William Gooding, a former superintendent on the Erie Canal. They must have felt right at home, listening to Dr. William Bradford Egan's stirring address on July 4, 1836. A native of County Kerry, Ireland, Egan had been in the city only two years, but showed all the signs of canal fever. Chicago historian A. T. Andreas claimed that the physician/real estate speculator once advised a patient to take her medicine "a quarter down, the balance canal time, one, two, and three years!"

Carving the 96-mile canal between Bridgeport and La Salle, Illinois, was dirty, backbreaking work and on payday Irish laborers often received scrip rather than currency. While some immigrants did take advantage of the opportunity to become farmers by exchanging canal scrip for land, according to William J. Onahan, a staunch advocate for Irish colonization, they did so "with great discontent, and in most cases because they had no alternative." Work stoppages on the canal had an immediate and profound effect on the city. In 1842, for example, unemployed Irish laborers flooded into Chicago, only to be joined in the next few years by immigrants from the Great Famine in Ireland. In addition to raising $2,600 (in four days' time in 1847) for famine relief efforts back home, the city's Irish contributed "considerable donations in corn, pork, flour, and other articles of food."

The lives of Jimmy Lane (1803–1897) and Margaret Higgins (?–1877) testify to the rapid social and economic mobility possible for Irish immigrants who cast their lot with the city, rather than the canal. Born in Charleville, County Cork, Ireland, James Lane settled in Chicago in 1835 where he found employment as a clerk in a real estate office. By 1836, he had opened the city's first meat market near the Dearborn Street bridge and in 1837 he hand-carried Chicago's first charter to residents in all six wards. So sparsely settled was the city that Lane accomplished the task in an hour. Shortly after his marriage to Margaret Higgins in 1838, the couple opened a grocery and tavern. Margaret Lane's experience as a domestic to wealthy merchant Ebenezer Peck was crucial to the success of the family business, which soon evolved into a popular boarding house at Dearborn and Illinois streets on the North Side. Although Lane served one term as an alderman in 1847, real estate investments near fashionable Lincoln Park proved more lucrative, and the couple retired from business in 1868. The mother of four daughters and two sons, Margaret Higgins Lane died in 1877 in the family's spacious home on Lane Place, renamed by the City Council in tribute to Chicago's oldest alderman.

Jimmy Lane was a founding member of the Montgomery Guards, an Irish militia that marched in the city's first St. Patrick's Day Parade in 1843. Fifty years later he was still participating in the annual event, which had become the largest political parade in the city. To the amazement of Chicagoans, in 1896, "Uncle Jimmy Lane" danced a three-handed reel at the crossroads of Adams and Desplaines streets in front of St. Patrick's, delaying the parade at Haymarket Square for an hour. The music, he told a reporter, reminded him of the Sunday dances of his youth at the crossroads in Ireland.

At the time Jimmy Lane was buried from St. Vincent's Church in 1897, Chicago had become one of America's largest industrial cities with a population of more than one million. Annexations in 1889 and 1893 had increased the city's territory to 185 square miles, much of it still prairie. Fully a quarter of Chicago's population was of Irish birth or descent in 1890, but its 70,000 immigrants constituted less than seven per cent of the city's total population (roughly the same percentage as Scandinavians). Historian Michael F. Funchion notes that after 1900, "Irish Chicago became a community dominated by three instead of two generations."

## Irish Catholic Identity

While Chicago's early Irish settlers included many prosperous Protestants, they quickly distanced themselves from their poorer Catholic countrymen, who swelled the ranks of the Democratic Party. In 1840, for example, Mayor William B. Ogden, Chicago's first mayor, complained bitterly that "the Irish entirely control'd the [recent election]." To make matters worse, police reports in the press in 1851 reminded Chicagoans on a daily basis that Irish men and women filled the city's new jail, nicknamed the Bridewell (after the famous London prison near St. Bridget's Well).

Joseph Medill, the son of Ulster Presbyterians, made his fortune as editor of the *Chicago Tribune* and claimed responsibility for "discover[ing] . . . Abraham Lincoln, and start[ing] him on the road which led to the presidency." But his newspaper also characterized Irish Catholics as "depraved, debased, worthless and irredeemable drunkards and sots" who blindly followed clerical leaders and contributed hard-earned nickels and dimes to the erection of beautiful churches and parochial schools. An 1857 *Tribune* editorial, for example, suggested that the unfinished Cathedral of Holy Name be converted "into a workshop for the unemployed" where "[t]he hum of satisfied industry" would replace lavish religious ceremonies.

Convinced that the Irish were "exceedingly ungovernable, and have no genius whatever for governing others," still the *Tribune* held out hope that Chicago's Fenians might soon free Ireland from British rule and escape the "real tyranny [of the Catholic priesthood]." Some immigrants and American-born Irish regarded enlistment in the Union and Confederate armies as a way to gain crucial military experience that could be turned against colonial rule in their homeland. But others answered President Abraham Lincoln's call for volunteers as a way to proclaim their loyalty as Americans. Indeed, when war broke out in 1861, James A. Mulligan, Chicago's most well-known Irish Catholic lawyer and Fenian, raised a regiment that gave new meaning to the term "Fighting Irish." The record of bravery compiled by members of the Mulligan Brigade and Rev. Denis Dunne's Irish legion did much to revise negative stereotypes about the Chicago Irish. Colonel Milligan was mortally wounded in the Second Battle of Kernstown in 1864, and his dying words, "Lay me down and save the flag," became a rallying cry for the Union troops.

## Rebuilding Chicago

During the period of heaviest Irish immigration in the 1850s and 1860s, Chicago began to emerge as the railroad center of the United States. The frontier town on the shores of Lake Michigan was fast disappearing as a new, modern city took shape. For civil engineers such as Michael McDermott (1810–1880) there was plenty of work to be done raising Chicago's street grade to provide better drainage and surveying vast tracts of prairie for real estate subdivisions. Few cities ever get the chance to recreate themselves on a grand scale, but in October 1871, a series of fires destroyed more than three square miles of Chicago's downtown and North Side. Flames engulfed "seventy-three miles of streets, eighteen thousand buildings, and the homes of one hundred thousand people."

Almost immediately, Catherine O'Leary, an Irish immigrant living at 137 DeKoven Street on the near west side, was blamed for the fire, a charge she denied until her death in 1895. The *Chicago Times* characterized her as "an old hag," and reporters descended on the frame-house neighborhood looking for the owner of the milk cow that had allegedly kicked over a lantern and burned the city down. According to the *Chicago Evening Journal,* the story "was caught up by the electric wires the next morning and flashed wherever telegraphy extends." As notary public and chief surveyor, Michael McDermott collected sworn affidavits from Catherine and Patrick O'Leary that they were in bed at the time of the fire. Legal documents painted a fuller picture of the couple, confirming that the O'Learys owned their home and lot as well as "five cows, a horse and wagon, on all of which they had not one cent of insurance." Although the official inquiry conducted by the Board of Police and Fire Commissioners exonerated Mrs. O'Leary, the urban myth lived on, generation after generation. The *Evening Journal* predicted, correctly, that "Mrs. O'Leary is in for it, and make no mistake. Fame has seized her and appropriated her, name, barn, cows and all." It

took more than 125 years, but in October 1997, the Chicago City Council finally absolved "Mrs. O'Leary and her cow from all blame in regard to the great Chicago fire of 1871."

Maintaining cultural identity was no easy task for the Chicago Irish since they were the most Anglicized of all European immigrants, the result of nearly three hundred years of British colonial rule. Unlike the city's Germans and Poles, for example, the Irish invested little energy in preserving their ancestral tongue, one of the traditional badges of ethnic identity. Although Gaelic speakers did settle along the north and south banks of the Chicago River, most had died off by the time the Celtic Revival in Ireland in the 1890s made the study of Irish language, music, and art fashionable. Moreover, the Irish did not create ethnically cohesive neighborhoods on the scale of the German "Nord-Seite" or "Polonia." As Funchion notes, the Irish were not only a "minority in the city as a whole, [they] were also a minority in most of the neighborhoods where they lived." Yet by the time of the Great Fire of 1871, Chicago's Irish had established an impressive network of Catholic parishes, schools, and charitable institutions.

## Parishes and Schools

In 1846, Chicago's first bishop, Irish-born Bishop William J. Quarter (1806–1848) pioneered a new concept in urban American Catholicism, establishing separate parishes for Irish and German Catholics on the city's north, west, and south sides. This pragmatic solution to the thorny problem of cultural diversity had long-term consequences for the Irish as well as for the city of Chicago. Whereas the national parishes of Germans, Poles, Bohemians, Italians, and Slavs tended to be concentrated in older city neighborhoods and industrial districts near the stockyards and steelmills, the English-speaking parishes of the Irish kept pace with Chicago's development. Between 1833 and 1900, sixty-two territorial parishes were established throughout the city, in residential neighborhoods and apartment districts along commuter railroads, streetcar, and elevated lines. These predominantly Irish parishes, with their circumscribed boundaries of one square mile, became a distinguishing feature of Chicago Catholicism, right down to the present day.

Irish investment in "brick and mortar" Catholicism yielded important dividends. Masonry churches became the symbolic center of Irish community life, visible proof that immigrants and their American-born children and grandchildren were creating a place for themselves in Chicago. St. Patrick's at Adams and Desplaines streets, for example, was the first Romanesque structure built in the city in 1856. Its resemblance to the original Smithsonian "castle" in Washington, D.C. was no accident: Asher Carter had worked with the famous James Renwick before moving to Chicago and setting up partnership with Augustus Bauer. But equally important for the future of the Irish in Chicago was their commitment to Catholic education.

On July 4, 1846, just ten years after work began on the Illinois & Michigan Canal, Chicago Catholics dedicated St. Mary of the Lake University, a three-story wooden structure "with brick basement and colonnade front," designed by Daniel Sullivan and built by James O'Donnell. The first institution of higher learning in the city, it was financed in part by contributions from such leading Protestants as William B. Ogden, Walter Newberry, and J. Y. Scammon.

In September 1846, 24-year-old Agatha O'Brien, a native of County Carlow, Ireland, arrived in Chicago with five Mercy Sis-

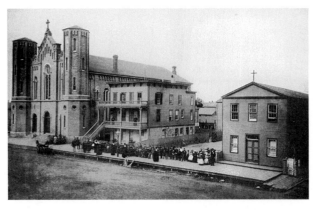

St. Patrick's Church, presbytery and schools, c.1865.

ters to establish the city's first Catholic school for girls, St. Xavier Academy. According to historian Suellen Hoy, Chicagoans, like Dubliners, called the Mercy Sisters "walking nuns." In addition to teaching school and catechism classes, they "set the pace for social reform," nursing cholera victims and staffing Chicago's first hospital, operating an employment bureau for Irish working girls, as well as the Catholic orphanage. Although she died in the cholera epidemic of 1854, Mother Agatha's purchase of property on the outskirts of the city guaranteed the survival of Mercy Hospital and St. Xavier Convent Academy (the forerunner of St. Xavier University).

In 1859, the Mercy Sisters were joined in Chicago by the Sisters of the Good Shepherd, a predominantly Irish religious order who cared for prostitutes and battered women released from the city's Bridewell. According to Hoy, "work and self-reliance, not marriage and dependence, were the watchwords of these Irish sisters." Destroyed by arsonists in 1859, the Magdalen Asylum was rebuilt in brick, not once, but twice. Following the Great Fire of 1871, the nuns expanded their complex on Hill and Orleans streets. At the time the House of the Good Shepherd moved to Grace Street in 1908, the sisters had cared for an estimated 18,000 young women of many different ethnic backgrounds.

Like St. Xavier's downtown, Sacred Heart Convent Academy on Taylor Street (1860) enrolled more Protestants than Catholics, evidence that these institutions met the needs of the expanding city. Jesuit Arnold Damen claimed that the Religious of the Sacred Heart had raised "at least $10,000" for the new Gothic church of the Holy Family on Twelfth Street and that they absorbed the entire cost of educating the girls of the parish. But more teachers were needed and in 1867, Damen invited the predominantly Irish Sisters of Charity of the Blessed Virgin Mary from Dubuque, Iowa, to make a foundation in the Jesuit parish. In keeping with their vocation as religious, the Religious of the Sacred Heart and the B.V.M. nuns maintained a low profile, but the results of their work in urban parochial schools were enormous. For example, in 1889, the same year Jane Addams and Ellen Gates Starr opened their Hull-House settlement on Halsted Street, the schools of Holy Family parish enrolled five thousand children.

Throughout the nineteenth century and well into the twentieth, Irish Catholics were eager, willing participants when it came to creating sacred space and putting their imprint on the urban landscape. Holy Family, for example, was the largest house

of worship in the city when it was dedicated in 1860. Ten years later, St. Ignatius College (the birthplace of Loyola University) opened its doors. According to one account, the building was constructed "on a large scale to make it possible to compete with the Protestant colleges and the public schools, which are like palaces." Likewise, in 1875, the Vincentian order began the work of establishing "a grand church and college" on the North Side, just blocks from the Presbyterian Seminary funded by Chicago's "reaper king," Cyrus McCormick. After years of worshiping in modest quarters, the Irish parishioners of St. Vincent's hired architect James J. Egan (1839–1914), a native of Cork City, to design a French Romanesque structure with twin towers that could been seen from all parts of the Lincoln Park neighborhood. A visible sign of the Irish presence in Chicago, St. Vincent Church (1897) and DePaul University (1898) quickly became landmarks in the city.

## IRISH LABOR LEADERS

Although Irish labor, first on the canal, then on the lumber wharves, railroads, stockyards and steelmills, contributed to Chicago's phenomenal growth and expansion in the nineteenth century, we know only very vague outlines of the story. And yet biographical sketches of prominent men published in the 1880s and 1890s confirm that many first and second-generation Irish achieved success in such diverse fields as meatpacking, furniture, contracting, brewing, drygoods, groceries, and baseball. John M. Dunphy, for example, was elected first president of the Bricklayers' Union in 1863 and his contracting business flourished after the 1871 fire. Among the notable structures he built were railroad magnate George M. Pullman's home on Prairie Avenue and the present Holy Name Cathedral (1875), designed by P. C. Keely of Brooklyn, a well-known architect of his day.

While much scholarly work remains to be done on rank and file union members, the record is clear that Irish men and women provided critical leadership in the fight to improve working conditions for Chicagoans of many different ethnic and racial backgrounds. John Fitzpatrick, for example, was born in Athone, Ireland, in 1870, but settled in Chicago after his parents died. Unable to continue formal schooling, the twelve-year-old boy took a job in the stockyards on the city's South Side, joining the International Union of Journeymen Horseshoers in 1886. Fitzpatrick soon found union organizing more to his liking. By 1899, he had emerged as a leader of the new Chicago Federation of Labor, serving as president from 1905 until his death in 1946. Historian Lizabeth Cohen estimates that in the Chicago area alone, 90,000 steelworkers supported Fitzpatrick's call for unionization in 1919.

Like so many Irish women of her era, Margaret A. Haley (1861–1939) began her career in a Chicago public school classroom in 1882. The daughter of an Irish-American surveyor, she recalled that her father "knew every stone along the [Illinois & Michigan] canal . . ." Haley learned her parliamentary skills as a member of the Women's Catholic Order of Foresters and turned them to good use as vice-president and later business manager of the Chicago Teachers' Federation. Together with Catherine Goggin, Haley championed the right of elementary school teachers to unionize and campaigned for women's suffrage, tax reform, teachers' pensions, and municipal ownership of public utilities.

IRISH NATIONALISM

Few American cities embraced the campaign for Ireland's freedom with as much fervor as Chicago, from the failed Fenian invasion of Canada in 1866 to the fall of Irish Parliamentary leader Charles Stewart Parnell in the 1890s. What is striking about the nationalist movement in Chicago is the way in which it cut across political, religious, class, and generational lines. Prominent businessmen such as furniture magnate John M. Smyth; candy manufacturer John Scanlan; contractor Francis Agnew; and coal merchant Daniel Corkery all contributed generously to the cause. Moreover, as Michael Funchion has demonstrated, the secret revolutionary group known as the Clan na Gael "took advantage of the city's decentralized political system to establish itself as a mini-machine that secured patronage jobs for its members."

In the 1880s, Chicago Clansmen were conspicuous in their support of the dynamite campaign in England that targeted such cherished sites as Whitehall, Victoria Station, and the Tower of London. Advocating "physical force" thousands of miles away from home was one thing. But when a bomb exploded on May 4, 1886, during a rally of German workers in Chicago's Haymarket, killing eight policemen and an equal number of civilians, the "massacre" took on new meaning for the Chicago Irish. Patrick Egan, president of the Irish National Land League, cabled Parnell in Ireland that "not a single Irishman was among the Anarchists at Chicago, while most of those who fell defending public order were of our nationality." During the trial of the Haymarket defendants, Dr. John B. Murphy, a surgeon at Cook County Hospital, offered graphic testimony about the injuries sustained by more than thirty police officers he had treated. Long after the collapse of the Irish nationalist movement in Chicago, the memory of Haymarket was kept alive through annual ceremonies at the monument erected by the city's business leaders in 1889. And as late as 1926, veterans were still sending funeral wreaths of roses and mums inscribed "May 4, 1886" to fellow officers and prominent Irish politicians. Increasingly, for the children and grandchildren of famine immigrants, the campaign for Irish freedom seemed to be a lost cause. In his famous "Mr. Dooley" columns in the 1890s, Chicago journalist Finley Peter Dunne (1867–1936) recounted the tragic story of Parnell's fall from power as well as painful memories of emigration.

SPORTS

Yet Dunne also knew from his experience as a young sportswriter that Irish-American identity had drawn new strength from sports, especially baseball. Historian Steven S. Riess notes that by the 1890s, "one-third of all major leaguers were believed to be Irish, and they soon comprised a large proportion of managers as well." The career of Charles Comiskey, the son of Irish nationalist leader Alderman "Honest John" Comiskey is a case in point. Born in historic Holy Family parish in 1859, young Charles learned to play ball in the prairies around Maxwell Street. After a stint in Dubuque, Iowa, he played for the St. Louis Browns, becoming manager in 1885. By 1900, the "Old Roman" was a nationally known figure in baseball and the owner of a team in the new American League. Comiskey's "White Sox" quickly drew a large following among the Chicago Irish and by 1910 the team played in a modern stadium at 35th and Shields— complete with an electric scoreboard. It was here, on Aug. 27,

The Irish Village at the 1893 World's Columbian Exposition was part of Chicago's Celtic Revival.

1911, that young James T. Farrell watched "Big Ed" Walsh pitch a no-hitter, defeating the Boston Red Sox 5 to 0. So memorable was this event that twenty-five years later, Farrell transformed it into literature in *A World I Never Made,* his second novel after the critically acclaimed *Studs Lonigan.*

THE CELTIC REVIVAL

Like the fictional "Studs," hundreds of young Irish-Americans who grew up in Chicago after the turn of the century held "green-bowed Irish history diplomas" on graduation day from parochial school. The Celtic Revival in Ireland had spread to America, focusing positive attention on traditional music, dance, and art, as well as the study of the Gaelic language. Beginning in 1901, for example, the Irish Music Club of Chicago sponsored annual Gaelic festivals that featured students from the McNamara Dancing School. And in 1908, the University of Notre Dame in South Bend, Indiana, established a chair of Irish history, the first of its kind in America.

By the time of the World's Columbian Exposition in 1893, Chicago's Lyon & Healy music company (1864) had become a leading manufacturer of harps, guitars, banjos, and mandolins. But without Francis O'Neill, the current American renaissance in traditional Irish music may not have been possible. Born in Tralibane, County Cork, in 1849, he settled in Chicago shortly after the Fire of 1871, where he quickly became known throughout the immigrant community as a piper. Trading railroad work for a police officer's uniform, O'Neill moved steadily through the ranks. During thirty years on the force, he collected several thousand Irish tunes played by immigrant musicians (including dance music that never had been written down before). And as Chief of Police from 1901 to 1905, he found jobs for talented flute players, fiddlers, and bagpipers! *O'Neill's Music of Ireland* (1903) and *1001 Dance Tunes* (1907) are now the standard reference works for musicians in Ireland as well as in America, Canada, and Australia.

The best-known example of the Celtic Revival in Chicago is still visible today at Old St. Patrick's at Adams and Desplaines streets. Between 1912 and 1922, Thomas A. O'Shaughnessy breathed new life and identity into the mother church of the Chicago Irish. Born in Mendon, Missouri, in 1870 and educated by the Sisters of Loretto and the Christian Brothers, O'Shaughnessy came to the World's Fair of 1893. There he saw close up, for the first time, replicas of ancient Irish treasures such as the Ardagh chalice, as well as the Celtic ornament on Louis Sullivan's Transportation Building. There was no turning back. O'Shaughnessy studied with stained glass and stencil expert Louis Millet (Sullivan's collaborator on Chicago's Auditorium Theater), and Alphonse Mucha, the most famous Art Nouveau artist of his day. During a trip to Dublin he received permission to sketch from the ninth-century illuminated manuscript known as the *Book of Kells,* an experience that had profound consequences for his art and the future of St. Patrick's Church. According to architectural historian Timothy V. Barton, O'Shaughnessy recovered the ancient method of making pot metal glass and created luminous windows in "brilliant pastel hues" that appear to imprison the color in light. He also decorated every surface in the church with elaborate Celtic stencils. O'Shaughnessy's masterpiece is the Great Faith window dedicated to the memory of Terence MacSwiney, the Lord Mayor of Cork and former commander of the Cork Brigade of the Irish Republican Army who died after a 74-day hunger strike in London's Brixton Prison on Oct. 25, 1920. In a tribute honoring "the youthful soldier of the Irish republic," Archbishop George W. Mundelein reminded Chicagoans that the Irish people had been betrayed by the League of Nations and he characterized MacSwiney as a new type of leader, "young men, not politicians, idealists . . . with the high purpose of martyrs. . . "

By the 1920s, however, the grandchildren and great grandchildren of the famine Irish thought of themselves as fully American. St. Patrick's had become the "old neighborhood parish," left behind in their move to fashionable boulevards, lakefront neighborhoods, and exclusive suburbs such as Oak Park, Evanston, and Wilmette where they built elegant Catholic churches and modern schools. That the public perception of the Irish had changed dramatically since the nineteenth century was clearly reflected in news coverage of the 1924 gangland slaying of Dion O'Banion, the notorious leader of Chicago's Irish gangsters, in his flower shop across the street from Holy Name. Indeed, as the *Chicago Daily News* pointed out, he was buried "without the blessings of the church" and the doors of the cathedral "where Dion was an altar boy twenty years ago, were closed to him."

## POLITICS

Throughout the city's history, the Irish have gained a reputation for their political skills in winning elections and creating a multi-ethnic Democratic machine. Ten mayors, beginning with Joseph Medill and John A. Roche, have been of Irish birth or descent: John P. Hopkins; Edward F. Dunne; William E. Dever; Edward J. Kelly; Martin H. Kennelly; Richard J. Daley; Jane M. Byrne; and Richard M. Daley. Journalists early on realized that Irish aldermen made for colorful copy and they created nicknames that have persisted down to the present day. Despite their popularity with the voters, election after election, "Foxy Ed" Cullerton; "Hinky Dink" Kenna; "Bathhouse John" Coughlin; and Johnny "de Pow" Powers became symbols of municipal corruption in the 1880s and 1890s. Jane Addams of Hull-House, for example, alone among social reformers, eventually conceded that there were good reasons "Why the Ward Boss Rules." Her nemesis, Johnny Powers (1852–1930), routinely secured employment for Italian immigrant newcomers; distributed tons of coal and hundreds of turkeys and ham at Christmas; and attended christenings, weddings, and wakes during the thirty-eight years he served as alderman of the old Nineteenth ward.

In recent years, scholars have begun to write the biographies of Chicago's Irish mayors, giving fuller portraits of reformers such as Edward Dunne and William E. Dever; New Deal "Machine Builder," Edward J. Kelly; millionaire businessman Martin Kennelly; and Jane Byrne, the city's first female mayor. But it is the Daley mayors, father and son, who continue to fascinate political scientists and journalists alike. Aside from their shared belief that "good government is good politics," Richard J. Daley and his son, Richard M. Daley, may well be remembered most for their vision of Chicago as the "City Beautiful."

## THE FUTURE

There is a message and a challenge to Irish-Americans in the following statistics on Irish immigration to Chicago over fourteen decades.

Chicago's Irish-born population, 1850–1990

|       | *Irish Immigrants* | *Total Chicago Population* |
|-------|--------------------|----------------------------|
| 1850  | 6,096              | 29,963                     |
| 1870  | 39,988             | 298,977                    |
| 1890* | 70,028             | 1,099,850                  |
| 1910  | 65,965             | 2,185,283                  |
| 1930  | 54,789             | 3,376,438                  |
| 1950  | 30,555             | 3,620,962                  |
| 1970  | 14,709             | 3,366,957                  |
| 1990  | 5,774              | 2,783,726                  |

*reflects 1889 annexation of the townships of Jefferson, Lake View, Lake and Hyde Park. Statistics based on U.S. Federal censuses.

So keeping a sense of Irish identity fresh and green will depend on Irish-Americans and those of some Irish lineage. The days of Irish immigration to Chicago are coming to a close and should cease in the early years of the new century.

*See* Illinois; Fiction, Irish-American; Nationalism, Irish-American (1800–1921)

Nicholas Carolan, *A Harvest Saved: Francis O'Neill and Irish Music in Chicago* (Dublin, 1997).

Charles Fanning, ed., *Mr. Dooley and the Chicago Irish: The Autobiography of a Nineteenth-Century Ethnic Group* (Washington, D.C., 1987).

———, *Finley Peter Dunne and Mr. Dooley: The Chicago Years* (Lexington, Ky., 1978).

James T. Farrell, *Studs Lonigan: A Trilogy* (1935; reprint [Urbana, 1993]).

Charles Ffrench, ed., *Biographical History of the American Irish in Chicago* (Chicago 1897).

Michael F. Funchion, *Chicago's Irish Nationalists, 1881–1890* (New York, 1976).

Paul M. Green and Melvin G. Holli, eds., *The Mayors: The Chicago Political Tradition* (Carbondale, 1995).

Melvin G. Holli and Peter d'A. Jones, eds., *Ethnic Chicago: A Multicultural Portrait* (Grand Rapids, 1995).

Suellen Hoy, "Caring for Chicago's Women and Girls: The Sisters of the Good Shepherd, 1859–1911," *Journal of Urban History*, 23:3 (1997): 260–94.

Richard C. Lindberg, *The White Sox Encyclopedia* (Philadelphia, 1997).

Lawrence McCaffrey, Ellen Skerrett, Michael F. Funchion, and Charles Fanning, *The Irish in Chicago* (Urbana, 1987).

Robert L. Reid, ed., *Battleground: The Autobiography of Margaret A. Haley* (Urbana, 1982).

Ellen Skerrett, ed., *At the Crossroads: Old Saint Patrick's and the Chicago Irish* (Chicago, 1997).

ELLEN SKERRETT

## CHICAGO, THE GREAT FIRE OF 1871

About 9:00 p.m. on the evening of October 8, 1871, a frantic neighbor awakened Mrs. Catherine O'Leary, a thirty-five-year-old Irish woman, a mother of three, and the wife of Patrick, a Civil War veteran. Daniel "Peg Leg" Sullivan had gone to the O'Leary's barn to feed his cow and likely dropped a match, pipe or lantern in hay or wood shavings. Kate O'Leary kept five cows and ran a small dairy at 135 DeKoven Street on the city's near West Side. Another version holds that Mrs. O'Leary had earlier gone into her pine board house to get some salt for an ailing calf, leaving a burning lantern in the barn. Recent scholarship supports the first version. In 1997, the Chicago City Council passed a resolution absolving her of blame. Whatever the case, the fire set off the worst disaster in American history to date. It could only be compared to the London fire of 1666 or the burning of Moscow by Napoleon in 1812. However, the legend of Mrs. O'Leary's cow refused to die. Twenty years after the fire, two reporters confessed that they had concocted the story, or at least doctored it to give the fire some dimension. Kate O'Leary was so harassed by the press that she had to move. She became a recluse, leaving her home only for daily Mass and to run errands. She died in 1895. The real reasons for the fire were much more complicated. Adequate fire protection could have contained the fire. But the city of 334,000 people had only 17 horse-drawn fire engines and 185 firefighters, most of them concentrated well away from one of the horrendous "patches" occupied by the city's heavily Irish poor. The 18-square-mile city had 530 miles of streets, only about 80 of which were paved. Sloppy building codes and enforcement tainted by corruption permitted pine board construction of match stick shanties, often two to a lot. It had rained only an inch in 95 days. Homes and hay barns were

Catherine O'Leary and her cow

tinderboxes. Once the fire got underway, winds reached 60 mph and flames as high as 500 feet, sending a red rain all over the city. Full city services were enjoyed by only the 10 percent of the population which held 94 percent of the wealth. The flames were so intense that sap-laden trees literally exploded, iron and steel melted, and stone turned to powder. The fire burned for one-and-one-half days. When it ended, 73 miles of streets and 17,540 buildings had been reduced to rubble. 90,000 people were left homeless and there was $190 million in lost property. One hundred and twenty bodies were recovered but careful estimates put the real number of dead at just under 300. The city was then about 20 percent Irish. They had been in Chicago since the 1830s, first as canal diggers, but by 1871 they accounted for one-third of the police force. More amazing than the destruction was the recovery. By 1893, the city held the World's Columbian Exposition. Chicago was substantially rebuilt within five years and by 1890 had a population of over one million.

*See* Chicago, Aspects of

Emmett Dedmon, *Fabulous Chicago: A Great City's History and People* (New York, 1981).

Donald L. Miller, *City of the Century: The Epic of Chicago and the Making of America* (New York, 1996).

R. TIMOTHY UNSWORTH

## CHICAGO POLITICS

The great nineteenth-century wave of Irish immigration to the United States began with the onset of the potato Famine in 1846. But the Irish weren't exactly strangers to the country, for advanced guards of Irish had reached these shores decades earlier. By the 1830s they had arrived in Chicago, where work had started on the Illinois-Michigan canal and soon after on the newly begun railroads. The railroads proved a special work magnet for the Irish laborer, and thousands of destitute Irish immigrants found employment with them, the Illinois Central Railroad most particularly. Gangs of Irish—laborers, sailors, squatters—settled on the city's borders and set up shanty villages along the main branches of the Chicago river. These ramshackle communities would become high-crime areas, and "hoodlum Irish" and "shanty Irish" became common terms for Irishmen arrested constantly for drunkenness and disorderly conduct. *The Chicago Tribune,* a leading anti-Irish newspaper at the time, would impatiently ask in 1874, "Why are the instigators and ring leaders of our riots and tumults, in nine cases out of ten, Irishmen?"

By 1850 the Irish composed almost forty percent of Chicago's foreign-born and over twenty percent of its total population. They were the city's second largest immigrant group and were to remain near the top throughout the century. They did not move quickly into professions or skilled jobs, and as late as 1870 the majority remained unskilled laborers or in domestic service. Nevertheless, many Irish managed to climb the socio-economic ladder by involving themselves in politics and municipal government. In 1853 the Irish constituted twenty-five percent of Chicago's public officials and they had elected political representation scattered through many local offices. Irishmen also gravitated toward the many politically related jobs, such as fire, police and sanitary positions. In 1865 one-third of the Chicago Police Department was Irish; by 1890 they were the dominant element, and they had six times as many officers on the force as the next highest immigrant group.

Meanwhile, local Democrats led by Mayor William B. Ogden, Chicago's first mayor, provided the Irish a political home. It was a maneuver that was bitterly resented by Ogden's political opponents, who believed the Irish to be uncivilized. Ogden and his followers, by contrast, viewed the Irish as a potentially manageable bloc of voters who would follow native Democratic leadership in return for petty favors and an occasional elected office. It was a patronizing attitude, and one year after Chicago's incorporation as a city in 1837 Ogden and others realized how they had misjudged their new friends' political ambitions. As one disgruntled and surprised Democrat wrote:

> The elections are over and all the Democrats are elected, Irish and all. I claim to be a Democrat myself but I do not go for electing Irish Democrats all the way from Ireland to legislate and to execute the laws, as though no one among ourselves is fit for such offices. Dr. Murphy for the Legislature and Issac Gavin for Sheriff are both elected, both Irishmen, as Irish as buttermilk and potatoes.

It would be some years, however, before Chicago was ready for Irish political leadership. To make a bad pun, the Irish were considered too "green" to take charge of the city. In the pre-Fire (1871) era, native Chicagoans were not impressed with the Irishman's political ability, and what today is considered Irish charm was then characterized as degenerate racial weakness. The Irish had to work for decades in Chicago's precincts and neighborhoods to climb the political ladder. It was not an easy climb, for in addition to coping with old-country factionalism and rivalries within their own ranks, they had to overcome scorn, bigotry and scurrilous attacks from the native Chicago establishment. Even those Irish who enlisted in the Civil War—an ambiguous act for many, as they would be fighting in a war to free black slaves, whom they feared as potential employment rivals—were not immune from criticism. When the Irish Brigade departed the city to join the war, *The Chicago Tribune* commented: "Although in material the men are a credit to every section, they are in outfit a disgrace to Chicago as a city, Cook as a county, and Illinois as a state."

Only after the Great Fire and the subsequent flurry of new immigrants from eastern and southern Europe did matters change. Second-generation Chicago Irishmen assumed the role of buffers between the strange-speaking newcomers and the native, older residents. The Irish, the city's oldest mass migrants, were pushed up the social, economic and political ladder because these newer and even more frightening groups were streaming into the city. In the process, the Irish became more acceptable to the city's Protestant establishment. Even the *Tribune* was mollified, remarking: "They are not cured yet, but around the city . . . we have seen them daily advancing in wealth, refinements, and worth. Faction and bigotry should belong only to savage tribes, and civilized beings should scorn to follow a man who represents no principle and who has none within himself."

Both older and new immigrant groups in Chicago marveled at the Irishman's political surge in the last quarter of the nineteenth century. The Bohemian newspaper *Svornost* believed Irish success rested on a strong sense of loyalty. "The Irish," it commented, "have their own political leaders whom they trust fully. The words of their leaders are law." Other nationalities, however, argued that the Irish politician's roughhouse tactics and election-day hooliganism gave him his advantageous position. The *Illinois Staats-Zeitung* followed this reasoning to explain why a city

that was one-third German did not have a comparable number of German officeholders: "It cannot be denied that the average German Americans . . . are indifferent towards public affairs, but they may offer as an excuse for their lack of activity . . . the wild doings of the political Irish gang." Nonetheless, all Chicago groups did marvel at the raw natural ability of the Irish in politics.

Nor did the Irish ability and desire to organize stop at local politics. Not having to face Protestant prejudice within their own religion, the Irish quickly took over the Catholic Church leadership in the city. Soon after their appearance in Chicago, the words "Catholic" and "Irish" became interchangeable. In 1854 there were seven Catholic churches in Chicago, three of which were Irish. By 1865, Chicago had sixteen Catholic churches, ten of which were Irish. Of the ten bishops, archbishops and auxiliary bishops who ruled over the destinies of Chicago's Catholics from 1844 until 1915, only two were of non-Irish birth or descent. The almost total domination of Chicago's Catholic hierarchy gave the Irish a tremendous moral influence over the ever-increasing Catholic population of the city. Irish political leaders in their wisdom closely allied themselves with their religious counterparts, and many times their separate roles became indistinguishable. Not only did the church become an important part of the Irish politician's control over his own people, but it helped him gain the respect and support of other Catholics. Most of Chicago's non-Irish Catholic newcomers quickly realized that anti-Catholic bigotry was actually anti-Irish bigotry and that their own attainment of religious equality rested squarely in the hands of the Irish.

Just as with their Catholicism, Irish leaders used newly formed Irish-American social organizations as effective political tools to gain and maintain power. The first settlers were homesick and alienated, lost in a large country and missing the closeness of their county and clan. They soon compensated for their lack of social outlets by starting numerous societies and clubs, such as the United Sons of Erin Benevolent Society, to complement religious and political activities. The friendships developed at these gatherings created personal bonds far stronger than any legal agreement or political alliance. Irish politicians, with clannish determination, distributed the spoils of city government—jobs, contracts and insurance—long before any political organization had set up a city-side patronage system to reward its members. No other ethnic group remained as steadfast to its own as the Irish; and whereas other newcomers marveled at this loyalty, the Irish merely looked on it as a fact of life.

In combining old-world traditions with new-world democracy, the Irish developed a unique political personality among Chicago's inhabitants. In their efforts to overcome political discrimination and ethnic prejudice, the Irish used muscle, their organizational skills, and their role as ethnic ambassadors to the city's native leadership to gain political leverage inside Chicago. In time the Irish became the major catalysts within the Chicago Democratic Party, and they caused much of the city's early history to center on their own quest for power and respectability. Local native Democratic leaders throughout the nineteenth century had to depend increasingly on Irish voting strength to keep their party viable. This reliance gave the Irish a strong voice in the selection of Democratic candidates as well as added prestige and control over the party's structure. To Chicagoans, every Irish saloonkeeper, undertaker and laborer seemed to possess political talent, and more important, the Irish were not afraid to use this ability for personal advantage. Summing up a political life-time of dealing with different nationalities, leading establishment figure Carter H. Harrison II, a five-term mayor of Chicago as his father before him, expressed the belief that, "among the Irish every grown-up was a leader, a potential leader or anxious to lead." Harrison's analysis was only half-correct; for besides wanting to lead, the Irish were willing to follow, and their loyalty to individuals with whom they identified and supported mattered more than the law or customs of their adopted country.

Unlike in other Eastern and Midwestern cities, however, the Irish takeover in Chicago was delayed. Splintered Irish loyalties and equally splintered Irish leadership, a legacy of discrimination, strong periodic reform movements, the diverse population make-up of the city, and the political wizardry of Republican Mayor William Hale Thompson all contributed to the lateness of Irish political control. But the key single obstacle to Irish domination of the local Democratic Party, and ultimately of the city, was the Carter Harrison family phenomenon. They dominated the scene for almost forty years, from 1879 to 1915, and even when out of office their personal magnetism kept followers loyal.

During that period, two Irish Catholics would be elected mayor of Chicago—John Hopkins in 1893 and Edward Dunne in 1905—but neither man represented the culmination of Irish efforts in city politics. Hopkins' election was a political accident and not the beginning of a political tradition. He was not an Irish ward leader nor one of the boys, but rather a suburban businessman. Dunne, by the same token, was a reformer who, though devoutly pro-Irish and pro-Ireland, acted more like a Union League Club "WASP" attorney than a politician from the neighborhood. Even though Dunne was elected governor of the state of Illinois in 1912 (and to this day remains the only Irish-Catholic Democrat ever elected to that office), neither he nor Hopkins was the new hero of the saloonkeeper-politicians, many of whom were Irish and all of whom were important political fixtures.

Successful Irish neighborhood saloonkeeper-politicians controlled their own community. Each neighborhooder was his own "ward lord," and the most ferocious political battles occurred in a party primary or party convention when aspiring challengers sought to take over a part of his kingdom. However, it was very difficult to dislodge the neighborhooder even if the community was undergoing an ethnic change or if the saloonkeeper-politician had the misfortune of having to answer to a judge or grand jury. The neighborhood saloonkeeper-politicians developed ward servicing techniques that became a model for future Chicago politicians. These men identified with their voters, they were accessible and reliable, and most of all, they seemed to care about people's needs. By 1915 the Irish takeover of the Democratic party was nearly complete.

Five years later another turning point in Irish Democratic politics took place, when George Brennan, an educator and assistant schools' superintendent whose wit and speaking ability allowed him to mingle comfortably with the city's social and economic elite, took command of the organization. A new breed of Irish politicians began to emerge. These men would be better educated, more discreet, less flamboyant and, especially important given that single-group ethnicity was weakening as a political determinant in party matters, they were better able to play multiethnic politics Chicago-style. Though their Irishness would be a factor, it would count less than loyalty to the organization, which more and more would become the vehicle of political survival and political glory.

Thus, from 1920 onward Irish political fortunes were almost solely encased within the city's Democratic party. Irishmen held elective and appointive offices, dominated leadership positions in the police and fire departments, and were now firmly anchored in business and labor circles. Furthermore, many Irish were moving into the board rooms of corporations, into the professions, as attorneys and physicians, as well as onto college and university faculties, beginning a trend that would accelerate with the decades. The economic advancement helped translate to geographical liberation, and Irish families were able to move into previously inhospitable and unattainable neighborhoods, such as Beverly on the city's far South Side.

But the ultimate political triumph, a firm lock on City Hall, remained elusive to Irish Democrats. In 1923, William E. Dever, a son of Irish immigrants who was born in Woburn, Massachusetts, was elected mayor, but he made no effort to work with Brennan or to use his office to bolster the local organization. Once again, as with Hopkins and Dunne, an Irish mayor had not exercised the power of Chicago's top office to consolidate party control over the city. Dever, in fact, may be the least-known Chicago mayor elected in the twentieth century.

Ironically, it would be no red-headed, silver-tongued son of Erin who would successfully challenge the old guard, unify the party, take over City Hall, and implement the political structure that Irish Democrats had worked generations to construct. It would be a stocky, street-smart Bohemian—Anton J. Cermak. Cermak was born May 9, 1873, in a Bohemian village fifty miles from Prague. His family emigrated to America the following year, settling in Illinois. Cermak had only an elementary school education, but one of his teachers happened to be George Brennan, the very one who was to become a leader in Democratic Irish politics. The political relationship between Cermak and Brennan within the Chicago Democratic party would run hot and cold, but there is little doubt that Brennan's influence gave Cermak a good start in big-city politics. With Brennan's help, Cermak was elected over two decades' time as state representative, Chicago alderman, chief bailiff of the municipal court, and in 1922 president of the Cook County Board of Commissioners. Then in 1931 Cermak was elected mayor, thus becoming the first new-breed Chicago mayor to occupy City Hall. It was a circumstance that found Irish new-breed politicians linking arms with the Bohemian leader and completing, in turn, the unification of the local Democratic party. Many factors contributed to Cermak's success, including his championing of the "wets" during Prohibition. But a key factor in Cermak's political takeover was his use of Irish new-breeders by elevating them to leadership positions in crucial managing committees. One could hardly call the latter action cynical or anti-Irish; rather, they reflected Cermak's view that political loyalty, competence and professionalism mattered more than simple ethnicity. It was a policy that also underscored his awareness that no successful Democratic leader in Chicago could afford to be anti-Irish.

Anton Cermak did not push the Irish out in order to gain power; instead, he won them over by persuasion, political muscle, and their own belief that he was a winner who could do what no other Democrat had ever done—unify the party. For the Irish to recognize this was insightful and also providential. If the Irish ward committeemen as a bloc had held firm against

Cermak in a kind of "ethnic Armageddon," they would have pushed the party back to its dark ages of factional feuding. New-breed Irish Democrats recognized the foolishness of divisive ethnocentrism and the importance of a multiethnic coalition. Although some Irish undoubtedly swallowed a little ethnic pride, they latched onto Cermak's fast-moving coattails.

Cermak died in a Miami hospital on March 6, 1933, the victim of an assassin's bullet apparently intended for President-elect Franklin D. Roosevelt, with whom he was meeting in Florida to discuss federal patronage among other matters. Cermak was also no doubt mending political fences, for he had supported former New York Governor and Irishman Alfred E. Smith at the national convention. There was a brief mourning period following Mayor Cermak's death, then an intensive month-long political struggle involving all the forces inside the local Democratic Party. At the end of this exciting and highly emotional period, Chicagoans saw Irish new-breed Democrats, loyal to Cermak and his memory, take over the party and the city leadership without breaking political stride. South Side Alderman Frank J. Corr, a political threat to no one, was elected interim mayor, and a month later former Sanitary District Engineer Edward J. Kelly, another non-threat to the Democratic organization and its leadership, was selected by the Chicago City Council to serve a full term. The vote for Kelly was 47-0.

The vaunted Chicago Democratic machine was thus born, and Chicago's Irish, after almost a hundred years of effort, were in command of city affairs. The mayor was Irish, the Cook County board president was Irish, the Cook County state's attorney was Irish, the tax assessor would be Irish in 1934, and the head of the Democratic Party was Irish. Late a half-century by Tammany Hall standards, Chicago's Irish had succeeded at last, and it had come to pass under a multiethnic coalition—a political organization built by new-breed Democrats eager to professionalize government and willing to share power with those who in turn were willing to work for the party. Unlike other political organizations, the late-arriving Chicago Democratic "machine" would not fight professional competence in government; rather, it would incorporate many administrative techniques usually associated with reform and reformers. However, the bottom line remained political control, and that now rested with the Democratic organization.

In the 1953–1955 period, the heights were scaled further for Chicago's Irish inside the Democratic Party. After six generations of political activity, the Irish found a man from the neighborhoods who not only took over the party, but the city as well. Richard J. Daley, the only Irish mayor of Chicago ever to have been a ward committeeman, became party chairman in 1953. Two years later he was elected mayor, a position he held until his death in 1976. For more than twenty years he ran the Democratic Party and the city of Chicago. He gained nationwide recognition as the ultimate political "boss" while he exercised enormous control over party and city. However, Daley did not operate as a chief of some ancient Irish clan or as a nationality leader from a narrowly based ethnic community; rather, he ran a multiethnic organization where politics and government became inseparable. Machine politics, Chicago style, evolved into an army that had the Irish controlling the officers but not the privates. The foot soldiers were Poles, Jews, Bohemians, Italians and eventually black Chicagoans; they accepted Irish leadership from Cermak's death to the end of the Daley years.

Mayor Richard J. Daley

On the other hand, Daley never hid his Irishness, and he used very many Irish in his daily dealings. As one associate explained things, this was because "when he needed someone to help or hire, he dealt with someone he knew and trusted . . . and most often that person was Irish." However, it would be a mistake to label Daley's rule an Irish regime because, like Cermak, Daley read precinct returns and demographics better than anyone else, and he knew which groups delivered the goods. Finally, Daley was not blind to potential adversaries, even if they were Irish, and he played them off against one another and against other ethnic groups, following the first political commandment in Chicago politics: "Don't make anyone who can unmake you."

Today a revolt against Chicago's Irish leadership would find Irish politicians hard-pressed to maintain control. Their city numbers have been reduced far below the totals of 1930, when Irish politicians had enough manpower to team up with Cermak and unify the party. Now, almost seventy years later, the Irish must cloak their political efforts in the guise of party unity or else make deals based on personal appeal, political trade-offs or political revenge. The Irish no longer possess enough numbers to trade in the urban political marketplace, and thus they can no longer make appeals to ethnic pride.

In a sense, then, current Irish politicians are the ultimate new-breeders: they have to avoid nationality—unless they express it in terms of general ethnicity—when attempting to garner white support in an increasingly black city. Irish political leadership, accordingly, is somewhat of an anachronism; the huge numbers are gone, and the building blocks, the neighborhoods, have all but disappeared. Economics and the search for the good life find Irishmen filling up suburban shopping centers, not ward meetings.

Daley's death tolled the end of a Chicago era and marked the demise of the traditional Irish political base. So it was an unsettled and transitional time when Jane Margaret Byrne (b. 1934) was inaugurated as the 41st Mayor of Chicago in April 1979. Her difficult four-year term was marked by high ideals but no great accomplishments.

Six years later Richard Michael Daley (b. 1942), the son of Richard J. Daley, won the mayoral election on April 4, 1989. A

Mayor Jane Byrne,
Chicago's first
female mayor

principled pragmatist, he dominated Chicago politics for the closing decade of the century. He won a fourth term in 1999.

He has surrounded himself with youthful administrators with graduate degrees who also possess a keen sense of mission to run Chicago better than it's ever been run before. The new political machine is fueled by steady leadership and a balanced budget not patronage; the new precinct captain is the taxpayer not the payroller; and the new political ideology is based on non-partisan economic development, not Democratic Party wins from the courthouse to the state house.

Since taking office in 1989 Rich Daley has down-played his Irish roots—even moving away from his parents' Bridgeport neighborhood. In an ever diversifying Chicago (the city holds an ethnic group parade downtown almost every Saturday) Daley has put together a political coalition of white ethnics, Hispanics, lakefront liberals, Asian Americans and some middle-class African Americans.

Still when things get rough—like a city worker goofing up or a reporter needling the mayor a bit too much—then and only then does the Irishness flow out of Daley's every pore. Like his father and countless other Chicago Irish politicians before him, Mayor Rich Daley fights back—words fly—his face reddens and though you might not know exactly what he is saying—you know exactly what he means. And when the explosion is over, Irish men and women, by birth and by marriage, living in Chicago and its suburbs, chuckle a bit, even smile sometimes, and generally feel damn proud of their heritage. Indeed they have arrived—and better yet, they're still kicking!

*See* Daley, Richard J.

Alex Gottfried, *Boss Cermak of Chicago, A Study of Political Leadership* (Seattle, 1962).

Paul M. Green, "Irish Chicago: The Multiethnic Road to Machine Success," in *Ethnic Chicago*. Peter d'A. Jones and Melvin J. Holli, eds. (Grand Rapids, 1981).

Lawrence McCaffrey, et al, *The Irish in Chicago* (Urbana and Chicago, 1987).

Harold Mayer and Richard Wade, *Growth of a Metropolis* (Chicago, 1969).

Mike Royko, *Boss: Richard J. Daley of Chicago* (New York, 1971).

PAUL M. GREEN

## CINEMA, IRISH IN

The Irish-American contribution to cinema is enormous. A recent filmography cites almost one thousand films made in the USA with an Irish theme or involving Irish individuals (Rockett 1996). Sadly, the majority of these films exist today only on paper or in archives in poor viewing conditions. Before 1951, cellulose nitrate was the substance used to record images on film. Nitrate films were (and are) notoriously prone to deterioration and even spontaneous combustion. Safer acetate copies are expensive to make, and most archives must make decisions to preserve one film at the loss of another. Any history of Irish-Americans in the cinema is hampered by these economic and technical imperatives.

Nevertheless, major trends can be outlined. The period from the beginnings of the cinema in 1895 to 1949 saw a constant stream of Irish-related films, with often fifteen to twenty features released each year. From the 1950s to the present, generally four or five notable films with an Irish interest were released. The reduction in the number of films is arguably indicative of the way the Irish, both Protestant and Roman Catholic, the former sooner than the latter, assimilated into the mainstream of American society. It seems that the further outside the pale the Irish in America were, the more films were made about them. By the turn of the century, depictions of the Irish in film were on the whole favorable, if not flattering. Stereotypical figures were common— the buffoonish idiot savant, the alcoholic with a heart of gold, the rough but kindly policeman, the wily but caring priest, the mother who would sacrifice everything for her children, and so on. The Irish sense of community was revealed as partly anarchic but fundamentally safe, commendable, and even desirable. Other, less frequent depictions stressed the Irish mobsters, but since these were offset by Irish-American law enforcement officials, Irish ethnicity was not unduly scapegoated.

### EARLY FILM

Although officially an Irish-Canadian, Sidney Olcott must rank as one of the most important figures in the early period of filmmaking. Sometimes credited for making the first American films that utilized foreign locations, he worked initially for the Kalem Company based in Florida, which flourished between 1907 and 1915. Olcott brought his crew to Ireland to shoot his "Irish" films, reckoning correctly that the large Irish immigrant population in the USA would enjoy images of the homeland. Olcott's films ran the full gamut from historical and political topics, *Ireland the Oppressed* (1912) and *Rory O'More* (1911), to more general melodramatic fare, such as *Come Back to Erin* (1914) and *The Colleen Bawn* (1911), based on the Dion Boucicault play. One of the marketing ploys for the latter films that Kalem engineered was to bring over crates of soil from Ireland for cinema patrons to stand in as they queued for their tickets.

Not all Irish-Americans were obsessed with making films of the "ould sod." Hal Roach and Mack Sennett both concentrated on contemporary comedy. Sennett is famous for his "Keystone Kops" series which may be said to have plundered the stereotype of the Irish cop for humorous ends. Roach worked successfully with Stan Laurel and Oliver Hardy on more complicated narratives, and much of his work still holds up well today. Other famous directors and actresses with Irish heritage in this silent period included Buster Keaton (whose father always claimed he was Irish) and Mary Pickford. On a more cere-bral level, the 1920s brought to prominence two other directors: Rex Ingram and Robert Flaherty. Ingram's contribution to cinema has often been underplayed, partly because his pictorial cinema is viewed as needlessly static. Born in Dublin, but immigrated to the USA in 1911, his *Four Horsemen of the Apocalypse* (1921) was a commercial success and brought Rudolph Valentino to stardom. Whereas Ingram has disappeared from the limelight (see O'Leary 1980), Flaherty's reputation has, if anything, increased steadily over the years, mostly due to the documentary issues his works raise. His "salvage ethnography" as depicted in *Nanook of the North* (1922) and *Man of Aran* (1934) have stimulated many academic debates about truth claims in documentary practice.

The 1920s was a decade where ethnic Irish appeared frequently in the cinema in mostly benign roles. Yet occasions of extreme stereotyping did cause offense, such as George Hill's comedy *The Callahans and the Murphys* (1927) which focused on two Irish tenement families. The film was banned in northeastern American cities, such as Rochester and Syracuse, in the face of protesting Catholic and Irish-American groups. They were offended by the portrayal of the Irish as argumentative and quick to fight. Interethnic comedy was explored in the series of seven films of *The Cohens and the Kellys* (1926–1933) which often revolved around the consequences of interethnic marriage. These films' social and cultural work appear to encourage the Jewish community to integrate more into the mainstream of American society, but they also show the eventual harmony between the two groups. Often overlooked in film surveys of this period is the contribution of craft workers and technicians. Willis O'Brien is famous for his special effects visible in Ernest Schoedsack and Merian Cooper's *King Kong* (1933), but he pioneered his technique for animating prehistoric creatures in Harry Hoyt's *The Lost World* (1925).

### 1930s AND 1940s

The 1930s cannot be discussed without reference to the Hollywood Production Code which laid down moral rules of conduct for movie producers in terms of their film's content. Unsurprisingly, one of the leading architects of the Production Code was Martin Quigley, editor of the *Motion Picture Herald* and a devout Roman Catholic. Irish Catholic groups were concerned that the movies would undermine church and family values. The censorship was exacerbated by the concentration of gangster films, and it was in this genre that the most famous Irish-American actor came to prominence. James Cagney burst onto the scene with *The Public Enemy* (1931) as a fearless gangster who was also charismatic. Perhaps his greatest Irish-American role of the 1930s, however, was in *Angels with Dirty Faces* (1938) in which he plays the criminal Rocky Sullivan, who is idolized by his juniors. The local priest (Pat O'Brien) convinces the condemned Sullivan to turn "yellow," once at the electric chair, so that his mythic nature will be undermined among impressionable youth. Nominated for an Oscar for this performance, Cagney ironically lost to Spencer Tracy, who won for a portrayal of a Catholic priest in *Boys Town* (1938). O'Brien and Cagney also played against each other in *The Fighting 69th* (1940). O'Brien plays Father Francis Duffy, the chaplain for the Irish regiment, while Cagney plays a frightened soldier who is persuaded by the priest to return and to die on the front line. O'Brien played numerous Irish-American roles over the years, including the Notre Dame football coach in *Knute Rockne—All American* (1940).

Priests were popular figures for Irish-American director Leo McCarey. His *Going My Way* (1944) starring Barry Fitzgerald, Bing Crosby and Frank McHugh—all acting priests—led to great financial success and many Academy Awards. This humorous film focused on the saving of a parish headed by an aging priest (Fitzgerald). Father Chuck O'Malley (Crosby) comes to the rescue with wit and charm. A sequel appeared as *The Bells of St. Mary's* (1945) with Ingrid Bergman as a nun teaming up with Crosby's Father O'Malley. In the 1930s and 1940s Irish ethnic characters did play major roles in screenwriters' minds—Mary Astor's Brigid O'Shaughnessy in John Huston's *The Maltese Falcon* (1941) and the two Irish leads, Rhett Butler (Clark Gable) and Scarlett O'Hara (Vivien Leigh) in Victor Fleming's *Gone With the Wind* (1939) are perhaps among the most memorable.

### JOHN FORD

From the 1930s to the 1950s, the major Irish-American director was John Ford, the son of Irish immigrants from County Galway. Ford's major work and successes were in producing westerns, such as *Stagecoach* (1939) and *The Searchers* (1956), but his early films examined Irish themes, which were explored in *Riley the Cop* (1928), *Mother Machree* (1928) and *Hangman's House* (1928). These are generally agreed to be run-of-the-mill films, and they do not match the tension and sophistication of his later *The Informer* (1935), which was based on Liam O'Flaherty's novel and starred Victor McLaglen as the man who betrays his IRA compatriot. What is significant about this film is Ford's unusual use of an expressionist style, in the manner of the German cinema of the 1920s, to convey the tragedy. Ford also brought Irish republican politics to the screen in 1936 with an adaptation of Sean O'Casey's *The Plough and the Stars*, but it was not successful, many citing discrepancies between the leads (Preston Foster and Barbara Stanwyck) and the rest of the mainly Irish cast, boasting Barry Fitzgerald, F. J. McCormick and Arthur Shields.

John Ford monument
in Portland, Maine

Although based on a Welsh mining community, many critics see Ford's *How Green Was My Valley* (1941) as effectively an "Irish" picture (it starred Irish actress Sara Algood in an Oscar-nominated role), just as others saw his *The Grapes of Wrath* (1940) as analogous to the Irish famine experience. Yet the key film that the "Irish Ford" is remembered for is *The Quiet Man* (1952) starring John Wayne as Sean Thornton and Maureen O'Hara as Mary Kate Danaher, the daughter of Red Will, played by Victor McLaglen. *The Quiet Man* celebrates the Irish rural community, its rites and rituals, and links Ireland and America together. Sean Thornton, though born in Ireland, emigrated to America as a young boy. There he worked in the steel mills and became a prize fighter. Now, he returns to reclaim his ancestral home. Just as Ford dealt with the myth of the West so well in his westerns, here Ford taps into the myth of the glorious return that many exiles and immigrants cherish. Critics have objected to the stereotyping found in the film—the dominant role of the church, the drinking rituals, the affirmation of manhood through physical fighting, but all of this is very consciously exploited by Ford for dramatic effect. It remains a popular film on both sides of the Atlantic. Irish-Americans as a specific subject did interest Ford in a few films, the most notable being *The Last Hurrah* (1958) starring Spencer Tracy as mayor Frank Skeffington of Boston involved in his last campaign for office. Ford is interested here to show how the practices and attitudes of one generation must gradually make way for the next.

### War and Postwar

The Second World War necessitated that films present upbeat or heroic images of Irish-Americans. In this vein, numerous films were produced that highlighted military endeavours, such as Lieutenant McMartin (Arthur Kennedy) in Howard Hawks' *Airforce* (1943) and "Boats" Mulcahy (Ward Bond) in John Ford's *They Were Expendable* (1945). Some films originated from actual tragic occurrences, such as Lloyd Bacon's *The Sullivans* (1944), which traced the lives of five brothers who died on the same ship during the war. Issues of community and patriotism emerge in these films, showing how well the Irish ethnic community had found its place in American society. Films did appear, however, which looked clearly at social problems. One of these is Elia Kazan's *A Tree Grows in Brooklyn* (1945) which examines urban tenement life for one Irish family. Johnny Nolan (James Dunn, who won an Oscar for his performance) is an alcoholic father who cannot seem to keep a steady job. His tragic death leads the family into poverty and a life of continuous struggle.

While the influence of the Production Code waned in the 1950s, a new Irish-American figure appeared on the scene to determine certain kinds of content: Republican Senator Joseph McCarthy. The latent fear of communism at the time of the Cold War was whipped up by McCarthy and spread to all areas of society, including the movie world. Screenwriters and producers were blacklisted, the "Hollywood Ten," and Irish-Americans were on both sides of the issue. Ronald Reagan (the future president) and Leo McCarey appeared to support McCarthy's views, whereas others, such as Philip Dunne and Gene Kelly, tried to resist the paranoia. We can see McCarey's anticommunist sympathies in his *My Son John* (1952) which traces how a young Irish Catholic (Robert Walker) joins the communist party and how this act apparently sets in motion the destruction of church, family and state values. This film starred one of the great Irish-American actresses, Helen Hayes, playing the concerned mother.

John Huston

By the 1950s, Irish-American actors did not find themselves typecast in specific roles. We do not, for example, look to films starring Grace and Gene Kelly for Irish-American representations. However, Irish environs or milieu continued to be useful for directors such as Elia Kazan. The latter's *On the Waterfront* (1954) is noted today for Marlon Brando's performance, but it is technically an Irish-American story about corruption.

### Recent Trends

Undeniably, gangster or mob pictures involving the Irish seemed to have a healthy life even beyond the heady days of the 1930s and 1940s. Irish gangster figures appear in Budd Boetticher's *The Rise and Fall of Legs Diamond* (1960), Richard Wilson's *Al Capone* (1959), George Roy Hill's *The Sting* (1973), Brian De Palma's *The Untouchables* (1987), Martin Scorsese's *Goodfellas* (1990), Joel Coen's *Miller's Crossing* (1990) and Phil Joanou's *State of Grace* (1990). One might also include Clint Eastwood's characterization of Harry Callahan in Don Siegel's *Dirty Harry* (1971), in which an unconventional police detective combats criminals with extreme violence. Less fiery Irish-American experience has been explored in Irving Lerner's *Studs Lonigan* (1960) from the fiction of James T. Farrell; Hector Babenco's *Ironweed* (1987) from the William Kennedy novel, starring Jack Nicholson and Meryl Streep; and Edward Burns' *The Brothers McMullen* (1995), which profiles three thirty-something brothers and their problematic relationships with the women they love.

Although having lived in Ireland for many years, John Huston made only one film with a specific Irish theme, and that was his final film, *The Dead* (1987). An adaptation of James Joyce's short story, Huston's film utilized many Irish and Irish-American actors, such as Angelica Huston, Marie Kean, Donal McCann and Dan O'Herlihy. Apart from gangster pictures and literary adaptations, there has of late been a tendency to bring in the figure of the Irish terrorist from Northern Ireland to strengthen or drive the narrative of American films. In this category, one must include Philip Noyce's *Patriot Games* (1992), starring Harrison Ford and Patrick Bergin; Stephen Hopkins's *Blown Away* (1994), starring Jeff Bridges and Tommy Lee Jones, and Alan Pakula's *The Devil's Own* (1997) starring Harrison Ford and Brad Pitt.

More traditional emigration and immigration films have not completely died away. The genre was revitalized to some degree by Matt Clark's *Da* (1988), from the play by Hugh Leonard. Starring Martin Sheen, the film follows the return home to Ireland of a successful Irish-American writer, Charlie Tynan, on the occasion of his father's death. Charlie must work through a host of conflicting emotions toward his dead father before he can return to America. Less introspective is Ron Howard's romantic adventure *Far and Away* (1992) starring Tom Cruise and Nicole Kidman as an Irish Catholic and Protestant who make it to the USA and solidify a new life together after many hardships. In the past thirty years, a few Irish-American films have defied easy categorization. One of these is Martin Ritt's *The Molly Maguires* (1970) featuring Sean Connery and Richard Harris. The film concentrates on a group of Irish Catholic miners in Pennsylvania in 1876 who violently resist the mine owners and their employees. Equally outstanding, but entirely different in tone, is John Sayles' *The Secret of Roan Inish* (1994), a modern fairy tale shot on location in County Donegal.

Where the 1930s to 1950s produced James Cagney, Pat O'Brien, Ronald Reagan, Maureen O'Sullivan and Spencer Tracy, the last twenty years has produced new actors with Irish surnames, if not specifically Irish roles, and this long list would include Micky Rourke, Meg Ryan, Elizabeth McGovern, and Brian Dennehy. Irish actors Liam Neeson, Pierce Brosnan and Gabriel Byrne have also made a name for themselves within American cinema, and may be regarded as now part of the Irish-American contribution. Although the Irish have assimilated well into the mainstream of American society, it seems likely that filmmakers will continue to use their diverse historical roles to construct filmic narratives. We may expect more films like Matt Clark's *Da* and Edward Burns' *The Brothers McMullen* if notions of heritage are still deemed important to American life.

*See* California; Huston, John

Richard Barsam, *The Vision of Robert Flaherty: The Artist as Myth and Filmmaker* (Bloomington, Ind., 1988).

Joseph M. Curran, *Hibernian Green on the Silver Screen: The Irish and American Movies* (Westport, Conn., 1989).

Tag Gallagher, *John Ford: The Man and his Films* (Berkeley, 1986).

Lee Lourdeaux, *Italian and Irish Filmmakers in America: Ford, Capra, Coppola and Scorsese* (Philadelphia, 1990).

Brian McIlroy, *World Cinema 4: Ireland* (Trowbridge, Wiltshire, 1989).

Liam O'Leary, *Rex Ingram: Master of the Silent Cinema* (Dublin, 1980).

Kevin Rockett, comp. *The Irish Filmography: Fiction Films 1896–1996* (Dublin, 1996).

Kevin Rockett, Luke Gibbons and John Hill, *Cinema and Ireland* (London, 1987).

Anthony Slide, *The Cinema and Ireland* (North Carolina, 1988).

BRIAN McILROY

# CIVIL WAR, THE

## BACKGROUND OF IRISH PARTICIPATION

During the American Civil War there were a number of identifiable ethnic units which served on both sides during the hard-fought battles that characterized America's only Civil War. Perhaps none were more famous than the Irish units that fought in this war, some for the Union, others for the Confederacy. This entry is designed to provide an overview of Irish participation in the American Civil War and to highlight the contributions of this ethnic group to the war effort.

European events in the 1840s resulted in a substantial influx of refugees/immigrants into the United States. Among those that came were a significant number of Irish. In fact between 1820 and the beginning of the Civil War, it is estimated that more than three million Irish immigrants arrived in the United States. The largest influx of Irish immigrants was immediately due to the Great Famine, which devastated the Emerald Isle in the wake of the crop failures from 1845–48, but it also resulted from the long-standing dissatisfaction with British rule. Thus, for both economic and political reasons, millions of disgruntled Irishmen settled in the continental United States. The largest concentrations centered in the area that stretched from Boston to Philadelphia. These new settlers were not always well received in the United States since they were often thought of as unskilled, uneducated people who competed with "citizens" for jobs. Furthermore, as Catholics in a largely Protestant country, they were often regarded with suspicion.

## INITIAL IRISH RECRUITMENT

When the Civil War began in 1861, the Irish willingly joined volunteer regiments and did so in significant numbers. It is estimated that some 150,000 men of Irish extraction fought in the Union Army alone. At least forty Union units were largely composed of Irishmen or had a substantial number of Irish soldiers in their ranks. Beyond these identifiable ethnic units, thousands of additional Irishmen were submerged in the main body of the Union Army in nonethnic units. Serving as well were significant numbers of Irish-Americans, citizens who were first-generation Americans of Irish extraction.

The preponderant number of Irish served with the Union, largely due to demographics more than an ideological bent. The majority of the Irish immigrants tended to settle in the North because the main ports of entry were all located in the north—Boston, New York, Philadelphia and Baltimore. Equally significant, there was a tendency for these new arrivals to seek employment in the immediate area where they entered the country. This factor made the North most attractive because the industrial expansion of the period was in the North and thus jobs were available there in greater numbers than in the largely agrarian south.

## NEW YORK'S 69TH REGIMENT/BRIGADE

While any number of Union states fielded Irish companies or regiments, the most famous of the Union Irish units and cer-

The most famous of the Union Irish units, New York's 69th regiment

tainly the largest was the New York Irish Brigade. To provide the nonmilitary reader with some appreciation for unit size, a Civil War regiment had authorized strength of 1,000 soldiers. A company was authorized 100 men. There was, however, considerable varience in strength for all Civil War units, depending on the state from which they originated and the fortunes of war. In actuality, company strengths were normally about 35–40 soldiers and a regiment, which consisted of ten companies, normally had about 350–400 soldiers. A brigade consisted of five regiments. The 69th had its roots in New York Irish Militia units founded in 1851. In 1857 two Irish regiments, the 9th and the 75th were consolidated to form the 69th Regiment of the New York Militia. When the war began and President Lincoln issued the call for volunteers from the states, the 69th New York State Militia was one of New York's volunteer elements that answered Lincoln's call for troops. Altogether 1,040 Hibernians volunteered to serve for a period of ninety days. Among the elements in this regiment was Captain Thomas F. Meagher's "Irish Zouaves," dressed in colorful uniforms trimmed with copious amounts of crimson or gold braid, but topped with the more traditional kepi, rather than the fez favored by many Zouave units.

This New York Regiment volunteered to assist in suppressing the rebellion, a task that most thought would last only a short period. The events of July 21, 1861, proved this assumption false. On that date at Bull Run, or Manassas Junction, the Union Army proved incapable of quickly accomplishing that task. At Bull Run the 69th was an element in Brigadier General William T. Sherman's Brigade and was actually in reserve until the middle of the afternoon. In reality, the 69th should not have even been involved in the fighting because it was a ninety-day volunteer regiment whose initial period of enlistment had already expired. Nonetheless, the Irish were willing to fight, and when Sherman's Brigade was pulled out of reserve to relieve regiments that had been in battle since morning, the 69th moved forward into battle. Commanded by Colonel Michael Corcoran, a well-known pre-war Irish leader, the regiment was thrown into battle in an attempt to take Henry House Hill, a task that had already stymied other Union regiments. The 69th successfully pushed Confederate troops from the Hill, resulting in words of praise from the Commander of Union forces, Major General Irvin McDowell. In the fighting that followed, however, Confederate reinforcements moved up and the Irish Regiment was caught up in the Union Army's retreat, which quickly turned into a rout. The 69th retreated in good order and though it suffered almost 200 casualties, the 69th's reputation as solid soldiers was established, a reputation which they would maintain throughout the war.

Following the engagement at Bull Run, the Irish regiment returned home and was treated as a victorious regiment by their fellow New Yorkers. For some of the Irish soldiers, however, the return to peacetime pursuits would be brief. Thomas Meagher, a bona fide Irish 1848 revolutionary, who had escaped British captivity and become a leader in the New York Irish community in the mid-1850s, began promoting the recruitment of a three-year Irish 69th Regiment. These recruiting efforts, encouraged by Meagher's considerable oratorical skills, resulted in the formation of a new 69th which enlisted many veterans from the old ninety-day regiment. This new regiment was not commanded by Meagher but by another prominent New York Irish leader, Colonel Robert Nugent. Thomas Meagher, though heavily involved in recruiting a new regiment, had set his sights much

Michael Corcoran

higher. He sought an all-Irish Brigade. Meagher had originally hoped to get Irish regiments from Massachusetts and Pennsylvania to fill out his five-regiment brigade, but the other states were unwilling to release their regiments to a New York outfit. They had their own quotas to fulfill and did not want to jeopardize the fulfillment of their quotas with a multistate brigade. Thus, the Irish brigade initially would be a New York unit composed of the 63rd, 69th and 88th New York and the 2nd New York Artillery battalion. The Chaplain of the 88th New York, Father William Corby, would later become president of the University of Notre Dame. Colonel Thomas Meagher, whose efforts were responsible for its creation, officially assumed command on February 5, 1862.

## Irish Brigade at War

The 69th departed from New York and proceeded to Virginia where it began training at Camp California, just west of Alexandria, Virginia. It was ultimately designated as the Second Brigade, First Division, 2nd Army Corps of the Army of the Potomac. After a period of initial training, it participated in General George B. McClellan's 1862 Peninsular Campaign and established its reputation as a hard-fighting unit at Malvern Hill in the summer. Prior to its commitment, in the spring the 29th Massachusetts (non-Irish) had been temporarily assigned to the brigade to augment its strength. In October 1862, following conclusion of the Peninsular campaign, the 116th Infantry, a regiment composed of Philadelphia Irishmen (sprinkled with a few "Pennsylvania Dutch") was added to the brigade. A short time later the 29th Massachusetts was traded to the Union 9th Corps for the 28th Mass., another Irish regiment. Thus, by year's end, the Irish brigade was close to reaching the configuration envisioned by Meagher, that is, a brigade consisting of five regiments of Irishmen from three different states.

In the latter part of 1862, the brigade entered into a series of hard-fought battles for which it is most remembered. During the second phase of the battle of Antietam, or Sharpsburg, it attacked Confederate positions in the now infamous "Bloody" or "Sunken Lane." The casualties by any standard (the 69th Regiment alone had 196 casualties out of 330 men) were appalling, but the bravery and discipline of the Irish regiments under

Thomas F. Meagher

murderous fire was recognized by soldiers of both armies. What was most impressive, the brigade remained organized and disciplined in the euphoria of attack and the disappointment of retreat. Much like its precursor, the 90-day New York 69th, this brigade had established a reputation as a crack brigade.

This reputation was furthered by the engagements at Fredericksburg. On December 13, 1862, at Fredericksburg, serving as a part of Edwin J. Sumner's Grand Division, the 69th Brigade had the task of assaulting the well-prepared defensive positions of the Confederate Army at Marye's Height and along a low stone wall and sunken road. Still commanded by now General Thomas Meagher, the Brigade attacked the Confederate positions which were virtually impossible to take by direct assault, as had been demonstrated by previous attacks by General W. H. French's Division and Colonel Samuel Zook's Brigade. In their traditional manner the Irish Brigade attacked, as ordered, and the resultant slaughter was unbelievable, even by Civil War standards. For example, all commissioned officers of the New York 69th and 112 of the 173 enlisted who assaulted the heights were casualties. At the end of the engagement, the five regiments of the brigade mustered 263 men; the remainder were either casualties or were detached from the brigade, due to the carnage. While the results of their attack were disappointing, through no fault of the brigade, their heroism on the field was never in question.

The Irish Brigade, though greatly diminished in strength and not yet rebuilt, was again required to participate in the next major engagement on the eastern seaboard. On May 3, 1863, it was employed in the Battle of Chancellorsville, yet another instance where the Union Army was badly handled by Robert E. Lee's Army of Northern Virginia. Following this engagement, Meagher requested the withdrawal of the Brigade to permit a badly needed reconstitution, but this request was refused. Meagher, disgusted by this decision, resigned in protest on May 19, 1863. The command of the Brigade was given to Colonel Robert Nugent, who had been a commander of the 69th Regiment. Thus, when the Gettysburg campaign began in the latter part of June 1863, the Brigade was under new but not unfamiliar leadership. The Brigade's service at Gettysburg was highlighted by their participation in the fighting on the second day at the Wheat-

field. In the bitter fighting which occurred there late on July 2, the Brigade again distinguished itself through the bravery of its soldiers, in bitter close quarters fighting for which the Brigade had become famous. It suffered accordingly, however. Approximately 532 soldiers entered the battle and at the battle's end, the Brigade had suffered about 198 casualties.

Following the Battle of Gettysburg, the Brigade was given a well-deserved furlough to rebuild from the devastating losses at Fredericksburg, Chancellorsville and Gettysburg. The campaigns of late '62 and 1863 had simply halved its strength. After reconstitution in its winter camp, in May 1864 it participated in the Wilderness campaign, and fought on that battlefield along with the Corcoran Legion, a unit from New York largely composed of Irish-Americans. It fact, the Irish Brigade continued to serve the Union for the remainder of the war, and in the Grand Review held in Washington May 23, 1865, the Irish deservedly took their place in the parade. Following the victory parade, the Irish made their way home, having established their reputation as the Union's best-known ethnic element.

## IRISH IN SERVICE OF THE CONFEDERACY

While the Union's Irish Brigade, as the largest Irish contingent in either army, has long captured the imagination of the Irish community and Civil War buffs, Irish units in southern service have often been overlooked. The 1860 census showed that some 85,000 Irish immigrants lived in the 11 states that would comprise the Confederacy. Even though the South had a smaller Irish population base from which to recruit, the Confederate states were successful in recruiting a number of Irish regiments. It has been estimated that some 30,000 Irishmen served as soldiers for the Confederacy and, in fact, records show that eight of the eleven Confederate states fielded Irish units of some sort. Mobile, Alabama, recruited the Emerald Guards, Savannah, Georgia, produced the Irish Jasper Greens and Charleston, South Carolina, fielded the Emerald Light Infantry.

One of the earliest and largest Irish southern units was the 6th Louisiana Volunteers, a regiment largely composed of Irishmen from one of the South's largest Irish communities, New Orleans. Organized on June 2, 1861, and mustered into Confederate service two days later, about half of the regiment's number were born in Ireland and many others were of Irish ancestry. The remainder of the regiment was filled out with a sprinkling of Germans and some with English and Scotch backgrounds. Claiming the Irish heritage for the entire regiment, during the course of the war the 6th Louisiana enlisted slightly over 1,200 soldiers. It was present on numerous battlefields from the Battle of Bull Run to Appomattox Court House, at which time the regiment had only some 55 exhausted veterans present for duty. These Louisiana Tigers fought in a number of significant engagements, including Gaines Mill, the Second Manassas, Antietam, Fredericksburg, Gettysburg, the Wilderness and Spotsylvania. The regiment's heroism under fire was noted on a number of occasions. Its only performance problem was its desertion rate, which was abnormally high for such a brave unit.

## FIRST VIRGINIA BATTALION (IRISH)

From another part of the Confederacy, Virginia recruited what may have been one of the Confederacy's least successful Irish outfits, the 1st Virginia Battalion, which became known as the Irish Battalion. This battalion was recruited in 1861 from the Covington area where many Irish had worked in the construction of the Virginia Central Railroad. Initially about 200 Irish were re-cruited into this unit where they served under largely non-Irish officers, many of whom were Virginia Military Institute gradu-ates. Despite professional leadership, the Virginia Irish Battalion was plagued by both discipline problems and by poor perfor-mance in battle. Their first real battle occurred on March 23, 1862, while they were a part of Major General Thomas Jackson's Army of the Valley at Kernstown, a short distance south of Win-chester, Virginia. In that battle the battalion retreated from the field in disorder and suffered nearly 150 casualties. It faired no better at Cedar Mountain, where it was still a part of Jackson's Army and where the battalion again retreated from the field in disorder. While Virginia did not dissolve the battalion, given its poor performance, in the fall of 1862 the Irish troops were as-signed to serve as the Provost Guard of the Confederate Second Corps. Ultimately, they would serve in the same role for the en-tire Army of Northern Virginia. Here they performed well and were successful in reducing straggling in the Confederate Army.

### THE TENTH TENNESSEE REGIMENT (IRISH)

A far better record was established by the Tenth Tennessee Regi-ment (Irish), recruited into Confederate service in the sum-mer 1861. The Tenth Tennessee consisted of approximately 730 soldiers who were either Irish-born or first-generation Irish-Americans. The regiment was both conceived and recruited by Randall W. McGavock, a Southerner of Scotch descent, but it had its origins with Company D Tennessee State Militia that had been recruited by then-Captain McGavock in the spring of 1861. The Tenth Tennessee was destined to spend its wartime service in the defense of Southern interests in the western theater. In February 1862 the Tenth was involved in the campaigns at Forts Henry and Donaldson. There it was a part of Lieutenant General Simon Buckner's Confederate force that achieved the dubious distinction of being trapped and forced to surrender to Gen-eral U. S. Grant. After the men and officers were paroled, they returned to duty and participated in the fighting in Missis-sippi. They were subsequently heavily involved in the fighting at Chickamaugua in September 1863 and at Missionary Ridge the following November. They were a part of General William J. Hardee's Corps during the bitter Atlanta Campaign and were still fighting with the Confederate Army during the last major engagement along the East Coast, the Battle of Bentonville, North Carolina. In all cases, they fought well and were consis-tently regarded as brave and dedicated soldiers on the battlefield.

### NOTABLE IRISH MILITARY LEADERS

Not all Irish soldiers served in identifiable Irish units and, fur-thermore, not all served as simple everyday soldiers. Some served in senior ranks for their respective causes. In Confederate gray there was Patrick Ronayne Cleburne, who was borne in County Cork, Ireland, and immigrated to the United States in 1849. Ulti-mately settling in Arkansas, where he first was a pharmacist and later a lawyer, Cleburne began his service to the Confederacy as a private in the 15th Arkansas Regiment. No stranger to military life (he had served in Her Majesty's 41st Regiment of Foot), Cle-burne quickly rose to command a regiment and ultimately to command a division, with the rank of major general. As a com-mander he was distinguished by his striking military bearing and the sound discipline and leadership he used on the battlefield, causing some to regard him as the "Stonewall Jackson of the West." When he died near Franklin, Tennessee, in November

General Patrick Cleburne leads his troops in battle.

1864, Confederate President Jefferson Davis stated that his death on the battlefield left a "vacancy that could not be filled."

At Gettysburg, the first general officer to fall in battle, on either side, was an Irish-American from Pennsylvania named Major General John F. Reynolds, commander of the Union First Corps. Reynolds, a West Point graduate from the class of 1841, was a well-respected professional Army officer who had served with distinction in the Mexican War. He participated in the Sec-ond Manassas, at Fredericksburg and Chancellorsville and had been discussed as a possible candidate for the position of Com-mander of the Army of the Potomac. His distinguished career, however, was cut short when, on the west side of Gettysburg in an area called Herbst or McPherson's woods, he was killed by a single shot by a Confederate infantryman.

On the other side of Gettysburg, at a place called Little Round Top, an Irish-born officer named Patrick Henry O'Rorke, the commander of the 140th New York, suffered a similar fate. Colonel O'Rorke, born in County Cavan, Ireland, was originally trained to be a marble cutter, that is, until he was given an ap-pointment to the U.S. Military Academy. He attended West Point and graduated in 1861. At the time of his graduation, he was first in his class and was first Captain of the Corps of Cadets. O'Rorke was a natural leader who fought at the first battle of Bull Run, and the Port Royal, South Carolina, expedition, prior to his asso-ciation with the 140th New York. He deserves credit, much like Colonel Joshua Chamberlain of the 20th Maine and Colonel Strong Vincent, Third Brigade, First Division, 5th Army Corps, for stopping General James Longstreet's drive to roll up the left of the Union line. In fact, had not a single Confederate bullet cut short the life of this promising officer, he would have likely con-tinued his outstanding military career, perhaps even to what his classmates had projected, i.e., that he would some day be the Commander of the U.S. Army.

In the western theater, Walter Paye Lane distinguished him-self as an exemplary leader in the uniform of Confederate gray. Lane was born in County Cork and came to Ohio at the age of four. As a young man he settled in Texas, where his sympa-thies switched to the South. As a Texan, he fought for his newly adopted state in the battle of San Jacinto, in the Mexican War as a Texas Ranger, and in Indian skirmishes. When the Civil War broke out, he became a Texas Cavalry officer, fighting at Wilson's Creek, Missouri, Pea Ridge, Arkansas, and at Mansfield, Louisiana, where he was severely wounded in 1864. He became a brigadier general during the last official meeting of the Confederate Senate, March 17, 1865, an appropriate day for an Irishman.

## Epilogue

What distinguished the Irish in the Civil War, whether serving as common soldiers, in distinctive regiments, or as ranking officers, is that so many served so well and were ranked as excellent soldiers in their newly adopted land. Why they fought and generally fought so well is difficult to answer to everyone's satisfaction. Like any volunteers, their reasons were certainly as varied as the backgrounds of the soldiers themselves. Some likely fought because they were caught up in the patriotic euphoria that gripped the nation and were carried away by the patriotic outpouring that affected many young men in the spring and summer of 1861. Others fought because it was an opportunity to visibly display patriotism and loyalty to their newly adopted country. One young Irish soldier stated that because he couldn't fight for Ireland he was fighting for the South. For whatever motivation, whatever purpose, Irish soldiers contributed significantly to their chosen cause during the American Civil War. In addition, their bravery and sacrifices likely changed, for the good, the attitudes of their non-Irish peers toward the Irish in America.

*See* Irish in America; Emigration: 1801–1921; Draft Riots

Robert G. Athearn, *Thomas Francis Meagher: An Irish Revolutionary in America* (New York, 1976).

Joseph G. Bilby, *The Irish Brigade in the Civil War: The 69th and Other Irish Regiments of the Army of the Potomac* (Conshohocken, Pa., 1998).

Irving A. Buck, *Cleburne and His Command* (Jackson, Tennessee, 1959).

William L. Burton, *Melting Pot Soldiers: The Union's Ethnic Regiments* (Ames, Iowa, 1988).

William Corby, *Memoirs of Chaplain Life: Three Years with the Irish Brigade in the Army of the Potomac (Lawrence Frederick Kohl, ed.)* (New York, 1992).

James P. Gannon, *Irish Rebels, Confederate Tigers: The 6th Louisiana Volunteers, 1861–1865* (Campbell, Ca., 1998).

Ed Gleeson, *Rebel Sons of Erin: A Civil War Unit History of the Tenth Tennessee Infantry Regiment (Irish) Confederate States Volunteers* (Indianapolis, 1993).

Jason H. Silverman, "Stars, Bars and Foreigners: The Immigrant and the Making of the Confederacy," *Journal of Confederate History,* no. 1 (Fall 1988): 265–285.

Peter Welsh, *Irish Green and Union Blue* (New York, 1986).

*Periodicals*
*Civil War: The Magazine of the Civil War Society.* March–April 1991 (Vol. IX, number 2), including the following articles:
Brian Benett, "The Ideal of a Soldier and a Gentleman," pp. 35–37, 64.
B. Franklin Cooling, "Patrick Ronayne Cleburne: Southern Citizen-Soldier," pp. 28–30, 44–46.
Jack McCormack, "The Fighting Irish," pp. 17–23.
Kevin C. Ruffner, "Virginia's Fighting Irish," pp. 65–71.

SAM J. NEWLAND

## CIVIL WAR, IRISH SEAMEN IN

Irish immigrants or men of Irish descent were significant participants in the War Between the States, fighting bravely for both the Union and the Confederacy. Although Irishmen during that period were more notably known for having fought in the respective armies, they also had a decisive role in the two navies.

### Union

Among those Irishmen who served on the Union side was Commodore Charles Stewart McCauley (1793–1869), who was born in Philadelphia, Pa. He was the son of John and Sarah (Stewart) McCauley; a nephew of Commodore Charles Stewart, first Senior Flag Officer and first Rear Admiral in the United States Navy; and a cousin of Charles Stewart Parnell.

During his early career, he saw action off the Virginia coast and on Lake Erie during the War of 1812. He headed the Washington Naval Yard during the Mexican War and was commander-in-chief of the Pacific Squadron from 1850–53. In 1855 McCauley was named temporary commander of the Home Squadron, which guarded American interests off the coast of Spanish-ruled Cuba.

Shortly before Virginia seceded from the Union, McCauley was put in command of the Norfolk Navy Yard and was instructed to refrain from provocative action. However, when the government ordered him to evacuate the most valuable ships from the yard, McCauley believed he should adhere to his earlier orders and failed to take necessary measures to protect the fleet, including the steam frigate *Merrimack*.

His refusal to act until he believed the yard was under threat of imminent attack brought about the fall of Norfolk in April 1861 and resulted in the virtual destruction of the Federal fleet. Under McCauley's orders, eight of the 11 ships in the yard, including the *Merrimack,* were burned or scuttled, and government buildings, docks and supplies were destroyed, while 3,000 guns and great numbers of shells were thrown into the water.

The Confederate Navy later salvaged the guns and ammunition, and raised and refitted the *Merrimack* and three other vessels. The *Merrimack* was transformed into the war's first ironclad vessel and renamed the CSS *Virginia.* As a result, McCauley may have had the dubious honor of making possible a Confederate Navy.

Stephen Clegg Rowan (1808–1890) was born in Dublin, Ireland, and emigrated with his family to America in 1818. They settled in Piqua, Ohio, and Rowan was appointed a midshipman from that state in 1826.

When the Civil War began, Rowan was in command of the Pawnee and helped defend Washington, D.C., during Abraham Lincoln's inauguration. He participated in the unsuccessful attempt to resupply Fort Sumter before the Confederate attack and towed the USS *Cumberland* safely from Norfolk before the base was dismantled. In May 1861 at Alexandria, Va., under the command of another Irishman, James Harmon Ward, Rowan made the first amphibious assault of the war on Confederate barriers that were positioned to prevent communication via the Potomac River between Union vessels and Washington, D.C.

In August 1861, Rowan participated in the attack on Hatteras Inlet, N.C. Aboard the USS *Delaware,* he commanded the squadron that cooperated with Major General Ambrose E. Burnside in the campaign that captured Roanoke Island, Elizabeth City, Edenton and New Brunswick, N.C. Those victories resulted in Rowan's promotion to captain and commodore on the same day, July 16, 1862. He ended the war in command of the Federal blockade of the Carolina coast. Before his retirement, Rowan was promoted to rear admiral and vice admiral.

Commander James Harmon Ward (1806–1861) from Connecticut was first commander of the Potomac fleet. He graduated from the American Literary Scientific and Military Academy, Norwich, Vt., and became a recognized authority on ordnance and naval tactics. His lectures on ordnance were published in 1845 and became the official textbook at the Naval Academy, Annapolis, which he had urged the government to establish.

Ward went on to command several ships and wrote scholarly works on naval tactics, as well as a treatise on steam. When the Civil War broke out, he proposed the use of a "flying flotilla" on the Chesapeake Bay and the Potomac River. The idea was approved and he was given command of a fleet of three steamers. Ward successfully silenced Confederate batteries at Aquia Creek, Va., but was killed while covering a landing party.

## CONFEDERACY

Confederate Navy Secretary Stephen Russell Mallory (1813–1873) was born in British Trinidad to Ellen Russell, who was from County Waterford, Ireland. He lived in Key West, Fla., where he practiced law and was a customs inspector and a judge.

In 1851 he was elected to the U.S. Senate from Florida, a position he held at the time of that state's seccession from the Union. During his time in the senate, Mallory served on the Committee for Naval Affairs. As chairman in 1855, he used the position to push for a larger and stronger navy.

Mallory was a reluctant seccessionist, even going so far as to try to prevent an outbreak of war in Pensacola Harbor. After Mallory resigned from the senate, Jefferson Davis appointed him Secretary of the Confederate States Navy.

The Confederate fleet had to be built from the ground up. Mallory sent naval officers and civilians to the North, to Canada, and to Europe to purchase vessels. To finance the purchase of cruisers, cotton was shipped through the blockades for sale in Europe.

Mallory supported the construction of ironclad vessels. He encouraged the manufacture of torpedoes, floating mines and the torpedo boat. He was criticized after the Confederacy lost New Orleans, Memphis and Norfolk, and particularly for the destruction of the ironclads CSS *Virginia* and CSS *Mississippi* to avoid their capture. His conduct was investigated by a joint committee of the Confederate Congress, and he was cleared of all charges.

The most famous naval man of the Confederacy was Matthew Fontaine Maury (1806–1873), whose parents were French Hugenot refugees who had settled in Ireland. Born in Spotsylvania City, Pa., Maury was reared in Tennessee. In 1825 he entered the U.S. Navy as a midshipman and was promoted to lieutenant in 1836.

Because of an injury to his leg, Maury was assigned to the Navy Department's Depot of Charts and Instruments in Washington, D.C. For 19 years he pursued meteorologic and oceanographic studies and eventually wrote several books on the subject of marine navigation. His work led to an international conference in Brussels, Belgium, in 1853 that benefited navies all over the world.

Maury resigned his post in 1861 when Tennessee seceded from the Union. He joined the Confederate Navy and was attached to the Office of Orders and Detail at Richmond, Va. He came in frequent contact with Mallory with whom he disagreed over the type of ships the South should build. Maury favored small gunboats with two to four guns each instead of the ironclad vessels.

Another of his duties was the devising and placement of submarine batteries in the James River. In 1862 he was sent to England to purchase ships and supplies. He served out the war in London. Maury was a leading hydrographer and, as founder of the science of oceanography, was known as "Pathfinder of the Seas."

Numerous seamen of Irish descent served under these officers and in naval battles during the Civil War. Two seamen, Irish-born John C. Cleary and William Healy, were killed when the CSS *Alabama* sank the USS *Hatteras* off the Texas coast on Jan. 1, 1863. Among those wounded were Edward McGower, Patrick Kane and John White. When the *Alabama* met its fate off Cherbourg, France, in 1864, one of the three casualties was an Irish seaman, John W. Dempsey.

*See* Civil War

John de Courcy, "Notes on Civil War Irish Seamen," *Éire-Ireland,* 6/1 (Spring 1971).

Patricia L. Faust, ed., *Historical Times Illustrated Encyclopedia of the Civil War* (New York, 1986).

Stewart Sifakis, *Who Was Who in the Civil War* (New York, 1988).

MARIANNA McLOUGHLIN

## CLAN NA GAEL

*See* Fenians and Clan na Gael.

## CLARK, DENNIS (1927–1993)

Historian, author, community activist. Born June 30, 1927 in Philadelphia, Clark was the eldest of three children of John Joseph Aloysius and Geraldine Hanson Clark, both of Philadelphia. Educated in Catholic elementary and secondary schools in that city, he graduated from St. Joseph's College there in 1952. On March 28 of that year he married Josepha O'Callaghan. Two daughters (Brigid and Conna) and four sons (Brendan, Patrick, Ciaran, and Brian) were born to the couple. Pursuing graduate studies in history at Philadelphia's Temple University, Clark completed an M.A. in 1966 and a Ph.D. in 1971.

### MANY-FACETED CAREER

Clark came from a family of working people hard hit by the 1930s depression. The preferential option for the poor became meaningful for him in his studies of the social encyclicals issued by the Vatican. Men like John LaFarge, S.J. inspired him. He was under no illusions that his native city was a model of equality for all. As a social and urban historian he viewed American history from the bottom up and was no admirer of power elites.

His activism began while serving in the U.S. Army (1945–47), in Utah, Texas, and New Mexico where he helped organize migrant workers to achieve decent living conditions. Clark worked as an information specialist for Philadelphia's housing authority in the early fifties when its facilities were being desegregated. A decade later he served as executive secretary of New York's Catholic Interracial Council and edited *Interracial Review* (1961–63). He was a founding member of the National Catholic Conference of Interracial Justice. In this period he published *Cities in Crisis: The Christian Response* (1960) and *The Ghetto Game* (1962). Later his activism led him to Appalachia for a time to engage in the war on poverty. From 1971 to 1993 he was with the Samuel Fels Foundation, initially as its secretary and then as its executive director—wherein he was responsible for evaluating applications for grants from Philadelphia's educational, cultural and community organizations—and from those in the arts.

## HISTORIAN OF THE AMERICAN IRISH

In addition to his activist roles and family responsibilities, Clark became a leading chronicler of Irish-Americans. Numerous journal articles, monographs and at least six books of his examined their story, beginning with *The Irish in Philadelphia: Ten Generations of Urban Experience* (1973). His last, *Erin's Heirs,* appeared in 1991. He demonstrated how Irish societies such as the Friendly Sons of St. Patrick, those based on county of origin in Ireland, fraternal, religious and labor associations eased the adjustment to America and preserved the identity of Hibernian immigrants. In Philadelphia, home ownership was achieved through creation of immigrant savings banks. He observed that Irish in Philadelphia fared better economically than those in Boston though less well politically due to division of their allegiance between Democratic and Republican parties. Pervasive bias against Catholic Irish persuaded the Archbishop of Philadelphia to build a cathedral without windows on the ground floor, realizing they could not withstand the frequent anti-Irish riots in the city.

## LEGACY

Writing was but one avenue of Clark's influence. He lectured at a number of colleges in the Philadelphia area including Villanova, St. Joseph's, and Temple, and taught full time at Chestnut Hill College for a year. He was a speaker with an abundance of earthy Irish stories, among them tales of his great-uncle Eddie "Bomb the bosses" McLean, a socialist—rabidly anti-clerical. Dennis Clark was a short, energetic, generous man who knew the cellar dwellers of the workforce from personal experience and documented their struggles in the best traditions of social science. He encouraged the work of numerous young scholars of ethnic and urban studies. His accomplishments were the product of a perceptive mind, a practical idealism and a disciplined life. His untimely death on September 17, 1993 was due to cancer complicated by diabetes.

*See* Historians of Irish America

*New York Times,* obituary (September 18, 1993).
*Philadelphia Inquirer* (July 4, 1988).
*Philadelphia Inquirer,* obituary (September 18, 1993).

L. A. O'DONNELL

## CLARK, PATRICK (1850–1915)

Miner, entrepreneur. Born on St. Patrick's Day, Patrick (or "Patsy," as he was called later in life) was one of a number of self-made Irish-American miner millionaires.

He arrived in the United States at age 20 and lived for a time with a sister in Pennsylvania. Like so many others, he headed out West to try his hand at finding a fortune in the ground. He struck out in California, Nevada, and Utah. But when he got to Montana, he met Marcus Daly and his luck began to change.

Impressing the Irish copper king with his knowledge, Clark became a junior partner and, in 1887, justified his mentor's confidence by helping Anaconda bring in the Poorman's Mine in Coeur d'Alene, Idaho.

The profits he earned allowed him to strike out on his own, buying a mine in British Columbia. After making improvements,

he sold the mine to another investor. Clark spent the rest of his life repeating that process, making himself a millionaire many times over in the process. His base of operations, Spokane, Washington, was the beneficiary of many of his charitable works.

John A. Barnes, *Irish-American Landmarks* (Detroit, 1995).

JOHN A. BARNES

## CLARKE, MARY ELIZABETH (1931–1980)

Martyr. Mary Elizabeth Clarke was born of Irish immigrant parents in New York City on January 13, 1931. While studying to be a teacher at Saint Joseph's College for Women, Mary decided to become a Maryknoll Sister. She entered in 1950 and later received the name Sister Maura John.

Her first assignment, in 1959, was to teach first grade in a parish school in the Bronx, a neighborhood so high in crime and low in income that it was classified by the Archdiocese of New York as "mission territory." After five years there, Maura was assigned to Siuna, Nicaragua, a gold mining town where the miners and their families lived in abject poverty at the mercy of company policies. Maura lived through poverty, floods, earthquakes and extreme injustice wrought upon the people. In 1962, Maura was named principal of the school and superior of the community in Siuna.

In 1976, Maura returned to the U.S. where she spent three years in mission education work in schools and parishes in the northeast. She endeared herself to all whom she met through her utter simplicity. She was eager to return to Nicaragua after finishing her time as a mission educator. Her response was called for and answered when the situation in El Salvador prompted the Maryknoll Sisters to consider how they could provide relief for the Sisters there. Maura said, "Since El Salvador has been made a priority for Maryknoll Sisters with Latin American experience, I may be going there." And she did, fully aware of the violence and confusion in that suffering country. She joined Maryknoll Sister Ita Ford in Chalatenango. Ita had survived a flash flood that took the life of her friend and co-worker, Sister Carol Piette, M.M., on August 23, 1980. Archbishop Romero had been shot and killed while saying Mass on March 24, 1980. Many of the poor had disappeared or were being killed or taken prisoner. The sisters' work with the poor put their own lives in danger. They had received death threats yet made a conscious choice to continue their work with and for the poor.

On December 2, 1980, Maura and Ita returned by plane from Nicaragua to El Salvador following a community meeting. Ursuline Sister Dorothy Kazel and Jean Donovan came to meet them at the airport. On the road from the airport, members of the Salvadoran National Guard intercepted the four women, Maura, Ita, Dorothy and Jean, took them to an isolated area, raped them and killed them with a shot in the head.

The words of Archbishop Romero (in a homily) resounded at this time: "Brothers and sisters, one who is committed to the poor must risk the same fate as the poor. And in El Salvador we know what the fate of the poor signifies . . . to disappear, to be tortured, to be captive, and to be found dead."

*See* Ford, Ita Catherine

Penny Lernoux, *Hearts On Fire, The Story of the Maryknoll Sisters* (Maryknoll, N.Y., 1993).

Judith M. Noone, M.M., *The Same Fate As the Poor* (Maryknoll, N.Y., 1984).

Phyllis Zagano, *Ita Ford, Missionary Martyr* (New York, 1996).

HELEN PHILLIPS, M.M.

## CLARKE, MARY FRANCES (c. 1803–1887)

Founder of the Sisters of Charity of the Blessed Virgin Mary (B.V.M.). Mary Frances Clarke, born in Dublin, Ireland, was the daughter of Cornelius Clarke and Mary Catherine Quartermas. After attending a "penny school," she and her friends opened a school in Dublin, Miss Clarke's Seminary, for girls who were too poor to attend the convent schools.

A Catholic missionary from the United States convinced Clarke and her four friends to begin a school for poor children of the Irish who had immigrated to Philadelphia, Pa. When in 1833 Clarke and the other young women arrived in the city, they met Rev. Terrence Donaghoe. While assisting them in establishing a school, he encouraged the small group to organize as a women's religious congregation, Sisters of Charity of the Blessed Virgin Mary (BVMs). Clarke was chosen by her friends to serve as the mother superior.

Bishop Mathias Loras invited the congregation to Dubuque, Iowa Territory, in 1843 to educate the children of the frontier's people. To escape the violence Catholics were experiencing from the Nativist Party and the ecclesiastical politics in Philadelphia, the group accepted his invitation. Clarke sent the young pioneer women who joined her congregation to open schools along the Mississippi River and near the westward trails. She kept in close contact with the sisters through extensive letter writing, encouraging them in their sufferings from the poverty and the harsh conditions of pioneer living. Her leadership style was compassionate and collaborative.

During her lifetime she accepted 440 women into the congregation. While serving fifty-four years as mother superior, she established forty parochial schools and nine boarding academies. In 1984 Clarke was inducted into the Iowa Women's Hall of Fame for her role in the education of the American frontier.

*See* Sisters of Charity

Jane Coogan, B.V.M., *The Price of Our Heritage* (Dubuque, 1975).

Lambertina Doran, B.V.M., *In the Early Days*. (St. Louis, 1911).

Laura Smith-Noggle, ed., *My Dear Sister: Correspondence and Notes of Mary Frances Clarke* (Dubuque, 1987).

KATHRYN LAWLOR, B.V.M.

## CLEARY, CATHERINE B. (1916– )

Banker, corporate director. Catherine Blanchard Cleary was born December 19, 1916, at Madison, Wisconsin. She was the daughter of Michael J. Cleary (1876–1947) and Bonnie Blanchard (1891–1970). Her paternal grandparents were born in Ireland: Michael Cleary (1823–1897) was a native of Coolaney, County Sligo, and Bridget Ducey (1839–1933) was born in County Wicklow.

Catherine Cleary was educated at the University of Chicago (B.A. 1937) and the University of Wisconsin Law School (LL.B. with highest honors, 1943). Upon graduation she served as a law clerk to Justice Edward T. Fairchild of the Wisconsin Supreme Court. Thereafter she practiced law in Chicago for several years before joining the First Wisconsin Trust Company in Milwaukee. In 1953–54 she served as assistant treasurer of the United States.

Cleary was elected president of the First Wisconsin Trust Company in 1969 and CEO the following year. In this capacity she was responsible for managing more than $1.25 billion in assets. She was the first woman to hold such a high position in the nation's banking industry. Her influential leadership positioned her to become a pioneer woman in the corporate boardrooms of some of America's largest businesses and charitable institutions. Cleary was named a director of General Motors, American Telephone & Telegraph, Northwestern Mutual Life Insurance Company, Kraft, and the Kohler Company. She has also served as a trustee of the University of Notre Dame, the Mayo Foundation, and the Johnson Foundation among others. Catherine Cleary's pathbreaking career significantly advanced the participation of women at the highest level of American business and finance.

Timothy R. Verhoff, "Catherine B. Cleary '43," *Gargoyle* (Winter 1991/92): 8–9.

Patricia Smith Wilmeth, "Catherine Cleary," *Wisconsin Women: A Gifted Heritage* (Madison: American Association of University Women, 1986): 186–88, 307.

THOMAS GILDEA CANNON

## CLEBURNE, PATRICK R. (1828–1864)

Military officer. Patrick Ronayne Cleburne was born March 16, 1828, County Cork, Ireland. After failing the medical exam, he joined the British Forty-First Regiment of Foot, which was half Irish. He served almost four years and was promoted to corporal. He purchased his discharge September 22, 1849 (Purdue, 5–14).

On November 5, 1849, after fifty days at sea, he and his family arrived in New Orleans. Cleburne lived in Cincinnati for a few months and then accepted employment with a drug store in Helena, Arkansas (Purdue, 23–26).

Mary Frances
Clarke

In December 1851, he bought half ownership in the store. In April 1854 the store was sold and Cleburne studied law for two years. He formed a law firm and later became a land speculator (Purdue, 37–55).

In 1860 he enlisted as a private in the Yell Rifles and was elected captain and later colonel of the First Arkansas Infantry. In March of 1862 he was promoted to Brigadier General. His troops were engaged at Shiloh where they suffered the highest casualties of any Confederate brigade (Buck, 79).

During the 1862 Kentucky Campaign, his command destroyed the Federal army at Richmond, where Cleburne was wounded in the left cheek. He later received the thanks of the Confederate Congress (Buck, 105–109). In the Battle of Perryville, October 8, his troops forced the enemy from their position. Cleburne was again wounded in the ankle (Purdue, 148–151).

In December of 1862, Cleburne was promoted to Major General. In the Battle of Murfreesboro, December 31, 1862, his division forced the Federals back three miles (Buck, 118–120). The division was engaged in the Chattanooga Campaign where they suffered heavy casualties at Chickamauga (Purdue, 227). In the Battle of Missionary Ridge, his division defeated Sherman, and Cleburne led several counterattacks. Cleburne commanded the withdrawal from the ridge and again received the thanks of the Confederate Congress for his defense of Ringgold Gap (Buck, 168–173 and Purdue, 243–263).

His division became known as some of the shock troops of the Army of Tennessee. Cleburne's Division carried a blue flag with a white moon. General William Hardee would later write that friends and foes soon learn to watch the course of the blue flag (Hardee, 17).

In January of 1864 he proposed the freedom of slaves and their families. Cleburne, who did not own slaves, felt one could not ask a man to fight as a slave. His staff told him it would kill him politically. He said that if they fired him he would reenlist as a private. He would never again receive a promotion (Purdue, 269–278).

His division fought in the battles of the Atlanta Campaign. In October of 1864 he spoke to his division. He compared their cause to Ireland under English rule, and their fate would be much worse if they lost. He said, "If this cause that is so dear to my heart is doomed to fail, I pray Heaven may let me fall with it (Purdue, 388).

In the 1864 Tennessee Campaign, November 30, near Franklin, Cleburne held his last meeting with his generals. After the meeting Cleburne replied, "Well, Govan, if we are to die then let us die like men." Cleburne had two horses shot out from underneath him and was on foot when he was killed fifty yards from the entrenchments (Purdue, 420–423). He was buried in Mount Pleasant, Tennessee until April 1870. He now rests in his adopted home in Arkansas. The Dublin newspaper *The Nation* wrote that "there were hearts that bled when its course was sped and Old Ireland felt your loss!" (Purdue, 430–434). General Robert E. Lee would state of Cleburne that on the field of battle "he shone like a meteor on a clouded sky!" (Pepper, 332–333).

*See* Civil War

Irving A. Buck, *Cleburne and His Command* (New York, 1908).

General William Hardee, "Sketch of Major General Patrick R. Cleburne," *Confederate Veteran*, vol. XII (January 1904).

Mark M. Hull, *A Meteor Shining Brightly: Essays on Major General Patrick R. Cleburne* (Milledgeville, Georgia, 1997).

Charles Edward Nash, *Biographical Sketches of General Pat Cleburne and General T. C. Hindman* (Dayton, Ohio, 1977).

Rev. George W. Pepper, *Under Three Flags or The Story of My Life as Preacher, Captain in the Army, Chaplain, Consul* (Cincinnati, 1899).

Howell and Elizabeth Purdue, *Pat Cleburne: Confederate General* (Hillsboro, Texas, 1977).

THOMAS Y. CARTWRIGHT

# CLEVELAND

Unlike most other nationality groups who arrived in the last century, the immigrant from Ireland to this country and to Cleveland specifically did not leave his homeland looking for a new opportunity for a better life. He would have remained in Ireland, a place he seems to have loved greatly. Immigration from Ireland was motivated by the absolute necessity to survive. The land in Ireland in the 1840s and 1850s was unable to sustain his life.

Some of these immigrants eventually came to Cleveland, Ohio which was founded in 1796. It had its origin in a venture called "The Connecticut Land Company." This company was the result of the pooling of land grants given by the Federal Government to individual states to compensate for financial losses to those states during the Revolutionary War. Northern Ohio constituted the land deeded to the state. It was called the Western Reserve of the State of Connecticut. The land was surveyed, subdivided and sold, mostly to people from Connecticut, the majority of whom left their life on the eastern seaboard, took a long journey to their land in the Western Reserve and tried to begin a new life.

The hardships, the painfully slow growth, and the desolation endured by the early settlers is a story in itself often told by wilderness historians. The fact was, however, that these people from Connecticut, enticed by vivid advertising which bore little resemblance to the reality of the frontier, came west to occupy the land which is the city of Cleveland today, grimly determined to make the city prosper. It did, but not during the lifetime of the original settlers who lived very short lives and who never saw what the city would become.

Central to the dynamic of the area was the theory of covenant which the early settlers made with one another. The idea was borrowed from the congregational Church of New England. For them to go home was to betray the covenant, so they stayed. To a great extent they exercised government, much of the time through a device they recalled from their earlier years on the East Coast, the town meeting.

All of this caused a very tightly-knit Yankee community to become extremely proud of itself, homogeneous and confident in its future in the Western Reserve. On the other hand, however, it all but guaranteed the failure of later non-Yankee arrivals to become an integrated part of the community for perhaps the entire remainder of the nineteenth century. These facts are important since they provide significant background to understand the several ways in which the Irish immigrants in Cleveland, confronted by the original Yankee community, turned in upon themselves and how these Irish struggled to maintain their ethnicity and how some failed to preserve any ethnic consciousness between the years 1845 and 1900.

With the opening of the locks in the St. Mary's River at Sault Ste. Marie, iron ore mined in upper Michigan could be carried by boat to the various iron and later steel mills on the South Side of Lake Erie. Cleveland was such a port. The city became quickly involved in the rapid growth of the Industrial Revolution.

Unskilled laborers were needed at once to unload cargoes arriving daily at the docks along the Cuyahoga River. Even stronger men, also unskilled, were needed to work in the mills. The jobs quickly fell into the hands of the Famine Irish immigrants, the least skilled of all the European immigrants.

By the time they arrived in Cleveland, Irish immigrants were already twice displaced. They had fled their homeland to avoid starvation; they found no opportunity for work in the cities along the Eastern Seaboard where they first tried to settle. The axiom "Go West Young Man," attributed to Horace Greeley in New York was an imperative for these people.

The vast majority of the Famine Irish who came to Cleveland to settle and work stayed. Their family names, mostly from Galway and Mayo and a few from Cork, are very much a part of the ethnic fabric of the city, one hundred and fifty years after their arrival. But in Cleveland, these Irish who were generally Catholic found a situation which resembled to a remarkable degree the same caste system they had known and fled from in Ireland. They had jobs but there was no hope for upward mobility—partly because of their lack of skills, and also because of their own lawlessness. Moreover, at the top of the system were the original settlers from Connecticut who reminded them of the Irish landlords from whom they sought escape back in Ireland. In places like Pottstown and Scranton in Pennsylvania and in Cleveland, the immigrant Irish firmly believed that the owners of the industries were close kin to the class of people who had oppressed them for close to two centuries in Ireland.

For their part, the third generation Yankees saw in the arrival of the Irish in Cleveland the beginning of a vast threat to their American enclave. Perhaps no city in the United States had its serenity broken as violently as did Cleveland by the arrival of the first great wave of Irish immigrants. The disparity between the newly arrived immigrant from Ireland and the native American was dramatic.

The Irish were at least culturally Roman Catholic. The native Clevelanders were not and they feared greatly the possibility of a segment of the people being dominated by the Papal States, the church of Rome and its Pope. The Irish were total strangers to the industrial revolution and were often illiterate, although they spoke the English language. This latter fact was to their advantage over later immigrants but to their disadvantage with the Yankees who were bewildered to find people who spoke English well but could neither read nor write the language. Apparently they never comprehended that it was their ancestors in England who were responsible for most illiteracy in Ireland. The Irish immigrants were the first large group who were not Anglo-Saxon and Protestant to arrive in Cleveland. Thus neither the Irish nor the Yankees had any previous memory of patterns of acculturation in which they could find hope of becoming "like us" or "like them" depending on one's point of view.

The Famine Irish in Cleveland were, at first at least, remarkably unruly. *The Cleveland Leader,* a notoriously anti-Irish newspaper, frequently proclaimed that 90% of the violent crimes done in Cleveland between 1850 and 1870 were done by Irish to Irish.

The Irish had no previous experience with representative government, orderly town meetings or consensus in decision making; still they were given the vote with very little knowledge of issues involved. The Yankees saw the Irish voting power and the Irish reputation for revolutionary tactics as a positive threat to the whole system of state and national political life. The immigrant Irish found, when they arrived in Cleveland, no organized societies of their kinsmen to welcome them nor was there any agency to help them through the trauma of immigration. Nearly every ethnic group that arrived in Cleveland after the Irish found such agencies or organizations. The voyage across the sea which took a minimum of six weeks was loaded with fear, and for so many, tragedy. It was hardly the passage the immigrants hoped for, and by the time they arrived in Cleveland, they may have wondered if the whole attempt at beginning a new life was worth it all.

Clearly, power was in the hands of the American-born Yankee from Connecticut in Cleveland. His reaction to the Irish had several predictable stages. First, he withdrew from any part of "his city" in which the Irish settled. Second, he consigned to the Irish the whole West Side of the Cuyahoga River bluffs. Here was begun the first ghetto of tar-paper shacks, pictures of which are easily discovered in the Archives of the Cleveland Public Library.

Soon enough the Cleveland newspapers began writing graphic descriptions of the ghetto, its squalor and its apparent hopelessness. The lack of any sanitation, the disease, the lack of any kind of adequate housing, all are described. But there is no sympathy, nothing to indicate that there was any hope for these immigrants to become useful citizens in their new city. In turn the Irish responded with more violence and with a deep interior despair.

On April 9, 1847, Pope Pius IX, at the request of Bishop John Purcell of Cincinnati, divided the Cincinnati diocese which, at that time included the entire state of Ohio, and gave the northern part of the State to a new diocese to be centered in Cleveland. A missionary French-born priest, Louis Amadeus Rappe, who had been working among the Irish who were digging the Maumee and Wabash Canal, was named Bishop of the new diocese.

Immediately, Bishop Rappe began to build for the diocese of Cleveland (which included all of northern Ohio from Indiana to Pennsylvania) a sense of community, with faith as the focal point. He borrowed rather large sums from his friends in France and began a remarkable building program. He began a seminary to train priests, an orphanage mostly for Irish children whose parents had died during the passage to America, a hospital which had a shaky start but when the bishop asked for funds to build a hospital closer to the center of the city and which would care for wounded union Army veterans returning from the battlefields in the South, the people of the city, regardless of religious affiliation, responded most generously to the appeal of the bishop for public funds. That hospital was called St. Vincent Charity; and today it bears that same name and is to be found at the location where it began.

Bishop Rappe, especially during his first years as bishop (1847–1860), directed much of his administration to aid the most urgent needs of the Irish immigrants. On the west side of the city, on the bluffs above the iron ore docks, he established the parish of St. Patrick in 1853. For more than forty years, this was the largest parish in the diocese, and during those years there were more than 1,000 children in the parish school. He appointed Fr. James Conlon, his vicar general, to be pastor of this parish.

On the East side, he founded the parish of St. John the Evangelist and the church he built there was his cathedral. It too was very large as was its parish school. Rappe himself was the pastor of the Cathedral parish, a position he held during the twenty-three years he was bishop of Cleveland. Rappe's concern for the Irish in Cleveland as well as the Irish in the larger cities of the diocese, Toledo, Sandusky and Youngstown, was remarkable.

For the Irish in the parishes he founded for them in the other large cities, he designated these parishes as English speaking and therefore as territorial parishes. During the years of the Great Famine in Ireland it was for these people who fled the Famine to come to Cleveland and northern Ohio that Rappe developed a specific policy.

The Irish immigrants were to acculturate with their non-Irish neighbors as best they could and as soon as possible. They were to seek steady jobs and home ownership. Only in the matter of temperance did the bishop permit the cathedral Irish to form their own ethnic society. That very popular temperance society took the name of Father Matthew, the Irish-born temperance crusader who had preached a mission at the cathedral in 1857. At that event, thousands took the temperance pledge. Among those taking the pledge was the French-born bishop himself. In later years he would say that he never broke that pledge, although he said he often found it rather difficult. It would seem that most people also kept the pledge. Crime among the Irish suddenly decreased. They began to work toward owning their own homes, tiny as these homes were; they were urged to save money trusting the local banks. In one generation, the Irish on the East side began to see themselves as upwardly mobile and capable of competing for jobs, not with one another but with the native-born Yankee Clevelanders. They accepted the urging of the Bishop that they should no longer see themselves as Irish or even Irish-American, but simply American.

Any priest stationed at the Cathedral during Bishop Rappe's time who saw himself as an Irish leader in an Irish parish was quickly transferred to the most rural parish that could be found where he was told to practice his nationalism among farmers. A case in point was that of Fr. T. P. Thorpe who, while at the Cathedral in 1864–65, became active in the movement of the Fenian Brotherhood. His efforts got him transferred in 1866 to Norwalk, Ohio. The Cathedral and two new parishes founded between 1855 and 1865—St. Bridget on E. 22nd St. near Charity Hospital and Immaculate Conception on E. 41st St. on Superior were comprised totally of Irish immigrants, who were encouraged to play down their nationalism and ethnicity.

This was not the case at all on the West Side. To be the first pastor of St. Patrick parish on Bridge Ave. in 1853, the bishop appointed Fr. James Conlon. Conlon was an Irish-born, quiet, conciliatory man whom the bishop seems to have trusted implicitly. He organized the new parish as an Irish parish from the very beginning. He encouraged the preservation of Irish culture more by tacit approval than by any other means, but he made it quite clear during the twenty-two years of his pastorate at St. Patrick's that his people were Irish Catholics. They were not to worship at the German Church of St. Mary's on West 30th St. nearby nor were they to mingle with their American born non-Catholic neighbors. Above all, Conlon felt, his people were not to marry nor even "keep company" (his words) with the Yankees. Catholics were to marry one another. In this he seems to have succeeded; in no year during his pastorate does one find more than two religiously "mixed marriages" in the parish records of St. Patrick's.

At St. Patrick's there were Irish literary, dramatic, cultural and musical societies as well as the hugely attended temperance society. There were Irish benevolent societies of all sorts as early as 1854, and, most importantly perhaps, the people of St. Patrick's were urged by Conlon to build their permanent church as an exact duplicate of one he had known as a boy in Ireland. It still stands today, a gaunt, high-ceilinged building although Conlon did not live to see it completed. It is in sharp architectural contrast to the warm French gothic design of the original St. John Cathedral.

If all of this meant that the people of St. Patrick's were to sacrifice upward mobility to preserve the clan-like neighborhood of the parish, Conlon seems to have said, "So be it." Thus not one but three or four generations of St. Patrick's men continued to work on the docks, unloading the ships coming to Cleveland laden with the recently discovered iron ore from Michigan and Minnesota. Others found work in the new iron and steel mills rising in the flats near the parish. This neighborhood remained tightly Irish nearly half-way into this century. It was proud, independent and aloof long after James Conlon died in Charity Hospital in 1875.

During the crucial years of the maturing of the Famine Irish on the East Side, that is to say during the years 1875 to 1895 when the children of the immigrants of the 1840s and 1850s were beginning to marry and move out of the parishes of their parents, they formed new parishes and neighborhoods which continued the logical consequences of Bishop Rappe's Americanist policies. These new parishes also embraced the children born of German parents whose arrival in Cleveland was begun about 1850.

The twentieth century has seen some remarkable changes in the ethnic consciousness of the Irish population of Cleveland. For some, recently discovered wealth and upward mobility had brought many third generation Irish to a position where they seem to have completely forgotten or denied their Irish heritage. For them the immigrant church era was ended. They moved to the suburbs but still gave considerable loyalty to their churches. However they no longer saw themselves as Irish-Americans but simply as Americans. There are great numbers of the descendants of the original East side Irish who live in the eastern suburbs. Many can trace their families back to the original founders of the first East side parishes. But for them, St. Patrick's Day (the ultimate litmus test) passes unnoticed. Or it might be briefly observed at a dinner at the Cleveland Athletic Club as they vaguely try to recall some heritage long since forgotten. For them a visit to the West Side Irish-American Club would be for most unthinkable; the connection is broken forever.

But for others, generally rooted in the original near West side parishes, acculturation and assimilation have not come so completely. St. Patrick's Day and its parade (a huge city event in Cleveland) belongs to them. They continue to support the several Irish-American clubs on the West Side. They keep alive much of their heritage in their dances, their radio programs, their contacts with relatives in Ireland and a sense of the community their ancestors had experienced in their neighborhoods of more than one hundred years ago. Seventy-five years ago, these ancestors poured considerable money toward the development of the Irish Free State. The West Side Irish are related to one another and are aware of these relationships. The weddings of their children, more often than not, have a tendency to show a familial focus on the transmission of a heritage. Funerals and the wakes that go with them continue to be the occasion of the gathering of a clan and remembering.

The Irish in Cleveland have been active in politics but on the county level, not the municipal level. There is no political "machine" like those found in other large cities. There have been no more than three or four mayors of Cleveland who were of Irish origin. There are however a disproportionate number of judges, over half of the judges working in the county, who are of Irish origin.

The Department of Urban Studies at Cleveland State University estimates that over 180,000 people in the greater Cleveland area of Northern Ohio are of Irish origin. Certainly those whose ancestors arrived in Cleveland prior to 1910 were in one way or another influenced by the Irish ethnic models of the East Side Irish or the West Side Irish. That dynamic is still operative. It continues to function even in the lives of those people who never heard of the distinction of West Side–East Side Irish.

Nelson J. Callahan and William Hickey, *The Irish and Their Communities in Cleveland* (Cleveland, 1978).

Michael J. Hynes, *A History of the Diocesee of Cleveland* (Cleveland, 1953).

NELSON CALLAHAN

## CLINTON, DeWITT (1769–1828)

*See* New York City: Irish-American Mayors

## CLINTON, GEORGE (1739–1812)

Soldier, statesman. Born of Irish Protestant lineage in Little Britain, New York, on July 26, 1739, Clinton studied and practiced law in New York after participating in Colonel John Bradsteet's campaign against Fort Frontenac. Elected to the provincial assembly in 1768, Clinton took a prominent role in the revolutionary movement and served in the Second Continental Congress. In December, 1775, Clinton became brigadier general of the militia, and he voted for separation from England though military duties precluded him from signing the Declaration of Independence. Despite the apparent lack of military skill displayed in his defense of the Hudson Valley, Clinton received a brigadier generalcy in the Continental Army in March, 1777.

In June of that year, Clinton won election as governor of New York, inaugurated on July 30, 1777, for the first of six successive terms in this office. Skillfully managing both the state's troubled finances and pressure from Indians, Clinton inspired New Yorkers to continue on despite the difficulties of Revolution. For this, he earned the sobriquet, "Father of New York."

Clinton later fought against ratification of the Federal Constitution, fearing a diminution of New York's commercial and political power, as well as his own, in the face of a strong national government. Under the name "Cato," he penned seven letters against adopting the Constitution and only when it had been ratified by the requisite number of states did Clinton assent to the New York convention's support of the plan.

Sensing defeat in 1795, Clinton declined to run for reelection but returned to serve a seventh term as New York's chief executive in 1801. In 1804, Clinton was elected vice president on the Republican ticket. While running for president as a Democrat in the 1808 election, Clinton was returned to the vice-presidency under James Madison, whom he openly disdained. On February 20, 1811, he broke the tie in the Senate to vote against rechartering the Bank of the United States and died in office on April 20, 1812.

*See* New York State; New York City

Elbert Herring, *An Oration on the Death of George Clinton* (New York, 1812).

John P. Kaminski, *George Clinton: Yeoman Politician of the New Republic* (Madison, 1993).

Ralph E. Prime, *George Clinton* (New York, 1903).

Ernest W. Spaulding, *His Excellency George Clinton: Critic of the Constitution* (New York, 1938).

*Public Papers of George Clinton,* 10 vols. (New York, 1899–1914).

CHRISTIAN G. SAMITO

## CLOSSY, SAMUEL (c. 1724–1786)

Founder of an American medical school. The exact date of Samuel Clossy's birth is unknown, but it is believed he was born in 1724. His father, Bartholomew Clossy, was a Dublin merchant who lived at 4 Suffolk Street.

Samuel Clossy received an education in the classics at the Reverend Alexander McDaniel Preparatory school in Cashel, County Tipperary. Later, he studied medicine at Trinity College, Dublin, obtaining a bachelor's degree in 1744 and a degree in medicine in 1751.

Following his graduation, Clossy was invited to perform postmortems on patients who died at Dr. Steevens' Hospital. During that time, he traveled to London to attend lectures given by William Hunter at Covent Garden and also worked at St. George Hospital. He also continued his studies at Dr. Steeven's and in 1775 received his doctor of medicine degree.

In 1761 Clossy became a fellow of the College of Physicians and a member of the Dublin Medico-Philosophical Society. He was then appointed physician at Mercer's Hospital and became a member of the hospital's board of governors.

During this time, he was organizing the information he had gained during his four years of post-mortem work at Dr. Steeven's Hospital. The book, *Observations on Some of the Diseases of the Parts of the Human Body,* was published in 1763 in London. When the book was reprinted in 1967, the editor, M. H. Saffron, pointed out how similar Clossy's method of case presentation was to modern-day clinical presentation.

In 1763 Clossy decided to immigrate to New York, hoping to take a post at a new military hospital that was being planned as a result of the French and Indian War. Although he had been mar-

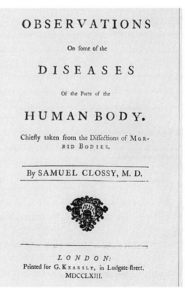

Title page of Samuel Clossy's book

ried four years and had a young daughter, Clossy didn't take his family to America.

Since plans for the hospital didn't materialize, Clossy began teaching a course in anatomy. However, he and his students found that the local people suspected them of body snatching. In 1763 Myles Cooper, second president of King's College (later Columbia University), invited Clossy to become his assistant. Clossy became the first professor of a medical subject in North America when he began a course in anatomy and was appointed professor of natural philosophy.

Although the population of New York at that time was about 20,000, the city had no hospital. Although Clossy and Cooper tried to establish a medical school at King's College, their plans were stymied by conservative elements in the college. Finally, on August 14, 1767, the governors of the college voted to proceed with the project, and Clossy became the first professor of anatomy. The opening ceremony for the school was held November 2, 1767, and the following year Clossy was awarded an honorary doctorate in medicine.

His academic career came to a halt in 1776 with the beginning of the American Revolution. Clossy gained enemies on both sides of the conflict through his refusal to join the rebels and his criticism of the loyalists. Clossy went to New Jersey when George Washington and his army occupied New York in April 1776 and converted the college into a hospital. The British, under Sir William Howe, took the city in September 1776. The soldiers broke into the college library and destroyed many valuable items, including Clossy's instruments and books.

After returning to New York in October 1776, Clossy once again began lecturing, only to have his health fail a year later. Because he was out of favor with the British authorities, who controlled the city, Clossy had been given the menial post of surgeon's mate. In December 1779, Clossy wrote to General Henry Clinton to ask for a promotion, listing his many qualifications.

When Clossy received no reply to his request, he decided to return to Ireland, once again requesting permission to do so from Clinton. Clossy noted that his presence in the colonies prevented him from helping his wife and daughter, who needed his assistance.

Clossy sailed for London in November 1780. However, his personal belongings, including an inscribed silver cup from his students, were lost when the ship carrying them sank off the French coast one year later. Clossy continued to receive military pay until June 24, 1784. He then received a pension, which allowed him to leave London and return to Dublin.

That same year Clossy's former colleagues elected him an honorary fellow of the Royal College of Physicians of Ireland. Two years later, on August 22, 1786, he died in Dublin.

Davis Coakley, *Irish Masters of Medicine* (Dublin, 1992).
M. H. Saffron, *Samuel Clossy, M.D.* (New York, 1967).

MARIANNA McLOUGHLIN

## COAL MINERS

The history of Irish coal miners in America is best exemplified by their experience in the anthracite coal regions of Pennsylvania. The hard coal fields were the first to be extensively exploited in the United States. Until 1869 they produced more coal than the rest of the nation. Moreover the Irish Diaspora coincided with the region's development. Anthracite production jumped from 34,893 tons in 1825 to 3,358,899 tons in 1850. The increasing number of mines fueled a rapid expansion of transportation services. Located within easy travel distance from the ports of Philadelphia and New York, this cornucopia of jobs attracted a large number of disembarking Irish.

Irish immigrants into the region fell into two groups. A minority were skilled miners who learned their trade either in the Castlecomer field or, most likely, in English, Welsh, or Scottish mines. The vast majority, however, knew nothing about mining coal. Skill level produced an important dividing line within the early Irish community.

Despite difference in skill levels, all Irish suffered from discrimination. They were denounced for being "clannish," described as "boors and brutes," and condemned as drunkards and criminals. "No Irish Need Apply" and "No Dogs or Irish Permitted" signs were as common as folklore would suggest, but the sentiment they proclaimed was widely shared.

Economic fear as well as religious intolerance informed anti-Irish prejudice. English, Welsh and Scotch miners had blamed Irish immigrants for the collapse of the wage structure in British mines which forced their emigration. In western Scotland, for example, the antagonism between Scottish mine workers and Irish "interlopers" led to the development of militant Orangeism and several riots. Many were determined not to permit "cheap" Irish labor to diminish their economic position in America.

Internal dynamics of the industry, not immigration, undermined labor's economic position. The rapid expansion of the mines created a capacity that easily outstripped demand by forcing down prices. During the 1830s the price of coal fell from $6.00 a ton to $4.00 a ton and would continue to slide until the Civil War.

Falling prices translated into lower wages. In 1829 a miner received a $1.25 per day. By 1842 the prevailing rate for a miner was 88 cents a day. Mostly laborers, the Irish received even less; in 1849 laborers earned between 60 and 66 cents a day. At the time it was estimated that at least $6.00 a week was necessary to support a comfortable life style. The truck system or company store eroded the purchasing power by forcing workers to buy goods from the operators at often inflated prices. Some rented housing from the mine owners who deducted the rent from their wages. In many cases payroll deductions left little or no cash in the pay envelope.

Workers protested the deterioration of their circumstances. The first united action occurred in July 1842. On July 9 a group of mostly Irish mine workers marched from mine to mine in the vicinity of Pottsville calling others to lay down their tools in an effort to end the truck system. Mine operators responded by

Irish coal miners

calling on the militia to put down this threat to their property and managerial prerogatives.

The 1842 suspension ended without bloodshed. But it established a pattern for labor-management struggles. Labor's response would be localized. Capital would call for and receive government aid. And, although other ethnic groups participated in the workers' collective protest, the "intemperate" Irish would be blamed for the strikes.

During the Civil War, labor protest and ethnic animosity combined with partisan politics to justify military occupation of part of the area. Inflation triggered a surge of new local union activity which, initially, enjoyed some success in increasing wages. But the new organizations also raised important work control issues and demanded that only union members be hired. Operators denounced the closed shop demand as another example of Irish clannishness. It was, they argued, nothing more than an attempt by the Irish to drive the English, Welsh, Scotch, and Germans from the mines.

The Irish propensity to support the Democratic Party added a more ominous color to the allegation. The war generated intense partisan feeling. Many democrats in the coal regions, as elsewhere, opposed the war arguing it was being fought for the benefit of only the Republican Party. The political debate generated violence. In July 1862, for example, John Kehoe, an Irishman and anti-war Democrat became involved in a heated political argument with a mine foreman, F. W. Langdon, at Audenreid. Later Langdon was found murdered and popular suspicion blamed Kehoe and/or his friends for the crime.

Opposition to the draft also produced violence which was blamed upon Irish Democrats. George K. Smith, a mine operator, was murdered in 1863 apparently because he gave a draft officer a list of his employees. Earlier that year a crowd stopped a Harrisburg bound train of conscripts, largely from Cass Township, Schuylkill County, and permitted those unwilling to be drafted to return home. To avoid disruption of the crucial anthracite industry, the federal government accepted bogus affidavits that the township fulfilled its quota for soldiers with voluntary enlistments. That Cass Township was heavily populated by Irish and a Democratic stronghold did not escape notice.

It was a simple matter to extend draft resistance to the labor strikes through their Irish connection. Hence, strikes became treason; they were obviously attempts by the Irish to disrupt vital war production. This logic justified court martialing and imprisoning union leaders as well as employing federal troops to protect strike breakers. The same reasoning gave credence to the notion of a secret Irish terrorist society in the coal regions.

Benjamin Bannan, the Whig editor of the *Miners' Journal* of Pottsville, first proposed the concept of a secret Irish society in the 1850s. To him, at that time, the society was a corrupt group of Irish Democratic politicians who collaborated with the liquor interests to control their more ignorant compatriots in order to loot the public treasury. During the Civil War, of course, the organization took on more sinister aspects including beatings and murder. After the war, however, such allegations disappeared.

But they were resurrected in 1871 by Franklin B. Gowen, President of the Philadelphia and Reading Railroad. Confronted by another wave of militant labor activity, Gowen complained of a secret organization which murdered people. He then claimed that the only people killed were those who disobeyed the directives of the union. Two years later he hired Alan Pinkerton's National Detective Agency to investigate crime in the coal regions.

The agency assigned James McParlan to the case. Born in Ireland, he emigrated to the United States in 1867. In 1871 he joined the Pinkerton Agency. Disguised as a tramp named McKenna, McParlan uncovered a number of groups in the coal fields reflecting current ethnic and intra-ethnic group tensions. The Modocs were a gang of Welshmen that flourished in the Mahanoy City area which preyed upon the Irish. Another group, the Sheet Irons or Chain Gang, consisting of "Kilkenny men" and "Young Irish-Americans," who were largely skilled miners, also targeted recent Irish immigrants.

McParlan, however, did not pursue either of these gangs. Rather, he focused on the organization he had previously identified as the culprit, the Molly Maguires. As a result of his investigation, twenty Irish Catholics were executed for a number of murders including those of Langdon and Smith during the Civil War. During the trial every effort was made to link the so-called Molly Maguires with organized labor. But the linkage could only be by innuendo; there was absolutely no evidence that those accused of being Molly Maguires ever influenced union policy or acted on its behalf.

The union which Gowen successfully tarred with the brush of terrorism was founded by John Siney in 1869. Siney was born in Bornos, County Queens (now Counties Offaly and Laois), Ireland on July 31, 1831. At the age of five he moved with his parents, who lost their holding, to Wigan, England. There he began working as a bobbin boy in the cotton mills and later became an apprentice bricklayer. He was a founder of the Bricklayers' Association of Wigan and served as president of that organization before emigrating to Saint Clair, Pennsylvania in 1863.

In 1868 Siney helped organize the Workingman's Benevolent Association of Saint Clair to resist pay cuts. Realizing that a local organization could do little to address the problem, he played a major role in the creation of the Workingmen's Benevolent Association (WBA), the first industry-wide labor union in anthracite, and served as its president until 1874. In 1873 he helped found the first national miners' union, the Miners' National Association. He also participated in the formation of the Greenback Labor Party.

Siney's labor philosophy was basically conservative. He visualized a harmonious relationship between labor and capital. Both were victimized by excessive production which reduced prices. The WBA would correct the problem by using the strike and other methods to maintain prices at a profitable level. The smaller mine operators embraced Siney's philosophy, but balked at the idea of sharing governance of work with their employee. Franklin B. Gowen, soon to establish a cartel with other railroad-mining companies, saw no need for a labor union. He forced the "Long Strike of 1875" which destroyed the WBA.

Improvement of wages was not the only concern of the WBA. The union also sought legislation to improve mine safety. In 1869 it secured an act "for the better protection of lives of the miners in the County of Schuylkill. The following year the law was extended to all anthracite mines. Despite safety laws, the anthracite mines continued to extract a frightful toll in limbs and life.

Most mine accidents kill or injure only one or two people. But occasionally, disasters killed many more. The first major disaster in anthracite occurred in September 1869 when a fire at the Avondale mine suffocated 110 men and boys. Siney's impassioned speech at the disaster site so moved a young Irish machinist, Terence V. Powderly, the future Grand Master Workmen of the Knights of Labor, that he dedicated his life to the cause of labor.

The victims of mine disasters reflected the changing ethnic composition of the industry's labor force. The majority of those killed at Avondale, for example, were Welsh and English. The Irish tragedy occurred on June 27, 1896 when almost 200 acres of ground above the Twin Shaft mine at Pittson "caved in" trapping approximately 135 men underground. Their bodies were never recovered.

By the 1880s the Irish-Americans had overcome discrimination, becoming highly skilled miners. Some had even become "bosses" or foreman. Others served as state mine inspectors. A large number, having learned mining in anthracite, moved west to the bituminous coal fields where they joined compatriots who had either migrated directly from Ireland or sojourned there from elsewhere in America.

Irish bituminous mine workers protested harsh working conditions with collective action. They participated in the "Great Strike of 1882" in the George Valley in Maryland. Two years later they were among the "core group" responsible for a 186-day strike in Texas. Both strikes occurred under the auspices of the Knights of Labor. After 1885, however, another union, the National Federation of Miners and Mine Laborers, competed with the Knights for their allegiance. After five years of competition the two unions merged to form the United Mine Workers of America (UMWA).

The new organization enjoyed initial success, but a depression and an ill-advised strike in 1894 depleted its treasury to less than $600. The union recovered under the leadership of Michael D. Ratchford. Born in County Clare, Ireland, Ratchford emigrated with his parents to Ohio in 1872 where he entered the mines at age twelve. After holding various union offices, he became the international president of the UMWA in 1897. Under his leadership the union waged a twelve-week strike which ended with the Central Competitive Agreement granting soft coal miners the eight-hour day, union recognition, and a uniform wage system. When he resigned the presidency in 1898 he was able to report that membership tripled and the treasury contained $11,000.

In 1898 the UMWA was primarily an organization of soft coal miners; only a small fraction of anthracite mine workers were members. Nevertheless, the union, under its Scotch Irish leader, John Mitchell, called a strike for September 17, 1900. Approximately 97 percent of the workforce obeyed the call. In October, the foiled mine operators ended the strike by posting notices of a 10 percent wage increase. Management's refusal to recognize the union caused another strike in 1902. The strike completely shut down the industry causing the federal government to intervene. The Anthracite Strike Commission awarded a wage increase, reduced the length of the work day for some, and established a grievance procedure.

Monsignor John J. Curran, pastor of Holy Savior Church in Wilkes-Barre, played a key role in the strike of 1902. His strenuous campaign on behalf of the mine workers gave the strikers a positive public image. He pleaded their cause before the mine owners. Rebuffed he took their cause to the White House where he formed a firm friendship with Theodore Roosevelt. Indeed, Roosevelt launched his Bull Moose presidential campaign with a mass meeting at Holy Savior Church!

Another non-miner played an important part in the development of the UMWA. Mary Harris (Mother) Jones was born in Cork, Ireland in 1830. By 1877 she was involved in labor activity and in 1890 became an organizer for the UMWA. She gained fame as an "agitator" for her "boys" in the bituminous and anthracite fields. In February 1913 she was court-martialed and convicted for her participation in the Paint Creek/Cabin Creek, West Virginia strike. Public outrage forced her release in May 1913.

Despite several setbacks over the next three decades, the UMWA would continue to be the dominate voice for labor in coal mining. The institution also provided another "ladder of success" for Irish-Americans who provided distinguished leadership at the local, district, and international levels.

John Brophy was one of the most able labor leaders in the twentieth century. Born in Dublin, Brophy's grandfather emigrated to Liverpool, England where he opened a shoemaking shop. The decline in demand for handcrafted shoes, however, forced his children into the mines; John's father, Patrick, entered the pits at the age of nine. In 1888 Patrick migrated to Philipsburg, Pennsylvania and two years later his family came to America. The family traveled from coal camp to coal camp for a decade looking for better working conditions. Finally they settled in Nanty Glo, Pennsylvania.

At Nanty Glo, John, already a dedicated labor unionist, became disenchanted with the condition of the UMWA local union. He considered its leadership ineffective and blamed them for apathy among the membership. At meetings he strongly criticized the incumbent officers and their policies. As a result he was elected to several offices in the local and finally was elected President of District Two of the United Mine Workers of America.

The strike of 1922 brought Brophy into open conflict with the strong-willed International President of the UMWA, John L. Lewis. During the strike Brophy, supported by his membership, fought to bring the previously unorganized miners in Somerset into the union fold. But the national contract Lewis signed with the operators excluded Somerset. For Brophy Lewis's actions was nothing less than a betrayal.

The outraged Brophy and other dissentients organized the Progressive International Committee to challenge Lewis. Lewis foiled the dissenters in the 1924 convention. Two years later Brophy launched another challenge under the slogan "Save the Union." Lewis won by an overwhelming majority which many complained was the result of fraud. Not content with his victory, Lewis drove the upstart out of the UMWA by suspending his membership.

The depression of 1929 and the opportunities presented to labor by the New Deal brought a reconciliation of the two. Lewis, realizing that he needed talented and dedicated people, permitted Brophy to rejoin the union. Brophy also accepted a job with the international offices UMWA. His first assignment was to investigate a rebellious dual union, Miners Progressive Association in Illinois, and then asked to organize the by-product coke industry. In 1935 Lewis turned to Brophy to lead the newly formed Committee for Industrial Organization (CIO). As the first and only Director of CIO, Brophy played an important role in organizing workers in the steel, rubber, automobile and other basic industries. Although the post of Director was eliminated in 1935, Brophy continued to play an important role in organized labor and government.

An Irish-American, Thomas Kennedy, from the anthracite region also gave prestigious service to labor and government. Kennedy was born in Lansford in 1887. He entered the mines at the age of twelve as a slate picker in the breaker. A year later he joined the UMWA. Although young, his leadership talents were recognized by the membership who elected him Secretary of the local union at the age 16. He remained in that post for seven years when he was elected President of UMWA District Seven. In that capacity he sat on the Anthracite Board of Conciliation and dominated contract negotiations with anthracite operators. He became the Secretary-Treasurer of the International UMWA in 1925. Although he retained his union positions, Kennedy, an ardent Democrat, played an active role in state politics in the 1930s. In 1934 he was elected Lieutenant Governor of Pennsylvania. His 1938 gubernatorial campaign, however, was unsuccessful.

Kennedy was more successful in union politics. In 1947 he was elected International Vice President and would hold that office until 1960 when he succeeded John L. Lewis. But Kennedy was too ill to fulfill the rigors of the office and William A. (Tony) Boyle was made Acting President of the UMWA in 1962.

"Tony" Boyle was president of the union' District Twenty-seven when John L. Lewis made him his administrative assistant in 1948. His primary function was to maintain the political machine that kept his boss in power. When he ascended to the presidency of the union in 1963 he continued the Lewis dictatorial style. But Boyle lacked Lewis's charisma and he failed to obtain favorable contracts from the operators. As a result of his indifference or incompetence wages in the coal industry fell below those paid the steel and auto industries. Discontent grew into open insurgency when Jock Yablonski challenged Boyle for the presidency in 1969. Not surprisingly, Boyle won the election by a two to one margin. Three weeks after the election, Yablonski, his wife and daughter were murdered. Outraged Yablonksi supporters formed an organization, Miners for Democracy, to wrest control of the union from Boyle. They were successful in 1972. Later Boyle was convicted of conspiring to murder Yablonski and his family.

Boyle's blemished career cannot tarnish the illustrious record of the Irish coal miners in America. The Irish supplied the labor necessary for the early rapid expansion of the industry and built the transportation lines to bring the fuel to market. Entering the mines as unskilled workers, they overcame discrimination to move up the occupational hierarchy to become miners and managers. And, they provided leadership in the miners' effort to end economic exploitation and secure industrial democracy.

*See* Labor Movement

Harold W. Aurand, *From the Molly Maguires to the United Mine Workers: The Social Ecology of An Industrial Union* (Philadelphia, 1972).

Perry K. Blatz, *Democratic Miners: Work and Labor Relations in the Anthracite Coal Industry, 1875–1925* (Albany, 1994).

John Brophy, *A Miner's Life, an Autobiography,* edited by John O. O. Hall (Madison, 1964).

Priscilla Long, *Where the Sun Never Shines: A History of America's Bloody Coal Industry* (New York, 1989).

Kevin G. Kenny, *Making Sense of the Molly Maguires* (New York, 1997).

Grace Palladino, *Another Civil War: Labor, Capital, and the State in the Anthracite Regions of Pennsylvania, 1840–68* (Urbana, 1990).

Edward Pinkowski, *John Siney: The Miners' Martyr* (Philadelphia, 1963).

Marilyn D. Rhinehart, *A Way of Work and a Way of Life: Coal Mining in Thurber, Texas, 1888–1926* (College Station, 1991).

Edward M. Steel, Jr., ed., *The Court Martial of Mother Jones* (Lexington, 1995).

HAROLD W. AURAND

## COCKRAN, WILLIAM BOURKE (1854–1923)

Lawyer, United States Congressman, and political gadfly. He was born on February 28, 1854 in Sligo, Ireland. He was the son of Martin and Harriet (Knight) Cockran. William spent his youth in Ireland and France, where his parents hoped that he would pursue what might have been a vocation to the priesthood. Instead, at age seventeen he emigrated to America and settled temporarily in Tuckahoe, New York. In Tuckahoe Cockran turned to law as his choice for a career. Teaching at a Catholic girls academy as well as serving as principal of a public school in Tuckahoe, the Irishman studied law at night. In 1876 he was admitted to the bar of the state of New York (Smith, *The Encyclopedia of American Catholic History,* 352).

Following a brief two-year stint as a lawyer in Mount Vernon, New York, Cockran moved to New York City where he entered into the political arena. This was a period in the history of the Irish in America, especially among recent immigrants, when their Roman Catholic identity seemed to be strengthening. Cockran, as a United States Congressman in 1886, 1890, 1892, and then for several years in the early twentieth century, used his well-known oratorical skills to consistently defend immigrants, in particular Irish Catholics (McCaffrey, *The Encyclopedia of American Catholic History,* 698–700).

It was in those days also that Cockran developed his reputation as a political gadfly, acting as a constructively positive stimulus for his Democratic Party and sometimes the Republicans as well. Cockran was willing to change party affiliations when required to do so because of his ideological convictions. But, he also was able to return to his original party if and when he deemed it ideologically necessary. At the Democratic national convention in 1884 Cockran gave an address in which he devastatingly assaulted his party's presidential nomination of Grover Cleveland. Later, in 1896, he broke with the Democratic Party in opposition to its support of William Jennings Bryan for President of the United States. Cockran disagreed on the free coinage of silver issue of that time. Cockran, in that election, favored William McKinley.

In 1900, though, Cockran rejected "the brutal imperialism of McKinley" (Smith, 353). Still, he later gave his support to President Theodore Roosevelt, who by all measures was even more imperialistic than McKinley. Cockran was to serve several more terms in the United States House of Representatives, 1904–1909 and 1920–1923. In the meantime, he strongly argued in support of Irish Catholic Governor Alfred E. Smith of New York for the Democratic Party's nomination for United States president in 1920. Always the voice of immigrants and a dependable gadfly, William Bourke Cockran died suddenly on March 1, 1923.

Thomas N. Brown, *Irish-American Nationalism, 1870–1890* (New York, 1966).

Lawrence J. McCaffrey, "Irish Catholics in America," *The Encyclopedia of American Catholic History* (Collegeville, 1997).

———, *The Irish Diaspora in America* (Washington, D.C., 1984).

———, *Textures in Irish America* (New York, 1992).

James McGurrin, *Bourke Cockran: A Freelance in American Politics* (New York, 1948).

Richard G. Smith, "Cockran, William Bourke (1854–1923)," *The Encyclopedia of American Catholic History* (Collegeville, 1997).

United States Sixty-Eighth Congress, First Session, May 4, 1924, House. "W. Bourke Cockran: Memorial Addresses Delivered in the House of

Representatives in Memory of W. Bourke Cockran, Late Representative from New York (Washington, D.C., 1925).

PATRICK FOLEY

## CODY, JOHN PATRICK CARDINAL (1907–1982)

Cardinal archbishop of Chicago (1965–1982). John Patrick Cody was born in St. Louis, Missouri, on December 24, 1907, 35 years after Cardinal George Mundelein (1872–1939), Chicago's first cardinal (1924). The two men defined a 67-year era marked by enormous progress but characterized by a consolidating authoritarianism. The triumphalist style changed with alarming speed following the Second Vatican Council (1961–1965), leaving a beleaguered cardinal who had just taken office and who had to serve for another 17 years, equipped only with the now ridiculed imperial style of his predecessors.

### EARLY CAREER

Cody was ordained for the Archdiocese of St. Louis on December 8, 1931. Named auxiliary bishop of St. Louis (titular bishop of Appollonia) in May 1947, he served in St. Louis until being named coadjutor bishop of St. Joseph, Missouri, in January 1954. In 1956 he was appointed bishop of Kansas City-St. Joseph, where he remained until 1961. In that year, he was named coadjutor archbishop of New Orleans to aging Archbishop Joseph F. Rummel. A year later he was appointed administrator, and by November 1964 he became archbishop of New Orleans. (It was the third successive diocese in which he had been named coadjutor with the right of succession to an aging bishop. Years later, in Chicago, the prospect of having a coadjutor appointed haunted him.)

In New Orleans, he took a strong stand in favor of integration, including the public excommunication of several prominent Catholic politicians when they refused integration within their parishes.

In June 1965 he was named eleventh bishop, sixth archbishop of Chicago succeeding Cardinal Albert Meyer (1903–1965). On June 26, 1967, Paul VI named him a cardinal priest, the fourth cardinal in Chicago history. He served as archbishop for seventeen years.

### THE PATH TO CHICAGO

Early in his career, Cody spent ten years in Rome, first as a seminarian (1927–31) and then as vice rector of the North American College and a staff member of Cardinal Eugenio Pacelli's (later Pius XII) Secretariat of State from 1932 to 1938. Another staff member at the time was a diplomat named Giovanni Battista Montini who would become Paul VI and who would appoint him to Chicago.

Recalled to St. Louis in 1938, Cody was made personal secretary to Archbishop (later Cardinal) John Glennon. He established his loyalties to the Church even before he was named a bishop. In February 1946, he accompanied Archbishop Glennon to Rome where the ailing prelate was to receive the cardinal's red hat. En route home, already near death, the 84-year-old cardinal visited his native Ireland where he died on the same day as Cody's mother in St. Louis. Cody chose to remain with Glennon.

When the see of Chicago opened, Cody enjoyed the support of Cardinals Francis Spellman of New York and James McIntyre of Los Angeles, together with the blessing of Egidio Vagnozzi, apostolic delegate, who was Cody's old Roman classmate.

Cody arrived in Chicago in a special railroad car that underscored his imperial style. He immediately dismissed a group of aging pastors and began to centralize all authority. (In fairness, the infirmities and ineptitude of some of the pastors was well known, but Cody's critics felt that he could have framed a more pastoral response.)

Under Cody's predecessors, Samuel Stritch (1939–58) and Albert Meyer (1958–65), Chicago became the center of liturgical reform, civil rights, labor movements, and family apostolates such as the Cana Conference and the Christian Family Movement. Known for its massive parishes, many of its pastors were de facto bishops who came to resent Cody's high-handed style. A chronic insomniac and micro-manager, he insisted on signing virtually every check, an impossible job in the massive archdiocese.

The Cardinal introduced many benefits for both clergy and lay employees. He instituted health insurance plans for priests and initiated a pension plan for both clergy and laity. However, he found himself with a rapidly shrinking clergy corps. He was faced with some 300 resignations from the active clergy. The clergy shortage forced Cody to close parishes, a reality that has continued.

By 1966 his high-handed style had so incensed his priests that they formed a de facto union, the Association of Chicago Priests (ACP). Initially, Cody tried to cooperate with them, but within a few years, tensions had grown so strong that he soon came to view appeals to his authority as challenges to it. When the ACP publicly censured both Cody and his auxiliary bishops, all contact was broken.

### THE FINAL YEARS

Although viewed as a restorationist, Cody had sensitive political radar. He sensed the mind of Rome on certain key issues, particularly those coming out of Vatican II. He revamped the seminary curriculum, established a permanent diaconate and promoted desegregation in the parishes and schools. He met with Martin Luther King, Jr., and gave generous subsidies to African-American and Hispanic parishes. However, he also drew sharp criticism for his lavish spending on the eventually aborted Catholic Television Network of Chicago (CTN/C) and the renovation of Holy Name Cathedral on which he lavished in excess of three million dollars. The first project underscored his vision but was severely hobbled by his autocratic style; the second was necessary but was carried out with such secrecy that clergy and laity rebelled.

By the early 1980s, Cody's administration began to unravel completely. His problems were compounded when rumors began to surface that he had diverted much of the archdiocesan insurance business to David Dolan Wilson, the son of Cody's stepcousin. There was no evidence that Wilson had cheated the archdiocese but the scandal was fueled by rumors of an affair with Helen Dolan Wilson who had relocated from St. Louis to a luxury apartment in Chicago and a home in Florida. The Cardinal held that she worked for the archdiocese but there was no evidence of any work product. She retired on a generous pension. It remains entirely possible that any support Mrs. Wilson received was from Cody's personal funds. Further, no one was able to substantiate any evidence of an affair.

The Cardinal's final days were spent fending off Internal Revenue Service charges that he had diverted church funds for personal use. Following his death, stories surfaced that Paul VI had hesitated from removing him from office and, allegedly, John Paul I had the necessary papers on his desk when he died after only 31 days in office. His subsequent support of Cardinal Karol Wojtyla, with whom he had received the red hat, insured his retention as archbishop. When as John Paul II, the Polish cardinal visited Chicago, Cody arranged a lavish welcome.

Now nearing his seventy-fifth year, Cody's health began to fail. His final days were spent with his lawyers. He died in his mansion on April 25, 1982, and was succeeded by Cardinal Joseph Bernardin.

*See* Chicago, Aspects of; Greeley, Andrew

Charles Dahm, *Power and Authority in the Catholic Church: Cardinal Cody of Chicago* (Notre Dame, 1981).
Ellen Skerrit, Edward B. Kantowicz, and Steven M. Avella, *Catholicism Chicago Style* (Chicago, 1993).

R. TIMOTHY UNSWORTH

## COHALAN, DANIEL F. (1865–1946)

Irish nationalist, Tammany politician, judge. The eldest son of Irish immigrants, Daniel Cohalan was born in Middletown, New York. He graduated from Manhattan College in 1885 before studying law and gaining admittance to the New York bar in 1888. By 1900, he was involved with the Democratic party, regularly attending state conventions and serving as a delegate to the 1904 and 1908 national conventions. Cohalan became a chief advisor to Tammany Hall leader Charles F. Murphy and was Grand Sachem of the Tammany Society from 1908–11. A political deal placed him on the New York Supreme Court in 1911, a post he held until resigning in 1924.

A prolific speaker and author, he proved one of the foremost Irish nationalists in America. In July, 1900, Clan na Gael reunited under leadership of Cohalan, John Devoy and Joseph McGarrity, calling for physical force to establish an independent Irish Republic. In August, 1907, a Sinn Fein League formed in New York under Cohalan's leadership, and he helped organize and was a major speaker at the March 4–5, 1916 Irish Race Convention held in New York City. From 1916–32, Cohalan was a leading member of the Friends of Irish Freedom as well.

During Eamon de Valera's United States tour in 1919–20, Cohalan and Devoy split with that leader, a move which seriously crippled the Friends of Irish Freedom. Among the issues in contention were their questioning of de Valera's right to make policy decisions for American Irish and the desire that much of the money being raised for revolution be spent on propaganda in the United States. There was also open hostility between Cohalan and President Woodrow Wilson based on personality and Cohalan's linkage with German activities before American involvement in World War I, his opposition to the League of Nations and his attempts to have the Ireland question discussed at the war settlement. Cohalan died on November 12, 1946, at the age of eighty.

*See* Fenians and Clan na Gael; de Valera, Eamon

The American Irish Historical Society in New York City has an extensive collection of Daniel Cohalan's papers.
John Devoy, *Recollections of an Irish Rebel* (New York, 1929).
Michael F. Funchion, ed., *Irish American Voluntary Organizations* (Westport, 1983).

Gustavus Myers, *The History of Tammany Hall* (New York, 1917).
Alan J. Ward, *Ireland and Anglo-American Relations 1899–1921* (London, 1969).

CHRISTIAN G. SAMITO

## COHAN, GEORGE MICHAEL (1878–1942)

Composer, dancer, lyricist, playwright, actor and producer. He was born on July 3, 1878, in Providence, Rhode Island. He was to be the only son of Jeremiah John "Jerry" Cohan and Helen Frances "Nellie" Cohan. Following his birth, George was baptized a Roman Catholic. Later on in his life, as his professional career began to mature, he became known simply as George M. Cohan. Jerry and Nellie also had two daughters. While the first died as an infant, the second, Josephine, went on to perform on stage with the family for many years (Birnbaum, 173).

The name Cohan is a modification of the Irish name Keohane, Cohan being the spelling which George's paternal grandfather adopted after his emigration from County Cork, Ireland, to Massachusetts. George had little formal education, attending elementary school in Providence for only three years before joining his parents and sister as entertainers on stage (Birnbaum, 173). The family act, which came to be called the Four Cohans, traveled throughout the land starring in theatrical productions. It was during that time that George M. Cohan developed his classic strutting dancing style and his famous phrase that he used at the close of performances, "My mother thanks you, my father thanks you, my sister thanks you, and I thank you" (Birnbaum, 173).

George M. Cohan was married twice, first in 1899 to Ethelia Fowler, who had the stage name "Ethel Levey" and who joined the Cohan family act. After their divorce in 1907, he married Agnes Nolan of Massachusetts. George and Ethelia had a daughter, Georgette; while George and Agnes became the parents of two daughters (Mary Agnes and Helen Frances) and a son named after his father.

As reflected in many of his stage performances and much of his composition, George M. Cohan's name became almost synonymous with American patriotism. His musical "Little Johnny Jones" (1904) gave the world the song "Yankee Doodle Boy." That production featured as well a less patriotic, but equally famous "Give My Regards to Broadway." Cohan's efforts also resulted in such classic works as "You're A Grand Old Flag" (1906), and the best known of all his patriotic compositions, "Over There" (written in 1917 as America entered World War I). In honor of "Over There" the United States Congress awarded him, and President Franklin Delano Roosevelt presented to him in 1940, a gold medal (Birnbaum, 174). After a long life of writing plays, composing songs and musicals, producing, and acting—interspersed with attending major league baseball games, his favorite sport—George M. Cohan died at his New York City home on 5 November 1942. He received a Roman Catholic burial from St. Patrick's Cathedral and was laid to rest in the Cohan family mausoleum in the Bronx (Birnbaum, 175).

*See* O'Neill, Eugene; New York City; Theater, Irish in

George Philip Birnbaum, "Cohan, George Michael," *Dictionary of American Biography,* Supplement Three: *1941– 1945* (New York, 1973).
George Michael Cohan, *Twenty Years on Broadway* (New York, 1924).
David Ewen, *Complete Book of the American Musical Theatre* (New York, 1958).

———, *Popular American Composers* (New York, 1962).
Ward Morehous, *George M. Cohan* (New York, 1943).

PATRICK FOLEY

## COLLINS, JOHN F. (1919–1995)

*See* Boston, Twelve Irish-American Mayors of

## COLLINS, PATRICK ANDREW (1844–1905)

*See* Boston, Twelve Irish-American Mayors of

## COLONIZATION AND IMMIGRANT FARMERS

The nineteenth-century Irish immigrant to America was primarily an urban creature. Most settled in the large eastern urban centers, the chief among these being New York, Philadelphia and Boston. Between 1870 and 1890, historian Carl Wittke has estimated, one out of every four Scandinavians in the upper Mississippi Valley was a farmer, and one out of every six Germans. Among the Irish, however, the number was somewhere around one in twelve.

Irish rural settlements developed in two ways: deliberately and accidentally. Irish canal and railroad workers, after their work was completed, stayed on in the surrounding areas. As a result impromptu Irish-American settlements arose near the Erie Canal and the Illinois and Michigan Canal, as well as the railroad lines such as the Union Pacific and other railroad lines. In other cases, the Irish were attracted by offers of cheap land, as the Mexican government offered in Texas in 1829. San Patricio and Refugio, two of Texas' earliest Irish settlements, emerged as a result.

During the nineteenth century, there were in fact a number of organized efforts to settle Irish Catholic immigrants in the West, in communities of their own. That is to say, most Irish colonies were planned, financed and organized by colonization societies in the East. In 1817, for example, the Irish Emigrant Society of New York petitioned Congress to set aside public lands in Illinois for an Irish settlement. The petition asked Congress to sell land on fourteen years' credit, but it was voted down in the House of Representatives, by a vote of 83 to 71.

Irish Catholic spokespersons, clergy and laity, were the main promoters (and sometimes detractors) of westward migration and settlement. The main impetus for this approach was the belief that immigrants could better preserve their faith, and protect themselves from anti-Catholicism, more effectively as groups than as individuals. In the 1820s Bishop John England of Charleston, and Bishop Benedict Fenwick of Boston, promoted Catholic colonization movements on a small scale.

The first nationwide effort at western colonization was the work of Thomas D'Arcy McGee, writer, speaker and Irish nationalist. McGee saw the urban environment as dangerous, and hoped to remove the Irish to a healthier region with greater opportunities. He organized the Irish Emigrant Aid Convention, which met in Buffalo in February 1856. The main opposition to McGee's plan, however, came from John Hughes, Archbishop of New York. Hughes saw emigration as impractical. He also disapproved of McGee because of his involvement with the Irish uprising of 1848. McGee's plans never fully materialized, partly because of Hughes' opposition and partly because most of the Irish preferred to stay in the East, especially after the decline of organized nativist movements by the late 1850s.

Individual Irish-Americans led colonization projects in the midwest. James Shields, soldier and senator from three states, established Shieldsville, Minnesota in 1857. In 1872 Civil War veteran General John O'Neil established O'Neil, Nebraska. The main leadership, however, came from the American bishops. Bishop John Lancaster Spalding of Peoria, in his writings, stressed the Church's duty to promote colonization, in order to remove Catholics from what he perceived as the deleterious effects of city life. Bishop John Ireland of St. Paul, Minnesota, took more practical measures.

In 1876 Ireland organized the Catholic Colonization Bureau. Within five years he bought 300,000 acres of land from the railroads (with which he had close connections) and established five settlements. In 1879 the Irish Catholic Colonization Society was incorporated in Chicago as a nationwide organization to promote western colonization. Some settlements such as DeGraff, Minnesota, developed successfully. Others, such as the attempt to settle Connemara peasants in Minnesota in 1880, were dismal failures.

One of the last colonization efforts was that of the Irish landowner John Sweetman. Sweetman established the Irish-American Colonization Company, Ltd., in 1880. He bought land from the railroads, financed immigration to America, and supplied them with all the farming necessities. The colony never stabilized, however, and a third of all the immigrants left within its first two years of existence. The colony finally dissolved in 1905, although some of Sweetman's descendants remain in Minnesota.

*See* Ireland, John

Marvin R. O'Connell, *John Ireland and the American Catholic Church* (St. Paul, 1988): Chapter 7.
Richard Shaw, *Dagger John: The Unquiet Life and Times of Archbishop John Hughes of New York* (New York, 1977): 309–311.
Thomas W. Spalding, C.F.X., "Frontier Catholicism," *Catholic Historical Review*, Vol. LXXVII/3 (July 1991): 470–484.
Carl Wittke, *The Irish in America* (Baton Rouge, 1956), Chapter 7.

PATRICK J. McNAMARA

## COLORADO

A legend, unfounded in fact, narrated that Celts visited Colorado as early as 450 A.D. In *Ancient Celtic America*, William R. McGlone and Philip M. Leonard suggested that scratches on rocks found in southeastern Colorado are ogham inscriptions, evidence of a Celtic presence perhaps a millennium before Columbus. Professional archaeologists, citing a lack of any corroborating evidence, rejected the hypothesis, leaving scholars to focus on more recent times for the arrival of the Irish.

Zebulon Pike, the first official U.S. explorer to enter the region, had a couple of Irishmen, Thomas Daugherty and Hugh Menaugh, with him when he visited Colorado in 1806. James Purcell of Scotch-Irish descent said that he discovered gold in central Colorado even before Pike arrived. Thomas Fitzpatrick, fur trader and Indian agent, hailed from County Cavan. Known among the natives as Broken Hand, he earned the thanks of Chief Little Raven who saluted him as the Arapaho's "one fair agent." Sir George Gore was less loved. The Sligo playboy baronet killed so much game that the natives, fearing for their food supply, considered killing him.

Far more threatening to the Indians were tens of thousands of gold seekers who rushed to the Rockies in 1859. Many of them were single, young men from midwestern and eastern states such as Illinois, Ohio, and New York where large numbers of Irish already lived. By 1860 the expanse of mountain, plain, and plateau that would soon be organized as Colorado Territory claimed 34,277 residents of whom 624 were Irish-born. With nearly two percent of the total population in 1860, the Irish constituted the area's second largest foreign-born group. In 1870 they moved into first place, but lost to the English in 1880. In 1910 when the Irish foreign-born population reached 8,710 and an additional 14,535 reported having two parents born in Ireland, the first and second generations combined amounted to less than three percent of the state's population.

Colorado's larger cities and its mining towns drew more than their share of Irish. Of the 35,629 people in Denver in 1880, nearly 2,000 were Irish-born. The same year, mineral-laden Lake County, dominated by Leadville, counted slightly more than two thousand, roughly eight percent of the population. By 1910 Leadville's glory had vanished, but nearly five hundred Irish still remained in Lake County. Pueblo, Colorado's number two city in 1910, tallied 491. Denver, five times larger than Pueblo, took the grand prize with nearly four thousand. Rural areas welcomed far fewer. Archuleta, Baca, Kiowa, and Kit Carson counties, for example, each had fewer than ten foreign-born Irish in 1900.

Denver and its Irish got off to a slow start. After the gold rush, the town stagnated. The Civil War, among other negatives, retarded development, but in the waning months of the conflict, Denver's Irish organized a Fenian unit which sputtered along into the late 1860s. Without the resources of either the English or the Germans, the Irish were often fated to play second fiddle to those groups. And if one separates Protestant Irish from the mass of Roman Catholics, the fractures within the community and the weakness of its economic underpinnings become even clearer.

Denver's first school master was a non-Catholic Irishman, Owen J. Goldrick. Pioneers knew he was learned because he could swear in Latin. James Archer, a developer of the city's water supply, Robert Morris, mayor from 1881 to 1883, and Thomas Patterson, U.S. representative (1877–1879), publisher of the *Rocky Mountain News,* and U.S. senator (1901–1907), were all prominent Protestant Irishmen. Fortunately for the Catholics the handful of wealthy Irish in their pews, particularly the miller John K. Mullen and the master-of-many-pursuits Dennis Sheedy, contributed generously to church building.

Organizations helped the Irish cushion the shocks of acculturation, gave them a sense of belonging, and let them flex their collective muscle. The Mitchel Guards, a private military company, paraded much during the late 1870s. Eventually more significant was the Michael Davitt Branch of the Irish Land League, the Denver chapter founded by Davitt himself in 1880. Admitting both Catholics and Protestants and drawing its membership from high station and low, the League wielded its clout to elect its president, Robert Morris, mayor in 1881. As David Brundage points out in *The Making of Western Labor Radicalism: Denver's Organized Workers, 1878–1905,* the League promoted labor solidarity by uniting Protestants and Catholics. Anxious to avoid religious squabbles, local Irish suspended parades on St. Patrick's Day in the early and mid-1880s. In 1887 the Catholic-centered Ancient Order of Hibernians, its first Denver chapter founded in 1879, restored the practice. By 1900 the city had five Hibernian units and a ladies auxiliary, the Daughters of Erin.

The temporary Catholic-Protestant rapprochement was perhaps fostered because Irish Catholics did not always bow to their

John K. Mullen

bishops. When in 1876 Bishop Joseph P. Machebeuf chided the Irish-American Progressive Association for inviting a Protestant clergyman to speak, Machebeuf was told to "stop making the altar a political platform in favor of England" and was accused of treating the Irish like children. Later, one of Machebeuf's priests, an angry Irishman named Michael Culkin, impiously greeted the bishop: "God damn you and your French priests."

Culkin did not speak for all the Irish. Many found a haven in their Roman Catholic parishes such as St. Leo's, where Irish-born William O'Ryan tended his flock for nearly half a century, and at St. Patrick's, where Joseph Carrigan celebrated Irish culture. Still tensions persisted. In 1910 Machebeuf's successor, Nicholas Matz, tried to remove Carrigan from his pastorate. Carrigan fought back, supported by the Hibernians who accused Matz of "jealousy, hatred and the spirit of revenge." John Reddin, a leading member of the fourth degree Knights of Columbus, and John K. Mullen cooled the dispute. Mullen wrote Reddin: "You know us Irish are impulsive and quick, and often stubborn and ugly. But we are also sympathetic and as quick to forgive and forget as we are to accuse or resent an alleged wrong." Matz forgave Carrigan, who fled to a mountain parish, 180 miles west of Denver.

The cooperation between Catholics and Protestants in the 1880s was made possible, in part, because the prosperous decade provided jobs for most everyone. The Irish were more likely to be laborers, policemen, or domestic servants than physicians, teachers, or lawyers. By 1900 many of them had gone beyond the world of picks and shovels to that of pencils and ledger books. Some did well in politics. Martin D. Currigan served five city council terms between 1874 and 1900 setting an example of Irish political success that continued in the early twentieth century when John McGauran became president of the board of supervisors, and Eugene Madden entrenched himself on the city council.

Yet Irish Catholic politicians had to leap hurdles of prejudice. Colorado's economy soured in the early 1890s and so did the spirit of toleration. With thousands unemployed, any job looked good. In 1894 the American Protective Association, an anti-Catholic organization, helped elect Republican Albert McIntire Colorado's governor. McIntire fed patronage spoils to the hungry bigots. His Fire and Police Board fired Catholic policemen in Denver. As one Irishman was being dismissed, he predicted that he would return to the force and that the governor would wind up picking weeds. The prophecy came true; McIntire died in poverty. But anti-Catholicism survived. In the mid-1920s the sons and daughters of Erin again faced organized anti-Catholic bigotry when the Ku Klux Klan grabbed power. Beholden to the Klan, Denver's mayor, Benjamin Stapleton, turned the police department over to a Klansman while Colorado's Klan governor, Clarence Morley, unsuccessfully tried to outlaw sacramental wine.

During the early 1880s Leadville rivaled Denver as a center of Irish strength. There, too, the Irish banded together, forming chapters of the Knights of Robert Emmet, the Wolfe Tone Guards, the Ancient Order of Hibernians, the Daughters of Erin, and the Irish Land League. After Michael Davitt visited Denver in October 1880 he braved Leadville's 10,000-foot elevation to speak to a packed hall, a worthwhile adventure because the Cloud City's Celts generously supported the League. Unlike Davitt, John Dillon, another leading Parnellite, did not have a political agenda when he came to Colorado in November 1883. Indicating that he planned to stay on his brother's ranch in Douglas County south of Denver, Dillon told a *Rocky Mountain News* reporter, "I came here solely for my health."

As in Denver, most of Leadville's Irish worked in unskilled or semiskilled occupations. Many were miners, prospectors, and laborers. In Leadville, as in Denver, they made their mark in law enforcement. Bill Convery, a University of Colorado at Denver graduate student, has found that two of Leadville's earliest marshals were Irish. George O'Connor lasted only a few weeks. He was killed by his own deputy. Another Irishman, Martin Duggan, succeeded O'Connor. Among 173 Irish women listed in the 1880 census, Convery reports that 75 listed their occupation as housekeeper, 38 as servant, and 33 as laundress. At least eight of them were Irish-born nuns, Sisters of Charity of Leavenworth, who staffed St. Vincent's hospital.

Politics and saloon keeping also attracted the Irish. In 1879 Irishmen dominated the city council. Kilkenny-born Peter W. Breene, a Republican, served as Colorado's lieutenant governor from 1885 to 1887 and as state treasurer from 1887 to 1889. In 1880 nearly a quarter of Leadville's 106 saloons were in the hands of men with Irish surnames. Helping supply those barkeepers was Henry W. Gaw, born in County Down, whose brewery near Leadville produced 155,000 gallons of beer in 1885. Denver also had plenty of Irish saloonkeepers with ten percent of its bars under Irish management in 1900. John K. Mullen, concerned about his fellow countrymen's drinking habits, tried to change their ways with the help of the St. Joseph's Catholic Total Abstinence Society.

Irish drinking mirrored Irish poverty. Many of Leadville's Irish, being poor, lived in the city's slums. Convery scrutinized the 1880 federal census to find that in the shanty-filled southeast sector the Irish made up twenty-one percent of the population. Denver data derived from surnames in the 1890 city directory shows relatively high numbers of Irish in older, cheaper neighborhoods where they mingled with natives and other foreign-born. Money made a difference. John K. Mullen and Dennis Sheedy resided in grand Capitol Hill mansions.

Mullen milled tons of wheat, amassing his millions a grain at a time. Sheedy cobbled together a fortune from banking, smelting, merchandising, and cattle raising. In Leadville, in the Cripple Creek-Victor district, and in other mining areas, an occasional lucky Irishman sometimes raced from the bottom rungs of the economic ladder to the top. Prospecting demanded neither a degree nor a pedigree.

Charles, Patrick, and John Gallagher located the Camp Bird mine near what would be Leadville on November 11, 1876, helping to trigger the silver rush. The brothers sold their claims for more than $200,000 and then, legend has it, spent the money. Robert Dillon from Tipperary, who worked with the Gallaghers, later discovered the Robert Emmet Lode. Edward Fitzgerald, born in County Waterford, made money from the Little Giant. Peter W. Breene owed part of his good fortune to the Colonel Sellers mine at Kokomo north of Leadville. Jack McCombe from King's County had four shillings and six pence to his name when he landed in New York City in 1873. His Maid of Erin mine, one of many he discovered, brought him $43,000.

In Cripple Creek, a decade and a half later, James Doyle, James Burns, and John Harnan, discoverers of the gold-filled Portland mine, outdid the Leadville Irish. Unfortunately Burns and Doyle spent a chunk of their treasure battling each other in court, a fight that put Doyle in jail for 209 days. Thomas Walsh, Clonmel born, was smarter. He retained enough of the fortune he made at the Camp Bird mine near Ouray to allow his daughter, Evalyn Walsh McLean, to shine as a Washington, D.C., socialite and owner of the Hope diamond.

Margaret Tobin Brown also laid siege to society, but her husband's Leadville lucre could not liquidate her social liabilities: second-generation Irish, Catholic, a garish wardrobe, faulty spelling. Her lot improved in 1912 when she enjoyed the strange good luck to be on the *Titanic* when it hit an iceberg. Her heroism in rescuing passengers brought her, if not full social acceptance, immortality of sorts as the subject of the play *The Unsinkable Molly Brown* which was later made into a motion picture. Denverites, liking her more dead than alive, made her overstuffed mansion into a house-museum in 1970.

Wearers of the green appeared robust in 1902 when the the Ancient Order of Hibernians held their biennial national convention in Denver. Their bile still flowed fiercely in 1914 when they declared war on green pigs and other "disgusting" novelties which demeaned Irish celebrations. In Boulder that year both Catholics and Methodists sponsored St. Patrick's Day programs. In Pueblo three hundred women and girls sold green ribbons to raise money for Sacred Heart Orphanage, and the United Irish societies sponsored a ball. Pueblo's Irish had another reason to celebrate because in 1912 their city had helped elect second-generation Irishman Edward Keating to the U.S. House of Representatives where he was to make a name for himself as sponsor of the Keating-Owen Child Labor Act (1916). And in 1919 Irish spirit still ran high as Denver's Brown Palace Hotel draped its balcony with Irish and U.S. flags to welcome Eamon de Valera, President of Ireland, who, recently escaped from an English prison, had come to the United States to raise money.

But times were changing. Denver's St. Patrick's Day parade died before World War I and the 1920 census revealed that less than one percent of the state's population was foreign-born Irish. During the 1920s the Ancient Order of Hibernians maintained their St. Patrick's Day practice of attending pontifical High Mass at the Cathedral of the Immaculate Conception, a French Gothic edifice John K. Mullen's money had helped build. That tradition ended in the early 1930s and by the decade's end the Order had disappeared from the city directory.

Hibernians hibernated. They were not dead. Many of the elderly foreign-born such as Katherine Halley, born near Dungarvan in 1847, were fading away. Yet their children and grandchildren—such as Katherine's daughter, Josephine, who delighted in reciting the "Our Father" in Gaelic and kept track of the Powers, Savage, Whalen, and Murray branches on the family tree—remained proud of their heritage. She was typical of many Irish families.

In the 1930s and 1940s John Carroll, Denver district attorney (1937–1941) and a U.S. representative (1947–1951), and William McNichols, Sr., Denver's auditor (1931–1955), kept the Irish political torch flickering. In the 1950s and 1960s Erin again awoke. Carroll took a seat in the U.S. Senate (1957–1963) and Stephen McNichols, the son of William McNichols, Sr., gained Colorado's governorship (1957–1963). Thomas G. Currigan, whose political roots stretched back nearly a century to Martin Currigan, became Denver's mayor in 1963. On his resignation in 1968 he was succeeded by William McNichols, Jr., who served until 1983. And from the 1970s into the 1990s state legislator and city councilman Dennis Gallagher demonstrated that an Irishman could succeed in North Denver. Gilding the shamrock from 1967 until his death in 1986 was Archbishop James V. Casey, who ended a century-long, Franco-German, episcopal monopoly.

Happy Irish-Americans formally revived the St. Patrick's Day parade in 1963. Chaired by James P. Eakins, it mushroomed into a major annual event, drawing tens of thousands of marchers and onlookers. And from 1980 into the late 1990s Denverites enjoyed listening to Irish debaters and speakers brought to Colorado by Gary Holbrook, a professor at Metropolitan State College of Denver.

Census Bureau statisticians estimated that in 1990 more than half a million Coloradans considered themselves to be fully or partially Irish. That many of them could not have identified de Valera, let alone Davitt or Dillon, may be true. Nevertheless, as the twentieth century neared its end, being Irish in Colorado was, at least and at last, fashionable.

David Brundage, *The Making of Western Labor Radicalism, Denver's Organized Workers, 1878–1905* (Urbana: University of Illinois Press, 1994).

Stephen J. Leonard, "The Irish, English, and Germans in Denver, 1860–1890," *The Colorado Magazine,* 54 (Spring 1977): 126–154.

Thomas J. Noel, *The City and the Saloon: Denver 1858–1916* (Lincoln: University of Nebraska Press, 1982).

STEPHEN LEONARD

## COLUM, MARY (1887–1957)

Literary critic. Mary Catherine Gunning Maguire was born on June 13, 1887, in Ireland. Raised by relatives, she attended St. Louis Convent Boarding School and, later, a German convent. After taking her B.A. at the Royal (later National) University, she became a teacher at Patrick Pearse's school, St. Ita's. Along with three teaching colleagues—Thomas McDonagh, James Stephens, and Padraic Colum—and a fourth man, David Houston, she founded The *Irish Review.* In 1912 she married Colum. In 1914, the couple moved to New York, where they would be firm fixtures in that city's literary circles for several decades.

### CRITICAL REPUTATION

Throughout her adult life, Mary Colum worked as a first-rate, forward-thinking literary critic. Her work was particularly characterized by an appreciation of modernist literature. According to Taura S. Napier, Colum's critical writings ". . . unlike the

Mary Colum

works of most of her contemporaries, were concerned with making inaccessible modernist literary styles comprehensible to the reading public." Colum's book *From These Roots* (1937) traced the early influences that led to the development of modern writing. Her work was praised by such luminaries as the playwright Eugene O'Neill and the critic Edmund Wilson. William Benet called her ". . . the best woman critic in America," (a somewhat backhanded compliment which reveals the sexism that female intellectuals of Colum's day had to deal with). In an article entitled "On Thinking Critically," she set forth her ideas on criticism:

> Criticism is a principle through which the world of ideas renews itself . At its highest . . . literary criticism is the creation of profound, informing, and transforming ideas about life as well as literature, for no man can understand literature without a comprehension of life, the subject of literature [qtd in Napier].

### EYEWITNESS TO HISTORY

Like her contemporary Oliver St. John Gogarty, Colum had a knack for knowing many of the key political and cultural figures of her age—people like Patrick Pearse, W. B. Yeats, and James Joyce. And, like Gogarty, she set down her memories of the Ireland of the early twentieth century in a memoir. Colum's book *Life and the Dream* (1947) traces her development as a young woman against the backdrop of the Irish Literary Renaissance's twilight years. Her last book, published posthumously, was *Our Friend James Joyce* (1958) which she wrote with her husband Padraic. It recounted the couple's friendship with the novelist. Mary Colum died in New York in 1957.

*See* Colum, Padraic; Joyce's *Ulysses* on Trial

Mary Colum, *Life and the Dream,* rev. ed. (Chester Springs, 1966).

Robert Hogan, et al., eds., *Dictionary of Irish Literature* (Westport, 1979).

Stanley J. Kunitz and Howard Haycraft, eds., *Twentieth-Century Authors* (New York, 1942).

Maureen Murphy, "Mary Colum," in *The Encyclopedia of American Catholic History* (Liturgical Press, 1997).

Taura S. Napier, "Mary Colum," *Modern Irish Writers: A Bio-critical Sourcebook.* Ed. Alexander G. Gonzalez (Westport, 1997).

Robert Welch, *The Oxford Companion to Irish Literature* (Oxford, 1996).

PETER G. SHEA

## COLUM, PADRAIC (1881–1972)

Poet, playwright, essayist, author of fiction, biography, and children's literature. An extremely prolific writer in a wide variety of genres, Padraic Colum was born in Ireland on December 8, 1881, to Patrick and Susan MacCormack Collumb of Collumbkille, County Longford. Padraic was the eldest child of eight; his father was a teacher in the workhouse in Longford, and the experience of that rural, relatively poor Catholic environment was to inform much of Colum's later work. In 1891, the family moved to Sandy Cove where Colum attended the Glastule National School. After examinations he went to Dublin where he was hired as a clerk in the Irish Railway Clearing House in Kildare Street.

### EARLY WRITINGS/CULTURAL NATIONALISM

In the Clearing House, between working long hours, Colum began to write his first poetry and plays. He became a member of the Gaelic League and joined the Irish Republican Army in 1901. Additionally, he began to establish relationships with the leading figures of the Irish Literary Renaissance—William Butler Yeats, George Russell (AE), Lady Gregory, Maud Gonne, and Arthur Griffith. Of these, Griffith was probably the most powerful influence on the young Colum. Under the older man's tutelage, Colum joined *Cumann na nGaedeal*, and much of his early work found publication in Griffith's fiercely nationalistic *United Irishman*.

Colum's first play, *The Children of Lir,* was published in *The Irish Weekly Independent and Nation* in 1901 under the pseudonym "Joseph P. Collumb." In the next year, four plays appeared in Griffith's paper: *The Foley's, A Play in One Act* (10 May, by "Padraig Mac Cormac Colm"); *The Kingdom of the Young* (14 June); *The Saxon Shillin'* (15 November); and *Eoghan's Wife, A Monologue for a Woman* (20 December). *The Saxon Shillin',* which won the paper's competition for a propaganda piece against enlistment in the British army, was the only one of these four plays produced. Having been rejected by William and Frank Fay's Irish National Theatre Society on artistic grounds, it was put up on patriotic ones by Maud Gonne's Daughters of Ireland (*Inghinidhe na hEireann*) on May 15, 1903.

### THEATRE BUSINESS

The Fay brothers were busy making their famous alliance with Yeats's and Lady Gregory's now-defunct experiment, the Irish Literary Theatre, soon to become the Irish National Theatre Society, Limited—the Abbey. Colum was offered membership and was favored by the older Yeats. Very quickly he began to establish a reputation as one of the company's more popular playwrights, being granted the title "our young Ibsen." Quite different from Yeats or John Millington Synge in his treatment of the Irish rural class, Colum's so-hailed "realistic" depictions of Irish life—in plays such as *Broken Soil* (1903, later rewritten as *The Fiddler's House*) and *The Land* (1905)—proved great successes among agrarian nationalists. Inevitable company bickering, however—due largely to taunts and insults from its benefactor, Annie Horniman, but also a result of that vexed issue, "Irish authenticity"—led to a number of resignations, including Colum's in 1906.

Colum joined forces with Edward Martin's Theatre of Ireland—the Abbey's most formidable rival for a time—where he

Padraic Colum

served as secretary. In 1907, the group produced *The Fiddler's House* in the Rotunda, Dublin, and that year his first book of poems was published (*Wild Earth*). In 1909 Colum met Mary (Molly) Catherine Maguire, a recent graduate of University College, Dublin, and the two were married in 1912. They were active for a time at Padraic Pearse's St. Enda's School and soon joined James Stevens, Thomas MacDonagh, and David Houston in forming *The Irish Review,* an influential monthly which ran until 1914. That year, under financial constraints, the Colums sailed to America.

### AMERICA

The trip to the United States seems to have been meant only as a visit, but the outbreak of the war, combined with the Americans' great interest in the Irish Literary Revival, forced a longer stay which became, as it happened, permanent. (It would not be until 1945, thirty-one years after their arrival in America, that the Colums would finally become United States citizens.) After a brief stay in Pittsburgh, the couple went to New York where they quickly established ties with the more eminent American writers of the time, including Robert Frost, who became a lifelong friend. In 1915, the two embarked on a lecture tour in the Midwest where they met Carl Sandberg, Sherwood Anderson, Vachel Lindsay, Edgar Lee Masters, and Harriet Monroe; later they became visitors at the MacDowell Colony in New Hampshire through the influence of Edwin Arlington Robinson. In 1915, having returned to New York, Padraic found work writing children's stories to supplement their meager income. In 1923, after a visit to Ireland, the Colums returned to the MacDowell Colony where Padraic completed his first novel, *Castle Conquer,* as well as a number of stories on Hawaii.

### FOLKLORE AND OTHER WRITING

Colum is known to many as a folklorist, specifically as an interpreter of Irish legend to a particular generation of Americans. Indeed, such work provided much of his income. After Macmillan read Colum's volume of children's stories, *The King of Ireland's Son* (1916), the company offered him a contract under which he produced in the ensuing years a number of children's books on Irish myth and saga as well as on the lore of other cultures. In 1922 Colum was hired by the Hawaiian legislature to gather a collection of Polynesian poems, stories, and legends to be studied by children in the Hawaiian schools. The contract resulted in two volumes: *At the Gateways of the Day* (1924) and *The Bright Lights* (1925), later combined into *Legends of Hawaii* (1937).

Following research in Hawaii, the Colums returned to the United States where they settled in Connecticut. Padraic's literary activity flourished in a remarkable line of books, including *The Voyagers* (1925), *The Forge in the Forest* (1925), *The Road Round Ireland* (1926), *Creatures* (1927), *The Fountain of Youth* (1927), *Balloon* (1928) and *Orpheus, Myths of the World* (1930). In 1930, the two left for Paris where they renewed their long-time friendship with James Joyce, and Colum completed two more books for Macmillan, *The Big Tree of Bunlahy* (1933) and *The White Sparrow* (1933) (He also helped Joyce type pages for what would become *Finnegan's Wake*.) Soon Mary was offered an editorship at *The Forum*, and the two moved back to New York where Padraic completed four more books: *The Legend of Saint Columba* (1935), *The Story of Lowry Maen*, a long narrative poem (1937), *Flower Pieces* (1938), and *Where the Winds Never Blew and the Cocks Never Crew* (1940).

In 1939, the couple received a joint appointment to the faculty at Columbia where they taught comparative literature until 1956. At various times they also taught at the University of Wisconsin (Madison) and at the University of Miami. In 1940, Padraic took a position as visiting professor of English at City College of New York and was in that year awarded the Poetry Society of America Medal. After the war, he set to work completing his long-planned biography on Arthur Griffith, *Ourselves Alone: The Story of Arthur Griffith and the Origin of the Irish Free State*, eventually published in 1959.

In 1957, following Molly's death, Colum began an extensive series of lectures across the United States. He edited *Poems of Jonathan Swift* (1962) and *Poems of Samuel Ferguson* (1963); his own literary output continued with three volumes of poetry—*Ten Poems* (1957), *Irish Elegies* (1958), and *The Poet's Circuits* (1960)—and a volume of lectures, *Storytelling, New and Old* (1961). In 1961, he again turned to the theatre with a series of Noh plays based on Irish historical figures: *Moytura*, on Sir William Wilde; *Glendalough*, on Parnell; *Monasterboice*, concerning Joyce; and *Cloughoughter*, about Roger Casement. The latter three form the trilogy, *The Challengers*, produced in Dublin in 1966. *Carricknabauna* was produced off-Broadway in 1967, and in 1969 he published *Images of Departure*.

Colum was active as a writer and lecturer until the end of his life. His long and distinguished career included such awards and positions as president of the Poetry Society of America (1938–39); Honorary Doctorate, National University of Ireland (1951); Fellowship Award, Academy of American Poets (1952); Lady Gregory Award, Academy of Irish Letters (1953); Honorary Doctorate, Columbia University (1958); and in 1963, membership to the American Academy of Arts and Letters. An esteemed and highly prolific writer in a variety of forms, Padraic Colum died in Enfield, Connecticut, on January 11, 1972, at the age of ninety. He was buried in Dublin.

*See* Poetry, Irish-American

Under the editorship of Sanford Sternlicht, Syracuse University Press has published three of Padraic Colum's works: *Selected Short Stories* (1985); *Selected Plays* (1986); *Selected Poems* (1989).

Zack Bowen, *Padraic Colum. A Biographical-Critical Introduction* (Southern Illinois University Press, 1970).

*The Collected Poems of Padraic Colum* (New York: Devon-Adair, 1953).

Padraic Colum, *Three Plays. The Fiddler's House, The Land, Thomas Muskerry* (Dublin: Maunsel, 1917).

Sanford Sternlicht, *Padraic Colum* (Twayne, 1985).

TODD HEARON

## COLUMBUS, CHRISTOPHER (1451–1506)

Navigator. Both oral and written traditions claim Irish connections for the Italian-born explorer in the service of Spain. A local belief in Galway, for example, holds that Columbus attended Mass there in St. Nicholas Church. According to historian David B. Quinn, Columbus certainly visited Galway prior to his first American voyage, most probably in 1477. On the Irish shore, the visitor viewed an exotic discovery: the drifting bodies of a man and woman of extraordinary appearance, who may have been Inuit (Eskimo) voyagers lost at sea.

An Irish sailor, who appears in Spanish records as Guillermo Ires, *natural de Galney*, was thought to have accompanied Columbus to America in 1492, and to have perished at the settlement left behind on the Caribbean island of Hispaniola. With his name variously translated as William Ayres, William Eris, William Harris, or simply William of Galway, the obscure seaman has appeared in many popular histories as the first documented Irishman in America.

This appealing story has not withstood rigorous scrutiny. The American scholar Alice Bache Gould, who spent decades researching the life stories of Columbus's crewmen in the Spanish archives, concluded that Guillermo Ires never sailed with Columbus. Although the Irishman's name did appear on an early—and unreliable—list of the men left on Hispaniola, Gould found that Guillermo Ires was still alive in Europe several years after his alleged death in America.

Alicia B. Gould, *Nueva Lista Documentada de los Tripulantes de Colon en 1492* (Madrid, 1984).

David B. Quinn, *Ireland and America: Their Early Associations, 1500–1640* (Liverpool, 1991).

BRIAN McGINN

Christopher
Columbus

## COMSTOCK LODE, THE (1859)

Washoe, Nevada Territory. The Comstock Lode lay in a three-mile-long ravine in the earth, 6,200 feet up on the side of Sun Mountain in the Washoe Desert out beyond the Sierras in a place called the Nevada Territory. In June 1859 Peter O'Riley and Patrick McLaughlin were digging a hole for the storage of water when they discovered the dirt in their shovels contained a yellowish sand mixed with bits of quartz and an unidentifiable black rock. As the Irish fellows dug deeper they discovered a richer conglomerate that they saved; later in Grass Valley, California, the substance was assayed as silver.

O'Riley and McLaughlin sold the Ophir mine to a group of Californians who managed to mine 38 tons of ore for a mill in San Francisco before the winter snows closed Nevada off from California. The bars were stacked in the front window of a bank and the spectacle drew large crowds of onlookers. By spring 1860, two towns were created by the influx of people up Mt. Davidson; by 1881 seven million tons of ore were dug from the lode and the yield profited $306 million worth of bullion. It was this ore that President Lincoln acknowledged as having saved the credit of the Union during the Civil War.

The Comstock's richest mine was the Consolidated Virginia; it was a combination of six previously sparse mines which was purchased by four Irishmen in 1871 for $100,000. Only four years later its worth had reached $160 million.

*See* Nevada

Dan DeQuille, *The Great Comstock Lode* (1998).
Internet: Historical Gazette.

JOY HARRELL

## CONN, WILLIAM DAVID (1917–1993)

Boxer. Often known as "Billy" or "The Pittsburgh Kid," William David Conn was a hot-tempered Irish youth from East Liberty, Pennsylvania, who became a first-rate boxer. By the age of 22 (1939), Conn had defeated Melio Bettina for the light-heavyweight championship, and defended the title three times. Three years later, Conn gave up the title to compete as a heavyweight. In his first fight with Joe Louis on June 18, 1941, Conn made a remarkable showing. Scoring point after point, Conn shuffled quickly around Louis until in the twelfth round Conn nearly knocked Louis out. In the thirteenth, however, the heavier Louis landed a knockout punch with only two seconds left in the round. A rematch was scheduled, but in a scuffle with his father-in-law, Conn broke his hand which kept him out of the ring for months until World War II brought both fighters into the Army. The rematch finally occurred after the war in June 1946. This time Louis knocked Conn out in the eighth round, but at a six-round exhibition fight in Chicago in 1948, Conn completed the match and lost only by decision.

Conn appeared in the film *The Pittsburgh Kid* in 1941 and, after his last fight with Louis in 1948, retired from boxing. Of his seventy-five fights, Conn won sixty-three; fourteen by knockouts with eleven losses and one draw. In 1965 Conn was elected to the Boxing Hall of Fame and spent his retirement in Pittsburgh, Pennsylvania, where he died on May 19, 1993.

*See* Boxing

Bob Burrill, *Who's Who in Boxing* (New Rochelle, N.Y., 1974).
Herbert G. Goldman, ed., *The Ring 1984 Record Book and Boxing Encyclopedia* (New York, 1984).
"Life of Billy Conn," *Boxing and Wrestling* 7 (August 1957).
David L. Porter, *Biographical Dictionary of American Sports: Basketball and Other Indoor Sports* (New York: Greenwood Press, 1989).
Bert R. Sugar, *The 100 Greatest Boxers of All Time* (New York, 1984).

DANIEL J. KUNTZ

## CONNECTICUT

The first Irish footprints in Connecticut, it turns out, may have been Irish paw prints. John Winthrop Jr. of Massachusetts, commissioned in 1635 to govern the settlements proposed along the Connecticut River, had studied at Trinity College in Dublin in 1632–33. After he returned to Massachusetts, a Dublin friend shipped him "three woolfe doggs and a bitch with an Irish boy to tend them." When Winthrop arrived at the Saybrook settlement at the mouth of the river in the spring of 1636, was he accompanied by his four Irish wolfhounds and their Irish attendant? History probably will never yield up the answer to that question. Nor will it divulge the identity of the first Irishman or woman who set foot in the Land of Steady Habits.

Certainly among the first were Irish soldiers who fought in the Pequot War in 1636, just a year after the towns of Wethersfield, Windsor, Hartford, and Saybrook were settled. John Dyer, a Windsor militiaman, was "a Catholic Irishman," according to Connecticut historian Albert Van Dusen. And Arthur Peach of Plymouth Colony, who reportedly did "good service against the Pequots" in Connecticut before being convicted of murdering an Indian in Rhode Island, was described as an Irishman by that colony's leader, Roger Williams.

Like Dyer and Peach, other Irish people drifted into Connecticut during colonial times. The most that can be said by way of generalization is that these Irish men and women began arriving early on, that they remained a small percentage of the population and that, in a staunchly Puritan colony, they were not always welcome.

In 1655, just twenty years after the founding of Hartford, for example, John Lyman brought an Irish servant with him when he came to settle there. Hartford authorities allowed him to remain only after he posted a £10 bond guaranteeing "his Irish boy Cornelius shall Carry Good behavior towards all the members of this Jurisdiction so long as he Continues his Servant in this Commonwealth." The next year the court settled a dispute between Matthew Allyn of Hartford and a Boston resident, Samuel Shore, over the price Allyn should pay for another Irish servant named Tobe, and fined "Edward King and Tobiah Redman, both ireshmen," ten shillings each for purchasing some stolen corn from another servant.

Also in the 1650s, an ironworks was established at New Haven by the same John Winthrop Jr. who had presided over the settlement of Saybrook. Winthrop brought to New Haven a number of laborers from the ironworks at Lynn, Mass., among them a clerk of the works named Patrick Moran and a workman named John Rylie. The ironworkers were an unruly lot, described as "unassimilable" by New Haveners.

It wasn't only Irish servants and laborers who caused raised eyebrows in early Connecticut. The Rev. James Lyon, an Anglican priest assigned to minister to people in Derby in the Naugatuck Valley, complained to his superiors in 1744 that as soon as his flock learned "from what country I came . . . they abused me, calling me 'an Irish Teague and Foreigner' with many other reflections of an uncivilized and unchristian kind . . ." Similarly, the Rev. Samuel Dorrance, a Scotch-Irish Presbyterian minister, became the center of a bitter dispute when he was called to be pastor of the Congregational Church in Voluntown in eastern Connecticut. Some church members filed a petition with the colonial legislature protesting the appointment, charging "we are informed he came out of Ireland and we do observe that since he has been in town, Irish do flock into town and we are informed that Irish are not wholesome inhabitants. . . ."

Despite Dorrance's difficulties, Scotch-Irish immigrants gradually established a substantial presence in the colony. In fact, the town of Union, in the state's northeast corner, has the distinction of being the only community in Connecticut actually settled by people from Ireland. Scotch-Irishmen James and William McNall, James Shearer and John Lawson arrived there about 1727, bringing with them, according to Union's historian, two things distinctly Irish, "the Irish potato as food for man and the foot-wheel for spinning flax." Perhaps the most celebrated of Connecticut's early Scotch-Irish settlers was Edward Pattison who came to Berlin around 1740 and went into the tinsmithing business, fashioning by hand and peddling for sale the first tin-plated kitchen utensils produced in the American colonies.

TRADE ENCOURAGED IMMIGRATION

A modest but steady transatlantic trade, in which Yankee ships carried timber and flaxseed to Ireland in return for Irish linens and other items, encouraged immigration to Connecticut seaports. The records of the Congregational Church in the port of Stonington attest to that with such entries as: "Nov. 28, 1736, John Moxleys and Mary his wife's dismission from Cork in Ireland was communicated to ye church and they were admitted to privileges with us . . ." and "April 17, 1737, Rose Alworth was admitted to ye privileges in this church belonging to members in full communion, we being certified of her profession and orderly conversation by a certificate from the pastor of a church in Bandon in Ireland."

The Moxleys and Alworths seem to have been of the Anglo-Irish Ascendancy and probably paid their own way to America. Irish peasants and commoners—Gaelic and Scotch-Irish alike—frequently secured passage across the Atlantic by agreeing to become indentured servants. The Connecticut Gazette reported in 1764: "Just imported from Dublin in the Brig Darby, a parcel of Irish Servants, both Men and Women, and to be sold cheap, by Israel Boardman, at Stamford."

A year later, Matthew Lyon, a native of County Wicklow, came to America and Connecticut as a "redemptioner." When Lyon's ship docked in New York, Jabez Bacon, a rich merchant of Woodbury, Conn., redeemed the Irishman's fare; in return, Lyon agreed to give Bacon three years of service. Lyon eventually gained his freedom, fought for American independence in the Revolutionary War, migrated to Vermont and was elected to Congress. He was one of the principals in the first rowdiness on the floor of the House of Representatives when he spat upon a fellow legislator who responded by striking him with a cane.

In at least one case, romance blossomed at sea for an Irish redemptioner. Mary Jordan caught the eye of the ship's captain, New Londoner James Rogers, during the voyage and they were married at New London on Nov. 5, 1675. Rogers, it was said, was fond of calling Mary the richest cargo he ever shipped and the best bargain he ever made.

Not all redemptioner stories had such happy endings, however, for early Connecticut papers contain numerous advertisements placed by masters seeking runaway Irish servants:

Robert Chambers, "an Irish man servant," sought by Nathaniel West of Tolland; Michael Shields sought by Abel Morse of New Haven; William Mosley, sought by Ichabod Fitch of Lebanon; stonecutters Andrew McDonagh and Thomas Craige sought by New Milford quarry owner Angus Nickelson.

In the Revolutionary War, the Irish, like their fellow colonists, were found on both sides of the argument, even within families. Nathaniel Fanning of Stonington, a descendant of Irishman Edmund Fanning who settled there in the 1650s, left a diary of his service in the American Navy under the legendary John Paul Jones. Another Edmund Fanning of Stonington had Tory inclinations, became a general in the British army and is credited with saving his alma mater, Yale College, from the torch when the British invaded New Haven in 1779.

A Scotch-Irishman, John McCurdy, helped establish the Sons of Liberty in Lyme and during the war hosted both George Washington and Lafayette at his tavern in that town. John Flynn, a blacksmith in Woodstock, and the grandson of an Irishman who immigrated to Massachusetts in the early 1700s, was a trumpeter with a Connecticut cavalry unit. Timothy Hierlihy of Middletown, an Irish immigrant who achieved the rank of major in the Connecticut militia during the French and Indian War, threw his lot in with the British, served with the Prince of Wales Regiment and when the war ended emigrated to Nova Scotia. Another Irishman, John Conderick, went the other way. Conderick deserted from the British ranks, served with distinction in the Continental Army during the assault on Stony Point, N.Y., and lived out his days as an honored patriot in Connecticut.

When the nation took its first census in 1790, 5,974 persons, 2.9 percent of Connecticut's 232,236 population, were of Irish stock, according to the Census Bureau. That total includes 3,708 with roots in Ulster, presumably mostly Scotch-Irish, and 2,266 from the other provinces of Ireland.

SOD-HAULERS ARRIVE

In the 1820s, when entrepreneurs proposed a canal from New Haven north into Massachusetts, they sent agents to Ireland to recruit workers. A New Havener recalled: "Vessel loads of lusty, sod-haulers were landed at New Haven . . . dressed neatly in their fair-day clothes, closely shaved, with blue-tailcoat, corduroy knee britches, woolen stockings, heavy brogans and stiff top hat, with short clay pipes roosting in the band . . ." The journal of a priest who visited these workmen contains the only record of their identities. In September 1828, on the canal near Hartford, Father Robert D. Woodley recorded that he baptized Mary, the daughter of James and Mary Sliney; Ann, the daughter of Austin and Ellen Doyle; Thomas, son of Owen and Mary Sullivan; Margaret, daughter of Thomas and Mary Haley; Mary, daughter of William and Bridget Doran; and Eleanor, daughter of Pat and Ellen Walsh.

As Connecticut moved from an agricultural to an industrial economy in the nineteenth century, thousands of other "sod-haulers" followed in the footsteps of the canal diggers. A correspondent for the *Boston Pilot* passing through the state in the 1840s wrote, "When manufactures began to penetrate (Connecticut's) . . . valleys and to creep up (its) mountain streams . . . Irishmen were called in to dig the deep foundations of huge factories, to blast the rocks, to build the dams, and when the great structures arose, the children of Irishmen were called to tend the spindles or the furnace."

In those years, enclaves of Irish people took seed in towns across Connecticut. In 1828, Michael Cooney, a hat dyer, brought his family to Norwalk. Soon they were joined by families named Donahoe, Burns, Gilhooly and Brennan. In the late 1830s, a hamlet of miners with names like Mike Martin, Patrick Duffy and Peter Casey grew up around a copper mine in Bristol. In the early 1840s, a traveler discovered in Chatham on the eastern side of the Connecticut River across from Middletown "a number of Irish Catholics constantly employed in quarrying stone who with their families and others residing in Middletown may amount to 150 or 200 souls."

Close on the heels of such settlers came Irish priests to minister to them and organizations to care for their social needs. In August 1829, Father Bernard O'Cavanagh, an Irish native, became the first resident priest in Connecticut when he was appointed pastor of Holy Trinity parish in Hartford. Four years later, another Irish native, Father James McDermot, became pastor of the state's second Catholic parish, Christ Church at New Haven. In January 1841, emigrants in New Haven founded that city's first Irish organization, the Hibernian Provident Society and in the same year, the state's first Catholic total abstinence society was organized by Irishmen in Hartford.

THE WATERSHED OF THE FAMINE

The Potato Famine of the late 1840s was a watershed for Connecticut as well as Ireland. In the early 1840s, there were between five and ten thousand Irish people of all persuasions in Connecticut. The 1850 U.S. census, the first in which the place of birth of every resident was recorded, revealed a tremendous increase with 26,689 Irish natives then living in the state. The floodtide triggered by the Famine continued through 1860 when there were 55,445 Irish natives in Connecticut and on up to 1890 when the census showed an all-time high of 77,880 Irish natives in the state. Throughout the second half of the nineteenth century, Connecticut continually ranked sixth or seventh among all the states—behind such far more populous states as New York, Massachusetts and Pennsylvania—in the number of Irish-born residents. It did so first because it was tucked conveniently between the two major eastern seaboard ports of New York and Boston, and, secondly, because it offered plenty of what the Irish needed most: jobs.

The Famine immigrants multiplied the number of Irish in cities like Waterbury and Hartford to more than twenty percent of the total population. But large numbers of Irish also settled in farming communities. The pastor of the Congregational Church in rural Newtown said of the 119 Irish families there: "Eighty-one . . . own real estate and it is a common remark that they stand ready to buy up all the land thrown on the market in the town . . . They buy poor land and by hard work improve it; and they buy good land and keep it good."

While generous in raising money for Ireland's suffering peasants, Connecticut residents grew increasingly disenchanted with the tidal wave of impoverished Irish families inundating the state. Conservative newspapers like the *Hartford Courant* railed against "this horde of Irish . . . besieging the workshops for work at less than living prices" and warned "Irish Catholics will soon be found in all our minor offices and like the Irish police in New York allow their countrymen the fullest liberty . . ." In 1855, the state elected a Know-Nothing governor who disbanded six militia companies composed mainly of Irishmen and lobbied for a law that would require a twenty-one-year waiting period for foreigners to be become citizens.

The Nativist paranoia faded before the overriding issue of slavery and the Civil War. In that conflict, Irish immigrants served in every Connecticut Army and Navy unit and even formed their own Irish regiment, the 9th Connecticut, which fought at the capture of New Orleans, in campaigns on the Mississippi River and in the 1864 campaign in the Shenandoah Valley of Virginia.

FENIAN DREAMS

When the war ended, the Irish in Connecticut, as in other states, were smitten with the Fenian dream of rescuing Ireland from English rule by attacking British-held Canada. In June 1866, hundreds of Connecticut Fenians, carrying knapsacks, bayonet pouches and canteens boarded trains for northern New England and participated in abortive attacks across the border. Some immigrants—Thomas J. Hynes of Hartford, John G. Healy and Lawrence O'Brien of New Haven, all Civil War veterans—returned to Ireland and were arrested as part of the Fenian conspiracy. In 1875, James Reynolds of New Haven was one of the driving forces and the treasurer for the successful effort to dispatch a whaling ship, the *Catalpa,* to rescue six Fenians imprisoned in western Australia.

Irish life in Connecticut in the nineteenth century wasn't all anti-British conspiracy; many first- and second-generation Irish were busy making their mark in their new homeland. In the 1840s, a Scotch-Irishman, Robert Bonner, developed a reputation as the fastest typesetter in the history of the Hartford Courant before moving on to become publisher of the *Merchant's Ledger* in New York City. Another Scotch-Irish immigrant, William W. Gillespie, a native of County Tyrone, became owner and managing editor of the *Stamford Advocate* in 1867. He was joined by his brothers, Edward T. and Richard H. Gillespie, and together they ran that newspaper for decades. In 1882, Father Michael McGivney, the son of Irish immigrants who settled in Waterbury, was the leading force in founding what today is an international fraternal insurance organization, the Knights of Columbus. In 1871, another New Haven Irishman, James Grogan, was elected president of Connecticut's first statewide labor organization, the Connecticut Labor Union. Grogan led a long line of Irish union leaders stretching well into the twentieth century and including two presidents of the Connecticut State Labor Council, Patrick O'Meara and John J. Driscoll.

Two nineteenth-century Connecticut Irish athletes, James O'Rourke of Bridgeport and Roger Connor of Waterbury, are honored in the Baseball Hall of Fame at Cooperstown, N.Y. Dennis Ryan of Waterbury and the Byrne family of Norwich earned national and international fame as acrobats. A Hartford Irishman, P. H. Reilly, was the state's foremost dance teacher. A Windsor Irishman, Edward J. Gavegan, worked his way through Yale playing the trumpet at dance halls before embarking on a legal career in New York City culminating in his appointment to the New York State Supreme Court.

ASSIMILATION AND INFLUENCE

Connecticut's Irish had come a long way by the turn of the twentieth century. Speaking at a St. Patrick's Day banquet in Bridgeport early in the century, Connecticut Gov. George Lilley told the Irishmen that he wasn't there just out of courtesy: "I claim a seat at your board by right of lineage for my great-grandmother was a McNamara; and while I am from the soil of New England and yield to none in my appreciation of the Yankee virtues, neither do I hesitate to say that it is with pride that I claim a strain of Irish blood in my veins."

The successful assimilation and the growing influence of the Irish were obvious in other ways too. In the late 1890s, voters in

Stamford and New Haven elected their first Irish mayors, William H. Bohannan and Cornelius Driscoll. Hartford followed suit in 1904 when Ignatius A. Sullivan became the first Irish mayor of the state capital. From the turn of the century to the 1920s, Jeremiah Donovan of Norwalk, James Glynn of Winsted, William Kennedy of Naugatuck, Bryan Mahon of New London, Thomas Reilly of Meriden and Patrick O'Sullivan of Derby all served in the U.S. House of Representatives.

An Irishwoman, Julia Corcoran of Norwich, was appointed the state's first female factory inspector in 1907. Another Irishwoman, Susan O'Neill of Waterbury, gained fame as one of the first women attorneys in the state. In a case which gained widespread attention, she represented an Irish musician, Myra Louise Gallagher, who claimed that her harp had been damaged by a shipping company. In 1909, in the midst of an outcry over the increasing number of injuries to high school football players, the Gaelic Athletic Association of Connecticut even lobbied to replace American football with Gaelic football in Connecticut schools.

In 1916, a young Irish-American who had spent much of his childhood in New London, entered on a career that would earn him acclaim as the nation's greatest playwright. Son of an actor born in Kilkenny, Pulitzer and Nobel Prize winner Eugene O'Neill filled his plays—from *Mourning Becomes Electra* to *A Moon for the Misbegotten* to *Long Day's Journey into Night*—with Irish characters, plots and themes.

FOCUS ON IRELAND

The World War I era refocused the attention of Connecticut's Irish on the land of their birth, or, increasingly, the land of their parents' and grandparents' birth. In the aftermath of the Easter Rebellion in 1916, three thousand Connecticut Irish met in New Haven to organize a state branch of the Friends of Irish Freedom. And in 1922, at another meeting in New Haven on St. Patrick's Day weekend, delegates from throughout the state unanimously opposed the proposed treaty with England, favoring complete independence for Ireland rather than free state status.

Not everyone agreed with such sentiments. The Orange Order remained strong in the Hartford area, several hundred members celebrating the anniversary of the Battle of the Boyne each July 12 with services in the First Presbyterian Church in that city. Nearby Manchester was headquarters for the one-hundred-member Washington Loyal Orange Lodge No. 117 which in 1908 hosted more than 450 delegates and guests at the national convention of the Order. Occasionally, conflict arose between the Orangemen and the Catholic or nationalist Irish. In 1914, for example, when Manchester decided to sponsor a gala Homeland Day to honor all the nationalities in town, the committee included one representative from each ethnic group except the Irish who, because of their differences, had two. As planning went forward, the Orangemen announced they would not march in the Homeland Day parade, causing the *Hartford Courant* to quip that they "didn't dare march in front of the green flags and wouldn't march behind them."

DWINDLING OF IMMIGRATION, FLOWERING OF IRISH LIFE

Irish immigration declined steadily throughout the twentieth century. From 70,994 in 1900, the number of Irish natives living in the state fell to 58,457 in 1910, 45,464 in 1920, 38,418 in 1930, 27,554 in 1940, 20,566 in 1950, 14,540 in 1960, 9,456 in 1970, 7,855 in 1980 and 5,765 in 1990. But as the number of immigrants declined, the number of Connecticut people who claimed Irish roots grew by leaps and bounds. In the 1990 census, 613,924 Connecticut residents said they were of Irish ancestry, and another 45,742 said they were of Scotch-Irish ancestry, a combined total of twenty percent of the state's 3.3 million people. The largest number of people claiming Irish ancestry was in Waterbury, 19,329 out of a population of 108,061, followed by Stamford with 15,383 of its 108,056 residents and Danbury with 14,504 of its 65,585 claiming Irish ancestry. Stamford also had the most residents—1,255—claiming Scotch-Irish ancestry, followed by Greenwich, 1,252 of a 58,441 population and Groton, 1,064 of 45,144.

Driven by the expansion of old and new Irish in the state, the latter years of the twentieth century witnessed a flourishing of all things Irish. The influence of the Irish in politics was at its peak. Hartford-born John Bailey was Democratic national chairman in the administration of President John F. Kennedy. Hartford area voters perennially returned Bailey's daughter, Barbara Kennelly, to Congress as U.S. representative from the 1st District. A succession of politicians with Irish roots—Robert A. Hurley, James C. Shannon, John Dempsey, Thomas J. Meskill, William A. O'Neill and John G. Rowland—served as governors. An immigrant whose family came from Cahir, Co. Tipperary, to settle in Putnam in the 1920s, Dempsey was the only naturalized citizen elected governor in the history of the state. In local politics, eight-term Irish Mayor Richard C. Lee won national recognition and election as president of the National Conference of Mayors for his urban renewal programs in New Haven.

Two Connecticut Irish politicians played key roles in the peace initiative in Northern Ireland in the 1990s. Former Congressman Bruce Morrison of Hamden, the son of an Irish-English father and an Austrian-American mother and the adopted son of a Scotch-Irish father and a German mother, was the chairman of Irish-Americans for Clinton in the 1992 presidential campaign. Already popular with the Irish-American community because of his "Morrison visas" which helped the immigrant Irish, Morrison was one of the Connolly House Group whose shuttle diplomacy between Washington and Ireland finally paid off in an Irish Republican Army cease-fire in August 1994. U.S. Sen. Christopher Dodd, the son of another senator, Thomas Dodd, with roots in Norwich stretching back to County Clare, was among the early supporters of an active American role in Northern Ireland and of a visa for Sinn Fein leader Gerry Adams.

Connecticut Irish people shone in other fields too. From his firm's headquarters in Hamden, Dublin-born architect Kevin Roche won international acclaim for buildings he designed in such far-flung places as Singapore, Madrid and Paris. Yale University history professor Paul Kennedy earned recognition as one of the era's most astute social scientists with such works as "The Rise and Fall of the Great Powers: Economic Change and Military Conflict, 1500 to 2000," and "Preparing for the 21st Century." Enfield native Michael Burke served behind enemy lines in the OSS in World War II, then went on to fame as a CBS executive and president of the New York Yankees before retiring to a farm in Aughrim, County Galway. An immigrant, John Whelan, a perennial winner of all-Ireland button accordion competitions, settled in Milford and entertained Irish-Americans from coast to coast with his music. Two Connecticut-born writers—Bridgeport native Maureen Howard and West Hartford native John Gregory Dunne—captivated readers with novels resonating with Irish characters.

Among a growing number of firms selecting Stamford for their corporate headquarters in the '90s were two Irish corporations: the Guinness Import Company and Telecom Ireland. Stamford also witnessed a renaissance of Irish attractions from a new AOH hall to the Fifth Province import store, and such pubs as Kennedy's, Tigin, Burns Bar and Cafe, Hickey's Bar and Grill and Fiddler's Green.

St. Patrick's Day paraders marched in New Haven, Stamford, Greenwich, Hartford, Milford, Meriden and other communities. A wide variety of organizations and events catered to all the interests of the various layers of Connecticut Irish: the Irish-American Home Society in Glastonbury, serving the Hartford area; the Irish-American Community Center in East Haven, the West Haven Irish-American Club and the Knights of St. Patrick, serving the New Haven area; the Gaelic-American Club in Fairfield; the Willimantic Irish Club; Ancient Order of Hibernian chapters in Danbury, Meriden, New Britain, Stamford and Waterbury; the Wild Geese in Greenwich; the Friendly Sons of St. Patrick in Norwich; Irish drama groups in New Haven and Fairfield; the Curry-Seery Branch of the Irish cultural organization Comhaltas Ceoltoiri Eireann; the Irish History Roundtable in New Haven; the Connecticut Irish-American Historical Society; and summer festivals in Danbury, Fairfield, Glastonbury, New Haven and New London.

Thomas S. Duggan, *The Catholic Church in Connecticut* (New York, 1930).

Neil Hogan, *The Wearin' O' the Green, St. Patrick's Day in New Haven, Connecticut, 1842–1992* (Hamden, 1992).

James H. O'Donnell, *History of the Diocese of Hartford* (Boston, 1900).

Frank Andrews Stone, *The Irish: In Their Homeland, in America, in Connecticut* (Storrs, 1975).

*The Shanachie,* newsletter of the Connecticut Irish-American Historical Society.

NEIL HOGAN

## CONNEMARA COLONIZATION SCHEME TO MINNESOTA

The subsistence crisis of 1879–81, brought about by the failure of the potato crop and the decline in remittances from seasonal work in Scotland and England, was one of the severest incidents of its kind in post-Famine Ireland and, especially, in the West of Ireland. In January 1880 the Catholic Administrator of Carna, Fr. Patrick Greally, wrote to the newspapers that half of the eight hundred families in his parish did not have enough to eat and that their holdings were too small and the land too sterile for them to survive. This letter alerted the Liverpool Irish Relief Committee to the crisis in Connacht and Fr. James Nugent was sent to report on the destitution in the region. While Nugent recommended relief as an immediate measure, he suggested that assisted emigration was the only long-term solution which could ameliorate the plight of the people.

In May 1880 Nugent secured the support of Bishop John Ireland of St. Paul, Minnesota for the settlement of fifty families under his Irish Catholic Colonization Association. Bishop Ireland had been bringing the Irish who had settled in the eastern cities to farms in Minnesota since 1875 and offering land to the settlers at low rents, payable over six years. Money for the transportation of the emigrants was secured from private subscriptions, the Liverpool Relief Committee, the Duchess of Marlborough Relief Committee and the *New York Herald* Relief Committee. Despite the opposition of Irish nationalists, the emigration proposal gained acceptance because it had the approval and the participation of the Catholic clergy in the West of Ireland and in Minnesota. Many Irish priests saw emigration as the only solution to the endemic poverty and distress and, while they opposed the exodus of the young and strong, they felt it could benefit the community if whole families left.

The 309 emigrants were chosen by the local clergy in Carna and Carraroe in Co. Galway and in Aughagower in Co. Mayo. They departed from Galway City on 11 June and arrived in East Boston ten days later, where they were met by Dillon O'Brien, the Secretary of the Catholic Colonization Society of Minnesota. O'Brien was the first to question the suitability of the emigrants since they appeared to be entirely unfit to cope with life on the American prairie. Most were settled at Graceville, Big Stone County, in northwest Minnesota, with the rest deciding to stay in St. Paul. Each of the twenty-four Connemara families who went to Minnesota were given 160 acres of land (five acres which had been cleared), a house, a yoke of oxen and two horses. They were assigned a host family in Graceville who would help them adjust to their new life. These emigrants were located in an area where the dominant agricultural emphasis was wheat growing, a practice of which they had no knowledge or experience. A further problem was loneliness since they had come from areas with large concentrations of population but were now on the frontier where population densities of 50 per square mile was the norm. Many were Gaelic speakers who found it difficult to communicate with their neighbours who were mainly German.

In late 1880 there were reports that the emigrants in Graceville were destitute and that they were maintaining that Bishop Ireland had neglected them. The winter of 1880–81 was very severe, a situation for which the new settlers were totally unprepared, having not insulated their homes against the long, harsh winter. At the same time settlers from Connemara were regarded by their neighbours as lazy, quick-tempered and with little inclination to look after themselves. Instead of securing work at harvest time they spent their time loitering around Graceville, arguing that there was no obligation on them to work. Perhaps Bishop Ireland had not emphasized sufficiently what he expected from the emigrants. He was annoyed that they had published their grievances in the national press, strengthening the hand of those who were opposed to the bishop and his colonization scheme. These particular emigrants added to the tensions and rifts by begging.

By the spring of 1881 Bishop Ireland realised that there was little permanent benefit to be gained by keeping the settlers in Graceville and arranged to have them transferred to St. Paul at his own expense. They were provided with jobs (mainly within the railway company). Most settled at Drayton's Bluff, which was also known as the Connemara Patch, in St. Paul. Only seven remained in Graceville on the farms that Bishop John Ireland had provided for them.

*See* Emigration: 1801–1921

Gerard Moran, "'In Search of the Promised Land': The Connemara Colonization Scheme to Minnesota, 1880," *Éire-Ireland,* vol. xxxi: nos. 3 & 4 (Fall/Winter 1996): 130–49.

———, "Near Famine: The Crisis in the West of Ireland, 1879-82," *Irish Studies Review,* no. 18 (Spring 1997): 14–21.

Marvin M. O'Connell, *Bishop Ireland and the American Catholic Church* (Minnesota, 1988).

James P. Shannon, "Archbishop Ireland's Connemara Experiment," *Minnesota History,* vol. xxxv, no. 5 (March 1957): 205–13.

GERARD MORAN

## CONNOLLY, JAMES BRENDAN (1868–1957)

Author, journalist, athlete. A Boston native, one of 12 children of Aran-born John and Ann (O'Donnell) Connolly, he was the first victor in Olympic competition in 1,500 years, winning Gold, Silver, and Bronze medals for track (triple, high, and long jumps) in the revived Modern Olympics at Athens in 1896. He published 25 books, an autobiography, countless articles, sea chanties, and more than 200 short stories, amassing a score of volumes on Gloucester and its intrepid fishermen. For the authenticity and power of his tales, he was likened to Homer, Kipling, Conrad, Cervantes, Bunyan, and Melville. Theodore Roosevelt was an admirer, as were Booth Tarkington and Kenneth Roberts. T. S. Eliot, who spent part of his youth in Gloucester, later (1952) declared Connolly's stories "the best tales . . . the only good tales" of the men Connolly described as "the greatest sailormen who ever lived." Connolly spent 1892–95 in Savannah with the U.S. Corps of Engineers, simultaneously writing sports for the *Morning News.* In 1895, he enrolled at Harvard but quit when denied leave to compete in the new Olympiad. The triple Medalist took part in the 1900 and 1906 Games, meanwhile serving with his State's 9th ("Fighting Irish") Infantry Regiment during the 1898 Siege of Santiago.

Connolly wed Elizabeth F. Hurley in 1904 (they had one daughter, Brenda), served in the Navy in 1907–08, ran for Congress in 1912, and covered Pershing's 1914 Mexico expedition for *Collier's.* During World War I, he sailed with U.S. destroyers based in Ireland as a stringer for three Boston dailies. In 1921, he was a U.S. Commissioner for the Relief of Ireland, filing 45 reports on "Tortured Ireland" during the Black-and-Tan War.

For his contributions to literature, he was awarded honorary doctorates by Fordham ('48) and Boston College ('52) plus honorary membership in the Gloucester Master Mariners. In 1948, he accepted Gold Medals from the American Irish Historical Society and Eire Society of Boston. In 1949, Colby College mounted a Connolly retrospective which published a brief biography containing an annotated list of his writings, many fea-

James Brendan
Connolly memorial

turing Irish themes, locales, speech patterns, and characters (some echoing family members) as well as illustrations by N. C. Wyeth and Howard Pyle. Connolly collections are kept at Colby, Boston College, Stanford, Harvard, Princeton, and Villanova. In 1987, Boston dedicated a Thomas Haxo sculpture of Connolly that depicts him landing at the 49-foot mark in his historic jump of 1896. Connolly died in Boston on January 20, 1957.

Gary Kissal, "New Life for an Old Salt? The Renaissance of James Brendan Connolly," *Eire Society of Boston Bulletin* (November 1991).

Stanley J. Kunitz, *Twentieth-Century Authors* (New York, 1942).

Colin Lacey and Kevin O'Neill Shanley, compilers, "Days of Glory: One Hundred Years of Irish Olympians," *Irish America Magazine* (July/August 1996): 39–40.

Bill Mallon and others, *Quest for Gold: The Encyclopedia of American Olympians* (New York, 1984): 287.

Ernest Cummings Marriner, *Jim Connolly and the Fishermen of Gloucester: An Appreciation of James Brendan Connolly at Eighty* (Waterville, 1949).

H. Ward McGraw, ed., *Prose and Poetry of America* (Chicago, 1934): 131, 159–73.

Kevin Shanley, O.Carm., "Tinker's Dam: First American Gold Olympic Medal," *Eire Society of Boston Bulletin* (December 1980).

GEORGE E. RYAN

## CONNOLLY, JOHN (1747/48 or 1751–1825)

Dominican friar, bishop. John Connolly, first resident Bishop of New York, was born in the parish of Monknewtown in the southeastern part of Upper Slane, County Meath, Ireland, at a time when church registers were kept at peril of life due to English rule in Ireland. The plate on his coffin gives his age in 1825 as seventy-seven years, but Dominican historian Victor O'Daniel determined in the 1930s from Belgian Cardinal Van Roey that he was ordained September 24, 1774 with a dispensation of thirteen months at the age of twenty-two years and eleven months. His parents, believed to be tenant farmers, sent John and his brother to study for the priesthood in Belgium. Family history reports that his brother returned to the family farm to marry and raise thirteen children; this brother was evicted for voting contrary to the landlord, and therefore sent twelve of his children to be raised by his bishop brother in New York. There is no official record confirming these matters.

John studied at the Dominican Holy Cross College, Louvain, and was ordained in Malines (Mechelin) in 1774. He was called in 1777 to Rome, to follow in the footsteps of his former teacher, Luke Concanen, as professor and Master of Students at the Irish Dominican twin convent churches of San Sisto and San Clemente. He would spend the next thirty-seven years there in administrative, diplomatic and teaching activities. Fluent in several languages, Connolly served as agent for the Irish bishops to the Vatican. In 1798 Napoleon's troops occupied Rome, holding Pope Pius VI prisoner, seizing and destroying religious properties and ordering away four thousand ecclesiastics. Connolly moved from San Sisto to nearby historic San Clemente, defying the troops and saving it from destruction. The French withdrew from Rome in October 1799 leaving the city in chaos, as Connolly became bursar, and later prior for a time, of the financially strapped San Clemente. As conditions in Europe stabilized somewhat, the Vatican could proceed with appointments for the New World: Luke Concanen was consecrated first Bishop of New York in 1808. Very ill, Concanen died in Naples while waiting passage to America. Delays from trans-Atlantic shipping embargoes and the War of 1812 (1812–1815) followed, but Pope Pius VII, who had also been imprisoned by Napoleon, was able finally to accept Connolly as Bishop of New York. He was consecrated November 6, 1814, in Rome.

On the way to America, Bishop Connolly performed episcopal services in Belgium, bereft of these for about fourteen years; he also stopped in Ireland to recruit, particularly in Kilkenny, for the New World. Thought lost at sea on a long crossing, Connolly arrived in New York on November 24, 1815, a week before Bishop John Carroll's death, to a diocese comprising all of New York State and northern New Jersey. The 15,000 Catholics in it were largely Irish and very poor, and served by only four priests. St. Peter's Church, the small St. Patrick's Cathedral (opened the previous May), both in New York City, and St. Mary's in Albany, were the only Catholic churches. Faced with heavy financial debt and few personnel, Connolly ordained several priests during his tenure, and saw churches established in Brooklyn, Paterson, Utica, Auburn, Carthage, Rochester, and elsewhere along the route of the Erie Canal, built from 1817 to 1825, largely by Irish labor. He opened a free school and an orphan asylum in 1817, bringing Sisters of Charity from Emmitsburg, Maryland, to assist. He left his diocese only once to be co-consecrator of Archbishop Ambrose Maréchal in Baltimore, who succeeded Carroll. Tensions rising from the lay trustee system, as well as ethnic strife between Irish and French, produced factions in several American cities: New York saw its bitterest effects from 1818 to 1820, but this subsided after Connolly and the Vatican took action to protect episcopal authority. Bishop Connolly was much loved by the people whom he served directly day and night, even during epidemics, as more pastor than prelate. In ill health for several years, John Connolly died February 6, 1825, and his funeral was attended by a reported thirty thousand persons; his remains, moved some time later to an unmarked vault, were not rediscovered until February 1976, and were reinterred in the crypt of Old St. Patrick's Cathedral.

Leonard E. Boyle, *San Clemente Miscellany I: The Community of SS. Sisto e Clemente in Rome* (Rome, 1977).
Florence D. Cohalan, *A Popular History of the Archdiocese of New York* (Yonkers, N.Y., 1983). [New edition in preparation].

ANNA M. DONNELLY

## CONNOLLY, MAUREEN CATHERINE (1934–1969)

Amateur tennis champion, first woman to win the Grand Slam in tennis. Connolly was born in San Diego, California, and her parents divorced while she was very young. Her tennis career began when the family moved to a home close to the University Heights playground and tennis court in San Diego. With her budding interest, her mother sent her to tennis pro Wilbur Folsom for lessons, and at the age of ten, Connolly entered her first tournament. Though initially left-handed, she trained her right hand and in 1947 entered the Southern California Invitational Tennis Championship and won.

Connolly began her serious tournament career in 1949 and won more than fifty championships before her fifteenth birthday. She was described as being an all-around player with a strong forehand and an acute focus. Eventually, as her popularity grew, she was nicknamed "Little Mo" by the sports writers of her day. Connolly's triumph came in becoming the first young lady

ever to become the national junior champion and to be simultaneously ranked among the adult women's top ten. Similarly, she was the first woman to win the Grand Slam in tennis: the British (Wimbledon), U.S., Australian and the French Opens in one year, 1953.

However, in July 1954, Maureen Connolly met with severe misfortune. Her career was ended by a horse-back riding accident that severely damaged her right leg. After announcing her retirement from competition, she resigned herself to her work as a tennis instructor until her death on June 21, 1969.

Anna Rothe, ed., *Current Biography Yearbook* (1951).
*Washington Post*, p. 16 S6 (D.C., 1951).
*Time Magazine*, 58:53 S 17 (1951).

JOY HARRELL

## CONNOR, JAMES EDWARD (1820–1891)

Union Army general, entrepreneur. A Kerryman, Connor immigrated to the United States when he was about 18 years of age and he quickly found himself in the uniform of his adopted country, fighting the Seminole Indian uprising in Florida. He also served in the Mexican War, being wounded at the decisive battle of Buena Vista, where U.S. forces were commanded by future Confederate President Jefferson Davis.

Following the gold strikes in California after the war, Connor headed west and founded the town of Stockton. When the Civil War began, he was once again in uniform, this time as a colonel in command of the 3rd California Volunteers. Both the Indians and the Mormons were showing signs of restiveness in the critical Utah Territory, so Connor and his men were dispatched there to secure the lines of communication between both coasts. They arrived on Sept. 4, 1861, establishing themselves at Camp Douglas, overlooking Salt Lake City.

Connor and his men participated in several small actions during their sojourn in Utah, but mostly they planned their postwar business careers. Connor was mustered out as a major general in 1866 and swiftly went into business in Utah. Although never terribly popular with the Mormon locals (he detested their religion), he nevertheless established the territory's first newspaper, opened its first silver mine, wrote its mining laws (he is called "the father of Utah mining") and operated the first steamship to navigate the Great Salt Lake.

*See* Civil War

John A. Barnes, *Irish-American Landmarks* (Detroit, 1995).

JOHN A. BARNES

## CONNOR, JEROME (1876–1943)

Sculptor. Patrick Jeremiah Connor was born in Annascaul, Co. Kerry. His father, a stonemason, took his family to Holyoke, Massachusetts, around 1890. Jerome ran away from home, obtaining work variously as a sign painter, boxer, machinist and stonecutter. Ultimately, settling on a career as a sculptor, he trained in Springfield, Massachusetts, with a local monument company. As early as 1893 he was noted as the sculptor of the life of the working man, and his sympathetic sculptures were exhibited in the Philadelphia Academy of Fine Arts.

Between 1898 and 1903 he worked with the Roycroft Institute of craftsmen at East Aurora near Buffalo, New York, where he married Anne Donohue in 1903. The Roycroft Institute (where he adopted the name Saint-Gerome) was run by Elbert Hubbard (of whom Connor later executed a statue) and pursued the arts and crafts ideals of William Morris. They lived initially in Syracuse where Jerome established a studio, working as a stonecarver and bronzecaster. This powerful, disciplined, figurative sculptor executed at least 200 works, ranging from small portrait heads to large civic commissions in bronze over a forty-five year career.

Although he was, in effect, the official sculptor of turn-of-the-century Catholic Irish-America, his work is essentially secular in conception. Among his most celebrated works in the U.S. are the Bronx *Victory Memorial* (1925); the *Archbishop John Carroll* monument on the campus at Georgetown University, Washington, D.C. (1912); the *Robert Emmet* statue—one of several Emmet pieces modeled from the Irish actor Brandon Taylor—at the Smithsonian Institute, also in Washington, D.C. (1917); as well as a number of Civil War memorials, including *Angels of the Battlefields* (1924) in commemoration of the nuns who served as nurses during the Civil War.

Connor's influences were primarily American, and secondarily Irish. His main interest was in designing public monuments, celebrating national ideals, ideals which he also wished to enshrine in the newly independent Irish state. In 1925, at the height of his powers and the peak of his reputation, he returned to Ireland to make the *Lusitania Peace Memorial* at Cobh, Co. Cork, which he worked on from 1925 till his death. This sculpture was to stand at the gateway between the old and the new worlds as a permanent and mute appeal for world peace. This was commissioned by a group of eminent Americans under the aegis of William H. Vanderbilt. In connection with this and other projects he traveled regularly between Ireland and the U.S. This, his *pièce de résistance,* centering on two mourning fishermen surmounted by the angel of peace, was not completed until 1968. Although the fishermen were cast in 1936, and the angel was ready for casting, Connor's backers had by this stage abandoned the commission in exasperation.

At the time of his return to Dublin, the city had no lost-wax foundry and so Connor introduced one. He was the first Irish artist to cast, chaste and patinate his own bronze work, including the bust of the poet and painter, his friend George Russell (AE) (1926), now at Limerick City Art Gallery. He exhibited at the Royal Hibernian Academy and at the Royal Academy. He is said to have been made an honorary chief of the Cherokee Indians, later appearing at a ball at the Royal Academy in London where he regularly exhibited his work, wearing an Indian headdress of feathers.

Although he was well received in Dublin art circles and did a series of relief portraits of the 1926 cabinet (including John Marcus O'Sullivan, Minister for Education, with responsibility for the arts), and submitted designs for the new coinage, post–Civil War Ireland was not financially or culturally inclined to accept his ideas. Most Irish stonecarvers worked on church commissions, and in this respect Connor differed from many of his compatriots in that he preferred a more heroic, secular conception of public sculpture, more akin to the work of the renowned French sculptor Rodin or the Irish-born American sculptor Augustus St. Gaudens. He was known for not completing his com-

missions, including the Tralee *Pikeman,* or the *Croppy Boy* (finished by Albert Power) and the Kerry *Poets* memorial. Such lapses contributed to his worsening financial situation. Despite the fact that he was a superb portraitist, and his public monuments were noted for their skill and virility, he ended his days in penury. In 1938 he was declared bankrupt, and although evicted from his studio on North Circular Road, he continued to return there to work. When he died, his friends, led by Domhnall O'Murchadha, R.H.A., then a young sculptor and art teacher, surreptitiously smuggled his work to safety. Before his own death in 1991, O'Murchadha arranged for the casting of eight bronzes from the estate to be completed for exhibition in Annascaul.

Connor died in 1943 and was buried in Mount Jerome cemetery in Dublin. Only one of his Irish memorials was executed during his lifetime and his *Robert Emmet* was financed by the Robert Emmet Statue Committee that later decided to present a cast of Connor's statue to Dublin, where it was placed in St. Stephen's Green in 1968. Patrick Kavanagh composed an elegy to him after his death; and the first, radical Irish Exhibition of Living Art devoted a special memorial section to Connor in 1943. The Hugh Lane Municipal Gallery of Modern Art hung his portrait by Gaetono de Gennaro.

National Gallery of Ireland, *Jerome Connor 1874–1943, Irish American Sculptor* (Dublin, 1993).

Theo Snoddy, *Dictionary of Irish Artists* (Dublin, 1996).

Lorado Taft, *History of American Sculpture* (New York, 1924).

NIAMH O'SULLIVAN

## CONSIDINE, ROBERT (1906–1975)

Journalist. Born in Washington, D.C., to William and Sophie (Small) Considine of Irish lineage, he attended Gonzaga High School and in 1923 became an employee of the government. Considine moved from entry level jobs such as messenger boy in the Census Bureau of Public Health to a clerk in the Department of the State. In the ensuing years, he worked on his budding interest in journalism and followed such interests by attending classes at George Washington University.

It was his extra-curricular interest in tennis that brought him the opportunity for employment in the newspaper field. In 1929, after having gained recognition with his many tennis victories in the surrounding communities of Washington, D.C., he began to write a weekly tennis column for the *Washington Post* and a year later was offered a full-time job in the sports department. In 1933, Considine was offered a higher paying position at the *Washington Herald* where he continued to cover major sporting events. Considine was transferred to New York's *Daily Mirror* in June 1937, where he began covering stories concerning political and cultural interests. During the U.S. preparations for the invasion of Normandy, Considine reported exclusively on the activities of the Eighth Air Force.

Considine wrote and co-authored several books, most notably: *MacArthur the Magnificent* (1942), *Madison Square Garden* (1942) and *The Babe Ruth Story* (1947) and the best-selling *Thirty Seconds Over Tokyo* and *General Wainwright's Story.* Considine also contributed many stories and articles to national magazines and became well known for his syndicated column, *On the Line,* which covered items of general interest. During World War II,

Considine served as a war correspondent and gained praise from noteworthy publications such as *Newsweek*.

*Newsweek* (29: 56 F3 '47).
*Who's Who in America* (1946–47).
*CAB* (1947).

JOY HARRELL

## CONSTITUTION OF THE UNITED STATES, THE

The Constitution of the United States was drafted in 1787, at the Constitutional Convention. All thirteen States had been invited to send delegates to the Convention, and only Rhode Island refused. The States sent outstanding individual delegates, including some who opposed a new form of government. Thirty-nine delegates signed the formal draft of the new Constitution. Four of these signers had been born in Ireland; several were descended from Irish-born settlers in America.

Pierce Butler (1744–1822), from South Carolina, was born in County Carlow, son of a baronet. He served as Royal Army officer, then settled in South Carolina, and became a prosperous planter. Butler argued for the fugitive slave clause (Article IV, Section 2) , and then argued that the South Carolina Convention should ratify the document.

Thomas FitzSimons (1741–1811) was a well-known Philadelphia businessman before the Revolution. He was one of the two Catholic delegates to the Convention (Daniel Carroll was the other). In debates, he recommended limits on the right to vote or hold office, and he favored giving Congress the right to tax both imports and exports. The status of this immigrant Irishman is indicated by his service as a founding trustee of the Bank of North America, and founding director of the Insurance Company of North America. He was a trustee of the University of Pennsylvania, and helped found Georgetown University.

James McHenry (1753–1816), representing Maryland, was born in Ballymena, and arrived in America in 1771. He studied medicine and became a physician. When war broke out, he joined a Pennsylvania regiment as surgeon, then became secretary to General Washington. He played a key role in getting Maryland to ratify the Constitution. Later he became Secretary of War in John Adams' Administration. Fort McHenry was named in his honor.

William Paterson (1745–1806) played the most prominent role of all Irish-born delegates to the Convention. Paterson was a legal scholar, and from 1776 to 1783 he served as Attorney-General in the revolutionary government of New Jersey. In the Convention, Paterson presented the "New Jersey Plan." This small-State plan would have kept the one-house Congress, where each State would have one vote. In fact, the Convention accepted the Connecticut Compromise, which provided for a Senate that would have equal representation of States, but a House in which the number of Representatives varied with the population of the States.

Paterson signed the Constitution, and worked hard to get it approved by New Jersey. Later he served as United States Senator, as Governor of New Jersey, and finally as Associate Justice in the U.S. Supreme Court. The city of Paterson, N.J. was named for him when it was established as a model industrial city in 1791.

Two delegates of Irish descent deserve special comment. Daniel Carroll (1730–1796) was a cousin of Charles Carroll of Car-

rollton. He used his family's great influence to help Maryland ratify the new Constitution. Richard Dobbs Spaight (1758–1802) represented North Carolina. His father was from Ireland, and became prominent in North Carolina's royal government. When Richard Spaight was quite young, both his parents died, and he was shipped back to Ireland to attend school. In 1778, aged only twenty, he returned to North Carolina, then in the midst of war. He joined the revolutionary forces, and soon began a political career.

At the Constitutional Convention, Spaight spoke in favor of two features that were not accepted: election of the President by Congress, and granting the President the power to fill vacancies in the Congress. The Constitution was not ratified by his State's 1788 Convention. North Carolina did not ratify the Constitution until 1789, after Washington was inaugurated and the first Congress proposed twelve Amendments making up a "Bill of Rights" (Ten were actually adopted by the States). Spaight's political career was mixed indeed: he supported the Constitution, but ran—and lost—as an Anti-Federalist candidate in 1789. Later he served four terms as Governor of his State.

### ANTI-FEDERALISM

After the Constitution was written, it was submitted to the States for ratification. Many States opposed it in whole or in part. Some leading Anti-Federalists had been members of the Convention, but would not sign. Other anti-Federalist figures included Patrick Henry of Virginia. All were worried that States would be swallowed up by the new United States.

Many Scotch-Irish, who had moved to the western frontiers, opposed any idea of a stronger central government. A fair number of politicians of Irish birth or descent were Anti-Federalists. The most prominent was surely George Clinton (1739–1812), Governor of New York, son of an Scotch-Irish immigrant who settled in Ulster County. Clinton tried to keep New York's Convention from ratifying the Constitution. After nine States ratified, the new Constitution was in effect. Then the New York delegates approved the Constitution by a split vote. George Clinton was later elected twice as Vice President of the United States.

Max Farrand, ed., *U.S. Constitutional Convention, 1787*, vol. 4 (New Haven, 1937).
Jackson Turner Main, *The Anti-Federalists; Critis of the Constitution, 1781–1788* (Chapel Hill, 1961).
*Dictionary of American Biography* (New York, 1936).

JOSEPH F.X. McCARTHY

## COOKE, TERENCE JAMES CARDINAL (1921–1983)

Cardinal archbishop. Born March 21, 1921, Cooke was baptized at Corpus Christi on Morningside Heights. Raised in Throgs Neck in the Bronx, he received his B.A. from Cathedral College in 1945. Ordained by Francis Cardinal Spellman December 1, 1945, Cooke worked at Saint Athanasius (1946–1947), left to earn his Ph.D. in social work at the Catholic University of America (1949), then returned to New York to teach at Fordham University (1949–1954) and to serve as procurator of Saint Joseph's Seminary (1954–1959). He entered chancery service as Spellman's secretary in 1957, then moved to vice chancellor (1958–1961), chancellor (1961–1964), and vicar general (1965–1967). With the vicar general position came appointment as auxiliary bishop on August 15, 1965, and consecration December 13, 1965. Apparently following Spellman's wishes, Pope Paul VI appointed Cooke Spellman's successor March 8, 1968. On April 4, 1968, Cooke was formally installed as archbishop and as Military Vicar of the United States Armed Forces. Paul VI created Cooke a cardinal April 18, 1969. On August 26, 1983, it was announced that Cooke had long been suffering from lymphoma, which had become terminal. He died October 6, 1983, and is buried beneath Saint Patrick's Cathedral. (Because the traditional red hat was no longer part of the cardinal's clothing when Cooke became one, there is no hat hanging from the ceiling for him.)

Cooke was noted for successful stewardship during difficult economic times. Attentive to pastoral care of new Catholics he appointed New York's first black and first Hispanic auxiliary bishops. In 1970, New York state became the first to permit non-residents of the state to have abortions, and Cooke became an advocate of right-to-life issues.

Michael and Margaret Gannon Cooke had emigrated from County Galway, and named their third child after Terence Mac-Swiney, Lord Mayor of Cork, who had died of the effects of a hunger strike in 1920. When Cooke went to Europe for his installation as cardinal, he visited his parents' birthplace, and vacationed in Ireland again in 1970. On September 4, 1975, he celebrated a memorial Mass at Saint Patrick's for the late Eamon de Valera, and in 1976 he was named honorary grand marshal of New York's Saint Patrick's Day Parade. Cooke combined loyalty to Ireland with a commitment to Christian morals. In 1981, he preceded the celebration of Saint Patrick's Day with calls to avoid "outrageous" (i.e., drunken) behavior. When in 1970 a 19–year-old Catholic was shot by police in a riot in Belfast, Cooke offered prayers for peace and justice. In 1972, British soldiers killed another 13 Catholics in Londonderry; Cooke offered Mass in memory of the deceased, called on New York Catholics to contribute to an Irish Relief Fund, and attended a Saint Patrick's Day Parade-turned-memorial march. In 1981, he twice wrote British Prime Minister Margaret Thatcher in vain attempts to end Bobby Sands' hunger strike; when Sands died, Cooke announced a Mass for peace in Northern Ireland. However, when in 1983, the Ancient Order of Hibernians named IRA supporter Michael Flannery grand marshal of the Saint Patrick's Day parade, Cooke announced the Church could not condone violence and refused to receive Flannery when the parade passed the cathedral. On September 30, 1983, he addressed a deathbed letter to the Irish-American community, expressing hope for peaceful resolutions to Irish conflicts.

The last testament of the Cardinal to the Irish-American community embodies his pastoral spirit.

September 30, 1983

Dear Brothers and Sisters of the
Irish-American Community,

At this grace-filled time of my life, I greet you in the name of the Lord Jesus, in the peace which He offers to us, and in the love of freedom and the common heritage which unites us. I offer to each one of you and your families my special love and affection.

In my years as a priest and bishop, God has given me the grace and the strength to serve His people of many beautiful national and ethnic groups. I thank God for this privilege and for the richness of the diversity of our Community of faith and love. I pray for fidelity to His sacred call, even in this time of serious illness.

I thank God especially that I have been able, with His help, to serve the people from which I myself have come. We, who are daughters and sons of Ireland, are descendants of a race which strives for goodness, truth and beauty and which has also known oppression, religious persecution, injustice and denial of human rights.

I am intensely proud of Ireland, our beloved Ireland, the small Nation which, despite centuries of suffering, "has never surrendered her soul." I rejoice in the tradition of faith and love, of learning, culture and freedom which we have received from the generations of her people. I pray that we will always remain faithful to the rich heritage which has been handed on to us.

Like you and so many sons and daughters of Ireland, I am profoundly grateful for the hope and for the freedom and opportunity which our beloved Nation, the United States of America, has offered to us, to our families, to those who have gone before us and to all who will come after us. When repression and starvation had all but crushed the spirits of our ancestors, they found here a welcome, a home, a place to worship God, to work and to be educated and to raise their families in freedom and in peace. May the Lord our God continue to bless our land and preserve it as a haven for the poor and the oppressed.

I offer to you, my brothers and sisters of the Irish-American Community, my heartfelt appreciation for all you have been to our nation and to our Church. Your contributions are ever so many—in education, in government, in public service, in the defense of peace and freedom, in the dedicated service of your sons and daughters who have entered the Priesthood and the Religious Life, in the close-knit and loving families in which moral and spiritual values are lived and handed on. For all this—and for so much more—I thank God with you and for you.

At this time of my life, I make a special plea to you. I make it from the depths of my soul. There have been circumstances which have caused misunderstanding and division among us, and I ask you now to work with all your hearts for healing, for reconciliation and for an end to violence here in our own community and in Ireland.

In a statement which I made last February, *The Quest for Peace in the North of Ireland*, I recalled the historic words of our Holy Father, Pope John Paul II, at Drogheda in 1979:

"I appeal to you, in the language of passionate pleading . . . turn away from the paths of violence and return to the ways of peace . . . I, too, believe in justice and seek justice. But violence only delays the day of justice. Violence destroys the work of justice."

I repeat now the call which I made then. May we work first for peace and reconciliation here in our own communities. Then may we help the situation in Ireland in very practical ways, especially:

- through our prayers for peace;
- through our assistance to families in need;
- through investment by our economic and industrial leaders in areas of vast Catholic unemployment and by substantial governmental assistance to depressed areas;

• and through a positive involvement of our government and public officials in insisting that Great Britain move toward a permanent, peaceful solution.

May I offer one last word to you. It is in the form of a farewell, for my physician has spoken very clearly to me about the nature of my illness.

I have absolute faith in the message of Our Lord and Savior Jesus Christ. I believe that He has indeed gone to prepare a place for us and that He calls us to eternal light and peace. I have tried to serve Him and His people faithfully and with love. I am confident of His mercy and His saving love. I beseech Him now to receive me, in the company of His Mother and all the angels and saints.

May Saint Patrick protect you. May Blessed Mary, the Queen of all Ireland, ever look upon you. And may Almighty God, the Father and the Son and the Holy Spirit bless you forever.

+Terence Cardinal Cooke
Archbishop of New York

*See* Catholicism, Irish-American

Benedict J. Groeschel, C.F.R., and Terrence L. Weber, *Thy Will Be Done: A Spiritual Portrait of Terence Cardinal Cooke* (New York: Alba House, 1990).
John J. Reardon, et al., eds., *"This Grace Filled Moment": Terence Cardinal Cooke, 1921–1983* (New York: Rosemont Press, 1984).

MARY ELIZABETH BROWN

## CORBETT, JAMES JOHN (1866–1933)

Boxer, "scientific" prizefighter. Often known as "Gentleman Jim," James Corbett was born September 1, 1866, to Irish parents in San Francisco, California. As a young man, Corbett found a job as a bank teller, but by age eighteen, his father had arranged his first boxing match with Frank Smith. The fight took place in Salt Lake City, Utah, where Corbett defeated Smith in just two rounds. In 1889 he fought three bare-knuckle fights with Joe Choynski, winning two of them and ending the third as "no-contest." In 1891, Corbett was still undefeated when he was matched against the black Australian Peter Jackson in San Francisco. The match became one of the greatest nineteenth-century fights with a bout that lasted sixty-one rounds and ended in a draw after neither of them could carry on. This match propelled him into the ring with "The Great John L," John L. Sullivan. Knowing that he had a weak "heavy punch," Corbett compensated by developing brilliant defensive tactics that made him a master of the perfectly timed fast punch. This led to Corbett's "scientific" approach against Sullivan which proved to be remarkably successful in the first U.S. World Heavyweight Boxing Championship with gloves and the new Queensberry Rules of 1892. The twenty-five year old Corbett defeated the elder Sullivan who landed only one punch in over an hour of fighting. Corbett next defeated the British champion Charley Mitchell in 1894 and gained worldwide fame as a heavyweight champion. In the same year, Corbett became the first boxer to appear in a movie at Thomas Edison's studio where he knocked out Peter Courney in six rounds. Corbett continued to defend the heavyweight title until 1897 when he was defeated by Robert Fitzimmons by a knockout punch in fourteen rounds at Carson City, Nevada on March 17. The prize-fighter tried to regain the title in two other attempts, but Corbett was defeated both times by James J. Jeffries. After the second defeat, Corbett retired with eleven wins (seven by knockout), four losses, two draws, and two no-contests.

Corbett is known for being the first fully successful fighter under the new Queensberry rules and developing the "scientific" approach to boxing. His fashionable attire and gentlemanly personality also helped him not only to popularize prizefighting for a wider audience, but also to land him leading roles in several plays, including George Bernard Shaw's *Cashel Byron's Profession*. Corbett died February 18, 1933, in New York City, and has been immortalized by the 1942 film, *Gentleman Jim,* starring Errol Flynn.

*See* Boxing

Henry Cooper, *The Great Heavyweights* (London, 1978).
James J. Corbett, *The Roar of the Crowd: The True Tale of the Rise and Fall of a Champion* (New York: Garden City Publishing Co., 1926).
David L. Porter, *Biographical Dictionary of American Sports: Basketball and Other Indoor Sports* (New York: Greenwood Press, 1989).
Bert R. Sugar, *100 Years of Boxing: A Pictorial History of Modern Boxing* (New York, 1982).
Bert R. Sugar, ed., *1983 Ring Record Book* (New York, 1983).

DANIEL J. KUNTZ

## CORCORAN, WILLIAM WILSON (1798–1888)

Businessman and philanthropist. His father was born in Ireland in 1754, and emigrated to Georgetown, D.C., in 1788 where he worked as a lawyer and also served as postmaster. William was privately educated and spent a year at Georgetown College (now Georgetown University). In 1815 he formed a dry goods and auction business with his brother, but the company went bankrupt in 1823. For the next seventeen years he worked at several banking and brokerage jobs.

In 1840 he formed the investment banking firm of Corcoran and Riggs. By 1854 Corcoran was a very wealthy man and retired to devote his time to art collecting and philanthropy. He donated generously to many varied charitable causes. He gave $550,000 for a home for gentlewomen who had met financial misfortune; and gave generously to religious and educational institutes of different denominations, including the Protestant Orphan Asylum of Washington and the Academy of the Visitation. But he is best remembered for his sponsoring the Corcoran Gallery of Art to which he donated his large personal collection. It was begun in 1859 but, owing to the Civil War, was not completed and opened until 1872 at Pennsylvania Avenue and Seventeenth Street (later moved to its present location in 1897).

Corcoran, like most of Washington's wealthy, sided with the South during the Civil War, and he spent the war years in France. There he could afford to live in style and he made influential friends, and the French ambassador intervened when some of his property was about to be seized by the U.S. government. He paid scant attention to Ireland and avoided any involvement with Irish nationalists. He is deservedly remembered for his charitable activities and for giving the nation the Corcoran Gallery of Art.

M. E. P. Bouligny, *A Tribute to W. W. Corcoran* (Washington, D.C., 1974).
*Evening Star* (Washington, Feb.24, 1888).

MICHAEL GLAZIER

Michael Corrigan

## CORRIGAN, MICHAEL AUGUSTINE (1839–1902)

Archbishop and educator. Michael Augustine Corrigan was born in Newark, NJ, on August 13, 1839, and died in New York City, on May 5, 1902. The son of Thomas and Mary (English) Corrigan, immigrants from Leinster, Ireland, he attended St. Mary's College in Wilmington, DE, and graduated from Mount St. Mary's College in Emmitsburg, MD, in 1859.

Sent to Rome by Bishop James Roosevelt Bayley of Newark, Corrigan was in the first group of twelve seminarians who entered the North American College when Pope Pius IX first opened its doors on Via dell'Umilità to the education of future priests on December 8, 1859.

Corrigan was ordained a priest on September 19, 1863, and returned to his home diocese in the following year with a doctorate in theology. Destined for a different ministry than that of a parish priest, Father Corrigan became deeply involved in the development of what is now Seton Hall University in South Orange, NJ, when it was an unknown college and seminary. From one of its professors, he rose to the presidency of Seton Hall College (1868–73) and, with the help of his three brothers, two priests and one doctor, Corrigan strengthened the financial base of that institution.

Recognized as a leader in the Diocese of Newark, Corrigan was appointed its vicar general in 1868 and administered the diocese when Bishop Bayley was attending the First Vatican Council (1869–70). With that background, when Bishop Bayley was elevated to Baltimore on July 30, 1872, Corrigan continued to care for the diocese (1872–73) until he himself was named Bishop of Newark by Pope Pius IX on February 14, 1873.

### New Jersey Catholic Bisop

Corrigan was consecrated a bishop on May 4, 1873, at St. Patrick's Pro-Cathedral in Newark by Archbishop John McCloskey of New York who was assisted by Bishop John Loughlin of Brooklyn, NY, and Bishop William George McCloskey of Louisville. Although Bishop Corrigan faced a number of problems in a diocese which covered the whole state, he brought his jurisdiction in line with the decisions of the Second Plenary Council of Baltimore (1866) through his diocesan reports, synods, and visitations. At the same time, Corrigan developed parochial schools within his diocese, provided for the spiritual care of youngsters confined to reform schools, supported such charitable works as hospitals and orphanages, and reflected a deep interest in the growth of St. Peter's College which, chartered on April 3, 1872, became the major ministry of the Jesuits in Jersey City.

Bishop Corrigan was particularly concerned about the faith of the immigrants, especially the Italians. This was a problem which he would face again in New York when Peter Paul Cahensly, an outspoken Catholic layman of German background, was warning the leaders of the Catholic Church that the process of Americanization of immigrants was leading to the loss of their religious faith.

### Archbishop of New York

Named Coadjutor Archbishop of New York by Pope Leo XIII on October 1, 1880, Corrigan did not became Archbishop of New York until October 10, 1885. Meanwhile, as a leading prelate at the Third Plenary Council of Baltimore (1883–84), Corrigan helped to shape the future of American Catholicism. Not long after his formal installation on May 4, 1886, the new archbishop clashed with Edward McGlynn, a priest who supported Henry George, an advocate of the single-tax theory on land. An enthusiastic believer in George, McGlynn campaigned for George in the 1886 campaign for Mayor of New York City against the wishes of his archbishop, who suspended the priest from his ministry and removed him from his pastorate. Though McGlynn was excommunicated for disobedience in 1887, he was reinstated as a priest in good standing by the pope's delegate to the United States in 1892. Since the single-tax theory was not contrary to Catholic social teaching, it appeared to some observers that Corrigan had acted rather precipitously in his handling of the priest.

### Leading Europeanizer

Archbishop Corrigan's various actions clashed with those liberal Catholics, especially Archbishop John Ireland of St. Paul, his major rival, who sought to Americanize Catholicism in his emphasis on the value of education in the public schools. Like Bishop Bernard Joseph John McQuaid of Rochester, a kindred spirit, Corrigan did not agree with Ireland over the value of public education. This was particularly true when the archbishop opposed Ireland in his support of Sylvester L. Malone, another priest, for a seat on the Board of Regents of the State University of New York. Understandably, Corrigan favored the candidacy of Bishop McQuaid who downplayed Ireland's view on the value of public school education and emphasized the importance of the conservative view on parochial school education.

Although Corrigan was the leading adversary of the Americanizers, no one could doubt the archbishop's sincerity. He founded many parishes, built churches, and developed the Catholic school system. And, with the support of the Jesuits, Corrigan was inclined towards Europeanization rather than Americanization of the Catholic Church in this country.

Despite all that, the crowning achievement of his legacy to New York is St. Joseph's Seminary at Dunwoodie, in Yonkers, which he opened in 1896. Archbishop Corrigan's remains rest under the high altar in New York's St. Patrick's Cathedral.

*See* Catholicism, Irish-American; McGlynn, Edward

Robert Emmett Curran, *Michael Augustine Corrigan and the Shaping of Conservative Catholicism in America, 1878–1902* (New York, 1978).

Stephen M. DiGiovanni, *Archbishop Corrigan and the Italian Immigrants* (Huntington, IN, 1994).

Joseph J. Mahoney and Peter J. Wosh, eds., *The Diocesan Journal of Michael Augustine Corrigan, Bishop of Newark, 1872–1880* (Newark, 1987).

Thomas T. McAvoy, *The Great Crisis in American Catholic History, 1895–1900* (Chicago, 1957).

VINCENT A. LAPOMARDA, S.J.

## COUGHLIN, CHARLES E. (1891–1979)

Controversial priest. Of Irish ancestry (a great-grandfather came to America in the 1820s to work on digging of the Erie Canal), Charles E. Coughlin was born October 25, 1891, in Hamilton, Ontario, son of Thomas and Amelia (Mahaney) Coughlin. He was ordained a Basilian priest in Toronto in 1916, but for most of his life he ministered as a diocesan priest in the United States, where as a radio presence he scaled the heights of fame and plumbed the depths of ignominy before settling to a life of relative obscurity as a pastor and director of the Shrine of the Little Flower in Royal Oak, Michigan.

Coughlin was educated in Canada, graduating from St. Michael's College, University of Toronto, in 1911. For several years he taught at Assumption College in Sandwich (now Windsor), Ontario, a boys' school run by the Basilians. He resigned from the order under an option provided by the 1918 Code of Canon Law revising the status of so-called sodalities (unattached religious communities of priests).

Crossing to the United States, Coughlin served as a curate in parishes of the then-Diocese of Detroit, and was incardinated into its priesthood in 1923. He quickly became a favorite of Detroit's Bishop Michael Gallagher for his "soaring rhetoric" and "fund-raising abilities," and in 1926 Gallagher gave him permission to establish a shrine honoring St. Therese of Lisieux in the rapidly growing suburb of Royal Oak, north of Detroit. The stage was thus set for one of the most remarkable—and notorious—clerical careers of the 1930s–1940s.

Commercial radio was in its infancy, and a Detroit station, WJR, founded in 1922, would become a keystone in the patching together of a nationwide CBS network. But in 1926 WJR was struggling for survival. Coughlin, only four months settled into Royal Oak, was invited to air a series of religious broadcasts, and so was launched "The Children's Hour," soon broadened in scope and renamed "The Golden Hour of the Shrine of the Little Flower." The program's success was phenomenal and Coughlin became a Sunday afternoon network fixture with a listening audience of some forty million persons across the country, and uncounted thousands more abroad through short-wave hookup via Philadelphia's WCAU. Mail began pouring into Royal Oak, reaching an estimated 80,000 letters a week, and the Post Office Department hurriedly built a new facility to handle the volume.

As Coughlin's popularity grew so did his confidence and his reach. No issue seemed beyond his competence, no goal beyond his dreaming. He pronounced on the roots of the Great Depression, monetary reform, the silver standard, redistribution of wealth, a guaranteed national wage, presidential politics, international diplomacy, banking, Bolshevism—with the texts of the broadcasts being reprinted in *Social Justice*, a weekly newspaper founded by Coughlin in 1936 whose circulation would eventually reach 200,000. So powerful was he that that same year he fielded a presidential candidate (Congressman William Lemke of North Dakota) under the banner of the National Union for

Charles E. Coughlin

Social Justice, an organization likewise of Coughlin's founding. Some speculated that he himself might have headed the ticket except that foreign birth precluded the possibility of his serving as president.

Coughlin cast himself as a social reformer, and initially his thought reflected the New Deal progressivism of President Franklin Roosevelt. Week by week, however, his ideology became more reactionary, and Coughlin evolved into an admirer of Hitler and Mussolini, a bitter anti-Semite and, as World War II erupted, a political isolationist. Reaction was predictable. Doors that were open to him, such as the White House's, began to shut tight. Government officials troubled over his loyalty and feared a link-up between Coughlin and his followers and Fascist elements at home and abroad. Church officials shared many of the same worries, as well as acute embarrassment over Coughlin's anti-Semitic views.

Coughlin's response to criticism was to raise the decibels and increase the dosages of hate. His favorite targets were the Roosevelt administration and Jewish leaders whom he felt no compunction about naming. President Roosevelt was branded a "liar," "anti-God" and the "Great Betrayer," while banking families such as the Kuhn-Loebs and the Rothschilds were defamed initially in code language ("international financiers"), then with blunt, ugly epithets ("modern Shylocks"). Coughlin even printed in *Social Justice* his own version of the notoriously fraudulent *Protocols of the Elders of Zion*.

A crisis point was reached with Coughlin's broadcast of November 20, 1938, discussing *Kristallnacht,* the infamous night of arson, looting and murder of Jews across Germany that occurred ten days before. Coughlin added a voice of protest to the outrage, but qualified it in such a way as to expose the depths of his own anti-Semitism. Among other things, he framed the action in the context of Nazi belief that "Communism and Judaism [were] too closely interwoven for the national health of Germany." The alleged link of Communism and Judaism was a familiar Coughlin theme.

There was great public revulsion. Coughlin lost his broadcasting outlet in New York and his radio audience, which had been in decline for several months, plummeted, though he was still left with an estimated 14.5 million listeners. Detroit's recently appointed archbishop, Edward F. Mooney, condemned the *Kristallnatcht* broadcast, saying through the diocesan newspaper: "Totally out of harmony with the Holy Father's leadership are Catholics who indulge in speeches or writings which in fact tend to arouse feelings against Jews as a race." (Gallagher died in January 1937; the see was elevated to an archdiocese and Mooney installed as its first archbishop the following August.)

For years Coughlin had enjoyed the patronage and indulgence of Bishop Gallagher, and he rewarded that favor by making Gallagher's image the model for the figure of St. Michael the Archangel carved into the tower of the shrine at Royal Oak. But with Mooney he would not have the same relationship. Mooney constantly confronted Coughlin on his anti-Semitism, charging that it was incompatible with the views of the church, and he demanded to review beforehand the scripts for Coughlin's radio broadcasts. It was a strong test of wills, which became the more pointed when the Vatican apparently declined to intervene directly into the case, indicating that the problem should be resolved locally. Coughlin was not to be easily silenced, and he continued to broadcast until being forced off the air waves in 1940 by a new code of the National Association of Broadcasters.

Coughlin still had *Social Justice,* however, and he managed to shield the weekly from church control on the basis that it was not a Catholic publication. War was raging in Europe and the paper's sympathies were so hostile to the Allies' cause that the U.S. military banned its distribution on military bases in March 1941 as detrimental to the national interests. The following year the government itself acted, threatening sedition proceedings and withdrawing the paper's second-class mailing privileges. The loss of postal privileges put *Social Justice* out of business and effectively drove Coughlin from the public arena.

Coughlin withdrew quietly to the life of a pastor in Royal Oak. In 1955, *Life* magazine visited and found "a man who had mellowed considerably, a man at peace." In 1976, on the fortieth anniversary of the Shrine of the Little Flower, Coughlin, now 85, was honored by friends and old associates. Among the speakers was Monsignor Edward J. Hickey, chancellor of the archdiocese during Mooney's tenure. Hickey looked back on the tumultuous years in Coughlin's life with an olive branch and an acknowledgment: "We think he made mistakes in economics and in his international relations . . . we condemned his attitudes toward the Jewish people. But when the showdown came, what so edified us all was his obedience. . . . I used to say if the bishop had told him to stand on his head . . . he would have done so." Coughlin died three years later, October 27, 1979.

*See* Ethnic Relations: The Jews and the Irish

Sheldon Marcus, *Father Coughlin: The Tumultuous Life of the Priest of the Little Flower* (Boston, 1973).
Donald Warren, *Radio Priest: Charles Coughlin, the Father of Hate Radio* (New York, 1996).

JOHN DEEDY

## CRAIG, JOHN (1709–1774)

Pioneer Scots-Irish clergyman and memoirist in eighteenth-century Virginia. Craig was born into a comfortable family of Presbyterian farmers in Donegore Parish, Co. Antrim. Educated at the University of Edinburgh (M.A., 1732), in 1734 he emigrated to Pennsylvania where he studied theology under the Irish-born Rev. John Thomson (d.1753) of Chesnut Level. In 1738 Craig was licensed to preach by the Presbytery of Donegal, and in 1740 he accepted a call to minister to the Scots-Irish settlers at the Triple Forks of the Shenandoah, in Virginia's Augusta County, thus becoming the first permanently-settled Presbyterian clergyman west of the Blue Ridge mountains. There he preached and farmed for the rest of his life, serving a congregation spread over 1,800 square miles, preaching alternate Sundays in two churches over ten miles apart—the Augusta Stone Church near Staunton and, until 1764, the Tinkling Spring Church near Fisherville. He also established and visited periodically at least thirteen other churches in western Virginia and North Carolina. Craig's long ministry weathered the Great Awakening, which split colonial Presbyterianism in 1741–1758 and subjected Craig, who adhered to the anti-evangelical Old Side, to attacks from itinerant, New Side revivalists; the French and Indian War (1755–63), when Craig fortified his churches and rallied his parishioners against Indian attacks; and, after 1763, the crisis in colonial-British relations, during which Craig became an outspoken champion of American rights. His memoir (written 1769–70) is a unique record of early Scots-Irish settlement and religion on the American frontier.

Craig's memoir is in the Historical Foundation of the Presbyterian and Reformed Churches, Montreat, N.C.
L. Chalkey, *Chronicles of the Scotch-Irish Settlement in Virginia,* I (Rossylin, Va., 1912).
L. K. Craig, *Reverend John Craig, 1709–74* (New Orleans, 1963).
W. H. Foote, *Sketches of Virginia, Historical and Biographical,* 2nd ser. (Philadelphia, 1855).
J. L. Peyton, *History of Augusta County, Virginia* (Bridgewater, Va., 1953 ed.).
J. A. Waddell, *Annals of Augusta County, Virginia, from 1726 to 1871* (Staunton, Va., 1902 ed.).
H. McK. Wilson, *The Tinkling Spring: Headwater of Freedom* (Fisherville, Va., 1954).

KERBY MILLER

## CRAWFORD, JOHN (1746–1813)

Physician and one of the first to introduce vaccination into the United States. John Crawford was born May 3, 1746, in the north of Ireland to the son of a Presbyterian minister. He studied medicine at Trinity College, Dublin, but before receiving a degree, he went to Leiden, Holland, and enlisted as a ship's surgeon for the East India Company.

His voyages took him twice to India and also to China. During those trips, he gathered information about the illness (probably beriberi) that affected sailors. Those observations were detailed in his first book, *An Essay on the Nature, Cause and Cure of a Disease Incident to the Liver,* which was published in London in 1772.

Crawford married a young lady named O'Donnell in 1778. He took her with him to Barbados when he was appointed physician-in-chief at a naval hospital there. After a hurricane in 1780, Crawford supplied medicine and assistance to those in need, expecting no payment for his services. When poor health afflicted him in 1782, Crawford, his wife and two young children left for Europe. However, his wife died on the voyage.

When his health had improved, Crawford returned to Barbados and in 1790 he was appointed surgeon major to the colony at Demerara. While in control of a military hospital there, he was able to study through autopsies the role of parasites in the formation of disease and the spread of infection.

In 1794 Crawford was again forced to return to Europe due to declining health. While in Holland, he obtained his medical degree from the University of Leiden. St. Andrew's University in Scotland had already granted him a degree in 1791. His time in Leiden also gave him the opportunity to discuss his ideas about infection with colleagues and to read the works of several distinguished scholars who had proposed similar views.

Instead of returning to the colonies, Crawford followed the advice of his brother-in-law, John O'Donnell, to join him in Baltimore, Maryland. In 1796 Crawford was appointed physician at City Hospital. One of his projects, with the collaboration of Benjamin Rush, was the establishment of a dispensary in Baltimore in 1801, the first of its kind in the city.

In 1800 Crawford received a sample of Edward Jenner's vaccine on a cotton thread, rolled up on paper and covered with a varnish to protect it from the air. He began to use it against smallpox at the same time that Benjamin Waterhouse was experimenting with it in Cambridge, Massachusetts.

Crawford was the first to propose a connection between insect contagion and yellow fever. He insisted upon cleanliness and isolation in hospital wards to help prevent the spread of contagious diseases.

In 1804 Crawford founded a weekly literary journal, *The Companion and the Weekly Miscellany*. Within two years, his daughter Eliza took over editorship and changed the title to *The Observer and Repertory of Original and Selected Essays*. She was the second woman to edit a journal in the United States. Crawford's paper "Remarks on Quarantines" was published in the journal in 1807. He also used the journal to publish a paper on his ideas about the development of infectious diseases.

Crawford found very little support during his lifetime from the medical community for his thesis on the transmission of disease. In 1809, however, his paper on contagion was published in the *Baltimore Medical and Physical Recorder*. Crawford held the theory that disease was caused by the introduction into the human body of some form of animal life so small that it can't be easily observed, and that each of these minute organisms caused its own disease.

It took seventy years for Crawford's theory to be proven correct. Scientists at that time found that elephantiasis develops in and is transmitted by a mosquito to humans.

Besides his medical interests, Crawford helped to begin the Baltimore Public Library, the Maryland Society for Promoting Useful Knowledge, and the Maryland Penitentiary. He was a member of, and an officer in, the Hibernian Benevolent Society. He was an active Free Mason and Grand Master of his Lodge in 1801.

Crawford died after only four days' illness on May 9, 1813. Evidently, Crawford had married a second time because his widow sold most of Crawford's library to the University of Maryland. The library contains about four hundred items and is the oldest private medical library in the United States.

Davis Coakley, *Irish Masters of Medicine* (Dublin, 1992).

E. F. Cordell, "Sketch of John Crawford," *Johns Hopkins Hospital Bulletin*, 102 (1899): 158–62.

Allan Johnson and Dumas Malone, eds., *Dictionary of American Biography*, vol. II (New York, 1930).

Francis R. Packard, M.D., *History of Medicine in the United States* (New York, 1931).

J. E. Wilson, "An Early Baltimore Physician and His Medical Library," *Annals of Medical History* (1942): 63–80.

MARIANNA McLOUGHLIN

## CREIGHTON, EDWARD (1820–1874)

Pioneer telegraph builder, banker, philanthropist. Edward Creighton was born in 1820 in Ohio to James and Bridget (Hughes) Creighton, American settlers from Ireland just after the turn of the century. At fourteen, Edward became a wagon driver. The magnetic telegraph equipment he often carried for the fledgling telegraph industry sparked his imagination and after acquiring a small sum of money, he secured contracts with the industry for stringing telegraph lines throughout the Middle and South West. His success and reliability brought him to the attention of Hiram Sibley, who recruited Creighton for the first practical venture of constructing a transcontinental telegraph system across the west. In 1854 Sibley put Creighton and his brother John Andrew in charge of managing the construction over the plains of the Nebraska Territory.

Sibley next sent Creighton out to search for suitable line trails through Omaha, Fort Kearny, Laramie, South Pass and over the Sierra Nevadas to the California coast. In the spring of 1861, Creighton's report reached Sibley who, after securing a congressional subsidy and a promise to complete the project within ten years, turned to Creighton to begin construction of the Pacific Telegraph Company. The project was started at both ends on July 4, 1861, and with unexpected speed the entire line from coast to coast had been completed by November 15—just four months and eleven days after its start.

Having invested in the company early, Creighton held the largest number of shares and became general manager of the Pacific Telegraph Company with considerable wealth. The entrepreneur also organized the first national bank of the Nebraska Territory and became its first president. As a devout Roman Catholic, Creighton often expressed a desire to establish a free Catholic school for higher education. This was never realized during his lifetime, but his brother, John Andrew, established Creighton University in his honor five years after Creighton's death in 1874.

M. P. Dowling, *Creighton University. Reminiscences of the First Twenty-Five Years* (Omaha, 1903).

J. Sterling Morton, *Illustrated History of Nebraska: A History of Nebraska from the Earliest Explorations of the Trans-Mississippi Region* (Lincoln, 1905).

Patrick A. Mullens, *Creighton: Biographical Sketches of Edward Creighton, John A. Creighton, Mary Lucretia Creighton, Sarah Emily Creighton* (Omaha, 1901).

James D. Reid, *The Telegraph in America: Its Founders, Promoters, and Noted Men* (New York, 1879).

DANIEL J. KUNTZ

## CREIGHTON, JOHN ANDREW (1831–1907)

Philanthropist. Although John Andrew Creighton began life in Licking County, Ohio, he was to gain fame and fortune in the West, cashing in on the businesses that developed as the United States steadily advanced its interests and horizon toward the Pacific coast.

He was the youngest of nine children, born Oct. 15, 1831, to James and Bridget (Hughes) Creighton, who emigrated to the

## CROWLEY, JOHN J. (1891–1940)

Priest, columnist, civic leader. John J. Crowley was born in Killarney, Ireland on December 8, 1891. John was the eldest of eight children. In 1903 the family emigrated to Worcester, Massachusetts. He graduated from Holy Cross College in 1915. During his college years he wrote many articles and poems for the college magazine.

### Desert Padre

Crowley entered the seminary in Baltimore and was ordained in 1918. After little over a year as assistant pastor in Los Angeles he was assigned to a desert parish which included Death Valley and Owens Valley with Mt. Whitney in full view of his little Santa Rosa Church in Lone Pine, California. His duties required driving over rough roads to the outlying areas where he ministered to Catholics who hadn't seen a priest in years.

In 1924 he was asked to serve as Chancellor for the diocese of Monterey-Fresno under Bishop MacGinley and was made a Monsignor the next year. He helped with many fund-raising activities which were quite successful until the Depression caused financial problems for the young diocese. In 1934 a new Bishop assigned him as pastor in Porterville. Shortly after, he became critically ill and on recovering asked the Bishop to return to Lone Pine where he served until his death in 1940. He also served as chaplain to the CCC boys in Death Valley. He preferred the title of "Father" to that of "Monsignor" and so he became known to all as Father Crowley, the "Desert Padre."

### The Writer

In 1934 Father Crowley began writing weekly columns for the Fresno diocesan newspaper, *The Central California Register,* under the byline of "Inyokel." "Sage and Tumbleweed" reflected his experiences in his everyday work and travels throughout the desert. The identity of Inyokel was known to only a few and the columns became so popular that the local Owens Valley newspapers asked permission to reprint them.

### The Citizen

During all this time Father Crowley could see that the residents of Owens Valley were suffering from economic problems, partly due to the fact that Los Angeles had built the Aqueduct in 1913 and appropriated much of the water needed by farmers and ranchers. There was much bitterness and despair, so he joined with other civic leaders to form the Inyo Associates which over time came to wrest concessions from Los Angeles and made life a little easier. The group attempted to relieve the financial problems of the area by promoting tourism. He was imaginative in having photographers handy for his Fisherman's Mass and for a huge pageant called the "Wedding of the Waters" when the Mt. Whitney-Death Valley highway was dedicated in 1937. The publicity engendered by these events and other efforts, plus a photo of Father Crowley saying Mass on the summit of Mt. Whitney, all attracted interest nationwide and brought tourism and renewed hope to the residents.

At the height of his influence, both as a priest and as a civic leader, he suffered a fatal accident on March 17, 1940. There is now a monument in his honor on the highway to Death Valley, and a memorial cross where he died. A reservoir and fishing lake built by Los Angeles was named Crowley Lake in his honor in 1941. He is still fondly remembered in the area.

Joan Brooks, *Desert Padre: The Life and Writings of Father John J. Crowley* (Desert Hot Springs, CA, 1997).
*Central California Register* (Fresno, 1934–1940).
Margaret Phillips, "Padre of the Desert," *Desert* (October 1947).
Irving Stone, "Desert Padre," *Saturday Evening Post* (May 20, 1944).

JOAN BROOKS

## CROWLEY, PATRICK FRANCIS (1911–1974), and PATRICIA (1913– )

Co-founders of the Christian Family Movement. Pat was born in Chicago, Illinois of Jerome J. Crowley, whose grandfather had immigrated from County Cork, Ireland, and Henrietta L. O'Brien whose father had immigrated from Tipperary, Ireland. Patty was born in Chicago, Illinois of Ovidas J. Caron and Marietta Higman, neither of Irish ancestry. Pat graduated from the University of Notre Dame in 1933, and received his law degree from Loyola of Chicago in 1937. He worked as a lawyer the rest of his life, taking care of the family businesses. In 1936, Patty graduated from Trinity College in Washington, D.C., where she was exposed to the progressive Catholic social thinker, Monsignor John Ryan. On October 16, 1937, Pat and Patty were married in Chicago. Together they raised 5 children of their own, acted as guardian to close to a dozen foster children, and hosted more than forty foreign students in their home. Together they formed one of the most significant lay couples, if not the most significant, in the history of the U.S. Catholic Church. Former University of Notre Dame President, Father Theodore Hesburgh, C.S.C., is fond of saying, that if they ever canonize a married couple, it should be the Crowleys.

Together they forged a movement that became one of the most dynamic in the U.S. church during the 1950s and 1960s—the Christian Family Movement (CFM). Though there is some debate as to who should be designated founder of CFM, there is no doubt that the driving force behind the success and spread of

Patricia and
Patrick Crowley

CFM was the Crowleys. Rightly, they have been called Mr. and Mrs. CFM.

In 1943, Pat and several other businessmen began meeting in Pat's father's office in the Chicago Loop. They formed a "businessmen's" Catholic Action cell. In 1944, Patty began meeting with a number of wives to form a "married women's cell." Out of these two groups Chicago Adult Catholic Action was formed. The men began sponsoring Cana Conferences and Pre-Cana Conferences were begun through the efforts of Patty. By 1948, the men's and women's Catholic Action groups had merged to form Adult Catholic Family Action. In June, 1949, family action leaders (59 lay, 12 clergy) from 11 cities met at Childerly Retreat Center in Wheeling, Illinois just outside of Chicago to form the national Christian Family Movement. At its peak, the movement claimed close to 50,000 couples in the United States and Canada.

In 1966, Pat and Patty assisted Jose and Luzma Alvarez Icaza of Mexico with the creation of the International Confederation of Christian Family Movements (ICCFM). In 1967, the Crowleys became ICCFM's president couple, a position they held until Pat's death. Patty remained president until 1977. In 1974, Pat and Patty were the driving force behind ICCFM's international family conference in Tanzania, Africa known as Familia '74.

In 1964, Pat and Patty were appointed to the Pontifical Commission for the Study of Population, Family and Births, popularly known as the Papal Birth Control Commission. The Crowleys were one of three lay couples on the Commission. They publicly sided with the Commission's Majority report, calling for a change in the Church's traditional teaching on birth control. Their view was rejected by Pope Paul VI in his encyclical *Humanae Vitae* in 1968.

The Crowleys received numerous awards including the Laetare Medal from the University of Notre Dame in 1966.

Jeffrey M. Burns, *Disturbing the Peace: A History of the Christian Family Movement, 1949–1974* (Notre Dame, 1999).
John Kotre, *Simple Gifts: The Lives of Pat and Patty Crowley* (New York and Kansas City, 1979).

JEFFREY M. BURNS

## CUDAHY, EDWARD ALOYSIUS, JR. (1885–1966)

Meatpacker. Born into Irish heritage in Chicago to Michael and Elizabeth (Murphy) Cudahy. Cudahy was raised in the shadow of his successful father and in his youth was victim of a bizarre kidnapping plot. In 1905 he became involved in the family's Omaha meatpacking plant and learned the trade. Cudahy worked with his father at the Chicago company headquarters and he became vice president in 1916.

After having served his time in World War I as captain of a machine gun company, he returned to the family business and began taking over many of his father's duties. In 1926, he became president of Cudahy Packing and his father retained the position of chairman of the board. At that time the company enjoyed a moderate success in the meatpacking industry and also manufactured such popular products as Old Dutch Cleanser, soap, and cottonseed oil. However, during the Great Depression the meatpacking industry suffered and Cudahy's company became intertwined in many competitive export deals.

Given the many struggles, Cudahy managed to sustain the company and it enjoyed a revival of net profits before World War II. By 1942 his company had earned over $3.4 million in profits and Cudahy began to spend less time in management functions. After the war the profits continued to increase to an all time high of $7.1 million. However, by 1948 profits declined to $1 million due to a strike against his monopoly on the meat market. The latter years of Cudahy's administration saw continuing decline. Cudahy resigned in 1962 due to the increasing problems and his decreasing health. He died on January 8, 1966.

William Kane, *The Education of Edward Cudahy* (1941).
The Cudahy Packing Company, *Yearbook* (1926–1931).
*Dictionary of American Biography,* supplement 8.

JOY HARRELL

## CUDAHY, MICHAEL (1841–1910)

Businessman, philanthropist, meatpacking pioneer. Born to Patrick and Elizabeth (Shaw) Cudahy in Callan, County Kilkenny, Ireland, Cudahy came to the U.S. with his parents and during his early teenage years left school to become involved in the meatpacking business. Cudahy prospered while employed for the company Layton & Plankinton. In 1866, he advanced through official ranks and three years later became superintendent at the Plankinton & Armour packing house in Milwaukee. Cudahy's advancement continued as he was promoted to trade inspector for several packing houses in Milwaukee and his abilities gained recognition. In 1875, he was made partner in the firm of Armour & Company of Chicago.

During the years of 1870–80, Cudahy made significant strides in his novel idea of summer curing of meats by way of refrigeration. While the meatpacking business had previously been restricted to winter salt curing methods, Cudahy's ideas regarding refrigeration inaugurated a new era in the history of the meat packing business. Merchandisers previously limited to winter marketing were then able to lengthen the period during which meat could be sold and consumed. Similarly, health and safety factors were buttressed by the lessening of dangerous decay in transportation between production and consumption. Cudahy became a leader in this new technology furthering his idea in the practical establishment of static refrigeration locations called "coolers" or cold storage warehouses. Similarly, the idea was later applied to transportation in cooler cars which became the hallmark for meat transportation.

In 1887, Cudahy joined his brother Edward in further marketing ventures which led to the establishment of a new business under the title of Armour Cudahy Packing Company. In 1890, Michael Cudahy purchased Armour's shares in the company and subsequently changed the name to the Cudahy Packing Company. He remained president of the company until his death on November 27, 1910.

Rudolf A. Clemen, *American Livestock and Meat Industry* (1923).
*Dictionary of American Biography,* 4.

JOY HARRELL

## CUDAHY, PATRICK (1849–1919)

Meatpacker, philanthropist. Patrick Cudahy was born on March 17, 1849, at Callan, County Kilkenny, Ireland. He was the son of Patrick Cudahy, Sr. (1810–1881) and Elizabeth Shaw (1814–1871), both of Callan. At the age of six months, Patrick emigrated to America with his parents and family. The Cudahys settled in Milwaukee, Wisconsin.

After completing grammar school, Patrick and his four brothers (Michael, John, William, and Edward) each found employment in the city's meatpacking yards. Patrick began his career in 1873 with the Lyman & Wooley firm. In the following year he succeeded his elder brother, Michael, as superintendent of the Plankington & Armour plant, earning a one-fourth ownership interest in 1885. Three years later, Patrick and his brother John formed Cudahy Brothers Company in Milwaukee. Michael and Edward established the Cudahy Packing Company in Chicago about the same time. All five Cudahy brothers helped each other out by loaning money and serving on each other's boards of directors. In 1893 Patrick moved his company to a southern suburb of Milwaukee named Cudahy in his honor. Cudahy's company loaned his workers the necessary funds to buy lots and build homes in Cudahy.

The Cudahy Brothers Company of Milwaukee and the Cudahy Packing Company of Chicago soon became national and international leaders in the meatpacking industry. A critical factor in the rise of the Cudahys was their pioneering use of cold storage facilities for meat. Prior to this innovation, meatpacking plants were shut down between March and October because of the lack of refrigeration. The Cudahys were able to do summer curing by freezing meat after the slaughter of animals. This innovation revolutionized the industry and enabled the Cudahys to market livestock year-round. As a result, the brothers' main business became the supply of domestic and foreign markets with cured pork. Cudahy Brothers Company had trade connections in Liverpool, Glasgow, Hamburg, Stockholm, Dublin, as well as every major American and Canadian city.

In 1877 Patrick Cudahy married Anna Madden (1852–1931), the daughter of Irish immigrants. Their son, John C. Cudahy (1887–1943) had a distinguished diplomatic career as United States Ambassador to Poland (1933–1937), Minister to Ireland (1937–1939), and Ambassador to Belgium (1939–1940). A grandson, Richard D. Cudahy, currently serves as a judge of the United States Court of Appeals in Chicago. Another grandson, Michael J. Cudahy, built Marquette Electronics, Inc. into a billion dollar business as one of the world's largest manufacturers of sophisticated medical technology.

Patrick Cudahy never forgot his Irish roots. He visited Ireland in 1891 and 1899. He was also active in various Irish organizations, including the American Irish Historical Society, Friends of Irish Freedom, and the Ancient Order of Hibernians. The Cudahys donated generously to a number of Catholic charities in Milwaukee. The Patrick and Anna Cudahy Fund continues to serve as a leading philanthropic institution. Patrick died on July 25, 1919, in Milwaukee. He is buried there in Calvary Catholic Cemetery. His obituary described him as the wealthiest man in Milwaukee.

Patrick Cudahy, *Patrick Cudahy: His Life* (Milwaukee, 1912).

Joseph Kennedy, *The Cudahys: An Irish-American Success Story* (Milwaukee, 1995).

THOMAS GILDEA CANNON

## CULLINAN, ELIZABETH (1933– )

Novelist, short story writer, writing program director. A native of the New York City area, Elizabeth Cullinan was born to Irish-

Elizabeth Cullinan

American parents, her grandparents having emigrated from Ireland. She was raised an Irish Catholic and graduated from the city's parochial schools and Manhattan's Marymount College. In 1955, she began working at *The New Yorker,* taking dictation from James Thurber, and working as secretary to William Maxwell, the fiction editor. It was during her tenure at *The New Yorker* that she began to write fiction, and it was in that publication that her work first appeared in 1960. Most of the stories published in *The Time of Adam* (1971), her first short story collection, initially appeared in *The New Yorker,* as have many of her collected and uncollected stories written later.

Cullinan's first novel, *House of Gold* (1969), won the Houghton Mifflin Literary Fellowship award along with critical praise. In 1977, while spending a term on the faculty of the University of Iowa's Writers' Workshop, she published her second short story collection, *Yellow Roses.* Her second novel, *A Change of Scene,* appeared in 1982. Cullinan continues to write fiction, and has served as Director of the Writing Program at Fordham University where she is on the faculty.

### LITERARY INFLUENCES AND COMPARISONS

Cullinan's fiction, clearly, comes out of her own Irish-Catholic experience and Irish-American background. Her identity was established within that context, and it is within that context that her fiction is created and her characters reside. The author writes about New York's Irish Catholics, and because of her concentration on both the scenes and characters she has derived from her own experience, reviewers and critics have often compared her to James Joyce, particularly when looking at such stories as "The Nightingale," "The Reunion," and "The Power of Prayer" (in *The Time of Adam*). While her writing style differs greatly from Joyce's, they do share a devotion to a particular environment. Joyce's writing focused on his Dubliners, while Cullinan's writing bears the influence of her New Yorkers.

Both writers have a gift for finding the extraordinary within the briefest, most ordinary of moments. Within their stories, there is always the sense of failed experiences, of missed opportunities, of loneliness, and of self-sacrifice. Their characters are often angry and guilt-ridden. Despite the similarities, Cullinan's fiction is not a rewriting of Joyce's. Within her own writing, writing that is often humorous and compassionate, without resorting to sentimentality, Cullinan found her own voice, her own way of exploring and defining the significance located within her characters' seemingly insignificant lives.

Considering the comparisons frequently made between Cullinan and Joyce, it is not surprising that her work is also compared to that of Anton Chekhov. Chekhov's stories often depict characters mired in lives filled with gloom, futility, and pessimism; they take note of the failure among people to communicate; and they focus on the reality of an experience, instead of what one might establish as an ideal. While Cullinan's stories are not entirely filled with despair, she is a writer of realism who often, especially in her early work, creates her stories around characters who have difficulty communicating, who feel as if they have been abandoned to lives of futility and hopelessness, or who resist the reality of their worlds.

Cullinan has acknowledged the influence William Maxwell had on her writing, and in addition to Joyce and Chekhov, her writing has been compared to that of Maeve Brennan, J. F. Powers, and Mary Lavin. (The title character of one of the stories in *The Time of Adam,* "Maura's Friends," is based on Mary Lavin.) In examinations of the characters and themes within her work, comparisons have also been made with James T. Farrell, Mary Anne Sadlier, Edwin O'Connor, and Tom McHale.

## THEMES

Many of these comparisons are made because of the themes that consistently appear within her fiction. Most noticeably within her earliest stories and *House of Gold,* the themes echo those found within the works of prior generations of Irish-American writers, and in them Cullinan helps to continue the tradition of early Irish-American fiction. Perhaps the most written about are those themes dealing with the dominant mother, whose overwhelming presence and constant search for respectability demands unwavering devotion to family, home, and church. In *House of Gold* and "The Voices of the Dead" (a story that was written early in Cullinan's career and published in *The New Yorker,* but was not collected until its inclusion in *Yellow Roses* because of its similarities to her first novel), characters define themselves by their role in the family and by the level of their adherence to the demands of Irish Catholicism. Many of these characters must confront the apparent emptiness of the church as an institutional entity and the emptiness of their own lives as they try to live according to codes established by family and church.

*House of Gold* and many of Cullinan's stories are most often described as "domestic fiction" because of their focus on family life. For instance, *House of Gold* takes place during the two days of the death and wake of an Irish-American matriarch, Julia Devlin, a woman for whom the possession of her house, devotion to her church, and sacrifice of four of her nine children to God (two are priests, and two are nuns) is a triumph. In this work, as well as many others, Cullinan examines closely the relationship between mother and children, despite the fact that Julia Devlin is never conscious during the course of the novel; her voice is heard only in "The Story of a Mother," Julia's brief yet idealized autobiography, read by her daughter-in-law while Julia is on her deathbed. The rest of Julia's story must be pieced together by readers as they hear about the fractured relationships and lives of her children. Julia Devlin, like other dominant mothers in Irish-American fiction, has molded her children into objects that define her to the community, and often more importantly, to the Church. She has inflicted her will upon her children, forcing them to live out her idea of who they should be, but her children pay a high price as they become trapped within the world she has made for them.

While Cullinan's first novel demonstrates how restrictive and isolating ethnic life can be, her second novel, *A Change of Scene,* and many of her stories set in Dublin depict young Irish-American women in search of an identity within their ethnicity. Because the novel and stories such as "Maura's Friends" and "A Good Loser" are set in Ireland, these characters search for an Irish-American identity within an Irish rather than American context. Cecilia Bell, a character in "Maura's Friends," comes to the conclusion that being Irish-American means that she is neither; she learns that her identity must be found somewhere in the ground between the two. In a sense, the return of Bell and Cullinan's other young female protagonists to Ireland represents a distancing of the present from the past, of the Irish-American from the Irish.

In much of her fiction, Cullinan allows her characters to explore their lives, including their ethnic background and religion, while trying to create and survive in worlds of their own making. Nora Barrett, a character who appears in three stories, "Le Petit Déjeuner," "The Old Priest," and "The Perfect Crime," aware that she has not lived up to the expectations of her mother, is caught between her desire to please her parents and her desire to be happy in her own life. But Nora and many other heroines in Cullinan's work become more certain of who they are; they have become survivors, able to live successfully outside of their childhood home, away from their families, and perhaps most importantly, away from their mothers. Essentially, they become able to forgive the oppression and isolation of the past and deal with the present. This does not mean, however, that these characters have forgotten their ethnic and religious heritage. They are stronger women, able to exist on their own, able to overcome and erase the limitations they inherited from their long-suffering mothers, but also able to bring together the best of the past and the reality of their present lives.

While many themes operate within her writing, the joy of Cullinan's work is found within the progression of her characters. Cullinan has stated that she enjoys picking up characters again at different parts of their story. Because of her willingness and ability to do just that, readers come face to face with not only characters who are making a journey toward personal awareness, but with an author who can lead her readers through the traditions of Irish-American fiction without removing herself or her characters from the demands and possibilities of a modern world.

Elizabeth Cullinan, *House of Gold* (Houghton Mifflin, 1969).

———, *The Time of Adam* (Boston, 1971).

———, "Idioms," *The New Yorker* (31 Jan., 1977).

———, "A Good Loser," *The New Yorker* (15 Aug., 1977).

———, *Yellow Roses* (New York, 1977).

———, "Echoes," *The New Yorker* (15 June 1981).

———, *A Change of Scene* (New York, 1982).

———, "Commuting," *Irish Literary Supplement* (Spring 1983).

———, "The Black Diamond," *Threshold,* Vol. 34 (Winter 1983–1984).

———, "The Promised Land," *Colorado Review,* 20/1 (1993).

Charles Fanning, *The Irish Voice in America: Irish-American Fiction from the 1760s to the 1980s* (Lexington, KY, 1990).

"The Heart of the Story: A Conversation on Writing Fiction Between Elizabeth Cullinan, Steve Heller, and Steven Schwartz," *Colorado Review,* 16/1 (1989).

Eileen Kennedy, "Bequeathing Tokens: Elizabeth Cullinan's Irish-Americans," *Éire-Ireland,* 16/4 (1981).

Maureen Murphy, "Elizabeth Cullinan: Yellow and Gold," *Irish-American Fiction: Essays in Criticism* (AMS, 1979).

Catherine Ward, "Wake Homes: Modern Novels of the Irish-American Family," *Éire-Ireland,* 26/2 (1991).

ELIZABETH BRYMER

## CURLEY, JAMES MICHAEL (1874–1958)

*See* Boston, Twelve Irish-American Mayors of

## CURTIN, JEREMIAH (1835–1906)

Internationally renowned ethnologist, linguist, folklorist, author and diplomat. Toward the end of his life, Jeremiah Curtin recorded in his memoirs that in the twenty-first year of his life, lying in a hay wagon on his family's farm in Greenfield, Wisconsin, he resolved to attend Harvard College and ". . . to find out all that is possible for me to find out about the world and this vast universe. . . . I will have, not the second best, but the best of all the knowledge there is. . . ."

Testimony to the success of the young frontier farm boy's quest was his friend President Theodore Roosevelt's observation on Curtin's passing in 1906 that death had "robbed America of one of its two or three foremost scholars."

Jeremiah Curtin was born on September 6, 1835, in Detroit, Michigan, the eldest of eight children of David Curtin of Bruree, County Limerick, Ireland, and Ellen Furlong of Buttevant, County Cork, Ireland. In 1836 the Curtins and a number of in-laws headed west to the Wisconsin territory, settling on adjoining farms in the Town of Greenfield in the southwestern part of Milwaukee County.

During his first full year at Harvard, Jeremiah mastered eleven languages and by his death he had a speaking knowledge of seventy languages. After graduating in 1863 with a bachelor of arts degree, Curtin was appointed secretary to the American legation in St. Petersburg, Russia (1864–69) by President Lincoln. Embarking on extensive European travel after leaving that post, Curtin returned to America and married Alma Cardell on July 17, 1872. The Cardell family had emigrated to America from County Tyrone, Ireland.

The Curtins formed a close literary team and for the next three decades traveled the world, with Jeremiah serving as lecturer, translator, newspaper correspondent, ethnologist, and linguist. Alma was his secretary, transcriber, editor, and photographer. From 1883 to 1891, Curtin served as an ethnologist with the Smithsonian Institution.

The prodigious literary production of Curtin's later years included sixteen published volumes of translations (from Russian and Polish into English) of novels, short stories, and poetry. His translation of Henry Sienkiewicz's *Quo Vadis* (1896) sold more than a million copies and made the Curtins financially independent.

Curtin also published thirteen volumes (many posthumously) of folklore and mythology collected in his travels. Included in this category were four major compilations of the rich folklore of his ancestral home: *Myths of Ireland* (1890); *Hero Tales of Ireland* (1894); *Tales of the Fairies and of the Ghost World Collected from Oral Tradition in South West Munster* (1895); and *Irish Folk Tales* (1943).

In the last full year of his life, Curtin served as an adviser to President Theodore Roosevelt at the Portsmouth (New Hampshire) Conference (1905) ending the Russo-Japanese War. His facility in both Russian and Japanese proved valuable in several sessions of the conference. Curtin then returned to his wife Alma's home in Bristol, Vermont, where he died on December 14, 1906. He is buried there alongside his wife of thirty-four years.

Three mementos to Curtin's extraordinary career stand in the Milwaukee area today. The Curtin home (built by his father in 1846) still stands on its original site and is operated as a museum by the Milwaukee County Historical Society. Curtin Hall on the University of Wisconsin-Milwaukee campus serves as the university's Foreign Language and Linguistics building. In 1953 the Milwaukee Public School Board dedicated Jeremiah Curtin Elementary School in his honor. Perhaps the most poignant tribute remains the words penned by President Theodore Roosevelt and inscribed on Curtin's tomb: "Historian, ethnologist, linguist, scholar of vast learning, humanitarian, Jeremiah Curtin traveled over the whole world, calling all men his brothers, and learning to speak to them in seventy languages."

Harry H. Anderson, "Jeremiah Curtin's Boyhood in Milwaukee County," *Historical Messenger of the Milwaukee County Historical Society,* Vol. 27/2 (June 1971): 30–50.

Thomas Gildea Cannon, "Jeremiah Curtin: Folklorist, Linguist," *Irish Genealogical Quarterly* 4/1 (1995): 3–10.

Frederick I. Olsen, "The Story of Jeremiah Curtin," *Historical Messenger of the Milwaukee County Historical Society,* Vol. 9/1 (March 1953): 3–7.

Joseph Schafer, ed., *The Memoirs of Jeremiah Curtin* (Madison, Wisconsin, 1940).

CHARLES W. COONEY

## CUSACK, MARGARET ANNE ("The Nun of Kenmare") (1832–1899)

She was born into a wealthy Protestant Dublin family in 1832 and her birthplace is now the College of Surgeons. A precocious and intelligent child, she grew up in an age of religious upheaval and questioning. Affected by the Oxford Movement, she became an Anglican nun in London in 1858, but her independence led to skirmishes with her superiors. She quit the convent and returned to Ireland where she became a Catholic and joined the Poor Clares in Newry. In 1862 she co-founded another Poor Clare convent in Kenmare in South Kerry.

She remained in Kenmare for nineteen years, years of tremendous activity and tumultuous conflicts. The convent, under her direction, became famous for producing elegant lace and won national recognition for its needlepoint. She produced scores of books, including popular works on Daniel O'Connell, Theobald Mathew, an illustrated history of Ireland and *The History of the Kingdom of Kerry*, published in 1871, which is again in print. Her frank political opinions and her nationalist activities brought her into conflict with the local clergy and the bishop of Kerry. In 1879, a year of crop failure and great deprivation, she used her organizational talents and energy to alleviate peasant poverty and her work was praised by Pope Leo XIII.

In 1881 she became a leading voice in the Ladies Land League and shared the uncompromising views of Fanny Parnell. She quit the Poor Clares and founded her own Congregation of St. Joseph of Peace. It failed and faded quickly, and her constant conflicts with bishops shadowed her activities. Eventually she left Ireland and went to America where she got involved in helping Irish immigrants. She was particularly interested in the problems of young Irish women and wrote *Advice to Irish Girls in America.* She split with the Catholic Church and renounced and denounced her former faith. She wrote two autobiographical works, *The Nun of Kenmare* (1889) and *Story of My Life* (1893). Embittered, she went to England and died at Leamington Spa in 1899.

Anne M. Brady and Brian Cleeve, *A Biographical Dictionary of Irish Writers* (Mullingar, Ireland, 1985).
Margaret Anne Cusack, *Advice to Irish Girls in America* (New York, 1886).
Irene French Eager, *The Nun of Kenmare* (London, 1970).

MICHAEL GLAZIER

## CUSHING, RICHARD J. (1895–1970)

Cardinal. Richard J. Cushing was a unique and memorable figure who in historical perspective towers above most churchmen of the twentieth century. He was not an eloquent preacher, nor was he a great theologian, but he was a Christian of extraordinary faith and wide vision. Rather than attempt, in a limited space, to portray the accomplishments of this simple and gifted prelate, it seems more appropriate to focus on the predominant aspect of his life, his charitable activities.

Richard James Cushing was born in South Boston, Massachusetts, on August 23, 1895, the third of five children and elder son of Patrick and Mary Dahill Cushing. His parents were Irish immigrants, and his father was a blacksmith. Cushing attended public elementary schools and graduated from Boston College High School in 1913. After two years of study at Boston College, Cushing entered the diocesan seminary, and was ordained a priest in 1921. He was almost immediately assigned to the diocesan office of the Society for the Propagation of the Faith where his exceptional ability to raise funds for the missions earned him wide recognition. In 1939 he was ordained an auxiliary bishop, and five years later he succeeded Cardinal William O'Connell as

Richard J. Cushing

archbishop of Boston. Cushing was named a cardinal in 1958. He died on November 2, 1970.

The appointment of Richard Cushing as archbishop in 1944 inaugurated a new era in Catholic charity in Massachusetts. In the early twentieth century, under Archbishop John Williams, Boston became one of the first dioceses in the country to place its charities under the aegis of an archdiocesan charitable bureau. William O'Connell, a staunch conservative in fiscal matters, radically expanded the domain and power of this central bureau. Richard Cushing, however, was from the start suspicious of bureaucratic practices in the delivery of charitable services. While he acknowledged that efficiency and accountability had merit, he argued that they hampered the spontaneity and personal involvement so essential in religious giving. "The individual must first be cared for," he cautioned, "and after that the bureau, card index, department and report. Modern philanthropy needs the spirit of St. Vincent de Paul, or else the individual is lost in a maze of records, social processes and philosophy" (Cushing, 1964, p. 60). Consonant with this perspective, Cushing preferred to initiate and supervise benevolent projects himself, leaving the archdiocesan charitable bureau to focus its attention mainly on foster home placement and family services.

Immediately upon assuming office, Cushing commenced the prodigious building program that was to make him an international legend in the field of philanthropy. In 1945 he established the Archbishop Cushing Charity Fund and called on Catholics of every social class to join in building it. "I ask you to think of our private, voluntary, educational, charitable and social institutions as your religious forefathers thought of the building of their cathedrals. Everyone sees in them a monument to the faith and the religious freedom, as well as the genius of those who built them. . . . Our hospitals, schools, asylums for the aged and underprivileged must be the cathedrals of the modern age" (Cushing, 1950, p. 88).

Because he devoted so much of his time to raising funds for a growing number of institutions and social agencies, Cushing frequently quipped that his episcopal motto really was: "Let's take up a collection." His definition of a "collection," however, was decidedly unconventional, extending as it did well beyond familiar appeals at Sunday Mass. Bostonians of all faiths supported the Archbishop's Charity Fund by collecting old automobile license plates for sale as scrap, and by participating in the Archdiocesan Waste Paper Drive, undertaken for the same purpose. Crowds filled Boston Garden for benefit performances by popular stage and screen stars. Fashion shows, horse shows, society balls, and parish bazaars raised substantial sums for the cause. These diverse events not only raised immense sums for charity, but they also offered citizens of every social class a chance to become involved in giving in ways that went well beyond simply making a financial contribution.

Throughout his long tenure as Boston's spiritual leader, Cushing's parishioners responded generously to his vigorous, and seemingly endless, calls for funds and volunteers. And religious communities, whose assistance was essential for the success of the work, gladly sent sisters and brothers to conduct Boston's many new homes, hospitals, social agencies, and schools. During his first five years as archbishop, Cushing brought twenty-eight new religious communities to Boston; by 1962 he had welcomed thirty more.

Several reasons explain Cushing's phenomenal success in fund-raising and in enlisting charity volunteers. In a description he once gave of St. Martin de Porres, he reveals the first reason: "The secret of his success," he maintained, "was his ability to touch the hearts of his benefactors. He was seldom refused, even when he asked for large donations. . . . The reason he was able to get it was that every one knew that whatever was given to him would be spent in its entirety for the purposes for which he begged it" (Cushing, 1962). Like St. Martin, Cushing could say: "When I became a priest, I made a promise never to take any money for myself and that is one promise I have kept" (quoted in Dever, p. 275). That simple statement meant a great deal to his people.

A second reason why Massachusetts citizens supported Cardinal Cushing's numerous benevolent projects lay in his personal example. His crowded schedule attested to his genuine respect and love for the poor, the sick, the elderly, and especially for children in need. For him, charity involved more than simply raising money for institutional support. He visited hospitals, schools, and charitable institutions of the archdiocese, day in and day out, giving freely of his time, his energy, and his renowned good humor. His powerful, personal presence profoundly influenced the level of charitable contributions. In Rome for the election of Pope Paul VI in 1960, he remarked that his absence would adversely affect charitable contributions. "When I'm home, I can raise it. But I've learned, on previous trips out of the country, that our charity alms are reduced to a very low level when I go away" (quoted in Fenton, p. 183).

A third reason for Cushing's success in drawing people to the cause of charity was his ceaseless reminder that religious giving had to be constant, and it had to embrace people in need of every race, religion, and ethnic background. "The obligations of charity are as real as getting up in the morning, and eating your breakfast, and going to work," he admonished parishioners. "They are not the abstract residue of long-forgotten penny catechisms. They are universal and cannot be denied" ("Cardinal Cushing Cries Out for Racial Justice," p. 140).

Throughout his tenure as archbishop, Cushing refused to divert funds contributed for charitable purposes to the building of a contingency fund for future projects or emergencies. He based his unorthodox position on his conviction that religious charity differed fundamentally from secular philanthropy. "All money given for charity in the Archdiocese should be used as it comes along," he contended, "without undue preoccupation with possible depressions or other future contingencies. Contrary practices . . . may be good business; they are not, however, good charity. Money given for charity should be used immediately—for charity. The Archdiocese is big enough and generous enough to take care of crises should crises come" (quoted in Oates, 134–35).

Cushing's original aim, to have every building paid for before it opened, seemed realistic in the post–World War II years, given the rapidly advancing socioeconomic status of Massachusetts Catholics. However, economic prosperity did not guarantee that donations would keep pace with the cardinal's widening charitable horizons and ambitious agenda. In 1967, he inaugurated a "Jubilee Fund Drive" for $50 million, the first appeal for so large a sum in the history of the archdiocese. Past giving records made him optimistic that this immense sum would readily be raised. However, contributions in cash and pledges never exceeded $42 million, and, more troubling, many donors did not honor their pledges. In 1969 a dismayed cardinal disclosed that the jubilee drive had raised only $20 million. At his death the following year, press reports indicated not only that he had raised over $300 million for charity, but also that the outstanding archdiocesan debt was an estimated $60 million. While this debt provoked some to discount his record in the field of charity, in the eyes of millions of Massachusetts citizens, whom he affectionately termed "the salt of the earth," Cushing's achievements were both amazing and unparalleled.

In 1958, Cardinal Cushing attempted to identify the outstanding characteristic of his episcopal predecessors. John Cheverus, he concluded, was best known for his "genial patience," Benedict Fenwick for his "urbane erudition," John Fitzpatrick for his "aggressive valor," John Williams for his "mellow stability, and William O'Connell for his "Roman cosmopolitanism" (quoted in Devine, p. 272). He left others to name his own outstanding virtue. In that regard, there has never been the slightest doubt or dispute. It was his all-encompassing charity.

*See* Boston; Catholicism, Irish-American

"Cardinal Cushing Cries Out for Racial Justice," *Interracial Review,* 37 (July 1964): 140.

"Cardinal Cushing Dies in Boston at 75," *New York Times* (November 3, 1970).

Richard J. Cushing, *Friends of God, Friends of Mine* (Boston, 1964).

———, *St. Martin de Porres* (Boston, 1962).

———, "The Survival of Our Private Charities," *Catholic Charities Review,* 34 (April 1950): 86–91.

John Henry Cutler, *Cardinal Cushing of Boston* (New York, 1970).

Joseph Dever, *Cushing of Boston: A Candid Portrait* (Boston, 1965).

M. C. Devine, *The World's Cardinal* (Boston, 1964).

John H. Fenton, *Salt of the Earth: An Informal Profile of Richard Cardinal Cushing* (New York, 1965).

Mary J. Oates, *The Catholic Philanthropic Tradition in America* (Bloomington, Ind., 1995).

MARY J. OATES, C.S.J.

# D

Larry Langman, *Encyclopedia of American Film Comedy* (New York, 1987): 158.

TOM DOWNEY

## DALEY, RICHARD JOSEPH (1902–1976)

Politician, mayor of Chicago. Born in Chicago on May 15, 1902, Richard Joseph Daley was the grandson of Irish immigrants. He attended Catholic schools and graduated from De Paul University Law School. Although he was admitted to the Illinois bar in 1933, he began a lifelong career in politics three years later, serving in the state assembly from 1936–38 and the state senate from 1939–1946.

He was director of revenue for the state of Illinois for one year, 1949–1950. Five years later, Daley was elected mayor of Chicago, a position he held for twenty-one years. For twenty-three years, he was chairman of the Cook County Democratic Party.

Daley was recognized for the effectiveness of his administration. Even though civil service had practically eliminated the patronage system in most cities, the city's fifty wards, which were directed by Democratic committee men, flourished.

Daley was a devout Catholic, and during his mayoral tenure, he used his influence to assist the Catholic Church and its schools whenever he could. He considered the church's social agencies a boon to the city.

Although Daley was considered to be a "dollar-honest" mayor, he tended to ignore the money-making schemes of those politicians who surrounded him. He believed that as long as the actions weren't immoral or illegal, they could be condoned, and referred to it as "honest graft."

Since many aldermen and appointees received generous contributions to their campaign chests and made money on the side through real estate deals or city-connected law business, Daley saw fit to pay them only modest salaries. He, himself, was more concerned with power than lining his pockets. As chairman of the Cook County Democratic Party, Daley collected almost $15 million in contributions. No evidence points to his using it personally.

Even though Chicago was governed smoothly during most of Daley's tenure, minority neighborhoods didn't fare as well as the white suburban areas. As a result, the civil rights movement brought about a great deal of tension in the city.

In 1960 Daley campaigned for Democratic presidential candidate John F. Kennedy. Through Daley's influence, both Cook County and the state of Illinois gave their votes to the nation's first Catholic president. Those electoral votes gave Kennedy a narrow victory over Republican Richard M. Nixon.

Daley's influence began to wane, both in the state and on the national level, after the 1968 Democratic National Convention, which was held in Chicago. During the convention, the Chicago police were accused of using brutal tactics to subdue demonstrators. Daley supported the police, but other politicians called the demonstrations "a police riot."

Even though Daley received fifty-eight percent of the vote in 1976, his last mayoral election, he began to realize that he was losing control. He also lost a bid to work closely with Jimmy Carter during the 1976 presidential election. Politics as Daley knew it was changing, and he eventually became the last of the big city bosses.

Daley was the first mayor of Chicago to be elected to consecutive four-year terms. He served six four-year terms and died while in office, December 20, 1976.

## DAILEY, DAN (1917–    )

Actor. Born Dan Dailey, Jr., on December 14, 1917, in New York City, his quick Irish smile and good looks, together with a wide range of singing, acting and dancing talents, won him roles in a number of hit films throughout the forties and fifties. Some of these include *The Mortal Storm* (1940); *Ziegfeld Girl* (1941); *Mother* Wore Tights (1947); *Give My Regards to Broadway* (1948); *You're My Everything* (1949); *My Blue Heaven* (1950); *The Pride of St. Louis* (1952); *Meet Me in St. Louis* (1952); *Meet Me at the Fair* (1952); *The Kid from Left Field* (1953); *The Wing of Eagles* (1957); and *Pepe* (1960).

J. Concannon and Frank Cull, *Irish American Who's Who* (New York, 1984).

Joseph Curran, *Hibernian Green on the Silver Screen* (Westport, CT, 1990).

EILEEN DANEY CARZO

## DALEY, CASS (1915–1975)

Comedienne. Born Catherine Daily in Philadelphia. As a child Daley began her entertainment career dancing and singing in the street in front of a neighbor's store. Moving to Camden, New Jersey, she graduated to local night clubs and theaters. Beginning as a singer and dancer, she gradually developed into a comedienne, capitalizing on her dancing ability to create a highly physical comedy routine heavily dependent on slapstick and sight gags. Her growing popularity attracted the attention of Broadway impresario Flo Ziegfeld. Seeing in Daley the possibility of another Fannie Brice, Ziegfeld signed Daley to a contract, shortened her name, and placed her in the lead role of his 1936–1937 Ziegfeld Follies. Daley became an immediate Broadway star, and later increased her popularity with radio appearances as well. By World War II, she had become one of America's favorite comic stars. A film career began in 1942 with Paramount, who starred Daley in a dozen movies from 1942 to 1954, all of which met with popular, if not critical, success. By 1948, Daley decided to scale back her career and start a family. Her only child, a son named Dale, was born later that same year. In the late 1960s, she began a comeback with the films *The Spirit Is Willing* and *Norwood: The Phynx*. She returned to Broadway in 1972 with *The Big Show of 1936*. Sadly, at the peak of her comeback, Daley died suddenly in 1975 as a result of an accident in her home in Hollywood.

*See* Cinema, Irish in

*Dictionary of American Biography*, Supplement 9: 215–16.

Ephraim Katz, *The Film Encyclopedia* (New York, 1994): 320.

The Daley legacy continued, however, when his son, Richard M. Daley, took over the city's reins a few years later. In 1999 his son was elected to his fourth term as mayor.

*See* Chicago, Aspects of; Chicago Politics

Paul M. Green, "Irish Chicago: The Multiethnic Road to Machine Success," *Ethnic Chicago,* ed. by Peter d'A. Jones and Melvin J. Holli (Grand Rapids, Mich., 1981).

Harold Mayer and Richard Wade, *Growth of a Metropolis* (Chicago, 1969).

Lawrence McCaffrey, et al., *The Irish in Chicago* (Urbana, Ill., and Chicago, 1987).

Mike Royko, *Boss: Richard J. Daley of Chicago* (New York, 1971).

R. Timothy Unsworth, "Richard Joseph Daley," *The Encyclopedia of American Catholic History,* Michael Glazier and Thomas J. Shelley, eds. (Collegeville, Minn., 1997).

MARIANNA McLOUGHLIN

## DALY, JOHN AUGUSTIN (1838–1899)

Playwright and producer. Born July 20, 1838, in Plymouth, N.C., John Augustin Daly was the son of Capt. Denis and Elizabeth (Duffey) Daly. His father was a shipowner and his mother the daughter of a lieutenant in the British army.

Following his father's death, his mother moved to New York with her two sons, Augustin (as he was known) and Joseph. Augustin became enthralled with the theatre and joined several amateur organizations.

Daly, however, was interested more in producing and directing plays than in acting. At the age of 18, he rented a hall in Brooklyn and produced a variety of plays, ranging from *Toodles* to *Macbeth.* Reviews of that venture were mixed, and Daly then began a 10-year career as a drama critic for several New York newspapers. During that period in his life, he also began writing his own plays.

After several rejections, *Leah the Forsaken,* an adaptation of the German play *Deborah* by S. H. von Mosenthal, was first staged at the Howard Athenaeum in Boston Dec. 8, 1862. Following that success, Daly began experimenting with adaptations of French and German plays and in dramatizations of novels.

His first original play, *Under the Gaslight,* was staged at the New York Theatre on Aug. 12, 1867. The story line introduced a scene that would be used in countless melodramas, the rescue of a person who was bound to a railroad track in the path of an oncoming train. His work, *The Red Scarf,* which premiered in 1869, used a similar technique with the hero bound to a log that was about to be sawed in half.

On Jan. 9, 1869, Daly married Mary Duff, whose father owned the Olympic Theatre. In August of that year, Daly leased the Fifth Avenue Theatre and established his own theatrical company. He began producing older English comedies of manners and worked toward productions of Shakespeare. His *Saratoga* in 1870 was a boost to American playwrights at a time when theatre managers were concentrating on foreign plays.

Daly's best play, *Horizon,* was performed March 21, 1871, at the Olympic Theatre. The play, which depicted Western American life, laid the foundation for realism in the work of American playwrights. In *Divorce* he attacked that growing social phenomenon in American society. The play, which began Sept. 5, 1871, at the Fifth Avenue Theatre, became one of that theatre's greatest successes, running for two hundred nights.

In 1873 Daly formed an organization among New York's producing managers by which actors would be loaned to the various theatres. That same year on Dec. 3, the New Fifth Avenue Theatre, which was built for him on Twenty-Eighth Street near Broadway opened.

In 1879 Daly began staging adaptations of French and German dramas and solicited works of American playwrights. At the Old Broadway Theatre, which was renamed Daly's Theatre, he assembled a company that included several prominent actors, including John Drew and Otis Skinner. However, Daly was known for casting ensemble performances without emphasis on stars.

In the 1880s Daly took the company to Europe, playing in London and Germany, where the first English-speaking company performed in nearly three hundred years. His efforts received mixed reviews in Berlin and Paris.

On June 27, 1893, Daly opened a theatre in London and staged *Twelfth Night,* which ran for one hundred nights. Upon his return to America, he continued productions of Shakespeare. During a business trip abroad to settle financial difficulties with his theatre in London, Daly died June 7, 1899, in Paris.

Daly wrote or adapted about ninety plays that were produced on stage. However, he never allowed any of his plays to be published, although many were privately printed. Daly was a skilled dramatist who achieved a unique role as manager, playwright and director in American theatre.

*See* Theater, Irish in

Joseph F. Daly, *The Life of Augustin Daly* (1917).

M. Felkeim, *The Theater of Augustin Daly* (Cambridge, Mass., 1956).

J. R. Towse, "A Critical Review of Daly's Theatre," and G. P. Lathrop, "The Inside Working of the Theatre," *Century* (June 1898).

MARIANNA McLOUGHLIN

## DALY, MARCUS (1841–1900)

Miner, copper king. Butte, Montana bills itself "the richest hill on earth," and Marcus Daly was the man who made it so. A native of Ballyjamesduff, Co. Cavan, Daly arrived in the United States still a teenager. For the first 20 years or so of his life, his story differed little from that of many Irish immigrants: manual labor at poor wages.

But much of his sweat was expended in the silver fields of Nevada, where he worked hard to learn the mining business. Eventually, he came to the attention of the Walker brothers, mine owners in Salt Lake City. They dispatched him to Montana to investigate the potential of the Alice Silver Mine. Daly not only recommended purchase, he threw $5,000 of his own savings into the deal. It was a good bet. He eventually sold out his interest for $30,000.

Geologists thought the Butte area exhausted, but Daly thought differently. He bought the Anaconda Silver Mine, and while the silver soon gave out, he sunk a shaft in what seemed like an unpromising area and struck an exceptionally rich vein of copper. Thus was born the legend of Marcus Daly and the fabulous Anaconda Copper Company.

Daly's fame spread far and wide, partly because, recalling his own roots as a low-paid laborer, he paid $3.50 for an eight-hour day. That was almost twice what industrial workers were making elsewhere. So many Irish immigrants flocked to Butte—and did so well once they got there—that Eamon de Valera made the city a stop on his periodic fund-raising tours of the United States early in the 20th century.

Building one of the greatest fortunes in 19th-century America, Daly used his money to make big improvements around Butte. He built power plants, irrigation stations, railroads, lumber mills and banks. He was the major contributor to the construction of the memorial at the Montana state capitol to Civil War Irish Brigade commander Thomas Francis Meagher.

A strong Democrat, Daly was one of Populist William Jennings Bryan's strongest supporters in his 1896 campaign. (An estimated 20 percent of all the money Bryan spent came from Daly.) The Irishman also engaged in a long-running and bitter feud with William Andrews Clark, a rival copper king who was a Republican. Clark very much wanted to be a U.S. senator, but Daly saw to it that his ambition was consistently thwarted. Clark finally won his Senate seat, but only after Daly's death in 1900.

*See* Montana

John A. Barnes, *Irish-American Landmarks* (Detroit, 1995).
David M. Emmons, *The Butte Irish: Class and Ethnicity in the American Mining Town* (Urbana: Chicago, 1990).

JOHN A. BARNES

## DAYTON, OHIO

Along with other local Midwestern cities, Dayton, Ohio, possessed a foreign-born population markedly lower than the mean for large American cities. Dayton—the ninth largest city in the Midwest—was almost last percentage-wise among major U.S. cities in 1870 and 1910 with Irish-born immigrants. In any decade, German-born outnumbered the native Irish by a minimum of three to one. Nevertheless, a primarily native-born population formed the most important ethnic fact about Dayton. The 1,252 native Irish in 1910 Dayton lived in a city of 117,000 that was eighty-four percent native-born. In what follows, the focus will be that of Famine-Irish Dayton, the years when native Irish had their greatest demographic impact on the city.

### THE ETHNIC CONTEXT

Some Protestant Irish figured prominently in the founding of Dayton. A significant portion of the inhabitants of early Dayton and the counties surrounding it was Scotch-Irish, often Irish Presbyterian. The Ireland-born George Newcom founded the first saloon and served as the first peace officer. Many of these families, such as the Pattersons of National Cash Register fame, continued to dominate much of the city's business, social, and intellectual life. Some unexplored percentage of Irish-born Protestants played roles later in Dayton's history. For example, John Breene, a carpenter-turned-politician and living in an area that had an important number of Catholic Irish, was both buried in the Episcopal church in 1881 and eulogized as "an impulsive Irishman, a Tipperary boy."

Few nineteenth-century Daytonians are linked or identified with counties in Ireland. In the (Catholic) Calvary records, nineteenth-century Irish Daytonians came from twenty-six of Ireland's thirty-two counties. Clare, Tipperary, Kerry, Mayo, and Dublin sired most of the nineteenth-century Dayton (Catholic) Irish. For most Daytonians, however, the Irish county of origin is known at the moment only to family genealogists.

For some decades, the largest concentration of Ireland-born was to be found among the retired and sick soldiers at the Soldiers' Home. The Home formed a geographic (but not political) arc of Irish influence with the rather small number of Irish west of the Miami River and with *the* Irish ward on the immediate east side. When, as so often happened, Dayton held no St. Patrick's Day parade, some Dayton Irish went the four miles west of Dayton to the Home to march and to celebrate. The commercial center downtown, the canal system which bisected Dayton, and the heavily German wards separated these Irish from the second largest Irish ward, which was centered from St. Joseph's church east to a burgeoning industrial area. South of Dayton, and almost touching the city boundaries, was another concentration of Irish working in the stone quarries of "Dayton Marble." Also in that area was St. Mary's, an institute that illustrated the decisive turn-of-the-century divide in the Dayton Catholic Church and in much of Dayton in general. This heavily German (and French) institution had in 1870 only one Irish teacher and no Irish-born among its 250 students. Just a few blocks north was the most concentrated Irish ward. However, at least half of the Irish there in 1870 had at least one German neighbor; in fact almost every Irish family had at least one German or American-born neighbor. Also here, African-Americans waited in one of their three churches for news of the Emancipation Proclamation and later for passage of the Fifteenth Amendment. (In the next decades they would go to these same churches to plan how to negate the votes of their Irish and German neighbors.) But the lack of substantial numbers made it impossible for the Irish to control either the Catholic Church or to dominate the various infrastructures of the city.

### DAYTON CATHOLICISM

Little is known of John McAfee, who after murdering his wife in 1825, was accompanied by a Catholic priest at Dayton's first hanging. The first acknowledged Catholic (and Irish) family arrived from Maryland in 1831, but soon found itself swamped by an influx of German Catholics whose Emmanuel church did not hear its first English sermon till 1903. St. Joseph Parish was founded in 1847 as the first English-speaking or "Irish" parish. Its founders included a number of French and German, particularly the Ohmers who were already prominent businessmen by 1850. The Dayton Famine Irish immigrants did not install an Irish-dominated Catholicism. In 1882, Sacred Heart, another Irish parish, started. Cordial relations continued between the two Irish parishes as the Hickey brothers pastored both parishes for many years.

The Dayton Irish had little interest in Irish nationalism. They gave no backing to the Fenians and disapproved of their raids on Canada. Fr. Richard Gilmour of St. Joseph's—later bishop of Cleveland—went so far as to excommunicate some women Land Leaguers. And Charles Steward Parnell ignored Dayton when he visited nearby Springfield.

Nevertheless, the 140-member Dayton AOH celebrated in 1903 its twenty-fifth anniversary with two hundred guests attending a banquet. By the 1890s and continuing into the early 1920s, there were three divisions of the AOH, two of the Ladies' AOH, as well as the Hibernian Rifles. At the 1910 state convention, the Dayton AOH reported a membership (excluding AOH men) of four hundred of the Ladies and 125 of the Hibernian Rifles. Today more than a hundred members continue the AOH tradition.

WAGE EARNERS

When John Breene came to Dayton to escape the Famine, 284 Ireland-born citizens lived in all wards of the city of nearly eleven thousand. Half of the family groups reported personal value to the 1850 census-taker ranging from $300 to $1,000. One-parent households reported a median value of $800. The 1870 census showed a town of 30,473 with 1,326 Irish-born of which one of three married working men was a laborer. Significantly, many older married laborers reported more substantial sums. One in eight married men filled factory jobs; one in eight worked on the railroad; and one in eight either toiled as a drayman or blacksmith. Ten percent were in journeymen trades such as carpenter, tailor, or shoemaker. Only one percent ran saloons, and one percent were in the city police.

Dayton's working Irish illustrate how success in America came more readily for adaptable individuals with some roots in an ethnic community. For example, Dennis Dwyer and William P. Callahan worked on the same bench in Ohmer's workshop in their first days in Dayton. Later Dwyer became a judge for decades and a pillar of St. Joseph's parish. Callahan died in 1903 as the "local prince of Industry," and—although "not conforming to any particular denomination"—was buried with Episcopalian rites. Less spectacularly, foreman William Turner facilitated communal and personal integration through his two-decade patronage of his Irish brethren at late nineteenth-century Barney and Smith Car Company. If one excludes young married couples, some eighty percent of Dayton Irish families reported enough personal wealth in the 1870 Census to be listed. Compared to the national figures found in an 1889 Department of Labor data, 1870 Dayton had a remarkably small number [.5%] of Irish wives working, and an average level [20%] of working children supplementing the family household budget. In 1870, ninety percent of the children of Ireland-born parents had been born in Ohio.

The 1850 census showed an Irish Justice of the Peace but no Irish city police. By 1870 there were three Ireland-born police, two others with Irish wives, and an Irish JP and a U.S. Marshal. In 1883, the Police Benevolent Association and the Police Commissioners Board had only one Irish officer each. Four Irish-born police worked in 1910 with colleagues, eighty-six percent of whom were born in Ohio. A more substantial Irish-ing of the Fire Department seems to have taken place in the same period. The number of fire department and police positions reflects the influence of Irish politicians who sought city jobs for their own but their influence was limited.

*See* Ohio

Emil Pocock, *Evangelical Frontier: Dayton, OH, 1796–1830* (Ph.D. diss., Indiana University, 1984).

LEROY V. EID

## DEASY, MARY MARGARET (1914–1978)

Author. Mary Deasy was born May 20, 1914, to William Paul Deasy and Clara Laura (Woelfel) in Cincinnati, Ohio of Irish and German ancestry. At age five she began piano study with her mother and went on to the Cincinnati Conservatory of Music, winning five scholarships, and graduating in 1935 with a Bachelor of Music degree. Deasy had also begun to write at the age of five. After a brief stint as a concert pianist, she opted against the demands of a music career and turned to the writing profession instead, having written a first novel at age eleven. She traveled throughout the United States for ten years studying, observing, and gathering subject material. Returning to Cincinnati after these travels, she began to publish well-received short stories, some of which were included in the *O. Henry Memorial Award Short Stories* (1945, 1947, 1962), and the *Best American Short Stories* (1945, 1946, 1953). Her stories, such as "A Sense of Danger," "Morning Sun," and "The People with the Charm," were lauded for their characterization, intensity, understanding, and narration skills, and appeared in *The Atlantic Monthly, New Yorker, Harper's, Virginia Quarterly Review,* and other literary reviews and magazines.

Deasy studied her favorite writers, among them George Meredith, Thomas Hardy, Henry James, James Joyce, along with the Russian novelists, and began to publish her own novels, beginning with *Hours of Spring* in 1948, which may be her best. Set in 1941, it concerns third-generation Irish-American Bride Joyce who rediscovers her County Kerry forebears through a series of interviews, and most closely resembles Deasy's own family background. Considered a regional realist, Mary Deasy was concerned with urban Irish-Americans living in the Ohio River Valley in Ohio and Kentucky; she studied the weaknesses, as well as the strengths, of multi-generational Irish-American family life. Other Irish-interest novels followed: *Cannon Hill* (1949), a Family Reading Club selection, *Ellen Gunning* (1950) which concerned marriage versus career, *Devil's Bridge* (1952), *The Boy Who Made Good* (1955), *The Corioli Affair* (1954), *O'Shaughnessy's Day* (1957), and *The Celebration* (1963). Family themes and politics were the focii of her work: *O'Shaughnessy's Day* centers on a ward boss and the impact of his death; *Devil's Bridge* revolves around an idealistic bridge builder faced with political corruption; and *The Boy Who Made Good* tells of a state official's return to politics. Deasy probes family complexities and these works are generally set in time from the 1890s to the 1920s, with a Celtic central figure. This fictional world is an orderly balance of triumphs and failures. Her writing from this period received superior critical reviews (several were book club choices), and were published in Belgium, Denmark, France, Germany, Great Britain, Norway and Spain.

But the very private Mary Deasy continued to produce in secrecy more than a novel a year from 1971 to 1978: eschewing publicity, she wrote under the pen name of Clare Darcy. Only her family and publishers (J. Walker & Co. and G. K. Hall) knew her identity until shortly after her death. In choosing anonymity Deasy turned from writing as a regional realist to creating Regency romances. The narrow historical Regency period in England lay from 1811 to 1820 when George III was king, but the country was ruled by his son George IV due to his father's insanity. The Regency fiction style was created in the nineteenth century by English novelist Jane Austin (1775–1817); Georgette Heyer (1902–1974) is considered a major modern Regency writer. The proper behavior of dashing men and well-mannered beautiful women, set within discreet romantic plots form the readable ingredients of Regency fiction. Deasy's very popular output (local librarians and neighbors were stunned to learn her true identity) included *Georgina* (1971), *Cecily; or, a Young Lady of Quality* (1972), *Lydia; or, Love in Town* (1973), *Victoire* (1974), *Allegra* (1975), *Lady Pamela* (1975), *Elyza* (1976), *Regina* (1976), *Cressida* (1977), *Eugenia* (1977), *Gwendolen* (1978), *Rolande* (1978), *A Clare Darcy Trilogy* (1979), *Letty* (1980), and *Caroline and Julia* (1982). Her novels were published in England, Italy, and Germany as well. Continuing to enjoy playing the piano daily, she lived with her sister, Dr. Clara L. Deasy, who was on the faculty of the College of Mount St. Joseph and the University of Cincinnati; her brother, Dr. George F. Deasy, was on the faculty of Penn State University. The Department of Special Collections at Boston University contains her manuscript material which includes novels, short stories, and articles, along with notebooks of research notes and scrapbooks of clippings and reviews of her work; it also includes correspondence covering 1936–1978 with publishers and agents concerning her novels, and some photographs of the author. Mary Deasy died of cancer on May 14, 1978, at the height of her hidden popularity, and was buried at Mother of God Cemetery in Covington, Kentucky.

*See* Fiction, Irish-American

*Biographical Dictionary of Contemporary Catholic American Writing,* ed. Daniel J. Tynan (New York, 1989).
*Contemporary Authors,* vols. 5–8 (Detroit, 1969).
*Current Biography* (1958).
Rosemary Davis, "Queen City Was Home to Author," *Cincinnati Enquirer* (May 19, 1978): D1, col.2, obituary.
Bonnie Kime Scott, "Women's Perspectives in Irish-American Fiction from Betty Smith to Mary McCarthy," in *Irish-American Fiction: Essays in Criticism* (New York, 1979).
*Who Was Who in America,* vol. 7 (1977–81).

ANNA M. DONNELLY

## DECLARATION OF INDEPENDENCE, THE

The Declaration of Independence stated America's major war aim: independence from Great Britain. When it was adopted, a large number of people in the thirteen States were of Irish birth or descent. A small number were Irish Catholics, for most colonies had banned Catholics. Scotch-Irish immigrants from Ulster, mostly Presbyterians, were the largest Irish group in British North America. Many of Irish birth or descent helped lead the Independence movement; others moved more slowly toward complete independence; some took no position, or opposed the idea of independence.

### THE CONTINENTAL CONGRESS

The Continental Congress which adopted the Declaration of Independence counted many of America's leaders among its members. The members of Congress had been appointed by their State legislatures, so membership showed their community standing. Fifty-six persons signed the Declaration, and have earned places among the founding fathers of the United States.

Three of these "Signers" were Irish-born, a strong indication that energetic and ambitious immigrants had become community leaders. All three were of Scotch-Irish descent. Matthew Thornton (1714–1803), who represented New Hampshire, was a physician and an active agitator against British misrule in America. He was elected to Congress in 1776, but stayed in New Hampshire to organize the Committee on Public Safety—the State's defense agency. He reached Philadelphia in November, long after the debates on the Declaration, but he signed it anyway!

Thornton was not the only late "Signer." Several Pennsylvania delegates signed late, because some original Pennsylvania delegates were removed from Congress for opposing the Declaration. Two new members were the other Irish-born signers: George

Taylor (1716–1781), an iron master, and James Smith (1719–1806), a lawyer. Both signed in August 1776. Delaware's Thomas McKean (1734–1817), of Scotch-Irish descent, insured that Congress would vote for Independence by getting his colleague Caesar Rodney to Philadelphia in time to vote. McKean wrote that nobody actually signed the Declaration on July 4. Matthew Thornton may well have been the last person to sign it.

Another late Signer was Charles Carroll of Carrollton (1737–1832), the only Roman Catholic signer. He was elected to Congress on July 4, 1776, and got to Philadelphia in time to vote for publishing the Declaration, which he signed on August 2. Carroll was descended from an old Gaelic family that moved to Maryland in the 1680s. He was one of the wealthiest men at the Congress, and risked a great deal when he joined in pledging his life, fortune, and sacred honor to the cause of independence. After independence, Carroll served as a Senator, and became one of the original directors of the Baltimore and Ohio Railroad.

### COMMITMENT TO INDEPENDENCE

The Declaration of Independence came about after long debate and preparation, both in and outside the Continental Congress. Public opinion was the first battleground for the Revolution. Men of Irish birth or descent helped establish an atmosphere in which a Declaration could be issued. Charles Carroll of Carrollton first became a public figure in the drive to form public opinion in Maryland. He published letters opposing Daniel Dulany (1722–1797), who was defending an arbitrary English Governor's actions. Dulany, son of an Irish immigrant lawyer, was charged as a Loyalist during the Revolutionary War.

The most dramatic commitment to independence was made by those who fought in the Revolutionary War. Substantial numbers of Irish names appear on Continental or State military rosters. A few may be cited as examples as well as many others.

Dublin-born Richard Montgomery (1738–1775) had served in North America as an officer in the British Army. He left royal service and settled in New York in 1772. Three years later he was one of the Continental Army's first Brigadier Generals, committed to defending American rights. He died months before the Declaration, leading his troops in a winter attack on Quebec.

Two of the Continental Army's Generals descended from families that had lived in Ireland. "Mad Anthony" Wayne's father had immigrated to Pennsylvania from Ireland. Wayne (1745–1796) won his nickname in several battles in which he seemed almost reckless at the head of his troops. After Independence, he was a civilian for only a short time. In 1791, he was appointed Major General in command of the newly organized, tiny regular army of the United States.

John Sullivan (1740–1795) was a lawyer whose family moved from Limerick to a Scotch-Irish area of New Hampshire. He helped lead the State's independence movement, sat in two Continental Congresses, but joined the Army before the Declaration of Independence. He had a mixed military career: captured at the Battle of Brooklyn, but successful at the battles of Trenton and Princeton, and as leader of an expedition to crush Iroquois power in western New York.

The small Irish-Catholic population provided numbers of volunteer troops and seamen. Two leading Irish-Catholic officers were, naturally enough, Philadelphia residents: Philadelphia was one of the very few places a Catholic could worship openly in the early 1770s. Stephen Moylan (1737–1811), born in Cork, was a successful merchant in Philadelphia before the war. He was on

Washington's staff as an aide with rank of Colonel in 1776, and later commanded the Continental cavalry, succeeding the Polish volunteer Casimir Pulaski.

John Barry (1745–1803), born in Tacumshane in Wexford, settled in Philadelphia in 1760, and had a successful career as a ship captain and trader. At the outbreak of war, he became a Captain in the infant U.S. Navy. He commanded the *Lexington,* the first American warship to capture an enemy vessel. After the British captured Philadelphia, he served on the *Delaware,* took part in the battles of Trenton and Princeton, then returned to sea as a combat captain. In 1794 he became Senior Captain in the Navy.

Bernard Bailyn, *The Ideological Origins of the American Revolution* (Cambridge, 1967).

Thomas Fleming, *Liberty* (New York, 1996).

*Dictionary of American Biography* (New York, 1936).

JOSEPH F.X. McCARTHY

## DELANTY, GREG (1958– )

Poet. Greg Delanty was born in Cork City, Ireland, on July 19, 1958. He was educated at Coláiste Chríost Rí and then at University College Cork, where he received his B.A. in English literature and history in 1980, followed by a higher diploma in 1982. While at U.C.C. he edited the arts magazine and published his first poems in *The Examiner.* The year following his graduation, in 1983, Delanty received the Patrick Kavanagh Memorial Award for poetry; in 1986 he was awarded the Allan Dowling Poetry Fellowship in the United States. His first book, *Cast in the Fire,* was published by the Dolmen Press in that year and was praised for the "fine sense of form" employed therein.

In subsequent collections, Delanty's poetry has adhered more or less to a "sense" of form, though the fineness and the compactness have roughened up and opened considerably. His poetry is characterized by the play of the personal voice (he is primarily lyrical) in an idiom of its own, one which draws abundantly on the dialect and "slanguage" of his native Cork. Delanty likes to twist the familiar turn of phrase even further, to buff the dulled and hackneyed till it alights in sudden clarity; in this he takes after a poet like Seamus Heaney. But Heaney's experience, that of the Irish "inner émigré," is expanded in Delanty's work by way of his own emigration to America, and by his facing and "fessing" up to the ambiguities of a split identity, "Irish-American."

Indeed, much of Delanty's work since his second volume, *Southward* (1992), has concentrated on the experience of exile (self-imposed), combined with the yearning for a sense of roots after self-extirpation (he emigrated to the U.S. in 1986). The conflicting strands of rootlessness and growth come together in a powerful way in Delanty's third book, *American Wake* (1995). Poems like "The Fat Yank's Lament (*to the Irish-Irish*)" and "Christopher Ricks's Oxford" articulate with wit and finesse the poet's attempt to fashion "home" out of its off-rhyme "poem." Delanty's grace is his sense of self-irony; many times it is humor that salvages him from the dreaded "wiles of nostalgia" ("In Search of the American Celts"). Indeed, the strength of the work thus far resides in his ability to press beyond the sentimental trappings of that word (nostalgia) into its original sense in English of a pathological condition. The poems, for all their wit, remain a witness to that pathology and poignancy.

Along with the experience of the emigrant, the tradition and lore of hot-metal printing has informed Delanty's work. He was born into a family of printers (his father, grandfather, uncles, and cousins all were compositors). As a youth he worked in the composing room of the Eagle Printing Company in Cork, and that experience finds ample treatment in his fourth book, *The Hellbox* (1998). The hellbox, a melting bin for worn or broken type, is an apt symbol for Delanty's own experience and heritage as he has and continues to recast it in his poems. He currently lives in Vermont with his wife, Patricia Ferreira, and teaches at St. Michael's College.

*See* Poetry, Irish-American

Greg Delanty, *Cast in the Fire* (Dolmen Press, 1986).

———, *Southward* (Dublin: Dedalus, 1992).

———, *American Wake* (Belfast: Blackstaff Press, Ltd., 1995).

———, *The Hellbox* (Oxford, 1998).

TODD HEARON

## DELAWARE

### The Colonial Era

The Irish in Delaware have received little scholarly attention, a fact that is surprising since their presence in the First State dates to the last quarter of the seventeenth century. According to the WPA Guide, the young colony had already changed hands four times by this point. In 1610 the directors of the Dutch West India Company claimed all lands west of the Delaware River and Bay for Holland, but with the exception of a short-lived settlement at Swanendael (now Lewes), near present-day Cape Henlopen, their primary concern was the trading post at New Amsterdam (now New York). As a result, the first permanent settlement in Delaware was established by the New Sweden Company in 1638. Peter Minuit, the same Dutch explorer who negotiated the purchase of Manhattan, led an independent Dutch-Swedish expedition and constructed a fort near the juncture of the Christina and Delaware rivers. By 1643 the Swedish investors had bought out their Dutch partners and sent their first governor, Johan Printz, to administer the small colony. Holland continued to press its original claim, however, and in 1651, Peter Stuyvesant, governor of New Netherland, sent two warships to establish a Dutch fort along the Delaware River, roughly six miles south of the Swedish settlement. Four years later, the Dutch finally forced the Swedes to capitulate, and their small encampment on the Delaware, renamed New Amstel, became New Netherland's southern capital.

Their victory was short-lived. In 1664, the English fleet sailed into the harbor at New Amsterdam and demanded that the Dutch surrender the entire colony of New Netherland to James, the Duke of York. Then, in 1682, James, in turn, ceded the lower portion of his claim to William Penn, who founded the colony of Pennsylvania (WPA, *Delaware,* pp. 21–41). Penn, a relative newcomer to the Society of Friends, had embraced the Quaker faith while managing his father's estate in northern Ireland, and he actively encouraged Irish dissenters to migrate to the New World. By the end of the century, Irish Quakers were safely ensconced in the old Dutch village of New Amstel, now New Castle, where their rising numbers began to affect the history of colonial Delaware. George Harland, for example, a native of County Down, settled in New Castle around 1687 and served briefly as colonial governor. After the three "Lower Counties" achieved their independence from Pennsylvania in 1704, New Castle served as Delaware's colonial capital. Because its quarantine regulations were less severe than Baltimore's or Philadelphia's, it also remained the chief port of entry for Irish immigrants into the mid-Atlantic region during this period (Purcell, "Irish Settlers in Early Delaware," p. 95).

The number of Irish immigrants in Delaware rose steadily through the eighteenth century. As time went on, they increasingly pushed inland from New Castle, establishing numerous small plantations and making ties with their Swedish, Finnish, Dutch, and English neighbors. In response to the westward-moving population, Andrew Justison and his Quaker son-in-law, Thomas Willing, laid out a new settlement adjacent to the old Swedish fort. Platted in several stages between 1730 and 1735, the settlement, called Willingtown, was intended to be "a farmer's town, a place of trade, and for the service of ships and mills" (WPA, *Delaware,* p. 267). Located at the juncture of the Christina River and the Brandywine Creek, the site was ideal for development. Settlers soon built a market house, a brewery, shipping wharves, warehouses, a ropewalk, a sail loft, and several shipyards. The level of commerce between Delaware, the West Indies, Ireland, and England also served as an early catalyst for local industry. Northern Delaware's landscape is characterized by gently rolling hills and swiftly flowing streams that once provided an abundant source of water power. By 1750 the flourishing community, rechristened Wilmington, was the most important flour milling center in the colonies. Rolling, slitting, saw, woolen, and snuff mills were in operation as well, and consequently, skilled artisans were in great demand. Evidence from daybooks and ledgers reveals that most of the men who filled these positions were Irish (Drescher, "The Irish in Wilmington, 1800–1845," pp. 16–19). Many came as redemptioners or indentured servants, but some were entrepreneurs. Francis Robinson, for example, an Irish Quaker, opened the first documented tanyard in Delaware in 1732 and became a prosperous merchant (Purcell, "Irish Settlers in Early Delaware," p. 96). The best-known Irish immigrant was Archibald Hamilton Rowan, a wealthy landowner who was imprisoned in Ireland for "plotting against the English government." In 1790 he escaped and came to Delaware, where he operated a calico printing and dying factory. English handbills offered ten thousand pounds reward for his recapture, but Rowan lived out his days in peace (WPA, *Delaware,* pp. 294–295).

As in the earlier period, most eighteenth-century Irish emigrants came to America hoping to better their condition, but refuge from religious persecution was another important motive. An early historian of Delaware's Irish community, Michael O'Brien, examined marriage and baptismal registers at Wilmington's Old Swedes (Lutheran) Church and discovered a dramatic rise in Irish membership beginning in 1714. Many of these individuals were identified as Presbyterians; in 1740 they finally organized their own congregation. Catholics were noted in the registers as well (O'Brien, "Irish Pioneers in Delaware," p. 187). Both groups were increasingly subject to penal laws in Ireland, and after the passage of a religious toleration act by the Delaware assembly in 1743, ships carrying refugees from Belfast were a regular sight at the New Castle wharves (Purcell, "Irish Settlers in Early Delaware," p. 97). The most prominent colonial Catholic was Cornelius Halloran, a well-to-do Irish emigrant who purchased a 250-acre tract in New Castle County from William

Penn's daughter, Letitia. The first documented Roman Catholic services in Delaware were held at his estate, Mount Cuba, now the site of an important observatory. As the number of Catholics in the vicinity grew, Halloran founded St. Mary's (Coffee Run) parish, a small, Jesuit mission served by circuit-riding priests from Maryland. Its little log church, built in 1790, was the first permanent Catholic church in Delaware (Mulrooney, "Labor at Home," p. 103).

Irish immigration necessarily slowed during the American Revolution, but those already settled here made important contributions to the war effort. As many as sixty percent of the soldiers recorded in New Castle County's militia rolls were of Irish extraction (O'Brien, "Irish Pioneers in Delaware," p. 188). A few, like Captain Robert Kirkwood, served with distinction. Born in Londonderry, Kirkwood led an independent regiment in the battles of Cowpens and Guilford Courhouse. After the war, some went on to achieve political success, including physician John McKinley (1721–1796), who became the first president of the state and was captured briefly by the British (WPA, *Delaware,* p. 48). The most prominent Irishman of the revolutionary era was lawyer George Read (1733–1798). The son of a native Dubliner, Read achieved fame as a signer of the Declaration of Independence and as a delegate to the Constitutional Convention (Purcell, "Irish Settlers in Early Delaware," p. 96).

## THE NINETEENTH CENTURY

The main impetus for Irish immigration during this period was the unprecedented economic growth of the region. Federalists in Delaware fully endorsed Alexander Hamilton's plan to finance internal improvements and facilitate trade. To that end, a detailed map showing the best transportation routes between Baltimore and Philadelphia was prepared and advertised between 1797 and 1801. The public works projects that resulted, including the Newport-Gap Turnpike, the Delaware and Hudson Canal, and the New Castle and Frenchtown Railroad, attracted thousands of unskilled Irish emigrants. By the time it opened in 1829, the Chesapeake and Delaware Canal, alone, had employed more than 2,000 Irish laborers (Drescher, "The Irish in Wilmington, 1800–1845," p. 21). Once their work contracts ended, the Irish fanned out across the state. Some made their way south to Dover, which had become the state capital in 1777, or to Delaware City, the eastern terminus of the Chesapeake and Delaware Canal. The majority of Irish laborers, however, gravitated towards the numerous industrial villages that were springing up in northern New Castle County.

The Irish in Delaware benefited greatly from the development of two new industries, textile and black powder manufacturing. The War of 1812 and the embargoes that preceded it stimulated the construction of cotton and woolen mills throughout the Brandywine valley. The growth of textile manufacturing, in turn, spurred the growth of iron foundries and machine shops to fabricate and repair the intricate carding, spinning, and weaving machinery. Surviving wage books at the Hagley Museum and Library confirm that emigrants from the British Isles made up the bulk of the local workforce, with families from northern Ireland still in the majority. The largest single employer of Irish immigrants during this period was E. I. du Pont de Nemours and Company, founded in 1802, just three miles west of Wilmington. Despite a slow and shaky start, the company secured a contract with the federal government in 1812 and began to expand. By mid-century, it operated three separate powder yards, five textile mills, a keg mill, and several farmsteads. This extensive property served as the firm's home plant until 1921 (Mulrooney, "Labor at Home," p. 39).

To recruit and retain the labor of Irish workmen, E. I. du Pont implemented an unusual array of direct assistance policies. These included high wages, interest-bearing savings accounts, free housing, free education for children, opportunities for advancement, pensions, and impressive benefits for widows. Believing that married men were more stable than single ones, du Pont also facilitated the emigration of wives and children, who were soon followed by siblings, parents, cousins, and friends. Company records provide dates of departure and arrival, names of passengers, names of ships, and information about the immigration procedure. These documents, coupled with oral histories and data from local graveyards, indicate that the majority of du Pont employees emigrated from Ulster, especially counties Donegal, Tyrone, and Fermanagh. Not surprisingly, the majority of the 1,200 known passengers (fifty-one percent) emigrated to Delaware between January 1, 1845, and December 12, 1849. In response to the crisis in Ireland, the du Pont Company extended its emigration services to Irish laborers employed elsewhere in New Castle County. Thus, by the time of the 1850 federal census, almost forty percent of the 2,000 or so individuals living in the powder mill community were natives of Ireland, and another twenty-two percent had at least one parent of Irish birth (Mulrooney, "Labor at Home," pp. 76–77). An equally large but as yet uncalculated number of Irish families inhabited other industrial villages in the area.

As their numbers rose, Irish immigrants soon affected the political life of the state. Under the 1792 Delaware constitution, all free, white men were eligible to vote if they were over the age of twenty-one, had resided in the state for two years, and had paid the required taxes. Many immigrants were thus entitled to the franchise, and politicians increasingly vied for Irish votes. The Democratic-Republicans, for example, ran on an anti-English platform in 1802 to solicit Irish support and successfully captured control of New Castle County. In response, Federalists, who dominated the rest of the state, leveled charges of political "chicanery" against their opponents, and castigated the Irish as "alien enemies" of the new nation. By the 1810s Republicans regularly countered that New Castle County manufacturers, most of whom were Federalists, exerted undue influence over the political process. Specifically, they accused the du Ponts and others of threatening to dismiss workmen who voted Republican. As it did elsewhere in the United States, this contest for Irish votes contributed to the rise of nativism in the 1840s and 1850s, but anti-Irish sentiment in Delaware never degenerated into open conflict. Not only did the Irish enjoy the support of local elites, but they "were never so numerous in New Castle County that they posed a threat to the existing order as they did in such cities as Boston or New York" (Drescher, "The Irish in Wilmington, 1800–1845," p. 125).

The Irish altered the religious character of antebellum Delaware as well. The Protestants among them were instrumental in founding Greenhill Presbyterian Church, Christ (Episcopal) Church, and Mount Salem Methodist Church, among others. Irish immigrants also contributed to the development of Delaware's Catholic parishes. In response to the growing Catholic population of New Castle County, the Reverend Patrick Kenny arrived from Dublin in 1804 to minister to his fellow Irishmen. Although based at St. Mary's (Coffee Run), the log church built by Cornelius Halloran, Kenny served a total of six missions in Pennsylvania, Maryland, and Delaware. These included St. Peter's in Wilmington, now the cathedral, which he founded in 1816. Within a few decades, the Irish community in Wilmington supported a Catholic orphanage, a female boarding school, a male academy, several benevolent associations, and at least three shops specializing in Catholic goods. The majority of Irish immigrants, however, lived several miles outside the city limits and maintained their faith through periodic visits from itinerant priests. Kenny's diary, for example, reveals that he not only administered the sacraments in private homes, but he occasionally held Mass outdoors, just as priests had done in rural Ireland. In fact, Catholics working in and around the du Pont powder yards did not resolve to build their own church, St. Joseph on the Brandywine, until 1841, one year after Kenny's death (Mulrooney, "Labor at Home," p. 110). A school and convent eventually followed.

As the nineteenth century progressed, the focus of Irish settlement shifted from the industrial villages of northern Delaware to Wilmington itself. Before the Civil War, the state's largest city had a specialized industrial economy based on iron, steel, shipbuilding, railroad car manufacturing, and carriage making. Because the demand for unskilled, immigrant labor was low, only nineteen percent of Wilmington's population was foreign-born in 1860, compared with twenty-five percent in Baltimore and twenty-nine percent in Philadelphia. The development of the leather tanning industry changed this pattern. Although tanyards had existed in Delaware since the eighteenth century, the industry expanded dramatically between 1825 and 1850 with the rising demand for glazed kid and moroccos for gloves and bookbindings. After the Civil War, Wilmington manufacturers perfected a new chrome process for tanning hides, and the city became one of the three leading production centers in the United States. The industry's rising demand for unskilled labor coincided with the increasing commercialization of Irish agriculture, and Irish immigrants began flooding into the city. By 1880, sixty-four percent of Wilmington's 5,674 foreign-born residents were Irish (Schreuder, "Wilmington's Immigrant Settlement, 1880–1920," pp. 143–145).

Following networks established decades earlier, the post-famine Irish settled primarily in the southeastern section of Wilmington, in what was then considered the sixth district (now the Eleventh Ward). There, within walking distance of the great leather factories, new arrivals crowded into small, brick row houses and struggled to make ends meet. Most were limited to unskilled positions, but a small percentage eventually secured skilled work. As they did in other cities, Irish immigrants established footholds on Wilmington's police force and in its fire companies during this period. Others opened small shops and businesses that catered to an exclusively Irish clientele. John D. Kelly III, for example, operated a well-known saloon called the Logan House, and parlayed his popularity in the Irish community into a successful bid for county sheriff. In other ventures, the Irish diverted a portion of their rising incomes to the construction of new urban parishes and parochial schools. The most prosperous among them, the so-called "lace curtain" or middle-class Irish, followed the city's expanding trolley lines and bought somewhat larger, but still modest, homes in northwestern neighborhoods like Forty Acres. The end of the nineteenth century also saw the emergence of Irish fraternal organizations, including the Ancient Order of Hibernians, which inaugurated an annual St. Patrick's

Day banquet. By 1900, the character of the city began to exhibit a distinctly Irish identity.

## THE TWENTIETH CENTURY

The prosperity enjoyed by Gilded Age Delawareans spilled over into the Progressive era. In 1902 E. I. du Pont's heirs formally reorganized the family firm and relocated its administrative offices to a new, thirteen-story structure in downtown Wilmington. As local tax laws changed, corporations from outside the state quickly followed suit, making Wilmington a center for big business and creating hundreds of new white-collar jobs. Manufacturing continued to expand too. By 1911, for example, F. Blumenthal and Company was the second largest tannery in the world. With the advent of World War I, the local shipbuilding and car-building industries received a boost as well. Attracted by these economic opportunities, immigrants from southern and central Europe, especially Italy and Poland, began to outnumber their Irish-born counterparts. Nevertheless, the early twentieth century constituted the peak period of Irish influence in Delaware.

One of the most prominent leaders of the Irish community at this time was Patrick R. Mulrooney. According to family records, Mulrooney emigrated from County Galway in 1883, settled in the sixth district of Wilmington, near the morocco shops, and arranged to bring out six of his eight brothers. Soon he opened a saloon and joined the city's two leading Irish fraternal organizations, the Tom Moore and Robert Emmet clubs. In 1903, under Mulrooney's direction, they were incorporated as the Irish-American Association of Delaware. Headquartered at Mulrooney's saloon, the ostensible purpose of this organization was to promote the "furtherance of the knowledge of the culture, history, and traditions" of Ireland, but the association also championed the cause of Irish nationalism in Delaware. Many of the members, including Mulrooney, the association's president, were active in the Clan na Gael. In 1916, Eamon de Valera made at least two documented trips to Wilmington. Oral histories maintain that de Valera visited Mulrooney's establishment on both occasions, and that the Delaware club regularly smuggled arms to Dublin. When Mulrooney died in 1943, Irish newspapers up and down the East Coast mourned his loss, and though the Irish-American Association eventually disbanded, Mulrooney's Tavern remains in operation under new ownership.

The Irish presence in Delaware decreased substantially after World War II, and today, Irish-Americans account for only about twenty percent of the population of New Castle County. Additional research is necessary to determine the exact cause of this decline, but the gradual acceptance of exogamous marriages and the movement of second- and third-generation families from the city to the suburbs undoubtedly weakened ties to a particular ethnic group. During the 1970s, however, the Irish community revived with the establishment of the Irish Culture Club of Delaware and the Emerald Society, as well as several informal organizations. The former hosts the city of Wilmington's annual St. Patrick's Day Parade, while the latter holds a lavish St. Patrick's Day banquet. The two groups also sponsor special lectures, trips, genealogical workshops, and films. Thus, while a detailed history of Delaware's Irish community remains to be written, these and other volunteer efforts are helping to preserve its heritage.

*See* Pennsylvania; Quakers from Ireland

Nuala McGann Drescher, "The Irish in Wilmington, 1800–1845" (M.A. thesis, University of Delaware, 1960).

Federal Writers' Project of the WPA, *Delaware: A Guide to the First State* (New York, 1938).

Margaret M. Mulrooney, "Labor at Home: The Domestic World of Workers at the du Pont Powder Mills, 1802–1902" (Ph.D. diss., The College of William and Mary, 1996).

Michael O'Brien, "Irish Pioneers in Delaware," *American-Irish Historical Magazine* 18 (1919).

Richard J. Purcell, "Irish Settlers in Early Delaware," *Pennsylvania History* 14/2 (April 1947).

Yda Schreuder, "Wilmington's Immigrant Settlement, 1880–1920," *Delaware History* 23 (1988–89).

MARGARET M. MULROONEY

## DEMPSEY, JACK (1895–1983)

Heavyweight boxing champion. Born as William Harrison Dempsey, Jack Dempsey was one of eleven children from Manassa, Colorado. At the age of sixteen, he left home and traveled west on the trains, stopping in mining towns to work and learning to fight to survive along the way. It was during these travels that Dempsey met Jack "Doc" Kearns whose admiration for the young man's remarkable strength led him to get Dempsey into the ring with boxers like Fireman Jim Flynn, Fred Fulton, the Battling Levinsky and Gunboat Smith—all of whom Dempsey knocked out.

In 1919, Dempsey challenged the reigning heavyweight champion Jess Willard in a Toledo, Ohio, outdoor ring. It was July 4, and in nearly 100 degree heat, Dempsey knocked Willard down seven times in the first round. The new heavyweight champion easily defended his title against challengers like Billy Miske, Bill Brennan, Tommy Gibbons and Georges Carpentier whose fight with Dempsey was boxing's first million-dollar ticket take.

Dempsey's fame spread beyond the United States when he was challenged by Argentina's "Wild Bull of the Pampas," Luis Angel Firpo in New York City, 1923. Dempsey sent him to the mat seven times in the first round. But Firpo came back toward the end to land a single punch that threw Dempsey through the ropes. A hush went through the crowd of 80,000 as Dempsey crawled back into the ring before the 10th count. Fifty-seven seconds into the second round, Dempsey won the match with a sensational knockout punch of the "Wild Bull."

For the next two years, Dempsey was inactive until Gene Tunney challenged the heavyweight champion in 1926. The younger fighter was quicker than the older Dempsey who was overtaken by Tunney's superior point score after ten rounds. Dempsey tried to retake the title the following year at Chicago's Soldier Field in what came to be one of the most controversial moments in boxing history. In the seventh round Dempsey knocked Tunney to the mat, but the referee refused to begin the count until Dempsey moved to a neutral corner. With several extra seconds to recover, Tunney pulled himself up on the ninth "long" count and then scored point after point over the next three rounds to win by decision. The estimated fourteen seconds of the "long count" thus became legendary in the annals of boxing history.

Dempsey's prowess was long remembered after his 1927 retirement from boxing. With a powerful two-fisted attack, Dempsey scored knockouts as early as fourteen and eighteen seconds into the match. Twenty-five of Dempsey's forty-nine knockouts occurred in the first round, and in his eighty-bout career, Dempsey had sixty wins. The heavyweight champion was inducted into the Boxing Hall of Fame in 1990, seven years after his death on May 31, 1983.

*See* Boxing

Jack Dempsey, *Dempsey* (New York, 1977).

Bruce J. Evensen, *When Dempsey Fought Tunney: Heroes, Hokum, and Storytelling in the Jazz Age* (Knoxville, 1996).

Nat Fleischer, *Jack Dempsey* (New Rochelle, 1972).

David L. Porter, *Biographical Dictionary of American Sports: Basketball and Other Indoor Sports* (New York, 1989).

Randy Roberts, *Jack Dempsey, the Manassa Mauler* (Baton Rouge, 1979).

DANIEL J. KUNTZ

## DESMOND, HUMPHREY J. (1858–1932)

Lawyer, legislator, author and journalist. He was born September 14, 1858 near Cedarburg, Wisconsin the eldest of nine children of Thomas Desmond and Johanna Bowe. His direct ancestor, Patrick Desmond of Bandon, County Cork, sired ten children by two marriages. One of these was Humphrey Desmond, the grandfather of the subject of this essay, who came to the United States in 1829.

In September 1877, Humphrey entered the University of Wisconsin and graduated three years later. In 1881 he was admitted to the Wisconsin bar and he almost immediately began a career in public service by serving on the Milwaukee school board (1883–1889). In 1890 he was elected to the Wisconsin State Legislature where he served one very productive term. Swept into office in a tide of opposition to the Bennett Law of 1889 which struck at parochial education and parental rights, Desmond helped to engineer the repeal of the hated statute and its replacement with a compulsory education law without state controls on parochial schools. Desmond was a strong supporter of public education as a pillar of American democracy and resisted attacks by Catholic leaders on them.

In 1898 at age forty he married Susan Ryan of Oshkosh, Wisconsin and sired six children. A gifted writer from childhood, Desmond was the author of twenty-five books on various topics. His enduring legacy was in the pages of the newspapers he controlled during his long journalistic career. He entered the ranks of Catholic journalism in 1880 when he became chief editorial writer for the widely circulated Catholic weekly, *The Catholic Citizen*. The *Citizen* was a paper that traced its origins back to 1869 and had gone through several name changes and different owners. In 1891, when the *Citizen* was legally incorporated, Desmond became the president and general manager of the Citizen Company. As editor, Desmond penned 15,000 editorial columns and 2500 columns of brief news. Unlike diocesan organs today, *The Catholic Citizen* was independent of hierarchical control and was one of the last great exemplars of lay-controlled Catholic journalism.

Desmond's association with his Irish past was complex. On the one hand he was a firm proponent of ethnic assimilation and deliberately moved his paper away from its former preoccupation with Irish affairs. He followed avidly the course of Irish nationalism, but insisted that American Irish do nothing more than encourage events unfolding overseas and avoid trying to influence them directly. Likewise, he cherished no romantic illusions about the "Old Sod," declaring that the Irish that emigrated to America were of a superior stock to those who remained in the old country. On the other hand, Desmond believed that the Irish

struggle for freedom had a great deal to teach the world about democracy. To this end he urged the study of Irish history in the United States. He was a great devotee of Irish culture and in *Why God Loves the Irish* (1918) he extolled the race for the spirit and humor that they injected into American society.

Desmond's *Citizen* was primarily a mouthpiece for American Catholic liberals who favored assimilation. He generally supported the efforts of prelates like Archbishop John Ireland, Cardinal James Gibbons, and Bishop James Keane who insisted that Catholicism more deeply integrate itself into the fabric of American life. He supported the work of the Paulist Isaac Hecker and highlighted the compatibility of American citizenship with Catholic identity (Scheiber, p. 78). He strongly defended the rights of American Catholics within the context of true religious freedom. As such he vigorously opposed the reading of the Protestant King James version of the Bible in public schools (the Edgerton Bible case) and excoriated the bigotry of the anti-Catholic American Protective Association as incompatible with the basic principles of liberty and justice which were the ideological bedrock of American life.

He was supportive of labor unions and mildly critical of American imperialist adventures in the wake of the Spanish American War of 1898. He also pressed temperance reform, a favorite hobby horse of late nineteenth-century reformers. He died February 16, 1932 at the age of seventy-three.

John O. Geiger, *H. J. Desmond, Catholic, Citizen, Reformer: The Quest for Justice Through Educational and Social Reform* (Ph.D. diss., Marquette University, 1972).

Richard J. Orsi, *Humphrey Joseph Desmond: A Case Study in American Catholic Liberalism* (M.A. Thesis, University of Wisconsin, 1965).

Richard Scheiber, *Humphrey J. Desmond, 'The Catholic Citizen' and Catholic Liberalism* (Ph.D. diss., Marquette University, 1990).

STEVEN M. AVELLA

## DETROIT

The Irish presence in the city of Detroit dates to the eighteenth century when the tiny settlement and garrison served as an anchor for French colonial interests in the lower Great Lakes. The city's early records include a few Irish soldiers and settlers in the outpost prior to its occupation by the British in 1760. The Royal Proclamation of 1763, The American Revolution, and Britain's reluctance to withdraw its military force from the Northwest Territory until 1796 retarded Detroit's growth, but a number of Irish were among those few who established homes and businesses near the post during the British occupation. The Macomb family, natives of County Antrim, founded a trading enterprise in 1772 (Denissen 1987:776–78). William, the son of immigrant entrepreneur Alexander Macomb, won a seat as Detroit's representative to Upper Canada's Assembly in 1792, thus becoming the first Irish-born resident of the city to enter politics (Dunbar 1970:153). Detroit-born grandson and namesake Alexander chose a career in military service, rising to Commanding General of the United States Army in 1828. The citizens of Michigan acknowledged the Macomb family contributions to state and nation by naming a county and a town in their honor (Malone 1933:155–57).

While Detroit served as territorial capital from 1805 to 1837, Irish immigrants and their descendants slowly increased in number. Although no statistical record of Detroit's foreign-born exists for this period, a wide variety of sources reveal information regarding the city's Irish population. Irishmen Joseph H. Patterson and Alpheus White served in the Territorial Legislature and both men were delegates to the Constitutional Convention of 1835. White, a veteran of the Battle of New Orleans, supported the provision that gave suffrage to alien residents of Michigan. Patterson suggested the names of four of the state's counties, Antrim, Clare, Roscommon and Wexford (Bingham 1888:540, 685). Irish-American George Bryan Porter served as governor of Michigan Territory from 1831 to 1834 (McMullen and Walker 1984: 192–93).

The history of the Catholic Church in Michigan provides a useful source of information about the Irish in Detroit during the territorial and early statehood periods. Father Gabriel Richard's 1822 census noted one hundred fifty Irish Catholics in the Detroit area. At least one hundred more arrived over the next four years. The rapid rise in the number of English-speaking Catholics in southeast Michigan led Bishop Fenwick to assign Irish-born Father Patrick O'Kelly to Detroit in 1829. The city's first Irish Catholic parish, Holy Trinity, was established by Father Bernard O'Cavenaugh in the mid-1830s; by 1840 there were more than two hundred families on the Holy Trinity roster (Paré 1983:366–67, 399, 407).

In addition to the highly visible population of Irish Catholics in Detroit there is strong evidence that suggests a similar number of Irish Protestants in the city. The records of the First Evangelical Society, an umbrella organization serving the spiritual needs of Detroit's non-Catholic residents, include several Irishmen. The Presbyterians, who constituted the majority of the Evangelical Society membership, began organizing First Presbyterian Church in 1819. The Methodists built a church in what is now Dearborn in 1818 and the Episcopalians formed St. Paul's Parish in 1824. A second Protestant Episcopal parish, Christ Church, was established in 1845 with Reverend William N. Lyster, a native of County Wexford, as its first rector. Baptists and Quakers of Irish origin were also well-represented on the membership rolls of Detroit's Protestant congregations (Burton 1930:1241–56; Woodford and Woodford 1969:152–57).

Detroit served as state capital from 1837 to 1847 when the seat of Michigan government was relocated to Lansing. Three factors influenced Irish immigration to the city during this period: Canada's Patriot Rebellion, improvements in the transportation infrastructure, and the economic opportunity associated with rapid urban expansion. During the Patriot War of 1837–38 a number of Canadian rebels fled to border cities in the United States to rest and regroup. Detroit was one of these sanctuaries. In the spring of 1838 the Patriots, augmented by a sizeable number of sympathizers recruited from Detroit's population, raided the city's arsenals and launched an invasion into British-held Canada. Michigan authorities prevented most of the rebel force from crossing the Detroit River, but about one-fifth of the Patriots reached Windsor where they were promptly defeated by a large Loyalist militia. Although the Patriot War continued for some months following the unsuccessful effort which embarked from Detroit, the revolt's ultimate failure stimulated a sharp rise in the city's population. Canadian emigrants dissatisfied with British-style rule and those fearing harsh reprisals included Irish settlers who had migrated to Canada prior to the rebellion (Dunbar 1970:353–54; Clark 1959:394–96, 402–03).

Detroit's location on a narrow strait between the upper and lower Great Lakes made the city an important transportation hub during the nineteenth century. Detroit became the major port of entry for Michigan's immigrants following its designation as the western terminus of the first regularly scheduled steamboat service crossing Lake Erie. Harbor improvements in the 1830s coincided with ambitious programs to expand road and railway service radiating from Detroit. Faced with periodic labor shortages, contractors employed on these public works projects recruited Irish laborers in cities along the Atlantic seaboard and transported them to Detroit where they constructed docks, warehouses, railroad terminals and the road network. Discoveries of iron ore and rich veins of copper in Michigan's Upper Peninsula during the mid-1840s spawned Detroit's industrial era. Employment opportunities in smelters, foundries, small manufacturing establishments, sawmills, and as laborers, tradesmen and professionals drew thousands of Irish from all walks of life to Detroit during the 1840s (Vinyard 1976:7–19). It is important to note that throughout the nineteenth century a significant number of Irish immigrants and their families resided in Detroit for a limited period of time. Close examination of census manuscripts reveals that many of these transmigrants eventually settled in other Michigan cities or among their countrymen in the state's rural areas.

A broad spectrum of push and pull factors influenced Irish settlement in Detroit in the years between the Great Starvation of the 1840s and the Great Depression of the 1930s. Biographical sketches of the city's leading Irish frequently allude to the ill effects of British colonial policy in Ireland as cause for emigration. Inadequate famine relief, land clearances, religious and cultural bias toward Irish natives, economic exploitation of Ireland's human and agricultural resources and political repression in one form or another are cited as primary push factors. Ireland's War of Independence and ensuing Civil War also prompted Irish to migrate elsewhere (Burton 1930:vols III and IV). Detroit, for those Irish who had knowledge of the city's opportunity, presented a reasonable choice among the cities considered suitable resettlement sites (Vinyard 1976:21–32, 48–49).

A number of Detroit's Irish immigrants received some form of assistance from Richard Elliott, the son of Tipperary-born architect Robert T. Elliott, who arrived in the city in 1834. Richard assumed responsibility for the operation of the Elliott Emigration Office when his father died in a construction accident in 1840. From that time until his death Richard Elliott arranged passage from European ports to the City of Detroit for thousands of Irish, German, Dutch and Scandinavian immigrants. Acting as travel agent Elliott sent bilingual instructions with tickets, met new arrivals and arranged for lodgings, employment, or emergency loans, and extended friendship and goodwill to all persons, native and foreign-born. In addition, Elliott contributed substantial financial support to Holy Trinity Parish and the *Catholic Vindicator,* Michigan's first Catholic newspaper. He also wrote a number of articles for the *Catholic Vindicator* supporting his perspectives on politics, religion and contemporary issues (Vinyard 1976:66–67).

The number of Irish in Detroit rose in proportion to the population growth and economic expansion in the city between 1850 and 1900. In 1850 one out of every six residents of Detroit had been born in Ireland. Ten years later census enumerators counted 5,994 Irish immigrants in the city, in addition to several thousand offspring of Irish parentage who had been born in the United States or Canada. The total number of Irish expatriates in Detroit reached a peak of 7,447 individuals in 1890. At the same census there were perhaps as many as fifty thousand Detroit residents who claimed an Irish ancestor. The number of Irish-born in Detroit decreased during the 1890s, falling to 6,412 in 1900. A portion of the decline may be attributed to increased mortality rates among refugees who fled Ireland during the 1840s, as well as the delayed effects of lower outmigration experienced by cities in the interior of the continent (U.S. Bureau of the Census, 1850–1900).

A large percentage of Detroit's Irish community was concentrated in a few enclaves until the 1860s when employment opportunities and the Civil War dispersed the immigrants over a wider area. Catholic Irish clustered near Holy Trinity Church in the 1840s. Corktown, with boundaries which roughly corresponded to the geographical limits of Holy Trinity Parish, contained one of the greatest concentrations of Irish, but not all of the Irish in this neighborhood were Catholic. Methodists, Anglicans and Presbyterians were not uncommon in Corktown, but nevertheless tolerated as at least Irish. Catholic immigrants established another neighborhood on the lower west side as Famine refugees arrived in the city in large numbers. A portion of the later arrivals settled near the docks and others migrated toward the suburbs. Wyandotte's Irish settlement arose in response to the demand for unskilled labor at the town's Eureka Iron Works. A few years later, the establishment of the Wyandotte Rolling Mill more than doubled the number of Irish who founded the parish that evolved into St. Patrick's Catholic Church (U.S. Bureau of the Census, 1850–1870; Vinyard 1976:96–97; Paré 1983:484–85). Industrial expansion during the Civil War drew more Irish to Detroit, some seeking work, others seeking relief from the social problems in the Eastern cities.

Detroit's Irish community was well represented among the approximately six thousand soldiers that the city sent to the battlefront during the Civil War. The First Michigan Infantry, among the earliest western regiments to arrive in Washington in 1861, suffered heavy casualties in the First Battle of Manassas. Mustered out and reformed, the regiment returned to the Army of the Potomac, where half its men were killed or wounded in the Second Battle of Manassas. The Twenty-Fourth Michigan, composed of Detroit and Wayne County volunteers, including a sizeable number of Irishmen, bought the Union Army precious time during the first day at Gettysburg, but four out of every five of its soldiers were lost to Confederate fire. Newly recruited men restored the regiment to fighting strength in the months following the battle, enabling the unit to continue serving until it was mustered out at war's end. Irish residents of Detroit also appeared on the rosters of other Michigan Infantry, Artillery and Engineer companies during the Civil War, displaying military prowess and patriotic fervor equal to any other segment of American society (Woodward and Woodward 1969:183–84; Williams 1994:50–55).

In the years following the American Civil War the occupational profile of Detroit's Irish began to shift as more men entered the skilled trades, moved into managerial positions or went into business for themselves. Irishmen headed Knights of Labor assemblies in the city, gaining experience that guided them in the early years of the trade union movement at the turn of the century. Detroit's first building trades unions included a high percentage of Irish and Irish-American among their charter members. Irish immigrants also led the struggle for industrial unionism in the city. Cornelius Patrick Quinn, a former member of the

Irish Republican Army, served as first president of United Auto Workers Dodge Local No. 3, in addition to holding the same office in the Greater Detroit and Wayne County Industrial Union Council. His colleagues in the city's UAW unions included Mike Magee, an Irishman whose experience in the 1913 Dublin Lockout helped guide the course of industrial unionism in Detroit during the 1930s (Dickerman and Taylor 1946:288; Babson 1983:75–96).

The rise to managerial ranks is impressive, but is eclipsed by the Irish and Irish-Americans who rose to national prominence while residing in Detroit. Thomas F. Griffin, a Limerick-born iron molder, established a foundry that evolved into a nineteenth-century industrial enterprise with an annual output of two hundred thousand boxcar wheels. Henry Ford, the son of a Corkman who farmed in suburban Dearborn, left home at age sixteen on the first step of a career path that led to success as the world's leading manufacturer of automobiles. Henry Ford is often praised for his 1914 industrial relations policy which introduced the eight-hour shift and five-dollars-a-day wage on Ford assembly lines. Others criticized his pacifist attitude during World War I and his alignment with Detroit's controversial radio priest, Father Charles Coughlin during the 1930s (Woodford and Woodford 1969:255–61; Tull 1965:89–92). Frank Murphy, whose father had fled Ireland to avoid prosecution for his involvement with the Fenians, rose from humble Huron County beginnings to become mayor of Detroit during the early years of the Great Depression. Murphy doled out the city's meager relief funds, buffered conflicts between starving workers and antagonistic employers and managed limited federal relief so skillfully that he was elected governor in 1936. In this post Murphy guided officials of General Motors and the United Automobile Workers into a landmark settlement that inaugurated an era of negotiations between automotive manufacturers and their employees. Frank Murphy resigned as governor in 1939, accepting Roosevelt's appointment as Attorney-General of the United States. During his short tenure in the Cabinet, Murphy waged a vigorous campaign against prominent lawbreakers including Kansas City's corrupt political boss, Tom Pendergast. Roosevelt recognized Murphy's fair-mindedness with a nomination to the U.S. Supreme Court in 1940. Jerome Cavanaugh, Detroit's other twentieth-century Irish-American mayor displayed equal talent for compromise during the race-based upheavals of the 1960s, but his political future was limited by changing attitudes generated by media coverage of the 1967 Detroit riots (Bald 1954:405, 422–25, 427, 432; Woodford and Woodford 1969:312–13, 349–52).

The Irish in Detroit have become successively more integrated into American society during the past two centuries but have not entirely forgotten their ancestral homeland. The city dispatched relief to Ireland during the Great Starvation, and at various times since the 1860s every major Irish-American organization established a branch in Detroit. The Fenian Brotherhood, the Irish Land League, Clan-na-Gael, and the American Association for the Recognition of Irish Freedom were among the most prominent of the political groups. The Ancient Order of Hibernians counted more than one thousand Irish Catholics in its Detroit divisions on the eve of World War I, but membership dwindled to less than one hundred men before John F. Kennedy's presidential candidacy inspired a mild resurgence in the ranks. The Gaelic League has encouraged the city's Irish to remember their heritage for over seventy-five years and at least a half-dozen smaller organizations focus their activities on preserving Irish dance, language and literature (Vinyard 1976:320–28; Ridge 1986: 95–97).

The number of Irish-born residing in Detroit has experienced ebbs and flows during the twentieth century but the overall trend has been one of decline. By 1910 there were 5,584 Irish natives living in the city, the lowest total since 1860. The 1920 and 1930 censuses indicate a rise in the number of Irish in Detroit. Examination of census manuscripts suggests that most of the expansion was related to the increasingly urban character of Michigan's population in response to mechanization of agriculture and the end of the "White Pine Era" as the last large tracts of virgin timber were harvested. Mortality and restrictive immigration laws contributed to the falling number of Irish-born residing in Detroit during the rest of the twentieth century. The records of the United States Immigration and Naturalization Service indicate that Irish emigration to Detroit has slowed to a trickle in the 1990s with less than fifty new arrivals documented each year (U.S. Bureau of the Census, 1910–1990; U.S. Immigration and Naturalization Service, 1990–1996). Though few, these immigrants continue to infuse Detroit's Irish community with new vigor, which has taken the form of wider participation in cultural events and additional material aid collected for suffering countrymen in Ulster.

*See* Michigan

Steve Babson, "Pointing the Way: The Role of British and Irish Skilled Tradesmen in the Rise of the UAW," *Detroit In Perspective* 7 (Spring 1983):75–96.

F. Clever Bald, *Michigan in Four Centuries* (New York, 1954).

Stephen D. Bingham, comp., *Early History of Michigan with Biographies of State Officers, Members of Congress, Judges and Legislators* (Thorp and Godfrey, State Printers and Binders: Lansing, 1888).

Clarence M. Burton, *The City of Detroit, Michigan, 1701–1922*, Vol. II (Detroit, 1930).

———, *The City of Detroit, Michigan, 1701–1922*, Vol. III and IV (Biographical) (Detroit, 1930).

S. D. Clark, *Movements of Political Protest in Canada, 1640–1840* (Toronto, 1959).

Father Christian Denissen, *Genealogy of the French Families of the Detroit River Region,* Revision 1701–1936, Vols. 1 and 2. Detroit Society for Genealogical Research (Detroit, 1987).

Marion Dickerman and Ruth Taylor, eds., *Who's Who in Labor* (New York, 1946).

Willis Frederick Dunbar, *Michigan: A History of the Wolverine State,* 2nd ed (Grand Rapids, MI, 1970).

Dumas Malone, ed., *Dictionary of American Biography*, Vol. VI, Part 2 (New York, 1933).

Thomas A. McMullen, and David Walker, *Biographical Dictionary of American Territorial Governors* (Westport, CT, 1984).

Michigan Adjutant General's Office, comp., *Record of Service of Michigan Volunteers in the Civil War, 1861–1865,* 46 vols. (1905).

George Paré, *The Catholic Church in Detroit, 1701–1888* (Detroit, 1983).

John Ridge, *Erin's Sons in America: The Ancient Order of Hibernians* (AOH Publications, Brooklyn, 1986).

Charles J. Tull, *Father Coughlin and the New Deal* (Syracuse, 1965).

U.S. Bureau of the Census, Seventh through Twenty-first Censuses of the United States, 1850–1990.

U.S. Immigration and Naturalization Service, "Immigrants Admitted by Metropolitan Area and Country of Birth," 1990–1996.

JoEllen Vinyard, *The Irish on the Urban Frontier: Nineteenth Century Detroit, 1850–1880* (New York, 1976).

Frederick D. Williams, *Michigan Soldiers in the Civil War.* Bureau of Michigan History (Lansing, 1994).

Frank B. Woodford, and Arthur M. Woodford, *All Our Yesterdays: A Brief History of Detroit* (Detroit, 1969).

RICHARD A. RAJNER

## DE VALERA, EAMON (1882–1975)

Irish leader and statesman. He was born on October 4, 1882, at the Nursery and Child's Hospital at 51st Street and Lexington Avenue in New York. His birthplace was a haven for the destitute and abandoned. His mother, Catherine (Kate) Cull of Knockmore Township near Bruree, Co. Clare, had emigrated to New York in 1879 and worked as a domestic with a wealthy French family named Giraud. Vivian de Valera, a Spaniard, was the family's music teacher and he and Kate Cull became romantically involved. Kate became pregnant, but de Valera vanished when the child was born. The boy was christened Edward and put in the care of a Mrs. Doyle, another Bruree immigrant. When he was three he was sent to be reared by relatives in Bruree. (His mother later married an Englishman named Charles Wheelwright, a livery driver, and lived in Rochester, New York.)

A reserved child, he was an adequate student in the two national schools he attended; and when he entered University College Dublin, he became a promising mathematician, and later became a competent teacher. He joined the Gaelic League in 1910 and in 1913 joined the Irish Volunteers; and despite his dislike for secret societies he joined the Irish Republican Brotherhood, which masterminded the 1916 Rising, of which he was one of the leaders. He was sentenced to death but was reprieved because of public revulsion at the British execution of the other 1916 leaders. He became a symbol for Irish republicanism and Eddie de Valera became Eamon de Valera. In 1917 he was elected member of parliament for Sinn Fein and was chosen leader of the party. He was imprisoned in 1918 in Lincoln Prison and escaped by the ingenious plan of Michael Collins and Harry Boland. When Sinn Fein members of parliament boycotted Westminster and created Dail Eireann as the legitimate parliament of the Irish Republic, de Valera became priomh-aire or president.

Eamon de Valera
on a trip to America

From June 1919 to December 1920 he toured America, seeking funds and recognition for the Irish Republic. He clashed with John Devoy and other Irish-American nationalists but made many supporters. In 1921, when a truce was reached in the War of Independence, de Valera held futile negotiations with Lloyd George. At the end of the year an Irish delegation, with a plenipotentiary status, was sent to London to enter formal peace negotiations with the British government. De Valera knew that the British were not going to recognize an Irish Republic or a united Ireland (partition was already an accomplished fact: in 1920 King George had opened Stormont, the Unionist dominated parliament) and he refused to be a negotiator. The delegation signed a treaty which the Dail narrowly approved on January 7, 1922, and the Irish Free State was founded. The opponents refused to accept the verdict which was approved by a good majority of the Irish people and they resorted to arms which led to the Civil War. It lasted until May 1923.

Eamon de Valera founded his own party, Fianna Fail, in 1926. Six years later he became the leader of the Free State and in 1937 he won a referendum which gave the country a new constitution that recognized the Catholic Church as the dominant religion. The country was defined as the thirty-two counties, ignoring the existence of a parliament in Belfast which had controlled and governed six counties in Ulster since 1920. And the name of the Free State was changed to Eire.

During World War II, Eire remained neutral despite much pressure to open Irish ports to Allied shipping. He was the dominant figure in Irish politics for decades, serving as Taoiseach or leader from 1932–48, 1951–54, 1957–59; and was elected president of Ireland twice.

An aloof and enigmatic character, de Valera thought more of Ireland's past and of the future of the Irish language—which was compulsory in primary and secondary schools—than of practical economic problems which made young men and women Ireland's most visible export. To modern historians, Eamon de Valera remains a shrewd idealist who led the Irish people for whom he was ever the reserved, confident and idealistic leader.

Tim Pat Coogan, *Eamon de Valera* (San Francisco, 1995).
E. F. Foster, *Modern Ireland, 1700–1972* (London and New York, 1988).
Maurice Moynihan, ed., *Speeches and Statements by Eamon de Valera, 1917–73* (Dublin, 1980).
J. P. O'Carroll and John A. Murphy, eds., *De Valera and His Times: Political Development in the Republic of Ireland* (Cork, 1983).
Frank Packenham, *Peace by Ordeal*, 3d ed. (London, 1972).

MICHAEL GLAZIER

## DEVOY, JOHN (1842–1928)

Fenian leader and journalist, was born in Kill, County Kildare, twelve miles from Dublin, on September 3, 1842. A grand-uncle was a United Irish rebel in 1798. Devoy's father, a laborer, broke stones for road construction and planted a half acre plot with potatoes and cabbage to feed his family. The family moved to Dublin in 1849 where the eldest son, aged fourteen, died of cholera. His father, a self-educated man who had been active in Daniel O'Connell's campaign for repeal of the Union, got work in a brewery and stayed there for the rest of his life. He retired as chief clerk.

Devoy's education was erratic due to rebelliousness. After a year at Kill national school he attended O'Connell's School and other schools in Dublin where he clashed with some teachers over politics. He defended John Mitchel and would not sing "God Save the Queen" and was expelled for throwing a slate at the teacher.

In 1861 he joined the Irish Republican Brotherhood and took an oath "to the Irish Republic, now virtually established, that I will take up arms . . . to defend its integrity and independence." He prepared for the struggle for Irish independence by joining the French Foreign Legion to learn the soldier's trade. He spent a year with the Foreign Legion in Algeria but wrote little in his memoirs about it. On his return to Ireland he worked full-time with the IRB preparing for rebellion against British rule.

### CHIEF ORGANIZER BRITISH ARMY

James Stephens, the founder of the Irish Republican Brotherhood, returned from America in 1864 with promises of funds, arms and officers for an Irish rebellion. Stephens appointed Devoy "Chief Organizer British troops in Ireland," the third IRB man to hold the position. His predecessors were in jail. His assignment was to recruit Irish soldiers in the British army in Ireland for the IRB. He claimed that of the 26,000 British troops in Ireland, "8,000 were sworn Fenians." An Irish historian, R.V. Comerford, says "research suggests that the actual figure may have been much lower." Whatever the figure, many British soldiers in Ireland were recruited into the IRB in the 1860s. Some were court-martialed and sentenced to death, reprieved and transported to Australia.

On September 14, 1865, Dublin Castle detectives raided the office of the *Irish People,* the IRB weekly, which also served as IRB headquarters. John O'Leary, the editor, Thomas Clarke Luby, the number two in the Fenian hierarchy, and Jeremiah O'Donovan Rossa, manager of the paper, were arrested. Stephens and Charles Kickham were captured six weeks later. The IRB leadership was in jail.

Devoy was assigned to organize Stephens' escape from Richmond Prison. His helpers were an IRB night watchman, Daniel Byrne, and a prison hospital orderly, John J. Breslin, who joined the IRB and was Devoy's close associate in America. An armed guard under Devoy conducted the operation. "It was the one proud day of the Fenian movement," Devoy recalled with justifiable jubilation.

### SECRET MEETINGS IN DUBLIN

On the evening of February 19, 1866, Devoy learned that his "Fenian soldiers" were threatening to seize a Dublin barracks and start a rising. Devoy reported the information to Colonel Thomas J. Kelly, the IRB Chief of Staff, who warned him to avoid "any premature movement . . . at all hazards." *Habeas Corpus* was suspended on February 17. "All the American officers in Dublin, except twelve, were arrested within two days after the first big swoop of the police," Devoy wrote in *Recollections of an Irish Rebel.*

On February 20 Colonel Kelly and Devoy attended a conference with Stephens in a "safe house" across the street from the Kildare Street Club. Stephens reported that the movement had no money and few arms. The U.S. Fenians were split. John O'Mahony, the head of the Fenian Brotherhood in America, had $125,000 in the treasury and Stephens sent a courier to ask him for the money.

When the conference resumed late on February 21, Colonel Kelly reported that the organization in Dublin was intact. There were 8,000 men in the city IRB, but arms for only a thousand. They had 800 rifles and 200 shotguns, revolvers and pikes. This was not enough to launch a general rebellion, Colonel Kelly declared. They should postpone the rising "and prepare for an insurrection under more favorable auspices in the future."

## THE DEVOY PLAN FOR A RISING

Devoy did not agree. He proposed an immediate attack on Richmond Barracks. He had the key to the back gate of the barracks and Fenian soldiers in the garrison. He could capture the barracks. "With Richmond in our possession, our next move would naturally be on Island Bridge barracks and the Royal Barracks across the King's Bridge." Devoy's call for rebellion was rejected by the senior Fenian officers present. "The last chance for a rising was thrown away," Devoy believed.

In the weeks that followed, hundreds were imprisoned, the IRB was shattered and Devoy was captured in a public house in James Street, a meeting place for Fenian soldiers. Edward Duffy, who was Stephens' deputy, ordered Devoy to plead "guilty" on the faint chance he might be released. He was sentenced to fifteen years penal servitude.

## NEW YORK

Devoy was in prison when the 1867 rising occurred. He was amnestied at the end of the decade after a British election in November 1868 brought William E. Gladstone, the Liberal leader, to power. Long term Fenian prisoners were amnestied on condition they did not return to Ireland before their terms had expired. The first five exiles to arrive in New York aboard the S.S. *Cuba* on January 18, 1871, included Devoy and O'Donovan Rossa.

Devoy got work as a reporter on James Gordon Bennett's *New York Herald* and later became foreign editor. His boyhood friend, James J. O'Kelly, who took the IRB oath on the same day as Devoy and also joined the French Foreign Legion, worked for the *Herald*.

The Fenian Brotherhood in America, Devoy learned, was split and demoralized. After June 20, 1867, there was a new Fenian group, Clan na Gael, which Devoy joined. At a Clan convention in July 1874, he urged the organization to raise money and rescue soldier prisoners in Australia. To his surprise, the delegates agreed. Following complicated planning and the purchase of the whaling ship, *Catalpa,* six Fenian prisoners were rescued and brought to the United States. They boarded the *Catalpa* on April 18, 1876, and "nearly four months later they were landed safely at New York," Devoy wrote. The sensational escape established Clan na Gael as the premier national organization of the American Irish.

## 1876-1928

Between 1875 and 1878 Britain and Russia seemed headed for war in the Balkans. The Clan sent a five-member delegation to interview the Russian minister in Washington in November 1876 and ask Russian support for an Irish rebellion. The minister told them the Irish people wanted reforms, not independence. Devoy founded a newspaper, the *Irish Nation,* to change that impression.

The most significant of Devoy's initiatives for Ireland was the "New Departure" of 1879 which he and Michael Davitt, recently released on ticket of leave from an English prison, persuaded Clan na Gael to adopt. The "New Departure" allied revolutionaries and constitutionalists behind the leadership of Charles S.

Parnell, to promote tenant right, self-government, peasant proprietary, the exclusion of sectarian issues from politics, and support for struggling nationalities. Two decades later, the Irish tenant had become a peasant proprietor following the land war.

When the First World War began in August 1914, Devoy asked the German ambassador to the United States for arms and "a sufficient number of capable officers" to aid a rebellion in Ireland. "But that we wanted no money." The arms ship *Aud* arrived in Tralee Bay on Good Friday, April 21, 1916, with 20,000 rifles, ten machine guns and ammunition for a rebellion to start on Easter Sunday. No one met the arms ship except British warships who ordered the *Aud* into Queenstown (Cobh). The skipper scuttled the arms ship at the entrance to the harbor and sent its cargo to the ocean floor.

Devoy, the key figure between the IRB in Dublin and Germany, charged the Wilson administration with passing information on Irish activities gleaned in a raid on a German office in Wall Street to the British which resulted in the capture of the *Aud.* He was wrong. British naval intelligence had broken the German code. All messages between Devoy and Berlin and Berlin and Devoy were read in London.

Devoy was a bitter enemy of Eamon de Valera's U.S. campaign in 1919–20 for recognition of the Irish Republic. He supported the Anglo-Irish Treaty of December 6, 1921, which granted Dominion status to three quarters of Ireland and retained the other quarter in the United Kingdom. "I am decidedly of the opinion that the British Government could not have been forced at that time to grant any more to Ireland than what was contained in the Treaty signed by Griffith and Collins," he told Colonel Maurice Moore.

In 1924 he visited the land of his birth for the second time since leaving it, as a guest of the Free State government. He died in Atlantic City, N.J., aged 86 on September 29, 1928. The *Times* of London called him "the most dangerous Irish enemy of Britain since Wolfe Tone," which was an accurate assessment of his importance.

*See* Fenians and Clan na Gael

Ryan Desmond, *The Fenian Chief* (Dublin, 1967).
John Devoy, *Recollections of an Irish Rebel* (New York, 1928).
T. W. Moody, *Davitt and Irish Revolution, 1846–82* (Oxford, 1982).
W. O'Brien and D. Ryan, eds., *Devoy's Post Bag,* vols. 1 and 2 (Dublin, 1948 and 1953).
Leon O Broin, *Fenian Fever* (London, 1971).
John O'Leary, *Fenians & Fenianism* (London, 1896).

SEÁN CRONIN

## DISNEY, WALTER (1901–1966)

Cartoonist, motion picture producer. The name of Disney is a household name to millions of Americans and families throughout the world, owing to the creative genius of a man who lives on in the spirit of Mickey Mouse, Donald Duck and dozens of other cartoon characters. Disney is responsible for technical innovations in sound, color and photography in the movies and on television, and for the creation of two of the world's most famous amusement centers, Disneyland in California and Disney World in Florida.

Walter Elias Disney was born on December 5, 1901 in Chicago, Illinois. When he was quite young, his father, a Canadian of Irish descent, moved his wife and five children to a farm in

Missouri where Walt acquired his love of animals and began sketching. His family later moved to Kansas City, and, though he never finished high school, he was an industrious young man, working at various jobs and studying in the evenings at the Chicago Academy of Fine Arts. After having served as a Red Cross ambulance driver during World War I, Disney returned to Kansas City and delved into the art of cartooning and filmmaking.

In 1923 Disney left for Hollywood and, in partnership with his brother Roy, set up a small studio and began developing short cartoons. Those were the beginnings of the great cartoon empire.

Disney's best known creation, Mickey Mouse, was an instant star in his first appearance in *Steamboat Willie* in 1928. In the some 100 cartoons produced over the next ten years, Mickey, together with friends, Donald Duck, Minnie Mouse, Pluto, Goofy and dozens of other characters, enjoyed international popularity; and Disney was recognized for his artistic innovations in the field of animated cartoons.

The Technicolor process was introduced in the Disney film, *Flowers and Trees* (1932), and the popular *Three Little Pigs* was released in 1933. The extraordinary *Snow White and the Seven Dwarfs* (1937), the first feature-length animated cartoon, delighted audiences young and old with its delightful characters and vivacious music; and it stunned Hollywood as the film industry's greatest moneymaker until *Gone With the Wind* four years later. *Fantasia* (1940), a combination of classical music and animation, was met with wild critical acclaim. This success was followed by *The Reluctant Dragon* (1941), *Dumbo* (1941), *Bambi* (1942), and a series of children's classics. Disney also produced a wildlife documentary series, "True Life Adventures," in which the animals had starring parts. Christmas Day, 1950, marked the debut of the familiar and well-loved Disney characters on television.

*See* Cinema, Irish in; California

*Newsweek,* 35 (February 13, 1950): 84.
*Readers Digest,* 41 (October 1942): 85–88.
R. D. Field, *The Art of Walt Disney* (1942).
*World Biography* (1948).

EILEEN DANEY CARZO

## DOHEN, DOROTHY M. (1924–1984)

Sociologist. A 1945 graduate of the College of Mount St. Vincent, Dohen cut her spiritual teeth on the Grail and Young Christian Workers. She published articles in two lay Catholic periodicals, *Commonweal* and *Integrity,* the latter of which she later became editor until it went defunct in 1956. Dohen wrote several books on spirituality, including *Vocation to Love* (1950) and *Journey to Bethlehem* (1958). The spirituality she described led to a life rooted in prayer, and balanced by ecumenical work and work for social justice; she taught that all three were essential practices. Several years ahead of Vatican II, Dohen espoused that Christians should look closely at the signs of the times. She regarded the church's relation to and role in modern society as the crucial issue of the era.

Dohen's ideas led her to pursue advanced degrees in sociology, earning an M.A. (1959) and Ph.D. (1966) at Fordham. In 1960 she published an analysis of women's rapidly changing role, *Woman in Wonderland.*

Her groundbreaking book, *Nationalism and American Catholicism* (1967), combined episcopal history and sociology and shed light on the Americanist controversies and on the contemporary "culture wars." By analyzing the words and deeds of six U.S. Catholic bishops, Dohen illustrated how each attempted to demonstrate the compatibility of faith and democracy. She argued positively that American religious pluralism precludes the establishment of a common religion, but warned that it also tends to dilute the distinctive contributions of particular religions.

From 1970–1972, Dohen edited *Sociological Analysis,* the Journal of the Association of the Sociology of Religion. She died of cancer in Manhattan, January 3, 1984.

Dorothy M. Dohen, *Nationalism and American Catholicism* (Sheed & Ward, 1967).
*New York Times,* obituary (January 1, 1984).

KAREN SUE SMITH

## DOHENY, EDWARD LAURENCE (1865–1935)

Oil producer. Born to Patrick Doheny (of Irish birth) and Eleanor Elizabeth Quigley, Doheny left home at age sixteen and worked for the government's geological survey of boundaries between Arizona and New Mexico and later began mining for gold in the western mountains. Doheny's good luck was made manifest in his accidental discovery of a plot of land rich with oil reserves. Doheny and his friend Charles Canfield leased a vacant lot nearby and began digging; they were rewarded with over 45 barrels of oil per day. Their work was a significant part of the oil boom in Los Angeles, California.

When the times yielded an excess of oil production in the United States, Doheny left the oil business and began producing asphalt. He developed a lucrative asphalt business in Mexico City. Later, the automobile transportation business demanded great amounts of gasoline; Doheny constructed the Mexican Petroleum Company of California and became a dominant figure in the Tampico field and Tuspan gasoline district. However, Doheny met with misfortune when in 1921 he was accused of conspiracy in conjunction with Albert B. Fall, secretary of the interior under President Harding. Doheny and Fall were charged with bribery and conspiracy to rob the nation of valuable property in exchange for personal gain. In 1926, both were acquitted of conspiracy; however, Doheny escaped the charge of bribery only to suffer great restitution charges and financial loss. In 1929, Doheny obtained from the U.S. Government a contract to build a naval fuel station at Pearl Harbor, Hawaii, and later the drilling rights in Elk Hills, California.

Doheny built a memorial library at the University of Southern California in Los Angeles for his son who was killed in 1929. Doheny later expressed interest in creating an Irish republic and served as president of the American society for the recognition of such an Irish state. Doheny died in Beverly Hills, California due to an ongoing illness which had incapacitated him for several years.

*Who's Who in America* (1932–33).
*Dictionary of American Biography,* supplement 1.

JOY HARRELL

## DOLAN, JAY PATRICK (1936–    )

Historian and educator. In the 1970s and 1980s Jay P. Dolan was the most influential historian of Roman Catholicism in the United

States. In the nineties the University of Notre Dame professor turned his attention to research and teaching on the Irish experience in America. Over the course of his career, Dolan authored pioneering studies of immigrant Catholicism and nineteenth-century Catholic revivalism, and he conceptualized, edited or co-authored several original volumes examining the historical evolution of the Catholic parish in the United States. A generation of undergraduate and graduate students relied on his monumental survey of American Catholic history from the first European arrival to the aftermath of the Second Vatican Council. Dolan's legacy also includes the Cushwa Center for the Study of American Catholicism, which he established at Notre Dame in 1977.

Jay Dolan was born in 1936 to Joseph T. and Margaret Reardon Dolan of Fairfield, Connecticut. He attended Georgetown University briefly before entering the seminary. Ordained in 1961, he served as a priest of the diocese of Bridgeport, Connecticut, until 1966, when he began doctoral studies at the University of Chicago. There he studied with Martin E. Marty, the eminent church historian and ecumenically minded Lutheran who had been an invited observer at Vatican II. Upon earning the Ph.D. in 1970, Dolan spent a year teaching at the University of San Francisco. In 1971 he joined the faculty of the University of Notre Dame, which became his permanent academic home. Having left the priesthood, he married the historian Patricia McNeal in 1973 and started a family.

As a young professor of history, Dolan made his mark on the discipline by advancing the development of social history, the study of the richly textured lives of ordinary people and communities—their ethnic backgrounds, jobs, family structures and kinship networks, neighborhoods, schools, religious beliefs and practices, and so on. Drawing on his Irish-American and Catholic heritages, Dolan explored the broader themes of social history as they found concrete expression in the lives of nineteenth-century Irish Catholic and German Catholic immigrants. Prior to Dolan's work, historians of Catholicism, with a few notable exceptions, had tended to focus on the careers of bishops, exemplary priests, and other elite Catholic leaders. This method reflected a preconciliar view which equated the Church and its (all-male) clerical and episcopal leaders. The American Catholic Historical Association recognized the significance of Dolan's research by awarding its highest award to his first book, *The Immigrant Church: New York's Irish and German Catholics, 1815–1865*, a comparison of three parishes that examined the role of religion and ethnicity in the building of urban neighborhood communities.

On display in Dolan's second historical monograph, *Catholic Revivalism: The American Experience, 1830–1900*, was the kind of innovative thinking that characterized his historical imagination. Borrowing a theme from the history of American Protestantism, Dolan used the term "revival" to shape his discussion of the parish missions, the religious order priests who conducted them, and the lay Catholics who participated in them. He demonstrated that the parish missions served as the Catholic counterpart to the waves of evangelical fervor transforming American religious sensibilities, public morals and civic institutions in the nineteenth century.

While the Irish occupied a prominent place in Jay Dolan's work, they were never depicted in isolation from the Germans, Italians, Poles, Lithuanians and other ethnic groups whose stories formed the rich mosaic of Roman Catholicism in the United States. Honoring the integrity of these separate and diverse eth-

nic experiences within one comprehensive and coherent historical narrative was the singular accomplishment of Dolan's most broadly influential work, *The American Catholic Experience: A History from Colonial Times to the Present* (1985). It was the first successful social history of Catholicism in the United States, and it remains the standard survey in the field fifteen years after its publication.

While Dolan continued to contribute chapters, essays, and articles that expanded on the themes covered in *The American Catholic Experience,* he also turned his energies to fostering the scholarship of other historians. In this regard he made a significant contribution in founding a national center for the study of American Catholicism, which was endowed in 1980 by the Charles and Margaret Hall Cushwa family of Youngstown, Ohio. The Cushwa Center, which Dolan directed from 1977 until 1993, sponsors publication series on American Catholicism and the Irish in America, conducts seminars on American religion, awards travel and research grants to historians and sociologists of Catholicism, and conducts long-term research and publication projects.

*See* Historians of Irish America

Jay P. Dolan, *The American Catholic Experience: A History from Colonial Times to the Present* (Garden City, N.Y., 1985).
———, ed., *The American Catholic Parish: The Northeast, Southeast and South Central States* (New York, 1987).
———, ed., *The American Catholic Parish: The Pacific, Intermountain West and Midwest States* (New York, 1987).
———, *Catholic Revivalism: The American Experience, 1830–1900* (Notre Dame, Ind., 1978).
———, *The Immigrant Church: New York's Irish and German Catholics, 1815–1865* (Baltimore, 1975).
———, general editor, *The Notre Dame History of Hispanic Catholics in the U.S.,* 3 vols. (Notre Dame, Ind., 1994)

R. SCOTT APPLEBY

## DOMESTICS

The identification of Irish immigrants, especially women, with domestic service resulted from a confluence of Irish and American factors. Irish culture did not cloister single women to the home until marriage. Instead, Irish economic strategies kept men on the farm to do the heavy labor and sent women to earn the cash for taxes. However, women were not equipped for skilled labor. Hence, they gravitated toward work they could learn on the job. In the United States, private households provided such work. The numbers of Irish women and their need for unskilled work drove down the price of their labor to the point where families could afford them much more easily than would be the case in other labor markets. Although there are no comprehensive figures, Irish women dominated domestic service in the northern United States from the rise of both immigration and the middle class after 1820 until the end of mass international migration and the rise of internal African American migration in World War I.

Irish women made domestic service serve their purposes. The nature of the job cut servants' personal expenses. Most servants had to live in the household; thus servants paid no rent. Most servants had to wear uniforms, which lowered their wardrobe expenses. Money not devoted to personal consumption was thus available for other purposes: remittances to maintain a farm

Washing dishes was just one of an Irish domestic's duties.

in Ireland, bringing a family to the United States, and donating to ethnoreligious causes. When the woman had met her family's needs, she was free to look to her own future, either by continuing to save for her old age or by marriage.

This economic strategy entailed personal sacrifice. "Unskilled" housework did require some education, especially if one came from a one-room cottage with little furniture, no floor or ceiling, and a peat fire, and entered a house with many rooms, more furniture, floors to mop, ceiling molding to dust, and a stove. In the absence of power appliances, cooking, cleaning, and laundering were time-consuming and arduous. Workdays were long, with servants stirring the fire and cooking the breakfast before the family awoke, and washing the dishes and banking the fire after the family retired. Work weeks were also long: nineteenth-century servants customarily got only a half-day off on Thursday and Sunday, and were on call throughout the night. Servants' control over their work was minimal, homeowners tried to get their money's worth by supervising servants minutely to insure constant work, thinking up extra tasks or asking servants hired for one kind of work to do another. Women who worked in isolation in a household and whose sex, ethnicity, and occupation lowered their status, were vulnerable to sexual abuse from men about the house. Relations with the women of the house required constant negotiation, as women might be united by sex but divided by ethnicity, religion, or class. A servant who lost her job also became homeless.

The popular theater and press unfairly depicted Irish women domestics in unflattering terms: slovenly, ignorant, and superstitious. Nor was the Irish or Catholic image of domestic servants a complete antidote to that stereotype, as women were expected to accept their lot without criticism of capitalism or gender inequity, to subordinate themselves to their families' needs, but somehow to overcome these admonitions and speak out when non- or anti-Catholic homeowners ridiculed Catholicism. However, rather than condemning working women for not fulfilling the ideal of the full-time homemaker, the Irish and Catholic press offered a counter-stereotype of home-bound women as unpro-

ductive, and praised their own women's independence, and support of their families and communities.

*See* Women, Nineteenth-Century

Hasia Diner, *Erin's Daughters in America: Irish Immigrant Women in the Nineteenth Century* (Baltimore and London: The Johns Hopkins University Press [Johns Hopkins Studies in Historical and Political Science, 101st Series, No. 2], 1983).

Faye E. Dudden, *Serving Women: Household Service in Nineteenth-Century America* (Middletown, Connecticut: Wesleyan University Press, 1983).

David M. Katzman, *Seven Days a Week: Women and Domestic Service in Industrializing America* (New York: Oxford University Press, 1978).

John Francis Maguire, *The Irish in America* (London: Longmans, Green, and Co., 1868; reprint New York: Arno, 1969): 333–344.

Timothy J. Meagher, "'Sweet Good Mothers and Young Women Out in the World': The Roles of the Irish American Women in Late Nineteenth and Early Twentieth Century Worcester, Massachusetts," *U.S. Catholic Historian*, V/3–4 (1986), 325–344.

Daniel E. Sutherland, *Americans and Their Servants: Domestic Service in the United States from 1800 to 1920* (Baton Rouge and London: Louisiana University Press, 1981).

MARY ELIZABETH BROWN

## DONAHOE, PATRICK (1811–1901)

Publisher. Patrick Donahoe was born March 17, 1811, in Munnery, Cavan, Ireland. In 1821 his parents emigrated to Boston.

At the age of fourteen, Donahoe became a printer's apprentice on the *Columbia Sentinel* and later on the *Transcript.* In 1832 when Bishop Benedict J. Fenwick bought the *Jesuit,* Donahoe began working on that paper and eventually entered into a partnership with Henry L. Devereux, its printer, to purchase the newspaper, which had been renamed the *Literary and Catholic Sentinel.*

In 1836 the newspaper became the *Boston Pilot,* a weekly newspaper devoted to Irish-American and Catholic affairs. It soon became the principal organ of Catholic opinion in New England and one of the most influential Catholic newspapers in the United States.

Donahoe also established a book publishing company, founded a bank, and began selling religious articles, becoming the largest religious articles dealer in New England.

His printing plant was destroyed in the 1872 great Boston fire. After the plant was rebuilt, it was destroyed again by fire the following year. These and other disasters, including the failure of his bank, forced Donahoe to declare bankruptcy in 1876.

He sold the newspaper to Archbishop John J. Williams and John Boyle O'Reilly in order to repay bank depositors. Donahoe then began publishing *Donahoe's Magazine* and began a travel agency. In 1890 he bought the *Pilot* from the diocese and managed it the rest of his life.

He received the Laetare Medal from the University of Notre Dame in 1893. He died March 18, 1901, in Boston.

M. A. Frawley, *Patrick Donahoe* (Washington, 1946).

MARIANNA McLOUGHLIN

## DONAHUE, PETER (1822–1885)

Entrepreneur. In the 19th century, engineers were known as "mechanics," for the simple reason that the internal combustion engine had not yet been invented. Peter Donahue was one of the most noted "mechanics" of the American West.

Born in Glasgow to Irish immigrant parents, he early tinkered with things mechanical and was working in a Glasgow factory by the age of nine. The family left for New York two years later and eventually settled in the factory town of Paterson, New Jersey. There, he was apprenticed to a locomotive builder and became an expert machinist.

The high quality of his work became well-known locally and in 1845 he was hired to work on a gunboat being built in New York for the government of Peru. Upon her completion, he elected to sail with her and spent several years in Peru. Upon the news of gold in California, however, he boarded a steamer and headed north. En route, however, the steamer's engines malfunctioned and Donahue offered to have a look. He fixed the problem so expertly that the captain of the ship offered him a job on the spot. Donahue declined politely, however. He had come for gold.

Initially, it looked like he should have stuck with the steamship company. Six months of unsuccessful panning was enough to convince him he would never find his fortune in a riverbed. Returning to San Francisco, he encountered his brother James and the two opened a blacksmith shop together.

From this humble beginning came the Union Iron Works, which eventually built Monitor-style gunboats for the Union Navy in the Civil War. In 1864, he sold the ironworks for $1 million and opened San Francisco's first gas works, which provided regular street lighting for the first time. More important, he founded the first omnibus street car railway, the forerunner of the cable cars that are the city's signature today.

Donahue was one of those who discovered that it was not necessary to find gold in order to find wealth in San Francisco. He also founded the first San Francisco to San Jose railway, as well as the San Francisco and North Pacific Railroad, which his son Mervyn headed for many years.

He is memorialized by the "Mechanic's Monument" at Market and Battery streets in San Francisco.

John A. Barnes, *Irish-American Landmarks* (Detroit, 1995).

JOHN A. BARNES

## DONGAN, THOMAS (1634–1715)

Colonial governor of New York, 2nd Earl of Limerick. Dongan was born the younger son of Sir John Dongan, Baronet in Castletown, County Kildare, Ireland, in 1634. After having spent time in the Irish regiment of the French army in England under Louis XIV, Dongan achieved the rank of colonel. However, in 1677 he left army service and was appointed lieutenant governor of Tangiers by Charles II, a post he kept until 1680. Owing to his friendship with the Stuarts, Dongan was appointed governor of New York by James, Duke of York.

Dongan left for New York in 1683 and executed his instructions from the Duke to convene an assembly. The Duke's order for Dongan required him to call a representative assembly which met in 1683 for the clarification of its organization and action which came to be known as the "Charter of Liberties." The charter provided for religious toleration and promoted a policy of cooperation with the Iroquois Confederacy against the French. This charter further served as a foundation for the future constitution of New York. Dongan forwarded the charter to the Duke, but it was rejected by the privy council after the Duke ascended the English throne as James II. New York then became a colony without assembled representation.

Dongan, however, continued to channel his energies toward the development of boundaries in the New York colony. He worked on defense strategies for the colony and conjured ideas about a postal system which would extend from Nova Scotia to the Carolinas, serving as a bridge between the English colonies in America.

Dongan's great achievement came in his awareness of the growing French power in the North and his insistence that the government keep such in check. He recognized the growing threat of the French as early as 1684 and was able to eventually convince the King of England that the French power must be contained if the English were to maintain cordial relations with the Iroquois Confederation. Dongan made many protests against the governor of Canada, De la Barre, and his successor, the Marquis de Denonville. In 1684, Dongan witnessed the disbursement of the arms of the Duke of York among the Iroquois villages, a step he felt commensurate with the establishment of a protectorate. In 1686, England established the Dominion of New England and later added New York and New Jersey. However, in 1687–1688 terse relations developed and Dongan succeeded in raising a force for the defense of Albany after hesitant approval from James II.

Later in 1688, James II appointed Sir Edmund Andros as successor to Dongan in the governance of New York. Dongan did not return to England but remained in New York until anti-Catholic outbreaks following the overthrow of James II in 1689 spurred his eventual return to England. Once back in England, Dongan succeeded his brother as the second Earl of Limerick in 1698. Dongan died a poor man on December 14, 1715, after failing to recover his ancestral lands from anti-Catholic confiscation.

*See* New York City; New York State

*Dictionary of American Biography*, 5.

T. P. Phlean, *Thomas Dongan, Colonial Governor of New York, 1683–1688* (New York, 1933).

J. H. Kennedy, *Thomas Dongan, Governor of New York, 1682–1688* (CUA studies in American Church History, vol. 9; Washington 1930).

JOY HARRELL

## DONLEAVY, J. P. (1926–   )

American-Irish writer "noted for characters who display heroism in the face of a mad universe and remain deeply attached to life despite its flaws," according to the *Merriam Webster Encyclopedia of Literature*.

### BACKGROUND

James Patrick Donleavy was born April 23, 1926 in Brooklyn, New York to Irish immigrants. During the Second World War, while working at the Naval Academy Preparatory School, he heard about the writer James Joyce for the first time. This, and descriptions of the festive life to be found among Dublin's many pubs, entranced the young Donleavy. At the war's end, he applied to many American colleges but was turned down because of his dismal academic record. He then applied to Trinity College in Dublin, which accepted him.

For three years, Donleavy attended Trinity, ostensibly studying microbiology, but spending a great deal of his time pub crawling, sometimes in the company of Irish writer Brendan Behan. Donleavy returned to the United States in the early 1950s to work on his first novel. The prejudices he had against the United States, as a country hostile to artists and sensitive spirits, were confirmed in his mind by the stifling climate created by McCarthyism and the pressure towards social conformity for which America during the Eisenhower years is best remembered. Donleavy returned to Ireland to live there permanently (he became an Irish citizen in 1967).

### THE GINGER MAN

His first novel—and the one for which he is still best known—is *The Ginger Man* (1950). The plot follows Sebastian Dangerfield, an appealing rogue in rebellion against social conformity. Dangerfield craves worldly success but is unwilling to make the compromises he perceives as necessary to fulfill his ambitions. Both lyrical and bawdy, *The Ginger Man* provided a compelling, passionate anti-hero for the postwar generation which embraced the novel.

Probably because of the frank sexuality portrayed in *The Ginger Man*, Donleavy had trouble finding a publisher for it. On the advice of Brendan Behan, Donleavy submitted his manuscript to Maurice Girodias who published it through Olympia Press, a publishing house which used revenue gained from selling pornographic novels to publish more respectable works by groundbreaking authors such as Samuel Beckett and Vladimir Nabokov. Donleavy believed that *The Ginger Man* would be grouped among Olympia's more respectable offerings. To his dismay, it was included in Olympia's infamous pornography collection, "Traveler's Companion Series." Because of the harm this might do to his literary career, Donleavy sued the company. A complex body of litigation then followed, concluding twenty-two years later when Donleavy purchased Olympia Press. (Donleavy recounts this experience in *The History of the Ginger Man*.)

### AFTER THE GINGER MAN

In the decades following *The Ginger Man*, Donleavy has written a number of other novels, such as *The Saddest Summer of Samuel S.* (1966), *The Destinies of Darcy Dancer, Gentleman* (1977), and *The Lady Who Liked Clean Rest Rooms* (1996).

Donleavy's work after *The Ginger Man* has received a mixed critical reception, prompting critic James Korges to observe, ". . . Donleavy is widely regarded as a one-book author whose claim to reputation rests entirely on his first novel" (Grant). Others have suggested that Donleavy's vision has grown darker after *The Ginger Man*. Charles G. Masinton suggested that ". . . a spirit of vigor or confidence is lost after *The Ginger Man,* and a pervasive gloominess begins to settle over his works" (Grant). Nonetheless, he remains an author who attracts both readers and continued critical scrutiny.

*See* Fiction, Irish-American

J. P. Donleavy, *The Ginger Man* (Atlantic Monthly Press, 1988).
———, *The History of The Ginger Man* (Houghton Mifflin, 1994).
"Donleavy, J. P.," in *Merriam Webster Encyclopedia of Literature* (Merriam Webster, 1995).
"J. P. Donleavy," in *World of Penguin* (Penguin Publishing, 1998). http://www.penguin.co.uk/Penguin/Authors/160.html(June 1, 1998).

William E. Grant, "J. P. Donleavy," in *Dictionary of Literary Biography,* Vol. 6: *American Novelists since World War II, Second Series* (Gale Research, 1980). Gale Literary Databases http://galenet.com (May 24, 1998).

PETER G. SHEA

## DONNELLY, IGNATIUS (1831–1901)

Politician, author, reformer. Youngest son of Philip Carroll Donnelly, Philadelphia-trained physician and immigrant from County Tyrone, who wed (Philadelphia-born) Catherine Francis Gavin in 1826. Donnelly was born November 3, 1831 in Philadelphia, and attended Ringgold Elementary School and Central High School in that city. Reading law under Benjamin H. Brewster, later Attorney General of the United States, he was admitted to the bar in 1852. Two sons and a daughter were born to his marriage to Katherine McCaffrey in September of 1855. In the following year the couple moved to Minnesota Territory. Relocation was inspired by his faith in limitless opportunities in the West, but reinforced by false rumors that he had misappropriated funds in his legal work for immigrant savings banks in Philadelphia. Prejudice against Irish Catholics was also a factor. Both issues resurfaced periodically throughout his career in politics in spite of their unjust character.

### SPECULATIVE PLUNGE

Unwary of any imminent collapse of the decade-long land boom in Minnesota Territory, Donnelly invested heavily and promoted settlement in a village called Nininger on the Mississippi River. The Panic of 1857 left him with empty lots and plentiful debt. Foreshadowing his future publishing ventures, he had brought out the *Emigrant Aid Journal* to attract settlers.

### POLITICAL ANIMAL

Down but not crushed he considered the crisis a test of his resilience. Blessed with a gift for electrifying oratory which typically drew large, enthusiastic crowds, he turned to politics. Moderately opportunistic, the young Philadelphia Democrat joined the Republican party and managed to win lieutenant governorship of the newly created state in 1858. He was twenty-eight. Elected to the U.S. Congress four years later, he served three consecutive terms. A member of the Committee on Public Lands, he was instrumental in engineering land grants for railroads in Minnesota. He sponsored the National Bureau of Education Act of 1866, supported the purchase of Alaska, and his tree-planting ideas gave impetus to what later became the Timber Culture Act of 1873. Along the way he became a Radical Republican opposing Andrew Johnson's reconstruction policy. He collected lifelong opponents in Elihu Washburne (an Illinois congressman), and his brother, William D. Washburn, wealthy Minneapolis miller and lumberman, who dispensed with the "e" in the family name.

Despite his boosterism and speculative period, Donnelly evolved into a reformer and rebel. Elected state senator on the Anti-Monopoly ticket in 1873, he fought for regulation of insurance companies and railroads in Minnesota. He charged timber firms with illegal lumbering on state lands. The *Anti-Monopolist,* a weekly he founded, gave voice to his crusades 1874–1879. A state usury law and legislation providing free textbooks for public schools were among his contributions during his five years in the state senate. A failed run for U.S. Congress in 1878 turned his substantial energies toward writing, for most of a decade.

## POPULIST

In 1886 he reentered the lists for the state house, and, with Farmers' Alliance and Labor support, won a seat. The year 1890 brought him to the state senate on the Farmers' Alliance ticket. Elected president of Minnesota's Farmers' Alliance, he propelled that organization into the Populist party which he helped to found and whose preamble for its platform he personally wrote. It was a rousing call to reform the evils of late nineteenth-century America—its railroad barons, powerful bankers and all those who enjoyed fortunes and power at the expense of impoverished working people "who are denied the right of self-organization for self-protection." Donnelly gave the keynote speech at the Populist party convention in Omaha in July of 1892, which chose James B. Weaver as its candidate for United States president. As Populist candidate for governor of Minnesota, Donnelly's innumerable fiery speeches were insufficient to elect him. He supported Eugene Debs, leader of the American Railway Union, in the Pullman strike of 1894, and lost an election for the state senate of Minnesota in the fall. Bowing to the inevitability of Populist fusion with the Democrats and William Jennings Bryan in 1896, he traveled his home state with Bryan and managed to win a seat in the Minnesota house of representatives. It was his last campaign.

## AUTHOR

Donnelly loved to read, acquired a substantial library and, to console himself after political setbacks, produced theoretical works and several novels. In 1882 Harper & Brothers published his *Atlantis,* a best seller postulating that the legendary island of that name was real and was the birthplace of civilization. One year later his *Ragnarok* appeared, arguing that the earth was sprayed with debris from an enormous comet ages ago. With *The Great Crytogram* (1888) he claimed that Francis Bacon had authored Shakespeare's plays.

Three novels of note followed. One, *Caesar's Column* (1890), a book depicting a vision of 1988 rising from the ashes of a corrupt nineteenth-century society; a second, *Doctor Huguet,* one year later, dramatized racism in the South; a third, *The Golden Bottle* (1892), was a story of tyrants overthrown by the people—reflecting his Populist activism.

Donnelly's wife Kate, perpetually anxious about the family's financial status and perceptively critical of his political ventures, died in June of 1894. In February of 1898, elderly and lonely, Donnelly married Marion O. Hanson his twenty-year-old secretary, a Norwegian immigrant of Methodist persuasion—to the dismay of his children. On January 1, 1901 Ignatius Donnelly died of a heart attack.

David D. Anderson, *Ignatius Donnelly* (Boston, 1980).

The Donnelly Papers, Minnesota Historical Society, Saint Paul.

John D. Hicks, *The Populist Revolt* (Minneapolis, 1931).

Martin Ridge, *Ignatius Donnelly: The Portrait of a Politician* (Chicago, 1962).

L. A. O'DONNELL

## DONNELLY, JAMES S., JR. (1943–  )

Historian, educator. He was born in Manhattan, N.Y., on January 19, 1943. After graduating (Cum Laude) in history from

James S. Donnelly, Jr.

Fordham College (1964), he attended Harvard University where he received an M.A. (1965) and Ph.D. (1971) in history, studying under H. J. Hanham and David S. Landes. He began his teaching career as an assistant professor at the University of Tennessee, Chattanooga (1969–72), after which he moved to the University of Wisconsin, Madison, where he has been a professor of history since 1980. His first book, *Landlord and Tenant in Nineteenth-Century Ireland* (Dublin, 1973), grew out of his early interest in Irish social and economic history and was a prelude to his masterful *The Land and the People of Nineteenth-Century Cork: The Rural Economy and the Land Question* (London and Boston, 1975; reprinted Dublin, 1985) which received the Herbert Baxter Adams Prize of the American Historical Association for 1975. The latter was the first book to examine a single Irish county over the course of the nineteenth century and it significantly altered many long-held assumptions about such topics as the Famine and the Land War. It, together with a series of pioneering articles that Donnelly published during the 1970s and '80s on agrarian secret societies in the eighteenth and nineteenth centuries and a jointly-edited book of path-breaking essays entitled *Irish Peasants: Violence and Political Unrest, 1780–1914* (Manchester, 1983), helped to establish him as one of the foremost historians of modern Ireland. His subsequent publications on the Famine, especially his chapters in the *New History of Ireland,* Vol. V, Part 1 (Oxford, 1989) contributed immensely to our knowledge of that calamity and have challenged those historians who downplay or ignore the culpability of the British government with regard to Ireland's plight during the late 1840s. He has also written on aspects of popular religion in modern Ireland, including a prize-winning essay, "The Marian Shrine of Knock: The First Decade," (*Éire-Ireland,* xxviii, 2 [Summer 1993]: 55–99) and he continues to publish extensively on agrarian secret societies and the Famine.

Donnelly was chosen a member of the School of Historical Studies at the Institute for Advanced Study in Princeton (1980–81), during which time he was a recipient of a Guggenheim Memorial Foundation Fellowship. He has received a number of other fellowships, including a Senior Fellowship at the Institute of Irish Studies at Queen's University, Belfast. During 1995–98, he served as Chair of the Department of History at the

University of Wisconsin, Madison. He received the University of Wisconsin Distinguished Teaching Award in 1975.

He has been prominent in the American Conference for Irish Studies, serving as treasurer (1985–87), vice president (1987–89) and president (1989–91) of that organization. He has served as a member of the editorial board of the journal *Rural History* and is currently senior consulting editor of the journal *Éire-Ireland* and sits on the board of advisors of the *Journal of British Studies*. He and his wife Joan have three children.

GARY OWENS

### DONOVAN, GERARD (1959–   )

Poet. Gerard Donovan was born in Wexford, Ireland, and grew up in Galway. He was educated at University College, Galway, Johns Hopkins University, and at the University of Arkansas. In 1993, he was the John Atherton Fellow in Poetry at the Bread Loaf Writers' Conference at Middlebury College, Vermont. Currently, he teaches English at Suffolk Community College, and Southampton College on Long Island. Donovan is also an accomplished classical guitarist who has performed professionally since 1983. As a poet, Donovan identifies John Montague, Patrick Kavanagh, Ian Chrichton Smith, and Hans Magnus Enzensberger as particular influences.

In many of the poems in his remarkable first collection, *Columbus Rides Again,* Donovan casts his eyes on America, his adopted home. In the title sequence, he imagines Columbus, who is something of the poet's alter ego, as a man who "keeps hanging around/the basketball courts, drinking whiskey/and dreaming of buffalo." Eventually, because he won't accept "the concept of ownership," or "act white," he is sent home. Donovan explores the pre-Columbian world to be better able to understand what has been lost to America by the process of colonization, and, in doing so, suggests ways in which Irish and Native Americans share a common historical experience. Also, in these poems, Donovan juxtaposes history with the present in order to describe those pressure points where contemporary America interacts with its complex past. He is aware though that the historical process can never be reversed as is made clear in a pointed poem, "Aborigine in Dover," when an aborigine is landed in jail after arriving in Dover and claiming England for the Aborigine nation.

Donovan's inventiveness and lyrical gifts are confirmed by his second collection, *Kings and Bicycles.* Here, he gathers some of the best poems from *Columbus Rides Again* and newer work. For the most part, the new work focuses on Ireland, and particularly on Galway, both the city, where he grew up, Connemara, and the Aran Islands. *Kings and Bicycles* is a homage to the Irish West, and a moving book of return. He explores mythology, landscape, and his connection to Synge, another Irish writer who had found inspiration in that part of the world. In "Two Seasons In Connemara," he is entranced by the powerful sense of place so deeply that "I leaned into the mesh of air/ and pitched, like water poured,/to every side but forward." This collection also features a sequence of love poems, "Love Scenes," which is a meditation on the many phases of love, as it is revealed to the lover both through lived experience and through a Christian upbringing. As a poet, Donovan is possessed of a powerful double vision, one which is simultaneously Irish and American, and he draws on these two literary traditions to great effect.

*See* Poetry, Irish-American

Gerard Donovan, *Columbus Rides Again* (Galway, Ireland, 1992).
———, *Kings and Bicycles* (Galway, Ireland, 1995).

EAMONN WALL

### DONOVAN, WILLIAM JOSEPH ("Wild Bill") (1883–1959)

Lawyer, diplomat, military hero and public servant. He was born to Timothy Patrick Donovan and Anna Letitia (Lennon) Donovan at Buffalo, New York, on January 1, 1883. While the nickname "Wild Bill" reflected his outgoing personality, Donovan always was a gentle and introspective man (Neal, 171). At age eighteen he entered the Vincentian-run Niagara University for the purpose of studying for the Roman Catholic priesthood. However, in 1904 Donovan matriculated to Columbia University, from which he earned a B.A. in 1905 and an LL.B. in 1907.

Returning to Buffalo after his graduation, Donovan established the law firm of Donovan and Goodyear. Later, in 1912, Donovan and Goodyear merged with Buffalo's leading law firm, O'Brian and Hamlin (Neal, 169). On 15 July 1914, Donovan married Ruth Ramsey. They eventually became the parents of two children.

As the United States became involved in the affairs of Mexico and then entered World War I under President Woodrow Wilson's interventionist policies, Donovan moved into the military phase of his life. He served on the Mexican border as a part of the New York National Guard in 1916, when the United States under General John J. Pershing pursued Pancho Villa. He eventually became a colonel in the New York 69th Regiment and ventured to France as a segment of Pershing's American Expeditionary Force sent to open American participation in World War I. In that conflict Donovan emerged an American hero, receiving the Distinguished Service Cross, the Distinguished Service Medal, and the Congressional Medal of Honor (Neal, 169).

After the Treaty of Versailles, Donovan's political life began to develop. In 1922 he was appointed United States attorney for the western district of New York. Later that year he failed in his bid to win the office of lieutenant governor of New York, losing to the Democratic ticket headed by another Catholic and future presidential candidate, Alfred E. Smith. Two years afterward, Donovan was appointed U.S. assistant attorney general.

In the presidential campaign of 1928, Donovan campaigned for Herbert Hoover, and in 1932 he unsuccessfully sought the office of governor of New York, to replace Franklin Delano Roosevelt who was running for the presidency of the United States. During the 1930s and 1940s, Donovan matured as a top level public servant and diplomat.

In his diplomatic ventures Donovan observed the 1935 Italian military invasion of Libya and Ethiopia, and in 1938 he traveled to Spain (during the final era of the Spanish Civil War). At the request of United States Secretary of the Navy Frank Knox, Donovan visited England to assess Britain's war activities during the early stages of World War II. Ultimately, at the urging of American President Franklin D. Roosevelt, Donovan threw himself into running the Office of Strategic Services, an organization that ultimately became the model for the domestic Central Intelligence Agency.

During 1953–1954 Donovan served as United States Ambassador to Thailand. The recipient of almost countless awards, including honorary doctorates and the French Legion of Honor, Donovan, due to ill health, began to pull back from public service after his time spent in Thailand. He died in Berryville, Virginia, on February 8, 1959.

Stewart Alsop and Thomas Braden, *Sub Rosa* (New York, 1964).

William J. Donovan and Edgar A. Mowrer, *Fifth Column Lessons for America* (New York, 1940).

J. L. Morrison, *New Catholic Encyclopedia,* vol. IV (1967).

Donn C. Neal, "Donovan, William Joseph," *Dictionary of American Biography,* Supplement Six: *1956–1960* (New York, 1973).

PATRICK FOLEY

## DOOLEY, THOMAS A. (1927–1961)

Physician, social activist, author. He was born on January 17, 1927, into a prominent family in St. Louis, where his paternal grandfather was a self-made Irish-American industrialist. After undergraduate studies at the University of Notre Dame, he moved on to St. Louis University Medical School where an active social life delayed his graduation until his fifth year.

### Navy Volunteer in Vietnam

In 1954 he enlisted in the United States Navy Medical Corps and was assigned to temporary duty in Vietnam. North Vietnam had just fallen to the Viet Minh following the French defeat at Dienbienphu, and the Geneva Accords mandated free passage for Vietnamese wishing to settle in the pro-Communist North or in the newly established pro-Western Republic of South Vietnam under its Catholic leader Ngo Dinh Diem. It was a time of great fear and confusion among the refugee population and of concern among anti-Communists, especially Catholics, in the West over the fate of those fleeing from the Communist North.

As part of the evacuation plan, the Navy was about to begin a refugee operation that would move some one million North Vietnamese Catholics southward to safety. The stage was set for

the making of a folk hero, and Lt. Dooley filled the bill. Operating out of Haiphong harbor in the north, he worked almost around the clock to help refugees in their flight. As a result of his efforts he was awarded South Vietnam's highest honor and was urged by American intelligence figures to write an account of his activities.

### Best-Selling Author and Hero

His first book, *Deliver Us from Evil* (1956), was condensed by *Reader's Digest* in fourteen foreign languages, and he became a celebrity and much sought-after spokesman for the Diem regime. Then at the height of his popularity he was forced to re-sign from the Navy after an investigation into his homosexual behavior. The intelligence community arranged for his voluntary service in "Operation Laos," a private medical mission. He quickly became once again an asset to American policymakers seeking to further U.S. interests in the region. The publication of *The Edge of Tomorrow* in 1958, an account of "Operation Laos," further added to his popularity and to the awards he received from colleges and other groups. After surgery for malignant melanoma, he went on a lecture tour that netted more than a million dollars for MEDICO, a medical aid program he helped start in Southeast Asia. He returned there in 1960 after publishing his third best-seller, *The Night They Burned the Mountain*, to supervise MEDICO's clinic programs. He died of cancer on January 18, 1961, one day after his thirty-fourth birthday.

Agnes W. Dooley, *Promises to Keep: The Life of Dr. Thomas A. Dooley* (New York, 1962).

Thomas A. Dooley, *Tom Dooley's Three Great Books* (New York, 1960).

James Terence Fisher, *Dr. America: The Lives of Thomas A. Dooley, 1927–61* (Amherst, Mass., 1996).

JAMES J. HALEY

## DORSEY, THOMAS FRANCIS ("Tommy") (1905–1956)

Musician and accomplished swing band leader. Born to Thomas Francis Dorsey and Theresa Langton, Tommy grew up in an Irish

Thomas A. Dooley

Tommy Dorsey

mining community in Pennsylvania where his father was determined to keep his boys out of the mines. Dorsey's father taught himself music in his spare time and organized a band in Shenandoah where his boys, Tommy and Jimmy, grew up learning to play the cornet. As teenagers, the brothers organized their own band, Dorsey's Wild Canaries, and performed throughout Shenandoah until 1922. The brothers next joined the Scranton Sirens for two years, but moved to the Jean Goldkette jazz band in Detroit, Michigan in 1924. Here they performed with talents like Bix Beiderbecke, Joe Venuti, and Eddie Lang. Jimmy began to play the saxophone and the clarinet, while Tommy turned to the trombone. In 1927, the entire Goldkette band was hired by the Paul Whiteman Orchestra of New York City which brought the Dorseys radio and recording jobs and performances with singers like Bing Crosby and the Boswell sisters. By 1934, the Dorsey's formed their own band, the Dorsey Brothers Orchestra, with the help of Glenn Miller.

A 1935 dispute, however, broke up the band. Jimmy and Tommy blew up at each other at a 1935 Memorial Day weekend performance and for the next eighteen years they led separate bands. Jimmy maintained the Dorsey Brothers Band, while Tommy took over a band from Joe Haymes. Tommy's high expectations led to a series of band member departures and replacements, but by the early 1940s, Tommy had assembled a group that became one of the most popular swing bands of the decade.

In 1953 Jimmy's band fell apart and became the occasion for the brothers' reconciliation. Tommy took Jimmy into his orchestra and they performed as Tommy Dorsey and His Orchestra, Featuring Jimmy Dorsey. The Dorsey brothers performed for the next three years until Tommy's sudden death on November 26, 1956. Tommy was survived by his wife, Jane New, and two children.

Richard English, "The Battling Brothers Dorsey," *Saturday Evening Post* (February 1946).

Obituary, *New York Times* (November 27, 1956).

Herb Sanford, *Tommy and Jimmy: The Dorsey Years* (New Rochelle, N.Y.: Arlington House, 1972).

DANIEL J. KUNTZ

## DOUGHERTY, DENNIS JOSEPH CARDINAL (1865–1951)

The sixth of ten children of Patrick and Bridget (Henry) Dougherty had an early vocation to the priesthood. Born in Ashland, Pennsylvania, and educated in public schools there and in Gerardville, he applied for admission to Saint Charles Borromeo, the archdiocesan seminary of Philadelphia, but was rejected because of his youth. He spent two years at Sainte-Marie College, Montreal, Canada, then transferred to Saint Charles; he finished his priestly education at the North American College in Rome and was ordained May 31, 1890, at Saint John Lateran by Lucido Cardinal Parocchi.

Dougherty returned to Philadelphia to serve as Saint Charles's comptroller and professor of dogmatic theology. His career took a new turn in 1898 when the United States acquired the Philippines from Spain. Pope Leo XIII, who had met Dougherty when the latter was in Rome and had asked he be granted a doctorate after listening to his discussions of scholastic theology, appointed him bishop of Nueva Segovia April 7, 1903; Francesco Cardinal

Satolli consecrated him in Rome June 14, 1903. He was transferred to the diocese of Jaro June 21, 1908. During his dozen years as a missionary bishop he reorganized two sees, raised funds in the United States, rebuilt physical structures, personally cared for lepers, and, in 1907, attended the provincial council of Manila, which was a major step in stabilizing the Filipino Church. He also set an important legal precedent. Prior to his coming to the Philippines, a Filipino priest named Greogrio Aglipay had requested the Vatican name a Filipino bishop. When an American was named instead, Aglipay apostatized. He claimed control of church property. Dougherty simply acted as though he were the rightful bishop and claimant to the church property, forcing Aglipay to apply to the courts for relief. The courts turned him down, establishing principles still used in determining who controls religious property when a schism occurs in the denomination.

Dougherty was transferred from the Philippines to Buffalo, New York, December 9, 1915, and transferred for the last time to Philadelphia May 1, 1918. He was enthroned as archbishop July 10, 1918, received the pallium May 6, 1919, and was elevated to cardinal March 7, 1921. He had just passed his thirty-third anniversary in Philadelphia when he died, on May 21, 1951. He is buried at the Cathedral of Saints Peter and Paul.

Although immigration to cities such as Philadelphia slowed after 1921, internal migration from city to suburb developed. Dougherty kept pace with this expansion, erecting 112 new parishes during his tenure. He also expanded the reach of other Catholic institutions, building a dozen hospitals and eleven rest homes for the elderly. He was particularly interested in improving Catholic education. He erected 145 parochial schools, 53 high schools, and 4 colleges, plus a preparatory seminary. He developed a system of archdiocesan high schools for boys and girls, the tuition for the students being paid by the parishes that sent them rather than by the families. Funds and personnel increased along with the number of institutions. Dougherty made the annual seminary collection the largest of its kind in the world and invited 25 new orders of women religious into his see to staff institutions. In short, he personified the brick-and-mortar prelate.

He also personified the powerful prelate who did not share power easily. And, in many ways, he had quite conventional opinions for his day, supporting the Legion of Decency and opposing communism. However, he could also harness his strong will to an independent mind. He opposed the local Christian Front, a right-wing group active in Pennsylvania in the 1930s, despite that group's support of the popular radio priest Charles Coughlin. He also opposed universal military training. He could be dictatorial where women religious were concerned—in 1922, fearing leakage among Peruvians who sent their daughters to Protestant schools, he ordered members of the Servants of the Immaculate Heart of Mary to Peru to found a school—but his strong will could also be of some help. He became devoted to Therese of Lisieux before she became a saint, and in fact promoted her canonization. As president of the National Commission for Catholic Missions among the Colored People and Indians (1921–1951) he worked closely with Katherine Drexel (now Blessed). In 1934 he invited Anna M. Dengel's Medical Mission Sisters to establish their headquarters in his see, and two years later was instrumental in having canon law altered so that the sisters could carry out their vision of being both women religious and practitioners of medicine. In 1945, he publicly endorsed the proposed Equal Rights Amendment to the U.S. Constitution.

*See* Catholicism, Irish-American

Philip Jenkins, "'It Can't Happen Here': Fascism and Right-Wing Extremism in Pennsylvania, 1933–1942," *Pennsylvania History,* 72/1 (1995): 31–58.

James J. Kenneally, "Women Divided: The Catholic Struggle for an Equal Rights Amendment, 1923–1945," *Catholic Historical Review,* 75/2 (1989): 249–63.

Hugh J. Nolan, "Cardinal Dougherty: An Appreciation," *Records of the American Catholic Society of Philadelphia* 62 (1951): 135–41.

Margaret Mary Reher, "Cardinal Dennis Dougherty and the IHMs: The Church as the 'Juridic'/Mystical Body of Christ," *Catholic Historian* 14/4 (1996): 53–62.

———, "Den[n]is J. Dougherty and Anna M. Dengal: The Missionary Alliance," *Records of the American Catholic Historical Society of Philadelphia,* 101/1–2 (1990): 21–33.

———, "Get Thee to a [Peruvian] Nunnery: Cardinal Dougherty and the Philadelphia IHMs," *Records of the American Catholic Historical Society of Philadelphia* 103/3–4 (1992): 41–51.

MARY ELIZABETH BROWN

## DOWLING, PATRICK J. (1904– )

Known in California and throughout the western states as the ambassador-at-large for all things Irish, Patrick Dowling stands apart for his tireless work to preserve the Irish past. He was born in 1904 in Camross, County Laois, and attended the local national school. He began his career as a messenger and laborer. Gifted with a sharp intelligence and a love of reading, he foresaw no future for himself in the new Irish Free State, and in 1926 he emigrated to San Francisco. There he worked at some menial jobs and attended school in the evening. Within five years he was the manager of a large branch of a national food chain. He eventually founded his own business and had the means to begin his life's great task—to research and trace the history of Irish immigrants in California.

In San Francisco he became a moving spirit in Irish-American activities, and was co-founder of the Irish Cultural Center in San

Patrick Dowling

Francisco in 1973, and two years later he established the All Irish Library and Archives at the Center. He toured the western states seeking gifts of books and artifacts for the library, and traveled to Ireland for the same purpose. Today it is one of the largest depositories of Irish Americana.

Patrick Dowling's vast knowledge of the Irish saga in California is reflected in his informative book, *California: The Irish Dream* (San Francisco, 1989); and its impressive bibliography gives an insight into the wide scope of his research and reading. In the twentieth century, few did more than Patrick Dowling to foster Irish culture and to make the descendants of immigrants aware of their roots and heritage.

*See* California

*The Dungannon Observor* (January 10, 1986).
*The Irish Echo* (August 28, 1998).
*The National Hibernian Digest* (July–August 1991).

MICHAEL GLAZIER

## DOWNEY, JOHN (c. 1765–1826)

Educator, essayist. John Downey was one of five children born to Captain John and Sarah Downey of Germantown, Pennsylvania. His father served as head of the English School at the famous Germantown Academy. Upon his father's death in battle at Crooked Billet in 1778, Downey's mother used her influence to gain her son entry into the Germantown Academy, where Downey distinguished himself in his studies. Moving to Harrisburg in 1795, Downey opened his own school there the following year. In 1798, he wed Alice Ann Beatty. Downey gained a reputation as an education reformer after proposing a public education plan to Governor Thomas Mifflin in 1797. The plan called for a multilevel education system to be established in each township, including at least two elementary schools, a school for advanced study, and an academy devoted to "more liberal science." All the schools would be supported by property tax assessments and other public funding sources. Attendance would be compulsory. While his plan was not enacted, Downey received praise for his efforts. He further gained fame as an essayist, particularly for his humorous political sketches under pseudonyms such as "Simon the Wagoner," "Simon Slim," and "Simon Easy" and published in a compilation entitled the *Justice's Assistant.* Downey also enjoyed local prominence in the economic and political life of Harrisburg. He served as justice of the peace, town clerk, and served in the Pennsylvania Legislature from 1817–1818. In business, he served as the first cashier for the Harrisburg Bank and played roles in turnpike and bridge ventures as well.

*Dictionary of American Biography,* Vol. III, part 1: 416–17.
John P. Ohles, ed., *Biographical Dictionary of American Educators,* 3 vols. (Westport, CT., 1978): I: 392–93.
James P. Wickersham, *A History of Education in Pennsylvania, Public and Private, Elementary and Higher* (1886; reprint, New York, 1969).

TOM DOWNEY

## DRAFT RIOTS (JULY 13–16, 1863)

A week of civil unrest in New York City which involved mostly Irish workers. The immediate cause of the riots was the institution of the first federally mandated draft, the Conscription Act of

March 1863, which was passed to bolster numbers in the Union Army. The new law extended the draft to all men between the ages of 20 and 35 and to unmarried men under 45. Lists were to be constructed by a thorough house-to-house survey and a lottery was to be held in each congressional district. Men whose names were chosen could present an "acceptable substitute" or $300 to escape conscription. This law fell especially hard on young Irish who were generally poor and unable to afford the cost of the waiver.

Many in New York believed that Democratic officials in Washington would protect them from the demands of the new draft law, and no organized demonstrations were planned as the first lottery was held on Saturday, July 11. Word quickly spread throughout the city on Saturday evening and Sunday in anticipation of further lotteries to be held Monday. The crisis began on Monday morning as workers failed to report for duty and began making their way to the site of the lottery drawing at Third Avenue at Forty-seventh Street. Mobs of workers looted stores looking for weapons and eventually began burning federal conscription offices, tearing down telegraph poles and upsetting railroad tracks, looting the homes of wealthy Republicans, attacking police and beating Blacks. Blacks were a particular target of Irish anger since April when Blacks had been enlisted to replace striking longshoremen. The Colored Orphan Asylum was destroyed on Monday afternoon and by the end of the uprising about eleven black men were lynched.

Although in a few instances priests were able to stop individual mob attacks, Catholic leaders were largely incapable of halting the violence. On Friday, July 17, Archbishop John Hughes addressed a crowd of about 5,000, composed mostly of Irish workers. He called for an end to the violence for the sake of religion and for the honor of Ireland and for use of peaceful methods for political change. Hughes was no supporter of abolitionism; however, he firmly supported the war to defend the union. Although the crowd listened to his words, the violence was mostly over thanks to the arrival two days earlier of Union troops hurried back from the recent battle at Gettysburg.

Initially brought upon by anger at the draft, these riots soon began to serve as a focus of Irish anger at Republican wartime policies and resentment at black competition in the workplace. Although popularly believed to have instigated the deaths of over one thousand, in reality about 105 (mostly Irish) people

Draft Riot, July 1863

were killed in all. Nevertheless, these urban riots still represent the worst mob violence in the nation's history.

*See* Civil War; New York City; Ethnic Relations: The African-Americans and the Irish

Iver Bernstein, *The New York City Draft Riots* (New York, 1990).

Florence D. Cahalan, *A Popular History of the Archdiocese of New York* (Yonkers, N.Y., 1983).

Alan P. Man, "The Church and the New York Draft Riots of 1863," *Records of the American Catholic Historical Association* 62 (March 1951): 33–50.

ANTHONY D. ANDREASSI

## DRINAN, ROBERT F. (1920–    )

Legal scholar, member of Congress, political activist. Drinan will always be remembered as "Our Father who art in Congress"; in 1970 he became the first Catholic priest elected to the U.S. House of Representatives. First elected on a peace platform, he served five terms from the 4th District of Massachusetts before Pope John Paul II forced him to cancel his 1980 campaign. The revision of Canon Law then underway (issued in 1983) barred priests from elective office.

Drinan remained active in Democratic politics, including a stint as president of Americans for Democratic Action (1981–84). But he is also a distinguished legal scholar, specializing in international human rights, professional ethics, and religious liberty.

Drinan's political battles often involved abortion. While in Congress, he opposed a constitutional amendment to reverse the U.S. Supreme Court's 1973 abortion decisions and supported Medicaid funding of abortion on the grounds that to do otherwise would discriminate against the poor. He later defended President Clinton's veto of a ban on "partial-birth" late-term abortions because the bill did not allow an exception for the mother's health. Church leaders sometimes forced Drinan to clarify his position, but while supporting the church's teaching on abortion, he never recanted his political positions.

In Congress, Drinan, who was dean of Boston University Law School from 1956 to 1970, served on the Judiciary Committee. He introduced the first impeachment resolution against President Nixon, based on the illegal bombing of Cambodia. He voted for articles of impeachment related to Watergate offenses, with no reference to Cambodia. He later argued that President Clinton's actions did not include an impeachable offense.

Since 1981, Drinan has been professor of law at the Georgetown University Law Center. He has held more than a half-dozen visiting professorships, received two dozen honorary degrees, and written scores of law journal articles and newspaper columns. He has been a columnist for *National Catholic Reporter* and a member of the editorial council of the *Journal of Church and State* since 1980. He regularly contributes to *America, Christian Century,* the *Boston Globe,* and the *London Tablet.*

Drinan's human rights activity includes leadership in the Lawyers' Committee for Human Rights, service on the U.S. Holocaust Memorial Council, and being an observer for elections in Panama (1985) and Armenia (1991). He was the only non-Japanese-American to serve on the Civil Liberties Education Fund (1996–98) which administered the Fund reimbursing Japanese-Americans interred during World War II. He has

Robert F. Drinan

also been a leader in the fight against world hunger, including being a board member of Bread for the World (1974–82).

Since 1996, Drinan has chaired the American Bar Association's Standing Committee on Professionalism. He chaired the ABA Standing Committee on World Order Under Law from 1982 to 1986.

Robert Drinan, *The Fractured Dream: America's Divisive Moral Choice* (New York, 1991).

———, *Stories from the American Soul: A Reader in Ethics and American Policy for the 1990s* (Chicago, 1990).

———, *Cry of the Oppressed: The History and Hope of the Human Rights Revolution* (San Francisco, 1987).

———, *God and Caesar on the Potomac: A Pilgrimage of Conscience* (Wilmington, 1985).

———, *Beyond the Nuclear Freeze* (New York, 1983).

———, *Honor the Promise: America's Commitment to Israel* (New York, 1977).

———, *Vietnam and Armegeddon* (New York, 1970).

JIM CASTELLI

## DUANE, JAMES (1733–1797)

Jurist, legislator, member of Continental Congress. James Duane was a son of Anthony Duane, an Irish immigrant and prominent New York merchant. Duane was admitted to the bar in 1754, quickly establishing a prosperous and prominent law practice. A prerevolutionary conservative, Duane assisted in efforts to quell Stamp Act rioters in 1765 and gained enmity later for defending a Tory assemblyman against radical charges of corruption. Despite radical opposition, Duane served as a delegate to the First Continental Congress, where he worked to moderate demands for colonial rights and supported Joseph Galloway's plan for a formal union with Britain. Duane was returned to the Second Continental Congress and served almost continually until 1783, distinguishing himself with service on a number of committees, especially finanacial and Indian affairs, despite accusations of Loyalist sympathies made in 1781. His final service with the Congress was to aid in drafting the Articles of Confederation. Returning to New York City in 1783, Duane became mayor and worked diligently to rehabilitate the city after years of British occupation. He also sat in the state senate from 1782–1790 and was an ardent supportor of the ratification of the Constitution. He resigned from the Senate after being appointed as the first federal judge of the district of New York by President George Washington. He spent much of his final years encouraging settlement in his vast landholdings in upstate New York and Vermont. He died in Schenectady, New York in 1797.

*See* New York City

*Dictionary of American Biography*, Vol. III, part 1: 465–66.

Edward P. Alexander, *A Revolutionary Conservative: James Duane of New York* (New York, 1938).

M. E. Bradford, "Free But Not Equal: James Duane of New York," *Continuity*, 15 (1991): 99–103.

TOM DOWNEY

## DUANE, WILLIAM (1760–1835)

Journalist, politician. Duane was born in upstate New York to Irish parents. Upon his father's death, Duane's mother moved the family back to Ireland. Disinherited after marrying a Protestant, Duane left home to learn the printer's trade. He emigrated to India in 1787 and established the *Indian World* in Calcutta, where his vocal criticism of the East India Company led to his arrest and deportation. First traveling to London, Duane became increasingly frustrated at his inability to procure justice from Parliament. Leaving England, Duane arrived in Philadelphia and joined Benjamin Franklin Bache in editing the *Aurora*. After Bache's death in 1798, Duane married his widow and became sole editor of the newspaper. The *Aurora* soon became the most influential organ of the Jeffersonians in their opposition to the Federalist administration of John Adams. Employing intemperate language and inflammatory attacks in advancing the Jeffersonian cause, Duane was often brought to trial under the Alien and Sedition Acts, but succeeded in avoiding prosecution. Upon the ascension of Jefferson to the presidency, however, the influence of the *Aurora* quickly faded. Disappointed in his efforts to gain federal patronage from the new administration, Duane gradually turned on many of the Jeffersonians he previously supported. Duane continued as editor of the *Aurora* until 1822. Upon his retirement, he spent his final years publishing accounts of his travels to South America and a number of mediocre works on military science.

*See* Philadelphia

*Dictionary of National Biography*, Vol. III, part 1: 467–68.

James Morton Smith, "The Aurora and the Alien and Sedition Laws, Part II: The Editorship of William Duane," *Pennsylvania Magazine of History and Biography*, 77 (1953): 123–55.

"The Letters of William Duane," *Proceedings of the Massachusetts Historical Society*, 2nd ser., XX (1906/1907): 257–394.

TOM DOWNEY

## DUFFY, FRANCIS PATRICK (1871–1932)

Scholar, military chaplain. His Irish parents, Patrick and Mary Ready Duffy, emigrated to Canada after the Great Famine. Living in a working-class district in Cobourg, Ontario, they reared eleven children of whom Patrick was the third. After a happy boyhood,

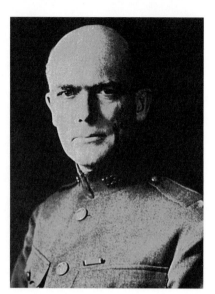

Francis Patrick Duffy

he won a scholarship to St. Michael's College, Toronto; and after graduation, moved to New York and earned his master's degree. He decided to study for the priesthood at St. Joseph Provincial Seminary at Troy and was ordained in 1896. Two years later he received a theological degree from Catholic University and began a teaching career at the new St. Joseph's Seminary (Dunwoodie) in Yonkers, New York. He was a scholar with wide horizons who felt a priestly education should be more than an unquestioning familiarity with some Latin textbooks by German or French writers, who left the message that philosophy and theology came to a full stop in the thirteenth century. In 1905 Francis Duffy, John Brady and James Driscoll founded *The New York Review* which acquainted its readers with the fresh work of European and American theological and biblical scholars. In Europe there was a crusade against Modernism, which began as a denunciation against a small group of scholars with heterodox opinions, but quickly evolved into an intellectual inquisition which did immense damage to the church and perpetuated lasting injustices. Duffy's column in the *New York Review* was suppressed and in 1908 the journal was forced to cease publication. The Modernist crackdown constricted Catholic intellectual life for six decades.

From 1916 to 1920 Duffy served as a military chaplain, and won fame in World War I for his service and courage in France with the "Fighting Sixty Ninth" Regiment of the New York National Guard. He was decorated by France and America and became a national hero. After the war he served as a pastor and became deeply involved in educational issues, fostered ecumenical dialog and civilized discussion on church and state relations.

Alfred E. Smith was the 1928 Democratic presidential candidate and, as a Catholic, he engendered widespread suspicion not only among the uneducated groups like the Ku Klux Klan but also among Protestant professionals and academics. Their suspicion was crystallized in an article in the March 1927 issue of the *Atlantic Monthly* in which Charles Marshall, a prominent Episcopalian lawyer, argued that it was incompatible for a Catholic to become president of the United States. Father Duffy was one of a trusted group which drafted Smith's cogent rebuttal. Smith lost the election in a landslide and bigotry was certainly a factor, but even had he been a fervent Baptist fundamentalist

he wouldn't have defeated Republican Herbert Hoover in a year of great prosperity.

In 1932 obituary notices across the country brought news of the death of Francis Patrick Duffy, the scholarly priest and patriot. Five years later, New York saluted his memory by erecting his statue in Times Square.

Francis Duffy, *Father Duffy's Story* (New York, 1919).
Ella M. Flick, *Chaplain of the Sixty-Ninth Regiment* (Philadelphia, 1935).

MICHAEL GLAZIER

### DUFFY, FRANK J. (1867–1950)

Banker, civic and religious leader. Frank J. Duffy was a Natchez, Mississippi, banker, businessman, planter, and Catholic leader who wrote a remarkable, perhaps unique page in American banking history. When the local Bank of Commerce of which he was president failed in 1929, Duffy felt a personal responsibility to his friends and customers. Over the next years (the depression years), "it was Mr. Duffy and only Mr. Duffy who dug into the personal fortune he had earned and saved to pay each depositor, dollar for dollar" (Natchez *Democrat*).

Frank J. Duffy was born in St. Louis, Missouri, in 1867. He came to Natchez around the turn of the century. He worked as a manager for the Southern Railway and Light Company and later entered the banking and hotel businesses, serving as president of the Bank of Commerce and owner of the Concord and later Duffy Hotels. He was also a successful planter in Concordia Civil Parish, Louisiana, across the Mississippi River from Natchez.

Duffy was an active civic leader and business adviser. He contributed generously to charitable causes, and was "a leading figure in all community work." Duffy served as president of the local Association of Commerce from 1915 to 1917. He was also a trusted adviser at St. Mary's Catholic Cathedral in Natchez, serving for many years on the Cathedral School financial advisory board and as an active member of the St. Vincent de Paul Society.

Duffy died in Natchez on January 5, 1950, after a long illness, and was buried in Calvary Cemetery in his native St. Louis. Duffy's actions toward his former banking customers after 1929 left a lasting memory of social justice and uncommon responsibility in the local community.

*See* Mississippi

Charles E. Nolan, *St. Mary's of Natchez: the History of a Southern Catholic Congregation, 1716–1988* (Natchez, 1992).
*Catholic Action of the South* (January 12, 1950).

CHARLES E. NOLAN

### DUGAN, ALAN (1923–   )

Poet. Alan Dugan was born in Brooklyn, N.Y., of Irish lineage and educated at Queen's College, Olivet College and Mexico City College (B.A., 1951). After serving in the United States Army Air Force during World War II, for about ten years he worked at various jobs in New York City in advertising, publishing and as a model maker for a medical supply house, all the while writing poetry. He served as poet-in-residence at Sarah Lawrence College (1967–1971) and then joined the faculty at the Fine Arts Work Center (1971–   ) in Provincetown, MA. He has received

Guggenheim Fellowships, a Rockefeller Foundation travel grant and other awards.

Dugan's *Poems* (1961), which won the Pulitzer Prize, the National Book Award and the Prix de Rome from the American Academy of Arts and Letters, virtually announced a new poetic voice in American poetry, and a style and tone that have remained consistent throughout Dugan's career.

Dugan sees life in unconventional ways and is honest, if limited, in how he treats what he sees. Nothing is sacred to him, his poems are self-contained, full of low-key and sometimes bitter humor, but always original and unlike anyone else's poetry. While Dugan cultivates a tone close to normal speech and has a narrow range of subjects, the muscular jolt of his diction and typographical experimentation in form can often contribute to a confusing style.

Initially one might think Dugan a nihilist or fatalist, but one is drawn back to his poetry to seek some clarity in the everyday objects and situations on which he focuses. He is a concerned observer who objectively describes the experiences—often fearful—of urban life. The speaker in "Untitled Poem," for example, says, "I am almost too old / to learn about human life / but I try to, I / watch it curiously and try / to imitate its better processes." And, as good poems do, Dugan's poems can universalize experience, even when the subject of that poem is often mundane and routine. The speaker in "Comment on 'Business Jacob, The Angel Wrestler,'" for example, says:

> You can't win, you can't draw,
> sometimes you can't even lose,
> but even to train up to such a fight
> is Victory.

And the reader frequently shares with Dugan a series of little victories over the routine fears of living. Boyers' observation is certainly right when he says that "One does not get terribly excited about [Dugan's] work but one nevertheless returns to it with increasing regularity. . . . In Dugan, at least, if one is able to hope at all, he hopes to endure rather than triumph."

Dugan's many ironic poses keep the reader at a distance. While honest, the poet's experiences in the poems are those of one who doubts, one who is subject to the workings of fate or chance, yet one who curiously observes and records. He deals frequently with the theme of war versus peace, for example, but the poet is neither hawk nor dove in his descriptions as with the hero who has become a statue, "to you the glory, brother, / and to us the girls."

In a real sense, Dugan is a moral poet concerned with making the best of the way things are, even when the odds are against one. It's what he refers to as the "other graffiti of the prisoners of this world," in the final lines of his first book and which, in his later books, is explored in the poet's own psyche.

*See* Poetry, Irish-American

Alan Dugan, *General Prothalamion in Populous Times* (Privately printed, 1961).
———, *Poems* (New Haven, 1961).
———, *Poems 2* (New Haven, 1963).
———, *Poems 3* (New Haven, 1967).
———, *Collected Poems* (New Haven, 1969).
———, *Poems 4* (Boston, 1974).
———, *New and Collected Poems, 1961–1983* (New York, 1983).
———, *Ten Years of Poems: from Alan Dugan's Workshop at Castle Hill Center for the Arts, Truro, Massachusetts* (Truro, 1987).
———, *Poems Six* (New York, 1989).

ANDREW M. McLEAN

## DULANY, DANIEL (1685–1753)

Lawyer, legislator, land speculator. Born in Queen's County, Ireland in 1685, the educated but impoverished Dulany immigrated with two brothers to Port Tobacco, Maryland, about 1703. After studying law with the former attorney-general of the colony, he gained admittance to the Charles County bar in 1709 and became a prosperous counselor. A land speculator, Dulany acquired thousands of acres in the Monocacy valley and encouraged German settlement of it, increasing its value tremendously. Dulany founded Frederick Town in 1745.

In 1721, Dulany moved to Annapolis and represented the city in the Maryland Legislative Assembly the following year. Appointed to the most important committee of the body, the Committee on Laws, he became a leader of those opposing the measures of the proprietor, governor and council, especially concerning the extension of English statutes to Maryland. In 1722, the proprietor vetoed a bill which seemingly introduced English laws into Maryland, claiming that no legislation should be promulgated without his approval. Dulany countered that Maryland's populace could not enjoy the rights and privileges guaranteed by the colony's charter without the protection of English statutes. In 1728, Dulany published a pamphlet on the issue, *The Rights of the Inhabitants of Maryland to the Benefit of the English Laws*.

In 1733, the proprietor appointed Dulany his agent and receiver general in order to remove him from his position as leader of the opposition that year, Dulany and Benjamin Tasker jointly held the office of commissary general. In 1734, Dulany was appointed judge of the admiralty and in 1736 was made sole commissary general, while ceding his position as agent and receiver general to Tasker. Dulany was sworn into the Governor's Council on September 25, 1742, and remained a member until his death in Annapolis eleven years later, on December 5, 1753.

*See* Maryland

Bernard Bailyn, *The Peopling of British North America* (New York, 1986).
Daniel Dulany, *The Right of the Inhabitants of Maryland to the Benefit of English Laws* (Annapolis, 1728).
Jacob Henderson, *The Rev. Mr. Jacob Henderson's Fifth Letter to Daniel Dulany, Esq. in Relation to the Case and Petition of the Clergy of Maryland* (Philadelphia, 1732).
Aubrey C. Land, *The Dulanys of Maryland: A Biographical Study of Daniel Dulany, the Elder (1685–1753) and Daniel Dulany, the Younger (1722–1799)* (Baltimore, 1955).
St. George L. Sioussat, "Economics and Politics in Maryland, 1720–1750, and the Public Services of Daniel Dulany, the Elder," in vol. 21 of *Johns Hopkins University Studies in History and Political Science* (Baltimore, 1903).

CHRISTIAN G. SAMITO

## DUNLOP, JAMES (1795–1856)

Lawyer, legal scholar. Born in 1795 at Chambersburg, Pennsylvania, James Dunlop descended from an Irish lineage dating back to his paternal great-grandfather. Dunlop's father was a prominent local lawyer. Dunlop's privileged upbringing provided him with a fine education. He graduated from Dickinson College in 1812 and gained admittance to the Pennsylvania bar in 1817. Upon graduation, Dunlop entered into practice with his father in Chambersburg. The practice flourished and Dunlop soon became active in the local business community as well, acting as a partner in a highly successful cutlery manufacturing firm. He served in the state senate from 1824–1827 and the house from 1831–1833. His political career ended abruptly in 1833 after he broke with the Jacksonian Democrats over the issue of the national bank, which Dunlop supported. Quitting his business ventures as well, Dunlop removed to Pittsburgh to concentrate full time on his law practice and legal studies. His first published work, *The General Laws of Pennsylvania, 1700–1846*, was very well received in the state legal community, establishing Dunlop as a leading legal authority in Pennsylvania. But while his practice and professional reputation grew, Dunlop's health failed him. He retired to Philadelphia in 1855, but continued writing. His most important work, *Digest of the General Laws of the United States*, was published shortly before his death in 1856.

*Dictionary of American Biography*, Vol. III, part 1: 518–19.
James Dunlop, *Digest of the General Laws of the United States* (Philadelphia, 1856).
*National Cyclopædia of American Biography*, Vol. XI: 360.

TOM DOWNEY

## DUNNE, DOMINICK (1925–  )

Journalist and novelist best known for writing about the often turbulent lives of the glamorous and wealthy. Dominick Dunne was born on October 29, 1925, the son of Richard E. and Dorothy Dunne. During the Second World War, he received a Bronze Star for his service in the Army during the Battle of the Bulge. After the war, Dunne received a B.A. at Williams College.

### EARLY SUCCESS

During the early years of his career, he worked extensively in television, serving as a stage manager on *The Howdy Doody Show* and as the executive producer of *Adventures in Paradise*. He also collaborated with stars like Humphrey Bogart and Frank Sinatra on film productions. In the early 1970s, Dunne worked as a film producer, making such films as *The Boys in the Band* (1970), *The Panic in Needle Park* (1971), *Play It As It Lays* (1972), and *Ash Wednesday* (1973). A number of Dunne's films were produced by Dunne-Didion-Dunne, a production company he formed with his brother and his sister-in-law, the writers John Gregory Dunne and Joan Didion.

### TURNING POINT

While Dunne enjoyed professional successes, his personal life was not so blessed. He was plagued by problems with alcohol and drugs. In the mid-1960s, his wife requested a divorce. His film *Ash Wednesday* was a financial failure. Dunne withdrew, seeking refuge in a cabin in Oregon. A supportive letter from the writer Truman Capote, as well as the death of one of his brothers, drew him out of his seclusion. Dunne moved to New York and completed a novel he had begun in Oregon entitled *The Winners* (1982). *The Winners* touches upon a subject which

Dunne would explore extensively in his subsequent career as a fiction writer and a journalist—corruption and intrigue among the wealthy and powerful.

His subsequent novels include *The Two Mrs. Grenvilles* (1985), *People Like Us* (1988), *An Inconvenient Woman* (1990), *The Mansions of Limbo* (1991), *A Season In Purgatory* (1993), and *Another City, Not My Own* (1997). Dunne has also worked as a writer and contributing editor at *Vanity Fair* magazine.

"Dominick Dunne," *Gale Literary Databases.* http://www.galenet.com (9 Sept. 1998).
Molly Leahy, "The Super Irish: Shining Stars of the Irish Diaspora," *The World of Hibernia*, Vol 4/1 (Summer 1998).
Michaela Swart Wilson, "Dunne, Dominick," *Contemporary Authors: New Revision Series*, Vol. 46 (New York: Gale Research Inc, 1995).

PETER G. SHEA

## DUNNE, FINLEY PETER (1867–1936)

Columnist and social commentator. Born on Chicago's Near West Side in the shadow of Old Saint Patrick's Church on July 10, 1867, young Peter Dunne was encouraged in reading and the life of the mind by his mother, Ellen Finley Dunne, a lover of Dickens, Scott, and Thackeray, and his older sister, Amelia, a teacher in the Chicago Public Schools. In June 1884, fresh out of high school and 16 years old, Dunne took a job as an office boy and cub reporter for the Chicago *Telegram*. Eight years and five increasingly responsible jobs later, he was editorial chairman at the Chicago *Evening Post*. It was there, at the ripe old age of 26, that Dunne created the voice of Mr. Martin J. Dooley, an aging immigrant saloonkeeper on Archer Avenue, in the South Side, Irish working-class community known then (and now) as Bridgeport.

In the *Post* of Saturday, October 7, 1893, the inaugural column opened with John McKenna, a genial politician, entering Dooley's place and greeting his old friend. Almost immediately, these weekly 750-word monologues (delivered to McKenna or long-suffering millworker Malachi Hennessy) became a Saturday evening Chicago tradition. The last in a series of dialect experiments for his creator, Mr. Dooley succeeded "Colonel Malachi McNeery," a fictional downtown Chicago barkeep whom Dunne had invented to provide weekly commentary in the *Evening Post* during the World's Fair of 1893. Dunne had modeled the Colonel on a friend of his, Jim McGarry, whose saloon in the downtown Loop was a gathering spot for newspapermen and visiting celebrities, including boxer John L. Sullivan and actor James O'Neill. In contrast to the cosmopolitan McGarry/McNeery location, Dunne placed Mr. Dooley's barroom as an outlying neighborhood institution where a regular clientele of Irish millworkers and draymen could find solace and companionship.

Between 1893 and 1900, some 300 Dooley pieces appeared in Chicago newspapers. Taken together, they form a coherent body of work, in which a vivid, detailed world comes into existence, a self-contained immigrant/ethnic culture with its own customs, ceremonies, "sacred sites," social pecking order, heroes, villains, and victims. The Chicago Dooley pieces constitute the most solidly realized ethnic neighborhood in nineteenth-century American literature. With the full faith of the literary realist, Dunne embraced the common man as proper subject and created sympathetic, dignified, sometimes heroic characters, plausibly grounded in a few city blocks of apartments, saloons, factories, and churches. The result of his labor was the great nineteenth-century Irish-American novel—in weekly installments. Importantly, all of these literary and historical riches were transmitted through the vernacular voice of an aging Irish immigrant, and Dunne's use of dialect was a major breakthrough.

Until Mr. Dooley began speaking, the brogue had been used pervasively in nineteenth-century drama, fiction, and journalism to portray the stereotypical "stage Irishman," a demeaning comic caricature of ignorance, belligerence, and garrulity, the purpose of which was mockery of supposed Irishness. But Mr. Dooley's brogue smashed the stereotypes for good and all. When he is being funny, he provokes laughter not because he knows so little, but because he knows so much. He is witty, satirical, cutting, and he exposes delusions rather than reinforcing them. Moreover, Mr. Dooley is funny in only half the Chicago pieces. He is just as often utterly serious, treating such subjects as starvation in Ireland and Chicago, wanton murder and grim retribution in the urban underworld, and heroic sacrifices by Bridgeport firemen in their tinderbox neighborhood, "consthructed f'r poor people out iv nice varnished pine an' cotton waste." Throughout the 1890s, Mr. Dooley gave Chicagoans pioneering weekly examples of the potential for serious fiction of common speech and everyday life.

Dunne's Chicago Dooley columns provide two precious and lasting contributions to our understanding of the Irish in America. First, Mr. Dooley is the custodian of urban, ethnic community memory stretching back to pre-Famine Ireland, in stories about Christmas visiting, crossroads dances, and being graduated "be th' toe iv th' hidge schoolmasther's boot." Harshest of all are the still vivid images of "our parish over beyant, whin th' potatoes was all kilt be the frost an' th' oats rotted with th' dhrivin' rain. . . . Musha, but 'tis a sound to dhrive ye'er heart cold whin a woman sobs an' th' young wans cries, an' both because there's no bread in th' house." He also preserves stories of the wrenching, turbulent crossing to America, the shattered dream of gold in the streets, the rough-and-tumble of life along the Illinois and Michigan Canal, and military service in the Union and Fenian armies. Second, Mr. Dooley is the historian of the community mores of Irish Chicago in the 1890s, in stories of stoic, exploited millworkers and day laborers, failed politicians who lose their money, successful ones who forget their friends, lace-curtain social climbers with pianos in the parlor, and voluble "pathriots" committed—rhetorically—to Irish freedom. He provides telling vignettes from the quotidian passing scene of the sufferings of the poor, the embarrassments and compromises accompanying the slow rise to middle-class respectability, and the painful gulf that often opens between immigrant parents and their American children.

Yearly holidays and commemorative events were often the catalyst for Dooley pieces that chronicle Irish and Chicago customs, from Memorial Day, Christmas, Thanksgiving, and the Fourth of July, to Orange parades on July 12, the United Irish Societies' "freedom picnics" on August 15, and, naturally, St. Patrick's Day. With much less advance notice than was provided by holidays, Dunne also wrote Dooley pieces in response to late-breaking news. When four Chicago firemen died in a Friday morning blaze, the Saturday *Post* contained Mr. Dooley's recollection of the tragic hubris of fireman Mike Clancy, the most admired man in Bridgeport, who feels himself slowing down and vows to quit after one more "rale good ol' hot wan." Clancy "was wan iv th' men undher whin th' wall fell. I seen thim bringin'

him home; an' th' little woman met him at th' dure, rumplin' her apron in her hands." Other pieces give us rare and colorful pictures of the activities that centered around a late nineteenth-century urban parish, among them the annual parish fair at "St. Honoria's" in 1895, featuring "Roddy's Hibernyun Band playin' on th' cor-rner," a shooting gallery, booths selling everything from rosaries to oyster stew, and a raffle for a doll, a rocking chair, and "a picture iv th' pope done by Mary Ann O'Donoghue." Other parish productions include a "temperance saloon" which lasts only one night, as the patrons have "dhrunk thimsilves into chollery morbus with coold limonade," a genealogy lecture in the school hall that erupts into a brawl over whose ancestors were kings and whose only dukes, and the staging of "The Doomed Markey" by the "St. Patrick's Stock Company" with Denny Hogan in the title role.

Written under deadline and often for specific occasions, the Chicago Dooley pieces are of extraordinary quality, for they create the illusion of a speaking voice grounded in place that still rings true across the hundred years since it first appeared. Their true greatness lies in the coming together in these newspaper columns of oral tradition and the written word. These are, after all, transcribed renderings of imagined conversational speech, much of it inspired by stories that had been told to the young Peter Dunne. It is as a speaking voice delivered through the medium of print that he has preserved the cultural memory and mores of Irish Chicago. Written out in longhand late on Friday nights for the Saturday *Post,* more often than not with a copy boy hovering at his elbow, the Chicago Dooley pieces combine virtually spontaneous composition and a minimal sense of *writtenness.* Moreover, as in the oral tradition, the Dooley pieces utilize a set of formal conventions: the entry of a patron into the saloon, ensuing episodic narratives, often introduced by a familiar phrase ("I see by th' pa-apers," or "D'ye mind th' Clancys that lived over be Halsted sthreet"), and a sharp, epigrammatic, closing pronouncement. In fact, the Chicago Dooley pieces constitute a rare and marvelous hybrid form. An early Dooley piece *is* closer to talk than writing. This body of work is truly transitional, bridging the gap between storytelling and printed short fiction to create, from fall 1893 through the end of 1897, an astonishing four-year window into the world of nineteenth-century Irish Chicago. There's a retrospective, piercing sense of urgency and great good fortune here, for the decade of the 1890s was virtually the last time when such a preserving endeavor was possible for Irish-Americans from the great post-Famine migration.

The literary situation changed dramatically for Dunne in 1898, when the popularity of Mr. Dooley's satiric perspective on the Spanish-American War led to national syndication and the publication of his first book of selected columns, *Mr. Dooley in Peace and in War.* From this point on, a Dooley piece was very much a *printed* text. Dunne moved permanently to New York City in 1900, and soon became the most popular humorist of the day, a position he held until World War I. Over this time, he put together seven more collections of his pieces, the last of them *Mr. Dooley on Making a Will and Other Necessary Evils* (1919). His tenure as resident American comic sage was remarkable both in its length and in the consistent high quality of the mostly occasional commentary on all manner of national figures and foibles. Mr. Dooley's lilting, skeptical voice remained blessedly lucid and rational to the end, and he gave the nation twenty years of intelligence, laughter, and perspective. He is still quoted extensively. What we find in these later pieces, however, is really only

Mr. Dooley's ghost—a rootless, disembodied voice, not all that different, except for the brogue, from its predecessors in the genre of American crackerbarrel dialect humor as established by Hosea Biglow, Artemus Ward, and Sut Lovingood, and exploited by the folksy, performing image of Mark Twain. Finley Peter Dunne's lasting achievement remains the Chicago Dooley pieces, which embody the truth of the creed of Patrick Kavanagh, whose own poetry is rooted in the small farms and fields of his native County Monaghan: "Parochialism is universal; it deals with the fundamentals." Dunne died in New York City on April 24, 1936.

*See* Fiction, Irish-American; Chicago, Aspects of

Finley Peter Dunne, *Mr. Dooley in the Hearts of His Countrymen* (Boston, 1899).

Philip Dunne, ed., *Mr. Dooley Remembers: The Informal Memoirs of Finley Peter Dunne* (Boston, 1963).

Elmer Ellis, *Mr. Dooley's America, A Life of Finley Peter Dunne* (N.Y., 1947).

———, ed., *Mr. Dooley at His Best* (New York, 1943).

Charles Fanning, *Finley Peter Dunne and Mr. Dooley: The Chicago Years* (Lexington, Ky., 1978).

———, ed., *Mr Dooley and the Chicago Irish: The Autobiography of a Nineteenth Century Ethnic Group* (Washington, 1987).

CHARLES FANNING

## DUNNE, IRENE MARIE (1898[?]–1990)

Motion-picture and stage actress and singer. Irene Marie Dunn (original name) was born to Joseph John and Adelaide Antoinette (Henry) Dunn Dec. 20, 1898, in Louisville, Ky. (Some accounts list her birth as 1901 and 1904.) Her father was a supervisory inspector of steamships for the U.S. government; her mother, an accomplished musician.

Her father died when Irene was eleven years old, and she and her mother moved to Madison, Ind., to live with Irene's grandparents. Dunne studied for a year at a music conservatory in Indianapolis. She then took a position as music and art teacher in an East Chicago, Ind., high school. Before reaching the school, however, she entered a scholarship contest to study voice at Chicago Musical College. Although competing against professionally coached singers, she won the scholarship.

Dunne turned to musical comedy and landed the leading role in a road company of *Irene*. She then went on to other road plays between 1922 and 1926, and sang with light opera companies in Atlanta and St. Louis.

In January 1927 she opened on Broadway in the role of Diana in *Yours Truly*. That same year, in July, she married Dr. Francis Dennis Griffin, a New York dentist. The turning point in her career came in 1929 when she was "discovered" by Florenz Ziegfeld while riding with him in an office elevator. Ziegfeld invited her to audition for *Show Boat,* and she won the leading role of Magnolia Hawks.

Her performance in *Show Boat,* which ran seventy-two weeks, led to offers from motion picture studios. In 1930 she accepted a contract from RKO. When her first picture, *Leathernecking,* wasn't critically acclaimed, she decided to pursue dramatic lessons. Six months later, she tested for the female lead in Edna Ferber's *Cimarron,* competing with several experienced actresses, and won the role. With that performance, she was hailed as "a new dramatic star" in 1931.

After the "tear jerker" *Back Street* in 1932, Dunne went on to star in several dramatic films, including *The Age of Innocence* (1934) and *Magnificent Obsession* (1935), in which Robert Taylor was her co-star.

When musicals returned to the screen, Dunne appeared in Jerome Kern's *Roberta* (1935) with Fred Astaire and Ginger Rogers. The following year, Universal cast her in *Show Boat.* That performance not only demonstrated Dunne's ability as a singer but also as a comedienne.

In 1939 RKO cast Dunne with Charles Boyer in *Love Affair,* and audiences viewed them as one of the most romantic teams in movies. Dunne noted that her appearance in 1941 with Bing Crosby in Columbia's *Penny Serenade,* the story of a childless couple who adopt an infant, was a reflection of her own life. She and her husband had adopted a one-year-old girl, Mary Frances ("Missy"), in 1936.

Among the forty-three feature-length movies she made, Dunne co-starred with many of Hollywood's leading men, including Rex Harrison, Spencer Tracy and Van Johnson. During the last decade of her career, she starred in *A Guy Named Joe* (1943), *The White Cliffs of Dover* (1944), *Anna and the King of Siam* (1946), *Life With Father* (1947), *I Remember Mama* (1948), and her last major film, *The Mudlark* (1950), in which she played Queen Victoria.

Dunne was nominated for an Academy Award as Outstanding Actress five times for her performances in: *Cimarron* (1930), *Theodora Goes Wild* (1936), *The Awful Truth* (1937), *Love Affair* (1939), and *I Remember Mama* (1948).

Known as the "First Lady of the Talkies," Dunne was honored by the University of Notre Dame with its Laetare Medal in 1940. With Norma Shearer and Greer Garson, Dunne was acclaimed a "First Lady of Hollywood." Dunne died Sept. 4, 1990, in Los Angeles.

*See* Cinema, Irish in

*Current Biography* (1945).
*Current Biography Yearbook* (1990).
*Encyclopaedia Britannica* (1996).
*International Motion Picture Almanac* (1943–44).
*National Cyclopedia of American Biography,* vol. F.

Irene Dunne

MARIANNA McLOUGHLIN

# DUNNE, JOHN GREGORY (1932– )

Novelist, journalist, essayist, and screenwriter respected for his sharp, gritty prose and incisive, unsentimental portraits of flawed but interesting people.

## BACKGROUND

John Gregory Dunne was born May 25, 1932 in Hartford, Connecticut, into a large family (he was the fifth of six children).

As a young adult, he attended Princeton (where he received an A.B. degree in English) and spent a two-year stint in the army before going to work at *Time* magazine as an editor and writer. According to Michael Adams in the *Dictionary of Literary Biography Yearbook 1980*, Dunne developed a dislike for the "assembly-line techniques of newsmagazines." No doubt this contributed to his embrace of "New Journalism," a brand of participatory reporting made famous by writers like Jimmy Breslin and Tom Wolfe. In 1958 he met the writer Joan Didion while she was an editor at *Vogue* magazine. They were married in 1964.

## EARLY WORK

Dunne's first book, *Delano: The Story of the California Grape Strike* (1967), centers on Cesar Chavez's National Farmworker's Association (NFWA) and the grape pickers strike the NFWA led in Delano, California. Dunne's eye for the revealing detail was praised, but he was also criticized for being distant from the events he covered. In the words of Martin Duberman, quoted in *Contemporary Literary Criticism*, ". . . he [Dunne] settles for presenting all available points of view instead of trying to discover where . . . the truth may lie." In *Quintana & Friends* (1978), a collection of previously published articles, Dunne attempted to explain his technique. "What I do is hang around. Become part of the furniture. An end table in someone's life. It is the art of the scavenger" (Adams).

*The Studio* (1969) is an inside look at a major film studio—Twentieth Century Fox—in the late 1960s. With his sharp eye for detail and attentive ear for the revealing quote, Dunne captured the chaos and small-mindedness of Hollywood. In *Vegas: A Memoir of a Dark Season* (1974) Dunne again looked at individu-

als living lives of quiet desperation. According to *Contemporary Authors*, "It is . . . the first book in which Dunne mines what he now routinely refers to as the 'Mother Lode'—his Irish-American heritage."

## MINING THE "MOTHER LODE"

Dunne's first novel, *True Confessions* (1977), set in 1940s Los Angeles, is about the relationship between two Irish-Catholic brothers, Tom Spellacy, a police detective, and Des Spellacy, an ambitious parish priest. The plot of the novel revolves around the murder of a prostitute. Critics praised *True Confessions* for, among other things, Dunne's success in creating vivid, idiosyncratic characters, particularly Tom and Des, two complicated men who develop, in the word of Michael Adams, "a growing awareness of the ambiguities of good and evil." In *Dutch Shea, Jr.* (1982) Dunne continues his examination of "corruption in an Irish-Catholic milieu" (*Contemporary Authors*). In *Harp* (1989), an autobiography, Dunne examines his ambivalence towards his Irish-Catholic background.

Aside from writing numerous articles and co-writing several screenplays, Dunne has also published other books such as *Crooning: A Collection* (1990), the novel *Playland* (1994), and *Monster: Living Off the Big Screen* (1998).

*See* Fiction, Irish-American

Michael Adams, "John Gregory Dunne," *Dictionary of Literary Biography Yearbook, 1980* (Gale Research, 1981).

John Gregory Dunne, *Harp* (Simon & Schuster, 1989).

"Dunne, John Gregory," *Contemporary Authors, New Revision Series*, Vol. 50 (Gale Research, 1996).

"Dunne, John Gregory," *Merriam Webster's Encyclopedia of Literature* (Merriam Webster, 1995).

"John Gregory Dunne," *Contemporary Literary Criticism*, Vol. 28 (Gale Research, 1984).

Hugh Kenner, "His Irish Is Up," *New York Times Book Review* (Sept. 10, 1989).

Raymond Schroth, "A Devotion to Rough Edges," *Commonweal* (Nov. 3, 1989).

PETER G. SHEA

John W. Lockington, *Robert Blair of Bangor* (Belfast, 1996).
Thomas M'Crie, ed., *The Life of Mr. Robert Blair, . . . with Supplement to his Life . . .* (Edinburgh, 1848).
J. S. Reid, *History of the Presbyterian Church in Ireland* (Belfast, 1867).
W. K. Tweedie, ed., "A Brief Historical Relation of the Life of Mr. John Livingstone" in *Select Biographies* (Edinburgh, 1865).
Thomas Witherow, *Historical and Literary Memorials of Presbyterianism in Ireland [1623–1731]* (London and Belfast, 1879).

JAMES E. DOAN

## *EAGLE WING* AND PRESBYTERIAN EMIGRANTS

The first attempted migration by Scotch-Irish Presbyterians to the American colonies was the ill-fated *Eagle Wing* expedition of 1636. They were led by two Scottish-born ministers, Robert Blair (1593–1666) and John Livingstone (1603–72), who had been active in the religious revival centered around Six Mile Water in northeast Ulster during the 1620s (Tweedie, 142–43). They were suspended for non-conformity in the early 1630s and by 1634 had begun considering emigration to New England. After receiving an invitation from the governor of Massachusetts, John Winthrop, as well as a visit from his son, John Winthrop, Jr., they began constructing a ship in Belfast, called *Eagle Wing* after the Exodus verse (19.4): "I bare you on eagles' wings, and brought you unto myself."

On September 9, 1636, 140 passengers departed from Groomsport, on the south side of Belfast Lough, but winds detained them in Loch Ryan, Scotland, and apparent leaks held them in the Kyles of Bute. Blair wrote an extensive account of the crossing, which was completed by his son-in-law, William Row (M'Crie, *The Life*). Livingstone also described the crossing and the hurricane which forced them to return home, indicating that it broke their rudder, as well as "much of our gallion-head, our fore-cross-tree, and tare our fore-sail, five or six of our chain-plates (strong links or plates on the ship's side, to which the shrouds are secured) made up, ane great beam under the gunner-roome door brake, seas came in over the round-house, and brake ane plank or two in the deck, and wett all them that were between decks" (Tweedie, 155). In the following year, the ministers were driven out of Ireland and took refuge in Scotland where many of their congregation followed them. Their attempts to settle in the New World, though thwarted by the adverse weather they encountered, were to bear fruit beginning in the 1680s and throughout the following centuries, when hundreds of thousands of their fellow Scotch-Irish countrymen successfully emigrated to America.

Since 1991 an annual *Eagle Wing* festival held in Groomsport, Co. Down, has commemorated the original attempted Scotch-Irish voyage to America. Including lectures and musical and dance performances, the festival, which takes place on the July 4 weekend, focuses on the contributions of Ulster people to American civilization as well as on the continuing cultural connections between Northern Ireland and the United States.

*See* Emigration: 17th and 18th Centuries

P. Adair, *A True Narrative of the Rise and Progress of the Presbyterian Church in Ireland, 1623–1670* (ed. W. D. Killen) (Belfast, 1866).

## EDUCATING IMMIGRANTS: A BOSTON CASE STUDY

In 1873, four Sisters of St. Joseph from Flushing, New York, led by 30-year-old, Irish-born Sister Mary Regis Casserly, arrived in Boston to open a parochial school. From this small beginning developed the Congregation of the Sisters of St. Joseph of Boston, a diocesan community that within a few decades became New England's largest sisterhood. By its fortieth anniversary in 1913, this sisterhood had increased to 211 members who staffed nineteen schools enrolling more than 9,000 children. The community's experiences in this period exemplify in important ways those of all sisterhoods whose members instructed children of Irish parentage in Massachusetts parochial schools. They reveal how, despite intense civic disapproval of their religion, their professional work, and their life style, women religious significantly advanced the social integration of the Irish in America.

Sisters working in the Boston archdiocese in the late nineteenth century forged their collective consciousness and professional commitments in an unfriendly social environment. Nowhere was mainstream opposition to the Irish and to parochial schools stronger than in Yankee Massachusetts. In 1850, Irish immigrants and their minor children comprised 43 percent of America's foreign-born population; in Massachusetts, however, the figure stood at 71 percent. The number of Irish-born and first-generation Irish-Catholic children in the state by the 1880s exceeded the total of other children by nearly 90,000. At this time, 21 percent of school-age Boston children, most of them Irish, were not attending school. A priority goal of the Sisters of St. Joseph was to reverse this distressing situation. Indeed, their first Boston school, which opened in October 1873, attracted many of these school dropouts. "A large number of girls," wrote the community annalist, "who had left the public school some time before, came because it was the Sisters' school" (Motherhouse Annals, 10/2/1873).

The anti-Catholic, anti-Irish spirit that characterized late nineteenth century Massachusetts had its roots in long-standing ties between the native stock Protestant majority, popularly termed "Yankees," and anti-Irish, Protestant England. Yankee leaders, or "Boston Brahmins," came from a small group of upper-class families that had controlled Massachusetts manufacturing and transportation industries, banks, insurance companies, and educational institutions for two centuries. A rapidly growing Irish-Catholic population led both groups to tighten ranks against the "outsiders," stereotyped simply as "'the Irish,'—Bridgets and Paddys; micks and harps; pot-wallopers, biddies, and kitchen canaries; greenhorns and clodhoppers—muckers all" (Trout, 170; Shannon, 185–86).

By the 1880s, Yankee critiques of Irish Catholics had begun to focus less on their religious beliefs than on their educational views. Relative to other major dioceses, Boston had few parochial schools when in 1884 the nation's bishops, meeting in the Third Plenary Council of Baltimore, decreed that Catholic children should attend parochial schools. The sudden school-building campaign that ensued in Boston in response to this mandate profoundly disturbed local Protestants. While the Catholic Church, in the words of a contemporary Yankee preacher, was acknowledged to be "the chief barrier against . . . the howling sea of an ignorant and unprincipled population" (quoted in Solomon, 53), its growing intrusion into the educational realm was intolerable. Public schools, after all, had long been the principal means by which Yankees controlled Irish-American children. If large numbers of these children were now to be educated separately, they would be even less acculturated than their parents. By withdrawing children from public schools, Irish Catholics were again exhibiting their deplorable lack of patriotism, their indifference to American democratic values, and their woeful intolerance.

Catholics ignored these charges and continued not only to open parochial schools but also to challenge traditional Protestant dominance of the public schools. However, victories over Yankee hegemony were rare in the nineteenth century. For example, in response to a vigorous Irish campaign to place more Catholics on the Boston School Committee, the British-American Association orchestrated a huge "mass indignation meeting" at Faneuil Hall. There, irate Protestants pledged to vote against all candidates allied to "any foreign power or potentate" (Kaufman, 147–48). As a result, the 1888 and 1889 elections routed every Irish Catholic from the school committee.

In 1888, Massachusetts Yankees mounted a major concerted attack on parochial schools in the form of a state legislative committee bill that would require state inspection of private schools. The provision that no school would receive state approval "unless *all* the teachers had certificates from the school committee" ("The Attack on Freedom," 547) posed a particularly grave threat, since virtually no Catholic school could meet such a standard. The bill was defeated, but only because a group of Boston's most influential Brahmins, including Thomas Wentworth Higginson, Rev. Edward Everett Hale, and Harvard and Massachusetts Institute of Technology Presidents Charles W. Eliot and Francis A. Walker, came forward to testify publicly against it. While these men strongly disapproved of parochial schools, they considered them a far lesser evil than the social chaos they expected the bill's enactment would spawn.

On a fundamental level, the opening of a Catholic school immediately affected the success of a town's public school. To defuse Protestant apprehensions in this regard, the Sisters of St. Joseph worked quietly to integrate every parochial school into its local community. Whenever possible, they held important school events in public halls, invited townspeople of all faiths to attend, and made these affairs as colorful as possible. The presence of Bishop John Lancaster Spalding of Peoria, Bishop John Ireland of St. Paul, and Archbishop John Williams of Boston at the dedication ceremony of a South Boston school in 1879, for example, attracted an impressive crowd of spectators and extensive press coverage. In the 1880s, sisters defused criticism that their new Stoughton school was "foreign" by making it the first school in town to fly the American flag. At the same time, they introduced an annual "visiting day" at the school so that town Protestants as well as Catholics could meet the sisters and observe classes in session. Such simple strategies generally allayed local fears. Within a few years, the Stoughton public school superintendent

himself presented diplomas to the pioneer graduating class of St. Mary's School.

Massachusetts town officials, nonetheless, perpetuated negative stereotypes about the intellectual abilities of Irish children and the quality of Catholic schools by requiring parochial school graduates, but not their public school counterparts, to pass special tests for admission to public high schools. The outcome of these tests, published in the press, became a topic of intense local discussion. Since the sisters prepared their pupils carefully for the examinations, the children passed them easily, and by 1913, most towns were admitting parochial and public school students to the public high schools on equal terms. For Irish Catholics, the abandonment of the high school admission tests represented a particularly gratifying Yankee acknowledgment of the quality of parochial schools and the proficiency of their faculties.

Despite such modest triumphs, perennial mainstream criticism that parochial schools were inferior to the public schools continued to distress Catholic parents. In an effort to counteract it, Sisters of St. Joseph scrupulously followed local public school standards and curriculum. They had never adopted the European disciplinary practices and "ornamental courses" very much in vogue in schools and academies conducted by other sisterhoods in the 1870s. Regular religion lessons and a Catholic atmosphere distinguished their schools, but in courses of study, textbooks, academic calendars, and pedagogical methods, they conformed as much as possible to public school policies. However, their commitment to the public school curriculum was not uncritical. When, for example, Boston public schools introduced industrial training programs in 1885, parochial schools did not follow suit. The sisters viewed the introduction of such programs in the elementary grades as seriously detrimental to the future career opportunities and professional aspirations of their working-class pupils.

A matter of increasing concern for Massachusetts Sisters of St. Joseph was the formal professional preparation of their members. To deflect Yankee criticism in this matter, the sisters had, from their first days in Boston, sought out prominent public school administrators to instruct young sisters in pedagogy. In 1879 the community annalist reported: "The services of Mr. Larkin Dunton, principal of the Normal School of the City of Boston, engaged to teach in the novitiate for two years— management of the classroom and technique of teaching. . . . We are all delighted and expect to reap great fruit from his instructions." The sisters benefited regularly from such in-house courses for many years. A 1907 annals entry, for example, indicated that Mr. McGrath, principal of the Eliot School, Bennet Street, Boston, would come to the convent to instruct the sisters on the teaching of fractions (Motherhouse Annals, 6/26/1879; 10/25/1879; 11/9/1907).

By the 1880s, however, teacher training had become a central political issue in Massachusetts, and the state's normal schools were improving swiftly. Public education officials argued that private as well as public school teachers ought to satisfy state certification requirements. The traditional informal approach to educating sisters for parochial schools came under mounting criticism, and the contentious 1888 debate over the private school inspection bill brought the issue dramatically to the fore. Although by the 1890s more Sisters of St. Joseph were high school graduates, few could yet meet state teacher certification standards. In this decade, Sisters of St. Joseph for the first time embarked upon formal, extra-convent, courses of study. Those destined for the faculty of the Boston School for the Deaf took courses at the Clarke Institution for the Deaf in Northampton, and another small cadre enrolled in a program in educational methods at the Harvard University Summer School. However, the community's meager financial resources made such opportunities the exception rather than the rule, and the troublesome problem of teacher certification for the general membership remained unresolved. For the most part, in 1913 young Sisters of St. Joseph, like their predecessors, were still "learning-by-doing," under the tutelage of experienced teachers.

Anti-Catholic ire in Massachusetts in the 1870s and 1880s focused not only on the Irish community, but, in a special way, on nuns and convent life. The sensational, anti-Catholic depictions of sisters that still appeared regularly in the regional press impeded efforts of Sisters of St. Joseph to be taken seriously as competent, progressive educators. Concluding that their most persuasive weapon was publicity, they decided to permit the press and the general public to attend the rites of reception of the religious habit and profession of vows. Curious Protestants as well as Catholics filled the church to behold young postulants exchange bridal raiment for the black habit of the Sisters of St. Joseph and hear novices pronounce the vows of religion. By welcoming the public to these hitherto private, time-honored ceremonies, the sisters dispelled considerable Yankee mistrust not only of nuns and convents but also of parochial schools.

Sisters of St. Joseph of Boston in the 1873–1913 period were typically native Bostonians of Irish families. Thus they were uniquely sensitive to Yankee descriptions of Irish Catholics as foreigners and "outsiders." As teachers of thousands of working-class Irish-American children in parish schools of the Boston archdiocese, they challenged Yankee ascendancy and enlarged the domain of common education to encompass parochial as well as public schools. The growing mutual regard that marked relations between Massachusetts Yankees and Irish Catholics after 1913 owed much to these resourceful women. By this date, Catholic convents and parochial schools were incontestable elements of New England's social fabric.

*See* Boston

"The Attack on Freedom of Education in Massachusetts," *American Catholic Quarterly Review* 13 (October 1888): 545–54.

Oscar Handlin, *Boston's Immigrants, 1790–1880* (New York, 1968).

Polly Welts Kaufman, *Boston Women and City School Politics, 1872–1905* (New York, 1994).

Motherhouse Annals, 1873–1913, Archives of the Congregation of the Sisters of St. Joseph of Boston, Brighton, Massachusetts.

Mary J. Oates, "Mother Mary Regis Casserly," in Maxine Schwartz Seller, ed., *Women Educators in the United States, 1820–1993: A Bio-Bibliographical Sourcebook* (Westport, 1994).

———, "Professional Preparation of Parochial School Teachers, 1870–1940,"in Michael F. Konig and Martin Kaufman, eds., *Education in Massachusetts: Selected Essays* (Westfield, 1989).

———, "Organized Voluntarism: The Catholic Sisters in Massachusetts, 1870–1940," *American Quarterly* 30 (Winter 1978): 652–80.

William V. Shannon, *The American Irish: A Political and Social Portrait* (New York, 1963).

A Sister of St. Joseph, *Just Passing Through, 1873–1943* (Boston, 1943).

Barbara Miller Solomon, *Ancestors and Immigrants: A Changing New England Tradition* (Chicago, 1956).

Charles H. Trout, "Curley of Boston: The Search for Irish Legitimacy," in Ronald P. Formisano and Constance K. Burns, eds., *Boston, 1700–1980: The Evolution of Urban Politics* (Westport, 1984).

MARY J. OATES, C.S.J.

## EDUCATION: IRISH-AMERICAN TEACHERS IN PUBLIC SCHOOLS, 1880–1920

By the turn of this century, Irish-Americans were the largest single ethnic group among teachers in American cities with large Irish-American populations. In Providence, Boston, New York, Chicago, and San Francisco, Irish-American women comprised one-quarter to one-half of all the teachers in the public schools at that time, and their numbers were growing. Many of these women were the American-born daughters of Irish immigrant mothers. Their entrance into white-collar work was unprecedented among any other second-generation female immigrant group, and their entrance into the lower middle class of white-collar work occurred at least a generation before that of most Irish-American men.

### Influx

The arrival of Irish-America's daughters into the classrooms of big city public schools was the result of a complex combination of factors in both Irish and Irish-American life in the late nineteenth century. In the decades after the Great Famine of the late 1840s, more and more Irish women lost their importance as co-producers on family-run farms in Ireland. As their employment and marriage opportunities at home decreased, however, their educational opportunities increased. By the late nineteenth century, girls outnumbered boys among the pupils in Ireland's national schools, the first state-supported school system in the British Isles, and throughout the late nineteenth and into the twentieth centuries, women were as apt (and in many years more apt) as men to leave their homeland permanently upon school-leaving. The vast majority of these women sailed to the United States.

The women leaving Ireland in the late nineteenth and early twentieth centuries were highly unusual in comparison to other female immigrants entering the United States in those years. Not only did the number of women leaving Ireland equal that of men, almost all of these young women were unmarried and traveling independently of husbands or fathers. Most were literate in the English language as a result of their childhoods spent in national school classrooms. They settled in America's cities, found jobs as domestic servants, eventually married, and gave birth to daughters destined to be the nation's schoolteachers.

Chicago teacher and principal Amelia Dunne Hookway

A connection between the unusual contours of Irish women's immigration and the entrance of so many of their daughters into public school teaching in America can be found by looking at the educational opportunities available to girls in rural Ireland and the propensity of the American-born daughters of these former national school pupils to enter teaching. Although primary school attendance was not made compulsory in Ireland until 1892, throughout the second half of the nineteenth century, figures collected by the Commissioners of National Education in Ireland indicate that girls in areas with the highest female emigration rates demonstrated higher levels of daily attendance and more years of schooling on average than did the boys. In addition to the literacy and numeracy they learned in the national schools, girls in classrooms observed, for the first time, a seemingly independent, educated, well-groomed lady not tied to family farm or shop. Teachers represented a new female aspiration: an independent woman with almost unimaginable grace and freedom. Furthermore, these ladies had achieved their status not through birth or marriage but through diligence at school, a diligence schoolgirls could imitate. Although few of these girls actually became teachers themselves, American census figures reveal the impact of their educational ambition on their American-born daughters. In 1900, for instance, over 70% of Irish-born women in the United States were employed in "service," and only slightly over 3% of them were classified as "professionals." In contrast, only one-quarter of American-born women of Irish descent were servants in that year, and over 14% of Irish-American women were counted as "professionals" by American census takers. Without doubt many of these profesional women were teacher-daughters of national school-educated immigrant mothers.

## BACKLASH

The entrance of Irish-American women into public school teaching did not go unnoticed by contemporary observers, and many of these onlookers were highly critical of the large numbers of Irish-Americans in the ranks of public school teachers. One such observer, Lotus D. Coffman of Columbia University's Teachers College, registered his criticism in terms of the cultural danger these newcomers represented to the nation's classrooms. In his influential book, *The Social Composition of the Teaching Population* (New York, 1911), Coffman launched a thinly veiled attack on the proliferation of Irish-Americans in the nation's teaching force. "[T]he differences in race . . . , social class, . . . economic station, . . . intellectual maturity, [and] . . . academic and professional training . . ." between the "American" teaching force of old and the new ethnic teachers were a major "problem" in contemporary education, Coffman warned his readers. "[T]he kind of people we get in teaching necessarily affects the kind of teaching we get" (14, 77, 71).

Coffman and others were especially concerned with the perceived inability of ethnic teachers to Americanize public school classrooms increasingly populated by children of immigrants from the non-English speaking world. Although Irish-American teachers came from English-speaking homes, their Catholicism was seen by critics as alien to mainstream American culture, and their presence in the public schools supposedly undermined the inculcation of those values. In San Francisco, for example, the Board of Education decreed that teachers would be immediately dismissed if they used any "sectarian or denominational" publications in the classroom. Instead, the Board reminded teachers that their mission was to "impress on the minds of their pupils the principles of morality, truth, justice, and patriotism, . . . to instruct them in the principles of free government, and to train them up to a true comprehension of the rights, duties and dignity of American citizenship." The Board was already preaching to the converted, however, as Irish-American teachers in San Francisco and other cities throughout the United States showed little interest in promoting self-consciously Irish or Catholic points of view in their classrooms. Despite the Boston School Committee's purchase of 605 Irish history textbooks for its schools in 1906, for instance, Irish-Americans in the public schools promoted American values, not ethnic ones, for the most part.

In fact, Irish-American teachers were often at the forefront of the Americanization process in the classroom. Chicago teacher and principal Amelia Dunne Hookway is one such example. The eldest sister of famed journalist Finley Peter Dunne and the daughter of an Irish-born mother, Hookway became nationally known as the founder and chief patron of a children's theater at her Howland School in Chicago. Her productions included dramatizations of popular children's literature, including Mark Twain's *The Prince and the Pauper,* as well as patriotic vignettes from early American history. Hookway's American culture, not her Irish roots, determined the curriculum she taught to her multicultural pupils in turn-of-the-century Chicago.

Much of the concern that many educational leaders felt about the influx of Irish-American women into the ranks of urban elementary school teaching was, therefore, based on misplaced fears. Despite the inability to pinpoint any cultural subversion among Irish-American teachers, however, these fears remained widespread throughout the early years of the twentieth century. One reason for the persistence of anti-Irish (and anti-Catholic) attitudes among influential educational leaders stemmed from the fact that many of the Irish-American women teaching in the public schools had been educated in Catholic schools, especially in Chicago.

By the turn of the century, Chicago had the largest Catholic school system in the country. Created in the 1840s as a haven for Irish and later Catholic immigrant groups seeking freedom from the Protestant values they believed were widespread in the public schools, Chicago's "separate but equal" Catholic schools seemed poised to undermine the city's public school system by the end of the century. Even though such obviously Protestant practices as the reading of the King James Bible in the public schools was outlawed in 1910, the city's Catholic schools were by then so well-established that few of Chicago's Catholic families with enough income to afford the fees for a Catholic education sent their children to the public schools. Nevertheless, although Irish Catholics had been among the primary founders of Chicago's Catholic school system and remained one of the single largest ethnic groups in its classrooms, Catholic school-educated Irish-American women were the largest ethnic group among the city's public Normal School graduates by 1908. By 1910, at least one-third of Chicago's public school teachers were Catholics.

The preponderance of Catholic school–educated Irish-American women in the city's Normal School and public school classrooms prompted a backlash from the Chicago school administrators who proposed a rule limiting the numbers of Catholic high school graduates eligible for entrance into the Normal School. While this rule was never enacted, largely because the board retreated in the face of a public outcry led by Cardinal Mundelein and other Chicago Catholic leaders, it illustrates the lingering unease non-Catholic civic leaders felt about Irish-American teachers in the public schools.

Boston's school officials had a similarly problematic relationship with their city's growing number of Irish-American teachers. Catholic education in Boston was never as widespread or as well-attended as Chicago's. Instead, Irish Catholics in the city were willing to send their offspring to the city's public schools, the oldest system in the nation. As the numbers of Irish-Catholic pupils grew throughout the later nineteenth century, Boston's school committees worried about the "Irish problem" confronting the city's educational infrastructure. Noting that, as usual, the Irish had the largest number of births of any ethnic group in the city, school officials watched the proliferation of Irish-Americans in the city's schools with dismay. As the number of pupils expanded, teacher recruitment and training necessarily became one of the school committee's highest priorities.

To meet the rising demand for more teachers, Boston's school authorities established a Normal School. In 1880, within a year of its founding, the school committee proudly reported that "the Normal School is doing a good work in affording to the children of the citizens of Boston an opportunity to prepare themselves in a profession. . . ." The Normal School was preparing these "children" so well that almost one-fifth of the school's first graduates were young women with Irish last names. Averaging fifty children in their classrooms, Irish-American women were an increasing proportion of Boston's public school teachers in the late nineteenth and early twentieth centuries, just as they were in Chicago and San Francisco, where they were one-third and one-half respectively of those cities' primary and grammar school teachers by the end of the twentieth century's first decade.

## SELF-HELP

Despite their cooperation in curriculum matters, however, Irish-American public school teachers were less tractable outside the classroom. Daughters of Irish-America, such as Margaret Haley and Catherine Goggins in Chicago, Kate Kennedy in San Francisco, and Grace Strachan and Kate Hogan in New York, were leaders in demanding job security, pension rights, and equal pay for teachers. Basing their demands on the same democratic American principles they taught inside the classroom, Irish-American women educators won hard-fought campaigns for teacher rights in cities throughout the country.

Writing in her posthumously published autobiography, *Battleground* (Urbana, Illinois, 1982), Haley credited her Irish-born mother with fostering her intellectual development, "as only the Irish, who had been denied the full measure of education, could value it," by teaching her daughter the Irish maxim, "Educate [yourself] in order that your children may be free" (14). Haley began her work in the Chicago public schools in 1882 after teaching in several rural schools in downstate Illinois. She remembered being "a tremendous conformist" at first, but as her career progressed she became increasingly critical of what she believed was the mismanagement of the schools and the oppression of their teaching staff. In 1897, Haley left teaching and became the paid business representative and vice president of the newly formed Chicago Teachers' Federation (CTF), the first teachers union in the United States. Throughout her long career as a union employee, Haley spearheaded successful campaigns to secure tenure and pensions for Chicago's public school teachers. Declaring that "only through the freedom of their teachers could the children remain free," Haley concluded that she "had no

choice to make. It had been made for me . . . Chicago is the proving ground of American democracy" (17, 40, 170).

When teacher Catherine Goggins, also the American-born daughter of an Irish immigrant mother, was nominated for the presidency of the CTF in 1899, her candidacy prompted a flood of anonymous letters attacking her "race and religion" (Haley, 37). Nevertheless, Goggins's strong voice for teachers' rights won her a victory. In her inaugural address she insisted that "the public school stands as a great barrier against [the] evils . . . of the sudden appearance of gigantic trusts [that] dominate . . . our municipal, state and national government [because the schools] teach . . . the fundamental principals of our government . . . [and] rest . . . on that bulwark of our liberties, the consent of the governed" (3, quoted in David Morrison, "Catherine Goggins," *Historical Encyclopedia of Chicago Women,* forthcoming).

Kate Kennedy of San Francisco also illustrates the American values of turn-of-the-century Irish-American public school teachers. Irish-born Kennedy reached San Francisco in the mid-1850s and started teaching in the frontier city's public schools in 1857. Until her death in 1890, Kennedy fought for teacher pensions, tenure rights, and equal pay for female teachers and principals. As a result of her work, California enacted the first equal pay for equal work law in the world in 1874.

Following in the footsteps of their counterparts in Chicago and San Francisco, New Yorkers Grace Strachan and Kate Hogan founded the Interborough Association of Women Teachers (IAWT) in 1906. Calling for equal pay for equal work, the IAWT soon attracted the majority of New York's elementary teachers as members and won important concessions from the school board and the state legislature in favor of teacher rights.

## LEGACY

The importance of Irish-American women in the public school classrooms of America's largest cities demonstrates a remarkable example of female advancement in an age when a group's mobility was measured mostly in male terms. Irish-American public school teachers (and their female-religious counterparts) were on the cutting edge of Irish-American educational progress at the turn of this century. Becoming a public school teacher in a large urban school system required years of preparation, which included a four-year academic high school course with classes in mathematics, foreign language, and literature, followed by teacher training in a Normal School. By the time they were hired by school systems in Chicago or Boston or San Francisco, Irish-American teachers had spent a minimum of thirteen years in school.

Like their mothers who had left Ireland armed with literacy and numeracy a generation before them, Irish-American teachers used their education to achieve economic self-sufficiency and social influence in an era that offered few options to women outside of marriage. The impact of these daughters of Irish-America on the public schools of the nation's largest cities insured that public education at the turn of the century maintained its democratic ideals, especially since these women were themselves beneficiaries of these principles. As a result of their educational achievements and political activism, Irish-American teachers were often leaders in their group's adjustment to American life. They were also transmitters of American culture to hundreds of thousands of even newer Americans placed under their care. Their role in the classroom made them the pioneers of Irish-America's entrance into the middle class, and their achievement inspired the daughters of other immigrant groups to embrace education for themselves.

*See* Women, Nineteenth-Century

Suellen Hoy, "Caring for Chicago's Women and Girls: The Sisters of the Good Shepherd, 1859–1911," *Journal of Urban History* 23/3 (March 1997): 260–294.

David Morrison, "Catherine Goggins," in *The Historical Encyclopedia of Chicago Women*, eds., Rima Schultz and Adele Hast (Bloomington, Indiana, forthcoming).

Marjorie Murphy, *Blackboard Unions: The AFT and the NEA, 1900–1980* (Ithaca, New York, 1990).

Janet Nolan, "The Great Famine and Women's Emigration from Ireland," in *The Hungry Stream: Essays on Famine and Emigration*, ed., E. Margaret Crawford (Belfast, 1997): 67–75.

———, "Irish-American Teachers and the Struggle Over American Urban Education, 1890–1920: A Preliminary Look," *Records of the American Catholic Historical Society of Philadelphia* 103/3–4 (Winter 1992): 13–22.

———, "Margaret Haley," in *The Historical Encyclopedia of Chicago Women*.

———, "The National Schools and Women's Mobility in the Late Nineteenth and Early Twentieth Centuries," *Irish Studies Review* 18 (Spring 1997): 23–28.

———, *Ourselves Alone: Women's Emigration from Ireland, 1885–1920* (Lexington, Kentucky, 1989).

———, "A Patrick Henry in the Classroom: Margaret Haley and the Chicago Teachers' Federation," *Éire-Ireland* XXX/2 (Summer 1995): 104–117.

———, "Saint Patrick's Daughter: Amelia Dunne Hookway and Chicago's Public Schools," in *At the Crossroads: Old St. Patrick's and the Chicago Irish*, ed., Ellen Skerrett (Chicago, 1997): 103–117.

Joel Perlmann, *Ethnic Differences: Schooling and Social Structure Among the Irish, Italians, Jews, and Blacks in an American City, 1880–1935* (New York, 1988).

James W. Sanders, "Catholics and the School Question in Boston: The Cardinal O'Connell Years," in *Catholic Boston: Studies in Religion and Community, 1870–1970*, eds., Robert E. Sullivan and James M. O'Toole (Boston, 1985): 121–169.

———, *The Education of an Urban Minority: Catholics in Chicago, 1833–1935* (New York, 1977).

Ellen Skerrett, "The Catholic Dimension," in *The Irish in Chicago*, eds., Lawrence J. McCaffrey and Ellen Skerrett (Chicago, 1987): 22–60.

David Tyack, *The One Best System: A History of American Urban Education* (Cambridge, 1974).

JANET NOLAN

# EDUCATION, PAROCHIAL

Irish-Americans have always been ambivalent about parochial education. To be sure, the Irish were the leaders of the movement to establish parish schools in the United States. But at no time in the history of American Catholic parochial education did a majority of Irish-American children attend parish schools. It is an incontrovertible fact of American history that a significant majority of Irish-Americans graduated from public schools.

Perhaps the best indicator of this ambivalence is the modest pace of Irish parish school establishment. A historical study of eighty-seven Irish immigrant parishes revealed that 27 percent had established a school within two years after parish formation and for almost half (46 percent), it took ten years. A comparable study of German Catholic parishes revealed that two thirds had schools within two years and 86 percent had a school within ten years (Dolan, 278).

The source of this Irish ambivalence was a lack of motivation to support parochial schools. Many ethnic groups such as the Germans eagerly established parochial schools in America to preserve their native language and cultural traditions, but not the Irish. Ireland had been under British domination for more than a century when the Irish began to emigrate to the United States in the 1820s. In truth, the Irish came to America not so much to find cultural freedom as to escape the poverty of their native land. Few gave much thought to preserving what little was left of their language and culture.

## OPPOSITION TO PUBLIC SCHOOLS

The Irish who did join the parochial school movement in the United States did so to preserve the Catholic faith of their children. In all the decades of oppression at the hands of the English, the Irish never abandoned the Church. Indeed, attending Mass and harboring priests were acts of defiance. More to the point, the Irish could well recall English efforts to use all manner of temptations—including education—to entice them to become Protestants. American public schools, many using the King James Bible as a text, seemed very much like the English institutions in Ireland.

Thus the conflict between the Irish and common school advocates was primarily catechetical. Protestant ministers and public schoolmen claimed that reading the Bible without comment or instruction was non-sectarian and non-dogmatic. Irish-Americans vehemently disagreed and charged that Bible reading without guidance was a Protestant concept and therefore unacceptable for the education of their children. No agreement could be reached because few Irish-American leaders were convinced that there was any common ground on which to compromise. To many Irish Catholics, education outside of their control was more dangerous than no education at all.

## AN EXPERIMENT IN MASSACHUSETTS

In this climate of disagreement there emerged in Lowell, Massachusetts, an Irish-American educational experiment that was to have important implications for the future of Catholic education throughout the United States. In an effort to "consider the expediency of establishing a separate school for the benefit of the Irish population," the Lowell town meeting of 1831 appropriated fifty dollars for the support of the local Irish Catholic school.

At the time, most Massachusetts schools were affiliated with religious denominations and the grant to the Catholic school seemed the most logical way of providing for the education of Lowell's small but growing Irish population. The relationship worked well and by 1835, three Irish Catholic schools in Lowell were being supported with public funds.

Even though educational cooperation ended in Lowell in 1852, the idea was too powerful and appealing to die. One small community in Massachusetts had solved the problem of public funding of parochial education and the plan worked well for almost twenty years. Other communities in other states also would try the Lowell plan with varying degrees of success in the later decades of the century. Before the end of the century, twenty-one communities in fourteen states would experiment with public support for private schools.

## NATIVISTS RESPOND TO IRISH-AMERICAN PROTESTS

But the cooperation that developed in Lowell was not typical of the relationship between the Irish and the native population in

Non-Catholics were suspicious of Catholic efforts to reform public education. In this 1871 cartoon by Thomas H. Nast, the bishops and the Vatican threaten American children.

other cities. In fact, tension was far more common than compromise, and in some communities—most notably Philadelphia—the tension led to violence. One might have thought that the so-called "City of Brotherly Love," with its moderate Irish-born bishop, Francis Patrick Kenrick, would have been able to resolve peacefully any differences over public education. But this was not the case.

The tension escalated in 1843 when Kenrick appealed to the public school officials to allow Catholic children to use their own version of the Bible in school. It seemed to be a reasonable request, but nativists saw dark designs in Kenrick's appeal to the board. Many were convinced that the petition was a diversion, the first step in a campaign to undermine the Christian curriculum of the public schools. In the nativist mind, Kenrick and his Irish Catholics were interfering with the will of the majority.

This tension festered for a year before exploding into the worst anti-Catholic rioting in American history in the spring and summer of 1844. A nativist rally on May 3 turned violent. Entire blocks of Irish homes went up in flames, but this was not enough for crowds as they moved on to destroy Catholic churches and a seminary. Throughout the Philadelphia Catholic community, priests, nuns, and lay people fled for their lives—refugees in a war of hate.

There was no resolution to the violence in Philadelphia, and few of the rioters were prosecuted. For many Irish-Americans, the violence in Philadelphia was proof that American society was anti-Catholic. Many Irish-Americans turned to parochial schools to protect their children.

## THE BISHOPS AND PAROCHIAL EDUCATION

It is surprising, therefore, that the Irish-American leadership, as reflected in the Catholic hierarchy, was not uniform in its support for parochial schools. Even though the majority of nineteenth century American Catholic bishops had been born in Ireland, each responded to the issue of parochial education in his own way. Some bishops chose to minimize their involvement in educational matters. Others were able to do very little because ethnic conflict and poverty had created far larger problems than the establishment of parish schools. Still other bishops were tireless advocates of parochial education, and in their dioceses their word was Church doctrine.

The personification of this last group was Bishop John Hughes of New York. Hughes' self image was that of an Irish chieftain. "I had to warn them against the dangers that surrounded them;" he wrote of his flock, "to contend for their rights as a religious community; . . . in short to knead them into dough, to be leavened by the spirit of the Catholic faith and of Catholic union" (Walch, 35). Hughes articulated and typified the ghetto mentality that set the tone for Irish-American Catholicism throughout the nineteenth century.

But Hughes and other parochial education leaders had only limited influence. Support for parochial schools was strongest in the cities where the Irish were isolated from the general population. But in other cities, Irish-Americans continued to chose public education for their children. This frustrated the bishops. "Listen not to those who would persuade you that religion can be separated from secular instruction," the bishops warned in 1852. "Listen to our voice, which tells you to walk in ancient paths; to bring up your children as you yourselves were brought up by your pious parents; to make religion the foundation of the happiness you wish to secure for those whom you love so tenderly. . . . Encourage the establishment and support of Catholic schools; make every sacrifice which may be necessary for this object" (Walch, 54). Much to the bishop's dismay, many Irish parents ignored this admonition.

## MARY ANNE SADLIER AND PAROCHIAL SCHOOLS

There was yet another way of convincing the Irish to support parish schools. Mary Anne Madden Sadlier, for example, used fiction to emphasize the importance of Catholic schooling and the dangers of public education. Born in Ireland, Sadlier was the foremost Catholic novelist of her time. Her stories were serialized in Irish Catholic newspapers and later compiled into popular novels.

Sadlier's fiction depicted the every-day lives of Irish-Americans in a melodramatic fashion. Each chapter touched upon the temptations, ambitions, problems, and issues that filled their lives. Many of the stories showed dramatically, if fictively, what would happen if Irish Catholic parents ignored the call for parochial schools. As literature, Sadlier's fiction was third-rate, but as propaganda it was a masterpiece.

Sadlier's novels with American settings—*Willie Burke, The Blakes and the Flanagans, Con O'Regan* and four other books—were the core of her popularity. *Willie Burke,* for example, sold seven thousand copies within a few weeks after publication. The response was gratifying, but Sadlier had a far more serious intention for her books than entertainment. Her goal was "to reach those who will not read pious or denominational books and to foil the spirit of the age with his own weapons. Such and no other have been the actuating motive of all the tales I have written" (Walch, 56). It is not surprising, therefore, that Sadlier was an important if not obvious leader in the campaign to establish parish schools.

## A NEW CAMPAIGN FOR PAROCHIAL SCHOOLS

The post–Civil War growth of Catholic parochial schools caused serious concerns among Irish Catholics. Most Irish-American leaders were pleased with the rapid growth of their parish schools, but some—conservatives for the most part—were not satisfied. In fact, conservatives were appalled with the large number of Irish-American parents who continued to send their children to public schools in spite of warnings to the contrary. The conservatives looked for a way to force reluctant pastors to build more schools and require recalcitrant Catholic parents to send their children to these schools. It was a frustrating experience with many false starts and few results except for an increase in acrimony.

The last two decades of the nineteenth century were years of upheaval and social change within the Irish community and the Catholic Church. A new generation of American-born Irish Catholics were attracted to the fruits of American life and hoped to prepare their children for increasingly productive lives in American society. The strong desire of these Irish-Americans to participate fully in American society provided a challenge and dilemma for Irish-American educators well into the twentieth century: Could parochial schools be both secular and Catholic?

## THE MODEL PAROCHIAL SCHOOL

The model most commonly utilized by Irish Catholics during those years to meet this challenge would become the prototype for the contemporary parochial school in the twentieth century. The Irish-American Catholic school was the result of a desire on the part of Irish-American-born prelates, pastors, and parishioners to establish parish schools that were fully competitive with local public schools. In fact, these Catholics desired to establish parish schools that were superior to public schools in secular as well as religious instruction.

It was a laudable goal fraught with difficulties. As Irish-American Catholic schools became increasingly similar to public schools, their independence and very reason for existence was threatened. As historian Howard Weisz has noted, the supporters of Irish Catholic schools were faced with the difficulty of arguing both that their schools were American and yet distinct from all other American schools. If these parochial schools were not demonstrably American, they would not appeal to Irish American parents; and if they were not different, then they had no reason to exist.

In fact, growing similarities between parochial and public schools caused concern among some Irish Catholics. One editor, Patrick Hickey of the *Catholic Review,* argued that the Irish-American parochial school, in its effort to Americanize, had strayed from the true path; to Hickey's way of thinking, the worst thing that could be said of parochial schools was that they were similar to public schools. Another editor, Maurice F. Egan, was critical of the growing number of different courses offered by Irish-American Catholic schools. In spite of these and other criticisms, advocates of the Irish-American Catholic schools were undeterred in their campaign.

In an effort to counter the arguments that parochial schools were inherently un-American, Irish-American Catholic educators mixed large doses of patriotism and civil piety into their parish school curriculum. "We have no flag but the stars and stripes, "noted one New York City pastor, "which we fly on every occasion over the school and rectory" (Walch, 73). In fact, Irish-American Catholic educators went so far as to claim that the establishment of a parish school was in and of itself, an act of patriotism and good citizenship.

## SCHOOLBOOKS

But flags and anthems were only one indication of the American undertone of the typical Irish-American parish school curriculum; better evidence can be found in the content of their school books. Even though these texts do not document the total classroom experience, such books necessarily made an impression on Irish-American children if only because long passages were com-

mitted to memory. A careful examination reveals very few differences between public and parochial texts in form and content.

The overwhelming majority of Irish-American Catholic school books were in complete thematic agreement with public school texts. Yet it would be erroneous to think of the two types as exactly the same. On one particular point, parochial school texts differed: the Catholic perspective on the American past was clearly partisan. Irish-American Catholic school books, to be sure, agreed that America was superior to other nations. Yet these texts also emphasized the continuing involvement and contributions of Catholics—particularly Irish Catholics in American history. Lesson after lesson recalled the exploits of American Catholic heroes such as Charles Carroll of Carrollton, Commodore John Barry and Bishop John Carroll.

Textbooks were only one indication of the values taught in the Irish-American Catholic classroom, but they provide a good impression of those values. Even though Irish-American Catholic schools remained distinct from the public schools in one important area—intensive religious instruction—they became increasingly similar in other areas. As Irish Catholic parents became concerned about their children's economic future, they pressured parochial school educators to emulate the curriculum used in public schools. Like all parents, Irish-American parents wanted the best for their children.

## BOTH AMERICAN AND CATHOLIC

This intense pressure to be both American and Catholic was not without controversy, however. In fact, it precipitated a new struggle among Irish-American Church leaders in the 1890s over the content and purpose of parochial schools and their relationship to American society. Liberal Irish-American Catholic bishops agreed with Irish-American parents that the purpose of the parish school was to preserve the religious faith of children and at the same time prepare them for productive roles in American society. Liberals, moreover, were inclined to acknowledge the positive contributions made by public schools to the general welfare of the nation.

Conservative Irish-American bishops wholeheartedly accepted the premise that parish schools should protect the religious faith of Catholic children, but these prelates disagreed with the liberals on the general value of public education and the specific role of parochial education in American society. Conservatives argued that the Church should be wary of making parish schools too American in tone and content, lest these institutions lose their distinctive Catholic qualities. In fact, the conservatives saw little in public schooling worth adopting. To their way of thinking, these institutions were hotbeds of materialism, hedonism, and immorality.

But the conservatives could do little to stem the tide of a distinctly American form of Catholic education. It was an extraordinary achievement for the liberals and marked an end to the combative educational policy instituted by John Hughes and his colleagues more than fifty years earlier.

## SCHOOL GRADUATES

Beginning in the 1890s, graduates of Irish-American parish schools began to seek additional education in area high schools. To meet this new demand, religious orders such as the Sisters of Mercy and the Society of Jesus established Catholic high schools in cities with large Catholic populations.

For the most part, these new Catholic high schools emulated local public high schools in their curriculum. The added benefit for most Irish Catholic parents was the fact that their youth would be molded by the fine hands of the nation's priests and nuns. Perhaps more than any other ethnic group, Irish-Americans worried that their children would lose their religious faith if they attended public schools.

There was great irony in this fear because upon graduation from these Catholic high schools, young Irish-American women frequently sought careers as teachers in the local public schools. In Chicago in 1902, for example, two-thirds of the candidates who passed the exam for admission to the local teachers' college were graduates of Catholic high schools. The archdiocesan paper, *The New World,* hailed this statistic as proof of the superiority of Catholic high school education.

It is not too much to say that teaching was the occupation of choice for single Irish-American women in the nation's largest cities. The Irish-American teacher joined the Irish-American policeman, fireman, and motorman as stereotypical civil servants in large American cities.

## BIG CITY SCHOOLS

The thirty-five years from 1915 to 1950 were years of consolidation in Irish-American Catholic education. After several decades of internecine warfare over the proper direction for parochial schooling and an exhaustive search for order that led to the establishment of diocesan school boards and professional standards for Catholic teachers, the predominantly Irish-American hierarchy sought to centralize and solidify their authority and control over parochial education in the middle years of this century.

This trend was particularly evident in the big cities on the eastern seaboard, the hometowns of the millions of Irish-American Catholics. In fact, it was the consolidation of authority in the largest American archdioceses such as Boston. New York, and Philadelphia that had the greatest impact on the future of parochial schooling.

The dean of these big city Catholic leaders during those years was William Henry O'Connell, the Irish-American cardinal archbishop of Boston from 1907 to his death in 1944. More than any other Catholic leader, O'Connell represented the changing of the guard, the arrival of a new generation of episcopal leaders. There was no aspect of Catholic life in Boston that went untouched after 1907.

Parochial education—primarily for the Irish-Americans—was an initiative of continuing interest to O'Connell. He increased the number of parish schools, reorganized the school board and the superintendent's office, and required regular examinations and inspections. Most important, O'Connell pressured religious orders to provide increasing numbers of classroom teachers. Thanks to O'Connell, the growth of the Irish-American parish schools in Boston had a momentum all its own.

O'Connell's interest in centralized control over parish education was in contrast with the attitude of Patrick Hayes of New York. At the time he became archbishop, Hayes inherited a project to unify the various Catholic charity programs in the archdiocese. He threw himself into this work and the result was a model program for other dioceses. When Hayes was made a cardinal in 1924, he was referred to as the "Cardinal of Charities," a title he bore proudly.

But Hayes' involvement in Catholic charities absorbed substantial portions of his time and he chose not to apply his experience in this area to other diocesan institutions. Unlike O'Con-

nell, Hayes did not establish his chancery office as the focal point of archdiocesan decision-making. As with other aspects of diocesan life, parochial education continued to grow of its own momentum without Hayes' direct involvement. By 1938, at the end of his 20-year tenure, Hayes could count 218 parish schools educating 91,000 students. Yet this was mediocre achievement for a diocese as large as New York. Of the five largest dioceses in the country during the first three decades of this century, New York had the lowest growth rate in parochial education.

If Hayes' passion for charity work limited his involvement in parochial education, his colleague to the south, Dennis Dougherty of Philadelphia, was just the opposite. Dougherty was second to no one in his interest and concern for parochial education. Indeed, his efforts to pressure recalcitrant pastors into establishing parochial schools were legendary. In fact, it was in this field that he did receive some national attention and recognition.

There is no doubt that Dougherty saw irony in the conditions of the 1930s and 1940s. Even though he was the master of his own archdiocese, events beyond his control—a major depression and a world war—prevented him from achieving a dream of placing every Catholic child in a Catholic school. To be sure, he made great progress toward this goal. The system grew from 174 elementary schools and 88,000 pupils in 1918 to 305 schools with 135,000 pupils in 1951.

Yet the development of the Irish-American model for parochial education, the norm in every diocese by 1930, would be undermined in the coming decade by economic conditions beyond the bishops' control. The hardship of the Great Depression stopped the progress of Irish Catholic school construction in dioceses large and small. And yet Catholics continued to send their children to these schools whenever possible. Classrooms were crowded and by 1950 it was not surprising to find major metropolitan areas in which fifty percent or more of the school children were enrolled in Catholic parochial schools. It was the drive and determination of men such as O'Connell and Dougherty that made such an achievement possible.

## PAROCHIAL EDUCATION IN THE 1950S

Dougherty's successor in Philadelphia, John O'Hara, was the foremost Irish-American advocate of parochial education in the United States in the 1950s. In fact, O'Hara's goal was to provide a parochial education for every Catholic child in his archdiocese. In only eight years, O'Hara oversaw the construction of 133 new parochial school buildings with 1,206 classrooms and 20 new diocesan high schools with 213 classrooms. These facilities provided for the total increase in the Catholic school population of over 102,000 pupils.

O'Hara was irritated by anyone who questioned the future of Catholic education. In 1954, for example, O'Hara was angered when another Irish-American, Monsignor William McManus of Chicago, published a pessimistic outlook on the ability of Catholic educational institutions to meet the enormous task of finding enough classrooms and teachers to meet the demand. O'Hara thought such doubts were scandalous ideas and the cardinal was quick to criticize McManus in letters to his fellow bishops.

Two years later McManus published another provocative article that further infuriated O'Hara. "How Good Are Catholic Schools?" McManus asked in the September 8, 1956 issue of *America*, a publication that O'Hara detested. O'Hara thought

John Cardinal O'Hara of Philadelphia made it his personal mission to promote Catholic school enrollment and would tolerate no pessimism about the future of Catholic education.

McManus and others who focused on the shortage of space in Catholic schools to be unduly negative. O'Hara believed that the Holy Ghost had sent the children and that God would provide the means of giving them an education. Few other Catholic leaders were willing to entrust the entire Catholic school system to divine intervention.

O'Hara died in 1960 and with his death came the end of the overt Irish-American influence over parochial education. The changes wrought by the second Vatican Council, the exodus of priests and nuns from the religious life, and the decline in the number of parochial schools and parochial school enrollment overwhelmed the Catholic Church in the United States. Although Irish-Americans continued to support parochial education, they no longer identified as leaders of the movement.

### THE LEGACY OF PAROCHIAL EDUCATION

Irish-American Catholic education is something of a misnomer. In truth, Irish-Americans never thought of their parish schools as anything but Catholic. "While these schools segregated Irish children from Protestants as well as Catholics of other ethnic backgrounds, they were not ghetto institutions," noted Ellen Skerrett. "On the contrary, the English-speaking Catholic schools of the Irish promoted integration into the larger society. They also played a crucial role in the formation of an American Catholic identity" (McCaffrey, Skerrett, et al., 44).

In truth, Irish-American educators—priests and nuns for the most part—did not see a need to stress Irish-American culture in the classroom. They simply assumed that Irish values and Catholic beliefs were intertwined. The former was subsumed into the latter. "Not only did Irish-American Catholic educators ignore the Irish dimension of their heritage," concluded historian Lawrence McCaffrey, "but they emphasized Catholic culture that was devoid of ethnic identity" (McCaffrey, Skerrett, et al., 150–51).

When Irish-Americans began to establish and promote parochial schools, their stated goals were to prepare their children for useful, productive roles in American society without compromising their religious faith. There was little mention or concern about Irish culture or language. Without doubt, they achieved their stated goals. Irish-Americans are among the most success-ful ethnic groups in the United States today. Parochial schools were an important building block in that achievement.

Patrick Blessing, *The Irish in America: A Guide to the Literature and the Manuscript Collections* (Washington, D.C., 1992).

Jay P. Dolan, *The American Catholic Experience: A History from Colonial Times to the Present* (Garden City, N.Y., 1985).

Thomas Donaghey, *Philadelphia's Finest: A History of Education in the Catholic Archdiocese* (Philadelphia, 1972).

Charles Fanning, *The Irish Voice in America* (Lexington, KY, 1990).

Michael Feldberg, *The Philadelphia Bible Riots of 1844: A Study of Ethnic Conflict* (Westport, CT, 1975).

Vincent P. Lannie, *Public Money and Parochial Education: Bishop Hughes, Governor Seward and the New York School Controversy* (Cleveland, 1968).

Thomas T. McAvoy, *Father O'Hara of Notre Dame: The Cardinal Archbishop of Philadelphia* (Notre Dame, IN, 1967).

Lawrence McCaffrey, Skerrett, Ellen, et al. *The Irish in Chicago* (Urbana, IL, 1987).

Brian C. Mitchell, *The Paddy Camps: The Meaning of Community among the Irish in Lowell, Massachusetts, 1821–1861* (Urbana, IL, 1986).

James M. O'Toole, *Militant and Triumphant: William Henry O'Connell and the Catholic Church in Boston, 1859–1944* (Notre Dame, IN, 1993).

Timothy Walch, *Parish School: American Catholic Parochial Education from Colonial Times to the Present* (New York, 1996).

Howard Weisz, *Irish American and Italian American Views of Education* (New York, 1976).

TIMOTHY WALCH

## EDUCATION, HIGHER

The historical role of the Irish in American higher education has never been studied in a systematic way. Hence this article will be more a review of topics in need of further research than a report on a body of knowledge previously investigated and reduced to intelligible form.

To account for this neglect, it should be noted first that higher education itself is not a subject that has attracted much attention from historians or other scholars, and its ethnic dimensions have been even more neglected. Nor has higher education occupied a prominent place on the horizon of popular consciousness—although its visibility was undoubtedly enhanced by the G.I. Bill of Rights, which sent multitudes of World War II veterans to college, by the campus riots of the 1960s, and by more recent controversies over affirmative action.

But leaving aside scholarly neglect and its relative obscurity in the national consciousness, higher education is not an area with which the Irish are automatically associated. In this it differs most obviously from politics. A certain amount of stereotyping is of course involved here, but there is more to it than that. Consider the works of two well-informed and sympathetic insiders. William Shannon's popular history, *The American Irish* (1963), devotes eight chapters to political affairs, two to religious leaders, and one each to literature and the theater, but none to higher education. Patrick J. Blessing's book-length bibliography, *The Irish In America* (1992), provides separate sections for politics, religion, labor, nationalism, and writers/literature/criticism, but includes no heading for education as such, much less higher education.

Given these circumstances, what can be said about this subject? One method of dealing with it would be simply to list Irish-American men and women involved in higher education. Woodrow Wilson, who came of Scotch-Irish stock, could be included in such a listing, although he is not primarily known for his academic career and presidency of Princeton University. The same is true of William Holmes McGuffey, also of Scotch-Irish background, who is remembered as the author of grade-school textbooks, not as a professor at three colleges in Ohio as well as the University of Virginia. William James is perhaps the most famous American of Irish derivation closely associated in the public mind with an academic institution, Harvard University, and remembered for his scholarly work in philosophy and psychology. Even if less well-known educators are included—such as William H. Kilpatrick, a collaborator of John Dewey's at Teachers College, Columbia, and one of the founders of Bennington College, and Charles McCarthy, whose "Wisconsin Idea" forged close links between state government and the state university in the Progressive era—this is a very short list. Many more Irish men and women of course contributed to American higher education. But to go beyond a distinguished few, such as those mentioned here, would require combing the published histories and institutional records of hundreds of colleges and universities. Nothing of this sort has been undertaken on a systematic basis. And though a simple listing would be valuable, it would not, of itself, give a satisfactory understanding of the scope and form of Irish involvement in American higher education.

A second way of approaching the topic would be to focus on two religious traditions, for Irish involvement in higher education was largely channeled through the Presbyterian and Roman Catholic churches. In the case of the former, Irish involvement is most conspicuous in the eighteenth and early nineteenth centuries when the Scotch-Irish were the leading element in the Presbyterian church in this country, and when it was most active in college founding. And though we tend to think of Irish-Americans as being Catholic, it is important to remember that until the late 1820s, emigration from Ireland was mainly from the predominantly Presbyterian northern part of the island.

The first notable Presbyterian educational foundation was the "Log College," founded in 1726 by Irish-born William Tennent, which became a nursery for "New Side" (i.e., evangelically oriented) ministers. It is regarded as the forerunner of Princeton (est. 1746), two of whose early presidents were products of the Log College, and which was heavily attended by Americans of Scotch-Irish derivation up through the time of Woodrow Wilson. The same was true of forty-nine other Presbyterian colleges, founded before the Civil War, that endured into the twentieth century. Moreover, Presbyterians were influential in the founding and early years of state universities in Delaware, North and South Carolina, Tennessee, Kentucky, Indiana, Ohio, and New York; in heavily Scotch-Irish western Pennsylvania, Presbyterians were among the promoters of the academy that evolved into the University of Pittsburgh. Religion clearly overshadowed ethnic consciousness in Presbyterian educational work, but the two were interwoven, and as Catholic immigration soared in the mid-nineteenth century, the Scotch-Irish grew more self-consciously "ethnic" as a way of distinguishing themselves from "Irish-Catholics."

The Catholic presence in American higher education dates from the founding of Georgetown in 1789. Its founder, Bishop John Carroll, was of Irish background, but its first student, William Gaston, later a distinguished jurist in North Carolina, was of mixed English-Catholic and Irish-Presbyterian (originally Huguenot) derivation. Planted as it was among the English Catholics of Maryland, and accepting large numbers of Protestants, it is

perhaps not surprising that students of English stock accounted for at least half of Georgetown's enrollment until after the Civil War. However, what Georgetown historian R. Emmett Curran, S.J., calls an "Irish-American troika"—three Roman-trained Jesuits of immigrant ancestry: Thomas Mulledy, William McSherry and James Ryder—provided essential leadership for the college in the antebellum years. The present university's noblest structure, Healy Hall, is named for Patrick F. Healy, S.J., Georgetown's president in the 1870s, whose father was an Irish immigrant, and whose mother was an African-American slave.

In the second half of the nineteenth century, Irish-American predominance was firmly established on Catholic campuses. It was most overwhelming where the Irish were concentrated in great cities, and not only at Boston College, which was all but exclusively Irish. In New York City, for example, Irish names dominated the 1847–97 graduation list of the College of St. Francis Xavier; in fact, just those beginning with "Mc" or "O'" constituted a sixth of the total. In 1908, statistics gathered by the Immigration Commission showed that the Irish accounted for three-fifths of the second generation (i.e., children of immigrants) in the student bodies of nine Catholic colleges for men. Analysis of more recent survey data reveals that the Irish Catholic proclivity for higher education grew even stronger over time. So much so that by the late 1970s twenty percent of the nation's Irish Catholics had attended graduate school and were, as Andrew M. Greeley put it in *The Irish Americans* (1981), "flooding into the academy" as faculty members. The most recent *National Faculty Directory* (1997) lists more than 2,200 names beginning with "O'," which offers suggestive, albeit anecdotal, evidence for Greeley's finding, and for his conclusion that "the emergence of a substantial Ph.D./intellectual class" is the most interesting development currently under way among Irish Catholics.

Catholic higher education was, until very recently, a strictly clerical operation in terms of leadership and control. On that account, nearly all the major administrators and leading scholars were priests, nuns, or brothers, and since the Irish furnished such a large proportion of vocations to the priesthood and religious life, they are likewise highly visible among those who attained distinction in the Catholic academic world. The case of the Catholic University of America, though perhaps extreme, illustrates the point. It was led through its first eight decades of existence (1889–1967) by clergymen named Keane, Conaty, O'Connell, Shahan, Ryan, Corrigan, McCormick, McEntegart, and McDonald. Irish-born or Irish-American nuns likewise played a prominent role in the foundation of the Catholic women's colleges that multiplied so rapidly after 1900. Conspicuous among these—to mention only a few associated with pioneer institutions—were Julia McGroarty, S.N.D. de N., of Trinity College; Pauline Kelligar, S.C., of the College of St. Elizabeth; Irene Gill, O.S.U., of the College of New Rochelle; Pauline O'Neill, C.S.C., of St. Mary's College (Indiana); Antonia McHugh, C.S.J., of the College of St. Catherine; and Mary A. Molloy (later Sister M. Aloysius, O.S.F.) of the College of St. Teresa. Among the brothers, Irish-born Patrick Francis Mullany, F.S.C., who was known as Brother Azarias, attained fame as an educator and writer in the 1870s and 1880s.

Among priests who taught in seminaries, James A. Corcoran and John B. Hogan were outstanding in the nineteenth century, and John Courtney Murray, S.J., in the twentieth. Singling out individual lay persons cannot help being arbitrary, but it is worth noting that Maurice Francis Egan, who taught at Notre Dame and the Catholic University of America, gained sufficient distinction to win an ambassadorial appointment from Theodore Roosevelt. Edward A. Fitzpatrick, who served as graduate dean at Marquette University and president of Mount Mary College in Milwaukee, and who wrote several books on Catholic higher education, was the outstanding layman in the field in the second quarter of the twentieth century. Three more recent scholars illustrate Greeley's point about the emergence of Irish Catholics on the broader academic stage: Helen C. White (d. 1967), a longtime professor of English literature at the University of Wisconsin, served as president of the American Association of University Women (1941–47) and of the American Association of University Professors (1957–58); Francis L. Broderick (d. 1992) became in 1968 the first chancellor of the University of Massachusetts at Boston; and David Herlihy (d. 1991) of Brown University served as president of the American Historical Association in 1990.

The study of Irish history, literature, and culture is another dimension of the subject that deserves attention. The Ancient Order of Hibernians underwrote the establishment of a Celtic chair at the Catholic University of America in the 1890s, when Harvard was the only other place in the country that offered the subject. However, Celtic failed to prosper at the Catholic University, being absorbed in the 1930s into a larger department of German and comparative philology. Harvard still boasts a department of Celtic language and literature, but has been joined in recent years by a number of other institutions featuring "Irish Studies" conceived on a broader interdisciplinary basis. According to the fourth edition of *A Guide to Irish Studies in the United States* (1995), the beginnings of the interdisciplinary approach may be dated from 1962 when the American Committee [now Conference] for Irish Studies was organized; course work in this area is now offered in some 400 of the nation's postsecondary institutions. Without attempting to identify the leaders of the movement, we can note that a number of schools in Boston and New York have strong offerings in Irish Studies; that a midwestern cluster extends from South Bend, Indiana, through Chicago, Illinois, to Madison and Milwaukee in Wisconsin; and that the San Francisco area harbors a similar concentration on the Pacific coast.

The vigorous development of these programs in recent years has given things Irish unprecedented visibility in American higher education. May they also give, in time, a better grounded appreciation of the Irish role in that phase of American life.

Mary Mariella Bowler, *A History of Catholic Colleges for Women in the United States of America* (Washington, 1933).

Robert Emmett Curran, *The Bicentennial History of Georgetown University,* vol. 1, *From Academy to University, 1789–1889* (Washington, 1993).

Philip Gleason, *Contending with Modernity: Catholic Higher Education in the Twentieth Century* (New York, 1995).

Andrew M. Greeley, *The Irish Americans: The Rise to Money and Power* (New York, 1981).

Howard Miller, *The Revolutionary College: American Presbyterian Higher Education, 1707–1837* (New York, 1976).

PHILIP GLEASON

## EGAN, EILEEN M. (1911– )

Member of the executive staff of Catholic Relief Services; writer; proponent of nonviolence; and co-founder, with Gordon Zahn, of Pax Christi-USA.

In working with persons displaced by World War II, Eileen Egan saw firsthand and early on the connection between violence and the plight of refugees. As a result, she devoted her life to performing works of mercy and promoting human rights, became skilled at peacemaking, and allied her efforts with two of the most notable women of the era, Dorothy Day and Mother Teresa.

The eldest daughter of Mary Agnes O'Sullivan-Bere and Jeremiah Egan, Eileen Egan was born (December 27, 1911) in Pontypridd, Wales. The family immigrated to New York City in 1926. Shortly thereafter, Jeremiah died, leaving six children. Egan attended Cathedral High School on scholarship and graduated from Hunter College in 1933. By the time she was twenty-three, her mother, too, had died, so Egan supported her siblings (assisted by an uncle).

In 1943, Egan joined the staff of the newly organized Catholic Relief Services, working in Mexico, Portugal, and Spain. For more than thirty years as a director of CRS programs in Germany, Italy, India, and Vietnam, she surveyed the conditions of refugees, reported her observations, and designed and implemented programs to alleviate massive human suffering. As director of the Barcelona office, Egan worked with Jews and Poles fleeing Hitler and Stalin. In postwar Germany, she faced an overwhelming problem: twelve million refugees, including Germans expelled from Eastern Europe. Her field reports were used in funding appeals, speeches, and in briefing the American Catholic bishops.

En route to Vietnam in 1955, Egan stopped in Calcutta and visited the slums to meet the sari-clad founder of the Missionaries of Charity, still unknown outside of India. Mother Teresa took Egan on a tour of her work in a city bursting with a million refugees from the "partition" wars. Later, Egan accompanied her on fund-raising trips to Germany, Switzerland, the Caribbean and Venezuela, and to Rome where Mother Teresa sought pontifical rank for her society of sisters. Egan accompanied Mother Teresa to Oslo where she accepted the Nobel Peace Prize. In *Such a Vision of the Street: Mother Teresa—The Spirit and the Work,* which won the Christopher Award, Egan draws on her long friendship with the nun.

In 1965, Egan took herself off the CRS payroll to lobby for peace at the Second Vatican Council in Rome. She and peace ac-

Eileen M. Egan

tivist Richard Carbray visited with the Council Fathers, urging them to make explicit the right to conscientious objection to military service, to validate the witness of Gospel nonviolence, and to condemn "the bomb." All three were achieved in the conciliar document, "The Church in the Modern World." Dorothy Day was also present, praying and fasting so that the bishops would support peace in Vietnam.

After retirement, Egan intensified her work for peace. In 1972, the American PAX association joined with the international Catholic peace movement; Egan and Gordon Zahn became co-founders of Pax Christi-USA, an organization with more than thirteen thousand members nationwide, including more than 100 U.S. bishops. A nongovernmental organization, it has consultative status at the U.N. Egan helped draft the statement "The Right to Refuse to Kill" for the U.N. Human Rights Commission, which in 1987, recognized conscientious objection as a human right.

Eileen Egan, *The Works of Peace* (Sheed & Ward, 1965).
————, *Such a Vision of the Street: Mother Teresa—The Spirit and the Work* (Doubleday, 1985).
————, *For the Life of the World: Catholic Relief Services, The Beginning Years* (CRS, 1988).
————, *For Whom There Is No Room: Scenes from the Refugee World* (Paulist, 1995).
————, *Peace Be With You: Justified Warfare or Nonviolence?* (Maryknoll, 1999).

KAREN SUE SMITH

## EGAN, MAURICE FRANCIS (1852–1924)

Journalist, teacher, author, diplomat. Maurice Francis Egan was a man of many professions but in sum he was a reflection of the growing influence of Irish Catholics in American society at the turn of the twentieth century. He associated with presidents and paupers with equal ease and, by his own recollection, his was "a happy life," a phrase he used to title his autobiography.

Egan was born in 1852 into a prosperous Philadelphia Catholic family. He was educated at parochial schools in that city and

Maurice Francis
Egan

at LaSalle College. He found his first career in journalism and, in addition to writing for a wide variety of publications, Egan also served as editor and part owner of the *Freeman's Journal,* an influential Catholic publication. He also was a frequent contributor to the *Century Magazine,* one of the most influential journals in the nation.

The need to support a growing family and the desire for a less hectic life led Egan to accept a professorship in English at the University of Notre Dame in 1888. Eight years later he accepted a similar position at the Catholic University of America, a move that brought him into contact with many of the political figures and diplomats of the era.

As a professor, Egan had more time to devote to his own writing than he had as a journalist and during the years from 1888 to 1907 he published 24 books and an unknown quantity of shorter works. Egan's prominence as a Catholic man of letters led to a 20-year friendship with Theodore Roosevelt. The president frequently called on Egan to advise him on matters of concern to the Catholic Church.

His friendship with Roosevelt led Egan to his career as a diplomat. In 1907, Roosevelt appointed Egan to be United States Minister to Denmark where he served with distinction through three administrations and successfully negotiated the sale of the Virgin Islands to the United States in 1917.

Egan returned to the United States in 1918 to a life of writing and semi-retirement. In addition to writing dozens of articles on every topic from foreign affairs to literary criticism, Egan also published three volumes of memoirs. Throughout his life, Egan received many awards and honors, but his greatest accolade came in 1919 when he was elected to the American Academy of Arts and Letters, an organization limited to 50 members and composed of the elite in the fields of music, arts and letters. Egan died a contented man in 1924.

Maurice F. Egan, *Recollections of a Happy Life* (New York, 1924).
Charles Fanning, *The Irish Voice in America* (Lexington, KY, 1992).

TIMOTHY WALCH

## EGAN, MICHAEL (1761–1814)

First Bishop of Philadelphia. Egan's place of birth is somewhat unclear, but he was probably born in Galway, although some report Limerick, Ireland. Egan entered the Franciscan Order of the Strict Observance at St. Anthony's College, Louvain, Belgium, and there received minor orders and the diaconate. He later went to Immaculate Conception College in Prague where he was ordained and awarded a degree in theology. In 1803, Egan was appointed pastor of St. Mary's Church in Philadelphia where he was later consecrated Bishop by Archbishop Carroll at St. Peter's Church in Baltimore in 1810. Archbishop Carroll is said to have reported Egan's character as one that was truly learned and humble, but deficient in the resoluteness and experience of the organization and direction of Episcopal affairs. Egan's legacy is indeed one that attests to his learned reputation (being fluent in both English and German). In addition to his failing health, Egan's last years were marred by financial difficulties and scandal spurred by trustee problems at St. Mary's where several administrators openly lead campaigns against him. Egan, however, opposed them and the schism was resolved when his opponents returned to England. Egan died of heart failure and nervous difficulty on July 22, 1814, only three years and nine months after his consecration as Bishop.

M. I. J. Graffin, *History of Right Reverend Michael Egan, First Bishop of Philadelphia* (Philadelphia, 1893).
*Dictionary of American Biography*, 6.

JOY HARRELL

## EIRE SOCIETY OF BOSTON, THE

Founded in 1937 by 82 adults fresh from a 16-lecture course in Irish history sponsored by the Massachusetts Department of Education, the Society is dedicated to spreading an awareness of the history and culture of Ireland, with emphasis on promoting "a consciousness of the influence of Irish thought and action in the advancement of American ideals." Because several similar organizations flourished in Boston at the time—Charitable Irish Society (1737), Ancient Order of Hibernians (1836), Clover Club (1883)—the Society avoided sponsoring events that would conflict with programs already fixed in the local American-Irish tradition. Instead, it chose to offer October-to-April films and lectures, tours to Ireland, publication of a monthly *Bulletin* featuring essays of Irish cultural interest, and an annual dinner at which the Society's Gold Medal would be given to someone deemed to have advanced Society ideals. This format makes the Society unique among scores of Irish groups in the New England Consular district. It has also allowed the Society to host hundreds of Irish and American writers, actors, public servants, musicians, teachers, and others, including presidents of Ireland and ambassadors to Washington and Dublin, to lead visits to all of Ireland and to Irish centers in the U.S. and Europe, to stage plays by Irish dramatists, to recognize artists, scientists, composers, scholars, philanthropists, jurists, etc., with the Gold Medal, and to encourage playwrights, poets, and other writers by regularly sponsoring readings, book signings, and opening nights—in short, to spread an appreciation of the cultural achievements of the Irish by any practical means. Over the years, the Society has sponsored numerous receptions, forums, exhibits, and essay contests for high schoolers, given art works, books, and legal materials to schools, museums, and libraries, funded the "Eire Suite" of Leroy Anderson for the Boston Pops, sent a delegation to Dublin for the 50th anniversary of the Easter Rising, arranged for the Boston Symphony to begin a European tour in Cork and Dublin, contributed to the support of several health-care, ecumenical, and peace-seeking efforts in Ireland, conducted in-house auctions to heal its chronically ailing treasury, and, in 1997, helped underwrite the $2M Famine Institute and Irish Famine Memorial erected along Boston's Freedom Trail. Lecturers have included Micheál MacLiammoir, Desmond Guinness, Brian Friel, Brendan Behan, Countess McCormack, and Grainne Yeats, while the Medal has been awarded to Siobhan McKenna, Seamus Heaney, the Chieftains, John Hume, and Sean MacBride, as well as to Richard Cardinal Cushing, John F. Kennedy, John Huston, Mary Lavin, Frank Patterson, John Ford, Padraic Colum, Eoin McKiernan, Maureen O'Hara, Cornelius Ryan, George Mitchell, Leon Uris, and more than 50 others. In 1996, full runs of the Society *Bulletin*, 54 volumes indexed, were bound and shelved in the research libraries of the Boston Athenaeum and Boston College. The Society logo was designed in 1937 by architect and first Medalist Charles Donagh Maginnis

The Eire Society of Boston, founded 1937

and modernized in 1998 by Boston artist and Permanent Deacon Gerard P. Rooney. The logo appears on all Society printings and is the obverse of the annual Gold Medal.

*See* Boston

Maureen Connelly, "Major Irish Societies," *Festival Bostonian Retrospective: Our Multicultural Heritage* (Boston, 1977): 18–21.
Paul J. Hennessy, "The Greening of Irish Studies," *Boston College Magazine* (Spring 1981): 10–14.
Michael P. Quinlin, ed., *Guide to the New England Irish* (Boston, 1987): 129.
George E. Ryan, "Looking Inward: The Eire Society of Boston," *Eire Society Bulletin* (January 1980): 1–3.
———, "Eire Society Archives Enrich Boston College," *Boston Irish News* (August 1981): 3.
Michael Ryan, *The Irish in Boston* (Boston, 1975).

GEORGE E. RYAN

## *ÉIRE-IRELAND*

Subtitled "A Journal of Irish Studies" and conceived in 1965 by Eóin McKiernan as a journal of criticism and enquiry for members of the Irish American Cultural Institute, the journal became a forum for the best of scholarship in North America concerning Ireland and Irish America. The journal was designed by Alfred Mullerleile—proprietor of North Central Press—and edited by McKiernan (1965–86), Lawrence O'Shaughnessy, and Seán McMahon. In 1966 each issue attained 150 pages in length, sewn in signatures.

From the start, *Éire-Ireland* was designed not only to represent Ireland's history, politics, and literature as the object of serious scrutiny, but also to inform and shape the literate culture of Irish America. The journal also presented regular commentaries by Charles Acton, on Irish classical music (1967–74); Antony Butler, on Irish art (1966–71); Seán O'Donnell on science in Ireland (1974–87); Nollaig Ó Gadhra, on the Irish Language (1967–78); Desmond Rushe on Irish drama (1971–80). Henry Beechhold edited the book reviews (1971–1986). Assitant editor in 1973 and then associate editor in 1976, Thomas Dillon Redshaw copyedited articles and conducted much of the editorial correspondence of the journal through June 1986. The 1985 issues of *Éire-Ireland* changed format from $2.28 \times 1.52$ cms in sewn signatures to $2.12 \times 1.35$ cms perfect bound, and thereafter the journal appeared perfect bound in the larger format.

In 1987, James J. Blake became editor of the journal, serving through the Fall, 1989, issue. Robert Ward served as book review editor (1989–92). Thomas Redshaw took on the editorship with the Winter, 1989, issue and, having appointed as advisory editors a board of Irish and American scholars, started a system of juried article selection, as well as the practice of publishing contemporary Irish poetry in the "Dánta Úra" section. In 1994, owing to growth of Irish Studies worldwide, each issue of *Éire-Ireland* became 190 pages long.

After the Irish American Cultural Institute moved its executive offices to Morristown, New Jersey, relations with the University of St. Thomas became difficult, and, eventually, Redshaw resigned his editorship, having completed the thirtieth volume in 1995. The editorial offices then moved to New Jersey and the editorship eventually became the responsibility of Vera Kreilkamp and Nancy J. Curtin, supervised by two "Senior Consulting Editors": James S. Donnelly, Jr. and Philip O'Leary. Later in 1996 the new editors produced the first double issue of *Éire-Ireland* (212 pages).

An essential guide to *Éire-Ireland* is Ed Marman's authoritative *Éire-Ireland: A Comprehensive Index, 1966–1988* (1992), published as issue XXVII: 1 of the journal.

*See* Irish American Cultural Institute

THOMAS DILLON REDSHAW

## ELLIS, JOHN TRACY (1905–1992)

Priest, historian, and educator. John Tracy Ellis was born on July 30, 1905, in Seneca, Illinois, to Elmer Lucien and Cecilia Murphy Ellis. Ellis completed his bachelor's degree at St. Viator College in Bourbonnais, Illinois, and then moved to Washington, D.C., to undertake graduate studies in medieval church history at The Catholic University of America. After earning his doctorate in 1930, Ellis spent four years teaching at small Catholic colleges in Illinois and in Minnesota. In 1935 he began preparation for the priesthood by enrolling in the Suplician Seminary in Washington, D.C. While studying at the seminary, Ellis taught history to undergraduate students at Catholic University. On June 5, 1938, John Tracy Ellis was ordained a priest by Bishop Francis M. Kelly of Winona, Minnesota.

After ordination, Ellis began teaching full-time at Catholic University. In 1941 he replaced Peter Guilday as Professor of American Church History. He also became the acting secretary of the American Catholic Historical society and managing director of the *Catholic Historical Review*, a position he held for over twenty years (1941–1963). During these years he became known as an outstanding scholar and teacher. His 1952 two-volume biography of James Cardinal Gibbons was a masterpiece of historical research and writing that set new standards of scholarship and clarity for ecclesiastical history. It proved to be a most reliable source not only for Cardinal Gibbons' life but for that whole period of early American Catholic history. Four years later Ellis published his best-selling historical survey, *American Catholicism*. A revised edition of the text was reissued in 1969.

An issue especially dear to John Tracy Ellis was the quality of scholarship and education being offered at Catholic universities. In 1955 he gave a lecture on "American Catholics and the Intellectual Life" that evoked a great deal of discussion and that resulted in increased attention to the quality of scholarship on Catholic campuses across the country. In this lecture Ellis ques-

tioned the academic quality of Catholic seminaries, colleges and universities, asking why they failed to produce their share of Rhodes scholars, prominent scientists and other intellectual leaders. He criticized American Catholic scholars for failing to uphold "the incomparable tradition of Catholic learning of which they are the direct heirs." He blamed them for adopting "a self-imposed ghetto mentality which prevents them from mingling as they should with their non-Catholic colleagues, and [for] their lack of industry and habits of work." In his 1965 Boniface Wimmer lecture, "A Commitment to Truth," Ellis called for honesty and integrity in the Catholic Church. He reasoned, "Nothing is gained by denying what is true. If we try to obstruct Catholic intellectuals, we obstruct the progress of the Church."

In 1964 Ellis moved to the University of San Francisco, where he continued teaching and publishing. From there he took leaves of absence to be visiting professor at Brown University (1967) and the University of Notre Dame (1971). He also served as a scholar-in-residence at the North American College in Rome from 1974 to 1976. Publications during this period included *Catholics in Colonial America* (1965), *A Commitment to Truth* (1966) and *Essays in Seminary Education* (1967), as well as contributions to the *New Catholic Encyclopedia* (1967) and *The Catholic Priest in the United States: Historical Investigations* (1971).

Ellis returned to Catholic University in 1976 as the initial occupant of the Catholic Daughters of America Chair of American Catholic History. He taught until failing health compelled him to retire in 1989. Three years later, on October 16, 1992, John Tracy Ellis died in Washington, D.C. He was 87 years old.

John Tracy Ellis, *Faith and Learning: A Church Historian's Story* (Lanham, MD, 1989).

Oscar H. Lipscomb, "John Tracy Ellis," *The Encyclopedia of American Catholic History*, 486–88.

Nelson H. Minnich and others, eds., *Studies in Catholic History in Honor of John Tracy Ellis* (Wilmington, DE, 1985), includes a bibliography of Ellis's publications compiled by Mark A. Miller, 674–738.

Thomas J. Shelley, "The Young John Tracy Ellis and American Catholic Intellectual Life," *U.S. Catholic Historian,* 13 (Winter 1995): 1–18.

———, "John Tracy Ellis," *The Modern Catholic Encyclopedia* (Collegeville, MN, 1994): 277–78.

PATRICIA DeFERRARI

## ELLIS ISLAND

A small island in upper New York bay near the New Jersey shore, Ellis Island is best known for its use as a federal immigration station, serving from 1892 to 1924 as the point of entry to the United States for over 14 million immigrants, representing 71% of total immigration. Included in that number were over 500,000 Irish immigrants, including fifteen-year-old Annie Moore, who traveled from Queenstown (now Cobh) County Cork, Ireland, and became the very first immigrant to be registered in the new station on January 1, 1892.

Named for its colonial owner, the Ellis family, Ellis Island was purchased in 1808 by the federal government and used as a fort and munitions arsenal. Designated an immigration station in 1890, the Island was increased in size by landfill from 2.5 acres to 27.5 acres. Consisting of several wooden buildings which were later destroyed by fire, the station was rebuilt in 1900 in French Renaissance style, with brick and limestone trim, designed by the New York firm of Boving & Tilton. In addition to

Annie Moore, a girl from Cork, was the first immigrant to enter New York through Ellis Island.

ence there. Also at Ellis Island is a statue of Annie Moore, dedicated in 1993 by the then-president of Ireland, Mary Robinson.

Four in ten Americans can trace their family roots back through Ellis Island, the "Gateway to America." Inextricably linked to the American story of immigration, Ellis Island remains an evocative symbol for immigrants and the descendants of immigrants, including, of course, the American Irish.

*See* Emigration: 1801–1921

Leonard Everett Fisher, *Ellis Island: Gateway to the New World* (New York, 1986).
Thomas M. Pitkin, *Keepers of the Gate: A History of Ellis Island* (New York, 1975).
Pamela Reeves, *Ellis Island* (New York, 1991).
Mary Shapiro, *Gateway to Liberty: The Story of the Statue of Liberty and Ellis Island* (New York, 1986).

KATHLEEN N. McCARTHY

## EMIGRANT RELIEF SERVICES (NEW YORK)

Migration is often conceived as a personal choice, which implies that the person or family would have the means to exercise that choice. Individuals or families obtained information, booked passage, arrived at the port of embarkation, arrived in good health and with funds in hand and luggage in tow, and negotiated the way from the point of debarkation to the first home and first job with the aid of relatives and friends. However, it is impossible to say how many immigrants to the United States fit that image, let alone how many in any one group such as the Irish, or how many in any one time period.

Descriptions of the travel arrangements indicate that sometimes some people might require some assistance. People always paid for their ocean voyages first, and some captains and crew took the money but exploited the poor passengers, denying them sufficient food and water. The poorest passengers traveled in steerage, in compartments that, on the journey to Europe, carried the bulky raw materials produced in the Americas. They had no privacy; observers constantly complained of the abuse of female passengers by male passengers or by sailors. People who did not bring their own bedding lay down on the wooden floors of their compartments to sleep, and ate wherever they could sit. Being below the waterline, steerage had no windows and depended on artificial light. Before electricity, all such light came from some kind of flame so a rough sea meant no light at all. It was difficult to bathe or to change clothes for the duration of the voyage, which could last eight weeks. Myriad vectors—rats, lice, poor sanitation, the passengers all in close contact with each other—spread contagious diseases. Remedies for these problems came not from societies but from legislation and from technology. An 1847 law required vessels to provide passengers a specific amount of space; an 1860 law attempted to protect women from abuse. In the 1860s, steam engines replaced sails, and increases in immigrant passenger trade led to the building of ships with accommodations for those traveling on limited funds.

Arrival in New York harbor brought new dangers. Until 1875, New York State legislated methods of immigrant reception, and imposed a head tax on immigrants in order to fund enforcement. Physicians boarded incoming ships and quarantined those who looked like they might have contagious diseases in the marine hospital on Staten Island until they got better or died. That hospital seldom had sufficient funds to maintain the patients in

the station, facilities on the Island grew to include a kitchen, bathhouse, laundry, contagious disease wards, carpentry house, bakery and ferry slip for transport to the City of New York.

At the center of the station was the Registry Room, where prospective immigrants were processed and either approved or rejected for admission to the United States. Federal law permitted the exclusion as undesirables those deemed by inspectors "idiots; insane persons; persons likely to become public charges; people convicted of crimes involving moral turpitude; polygamists; and those with loathsome, contagious diseases." Later restrictions on immigration included a literacy test, and a quota system, which placed an overall annual ceiling on immigration, and established limits by country of origin.

Conditions on Ellis Island were often difficult. Immigrants faced a bewildering medley of people and procedures; congestion, confusion, corruption and delay, combined with the risk of rejection by the inspectors to make the experience at the station arduous for most. Reforms implemented after 1914 alleviated some of the difficulties.

Changes in immigration law after 1924, including the requirement that immigrants obtain visas in their country of origin before traveling to the United States, reduced the number of immigrants passing through the station. After years of declining use, Ellis Island closed in 1954.

Declared part of the Statue of Liberty National Monument in 1965 by President Lyndon Johnson, Ellis Island was restored and opened to the public in 1990. Today it features an historical museum, library and exhibits which recreate the immigrant experi-

comfort, let alone treat their ailments, and it was unpopular with its neighbors, who objected to the expense (even though it was funded by its users) and to the presence of contagious disease. Thieves picked the pockets and stole the luggage of those healthy enough to land. "Runners" drummed up business for lodging houses by grabbing luggage or family members and forcing the migrants to follow them. Lodging house keepers overcharged them; employers underpaid them, and subjected them to hours or working conditions considered atrocious in America.

New York Irish organized societies: the Friendly Sons of Saint Patrick in 1784, the Irish Emigrant Association in 1817, the first U.S. unit of the Ancient Order of Hibernians in 1836, and the Irish Emigrant Society in 1841. Such groups provided services ranging from business contacts to charity and occasionally aided migrants in transit. Their services could benefit themselves as well. Realizing a new opportunity for banking services among this population, the Irish Emigrant Society organized Emigrant Industrial Savings Bank in 1850.

The potato famine of the late 1840s and early 1850s meant more Irish, more poor, more Catholics, and more people who needed specialized assistance with landing in the United States. In 1846, the New York City Board of Aldermen investigated private institutions established for impoverished Irish in the city (which then was limited to Manhattan) and Brooklyn. They found numerous examples of exploitation. The next year, the state legislature appointed a Board of Commissioners of Emigration composed of Irish- and German-Americans who agreed to serve without pay and to monitor businesses catering to migrants. The Board then lobbied until New York State agreed to use Castle Garden (q.v.) as an immigrant station. Thereafter, after physicians cleared international passengers for entrance into the United States, small boats carried those coming as immigrants (as opposed to visitors) to Castle Garden at Manhattan's southern tip. Agents of the Board collected statistics (records which were later stored at Ellis Island and were destroyed in a fire there). Castle Garden had facilities for washing and eating; and people could sleep on its benches. More important, they got advice regarding changing their money to U.S. currency, arranging inland transportation, meeting relatives, finding lodging, and job-hunting. When they heard reports of abuse or noticed examples of it, the Board investigated and tried to punish the guilty and to propose more effective legislation. Among their accomplishments was the 1864 erection of a new marine hospital on Ward's Island.

Some people had more ambitious plans for migrant assistance. The colonization movement encouraged Irish-Catholics to settle on the frontier, where they could escape wage dependency through farming and where they could maintain their faith far from the temptations of the big cities. Practical and political problems beset colonization. It proved difficult to raise funds and to convince migrants to trade the devil they knew in the city for the one they did not on the frontier. Also, urban leaders wanted promising migrants to stay in the cities, where their success benefited struggling Irish communities. As a way to fix the different arguments about colonization in the mind, one might note that among its advocates was Bishop John Lancaster Spalding of Peoria, Illinois, and among its detractors Archbishop John Joseph Hughes of New York.

The 1875 Supreme Court decision *Henderson* v. *Mayor of New York* ruled that the federal government, not the states, had primary responsibility for immigration. As the Board of Com-missioners of Emigration was authorized by state charter, it had to be phased out. However, the federal government did not replace it, and thus new emigrant relief services developed. An example was Our Lady of the Rosary, a parish erected by the Archdiocese of New York at the southern tip of Manhattan in 1882. The parish followed the work of Charlotte Grace O'Brien in that it was intended to support a new immigration station expressly for Irish women traveling alone. The federal government received immigrants at Castle Garden until 1891 and thereafter (except when it was rebuilding after a fire) at Ellis Island. In either case, Irish women admitted to the United States could easily get to Holy Rosary, where they could attend church, make complaints about ill-treatment aboard ship, receive advice, and take advantage of an employment office specializing in the placement of domestic servants. The workload at Holy Rosary declined in the 1920s, when southern Ireland became independent, the United States sought to limit migration (although the Irish were not as handicapped by this as other nationalities were), and modern appliances took the jobs of many domestic servants. However, the parish continues, and now houses a shrine to Saint Elizabeth Ann Bayley Seton.

Until 1922, migrants took responsibility for their own relief, with each ethnoreligious group helping itself. That year, American Catholicism began to claim responsibility for migrant care. The new National Catholic Welfare Conference established a Bureau of Immigration with a Port Office in New York. Thus, care of the Irish became part of the general care of migrants. The type of aid offered also changed until it became focused almost exclusively on leading the prospective migrant through the maze of U.S. immigration law and on protecting Irish interests whenever changes in the law were proposed. An example of the new definition of emigrant relief is the provisions in the 1990 law for a category of visas set aside to insure the diversity of the immigrant stream; Irish Americans had lobbied for that provision on the grounds that the previous (1965) law, which gave priority to family reunification, prevented many Irish from obtaining visas.

*See* Emigration: 1801–1921

Ronald H. Bayor and Timothy J. Meagher, eds., *The New York Irish* (Baltimore and London: The Johns Hopkins University Press, 1996).

John Francis Maguire, *The Irish in America* (London: Longmans, Green, and Co., 1868; reprint New York: Arno Press, Inc., 1969): 179–213.

Maureen Murphy, "Charlotte Grace O'Brien and the Mission of Our Lady of the Rosary for the Protection of Irish Immigrant Girls." *Mid-America*, LXXIV/3 (October 1992): 353–370.

John Lancaster Spalding, *The Religious Mission of the Irish People and Catholic Colonization* (New York: Catholic Publication Society, 1880; reprint New York: Arno, 1978).

MARY ELIZABETH BROWN

## EMIGRATION: 17th AND 18th CENTURIES

The burden of evidence available and the fruits of continuing research continue to support the view that emigration from Ireland in the seventeenth century was greatly overshadowed by the numbers who emigrated, particularly to colonial America, in the eighteenth century, or at least from the end of the first quarter of the eighteenth. The migratory patterns that can be detected with any degree of certainty would suggest that, if anything, there may even have been an overall net inflow of immigrants in the first three quarters of the seventeenth century. Nevertheless, L. M.

Cullen makes the point that, in relative terms, the proportion of emigrants, certainly in the period 1675–1700, compared favourably with the ratios per 1,000 of the population in the succeeding century.

Departures from Ireland at this time generally took the form of exile, voluntary or forced; indeed, in many cases, those who left, particularly the principal Catholic Irish families who left in significant numbers at either end of the century, felt that they were in a position where they had no choice but to remove themselves from their native land. The series of planned and gradual plantations, evident in Munster in the sixteenth century, had continued in the early years of the seventeenth, particularly in Ulster. The consequent exile of the Gaelic Irish which this development heralded, the consequence of the rebellion of 1641 which betokened the end of the first phase of seventeenth-century settlement, and the expulsions following the Williamite war in Ireland at the end of the century all form the background against which migration from and to Ireland in the seventeenth century should be set.

By the end of the sixteenth century, "the number of English in Ireland had increased from some hundred to several thousands." This quota was increased in turn in the early years of the seventeenth century when the English government embarked on the plantation of Ulster. Between then and 1641, the English settlers in the six escheated Ulster counties should be added to the immigrants, mostly from the Scottish Lowlands, who migrated at the same time to the Ulster counties not included in the official plantation, Antrim and Down. R. Gillespie calculates a "settler population of 3,329 persons for Antrim and 6,080 for Down," a total of 9,415 by 1630. These figures, as Gillespie acknowledges, are commensurate with Perceval-Maxwell's estimate of "4,000–5,000 male Scots or 2,000 families" who featured in the assimilated plantation of these two counties in eastern Ulster, closest to Scotland. It was from these two counties that much of the emigration that developed in the eighteenth centuries would emerge. There was at the same time a "substantial migration" from England into the areas of Ireland planted earlier, particularly into Munster.

By 1641, even though the total population of Ireland was still small, the population had probably doubled from what it had been in 1600. Munster even had sufficient surplus population to supply migrations for America, perhaps the first instance of recorded transatlantic emigration, as opposed to migration from say the fishing areas of Waterford to Newfoundland which only infrequently resulted in more permanent settlement.

The plantation of the province of Ulster in the early years of the seventeenth century created a displacement of native population, best represented by the Flight of the Earls from Rathmullan, County Donegal, in 1607. Chieftains of prominent Ulster families took flight in response to the usurpation of their land and their authority which the plantation of Ulster brought. Europe was the destination of this migration which, in many ways, signalled the end of one thousand years of the old Gaelic order and announced the arrival of the "civilising" influence of the English planter.

At the end of the seventeenth century, in the wake of the decisive War of the Two Kings, between William of Orange, the recently-imposed king of England, and the deposed Catholic king James II, there was a similar departure of many leading Catholic families, and on a greater scale. Following the Treaty of Limerick in 1691 Europe, particularly France, was again the principal des-

tination of those Irish soldiers, led by Patrick Sarsfield, who had supported the Jacobite cause in attempting to regain the throne of England. This struggle has been best remembered by the Battle of the Boyne fought on 1 July 1690, and remembered to the present day by thousands of Orangemen on 12 July each year. However, it was the more decisive defeat inflicted on the Jacobites at the Battle of Aughrim in 1691 which put paid to Irish hopes of regaining their land and status and which prompted their flight.

Some 15,000 Irish soldiers were allowed to leave Ireland and to sail to France to serve in the army of Louis XIV, who had supported the Jacobite cause against William. At a stroke, almost, the cream of Catholic Irish society was banished and on such a scale as to create the conditions for the rise of the Protestant Ascendancy, as it would in due course be called, which would continue to exert its authority under the series of repressive laws known as the Penal Code.

In the early 1680s, a period of distress caused by a combination of epidemic diseases and banditry exacerbated by the severe winter of 1683–84, there is evidence of a movement from Ulster which took up to at least 2,000 people to the eastern Chesapeake Valley by 1692. A number of ministers in the depressed Laggan valley in County Donegal in the north-west of the country announced their intention to emigrate in, 1684, citing both "persecutions" and the "general poverty abounding in these parts." Edward Randolph observed in 1692 that Somerset County, Maryland, was "a place pestered with Scotch and Irish."

This presaged a gradual and growing pattern of migration particularly from Ulster, significant examples of which first became evident in the early years of the eighteenth century. Much has been made of the claim that these instances of Presbyterian congregations, or Presbyterian-dominated communities, quit Ireland in response to the iniquities inflicted on them by the Penal Laws. Designed, as the title of one of them baldly stated, "to prevent the further growth of popery," the restrictions imposed weighed heavily against the freedom to practice any religion other than that of the official Church of Ireland. However it is clear that the impulse which prompted the emigrations in the 1680s and early 1690s took account not only of religious, political and economic factors but was also a response to the activities of colonial undertakers and new developments in maritime commerce.

These were undoubtedly factors which materialised in the first two decades of the eighteenth century. One of the earliest documented cases was of the group of Presbyterians who left Lifford in County Donegal in 1705 and found their way, probably taking ship at the nearby port of Derry, for Newcastle near Philadelphia. On arrival in Philadelphia, the Lifford congregation sent back a plea for funds to support the establishment of a place of worship:

> We undersubscribers and the greatest number of us born and educated in Ireland under the ministry of Mr. William Traill our Presbyterian minister formerly at Liford are by a divine Providence setled with our families at Newcastle and about it in the province of Pensilvania. . . . We do most humbly address ourselves to you as onto our mother church and to intreat your advice in this our uncertaine condition and if there can be any supply granted for our small congregation. . .

This is representative evidence for confirming the somewhat stereotypical image of early eighteenth-century migration, of

Ulster Scots fleeing in protest at the suppression of their freedom of worship to a New World where they could establish their independence of thought and worship. From 1718 an exodus of Presbyterian congregations took shape. In that year alone eleven Presbyterian ministers and nearly three hundred members of their congregations petitioned the governor of New England, Samuel Shute, for a grant of land. Responding to his encouragement, five ships left Derry quays that summer for Boston.

This transatlantic migration got under way just as the post-Williamite war arrival of Scots into Ulster had almost completely ceased. Catholics had neither the resources nor the inclination to go to colonies which were themselves predominantly Protestant. The momentum of Presbyterian emigration gathered pace. Thomas Whitney, a seaman waiting to sail from Larne in County Antrim, wrote in July 1727:

> Here are a vast number of people shipping off for Pennsylvania and Boston, here are three ships at Larne, 5 at Derry, two at Coleraine 3 at Belfast and 4 at Sligo, I'm assured that within these eight years there are gone above forty thousand people out of Ulster and the low part of Connaught.

Around 3,500 are estimated to have left Ulster 1725–27, a movement which reached a peak in 1729. In that year, the Address of Protestant Dissenting Ministers to the King argued that the sacramental test was found by Ulster Presbyterians to be "so very grievous that they have in great numbers transported themselves to the American plantations for the sake of that liberty and ease which they are denied in their native country."

There are, however, a number of other characteristics of the early eighteenth-century diaspora from Ireland which provide an appropriate balance of a consideration of the causes. The rents paid by tenants to their landlords were, as they were to be throughout the rest of the century, a crucial factor propelling emigrants abroad. By the years immediately before and after 1720, the first leases granted to the several thousands who had arrived from Lowland Scotland had reached the end of their first terms. Landlords took the opportunity, in renewing them, to raise rents to a more competitive level. Archbishop King described it thus in 1719:

> Nor do only Dissenters leave us, but proportionally of all sorts, except Papists . . . after the Revolution, most of the Kingdom was waste and abundance of people destroyed by war. The landlords therefore were glad to get tenants at any rate and set their lands at very easy rents . . . but now their leases are expired and they [are] obliged not only to give what was paid before the Revolution but in most places double and in many places treble, so that it is impossible for people to live or subsist on their farms.

As the first quarter of the century wore on, economic factors associated with land and the level of rents assumed a greater significance in the emigrants' decision-making.

Even in the late 1720s, when the Presbyterian exodus was gathering a momentum of its own, there is sufficient evidence to suggest that, inevitably almost, the harsh economic circumstances which provoked Archbishop Boulter to contribute £500 to an appeal sponsored by the Merchant Taylors to relieve distress in Ulster could increasingly be seen influencing decisions to emigrate. In 1729 the Justices of Assize for the North-West Circuit of Ulster recorded that those preparing to emigrate

complain that several gentlemen have lately raised their rents above the value of their lands . . . The Protestant tenants complain that many landlords turn them out of their farms and give them to Papists for the sake of a little increase in rent . . . They likewise complain of vigorous methods in payment of their tithes, the clergy generally setting their parishes to lay farmers, who they allege demand more than the value of their tithes.

The same report remarked on the effect of land agents sent by ships' captains, who scoured the country assuring tenants in shortened circumstances that "in America they may get good land to them and their posterity for little or no rent without either paying tithes or taxes." Archbishop Boulter, who deplored the drain of good Protestant stock in such alarming numbers, nonethelesss acknowledged the success of these agents who had "deluded the people with stories of great plenty and estates to be had . . . and they have been better able to seduce people by reason of the necessities of the poor of late."

Whatever their circumstances, even when economic troughs were replaced by better times in the 1750s and 1760s, land remained the most enticing attraction of America for the tenant farmer in Ireland. The availability of large tracts of land in the American colonies in the 1750s and 1760s was increasingly advertised in Ulster. The *Belfast Newsletter,* begun in 1737, regularly carried notices of the availability of land.

> David Waugh, being just arrived from America, takes the opportunity of acquainting his countrymen that he can accommodate any of them that incline to go over with their families with farms of as good land as ever they enjoyed or saw in Ireland or perhaps better . . . Settlers shall have deeds of said land forever free for the first five years and after . . . to pay only one shilling sterling the acre yearly.

The temptation to remove to America where, as another advertisement phrased it, "instead of tenants they become landlords," proved irresistible for tenants whose rents continued to rise and who, additionally, continued to pay tithes to the Church of Ireland. Stronger still was the example of friends and relatives who had made the move and whose reports home of their progress encouraged the intending emigrant to embark on the journey. Many dithering minds were made up when they received a letter which read:

> I now live upon the waters of Juniata, province of pensylvania . . . about one hundred and fifty miles from Baltimoar and I folow farming now. Land can be purchased hear for twenty shillings a Acre which is then free paying only the tax. I have given a small account of the country to you and if you thought it answerd you to come I would be fond to see you hear . . .

The example of a friend or relative doing well and their offer of a place to stay on arrival until the new immigrants became established was the assisted passage many sought. This form of chain-migration, which was to reach very sophisticated levels at the height of the massive famine-induced emigration from the mid-1840s, took root from the middle of the eighteenth century. Between this coordinated and organised migration and the transfer of congregations earlier in the century, there developed two principal means of assisting emigrants.

One was offers by land speculators enticing communities or neighbourhoods to transplant themselves to North America.

Schemes for land in Nova Scotia, following the removal of the threat of French dominance after the Seven Years War, as well as for the thirteen colonies, were widely advertised. Throughout the 1760s, Colonel Alexander McNutt and Thomas Debrisay undertook a vigorous promotional campaign to attract settlers, preferably in family units, to Nova Scotia. Agents appointed throughout counties Donegal, Antrim, Londonderry, Monaghan and in Belfast participated in a scheme which, says Dickson, "encouraged between four hundred and five hundred people to emigrate from Ireland to Nova Scotia in the 1760s." Arthur Dobbs, while Governor of North Carolina, 1754–65, though his stated preference was for European settlers of German origin, selected suitable tenants on his County Kildare and County Antrim estates and arranged their removal to the Carolinas where he himself had obtained nearly half a million acres of prime land.

The number of references to "families" in early-eighteenth-century emigration sources confirm that migration, particularly from Ulster was dominated in this period by the removal of household units, indeed often groups of households, representing whole or partial communities. For individuals, travelling with no other family members, the route to America was often as an indentured servant. For a free passage, the "servant" was contracted to work for whoever purchased his services on arrival from the ship's captain. This arrangement suited many unmarried men, particularly Catholics from counties outside Ulster. However much it may have many of the hallmarks of a white slave trade, there is no doubt that this arrangement suited many who could not have raised the money for the passage. The five years' "servitude" in fact allowed many to form an idea of what they were best equipped to do in this new world and where they might go to do it. A considerable number of Irish emigrants who began life in America as indentured servants progressed to a position of importance. William Killen from County Clare, indentured to work in Maryland, became Chief Justice of Delaware; Charles Thomson from Maghera, County Londonderry, who had been indentured at the age of ten, his father having died on the voyage, went on to become Secretary of the First Continental Congress.

Another Ulster-Scot who played a prominent role in early American political development was John Dunlap. Born in Strabane, County Tyrone, he had emigrated at the age of ten and trained as a printer. He printed the American Declaration of Independence and, in 1784, started the *Pennsylvania Packet,* the first daily newspaper to be printed in the United States. He maintained a constant correspondence throughout this period with his family in Strabane which may be taken as representing the impact with kith and kin of emigrants' letters in maintaining the momentum of the emigration movement.

> . . . the young men of Ireland who wish to be free and happy should leave it and come here as quick as possible. There is no place in the world where a man meets so rich a reward for good conduct and industry as in America.

Dunlap's letter may be taken to exemplify one of the characteristics which L. M. Cullen identified as marking the transatlantic migration in the 1760s and 1770s as a "watershed." The "pull" of America became more irresistible for individuals by the arrival of such letters, one of the forms of "improved communications which made new opportunities much better known," identified by Cullen in the period immediately prior to the Declaration of Independence.

Ironically, even though the accelerating pace of emigration in the 1760s coincided with a period of relative amelrioration in the rural economy, the sustained mushrooming of emigrant totals in the years immediately preceding the War of Independence can be attributed to a series of economic and social difficulties. Not the least of these was the depression in the linen market which affected farm incomes generated by domestic spinning and weaving. Of equal concern was the widespread raising of rents on the great estates in counties Antrim, Down, Londonderry and Tyrone. Not only did this broaden the general predisposition to emigrate, it also gave rise to another factor which influenced would-be emigrants. A series of rural disorders was perpetrated by the "Hearts of Steel" whose complaints must have been echoed by a considerable proportion of emigrants from 1770–1774:

> the deplorable state to which depression has brought us, by reason of heavy rents which are become so great a burden to us that we are not scarecely able to bear . . . so that, between landlords and rectors, the very marrow is screwed out of our bones.

One estimate of the numbers who emigrated during 1770–74, in what was clearly the climax of emigration to colonial America, puts the total at an overall 40,000 or an average of 10,000 per year. There is no doubting that there was an emigration hemorrhage in these years and contemporary sources commented on it in graphic terms. The claims and counter-claims of the numbers of emigrants in this period are echoed throughout the main period of emigration in the rest of the eighteenth century. There is now general acceptance that R. J. Dickson's 100,000 and D. N. Doyle's 120,000 err on the side of generosity, It might equally be argued that Cullen and Wockek's lower estimates do not take full account of the different ports through which immigrants could arrive in colonial America. Even for the period after the Treaty of Paris there is evidence of a renewed and heavier stream of emigration.

One of the features which is worth commenting on in the debate about the quantifcation of the transatlantic traffic is the extent to which emigration continued to be a direct response to the circumstances created by difficult economic years. Kirkham states that the "crisis" characteristic continued over much of the eighteenth century, and there is good reason for seeing it in the glut of emigrations in the period 1770–74. It is however more appropriately associated with the years up to 1750. Kirkham's point is that the years before 1750 in which sailings of emigrant ships peaked—1718–19, 1727–29, 1735–36, 1740–41 and 1745–46—were all years of poor harvests, disease or economic crisis. Furthermore, although these years only account for one quarter of the time span of the period to 1750, they "account for more than half of the sailings identified."

The increased rates of emigration from Ireland in the 1750s and 1760s are significant, says Cullen, because in these decades of "powerful economic expansion . . . the . . . pressure for employment outlets and the crisis mobility associated with it had greatly eased." "Pull" had replaced "push" as the predominant factor underlying individual cases of emigration.

Doyle's work in extrapolating from the statistics of the 1790 census leads him to "conclude that the Irish stock population of the infant United States in 1790 was around 447,000, up to two-thirds of which (some 295,000) was of Scotch-Irish extraction." By the same calculation, "116,000 may stand as the figure of southern Irish background." Maldwyn Jones estimates that some 100,000 emigrated from Ireland 1783–1814, effectively from the end of the War of Independence until the end of the Anglo-American War in 1814. The uncertainty that has characterised the ongoing discussions about the numbers who emigrated between 1600 and 1800 continued until the end of the eighteenth century. Moreover, the most recent estimate for the numbers involved in the United Irishmen's failed rising of 1798 who took voluntary or forced exile in the United States, 2,000–2,500, indicates the extent to which Ireland's first republicans found ready accommodation in the United States.

*See* Scotch-Irish and American Politics; Scots Irish

Jonathan Bardon, *A History of Ulster* (Belfast, 1992).

H. Tyler Blethen and Curtis W. Wood, Jr., eds., *Ulster and North America: Transatlantic Perspectives on the Scotch-Irish* (Tuscaloosa and London, 1997).

N. P. Canny, ed., *Europeans on the Move: Studies on European Migration 1500–1800* (Oxford, 1994).

David Noel Doyle, *Ireland, Irishmen and Revolutionary America, 1780–1820* (Cork, 1981).

R. J. Dickson, with a new introduction by G. E. Kirkham, *Ulster Emigration to Colonial America 1718–76* (Belfast, 1966, 1988).

R. G. Gillespe, *Colonial Ulster: The Settlement of East Ulster 1600–1641* (Cork, 1985).

E. R. R. Green, ed., *Essays in Scotch-Irish History* (Belfast, 1992).

Kerby A. Miller, *Emigrants and Exiles: Ireland and the Irish Exodus to America* (New York, 1985).

TREVOR PARKHILL

## EMIGRATION: 1801–1921

### I. Scale

Throughout Ireland's long nineteenth century of social, economic, and political turmoil between the Union with Great Britain in 1801 and the partition settlement of 1921–22, emigration was a distinctive and disturbing element of Irish life. Even before the Great Famine, precipitated by the potato blight of 1845, Ireland was noted for its exceptional outflow, which was widely regarded as proof of "over-population" and a symptom of chronic impoverishment. Emigration was no less important than mortality in depopulating Ireland during the Famine, peaking during the period of recovery in the early 1850s. Thereafter, relentlessly intense emigration has persisted with only brief and partial remissions, even in the absence of life-threatening disaster and dire poverty, contributing critically to Ireland's unique pattern of continuous depopulation during the post-Famine century. Most of Ireland's human export trade after 1850 was directed towards the United States; but the origins of the American Irish can only be understood by an enquiry into the scale, composition, constraints, agencies, and dynamics of Irish emigration as a whole.

Long before the Famine, the intensity of Irish emigration had become remarkable in the context of contemporary Europe. The pre-revolutionary movement to America, dominated by Ulster Presbyterians and indentured servants, had already given place to a broader emigration between the treaty of Versailles in 1783 and the renewal of Anglo-American hostilities in 1812. Despite interference from wars, prohibition of artisan emigration, and the severe passenger legislation of 1803, 100,000 people are thought to have left Ireland for North America during those three decades. Most of them were paying passengers rather than servants imported under contract, while many were southerners and Catholics. Even more made for Britain, where recognisable Irish enclaves developed in cities such as London, Manchester, and Glasgow. After the resumption of peace in 1815, emigration resumed and intensified. One million Irish emigrants are estimated to have crossed the Atlantic between 1815 and 1845, with half that number taking the cheaper British alternative and some 30,000 obtaining state assistance to undertake the much longer journey to Australia. Before the Famine this huge egress curtailed, but did not reverse, population growth: the century-long decline began in about 1847, when emigration and famine-related mortality were of comparable importance as agents of depopulation. Movement out of Ireland probably exceeded one million between 1846 and 1850, yet did not peak until 1851 when the worst ravages of dearth, death, and disease had passed in most regions. Between 1851 and 1870, recorded outward movement oscillated about a slowly declining axis; yet even years of Irish prosperity such as 1857 and 1866 generated more emigration than any but the most desperate pre-Famine years. Estimates of net outward movement suggest that the probability that a young person would "disappear" from Ireland in the course of a decade was close to a third in the 1850s and 1860s. This index of "cohort depletion" refers to the group aged 5–24 years at the beginning of each intercensal decade. Various measures suggest that the volume of out-migration between 1851 and 1871 lay between 2.1 million and 2.6 million. All told, at least five million people left Ireland during the first seven decades of the century. More than two and a half million others were to emigrate between 1871 and 1921.

Throughout the later nineteenth century, Ireland's rate of emigration was easily the highest in Europe. Even in the sluggish

Cohort Depletion, 1821–1911

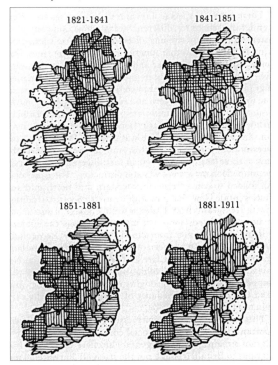

Counties are shown in descending order of depletion: cross-hatching, verticals, horizontals, dots.

1890s, the decade's emigration from Ireland amounted to a tenth of Ireland's mean population. About a quarter of each youthful cohort "disappeared" from Ireland during each intercensal decade from the 1870s to the 1910s, and still others would have emigrated later in their lives. Other estimates of net out-migration suggest that in the 1870s the Irish rate tripled its nearest rivals (Norwegian, Swedish, and Scottish); while even at the height of the "new immigration" of the 1890s, net movement from Italy was less than half as brisk as that from Ireland. No German state approached Irish rates, though provinces such as Pomerania, Posen, and East Prussia sometimes drew close. Ireland's persistent predominance was masked by its decreasing weight among European populations, which meant that the absolute volume of Irish emigration declined while that from the expanding populations of central and southern Europe increased. Ireland's share of the population of the British Isles declined from a third in 1841 to a fifth in 1871, and to a mere tenth in 1911: consequently, net emigration from Ireland between 1871 and 1911 only just exceeded that from Britain despite the much higher Irish rate *per capita.* By the early twentieth century, twice as many British as Irish passengers were leaving for the United States, while Irish emigrants comprised only a twentieth of the movement to Canada and Australasia.

The relentless movement out of Ireland was only occasionally interrupted, and the temporary retention in Ireland of thousands of young people had significant social and political consequences. The American recession of the mid-1870s caused a sharp drop in emigration which was only partly absorbed by relative prosperity in Ireland. The creation of a surplus of young men and women with little prospect of advancement at home, and frustrated in their expectation of a foreign career, contributed to the social unrest of 1879–81 until American recovery reopened the floodgates. This pattern was repeated during the Great War and the War of Independence, when the requisitioning of passenger vessels and the menace of mines and torpedoes reduced trans-Atlantic movement to a trickle. Athough much of Ireland's surplus youth was absorbed by wartime industries, military recruitment, and increased agricultural employment, under-employment became serious in western counties and was often cited as a major factor in swelling revolutionary organisations. When the transoceanic passenger trade was restored in 1920, emigration immediately reached the pre-war level despite the best efforts of Dáil Éireann to keep the people at home through propaganda, permits, penalties, and prohibitions. The experience of the wartime and revolutionary period offers persuasive evidence of the social and political importance of emigration. The decision to leave Ireland was essentially the outcome of economic and social factors, impervious to the rhetoric of politicians; but the organisation of politics was profoundly affected by the extent, timing, and composition of the emigrant stream.

Where did the migratory Irish settle? Relatively few moved county within Ireland, despite the drift of population from rural areas to Dublin and especially Belfast: even in 1851, the population born in one county and living in another was only 550,000. By contrast, over three million natives of Ireland were living overseas by 1871, a number close to the entire adult population still at home. The chief country of settlement over the next half century was invariably the United States, followed by Britain, Canada, and Australia; but the regional distribution altered significantly over time. The United States became the majority

destination only in the 1860s, and probably housed fewer Irish migrants than Britain until the late 1840s. After the Famine, Australia also took an increasing share of the displaced Irish, whereas the number of first-generation residents in Britain and Canada declined, at first relatively and after 1861 absolutely. These figures mask the impermanence of foreign residence for many Irish migrants, who moved on freely from country to country as well as town to town, thinking nothing of crossing the Pacific in pursuit of the latest goldrush in Victoria, New Zealand, or California. Particularly in mid-century, the census returns for Irish-born residents in Canada and Britain were vastly inflated by the temporary presence of emigrants expecting to move on to the United States. Smaller pockets of Irish settlement developed in every Anglophone country and throughout the British Empire, but the only other major countries of settlement were New Zealand and South Africa. Argentina, which received about 7,000 Irish emigrants between 1801 and 1870, was the only non-Anglophone country to attract a significant Irish intake, though speculators promoted several schemes to bring Irish settlers to Latin America including Edward Cullen's dream of creating an Irish "New Granada" in Panama in 1858. America was not the only major destination for Irish emigrants, whose experience varied according to the social, economic and political conditions in each place of settlement.

The distribution of the Irish overseas changed little between 1871 and 1911, some three-fifths of these being resident in the United States. The proportion in Britain was never far from a fifth, with Australia overtaking Canada as the next most important destination. The various series recording extra-European passenger movement from the United Kingdom agree that the United States consistently attracted four-fifths of all Irish passengers. In this respect Ireland resembled Germany, which often sent more than nine-tenths of its emigrants to the United States. Everywhere Irish immigrants became rapidly less conspicuous as a proportion of the local population, though this loss was counterbalanced by proliferation of the descendants of Irish settlers. In 1871, when the Irish population overseas was most numerous, the Irish-born component of the local population was only three percent in Britain and five percent in the United States, but six percent in Canada and thirteen percent in Australia. These proportions had declined sharply by 1921, when one Australian in fifty was Irish-born, while Irish natives accounted for only about one percent of the population in Britain, Canada, and the United States. Ireland's overseas population still exceeded one and three-quarter million; yet the impact of Irish emigration, once so important for all the major countries of settlement, was by 1921 largely confined to the country of origin.

The choice of destination was affected by many factors, including the availability of state assistance and private enticements, the relative prosperity of different host economies, and the choices of earlier Irish settlers who played a crucial part in subsidising and governing further movement. The shift of preference from Britain to the United States in the 1840s was largely an accident of the timing of the Famine, which coincided with economic crisis in Britain and Australia and relatively strong demand for employment in the United States. Once the Famine exodus had crossed the Atlantic in pursuit of life and a livelihood, its presence acted as a magnet for future generations of prospective emigrants. Nevertheless, the number and also the proportion choosing the United States varied according to cyclical variations in the American economy. Thus peaks in one index of American economic growth in 1873, 1882, 1892, and 1907 were reflected in 1873, 1883, 1895, and 1907 by peaks in Irish movement to the United States. Likewise, the economic troughs of 1878, 1885, and 1896 were echoed in the diminished emigration of 1877, 1885, and 1898. It was in periods of economic downturn in the United States that emigrants were most easily diverted elsewhere, as to Britain and Australasia in the later 1870s, Britain at the turn of the century, and Canada just before the Great War. The oscillation in roughly opposite directions of the American and British economies cushioned the impact of American recession by offering Irish emigrants the alternative prospect of employment in Britain. Most emigrants, however, were restricted in their choice of destination by ignorance, precedent, and links with previous emigrants: their response to American recession was often to postpone rather than redirect their outward movement. Cultural constraints may also have dissuaded some emigrants from choosing the British colonies and dominions, just as ignorance of language ensured that South America would remain only a minor site for Irish settlement. High opportunity-costs as well as fares impeded emigration to Australasia, while movement to Canada was restricted by the widespread belief (reported in 1882) that "it was a great iceberg."

Undoubtedly the most important factor in determining emigrant destinations was the location of previous emigrants. The networks of friendship, marriage, residence, and employment built up by earlier Irish settlers and their descendants exercised a powerful attraction on their Irish connections, creating a system of "chain migration" which reinforced existing patterns of settlement. After arriving overseas many emigrants continued their rambling in search of a better life, but even their rambling was often directed by information gleaned from other Irish settlers and their networks. These influences account for several highly localised migrations from pre-Famine Ireland, whereby chains of emigrants from certain counties in Ireland selected rather obscure destinations such as Nova Scotia, Newfoundland, and Argentina. The importance of chain migration is evident in the distinctiveness and the persistency of the patterns of regional origin of Irish settlers in each major host country. In some cases, these distributions were largely determined by the origins of pre-Famine pioneers; but in the major countries of settlement, the formative period was the Famine-driven migration of the mid-century. The force of precedent in determining the patterns of Irish settlement is manifest in statistics showing the Irish-born component of the migratory population of the American states and also the British counties. In both England and Scotland, over nine-tenths of the regional clustering of Irish immigrants in 1901 is statistically "explained" by the clusters recorded in 1871. Despite massive turnover of population and internal migration, a similar degree of stability applies to the distributions of Irish settlement in the American states in 1870 and 1910. Emigrants were guided in their movements out of Ireland by a mental map, framed by the long succession of earlier Irish explorers.

## II. Composition

Emigration, though touching every locality in Ireland, was far from uniform in its impact. For the pre-Famine period, the best available index of net outward migration is "cohort depletion," defined above. Between 1821 and 1841, depletion was greatest in a cluster of Ulster and Leinster counties, though even then virtually every county was subject to considerable out-migration. During the 1840s the epicentre of depletion moved westwards,

Bound for New York

and Connaught lost nearly half of its youthful population as a result of massive outward movement as well as mortality (in uncertain proportions). Over the following decade emigration from Munster and the south-west probably increased slightly, whereas movement out of other provinces diminished. By the 1860s, the regional distribution of the Famine decade had been mainly restored, emigration from the less "backward" eastern counties having been relatively minor at all periods. The catastrophe of the Famine thus generated an immediate and lasting transformation in the regional patterns of outward migration. The counties most devastated by the Famine were also those in which the "adjustment" of heavy emigration was most emphatic.

Between 1871 and 1911, the highest rates of net outward movement continued to be recorded for the counties of the west and the north midlands. After about 1880, Connaught's preeminence was reflected even in the defective returns of gross emigration, despite their exclusion of numerous Connaught emigrants who travelled undetected to Britain via Dublin. The northeastern and southeastern counties continued to record relatively low rates of cohort depletion, though even these usually exceeded comparable figures for net emigration from Britain. Munster, so often depicted as the hub of Irish emigration, fell far short of the poorer province of Connaught in the rate as distinct from the volume of its emigration. These disparities were gradually accentuated in the decades leading up to the Great War. Emigration rates from Connaught declined only slowly after the 1880s, the reduction being greater for Munster and Ulster, and precipitate in the case of Leinster. Thus emigration became increasingly a regional phenomenon, yet never to the extent of eliminating its social importance even in Antrim, Kildare, or Wexford.

From the Famine onwards, emigration was consistently most intensive from counties with little employment outside agriculture, counties which also tended to be heavily burdened with small farms of low valuation. The association between heavy emigration and rural poverty was accentuated in the movement to the United States: thus Connaught was not merely over-represented in emigration but also overwhelmingly "set towards the west" rather than towards Britain or Australia. These statistical findings challenge the still widespread belief that lack of means, ignorance, and attachment to the Irish sod continued to block movement out of the most "backward" regions until the last years of the century. Nor is it generally true that out-migration was sluggish from poorer districts within counties: even before the provision of state and private assistance for emigration from "congested" areas in the 1880s, cohort depletion was heavier from the impoverished coastal unions of Donegal than from the county's inland region. It is less clear that the group most prone to emigrate were the poorest inhabitants of the poorest localities. But in terms of neighbourhood if not personal background, the emigrants emerged disproportionately from economic contexts of rural poverty, where demand for labour and living standards (at least by the conventional measures of mean income and quality of housing) fell far short of those prevailing in Britain, Australasia, or America. The regional origins of Irish emigration strongly suggest that it did indeed act as a palliative for poverty from the Famine onwards.

By 1850, alone among the European countries populating the New World, Ireland was generating "an equal emigration of the sexes," which Edward Gibbon Wakefield in 1849 had deemed "one essential condition of the best colonisation." In Britain and Europe (with the occasional exception of some Scandinavian countries), male emigrants regularly outnumbered women despite the roughly equal economic and social pressure on both sexes to venture overseas in order to better themselves. The Irish exception should probably be ascribed to the shock of the Famine, which made the need to leave Ireland seem so urgent that many families abandoned conventional constraints against sending unprotected girls on a dangerous voyage to an uncertain future. As favourable reports multiplied of the fate of these pioneers, and as networks of friends and relatives developed in the host societies, the Irish at home became less apprehensive about the moral, social, and physical risks entailed by female emigration. Until the Famine, the majority of transatlantic emigrants from Irish ports were male, although the female component had risen steadily from a third in 1803–5 to nearly half by the early 1840s. This trend was temporarily reversed between 1846 and 1848, but by the early 1850s there was a slight female excess, the male majority being restored after 1856. By about 1870, these fluctuations had balanced out, leaving only a slight female majority in the residual population at home. The sex of Irish residents in North America was not returned in the census reports, but in England and New South Wales parity had been attained. The female component in recorded emigration from Ireland was usually greatest in the vicinity of Connaught, with its high emigration rates overall, while men predominated in movement out of the urbanised east and particularly the Belfast region. During the four decades preceding the Great War, there was usually a small male majority, reversed during the years 1893–1904. This female excess at the turn of the century was a consequence of the rapid decline in demand for paid female labour in rural Ireland, coupled with the persistent demand for domestic servants in the United States even after the slump of 1893 had curtailed the demand for male labourers.

The unusually even balance of the sexes in Irish emigration was achieved not by universal movement in family groups, but through a steady flow of unattached girls as well as youths. Although sampled passenger lists indicate that the majority of pre-Famine emigrants travelled with others of the same surname, the proportion exceeded three-fifths only in 1803–5. In

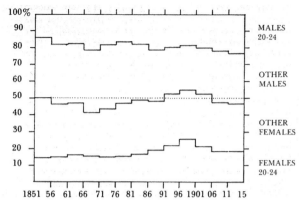

Emigration from Irish ports, May 1851–1914: Percentage distribution by sex, distinguishing emigrants aged 20–24, for each quinquennium.

1831, the family component in Irish emigration to the United States was much smaller than for British emigrants, probably reflecting the lower proportion of prospective emigrants capable of raising the fare for a family passage. Even before the Famine, over four-fifths of transatlantic emigrants from Irish ports were "statute adults" (required to pay full fare, being over 14 or 15 years). The adult component fell slightly in 1847–48 as tenant farmers responded to the Famine by selling their remaining assets in order to emigrate as a family group. Various returns show that the importance of family and child movement declined significantly after the Famine. Between 1851 and 1914, the proportion of children declined fairly steadily from nearly a quarter in the early 1850s to an eighth in the late 1860s, subsiding to a mere twelfth by the eve of the Great War. The registrar-general's returns show that emigration was increasingly concentrated in the age group 20–24. This group had reached a critical point in the life-cycle, having recently entered the labour market but not yet the marriage market. Emigration offered them the promise of employment overseas followed by marriage; whereas delay in departure threatened them with exclusion from both markets, first in Ireland but before long in the world at large. By the 1860s, over a third of all Irish emigrants were aged between 20 and 24, the median age at departure being slightly lower for women than for men. After the mid-1880s, about two Irish emigrants out of every five belonged to this age group; while the proportion of married emigrants hovered around one in ten. Emigration had become a young man's and a young woman's game, the rules of which were well known to every cohort of Irish people reaching adulthood after the Famine.

Most emigrants, when asked to state their calling on embarkation, claimed neither status nor skills. From about 1830 to the Famine, the majority of Irish emigrants to Boston and New York were returned as "labourers" or "servants." The unskilled component grew fairly steadily from under a third in the early 1820s to about three-fifths in the 1840s. Farmers, who had accounted for about a third of a sample of occupied emigrants before 1825, remained a substantial but decreasing minority. Yet farmers and labourers together were no more predominant among male emigrants than in Ireland's pre-Famine population. Textile, clerical, and commercial personnel were underrepresented; but industrial and construction workers, as well as artisans, were prominent in movement to New York. After 1850, labourers overwhelmed all other categories of male emigrants, outnumbering farmers by at least ten to one. With the exception of clerks, no other group was over-represented among emigrants of the early 1850s, when compared with the Irish male work-force in 1851. By comparison with British emigrants in 1857 and 1867, the Irish outflow had a much greater component of labour-ers and fewer farmers, despite Ireland's far larger agricultural sector. In 1857, virtually all female emigrants of both nation-alities were either servants or without occupation; but a decade later this remained true only of the Irish. The predominance of labourers and servants persisted into the twentieth century, with servants accounting for nine-tenths of female emigrants up to 1910. Around the turn of the century, the proportion of occupied male emigrants returned as labourers had dropped from four-fifths to two-thirds, the change being caused by increasing emi-gration of farmers, clerks and shop assistants rather than trades-men. Whereas Canada and especially Australasia attracted an increasing proportion of professional, commercial and skilled emigrants from Ireland, this trend was only faintly perceptible in the case of movement to the United States.

It is tempting to cite the apparent predominance of menial workers as evidence that relatively little "human capital" was transferred from Ireland to the New World through emigration. In fact, the occupational labels recorded by enumerators reveal little about the emigrant's class background or likely efficiency as a settler. Most youthful sons of farmers and shopkeepers would have described themselves as "labourers," even if they had some prospect of succession to land or a shop in later life. Like-wise, employment as a "servant," often unpaid within the family household, was a common phase of the life-cycle for young women of all but the highest social strata. Ireland's endemic under-employment ensured that these occupational descriptions were often assertions of intention rather than fact: those about to enter the regular workforce through emigration tended to choose occupations accessible to them abroad rather than those of their parents. The occupational returns therefore embody a tangle of incongruous factors such as the "life-cycle effect," future hopes, past experience, and also the guesswork of shipping clerks or po-licemen making out registers in a hurry. Since versatility, energy, and adaptability were more important than conventional skills in winning a livelihood for new arrivals in America or Australia, there is no good reason to suppose that the human capital repre-sented by Irish "labourers" and 'servants" was inferior to that for British emigrants, who were more likely to claim trades and skills of dubious utility in the New World.

Literacy in English is probably a more useful index than occu-pation of the Irish emigrant's human capital, since this achieve-ment vastly extended the range of occupations and services open to the emigrant in the Anglophone world. Since almost all Irish emigrants could speak English, even if to some ears impenetra-bly, they enjoyed a marked comparative advantage over many of their European competitors at the time of arrival. Though many emigrants from the west of Ireland must have spoken and under-stood Irish, there are few references to its public use by emi-grants, for the language was an incubus rather than an asset in the countries of Irish settlement. Irish was even less common as a written medium, virtually all surviving emigrants' letters being written in English or in various Hiberno-English dialects. The capacity to read a newspaper or write an application was no less important than mastery of spoken English in securing a liveli-hood, and here the Irish were initially at a marked disadvantage by comparison with English and Scottish emigrants. By the turn of the century, Irish census returns indicate that illiteracy had been virtually eliminated among young adults—a tribute to the impact of the national education system founded in 1831. Those contemplating emigration were keenly aware that basic literacy was essential for success overseas, and this was often cited as a significant factor in whetting the Irish appetite for education (especially among girls hoping to take up domestic service). For most of the nineteenth century, however, illiteracy was wide-spread among the Irish population; and indirect calculations suggest that emigrants were more likely than those remaining at home to be illiterate, until the 1860s but not thereafter. In the case of state-assisted emigrants to New South Wales, only two-fifths of those arriving in 1848–50 could read and write, a proportion which rose to two-thirds by 1866–69. The patterns of emigrant literacy thus suggest that the emigrants differed little from their Irish contemporaries in this index of their "human capital," and also that their disadvantage by comparison with British emigrants diminished rapidly from the Famine onwards.

Though Catholics dominated Irish emigration after the eigh-teenth century, Protestant movement was never negligible. Early in the century, there was extensive emigration from northern counties with large Protestant populations, but from the 1840s onwards the continuing northern emigration was swamped by that from the Catholic-dominated south and west. Evidence from Antrim and Londonderry in the 1830s indicates that Pres-byterians were more disposed to emigrate than either Catholics or Churchmen. Even in 1851, up to a third of passengers leaving Derry were identified as Protestants, and a year later an Armagh priest testified that the intensity of emigration from the Cross-maglen district did not vary according to denomination. The pre-Famine influx of Irish Protestants into Canada left an en-during imprint, and in Ontario the Protestant proportion of those claiming Irish stock remained static around two-thirds be-tween 1842 and 1871, a similar figure being recorded in 1931. The Australian census for 1911 shows that twenty-nine percent of the Irish-born population were non-Catholics, the proportion being highest in Tasmania and lowest in South Australia. Unfor-tunately, no comparable records of religious affiliation were com-piled in either Britain or the United States, so that the widespread supposition of an overwhelming Catholic majority among Irish settlers is impressionistic and speculative.

Nevertheless, it seems clear that the general preponderance of Catholic emigrants masked important variations by region of set-tlement as well as origin. Despite the contrary opinion of many hostile observers, the vast and variegated human stream which poured out of Ireland under the Union cannot usefully be re-duced to a simple stereotype of "Paddy" or "Biddy."

## III. CONSTRAINTS

In a world of unfettered mobility and universal access to in-formation, the rational actor would be always on the move in pursuit of a superior quality of life attainable somewhere else. From this perspective, the puzzle for historians is not to explain migration, but why people fail to migrate. The constraints in-hibiting long-distance emigration from Ireland, as from every country in nineteenth-century Europe, included ignorance, ex-pense and danger, as well as attachment to the familiar "home" environment. As demonstrated by the rapid diffusion of practi-cal knowledge about emigrant opportunities during the Famine, the constraint of ignorance may be easily overcome in a crisis. Yet the readiness with which hundreds of thousands of unlettered, poor, and "backward" Irish people acquired the emigrant mentality also reflected a prolonged process of pre-Famine propaganda and marketing. The passenger-brokering business, initiated in Dublin and Belfast by Francis Taggart, got underway immediately after the peace of 1815. By 1827, the Canada Company had agents in Dublin, Cork, Limerick and Omagh, as well as in Liverpool and New York; and fifteen years later, the Cork agent of a single "bounty" contractor for Australia retained no less than thirty-eight sub-agencies in all four provinces. Local newspapers (whose circulation was further extended after the abolition of stamp tax in 1855) carried notices of forthcoming sailings to the New World, while bills and posters began to decorate walls, shopfronts, and even schoolrooms. As early as 1834, Henry Inglis "noticed in one of the poorest cabins, in the neighbourhood of Youghal, where scarcely any furniture was to be seen, one of the printed bills, announcing the approaching departure of a ship for Canada, stuck upon the wall." The larger passenger trade to the United States gave rise to even denser networks of local agents, often merchants and shopkeepers in small towns, whose advertisements and advice on current bargain fares made emigration seem a routine and attractive option. Those whose interest had been aroused were inundated with guides and manuals offering practical advice, often with an obvious commercial motive but sometimes in the disinterested hope of redirecting emigrants from foreign urban slums to "the interior." During and after the Famine, the flood of information expanded, along with the scale and sophistication of the emigration industry. Even in the remotest localities, the Irish had ready access to detailed reports of wages and living conditions throughout North America and Australasia, and ample guidance in the cheapest and safest routes for reaching the most advantageous destinations.

The most important source of practical guidance was the correspondence of the emigrants themselves. The "American letter" was already an institution in much of rural Ireland before the Famine, though the prevalence of illiteracy meant that many letters had to be dictated abroad and read aloud at home. Apart from enclosing money (the most eloquent argument for emigration), these letters served to convey information, nominate or discourage further emigrants, and reinforce the bonding of separated kinsfolk. In the 1830s, transatlantic postage was still expensive and slow, often being entrusted to agents who negotiated with captains or passengers to act as couriers. Yet between 1833 and 1835, over 700,000 letters from New York passed through Liverpool post office, eleven times the reverse correspondence; the bulk of these were probably letters from Irish settlers. The temperance advocate Fr. Theobald Mathew testified in 1847 that he had forwarded "hundreds and hundreds" of emigrant letters: "being so well known I am a kind of agent." Three years earlier, the parish priest of Schull, Co. Cork, had remarked that "when they write home, the friends come to me to read them. The accounts are very flattering. The general observation they make in the letters to friends is, that there is no tyranny, no oppression from landlords, and no taxes." After the Famine, the volume of emigrant correspondence vastly expanded with the diffusion of literacy and reductions in the expense and transit-period of postage. The letters home often provided statistics of wages, prices, rents, and transportation costs, so conveying to Irish readers and auditors not merely an often favourable vision of life abroad, but also precise indications of where to go and what to do after arrival. Though despair and discontent occasionally intruded,

those who "failed" as emigrants typically ceased to correspond with their connections at home except, on occasion, to solicit reverse remittances.

During the first half of the century, the obstacles raised by the workings of the passenger trade had been formidable: one can but wonder at the alertness and ingenuity with which so many Irish people circumvented them. The removal from Ireland of several million people naturally required massive provision of shipping, yet specialised passenger transportation was slow to develop. People long remained a rather unwelcome substitute for more profitable cargoes on both the cross-channel and transatlantic routes, filling empty holds in ships returning to pick up further merchandise. Since few passengers so far sought to travel eastwards across the Atlantic, it is not surprising that pre-Famine passenger vessels typically carried fish and oil from Newfoundland, timber from Canada, flaxseed from New York and Philadelphia, or cotton from Baltimore. During the Famine, a three-way trade developed for ships plying between Liverpool, New York, and New Orleans, with coal or manufactures replacing people at New York and cotton being transported between New Orleans and Liverpool. The extension of specialist passenger shipping was progressively encouraged from the 1840s onwards by the increasing predictability of demand as emigration from Europe became endemic rather than episodic; by increasingly rigorous passenger legislation that made it more difficult to convert cargo holds into human quarters; and finally by the expanding reverse movement of passengers from America. The reverse movement of tourists, businessmen, and emigrants from the United States had become considerable by the turn of the century: between 1895 and 1913, no less than forty-three Irish passengers entered the United Kingdom for every hundred who left it.

The entrepreneurial risks associated with passenger shipping, whether in one or both directions, were invariably greater in the case of Irish than of British ports. Since the "ceiling" for pre-Famine annual movement from Irish ports was only about 35,000, most Irish passengers bound for the United States were obliged to travel indirectly via Liverpool. In 1843, about ninety-three per cent of these passengers are estimated to have chosen Liverpool, which remained the most popular port of embarkation until the late 1860s. Even during the Famine exodus, shippers had been reluctant to embark from Irish ports, predicting an early end to massive emigration. Nonetheless, Irish emigration eventually proved sufficiently regular to sustain a flourish-

The U.S. Postal Service issued a stamp commemorating Irish immigration, February 26, 1999.

ing passenger trade using Irish ports: by 1872, less than two-fifths of emigrants to the United States followed the precedent of their Famine-driven predecessors by boarding at Liverpool. Queenstown (Cobh) became the major port of embarkation for emigrants from Munster and Connaught, while Leinster was served by Dublin, and Ulster by Belfast and Derry or Moville.

The direct costs of emigration were influenced by legislation as well as market factors. Statutes restricting the ratio of passengers to tonnage tended to increase the price as well as the comfort and safety of emigration. The harsh British legislation of 1803 gradually gave place to virtual deregulation by 1828, and the appointment of the Colonial Land and Emigration Commissioners in 1840 did not lead to any rapid and effective regulation of passenger traffic. This was achieved only between 1847 and 1855, while the application of statutory controls to cabin passengers and to shipping within the British Isles was negligible until 1863. The Merchant Shipping Act of 1894 introduced compulsory medical certification, licensing of passage brokers and runners, and detailed entitlements for cabin passengers (who accounted for nearly a third of all passengers from the United Kingdom to extra-European destinations between 1877 and 1900). In 1819, supervision of shipping had been initiated in the United States, whose more rigorous requirements ensured that fares generally exceeded those to British North America until the 1850s. Irish bargain-hunters adeptly exploited the wild fluctuations in fares to America according to demand, shipping line, and ports of departure and arrival, although the average fare probably changed little between the 1830s and mid-century. In 1832, a steerage passage from Ireland to New York cost ninety shillings, a pound less than the fare from Bristol, but three times the fare from Irish ports to Quebec. During and just before the Famine, tickets might often be had for less than £3, and even in the mid-1850s the price was only a few shillings higher. This was nevertheless a substantial sum even for a small farmer, comparable with half the price of a heifer, a summer's earnings, or the annual rent for a typical western holding. Since a similar additional outlay was normally required for "outfit," inland transportation, landing money, and often port taxes, emigrants without funding from their predecessors had to show resourcefulness in order to escape Ireland. Those bound for Australia, for which the full fare was between £10 and £15 in 1848, could seldom hope to travel without state assistance. But the majority making for the United States displayed a keen market sense, travelling to distant ports in search of cheap or discounted tickets, and often taking the cheaper routes via Canada despite the arduous onward journey to the United States that this might entail. In the less frenzied conditions of the later nineteenth century, discounts were less readily available except from continental ports or in years of intense competition such as 1885. By 1883, all the regular shippers were charging four guineas for a steerage passage on the route from Liverpool to New York, a quarter the price of a ticket to Australia.

The indirect costs and risks associated with emigration were more apparent than prohibitive. Until 1850, when the introduction of iron-hulled screw steamers reduced the emigrant's passage to about a fortnight, the Atlantic crossing typically took about six weeks. For emigrants forgoing employment at home the opportunity-cost was therefore considerable; but since most were either unemployed or underemployed in Ireland, the duration of transit imposed little extra burden except for the cost of provisions beyond the statutory requirement, and the risks of

discomfort, seasickness, susceptibility to infection, and shipwreck. Only about fifty-nine passenger vessels plying between the British Isles and America were wrecked between 1847 and 1853; but public fear of a watery death was enhanced by the wide publicity given to those disasters. The same applied to shipboard mortality, which was only a severe risk in the case of the "coffin ships" making for Canada in 1847. The fetid holds of these almost unregulated vessels provided a congenial breeding ground for lice-borne fever bacilli, and "ship fever" ravaged the Famine-weakened emigrants both during and after the voyage. Of nearly a hundred thousand emigrants who embarked for Quebec in 1847, over a sixth died on board ship, in the hospital on Grosse Isle, or elsewhere in Canada East or West while still under official scrutiny. A medical officer at Grosse Isle observed "a stream of foul air issuing from the hatches as dense and as palpable as seen on a foggy day from a dung heap." By contrast with this appalling carnage, the risk of death in other seasons and on other routes seldom exceeded two per cent. Between 1842 and 1846, recorded shipboard mortality among all overseas emigrants from the United Kingdom was one in 160, and by 1858 it had fallen back to one in five hundred. The lingering nightmare of the coffin ships did not demonstrably impede emigration, serving merely to divert it elsewhere and to instil a lasting distaste for Canada as a destination. And if the urgent desire to leave Ireland could overcome that horror, it is scarcely surprising that emigrants brushed aside the more humdrum inconveniences of seasickness, infestation, cramped and insanitary accommodation, despotic ships' officers, and hostile fellow passengers; not to speak of the predatory crooks, touts, runners, or sharpers who preyed upon them before, during, and after the voyage. Neither death nor discomfort could staunch the flow out of Ireland. For post-Famine emigrants, the voyage was no longer a hazardous and unsupervised probe into the unknown. Most travelled by steamer rather than sailing vessel, with a resultant reduction of transit time and risk of wreck. Between 1867 and 1914, the length of the transatlantic voyage was progressively reduced from over a fortnight to less than a week. By the end of the century, an unaccompanied girl could travel to America without serious risk of being insulted, raped, or robbed; the worst hazard encountered by most passengers was seasickness. For many, as personal diaries attest, the transoceanic passage had become an agreeable form of tourism.

## IV. AGENCIES

If the constraints of ignorance, expense and danger proved ineffectual in blocking emigration, the impact of organised promotion was equally marginal. Throughout the early nineteenth century, systematic colonisation had been repeatedly proposed as a cure for Irish and indeed British poverty, offering equal benefit to the home and host societies. Yet the vast expense of these schemes restricted their application to a few experiments, such as those organised by James Buchanan from Ulster to Upper Canada via New York (1817), by Richard Talbot from Cloughjordan, Co. Tipperary, to London in Upper Canada (1818), and by John Ingram from Cork to the Cape of Good Hope (1823). The first major scheme was implemented in 1823 and 1825, when Peter Robinson took 2,592 emigrants from Munster to the Bathurst and Newcastle districts in Upper Canada. Despite encouraging reports of the settlers' performance, repetition was discouraged by the vast expense to the state: over £20 per capita, four times the amount typically spent by later private benefactors. The state's second experiment in clearing a locality of its "surplus" population was undertaken on various Crown estates in Roscommon, Galway, Cork, Kerry, and King's County (1847–52), from which over a thousand emigrants in 240 households were removed to the United States at the cost of six guineas a head. No further local clearances were attempted with state involvement until the 1880s, when hardship reminiscent of that in 1847 momentarily restored the issue to practical politics. Under statutes of 1882 and 1883, some 24,596 emigrants received free grants of up to £8 per capita, mainly allocated to complete family households in thirty-six western unions with the collaboration of private philanthropists. Contrary to the government's intention, most of these families of assisted emigrants went to the United States rather than Canada or Australia.

In addition to these schemes of "social engineering," official assistance was provided to various special groups of emigrants, including convicts transported to Australia, the "free settlers" who joined them, Crown witnesses, and military pensioners. Subsidies were also offered to individual paupers in order to reduce the recurrent burden of poor relief. Only about twenty-seven paupers benefited from relevant statutes between 1838 and 1843, but 306 paupers left in 1844–46, mainly from northern Poor Law Unions. Later amendments made the provision less repugnant to ratepayers, 965 emigrants being assisted in 1848–49 (mainly from Wicklow and Clare), and 871 in the following year. Over the next two decades, some 26,000 recipients were helped to British North America and elsewhere, the Poor Law Guardians typically providing outfit and transportation to the port of departure for paupers whose passage was sponsored by friends or landlords. Under a special scheme implemented between May 1848 and April 1850, 4,175 "female orphans" were despatched to Australia with the help of free passages and contributions of £5 per head from the Unions. All told, these schemes removed 33,000 emigrants from Ireland between 1818 and 1870. Australia was the only destination to which extensive colonisation was attempted, using revenues raised from colonial land sales. Under numerous schemes, often involving a combination of public and private funding, about 150,000 emigrants were assisted to the Australian colonies between 1832 and 1870, after which the flow diminished to a trickle (except to Queensland) as colonial demand for unskilled labour and service diminished. Colonial governments continued to offer sporadic inducements to particular categories of emigrant, whether in the form of assisted passages, assistance with inland transportation, or land grants. Yet the stringent criteria for direct official assistance ensured that the only extensive schemes were those involving nominations and contributions from friends or relatives already overseas, so tending to reinforce established axes of migration. State intervention never exercised more than a minor influence on the scale or direction of Irish emigration, mainly because administrators had discovered during the Famine that a vast and self-perpetuating movement could be generated without expense to the public purse.

Since "improving" landlords had a clear interest in promoting systematic emigration to cushion the impact of "clearances," it is not surprising that some of the major architects of state assistance were Irish landlords and their numerous representatives in both houses of parliament. Landlord collaboration with the state was overt in the Talbot, Robinson, and Crown estate ventures; implicit in the assistance administered by Poor Law Guardians; and informal in the selection of emigrants for Australia,

where the Monteagles' personal interventions with T. F. Elliott enabled several hundred inhabitants of the Foynes estate in Co. Limerick to obtain subsidies from the Emigration Commissioners. But most "clearances" were accomplished without state aid, a fact which dissuaded all but the richest landlords from using subsidised emigration as a tool for estate reorganisation. In Quebec, the emigration agent recorded 14,213 Irish passengers travelling with private assistance on 216 ships, over a twelfth of all Irish arrivals at Quebec and Montreal. A more wide-ranging but impressionistic guide to the scale of private assistance is provided by a medley of memoirs, estate records, newspaper articles, and parliamentary reports. These make reference to 175 cases of assistance by individuals or groups, who probably aided at least 12,000 emigrants between 1826 and 1845; 22,000 between 1846 and 1850; and 14,000 between 1851 and 1870. Private sponsorship by landlords and entrepreneurs became less common later in the century, though many Catholic clergymen continued to believe that the creation of Irish colonies in the United States was the best strategy for propagating the faith and regulating the flock in the New World. Irish-Catholic colonisation schemes were promoted in Minnesota, Arkansas, Nebraska, and Mississippi, the model being Bishop John Ireland's settlement programme initiated in St. Paul, Minnesota. The craze for Catholic colonisation peaked in 1879–81, before faltering after the reported failure of many colonists and the financial collapse of unsound enterprises. Otherwise, the only major private attempts to interfere with the free flow of migration were those undertaken by two philanthropists, James Hack Tuke (1882–84) and Vere Foster (1880–84). Tuke's fund raised nearly £70,000 in Britain and assisted 9,482 emigrants, most of whom left in family groups from Mayo, Galway, and Donegal to the United States. Foster, an initially rich bachelor of limitless energy and practicality, was unique in sponsoring individual rather than family emigration, providing a pound or so towards the passage of no less than 20,250 unmarried girls. His outlay of £30,000 was undoubtedly a key factor in reviving female emigration to the United States from the poorest regions of western districts stretching from Donegal to Kerry. The effect of such schemes was to clear bottlenecks rather than to initiate emigration from districts already heavily embroiled in emigration.

Of the five million emigrants who left Ireland between 1801 and 1870, only about one in twenty appears to have received organised state or private assistance. Most "pioneers" from localities not yet used to emigration had therefore to rely on their own sparse resources of cash, derived from dowries, tenant right payments, sale of livestock, wages, or thefts. Thereafter, remittances from friends and relatives already settled overseas became the main agency for continued emigration. The flood of "American money" to rural Ireland, subsidising local households as well as funding emigration, was widely reported in the decade before the Famine. From 1848 onwards, incomplete official statistics were collected from shippers and bankers dealing with the North American passenger trade. From half a million pounds in 1848, the stated volume of remittances rose to a million in 1850 and to a peak of a million and three-quarters in 1854. It declined fairly steadily over the following decade but recovered to three-quarters of a million pounds in 1870 and a million and a half in the 1880s. In 1868, as in 1848, about two-fifths of these payments were through prepaid passages, enough to bring out perhaps three-quarters of all emigrants from the British Isles to North America. Assistance from previous settlers remained important in 1904–15, when official returns indicated that a third of all Irish steerage passengers to the United States had travelled on prepaid warrants. "Emigration begets emigration," as the Emigration Commissioners observed in 1849; and within a few years the "stream of gold" had penetrated even the most remote districts of Ireland.

## V. DYNAMICS

What drove nearly eight million people to leave Ireland for Britain and the New World between 1801 and 1921? That mass movement was the outcome of innumerable private decisions, only marginally influenced by constraints on mobility or schemes of social engineering. The year-by-year fluctuation in emigration reflected variations in the relative performance of the Irish and foreign economies; yet economic pressure alone cannot explain the persistence from generation to generation of habits diffused during the Famine crisis. Irish emigrants were to some extent "rational actors," responding to changes in income and employment opportunities abroad by postponing or redirecting their departure. More profoundly, their decisions were influenced by collective rather than individual self-interest. Emigration became an almost universal strategy whereby Irish families secured a livelihood for more children than Ireland itself could provide for, through either land, employment, or marriage. The assumption that half of each cohort would depart was built into the politics of the family, and decisions about the selection of emigrants and timing of departure were typically made after negotiation between family members. By facilitating emigration for some offspring, and access to land or employment for others, families attempted to achieve an equitable resolution of competing claims on scarce resources. Emigrant children participated in these negotiations through correspondence and through remittances, which affected the selection of their successors and also provided a "pension" or subsidy for struggling parents. Irish emigration is best pictured not as the outcome of expulsion or selfishness, but as a collective accommodation to the chronic incapacity of Irish society to provide for each new generation. The twin effects of emigration were to ameliorate poverty in the short term, and to discourage radical economic and social transformation by facilitating the maintenance of large families, small farms, and other "archaic" but homely elements of Irish life. For better or for worse, most Irish children of the nineteenth century were "reared for emigration." Even those who remained in Ireland would in most cases have contemplated departure, and their awareness of an alternative and seductive way of life permeated Irish thought and behaviour in ways not yet fully understood.

How did the five million or so Irish emigrants who settled in the United States compare with the minority who chose other destinations, mainly in the British Empire? This article has highlighted certain distinctive elements of the movement to America, though the paucity of reliable statistics for most of the nineteenth century makes comparison hazardous. By the late nineteenth century, those choosing America were more likely to emanate from the poorest counties of Connaught and the west, and more likely to be described as mere "labourers" or "servants." It seems likely that the Protestant proportion was relatively low, though the ever multiplying descendants of the early Ulster settlers, spreading out from Philadelphia, guaranteed a substantial "Scotch-Irish" population of Protestant native-born Americans with Irish origins. Yet studies of the Irish in Australasia, for example, suggest that these came from a stock almost indistin-

guishable from that supplying America. Many families sent members to both destinations, and emigrants moved freely between different countries of settlement in response to competing opportunities. Neither official "quality controls" on assisted emigration nor political preferences seem to have had significant influence on the choice between America and Australia: prospective emigrants proved adept at redescribing their careers to match the official criteria, and most Catholic nationalists had no quarrel with the British Empire once outside Ireland. There was no clear distinction in origin between the movements to the United States and the Empire, both of which were primarily determined by economic and social factors, rather than political or administrative influences. The major contrast between Irish emigration to the United States and elsewhere lay not in its genesis, but in the emigrant's subsequent experience. The American Irish were far more likely than their Australian or Canadian contemporaries around 1870 to reside in cities, to congregate in restricted regions (particularly the north-eastern states), and to have menial employment. In these respects, the Irish in America (as in Britain) were markedly disadvantaged by comparison with the minority settling in the colonies, where the Irish formed a substantially larger component of the population. As the Australian and Canadian examples suggest, the Irish emigrants were not doomed to failure by ignorance, lack of skills, or any crippling "Gaelic world-view." It was conditions in the United States which initially inhibited the success and social mobility of its Irish population. By 1900, the economic disadvantage of the Irish emigrants (and especially their children) had virtually disappeared. A new wave of emigrants from southern and eastern Europe had arrived to experience the privation and discrimination formerly reserved for the American Irish.

*See* Famine, The Great; Irish in America; Foster, Vere

William Forbes Adams, *Ireland and Irish Emigration to the New World from 1815 to the Famine* (New Haven, 1932).

Donald Harman Akenson, *The Irish Diaspora: A Primer* (Toronto and Belfast, 1993).

R. D. Collison Black, *Economic Thought and the Irish Question, 1817–1870* (Cambridge, 1960).

K. H. Connell, *The Population of Ireland, 1750–1845* (Oxford, 1950).

David Fitzpatrick, "Emigration, 1801–70" and "Emigration, 1871–1921," in W. E. Vaughan, ed., *A New History of Ireland*, vol. 5 (Oxford, 1989): 563–622; vol. 6 (Oxford, 1996): 606–52 (these chapters cite the sources for many of the facts and statistics appearing in this article).

———, *Oceans of Consolation: Personal Accounts of Irish Migration to Australia* (Ithaca, N.Y., 1995).

Timothy Guinnane, *The Vanishing Irish: Households, Migration, and Rural Economy in Ireland, 1850–1914* (Princeton, 1997).

Robert E. Kennedy, *The Irish: Emigration, Marriage, and Fertility* (Berkeley, 1973).

Oliver MacDonagh, "The Irish Famine Emigration to the United States," *Perspectives in American History*, x (1976): 357–446.

Kerby A. Miller, *Emigrants and Exiles: Ireland and the Irish Exodus* (New York, 1985).

Joel Mokyr, *Why Ireland Starved* (London, 1983).

Cormac Ó Gráda, *Ireland: A New Economic History, 1780–1939* (Oxford, 1994).

Patrick O'Sullivan, ed., *The Irish Worldwide*, 6 vols. (Leicester, 1992–97).

Arnold Schrier, *Ireland and the American Emigration, 1850–1900* (Minneapolis, 1958).

DAVID FITZPATRICK

## EMIGRATION: 1922–1998

The coming into existence of the Irish Free State in 1922 might appear at first sight to have heralded a new era in the history of emigration. Had not the Sinn Féin leaders who, under whatever party designation, would rule the independent Irish state for nearly half a century, denounced "the curse of emigration" as the single most serious obstacle to the prospects of social regeneration in Ireland? Did not solving the emigration problem take precedence virtually over all others in the hierarchy of material challenges which Irish nationalists, of all shades of opinion, had identified as crucial to the vitality, even the viability, of any form of self-governing Ireland?

All this was indeed true. But the realities confronting the new rulers of the Free State turned out to be very different indeed from the circumstances envisaged in the inherited rhetoric. That rhetoric contained little systematic socioeconomic analysis, preferring to axiomatically attribute emigration to British misrule in Ireland. The implication was that once Ireland wrenched herself free from the paralysing grip of Britain, then emigration would simply wither away. The consequence was that the first rulers of the new state found that little concrete thinking about the economics of an independent Ireland had actually occurred prior to independence.

They were, in any event, soon plunged into Civil War. Little attention could be devoted to the emigration problem until that war ended in May 1923. By then, the two most dynamic personalities of the new government, Michael Collins and Arthur Griffith, were both dead. Griffith was the main economic thinker in Sinn Féin, and Collins the pro-Treaty leader of greatest natural ability and with most fire in his belly. When allied to the defensive mentality fostered by the Civil War in any case, the deaths of the two most prominent leaders reduced the sense of urgency about tackling the problem, which continued unabated during the 1920s.

In analysing developments, allowance must be made for the vagaries of the statistical coverage, which make it virtually impossible to be certain about precise figures in any year, right down to the present. Problems arise, inter alia, from the discontinuities deriving from the imposition of partition in 1921, including variations in statistical coverage between North and South, difficulties in distinguishing between gross and net emigration, and inconsistencies between Irish emigration and American immigration figures. Nevertheless, it is possible to establish the main trends clearly enough. In the immediate pre-war period, between 1909 and 1913, emigration to the USA from the 32 counties averaged about 35,000 per annum. The 26 counties that would constitute the Free State accounted for more than 30,000 of this. The numbers fell to virtual vanishing point in 1918, when only 136 emigrants to the USA were recorded. After a slow rise to 2,319 in 1919, the figure jumped to 23,612 in 1920, of which more than 20,000 came from the 26 counties.

Although numbers from the Free State fluctuated for the rest of the decade, they exceeded 26,000 in both 1925 and 1926, before declining to just under 24,000 in 1927 and 22,000 in 1928, and about 18,000 in 1929. Despite the deepening slump in America, they still exceeded 14,000 in 1930, but than collapsed to only 801 in 1931, and would never exceed 1,000 again until after the Second World War (Commission on Emigration, pp. 316–17).

While bearing in mind the uncertainties in the statistics, it seems clear that by the mid-1920s the emigration rate to the USA

had recovered almost to the level of the immediate pre-war years. If it began to decline somewhat from 1927, it is clear that it is 1931 that brings to an end the era not only of post-Treaty, but of post-Famine, emigration. That era had lasted just seventy-five years, if we take it as beginning in 1856, which recorded the first sharp fall in the flow that could be attributed directly to the famine and its consequences. Emigration to the US during the entire 1930s accounted for less than any single year in the 1920s. Not 1921, but 1931, marks an almost unnoticed watershed in Irish social history in general, and in the history of Irish emigration to America in particular. It ought to loom much larger than it does in our consciousness of emigration history.

It is striking how many of even the best works on the history of Irish emigration to the USA end in 1921. Kerby Miller's classic *Emigrants and Exiles: Ireland and the Irish Exodus to North America* (New York, 1985), one of the truly great works on the emigration experience of any people, is only the most obvious case. The reasons for ending at 1921 are self-evident. But this in fact is to impose a false closing date on the history of emigration to America. The 1920s, therefore, tend to dangle in a vacuum. They are omitted from studies of the long nineteenth century, and merit only a fleeting flashback in studies devoted to the spectacular developments of the 1980s. This is to grossly underrate not only their intrinsic interest in telling us much about the Ireland of the 1920s, but also to undervalue their potential for casting retrospective light on aspects of the pre-1914 emigration experience. Much worthwhile research remains to be done on this neglected decade.

It also seems clear from these figures that restrictive American legislation, which is often blamed for the alleged decline in Irish emigration during the 1920s, had little influence in reality. The annual quota of 28,567 allocated to the Irish Free State in the Immigration Act of 26 May, 1924, was never actually reached, the highest recorded emigration of 26,431 in 1925 falling more than 2,000 below the ceiling. The quota would be reduced to 17,853 in the course of 1929, but the fall in emigration in 1930 to nearly 4,000 below the quota derived from purely economic circumstances, paralleled as it was by the decline in emigration to Canada and Australia also, both likewise suffering from severe slump, and indeed by a dramatic decline in total overseas emigration from Northern Ireland from 9,217 in 1930 to only 1,086 in 1931 (Vaughan and Fitzpatrick, *Irish Historical Statistics*, p. 267).

Emigration from Northern Ireland tends to be seriously neglected in the study of Irish emigration. In the decade before the First World War, emigration from the six counties that would become Northern Ireland was running at about one-quarter to one-third of all Irish overseas emigration, a ratio that seems to have also prevailed in the 1928–31 period, for which figures are available. (Commission on Emigration, pp. 118, 125, 319). The emigration rate from Northern Ireland, contrary perhaps to assumptions derived from its assumed superior economic performance, seems to have been broadly similar to that from the twenty-six counties of Southern Ireland. Nevertheless, it can be justifiably neglected in the study of emigration to the USA, for the direction of Northern emigration diverged dramatically from that of the South. Or perhaps, one might surmise that the direction of Protestant/Unionist emigration diverged sharply from that of Catholic/Nationalist, even within Northern Ireland. In contrast to the eighteenth-century experience, Protestant emigration seems to have gone not to America, but predominantly to Britain and Canada. In the 1901–21 period, Canada and Britain together took 68,000 emigrants from the North, compared with the 43,000 who departed for the USA. The comparable figures for the South were 36,000 and 336,000, respectively. Psychologically, partition already seems to have existed long before the establishment of Northern Ireland, although it may be that the real partition came within the North rather than strictly along the line of the border. There is scope for much further research on this entire issue.

While the causes of emigration remained overwhelmingly economic, as the virtual cessation in 1931 and the following years suggest, there is plenty of anecdotal evidence that among the emigrants of the 1920s were many who couldn't get a job in Ireland because of their anti-Treaty political activity. Many of the 10,000 anti-Treaty IRA prisoners captured in the Civil War had few prospects at home on their release, and duly sought refuge in the USA. Many who may have fought in the belief that independence would bring them employment in Ireland found themselves involuntary emigrants as a result of their efforts. Some would flourish in America, for they tended to be men of drive and determination. But many of even the most successful would retain bitter memories and would remain available for support for anti-Treaty movements, ranging from the IRA to Fianna Fáil, for long afterwards. Their experience forms a fascinating facet of the emigration of the 1920s, and remains to be adequately reconstructed.

If the Great Slump brought an end to the era of post-famine emigration to America, this did not of course mean that emigration from Ireland ceased forever. In fact, it ceased for no more than five years. But when it resumed it was no longer to America, but to Britain. Numbers to Britain having dwindled since the 1870s, they now surged upwards in the mid-1930s. The reason was simple. The British economy revived far more vigorously than the American economy in the second half of the 1930s. Despite the New Deal, American unemployment remained exceptionally high, particularly in those sectors in which Irish emigrants had traditionally sought their first jobs, the building industry, the docks, transport, and domestic service. In Britain, on the other hand, the building industry recovered significantly, particularly in London and southeast England, to which footloose Irish emigrants now increasingly wended their way. Emigration to Britain increased further during the Second World War, with the insatiable British demand for labour, whether in the armed forces or in the war economy.

It would have been intriguing to see what would have happened after the war if the British economy had plunged into slump, as many anticipated, on the basis of post–First World War experience, while America boomed. Perhaps the flows would have reversed themselves once more. But that did not happen. A Labour government committed to sustaining demand, and to the welfare state, helped ensure full employment in post-war Britain. The exodus from Ireland surged to new twentieth-century heights over the next fifteen years, with the 1950s recording the highest rates of emigration since the 1880s. The difference was that emigration during the 1950s was overwhelmingly to Britain, whereas during the 1880s it had been overwhelmingly to America.

Some emigration did of course resume to America after the war. While the statistics, as ever, vary according to the sources, the most reasonable conclusion seems to be that the numbers leaving for America averaged about 5-6,000 a year between 1945

and 1960, before declining, broadly in line with a general fall in emigration, to under 4,000 a year in the 1960s, and little more than 1,000 a year in the 1970s.

Indeed, the 1970s appeared to be a historic decade in the history of emigration. They recorded the first net immigration movement in Irish history since the seventeenth century. As the Irish economy flourished relative to Britain, a reverse movement set in across the Irish Sea. But the 1980s would see the prospects blighted. As the Irish economy plunged into depression, recorded unemployment rose from 7.1% in 1978 to no less than 17.7% in 1987. Gross emigration between 1980 and 1984 may well have exceeded 50,000, before surging to more than 150,000 between 1985 and 1990. While about 70% of these went to Britain, substantial numbers turned towards the USA once more. However, they now found the legislative situation much more restrictive than ever before.

While Irish emigration during the 1950s had lagged far below the Irish quota of 18,700 annually, under the 1965 Immigration Act, the Irish quota was dé facto slashed drastically. In principle any individual country, including Ireland, could be allocated a quota of 20,000 visas. But the allocation of the global annual total of 270,000 visas depended largely on having close relatives already resident in the USA. Relatively few Irish could avail of this advantage by the 1980s, given the very low levels of post-war emigration to the USA, which had dwindled to virtually nothing during the 1970s. The number of Irish-born in the USA had already fallen steadily during the century, from its peak of 1.872 million in 1890 to 1.037 million in 1921, to 678,000 in 1951, and only 251,000 in 1971. Fewer than 8,000 Irish were admitted legally to the US between 1981 and 1986, even if the annual numbers doubled from 902 to 1,839 over those years. The number of illegals rose sharply, however, although the exact number itself became a matter of intense dispute, ranging from a lower estimate of "under 40,000" (Mulholland and Keogh, p. 92) to an upper estimate of 136,000 (Corcoran, *Irish Illegals*, p. 11). The view of Mary Corcoran, the leading authority on the subject, is that there were probably at least 50,000 illegals resident in the USA in 1986 (ibid., p. 11), which suggests a substantial emigrant movement in the early eighties.

If American immigration legislation had made little difference to Ireland before 1965, it was now having a major impact. The Irish government mounted a vigorous campaign to have the restrictions relaxed, the Irish Embassy in Washington working particularly closely with Senator Edward Kennedy and Congressman Brian Donnelly, who sponsored the Immigration Reform and Control Act of 1986, which allowed more than 20,000 Irish emigrants into the USA between 1987 and 1990, over 16,000 on NP-5 Visas, colloquially known as the Donnelly visas. That Irish applicants secured 41% of the 40,000 special visas issued owed not a little to a vigorous information campaign in Ireland and among illegals themselves in America, who sought to regularise their position under this legislation. (Sen. Edward Kennedy, in Mulholland and Keogh, pp. 11–12; Corcoran, p. 10). Building on this foundation, the subsequent Morrison visas allocated a further 16,000 more places to Ireland annually for a further three years (Corcoran, p. 189).

With the astonishing economic growth of the 1990s in Ireland, net migration actually became positive once more. Whether this will continue to be the case, or will prove merely an interlude, like the 1970s, in the centuries-old history of emigration, remains to be seen. Although the economy is probably in many respects more robust than it ever was, it remains so open, with one of the highest ratios in the world of trade to national product, that it must always prove vulnerable to adverse global developments. While the long-term prognostication may be more optimistic than ever before, sharp short-term reverses could certainly occur, leading to resumed emigration.

Nor does a net positive balance mean that emigration necessarily ceases. That balance can be the consequence of substantial movements in both directions. Irish emigration to the USA continues in the mid-1990s, if at a significantly lower level than during the 1980s. The difference is that much of it is now voluntary, as emigrants increasingly move deliberately to acquire skills and education with a possible view to returning home in due course.

Nevertheless, one must resist the temptation to romanticise the recent Irish emigrant experience, different though much of it has undoubtedly been from that of earlier generations. This was a trap into which the then Tánaiste (Deputy Prime Minister) and Minister for Foreign Affairs, the late and much loved Brian Linehan, partly fell when, in America in 1987, he projected an image of new Irish emigrants as the incarnation of enterprise culture, intrepid adventurers in a drive to hone their skills and acquire the expertise that would enable them to return to Ireland to participate in a thrusting new economy, from which both themselves and the country would benefit. There was certainly an element of this, particularly in the case of graduate emigrants, a growing but still minority percentage of all emigrants. But the bulk of the immigrants of the eighties, especially the illegals, came with no such overvaulting ambitions. They were often those who could find no jobs in the stagnating Irish economy of the 1980s, and would in turn often find themselves opportunistically exploited by employers, not least Irish employers, who took advantage of the lack of bargaining power often attendant on their illegal status.

Both continuities and discontinuities can be detected in a number of the key variables associated with emigration throughout the century. The vast majority of emigrants, male and female, were at all times under thirty years of age, and unmarried, on arriving in America. The sex ratio, remarkably balanced in comparative European terms, remained broadly stable over the period as a whole, although with some fluctuations, usually within the 45–55% range, over shorter periods. The female surplus among overseas emigrants during the 1892–1904 period turned into a slight male surplus in the decade immediately before the First World War. The female to male ratio reached an exceptionally high level in 1920 and 1921, perhaps reflecting to some extent the death in the First World War of males who might otherwise have become emigrants, and a relatively low rate of emigration among males active in the IRA during the War of Independence, perhaps nursing hopes of better times to come in Ireland, or influenced by an IRA General Headquarters edict which actually forbade the emigration of Volunteers in 1920, deemed tantamount to desertion.

There was a small female emigrant surplus to the USA in the 1924–30 period, although this was more than balanced by male surpluses in emigration to Canada and elsewhere overseas. The USA tended to be slightly more popular as a destination of female emigration than other overseas countries, presumably because of the closer family connections, which probably counted even more for females than for males, important though they were for nearly everyone. The 1950s also recorded a female to male ratio of about 55% to 45%, but the illegals of the 1980s had a roughly similar male surplus.

In occupational terms, the bulk of Irish male emigrants until the 1950s–1960s continued to come from agricultural labouring and general urban labouring backgrounds. The biggest single change in occupational roles at the American end has been the dramatic decline in domestic service as the main occupation for females, which has dwindled from probably 50% at the outset of our period to virtually vanishing point today.

While the occupational spectrum of Irish emigrants has become more diversified, the geographical destination of emigrants has tended to become more concentrated, with a small number of big cities, Boston, Chicago, San Francisco, and, above all, New York, accounting for the vast majority of recent immigrants.

The history of Irish emigration to the USA since 1922 remains badly underresearched. Until that research is done, generalisations of the type that can be advanced confidently for the nineteenth century, concerning decisions to emigrate from Ireland, as well as settlement patterns, marriage patterns, social mobility, return rates to Ireland, etc., must remain uncertain.

Whereas the low rate of return migration, for instance, was a distinctive characteristic of the Irish experience down to the Second World War, the growing affluence of the Irish in America, and in particular the growth of air travel from the second half of the 1950s, began to make frequent return a much more normal aspect of emigrant lives. This marks another significant discontinuity in the life experience of emigrants and of those they left behind. There are no more American "wakes."

Numerous other questions suggest themselves for further research in the shifting scenario of the Irish emigration experience. To what extent has a transatlantic culture emerged among Irish emigrants? If so, how far has this begun before they leave Ireland, influenced by their growing exposure to American media, and the consequent increasing internalisation of American values—if indeed they are internalised? Here is another subject for research. How far does the growth in seasonal emigration, with students flocking to earn summer money now a regular part of the third level education scene in Ireland itself, influence subsequent decisions to try to return to America for longer periods?

If emigration today connotes nothing like the same sense of finality, of rupture with "home," that it did for so many for so long, how are the final decisions made as to whether they will opt to become Americans, or to return to Ireland? Can any patterns be detected in this regard, or does the host of individual decisions involved resist the imposition of any pattern? All this requires further intensive research.

So does the difference that returned emigrants make to Ireland. How far, for instance, are they at the cutting edge of social and technological change in Ireland, as the Brian Lenihan model postulates? How far do they return with an enhanced self-confidence, based on their realisation that they have performed successfully in the most competitive market in the world?

The whole impact of the Northern question on first-generation Irish emigrants, in particular, requires detailed research. It has been argued, for instance, that many of the emigrants of the 1950s felt little loyalty to the government of the Irish Republic, which they believed had virtually betrayed them by its failure to foster economic development more successfully, thus compelling them to become emigrants against their will. Why should they feel a sense of gratitude to a state which in their view had failed them? Did something of this sentiment undergird their degree of support for Sinn Féin and the IRA in Northern Ireland? There is an intriguing research subject!

The psychology of emigration, in all its facets, both among those who choose to remain in America, and those who return to Ireland, offers a rich laboratory for the study of human relations in all their manifold variety. Although the numbers of Irish emigrants to America are far lower than a century ago, connections continue at a generally relaxed and intimate level. Whether that will remain the case, especially now that intense Irish-American involvement in finding a solution to the Northern Ireland question may be expected to decline, remains to be seen.

Another major research area must concern relations between the new immigrants and the longer settled ones, of whatever generation. Differences between the generations are graphically, and to some extent poignantly, captured in differences in style and tone between the old established, rather sedate *Irish Echo* in New York, attuned to the needs and assumptions of those well-settled in America, and the *Irish Voice*, launched in December 1987, appealing to the younger emigrants in very different tones, alert to the more uncertain but often more assertive instincts of the younger generation, many of whom remained in close contact with home, and remained open as to where their future might lie, nursing an image of themselves as "an extension of community abroad" (Corcoran, p. 170).

The future of Irish emigration to the USA remains unpredictable. What is clear is that the issues raised by the emigrants since 1922 and not least by the events of the last two decades ensures that the subject will retain its fascination for all those interested in Irish-American relations, and in the study of culture contact between generations and between peoples.

Commission on Emigration and other population problems: 1948–1954, *Reports* (Dublin, 1956).

Mary P. Corcoran, *Irish Illegals: Transients Between Two Societies* (Westport, Connecticut, 1993).

W. D. Griffin, *The Irish in America* (Dobbs Ferry, N.Y., 1973).

Richard Kearney, ed., *Migrations: The Irish at Home and Abroad* (Dublin, 1990).

Lawrence J. McCaffrey, *The Irish Diaspora in America* (Bloomington, 1976).

———, "The recent Irish Diaspora in America," in D. L. Cuddy, ed., *Contemporary American Immigration* (Boston, 1982).

Joe Mulholland and Dermot Keogh, eds., *Emigration, Employment and Enterprise* (Cork, 1989).

W. E. Vaughan and A. J. Fitzpatrick, *Irish Historical Statistics: Population, 1821–1971* (Dublin, 1978).

J. J. LEE

# EMIGRATION:
# THE END OF THE IRISH WAKE

## A Pattern of Return Migration

Current migration trends suggest a radical departure from the pattern of migration which characterised the 1980s in Ireland. In that decade net outward migration rose to levels reminiscent of the bleak 1950s. The outward migratory flow was almost twice what it is now, and the numbers returning were substantially lower. Nowadays, more people are entering Ireland than leaving, bringing the country's migratory profile into line with the other member states of the European Union. Irish immigration rather than Irish emigration is symptomatic of the demographic changes being wrought by the unprecedented growth in the Irish economy.

Between 1991 and 1996 there were an estimated 177,000 in-migrants compared with 174,000 out-migrants (Central Statistics Office). These figures contrast sharply with those for 1987–1991 when the excess of emigrants over immigrants exceeded 100,000. The 1996 Census showed that almost eighty percent of those born in 1970 (twenty-six year olds) were alive and in Ireland. Forty years previously in 1956, the equivalent figure for twenty-six-year-olds was fifty-seven percent. Half of that difference may be attributed to the fall in death rates among infants and young people, and half by reduced emigration (Fitzgerald, 1997).

## Interpreting Current Return Migration

Although Ireland is now a country of net immigration, this does not mean that all outward flows have ceased. Preliminary figures for 1996 show that 32,800 people left Ireland in that year, two thirds of whom were in the 15–24 year age band (Central Statistics Office). Just under half of those travelled to the United Kingdom. Service providers in London have noted no falloff in the number of people availing of their services, which would suggest that poverty emigration continues unabated. But the numbers leaving are now masked by the fact that at least as many people are immigrating to Ireland. Crucially, the incoming migrants tend to be older, to have educational credentials and have amassed a wealth of career experience. Barrett and Trace have demonstrated that upward of fifty percent of those in the 25–39 age band, who returned to Ireland in the year ended April 1996, had a third-level educational qualification (1998: 12–13). Thousands more aspiring returners are waiting in the wings. The Higher Skills Pool established jointly by FAS (State Training Agency) and the IDA (Industrial Development Authority) as a mechanism for linking graduates abroad seeking to return with companies in Ireland has over 8,000 people on its database. About fifty percent of those fall into just three job categories: Engineering, Computers and Accountancy. There is conclusive evidence that the brain drain which concerned policy makers in the 1980s has declined dramatically in recent years. In 1988, almost twenty percent of Irish graduates emigrated. By 1996, this figure had fallen to nine percent (Higher Education Authority, Annual Reports).

Not only has Ireland's migratory pattern changed, but the entire context which has traditionally provided a framework for understanding those population flows has been transformed. An earlier exploration of the lives of undocumented Irish emigrants in New York City in the 1980s (Corcoran, 1993) called into question the usefulness of conventional migration theory in conceptualising their experiences. While some fell into the traditional category of economic refugees, many could be more accurately classed as adventurers, people seeking an escape route from Ireland, engaged on a quest for personal self-development or a combination of both. A paradigm which takes account of the contingent, reflexive and often transient nature of contemporary migratory flows seems to better express the migratory trajectory of more recent Irish emigrants. They are deeply ambivalent about identifying themselves as emigrants, in the traditional sense. As transnational workers they participate in an increasingly globalised labour market. However, their self-identity remains remarkably local and avowedly Irish. Many of those who left in the 1980s expressed a desire to return home. In stark contrast to their forebears, they could be classified as sojourners rather than settlers. In the 1990s that desire to return seems to have become not just an aspiration but a reality for growing numbers of Irish emigrants.

## The Lure of the Celtic Tiger

The decline in net outward migration is mirrored by a concomitant growth in prosperity at home. As recently as the early 1970s, the last decade in which net in-migration was recorded, gross domestic product (GDP) per head of population in the Republic was half that of the UK. In 1996, Ireland produced more wealth per capita than the United Kingdom. Taking an EU average as 100, Irish GDP stood at 100.7 while the equivalent figure for the UK was 98.9. According to economic forecasters, this disparity is set to widen further as we move toward the end of the century, (O'Toole, 1996: 1). The much vaunted Celtic Tiger is now exerting a magnetic attraction on the diasporic community. Ireland—the touchstone of tradition and folk ways and the bastion of trust-relations between people embedded in intense social networks—still fuels the imagination of our emigrants. The current wave of return may be understood as a quest for anchorage. These returning emigrants seek a more family- and community-oriented style of life to replace the commodified and compartmentalised experiences which characterised their lifestyle in world cities like London and New York. In effect, they are seeking an anchor in an increasingly atomised world. The factors key to the decision to return include the provision of a better quality of life for children, having more time, the ease of Irish sociability, the quality of friendship and the slower pace of life. Ironically, the slower pace of life which caused the most serious adjustment problems for the returned emigrants surveyed by Gelmch (1986) in the 1970s and McGrath (1991) in the 1980s, is eulogised by those returning in the 1990s. Paradoxically, the rise of the Celtic Tiger which has facilitated the return of emigrants in such significant numbers is inextricably bound up with a creeping individualism in Ireland. The country has itself been incorporated into the project of modernity. Life has become faster, more competitive and more stressful in the larger cities to which the returners migrate. The private sector now demands the same level of commitment from Irish-based employees as is demanded of employees of the parent company and its international counterparts. This puts at risk precisely those characteristics which the returning emigrants covet. The very aspects of Irish life which attract them back, are in the process of disappearing. Contrary to their expectations it is difficult to acquire reasonably priced housing, commuting times are considerably longer than they anticipated and there is less time than they hoped for a social life. Indeed, as the recently returned poet, Michael O'Loughlin has pointed out, the boom in return emigration has itself become part of the problem: "Fact is returning hurts more than leaving. And returners are awkward for the mother country. Ireland is proud of its diaspora, as long as it stays where it bloody well is and doesn't push up house prices and confuse banks," (*Irish Times*, Aug 23, 1997). As Fred Hirsch argued in his classical text, *The Social Limits to Growth*, the choice facing the individual in a market type transaction in the positional sector, in the context of material growth, always appears more attractive than it turns out be after others have exercised their choice (1976: 52). The positional economy is defined by Hirsch as all aspects of goods,

services, work positions, and other social relationships that are (1) scarce in some absolute or socially imposed sense; (2) subject to congestion or crowding through more extensive use. In other words, the satisfaction that returning emigrants may derive from goods and services depend increasingly not only on their own consumption but on the consumption of others as well. In a booming economy, characterised by net immigration rather than net emigration, where the demands of an expanding middle class are outstripping supply, the acquisition of positional goods becomes ever more difficult. The returning emigrants find themselves caught in a bind. Ireland's exemplary economic performance makes the dream of return a reality, but the economic performance is based on the very values and practices which these emigrants are attempting to escape.

Estimated Net Migration
*(The number of out-migrants less the number of in-migrants)*

| Year Ending | |
|---|---|
| April | Net migration |
| 1980 | –8,000 |
| 1981 | +2,000 |
| 1982 | –1,000 |
| 1983 | –14,000 |
| 1984 | –9,000 |
| 1985 | –20,000 |
| 1986 | –28,000 |
| 1987 | –23,000 |
| 1988 | –42,000 |
| 1989 | –44,000 |
| 1990 | –23,000 |
| 1991 | –2,000 |
| 1992 | +6,000 |
| 1993 | –1,500 |
| 1994 | –5,500 |
| 1995 | –1,700 |
| 1996 | +5,700 |
| 1997 | +15,000 |

*Source:* Central Statistics Office.

*See* Emigration: 1922–1998

Alan Barrett and Feargal Trace, "They're Coming Back: Return Migration into Ireland in the 1990s. Conference Paper, 'Immigrants and Their Transition to a New Labour Market'" (Tel Aviv University, March 23, 1998).

Central Statistics Office. *Annual Population and Migration Estimates 1991–1996* (Cork: CSO).

Mary P. Corcoran, *Irish Illegals: Transients Between Two Societies* (Westport, CT, 1993).

G. Fitzgerald, "Latter-day emigrants opt for short-term stay-away," *Irish Times* (August 9, 1997).

George Gmelch, "The Readjustment of Return Migrants in Western Ireland," in R. King, ed., *Return Migration and Regional Economic Problems* (London, 1986).

Higher Education Authority, *Annual Report* (Dublin: HEA, 1997).

F. Hirsch, *Social Limits to Growth* (Twentieth-century Foundation, 1976).

Fiona McGrath, "The Economic, Social and Cultural Impacts of Return Migration to Achill Island," in R. King, ed., *Contemporary Irish Migration* (Geographical Society of Ireland Special Publications, Number 6, 1991).

Michael O'Loughlin, "The Return of the Native," *Irish Times* (August 23, 1997).

F. O'Toole. "In the Land of the Emerald Tiger," *Irish Times* (December 28, 1996).

MARY P. CORCORAN

## EMIGRATION, LAWS COVERING

### LAWS IN IRELAND AND THE UNITED KINGDOM

At the time the United States became independent, and thus able to control its own immigration law, Ireland was a colony of the United Kingdom (U.K.), which therefore governed emigration out of it. U.K. law neither encouraged nor discouraged migration out of Ireland, but did try to direct it to other parts of the British Empire rather than lose population. Usually it did so by regulating the passenger trade; an 1803 law permitted ships traveling within the empire to carry one passenger for every two tons of burden (that is, a two-ton ship could have one passenger) but requiring ships going outside the empire to carry only one passenger for every five tons of burden. The methods were unsuccessful; Irish migrants went to the United States directly, or went to Canada and crossed the border.

The War of 1812 roused fears of a U.S. invasion of Canada. The War Office began to assist soldiers willing to settle in Canada, thus hoping to build up a population that could defend the place against U.S. attack. In 1816, after the United States and United Kingdom had signed the Treaty of Ghent, the Colonial Office extended the same offer to civilians. In neither case did much migration result.

In the 1830s, British authorities began to encourage Irish emigration specifically. The case of Irvilloughter in County Galway may serve as an example of how this came about. In the seventeenth and eighteenth centuries, the British crown leased land to non-Irish families who in turn collected rents from the native Irish who worked their land and who took out subleases on little plots which they used to build their huts and raise their food. The subleases lasted longer than one generation, and the landowners never put more land on the rental market, so over time the tenants' plots were subdivided to the point where they were too small to support the families that lived on them. In 1836, the leases began to expire, and the Commissioner of Woods offered to relocate the excess tenants. The tenants refused. When the potato famine pushed the tenants over the edge of privation into desperation, Irvilloughter's residents applied for relocation assistance. At this point, the Commissioners of the Treasury approved expending funds to transport them to Canada. The first party left County Galway June 10, 1848, and arrived in Quebec July 23 of the same year. In other cases, authorities even spent money to send migrants outside the British empire; in Ballykilcline in 1848, County Roscommon, the Commissioners of the Treasury funded emigration to New York City.

After the emergency of the potato famine, the United Kingdom reverted to laissez-faire migration policies. When Eire became independent in 1922, it continued these policies. Overall, Irish migration to the United States has not been shaped so much by Irish law as by U.S. law.

### 1776–1880: RELATIVELY OPEN MIGRATION

When the United States declared its independence, individual states made their own laws regarding immigration and naturalization. The federal government entered the field March 26, 1790, with a law that established a residence requirement of two years for naturalization in any one state. It repealed this law January 29, 1795, and replaced it with a new law requiring a five-year residency and a declaration of intent to become a citizen, the latter to be filed three years prior to naturalization.

A flurry of legislation occurred in 1798. The Naturalization Act of June 18 raised the residency requirement from five to fourteen years. The Aliens Act of June 25 permitted the president to detain resident aliens deemed dangerous to the United States; it was also the first to require ship captains to report the arrival of aliens aboard their vessels. The Alien Enemy Act of July 6 permitted the president to deport or confine males over 14 years of age if the United States went to war against their home countries. Together with the Sedition Act of July 14, these laws were designed in part to convince France that the United States was serious about protecting its shipping from the effects of the Anglo-French naval war then raging, and to drive France to negotiations. There were also political motives. The High Federalists who passed the Alien and Sedition Acts thought that immigrants voted for their opponents, the Democratic Republicans, and thus controlling immigration was a step in reducing the Democratic Republicans' strength. Finally, the legislation bespoke a certain attitude toward immigrants, including the Irish. The High Federalists assumed the immigrants supported revolutionary France. This was not because they were from that place; most French migrants were in fact refugees from the revolution's attempts to separate church and state and to abolish the class system. The migrants most supportive of the French Revolution and the Democratic Republican party were the Irish, who had a rebellion of their own in 1798. The crisis passed in 1800, after Napoleon took power and chose to negotiate rather than to fight.

During the first four-fifths of the nineteenth century, what laws the federal government passed either established administrative procedures or protected travelers. Sometimes the same law did both. A March 2, 1819, law required keeping an annual count of arrivals, and also restricted the number of passengers on vessels entering or departing the United States. Laws passed on February 22 and March 2, 1847, established safety regulations on passenger vessels and specified the amount of space each passenger was to have. A March 3, 1855, law replaced these two laws with a safety code and refined the procedures for reporting arrivals by sorting the travelers into temporary and permanent migrants. These laws were at least partly in response to a phenomenon associated with the famine migration. Most ships that went between the United States and the United Kingdom were freight ships, with storage structures in the hold below the waterline, where the steering mechanism was (hence the term "steerage"). They were fully loaded when bringing raw goods from the United States to England, but until the famine might sail west in ballast. During the famine overcrowding in steerage raised the specter of uncontrollable contagious diseases reaching U.S. shores.

Individual states passed various immigration laws. States along the frontier wanted to increase white population vis-à-vis the Indians, develop local economies, and build up sufficient population to justify larger delegations to the House of Representatives. Conversely, states along the Atlantic Coast feared the influx of the culturally different Irish Catholics. A cholera epidemic in 1832 provided another reason to fear immigrants. As early as 1837, Massachusetts began to levy a $2.00 head tax on immigrants. The Irish potato famine increased the number of impoverished migrants and contributed to another cholera epidemic in 1849. During the 1850s, New York and Massachusetts created state boards to provide for orderly admission processes.

During the 1850s, states also passed a barrage of laws aimed at immigrants settled within their borders. Most of these laws were directed at two characteristics of the famine migration. Most of the famine migrants were at least nominally Catholic. Ironically, a nation that in 1798 feared the Irish as radical revolutionaries now began to fear them as conservatives who voted at the will of their clergy. Americans also feared Catholic influence on gender roles; while most U.S. Protestant denominations had no place for single adult women, Catholics had institutes of female religious, in which women spent their lives teaching, nursing, or caring for groups with special needs such as the elderly poor or unmarried mothers. Americans also had unfavorable views of Irish drinking habits, and opposition to Irish (and German) drinking reinforced a crusade against native alcohol consumption.

Different states passed laws reflecting different aspects of native opposition to Irish Catholics. In 1851, Maine became the first to prohibit the manufacture and sale of intoxicating beverages, and in 1855, many nativist-dominated legislatures followed suit. In 1854, nativist candidates swept the Massachusetts elections. In 1855, the new legislature passed laws to inspect Catholic convents to ensure no women were held there against their wills, and appointed a committee of legislators to travel the commonwealth conducting the inspections. New York state dealt with another issue that reflected Protestant-Catholic tensions, the ownership of religious property. Catholicism's canon law made bishops, the "ordinary" authorities in their dioceses, responsible for diocesan property, and some states accommodated this arrangement by permitting bishops to be the sole trustees of property-owning corporations. In 1855, though, New York began to require that each piece of local parish be incorporated separately, and that two laymen be on the boards of trustees.

The laws' major effect on migration was the ability to see it; until ports began counting immigrants in 1820, there were no records regarding Irish migration. Between 1820 and 1834 migration out of what is now Eire and Northern Ireland stayed in the 1,000s, with two bursts of 12,000 migrants (1828 and 1832). In 1834, it jumped to 24,474, and remained over 10,000 per annum until the famine. In 1847, it jumped to 105,536, and remained over 100,000 per annum until 1854.

## 1880–1921: Increasing Federal Regulation

It was New York's experience with the care of incoming migrants that led to a major change in U.S. immigration law. In 1851, New York created a state board of volunteer immigration commissioners. This board had use of an old fort turned entertainment center, Castle Garden, in Manhattan's Battery Park. Barges brought incoming steerage passengers there from East River ship docks. Commissioners collected statistical information on immigrants and tried to help them make post-voyage plans. However, the question came up as to the degree to which a single state could regulate commerce that in turn impacted other states. In the case of *Henderson* v. *Mayor of New York* (1875), the Supreme Court ruled that immigration was subject to federal, not state, regulation.

In 1882, the federal government began to exercise its power. Insofar as Irish immigration was concerned, the federal government entered a period in which immigration was heavily regulated, meaning that there were a number of requirements individual immigrants had to meet before admission to the United States. Beginning August 3, 1882, persons who were deemed likely to become public charges, that is, to require welfare, were not permitted to enter the United States. After February 26, 1885, contract laborers—those who had already agreed to take particular jobs—were forbidden entry. A law of March 3, 1891, denied admission to persons suffering from certain contagious diseases, persons convicted of felonies and also persons convicted of some misdemeanors, and polygamists. A March 3, 1903, law excluded those advocating certain political opinions, including the violent overthrow of the rule of law, governments, and the U.S. government in particular. A February 20, 1907, law excluded persons with certain mental disabilities, persons with tuberculosis, minors unaccompanied by their parents, persons with criminal records involving moral crimes, and women coming or being brought to the United States for prostitution. (This last regulation was reinforced by the Mann Act of June 25, 1910.) These laws were applied to all migrant groups equally, and had little effect on Irish migration. From the end of the famine migration until the onset of World War I, that is from 1854 to 1914, Irish migration remained constant at tens of thousands each year.

With the Immigration Act of February 5, 1917, the federal government entered a new phase, emphasizing restriction of immigration to certain favored groups. The architects of this new policy were generally well-born, well-educated persons with some professional qualifications in addition to careers in politics and public service. Their education may have done them a disservice, for this was a time in which scholars emphasized nature over nurture. Science and social studies taught that one's genetic inheritance determined one's life. Emphasis on the proper gene pool, ethnic group, or, in the parlance of the day, "race" provided a way to identify immigrants least likely to succeed and to exclude them from the United States. The Irish were not considered among the most promising gene pools, and many restrictionists would have liked to prohibit Irish immigration along with the rest. However, it was politically unwise to advocate the restriction of white immigrants on racial grounds, as there were already too many among the electorate. The trick then was to devise laws which sounded even-handed while restricting immigration only to desirable races.

The laws devised permitted continued Irish migration. The 1917 law established a literacy test for admission to the United States, but almost all Irish were literate, and in English (which was not a requirement). The federal government began to try to restrict immigration by basing the laws on the proportion of the immigrant ethnic or racial group already in the U.S. population. The first law openly embodying the restrictionist principle to Europeans was passed May 19, 1921. It limited the number of immigrants from any one country to a number equal to 3 percent of that country's representation in the United States in the 1910 census. The May 26, 1924, law refigured the quotas so as to favor preferred ethnic groups. From 1924 to 1927, each country received a quota based on 2 percent of the number of persons of that country in the 1890 census. After 1927, each country got a third and final quota. This time, the federal government set a cap of 150,000 on the total number of admissions to the United States in any year. Each country got a quota the number of which bore the same relation to 150,000 that people born in that country and living in the United States bore to the total U.S. population in the 1920 census.

## 1921–1965: The Irish Under the Quota Laws

It was during this period (1922) that Eire, or the Irish Free State, became independent, requiring U.S. authorities to establish separate quotas for Great Britain and Northern Ireland, and for Eire. From 1924 to 1929, the U.K. had a quota of 34,007, and Eire a quota of 28,567. After 1930, the figures were 65,721 and 17,853, respectively. The actual number of visas available varied by about 100 each year, because occasionally individuals admitted as non-immigrants one year adjusted their status the next. The United States counted Irish immigrants on a different basis than it counted the issuing of visas, counting Eire and Northern Ireland together. During the 1920s, the Irish used almost all the visas available to them. The maximum number from Ireland in any one year in the decade of the 1920s was 28,435 (1921); the minimum was 19,921 (1929). Thereafter, the Great Depression probably did more to reduce immigration than the restriction of visas did. During the 1930s, Irish migration went from a high of 23,445 (1930) to a low of 338 (1933). World War II prevented migration even more effectively; during the 1940s, Irish migration sank to a low of 83 (1942), and reached a high of 8,678 only after the war was over (1949).

During the period between 1945 and 1965, the most notable feature of U.S. immigration legislation as far as the Irish are concerned might be Irish-American leadership in that field. Patrick Anthony McCarran (1876–1954), himself the son of an Irish immigrant, was the sponsor of the Immigration and Nationality Act of June 27, 1952. McCarran's law eliminated race discrimination in the matter of naturalization and sex discrimination in the matter of immigration. It maintained the national quotas of the 1920s, adding new ones for countries that had become independent since World War II and in order to eliminate the previous exclusion of Asians. McCarran's law was unpopular among many Americans, including an up-and-coming politician of Irish extraction, John F. Kennedy. Kennedy argued that the law reflected a racism that was unfair in itself, that hurt members of various ethnic and racial groups, and that damaged world opinion of the United States at a point in the Cold War when the country wanted as many allies as possible. Irish immigrants, though, do not seem to have been adversely affected by the quotas at this time. They never used all available visas. During the 1950s, Irish migration ranged from 3,144 (1951) to 9,134 (1958).

Kennedy's suggestion that the United States revise its immigration laws in a more egalitarian direction was not taken up during his lifetime. After his assassination, his successor in the presidency, Lyndon Baines Johnson, pressed for immigration reform on the grounds that it had been part of the Kennedy program, which he himself fully supported. The Immigration and Naturalization Act Amendments of October 3, 1965, were the result. This law is also known as the Hart-Cellar Act, after its Senate sponsor Philip A. Hart (D-Michigan) and its House sponsor Emmanuel Cellar (D-Brooklyn), and it was passed partly due to the leadership of John Kennedy's younger brother Edward M. (D-Massachusetts). Under this law, the Western Hemisphere (North and South America) got a maximum of 120,000 immigrants per year. The Eastern Hemisphere (Africa, Asia, Australia, and Europe) got a maximum of 170,000, with no one country to get more than 20,000 visas. The applicants for these 20,000 visas per country could be ranked, with preference going to those rejoining their families, then to people who met certain U.S. eco-

nomic needs, and then to refugees. Some family members of U.S. citizens and legal residents were admitted outside the quota system. On October 20, 1976, the federal government gave each country in the Western Hemisphere the same 20,000-visa limit the Eastern Hemisphere had. On October 5, 1978, the government abolished the distinction between hemispheres and established a global ceiling of 290,000 immigrants.

The visas available to Eire thus increased slightly while those available to Northern Ireland were reduced. Neither change affected Irish immigration right away. During the 1960s, U.S. migration from Ireland ranged from a high of 6,918 (1960) to a low of 1,981 (1969). During the 1970s, the figures were 2,000 (1973) and 982 (1979). The real impetus to change in Irish-American migration patterns came when Ronald Reagan was president (1981–1989) and Margaret Thatcher prime minister (1979–1990). Political violence in Ireland was one factor. The major factor was economic. Opportunity decreased in Great Britain and in Ireland. However, opportunities, especially for English-speaking laborers such as waiters, nannies, and construction workers, increased in the United States. Officially, migration did not increase much during the 1980s; the high was 6,983 (1989) and the low 949 (1982). However, the trend was upward.

It was at this point that the 1965 law began to be perceived as working a hardship on the Irish. If there were 20,000 visas per country and 290,000 worldwide, then fourteen countries sending 20,000 immigrants and one sending 10,000 would exhaust the available U.S. visas. And other countries found it easier to send migrants. During the late 1960s, migration from the Western Hemisphere and the Pacific Rim far exceeded Irish migration. As those migrants became legal residents and U.S. citizens, their relatives had preference among those waiting for visas. This chain migration of relatives diverted the supply of visas to a few countries. The Irish did not have the numbers to start a substantial chain migration.

## Since 1965: Championing Irish Opportunities for Migration

The political situation that had unintentionally benefited the Irish during the most restrictive period of immigration legislation now loomed as a potential threat. One could not argue for special consideration for Irish immigrants, because too many voters would object to preferential treatment for any one nation. The Irish Immigration Reform Movement and Irish American politicians, such as House Representative Brian Donnelly (D-Massachusetts) and Bruce A. Morrison (D-Connecticut) and Ted Kennedy, led the effort to insert into U.S. immigration law language that would diversify the source of migrant flows, and they hoped to benefit Irish migration thereby. However, the legislation was drawn up without specific reference to the Irish. The Immigration Reform and Control Act (IRCA) of November 6, 1986, set aside from the total number of visas available 10,000 for persons from countries adversely affected by the 1965 law. During 1987, such persons could apply for admission to the United States. Reviewers gave each applicant points for various characteristics: education, potential labor contribution, ability to speak English, etc. After that, applications were selected at random; hence the colloquial name for the procedure, the "lottery." IRCA set aside another 10,000 visas for a 1988 lottery.

The Immigration Act of November 29, 1990, incorporated the idea of considering the needs of nations without substantial family chain migration. This law established a ceiling of 700,000 immigrants per annum for the years 1992–1994, and a ceiling of 675,000 immigrants beginning in 1995. Of the 675,000 visas, 480,000 went to individuals reuniting with their families; 140,000 to those meeting U.S. employment needs. Another 55,000 were for "diversity immigrants."

Other legislation regulates the behavior of migrants within the United States. Migrants suspected of connection to the Irish Republican Army (IRA), for example, fall under antiterrorist law. The largest body of law regarding settled immigrants is probably the September 30, 1996, Illegal Immigration Reform and Immigrant Responsibility Act (IIRIRA). The law sets forth various categories of migrants, such as naturalized citizens, legal residents, and refugees, the types of federal welfare benefits available to each, and the duration of such benefits, and also regulates what states may offer naturalized citizens, legal residents, and refugees in the way of state-level welfare benefits. In this case, the lack of chain migration among the Irish may work to their favor. Ireland itself has a level of benefits such that persons do not need to migrate in order to receive decent care; they can get the care in Ireland, and, if necessary, their relatives can help to support them by remitting money from overseas. Migrants who do not bring children, the elderly, or handicapped family members have less need of public education services, public medical services, Supplemental Security Income (SSI), Temporary Assistance to Needy Families (TANF), or other benefits.

*See* Emigration (5 entries)

William Forbes Adams, *Ireland and Irish Emigration to the New World from 1815 to the Famine* (Baltimore, 1980).

William S. Bernard, "Immigration: History of U.S. Policy," in Stephen Thernstrom, Ann Orlov, and Oscar Handlin, eds., *The Harvard Encyclopedia of American Ethnic Groups* (Cambridge, Massachusetts, 1980): 486–495.

William S. Bernard, Carolyn Zeleny, and Henry Miller, eds., *American Immigration Policy: A Reappraisal* (New York, 1950).

Eilish Ellis, *Emigrants from Ireland, 1847–1852: State-Aided Emigration Schemes from Crown Estates in Ireland* (Baltimore, 1977).

John Higham, *Strangers in the Land: Patterns of American Nativism, 1860–1925,* corrected and with a new preface (New York, 1969).

*Historical Statistics of the United States,* 2 volumes (Washington, D.C., 1975), volume 1, pp. 105–107.

E. P. Hutchinson, *Legislative History of American Immigration Policy, 1798–1965* (Philadelphia, 1981).

David M. Reimers, *Still the Golden Door: The Third World Comes to America,* second edition (New York, 1992).

*Statistical Yearbook of the Immigration and Naturalization Service* (Washington, D.C., 1997).

Philip Taylor, *The Distant Magnet: European Emigration to the USA* (New York, 1971).

Reed Ueda, "Naturalization and Citizenship," in Stephen Thernstrom, Ann Orlov, and Oscar Handlin, eds., *The Harvard Encyclopedia of American Ethnic Groups* (Cambridge, Massachusetts, 1980): 736–748.

MARY ELIZABETH BROWN

## EMMET, THOMAS ADDIS (1764–1827)

Doctor, lawyer, Irish patriot. Born in Cork, Thomas Addis was an older brother of Robert Emmet, famous for his 1803 Dublin insurrection. Thomas Addis Emmet was graduated from Trinity College, Dublin, in 1782 and then left Ireland to study medicine at Edinburgh University, where he finished his degree in

Thomas Addis Emmet, 1764–1827

1784. While in Scotland, Emmet's oratory skills matured, and he presided over five debating societies (*The National Cyclopaedia of American Biography,* Vol. V).

After taking his medical degree, Emmet traveled at length on the Continent, and, on the death of his brother, a lawyer, he returned to London to begin to study law. He was admitted to the Dublin Bar in 1791, the same year Wolfe Tone founded the Society of United Irishmen. Emmet joined the United Irishmen in 1795, eventually serving on its grand executive committee, which allegedly supervised the activities of more than half a million members. Apprehended by authorities in March 1798 for subversive political activity during martial law, Emmet served time in Dublin's Kilmainham Jail. Having been promised his liberty, Emmet confessed his guilt before the Irish House of Commons but managed to avoid implicating his compatriots (Wilson and Fiske).

Unmoved authorities rescinded their promise of freedom, however, and Emmet was subsequently removed to a prison in Scotland, where he served three years. During his imprisonment Emmet began to write about Irish history and politics, including his firsthand experiences within the upper ranks of the United Irishmen and the activities of 1798. By 1807 his collection had been published in New York, entitled *Pieces of Irish History.* Emmet eventually earned his freedom—but at the ultimate price of exile from his homeland.

Attempting a fresh start, Emmet and his wife, Jane Patten, traveled to Brussels and then set off for New York City, settling there in 1804 (ibid). Emmet quickly established himself by joining the ranks of the New York Democratic party and, by 1812, having gained a reputation as an outstanding Supreme Court lawyer, held the office of attorney general of New York. Hamilton College awarded Emmet an honorary degree in 1822, as did Columbia in 1824. In 1829, Charles Haynes wrote and published Emmet's memoirs in London. Throughout his life Emmet was best remembered as a driven man: "While he was a brilliant orator and able and logical in argument, he nevertheless depended upon hard labor for his success, and is said to have worked thirteen hours a day, mixing but little with the fashionable world, [and] often amusing himself with mathematical calculations. . ." (ibid).

Having established both his credentials and popularity as a political hero in Ireland, Emmet worked doggedly to secure a similiar life in the New World. In New York, he was revered lifelong for helping fellow Irish immigrants assimilate into their adopted homeland and its foreign culture. A monument was dedicated to Thomas Addis Emmet in Saint Paul's churchyard in New York City after his death in November 1827.

*See* New York City; United Irishmen
and America

Rossiter Johnson, ed., *The Twentieth Century Biographical Dictionary of Notable Americans,* Vol. III (Boston, 1904).
*The National Cyclopaedia of American Biography,* Vol. V (New York, 1897).
*Who Was Who in America,* Historical Volume: 1607–1896 (Chicago, 1963).
James Grant Wilson and John Fiske, *Appleton's Cyclopaedia of American Biography,* Vol. II (New York, 1888).

JAMES P. LEONARD

## EMMET, THOMAS ADDIS (1828–1919)

Physician, writer. Born in Charlottesville, Virginia, Emmet was a grandson of Irish expatriate Thomas Addis Emmet, who emigrated to New York in 1804. Emmet was graduated from Jefferson Medical College, Philadelphia, in 1850 and became resident physician in the Emigrants' Refuge Hospital, Ward's Island. He specialized in women's health issues, working as assistant at Woman's Hospital until 1861, when he earned the job of surgeon-in-chief and, later, visiting surgeon. During his tenure, Emmet invented a procedure to repair ulcerations of the womb (Johnson and Malone). In 1879 he published *The Principles and Practice of Gynecology,* reprinted in three editions and translated into German and French; moreover, he contributed dozens of monographs to medical journals in the U.S. and abroad.

Emmet demonstrated additional talents and interests, as well. More than 150 of his illustrations appeared in published works. Like his grandfather, Emmet supported home rule for Ireland. He wrote and published works on Irish history and politics, including *The Emmet Family with Some Incidents Relating to Irish*

*History* (1893) and *Ireland Under English Rule* (1903), which documented English mismanagement of Ireland (*The National Cyclopaedia of American Biography,* Vol. X). Emmet served as president of the Irish National Federation of America from 1891 to 1901. In 1898 the University of Notre Dame awarded Emmet the Laetare Medal, and in 1906 Pope Pius X named him a Knight Commander of the Order of Gregory the Great. In 1854 Emmet married Catherine Duncan, with whom he had six children.

Allen Johnson and Dumas Malone, eds., *Dictionary of American Biography,* Vol. 3 (1931). CD-ROM (New York, 1997).
Rossiter Johnson, ed., *The Twentieth Century Biographical Dictionary of Notable Americans,* Vol. III (Boston, 1904).
*The National Cyclopaedia of American Biography,* Vol. X (New York, 1909).
*Who Was Who in America,* Volume I: 1897–1942 (Chicago, 1963).
James Grant Wilson and John Fiske. *Appletons' Cyclopaedia of American Biography*, Vol. II (New York, 1888).

JAMES P. LEONARD

## EMMONS, DAVID MICHAEL (1939–   )

Historian of the Irish in the West. David Michael Emmons was born March 28, 1939 in Denver, Colorado, the son of Waltman Oliver and Irene Yolanda Celantano Emmons. He attended the University of Colorado where he majored in Classics and Philosophy. He graduated in 1961 and immediately commenced graduate study in Western American history under the direction of Professor Robert G. Athearn at Colorado.

In 1984 Emmons stumbled across the records of the two largest Irish-American associations in Butte, Montana, the most Irish city in America. Almost irretrievably lost when the Model Cities program mandated the destruction of Butte's Hibernia Hall, these many thousands of pages of records were deposited at the World Museum of Mining in Butte and made available for microfilming. The filming filled 12 reels of 1,000 frames each; the Irish Collection as it came to be called, remains the largest and richest collection of primary material on any Irish American community in the United States. It is available to scholars at the Butte/Silver Bow Archives, the University of Montana, and the University of Notre Dame.

Thomas Addis
Emmet,
1828–1919

David Emmons

Based principally on this collection, he wrote a book on the Butte Irish and in 1987 sent it to the University of Illinois Press. Richard Wentworth, the press's director, persuaded Emmons to allow the Press to submit the manuscript for the Ellis Island/ Statue of Liberty Centennial Prize and publication in the Illinois series of the same name. He agreed. It won the prize and in 1989 appeared as *The Butte Irish: Class and Ethnicity in an American Mining Town, 1875–1925.* Now in its fifth printing, the book won the Robert G. Athearn Prize of the Western Historical Association and was cited for honorable mention by the American Committee for Irish Studies for its James B. Donnelly Award. It appeared in paperback in 1990 and in 1995 the Irish American Cultural Institute named it one of the fifteen best books written on the Irish experience in America.

Emmons is presently Professor of History at the University of Montana in Missoula. His articles have appeared in *Labor History, The Journal of American Ethnic History, Éire-Ireland,* and *The Western Historical Quarterly,* among other journals. He is married to the former Caroline Dollard and is presently engaged in the writing of *A Better Country: Irish Catholic Settlement and Survival in America's West, 1845–1945.*

*See* Montana

*Garden in the Grasslands: The Boomer Literature of the Central Plains* (Lincoln, 1971): 220.

———, *The Butte Irish: Class and Ethnicity in an American Mining Town, 1875–1925* (Urbana and Chicago, 1989): 443.

———, "An Aristocracy of Labor: The Irish Miners of Butte, 1878–1914," *Labor History,* vol. 28 (Summer 1987): 275–306.

———, "Faction Fights: The Irish Worlds of Butte, Montana, 1870–1930," in Patrick O'Sullivan, ed., *The Irish World Wide: History, Heritage, Identity,* vol. II *The Irish in New Communities* (Leicester and New York, 1992): 80–104.

## ENGLAND, JOHN (1786–1842)

First Catholic Bishop of Charleston, South Carolina (1820–1842). England was born on September 28, 1786 in Cork, Ireland, the son of Honora Lordan and Thomas England, a successful tobacco merchant and a representative of the new late eighteenth-century middle-class Catholics. As a member of a relatively prosperous family, England had the advantages of a good education during the early days of the relaxation of the penal laws against Irish Catholics. From 1792 to 1800, he received his primary education in the Cork Protestant schools, where the leading members of Cork society sent their children. Two years after his early classical education, he apprenticed himself to a Cork lawyer, intending to enter the bar, a profession open to Irish Catholics after 1793. He abandoned the study of law, however, in 1802 and went to St. Patrick's College in Carlow, Ireland, where he studied for the priesthood.

After ordination in 1808, England returned to Cork where he assumed a number of pastoral services. From 1808 to 1812, he was a preacher and lecturer at St. Finbar's Cathedral, a chaplain to the Presentation Sisters, an inspector of schools, a writer of school textbooks, and a Lancasterian educational reformer. He became president of Cork's newly established College of St. Mary in 1812 and remained at that position until 1817. From 1814 to 1818, moreover, he was editor and contributor to *The Cork Mercantile Chronicle,* a leading Irish newspaper that became during

John England

England's trusteeship a strong defender of Irish civil and political rights and an opponent of British attempts to obtain a governmental veto over the nomination of Catholic bishops in the British Isles.

During the so-called veto controversy, England rose to prominence in Cork as a fiery advocate of religious liberty, separation of church and state, and a voluntary (not a state-financed or supported) church, relying considerably on arguments for religious toleration that were first articulated by Arthur O'Leary and brought to prominence in early nineteenth-century Ireland by fellow anti-vetoist Daniel O'Connell. England's involvement in the veto crisis was part of the new activism among the Irish clergy and manifested a new Irish-Catholic appropriation of some eighteenth-century Enlightenment values.

In 1818, after his initial engagement in the veto controversy, England was appointed pastor of Bandon, Ireland, where he remained until he was ordained Bishop of Charleston, South Carolina, in 1820. Pope Pius VII (1740–1823) chose England as the first bishop of Charleston for two reasons. First and foremost was the fact that Irish Catholic lay trustees in Charleston, Norfolk, Virginia, Philadelphia, and New York had complained to Rome during the previous five years about the French hegemony of the American Catholic hierarchy and petitioned the papacy for Irish bishops to represent their own interests in the church. Many of the prominent Irish-American laity thought that the French clergy and hierarchy were not sympathetic with the Irish Catholic nor with American republican values. Second, Irish clergy, some of whom were in the United States, had suggested to the Vatican that England was a exceptional candidate for the episcopacy and would be able to bring peace to the American Church which was in the midst of a series of ethnic and ideological conflicts. England was chosen to be the first bishop of Charleston and was given the mandate of bringing peace to the distracted congregations. The Vatican was also aware that in making the appointment of England, it was meeting the aspirations of the Irish laity, as Vatican letters to the laity clearly indicated in the appointment of three Irish bishops to Charleston, Norfolk, and Philadelphia.

The thirty-four-year-old Bishop England brought peace to his new diocese and represented the voice of Irish-American

Catholicism not only in his diocese of Charleston, comprising South and North Carolina and Georgia, but also in the nation as a whole. In fact, in the course of his twenty-two year tenure as bishop he was the most prominent national voice of Catholicism and of Irish concerns. In his own diocese, he was able to secure peace among the contending factions by force of his personality and by creating a number of measures that endeared him to his own Catholic people and to the democratic people of the United States. The most important measure for obtaining peace and the participation of his people in the administration of his diocese was the establishment of a diocesan republican-like constitution (1822) that incorporated laity and clergy in the management and supervision of parish and diocesan life. He also erected a seminary for the education of native American clergy (1825), a philosophical and classical school for Charleston's white students (1832), a school for Blacks (1835) that was forced to close because of resistance from prominent Charleston city fathers, and founded the Sisters of Our Lady of Mercy in Charleston (1827), an order of nuns of Irish heritage that became a major support for the educational and health concerns of the Catholic people of his diocese. He also founded the Brotherhood of San Marino, the first Catholic society for working men in the United States, organized the Anti-Duelling Society of Charleston, edited catechisms, and prepared a new edition of the missal.

As a young priest in Ireland and as a bishop in the United States, England represented that side of late eighteenth- and early nineteenth-century Catholicism that was open to and accommodating toward an Enlightenment mentality that prized reason, democracy, religious liberty, voluntaryism in religion, and separation of church and state. Like many Gallican-influenced clergy and bishops of his day, moreover, he emphasized the rights, dignity, and integrity of the national church, pressuring the archbishops of Baltimore to convoke national councils of bishops to symbolize the unity of the national church and to provide a forum for an efficient and effective episcopal governance of the American church. Although he considered Southern slavery personally repugnant, he defended the institution itself as compatible with Scripture and the Christian tradition. His ideological support of slavery and his view of the compatibility of Catholicism and American democracy won him many friends in the city of Charleston, but also demonstrated clearly the difficulties inherent in his accommodationist stance toward the world in which he lived.

From 1820 until his death in 1842, England became something of a national spokesman and apologist for the compatibility of Catholicism and American democratic traditions, as well as a representative of an Irish-Catholic tradition of abhorrence for the British union of church and state that made of Irish Catholics second-class citizens. He was frequently called upon to preach in Protestant as well as Catholic churches in his own diocese and in numerous other churches from Boston to New Orleans. In 1822, he established the first national Catholic newspaper, the *U.S. Catholic Miscellany,* to provide information on national events, to defend the church, to give Catholics a voice in national affairs, and to report on events in Ireland that were of concern to an American-Catholic Irish readership. His national prominence was acknowledged in 1826 when he was invited to address the United States Congress, the first Catholic clergyman to do so. The Vatican, too, acknowledged his skills when it appointed him apostolic delegate (1833–37) to Haiti to reestablish diplomatic relations between Haiti and the Vatican.

England was never able to adjust fully to the climate in Charleston and died on April 11, 1842 at the early age of fifty-four. With England's death the baton of Irish clerical leadership passed to a *very* different Irish cleric, Bishop John Hughes of New York City.

*See* Catholicism, Irish-American

England's letters and unpublished correspondence are located primarily in the Archives of the Archdiocese of Baltimore, the Diocese of Charleston, Propaganda Fide (Rome), and the University of Notre Dame. *The Works of the Right Reverend John England, First Bishop of Charleston,* ed. Ignatius A. Reynolds, 5 vols. (Baltimore, 1849); ed. Sebastian G. Messmer, 7 vols. (Cleveland, 1908); Peter Guilday, *The Life and Times of John England, First Bishop of Charleston (1786–1842),* 2 vols. (New York, 1927; rpt. New York, 1969); Patrick Carey, *An Immigrant Bishop: John England's Adaptation of Irish Catholicism to American Republicanism* (Yonkers, N.Y., 1982); Peter Clarke, *A Free Church in a Free Society* (Greenwood, S.C., 1982).

PATRICK W. CAREY

## ENVOYS AND AMBASSADORS

The Anglo-Irish Treaty, which was supposed to bring a final peace to Ireland, was signed in London on December 6, 1921. The treaty recognized *de facto* division of Ireland into twenty-six counties which would become the Irish Free State and the six Ulster counties which already had its own parliament that had been opened by George V in June 1921.

The acrimonious debate on the treaty began in the Dail in Dublin on December 14, 1921, and lasted until January 7, 1922. Led by Michael Collins and Arthur Griffith the pro-treaty party won the open vote against Eamon de Valera and his allies who were dissatisfied with anything less than a 32-county republic. On June 16 the people voted overwhelmingly for pro-treaty candidates. On June 28 the provisional government attacked the Four Courts occupied by republican dissidents, and the Civil War began. It lasted until June 27, 1923, when De Valera asked his republican allies to lay down arms. In October 1924, the Irish Free State established formal diplomatic relations with the United States. The following diplomats have represented Ireland in America:

*Envoy Extraordinary & Minister Plenipotentiary*

| | | |
|---|---|---|
| Timothy A. Smiddy | October 1924 | – January 1929 |
| Michael A. McWhite | March 1929 | – March 1938 |
| Robert Brennan | October 1938 | – March 1947 |
| Sean Nunan | June 1947 | – April 1950 |

*Ambassador Extraordinary & Plenipotentiary*

| | | |
|---|---|---|
| John Joseph Hearne | April 1950 | – August 1960 |
| Dr. Thomas J. Kiernan | September 1960 | – April 1964 |
| William P. Fay | May 1964 | – September 1969 |
| William Warnock | March 1970 | – August 1973 |
| John Molloy | November 1973 | – September 1978 |
| Sean Donlon | October 1978 | – October 1984 |
| Padraig MacKernan | September 1985 | – August 1991 |
| Dermot Gallagher | September 1991 | – August 1997 |
| Sean O'Huiginn | September 1997 | – |

JOAN GLAZIER

# ETHNIC RELATIONS:
# THE AFRICAN-AMERICANS AND THE IRISH

Many elements are involved in a consideration of Irish/African-American relations. There are time periods which exert their influence on these relationships. There are geographical areas with their varied points of emphasis on racial conditions. Under these two conditioning factors, the Irish and the African-Americans may be considered as "Common Targets," competitors or cooperators, or an admixture of all three at the same time. The Irish-Americans cannot logically be taken as a single psychological entity, nor should the African-Americans. Generalities may be expressed, but each group is composed of individuals who have individual reactions, which again may vary with time and place. Not all Irish-Americans were Catholic, but a growing number of Catholics from the early Colonial Period were Irish. With predominantly white Protestant culture in control in the English Colonies of America, all other groups assumed an inferior and dominated position. This included Catholics, Native Americans, African-Americans, and especially the inhabitants of the bordering French- and Spanish-controlled colonies, who were also at least nominally Catholic.

## COLONIAL PERIOD

In the earliest stages of colonization in Virginia and Maryland neither colony had statutory slavery. Indentured servitude included white, African-American and Native American men and women. Statutory recognition of slavery was established in Virginia in 1661. Maryland gave statutory recognition of slavery in 1663. After that time period, slavery was generally restricted to the African-American and not to the white servants. By a Maryland law of 1681, children born of a white woman were free, even if the father was an African-American slave. There were several instances of mixed Irish-American and African-American families in this period.

The fact that these two groups functioned as a common target is shown in an act passed by the Maryland Legislature in 1704: "an act imposing three cents per gallon on rum and wine, brandy and spirits, and twenty shillings per poll for Negroes, for raising a supply to pay the public charge of the province, and twenty shillings per poll on Irish servants, to prevent their importing too great a number of Irish papists into this province" (*History of the Negro Race in America,* George Williams, Volume I, New York, 1882). The amount was later raised to forty shillings. After 1732, Protestant servants from Ireland and elsewhere could be imported duty free. Georgia, from its first settlement, was intended to be a buffer against Spanish Florida. As such, it was to be slave-free, as well as a rehabilitation center for Englishmen released from prison to do the farm work and other labors. It was for that reason that slavery, rum and Catholicism were forbidden. Alcoholic drinks were permitted in 1742 and Negro slavery in 1750. Anti-Catholicism and, implicitly, anti-Irish Catholicism remained strong in many areas, at least until well into the middle of the twentieth century.

## POST-REVOLUTIONARY PERIOD

The Revolutionary War began an amelioration of some of the previously dominant English Protestant culture. With the swelling ranks of Irish immigrants from the repression of the Rising of 1798, the problems before and after the parliamentary union of Great Britain and Ireland in 1801, and especially the famine of 1845, a new reaction on the part of the dominant culture took place. Nativism in its various aspects, as well as anti-abolitionism, arose to meet perceived threats to the economic and political establishments. In the economic field the Irish and African-Americans became competitors. In the jobs that were dangerous to health and life, the Irish, who were paid a salary, replaced the African-Americans, who had been purchased. An Irishman lost would mean an immigrant lost, whereas a slave lost would mean an investment lost. On the other side of the scale, skilled and semi-skilled labor, such as carpenters, coopers, ship-fitters and the like, previously held by free or slave African-Americans, was appropriated by the swelling immigrant ranks. In the mills and factories of the Northeast, labor was being supplied by a transition of home workers and farm hands to the factories. Recent immigrants and African-Americans were not welcomed as competitors for these jobs. Up to the time of the Mexican War, the major effort on the political side was to develop a cohesive voting group to hold in check various suspected conspiracies seeking to threaten the Anglo-Saxon superiority. This occasioned the Alien and Sedition Acts of 1798, which included extending the pre-naturalization period from five to fourteen years, although it only lasted until 1802. This move was paralleled by increasing activity in the South restricting African-American freedoms because of Abolitionist activities. While both groups were targets of ire, they did not react in common.

While there was not a group activity, there was individual activity. John England became the first Bishop of Charleston in 1821. It had been reported that the Catholic chapel there had 300 white and 150 African-American members. Bishop England gave his personal care to the African-Americans in his diocese and reported in 1833 that there were 40,000 Negro slaves in his diocese and 5,000 of these were Catholic. He established the Sisters of Our Lady of Mercy (mainly Irish background) to instruct both the African-American girls and the poor white girls of the city. In the summer of 1835, he opened his school for African-Americans. In January of 1836, mobs arose in Charleston, attacked the post office, removed Abolition papers and burned them before a large crowd. Warned by friends that he was next, because he was suspected of having Abolitionist tendencies, John England was able to gather a group of loyal Catholics as guards, and escaped harm. The eventual outcome of the troubles was that all schools for African-Americans in the city were closed.

Another individual instance is offered by the action of Father William Byrne, founder of St. Mary's Seminary in Kentucky. During the cholera epidemic of 1833, although sick himself, he answered a call to the sickbed of a dying African-American woman and prepared her for death. The next day, Father Byrne died of the same disease. Unfortunately, on the other hand, many Irish-Americans owned slaves, sold slaves—even members of the hierarchy and religious organizations did so.

One Irish immigrant came to Georgia about 1816. Eventually he purchased almost 400 acres of land north of Macon. He became a slave owner and chose a light-skinned slave woman to become the mother of his ten children. Unable to marry in Georgia, he remained monogamous until his death. Three of his sons, under the tutelage and protection of Bishop John Fitzpatrick of Boston, became priests. James Augustine Healy, ordained in 1854 in Paris, became the Bishop of Portland, Maine in 1875. Alexander Sherwood Healy was ordained in Rome in 1858 as a priest for Boston. Patrick Francis Healy was ordained in Belgium as a Jesuit in 1864. He became President of Georgetown in 1874. Two sisters became nuns, and one brother became a Captain in the United States Coast Guard.

There were race riots in the period before the Civil War in 1829 in Cincinnati; in 1830 in Portsmouth, Ohio; in Philadelphia in 1834, 1835 and 1842; and in Pittsburgh in 1839. These were not specifically Irish in origin, but many Irish-Americans participated in the violence, and these riots foreshadowed other riots to come during the Civil War period.

## CIVIL WAR AND AFTER

Know-Nothing agitation continued to keep immigrants and African-Americans on edge. When the Civil War came much ill will among Northern whites was caused by the government's delay in forming African-American troops. There was expressed a willingness to defend the Union, but not to fight for the African-Americans when they were not fighting for themselves. White workers feared the emancipated slaves would flood the North and that this would lower wages and cause unemployment. The experience of African-American strikebreakers being used made the situation even more volatile. In New York City, Irish-Catholic workers clashed with African-Americans over menial jobs. A combination of a longshoreman's strike, coupled with new draft regulations which the Irish believed were aimed at them, gave rise to the Draft Riots in New York in July of 1863. African-American homes and businesses were burned, along with the Colored Children's Orphanage, as well as the nativist New York Tribune. At least 120 people were killed. New York Irish-led police, backed by troops, withdrawn from Gettysburg after the battle, brought an end to the fighting in New York City, but hardly peace.

The post–Civil War period ushered in a time of rising American economic imperialism, rapidly swelling immigration, land expansion into the territories, Reconstruction governments in the former Confederate States, and party frictions in the other states. In all of these situations, the most perduring agitation for Irish-Americans and African-Americans was the Ku Klux Klan in its various forms, not only in the Reconstruction period, but to the present day. Both groups were targets for the Klan. The first Klan between 1866 and 1871 mainly concentrated on re-establishing white supremacy, not just in government but in all aspects of Southern life. That life was to be white, Anglo-Saxon, and Protestant. The political affiliation was mainly Democratic. The African-Americans, under the aegis of the Freedmen's Bureau and the Union League of America, were staunch supporters of the Republican Party, which in their point of view had freed them from slavery. Relatively few Irish-Americans were Republicans. The Irish swelled the ranks of the Democratic machines of the cities in the North and West. Politically, there would be very little cooperation between the two groups.

Migration patterns showed the African-Americans moved mainly from the country to the city, from the South to the North and to the West. The pattern of Irish migration was likewise to the cities of the Northern Atlantic seaboard, as well as to the Midwest and West. The two groups immediately were in competition for housing and jobs. Between 1851 to 1921, 3,750,000 Irish immigrants came to the United States. By 1900, Washington, Baltimore, Philadelphia and New York each had well over 50,000 African-American residents. Housing patterns were quickly established. Initially this was somewhat by chance and the circumstance of available space. Eventually, where growing affluence led to property buying instead of rental, it was by restrictive covenant and after 1912, by law. These established housing patterns created both an African-American and an Irish-American ghetto. They remained in effect until job opportunities gave increasing income that allowed some to move out of the slums to which they had been confined.

Developing unionization was one means of opening up job opportunities, but few of the developing unions accepted African-American members. One organization that did, the Knights of Labor, had approximately 60,000 African-American members by 1886. The Knights had many Irish-American members, but it reached its zenith in 1886 and was eventually replaced by the American Federation of Labor. While initially this organization opposed discrimination, by the turn of the century they had practically ignored this proviso. They did charter a limited number of locals of all African-American membership.

If there was little interrelationship with the groups, there were individual efforts that stand out. The O'Connor brothers, Michael and James, from County Cork, were outstanding in their work for the African-American community. Michael, the elder, born in 1810, was ordained in Rome in 1833. He spent time in the College of Propaganda in Rome and in Ireland before coming to the Diocese of Philadelphia. He became the first Bishop of Pittsburgh, then the first Bishop of Erie, and then back again as the third Bishop of Pittsburgh. While at Pittsburgh he started a chapel for African-Americans in 1844. While the chapel was short lived, it foreshadowed what he would do. O'Connor resigned the episcopacy and became a Jesuit in 1860. At Loyola College in Baltimore, he gathered funds to buy a former Unitarian church and make it into St. Francis Xavier Church for African-Americans. In 1863 this became the first African-American Catholic Church in America, dedicated to the Catholic community that had been in existence in Baltimore since 1793. Michael O'Connor was instrumental in bringing the Mill Hill Fathers from England in 1871 to take on the mission to African-Americans in the United States. While Mill Hill was English in origin, a large proportion of its members were Irish or of Irish descent. The American community, the Josephites, that separated in 1892–1893 to dedicate themselves to the African-American community, consisted of two Irish, one African-American and two men from Holland. As years went by, in the early stages of the community, there was a strong Irish-American influence.

James O'Connor was born in 1823, ordained in Rome in 1858, and eventually became first Bishop of Omaha. He was a spiritual director of Mother Katharine Drexel, the foundress of the Sisters of the Blessed Sacrament, who dedicate themselves to the African-American and Native American missions. In the early years of the Sisters of the Blessed Sacrament, many of the Sisters were Irish and Irish-American. Many of them still are of Irish descent.

Michael and James O'Connor were involved with the development in the United States of the Mercy Sisters, founded in Dublin in 1831 by Mother Catherine McAuley. Michael had brought Sister Xavier Warde to America in 1843 and continued to be interested in their work the remainder of his life. One of the Sisters of Mercy, Mother Austin Carroll, was born in Clonmel, Tipperary in 1835, entered the convent in Cork in 1853 and came to the United States in 1856. She was a versatile historian, writer, teacher, administrator, and interested in the spiritual and temporal welfare of all those around her. She came to New Orleans in 1868 and helped to found schools, homes of refuge and centers for medical attention for all people, regardless of color or race. Much of the work she financed from her writings. She authored twenty books, translated or compiled eighteen more books and had thirty-nine published articles. These writings supplied the funding for much of the work of her Sisters of Mercy. Her hunger for justice drove her to make education available for African-American children. When the Bishop of Natchez wrote her that he had no funds for an African-American school in Biloxi, she was able to supply the funds from her own resources and friends. Her Biloxi school was the only one available for African-Americans in that city until almost 1890, when the first public schools for Negroes were opened there. Bishops like John Quinlan and Jeremiah O'Sullivan of Mobile gave generous encouragement for African-American schools. New Orleans had problems in keeping African-American Catholic schools. One was opened in the Redemptorist directed area on September 14, 1874 and a week later an arsonist reduced it to ashes. The two following attempts lasted a bit longer before they also were put to the torch. Carroll did finally get a permanent school established in 1883 in St. Michael's Parish. Besides schools for African-Americans in New Orleans, Biloxi and Mobile, she established them also in Pensacola and Warrington, Florida; St. Martinville, Louisiana; Birmingham, Alabama and Gulfport, Mississippi. One source of encouragement came from Bishop James O'Connor, who served as an advisor in her literary work, as well as in problems with the hierarchy and as a general spiritual support.

Another individual to note was Mrs. Margaret Mary Healy Murphy. This fairly wealthy widow gave up her home in Corpus Christi, Texas, that it might serve as a hospital. In San Antonio she built a church and a school for African-Americans. She gathered teachers and eventually founded the Sisters of the Holy Spirit and Mary Immaculate in 1893. Many of the Sisters were and are Irish-Americans, and they still dedicate much of their time and efforts to the African-American community.

The Catholic Church through the Baltimore Second Plenary Council (1866) and the Third Plenary Council (1884) began to present a common rallying ground for involvement in race relations. One establishment was the Commission for Catholic Missions among the Colored People and the Indians. A yearly national collection in all American parishes resulted in extended funding to establish missions, schools and other training facilities. These were located particularly·in Southern and Western dioceses, supported by the contributions of Northern and Midwest Catholic parishes, heavily Irish in population. The development of a Congress of Colored Catholics, between 1889 and 1894, brought together African-American Catholic leaders and outstanding leaders of the hierarchy and clergy. Among these were Cardinal James Gibbons, Archbishop John Ireland, Bishop John Keane and many clerics of Irish origin. One of the supporters of the men and this movement of the African-American laity was John Boyle O'Reilly, editor of the Boston Pilot.

TWENTIETH CENTURY

The new century brought with it not an end to extensive lynchings (more than 2,500 in the final sixteen years of the century ending) but an increase in race riots and further lynchings. Georgia had race riots in 1904 and 1906. Brownsville, Texas in 1906 had a riot involving an African-American regiment of soldiers. Other riots occurred in Ohio in 1904, Indiana in 1906 and Spring-field, Illinois, in 1908. To counteract these attacks, a group of young African-Americans banded together to form the Niagara Movement. This, in turn, grew into the National Association for the Advancement of Colored People. In African-American Catholic circles, the clergy and laity were developing an organization, the Knights of Peter Claver, to provide "Catholic fraternalism, Christian charity and insurance protection for Negro Catholics." Four Josephites, of whom one was African-American, one who was named Father Samuel Kelly and three African-American laymen were the founders of the Knights in 1909. Another practical effort that became biracial was the Catholic Student Mission Crusade established in 1918. Its function was to interest students in assisting the missions. For at least forty years it was effective, especially in assisting African-American missions, and helped greatly to strengthen inter-racial relations, particularly in the high school, college and seminary age groups.

One further case where African-Americans and Irish Catholics were common targets occurred in Florida. The so-called "Guardians of Liberty" pushed through a state law in 1913 "forbidding whites to teach colored in colored schools." The law was not applied until Easter Monday, 1916, when three Sisters of St. Joseph of St. Augustine were arrested for teaching African-Americans in the Catholic school in St. Augustine. Bishop Michael Curley fought for the cause and the result was that the law was declared unconstitutional. Before Curley left to become Archbishop of Baltimore in 1921, he had six schools for African-Americans in his diocese.

To supplement the work of the Knights of Columbus in Army camps in the First World War, a group developed in the Maryland and Washington area to secure appointments of Catholic Negroes to the camps. This evolved into the Federated Colored Catholics in 1925. A split between eastern and western factions in 1932 eventually led Fr. John LaFarge, S.J., to combine the Catholic Laymen's Union, the Federated Colored Catholics, together with a group of Negro Catholic professionals and businessmen in Harlem, to form the Catholic Interracial Council of New York. This took place in 1934 under George Hunton as Director. Also evolving during this time period were Clergy Conferences on Negro Welfare. The parent Northeast Clergy Conference added the influence of the Richmond Clergy Conference, the Mobile Clergy Conference, and the Mid-West Clergy Conference. A broader based Catholic Conference of the South was formed in 1940 to apply Christian principles to eliminate segregation and gain broader democracy. All these activities made it possible for the Catholic Interracial Council to spread throughout the nation. By 1965, there were more than 110 Councils in operation. To coordinate these activities and develop a centralized fact-gathering and evaluating group, the National Catholic Conference for Interracial Justice was established in 1960. Leaders in this group, among others, were R. Sargent Shriver and Monsignor Daniel Cantwell. All this organizing created an atmosphere of interest and understanding on the part of the clergy and laity to raise up Christian principles and overcome the barriers of nationalism and sectional interests.

WORLD WAR II AND BEYOND

The American Bishops statements in 1943 and 1958 stressed the religious and moral character of the race question. Not all Catholics embraced these statements with their full support. Many Baltimore Catholics, including Irish Catholics, reacted strongly to Cardinal Lawrence Shehan's pastoral letter of March 1, 1963. He pointed out that Catholics had been all too slow in correcting their shortcomings in the field of racial justice, and therefore they had a special obligation to place themselves in the forefront of movements to remove the injustices and discriminations that still remained. Other bishops had spoken and acted. One was Archbishop Robert E. Lucy of San Antonio, where there were both Mexican and Negro minorities under his jurisdiction. In 1942, he stressed that democracy had no meaning where special privilege and injustice prevailed. In 1945 he attacked the Texas poll tax law. In 1951 he rebuked those who tolerated race prejudice. He backed his words by integrating all phases of his Archdiocese. Chicago had the input of Bishop Bernard J. Sheil and Cardinal Albert Meyer, who integrated parishes, schools, hospitals and social service. When Archbishop Patrick A. O'Boyle took over the Archdiocese of Washington in 1946, he began and carried through African-American participation in all phases of parochial and diocesan life. In his 1963 pastoral he stressed that no Catholic with a good conscience could deny the Negro the legitimate opportunity for a job, proper and adequate welfare assistance and full participation in public and private educational facilities. He spoke out also in Vatican II, asking for forthright and unequivocal condemnation of racism in all forms.

In the general push for Civil Rights that developed under the leadership of Reverend Martin Luther King, Jr., beginning in Montgomery, Alabama in 1955, there was a very mixed Catholic participation. The local Bishop Thomas J. Toolen forbid any priests or sisters in the diocese to participate in the demonstrations. He also instructed religious communities who worked in the diocese not to allow any of their members from outside the diocese to come within his territory to participate in demonstrations, and many bishops and superiors felt obligated to carry out his instructions. After the police cruelty on the Edmund Pettus Bridge in Selma, Alabama, Catholic support for the protesters grew significantly. The National Catholic Congress for Interracial Justice responded to Martin Luther King's invitation to participate in the Selma Marches. The Catholic Church participation made a significant visible declaration with the presence of priests in roman collars and nuns in their habits. The impetus carried over to extended Catholic activities in many dioceses, especially Milwaukee, Detroit, Pittsburgh, Baltimore, Omaha, San Francisco, Houston, New Orleans and Chicago. Jesuit Father Louis Twomey appealed to the Superior General in Rome to issue a decree ordering all Jesuits to get involved in civil rights. Another outstanding Jesuit civil rights activist was Joseph Fichter, who lectured and wrote on the needs for a multicultural church.

The federal government under Truman, Kennedy and Johnson, with the support of the heavily Irish Democrats, put into effect the new programs to extend civil rights broadly throughout the nation. There were no immediate solutions to the long-standing problems, but at least a significant start had been made, and hopefully, the process will continue to a just and happy solution. There is no one resolution that may legitimately be made in regard to Irish/African-American relations. One major element of change has been the fact that Irish-Americans, for all practical purposes, have ceased to be in the classification of a minority since the 1970s. Minority groups now are African-Americans, Latin Americans and Asian Americans. These now bear a common target designation. Between the African-American and the Irish-American there is a different type of competition as social, economic and political conditions improve. Cooperation is be-

coming more frequent, even if still on the basis of individuals rather than groups.

*See* Labor Movement; Civil War; Draft Riots

Patrick Corish, *The Irish Catholic Experience: A Historical Survey* (Wilmington, 1985).

Cyprian Davis, O.S.B., *The History of Black Catholics in the United States* (New York, 1990).

John Tracy Ellis, ed., *Documents in American Catholic History,* Vol. 1: 1493–1865; Vol. 2: 1866–1966 (Wilmington, 1987).

John Hope Franklin, *From Slavery to Freedom* (New York, 1963).

Madeline Hook Rice, *American Catholic Opinion in the Slavery Controversy* (New York, 1911).

John LaFarge, *No Postponement: U.S. Moral Leadership and the Problem of Racial Minorities* (New York, 1950).

Sister Mary Hermenia Muldrey, R.S.M., *Abounding In Mercy* (New Orleans, 1988).

Stephen J. Ochs, *Desegregating the Altar: The Josephites and the Struggle for Black Priests* (Baton Rouge, 1990).

PETER E. HOGAN, S.S.J.

## ETHNIC RELATIONS: THE GERMANS AND THE IRISH

Given the fact that Irish and German immigrants of the nineteenth century formed the two largest ethnic groups in America, surprisingly little has been written concerning their interrelations. As the size and complexity of this topic has seemingly deterred the composition of more ambitious works, this sketch must rely to a great extent on information extracted from the separate histories of these two peoples. Of course, neither group could ever isolate itself entirely from the other as much as they at times wanted to. Yet, the history of the Irish and the Germans in the United States very often appears as two separate narratives running concurrently, with only occasional cameo appearances in each other's story. The major exceptions to this pattern were the Irish and German Catholics in America who were bound together by a mutual faith. As they share a common and well-documented history within the larger history of their ethnic communities, this article will devote particular attention to Irish and German relations within the Catholic Church in America. Additionally, as information on the Irish in America may easily be gleaned from other articles in this volume, this essay will concern itself primarily with presenting information relevant to the German side of this interrelationship.

### COLONIAL PERIOD UNTIL 1820

The first large scale encounter between the Irish and the Germans in the American colonies occurred in Pennsylvania. Here, in 1683, German Mennonites started an influx of immigrants from the German states at the invitation of William Penn. Pennsylvania's religious tolerance made it an attractive destination for various groups of German Protestants seeking religious freedom and economic opportunities during the eighteenth century. From the first community at Germantown near Philadelphia, German-speaking immigrants spread west across the colony. By mid-eighteenth century, the German immigration into Pennsylvania had become so large that some voiced fears of it becoming a German colony. It is estimated that on the eve of the Revolution there were one hundred thousand German settlers in Pennsylvania. Once in America, many Germans travelled south from

Pennsylvania along the Appalachian mountain range into Maryland, Virginia and the Carolinas. German settlements were also established in the Mohawk Valley of New York during this period. Simultaneous to this migration of Germans was the movement of Scotch-Irish Presbyterians from Ulster into these same regions. As the German colonists tended to form their own distinct, rural settlements, their interaction with the Scotch-Irish was limited. However, when contact did occur, German and Irish relations were not cordial and numerous. "Dutch"-Irish riots were reported during elections in the colony.

Even in these early days of immigration to North America, while the Protestants in each group could largely ignore each other, Irish and German Catholics as were being forced to relate with one another whether they liked it or not. Although Catholics formed a small minority of the German immigrants in Pennsylvania, by the mid-eighteenth century there was a sufficient number of German Catholics in the colony as to require the ministrations of several German-speaking Jesuit priests. In fact, in the decades immediately surrounding the Revolution, the Catholic population in Pennsylvania was predominately of German origin. In 1788, the German-speaking Catholics of Philadelphia separated themselves from predominately Irish St. Mary's parish to establish Holy Trinity church as the first German national or ethnic parish in America. By doing so they were trying to retain their religious traditions and cultural identity against the perceived threat of forced accommodation to Anglo-American or Irish religious practices. To German Catholic sensibilities the Catholicism which had developed under British penal codes both in the British Isles and in America was a pale shadow of the richly devotional faith they practiced in the fatherland. German Catholics were accustomed to beautifully decorated churches with music at most Masses and public processions. By erecting their own parishes staffed with their own clergy, German Catholics wished to replicate their religious life as it existed in the old country.

Not long after its establishment, Holy Trinity parish was in open schism, rejecting the authority of Bishop John Carroll. This schism owed as much to disputes over trusteeism as it did to ethnicity. However, in a pattern that was quickly repeated in Baltimore, and continually throughout the nineteenth century, German Catholic clergy and laity began complaining to the authorities in Rome that the hierarchy in America was neglecting their needs, as the nineteenth century unfolded, and bishops in the United States came in increasing proportions from Irish stock. As a result, controversies, which appeared to the bishops to be clear matters of church governance, were frequently perceived by German Catholics as efforts to maintain Irish dominance.

## 1820 to 1865

Following the end of the Napoleonic wars, the Germans, like the Irish, began emigrating to America in ever-increasing numbers. By 1830 the tide of immigration became a continuous flood. It is estimated that during the nineteenth century five million German-speaking emigrants arrived in the United States, with their numbers being exceeded only by the Irish. The German immigrants differed in a number of important ways from the Irish. The German immigrants of the nineteenth century were much more diverse than their Irish counterparts. To begin with they were divided by religion, being roughly 60% Protestant and 40% Catholic. Since Germany remained divided into a number of states until 1870, the German immigrants did not share as

strong a sense of national identity as the Irish. The common bond for German immigrants within America was their language but even here differences of regional dialect divided German immigrant communities in ways that were imperceptible to outsiders. Coming from a broader range of occupations than the Irish immigrants, the German immigrants were also more divided by class distinctions.

Additionally, the German immigrant community lacked the political unity enjoyed by the Irish. The Germans in America were divided, broadly speaking, into the rather conservative Lutheran and Catholic "church" Germans and the liberal "Forty-eighters" and socialistic Turnerverein men. While these latter two groups were numerically small, they were influential in German-American intellectual circles and their vocal hostility to organized religion contributed to the self-segregation of both Lutheran and Catholic Germans. These frustrated German revolutionaries were also strongly anti-Irish for, as one wrote, "The Irish are our natural enemies because they are the truest guards of Popery." Reflecting their anti-Catholicism, the Forty-eighters had a prominent role in the riots in Cincinnati which accompanied the visit to that city in 1854 of the pope's emissary, Msgr. Cajetan Bedini. The "church" Germans, like the Irish, gravitated to the Democratic party because of its opposition to nativism and its reluctance in the nineteenth century to seek unwelcome social reform through government coercion, as exemplified by the temperance movement and Sabbath laws. The Forty-eighters and German evangelical Protestants favored the Republican party, the end of slavery, and women's suffrage. Commenting on the fierce antipathies that divided the Germans in America, one German newspaper editor, writing in the 1850s, remarked on their tendency to isolate themselves from one another and nourish their strongest passions, their love of beer and hatred for the Irish. While they would band together against the temperance movement and Sabbath laws that threatened their beer gardens, on other issues Germans in America had little motivation to act in unison and rarely did so.

The settlement patterns of the Germans also distinguished them from the Irish. The tenant farmers of Ireland largely abandoned agricultural life when they reached American cities. Most Germans also lived in American urban areas where the unskilled workers among them competed with the Irish for jobs. But fully a third of the Germans in America were farmers who settled in the rural communities of the Midwest. The interest in pursuing agriculture among so many of them resulted in the preponderance of German settlements being established within the triangle formed by the cities of Cincinnati, Milwaukee and St. Louis. By the mid-nineteenth century, more than half of all German-born Americans lived in the states of Ohio, Illinois, Wisconsin and Missouri. This area and its cities also had a significant Irish population, but the Irish did not dominate the immigrant community here as they did in the cities along the eastern seaboard.

The Irish and the Germans were also received differently in the Anglo-Saxon Protestant culture. While the Irish were scorned and feared by many for their poverty, perceived vices and their Catholicism, the Germans were the beneficiaries of a more positive stereotype in the eyes of the general public. The Germans were credited with many of the virtues that the Irish purportedly lacked. They were considered industrious, thrifty and honest, although some criticized their separatism and their tendency toward authoritarianism in their familial and social relationships. The cultural heritage of the Germans in the fields of science, art, music and literature contributed greatly to their positive image. Additionally, because the majority of Germans in America were Protestants, as an ethnic group the German-speaking immigrants were not as readily identified with "Romanism" as were the Irish. Still, German Catholics in America did not escape attack during the anti-Catholic nativist campaigns of the 1820s and 1850s. In fact, nativist hostility unwittingly drew Irish and German Catholics together in common defense.

But the hostility of outsiders was a poor basis on which to establish unity within the Catholic Church in America, and Irish and German tensions continued to grow along with the Catholic population. These tensions centered around the continued use of the German language within church-sponsored institutions. Bishop John Martin Henni, who was an influential leader of German Catholics in Ohio and Wisconsin through the middle decades of the century, is credited with coining the German Catholic rallying cry, "language saves faith." Under this motto, German Catholics in the Midwest founded scores of their own parishes and schools during the years leading up to the Civil War. As long as American bishops supported, or at least tolerated this separatist impulse, there were few conflicts. However, some English-speaking Catholics resented the Germans' insistence on the use of their language as an easy target for the nativists and an obstacle to Catholic acceptance in the United States. Additionally, as the Church in the United States could not meet the religious and educational needs of its swelling immigrant membership, there were inevitable squabbles over the allocation of personnel and resources to meet these demands. As early as 1836, the saintly John Neumann, later bishop of Philadelphia, expressed concern that Germans in New York would not receive due attention if Bishop John Dubois was succeeded there by an Irishman. As it happened, some German Catholics in New York did complain that Archbishop John Hughes favored his fellow Irishmen.

German Catholic resentment of Irish domination of the Church was fueled by the fact that half of the American bishops appointed in the nineteenth century were either Irish born or of Irish descent while the proportion that were of German lineage never reached even 20 percent. German Catholic resentments against their Irish brethren were further exacerbated before the Civil War when funds sent to the Church in America by Austrian and Bavarian mission aid societies, under the patronage of the Hapsburgs and King Ludwig, were used by the American bishops for non-German speaking communities. Another cause of tension between Irish and German Catholics was the strong support that the Irish clergy gave to the temperance movement. The different attitudes the two groups had toward the question of drink was epitomized by the struggle in the 1850s between Bishop Michael O'Connor of Pittsburgh and Boniface Wimmer, O.S.B., founder of the American Benedictines, over the latter's desire for the canonical independence of his abbey in Latrobe and its operation of a brewery. To the Irish bishop, mindful of the debilitative effect that alcohol had on so many of the Irish poor and the American stereotype of the dipsomaniacal Irishmen, a brewery under Church auspices was a cause of scandal. For the Germans, beer was simply a part of their culture which they were not going to shed out of fear for anti-Catholic bigotry. In a victory for culture and beer, Wimmer succeeded in getting papal approval for the operation of his brewery. In making his appeal to Rome, Wimmer had enlisted the support of King Ludwig of Bavaria. This was not the first time German Catholics in

America had sought European intervention for their cause. In 1846, Ludwig's ambassador to the Holy See and personal friend of Pius IX, Graf von Spaur, had complained in Rome about the lack of interest shown by the Irish bishops in America for the needs of German Catholics. At Ludwig's behest, he also pressed for the appointment of more German-speaking bishops in America and would later take credit for the appointment of John Neumann as Bishop of Philadelphia. The Irish-American bishops not only resented the Germans' propensity to go over their heads, but they were also angered that foreign princes were exercising their influence in the internal affairs of the Church in the United States. They were further incensed that they were being depicted in Rome as negligent of their flocks and biased against the Germans. These fissures, which remained largely below the surface in the years prior to the Civil War, would widen and become public in the 1870s and 1880s.

## 1865 TO 1900

The historian Kathleen Neils Conzen has perceptively noted a cartoon published in 1883 in the German-American humor magazine *Puck* as indicative of German-American perceptions of themselves and American society in the latter half of the nineteenth century. The illustration, suggestive of the Last Supper scene, celebrates the bicentennial of German immigration to America and proclaims the German-American, sitting in the center of the table, to be the "Healthiest Lad Among Uncle Sam's Adopted Children." Eleven other ethnic groups, depicted in stereotypical fashion, are arrayed around him at the feast with a simian featured Irishman in the place customarily reserved for Judas. Similar depictions of the Irish as apelike and treacherous are frequently found in the work of the German-American cartoonist Thomas Nast.

Without a great deal more research it is difficult to say how much these mean caricatures reflected the general attitude of German-Americans toward the Irish. However, historians of the Germans in America have consistently noted their confidence in the superiority of German culture above all others. This chauvinism increased after the Civil War in which they had proven their loyalty by their contributions to the Union cause. The unification of Germany, its victory in the Franco-Prussian War, and its expanding empire provided German-Americans, even the most liberal, with further indications of the superiority of German culture. At a time when many subscribed to the notion of "manifest destiny" and racial supremacy as a result of evolution, German-Americans saw themselves on an equal footing with the "Wasps" in America and co-creators of its culture and institutions. Concomitant with this sense of superiority was a disdain for other ethnic groups. The cartoons mentioned above suggest that at least some German-Americans had a special loathing for the Irish who were an equally strong immigrant group and who, in the last decades of the century, were now pushing their way into political power. Yet, despite what may have been an attitude of condescension toward the Irish, the Germans in America, for the reasons stated previously, had learned to live with their immigrant rivals by keeping them at a safe distance. But this was becoming increasingly more difficult to do within the Catholic Church.

The decades following the Civil War were years of phenomenal growth for the Catholic Church in the United States as European immigration transformed both the nation and the Church. The Catholic population more than doubled from 6,259,000 in

1880 to 16,363,000 in 1910 while the country's overall population went from approximately 76 million to 92 million. Population growth of this magnitude posed enormous challenges for the Church. This growth also intensified debate among the leadership of the American Church over the question of "Americanization." It was commonly recognized by Catholic leaders that if the immigrants were to survive in this country they must be assimilated into the social life of their new home. However, there was sharp disagreement, along both ideological and ethnic lines, as to how far and how fast this process of Americanization should go. The more conservative view was that since the United States was essentially a Protestant country, driven by a materialistic economic system and pervaded by bigotry against Catholics and immigrants, an extensive and rapid Americanization of the immigrants posed a real threat to their Catholic faith while bringing few rewards in return for their assimilation. This view was characterized by an inherent distrust of contemporary society in general and the secularizing trends in American society in particular. German Catholics generally subscribed to this view, but it was also shared by conservative Catholics among other ethnic groups, including the Irish.

The liberal view was based on a much more positive assessment of American society. In fact, enthusiastic about the potential of the growing nation, the leading adherents of this view, who came to be known as the "Americanists," were ardent nationalists who believed that the United States had a God-given mission to convert the world to the American understanding of liberty and justice. All the leading Americanists, Archbishop John Ireland of St. Paul, Bishop John Keane, first rector of the Catholic University of America, Msgr. Denis O'Connell, rector of the North American College in Rome, and Cardinal James Gibbons, archbishop of Baltimore and *de facto* head of the American hierarchy, were either born in Ireland or of Irish stock. From their perspective, not only should the immigrants be assimilated as rapidly as possible, but also the Church should take an active role in promoting their Americanization. The Americanization of the Catholic immigrants would both upgrade their social status and eliminate the stigma of being foreign. The Americanists were anxious to change the foreign image of the Church because they believed that this image was an obstacle to the conversion of America to Catholicism, which they envisioned. They believed that the Holy Spirit was at work in the founding of the American republic and that the compatibility between American civic ideals and Catholic anthropology and social teaching made the country ripe for conversion.

Contrary to the guarded outlook of the German Catholics and other conservatives who saw the "American experiment" as the offspring of Enlightenment rationalism with its hostility to revealed religion, the liberal Americanists believed that contemporary American society presented a wonderful opportunity for the Church to prosper. The secular character of the nation's public life, with its separation of church and state, meant that the Catholic Church could preach its message without competing against the privileges of a state Protestant church like the Church of England, and without the burden of the anticlericalism of civil authorities that existed in Germany, France and Italy. For the Americanists, America was not just a tolerable place for Catholicism to survive, America was God's gift to the Church and a Catholic America would be His gift to the world.

Throughout the late 1880s and the early 1890s the German Catholics and the Irish Americanists engaged in increasingly bitter struggles as to which view would dominate the life of the Church in America. These were not struggles over theory, but over the application of these conflicting views on specific issues that related to ethnicity and Americanization. From 1878 to 1880 the two factions were in a contest to see which group would have its candidate selected as the new archbishop of Milwaukee. The prize finally fell to the German-born Michael Heiss, much to the disappointment of non-German clergy of Wisconsin. In 1884, eighty-two mostly German priests of the Archdiocese of St. Louis petitioned Rome for canonical recognition of their German-language missions so that they and their congregations would not have to continue their subjugation to the pastors of the local, English-speaking parishes. The petition was never seriously addressed. About this same time the authorities in Rome informed the American bishops that they were receiving numerous letters and petitions from German Catholics requesting the Holy See protect their interests from the aggression of English-speaking and Irish Catholics. As several important clerics in Rome were supporting these claims, Bishops Richard Gilmour and John Moore responded with a letter of their own. The bishops rejoined that it was the Germans who were the aggressors in pushing the German language in the parishes and schools where there were significant numbers of non-Germans. They also contended that, in several Midwestern dioceses, priests of Irish origin were effectively barred for consideration as bishops even though half the local population was Irish. And on it went. In 1886, Father Peter Abbelen, theological adviser to Archbishop Heiss, took a petition to Rome on behalf of the German priests of Cincinnati, Milwaukee and St. Louis, repeating the requests of the 1884 petition and asking also that there should be proportional representation of Germans in the selection of pastors. Abbelen's memorial depicted the situation as one of the Germans being oppressed by the Irish. The following year, at the urging of most of the American bishops, the Roman authorities rejected most of the items in Abbelen's petition. That same year, 1887, three-hundred German priests gathered in Chicago and formed their own union, the German American Priests Society or "Priesterverein." In 1890, there was another contest over the archbishopric of Milwaukee and again, the German candidate eventually was appointed. In 1891, the German emigrant aid society, the St. Raphael Society led by Peter Paul Cahensly, petitioned Pope Leo XIII on behalf of non-English speaking immigrants in America with the Lucerne Memorial. This petition asserted that some ten million Catholics had been lost to the faith in America due primarily to the lack of opportunities for instruction and worship in their own languages. This petition added to the previous requests by asking for proportional representation in the appointment of American bishops. The Lucerne Memorial was roundly denounced by all but the German bishops in America as dangerous foreign meddling in the affairs of the Church in the United States. Cahensly was falsely portrayed by his Americanist opponents as a tool of the Prussian imperialists and after skillfully manipulating the press, they succeeded in having him denounced on the floor of the U.S. Senate. The demonizing of Cahensly by his Americanist opponents embittered the German Catholics as they regarded him as a benevolent father to the German Catholic emigrant.

Other issues besides clerical authority and "language parishes" were brought into the fight between the Germans and the Irish over the direction of the Church. These included mandatory attendance at parochial schools or acceptance of the public school system, the temperance movement, the administration of the Catholic University of America and Catholic involvement in secret societies and the labor movement. On all of these issues the German Catholic bishops, clergy and press took a conservative position while most of the Irish Catholic bishops, clergy and press, led by the Americanists, took the opposite view. Matters finally came to a head with the papal condemnation of Americanism in 1899, which essentially endorsed the German and conservative Catholic position in regard to the Church's adaptation to American society. However, by this time, the heavy German immigration of the 1880s had slowed to a trickle; and with the inevitable Americanization of German emigrants and their descendants, the conflicts with the Irish over language use in the Church, and its corollaries, was effectively ended.

## THE TWENTIETH CENTURY

The outbreak of World War I brought about a unique period of cooperation between many of the Irish and Germans in America. Inflamed by the Easter Rebellion of 1916, which had been aided by Germany, Irish-Americans with nationalist sympathies joined German-Americans in their fierce hostility towards Great Britain. Large numbers of both groups left the Democratic party in 1916 to vote for the Republican Charles Evans Hughes and continued neutrality. There are reports of joint celebrations of St. Patrick's Day and Bismarck's birthday during the period of American neutrality. However, when hostilities were declared on Germany, both Irish- and German-Americans rallied to the cause. Their doing so is indicative of how truly American both groups had become, and whatever differences remained between them were based more on communal memories than on contemporary issues.

Perhaps reflecting the positive turn in Irish and German relations is the fact that more intermarriage occurred between the Irish and the Germans than between any other immigrant groups. Well-known Irish-Americans such as the anti-communist crusader, Senator Joseph R. McCarthy, the priest-activist, Father Daniel Berrigan, S.J., presidential candidate Senator Eugene McCarthy, and the Archbishop of New York, John Cardinal O'Connor, are among those with one parent of Irish and one of German descent.

Colman J. Barry, O.S.B., *The Catholic Church and German Americans* (Milwaukee, 1953).

Kathleen Neils Conzen, "German-Americans and the Invention of Ethnicity," in *America and the Germans: An Assessment of a Three-Hundred Year History*, eds., Frank Trommler and Joseph McVeigh, Vol. I, *Immigration, Language and Ethnicity* (Philadelphia, 1985).

Philip Gleason, *The Conservative Reformers: German-American Catholics and the Social Order* (Notre Dame, 1968).

La Vern J. Ripley, *The German-Americans* (Boston, 1976, 1983).

RORY T. CONLEY

## ETHNIC RELATIONS:
## THE ITALIANS AND THE IRISH

For years Italian-American and Irish-American relationships have intrigued both general observers and social scientists who have found the interaction one of an amalgam alternating between violence and conflict during early stages, to one of toleration and acceptance and even a blending in later stages. Forming two of the largest Catholic ethnic groups in the United States,

they offer concrete examples of subgroups that have had significant impact upon each other even while also dealing with the demands and challenges presented by the mainstream culture. To examine this in a meaningful manner, it would be useful to compare Italian-Irish relationships in the areas of immigration, residential choices, work, education, religion, marriage and politics.

Centuries of poverty, misrule, and persecution at the hands of English overlords found Ireland entering the nineteenth century a backward, suppressed, and forlorn nation. Although some Irish immigration can be traced to the colonial period, it accelerated significantly in the 1820s and reached massive proportions during the 1840s in the wake of the Irish potato famine. Three continuous years of disease to the ubiquitous, all-purpose food was a scourge that forced millions of Irish to emigrate for survival. As immigrants to the United States they became the first mass subgroup of Catholic immigrants to challenge America's assimilative capabilities.

Discrimination against their "foreign" Catholic religion inveighed heavily against these newcomers as they sought to improve their lot in the new land. Seared by devastating experiences of working the soil in the old country, possessing little capital with which to buy land in America, and working consciously to create a degree of cohesion among the Catholic Irish resulted in settlement primarily in the eastern part of the United States. Ongoing immigration from the Emerald Isle augmented Irish residential concentrations so that by the turn of the nineteenth century they formed major groups in the large cities of the east such as Boston, Philadelphia, and New York.

Italian immigration to this country became of significant proportion two to three generations later. Commencing in the 1880s against a background of poverty, class discrimination, ignorance, and exploitation at the hands of the upper class and the church hierarchy, Italians formed the largest single body that comprised the "New Immigration" from southern and eastern Europe. In time they would constitute the second largest number of all immigrants entering this nation.

While there are obvious similarities in the background of the two groups, notably with regard to deprivation, residential choices, and religion, there were important differences. Notwithstanding a heritage of the Gaelic language, the Irish were adept in the English language which was a virtual prerequisite to progress in this country. Arrival in the United States generations earlier than Italians provided the Irish with more time to assimilate. Because of centuries of religious persecution in their Irish homeland, the Catholic religion was tantamount to political loyalty. To be Irish and Catholic was axiomatic. The Irish established the Catholic Church as a powerful institution in this nation. In time, an amalgam of the old and the new became evident in urban Irish neighborhoods as parishes became the centers of community life. Interaction between parish priests and parish members was close as family and community activities revolved around the church calendar. Thus the church acted as a supporting arm of Irish family life and Irish families strongly upheld the church.

Because they arrived at a time of an accelerating industrial revolution, and because of their poverty, Italians were even more inclined than the Irish to settle in congested cities, frequently moving into areas previously inhabited by the Irish or in close proximity, thereby provoking turf wars. In the prevailing pecking order of the late nineteenth century, the more Americanized Irish occupied a higher socioeconomic position. Not surprisingly they perceived Italians as intruders who threatened their homogeneity and from whom they sought to protect themselves by attempting to maintain residential segregation. For example, regarding the large influx of Italians into their neighborhood as a threat, the Irish of New York's Greenwich Village moved into the western part of the neighborhood where they were separated by a rough dividing line, as each ethnic community developed its own institutions: political clubs, social/athletic clubs and churches. Endogamous marriages characterized marital relations into the early decades of the twentieth century. Notwithstanding this background, change was inevitable because in fact the lines between the two were never hard and fast. An investigation into marriage patterns in Middletown, Connecticut, is instructive. Whereas 100 percent of Italian marriages were endogamous in 1900, the following decades witnessed a weakening of endogamy. Ninety percent of Middletown's Italians married within their ethnic group in 1920, with the figure dropping to 50 percent in 1940, and even more to 21.8 percent in 1970.

Studies of the interrelationship between the Irish and Italians indicate that each suffered in the estimation of the other. In Philadelphia, for example, Italians looked upon the local Irish as unsympathetic, uncongenial and pigheaded, while the Irish reproved Italians as ignorant, dirty and superstitious. Accordingly, while the local Catholic press covered church activities of both groups, it also seemed to contain more items derogatory to Italian newcomers, undoubtedly due to the greater role played by writers of Irish ancestry.

The interrelation between Italians and Irish in the Catholic Church in America merits special consideration. As both were followers of the same religious creed, there would seem to be the basis for sharing in common a fundamental socio/cultural characteristic. This, however, was not to be the case. As earlier arrivals who had achieved a measure of success and assimilation, Irish-Americans saw little benefit in being associated with Italians who were regarded with substantial hostility and suspicion not only by themselves, but also by native Americans. There also existed significant differences in religious mentality that were cultural and historical in nature. Furthermore, by the time of the coming of the Italians, Irish-Americans dominated the American Catholic Church, especially in its hierarchy. Sociological literature stresses some points of difference between the ethnic groups in the areas of church attendance, mistrust of people, and gender roles. While regular attendance at Sunday Mass was a distinctive feature of Irish-American life, it was noticeably less customary among Italian immigrants. The latter's infrequency was attributable to differences in cultural attitudes—while Italy was overwhelmingly Catholic, Italian attendance at Sunday Mass seemed to give lie to this attachment. Due to nationalistic and political developments peculiar to nineteenth-century Italy, there existed a strong current of anti-clericalism that some Italian immigrants transplanted to these shores. This attitude was in marked contrast to Ireland where clergymen were highly respected and were acknowledged as unquestioned leaders of the community. There was considerable difference between the two ethnic groups regarding financial support for the church. In the absence of state support for the Catholic Church in Ireland, and because of a heritage of discrimination, Irish lay people took it upon themselves to see to it that their churches received adequate monetary maintenance. The situation was quite different in Italy where state support for churches was the rule and people were not accustomed to providing financial support for the church from

their own private resources. This attitude was regarded by native American and Irish Catholics as illustrative of the weakness of Italian adherence to Catholicism. Add to this background the Italian immigrants' preoccupation with earning a living, even when it conflicted with religious duties, and their difficulties with understanding the English language, and one can begin to comprehend a seemingly feeble affiliation to church doctrine, discipline, and practice.

Italian predilection for elaborate *festas* and saint celebrations, while deemed essential marks of their religious devotion to Italians, were regarded as poor substitutes for genuine piety as expressed in regular Mass attendance and church support. For many Italian immigrants, worship in American Catholic churches seemed to be so foreign that it was almost that of another religion. Much of the strangeness in religious worship was alleviated with the coming of an Italian clergy and establishment of national/ethnic parishes which incorporated their familiar language, liturgy and saint devotions. In this regard, while some Irish-American members of the hierarchy discouraged the concept of national parishes, others were more receptive. Much has been written about the evolution of Catholicism among Italian-Americans to a point where by the second half of the twentieth century their practices have become Hibernicized. Thus, although some differences between the religious practices of Irish-Americans and Italian-Americans are still discernible, they are not as significant as formerly. Furthermore, whereas previously there was a dearth of Italian-American members in the American Catholic hierarchy, such no longer is the case in the second half of the twentieth century. Indeed, Italian-Americans such as Cardinal Joseph Bernardin and Bishop Anthony M. Pilla have served as presidents of the American Catholic bishops.

The relationship of Irish-Americans and Italian-Americans in the realm of politics is another important dimension for consideration. The prominence of people of Irish descent in American politics is legendary not only because of their command of the English language and their earlier entry into American society but also because of their attraction to political life. Students of ethnic politics have observed that their natural gregariousness, their urban concentration, and their realization that politics was a road to influence and power, rendered them uniquely qualified to enter and quickly emerge as powerful political forces. In a word, they seemed to be born to the profession. This impression is expressed by students of the subject such as Edward M. Levine, who described Irish-American involvement in Chicago as follows:

> The more I became aware of the Irish, the more curious it seemed that so many of them were in urban government and that they found politics so congenial. Politics appeared to suit them as a comfortable and familiar way of life. And quite unlike any of the other immigrant Americans, the Irish were and still are counted in urban politics in the North and East far beyond their proportion of the population. They are also the only ethnic group which has been identified with politics, as the term "Irish politician" signifies."

Throughout the nineteenth century, Irish-American political life was encompassed within the Democratic party. This was especially true in local politics where the saloon and the fire department served as influential neighborhood fixtures. Control over these institutions evolved into a politicization that was abetted by virtual exclusion from the Republican party and a heartily receptive Democratic party. The symbiotic relationship between Irish Catholics and the Democratic party was regarded as an unalterable conjunction. Paul O'Dwyer, spirited New York liberal Democrat, was famous for a humorous story that symbolized the tie. Thus the tenement clubhouse boss was scandalized at the news that O'Brien had turned Republican. "That's a damned lie," the boss thundered. "I saw O'Brien at Mass last Sunday." Although this association continued well into the twentieth century, a gradual shift away from the early ties has taken place and, by the end of century, to be Irish, Catholic and Democrat was no longer axiomatic.

Italian immigrants, by contrast, were destined to traverse a much slower ascendancy along the political ladder. Their later arrival, ignorance of the English language, limited funds, unfamiliarity with American political practices, and seeming torpidity regarding naturalization, constituted part of the explanation for this. Not to be overlooked was the fact that since most Italian immigrants of the late nineteenth and early twentieth centuries did not expect to remain as permanent residents of the United States, they did not take out citizenship. Gradually as more and more Italian immigrants became naturalized Americans and obtained the franchise, they began to participate in the American political enterprise. The political aspirations of Italian-Americans had an additional obstacle to overcome, namely the Irish who lived in and politically dominated the immigrant neighborhoods that would also be their places of settlement. The Irish preceded them and Irish-American political bosses controlled local politics. When in some instances the Irish did not seem amenable to the sharing of power, this had the effect of driving Italian-Americans to the Republican party in protest. This was clearly the case in 1894 when a local Chicago Italian-American openly encouraged his fellow ethnics to look to the Republican party for true democratic leadership.

Accordingly, only when they were accommodated by the Irish political leadership could Italian-Americans begin their political upward mobility, and only after some experience at lower and middle echelon levels in the political hierarchy, could they strive for real power and leadership. This background was evident in numerous cities. Thus the significance of Carmine DeSapio's elevation as Tammany Hall leader in 1949 was important not only because it was the first time an Italian-American had achieved this powerful post within the New York Democratic party, but also because it marked the end of a decades-long control by Irish-Americans. Likewise, Thomas Mennino's election as mayor of Boston in 1993 proved a turning point to an extended Irish-American political dominance in that city.

Politics and work were unmistakably linked. Influence in local political affairs opened the doors to the civil service field, thereby providing many Irish-Americans with opportunities for steady and secure jobs within the police and fire departments, the court systems, and teaching in the public schools. It was not unusual for Italian-Americans to reside in neighborhoods that were patrolled by Irish policemen and for their children to have teachers of Irish descent. It would take decades before Italian-Americans entered these civil service occupations in significant numbers. The Frank Hague years (1917–1949) illustrates the attachment the local Jersey City, New Jersey, Irish had for their mayor who was one of their own. He was a hero to the working-class ethnic group who did not begrudge him his wealth, appearance or attitude because he demonstrated an unabashed preference for them in municipal jobs. Even after dramatic population shifts had propelled Italian-Americans to the top numerically, Hague refused

to give them proper political recognition, consenting only to a few token posts. Although some local Italian-Americans tried to challenge Hague's political stranglehold, they were usually met with retribution. It was only after his retirement in 1949 that they succeeded. By the 1980s and 1990s Italian-American names in cities like Jersey City and New York began to replace Irish names as police sergeants, chiefs of detectives, precinct captains, superior officers of fire brigades and even presidents of police and fire department unions.

Irish and Italian paths crossed in private industry as well. Middletown, Connecticut, was a case in point. During the latter part of the 19th century, Irish immigrants, although encountering some incidents of prejudice, nevertheless, were welcome as laborers in the city's development of manufacturing, mills, and foundries. A significant minority in Middletown, by the early 20th century, the Irish felt the pressure of a burgeoning Sicilian/Italian population that would compete with them for jobs and housing. The newcomer Italians met with animosity and prejudice from old stock Americans and the Irish element. Just as the earlier Irish immigrants had to contend with unsympathetic Protestant Scotch-Irish foremen in the 19th century Pennsylvania mines, Italian laborers frequently worked under Irish foremen in construction jobs such as building roads and subways.

Sometimes they clashed as in an 1870 sanguinary incident in Mamaroneck, Westchester County, New York, which revealed how deep indeed was the competition over jobs between Irish-Americans and Italian-Americans. The local sheriff reported that whereas Irish laborers employed in grading and laying out a park domineered Italians in an earlier period, in time the Italian element grew so large that the competition spilled over into serious fights between hundreds from each ethnic group. Much the same pattern attended incidents involving Brooklyn and New York longshoremen of the late 19th and early 20th century. The dominant ethnic group in this line of employment, by the early twentieth century, the Irish longshoremen saw the tremendous growth of the Italian populace not only as residences in adjoining neighborhoods, but also as competitors with them for jobs on the docks. Whereas the Irish represented 95% of the New York longshoremen in 1880, by 1912, the Italian element ranked a close second with indications that they would soon surpass them. When the predominantly Irish-controlled International Longshoremen's Association refused to accommodate the Italians, the latter formed their own locals. In October 1919, the ethnic cleavage manifested itself in a violent clash in which shots were fired and men beaten up as 1,000 Brooklyn Italian longshoremen attacked 200 Irish. In time, especially after a period of enforced interaction in housing and public schools and in churches, and most particularly after an increase in Irish-Italian marriages, friction subsided.

In retrospect, the period of early interaction between Irish- and Italian-Americans was characterized by a degree of animosity, friction, and even violence. It would be incorrect, however, to leave the impression that this was the totality of the experience. More than a few Irish clergy, for example, were supportive of the need to try to understand and accommodate Italian religious customs. Archbishop Michael Corrigan and Cardinal John Farley of New York, for example, agreed to the creation of numerous Italian national parishes and gave from their personal funds to these parishes. Annie Leary was known as a generous and long life donor to New York's Italian parish of Our Lady of Pompeii and to the Cabrini Missionaries. Likewise, notwithstanding the invisible borders between the groups in neighborhoods, marriages between the ethnic groups took place slowly among first generations, but increasing with each generation so that it is no longer unusual to learn of marriages between Irish-Americans and Italian-Americans. Although more research would be needed to bear this out, the impression is that marriages between these ethnic groups probably constitutes the largest number of exogamous unions for both Irish- and Italian-Americans. Television personality Regis Philbin, writer/journalist Anna Quindlen and movie actor John Travolta are among the more well-known Irish-Italian personalities.

The sharp differences with regard to religious customs, evident in the previous phase of contact, have also undergone significant evolution. Indeed, Louis Gesualdi's study of religious acculturation indicates that in the late twentieth century among higher socioeconomic Italian-Americans, religious practices conform to Irish-American Catholics. Although this is not the case with blue collar and less educated Italian-Americans, whose church attendance continues to be relatively low and where churchgoing is more predominantly a woman's trait, the expectation is that these differences will continue to decrease with the attainment of increased education and higher socioeconomic levels.

By the end of the twentieth century most Americans of Irish and Italian descent live in American suburbs that no longer are characterized by sharp delineations between ethnic neighborhoods as in the inner cities. Along with other ethnic groups, Irish and Italian neighbors live in close proximity to each other, children attend the same schools, worship in the same churches, participate in similar religious and civic organization activities, and function in integrated political movements. Thus within the span of two or three generations, the early era of hostility has been replaced with accommodation, cooperation and association.

Mary E. Brown, *Churches, Communities and Children: Italian Immigrants in the Archdiocese of New York 1880–1945* (New York: Center for Migration Studies, 1995).

Lawrence Costello and Stanley Feldstein, *The Ordeal of Assimilation* (Garden City, N.Y., 1974).

Francis X. Femminella, ed., *Italians and Irish in America* (New York: American Italian Historical Association, 1985).

Louis Gesualdi, "The Religious Acculturation of the Italian American Catholics: Cultural and Socio-Economic Factors," *The Italian American Review*, Vol. 6/1 (Spring/Summer 1997): 100–124.

Salvatore J. LaGumina, "Paul Vaccarelli: The Lighting Change Artist of Organized Labor," *Italian Americana*, Vol. XIV/1 (Winter 1996): 24–45.

Edward M. Levine, *The Irish and Irish Politicians* (Notre Dame, Ind., 1966).

Humbert Nelli, *The Italians of Chicago: 1880–1930* (New York, 1970).

Jill S. Quadagno, "The Italian American Family," *Ethnic Families in America* (New York, 1881): 61–85.

SALVATORE J. LAGUMINA

## ETHNIC RELATIONS: THE JEWS AND THE IRISH

Irish-Jewish relations in the United States date primarily from the period of large-scale East European Jewish immigration beginning in the 1880s. From that point on, contact in politics, neighborhoods, and occupations generally have determined the parameters of that relationship. Generally, this intergroup contact has followed the usual American pattern of occasional minor hostility or temporary cooperation based on the needs and aspirations of each group at that moment. However, during the late 1930s and early 1940s in New York and Boston, that pattern faded during a period of intense Irish-Jewish conflict, which illustrated some of the most serious animosities evident among the European immigrant groups. But eventually, those tensions abated as the situation changed. Conflict, like cooperation, was always the result of the conditions of a particular time and place.

### EARLY YEARS

The initial contact was both positive and negative. Jews saw the Irish as an American group, speaking English and achieving political power. As an example of Jewish perceptions of the Irish as assimilated, and truly American, many Jewish boxers in New York fought under Irish names (Rischin, 263). Irish control of the city's politics also indicated an acceptance in America that Jews wished to emulate, but it also eventually frustrated and angered the city's Jews. For the Irish, the Jews represented another competing group, with strange cultural traditions, who could challenge the Irish in a variety of situations. At first, the challenge was to the very neighborhoods in which the Irish lived in cities such as New York and Boston (Ryan, 137). The incident that illustrates the intergroup tensions already brewing by 1902 is the riot that accompanied the large funeral procession of Rabbi Jacob Joseph as it went through New York's lower east side Irish areas. As the funeral crowd passed into Irish territory, Irish factory workers from a nearby building began pelting the crowd with various objects. The Jews counterattacked and rushed the building. The riot that ensued was the flash point of rising tensions due to ethnic succession in these neighborhoods as Jews replaced the Irish. Other Jewish funeral gatherings had been attacked earlier and both groups were at the breaking point when the riot took place. Adding to Jewish frustrations was the one-sided policy of the largely Irish police force which also proceeded to attack the Joseph funeral mourners. The police involvement in the riot against the Jews related not only to ethnic favoritism but to the burgeoning political competition. In this case the Jews during the 1901 mayoral campaign had rejected Tammany control due to issues of police corruption, and the police clearly resented the Jewish position (Higham, 227–228; Rischin, 91).

Although politics could be a divisive force, it also worked to pull these groups together in mutual support of the Democratic party's social goals. In Boston, Irish and Jews often worked together in the Democratic party and in support of James Michael Curley's mayoral campaigns beginning in 1913. But Jews rarely were chosen for high-level positions. These positions stayed under Irish control. Ward boss Martin Lomasney and other Irish leaders carefully manipulated the Jewish vote. Symbolic gestures were plentiful; positions of power were not. Jews also worked within the Democratic machine in Chicago but were not awarded important positions until the Republican party under William Hale "Big Bill" Thompson began competing for this group's support in the World War I period (Erie, 101–104, 127–128). New York's much larger Jewish community presented similar issues for the Democratic party's Irish leaders. Jewish voting in New York was also not solidly Democratic; the Socialists and Republicans continued to attract considerable Jewish support. Irish Democratic leaders needed the Jewish vote to keep their party in power. Yet, there was a reluctance to share power. To win and keep Jewish support meant not only appealing to Jewish social concerns but providing political positions to this group.

the history of the Irish and the Poles in America was shaped not by these similarities, but by their competition in the fields of employment, politics, and religious affairs.

## EMPLOYMENT

Upon their arrival in America, most of the Irish laborers were forced to take the lowest paying unskilled jobs available and to settle for the least expensive accommodations in the overcrowded urban slums. By the time the Poles arrived in large numbers after the Civil War, the Irish had been in America en masse for two generations, many beginning during that time the slow, difficult climb up the socioeconomic ladder. With the arrival of the Poles, the remaining Irish came under increasing socioeconomic pressure as the newcomers began to compete for low paying jobs and cheap urban tenements. Soon, Irish lips began to utter complaints about low-paid Polish workers taking their jobs in the mines and manufacturing industries. In postbellum America, Irish miners complained bitterly about competition from Polish and other Slavic workers, charging that the "durrty furruners," as they called them, took "bread from the lips of decent, law-abiding Americans." Although both the Irish and the Poles were early supporters of the labor movement, they seldom joined forces in that arena until after the First World War. Instead, in the nineteenth century frequent violence occurred, including struggles between groups of workers as well as clashes between Irish police and Polish workers in the coal fields, the textile mills, and other places of employment for unskilled laborers. The Haymarket Riot and the Lattimer Massacre were but two examples of the more deadly of these confrontations between Slavic workers and Irish authorities.

Despite these historical conflicts, Andrew Greeley found that the Irish and the Poles took from their working-class backgrounds remarkably similar traits. On a personality scale designed to determine "fatalism," for example, the Irish rank highest in "fatalism" and Slavs second. The Irish rank second of the groups examined in terms of emphasis on pay, benefits, and hours, while the Slavs are third. Similarly, in terms of "self-reliance" the Irish are also second and the Slavs third. Through thrift and economic solidarity, both the Irish and the Poles were able to accumulate capital, but whereas the Irish sought to accumulate family "nest eggs," the Poles pursued their cultural ideal of home ownership, eventually ranking among the most successful ethnic groups in attaining that status.

## POLITICS

Irish immigrants enjoyed two major advantages over the Poles in America—they spoke English and they arrived in large numbers a half-century earlier. These advantages can clearly be seen in the political development of the two groups. By the time the Poles arrived in large numbers, the Irish had largely negotiated the political barriers to participation, forming ethnic voting blocs that captured political control of many of the urban areas into which the newly arriving Poles flocked. Through support for Tammany Hall in New York City, and similar Democratic political machines in Boston, Chicago and other northeastern cities, the Irish gained local and regional political power, and with it opportunities for public employment and other benefits of the spoils system of government.

As the newest arrivals, the Poles entered an urban life controlled largely by Irish politicians and their allies. Initially, many reacted by joining the rival Republican party, but over time Poles began to seek alliance with the Irish city bosses. In return for their votes, political bosses provided spoils to local Polish leaders. Although the Poles were clearly the junior partners in the relationship, they tended to be one of the more insular immigrant groups and were generally content with the relationship as long as they felt a sense of control over their own ethnic neighborhoods.

Although urban ethnic politics provided short-term gains and access to at least the illusion of power, Poles were generally unsuccessful in obtaining real control over major cities. In Chicago, which boasted the largest Polish population outside Warsaw, most Poles supported the Democratic Party but were in the peculiar position, as Edward Kantowicz explained, "of possessing the largest new immigrant group in Chicago yet falling short of a numerical majority in the city." By stressing group solidarity, the Poles in Chicago were looked upon as a threat by other groups who, when combined, possessed greater voting power. Successful politicians in ethnically divided Chicago were able to build bridges to other hyphenated groups, Kantowicz argues, while the Poles "used the hyphen as a bludgeon rather than a bridge and Polonia's capital remained in the stage of hyphenated politics far too long." The result was that in most urban areas Poles, despite their sometimes significant numbers, only rarely attained political ascendancy. This failure led to considerable frustration on the part of the more politically aware within the Polish community, as seen in this complaint published in 1922 in *Dziennik Chicagoski* [Chicago Daily News] which blamed Polonia's lack of political success on the Irish: "Whoever is familiar with our city politics knows only too well how the Irishmen, the most notorious political tricksters in the entire country since the earliest times, manipulate continually and invariably the divergent ambitions of private groups or individuals within the non-Irish nationalities against one another in order to promote thereby their own selfish interest."

A similar pattern emerged in most of the other major northeastern metropolitan areas as Poles were successful in electing their own at the local ward level, but generally unsuccessful in electing mayors or other city-wide officers. In Milwaukee, Donald Pienkos found that the limited success of Polish Americans in local politics was due to a combination of the dominance of German Americans and internal conflicts within Polonia. An exception to the general portrait of Polish urban political limitations can be seen in Buffalo where the local Polish community maintained a strong political presence, electing mayors, state representatives, judges, and other city and county-wide officials. The difference between Buffalo Polonia's general success in obtaining political influence, and the relative failure of Polonia in other large cities, rests, according to Walter Borowiec, with the Buffalo Poles' propensity for voting for their own regardless of party affiliation. Indeed, his studies indicate that "of all the ethnic groups, Poles rank first in supporting their own."

On the national level, during the interwar period the support of Poles for the Democratic Party began to crystallize in 1928 when Alfred E. Smith, a Catholic, proved very popular as the Democratic standard bearer. Before Smith, the "Polish vote" might have been very real at the local level, but there was little evidence that it was solidified at the national level. Smith's background, coupled with his advocacy of policies favorable to the working class and his opposition to Prohibition, won a clear and significant majority of Polish votes. In a sense, Smith's candidacy presaged the urban-ethnic-working class–Black coalition that later provided the basis for Franklin D. Roosevelt's ascendancy. In Chicago, for example, Kantowicz found that 79.95% of the Polish vote went to Smith. By 1960, only Poles and African-Americans were more solidly Democratic than the Irish.

## RELIGIOUS AFFAIRS

When the Irish arrived in America it did not take the staunch Roman Catholics long to denounce control of the American ecclesiastical hierarchy by French clergy. Within a short period of time, by force of numbers and ethnic solidarity, they succeeded in gaining such complete control of the American church that Bishop John Lancaster Spaulding of Peoria, in his *The Religious Mission of the Irish People,* published in 1880, could claim that "The general truth is that the Irish Catholics are the most important element in the Church of this country. . . . Were it not for Ireland Catholicism would today be feeble and non-progressive." At the Third Plenary Council in 1884, Bishop Bernard J. McQuaid of Rochester, New York, claimed boldly of his Irish ancestors that "All the other nationalities of Europe can kneel at their feet and imbibe salutary and profitable lessons." The Poles who arrived en masse during the same decade thought otherwise.

Poland became a Christian nation in 966 when Mieszko I accepted religious conversion in the vain hope of arresting Prussian invasions. From that time on, despite a history of national religious toleration, Catholicism became increasingly linked with nationalism and patriotism. The successful defense of the monastery at Częstochowa by a few hundred Poles against thousands of invading Swedes in 1655 was looked upon as a miracle of sufficient import to make the icon of the Black Madonna, housed in the monastery, into a national shrine. Throughout the centuries, the Poles portrayed themselves as the eastern bulwark of Christendom, protecting it from Mongols, Tatars, Turks, and other non-believers. The victory of a multinational Christian army under King Jan III Sobieski over the Ottoman Empire at Vienna in 1683 solidified this notion in the national psyche. Later, when Poland was erased from the face of Europe through partition, national customs, heritage, and patriotism were kept alive largely through illicit classes, social activities, and patriotic meetings held in local parish churches. Thus, by the time of the mass migration of Poles in the years after the American Civil War, Catholic Poles felt their church was a vital part of national patriotism.

In America, the early Polish settlers usually attended Irish and German parishes until they were sufficient in number to form their own. In Poland there was a tradition of lay involvement in the founding of parishes. The *ius patronatus* was a long-established "right of patronage" under which a member of the gentry whose ancestors endowed a parish might nominate a pastor. Although this right did not directly involve parishioners, it was well-known among Polish immigrants and established a precedent of lay involvement in parish affairs. As a result, most of the early Polish parishes in America were established by lay persons rather than by religious authorities. The normal scenario was for a lay committee to collect funds, purchase land, construct a building, and petition the local bishop for authorization to form a parish. A priest usually entered the picture somewhere after the first step. Thus, most Polish parishes began as lay initiatives and continued to have lay involvement in the administration of parish affairs.

The Polish parish in America was both a reflection of Polish religious conviction and pride in their group accomplishment. Andrzej Brozæek suggests that individual contributions to the local parish "became as important a source of prestige as land holdings had been in the Old Country." By 1908 per capita church support among Poles in Chicago was $3.51, or $17.55 for a family of five. This was about one and one-half week's wages for an unskilled worker, or about two months' rent in a tenement. The rate of Polish contributions was among the highest of the post–Civil War immigrant groups.

But there was a significant difference between the Catholic Church in America and that in Poland. The hierarchy in America was controlled by largely Irish bishops rather than co-nationalists as in Poland. By 1900, Irish prelates held all the seats of ecclesiastical power in the United States and a majority of the priests were Irish, with the result that the hierarchy became almost a closed ethnic caste and local parish celebrations focused on St. Patrick's Day and other Irish national and religious manifestations. Thus, during the immigrant generation Polish Catholics generally received unsympathetic, if not outrightly hostile treatment from the American Catholic hierarchy and local priests who displayed little understanding of the new arrivals, choosing instead to ignore them, or in some instances make them the focal point for derision and discrimination. It was not long before the Poles began to derisively refer to the American hierarchy as "One, Holy, *Irish,* and Apostolic Church."

Yet, as Polish immigration increased, the Catholic hierarchy quickly came to see that the Poles formed a large and growing percentage of Catholics in America, and as such some effort to retain their religious loyalty was in order. One policy adopted by the Church was the creation of "national parishes." Under this principle parishes were organized not along geographic lines, but on the basis of the "particular character" of the people—in this case usually language. By 1912 there were almost 1,600 "official" national parishes, including 346 German, 336 Polish and 214 Italian. From the perspective of the Catholic hierarchy the movement to national parishes was designed specifically to preserve the faith among immigrant communities. The Polish immigrants, however, did not see it that way.

Most of the Poles' complaints involved their desire for democracy and equality in parish and Church governance. Since most parishes began through lay initiative, the Poles, relying for justification on both the Polish precedent of lay involvement and their view of American democracy, sought some control over parish finances, the right of parish councils to hold title to property purchased with the parishioners' money, and increased authority for the parish councils. Additionally, Polish priests, often frustrated by lack of career mobility in the national parishes, voiced their own complaints over inequities in assignments and promotions. These grievances crystallized around the demand for appointment of Polish bishops. Not all of the Polish clergy supported this, but few if any opposed it.

In 1896 a Polish Catholic Congress convened in Buffalo under the leadership of Rev. Jan Pitass to discuss concerns about the American Church. A second Congress in Buffalo in 1901 convened to develop a strategy to promote the appointment a Polish bishop to minister to the immigrants in America. Acutely aware of their inferior status within the Church, their slogan was not *representacja* [representation] but *rownouprawnienie* [equality]. Rev. Wacław Kruszka, a strong voice for Polish rights within the Church, made an emotional appeal for "unity in diversity," a view of cultural pluralism within the American Catholic Church that was clearly ahead of its times. Largely through Kruszka's influence, the conference decided to send letters of appeal to the Apostolic Delegate, Archbishop Satolli, to Cardinal Gibbons, and to the American bishops asking for the creation of Polish-speaking auxiliary bishops in twelve dioceses whose population numbered between 25% and 50% Polish Americans.

When their letters were ignored, the Poles sent delegates to plead their case directly with the Vatican. As a result, Rev. Paul Rhode was appointed Auxiliary Bishop of Chicago in 1908, the first Polish American to attain this status. Despite Rhode's elevation, the Poles remained dissatisfied. They did not view the position of Auxiliary Bishop, with its limited influence and lack of real authority, as in any way fulfilling their desire for real equality.

While most Poles attempted to work within the Roman Catholic Church to secure equality, by the mid-1890s a serious movement toward the establishment of "independent" parishes had already begun. The complaints of these local parishioners were articulated in *Kuryer Polski* whose editor stated emphatically: "The founders and benefactors of Polish churches in America are not priests nor American bishops. The founders and benefactors of Polish churches in America are the Polish parishioners. Polish parishioners give their hard-earned pennies for the founding and support of the churches. . . . But the priests and bishops are only the servants of the church. Therefore the bishops and priests should honor the founders and benefactors of the church, not tyrannize them. In the old country, the founders and benefactors had a voice not only in the running of church affairs, but in the selection of the pastor. Here in America, the founders and benefactors of the Polish churches, that is, the Polish people, should certainly have the same rights and privileges."

Irish authorities within the Roman Catholic hierarchy responded quickly and dramatically against the *niezależnicy* [independents], equating "lay rights" with heresy and labeling them pagans, heathens, atheists, revolutionaries, lawbreakers, and worse. In a concerted effort to crush growing dissent, Irish bishops used discipline and excommunication to enforce obedience from parishioners and priests alike. Gradually, the independent movement crystallized around Rev. Francis Hodur, a strongly nationalistic priest in Scranton, Pennsylvania. Serious trouble began when Hodur demanded that church property in his parish be held by the laity, and that the laity have a voice in the appointment of pastors—classic demands of those advocating "trusteeism." When Hodur refused to relent he was excommunicated, but even this drastic action failed to sway him. In 1897 he founded the newspaper *Straż* [The Guard] to disseminate his perspective, a move quickly countered by the Roman Catholic publication of *Przegląd* [The Review]. As the bitter public debate continued, Hodur became the acknowledged leader of several independent parishes in central Pennsylvania.

As support for Hodur increased he moved to consolidate support by organizing the independent parishes into the Polish National Catholic Church. The new church's constitution, adopted in 1904, provided the following rationale for separatism: "Should we Poles renounce today our rights and our national character given to us by God? Should we disinherit our souls, and deprive ourselves of independence, in order that we might please the Pope and the Irish bishops? No, never! If our nation has any mission in humanity's reach for higher goals, then it must also have its own distinct, Polish faith, its National Church, as all creative peoples of the world have. Our Polish National Church in America is the first step in the work of forming an independent life in emigration, and, God grant, for the future of our entire people."

Under Hodur's leadership, PNCC membership rose steadily to between 60,000 and 85,000 in more than fifty parishes by 1926. By the time of Hodur's death in 1953 it numbered more than 130,000 members, but this was less than 5% of the membership of organized Polonia. Although numerically small, the PNCC movement provided an outlet for Polish religious nationalism and eventually influenced the Roman Catholic Church to adopt a more conciliatory attitude toward its ethnic minorities in America.

Despite Hodur's schismatic movement, and further inroads by Poles working within the American hierarchy, by 1970 although only 17% of Roman Catholics in America were Irish, they still accounted for 35% of the priests and held 50% of bishoprics. At the same time, with approximately the same number of Catholics—about 17%—Poles accounted for only 3% of the cardinals, archbishops, and bishops in the American hierarchy. This discrepancy accounts in large measure for a legacy of distrust among Polish Catholics that, despite their continued religious faith, remains to this day.

John J. Bukowczyk, *And My Children Did Not Know Me: A History of the Polish-Americans* (Bloomington and Indianapolis, 1986).

Frank Mocha, ed., *Poles in America: Bicentennial Essays* (Stevens Point, WI, 1978).

James S. Pula, *Polish Americans: An Ethnic Community* (New York, 1995).

JAMES S. PULA

# EUROPEAN IRISH EXILES AND AMERICA

During the late seventeenth and throughout the eighteenth centuries a flow of Irish people dealt with defeat at home with emigration to continental Europe. This movement was considerably smaller than that to North America but of serious consequence in the history of Ireland. It was made up initially of the leaders and soldiers of defeated armies and, only to a limited extent, of their families. But also included were priests and students seeking a form of education prescribed at home, together with the sons of Catholic gentry following military careers likewise barred to them in Ireland, as well as a flow of army recruits. Displaced merchants from Irish towns moved to ports in France and Spain.

This was an emigration of an upper social stratum of Catholic Irish society and of young talent against whom doors were closed at home, but it is not the whole story. Three institutions provided a loose spine to this scattered migration. One was a series of long-lasting Irish regiments in the service of France and Spain which provided military careers and an opportunity for further military and political advancement. Individual soldiers could be found elsewhere right across Europe but not in continuing Irish establishments. A second component was the ring of Irish Catholic colleges in university cities and other places in the Low Countries, France, Spain and beyond. And a third element could be seen in a network of merchants and shippers in ports such as Nantes and Bordeaux, Cadiz and Lisbon. Spain had a long history of providing a refuge and an opportunity for Irish exiles from the time of the wars at the end of the sixteenth century. This had included employment in the New World, and in the eighteenth century Irish officials could be found in Florida, Louisiana and Mexico which at the time included parts of what is now the southwest of the United States. Perhaps the most notable, if not the most popular, of these was Alexander O'Reilly, born in County Meath in 1722 and who was sent in 1769 to settle the government of New Orleans and surrounding Louisiana territory. He punished dissidents severely and drew up a series of laws and regulations for the territory. He brought with him to Louisiana a number of Irish officers, one of whom was Hugh O'Connor, born in Dublin in 1734 and, according to a certificate from the Archbishop of Dublin, a descendant of Rory O'Connor, a celebrated medieval Irish king. Hugh O'Connor spent time on the frontiers of Louisiana confronting the Apache inhabitants.

Two of the traditionally Irish regiments of the Spanish army have also been traced in North America in the latter half of the eighteenth century. In 1768, a battalion of the Ultonia (Ulster) regiment under the command of the Kildare-born Diego Aylmer was sent to Mexico for a few years. The officers of this unit were predominantly Irish, and Aylmer himself was the nephew of the once celebrated Jacobite exile and correspondent, Charles Wogan. The other unit was a battalion of the regiment of Hibernia which formed part of the Spanish force which successfully captured Pensacola in Florida from the British in 1779–81 during the American War of Independence. Arturo O'Neill, who commanded the battalion, was the son of Henry O'Neill of County Mayo, and he went on to become commandant of that region of Florida and afterwards captain-general of Yucatan, a lieutenant general and, before he died in 1814, Marques del Norte.

There were other Spanish-Irish officers active in the region such as the Irish-born Charles Howard who was for a time acting governor of West Florida or Enrique White of the Hibernia regiment who became governor of East Florida in 1796. And although he was of a slightly later generation, Juan O Donoju, born in Seville in 1762, deserves mention as the sixtieth and last Viceroy of New Spain. With the Mexicans seriously in revolt, he was sent over in 1821 and quickly decided to sign a treaty which envisaged the virtual independence of Mexico. An apparently infuriated Spanish government recalled him, but O Donoju became ill and died in Mexico City.

It was not only from Spain that Irish military figures found their way to North America. The French had long made settlements in what is now eastern Canada and had penetrated into the present Ohio and Illinois territory, and down along the Missouri-Mississippi to Louisiana. No significant number of Irish seemed to have settled in areas still under the control of the French, but some individuals can be traced and the American War of Independence led to some curious encounters.

One controversial figure of the mid-century is remembered as the commandant of the Illinois territory and the man who built the stone fort where later the city of St. Louis grew up. He was Barthelemy McCarty-McTeigue, the French-born son of an Irish officer. He had served for a time in the Franco-Irish regiment of Clare, and came to America in his twenties. After the French defeat in the 1760s he retired to Louisiana.

By the time of the American War of Independence, the movement of Irish people to continental Europe had greatly diminished, and in Ireland itself new political situations and priorities had developed. Yet exiles in France remained active and contributed to Britain's difficulties when the American war got under way. Count Patrick Wall from Carlow, for example, a general in the French army, began presenting memoirs and plans in 1778 for the invasion of Ireland. The fear of French invasion of Ireland kept some British naval forces away from the North American war. Of course, the French did not threaten only because of Irish prompting, but the prompting took place.

To America itself went a battalion of Dillon's Franco-Irish regiment and a section of Walsh's. These took part in the siege of Savannah and in various episodes in the West Indies. Various individuals served with Rochambeau's army further north, and altogether about a hundred Irish or Franco-Irish officers are known to have taken part in the war. None served in the highest ranks with the exception of Thomas Conway, born in Kerry in 1733, who was made a major-general in the American continental army but who became involved in a controversy concerning the role of George Washington. This led to his resignation and return to France, from where he later moved to become governor of French territories in the Indies. While it is interesting to speculate about how the Americans viewed these officers, perhaps the more surprising point is the curious role played in history by many of them after the American war ended. At least ten of them became generals, most of them serving the new regime emerging in the French revolution but with fatal results for four of these. Arthur Dillion and James O'Moran, both senior generals, were guillotined in 1794. Likewise Thomas Ward, a Dublin-born brigadier-general; while another Dubliner, Theobald Dillon, was earlier killed by his own troops near Lille in 1792.

Three others also stayed with the new regime. Isidore Lynch became a major-general but refused to fight against the Catholic insurgents in the Vendee, while Patrick O'Keefe from Kilkenny went on to retire as a general of brigade. The third, Charles Jennings, who used the name Kilmaine in France, was probably the best known of the Franco-Irish veterans of the American war. He held various military commands, and was Bonnaparte's cavalry commander in the Italian campaign of 1796. He took a close interest in Irish affairs and in the fate of his friend, Wolfe Tone, but he died at the age of 48 in 1799.

Two of the best known Irish figures in the colonies at the end of the seventeenth century had French or Jacobite links. Charles Carroll who came from Ireland to Maryland in the 1680s as attorney general may not have spent time on the continent but certainly did his legal studies in London. He was the son of Daniel Carroll of Aughurty in what is now County Offaly, and it is known that two Carrolls of Aughurty were attained for High Treason in 1691 at the time of the Jacobite war. Elsewhere Daniel Carroll is described as of Litterluna and that both a grandson and a son of his were killed at the Boyne. Various Carrolls went off to the continent, and one can only note that the Daniel Carroll who became a Knight of Santiago in Spain in 1706 was the son of a John and the grandson of a Daniel Carroll.

An older contemporary of Charles Carroll certainly spent considerable time in France and North Africa. Thomas Dongan from Kildare was colonel of an Irish regiment in France in the 1670s, and was later made first Governor of New York and district by Charles II. Ironically his activities there upset the French and this contributed to his being recalled from the post. He had shown interest in bringing over Irish people who had lost estates in the troubles at home, but this does not seem to have had any large–scale result.

One cause of confusion was that an important proportion of the Irish who went to the continental countries did not have Gaelic family names. They were the descendants of the Normans, English and others who had settled in Ireland from medieval times. By 1700 some of these families had been in Ireland for 500 years, and names such as Butler, FitzGerald, Barnewall or Plunkett would be recognized as distinctively Irish in Ireland, but less so in places of migration such as North America. Unless the families retained a Catholic religious affiliation, it was easy for other people to mistake their background and country of origin.

The Meade families (even if there is some discussion about the origin of the name) are a case in point. George Meade of Philadelphia, active in Revolutionary politics, was well known as a Catholic and it is said that his father was a merchant from Limerick. But one genealogical account of the widely known Meade family of Virginia, also prominent in the Revolution, tells of the founder of the family, Andrew Meade, arriving from Ireland in the 1680s and acquiring much land—and that his mother was a Sarsfield of Kilmallock, a noted Jacobite family, and that he had close family relations among Irish officers in France. The Dongans and the Dillons came to America as established officers, even as aristocrats, but the largest number of Irish who had gone to France or Spain were soldiers of lower rank or relatively poor scholars. It is unlikely that a large number of these re-routed themselves across the Atlantic, but some did. John Mullanphy who came over in 1792 and established himself as a businessman and philanthropist in St. Louis kept up French connections and is said himself to have lived in France and served in the Irish Brigade. Owen O'Sullivan was born in France about 1692, the son of an officer in the exiled Jacobite army, but later went to Ireland from where he emigrated with his wife to New England. He worked as a teacher of languages in Maine, and among his sons were a later major–general in the Revolutionary army and a governor of Massachusetts.

Owen O'Sullivan was undoubtedly an exception rather than a rule. Yet one might expect that some of the many Irish and other colleges on the European continent would at least appear in the New World; and some certainly did. The jurist Aedanus Burke (1743–1802) is reported as having studied at St. Omer before coming to Virginia. James O'Hara (1752–1819) who was Quarter-Master of the United States Army in 1792 is likewise said to have been a student at St. Sulpice in Paris. And a French education must have been part of the background of at least some of the Irish schoolmasters known to have been active in the colonies.

The typical products of the Irish colleges were Catholic priests, but virtually all the colonies had legal restrictions on Catholic practice and there were thought to be only 25,000 practicing Catholics in the United States in 1785 and according to the later Archbishop John Carroll, there were only 30 priests, mainly Anglo-American Jesuits. Yet there must have been many more Catholics or near descendants of Catholics, and some Irish priests with continental training were to be found particularly in the last quarter of the century.

The names of a number of Irish priests who came as chaplains with the French armies and fleet are recorded. One was Fr. Michael Glennon (1739–45) who served both as a chaplain and interpreter and later made a claim back in France for property stolen at Williamsburg in 1782. In Philadelphia, an Augustinian who had studied at Toulouse, Fr Mathew Carr (1750–1820) started a church to which George Washington contributed funds; he is reported to have been a chaplain with Rochambeau's force. And two bishops may be mentioned. In the 1790s, Edmund Burke, a product of the Irish College in Paris, was active in areas of Michigan and Ohio, then under Canadian jurisdiction, and was later a bishop in Nova Scotia, and although he worked outside the United States, James O'Donnell (1737–1811), a Franciscan, can be noted not least because he was ordained from the Irish College at Prague and was the first English-speaking Catholic bishop in Canada.

There remains the other element in the Irish continental migration—the scattered community of merchants in French and Spanish ports and a considerable presence in the West Indies. The links with North America cannot be claimed to have been extensive, nor indeed much investigated. Two particular cases, however, can be cited which convey something of the nature of the whole European connection. Stephen Moylan (1737–1811) who held various prominent posts under Washington in the American Continental army, if not without ups and downs, came from a Cork merchant family with commercial links overseas including Lisbon where Stephen spent a period of time. Later in Philadelphia he developed shipping links with the West Indies and Lisbon; and his brother James became the U.S. agent at the French port of L'Orient.

He had another brother, however, who was not a merchant but a bishop. This Francis Moylan made a lifelong friend of one Henry Edgeworth from their student days at the Irish College in Toulouse. Francis Moylan became Bishop of Cork and the Abbe Edgeworth was the priest who attended Louis XVI of France at his execution and was later chaplain to the exiled royal family. Thus unrolled the complicated links of this scattered family.

The other case relates to a letter written in 1745 by a member of the Irish merchant family of Colgan in Tenerife in the Canary Islands. It was about the attempt of the young Prince Charles Edward Stuart to overthrow the regime of King George in England and Scotland. The letter was to one Bernard Murphy "in America." Over thirty years later, a noted American colonel had been captured by the British and taken across the ocean. The ship called at Madeira, and Ethan Allen wrote later in his diary: "Irish generosity was again excited, for a gentleman of that nation sent his clerk on board to know of me if I would accept a sea store from him, particularly of wine." It is stretching coincidence to imagine that the benefactor was linked to the Colgan family of Tenerife. But the old merchant community was still in business.

Taken together, it cannot be said that the connections were extensive between the soldiers, merchants and colleges of the Irish migration in Europe and the lives of their fellow countrymen who had emigrated to North America. The two phenomena were different in character and scale. Yet it is fair to argue that an awareness of both linkages adds to the understanding of each one in turn.

Louis Cullen, "The Irish Diaspora of the Seventeenth and Eighteenth Centuries," in Nicholas Canny, *Europeans on the Move* (Oxford, 1994).
D. N. Doyle, *Ireland, Irishmen and Revolutionary America* (Dublin, 1981).
Kerby A. Miller, *Emigrants and Exiles* (New York, 1985).
*The Irish Sword,* 1954, et seq. (Dublin).

FRANK D'ARCY

one and all as "Tessie," she named it for her father. It burned in the 1906 earthquake, but was rebuilt and remains one of the city's landmarks to this day.

John A. Barnes, *Irish-American Landmarks* (Detroit, 1995).

JOHN A. BARNES

## FAIR, JAMES (1831–1894)

Mining entrepreneur, U.S. senator. A native of Belfast, James Fair was 12 when his parents immigrated to the United States and settled in Geneva, Illinois. Unlike many Irish immigrants of that period, young James received a solid education, first in the local public schools and later in Chicago. Records show him to have been exceptionally well-versed in mathematics and chemistry, two disciplines that would later stand him in good stead in the world of business.

Like much of the rest of the country, Fair headed west in 1849 upon the news of gold in California. He attained enough success to buy a farm in Petaluma four years after his arrival, but he found that he missed mining and soon returned to it. Completely self-taught, he soon achieved recognition as one of the best mining engineers in the state.

News of the Comstock Lode silver strike in 1860 brought Fair and many others across the mountain passes into Nevada. His mining knowledge was in demand and he soon found himself manager of the Ophir silver mine.

It was around 1864 that he met John Mackay. It was Fair's keen executive eye that noticed William Sharon's Bank of California empire was overextended and that the Hale and Norcross mine that it controlled was vulnerable to takeover. In partnership with James Flood and William O'Brien they won control of the Hale and Norcross in 1867.

It was also Fair who convinced the other three that the Virginia Consolidated mine, which many thought played out, still contained valuable ore that could be extracted with the right technology. He proved to be correct, and the Virginia Consolidated became the source of the fabulous wealth of the so-called "Irish Four."

Fair was a natural choice for public office and in 1880 he won election from Nevada to his first and only term in the U.S. Senate. He was a well-regarded senator, serving on several important committees. His floor speeches were characteristically informed, thorough and pertinent.

One of his great business achievements came in the late 1880s when he rescued the Nevada Bank, which he had helped found but which became insolvent after his departure. In what has been described as one of the great feats of financing of the 19th century, he singlehandedly reestablished the bank's credit on a sound footing. Fair's relatively early death in 1894 was attributed by many to his forceful desire to continue working long hours.

His monument, even though he had nothing to do with its construction, is the magnificent Fairmont Hotel crowning San Francisco's Nob Hill. Built by his daughter Theresa, known to

## FAMINE, THE GREAT

The Great Irish Famine of 1845–52 was a pivotal event in the history of modern Ireland. Its reverberations also influenced the development of Britain, America, Australia and the numerous other countries to where famine victims or their descendants emigrated.

As a crop failure, the Irish Famine was unprecedented in the history of modern Europe. By the 1840s famine had disappeared from western Europe with few exceptions. It had receded from England and Wales by the seventeenth century and Scotland by the eighteenth century. The Irish Famine, therefore, occurred late within British and European development. Moreover, it took place within the jurisdiction of the most industrially and commercially advanced economy in the world. As a result of the Act of Union of 1800, Ireland had been joined politically with Britain to form the United Kingdom. Consequently, Ireland lost its own parliament in Dublin and, throughout the Famine years, was governed directly from London.

The impact of the Famine also made it unique. Within the space of five years Ireland lost twenty-five percent of its population, through death or emigration. Although more people died in other famines (China, 1877–78; Ukraine, 1932–33; Bengal, 1940–43) in relation to the total population, more lives were lost during the Irish Famine than in any other modern subsistence crisis. The heavy losses were to some extent due to the longevity of the crisis. But even when good harvests returned to Ireland after 1851, the indicators of distress remained high. Moreover, the Irish population continued to decrease due to sustained emigration, later marriages and higher rates of celibacy. By 1900 it had fallen to four-and-a-half million, compared with its pre-Famine level of eight-and-a-half million. This fact led some Irish nationalists to lament that, by the end of the nineteenth century, there were more Irish-born people living in America than in Ireland. For nationalists also, the Famine deepened the existing political divisions between Britain and Ireland by demonstrating that the United Kingdom was a union in name only.

### Pre-Famine Ireland

The immediate cause of the crisis was a mysterious blight or disease, *phytophthora infestans,* which destroyed the potato crop in varying degrees over a period of seven consecutive years. Although the same blight had destroyed the potato crop in America and Europe, it was only in Ireland that the population had such a high dependence on this single foodstuff. Potatoes were not indigenous to Ireland. They had been introduced in the sixteenth century and were initially consumed as a vegetable for the gentry. By the eighteenth century, potatoes had become the staple diet of labourers and small farmers. As the Irish population grew after 1750, so did dependence on the potato. Potato growth was suited to Ireland's damp, moderate climate and acidic soils. They were easy to prepare and required no processing. Potatoes eaten in their skins were highly nutritious and, when taken with buttermilk, they provided a balanced diet. From the total crop yield,

Woman begging
at hard-hit
Clonakilty
in Cork

The tardiness in establishing the works was due to a combination of local landlord inertia and central governmental bureaucracy, which included the hiring of twelve thousand relief officials. In County Tyrone, for example, where only two percent of the population was employed on the public works, it took almost two months before works could be commenced and an initial grant issued. The projects undertaken were deliberately intended to be of a useless nature, resulting in their description as "roads that led nowhere and walls that surrounded nothing." More seriously, their utility as a mechanism for saving lives was defective which was evident from the fact that in the six-month period after October 1846, disease and mortality soared. Although official records were not kept, an unofficial estimate was that during this period, 400,000 people lost their lives through disease or starvation.

The response of the Whig government and its supporters was motivated by a desire to bring about changes in Ireland. The reorganisation of Irish society remained a constant aspiration of politicians and administrators in London. This ambition had been evident even under Peel who had chosen Indian corn as a substitute foodstuff in the hope that it would permanently replace potatoes in the Irish diet. As the Famine progressed, the political response was driven increasingly by reasons that were rooted in social engineering and short-term political and budgetary considerations, rather than in the alleviation of suffering and the maintenance of lives. The approach of a general election in 1847 also meant that the minority Whig government was cau-

A Famine funeral

tious about alienating its middle-class support base. At the same time, the Whig Party wanted to lose the reputation of being the party of high expenditure, especially as Britain was entering a deep industrial recession. Increasingly after 1846, policy formulation was shaped by a mixture of political economy, Christian providentialism (which decreed that the blight was a "punishment" by God on the improvident Irish people) and political opportunism. Christian providentialism, in particular, was a powerful tool in providing an interpretative framework for policies which placed social change above saving lives. The fact that the majority of the Irish poor were Catholic provided an added justification for a number of Protestant politicians to suggest that a period of atonement was necessary for Ireland. In the wake of the first appearance of blight, the Home Secretary, Sir James Graham, remarked, "It is awful to observe how the Almighty humbles the pride of nations. The sword, the pestilence and famine are armies of his displeasure." This viewpoint was most evident amongst an influential "moralist" grouping within the Whig Cabinet, which included the Chancellor of the Exchequer, Charles Wood, and Lord Grey. They were supported enthusiastically by Charles Trevelyan in the Treasury, who played a key role throughout the Famine. Trevelyan claimed that the food shortages were "a judgement of God on an indolent and unself-reliant people." Within Westminster and Whitehall, changes which had seemed so desirable before the Famine, finally, with God's support, appeared to be achievable.

### "BLACK '47"

The year 1847 is remembered as "the Famine Year" or "Black '47" due to the high levels of distress, disease, evictions, emigration and mortality. One aspect of the Whig government's relief policy which proved to be controversial was its decision not to intervene in the import and export of food but to leave it to market forces. One of the consequences of this measure was that food and a wide variety of other goods continued to leave Ireland following the second failure of the potato crop. In 1847 alone, over 4,000 Irish ships were used to carry cargoes from Ireland to Britain. Some of these vessels were bringing food from ports situated in the poorest parts of Ireland, such as Skibbereen in west Cork, Kilrush in County Clare, and Killala and Westport in County Mayo. Apart from corn, other foodstuffs exported included butter, bacon, eggs, fish, whiskey, livestock and even potatoes and Indian corn. The quantities involved were large. In the first week of 1847, 4,455 firkins (barrels with nine gallons capacity) of butter were exported from Ireland to the port of Liverpool and this quantity increased to 4,691 during the following week. In the first nine months of 1847, 183,392 gallons of whiskey (made from grain) were exported to Liverpool. The export of cattle from Ireland to Britain increased by one-third in 1847 compared with the previous year.

In comparison to the brisk export trade, the import of food during the winter of 1846–47 proved to be slow and erratic. Despite the government's apparent commitment to free trade, food coming into Ireland was hampered by the Navigation Acts, which stipulated that all imported merchandise had to be carried on vessels registered in Britain. More significantly, the alacrity with which merchants were exporting goods from Ireland was not matched by their commitment to bring foodstuffs into the country. Irish merchants appeared to be more interested in the high profits that could be obtained from exports rather than in supporting the less developed import trade. At the beginning of

An eviction

After the eviction

1847, the Lord Lieutenant in Dublin informed the Prime Minister that the merchants had not behaved responsibly. He accused them of having "done as little as they could" to bring food into the country whilst at the same time doing "their best to keep up prices." He concluded his report pessimistically by saying, "It is difficult to persuade a starving population that one class should be permitted to make fifty percent profit by the sale of provisions whilst they are dying in want of these."

In an attempt to encourage additional food imports, at the beginning of 1847, the government relaxed the Navigation Laws and removed a number of import duties from goods coming into Ireland. They also announced that the failed system of public works was to be replaced with soup kitchens. Although large amounts of corn began to arrive in Ireland in the spring of 1847 during the critical winter months, a "starvation gap" had existed in parts of Ireland as the wages paid on the public works had proved insufficient to purchase food in a period of inflated prices. The main beneficiaries of this policy had been Irish and British merchants, who made unusually high profits. The decision to allow food to be exported whilst people starved aroused criticism from a diverse group of people, ranging from the Irish nationalist John Mitchel to the Lord Lieutenant, the Earl of Clarendon, the highest ranking government official in Ireland. At the end of 1847, Clarendon admitted in private correspondence to the Prime Minister that financial greed and political opportunism had dictated policy in Ireland, regardless of the human cost. He concluded by saying, "No one could now venture to dispute the fact that Ireland had been sacrificed to the London corn dealers because you were a member for the city, and that no distress would have occurred if the exportation of Irish grain had been forbidden."

Whilst ideological debates raged between high-ranking officials in London and Dublin, in many parts of Ireland the deficiencies of the relief policies were palpable. By the beginning of 1847, the name of a small town in County Cork, Skibbereen, had become synonymous with suffering and starvation. The first famine death had occurred there on 24 October 1846 and these continued to rise sharply. A number of journalists and philanthropists visited Skibbereen and, through their accounts, they brought the place to the attention of people throughout the world. But words or even sketches were inadequate to portray the depth of suffering. Thus William Bennet, a Quaker who visited cabins of the poor in the west of Ireland in March 1847, admitted, "language utterly fails me in attempting to depict the state of the wretched inmates." Nonetheless, he went on to say, "We entered a cabin. Stretched in one dark corner, scarcely visible, from the smoke and rags that covered them, were three children huddled together, lying there because they were too weak to rise, pale and ghastly their little limbs—on removing a portion of the filthy covering—perfectly emaciated eyes sunk, voice gone and in the last stage of actual starvation. Crouched over the turf embers was another form, wild and all but naked, scarcely human in appearance. It stirred not nor noticed us."

The horrors of famine were not just confined to the west of the country. Areas in the northeast were also being ravaged. In 1846 and 1847, there was a severe industrial recession throughout Europe which had repercussions on the textile industry in Ulster. Many mill workers were either laid off or put on shorter working hours. The confluence of an economic recession and a bad potato and oats harvest meant that people in the most industrially advanced region of Ireland also began to feel the impact of starvation. In Newtownards in County Down, which was one of the wealthiest towns in Ireland, the poor were described as being "emaciated and half-famished souls" who lacked even "sufficient clothes to cover them." In Lurgan, County Armagh, which lay at the center of the linen-producing region of Ireland, mortality in the local workhouse was second only to mortality in the Cork workhouse. A member of the Society of Friends who visited Armagh at the beginning of 1847 gave his opinion that "It would be impossible to find more distressing cases, short of the horrors of Skibbereen." It was evident that Skibbereen had become the benchmark for suffering of the Irish people and, at the same time, a symbol of the failure of the British state.

The wretchedness of the people in 1847 was manifested not only by a growth in disease and mortality but also through a sharp increase in crime. In 1847, the number of recorded offenses was sixty percent higher than in the previous year. Yet, traditional agrarian crimes declined but they were replaced by petty crimes which appeared to have been motivated by hunger. The offenses also reflected a breakdown in traditional social relationships. Crimes which were categorised as "theft" or "social protest" (such as food riots) accounted for 85 percent of all crimes in 1847, whereas before the Famine, they were responsible for less than a third of total crimes. For example, over 10,000 reports of cattle and sheep stealing and 1,200 cases of plundering of provisions were reported. Notwithstanding the perception of widespread lawlessness, cases of physical violence were lower in 1847 and 1848 than they had been in 1844 and 1845. Recorded crimes peaked in 1847 when they reached almost 21,000, compared with over 6,000 in 1844. They did not fall to their pre-Famine level again until the mid-1850s.

Offences relating to destitution were also apparent in areas which were generally regarded as being prosperous and law-abiding. In January 1847, the police in Portadown, County Armagh, reported that between twenty-five and thirty men had stolen fifty bags of flour from a nearby barge. Similar crimes were reported in the weeks that followed. No other items of value were removed from the boats, only food. To prevent this, additional troops were stationed near to the canal. In Belfast, bread shops were attacked by labourers who could not find employment. As was the case elsewhere, the purpose of the attack was not simply to steal, but to regulate prices and to force a sale at what was considered to be a fair market price. These instances of direct, collective action became less frequent in the later years of the Famine.

Those people who owned land and provisions, no matter how small, felt threatened by the apparent growth in lawlessness and many requests were made for either additional constabulary or the military to be stationed in their areas. In the middle of 1847, the Prime Minister agreed to send 2,000 mounted police and armed forces to Ireland. Between 1845 and 1850, the size of the constabulary was increased from 9,100 to 12,500, yet it still did not keep up with demands for more policing. In the initial stage of the crisis, one of the main tasks of the police had been to record the extent of crop lost and the consequent need for relief in their localities. Increasingly, they were used as a buttress for policies which exacerbated rather than alleviated the suffering. For example, after 1847, the main duty of both the constabulary and the army was to assist in evictions, especially mass evictions. They were also frequently called upon to assist or protect collectors of local rates and taxes and, if this was not successful, they provided support for the bailiff to seize the crops and livestock of the defaulter. Many of the latter were small tenant farmers, rather than potato cultivators, whose livelihoods had also been put at risk largely due to a sharp increase in local taxation. In the early years of the Famine, the army was frequently called on to guard food which was either leaving or being moved about the country. Inevitably, there were a number of violent confrontations between the police and the people, most frequently in counties Clare, Galway, Mayo and Tipperary.

Emigrants sail for Liverpool, the main port of embarkation for America, hoping to escape the Famine.

The priest blesses emigrants before they leave for America.

The desperation of the Irish people was further demonstrated by their desire to flee from Ireland. Even before the Famine, emigration from the country had been amongst the highest in Europe. But those who fled after 1846 were drawn from the poorest sections of society and they possessed few resources or skills. The ultimate destination of many famine emigrants was America, but large numbers also went to Canada, Australia and Britain. Leaving Ireland did not mark an end to the misery. There was little regulation of the passenger trade, which meant that conditions on board ships were often squalid and insanitary, leading to the sobriquet "coffin ships." The *Liverpool Mercury* described the journey as a "human cattle trade," but cattle were regarded as a valuable economic commodity and thus treated with more respect than human cargoes.

It was generally the poorest emigrants who remained in Britain as it was the closest and cheapest destination. Even those who did not intend to settle in Britain usually travelled there first, usually to Liverpool, which was the main port of embarkation for America. The influx of immigrants to Britain was regarded with increasing hostility. The Irish poor were viewed not only as a financial burden on British tax-payers, but as carriers of disease, especially fever. Moreover, the local authorities in the towns in which the Irish poor congregated did not possess either the administrative machinery or the financial resources to provide the high levels of emergency relief required after 1846. Some local authorities in Britain asked the central government for assistance to cope with the increased demand for relief and medical aid. When this request was refused, many local authorities implemented draconian steps to exclude Irish immigrants. In Cardiff in Wales, for example, ships carrying Irish poor were not allowed to come into the port. This led to some ships docking farther up the Welsh coastline, but this practice was ended when it was found that a number of the Irish passengers drowned in quicksands as they attempted to get to the shore. Under the provisions of the English and Welsh Poor Laws, the English authorities did not have to give relief to newcomers to their area. This law had been little used before 1846, but in 1847, the Liverpool authorities deported 15,000 paupers back to Ireland under its provisions. At the same time, the threat of removal to Ireland deterred other paupers from applying for relief in England which, in turn, contributed to higher levels of mortality. In 1847, 7,000 Irish paupers died in Liverpool from hunger or disease. The high mortality led a local newspaper to describe the situation as "a Skibbereen in Liverpool."

Bridget O'Donnel and her children face a fourth year of the Famine.

## Soup Kitchens and Souperism

The government responded to the failure of its policies by announcing, at the beginning of 1847, that the measures introduced only a few months earlier were to be abandoned and replaced by the Temporary Relief Act. In the place of public works, soup kitchens were to be established where free food would be available. The use of soup kitchens had already been pioneered with great success by the Society of Friends at the end of 1846. This new policy meant that for the first time the government was tackling the problem of hunger directly, and without requiring either payment or labour in return. It also meant that the government was contravening the principles on which their previous responses had been based. From the outset, however, the soup kitchens were regarded as a temporary expedient, to provide interim relief until a more permanent solution could be made available.

To make the new scheme more acceptable to those tax-payers who were ideologically opposed to gratuitous relief, soup was chosen because it was cheap and had little exchange value. The government persuaded a French society chef, Alexis Soyer, to visit Dublin for the purpose of devising a number of cheap but nutritious soup recipes and to devise a strategy for its distribution. Amidst a flurry of publicity, Soyer's "model" soup kitchen was opened in Dublin on 5 April and a number of dignitaries, including the Lord Lieutenant, were invited to sample the fare. They declared the soup to be "delicious." The destitute were only allowed to taste the soup after the dignitaries had left. To expedite the transition to the new system of relief, the Treasury insisted on a quota of reduction of employment on the public works, even before the soup kitchens were operative. This forced closure of the relief works contributed to an increase in mortality in the spring of 1847. A number of soup kitchens, including the one in Skibbereen, only became operative in June. The Society of Friends played an important role in expediting the opening

of the government soup kitchens, as it was they who imported and paid for many of the large cauldrons needed for making the soup.

By July 1847, soup kitchen relief was at its peak and over three million people each day were receiving free rations of food. In parts of County Mayo, entire communities were dependent on this form of relief. In Belfast and its hinterland, no government soup kitchens were opened, despite widespread destitution. In the Belfast area, the local residents decided to rely on private soup kitchens on the grounds that they would be less expensive to operate. The quality of the soup provided varied from place to place. In the worst instances it was described as little more than flavoured water. Yet, regardless of its limitations, the soup kitchen system was the most successful of all of the government's schemes and mortality did begin to fall in the summer of 1847. It was also relatively cheap to operate, especially in comparison to the public works; a daily ration of relief cost two old pence which, in total, cost two million pounds which was less than the government had anticipated. Although most of this money was initially provided by the government, it was to be repaid by the local taxpayers in Ireland. Significantly, the soup kitchen programme demonstrated that the British state did possess the logistic and the administrative ability to feed the people of Ireland.

Throughout 1847 the role of private charity was important in saving lives. As news of the situation in Ireland spread—through newspapers, church pulpits, letters and word of mouth—charitable collections for Ireland commenced. The scale of fundraising activities was unprecedented as donations were made from all five continents and cut across traditional religious, national, cultural and economic divisions. The first collection for Ireland took place in Calcutta in India at the end of 1845, at the initiative of members of the British army stationed there (a large portion of whom were Irish). They raised almost £14,0000. The majority of fund-raising activities took place following the second, more serious crop failure. One of the first groups to become involved in private relief was the Society of Friends, or Quakers. They were known for their philanthropic activities and were respected for not attempting to use their work to gain religious converts. In total, the Quakers raised over £200,000, mostly from contributions from Britain and America, including a donation from the Choctaw Nation in Oklahoma. Members of the Society of Friends travelled to the poorest districts in Ireland to help to oversee the distribution of aid. Their reports, which were widely published, gave authenticity to the earlier accounts of the suffering in Ireland. The Quakers were critical of both absentee landlords and of the minimalist approach of the government. They suggested that the British state needed to place humanitarian considerations above ideology. In 1848 the Quakers withdrew from providing direct aid, arguing that the scale of the problem was so great that only the resources of a government could redress it.

The largest relief organisation was the British Relief Association for the Relief of Distress in Ireland and Scotland (Scotland had also suffered potato failure although not on the scale of Ireland). It was founded on 1 January 1847 by the noted Jewish banker and philanthropist, Lionel de Rothschild, with the support of a number of wealthy British businessmen. A Polish Count, Paul de Strzelecki, was appointed to supervise the distribution of their money. The association received donations from many influential British people, including members of the royal family and members of parliament. The most famous—and largest—donation was made by Queen Victoria, who gave

Miss Kennedy distributes clothing to the poor.

£2,000. They also received assistance from overseas, including £1,000 from the Sultan of Turkey. But the majority of the association's donations were made by ordinary British people who had been moved by the reports of suffering in Ireland. In total, the British Relief Association received over 15,000 individual donations which amounted to over £400,000.

The Catholic Church also provided significant levels of relief, although they possessed no official relief organisation. Its success in fund-raising was helped by the early and public involvement of the Pope, Pius IX. The Pope not only made a private contribution to famine relief, he took the unusual step of issuing an encyclical in which he asked the international Catholic community to pray for Ireland. Throughout 1847, large amounts of aid were also provided from America. Even before the Famine, large numbers of Irish people had emigrated there and the links between the two countries were felt to be strong. Although a proposal by the American Congress to send $500,000 in direct state aid to Ireland was rejected, they did give permission for a number of warships to be used to take supplies to Ireland. This decision did evoke some criticism as America was at war with Mexico at the time. Two of the most famous vessels to take food and other necessities were the *Jamestown* from Boston and the *Macedonian* from New York, both of which sailed to Cork. In total, over 100 ships carrying aid were sent from America in 1847. Although the bulk of charitable assistance arrived too late to prevent mass mortality, private aid did provide a vital life line for many Irish people in 1847. But, by 1848, most of the charitable efforts had dried up.

Private charity was partly discredited by the attempts of a few organisations to use the existence of hunger as an opportunity to proselytise, that is, convert the poor from Catholicism to Protestantism. This activity was known as "souperism" and those people who accepted the food or soup were known as "soupers" or *Cat Breacs*. The largest proselytising group was the Irish Relief Association which mostly operated out of Belfast although their activities spread as far as Connaught. They regarded the famine as "a favourable crisis" which was allowing them to "bring the light of the Gospels to the darkened mind of the Roman Catholic peasantry." Women were particularly active in the association and many of them learned the Irish language to enable them to converse more easily with the peasantry. Although the number of converts appeared to be relatively small, the existence of proselytism left a legacy of bitterness against private philanthropy.

## PROPERTY SUPPORTING POVERTY

The harvest of 1847 was virtually free from blight but the overall crop yield was small. After two years of disease, the potato economy had collapsed and the people who had depended on them had few resources remaining. Moreover, the cumulative effects of malnourishment and disease were manifest. Nonetheless, the British government took advantage of the absence of blight to pronounce that the Famine was over and that, in future, Ireland had to rely on its own resources. At the same time, a new system of relief was to come into effect, based on the Poor Law system, which was to provide a permanent and final solution to the relief of destitution. The Whigs had been responsible for introducing a Poor Law system to Ireland in 1838 (modelled on the English workhouse system). They favoured this model of relief because it compelled each area to be responsible for financing its own poverty, thus forcing local proprietors to take an active interest in keeping relief provision as stringent as possible. But for the victims of the subsistence crisis, the change to the Poor Law resulted in a loss of status: people who a year earlier had been classed as workers on the public works were now officially designated "paupers."

In the summer of 1847 there had been a general election in Britain. The Whig Party had been re-elected, but with a small majority, and their success was largely due to the support of the influential merchant and middle classes. During the election campaign, it had become apparent that giving any further financial assistance to Ireland was viewed as a drain on British taxpayers' resources, whilst helping to perpetuate a backward system of agriculture. The election coincided with a severe industrial and commercial depression which hit the British middle classes. Promises of financial retrenchment in Ireland became a key component of the Whig government's policies. The extent to which this course of action had popular support was evident in October 1847 when Queen Victoria, through the medium of a published "Queen's Letter," attempted to raise more private aid for Ireland. She and her proposal were publicly condemned, the influential *Times* newspaper leading the assault.

By the end of September the soup kitchens had closed and private assistance had begun to diminish, which left the poor with little alternative but to seek relief from the Poor Law. Under the provisions of the 1838 Poor Law Act, relief could only be given to the destitute who became inmates of a workhouse. But the strict regulations which governed work, dress, discipline, classification and family segregation meant that workhouses were disliked by poor people and used only as a last resort. On the eve of the Famine, no workhouse was full and some contained as few as five inmates. But in 1846, as the public works proved deficient, demand for admission to the workhouses grew and by the end of the year, half of the 130 workhouses were full and refusing to allow any further admissions. To cope with the additional claims, some emergency accommodation was provided, but much of it was inappropriate or insanitary, which had fatal consequences for paupers who were already ill. The workhouses, regardless of their limitations and harsh regimes, increasingly became last refuges for a desperate people, especially those who were sick or infirm, and for the thousands of children who had been abandoned or left orphaned.

To enable the Poor Law to provide for both ordinary and famine relief, the existing legislation was amended. The new Poor Law of 1847 marked a radical break with the principles on which the original law had been established. For the first time, outdoor relief, that is, the giving of relief to people who were not inmates of the workhouse, was permitted. But local relief officials were also urged to rent additional accommodation so that indoor relief could continue to be used as the main test of destitution. The original workhouses had been designed to cope with approximately 100,000 paupers, but by the beginning of 1849 they had expanded to accommodate 250,000 inmates, which still proved to be insufficient for the demands being placed on them. Although the new system of relief was intended to be self-financing, the most insolvent twenty-two unions were given special category status and officially designated "distressed" by the government. In effect, this status meant that they could receive limited funds from the government.

To make outdoor relief as disagreeable and cheap as possible, rations were given only in the form of cooked food. The government had recommended a pound of food per day for each adult, but often rations fell far short of this amount. The infrastructure of the Poor Law also proved less effective than that of the dismantled soup kitchens in getting relief to the most isolated townlands. To deter people from applying for assistance, all "able-bodied" paupers were expected to break stones for up to ten hours daily. Notwithstanding the reluctance of the government to sanction outdoor relief, by the middle of 1848, over 800,000 people were receiving it daily. In total, over one million people were dependent on the Poor Law, despite its harsh requirements and minimal levels of assistance. Demonstrably, the Irish Famine was far from over.

The Poor Law had been chosen as the medium to alleviate both customary and famine relief after 1847 because it was regarded as a way of forcing landlords to take financial responsibility for poverty in their localities. Yet one of the main weaknesses of the Poor Law was its inability to meet the financial demands placed on it during a subsistence crisis. Even before 1847, many unions were already under extreme financial pressure and this intensified as other forms of relief disappeared. Because each local unit of Poor Law administration (union) was a self-financing unit, the fiscal burden was heaviest in areas where poverty was most acute. A large number of ratepayers were either unwilling or unable to meet the financial demands placed on them. Local relief officials who experienced difficulty in collecting rates were given extensive military and police support. If rates continued to be uncollected, the officials were forcibly removed from office and replaced by paid administrators appointed by commissioners in Dublin. By 1848, the system was beginning to collapse under the strain of too few resources in the face of unremitting demand for relief. Relief administrators in Dublin, including Edward Twistleton, the Chief Poor Law Commissioner, citing the high levels of starvation, pleaded with government and Treasury officials in London to make more money available. Such requests were refused, reflecting a determination that Ireland had to be forced to depend on her own resources, regardless of the high human cost.

A particularly harsh component of the amended Poor Law was the Quarter Acre Clause, also known as the Gregory Clause, after its originator. This enactment stipulated that no person who occupied more than a quarter of an acre of land was eligible to receive relief. For numerous small tenants this requirement was the final straw as it forced a stark choice between surrendering their land or starvation. Many landlords also found themselves under financial pressure from reduced rents and mounting taxation

after 1847, especially those whose estates were already indebted. Leading members of the government viewed the crisis as an opportunity to rid Ireland of proprietors who had invested little time or capital in their properties and had become a hindrance to modernization. To facilitate the removal of such landlords, Encumbered Estates Acts were passed in 1848 and 1849.

A number of landlords used the non-payment of rents as an excuse to evict their tenants. Some landlords attempted to cushion the impact of eviction (whilst ensuring that it was permanent) by assisting the tenants to emigrate, but others took advantage of the existing social dislocation to enforce mass removals of their small- and medium-sized tenants—especially those who were renting good quality land. The scale of evictions was vast. From 1849 (when official records commenced) to 1854, one-quarter of a million people were officially and permanently removed from their holdings. This figure only represented a portion of all evictions as it did not include those who had been ejected illegally or who had voluntarily surrendered their properties. Many of those evicted who had nowhere to go dug "scalps"—holes which were covered with sticks and earth—but they were even forcibly removed from these.

After 1847, homelessness became as much a cause of mortality as hunger. Reports from local relief officers in Ireland to government officials in London stated the extent of the problem clearly. The government refused to interfere, arguing that such land clearances would ultimately benefit Ireland. One report to Trevelyan, from Kilrush in County Clare, recounted that 1,200 people had been evicted within a period of two weeks. It went on to say, "As soon as one crowd of homeless or naked paupers are dead or provided for in the workhouse another wholesale eviction doubles the number who, in their turn, pass through the same ordeal . . . until, broken down by privation and exposure to the elements, they seek the workhouse or die by the roadside." Clarendon, the Lord Lieutenant, had also become disillusioned with the indifference of his Whig colleagues to the suffering. This unconcern led him to assert, "I don't think there is another Legislature in Europe that would disregard such suffering as now exists in the west of Ireland, or coldly persist in a policy of extermination."

### Rebellion, Revolt and Loyalism

The year 1848 was one of revolution and uprisings throughout Europe, triggered by events in France in February. Within Ireland, a political vacuum had been created by the death of Daniel O'Connell in the previous year. It was filled partly by a group of radical nationalists who added the starvation of the Irish peasantry to their existing political grievances, arguing that the solution lay in the overthrow of the existing landlord system and in ending the political connection with Britain. A group of these men, who had been part of the Young Ireland movement, reconstituted themselves as the Irish Confederation at the beginning of 1848 and began to plan an armed rebellion. The British government was aware of their plans in advance. The passing of a Crime and Outrage Act in the previous year had given the Irish Executive extensive powers which they used to place the country under virtual martial law and to arrest leading members of the Confederates. Regardless of the absence of many of their leaders, an armed uprising took place in County Tipperary in July 1848. It was led by William Smith O'Brien, a Protestant landlord who was also a member of the British parliament. He was actively supported by less than 100 men and the insurrection was easily defeated. Its leaders were subsequently transported to Tasmania. Overall, the rising lacked mass support, as food, shelter and survival continued to be the primary concerns of many Irish people. Nevertheless, the uprising was significant because the British press used it as proof of the disloyalty and ingratitude of the Irish people. A number of British newspapers also suggested that the Irish were using the money that had been sent for aid for the purchase of weapons.

Within Ireland, the uprising was overshadowed by early reports that the blight had again appeared in the country. These initial fears were not unfounded. In 1848, over half of the potato crop was destroyed and, along the western seaboard, the blight was as destructive as it had been in 1846. A further year of famine was inevitable but again the British government decided that the Poor Law alone should provide the necessary relief. By the beginning of 1849, over one million people—approximately one in every six people—were in receipt of either indoor or outdoor relief. But the Poor Law was showing the strains of such unremitting pressure. The indebtedness of many unions had grown and their lack of capital meant that they were unable to provide the poor with medical assistance, clothes, bedding, coffins, or sometimes even food. Mortality in the workhouses reached 2,500 per week, although in some western workhouses the rate was far higher. The system could not keep count of those who died outside the confines of the workhouse. The appearance of a cholera epidemic in the country, especially in the vicinity of seaports, also contributed to an increase in excess mortality. In three of the four provinces of Ireland mortality was higher in 1849 than it had been two years earlier, in so-called "Black '47." In a number of districts, the cumulative effects of years of shortages were taking a dreadful toll. In 1849, alleged cases of cannibalism were reported in County Mayo. In Kilrush in County Clare, the suffering of the population was being likened to Skibbereen two years earlier. A parliamentary enquiry was set up to find out why the area was continuing to suffer so badly. Its report estimated that the local population had fallen by almost fifty percent in four years with little sign of recovery. The enquiry was critical of both local landlords and the policies of the central government. The report concluded by saying, "a neglect of public duty has occurred and has occasioned a state of things disgraceful to a civilised age and country, for which some authority ought to be held responsible and would long since have been held responsible had these things occurred in any union in England."

Despite compelling evidence of genuine suffering in many parts of Ireland, the British government remained committed to the principle that Irish property should support Irish poverty. Instead, a further policy modification was introduced. In May 1849 the Rate-in-Aid Act was passed which imposed an additional rate on solvent unions in the north and east of the country, for immediate transfer to impoverished unions in the rest of the country. This response demonstrated the determination of the British government that famine relief was to be an Irish and not a British responsibility. Public opinion in Britain also appeared to be firmly opposed to providing further assistance to Ireland. In February 1849, when a small and final grant of £50,000 was given to the poorest Irish unions as an interim measure until the new rate was available, the British press responded angrily. A cartoon in the satirical journal, *Punch*, depicted an English labourer struggling to carry a plump, grinning Irish peasant with a bag

containing £50,000. The caption read: "The English Labourer's Burden." Adopting a similar interpretation, *The Times* described the grant as having "broken the back of English benevolence."

The decision to introduce the Rate-in-Aid was rigorously opposed by taxpayers in unions in the northeast of Ireland who viewed the tax as a direct transfer of their resources to the impoverished unions in the west of Ireland. They also argued that the northern unions were being penalised for their good management, which they contrasted with the ineptitude of the relief officials in the western unions. Some of the opposition was expressed in divisive, sectarian terms, a clear distinction being drawn between the people of Ulster and those in the south and west of the country. At one public meeting the latter were described as "an army of beggars." One Ulster landlord, Robert Dolling, asserted that the reason why Ulster had not suffered during the preceding years was because "We are a painstaking, industrious, laborious people, who desire to work and pay our just debts, and the blessing of the Almighty is upon our labour. If the people of the south had been equally industrious with those of the north, they would not have so much misery among them."

Some of the opposition to the Rate-in-Aid was on the grounds that the new tax was a denial of the responsibilities engendered by the Act of Union. One Belfast newspaper warned that "this measure will dangerously affect the loyalty of the people of this province." The most determined opponent of the tax, however, was the English Poor Law Commissioner, Edward Twistleton. He had regularly asked the Treasury for additional funds for the destitute and had become increasingly critical of the policies which he was in charge of implementing. Twistleton resigned in protest at the imposition of the Rate-in-Aid, arguing that the west of Ireland should be treated as if it was "locally joined to Devonshire or Cornwall."

The opposition to the new tax in Ulster was intense but short-lived. Following the introduction of the Act, the northern unions agreed to end their campaign of opposition. The expressions of dissent were replaced by public professions of loyalty a few months later when Queen Victoria visited Ireland, in August 1849. She was the first British monarch to visit Ireland since 1821 and the first to visit Belfast for almost two hundred years. The government viewed Victoria's visit as a publicity exercise which would demonstrate that the famine was finally over and which would result in more British capital being invested in the country. Her stay in Ireland was brief and she saw only the east of the country which was beginning to recover from the Famine. She visited Cork, Dublin and Belfast and travelled between the three cities by yacht and not overland. Victoria noticed that many of the women were "dressed in rags" but she attributed this to the fact that "they never mend anything." Although there was some opposition to the visit, for the most part she was greeted warmly and she promised to return again soon. However, during Victoria's long reign of over sixty years, she visited Ireland only two additional times. Increasingly, she became a symbol of Britain's callousness during the famine years and she was given the epithet "Famine Queen." In 1900, at the age of 81, when Victoria was contemplating a final visit to Ireland, the Irish nationalist Maud Gonne observed "however vile and selfish and pitiless her soul may be, she must sometimes tremble as death approaches when she thinks of the countless mothers who, shelterless under the cloudy Irish sky, watching their starving little ones, have cursed her before they died."

CONCLUSION

In 1850 and 1851 there were some instances of potato blight in Ireland but they were increasingly localised. Yet the impact of famine did not end when good harvests returned to Ireland, and events set in train by the potato blight continued to have repercussions in the following decades. Within the space of six years the social structure of Ireland transformed. Many victims of the Famine were drawn from the very poorest groups in society. They were also predominantly from the west of the country and had been potato growers, Irish speakers and Catholic. But the impact of the Famine also cut across geographic and religious boundaries. Approximately three thousand Baptists had lost their lives, and in parts of counties Donegal and Armagh, the Famine had wiped out large numbers of Protestants. Other by-products of the crisis, such as emigration, evictions, disease and high taxation, also had an impact on other social groups, including landlords. In total, over twenty-five percent of land changed hands during the Famine. But the modernisation of Irish agriculture, which had been an objective of many politicians, proved to be ephemeral. Although agricultural production did change, it never followed the anglicised model that was held up as the ideal. Irish society also changed, but again not in the way hoped for. In the post-Famine decades, Catholicism became more deeply embedded in Irish society and potatoes continued to be the staple food of poor people who continued to reside on small plots of land. However, mass mortality and sustained emigration had brought to an end the rich communal life of pre-Famine Ireland. Also, the fact that the majority of emigrants were young and amongst the healthiest and most enterprising members of society, contributed to a social torpor amongst those who were left behind.

The Famine also proved to be a political watershed. For nationalists, the events of 1845–51 clearly demonstrated the failure of the Act of Union and reinforced the desire for political independence. For unionists, the Famine was viewed as a southern and western phenomenon which provided further evidence of the differences between Ulster and the rest of the country. Nevertheless, one of the consequences of mass emigration was that the memory of the Famine was carried beyond the shores of Ireland, and Irish politics were increasingly conducted on an international stage.

*See* Emigration: 1801–1921

Rob Goodbody, *A Suitable Channel. Quaker Relief in the Great Famine* (Bray, 1995).

Margaret Kelleher, *The Feminization of Famine. Expressions of the Inexpressible?* (Cork, 1997).

Christine Kinealy, *This Great Calamity. The Irish Famine 1845–52* (Colorado, 1995).

Christine Kinealy and Trevor Parkhill, *The Famine in Ulster* (Belfast, 1997).

Gerard MacAtasney, *'This Dreadful Visitation'. The Famine in Lurgan/Portadown* (Belfast, 1997).

Cormac Ó Gráda, *Ireland before and after the Famine. Explorations in Economic History* (Manchester, 1993).

Patrick O'Sullivan (ed.) *The Meaning of the Famine* (Leicester, 1997).

Michael Turner, *After the Famine. Irish Agriculture 1850–1914* (Cambridge, 1996).

CHRISTINE KINEALY

## FAMINE: AMERICAN RELIEF MOVEMENT (1846–1850)

The troubles in Ireland, and the oppression under which the people of that island suffer, form the topics of conversation in every quarter of the globe. They are heard of at St. Petersburgh and at Constantinople; are discussed in the log cabins of the Far West; and are mooted in the Parisian Clubs. America transmutes her weapons of defense into messengers of relief, and under the smiles of the stars and stripes, pour upon the shores of Green Erin food for her famine-struck cottiers.

*Merchant's Magazine,* 1848

On the eve of the Great Irish Famine, thousands of Irish had already left the troubled shores of Ireland with hopes of prospering in the land of plenty—America. Although these early Irish emigrants faced much adversity, by the mid-nineteenth century they materialized as a part of the American social and economic fabric. Thus, when American newspapers first reported that a famine was ravaging Ireland, the response was immediate and overwhelmingly generous. Americans across the Union joined hands to establish a famine relief movement that would unhesitatingly contribute millions of dollars in both provisions and monetary funds to mitigate Ireland's suffering.

In recent years, an explosion in famine scholarship has produced a vast amount of important research, yet the American response to the famine has received hardly any critical attention. Most famine relief accounts tend to concentrate solely on the British government's response. The most comprehensive reviews of relief, James S. Donnelly's work in *A New History of Ireland* and T. P. O'Neill's research in *The Great Famine,* devote all their attention to how the British government handled the question of relief, analyzing and criticizing Britain's misguided attempts to provide aid for a most complicated tragedy. Yet, as more scholars are drawn towards reconsidering the Great Irish Famine, they have begun to consider seriously the enormous amount of international sympathy that Ireland's calamity generated. The Irish Government's Famine Commemoration publication, *Ireland's Famine: Commemoration and Awareness,* is a testament to this new surge in research as within it is Christine Kinealy's short, but important, piece of research that succinctly summarizes the foreign aid donated to Ireland during the Great Famine. Kinealy's work has opened a new door through which scholars can consider exactly how this newly uncovered international response shaped the famine experience.

This article adds to Kinealy's research by providing an overview of the American famine relief movement as evidenced in New England periodicals and newspapers. It is an overview that reveals an America on the verge of becoming the global leader in volunteerism. As the famine began to take its toll on Ireland in 1846, America was still an isolationist nation concerned only with solving her own internal struggles and dissipating the sectarianism that threatened to destroy the newly sanctioned Union. However, the desperate Irish famine victims' cries so powerfully affected America that her gaze turned from inward to outward. The famine caused America to cast aside her isolationist ideology and respond to the distressed famine victims with a relief movement that would mark America's entrance onto the international stage for humanitarian acts.

Initially, America's relief movement was a grassroots effort with donations coming in from far-flung parts of the Union. Not surprisingly, the Irish inhabitants of Boston were some of the first Americans to solicit relief donations. The *Boston Pilot* reports that the initial famine relief collection meeting was held in early January 1846. To facilitate donations, the chairman opened the meeting by declaring that the evening's discussion topic was the injustices and oppressive nature of British rule over Ireland, and anyone who wished to speak had to pay one dollar per minute. Donation amounts climbed steadily, eventually totaling twenty-three hundred dollars, as the mainly Irish-American participants ignored the passing minutes and presented one impassioned dissertation after another.

However, not all the early relief donations originated from Irish-Americans. In fact, the majority of the contributions came from cities and townspeople who had no ties to Ireland at all. Relief came from cities as far west as Madison, Wisconsin and Knoxville, Illinois, as far north as Rochester and Utica, New York, and as far south as New Orleans, Louisiana. And the collection of the aid was as eclectic as the places from which it came. As the *Niles National Register* records in early 1847, Baltimore residents paid generously to attend a Relief Ball, which raised over twenty-two hundred dollars to benefit the starving Irish. When one Genosee, New York farmer contributed 1,000 bushels of corn, his donation provoked a ship owner of this same town to subscribe to the relief effort by offering to convey the corn free of charge.

Still, many Americans chose more traditional means of donation, contributing whatever amount of their private funds they could afford to send. In February, 1847, the *Register* reports that both the Philadelphia Board of Brokers and the cadets at West Point Military Academy donated three hundred dollars, the hands at the Brooklyn Dry Dock contributed seven hundred dollars, a random Saturday night collection in Providence, Rhode Island raised $5,856, and over twenty thousand dollars was donated in New York from several private sources: sixteen different New York City firms, the Stock Exchange, and the residents of Albany, Utica, and Rochester.

The erratic nature of the relief collection makes its success seem particularly unlikely. And, the relief movement appears even more fruitless in light of the fact that, according to a November 1846 *Register* edition, Ireland would need well over ten million dollars to recover the losses incurred from damaged crops. However, Americans seemingly chose to ignore such dismal statistics and continued to give freely, leading the *Register* to report on January 30, 1847 that through private donations alone over $1,200,000 had already been sent over to relieve Ireland's distress.

Although these grassroots, private donations continued to be collected throughout the famine years, the relief movement transformed in February 1847 into a more officially organized effort under the auspices of the United States government. On February 20, 1847, the *Register's* National News section reported that then Vice President George M. Dallas called a meeting to create a national structure from which to call, collect, and transport aid to those suffering in Ireland. Congress immediately expressed its avid support of Dallas' endeavor by quickly sending a congressional representative from every state and territory in the Union to help establish an organized and effective relief movement. Congress accomplished its goal as this historic meeting built the structure for America's first national relief movement. The meeting established that two centralized relief committees, one in New York and the other in New Orleans, would be responsible for collecting, tallying, and transporting the aid

donated from across the Union to ports and places throughout Ireland. Additionally, representatives resolved to transmit the contributions in the forms of flour, Indian corn and meal, and other provisions, as well as to publish periodically the progress of America's relief movement in periodicals and newspapers. The latter resolution held much importance because it allowed the American people to understand that even the smallest contributions helped to raise the millions that were needed. Yet, probably the most important resolution of the entire meeting was a formal call to each city and town across America to form relief committees that would solicit donations and forward them to the Central Relief Committees in New York and New Orleans.

The response to this meeting was overwhelming. Within a week of Vice President Dallas' call for relief, the *Register* reported that receipts from the New York Relief Committee had reached nearly $40,000. Throughout 1847, the amount of aid continued to pour in week after week as Americans unabatedly gave donations to the newly formed relief committees in such cities as Baltimore, Philadelphia, Boston, New York, New Orleans, Albany, Madison, Lynchburg and Rockingham, Virginia; Jersey City, New Jersey; and Montgomery, Mississippi. Within the cities, the church became the most common site for collection. In just one week of masses and services, the Philadelphia and Albany churches raised a total of six-thousand and five-thousand dollars respectively. Private donors also continued to submit contributions, like in Washington where donations totaled $2,205.50 when a smattering of law offices and congressional representatives made subscriptions, and in Boston where three individual households, as anonymous donors, single-handedly sent $4,000, $12,000 and $24,500 respectively. By May 1, 1847 the *Register* reported that the total amount received and shipped to Ireland was $581,893.00, and by the end of Black '47 the grand total of contributions donated by Americans amounted to over $1.5 million. An astounding fact and a testament to the power of America's first organized relief movement.

While collecting the aid made up only one half of the process, transporting it made the movement whole. The United States government took the helm in this area by offering two naval war vessels, the USS *Jamestown* and USS *Macedonia,* to convey the much needed provisions to Ireland. And with this agreement, history was made as these two ships became the first war vessels ever to sail strictly in the name of charity. It appeared that with each new development of the relief movement, America continued to prove herself as a world leader in volunteerism. Yet, America's new role in global politics did not come without challenges since prior to these vessels successfully conveying their goods to the Irish, they encountered several obstacles.

Initially, the employment of the *Jamestown* and the *Macedonia* was presented as part of a congressional Irish Relief Bill that called for the use of these ships, as well as a U.S. government contribution of $500,000. The use of these vessels was put in jeopardy when, after a desperate attempt in Congress to successfully pass the bill, it was defeated 82 nays to 75 yeas. Luckily, the Secretary of the Navy recognized the importance of this mission and quickly offered the use of the *Jamestown* and *Macedonia.*

Additionally, this mission of charity incurred more challenges when Congress chose Boston and New York as the sites to outfit these two ships. While the Boston volunteers set to work immediately, packing the *Jamestown* with relief goods, the New York Relief committee protested using the *Macedonia* since the British captured her during the late war. The committee saw her as damaged colonized goods that would only add insult to injury if she were used to transport provisions to help relieve those still suffering under Britain's colonial rule. After a bitter struggle, this impasse was overcome when the needs of the starving Irish overruled ideological misgivings.

Success was achieved, finally, on April 2, 1847 when the USS *Jamestown* left Boston for Cork laden with 8,000 barrels of breadstuffs and manned by over fifty volunteer crewmen. While the USS *Macedonia's* departure was delayed until late in the summer of 1847, she eventually sailed carrying over $50,000, or around 15,000 barrels, in provisions. The November 6th issue of the *Friend's Review* captured the success of both these missions when it reported that as the *Macedonia* prepared for her return to America, the Lord Alderman of the city of Cork came aboard the ship to let Captain De Kay know that the Irish councilmen alleged that "many thousand lives had been saved by the timely aid brought out by this ship . . . in one county 9,000 persons had been saved; and it was estimated that over 25,000 persons owed their preservation to the alms of the American people forwarded by this single ship." This mission of charity, despite its many problems, not only accomplished its goal of relieving Ireland of her distress, but it also underscored America's commitment to global volunteerism.

In the spirit of the *Jamestown's* and *Macedonia's* missions, many Americans contributed to the relief movement by offering to transport provisions to Ireland. The week after Vice-President Dallas' meeting in February 1847, the Baltimore and Ohio Railroad Companies resolved to carry all relief donations to the Central Committees free of charge, and the packet ship *Virginia* sailed from America's shores carrying 15,000 bushels of corn, 2,000 barrels of flour and meal, 200 barrels of onions, and 340 packages of cheese. In total, between the months of February and May 1847, the *Register* accounted that over 64 ships set sail from the Eastern seaboard conveying over 243,000 bushels of corn, 90,000 barrels of flour, 12,000 feet of pine lumber, 8,880 bushels of wheat, 5,200 barrels of corn meal, 250 barrels of navy bread, 500 kegs of lard, and 1 barrel of ham. The single greatest amount of relief transported, according to the *Register*, was on March 27, 1847 when twelve separate ships sailed from Baltimore laden with a total amount of 129,809 bushel of corn, 31,894 barrels of flour, 8,893 bushels of wheat, and 850 barrels of corn meal. Additionally, waiting in the Baltimore ship docks were twenty-two other vessels with upwards of 30,000 barrels of flour. Although these records do not include the vessels which left from the Southern seaboard docks, just these accounts alone enforce the vastness of the American relief movement. It was a movement that truly hoped to save a nation and her people.

Probably one of the most important elements of the famine relief movement was not the dollar amounts contributed or total barrels of provisions transported, but the sense of unity the relief movement created in America. History has shown us that pain and suffering breeds compassion, volunteerism and unity. Relief came from such disparate religious societies as the Jewish population in New York, the Shakers of New Lebanon, the Catholics and Protestants throughout the country, and the Quakers of Pennsylvania. The new Irish immigrants joined hands with the slaves of the South and the Choctaw Indians of Oklahoma to provide relief for their impoverished brethren. What is most poignant about the aid provided by these latter groups is that they represented the oppressed helping the oppressed. When the Choctaw Indians, who had been forcibly moved to inhabit Oklahoma by the U.S. government, learned of the destitution in Ireland, they immediately responded with a donation of $710. It was as if their own history of suffering in America allowed them to understand more fully Ireland's desperate need. And so, the Choctaw Indians joined the very Americans who had caused them so much pain and donated to the American relief movement. Their effort seems to highlight that even during a time of horrid oppression and sectarianism in American history, Americans of all shades could momentarily ignore their internal divisions and unify to help provide relief for those so desperately in need.

Within the periodicals and newspapers, reports of relief contributions came to an almost abrupt end in early 1848. Although some Americans continued to donate relief right through 1851, the Central Relief committees took their cue to dismantle the national relief effort in 1848 when the British government signaled the end of the famine by deconstructing its soup kitchens and public works projects. In a sense, however, the legacy of this relief movement has lived on long past the famine's end. The famine relief effort allowed America to develop itself as the savior of the destitute and oppressed. In the words of an Irish journalist found in the May 8, 1847 *Register*:

> Honor, then, to America. In it the cause of humanity needs no spur from shame, hypocrisy, or "state policy." In her bosom we knew that our exiles found a refuge where they were safe from exterminating landlords and class legislation—where the motto for all was "live, and let live!"—and not; "live ye, the many—or—die for the few—the unprivileged for the privileged!" But never, much as our hearts yearned towards America as the asylum of our hopeless cast out thousands, never, we say, great as was our experience of the generosity with which our countrymen were received on its shores, were we prepared for the surprising acts of humanity and benevolence towards this stricken nation, which mail after mail enables us to record, and to bless.

A. B. and Richard L. Allen, eds., *The American Agriculturist*, vol. 5–9 (New York, 1846–1850).

D. George Boyce, *Nineteenth-Century Ireland* (Dublin, 1990).

L. Perry Curtis, *Apes and Angels: The Irish Man in Victorian Caricature* (Washington D.C., 1971).

Patrick Donahoe, ed., *The Boston Pilot*, vol. 9–13 (Boston, 1846–1850).

James S. Donnelly, Jr., "The Construction of the Memory of the Famine in Ireland and the Irish Diaspora, 1850–1900," in *Éire-Ireland* (Spring/Summer 1997): 20–55.

R. Dudley Edwards and T. Desmond Williams, *The Great Famine: Studies in Irish History, 1845–52* (New York, 1957).

R. F. Foster, *Modern Ireland, 1600–1972* (London, 1988).

Freeman Hunt, ed., *Merchant's Magazine and Commercial Review*, vol. 17–29 (New York, 1846–1850).

Christine Kinealy, "Foreign Aid to Ireland during the Great Famine," in *Ireland's Famine: Commemoration and Awareness* (Dublin, 1997).

Enoch Lewis, ed., *Friend's Review*, vol. 1–4 (Philadelphia, 1846–1850).

Eliakim Littell, ed., *The Living Age*, vol. 11–28 (Boston, 1846–1850).

William Lloyd Garrison, ed., *The Liberator*, vol. 15–20 (Boston, 1845–1850).

F. X. Martin, F. J. Byrne, and W. E. Vaughan, eds., *A New History of Ireland.* Volume V: *Ireland under the Union, I 1801–70* (Oxford, 1989).

Kerby A. Miller, *Emigrants and Exiles: Ireland and the Irish Exodus to North America* (New York, 1985).

Brian C. Mitchell, *The Paddy Camps: The Irish of Lowell, 1821–61* (Urbana, 1988).

Frank Luther Mott, *American Journalism. A History: 1690–1960* (New York, 1962).

Hezekiah Niles, ed., *The Niles National Register*, vol. 69–73 (Philadelphia, 1846–1850).

J. G. Palfrey, ed., *The North American Review*, vol. 62–67 (Boston, 1846–1850).

Cathal Póirtéir, ed., *The Great Irish Famine* (Cork, 1995).

Arthur M. Schlesinger, Jr., John Blum, and C. Vann Woodward, eds., *The National Experience.* Part One: *A History of the United States to 1877* (New York, 1993).

DIANE HOTTEN-SOMERS

## FAMINE COFFIN SHIPS, THE

The "coffin ships" are an evocative symbol of the Great Famine and its ensuing Diaspora. Their fetid holds have been compared to the boxcars of the Holocaust. But the coffin-ship era belongs mainly to the panic-driven exodus from Ireland to British North America during 1847. Some 20 percent of 100,000 emigrants perished on this route—a small but significant minority of the 2.1 million who emigrated between 1845 and 1855.

As starvation and disease devastated Ireland, tens of thousands of people embraced emigration as their only escape from destitution or death. Neither reports of adverse conditions abroad, nor the lack of provisions aboard unsafe vessels could check the lemming-like march to the ports. Departures under such conditions were bound to produce disasters at sea or on landing. Black '47 was by far the worst year in this respect, with the mortality rate among Irish emigrants to Canada reaching 17 percent. It fell to 1 percent the following year (James S. Donnelly, "Excess Mortality and Emigration" in *A New History of Ireland*, V, Oxford 1989, pp. 353–56).

In 1847, the headlong flight of refugees to North America reached 214,000: more than 100,000 of the poorest took the cheaper route to the British provinces, where they overwhelmed the authorities in Quebec and New Brunswick. The remainder sailed directly to the United States (Kerby A. Miller, *Emigrants and Exiles: Ireland and the Irish Exodus to North America,* New York 1985, pp. 292–98; Michael Quigley, "Grosse Ile . . ." in *The Hungry Stream,* E. Margaret Crawford, ed., Belfast 1997, p. 36).

Already weakened by malnutrition, the Irish were crowded aboard ships unfit for human transportation. Unscrupulous shipowners provided no sanitary facilities. Emigrants arrived sick and miserable at Grosse Ile quarantine station, Quebec, where typhus spread quickly to epidemic proportions despite outstanding humanitarian efforts.

The latest Canadian research puts the number of deaths among emigrants arriving through Quebec in 1847 at 17,477 (Andre Charbonneau and Andre Sevigny, *Grosse Ile: A Record of Daily Events,* Canadian Heritage Ottawa, 1997; a companion volume, *A Register of Deceased Persons at Sea and on Grosse Ile in 1847,* contains the names of 8,308 who died on the coffin ships or at the quarantine island). Of the 98,649 emigrants, mostly Irish, who sailed for Quebec, 5,293 perished on board ship, either during the crossing or in quarantine, and 3,452 while detained on Grosse Ile; the remaining deaths occurred in Quebec, Montreal, Lachine, Toronto and other Canadian towns.

Emigration to New Brunswick followed the same calamitous course on a smaller scale. One-seventh of the 16,000 Irish immigrants who passed through Partridge Island and Middle Island quarantine stations died before the year was out. The cumulative

Irish immigrants aboard a coffin ship

effect of federal and state legislation in the spring of 1847 had been to turn the worst of the emigration northwards; and, although the season was among the worst experienced by the United States, New York and Boston avoided the epidemics of Quebec and Montreal (Oliver MacDonagh, "Irish emigration . . . during the Famine" in *The Great Famine,* R. D. Edwards and T. D. Williams, eds., Dublin 1994 edn., pp. 371–79).

About 400 sailing ships took part in this tragic odyssey; the average age of those who died was twenty. While the Atlantic crossing was made normally in forty-five days, twenty-six vessels took over sixty days to reach Grosse Ile. Liverpool and Cork were the main ports of embarkation. Refugees from western counties generally walked to Dublin and crossed to Liverpool—"the gateway to the Atlantic"—on the decks of cattle boats. Thousands who had escaped typhus in Ireland picked up infection in that city's notorious lodging houses. The holds, in turn, provided a congenial breeding ground for lice-borne bacilli, and fever ravaged the emigrants during and after the voyage to North America.

"Before the emigrant is a week at sea he is an altered man," wrote the philanthropist Stephen de Vere, of Curraghchase, County Limerick, who traveled to Quebec as a steerage passenger. "Hundreds of poor people, men, women and children, of all ages from the drivelling idiot of ninety to the babe just born, huddled together, without light, without air, wallowing in filth and breathing a fetid atmosphere, sick in body, dispirited in heart; the fevered patients lying between the sound . . ." (Noel Kissane, *The Irish Famine: A Documentary History,* National Library of Ireland 1995, pp. 162–63).

### GROSSE ILE

He noted the chaos and suffering at Grosse Ile: "Water covered with beds, cooking vessels etc. of the dead. Ghastly appearance of boats full of sick going ashore never to return. Several died between ship and shore. Wives separated from husbands, children from parents" (David Fitzpatrick, "Emigration" in *A New History of Ireland,* V, p. 582; "Flight from Famine" in *The Great Irish Famine,* Cathal Póirtéir, ed., Dublin 1995, p. 179).

One of the priests attending the sick, Bernard McGauran, declared: "It would be better to spend one's entire life in a hospital than to spend just a few hours in the hold of one of these vessels."

By May, more than 12,000 refugees were detained at Grosse Ile. Dr. George Douglas, the medical superintendent, said the Cork and Liverpool passengers were "half dead from starvation and want before embarking" (HC 1847–48 [50], xlvii). Disoriented, passive and fatalistic, many were drained of hope. On the other hand, such was de Vere's admiration for the patience of the poor, which he attributed to their faith, that he became a Catholic later in the year.

At the height of the disaster, 3,000 people lay ill on Grosse Ile and up to 86 burials took place each day. Imposing a quarantine on the small island was physically impossible, according to Dr Douglas. His decision that "healthy" passengers be quarantined on board contributed to the tragedy. A fatal delay of several days occurred before fever victims were removed. Infection enveloped the emigrants as healthy and ill, dying and dead were confined together in the sweltering heat.

Fr. Bernard O'Reilly said it was unacceptable that thousands of his fellow countrymen should be sacrificed through neglect and lack of foresight. Another priest, Elzéar-Alexandre Taschereau— later archbishop of Québec—observing how numbed to horrors the victims had become, saw "this as a new mark of degradation caused by an excess of suffering" (Charbonneau and Sevigny, *Grosse Ile*, p. 152; Donal A. Kerr, *The Catholic Church and the Famine*, Dublin 1996, pp. 43–50, 90).

The *Virginius,* one of the most notorious coffin ships, reached Grosse Ile in August after a nine-week voyage; 158 of its 476 passengers had died at sea; 180 were sick with typhus or dysentery. Those able to come on deck, Dr Douglas reported, were "ghastly yellow-looking spectres . . . not more than six or eight were really healthy." Douglas went on to describe the arrival of the *Naomi,* "another plague ship" chartered by Major Denis Mahon of Strokestown to deport one-third of the 3,000 tenants he had evicted from his Roscommon estate. Seventy-eight of its 331 passengers had died during the voyage and 104 arrived sick. The filth in the hold made it difficult to breathe. Some of the dead had to be dragged out with boat hooks, since even their own relatives refused to touch them.

The shipping of the destitute and diseased to Canada continued until perilously late in the season. Lord Palmerston, the British Foreign Secretary, had chartered nine ships to clear his Sligo estates of 2,000 tenants. One of these, the *Lord Ashburton,* was the last vessel to be inspected at Grosse Ile during the 1847 navigation season. The *Quebec Gazette* described its condition as "a disgrace to the home authorities." 107 passengers had died during the crossing and another sixty were ill. The *Canadien* denounced the British government's negligence in allowing passenger ships to leave so late in the season.

Two other ships chartered by Palmerston unloaded their human cargoes in St. John—as the St. Lawrence was closed by ice. An indignant city council censured him for having "exposed such a numerous and distressed portion of his tenantry to the severity and privations of a New Brunswick winter . . . unprovided with the common means of support, with broken-down constitutions and almost in a state of nudity." St. John was filled with "swarms of wretched beings going about the streets imploring every passer-by, women and children in the snow, without shoes or stockings and scarcely anything on."

A member of the Legislative Council asserted, in a letter to the British Colonial Secretary, that conditions aboard the ships bringing Irish paupers to Canada were "as bad as the slave trade" (Cecil Woodham-Smith, *The Great Hunger,* New York 1989 edn, pp. 228–29).

## 20,000 DIED

At least 20,000 immigrants had perished by the close of 1847, and 30,000 of the most able-bodied crossed to the U.S.; of those bound directly for the States between 8,000 and 9,000 died en route or shortly after arrival (including 500 on Deer Island quarantine station, near Boston). Some 453 orphaned children were adopted by French-Canadian families. Thousands died in the fever sheds on Grosse Ile. Others, released after cursory medical inspection, spread disease and death up the St. Lawrence. At Lachine, the dying Irish crawled through the streets, in vain begging shelter from the frightened inhabitants. Similar scenes were re-enacted in St. John, Boston, New York, New Orleans, and along inland routes.

In his haunting book, *The End of Hidden Ireland: Rebellion, Famine and Emigration* (New York 1995, p. 230), Robert James Scally says the migration in coffin ships "bears more resemblance to the slave trade or the boxcars of the Holocaust than to the routine crossing of a later age." For many refugees they were floating charnel houses to a land of false promises.

Although 95 percent of Famine emigrants survived the crossing with ingenuity and determination, their lifespan was often short. Reaching North America did not end their nightmare; bigotry and fear of disease inflamed anti-Irish prejudice. Nativism, poverty and the need for cohesion decreed that they settled initially in shantytowns in the east. While many remained in essentially Irish surroundings, those drawn outward by the lure of wages would eventually make up the main flow of immigrants, completing the transformation from Irish peasant to American worker.

The overcrowded and insanitary housing conditions contributed to severe social problems and a high mortality rate. Bishop John Hughes of New York compared Irish ghettos to the hovels from which most of their inhabitants had been transplanted. Irish immigrants made up 87 percent of that city's unskilled labor force by 1855.

In general, the Famine Irish experience in the New World was one of poverty and hardship or, at best, gradual improvement. The average emigrant, one exile wrote, "toils on, year after year, under a burning sun in summer and intense cold in winter, to earn a miserable subsistence, and is not so happy in his position as he would be in his own country with a single acre to raise potatoes for himself and family." He entered the American workforce at the bottom, competing only with free Blacks, frequently encountering "No Irish Need Apply" notices.

*See* Emigration: 1801–1921; Famine, the Great

BRENDAN Ó CATHAOIR

## FANNING, CHARLES (1942– )

Irish studies scholar. Born and raised in Norwood Massachusetts, Charles Fanning earned his B.A. from Harvard College in 1964 and his Ph.D. from the University of Pennsylvania in 1972, writing a dissertation entitled "Finley Peter Dunne and Mr Dooley: The Chicago Years." Since then he has taught at Bridgewater State College in Massachusetts, the University of Canterbury in New Zealand, the American Antiquarian Society in Massachusetts, the University of Missouri, and is currently a professor of English and History and Director of the Irish and Irish Immigration Studies Program at Southern Illinois University at Carbondale. His current teaching and research interests include Irish Studies and literature, American Studies and literature, British literature, and Post-Colonial literatures in English.

Fanning has received, among others, grants from the National Endowment for the Humanities and the U.S. Department

Charles Fanning

of Education, funding which has helped him to further his own research and to create opportunities for others to learn about and participate in Irish Studies. Among the honors and awards bestowed on Fanning for his work in Irish Studies are two American Irish Foundation Research Awards; the American Book Award of the Before Columbus Foundation for *The Exiles of Erin;* the Prize for Literary Criticism and Related Fields of the American Conference for Irish Studies for *The Irish Voice in America;* the Frederick Jackson Turner Award of the Organization of American Historians for *Finley Peter Dunne and Mr. Dooley;* the Hibernian Research Award from the University of Notre Dame; in addition to a fellowship and stipends from the National Endowment for the Humanities, the Newberry Library Research Fellowship, the Rockefeller Foundation Humanities Fellowship for Independent Study, and the American Council of Learned Societies Fellowship, among others.

In his field, Fanning is considered a leading scholar and has published heavily. Central to his research and publication interests are the "Mr. Dooley" writings of Finley Peter Dunne, the works of James T. Farrell and numerous other Irish-American authors and poets, the Chicago Irish, and the Irish-American immigrant experience. Fanning's most recent publication is the *Chicago Stories of James T. Farrell,* a collection he both edited and introduced. Also forthcoming is the second edition of *The Irish Voice in America,* in which Fanning adds a chapter on Irish-American literature since 1990. In addition, Fanning is presently researching writers of Irish ancestry in Australia and New Zealand.

Beyond the pursuit of his research and publication interests, Fanning, upon his arrival in 1993, created a continually evolving program in Irish and Irish Immigration Studies at Southern Illinois University at Carbondale. Not only does he direct the program, but he teaches many of the courses within the program as well. He encourages participation by students in a wide-range of activities relating to Irish Studies, supporting their academic endeavors well beyond the formal classroom. Toward that end, under Professor Fanning's direction, an exchange program with University College Galway was established, a program in which both graduate students and faculty continue to participate. These and numerous other activities provide tangible representation

of Charles Fanning's continued devotion to the advancement of Irish Studies.

Charles Fanning, *Chicago Stories of James T. Farrell* (Illinois, 1998).
———, *The Exiles of Erin: Nineteenth-Century Irish-American Fiction* (Notre Dame, 1987; Dufour Editions, 1997).
———, *Finley Peter Dunne and Mr. Dooley: The Chicago Years* (Kentucky, 1978).
———, *The Irish in Chicago,* with L. J. McCaffrey et al. (Illinois, 1987).
———, *The Irish Voice in America: Irish-American Fiction from the 1760s to the 1980s* (Kentucky, 1990).
———, *Mr. Dooley and the Chicago Irish: The Autobiography of a Nineteenth-Century Ethnic Group* (Washington, D.C., 1987).
———, *Nineteenth-Century Chicago Irish* (Chicago, 1980).
———, *The Woman of the House: Some Themes in Irish-American Fiction* (Boston, 1985).

ELIZABETH BRYMER

## FARLEY, JAMES ALOYSIUS (1888–1976)

United States Postmaster General, businessman and politician. He was born on May 30, 1888 at Grassy Point, New York. Farley graduated from Packard Commercial School in New York City and, in 1906, began working as a bookkeeper for Universal Gypsum Company, thus commencing his involvement in the business world (McLoughlin, 497). Between 1912 and 1919 Farley served as town clerk at Stony Point, New York. But then he returned to New York City to develop his building materials interests and to enter the political field.

Serving first as a port warden for the New York Port Facility and then on the board of the New York Athletic Commission, Farley afterwards was elected a member of the New York State Assembly (McLoughlin, 497). While his business enterprises expanded in New York City during the late 1920s and 1930s, Farley's political presence within the Democratic Party, locally and nationally, began to become more prominent.

In rapid succession from 1928 through 1932, Farley organized Franklin Delano Roosevelt's successful 1928 campaign for governor of New York, was named chairman of the New York State Democratic Committee after having served as that group's secretary, and in 1932 headed up Roosevelt's campaign for President of the United States as chairman of the Democratic National Committee. Roosevelt, upon assuming the presidency, named Farley to the office of United States Postmaster General.

In 1936, Farley spearheaded Roosevelt's successful reelection effort. But when Roosevelt sought a third term as President in 1940, Farley opposed him and in fact himself stood for the nomination. In her book, *Times To Remember* (1974), Rose Fitzgerald Kennedy quotes her son Joseph Kennedy, Jr. as writing to his father that, regarding the 1940 election, "Farley has come out and said that his name will be presented at Chicago regardless of what happens" (p. 240). As it was to develop, Joseph Kennedy, Jr. was selected as a Massachusetts Farley delegate to that Democratic National Convention at Chicago and remained loyal to the Postmaster General in his disagreement with Roosevelt's quest for a third term to the very end. Not surprising perhaps, when another Roman Catholic, Frank Comerford Walker, helped Roosevelt attain the nomination, he was named to succeed Farley as Postmaster General (31 August 1940).

James A. Farley remained in politics through the national elections of 1944, serving as New York State Democratic Committee chairman a second time and continuing in his disagreement with Roosevelt's being nominated once more for the presidency. Moving away from politics after that, Farley retired to his New York City apartment and turned his attention again to the world of business. He died on June 9, 1976 in New York City.

James A. Farley, *Behind the Ballots* (New York, 1938).

———, *Jim Farley's Story* (New York, 1948).

Rose Fitzgerald Kennedy, *Times to Remember* (New York, 1974).

Marianna McLoughlin, "Farley, James (1888–1976)," *The Encyclopedia of American Catholic History* (Collegeville, 1997).

J. P. Shenton, "Walker, Frank Comerford," *New Catholic Encyclopedia*, vol. XIV (Washington, D.C., 1967).

PATRICK FOLEY

### FARLEY, JOHN MURPHY CARDINAL (1842–1918)

Cardinal archbishop. Born April 20, 1842, in Newton Hamilton, County Armagh, to Philip and Catherine (Murphy) Farelly, Farley changed his surname to conform to its pronunciation in 1872. He left Ireland in 1864 when his parents died, came to New York where his merchant relatives were, and entered Saint John's (now Fordham). He received his priestly education at the North American College in Rome, where he was ordained June 11, 1870. He was consecrated a bishop December 31, 1895, made New York's fourth archbishop September 15, 1902, and created a cardinal November 27, 1911. He died September 17, 1918, and is buried in the prelates' crypt of Saint Patrick's Cathedral.

Farley created a series of boards, composed of chancery representatives and pastors for each ethnic group, to coordinate relations between the growing number of varied language groups and the chancery. Modernism led Farley to cut short Saint Joseph's Seminary's publication of the *New York Review,* but Farley left permanent marks on archdiocesan higher education in other ways: transferring the seminary from Sulpician to archdiocesan priests, helping to raise Fordham to university status, founding of Cathedral College for young men, and supporting three women's colleges: the College of New Rochelle, the College of Mount Saint Vincent, and Manhattanville College of the Sacred Heart. Farley was also interested in Catholics and the theater. Nationally, Farley was associated with the Catholic University of America, the *Catholic Encyclopedia,* and coordination of Catholic efforts to support World War I.

Farley's work with the Irish was complicated by the events of World War I. In 1916, a split in the Ancient Order of Hibernians threatened to politicize the Saint Patrick's Day parade. Farley's influence led factional leaders to compromise in order to conduct the parade, but Farley declined to review it. In 1918, Farley became caught between those who complained about Catholic support for Sinn Fein and those who thought opposition to Sinn Fein meant Farley was bowing to anti-Irish bigots. After the Easter Rebellion, Farley appealed for Irish Relief, but consciously or not, he balanced that interest with appeals for other charities. His own opinions were best expressed in 1912, when he renounced visiting Ireland until the British granted home rule, a vow that, with inadvertent help from wartime travel restrictions, he kept.

John M. Berry and Frances Panchok, "The Catholic Literary Imagination: Church and Theatre." *U.S. Catholic Historian,* 6/2–3 (Spring–Summer, 1987): 151–179.

Thomas J. Shelley, "John Cardinal Farley and Modernism in New York." *Church History,* 61 (1992): 350–361.

James J. Walsh, *Our American Cardinals* (New York and London: D. Appleton and Company, 1926).

MARY ELIZABETH BROWN

### FARRELL, JAMES AUGUSTINE (1862–1943)

Steel executive. Farrell was born in New Haven, Connecticut, to John Guy Farrell, an Irish Catholic from Dublin, and Catherine (Whalen) Farrell. Early in life, Farrell continued his father's interest in the merchant business after his father was lost at sea. In 1888, he moved to the United States and began working for the Pittsburgh Wire Company as a laborer. Farrell sought to further his position and began studies in the wire-drawing trade. In 1889 he was rewarded for his efforts with a promotion to salesman.

Farrell continued his interest in the trade and began increasing his knowledge of foreign markets. His advancement continued and in 1903 he became president of the U.S. Steel Products Corporation; in this position, he advanced the corporation's net gain threefold. In 1911, he was nominated and became president of United States Steel and held the position until 1932. Farrell's position in international foreign trade led him to the position of chairman of the Foreign Relations Committee of the American Iron and Steel Institute from 1910–1932, as well as to the position of chairman of the National Foreign Trade Council.

Farrell was known for his prudence and keen business relations. He resigned his position at U.S. Steel in 1932 and traveled between New York City and South Norwalk, Connecticut, enjoying sailing and other hobbies. He died of heart disease on March 28, 1943, at the age of eighty-one.

*Authentic History of the U.S. Steel Corporation* (1916).

Frank C. Harper, *Pittsburgh of Today,* 4 vols. (1931).

*Dictionary of American Biography,* supplement 3.

JOY HARRELL

### FARRELL, JAMES T. (1904–1979)

Novelist, short story writer. When James T. Farrell left his Chicago South Side Irish-American neighborhood in 1931 to live in New York and Paris, he took with him a prodigiously detailed memory of a boyhood, youth, and young manhood steeped in the hyphenate culture of that neighborhood. In fact, Farrell not only recollected the often grim, brutal details of Irish ghetto living, he recounted the challenges of its rough-and-tumble street life and its suffocating anti-intellectualism.

He was born February 27, 1904, one of fifteen children of James Francis Farrell and the former Mary Daly, and reared by his maternal grandmother and an uncle in lower-middle class circumstances. "It wasn't that there was anything wrong with my own parents," he once said, explaining the arrangement, "but when a new sister was born, I was sent to live with my grandmother for two weeks and I was the cock of the walk; when I went back home I threw a tantrum, so my mother said to my father, 'You might as well take him back to my mother.'"

Young James attended St. Anselm's Grammar School and had his first fistfight within two weeks of stepping on the playground. He reports that, when a bigger boy swore at him, "I went at this kid and knocked him down, bamming his head on the sidewalk. I sat on his chest, punching him. I almost massacred him." The son and grandson of teamsters, Farrell confessed, "I was supposed to go out on the wagons, too"; but he began writing early and narrowly escaped entering the family trade. He was, he claimed, a chip off the old block. The elder Farrell was something of a brawler, too, and, as James told it, "Periodically, he would get drunk, get into a fight which he would inevitably win and come home late, sometimes with a bruise on his face."

As an author, James T. Farrell gave that sort of street-toughness powerful expression, especially in the Lonigan saga and other autobiographical stories, novels, trilogies, and a pentology. *Young Lonigan* (1932) began with this memorable description of the hero leaving grammar school on graduation night:

> Studs Lonigan, on the verge of fifteen, and wearing his first suit of long trousers, stood in the bathroom with a Sweet Caporal pasted in his mug. His hands were jammed in his trouser pockets, and he sneered. He puffed, drew the fag out of his mouth, inhaled and said to himself, "Well, I'm kissin the old dump goodbye tonight."

After elementary school, Farrell went to St. Cyril's High School, where he showed promise as a writer and won letters in baseball, football, and basketball. His fiction is full of exaggerated athletic heroism and brims with abundant self-pity. Like Joyce, he decided "to fly the nets" of his neighborhood; and, like Joyce, he remained always aware of his origins and the consequences of his origins: "I am a second-generation Irish-American," he wrote later. "The effects and scars of immigration are upon my life. The past was dragging through my boyhood and adolescence. Horatio Alger, Jr., died only seven years before I was born. The 'climate of opinion' (to use a phrase of Alfred North Whitehead) was one of hope. But for an Irish boy born in Chicago in 1904, the past was a tragedy of his people. . . ."

The short story "Studs," written in 1929, before he had published any other fiction, is particularly important as an introduction to Farrell, and not just to his most famous work, the Studs Lonigan trilogy. He wrote:

> This, one of my first stories, is the nucleus out of which the Studs Lonigan trilogy was conceived, imagined, and written. It should suggest the experience and background of these books and my own relationship to their background. But for the accident of this story, and of the impressions recorded in it, I should probably never have written the Studs Lonigan series.

And one might reasonably speculate that few, if any, of the subsequent fifty-one volumes that provide a panorama of urban Irish-America in the first three-quarters of the century probably would have been written. Farrell forgot nothing, he reported everything.

Though he attended the University of Chicago on and off for three years and went nights to De Paul University after that, Farrell was never graduated from either. He was a voracious reader with a bent for social history and political philosophy. He learned on the job—in fact, on a variety of jobs that helped shape his life, his fiction, and his politics. Among other employments, he worked as a gas-station attendant, an express company clerk, and a salesman of shoes, cigars, and advertising. It was in 1929, "the Year of the Crash," that he began to write stories.

From the nucleus of the story "Studs" came Farrell's most famous trilogy, *Young Lonigan* (1932), *The Young Manhood of Studs Lonigan* (1934), and *Judgment Day* (1935). Significantly, the nar-

James T. Farrell

rator of the trilogy is Danny O'Neill. Through the eyes of Danny, Farrell not only records an Irish-American wake but reveals the shallowness and emptiness of the dreams and fantasies that lead to Studs' death at age twenty-six. In the trilogy, Studs is survived by Danny O'Neill, whose story—in many ways, Farrell's own—is set down in the O'Neill-O'Flaherty pentology: *A World I Never Made* (1936), *No Star Is Lost* (1938), *Father and Son* (1940), *My Days of Anger* (1943), and *The Face of Time* (1953).

In addition to these eight novels, which comprise his most significant works, Farrell published over twenty other novels, including the Bernard Clare trilogy and eight volumes of the *Universe of Time* series, originally projected for some thirty volumes. In an active writing career that spanned more than fifty years—in decades that saw considerable political activity and writing—ending with his death in 1979, Farrell wrote 250 or more short stories that extended his extraordinary range of types and incidents and which were collected in such volumes as *Calico Shoes and Other Stories* (1934), *Guillotine Party and Other Stories* (1935), *Can All This Grandeur Perish? and Other Stories* (1937), *$1,000 A Week and Other Stories* (1942), *To Whom It May Concern and Other Stories* (1944), *When Boyhood Dreams Come True* (1946), *The Life Adventurous and Other Stories* (1947), *An American Dream Girl* (1950), *French Girls Are Vicious and Other Stories* (1955), *A Dangerous Woman and Other Stories* (1957), *Side Street and Other Stories* (1961), *Sound of a City* (1962), *Childhood Is Not Forever* (1969), and *Judith and Other Stories* (1973).

In addition to his fiction, Farrell produced a body of critical essays that are at times acute and penetrating in their judgments of the literature of the century and in their understanding of the political and social tenor of the period. His *League of Frightened Philistines* (1945), for example, set out unorthodox theories based on Marxist principles that he believed should govern literary criticism and publishing.

With pardonable chagrin, Farrell felt that too many of his readers dwelt too long on the Studs Lonigan trilogy at the expense of other works and that this narrow approach kept him in a kind of critical limbo. "As the story grew into a novel, I asked myself what Studs's life had been like during his short years," he once wrote. "I had planned a novel of one volume, beginning with the night of Studs's graduation from grammar school in

June of 1916. But as I wrote—for some twenty months I had written most of what was to become the first two volumes of this trilogy revising and rewriting some chapters a number of times." Studs enters life as a young man of enormous potential but, over twelve years, deteriorates into a drifter and wastrel, a petty criminal, an alcoholic and a gambler.

Vanguard Press in New York cautiously put out the first volume in a plain brown paper dust jacket with the warning: "This novel is issued in a special edition the sale of which is limited to physicians, surgeons, psychologists, psychiatrists, sociologists, social workers, teachers and other persons having a professional interest in the psychology of adolescence." It attracted widespread praise, particularly for the accuracy and honesty that its blunt style and gritty vividness conveyed. A *New York Times* critic said it was certain "this book is no novel," that the publishers must have called it fiction "for lack of a better classification." A *Nation* critic hailed it for its "honest, unspectacular realism."

What is certain is that the Studs trilogy had an enormous impact on the literary world of the '30s: H. L. Mencken called Farrell "the best living American novelist," and many readers and critics were deeply moved by what they saw as the absolute honesty and realism of his account of Studs' boyhood. Herschel Bricknell, in *The Review of Reviews,* called the trilogy "the most considerable contribution to proletarian fiction that has yet been made in this country."

The trilogy won Farrell a "Book-of-the-Month Club Award" in 1937, but in later years he grew to resent the fact that the critics continued to prefer Studs to the subsequent works. He once told an interviewer bleakly that "Studs's been a chain around my neck." Nevertheless, even he must have felt the staying power of the trilogy when, shortly before his death, it was dramatized as a six-hour miniseries in March 1979.

The first volume of his next novel cycle recounted the rise of Danny O'Neill. In *A World I Never Made* (1936) and the rest of the O'Neill autobiographical saga, Farrell traced the by-now familiar story of his protagonist's progress from Chicago's South Side to a sophisticated literary life in New York. If Studs inherited Farrell's penchant for aimless drifting, Danny O'Neill inherited his sensitivity, intellectual curiosity and passion for language. Though the O'Neill series carries the style and tradition of Studs, Farrell's obvious sympathy for O'Neill blunts his realism; nothing after the Lonigan trilogy captivates readers and critics in quite the same way.

Farrell brought a Dreiser-Zolaesque realism to the fore against an Irish-American background and literally shocked an American public unused to such callous brutality and sexual explicitness. In 1937 Farrell was cleared of writing "obscene novels" in a suit brought by John S. Sumner of the Society of the Suppression of Vice in New York and cleared in a second suit, filed in 1949 in Philadelphia against several writers, for "pornography arising from their novels." The effect of the censorship was a renewed popularity that vaulted Farrell into international critical prominence. Millions of copies of the Lonigan books were sold.

Farrell's political views were also suspect. Like many other authors writing out of the Depression and post-Depression periods, he stood politically far to the left. And, though he denounced Stalinist Communism, he became an outspoken critic of capitalism as chairman of the American Committee for Cultural Freedom from 1954–1956. Unfortunately, his fiction was often marred by long, disjointed propagandistic runs that were repetitious and tedious.

Farrell once said, "I don't have a method; I sit down and write." And, during the lean years, he kept on writing, mostly novels, criticism, and poetry. His later work had relatively little critical or commercial success. The sales of nine novels that Doubleday published in the '60s and '70s averaged only 8,000 copies each. Though he was frustrated at the critical apathy his work had received over those decades, Farrell fought back. In 1967 he wrote to the editor of *The Times Book Review* saying, "As a matter of data 'for the files' I wish to give you a partial list of names of those who have found some merit in my various writings." Five pages of double columns listing admirers, from H. L. Mencken to Mercedes McCambridge, followed. Farrell admitted in an interview that he had vast ambitions and an incurable ego. "When I was working in a gas station as a boy, they thought I was a genius and I've never believed in failure. And then, I always wanted to write about my family; I think that had much to do with it."

Farrell's critics have called him "a master of naturalism" and variously compared him to Dreiser, Flaubert, Zola, and other European realists, but Farrell rejected such labeling; he preferred to go his way unimpeded by comparisons to the literary lions. He sought to promote social reform through his writing: "If there is any hatred in my books, it is not directed against people but against conditions that brutalize human beings and produce spiritual and material poverty," he said. His writing embodies an environmental determinism that is derived from philosophical Marxism, but the core experience out of which he writes and the language of his most memorable characters is lower-class Irish-American from Chicago's South Side.

In 1931 Farrell married Dorothy Patricia Butler, but they were later divorced, and he married the actress Hortense Alden. He had a son by Alden. When that marriage ended in divorce, he remarried his first wife, in 1955, though they separated three years later. Cleo Paturis, a New York editor, was after that Farrell's longtime live-in companion.

Farrell died in New York at age 75 on August 22, 1979. A cantankerous old man with little faith in the critics, he composed his own verse obituary.

> My Obituary
> One James (T. for Thomas)
>   Farrell
> Who might have been this,
> And who might have been that,
> But who might have been
> Neither this nor that,
> And who wrote too much,
> And who fought too much,
> And who kissed too much,
> For all of his friends,
> (He needed no enemies)—
> That man, J. T. F.
> Died last night
> Of a deprivation of time.
> He willed his dust
> To the public domain.
>         —James T. Farrell, 1962

*See* Fiction, Irish-American

Daniel J. Casey and Robert E. Rhodes, eds., "James T. Farrell," in *Modern Irish-American Fiction: A Reader,* (Syracuse, N.Y., 1989).
Donald Heiney, *Recent American Literature* (Great Neck, NY, 1958).

Barry O'Connell, "Lost World of James T. Farrell's Short Stories," in *Irish-American Fiction: Essays in Criticism,* eds., Casey and Rhodes (NY, 1979).

Eric Pace, "James T. Farrell, Realistic Novelist, Dies . . .," *New York Times* Obituary (August 23, 1979).

DANIEL J. CASEY

## FARROW, MIA (1945–   )

Actress. Born Maria de Lourdes Villiers Farrow to Maureen Paula O'Sullivan (actress) and John Villiers Farrow (director), Farrow survived a childhood which included a bout with polio at age nine and the pursuit of a vocation as a nun at age twelve, only to discover her talent as an actress in film at age fourteen. Farrow visited New York and soon found a place in her first role in an off-Broadway production of *The Importance of Being Earnest* in 1963; she was then recruited by Twentieth Century-Fox for a role in the popular television series *Peyton Place.*

Farrow attracted media attention when at age twenty-one she married Frank Sinatra. However, the marriage was short-lived and the couple separated in 1967. Farrow's career blossomed after the success of her third major motion picture, *Rosemary's Baby.* In 1969 she starred in *John and Mary* with Dustin Hoffman. She then enjoyed many leading roles in films such as *Hannah and Her Sisters* (1986), *The Great Gatsby* (1973), *Husbands and Wives* (1992), *Widow's Peak* (1994), and *Reckless* (1995).

Farrow's personal life took yet another turn when she became involved with conductor André Previn and in 1970 she gave birth to their twin boys; she married Previn later that same year. Farrow, at age twenty-nine, continued her career and starred in *The Great Gatsby,* had another son and adopted three Asian children. Farrow then divorced Previn and had an affair with cinematographer Sven Nyquist. At age thirty-four she became Woody Allen's girlfriend and leading lady and starred in thirteen of Allen's pictures. She gave birth to his son and adopted two more children with him before their marriage ended in divorce and a bitter custody battle in which Farrow charged Allen with sexual abuse of their children, particularly Soon-Yi. The court awarded custody to Farrow and she has since chronicled her relationship with Allen in a book entitled *What Falls Away.*

*See* Cinema, Irish in

*Life,* 62 (May 5, 1967): 75.
*New York Times* (June 23, 1968).
*Newsweek,* 65 (January 4, 1965): 31.
*International Motion Picture Almanac* (1969).

EILEEN DANEY CARZO

## FAY, FRANCIS ANTHONY ("Frank") (1897–1961)

Actor, vaudevillian. Fay was born in San Francisco, California, to Irish descendants William and Molly (Tynan) who were both performers. He attended school in New York until fifth grade and then left to work in a Shakespearean company before choosing vaudeville as a profession. In 1917 Fay struck out on his own and performed comedy sketches before winning roles in the Broadway musical *Girl o' Mine* (1918) and several other productions during the following years.

In 1926, Fay wrote and produced the play *The Smart Alec* that was not very successful and caused financial strain. Better fortune was had when Fay married Barbara Stanwyck, a young aspiring actress, on August 26, 1928. Fay and Stanwyck moved to Hollywood and made movies together. By 1933, Stanwyck had gained much recognition and by 1935 the marriage had dissolved and ended in divorce. During this period Fay became known for his heavy drinking, but he continued to struggle in show business.

In 1936, Fay initiated a very successful radio program in which he recited lyrics to popular songs and then made satirical comments on them and the issues of the day. He continued to appear in movies, and a decisive break in his luck came when he was asked to star in the role of an eccentric alcoholic, Elwood P. Dowd, in a Broadway production of *Harvey.* Towards the end of his life, Fay worked only nightclubs and a few television offers. He died in Santa Monica, California, on September 25, 1961.

*See* Theater, Irish in

The Billy Rose Theatre Collection in the Library and Museum of the Performing Arts at New York Public Library at Lincoln Center.
"Frank Ray Returns," *New York Times* (October 27, 1957).
*Dictionary of American Biography,* supplement 7.

JOY HARRELL

## FAY, SIGOURNEY WEBSTER (1875–1919)

Priest, teacher, diplomatist. Fay was born on June 16, 1875, into a prominent Philadelphia family of Irish lineage. His mother was a descendant of Dr. James Hutchinson of Revolutionary War fame, his father a decorated veteran of the Civil War. Fay graduated from the University of Pennsylvania in 1897 and the Episcopal Divinity School in 1903. That same year he was ordained by Bishop Charles C. Grafton for the Episcopal diocese of Fond-du-Lac, Wisconsin, where he served as Grafton's archdeacon and later as professor of dogmatic theology at Nashotah House, a seminary famous for its Anglo-Catholic teachings.

Fay was a stalwart of the Anglo-Catholic wing of the church. He represented the High Church faction at the 1907 Richmond Convention, which identified a sharp division among American Episcopalians and led ultimately to the defection of more than twenty clergymen to the Catholic Church in what became known as the American Oxford Movement. Fay himself was received into the Catholic Church in 1908 and ordained by Cardinal James Gibbons in 1910. He quickly gained notice as a preacher and spiritual adviser and served as a confidential assistant to Gibbons. He also resumed his teaching career, first as professor of sacred theology at Catholic University of America and then as headmaster of the Newman School for Boys in Hackensack, New Jersey. The socially connected Fay's erudition, wit, and patrician charm strongly influenced Newman's most famous alumnus, F. Scott Fitzgerald, who dramatized their friendship in his first novel, *This Side of Paradise.*

Fay's extensive acquaintance among prominent British and Anglo-Irish diplomats and politicians led to special duty during World War I. Service in Italy as a uniformed officer in the American Red Cross in 1918 allowed him to meet secretly with Pope Benedict XV and to devise with Vatican officials an orchestrated effort to expunge from ongoing treaty negotiations a clause introduced by the Italian government to exclude the Holy See from any peace conference. Facing strong European opposition, Fay realized that he could work more effectively through his friends on the British Commission in Washington and with Arthur Balfour, the British Foreign Minister, in London.

Fay was also determined to use his international connections in the cause of Irish liberty. He had always celebrated his Irish ancestry, and in conjunction with his friend the Anglo-Irish writer and diplomat, Shane Leslie, he pressed his allies in the British government to support Irish aspirations for freedom in exchange for his help in winning support for the allied cause among American Catholics.

Created a monsignor by a grateful pope, Fay returned to the United States to prepare for a new round of diplomatic initiatives, only to succumb to influenza. He died in New York City on January 10, 1919.

*See* Fitzgerald, F. Scott

MORRIS MacGREGOR

## FEEHAN, PATRICK (1829–1902)

First archbishop of Chicago. Born in County Tipperary, Ireland, he entered the seminary at Maynooth, but completed his studies in St. Louis, Missouri, where he was ordained in 1852. In 1865 he became bishop of Nashville and worked diligently to meet the pastoral needs of the diocese, despite the loss of more than seventy priests and sisters to yellow fever in the 1870s.

He was made archbishop of Chicago in 1880 and during his tenure the Catholic population grew to 800,000. He was a man of prudence with fine administrative skills and a lifelong interest in education, all of which contributed to his being chosen head of the committee on schools at the Third Plenary Council of Baltimore in 1884. Although not given to public speaking appearances, he at times could be eloquent, as in his defense of the Ancient Order of Hibernians at a meeting of the American archbishops. He was also active in religious activities held in conjunction with the 1893 World's Columbian Exposition in Chicago.

In the later years, he was embroiled in controversies involving priests of the diocese. The first concerned a conflict with parishioners of St. Hedwig's parish over replacing their pastor, Anthony Kozlowski. The archbishop refused their demands, and some one thousand parishioners joined the excommunicated Kozlowski's Independent Catholic Church.

The other controversy involved Irish-born and American-born priests of Irish descent over the choice of an auxiliary bishop. When the archbishop chose his chancellor, Peter Muldoon, some twenty Irish-born priests wrote a defamatory letter to the apostolic delegate concerning Muldoon. When the delegate dismissed the charges, Fr. Jeremiah Crowley refused to submit to the archbishop and was excommunicated. Weakened by three bouts with pneumonia, Feehan died on July 12, 1902.

*See* Chicago, Aspects of

Cornelius J. Kirkfleet, *The Life of Patrick Augustine Feehan* (Chicago, 1922).

Charles Shanabruch, *Chicago's Catholics: The Evolution of an American Identity* (University of Notre Dame Press, 1981).

JAMES J. HALEY

## FEENEY, CHARLES (1931–  )

Philanthropist. In 1996, listing him as one of the four hundred richest people in America, *Forbes* magazine described Charles (Chuck) Feeney as "reclusive." It's a word that is often used in conjunction with the generous benefactor.

Charles Feeney

Over recent years, Feeney gave away over 650 million dollars anonymously to various charities and educational institutes. In 1996, the sale of Duty Free Shops, the billion-dollar multinational chain he co-founded in 1960 with a Cornell University classmate, forced Feeney into the open and he was revealed as the man behind a host of incredibly generous donations. *The Washington Post* described him as "a man who wanted to remain a nobody . . . [who] had financed a secret philanthropic organization . . . the fourth-largest charity in the United States."

*New York Times* columnist Maureen Dowd, writing about Feeney after he accepted an award at *Irish America* magazine's Business 100 luncheon in 1998 and, in a rare move for Feeney, spoke to the assembled guests, said his "desire for anonymity is startling in an age when people stamp their names on every available surface."

A native of Elizabeth, New Jersey, Feeney has roots in County Fermanagh and is a citizen of both the U.S. and Ireland. He was a leading member of the Irish-American peace delegation which helped secure the first IRA ceasefire in August 1994, and he also financed the establishment of the Sinn Fein office in Washington, D.C.

He also included a number of Irish colleges and third-level institutes among the various educational bodies he has given money to. As well as being a staunch supporter of Cornell University, his alma mater, Feeney gave $15 million to the University of Limerick and $10 million to Trinity College, Dublin. In all, he donated over $100 million to Irish universities.

In various interviews, Feeney has summed up his philanthropic bent very succinctly. He told the *New York Times* that one of the primary motivations behind his generosity was that "you can only wear one pair of shoes at a time." Another time, indicating his feelings on wealth accumulation, he notably asked, "Just what are people going to do with all this money? It's not like they can take it with them."

As a businessman, Feeney has an extremely diverse portfolio of interests, including investments in real estate, retailing, energy, hotels, venture capital and information technology.

He is married and has five children.

*Irish America Magazine*, vol. xii/4 (July/Aug. 1996); vol. xiv/2 (Mar./Apr. 1998).

DARINA MOLLOY

## FEENEY, LEONARD (1887–1978)

Author and controversial priest. For decades Father Leonard Feeney commanded headlines, favorable and unfavorable, as a darling and later a hairshirt of the church. Born in Lynn, Massachusetts, February 14, 1887, the son of Thomas B. and Delia A. (Leonard) Feeney, both Irish immigrants, he joined the Jesuit order in 1914 and was ordained in 1928. He won early recognition as a poet, essayist and lecturer. He served as president of the Catholic Poetry Society of America and as literary editor of *America*, writing a dozen books, including such bestsellers as *In Towns and Little Towns* (1927) and *Fish on Friday* (1934). In 1943 Sheed & Ward brought together the best of his work in a *Leonard Feeney Omnibus*. Feeney delivered the 1937 Advent sermons in St. Patrick's Cathedral with Cardinal Patrick Hayes presiding and *Time* magazine sitting in and quoting extensively. By his mid-forties he was a genuine celebrity.

The glamorous image began to unravel a few years after Feeney became associated with St. Benedict's Center, a gathering place for Catholic students at Harvard and Radcliffe that opened in 1940 in a former Cambridge furniture store, hard by Harvard Yard. Feeney, now teaching at a Jesuit seminary in suburban Weston, dropped by one day out of curiosity and was impressed by the Center's apostolic initiatives. Occasional trips became daily ones, and in 1943 he was named full-time chaplain. Feeney counseled, presided over afternoon teas, and gave Thursday evening lectures to crowds that overflowed the premises, forcing some to listen from the sidewalk by open windows. His standing as a literary figure enhanced St. Benedict's reputation, and the Center grew in renown. By the late 1940s it boasted 200 converts, 100 persons channeled into religious life, and 250 students enrolled in a variety of academic courses.

Meanwhile, Feeney was fixing on the principle that there was no salvation except through the Catholic Church. He based his theology on the Latin maxim *Extra ecclesiam nulla salus*, "outside the church no salvation," which he traced from the church Fathers, through Boniface VIII's *Unam Sanctam*, to the profession of faith taken by the Fathers of Vatican Council I. His theology was uncompromisingly severe and out of line with a growing Catholic ecumenism. It put him on a collision course with church authority. Admirers turned away, leaving him with a small, albeit rabid group of followers.

Triggering preoccupation with salvation theology was the atomic bombing of Japan in 1945. For Feeney it was an apocalyptic happening confirming the vice and corruption of the world, and it launched him on an aggressive evangelism fueled by vindictiveness and hate—against Jews and Protestants, institutions such as Harvard and Boston College, individual Jesuits and Boston archdiocesan officials, including Archbishop Richard J. Cushing. "Prodigy" had become "problem," and a very public one once Feeney took his crusade to the Boston Common for Sunday meetings marked by shouting matches, vicious heckling and near riots. The media dubbed the spectacle the Boston Heresy Case.

In 1949 church authorities cracked down. St. Benedict's Center was placed under interdict, Feeney was silenced by Cushing, then dismissed by the Jesuits from their order. The Vatican's Holy Office summoned him to appear in Rome, but Feeney ignored the summons. In 1953 Rome finally declared him excommunicated. Paradoxically, the excommunication was based not on the dogmatic questions raised by Feeney's insistence on the *Extra ecclesiam nulla salus* principle, but rather on disciplinary grounds, specifically "stubborn disobedience" in failing to appear "before the authorities of the Sacred Congregation."

Feeney and his followers, now grouped into a religious order called the Slaves of the Immaculate Heart of Mary, lived for a time in Boston-area tenements, then in 1957 they relocated to a 146-acre farm in the Central Massachusetts village of Still River. They named the property St. Benedict's. There they farmed and slipped gradually from sight and mind, except for occasional forays by individual members to various parts of the country where they hawked salvation tracts and Feeney books, often being arrested for peddling without a license and trying to incite a riot.

During the turmoil, long-time friends of Feeney and patrons of the old St. Benedict's—notably, Cardinals Humberto Medeiros of Boston and John Wright of the Vatican's Congregation for the Clergy—worked to affect a reconciliation. They achieved success when Feeney and twenty-nine of his followers were formed into a new community, the Pious Union of Benedictine Oblates. No recantation of dogmatic principles was demanded.

The Feeney reconciliation took place in 1972, but was not announced until 1974, the delay being due largely to questions over property rights spawned by the refusal of eighteen others of the community to accept reconciliation. The legal complication was that Feeney had placed ownership of the Still River property in the names of all members of the community, opening the door to numerous claims and counterclaims. The dissidents splintered off into a group of their own, the first of several such splits.

Feeney died January 30, 1978, at Nasoba Community Hospital, Ayer. He was 80. His funeral Mass was celebrated by two priest-brothers, Thomas Feeney, S.J., and John, a priest of the Boston archdiocese. Burial was at St. Benedict's in Still River.

John Deedy, "An Update on Leonard Feeney," *Commonweal*, January 7, 1977.

———, *Seven American Catholics* (Chicago, 1978).

JOHN DEEDY

## FENIAN RAIDS (1866; 1870; 1871)

After the Civil War in the United States the Fenian Brotherhood split into two factions. One faction led by John Devoy and John O'Mahoney wanted to send money, men and arms to Ireland to aid the freedom struggle. However, the other faction led by Colonel William Roberts wanted to attack British imperialism in Canada and hold it ransom in exchange for Ireland's freedom.

In May of 1866 the Roberts faction invaded Canada from Buffalo, when 800 men under General John O'Neill crossed the Niagra River and occupied Fort Erie. After some initial success at Ridgeway where they routed Canadian militia with an ambush and a fierce bayonet charge, they ran short of supplies and returned to Ft. Erie. They were arrested by American authorities. President Andrew Johnson issued an order forbidding further Fenian activities and confiscating their supplies. On June 7, 1866, a thousand Fenians commanded by General S. P. Spears crossed the border and occupied Pigeon Hill in Quebec. However, they retreated to the United States after American troops seized their supplies at St. Albans, Vermont when reinforcements camped at Malone, New York did not arrive. Other brief invasions occurred in New Brunswick near Campo Bello Island in

1866, Quebec in 1870 and Manitoba in 1871 but were countered by effective force. The Fenians apparently fought well but had supply problems that led to military failure. The Fenians had also counted on substantial help from Canadians, which obviously did not materialize. The Fenians assumed they would be exempt from the neutrality laws in the United States and many felt double-crossed when American authorities intervened.

It is well to remember that American authorities used the Fenians as threat for leverage in their negotiations with Britain in the Alabama Claims dispute and the recognition of naturalized United States citizens. The Fenians did strike fear into Canadians and many believed the Fenians were about to cross the border at any time. Canadian authorities followed Fenian movements and began to prepare for invasion. It is estimated that the Canadian government spent $1,000,000 related to the Fenian raid. A number of spies including "Red Jim" McDermott, a Fenian, supplied information to the Crown about Fenian operations. At its peak, the Fenians had possibly 50,000 members, most of whom had military experience and therefore had the potential to do a great deal of damage.

Although the raids failed to free Ireland from British rule, they had a significant effect in Canadian history. The Fenian threat promoted Canadian nationalism as the provinces had to unite for a common defense. In 1867, only a few months after the 1866 Raids, the separated provinces united in a confederation under the British North America Act, establishing the modern Nation of Canada. As a postscript, in 1868 Thomas D'Arcy McGee, the Father of Confederation, was assassinated while en route to his Ottawa home and Fenians were suspected as the assassins by many Canadians.

*See* Fenians and Clan na Gael

S. J. Connelly, ed., *The Oxford Campanion to Irish History* (New York, 1998).
Desmond Ryan, *The Fenian Chief: A Biography of James Stephens* (Dublin, 1967).

SEAMUS METRESS

## FENIANS AND CLAN NA GAEL, THE

### The Fenians

The Fenian Brotherhood was founded in New York in 1854 or 1855 as the Emmet Monument Association. The name explained its purpose: the overthrow of British rule in Ireland. In his famous speech from the dock on being sentenced to death in 1803, Robert Emmet said his epitaph should not be written until Ireland had taken her place among the nations of the earth. John O'Mahony and Michael Doheny, the founders of the Emmet Monument Association, which became the Fenian Brotherhood in 1858, refugees from the Young Ireland rebellion of 1848, were determined to make the writing of Emmet's epitaph a reality. They were aided by Joseph Doheny.

### The Irish Republican Brotherhood

O'Mahony and Doheny discussed sending an expeditionary force of exiles to Ireland in 1855, but it was impractical. O'Mahony sent a letter by courier to James Stephens in Dublin.

This letter from New York asked Stephens to start a new movement for Irish independence with Irish-American support. Stephens agreed to establish a revolutionary organization and set

conditions. Financial support on a monthly basis was essential. He called the new organization the Irish Revolutionary Brotherhood, later the Irish Republican Brotherhood, or IRB. The first members were John O'Leary and his friend Thomas Clarke Luby, a Protestant. They had worked with James Fintan Lalor who was trying to start a rising by seizing Dublin Castle before his death in 1849.

"Stephens had the root idea," O'Leary recalled, and consequently was the real founder of Fenianism. It began on March 17, 1858, in Dublin and spread fairly rapidly. As the Fenian Brotherhood grew in America and the IRB in Ireland both movements worked in tandem up to the split over the invasion of Canada which tore them apart. Many Fenians felt that Ireland, still prostrate after the Great Famine and its consequences, could not mount a successful insurrection, and argued that an invasion of Canada might be a bargaining chip with the British government.

When the U.S. Civil War ended in April 1865, thousands of soldiers in the Union armies who wanted to establish an independent Ireland joined the Fenian Brotherhood. Britain aided the Confederacy, materially and diplomatically, in the Civil War. This caused bad feeling toward Britain in the northern states.

John O'Mahony opposed the Canadian adventure because Ireland's battle for freedom would have to be fought in Ireland. The Irish in America, if they wished to join it, should go to Ireland to fight. The IRB and Stephens would decide when, where and how that would be done. The Fenian Brotherhood should support the IRB with money, arms and training officers, as had been agreed. But the siren song of crossing into Canada to free Ireland was tempting.

### An International Movement

Fenianism in the 1860s was an international movement. There were Fenians in Britain, Australia, New Zealand, Canada, the United States, South America and of course Ireland. O'Mahony, a Gaelic scholar, had translated Geoffrey Keating's *Foras Feasa ar Eirinn,* a survey of Irish history, into English. His interest in Irish mythology led to his adoption of the term "Fenians," from the Gaelic *Fian,* a warrior who guarded the shores of pre-Christian Ireland. Although a colonel in the New York National Guard O'Mahony was more literary man than soldier.

John O'Mahony

He lost control of the Fenian Brotherhood to advocates of war against Canada. A Fenian Brotherhood convention in November 1863 established an Advisory Council to limit his authority. In October 1865, the Advisory Council was replaced by a "Senate" and "House of Delegates," an Executive Government in exile, as the Foreign Office in London charged.

William R. Roberts, a millionaire dry goods merchant, was president of the Fenian Senate. O'Mahony controlled the treasury. In October 1865, Roberts appointed General Thomas W. Sweeney, an officer on the active list of the U.S. army, Fenian Secretary of War. A native of Dunmanway, County Cork, Sweeney was a professional soldier who commanded the Second Division of the Army of the Tennessee at the decisive battle of Atlanta in July 1864 under General William Tecumseh Sherman.

Sweeney drafted a war plan for the invasion of Canada. It was too ambitious for the resources of the Fenians, but he trusted the veterans he commanded to implement it. Victory or defeat depended on the U.S. attitude to an attack on Canada. With the United States neutral, an attack might succeed. Otherwise it would fail. After four years of civil war, the administration of President Johnson, Lincoln's successor, was not in a position to challenge Britain in North America, even for payment in Irish Democratic votes.

### A President's Guarantee

The Fenian Council continued to debate the proposed attack on Canada which O'Mahony and his ally, B. Doran Killian, opposed. Roberts accused O'Mahony and Killian of paying out "about $26,000—willfully and criminally expended by the above named individuals—for the hiring and purchase of an elegant mansion," the Moffat mansion, in Union Square, near Tammany Hall. O'Mahony was replaced as Head Center of the Fenian Brotherhood by Roberts who changed his title to the more American sounding "President of the Fenian Brotherhood." Following British protests over his role as Fenian Secretary of War, Sweeney was dismissed from the U.S. Army.

In the fall of 1865 Killian went to the White House to discuss with President Johnson and his Secretary of State, W. H. Seward, who was considered pro-British by the Irish and "reasonable" by the British, the administration's response to a Fenian raid on Canada and the occupation of British territory. Would the United States recognize the Fenians as belligerents if they attacked Canada? Johnson's enigmatic reply was that he would acknowledge the *fait accompli*.

Although O'Mahony opposed an attack on Canada as against his principles, he needed an alternative to Sweeney's operation and Killian's proposal that they buy a ship for $40,000 to ferry a small expedition to Campobello Island in the Bay of Fundy, between the province of New Brunswick, Canada, and the state of Maine; it sounded easy to carry out. They would land a few Fenians, fly an Irish flag and occupy the tiny island.

The United States had its own claim on Campobello because of its location directly off the Maine coast. If the Fenians seized the island as a base they would hand it over to Washington when their work was done. Killian commanded the expedition to Campobello on the wreck of a ship they had purchased with their treasury. Six British warships guarded the island; they knew they were coming, obviously, and occupation was out of the question and Killian surrendered to the U.S. army on the frontier. No shots were fired. The $40,000 purchase price of the ship left the Fenian treasury empty without a victory to celebrate.

### General Sweeney's Strategy

On taking command of the Fenian army in October 1865, General Sweeney wrote: "The most reliable accounts from Ireland have convinced me that our friends there are totally unprepared with the material means, necessary to contend, with any show of success, against the British troops, and that to excite an insurrection, at present, would be but to provoke a wholesale massacre, in which thousands of brave lives would be sacrificed in a useless struggle." Since he found no Fenian operations plan other than "to wait until something should turn up," he drafted his own Canadian plan.

A column from Detroit would cut the Great Western Railroad "to menace and occupy Port Stanley, Ontario, securing us a port on Lake Erie where we could receive supplies and reinforcements. . .

"A second column would cross the Niagara River against Hamilton, Ontario, which would hold or destroy the Welland Canal, interrupting all naval communication between Lakes Erie and Ontario. . . . A third column from Ogdensburg would seize and hold Brockville and Prescott and along the railroad up to Ottawa which has no fortifications and is defended by only five companies of Volunteers recruited from Government clerks and employees and known as the Civil Service Battalion . . ."

Sweeney's directive concluded: "Here [in Ottawa] we shall secure a number of important personages who will serve as hostages for our brothers lying in English jails." He suspected the Fenians would have to live off the land, but that would not be a problem for veterans. He anticipated no opposition in Quebec because its people resented English rule."

### The Battle of Ridgeway

Some 600 Fenian veterans under Colonel John O'Neil, a native of County Monaghan, who commanded a battalion of African American troops in the civil war, crossed the Niagara River near Buffalo, New York, on the night of May 31, 1866, and occupied Fort Erie, Ontario. Next day Ottawa put the number of "well armed" Fenians in Fort Erie at between 800 and 900. British regulars and Canadian Volunteers were dispatched by rail to Chippewa, sixteen miles from Fort Erie, with artillery. From Chippewa on June 2 they moved toward Fort Erie, detrained at Ridgeway and "came upon the Fenians encamped in the bush and immediately attacked them," Ottawa said. "This occurred some time on Saturday, June 2."

O'Neil moved in the darkness from Fort Erie to Ridgeway where the battle was joined almost immediately. O'Neil commanded a battalion of the Irish Republican Army. Eight Fenians were killed, sixteen wounded. Combined British-Canadian losses were ten dead and thirty-seven wounded. A diversion ordered by Sweeney did not take place. He accused the officer in charge of cowardice and dismissed him.

Without reinforcements or food, both of which were necessary, O'Neil withdrew to the shore of Lake Erie where his men were taken aboard the U.S. warship *Michigan* patrolling the lake and surrendered. The Fenians were disarmed and sent home. On June 5, 1866, President Johnson ordered the arrest of "all prominent, leading or conspicuous persons called 'Fenians' who . . . may be guilty of violations of the neutrality laws of the United States."

Florence E. Gibson in *The Attitudes of the New York Irish Toward State and National Affairs* [Columbia UP: 1951] comments: "The delay in the issuance of these documents from May 31 to

John Devoy

June 5 would indicate that the President was not too enthusiastic about stopping the Fenian invasion."

She quotes the British agent, Thomas Miller Beach [*alias* Henri Le Caron], an army companion who accompanied O'Neil to the White House in 1868 to meet the President. Johnson received O'Neil as "an old friend from Civil War days", saying: "General, your people unfairly blame me a good deal for the part I took in stopping your first movement. Now I want you to understand that my sympathies are entirely with you, and anything which lies in my power I am willing to do to assist you. But you must remember that I gave you five full days before issuing any proclamation stopping you. What, in God's name, more did you want?"

## PAPAL EXCOMMUNICATION

It was neither O'Neil's fault nor Sweeney's that the Fenians failed to achieve their goals in Canada. In 1870 O'Neil's adjutant, the British secret agent, Thomas Miller Beach, alias Henry Le Caron, was in charge of the Fenian arms dumps. O'Neil did not cross the border. The federal government struck first and arrested the Fenians. Federal marshals seized O'Neil at St. Albans, Vermont, on May 25, 1870, for violating the neutrality laws. Gibson calls his final Fenian raid a "debacle."

1870 was a bad year for Fenianism. On January 12, 1870, Pope Pius IX decreed that membership in the Fenians was subject to excommunication. This decree was promulgated in every American diocese and it struck at Fenians and their supporters all over America. The Fenians were condemned from pulpits and they splintered and waned. Without military success and hit by a papal condemnation, the influence of the Fenians faded.

Stephens, the Chief Organizer of the Irish Republic, was in New York during the Fenian attack on Canada which he condemned. He took control of the O'Mahony faction of the Fenian Brotherhood, and was dismissed himself at a meeting of American IRB officers in New York on December 15, 1866. They demanded a date for a rising in Ireland. When he refused to give it they fired him and even threatened to shoot him. He returned to France, as he was still a wanted man in Ireland.

Colonel Thomas J. Kelly, the IRB Chief of Staff, took command of the IRB and moved to Manchester, England, to hold a conven-

tion and reorganize the movement. He was arrested on September 8, 1867, and rescued from the van taking him to prison. A police sergeant was shot dead, Kelly escaped and was not caught again. Three Fenians in the rescue party, Allen, Larkin and O'Brien, called "the Manchester martyrs," were hanged. An attempt to free a Fenian officer, Colonel Richard O'Sullivan Burke, from Clerkenwell prison, London, using explosives to blow in a wall, killed a dozen people and wounded 120. A man was hanged for it.

The heavy defeats suffered by the American and Irish wings of the Fenian movement in the 1860s undermined the morale of members who had sacrificed themselves in prisons or on the run and sometimes in battle without expectation of recognition or reward.

The Fenian rising in Ireland in March 1867 was a "military fiasco," according to John Devoy, who was in prison at the time with most of the IRB leadership, except Stephens who escaped to France. That chapter of Irish history closed and another opened.

## CLAN NA GAEL

Clan na Gael, a secret Irish-American revolutionary society, began life in Hester Street, New York, on June 20, 1867, the anniversary of the birth of Wolfe Tone, the father of Irish Republicanism. The Clan was a Fenian organization without ever talking about it. Its chief figures were Fenians. Within ten years of its founding it was the only effective Irish body in America. "The chief figure at the [Hester Street] meeting," which founded Clan na Gael, John Devoy wrote in the *Gaelic American* of November 29, 1924, "and the inspirer of the movement was Jerome J. Collins, a very able man, a civil engineer who had to flee from London in 1866 because a plot to rescue the newly convicted Fenian prisoners, then in Pentonville Prison, became known to the Government."

Collins, who was not then a Fenian, was working for an iron construction firm in London which permitted him to inspect the prison blocks and locate the cells of the Fenian prisoners, who included leading figures of the movement such as John O'Leary, Thomas Clarke Luby, Charles Kickham, O' Donovan Rossa, Denis Dowling Mulcahy, among others. They had been transferred from Mountjoy Prison, Dublin, to London.

When the authorities became aware of what was afoot, the rescue attempt was abandoned. Collins, a native of Dunmanway, County Cork, fled to the United States and joined the Fenian Brotherhood. Some days after the founding meeting of Clan na Gael, Collins joined an expedition to the Arctic, and perished of cold and hunger.

The founding of Clan na Gael was not intended to create a rival organization to the Fenian Brotherhood, then hopelessly split and ineffectual. It originated in a plan of Collins to kidnap Prince Arthur of Connaught, then on a visit to America, and hold him as a hostage in exchange for the release of the Fenian prisoners.

An engineer in New Jersey, Collins employed many Fenian workers. The men selected for the operation belonged to both sides of the Fenian divide. The plot failed because of a change in the prince's plans, which was probably just as well for the nascent Clan and the Irish of New Jersey and New York.

The organization was divided into camps or clubs. It grew slowly at first. The camps were numbered in the order of organization, John Devoy explained. Number 1 was in New York, Number 2 in Jersey City, Number 3 in Buffalo, Number 4 in New

York, Number 5 in Boston, Number 6 in Jersey City, and so on to Number 64 in San Francisco. An early Clan chairman was Dr. William Carroll of Philadelphia, a Donegal Presbyterian who had been a major in the Union Army.

## The Dynamite War, New Leaders

Clan na Gael set up a Revolutionary Directory of seven members: three nominated by the Clan Executive, three by the Supreme Council of the IRB, and one by the executive of the Fenian movement in Australia and New Zealand.

But in December 1875, O' Donovan Rossa, who did not join Clan na Gael, established a "Skirmishing Club" to conduct uninhibited underground warfare against Britain for her conduct in Ireland. His inspiration came from Patrick Ford, editor of *The Irish World*. The Clan took over the fund and in 1881 three men called collectively the Triangle, Alexander Sullivan, Michael Boland and Denis Feely, were in control of Clan na Gael.

The new leadership initiated a dynamite campaign against London, as a reprisal, it was claimed, to coercion in Ireland. Lives were lost. Dedicated volunteers placed bombs in public buildings and the Houses of Parliament. The latter was the most successful operation of the campaign: the man responsible was Luke Dillon, born in Leeds of Irish parents, raised in the United States, a resident of the city of Philadelphia. During the Boer War he tried to blow up the Welland Canal in Canada, was arrested as he walked away and spent fourteen years in prison for a deed that took no lives.

Devoy denounced the dynamite campaign, but worked for those who suffered imprisonment because of it. One such was Tom Clarke, his close collaborator later in New York and Dublin. Clarke spent sixteen years in English prisons under the direst conditions. The experience did not dampen his ardor for the cause in any way.

While the Davitt-Parnell Land League was waging a campaign of passive and sometimes active resistance to landlordism throughout Ireland, with the backing of Devoy whose New Departure policy was attempting to bring about a social revolution, the Triangle leadership of the Clan, Devoy and others charged, was "substituting a dynamite policy for one of insurrection; of terrorism to force concessions from the British Government rather than starting a fight for independence to drive the English out of Ireland."

## Split in Clan na Gael

One result of the dynamite campaign was a split in Clan na Gael which retarded progress for fifteen years, according to Devoy. Another was the murder of Dr. Philip Henry Cronin, which was "the direct result of branding all critics as British agents." [*Devoy's Post Bag,* vol. 2, eds. William O'Brien and Desmond Ryan, p. 233.]

To make peace with the IRB Supreme Council, Alexander Sullivan sent General F. F. Millen, the British agent, a fact unknown until recently, as his delegate to Ireland. Millen also accompanied Devoy to Ireland in 1879 when they met members of the Supreme Council and Parnell. He was present, too, as a member of the delegation that interviewed M. Shiskin, the Russian Minister at Washington, in 1876. The other Clan delegates were Dr. Carroll and Devoy.

Shiskin impressed Devoy when he said there was no public demand in Ireland for separation from Britain, that representatives of the British Crown were well received wherever they went in Ireland. Devoy could not disagree with these statements. He was determined to do something about it.

Two years after his meeting with Shiskin, Devoy founded *The Irish Nation* to educate Irish-Americans on the issues in Ireland and America, as Clan na Gael saw them. It began publication in November 1881. It boosted Parnell, the Land League and the Irish Home Rule Party among Irish-Americans.

It spotlighted coercion in Ireland after the Phoenix Park assassinations of the new Chief Secretary for Ireland, Lord Frederick Cavendish, and the permanent Under Secretary Thomas Henry Burke on May 6, 1882, by the Invincibles, five of whom were hanged. Pat O'Donnell, who shot Carey, the Invincible informer, en route to South Africa, was also hanged. A Donegal man, he had worked in the Pennsylvania coal mines with the Molly Maguires, twenty of whom were hanged for labor-related crimes.

## Rule of the Triangle

Under the direction of the Triangle, a hand-picked executive board held absolute power to run Clan na Gael from 1881. Expenditures were not accounted for and one consistent critic, Dr. Philip Cronin, was accused of treason for demanding explanations for monies spent. Cronin, who was a friend of Devoy, was expelled from Clan na Gael. Devoy himself always went armed in Chicago where Alexander Sullivan was a dominant figure. At a joint convention of the Devoy and Sullivan factions in June 1888 to reunify the Clan, Dr Cronin repeated his charges. At a trial of two Triangle backers in August 1888 it was revealed that the leadership had destroyed its financial records. A majority report exculpated Sullivan and his colleagues. A minority report found $85,000 in Clan funds missing.

Dr. Cronin, who sought to have the record published, disappeared on May 4, 1889. On May 22 his body was found in a sewer. Three men charged with conspiracy to murder Dr. Cronin were members of Camp 20 of Clan na Gael in Chicago. Sullivan was charged with complicity in the conspiracy to murder Dr. Cronin, but there was insufficient evidence to indict him. The murder of Dr. Cronin was a low point in the history of Clan na Gael.

Devoy reunited the Clan, established firm relations with the IRB, and at the start of the twentieth century launched the weekly *Gaelic American*.

## Clan-IRB Relations

Clan na Gael largely financed the Supreme Council of the IRB after reunification. The IRB was small and compact. It operated secretly, and had few resources. It depended on the Clan for financial aid. The Clan was large, relatively affluent and politically sophisticated and influential.

The Clan gave the IRB a subsidy of about 350 pounds a year, between 1905 and 1916, when the pound was worth five dollars. It kept the IRB in business. The Clan supported leaders it had confidence in and ignored others who quickly got the message and quit. In 1912 Devoy was responsible for tilting the balance in the IRB leadership to Tom Clarke and his *protege,* Sean McDermott. They were elected to two key positions on the Supreme Council: Secretary and Treasurer. Clarke, who transferred from New York to Dublin in 1907, was elected to the Supreme Council. He was the key man of the IRB from 1912 to 1916 with Sean McDermott. When the Irish Volunteers were organized in November 1913, several sums of one thousand pounds were specially sent over on urgent appeals from the IRB.

## DEVOY MEETS GERMAN ENVOY

Devoy was a keen student of international affairs. In 1914 he knew war was on the way. He planned to make England's difficulty Ireland's opportunity. He was in "constant communication through Tom Clarke" with the IRB. "Soon after the outbreak of the World War, a special committee of the Clan na Gael presented Ireland's case to the German ambassador, Count von Bernstorff," Devoy wrote in *Recollections* published in 1929, a year after his death,

Franz von Papen, Chancellor of Germany immediately before Adolph Hitler took power, was Germany's military *attache* in Washington in 1914. He was present at the meeting between Devoy and the German ambassador. Devoy said "our friends in Ireland intended to use the opportunity presented by the war to make an effort to overthrow English rule in Ireland and set up an independent government; that they had not an adequate supply of arms, had no trained officers, and wanted Germany to supply the arms and a sufficient number of capable officers to make a good start, but that we wanted no money. We needed military help only. This was stated with clearness and emphasis."

## 1916 AND AFTER

From this meeting grew the decision of the IRB to stage a rebellion in Dublin if Germany landed sufficient arms to give the rebels a chance of success. Germany sent a shipload of arms and ammunition for 20,000 men. The rising was to be an all-Irish affair. The British Navy intercepted the arms ship *Aud* which its skipper scuttled, sending its cargo of arms to the Atlantic floor. British Naval Intelligence tracked the ship to Ireland. Devoy wrongly blamed the Wilson administration for passing the information.

The Dublin rebellion lasted from Monday to Saturday of Easter Week 1916. The IRB declared an Irish Republic, fought to defend it, and changed history in the process. Devoy was still active a year after the rising, attempting to get German aid for a repeat performance. The Germans would have sent arms but with the executions the IRB was left leaderless. There was no one left to handle an arms shipment on the scale of 1916.

There followed the rise of Sinn Fein with the elections of December 1918, and the establishment on January 21, 1919, of Dail Eireann, the Parliament of the Irish Republic. On the same day, an ambush at Soloheadbeg, County Tipperary, ushered in the kind of guerrilla warfare that is referred to when one speaks of the Irish War of Independence.

The IRB, whose leadership perished in the Easter Rising, was reorganized under a series of Supreme Councils between 1916 and the ratification of the Anglo-Irish Treaty in January 1922. Ireland was partitioned. The IRB by secret majority vote backed the Treaty—and so did John Devoy.

See Devoy, John; Kelly, Thomas; Nationalism,
   Irish-American (2 entries); Republicanism, Irish American

Florence Gibson, *Attitudes of the NY Irish Towards State and National Affairs, 1848–1892* (New York, 1951).

Leon O'Broin, *Fenian Fever* (London, 1971).

———, *Revolutionary Underground* (Dublin, 1976).

John Devoy, *Recollections of an Irish Rebel* (New York, 1929).

Sean Cronin, *McGarrity Papers* (Tralee, 1972).

William O'Brien and Desmond Ryan, *Devoy's Post Bag*, vols. 1 and 2 (Dublin, 1948/1953).

Desmond Ryan, *The Fenian Chief* (Dublin, 1967).

John O'Leary, *Fenians & Fenianism*, vol. I (London, 1896).

T. W. Moody, ed., *The Fenian Movement,* Thomas Davis Lectures (Cork, 1968).

———, *Davitt and the Irish Revolution* (Oxford, 1982).

SEÁN CRONIN

## FENIANS AND THE ARMY

Commanders of Western posts found Fenianism a popular expression among their Irish troops. In 1868, a soldier stationed at Fort D. A. Russell, Dakota Territory, claimed that "seven-eighths of the men of this Regiment are Sworn Fenians." Fort Whipple, Arizona Territory, also had a considerable Fenian presence; however, here as elsewhere, soldiers expressed their political sentiments by attending meetings and collecting donations. Soldiers stationed at Fort Pembina, Dakota Territory, actually "apprehended" a Fenian raiding party led by John O'Neil. This group, thinking they had captured a Canadian-based Hudson Bay Trading Post, were arrested by Captain Wheaton of the Twentieth Infantry when he determined the post was on the American side of the border. None of these Fenians were ever punished for the infraction as no jury in that country would convict them.

The ambitions of Irish soldiers who desired a direct U.S.-Anglo confrontation escalated when the U.S. Senate and House rejected an initial British offer to settle the "*Alabama* Claims." The *Alabama* was a British-built battleship that destroyed sixty-eight Union ships during the Civil War. American animosity toward Britain remained high in the post-war years and Fenian sympathizers among the soldiers at Fort Fred Steele, Dakota Territory, hoped that war with Britain would not only help the cause of Irish freedom but would give them a "chance of a brush with the English Red Coats." These aspirations never materialized and Fenianism declined among Irish soldiers after the U.S. and Britain sucessfully arbitrated differences. However, Irish culture and sympathy for a "free Ireland" remained dynamic among the soldiers serving in the U.S. Army during the nineteenth century.

See Fenians and Clan na Gael

"Fenians in Dakota," *South Dakota Historical Collections*, Volume 6 (1912): 117–30b.

Maurice Woulfe, Fort D. A. Russell, Dakota Terr., to cousin, Maurice Woulfe, Bruff, Co. Limerick, 3 Sept. 1868, Kerby Miller Collection.

———, Fort Fred Steele, Wyoming Terr., to cousin, Maurice Woulfe, Bruff, Co. Limerick, 30 April 1869, Kerby Miller Collection.

KEVIN STANTON

## FICTION, IRISH-AMERICAN

Historically, the Irish have been an extremely articulate people, the creators of one of the oldest and richest literatures in Europe, uniquely impressive, perhaps, in proportion to their numbers. This legacy surely helps explain the many fascinating and accomplished Irish literary responses to American immigration and ethnicity. Taken together, these hundreds of texts establish the existence and persistence of a specifically Irish-American tradition of written self-expression. Rooted in the eighteenth century, expanding in the nineteenth, and blossoming in the twentieth, Irish-American writing is the most extended, continuous body of literature by members of a single American ethnic group available to us—a wonderful resource for understanding the human dimension of the Irish diaspora and its American aftermath.

This remarkable fiction gives us vivid insights into Irish immigrant and ethnic life, especially valuable for the earlier years. We learn about the crossings—in the pre-Famine cabin class for bright young Trinity College graduates on the make, in the overcrowded, unhealthy bowels of the Famine-generation "coffin ships," and in the much faster steam-powered vessels of the late nineteenth century. We learn what life was like in the first American urban ghettoes of Boston's North End, of Hell's Kitchen in Manhattan, and on the South Side of Chicago. We see what a boarding-house and rented rooms looked like and how they were furnished. We discover the conditions of employment as domestic servants, millworkers, pick-and-shovel laborers, and watch the gradual move to better jobs—at first through civil service as police and firemen, and then into the white-collar ranks of retail sales, office work, teaching, and nursing—and beyond. We mark the painful gulf that so often opened up between immigrant parents and their American children. We come to understand how ethnic parishes, schools, and neighborhoods cohered and evolved. In short, we experience through fiction what it has felt like to be Irish in America—all along the way.

There have been two separate cycles of Irish-American fiction—one in the nineteenth century and one in the twentieth. In the nineteenth century, Irish-American writers formed into three distinct literary generations: those who came before the catastrophe of the Great Hunger of the late 1840s; the Famine generation, who came between 1850 and 1875, the period of greatest immigration and upheaval; and the children of the Famine immigrants, who chronicled the growth of an Irish-American middle class between 1875 and World War I. A useful way to understand these three generations is to consider the intended audience for the writers in each. The pre-Famine Irish-American community contained a large number of educated professionals, and here there was already in place an inclusive sense of audience—the general American reading public. In the second generation, in response to the catastrophe of the Great Hunger, that sense of audience shrank to become exclusively Irish-American. In the third generation, the sense of audience opened out again in an embrace—with qualifications—of the tenets of literary realism.

The pioneering Irish-American novelists of the 1820s and 1830s saw themselves as American writers with an American audience. James McHenry, the first Irish immigrant to attempt to support himself as an American literary man, wrote novels in the 1820s with protagonists who were Ulster Presbyterians like himself. His purpose was the education of the general public in America, where, as he says in one preface, "it is imagined that the Irish are all Papists and bog-trotters. It is forgot, or rather in most instances it is not known, that in the province of Ulster alone, nearly two millions of people, at least one-fourth of the population of the whole Island, are neither the one or the other." McHenry also casually appropriated American historical settings and characters. He worked Braddock's campaign in the French and Indian War, about which he claimed special information, into his novel *The Wilderness* (1823), and in the same book he brought in Colonel George Washington as a fairly prominent character, making young George an unsuccessful suitor for the hand of his Ulster immigrant heroine. An ambitious, confident man of letters, McHenry was also founding editor of the *American Monthly Magazine* in Philadelphia. The son of Irish Catholic

immigrants and the author of nine works of fiction, Charles James Cannon traveled in New York intellectual circles, championed the poetry of "our own Poe," and dedicated his first novel, *Oran the Outcast* (1833) to James Fenimore Cooper. In the preface to one novel Cannon declares that although he is proud of his heritage, he wants reviewers to judge him as a "NATIVE AMERICAN" (his emphasis), rather than as "an Irish Roman Catholic." Both Cannon and McHenry also had plays produced on the American stage, as did another immigrant writer, John McDermott Moore, a New York journalist who started two short-lived newspapers of his own in the 1830s, and published essays and fiction in the mainstream literary periodicals *The Dollar Magazine* and *Brother Jonathan*, edited by N. P. Willis. Moore's novel of Irish New York political and social life, *The Adventures of Tom Stapleton*, was serialized in *Brother Jonathan* in 1842 and had three editions in book form, including one in London, where its title was *Life in America*.

The writers of pre-Famine Irish America also produced a significant amount of fiction in which satire and parody dominate. The targets of this cluster of mostly humorous writings included various kinds of literary propaganda: political campaign biographies, anti-Catholic "convent revelations," anti-Irish character stereotyping, and the simplistic moralizing plots of popular sentimental fiction. The audience for such works was conceived as not exclusively Irish-American, but as a wider and well-read public, appreciative of sophisticated literary effects. If the reader were Irish, it was assumed that he was sure enough of his identity and position to be able to laugh at himself. If a member of the host American culture, it was assumed that he could laugh at his own stereotyping and misconceptions of the Irish.

In the twenty-five years before the Great Famine, several writers published fascinating books that echo the traditional Irish satiric vein that can be traced from Swift and Sterne all the way back to the bards. *The Life and Travels of Father Quipes, Otherwise Dominick O'Blarney* (1820) and *The Life of Paddy O'Flarrity* (1834) are engaging picaresque tales which satirize the immigrant's dream of success and the venality of political aspiration by parodying American campaign biography. *Six Months in a House of Correction; or, The Narrative of Dorah Mahoney* (1835) parodies the fiction of "awful disclosures" about religious life and satirizes the nativist impulse as it was manifested in the 1834 burning of the Ursuline convent in Charlestown, Massachusetts. And John M. Moore's *The Adventures of Tom Stapleton* (1842) pokes good-natured fun at many aspects of American and Irish-American life, while parodying a range of New York dialects and the conventions of popular, sentimental fiction. All of these books also satirize native American stereotypes of the Irish by reproducing them in exaggerated comic versions, and the nature of this material dictates a further dimension of comic self-satire, and acknowledgement that the Irish do, in fact, drink, fight, blarney, and backbite, perhaps to excess. As a group, this cluster of primarily entertaining treatments of potentially sensitive subjects (Catholicism, nativism, political corruption, and unattractive aspects of Irish identity) suggests that this first Irish-American literary generation and its audience were sophisticated, highly literate, confident, and unthreatened by the strange, new American culture in which they found themselves.

With the coming of the Great Famine, all such laughter stopped. Nothing could be further from the playful sophistication of the pre-Famine satirists than the grimly serious and didactic fiction produced by Irish-Americans of the Famine generation. The reversal is so dramatic because the writers who emerged after the Famine were not a second generation, not the children of immigrants, but a new first generation. Most of these new novelists were themselves immigrants who had come to the United States as adults in the later 1840s. And the great weakness of this generation's fiction was the constriction of the assumed audience. As Famine immigrants themselves, these new writers wrote only for their own kind, the audience of traumatized refugees with whom their own experiences allowed them to identify. Perceiving that audience to be desperately in need of guidance, they turned out utilitarian, practical novels with three major purposes: Catholic-tract fiction to exhort the immigrants to keep the faith on alien soil; immigrant-guidebook fiction to instruct the newly arrived on how to get along in America; and nationalistic-political fiction to aid the cause of freedom from British rule back in Ireland. Thus, in a matter of a few years, the fictional norm had been overturned: from critique of propaganda to propaganda itself; from lively engagement in aesthetic and stylistic matters to frequent avowals (in prefaces, mostly) of suspicion of fiction as a morally subversive medium whose appropriation was justified only by the didactic goals of the work at hand; from parody and exposure of fictional conventions that have been manipulated for extra-literary purposes to humorless embrace of those same conventions—sentimental rhetoric, stereotyped characters, simplistic conflicts, and moralizing themes.

Between 1845 and 1875, six people wrote three or more novels in which being Irish in America is of central concern. All six were themselves immigrants, all six came to America as adults (the youngest was twenty-four), and the four for whom accurate dates exist all came between 1844 and 1850. Two of these novelists were priests, Fathers John Boyce and Hugh Quigley; two were primarily journalists, Peter McCorry and Dillon O'Brien; one, David Power Conyngham, was a veteran of both the 1848 Irish rebellion and the American Civil War; and one, Mary Anne (Madden) Sadlier, was the first lady of Irish-American publishing. In addition, most of the authors who wrote only one or two novels were also immigrants.

Famine generation Irish-American fiction contains a few recurrent themes, often organized into a predictable pattern. First, a hard life of great suffering in Ireland is presented, marked by landlord exploitation, famine, painful eviction from the old home, and the reluctant decision to emigrate. Second, the crossing to America is seen as a wrenching rite of passage, the violence of which is often symbolized by a fierce storm at sea. Third, the disorientation of the first months in the new world is evoked, with swindles, humiliation, and the most dangerous threats to morality and the faith. Fourth, right and wrong ways of meeting these challenges are exemplified in the contrasting careers of Irish Catholics who keep the faith and those who lose it. Failure most often means succumbing to drink, dissolution, and early death. Success means working hard, holding a job, and keeping one's family together and Catholic. One convention recurs in novel after novel as a means of illustrating the points being made: the death-bed scene. The good die peacefully, surrounded by a loving family, and not without occasional angelic music and lighting; the bad die horribly, weeping, gnashing their teeth, and calling—too late—for a priest. An important crux of feelings for Irish and Irish-American cultures, this convention remained strong through the rest of the nineteenth century. Indeed, it was not fully exorcised until the final page of James T. Farrell's third Studs Lonigan novel, *Judgment Day,* published in 1935.

Mary Anne
Madden Sadlier

The most prolific of the Famine-generation novelists was Mary Anne (Madden) Sadlier, who came over from County Cavan in 1844 and married Catholic-book publisher James Sadlier two years later. She published some sixty volumes in a variety of literary modes, many of which were in print for the entire second half of the nineteenth century. These include eighteen novels of Irish and Irish-American life published between 1850 and 1870, all of them organized around the Manichean opposition of right and wrong ways of living. Although they are predictably and inexorably moralistic, these books lavishly document many features of nineteenth-century immigrant life. Mrs. Sadlier tended to deal with one key ethnic issue per novel: for example, entrance into the business world in *Willy Burke; or, The Irish Orphan in America* (1850), the controversy about sending Catholic children to the public schools in *The Blakes and Flanagans* (1855), the working conditions of servant girls in *Bessy Conway* (1861), the plight of Irish children in public orphanages in *Aunt Honor's Keepsake* (1866), the dangers of making it into the upper classes in *Old and New; or, Taste vs. Fashion* (1862), and the generally pernicious effects of the urban environment (overcome by the protagonists moving to near-idyllic Iowa) in *Con O'Regan; or Immigrant Life in the New World* (1864). Sadlier also wrote ten novels with Irish historical settings, from *The Red Hand of Ulster* (1850) to *Maureen Dhu* (1870).

As a number of historians have shown, late nineteenth-century Irish America was a complex, anxious, transitional culture, an uneasy mix of recent immigrants, older settlers still stuck in the working class, and the new "lace curtain" bourgeoisie. The fiction produced by this divided generation reflects these same unresolved internal conflicts. It is a literature of ambivalence, the poles of which are the two opposed concepts of literature that were at war in the American literary marketplace of the day: respectable romance and disreputable realism. The inability of Irish-American writers to decide between these two aesthetic (and as some saw it, moral) imperatives constitutes the most pervasive characteristic of the fiction of this, the third nineteenth-century Irish-American literary generation. This ambivalence took every possible form. Some individual novels and stories begin realistically and end romantically. Or vice versa. Some writers produced first novels of considerable realistic power, only to turn in subsequent fiction to the bland formulas of popular romance. Or vice versa. Not that there were no consistently respectable Irish-American writers. The creators of popular romance we have always had with us. It is just that no promisingly realistic Irish-American novelist was able wholly to abjure genteel literary values in favor of hard-nosed cultural self-assessment.

The writers of this third generation were actually second-generation Irish, because they were the children of the Famine immigrants. Many writers never wavered from the decorous dictates of the Gilded Age. After all, this new literary generation coincided with the emergence of an Irish-American middle class. Themselves charter members, many novelists consciously wrote for this audience of new bourgeoisie and promulgated through their fiction the values of genteel respectability. In addition, Irish-American fiction of the previous, Famine generation had been predominantly romantic, didactic, and sentimental, thereby providing precedents and models. Thus, the new "respectable" writers were the true heirs of Mrs. Sadlier, and the result of their labors was a new wave of didactic propaganda fiction, aimed exclusively at Irish-Americans. Like their Famine-generation predecessors, these writers used fiction to defend the Catholic faith and to instruct their readers in how to live in the New World. The main difference is a raising of the tone and level of expectation of what constitutes a proper, successful life. The Famine generation had written survival manuals; the following generation wrote etiquette books. The essential figure here is Notre Dame professor Maurice Francis Egan, whose dozen works of fiction, including *The Success of Patrick Desmond* (1893) and *The Vocation of Edward Conway* (1896) mirror the Irish-American genteel mind in its nascent state.

From our perspective, this may seem a turgid and dreary vein, but it is important not to ridicule the efforts, including literary, of this culture to become respectable. Although the effort led many writers away from the aesthetically more promising path of the realistic movement, it was part of a much larger, thoroughly understandable, and even laudable set of changes. The virtues of respectability were necessary for any sort of advancement in America for oneself or one's children. Caught in the throes of the transformation from a pre-industrial society in Ireland to an urban, industrial American world, Irish immigrants needed to develop new habits of reliability at work and in the home. With such steadiness came new opportunities and aspirations. For all of this, the blanket term "respectability" applies, and in a wholly positive way. We should not lose sight of that. On the other hand, respectability in literature meant a number of things detrimental to the development of the kind of honest self-assessment of one's culture that informs any generation's most valuable literature.

A significant number of later nineteenth-century Irish-American writers did, however, embrace the tenets of the realistic movement to varying degrees. In the best work, there is once again, as in pre-Famine fiction, an expansion of possibilities: a sense of literature as realistic cultural criticism beyond didactic moralizing or pure escape, and a sense of a larger American audience beyond one's own kind. The writers who produced this generation's most consistently realist fiction came from a variety of backgrounds and places. Most often, their novels and stories contain a familiar ambivalent pattern consisting of realistic settings, characterizations, and incidents marred by concessions to sentimental romance in the form of implausible resolutions of plot. Most important, though, was the fact that these writers began to write genuinely critical fiction. They began to criticize

their culture and its "rise" by asking for the first time a number of questions: what had been the price of achieving respectability, of having had to work so hard and long at backbreaking jobs, of having used politics as a way out, of having grown up in insulated and isolating ghetto communities and families? They also joined other late-nineteenth-century American writers to explore the effects on the human spirit of urban "slum" life. And they began to criticize their culture's literary heritage as well, by including in their own fiction alternatives to such conventions as the triumphant Irish Catholic hero and the climactic, sentimental death-bed scene. However tentative and incomplete their accomplishments, what Ezra Pound said of Walt Whitman is true of these ethnic literary pioneers: "It was you that broke the new wood. Now is a time for carving."

By 1880 over a third of America's Irish-born citizens were living beyond the East Coast, and the significant dispersal is reflected in this generation's fiction. Notable proto-realist writers and their fictional locales include the following: John Boyle O'Reilly's Australian convict-labor colony (in *Moondyne,* 1879), the Rochester (New York) of Henry Keenan (*The Aliens,* 1886) and Katherine Conway (*Lalor's Maples,* 1901), James W. Sullivan's *Tenement Tales of New York* (1895) and the Manhattan of stories by Myra Kelly, Harvey J. O'Higgins and Eugene Clancy, the New York City and state of William A. McDermott (*Père Monnier's Ward,* 1898), John Talbot Smith's Connecticut and Adirondack towns, John T. McIntyre's South Philadelphia, Kate Cleary's Nebraska prairies, and George Jessop's San Francisco.

Finley Peter Dunne of Chicago is a very special case. Although he wrote column-length newspaper sketches, his "Mr. Dooley" pieces are the only body of work at this time in which a realist perspective is sustained throughout, and thus he is Irish-American literature's first genius. Born to immigrant parents on Chicago's Irish West Side, Peter Dunne took a job as a cub reporter for the Chicago *Telegram* at age sixteen in 1884. Eight years and five increasingly responsible positions later, he was editorial chairman at the Chicago *Evening Post.* It was there, in October 1893, that he imagined himself into the character of Martin Dooley. Almost immediately, his 750-word monologues (delivered to genial politician John McKenna or long-suffering millworker Malachi Hennessy) became a Saturday evening Chi-

Finley Peter Dunne

cago tradition. Mr. Dooley was located firmly behind the bar of a saloon on Archer Avenue on the city's South Side, in the Irish working-class neighborhood known as Bridgeport. Between 1893 and 1900, when Dunne moved on to New York and a different sort of career as a satirist of our national life, some 300 Dooley pieces appeared in Chicago newspapers. Taken together, they form a coherent body of work, in which a vivid, detailed world comes into existence—a self-contained immigrant/ethnic culture with its own customs, ceremonies, "sacred sites," social pecking order, heroes, villains, and victims. With the full faith of the literary realist, Dunne embraced the common man as a proper subject and created sympathetic, dignified, even heroic characters, plausibly grounded in a few city blocks of apartments, saloons, factories, and churches. Moreover, characters, places, and communities are all embodied in the first dialect voice to transcend the stereotypes of "stage Irish" ethnic humor. The Chicago Dooley pieces constitute the most solidly realized ethnic neighborhood in nineteenth-century American literature.

At this point, the first cycle of Irish-American fiction ended in a dramatic hiatus. In the literary generation that came of age just after 1900, no Irish-American writer built a career based on the realist aesthetic precedents set in the previous generation. Nineteenth-century Irish-American fiction, including the period of heightened literary activity at the turn of the century, was abruptly forgotten. The second, twentieth-century cycle of Irish-American fiction eventually began and ran on its own, independent of the nineteenth-century cycle. What happened can only be described as wholesale cultural amnesia. There had been dozens of writers and hundreds of books that explored Irish-American immigration and ethnicity. There was "new wood" broken by writers in the last quarter of the old century, ready to be "carved" in the new. There certainly still continued to be an Irish-American ethnic life through the first three decades of the twentieth-century. Although some Irish-Americans did begin literary careers in the new century by exploring their own ethnic experience, most either went on to other subjects or else stopped writing entirely. Those who left for the greener pastures of sentimental romance, juvenile fiction, or mystery stories included John T. McIntyre, who published a first novel (*The Ragged Edge*, 1902) of Philadelphia Irish politics and neighborhood life; Kathleen Thompson Norris, who wrote promising stories (collected in 1909) of Irish middle-class life in her native San Francisco; and Clara Laughlin, whose novel "*Just Folks*" (1910) contains solid detail about Chicago's Irish working-class.

Probably the best-known writer whose career embodies this literary generation's rejection of its realistic ethnic dimension is Brian Oswald Donn-Byrne. Born in 1889 to an itinerant Irish family temporarily living in New York, Byrne was raised in South Armagh and educated in Dublin. He returned to America in 1911, married an Irish girl in Brooklyn, and began to write fiction. His earliest work suggests that he could have become a significant realist writer. His first novel, *The Stranger's Banquet* (1919), deals with labor unrest in an American shipyard run by an Irishman. It contains portraits of socialists, anarchists, and IWW agitators, and also touches on the perils of American success through the character of the shipbuilder's dissipated son. Complaining of the novel's unevenness, the *New York Times* reviewer of *The Stranger's Banquet* counseled its author toward a promising future, "provided he is willing to leave realism to others and devote himself to the sort of mystic romance which would seem to be his proper métier." Byrne took this advice to heart,

and had a huge success in 1921 with *Messer Marco Polo,* a love story of Marco Polo's journey to China, as narrated by an Irish storyteller. Subsequently, he made his very lucrative way as a purveyor of popular romance, including large doses of Celtic-twilight Irishry. And so it went.

Certainly, McIntyre, Norris, Laughlin, and Byrne would have known about the nineteenth-century Irish-American writers who were being published as they were growing up. It is also more than likely that the first, ethnic works of some of the younger writers were modeled on the older. But no one continued in that vein. Thus, when the next group of slightly younger writers of Irish background came up in the 1920s, and these included F. Scott Fitzgerald and John O'Hara, there was precious little left in the way of ethnic literary awareness for them to build on. A partial explanation lies in historical events. With the approach of World War I, European ethnic identifications (other than ties to England) became positively unsavory in the eyes of many Americans. Moreover, in the context of increasing support for United States entry into the war, the Easter Rising in Dublin in April 1916 was less than popular in mainstream America. Also, in 1914 President Woodrow Wilson made his famous "hyphenated Americans" speech at the unveiling of a monument to Commodore John Barry, whom Wilson praised as "an Irishman [whose] heart crossed the Atlantic with him," unlike "some Americans" who "need hyphens in their names, because only part of them has come over." Wilson and Theodore Roosevelt became the leading spokesmen in the hue and cry over "divided loyalties" which intensified with United States entry into the war in April 1917. This public rhetoric, America's alliance with England, and the negative perception of Irish nationalism after the Easter Rising all contributed to an emphatic lessening of Irish-American ethnic self-assertion during these years. Two further blows to Irish ethnicity, literary and otherwise, were the bitter conclusion of the Irish Revolution and the passage of immigration restriction laws. First, the treaty signed in December 1921 to end the Revolution created the problematic partition of Northern Ireland and the Irish Free State, which, in turn, led to the heartbreak of civil war for two more years. This prolonged strife worked to destroy the powerful nationalist component of Irish-American self-consciousness. To many, the "Troubles" were an extremely painful coda, much better left unexplored. Second, the agitation for immigration restriction eventually brought about severely limited quotas which affected Ireland along with the rest of Europe. The Johnson-Reed Act of 1924 established small and decreasing quotas for admission to the United States, and with new blood from Ireland severely curtailed, Irish America was transformed from an immigrant to an ethnic culture. It is my sense that cultural politics also played a part in Irish America's literary hiatus, especially early on. During the crucial decade 1900–1910, while the works of the preceding generation were still fresh, aspiring writers were somehow discouraged from exploring the ethnic dimension. I believe that the American publishing-editing-reviewing-distribution network at the turn of the century exerted negative pressure, and that the Anglophile and anti-Catholic orientation of this controlling group was a root cause of decisions by new Irish-American novelists not to write about their own backgrounds—the communities, customs, and characters that made up their world.

Irish-American fiction began over again in 1932 with the publication of *Young Lonigan: A Boyhood in Chicago Streets* by James T. Farrell. The Farrell generation had to establish anew the precedent of creating an American fictional world from Irish ethnic materials. Farrell himself spoke often of having had to invent his literary self from nothing, and he certainly stands out as singularly committed to the writer's life and to Irish-American materials by the late 1920s. (He was born in 1904 the son of a Chicago teamster and a former housemaid and the grandson of Irish immigrants.) There was no question in his own mind about the nature of the world he was creating. In a 1932 letter to Ezra Pound, who had just read the galleys of *Young Lonigan,* Farrell declared: "As to the Irishness of it, I generally feel that I'm an Irishman rather than an American, and the book was recommended at [its French publishing house] as being practically an Irish novel." Nor was there any question in Farrell's mind about the nature of the job that needed doing, for his earliest literary reviews remark on the absence of critical realism in Irish-American fiction.

James T. Farrell brought two crucial elements to Irish-American fiction: a criticism of life and a voice for the inarticulate. Farrell's fiction contains the first clear-eyed critique of the social and moral failings of the Irish-American subculture. It also contains his brilliant solution to the problem of narrative voice that he set himself: how to render the thoughts of people for whom self-expression comes hard. Farrell created a style consistent with what he saw as "my constant and major aim as a writer—to write so that life may speak for itself." It is a style of scrupulous plainness, a medium capable of a hard-won, minimal eloquence that embodies his faith in the ability of ordinary people to clarify and bless their own lives, even if only in their own minds. This is his greatest gift to American literature. One example of how Farrell's criticism of life emerges from a specifically Irish-American context is the powerful subversion in the *Studs Lonigan* trilogy of the character of the Irish-Catholic matriarch and the plot device of the happy death. As her son lies dying, Mary Lonigan is revealed as wholly bereft of charity. In place of a moral center, she reveals only the acquisitive drives to possess her children permanently and to achieve social prominence in the community. Catholicism has become a set of forms whose main relevance is its contribution to her dream of herself as a respectable mother. Further, with the climactic but meaningless death of the hapless Studs, Farrell emphatically counters the death-bed convention. Moreover, this is the final step in a more general accomplishment—the wholesale critique in *Studs Lonigan* of distorting mythologies of character and aspiration that were dominant in Farrell's Irish-American Catholic culture, and of the rags-to-riches, Horatio-Alger plot line so prevalent in nineteenth-century popular fiction, Irish-American and otherwise.

In Farrell, the flawed but persistent nineteenth-century Irish-American tradition of literary self-scrutiny finally had its first worthy twentieth-century inheritor. His considerable body of work constitutes one of the great sustained accomplishments of twentieth-century American literary realism. Filling over fifty volumes, this corpus includes hundreds of stories and four large fictional cycles: the *Studs Lonigan* trilogy, the O'Neill-O'Flaherty pentalogy, the Bernard Carr trilogy, and the *Universe of Time* sequence, of which ten volumes were published before Farrell's death in 1979. The first two major cycles, the Studs Lonigan and O'Neill-O'Flaherty novels, share a setting (Farrell's childhood neighborhood around Washington Park on Chicago's South Side), a time frame (roughly 1900 to 1930), and several characters. The extremely impressive and moving O'Neill-O'Flaherty series consists of *A World I Never Made* (1936), *No Star Is Lost* (1938), *Father and Son* (1940), *My Days of Anger* (1943), and *The Face of Time* (1953). Farrell's own youth had much more in common with the experience of Danny O'Neill in the second series than with that of Studs Lonigan. Indeed, the eight Washington Park novels comprise one coherent grand design with two contrasting movements: the downward, negative alternative embodied in the passive, doomed Studs, and the upward, positive possibility embodied in Danny O'Neill, who grows up to become a writer. Farrell's Washington Park novels and the many short stories that share the same setting (some fifty are about Danny O'Neill) make up a thoroughly realized fictional depiction of three generations of urban Irish-Americans—from nineteenth-century immigrant laborers to Depression-era intellectuals. Farrell's fifty years of fierce dedication to his craft would surely have been appreciated by the nameless or forgotten Irish-American writers who preceded him.

There is one other writer who stands with Farrell at the beginning of the twentieth-century cycle. This is Jim Tully, whose first novel, *Emmet Lawler,* appeared in 1922. Tully's dozen autobiographical books and novels about the Irish underclass of bums and drifters, including *Beggars of Life* (1924) and *Shanty Irish* (1928), stake out a piece of ethnic turf that has been explored more recently by William Kennedy.

Writers of the new, second cycle shared one large advantage: the problem of audience did not have to be solved over again. Farrell and Tully wrote for the general American reading public right from the start. What defines the new cycle's turns is not, then, the question of audience, but changing attitudes toward the formal conventions of realism consistent with the development of American literature in general. Farrell's plain style and critical realism were clearly the models for the next literary generation, the "Regional Realists" who wrote first books of Irish-American life in the later 1930s and the 1940s, among them Joseph Dineen (*Ward Eight,* 1936), Thomas Sugrue (*Such Is the Kingdom,* 1940), Leo Ward (*Holding Up the Hills,* 1941), Richard Sullivan (*Summer after Summer,* 1942), Charles Driscoll (*Kansas Irish,* 1943), Jack Dunphy (*John Fury,* 1946), Harry Sylvester (*Moon Gaffney,* 1947), and Mary Deasy (*The Hour of Spring,* 1950). The most accomplished of these are Edward McSorley's *Our Own Kind* (1946), a lyrical recollection of the family of a foundry worker in Providence, Rhode Island, in the 1910s, Mary Doyle Curran's *The Parish and the Hill* (1948), a sharp delineation of the contrast between "shanty" and "lace-curtain" Irish in Holyoke, Massachusetts, and Brendan Gill's *The Trouble of One House* (1950), a moving evocation of the mystery and power of the home as threatened by early death in Hartford, Connecticut.

Since World War II, Irish-American life has changed in many ways. After 1945, the G.I. Bill of Rights provided higher education and opportunity for white-collar work for thousands of Irish-Americans. Many of these signaled their entry into the middle class by moving from old city neighborhoods out to the suburbs. John Kennedy's election to the presidency in 1960 was a dramatic symbol of Irish postwar accomplishment. The late 1960s saw the beginning of a resurgence of ethnic self-awareness among descendants of European immigrants in both universities and the wider culture. Among Irish-Americans, two specific causes of renewed attention to the old country have been the rekindled "Troubles" in Northern Ireland and the "New Irish" immigrants, both illegal and legal and mostly well-educated, of the 1980s and 1990s. Certainly, there continues to be an ethnic dimension to many Irish-American lives, of which some 44 million were estimated in the 1990 census. Often the self-identification is attached to Catholicism and stoked by interest and instruction in Irish arts, including literature, music, and dancing.

There have been at least two generations of Irish-American writers since the 1940s, and it may be useful to place their fiction into four groups: past lives, those chronicled in historical novels; public lives, those concerned with the outer world of work; private lives, where the focus is home and family; and stylized lives, novels in modernist and experimental literary modes.

Irish historical fiction has had many erstwhile American laborers. Since the extraordinary two-year bestsellerdom of Leon Uris's *Trinity* (1976), there has been more than a generation's worth of such books of varying interest, by writers including James Carroll, James F. Murphy, and Joan Bagnel. The outstanding accomplishment has been the trilogy of deeply considered, scrupulously authentic novels by Thomas Flanagan. In *The Year of the French* (1979), *The Tenants of Time* (1988), and *The End of the Hunt* (1994), Flanagan has given us memorable renderings of the impact on ordinary people of Irish nationalism during, respectively, the Rebellion of 1798, the 1867 Fenian Rising, and the Irish Revolution of 1916–1921. For nineteenth-century Irish America, we now have as well the achievement in historical fiction of Peter Quinn, whose *Banished Children of Eve* (1994) re-creates Irish New York in the season of the Draft Riots of 1863. The novel provides complex, clarifying insight into several interlacing urban worlds: New York's criminal underbelly, domestic service by immigrant women, music-hall minstrelsy, the political scene at Tammany Hall, and gang life among the "Plug Uglies" and "Dead Rabbits." Quinn's book is full to bursting with information and insight.

Public lives are books mostly dealing with Irish-American life on the job and outside the home, novels about priests, politicians, business leaders, police, firefighters, and other civil servants. Here the early, exemplary figure is Edwin O'Connor, whose death at age 49 was a great loss to Irish-American letters. O'Connor wrote one accomplished novel on each of three obsessive Irish-American subjects—politics (*The Last Hurrah,* 1956), religion (*The Edge of Sadness,* 1961), and family (*All in the Family,* 1966). And in the best of his novels, *The Edge of Sadness,* he also began to expand the formal possibilities of Irish-American fiction. Along with its spiritual focus, this is a novel about the character of the old Irish-American talk, and O'Connor comments brilliantly on the relationship between conversation and ethnic community. One of the most versatile novelists of the public lives of Irish-Americans has been Thomas J. Fleming, whose political novels, beginning with *All Good Men* (1961), chronicle the transfer of power from the old boss system to a new liberal leadership in Jersey City. Fleming has also written of similar transitional tensions in the Catholic church, notably in *The Good Shepherd* (1974). The great chronicler of American Catholic clerical life has been J. F. Powers, whose mid-century stories, pioneering in their depiction of priests and nuns as human beings, have been followed by a life work of beautifully crafted fiction, including the novels *Morte D'Urban* (1962) and *Wheat That Springeth Green* (1988). Latter-day Irish-American political novelists include Edward R. F. Sheehan, Wilfrid Sheed, Jack Flannery, and James Carroll; and chroniclers of the religious life include Andrew M. Greeley, Ralph McInerny, Francis Phelan, and Mary Gordon. Cops and robbers, firemen, and other civil servants have continued to appear in a considerable array of fictional forms in books by George V. Higgins, John Gregory Dunne, Vincent Patrick,

Edwin O'Connor

Jimmy Breslin, Joe Flaherty, Alan Dennis Burke, Tom Molloy, and Dennis Smith.

It is only natural that private, domestic life continues to have a central position in Irish-American fiction because ethnic identity has always begun as a family affair, emerging from customs and attitudes grounded in the home. Here a model of clarity and craft is the fiction of Elizabeth Cullinan, whose depiction of an emotionally impoverished matriarch and her fortress *House of Gold* (1970) in suburban Long Island is powerful and definitive. At the end of this first novel, there is only minimal hope—in the persons of a ne'er-do-well son whose failure has absolved him of the weight of family responsibility, and two teen-aged granddaughters whose skeptical perspective bodes well for their generation. However, in her more recent fiction, the Cullinan narrative voice has become that of one of those skeptical granddaughters grown into a reasonably assured and independent adulthood. In the collection *Yellow Roses* (1977) and the novel *A Change of Scene* (1982) this is a sane, sensible voice balanced between then and now, the ethnic and the worldly, and better able to judge self and others because of the double vision. Cullinan stories follow a pattern of incisively observed encounters and emotional consequences that build in seemingly casual movement to climactic generalizations so appropriate and valid as to be immediately recognizable as wisdom.

In the context of Cullinan's shaping example, other useful domestic fiction of Irish America (with settings from Boston and New York to Hawaii and San Francisco) of the generation that began publishing in the early 1970s includes Edward Hannibal's *Chocolate Days, Popsicle Weeks* (1970), Arthur Cavanaugh's *Leaving Home* (1970), Philip F. O'Connor's *Old Morals, Small Continents, Darker Times* (1971), Elizabeth Savage's *A Good Confession* (1975), Julian Moynahan's *Where the Land and Water Meet* (1979), and Susannah Moore's *My Old Sweetheart* (1982).

The stylized, modernist mode has an extremely impressive twentieth-century Irish lineage back through Samuel Beckett and Flann O'Brien to that fabulous artificer James Joyce. The pioneering, post-war Irish-American practitioner on the dark side of this satiric vein was J. P. Donleavy, whose 1955 novel of boozy charm and cruelty, *The Ginger Man,* helped establish the term "black humor." Subsequent worthy contributors and their inaugural works include Tom McHale (*Principato,* 1970), Mark Costello (*The Murphy Stories,* 1973), and John Kennedy Toole (*A Confederacy of Dunces,* posthumously published in 1980). A younger generation of darker stylists is well represented by Thomas McGonigle, whose *Going to Patchogue* (1992) is the extended stream-of-consciousness narration of a journey from the narrator's Lower East Side apartment to his hometown of Patchogue, Long Island, and back. This one-day pilgrimage is a compelling figure for American as well as Irish-American migratory restlessness. McGonigle's kindred spirit, wilder and closer to the edge, is Michael Stephens, whose painful chronicle of movement between Brooklyn and Long Island takes place over two novels, *Season at Coole* (1972) and *The Brooklyn Book of the Dead* (1994).

On the other hand, Irish-Americans have also written some of the most accomplished fiction on the light, comic, essentially Joycean side of the modernist street. In *Bridgeport Bus* (1965), Maureen Howard explores the thematic roots of her own Irish Catholic upbringing through a risky, ebullient mixture of styles and forms that expresses her impatience with conventional narrative. In several subsequent novels she has continued to chart the growth toward understanding and possibility of Irish-American women in vibrant and various fictional forms that both expose and celebrate the qualities of the storyteller's art. *Natural History* (1992) is a full realization of Howard's trademark and identifiably Irish-American literary concerns with the presence of the past, the spirit of urban place, and Joycean technical wizardry, all in the service of emotional truth. The genius loci is her native Bridgeport from the 1940s through the mid-1980s, and the novel charts the involvement with local history and personal memory of one family's quest for the the American dream.

William Kennedy's Albany is as rich a source as Farrell's Chicago or Faulkner's Mississippi, and his continuing cycle of novels demonstrates that he carries around in his head a whole Irish-American world—from the Famine immigration up through the 1950s—vivid, coherent, and available for imaginative appropriation. The Albany cycle is centered in the Pulitzer-Prize novel *Ironweed* (1983), which takes place at Hallowe'en of 1938, and charts the life and hard times of Francis Phelan, homeless drifter and pilgrim soul, in a prose that melds the realist tradition and visionary flights akin to South American magic realism. *Legs* (1975) and *Billy Phelan's Greatest Game* (1978) share with *Iron-*

*weed* the Albany setting, the time frame of roughly 1925 to 1938, and a vivid cast of characters both dead and alive, bums and bootlickers and honest working men, journalists, politicians, gamblers, and gangsters. Set in the mid-nineteenth century, *Quinn's Book* (1988) involves ancestors of characters from the other novels and several shaping events of Irish-American history, among them the Famine immigration and the Civil War. *Very Old Bones* (1992) continues more explicitly the engagement with the mysteries and challenges of art in *Quinn's Book,* this time by focusing on Francis's brother, the painter Peter Phelan. Here Kennedy spools backward in time from a crucial family gathering in 1958 to a harrowing saga from the 1880s involving the immigrant generation of Phelan ancestors. In *The Flaming Corsage* (1996), the time frame is 1884-1912, and Kennedy brings to the fore playwright and immigrant's son Edward Daugherty and his enigmatic, doomed wife Katrina Taylor, an Albany Anglo-Dutch aristocrat, both of whom have played important though minor roles in earlier novels. Thus, the life work that has sprung, however improbably, from New York's down-at-heels capital city expands and deepens and continues to amaze.

A view of ethnic otherness not as destructive self-estrangement but as creative expansion of possibility has been in the ascendant in Irish-American fiction in more recent years. This constructive, functional way of looking at one's ethnic world, a movement from constriction to openness, is observable between the earlier and later fiction of a number of Irish-American writers who began in the 1960s and early seventies, among them Maureen Howard, Jimmy Breslin, Joe Flaherty, Pete Hamill, Dennis Smith, and Ellen Currie. Invariably, their later work presents a more positive evocation of the spirit of place, a deeper sense of the value of ethnic doubleness, and protagonists who find their voices, articulate their troubles, and move toward the light of resolution and change for the better. In the next generation, many writers begin with that positive orientation and move on from there.

In the continuing tradition of Irish-American realist fiction, there are four salient elements: the inclusion of religion, usually Catholicism, as a still consequential part of American life; further consideration of domestic experience, of home and family; the now availably familiar location of middle-class suburbia; and a marked increase in women's voices. This entry concludes with a brief survey of emergent writers, along with their settings and some of their chief concerns.

The seven connected stories of Maura Stanton's *The Country I Come From* (1988) trace an Irish Catholic coming of age in the upper Midwest with a poet's eye for imagery and ear for rhythms. Ellen Currie's New York novel *Available Light* (1986) and her stories, collected as *Moses Supposes* (1994), illustrate the range of her astute, comic vision of domestic life from the cradle to old age. Edward J. Delaney's stories mark the still solid connectedness of Ireland and Irish Boston in the 1950s. Terence Winch's collection *Contenders* (1989) is full of subtle, defining ethnic traces in post-Vietnam New York City. Kristina McGrath's *House Work* (1994) is a family story of the children of immigrants set in working-class Pittsburgh which conveys the centrality of home for this generation in a style of dramatic lyricism. Anna Quindlen's *One True Thing* (1994) also focuses intensively on the domestic by exploring the growth of a daughter's sense of the profound challenges of "homemaking" over the course of her mother's terminal illness. In *Chelsea Girls* (1994), Eileen Myles's straight-on, laconic voice provides a steady purchase for the emotional rendering of a Boston-area childhood marked by the suffering and death of

William Kennedy

an alcoholic father. In its focus on house and home, the weight of family history, and the difficulties of communicating emotion, Thomas E. Kennedy's *Crossing Borders* (1990) is squarely in the mainstream of Irish-American culture, and it, too, is a novel that credits, in commuting Westchester County, the spiritual dimension of the everyday. Small-town New England is the setting for Michael Downing's *A Narrow Time* (1987), which probes the familiar disjunction between illusion and reality about mothers, and in *Mother of God* (1990), Downing extends his exploration of motherhood and pathology with a portrait of a Pittsfield, Massachusetts, family dominated by a woman of surpassing self-delusion and selfishness.

Alice McDermott's creative work has been the imaginative reconstruction of the lives of lower-middle-class Irish New Yorkers, mostly the children and grandchildren of immigrants, who came out of World War II into the possibilities opened by the G.I. Bill. McDermott has truly a historical imagination, fully engaged with New York City and environs from the 1940s through the 1970s. Her novel *At Weddings and Wakes* (1992) presents four daughters of Irish immigrants whose lives are centered in the top-floor Brooklyn apartment, weighted down with family history, where three of them still live with "Momma," their mother's sister. The salient events in the present are the courtship and marriage of middle-aged May Towne, a former nun, but the past is never far from consciousness, and family happenings all the way back to immigration remain vivid and defining. In *Charming Billy* (1998), McDermott creates the connected lives of Billy and Dennis Lynch, two cousins who emerge from the War in Europe to "steady jobs at Con Ed." The crucial events here are Billy's experience of first love in eastern Long Island in July 1945, the revelation that comes to him while in Ireland taking "the pledge" to stop drinking in the summer of 1975, and his own funeral in Queens in April 1983. The greatness of this novel is in McDermott's direct yet compassionate exploration of two central Irish-American issues: sincerely held Roman Catholic faith and the curse of alcohol abuse.

Irish-American writers in the past twenty-five years have had the luxury of two generations of identifiable ancestors, and the examples of forerunners such as James T. Farrell and Edwin O'Connor have enabled the younger writers to strike out on their own with conviction and with admirable results. We need look no further than the work of Thomas Flanagan, Elizabeth Cullinan, Maureen Howard, William Kennedy, and Alice McDermott for evidence of the persistence late into the twentieth century of a distinctive and accomplished Irish-American fiction.

*See* Poetry, Irish-American

Daniel Casey and Robert Rhodes, *Irish-American Fiction: Essays in Criticism* (New York, 1979).
———, *Irish-American Fiction: A Reader* (Syracuse, 1989).
Elizabeth Cullinan, *House of Gold* (Boston, 1970).
J. P. Donleavy, *The Ginger Man* (Paris, France, 1955).
Finley Peter Dunne, *Mr. Dooley and the Chicago Irish.* Ed. Charles Fanning (Washington, 1987).
Charles Fanning, ed., *The Exiles of Erin: Nineteenth-Century Irish-American Fiction* (Chester Springs, Penn., 1997).
———, *The Irish Voice in America: Irish-American Fiction from the 1760s to the 1980s* (Lexington, Ky., 1990).
James T. Farrell, *Studs Lonigan: A Trilogy* (New York, 1935).
———, *Father and Son* (New York, 1940).
———, *Chicago Stories of James T. Farrell.* Ed. Charles Fanning (Urbana, Ill., 1998).
Maureen Howard, *Natural History* (New York, 1992).
William Kennedy, *Billy Phelan's Greatest Game* (New York, 1978).
———, *Ironweed* (New York, 1983).
Alice McDermott, *Charming Billy* (New York, 1998).
Edwin O'Connor, *The Last Hurrah* (Boston, 1956).
———, *The Edge of Sadness* (Boston, 1961).
Mary Anne Sadlier, *The Blakes and Flanagans* (New York, 1855).

CHARLES FANNING

## FINDLEY, WILLIAM (1741–1821)

Politician. The preeminent Irish-born leader of western Pennsylvania's democratic forces in the late eighteenth and early nineteenth centuries, Findley was born in east Ulster into a Presbyterian family of Scots Covenanter descent. In 1763 he immigrated to Pennsylvania and settled in Waynesboro, where he worked as a weaver and schoolmaster. Like his Ulster-born political associates, John Smilie and David Redick, Findley acquired political influence and economic independence through the upheavals of the American Revolution, during which he served on the local committee of observation and as a militia captain. In 1783 Findley moved his family across the Alleghenies and settled in Unity Township, Westmoreland County, where his neighbors elected him to the Pennsylvania Council of Censors (1783), the General Assembly (1785–88), and the Supreme Executive Council (1789). As George Bryan's most important "Irish colonel" in western Pennsylvania, Findley was a staunch Anti-Federalist and defender of Pennsylvania's ultra-democratic 1776 constitution. Elected as delegate to the state ratifying convention of 1787, Findley strongly opposed the U.S. Constitution, but adopted a more conciliatory approach in the state constitutional convention of 1789–90. In 1790 Findley was elected to the state legislature under the new constitution, but resigned to serve in the U.S. House of Representatives in 1790–99 and again in 1804–17. A founding member of Mathew Carey's Hibernian Society (1790) in Philadelphia, in the 1790s Findley championed the French Revolution, opposed the Washington administration's financial and pro-British foreign policies, became a leader of western Pennsylvania's Jeffersonian Republicans, and weathered Federalist accusations of "treason" during the Whiskey Rebellion (1794), in which he played a major but ambiguous role. His political positions moderated in later years: e.g., from fierce opposition to Federalist banking schemes in the late 1780s and early 1790s, to firm support for the Second Bank of the United States in 1816. Findley's Irish origins and early plebeian occupations were scorned by Federalist and conservative Republican opponents, such as Hugh Henry Brackenridge, who satirized Findley as an uncouth, hard-drinking "Irish Teague" in his novel, *Modern Chivalry* (1792–1815).

*Dictionary of American Biography.*
J. H. Campbell, *History of the Friendly Sons of St. Patrick and of the Hibernian Society for the Relief of Emigrants from Ireland* (Philadelphia, 1892).
C. Schramm, "William Findley in Pennsylvania Politics," *Western Pennsylvania Historical Magazine,* 20 (1937): 31–40.

KERBY MILLER

## FITZGERALD, BARRY (1888–1961)

Actor. Born William Joseph Shields on March 10, 1888, in Dublin to Adolphus William and Fanny Ungerland Shields, he became one of the best comedic character actors of stage and screen of his day.

He attended Merchant Taylors Endowed School and Skerrys College in Dublin, and began a career in the Civil Service. In a secure but dull job, he spent his free time playing sports—boxing, swimming and football—and often visited the famed Abbey Theatre, where he had the opportunity to take walk-on parts when needed beginning in 1915. In a few years he was playing major parts (under the name of Barry Fitzgerald), but it wasn't until 1929 that he felt secure enough to give up his day job at the Unemployment Insurance Division. As a leading member of the Abbey Theatre he learned his craft and played a variety of characters in the plays of O'Casey, Synge, Yeats and Dunsany, among others.

He came to America with the Abbey Players in 1932; and in 1936 John Ford brought him to Hollywood to do the film version of *The Plough and the Stars.* Fitzgerald remained in America, alternating between his film and stage career. He maintained a first-rate reputation on stage, playing on Broadway in *The White Seed, Juno and the Paycock,* and *Tanyard Street.* He contributed significantly to such films as *The Long Voyage Home* (1940), *How Green Was My Valley* (1941), and *None But the Lonely Heart* (1944).

After many years of crafting insightful characterizations in supporting roles, Fitzgerald was catapulted to stardom with his portrayal of the lovable, petulant old priest in Paramount's *Going My Way* with Bing Crosby. Critics were unanimous in their praise of his work, and one called it "one of the great performances of our time." (It was surprising to many people to learn that, despite his heartwarming rendition of this Roman Catholic priest, Fitzgerald was himself a Protestant.) The film won nearly every major award in 1944, including an Academy Award for Fitzgerald as Best Supporting Actor. Almost overnight, he was in demand from the major film studios, and continued working in numerous films such as *And Then There Were None* (1945), *California* (1947), *Easy Come, Easy Go* (1947), *Top o' the Morning* (1949), and *The Quiet Man* (1952), among others.

With his intelligent characterizations, Fitzgerald was an ingenious comic actor who always brought a laugh to the audience the moment his squinting face appeared, jutting out his pride-filled jaw, mangling his words, and always at the ready to escalate a barroom discussion into a fistfight (striking one of his "Put up your dukes" poses).

Fitzgerald was a simple man who never got caught up in the Hollywood life. Even in stardom, he continued to ride his motorcycle to work, enjoyed a casual game of golf, and took up the piano when he was fifty.

*See* Cinema, Irish in

J. Concannon and Frank Cull, *Irish American Who's Who* (New York, 1984).

Joseph Curran, *Hibernian Green on the Silver Screen* (Westport, CT, 1990).

*Hollywood Album, Lives and Deaths of Hollywood Stars from the Pages of The New York Times* (New York, 1977).

EILEEN DANEY CARZO

## FITZGERALD, EDWARD (1833–1907)

Bishop. He was born in Limerick, Ireland, in 1833. His father was born in Ireland, while his mother was from Germany. At age 16, his family emigrated to America, where they settled in Ohio. In 1850, he began priestly studies, and was ordained for the Cincinnati archdiocese in 1857. He served as a priest in Ohio until June 1866, when he was appointed bishop of the Little Rock diocese, covering all of Arkansas. He initially refused the appointment, finally accepting under religious obedience. At age 33, he was the youngest bishop in America. He arrived in his diocese on March 17, 1867.

In the antebellum era, there were approximately 84,000 Irish-born in the South. Only in Tennessee, Missouri, Louisiana and Virginia did they number more than one percent. The Catholic church's institutional development was uneven and sparse, especially compared with the Northeast. Many priests refused to work in the South because of bad weather, poverty, Protestant hostility and long hours of circuit riding. By the mid-nineteenth century, Arkansas's Catholic population was less than one percent. These considerations may have been in Fitzgerald's mind when he first declined the appointment.

The defining characteristics of nineteenth-century American Catholicism were immigration and institutionalization, with the Irish dominating both. While these trends were especially pronounced in major urban centers, they were also present during Fitzgerald's forty-year tenure in Arkansas. By the turn of the century the number of churches and chapels rose from 9 to 51; three Catholic hospitals were established; the number of priests rose from 6 to nearly 50 (including religious), while women religious increased from 20 to nearly 150.

When Fitzgerald arrived in 1867, the predominant ethnic group among Arkansas Catholics was the Irish. During his rule, however, the Irish component was actually outnumbered by newer immigrant groups. These included the Germans, Swiss-Germans, Poles and Italians; smaller groups included Czechs and Austrians. Fitzgerald also made concerted efforts to minister to African-American Catholics. By 1890, the United States had a foreign-born population of 16%, at its highpoint, the percentage in Arkansas was 1.7%. In this sense Fitzgerald's experience differed from that of his fellow bishops in the North, the majority being of Irish descent or birth during this period.

Fitzgerald is probably most remembered for his participation in the First Vatican Council (1869–1870). He was one of two bishops in the entire Roman Catholic Church to vote against Pope Pius IX's declaration of papal infallibility. He did not get into trouble, however, because at the end of the vote he immediately went before Pius and submitted to the declaration. As he later told a French priest visiting Arkansas, he voted against the declaration because he believed it would hinder his own evangelization efforts in Arkansas, where Catholics were a tiny minority. In the end, his stance at Rome seems to have increased his stature among his Protestant neighbors.

Ironically, although Fitzgerald refused the Little Rock appointment, once he got there he determined to stay. He was considered for a number of other dioceses, but refused to transfer. In 1893 he served as interim administrator of the recently erected Dallas diocese. In January 1900 he suffered a stroke that confined him to a hospital until his death on February 21, 1907.

Fitzgerald's experience was atypical of most Irish-American bishops. He administered to a flock unevenly scattered throughout a rural state, where at their height they composed almost two percent of the overall population. Like other Irish-American bishops, however, he applied the same principles of organization and management that proved so successful in the larger urban areas where Catholics, especially Irish ones, were far from being a minority.

*See* Catholicism, Irish-American

Dennis Clark, "The South's Irish Catholics: A Case of Cultural Confinement," in Randall M. Miller and Jon L. Wakelyn, eds., *Catholics in* the Old South: Essays in Church and Culture (Macon, GA, 1983): 195–209.

James M. Woods, "Arkansas, Catholic Church in," in Michael Glazier and Thomas J. Shelley, eds., The Encyclopedia of American Catholic History (Collegeville, MN, 1997): 113–16.

———, "Fitzgerald, Edward," in Ibid., 510–12.

———, Mission and Memory: A History of the Catholic Church in Arkansas (Little Rock, 1993).

PATRICK J. McNAMARA

## FITZGERALD, F. SCOTT (1896–1940)

Novelist, short story writer. Francis Scott Key Fitzgerald was born to Edward and Mollie McQuillan Fitzgerald in St. Paul, Minnesota, on September 24, 1896. His maternal grandparents were Philip F. McQuillan, a successful businessman born in County Fermanagh, Ireland, and Louisa Allen McQuillan, the daughter of an Irish immigrant carpenter. Little is known about his paternal grandfather, Michael Fitzgerald, but his maternal grandmother, Cecilia Ashton Scott Fitzgerald, could trace her family back to the seventeenth century in Maryland.

F. Scott Fitzgerald analyzed his family heritage and his social insecurity in a 1933 letter to John O'Hara:

> I am half black Irish and half old American stock with the usual exaggerated ancestral pretensions. The black Irish half of the family had the money and looked down upon the Maryland side of the family who had, and really had, that certain series of reticences and obligations that go under the poor old shattered word "breeding" (modern form "inhibitions"). So being born in that atmosphere of crack, wisecrack and countercrack I developed a two cylinder inferiority complex. So if I were elected King of Scotland tomorrow after graduating from Eton, Magdalene to the Guards with an embryonic history which tied me to the Plantagonets, I would still be a parvenue. I spent my youth in alternately crawling in front of the kitchen maids and insulting the great (A Life in Letters, p. 233).

Fitzgerald served his literary apprenticeship by writing for publications at the schools he attended. His first appearance in print came at age thirteen with the publication of a short story, "The Mystery of the Raymond Mortgage," in The St. Paul Academy Now and Then in October 1909. From 1911 to 1913 he attended the Newman School, a Catholic prep school in Hackensack, New Jersey.

In September 1913, Fitzgerald entered Princeton University with the Class of 1917. He wrote for The Nassau Literary Magazine and The Princeton Tiger, wrote lyrics for the Triangle Club's musical comedies, and was elected to Cottage Club. His college friends included Edmund Wilson and John Peale Bishop. Fitzgerald left Princeton in fall 1917 to join the army, where he began writing "The Romantic Egotist," an early version of his first novel which Charles Scribner's Sons declined to publish the next year.

In July 1918, while stationed at Camp Sheridan near Montgomery, Alabama, Fitzgerald met Zelda Sayre, a celebrated belle with whom he quickly fell in love. They talked of marriage, but she was hesitant to commit herself until he proved he could support her financially. After his discharge from the army in February 1919, he sought success in New York, where he worked for an advertising agency and, he claimed, wrote 19 stories and

F. Scott Fitzgerald

received 122 rejections. His first commercial story sale was a revision of his 1917 story "Babes in the Woods" for The Smart Set (September 1919). That summer, Zelda broke their engagement, and Fitzgerald quit his job and returned to St. Paul to rewrite his novel.

On September 16, 1919, Maxwell Perkins of Scribners accepted This Side of Paradise, and in November Fitzgerald became a client of literary agent Harold Ober at the Paul Revere Reynolds Agency, which specialized in placing fiction with mass-circulation magazines. Fitzgerald made his first sale to The Saturday Evening Post ("Head and Shoulders," February 1920), which quickly became his primary story market. His early stories were distinguished by the seriousness with which he treated the concerns of youth. He came to begrudge the time that story-writing took from work on his novels, but in addition to supporting him financially, the stories served as a place to work out ideas and themes he used in his novels. His stories and novels alike deal with themes of aspiration and mutability and are characterized by a rich evocation of the details of time and place. His life and work are identified with the Jazz Age, which he named.

In January 1920 Fitzgerald moved to New Orleans, Louisiana, for less than a month before returning to New York. During his visits to Montgomery, he and Zelda resumed their engagement. This Side of Paradise, which Fitzgerald described as a "quest" novel, was published on March 26, 1920 and brought him fame almost overnight. Set mostly at Princeton, the novel tells the story of ambitious Amory Blaine's life and loves. Fitzgerald and Zelda married on April 3 in New York, then spent the summer in Westport, Connecticut, where he began his second novel. His first story collection, Flappers and Philosophers, was published in September.

The Fitzgeralds returned to New York in October, and after their first trip to Europe in summer 1921, they moved to St. Paul, where their only child, Frances Scott ("Scottie") Fitzgerald, was born on October 26. Fitzgerald's second novel, The Beautiful and Damned, was published by Scribners on March 4, 1922. Like his story "May Day" (The Smart Set, July 1920), the novel is influenced by literary naturalism; it traces the dissipation of Anthony and Gloria Patch.

Fitzgerald's second story collection, Tales of the Jazz Age, was published in September 1922. In October he and Zelda moved to Great Neck, Long Island, New York, where he developed a close friendship with Ring Lardner, increased his drinking, and began writing a play that he hoped would make his fortune. *The Vegetable,* a political satire, was published on April 27, 1923. It failed at its Atlantic City tryout in November, and Fitzgerald returned to writing short stories for ready cash.

In May 1924 the Fitzgeralds sailed for France, attracted by a lower cost of living and the expectation of few distractions from writing. They settled on the Riviera, where they met Gerald and Sara Murphy and where Zelda became involved with a French aviator, Edouard Jozan, a situation which influenced the writing of Fitzgerald's third novel, *The Great Gatsby,* begun that summer and revised in Rome that fall. In it Fitzgerald explored the American Dream through the aspirations of Jay Gatsby, a self-made man who achieves financial success but fails to understand how wealth works in society. Gatsby believes in the promises of America, but his ambitions are undermined by and confused with his illusions about Daisy Fay Buchanan, whom he loves. *The Great Gatsby* was published on April 10, 1925; sales were disappointing, but reviews were excellent, and today it is regarded as a prime contender for the title "the great American novel."

Fitzgerald met Ernest Hemingway in Paris in May 1925, beginning his most important literary friendship; and that summer he began planning the novel that would become *Tender Is the Night.* His novelette "The Rich Boy" was published in *Redbook Magazine* in January–February 1926, and his third story collection, *All the Sad Young Men,* appeared in February. The Fitzgeralds returned to America in December and traveled to Hollywood in January 1927 for a two-month stint at screenwriting. In March they settled at "Ellerslie" near Wilmington, Delaware, where they spent two years, interrupted by a summer 1928 trip to Europe. Fitzgerald made little progress on his novel; Zelda began ballet lessons, and her intense work damaged her health and caused strife in their marriage. The Fitzgeralds returned to France in March 1929, and Zelda suffered her first breakdown in April 1930. After brief stays at clinics in France and Switzerland, Zelda entered Prangins Clinic at Nyon, Switzerland, in June 1930. Fitzgerald traveled between Paris and Switzerland while writing stories to pay Zelda's medical expenses. One of his best stories, "Babylon Revisited," was published in *The Saturday Evening Post* in February 1931.

In September 1931, Zelda was discharged from Prangins, and the Fitzgeralds returned to America, renting a house in Montgomery, Alabama. Fitzgerald traveled to Hollywood alone in November for a two-month screenwriting job with Metro-Goldwyn-Mayer. Zelda suffered her second breakdown in January 1932, and in February she entered the Phipps Psychiatric Clinic of the Johns Hopkins University Hospital in Baltimore, Maryland, where she quickly wrote her novel, *Save Me the Waltz,* which was published by Scribners in October. Her writing was a source of conflict with her husband, who believed she was using up material he intended for his novel-in-progress. Zelda was discharged from Phipps in June, but she was a resident or outpatient of psychiatric clinics for the rest of her life.

Fitzgerald, who had rented a house outside Baltimore to be near Zelda, completed *Tender Is the Night,* which was published on April 12, 1934. The novel, an account of the decline of Dick Diver, a brilliant psychiatrist who marries a wealthy mental patient, met with mixed reviews; and Fitzgerald believed that the nine-year interval between it and *The Great Gatsby* had damaged

his reputation "almost beyond repair." His fourth story collection, *Taps at Reveille,* was published in March 1935.

The years 1935–1937 are known as "the crack-up," taking the name of a 1936 confessional essay Fitzgerald wrote for *Esquire.* He was ill, alcoholic, and no longer able to write commercial stories to pay off his mounting debts. He lived in various hotels near Asheville, North Carolina, where Zelda entered Highland Hospital in April 1936.

In July 1937 Fitzgerald moved to Hollywood, where he worked for MGM for eighteen months, receiving his only screen credit for *Three Comrades* (1938), then freelancing for various studios. In Hollywood he fell in love with columnist Sheilah Graham, who remained his companion for the rest of his life. He wrote seventeen of his planned thirty episodes for his fifth novel, set in Hollywood, before his death on December 21, 1940. The uncompleted novel was edited by Edmund Wilson and published as *The Last Tycoon* on October 27, 1941. Zelda Fitzgerald died in a fire at Highland Hospital on March 10, 1948.

In college F. Scott Fitzgerald had told Edmund Wilson, "I want to be one of the greatest writers who ever lived, don't you?" At the time of his death, Fitzgerald believed himself a failure, and most of the obituaries were condescending. But the Fitzgerald "revival" which began in 1945–1950 resurrected his reputation so that now he is considered to have achieved his 1920 pronouncement that "An author ought to write for the youth of his own generation, the critics of the next, and the schoolmasters of ever afterward."

*The Cambridge Edition of the Works of F. Scott Fitzgerald* (Cambridge, 1991– ). *The Great Gatsby*, ed., with intro. by Matthew J. Bruccoli, 1991; *The Love of the Last Tycoon: A Western*, ed., with intro. by Bruccoli, 1993; *This Side of Paradise*, ed., with intro. by James L. W. West III, 1995.

*F. Scott Fitzgerald: A Life in Letters.* Ed., with intro. by Matthew J. Bruccoli, with Judith S. Baughman (New York, 1994).

*F. Scott Fitzgerald In His Own Time: A Miscellany.* Ed., with intro. by Matthew J. Bruccoli and Jackson R. Bryer (Kent, OH, 1971).

*F. Scott Fitzgerald Manuscripts.* Ed., Matthew J. Bruccoli, 18 vols. (New York & London, 1990–1991).

*The Notebooks of F. Scott Fitzgerald.* Ed., with intro. by Matthew J. Bruccoli (New York & London, 1978).

*The Short Stories of F. Scott Fitzgerald.* Ed., with preface by Matthew J. Bruccoli (New York, 1989; London, 1991).

*Tender Is the Night*, Centennial Edition. Ed., with intro. and notes by Matthew J. Bruccoli (London, 1996).

Matthew J. Bruccoli, *F. Scott Fitzgerald: A Descriptive Bibliography*, revised and augmented edition (Pittsburgh, 1987).

———, *Some Sort of Epic Grandeur: The Life of F. Scott Fitzgerald,* revised edition (London, 1991; New York, 1993).

Scottie Fitzgerald Smith, Matthew J. Bruccoli, and Joan P. Kerr, eds., *The Romantic Egoists: A Pictoral Autobiography from the Scrapbooks and Albums of F. Scott and Zelda Fitzgerald* (New York, 1974).

Mary Jo Tate, *F. Scott Fitzgerald A to Z: The Essential Reference to His Life and Work* (New York, 1998).

MARY JO TATE

## FITZGERALD, JOHN FRANCIS (1863–1950)

*See* Boston, Twelve Irish-American Mayors of

## FITZPATRICK, JOHN (1871–1946)

Labor leader, Progressive, Irish nationalist. John Fitzpatrick was born April 21, 1871, in Athlone, County Westmeath, where he attended a national school. He was the youngest son of a retired British Army sergeant and Adelaide Mingey of Suffolk, England, whom the father had met there while on active duty. When the boy was two his mother died and his father married Mary Coughlin, who, unlike his birth mother, was a Catholic. She raised the children in that faith.

## ATHLONE TO CHICAGO

Orphaned at age ten, John Fitzpatrick was taken to live with an uncle, Patrick Fitzpatrick, in Chicago where he attended public school until his uncle died in 1884. At that point he began work at Swift and Company to help support his foster family. For three years at Swift he shared with Slavic immigrants, Black employees and others, harsh work in the packinghouse. It left a vivid impression. Thereafter, he apprenticed in the horseshoers trade. On completion he joined Local Four of the Journeymen Horseshoers Union. Elected to various offices in Local Four, he served as its business agent for five years. In 1892 he married a cousin, Katherine Fitzpatrick, a school teacher. They lived in Bridgeport, a traditional Irish neighborhood in the city. They had one child, John Patrick, who served in the army in World War II and later became an engineer.

## CHICAGO LABOR LEADER

Fitzpatrick was first elected president of the Chicago Federation of Labor (CFL) in 1899. He resigned in 1901 to become an organizer for the CFL. Asked to run again for president in 1905 after the notorious Martin B. "Skinny" Madden had taken over as its leader, Fitzpatrick defeated Madden in a closely monitored election. Except for the year 1908, he led the Federation until his death in 1946. Known for his honesty and dedication to "organize the unorganized," he became a revered figure in the trade union movement.

He saw to it that CFL backed a fledgling organization engaged in a strike in the men's clothing industry in 1910. The result was the Amalgamated Clothing Workers of America, led by militant Sidney Hillman—outside the AFL which refused it a charter. Collaborating with William Z. Foster Fitzpatrick promoted organization of the stockyards in 1917 culminating in a favorable award by government-appointed arbitrator Judge Samuel B. Altschuler which provided wage increases, an eight-hour day, and other benefits for employees.

With Foster, Fitzpatrick undertook to organize the steel industry in 1918. The campaign succeeded in drawing thousands of employees from a wide variety of ethnic groups into its ranks, but these encouraging developments were insufficient to overcome the intransigence of Elbert H. Gary, chairman of the United States Steel Corporation, who steadfastly refused to deal with any labor organization—forcing a strike which ultimately failed. Concerned for Black workers, Slavic immigrants and other ethnics, Fitzpatrick also opened opportunities for women. Public school teachers, mostly women, organized a union with his help, and officers of it, like Margaret Haley, sat on the CFL's executive board, as did Margaret Dreier Robins, founder of the Women's Trade Union League. Jane Addams, founder of Hull House, a pioneer settlement house, was a close friend of Fitzpatrick as well. Their influence reinforced Fitzpatrick's Progressive inclinations.

## POLITICAL VENTURES

The CFL leader endorsed Progressive reforms. He was convinced of the need for a third party and in fact stood for election on the Labor party ticket for mayor in 1919 and for U.S. senator in 1920. Results were disappointing in both cases. A final third party venture took place in July 1923, when Fitzpatrick invited all labor, farmer, liberal and socialist elements to convene in Chicago to form a national party. It was torpedoed by William Z. Foster, who, having secretly joined the Communist party in 1921, arrived heading the Workers party (a communist front) and, using well-planned tactics, took control of the proceedings. Exasperated, Fitzpatrick denounced his old collaborator and abandoned third party endeavors. Foster's treachery also changed Fitzpatrick's initially favorable response to the Russian Revolution to one of distrust if not disgust.

## DEVOTION TO IRISH INDEPENDENCE

Another of Fitzpatrick's long-time concerns was freedom for Ireland. The CFL's publication "New Majority" regularly carried news of developments in Ireland and criticism of the British goverment. Fitzpatrick held membership in Friends of Irish Freedom (FOIF), established to aid preparations for the Easter Rising of 1916. In 1919 Eamon de Valera came to the United States seeking funds for the newly announced Irish Republic as well as recognition of it. Finding he disagreed with FOIF leaders, he organized the American Association for Recognition of the Irish Republic (AAIR). He recruited Fitzpatrick to join the AAIR and to speak often in favor of recognition and also to promote sale of its bonds. The CFL leader enthusiastically fulfilled the request. He also contrived to get the 1920 AFL convention to pass a resolution in support of the Republic of Ireland, and he organized a Labor bureau to spread the word to central labor councils in communities around the country. He asked them to boycott British goods as well.

Irish labor leader James Larkin, in the United States from 1914 to 1923, became a good friend of Fitzpatrick and shared numerous speaking engagements with him. Fitzpatrick devoted strenuous efforts to obtain release for Larkin after the man's imprisonment for criminal syndicalism. It came in January 1923 when New York Governor Al Smith pardoned Larkin as one of his first acts on taking office.

John Fitzpatrick was a true Progressive, not a Socialist. He fought for a strong labor movement open to women and workers of all ethnic backgrounds regardless of color, for industrial unions in manufacturing, for wage and hour laws, protective legislation for women and children and health and safety regulations for industry. On September 27, 1946, this humanitarian leader, faithful to the causes which inspired his career—the labor movement, social justice and freedom for Ireland—died at age seventy-five.

*See* Labor Movement

John Fitzpatrick Papers, Chicago Historical Society.
John H. Keiser, "John Fitzpatrick and Progressive Unionism, 1915–1925" (Ph.D. Diss., Northwestern University, 1965).
Barbara Warne Newell, *Chicago and the Labor Movement* (Urbana, 1961).

L. A. O'DONNELL

## FITZSIMMONS, JAMES EDWARD ("Sunny Jim") (1874–1966)

Horse trainer. Fitzsimmons was born of Irish heritage in Brooklyn, New York, to George and Catherine (Murphy). At age eleven, he began working for Brennan Brothers Stable, during which time he met George ("Fish") Tappan, who in later years became his loyal life-long assistant. In 1889 Fitzsimmons became a jockey and in 1890 rode his first winning horse named Crispin. During this time, it is rumored that he even rode for Frank James, Jesse James' brother.

Fitzsimmons encountered problems in maintaining a low enough weight to qualify for riding and was forced to give up riding for horse training in 1894. The following years brought many trials and career struggles. It was not until in his early thirties that his luck, as he fashioned it, began to change. In 1914, he gained attention as a trainer for the Quincy Stable and later for the Belair Stud Farm in 1924. This attention led him to a job position at the Wheatley Stable of Mrs. Henry Carnegie Phipps and her brother Ogden L. Mills, who later became secretary of the treasury in Herbert Hoover's cabinet. At Wheatley Stable he began working with the yearlings, Dice and Diavolo, and in 1927 Dice won five starts.

However, it was the horse Gallant Fox who brought Fitzsimmons' career to its pinnacle. Gallant Fox won $308,165 and made Fitzsimmons a leading trainer. In 1930 the horses he trained won a total of $397,355 thereby securing a lucrative future for him. Gallant Fox won the Triple Crown—the Kentucky Derby, the Preakness, and the Belmont Stakes. In 1932, another prize winner, Dark Secret won fifteen stakes races and became a renowned distance horse. Other notable horses trained by Fitzsimmons include: Omaha, who won the Triple Crown in 1935, Dwyer, and the Arlington Classic; Granville, who won the Belmont Stakes, Arlington Classic, the Lawrence, Realization, Travers, and Saratoga Cup; and Johnstown, who won the Kentucky Derby and Belmont Stakes.

Fitzsimmons also raced in Florida and owned a company which manufactured Bigeloil (a cure-all for horses) and several devices for various horse injuries. It was George Dailey of the *New York World* who gave him his nickname "Sunny Jim" and he was also known as "Mr. Fitz." His gregarious demeanor earned him a popular reputation even among his opponents. At the spunky age of eighty Fitzsimmons was still working and admired as a top trainer in his field. He is reported to have suggested that longevity consists of a life of regular work, simple eating and fresh air. However, it was severe arthritis, caused by the early years of battling his weight with various rigid diets, that left him with a stooped posture and struggles with pain. In 1963 he retired from a seventy-eight year career span that was composed of some luck and great skill. He was celebrated for his many winnings: the Kentucky Derby three times, the Preakness four times, the Belmont Stakes six times, and the Wood Memorial eight times. He died in Miami, Florida, on March 11, 1966.

Jimmy Breslin, *Sunny Jim* (1962).
Red Smith, "Mr. Fitz," *To Absent Friends from Red Smith* (1982).
*Dictionary of American Biography,* supplement 10.

JOY HARRELL

## FITZSIMMONS, or FITZSIMINS, THOMAS (1741–1811)

Merchant, congressman, philanthropist, signer of the U.S. Constitution. Fitzsimmons was born the son of Thomas Fitzsimmons in Ireland, but the exact birthplace and date of arrival in America has yet to be established. The earliest records indicate that Fitzsimmons and his father were members of St. Mary's parish in Philadelphia in 1758. In November of 1761, Fitzsimmons married Catharine Meade, daughter of a wealthy and successful merchant, Robert Meade. Fitzsimmons eventually became involved in his wife's family business and became a partner in the mercantile business.

Fitzsimmons quickly became established in the community where he served on the Navy Board and the Council of Safety. In 1782, Fitzsimmons was elected to the U.S. Congress under the Articles of Confederation and served as a member of the Pennsylvania Board of Censors and the state legislature. Fitzsimmons was concerned with many commercial issues and allied himself with those who advocated strong Federal government, a suffrage limited to freeholders and a ratification of the Constitution. From 1789 to 1795, after ratification of the Constitution, Fitzsimmons was elected to the House of Representatives, where he aligned himself with the supporters of Hamilton and the Federalist party. As a representative, Fitzsimmons worked tirelessly in favor of creating provisions for relief of the U.S. debt and the introduction of tariffs that would aid in manufacturing and industrialization.

In 1794, Fitzsimmons lost his position in the House of Representatives and he retired to varying civil projects. He continued his efforts of opposition in the matter of the establishment of an embargo because he believed it was both inefficient and unfair. Fitzsimmons became especially successful and noteworthy in his efforts with the establishment of the first bank in America, where he became one of its trustees. Similarly, he was the founder, director and president of the Insurance Company of North America as well as president of the Philadelphia Chamber of Commerce and the Delaware Insurance Company.

In later years Fitzsimmons became involved in such civic causes as the board of the University of Pennsylvania, where he worked on various educational issues. His philanthropic pursuits included membership in the Hibernian Society, and he made large contributions to the construction of St. Augustine's parish in Philadelphia. While very successful for the majority of his business career, he eventually fell sway to a bad business deal involving several associates. Bankruptcy followed, but Fitzsimmons was able to resurrect himself from the difficulties in due time. However, due to the setback of several land investments in 1805 as well as the bankruptcy, Fitzsimmons never enjoyed complete recovery financially. He died in Philadelphia on August 26, 1811.

J. T. Scharf and T. Westcott, *History of Philadelphia* (1884).
Henry Simpson, *Lives of Eminent Philadelphians* (1859).
*Dictionary of American Biography,* 6.

JOY HARRELL

## FIVE POINTS: AN INFAMOUS IRISH SLUM

New York's Five Points neighborhood was one of the most infamous slums in nineteenth-century New York. The neighborhood was named for the five-cornered intersection at its center, where Anthony (now Worth), Orange (now Baxter), and Cross (now Mosco) Streets converged. Almost as soon as the neighborhood was laid out in the early nineteenth century, the Five Points was home to an especially high concentration of Irish immigrants. By 1855, about two-thirds of the Five Points adult population was Famine Irish.

Five Points was best known to contemporaries as the site of the filthiest, most decrepit tenements in the United States. The most famous was the Old Brewery, so called because it had been used to manufacture beer before being converted to a residence in the 1830s. One newspaper called the Old Brewery "the wickedest house on the wickedest street that ever existed in New York." Many of the Irish living in the neighborhood, especially those recently arrived and trying to save money to bring over other family members, resided in the Five Points dismal basement boarding houses. "Without air, without light, filled with damp vapor from the mildewed walls, and with vermin in ratio to the dirtiness of the inhabitants," commented the *New York Tribune*, "they are the most repulsive holes that ever a human being was forced to sleep in." Other Irish immigrants lodged in slightly better conditions in private apartments with countrymen already established at the Five Points. It was not uncommon to find eight Irish immigrants squeezed into a two-room, 225-square-foot Five Points apartment.

The Five Points was also known for its saloons and some bordellos. "Grog shops, oyster cellars & close, obscure & suspicious looking places of every description abounded," wrote author Richard Henry Dana after visiting the neighborhood and sampling a brothel in the early 1840s. "All the houses in this vicinity [near the Old Brewery], and for some considerable distance round—yes, every one—are of the same character, and are filled in precisely the same manner," observed journalist George Foster at mid-century. Some police records confirm Dana's and Foster's charge of rampant prostitution. The area surrounding the Five Points was also impoverished with its quota of crime. In the two decades before the Civil War, virtually every building on the blocks of Anthony and Cross Streets that led to the Five Points housed residents charged with operating a "disorderly house."

All in Five Points were poor, but the majority were decent, honest people. There was more to the Five Points than misery and vice. In the neighborhood's dance halls, Irish steps such as the jig were combined with American dance forms such as the "shuffle" to create modern tap dancing. The early domination of the Irish in the neighborhood also allowed it to produce the city's first important Irish Catholic political leaders. John Clancy and Matthew T. Brennan, both New York-born children of Irish immigrants, built their political strength in the Five Points area. They used that base of support to become the first two Irish Catholics to hold important citywide elective offices, with Clancy serving as county clerk in the late 1850s and Brennan as comptroller during the early years of the Civil War. By that point, many Irish immigrants and their children had improved their circumstances enough that they could afford to move to cleaner and safer parts of New York City. As a result, Italians by 1880 far outnumbered the Irish in the Five Points district. Nonetheless, the Five Points by that point had played an important role in shaping the reaction of some Irish to American life, while at the same time helping (through its reputation) Nativists to damn Irish immigrants.

*See* New York City

Carol Groneman, *"The Bloody Ould Sixth," A Social Analysis of a New York Working-Class Community in the Mid-Nineteenth Century* (Ph.D. diss., Rochester, N.Y., 1973).

K. Spann, *The New Metropolis: New York City, 1840–57* (New York, 1981).

TYLER ANBINDER

## FLANAGAN, BERNARD J. (1908–1998)

Bishop. Bernard J. Flanagan was born in Proctor, VT, on March 31, 1908, and died in Worcester, MA, on January 28, 1998. His ancestry went back to the Flanagans of Roscommon, Ireland, with John, Bernard's father, the son of an Irish immigrant, and Alice (McGarry), his mother, the granddaughter of Irish immigrants. After graduating from Proctor High School in 1924 and the College of the Holy Cross in 1928, Bernard was sent to Rome to study for the priesthood and was ordained there by Francesco Cardinal Marchetti-Selvaggiani, on December 8, 1931.

Father Flanagan returned home and took up his first priestly assignment among the Italians of St. Monica's in Barre, VT, from 1932 to 1940. Then, after less than six months at St. Louis in Highgate in 1940, Flanagan was sent to the Catholic University in Washington, D.C., where he earned a doctorate in canon law in 1943. Thus, equipped for administrative duties, Father Flanagan was appointed chancellor and, in 1945, promoted to monsignor.

Since Flanagan's career in the Diocese of Burlington was so exceptional, Pope Pius XII appointed him, on September 1, 1953, first Bishop of Norwich in Connecticut. He was consecrated bishop in the Cathedral of the Immaculate Conception in Burlington, VT, by Bishop Edward Francis Ryan, assisted by Bishop Vincent S. Waters and Bishop John P. Cody. Under Bishop Flanagan, Catholics in the new diocese increased by 25,000 and school enrollment by 2,000 while religious orders and congregations even established novitiates there.

After six years as Bishop of Norwich, Flanagan was named by Pope John XXIII as the second Bishop of Worcester, MA, on August 8, 1959. Completely absorbed in the changes that swept through the Catholic Church during the Second Vatican Council, Bishop Flanagan implemented them in his diocese so successfully that he became a model for other bishops in introducing liturgical reform. Trained as a canon lawyer and having served as a prosynodal judge of the marriage tribunal as a young monsignor, Bishop Flanagan proved to be such a wise leader in defending the principles governing marriage annulments that he won the respect of Pope Paul VI because of the soundness of his rationale.

That same distinction was evident in Bishop Flanagan's approach to ecumenism, which led his peers inside and outside his church to elect him as the first President of the New England Consultation of Church Leaders. It was no wonder that, when Bishop Flanagan celebrated his silver jubilee as a bishop in 1978, people were unanimous in their esteem of one who had even taken an unusual step, at least for a bishop in that era, to go to Washington and speak out against the War in Vietnam during March of 1972.

As a church leader in three states, then, Flanagan left his imprint on American Catholicism. Although he resigned as Bishop of Worcester, on April 12, 1983, he continued to serve the people of his diocese until his death in his ninetieth year. Bishop Flanagan's body now rests in St. John's Cemetery in Worcester, but his memory lives on in the people of that city.

Archives, Dioceses of Burlington, Norwich, and Worcester

*Catholic Free Press*, *Bishop Bernard J. Flanagan Memorial Supplement* (Worcester, March 20, 1998).

Bernard J. Flanagan, *First Synod of the Diocese of Worcester* (Worcester, 1962).

particular, Flannagan focused on themes of birth and rebirth, as well as mother and child motifs. His work drew increasing attention and acclaim by New York City art galleries. In the early 1930s, Flannagan spent several years working in Ireland which constituted perhaps the most prolific period of his artistic career. Emotional and physical problems, however, lent a tragic air to the final decade of his life. Upon his return from Ireland, he suffered a mental breakdown and spent several months recovering in a sanitarium. Serious automobile accidents in 1936 and 1939 led to a series of operations which left him debilitated and depressed. Shortly before a major exhibit of his work at the Museum of Modern Art in New York, Flannagan committed suicide in January 1942.

"The Sculpture of John B. Flannagan," in Museum of Modern Art, *Five American Sculptors* (New York, 1942, 1969).
Robert Joseph Forsyth, "John B. Flannagan: His Life and Works" (Ph.D. diss., University of Minnesota, 1965).
Jane Turner, ed., *The Dictionary of Art* (London, 1996): XI: 160–61.

TOM DOWNEY

## FLANNERY, JOHN (1835–1910)

Banker and cotton merchant. Flannery was born in Nenagh, County Tipperary, Ireland, to Johan and Hannah (Hogan) Flannery. Due to the harshness of the famine and revolutionary troubles, the young Flannery and his father emigrated to the United States in 1851 where they sought employment. Flannery obtained several clerical positions before settling permanently in Savannah, Georgia, in 1854, where he joined a military organization, the "Irish Jasper Greens." When the Civil War broke out, he joined as a volunteer and served in several positions during the war. When he returned home, he became partner in a cotton-commission firm which he eventually reorganized under the title John Flannery & Company.

Meanwhile, Flannery engaged in many social and cultural interests; he was director of the Southern Bank, organizer of the Savannah Hotel Company, participant in the construction of the De Soto Hotel, vice president of the Hibernian Society and also a member of several other civic and religious organizations. As a devoted Catholic, he supported many Catholic events in Georgia. He was married to Mary Ellen Norton in 1867 and they had six children. Flannery died on May 9, 1910.

A. D. Candler and C. A. Evans, *Cycle of Georgia* (1906).
*Who's Who in America* (1912–1913).
*Dictionary of American Biography*, 6.

JOY HARRELL

## FLATLEY, MICHAEL (1958– )

Dancer, choreographer. Born in Chicago to Irish immigrant parents from Counties Carlow and Sligo, Michael Flatley was just four years old when he took his first dancing steps, but it would be another seven years before his natural talent was harnessed and encouraged through lessons.

The first American-born dancer ever to win the All-World Championships in Irish dancing, Flatley retired from competition in 1976 but not before winning hundreds of trophies in over a dozen countries.

He danced on tour during the late 1980s and early '90s with the internationally famous traditional music group The Chieftains, but it was 1994 when Flatley truly exploded onto the worldwide stage. A seven-minute act during the intermission of that year's Eurovision Song Contest became the inspiration for *Riverdance*, the hit show which has played to millions of people worldwide. After a much-publicized split from Riverdance in 1995, Flatley quickly put together his new show, *Lord of the Dance*, which has played stages from New York to Sydney and Tokyo.

Described by *National Geographic* magazine as a "national treasure," Flatley is listed in the *Guinness Book of Records* for the fastest number of taps per second—he was recorded doing an astonishing twenty-eight taps per second.

*See* Chicago, Aspects of

*Irish America*, vol. xiii/2 (Mar./Apr. 1997); vol. xiv/2 (Mar./Apr. 1998).

DARINA MOLLOY

## FLATLEY, THOMAS J. (1932– )

Real estate developer. Born on a farm in Kiltimagh, Co. Mayo, son of John and Margaret Flatley, he attended St. Colman's College and was an insurance agent before emigrating aboard a cargo ship in 1950. While en route from Baltimore to New York and Boston, he enlisted in the Army's Signal Corps during the Korean War, then studied mechanical trades and labor law at Northeastern University, Wentworth Institute, and Boston College. In 1958, he founded the Flatley Company, builders, which by 1990 had become a real estate enterprise with 75 properties—Sheraton Tara hotels, office parks, shopping centers, residential complexes, "Mayo Health Facilities," and a TV station, most in New England. An avid sportsman and ex-boxer, the non-smoking, non-drinking 6-footer jogs, skis, bicycles, swims, and plays tennis, handball, and squash. He and the former Charlotte McLeod have 5 children and 13 grandchildren. In 1996, Boston Mayor Thomas Menino asked Flatley to chair an Irish Famine Memorial committee that would both erect along Boston's Freedom Trail a monument to the famine Irish and other immigrants to the region, and establish a permanent Famine Institute to recognize relief efforts throughout the world. Bronze sculptures by Robert Shure depict two family groupings, one of parents and a child fleeing the Great Hunger, the other of a similar threesome setting off confidently in their adopted land. With Flatley as master of ceremonies, assisted by new immigrants from Ireland, Rwanda, and Vietnam, the $2M memorial was dedicated June 28, 1998, in the heart of downtown Boston.

Scott Allen, "7,000 hail unveiling of Irish memorial," *Boston Globe* (June 29, 1998): B1.
Charles Claffey, "The Flatley formula: persistence," *Boston Sunday Globe* (February 23, 1975): A-49.
Thomas J. Flatley, "Memorial is a symbol of city unity," *Boston Herald* (June 26, 1998): F10.
"Mayoman Flatley sells 15 hotels for $470M," *Irish Echo* (August 13–19, 1997).
"The World According to Flatley," *s/f* (Square Footage: New England's Real Estate Magazine), (January–February, 1990): 32–37.

GEORGE E. RYAN

## FLEMING, THOMAS JAMES (1927– )

Writer. Thomas Fleming was born July 5, 1927 in Jersey City, N.J. to Thomas James Fleming and Katherine (Dolan). His father,

Thomas Fleming

a first generation Irish-American, became a popular political ward leader in Jersey City, whom his son has touchingly remembered in an *American Heritage* article, "Visions of My Father" (July/August 1991). The Catholic-educated younger Fleming served in the 1950s as a reporter, as assistant to writer-editor Fulton Oursler, and as associate, and later executive editor for *Cosmopolitan* magazine, 1954–1961. He became a full-time writer in 1961 and has since produced over fifty books of fiction, history, and biography, and contributed to a variety of other publications and media. His wife, Alice Mulcahey Fleming, is also a writer.

Fleming has focused particularly on the American Revolution and on the experience of the Irish immigrants of the twentieth century, illuminating historical facts with the deeply personal issues of his subjects. His first published novel, *All Good Men* (1961), dealt with post–World War II Irish-American machine politics, and the year before he had produced a Literary Guild Selection, *Now We Are Enemies,* a historical study of the Battle of Bunker Hill. Since then his literary output generally alternated between writing historical fiction, which he preferred, and non-fiction works of history and biography. His biography of Thomas Jefferson, *Man from Monticello* (1969), won a Christopher award, while his 1970 novel *The Sandbox Tree* (seventeen years in the writing) aroused controversy with its sharply critical stance on the pre–Vatican II Catholic Church: its point of view was that of the women characters, as was his later novel *Officers' Wives* (1981). *The Good Shepherd* (1974) centered on a fictional archbishop and questions of faith and conscience in the post–Vatican II era. Fleming stated in an interview that he would like to be recognized as an American writer who happened to have been born Catholic, rather than as a Catholic writer, and has felt that he had been cut off from the American experience, given his Irish background and religious experience. His fiction evokes a strong sense of history in the reader, and his well-researched non-fiction utilizes contemporary accounts of his subjects from their letters and diaries. He published a history of New Jersey in 1977, and has written impressive biographies of George Washington, Benjamin Franklin, and Harry Truman. His historical books and articles for younger audiences cover a wide range of subjects, such as immigration, African Americans, West Point, and American newspapers. World War II was the subject of the novels *Time and Tide* (1987), *Over There* (1992), and *Loyalties*

(1994). Several novels chronicle the fictitious Stapleton family from frontier colonial life into the nineteenth century, including *Remember the Morning* (1997) and *The Wages of Fame* (1998). *Liberty! the American Revolution* (1997) is Fleming's companion volume to the PBS television series on the Revolution, and he contributed to PBS's *The Irish in America: The Long Journey Home* which aired in 1998. He has been the recipient of a number of literary and history awards, and lives in New York City.

*Contemporary Authors, New Revision Series*, Vol. 10 (Detroit, 1983). *Who's Who in America*, Vol. 1. (1998).

ANNA M. DONNELLY

## FLOOD, JAMES CAIR (1826–1888)

Entrepreneur. The one American-born partner of the so-called "Irish Four" silver kings, Flood's forte was finance. He was the financial genius who helped make himself and his three partners—James Fair, John Mackay, and William O'Brien—all rich.

Born in New York City of Irish immigrant parents, James C. Flood was apprenticed to a carriage maker. Arriving in San Francisco to seek his fortune, he opened a livery stable. It prospered for a time, but went bankrupt when the gold bubble burst temporarily in 1854.

Along with partner William O'Brien, Flood opened the Auction Lunch, a bar that offered a free sandwich with every drink. He listened closely as his clientele, mostly stockbrokers and traders, described the ways of the financial markets. Eventually, he and O'Brien opened their own brokerage. One day, they were approached by two Nevada miners—Fair and Mackay—with a proposition for taking over the Hale and Norcross mine, which was thought to be worthless but which Mackay's skilled eye thought was profitable. It was their first step toward bringing in the Virginia Consolidated in 1873, which eventually produced over $100 million in silver ore.

Flood built two magnificent mansions for himself, one on Nob Hill (which burned in the San Francisco earthquake of 1906 and subsequently became the Pacific Union Club) and one in Menlo Park (which also eventually burned). The onetime carriage maker toured San Francisco in a silver-trimmed carriage driven by a footman in plum-colored livery. His opulent lifestyle and aloof manner attracted considerable unfavorable comments in the press.

John A. Barnes, *Irish-American Landmarks* (Detroit, 1995).

JOHN A. BARNES

## FLORIDA

### THE COLONIAL PERIOD, 1565–1821

The first Irish to settle in what would become the United States did not arrive in the 1700s, or in the mid-1800s, but migrated to Spanish Colonial Florida in the late 1500s.

St. Augustine, the first permanent settlement and the first parish in what would become the United States, was founded by the Spanish in 1565, forty-two years before England's founding of Jamestown and sixty-nine years before Lord Baltimore established St. Mary's, Maryland. Unlike Maryland, where Catholics were at best a tolerated small minority, St. Augustine was a Catholic colony from its inception.

The first recorded Irish immigrant arrived in St. Augustine in June 1597: Fr. Richard Arthur, a native of Limerick. Michael V. Gannon speculates that Arthur as a layman served with the Irish Brigade (first allied in 1586 with the Dutch, then, switching sides, with Spain). After the Dutch Revolt, Arthur studied for the priesthood in Spain. Appointed pastor of St. Augustine Parish in February 1598 by the Bishop of Santiago de Cuba, Arthur was also named Florida's Vicar General, its ecclesiastical judge, and its episcopal visitor to the Franciscan missions to Native Americans. His parishioners were colonists, creoles, and soldiers (some of whom would also have been Irish). Arthur remained St. Augustine's pastor until his death around 1606.

During Florida's Second Spanish Colonial Period from 1783 to 1821, documents reveal the presence of other Irishmen. Captain Charles Howard was dispatched to St. Augustine in 1784 to reclaim Florida for Spain (England possessed Florida from 1763 to 1783). Howard, a skilled diplomat who spoke English, Spanish, and French fluently was a member of the Spanish army's all-Irish regiment, the Hibernians. Commanded by Irishmen Lieutenant Colonel William O'Kelly and his adjutant, Captain Edward Nugent, the Hibernian Regiment garrisoned St. Augustine from 1784 until 1821. The last British Governor, Major General Patrick Tonyn (an Anglo-Irishmen), formally surrendered St. Augustine to Spain on July 12, 1784, a date not lost on Howard, O'Kelly, Nugent, and the other Irish-born soldiers there that day, since it marked the anniversary of the Battle of the Boyne (1690).

Along with the Hibernian Regiment came Irishman Fr. Thomas Hassett, appointed pastor of St. Augustine Church and chaplain to the military garrison. Recently ordained Fr. Michael O'Reilly, a native of Longford, accompanied Hassett as assistant pastor. Both priests attended the Irish College at Salamanca; that college, part of the University of Salamanca, was founded in 1593. In 1787 Hassett started a free parish school with O'Reilly in charge. Aware that on the frontier north of St. Augustine were Anglo-Americans who had agreed to become Catholics in return for taking up residence in Spanish Florida, Hassett set out on a pastoral visitation to these frontiersmen in mid-April 1790. Traveling along rivers and covering 600 miles in five weeks, he discovered isolated homesteads whose residents never saw either a priest or a Protestant minister in their entire lives. During the trip, Hassett instructed children, handed out English-language Catholic catechisms to adults, and baptized seventy-eight children and fifty-one black slaves. Upon returning to St. Augustine in May, Hassett requested more priests to help evangelize Florida's frontiersmen. In December 1791 three newly ordained Irish priests arrived from Spain. But Hassett's ambitious plans to evangelize Florida's frontiersmen never materialized. In 1795 Hassett was transferred to New Orleans, where he died in 1804. Meanwhile, two of the new priests took ill and were sent to Havana by 1796. However, the third, Fr. Michael Crosby of Wexford, an alumnus of the Irish College at Salamanca, remained on, eventually replacing Fr. O'Reilly as St. Augustine's pastor in 1812.

But another of Hassett's dreams did materialize. St. Augustine had no parish church since 1702, when it was burned to the ground by invaders from Charleston. For almost a century Mass was said in a hospital chapel or in a house. Both Hassett and O'Reilly pushed the Crown for the construction of a church. Finally the King of Spain financed the construction of a new coquina rock church which was begun in 1793 and completed in 1797, after Hassett's departure.

Meanwhile in Pensacola, St. Michael Parish was impoverished. The only priest in town, Fr. James Coleman, also a graduate of the Irish College at Salamanca, said Mass in a dilapidated building. Nevertheless, he remained as pastor of a mixed population of 1,796 Spanish, French, and Irish until his retirement in 1822.

In the political sphere, three Irishmen served as colonial governors during the twilight years of Spanish Florida. Henry White, a Dubliner, held office from 1796 to 1811; Sebastian Kindelan governed from 1812 to 1815; José Coppinger, born in Havana to an Irish father and a Cuban mother, administered from 1816 to 1821.

As can be seen, the Irish played a prominent role in the ecclesiastical, political, and military life of the Second Spanish Colonial Period which concluded in 1821.

### Frontier American Catholicism, 1821–1880

The story of the Irish in Florida is intimately linked to the Catholic Church. When Florida became a U.S. Territory in July 1821, the Irish pastor of St. Augustine, Fr. Michael Crosby, who arrived thirty years before, became disheartened and considered resigning his pastorate because he believed that the departure of the Spaniards and the growing presence of American Protestants would make the exercise of Catholicism untenable. Crosby died in 1822, the same date that the Bishop of Charleston, Irishman John England, began to "look after" Florida. Bp. England estimated that only 300 to 400 Catholics remained in St. Augustine, maybe another 100 on the St. John's River, and 100 on Amelia Island. The largest ethnic groups in the region were Spanish Minorcans, followed by a few Italians and Mexicans; the Irish presence was negligible.

Although Bp. Michael Portier of Mobile technically had jurisdiction over Florida from 1825, in fact Bp. England oversaw the pastoral care for St. Augustine since Portier was too far away to have any effect. As early as 1823, Bp. England sent one newly ordained Irish-born pastor after another to St. Augustine. None stayed more than a few months. Irish-born Fr. Timothy McCarthy arrived as pastor in June 1825. By February 1827 McCarthy vacated the city because of a lack of financial support by the church wardens, a six member board of lay trustees incorporated in 1823 to oversee parish temporalities. In November 1828 Bp. England sent twenty-six year old Fr. Edward Francis Mayne of County Atrium to St. Augustine. By August 1829 Mayne was ousted by the wardens, who docked his salary and locked him out of the church. Nevertheless, Mayne hung on and was finally accepted by the wardens in 1832. But it was a Pyrrhic victory since he died in December 1834. St. Augustine was a revolving door for pastors until 1836 when Bp. Portier sent a French priest who stayed seven years.

Pensacola's St. Michael's Parish also had wardens, but the parish was too impoverished for lay trustees to leverage pastors. The presence of the Irish in Pensacola was also negligible.

Key West was the only other city in Florida at the time. Incorporated in 1828, this port city was settled by just about every nationality. In 1835 its population was 582; by 1870 it had 5,016 residents. During two-thirds of the 19th century it was Florida's largest city. When the Bishop of Savannah was charged with overseeing Florida in 1850, he sent Irishman Fr. John Kirby to Key West in 1851. Key West's first Catholic church, Mary, Star of the Sea, opened in February 1852. At that time about 300 Catholics lived amidst a total population of 2,000. Seven of Key West's eight pastors from 1851 to 1857 were Irish-born, as were the majority of their parishioners.

From 1847 through 1854 over 100,000 Irish immigrants came to the U.S. annually. But by 1850 only 4.2 percent of whites in the South were foreign-born. Except for the port cities of Apalachicola and Key West, no antebellum Florida town had appreciable concentrations of Irish, unlike the urban centers of Boston, New York, Philadelphia, Chicago, or the Southern port cities of Charleston, Savannah, and New Orleans. Florida was not very attractive to any immigrant, especially the Irish. Most of the state was unsettled and uninhabitable; in 1860 Florida had only 2.6 persons per square mile and a population of 140,000. Its cities were too small with too few jobs. Free laborers competed with slaves. Immigrants could only reach Florida from Northern cites connected to European ports; few could afford the cost of transportation South. Besides, the Southern half of antebellum Florida was disturbed by two Indian wars: the Second Seminole War (1835–1842) and the Third Seminole War (1855–58). For a devout Catholic, parishes and priests were too few and far between. For example, in 1855 the entire state had six priests: two in Pensacola; one in Apalachicola; two in St. Augustine (one to cover the parish and one to range the frontier); one in Key West. By 1860 over 1.6 million Irish lived in America, but Florida (a state in 1845) had no Irish neighborhoods, no Irish parishes, no Irish political organizations. After the Civil War, Florida's economy was in shambles, making it even less attractive to immigrants.

Frenchman Augustin Verot arrived in St. Augustine in June 1858 as the Bishop of the Vicariate of Florida (territory east of the Apalachicola River). Parishes in Pensacola and Apalachicola now belonged to the Diocese of Mobile. Upon arriving, he found three parishes and three priests: two Frenchmen in St. Augustine and one Irish alumnus from All Hallows Seminary, Fr. William Hamilton, in Jacksonville (the pastorate in Key West was vacant). In May 1859 he sailed to France where he recruited six diocesan priests and five seminarians. On his way back to America, Verot stopped off in Ireland, visiting All Hallows Seminary, Dublin. There he enlisted one seminarian, James O'Hara, the only Irishman he ever recruited. Despite the Union Blockade of Southern ports during the Civil War, O'Hara slipped through in 1863 and remained in Key West as pastor until 1866. Verot became the first Bishop of St. Augustine in 1870.

## Irish Clergy, American Parishioners, 1880–1970

When Bp. John Moore of County Meath succeeded Bp. Verot in 1877, he turned to his native land to recruit priests for his missionary diocese. By 1885, ten of his eleven clergy were Europeans, three of whom were Irish; by the 1890s he had six Irish-born seminarians studying in Rome. Before he died in 1901, Moore ordained at least ten Irish priests for the Diocese of St. Augustine. This trend of recruiting priests from Ireland was continued by Moore's successors. As late as 1940 close to 60 percent of Florida's diocesan priests were Irish-born.

From the mid-19th century to the mid-20th century Ireland's supply of priestly vocations exceeded domestic demand. Ireland exported priests to missionary lands. Beginning with the foundation of All Hallows in Dublin in 1842, five other Irish seminaries earmarked their seminarians for English-speaking missionary countries, mostly where Irish people had immigrated. Yet unlike the 19th century urban centers of Boston, New York, Philadelphia, or Chicago where Irish priests ministered to Irish immigrants in Irish parishes, Florida had no concentrations of

Irish in its few small cities. Nevertheless, Irish priests came as missionaries to Florida's few Catholics scattered in small towns and on frontier homesteads.

The Irish were also well represented in two religious congregations who worked in Florida. Desperately short of priests, Bp. Moore in 1889 invited the New Orleans Province Jesuits to care for Catholics scattered throughout the lower third of the state. With their multi-lingualism and specialization in missionary work, the Jesuits from 1889 to 1921 had the exclusive pastoral care of South Florida. During that period, about 20 percent of the Jesuits who served there were Irish. In 1921, except for a few urban parishes, the Jesuits handed back the pastoral care of South Florida to diocesan priests. By that time the bishop had enough Irish priests to cover the territory; by then 70 percent of Florida's diocesan priests were Irish-born.

The Sisters of St. Joseph were brought over from Le Puy, France, to St. Augustine by Bp. Verot in 1866. In 1899 Bp. Moore severed their ties with France and began recruiting candidates for the congregation extensively from Ireland. In the years that followed Irishwomen dominated the diocesan congregation's leadership.

Florida continued to be unattractive to Irish immigrants. As before, much of it was either uninhabitable or too tropical or too isolated to entice Irish immigrants. Nor was there much employment. Only in the late 1880s and 1890s were railroads built along Florida's East and West Coasts, accompanied by the construction along coastal routes of luxury hotels to attract wealthy vacationers. Irish laborers constructed both the railroads and the hotels, but when these projects terminated most moved to other places where work was more plentiful.

What follows are a few examples of Florida settlement patterns as they relate to parish life and the Irish. In 1834 Hillsborough County was organized with Tampa as its seat. Tampa's population was 885 persons in 1860, the year Tampa's first parish was established with its French pastor and forty-one households, about half of whom were foreign-born. Typical of many American frontier settlements, no one ethnic group predominated in the parish which had six Hispanics, five Irish, four French or French-Canadians, two Italians, and several other nationalities. With the coming of the cigar industry to Tampa in the mid-1880s, Spaniards, Cubans, and Sicilians dominated Tampa's Catholic ethnic community for decades. By 1900 Tampa had a population of 15,836, but fewer than 200 (that is, 1 percent) were born in Ireland. The *Tampa Tribune* remarked in 1896 that it was strange that an American city the size of Tampa did not have a St. Patrick's Day Parade. Nor did any other city in Florida have such a parade until the 1980s.

San Antonio (incorporated in 1885) is thirty miles north of Tampa. St. Anthony Parish was founded there in 1884. Its first pastor was Irish, but the parish was comprised of Germans, Irish, French, and Americans. From the beginning German parishioners were at odds with their pastor over the language of pastoral care. By mid-1885 they founded their own German parish (Sacred Heart in nearby St. Joseph) and were attended by German-speaking Benedictines. But St. Anthony never became an "Irish parish"; its second pastor, who came in 1886, was a Bavarian-born Benedictine.

The few Irish who resided in Florida in the 19th and early 20th centuries were as likely to settle on frontier homesteads as in towns. Bartholomew Forgarty resided at the mouth of the Manatee River south of Tampa since 1867 and constructed a chapel near his house in 1888. When a missionary Jesuit visited his homestead in 1889, he made his First Communion. The last time he had seen a priest was in 1871! His brother John who lived nearby was typical of what happened to some Catholics when isolated on the frontier; first he became a Methodist, then an Episcopalian. Although the abandonment of the Catholic faith on the frontier was always a real possibility when separated from priestly ministrations and parish life, some preserved their Catholicism within the domestic church. A Jesuit missionary came across Irishman Patrick Bannon and his family living in a large chicken coop near Haines City in 1916. The Jesuit visited the family, said Mass, and taught the children a catechism lesson. He later wrote how amazed he was at how well the children knew their catechism and how well the family kept alive their faith under such inimical conditions.

### 1970 AND BEYOND

It is impossible to imagine Catholicism in Florida without the contribution of Irish-born priests. They came at a time, from the 1880s to the 1960s, when their presence and skills were much needed. Native vocations were few and new parishes were needed as new communities formed from the waves of new residents flooding Florida. Irish priests started new parishes, raised money, built churches, and paid off debts. They brought with them their experience of the Church of Ireland, transplanting some of its characteristics into Florida's ecclesiastical soil. Priestly fraternity in Florida was an Irish brotherhood, at times supported by an Irish-born bishop also.

However, by the 1950s things began to change. The Irish-American diocesan bishop put more effort into recruiting American-born priests. By 1978 about 35 percent of Florida's priests were Irish-born; by 1996 only about 20 percent were.

In 1940 Florida had almost 1.9 million residents, making it the twenty-seventh largest state. The Catholic population was about 73,181 or 4 percent of the state's population. About 60 percent of Florida's eighty-eight diocesan priests were from Ireland. In 1996 Florida's population was 14.3 million, making it the fourth largest state. Florida had 1.98 million Catholics, or 14 percent of the total. Now about 20 percent of Florida's 849 diocesan priests were Irish-born.

As in the past, only a small number of Irish immigrants found their way to Florida's major cities. With the post-1960s emphasis on multi-culturalism and ethnic pride, Irish-Americans gained a new interest in Celtic culture, as expressed, for example, in the institution of a St. Patrick's Day Parade in Delray Beach, the airing of Irish music radio programs and the opening of shops featuring Irish goods. Celtic consciousness may be stronger now in Florida than it ever was before, although it was always potent among Florida's Irish-born clergy.

*See* St. Augustine; Spanish Florida: Irish Connections

Charles S. Coomes, "The Basilica-Cathedral of St. Augustine, St. Augustine, Florida, and Its History," *El Escribano* 20 (1983): 32–44.

Patrick Corish, *The Irish Catholic Experience: A Historical Survey* (Wilmington, 1985).

Michael V. Gannon, *The Cross in the Sand: The Early Catholic Church in Florida, 1513–1870* (Gainesville, 1989).

Brian McGinn, "The Irish in St. Augustine," *Ducas* (Summer 1997): 8–9.

Michael J. McNally, *Catholicism in South Florida, 1868–1968* (Gainesville, 1984).

———, *Catholic Parish Life on Florida's West Coast, 1860–1968* (St. Petersburg, 1996).

Grady McWhiney, *Cracker Culture: Celtic Ways in the Old South* (Tuscaloosa, 1988).

Patrick O'Sullivan, "Catholic Irish in the Deep South," *Ecomene* 8 (1981): 42–48.

MICHAEL J. McNALLY

## FLYNN, EDWARD JOSEPH (1891–1953)

Lawyer, politician. Ed Flynn's father, Henry Timothy, a graduate of Trinity College, Dublin, came to New York from Ireland in the 1870s with Ed's mother Sarah (Mallon). Growing up comfortably in the Bronx as the youngest of five children, Flynn received his law degree from Fordham University in 1912, and by 1927 had married Helen Margaret Jones with whom he had three children. His political career started with his Tammany Hall endorsement as New York State Democratic assemblyman for the Second District in 1917. By 1921 he was elected Sheriff of Bronx County, and in 1922 became chair of the county executive committee. Thereafter, he controlled the Bronx Democratic Party until his death. Flynn played an important part in the elections of New York City mayors Jimmy Walker (1925), William O'Dwyer (1949), and Robert Wagner (1953). He supported governors Franklin Roosevelt and Herbert Lehman with both of whom he served as secretary of state (1929–1939). He also served as commissioner general of the 1939 World's Fair. In 1940 he was Roosevelt's choice as national chairman of the Democratic party, and helped secure Harry Truman as vice president in 1944. Roosevelt appointed him minister to Australia in 1944, and he was involved in high-level Moscow and Vatican discussions on religious freedom under communism in Russia and the Balkans. Flynn was a practicing Catholic and Knight of Malta. Publicity surrounding allegations of petty graft in 1942 contributed to his resignation as Democratic national chairman, but he continued in local and state politics. With legal partner Monroe Goldwater from 1924 on, he built a large law practice over the years. His health diminished after a heart attack in 1950, and in 1953 while on vacation in Dublin, he was stricken and died August 18; he was buried from St. Jerome's Church in his beloved Bronx where he was said to have known personally thousands of voters.

*See* New York City

*Dictionary of American Biography,* Supplement 5, 1951–1955 (New York, 1977).

Edward Joseph Flynn, *You're the Boss* [Autobiography] (New York, 1947).

ANNA M. DONNELLY

## FLYNN, ELIZABETH GURLEY (1890–1964)

Labor organizer, communist official. Born in Concord, New Hampshire, August 7, 1890, she was the daughter of Tom Flynn whose father came from County Mayo in the 1840s, and Annie Gurley, who emigrated from Galway in 1877. Elizabeth was the first born of the family's three daughters and one son.

### FAMILY HERITAGE

The family had a rebellious heritage dating back to the United Irishmen and the Rising of 1798 when French General Humbert

Elizabeth Gurley
Flynn

landed at Kilalla Bay with his troops. All of Elizabeth's great grandfathers—Flynn, Gurley, Ryan and Conneran—were United Irishmen by her account. Great grandfather Flynn of County Mayo, she said, guided a force of French and Irish from Ballina to Castlebar—where they routed the British. He was known as "Paddy the Rebel," father of eighteen, one of whom was Elizabeth Flynn's grandfather, who left Ireland during the Great Famine, settled in Maine and participated in the Fenian invasion of Canada.

All of this was related to the Flynn children by their Irish nationalist parents. Tom Flynn had been blinded in one eye working in a quarry in Maine. A socialist, he found his eldest daughter receptive and weaned her on Marxism. Her father had a talent for mathematics and studied civil engineering at Dartmouth College though financially unable to complete a degree. He became an itinerant maker of city maps—moving his family from town to town in New England and elsewhere until they settled into a flat in the South Bronx.

In Public School Number 9 Elizabeth proved a bright student. Appreciation of the Bill of Rights was instilled in her by J. A. Hamilton, who drilled everyone in the American Constitution. Joining the debating society, she won honors. Blossoming as a public speaker, she left school to stump for socialism. Early on Flynn met James Connolly, Irish socialist (and later nationalist hero), then living in America. Becoming friends, Connolly provided advice for the apprentice radical.

## LABOR ORGANIZER

Known as Gurley Flynn, she had begun her life's work—that of an agitator. An attractive, dark-haired, blue-eyed young woman, she was well-equipped with a strong voice, fighting spirit and an Irish way with words. David Belasco, the producer, wanted to put her on stage in a drama about working people. Then an obscure magazine editor, Theodore Dreiser, called her "an East Side Joan of Arc." The Industrial Workers of the World (IWW), formed in 1905. She joined the following year. Meeting a copper miner at the IWW convention in Chicago in 1907, she accepted his invitation to tour the mines in Michigan's upper peninsula. John A. Jones, her guide on this happy speaking excursion, proposed. Again she accepted. The marriage failed, but two children were born—but one died shortly after being born.

Flynn was highly visible in IWW free speech fights in Missoula, Montana and in Spokane, Washington, where she spent time in jail before being acquitted. As a national organizer for IWW she aroused mass demonstrations at the textile strike in Lawrence, Massachusetts in 1912 (in association with Joseph Ettor and Arthuro Giovannitti), and in the silk strike in Paterson, New Jersey in 1913. In Paterson she met Carlo Tresca, an Italian anarchist refugee with whom she entered a common-law relationship in New York City lasting thirteen years.

She was equally in evidence at the 1916 strike of miners in the Mesabi Range and at the textile strike in Passaic, New Jersey in 1926. But the IWW had lost many of its leaders in 1917 when they were arrested for violating espionage and sedition laws. Most of them were convicted, but Flynn contrived to have her case (and that of Tresca, Ettor and Giovannitti) separated from the others. Helped by influential friends, she hired expensive lawyers who managed to have the charges against her (and the other three) dismissed.

During the red scare of 1919–1920, the Workers' Defense Union, begun in 1918 by Flynn and others, provided legal aid for numerous immigrants arrested and threatened with deportation. She was also a founder of the American Civil Liberties Union in 1920. It worked on behalf of anarchists Nicola Sacco and Bartolomeo Vanzetti, who were convicted of murder—arguably a verdict heavily influenced by prejudice against their radicalism. Flynn devoted years to marshalling support for their release—and later, to prevent their execution. When they were electrocuted, Flynn had a breakdown from which she required ten years to recover. Estranged from Carlo Tresca after 1925, she sought refuge with an old radical comrade, Dr. Marie Equi of Portland, Oregon, who nursed her for a number of years. In 1937 she returned to New York City. Sponsored by her old friends, William Foster and Mother Bloor, she joined the Communist party. Originally, she had applied for membership in 1926, but due to factional strife the application had never been processed.

## COMMUNIST OFFICIAL

The last twenty-seven years of Flynn's life were dedicated to the Communist party. Becoming a national organizer for the party, she renewed her contacts with labor under the "United Front" policy. Her column "Life of the Party" became a regular feature of the *Daily Worker*. She was elected to the party's national committee in 1938. However, the ACLU expelled her from its national committee in 1940 because of her membership in the Communist party.

In 1951 she was indicted for violating the Smith Act of 1940, which made it illegal to advocate overthrow of the government by force. She was convicted in 1953 in spite of a passionate defense she made during the nine-month trial. Sentenced to three years in the Federal Penitentiary for Women in Alderson, West Virginia, she was held there from January 1955 to May 1957. While awaiting incarceration she wrote an autobiography covering the first thirty-six years of her life. It was published in 1955. After release she published a memoir, *The Alderson Story*.

Returning to action in the Communist party, she found it in the throes of another factional struggle, but persevered nevertheless. In 1961 she became the first woman to chair the American Communist party. She went to Moscow in 1964 for a vacation and to write a second volume of her autobiography, but it was never written as death intervened on September 4, 1964. She was accorded a state funeral in Red Square.

Rosalyn Fraad Baxandall, *Words of Fire* (New Brunswick, N.J., 1987).
Elizabeth Gurley Flynn, *The Rebel Girl* (New York, 1973).
*New York Times,* obituary (September 6, 1964).

L. A. O'DONNELL

## FLYNN, ERROL (1909–1959)

Actor. Born on June 20, 1909 in Tasmania, Australia, of Irish parents, Marelle Young Flynn and Theodore Thomson (who had served as Professor of Marine Biology at Queen's College, Belfast), Errol Leslie Flynn became the king of the swashbuckler movies of the 1930s.

An adventurer at heart, Flynn was living the romantic life in the South Seas when a group of American movie makers rented his small schooner and included its skipper in a film which was shown in Australia. He immediately set his sights on an acting career in the motion picture business.

Flynn made his film debut in an Australian semi-documentary in 1933 before going to America where he began making Warner Brothers films for Michael Curtiz, the director most responsible for developing his screen persona as a dashing, devil-may-care, light-hearted hero, beginning with his starring role in *Captain Blood.* Whether dueling with Basil Rathbone in *The Adventures of Robin Hood* (the best of the swashbucklers) or romancing Olivia de Havilland in *They Died With Their Boots On,* Flynn thrilled audiences with his graceful yet athletic sword fights and mock-heroic seriousness that these films required.

In the 1940s, he starred in war films such as *Desperate Journey* and *Northern Pursuit;* and, in *Objective, Burma!* he practically won the war singlehandedly for America. Later, he became quite good playing personable drunks in *The Sun Also Rises* and *Too Much Too Soon,* among others.

Off screen, Flynn's high adventures in Hollywood as a charming rogue kept the public riveted to the gossip columns. After three marriages and four children, his romantic adventures were as legendary as his screen personae. His misdeeds often brought him to court on charges from minor fistfights to a famous statutory rape trial at which he was acquitted. As on the screen, Flynn always seemed to land on his feet, and he will remain immortal as long as there are fans who delight in sword fights, war adventures, and booze. His autobiography, *My Wicked, Wicked Ways,* was published in 1960, a year after his death.

*See* Cinema, Irish in

J. Concannon and Frank Cull, *Irish American Who's Who* (New York, 1984).
Joseph Curran, *Hibernian Green on the Silver Screen* (Westport, CT, 1990).
*Hollywood Album, Lives and Deaths of Hollywood Stars From the Pages of The New York Times* (New York, 1977).

EILEEN DANEY CARZO

## FLYNN, RAYMOND L. (1939– )

*See* Boston, Twelve Irish-American Mayors of

## FOGARTY, GERALD P. (1939– )

Historian, professor, Jesuit. Gerald Fogarty was born in Baltimore, Maryland, January 7, 1939, son of Gerald P. and Ellen T. (McHugh) Fogarty. He studied chemistry at Loyola College, Baltimore, before entering St. Mary's Seminary in that city. He studied subsequently at St. Isaac Jogues Novitiate in Wernersville, New York, as well as at Fordham and Yale Universities, receiving bachelor's and master's degrees from Fordham in 1964 and 1967, respectively, and a doctorate from Yale in 1969. At Yale he won the George Washington Egleston Prize for the best essay in American history, and the Theron Rockwell Field Prize for the best dissertation in religion, literature and poetry. Fogarty also holds degrees from Woodstock College and Union Theological Seminary. He was ordained as a Jesuit in 1970.

Fogarty has held academic positions at a number of universities, including Fordham, the Catholic University of America and Boston College, and is presently the William R. Kenan, Jr., Professor of Religious Studies and History at the University of Virginia in Charlottesville. He has published a number of books and scholarly articles, many dealing with relationships between the Vatican and the American hierarchy. He is considered one of the foremost authorities on the Americanism controversy of the late nineteenth century.

Fogarty's books include *The Vatican and the Americanist Crisis: Denis J. O'Connell, American Agent in Rome, 1885–1903* (1974), *The Vatican and the American Hierarchy from 1870 to 1965* (1982), and *American Catholic Biblical Scholarship: A History from the Early Republic to Vatican II* (1989).

Currently Fogarty is completing a history of the Catholic Church in Virginia with the working title *Commonwealth Catholicism.* Other research projects include studies of Vatican-United States relations during World War II and, for the Instituto per le Scienze Religiose in Bologna, the American hierarchy's preparation for Vatican Council II.

Since 1971 Fogarty has been archivist for the Maryland Province of the Society of Jesus.

Gerald P. Fogarty, *The Vatican and the American Hierarchy from 1870 to 1965* (Wilmington, DE, 1985).
———, *The Vatican and the Americanist Crisis: Denis J. O'Connell, American Agent in Rome* (Rome, 1974).

JOHN DEEDY

## FOLEY, THOMAS S. (1929– )

Congressman, Speaker of the House, ambassador. Thomas S. (Tom) Foley was born March 6, 1929, in Spokane, Washington, the son of Ralph E. and Helen (Higgins) Foley. His father was a superior court judge. Foley attended Catholic high school, then entered the University of Washington, receiving a bachelor's degree in 1951 and a law degree in 1957. Over the next three years he practiced law, taught law at Gonzaga University, served as a deputy prosecuting attorney and as a state assistant attorney general. In 1961 he went to Washington, where he became counsel to the Senate's Interior and Insular Affairs Committee. He served in the position until 1964.

A Democrat, Foley stood for Congress in 1964 and was elected from the Fifth Washington District, a sprawling agricultural area in the eastern part of the state. He rose to majority whip in 1981, majority leader in 1987, and in 1989 to Speaker of the House, succeeding Jim Wright (D-Texas), who resigned under pressure for alleged ethics violations. He was the first Speaker of the House to come from west of the Rockies. Some viewed his elevation to the Speakership skeptically because of his penchant for cautiousness. (Former Speaker Thomas P. O'Neill once commented that Foley could argue three sides of every issue.) But Foley was an effective consensus builder and skilled parliamentarian, and he won respect from Democrats and Republicans alike for fair-mindedness. As Speaker he steered the House in essentially liberal directions.

Foley served as Speaker until 1994, when he was defeated for reelection to Congress in his home district. The defeat, coming after thirty years' service in the House, was a stunning one, and was attributed by analysts not to questions of leadership or performance, but rather the increasingly conservative composition of his district and the Republican tide that swept the nation that year. Foley's strenuous opposition to term limits and his support of a ban on assault weapons, both popular conservative causes, were seen as factors in his defeat. He was also targeted by H. Ross Perot, the quixotic third-party presidential candidate of 1992 with many followers listening yet to his words. The defeat was the more remarkable as no Speaker of the House had lost his congressional seat since the elections of 1860.

Foley returned to the practice of law, but soon was back in public life as United States Ambassador to Japan, being named by President Clinton in 1997. He quickly won praise in Tokyo for his role in mediating problems between the United States and Japan over economic policies. In a 1998 interview with the *Washington Post,* Foley said he loved his job as ambassador and that it passed the so-called McCormack Test, a reference to advice then-Speaker of the House John McCormack gave him as a House freshman back in 1964: "If you don't have a sense when you come to work in the morning that it is a rare privilege to be representing [your constituents], if you are not thrilled—just quit."

In 1968 Foley married the former Helen Strachan, who was the long-time unofficial (and unpaid) chief of staff in his congressional office.

*Collier's Year Book* (New York, 1990).
"Mr. Foley Goes to Tokyo," *Washington Post,* March 22, 1998.

JOHN DEEDY

## FORD, FRANCIS XAVIER (1892–1952)

Missioner, bishop. Francis X. Ford was born on January 11, 1892, in Brooklyn, New York, the son of Austin B. Ford of Ireland, and Elizabeth A. Rellihan, originally of Keokuk, Iowa. The elder Ford settled in New York where he became publisher of the *Irish World* and editor of *The Freeman's Journal.* Elizabeth was a writer for both publications and reported on Irish matters for the New York *Times.* In 1912 Francis was the first student accepted for the seminary of the recently founded Catholic Foreign Mission Society of America (Maryknoll). He was ordained a priest December 15, 1917. Named to the first group of four Maryknoll missioners assigned overseas, he began work in Kongmoon, China, in 1918. In 1925 he was named superior of a new mission, Kaying, becoming its first bishop in 1935. His missionary leadership was distinguished by an emphasis on development of Chinese clergy, religious sisters and catechists. With the creative collaboration of Maryknoll sisters and others, he introduced the practice of having religious sisters engage in a direct apostolate among Chinese women—traveling in pairs from village to village, visiting them in their homes. It was a successful innovation formally commended by the Vatican in 1939.

Ford remained with his people in Kaying throughout World War II. Civil war after 1945 brought a more severe challenge. Communist forces under Mao Ze-dong gained control of China in 1949; arrests and deportations of foreign religious personnel began in 1950. Falsely accused of being a spy for the United States, the bishop was placed under house arrest. In April 1951, following a staged trial, he and his secretary, Maryknoll Sister Joan Marie Ryan, were dragged through the streets of Kaying and other towns and finally imprisoned in Canton where Ford died, broken in health, February 21, 1952. Sister Joan Marie was deported.

John F. Donovan, *The Pagoda and the Cross: The Life of Bishop Ford of Maryknoll* (New York, 1967).
Raymond A. Lane, ed., *Stone in the King's Highway: Selections from the Writings of Bishop Francis Xavier Ford* (New York, 1953).
Jean-Paul Wiest,"The Legacy of Francis X. Ford, M.M.," *Mission Legacies,* ed. G. H. Anderson (Maryknoll, N.Y. 1994): 232–240.
———, *Maryknoll in China: A History 1918–1955* (rev. ed. Maryknoll, N.Y., 1997).

WILLIAM D. McCARTHY, M.M.

## FORD, HENRY (1863–1947)

Automobile manufacturer, philanthropist. Henry Ford was born July 30, 1863, on his parents' farm near Dearborn, Michigan. His father, William Ford (1826–1905), had been born on the Madame estate in the townland of Crohane, near Ballinascarty, County Cork, Ireland. The senior Ford emigrated to America in 1847, the worst year of the Great Famine. Henry's mother, Mary Litogot O'Hern (1839–1876), was born in America, orphaned in infancy, and adopted by Patrick and Margaret O'Hern, an Irish immigrant couple from Fair Lane (now Wolfe Tone Street) in Cork City.

Henry Ford attended rural schools and worked on his parents' farm until the age of fifteen. He was a mechanically gifted youngster who repaired watches and clocks in his spare time. Averse to farmwork, Henry found a job as a machinist's apprentice in Detroit in 1878. A few years later he returned to Dearborn and built a machine shop and sawmill on his parents' farm. In 1888 Henry married Clara J. Bryant of Greenfield, Michigan. The marriage produced one child, Edsel Bryant Ford (1893–1943).

Henry Ford took a position as chief engineer of the Edison Co. in Detroit in 1888. The recent invention of the gasoline-fueled internal combustion engine fascinated him. In 1899 he organized

Henry Ford

the Detroit Automobile Co., a manufacturer of custom cars. He left that position to build racing cars. In 1903 he launched the Ford Motor Co. After experimenting for a few years, the company built its first Model T automobile in 1908. Sales were lively (1,700 the first year), but Ford pondered how to develop a larger scale manufacturing business. The ideas he came up with revolutionized all facets of American industry.

In 1913 Ford originated the famous assembly line technique. This allowed him to improve production efficiency that led to a reduction in the price of his product, a shift that led in turn to vastly increased sales volume. The net result of Ford's business tinkering enabled Ford Motor Co. to offer the Model T for $500, a sum reachable by a vast segment of the American market. Between 1908 and 1927, the company sold fifteen million automobiles. The automobile became so popular that Herbert Hoover was elected president in 1928 on a prosperity platform promising "a car in every garage." Ford Motor Co., which initially had been capitalized at the nominal sum of $100,000 in 1903, reported surplus profits of $700 million in 1927. The phenomenal success of Ford's production and marketing ideas made him a multi-billionaire. In recognition of his Irish ancestry, Ford built his first overseas plant in 1917 in Cork City.

Ford proved to be a demanding, paternalistic, and contradictory boss. He paid above-market wages to his laborers and started a profit-sharing program for his employees. On the other hand, he opposed the formation of labor unions, demanded sobriety on the part of his workers, and required thrift as a condition of participation in the company's profit-sharing. The inherent contradictions in Ford's personality became apparent in his quixotic "peace ship" effort to avert World War I. When this endeavor failed, his pacifist principles gave way to Ford Motor Co. becoming a major producer of war materiel. He continued to tinker with his prize product. This led to the replacement of the Model T by the Model A and the development of the V-8 engine.

Henry Ford died April 7, 1947, at Dearborn. He was succeeded by his grandson, Henry Ford II. A sizeable portion of Ford's estate was bequeathed to the Ford Foundation (established in 1936), one of the largest ($4 billion in assets) and most influential philanthropic institutions in America.

Robert Lacey, *Ford: The Men and the Machine* (Boston and Toronto, 1986).
Allan Nevins, and Frank Ernest Hill, *Ford: The Times, the Man, the Company*, 3 vols. (New York, 1954–63).

THOMAS GILDEA CANNON

## FORD, ITA CATHERINE (1940–1980)

Martyr. Ita Catherine Ford was born in Brooklyn, New York, of Irish ancestry on April 23, 1940. During her high school years she began sharing with her best friend the desire to enter the Maryknoll Congregation. Her father's cousin was Bishop Francis Xavier Ford, M.M., who died in prison in China in 1952.

She attended Marymount College, obtaining a B.A. in English literature in 1961. During her senior year, she went on a student tour to Russia and Poland. Her experience of the deep faith of a people who were denied freedom of religion helped her to clarify her own values and her desire to be a missioner.

Ita entered Maryknoll on September 6, 1961. Prior to taking her first vows, nearly three years later, a health problem forced her decision to leave. She kept in close contact with friends in

Ita Catherine Ford

Maryknoll. She was soon teaching catechism to Puerto Rican children and reading for the blind in her neighborhood. She worked for Sadlier Publishing Company as an editor of high school English and religion textbooks. She lived a very simple life, concentrating on essential values. Ita reentered Maryknoll on September 2, 1971, making her first promise on April 29, 1972.

In September of that year, Ita was assigned to work in Chile, arriving there just before the CIA-inspired military coup which toppled the government of Salvador Allende. She worked with the very poor during years of great hardship and persecution. Ita returned to Maryknoll in New York for a year of study and reflection. She never realized how completely drained she was from her experience in Chile. Spiritual direction helped her regain her confidence and her ability to pray.

The situation in Nicaragua and El Salvador prompted the Maryknoll Sisters in Latin America to consider how they could provide relief for the sisters there. Ita arrived in El Salvador on the day of Archbishop Oscar Romero's funeral. After consulting the local church about their ministry, the sisters decided to organize relief for rural peoples who were suffering human rights abuses and to document those abuses, knowing this would put their lives in danger. The work that Maryknoll Sisters Ita Ford, Maura Clarke, Ursuline Sister Dorothy Kazel and lay missioner Jean Donovan shared brought them together on the road from the airport on December 2, 1980. Together they shared the brutality and indignity of rape and death at the hands of the Salvadoran National Guard.

*See* Clarke, Mary Elizabeth

Penny Lernoux, *Hearts on Fire, The Story of the Maryknoll Sisters* (Maryknoll, N.Y., 1993).
Judith N. Noone, M.M., *The Same Fate As the Poor* (Maryknoll, N.Y., 1984).
Phyllis Zagano, *Ita Ford, Missionary Martyr* (New York, 1996).

HELEN PHILLIPS, M.M.

## FORD, JOHN (1895–1973)

Film director. John Ford was born B. Sean Aloysius O'Feeney on February 1, 1895, at Cape Elizabeth, Maine, the thirteenth and youngest child of Irish immigrants. He grew up in Portland, Maine, where he graduated from high school in 1913. Just after graduation, the young man traveled across the country to join his brother, Francis, who worked as an actor, writer and director at Universal Studios in Hollywood and who had changed his surname to Ford. Sean did the same, and went as Jack Ford until 1923 when he became known as John Ford. He began first as a set laborer, a propman, and as a double occasionally for his brother. In 1915, according to one author, Ford appeared in *The Birth of a Nation* as a hooded Ku Klux Klan rider. Soon after this film, Ford began to help direct his brother's films and act in some of them. By 1917, Ford had completed his very first feature film entitled, *Straight Shooting,* and by 1920 had made more than 30 films before moving from Universal to Fox. It was there that Ford became one of the greatest directors in American cinema history. He directed such durable silent film classics as *The Iron Horse* (1924) and *Four Sons* (1928), and over the next two decades, *The Informer* (1935), *Young Mr. Lincoln* (1939), *The Grapes of Wrath* (1940), *My Darling Clementine* (1946), *The Rising of the Moon* (in Ireland) (1957), *The Searchers* (1956), *The Fugitive* (1947), and *The Man Who Shot Liberty Valance* (1962).

Ford's style and vision of film was perhaps the most personal and the most consistent of American directors in the twentieth century. His movies often explored the themes of the American experience in heroes who were often loners, separated from society, and given more to action than to words. He often highlights the tensions in American history by contrasting, for example, the "wanderer" against the "settler," the "mind" with the "gun," or the "individual" with "society."

During the Second World War, Ford served as a lieutenant commander in the Navy as chief of the Field Photographic Branch of the OSS with the task of directing a number of propaganda documentaries. Later promoted to rear admiral, Ford explored the camaraderie of the group and seemed to reflect this in his real-life friendships with actors like Ward Bond and John Wayne. (One author credits Ford with having taught John Wayne his famous walk.)

Ford won four Academy Awards as director, two Oscars for his wartime documentaries, and the New York Film Critics Award four times. Several documentary films have been made on his life

John Ford

and work. Ford died from cancer at the age of 78 at Cape Elizabeth, Maine, on August 31, 1973.

*See* Cinema, Irish in

Peter Bogdanovich, *John Ford* (Berkeley: University of California, 1967).
Ephraim Katz, ed., "John Ford," *The Film Encyclopedia* (New York: HarperPerennial, 1994).

DANIEL J. KUNTZ

## FORD, PATRICK (1837–1913)

Journalist, editor. Patrick Ford earned his living as a journalist and editor, but the passion of his life was to the cause of Irish independence. Ford was born in Galway in 1837 but was soon left an orphan. Family friends brought him to Boston in 1844 where he was educated in local public schools and at the famed Boston Latin School.

Although Ireland would come to dominate his latter life, Ford had no memories of his youth in that country. "I might as well have been born in Boston," he told one reporter. "I brought nothing with me from Ireland . . . Nothing tangible to make me what I am" (Brown, 22). Indeed, it was the anti-Irish hostility of antebellum Boston that molded Ford into an Irish patriot. "I was not yet awake about Ireland," he later wrote, "but I began to think early, to read whatever I could lay my hands on . . . And to think over what I had read" (Brown, 22).

Ford also was influenced by the well-known abolitionist, William Lloyd Garrison. By chance, Garrison hired Ford to work as a printer and journalist in the offices of his paper, *The Liberator.* The doctrinaire tones that Garrison used to champion the abolition of slavery would later be found in the rhetoric of Ford's campaign to win Irish independence.

Ford began to write and edit in earnest in 1855 and would become editor and publisher of the *Boston Sunday Times* in 1859. Duty to the union cause called him, however, and Ford served with the Ninth Massachusetts Regiment during the Civil War. Following the war, Ford spent two years in Charleston, South Carolina as the editor of the *Charleston Gazette,* but by the end of the decade, he had moved to New York.

It was in New York that Ford started *The Irish World,* the foremost Irish-American newspaper of the 1870s and 1880s. In its pages, Ford published sensational stories and drawings of Irish tragedy at the hands of English tyranny. "He was moralistic and shrill," noted historian Thomas Brown, "given to expressions of righteous violence that were thick with the Old Testament. He oscillated wildly between the two extremes of universal humanitarianism and Irish terrorism" (Brown, xvi).

Ford's doctrinaire approach to Irish independence left little room for him to cooperate with other Irish-American nationalists. He fought bitterly with Michael Davitt, John Devoy and other nationalists over a range of tactics and issues.

He remained active in both American and Irish politics the rest of his life. In 1881, he published *A Criminal History of the British Empire* and four years later, *The Irish Question and American Statesmen,* two books that fanned the flames of anti-British hostility.

Beginning in 1886 Ford joined with Henry George and others who worked for social justice. Indeed, it can be argued that Ford should not only be remembered as an Irish nationalist, but also as an early social welfare activist. Ford remained editor of *The Irish World* until 1911 and died at his home in Brooklyn in 1913.

Thomas N. Brown, *Irish American Nationalism, 1870–1890* (Philadelphia, 1966).

William L. Joyce, *Editors and Ethnicity: A History of the Irish American Press, 1848–1883* (New York, 1976).

TIMOTHY WALCH

### FOSTER, STEPHEN COLLINS (1826–1864)

Composer. Born into Scotch-Irish ancestry, Foster was the son of William Barclay and Eliza (Tomlinson) Foster. Foster received training at the Allegheny and Athens academies and then went to Jefferson College in 1841; it was during his first college year that he discovered his overriding passion for music. Foster abandoned a college career to pursue his talent and continued his education with private tutors in Pittsburgh, Pennsylvania. He produced several early pieces including "The Tioga Waltz" for flutes, performed at the Athens Academy Commencement, and "Open Thy Lattice, Love," which was published in 1844.

However, he did not receive support for his musical ambition and was sent to Cincinnati to help his brother with accounting practices in his business. Foster continued to compose several ballads including "Louisiana Belle," "O' Susanna," "Uncle Ned," and "Away Down South," all of which were published in *Songs of the Sable Harmonists* in 1848. Realizing the lucrative potential of his talent, Foster soon returned to his family's home in Allegheny City and worked on a musical career. Foster composed several pieces considered "Negro minstrels" and was able to sell the privilege of singing his songs as well as publishing some of his popular selections like "Old Folks at Home" and "Massa's in the Cold, Cold Ground" in 1852.

Foster stayed in Pittsburgh and worked tirelessly. His efforts brought him another publication in 1860 of "Old Black Joe" but he soon hit hard times. Foster spent his last years living in impoverished conditions, drinking heavily and selling his pieces for less than sufficient remuneration. He died in the charity ward of Bellevue Hospital. Foster is remembered for his contributions to the folk literature of American music.

Morrison Foster, *Biography, Songs and Musical Compositions of Stephen C. Foster* (1896).

H. V. Milligan, *Stephen Collins Foster* (1920).

*Musical America,* (July 1921).

*Dictionary of American Biography,* vol. 6.

JOY HARRELL

### FOSTER, VERE (1819–1900)

Friend and benefactor of Irish immigrants, children and teachers. He was born in 1819 into wealth in Copenhagen where his father, Augustus Foster, was the British ambassador and his mother, the niece of the Earl of Buckinghamshire, was the leading social hostess. After distinguished academic years at Eton and Oxford, he joined the Foreign Office and served as a diplomat in Brazil and Uruguay. He was 28 in 1847 when he first visited Ireland, the land of his Anglo-Irish forebears, which was in the throes of the Great Famine.

Over the next half-century Vere Foster was perhaps the greatest benefactor of Irish immigrants and underpaid Irish teachers.

Vere Foster

He was a generous pragmatist who put his private fortune into the hands of over 22,000 emigrants, mostly young women, who wanted a better deal and a better life in America. In 1850 he boarded the *Washington* with emigrants bound for New York. His report of the appalling conditions on board was responsible for parliamentary legislation which specified minimum standards for emigrant ships. He spent a year in America, traveling over 10,500 miles to get a first-hand view of the new life of the Irish exiles. He made a diligent study judiciously interviewing people like Horace Greeley, police chiefs, and clergy, and examined the working conditions of the young exiles. He concluded that, as a short-term solution, emigration was the best policy. Upon his return, he helped thousands to buy passage to America. (It cost a pound and a half, plus food and clothing for the trip to America in the middle of the nineteenth century.)

Again in 1857, he accompanied 140 emigrants on the *City of Mobile*, and judged the behavior of some of the crew as reprehensible and the conduct of some of the young women as disgraceful. On his return he did not share the aims and methods of Irish nationalists who gave little thought to education, which he deemed was the rite of passage for children who were to stay in Ireland and for those destined to emigrate. He raised money for the poorer schools and subsidized the famous Vere Foster Copy Books, which aided thousands of children to write legibly. The Irish National Teachers Association was founded in 1868, and the grateful poorly paid teachers elected Foster as the first president of their union.

Few gave so much to Ireland's children and its poor. And it was tragic that Vere Foster died alone and in poverty in a shabby rooming house on Great Victoria Street, Belfast, on December 21, 1900.

*See* Emigration: 1801–1921

Art Byrne and Sean McMahon, *Great Northerners* (Dublin, 1991).

Mary McNeill, *Vere Foster* (Tuscaloosa, Ala., 1971).

MICHAEL GLAZIER

### FOSTER, WILLIAM ZEBULON (1881–1961)

Union organizer, Communist official. Born in Taunton, Massachusetts February 25, 1881, William Z. Foster was the child of

James Foster (a Fenian from County Carlow, who fled Ireland after a failed plot in the British Army), and Elizabeth McLaughlin of Carlisle (NW England). Of their twenty-three children, five survived beyond infancy. In 1886 the family moved to Philadelphia to an Irish ghetto called "Skittereen" with the usual corrupting influences. According to Bill Foster, the neighborhood had few if any redeeming aspects. His father, a stableman, urged him to the cause of Irish independence. His mother wanted him to become a priest. The boy rejected both ideas, but became a precocious reader of literature on revolution. Leaving school at age ten to help support the family, he worked in several poisonous lead plants, was apprenticed to a sculptor, but abandoned art to see the world as a seaman and also restore his lungs. He joined the Socialist party immediately after hearing a soapbox lecture on it during a warm evening in June 1900 at Broad and South streets in Philadelphia.

## Conversion to Radicalism

The streetcorner lecture permanently affected his life. He had never before been exposed to a book or a speaker espousing socialism. The explanation of socialism on that evening in Philadelphia made a deep impression on the young man. His objections to the society in which he lived crystallized and the solutions offered by the speaker were convincing for him. Workers should gain government power and abolish the capitalist system. He proceeded to devour socialist literature. His new belief would persist for a lifetime, though it would evolve through a number of mutations. After his return from seafaring, Foster continued to exhibit a penchant for manual work of all kinds—mainly in the American West. By turns he was a muleskinner, shepherd, metal miner, lumberjack, harvest hand, construction worker, railroader, tent show canvasman and trolley car motorman. This resume later became a basis for Communist party literature depicting him as a "working-class giant," a kind of living, breathing embodiment of proletarian experience.

Traveling around the country from job to job, he came across the Industrial Workers of the World (IWW), and became an active member in Spokane. During a sojourn representing IWW in Europe in 1910, he was converted to syndicalism by French trade unionists in Paris. On his return, efforts to persuade IWW to adopt the French version of syndicalism failed. Foster then organized the Syndicalist League of North America (SLNA) and, with a few followers, set out to infiltrate AFL unions with a revolutionary spirit. His campaign was not successful.

## Organizing Drives

Always on the move, Foster turned up in Chicago in 1915 as a railway car inspector in the stockyards. He convinced John Fitzpatrick to attempt organizing employees in the meatpacking industry in 1917, using an approximation of an industrial union. The operation was effective in overcoming numerous obstacles and won an important government-directed arbitration award giving many benefits to employees.

A similarly designed campaign in the steel industry in 1918 undertaken by Foster and Fitzpatrick ended in a long strike. In spite of signing up 365,000 members early on, steel corporations refused to recognize or negotiate with the union. In both efforts the two leaders displayed a remarkable ability to appeal to immigrant workers from eastern Europe, Italy and also Black employees. At loose ends for several years thereafter, Foster organized the Trade Union Educational League (TUEL), to radicalize labor organizations.

## Embracing Communism

Accompanying Earl Browder to Moscow for a meeting of the Red International of Labor Unions (Comintern) in 1921, he secretly joined the Communist party and was directed to use TUEL to "bore from within" American unions. Keeping his membership secret, Foster contrived to take control of a third party farmer-labor convention in 1924 with a Communist front called the "Workers' Party." By doing so he alienated Fitzpatrick and other union friends. Foster was the Communist party's candidate for president of the United States in 1924. Again in 1928 and in 1932 he was its candidate for that office.

In 1928 the Comintern dictated an end to "boring from within." The new policy was dual unionism—Communist unions to compete with established labor organizations. Foster detested this approach, but swallowed his pride and embraced it, replacing TUEL with the Trade Union Unity League (TUUL) for that purpose. He persisted obediently for three years until rocked by a serious heart attack amidst his presidential campaign of 1932.

Recovering from his affliction he discovered that "popular front" had become the new orthodoxy and dual unionism was scrapped in favor of cooperating with the Congress of Industrial Organizations (CIO), and gaining a foothold in it. "Popular front" also meant collaborating with all anti-fascist groups—until the Hitler-Stalin Treaty of 1939. At that time a quick about-face followed. Now the policy was to oppose military preparedness efforts in the United States and instigate strikes at defense plants. When World War II broke out in September of 1939, it was an "imperialist war" according to party-liners, but only until Germany invaded Russia in June of 1941, when another turnabout favored all-out production, no strikes and conceding hard-won gains to speed output. Foster faithfully observed all of these twists and turns and his attempts to justify them caused him to be called William Zigzag Foster by some critics.

Finally, in 1945 party leader Earl Browder was denounced for "right deviationism," and defrocked. Foster was given command. An uncritical adherent of the party line, he presided over a catastrophic loss of membership due to the Cold War. He was unseated in 1956.

William Z. Foster married Esther Abramovitz on March 23, 1918.

In January of 1961, seriously ill, the old Marxist warhorse traveled to Moscow for medical treatment. William Z. Foster died there on September 1, 1961. He was accorded a state funeral in Red Square.

*See* Labor Movement

Bert Cochran, *Labor and Communism* (Princeton, 1979).
William Z. Foster, *Pages from a Worker's Life* (New York, 1939).
Edward P. Johanningsmeier, *Forging American Communism* (Princeton, 1994).

L. A. O'DONNELL

## FOWLER, GENE (1890–1960)

Author, journalist. Born Eugene Parrott Devlan March 8, 1890, in Denver, Colorado, to Charles Francis Devlan, Jr., and Dora Grace Parrott Devlan, he was deserted by his father before birth. His mother later married Frank Fowler who adopted him, but he was raised primarily by his maternal grandmother, Elizabeth Wheeler. His ancestry was a mix of Irish and Pennsylvania Dutch on his mother's side, and Irish and some French on his father's. A variety of jobs in taxidermy, telegraph office work, printing, and produce wagon driving brought him experiences that contributed to the tough, florid language of his offbeat fiction writing later. In 1912 he became a reporter for the *Denver Republican,* and in 1913 worked for the *Rocky Mountain News,* covering crime, sports and local government. Fowler married Agnes Hubbard in 1916 with whom he had three children. Helped by his friend Damon Runyon, also of Colorado, he moved east in 1918 to become sports reporter for William Randolph Hearst's *New York American;* he joined the *New York Daily Mirror* in 1924, becoming managing editor of the *American* a year later. As managing editor of *The New York Morning Telegraph* in 1928 he hired writers such as Ring Lardner, Ben Hecht, Westbrook Pegler and Walter Winchell, but ended his newspaper career in 1931, being fired for paying a top-flight staff excessively high salaries.

Turning to Hollywood, he made the thirties his best decade as both a fiction and screenwriter. He produced over a dozen books and more than twenty motion picture scripts. Successful scripts and film stories for eight major studios include *State's Attorney* (1932), *Call of the Wild* (1935), *White Fang* (1936), *Earl of Chicago* (1940), *Billy the Kid* (1941), and *The Oregon Trail* (1959). Fowler served as press agent for Queen Marie of Rumania, and managed prize fighters and wrestlers. He wrote lively biographies, including the best-selling *Good Night Sweet Prince* (1944) on his close friend John Barrymore, *Schnozzola: The Story of Jimmy Durante* (1951), and an autobiography *Solo in Tom Toms* (1946). Gene Fowler died July 2, 1960, of a heart attack at age 70 in his Brentwood, California, home.

*Current Biography 1944* (New York, 1944).

*Dictionary of American Biography*, Supplement 6, 1956–1960 (New York, 1980).

H. Allen Smith, *The Life and Legend of Gene Fowler* (New York, 1977).

*World Authors 1900–1950*, Vol. 2 (New York, 1996).

ANNA M. DONNELLY

## FRANCISCAN BROTHERS

### ORIGINS

The Franciscan Brothers who emigrated from the west of Ireland to North America in the nineteenth century can trace their origins and identity to medieval Italy and pre-Reformation Ireland. Franciscan Brothers of the Third Order Regular were founded because of the desire of secular Franciscans to live a religious life in community. Shortly after the Third Order Secular was founded by St. Francis of Assisi in the thirteenth century in Italy, communities of these Third Order members were created between 1214 and 1221.

### FRANCISCAN BROTHERS IN IRELAND

The first foundation of the community in Ireland was at Killeenbrenan near Shrule in County Mayo, *c.* 1426. Patrick Conlon, O.F.M., in his *Franciscan Ireland* (pp. 94–95), notes that by 1450, the Third Order Regular had twelve houses, primarily in the Gaelic-speaking areas of the west and north. By the time of the Suppression there were forty friaries of the Third Order Regular in Ireland, principally involved in the education of poor boys in the provinces of Ulster in the north and Connacht in the west.

After the Flight of the Earls in 1607, all of these friaries were suppressed.

In 1817, a few pious men who were members of the Franciscan Secular Third Order attached to Adam and Eve's Church, Merchants Quay, Dublin, came together in community and took religious vows. In 1818, two of these Brothers went to Mountbellew, County Galway at the request of Christopher Dillon Bellew and founded the friary and school which is now the Franciscan Brothers' Agricultural College. By the mid-nineteenth century the Brothers had founded over ten "monasteries" in the west of Ireland, earning their popular name, 'Monks of the West.'

### LOUISVILLE, KENTUCKY

Two Franciscan Brothers from Tuam, County Galway, Ireland, first arrived in America in Louisville, Kentucky in August, 1846, just before the Great Famine. They were sent by their ecclesiastical superior the famous Archbishop John McHale, called the "Lion of the West," for his fervent Irish patriotism. One of the most important prelates in Ireland in the nineteenth century, McHale was very influential in the development of Catholic education for Irish emigrants in the Americas because of the religious communities he sent to America at the request of American bishops. They opened a free school for boys, which was enthusiastically received by the Catholic population. By 1847, they had sixty students in their school on Market Street. However, they were replaced by the Jesuit Fathers, who returned to Louisville in 1848.

### ST. JOHN'S, NEWFOUNDLAND

Four Irish Franciscan Brothers arrived in St. John's, Newfoundland, Canada, in 1847. They were also sent by Archbishop McHale at the request of Bishop Michael Anthony Fleming, O.F.M. They began operation of an orphan asylum and school with the financial support of the Irish Benevolent Society. However, by 1852, "friction" with local officials was interfering with the Brothers' operation of their school. As the Irish Brothers Archives note: the "friction arose from a new system of education involving right of entry and supervision established by local officials whose prejudices against Catholic Education were well known." Two of the Brothers, John Hanlon and Bernardine Rogers, went back to Ireland in 1850, but eventually settled in Loretto, Pennsylvania in the 1850s.

### LORETTO, PENNSYLVANIA

The third community of Brothers in America was more successful. Invited by Michael O'Connor, the first Bishop of Pittsburgh, John Gilmary Shea writes in *The History of the Catholic Church in the United States, 1844–1866,* (vol iv, pp.75–76), that: "Six Brothers of the Third Order of St. Francis, three from the communities of Clifden and Roundstone [part of John McHale's Province of Tuam in the west of Ireland], and three from [St. John's] Newfoundland, came over in 1847 and began their labors in Loretto.... [Under the leadership of Brother Lawrence O'Donnell, the first superior] the Brothers proved themselves able instructors. Their community prospered, the academy was incorporated as a college [St. Francis College] in 1854, and the Brothers continued to do good service in parochial schools."

### BROOKLYN, NEW YORK

Many of the Irish who arrived in New York after the Great Famine eventually settled in Brooklyn, just across the East River from Manhattan and connected by many ferries. Bayor and Meagher's *The New York Irish* (Appendix 1, Statistical Table, pp. 554–555) states, that by 1855, the Irish-born population of Kings County, the present borough of Brooklyn, was 59,308, or 27.4% of the total population of 216,355. By 1875, the total Irish-born in Brooklyn rose to 83,069; but this figure does not account for the many American-born children of their Irish-born parents. An estimate of 200,000 Irish-born and first-generation Irish-Americans would raise the number of the Irish-connected population in Brooklyn to almost 40% of the total of 509,154 persons listed in *The New York Irish* statistics for that year. Brooklyn had a ready population of students needing the services of the Irish Franciscan Brothers.

In 1858, Brothers John McMahon, Vincent Hayes and eight young men desiring to be Brothers, arrived in Brooklyn at the request of John Loughlin, the first Bishop of the newly created diocese of Brooklyn. These Brothers, who were also sent by Archbishop John McHale, were from Roundstone in the west of Ireland. Their first duty was to take charge of the newly built Male Orphan Asylum, which was to burn to the ground in a tragic fire in the morning of November 9, 1862. They also founded St. Francis Academy in 1859, the first Catholic secondary school in Brooklyn, which received its charter to award degrees in 1884, when it become St. Francis College. In 1859, the Brothers requested a Rescript from the Holy Father granting the new community permission to be subject for the time being, *pro tempore*, to John Loughlin, the Bishop of Brooklyn, "and to make other foundations, when the proper authorities appprove it." The Rescript was granted by Pope Pius IX on 15 December 1859.

### California

Although the Brothers had plenty of work in Brooklyn, evidence from the Santa Barbara Archives of the Friar Minor Franciscans suggests that Brother John McMahon, the Superior of the small Brooklyn community, took the phrase, *pro tempore,* at its face value. He wrote to these First Order Franciscans in Santa Barbara, California in late 1859 or early 1860, seeking their assistance to establish a house and college in Santa Barbara. Father Gonzales Rubio, the President of the Franciscan Apostolic College in Santa Barbara, wrote in 1860 discouraging the Brooklyn Brothers from travelling to California because of a long-standing difficulty between the Franciscans and Thaddeus Amat, C.M., the Bishop of the Monterey diocese. Despite Father Rubio's letter, Brother John McMahon and four Brothers did travel to Santa Barbara in the summer of 1862, without Bishop Loughlin's permission, to begin a long, unsuccessful effort to establish a college in California.

### Clontarf, Minnesota and Spaulding, Nebraska

In 1880, Bishop John Ireland of St. Paul, Minnesota, sought Brothers from Brooklyn to open a school for Native American boys in Clontarf, Minnesota. Two Brothers, Malachy Shields and Alphonsus Maroney, arrived in 1880, and were followed by three Brothers in 1881 and three more in 1882. However, by 1882, Shields and Maroney had returned to Brooklyn, when, community legend tells us, "the cows died of the cold". The small community received new members, the most famous being Brother Joseph Fielding, a native of Ireland, who joined from Massachusetts when his wife died. He was called "Injun Joe" by the Native Americans because of his friendship with Chief Sitting Bull. When the mission was forced to close because the federal fund-

ing was withdrawn in 1895, five Brothers transferred to Spaulding, Nebraska to begin a new mission.

### Successful Educators

By the turn of the century, the Brooklyn Brothers had taught in seventeen parochial schools in Brooklyn, Roundout, New York and Jersey City, New Jersey, two high schools and St. Francis College. Some Brothers also went to Olean, New York in 1873, to assist the Franciscans Friars to start St. Bonaventure's College. The Franciscan Brothers currently teach and are administrators in St. Francis College, Brooklyn, New York; and conduct four high schools, St. Anthony's in South Huntington, New York; St. Francis Preparatory in Fresh Meadows, New York; St. John the Baptist in St. Louis, Missouri; and Cardinal Gibbons High School in Raleigh, North Carolina. The Brothers administer Mount Alvernia on Long Island, which has the oldest Catholic summer camp in the country, and serves as a Conference Center throughout the year. They also teach in schools and work in ministries in New York, New Jersey, Brooklyn, Long Island, and North Carolina.

Ronald H. Bayor and Timothy J. Meagher, *The New York Irish* (Baltimore, 1996).

Patrick Conlan, O.F.M., *Franciscan Ireland* (Mullingar, Westmeath, 1988).

John Gilmary Shea, *History of the Catholic Church in the United States,* 4 vols. (New York, 1892).

EMMETT CORRY, O.S.F.

## FRIENDLY SONS OF ST. PATRICK, THE

A collection of independent, charitable, fraternal, and social organizations, the various Friendly Sons societies find their beginning in the Friendly Sons of Philadelphia which held its first meeting on March 17, 1771. That organization included several prosperous merchants and military leaders who were to play prominent roles in the American struggle for independence. Its first president was Stephen Moylan. Commodore John Barry was a member and George Washington was adopted as a member in 1781. With its focus primarily fraternal during the war, by the end of that conflict its membership declined. In 1792 a new organization, the Hibernian Society for the Relief of Emigrants, was organized which included several of the former society's members. It would adopt the Friendly Sons name for itself in 1897 and continues its activities to the present day.

Two original members of the Philadelphia organization relocated to New York and organized the Society of the Friendly Sons in that city in the winter of 1783, holding its first dinner on March 17, 1784. That organization, which is still in existence, would strongly influence future groups and chose as its first president Daniel McCormick, an industrious merchant, civic leader, and generous public benefactor.

In the eighteenth century, the word "friendly" denoted not only social activity but involved charity as its primary meaning. At that time, there were no municipal welfare systems and the Friendly Sons came to the aid of impoverished and displaced Irishmen in their cities. They provided money, food, shelter, and employment for their less fortunate countrymen. Similar organizations existed for those of English, Scots, Dutch, German, and Welsh descent.

In addition to its charitable function, the Society also existed to promote a spirit of friendship among the members and to foster a knowledge and devotion to their common Irish heritage. Four meetings were held each year, the most popular of which was the Saint Patrick's Day Anniversary Dinner. Initially membership was limited to natives of Ireland or their sons, although the sons of members could qualify for membership, even if their Irish heritage was more remote. Membership was at first restricted to one hundred (and now 1,000) and although not stated in its constitution or by-laws, membership was usually only for the city's elite. Many socially prominent figures such as George and De Witt Clinton and James Duane, the first mayor of New York after the British evacuation of the city, joined the Society. President Daniel McCormick, along with another founder, William Constable, and Alexander Hamilton, organized and opened the Bank of New York in 1784. In later years, Presidents Theodore Roosevelt and Richard Nixon would join the Society, as would major industrialists such as William R. Grace and merchants such as John S. Burke and John Phelan, the president of the New York Stock Exchange.

In the early years, most members of the Friendly Sons were Presbyterians, since most upper-class Irish merchants were of that faith. But membership also included Episcopalians, Quakers, and Roman Catholics, a group that would come to dominate in the twentieth century.

Tradition also maintains that at one of the early meetings of the Society, it was decided that religious and political discussions would be avoided, and that no question be raised at meetings which would cause discord or disunity. Such a policy has generally been maintained.

As a fraternal organization, the Society adopted a number of customs. Badges of membership are issued and expected to be worn at meetings. Memorial tributes are composed and distributed. Dues are collected which form the treasury for their charitable activities. In the early days, the distribution of benefits was handled on an individual basis to those in need. By the twentieth century, grants were made by the almoner to a variety of social welfare organizations devoted to assisting the poor.

The Anniversary Dinners held on March 17th became elaborate formal affairs whose proceeds were used to fund the charitable activities. The menu could be extensive and the speakers are drawn from among the most prominent political, educational, and business leaders. The speeches are given in response to "toasts" which have been as many as thirteen in number, but in the 20th century, had stabilized at three. Among the featured speakers and guests have been Daniel Webster, Henry Ward Beecher, Presidents Cleveland, Taft, Theodore and Franklin Roosevelt, Truman and John F. Kennedy, several Supreme Court Justices, Governor Al Smith, Reverends Robert I. Gannon, S.J., and Fulton Sheen, Ireland's President Eamon de Valera and Judge William Hughes Mulligan of the U.S. Court of Appeals. The speeches are reproduced in a hardcover yearbook. The attendance in New York typically exceeds 2,000.

The Glee Club was founded in 1913 by Victor Herbert, the famous conductor and composer of operettas. They perform "The Hail of the Friendly Sons," composed by Herbert, at all meetings and give concerts at hospitals and nursing homes.

Although the Society began quite auspiciously, its members were sorely tested when a fire devastated New York in 1835 destroying the businesses of most of its members. This was followed by the depression of 1837 and the enormous influx of poor Irish in the 1840s as the Famine took its course. The Society cancelled its dinners in 1847 and 1848, sending the money to Ireland to help with famine relief. As the century continued and the Irish immigrants became more established in the new world, the Society resumed its position of influence and prosperity. During the 20th century, an invitation to the Anniversary Dinner became a mark of social prominence.

As New Yorkers relocated to other parts of the nation, they carried with them a desire to continue the spirit of charity and comraderie they found in the New York Society. Independent organizations have grown up in Cincinnatti, Ohio (founded 1868), Lackawanna County, PA (1906), Honolulu, HI (1939), Los Angeles, CA, San Diego, CA, Seattle, WA, Warren, MI (1940), and more than twenty other locations. The Friendly Sons of Westchester County, N.Y., in particular have established a distinguished reputation for their financial support of charitable projects both in Ireland and in the New York area.

Thomas A. Daly, *The Friendly Sons of St. Patrick* (Philadelphia, 1920).

Michael Funchion, ed., *Irish American Voluntary Organization* (Greenwich, CN, 1983).

Richard C. Murphy and Lawrence J. Mannion, *The History of the Society of the Friendly Sons of Saint Patrick in the City of New York, 1784 to 1955* (New York, 1962).

———, *Yearbooks* (The Society of the Friendly Sons of St. Patrick in the City of New York, 1956–1997).

ROBERT REILLY

# G

## GAELIC ATHLETIC ASSOCIATION, THE

While the games of hurling and Gaelic football have evolved as the most popular in Ireland, the history of the Gaelic Athletic Association in America has been a difficult one for the exiles and their descendants. This story of the GAA in the U.S. centers mainly on the unit of the Association in New York which, because of the large numbers of Irish who immigrated to that city, has proven to be the one where newspaper accounts are more readily available through the columns of writers such as Liam O'Shea (*Irish Advocate*), Wedger Meagher (*Irish Echo*), and more recently the *Echo*'s John Byrne whose weekly reports in "The Game Of The Gael" became the most popular ever for followers of the games in the U.S.

It may come as something of a surprise to GAA enthusiasts to learn that the first known players to bring the uniquely Irish sport of hurling to America were in fact emigrants from the northern province of Ulster. Tavern owners such as Thomas McMullin and Charles Loosely imported hulrs and hurling balls for the use of their patrons as early as 1781, and the composition of the teams of that era were almost exclusively Irish-born soldiers serving in the British army.

Outside of New York, the earliest references to organised hurling in the U.S. was of a team in San Francisco in 1853, while in Boston a competition for the John Boyle O'Reilly hurling cup was in existence during the 1890s.

Chicago became the first American city to affiliate in 1893 with the parent body in Ireland when it was reported that the GAA in that city had fifteen clubs in competition with a membership of some 2,000.

The so-called invasion of 1888, the brainchild of Maurice Davin, had hoped that by bringing the cream of Irish athletes to America that financial assistance would be forthcoming to the fledgling Irish organisation, but a number of factors combined to leave it far from the success which had been the hope of the organising body. Being an election year in the U.S. political world, the attention of the general public was focused in that direction, and with the publicity afforded to the Gaelic contests far from what was required to stimulate interest, the tour failed to generate the attention of the public. When the touring party had completed their series of exhibition games in Brooklyn, Boston, Trenton, Lowell, Yonkers, Newark, Patterson and Philadelphia, not all of the Irishmen returned to their native land, as a sizeable proportion elected to make a new life in America.

On 12 December 1914, Snow's Hall in New York was the setting for an historic meeting which heralded the beginning of the Gaelic Athletic Association in the city. Representatives of 24 football and hurling clubs (including 3 from Philadelphia) decided that the appropriate time had arrived when Gaelic athletes should control their own activities. Prior to this, it was the organisations who had control of the sporting events at Celtic park in the Sunnyside area of Queens.

The first championships commenced in 1915, and when all of the fixtures had been completed, it was the Cavan club that had the honour of being crowned the first official GAA champions in football, with Cork garnering the honours in hurling.

A year later, officials of the four attended a meeting of the association at which they were persuaded to participate in the leagues of that year, and from there the GAA went from strength to strength in New York with the weekly schedules at Celtic park often attracting atttendances of well over 10,000.

The first county visitors to the U.S. would be the All Ireland hurling kingpins from Tipperary who made an unbeaten cross-country tour, with games played in New York, Chicago and San Francisco during 1926, and such was the appeal of these outstanding young athletes that the Irish immigrants clamoured for further such visits.

The parent body of the GAA based in Dublin and its counterpart in America were separated by more than the vast expanse of the Atlantic Ocean, with their political preferences the most recognisable. New York had for long been the refuge of Irish republicans seeking to escape both the war of independence and the civil war in their homeland, while during the 1920s, the vast majority of those who controlled the unit in the homeland would have favoured the opposite end of the political spectrum. Consequently there was a deep mistrust between the two, and in Dublin an unwillingness to accept the Gaels in America as totally sincere about the promotion of the games.

In 1927, the All Ireland champion footballers in Ireland were invited by the Gaels of New York to undertake a tour of a number of U.S. cities, but this proposition was not readily sanctioned by the people in control on the Central Council of the GAA, and before they would agree to permit Kerry, the eventual champions, to travel, they insisted that the tour be under the direction of a professional American sports promoter. In the hope of ensuring that Kerry would be granted the required permission to travel, the American Gaels acquiesed to this demand and the tour was then given the approval of the Council. However, there was one further demand from the governing body, and that was that the players would sign a statement to the effect that upon completion of the tour they would return to Ireland. And during the following May and early June, Kerry arrived in America.

No one really felt that the New York representative selection would be up to the lofty standard of the All Ireland winners of 1927, and it came as a major shock to everyone when the visitors were defeated in the two scheduled contests with the Big Apple team.

A third game was neccesitated when the visitors went looking for the tour promoter to receive the monies agreed to be paid to them upon completion of the stipulated schedule, but this gentleman was not to be found, having departed from New York in the dead of night. The teams agreed to another game at Celtic park where the receipts were divided between the Kerrymen and the New Yorkers, who won the match.

Unlike the winning GAA champions in Ireland, this magnificent New York team received little acclaim for their achievements, and indeed, many of the leading Irish newspapers of the time belittled their conquest of the Kerrymen. The victorious

Americans' names have never appeared in any GAA publication where the sporting heroes of years gone by are immortalised, so here we list those men who proved to everyone that the Gaels of America were in every way as competent in their sport of choice as any back in the land where the game had originated: Eddie Roberts (Waterford), Paddy Ormsby (Mayo), Andy Furlong (Wexford), Bertie Graham (Kildare), John "Peck" Tuite (Louth), Johnny McGoldrick (Leitrim), Jim Jermyn (Cavan), Martin Shanahan (Tipperary), Mike Bolger (Wexford), Dan Henry (Sligo), Eddie "Sapper" O'Neill (capt. Kildare), Paddy Lenihan (Cork), Joe Stynes (Kildare), Tommy Flynn (Leitrim), Sean Carr (Roscommon). Reserves—Dan Sullivan (Cork), Martin Cody (Kilkenny), Rusty Ormsby (Mayo), John Keeley (Kildare). Manager—Mike Hanrahan (Kilkenny).

A year later, further conflict arose between the Americans and the Central Council when, following the former's elimination from the Tailteann games at Croke Park, they were granted permission to play a number of exhibition games with county teams in an attempt to recoup some of the huge costs of sending the two representative American teams to that particular competition. However, when the visiting football squad went along to the Garda ground in the Phoenix Park where they had been assured that training facilities had been provided for their needs, they found the gates locked, and so were forced to seek alternative facilities. These were granted by the Bohemians soccer club who put at their disposal the Dalymount Park pitch, but by accepting this offer, the New Yorkers had unwittingly broken a cardinal rule of the time whereby playing, attending, or using the ground of a soccer or rugby club was punishable by suspension from the association. After a meeting of the Central Council, they were told that permission for them to play further challenge games in Ireland had been withdrawn, and so they had to bid an ignominious farewell to the land of their birth.

During the 1940s, World War II saw the call to arms of so many Gaelic players that the games at Innisfail Park in the Bronx teetered on the verge of extinction, and with the gate receipts from the Sunday programme of games insufficient to maintain the upkeep of the ground, leaseholder P. J. Grimes was forced to terminate his contract with the municipal body that owned the playing field. A local soccer league had designs on the facility, but just when it seemed inevitable that the GAA would have to seek alternative locations for their games, John Kerry O'Donnell stepped forward to save the day when he sold several of his Manhattan bars to accrue the funds required to keep Innisfail available for the exclusive use of the GAA.

Undoubtedly the biggest event in the annals of the GAA in America was the decision to play the 1947 All Ireland football final in New York. While the concept was the brainchild of John Kerry O'Donnell, it was mainly through the efforts of Clare-born Central Council delegate Canon Michael Hamilton that the final was reluctantly taken outside of Ireland for the one and only time. Cavan 2-11; Kerry 2-7 was the outcome of that historic match and while the attendance was somewhat disappointing at 34,941, the monetary receipts were the highest ever returned for an All Ireland final up to that time.

In the late 1940s emigration from Ireland to the U.S. rose dramatically, and with such an influx of new playing talent arriving in New York, it heralded a rise in the fortunes of the Association in the area. Having unsuccessfully applied on a number of occasions for admittance into the All Ireland competitions, New

York's request for inclusion in the National Leagues was more favorably considered and in 1950 both hurling and football teams made their inaugural appearances in the finals of these competitions.

The hurlers had the opportunity of playing Irish winners Tipperary in the Polo Grounds, but lost to Tipperary by the narrow margin of two points.

For the footballers, the journey back to Dublin to face the mighty Cavan selection was predicted to end in an embarrassing reverse for the Americans, but led by Mickey O'Sullivan, a native-born New Yorker, they created one of the greatest upsets ever in the history of the competition to triumph by 2-8 (14 points) to 0-12.

New York's relationship with the Central Council in Dublin was to be a very strained one throughout the 1950s and 1960s and while their footballers added a further two NFL titles to their honour roll in 1964, the majority of the Irish counties were unhappy with their participation in the competitions.

In 1970 the visit of Cork hurlers to New York for the decider of the hurling league ended in a narrow two-point victory for the Leesiders, but it was the after-match fight when referee Clem Foley sustained a broken jaw that finally led to the end of the American's participation in these competitions. However, they were afforded a token admission to the series at the end of the 1980s, as a gesture of good faith for affiliating with the parent body in Dublin.

Today the GAA in America is played in virtually every city where there is a sizeable Irish population, and while the New Yorkers continue to administer their own affairs, the remainder of the cities throughout the U.S. have banded together to form the North American Board.

Every two years, teams representative of both bodies travel over to Ireland to compete in what is known as the International Competition, with teams from Australia, England and Scotland also in attendance. Perhaps it is a reflection of the current strength of the game on the American continent that in this particular competition the NAB has emerged victorious in both 1994 and '96 by overcoming the New York selection in the finals of both these years.

The future of hurling and Gaelic football in America depends on new immigrants and their willingness to participate—and to devote time to train and prepare; and, by their professionalism, to attract people to Gaelic playing fields across America.

Fergus Hanna, *The Lost Green Field* (New York, 1999).

FERGUS HANNA

## GALLAGHER, TESS (1943– )

Tess Gallagher, poet, essayist, and fiction writer, was born on July 21, 1943, in Port Angeles, Washington, where she still lives in a home she designed and built for herself. She is of Irish, Cherokee, and Blackfoot descent. Her parents, Leslie O. and Marie Bond, were both loggers; her father also worked as a longshoreman. Tess had a difficult childhood: her father was an alcoholic who beat her with a belt, her parents argued, and the mother and the children often waited in the car outside bars to take the drunken father home. But Tess grew to connect womanhood with strength. As she has written of women, "they learn more readily what the slave, the hostage, the prisoner, also

Tess Gallagher

know—the ultimate freedom of the spirit" ("My Father's Love Letters," *A Concert of Tenses: Essays on Poetry*).

Though her father told her that education was wasted on girls, Gallagher graduated from the University of Washington in 1963. That same year she married Lawrence Gallagher, a sculptor and a marine pilot. While he served in Vietnam, Tess spent time in Ireland and Europe. Her growing anti-war sentiment, she claims, finally caused her to begin her life as a poet. Her visit to Ireland produced some very fine poems, including "Under the Stars," where she says:

> Again I walk into the wet grass
> toward the starry voices. Again, I
> am the found one; ultimate, returned
> by all I touch on the way. (Stanza IV, ll.3–6)

Gallagher has returned to Ireland, to the Sligo area in particular, many times over the years. She says leaving Ireland makes her homesick: "There's a preciseness you get in Irish wit that we don't often meet in America" ("A Concert of Tenses: An Interview With Jeanie Thompson," in *A Concert of Tenses*).

In 1974 she received her M.F.A. from The University of Iowa Writer's Workshop. Over the years she has taught at many universities, including Syracuse University, The University of Missouri, The University of Arizona, and Bucknell University. She has received numerous literary awards, including grants from the Guggenheim Foundation and the National Endowment for the Arts.

From 1973–77, Gallagher was married to the poet Michael Burkart. In 1977 she met fellow poet and fiction writer Raymond Carver at a writer's conference. They fell in love. When they first met, Carver was a recovering alcoholic and had not written anything for ages. But their eleven years together, until his death from lung cancer in 1988, were wonderfully productive: they published eleven books between them. Carver and Gallagher were married shortly before he died. In the following years much of Gallagher's time was spent managing Carver's literary estate and related lawsuits. *Moon Crossing Bridge* (1992) is a collection of poems dealing with the long process of grieving.

Carver and Gallagher became one of the most famous couples in contemporary American letters. Both were drawn to the world they grew up in—the Great Northwest—a world of blue-collar, hard drinking, financially insecure characters. Carver's reputation skyrocketed after his death, but as their friend Harold

Schweiger has said: "For whatever fame she gained on his coat-tails also belittled her own talent. . . . Tess was given that inferior role, which she was gracious enough to accept, but she also has tremendous talent" (qtd. in "Widow's Work," by John Douglas Marshall, *Los Angeles Times,* Jan. 12, 1992, Magazine, p. 18).

Gallagher has been a prodigious writer throughout her career, equally at home in poetry and prose. Her most recent book, *At the Owl Woman Saloon* (1997), is highly acclaimed collection of short stories. She has said, "I like the language of fiction to be very transparent, conventional even—the fish to the water . . ." But she claims poetry is "deep-sea diving" ("A Conversation with Tess Gallagher," *Atlantic Unbound,* July 10, 1997). She is widely regarded as one of the best contemporary American poets. Her most recent book of poems is *Portable Kisses* (1996). In all her work, as critic Michiko Kakutani has noted, "Tess Gallagher has written movingly of damaged relationships, misplaced selves and the losses incurred by time and death" (rev. of *The Lover of Horses,* The New York Times, Sept. 6, 1986, Section 1, p. 12).

Other books by Tess Gallagher include *Under Stars* (1978), and *My Black Horse: New and Selected Poems* (1995).

*See* Poetry, Irish-American

KATHLEEN OCHSHORN

## GARLAND, JUDY (1922–1969)

Actress, singer. Born Frances Gumm in Grand Rapids, Michigan, on June 10, 1922, Judy Garland was raised in the entertainment business and was one of the world's most beloved and talented stars of film and stage spanning four decades.

By the age of four, Garland was singing on the vaudeville circuit with her two older sisters in The Gumm Sisters Kiddie Act. As a teenager, she gained popularity in the Andy Hardy film series for MGM Studios, and won international stardom as Dorothy in the 1939 classic *The Wizard of Oz,* for which Garland won the Academy Award for her rendition of its theme, "Over the Rainbow." She went on to star in such successful films as *Strike Up the Band* (1940), *Meet Me in St. Louis* (1944), *Easter Parade* (1948), *A Star Is Born* (1954), and *Judgment at Nuremberg* (1961). Throughout the 1960s, Garland received international acclaim as a concert singer, bringing to the stage not only her extraordinary talent, but the personal magnetism and vulnerability which earned her the loyal devotion of her fans. Her "It's a Great Day for the Irish" is a standard St. Patrick's Day song.

But Judy Garland's life was not a happy one. As a child super-star, her talent and good nature were exploited by her mother and the other adults in her life; and the same naivete and help-lessness which captivated audiences led her to depend heavily on others to run her life and to four unhappy marriages. For most of her career, Garland relied on pills—to get her going in the morning and to put her to sleep at night—until she was hopelessly addicted. Her film career suffered as a result of the pills, and eventually her voice and on-stage performances became erratic. She seemed to find happiness with her fifth husband, Mickey Deans, who found her at home, victim of an apparent accidental overdose. Thousands of fans attended her funeral in New York City.

Garland was proud of her Irish heritage and spoke often of her grandmother, Eva Milne, who was born in Dublin, Ireland. Eva Milne's father, Hugh Fitzgerald, was a first cousin to Ulysses S.

Grant. Garland had two children (Joey and Lorna) by her third husband, Sid Luft; and her daughter, Liza Minnelli, by her second husband, Vincente Minnelli, is herself a star entertainer, and her energy, style and magnetism is reminiscent of her mother's.

*See* Cinema, Irish in; California

J. Concannon and Frank Cull, *Irish American Who's Who* (New York, 1984).
Joseph Curran, *Hibernian Green on the Silver Screen* (Westport, CT, 1990).

EILEEN DANEY CARZO

## GARSON, GREER (1908–1996)

Actress. Born on September 29, 1908 in County Down, in Northern Ireland. Garson became one of Metro Goldwyn Mayer's most glamorous leading ladies. Garson made her stage debut in 1932 with the Birmingham Repertory Theatre in *Street Scene,* and appeared in numerous leading roles in the London theatre until her discovery by Louis B. Mayer in 1938. Mayer was struck by her beauty and refinement and cast her in some of his classiest films through 1954.

During her sixteen years (and twenty films) at MGM, Garson showed a versatility uncommon at the time, playing leading roles in everything from light comedies to heavy dramas. She captivated audiences and won Academy Award nominations for her performances in *Goodbye, Mr. Chips* (1939), *Blossoms in the Dust* (1941), *Madame Curie* (1943), *Mrs. Parkington* (1944), *The Valley of Decision* (1945), and as Eleanor Roosevelt in *Sunrise at Campobello* (1960). But perhaps her best known role, for which she won the Academy Award in 1942, is that of the title character in *Mrs. Miniver,* the indomitable British housewife who bravely carries on in the midst of World War II.

Garson returned to the live stage, making her Broadway debut in the musical comedy *Auntie Mame* in 1958; and she appeared in a number of television dramas before her death in Dallas in 1996.

*See* Cinema, Irish in; California

J. Concannon and Frank Cull, *Irish American Who's Who* (New York, 1984).
Joseph Curran, *Hibernian Green on the Silver Screen* (Westport, CT, 1990).

EILEEN DANEY CARZO

## GAVIN, IGNATIA (1889–1966)

Religious, pioneer worker with alcoholics. Born in County Mayo on January 2, 1889 to Patrick, a farmer, and Barbara Neary, Bridget Della Mary Gavin and her family immigrated to the United States and settled in Cleveland in 1896. In 1914 she entered the Sisters of Charity of St. Augustine and took the name "Ignatia." She soon began working in a hospital where she met Dr. Robert Smith and Bill Wilson, co-founders of Alcoholics Anonymous. Beginning in 1939, these two men and Sr. Ignatia set up the first treatment center for alcoholics in St. Thomas Hospital in Akron, Ohio. She argued for the care of the soul, as well as the mind and body, in the rehabilitation of the alcoholic person and worked for the expansion of care for those addicted to alcohol. By the time of her death, Sr. Ignatia had personally

Ignatia Gavin

counseled over 15,000 alcoholics and their families. Her funeral attracted hundreds, including Bing Crosby, who came to pay their last respects to the "angel of Alcoholics Anonymous."

Mary C. Darrah, *Sister Ignatia: Angel of Alcoholics Anonymous* (Chicago, 1992).

ANTHONY D. ANDREASSI

## GAYNOR, WILLIAM J. (1848–1913)

*See* New York City: Irish-American Mayors

## GEORGIA

Georgia was neither a significant entrepôt for Irish migrants to North America, nor a prominent destination of eventual settlement. The few who did settle there played a series of important social and economic roles, which evolved as Georgia developed from a frontier outpost into a settled society. During the eighteenth century the Irish helped to populate the frontier settlements of this southern-most British colony. In the nineteenth century, they filled vital niches in a labor-short economy. Twentieth-century Americans may see the Georgia-Irish in terms of the fictional, doomed Gerald O'Hara of the onamatopoeic Tara; but this is no more accurate or meaningful a view than the vernal bacchanalia of Savannah's St. Patrick's Day festival. To understand the Irish experience in Georgia we must recognize the changing patterns that brought them there and the communities they constructed once they arrived.

Colonial Georgia, first conceived as a receptacle for undesirables, took a dim view of improvident Celts and Catholics of any description. The Irish were not universally welcomed as prospective settlers. The colony' first charter banned Roman Catholics (as well as rum and slaves) in the interests of creating a model society. Once launched on the American frontier, the governing trustees soon had to weigh their philanthropic and reforming ideals against the practical problems of survival. Catholics might be viewed as potential traitors in ideological sympathy with Spain and France, and the Irish might be reputedly too drunk and disorderly for a new community intended to eliminate old human failings. But the fact quickly emerged that the colony would not survive at all without more settlers. Therefore, in December, 1733, a shipload of forty Irish convicts received grudging permission to land at Savannah on condition that the passengers commit themselves to the defense of the settlement.

The majority of the early Irish arrivals in Georgia had only one bar of prejudice to hurdle, for they were mostly Ulster Presbyterians who descended from Stuart Scotland. The economic crisis of the 1740s drove them from northeastern Ireland to the American colonies, where they trickled down the Appalachian trails to the Georgia back country. William McWhir's trek was in many ways characteristic of these migrants. Born in County Down in 1759, he came to America at 24 years of age and arrived at Alexandria, Virginia. Within ten years he moved to Savannah, where he followed the atypical career of a Presbyterian minister. His selection of Georgia as a secondary destination after first landing elsewhere in America would be the path of the great majority of Irish who ever reached the state.

The traces of the Scotch-Irish newcomers appear in unpredictable places. A handful settled in what later became Laurens County, on the Oconee River roughly halfway between Savannah and Macon, during the 1780s. Entering the lumber trade, which suited the available means of transport, they came to own enough property and clout that the county seat, founded in 1812, was called Dublin in their honor. (There is no evidence for the old story that the land for Dublin was donated to the county by one of the more successful pioneers.) The flow of Ulster migrants and their descendants filled in a back country that by 1790, according to some estimates, was fifty percent Ulster and Presbyterian in its heritage.

The Scotch-Irish were by reputation stubborn individualists with a strong anti-authoritarian streak. Ironically, they were also the beneficiaries of an early public-private partnership in assisted emigration designed to promote frontier development. Colonial Governor James Wright formulated the plan in 1763, after securing land through a treaty with the Creek Indians and extracting a promise from the colonial Assembly to provide funds for assisting immigrants. In early 1765, a pair of Irish Indian traders who operated in the Augusta region petitioned the Assembly for a grant of 50,000 acres to establish a township, to be populated by Irish Protestants recruited from Belfast and its hinterlands. One of the plan's proponents, John Rea, had come to Georgia from Ireland three decades before and established a dominant position in the deerskin trade with the Creeks. With the Governor's backing, he now contacted his brother Michael, in Belfast, to promote the new opportunities. Michael Rea wrote the material for the Belfast press highlighting Georgia's attractions as described in John Rea's correspondence. John Rea meanwhile urged the Assembly to allot money to assist such recruits as might be assembled. His aims coincided with Governor Wright's plan to strengthen the frontier defenses by rapid expansion of the settlements. The Reas, of course, stood also to profit by the success of the plan.

None of the promoters of this scheme succeeded in convincing the Board of Trade of its wisdom. The Board felt that the drain of Protestants from troublesome Ireland was a risky proposition. Moreover, they anticipated that the large proportion of recession-driven linen weavers among the prospective migrants might become the foundation of a competing manufacture in America. In 1767 the Board of Trade vetoed the Assembly's plan to help Protestant families settle in Georgia.

The Reas were undeterred. From 1768, when 107 Belfast emigrants arrived at Savannah in December, the Reas orchestrated the passage of seven boatloads in the nine years remaining before the Revolution. More than seven hundred emigrants were delivered by this means, and a substantial number got cash assistance as well as land grants in spite of London's opposition to the idea. The township created for them, Queensborough, was an isolated spot a hundred miles from Savannah and fifty from Augusta. While far from help, Queensborough was close to the Creeks. Relations with these native Americans deteriorated after 1773; the Creeks attacked the frontier settlements on Christmas of that year, and spread panic widely as they continued the offensive into 1774. Town-building was retarded and new settlers were deterred by the Indian troubles. In 1770 it was estimated that perhaps 270 of the immigrant families occupied Queensborough township and the surrounding area. When the Revolution exploded, though, the Scotch-Irish outpost proved too exposed and underpopulated to avoid looting and eventual destruction.

Emigration from Ireland was inhibited first by the Revolution, and then by the combination of domestic prosperity and international upheaval caused by the Napoleonic Wars. When the flow of Irish arrivals into Georgia resumed in the 1820s, they were different sorts of people who came to play a new role in the state's growth. The most urgent economic need Georgia faced in the early nineteenth century was for infrastructure that would link its commodity-rich interior to the coastal trade centers. The new wave of Irish immigrants played a key part in these efforts.

Canals to connect the state's rivers and ports were the first projects to attract Irish hands. The canal planned to link the port of Brunswick with the Altamaha River, begun in 1830 using state capital and slave labor, illustrates one version of the Irish experience in public works. After the first four years, with limited progress to show for its investment, the state pulled out of this project. New backers with Boston money came in and brought Irish hands to the scene. The new arrivals were heavily-Catholic work gangs whose roots lay in the south of Ireland and whose recent background was with the canals and railroads of the northeastern United States. The Irish worked on the Brunswick and Altamaha Canal until it finally went bankrupt in 1839. Some of them stayed along the lines of their labors; some went back north for work; many drifted back to the region's dominant city, Savannah.

By the 1840s Savannah functioned as a labor depot on the regional level, much as New York or Boston did on the national level. The resource, mobile skilled hands, was almost entirely Irish in background. Entrepreneurs or contractors with ditches to be dug or land to be cleared looked in Savannah for the work force they needed when local labor was too scarce or a district's slaves too dear.

The railroads were the next great beneficiaries of the new labor market. The Central of Georgia, which linked Savannah with Macon and the rich hinterlands between, was built between 1836 and 1843. Its first workers were predominantly Irish, many recruited for their expertise honed on the roads of the North. The Georgia Railroad began in the same years to introduce Irish contract laborers to the Augusta region (where many still under contract to the railroad went to work in 1845 on the Augusta Canal). The Western and Atlantic, the third great Georgia line, used Irish muscle to establish rail connections between Atlanta (the terminus of the Georgia Railroad) and Chattanooga; it began to recruit for workers in Savannah in 1838.

Relations between the immigrants and their employers were often tense. Canals and railroads sent men into the wilderness for eighteen to thirty dollars a month. The companies paid little attention to the web of rivalries among gangs from different counties in Ireland, and made at best ineffective efforts to keep strong drink out of the swamps and woods. Supervisors complained constantly of the fighting and drinking among the men. Contractors near Savannah got Father Jeremiah O'Neill, a Kerry native who was the city's Catholic pastor for more than thirty years, to ride circuit from camp to camp, bringing the men the sacraments and urging them to behave. (O'Neill had a vested interest in the success of these adventures, since he was one of the regular brokers between recruiters looking for hands and Savannah laborers looking for work.) In the long term, this tactic failed. By 1840 the Central railroad was trying to hire slaves from planters along its path so it could get rid of the erratic Irishmen. All the lines in these years struggled with the problem of Irish combativeness compared with the malleability (but greater scarcity and expense) of hired slave labor. In most of the road-building districts, there were no other choices.

The immigrants were not the only parties to these projects to misbehave. Contractors could also be unscrupulous, or merely inept, as is illustrated in the case of the Ocmulgee and Flint River Railroad. This line was planned to run from Mobley's Bluff, on the Ocmulgee River in Irwin County, to Albany on the Flint. It was chartered in 1827, and after a decade of money troubles contractor Abbot H. Brisbane introduced Irish hands to the job in 1841. The work may have moved faster but the money did not. Brisbane was obliged to scramble among business, ethnic, and religious backers as far off as New York and Charleston to raise money to pay and feed his crews. Finally his luck ran out. In September, 1843, work gangs besieged the promoter and his family in their cabin; a corp of militia volunteers marched to the scene to disperse a gang of sixty or more, many armed for the occasion. Brisbane fled, only to resurface a decade later with new backers and a new scheme to build a railroad in southwestern Georgia.

These episodes should not obscure the fact that hundreds of the new wave of immigrants made quiet contributions to their communities, settling on or near the routes they helped to clear. The unskilled met the rising demand for stevedores and other muscle work; the skilled had chances to practice their crafts; the few with capital established themselves as general merchants or broke into the cotton trade. As the agriculture-based economy grew, slaves became too valuable to disperse into other activities. The Irish stepped into this labor gap.

By the middle of the nineteenth century, the Irish communities in Georgia differed according to how recently the immigrants had arrived and what they had come to do. Savannah was home to the richest mix, as a largely Presbyterian group of early arrivals, with property and an established place in local society, viewed with mixed feelings the mass of largely Catholic, working-class newcomers struggling for their fortunes. Atlanta, by contrast, was a new town with no preexisting hierarchy, and no established Scotch-Irish merchant class, where the later arrivals found entrepreneurial opportunities more readily.

As more and more Irish immigrants came to Georgia they arranged to send more and more in remittances home to their families in Ireland. Agencies appeared to handle these increasingly lucrative transactions, often through companies with family members on both shores. For example, Savannah had a substantial Wexford population by the early 1850s. The merchant shippers William Graves and Son, of New Ross, handled cash exchanges and arranged passages in Ireland for immigrants who contacted them through the Bay Street offices of James Graves, in Savannah. These commercial connections reinforced the networks of families and friends that told old-country relations about the new world opportunities to be had in Georgia.

Wherever they settled in significant numbers, the Irish built a framework of voluntary associations and religious societies within which they helped each other confront the problems of life in America and kept some contact with the upheavals of Ireland. The Hibernian Society was formed in Savannah in 1812 by gentlemen of property and standing (its first charter limited membership to no more than one hundred individuals of Irish birth), and it served as a keystone of south Georgia Irish social life. The Hibernians existed, they said, for benevolent and social purposes, and to cultivate their members' ties with Ireland. Charity was a year-round concern, but the other objectives were met in the Hibernians' great civic festival, St. Patrick's Day. The antebellum version of this event was restrained by modern standards, featuring a parade and one or more banquets but no flood of tourists by the thousands and no streets awash in green beer. The Hibernians represented Irish Savannah during the rest of the year at other civic observances including funerals, patriotic holidays, and other public events that called for an organized expression of Irish engagement.

Among other things, the Hibernians illustrated the relationship of religion and class among Savannah's immigrants. The organization had twelve presidents during its first century, including nine Protestants and three Catholics. The reason for this distribution was property, not prejudice. Catholic and Protestant coexisted peacefully in the Society, but it was above all else an organization of propertied Irish men. They selected leaders from among the successful regardless of religious affiliation; the Protestant members, being among the earlier and better-established arrivals in the city, tended as a rule to be more materially successful. This difference is not known to have been a source of friction within the organization.

Each community with a significant Irish population developed its own network of benevolent and charitable organizations. These included groups concerned with local charitable issues (relief of widows, orphans, and indigent countrymen), trans-Atlantic benevolence (especially during the Famine years), and Irish politics. Milledgeville and Savannah both supported chapters of the Irish Repeal Association, which functioned to raise American money for Daniel O'Connell's cause in Ireland during the 1840s. There was no limit to these groups' memberships, of course, and they included the occasional native southerner willing to twist the lion's tail by contributing to an anti-British program. In 1843, though, O'Connell came out against slavery. The Milledgeville branch of the Association fell apart in internal bickering, as did most other chapters in the South. Savannah's Repealers distinguished their support for Irish independence from a complete agreement with all of O'Connell's views, and stayed focused on the primary goal while recommending that the leadership in Ireland do likewise.

A more directly activist turn was taken by the Irish militia companies. The Jasper Greens of Savannah, probably the oldest of these groups, were named after Sgt. William Jasper, a legendary hero of the Revolution in Savannah. When Georgia formed a volunteer infantry regiment to send to the Mexican War, the Jasper Greens won a lottery among Savannah's six companies to earn the right to go. They also fought in the Civil War, as did an impromptu company of eighty Augusta Irish and comparable bands from all over the state. Where the benevolent and political societies were intended mainly to meet Irish needs, the militias engaged the Irish with the larger communities in which they lived, and showed the depth of the immigrants' commitment to the new, southern way of life.

The militias also showed, as did the behavior of the Irish in other venues, the immigrants' pro-slavery outlook. Most of the new arrivals after the 1830s were workers who saw black hands as potential competitors and threats to their livelihoods. Race feelings reinforced the acute Irish distaste for African-Americans which was axiomatic among contemporary observers. And the Irish definitely recognized that if they desired to make a place for themselves in white southern society, they must adopt white southern mores on this critical issue. The Catholic Church did nothing to dissuade them here, calling for humane treatment for the enslaved but defending the institution of slavery as an essential bulwark of the existing social order.

By the mid-nineteenth century the Catholic Church was becoming a major emblem of spreading Irish settlement throughout Georgia, a fact which reflects the numerical weight of Catholic southern Irish migrants among the late antebellum arrivals. A look at the hierarchy of Georgia Catholicism shows the Irish influence. In 1850, Georgia became an independent Catholic diocese; the first bishop was Francis X. Gartland, who was born in Dublin. Veteran parish priests at the time included the Kerryman, O'Neill, in Savannah, with Kerry transplant John F. Kirby as his assistant; John Barry, born in Wexford, at Augusta; and Peter Whelan, also Wexford-born, who pastored the church at Locust Grove for fifteen years. The same band tended to move from assignment to assignment; thus, Whelan was the chaplain at Fort Pulaski, outside Savannah, when it came under siege during the Civil War. After the garrison finally surrendered the troops were imprisoned on Governor's Island, New York, and Whelan went with them. He returned to Georgia in a prisoner exchange and by the summer of 1864 had become the stockade chaplain at Andersonville Prison. All these priests rode circuit among chapels all over Georgia and the near parts of the Carolinas, which probably reinforced the identification of Catholicism as an Irish trait among rural as well as urban Georgians.

Anti-Irish, anti-Catholic sentiments intermittently colored popular thought and public discussion in nineteenth-century Georgia, but they never amounted to much at the ballot box. The appeal to Protestant bigotry and fears of popery never overcame demonstrable Irish loyalty to local or regional social and political standards. The Know-Nothings adopted temperance as one of their key issues in Georgia, and temperance agitators could and did speak to the well-publicized Irish failings involving alcohol. But the Catholic Church tried to lead the way on this problem, following even in the early 1840s the example of Father Matthew's total abstinence crusade in Ireland. Georgians before the Civil War may have harbored suspicions or ill opinion of the new Irish Catholic neighbors. But they also suspected the nativist factions of being soft on the slavery issue, and no amount of ethnic or religious prejudice could overpower Georgians' views on slavery.

By the end of the antebellum era, the 6,586 Irish-born residents of the state comprised over half of the foreign-born in Georgia—and six-tenths of one percent of the total population. To many Georgians, the Irish immigrants of these years were literally invisible. Settled mainly in the towns, the immigrants entered into southern social life as far as their often limited means would allow. They constructed an ethnic world-within-a-world, with social, charitable, and religious associations, and maintained some increasingly tenuous ties to Ireland. They were numerous and active enough to influence local politics in some towns, but their more important achievements were to build a place for themselves as citizens in the southern social and economic order.

Georgia was not an important port of entry for immigrants to the United States. From the colonial years on, the common experience of its free immigrants was to enter the country at one of the prominent northern ports and then make their way south. The outbreak of the Civil War in 1861 stopped the streams of Irish arrivals, and after the war the migrations never resumed. The defeated South lacked the economic opportunities of the antebellum years, and the Irish had little desire to compete for work with the freedmen crowding into southern cities. The foreign-born population of Savannah in 1860 was 21% of the total; by 1900, foreigners made up only 6.3% of the urban masses there. The 1940 Census revealed that no county in Georgia had even as many as one thousand Irish-born residents. Georgia's Irish communities remained distinctive as long as they received fresh influxes of the Irish-born. But by the present century, the days of those new arrivals vitalizing the state's immigrant communities were over.

Helen Callahan, "A Study of Dublin: The Irish in Augusta," *Richmond County History,* 5 (Summer 1973): 5–14.

Fussell Chalker, "Irish Catholics in the Building of the Ocmulgee and Flint Railroad," *Georgia Historical Quarterly,* 54 (Winter 1970): 507–516.

E. R. R. Green, "Queensborough Township: Scotch-Irish Emigration and the Expansion of Georgia, 1763–1776," *William and Mary Quarterly,* 3rd series, 17 (April 1960): 183–199.

Carol Louise Hagglund, "Irish Immigrants in Atlanta, 1850–1896" (M.A. thesis, Emory University, 1968).

John M. Harrison, "The Irish Influence in Early Atlanta," *Atlanta Historical Bulletin,* 7 (October 1944): 196–211.

Edward M. Shoemaker, "Strangers and Citizens, The Irish Community in Savannah, 1837–1861," (Ph.D. diss., Emory University, 1990).

Fred Siegel, "Artisans and Immigrants in the Politics of Late Antebellum Georgia," *Civil War History,* 27 (September 1981): 221–230.

Herbert Weaver, "Foreigners in Antebellum Savannah," *Georgia Historical Quarterly,* 37 (March 1953): 1–17.

EDWARD M. SHOEMAKER

## GIBBONS, JAMES CARDINAL (1834–1921)

Cardinal-archbishop of Baltimore. James Gibbons was born July 23, 1834, in Baltimore and baptized in the Cathedral of the Assumption. He was the son of Thomas Gibbons, a native of Gortnacullin, Tourmakeady, County Mayo, where he had been a small farmer, and of Bridget Walsh of Tooreen of the same county. James was probably named for his maternal grandfather, James Walsh, the village schoolmaster. His parents and two older sisters had immigrated to Canada probably in 1829. The following year they had moved to Baltimore, where the father found work as a clerk in a commercial firm. In 1837, however, for reasons not clear, the parents and their now five children returned to Ireland.

James Cardinal
Gibbons

There Thomas Gibbons purchased land and opened a grocery store in Ballinrobe, County Mayo, which he ran until he died of cholera in 1847. In Ballinrobe James attended a small private school, where he was well grounded in the classics and where his closest friend was the only Protestant boy in town. Worsening conditions in Ireland, however, determined the mother to return to America, but not to Baltimore. In the spring of 1853 the family established residence in New Orleans. There James found employment in a grocery store, whose Presbyterian owner took a paternal interest in him.

### PRIEST, BISHOP, AND ARCHBISHOP

In 1854 young Gibbons attended one of the early missions conducted by the Redemptorists, during which he was inspired to become a priest. In 1855 he entered St. Charles College, the minor seminary for the archdiocese of Baltimore, and was accepted into the archdiocese by Archbishop Francis Patrick Kenrick. In 1857 he moved to the major seminary, St. Mary's, where he was an exceptional student and seminarian, well liked by fellow students and faculty alike. On June 30, 1861, he was ordained by Archbishop Kenrick in the seminary chapel. Six weeks later he was appointed pastor of a new parish, St. Bridget's, from which he served as chaplain to nearby Fort McHenry during the Civil War.

Gibbons' gentle but winning personality drew the attention of two important patrons, the two succeeding archbishops of Baltimore: Martin John Spalding and James Roosevelt Bayley. Spalding made him his secretary in 1865 and at the Second Plenary Council of Baltimore persuaded the bishops to recommend Gibbons for the newly-established vicariate apostolic of North Carolina, a title conferred by Rome on March 3, 1868. On August 16 Spalding raised his protégé to the episcopacy, the youngest bishop in the Catholic world. As a result of one of Spalding's last requests to the Holy See, Gibbons was chosen administrator and then bishop of the diocese of Richmond, Virginia, in 1872. In both North Carolina and Virginia he proved an able administrator. On May 25, 1877, at the request of Archbishop Bayley, Gibbons was named the latter's coadjutor with right of succession. At Bayley's death on October 3, he became the ninth archbishop of Baltimore, America's oldest and most prestigious see.

At this point in his life Gibbons was not a man of great ambition or large plans. Rightly, he considered the archdiocese well endowed in institutions and personnel. Nothing beyond its borders was of overriding interest to him. He was thrust into a role of leadership in the American church by his appointment to preside over the Third Plenary Council, the poor health of Cardinal John McCloskey of New York, the ranking prelate, precluding the latter's assumption of that honor. For its convocation Gibbons had initially shown little enthusiasm, but he played his part well both in its preparation and in the proceedings of November 9 to December 7, 1884. In consequence of this most productive of the councils of Baltimore, legislating such important matters as Catholic schools, a Catholic university, a uniform catechism, diocesan curias, and the support of Indian and Negro missions, Gibbons was named America's second cardinal on June 7, 1886. A week after receiving the red hat in Rome on the feast of St. Patrick in 1887, he delivered in his titular church of Santa Maria in Trastevere a ringing paean to his native land, which caused Father Isaac Hecker, founder of the American Paulists, to observe how well suited the new cardinal was by his "thorough-going American spirit to interpret us to the peoples and powers of the Old World" (*Catholic World* 45 [June 1887]: 331).

In Rome Gibbons also developed a close bond and working relationship with three American churchmen, all Irish born, whose ambitions for the church in the United States would fuel Gibbons' own: John Ireland, bishop and soon archbishop of St. Paul; John Joseph Keane, rector designate of the recently established Catholic University of America; and Denis O'Connell, rector of the North American College in Rome. Together they won the unqualified endorsement of the Holy See for the establishment of the Catholic University in Washington, D.C., a part of the archdiocese of Baltimore, over objections raised by the archbishop of New York and the Jesuits. Together they forestalled a Roman condemnation of the Knights of Labor, the largest workingmen's association in the United States, for which action Gibbons was acclaimed champion of the working class. And together they successfully countered the Abbelen petition, a series of demands that would have granted a greater autonomy to German Catholics in America. The latter, however, was but the opening skirmish of an ethnocultural conflict within the Catholic Church in the United States.

### AMERICANIZER

Despite his Irish background Gibbons became an ardent advocate of the rapid assimilation of Catholic immigrants, as were Ireland, who was even more outspoken on the subject, Keane, and O'Connell. In his own archdiocese the most distressing problems Gibbons encountered were with the national (ethnic) parishes of his see city, especially the Slavic and Italian ones. A Polish parish effected a defiant schism. While the Redemptorists kept the German parishes of the oldest archdiocese submissive, a challenge more ominous than the Abbelen petition was posed by the Lucerne Memorial presented to the pope in 1891 by Peter Cahensly, founder of the German St. Raphaelsverein, which deplored the sad neglect of German immigrants to the United States on the part of the American (preponderantly Irish) hierarchy. Many perceived a plot to Germanize America, including Archbishop Ireland, who had Cahensly denounced on the floor of the U.S. Senate. Gibbons was able to blunt the spread of what was termed "Cahenslyism" by a forceful sermon in the cathedral of Milwaukee itself before its German-speaking archbishop, denouncing those who would "sow tares of discord in the fair fields of the Church in America."

In their opposition to German demands, Irish members of the American hierarchy were solidly united. In other matters, however, they were seriously divided. By the early 1890s liberal and conservative blocs had developed. The liberals, or Americanists, looked to Gibbons, Ireland, and Keane as their standard bearers, the conservatives to Archbishop Michael A. Corrigan of New York and his outspoken suffragan, Bishop Bernard J. McQuaid of Rochester. The conservatives had the support of the Germans and Jesuits, particularly on the school question. When Archbishop Ireland proposed his Faribault Plan for the incorporation of parochial schools into the public school system, the conservatives reacted loudly and, despite the initial support of an apostolic delegate named by the pope in 1893, ultimately brought about its rejection. The two sides differed also on such matters as secret societies, interfaith gatherings, and social programs, the latter highlighted by Corrigan's suspension of the popular Edward McGlynn, one of his social-minded priests. In general the conservatives were uneasy at the liberals' active promotion of such American principles as religious toleration and the separation of church and state.

When the first apostolic delegate, Archbishop Francesco Satolli, turned against the liberals, the Vatican itself revealed its displeasure with their views and actions by the dismissal of Denis O'Connell as rector of the North American College in 1895 and John Keane as rector of the Catholic University in 1896. When Ireland, Keane, and O'Connell, with Gibbons' support, advanced in Europe their agenda for Americanizing the church there, conservatives abroad combined, focussing on a biography of Isaac Hecker, to bring about the papal condemnation of a heresy labeled "Americanism." Condemned were a medley of beliefs such as a reliance on the Holy Spirit rather than external guidance, the superiority of active over the passive or supernatural virtues, a depreciation of religious vows, and, most importantly, a need for the church to adapt itself to new theories and methods in order to win converts. The papal letter *Testem benevolentiae,* dated January 22, 1899, was addressed to Cardinal Gibbons alone.

## CATHOLIC LEADER AND SPOKESMAN

Despite the eclipse of the Irish-born Americanizers, Gibbons continued to exercise an undisputed leadership in the Catholic Church in the United States. As ranking prelate he presided over the annual meetings of the archbishops begun in 1890 and over the transformation of the National Catholic War Council into the permanent National Catholic Welfare Council in 1919. In his later years he was revered even more by Americans generally as the nation's most distinguished churchman. His *Faith of Our Fathers,* first published in 1876, remained the most-read work by an American Catholic author. His frequent appearances at important national events were fully covered by the press, as were his opinions on timely and controversial topics, political and religious. His opinions on religious matters were always calculated to allay antipathies between Catholic and non-Catholic Americans. Gibbons' opinions were not always consistent. At the time of the Spanish-American War he was a pacifist, branding militarism as unchristian. During the first World War he urged Catholic men to fight bravely for their country and be proud of their wounds. At the local level Gibbons supported such Progressive measures as city planning, public health, consumer protection, and the regulation of sweat shops. At the national level he opposed the Seventeenth, Eighteenth, and Nineteenth Amendments.

Despite his progressive inclinations, therefore, Gibbons can not be lodged squarely in the liberal spectrum of the Irish Catholic experience. He was far from enthusiastic about the lay Catholic congresses of 1889 and 1894. His reputation as a friend of the workingman notwithstanding, his support for union labor in diocesan contracts left much to be desired. Though he favored the vote for Maryland's African Americans, he never seconded the attacks of his friend in St. Paul on the color line. And he made no effort to hide his disdain for feminists.

On one issue Gibbons was conspicuously silent: the Irish question. Although he admitted privately to Cardinal Michael Logue, primate of Ireland, that he preferred Irish control of internal affairs under English dominion rather than absolute independence, he refused to take a public stand on the matter of home rule. Gibbons rarely alluded to his Irish ancestry. He deplored, in fact, the hyphenated "Irish" and other such national designations in the title of many societies, wishing such organizations to be "more American in name and spirit." He advised the Irish not to immigrate to the United States, and those who did he urged to practice the virtues of thrift, honesty, and fidelity to contracts so honored in America. An explosion of lay societies occurred under Gibbons, some of which he favored, especially the young men's literary societies and the Knights of Columbus to which Irish Catholics were attracted.

The ninth archbishop of Baltimore was very much in the Maryland tradition, of which the first archbishop was the principal architect. In his all-embracing ecumenism, his civic sense, his devotion to American principles, his deep-felt patriotism, and in the esteem with which he was held by all, Gibbons more closely resembled Archbishop John Carroll than any other member of the American hierarchy. Also like Carroll he was able to interpret broadly Roman directives or ignore them altogether. Gibbons was not an institution builder because he was not a wall builder, desiring his immigrant flock to move as rapidly as possible into the mainstream. Under Gibbons the archdiocese of Baltimore declined gradually in population, institutions, and personnel in proportion to the growth of such major sees as New York, Philadelphia, Boston, and Chicago.

Shortly after Gibbons' death, the apostolic delegate Giovanni Bonzano reported to Rome that the archdiocese of Baltimore was not in a flourishing condition. The cardinal, he claimed, had shunned acts of administration of an odious nature and had paid small attention to the decrees of the council over which he had presided. His curia was one of the most poorly organized. Still the apostolic delegate was prepared to admit that Gibbons had served the church well in assuaging intolerance and bigotry. With consummate tact, Bonzano claimed, he had become the friend of people of every condition, race, and faith, so that at his death he was exalted as a patriot, citizen, and statesman, a man of great vision whose words on national questions were always peaceful and just.

Gibbons enjoyed remarkable health until a few days before his death on March 24, 1921, after having reigned in Baltimore for forty-three and a half years, one of the longest in the history of the American hierarchy. He was buried in the crypt of the cathedral in which he had been baptized.

Archives of the Archdiocese of Baltimore.

John Tracy Ellis, *The Life of James Cardinal Gibbons, Archbishop of Baltimore, 1834–1921,* 2 vols. (Milwaukee, 1952).

Gerald P. Fogarty, ed., *Patterns of Episcopal Leadership* (New York, 1989).

Thomas W. Spalding, *The Premier See: A History of the Archdiocese of Baltimore, 1789–1989* (Baltimore, 1989).

Allen Sinclair Will, *Life of Cardinal Gibbons, Archbishop of Baltimore,* 2 vols. (New York, 1922).

THOMAS W. SPALDING

## GILL, BRENDAN (1914–1997)

Urbane man of letters whose six decades of work at *The New Yorker* magazine as a critic, interviewer, and fiction writer helped shape American literary tastes and trends during the latter half of the twentieth century.

### BACKGROUND

Gill was born in Hartford, Conn. His upbringing and education (he attended Yale) were quintessentially WASP, although he possessed traces of his ethnicity in his speech which had ". . . an Irish deliciousness, a pleasure in the speaking that prolonged the key phrases," according to his friend, the writer John Updike (in a final tribute published in *The New Yorker*).

Gill joined the staff of *The New Yorker* shortly after leaving college in 1936. He worked with four different editors of the magazine during the decades when American writing, both fiction and nonfiction, acquired an international stature and influence that mirrored the rise of the United States as one of the chief global powers.

Apart from magazine writing, Gill wrote fifteen books whose range reflected his own wide and varied tastes. Among his works were biographies of the actress Tallulah Bankhead, the architect Frank Lloyd Wright, and the aviator Charles Lindbergh. He also composed a study of creative men and women whose gifts bloomed in the latter part of their lives, entitled *Late Bloomers*.

Gill had passions other than writing. Aside from being a vice president of the American Academy of Arts and Letters, he was also chairman of the Andy Warhol Foundation for the Visual Arts and "a founder of the P.S. 1 Center for Contemporary Art in Long Island City, Queens," according to the *New York Times*. A crusader on behalf of the preservation of architectural landmarks, he fought to preserve Grand Central Terminal.

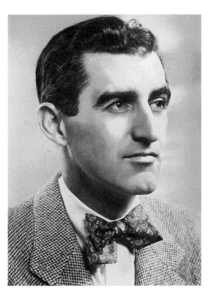

Brendan Gill

### RUFFLING FEATHERS

The book for which Gill will be probably best remembered is *Here at the New Yorker* in which he reminisced about the literary institution which had long employed him. First published in 1975, his account of the magazine, its history and its inner workings, did not draw universal praise. A few people thought he had violated an unspoken rule of privacy by writing about *The New Yorker* and its staff, which, in the eyes of some, represented a cultural elite whose members valued their privacy.

This was not the only time the normally genteel Gill courted controversy. After scholar Joseph Campbell acquired posthumous fame—as the subject of journalist Bill Moyer's public television series, *The Power of Myth*—Gill attacked Campbell's ideas and his character. According to *People Magazine,* Gill "accused Campbell of being a racist and a reactionary and denounced Campbell's call to 'follow your bliss' as a slogan 'sanctioning selfishness on a colossal scale.'" Gill published his criticisms of Campbell in the *New York Times Review of Books* and even argued with Moyers over the merits of Campbell's work in a televised debate. Gill died in New York on December 27, 1997.

Andrea Chambers, "Bill Moyers Angrily Defends Joseph Campbell Against Charges That His Wisdom Was Only a Myth," in *People Weekly* (Nov 27, 1989).

"Citizen Gill," in *Postscript. The New Yorker* (Jan 12, 1998).

Herbert Muschamp, "Brendan Gill Dies at 83; Author and Preservationist," in *The New York Times* (December 29, 1997).

PETER G. SHEA

## GILMORE, PATRICK SARSFIELD (1829–1892)

Bandmaster. Gilmore's Irish parents from Athlone encouraged their son toward the priesthood, but his interests quickly developed in the area of music. Intrigued by the local regimental band, Gilmore became a student of the conductor who taught him to play the cornet and music theory until he joined the band himself. The band was transferred to Canada and Gilmore went with it. Just before his twenty-first birthday, Gilmore struck out on his own, securing the leadership of a military band in Salem, Massachusetts. "Gilmore's Band" quickly became famous and it toured throughout the United States. When the Civil War broke out, Gilmore was mobilized with the 24th Massachusetts Regiment as bandmaster. His success there brought Gilmore to the leadership of all army bands at the Department of Louisiana in 1863.

After the war, Gilmore became famous for his "monster band." With a 5,000 member chorus and 500 instruments, Gilmore helped to celebrate Governor Hahn's inauguration at New Orleans where he created a sensation. Boston's 1869 "National Peace Jubilee" witnessed Gilmore's chorus of 10,000 and an orchestra of 1,000 which included canon fire, church bells, anvils, and members of the local fire department. Feeling the possibilities of the "monster band" exhausted, Gilmore next took charge of the 22nd Regiment band of the New York National Guard. Gilmore's brilliant leadership there brought this band on tour throughout the United States, Canada, and Europe with electrifying drill performances. It was while conducting his band at the St. Louis Exposition of 1892 that Gilmore suddenly died on September 24, leaving his wife and daughter behind.

Marwood Darlington, *Irish Orpheus, the Life of Patrick S. Gilmore, Band Master Extraordinary* (Philadelphia: Oliver-Maney-Klein, 1950).

L. C. Elson, *The History of American Music* (New York: The Macmillan Company, 1904).

*Metronome* (September, October 1907, and Anniversary Supplement, February, 1910).

*St. Louis Globe-Democrat, N.Y. Herald* (September 25, 1892).

G. P. Upton, *Musical Memories* (Chicago: A.C. McClurg, 1908).

DANIEL J. KUNTZ

## GLEASON, HERBERT JOHN ( "Jackie") (1916–1987)

Actor, comedian, and composer. Jackie Gleason was born in Brooklyn, N.Y., on February 26, 1916, to Herb Gleason, an insurance auditor, and Mae Gleason (née Kelly). Jackie's older brother, Clemence, died in 1919. When Jackie was nine years old, his father abandoned the family and his mother began working as a subway booth attendant. She died seven years later in 1932.

At age 15 Gleason won his first prize at an amateur night contest in a Brooklyn theater. He then began working as a carnival barker and as an emcee in resorts and other clubs. In 1938 he made his broadway debut in "Hellzapoppin." More than ten years later, Gleason launched his television career by signing on with NBC to star in *The Life of Riley* in 1949. Although he left the show after a year because he was unhappy living in Los Angeles, the move actually served to advance Gleason's television career. Upon returning to New York City, Gleason became host and performer in the variety show "Cavalcade of Stars," where he first teamed up with Art Carney. This show also introduced Gleason to June Taylor and the June Taylor Dancers. In 1952 Gleason signed a two-year, multimillion dollar contract with CBS for his own variety show on television. A regular feature of Gleason's show was a sketch based on a Brooklyn couple, bus driver Ralph Kramden and his wife Alice (Audrey Meadows), and their neighbors Ed and Trixie Norton (Art Carney and Joyce Randolph). In 1955 Gleason abandoned the hour-long format in favor of a half-hour sitcom focused solely on *The Honeymooners*. After only 39 episodes, CBS persuaded Gleason to return to the hour-long format. Since then, these 39 episodes have become TV classics and were packaged for Showtime and for video in the 1980s.

After his show ended in 1959, Gleason returned to Broadway to star in the musical *Take Me Along,* adapted from Eugene

Jackie Gleason

O'Neill's *Ah, Wilderness!* His performance won him a Tony Award for Best Actor (1960). In 1961 Gleason earned an Oscar nomination as Best Supporting Actor for his role as Minnesota Fats in *The Hustler* (1961). The following year he starred in the films *Gigot* and *Requiem for a Heavyweight.* Many fans remember Gleason for his performance as Burt Reynolds' nemesis, Sheriff Bufford T. Justice, in *Smokey and the Bandit* (1977) and its two sequels. His final movie role was to play Tom Hanks' father in *Nothing in Common* (1986). That same year Gleason was inducted into the Television Academy Hall of Fame.

In addition to his success in comedy and in serious acting, Jackie Gleason was known for his singing ability. He recorded close to 40 albums with the Jackie Gleason Orchestra. He died of cancer on June 24, 1987.

*See* Cinema, Irish in

William A. Henry, III, *The Great One: The Life and Legend of Jackie Gleason* (Doubleday, 1992).

W. J. Weatherby, *Jackie Gleason: An Intimate Portrait of the Great One* (Pharos Books, 1992).

PATRICIA DeFERRARI

## GLENDON, MARY ANN (1938–   )

Law educator. Mary Ann Glendon was born October 7, 1938, in the Western Massachusetts town of Pittsfield, and raised in nearby Dalton. She was the daughter of Martin F. and Sarah (Pomeroy) Glendon. Her father, a reporter for the *Berkshire Eagle,* served as chairman of the local board of selectmen, the first Irish-American Democrat to hold the post. Her mother, on the other hand, belonged to one of the nation's earliest families. Pomeroys fought in both the Revolutionary and Civil wars, and grandfather Theodore Pomeroy was chairman of the town's Republican committee. Glendon describes herself, accordingly, as a "true hybrid," telling the *Boston Globe* that "a big part of who I am is half-Irish and half-Yankee."

Glendon attended Mount Holyoke College in 1955–1956, then transferred to the University of Chicago, where she received a bachelor's degree in 1959. A law degree followed in 1961. She was a foreign-law fellow at the Universite Libre de Bruxelles and legal intern to the European Economic Communities in Belgium in 1962–1963. On her return to the United States she acquired a master's degree in comparative law from the University of Chicago, then joined the Chicago law firm of Mayer, Brown and Platt as an associate.

Meanwhile, Glendon immersed herself in the civil-rights movement. She took part in the 1963 March on Washington addressed by Dr. Martin Luther King, Jr., and the following summer worked on the voter-registration drive in Mississippi. While in Mississippi, she met an African-American attorney, also engaged in civil-rights activities, and the two subsequently married in a civil ceremony. They conceived a daughter, Elizabeth, before the marriage broke up in 1966.

Glendon's civil-rights involvements stemmed from ingrained Democratic Party social convictions of her youth. She is still a social liberal, but she describes herself now as a political independent.

From 1968 to 1986 Glendon was a member of the faculty at Boston College Law School, except for the 1974–1975 academic year when she was a visiting professor at Harvard Law School.

Mary Ann Glendon

She has held other visiting professorships at University of Chicago Law School and the Gregorian University in Rome. In 1986 she formally joined the Harvard Law School faculty and is now its Learned Hand Professor of Law. Her specialty areas are human rights, comparative and constitutional law, and legal theory.

Glendon has written nine books, among them *Abortion and Divorce in Western Law: American Failures, European Challenges* (1987), wherein she forcefully states opposition to abortion and to the Supreme Court's 1973 *Roe v. Wade* decision. "Not only did the court get the story wrong," she wrote of the 1973 decision, "but it foreclosed the possibility of working out a better story." Glendon's book won the 1988 Scribes Book Award. Another book, *The Transformation of Family Law,* won the Order of the Coif Triennial Book Award in 1993.

In 1994 Glendon was appointed by Pope John Paul II to the recently created Pontifical Academy of Social Sciences, and the following year she was named to the Holy See's Central Committee for the Great Jubilee 2000. She also serves on the Pontifical Council for the Laity.

In 1995 Glendon was chosen to head the Vatican delegation to the United Nations Fourth World Conference on Women in Beijing, China, and thus became the first female in history to lead a Vatican delegation to a major international gathering. Under her leadership, the delegation extended qualified endorsement to the conference's Platform for Action, dissenting on the women-health section dealing with the treatment of sexuality, motherhood and family.

Glendon serves on the Advisory Committee on Social Justice of the Archdiocese of Boston. She has numerous honorary degrees, including from the universities of Chicago and Louvain.

In 1970 Glendon married Edward R. Lev, a labor lawyer. In addition to Elizabeth Glendon Lev, she has two other daughters, Sarah Pomeroy Lev and Katherine Glendon Lev.

Dick Lehr, "Mary Ann Glendon: Writing Her Own Party Line," *Boston Globe* (December 11, 1996).
Ann Evory, ed., *Contemporary Authors,* vols. 41–44 (Detroit, 1979).

JOHN DEEDY

## GLENNON, JOHN JOSEPH CARDINAL (1862–1946)

Cardinal Archbishop of St. Louis. Born to Matthew and Catherine Rafferty near Kinnegad, County Meath, Ireland, June 14, 1862, Glennon attended the diocesan college of St. Mary's in Mullingar. He completed further studies in philosophy and theology at All Hallows College in Dublin until 1883, when Bishop John Hogan of Kansas City invited the theology student for ordination at the Kansas City diocese. Beginning at age twenty-two, Glennon spent the next three years as assistant pastor at St. Patrick's Church in Kansas City. Glennon next attended the University of Bonn where he studied German in order to minister more effectively among the growing number of German Catholic immigrants in Missouri. On his return, Glennon was appointed secretary and then rector of the cathedral, and in 1892 he became vicar-general. Bishop Hogan requested a coadjutor as his health began to fail, and the pope appointed Glennon. In 1903, Glennon was moved to the St. Louis Diocese as coadjutor to Archbishop John Kain who died in that year and whom he succeeded as archbishop. An extraordinary and gifted builder, Pope Pius XII called Glennon to Rome for his investiture as cardinal on February 21, 1946. On his way back to the U.S., however, Glennon contracted pneumonia and uremic poisoning on his way through Ireland and died at the home of President Sean O'Kelly in Dublin. Glennon's body was returned to the U.S. on March 13, 1946, where he lays in the crypt under the Chapel of All Souls in St. Louis.

*See* Catholicism, Irish-American

Cyril Clemens, "Cardinal Glennon of St. Louis," *Ave Maria* (1947).
Brendan A. Finn, *Twenty-Four American Cardinals* (Boston: B. Humphries, 1947).
Nicholas Schneider, *The Life of John Cardinal Glennon, Archbishop of St. Louis* (Liguori, Mo.: Liguori Publications, 1971).
Martin G. Towey, "Glennon, John Joseph," *The Encyclopedia of American Catholic History,* Michael Glazier and Thomas J. Shelley, eds. (Collegeville: The Liturgical Press, 1997): 593–594.

DANIEL J. KUNTZ

## GLOVER, ANN (d. 1688)

Ann ("Goody") Glover, widow and martyr, was born in Ireland (the place and year are not known) perhaps in the first half of the seventeenth century, and died in Boston, Massachusetts, on November 16, 1688. Little is known about her life before her arrival in Boston around 1680. She had been deported from Ireland, like many Catholics, including her husband, by Oliver Cromwell, Lord Protector of England (1653–1658), to Barbados, an English colony that had been linked with Boston since the time of John Winthrop. After the death of her husband in that sugar producing center of the British Empire, Goody and her daughter, Mary, came as servants to Boston where they resisted efforts of the Puritans to convert.

As a widow in a Puritan society, Glover was particularly vulnerable to the charge of witchcraft, a situation that was further compounded by her being both Irish and Catholic. She and her daughter were employed by John Goodwin, a Boston mason, until she was blamed for linens missing from the family laundry. Dismissed from the household staff, the reputation of the Glovers was tarnished, though there was no proof of the theft (the linens were later found to have been misplaced).

Later, when his four children began to act strangely, Mr. Goodwin consulted a physician, Dr. Thomas Oakes, whose diagnosis was that the nature of the malady afflicting the Goodwin children was not physical but spiritual, that is, they were under the influence of a witch. The children, Benjamin, Mercy, John, and Martha, were between the ages of five and thirteen, and their bizarre behavior astounded those who witnessed their actions. In his work, *Memorable Providences* (1689), Cotton Mather, pastor of the church where the Goodwins worshipped in Boston's North End, wrote: "they were all four tortured every where in a manner so very grievous, that it would have broke an heart of stone to have seen their Agonies."

After a day of prayer by the clergy had failed to bring relief to the children, the Puritan community turned its attention to Ann Glover as the prime suspect. Jailed without any evidence against her, Glover had to await her trial in chains and without adequate food. Meanwhile, she was subjected to interrogations under the supervision of Cotton Mather who used translators to understand Glover's Gaelic. Without regard to the nuances or accuracy of the translation, Mather, the guardian of the integrity of a Puritan society against witches and Catholics, allowed his preconceived ideas to distort what was translated. Consequently, Mather alleged that Ann had confessed that she was a witch.

Even if she was a witch, Glover should not have been hanged because no person who had confessed to witchcraft in the history of Massachusetts previous to her time had ever been executed. Glover's condemnation, approved and witnessed by Mather, shows how really prejudicial he was regarding her cause. The contemporary testimony of Robert Calef, a Boston merchant, set forth in his work, *More Wonders of the Invisible World* (1700), stated that "the proof against her was wholly deficient." In considering the persons involved and the circumstances of her trial, it becomes clear that Glover was a victim of injustice.

Consequently, three hundred years after her death, the Boston City Council, in declaring November 16, 1988, "Goody Glover Day," condemned what had been done to her and formally restored her good name. Thus, Goody Glover can be regarded as perhaps the first and only martyr of Irish descent in what is now the United States of America.

James Bernard Cullen, "The Irish Witch," in *The Story of the Irish in Boston,* chapter 2 (1889): 25–30.
Harold Dijon, "A Forgotten Heroine," *The Ave Maria,* 60 (1905): 266–271.
Vincent A. Lapomarda, "A Catholic in a Puritan Society," *The American Benedictine Review,* 41 (1990): 192–208.
George Francis O'Dwyer, "Ann Glover, First Martyr to the Faith in New England," *Historical Records and Studies,* 15 (1921): 70–78.

VINCENT A. LAPOMARDA, S.J.

## GOGARTY, OLIVER ST. JOHN (1878–1957)

Writer, medical doctor and renowned conversationalist who personified the wit and brilliance of the Irish Literary Renaissance.

### BACKGROUND

Gogarty was born in Dublin, the son of Margaret Oliver Gogarty and Henry Gogarty, a medical doctor whose father (and grandfather) had been physicians as well.

Gogarty received his early education at schools in Ireland and England. He received his collegiate education first at Royal University (University College, Dublin), then transferred to Trinity. He completed medical studies at Trinity in 1907.

### EARLY FAME

During his college years, Gogarty was an accomplished scholar-athlete whose exceptional wit and conversational skill became quickly recognized. An abiding influence on him was J.P. Mahaffy, one of his professors at Trinity. Mahaffy was one of the leading conversationalists of his day (Oscar Wilde had been one of his pupils) and he even wrote a book, *Art of Conversation,* a copy of which Gogarty kept until his death. Gogarty's verbal ability extended into composing poetry (he wrote copious amounts of verse). His ability as a poet led him to attend Oxford where (according to Ulick O'Connor) he hoped to compete for the Newdigate Prize for English verse.

During his years as a medical student, Gogarty became friendly with the writer James Joyce, who would recreate Gogarty as the character "Buck Mulligan" in *Ulysses.* Gogarty resented the character (who betrays the novel's protagonist, Stephen Dedalus), yet could never fully escape identification with it due to the novel's fame.

Joyce wasn't the only famous Irishman with whom Gogarty was intimate. Thanks to his interest in art and politics, Gogarty was a valued friend of such luminaries as the poet William Butler Yeats, the painter Augustus John, and the Irish political leaders William T. Cosgrave, Arthur Griffith, and Michael Collins. (After their untimely deaths, Gogarty had the melancholy task of embalming both Griffith and Collins.)

Apart from his writing and his medical practice, Gogarty was an active participant in politics, serving several years as an Irish Free State senator. Gogarty abandoned his involvement in Irish politics in the 1930s after the rise of Eamon de Valera as head of the Irish government. Gogarty detested de Valera and saw in him a politician whose small-mindedness would betray the aspirations and hopes of Gogarty's generation.

### REMEMBRANCE OF THINGS PAST

Ireland under de Valera was proving to be a different place from the Ireland in which Gogarty had spent his youth. The Ireland of the early twentieth century, which had pulsed with creativity, first in art (the Irish Literary Renaissance) and then in politics (the independence movement), was fading away. In the late thirties Gogarty published *As I Was Going Down Sackville Street* 1937), an imaginative memoir of his younger days, for which, among his published works, he is best remembered.

After the beginning of the Second World War, Gogarty attempted to enlist in the British armed forces as a medic. Unsuccessful at this, Gogarty moved to America. Thereafter, he returned to Ireland only intermittently until his death.

In his last years, Gogarty supported himself by writing articles and books, as well as giving speeches. His conversational skill had not abandoned him and he found his company as sought after as it had been in Ireland and Britain. The hustle and bustle of America fascinated him, but he found some aspects of its culture distressing. In one anecdote mentioned by Ulick O'Connor, Gogarty was entertaining friends at a bar in New York, in the middle of telling one of his many stories, when a young man dropped a coin into a nearby juke box, causing it to blare loudly over the bar. According to O'Connor's source, an annoyed Gogarty said, "Oh dear God in heaven, that I should find myself thousands of miles from home, at the mercy of every retarded son of a bitch, who has a nickel to drop into that bloody illuminated coal-scuttle."

He died in New York on September 22, 1957. His body was returned to Ireland and buried in Connemara.

*See* De Valera, Eamon

James F. Carens, "Oliver St. John Gogarty," *Dictionary of Literary Biography,* Vol. 15 (Gale Research, 1983).

———, "Oliver St. John Gogarty," *Dictionary of Literary Biography,* Vol. 19 (Gale Research, 1983).

"Gogarty, Oliver St. John," *Contemporary Authors,* Vol. 150 (Gale Research, 1996).

"Gogarty, Oliver St. John," *Merriam Webster's Encyclopedia of Literature* (Merriam Webster, 1995).

"Gogarty, Oliver St. John," *20th Century Authors: A–K* (H. W. Wilson, 1942).

Ulick O'Connor, *Oliver St. John Gogarty* (Jonathan Cape, 1963).

PETER G. SHEA

Doris Kearns Goodwin

## GOODWIN, DORIS KEARNS (1943–  )

Historian, educator, author. Doris Kearns Goodwin was born January 4, 1943, in Rockville Centre, New York, where she grew up absorbed in the affairs of family, the rituals of Catholicism, and the fortunes of the Brooklyn Dodgers baseball team, an experience she later turned into a best-selling memoir, *Wait Till Next Year.* She is the daughter of Michael A. and Helen W. (Miller) Kearns, her father being a bank examiner for the State of New York. She attended public schools before graduating magna cum laude from Colby College in 1964. A doctoral degree followed from Harvard University in 1968.

In the early 1960s Goodwin worked in Washington, D.C., as a State Department and House of Representatives intern. She became a research associate in the Department of Health, Education and Welfare in 1966, and in 1967 a special assistant to Willard Wirtz, Secretary of the Department of Labor. Invited that year to a White House dance, she met President Lyndon Johnson and found her life dramatically altered. Goodwin had recently co-authored a *New Republic* essay severely critical of Johnson's foreign policy, but instead of contesting the thrust of the article with her, Johnson asked her to dance. At evening's end, he suggested that she come to work in the White House as a special assistant. Johnson subsequently asked her to help him organize his memoirs. In 1977, four years after Johnson's death, Goodwin published *Lyndon Johnson and the American Dream,* a political and psychological study that received wide acclaim.

Shortly after, Goodwin contracted to do a biography of John F. Kennedy, a project that expanded in the writing from focus on an individual into a multi-generational study of the interlinked Kennedy and Fitzgerald families, arguably the nation's most famous Irish-American political clans. Appearing in 1987 under the title *The Fitzgeralds and the Kennedys: An American Saga,* the book chronicled the families' history from the baptism in 1863 of John Francis (Honey Fitz) Fitzgerald, in time the first American-born Irish-Catholic mayor of Boston, to the inauguration of his grandson, John Fitzgerald Kennedy, as president in 1961, the first Catholic to hold the office. One of Goodwin's principal sources in writing the book was her husband, Richard, at one time a speechwriter and adviser to John Kennedy, his brother Robert, as well as to President Johnson, Kennedy's successor.

Critics praised the book and Goodwin's objectivity, deeming the latter a special feat given her husband's close association with the Kennedys over three decades' time.

Goodwin's next book focused on another presidential family, the Franklin Delano Roosevelts, and was entitled *No Ordinary Time: Franklin and Eleanor: The Home Front in World War II.* It was published in 1994 and hailed for its remarkable grasp of people and events—such as, in *The Christian Science Monitor's* words, President Roosevelt's "struggle to push his isolationist nation toward a war even before a declaration of hostilities." The book was awarded the 1995 Pulitzer Prize for history.

Goodwin has been connected to Harvard University faculty since 1969, serving most recently as associate professor of government. She has also been assistant director of the Institute of Politics, and beginning in 1971 a member of the Faculty Council. She appears frequently as a political analyst on national television, and at one time hosted her own show, "What's the Big Idea," on WGBH-TV, Boston.

She and her husband live in Concord, Massachusetts. They have three sons.

*Contemporary Authors,* CD-ROM, Gale Research Inc. (Detroit, 1996).

Doris Kearns Goodwin, *Wait Till Next Year: A Memoir* (New York, 1997).

JOHN DEEDY

## GORDON, MARY (1949–  )

Novelist, critic, and essayist, best known for writing fiction which explores the emotional and spiritual lives of women.

### BACKGROUND

Gordon was born December 8, 1949 in Far Rockaway, New York. Her parents were David Gordon, a Lithuanian-Jewish immigrant who converted to Catholicism, and Anna Gagliano Gordon, a legal secretary whose roots were Sicilian-Irish.

Mary Gordon revered her father, a charming, highly literate, multilingual man who died of a heart attack when she was seven years old. Years later she would discover that her father had fabricated many details about his life, such as his claim to have been born in America and to have attended Harvard. In her memoir/

biography *The Shadow Man* (1996) Gordon explored her father's true history (which included mention of several anti-Semitic articles he had written).

Mary Gordon received her primary and secondary education at Holy Name of Mary School in Valley Stream, N.Y. and Mary Louis Academy in Jamaica Estates, N.Y. In 1967 she began attending Barnard College of Columbia University having received a scholarship. At Barnard, Gordon met the novelist Elizabeth Hardwick, who encouraged her to switch from writing poetry to prose.

Gordon began writing her first novel, *Final Payments,* in 1975. At first publishers rejected her manuscript. Elizabeth Hardwick then suggested that Gordon revise the novel by changing the narration from third-person to first-person, making it more personal. After this and a few other changes, the novel was picked up by Random House, which published it to considerable critical and financial success in 1978.

Gordon's subsequent writing career has been very productive. Apart from *Final Payments,* her novels include *The Company of Women* (1980), *Men and Angels* (1985), *The Other Side* (1989), *The Rest of Life: Three Novellas* (1993) and *Spending: A Utopian Divertimento* (1997). Additionally, she has written a collection of short stories, *Temporary Shelter* (1987), an assortment of critical essays, *Nice Boys and Dead Girls* (1991), and her memoir/biography *The Shadow Man* (1996), as well as numerous articles and book introductions.

## CRITICAL RECEPTION

Since the publication of her first novel, Mary Gordon has received considerable critical attention. Critics have praised her lyrical, metaphor-rich prose (which recall her early years as a poet), and her sensitive treatment of the interior lives of contemporary women who struggle to succeed in the world while maintaining a core set of values.

Despite the religious themes of her early novels, Gordon has resisted the classification "Catholic novelist" because she finds the term too limiting. According to *Contemporary Authors, New Revision Series,* Gordon gave an interview published in *U.S. News and World Report* where she says, "You wouldn't call John Updike a Protestant novelist. There are things I wrote about that

came out of my past that had to do with Catholicism, but that's not all I do."

## THINKING ABOUT THE IRISH IN AMERICA

Irish-Americans appear frequently in Mary Gordon's work. In her stories, Irish-Americans struggle with their unique cultural and religious legacies, confronting how those forces shape their perception of themselves and the world. In *The Other Side* Gordon examines five generations of an Irish family, the MacNamaras, with one generation set in Ireland and the subsequent four in America.

In her essay "'I Can't Stand Your Books: A Writer Goes Home," published in the collection *Nice Boys and Dead Girls,* Gordon admits that many members of her extended family disapprove of her work. Using her relatives' disapproval as a departure point, Gordon explores the ambivalent feelings many immigrant Irish have about writing which unveils the self. In Gordon's view,

> The American Irish . . . arrived in America already knowing the language. Yet this knowledge . . . didn't spare them from the hatred and contempt of the natives . . . Did it, perhaps, create in them [Irish-Americans] the illusion that if they behaved, didn't make waves, didn't stand out, they might be accepted? (205)

Gordon suggests that this desire to be accepted, to mix in with the native WASP population, led Irish-Americans to censor themselves, to resist telling their own distinct stories, in the hope that this would accelerate their acceptance into the American mainstream. However, despite this group inhibition, Gordon sees in the Irish-Americans a special strength, the paradoxical ability to grow strong from failure.

> . . . Irish-Americans are nearly always defending the wrong thing; nevertheless, most people find nothing worth defending, and the posture of the mistaken defender is compelling to the spirit . . . The Irish have always in the back of their eye the vision of the ideal. Therefore, they must always be failures. For it is impossible to live up to the ideal; but to be attracted to it, to keep it in the back of one's eye, to know that one's endeavors are, however successful, inevitably failures, is to see the human condition in its clearest, most undiluted colors, to feel its starkest music in the bone. (206)

*See* Fiction, Irish-American

John Auchard, "Mary Gordon," *Dictionary of Literary Biography,* Vol. 6 (Gale Research, 1980).

Robert H. Bell, "All Expenses Paid," *Commonweal* (April 10, 1998).

Alma Bennett, *Mary Gordon* (Simon & Schuster, 1996).

Diana Cooper-Clark, *Interviews with Contemporary Novelists* (St. Martin's Press, 1986).

Joan Goldsworthy, "Mary Gordon," *Contemporary Authors, New Revision Series,* Vol. 44 (Gale Research, 1994).

"Mary Gordon," *Contemporary Literary Criticism,* Vol. 22 (Gale Research, 1982).

Mary Gordon, "My Mother is Speaking from the Desert," *New York Times Biographical Service* (March 1995).

Mary Gordon, *Nice Boys and Dead Girls and Other Essays* (Viking, 1991).

———, *The Shadow Man* (Random House, 1996)..

John R. May, "Mary Gordon," *Dictionary of Literary Biography Yearbook, 1981* (Gale Research, 1982 ).

Mary Gordon

PETER G. SHEA

## GRACE, THOMAS (1841–1921)

Second bishop of the Diocese of Sacramento, California. He was born in County Wexford on August 2, 1841, the son of James and Ellen Armstrong Grace. He was educated in local schools and when he chose a priestly vocation, he attended St. Peter's College in County Wexford and afterwards completed his education at All Hallows College in Dublin. Ordained June 24, 1867, by Bishop David Moriarity of Kerry, he was sent to California and presented himself for service to Bishop Eugene O'Connell of the Vicariate of Marysville. The Marysville jurisdiction encompassed much of northern California as well as a good portion of western Nevada. In 1867 he got his first assignment. Grace was sent to the city of Red Bluff at the head of the Sacramento Valley, where he established a parish and built a convent for the Sisters of Mercy.

By the 1880s, the mining frontier was declining in the West and the city of Grass Valley was losing population. At the direction of coadjutor bishop Patrick Manogue, Grace went to Sacramento in 1862 to prepare the ground for the eventual transfer of the city from the jurisdiction of the Archdiocese of San Francisco to become the headquarters of a new diocesan central moved from Grass Valley to the state capital of California. The move was finally made in May 1886, and shortly afterwards, Manogue began construction on the monumental Cathedral of the Blessed Sacrament located on land Grace had helped secure with the help of a fellow native of Wexford, Captain Thomas Dwyer, one block north of the state capital building. After years of devoted pastoral service, Grace was consecrated the second bishop of Sacramento on June 16, 1896.

The years of Grace's episcopacy (1896–1921) were years of growth for the city of Sacramento and the Sacramento Diocese. For a supply of priests, he continued to rely heavily on graduates of All Hallows and other Irish seminaries. He also was an unflinching supporter of Catholic assimilation and for a time resisted pressures from various nationality groups within the city of Sacramento and the diocese at large for their own parishes. However, the growing ethnic diversity of the diocese compelled him to approve new churches for the Italians and the Portuguese and to make pastoral provisions for a growing number of other nationalities.

His dedication to a free Ireland never waned and he listed himself as a strong supporter of Irish nationalist movements. In 1908 he approved the establishment of *The Catholic Herald* as an independent Catholic newspaper in his diocese under the ownership and editorial pen of Thomas A. Connelly. Connelly was also an unabashed Irish patriot and devoted numerous columns in *The Catholic Herald* to the cause of Irish freedom. Grace's devotion to Irish nationhood was strong even to the end of his life. In July 1919 Grace was on hand to welcome Eamon de Valera, President of the Irish Republic, who visited the Capital City, and he escorted the Irish leader to an enormous rally in Sacramento's Plaza. After World War I, Grace's health began to decline and he died on December 27, 1921.

John T. Dwyer, *Condemned to the Mines: The Life of Eugene O'Connell, 1815–1891* (New York, 1976).

"Thomas Grace" in John J. Delany, *Dictionary of Catholic Biography* (Garden City, N.Y.): 221.

"Thomas Grace" in William L. Willis, *History of Sacramento County with Biographical Sketches* (Los Angeles, 1913): 427–433.

STEVEN M. AVELLA

## GRACE, WILLIAM RUSSELL (1832–1904)

First Roman Catholic Mayor of New York City, Irish philanthropist, shipping magnate and co-founder of Grace Brothers and Company. He was born on May 10, 1832, in Queenstown, Ireland. His parents were James and Mary Ellen (Russell) Grace, William himself carrying his mother's maiden name as part of his own moniker. Going to sea early in his life and then working for two years in Liverpool, England, young Grace in 1850, through the influence of his father, settled in Peru.

During the ensuing ten years he labored with his brother Michael in providing supplies for ships. It was as a partner in Bryce and Company—a position he had earned through his decade of conscientious effort—that he, along with Michael, formed that business into Grace Brothers and Company. In the meantime, William married Lillius Gilchrest (1859). Over the years the two of them parented eleven children (Kelly, *The Encyclopedia of American Catholic History*, 597–98). Eventually Grace moved his family to New York City, where he continued to develop his entrepreneurial interests. Adding shipping to his commercial vision and entering the export world, he increasingly focused on the tremendous economic opportunities that Peru offered. Grace accumulated such a vast fortune that at one point in time, in an uneasy alliance with British investors, he was able to assume the Peruvian national debt. That development brought Grace even greater wealth opportunities. Thus in 1895 he formed W. R. Grace and Company to oversee his almost incomprehensibly immense holdings (Kelly, 598).

Meanwhile, in 1880, Grace was elected the first ever Roman Catholic mayor of New York City. He served in that office for two terms. It has been suggested that Grace's election may have reflected a growing public acceptance of Roman Catholicism in New York City, what with his election following by five years Archbishop of New York John McCloskey's being named a Cardinal Priest of the Church and by one year the dedication of that archdiocese's new St. Patrick's Cathedral.

Grace, however, returned to private business in 1887, even though the Democratic Party wanted to elect him governor of New York. Continuing to guide his business ventures, to support causes such as Irish relief and the Grace Institute—which he founded to help in the education of poverty-stricken young women—and to remain a devout Roman Catholic layman and devoted family man, William Russell Grace died in New York City on 21 March 1904 (Kelly, 598).

*See* New York City; New York City: Irish-American Mayors

Jay P. Dolan, *The Immigrant Church: New York's Irish and German Catholics, 1815–1865* (Baltimore, 1975).

Joseph Peter Grace, *W. R. Grace, 1832–1904 and the Enterprises He Created* (New York, 1953).

Peter Hevner, *A One-sided History of Wm. R. Grace, The Pirate of Peru* (New York 1888).

Joseph F. Kelly, "Grace, William Russell (1832–1904)," *The Encyclopedia of American Catholic History* (Collegeville, 1997).

*New Catholic Encyclopedia*, vol. X (1973).

*The Official Catholic Directory* (Wilmette, Illinois, 1989).

PATRICK FOLEY

## GRADY, HENRY FRANCIS (1882–1957)

Educator, diplomat, businessman. Born one of seven children February 2, 1882 in San Francisco, California, to John Henry

Grady and Ellen Genevieve (Rourke), both native Californians, Henry Grady would fuse teaching, diplomacy, and commerce in service to government and international trade. He studied at St. Mary's University, Baltimore, Catholic University, University of California, and Columbia University, writing his doctoral dissertation at Columbia on *British War Finance, 1914–1919* (1927). In 1917 he married Lucretia del Valle; they had four children. Grady taught economics and finance at City College and Columbia in New York, and entered government service with the U.S. Shipping Board in 1918. Following this he became the first U.S. trade commissioner to Europe, reporting as commercial attaché in London and Holland on postwar financial conditions (1919–1920). In 1921 he was acting chief of the Bureau of Foreign and Domestic Commerce's research division and teaching at Georgetown University. Later that year he returned to the West as lecturer, and afterward, professor and dean, at the University of California, Berkeley until 1937. As trade advisor to the San Francisco Chamber of Commerce 1922–1934, he advocated reduced trade tariffs and repeal of Chinese immigration restrictions. Acquiring a reputation for getting difficult things done with superior technical knowledge and good people skills, Grady aided the federal government in developing the reciprocal trade agreements program in 1934. He became Vice-Chairman of the U.S. Tariff Commission in 1937, and held numerous government posts, including that of Assistant Secretary of State, while working toward the goal of world free-trade which he described in a variety of economic and trade journal articles. As head of the American President Line (1941–1947), he directed strategic defense materials from the Far East to the U.S. in his ships prior to Pearl Harbor, serving as President Roosevelt's personal representative. Henry Grady supported economic aid to the Third World as a deterrant to communism, assisted in implementing the Truman Doctrine and the Marshall Plan, helped supervise elections in Greece (1945–1946), became the first U.S. ambassador to India (1947), and was ambassador to Iran (1950–1951). Though a Democrat, Grady differed with the administration in handling the Palestinian and Iranian situations of the time. He resigned from government service in 1951, but remained active on many fronts, in particular, as foreign adviser to Adlai Stevenson, and heading a group opposing Senator Joseph McCarthy. Ever advocating a more open trade policy, he died on board the *President Wilson* while cruising between Hong Kong and Japan on September 14, 1957.

*Current Biography 1947* (New York, 1947).
*Dictionary of American Biography,* Supp. 6 (New York, 1980).
*Encyclopedia of U.S. Foreign Relations,* Vol. 2 (New York, 1997).

ANNA M. DONNELLY

## GREELEY, ANDREW M. (1928– )

Priest, sociologist, novelist. He was born on February 5, 1928, in Oak Park, IL, to second-generation Irish immigrant parents with County Mayo roots. He and his two younger sisters, Grace and Mary Jule, grew up on Chicago's West Side. A studious dreamer, he attended St. Angela's grammar school and Quigley Minor Seminary. In 1947—ten days before his father's death—he entered St. Mary of the Lake Seminary at Mundelein, IL, where he earned a B.A. in philosophy (1950) and an S.T.L.—licentiate in theology—(1954). His mother returned to work to support the family.

Andrew M. Greeley

Greeley was ordained on May 5, 1954, and appointed assistant pastor of Christ the King parish in Beverly Hills. He worked with young people; and, under the pseudonym Laurence Moran, started to write brief pieces for the teen magazine *High Times.* A voracious reader, he was better prepared than most of his contemporaries for the Second Vatican Council (1962–65), which opened the Church to dialogue with science, democracy, and ecumenism. It also separated, as Greeley would say thirty-three years later, the old "Confident Church" from the new "Confused Church." Much of Greeley's life work has involved demonstrating that the Confused Church is preferable to the Confident Church.

### SOCIOLOGIST

Archbishop Albert Gregory Meyer encouraged Greeley to do graduate work in sociology at the University of Chicago. When he enrolled in September 1960, he had already published his first book, and a second one was in press. While continuing full-time parish work at Christ the King, he completed the M.A. (1961) and Ph.D. (1962) in twenty months with a straight A average. His dissertation research established that four of seven "expert assumptions" concerning Catholics were totally or partially wrong. He had mounted Rosinante and set out on his lifelong mission of tilting at academic and ecclesiastic windmills and bursting the bubbles of the establishment with the sharp lance of empirical evidence. In 1964 Greeley was reassigned to St. Thomas the Apostle in Hyde Park. The following year, shortly before Meyer's death, he was granted special, non-parish status by the Archbishop. Hence, Greeley was at the margins of parish work and active in writing and research when Archbishop (later Cardinal) Cody arrived in Chicago.

From then on Greeley would do parish work on weekends and be priest in, through, and alongside other careers in the secular worlds of quantitative research, higher education, journalism and publishing. He has been with the National Opinion Research Center (NORC) at the University of Chicago since 1961, serving at various times as Director of the Center for the Study of Pluralism, Senior Studies Director, and Research Associate. In the 1960s and early '70s he taught higher education at the University of Illinois, Chicago Circle. Since 1978 he has been

Professor of Sociology at the University of Arizona, Tucson (Spring), and since 1991 Professor of Social Science at the University of Chicago (Fall). He now travels regularly to Ireland and Germany to lecture and collaborate with colleagues on such projects as the International Social Survey Program.

As a sociologist, Greeley's main interests have fallen into three categories: (1) Catholic schools (four studies in three decades), (2) ethnic subcultures in the United States (especially the Irish), and (3) sociology of religion. As of 1998, of Greeley's 149 books, 43 deal primarily with sociology.

*The Priest Study.* In 1967 the U.S. Bishops' Conference authorized a scholarly investigation of the U.S. Church, consisting of historical, psychological, and sociological components. Joseph Bernardin served as liaison between the bishops and the researchers, including John Tracy Ellis (history), Eugene Kennedy (psychology), and Andrew Greeley (sociology). The NORC team conducted the mammoth sociological study, initially involving a sample of 7,474 priests. As has happened so often, the findings were controversial. The U.S. hierarchy didn't want to be told that only thirteen percent of younger priests still accepted *Humanae vitae.* Radical priests were upset that so many priests were shown to be well-adjusted and celibate. Conservative bishops were appalled that not all priests were satisfied in their work. In the ensuing fracas Greeley accused the bishops of moral bankruptcy for trying to discredit the study they had sponsored.

*From Sex as Sacrament to God Images.* Survey research was reinforcing Greeley's suspicion that the notion of the "sacramentality" of sexual love lurked in a unique way in the Catholic preconscious. In other words, if we believe in the Incarnation, then making love is a way of sharing God's passion. He elaborated on those connections in *Sexual Intimacy* (1973) and *Love and Play* (1975). In *Catholic Schools in a Declining Church* (1976), he argued that by issuing the birth control encyclical, Rome had unwittingly empowered the laity to turn into "do it yourself Catholics" who remained affiliated with the Church, but on their own terms, without paying attention to official rules concerning sexual practice. Eventually, these intellectual pathways led Greeley to focus on divine androgyny with special emphasis on the long neglected feminine aspects of God—first clearly enunciated in *The Mary Myth* (1978). All of this engendered further quantitative studies involving people's God-images, published in such works as *The Religious Imagination* (1981). Using statistical methods and a "grace scale," he demonstrated that Catholics are more likely than Protestants to imagine God as primarily "Mother-Lover-Friend" (in contrast to "Father-Master-Judge"), reinforcing David Tracy's theological distinction between the analogical and the dialectical imagination. In 1995 he published *Religion as Poetry,* the synthesis of twenty-five years of sociological theorizing. In the book he argues (1) that religion does matter in modern society, (2) that religious imagery is the most powerful religious predictor variable currently available to us, and (3) that differences between Catholics and non-Catholics in political and social attitudes can be accounted for by different Catholic religious images.

Seanachie

In the late 1970s Greeley's sociological focus on the religious imagination and the womanliness of God combined with his Parish-Priest and Irish-Leprechaun identities to emerge as Andrew Greeley, Seanachie-Homilist. Almost overnight—after the 1981 runaway success of *The Cardinal Sins*—Greeley became pastor of a global congregation without walls, the readers of his novels. Profits from the sale of the novels went to such causes as a Chair in Catholic Studies named for Greeley's parents at the University of Chicago (1.5 million dollars) and a foundation to support Chicago inner-city Catholic schools (1 million dollars).

*Romances of Renewal.* His first published novel (1979), *The Magic Cup,* based on the Irish Grail legend of Art the Son of Conn, set the fundamental theme for Greeley's future stories. His male protagonists are generally baptized reincarnations of such wayfarers as Conn, Bran, Fann, Maelduin, and Saint Brendan in search of the "Blessed Land of the Ever-Living Women" whose adventures were spun out in countless variations by popular bards. Greeley's characters evoke, beyond the Celtic realm, such figures as Faust, Don Quixote, Dante, Parzival, Odysseus, and the progenitor of them all, Gilgamesh in search of the plant of life. Unlike most non-Celtic heroes, Greeley's men discover that the object of their desire is pursuing them with equal (or greater) vigor and turns out to be a manifestation of the Celtic triple goddess Brigid—maiden-mother-crone—who outwitted the ire of Saint Patrick and entered Christian sainthood as Abbess and Bishop Brigid of Kildare, whose feast day is February 2, coincidentally, James Joyce's birthday. Greeley claims her as his patron saint and begins his autobiography with a Gaelic prayer to St. Brigid. As of 1998, Greeley has published 38 novels, most set in an American-Irish milieu, and all in some way stories of hope—of God's implacable love, of sin and grace, of resurrection and second chances, of old love lost and found anew, of Ulysses and homecomings.

Coda

Greeley's mission can be summarized in the conclusion of the "platform" speech of Don Luis, the fictional contender for the papacy in his novel, *White Smoke:* "So many of our lay people believe that ours is a Church of rules, that being Catholic consists of keeping rules. They do not find an institution which is like that very appealing. Nor should they. In fact, we are a Church of love. . . . [W]e exist to preach a God of love, we try to be a people of love, and we want our church to be, insofar as we poor humans can make it, a Church of radiant love. Does such a Church have a future? How could it not?"

Andrew Greeley, *The Catholic Priest in the United States: Sociological Investigations* (Washington, D.C.,1972).

———, *Unsecular Man: The Persistence of Religion* (New York, 1972).

———, *The Irish Americans: The Rise to Money and Power* (New York, 1981).

———, *Confessions of a Parish Priest* (New York, 1987).

———, *The Catholic Myth* (New York, 1990).

———, *Religion as Poetry* (New Brunswick, N.J., 1995).

———, *White Smoke* (New York, 1996).

———, "Retractions of a Parish Priest" (Unpublished Manuscript, 1998).

Elizabeth Harrison, *Andrew M. Greeley: An Annotated Bibliography* (Metuchen, N.J., 1994).

John N. Kotre, *The Best of Times, The Worst of Times* (Chicago, 1978).

Ingrid H. Shafer, *Eros and the Womanliness of God* (Chicago, 1986).

*The Discovery Deposition of James Winters* (http://www.usao.edu/~facshaferi/winters.html).

INGRID SHAFER

## GRENNAN, EAMON (1941– )

Poet, essayist, translator. Born in Dublin and educated in Ireland and America, Grennan belongs to a generation of Irish emigrants who live in America but maintain close ties with Ireland. The style and themes of his poetry reflect his dualistic culture and multiple traditions. His striking portraits of nature and family have won him international recognition.

## BACKGROUND

Grennan enrolled in a Cistercian boarding school, moving from Dublin to rural Roscrea, Tipperary, in 1955. He took interest in sports, literature, and theater. At University College, Dublin, he majored in English and Italian, finishing his B.A. in 1963 and M.A. in 1964. After a year in Italy, he enrolled in Harvard's Ph.D. program in English. Before completing his degree, however, he returned to Italy (Florence) for a year, then taught in Dublin and New York. He finished his Ph.D. in 1973 with a dissertation on Shakespeare's history plays. By then, he was married and had two children. Since 1974, he has taught at Vassar College, where he is the Dexter M. Ferry Jr. Professor of English. He also spends time in his cottage in the west of Ireland.

While in Dublin, Grennan had been marginally involved in the burgeoning literary scene, but he did not begin writing poetry seriously until 1977, when he took a leave of absence and returned to live for a year in a coast guard house in County Wexford. Studying both Irish and American poetry, Grennan began to seek and express the conjunction of these traditions.

## POETRY

Grennan is part of the resurgent wave of Irish emigrants, the "New Irish," who came to the U.S. during the 60s and 70s. Poet Eamonn Wall has called this generation "commuters" rather than exiles or emigrants because they frequently return "home" to Ireland. The writers of this generation, and Grennan in particular, have neither ceded their Irish heritage nor ignored their experiences outside Ireland, unlike earlier Irish exile writers. Rather, they have engaged both cultures and traditions, with "a mixture of alienation and excitement" (Wall, "Exile, Attitude, and the Sin-é Café: Notes on the 'New Irish,'" *Éire-Ireland,* Winter 1996). Grennan has commented on his own sense of "doubleness," which he experiences as a result of his dual heritage, as he noted for a Prague journal, "it is the movement back and forth between over here and over there that's important to me" (*Metre; A Magazine of International Poetry,* Autumn 1997).

His poetry owes much to the influence of Irish and American writers: Patrick Kavanagh, Thomas Kinsella, John Montague, James Wright, Elizabeth Bishop, Robert Lowell, Gary Snyder, and many of Grennan's contemporaries. Furthermore, his poems echo such diverse writers (from Basho to Rilke) that one can find references to Shakespeare and Lowell and hear echoes from Ted Hughes and Thoreau in the same poem, as in "Towards Dusk the Porcupine."

Grennan's main themes include: family (marriage, parent-child relations, divorce); the duality of (what he calls) "settlement and break-up"; and animals and landscapes of Ireland and America. His animal portraits are notable achievements, especially in later volumes. Also, in the tradition of William Carlos Williams, Grennan has found the knack of revealing profundities through simple and natural language, but his lyrical directness is all his own. He has been awarded NEH and NEA grants, a Guggenheim Fellowhip, a Shenandoah Award, a Pushcart Prize and a PEN Award for Poetry in Translation.

*See* Poetry, Irish-American

Grennan's work:

Poetry: *Wildly for Days* (Gallery, 1983), *What Light There Is* (Gallery, 1987), *Twelve Poems* (Occasional Works, 1988), *What Light There Is and Other Poems* (North Point, 1989), *As If It Matters* (Gallery, 1991, Graywolf, 1992), *So It Goes* (Gallery, Graywolf, 1995), *Relations: New & Selected Poems* (Graywolf, 1998).

Translations: *Selected Poems of Giacomo Leopardi* (Dedalus, 1995, Princeton, 1997).

Criticism: *New Irish Writing,* eds., James Brody and Eamon Grennan (Twayne, 1988).

JOSEPH LENNON

## GUINEY, LOUISE IMOGENE (1861–1920)

Author. Louise Imogene Guiney, poet, essayist and literary historian, was born in Roxbury, Massachusetts, January 7, 1861, daughter of Patrick and Janet Doyle Guiney. She was educated by private tutors and at the Academy of the Sacred Heart ("Elmhurst") in Providence, Rhode Island, an elite convent school. Prospects of a genteel life disappeared, however, when her Tipperary-born father, a famed Civil War general, died prematurely of war wounds, leaving the family with "more glory than dollars." Louise was 16 at the time.

At age 19 Guiney's verses were appearing in the *Pilot,* and soon after in *Atlantic Monthly, Scribner's, Catholic World* and other leading periodicals. The first of some 30 books of poetry and prose was published in 1884. She was an exciting, blossoming talent, but income from independent writing was insufficient to sustain her and her mother. She applied for the position of postmaster at Auburndale, a Boston suburb, and was named to the post by President Grover Cleveland in 1894. Nativists objecting to the appointment of an Irish Catholic launched a boycott against the purchase of stamps at the facility, the sale of stamps then being a postmaster's major source of income. Guiney weathered their protest, but resigned in 1897 when diagnosed with meningitis. She worked briefly at the Boston Public Library before sailing for England in 1900 to devote herself to writing and scholarship, returning but twice to the United States.

As a writer, Guiney occupied herself with dusty figures of literary history—Lady Danvers, Henry Vaughan, Topham Beauclerk, James Clarence Mangan, George Farquhar, William Hazlitt, *et al.*—then fixed on the recusant poets of the English Reformation, intending to rescue what she felt was a lost chapter of Catholic heritage. The recusants project consumed the last seven years of her life and the exertions, it is said, quickened her demise. Only one of two projected volumes was published, that in 1938, eighteen years after her death. On September 8, 1920, Guiney suffered a stroke. She died the following November 2 at Chipping Campden and was buried in Wolvercote Cemetery, Oxford, beneath a Celtic cross of her own design.

*See* Fiction, Irish-American

Henry G. Fairbanks, *Louise Imogene Guiney: Laureate of the Lost* (Albany, N.Y., 1972).

Paula M. Kane, *Separatism and Subculture: Boston Catholicism, 1900–1920* (Chapel Hill, 1994).

Eva Mabel Tenison, *Louise Imogene Guiney, Her Life and Works, 1861–1920* (London, 1923).

JOHN DEEDY

## GUINEY, PATRICK ROBERT (1835–1877)

Soldier, lawyer, politician. Born on January 15, 1835, in Parkstown, County Tipperary, Guiney immigrated to Maine at age seven. After working in factories and machine shops in boyhood, Guiney attended the College of the Holy Cross in Worcester, Massachusetts, for a year before studying law. In 1858 Guiney relocated to Boston where he practiced law and wrote for the Boston *Times*. He married on January 8, 1859, moved to Roxbury, Massachusetts and won a seat on the town's Council. His only child, Louise Imogen Guiney, was soon born and she grew up to be an eminent poet.

When the Civil War erupted, Guiney enlisted in the Ninth Massachusetts Volunteer Infantry, an Irish regiment commanded by Colonel Thomas Cass, and accepted a captain's commission on June 11, 1861. He befriended Thomas F. Meagher and, despite Irish-Americans' strong political allegiance to the Democratic party, Guiney became an outspoken supporter of Lincoln, abolitionism and the Republicans. He rose in rank to lieutenant colonel and during the battle of Gaines' Mill on June 27, 1862, Cass fell ill and relinquished command to Guiney. The "Fighting Ninth" formed the retreating Federal column's rearguard and Guiney led its nine charges against attacking Confederates. When Cass fell mortally wounded a few days later, Guiney received promotion to colonel and commanded the regiment until receiving a bullet in the eye while leading a charge at the Wilderness on May 5, 1864.

Guiney recuperated and accepted appointment as assistant district attorney for Suffolk County in 1865. Honored as a war hero, he received brevet promotion to brigadier general and ran for Congress for the Workingman party. Troubled by his wound, Guiney resigned from the district attorney's office in 1869 and won election as Register of Probate and Insolvency for Suffolk County in 1871. Guiney held this position until his death on March 21, 1877, honored by a large funeral cortege which laid him to rest at Holyhood Cemetery in Brookline.

Louise Imogen Guiney, "Patrick Robert Guiney," in *The Holy Cross Purple*, vol. 3 no. 1 (June 1896).

Patrick Robert Guiney Military Service and Pension Records, National Archives, Washington, D.C.

Christian G. Samito, ed., *Commanding Boston's Irish Ninth: The Civil War Letters of Colonel Patrick R. Guiney, Ninth Massachusetts Volunteer Infantry* (New York, 1998).

CHRISTIAN G. SAMITO

## GUNN, JOHN EDWARD (1863–1924)

Bishop and educator. John Edward Gunn was born on March 15, 1863, in Fivemiletown, County Tyrone, Ireland, the son of Edward Gunn and Mary Grew. The family came originally from Caithness, Scotland.

Gunn was educated at St. Mary's College in Dundalk; the Marist House of Studies in Paignton, Devonshire, England; the Catholic University of Ireland; the Marist House of Studies in Belley, France; and the Pontifical Gregorian University in Rome. He joined the Marist Fathers, a religious community, on August 15, 1881, professed his vows on August 23, 1884, and was ordained to the priesthood in Rome on February 2, 1890, and taught for eight years.

From 1898 to 1911, he served as pastor of Sacred Heart Parish in Atlanta, Georgia, where he helped mitigate anti-Catholic bigotry. He was named the sixth bishop of the Diocese of Natchez, Mississippi, on June 29, 1911, and was consecrated in Atlanta on August 29, 1911.

Gunn spent much of his episcopate in Mississippi on the road. "Mile after mile of Mississippi territory he traveled, breaking the bread to the lowly, preaching, teaching and confirming. Every little mission had its visit; every parish had its frequent call." Gunn also became known as "the bishop of poor churches and especially of the colored, the Indians and the abandoned white Catholics of the distant parts of Mississippi." During his tenure in Mississippi, more than fifty small chapels were built throughout the state so rural Catholics would have "a little place of worship." He believed that education was "the foundation of all things diocesan" and guided the expansion of the Mississippi Catholic schools so they were serving over 7,000 children at his death in 1924. Gunn spent much time at Pass Christian where he found the Gulf Coast climate beneficial to his poor health. Gunn died at Hotel Dieu in New Orleans on February 19, 1924.

*See* Mississippi

Joseph Bernard Code, *Dictionary of the American Hierarchy, 1789–1964* (New York City, 1964).

"Diary of the Diocese, 1911–1922," and Gunn Papers in Archives, Diocese of Jackson.

Richard O. Gerow, *Catholicity in Mississippi* (Natchez, 1939).

Charles E. Nolan, *St. Mary's of Natchez: the History of a Southern Catholic Congregation, 1716–1988* (Natchez, 1992).

CHARLES E. NOLAN

# H

can Rainbow: Early Reminiscences (1971), fragments written 1922–1955. Ever independent and his own person, Hackett died on April 25, 1962, in Virum, Denmark.

Dictionary of American Biography, Supplement 7, 1961–1965 (New York, 1981).
Dictionary of Irish Literature. Rev. ed. Robert Hogan, ed. (Westport, CT, 1996).
World Authors 1900–1950, Vol. 2 (New York, 1996).

ANNA M. DONNELLY

## HACKETT, FRANCIS (1883–1962)

Author, editor, critic. Francis Hackett was born on Jan. 21, 1883, to John Byrne Hackett, a doctor, and Bridget (Doheny) in Kilkenny, Ireland where he received a Catholic school education and studied at the Conglowes Wood College, a prestigious Jesuit secondary school. He also attended the Royal University without taking a degree. Hackett developed a strong admiration for the Irish nationalist patriot Charles Stewart Parnell (1846–1891), and an antipathy for the Catholic Church, British imperialism, and upper-class distinctions. He came to New York in 1901 to further himself, and began to publish articles in Irish reviews while working a variety of jobs and helping found an Irish literary society. Being rejected for enlistment in the U.S. Navy, he found work in Chicago as a railroad clerk, and began to meet Chicago's political and cultural leaders. He was a reporter briefly for William Randolph Hearst's *Chicago American* (he was fired for exaggerating stories) and wrote reviews and articles in 1906 for the *Chicago Evening Post*. That same year he moved into Jane Addams' Hull House and taught English to Russian immigrants. Contact with Addams and such persons as Thorstein Veblen, William James, and British intellectual socialists moved him toward more democratic and radical views. In 1908 he became literary editor of the *Post*. By 1909 Hackett was editor of the *Post's* new literary supplement, *Friday Literary Review*, which became a vehicle for literary realism and cultural radicalism. Hackett assisted in creating the magazine *New Republic* in New York at the invitation of its editor-founder and political theorist Herbert Croly, becoming literary editor in 1914. He married Danish-born *New Republic* editor Signe Kirstine Tolksvig in 1918. His strong support of Irish nationalism and the League of Nations put him at odds with Croly, and led him to move to southern France with his wife in 1922, where he became a freelance writer for some years, returning only briefly to the United States. He lived in Ireland from 1929, but left for Denmark in 1936 when the Irish censored his autobiographical novel *Green Lion*. In 1940 Hackett and his wife avoided the Nazi threat there and returned to the United States, remaining until 1946, when he went back to Denmark. Francis Hackett's two main focal points were literature and Ireland. Among his published works are *Ireland: A Study in Nationalism* (1918), *Horizons: A Book of Criticism* (1918), *Henry the Eighth* (1929)—a biography six years in the making and highly praised, *Francis the First* (1934), the historical novel *Queen Anne Boleyn* (1939), *The Story of the Irish Nation* (1939)—written in three months, the autobiographical *I Chose Denmark* (1940), *What "Mein Kampf" Means to America* (1941), *On Judging Books, in General and in Particular* (1947), and the posthumous Ameri-

## HALEY, JACK (1899–1979)

Actor. Born John Haley of Irish heritage to John Joseph and Ellen (Curley) Haley, he was educated at Dwight Grammar School and Boston English High School in South Boston. Early on Haley departed from his mother's wish for him to pursue a career as an electrician; instead, he left home for New York to pursue his dream of being an actor. From New York he moved to Philadelphia and found a job as a song plugger for the McCarthy Fisher Music Publishing Company and later found subsequent interest and employment in vaudeville.

Haley was successful on the vaudeville circuit, particularly in his part in "Haley Crafts" in 1920. This performance at the Palace Theater in New York City ran for six months and allowed him to move on to Broadway for a role in *Around the Town*. Having made many contacts on the vaudeville circuit, he worked for over ten years, during which he met his future wife, Florence McFadden, and was married in 1921. Together, the Haleys worked with several vaudeville troupes and eventually moved to Los Angeles, California, where Jack began work as master of ceremonies at a local theater. Haley gained his first big break in the Broadway musical revue *Follow Thru* in 1929 and from there took several lead and secondary roles in various song-and-dance routines. His career reached an unexpected high point when Metro-Goldwyn-Mayer gave him the part of the Tin Man in *The Wizard of Oz* (1939) after Buddy Ebsen resigned from the part. The success of the film made Haley into an American icon and his memorable portrayal of the Tin Man became a celebrated part of film history.

Though he enjoyed the popularity due to *The Wizard of Oz,* the following years did not bring many more roles for Haley. He soon realized that the era for which his talent was designed had come to an end; he then retired to secondary interests in real estate and various charitable causes.

On June 6, 1979, he died of a heart attack.

*See* Theater, Irish in

Douglas McClelland, *Down the Yellow Brick Road: The Making of the Wizard of Oz* (1989).
The Academy of Motion Pictures Library in Los Angeles.
*Dictionary of American Biography,* supplement 8.

JOY HARRELL

## HALLE, KAY (1904–1997)

Socialite. Born in 1904 in Cleveland, Ohio, Kay Halle was the daughter of the romantic union of a wealthy German-Jewish merchant and an Irish-Catholic working-class girl. Raised in the privilege afforded by the success of her father, a founder of the old Halle Brothers department store in Cleveland, Ohio, Halle moved comfortably amongst the intellectual, social, and political elite of her day. An heiress of independent means, and reputedly both beautiful and glamorous, Halle never married, despite an apparent range of suitors.

After briefly attending Smith College in Massachusetts, Halle worked intermittently as a journalist, writing for the *Cleveland Plain Dealer* and other publications, and conducting radio interviews with public figures. Halle's most prominent role, however, was that of a member of society, who had a talent for intimate friendships with powerful people in politics and the arts. Her circle of confidantes included, at various times, Winston Churchill, his son Randolph Churchill, composer George Gershwin, statesman W. Averell Harriman and President Franklin D. Roosevelt, among others.

Halle published two volumes of the collected sayings of Winston Churchill, and was said to be instrumental in persuading the United States Congress to confer on him honorary American citizenship. Halle died on August 7, 1997, in Washington, D.C., at the age of 93.

"Kay Halle, an Intimate of Century's Giants," *The New York Times* (August 24, 1997).

KATHLEEN N. MCCARTHY

### HALPINE, CHARLES GRAHAM (1829–1868)

Journalist, politician. Halpine was a journalist who supported both American and Irish governmental reform. Born in 1829 in County Meath, Ireland, Halpine attended Trinity College in Dublin where he studied both medicine and law. Neither profession interested Halpine very much and he soon turned to journalism as his career.

The growing burdens of raising a family led Halpine to emigrate to the United States in 1851. Halpine first found work writing advertisements for P. T. Barnum, but later took on the task of editing a humorous weekly known as *The Carpet Bag.* He went on to serve as correspondent and associate editor of the *New York Times.*

Halpine was keenly interested in both Irish and American politics. He had been a member of the "Young Ireland" reform movement in the late 1840s and became an ardent Democrat and secretary to Senator Stephen A. Douglas in this country in the 1850s. In New York City, he was among the Democrats who sought to reform the Tammany political organization.

At the outbreak of the Civil War, Halpine joined the 69th New York Regiment, the so-called "Irish Brigade." Although he proved himself an able soldier in the field, and was promoted several ranks, Halpine's greatest value to the war effort was as a writer and satirist.

Writing in the character of an ignorant Irish private named "Miles O'Reilly," Halpine penned humorous yet biting letters to the press that criticized northerners who would not support the war effort. These war letters became so popular that they were compiled into two best selling books entitled *The Life and Adventures of Private Miles O'Reilly* (1864) and *Baked Meats of the Funeral* (1866).

Failing eyesight forced Halpine to resign from the army in July of 1864 and he returned to New York to pursue his twin passions of journalism and local politics. In the Spring of 1865, Halpine became editor of the *New York Citizen* and greatly increased its influence and circulation. In this effort, Halpine allied himself with Robert B. Roosevelt, uncle of Theodore Roosevelt, the future president of the United States.

Halpine was a controversial figure in both American and Irish political circles years immediately after the war. He supported President Andrew Johnson's efforts to bring the southern states back into the union and in that effort ghost-wrote *The Prison Life of Jefferson Davis* to generate sympathy for the former president of the confederacy. Halpine also championed the efforts of the Fenian Brotherhood to win Irish independence which led to protests from the British government.

With the help of Roosevelt and others, Halpine was elected Register of the County and City of New York in 1866, a position that made him responsible for the registration of deeds and other legal documents. But this success was too much for Halpine. His insomnia and alcoholism, combined with frequent bouts of depression, led Halpine to commit suicide on August 3, 1868. With his troubled death, an important voice for both American and Irish governmental reform came to an end.

William Hanchet, *Irish: Charles G. Halpine in Civil War America* (Syracuse, N.Y., 1970).

Robert B. Roosevelt, *The Poetical Works of Charles G. Halpine* (New York, 1869).

TIMOTHY WALCH

### HAMILL, PETE (1935–   )

Journalist, author. Pete Hamill, a best-selling author, screenwriter and journalist, was born in Brooklyn to immigrants from Belfast. Hamill grew up in the then-working class neighborhood of Park Slope adjacent to Prospect Park. He was a child of New York during its mid-century Golden Age, before suburbanization tore a hole in Brooklyn that has yet to be repaired. Among the lessons he learned from his parents was that work was its own reward, the reason why the family lived in Brooklyn and not Belfast. His father worked to feed his large family despite what would now be called a physical challenge—he lost a leg as a young man. His mother so valued work that long after her children were reared and had attained success, she took a job as a clerk in an off-track betting office. The Brooklyn of his childhood and young adulthood appears often in Hamill's fiction and journalism.

After working on the Brooklyn docks, Hamill joined the Navy as a young man and, after serving his stint, set out for Mexico to pursue what became a lifelong interest in art. It was there that this child of Brooklyn, of comic books and radio serials and the beloved Dodgers, began to appreciate the enormity of his parents' journey to America. In Mexico, he was an outsider, just as immigrants were and are in America. It was then, too, that Hamill began to dwell on what he would call the "interrupted narrative" of the immigrant experience of his family's experience. His parents grew up on tales of the heroes and martyrs of Irish history. As an American growing up in the middle of the American Century, Hamill's heroes were Jackie Robinson and Captain Marvel. This appreciation of his family's experience has made Hamill an eloquent voice for modern American immigrants.

Hamill started his journalistic career in the early 1960s at the *New York Post,* then an earnest, liberal afternoon newspaper perennially on the verge of closing. As American society teetered on the edge of a collective nervous breakdown during the tumultuous sixties, Hamill made his name as a passionate opponent of the Vietnam War and an advocate for the civil rights movement. It led to the publication of *Irrational Ravings,* a collection of his journalism from the 1960s. In the early months of 1968, Hamill and two New York colleagues, Jimmy Breslin and Jack Newfield, befriended presidential candidate Robert F. Kennedy. Indeed, it was a letter from Hamill, then living in Belfast and witnessing first-hand the outbreak of the Troubles there, that persuaded Kennedy to declare his candidacy. Hamill was among those in the kitchen of the Ambassador Hotel in Los Angeles on June 6, 1968, when Robert Kennedy was mortally wounded. Hamill returned to the daily newspaper business in the early 1970s when the *New York Daily News* hired him and Breslin in tandem. As their fellow Irish-Americans streamed out of the cities and the Democratic Party, Hamill and Breslin remained unapologetic liberals. Hamill once again left daily journalism in the early 1980s. He became a regular columnist for *Esquire,* the monthly men's magazine, continued his screenwriting career and built up a large national following with a series of novels, many of them reflecting his Irish upbringing.

In the early 1990s, his memoir of his days as a young newspaper columnist, *A Drinking Life,* became a huge bestseller. He followed up that success with a novel entitled *Snow in August,* a work featuring the friendship between an aging rabbi and a young Irish Catholic boy in the post-war Brooklyn of Jackie Robinson's rookie season with the Dodgers. Like *A Drinking Life,* it was a smashing success.

Hamill also won national attention for his three-month tenure as editor of the *New York Post* in 1993 at a time when the newspaper that launched his career was yet again on the verge of closing. When an eccentric millionaire named Abe Hirschfeld found himself as temporary owner of the newspaper, he fired Hamill, touching off a hilarious and yet determined rebellion by the *Post's* editorial staff. Hamill eventually returned to the newsroom to a welcome usually reserved for rock stars. His tenure, however, didn't last much longer. A few years later, he was hired to edit the *Daily News.* He improved the paper's coverage of immigrants and beefed up its investigative unit. To no avail; he and the paper's owner parted ways after less than a year.

*See* Fiction, Irish-American

Pete Hamill, *A Drinking Life* (Boston, 1995).
———, *Loving Women* (Chicago, 1990).
———, *Piecework* (Boston, 1996).
———, *Snow in August* (Boston, 1997).

TERRY GOLWAY

## HARNETT, WILLIAM MICHAEL (1848–1892)

Painter. Son of a shoemaker, born in Ireland in 1848, Harnett's family moved to Philadelphia where he practised engraving from 1865 until the early 1870s when the mechanisation of his job rendered him unemployed. In 1871 he moved to New York to study at the National Academy of Design and Cooper Union, returning to Philadelphia in 1876 where he continued his studies at the Pennsylvania Academy of Fine Arts. In 1880 he went to London, Frankfurt and Munich, remaining in Munich until 1885, and returned to the U.S. via Paris where he had exhibited at the Paris Salon.

Although his favoured objects—initially fruit and vegetables, and later beer mugs and tobacco, books and musical instruments, writing materials and skulls—may be easily dismissed as ordinary, everyday ones, their symbolic qualities should not be underestimated. Even paintings which at first glance appear to be neutral usually carry a symbolic resonance, such as the life-sized components of *The Artist's Letter Rack* (1879) in the Metropolitan Museum of Art.

This tradition of still-life painting, which includes Raphaelle Peale and William Harnett, purports to suppress the authorial presence where conceptual realism is deployed to explore tactile and intellectual considerations, as opposed to another still-life tradition, which includes Chardin and Cézanne, in which the object is a vehicle for the exposition of formal, optical and perceptual considerations which interest the artist. *Trompe l'oeil,* at which Harnett excelled, is a further refinement of the former category of still-life painting in which the artist seeks to identically recreate material reality.

In one of Harnett's rare figurative paintings, *Attention Company!* (1878), he paints a "piccaninny," playing up the stereotypical characteristics in a display of virtuosity. Such was Harnett's skill in hyperrealism that anecdotes abounded about the need to place guards beside his paintings to prevent, for example, anyone trying to take down the fiddle and bow, so illusionistically painted in *The Old Violin.* On another occasion, disturbed by its remarkable illusionism, Harnett's painting of treasury bills provoked federal agents to confiscate one of his paintings of a five-dollar bill in a New York saloon in 1886.

He himself described his work as one of "selective imitation," reserving the right to compose at will, to add and subtract, and to imbue the objects not only with narrative but also with romantic and emotional qualities, insisting in an interview with the *New York News* that thereby he did not closely imitate nature. In that interview he made it clear that the selection of objects was intended to convey states of mind. One such state was nostalgia and, of course, nostalgia in the late nineteenth century was often understood as a way of either creating a sense of the past or holding on to values that were under threat. The choice of the objects depicted focuses on a pre-industrialised age, handmade objects that are given added significance in the knowledge that they will soon be obsolete, amounting to what Robert Hughes called "a virtual fetishization of the mundane." It has also been noted that Harnett is concerned with predominantly male objects—drinking utensils, revolvers, briar pipes and horseshoes. His audience was predominantly not only white, male and middle-class but also intelligent enough to appreciate the visual deception.

Other Harnett paintings include *After the Hunt* (1885); *Old Models* (1892); *Golden Horseshoe* (1886); and *The Faithful Colt* (1890). His work is found in collections such as the Fine Arts Museum, San Francisco; the Metropolitan Museum, New York; the Museum of Fine Arts, Boston; the Addison Gallery, Andover, Massachusetts; and the Graves Art Gallery, Sheffield.

Doreen Bolger, et al., eds., *William M. Harnett* (New York, 1992).
Alfred Frankenstein, *After the Hunt: William Harnett and Other American Still-life Painters, 1870–1900,* rev. ed. (Berkeley, 1969).
David M. Lubin, *Picturing a Nation: Art and Social Change in Nineteenth-Century America* (New Haven, 1994).

NIAMH O'SULLIVAN

## HARPER, ARTHUR (1835–1897)

Prospector. Arthur Harper, and men like him, were the muscle, sinew and grit that opened the western mining frontier. Born in County Antrim in 1835, Harper was described as "an Irishman with a square face, shrewd eyes, and a great beard that later turned snow white and gave him the look of a frontier Charles Evans Hughes." He, along with millions of his countrymen, immigrated to New York in 1847. Urban life, however, bored him and by the late 1850s he was in British Columbia, panning for gold during the Fraser River excitement. His wanderlust led him farther north, to the Cariboo in the 1860s and later to the Cassiar gold diggings.

In 1872, he decided to abandon civilization altogether when he, along with two other prospectors, invaded the vast expanse of the Yukon River valley. In this remote wilderness, the sober, industrious Harper found a home; as historian Pierre Berton noted, "for the next quarter century the river was Harper's highway; he roamed it, seeking the will-o-the-wisp in every tributary stream, testing the gravels, panning the sidebars, always hoping to find the treasure." Try as he may, however, he never "struck it rich" as a miner. Seeking a means of support, he became an agent for the Alaska Commercial Company; in that capacity, he and his partners welcomed new prospectors into the country and encouraged their efforts. Over the years, Harper ran stores at Fort Reliance, Fortymile, Stewart River, and Fort Selkirk. His generosity was legendary; he "grubstaked" (outfitted) scores of prospectors, some of whom made rich gold strikes.

He was still on the river in August 1896 when a trio of prospectors discovered the gold that launched the fabulous Klondike stampede. During the year that followed, thousands descended on Bonanza and Eldorado creeks, and by the summer of 1897, "Klondike" was a magical word known around the world. By that time, however, life on the frontier had taken its toll on Arthur Harper. His constitution weakened by tuberculosis, he sailed south to San Francisco and headed to the desert to recuperate. But it was too late; in November 1897, the 62-year-old Harper died in Yuma, Arizona. Harper never got rich from his efforts, but he could take immense satisfaction in opening up the Yukon River valley to the thousands that followed in his footsteps.

*See* Alaska

Frank Norris, "North to Alaska: An Overview of Immigrants to Alaska, 1867–1945," *Alaska Historical Commission Studies in History*, No. 121 (Anchorage, 1985).

FRANK NORRIS

## HARRIGAN AND HART

Actors, playwrights, producers. Edward (Ned) Harrigan (1845–1911) and Tony Hart (1855–91) were household names to immigrants in the closing decades of the nineteenth century and beyond. Harrigan was born on the Lower East Side of New York and began his stage career in California but returned to New York where he formed a partnership with Hart, which lasted for fourteen years. They humorously depicted multiethnic immigrant life in New York with plays, sketches and burlesque. Harrigan was the more gifted writer, but Hart, a versatile actor with a superb touch of timing, was the ideal partner; and together they made New York laugh and sing. They delighted audiences with over three dozen original productions. Their most memorable hits were *The Mulligan Guards* (1873), *Cordelia's Aspirations* (1883) and *Dan's Tribulations* (1884).

Ely Jacques Kahn, *The Merry Partners, The Age and Stage of Harrigan and Hart* (New York, 1955).

JOAN GLAZIER

## HARRINGTON, DANIEL J. (1940–  )

Jesuit, biblical scholar, linguist, editor. He was born on July 19, 1940, in Arlington, MA. His father had emigrated from County Cork and his mother's parents hailed from Dublin and Cavan. In 1970 he received his doctorate in Near Eastern languages and literatures from Harvard University. The following year he was ordained a Jesuit priest, and continued his studies at the Hebrew University of Jerusalem and at the Ecole Biblique de Jerusalem. He then began his teaching career at the Weston Jesuit School of Theology where he is professor of New Testament studies. Over the years Daniel Harrington has earned an international reputation for his versatile scholarship, and he strives to link his learning to contemporary questions and problems. Since 1972 he has been editor of *New Testament Abstracts* and one of his recent books, *The Gospel of Matthew*, appears in the *Sacra Pagina* series which he also edits. A man of deep courtesy, he can discuss and elucidate the latest insights into the Aramaic Targums and The Dead Sea Scrolls with the same ease as he can talk about baseball and share his extraordinary knowledge of the history of the game. The author of over twenty books, his erudition has been acclaimed by Jewish and Protestant scholars alike.

Daniel J. Harrington, *A Manual of Palestinian Aramaic Texts* (Rome, 1978).
———, *Interpreting the New Testament* (Wilmington, Del., 1979).
———, *Interpreting the Old Testament* (Wilmington, Del., 1981).
———, *The Maccabean Revolt: Anatomy of a Biblical Revolution* (Wilmington, Del., 1988).
———, *Wisdom Texts from Qumran* (London, 1996).

MICHAEL GLAZIER

## HARRINGTON, EDWARD MICHAEL (1928–1989)

Socialist, writer, organizer, activist, and teacher; co-chair with Barbara Ehrenreich of the Democratic Socialists of America. By the time of his widely mourned death in 1989, Michael Harrington had written sixteen books and scores of articles, keeping the Socialist agenda alive in American politics and policies in the era after Norman Thomas. Harrington's most significant book, however, remained his first, *The Other America: Poverty in the United States* (Macmillan, 1962), written while he was still in his thirties. It won the George Polk Award and the Sidney Hillman Award. Its reception by the American public not only catapulted Harrington into the public eye and into the White House as a consultant, but also served as the basis for policies that improved the lives of millions of Americans living in poverty, especially the elderly.

Harrington's thesis contradicted the optimistic projections, made popular by writers such as John Kenneth Galbraith in *The Affluent Society,* that poverty was being eradicated in the postwar economic boom. Harrington argued that prosperity had not reached a quarter of Americans who remained poor even though many worked full-time; nor would their lot improve without the active intervention of government. Harrington sprinkled his social theory with clearly put policy prescriptions and compelling thumbnail portraits of real persons trapped in poverty. Like an American Charles Dickens, he described the reduced circumstances of workers in sweatshops, migrant camps, mining towns, and isolated farms, as well as those working for sub-minimal wages, workers held back by racism, and the elderly not covered by pensions and unsupported by family. These were the "other Americans" whose cause he championed.

The book caught the eye of Dwight MacDonald, whose lengthy, positive review of it in *The New Yorker* sparked a national discussion about hidden poverty, its causes and remedies, that reached the Oval Office. President John F. Kennedy was given a copy after he asked an aide whether there was anything to it. The president was convinced enough by the book to put the elimination of poverty high on his domestic priority list. When the president was killed in Dallas not long afterward, the mantle passed to Lyndon B. Johnson, who declared a War on Poverty.

Harrington, meanwhile, a well-educated, pacifist Socialist, impassioned about human rights, had gone to Paris where he married Stephanie Gervis. On returning to New York in 1964, he was stunned to be summoned to the White House to help President Johnson prepare the anti-poverty portion of his State of the Union address.

In later writings, Harrington analyzed what worked well (expanded Social Security, Aid to Families with Dependent Children, food stamps, housing and medical care programs) and went wrong with the War on Poverty (money siphoned off for the Vietnam War; later allocations too small to make a difference). His last work, *Socialism Past and Future* (Arcade, 1989) outlined what could yet usher in a new progressive society: an international scope, tax policies that redistribute wealth and increase growth, and control from below.

Asked how his brand of socialism differed from Eastern European and Soviet models, Harrington said in an interview: "Marx was a democrat with a small d. The Democratic Socialists envision a humane social order based on popular control of resources and production, economic planning, equitable distribution, feminism and racial equality."

The son of a patent lawyer father and teacher mother, Harrington (b. February 24, 1928) grew up during the Great Depression in what he considered to be a middle-class, Irish-Catholic ghetto. He was Jesuit-educated at College of the Holy Cross in Worcester, Massachusetts, briefly studied law at Yale, but left to earn an M.A. in English Literature at the University of Chicago (1948). During the Cold War years, he blundered on Bohemia in New York, where he joined Dorothy Day at the *Catholic Worker,* and in Paris, where he befriended Alexander Calder and a circle of other artists and intellectuals. In his autobiography, *The Long-Distance Runner* (1988), Harrington writes that he later distanced himself from the Catholic faith, but considered himself "an atheist fellow traveler of moderate Catholicism."

Most of his life Harrington was active in organizing and served on the executive board of the Socialist Party from 1960 to 1972. In 1973, Harrington founded the Democratic Socialist Organizing Committee, which merged a decade later with the New American Movement to become the Democratic Socialists of America. It remains the nation's largest Socialist organization.

A member of the editorial board of *Dissent* magazine, Harrington wrote widely on contemporary politics, including *The Next Left* (1987), *The Politics at God's Funeral* (1983), *The Next America* (1981), *Twilight of Capitalism* (1976), *Toward a Democratic Left* (1968), and *The Accidental Century* (1965).

Harrington died of cancer of the esophagus in 1989 at the age of sixty-one.

*Current Biography Yearbook,* 1988.
Arthur J. Moore, "Rembering Mike," *Christianity and Crisis,* 49 (September 11, 1989): 253–54.
*New York Times,* obituary (August 2, 1989).
Peter Steinfels, "A Man Who Made a Difference: Michael Harrington in Our History," *Commonweal,* 116 (September 8, 1989): 466–69.

KAREN SUE SMITH

## HAUGHERY, MARGARET GAFFNEY (1813–1882)

Immigrant philanthropist. Native of Carrigallen, County Leitrim, Ireland, daughter of William Gaffney and Margaret O'Rourke. Her parents and their three youngest children migrated to Baltimore in 1818. Margaret was orphaned in 1822, received no formal education, and married Charles Haughery in the Baltimore Cathedral in 1835. The couple moved to New Orleans the same year; a daughter Frances was born in 1836. Margaret's husband and daughter died shortly afterwards.

Margaret worked in a hotel laundry and then at Poydras [Orphan] Asylum. She moved in with the Sisters of Charity at the asylum. She borrowed money to purchase two cows to provide milk for the orphans and soon developed a thriving dairy business. She also began her daily visits to the markets to beg food for the orphans. In 1859, Margaret sold her dairy business and took over a failing bakery. The bakery also provided her with her own apartment, the first place of her own since 1836. She soon turned Margaret's Steam and Mechanical Bakery into a flourishing enterprise, always providing free bread to the orphanages and the Little Sisters of the Poor.

Margaret devoted her widowed life to assisting the orphans, the sick, and the poor. In 1836, she helped the Sisters of Charity move their program to St. Patrick Asylum and, in 1840, to a newly-built facility renamed the New Orleans Female Orphan Asylum in 1843. She helped raise funds to build St. Teresa of

Margaret Haughery

Avila Church (1849), St. Elizabeth's House of Industry (1855), and St. Vincent Infant Asylum (1858). She aided the yellow fever victims and helped the poor and homeless after the Civil War. She herself lived a simple life.

Margaret died in New Orleans on February 9, 1882, and was buried in St. Louis Cemetery #2. She bequeathed her estate to the city's Catholic, Protestant, and Jewish orphanages as well as the Little Sisters of the Poor. In 1884, a statue of Margaret was unveiled in front of New Orleans Female Orphan Asylum, the second statue of a woman erected in the United States.

M. Catherine Joseph Haughery, "A Candle Lighted: A Capsule Biography of Margaret Gaffney Haughery (1813–1882)," *Records of the American Catholic Historical Society of Philadelphia*, 64 (June 1953): 113–120.

Raymond J. Martinez, *The Immortal Margaret Haughery* (New Orleans, 1956).

Edward F. Murphy, *Angel of the Delta* (Garden City, N.Y., 1958).

Mary Lou Widmer, *Margaret, Friend of Orphans* (Gretna, Louisiana, 1996).

CHARLES E. NOLAN

## HAWAII

According to the 1990 United States census, at least 65,587 residents in Hawaii claimed at least one Irish ancestor. There is no way of knowing how many were descendants of the *kamaaina* (early residents). Therefore, a broad definition of Irish, meaning born in Ireland, whether Gaelic-Irish, Scotch-Irish or English-Irish is used here.

The Irish who came to Hawaii in the nineteenth century differ from other national groups in the fact that they came as individuals, not as contract laborers nor through family or geographical ties. Nor did the Irish come to Hawaii during the years of the famine. However, those who arrived later in the century from Boston or New York, Canada or Australia, were probably descendants of Famine immigrants.

It is the individual Irish men and women who made contributions to Hawaii. Vignettes of some of those Irish and their contributions are detailed here.

### EARLY IRISH ARRIVALS

The first Irish to arrive in what was known as the Sandwich Islands came with the English explorer Captain James Cook in 1778. The ship's roster listed seven Irishmen, including Thomas Quin, Patrick Whelan, Matt Daley and others with equally Irish names. There are no known descendants of these men. Of eleven foreigners living with King Kamehameha I in the 1790s, one is identified as Irish but not named.

The first Irish who had an impact on Hawaii were three Irish priests who had joined the French order of the Congregation of the Sacred Heart and arrived as missionaries in 1836. One of them, Father Arsenius Walsh who was a British subject, served for more than 30 years and built the first Catholic churches on the islands of Kauai and Hawaii. These early Catholic missionaries did not receive an enthusiastic welcome by the authorities because of the influence of American Protestant missionaries who had arrived in 1820.

Henry (or Harry) Purdy was known to have arrived in the islands by 1838. He took advantage of his British citizenship in 1843 to claim 640 acres of land through the British Commission. The land was later awarded to him by the Great Mahele. Purdy had two notable descendants, Ikua Purdy, a world champion cowboy, and Governor John Waihee.

Another Irishman who claimed land from the British Commission was Benjamin Thompson of Kauai, who claimed to have been given his land by King Kaumualii of Kauai for services rendered between 1819 and 1823.

### GAINING A FOOTHOLD

Alexander James Campbell and his wife, Mary Gehegan, were the first of two Scotch-Irish Campbells from Londonderry to arrive in Hawaii, about 1855. Campbell was a lawyer, but following a disagreement with a local judge, he decided to make his living as a tailor. Today's *kamaaian* Campbells are descended from him through his son.

The second and better known Campbell, also James, arrived in 1861. The land he purchased became the basis of the present-day Campbell Estate. He married Abigail Maipinepine, a Hawaiian. When he died in 1900, the estate was left to his daughters in equal shares. Today, his descendants are the families of Kawananakoa, Shingle, Beckley and MacFarlane.

George Galbraith arrived in Hawaii in 1849 from Belfast and became a rancher. He acquired 2,300 acres of land in Wahiawai on Oahu. He never married and when he died in 1904, he left his estate, primarily land, to relatives and friends in Hawaii and County Down. Specific sums were left to forty-nine persons and their heirs as annuities. The heirs to those forty-nine now number more than four hundred. In the year 2000, several million dollars will be distributed to hundreds of heirs throughout the world.

The McInerny name has meant the best in clothing in Hawaii for more than one hundred years. Michael McInerny, a ship's carpenter, arrived in Hawaii in 1857. In 1860 he married Mary Brady, who had come to the islands as a nanny. There is a strong suspicion that Mary was the driving force behind the clothing business that the family established. The McInerny Foundation still exists today.

Among the several Irish named Hughes who came to the islands, the one with a major impact was John A. Hughes from County Louth. He was brought to Hawaii from San Francisco by Benjamin Dillingham in 1889 to design and build railroad cars for Oahu Railway and Land Company. He was followed twenty years later by his brothers, Patrick and Gerald.

Other instances of families who came to Hawaii have been recorded. Christopher Lewers arrived in 1850 and was one of the founders of Lewers & Cooke. His cousin, Robert Lewers, arrived in 1856 and developed the company, which has been Hawaii's primary building supply business for more than one hundred years. At least three members of the McCorrison family were notable for developments on the island of Molokai. The Doctors Robert McKibben, father and son from Belfast, served Hawaii's residents, including the royal family, from 1856 until the end of the nineteenth century.

Many businessmen of Irish ancestry have been successful in Hawaii. One that stands above the rest, however, was Maurice Sullivan of County Clare. He came to Hawaii from New York as a soldier during World War II and stayed on to found Hawaii's first supermarket chain, Foodland.

Although the Irish in Hawaii were never recruited as plantation laborers, that does not mean the idea was not proposed. A letter to the editor of the *Hawaiian Gazette* in 1882 suggested that the Board of Immigration look into paying the passage for Irish peasants who were as "industrious as any other race on earth" and would probably be willing to work for $10 or $12 per month. Nothing ever came of this suggestion, perhaps because of the Protestant missionary opposition to Roman Catholics.

While most of the Irish mentioned are remembered for their economic and social contributions, Marcus Cummins Monsarrat had another role in Hawaii's history—the Royal Scandal. Monsarrat was an auctioneer and arrived in Hawaii about 1850. One evening in 1857 he was seen leaving the room of Princess Victoria Kamamalu, sister of King Kamehameha IV, at an improper hour. He was arrested for "inflicting a deep injury on the king and his family" and banished for life. The king later relented and allowed Monsarrat to return to his family, which included two sons who become well known as a surveyor and an attorney.

### POLITICAL INVOLVEMENT

Many Irishmen and, eventually, their sons married Hawaiian women. Therefore, some of today's prominent families, such as Chillingworth, Lucas, Gleason, Toomey, Bolster, Richardson, Cullen and Markham, are descendants of those early Irish-Hawaiian marriages.

One of these Irish-Hawaiian families was notable for actively supporting the monarchy after its overthrow. The sons of William Carey Lane of County Cork and his Hawaiian wife, John, Lot and Patrick, joined Robert Wilcox in 1895 in his attempt to restore Queen Liliukalani to her throne. The rebels were quickly caught and given long jail sentences, but were soon released. John Lane later became mayor of Honolulu and high sheriff of the territory.

Since annexation of the islands in 1898 by the United States as a territory, Hawaii has had three governors of Irish descent. Charles McCarthy was territorial governor from 1918–1921. His most notable achievement, however, came after he left office and supervised the reclamation of Waikiki.

President Dwight D. Eisenhower chose William F. Quinn as territorial governor in 1957. When Hawaii became a state, Quinn became the first elected state governor in 1959 and served until 1962. John A. Burns was Hawaii's last delegate to Congress (1957–1959) when Hawaii was admitted as a state. He organized the Democratic party in Hawaii and served as chairman of the County Democratic Committee from 1948–1952. In 1959 he was named Outstanding Catholic Layman. He was state governor from 1962–1974.

### IRISH CATHOLIC INFLUENCE

One group of Irish who arrived in Hawaii has seldom been recognized. In 1883 a group of Franciscan sisters from Syracuse, New York, under the leadership of Sister Marianne Kopp, arrived to care for lepers. Five of the six women in that group were Irish—Sister Renata Nash from County Limerick; Sister Ludovica Gibbons, County Donegal; Sister Rosalie McLaughlin, County Leitrim; and Sisters Bonaventure Caraher and Antonella Murphy, born in the United States of Irish parents. The sisters served for many years at the Kakaako Receiving Hospital, the first hospital on Maui, and at Kalaupapa, the isolated leper settlement.

The first two bishops of the Diocese of Honolulu, which was created in 1941 and includes all the islands of Hawaii, were Irish. Bishop James J. Sweeney (1941–1967) was a native of San Francisco. His association with Hawaii began when he was assigned to assist with the spiritual care of military troops on the islands during World War II. In 1946 Sweeney founded St. Stephen's Seminary in Kaneohe, Oahu, and convened the first and only synod of the diocese in 1957. He retired in 1966 due to illness and died in San Francisco in 1968.

Bishop John J. Scanlon (1967–1982) was Irish-born. A priest in San Francisco since 1930, he was appointed auxiliary bishop for Honolulu in 1954. During his bishopric, he brought in nine religious communities to serve schools, hospitals, and various ministries in the diocese. He was outspoken against abortion and a proponent for respect for life. He opened the Mary Jane Pearson Center for unwed mothers in 1976. He retired at the age of seventy-five and died January 31, 1997.

A. Gavan Daws, *The Shoal of Time, A History of the Hawaiian Islands* (Honolulu, 1974).

Michael Glazier and Thomas J. Shelley, eds., *The Encyclopedia of American Catholic History* (Collegeville, Minn., 1997).

Ralph S. Kuykendall, *The Hawaiian Kingdom, 1778–1893*, 3 vols. (Honolulu, 1937–1967).

Robert Schoofs, *Pioneers of the Faith, A History of the Catholic Mission in Hawaii* (Honolulu, 1978).

AGNES C. CONRAD

## HAYES, HELEN (1900–1993)

Actress. Helen Hayes was born in Washington, D.C. on October 10, 1900 to Francis van Arnum Brown, a pork and poultry salesman, and Catherine Estelle Hayes and was the couple's only child. Her maternal great aunt was the Irish-born singer, Catherine Hayes, who gained fame as the "Swan of Erin" during the Gold Rush in California. Her mother, who once unsuccessfully tried her luck at acting, initiated Helen into dramatics at the tender age of six, and the girl played a role in a Shakespearean play in a local Catholic school. Soon after, her mother took Helen to New York where she had roles in both an off-Broadway play and a short film.

After graduating from Sacred Heart Academy in Washington, she moved to New York at the age of 20, took her mother's surname, and made her debut on Broadway as a flapper in the play *Bab*. Though her performance received poor reviews, she

Helen Hayes

remained undeterred and worked on improving her voice as well as standing taller on the stage (she was five foot even). After meeting the playwright Charles McArthur, she fell in love, but she hesitated to wed as McArthur was already married. But they eventually married, and in 1930 she had her only child, Mary. In 1938 the couple adopted a son, James McArthur, who went on to fame as a television actor and is best remembered for his role in "Hawaii Five-O." In 1949 Mary tragically died of polio. Her death destroyed her father, and in later years Helen Hayes remarked that she helplessly watched her husband drink himself to death. He died in 1957.

Helen Hayes is remembered as an actress for both her skill and versatility, and her more famous plays on stage include *Mary of Scotland* (1933), *Victoria Regina* (1935), *The Glass Menagerie* (1948, 1951, 1961), and *Harvey* (1970). In film she appeared in *The Sin of Madelon Caludet* (1935) and *Airport* (1970) (for both of which she won Oscars), and in several Walt Disney films as well as some roles on television.

Helen Hayes devoted time to charitable causes and was awarded the Laetare Medal of the University of Notre Dame in 1972 for her contributions to Catholic culture in America. In 1979 she acted as a lector for the mass celebrated by Pope John Paul II in Yankee Stadium. In 1986 she was awarded the Presidential Medal of Freedom by President Ronald Reagan, the highest award given to a civilian. Her autobiography, *My Life in Three Acts* (1990) details the life of a woman who maintained a sense of dignity while making extraordinary achievements and experiencing intense sorrows. She died on St. Patrick's Day in Nyack in 1993.

*See* Theater, Irish in

Eric Pace, "Helen Hayes, Flower of the Stage, Dies at 92," *The New York Times* (March 18, 1993): 1.

ANTHONY D. ANDREASSI

## HAYES, PATRICK JOSEPH CARDINAL (1867–1938)

Born on the site of Saint Andrew's church rectory in Manhattan to Daniel and Mary (Gleason) Hayes, formerly of County Killarney, Hayes received his education at Christian Brothers' schools in New York City, Saint Joseph's Provincial Seminary in Troy, New York, and at Catholic University, where he received his S.T.L. in 1894. Ordained September 8, 1892, he began his priestly career in 1894 at Saint Gabriel's on East 37th Street, where John Murphy (later Cardinal) Farley first noticed his abilities. In 1903, Farley advanced Hayes to chancellor and the presidency of Cathedral College. Hayes was consecrated a bishop October 28, 1914, and from 1915 to 1917 was pastor of Saint Stephen's on East 29th Street. On November 24, 1917, the Vatican appointed Hayes Military Ordinary; he brought that office with him when he became archbishop of New York March 10, 1919, and his successors have held it since. Elevated to cardinal March 24, 1924, Hayes died September 4, 1938, and is buried in Saint Patrick's Cathedral prelates crypt.

Hayes was friendly with politicians such as Alfred E. Smith, another Irish-American New York Catholic born in poverty who worked his way up, but he avoided shows of political leadership. He also avoided using his pulpit to comment on politics; the one exception came in 1935 when he preached against Margaret Sanger's suggestion that poor people be urged to use birth control, arguing against the notion that children ought to be considered commodities one had if one could afford them. His most enduring reputation has been that of the "Cardinal of Charities," who organized New York's Catholic Charities.

Regarding his leadership in Irish issues, Hayes presided over a Memorial Mass for hunger striker Terence MacSwiney in 1920, appealed for Irish relief and gave $5,000 himself to the cause, and warned that the violence of the 1922 independence campaign would cost Ireland many American friends, but he did not make a point of public leadership. Hayes often spent the period from mid-January to mid-March in the Bahamas, of which the archbishop of New York was traditionally vicar, and thus was not always available for the Saint Patrick's Day parade.

John Bernard Kelly, *Cardinal Hayes: One of Ourselves* (New York and Toronto: Farrar and Rinehart, Inc., 1940).
James J. Walsh, *Our American Cardinals* (New York and London: D. Appleton and Company, 1926).

MARY ELIZABETH BROWN

## HEALEY, ARTHUR D. (1889–1948)

Congressman and judge. Arthur Daniel Healey was born in Somerville, MA, on December 29, 1889, and died in his native city on September 16, 1948. The son of Dennis and Mary (Ireland) Healey, he began his studies at Dartmouth College in 1910 and concluded them at Boston University with a law degree in 1913. In the following year, with his brother, Robert, he was practicing law in the firm of Healey & Healey. However, Arthur's legal career was interrupted by World War I, during which he rose to a second lieutenant in the Quartermaster Corps. Thereafter, Arthur served as the Chairman of the Democratic Party in Somerville until he was elected to the United States Congress in 1932.

Coming from a district, part of which was later represented by James Michael Curley, John Fitzgerald Kennedy, and Thomas P. O'Neill, Jr., Healey went to Washington and became a significant player in the legislation of the New Deal. His name became fixed to the Public Contracts Act of 1936, which established the minimum wage for manufacturing products purchased by the federal government. For a decade in Washington, Healey was a vigorous advocate of economic and social reform in favor of the worker and the farmer.

Appointed to the federal bench on August 3, 1942, by President Franklin D. Roosevelt, Healey returned to Boston where he spent the last years of his life as a trial judge. Survived by his wife, Tresla (Fisher) Healey, and their four children, among whom was Robert Fisher Healey (1924–87), later a Jesuit priest and professor, Judge Healey was buried in Oak Grove Cemetery, in Medford, MA. Judge Arhur D. Healey's native city dedicated an elementary school in his memory, on October 28, 1956.

Arthur D. Healey Papers, Special Collections, College of the Holy Cross (Worcester, MA).
United States Government, *Biographical Directory of the American Congress, 1774–1961* (Washington, 1961): 1033.

VINCENT A. LAPOMARDA, S.J.

## HEALY, JAMES AUGUSTINE (1830–1900)

First Black Catholic bishop. James Augustine Healy was born on a plantation not far from Macon, GA, on April 6, 1830, and died in Portland, ME, on August 5, 1900. His father, Michael Morris

Healy, an immigrant from County Roscommon in Ireland, took Mary Eliza Smith, a slave girl from Georgia, as his wife in 1829. Since that action deprived their children, James and his five brothers and four sisters, of an education in the South, their father sent the boys in 1837 to be educated by the Quakers, first to Flushing, on Long Island, NY, and then to Burlington, NJ.

Later, in his travels, Michael met Bishop John Bernard Fitzpatrick of Boston who persuaded the father to send his sons to the College of the Holy Cross in Worcester, MA. Here the younger boys, Patrick and Sherwood, could continue their grammar school education, and the older boys, James and Hugh, could finish their secondary education and go on to college. Enrolled at Holy Cross, the Healys were baptized into the Catholic faith on November 14, 1844, and James proved to be an exceptional student by graduating first in his class from Holy Cross in 1849.

### BLACK PRIEST

Since James was interested in the priesthood, he went to the Grand Seminary in Montreal to study under the Sulpicians before continuing his studies at St. Sulpice in Paris. Ordained a priest by Archbishop Marie Dominique Auguste Sibour of Paris in Notre Dame Cathedral on June 10, 1854, James returned to Boston where he engaged in priestly work among the Irish immigrants.

Some of the Irish were orphans at the House of the Angel Guardian and others the parishioners of St. John's in the North End. The Irish orphans loved Healy who organized them in a choir that won the hearts of their audience on St. Patrick's Day. And the Irish parishioners found in Father Healy a true friend of the poor as he devotedly and fearlessly ministered to them despite the cholera that plagued their area of the city.

Within a year of his ordination, Father Healy was making such an impression in Boston that Bishop Fitzpatrick chose him as his secretary, in 1854, and his chancellor, in 1857. Father Healy proved very effective in reorganizing the diocese and was very helpful in defusing the draft riots among the Irish during the Civil War. Then, Bishop John J. Williams, Bishop Fitzpatrick's successor, appointed Father Healy as the pastor of St. James Church in Boston's South End in 1866, a position which he held for almost ten years in a city where the Irish population was constantly increasing.

### BLACK BISHOP

On February 12, 1875, Pope Pius IX appointed Healy as the second Bishop of the Diocese of Portland, ME, a jurisdiction that included both Maine and New Hampshire until June of 1884. A frequent visitor to the Irish enclave at Damariscotta, ME, before his appointment, Healy was consecrated bishop, on June 2, 1875, in the Cathedral of the Immaculate Conception in Portland, ME, by Archbishop Williams who was assisted by Bishop Francis McNeirny of Albany, NY, and Bishop Patrick Thomas O'Reilly of Springfield, MA.

Bishop Healy contributed to the growth of the Catholic Church in Maine for a quarter of a century by extending Catholicism into the smaller towns and cities of his diocese. He was particularly mindful of the Irish, especially those on Munjoy Hill, not too far from his cathedral, and of the French Canadians. The latter, whose language he spoke, resided mainly outside of Portland and were spread throughout his vast diocese. Bishop Healy even helped to found St. Mary's College (1886–1926) in Van Buren, an Americanizing institution for the French Canadians.

While he helped to establish orphanages and schools and provided chaplains for children in public institutions, Bishop Healy's tenure was marked by an increase in convents (eighteen), missions (sixty-eight), parishes (sixty), and schools (eighteen). In these developments, he had his own administrative problems with Mother Mary Xavier Warde (1816-1884), foundress of the Sisters of Mercy in the United States, who provided the personnel for many of these institutions.

On the national scene, Bishop Healy was recognized as an exceptional speaker among the American bishops. Though some of his critics find that he remained silent on the issue of race, Albert S. Foley, his biographer, does not agree. Bishop Healy moved other bishops to eliminate discrimination in the churches just as he did for the three hundred Black Catholics within his own diocese. Not unmindful of his own shortcomings, "I pray," he said of those who would scrutinize his life, "that they will be kind in judging my numerous faults, mistakes and errors of judgment."

Twice within a period of five years, when he was confronted with the opposition of one of his priests, Jean François Ponsardin, who tried to turn an administrative problem into a personal one for his ordinary, Bishop Healy had offered the Vatican his resignation. It was not accepted and Healy was appointed an Assistant to the Papal Throne in 1900.

Despite racial prejudice, Bishop Healy was much loved by his flock as became evident in the outpouring of sympathy manifested following his sudden death. Bishop Healy's remains rest among his people in Calvary Cemetery in South Portland under a rather large Celtic Cross recalling his Irish origins. At the College of the Holy Cross in August of 1962, Healy Hall was dedicated in his memory and, in March of 1998, a state panel suggested that his portrait be among those honored in the State House in Augusta, ME.

Archives of the Archdiocese of Boston (MA); College of the Holy Cross, Worcester, MA; and Diocese of Portland (ME).

Albert S. Foley, *Bishop Healy: Beloved Outcaste* (New York, 1954).

Josephine Kelly, *Dark Shepherd* (Paterson, 1967).

William Leo Lucey, *The Catholic Church in Maine* (Francestown, NH, 1957).

James M. O'Toole, *Passing* (Notre Dame, 1996).

VINCENT A. LAPOMARDA, S.J.

## HEALY, MICHAEL MORRIS (1796–1850)

Irish immigrant, plantation owner. Born in Ireland on September 20, 1796, Healy emigrated to America in 1815 and settled in Jones County, Georgia, just outside the city of Macon. Successfully engaged in cotton farming, he eventually owned 1500 acres and 50 slaves. One of his slaves, Eliza Clark (1813–1850), became his common-law wife, in spite of the social taboos in the antebellum South which proscribed interracial marriage. Together they produced nine surviving children, most of whom built successful careers in spite of the disabilities imposed on Americans of mixed racial heritage; several of these found vocations as Catholic priests and nuns. These included: James Augustine (1830–1900), the second bishop of Portland, Maine (1875–1900); Hugh Clark (1832–1853), setting himself up in the hardware business in New York City when killed in a boating accident; Patrick Francis (1834–1910), the president of Georgetown University (1878–1883); Alexander Sherwood (1836–1875), rector of

Boston's Catholic Cathedral of the Holy Cross; Martha Ann (1838–1920), a housewife in suburban Boston; Michael Augustine (1839–1904), a captain in the U.S. Revenue Cutter Service, precursor to the Coast Guard; Amanda Josephine (1845–1879), a sister in the Religious Hospitallers of Saint Joseph, Montreal; Eliza Dunamore (1846–1919), a sister in the Congregation de Notre Dame, Montreal; and Eugene (1849–1914), a salesman.

*See* Healy, James Augustine; Healy, Patrick Francis

JAMES M. O'TOOLE

## HEALY, PATRICK FRANCIS (1834–1910)

Priest and university president. Patrick Francis Healy was born on February 27, 1834, near Macon, GA, and died at Georgetown in Washington, D.C., on January 10, 1910. His father, Michael Morris Healy, came to the United States from County Roscommon in Ireland not too long after the War of 1812. The father, who established himself in Georgia as a plantation owner, took as his wife a mulatto girl and they became the parents of four girls and six boys, among whom was Patrick. Originally enrolled in a Quaker school with his brothers, James and Hugh, in Flushing, NY, Patrick and his brothers, including Sherwood, were enrolled at the College of the Holy Cross in Worcester, MA, on August 14, 1844, where they were baptized in the Catholic faith three months later, on November 14.

After he had completed his studies at Holy Cross, Patrick entered the Society of Jesus on September 16, 1850. As a young Jesuit, he taught at St. Joseph's College in Philadelphia for a year (1852–53) before he was sent to Holy Cross where he taught for five more years (1853–58). Continuing his studies for the priesthood in Europe, first in Rome and then at Louvain, Patrick was ordained at Liége, on September 3, 1864, by Bishop Johann Theodor Laurent, former Vicar Apostolic of Luxembourg. When, on July 16 of the following year, he had successfully passed his graduate examination, Father Healy became the first American Black to hold a doctorate.

### PRESIDENT OF GEORGETOWN

Returning home, Patrick was sent to teach philosophy at Georgetown University (1866–68) where he became its Dean (1868–69), Vice President (1869–74) and President (1874–82). Father Healy's leadership as the first American Black to head a major American university was marked by such a transformation of Georgetown into a major university that his biographer regarded the Jesuit as Georgetown's second founder. During his tenure there, Father Healy Americanized Georgetown by constructing new buildings, restructuring its curriculum, expanding its library, and improving its alumni relations. At the same time, he did not abandon the European academic ideals which he had valued when he was at a university like Louvain.

### HIS LATER YEARS

Many of Father Healy's last years after Georgetown were associated with his brother, Bishop James Augustine Healy of Portland, ME. During these years, the Society of Jesus assigned Patrick to St. Joseph's Church in Providence, RI, (1891–94) and to St. Lawrence Church in New York City (1895–1906) so that he could be geographically closer to the bishop with whom he spent most of his time in ministry and travel. In 1881, for example, Patrick dedicated the cornerstone for the new St. Dominic's Church in Portland, ME, the center of the oldest Irish parish in that city. Thus, in such proximity, Patrick was in a position to return to Holy Cross on November 9, 1893, to celebrate the jubilee of his alma mater which he and his brother had honored by their distinguished careers.

### THE HEALY LEGACY

Today Patrick Healy's memory is perpetuated at Georgetown where he was interred in the Jesuit Cemetery and in the building named for him when he was still serving as President of Georgetown University. In addition to James, Patrick's brother Sherwood became a priest and seminary professor, Michael left his mark on history as a commander in what is now the Coast Guard, and two of his sisters, who had been educated by the Sisters of Notre Dame in Montreal, joined religious congregations in Canada.

Archives of the College of the Holy Cross (Worcester, MA), and Georgetown University (Washington, D.C.).

Robert Emmett Curran, *The Bicentennial History of Georgetown University,* 2 vols. (Washington, D.C., 1993–97).

Albert S. Foley, *God's Men of Color* (New York, 1955).

———, *Dream of an Outcast* (Tuscaloosa, 1989).

Thomas J. O'Donnell, "For Bread and Wine," *Woodstock Letters*, 80 (1951): 99–142.

VINCENT A. LAPOMARDA, S.J.

## HEFFERNAN, MICHAEL (1942–   )

Poet. Michael Heffernan was born and raised in Detroit where he attended Catholic schools. He received degrees from the University of Detroit (B.A.) and the University of Massachusetts (M.A. and Ph.D.). He has taught at Oakland University, Pittsburg State University, and is currently Professor of English at the University of Arkansas. He cites his parents as particular influences on his writing as they instilled in him a love for the spoken and written word in their urban Detroit home. Heffernan fell in love with poetry at age thirteen through an edition of Whitman's *Leaves of Grass,* which he found on one of his mother's bookshelves.

Heffernan's poetry has been published in many of America's most prestigious literary journals, and five collections of his work have appeared in book form. *Love's Answer* (1994) was awarded the Iowa Poetry Prize. X. J. Kennedy has said that Heffernan's work "has feeling, intelligence, and musical skill in all the right amounts, and [that] he writes always in a disarming personal voice." At the core of his poetry is a deep reverence for the everyday world which, perhaps as a result of his immersion in Catholicism as a child, is treated with sacramental importance. In this respect, his work is similar to Philip Levine's, another poet who emerged from a working-class area of Detroit. For the most part, Heffernan's chosen form is the lyric and he is equally dexterous with both the traditional, closed lyric and with the more open, free-flowing contemporary form. His ability to move easily across formal boundaries is exemplified in *Love's Answer.* In the opening poems, the collection's purpose is established formally before it gives way to a more informal voice which suits so well the poet's journey across a variety of physical, psychological, and historical landscapes. His most resonant themes are family, place, love, and the search for points of contact, not only with mothers, fathers, lovers, and landscapes, but also with other writers. Frequently, Heffernan strikes a tragic note, at once both elegiac and hopeful.

In his recent work, Ireland has become a central presence in Heffernan's work. In his remarkable Irish poems, he is engaged in many dialogues with place, particularly with rural Ireland to which he is particularly drawn, and with the writers and ordinary folk who have peopled the Irish landscape. In "The Land of Heart's Desire," he celebrates with Eriugena the complex spirit of Ireland: "This was the music light makes over Ireland,/as jackdaws toss themselves like chips of slate/over gray lake water under a smear of sky,/their cursive wingbeats writing nothing down." Throughout his career, Heffernan has succeeded in a powerful, moving, and eloquent way, in providing humanity's quiet multitudes with proud and living voices.

*See* Poetry, Irish-American

Michael Heffernan, *The Back Road to Arcadia* (Galway, Ireland, 1994).
———, *The Cry of Oliver Hardy* (Athens, Georgia, 1979).
———, *Love's Answer* (Iowa City, Iowa, 1994).
———, *The Man at Home* (Fayetteville, Arkansas, 1989).
———, *To The Wreakers of Havoc* (Athens, Georgia, 1984).

EAMONN WALL

## HENEY, MICHAEL (1864–1910)

Railroad builder. Michael J. Heney, the "Irish prince," was one of the north country's most legendary characters, a man of action who, during his relatively short life, was largely responsible for the construction of two major Alaskan railroads.

Heney was born in 1864 in Ontario, Canada, the son of an Irish immigrant farmer. Bored with school, he ran away from home at age 14 and began working for the Canadian Pacific Railroad. By 1885 he was a well-established contractor, and for the next dozen years he plied his craft in British Columbia and Washington state.

Alaska called him north in 1897, and the following March he joined the Klondike throng and visited Skagway. He hiked both the Chilkoot and White Pass trails and was soon convinced that a railroad could be built over White Pass, but he had no money to put his plan to work. Fate shined kindly upon him, however, when on April 21 he met a group of British financiers in a Skagway hotel and convinced them to construct the line he envisioned. By the end of May, hundreds of men were at work, preparing the right-of-way and laying rails for the newly christened White Pass and Yukon Route railroad. Heney was initially tapped to be labor contractor, but Chief Engineer E. C. Hawkins got so bogged down with other affairs that within a few months, Heney was effectively directing the construction effort as well.

Heney got along enormously well with the railroad construction crews, and under that arrangement rails were laid up the dizzying, dangerous Skagway River valley. Winter, with huge snowstorms and bone-numbing cold, slowed work, but Heney and his men soldiered on. By February 1899, rails had been laid 20 miles to White Pass summit, 2,900 feet above sea level; five months later, the line had been extended another 20 miles to the shores of Lake Bennett. A new era in transportation was born; no more would travelers have to brave the rigors of the White Pass or Chilkoot trails. During the next year, the White Pass and Yukon Route was extended another 70 miles to Whitehorse, on the Yukon River. When the line was completed, one and all hailed "Big Mike" Heney for having made it all possible.

Heney remained active in Alaskan affairs. In 1901, he hiked from Valdez to Eagle, but concluded that constructing a railroad along that route would be premature. But in 1905, friends convinced him to return to the area and help build a rail line to a huge proposed copper mine in the Copper River valley. Heney, alone among contractors, felt that a line up the river valley was feasible, and in 1908 construction began. The odds—financial, topographical, and logistical—were enormous, but Heney pushed on. By 1910, the 200-mile line from Cordova to Kennecott was well on its way to completion. Heney, however, began to suffer from the effects of an August 1909 shipwreck. His legendary energy began to ebb and on October 11, 1910, the 45-year-old Heney died of pulmonary tuberculosis. The line to Kennecott was completed the following March. His fame and admiration were such that soon afterward, Rex Beach wrote *The Iron Trail,* a best-seller that told, in fictional form, of his heroism and accomplishments.

*See* Alaska

Elizabeth A. Tower, *Big Mike Heney, Irish Prince of the Iron Rails* (Anchorage, Alaska, 1988).

FRANK NORRIS

## HENRY, JOHN (1746–1794)

Actor and successful theatrical manager. Born in Dublin, Ireland, Henry received his education in the liberal arts and arrived in the U.S. where he made his debut at the Southwark Theatre in Philadelphia, 1767. Henry quickly gained popularity owing to his good looks and his talent in such accomplished roles as Othello. Henry married an actress, Maria Storer, and worked to establish himself in theatrical creations such as his adaptation of the French play *The School for Soldiers,* or *The Deserter.* Henry eventually became partners with Lewis Hallam who had managed a small troupe in the U.S. The alliance of Henry and Hallam allowed the power and popularity of theatrical rule from New York to Annapolis. However, after management disputes, Henry resigned from the company and returned to England so as to solicit and reorganize his own group. With great misfortune, Henry eventually lost his primacy in this troupe to one of the actors he had hired while in England. Shortly after this loss, Henry suffered great duress and eventually died from consumption in October of 1794.

*See* Theater, Irish in

William Dunlap, *A History of the American Theatre* (1832).
W. B. Wood, *Personal Recollections of the Stage* (1855).
*Dictionary of American Biography,* 8.

JOY HARRELL

## HERBERT, VICTOR AUGUST (1859–1924)

Musician, composer. Born in Dublin, Herbert was a grandson of novelist, poet, and dramatist Samuel Lover. At age seven, Herbert's widowed mother accompanied her son to Germany, where he studied Latin and Greek and played piano, flute, piccolo, and cello. From 1876 to 1880 Herbert made his living playing cello in various orchestras. By 1881 he had become first cellist for the Court Orchestra in Stuttgart under Max Seyfritz, who encouraged the young musician to compose (Ewen, *American Composers*). Under Seyfritz's tutelage, Herbert completed *Suite for Cello and Orchestra* (1883). In 1885 Herbert joined the Neue Stuttgarter Musikschule, where he met opera singer Therese For-

Victor Herbert

ster, whom he married in 1886 in Vienna; thereafter the couple moved to New York to perform with the Metropolitan Opera. Herbert played in a variety of chamber groups in New York and Boston and, from 1898 to 1904, conducted the Pittsburgh Symphony (Greene). In 1904 he founded the Victor Herbert Orchestra.

Composing operettas gained Herbert preeminence in the music world. His first piece, *Prince Ananias* (1894), made its debut in Boston; and his first major success, *The Wizard of the Nile* (1895), played at the Casino Theatre in New York. Herbert is best known for *Babes in Toyland* (1903), *Mlle. Modiste* (1905), *The Red Mill* (1906), and *Naughty Marietta* (1910). He produced two full-length operas, *Natoma* (1911) and the failed *Madeleine* (1913); the former was alternately praised and criticized for its incorporation of authentic Native American music (Ewen, *American Composers*). Parody was a hallmark of many of Herbert's works, even when audiences remained oblivious to its intent, particularly in songs such as "Rock-A-Bye Baby" for *Babes in Toyland* and "Kiss Me Again" for *Mlle. Modiste.*

In 1913 Herbert filed suit in New York against a restaurant orchestra, which he believed should pay royalties for using his original score. In 1917 the U.S. Supreme Court ruled in Herbert's favor. As a result Herbert banded together a number of associates—composers, lyricists, and publishers—to form a consortium, later named the American Society of Composers, Authors, and Publishers (Ewen, *Popular American Composers*).

In 1902 Herbert became an American citizen; however, he retained a love of his homeland and was active in Irish societies, serving as president of the Friendly Sons of St. Patrick and the Sons of Irish Freedom (Malone). On Herbert's death in 1926, Judge Daniel Cohalan noted that the composer zealously advocated Irish freedom from England, even when it was a politically unpopular position to take (Callahan).

Jack Callahan, "The Great Victor Herbert," *Irish America* Magazine (March/April 1998).

David Ewen, ed., *American Composers: A Biographical Dictionary* (New York, 1982).

———, ed., *Popular American Composers: From Revolutionary Times to the Present* (New York, 1962).

David Mason Greene, *Greene's Biographical Encyclopedia of Composers* (New York, 1985).

Dumas Malone, ed., *Dictionary of American Biography,* Vol. III (New York, 1932).

JAMES P. LEONARD

## HERON, MATILDA AGNES (1830–1877)

Actress. Heron was born in County Londonderry, Ireland, to John and Marly Laughlin Heron in 1830. She left Ireland and was raised by her brother Alexander in Philadelphia. Heron attended school and became a student under the tutelage of actor Peter Richings and made her debut in 1851. Her experiences and talent eventually afforded her leading roles at the Bowery Theatre in New York. Heron then migrated to the West Coast where she arrived with next to nothing other than her budding talent. She made her second debut in San Francisco in 1853 and again gained local popularity. After her successes in California, she traveled to Paris where she viewed popular theatre and began work on translating French productions into English. She translated *La Dame aux Camelias* and took the leading role upon her return to the U.S. Audiences enjoyed her versatility that bore itself in an irresistible intense spontaneity in the role of Camille and later in her role in *Oliver Twist*. Heron's popularity was made by adherence to familiar roles which provided steadfast displays of her artistry. However, her popularity eventually faded and she found herself destitute after a life of monetary squandering. Heron barely managed in the latter years of her life by engaging in the theatrical instruction of interested pupils. Her most notable student was her own daughter, Helene Stoepel, who took the stage name of Bijou Heron. Heron died March 7, 1877, after having failed to recover from an operation.

William Winter, *Vagrant Memories* (1915).

Laurence Hutton, *Plays and Players* (1875).

*Dictionary of American Biography*, 8.

JOY HARRELL

## HICKEY, JAMES A. CARDINAL (1920–  )

Cardinal archbishop. The Hickey family's experience mirrored that of many twentieth-century Americans of Irish heritage. It could trace its Irish ancestors to the pre-famine immigration. Yet even as these long ties to the old country weakened, lingering isolation in a still largely non-Catholic environment bolstered the Irish-American's sense of community and loyalty to parish and Church.

Born in Canada where he was trained as a dentist, Dr. James P. Hickey, himself the son of Irish immigrants, emigrated to Midland, Michigan, in 1903 where he met and married Agnes Ryan, a third-generation American whose family was closely involved in the local Irish-American community. Hickey's successful practice and growing involvement in business affairs provided a secure home for his wife and two children, Marie and James Aloysius, who was born on October 11, 1920.

PRIEST

After training at St. Joseph's Seminary in Grand Rapids, Sacred Heart Seminary in Detroit, and Washington's Catholic University, Hickey was ordained a priest for the Diocese of Saginaw in June 1946. Two of the future cardinal's abiding interests emerged during the early years of his priesthood. His concern for the welfare of Hispanics, first expressed in Hickey's article on the plight of migrant farm workers in the Saginaw Valley written during seminary days, prompted Bishop William F. Murphy to assign the new priest to organize the diocese's first Hispanic apostolate. Unusual in those times, Hickey became conversant in Spanish so that he might better address the physical and spiritual concerns of this increasingly important element of the American Church.

Hickey was consecrated as auxiliary bishop of Saginaw in April 1967 and appointed as diocesan administrator. This also led to service as chairman of the National Conference of Catholic Bishops' Committee on Priestly Formation and as consultor to the Vatican's Congregation for Catholic Education. Finally in 1969, Hickey became rector of the North American College in Rome where he was responsible for training seminarians from all parts of the United States.

In 1975 Pope Paul VI named Hickey bishop of Cleveland, a community then strongly divided over school busing and the economic dislocation besetting many American industrial cities. Hickey's administrative skills—his use of urban vicars and a new office of Black Catholics, for example—along with his very public commitment to racial and ethnic harmony helped ameliorate tensions in the region. True to his concern for Hispanic Catholics, Hickey also inaugurated a sister-parish program between churches in Cleveland and El Salvador and sent workers to minister to the poor of that war-wracked nation. The death of two of those missionaries and the assassination of his friend Archbishop Oscar Romero (which occurred after his arrival in Washington) only deepened his commitment to justice in El Salvador. It would also mark the beginning of his appearances before congressional committees and at other public meetings where he reiterated the Church's demand that the United States increase humanitarian aid while diminishing its military assistance to Central America.

### In Washington

Experience gained in dealing with Cleveland's manifold social problems served Hickey well when he became the third archbishop of Washington in 1980. There, too, he was expected to assume a prominent role in national Catholic affairs. He increasingly came to serve as a spokesman for his fellow bishops, joining in the national debate on diverse social and political issues and providing the president and congress with the Church's views on abortion, civil rights, physician-assisted suicide, and the arms race, among others. His role in these debates was given more weight when Pope John Paul II raised him to the College of Cardinals in 1988.

His work with the leaders of the city's large Latino community and his sympathetic support for the needs of African-American Catholics set the tone for his administration of the multiethnic archdiocese. His pragmatic approach to poverty was reflected in his active sponsorship of the John Carroll Society's *pro bono* program that enlisted Washington's Catholic health care workers and attorneys on behalf of those needing assistance. In a similar manner, and against considerable local opposition, he brought in Mother Teresa's missionaries to minister to the city's growing AIDS population.

Hickey often makes reference to his Irish ancestry. Rather than serving to isolate him from the concerns of his diverse archdiocese, however, that heritage has led him to champion its causes with sympathetic and practical leadership.

MORRIS MacGREGOR

## HIGGINS, GEORGE G. (1916– )

Social action leader and scholar. AFL-CIO president Lane Kirkland once described Msgr. Higgins as "the labor movement's parish priest," but Higgins is more than a "labor priest." Higgins described his father, Charles, a postal clerk who poured over *America* and *Commonweal,* as a "blue-collar intellectual." The phrase describes Higgins himself—once described by church historian Msgr. John Tracy Ellis as "the best informed Catholic priest in the United States"—in a different way. With a doctorate from the Catholic University of America, he is far more educated than his father, but he never lost touch with working men and women.

George Higgins has been a human bridge connecting the Catholic Church and the labor movement, intellectuals and working people, and Catholics and Jews. Higgins' father's respect for the people and culture of Chicago's Jewish ghetto and Higgins' contact with Jews in the labor movement sparked his concern for Catholic-Jewish relations.

A Chicago native, Monsignor Higgins graduated from Saint Mary of the Lake Seminary in Mundelein, Ill. He came to Catholic University in Washington in 1940 and became a student of the church's social action leaders, including Msgr. John A. Ryan and Msgr. Francis Haas. Higgins praises the rich intellectual life in Washington that was a by-product of World War II; many priests who normally would have gone to graduate school in Europe congregated at CUA.

Higgins joined the social action department of the National Catholic Welfare Conference (later the National Conference of Catholic Bishops) in 1944 and remained on staff there until 1980. In the late 1970s, conference officials could not fit Higgins into a neat bureaucratic slot during a reorganization and tried to push him into retirement, but Catholic social action leaders, including many bishops, virtually rebelled, winning his reinstatement.

Higgins' most visible role was in guiding the bishops into a mediating role between California grape growers and Cesar Chavez's United Farm Workers Union. He has been a member of the United Auto Workers' Public Review Board for more than 30 years. Higgins described his role with typical modesty in a 1995 Interview with Catholic News Service: "I've been quite content to exercise what you might call a ministry of presence, of being helpful, of giving encouragement. If I can manage it I will never turn down an invitation to go to a labor meeting."

While Higgins is devoted to the church and the union movement, he freely criticizes both when they do not live up to their ideals. He has particularly criticized Catholic hospitals, schools, and other institutions when they treated workers and unions unfairly. He told CNS that criticizing Catholic institutions has "often been one of the least pleasant things that I've been involved in, because it sometimes leads to hard feelings. . . . But I'm quite willing to do it whenever I'm called upon to do it." In an October 1998 speech before the National Catholic Educational Association, he criticized Catholic schools for opposing efforts to unionize teachers.

Higgins was a major adviser to the U.S. bishops and the Vatican during Vatican II. He was a member of the Preparatory Commission on the Lay Apostolate and a consultant to the council. He attended all four sessions of Vatican II and was a leading figure in interpreting the council to the English-speaking world at the U.S. bishops' daily press briefings.

Higgins has received awards from the Catholic Press Association, the Washington Theological Union, and the American Labor History Museum. He received the David A. Morse Humanitarian Award, the highest honor bestowed by the Washington office of the International Labor Organization.

Gerald M. Costello, *Without Fear or Favor: George Higgins on the Record* (Mystic, Conn., 1984).
George G. Higgins, with William Bole, *Organized Labor and the Church: Reflections of a "Labor" Priest* (Mahwah, N.J., 1993).

JIM CASTELLI

## HIGGINS, GEORGE VINCENT (1939– )

Journalist, lawyer, novelist, instructor. Born in Brockton, Massachusetts, George Higgins has made a career of merging multiple talents. He worked as a journalist after completing his undergraduate degree at Boston College in 1961. He earned an M.A. from Stanford University in 1965, and went on to receive his J.D. from Boston College Law School (1967) and was admitted to the Massachusetts Bar the same year. From the late 1960s, Higgins worked for the Office of Attorney General and the U.S. District Court in Boston. He also taught as an adjunct university instructor and published regular newspaper columns. Beginning in 1972, he published at least one novel almost every year until 1995. (For a comprehensive list of works, see Chapman, p. 212.) Adding to that list are *Swan Boats at Four* (1995), *Sandra Nichols Found Dead* (1996), *A Change of Gravity* (1997), and *The Agent* (1998).

Intermingling careers fostered Higgins' literary talents. While working stints as both prosecutor and defense lawyer during the 1970s, Higgins published works focusing on organized crime, thugs, and the groups with which they interact in the court system: judges, lawyers, and politicians. In *The Friends of Eddie Coyle* (1972), *The Digger's Game* (1973), and *Cogan's Trade* (1974), Higgins documents "the obscure world of the criminal . . . which is realistically depicted as a pitiless jungle where self-preservation depends on constant vigilance, and everyone leads a twitching knife-edge existence" (ibid).

Rather than sketching a predictable, one-dimensional world where criminals and prosecutors take turns manipulating the justice system, Higgins' characters demonstrate that corruption—in various forms—infiltrates the DA's office, police precincts, and the courtroom. Consequently, notes one critic, Higgins' prose leaves readers "with the satisfaction of a puzzle naggingly left open in spite of all pieces being accounted for, the feel, almost, of real life and biography" (Tynan). Moreover, the "authentic" street dialogue Higgins employs relies on unclear pronoun references, repetition, and lengthy run-on sentences (ibid). The effect forces readers to stop and reread, struggling to make out who is telling the truth, concealing it, and then questioning why.

Higgins did not focus solely on criminal justice issues. His nonfiction *The Friends of Richard Nixon* appeared in 1975, followed by *Style versus Substance: Boston, Kevin White, and the Politics of Illusion* (1984), *The Progress of the Seasons: Forty Years of Baseball in Our Town* (1989), and *On Writing: Advice for Those Who Write to Publish (Or Would Like To)* (1990). Higgins contributed various works to anthologies such as the *Best American Short Stories* (1973) and *They Don't Dance Much* (1975), as well as

*Arizona Quarterly, Cimarron Review, Esquire, Atlantic Monthly, Playboy, GQ, New Republic,* and *Newsweek* (Chapman).

In the late 1960s and early 1970s, Higgins taught law enforcement courses at Northeastern University in Boston and at Boston College Law School and consulted for the National Institute of Law Enforcement and Criminal Justice. He has been a columnist for the *Boston Herald American* (1976 to 1979), the *Boston Globe* (1979 to 1985), and the *Wall Street Journal* (1984 to 1987). In the late 1980s he began teaching creative writing at Boston University. Higgins is a member of the Writers Guild of America. Throughout his career, the author has remained pragmatic: "I want to continue to deal with the real world, and the only way to do so is to butt up against it every so often no matter how soiled you get in the process" (Metzger).

*See* Catholicism, Irish-American

Jeff Chapman and Pamela Dear, eds., *Contemporary Authors: A Bio-Bibliographical Guide*, New Revision Series, Vol. 51 (Detroit, 1996).
Linda Metzger and Deborah Straub, eds., *Contemporary Authors: A Bio-Bibliographical Guide* (Detroit, 1986).
Daniel Tynan, ed., *Biographical Dictionary of Contemporary Catholic American Writing* (New York, 1989).

JAMES P. LEONARD

## HIGGINS, MARGUERITE (1920–1966)

Journalist and war correspondent. Higgins was born in Hong Kong to Lawrence Daniel Higgins (of Irish descent) and Marguerite de Godard. Higgins' early years were spent in California where she received her B.S. at the University of California. Higgins then moved to New York where she received her M.S. from the Columbia University School of Journalism in 1942. One of her first achievements was an interview with Madame Chiang Kai-shek in which Higgins demonstrated her exceptional journalistic abilities. Higgins was eventually transferred to the *Herald Tribune's* Paris office were she covered the capture of Munich and the American entry into Dachau and Buchenwald concentration camps. In 1947, Higgins became chief of the Berlin bureau and continued to display her excellence in reporting.

Marguerite Higgins

In 1950, Higgins became engaged in coverage of the United States Army in Korea where she petitioned General Douglas MacArthur to rescind an order which forbade female correspondents, a petition which he granted. In 1951, Higgins won the Pulitzer Prize for international reporting, especially for her candor and courage in front-line war coverage. Later the same year she published *War in Korea: The Report of a Woman Combat Correspondent,* for which she received further recognition. Higgins career was quite successful and brought her many rewards and honors. In 1958, she returned to the United States to serve as a correspondent for the *Herald Tribune* and remained there until accepting a lucrative position with the Long Island *Newsday.* Higgins continued to cover national issues and authored several books including *Our Vietnam Nightmare* (1965). She encountered misfortune when she contracted a rare tropical disease from the bite of a sandfly in her travels between Saigon and Karachi. Higgins died from ensuing complications on January 3, 1966.

*See* Journalism, Irish-American

Marguerite Higgins and Peter Lisagor, *Tales of Foreign Service* (1963).
"Girl War Correspondent," *Life* (October 2, 1950).
*Dictionary of American Biography,* supplement, 8.

JOY HARRELL

## HILL, WILLIAM (1741–1816)

Ironmaster, Revolutionary War officer, state senator. Born in Ireland in 1741, William Hill emigrated to Pennsylvania by 1762 and then traveled to South Carolina, where he and his partner, Isaac Hayne, secured several large land grants and produced iron on Allison's Creek. By 1799 Hill was advertising such products as farm tools, swivel guns, cannon and cannon balls, and kitchenware. Hill's enterprise, in fact, produced most of the cannon balls during the 1780 siege of Charleston. The British, however, burned down his plant, which drove Hill into the Revolutionary army where he became a lieutenant colonel. There he led militias through Williamson's Plantation, Rocky Mount, Hanging Rock, King's Mountain, Fishdam Ford and Blackstock's. After the Revolutionary War, Hill served several terms in the South Carolina state legislature, served as justice for the Camden district in 1783, and as member of the county court of York from 1785 to 1799. By 1787, Hill restruck his partnership with Hayne and together they rebuilt the Aetna furnace which became one of the most important in South Carolina at the time. Hill had six children with his wife, Jane McCall, and died near York, South Carolina, on December 1, 1816.

*See* Scots Irish

*The National Cyclopedia* (New York: J. T. White, 1898).

DANIEL J. KUNTZ

## HISTORIANS OF IRISH AMERICA

Although Irish people were a lively element of the population in colonial times and were actively involved in the War of Independence, no substantial treatment of their history in America was produced until much later. In their narratives of the American Revolution, David Ramsay, Alexander Graydon and others noted their extensive presence and participation. In his study of political conflict in the era of the War of 1812, *The Olive Branch,* Matthew Carey devoted a couple of pages to extolling the contributions of Irish people in the revolutionary period and after.

The first book-length history of the subject was provided by the irrepressible Thomas D'Arcy McGee, who produced his *History of the Irish Settlers in North America* in 1852. Based on a series of lectures and containing readily available information, the book took a most favorable view of the various activities of the natives of Ireland in America. He took the same approach in his *Catholic History of North America,* which appeared in 1855. In *Civilized America* (1859), Thomas Colley Gratton included a variety of incisive comments on the position of Irish people at the time.

For the next thirty years this history was only treated in articles and excerpts from speeches either appearing in Irish-American newspapers or in ranting nativist publications. Irish involvement in the Civil War produced memoirs and biographies of individuals but no general assessment of Irish participation in the conflict. A partial exception to this situation was provided by the Irish M.P. John Francis Maguire, whose *The Irish in America,* published in 1868, while supplying some background, concentrated on the contemporary social and economic status of Irish people in the United States.

In his work, *The American Irish and Their Influence on Irish Politics,* published in 1882, the English journalist Philip Bagenal gave a treatment to the Irish involvement in the American Revolution which would have warmed the heart of the most fervent Irish-American patriot. Controversy surrounding the Irish role in that struggle flared up in the pages of the *North American Review* in 1887 when an article by Duffield Osborne argued that the Irish played only a very marginal part in the conflict; Thomas F. Meehan provided a vigorous reposte. The same year Edward M. O'Condon published a short, laudatory survey of the Irish in this country.

The event that sparked considerable historical activity among some Irish-Americans was the appearance of Charles A. Hanna's history of the Scotch-Irish in 1902, which claimed that almost all the people who came from Ireland up to 1775 were Ulster Scots, who, because they originated in Scotland, were not Irish at all. The battle over the "Scotch-Irish" was on. The supporters of the Scotch-Irish thesis won the academic contest as they produced a series of books, written by at least semi-professional historians and published by university presses, which gained general acceptance from the academic community and writers of text books.

The advocates of a substantial purely Irish presence in the colonial and revolutionary eras were committed but amateur advocates. Among those writing booklet-length works were Frank Reynolds, Thomas Magennis, John C. Linehan, Martin Glynn, James Haltigan, T. H. Murray and Thomas H. Mahony. Their assumptions were identical: the Irish were wonderful and without them we would all be singing "Rule Brittania." Martin I. J. Griffin self-published two volumes of annotated documents on Catholics in the Revolution in 1907.

The American Irish Historical Society, formed in 1897, published an annual journal whose contributors were the same type of amateur historians; nary a critical word about the Irish appeared in any of its proceedings. Rising to be the society's historiographer was the remarkable Michael J. O'Brien, whose articles came to nearly monopolize the annual publication. Irish-born and a traveling accountant by occupation, O'Brien demonstrated great energy and commitment in assembling a vast array of data which indicted a wide range of Irish involvement in the Revolution. He pulled much of this information together in a book, *A Hidden Phase of American History: Ireland's Part in America's Struggle for Liberty.* Published in 1919 in the midst of the successful Irish struggle for self-government, the work was provocative, claiming that a third of the Patriot forces were Irish, and abusive towards established historians who had apparently deliberately overlooked the Irish contribution.

Although O'Brien's book was the result of considerable scholarship and included many reference notes, his exaggerated claims cut no ice with the academic historians. The denoucement of his work was provided by the eminent J. Franklin Jameson, President of the American Historical Society, who noted O'Brien's over-ambitious claims and was generally dismissive of the work. One small but significant accomplishment for those who argued that there were many more Irish in the country than noted by the first national census in 1790 was substantiated in 1931 when a committee of the American Historical Association found that this was the case.

For many more years O'Brien continued to produce a mass of articles and several books on the subject, but no academic historian examined the general subject for the next half century. The time of a broad recognition of ethnic diversity and involvement in the nation's history was yet to come. As well, for many years there was no serious work about the general subject of the Irish in this country. The many Catholic colleges and universities, generally products of Irish origination and support, did not produce any historians to address this specific subject.

Meanwhile the advocates of the "Scotch-Irish" agenda were strengthening their linkages with academe. There was Henry J. Ford's *The Scotch-Irish in America* in 1915, Wayland Dunaway's *The Scotch-Irish of Colonial Pennsylvania* in 1944 and James G. Leyburn's *The Scotch-Irish: A Social History* in 1962. Leyburn's book is interesting in that it compares the colonial Scotch-Irish with the Scots and the Germans, but never with their fellows from Ireland. A brief, balanced assessment of the controversy is provided by R. J. Dickson in his *Ulster Emigration to Colonial America, 1718–1775* (pp. 296–97).

A tentative step towards an assessment of the Irish in nineteenth-century America was provided in 1941 with the publication of Oscar Handlin's *Boston's Immigrants.* In a city overwhelmingly Irish and "Yankee," Handlin observed that the Irish had declined to follow the trend towards accommodation with those of English stock.

Having examined the history of German-Americans, Carl Wittke in 1956 produced the first academically respectable history of the Irish in America. Four years later Professor George Potter published his zestful, largely uncritical study of the Irish in the Civil War. The election of John Fitzgerald Kennedy to the Presidency in 1960 sparked public interest in the Irish-American phenomenon. A mass of books about the Kennedy clan and their Irish-American cohorts followed, probably the best of which was Doris Kearns Goodwin's *The Fitzgeralds and the Kennedys.*

The appearance in 1963 of William V. Shannon's *The American Irish* provided a balanced, broad and engaging view of many aspects of the Irish experience. In the same year in the book he co-authored with Nathan Glazer, *Beyond the Melting Pot,* Daniel P.

Moynihan presented a baleful picture of the Irish in New York City: having lost most of their political power, the Irish had failed to compensate for this by social and economic achievement. Moynihan's theory was obsolete within fifteen years.

The formation of two scholarly organizations gave a new footing to Irish studies in this country. The American Committee (later Conference) on Irish Studies (1962), organized by Lawrence McCaffrey, Emmet Larkin and Gilbert Cahill changed and elevated the course of Irish studies. The Irish American Cultural Institute (1966), led by Eoin McKiernan, with its valuable journal *Éire-Ireland,* made a significant contribution. Although both groups originally centered their attention on the literature and history of Ireland, increasing emphasis has been given to the Irish cultural contribution in America.

Studies of Irish America fanned out in all directions. Among the works produced in this period was a facinating study of the Irish in New Orleans by Earl Niehaus. Dennis Clark began publishing a series of books on the Irish in Philadlphia. Thomas Brown published his succinct and bracing *Irish-American Nationalism.* Fictional and literary treatments of the Irish-American experience were assembled and edited by Charles Fanning, Daniel Casey and Robert Rhodes. Several short surveys appeared. In 1966 James E. Johnson, in a book for young readers, Joseph P. O'Grady and John B. Duff published excellent brief studies of Irish-American history. In 1976 Lawrence McCaffrey's *The Irish Diaspora in America* was published and became the most used, respected text for college courses. McCaffrey's books, articles, lectures and his constant encouragement of students made him America's Dean of Irish Studies.

With the rise of ethnic studies in the 1970s came the introduction of Irish history and literature courses and programs in colleges and universities, rising to a total of five hundred such. Even the Catholic institutions joined the flow. This development greatly expanded the readership of works in the field. Historians in Ireland generated fresh scholarship. Commemorating the American bicentennial, David Noel Doyle and Owen Dudley Edwards edited a superb collection of articles in *America and Ireland, 1776–1976.* Of similar quality was the collection edited by P. J. Drudy, *The Irish in America.* In 1976 Arno Press began publication of a set of forty-two books, some reprints and others original works, on the Irish saga in America.

In the 1980s came a wealth of incisive studies. Andrew Greeley unfolded a series of sociological studies backed by an array of statistics about Irish-Americans. Marjorie Fallows contributed with a sociologically orientated study of the descendants of Biddy and Paddy. Their evidence indicated those of Irish Catholic stock had risen to second place in both education and incomes. These facts would take some getting used to in certain circles. In *Rainbow's End; Irish-Americans and the Dilemmas of Urban Machine Politics, 1840–1985,* Steven P. Erie forged a comprehensive study of the subject. Forrest McDonald and Grady McWhiney introduced their "Celtic South" theory, arguing that when the numbers of people from Ireland, Scotland, Wales and northern England are added up, the interior region of the South was shaped by the values and customs of these people. Hasia Diner gave evocative and revealing treatment to the story of Irish female domestic servants in *Erin's Daughters in America.* In *Being Had: Historians, Evidence and the Irish in North America,* Donald H. Akenson asserted that, in fact, most Irish in the U.S.A. and Canada were historically rural and Protestant.

It was David Noel Doyle of the National University of Ireland, Dublin whose dissection of census figures brought a new perspective to the position of nineteenth-century Irish-Americans in his robustly titled *Irish-Americans, Native Rights and National Empires*. Doyle also marched confidently onto treacherous ground, abandoned since the time of Michael J. O'Brien, in his *Ireland, Irishmen and Revolutionary America, 1760–1820,* in which he wove a mountain of data into a fist of analysis. Kerby Miller wrote a six-hundred page master work in his *Emigrants and Exiles* (1985) in which he argued, among other matters, that the Irish had a very minor part in the revolutionary upheaval and demonstrated a marked inability to compete in nineteenth-century Americana. In 1995 Noel Ignatiev recapitulated conclusions about the relationship between the Irish and Blacks in *How the Irish Became White*.

Jay P. Dolan set the study of American Catholicism on a new course with *The American Catholic Experience* (1985); and his well-researched work *The Immigrant Church: New York's Irish and German Catholics, 1815–1865* (1978) is a classic study.

To accompany this torrent of publications came supportive bibliographical works. The pioneer in this field was Seamus Metress who produced an invaluable trilogy of bibliographies from 1981 to 1998, the last of which was *The Irish in North America: A Regional Bibliography*. Patrick J. Blessing's *The Irish in America: A Guide to the Literature and Manuscript Collections* is invaluable. There is a wealth of information in Michael Funchion, editor, *Irish-American Voluntary Organizations*.

Donald H. Akenson, *Being Had: Historians, Evidence and the Irish in North America* (Ontario, 1985).

Patrick J. Blessing, *The Irish in America: A Guide to the Literature and the Manuscript Collections* (Washington, D.C., 1992).

David N. Doyle, *Irish-Americans, Native Rights and National Empires* (New York, 1976).

———, "The Regional Bibliography of Irish America, 1800–1930," *Irish Historical Studies*, xxiii, 91 (1983): 254–83.

Lawrence J. McCaffrey, *Textures of Irish America* (New York, 1992).

Forrest McDonald and Grady McWhiney, "The Celtic South," *History Today* (July 1980).

Seamus Metress, *The Irish in North America: A Regional Bibliography* (Ontario, 1998).

Kerby Miller, *Emigrants and Exiles: Ireland and the Irish Exodus to North America* (New York, 1985).

ARTHUR MITCHELL

## HOBAN, JAMES (1762–1831)

Architect of the White House. Born outside Callan, County Kilkenny, Hoban became a student of Thomas Ivory at the school of Dublin Society where he studied art and drawing. In 1780, he was awarded a premium for his drawings and was then employed by the Dublin buildings commission to work on various building projects, particularly the Royal Exchange which is now the City Hall. Hoban also served as an artist in the drawing and architecture of the bank of Glendower, Newcomen and Company and the Custom House built in 1781. Hoban established a popular reputation with those in the architecture business and prospered in his homeland of Ireland.

After having exhausted his opportunities in Ireland, Hoban emigrated to the United States in 1785. Hoban settled in Philadelphia first and then later moved to South Carolina where he was awarded recognition for his design of the state capital at Columbia in 1791. Hoban's design of the Columbia capital resembled the design of L'Enfant as it is portrayed in the Federal Hall in New York. In 1792, he also won a competition for a design of the president's house in Washington, which later became known as the White House. Hoban's reward comprised both five hundred dollars and a lot in the city.

Hoban gained notoriety for his work on the White House plans. When the White House was finished, it showed remarkable similarities to the Leinster House in Dublin. Hoban was then hired to further supervise the complete construction of the White House. When the cornerstone was laid at the White House by President Washington on September 13, 1793, Hoban assisted as a representative of the Federal Masonic Lodge.

Hoban's career continued to blossom. In 1793, he began the design and construction of the Great Hotel at Washington, with the construction of the Little Hotel following in 1795. Hoban also assisted as master architect of the Federal Masonic Lodge until it was occupied by Adams and Jefferson in 1800. In addition to these tasks, Hoban was made superintendent at the Capitol where he was very active until the appointment of Latrobe as surveyor of public buildings in 1803.

Hoban's achievements in the architect business made considerable strides in the expansion of the industry. Success treated Hoban with a favorable reputation for both his skill and his personal demeanor: he was known to be reserved, but tenacious in his insight and in the execution of his business. Overall, Hoban provided the Federal City with a stable locus of architectural and professional resources. When in 1814 the British destroyed the White House, Hoban was elected once again to draft and rebuild it. In addition to this project, Hoban also took on the commission to build the State and War Offices. Later in Jefferson's administration, Hoban's employment decreased, but by that time his land holdings provided him with a sufficient salary.

Hoban married Susannah Sewell in 1799 and had ten children. He died in Washington on December 8, 1831 and left an extensive estate and legacy both in his private life and in his architecture.

M. J. Griffin, "James Hoban, The Architect and Builder of the White House," *American Catholic History Researches* (January 1907).

"The Genesis of the White House," *Century Magazine* (February 1918).

*Dictionary of American Biography*, 9.

JOY HARRELL

## HOGAN, BEN (1912–1997)

Golfer. William Benjamin Hogan was born of Irish lineage in Dublin, Texas, on August 13, 1912, to Chester and Clara Hogan. His father committed suicide when Ben was nine, and three years later he started his golfing career as a caddie. At 17 he was playing professional golf; and he became one of the greatest golfers of all time, even though Sam Snead and Jack Nicklaus won more major tournaments.

Experts on the game agree that what distinguished Hogan was his concentration and determination to win. Jimmy Demaret noted: "What set Ben apart from everybody else in the game—the unbelievable will to win, the quiet determination, the intense concentration." A small compact man—he was 5'8"—he valued his game and his privacy, and made few close friends. Yet his

Ben Hogan

fellow professionals held him in exceptionally high regard and affection, and felt that he deserved every victory he won, and he won many—PGA Championship 1946, '48; British Open 1953; U.S. Open 1948, '50, '51, '53; The Masters 1951, '53.

*New York Times* (July 26, 1997).

JOAN GLAZIER

### HOGUN, JAMES (d. Jan. 4, 1781)

Revolutionary soldier. James Hogun emigrated from Ireland by 1751 and settled in Halifax County, N.C., where he became a member of the Halifax County Safety Committee in 1774. In the following year, he represented the Provincial Congress of April 4 and November 12, 1776, and became interested in military affairs. Hogun soon became first major of the Halifax militia, which he organized and reported on to the Provincial Council. The Council later appointed him 7th colonel of the North Carolina Continental Line. In the following July, Hogun's militia joined Washington's army in the battles of Brandywine and Germantown. By 1778, Congress had demanded four new regiments from North Carolina, and Hogun was assigned the duty of raising and organizing them. Commanding the first regiment himself, Hogun joined the Continental Army at White Plains in August 1778, and in the following year was transferred to fortification duties at West Point and Philadephia. In 1779, after being promoted to the rank of brigadier general, Hogun was ordered to lead a brigade to help defend Charleston, S.C., under General Lincoln. The city fell to the British, however, and Hogun's troops were incarcerated at Haddrell's Point as prisoners of war. As a brigadier general, Hogun was offered better treatment, but he refused it in order to share the same fate as his men. His health failed under the strain and Hogun died at Haddrell's Point on January 4, 1781, leaving behind a wife, Ruth Norfleet, and a child, Lemuel.

*See* American Revolution

S. A. Ashe, *Biographical History of North Carolina,* Vol. IV (1906): 196–202.

William L. Saunders, ed., *The Colonial Records of N.C.,* Vols. IX and X (Raleigh: P.M. Hale, 1886–1914).

William L. Saunders and Walter Clark, eds., *The State Records of N.C.,* Vols. XI–XXII (Raleigh: P.M. Hale, 1895–1907).

DANIEL J. KUNTZ

### HOLLAND, JOHN PHILIP (1840–1914)

Inventor, "father" of the modern submarine vessel. John Holland was born at Liscanor, County Clare, Ireland, on February 29, 1840, to John and Mary (Scanlon) Holland. As a youngster, Holland was educated with the Christian Brothers in Ennistymon, Ireland, and later at Limerick. When he was eighteen, Holland began teaching throughout Ireland for the next fifteen years. It was during this time that Holland became interested in underwater transport and read about the relative successes and failures of inventors like Bushnell, Bourne, and Fulton. They inspired Holland to pursue the problem further until by 1870 he had put together plans for an undersea boat. Without the financial means to construct it, however, Holland abandoned his plans until his arrival in the United States in 1873. Settling in Paterson, New Jersey, Holland taught at St. John's Parochial School until 1879. He took his plans to the Irish Fenian Society (the Irish Republican Brotherhood), which supported his idea and provided him with $23,000 for a submersible vessel that they hoped to use one day against England. Two years later, the *Fenian Ram* showed promise in its Hudson River test runs. Measuring more than thirty feet long and six feet wide, the submersible supported a crew of three and by 1883 had reached a depth of sixty feet where it remained for an hour. The main principles of submarine construction having been proven with the *Fenian Ram,* Holland began to work with Lieutenant L.G. Zalinski in 1886 to construct an improved submersible. This was constructed without Holland's direct supervision, however, and the result was a badly damaged hull in a launching accident. Holland continued to tinker with designs until he was befriended by Lieutenant W. W. Kimball, who, for twenty-five years advocated Holland's ideas in Washington. Holland offered plans to the Navy Department after 1888, and, by 1895, his Torpedo Boat Company won a contract from the United States Navy to build a submarine. With $150,000, Holland began construction on the *Plunger* at the Columbian Iron Works in Baltimore. But again, supervision of the project was taken from Holland and given to Admiral George W. Melville, whose traditional ideas and dismissal of Holland's principles produced an overpowered failure. With only $5,000 left in his private funds, therefore, Holland began to construct the *Holland* at the Crescent Shipyards in Elizabeth, N.J. More than fifty feet long and ten feet wide, this gasoline-engine powered vessel was launched in 1898 and succeeded in rigorous testing. The federal government purchased the submersible and ordered six more. Orders for his submarines quickly came from England, Japan, and Russia. Holland was later commissioned to design two submarines for the Japanese during the Russo-Japanese War and in 1910 was awarded the Mikado's Order of the Rising Sun for his efforts. Financial disputes between Holland and his backers remained with Holland for the rest of his life, but he was successful in privately developing a system of escape for sailors in damaged submarines in 1904. Married to Margaret Foley of Paterson, N.J., on January 17, 1887, Holland died on August 12, 1914, leaving four children.

*American Inventor* (October 1, 1900, March 1, 1902).
*Army and Navy Journal* (April 2, October 29, December 3, 1898).

Charles W. Domville-Fife, *Submarines and Sea Power* (London, 1919).

Edward Byrn, *The Progress of Invention in the Nineteenth Century* (New York: Russell & Russell, 1970).

*Newark Evening News* and *Newark Star* (August 13, 1914).

*Report of the Secretary of the Navy* (1895–1900).

*Ships' Data, U.S. Naval Vessels* (1929).

Simon Lake, *The Submarine in War and Peace* (1918).

DANIEL J. KUNTZ

## HOLY CROSS COLLEGE (Massachusetts)

Holy Cross College opened in November 1843 with twelve students and three Jesuit priests and three laymen as administrators and faculty. The College of the Holy Cross in Worcester, Massachusetts, has paralleled in its history the great wave of Irish immigration and settlement in southern New England and in the Northeast USA in general. Through roughly the first 125 years of its existence, the college followed the classical Jesuit liberal arts curriculum (languages, literary studies, poetry, rhetoric, mathematics, philosophy, and theology). Though in its early days (until 1914) it combined preparatory and college programs, and later sponsored a small master's program in chemistry (since discontinued), Holy Cross has been and remains primarily an undergraduate institution.

In the context of Irish-American history, it has been especially significant in preparing its graduates for careers in various "professions": clergy, law, military, education, business, and medicine. Given the great influence of Irish-Americans in southern New England Catholicism (Massachusetts, Connecticut, Rhode Island), it is not surprising that many of the most distinguished graduates of Holy Cross should be of Irish (at least in part) extraction.

Benedict J. Fenwick, a Jesuit until named bishop of Boston in 1825, founded the institution to be both a college and a seminary. From its earliest days many of the school's graduates became Roman Catholic priests, serving especially in central and western Massachusetts, and providing candidates for men's religious orders (especially the Society of Jesus). Two of the most prominent early graduates were Rev. Patrick F. Healy, S.J. (who became president of Georgetown University) and Bishop James A. Healy (of Portland, Maine)—brothers born of an Irish-American father and an African-American mother. Two recent bishops of Worcester, Bernard J. Flanagan (class of 1928) and Timothy J. Harrington (1941), were graduates of Holy Cross.

The first Irish Catholic governor of Massachusetts (later a senator) was David I. Walsh (1893). Rev. Joseph T. O'Callahan, S.J. (a professor at Holy Cross before World War II) was awarded the Congressional Medal of Honor in 1946 for his courage on the carrier U.S.S. *Franklin* and achieved the rank of commander in the navy. Joseph E. Murray (1940) received a Nobel Prize for physiology and medicine in 1990. The famous trial lawyer, Edward Bennett Williams (1941), served as chairman of the board of trustees in the 1980s. E. Michael Harrington (1947) opened the eyes of the world to "the other America." And Holy Cross awarded an honorary degree to Eamon de Valera as early as 1920.

In the late 1960s and early 1970s three events changed Holy Cross: The curriculum became elective rather than required; the college was separately incorporated and no longer directly controlled by the Society of Jesus; and women were admitted as students. Efforts at diversifying the faculty and student body have not deterred Irish-Americans from continuing to be the main ethnic group. Indeed, one national magazine described attending Holy Cross as going to a "family reunion" (though some current students complain that not enough attention is given to Irish culture).

Vincent A. Lapomarda, *The Jesuit Heritage in New England* (Worcester, 1977).

Walter J. Meagher and William J. Grattan, *The Spires of Fenwick* (New York, 1966).

DANIEL J. HARRINGTON, S.J.

## HORGAN, PAUL GEORGE (1903–1995)

Writer, historian, instructor. Born in Buffalo and educated in Albuquerque, Paul Horgan's professional career spanned almost seven decades. He produced more than a dozen novels; won awards for meticulously researched historical and biographical works; and published more than one hundred short stories and novellas, three books of poetry, as well as drama and essays. His 1954 historical work, *Great River*, and 1975 *Lamy of Santa Fe*, a biography, won Horgan two Pulitzer Prizes (Tynan); *The Fault of Angels* (1933) won the Harper Prize Novel Contest, and *The Saintmakers' Christmas Eve* (1955) won a Bancroft Prize. Horgan also taught and experimented with painting and illustration—some of which became cover art for his published texts.

Critics frequently label Horgan a regionalist writer because he focused primarily on the people and culture of the southwestern U.S., where he moved at the age of twelve. However, Horgan worked with myriad subjects, publishing nonfiction, such as *Conquistadors in North American History* (1963), *The Heroic Triad: Essays in the Social Energies of Three Southwestern Cultures* (1970), *Encounters with Stravinsky* (1972), and *Approaches to Writing* (1973) (Graham). Horgan expended great amounts of time in research, often spending years collecting information before writing. Preparing for *Great River*, the author traveled the 1,800-mile length of the Rio Grande three times and made dozens of shorter trips in the ten years preceding publication of the two-volume work. While preparing for his other Pulitzer Prize-winning work, *Lamy of Santa Fe*, which took almost twenty years, Horgan visited the Vatican archives, the University of Notre

Paul George Horgan

Dame, and Mexico to secure information on Bishop Jean Baptiste Lamy (Lesniak). The author did not require such preparation for his fiction, however. *Far From Cibola* (1938) took twelve days to complete and ranks as one of the author's favorite texts (Graham).

Beyond perfecting his talent for fastidious research and writing, Horgan also dabbled in the visual arts, producing sketches, illustrations, and watercolors. Admitting that combining text and image heightened the authenticity and descriptive power of his writing, Horgan noted that such efforts helped evoke the essence of his subject: "In works of history I must see the plans I write about" (Commire). Horgan frequently achieved that effect; one critic notes that the author's characters "disturb by their simple verisimilitude and what they tell us about ourselves" (Glazier). As an individual with spiritual conviction and faith, Horgan often wrote to expose human weakness, not for tragic effect but to reinforce the dignity of the human spirit, particularly via the Catholic faith (ibid).

In 1960, Horgan became a fellow at Wesleyan University in Connecticut. During his thirty-five-year tenure, he was adjunct professor of English, director of the Center for Advanced Studies, and permanent author in residence. Horgan also held a Guggenheim fellowship (1945), served in the U.S. Army, and was a member of the National Institute of Arts and Letters. He was created a Knight of St. Gregory in 1957 and served as president of the American Catholic Historical Association in 1960 (Lesniak). Honoraria include nineteen D.Litt. degrees conferred by universities across the U.S. Horgan's shorter works appear in multiple anthologies and in periodicals such as *Atlantic Monthly, Harper's, Vanity Fair, Saturday Evening Post, Southwest Review,* and *Good Housekeeping.*

*See* Fiction, Irish-American

Anne Commire, *Something about the Author,* Vol. 13 (Detroit, 1978).

Michael Glazier and Thomas Shelley, *The Encyclopedia of American Catholic History* (Collegeville, MN, 1997).

Judith Graham, *Current Biography Yearbook* (New York, 1995).

James Lesniak, *Contemporary Authors: A Bio-Bibliographical Guide* (Detroit, 1992).

Daniel Tynan, ed., *Biographical Dictionary of Contemporary Catholic American Writing* (New York, 1989).

JAMES P. LEONARD

## HOVENDEN, THOMAS (1840–1895)

Painter and etcher. Thomas Hovenden was born in the village of Dunmanway, Co. Cork, to an English Protestant father and an Irish mother who tragically died in the Great Famine of the 1840s, resulting in his placement in an orphanage. At fourteen he was apprenticed to George Tolerton, a carver and gilder who referred him to the Cork School of Design in 1858. He emigrated to New York in 1863 where he entered the school of the National Academy of Design, and was elected a member in 1882. With Hugh Bolton Jones he moved to Baltimore in 1868. He worked in history painting and genre painting in which he painted anonymous ordinary people doing ordinary things, paintings of literary themes, landscapes, and portraits. He was one of the rare artists of his time who could competently etch his own works.

In 1874 Hovenden went to France for six years, and in Paris he studied at the prestigious Ecole des Beaux-Arts under Alexandre Cabanel, and went to Pont-Aven in Brittany, returning to the U.S. in 1880. The period was crucial in bringing his work to the level of technical and conceptual sophistication. In Pont-Aven Hovenden, joined by two other Irish artists, Aloysius O'Kelly and Augustus Burke, was embraced by the circle of American painters under the paternal influence of Robert Wylie. In this tiny rural village Hovenden met Helen Corson whom he married in 1881.

A two-day journey from Paris, Pont-Aven embodied all the qualities admired by Hovenden: rurality, simplicity and communality. There he painted *The Hunter's Tale, The Poacher's Story* (1880), *The One Who Can Read* (1877), and *In Hoc Signo Vinces* (1880). The latter, based on the wars of the Vendée (1793–95), recalled the peasant uprisings against the revolutionary government in western France. The painting was exhibited at the Paris Salon in 1880 and, notwithstanding its allegiance with the forces of tradition, made his name. The Chouan (a Breton royalist insurgent), as Ann Terhune notes, "became a symbol of loyalty and faith, a noble victim, a natural man living close to the soil, and, by inference, a staunch and hardy survivor holding fast against the forces of industrialisation"—in other words, he embodies all the classic ingredients of a Hovenden painting. Hovenden returned to New York, showing the picture at the National Academy of Design to great acclaim, and particular note was made of his accomplished handling of the figures. He was elected a member of the Society of American Artists; he became a member of the New York Water Color Society, the New York Etching Club, the Philadelphia Society of Artists, and the National Academy of Design. In 1881 he and Helen Corson moved to Plymouth Meeting, Pennsylvania, where the Corsons were known as Quakers and abolitionists. The expectation that he would begin painting American national ideals took an unexpected turn when he chose African-American subject matter. This was consistent with his earlier interest in Breton peasantry, as both communities were deprived and marginalised, spoke in dialect and struggled to maintain their traditions against the prevailing forces of change. Hovenden was commissioned by Robbins Battell to paint the renowned abolitionist in *The Last Moments of John Brown,* now in the Metropolitan Museum of Art, New York. The painting resonates with Hovenden's own abolitionist conviction. His wife's family were also involved in the abolitionist movement and Hovenden's studio had once been used as a stop along the Underground Railroad. Hovenden extended his interest in African-American culture in other works which, to our eyes, are somewhat inaccurate in their characterisation—depicting African-Americans as happy with their lot in the face of all adversity. While these images may be perceived as patronising, he did have significant links with the Black artist Henry Ossawa Tanner, both of whom produced visually defining images which did challenge racial stereotypes. Similarly, *In the Hands of the Enemy* (1889) depicts a Union family caring for a wounded Confederate soldier after the battle of Gettysburg. The theme of Christian, fraternal reconciliation, transcending political or racial difference, is thus further developed in this painting for which Hovenden earned a record $5,500. His largest and last painting, *The Founders of a State* (1895), remained unfinished at his death. It shows the opening of the Southwest in response to the pressure from frontiersmen for occupation of former Indian territory, resulting in the occupation of the best Cherokee land by homesteaders.

Although well-known as a major artist in his own time, he was subsequently overshadowed by painters such as Thomas Eakins and Thomas Anshutz who also taught at the Pennsylvania Academy of Fine Arts where Hovenden taught from 1886–1888. In fact, Hovenden succeeded Eakins as Professor of Painting and Drawing. His brand of history/narrative/genre painting went largely out of critical favour; his reputation declined but revived with the major exhibition at the Woodmere Art Museum, Philadelphia, in 1995 which characterised Hovenden as the master of home, hearth and humanity.

The underlying concerns of his work embrace issues of identity and belonging, nostalgia and hope, patriotism and heritage. He set out to enshrine traditional values, maintaining the bonds of family and country as he struggled to visualise the tensions of a rapidly industrialized society. He sought to uphold traditional American values, and his work is imbued with a fervent sentimentalism which greatly appealed to the taste of his age. The quintessentially American *Breaking Home Ties* (1890) enshrined his ideas about hearth and home, where the perennial virtues of family loyalty in a sober, God-fearing environment appealed to a receptive audience. But his work began to receive a less rapturous reception as Impressionism increasingly became the norm. If the critics were less than enthusiastic, the public was still ecstatic. The picture was exhibited at the World's Columbian Exposition in Chicago in 1893 and it was considered the most popular of all the thousand paintings on view.

He died prematurely at Plymouth Meeting, Pennsylvania, killed by a locomotive at a railroad crossing.

Woodmere Art Museum, *Thomas Hovenden (1840–1895): American Painter of Hearth and Homeland* (Philadelphia, 1995).

NIAMH O'SULLIVAN

## HOWARD, MAUREEN (1930– )

Novelist. Maureen Howard is an innovative writer, a prominent and important voice in American literature, not to mention Irish-American writing. Born June 30, 1930, Howard was raised in an Irish Catholic family in the industrial city of Bridgeport, Connecticut. She is married and lives with her husband in Manhattan. Her only child, Loretta, also resides in New York City.

Howard's father was a county detective and her mother remained at home enhancing Maureen and her brother's cultural educations with a variety of activities including, for Maureen, lessons in elocution. Her mother wanted her children to gain an appreciation for the arts, which were a limited aspect of life in Bridgeport. Howard was educated at Smith College, as was her mother, and after graduation she worked in publishing and advertising before she began to write full time. She published her first book, *Not a Word About Nightingales,* in 1960 and six additional novels followed. The most recent among them is *A Lover's Almanac* (1998). Critically well received, Howard's novels *Grace Abounding* (1982), *Expensive Habits* (1986), and *Natural History* (1992) were all nominated for the Pen/Faulkner Award.

Though she is a consummate novelist and stylist, her nonfiction is also noteworthy. In 1977, she edited *Seven American Women Writers of the 20th Century* and her memoir, *Facts of Life* (1978) won her the National Book Critics Circle Award for general nonfiction. *Facts of Life* details her childhood and early adulthood in honest and unflinching prose. An essayist as well

Maureen Howard

as a fiction writer, Howard has contributed to a large number of publications including the *New Yorker,* the *New York Times* and the *Yale Review* and has been awarded fellowships by the Guggenheim Foundation and Radcliffe Institute. She also received the Academy Award from the American Academy of Arts and Letters.

Howard has not received due credit for her influence on the structure of the American novel. Her almost stream of consciousness narrative and seemingly effortless melding of history and fiction are deceptive as Howard pays close attention to her craft. Her second novel, *Bridgeport Bus* (1965), was especially groundbreaking for its time. Daring and inventive, the narrative shifts between the first and third person and details the story of a thirty-five year old Mary Agnes Keely, a virgin, who flees her constrained life with her mother in Bridgeport to discover herself in New York City. The tension between life with her mother in Bridgeport and the freedom Mary Agnes finds in New York City is powerful. Mary Agnes faces an essentially Catholic moral dilemma: does she return to her ailing mother or embrace the pleasures of her new life?

Howard has contributed to American literature for almost forty years. Along with Elizabeth Cullinan, she is a bridge between early Irish-American women novelists, Ellin Mackay Berlin, Mary Deasy and Mary Doyle Curran, and the contemporary works of Anna Quindlen, Mary Gordon and Alice McDermott. Her influence on Irish-American writing cannot be underestimated. In her forward to *Cabbage and Bones: An Anthology of Irish American Women's Fiction,* she writes, "I am an old party, the Irish kid with a mouth on her, from a mostly Irish parish where we combined the Puritan past with mockery of our cut-glass station. Like many women who are included in *Cabbage and Bones,* I have had to reach back to Ireland, to the strong pull of that legendary soil, rocky and generative."

In addition to her own writing, Howard is a generous and passionate teacher. She has taught for years at a number of colleges and universities including Princeton, Amherst and Yale. She is on the faculty of the writing program at Columbia University where she encourages developing writers to hone their craft. About her own work she says, "Why do I go on writing? Because

I enjoy it as my life, and in the hope that if I try again I will choose the right word or a tone, a gesture that will open the door of a closed room, connect to the world, give another small revelation."

*See* Fiction, Irish-American

*Dictionary of Literary Biography Yearbook,* "Maureen Howard," by David M. Taylor (1983).

Maureen Howard, "Before I Go I Have Something to Say," *New York Times Book Review* (April 25, 1982).

Caledonia Kearns, ed., with a Foreword by Maureen Howard, *Cabbage and Bones* (1997).

CALEDONIA KEARNS

## HUGHES, ANGELA (1806–1866)

Foundress. She was born in Annaloghan, County Tyrone, in 1806, the daughter of Patrick and Margaret McKenna Hughes and the younger sister of the future archbishop of New York, John Hughes. At the age of thirteen her family emigrated to the United States and settled in Chambersburg, Pennsylvania. She attended St. Joseph's Academy in nearby Emmitsburg, Maryland, from 1823 to 1825 and then joined the Sisters of Charity there, taking the name Sr. Mary Angela. After her profession in 1828 she was given assignments that ranged from St. Louis, Missouri, to New York City, mostly serving the needs of orphaned children. From 1833 to 1837 she served at Mullanphy Hospital in St. Louis, the first Catholic hospital in the United States, founded in 1828 by the Sisters of Charity.

Then in 1846 the Sisters of Charity in New York, unable to resolve a dispute with Bishop Hughes to everyone's satisfaction, split into two groups, twenty-nine sisters returning to Emmitsburg to the original foundation by Mother Elizabeth Seton. The remaining thirty-three sisters (including Angela Hughes) formed a new community, the Sisters of Charity of New York. In December 1846 at the first election of the New York community, Bishop Hughes forbade the selection of his sister as first mother general. In 1849 as assistant to the mother general, she was given the task of establishing St. Vincent's Hospital, the first Catholic hospital on the eastern seaboard.

In December 1855 she gave up her post as superior of the hospital upon her election as the third mother general of the community. During her time in office, she moved the site of the motherhouse to an estate on the Hudson River in the Riverdale section of the Bronx. After her second term as mother general ended in 1861, she again became superior of St. Vincent's Hospital until her death on September 5, 1866.

*See* Sisters of Charity; New York City

Marie de Lourdes Walsh, S.C., *The Sisters of Charity of New York, 1809–1959* (New York, 1960).

————, *With a Great Heart: The Story of St. Vincent's Hospital and Medical Center* (New York, 1965).

JAMES J. HALEY

## HUGHES, JOHN JOSEPH (1797–1864)

New York's first archbishop. Hughes was born June 24, 1797, in Annaloghan, County Tyrone, Ireland, to Patrick and Margaret Hughes, and emigrated to the United States in 1817. Receiving his priestly education at Mount Saint Mary's in Emmitsburg, Maryland, he was ordained for service in the Diocese of Philadelphia on October 15, 1826. On January 7, 1838, he was appointed coadjutor to the Bishop of New York. Upon the bishop's death on December 20, 1842, Hughes became bishop. When on July 19, 1850, the Diocese of New York was named an archdiocese, Hughes was made its first archbishop. He died in office in New York on January 3, 1864. In 1883, his remains were placed beneath Saint Patrick's Cathedral on Fifth Avenue, the cornerstone of which he had laid on August 15, 1858.

One of Hughes's memories of Ireland was how, when his sister Catherine died, the family had to conduct their religious service outside the cemetery walls because penal laws forbade Catholic worship at her graveside. Nor was the family economy, based in farming and linen weaving, secure. When John showed an interest in the priesthood, his parents were able to provide schooling. Then, in 1814, the crops failed and the Napoleonic War ended, which meant that linen weavers resumed international competition. His parents pulled John from school and apprenticed him to a gardener. Even that was not enough, and the family migrated when John was about 20.

Hughes found a new path to the priesthood. Securing a laborer's job at Mount Saint Mary in Emmitsburg, Maryland, where there was a seminary, he approached the rector, John Du Bois, to enter the seminary. When Du Bois, dubious about his scholarly background, refused him, Hughes enlisted the sympathies of Mother (later Saint) Elizabeth Ann Seton, whose Sisters of Charity had their motherhouse at Mount Saint Mary's. Seton prevailed upon Du Bois to offer Hughes a deal: a job as a gardener in exchange for remedial tutoring. By 1820, Du Bois had relented and Hughes was a regular student.

When Hughes became a Catholic priest, Protestant Americans had philosophic objections to Catholic teachings, and Americans interested in politics questioned its governance system and its acceptance of the separation of church and state. While migration added to the number of Catholics, it also reinforced the idea that Catholicism was a religion of foreigners and the poor, triply marginalized from the mainstream of U.S. life. It was Hughes's life work to bring Catholic migrants into that mainstream.

John Joseph Hughes

## A CATHOLIC IDENTITY

Hughes early emerged as a defender of his faith. In 1829–1830, he used a pseudonym to send to a virulently anti-Catholic newspaper a series of fake news reports on the Catholic invasion of Pennsylvania, then (July 3, 1830) revealed in a Catholic paper how he had hoodwinked the nativists. His first impressive appearance on the debating platform came January 29, 1836, against John C. Breckenridge, son of Thomas Jefferson's attorney general and graduate of Princeton. Nor did Hughes eschew politics. On October 29, 1841, he chaired a meeting at New York's Carroll Hall to select a slate of thirteen candidates committed to supporting Governor William Henry Seward's proposal to distribute tax monies to Catholic schools, and ten of the candidates (the ones who had also been nominated by the regular Democratic party) won their elections that November, leading to the creation of a truly public, and more secular, school system and a system of Catholic schools. When in 1844 anti-Catholicism turned riotous, Hughes called on New York Mayor Richard Morris and advised him to work closely with mayor-elect James Harper (who had won with a large nativist vote) to prevent violence in the city, apparently preventing civil unrest.

Hughes emphasized the development of Catholic institutions and religious communities. In 26 years as prelate, he opened 23 parishes on Manhattan alone, and more throughout the whole diocese. He welcomed religious communities into the diocese: the Jesuits and Ladies of the Sacred Heart in 1841, the Sisters of Mercy in 1846, and the Christian Brothers in 1853. In 1849, Hughes's sister Eileen, in religious life Mother Mary Angela of the Sisters of Charity, founded Saint Vincent's Hospital.

Among the institutions Hughes built up was the episcopacy. When in 1846, the Sisters of Charity informed him of their intention to follow a rule promulgated by their international headquarters in France, which prohibited their care of boys over a certain age, Hughes developed an alternative: a diocesan-based community of Sisters of Charity more directly under his control. Such exertions of episcopal authority could have ethnic overtones. In the late 1840s and 1850s, Hughes faced opposition from a corporation of church trustees at Saint Louis, Buffalo, who feared Hughes's management might undermine their parish's German nature.

## AN ETHNIC IDENTITY

Hughes seldom supported displays of Irish ethnic identity. He arrived in New York in the midst of a trustee controversy with ethnic overtones, in which the Irish laity of Saint Patrick's Cathedral opposed their bishop, John Du Bois (the same man Hughes encountered at Mount Saint Mary's), partly on ethnic grounds. In this conflict between religious authority and ethnic loyalty, Hughes sided firmly with the former. When other prelates suggested that Irish Catholics might better preserve their faith and advance their fortunes if they were placed in ethnic agricultural colonies on the frontier, Hughes refused to cooperate. He regarded the followers of Daniel O'Connell as well-meaning but held aloof from them, and he positively condemned violent efforts to free Ireland from England.

Hughes encouraged the adoption of an American identity, and he adopted that identity himself. During the Mexican-American War, he worked to provide Catholics in arms with priestly service. In 1847, he refused a request from the federal government that he serve as an unofficial representative to Mexico. However, when the Civil War broke out, he accepted another such request, and toured Paris, Rome, and Ireland on behalf of the Union cause. He last appeared in public July 17, 1863, belatedly calling for a halt to the New York City draft riots.

## ASSESSMENT

Hughes has come to symbolize a type of Catholic leader who energetically defended and protected the faithful. He has also come to symbolize the privileging of the episcopacy at the expense of other sources of Catholic leadership. His contribution to American Catholicism has been characterized as creating a Catholic ghetto that rejected much of the American surrounding, and also as accepting the American surrounding to the point of avoiding a Catholic critique of society. (Hughes was a person of his times insofar as slavery was concerned.) Although one may discuss theories of assimilation, Hughes pioneered the method that immigrants actually used, in which they developed parallel structures—their own ethnoreligious institutions—that promulgated many of the values of American society.

*See* New York City

Charles P. Connor, "Archbishop Hughes and the Question of Ireland, 1829–1862," *American Catholic Historical Society of Philadelphia Records and Studies* 45 (March–December 1984): 15–26.

Andrew M. Greeley, *The Catholic Experience* (Garden City, New York, 1969): 102–126.

John R. G. Hassard, *Life of the Most Reverend John Hughes, D.D., First Archbishop of New York* (New York, 1866).

Richard Shaw, *Dagger John: The Unquiet Life and Times of Archbishop John Hughes of New York* (New York, 1977).

MARY ELIZABETH BROWN

## HURLEY, PATRICK JAY (1883–1963)

Lawyer, diplomat. Hurley was born and raised in the Choctaw territory (later Oklahoma). After earning a law degree in Washington, D.C., in 1908, he returned to Oklahoma and established a successful law practice in Tulsa, gradually becoming influential in the state's Republican Party. Herbert Hoover rewarded his party service by appointing Hurley as Secretary of War in November 1929. After Hoover's defeat in 1932, he returned to his legal and business activities. His diplomatic career began in 1940, when Hurley served as private emissary for the Sinclair Oil Company and negotiated a settlement with Mexico for company property seized in 1938. In 1942, Franklin Roosevelt made Hurley a brigadier general and gave him a number of military and diplomatic assignments in the Pacific theater. Late that year, General Hurley made a good will tour of the Soviet Union and was present at the Teheran Conference in November, 1943. In 1944, Roosevelt made Hurley special envoy to China to reconcile differences between American General Joseph Stillwell and Nationalist leader Chiang Kai-shek, and also to create a settlement between Nationalist and Communist forces. Made ambassador to China in November 1944, Hurley worked over a year to reach a solution, but failed and resigned his post in frustration at the end of 1945. He spent his later years as an outspoken anti-Communist and critic of Truman's China policy, tarnishing some of the reputation he earned from his earlier diplomatic career. He died in Santa Fe, New Mexico, in 1963.

*Dictionary of American Biography*, Supplement 7: 376–77.

Russell D. Buhite, *Patrick J. Hurley and American Foreign Policy* (Ithaca, 1973).

Xiansheng Tian, "Patrick J. Hurley and Chinese-American Relations, 1944–1945" (Ph.D. diss., Oklahoma State University, 1995).

TOM DOWNEY

## HUSTON, ANJELICA (1951–   )

Actress. The daughter of John Huston (son of Walter Huston, well-known actor of Irish heritage) and Enrica Soma, Huston was born in Los Angeles, California; five months later her family moved to County Galway, Ireland. Huston spent an ideal childhood there at her father's mansion, St. Clerans, a Georgian 110-acre estate. Early on, she aspired to playing the role of Juliet in Franco Zeffirelli's *Romeo and Juliet* but her father insisted that his daughter take the lead in his film *A Walk with Love and Death*. Nevertheless, Huston grew in experience, grace, and stature. In 1973, she moved back to Los Angeles where she eventually met Jack Nicholson with whom she found an inspiring mutual attraction.

Huston's career is a testimony to her skill and vivid performances; some of her more memorable films include *Prizzi's Honor*, for which she won an Academy Award in 1986, *The Dead*, *Crimes and Misdemeanors*, *A Love Story*, *The Postman Always Rings Twice*, *A Rose for Emily*, *The Cowboy and the Ballerina*, *Tamara*, and *Captain Eo*. It was *Prizzi's Honor* which gave Huston a role that showcased her acting while allowing her to work with the two most significant men in her life, her father and Jack Nicholson.

Huston's father died in 1987 and she was deeply affected by the loss. Nevertheless, her career continues to prosper and she is known as a woman of grace, a towering beauty both delicate and strong.

*See* Cinema, Irish in; California

*New York Times*, C, p. 19 (June 27, 1985).
*People*, 24 (July, 1985): 51.
*Contemporary Theatre, Film and Television* (1987).
*Who's Who of American Women* (1989–1990).
*CAB* (1990).

JOY HARRELL

## HUSTON, JOHN (1906–1987)

Director and writer. Born into Irish ancestry as the son of famed actor Walter Huston and Rhea (Gore), Huston was raised in Nevada and Missouri during the years his father worked in engineering and various water and power plants. He attended various schools while young and his education became unstable when his father began acting again on the vaudeville circuit. Huston left high school during his second year and became a lightweight professional boxer. However, by the age of eighteen, he had ventured into theater and was acting in the lead role in Sherwood Anderson's *Triumph of the Egg* in Greenwich Village.

Huston became frustrated with acting and joined the Mexican cavalry where he remained for two years. After resigning, he began a series of jobs, eventually trying his hand at writing. He wrote several short stories and was encouraged by H.L. Menken, editor of the *American Mercury*, to continue his pursuits in this arena. Huston then took a job as a reporter for the old New York *Graphic* where his mother was also employed. His success as a writer continued and he was hired by Samuel Goldwyn as a writer at the Goldwyn studios; his first script was that of *A House Divided* in which his father had an acting role.

Soon after, Huston became frustrated with Hollywood and he moved to England and became a writer; he moved from there to Paris and studied art for two years. Eventually, he returned to New York and became an editor of the magazine *Mid-Week Pictorial* and also reimmersed himself in acting in the lead role for the WPA's Chicago presentation of *Abe Lincoln In Illinois*. In 1938, he returned to Hollywood and became a writer for Warner Brothers. There he worked on such projects as *The Amazing Dr. Clitterhouse, Juarez, Dr. Ehrlich's Magic Bullet, High Sierra* and *Sergeant York*. In 1939 he directed *A Passenger to Bali* and the Broadway play *In Time To Come*, the latter being a biography of Woodrow Wilson. In 1941, Warner Brothers assigned Huston to the picture *The Maltese Falcon* which became a high point in his career; his father appeared in this picture as well and joined his son's rising success. The family duo continued in movies such as *In This Our Life, Across the Pacific*, and *The Treasure of Sierra Madre*.

Huston enlisted in the U.S. Army and was given the task of filming World War II documentaries. He produced *Report From the Aleutians* and *Battle of San Pietro*, followed by a psychiatric documentary titled *Let There Be Light*. After he was discharged from the Army in 1945, Huston returned to New York and began work on Jean-Paul Sartre's play *No Exit*, followed then by the movie *Three Strangers*. In 1948, with the release of *The Treasure of Sierra Madre*, Huston's occupation as director was once again recognized and celebrated among the Hollywood crowd. Later the same year, he won the New York Film Critic's award for best director in his production of *The Treasure*. Similarly, in 1947–48 he was voted best director by *Film Daily*. In 1948, he went on to found Horizon Films and released the film *We Were Strangers* and later a screen version of *Quo Vadis*.

Huston was celebrated for his work in many fine productions, particularly *The Maltese Falcon* and *The Treasure of Sierra Madre*, both of which brought awards for his superb direction. He died in 1987.

*See* Cinema, Irish in; California

*American Mercury*, 23 (May 1931): 113–115.
*New York Herald Tribune*, II (January 1949): 5.
*International Motion Picture Almanac* (1947–1948).
*CAB* (1949).

JOY HARRELL

## HUSTON, WALTER (1884–1950)

Stage and screen actor. Huston was born in Toronto, Canada, to Robert Moore and Elizabeth (McGibbon) Houghston of Scots-Irish lineage. Huston's career began early in drama classes which drew his interest while he attended the Toronto College of Music. He acted in his first play at age eighteen and then decided to join a road company producing the melodrama *In Convict Stripes*. He soon met and married Rhea Gore, a newspaper woman, in 1905 and their only child was John Marcellus Huston. During this time, Huston abandoned his career on the stage and worked as an engineer.

His marriage did not last very long and he divorced in 1914 and then pursued the vaudeville circuit with his new wife, Bayonne Whipple. His career met with prosperity in 1924 when he was cast in a Broadway production of *Mr. Pitt* and eventually gained fame in his role as Ephraim Cabot in Eugene O'Neill's *Desire Under the Elms.* Huston continued acting in several plays and screen roles such as *The Commodore Marries, Gentleman of the Press, Lady Lies, The Virginian, Abraham Lincoln, Dodsworth* and *Rhodes.*

Huston divorced once again and married Ninetta Eugenia Sunderland in 1931 while performing *Othello* on Broadway which had mixed reviews; however, the next season he took the role of Peter Stuyvesant in *Knickerbocker Holiday,* a musical in which his fine voice was recognized. Huston continued to make appearances in films such as *All That Money Can Buy* (1941) and also starred in all of his son's films, such as *The Maltese Falcon* (1941) and *The Treasure of Sierra Madre* (1948), for which he won an Academy Award for best supporting actor.

Huston also participated in a very successful radio broadcast show. His most popular performances were with the Theatre Guild On The Air, *On Borrowed Time* (February 17, 1946) and *Our Town* (March 12, 1950). Also, he provided documentary narration during World War II while urging those involved in American theater to boycott the Germans and their products. He continued to act and perform in various films and enjoyed vacation time at his mountain home and cattle ranch. Huston died of a ruptured abdominal aneurysm in Beverly Hills, California, on the day following his sixty-sixth birthday.

Huston's legacy is a testament to his persistence, to his talent and natural drive for success. Many commentators have expressed tribute to his personal accomplishments in the acting industry. Primarily, he is remembered for his ruggedness, virility, and pioneering spirit which revealed the essence of America. His most successful roles were those of larger-than-life characters who were wearied but not worn, lonely figures searching for renewal and inspiration. Above all, Huston became a living symbol on stage and that reality lives on in those who remember and continue to enjoy his work.

*See* Cinema, Irish in; California

The Theatre Collection of the New York Public Library at the Lincoln Center.
Walter Huston, "In and Out of the Bag," *Stage* (March 17, 1937).
*Dictionary of American Biography,* supplement 4.

JOY HARRELL

## HYLAN, JOHN F. (1869–1936)

*See* New York City: Irish-American Mayors

## HYNES, JOHN B. (1897–1970)

*See* Boston, Twelve Irish-American Mayors of

I

## IDAHO

### "A Look to Green Pastures Elsewhere"

Irish immigrants and their later descendants were attracted to Idaho by the economic opportunities available in mining, on the railroads, supplying the needed labor and meeting the religious needs of those in the state. John O'Farrell of County Tyrone, Ireland, mined in California before settling in Boise City in 1863. He married another Irish native, Mary Anne Chapman, and built the "first log cabin" in Boise, where the first Catholic Mass was celebrated. John worked as a blacksmith and was one of the promoters of the New York canal which provided irrigation water for the valley between the Boise and Snake rivers. A north end neighborhood street, not far from their log cabin, bears his name (Rahder 68).

In 1862, Martin Cathart, who moved from California to Florence, Idaho, became a shoemaker in Centerville and later moved to Placerville where he had a shoe, boot and saddle business. John Cuddy, from Tipperary, Ireland, settled on Rush Creek in Washington County in 1869 where he built a two-story lumber and grist mill. "Cuddy's Flour" became an important source of food for mining camps in the Boise Basin. Robert Dempsey mined and later worked as an Indian interpreter at a trading post near Blackfoot in the southeastern part of the state. He eventually settled Dempsey, which later became Lava Hot Springs (Rahder 69).

The story continued in other parts of the state with other characters that played leading roles. John Kennedy settled in the north, near Lapwai, and John McMonigh ranched in central Idaho near Hailey, along with Ben Darrah who became one of the leading stockmen in the Shoshone-Gooding area. William Conrad Hawkes worked below Pocatello in the southeastern corner near Hawkins Basin. And Jean Heazbe, an Irish woman who donned men's work clothes, ranched near Delamar near Owyhee County in the southwestern portion of Idaho (Rahder 69).

In 1847, Ireland had a population in excess of 8 million, or 251 people per square mile. Abject poverty and the potato famine forced them to arduous canal digging, railroad building or jobs few others wanted. The discovery of gold in California coincided with a surplus of Irish labor in the great Eastern cities and by 1860 an Irish priest writing home would estimate that San Francisco was one-third Irish in population. Besides the opportunities of the gold strike, thousands of Irish provided railroad companies the labor needed to excavate routes, smooth grades and lay track. The Irish spread throughout the West following these opportunities as they played themselves out (Dwyer

224–225). "To some few it would bring wealth, and social esteem; to the majority it was only a means of livelihood, and the rapid and unpredictable fluctuations of the economy would in time prove disheartening to most of them. Without permanent roots in what was to them always more or less of an alien soil, they tended to look to greener pastures elsewhere—California, Montana, Colorado, wherever the new mining centers opened" (Dwyer 232).

The discovery of gold in the summer of 1862 attracted thousands that lived by the rhythm of the boom-bust cycle. They set up camp in Centerville, Idaho City, Pioneer, and Placerville which were part of the Mores, Grimes, and Granite creeks, a subset of the Boise River drainage. The word of a gold strike worked like a magnet and by 1863, perhaps as many as 25,000 had been attracted to the area. However, as the reality of available opportunity became apparent, most moved, leaving fewer than a few thousand in these towns (West 109).

Between 1863 and 1872 more than 1.7 million ounces of gold were produced in Boise county. The Irish were the single largest ethnic group to work in the extraction of this gold. Of the 885 Irish listed in the Idaho Territorial Census of 1870, 623 of them were engaged in mining or related mechanical trades. Idaho City became the central hub of the mining community rivaled only by Boise for population and influence in the state. Information from two counties in Idaho in 1870 provides a profile for the Irish at this time. Of 141 Irish, 75 of them were working in mines, with an average age of 37, and nearly all had lived elsewhere in America before coming to Idaho. The highest percentage of these were coming from California, Oregon, New York and Massachusetts, but foreign countries included Australia, New Zealand, and Canada. Irish men outnumbered Irish women 285–37 in 1870. Consequently, few women were working and not many of the men had families (West 110, Hart 1, Rahder 61).

While most were miners, there is evidence to suggest that the Irish had taken advantage of other opportunities. In a study of five mining towns dating back to the 1870s, one out of four were miners; however a quarter of all shoemakers, grocers, saloonkeepers, butchers, and livery operators as well as two of the towns' engineers were from Ireland. The communities these Irish lived in were overwhelmingly inhabited by male and transient populations. Perhaps as few as 10% of the 2,010 stayed there from 1870–1880 (West 112–118).

The disparity in property ownership would have caught one's eye, but perhaps even more glaring would be the ethnic mix that these mining camps contained. Foreign-born made up 68.1% of the total population of the camps in 1870. This percentage exceeded and in some cases doubled that in cities such as Brooklyn, Boston, Pittsburgh, Philadelphia, Baltimore and New Orleans. "Even in 1880, Placerville and Pioneer had proportionately more immigrants than the most polyglot precincts of Chicago, and the most ethnically diverse wards of cities like South Bend, Indiana, at the turn of the century" (West 111–118).

Language, custom, tradition and many other traits separated these immigrants from each other. However, one choice all held in common was the decision about staying. Significantly, between the years of 1869 and 1872, citizenship papers show that of sixty-four men in the Boise Basin choosing to become permanent residents, twenty-seven were from Ireland. However, this trend waned as less gold was removed from the mines. Between the years 1872 and 1880 only 250,000 ounces were unearthed and the number of permanent Irish residents also began to decline (Rahder 66).

A profile of early immigrants describes the lot of those few that did make it. John D. Carroll of Dublin left California for Idaho in 1860. In three weeks time, he amassed nearly 4,000 dollars, but that opportunity quickly ran its course and he later went back to California and Nevada in search of other strikes. Eventually, he returned to Idaho and was appointed city marshall in Bonners Ferry in northern Idaho. By 1865, Mike Leary became known as the "Placer King of Idaho." He accumulated claims totaling more than 1,000 acres by 1898. He extended his wealth by acquiring 55% of findings of the Chinese miners who were leasing his claims and Leary and his wife raised nine children at Granite Creek in Boise basin.

The 1880s shifted the focus of mining from gold to ore which brought the greatest number of Irish to the northern portion of the state. Shoshone County then replaced the Boise Basin as Idaho's principal mining region. Phil O'Rourke helped Noah Kellogg in discovering one of the largest silver mines in the nation. Described as an "irrepressible, irresponsible, happy-go-lucky Irishman," he helped Kellogg identify the heavy rock as rich samples of galena, a mixture of silver and lead. The two went back to the spot where Kellogg had found it and posted two mining claims on either side of the gulch. One was named Sullivan and the other Bunker Hill. They took more samples and returned to Murrayville on September 10, 1885 which initiated a stampede as word got out about the rich deposits (Rahder, 62–63).

As Irish worked the mines in this region, unions formed to support the workers and the Irish played many of the leading roles. The union membership of Burke, Idaho, was 130 in 1890 with the Irishmen Thomas Doyle and Hugh McGee serving as President and Vice-President. Richard Magnuson, remarked, "being an Irishman was a necessity for election in this union." While they remained active in unions and hoped to improve their new lives in America, many maintained support for the political struggle in Ireland (Hart 5, Rahder 64).

## "FROM IDAHO, GEM OF THE MOUNTAIN, TO ERIN GEM OF THE SEA"

The following poem appeared in the *Idaho World* of August 1865:

> "From Idaho, Gem of the Mountain,
> to Erin gem of the Sea.
> A fraternal greeting we send you
> on joining the famous F. B.
>
> To the Patriots, Statesmen and Soldiers,
> whose hearts beat dear Erin for thee,
> and who watch thy star rise in the horizon
> to proclaim thee great glorious and free;
>
> Lo our bretheren in the cause of old Ireland,
> wherever their footsteps may stray.
> God speed you, when the "green"
> to the breezes you'll throw.
> Men, money and prayers will assist you
> from the miners of Idaho.

The Fenian Brotherhood had an active membership in the Boise Basin mining camps in the 1860s and 1870s. Local lodges included the Emmet Circle at Pioneer city, named for Robert Emmet (1778–1803), an Irish patriot hanged for treason; the Sars-

field Circle at Centerville, named for Patrick Sarsfield (d. 1693), an Irish general; and the Idaho and Emerald Circles at Idaho City. The following ad appeared in the *Idaho World,* Idaho City's newspaper on January 20, 1870. "That all respectable citizens of Irish, American or European birth or lineage (apparently excluding Chinese), who are kindly disposed to the sacred cause which united us in heart and sentiment are respectfully invited to join our fraternity."

The brotherhood demonstrated their force. According to the July 7, 1866 *Idaho World,* "Pioneer City's circle paraded in Idaho City on the Fourth of July that year, led by the Emmet Life Guards wearing green uniforms and bearing rifles. The Guards marched to Buena Vista Bar later in the afternoon 'to test their skill at target shooting. Some very fine shots were made—the target being totally riddled.'" In the evening a grand Fenian Ball was hosted by the Guards.

Many Irish patriots found allies in America and her past. The experiences of the Revolutionary War, the War of 1812, and British support for the Confederacy created numerous sympathizers of the Irish cause. On a local note, as Idaho prepared for admission to the Union a year later, Boiseans paraded and listened to orators. July 4, 1889, the day the constitutional convention was called, J. W. Reid of Lewiston, Vice Chairman of the Convention, delivered what the *Statesman* described as "a beautiful and touching tribute to the Irish nation, its brave and patriotic people and its present oppressed condition. The remarks affected many, who are neither Irish nor of Irish descent almost to tears" (*Idaho Daily Statesman,* July 6, 1889). The Fourth of July parade featured "two citizens on foot, one bearing the star spangled banner and the other the green flag of Erin, adorned with a picture of the harp that once through Tara's halls, the soul of the music shed" (Hart 3, Rahder 66).

The years between 1865–1868 marked the greatest involvement of the Fenian movement in Idaho but after the uprising failed in 1867 in Ireland, the movement lost its momentum and mostly faded away. However, these organizations were often focused socially as they were politically and often continued in this manner. They continued to raise money, and sponsor social affairs and parades. Dances and balls took place in Pioneer City, Wallace, and were commonplace in communities throughout the Salmon River and Sawtooth Country in the early 1900s. Irish in Custer and in Boise regularly celebrated St. Patrick's Day and other Irish events (Rahder 66).

Besides working as miners and other laborers, Irish outnumbered other ethnic groups in most western military posts. For example, they made up the largest ethnic block at Camp Howard in the 1870s. At the 1877 battle against the Nez Perce Indians in White Bird Canyon, Companies F and H were predominantly Irish, and a full third of the thirty-three fatalities were Irish. A few of these soldiers had earlier military service, chiefly in the American Civil War, but for most the military represented their best opportunity for steady work (Hart 6, McDermott 57–68).

### CULTURE AND CATHOLICISM

While there may have been some difference in employment, nearly all had a common connection to the Roman Catholic Church. As the Irish settled with the extension of the railroads and the opening of mines, the Catholic Church moved with them, which allowed the immigrants to maintain religious practices. In Boise City, "the new cabin [of the O'Farrells] was quickly converted into a chapel, and for many years served as such." When a

Catholic church was begun in January of 1870, Irish soldiers Hennessy and O'Keefe from Fort Boise were among the four volunteers who did carpentry. In order to meet the needs of the growing population of the eastern city of Pocatello, Catholic services were held there beginning in 1884 (Hart 8–9).

In northern Idaho, Father James Kelly arrived in 1902 and served the mining camps in that area. In March of 1903, he conducted the first Catholic Mass in Sandpoint, Idaho, and built St. Joseph's church in 1907. He served as pastor there until he retired in 1928. Many of Idaho's early hierarchy were of Irish descent. Daniel Gorman, Bishop of Boise from 1918 until 1927 was born in Iowa of Irish parents. His successor, Bishop Edward Joseph Kelly, was the son of pioneer Irish from Wasco County in Oregon. It appears that Catholic allegiance remained steady. Although there was a very heavy Mormon influence that settled in southern Idaho, few of the Irish converted to the Church of Latter Day Saints. "Of the many immigrants from the British Isles who became Mormons and settled in Utah and southeastern Idaho, the Irish were the fewest in number among them" (Hart 8–9, Rahder 72).

Mostly, the Irish lived among the residents of Idaho with little discrimination. A majority of the prejudice that did exist was targeted at Catholics in general and rarely aimed directly at the Irish. The revival of the Ku Klux Klan in the West between 1922–1925 led to cross burning near Catholic churches. "The Italians and Irish were targeted for special hostility because of their Catholicism." In some communities new chapters of the Knights of Columbus were formed as a defensive countermeasure (Gerlach 97–98, 116).

While Catholicism may have provoked prejudice against the Irish, their ability to speak English did provide a key advantage over many other immigrants. Their language ability allowed them to communicate easily and fit into the broader culture and some Irish even worked as entertainers. In Idaho, perhaps no performer was better known or appreciated than John Kelly, violinist and reader of sentimental ballads. He performed *My Mother's Grove* at Idaho City on January 7, 1865. "He could make his pet instrument tell a plaintive tale of home and mother or of tearful ones who waited, oft in vain, the return of father, brother or lover; again he would arouse the reckless instincts of his hearers by some rollicking time which told of wine and song. He could captivate the most difficult of audiences—and many of them were" (McConnell 140).

The performances continued in other venues. A company that played in Idaho City in May 1866 performed the comedies *Katty O'Shea* and *Wild Irish Girl,* and a farce called *The Irish Dragoon.* An amateur variety show in Boise in 1871 featured soldiers from the Fort. Murphy and Brobbin performed " a double Irish jig" and another sang Irish songs. Along with theater came Irish humor in the newspapers. The pages of Idaho newspapers often featured Irish jokes, usually employing phonetic spelling to recreate the sound of the spoken language (*Idaho Tri-Weekly Statesman,* January 5, 1871, *Idaho World,* May 19, 1866, Hart 10).

However at times, during the Prohibition Era for example, Irish cultural values clashed with American movements. For some, it presented a profitable opportunity. Anna, Margaret, and Mary O'Gara ran a rooming house and a couple of restaurants in St. Maries in northern Idaho. It was said that their biggest source of income was bootlegging whiskey. During one raid, Margaret, "brought her small whiskey keg into the kitchen and spread her voluminous skirts around it. There she stood adament while officers searched the quarters" (Rahder 69).

The Prohibition Era paralleled another movement in America, the desire to limit immigration. In 1900, there were 1,600 Irish-born residents in Idaho, 20% of them living in the northern Idaho mining towns. By 1910 there were almost 1,800 Irish which comprised over 6% of the total state foreign-born population. By 1920, the number had dropped to 1,400 and by 1930 there were just 616 Irish-born residents in the state. Clearly, immigration restrictions and fewer economic attractions reduced the number of people coming to Idaho (Rahder 68).

## Religious Emigrants and Later Generations

While this was true for large-scale Irish immigration, missionary priests were one exception to this overall decline in numbers. Young Irish men were flocking to seminaries in record numbers in the early years of the twentieth century, far more than the Church in Ireland itself needed. Special seminaries were organized especially for those who wished to take the risk and adventure involved of being mission priests. Idaho's Bishops Glorieaux and Gorman found in the Irish a source to meet the needs of the growing population. The largest number of Irish priests came during the 1940s, with over twenty-five arriving in just seven years. These men brought with them a level of education and dedication which, despite often parochial attitudes, allowed many to become highly respected members in the community. These priests pushed for education and established Catholic schools in many cities throughout the state which continue to function to the present day. Although small in number, this group of almost fifty men formed the most educated specific group of immigrants to Idaho and made considerable contributions to its development (Faucher interview).

Besides these missionary priests, the number of Irish immigrants continued to decline over the years. However, these individuals left many marks of their presence around the state. Some of these reminders are evident in geographical locations around the state. Irish immigrants named Irish Creek in Clearwater County, Irish Canyon in Lemhi County, Maloney Creek in Lewis County, and Kootenai County is dotted by O'Gara Bay, O'Rourke Bay and Killarney Lake. In addition to these identifiers and the contribution that the Irish have made in the development of the state remains the lineage of these pioneers. Although the numbers had declined by the 1920s, that same year, 3,387 people had at least one Irish-born parent (*Idaho World,* May 19, 1866, Hart 10).

This legacy has continued to today. These descendants of the Idaho-Irish and dozens of other Irish descendants that have moved to Idaho have continued to preserve their Irish heritage. Paralleling the ethnic revival in many American communities, the Irish in Idaho have formed the Irish-American Club and the Hibernia Institute to ensure that the Irish presence in Idaho remains (Delaney interview).

Cyprian Bradley and Edward J. Kelly, *History of the Diocese of Boise, 1863–1951* (Boise, 1953): 88–93.

Frederick S. Buchanan, "Imperial Zion: The British Occupation of Utah," *The Peoples of Utah.* Helen Z. Papinikolas, ed. (Salt Lake City, 1976).

Robert J. Dwyer, "The Irish in the Building of the Intermountain West," *Utah Historical Quarterly* ( July 1957): 224–230.

Larry R. Gerlach, *Blazing Crosses in Zion: The Ku Klux Klan in Utah* (Logan, 1982): 97, 98, 116.

William J. McConnell, *Early History of Idaho* (Caldwell, Idaho, 1913).

Robert McCrum, William McCrum, and Robert MacNeil, *The Story of the English* (New York, 1986).

John D. McDermott, *Forlorn Hope: The Battle of White Bird Canyon and the Beginning of the Nez Perce War* (Boise, 1978): 57–68.

Bobbi Rahder, "Idaho's Irish Americans," *Idaho's Ethnic Heritage: Historical Overviews* (60–79).

Elliott West, "Five Idaho Mining Towns, A Computer Profile," *Pacific Northwest Quarterly* (July 1982):108–120.

Interview with Reverend W. Thomas Faucher, April 15th, 1998, Boise, Idaho.

Interview with Ms. Carroll Delaney, April 19th, 1998, Boise, Idaho.

JOHN BIETER

# ILLINOIS

As a frontier state in the early nineteenth century, Illinois had no established privileged or entrenched ethnic or religious group. Settlers from a variety of backgrounds, particularly Yankee Protestants, southern Protestants, German Lutherans and Catholics, Swedish Lutherans, and Irish Catholics, came to the prairie state and competed for jobs, land, and resources, as well as political, religious, and social dominance. The pecking order they created was determined by resources and skills they arrived with as well as their values and attitudes towards others.

The Irish migrated to Illinois poor and without adequate farming or industrial skills to begin on an equal level with other groups. They began at the bottom of the economic order and fought their way up. Social and religious prejudice plagued them along the way. Their economic, political, and social success in Illinois depended upon which towns and rural communities they settled in and how many settled there in order to give them the power to influence community affairs to benefit themselves.

The Illinois territory was claimed by the French after Father Marquette's and Louis Joliet's historic exploration of the region in 1673. It was as officers in the French army that the first Irish set sight on its prairies, its forests, and its bluffs along the Mississippi River. These Irish soldiers were the Wild Geese of Ireland who fled to France after James II, backed by the French, was defeated at the Battle of the Boyne by William of Orange in 1692. They established a tradition for Irish men to fight for France. These Wild Geese served at every European battlefield for over a hundred years. For lack of alternative employment in Ireland, many Irish men also joined the British military. As France and Britain fought for an empire in eighteenth-century North America, the Irish would lend their hand.

One of the Wild Geese, Chevalier Charles MacCarthy, born in Ireland in 1706, served as an officer in the French army. In 1731 he was sent to Louisiana, and in 1751 he took command of Fort de Chartres on the Illinois banks of the Mississippi, approximately fifty miles south of St. Louis. From 1760 to 1763 when the Treaty of Paris was signed giving French North American territory to the British, MacCarthy acted as governor and commander of Illinois. In 1764 he was given posthumously the Cross of St. Louis for his services.

When the British assumed control of the territory between the Appalachian Mountains and the Mississippi River, the Indians of Illinois under the leadership of the Ottawa chief, Pontiac, resisted British occupation of French forts. In 1764 the Twenty-second British regiment, comprised mainly of Irish soldiers,

headed toward the Illinois territory through Indiana. They were attacked near the Wabash River by the Kickapoo and Mascoutens Indians. Many in the party were killed. Colonel George Croghan, a native of County Sligo, was chosen as negotiator for the British because of his diplomatic skills and his previous experience with local Indians during the wars with the French. He was instrumental in securing the territory for the British.

In 1773 Patrick Kennedy explored the Illinois River for copper mines. His journal was later published in 1797 in Gilbert Imlay's *Topographical Descriptions of the Western Territory*. Imlay was a captain in the American army and was commissioned by the U.S. government for laying out lands on the frontier.

During the American Revolution, the Irish figured prominently in the contest with the British over Illinois. Colonel George Rogers Clark led an army made up of mostly Irishmen recruited from the territory west of the Allegheny Mountains. This outfit has been described as being full of anti-English sentiment and glad to have the chance to strike a blow against an old oppressor.

The state of Virginia had laid claim to much of Illinois and ordered Clark to conquer the Northwest Territory. Virginia, however, did not provide money for Clark. Clark's unit appealed to Oliver Pollock, an Irish Catholic from New Orleans for funds. Pollock, an ardent supporter of American freedom, gave thousands of dollars of his own money to Clark's army. Pollock also enlisted the monetary aid of his friend, Count Alexander O'Reilly, the Irish governor of Cuba, for the Illinois campaign. O'Reilly obtained a seventy-thousand dollar loan from Spain, and gave orders that no one in Spanish territory west of the Mississippi give aid to the British.

After the Revolution many of Clark's men settled in Illinois, particularly Monroe, Randolph, and St. Clair counties which stretch along the Mississippi River between Fort de Chartres and St. Louis. The Irish comprised the majority of settlers. Perhaps having nothing to return home to, they found life among the earlier French Catholic settlers comfortable. Some Irish also settled in and around Cairo at the very southern tip of Illinois at the confluence of the Ohio and Mississippi rivers. Irish folksongs, such as "Willy Reilly," were popular at pioneer gatherings. At the northern end of the Illinois territory, Captain John Whistler, another son of Erin, was the first commander and builder of Fort Dearborn which was established at the mouth of the Chicago River in 1803.

The Irish were prominent in politics from the beginning of Illinois history. John Edgar, a Catholic and native of Ireland, joined the British navy which brought him to the Great Lakes region. When the American Revolution broke out, Edgar gave up his command of a British vessel to join the American cause. Edgar was so popular that when the government was organized for the Northwest Territory in 1798, Edgar was elected to represent Randolph County in the first legislature as well as a judge for the territory. He also was appointed Major General of the United States for the Illinois Militia. Edgar's wife was very involved in parish activities. Samuel O'Melvany, a native of Ireland, served as a member of the first Constitutional Convention of Illinois in 1818.

Many of the earliest school teachers and lawyers in the region were Irish. Most notably was James Shields. He left Ireland for America and then traveled to Illinois on foot. When he arrived at Fort Kaskaskia, fifteen miles south of Fort de Chartres, he secured a position as a school teacher. By 1832 he began practicing law, and launched a political career in the state legislature in

1836. From there his political fortune led him to Washington as a land commissioner. When the Mexican War broke out, President James Polk gave him a commission as colonel. He returned to Illinois to raise a regiment. He emerged from the war a general and hero. From 1849 to 1855 he served as a Democratic senator for Illinois.

Many of Illinois' earliest settlers migrated from the Upper South, particularly Kentucky, to southern Illinois in the early nineteenth century. While many of these were Protestants, Irish Catholics also made up a notable part of this migrant group. In these early years they lived as subsistence farmers. They took up residence in southeastern Illinois in Shawneetown near St. Patrick's Mission, as well as Waltonboro, New Haven, Piopolis, and Enfield. Itinerant priests from St. Vincent parish in Uniontown, Kentucky, fourteen miles to the east of Shawneetown, served their spiritual needs. Most notable was Father Elisha Durbin, referred to by Protestants as "Daddy Durbin," who arrived in the 1840s.

In 1843, the Chicago Diocese was created, which extended throughout the state until the Diocese of Alton was created to serve the southern half of Illinois. In 1847 Shawneetown welcomed its first resident priest, Reverend J. A. Drew, sent from the Chicago Diocese. Mass was celebrated in private homes until a log cabin church was erected in 1853 dedicated to St. Patrick. Worshippers often arrived the day before services and left the day after, thus creating an opportunity to bind the Catholic community together. A small frame church of St. Patrick's was constructed in 1860 to accommodate the fifty families of the parish. Many Protestants contributed financial support to its erection. This area remained an economic backwater until improvements were made in drainage and transportation for agricultural produce and access to markets. Later in the nineteenth century the coal fields southeast of Shawneetown were developed.

While Illinois has a number of navigable rivers that flow into the Mississippi River, most notably the Illinois River, they do not naturally connect with Lake Michigan. For the state to take advantage of its position between the Mississippi River and the Great Lakes and promote itself as the entrepot of the Midwest, it needed to establish connecting links between these major waterways. In 1827 Congress donated a ten-mile stretch of land for a canal to be built from Chicago to La Salle. Congressman Zadoc Casey of Jefferson County whose father was from County Tyrone, Ireland, played a key role in ushering the legislation for the Illinois and Michigan Canal through Congress. In 1829 the Illinois General Assembly appointed a Board of Canal Commissioners to select the route and plan out towns along the proposed route. By 1836 the financing was complete and the digging began. However, there were not enough local laborers to do the job.

Taking their cue from eastern canal builders who ran ads in Irish newspapers, Illinois canal entrepreneurs recruited Irish and other immigrants from Canada and the eastern states. Irish communities with makeshift shanties soon dotted the canal route. By 1838 an Irish Catholic contractor in La Salle asked the bishop of St. Louis to send a priest to serve two thousand Irish, German, and French Canadian Catholics there. Two priests arrived on March 29, 1838, greeted by a fife-and-drum corps playing the Irish tune "Garry Owen." Ottawa opened St. Columba's that year. The majority of the parishioners were Irish.

The Bank Panic of 1837 jeopardized the value of Illinois currency to the point that by 1842 the state treasurer only accepted payment in gold and silver. Funding for the canal evaporated. Canal contractors paid workers with Michigan bills or canal scrip which were not readily accepted by provisioners nor could they be cashed for full value. Therefore, workers suffered reduced to nonexistent wages. The state then offered canal workers the option of redeeming the scrip for state land. Many Irish contractors and workers established themselves as permanent residents along the canal route by this means.

Economic hard times pitted ethnic groups against each other. In the summer of 1838 violence broke out between Irish Catholic "Corkonians," who made up the majority of workers, and Protestant "Fardowners," whom the Irish resented because American contractors gave them special preferences in hiring. Irish Catholic gangs roamed the canal corridor from Chicago to La Salle beating up Protestants along the way. The sheriff of Ottawa arrested sixty men, but later released them since the town jail could not house so many prisoners.

By 1845 the canal project received new injections of loans and the digging resumed. In the meantime, however, many of the original laborers had settled into farming or other occupations or drifted elsewhere. New workers had to be recruited. Once again Irishmen responded. Irish "Pats" found the hours long, the wages low, conditions miserable, and foremen harsh. After an unsuccessful strike in 1847 some Irish left for farm work. More Irish were brought in from the East. By 1848 their job was finished. The canal made Chicago, rather than St. Louis, the economic focus of the state and the central Illinois prairie along these water routes was opened for settlement.

While the Illinois and Michigan Canal was being dug, the first railroad lines were planned to cross Illinois prairies to further facilitate access to markets for Illinois farmers. In 1835 the Illinois General Assembly granted twelve railroads charters, such as the Quincy to Springfield line, the Chicago Rock Island line, and the Galena and Chicago Union Railroad.

During the 1840s and 1850s the nation zealously pursued internal improvements. Illinois Senator Stephen Douglas conceived of a railroad project that would connect the state's existing lines and water routes and further the development of Illinois, as well as unite East and West and mitigate sectional differences between North and South. This ambitious plan resulted in the seven-hundred-mile Illinois Central from Galena and Chicago to Cairo, and ultimately to Louisiana and the Gulf of Mexico. Existing lines were tied into this railway system and bridges were built across the Mississippi to connect Illinois railroads with those leading to western states. Ground breaking ceremonies were held on December 23, 1851, both in Chicago and Cairo.

The same labor shortage which plagued canal construction affected railroad building. Therefore, advertisements went out to Irish newspapers and recruiters were dispatched to the Emerald Isle claiming ten thousand workers were needed at a dollar a day. German immigrants were also brought in. German immigrants came from the peasant class and were more attracted to the prospect of cheap land in the West. When they made enough money, they bought farm land. The Irish, on the other hand, needed the wages and were generally less interested in farming. When one section was completed, the Irish were willing to move on to the next.

Working conditions were harsh in the intense heat of summer and the bitter cold of winter. New and untested machinery was an occupational hazard. Illinois land was poorly drained and stagnant waters bred ague, a form of malarial fever. Cholera epidemics spread from immigrant ships along the paths immigrants traveled to Illinois. It killed hundreds as it quickly spread through the shantytowns along the canal and railroad lines where sanitation was poor and water supplies easily contaminated. A priest from La Salle deplored the fact that the "plague-stricken region was, with hardly an exception, Catholic."

Illinois natives and railroad employers developed an antipathy toward the contentious Irish. Poor camp conditions, wage disputes, bad food combined with whisky, and Irish-German competition often led to riots, bloodshed, and murder. There was a saying that "a murder a mile" marked the Illinois Central line. Contractors also lured workers away from each other, causing high labor turnover. New recruits were constantly in need.

Illinois Central recruiting agents sought in Ireland married men with families who they thought would be more sober and industrious and would eventually buy land from the company and settle the region. Many thousands of acres in Illinois were indeed purchased by the Irish. They settled in Will County, south of Chicago, and joined former Irish canal workers in La Salle. However, even though Germans were considered less physically suited to railroad work, they were considered steadier and more docile than the Irish and, therefore, a better long-term investment. While the Irish remained an important component in the Illinois Central labor pool, German workers gradually supplanted the Irish. In 1856 the Illinois Central was completed. By 1860 Illinois had more railroad mileage than any other state except Ohio. Chicago was the terminus for eleven major lines making it the railroad center of America.

In 1850 Illinois' Irish population was twenty-eight thousand. One third of these were in agriculture. By 1870 the Irish-born population of Illinois numbered 163,625. Of those 43,463 or 36.1 percent lived in rural counties. The majority of Irish in Illinois clearly preferred city life. However, the number who lived in rural areas increased over this twenty-year period. Historians, such as Lawrence J. McCaffrey, have argued that the Irish-American experience is an urban one. While these figures for Illinois do not refute the predominance of an urban Irish-American culture, they do create a more complex portrait of the Irish in America. Many of the same themes of industrial exploitation and strife, nativism, the importance of Catholicism in sustaining the community, and ultimately success and acceptance can be found in the small towns and rural communities of Illinois.

Although it was the promise of employment on the canal and railroads that brought the Irish to Illinois, the opportunity to purchase land along these routes lured many Irish to farming. Due to the ease of obtaining land, the majority of the farming population along the Illinois and Michigan Canal was Irish. Some Irish came to farming in Illinois through the efforts of William Scully who bought up land scrip from canal workers who went to fight in the Mexican War. Scully acquired two hundred thousand acres of land, most of which was in Illinois. He then sent recruiting agents to Ireland who brought over many Irish to settle on his lands. About this time Thomas D'Arcy McGee, a former Young Irelander and poet, wrote of the Irish prairie farmer in Illinois:

> 'Tis ten long years since Eileen bawn
> Adventured with her Irish boy
> Across the seas and settled on
> A prairie farm in Illinois
>
> Sweet waves the sea of Summer flowers
> Around our wayside cot so coy

> Where Eileen sings away the hours
> That light my task in Illinois
>
> Chorus—
> The Irish homes of Illinois
> The happy homes of Illinois
>    No landlord there
>    Can cause despair
> Nor blight our fields in Illinois

It has also been argued that if the Irish did initially take up farming, they quickly abandoned it due to poor farming skills and the loneliness of large-scale American farms. However, the Irish rural population between 1850 and 1870 increased in numbers and percentage from one-third to thirty-six percent. In his study of Irish farmers in the canal town of Lemont, southwest of Chicago, and the largely Irish town of Hartland in McHenry County on the northern border of Illinois, Paul Connors found that the Irish adapted successfully to farming life and compared well to more experienced Yankee and German farmers. The Irish saw farming as an opportunity for economic advancement. Their farms were larger than average and production was commercially oriented, compared to Germans who were more prone to see farming as a means to sustain a traditional lifestyle. "The frontier of Cook and McHenry counties," Connors states, "offered the Irish something very valuable that did not exist for many of them in the American urban ghetto—a chance to bury their past and seed their future."

The Irish farmers of Hartland stayed with farming longer than those in Lemont. Fifty-three percent of the original Irish farmers there in the 1850s were still farming in 1892. They loaned farm tools, seed, cows, and pigs to newly arrived Irish to make a successful transition to the Illinois frontier. The stability of the Irish there could in part be attributed to the higher quality of the soil, and also because Hartland was predominantly Irish compared to the more ethnically diverse Lemont. Lemont was also on the canal corridor and had greater proximity to industrial jobs. Improved farms could fetch a tidy profit. Hartland residents considered their town to be an "island" in a hostile Yankee sea. By the turn of the century, many Irish farmers in Hartland were able to send their sons to the University of Notre Dame. This further suggests that the Irish saw farming as an opportunity rather than a calling.

The Irish who did not turn to farming struggled to make their way in new industrial towns that sprang up near the canal and railroad lines. Ottawa on the Illinois and Michigan Canal became an important shipping and manufacturing center. Job opportunities attracted many immigrants. In 1850 the Irish were the largest ethnic group in the town with its foreign-born population numbering twenty percent of the total. By 1860 the foreign-born Irish were eighteen percent of Ottawa's population. Native Americans, however, dominated the economic life of Ottawa with sixty-eight percent in the professional and commercial class. Germans numbered thirteen percent of Ottawa's population, but dominated nearly a third of its manufacturing. The Irish, on the other hand, made up sixty-five percent of the laboring class and forty-two percent of unskilled workers. Only eight percent of proprietors were Irish. The richest man in Ottawa, however, was Irish.

Besides being economically stratified, ethnic groups in Ottawa worshipped and socialized separately. Yankees were aloof in their dealing with others, and did not consider these ethnic groups, especially the Irish, as equal partners in community building. The Ottawa Irish, however, refused to be marginalized. They staged an annual St. Patrick's Day parade to make their presence known, and in 1848 they sponsored a short-lived Irish newspaper, the *United Irishman,* which advocated the repeal of the Union of England and Ireland. The Irish also used their numbers to build political power to serve the interests of the economically disadvantaged.

Ottawa's schools became the main issue of contention between the Irish and the Yankees. In the early years of the town, native Americans sent their children to private schools. In 1855 Illinois law mandated local public schools. The Irish recognized the advantage of education for economic mobility and quickly moved to capture control of the school board. They battled Yankees who preferred to spend money on high schools rather than invest in the primary grades. In mid-nineteenth-century America, high schools were for the privileged elite. Since the Irish used and needed the grade schools more than the Yankees, they wanted money invested there and they succeeded.

Irish political power in Ottawa brought the familiar charges of corruption. In the 1856 presidential race the Republican candidate, John C. Frémont, lost by a slim margin in Ottawa to the Democrat James Buchanan. The local newspapers complained that there was illegal voting, and that the Democrats won because "unlike the masses of intelligent, industrious freemen" and "the Germans [in Ottawa who] did nobly vote for freedom, most of the Irish voters were not able to break loose from the party that has so long cajoled them." It claimed that Irish votes were bought by buying new equipment for the firehouse and promising the "Irish schoolmarm" employment in the schools. By 1859 Ottawa Republicans gave up hope of ever politically controlling the town.

Illinois' rich deposits of lead and coal invited industrialization. During their occupation of the region, the French had mined lead in Galena. Their main commercial interest, however, was the fur trade with the Indians. The commercial potential of lead was not developed until Illinois reached statehood. By 1823 Irishmen were digging in its lead mines, as well as working the wharves on the Mississippi. By 1828 there was a notable Irish community in Galena.

Illinois' rich and abundant coal deposits stretch from central to southern Illinois in the shape of a subterranean saucer. While inferior quality coal had been surface mined from the mid-nineteenth century for local use, to mine higher grade coal required deeper shafts, mechanized equipment to mine it, and capital to make it happen. By the late 1880s the industrial demand for coal in the United States encouraged investors to look beyond Pennsylvania and Kentucky to Illinois. By 1890 coal was mined in three areas of Illinois—Spring Valley and Coal City in the north-central region, St. Clair county south of St. Louis, and throughout southern Illinois in the region known as "Little Egypt." After 1890 mines were sunk in Macopin and Montgomery counties northeast of St. Louis.

In the early years of mine operations, English, Welch, Scots, and Irish labored in the mines. Many Irish came to work in these mines after building the railroads that led to them. Shawneetown's Irish Catholic population received a boost when mines opened there. After 1900 many miners were East Europeans.

The Irish were often the most active in mine union organizing. One of the most famous union organizers was Mother Jones, who founded the International Workers of the World, or Wobblies. Mary Harris was born in Ireland to poor peasant parents sometime between 1830 and 1835 in County Cork. She came to America in 1840 where she became a school teacher and married George Jones, who was active in unions in Memphis. In 1867 a yellow fever epidemic spread through the city, killing her husband and all of her children. Unable to bear her surroundings, she left Memphis for Chicago in 1868 and opened a dress shop which was later destroyed in the Great Chicago Fire of 1871. Rather than break her spirit, these tragedies encouraged her to turn her life's work to the suffering of others and the plight of the poor and exploited. She joined the Chicago Knights of Labor and from there extended her union organizing across the country, giving support to many union activities including those of the United Mine Workers (UMW) in Illinois Coal fields. When she died in 1930, she was buried at her request in Mt. Olive, Illinois, in a UMW cemetery, which was the only union-owned cemetery in the country.

Many Irish were attracted to the burgeoning steel industry, quarry mining, and stone cutting in Joliet. It was situated on the I & M Canal and Des Plaines River, and coal and limestone were close by and plentiful. In 1870 Joliet Iron and Steel Company, shortly thereafter renamed Joliet Steel Company, opened its mill for operation. It produced steel rails, barbed wire, and sheet metal, and other steel products. By 1872 the Associated Brotherhood of Iron and Steel Heaters was organized.

Stephen Freeman has argued that the early development of union organizing in Joliet steel mills was probably due to the common ethnic background of the workers. Most were first- and second-generation immigrants from England, Ireland, Wales, and Scotland. While one could argue that there were cultural differences and even animosities among this group, their common language and work situation reduced these differences. Union organizing in Joliet also received the support of other mining and industrial workers in nearby counties. In addition, the Irish, who were found at every skill level, were able to bridge the divide between skilled and unskilled work due to their common affiliation with the Ancient Order of Hibernians and the Irish Land League.

Joliet's business community also gave unions a boost by their shared Irish identity. Irish businessmen who had established themselves as blacksmiths, furniture dealers, dry goods merchants, and marble and stone manufacturers made common cause with union workers in supporting Irish Home Rule. Between 1879 and 1881 four mass meetings were held in which British landlords were vilified. Leading citizens gave speeches condemning the hereditary land system and committed themselves to oppose the "rich trying to crunch out the poor" anywhere. When steel workers went on strike, one thousand Joliet residents showed their support by holding a mass meeting. Catholic priests and union officials together made appeals to the crowd. Business and unions also worked together to eliminate the use of convict labor for commercial employment which was supplied by the Joliet State Penitentiary.

However, despite this early success, unions declined and were disbanded by 1885. They failed to gain control over the work process. Labor-saving machinery, diversification of production, and the introduction of East European workers made it increasingly difficult to devise a common strategy. Skilled and unskilled workers looked to protect their own interests. By this time, however, the Joliet Irish had access to other economic opportunities.

Not all the Irish who settled in Illinois towns were as successful economically or politically as powerful as those who settled in towns like Ottawa or Joliet. In the towns of Belleville, which is southeast of St. Louis, and Galesburg, between Peoria and Davenport, Iowa, the Irish were a marginalized minority, not part of a large and rising community like their counterparts in Joliet, Ottawa, and Chicago. Belleville was mostly settled by Germans. Galesburg was settled primarily by evangelizing Native Americans. The small Irish population was relegated to the bottom rung of the economic ladder in unskilled and laboring jobs. In Galesburg two-thirds of servants were Irish and Swedish. Their weak position in the town is evident by their not being able to have regular Catholic services until 1863, nearly thirty years after the town was founded. As a Republican stronghold, Galesburg residents did not view the Irish sympathetically. While they welcomed the Swedes, their newspapers printed disparaging comments of Irish railroad workers.

Yankee New England Protestants and immigrants competed for dominance in these frontier communities. Many native Americans were infused with the reforming zeal of the 1830s and 1840s which embraced the belief in the perfectibility of the human race. Sin did not have to be tolerated since it could be eliminated. Protestant clergy from various denominations, such as the Congregationalists, Presbyterians, Methodists, and some Baptists led the campaign for the perfect society. These Protestant denominations faced stiff resistance from Catholic immigrants.

For many Protestant missionaries their brand of Christianity was fused with American nationalism. Catholics could not be true Americans since they were followers of a religion that did not equip them for self-government or independent thinking. They also speculated that the pope was plotting to take over the country and destroy American freedom and government. They aimed to convert Catholics to Protestantism and Americanism. Protestant reformers in Illinois were horrified by what they considered un-Christian lifestyles in Irish settlements along the canal and railroad lines. Irish saloons did a thriving business on Sundays. One Protestant reformer in the heavily Catholic town of Lockport commented that the people were living without God and happy to remain so.

Catholic missionaries, on the other hand, were overwhelmed by ministering to the Catholic immigrant population and less interested in converting Protestants. Their goals were to keep Catholics loyal to Mother Church. The Irish who had faced Protestant hostility in Ireland turned a deaf ear to their moral crusades.

Unable to persuade immigrants to follow the righteous path, Protestant reformers aimed their efforts at Americanizing and Protestantizing Illinois residents through the common schools. In 1855 Illinois teachers agreed that the Protestant Bible be adopted as a textbook in public schools and that readings from scripture begin the school day. Irish and German Catholics resented this insult to their faith. In response Irish Catholics established their own newspaper, the *Western Tablet,* published out of Chicago. It became the voice of Catholicism in the state. The paper denounced public schools as heathen dens and oppressive to Catholics. Catholic communities throughout Illinois formed their own parochial schools rather than send their children to Protestant schools.

Irish immigrants in Illinois were resentful of reform efforts that tried to change not only their religion, but their social customs, particularly alcohol consumption. In 1855 reformers launched a statewide campaign to prohibit the manufacture and sale of alcoholic beverages in the state. Immigrants, particularly the Irish, were, in the Yankee Protestant mind, violent drunks. The only way to curb this behavior was to outlaw spirits.

The root, however, of Irish problems with drink and violence came from harsh working conditions and contractors reneging on promised wages. Irish canal workers had to contend with long periods without pay. Irish railroad workers in the 1850s often faced the same problems. The Irish were particularly irked when wages were withheld because many of them came to Illinois lured by the promise of high wages. In Dixon, Illinois, when an outraged Irish railroad laborer protested against wage cuts and delays in payment, a contractor put a gun to his head and told him he would blow his brains out if he continued to complain.

The most famous incident of Irish violence was in La Salle in 1853. The largely Irish crew of 450 laborers, who were recruited by the Illinois Central with the promise of $1.25 a day, were at work on a bridge over the Illinois River. In the midst of December their wages were cut to one dollar. Albert Story, the contractor, said anyone who was unwilling to accept this would be dismissed. On payday, December 15, a payroll error was discovered and wage distributions were stopped. Angry workers stormed the contractor's office. Story fired his gun and fatally shot one of the men. He fled home, but a mob caught him and beat him to death with their picks, shovels, and stones. Later the local sheriff and a posse arrested several Irishmen. Governor Joel A. Matteson later pardoned them because the evidence against them was weak. The governor also noted that Story had fired the first shot. The Yankee community of La Salle was outraged by the pardon, claiming he "bowed to Irish arrogance and outrage."

Throughout Illinois the incident was denounced as an Irish riot and Story was hailed as a man defending his property. Only the *Western Tablet* described the slain Irishman as a peaceable man and the father of two. The La Salle riot provided a shot in the arm to the temperance movement. Throughout Illinois "liquor riots" broke out as women smashed up saloons. Many cities and towns passed Sunday closing laws. Illinois immigrants and backcountry southerners in Little Egypt rose to resist it. On June 4, 1855 Illinois residents voted on the Maine Law which would prohibit the manufacture and sale of liquor. In the largest turnout in Illinois up to that time, voters rejected prohibition. While the temperance movement intended to control and Americanize immigrants, it instead politically united the German and Irish communities in the state in resistance to nativist campaigns.

Nativist hostility made the Irish of Illinois confirmed Democrats. The Democratic party welcomed immigrants and championed the common man. In Illinois, as elsewhere in the country, the Whig Party was the political arm of Yankee reformers. The hegemony of the Whigs was challenged in the 1850s by sectional strife and by the Know-Nothing Party which sought to exclude immigrants from American political life. The Whigs and Know-Nothings later merged with the new Republican party. When slavery came to dominate political discussion in the decade, the Republican press in Illinois wrote that slavery and Catholicism were "two despotisms" threatening American freedom. Because of these attacks, many Irish unfortunately became defenders of slavery and supported Senator Stephen Douglas over Abraham Lincoln.

Well into the twentieth century, tension over religion and economic competition continued to divide downstate Irish-Americans from their Protestant neighbors. The Irish remained loyal to Mother Church and the Democratic party which championed the needs of the common man. Illinois Catholics found a defender in Bishop John Lancaster Spalding of Peoria. Peoria, located on the Illinois River, was the state's second city to Chicago. It was a prosperous trading center and a hub for nine railroads. The first Catholic Church of St. Mary's was established there in 1846. The growth in number of Catholics in Illinois and the prominence of Peoria prompted the Catholic Church in 1875 to create the Diocese of Peoria to oversee twenty-two counties of northern Illinois and forty thousand Catholics. In 1877 Spalding was installed as bishop.

Spalding came from an old Maryland Catholic family, yet he had an affinity for the Irish. They were "providential instruments" in the revival of the Catholic Church in America. He said:

No other people could have done for the Catholic faith in the United States what the Irish people have done. Their unalterable attachment to their priests; their deep Catholic instincts, which no combination of circumstances has ever been able to bring into conflict with their love of country; the unworldly and spiritual temper of their national character; their indifference to ridicule and contempt, and their unfailing generosity, all fitted them for the work which was to be done, and enabled them in spite of strong prejudices against their race which Americans have inherited from England, to accomplish what would not have been accomplished by Italian, French, or German Catholics.

Spalding vigorously defended the Irish against attacks of disloyalty, saying their love of freedom in this country was a direct reaction against English tyranny in Ireland. If anything, the Irish were ultra-Americans often blind to the defects of America. Spalding also endeared himself to the Irish for his sympathetic views on the Irish Land League, Charles Stewart Parnell and the Irish Constitutional Party, and Irish independence.

Spalding was also a supporter of the Irish Catholic Colonization Association founded in 1879. Its goal was to settle Irish from eastern cities where poverty and vice reigned to the wholesome farms in the Midwest. Spalding argued that not only would it be a healthier environment for the Irish, but the Irish would fulfill their special mission of championing Catholicism in the English-speaking world. Some successful settlements were established in Minnesota and Nebraska. However, the organization could never raise enough funds to continue this migration. No settlements were formed in Illinois.

Despite their defiant stand against Anglo-Protestants, the Yankee sense of superiority still permeated towns throughout Illinois into the twentieth century and influenced the writings of J. F. Powers. Powers was born in Jacksonville, thirty miles west of Springfield. His family later moved to Quincy where Powers attended high school at Quincy Academy staffed by the Franciscan fathers. His 1962 novel *Morte D'Urban* won the National Book Award. In his books Powers explores the Catholic world of Midwestern small towns. In *Morte D'Urban* the central character is a Catholic boy who enters the priesthood. He recalls the Protestants in the small Illinois town he grew up in "felt that it was their country, handed down to them by the Pilgrims . . . and that they were taking a risk in letting you live in it." Powers himself said of Jacksonville that the "town was Protestant. The best people were Protestants and you felt that . . . It made me mad."

By the mid-twentieth century the Irish community lost its immigrant flavor. World War I, the National Origins Act of 1924, and the Great Depression ended America's first great age of immigration. The 1990 U.S. Census reported 1,861,107 persons claiming Irish ancestry in Illinois. The metro-Chicago area claims 600,000 of these. Chicago itself claims 250,000. The hinterland of Illinois clearly has a substantial portion of its population identifying themselves as Irish. The prairie Irish fought marginalization by Yankee Protestants, but still claim an Irish heritage. They, however, have been marginalized in the historical record by twentieth-century historians who have been more interested in the urban Irish experience. How they have continued to maintain their Irish identity is a story that has yet to be written.

*See* Chicago, Aspects of; Chicago Politics; Labor Movement

Clarence Walworth Alvord, *The Illinois Country, 1673–1818* (Chicago, 1965).

P. T. Barry, "The First Irish of Illinois," *Transactions of the Illinois State Historical Library*, 1902.

Frederic Beuckman, "Catholic Beginnings in Southern Illinois: Shawneetown," 14(2) *Mid-America: An Historical Review* (1931).

Dennis Clark, *Hibernia America: The Irish and Regional Cultures* (New York, 1986).

Kay J. Carr, *Belleville, Ottawa, and Galesburg Community and Democracy on the Illinois Frontier* (Carbondale, 1996).

Paul Connors, "The Irish in Lemont and Hartland," Unpublished paper. Loyola University Chicago, December 1991.

Kathleen Cook, "A Study of the Hartland Irish and Johnsburg Germans, 1840–1890," Unpublished paper. Loyola University Chicago, December 1991.

Stephen Freeman, "Organizing the Workers in a Steel Company Town: The Union Movement in Joliet, Illinois, 1870–1920," *Illinois Historical Journal* 79 (1986).

Paul Wallace Gates, *The Illinois Central Railroad and Its Colonization Work* (Cambridge, 1934).

Joan C. Hawxhurst, *Mother Jones Labor Crusader* (Austin, Texas, 1994).

Charles W. Mayer, "J. F. Powers and the Catholic Clergyman," 12(1) *Western Illinois Regional Studies* (Spring 1989).

Judge John P. McGoorty, "The Early Irish of Illinois." *Transactions of the Illinois State Historical Society*. 1927

David Francis Sweeney, *The Life of John Lancaster Spalding First Bishop of Peoria, 1840–1916* (New York, 1965).

Mark Wyman, *Immigrants in the Valley Irish: Germans, and Americans in the Upper Mississippi Country, 1830–1860* (Chicago, 1984).

EILEEN M. McMAHON

## INDIANA

Immigrants from Ireland initially entered Indiana in the 18th century when the country north and west of the Ohio River was occupied by the Miami, Shawnee, Ottawa, and other Native American people. George Croghan, an Irish immigrant, played a remarkable role in the history of mid-18th century contacts between people of Native American and European backgrounds in Indiana and elsewhere south of the Great Lakes. Shortly after emigrating from Dublin to Philadelphia in 1741, Croghan established a fur trading business with several Pennsylvania traders. During the decade, Croghan's trading enterprise extended ever westward ultimately reaching the Wabash River in Indiana. Croghan was the first fur trader based in the English colonies to establish successful business ties with Native Americans in that western region claimed by France. Previously, the French had completely dominated the fur trade in Indiana and in other parts of France's colonial empire.

Recognizing that many native people held the Irishman in high esteem, English colonial authorities gave Croghan assignments in Anglo-Indian diplomacy. During the 1740s and 1750s Croghan urged his Native American associates to ally with Great Britain in its intercolonial rivalry with France. English colonial officials again called upon Croghan's diplomatic skills after France had been eliminated from North America by the Treaty of Paris (1763) at the conclusion of the French and Indian War. In 1765 Croghan met the Ottawa leader Pontiac at Fort Ouiatanon on the Wabash River in Indiana. The Irishman negotiated the end of Pontiac's War, during which British posts in the Great Lakes region had been captured by Native Americans.

A very large proportion of the migrants who settled in Indiana before 1800 consisted of people with family origins in northern Ireland. Immigrants from Ulster composed the largest non-English foreign born group in the English colonies in the 18th century. These newcomers were largely people of Scottish ancestry. Throughout the century, the Scots-Irish settled on colonial frontiers. Consequently populations were predominantly Scots-Irish in the western districts of Pennsylvania, Virginia (including Kentucky), and the Carolinas. Eventually, as the frontier moved further westward, some of the Scots-Irish from those areas removed to Indiana, thereby changing its ethnic composition. Only Native Americans and French inhabitants had lived permanently in Indiana in colonial times. The first newcomers entering Indiana from the United States arrived during the War for Independence, when George Rogers Clark led an American army to Vincennes where it defeated a British military unit in 1779. Undoubtedly, a number of Clark's troops were of Irish ancestry, given the fact that Clark had recruited his men in Scots-Irish areas of western Pennsylvania and western Virginia.

The Scots-Irish were among the migrants who settled in southern Indiana when it was part of the Northwest Territory, 1783 to 1800. The Scots-Irish frontiersmen of that time were stereotyped as hard drinking, aggressive, and even violent, especially toward Indians. By 1786 a few hundred recently arrived English speakers, undoubtedly including many of the Scots-Irish, were living in the area of Vincennes on the lower Wabash River. The town's French inhabitants, who were still the majority of the local population, regarded some of the newcomers as outlaws whose behavior was intolerable. Daniel Sullivan, surely an Irishman, was especially objectionable according to Colonel LeGras, a Vincennes magistrate. The Ohio River was the southern boundary of other late 18th century Indiana settlements areas. Clark's Grant was located near the falls of the Ohio River in present Clark and Harrison Counties. The Gore was near the current Ohio/Indiana boundary and it included present Dearborn County. A great proportion of the old stock settlers of those areas were of Irish ancestry. The Irish stock settlers were largely related to persons who had emigrated from northern Ireland and who had settled earlier in the Carolina back country or in Kentucky.

The Irish were present in the Indiana Territory during its sixteen-year history beginning in 1800 when the territory was created by an act of Congress. During that period Native Americans were removed from southern Indiana which was increasingly settled by pioneer families living in log cabins and growing corn and raising hogs as subsistence farmers. The first settlers of some areas of the Indiana Territory were natives of Ireland. James McGuire was the first settler of Laughery Township, Dearborn County. McGuire was born in Dundalk in Ireland's Leistner province. John Kelso, also an immigrant from Ireland, was the first settler in an area which became Kelso township, Dearborn County.

Some natives of Ireland played prominent roles in the public life of the Indiana Territory. An Irish immigrant, William Prince, resided at the territorial capital of Vincennes in Knox County. At different times he was county sheriff, town postmaster, and county justice of the peace. Also, Prince was appointed to the territorial Council in 1809 and as territorial auditor (1810–1813). James Dill, also a native of Ireland, created a memorable reputation as prosecuting attorney in the courts of Dearborn County. The Irish participated in the transitional process leading from territorial status to statehood for Indiana. Patrick Beard, James Dill, William Graham, and David Robb, all natives of Ireland, were four of the six foreign-born delegates elected to the state constitutional convention meeting in Corydon, Indiana, 1816.

The United States was beginning to experience immigration on a massive scale for the first time when Indiana became a state in the Union. Approximately five million immigrants arrived in the United States during 1815–1860 and about two million of them were natives of Ireland. In contrast to earlier times, only a small fraction of the 19th-century Irish immigrants came from Ulster. By 1860 the states with the largest Irish immigrant populations were in and near the New England region. Meanwhile, significant numbers of Irish newcomers were found in cities in all regions of the country. Fewer Irish newcomers resided in Indiana than in other Great Lakes states. Even so the number of Irish immigrants in Indiana almost doubled during the 1850s, increasing from 12,787 in 1850 to 24,495 in 1860, when the total Indiana population was 1,350,428. Irish immigrants comprised twenty-one percent of the state's foreign born population in 1860. Only German immigrants exceeded that percentage.

Indiana moved through the pioneer phase of society during the 1815–1860 period of immigration history. The state's social-economic development was facilitated by the construction of roads, canals, and railroads linking previously isolated pioneer farms and communities to outside markets. All regions of Indiana were well settled by 1860. Commercial farming was beginning to replace subsistence farming, manufacturing establishments using farm commodities were appearing, and towns were growing in number and size. Yet Indiana was still a largely rural and agricultural state on the eve of the Civil War.

Irish immigrants were instrumental in making the transportation improvements that advanced modernization in early 19th-century Indiana. Thousands of Irish aliens, recruited in eastern states, worked as laborers constructing the Wabash and Erie Canal, the Whitewater Canal, and the Central Canal in Indiana during the 1830s. Other Irish immigrants were among the construction workers building the National Road from Richmond to Terre Haute in the same decade. Also, Irishmen were employed in Indiana canal construction in the 1840s and 1850s. Meanwhile, Irish immigrants helped build early rail lines in Indiana, including the state's first significant railroad; it was completed from Indianapolis to Madison in 1847.

Before 1860, only a fraction of Indiana's Irish immigrants were road, canal, and railroad laborers. Undoubtedly, most of the Irish construction workers departed Indiana upon the termination of their employment. The majority of the Irish laborers in canal construction camps were single males or married men temporarily separated from their spouses. Yet some Irish married women were present in the camps. Father Lalumiere, a

Catholic priest serving in Terre Haute, wrote that he attended many families and single men when he visited Catholics on the Wabash and Erie Canal between Lafayette and Coal Creek in 1842. Nevertheless, often canal laborers returned to their families in the East after a period of hard living in canal shanty towns in Indiana. An Irish exodus following the completion of canal building in Pike County, Indiana, was a manifestation of the transience of canal laborers; the number of persons born in Ireland fell in Pike County from 683 in 1850 to 261 in 1860.

Yet some of the Irish construction laborers eventually settled along road, canal, and railroad routes where they had worked in Indiana. For instance, a number of the Irish immigrants who had been involved in railroad construction at Indianapolis subsequently settled there. But, only a small proportion of the state's Irish settlers had come to Indiana to be employed on transportation projects. Most of the Irish who located in Indiana at the time were drawn by the promise of other economic opportunities in the state. Many other Irish immigrants took residence in Indiana towns where recently completed transportation lines were facilitating economic development and thereby creating a demand for labor or in the state's sparsely settled areas where land was cheap.

The geographical distribution of the Irish foreign-born population in Indiana was only in some ways unlike that of the state's general population, 1816–1860. Indiana's Irish population was much more urban than the state's general population by 1860. At least one third of the Irish foreign-born lived in Indiana's urban places, while less than ten percent of the total state population was urban in 1860. Reflecting the whole population, most Irish immigrants in Indiana were located in rural areas where they lived on farms or in villages. For example, Irish immigrants were among the earliest settlers in the vicinity of Little Indian Creek, Lafayette Township, in Floyd County, bordering on the Ohio River. During the 1820s, Irish Catholic families there established farms and erected a log edifice that became St. Mary's Church. Likewise, according to a demographic study, farming was the occupation of fifty-three percent of the Irish immigrants in the northern third of Indiana in 1850.

While natives of Ireland resided in every Indiana county, the concentration of Irish newcomers was greatest in the southern third of the state in 1850. A disproportionate percentage of the Irish lived in a few Indiana counties. The ten counties with the greatest numbers of persons born in Ireland contained fifty-three percent of the Irish immigrants. Seven of these counties with high Irish populations in 1850 were in the southern third of Indiana. Irish immigrants tended to locate in counties on new transportation routes in all sections of the state during the 1850s. The Wabash and Erie Canal, the Indianapolis and Madison railroad, and the National Road passed through nine of the ten Indiana counties containing the greatest numbers of Irish immigrants in 1860.

In the antebellum era, newcomers from Ireland formed cultural institutions including churches and schools in efforts to maintain their Irish heritage. The Irish in the state were much involved in the organization of Catholic parishes and in the erection of Catholic church edifices between 1830 and 1860. The arrival of Irish immigrants contributed to an increase of communicants of the Catholic Church in towns located on recently constructed canals, roads and railroads. Catholic congregations were initially composed of ethnic mixtures including Irish and German. Often a largely Irish congregation remained in the ini-

tial Catholic church of an Indiana city when the German communicants withdrew to form a separate parish. This occurred in a number of Indiana cities, including Fort Wayne, Evansville, Indianapolis, Lafayette, Madison, and New Albany. Some Catholic parishes were principally Irish when they were organized, for example, North Madison's St. Patrick's Church which was built near the Irish neighborhoods there. By 1860, at least one parochial school existed in almost every predominantly Irish Catholic parish in urban Indiana.

Many of the Irish in Indiana were active in politics and government, 1816–1860. Most Irish voters supported the Democratic Party, whose policies were sympathetic to immigrants, and most rejected the Whig Party for its nativist positions. The nativism and the anti-Catholicism of the Know-Nothing movement of the 1850s largely were responses to the growing presence of the Irish in Indiana's population and party politics. Natives of Ireland were elected to Democratic Party positions and to public offices in Indiana before 1860. Cornelius O'Brien was Dearborn County Clerk and delegate to the Democratic national convention in 1856. At least twenty-five Irish immigrants were among the 1,513 legislators who served in the Indiana General Assembly, 1816–1850. Most of the foreign-born Irish legislators were from Ulster. There were only nine Catholic legislators during that period. Also, Irish immigrants in Indiana were interested in public affairs in Ireland. In some cities, including Fort Wayne, Irish immigrants organized relief efforts to aid Ireland during the terrible potato famine of the 1840s.

The Irish presence in Indiana grew as the modernization of the state accelerated, 1860–1920. Indiana's population had become predominantly urban by 1920 and its economy then had become diversified with modern industry and agriculture. The Irish immigrant population of Indiana increased after 1860, reaching its largest figure (28,698) in 1870. The number of Irish aliens in Indiana was greater during 1860–1920 than ever before or after. There were more than twenty thousand Irish immigrants in Indiana from 1870 through 1890. At least a few Irish immigrants lived in every Indiana county, excepting one, through 1920. But, nine of the ten Indiana counties with the greatest populations of persons born in Ireland were in the state's central and northern sections in 1900. This distribution of the foreign-born Irish population echoed a larger phenomenon involving the growth of industries and city populations in the central and northern counties of Indiana in the late 19th century and early 20th century. The Irish immigrants were more urban than Indiana's general population, 1860–1920. Thus, almost seventy-two percent of the Irish foreign born was urban in 1920 while that figure was only about fifty-one percent for the total state population.

Many of the Irish were employed in factory and construction work in Indiana cities, 1860–1920. The employment experiences of the Irish who located in Indiana in the late 19th century were different than those of the Irish who entered the state before the Civil War. Earlier the urban Irish were largely restricted to low-paying jobs, unskilled labor for men and domestic service for women. But according to a study of census records, a large proportion of the Irish working in South Bend were factory employees or skilled workers in 1880. The Irish worked in factories elsewhere, for example, Irish women were employed by the Starch Works located on the near south side of Indianapolis. Irish men were hired as construction workers, erecting buildings and constructing streets in burgeoning Indiana towns and cities.

Indiana's Irish community was most identifiable during 1860–1920 because there were more Irish aliens in the state during that era than in any other period. Irish residential areas in some cities became increasingly visible as immigrants formed largely, but not exclusively, Irish neighborhoods that were sometimes known by ethnic nicknames, such as "Dublin" in South Bend, "Irish Town" in Fort Wayne, and "Irish Hill" in Indianapolis. Also, the Irish in Indiana were known by their identification with cultural institutions, 1860–1920, most notably churches and schools in predominantly Irish Catholic parishes. Among the congregations that became largely Irish in that era were those of St. Joseph's Church in Terre Haute, St. Patrick's Church in South Bend, and St. Patrick's (initially St. Peter's) Church in Indianapolis. Parochial schools that were started in predominantly Irish parishes before 1860 still offered Catholic education and new ones were opened during that period.

The proliferation of Irish associations in Indiana after 1860 called attention to the existence of the Irish community in the state. The Irish in Indiana founded military, benevolent, fraternal, temperance, and musical organizations. Two Irish regiments were formed in Indiana during the Civil War, the Thirty-fifth regiment and the Sixty-first regiment. Numerous Irish mutual aid societies in Indiana included the United Irish Benevolent Association in Indianapolis. The Ancient Order of Hibernians was the largest and most enduring of the Irish fraternal organizations established in Indiana, 1860–1920. Among the Irish women's organizations appearing in Indiana after 1860 were the Maids of Erin in Indianapolis, the Sodality Society of the Church of the Assumption in Evansville, and local female units of the Ancient Order of Hibernians in Fort Wayne and Terre Haute. Still other examples of Irish organizations in Indiana were the Emmet Guard Band that marched in Indianapolis and the St. Joseph Total Abstinence Society of Terre Haute. Many Irish ethnic organizations had ties with churches in Catholic parishes that were chiefly Irish. The significant social role of the Catholic Church was exemplified by St. John's Church which was at the center of Irish social life in Indianapolis, 1870–1900. Furthermore, awareness of the Irish in Indiana was raised by observances of St. Patrick's Day, which the Irish saw as an occasion for religious observance and as a time of great celebration.

The pace of economic advancement was slow for most of the Irish living in Indiana in the late 19th century. At the turn of the century a large proportion of the Irish were still tied to relatively low paying jobs in Indiana. Yet, a number of the Irish were employed in Indiana's businesses and professions. Construction companies were started by many Irishmen, including Daniel Foley who founded the American Construction Company in Indianapolis. Also, the Irish were involved in grocery, drug store, furniture, saloon, hotel, manufacturing, and other enterprises in Indiana. The professions entered by the Irish in Indiana included law, teaching, medicine, and the clergy.

The church and politics were the means of social-economic advancement for some of the Irish in Indiana, 1860–1920. The Reverend Denis O'Donoghue, an Indiana native of Irish ancestry, was appointed auxiliary bishop of the Indianapolis diocese in 1900 and then named bishop of Louisville in 1910. Meanwhile, other Irish men and women in Indiana devoted their lives to the Catholic Church. Many Irish priests were assigned to Catholic parishes in Indiana. Also, many of the Irish women teaching in Indiana were on Catholic parochial school faculties. The careers of some Irish lawyers in Indiana were advanced in politics. A large proportion of the Indiana legislators of Irish antecedents were attorneys. Also, the Irish who were successful in business in Indiana were often involved in politics. Irishmen with political connections sometimes became policemen and firemen in Indiana cities and some of them became chiefs.

Irish voters in Indiana backed the Democratic Party and Irish candidates for office in the state usually were on the Democratic ticket, 1860–1920. Thomas Taggart of Indianapolis was one of Indiana's Irish politicians who played important roles in Democratic party leadership. Taggart, a native of northern Ireland, was Democratic state chairman (1892–1894) and Democratic national committee chairman (1904–1908). Taggart was one of five Protestants of Irish ancestry elected mayor in Indianapolis during 1860–1900. There was a significant increase in the participation of Irish Catholics in Indiana politics and government during 1860–1920. Irish Catholics were elected to a great variety of offices in Indiana municipal, county, and state governments. David J. Hefron, who was mayor of Washington (1871–1875), and Patrick H. McCormick, who was mayor of Columbus, were examples of Irish Catholic Democrats elected at the municipal level before 1900. Irish Catholic Democrats holding Indiana county positions during the 1860–1920 years included Perry County Sheriff John Sweeney, who was born in County Cork, Ireland. Among the Irish Catholic Democrats elected to state offices in Indiana were Matthew L. Brett of Washington, who was state treasurer (1863–1865), and James H. Rice of New Albany, who was state auditor (1883–1887). According to a study of the Indiana General Assembly, there were at least 125 legislators of Irish ancestry (five of whom were natives of Ireland) among the 1,712 members of the General Assembly during the 1890–1930 era. The Irish legislators formed a large proportion of the ninety-three Catholic members of the Assembly during 1891–1929.

Also, some of the Irish in Indiana were interested in political activities concerning Ireland, 1860–1920. For example, some of them joined the militant Irish republican Fenian movement. The Indianapolis Circle of the Fenian Brotherhood was active in the 1860s. Later, some of the Irish in Indiana were involved in other Irish nationalist movements, such as the Irish National Land League which was organized in Indiana during the 1880s. Irish nationalism appeared in Indiana during World War I when Irish nationalists, who did not want the United States to join Great Britain in the war in Europe, participated in joint German-Irish rallies held in several Indiana cities in 1915 to protest American favoritism toward the Allies.

The 20th-century Irish experience in Indiana was a departure from the past. During 1920–1998 most of the Irish in Indiana were descendants of immigrants from Ireland. The number of natives of Ireland in Indiana declined from 7,271 in 1920 to 2,352 in 1950 to 825 in 1980. Over half of the Irish newcomers lived in Lake and Marion counties, 1900–1950. Awareness of the Irish as an Indiana ethnic group lessened after 1920. Irish neighborhoods disappeared in Indianapolis, South Bend, Fort Wayne, Madison, New Albany, and in other Indiana cities as their residents moved elsewhere. Likewise, as the Irish dispersed residentially, Irish predominance ended in some urban Catholic parishes. Many Irish benevolent and fraternal organizations faded away. During the 1930s some observers of ethnic life in the state mistakenly concluded that the Irish in Indiana were entirely assimilated in the greater society and that there no longer was a distinctive Irish identity in places like Indianapolis.

The descendants of Ireland made significant social-economic progress in the 20th century, especially after World War II when the Irish entered the middle and upper-middle classes. The numbers of professional and business people of Irish background increased as the children and grandchildren of Irish immigrants graduated from professional schools and graduate schools as well as from colleges and universities. Among them were technicians and insurance company entrepreneurs, physicians and professors, and lawyers and bankers, such as William P. Flynn, who was board chairman of the Indiana National Bank. By 1980 Irish Catholics enjoyed an occupational distribution similar to that of urban Anglo-Saxon Protestants.

Maintaining a tradition, the Irish were active in Indiana's government and Democratic Party politics from 1920 to the end of the century. William J. Mooney was Indiana state campaign director for Democratic presidential candidate Al Smith in 1928. Frank E. McKinney was national chairman of the Democratic party when Harry Truman was president of the United States. At mid-century, Al Feeney was mayor of Indianapolis; he was the first Irish Catholic Democrat elected to that office. A study of the Indiana General Assembly reported that 83 of the 1,258 legislators were of Irish ancestry during 1930–1970. Women with Irish forbearers were elected to the General Assembly in the 1960s. Anna Maloney represented Lake County in the House of Representatives (1961–1972). Kathrine Margaret O'Connell Fruits and Cecilia M. Logan held Marion County seats in the House of Representatives (1966–1967). Tippecanoe County was represented in the House by Sheila Ann Johnston Klinker (1983–1984). Frank Lewis O'Bannon, a Methodist, was elected Governor of Indiana in 1996. His forbears were Irish, English, Dutch, German, and French.

While the number of Irish living in Indiana fell and many of the state's Irish neighborhoods, parishes, organizations, and institutions faded into the past, the Irish identity survived in Indiana among the descendants of Irish immigrants, 1920–1998. Irish group consciousness was sharpened in the 1920s by the anti-Catholic campaign of the Ku Klux Klan which rose to power in Indiana in that decade. Irish critics of the Indiana Klan included Dennis John O'Neill, who shared a Pulitzer Prize for an *Indianapolis Times* series of articles which exposed the Klan's corrupt political activities in Indiana and contributed to its decline. Surely the "Fighting Irish" raised Irish group awareness in the decades after World War I when the University of Notre Dame's football team was achieving fame. Some Irish ethnic associations continued their activities in Indiana through the 1920s and the Depression decade and afterwards. For example, the Ancient Order of Hibernians remained vital in Indianapolis through the 1990s. Founded in 1959, the Friendly Sons of Erin was active for decades in Lake County. The Irish in Indianapolis supported a number of ethnic organizations in the last decade of the 20th century, including the Irish American Heritage Society, the Irish Step Dancers, and the Indiana Irish Culture Society.

At the end of the 20th century, most of the Irish in Indiana were separated from their immigrant forbears by generations. Often Irish Hoosiers had one parent who was not of Irish descent or who was not Catholic because of marriages made across lines of nationality and religion. Nevertheless, surnames and family histories continued to link many Hoosiers to the heritage of immigration from Ireland. For example, a family tradition was kept by Captain David T. Shea and five of his brothers, who were members of the Indianapolis fire department in the 1970s. Their immigrant grandfather had been an Indianapolis firefighter. Likewise, the Irish family's traditional commitment to the Catholic Church was manifested in the career of Edward T. O'Meara, who was archbishop of the Archdiocese of Indianapolis (1980–1992). Certainly, the Irish in Indiana were reminded of their ties to Ireland each year when St. Patrick's Day was celebrated in gatherings and parades across the state and the nation. A remarkable percentage of Hoosiers thought of themselves as being Irish near the century's end. The 1990 census stated that Indiana's total population was approximately five million and that almost one million Hoosiers reported that they were Irish.

*See* Emigration: 1801–1921

This essay draws much from *Peopling Indiana: The Ethnic Experience,* edited by Robert M. Taylor, Jr. and Connie A. McBirney (Indianapolis, 1996). Also see:

Herman J. Alerding, *A History of the Catholic Church in the Diocese of Vincennes* (Indianapolis, 1883).

Herman J. Alerding, *The Diocese of Fort Wayne, 1857–1907: A Book of Historical Reference, 1669–1907* (Fort Wayne, IN, 1907).

John Aylward, "Immigrant Settlement Patterns in South Bend, 1865–1917" [typescript, Dec. 9, 1971, Northern Indiana Historical Society].

John D. Barnhart and Donald F. Carmony, *Indiana, From Frontier to Industrial Commonwealth,* 2 vols. (New York, 1954).

John D. Barnhart and Dorothy L. Riker, *Indiana to 1816, The Colonial Period* (Indianapolis, 1971).

Charles Blanchard, ed., *History of the Catholic Church in Indiana,* vol. 1. (Logansport, IN, 1898).

Carl F. Brand, "History of the Know Nothing Party in Indiana," *Indiana Magazine of History,* 28 (March 1922): 47–81 and (June 1922): 177–206.

Hasia R. Diner, *Erin's Daughters in America, Irish Immigrant Women in the Nineteenth Century* (Baltimore, 1983).

Leonard Dinnerstein and David M. Reimers, *Ethnic Americans, A History of Immigration and Assimilation* (New York, 1982).

Dean R. Esslinger, *Immigrants and the City, Ethnicity and Mobility in a Nineteenth-Century Midwestern Community* (Port Washington, N.Y., 1975).

Paul Fatout, *Indiana Canals* (West Lafayette, IN, 1972).

Sharon B. Hinkle, "Irish Immigrants in Terre Haute, Indiana in 1860: A Comparative Study" (Thesis, Indiana State University, 1987).

Maldwyn A. Jones, *American Immigration* (Chicago, 1974).

Elfrieda Lang, "Irishmen in Northern Indiana Before 1850," *Mid-America: An Historical Review,* 36 (1954): 190–98.

Edward A. Leary, *Indianapolis, The Story of a City* (Indianapolis, 1971).

William McNamara, *The Catholic Church on the Northern Indiana Frontier, 1789–1844* (Washington, D.C., 1931).

James H. Madison, *Indiana Through Tradition and Change: A History of the Hoosier State and Its People, 1920–1945* (Indianapolis, 1982).

Kirby A. Miller, *Emigrants and Exiles, Ireland and the Irish Exodus to North America* (New York, 1985).

John H. O'Donnell, "The Catholic Church in Northern Indiana: 1830–1857," *The Catholic Historical Review,* 25 (July 1939): 135–45.

Rebecca A. Shepherd, Charles W. Calhoun, Elizabeth Shanahan-Shoemaker, and Alan January, eds., *A Biographical Dictionary of the Indiana General Assembly, Vol. 1, 1816–1899* (Indianapolis, 1980).

Emma Lou Thornbrough, *Indiana in the Civil War Era, 1850–1880* (Indianapolis, 1965).

Philip R. VanderMeer, *The Hoosier Politician, Officeholding and Political Culture in Indiana, 1896–1920* (Urbana, IL, 1985).

Justin E. Walsh, *A Biographical Directory of the Indiana General Assembly, Volume 2, 1900–1984* (Indianapolis, 1984).

Justin E. Walsh, *The Centennial History of the Indiana General Assembly, 1816–1978* (Indianapolis, 1987).

Carl Wittke, *The Irish in America* (Baton Rouge, LA, 1956).

WILLIAM W. GIFFIN

# IOWA

## First Settlers and Missionaries

The Irish are storytellers, not statistic-keepers. Perhaps nowhere has this been more true than among the Irish who have lived their lives on the seeming sameness of the gently rolling plains of Iowa. The first Irish to set foot in what is now the state of Iowa were among a group of miners who came in 1830 to work in the lead mines in a tiny settlement known as Dubuque Mines, a few miles outside the present city of Dubuque. They probably came from the mining town of Galena, on the Illinois side of the Mississippi. The territory opened up to more settlers after the so-called Black Hawk Purchase of 1832, following the war in which the Indians lost title to their lands in eastern Iowa. Dubuque became the main entry point for the Irish. In those early years a number of Irish held important positions in Dubuque. Patrick Quigley, who ran a store in partnership with Alexander Butterworth, both from Ireland, was the first justice of the peace. Later he was elected to the Territorial Legislature of Wisconsin. In this mixed community of Irish, German, Dutch, and French, John Foley was elected to the Wisconsin Territorial Council, F. K. O'Farrell, a merchant and realtor, was mayor from 1844 to 1846, and Charles Corkery was probate judge of Dubuque County from 1844 to 1857.

The first missionary to minister among the Irish settlers was Rev. John McMahon, who became pastor of Galena, Illinois, and the surrounding area including Dubuque. Early in 1833 he celebrated Mass in the home of Patrick Quigley and from that time until 1836 the Quigley house was used as a church. Father McMahon died of cholera after ministering to the miners for about nine months. Father Charles Felix Van Quickenborne, S.J., was sent by Bishop Rosati of St. Louis to serve the Catholics in Galena and on July 10, 1833 he crossed the Mississippi to Dubuque and baptized the eight-month-old child of Patrick and Mary Sullivan Monaghan. Although he remained only a week in Dubuque, staying at the home of a Mrs. Brophy, he made arrangements for construction of the first church of any denomination in Iowa. In the following year Rev. Charles Francis Fitzmaurice, a native of Ireland, arrived in Galena and alternated on Sundays between Galena and Dubuque. He pushed ahead with the plans for the new church. Although the cholera also took Father Fitzmaurice after only three short months of ministry, it was he who involved himself in the case of the first murder and subsequent execution to take place in Iowa.

Patrick O'Connor, a one-legged miner from Cork, entered into a mining partnership with a young man, George O'Keaf, also from Ireland. Together they constructed a cabin close to Dubuque along the Mississippi near the mines. Having gone into Dubuque to buy provisions, O'Keaf returned with an acquaintance to find the door of the cabin fastened on the inside. He called to O'Connor to open it. With the comment from inside, "I'll open it when I get ready," and rain beginning to fall, O'Keaf leaned against the door and forced it open. O'Connor, sitting on a bench opposite the door, leveled a musket and fired at O'Keaf. Five slugs entered his breast and he fell dead. The young man ac-

companying O'Keaf ran for help. A crowd soon assembled and some wanted to hang O'Connor on the spot from a tree near the cabin. Others counseled that he should be taken to Dubuque and given a trial.

A jury was chosen and after hearing testimony, some of which challenged the legality of a trial so constituted, O'Connor was found guilty of first degree murder and sentenced to be "hung by the neck until he is dead." Shortly before the execution, Father Fitzmaurice inveighed against the decision of the people calling it illegal and unjust. (Jurisdiction in the territory which later would be the state of Iowa was at the time unclear.) The execution took place on June 20, 1834, before a crowd of about one thousand people. Father Fitzmaurice rode with the condemned one on the cart carrying the casket to the place where the hanging was to take place. The priest prayed with O'Connor and before he died O'Connor told the people that he had killed O'Keaf, that he was sorry for it, and he hoped that all would forgive him. At the signal the hangman drove the cart out from under the hanging man. The body was cut down and placed in the coffin, along with his wooden leg, and deposited in a grave. Eight days after the execution of Patrick O'Connor, Congress placed the tract of land including modern Iowa under the jurisdiction of the Territory of Michigan.

## Missionary Mazzuchelli ("Matthew Kelly") and First Bishop Loras

Especially beloved among the early Irish settlers in Iowa was the Italian Dominican missionary, Samuel Charles Mazzuchelli. As described by M.M. Hoffmann, a historian of the early Church in Iowa (*Church Founders of the Northwest,* p. 69) he was a "saint and scholar, architect and artist, priest of God and gentleman of the frontier world; he personified physical and spiritual courage; his tongue was a fire of eloquence; his brain was a vehicle of the wisdom of the Lord" (68). In Iowa he formed or helped form almost every early mission along the Mississippi from Dubuque to the Missouri border, and inland as far as Iowa City.

One story will suffice to show how the Irish claimed this remarkable Italian priest as one of their own. At a gathering after the christening of the firstborn to an O'Connor family (not to be confused with Patrick O'Connor mentioned above), Father "Matthew Kelly" was invited to take part in the festivities. When they saw "his reverence" coming, Mrs. Beacom let go with a Gaelic greeting, "Caed Mille Failthe."

"Arrah, what's that you're sayin' to him?" said Mrs. Murphy, coming forward with outstretched hand, "and him an Eyetalian."

"Sure it's fettin' I was. He seems so like our own."

"And I am your own," said the priest. "Don't good Christians the world over, belong to each other? And indeed, am I not just as much Father Kelly as Father Mazzuchelli?"

In June of 1837 a new Catholic diocese of Iowa was created with Dubuque as the bishop's residence. Mathias Loras was named the bishop. A native of France, Loras had been ministering in New Orleans. He wrote to the bishop of St. Louis, who previously had responsibility for the area of the new diocese, that he would return to Europe and France before assuming his duties in Dubuque. He hoped to recruit an Irish, a German, and three or four French priests to help with his mission. He also was anxious to get sisters to start a school, and his dream was to establish a college. Disappointed by the reaction of the bishop of Dublin about sending an Irish priest to Dubuque, Loras, after he arrived home, wrote to the bishop of St. Louis imploring him to send a pastor to Galena so Father Mazzuchelli could dedicate his whole work to the new diocese of Dubuque. "I have an absolute need of 'M. Kelly,'" the French bishop wrote.

Because of Mazzuchelli's familiarity with the English language and his great popularity among the Irish people, the bishop sent him to a new mission about twenty miles from Dubuque called Maquokiti, later known as Garryowen. (More will be said about Garryowen later.) Mazzuchelli decided to build a church and because of the abundance of timber there he distributed among the forty-two men of the settlement the labor of preparing a great number of beams, from twenty to forty feet long. In the spring each of these men carried to the building site his own handiwork. As they were not in a position to contribute money, they gave their assistance in many other ways. In 1840 when Father Mazzuchelli celebrated the first Mass in the new church, dedicated to St. Patrick, there were scarcely one hundred Irish in the parish. Three years later there were six hundred and the parish had a school. By 1850, of the sixty-five families in Butler Township around Garryowen, all but four were farmers. There were two laborers, a shoemaker and a country school teacher named Dennis Mahoney. In addition there were fourteen single men, two single women and three widows living in the neighborhood ("The Irish in Iowa," *The Palimpsest* XLV/2, Feb. 1964, p.57).

The earlier plans for a church in Dubuque having not been carried out, Bishop Loras engaged Father Mazzuchelli to build St. Raphael Cathedral. Using stone rather than the earlier designated wood, the church was completed in 1837. Mazzuchelli also supervised the erection of a large building to the rear of the cathedral which served as the bishop's residence as well as St. Raphael's Seminary. (Later, Loras began St. Bernard's Seminary that eventually became Columbia College and then the present Loras College, the first diocesan college in Iowa.) Dubuque at the time had some three thousand inhabitants, fifteen hundred of whom were Catholics. Both Protestants and Catholics contributed to the building fund of the first cathedral and likewise participated in the ceremony of the cornerstone laying. Twenty years later this church was replaced by another and Bishop Loras celebrated Mass in the new cathedral just two months before his death. The formal dedication of the new cathedral took place in 1861 with Bishop Smyth, Loras' successor, presiding.

## An Irish Trappist Monastery on the Frontier

In 1849 the Cistercian Trappists arrived in Dubuque, a contemplative order of Irish monks from Mt. Mellary Abbey in County Waterford, Ireland. Bishop Loras had struggled long and hard to have a community of men religious settle in his diocese. Father Clement Smyth and Brother Ambrose became the representatives from the Irish monastery to select a place for a new foundation. They had been preceded by a Brother Marcarius (Patrick Keegan) who had not made a favorable impression on the bishop of Dubuque. Father Smyth later would become auxiliary bishop of Dubuque and succeed Bishop Loras as the second bishop of the diocese. A site twelve miles from Dubuque was selected for the new monastery where 1,260 acres were bought from the local farmers. Word was that the farmers raised the price per acre when they found out this was the site that the monks really wanted for their monastery. In 1849 when the Abbot of Mt. Mellary in Ireland arrived in Dubuque with four more brothers, he was pleased with the site and ordered construction of a two-story frame building that served both the monks and a school for boys.

The Abbot appointed Father James O'Gorman as superior of the new monastery and returned to Ireland. Soon sixteen additional brothers joined the small group at New Mellary, as the Iowa foundation was called. Twenty-two had left Ireland together and only sixteen reached Dubuque. After seven weeks crossing the Atlantic, the brothers arrived in New Orleans and began a steamboat journey up the Mississippi to St. Louis. Cholera struck and six of the brothers died and were buried along the way. The last to die, Brother Victor, was heard to say shortly before he died, "Oh my! Oh my! Will any of us live to reach Dubuque?" The monks at New Mellary were astonished and saddened to hear of the loss of their brothers. By 1851 the number of members of the order had grown to forty.

It is rare for a Trappist monk to be named bishop, but two priors from New Mellary were named bishops within two years. Prior Clement Smyth was named coadjutor with right of succession to Bishop Loras of Dubuque in 1857, and his successor at the monastery, Prior James Myles O'Gorman, was named Vicar Apostolic (the name for a missionary bishop before a diocese is established) of Nebraska in 1859. Bishop Smyth persuaded his friend, Bishop O'Gorman, to care for the Catholics living on the western edge of the Iowa diocese across the Missouri River from Omaha. This sharing of the episcopal care of Iowa by two former Irish priors of New Mellary continued until Bishop Smyth's death in 1865.

## Irish Women Religious Make Their Lasting Mark

Irish priests came in droves to minister to their Irish brothers and sisters in the towns and countryside of the new frontier that was Iowa. But religious sisters also came and endured the difficulties of the rustic pioneer life for the sake of education (first for the children in schools, and later through colleges for young women) and care of the sick. The Sisters of Charity of the Blessed Virgin Mary, which first consisted of four women from Dublin determined to provide education for the young in America, arrived in Philadelphia in 1833 and found a protector and spiritual guide in Father T. J. Donaghue. After ten formative years in Philadelphia, during which the community grew, five of the sisters ventured westward to Dubuque at the request of Bishop Loras. Upon arriving, and under primitive living conditions, the sisters began St. Mary's Academy in Dubuque. Eventually the entire community, along with their protector, Father Donaghue, moved to Dubuque. Under the able leadership of Mother Mary Francis Clarke, the growing band of Irish sisters set out establishing schools not only in Dubuque, but by the early 1850s in Davenport, Garryowen, Burlington, Iowa City and Muscatine. In the following years the sisters opened fifty-nine schools throughout the state. In addition they founded what today is called Clarke College in Dubuque.

In 1869 the Sisters of Mercy went to DeWitt, Iowa, to establish a school. Three of them journeyed to Davenport to St. Anthony's parish to solicit funds for their project. Certain parishioners implored them to begin a hospital in Davenport "for the sick, the poor and the insane." Mother Mary Boromeo Johnson, who had brought the small group of sisters to DeWitt to start a school, was the first of three Irish-born sisters whose skills and labor laid the ground work for hospital care in Iowa. She with two of her associates had come to Chicago and had become affiliated with the Sisters of Mercy whose founder, Catherine McAuley, was also from Ireland. In 1861 Mother Mary Boromeo left Chicago to follow the "Irish Brigade" of the Union Army to Missouri where she ministered to the wounded of both the North and the South. Later she worked on the hospital ship *Empress* that brought the wounded from Shiloh to Keokuk, Iowa. Her brave service brought praise from President Lincoln. The two other sisters who had come from Ireland with her also performed this Civil War service before they came to Iowa.

In a short seven years of ministry in Iowa, Mother Boromeo, in addition to founding the hospital in Davenport, successfully established a convent in DeWitt and staffed the school. In the DeWitt novitiate she admitted seventeen postulants in two years, and started two convents and schools in Independence and Cedar Rapids. Mount Mercy College would eventually grow out of the Cedar Rapids mission. Cancer took the life of Mother Boromeo when she was only forty-two. Her two early associates followed her as leaders of the Sisters of Mercy in Iowa ministering to the sick and educating the young. In 1893 the sisters opened a hospital in Des Moines.

When John McMullen was named the first bishop of the newly formed Diocese of Davenport in 1881, he was greeted by the Mercy Sisters who had known him in Chicago. McMullen was born in County Down, Ireland, and as an infant emigrated with his family to Canada and then the United States, finally settling in Chicago. Shortly after his ordination, well-educated and creative, he was named the president of the University of St. Mary of the Lake in Chicago and rector of the seminary. The closing of the university in 1866 was a great disappointment to McMullen. Once in Davenport it is not surprising that one of his first acts, after having confirmed some 13,000 people as he traveled through his diocese in his first years as bishop, was to look for a place to begin a college. Two rooms were found at St. Margaret's Cathedral (later renamed Sacred Heart) and in 1882 St. Ambrose College was born. It was named by McMullen after the scholarly fourth-century bishop of Milan, Italy. It continues today as a thriving university of nearly 3,000 students.

Another group of religious women of Irish descent that have labored in Iowa from early days is the Sisters of the Presentation founded by Nano Nagle in County Cork in 1777. John Hennessey, the third bishop of Dubuque, visited the Presentation convent at Mooncoin in County Kilkenny on his return from Rome in 1870 and invited Mother Vincent Hennessey to come to Dubuque. In 1874 Mother Vincent and three novices arrived in Dubuque. They found a home in a parish residence at Key West, three miles south of Dubuque, because the house in Dubuque was not ready for them. There they opened a school and began teaching young children. Two years later a school was opened in West Dubuque. A motherhouse was completed in Dubuque in 1879 and from there the sisters spread out through the small settlements and growing cities of Iowa as teachers. When the community celebrated the golden jubilee of their coming to Iowa in 1925, they had almost 200 members and schools in some twenty Iowa towns.

With the changes of Vatican II, and the subsequent diminishing number of sisters and small parochial schools, the Presentation Sisters, like those of other religious communities in Iowa, turned more and more to parish ministry to serve as religious education directors, ministers to the elderly, and as pastoral associates.

IRISH IMMIGRANTS AND IRISH SETTLEMENTS

In the 1850s there were 4,885 Irish-born people in Iowa. In ten years the number had jumped to 28,072, reflecting the plight of the Irish people during the potato famine at home. By 1870 the Irish numbered 40,124. The number increased slightly to 44,061 by 1880 and then began to decline as the original settlers either died or moved farther west, and the Irish immigrants who did come tended to stay in the larger cities. Earlier, when the Iowa territory first opened, there was a definite attempt to attract the immigrants to the rich farm land of Iowa. This is reflected in an article by Charles Corkery, one of the early settlers in Dubuque and an advocate of Irish immigration. In 1841 he wrote to the Philadelphia *Catholic Herald*: "My sole desire is to direct the attention of Catholics (Irish Catholics more particularly) to the country little known, and less appreciated in the East. . . . I have had ample opportunities of bearing witness to the testimony of many able and respectable writers (travelers and others) who unite in giving Iowa the happy cognomen of 'the garden of America,' the Eldorado of the West. . . . Irishmen unite in saying that our wheat and oats are nothing inferior to those of Ireland, and I have never seen better potatoes in Ireland . . . than those raised in the mining district" ("The Irish in Iowa," *The Palimpsest*, XLV/2, Feb. 1964, p. 43).

The majority of the early Irish settled in the growing communities along the Mississippi—Dubuque, Davenport, Bloomington (Muscatine), Burlington, Fort Madison and Keokuk. They were for the most part poor, but the Burlington *Territorial Gazette* spoke favorably toward the Irish settlements: "Of all the foreigners who come among us, the natives of the Emerald Isle are the most enthusiastic in their admiration of our institutions." The Irish worked in mills and drove drays, hauling merchandise and passengers to and from the steam boats. They also were involved in trades connected with building. The coming of the railroads was a boon to Irish laborers and often after completing a job they would 'settle out' in the towns along the railway and begin farming. When in 1866 the *Des Moines Register* felt progress was not what it should be in the construction of the Des Moines Valley Railroad it proclaimed, "Call Ireland to the rescue! Shovel and pick-ax, do your duty!"

Not all publicity was so complimentary, however. In the *Davenport Gazette* there appeared, "This city contains all kinds of people and from all nations of the human race, and some that are scarcely human, among whom are some of the wild red-mouthed Irish, with hair on their teeth, that are a pest to society." The Irish women who came often did domestic work or took in washing. In 1846 the *Dubuque Herald* said that nearly all the Irish in the First Ward, called Dublin, were guilty of the crime of being poor ("The Irish in Iowa," *The Palimpsest* XLV/2, Feb. 1964, p. 66).

The Boston *Pilot* reported the "West is full of colonies of Dutchmen, Norwegians, Portuguese and Hollanders, while the Irish though they are *everywhere* in units are nowhere together." There were, however, a number of typical Irish communities. Garryowen (originally called Makokiti), as discussed earlier, was one such place. Its settlers came primarily from Counties Cork and Limerick. Dennis Mahoney, the school teacher, was the one instrumental in getting the name of the village changed from Makokiti to Garryowen. Being from Limerick, he wanted the name of the town to commemorate the finest soccer team in Ireland—Garryowen, which happens to be in County Limerick. Mahoney later became a lawyer and in 1848 was elected to the state legislature. In his position as chair of the House Committee on Schools, he helped draft the bill that became the Public School Law of Iowa. As a legislator, treasure and later sheriff of Dubuque

County, and as an articulate Democrat newspaper editor who opposed Lincoln and the Civil War, Mahoney provides some colorful pages in Iowa history.

Another area that still goes by the name Irish Settlement is south and west of Des Moines. Rev. Timothy N. Mullen brought a number of Irish families to the area in 1853. Among them were immigrants from Counties Down, Roscommon, Derry, and Cavan. The settlement spread over areas of Madison and Jefferson counties. Drawn by the rich Iowa soil, the families prospered even though a number of them could not read or write. By 1860 a certain John Cunningham possessed $11,000 of property, but by 1870 he had land holdings worth $57,000. St. Patrick's Parish of Irish Settlement in Madison County was made doubly famous in October of 1979 when Pope John Paul II chose to visit this little church when he came to Iowa and celebrated with thousands of Iowan and other Midwesterners of various religious backgrounds at the Living History Farms outside of Des Moines. In his message to the people of Irish Settlement, he captured the spirit of this rural Iowa community and so many like it: "On your farms you are close to God's nature; in your work on the land you follow the rhythm of the seasons, and in your hearts you feel close to each other as children of a common Father and as brothers and sisters in Christ."

Emmetsburg in Palo Alto County, named after the Irish patriot Robert Emmet, was another early Irish settlement. In 1856 a number of Irish families from Illinois with six ox-drawn wagons crossed the Mississippi at Dubuque and followed the old trail through Manchester, Independence and Waterloo. Their destination was somewhere near Sioux City. When they reached Ft. Dodge they were advised by an Irishman named Lynch that good land, abundant water and plenty of timber could be found up along the west fork of the Des Moines River near Medium Lake. There they settled and soon were joined by others. In 1858 three speculators from Fort Dodge, Hoolihan, Cahill and Cavanaugh, came to the area on the west side of Medium Lake and staked out a town. Hoolihan suggested it be named after Robert Emmet. Although the speculators built a log court house, store, blacksmith shop and post office, when the county government was organized in that same year, another location was chosen for the county seat but the name followed to the site of the present town. The county officials with names like McCosker, Mulroney, Shea, and Tobin all came from the surrounding Irish colony. Emmetsburg has continued to this day to celebrate its Irish heritage. It has Dublin as its sister city and St. Patrick's Day often brings official guests from Dublin to help the town celebrate.

In 1849 Bishop Loras had strongly recommended the Des Moines River valley to immigrants. Irish settlers coming through Keokuk, at the southeast tip of the state where the Des Moines River enters the Mississippi, settled in Staceville (later called Georgetown), in Monroe County. A log church was build in 1857 but was replaced by a beautiful stone church in 1868, built from stone quarried close by with the help of parishioners. In nearby Melrose, still known as "Little Ireland," the earliest settlers were Methodists, and when the Irish came into the valley, tension developed between the two groups. In the early 1900s the Methodists began to move out of Melrose, some even digging up their dead and taking them with them. Eventually the Methodist-Episcopal Church was abandoned and later torn down. (Some Methodist families remained, however, and from one such family came United States Senator Thomas E. Martin. On the Irish side, Melrose's favorite son was the Rev. Leo Ward, philosopher and author at the University of Notre Dame.) Typical of so many Irish communities, the railroad brought many young Irish workers into the area: "There was a group of hardy men who helped build the first railroad west of the Des Moines River. Lured by the desire to have a farm in Monroe County, they returned after the railroad was finished to Keokuk" (M. M. Schmidt, *Seasons of Growth,* p. 72).

## A Railroad That Never Came: The Saga of Lytle City

Some Irish entrepreneurs, thinking they would strike it rich, anticipated the coming of the railroad by staking out towns along its supposed path. In one case, at least, the railroad chose another route. Lytle City in Iowa County was the village. In 1857 when the Mississippi and Missouri Railroad (later to become a part of the Chicago, Rock Island and Pacific) was about to be constructed from Iowa City to Des Moines, John Lytle and his sons conceived a project of locating a town site on the proposed railroad. A site was selected that lies about twenty miles due west of Iowa City passing through the Irish settlement of Holbrook. The three founders and their families settled in and began to erect wooden houses and a general store. A large area was even designated as a city park! Soon others joined them including a blacksmith, a shoemaker, a carpenter, a wagon maker, a plasterer, a saloon keeper, and several merchants. All hoped for the arrival of the railroad. Their hopes were dashed, however, when the railroad route was moved some twenty miles to the north so that it would go through the county seat at Marengo.

The inhabitants probably heard the disappointing news by 1860, but continued to hope that somehow the railroad would come and lead them out of their wilderness. The motto "If you build it, they will come" found its roots in Iowa long before the movie hit, *The Field of Dreams,* suggested "Is this heaven? No it's Iowa!" From 1857 until 1884 they waited and they hoped. Harry Eugene Kelly, a native son of Lyle City, told of the ordeal in the Williamsburg *Journal-Tribune* in 1936. Ironically, and unexpectedly, a railroad finally came to Lytle City, but it brought disaster. In 1884 the Milwaukee Railroad did come through a few miles to the west, but running north and south between Marion and Ottumwa, not east and west. The village of Parnell was established along the new railroad and to the new town the remaining inhabitants of Lytle City promptly moved, taking with them their residences, stores, buildings and families!

Parnell was named after the Irish statesman who had come to the American people to plead the cause of Ireland's land-impoverished peasants. (He spoke in Dubuque in 1879.) The earliest Irish settlers came in the late 1840s and early '50s. Many of the people who moved from Lytle City had come directly from Ireland but others, first-generation Irish, came from Ohio and other states further east. Today, in addition to the many citizens of Irish descent, Parnell has a number of Mennonites and a Mennonite church. What used to be exclusively Parnell Irish must now share a place with Parnell Amish. A number of young women from Parnell and the surrounding area joined the Sisters of Humility who taught in the school from 1901 until 1953. The Humility Sisters, whose roots were French, came to Ottumwa, Iowa, from Missouri, and became an important part of parochial education in the state. Many second- and third-generation Irish young women joined the order. Sister Ritamary Bradley, SFCC, while a member of the community, was instrumental in founding the Sister Formation Conference, which promoted professional preparation and advancement for women religious. The Humilities started not only Ottumwa Heights College, which prepared many young laywomen as teachers, but also Marycrest

College in Davenport (now Marycrest International University). The present bishop of Davenport, William Franklin, whose predecessor was Gerald O'Keefe, received his early education from the Humility Sisters in the Parnell school.

## IOWA'S IRISH HEROES AND LEGENDS OLD AND NEW

One of the able administrators of the Parnell school (1925–1941) and a legend in himself was J.B. McAreavy. Born in 1900 and raised in the Irish settlement of Ryan in Delaware county, "J.B.," "Mac," or as he was known in his early days, "Highball," was principal for three years and superintendent for thirteen. In addition he coached some excellent teams in basketball and baseball. A fine athlete himself, the nickname "Highball" was attached by another Irishman, Fritz McPartland. As related by the beloved eastern Iowa sportscaster, Tait Cummins, himself Irish, "Mac" was pitching in a Valley League game in Dubuque in the early 1920s and McPartland was umpiring. One pitch looked high to Fritz, so he called out, "Ball one." McAreavy glared at the ump. The next pitch was also called a ball and this time McAreavy gave McPartland some heated advice. The next pitch was also a ball—high. At that point McAreavy returned to the mound, wound up and threw the ball completely over the grandstand. He turned to McPartland who was working behind the mound and shouted, "Now you s.o.b, that ball is high!" as he stormed off the field, the umpire in hot pursuit. Irish in Iowa, as elsewhere, can at times have short tempers!

After serving in the Seabees during World War II, "Mac" began a distinguished career as teacher, principal and then superintendent in Oxford (on the Rhine), in Johnson County, a community of English, Welsh, German, and Bohemian, but with a solid core of Irish centered around the McDonough family from Galway. There "Mac" encountered another hotheaded Irishman, Rev. P. J. Ryan, the local pastor for some twenty-seven years who was from Tipperary. Father Ryan and "Mac" squared off on a number of issues concerning church and school, but the pastor had the advantage when it came to the pulpit. The parishioners, not yet introduced to television, would have the week to dwell on Fr. Ryan's colorful and pointed sermons. With his eye on McAreavy, he ended one of his memorable sermons with, "I don't know what to do mitcha. You're too dumb to understand your religion, you're too cheap to pay for it, and you're too weak to fight for it. You're just tummin' your way to heaven!"

One of the teachers that McAreavy hired to teach music in the Oxford school was Imogene O'Brien from Ryan. Having just married John W. Eckstein, who also was from Ryan, and who was in medical school in Iowa City, Imogene O'Brien Eckstein went on to become an outstanding lay leader in the post–Vatican II church. She was elected first president of the Davenport Diocesan Pastoral Council, president of the National Council of Catholic Laity, and in that capacity served with a number of others from the United States as representatives to the World Consultation of the Laity in Rome in 1975. In 1977 this very Irish mother of five was awarded the *Pro Ecclesia et Pontifice* medal by Pope Paul VI, one of the highest awards in the church.

Her husband, Dr. John Eckstein, Annie Cody's grandson whose father came from County Kilkenny, Ireland, had a distinguished career in medicine at the University of Iowa where he served as dean of the Medical School from 1970–91. In addition he has been recognized for his outstanding work in heart research for which he has received numerous honors and awards.

If famine in Ireland and hope for a better life brought to Iowa many farmers, tradesmen, laborers—and religious women and men to serve their spiritual needs—during the latter part of the twentieth century, education and research in the field of medicine seem to have attracted a considerable number of Irish physicians to the Iowa City-Cedar Rapids area near the University of Iowa Hospitals. Chipper Kearney, an Iowa City Irish tailor from County Tyrone, full of Irish stories, keeps a tab on many of the recent Irish immigrants to the Iowa City area. There are some eight or ten doctors in the area with roots in Ireland. One young doctor, Joseph Murray, with his wife, Imelda, and three children have found in Iowa City an ideal place for the children to receive an excellent education in safe surroundings, a vibrant faith community in which to worship, a lively intellectual community where serious issues are always open for discussion. (The famous Iowa Writers' Workshop has also attracted a number of fine writers, including Flannery O'Conner, Bill Murray, and Frank Conroy, the current director of the school.) The friendliness of the people and the varied greens of spring and summer remind the couple of home and Galway where they met. Being a member of the staff of the noted University of Iowa Hospitals has fulfilled the dream of Dr. Murray of being able to do research, practice medicine, and teach at the same time. One great advantage the contemporary Irish immigrants enjoy is being able to keep in contact with family back home by means of the Internet. Dr. Murray and his wife have also been instrumental in establishing in their community Project Children that brings young people from the North and the South of Ireland for a summer in the United States with the hope that the divisions in their homeland may lessen as the youth begin to know one another.

Like Irish everywhere, the Iowa Irish have had a yen for politics. Being a minority, mostly Democrats and Catholics, and in some places discriminated against, still the Irish have made and continue to make their mark in the political arena. State Senator Pat Deluher of Davenport (with maternal roots in the Donovan family from Bernard near Garryowen) says that the Irish continue to make their presence known in both houses of the legislature as well as in judgeships and state offices. The first governor of the state, Kirkwood, has some Irish roots. The Irish have partial claim on the popular governor in the 1960s and U.S. Senator in the 1970s, Harold Hughes, whose mother was a Kelly.

In the area of organized labor the Irish often took the lead. The two O'Conner brothers, Ed and Bill, priest professors at St. Ambrose College, were outspoken activists in the labor movement in the Davenport area during the late twenties and thirties.

One of the early heroines of Irish ancestry, known to school children who study Iowa history, is Kate Shelly. On the late evening of July 6, 1881, a severe thunderstorm and torrential downpour struck the little mining town of Honey Creek on the east side of the Des Moines River in Boone County. Kate, a young Irish woman, heard from her cabin near the tracks the railroad bridge collapse. Knowing that a passenger train would be passing within hours, she braved the storm and made her way along the train tracks to the adjacent village to warn the station master to stop the train before it reached the collapsed bridge. She has her place in Iowa history for her heroic deed.

It was not only the railroads that provided fodder for Irish legends in Iowa. Roads and highways did the same. When the territorial government was moved from Burlington to Iowa City in 1841 (Iowa became a state in 1946), the new stone capitol was not yet completed. The legislature had to meet in a frame building named after its builder, the Irishman, Walter Butler. A road from Dubuque to Iowa City, a distance of 100 miles, was authorized and another Irish settler, Lyman Dillon, was employed to break the trail for such a road by "ploughing a furrow as straight as a team of oxen could be driven and the topography would allow." ( Sage, *A History of Iowa,* pp. 63–64). Whether the oxen or the topography was to blame, the road to this day resembles a snakepath.

The railroads opened Iowa farmland to Irish immigrants, but roads from farms to the railroad became a major problem. Thomas Harris MacDonald, who grew up in Montezuma, Iowa, pulled Iowa out of the mud as the chief builder of Iowa's highway system from 1904–1919. He then became chief of the U.S. Bureau of Public Roads, holding various positions related to the federal highway system until his retirement in 1957.

A recent PBS documentary, *Divided Highways,* said that Mac-Donald, who created the interstate system, did as much as Henry Ford to put Americans on wheels. The momentous decisions of this very proper, but private Scotch-Irishman "transformed the American landscape and affected the daily lives and movements of almost every citizen" (The companion to the PBS documentary, "Divided Highways," by Lawrence Hott and Tom Lewis).

Although the time is past when hundreds of young Irish women either directly from Ireland or with Irish parentage were filling the ranks of religious orders as teachers, nurses, and administrators, a few still follow the path of the vowed life. One is Sister Bernadette Kett, OCD, a native of Tullamore, County Offaly, Ireland, who recently entered the Carmelite Monastery in Eldridge, Iowa.

In Iowa one cannot think about World War II without remembering the Sullivan brothers from Waterloo. The five brothers gave up their lives together when the cruiser *Juneau* on which they were all crew members, was sunk in the South Pacific in 1942. The Vietnam War is memorialized in the death of Michael Mullen, son of Peg and Gene Mullen, by "friendly fire." Michael, who would have been fifth generation of Irish settlers who had farmed the same land, was killed by mortar fire from the American side. In what they believed to be a coverup, his parents persisted in attempting to find out what really happened to their son. The whole episode, which merely fueled the growing opposition to the war, was recounted in the book by C. D. B. Bryan, and subsequently a movie, *Friendly Fire.*

The eyes of the world turned on Iowa in 1997 when septuplets were born to Bobbi and Ken McCaughey of Carlisle. The McCaughey roots are found in Ireland where Joseph McCaughey was born at Newtown (Limavady) Ireland. One of his sons, William, married Margaret Jackson who was the sixth generation in direct descent from Robert Bruce, King of Scotland. The Mc-Caugheys emigrated to America in 1773. The McCaughey family arrived in Iowa in 1850. The grandfather of the septuplets, Kenneth Paul McCaughey, married Mary Martesy McKissick, so, according to the grandmother, from their side of the family the septuplets have " a double shot of Irish!" One of the two doctors that delivered the septuplets, Paula Renee Mahone, who came to Iowa in 1993 from Ohio, is African-American, but with a name like Mahone, it is little wonder that the Iowa Irish would want to claim her as their own, even as the early settlers in Dubuque and Garryowen claimed the Italian missionary (Matthew Kelly) Mazzuchelli as one of theirs.

Jo Barbels Anderson and J. Michael Anderson, *The Man Mazzuchelli* (Madison, 1974).

C. D. B. Bryan, *Friendly Fire* (New York, 1976).

Homer L. Calkin, "The Irish in Iowa," *The Palimpsest* (XLV/2, 1964).

M. M. Hoffmann, *Arms and the Monk—The Trappist Saga in Mid–America* (Dubuque, 1952).

———, *Centennial History of the Archdiocese of Dubuque* (Dubuque, 1938).

———, *The Church Founders of the Northwest* (Milwaukee, 1937).

Lawrence Hott and Tom Lewis, The companion to the PBS documentary, "Divided Highways."

Eliphalet Price, "The Execution of Patrick O'Conner," *The Palimpsest* (I/3, 1930).

Leland L. Sage, *A History of Iowa* (Ames, 1974).

Madeleine M. Schmidt, CHM, *Seasons of Growth: History of the Diocese of Davenport* (Davenport, 1981).

EDMOND J. DUNN

## IRELAND, JOHN RICHARD (1838–1918)

Archbishop of St. Paul. A nationally known religious leader in Gilded Age America, John Ireland was born September 11, 1838, to Richard and Judith (Naughton) Ireland at Burnchurch in County Kilkenny, Ireland. In 1849, young John came to America, an exile from the Famine, with the rest of his family. After several rapid moves, they settled in Minnesota.

Sent by his bishop to study in France at Meximieux and Montbel, seminarian John Ireland returned to be ordained a priest in St. Paul, December 22, 1861. He served in 1862–63 as Civil War chaplain to the Fifth Minnesota Volunteers and saw action most notably at the Battle of Corinth. During 1869–70 he attended the First Vatican Council in Rome as a delegate of his bishop. Ireland was himself consecrated coadjutor bishop of St. Paul on December 21, 1875. One of his earliest projects, in conjunction with railroad financier James J. Hill, involved bringing some 4,000 immigrant families from crowded Eastern cities to settle the farmlands of Minnesota.

By the time he was named first archbishop of St. Paul in 1888, Ireland was a rising star in American Catholic circles. A Baltimore sermon in 1889 clearly identified him with other prelates who favored an optimistic view of the age and a conviction that American government and liberty were natural allies of the Catholic Church and its culture:

> I love my age. . . . I revel in its feats of valor, its industries and its discoveries. . . . I believe that God intends the present to

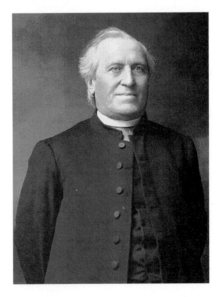

John Ireland

be better than the past, and the future to be better than the present . . . (O'Connell, 280–81).

The archbishop's progressive views were summarized in his 1897 work, *The Church and Modern Society.*

Ireland was instrumental in the establishment of the Catholic University of America at Washington. He served as an invaluable assistant to Cardinal Gibbons in his successful battle to prevent Rome's condemnation of the Knights of Labor, an early labor union. The Minnesota prelate pioneered innovative approaches to Catholic education that sought greater partnership with public schools. He also supported and attended the premier American interfaith gathering, the World Parliament of Religions at Chicago in 1893 (though by latter-day standards he was far from ecumenical in his attitude toward Protestants or Eastern Rite Catholics).

A vocal and progressive Republican, Ireland met with President McKinley at the White House in April 1898 in a fruitless attempt to prevent the Spanish-American War. In 1901, he received an honorary doctorate from Yale University.

Ireland battled with many Catholic German-Americans whom he faulted for not entering adequately into the mainstream of U.S. culture. His lifelong campaign against alcohol alienated the archbishop from many of his other coreligionists as well. He was an early and strong supporter of civil rights for African Americans; but he was an opponent of woman's suffrage. In his home archdiocese, he was a major builder, being responsible most notably for the Cathedral of St. Paul and the Basilica of St. Mary in Minneapolis that were under construction simultaneously in 1915.

Ireland died September 25, 1918, without receiving a cardinal's hat, an honor that he had hoped for much of his professional life.

*See* Catholicism, Irish-American

Gerald P. Fogarty, "Ireland, John," *Encyclopedia of American Catholic History* (Collegeville, Minn.: Liturgical Press, 1997): 687–89.

James Moynihan, *The Life of Archbishop John Ireland* (New York: Harper and Bros., 1953).

Marvin R. O'Connell, *John Ireland* (St. Paul: Minnesota Historical Society, 1988).

J. P. Shannon, "Ireland, John," *New Catholic Encyclopedia* VII (New York: McGraw-Hill, 1967): 610–13.

CLYDE F. CREWS

## IRELAND: 1798–1998

### THE 1798 INSURRECTION

If 1998 heralds the dawn of peace and agreement in all of Ireland, as so many people hope, then it will be an appropriate bicentenary of a national uprising organised by the United Irishmen, who sought not only to end British rule but to replace old sectarian animosities by "a brotherhood of affection, an identity of interests, a communion of rights and a union of power."

The decade of the 1790s, beginning in hope but ending in heartbreak, holds the key to understanding the two subsequent centuries of Irish history. The major themes of modern Ireland were already set in dramatic interplay—the emergence of nationalism and the idea of a Republic; the attempt to ally Catholic, Protestant and Dissenter; the foundation of the Orange Order, and of Maynooth College; the granting of substantive relief to

Catholics from the penal laws; and the frustrated hope of full Emancipation.

The insurrection of 1798, inspired by American and French revolutionary ideas, was complicated by sectarian passions, and had civil war dimensions as well as those of a liberation struggle. It was the bloody climax of a tumultuous decade, and the most convulsive political event in modern Irish history. In the violent summer weeks of 1798, 30,000 or so perished (in Wexford and the southeast, in the Midlands, in Antrim and Down, and in Connaught), more than in all subsequent rebellions and "troubles" *combined* down to our own day. The rebellion was crushed by ruthless, superior Crown forces, by widespread infiltration of spies and informers and by the failure of French military aid to arrive at an appropriate time. There followed reprisals, transportations and executions, particularly in the southeast. Theobald Wolfe Tone (1763–98), the leading spirit of the United Irishmen and the so-called father of Irish republicanism, committed suicide while in jail under sentence of death.

In the aftermath of 1798, there took place a realignment, or perhaps a polarisation, of forces in Ireland. The "Protestant nation," which had flirted with "patriotic" ideas from the 1770s to the 1790s but which had failed to deliver equality to their Roman Catholic fellow-countrymen, now returned to the sheltering arms of Mother England. Erstwhile Presbyterian Republicans also sought economic and religious security in closer links with Britain. The Roman Catholic majority was to be mobilised in various ways throughout the nineteenth century to become the modern Irish nation.

### THE UNION

The Act of Union (1800) was Britain's security response to Irish political and military instability, as evidenced particularly by the 1798 rebellion. The Irish parliament was abolished, the United Kingdom of Great Britain and Ireland was created and it was to last "forever." Ireland would be represented at Westminster by four bishops and twenty-eight "temporal" peers in the House of Lords, and a hundred MPs in the House of Commons. Within two or three decades, there was also to be financial union, and the two exchequers were amalgamated.

The proposed Union was a matter of intense debate. Its Protestant opponents were motivated partly by "patriot" feeling, partly by fear of an adverse impact on Irish commerce but also by the desire to retain political patronage and ascendancy. Catholic leaders, both episcopal and lay, generally backed the proposed Union, encouraged by the government to believe it would be the best framework for the accomplishment of complete Emancipation and the promotion of their interests. So, not all Irish "baddies" were for the Union and not all "goodies" against it!

Generations of Irish children were to be taught that the Union was passed "by perjury and fraud, by men who sold their land for gold as Judas sold his God." The government certainly pressured and seduced anti-unionists but such strategies were common enough eighteenth-century parliamentary practice.

The Union conditioned the course of Irish history down to 1922 and after. In theory, Ireland was to be governed after 1800 as part of one British state, and was supposed to be treated equally with other components of the United Kingdom. But because Ireland *was* different, in terms of religious and political grievances, rapid population growth, agrarian discontent, and poverty, it continued to be governed in colonial style by a Dublin

Castle hierarchy—lord lieutenant, chief secretary and under-secretary—answerable to the imperial government of the day in London. Moreover, Ireland's problems resulted in a degree of state intervention remarkable for the nineteenth century. Examples of this were the national school system (creating high literacy levels which, ironically, contributed to popular nationalism); public health; the poor law; and centralisation of agencies such as the constabulary.

While the Protestant minority saw the United Kingdom as the guaranteed framework of their religious, economic and social ascendancy, the Union was anathema to the nationalist spokesmen for the Catholic majority. The orthodox nationalist view was that pre-Union prosperity under a Dublin parliament was followed by post-Union economic decline. The simplistic corollary was that restoration of an Irish parliament would bring back Irish prosperity, a myth that endured down to the post-independence period. Opposition to the Union was mobilised on a mass basis in the Repeal agitation of the 1830s and 1840s and the Home Rule movement of the 1880s and 1890s. Yet, it can be argued that it was the wider Union context which made peaceful reforms, like Catholic Emancipation and land legislation, possible—reforms which would have met with fierce resistance from a Protestant-dominated Irish parliament after 1800. Conversely, the security which Protestants sought in the Union proved illusory: their church was disestablished in 1869, their rôle as landed gentry was undermined shortly thereafter and their monopoly of public office was gradually broken by continuing political and electoral reforms.

### PRE-FAMINE RURAL ECONOMY

Irish poverty, which was to have such a tragic expression during the Great Famine (1845–49), was the consequence of the economy and society. A phenomenally growing population was hugely dependent on a ramshackle land system. The population rose from 4.4 million in 1791, to 6.8m in 1821, to 7.8m in 1831 and (with the *rate* of increase slackening) to 8.2 m in 1841. Such growth was originally based on increased agricultural output meeting markets in Britain and overseas, early marriages linked to subdivision of holdings and subsistence diet precariously based on the ubiquitous potato. Population growth and the potato economy particularly characterised the rural underclass, the cottiers and agricultural labourers, some of whom were landless and vagrant while others depended on subsistence plots. Tenant farmers and middlemen were farther up the social pyramid while several thousand landlords, Protestant in religion and English in culture, formed the apex.

Landlords traditionally have had a bad press, understandably in many cases. But even improving landlords, in the early nineteenth century, were faced by formidable difficulties. There was intense resistance among land-hungry tenants to attempted consolidation of smallholdings. Tenant grievances often found expression in violent agrarian unrest. From the late eighteenth century to the Famine, rural secret societies such as the Whiteboys, the Rightboys, the Rockites, the Hearts of Steel and the Molly Maguires were particularly active at times of economic depression. By maiming livestock, injuring property, intimidation and personal violence, these societies made effective protests against enclosures of common land, tithes and local tax burdens. All this was not simply a straightforward confrontation between tenants and landlords. In a complex system of land tenure, agrarian protest was often conducted by labourers and cottiers against the tenant farmers. More generally, agrarian unrest was aggravated

Daniel O'Connell

by depression and slump after the ending of the revolutionary and Napoleonic wars in 1815. For the previous forty years, Ireland had benefitted from the demand, and consequent high prices, for grain and foodstuffs.

### EMANCIPATION: DANIEL O'CONNELL

The great political drive of the 1800–30 period was towards the achievement of Catholic Emancipation. Irish Catholics had been disappointed and embittered by the British government's failure to deliver full emancipation with the Union, as had been promised. Parliamentary petitions proved fruitless, and some kind of agitation was indicated. Catholics had been relieved from many of their disabilities in the 1780s and 1790s and had been given the parliamentary vote (on the limited franchise basis then prevailing) in 1793. But they were still second-class citizens, being denied the right to sit in parliament and to hold the highest offices in government, the public service, the army and the law. These remaining penal laws directly affected only the professional classes but they demeaned the status of *all* Catholics.

In 1823 the foundation of the Catholic Association marked a new phase in the struggle for equal rights for Catholics and, as things turned out, in popular mobilisation and mass politics. The spread of the Association was linked with the Catholic "rent" whereby members paid a small but regular subscription, thereby not only providing campaign funds, but supplying a strong psychological sense of identification with the cause. This extended to the poorest classes whose widows' mites tied them into the Association as well, even though they lacked the franchise, and would not gain directly from emancipation. In addition to these pioneering techniques of democratic organisation, the Association drew popular support by publicising various popular grievances, exposing the partisan workings of the law and the courts, and making the fullest use of propaganda outlets such as newspapers. Two other novel features deserve mention: the organisation of mass meetings, and the recruitment of the Catholic clergy as agents and organisers throughout the parochial network of Ireland. The Catholic Church had been traditionally cautious where agitation was concerned, even for Catholic relief, and clerical involvement now was a new departure, but one undertaken with alacrity and enthusiasm. The "priest in politics" had arrived, and stayed for the best part of a century.

The inspiration and embodiment of the new agitation was Daniel O'Connell (1775–1847), the first and arguably the most significant of Ireland's popular leaders, and the father of Irish democracy. The O'Connells of Derrynane, on the remote south Kerry coast, were Catholic petty gentry who had survived the penal laws by keeping their heads below the parapet, enjoying good relations with Protestant fellow-landlords and not falling foul of the law. The O'Connells had strong links with *ancien régime* France, through soldiering and commerce.

O'Connell became a brilliant barrister and won popular fame because of his defence of Catholic clients in the courts against a partisan magistracy and police system. In fact, his soubriquet of "the Counsellor" had much greater currency in his own time than the later one of "the Liberator," and tales of his forensic cunning abounded in the rich folklore that surrounded him. His political involvement partly stemmed from his resentment at the legal constraints that prevented him, as a Catholic, from reaching the heights of his profession.

As Ireland's first populist politician, he was a splendid orator and demagogue. Though he did not pioneer the strategy of putting up pro-Emancipation candidates in parliamentary elections, he brought it to a successful conclusion, daringly standing himself, as a Roman Catholic, in the Clare election of 1828, and winning a resounding victory with the backing of the "forty-shilling freeholders" who courageously defied their landlords' directions in open ballot at the hustings. The Protestant establishment in England and Ireland feared rebellion and anarchy should the Catholic demand continue to be refused. Accordingly, the Catholic Emancipation Act became law on 13 April 1829. While the Act removed virtually all remaining legal and civil restrictions on Roman Catholics in the United Kingdom, in the nature of things only the well-off reaped the rewards in the short term. Yet psychologically *all* Catholics were liberated by this great landmark in hard-won civil rights. In Ireland, the Act was a significant step in eroding Protestant dominance in the professions and public life.

Genial and extrovert in personality, O'Connell's philosophy was pragmatic and utilitarian. For him, human rights resided in the individual and not in the nation: indeed, he was a liberal rather than a nationalist. As a matter of realpolitik, he was opposed to the use of violence in the achievement of political aims. He certainly had no interest in what would later be called cultural nationalism and, though himself a native Irish speaker, shed no tears at the "gradual disuse" of the language. He was passionately committed to human rights at home and abroad, and opposed slavery in the United States as well as discrimination against Jews in Britain and Europe. In an age when throne and altar were still closely intertwined, O'Connell argued for the separation of church and state. By showing in his own career that there was no inherent contradiction between Catholicism and democracy, he was the forerunner of the European Christian Democrat tradition. Since he was a practitioner of ward boss politics, croneyism and nepotism, he was also the prototype of welfare mayors in modern American cities. In short, Daniel O'Connell's historical significance far transcends the Irish context.

## REPEAL

After Emancipation, O'Connell, now a parliamentarian with his own following or "tail," seemed to alternate between seeking reform under favourable British administrations—the "justice for Ireland" policy—and agitating for Repeal of the Act of Union. The 1830s saw advances in the provision of primary education,

A poster issued by Daniel O'Connell in support of the Repeal of the Act of Union, July 1841

the effective solution of the tithes grievance, and the introduction of a well-intentioned (albeit inadequate) poor law system. Much of this spirit of reform was personified in Thomas Drummond (1797–1840), under-secretary at Dublin Castle (1835–40), whose progressive policies were best expressed in his celebrated reminder to Irish landlords: "property has its duties as well as its rights."

However, O'Connell became convinced that Irish Catholic rights would never realise their true potential in a predominantly Protestant United Kingdom. His later career was dedicated to a campaign, peaking in 1842–43, to secure Repeal of the Union and self-government for Ireland. The tactics adopted were similar to those used in the Emancipation agitation, but Emancipation was only a sectional or civil reform whereas no London administration would give in to a movement threatening the fabric of the United Kingdom. When O'Connell accepted a government ban on a proposed "monster" meeting at Clontarf in October 1843, the Repeal movement was effectively at an end. It was also damaged by a split between O'Connell and his "Young Ireland" followers who espoused a more radical brand of nationalism through the talented pens (notably used in *The Nation* weekly newspaper) of such journalist-nationalists as Thomas Davis (1815–45) and John Mitchel (1815–75).

Thomas Davis, Charles Gavan Duffy, and John Blake Dillon co-found *The Nation,* a newspaper that published the views of the Young Ireland Party.

O'Connell died in 1847, his last years clouded by the Great Famine. His impotence in the face of this catastrophe—he could only utter pathetic parliamentary pleas for help—revealed the limitations of his political philosophy, which lacked any meaningful social or economic analysis. Proposing that absentee landlords be taxed was a totally inadequate response to Ireland's grievous socioeconomic problems.

## THE FAMINE

Extensive historical research has deepened our understanding of the Great Famine (1845–49) but has not changed its central significance in modern Irish history. It is at once *the* great catastrophe and the great watershed. It set in train fundamental social, economic and cultural changes, or at least accelerated changes already happening. The Famine cut to the heart of the Irish psyche, and popular perceptions of the event greatly influenced the course of Irish and Irish-American nationalism and of Anglo-Irish relations.

The immediate cause of the Famine was destruction of the potato crop by blight in successive years. Potatoes were the staple diet of at least one-third of the population, notably agricultural labourers and cottiers, but typhus and fever accounted for more deaths than starvation, in all totalling over one million. Some relief was undertaken by private sources, such as the Quakers, but governmental response was totally inadequate despite the efforts of concerned public servants. A supply of Indian meal, a programme of public works, and the provision of soup kitchens were all insignificant given the huge dimensions of the suffering, and the overcrowded "workhouses" were completely unable to cope.

Nationalist recriminations imputed callous negligence, if not genocidal intent, to the British administrations of the day, which were blamed not simply for the catastrophe but for the land

The Famine endures: a widow and her dying child

system which facilitated it. Government economists were hidebound by *laissez-faire* principles, which prohibited interference with the food market and the export of agricultural produce: it was the sight, and the subsequent memory, of grain leaving Irish ports while the population starved that stuck in the craw of Famine survivors and their descendants, especially in the United States. Another bitter Famine recollection was of increasing evictions by apparently ruthless landlords. Some politicians and public servants saw the crisis in Ireland as an opportunity for a belated overhaul of land structures and a chance to consolidate smallholdings, now that excessive population was being reduced. And not a few in church (established) and state (British) saw the hand of God at work, chastening and correcting a feckless and improvident people.

The population of Ireland fell by one-fourth between 1845 and 1851, to 6.5 million in the latter year (the *rate* of population growth had been slackening before the Famine). The virtual decimation of the cottier class, and the sharp reduction in the number of agricultural labourers, meant a new emphasis on the family farm and the replacement of improvidently early marriages by prudently late nuptials (generally an arranged marriage or "match") or by none at all in many cases. Accordingly, as pasture regained its traditional supremacy from pre-Famine intensive tillage, population was proportionately surplus to requirements, with emigration taking care of the overflow.

The result of all this was a continuing population decline (particularly in rural areas) down to 4.4 million in 1911, and a relatively stagnant level thereafter. Under native government from 1922, population still fell gradually but began to pick up with an improved economic situation from the 1960s.

In the desperate attempt to escape a stricken land, over one million people emigrated during and immediately after the Famine. Emigration had been a phenomenon of Irish life from the early 1800s but the pattern now quickened, women emigrating as well as men (which didn't happen with other European emigrants). The United States was the favourite destination, with far-reaching consequences for Irish nationalism. For some, emigration was a personal and cultural upheaval, subsequently sentimentalised as "exile" in the nationalist perspective. For others,

Ireland in 1845

as for millions of Europeans, it was a pursuit of a better life. In any case, it is estimated that, in the century from 1815 down to 1914, eight million Irish people left their native land for good. This resulted in the phenomenon of "the sea-divided Gael" and "the Irish race," a global constituency or diaspora (some forty million of Irish descent in the United States? seventy million world-wide?), a potential source of goodwill or more material succour for the Irish at home.

Depopulation and evictions led to the consolidation of sub-sistence smallholdings, a more simplified land structure and the emergence of the tenant farmer as the dominant representative stock of rural Ireland. In turn, this advanced the cause of tenant rights and, later on, in the 1880s, the mobilisation of tenant power in the successful fight against landlordism. In this as in other areas, the Famine cleared the way for modernisation.

The Catholic Church had found it difficult to service the pastoral needs of an exploding and poverty-stricken pre-Famine population and to make disciplinary headway against a rural underclass strongly influenced by quasi-pagan folk beliefs. In the improved economy of post-Famine Ireland, and with the wiping out of this underclass and the weakening of this "pagan" underlay, the Church entered a new phase of strength and power (to last for over a century) through institutional buildings, a high priest-people ratio, tight clerical discipline, obedience to Rome, streamlined organisation all round and, above all, involvement in education. Paul Cardinal Cullen, archbishop of Dublin (1852–78), personified this new development.

English was the language of conquest and colonisation in Ireland, and also of public life and formal education. The Irish language was well in decline long before the mid-nineteenth century but it was still the everyday language of perhaps four million people on the eve of the Great Famine. But these were predominantly the poorest classes who were most heavily affected by Famine fatalities and subsequent large-scale emigration. In the 1851 Census, Irish speakers accounted for only 1.5 million, or a quarter of the population. The language shift to English, the perceived language of social advance and material betterment, continued inexorably for the rest of the century and into the next.

The Famine quickly radicalised nationalist sentiment, as is evident from the writings of James Fintan Lalor (1807–49) and John Mitchel (1815–75). Anti-British, separatist and occasional "socialist" notes were sounded, and even in more moderate and constitutional political circles, the dominant feeling was that a remote and uncaring London government bore a large responsibility for the calamity.

There were other, indefinable ways in which memories of the Great Famine deeply affected the Irish mind. There was the half-suppressed realisation that not everything could be blamed on British misgovernment and incompetence, and that some Irish people had callously prospered at the expense of their starving fellow countrymen. Post-Famine generations suffered a deep sense of insecurity about the possible reoccurrence of such a catastrophe, or through the fear of being driven by poverty to have recourse to the dreaded "workhouse." More happily, historical consciousness of their own Famine has made Irish people generously responsive to appeals to help alleviate famine suffering in various twentieth-century calamities.

## EDUCATION

Though cultural nationalists rightly deplored the national loss experienced through the decline of the Irish language, English

Thomas Davis

was the indispensable language of educational advance, of political sophistication and, ironically, of the growth of popular nationalism eventually leading to independence. "Educate that you may be free" was the great political slogan of the Young Ireland nationalist philosopher Thomas Davis (1815–45) but education was, in the first instance, a liberation process for the individual. Whatever the motivations of those who set up the national schools system from 1831, the schools supplied the powerful tool of literacy to the people as well as providing a surprisingly wide curriculum. The proportion of Irish people able to read (English, of course, since literacy in Irish was rare) rose from 47% in 1841 to 88% in 1911, an increase of far-reaching implications in all areas of life.

Secondary education in the nineteenth century was available only to a privileged minority, with financial support being provided by the government through the Intermediate Education Act (1878). University education was even more elitist as well as being a highly controversial matter, because of the conflicting attitudes of the state and the churches. The Queen's Colleges Act (1845) provided higher education in colleges at Belfast, Cork and Galway, while University College Dublin and Trinity College Dublin had different histories and developments. By and large, the native language and culture were ignored in schools at every level, and had to await the arrival of an independent Irish state to secure proper attention.

### THE FRANCHISE

The myth still persists that violence was the dominant mode of political action in Ireland down to independence. In fact, the Irish pioneered mass electoral politics and the development of parliamentary parties. Political mobilisation was, of course, predicated on the slow but sure extension of the right to vote and the elimination of privileged borough franchises. The march to democracy was marked by successive milestones, weakening and finally eliminating the link between property and franchise. The Reform Act of 1868 and the Representation of the People Act (1884) were precursors to the great widening of the franchise in 1918, when another Representation of the People Act gave the vote to men over 21 and women over 30, thus facilitating the Sinn Féin electoral landslide in that year.

## The Fenians

In the 1850s, there was an attempt to promote an Independent Opposition Party linked to tenant right agitation but the times were not propitious for such developments which faintly foreshadowed the powerful parliamentary-land movement of the 1880s. Meanwhile, Fenianism dominated the nationalist stage. It could be regarded as the most significant of the dragon's teeth sown by the Great Famine, and the first major expression of post-Famine Irish-America whose bitterness is encapsulated in the ballad phrase, "revenge for Skibbereen." Organised by such Young Ireland survivors as John O'Mahony (1816–77), James Stephens (1824–1901) and Michael Doheny (1805–63), the Fenian Brotherhood or Irish Republican Brotherhood was founded as a revolutionary, secret society in 1858 on both sides of the Atlantic, with the specific aim of establishing an Irish republic by force of arms. (The term "Fenian" was inspired by the "Fianna," legendary warriors of early Ireland.) It had a vast membership network, on paper at any rate, particularly in the United States but also in Britain and Ireland. Despite its secrecy ethos, it organised openly and preached the gospel in its own newspaper, *The Irish People.* Opposed by the Catholic Church and by constitutional nationalists, it sought to infiltrate the British Army but was in turn infiltrated by spies and informers. Prominent leaders were arrested in 1865, and a rising in March 1867 only amounted to a few skirmishes.

Nevertheless, the movement had a lasting impact on the revolutionary and republican tradition. There was great popular regard for "the bold Fenian men," an amnesty movement for Fenian prisoners focused nationalist attention, and the execution of three Fenian activists, the "Manchester Martyrs," provoked widespread and enduring sympathy. The IRB maintained an intermittent but significant conspiratorial existence during the following decades, being the prime mover in planning the Easter 1916 Rising. On the Protestant unionist side of the coin, "Fenian" remains to this day a term of abuse for Catholics in Northern Ireland, and in Victorian England it connoted a threatening bogeyman. Finally, in terms of practical consequences, Fenianism helped William Ewart Gladstone (Liberal party prime minister, 1868–74 and later periods) to realise the need for "justice for Ireland." This was expressed in such reforming measures as the disestablishment of the Church of Ireland (1869) and the Land Act of 1870, and later in attempts to enact Home Rule for Ireland.

## Railways

Despite (or perhaps because of) population loss and emigration, living standards rose, and business activity increased in the later nineteenth century. There was a lively trade in foodstuffs, both for the home and export markets, though industrial development in the south of Ireland was largely centred in Dublin. Belfast and east Ulster were the heartland of Ireland's industrial revolution, with the emphasis on shipbuilding and factory-based textiles.

All these developments, north and south, were greatly facilitated by the railway age. The opening of the Dublin-Kingstown line in 1834 ushered in twenty years of extensive railway building. The travel revolution modernised people's lives in various ways, in the provision of cheaper commodities, for example, in standardising timekeeping, and in easier access to seaside resorts. But Ireland's low population density could not sustain an extensive rail network, and the popularity of road transport in the age of the motor car was to lead by the mid-twentieth century to a ruthless paring back of the number of rail lines.

## Land, Home Rule and Parnell

Between 1870 and 1903, the ownership of Irish land was transferred from some thousands of landlords to some hundreds of thousands of tenants. This dramatic shift, which totally undermined the Ascendancy class, was accomplished by a combination of political leadership, parliamentary legislation and mass action. While the strategies employed were generally within the law, intermittent violent pressure helped to "secure a hearing for moderation," as the phrase went. IRB activists combined with Irish parliamentarians in a "New Departure" compact that was designed to promote the "national" as well as the "land" question. Home Rule and peasant proprietorship went hand in hand.

The Land League was the mass organisation whose aims extended from tenants' rights and rent reductions to peasant proprietorship and, in the case of founding father Michael Davitt (1846–1905), to the dream of land nationalisation. Charles Stewart Parnell (1846–91) was president of the League—and its inspiration—during its most influential period (1879–82) but he then replaced it by the National League, reflecting his move away from the volatile and semi-violent agrarian struggle to the constitutional pursuit of Home Rule. (There was also a short-lived Ladies' Land League, led by Parnell's sister, Anna.)

The land war used a variety of strategies—rent witholding (as in the Plan of Campaign), physical resistance to evictions, and boycotting, combined with effective anti-landlord and anti-British rhetoric at mass meetings. Government coercion simply stimulated the movement to greater efforts. Reforming land acts, notably Gladstone's 1881 Act and Wyndham's 1903 Act, satisfied the substance of the land movement's claims, mainly through the mechanism of government-advanced land-purchase loans to the tenants. Nevertheless, the poorer rural classes continued to have their grievances, and agrarian agitation rumbled on intermittently down to the foundation of the Irish Free State.

In conclusion, two general observations may be made about the restructuring of the land system: first, the small family farms of Ireland remained economically unviable down to the late twentieth century, with consequent rural stagnation and continuing

Michael Davitt

emigration—this situation was transformed only by European Community membership in 1973 and the benefits of the Common Agricultural Policy; secondly, the new peasant proprietors comprised a fiercely individualist and conservative bloc, adamantly opposed to any radical "isms" of a socialist or secular kind.

The passions stirred by the land war were as much nationalist as agrarian, and this redounded to the benefit of the Home Rule movement. Initially espoused by some middle-class Protestants and led by the conservative and moderate nationalist Isaac Butt (1813–79), Home Rule really took off as a national movement under the leadership of Parnell in the late 1870s. A County Wicklow Protestant landlord who became leader of a largely Catholic "tenant" people, Charles Stewart Parnell remains somewhat of a paradox. Rather aloof in temperament, he was a superb political and parliamentary strategist, and inspired fierce loyalties as well as intense hostility. He welded his followers in the House of Commons into the first disciplined and organised political party in the United Kingdom, thereby leaving an indelible mark on the development of Irish democracy. The quality of the Irish parliamentary party, comprising eighty-six members after the 1885 election, was reflected in the calibre of Parnell's foremost lieutenants, John Dillon (1851–1927) and William O'Brien (1852–1928).

Strictly speaking, "Home Rule" meant an unspecified measure of self-government under continuing Westminster sovereignty but like similar dynamic catch cries from the past, "Emancipation" and "Repeal," it could be interpreted variously and ambitiously to mean the essence of Irish independence. Its very ambiguity was a source of strength to the enigmatic Parnell who was thus enabled to lead a remarkable common front in the 1880s, which included an IRB or Fenian element, influential Catholic bishops, agrarian radicals and, of course, the powerful parliamentary party.

Gladstone's Home Rule Bill of 1886 ran into opposition not only from the Conservatives and unionists but also from a powerful section of his own followers, thereby seriously splitting the Liberal party. Meanwhile, Parnell seemed to have withdrawn somewhat from the centre of events, though he reached a new pinnacle of popularity when the accusations by *The Times* newspaper, that he had connived at terrorist crime, were proved (in 1890) to be false. Shortly afterwards, his affair with Katherine O'Shea became public, with Parnell being cited as co-respondent in a divorce petition. He was now disowned by the Catholic bishops as national leader, and the Irish parliamentary party became grievously split on the issue. With his career in ruins, Parnell fell ill and died in October 1891.

In the circumstances, it is hardly surprising that an aura of tragic romance long surrounded his name: his followers cast him in the rôle of blameless hero, brought low by malicious and vindictive enemies—"the bishops and the party that tragic story made," to quote Yeats. But Parnell was very much the author of his own misfortunes, first, through his neglect of Ireland, politics and parliament in the late 1880s, and ultimately through his refusal to accept that his leadership after the divorce scandal was an embarrassing liability to the Nationalist-Liberal alliance and therefore to any renewed prospect for Home Rule.

Like other nationalist leaders since his time, Parnell underestimated the strength of Ulster unionist resistance to Irish self-government. Nevertheless, his importance as a great nationalist leader endures. He made self-government for Ireland a central issue in British politics. What "the Chief" seemed to stand for in terms of Ireland's independent destiny, appealed to constitutionalists and republicans alike in the decades after his death.

## Renaissance and the "New Nationalism"

While Gladstone's second attempt to enact Home Rule also failed (1893) and while Parnell's once great party consumed itself in factional squabbles, Ireland at the turn of the century was characterised on the one hand by relatively benign government from the Conservative party ("killing Home Rule by kindness") and on the other by a remarkable literary and cultural renaissance. Poets (e.g., William Butler Yeats, 1865–1939) and dramatists (e.g., John Millington Synge, 1871–1909), often from Protestant backgrounds, sought inspiration from folklore and mythology to create a new literature and drama in English. The movement, variously called the "Anglo-Irish revival" or "the Celtic twilight" and closely associated with the Abbey Theatre in Dublin, did not always meet with the approval of a strongly conformist and conservative Catholic public opinion. Neither did it harmonise with the philosophy of the Irish language revival whose advocates argued that no true Irish literature could be created in English. D.P. Moran (1869–1936) preached the (often intolerant) doctrine of "Irish-Ireland" in his *Leader* weekly newspaper.

The Gaelic League was founded in 1893 by Eoin MacNeill (1867–1945) and (the Protestant) Douglas Hyde (1860–1949, first president of Ireland, 1938–45) with the aim of restoring the Irish language as the vernacular. Though Irish was arguably too far in decline ever to stand a realistic chance of being revived as a nation-wide everyday language, the League became a powerful educational and cultural movement. Hyde wished it to be non-political as he wanted to retain Protestant and unionist interest but the League inevitably attracted radical nationalists who eventually took it over. As a cultural force, it contributed enormously to the formation of the Irish revolutionary mind and the struggle for independence.

Most popular and successful of all the "new nationalist" organisations was the Gaelic Athletic Association founded in 1884 by Michael Cusack (1847–1906). Though the GAA was enthusiastically supported by Archbishop T.W. Croke of Cashel (1824–1902) and other Catholic clergy, the IRB or Fenians dominated it in the early years and it was riven by disputes. By the early 1900s however, the Association began to prosper as an organised spectator sport in the games of hurling and Gaelic football, even though the founders' intentions were that Irish youth would undergo social and national regeneration by active participation in athletics.

The GAA both reflected, and contributed to, the strongly nationalist atmosphere of the period. It banned its members from playing or even watching "foreign" games (rugby and soccer in particular) and it excluded—under Rule 21—policemen and armed forces, representing British rule, from membership. The "foreign games" ban was to be abolished in 1971 but Rule 21 is still (1998) in force. In healing the wounds of the Civil War (1922–23), the GAA was an important reconciling force. As a great social and recreational movement in modern Ireland, the GAA went from strength to strength after independence.

The organisation which did most to focus the "new nationalism" was Sinn Féin—"we ourselves"—(1905). It was far more successful, before 1916, as a nationalist mind-moulder than as a political party. Its chief founder Arthur Griffith (1871–1922) was also its leading polemicist and propagandist. Its dominant

Edward Carson speaks at an anti–Home Rule meeting, 1912.

political idea, a dual monarchy with an independent Ireland under the British crown, was soon superseded but its socio-economic policy was to have a central influence for decades. This was the notion of self-sufficiency, which had a long lineage in economic nationalism. Ireland's resources (afforestation, for example) would be exploited in the interests of its people, and tariffs would protect native industries, thus creating employment and ending the haemorrhage of emigration. Sinn Féin advocated civil disobedience, withdrawal from Westminster and institution of a native parliament, rather than a physical force strategy.

### VOLUNTEERING, NORTH AND SOUTH

Events as well as movements, together with the moribund state of post-Parnell faction-ridden parliamentary politics, strengthened the new nationalism as the century turned. One of these events was the centenary of the 1798 insurrection, widely observed throughout the country; another was the struggle in South Africa of the Boers against British rule (1899–1902) which evoked great interest and sympathy in nationalist Ireland; and yet another catalyst was the protest movement against Queen Victoria's visit in 1900.

However, it was the controversy over the third Home Rule Bill (1912–14) that initiated the turbulent happenings of the decade which followed. While the bill dragged its slow length through parliament, unionists in the northeast (under the leadership of Dublin-born Edward Carson, 1854–1935, and James Craig, 1871–1940) were mobilised for resistance on the grounds that "home rule was Rome rule," that it betrayed their British and imperial heritage, and that Irish self-government would be disastrous for the Ulster economy. The Ulster Volunteer Force (UVF) was founded in January 1913 to give paramilitary teeth to the unionist campaign and the Larne gun-running the following April made the 90,000-strong militia a formidable factor. Meanwhile, nationalists reacted in November 1913 by forming the Irish Volunteers in Dublin to defend the apparently imminent granting of Home Rule. The IRB had placed itself in strategic positions in all the nationalist movements, and the Volunteers were no exception, though John Redmond (1856–1918), moderate leader of the reunited Irish parliamentary party, seemed to have secured overall control of a force which was to grow to about 160,000.

This tense situation took a further critical turn with the outbreak of the Great War (1914–18). The Home Rule Act had eventually become law but its implementation was deferred to the end of the war. To many nationalists, this postponement was proof of British duplicity on the issue, and the last straw was Redmond's appeal to the Volunteers to support the British war effort and go "wherever the firing line extends." There ensued a split in the Volunteers, with the great majority (the National Volunteers) supporting Redmond and heeding his call. The minority (the Irish Volunteers) under Eoin MacNeill became an intensely nationalist corps dedicated to defending Ireland's right to self-government.

### EASTER RISING 1916

While the UVF and many National Volunteers fought on the Western front, the IRB set about using the manpower of the 15,000-strong Irish Volunteers to mount a rebellion, exploiting "England's difficulties" as Ireland's opportunity. Though organisational plans were confused and the expected German help never materialised, the Easter Rising broke out in Dublin on 24 April 1916 with the seizure of the General Post Office and other locations by approximately 1,000 Volunteers and 200 members of the Irish Citizen Army, a socialist-nationalist militia under the labour leader, James Connolly (1868–1916). Though some skirmishes took place in provincial areas, the 1916 Rising, as it eventually took place, was less of a military operation with some prospect of success than a staged demonstration of militant nationalism and a "blood sacrifice." The rebels formed a Provisional Government which declared an Irish Republic to be established and issued a Proclamation "in the name of God and the dead generations," demanding the allegiance of the Irish people. The commander-in-chief of the Volunteers in the Rising and the president of the provisional government was Patrick Pearse (1879–1916), teacher and revolutionary, whose writings had exalted the concept of bloodshed and "blood sacrifice" and who had declared the year before that "Ireland unfree shall never be at peace."

The fighting against Crown forces continued for a week and ended in the surrender of the insurgents, the devastation of Dublin city centre and the deaths of some 200 combatants and 230 civilians. The Rising was seen as a stab in the back from the standpoint of the British authorities and the Ulster unionists, many thousands of whom were to die in the battle of the Somme some months later. Moreover, the Rising was regarded as mad-

Patrick Pearse

Sir Roger Casement

ness or sabotage by the thousands of "southern" Irish who also suffered heavy casualties at the front, by most clerical leaders, by mainstream constitutional nationalists and by commercial and farming interests who were "doing well out of the war."

Hostile public opinion soon changed to sympathy and even admiration, as dormant nationalism was stirred by the courage and idealism of the insurgents, and the perceived martyrdom of the fifteen leaders executed by the British authorities. (A sixteenth, Sir Roger Casement, 1864–1916, was added in August when he was hanged for treason in trying to secure German aid.) Nineteen-sixteen became the mystic year of Irish republicanism, exerting a mesmeric influence on nationalists for decades to come, with the Proclamation being seen and read as a sacred text.

## POST–1916 RESURGENCE

Widespread arrests of insurgents were followed by internment but a general release within a short period enabled surviving 1916 leaders to organise a new resistance. Two of the most prominent of these were Eamon de Valera (1882–1975) and Michael Collins (1890–1922). Sinn Féin, as such, was not involved in the Rising, but as the best-known national organisation, it now became the vehicle and the framework for post-1916 nationalist resurgence. However, the "new" Sinn Féin was a never-quite-harmonious common front of old-style Griffith moderates, militant Volunteers and others. The organisation's October 1917 Ard-Fheis (convention) declared its aim to be "the international recognition of Ireland as an independent Irish Republic" and elected Eamon de Valera as its president. De Valera was also appointed president of the Volunteers and was elected MP for East Clare. He trailed clouds of glamorous glory as a surviving 1916 commandant, and was seen as an exotic name and personality. Thus began the turbulent and chequered career of the predominant nationalist leader of twentieth-century Ireland.

Sinn Féin grew in numbers and popular support during 1918, deriving particular credit from its rôle in the successful campaign of opposition to the British government's plan to impose conscription on Ireland. In the U.K. general election of December 1918, the first since 1910, Sinn Fínn greatly benefitted from the new nationalist mood and from the three-fold increase in the electorate through the post-war extension of the franchise. In a

sweeping victory, it secured 73 out of 105 parliamentary seats in Ireland, leaving only a solid unionist bloc in the northeast, and a handful out of the now decimated Irish parliamentary party. That party was the victim not only of radical nationalism but of generational and social change. John Redmond, its leader, had died a broken and discredited man, having failed to realise his dream of Home Rule within the British Empire and of harmony between nationalist and unionist in a common war effort. In the demonology of Irish nationalism, he would (unfairly) be remembered as a West Brit, a stooge, and an ignominious compromiser.

## DÁIL ÉIREANN: THE ANGLO-IRISH STRUGGLE

The elected Sinn Féin members did not take their seats at Westminster but convened their own parliament, Dáil Éireann, in Dublin in January 1919. Ignored by unionists and the rump parliamentary party, it reaffirmed the Republic "established in 1916," issued a Declaration of Independence and a socially radical "Democratic Programme," and elected de Valera president of a Westminster-style cabinet government. The Dáil was eventually proscribed but its ministry tried to function, with some success, in opposition to the British regime. The new administration unsuccessfully tried to secure international recognition at the Versailles peace conference on the much-proclaimed principles of national self-determination and the rights of "small nations." It was this failure, as well as the militancy of Volunteers within and without the Dáil, that lay behind the gradual recourse to violence which, when met with state counterviolence, constituted the Anglo-Irish War or "War of Independence," 1919–21. The vote for independence in 1918 had not been intended as a mandate for violence.

The struggle conducted by the Volunteers (coming more and more to be known as the Irish Republican Army or IRA) consisted initially of arms seizures and attacks on policemen (Royal Irish Constabulary) and police barracks. The succeeding phase was guerrilla warfare which highlighted the rôle of "flying columns" specialising in ambushing Crown forces. The British government retaliated with counterterror measures through the agency of the notorious "Black-and-Tans" and Auxiliaries. IRA activity was sporadic and local, with the initiative generally taken by local leaders, and large areas of the country remained rela-

Eamon de Valera

tively unaffected. Popular support for the struggle was partly genuine and voluntary, partly the consequence of IRA intimidation and the fear of suffering the well-known fate of the "informer" and the "collaborator." Some Dáil members were unhappy with the strategy of violence, and the IRA, in turn, was wary of allowing civilian politicians to control or limit their activities.

Two dramatic events generated widespread interest and sympathy. Tomás MacCurtain, commandant of the local IRA brigade, was elected Sinn Féin Lord Mayor of Cork in January 1920 and was murdered in his home by the RIC six weeks afterwards. He was succeeded as Lord Mayor by Terence MacSwiney who, on being imprisoned on a technical charge, went on a hunger-strike which resulted after seventy-four days in his death in Brixton prison, London, on 25 October 1920. MacSwiney's sacrifice gained valuable international support for the Irish cause.

A remarkable feature of the Anglo-Irish struggle was the commanding rôle of Michael Collins. He was particularly influential with the secret IRB. As Dáil Minister for Finance he successfully organised the Dáil loan which funded the workings of the revolutionary government. More importantly, as IRA director of intelligence, he masterminded the campaign and organised the "squad" which ruthlessly smashed the Castle intelligence system. Renowned for his "scarlet pimpernel" adventures, his forceful and energetic personality won him a loyal following but also made him enemies within the movement. Eamon de Valera, who returned to Ireland in December 1920 having spent eighteen months in the United States seeking moral and financial support for Irish independence, was critical and perhaps jealous of the "Big Fellow's" dominant rôle.

## Partition

Meanwhile the Government of Ireland Act (1920) entirely failed to meet nationalist aspirations but brought Northern Ireland into being. Having failed to prevent Home Rule, the Ulster unionists' fall-back strategy was to opt out of it. Unionists used their influence at Westminster to get a six-county bloc (Antrim, Armagh, Down, Fermanagh, Londonderry and Tyrone) as the excluded territory, the largest area possible consistent with a comfortable unionist majority and secure dominance. The 1920 Act provided for two subordinate "home rule" parliaments, one with jurisdiction over the six counties (Northern Ireland) at Belfast and the other for the remaining twenty-six (Southern Ireland) at Dublin. A Council of Ireland would deal with matters of common concern, north and south, and would hopefully encourage unity. Sinn Féin and the Dáil ignored the Act, simply using the machinery of its elections to constitute an uncontested Second Dáil. In Northern Ireland, the Unionists led by Sir James Craig took 40 of the 52 seats in the new parliament there, which was formally opened in June 1921.

## Treaty and Civil War

Meanwhile, the two-and-a-half years of the Troubles accounted for the deaths of 750 IRA and civilians, some 150 Crown forces and 400 (mostly Irish and Catholic) policemen. By the spring of 1921, the IRA had made much of Ireland ungovernable by the Crown, and a truce in July began complicated preliminary moves leading to treaty negotiations in London in the late autumn between an Irish delegation, headed by Arthur Griffith and Michael Collins, and a high-powered British government team, led by prime minister David Lloyd George. (By that time, partition was already established, and Northern Ireland a going con-

Michael Collins

cern.) De Valera's absence from the Irish side and his appointment of a reluctant Collins remain controversial points.

On 6 December 1921, in a tense atmosphere of pressure, the Irish negotiators signed the best deal they thought they were going to get, only to have it rejected out of hand by de Valera and intransigent cabinet colleagues in Dublin. This Anglo-Irish Treaty provided for an Irish Free State as a dominion within the British Commonwealth, on the model of Canada. It would have the substance of independence, though its members of parliament (Teachtaí Dála) would have to swear fidelity to the Crown, and it was by no means clear in an evolving Commonwealth how far foreign policy would still be controlled by Westminster. Also, under the Treaty, certain naval bases or ports would remain under British control. Moreover, should Northern Ireland wish to opt out of the Irish Free State (which it was certain to do), a Boundary Commission would delineate the border.

The Dáil engaged in bitter and divisive debate on the Treaty. Its supporters argued it was the stepping-stone to full independence, whereas its opponents maintained it was a betrayal of the "Republic" and denounced the oath of fidelity as unacceptable. Neither side paid much attention to the Northern Ireland clauses (presumably on the facile assumption that the Boundary Commission would reduce the partitioned area to an unviable corner, and so facilitate unity) or to the Treaty ports issue. On 7 January 1922, the Dáil ratified the Treaty by 64 votes to 57.

There followed months of turbulence and mutual antagonism, as the anti-Treaty group in Sinn Féin and the IRA refused to accept the majority decision and opposed the transitional moves to bring the new State into existence, or as they would see it, to illegally disestablish the Republic. Eventually, in June 1922, hostilities broke out between the two factions—the Free Staters, now constituted as a provisional government in charge of a newly formed army, and the Republicans, or "Irregulars" or anti-Treaty forces. The government had superior resources and employed ruthless measures, and the old guerrilla strategy did not work this time for the Republicans. The Civil War was small in scale, short in duration—ending in April 1923—and low in fatalities, probably not exceeding 1,000. The latter included talented and dedicated leaders on both sides—the Republicans Cathal Brugha and Harry Boland, and, most notably, the pro-Treaty Michael Collins, commander-in-chief of the Free State army, killed in an ambush in his native West Cork by his erstwhile comrades. Eamon de Valera, though president of the shadowy Republic, played no significant rôle on the anti-Treaty side.

The Civil War can be interpreted in various ways—a struggle by idealists against pragmatists, or militarists against civilian politicians, or even radicals against a new establishment: the Treaty was supported by big business, the press and the Churches but also, it must be said, by the mass of public opinion, as was evident in the general elections of 1922 and 1923. In any event, such was the bitterness of the struggle and the enduring memory of atrocities on both sides, that Irish politics and society suffered the wounds for decades, as a great national movement permanently divided into political parties perpetuating the Civil War division.

The defeated republicans, appropriating the magic names of Sinn Féin and the IRA to themselves, subsided for the moment into sullen and abstentionist opposition, refusing to recognise the new State and its institutions. The victorious pro-Treaty faction formed itself into a political party called Cumann na nGaedheal ("the band of the Gaels"), which governed the Irish Free State from its inception (formally, on 6 December 1922) for the next ten years. Eamon de Valera ended his abstentionist policy in 1927, having broken with Sinn Féin and having founded a new party, Fianna Fáil ("army of Ireland"). Sinn Féin-IRA were now an extra-parliamentary republican rump, looking back to the 1918–22 years as the only valid expression of national self-determination, and maintaining a fitful and harassed existence for decades to come.

## Native Government from 1923

Despite the unpromising beginnings of the independent State, Cumann na nGaedheal, under W. T. Cosgrave (1880–1965), provided efficient, if somewhat repressive and increasingly unpopular government. Its conservative economic policy gave priority to agricultural and livestock exports, with low taxation and minimum social welfare. Constitutionally, the emphasis was on developing the Treaty settlement within the Commonwealth. Culturally and socially, a pattern was set which was to endure, with some modifications, down to the 1970s. The revolutionary hopes of the independence struggle gave way to social reaction, to a class-divided, if nominally casteless, society, to a dominant Catholic ethos reflected in censorship and sexual repression, and to the return of Irish women to their traditional "station in life," in kitchen and bedroom. (Women had played an active rôle in the 1916–23 period: Countess Constance Markievicz, 1868–1927, was the first woman elected to the House of Commons and appointed as an Irish government minister.) Still, the new State laid down, in adverse circumstances, solid and durable institutions, such as a civil service of integrity and competence and, most remarkably, an unarmed and popular police force, the Gárda Síochána ("guardians of the peace").

## Fianna Fáil in Power

Less than ten years after their crushing defeat in the Civil War, de Valera and his followers came peacefully and democratically to power in 1932. Though relying on the small Labour party to form its first administration, Fianna Fáil was able to govern on its own for much of the 16–year period during which it held continuous office down to 1948. Over that time, the Cumann na nGaedheal opposition, name-changed into Fine Gael from 1933, never looked like returning to power, its image ever more associated with the past and not helped by its short flirtation with an ineffectual paramilitary wing, Irish-style fascists popularly known as the "Blueshirts" (1932–34).

The most important party in the history of the State, Fianna Fáil was to enjoy power, either as the sole or the dominant party in government, for 45 of the 72 years from its foundation down to 1998. Initially, it owed its success to a charismatic leader, Eamon de Valera; to able lieutenants like Seán Lemass, who was to succeed "the Chief" from 1959 to 1966, and Seán T. O'Kelly (President of Ireland, 1945–59); to a highly professional grass-roots organisation, and to party discipline and loyalty; to an appealing mix of nationalism and populism; and to a socio-economic policy based on tillage and the small farmer, on the creation of tariff-protected industries, and on relatively generous social welfare. Despite its earlier links with the IRA, in power it acted as ruthlessly against subversives as Cosgrave's government had done. At the same time, other republican dissidents were conciliated by de Valera's unilateral and progressive undoing of such Treaty shackles as the oath of fidelity and the governor-generalship; his tough conduct of an "economic war" with Britain, 1932–38; and his introduction in 1937 of a new Constitution, *Bunreacht na hÉireann*, which unequivocally affirmed the sovereignty of the State and its *de iure* anti-partitionist claim to jurisdiction over the "Six Counties" of Northern Ireland. The Constitution also created the title and office of Taoiseach (chief) for the head of the Irish government, as well as the ceremonial post of President of Ireland. Finally, the Anglo-Irish Agreement of 1938 ended the "economic war" on favourable terms to Ireland, and returned "the Treaty ports" to Irish control.

## Neutrality

The latter concession made Irish neutrality in World War II ("the Emergency") possible. Neutrality was the acid test of the State's sovereignty, as well as the only feasible policy at a period when formal participation as a belligerent on the Allied (effectively, the British) side would have wrecked a new-found consensus and invited republican sabotage of any war effort. In the event, there was considerable behind-the-scenes cooperation by the Irish authorities with the Allies while thousands of Irishmen and women worked in British hospitals and munition factories and enlisted in her armed forces. On the surface, however, the diplomatic proprieties of neutrality (strict censorship of military news, for example) were meticulously observed, in particular the notorious visit of the Taoiseach, Eamon de Valera, to the German legation to express his condolences on Hitler's death. In the Dáil and in the country, neutrality had enthusiastic and virtually unanimous support. Old civil war animosities were transcended, and national morale was high, in a common resolve to defend the State against any invader and in a common endurance of austerities.

The "Emergency" period was significant for the development of a Twenty-Six County "national" identity. There was tremendous pride in de Valera's dignified and eloquent response on radio to Winston Churchill's caustic criticism of Irish neutrality in his victory speech. Popular attachment to neutrality developed in the 1950s and 1960s into a desire to observe military detachment from the Cold War, to play an independent and active rôle at the United Nations and to contribute to its peace-keeping missions.

## NORTHERN IRELAND, 1920S TO 1960S

Northern Ireland, as part of the United Kingdom, was involved in World War II, and Belfast suffered severe German air raids. The North's wartime experience was only one reflection of its very different and diverging history from the South since 1920. Born in bloodshed and sectarian violence, with the expulsion of Catholic workers from the Belfast shipyards, Northern Ireland (ironically given Home Rule) never achieved the consensus so quickly forthcoming in the South by the mid-1930s. The Boundary Commission's proceedings ended in a debacle in 1925, and partition was copperfastened. (Its effect on the South was to create a 95% Catholic State, thereby ensuring an oppressive homogeneity but also political stability). In settling for the six-county area, the unionist leadership effectively abandoned their Protestant brethren in the other three Ulster counties and in the nationalist South. With their comfortable and permanent artificially built-in majority, the unionists ruled the roost for fifty years. The Northern government and parliament (housed in splendid new buildings at Stormont, near Belfast, since 1932) were nominally subject to Westminster which in practice did not interfere in Northern Ireland. There was a small but impotent nationalist party in chronic opposition.

A sullenly dissenting Catholic/nationalist minority of more than one-third (increasing to over two-fifths by the end of the century) resented not only partition in itself but the rough injustice of the border as drawn. They never gave their allegiance to the Stormont regime, which accordingly treated them as untrustworthy rebels and fifth columnists (in popular Protestant parlance, "taigs" and "fenians"). The nationalists perceived themselves as being discriminated against all along the line—in policing (overwhelmingly Protestant), in the public service (ditto), in employment, in housing and in local government where the constituencies, notably in Derry City, were often gerrymandered.

Another source of grievance for Northern nationalists was their sense that the people of the South were indifferent to their fate. Their seemingly fatalistic acceptance of the constitutional status quo was indicated by their lack of response to the IRA border campaign of 1956 and after. However, the potential for change was inherent in the extension to Northern Ireland of British welfare state provisions in the late 1940s, in the areas of health and social services, but above all, in education. Working- and lower-middle class Catholics who were the beneficiaries of "free" education were to ably articulate their grievances in the years ahead in the civil rights movement, with momentous consequences.

## THE SOUTH, 1945–66

The policies of all parties in the South towards Northern Ireland boiled down to irredentist rhetoric and bluster, with little attempt to understand the underlying realities. This typified the anti-partitionist movement of the late 1940s, when there was angry reaction to the British reaffirmation (Ireland Act, 1949) of Northern Ireland's status within the United Kingdom. The Ireland Act, in turn, was a response to Dublin's decision to end constitutional ambiguity by passing the Republic of Ireland Act (1948). This severed any remaining tenuous links with the Commonwealth, and declared the State to be a Republic.

For the most part, however, the South got on with its own business. Disenchantment with Fianna Fáil's long rule led to its alternation during the 1950s with interparty governments, led by Fine Gael's John A. Costello (1891–1976) as Taoiseach (1948–51, 1954–57) and comprising virtually every party but Fianna Fáil. Costello was a loyal son of the Catholic Church, and meekly acquiesced in the Church's successful objection in 1951 to a proposed health plan, known as the "Mother-and-child" scheme, promoted by a crusading young government minister, Noel Browne. The episode revealed the extent of episcopal power, and was subsequently seen as a crucial event in Church-State relations.

The 1950s were a bleak decade, with governments being unable or unwilling to solve the chronic problems of poverty, rural depopulation, unemployment and massive emigration to Britain and the U.S. People wondered whether the struggle for independence had been worthwhile. But better winds began to blow, coinciding—and not entirely unconnected—with the departure of the aging de Valera to graze in the tranquil pastures of the presidency (1959–73), and the accession of the pragmatic Seán Lemass, long Taoiseach-in-waiting, to power in 1959. In the 1960s, Ireland (as the State is often ambiguously called) enjoyed a modest measure of prosperity partly based on an economic plan devised by T.K. Whitaker, a gifted public servant. It also underwent an enlivening and enriching cultural experience, exemplified in the musician Seán Ó Riada (1931–71) who was the inspiration of the vibrant revival of Irish traditional music in the decades that followed. The enthusiastic reception for President J. F. Kennedy in 1963 symbolised the advance of the Irish at home and abroad.

Other instances of a new spirit of pride and self-confidence were a modestly successful independent foreign policy and a sharpened consciousness on social issues such as housing. The Second Vatican Council (1962–65) began the slow process of

Partition of Ireland

liberating Irish Catholicism. Educationally, the advent of "free" secondary schooling was a break in the ramparts of social privilege. Two-way tourism helped to broaden Irish attitudes in general. But the most radical influence in maturing mindsets was Irish television, where "chat" programmes, notably *The Late Late Show*, broached erstwhile taboo topics (analysis of the Catholic Church's rôle in Irish society, for example) and helped to end the inhibitions encapsulated in the phrase "say what you like but say nothing."

Other new departures were evident in the Anglo-Irish free trade agreement (1965); in the exchange of visits, also in 1965, between Taoiseach Seán Lemass and Northern Ireland Prime Minister Terence O'Neill; and in preliminary moves to join the European Economic Community. In the context of all this self-confident modernising process, it seemed appropriate and safe to publicly celebrate the 50th anniversary of the 1916 Rising with an almost triumphalist enthusiasm. But, never surprisingly in Ireland, history was soon to reenter politics with a vengeance.

## CONFLICT IN THE NORTH

In the late 1960s the Northern Ireland Civil Rights Association (NICRA) was founded to seek political and social reform and the ending of discrimination in housing allocation and public employment. A further grievance was the siting of the new University of Ulster (1968) in unionist Coleraine rather than nationalist Derry. NICRA was not primarily anti-partitionist and was based on American and British models. Its songs ("We shall overcome") and slogans ("one man one vote," i.e., universal adult suffrage in local elections) were universal rather than nationalist. Its street protests and marches were met by Royal Ulster Constabulary (RUC) repression and by an extremist Protestant backlash. Violent rioting in Derry and Belfast in August 1969 led to several lives—mostly Catholic—being lost. British troops were rushed to Northern Ireland and the Fianna Fáil Taoiseach, Jack Lynch (1966–73, 1977–79) announced that Dublin could not stand idly by, though this assertion was not followed by interventionist action.

The IRA's failure to defend nationalist areas in Belfast was attributed by "purists" in the movement to the leadership's involvement in political and social activism during the 1960s. Accordingly, a split took place in December 1969 between the Officials (favouring politicisation) and the Provisionals (traditionalist or militarists), with a corresponding rupture in Sinn Féin, the political wing of the IRA. The Northern situation deteriorated in 1970–71 as British political and military blunders enabled the Provisionals to fill a rôle as protectors of the nationalist people. In February 1971 they killed the first of hundreds of British soldiers to die in the "Troubles" and in April they began a systematic and lengthy bombing campaign. A hamfisted and one-sided internment operation in August 1971 bitterly alienated virtually the whole Catholic population and resulted in massive civil disobedience.

As the turmoil continued, one event was to leave a particularly indelible mark. On "Bloody Sunday," 30 January 1972, British Army paratroopers shot dead 13 unarmed civilians during a civil rights demonstration in Derry. Two months later, the Stormont Parliament was prorogued (in effect, abolished), to be replaced by direct rule from Westminster administered by a Secretary of State for Northern Ireland, and the half-century of unionist ascendancy had ended forever. But the violence continued as the Provisional IRA pursued their aim of a united Ireland through terrorist bombings and shootings, countered by assassinations and atrocities from such loyalist terror groups as the Ulster Defence Association and the Ulster Volunteer Force.

Various attempts at an internal settlement failed in the 1970s and 1980s—the Sunningdale Agreement (1973–74), the Constitutional Convention (1975–76), the Northern Ireland Assembly (1982–86). Another critical development was the hunger-strike action of IRA prisoners seeking the restoration of political status, resulting in the deaths of Bobby Sands MP and nine others in 1981. Around this time Sinn Féin/IRA adopted a new dual strategy of seeking power "with a ballot paper in one hand and an armalite in the other," thereby introducing Sinn Féin as a successful electoral force in Northern politics. Meanwhile, political and diplomatic links between London and Dublin provided a new framework for the problem as expressed in the Anglo-Irish Agreement of 1985.

## THE PEACE PROCESS

From the late 1980s, a peace process took slow and laborious shape, meeting with many setbacks. One strand consisted of contacts between John Hume, leader of the moderately nationalist Social Democratic and Labour Party, and Gerry Adams, president of Sinn Féin. Hume sought to persuade Adams that physical-force nationalism was obsolete and that the real obstacle to peace and unity was the deep division in the Northern community.

Meanwhile, the outlines of a possible settlement were becoming clear. The governments in Dublin and London, encouraged by the European Union and, increasingly and much more significantly, by the United States, worked to bring about the end of IRA violence and the involvement of Sinn Féin in the political process. However, mainstream unionism had also to be reassured. The grand plan was to have a genuinely power-sharing Northern assembly, and to retain the UK link while setting up cross-border institutions, and developing closer links between the Republic and Britain, now moving toward devolved governments in Wales and Scotland. Thus, it was hoped, all the divergent interests could be moved towards multifaceted cooperation, genuine trust and ultimate reconciliation. (The British, it should be pointed out, were vitally concerned to end the IRA threat of destructive bombings in London and "the mainland" generally.)

The death toll in the "Troubles" (peaking at their bloodiest in the mid-1970s) down to the late 1990s amounted to nearly 3,300 with twelve times that many injured, and countless lives shattered. Republican and loyalist terrorists, as well as the security forces, were at once perpetrators and victims. About three hundred RUC members died, and over six hundred British soldiers. Many of the remaining 2,300 casualties were innocent civilians—men, women and children. The Protestant and Catholic working classes, segregated in their ghettoes and locked in their mutual hatreds, suffered disproportionately. Though the republican groups sought to portray the struggle as one of liberation, it had much more the appearance of a civil and sectarian conflict, and the great majority of those who died were Northern Ireland people. After nearly thirty years, there was no mistaking the popular yearning for peace.

## THE BELFAST AGREEMENT, 1998

With IRA and loyalist ceasefires more or less in place by the mid-1990s, the protracted and torturous political negotiations ended in a deal on 10 April 1998, the so-called Good Friday or Belfast Agreement. It was a programme for a settlement rather than a settlement in itself. The participants comprised the British and Irish governments, the SDLP and Sinn Féin on the nationalist side, the mainstream Ulster Unionist Party (UUP), as well as the fringe loyalist parties representing *their* terrorist factions, and middle ground groups such as the Alliance Party and the Women's Coalition.

The Agreement was opposed by nationalist and unionist right wings who, from opposite ends of the spectrum, shouted "betrayal" and "no surrender." Leading personalities involved in all this historic development included the politically strong British Labour leader and Prime Minister Tony Blair, the popular Taoiseach Bertie Ahern, John Hume, Gerry Adams and David Trimble (UUP), who had to deal with substantial dissent within his own party. Encouragement was provided from the chair by former U.S. Senator George Mitchell and from the sidelines by an intensely interested U.S. President Bill Clinton. (Irish-American opinion about Northern Ireland had become informed and sophisticated.) The personification of the opposition to the Agreement was the Rev. Ian Paisley, MP, political and religious Protestant fundamentalist, leader both of the Democratic Unionist Party (DUP) and of the Free Presbyterian Church, a demagogue stoker of anti-popery fires. The 200–year old (Protestant) Orange Order also regarded the Agreement as a sellout.

The deal provided for the consent principle, that is, the retention of the Union unless and until the people of Northern Ireland decided otherwise; the pursuit of political aims through exclusively nonviolent means; the replacement of the territorial claim in the Republic's Constitution; an elected Northern Assembly and a power-sharing executive, with provisions for "parallel consent" and weighted majorities; cross-border bodies to deal with matters of common interest, North and South, as well as symbolising an all-Ireland dimension for Northern nationalists; the development of parliamentary and institutional contacts between Ireland and the regions of Great Britain; a radical review of policing; and, most controversially, the release of "political" prisoners.

In an unprecedented expression of self-determination, the Agreement was put by referendums, North and South, to the people for endorsement, on the same day, 22 May 1998. There was a massive Yes vote in the Republic of 95% and a less emphatic but impressive Yes answer, 71%, given by Northern Ireland voters as a whole, though argument raged as to whether a majority of unionists had said Yes. At any rate, there could be no doubt but that a green light had been given island-wide to the Agreement and, equally, that numerous obstacles lay ahead before its spirit and its letter could be implemented. It was by no means clear, for example, that the republican and loyalist paramilitaries would "decommission" their arms, let alone go out of business.

Elections for the Assembly, held in June 1998, resulted in a pro-Agreement majority, and in the appointments of David Trimble (UUP) and Séamus Mallon (SDLP) as First Minister and Deputy First Minister, respectively. The new dispensation was immediately threatened with violence and instability, as the controversial "marching season" of the anti-Agreement Orange Order began.

### THE SOUTH: REACTION TO NORTHERN CONFLICT

The reaction of the Republic to the Troubles in the North is a complicated topic. In theory, the aspiration to a united Ireland was shared by all parties (for Fianna Fáil, it was one of their "twin" aims, the other being the restoration of the Irish language) and the great majority of the people. In practice, Dublin governments had never been at ease with Northern nationalists, let alone unionists, and had been ruthless with republican groups pursuing the national objective by force of arms.

By the 1960s, the North had been virtually forgotten and the violence of 1968–69 was as much a shock to Southern citizens as it was to the world at large. At the beginning, there was strong nationalist sympathy and identification with "the kith and kin" north of the border. Two government ministers were dismissed by Taoiseach Jack Lynch in 1970 for alleged use of public funds to import arms for beleaguered Northern Catholics or, putting it another way, for the IRA. One of the ministers, the controversial Charles J. Haughey, was a defendant (but acquitted) in a subsequent arms trial. Lynch acted carefully and cautiously in these critical early years, and the Republic avoided direct involvement in the Northern crisis. Public fury at the events of Bloody Sunday expressed itself in the burning of the British Embassy in Dublin. Car bombings by loyalists in Dublin and Monaghan in 1974 resulted in the worst fatalities of any single episode in the Troubles. Over the years, some few Gardaí died at the hands of terrorists.

Apart from such incidents, however, the Republic generally escaped unscathed in terms of death and injury. By the mid-1970s, people in the South had been revolted by terrorism in Northern Ireland, particularly where it was being carried out in their name. It was noticeable that, during the IRA hunger-strike campaign in 1980–81, and in contrast to spontaneous public reaction in 1969–72, public support in the South had to be mobilised and orchestrated. The realisation also grew that the Northern conflict was bad for tourism in the Republic (especially for the dependable and profitable tourist trade from Britain which had just taken off before the Troubles) and for inward investment generally. The exchequer had to bear the costs of extra security along the border and in the prisons. Inevitably, the ongoing crisis meant a restriction of civil liberties. Apart from border counties and republican pockets elsewhere, the South (people as distinct from media) tended to "switch off" the North, as the seemingly endless Troubles continued. The aspiration to a united Ireland went sour, as surveys showed, particularly if unification meant extra taxation, and the transfer of responsibility for community conflict to the Republic. Southern reservations gradually came to apply to Northern nationalists as well as to unionists.

Nonetheless, the Northern conflict would not go away and successive governments built up a relationship with London in the promotion of a peace process. Paradoxically, the Northern problem eventually led to an unprecedented rapport in British-Irish relations with the British Prime Minister being invited in 1998 to address the Houses of the Oireachtas (parliament). Meanwhile, the Republic's strong referendum endorsement of the Good Friday Agreement reflected a genuinely disinterested wish to support the chance for peace in Northern Ireland rather than to push the prospect of unification. After decades of feeling frustrated and impotent, people were glad to be doing something to help. But there was also an unworthy but realistic sentiment at work about hoping to get "the North off our backs."

### THE REPUBLIC'S ECONOMY, 1970S TO 1990S

It is highly significant that the Northern conflict was never a major issue in the Republic's elections during nearly three decades. A wide range of other issues preoccupied the citizens in years of profound social, cultural and technological change. In the economy, the ephemeral success of the 1960s gave way to recession, partly reflecting the 1970s oil crises but also caused by domestic factors. Heavy taxation, over-generous pay settlements, serious inflation, poor management and uncontrolled foreign borrowing dogged the economy into the 1980s when the national debt, unemployment and emigration reached crisis proportions, as successive governments appeared to be unable to provide a living for a huge young population.

The problems were that the Irish economy was marginal and vulnerable in modern trading conditions; that the Republic aspired to First World living standards while her resources seemed to be those of a (admittedly well-off) Third World country; and that the prolonged Northern conflict added to the strains on the Southern economy. Moreover, Irish society seemed increasingly polarised around extremes of wealth and poverty.

In the late 1980s when a Fianna Fáil government undertook the unpopular task of cutting public expenditure, the Fine Gael opposition gave it support in a new climate of fiscal rectitude. Slowly, the economy improved and then blossomed in the mid- to late-1990s. Emigration slowed down, and former emigrants returned to work at home. A skillful and expert workforce was developed in the new "sunrise" industries—pharmaceuticals and electronics—while Irish foodstuffs established various export niches. There was a boom in housing and the construction industry, always a barometer of fair economic weather. Substantial reductions were made in the still high unemployment figures, down to 10% of the workforce by 1998.

Multinationals were attracted to Ireland by liberal tax incentives but were sometimes criticised for repatriating their profits and for suddenly taking flight to countries of cheaper labour. In spite of some volatility, however, and warning notes being sounded about inflation and the economy "overheating," the "Celtic Tiger" seemed in excellent health in 1998, as a possible average growth rate of 6% per annum over the next ten years was being predicted.

IRELAND, EUROPE AND THE WIDER WORLD

The country's accession to the European Economic Community (subsequently renamed the European Community and then the European Union) was a milestone in Ireland's history. It marked the end of the old economic nationalism, with textiles, car assembly and footwear bearing the brunt of the removal of tariffs. But membership proved a huge benefit in terms of diversified markets (exports to Britain declined from 75% in 1960 to 43% in 1980), Community-funded development projects (notably in road modernisation), direct financial transfers to the Dublin exchequer, remarkable agricultural prosperity and immeasurable improvement in the living standards of farmers (but not of fishermen).

The obverse side was an unhealthy "dependence" or begging-bowl mentality towards "Brussels" (shorthand for the EU). At any rate, Ireland moved irreversibly towards closer European union, with popular endorsements of the Single European Act (1987) and the Maastricht and Amsterdam Treaties (1992 and 1998, respectively), and impending participation in a single European currency by 1999. Directives from Brussels increasingly affected many areas of Irish life, and European courts made a progressive impact on Irish conservatism in human rights, social legislation and the status of women.

A significant minority of citizens remained uneasy about the gradual erosion of national sovereignty, and the bureaucratic and undemocratic nature of many Community institutions. In particular, reservations were expressed about the effect of membership on the remnants of an independent foreign policy and on "traditional neutrality." However, the blunt facts were that world views were a luxury for a small dependent country and that membership (and benefits received) committed Ireland to participation in common defence, as European union deepened into integration.

Outside of the EU, there were areas where modern Ireland had a distinctive and not unimportant presence. The Irish Catholic missionary tradition in Africa and elsewhere took a radical turn in the 1970s and 1980s as many priests and nuns espoused the cause of oppressed peoples suffering poverty and injustice under neo-colonialist regimes. This was seen as the proper world rôle of a small nation, which had long thirsted for justice. For similar reasons of historical self-awareness, the generosity of individual Irish people towards famine-afflicted countries was remarkable. At another level, teachers, social workers, research experts, engineers and nurses made a special contribution to developing countries in Africa, Asia and the Middle East. What Ireland offered here was a certain temperamental affinity, a rapport based on ex-colonial experiences and a special small-scale expertise developed under native government in such areas as peat production and rural electrification. Irish entrepreneurs also made their mark not only where the free market offered opportunity in Europe but much farther afield in such spheres as the retail trade, the food industry and fashion.

POLITICS AND SOCIETY, 1970S TO 1990S

Whatever about economic fluctuations and cultural change, the Republic's political system looked remarkably durable and stable from the 1960s to the 1990s, given the fragmenting tendencies of the proportional representation electoral system, increasing socioeconomic pressures and the potentially destabilising effect of the North. The two larger parties alternated in government with Fianna Fáil forming single-party and, from 1989, coalition administrations under Taoisigh Jack Lynch, C. J. Haughey and Albert Reynolds successively; and a much weaker Fine Gael holding office with the aid of smaller parties (notably Labour, making substantial electoral gains in 1992 on its traditionally modest base but falling back in 1997) under Taoisigh Liam Cosgrave, Garret FitzGerald and John Bruton.

Irish politics continued to be cautious, solidly parliamentary, extraordinarily (by English and American standards) intimate and personal and an unrivalled spectator sport. In the 1990s, revelations about the dubious relationships of some politicians with the world of business, and stories of bribery and backhanders, intensified public cynicism but by no means diminished public interest. Another notable feature of Irish politics in the 1990s was a general move of the parties, under various influences, towards the middle ground of "social democracy." Similarly, most parties now favoured the market economy, with a consequent downgrading or proposed privatisation of semi-state bodies which had played a dominant rôle since independence.

In 1990 the surprise election of radical and feminist Mary Robinson to the largely ceremonial post of President of Ireland was both a symbol and a catalyst of further change. She transformed the office by her (relative) youth, her charm and warmth, her meet-the-people policy, her intellectual distinction and her compassionate devotion to humanitarian causes at home and abroad. Her ubiquitous presidential presence enhanced the esteem of every Irish woman. She chose to serve only one seven-year term, being then appointed U.N. Commissioner for Human Rights, and she was succeeded as president by another woman of distinction, Mary McAleese (1997– ).

In a conservative, patriarchal Catholic state, the emphasis had been on women's domestic rôle and indeed this was articulated in the Constitution (Art. 41.2). From the early 1960s there was a radical shift in women's work from farms and domestic service to teaching, nursing, shop and office work and employment in light industries. The establishment of the Council for the Status of Women in 1973 was an important milestone in advancing women's rights. Feminist groups and various women's organisations sought to increase the rôle of women in politics, parliament and public life, with a considerable degree of success. But whatever the law might say about equality, in-built male dominance, as well as inertia in the system, meant that women had still to scale the commanding heights of managerial and academic appointments.

### LANGUAGE, CULTURE AND MORALITY

By the 1990s Eamon de Valera's much-derided Gaelic, rural idyll (given preeminent expression in his St Patrick's Day 1943 radio broadcast) was a fantasy of the past. The revival of Irish as a spoken language had been a primary objective of the State's founding fathers, and much money and energy had been poured into revival strategies, particularly the gaelicisation of education. Later in the century, the language was given its own radio and television stations.

Perhaps the national aim was never realistic: in any event, the language revival or "language replacement," was a failure, as was the second-best or fall-back objective, a bilingual Ireland, and by the century's end the ever-dwindling Gaeltachts, or native-speaking areas, appeared doomed. Whatever the popular goodwill towards the language, the great majority simply preferred to speak English and never learned to speak Irish properly. The value of Irish as a distinguishing mark of identity was widely recognised and underlay the expansion of Gaelscoileanna, or Irish language schools, from the 1970s, but all the evidence was that in the future, Irish would be no more than an agreeable cosmetic gloss on the national life.

Rural Ireland was also in the grave as the farming population aged and the younger generation deserted the land. With the evergrowing homogenisation of popular culture, Irish country folk no longer had a distinctive way of life. On the other hand, provincial towns acquired a colour and vitality unknown in the past. A similar vitality was also evident in the ever-growing popularity of Gaelic games and Irish traditional music. At the same time, Ireland seemed to excel in pop and rock culture, and Irish musicians of all kinds achieved international acclaim, as indeed did Irish poets (like Nobel laureate Séamus Heaney), novelists, playwrights, film producers, actors and dancers.

Within Irish Catholicism from the 1960s and 1970s, there developed a critical attitude towards the clerical establishment, a new lay independence in matters of sexual morality and an *à la carte* approach to what had been a no-choice menu of obligatory doctrinal and moral items. There was also a growing tolerance of other Christian denominations and even of exotic non-Christian sects. In attitudes towards social or moral legislation, traditional views had to contend with the new liberal climate, and this had confusing and inconclusive results. A referendum in 1983 inserted a "pro-life" clause in the Constitution but in 1992 the people affirmed the rights to information (on abortion) and to travel (for abortion, mostly to England). By the century's end the abortion debate raged unresolved, as it did in the U.S. and elsewhere. Liberal attitudes prevailed over conservatism (under European court pressure) in the decriminalisation of homosexuality and in making contraceptives widely available. In 1995, a referendum by the narrowest of majorities allowed for a measure of divorce in strictly defined circumstances.

From the 1960s, the puritanical obsession with sexual morality—which for economic and other reasons had preoccupied Irish Catholics from the Great Famine era—gave place to a continuing public debate on the social injustices endemic in Irish society (extremely caste-conscious though nominally classless), and on how best to distribute the, initially frugal but ever richer, national cake. Social welfare provisions and public health services gradually improved.

### EDUCATION: SOCIAL PROBLEMS

From the 1960s, though full equality of educational opportunity remained down the road, second-level access was improved through the provision of free school transport and the (partial) abolition of school fees. There were rapid advances in technological education and, with the extension of third-level grants and—in the mid-1990s—the rather illusory benefit of fees abolition, the universities were no longer the exclusive preserves of the affluent professional and commercial classes. In general, the high levels of education, which could be seen as a heritage of British rule, were further developed. Two new universities in Limerick and Dublin (1989) again reflected the emphasis on technology while, under the 1997 Universities Act, the National University of Ireland colleges at Cork, Galway, and Maynooth became independent universities.

Foremost among Ireland's problems in the 1980s and 1990s was violent crime, much of it drug-related. Traditionalists attributed its widespread nature to the breakdown of individual morality and of religious sanctions. There was also a chronic failure to face the problem of the country's 10,000 quasi-nomadic travelling community and their troubled relations with the settled population. Popular hostility was also expressed to the 1990s influx of refugees from Eastern Europe (especially Romania) and the Middle East who were seeking asylum, or work, or relatively attractive social welfare benefits.

Environmental concerns (including traffic problems and road fatalities) became a matter of intense debate in late twentieth-century Ireland. The competing claims of development and conservation gave rise to arguments in other countries, of course, but in Ireland the issue was centrally important, since the absence of an industrial revolution had helped to keep a richly scenic country relatively unpolluted and extremely attractive to tourists. There were fears that the landscape was being blighted by masts and pylons, unattractive conifer plantations, ribbon development and ugly housing. A variation on the main debate was the argument between the champions of interpretative centres (liberally funded with EU money) and the critics of these centres as vulgar intrusions on nature's beauty.

### IRISH CATHOLICISM TRANSFORMED

In an era of multifaceted change, the most remarkable (and most rapid) change of all was the decline of institutional Irish Catholicism. For various historical reasons, among them being partition, the ethos and very identity of the Irish Free State had been

Catholic from the outset. There was a close, almost instinctive, liaison between church and state, which were both paternalistic and authoritarian. Politicians deferred to churchmen in the drafting of laws and in the observation of protocol on public occasions. The Catholic Church in the Ireland of the 1920s to the 1960s was streamlined in terms of organisation and discipline, exercised control over education, and could rely on an obedient and numerous clerical force of priests, nuns and brothers. The laity seemed the most faithful in Europe in terms of regular observance of their religious duties, with Sunday Mass-going at over 90%.

The Patrician congress of 1962, evoking the atmosphere of the great Eucharistic congress of 1932, made it appear that the Catholic ethos would endure indefinitely. Yet the imposing edifice was rocked to its foundations within the next three decades. Various modernising and secularising factors were at work; the optimistic spirit of Vatican II undermined the morose ambience of post-Famine Catholicism; the state began to distance itself from the church; the independent lay mind was in the ascendant; the "simple faithful" was a vanishing species, with the extension of education; the age of deference and ring-kissing was over; women expressed resentment at an exclusively male priesthood; and the heretofore unquestionable (clerical celibacy, for example) was now subjected to critical scrutiny.

By the 1990s vocations to the religious life, particularly priestly vocations, had declined to crisis point. Staffing and control of secondary schools were passing rapidly to lay teachers. The wide publicity given to the misbehaviour of certain religious (even if only a small minority) greatly diminished the respected standing of priests and nuns in the eyes of Irish Catholics. Particularly damaging were the revelations that Bishop Casey of Galway had had an affair and had fathered a son, and that some other priests had behaved similarly. Worst of all were the widely publicised cases of child sexual abuse by clerics, and the past ill-treatment by nuns of girls in orphanages and "magdalen laundries."

Sunday Mass-going fell from 91% of Catholics in 1973, to 87% in 1983, to 77% in 1994 and to 60% in 1998. The accelerated rate of decline in the mid-1990s was particularly notable. A survey in February 1998 revealed that 40% of Catholics questioned rarely or ever went to confession. Yet 82% considered religion an important factor in their lives. 70% felt priests were in touch with local issues, and were satisfied with the quality of spiritual and community services priests were providing. It was also clear that Catholicism was still a considerable social and cultural force (centrally involved in the rites of passage, for example) and that declining Mass attendances were still high by continental standards.

Episcopal pronouncements now reflected the Catholic Church as the conscience of society rather than the dictatorial controller of (generally sexual) morality. Religious personnel, no longer running middle-class schools, were now involved in social ministries, working with the poor and the marginalised. All in all, Irish Catholicism was undergoing profound transformation rather than experiencing terminal disintegration. Conformity, intolerance, toeing-the-line were giving way to honest and generous spiritual experience.

### A VISIONARY FUTURE?

Perhaps the nation at large was now open to similar experiences in the secular sphere. In the new clauses proposed for the Con-

stitution, and hugely endorsed in the 1998 referendum, "the Irish nation" was envisaged in voluntary, flexible, generous and, above all, inclusive terms. Two centuries after the United Irishmen, was their vision being defined anew?

*See* Emigration: 1801–1921; Emigration: 1922–1998; Famine, the Great; Catholicism, Irish-American; Irish in America

Jonathan Bardon, *A History of Ulster* (Belfast, 1992).
D. G. Boyce, *Ireland, 1828–1923* (Oxford, 1992).
T. Brown, *Ireland: A Social and Cultural History, 1922–79* (Glasgow, 1981).
R. Fanning, *Independent Ireland* (Dublin, 1983).
R. F. Foster, *Modern Ireland, 1600–1972* (London, 1988).
K. T. Hoppen, *Ireland since 1800: Conflict and Conformity* (London, 1989).
D. Keogh, *Twentieth-Century Ireland* (Dublin, 1994).
J. J. Lee, *Ireland 1912–85: Politics and Society* (Cambridge, 1989).
John A. Murphy, *Ireland in the Twentieth Century* (Dublin, 1975 and 1989).
*A New History of Ireland, V, 1801–70*, ed. W. E. Vaughan (Oxford, 1989).
*A New History of Ireland, VI, 1870–1920*, ed. W. E. Vaughan (Oxford, 1996).
C. Ó Gráda, *The Great Irish Famine* (London, 1991).
G. Ó Tuathaigh, *Ireland before the Famine* (Dublin, 1972 and 1990).
*The Oxford Companion to Irish History*, ed. S. J. Connolly (Oxford, 1998).
*The Oxford Companion to Irish Literature*, ed. Robert Welch (Oxford, 1996).

JOHN A. MURPHY

## IRELAND: PLANTATIONS (1548–1700)

It is generally agreed among historians that Ireland between 1580 and 1700 underwent a revolution. From the point of view of the outsider Ireland in the middle of the sixteenth century was, at best, a curiosity and at worst barbaric. By 1700 it was recognisable as a society governed by the norms of ancien régime Europe. It would be more accurate to characterise this change not as the product of a single dramatic change but rather as the result of a series of interrelated revolutions. Some of these changes are paralleled by developments in other parts of Europe. The centralisation of authority in Dublin and the undermining of powerful local magnates, for instance, happened elsewhere in Europe also. Similarly the economic transformation of Ireland with the rise of a market economy and the greater commercialisation of economic life echoed a wider European process. In religious terms too, the progress of the Reformation and Counter-Reformation in Ireland must be seen in a European context.

In one area, however, the change which took place in early modern Ireland was almost unique in Europe. The composition of the social and political elite of early modern Ireland underwent a dramatic shift in the years between 1580 and 1700. The Irish peerage summoned to the parliament of 1585 was drawn from five Gaelic or Gaelicised families and twenty Old English landed families, the descendants of the medieval Anglo-Norman settlers. By the end of the seventeenth century, of the fifty-nine elite families who were summoned, thirty-nine (or about two thirds) were drawn from New English settler families who had arrived in the country in the half century before 1641 and a further five were settler families of post-1641 origin. Old English families had thirteen representatives while just two were of native Irish extraction. The composition of this parliament reflects a major transfer of power, and ultimately land, from one social group to another.

Estimates of the scale of land transfer in the seventeenth century are hazardous. J. G. Simms has estimated that land held by Catholics fell from fifty-eight percent in 1641 to twenty-two percent by 1688 with a further slide to fourteen percent by 1700. Identification of religion with ethnic origin is problematical. One of the largest settler landlords in Ireland, the earl of Antrim, was a Catholic while the native Irish earl of Thomond and the Old English duke of Ormond were Protestants. However, estimates, such as those of Simms, do provide one indication of the scale and timing of the transfer of land between social groups in Ireland.

It is possible to identify four elements in the mechanism of the transfer of land. First, there were formally organised plantations which included not only transfers of land but also attempts to re-order the social structure of the settled lands. In this class the plantations of Munster in the 1580s and Ulster in the early seventeenth century provide the most dramatic examples. Secondly, there were less organised colonisation schemes which did not require the introduction of settlers but did involve transferring the ownership of land. These included the early seventeenth-century plantations of Wexford, Longford and Leitrim. Thirdly there were large-scale land transfers as a result of warfare, largely the spoils of war moving from vanquished to victor, in the 1650s and again after the Williamite wars of the 1690s. Finally, and probably more important in the longer term there was informal colonisation in which local native Irish landowners fell into debt and sold their lands to Old English or New English settlers. Areas such as Antrim and Down fell into settler hands in this way and large parts of Connacht passed from native Irish ownership to that of the Old English by purchase in the early seventeenth century. One fifth of Sligo and almost half of Mayo were in Old English hands by 1641 as a result of such stratagems.

Of all these mechanisms of land transfer undoubtedly the most spectacular were the formal plantations of Munster in the 1580s and Ulster after 1609.

## Early Plantations

Plantations were not new features of Irish life in the late sixteenth century. Throughout the sixteenth century the Dublin administration, increasingly in the hands of New English officials after 1534, was faced with a twin problem. First, they wished to eliminate the fragmented political authority which bedeviled sixteenth-century Ireland. To achieve this the near-autonomous indigenous Irish lordships had to be bound together into what both Old and New English administrators termed a "commonwealth" held together by common bonds and assumptions about language, authority and the law. Such changes could not be implemented in the short term. The second set of problems, however, did call for more immediate solutions. How were the borders of the area of English authority, the Pale, to be secured while the more ambitious schemes were effected?

The first solution to the immediate security problem was simple: strategically placed garrisons which were to be maintained as cheaply as possible. In 1548 a solution presented itself. The marshal of the army, Nicholas Bagenal, was granted the lands of the newly dissolved monastic house at Newry with the injunction that he establish a fort there to protect the northern edge of the Pale. Bagenal complied and introduced Welsh and English settlers to his newly founded town at Newry. A second, roughly contemporaneous scheme was planned following the local ris-

ing of O'Connors, O'Mores and O'Dempseys in Leix and Offaly. This met with less success despite offers from individuals, such as Edward Walshe, to organise private settlements in the area. It was 1557 before a more systematic approach was applied to this area. Leix and Offaly were transformed into King's and Queen's counties (named after Mary I and her husband Philip) and set aside for a settlement of soldiers and others from within the Pale and from England. The aim was to provide security for the western edge of the Pale and also to generate royal income through rents and other payments to the Irish Exchequer.

The idea of defence by contracting work to private enterprise immediately proved a success in the eyes of government. In 1571 and 1572, for instance, Sir Thomas Smith and the earl of Essex, both English courtiers, were granted large parts of east Ulster. This was intended to create bulwarks against highland Scots, whose recent arrival in large numbers was feared as a destabilising force in Ulster politics. These settlements had mixed fortunes. There was no guarantee that they would provide the necessary security. Bagenal may have succeeded at Newry but the ventures of Smith and Essex were miserable failures. In the midlands the effect of plantation was to institutionalise violence as soldiers found it profitable to harass the native Irish and to maintain a large military presence for which captains could draw allowances. Such settlements simply replaced overmighty Irish lords with violent English ones.

## Munster

Such military settlements may have gone some way toward providing cheap security but they did little to implement the longer term strategy of creating an English-style commonwealth in Ireland. The opportunity to do this presented itself in November 1583 when the earl of Desmond, in rebellion since 1579, was taken by surprise and decapitated in a glen near Tralee. A rebel under common law, his lands had been confiscated four years earlier. The end of the war provided the government with an opportunity to reorganise the social order in a large part of Munster. It took two years and a large scale survey to produce the plan which emerged in 1585. The moving force behind it was almost certainly Elizabeth's principal secretary of state, Lord Burghley. It was 1586 before the final details emerged and it was soon apparent that this plan was unlike anything else that had been tried in Ireland. It was nothing less than a scheme for social engineering, aimed primarily not at defence but to re-create the world of south-east England in southern Ireland. An estate system was to be formed by making grants ranging from 4,000 to 12,000 acres to thirty-five English landlords. They were to be agents for the introduction of English lifestyles by building villages and settling on their lands, within seven years, freeholders, copyholders and cottagers. Each estate was to have ninety households by 1593. The scheme also introduced the English law of landlord and tenant to regulate the settlement. The allocation of the different tenures to the settlers was designed to produce a social hierarchy with powerful freeholders at the top and cottagers, with no security of tenure, at the bottom. The landlords were to practice English style agriculture based on grain growing. This was labour intensive and, it was hoped, would produce stable settlement, replacing the more mobile cattle raising favoured by the native Irish.

## Ulster

By 1594 many of the government officials who had planned the Munster scheme were disappointed with the results but further consideration of the problem was postponed by the outbreak of the Nine Years War in 1594. At the end of that war in 1603 they were reluctant to become involved in another plantation scheme on the scale of that in Munster and they were prepared to offer Hugh O'Neill an advantageous peace rather than confiscate his lands as a traitor. The administration's hand was forced when in September 1607 O'Neill and his principal followers unexpectedly left Ulster for continental Europe never to return, although O'Neill himself wished to. The government confiscated (or escheated) their lands comprising the modern counties of Armagh, Tyrone, Fermanagh, Londonderry, Cavan and Donegal. A dangerous power vacuum now existed in Ulster. This time London, in the person of the king and the Irish committee of the Privy Council, prepared a scheme for the settlement of Ulster which was ready by 1609. It was influenced not only by the Munster experience but also by the earlier attempt of James I to plant the island of Lewis in Scotland. Land was to be allocated to English and Scottish landlords, as well as former soldiers and some native Irish, lots of 2,000, 1,500, and 1,000 acres, rather smaller than those in the Munster scheme. The entire county of Coleraine was set aside not for individuals but for that new invention of seventeenth-century entrepreneurs—the joint stock company. The shareholders (and providers of capital) were to be the twelve London livery companies who set up a new body, the Irish Society, to manage their asset which was newly renamed county Londonderry. The Ulster planation scheme also contained provisions for reshaping the social world. The number and type of tenants which each landlord had to find were stipulated and land was also assigned to the established church. Landlords were to build houses, improve their lands and remove native Irish tenants within a specified time, replacing them with Scottish or English settlers. Towns were to be built and artisans encouraged to settle in them.

There were two innovations over the older Munster scheme. First, native Irishmen were to be among the grantees in the scheme, receiving about a fifth of the land granted, whereas in Munster all the Irish had been excluded. Secondly, provision was made for the building of schools in Ulster with land in each county being set aside for "Royal Schools": an indication that education was considered an important agent of social change.

## THE RESULTS

Measuring the impact of these settlement changes in the sixteenth and seventeenth centuries is a difficult task. It is clear that gaelic Irish society in the early modern period was changing as a result of its own dynamic and many of the changes which were introduced by settlers may have occurred in any case, though at a much slower rate. Moreover even without formal plantation schemes or land redistribution Ireland was certainly an attractive location for settlers from England and Scotland. Between 1580 and 1640 about 370,000 Englishmen and 100,000 Scots left their homes and families to make their fortunes abroad. Rising population and demand for increasingly expensive land along with diminishing opportunities in the church or the law for younger sons made self-imposed exile a fate for many. Some, such as those from the east coast of Scotland, went to Europe as mercenaries in the armies engaged in the Thirty Years War. From south and west England others, fired by religious zeal, travelled west to New England. Yet others from the same areas were lured to other newly discovered parts of America by stories of fabulous fortunes to be made in the more commercially minded colony of Virginia. Others saw in Ireland, only a short sea journey away

whose inhabitants were already well known as a result of trade, under-exploited natural resources which they could develop. Informal colonisation in this context was a fact of life rather than a dramatic new innovation.

In the short term, however, the social changes hoped for by central government in its framing of the formal plantation schemes in Ireland were not achieved. In the case of the Munster plantation, by 1592 the targets for the introduction of settlers had not been achieved and landlords were less effective than it was hoped in building villages and introducing agricultural change. London may have had good social reasons for wishing to introduce wheat growing in Munster but the settlers soon had the evidence of climate and soils to realise this was impracticable. In Ulster too expectations fell short of realities. Surveys of the plantation in 1611, 1615 and 1619 all revealed that the targets set were not being met. Settler landlords had not completed the required buildings and had not removed the native Irish from their estates. Towns were poorly developed and many existed only on paper. Most importantly, from the perspective of the London government, the new settlements had not generated much revenue for the Exchequer. A major enquiry on the state of the plantations, and the state of the government of Ireland generally, was undertaken in 1622. This resulted in threats of confiscation of land from those who had not fulfilled the requirements of the plantation scheme. Indeed it was this threat which made some of the Ulster planters uneasy bedfellows with the Old English in demanding security of tenure during the episode of the Graces in the 1620s. The rebellion of the 1640s saw the destruction of much of what had been achieved in the early plantation schemes and the late seventeenth century saw a significant restructing of Ulster society.

If the government was unhappy about the progress of settlement in the sixteenth and seventeenth centuries, the native Irish population were more ambivalent. There is little evidence of discontent among the Irish of Ulster or Munster before the middle of the seventeenth century. Some may have been fatalistic. The surviving Irish poetry of the period tends to view the fall of the old order as a judgement of God on the Irish for their sins. Some left Ireland. Troublesome Kavanaghs from the Wexford plantation were shipped to Virginia but many others opted to travel to continental Europe. Some became mercenaries in the Spanish armies of the Low Countries while a select few became students in the newly established Irish seminaries in Spain, France or the Spanish Netherlands. However, given the very low population levels which characterised especially Ulster, it is likely that the introduction of numbers of new settlers did not generate tensions over land ownership. Indeed many native Irish lords of the second rank became integral to the new order. Those who planned the rising of 1641 were not those dispossessed by the plantation schemes but rather were key figures in the new order. Most were members of parliament or officials in local government such as sheriffs or justices of the peace. Their concerns were those of high politics rather than local realities and it was late in the rising before the discontents generated by plantation were raised. It was the Cromwellian and later land redistributions which upset the native Irish to a much greater extent. First, these took place in a changed economic climate. Population levels were higher and therefore demand for land greater so that the possibilities of friction between competing interests more likely. Secondly, the native Irish literati of the late seventeenth century repeatedly cited the social origins of the Cromwellian and later settlers as a cause of friction. Whereas in the early part of the seventeenth century most of the settler landlords had come from gentry backgrounds, those who arrived later in the century were of much more humble origins, many of them being soldiers. While the social bond of gentility might make a *modus vivendi* possible in the early seventeenth century this was less probable later in the century.

Not surprisingly, those who viewed the settlement changes as successful were the new landowners. Most were younger sons, government officials or, more frequently as the century progressed, soldiers. They had acquired at little cost substantial estates. Moreover Ireland was a world of low rents and abundant land, although this was less true by the end of the century. The result was that there was a thriving land market which would not stabilise until the beginning of the eighteenth century and would allow some, such as Richard Boyle, earl of Cork, to build large landed estates. However, managing these estates was not easy. Their social backgrounds meant that most landlords did not have the resources necessary to develop their lands and the accumulation of capital took time. Hence many landlords were reluctant to remove rent-paying native Irishmen from their estates.

Plantation and colonisation did have a dramatic effect on Irish life. The population of Ireland rose from probably about a million in 1600 to 2.8 million by 1712, largely as a result of immigration. This dramatically expanded labour force increased agricultural output in the early part of the century although in the later part of the century both economic and governmental pressures saw a move to more processed goods. Here the skills which settlers provided were of crucial importance to economic life. While in the short term seventeenth-century plantations may have proved disappointing for the governments which promoted them, the wider process of colonisation proved to be one of the main engines of social and economic change, although not the sole one, by which Ireland moved from a medieval to a recognisably more modern world by 1700.

---

Raymond Gillespie, *Colonial Ulster: the Settlement of East Ulster, 1600–1641* (Cork, 1985).

———, *The Transformation of the Irish Economy* (Dundalk, 1991).

———, "Explorers, Exploiters and Entrepreneurs: Early Modern Ireland and its Contexts," in B. J. Graham and L. J. Proudfoot, eds., *An Historical Geography of Ireland* (London, 1993).

Michael MacCarthy-Morrogh, *The Munster Plantation: English Migration to Southern Ireland, 1583–1641* (Oxford, 1986).

Philip Robinson, *The Plantation of Ulster* (Dublin, 1984).

J. G. Simms, "Land Owned by Catholics in Ireland in 1688," in *Irish Historical Studies,* vii, no. 27 (March 1951).

RAYMOND GILLESPIE

## IRELAND: THE PENAL LAWS (1695–1709)

After the defeat of James II by William of Orange, his son-in-law, at the Battle of the Boyne in July 1690, James and his army fled. But the Irish, led by Patrick Sarsfield, fought on, until they were eventually forced to seek and sign the treaty of Limerick in October 1691. Sarsfield and 14,000 Irish soldiers were allowed to emigrate to Europe, and they were the forerunners of the legendary "Wild Geese" who later won fame on the battlefields of Europe. The treaty promised those who did not emigrate the right to own property, freedom of religion, and the right to enter the professions and to practice law.

But the Irish parliament, then totally controlled by members of the Church of Ireland (Episcopalian), objected to the terms of the treaty and enacted the "popery code" of stringent and repressive laws aimed primarily at Catholics. But in several ways, they also penalized nonconformists, principally the Presbyterians. Even though the Tolerance Act of 1719 brought them some relief, those who emigrated during the eighteenth century harbored memories of discrimination and persecution.

### THE PRINCIPAL LAWS

Penal laws enacted in 1685 and 1687 banned Catholics from operating schools, becoming teachers or educating their children abroad. The Bishops' Banishment Act of 1697 ordered all bishops and ecclesiastical administrators out of the country, and also forced members of religious orders into exile. It allowed one priest from each parish to remain, but prohibited any replacements.

The estates of deceased Catholic landowners were to be divided among their male heirs; and Catholics were forbidden to hold leases for over 31 years. The legal profession was closed to them as were all government posts, big and small, and they were banned from the army and navy. Under an English law of 1691, Catholics were already barred from serving in parliament, but punitive legislation in 1728 stripped them completely of the right to vote and excluded them from local and national government.

It was physically and practically impossible, and often politically inexpedient, to consistently enforce these laws, decade after decade. Rising popular resentment and agitation led to the formation of the Catholic Committee in 1760. Influenced by domestic discontent and British foreign policy, relief for Catholics was enacted in 1778, 1782 and 1792–93. The penal era ended when Daniel O'Connell won Catholic Emancipation in April 1829 when Catholics were permitted to sit in parliament at Westminster.

### THE AFTERMATH

The penal laws had lasting economic, educational, religious and psychological consequences for the majority of the Irish people. Emigrants, mostly Presbyterian, who sailed for America in the eighteenth century brought with them a resentment toward the Church of Ireland and an abiding distrust of the English government. While the penal laws were primarily aimed at Catholics, their purpose was not to convert but to subjugate them, economically and culturally. The prescribed division of farms at the death of their Catholic owners had dire economic consequences on a country with a growing population and where, by 1780, Catholic ownership of arable land was merely 5 percent. And the deliberate curtailment of educational opportunities had long-distance consequences for the majority of the Irish people.

Those who emigrated to America in the 1830s, and especially after the Great Famine in the awful 1840s, traveled with few possessions. They crossed the Atlantic with miserable personal memories and a communal legacy of injustice which bonded them in a new land, and profoundly influenced their social and political attitudes in American life for more than a century.

---

S. J. Connolly, ed., *The Oxford Companion to Irish History* (Oxford and New York, 1998).

T. W. Moody and F. X. Martin, eds., *The Course of Irish History* (New York, 1967).

Fergus O'Farrell, *Catholic Emancipation and the Birth of Irish Democracy* (Dublin, 1985).

T. P. Power and Kevin Whalen, eds., *Endurance and Emergence: Catholic in Ireland in the Eighteenth Century* (Dublin, 1990).

MICHAEL GLAZIER

## IRELAND: THE LAND LEAGUE

The Mayo Land League was founded by Michael Davitt in 1879. Shortly after, it became the National Land League headed by Charles Parnell. The Land League demanded the end of the landlord system and advocated the three F's: fair rent, fixity of tenure and free sale of tenancy.

The League enlisted massive support and conducted a Land War between 1879 and 1882, which was a period of intense and elaborate use of moral force. Embargoes were placed on evicted farms which would not allow anything to move in or out of them. The boycott was effectively used to socially ostracize collaborators and evictions were accompanied by huge demonstrations. Social welfare support in the form of shelter and money was provided for families evicted for nonpayment. The League defended those who were prosecuted and cared for the families of those who were sent to prison.

In 1879 Michael Davitt had traveled to America and met with John Devoy of the Clan Na Gael. They reached an agreement known as the New Departure. The Clan Na Gael would agree to support land reform and constitutional nationalism while continuing to prepare for revolution. At the same time Parnell and Davitt would not interfere with the promotion of revolutionary nationalism. In 1882 Parnell would call for home rule and when Britain refused, a revolt of the masses would occur. Many in the Clan Na Gael did not agree with this strategy initially but eventually came to embrace it.

In early 1880 Parnell participated in a ten week fund-raising tour of the United States. During his tour Parnell was also able to address the United States Congress about the conditions in Ireland and the potential role of American political pressure for change. At the end of his tour Parnell urged the founding of the American wing of the Irish National Land League.

In May of 1880 the Irish National Land and Industrial League was founded by Clan Na Gael as a front to raise money and press political issues. The League was more commonly known as the

Charles Stewart<br/>Parnell

Irish National Land League of America. The Land League attracted many Irish-Americans who were hesitant to be involved in organizations that advocated physical force and violence. Land League branches were organized across the United States. After Parnell's sisters, Anna and Fannie, traveled to America to raise funds, American women formed The Ladies Land League. In Cleveland, Ohio, The Ladies Land League defied the Anglophile Bishop, Gilmour, who opposed their efforts as well as the cause of the Irish freedom.

American money funded the National Land League in Ireland in order to aid evicted tenants and purchase legal aid for families. Americans also publicized the anti-landlord case in America and gained much sympathy and support.

However, an ideological split in the Irish-American community led to the division of fund-raising activities between the Irish National Land League and the Irish World Land League led by Patrick Ford, editor of *The Irish World*. Ford, who was a socialist, wanted to nationalize land instead of promoting peasant proprietorship. The Clan Na Gael-led Irish National Land League did not support Ford's radical agrarian ideas.

The Irish National Land League voted itself out of existence in April of 1883. The League was constantly plagued by disputes between radical Clan Na Gaelers who wanted self government for Ireland through revolution and pacifists who merely wanted land reform. At its peak the League had branches in almost every state and probably about 50,000 members.

J. Donnelly, Jr., *The Land and the People of Nineteenth-Century Cork* (London, 1975).

T. W. Moody, *Michael Davitt and the Irish Revolution 1846–82* (Oxford, 1981).

W. E. Vaughan, *Landlords and Tenants in mid-Victorian Ireland* (Dublin, 1994).

SEAMUS METRESS

## IRELAND: NINETEENTH-CENTURY PRIMARY EDUCATION

From a comparative perspective, Ireland presents a fascinating case study of the development of primary education in the nineteenth century. While the Act of Union of 1800 bound Ireland more tightly into the United Kingdom, Ireland was a very divided society in terms of religion, political allegiance and material well-being. The mass of the population experienced great degrees of poverty, but one of the phenomena of the ordinary people, noted by many contemporary observers, was the regard in which they held learning and the sacrifices they would make to attain it. It was a concern by the state to control and shape the type of schooling provided which was one of the main reasons for the establishment of a state-supported system of primary education decades before such an initiative took place in England or France. One of the great crusades of the nineteenth century was the spread of mass popular education and the promotion of literacy and numeracy. The Irish experience was one of the most impressive, and elements of the Irish system were transplanted to other regions of the English-speaking world in the nineteenth century. In dealing with this experience in a short article it may be beneficial to approach it through a series of questions:

- What was the schooling situation in the first third of the century?
- Why was a state-controlled system established in 1831?

- How was this system administered?
- How did the system progress?
- What were the curricular patterns and teaching styles?
- How did nonaided schools fare?
- What was the image of the teachers' role?

## What Was the Existing Schooling Situation?

By the early nineteenth century, Ireland had inherited various types of schools such as parish, diocesan, royal and charter schools, which had been designated by state legislation as agencies of colonial conquest to spread the use of the English language and the Protestant faith, but these schools failed to reach the mass of the people. Since the late seventeenth century, Catholics and Presbyterians had suffered from harsh penal legislation which prohibited them from setting up schools or sending their children abroad for education. Despite this, Catholics had succeeded in setting up numerous unofficial schools which became known as "hedge schools" and these were widespread by the early nineteenth century. These schools were truly of the people, by the people and for the people, as the impoverished populace provided the shelters for the schools, employed their own masters, coming from the people, and supported them in whatever way they could, often in kind. Of great value to the teachers was the respect in which they were held by the people.

The relaxation of penal legislation through the relief acts of 1782, 1792 and 1793 allowed greater official tolerance, and religious orders began their educational/pastoral activities by founding schools. The early nineteenth century also saw much evangelising zeal with a proselytising intent by a number of Protestant religious groups (Bowen, D., *The Protestant Crusade in Ireland, 1800–70,* Dublin: 1974). The fact that some of the societies benefited from public funds added to the annoyance of Catholics. One particular society, the Society for Promoting the Education of the Poor of Ireland, popularly known as the Kildare Place Society, got particular government support from 1816. It was educationally progressive and it set out to be religiously neutral "divested of all sectarian distinctions in Christianity." At first Catholics accepted the Kildare Place Society but from 1820 they became disillusioned and dissatisfied with it and they pressed the state to provide a system congenial to Catholic requirements.

Thus, at the outset of the nineteenth century there was much educational activity in Ireland, and many and varied schools were provided by individuals and voluntary societies. By the year 1824 an official commission calculated that there were about 11,000 schools in Ireland catering for upwards of half a million children, and staffed by about 12,000 teachers (*Reports of the Commissioners of Irish Education Inquiry,* House of Commons [H.C.], 1826–27 [516], xiii, p. 1,058). By far the largest category of schools was the hedge schools which numbered about 9,000 and catered for almost 400,000 children. The number of pupils enrolled in all schools but whose attendance could often be sporadic and short-lived, amounted to two out of every five children of school-going age at that time. With this level of voluntary activity, some of it with state support, the question presents itself as to why the state intervened to set up a centrally controlled system?

## Why Set Up a State-Controlled System in 1831?

At first sight, Ireland would not seem to have been a likely place for large-scale direct intervention by the state. Many factors which in other countries acted as a propelling force, such as the Industrial Revolution and moves to urbanisation, were not striking issues in the Irish context. Ireland was also a difficult case in that strong hostilities existed between the denominations. On closer examination, however, there were many reasons which favoured the state action of 1831. There had been a long tradition of British state legislation relating to education in Ireland. The work of various commissions in previous decades as well as highlighting debate on educational issues, had also indicated a path forward for state action on which, at least at official level, there was general agreement. The gathering official consensus was that a state-supported system of parish schools should be organised under the supervision of a Government Board. The leading principle of the system should be "that no attempt be made to influence or disturb the peculiar religious tenets of any sect or description of christians" (*Fourteenth Report of the Commissioners of the Board of Education in Ireland,* H.C. 1812–13 [21], vi).

In the context of post–Act of Union politics, the government felt that the schools could serve politicising and socialising goals, cultivating attitudes of political loyalty and cultural assimilation. The danger of separate school systems operating without official supervision needed to be countered. The fear of political subversion through the hedge schools was very real. Further, theorists in England, such as Adam Smith, had urged that the state should promote literacy and numeracy at elementary level as an essential factor for industrial progress. Ireland, as a colony, could be used as an experimental milieu for social legislation which might not be tolerated in England where *laissez faire* politico-economic policies were more rigid and doctrinaire.

The achievement of Catholic Emancipation in 1829, following the mass movement master-minded by Daniel O'Connell, was a practical demonstration that Catholic demands for fair treatment could not be suppressed, and the national school system under state control seemed to the government the best way of directing educational provision. Further, a number of influential, informed and respected Irish members of the English Parliament, such as O'Connell, Thomas Spring-Rice, and Thomas Wyse, kept up the pressure for action. Members of the new reforming Whig government of 1830, such as Lord Anglesey, the Lord Lieutenant of Ireland and Lord Stanley, the Chief Secretary for Ireland, judged the time to be ripe for action, and so this highly significant government initiative was undertaken.

It was the state's intention to operate a multidenominational or "mixed" primary system wherein children of all denominations would be educated together in secular subjects while separate arrangements would be made for doctrinal instruction according to different denominational tenets. This effort to draw a distinction between secular and purely religious instruction was to prove a most contentious one. Each of the denominations disputed this distinction, seeing the whole schooling process as an extension of pastoral care with religion interpenetrating all facets of education. Moreover, in the context of strong denominational animosities and a live tradition of proselytism, the concept of a mixed education system would prove difficult to realise. The churches were anxious to benefit from state finance in support of schooling but each denomination strove to shape the national school system towards its denominational requirements. This conflict between state and church on the control of schooling pursued a tortuous and labyrinthine path resulting in the state's retaining the concept of a *de facto* mixed system which from mid-century onwards became increasingly denominational at the local level in terms of management, pupil clientele and teaching staff.

## How Was the System Administered?

The ideals and structure of the new national system were set out in a letter from Lord Stanley to the Duke of Leinster, a liberal Protestant, inviting him to become chairman of the new Board of Commissioners for National Education. The following were the chief points in this foundation document of the Irish national school system. Following a historical review of proposals of earlier commissions, Stanley rejected the mode of applying state funds for education through voluntary societies such as the Kildare Place Society. Instead he proposed a government-appointed, mixed denominational board comprised of men of high personal character, including individuals of exalted station in the churches. This board was to exercise authority over schools erected under its auspices or placed under its control. Local funds had to be forthcoming in aid of teacher salaries, the cost of furniture and maintenance, and the school site. The Stanley Letter also stated that the Board was to have complete control over textbooks used and, by means of inspection, ensure that regulations were enforced. Funds approved by Parliament were to be disbursed by the board for such things as aid for school building, payment of inspectors, gratuities to teachers, providing a model school for teacher training, and publishing textbooks for schools.

At the local level, the school manager, who in practice became almost always a clergyman, had the right to hire and dismiss teachers, to distribute teacher salaries, to arrange the timetable, to oversee the general work of the school and to be responsible for the general maintenance and equipment of the school. From this division of powers it can be seen that the most important remained with the central authority, though at the local level the manager had considerable power over the teachers.

## How Did the System Progress?

While much controversy surrounded the control exercised by the Board and its policy on mixed denominational education, it was striking how, at local level, the people utilised the system on such a wide scale for the education of their children. In the course of a generation, the national school system had been adopted generally, as is clear from the following table.

Table 1. Expansion of the National School System, 1833–1860

| Year | Parliamentary Grant | Number of Schools Associated with Board | Number of Pupils on Rolls |
|---|---|---|---|
| 1833 | £25,000 | 789 | 107,042 |
| 1840 | £50,000 | 1,978 | 232,560 |
| 1850 | £125,000 | 4,547 | 511,239 |
| 1860 | £294,000 | 5,632 | 804,000 |

Thus, by 1860 there were about 800,000 pupils (the great majority of children of school-going age in the population) attending the 5,600 schools associated with the Board at a state financial cost of almost £300,000. The localities never provided the level of local funding which was envisaged, though small school fees were sporadically paid until their abolition in 1892. The majority of schools were conducted by lay teachers, but the schools of religious communities, particularly nuns, which accepted the regulations of the Board also qualified for state financial support. The Board had also established both male and female denomina-

tionally mixed training colleges in Dublin as well as a scheme of "district model" schools under the direct control of the Board wherein pupil teachers did an apprenticeship. This system of teacher training became anathema, particularly to the Catholic Church authorities, who eventually set up their own colleges and got state support starting in 1884.

The National Board began in 1832 to establish an impressive state school inspectorate which acted as a vital link between the Board and the growing network of schools throughout the country. The scheme of textbooks envisaged in the Stanley Letter proved a considerable success. The commissioners published a set of reading books for five different grade levels which quickly established a high reputation for themselves in Ireland, and they even enjoyed a considerable export demand in England and some of its colonies. There was a strong moralistic and socialising aura to the books. The Irish language was not acknowledged as a national school subject, even in areas where the living and sole vernacular of the people was Irish. Indeed, for much of the century the books contained very little material relating to a distinctively Irish environment and were geared towards the British cultural policy of the time.

## What Were the Curricular Patterns and Teaching Styles?

The curriculum was based mainly on the textbooks produced by the Board of Commissioners. The promotion of literacy and numeracy formed the core concern, but a surprisingly wide range of subjects was approved in the early decades. Having been established in late 1831, the Board had published its five Reading Books by 1835, as well as a book on arithmetic, bookkeeping, a geometry book, and two selections of scripture readings. By 1841, the Board had produced further books on grammar, the "art of reading," a girls' reading book, a book on mensuration and one on needlework. It produced school slates, maps, stationery, and such requisites.

The Board did not compel schools to use its texts, although it retained the right to sanction any books being used. An important incentive was that schools received an initial stock of books free of charge and, subsequently, at half-price. In November 1832, the Board appointed an official bookseller and book depositor. It also organised distribution through regional book depots and teachers benefited from a discount on the sale of textbooks and school materials. The Board showed further initiative by appointing agents in 1836 for the sale of its books in London and Edinburgh, a move which was to prove very lucrative. As well as reading, writing and arithmetic, the national schools at this time were to promote instruction in elements of history and geography, leading subjects of "useful knowledge," as well as bookkeeping, geometry, surveying/mensuration, political economy, while girls were to be taught sewing or knitting. In the Report of 1840, the Board remarked: "We attach much importance to the cultivation of vocal music as a branch of general education" (20, p. 87).

Interestingly, the National Board also sought to promote agriculture in association with its school system. In 1838 it set up its first model agricultural school in Glasnevin, Dublin. The Report for 1837 stated: "Considering the very backward state of agriculture in Ireland, and that it forms the only source of employment for a vast portion of the labouring poor, we think it particularly desirable that a better knowledge of it should be promoted: and that the schools under us should tend, as far as practicable, to

Ulster was part of that unit, and that any Home Rule settlement had to be for the historic entity of Ireland.

His appeal fell on totally deaf ears. Ulster unionists, under the parliamentary leadership of Colonel Edward Saunderson, wanted no truck with Home Rule in any shape or form. Had Home Rule become a real threat—had it not fallen at the first hurdle but been carried through the Commons into the Lords—it is possible that the question of partition would have loomed much larger, although it seems improbable that there would have been military resistance at that time.

There the matter rested until the Second Home Rule Bill, introduced again by Gladstone in 1893. This time he carried the bill through the Commons, only to have it thrown out by the massive Conservative majority in the Lords. Ulster unionist resistance had in the meantime become more organised, with certain overtones of paramilitary organisation, still under the leadership of Saunderson. Had the Bill passed, it is not inconceivable that conflict would have resulted.

Nevertheless, despite the heightened profile of the Ulster dimension in 1893, the unionist argument was not yet an essentially partitionist one. They believed that their opposition would protect not only Ulster unionists but also Irish unionists from the dreaded scourge of Home Rule.

It would be more than a decade before this perspective began to decisively alter. With Conservatives in power from 1895 to 1906, there was no immediate threat. Once Conservative fortunes began to wane, however, and a Liberal government looked likely after the next election, a specifically Ulster Unionist Council was formed in 1905 to defend the essential interests of Ulster unionism in the face of an anticipated Home Rule Bill, following a Liberal return to office.

Confrontation was postponed for six years, simply because the victorious Liberals in 1906 were not dependent on Home Rule support in parliament. It wouldn't be until they became dependent on that support, after two close elections in 1910 reduced their own majority, that the government of H. H. Asquith introduced the third Home Rule Bill in April 1912.

The alarm this created amongst Ulster unionists was not because the terms of the bill were more ambitious than those of 1893 or 1886. The bill was still little more than a glorified form of local government, with a Home Rule parliament having no control over its own income, or over defence or foreign policy. Rather was it because the potential for parliamentary resistance had been greatly weakened when the Liberals broke the power of the House of Lords, in the Parliament Act of 1911, to block Commons legislation. Hitherto, as in 1893, the Lords, with their inbuilt Tory majority, had presented an impregnable barrier against Home Rule. Now, they could reject Commons legislation only for a maximum of three years. A Home Rule Bill passed by the House of Commons for the first time in 1912 could therefore become law after its third passing in 1914.

Once Asquith introduced the third Home Rule Bill in April 1912, the unionists had lost the constitutional game. Having denounced Irish rebelliousness for more than a century, they now found themselves tempted in the same physical force direction. And this was precisely what the new Unionist leader, Sir Edward Carson, and the new Conservative leader, Andrew Bonar Law, embarked upon in 1912. Their perspectives and motives were, however, somewhat different. Carson, a Dubliner, an Irish rather than an Ulster Unionist, still clung to the belief that Home Rule could not work economically without unionist Ulster, the most industrialised part of the country, whose resistance could therefore sabotage the entire project. However radical in method, his perspective was traditionalist. Bonar Law, the Canadian son of an Ulster Presbyterian minister, although also opposed to Home Rule for Ireland, thought rather more in Ulster than in Irish terms.

Much debate has revolved around their ultimate intentions. Would they have launched a campaign of violence against the actual implementation of the Home Rule Act, as their more extravagant rhetoric implied, Bonar Law assured his audience at Blenheim Palace in the summer of 1912 that if an attempt were made to foist Home Rule on Ulster Protestants, "they would be justified in resisting such an attempt by all means in their power, including force . . . I can imagine no length of resistance to which Ulster can go in which I should not be prepared to support them. . . ." In a Solemn Covenant signed by virtually all Ulster Protestant adult males, and affirmed by females in September 1912, they assured the world that they would take any measures necessary to defeat this "conspiracy" to force them out of the United Kingdom and place them at the mercy of their hereditary enemies.

Nor did unionists confine themselves to rhetoric and resolutions. The Ulster Volunteer Force was established in 1913, rapidly training 100,000 men in military manoeuvres, and gaining credence from the illegal gunrunning of 25,000 rifles and 3,000,000 rounds of ammunition from Germany into Larne, Donaghadee and Bangor in April 1914. Although the weapons may not have been of the highest quality, they ensured that the UVF was incomparably better armed than the National Volunteers, founded in imitation of them in November 1913. The military threat acquired further credibility from the fact that the previous month British officers, in the so-called Curragh Mutiny, had offered to resign their commissions rather than obey any putative order to suppress Ulster unionist revolt.

The Home Rule leader, John Redmond, scoffed at this exhibition of physical force Ulster unionism. Having built his whole political career on constitutional behaviour, he had no choice but to dismiss any alternative as inconceivable. He could not bring himself to contemplate the possibility that, having played the game and won, he could find his enemies unilaterally changing the rules. It was both psychologically and politically necessary for Redmond to cling to the belief that unionist threats were bluff, and that Conservatives and Unionists would ultimately abide by a parliamentary decision.

There is a view that Bonar Law, no matter about Carson, was indeed using the Ulster crisis to strengthen the Conservative position in Westminster, that he saw it as a means to the end of destabilising the government, and would not have pushed matters to open rebellion. We simply cannot know. By 1914, however, even if Bonar Law and perhaps Carson were to seek a safe retreat behind the rhetoric of confrontation, there could be no guarantee that the Ulster Volunteer Force would abide by the instruction to march back down the hill again.

Redmond sought to stiffen Asquith's resolve against any possible compromise. He thus rejected out of hand the first concrete scheme for partition, by Thomas Agar-Robartes, a Liberal MP, who in June 1912 proposed a four-county Northern Ireland, consisting of the counties with Protestant majorities, still as in Parnell's day, Antrim, Down, Armagh and Londonderry.

Redmond responded with outrage. Partition presumed two nations in Ireland, an idea he denounced as "blasphemy." For

Redmond, there could be only one Irish nation, and he could never consent to its partition.

But if Redmond could not, the embattled Asquith was increasingly attracted by the idea as an escape route from the impending confrontation that could bring Britain to the brink, or even over the brink, of civil war.

Carson contemptuously rejected the four-county "Ulster," but intimated in December 1912 that he might settle for the nine counties of "historic" Ulster. This was an agile adaptation of unionist argument. Having denied that Ireland enjoyed any historic unity, it now suddenly discovered that "Ulster" had a historic unity all of its own. This made political sense. Carson was still intent on blocking Home Rule altogether. If he was forced to retreat on the prinicple for Ireland, the most effective blocking tactic was to claim exemptions for the largest possible amount of territory, in the hope that this would frustrate the entire scheme.

The momentum for partition as an escape route for the government from the awful vista confronting Britain led to the Buckingham Palace Conference of July 1914, in which both sides wrestled each other to a standstill, the negotiations breaking down after three days of futile wrangling.

However, in the changed political circumstances following the outbreak of the First World War in August, Redmond arrived at a compromise with Asquith which contained the potential seeds of a partition settlement. Asquith agreed to put the Home Rule Act on the statute book in September as it now passed through the Commons for the third time, but only on condition that implementation would be deferred for a year, or until the end of the war, when the question of Ulster would be considered again.

Redmond has often been criticised for accepting this arrangement. But he had little choice. The overwhelming assumption at the time was that the war would be over within months. Deferral therefore would be for a maximum of a year. Getting the Act on the statute book was more important than immediate implementation, if postponement meant only a year. Had Redmond refused to support the British war effort, while Carson's U.V.F. were flocking to the colours, partition would have been inevitable, for how could the British government renege on its kith and kin in Protestant Ulster who had stood loyally by Britain in her hour of need, while Home Rulers had skulked in their noncombatant tents?

Redmond's calculation was quite rational in the circumstances of August 1914. But the politics of partition turned against him in the course of the war, simply because the war lasted so long. First, Carson entered the Cabinet in May 1915, thus strengthening his hand in any putative postwar settlement. Then came the Easter Rising, which allowed unionists to paint all Irish nationalists as enemies of Britain. Lloyd George, whom Asquith deputed to negotiate an Irish settlement in the aftermath of the Rising, persuaded Redmond to accept Home Rule on condition of temporary exclusion of six counties, while simultaneously guaranteeing Carson that exclusion would be permanent. Redmond was exposed as a dupe of British duplicity.

Home Rule remained in cold storage until the end of the war. Noone could have envisaged the postwar circumstances. Redmond, perhaps the most staunch antiparititionist of all, had died in March 1918, his Home Rule party soon to be superseded by the Sinn Féin of Eamon de Valera which won 73 of the 105 Irish seats, compared with 6 Home Rule and 26 Unionist seats, in the December general election. But that same general election brought a Conservative triumph in Britain. Even if Lloyd George, "the man who won the war," remained as prime minister, his Cabinet was predominantly Conservative, the Tory leader being none other than Andrew Bonar Law, and the Secretary of the Irish Situation Committee, Walter Long, a previous Conservative Chief Secretary for Ireland and leader of the Unionist party in parliament between 1906 and 1910.

Two basic changes had occurred since 1914 in British attitudes. First, the Conservatives finally accepted the idea of Home Rule, which they had previously opposed in principle. But it would be Home Rule for Southern Ireland only. What was Southern Ireland? From a Conservative perspective, it was whatever was left over after Northern Ireland was established. What then was Northern Ireland? The Cabinet Committee on the Irish Situation preferred a nine-county Ulster. But Ulster Unionists, increasingly guided by Sir James Craig, a staunch Presbyterian from Co. Down, an outstanding organiser, hitherto Carson's main lieutenant, rather than Carson himself, who still thought in Irish rather than Ulster terms and felt betrayed by any concession of Home Rule, sought a six-county border. As Walter Long reported on February 3, 1920, the Ulster Unionist leadership was opting for a six-county rather than a nine-county Northern Ireland, because "the inclusion of Donegal, Cavan and Monaghan would provide such an access of strength to the Roman Catholic party, that the supremacy of the unionists would be seriously threatened."

That was the border the Cabinet duly imposed in the Government of Ireland Act of December 1920, which established two parliaments, subordinate to Westminster, in Belfast and in Dublin. As the Dublin parliament was boycotted by Sinn Féin, the Government of Ireland Act was in effect the founding charter of Northern Ireland. The establishment of Northern Ireland took precedence over that of Southern Ireland, for the South was simply the residual after the British decided where the North's border would be.

Although the IRA was achieving some military success during the War of Independence in the South, it could not thwart the establishment of Northern Ireland. Even in the areas with Catholic majorities, the superior military power of British and unionists successfully sustained unionist rule. Tyrone and Fermanagh had county councils with Irish nationalist majorities, elected in 1920. Their protests against their incorporation in Northern Ireland were in vain. Dissolved by the government, their resistance proved ineffectual against the combination of the British army and the Ulster Special Constabulary, often composed of U.V.F. veterans returned from the First World War.

The general election of May 1921 in Northern Ireland returned 40 unionists and only 12 demoralised nationalists. The Northern Ireland parliament, opened by King George V in June, and with Craig, who formally succeeded a disillusioned Carson as Unionist leader in February, as Prime Minister, heard an eloquent appeal from the king to his Irish subjects to live in peace—now that Northern Ireland was safely in existence.

It was in response to this appeal that Lloyd George then embarked on the negotiations that led to the Truce of July 11, 1921, and eventually to the negotiations that culminated in the Anglo-Irish Treaty of December 6, 1921.

It is important to stress that Northern Ireland was already in existence before the truce. It is still asserted with monotonous regularity that it was the Treaty of December 6, 1921, that partitioned Ireland. It wasn't. Ireland was already partitioned. The treaty delegation was well aware that the IRA was unable to prevent the imposition of partition earlier in the year, along a six-county border, despite there being a majority of Catholics to the immediate northern side of most of that particular line. They were in no position to reverse a military defeat by diplomacy, given the continuing disparity between unionist and Irish nationalist forces.

Nevertheless, the Sinn Féin delegation negotiated vigorously on the issue of partition. The British representatives were confronted with an Irish team that contested every square mile of territory inhabited by a nationalist majority on the northern side of the border.

It was in response to this that the idea of the Boundary Commission was incorporated into Article 12 of the treaty, which proposed that a Commission, to consist of one representative each representing South and North, and a chairman appointed by the British government, would determine the boundary "in accordance with the wishes of the inhabitants, insofar as may be compatible with economic and geographic conditions."

In the event, the chairman of the Boundary Commission, Mr. Justice Feetham, a judge of the South African High Court, who effectively had the casting vote, laid most emphasis on "economic and geographic conditions," to the ineffectual chagrin of Eoin MacNeill, the Free State representative. The Commission recommended only minor changes in the border in both directions. When the findings were leaked to the *Morning Post* in November 1925, the President of the Executive Council of the Free State, W. T. Cosgrave, hastened to London to have the report suppressed and to accept the status quo.

"Economic and geographic conditions" were highly subjective concepts. They were determined essentially in the context of military realities, which allowed the unionist position of "what we have we hold" to triumph. It seemed as if the issue was settled. But the logic of a solution based essentially on military criteria would be brutally exposed fifty years later, and peace and conciliation would not finally come, if then, until another horrible chapter was written in blood. Everything else was rationalising rhetoric.

Despite the fact that "the wishes of the inhabitants" to the immediate north of the border had been largely ignored, there was an indisputable 2:1 unionist majority in Northern Ireland, even if it did not stretch as far as the border itself. As Irish nationalists within Northern Ireland could not hope to achieve military success—despite the substantial disruption caused by the IRA military campaign after 1970—and as any irredentist aspirations the Irish Free State might harbour were patently futile in the face of superior British military strength, Northern Ireland was effectively secure as long as it was protected by Britain. The areas of Protestant majority, particularly in the inner four counties, were probably secure against the worst threats either the Free State or internal rebels could pose, given their large unionist majority and their determination, reflected ever since the founding of the U.V.F. in 1913, to resolutely defend their position. Of their courage, demonstrated with conspicuous gallantry on the Somme in July 1916, there could be no question.

And threat there was, if largely rhetorical, until 1970. The 1937 Constitution of the Irish Free State denied the legitimacy of not only the line of the border, but the very existence of Northern Ireland, even if it also denied the legitimacy of any IRA campaign against either the border or the polity, which allowed the government to move firmly against revived IRA activity during the 1939–45 period. This was further compounded by the procla-

mation of an Irish Republic in 1949. The response of the British government was the Ireland Act, declaring "that in no event will Northern Ireland or any part thereof cease to be part . . . of the United Kingdom without the consent of the parliament of Northern Ireland." The Northern government dealt effectively, in cooperation with the government of the Republic, against an IRA border campaign during 1956–62, but the Provisional IRA campaign after 1970 proved far more difficult to counter.

What followed was a protracted and convoluted search for a solution to the Northern troubles, which included the effective abolition of the parliament of Northern Ireland at Stormont in 1972; the abortive Sunningdale Agreement of 1973, which instituted a power-sharing executive between unionists and nationalists, but quickly collapsed in the face of a unionist strike in 1974; the Anglo-Irish Agreement of 1985, by which the government of the Republic secured a degree of influence in Northern Irish affairs, but effectively recognised partition in acknowledging that no change could occur in the constitutional status of Northern Ireland without the consent of the majority within Northern Ireland; and the Good Friday Agreement of 1998, which provided for an amendment in the Republic's constitution, translating the territorial claim on Northern Ireland into an aspiration for unity with the consent of the majority in the North, an agreement ratified by an overwhelming majority in a referendum in the Republic, in return for restoring a power-sharing executive in the North, and the establishment of a number of cross-border bodies.

Whether this will resolve a problem that can be traced back nearly four centuries to the first settlement of Protestant planters in Ulster, in a more permanent manner than the Government of Ireland Act of 1920, remains to be seen. Whatever its fate, it can claim to be the first Northern Ireland settlement that has received the support of a majority of both ethno-religious groups in the North and of the Southern electorate. Its critics would argue that it legitimises a partition imposed without consent through superior military force in 1920, and thus retrospectively justifies the principle of force majeure. Its supporters, now the overwhelming majority of the people on the island, would respond either that partition was perfectly justified in the first place, or that it is the settlement which now least divides both the people/peoples of Northern Ireland, and the people/peoples of the island of Ireland least, and therefore has most prospect of solving a hitherto intractable problem, on the basis of what may be christened "partition with a human face."

Jonathan Bardon, *A History of Ulster* (Belfast, 1992).

Paul Bew, *Ideology and the Irish Question: Ulster Unionism and Irish Nationalism, 1912–1916* (Oxford, 1994).

Patrick Buckland, *Irish Unionism*, 2 vols. (Dublin, 1972–73).

Mary Harris, *The Catholic Church and the Foundation of the Northern Irish State* (Cork, 1993).

Michael Laffan, *The Partition of Ireland, 1911–1925* (Dundalk, 1983).

James Loughlin, *Gladstone, Home Rule and the Ulster Question 1882–93* (Dublin, 1986).

Nicholas Mansergh, *The Unresolved Question: The Anglo-Irish Settlement and Its Undoing, 1912–1972* (New Haven, 1991).

D. Mansergh, ed., *Nationalism and Independence: Selected Irish Papers of Nicholas Mansergh* (Cork, 1997).

Eamon Phoenix, *Northern Nationalism: Nationalist Politics, Partition and the Catholic Minority in Northern Ireland, 1890–1940* (Belfast, 1994).

A. T. Q. Stewart, *The Ulster Crisis* (London, 1979).

JOSEPH J. LEE

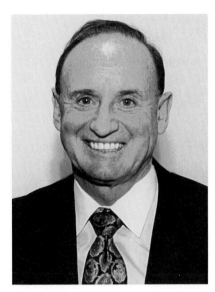

ICCUSA President
Maurice A. Buckley

## IRELAND CHAMBER OF COMMERCE IN THE U.S.

The Ireland Chamber of Commerce in the U.S. (ICCUSA) is the nonprofit membership organization promoting the business interests of its members and the development of mutually beneficial economic, financial, commercial and educational relationships between the United States and Ireland.

Founded in 1988, ICCUSA is comprised of business executives, professionals and individuals in the U.S., the Republic of Ireland, and Northern Ireland. Without political or sectional affiliations, the Ireland Chamber promotes development opportunities for businesses on both sides of the Atlantic. It has a membership of more than 500 corporations and individuals.

ICCUSA maintains an extensive communications program through advertising, publications, mailings, seminars and other means, to facilitate the exchange of useful information and ideas concerning the many benefits of doing business in or with Ireland. The Ireland Chamber assists firms and individuals seeking contact with government agencies and officials in Ireland and the U.S., serving as a coordinator on business-related matters of every kind.

The "Ireland FAX Library," created by ICCUSA, provides information about doing business in Ireland, available by fax twenty-four hours a day from anywhere in the world. This electronic data retrieval system also includes a website: "www.iccusa. org." The Ireland Chamber also publishes the *U.S./Ireland Trade Directory,* the only reference work of its kind available.

*See* Achievement of the Irish

FRANK CORBIN

## IRISH AMERICA MAGAZINE

In his inaugural *Irish America* magazine editorial in October 1986, founding publisher Niall O'Dowd expressed his hope that the publication would be "a powerful vehicle of expression for Irish Americans."

That first magazine also contained a listing of the top one hundred Irish-Americans, with Senator Edward Kennedy, tennis star John McEnroe and then-U.S. president Ronald Reagan featured on the front cover alongside the proud boast of "Irish America's finest."

In the intervening years, the top one hundred listing has gone on to be an annual feature, along with a listing of the top hundred business men and women achieving remarkable success in Irish America. In 1998, the magazine launched the first-ever listing of Irish-American achievers in the heart of New York's financial district—the Wall Street top fifty.

But *Irish America* magazine prides itself on being about much more than annual listings—the publication features heartwarming, and often thought-provoking, stories and interviews on all manner of topics.

A popular reader feature is the ancestor tracing section, which regularly receives letters from people trying to obtain further information on their family history. In 1997, a young man in Puerto Rico, who had just discovered that he had been born to an Irish mother in New York City, wrote to *Irish America*. Within just a few months of the publication of his letter, his extended family throughout the United States had made contact, and the following year he traveled to meet with them for the first time.

Editor-in-chief Patricia Harty recalls the factors which spurred the founding of the magazine. "Well, it was 1985 and we had an Irish president back in the White House, U2 was beginning to break on to the American music scene and we felt it was time to keep Irish Americans up-to-date with all these developments," she says.

Thus, *Irish America* was born—with the twin aim of informing Irish-Americans of the latest happenings in Ireland, and especially Northern Ireland, while also spotlighting the rich and varied history of the Irish in the United States.

The magazine quickly became a focal point for those who had previously had no outlet for their dreams and ideas. Interviews with Irish-Americans from all walks of life—business, the arts, religion, politics, medicine, education—showcased talent after dazzling talent. Other areas of the magazine focused, and still do, on Irish and Irish-American history, genealogy, book and music reviews and other features.

*See* Journalism, Irish-American

DARINA MOLLOY

## IRISH AMERICAN CULTURAL INSTITUTE

The Irish American Cultural Institute (IACI) was founded in St. Paul, Minnesota, in 1962 by Dr. Eoin McKiernan, then chairman of the English Department at the College (now University) of St. Thomas; his wife Jeannette; and philanthropist Patrick Butler, who provided major financial support. Although the school provided space for the organization, the IACI was from its inception an independent group that aspired to a national presence. The IACI was officially incorporated in 1964 as a nonprofit educational foundation.

In the early 1960s, McKiernan wrote and hosted a series of programs about Ireland that were broadcast on educational television. Buoyed by the series' success, McKiernan and his associates established the Institute because they felt that Americans, including Irish-Americans, knew little about Irish culture and contributions to American life. The organization sought to provide programs that would, first, educate Irish-Americans and the general public and, second, show appreciation to Ireland by providing grants to the arts in Ireland, including theatre, literature, music, and visual arts. In 1972, McKiernan resigned from the faculty of St. Thomas to devote himself full-time to the Institute.

The establishment of the IACI was significant in that it was a new kind of Irish organization. Where others shared a religious, fraternal, political, mutual aid, or similar purpose, the IACI attempted to establish a national Irish organization strictly along cultural lines with no religious or political point of view. Its origins in the Midwest, away from the East coast locus of most other Irish organizations, also set it apart. The Institute's approach was comprehensive. Rather than concentrate on only one facet of Irish culture, such as dance or music, it dealt with all aspects of Irish and Irish-American life. In 1981 the National Endowment for the Humanities awarded the Institute a $375,000 Challenge Grant to extend its educational work, which was successfully matched 3 to 1.

In addition to awards to Irish artists, the Institute publishes the quarterly *Éire-Ireland*, the first American scholarly publication devoted to Irish Studies and a major influence in advancing the discipline in North America and elsewhere. "Dúcas," an occasional membership newsletter, provides popular writing on Irish matters. In 1976, the IACI launched The Irish Way, an annual summer program in Ireland for American high school students. The Irish Perceptions lecture series and its predecessor, the Irish Fortnight, have brought more than 200 speakers to tour the United States. The Institute has also supported tours in the United States of professional theatrical productions and of Irish art and photography exhibitions; has offered an annual IACI Visiting Fellowship in Irish Studies at NUI-Galway since 1992; and makes grants from its Irish Research Fund to support scholarship on the Irish in America. From 1984 to 1993, its "Trees for Ireland" program provided funds for reforestation efforts in Ireland. In 1994, the Institute spearheaded the Annie Moore Project commemorating the first Irish-born immigrant to go through Ellis Island.

McKiernan directed the operation of the Institute until 1985. He remained Chairman of the Board until 1988, when New Jersey businessman John P. Walsh took up the dual position of Chairman of the Board and CEO of the Institute. In 1995, the Institute moved its headquarters from St. Paul to Morristown, New Jersey. It currently has chapters in 19 cities in the United States.

*See* Irish Studies

EDWARD D. MARMAN

## IRISH BRIGADE

The Irish Brigade has been deemed "the best known of any brigade organization, it having made an unusual reputation for dash and gallantry. The remarkable precision of its evolutions under fire; its desperate attack on the impregnable wall at Marye's Heights; its never failing promptness on every field; and its long continuous service, made for a name inseparable from the history of the war" (Fox 118). The unit suffered staggering casualties, losing over four thousand men killed or wounded in the course of its service, more than ever served with it at any given time. Two of its regiments, the 69th New York and 28th Massachusetts, ranked among the top ten out of over two thousand Federal regiments in the number of combat deaths they endured.

After the battle of First Bull Run, the colorful Thomas Francis Meagher began recruiting a brigade to be composed of Irish regiments, proposing that three be from New York and one each from Massachusetts and Pennsylvania. He intended to lead one of its New York regiments while James Shields would command the brigade, but Meagher received the appointment when that officer declined the commission.

In light of nativist prejudice and Irish-American hostility to the Republican party and its abolitionist ideals, it seemed unlikely that the Irish would turn out as staunch supporters of the Union. Yet, many volunteered and shed blood for their adopted country. Some were motivated by devotion to the Union and its Constitution, while others hoped Irish valor would prove their loyalty and surmount the misgivings and disdain of nativists. England's pro-Confederate stance antagonized Irishmen who refused to be on the same side as Ireland's oppressor and the Catholic Church's position that a government must be legitimate cast doubt on the validity of Confederate authorities. Economic conditions also made army service a viable option for many struggling laborers.

The Irish Brigade deployed near Washington, D.C. shortly before Christmas, 1861, composed at the time of only the 63rd, 69th, and 88th New York Infantry Regiments. On February 5, 1862 Meagher formally took command as the men of the Irish Brigade turned out in full dress. The brigade participated in McClellan's Peninsula campaign as part of the First Division, Second Corps, with which it would serve throughout the war. Although predominantly a Yankee regiment, the 29th Massachusetts Infantry was added to the brigade during the Peninsula campaign before being replaced by the Irish 28th Massachusetts Infantry in November, 1862. At Gaines' Mill on June 27, 1862, the brigade reinforced a collapsing Union line and covered its retreat and fought well at Malvern Hill a few days later.

At Antietam on September 17, 1862, Meagher personally led his brigade in a charge on the center of the Confederate line at the Sunken Road. The attack was repulsed with heavy losses, as Meagher's horse was shot out from beneath him and the 69th New York lost eight colorbearers. Although not completely composed of Irishmen, the 116th Pennsylvania Infantry joined the Irish Brigade in October, 1862, and served with it until transferred in June, 1864.

On the morning of December 13, 1862 Meagher ordered green sprigs placed in the caps of all twelve hundred officers and men of his brigade and addressed each regiment individually before the battle of Fredericksburg. After passing through the town, the Irish Brigade deployed for battle and charged through a fearful fire of artillery and small arms in an unsuccessful attempt to reach Confederates entrenched atop Marye's Heights. One soldier wrote that the storm of shot and shell was "terrible" and mowed "whole gaps out of our ranks and we having to march over their dead and wounded bodies" (Welsh, 43). The next day, only 280 men appeared under arms to represent the brigade, and one of the 69th New York's colorbearers was found dead with the regiment's national colors concealed and wrapped around his body to prevent its capture, a bullet having pierced both the flag and his heart.

After Chancellorsville in May, 1863, Meagher applied for permission to recruit the brigade back to strength but he resigned when the request was denied. The four hundred men of the Irish Brigade assembled and took leave of their commander on May 19, 1863 and Colonel Patrick Kelly assumed leadership. Due to their small numbers, the Irish Brigade's three New York regiments were consolidated into two companies each and the 116th Pennsylvania into four companies prior to Gettysburg.

In the afternoon of July 2, 1863 the brigade neared Gettysburg's Wheatfield, where a powerful Confederate attack had shattered an exposed portion of the Federal line. The Irishmen halted momentarily, knelt and uncovered their heads as the 88th New York's chaplain Father William Corby gave them benediction. The men then rose to their feet and, charging the Confederate line, helped stem the gray surge. The Irish Brigade reached the Stony Hill before having to retreat in the face of mounting Rebel pressure, having lost over two hundred of the 530 troops it brought into combat.

During the winter of 1863–1864, a large number of Irish Brigade veterans re-enlisted in their regiments and recruitment efforts helped fill the units' ranks. Colonel Thomas A. Smyth, an Irishmen from outside the Irish Brigade, commanded it from February to May, 1864, through the battles of the Wilderness and Spotsylvania. Colonel Richard Byrnes took over direction of the Irish Brigade in mid-May but only led it for a few weeks. While leading its charge at Cold Harbor on June 3, 1864, Byrnes was hit in the back with a minie ball which lodged in his spine, and he died on June 12.

Colonel Kelly reassumed leadership of the decimated brigade, but when he was killed in an attack on Petersburg on June 16, 1864, the Irish Brigade was broken up, its units transferred to other organizations. However, by November 1, 1864 recruits had partially restored the Irish regiments' strength, and the three New York units joined with the 28th Massachusetts to once again constitute the Irish Brigade. Colonel Robert Nugent accepted command to direct the Irishmen through the Appomattox Campaign and lead it down the streets of Washington in the Grand Review on May 22, 1865.

The Irish Brigade was known not only for its fighting spirit but its dash and Irish-Catholic identity. Many of its regiments carried flags of Irish green emblazoned with the Irish harp, and the 28th Massachusetts' Gaelic motto was "Fag an bealac," or "Clear the road." The unit became the center of Fenian activity in the Army of the Potomac, hosting the group's monthly meetings in which political business mixed with social camaraderie. The Irish Brigade's Saint Patrick's Day celebrations were especially jovial occasions, marked with freely flowing liquor and much food to accompany horse races and other contests. Furthermore, its camp became the focus of Catholics within the entire Army of the Potomac, and there were times when the only chaplain of that faith serving with the army was located in the Irish Brigade.

The Irish Brigade served for over three years, found itself in the hottest fighting on many a battlefield, and became one of the most renowned organizations of either army. While most units lost two soldiers dead to disease or accidents for every combat death during the Civil War, the Irish Brigade had two killed from battle for every man lost to illness. In enduring fearful casualties and performing brave feats, its men defended the Union and provided a testament to Irish valor.

Robert G. Athearn, *Thomas Francis Meagher: An Irish Revolutionary in America* (Boulder, Co., 1949).

Joseph G. Bilby, *Remember Fontenoy! The 69th New York and the Irish Brigade in the Civil War* (Highstown, N.J., 1995).

Boston *Pilot*. David Power Conyngham, *The Irish Brigade and its Campaigns* (New York, 1867).

William Corby, *Memoirs of Chaplain Life: Three Years with the Irish Brigade in the Army of the Potomac* (Chicago, 1893).

William F. Fox, *Regimental Losses in the American Civil War, 1861–1865* (Albany, 1898).

Francis Galwey, *The Valiant Hours* (Harrisburg, 1961).

Lawrence Frederick Kohl, ed., *Irish Green and Union Blue: The Civil War Letters of Peter Welsh* (New York, 1986).

St. Clair A. Mulholland, *The Story of the 116th Regiment Pennsylvania Volunteers in the War of the Rebellion* (Philadelphia, 1903).

New York, *Irish-American*.

Kevin E. O'Brien, ed., *My Life in the Irish Brigade: The Civil War Memoirs of Private William McCarter, 116th Pennsylvania Infantry* (Campbell, Ca., 1996).

*The War of the Rebellion: A Compilation of the Official Records of the Union and Confederate Armies*, 128 vols. (Washington, D.C., 1880–1902).

CHRISTIAN G. SAMITO

## IRISH CHRISTIAN BROTHERS, THE

Today, paradoxically, there are no Irish Christian Brothers in the United States. The official name of the worldwide group of religious men once called by that title was Brothers of the Christian Schools of Ireland (F.S.C.H.). In 1966 the name was changed to Congregation of Christian Brothers (C.F.C.).

### BACKGROUND

The congregation was founded in 1802 by a wealthy Waterford businessman, Edmund Rice (1762–1844), to teach poor Catholic boys in tuition-free schools. His first school was set up in 1796 in Waterford, but Mt. Sion School (1804) in that port city is traditionally seen as the foundation school of the new teaching society. Seeing hordes of poverty-stricken boys denied an education, let alone an Irish-Catholic education, Edmund donated all of his material wealth and all of his gifts and talents to bring about systemic change in the structure of the times. Although the poor spoke only Gaelic, he realized that they also had to learn English to begin on the road to prosperity. "At the beginning of the nineteenth century, the condition of the poor, in both town and country, was deplorable" (O'Toole, 184, 187). Edmund was a man of fervent prayer and of unrelenting faith in Divine Providence, as well as one who possessed an enduring compassion and commitment to the marginalized people of his time (Houlihan, 140).

The unique character of Brother Rice's Catholic schools was not that they were tuition-free, but that the boys were taught by vowed male religious in a congregation that was granted papal status. There were other prominent religious contemporaries who had founded schools for the poor. One was Honora (Nano) Nagle (1718–1784), educated in France, who founded the Sisters of the Presentation of the Blessed Virgin Mary (Cork, 1775). This group was to play an important role in the development of the first society of male, lay-religious teachers in Ireland (*Nano Nagle's Ireland*). Another was Mother Mary Aikenhead, a good friend of Brother Rice, foundress of the Religious Sisters of Charity (Dublin, 1815), originally begun for the poor and the sick (Normoyle, *Memories,* 158). Catherine McAuley (1778–1841), who founded the Sisters of Mercy (Dublin, 1831) is another example. However, these schools were taught by religious sisters, who were tolerated by most of the priests and bishops in educating poor boys and girls, including teaching them religion. In the eighteenth century, the priest had the major responsibility to instruct boys, albeit furtively, in their religious learning. For many Irish clerics, having a male lay-religious—a brother—do so was quite revolutionary and, for some, including bishops, quite threatening.

How did Brother Edmund's followers, having taken a vow of strict poverty, live, and the tuition–free schools they operated, function? Their meager personal expenses and the cost to run the schools were obtained entirely by begging, church collections and from benefactors, both secular and diocesan. It was not until 1838 that Brother Edmund allowed some of the schools to charge tuition and thus make it possible to conduct more tuition-free schools for the poor (Houlihan, 49), although the question of pay-schools was not settled until many years later. Archbishop Murray of Dublin said to Edmund, "The rich have high schools and colleges and the poor have free schools, but my dear middle class people, where can they send their children?" (Fitzpatrick, 317). Wrote Edmund to his brothers, ". . . There is but one alternative left for the support of some of our houses already established and the further propagation of our Institute . . . the gradual establishment of pay-Schools . . ." (Normoyle, *A Companion,* 515). As a result, a fourth vow of gratuitous instruction was no longer taken by the brothers.

Teaching the Roman Catholic faith during the early part of Brother Edmund's lifetime was actually illegal and had been for more than a century. This was because of the British Penal Laws, begun in 1679 in Ireland against Roman Catholicism, which forbade the establishment of Catholic churches as well as schools where that faith and the Gaelic tradition could be taught. In fact, anti-Irish (Roman Catholic) sentiment and discriminatory laws began as more of a political threat (e.g., Catholics could not own property) than as a religious one, as early as the Protestant Reformation in England (1534) under Henry VIII (Houlihan, 148). As a result, the majority of the people affected in Ireland became poor or seriously impoverished. "The British Penal Laws had reduced the Catholic majority to destitution and ignorance" (Dunkak, 326). However, the Penal Laws, by the end of the eighteenth century, were being relaxed—happily for the lower Roman Catholic classes, unhappily for most of the upper class, Church of Ireland minority.

In 1808 Edmund and his followers donned a religious habit (worn only inside the house). They each took a religious name; Edmund chose Ignatius after St. Ignatius Loyola (1491–1556), founder of the Society of Jesus. From 1809, when Edmund's group took perpetual vows of poverty, chastity, obedience and gratuitous instruction of youth, to 1822, the society was called the "Monks of the Presentation" since they took most of their Rule from the Presentation Sisters. In 1820 Brother Edmund's Institute was officially sanctioned by Pope Pius VII (1799–1823) as a papal institute of teaching brothers. This meant that they were free to establish schools in any diocese or any country, with the permission of the bishop, but were not under the direct authority of any bishop.

In the mid-1820s among emerging emancipation legislation and the leadership of Brother Edmund's good friend, the Great Emancipator, Daniel O'Connell (1775–1847), the Irish were freed from many educational, political and financial shackles. However, freedom to establish religious groups of brothers and to recruit religious vocations for existing ones were still illegal. This was a difficult time for the congregation, even with the support of many Irish bishops (e.g., Hussey, Power, Murray) as well as O'Connell, who called Brother Edmund the "Patriarch of the Monks in the West" at the 1828 dedication of a school in Dublin (Normoyle, *Tree,* 214).

## North America

During these decades, many Irish people left their country to go to North America, especially to Newfoundland and the middle Atlantic area of the United States. By mid-century, however, as a result of the Great Famine (1845–1850), the Irish were flooding into both Canada and the U.S. The bishops of the American church at that time were predominantly Irish-born. They began to address the religious and educational needs of the growing Irish population in their expanding dioceses. However, ". . . often Irish immigrants reacted negatively to French priests trying to minister to them. They demanded clergy of their own . . ." (McCaffrey, 697).

In meeting the need for a Catholic educational system, schools had been established for some time. Among other foundresses, the New York-born saint, Mother Elizabeth Seton (1774–1821), had opened schools primarily for Catholic girls in Baltimore (1809), but there were few Catholic schools for boys. In addition, the bishops felt that a group of male religious teachers, who spoke the same language as, and who could identify with, the Irish immigrant was needed to address the educational vacuum. For most bishops, the Christian Brothers of Ireland was their first choice (Normoyle, *Tree,* 237).

As early as 1828, Brother Edmund had received requests for Christian Brothers to teach in North America. The first petition was from Archbishop James Whitefield of Baltimore (d. 1834), ". . . I hope, therefore, you will send me . . . zealous cooperators . . ." Brother Patrick Ellis, an assistant of Brother Rice, wrote that there were no brothers to send (Normoyle, *Companion,* 224). There were also similar requests from Bishop John Dubois of New York (1764–1842) and Bishop Michael Fleming of Newfoundland, born in Carrick-on-Suir, as well as from Bishop John England of Charleston (1762–1842), born in Cork (Scanlan, I, 43–44). While visiting the U.S. in 1832, Father Peter Kenney, S.J. (1779–1841), an Irish theologian, friend and adviser of Brother Edmund and the congregation, wrote him, ". . . I do not see anything (in the U.S.) like your schools for the instruction of poor boys. Would to God that Bishop England could bring a few of you here" (Normoyle, *A Companion,* 407). This was not to be, however.

John Hughes (1797–1864), born in County Tyrone, the first archbishop of New York (1842–1864), returned to Ireland for a visit in 1841. He was much impressed with Brother Rice's schools. He tried to arrange for a group of brothers to come to New York. As with earlier requests, it did not happen.

In the late 1850s and early 1860s, with vocations increasing as the result of a better climate of toleration for priests and religious groups, Edmund's society did expand, but in other directions, including Melbourne, Australia (1868). They finally arrived in the New World, in St. John's, Newfoundland, in 1876. Expansion during the last decade of the century included India (1890) and South Africa (1897). A school was even begun in Rome (1901).

## To America

The first of Edmund Rice's brothers to arrive in the U.S. did not come to teach but to raise money. Brother Edward A. O'Donnell (1834–1886), born in Dingle, arrived in the U.S. in 1881 to solicit funds for a new Irish novitiate in Dublin. After a year, he returned to Ireland but came back to the U.S. in 1884 to continue fund-raising. He became sick while soliciting and died at his sister's home in Easthampton, Massachusetts. He is buried in Holyoke.

Requests to come to the U.S. started in 1828; the brothers finally came sixty years later. Negotiations began in the mid-1880s. A Massachusetts bishop wanted the brothers to teach in a school for very poor boys. He wrote to Brother Richard A. Maxwell, the fourth superior general (1880–1900) in Dublin. As a result, in 1888 four brothers were sent to Worcester, Massachusetts, to St. John's Elementary School. One, Brother James G.Hughes (1851–1926), was appointed the superior/principal. Sadly, they remained there less than two years and returned to Ireland because of administrative differences with the local pastor. Ironically, at this time, the bishop of the diocese of Springfield had invited them to come into his diocese. Edmund's brothers would not return to the U.S. until sixteen years later, not at the request of a bishop but of an Irish-born priest (Scanlan, I, 47).

## JAMES W. POWER

The success of the final effort to bring the Christian Brothers to the U.S. was due to two men: Father (later Msgr.) James W. Power (1849–1926), born in Newton, County Waterford. He had come from Ireland to New York City in 1868 (Cox, 163–164). The other was Brother George T. Frisby (1863–1927), born in County Kilkenny. Brother Frisby, like Brother O'Donnell decades before, was in the U.S. to raise funds for the brothers in Ireland. He made his headquarters at Father Power's church, All Saints, on 129th Street and Madison Avenue, in the Harlem section of New York City. Father Power was impressed with Brother Frisby and his educational mission. At Frisby's urging, he requested Brother James C. Whitty (1849–1930), the superior general (1905–1920), to send brothers to teach boys in his elementary school on 130th Street which was then staffed by Mother Seton's Sisters of Charity (Scanlan, I, 47).

Father Power, a life member of the American Irish Historical Society, also wanted his Irish-American boys to be educated in the history, culture and traditions of Ireland. He needed the Christian Brothers in order to accomplish these aims. When requesting the permission of New York's archbishop (later cardinal) John Farley (1902–1918) to bring the brothers to his parish school, he wrote, on May 5, 1906, in part, ". . . I beg to petition Your Grace . . . for the acceptance of the Irish Christian Brothers to teach in the boys' parochial school of All Saints. . . ." As an incentive, he also wrote: ". . . Mother Melita refuses to give me sisters for classes in the boys' grammar department longer than this year . . ." (Scanlan, I, 48).

James W. Power

On August 29, 1906, four of Edmund's Christian Brothers arrived in New York City from Queenstown, Ireland, after a six-day voyage on the S.S. *Majestic*. They were met at the dock by Father Power and Brother Frisby.

## THE FOUNDING COMMUNITY

Patrick J. Ryan (1867–1947), born in Annagh, had been appointed the superior of the new community. He was accompanied by Michael S. Curtis (1874–1936), born in Dundalk, and two novices. One was John A. Kelly (1882–1959), born in Dunmore. [Brother Kelly was to be the founder of Sacred Heart School, New York City (1924), and provincial (1943–47).] The other novice was John G. Molloy (1885–1970), born in County Carlow. Brother Molloy stayed only one year and then returned to Ireland, eventually going to Australia (Scanlan, II, 55).

The four began teaching in the boys' division at All Saints School in September 1906 and resided at 2081 Fifth Avenue. "It ended a period of seventy years when the entire focus of the Congregation was on Ireland and on the British colonies overseas. It was, at last, a solid response to repeated requests from American bishops and pastors dating from the time of the Founder" (Scanlan, I, 41).

Edmund's Christian Brothers who came to All Saints Parish quickly realized that the Brothers of the Christian Schools—the de LaSalles—were known in the U.S. as "Christian Brothers." So the Brothers of the Christian Schools of Ireland adopted with ease the unofficial title of the "Irish Christian Brothers" in America. Although Irish, "indicative of their determination to remain in the U.S., the pioneers sought and got legal incorporation as the Christian Brothers' Institute (and) took initial steps to becoming citizens . . ." (Scanlan, I, 51).

## BROTHER PATRICK J. RYAN

When the Christian Brothers' General Council in Dublin chose Patrick J. Ryan to lead a successful foundation in the United States, they picked the ideal man to do so. Brother Ryan was deeply spiritual, intelligent, a born diplomat, a wonderful public relations man and a shrewd fund-raiser. He had served for twenty years in Gibraltar and had just completed one year as superior-principal in Naas, Ireland (Scanlan, I, 50; II, 43). After serving as superior at All Saints (1906–1915), Brother Ryan was appointed the first novice master for the incoming religious vocations to the brothers in New Rochelle, NY.

By 1916 an American Province, encompassing all of the United States and Canada, was established, with Brother Ryan as the first provincial (1916–1930). By 1920 there were sixty-two professed brothers, sixteen annually professed and eleven novices and a number of postulants. The new province did not restrict its work to the northeast coast but soon established schools across the country (and Canada). During Ryan's leadership in 1923, O'Dea High School was founded in Seattle, Washington; in 1924; Boys Central High School in Butte, Montana; and in 1926, Leo High School in Chicago. After Brother Ryan completed his term as provincial, he remained a province consultor for thirteen years (1930–1943).

During the first thirty years that the Christian Brothers were in the U.S. (1906–1936), most of them under Brother Ryan's leadership, ten communities/schools were established in the Archdiocese of New York. Even after his province leadership responsibilities ended, Brother Ryan remained vigorous and active as the province vocation director (1943–1947).

## Brother Joseph I. Doorley

The de LaSalle Brothers had schools for boys in New York City since 1848, but they were forbidden, at that time, by their Rule to teach Latin. This was because Father John de LaSalle feared that, the brothers having learned Latin, they would be recruited to become priests. New York's Archbishop John Farley wanted more boys' schools that included Latin in the curriculum—"classical academies" (probably to increase interest in the priesthood as well as a foundation for those who did enter the seminary). Although the archbishop was not completely favorable, at first, to having two schools in the same parish, the Irish Christian Brothers, who taught Latin and who also wanted a school of their own, founded All Hallows Institute in 1909 (Scanlan, I, 52). First established in All Saints parish on West 124th Street, it is now located in the Bronx, NY, on 164th Street and the Grand Concourse. The superior general, Brother Whitty, selected his nephew, Brother Joseph I. Doorley (1878–1963), born in Cloneen, County Carlow, to found All Hallows.

As the reputation of All Hallows grew around New York City, influential families in Westchester County, about fifteen miles north of the city, led by State Supreme Court Justice Keogh, petitioned the brothers to establish a school in that county. The result was the Iona School (1916), which today is two separate schools—Iona Grammar and Iona Preparatory in New Rochelle.

As a result of a conversation at dinner with George Cardinal Mundelein (1872–1939), Brother Doorley founded Leo High School in Chicago (1926). He also served from 1922 to 1939 as a provincial consultor. The brothers in America assumed that Brother Doorley would be the next provincial, but, in late 1938, he was appointed an assistant general in Dublin to take the place of a brother in that position who had died. After this assignment, in 1947, at age 69, he again opened another school, Cardinal Newman College, in Buenos Aires, Argentina. In 1963 he died and is buried in Buenos Aires.

When Brother Doorley founded Iona Grammar and Iona Preparatory Schools, he envisioned some day to open a college also known as Iona. It was not until 1940, however, that the brothers founded Iona College in New Rochelle, NY, with Brother William B. Cornelia (1885–1955), born in Dublin, as its first president (1940–46) (Scanlan, I, 75). The college continues to serve young adult men and women in the tradition of the brothers and has expanded rapidly in the past fifty years. Brother Doorley's dream had been fulfilled.

## Brother Eugene F. Ryall

Brother Doorley founded schools which were far apart (New York, Chicago, Buenos Aires). Brother Eugene F. Ryall (1880–1953), born in Ballindangan, County Cork, founded Power Memorial Academy (1931) and Rice High School (1938), both in New York City. He also held the position of province consultor for twenty years.

Brother Ryall was among the second wave of brothers who came to the U.S. and began teaching at All Saints School in 1907. Brother taught at All Saints Elementary School for twenty-four years. He was a shrewd fund-raiser and a practical but faith-filled brother. While at All Saints, he realized that there were thousands of Catholic parents with boys graduating from New York City elementary schools who could not afford the tuition to send them to the existing Catholic high schools (Scanlan, II, 45).

When All Hallows moved to the Bronx (1931), Brother Ryall began a high school, charging modest tuition fees, in an empty building. He called it Power Memorial Academy, after Msgr. James Power, and was its first principal (1931–1937). Power Memorial moved from 124th Street (1936) to 61st and Amsterdam Avenue in Manhattan. (The school closed in 1984.) Two years later (1938), Brother Ryall founded Rice High School, the first school to be named after Brother Rice, in the former All Hallows/Power Memorial building. In 1940 Rice High School moved into 74 West 124th Street. It is still there, the only remaining Catholic boys high school in New York's Harlem (Scanlan, I, 68). It is to Brother Ryall's great credit that he founded two schools in the depths of the Depression under very difficult financial circumstances.

## Brother Michael C. Ryan

If the other leaders of the province are remembered for their dynamism, leadership and educational vision, Michael C. Ryan (1879–1964) born in Murroe, County Limerick, is revered as the founder of the spiritual life of the province. He came from Ireland to St. John's, Newfoundland in 1902 where he taught for seventeen years. As novice master for twenty-six years (1919–1945), Brother Ryan personally molded the spirit of Edmund Rice into the majority of the 174 brothers who were in the province in 1944 (Scanlan, I, 77; II, 32). After decades as novice master at the province formation center in West Park, he accepted the position of superior and principal of Sacred Heart School in New York City (1946–1951).

## Brother Arthur A. Loftus

Arthur Loftus, a son of John (born in Mayo) and Elizabeth Thiel Loftus, entered the Christian Brothers in 1918, at age 14, only twelve years after the first U.S. community opened. Over the next fifty years, this "man on the move" continued the spirit, determination and tone of the Irish-born founders in America. He became president of Iona College (1946–1952); provincial consultor (1947–1953), provincial (1953–1960), principal of Essex Catholic High School, Newark, N.J. (1963–1966) and superior general (1966–1972) of the worldwide congregation, then numbering nearly three thousand brothers (Scanlan, II, 46).

Somewhere along this busy road, he earned a doctorate from Fordham University. During his leadership, in part especially due to a significant increase in vocations, the Congregation of Christian Brothers founded fifteen additional communities around the world, and, in the American Province, schools in South Africa (1951), the West Indies (1954) and Peru (1966) which still flourish today. Few brothers have made such a dramatic impression on the American Province or the Congregation as Brother Loftus.

## The Legacy

By 1966 the American province had grown to such a degree that Canada became its own province and the U.S. divided into two, the Western American and Eastern American provinces. In that year, to better reflect the international ethnic mix of the brothers and their worldwide ministries, the Brothers of the Christian Schools of Ireland (F.S.C.H.) changed their name to Congregation of Christian Brothers (C.F.C.). Now, throughout the world, the brothers no longer refer to themselves as the Irish Christian Brothers but as the Christian Brothers.

At the end of the twentieth century, in the U.S. and in the other thirteen provinces around the world, the Christian Brothers are proud of their Irish religious roots. They continue Edmund's charism: to address the challenges of the poor and marginalized. Now, however, they minister internationally around the world, from Ireland to South Africa, from the United States to Peru and from China to Australia. As a testament to Brother Rice and the work of the Congregation of Christian Brothers, Edmund Ignatius Rice was declared Blessed by Pope John Paul II on October 6, 1996. His feast day is May 5. Edmund's cause for canonization progresses.

Today, there are 300 Christian Brothers in the U.S. and Peru. Together with the Rice Associates and lay colleagues in the ever-expanding Edmund Rice family, the brothers continue to answer the educational call, especially of the poor and the needy, with faith and joy, begun almost two hundred years ago by Blessed Edmund Rice in Ireland.

Brother Gordon R. Bellows, C.F.C., "Characteristics of Christian Brother Schools," *Christian Brothers' Educational Record-1988* (Private Circulation, 1988): 184–191.

*Christian Brothers' Educational Record-1907,* "Our Foundation in New York" (Private Distribution, Dublin: Fowler Printers, 1907): 63–67.

*Constitutions of the Congregation of Christian Brothers* (Rome: Private Circulation, 1996).

E. R. Cox, "Rt. Rev. Monsignor James W. Power," *1926 Journal of Irish-American Historical Society,* quoted in *Christian Brothers Educational Record-1927* (Dublin: Dollard Ltd., 1927): 163–169.

Brother Harry M. Dunkak, C.F.C., "Congregation of Christian Brothers," *The Encyclopedia of American Catholic History,* eds. Michael Glazier and Thomas J. Shelley (Collegeville, MN, 1997): 325–326.

Brother J. David Fitzpatrick, C.F.C., *Edmund Rice* (Dublin: M.H. Gill & Son, Ltd., 1945).

Brother Angelus Gabriel, F.S.C., *Christian Brothers in the U.S., 1848–1948* (New York: Declan McMullen Co., Inc., 1948).

Brother James A. Houlihan, C.F.C., *Overcoming Evil With Good: The Edmund Rice Story* (New York, 1997).

Lawrence J. McCaffrey, "Irish Catholics in America," *The Encyclopedia of American Catholic History,* eds., Michael Glazier and Thomas J. Shelley (Collegeville, MN, 1997): 696–705.

Brother Michael C. Normoyle, C.F.C., *A Companion to* A Tree Is Planted (Ireland: Private Circulation, 1977).

———, *A Tree Is Planted,* 2nd ed. (Ireland: Private Circulation, 1976).

———, *Memories of Edmund Rice* (Ireland: Private Circulation, 1979).

Brother Anthony L. O'Toole, C.F.C., *A Spiritual Profile of Edmund Ignatius Rice,* I (Bristol: Burleigh Press, 1984).

Desmond Rush, *Edmund Rice: A Man and His Times,* 2nd ed. (Dublin, 1995).

Brother Robert V. Scanlan, C.F.C., "The Christian Brothers in the United States, Part I," *Christian Brothers' Educational Record-1982* (Private Circulation, 1982): 41–79.

———, "The Christian Brothers in the United States, Part II," *Christian Brothers' Educational Record-1983* (Private Circulation, 1983): 27–68.

BROTHER SALVATORE A. FERRO, C.F.C.

## IRISH HERITAGE OF THE SOUTH

Southerners are not like other Americans, and they never have been. Sociologist John Sheldon Reed insists that even today significant cultural differences separate Southerners from Northerners, and that many of these differences are as prevalent now as they have ever been.

The authors of this essay contend that Americans have been divided culturally for more than three hundred years—that Southerners and Northerners have always been significantly distinct from one another. Their ways and values have never been the same because their cultural heritages are different. More specifically, the North was settled mainly by English and Germanic peoples, who culturally dominated the area, and the South was settled primarily and culturally dominated by Celtic peoples—from Ireland, Scotland, Wales, and the "Celtic fringe" of England.

In using the term "Celtic," we do not mean to suggest a common genetic pool, for the people under discussion were clearly of different genetic mixtures. The Welsh are obviously of different genetic stock from the Irish, for instance, and Highland Scots have different bloodlines from Lowlanders. Rather, we are speaking of peoples who shared a common cultural heritage—customary lifestyles, attitudes, and ways of doing things. Even in that sense, of course, the various peoples we treat as Celts were far from identical. But after a great deal of study, we have concluded that it is legitimate to consider them as a single general cultural group, different from the English—much in the same way that Western culture is seen as distinct from Islamic culture, while recognizing that Italians and Swedes differ from one another even as do Libyans and Pakistanis. A more accurate phraseology than Celtic, in the sense that we use the term, would be "people from the British Isles who were historically and culturally non-English"—but that phrase seems less catchy.

For too long historians have accepted the myth that Anglo-Saxons settled and dominated the antebellum South; that the region was and is what George B. Tindall calls "the biggest single WASP nest this side of the Atlantic." Actually, the overwhelming majority of the people who settled the South were not Anglo-Saxons but Celts.

Just the opposite was true in the Old North, where people of English as well as of other Anglo-Saxon heritage dominated throughout the antebellum period. The importance of all this is that the cultural antagonism that had, for centuries, divided Celts from Englishmen in the British Isles continued in America. Of course, neither the Old North nor the Old South was homogeneous, but the tendency, by and large, was for Celts who settled in the North to become Anglicized and for Englishmen in the South to be Celticized.

Establishing who settled when and where in America is more difficult than one might imagine; determining the national or ethnic composition of a sizable number of Americans is arduous. Ideally, the information would be recorded in the census, but such was not done until later in the nineteenth century. Alternatively, the ethnic composition of the population might be reconstructed from lists of arriving immigrants, but only fragmentary records exist for the colonial and early national periods. No systematic recording of the arrival of immigrants was required by law until 1819. The resulting records are useless in analyzing the ethnic makeup of the southern population because so few migrants came to the South after 1819. Only about 4.2 percent of the white people in the South in 1850 were foreign-born, and most of them were concentrated in such urban places as New Orleans, Mobile, and Charleston.

Since records of early settlers are either unavailable or sketchy, we have relied on name analysis. Tracing ancestry is both complex and inexact, but fairly reliable approximations can be reached if the list of European names is full and accurate, if the body of American names being analyzed is large enough to absorb the invariable flukes and exceptions, and if a rigorous methodology is formulated.

Wherever possible, we have relied on the work of other scholars, but we have developed, thus far, three methods of name analysis. None is foolproof, but each provides a useful check on the other, and together they offer what we consider a reasonable approximation of the ethnic composition of the areas analyzed.

The focus here is on what these methods of name analysis reveal rather than on the techniques involved. Anyone interested in the specifics of our methodology may consult our articles listed in the attached bibliography.

One of our methods, a projection technique, reveals that sectionalism based upon settlement patterns existed throughout the United States at the time the first federal census was taken in 1790. Well over three-quarters of the people living in New England were of English origins. New York, having originally been a Dutch colony, retained a large Dutch component in its population; but the single largest group, comprising something over two-fifths of the people, was English. Pennsylvania was heterogeneous: two-fifths of the people were of Celtic origins, a third were German, fewer than a fifth were English. Elsewhere, the farther south and west from Philadelphia, the more Celtic the population: in the upper South, Celts and Englishmen each constituted about two-fifths of the population; in the Carolinas, more than half the people were Celtic and Celts outnumbered Englishmen five to three.

Even more significantly, Celts completely dominated the frontier from Pennsylvania southward, where they constituted from three-fifths to nearly a hundred percent of the total population. In such interior North Carolina districts as Hillsborough, Celts composed nearly a hundred percent of the population, and in some western Virginia counties, Scots and Irish alone numbered almost eighty percent of the population.

Using our projection technique, we have also analyzed the censuses of 1810, 1830, and 1850 and found that the Celtic portion of the southern white population stabilized at about sixty percent; the English portion stabilized as about a third of the total; the remainder were largely of German, French, or Spanish origins. In New England and the upper Middle West, the English continued to constitute about three-quarters of the population until the 1840s, when the arrival of numerous refugees from the Irish potato Famine changed the ratio to about sixty to forty percent English.

Our conclusions on settlement patterns are supported by other works. Charles Banks, for instance, in his study of English immigrants in New England between 1620 and 1650, indicated that none came from Ireland, Scotland, or Wales, and only 185 of 2,885 originated in the Celtic fringe; seventy-one percent came from the east and southeast of England. Conversely, in an analysis of 7,359 references to seventeenth-century Virginians, John E. Manahan found that ninety percent came from Cornwall, Wales, Ireland, or the Celtic fringe.

Additional studies confirm that many more Celts settled in the antebellum South than traditional sources acknowledge. In 1850 some 25,000 or more Irish, a quarter of the city's population, lived in New Orleans, and even in Apalachicola, Florida, the Irish were the largest foreign-born element in the population.

Not all the Irish in the South arrived in the late antebellum period, nor were they confined to urban areas. One investigator has found records of "a great infusion of Irish" into the South throughout the colonial period. Another writer concluded that thousands of Irish were transported to America between 1703 and 1775 and that many settled in Virginia, the Carolinas, and Georgia. Yet another scholar estimates that in 1790 Irish settlers

constituted twenty-six percent of the population of South Carolina and twenty-seven percent of that of Georgia.

Many of these Irish have been overlooked by historians who have assumed incorrectly that during the colonial period of American settlement all natives of Ireland outside Ulster were devout Catholics. "The passionate and exemplary attachment of the Irish nation to the Catholic faith dates from a later time," writes Emmet Larkin about the seventeenth and eighteenth centuries; "the real contest was between Englishmen and Irishmen rather than Protestants and Catholics. . . . In Ireland in the seventeenth century . . . the Irish laity were still for the most part only passively and traditionally Catholic."

Nor did the situation change during the first part of the nineteenth century. In pre-Famine Ireland only thirty-three percent of the Catholic population went to Mass. Most of the two million Irish who emigrated between 1847 and 1860 were part of the pre-Famine generation of nonpracticing Catholics. Not until the later part of the nineteenth century, long after most of the Irish who came to the South had made the move, did the "devotional revolution" turn Ireland into a country of churchgoers who equated Irish Nationalism with Catholicism.

Irish settlers in the South, especially those who arrived in the seventeenth and eighteenth centuries, suffered little cultural shock; they mixed easily with the Scotch-Irish and Scots—people with whom they had shared traditions and ways for centuries—feuded and stole each other's livestock, just as they had always done, and helped to spread Celtic culture across the southern backcountry. The evidence indicates that large numbers of Irish simply adopted the religion of their southern neighbors. For example, Andrew Leary O'Brien, who was born in County Cork, Ireland, in 1815, migrated to South Carolina, married a local girl, and converted to her Methodist faith. A Catholic bishop, after traveling in the antebellum South, maintained "that, calculating from the names of the people, no less than forty thousand had lost the Faith in the Carolinas and Georgia." Later a British Catholic observed that the South was full of Irish names. "No doubt," he wrote, "the [Protestant] missionaries on circuit baptized the children and grandchildren of Irish who had not brought their women or their priests. [Baptist ministers], Wesleyan ministers, Methodist bishops, bear Irish names—Healy, Murphy, Conner. Their blood could only have come from Ireland. One of these Irish patriarchs . . . did meet a priest after fifty years, and could only present two grownup generations of Methodists."

A second method of name analysis, an apportionment system that we have developed, also suggests that a Celtic cultural hegemony existed in the South. Some sample results: An examination of the names recorded in the early censuses of three Georgia counties reveal that fewer than a third of the families listed were English; more than half were Celtic. Of the families identified as being of British extraction, sixty-two percent were Celtic and thirty-eight percent were English. A similar pattern was found in Lowndes County, Mississippi, where an examination of the 1,616 families listed in the 1850 census revealed that more than half were Celtic and only a third were English. Of the families identified as British, sixty-one percent were Celtic and thirty-nine percent were English.

The significance of these figures from Georgia and Mississippi becomes clear when we look at the ethnic pattern in a comparable northern area. For example, Eaton County, in central Michigan, was settled between 1834 and 1860 primarily by people from New England, New York, and Ohio. Nearly half of the first 2,175 families to acquire land in the county were of English ancestry; fewer than a third were of Celtic ancestry. Of the families identified as British, fully sixty-one percent were of English extraction and only thirty-nine percent were Celtic. This is the exact reverse of the southern pattern.

In an effort to overcome some of the biases inherent in our apportionment technique, we have experimented with a third method of name analysis. We compiled a list of 2,468 names that are common to, and peculiar to, the shires of the south and east of England. To see just how many of these names, supposedly the most English of English names, could be found in the deep South in the late antebellum period, we compared them with the 20,000 or so names listed in the United States Census of Alabama in 1850. We also compiled a list of 1,087 different names, almost all of them Celtic, found on gravestones in the counties of Antrim and Down in northern Ireland, which we then compared with the Alabama census of 1850. The results: eighty-four percent of the Celtic names but only forty-three percent of the English names were found in Alabama.

Such ratios of Celts to Englishmen as our various name analysis methods reveal suggest that the North and the South were settled and dominated numerically during the antebellum period by different peoples with significantly different cultural backgrounds. This is not to suggest that either North or South was homogeneous: there were hustlers, go-getters, eccentrics, hard workers, and even literate people sprinkled throughout the South. Similarly, there were individuals and groups in the North that resisted amalgamation. Some Scotch-Irish in New England, for example, refused from the outset to fit into Puritan society. But the tendency, by and large, was for Celts in the North to become Anglicized and for Englishmen in the South to become Celticized.

The persistence of Celtic and English cultural traits over time and distance is evident in the observations of travelers and other contemporary writers. The ways and values which they found characteristic of antebellum Southerners were the same that seventeenth- and eighteenth-century observers reported as being peculiar to the Celtic people of the British Isles; conversely, the observed ways and manners of antebellum Northerners were precisely those that seventeenth- and eighteenth-century writers found typical of the English people of the British Isles. In other words, Celts in the South and Englishmen in the North retained most of their folkways, imposed in large measure their traditions and habits upon their New World environment, and acculturized within a generation or so the greater number of outsiders who settled among them.

The Celtic ways that Southerners adopted from their British ancestors—which we call Cracker Culture—spread from the Southeast to Texas and shaped habits and manners, especially in the backcountry South, throughout the antebellum period. It was the predominant but not the only culture of the Old South.

Besides Crackers, the Old South produced some Cavaliers. If Andrew Jackson and Nathan Bedford Forrest were outstanding representatives of Cracker Culture, then Jefferson Davis and Robert E. Lee represented equally well Cavalier Culture. But the cultural differences between Crackers and Cavaliers were often more apparent than real; they shared many traits, especially those of courage and honor.

A wide range of eyewitnesses noted the similarities between the culture of Celtic peoples of the British Isles and those of southern Crackers. Both were more hospitable, generous, frank, courteous, spontaneous, lazy, wasteful, lackadaisical, impulsive, careless, rustic, impatient, extravagant, sensual, rural, romantic, militaristic, violent, and lawless than Englishmen and Northerners, who were in turn more frugal, ambitious, shrewd, aggressive, enterprising, zealous, stingy, meddlesome, methodical, conscientious, practical, tenacious, calculating, reserved, Puritanical, urban, progressive, bookish, peaceful, cautious, disciplined, orderly, and law-abiding than Celts and Southerners.

Celtic Britain and the Cracker Culture of the Old South were leisure-oriented societies that fostered idleness and gaiety, where people favored the spoken word over the written and enjoyed such sensual pleasures as smoking, drinking, fighting, gambling, fishing, hunting, talking, and loafing. Family ties were much stronger in Celtic Britain and in the antebellum South than in England and in the North; Celts and Southerners, whose values were more agrarian than those of Englishmen and Northerners, wasted more time and consumed more tobacco and liquor and were less concerned with the useful and the material. Englishmen and Northerners, who favored urban-villages and nuclear families, were just the opposite; imbued with a work ethic and commercial values, they were neater, cleaner, read and wrote more, worked harder, and considered themselves more progressive and advanced than Celts and Cracker Southerners.

*See* Scots Irish; Irish in America

Forrest McDonald and Ellen Shapiro McDonald, "The Ethnic Origins of the American People, 1790," *William and Mary Quarterly,* 37 (1980): 179–199.

Forrest McDonald and Grady McWhiney, "The Antebellum Southern Herdsman: A Reinterpretation," *The Journal of Southern History,* 41 (1975): 147–166.

John S. Reed, *The Enduring South: Subculture Persistence in Mass Society* (Chapel Hill, 1974).

———, *One South: An Ethnic Approach to Regional Culture* (Baton Rouge, 1982).

Grady McWhiney, *Cracker Culture: Celtic Ways in the Old South,* with a Prologue by Forrest McDonald (Tuscaloosa, 1989).

Grady McWhiney and Forrest McDonald, "Celtic Names in the Antebellum Southern United States," *Names: The Journal of the American Name Society,* 31 (1983): 89–102.

GRADY McWHINEY AND FORREST McDONALD

## IRISH IN AMERICA, THE

Irish movement to the United States was part of a great dispersal of European peoples to all parts of the world in which the Irish held first place. Ireland, with around two million people in 1687, sent at least ten million people overseas over the next three hundred years. Ireland sent a larger proportion of her sons and daughters into exile in the New World than any other country. In the early nineteenth century this steady stream of transatlantic travelers grew into the first of the great mass migrations to the United States. The high level of emigration from Ireland has been essential for the preservation of the social and economic order of the home society to an extent unknown in other parts of Europe. In turn the Irish provided the strong backs to spur the rapid expansion of the United States and became the first major immigrant group to challenge and transform political and social institutions during the most formative years of the new nation. The story of the Irish people is the story of emigration; the story of the American people is the story of immigration.

This essay attempts to provide an overview of our present understanding of Irish migration and adjustment to the United

States. It takes advantage of the considerable advances made by historians of Irish migration on both sides of the Atlantic over the past two decades who recognize the necessity for understanding the full range of factors involved in the process at the origin and at the destination. Equally as important in recent studies of Irish movement to America is the gradual recognition of the extent to which immigrants themselves made decisions during all phases of the transatlantic journey and of their adaptation to the New World. The journey was selective of individuals, the great majority of whom had never been ten miles from home, with the vision and the drive to make momentous decisions regarding their future. The sadness of departure was counterbalanced by planning and preparation for the transatlantic journey and by anticipation for the future. The initial shock of arrival in the New World was mitigated by contact with fellow countrymen and women in Irish enclaves usually in American cities. Although the variation in social conditions and the structure of opportunity confronting Irish immigrants in communities all across the United States at different times was impressively wide, at some stage newcomers and their children began to display evidence of adaptation to various critical facets of life in American society: job selection, income, movement up and down the social scale, housing, patterns of residence, marriage, family life, education, attitudes on social issues, and patterns of retirement, to name some of the more common and measurable. Outside observers often reflected on the meager achievements of a great many Irish newcomers, but the degree to which any measurable change on the indicators of life in the larger society represented a major and welcome transition in the lives of the newcomers is reflected in the low rate of return home. Fewer Irish returned home than any major European immigrant group in America.

Who are the Irish in America? We can define the Irish in America as those born in Ireland, their children and grandchildren and, to the extent that we can trace them, their descendants. The group roughly corresponds to the 45 million people, almost one in five of the American population, Irish-Americans or Irish ethnics as they are often called, who claimed Irish ancestry on the 1990 U.S. census. This group can be further broken down into the 39 million people who identified themselves as Irish and the almost 6 million people who identified themselves as Scotch-Irish. Many historians of American immigration have assumed that Americans identifying themselves as Irish are Catholic. While such an assumption was true for the nineteenth century, at present only about one in three of the 39 million Irish in America claim to be Catholics, the remainder profess adherence to the Protestant faith or claim no religious affiliation. The 6 million Americans of Scotch-Irish ancestry are overwhelmingly Presbyterians or other Protestant denominations. As indicated in Table 1, beginning with the 1820 U.S. census, the first to record nationality, immigration from Ireland grew slowly with each passing decade until almost one million made the journey during the 1850s. The arrival in America of vast numbers of newcomers from throughout the world over the last half of the nineteenth century, coincidental with a gradual slowing in the rate of movement out of Ireland, diminished the Irish importance in the immigrant stream: in 1850 the Irish provided almost half of all newcomers; by 1920 the Irish provided only one in forty. In 1920 almost 5 million Americans were either Irish-born or boasted at least one Irish parent. As indicated in Table 1, from a peak of 1.9 million in 1890 the Irish-born population has declined steadily to 169,827 in the 1990 U.S. census of population.

Table 1. Irish In America for Period Indicated or at End of Decade Indicated

| | 1<br>*Arriving from Ireland over Census Period* | 2<br>*Irish-born at End of Decade* | 3<br>*Irish Parentage at the End of Decade***  |
|---|---|---|---|
| 1821–1830 | 50,724 | N/A | N/A |
| 1831–1840 | 207,381 | N/A | N/A |
| 1841–1850 | 780,719 | 961,719 | N/A |
| 1851–1860 | 914,119 | 1,611,304 | N/A |
| 1861–1870 | 435,778 | 1,855,827 | N/A |
| 1871–1880 | 436,871 | 1,854,571 | 3,238,580 |
| 1881–1890 | 655,482 | 1,871,509 | 2,924,172 |
| 1891–1900 | 388,416 | 1,615,459 | 3,375,546 |
| 1901–1910 | 339,065 | 1,352,251 | 3,304,015 |
| 1911–1920 | 146,181 | 1,037,234 | 3,122,013 |
| 1921–1930 | 210,024 | 744,810 | 2,341,712 |
| 1931–1940 | 10,973 | 572,031 | 1,838,920 |
| 1941–1950 | 19,789 | 505,285 | 1,891,495 |
| 1951–1960 | 48,362 | 338,722 | 1,434,590 |
| 1961–1970 | 32,966 | 251,375 | 1,198,845 |
| 1971–1980 | 14,230 | 198,943 | N/A |
| 1981–1990 | 33,829 | 169,827 | N/A |
| 1991–1996 | 54,425 | N/A | N/A |

*Source:* Column 1 was computed from the *1985 Statistical Yearbook of the Immigration and Naturalization Service.* (Washington, D. C., Department of Justice: Immigration and Naturalization Service, 1985). Table Imm, pp. 2–5. For years after 1985 see respective *Statistical Yearbook of the Immigration and Naturalization Service.* It should be remembered that figures in Column 1 appear to cover only those whose last residence was Ireland and thus exclude Irish arrivals who had made an interim stop in another country; Columns 2 and 3 were developed from the following sources: *Historical Sources of the United States: Colonial Times to 1970.* Bureau of the Census, 1975, pt. 1, pp. 116–18 for all statistics with the following exceptions: Irish-born for 1940 from *Census of Population, 1950, II, Characteristics of the Population* (state volumes, Table 24); native of Irish parents for 1880 was computed from *Statistics of the Population at the Tenth Census,* June 1, 1880 (Washington, D. C., 1883), pp. 674 ff; for 1890 the figures were computed from *Report of the Population of the U.S. at the Eleventh Census, 1890, pt. 1,* (Washington, D. C., 1895), pp. 686 ff.

**Parentage means one or both parents born in Ireland. Since 1930 total applies only to the 26 counties of Ireland.

Nonetheless, a fairly significant revival in Irish movement to the United States has taken place over the past ten years.

### Irish Movement to Colonial America

As Europeans struggled to colonize the New World after 1600, Ireland underwent an intense social transformation that destroyed forever the old Gaelic society, dispossessed Catholic landholders, and replaced many of them with a variety of English and Scots newcomers. Ireland's tradition of migration and its location on the far western edge of the known world ensured an impressive rate of movement throughout Europe and across the Atlantic before and after Columbus's voyage. History had prepared the Irish to travel, to live among strangers, and to accommodate to a form of government at home which, like the government emerging in the American colonies, was unmistakably English.

For over three centuries after the first settlement of the New World, Ireland sent large groups of newcomers to the colonies and to the United States. In 1586 Irishman Edward Nugent stopped raids on the English camp in present-day North Carolina by killing the Indian Chief Pemispan. Many Irish traveled across the Atlantic as voluntary migrants, either as paying passengers, or indentured servants—generally unmarried people who contracted with a ship's captain to be sold into service in lieu of paying their passage. Some traveled involuntarily as convicts or prisoners of war especially during Cromwell's campaign as thousands of political, military and Catholic prisoners captured in Irish campaigns were sold into servitude. The passage of a spate of laws in the late seventeenth century restricting the rights of "papists" in South Carolina, Maryland and Virginia suggests their arrival in increasing numbers over the period. Nor does it appear that the movement of impoverished Irish declined over the eighteenth century, many of whom migrated as a result of acts passed by the Irish Parliament authorizing a sentence of transportation for a variety of offenses and providing bounties for ship captains involved in the trade. Steady trade in Irish Catholic indentured servants continued until the decade after the American Revolution. A Catholic bonded servant could expect to be sold at the dockside to the highest bidder and stood a far greater chance than a Protestant newcomer of having to spend the difficult period of "seasoning"—adjusting to the New World—working for an employer who did not share his religion and who detested him for his. These circumstances may well explain the large numbers of Irish listed as runaways in colonial newspapers. At the same time a small but significant movement took place of Catholic migrants who paid their own passage and arrived with sufficient funds to establish a respectable existence. New York had a contingent of prosperous Irish Catholics from around 1650; colonies of prosperous Irish Catholics from Tipperary and Waterford began settling in New Jersey in 1683. Catholic Charles Carroll moved to Maryland in 1681 and established a family that produced a signatory to the Declaration of Independence. Philadelphia had a group of prosperous Irish Catholic residents by the mid-eighteenth century. At about the same time, the Protestant Charitable Irish Society of Boston recognized the existence of a significant body of prosperous Catholic Irish by opening up the Society to them. By the time of the American Revolution, a number of affluent Catholics and ex-Catholics, either Irish-born or of Irish background, emerged with considerable fortunes in the ranks of prominent Americans throughout the colonies.

After they began arriving in large numbers in the American colonies after 1680, Presbyterians from Ulster vastly outnumbered Irish Catholics for the remainder of the colonial period. The majority of Irish Presbyterian immigrants in the early eighteenth century headed for New England where they were directed to frontier areas by colonists anxious to establish a buffer against Indian attacks. Despite the success of Presbyterian newcomers in establishing a chain of settlements along the Western frontier of the colony of Massachusetts, New Englanders found them a troublesome and difficult lot. Hostility between the groups, and the growth of trade between Pennsylvania and Irish ports, led to a diversion of the Scotch-Irish movement to William Penn's colony after 1725. For the century that followed, Scotch-Irish newcomers dominated the transatlantic stream from Ireland. Although a significant number of Irish Presbyterians settled around Philadelphia, the great majority headed for frontier areas and out into the newly settled Cumberland Valley. As land became increasingly difficult to acquire in Pennsylvania,

the Scotch-Irish spread southwards along the frontier into Virginia and the Carolinas. Their establishment by 1750 of a chain of settlements, stretching along the Great Wagon Road that ran from Pennsylvania to Georgia, exposed them to the brunt of Indian raids, and they played a major part in military operations including the French and Indian War. As English-speaking Protestants, some of relatively high economic standing and with a tradition of direct interaction with English government, the Presbyterian Irish played a significant role in all aspects of the development of Colonial America. In addition to their fighting prowess and their social turbulence, they spearheaded westward expansion, played an important role in American politics long before the mass involvement of their Catholic countrymen, and established American Presbyterianism as well as a network of schools and universities all across the country.

Irish Quakers, predominantly converts of English or Scotch background, moved to the American colonies between 1682 and 1750. Armed with a "certificate of removal" attesting to their membership in good standing in the home meeting (congregation), a Quaker immigrant was readily accepted by Friends in the New World, most often in Pennsylvania, but on occasion in Maryland, West Jersey, or the Carolinas. The majority of Irish Friends, farmers or businessmen at home, crossed the Atlantic in their prime producing years. There was, however, a sizable representation of younger individuals starting out in life who, to pay costs of passage, either borrowed money from members of their home meeting or sold themselves as bonded servants, usually to fellow Quakers. Some wealthy Quakers improved their financial position by bringing over non-Quaker indentured servants and selling them in the New World. Descendants of early Irish Quaker settlers, together with newer arrivals, eventually moved south into the Shenandoah Valley of Virginia and into South Carolina and Georgia during the first half of the eighteenth century. By the time of the American Revolution, Irish Friends or their descendants could be found in Pennsylvania, Delaware, Virginia, South Carolina and Georgia.

Since they appear to have blended into the colonies with a minimum of friction, little detailed information is available on the experiences of Irish immigrants from the Established Anglican Church. But it is obvious that they were a significant and impressively diverse group. Many came as indentured servants, particularly to Virginia, but also to Georgia and the Carolinas, areas where there were few obstacles other than economic ones to their acquisition of land after indenture. Others, arriving as paying passengers, remained in urban areas where some became prominent: Hugh Gaine founded a newspaper in New York; John Daly Burk served as editor of Boston's first daily newspaper and was an important spokesman for the new United States. The Declaration of Independence was signed by three Irish-born members of the Anglican Church, and five individuals of Irish Episcopalian background.

By the time of the American Revolution the Irish population of the American colonies was as heterogeneous as the population of Ireland. Most prominent all across the new country were settlements of Irish Presbyterians. The striking feature in the adjustment of this diverse people to the New World was the lack of friction between Presbyterians and Catholics who had regarded each other with enmity in Ireland. This peacefulness during the early years of settlement resulted from the physical isolation of different religious groups from each other, occasioned by settlement in different areas. When Catholics and Presbyterians did clash in later years, these contacts took place in the more diverse cities and towns. Although there are scattered references to the use of the term "Scotch-Irish," Irish Presbyterians still called themselves "Irish" and displayed as much pride and nostalgia for their homeland as their Catholic countrymen, often naming settlements all along the Great Wagon Road after areas of origin in Ireland. Moreover, in Boston, New York, Philadelphia, and Charleston, Presbyterians joined Catholics, Quakers and Episcopalians from Ireland in fraternal organizations to provide assistance to impoverished newcomers from Ireland regardless of religion.

## REVOLUTIONARY AMERICA

The American Revolution intensified this ecumenical spirit and led to common participation by Irishmen of all religions in military units, both loyalist and rebel. Presbyterian and Catholic Irishmen proved such ferocious fighters for the American rebels that in 1778 the British Commander-in-Chief, Sir Henry Clinton, proposed to augment his forces from "whence the rebels themselves drew most of their best soldiers—I mean the Irish." Subsequently, an Irish loyalist regiment, the Volunteers of Ireland, consisting of Irishmen of all religions, was raised in Philadelphia and served for the remainder of the war. Catholic and Presbyterian Irish could be found on the loyalist side in all areas, but the great majority of Sons of Erin backed the rebels. The French armies which aided the American forces had a great number of Irish Catholic soldiers. Presbyterians in Pennsylvania served so well, despite a minor mutiny, that their "Line of Ireland" was credited with playing a major role in the victory of the Americans. There was much justification for the statement in the Irish Parliament in 1784, "America was lost by Irish Emigrants."

It is impossible to discern the national origins or the religions of the American population during the colonial and early national periods. It is possible to say, however, that the Irish were the largest of the non-English arrivals during the colonial years and that about half of all Irish in the New World came from Ulster, the remaining half from the other three provinces of Ireland. By 1800 the city of Philadelphia was the most important Irish city in the new United States with about 6,000 inhabitants claiming Irish birth, among them Catholics, Quakers, Presbyterians, and Episcopalians. Prominent publisher Mathew Carey and linguist Matthias O'Conway joined a number of their countrymen at the top of the social scale. One of Philadelphia's leading merchants, Irish Presbyterian Blair McClenachan, led a mob to the residence of the British minister during the agitation against Jay's Treaty in 1795.

That many Irish could be found at the bottom of the social ladder is suggested by crime statistics: although they made up only 7 percent of the population between 1794 and 1800, the Irish provided 36 percent of all criminals, convicted mostly for theft of food or clothing. The increasing number of Catholics among the Irish population of Philadelphia is suggested by the expanding numbers of Catholic burials and by the development of Irish shantytowns in proximity to Catholic churches and to taverns catering exclusively to Irish immigrants. It was in fact the first example of a distinctly Irish urban community which eventually appeared in every major city in the country over the nineteenth century.

## PRE-FAMINE IRELAND

The peace of 1815 marked the end of the agricultural prosperity of the Napoleonic Wars as the war-inflated price of wheat dropped sharply to 50 percent of the price in 1812. The benefits from such a system were unevenly distributed, especially to the great majority of the rural population on the bottom of the social structure, that is, cottiers and conacre holders (sharecroppers) and landless laborers, all of whom lived in smoke-filled, one-room mud cabins—class IV houses on the census. The famines of the period, 1817, 1822, 1831, 1835–37, 1839 and 1842, hit hardest among the expanding population on the bottom of the social structure. Small farmers too were terrified by the prospects of famines and economic fluctuations and saw little hope for the future. Nor could the nonagricultural sector of the economy absorb the growing surplus of rural workers; for as population expanded industry remained steady or declined particularly in the textile industry which had involved large segments of the population. By 1830 the woolen industry was dying; cotton was declining rapidly; while linen moved out of homes and relocated to the newly appearing factories in the Northeast.

These changes took place in the midst of a striking demographic transition. From 6.8 million in 1821 the population grew to about 8.3 million in 1841 even though the rate of increase was slowing in response to the changing conditions. An almost twofold increase took place in the numbers of agricultural laborers and farm servants—from 665,000 to 1.3 million between 1831 and 1841, while changes in the numbers of tenants farming both large and small holdings were insignificant. Between 1800 and the Great Famine of 1845 the most obvious cause of the slowdown in the rate of population growth was the development of widespread emigration, together with increases in the rate of permanent celibacy and delayed marriage. The migration flow to the United States was slow for the first decade and a half of the nineteenth century, with the exception of the years 1800 to 1802, when around 6,000 Irish per year crossed the Atlantic. In 1816, over 6,000 Irish emigrated to the United States, while 9,000 made the same journey in the following year. In 1818 an astonishing 20,000 crossed the Atlantic. Thereafter departures grew steadily until they reached almost 93,000 in a single year, 1842. Altogether, at least 1.3 million Irish departed for the United States over the years from 1815 to the Great Famine. The majority of emigrants in the century after 1820 were unmarried and under 35 years of age. Three out of four were under 35 years of age between 1803–1805. In the early decades of the nineteenth century, skilled artisans were most numerous and by the late 1830s the majority were unskilled rural laborers from the subsistence sectors of the society. For a great many Irish, movement across the Atlantic became a realistic alternative to remaining at home. Although Catholics were well represented in the early years of the nineteenth century, not until the late 1830s did they dominate the movement. The foundation was laid for the massive outpouring of Catholic emigrants of later years.

After the Napoleonic Wars the pressure of an expanding population on a sluggish economy forced a transformation in peasant families. Fathers were no longer able to provide a patch of land to each son on marriage, usually by subdividing a family's meager holding. Thus increasing numbers of children joined the expanding ranks of landless laborers or left the country. Concurrently, the peasant outlook changed. With the expansion of communications and transportation routes, the establishment of a police force, and the appearance of a rapidly growing and popular school system, the entire country began to feel the impact of administrators and police. Rural children flocked to the new schools which provided an education in English, a language increasingly necessary for survival—as opposed to Irish which many saw as the "language of poverty and want."

Eventually a generation of English-speaking peasants appeared whose knowledge of the outside world was no longer restricted to the oral Irish (Gaelic) culture. Instruction in geography in the schools, widespread advertising campaigns by emigrant agents, the impressive circulation of newspapers, and widely distributed letters from emigrants in America, combined to expand the peasants' consciousness. At that critical stage in a family's life cycle when children elsewhere move out of the home, the Irish young, male and female, came to see moving out of the country as a desirable option. A growing proportion of young literate peasants turned to emigration to the United States as an alternative to the traditional patterns of marriage and land acquisition accepted by their fathers. Common sense would tell us that they were more likely to take risks than their fellow countrymen and women who stayed at home.

## GREAT FAMINE

The potato fungus which first struck Ireland in late August 1845 was unprecedented and unexpected as previous potato failures had been comparatively small. However, the entire crop failed in the following year and despite some lessening of the disease in 1847, starvation was widespread since most of the seed potatoes had been eaten or destroyed by disease. The 1848 crop was a total disaster, but 1849 saw a gradual improvement and by 1850 the worst was over. A number of factors slowed the reaction of the British government to the disaster: a lack of reliable information in the initial months of the crisis, transportation difficulties, and a widely shared consensus among the best economic minds of the day, both in Europe and America, that free markets could achieve far more than any government agency and that interfering in the workings of the free market would bring greater disaster. Furthermore, many English preferred to view the potato as an inferior food, cultivated by a feckless race of Irish paupers in "lazy" beds, ignoring the fact that, apart from a few exceptional years, the potato had provided sufficient food for a rapidly expanding population for some time and that Irish potato eaters who served in the English army at this time were the tallest military men in Europe. To these individuals, the "Potato, Paddy and Popery" explained what they considered as the Irish place at the bottom of the cultural ladder. Many who shared the view of the Famine as a moral problem believed that any intervention to alleviate the starvation would thwart God's plan to deal with the Irish.

In 1845 a limited scheme of public works and a restricted food distribution system was initiated by the government to deal with the disaster. By late 1846 recognition of the unprecedented scale of the disaster could no longer be avoided and the British government initiated a large scale program to deal with the starvation and deprivation. By the spring of 1847 almost three-quarters of a million Irish were employed on relief projects and by August 1847 over three million people were being fed daily in addition to a broad program of assistance from private charities both British and American.

The impact of the Great Famine has been accurately compared to the impact of a major war: it brought about the most revolutionary change in Ireland for several hundred years. Most obvious is the demographic change: the Irish population quadrupled in the century before the Famine, after the Famine the population dropped until the 1960s when it began a slight rise. Between 1845 and 1851 about 2 million Irish disappeared—at least one million died, the remainder emigrated. In 1845 some 77,000 people left Ireland and 106,000 did so in the following year. Almost a quarter of a million left in 1851. Overall, the majority left from the Midland and the Northwest: Mayo, Leitrim, Fermanagh and Meath lost between 15 and 17 percent of their population, while Roscommon, Sligo, Longford, Cavan and Monaghan saw between 18 and 22 percent of their population depart. In striking contrast the relatively small emigration took place from two widely dissimilar areas, Ulster and the West of Ireland south of Mayo. In Ulster, alternate sources of income, industrial development and progressive farming mitigated the impact of the disaster, while the West maintained traditional patterns of community organization where there had always been a hesitancy to depart for distant parts.

Who were the Famine refugees? The 1851 census showed the disappearance of landholders from 100,000 plots of under one acre and approximately the same number of plots from one to five acres together with 120,000 between five and fifteen acres. Almost 400,000 farm laborers and farm servants left over the same period. Finally, 341,000 fourth-class houses, smoke-filled, one-room sod huts disappeared. Applying the conservative figure of slightly less than six family members occupying each sod hut, this disappearance represents the loss of around 2 million people. The evidence is unmistakable that the Famine struck the lowest levels of society with unprecedented fury. Almost eight out of ten emigrants during 1851, one of the few years for which we have such information, claimed previous employment as farm laborers, a mere 8 percent claimed to be full-time farmers. The Great Famine exodus was overwhelmingly a movement of the more impoverished Irish rural dwellers to various parts of the world, particularly to the United States.

## IRELAND 1851–1920

The traditional view of the years from the Great Famine to the successful struggle for independence as one in which Irish tenant farmers struggled in vain with predatory landlords who eventually drove many of them into emigration obscures far more complex and ambiguous facts. In fact, the Famine initiated a reordering of the agricultural community which saw the appearance of an extensive class of respectable farmers together with a more prosperous landlord class and the steady disappearance of that great army of landless laborers and cottiers which had been enumerated in the 1841 census. Landlords did well over this period; middle and upper level farmers also did well; but small farmers and laborers did very poorly, especially in the West. The electorate became socially and economically more homogeneous and a new political and social order emerged in which farmers (and small town shopkeepers) came to dominate politics in an alliance that continued until long after the independence struggle. As the more prosperous farmers with 30 acres or more focused their political energies on improving their lot relative to the landlords in the various land movements, very little was done for those on the lower level of the society. Efforts by the British government to provide relief for the destitute on road-building projects produced an advanced communications network during and following the Great Famine. Along the new highways moved the products of England's expanding factories, thus accelerating the decline of rural crafts and smothering industrial development and further compounding the misery of the poor. As the century progressed, the new highways facilitated the movement to "disturbed areas" of the expanding numbers of armed constabulary and military forces which in turn produced an increasingly tractable society. Nevertheless, emigration remained the most important factor in keeping down disturbances throughout rural Ireland. The importance of emigration as a safety valve is clear in the difficulty of keeping the peace whenever emigration was constrained, as it was by the American slump of 1874–79 and the period during and immediately following World War I when unemployed young men supplied many of the recruits for the Irish Republican Army.

The post-Famine transition was made possible by an extraordinary exodus of the economically less fortunate, made all the more impressive by the dramatic overall decline in the population from 6.3 million in 1851 to 4.1 million in 1921 and the accompanying increase in the number of farmers—from 40 percent to 60 percent of the population between 1850 and World War I. In the three-quarters of a century after the Famine, between 4.5 and 5 million people left Ireland, about a quarter to Great Britain and the remainder to the United States, the overwhelming majority of them claiming a background as rural laborers. These departures reflected a wider demographic transition. As the increasing consolidation of agriculture depressed the demand for rural laborers, periodic famines still made life precarious in rural areas, especially for those on the lower levels of society. While high marriage rates, high marital fertility and traditional land-use patterns could still be found along the western seaboard for some decades after the Great Famine, in general, permanent celibacy and delayed marriage spread throughout rural Ireland and the urge to emigrate to the New World became general. A slow but steady increase took place in age at marriage, and the proportion of individuals who never married expanded as more and more men, without land and lacking the resources or the will to emigrate, found it impossible to get wives: the percentage of men aged 45–54 who had never married rose from one in ten in 1841 to almost one in three in 1911. Over the entire period men and women left in roughly equal numbers, although females slightly outnumbered males in twenty-five of the years between 1869 and 1920. Irish female emigrants, who tended to be slightly younger than departing males, made up a larger proportion of emigrants from Ireland than from any other country in nineteenth-century Europe, apparently preferring to take their chances among what folklore and common sense told them was a more enterprising type of Irish male on the Irish-American marriage market as an alternative to the harshness of life for women in the more remote areas of the rural countryside.

Irish kinship networks facilitated the movement to the New World. Rare indeed was the peasant emigrant who traveled alone across the Atlantic. Many emigrants shared surnames with fellow passengers or traveled with individuals from the same areas of origin. A relatively small number of emigrants traveled in family groups to the United States on "assisted passage" paid for by landlords or the government. For the vast majority, kinship networks were vital to providing the money to pay fares. At home groups of related individuals often pooled resources to send out younger and more energetic members who earned and sent home sufficient funds to pay fares of those who remained behind. The enormous amounts of money sent from the United States to Ireland attests to the continued strength of kinship networks after departure. The Irish sent home far more money than any other immigrant group in the United States. In addition to paying the fares of a great number of emigrants, the massive sums of money or "remittances" sent home were vital in ensuring the survival of the smallest and most unproductive landholdings in rural areas of Ireland, particularly in the West. Large-scale

Irish peasant movement to the New World, therefore, was not a mindless flight from intolerable home conditions but, given the limited range of alternatives within the system, a deliberate departure of generally literate individuals who were very much concerned with the survival and well-being of family and friends remaining at home.

The massive Protestant emigration of the early days had by the mid-nineteenth century declined to about 10 to 15 percent of all departures from Ireland, and this percentage held for the remainder of the century. While departing Protestants were more likely to come from the more prosperous element of the home society, there was at all times a significant number of Catholics who had worked as artisans, merchants, and professionals at home. Overall, the proportion of emigrants, both Protestant and Catholic, from the more qualified elements of the workforce ranged from a high of 75 percent in 1820 to a low of 9 percent in 1900. In adjusting to the New World, immigrants from the higher levels of the social scale at home, Catholic or Protestant, were better prepared to deal with life in the United States, and generally put some distance between themselves and the great masses of impoverished Catholics.

### Old and New Worlds

Although Irish society was becoming more commercialized and modern throughout the nineteenth century, it was a transition that took a uniquely Irish direction in critical ways very much at variance with life in the United States. Much of the expanding commerce in pre-Famine society involved periodic contacts with wandering traders who worked on a barter basis and who appeared on fair days often camping on the streets: the 1841 census showed 27,000 "huxters" and dealers operating throughout the country. Cash was scarce and infrequently used by most rural dwellers in contrast to the universal use of money in the United States. The small amount of cash necessary for survival on the level of society that produced the vast majority of emigrants was usually earned by keeping a pig or a farm animal, which was then sold at the proper time, or by seasonal migration by family members. Landless laborers, often sharecropping on small conacre or rundale holdings, were paid in a "potato wage" by farmers who in return for work gave them access to a small patch of land on which they could grow enough potatoes to survive. While many of the wandering dealers were replaced by small shops after the Great Famine, the relationship between traders and their customers was slow to change. Well into the twentieth century it was possible in many of the more congested rural areas to exchange farm products, especially eggs or peat, and labor, for goods or to repay debts to storekeepers. At the same time on middle levels of the rural society, "strong" farmers frequently paid their bills by exchanging one or more farm animals with local shopkeepers in lieu of cash, generally at the end of harvest time.

Particularly significant was the gap between work values throughout Irish rural society and in the United States. Irish peasants disdained the strong emphasis on the individual competitive work ethic common throughout American society. Attempts by overseers on Famine relief projects to change "inefficient" Irish work-sharing practices by encouraging rural dwellers to compete with each other failed dismally. Announcements by overseers that some members of a work gang would be let go as funds were insufficient to continue the employment of the entire group were invariably met by the group uniting and making a common decision to take a reduction in pay so that all might share equally in whatever work and funds were available. Similar "peasant combinations" operating as a group were common among Irish workers building canals and railroads in the United States as early as the 1830s. Throughout Irish rural society it was commonly believed that a move up the economic scale could only be accomplished at the expense of family and kin, not an unrealistic attitude in view of the limited amount of land and other resources available to them. Closely related to the disinterest in efforts to improve one's position was the respect for cooperation between kin and neighbors and the traditional belief that food and shelter should be provided to all strangers—a belief which partly explains the vast numbers of beggars in the society. Irish peasants preparing to depart frequently defined the United States in terms of a purified version of their own society, a land in which "everyman's duty is to lend a helping hand to his fellow, particularly if he is a stranger." The shock of arrival for such people can only be imagined.

To American society an Irish newcomer could offer only his labor. To the newcomer American society offered the opportunity to undertake the precarious task of making one's own future in a society lacking all of the familial supports and restraints of home. Gone was the network of family and friends of the townland and village. Gone too were the landlords, clergymen, tithes, taxes, churches, and the pervasive evidence of the power of the national government with the militia-like armed national police force and the numerous army garrisons. On the eve of the Great Famine a parish priest in County Cork reported that the most common observation in the letters of his former parishioners in America was their astonishment that there was "no tyranny, no oppression from landlords, and no taxes." In America, apart from federal elections, a Fourth of July parade, or the arrival of a new postmaster, the federal government was a distant stranger fulfilling more a symbolic than a governmental role. Indeed, governmental and other restraints were so limited that Americans were continually forced to consider the implications of their actions both as individuals and as members of a community in a manner unlike any other people in the world.

Immigrant anxiety over the absence of familiar social institutions was intensified by the merciless pressure to make individual decisions. Already by 1850 a resident of this new American world could choose to become an inhabitant of any one of thirty-one states stretching 3,000 miles across the continent, claim membership in any one of at least 100 religious denominations, or seek employment in one of the expanding pools of thousands of jobs. The unremitting transformation of the economic structure led to the disappearance of a great many jobs to be replaced by others, frequently in different states or regions; the average worker was forced on numerous occasions to leave one occupation and to choose another. In contrast to home where the costs of failure could be catastrophic, America was the land of the first chance, the second chance, and indeed of as many chances as an individual decided to attempt in the struggle to survive and to prosper. Vast hoards of strangers invaded local communities: Irishmen seeking work on turnpikes and railroads, uprooted Americans moving in straitened circumstances to new places where they dreamed of finding better jobs or settling good land. Day-to-day activity for an American urban dweller involved contact with an array of racial and national groups unknown throughout most of the remainder of the world. Geographic turnover rates over the 1850s reached the highest levels in American history and diluted the old sense of belonging fondly remembered by older citizens. The most striking

theme in nineteenth-century American thought is the concern over possible disunion: society appeared about to come apart at the seams.

Yet American society endured—despite the temporary sundering over the slavery issue during the Civil War. Population expanded, new territory was acquired, the economy grew steadily, and politics flourished on the local, state and national levels among the most kaleidoscopic mix of people on the face of the earth. A newcomer quickly sensed that the American system functioned in a manner unlike any other in the world. But how? Despite the vastness of America, the scale of life centered on the individual. French traveler, Alexis de Tocqueville, one of the most astute of nineteenth-century observers, concluded that the great and uniquely American achievement had been to join personal conduct to social benefit, that is, to make every person feel that he was a vital cog in the system and that his personal good conduct was essential to the smooth functioning of the entire society; self-interest was joined to social perfection. He called this belief the "principle of interest rightly understood" and claimed that Americans somehow seemed to have struck on a system of values perfectly suited to the times. Being American was a state of mind. Every American seemed to have the ability to join with other Americans and re-create America everywhere they settled. The strength of this special and enduring American culture is obvious in the degree to which isolated communities thousands of miles from each other were able to maintain remarkably similar and interchangeable ways of life. The emphasis on the power and importance of the individual in all areas of national and local public life was clear. The unique ungarrisoned city of Washington, with its broad boulevards fanning out in all directions designed to encourage the inhabitants to visit *their* government, stood in striking contrast to the heavily guarded capital cities throughout the remainder of the world—the perfect symbol of the confidence of Americans in the individual. It was common up until the Civil War for citizens to enter the White House and approach the president for a personal loan or political favor. Poet Walt Whitman's belief that the secret of the success of the American experiment lay in the unleashing of "the great pride of man, in himself" was well said, albeit a touch pedantic for a struggling immigrant, Irish or other, who saw the differences in a far more personal light. The words of an Irishman writing home in the mid-nineteenth century who discovered himself in a society where "labor is prized and rewarded, and where every man is the equal of his fellows" were echoed in the 1980s by the observation of an illegal Irish immigrant that in America "everyone is equal because of the jobs people do."

## Settlement/Family/Community

Despite their rural background, Irish immigrants settled overwhelmingly in urban areas in the United States. In 1850 almost four out of five newcomers settled in the more urbanized East Coast states. As indicated in Table 2, by 1920 almost half of all Irish-born Americans resided in fifteen American cities. Indeed almost 90 percent of all Irish immigrants resided in U.S. cities, making the Irish almost twice as likely to live in a city as the American population as a whole. In the cities, Irish families generally resided in clusters, frequently consisting of families or individuals from similar homeland areas of origin in distinctly Irish neighborhoods of which the notorious Five Points in New York provided the archetype. Although all Irish neighborhoods had a substantial non-Irish population, Irish residents were drawn together by a tradition of supporting individuals and in-

Table 2.  Irish-Born for Selected Years in Fifteen Cities of Largest Irish Population in 1890

| | 1850 | 1860 | 1870 | 1880 | 1890 | 1900 | 1910 | 1920 |
|---|---|---|---|---|---|---|---|---|
| New York | 133,730 | 260,450 | 275,984 | 277,409 | 275,156 | 275,102 | 252,672 | 203,450 |
| Philadelphia | 72,312 | 95,548 | 96,698 | 101,808 | 110,935 | 98,427 | 83,196 | 64,590 |
| Boston | 35,287 | 45,991 | 56,900 | 64,793 | 71,441 | 70,147 | 66,041 | 57,011 |
| Chicago | 6,096 | 19,889 | 39,988 | 44,411 | 70,028 | 73,912 | 65,969 | 56,786 |
| San Francisco | N/A | 9,363 | 25,864 | 30,721 | 30,718 | 15,963 | 23,153 | 18,257 |
| Pittsburgh | N/A | 9,297 | 13,119 | 17,110 | 26,643 | 23,690 | 18,873 | 13,989 |
| St. Louis | 9,719 | 29,926 | 23,329 | 29,536 | 24,270 | 19,421 | 14,262 | 9,244 |
| Jersey City | N/A | 7,380 | 17,665 | 30,390 | 22,159 | 19,314 | 16,124 | 12,451 |
| Providence | 7,635 | 9,534 | 12,085 | 13,939 | 19,040 | 18,686 | 15,801 | 11,900 |
| Cleveland | N/A | 5,479 | 9,964 | 11,958 | 13,512 | 13,120 | 11,316 | 9,478 |
| Baltimore | 12,057 | 15,536 | 15,223 | 14,238 | 13,389 | 9,690 | 6,806 | 5,074 |
| Newark | 5,564 | 11,167 | 12,481 | 13,451 | 13,234 | 12,792 | 11,225 | 8,840 |
| Cincinnati | 14,393 | 19,375 | 18,624 | 15,077 | 12,323 | 9,114 | 6,224 | 3,887 |
| Buffalo | N/A | 9,279 | 11,264 | 10,310 | 11,664 | 11,292 | 9,423 | 7,264 |
| New Orleans | 20,200 | 24,398 | 14,693 | 11,708 | 7,923 | 5,398 | 2,996 | 1,543 |
| Total | 316,993 | 572,612 | 643,881 | 686,859 | 722,435 | 676,068 | 604,081 | 483,764 |
| U.S. Total Irish | 961,719 | 1,611,304 | 1,855,827 | 1,854,571 | 1,871,509 | 1,615,459 | 1,352,251 | 1,037,234 |
| % Irish In 15 Cities | 33 | 36 | 35 | 37 | 39 | 42 | 45 | 47 |

*Source:* Computed from data given on U.S. census reports for respective decade.

stitutions. The activities of grocers and saloon keepers, who acted as cultural brokers by providing advice and extending credit particularly to new arrivals, were augmented by the work of politicians, priests, and members and leaders of Irish fraternal, charitable, county and religious organizations.

Most Irish immigrants lived in a nuclear household, that is, parents and children. Grandparents occasionally crossed to join children, usually on the East Coast. The Irish tended initially to marry within their own group: the Famine generation in Boston had higher rates of in-group marriage than all other groups in the city. In the Midwest and the Far West between 1850 and 1880, the Irish usually selected spouses of the same national background. Those Irish who married outside the group were most likely to be found on the middle and upper reaches of the social scale. In the four decades after 1880 these high rates of in-group marriage dropped sharply in all regions of the country. By 1920 only 73 percent of married Irish males in the United States claimed Irish-born partners. But the same evidence suggests that two out of three of the non-Irish-born spouses were second-generation Irish. Thus, the apparent assimilation suggested by the rates of marriage outside of the group is of a decidedly limited kind.

Despite considerable variation between Irish at different locations and on different levels of the society, the group had a larger proportion of missing fathers than that of other immigrant groups, overwhelmingly the result of high mortality in dangerous jobs associated with the western movement. The West is dotted with the graves of Irish fathers who died in accidents, cholera epidemics or other illnesses as they worked their way west, often with railroad construction gangs, in advance of their families. Irish families, especially those without a father, often took in boarders, usually individuals related to the family or who came from the same area of origin in Ireland. Girls and boys were equally likely to attend school. Although children usually went to work at an early age, children of Irish immigrants attended schools as often as other immigrants and were more likely to be holding jobs at the same time. The uniqueness of these co-operative family patterns is reflected in the fact that by 1910 the

*Reports of the Immigration Commission* showed that, despite the Irish confinement to unskilled and poorly paid jobs, the average income of Irish-American families surpassed that of other immigrant groups.

As measured by the level of persistence in the U.S. Census—the proportion of a group remaining in a community for a decade or more—the Irish displayed the same level of movement in and out of communities as Americans on similar levels of the occupational ladder, suggesting that the movement was the result of patterns of economic development rather than any cultural legacy. Significantly it seems that for a great many the process of migration accelerated the process of assimilation and achievement. Many Irish improved their position by moving to the frontier. All across the country Irish immigrants moved within groups of other Irish: A lone Irish traveler was a rare figure. Much of the Irish movement reflected their concentration in many of the most menial tasks all across the country, especially in transportation. The Irish were prominent in building the network of highways and railroads which stretched to Wisconsin and Missouri by 1860. They worked with the Chinese to place the railroad tracks which linked the continent in 1869. The Irish predominated among immigrant groups in the vast and forgotten "Foreign Legion" who drove freight wagons all across the Great Plains and the Far West.

The Irish pioneered the establishment of scattered communities on the various mining frontiers, from the California Gold Rush of 1849; into the Pacific Northwest and the Southwest for gold in 1858; to Nevada for silver in 1859; to Colorado for gold in the same year; into the Black Hills of Dakota for gold in the mid-1870s. On the last of the western mining frontiers, Butte, Montana, with 12,000 Irish inhabitants out of a total population of around 47,000 in 1900, had the largest proportion of Irish inhabitants of any city in the country. The Irish provided the largest foreign-born group in the Army of the West: Thirty-two Irishmen died in 1876 with General George A. Custer at the Battle of Little Bighorn. The Irish were as close to the cutting edge of the drive west as any other group. As indicated in Table 3, the Irish were well represented all across the country: over a third of all

Table 3. Irish-Born in the United States, by U.S. Census Region and State, 1850–1920

| NORTHEAST | 1850 | 1860 | 1870 | 1880 | 1890 | 1900 | 1910 | 1920 |
|---|---|---|---|---|---|---|---|---|
| *New England* | | | | | | | | |
| Connecticut | 26,689 | 55,445 | 70,630 | 70,638 | 77,880 | 70,994 | 58,457 | 45,464 |
| Maine | 13,871 | 15,290 | 15,745 | 13,421 | 11,444 | 10,159 | 7,890 | 5,748 |
| Massachusetts | 115,917 | 185,426 | 216,120 | 226,700 | 259,902 | 249,916 | 222,862 | 183,171 |
| New Hampshire | 8,811 | 12,737 | 12,190 | 13,052 | 14,890 | 13,547 | 10,613 | 7,908 |
| Rhode Island | 15,944 | 25,285 | 31,534 | 35,281 | 38,920 | 35,501 | 29,715 | 22,253 |
| Vermont | 15,377 | 13,480 | 14,080 | 11,657 | 9,810 | 7,453 | 4,938 | 2,884 |
| Subtotal | 196,609 | 307,663 | 360,299 | 370,749 | 412,846 | 387,570 | 334,475 | 267,428 |
| *MidAtlantic* | | | | | | | | |
| New Jersey | 31,092 | 62,006 | 86,784 | 93,079 | 101,059 | 94,844 | 82,749 | 65,971 |
| New York | 343,111 | 498,134 | 528,806 | 499,445 | 483,375 | 425,553 | 367,877 | 284,747 |
| Pennsylvania | 151,723 | 201,939 | 235,798 | 236,505 | 243,836 | 205,909 | 165,091 | 121,601 |
| Subtotal | 525,926 | 762,079 | 851,388 | 829,029 | 828,270 | 726,306 | 615,717 | 472,319 |
| N.E. TOTAL | 722,535 | 1,069,742 | 1,211,687 | 1,199,778 | 1,241,116 | 1,113,876 | 950,192 | 739,747 |
| NORTH CENTRAL | | | | | | | | |
| *East North Central* | | | | | | | | |
| Illinois | 27,786 | 87,573 | 120,162 | 117,343 | 124,498 | 114,563 | 93,451 | 74,274 |
| Indiana | 12,787 | 24,495 | 28,698 | 25,741 | 20,819 | 16,306 | 11,266 | 7,271 |
| Ohio | 51,562 | 76,826 | 82,674 | 78,927 | 70,127 | 55,018 | 40,057 | 29,262 |
| Michigan | 13,430 | 30,049 | 42,013 | 43,413 | 39,065 | 29,182 | 20,434 | 16,531 |
| Wisconsin | 21,043 | 49,961 | 48,479 | 41,907 | 33,306 | 23,544 | 14,049 | 7,809 |
| Subtotal | 126,608 | 268,904 | 322,026 | 307,331 | 287,815 | 238,613 | 179,257 | 135,147 |
| *West North Central* | | | | | | | | |
| Iowa | 4,885 | 28,072 | 40,124 | 44,061 | 37,353 | 28,321 | 17,756 | 10,686 |
| Kansas | — | 3,888 | 10,940 | 14,993 | 15,870 | 11,516 | 8,100 | 4,825 |
| Minnesota | 271 | 12,831 | 21,746 | 25,942 | 28,011 | 22,428 | 15,859 | 10,289 |
| Missouri | 14,734 | 43,464 | 54,983 | 48,898 | 40,966 | 31,832 | 23,290 | 15,022 |
| Nebraska | — | 1,431 | 4,999 | 10,133 | 15,963 | 11,127 | 8,124 | 5,422 |
| North Dakota | — | 42 | 888 | 4,104 | 2,967 | 2,670 | 2,498 | 1,660 |
| South Dakota | — | — | — | — | 4,774 | 3,298 | 2,980 | 1,954 |
| Subtotal | 19,890 | 89,728 | 133,680 | 148,131 | 145,904 | 111,192 | 78,607 | 49,858 |
| N.C. TOTAL | 146,498 | 358,632 | 455,706 | 455,462 | 433,719 | 349,805 | 257,864 | 185,005 |
| SOUTH | | | | | | | | |
| *South Atlantic* | | | | | | | | |
| Delaware | 3,513 | 5,832 | 5,907 | 5,791 | 6,121 | 5,044 | 3,984 | 2,895 |
| Florida | 878 | 827 | 737 | 652 | 1,056 | 797 | 1,069 | 1,304 |
| Georgia | 3,202 | 6,586 | 5,093 | 4,148 | 3,374 | 2,293 | 1,655 | 1,112 |
| Maryland | 19,557 | 24,872 | 23,630 | 21,865 | 18,735 | 13,874 | 9,701 | 6,580 |
| North Carolina | 567 | 888 | 677 | 611 | 451 | 371 | 304 | 301 |
| South Carolina | 4,051 | 4,906 | 3,262 | 2,626 | 1,665 | 1,131 | 675 | 442 |
| Virginia | — | — | 5,191 | 4,835 | 4,578 | 3,534 | 2,450 | 1,732 |
| West Virginia | 11,643 | 16,501 | 6,832 | 6,459 | 4,799 | 3,342 | 2,290 | 1,459 |
| District of Columbia | 2,373 | 7,258 | 8,218 | 7,840 | 7,224 | 6,220 | 5,343 | 4,320 |
| Subtotal | 45,784 | 67,670 | 59,547 | 54,827 | 48,003 | 36,606 | 27,471 | 20,145 |
| *East South Central* | | | | | | | | |
| Alabama | 3,639 | 5,664 | 3,893 | 2,966 | 2,604 | 1,792 | 1,167 | 809 |
| Kentucky | 9,466 | 22,249 | 21,642 | 18,256 | 13,926 | 9,874 | 5,913 | 3,422 |

Table 3  (*cont.*)

| SOUTH | 1850 | 1860 | 1870 | 1880 | 1890 | 1900 | 1910 | 1920 |
|---|---|---|---|---|---|---|---|---|
| *East South Central (cont.)* | | | | | | | | |
| Mississippi | 1,928 | 3,893 | 3,359 | 2,753 | 1,865 | 1,264 | 747 | 412 |
| Tennessee | 2,640 | 12,498 | 8,048 | 5,975 | 5,016 | 3,372 | 2,296 | 1,291 |
| Subtotal | 17,673 | 44,304 | 36,942 | 29,950 | 23,411 | 16,302 | 10,123 | 5,934 |
| *West South Central* | | | | | | | | |
| Arkansas | 514 | 1,312 | 1,428 | 2,431 | 2,021 | 1,345 | 1,077 | 676 |
| Louisiana | 24,266 | 28,153 | 17,068 | 13,807 | 9,236 | 6,436 | 3,753 | 2,000 |
| Oklahoma | — | — | — | — | 329 | 1,384 | 1,800 | 1,321 |
| Texas | 1,403 | 3,480 | 4,031 | 8,103 | 8,201 | 6,173 | 5,355 | 4,333 |
| Subtotal | 26,183 | 32,945 | 22,527 | 24,341 | 19,787 | 15,338 | 11,985 | 8,330 |
| SOUTH TOTAL | 89,640 | 144,919 | 119,016 | 109,118 | 91,201 | 68,246 | 49,579 | 34,409 |
| WEST | | | | | | | | |
| *Mountain States* | | | | | | | | |
| Arizona | — | — | 495 | 1,296 | 1,171 | 1,159 | 1,550 | 1,206 |
| Colorado | — | 624 | 1,685 | 8,263 | 12,352 | 10,132 | 8,710 | 6,191 |
| Idaho | — | — | 986 | 981 | 1,917 | 1,633 | 1,782 | 1,410 |
| Montana | — | — | 1,635 | 2,408 | 6,648 | 9,436 | 9,469 | 7,260 |
| Nevada | — | 651 | 5,035 | 5,191 | 2,646 | 1,425 | 1,702 | 970 |
| New Mexico | 292 | 827 | 543 | 795 | 966 | 692 | 644 | 434 |
| Utah | 106 | 278 | 502 | 1,321 | 2,045 | 1,516 | 1,656 | 1,207 |
| Wyoming | — | — | 1,102 | 1,093 | 1,900 | 1,591 | 1,359 | 956 |
| Subtotal | 398 | 2,380 | 11,983 | 21,348 | 29,645 | 27,584 | 26,872 | 19,634 |
| *Pacific States* | | | | | | | | |
| California | 2,452 | 33,147 | 54,421 | 62,962 | 63,138 | 44,476 | 52,475 | 45,308 |
| Oregon | 196 | 1,267 | 1,967 | 3,659 | 4,891 | 4,210 | 4,995 | 4,203 |
| Washington | — | 1,217 | 1,047 | 2,243 | 7,799 | 7,262 | 10,178 | 8,927 |
| Subtotal | 2,648 | 35,631 | 57,435 | 68,864 | 75,828 | 55,948 | 67,648 | 58,438 |
| WEST TOTAL | 3,046 | 38,011 | 69,418 | 90,212 | 105,473 | 83,532 | 94,520 | 78,072 |
| UNITED STATES TOTAL | 961,719 | 1,611,304 | 1,855,827 | 1,854,570 | 1,871,509 | 1,615,459 | 1,352,155 | 1,037,233 |

*Source:* Computed from the following: 1850, J. D. B. DeBow, *Statistical View of the United States,* Washington, D.C.: A. O. P. Nicholson, public printer, 1854, p. 116; 1860–1920, *Census of Population, 1950,* Vol II, *Characteristics of the Population,* Table 24 of respective state volume.

The total Irish in Dakota for 1860 was developed by comparing the 1860 *Census of Population* figures, which gave a total of 5,070 Irish for all seven territories, with the 1950 *Census of Population* cited above which gives a breakdown by territories for 1860 but leaves out "Dakota" and also leaves unexplained 42 "missing" Irish immigrants in the territories at that time. It seems reasonable to assume that for 1860 the "missing" 42 are in the "missing" Dakota territory.

Irish in the United States resided in areas off the East Coast according to the U.S. Census of 1880 when they were among the three largest immigrant groups in all western states and territories with the exception of Utah.

## QUALITY OF LIFE

The poor preparation of most Irish newcomers for life in urban America is reflected in their dismal health experience. Mortality statistics on Irish immigrants in the United States starkly reflect their poor living conditions and their penchant for alcohol. Nineteenth-century Americans rarely saw a gray-haired Irish-

man. Boston's death rates rose dramatically over the 1850s with the arrival of the Irish. Accidents and work injuries were the primary causes of Irish male deaths throughout the country in 1880, especially in the Central Appalachians and the Far West—the newspapers in these areas carried long columns of poignant letters from wives and families in the East trying to locate a missing Irishman who had gone west in search of a job. Alcohol and alcohol-related diseases were more pervasive among the Irish than any other group. Male death rates generally surpassed female rates, but as late as 1920 Irish-born females were particularly susceptible to death from tuberculosis and problems of the circulatory system—diseases most likely to be caused by deprivation. Infant death rates were higher than for any other early immigrant group. By the early twentieth century overall immigrant mortality rates appear higher than in Ireland.

But it is clear from the impressive growth in numbers of second-generation Irish that high levels of mortality were offset by high rates of fertility. In 1880 Boston, Irish women were more fertile than other immigrant women. In 1910 the Irish rate of reproduction was the second highest among major immigrant groups, surpassed only by French Canadians. High rates of Irish fertility were achieved despite the survival of pre-migration patterns of permanent celibacy and later marriage. One extensive survey of Irish female workers in 1910 found that one in four remained unmarried, a proportion higher than any other major immigrant group.

RELIGIOUS CONFLICT

The key to understanding everyday life in the American society encountered by Irish immigrants, especially in the nineteenth century, lies in recognition of the unique perspective and "moral stance" of its inhabitants. Protestantism and a Protestant-based morality was infused into all important aspects of life: politics, family life, personal behavior, even business dealings, were regarded as moral activities especially with the rise of crusading evangelicals as the Civil War approached. Struck by the absence of an established religion in 1831, English visitor Francis Trollope discovered that Protestantism in fact served the same purpose in that it imposed "a religious tyranny which was exerted very effectively without the direct aid of government." Alexis de Tocqueville agreed in his classic *Democracy in America:* "Religion [Protestantism]," he declared, was "foremost of the political institutions of the country." But beneath the facade of moral certainty to which Americans desperately clung, the cultural, economic and political foundations were shifting and the most disturbing evidence of the shift was the expanding numbers of Catholic Irish.

As the numbers of impoverished Irish Catholic newcomers began to overwhelm earlier more skilled and often Protestant arrivals from Ireland in the late 1830s, American Protestants began to see themselves as under siege. The Irish had a similar view of the larger American Protestant society. Throughout Ireland and the United States around this time, sectarian tensions were increasing. At home many of the areas of origin of Catholic immigrants had been the target of Protestant proselytizing efforts; in the United States an earlier tradition of anti-Catholicism, obvious at some time or another in all of the colonies, began to assume a new importance with the arrival of increasing numbers of Catholic immigrants. Many Americans believed that the Roman Catholic Church was clearly bent on a takeover of the promised land and its agents were the Irish. A great variety of anti-Catholic societies and organizations appeared with the dramatic expansion in the Irish Catholic presence. At the same time Protestant nativists began a series of violent depredations against the Irish, beginning with the burning of the Ursuline Convent in Charlestown, Massachusetts, in 1834. The 1847 Mexican-American War defection of a battalion of Irish to the enemy, who called them the San Patricios, had been somewhat inspired by the sight of Americans burning Catholic churches and maiming helpless Mexicans, and it intensified the divisions between Irish Catholics and native Protestants. Further exacerbating the divisions between the Irish and the larger American society was the Battle of Chapultepec Castle where the San Patricios, under the command of John Reilly from Clifton, County Galway, were the last unit in the Mexican Army to surrender to the Americans. The bravery of the San Patricios is still widely celebrated throughout Mexico each year.

The terms Irish and Catholic became synonymous and the Presbyterian Irish began to identify themselves as Scotch-Irish and to participate in anti-Catholic, anti-Irish activity, particularly in places where the newer immigrants threatened their livelihood by taking jobs at lower wages. Anti-Catholic riots in Philadelphia in 1844 in which two churches and scores of Irish homes were burned began as inter-Irish disputes, Presbyterian versus Catholic, and the rioters appear to have had both economic and religious motives. The introduction in 1867 to the U.S. of the Loyal Orange Institution—founded in Armagh in 1795, to confront the Catholic Church and to maintain loyalty to the British Crown—intensified Scotch-Irish activity against Irish Catholics. From its founding the Orange Order formed the backbone and, in some cases, inspired the foundation of many of the numerous anti-popery organizations of the day throughout the U.S. In 1870 in New York City the annual Twelfth of July parade resulted in a clash between Scotch-Irish Protestants and Irish Catholics in which eight people were killed and scores injured. The following year the event and the riot were repeated with more disastrous results: two policemen and thirty-one spectators were killed. The Order was particularly prominent in the nationwide American Protective Association, founded in the 1890s to curb the political influence of Irish Catholics. By 1914 the Orange Order reached a peak with 364 lodges and over 30,000 members before going into rapid decline. The last sizable Twelfth of July parade in New York City was held in 1919.

THE CATHOLIC CHURCH

Irish immigrants and their descendants had a profound impact on all levels of American Catholicism. In 1800, that is prior to the massive influx of Irish Catholic immigrants, the American Catholic Church was in its infancy. The only bishop, John Carroll, a descendant of an illustrious Irish Catholic family, was joined by four Irish-born bishops with the creation of new dioceses in 1808. The numbers of arriving Irish clergy increased steadily: over the 1840s the total number of priests jumped from 480 to over 1500—about 35 percent of whom appear to have been Irish. Irish prelates defined the position of the Catholic Church on every major issue during the nineteenth century: trusteeship of Catholic parish churches and the Catholic position on slavery as a political problem outside of the purview of religious doctrine. During the Civil War priests and nuns from Ireland operated on both sides. Bishop Patrick N. Lynch of Charleston toured Europe in support of the Confederacy while Archbishop John Hughes of New York attempted to change the opinions of European supporters of the South. Donegal-born Bishop John J. Keane persuaded the Knights of Labor to drop their secret oath, thus avoiding censure of the organization by the Vatican and allowing Catholics to join. Their early arrival and their facility in the English language had assisted the Irish in becoming the leading spokesmen of nineteenth-century American Catholicism. By the end of the century about 50 percent of all bishops were of Irish extraction, and only four out of seventeen cardinals had not been Irish.

As Catholic Irish and German immigrants arrived in great numbers, the church began the establishment of a vast network of ancillary services—elementary schools, high schools, universities, hospitals, asylums, and orphanages—all across the country. The uniquely Irish parish developed over the same period, each led by Irish priests who went to heroic efforts to provide their flocks with a variety of services. The cornerstone of the parish was the school, established to guard children against exposure to Protestant teaching. But Catholic schools met only limited success in educating immigrant children. In New York, the great center of Catholic education, by the late 1850s the Catholic school system was valued at two million dollars, yet only one in three of all Irish immigrant children was attending. By the time the Irish and others succeeded in forcing laws limiting the use of the Protestant Bible in public schools, shortly after mid-century in most places, Irish church leaders continued to expand the number of Catholic schools, adding a network of high schools and colleges, in the belief that such schools offered a better preparation for life. By 1900 Catholic institutions of higher education were providing a substantial proportion of the advanced education of Irish Catholic children.

Despite heroic efforts by the Catholic Church to assist Irish immigrants, the evidence suggests a high rate of departures from the church. As was the case in pre-Famine Ireland, Irish attendance at Sunday Mass in the New World was less than perfect. It has been estimated that only about 50 percent, at best, of Irish Catholics attended Mass regularly even in areas of their heaviest representation in East Coast cities. Nevertheless, for the great majority of Irish the church was the most important and familiar institution in their lives. Irishmen working in mining camps, on railroad construction crews or serving in the military on remote frontier outposts, who rarely attended Mass, invariably sent for a priest when one of their comrades was sick or dying. And their priests responded: one Irish priest from the Sacramento, California, diocese in the 1860s rode over a thousand miles through dangerous country to aid a dying Irishman. In addition to their regular parish duties, Irish priests in the Far West and elsewhere spent much of their time providing an extensive network of support for Irish immigrants: they ran a location service which in response to queries from Irish families throughout the United States or in Ireland attempted to find Irish immigrants who had disappeared on the journey west. They also sought out good land at the request of prospective Irish settlers; they buried the dead, especially after the periodic cholera epidemics, and did their best to inform relatives at home or in Ireland; and they collected funds for the poor in Ireland.

## Politics/Nationalism

The background in Ireland was a decided advantage in preparing newcomers for American politics. Increasing literacy in English, participation in Daniel O'Connell's Catholic Association, and the tithe war against the British government and the established church brought politics into the lives of the vast majority of the rural population. The entire rural population became intensely involved in campaigns: voter and non-voter turned up at the hustings to encourage their candidate and to intimidate political opponents. The expansion of the franchise in American cities in the early nineteenth century, in many ways a direct result of Irish participation in politics, and the emerging spatial divisions of the industrial city created neighborhoods that could be exploited politically. The personal reciprocal relationships on which the power of the Irish political boss and his political machine were based harked back to the face-to-face world of the Irish village with their enduring loyalties to one's neighbors and customary bonds based on obligations of dependency between individuals and families. As Irish political leaders moved to take advantage of the situation, they were confronted, often violently, by Americans determined not to lose control of their communities. The most extreme, and to date one of the most ignored, reactions to Irish political success in any American city was that of the 7,000-strong private army of the Grand Committee of Vigilance of San Francisco, which included the bulk of the respectable citizens and all of the Protestant ministers in the city save one. The committee seized power in 1856 in the only armed *coup d'état* in American history, executed four individuals and deported or "warned out" hundreds of others from the city. The great majority of its victims were Irish-American political organizers and their confederates. Through their political arm, the People's Party, the vigilantes monopolized San Francisco city government for twenty years. The widespread support for these activities across the country, coupled with the enthusiastic approval of the violence by almost all nineteenth-century writers, suggests that the committee tapped an impulse deep in the psyche of members of the larger society.

The Irish used their power in politics to project their concern for developments in their native land. Throughout the 1790s the American Society of United Irishmen established branches in all major cities. Daniel O'Connell received a great deal of support from a variety of Irish-American associations in his campaign for Catholic Emancipation during the 1820s and in his 1840s campaign to repeal the Act of Union joining Ireland to Great Britain. The Young Ireland Rebellion of 1848 inspired Irish Republican clubs in many Irish cities. But it was the Famine refugees who established the most lasting and effective nationalist organization, the Fenians, named after a mythical band of Irish warriors and dedicated to freeing Ireland by military means if necessary. It was founded in 1857 by two former Young Irelanders, John O'Mahony of New York and James Stephans of Dublin. The coming of the Civil War provided the young Fenians with an opportunity to gain valuable military experience, to win the respect of the United States government, and, for the great numbers of Irish in the North, to strike a blow against England which was widely seen as advocating the Southern cause.

There are no exact figures on the Irish-born who served in the Civil War. It does appear however that Ireland provided the largest number of foreign-born troops in the Southern or Confederate Army and tied with Germany as the source of the largest immigrant group in the Northern or Unionist forces. The Irish overwhelmingly served the Union. Irish regiments were raised in Pennsylvania, Ohio, Indiana, Illinois and Iowa. At least nine Irish-born generals served the North: Curtin, Sweeny, Mulholland, Smyth, Shields, Kearney, Corcoran, Guiney and Meagher. On the Southern side, Alabama, Georgia, Missouri, North Carolina, South Carolina, Tennessee, Texas and Virginia raised Irish units and at least five generals were Irish-born: Cleburne, Finnegan, Hagan, Land and Moore. Most Irish on both sides served in units of mixed nationality. The Irish were noted as fierce fighters in both North and South. The courage of the Irish Brigade in the Union Army at the bloody Battle of Fredericksburg, where two-thirds of the unit were lost, was admired even by the *London Times*. They frequently went into battle with sprigs of green in their caps. And they often recognized each other across the battle lines. As they buried their dead on the night after the carnage at Fredericksburg, the Irish on both sides joined across the hills in a common chorus of "Dear old Ireland! Brave old Ireland! Ireland! boys hurrah!"

The Fenian attempts to free Ireland following the Civil War were anticlimactic and handicapped by a split in the organization. By 1870 the Fenians had faded into insignificance to be replaced by Clan na Gael or United Brotherhood that in 1877 joined with the Irish Republican Brotherhood in the United Kingdom to organize a joint revolutionary directory which attempted to form alliances with England's enemies. Various nationalist groups in the United States joined with peasants and Home Rulers in Ireland to support Charles Stewart Parnell in his New Departure in the 1880s. When this alliance floundered towards the end of the decade, Irish nationalists spent the next two decades restoring the bonds that underlaid the New Departure. The Easter Rising of 1916 in Dublin and the British executions of the ringleaders led to widespread attacks by the Irish-American press on President Wilson, which had little overall impact. Irish-American voters ignored the issue and supported Wilson in the 1916 campaign. In 1919–1920, Priomh Aire (first minister) Eamon de Valera of Sinn Fein's governing body, Dail Eireann, traveled to America to raise funds and to mobilize Irish-American support for the cause at home and did much to advance his own position at the time when his fellow countrymen were fighting the Black and Tan war at home. Overall, de Valera's visit intensified divisions among Irish-American organizations and greatly weakened Irish-American influence on President Wilson and in American political affairs.

## Labor Unions/Occupations

Heavy Irish involvement in labor unions was facilitated in the early days by their penchant to band together in secret societies to project their interests. Already by the 1830s Irish workers on the Chesapeake and Ohio Canal banded into secret societies and fought each other. Similar secret societies caused much violence among Irish laborers working on the Illinois Central Railroad in the 1850s. Irish-born Martin Burke became a co-founder of the first national organization of coal miners in 1861, the American Miners Association. Other Irish labor leaders rapidly followed: William McLaughlin of the Shoemakers Union; John Siney of the Anthracite Miners Union; J. P. McDonnell of the International Labor Union; and Dennis Kearney of the California Workingmen's Union. About one-third of all employees who struck against major East Coast railroad lines in 1877 were Irish, thus underscoring the popularity of labor unions with Irish immigrants. The use of the boycott by New York labor in the 1880s was credited to Irish immigrants who had used the weapon as a form of social ostracism at home. Labor violence involving the Irish over the 1870s and 1880s shocked the prominent Irish into a recognition of the dire needs of many of their countrymen.

In the Pennsylvania coal fields a secret organization, the Molly Maguires, resorted to violent methods to deal with frightful working conditions. A series of spectacular trials followed in which the Mollies were credited with murdering nine men and twenty Irishmen were convicted and executed. But labor conditions slowly improved, to a large degree due to men and women of Irish birth or extraction who in the early twentieth century could be found across the entire spectrum of the American labor movement. By 1900 Irish immigrants or their descendants held the presidencies of over 50 of the 110 unions in the American Federation of Labor.

The prominent and expanding Irish role in labor organization over the nineteenth century went hand-in-hand with discernible, though modest, progress of the group up the occupational scale. Irish immigrants in 1850 were confined to a relatively small number of occupations. The great majority on the lower levels of society worked as casual laborers; in the middle ranges some more fortunate Irish worked as bartenders, soldiers, carpenterers and blacksmiths or in the ranks of small proprietors, most often as liquor dealers or owners of boardinghouses; the few Irish on the white-collar levels generally worked as clerks, clergymen or schoolteachers. By the turn of the century, reflecting the expansion in the job market, the Irish had scattered into a wide variety of jobs, the majority above the unskilled laboring level which now employed only one in five Irish. Eleven percent of America's policemen and longshoremen were Irish-born and 6 percent of all Irish owned their own businesses. Overall, one in ten Irish were employed as farmers in 1870 and 9 percent of the group worked as farm laborers.

Despite the rapid movement of large numbers of impoverished Irish in all parts of the country, migration from the East Coast, across the entire continent, was generally composed of the young, skilled, literate and generally resourceful newcomers. In 1850 San Francisco 14 percent of Irish immigrants were in white-collar jobs compared with 6 percent in Boston. Irish women were more likely to remain on the East Coast. Sacramento and Los Angeles had about ten Irishmen for every Irishwoman. In Butte, Montana, in 1900 Irish men outnumbered Irish women by three to two. Everywhere, Irish women were concentrated in a narrower range of jobs than men. In 1850, Irish women on the East and West coasts were most often employed in domestic service. In 1900, almost 2 percent of all employed Irish women, including many Catholic nuns, worked as teachers. By 1920 Irish women displayed little of the occupational diversity of their menfolk, as they provided 81 percent of all domestic servants in the United States.

The Irish concentration on the bottom of the occupational scale and their dismal record of improving their jobs further underscored the poor preparation of most Irish newcomers for life in the United States. The Irish were the only immigrant group whose record of occupational mobility was as poor as that of American Blacks during the late nineteenth century. In Boston, the native-born and other immigrant groups outperformed Irish immigrants in the rate of movement up the occupational scale. Those Irish who did well from the day of arrival, and the great majority of those who moved up the occupational scale, almost invariably came from the more prosperous element of the home society. Many of the Irish who moved from the East Coast improved their occupational status, generally by becoming farmers or proprietors of small businesses. Although we lack studies of the job experiences of Irish women, scattered reports show that Irish women who moved from the East Coast frequently improved their social standing by marrying wealthy non-Irishmen, especially in the Far West.

## Theater/Literature/Sports

Dublin-born playwright and actor Dion Boucicault, the most popular playwright of his day, made a significant contribution to the improving Irish image when he launched a campaign all across the United States to reverse the long-established English theater stereotype of the stage Irishman to a charming and beguiling person with a native intelligence and resourcefulness—an image which achieved an enormous and permanent popularity with American audiences. With their humorous portrayal of the New York Irish in the popular "Mulligan Series," Edward Harrigan and Anthony Hart made a major contribution to the development of the American musical. Irish-born Victor Herbert became the most prominent composer of American light opera in the 1880s. By 1910 Irish plays and musicals retained their popularity, but the stage Irishman was gone, the victim of Boucicault and other playwrights and an all-out campaign by the Ancient Order of Hibernians. The award of the 1920 Pulitzer Prize to the son of an Irish immigrant, Eugene O'Neill, for his play *Beyond the Horizon* signaled the end of an era. And in 1936 O'Neill won the Nobel prize for literature.

In literature by the middle of the nineteenth century, defensive works like William James MacNeven's *Pieces of Irish History* (1807) and Mathew Carey's *Ireland Vindicated* (1819), both of which had attempted to refute Protestant accusations of Catholic inferiority, were gone. Writers of Irish birth or Irish parentage now began to respond to the divisions between Irish immigrants and the host society by producing a "literature of accommodation"—novels and poems covering Irish themes and widely read by Americans. Mary Anne Sadlier, a native of County Cavan, expressed satisfaction with the misfortunes of a lapsed Catholic in *The Blakes and the Flanagans* (1855). Less bitter was the popular work *Shandy McGuire* (1851) by Donegal-born Father John Boyce (pseudonym, Paul Peppergrass). Equally as popular were the poems of Irish-born John Boyle O'Reilly, *Songs, Legends, and Ballads* (1878) and *The Statues in the Block* (1881). Among the second-generation Irish writers who made a remarkable impact were Louise Imogen Guiney with *Roadside Harp* (1893) and *Patrins* (1897); and Katherine Eleanor Conway with *On the Sunrise Slope* (1881). O'Reilly, Guiney, and Conway played an important role as cultural ambassadors from the Irish-American society to the more literate segment of society.

Respect for physical endurance in Irish society made sports popular with Irish-Americans. The Irish played a prominent role in boxing since its inception as an organized sport. Tipperary native John Morrissey became heavyweight champion of America after a career as a street fighter. Irish-born Paddy Ryan, the first boxer ever to win the heavyweight championship in his first fight, was defeated in 1882 by John L. Sullivan, a second-generation Irish-American who was defeated in turn ten years later by a San Franciscan of Irish parentage, James J. Corbett. Irish boxers were so popular by the end of the nineteenth century that other immigrant groups assumed Hibernian names before embarking on a career in the ring. Irish players and managers of Irish ancestry contributed to the development of baseball as a national sport. In the twentieth century, Catholic colleges with large Irish student bodies, such as Notre Dame, Fordham, Holy Cross and Boston College, earned football fame.

### IRISH AND AMERICAN: ACCEPTANCE

By 1920 the Irish were accepted members of the American social family. Despite the initial concentration of the great majority of Irish newcomers over the late-nineteenth century on the bottom of the occupational scale and their role as the only immigrant group whose record of occupational mobility was as poor as that of American Blacks, Irish immigrants made choices which even-

tually ensured that their children would move up the occupational scale far more rapidly than American Blacks and that their descendants would enjoy the same patterns of achievement as members of the larger society. By 1920 a great many descendants of earlier Irish arrivals were scattered throughout the country as Americans of Irish descent came to outnumber the Irish-born by three to one. Immigrants or their children could be found on all levels of American society, a significant proportion of professional and white-collar Americans boasted an Irish background. A great many Irish-American families had made the journey from Irish neighborhoods to the expanding white-collar suburbs, albeit over at least two generations, probably the slowest such journey among all nineteenth-century immigrants. Men of Irish background were well represented in Catholic colleges such as Notre Dame, Fordham, Holy Cross and Boston College. The Irish sportsman was synonymous with the American sportsman, particularly in boxing and baseball. Unnoticed by the majority of the larger society was the steady stream of post-World War I Irish immigrants, six out of ten from an unskilled rural background at home, who settled among the "shanty" Irish neighborhoods. Although these newcomers left a far more developed home society than the Famine refugees, the shock of arrival in a society rapidly becoming the most highly developed industrial society in the world was no less formidable. By 1920 the improved acceptance of the Irish in America and the wide range of well-developed organizations in Irish neighborhoods made the lot of new arrivals far less difficult than the experience of their countrymen and women who had arrived earlier.

### IRELAND, 1922–1965

The great agricultural boom of the World War I period collapsed in 1920. The expectation that independence would improve conditions of life throughout Ireland proved ill-founded. Members of the more respectable society generally held their own economically, with larger farmers improving their situation. The increase in scale of farm operations which began with the Great Famine continued: The percentage of holdings over fifty acres increased over the 1920s to reach 23 percent in 1931, 29 percent in 1960, and finally 33 percent in 1980. Those on the low end of the occupational structure confronted an increased level of deprivation and poverty. Poet William Butler Yeats' pre-Independence warning to a roadside laborer that after the struggle for freedom "you shall still break stone" proved remarkably prescient. Attempts by the diminishing but still substantial group of landless rural laborers to unionize in the 1920s failed dismally in the face of hostility by the government, denunciation by the Catholic Church, the opposition by middling and larger farmers, and by elements of the Irish Republican Army (IRA), especially in County Cork, who successfully fought efforts by small farmers and laborers to "cash in on the work of the IRA."

Between 1921 and 1961, with the exception of a modest increase of around 5,000 persons between 1946 and 1951, the decline in population that began with the Great Famine continued unabated. The patterns of late marriages which had begun with the Great Famine, high birth-rate within marriage and advanced age at marriage continued. By 1929 the Irish age of marriage was the highest in the world, reaching almost 35 for men and 29 for women. Twenty-four percent of the female population of the Irish Free state were not married by the age of 45, that is, when they were past the age of child-bearing. This was offset by the birth-rate, which in the late thirties was the highest in the developed world. Despite a small decline in these figures by 1946 Ireland still led the world in age at marriage and in the proportion of individuals unmarried at all ages; and at the same time one-third of all farmers were over 65 years of age. This was not a recipe for modernization or change. Nevertheless, the birth rate remained consistently higher than the death rate. A positive natural increase took place which was in turn more than offset by a high rate of emigration. Thus the population continued to decline from 2.97 million in 1926 to 2.81 million in 1961.

Poverty, lack of jobs, housing shortages, the increasing age at marriage, and the departures overseas of the young were all related. The worldwide economic collapse of 1929, which took some time to reach Ireland, produced mass unemployment in many areas of the country. Between 1926 and 1961 jobs in agriculture declined by 272,303 while 101,828 new jobs were created in other sectors of the economy, for a net loss of 170,475. The impact on rural and urban areas was obvious. By 1935 unemployment was twice as high as it had been a decade before. After a period of decline in the late 1930s which lasted up to 1945, the economy expanded rapidly with the end of the war. But the 1950s saw the beginning of a period of economic stagnation and the lack of jobs became critical in both rural and urban areas. As had been the case since independence, government ministers remained on the sidelines "watching the situation carefully." Nevertheless, an expanding network of self-help clubs and unemployment organizations appeared—the most well-known of which were the Mount Street Club, the Dublin Unemployed Association, and the Unemployed Protest Committee. Few were moved by the frequently published newspaper pictures of Mount Street Club members, with emaciated physiques and missing teeth, digging ditches in desolate fields in scenes strikingly reminiscent of Maguire and his men in Patrick Kavanagh's stunning poem of the period, *The Great Hunger*. Despite the initiation of efforts to move Dublin's poor out of frightful tenement conditions to new suburban estates in Drimnagh, Crumlin and Cabra, and an attempt to eliminate one of the highest rates of tuberculosis in the world, no Irish government before the late 1950s saw fit to significantly expand the Victorian health services, increase the meager old-age pensions (indeed they were cut for several years) or to extend the minimal unemployment insurance program. It was clear that politicians of all the major parties had come to accept emigration rather than governmental action as the solution to a national problem.

UNITED STATES, 1920–1965

A strong surge in emigration to the U.S. took place from 1920 to 1927, the result of delayed departures following the abandonment of World War I restrictions and a decline in domestic jobs because of a slump in agricultural prices in Ireland which lasted until 1927. An improvement in the Irish agricultural market provided jobs at home just as conditions for newly arrived Irish in the United States became increasingly difficult. By 1930, the movement of American Blacks from the rural South to industrial cities, the arrival of immigrants from Southern and Eastern Europe and intensified restrictions on emigrants to the United States over the Great Depression affected the Irish. And during the Great Depression more Irish went home than arrived in the United States, a reversal of movement not seen again until 1996 and 1997. During World War II the great majority of Irish emigrants moved to England to serve in the armed forces or to work in war-related industries. The level of departures grew rapidly over the 1950s to reach its highest levels since the 1880s. Of the 502,000 persons between the age of 10 and 19 in the 1951 census, only 303,000 remained in the country ten years later. In all, between 1921 and 1961 about 900,000 Irish emigrated.

Nevertheless, Americans of Irish birth and of Irish parentage declined steadily after 1920. The traditional concentration of Irish in urban areas increased over the twentieth century. New York remained the largest Irish city in the country. By 1970 three out of four Irish immigrants resided along the East Coast. The 10 percent of the group who lived on the West Coast by 1970 were significantly better educated than their countrymen on the East Coast. Irish-born males over twenty-five years of age in major California cities boasted an average of twelve years of education as compared with nine years of education for the same age group in East Coast cities.

The dispersal of Irish immigrants and their children throughout the occupational structure and up the occupational ladder continued apace after 1922. As noted in Table 4, by mid-century 24 percent of Irish-born men were in white-collar jobs. As had been the case for some time, clergymen were well represented in the slightly more than 4 percent of Irishmen in the professional ranks. About 73 percent of all Irishmen in America in 1950 labored on the blue-collar levels. Among the semi-skilled and service workers the Irish provided a great many porters, cleaners, firemen and policemen. While the children of Irish parents seemed to have achieved significant upward mobility, as noted in Table 4, compared with other immigrant groups, especially English-speaking newcomers, the achievement of this second generation was in fact rather modest. One of the more striking achievements was the significant movement of the children of Irish newcomers into professional jobs, generally as accountants, clergymen or lawyers. Second-generation women, scattered throughout the occupational structure, were well represented in law, engineering, teaching and clerical work. The Irish and their children were making significant inroads into American society.

The impact of Irish culture on the Irish-American family is discernible up into the twentieth century, but falls off signifi-

Table 4. Occupational distribution of Irish-born males and their sons in 1950, compared with males of Irish ancestry and the U.S. male population in 1969, by percentage.

|  | 1950 | | 1969 | |
|---|---|---|---|---|
|  | *Irish-Born* | *Sons: Second Generation* | *Irish Ancestry* | *U.S. Population* |
| Professional | 4.2 | 9.5 | 14.1 | 13.6 |
| Managers | 7.6 | 11.6 | 19.1 | 17.0 |
| Clerks | 8.3 | 13.0 | 8.5 | 7.0 |
| Salesmen | 3.8 | 7.5 | 6.3 | 5.4 |
| Craftsmen | 20.6 | 19.3 | 20.8 | 20.1 |
| Operatives | 19.1 | 16.5 | 17.9 | 20.4 |
| Service Workers | 18.8 | 11.0 | 6.0 | 6.7 |
| Farm Laborers | 0.8 | 0.9 | 1.0 | 2.0 |
| Laborers | 13.7 | 5.9 | 6.1 | 7.5 |

*Source:* Data for 1950 are computed from special samples from the 1950 U.S. Census; for 1969 from the U.S. Bureau of the Census, *Current Population Report,* Series P-20, no. 221, *Characteristics of the Population by Ethnic Origin, November 1969* (Washington, D.C., 1971), Table 15; U.S. male sample for 1969 computed from U.S. Department of Labor, Bureau of Labor Statistics, *Handbook of Labor Statistics* (Washington, D.C., 1973), Table 6.

steadily increased for other groups over the past quarter century. It is significant in any evaluation of the relative strength of Irish migrant streams across the Atlantic that the overwhelming majority of Irish immigrants since 1986 have remained in the United States and are now in a position to encourage further emigration by arranging the follow-up movement of members of their immediate families under the various immigrant preferences in U.S. immigration law. The Irish influx since 1986, therefore, has succeeded not only in reviving the Irish community in America but also in setting up the conditions for a steady follow-up of Irish emigration to the U.S. for the foreseeable future.

### CONCLUSION

The Irish presence in the United States has been so long and so varied that it touches all aspects of the American world. The background and education of Irish immigrants at the point of origin, the social and economic structure of the host community at the destination, and the timing of their arrival are among the factors explaining the wide variations we encounter in trying to summarize the Irish-American experience. On the high end of the social ladder we see the grandson of a Famine immigrant move to the White House, while Americans of Irish ancestry are more likely than other Americans to be found in the professional and managerial ranks of the job structure. On the other end of the ladder, however, 9 percent of Americans of Irish ancestry live below the poverty level—the highest such rate for Americans of any European background. Similarly, the range of assimilation by Americans of Scotch-Irish ancestry is reflected in the fact that, in addition to their remarkable contributions to community formation, politics and education in early America and the fact that fourteen American presidents, including the present occupant of the White House, Bill Clinton, claim a Scotch-Irish background, many of the poorest and most disadvantaged members of the white American population, the people of the Appalachian mountain states, quite validly claim the same ancestry. We have barely scratched the surface in attempting to understand the complexity of the process that produced such variations.

Irish emigration at once fostered the preservation of the social and economic order at home just as it helped the transformation of society in America. In Ireland, emigration allowed the maintenance and strengthening of the status quo despite the Great Famine, the elimination of the landlords, the successful struggle for independence, the vicissitudes of life in the 1930s and 1940s in Ireland, the social and economic crisis of the 1950s and—to an extent that has yet to be fully realized—the downturn of the 1980s. In the United States, the Irish became the first major immigrant group to transform American society. Their facility in the English language and their familiarity with representative politics allowed them to translate cultural and religious cohesion into organizations that profoundly influenced American politics, labor organizations, the Catholic Church and the Presbyterian Church at a time when these institutions were in the early stages of development. At home, emigration was vital in allowing the postponement of fundamental social and economic change. In America, the interaction between the Irish and the host society accelerated the emergence of a diverse and democratic America, capable of melding the world's most kaleidoscopic collection of races and peoples into the most powerful nation in the world.

Given the increasing level of contact between Ireland and the U.S., the broad and expanding U.S. participation in the Irish economy, the growing numbers of students and visitors who cross the Atlantic, the rapid improvements in the range and speed of electronic communications best seen in use of the internet, the increasing availability of American literature, films, news programs and other media in Ireland, it is possible that the idea of America may be as important to future generations in Ireland as America the place was to past generations. We already saw the seeds of such a development in the economic forces unleashed by the acceptance of American ideas as a result of the Marshall Plan, in the importance of the American Civil Rights movement in inspiring disadvantaged Catholics in Northern Ireland, in the key role played by the grandson of a Protestant emigrant from County Antrim, former U.S. Senator George Mitchell, in bringing all factions on the island together to make peace, and in the January 1999 passage of a law providing 12,000 U.S. visas for a period of three years to Irish nationals from disadvantaged counties on both sides of the border to allow them to "kick start" their lives by learning American job skills. As Ireland moves to confront the challenges of the millennium in an increasingly diverse European Community, it is fitting that the Irish at home and abroad should welcome, in the words of former Irish President. Mary Robinson, "a dialogue with our own diversity" and strive to come to grips with the critical role emigration has played in the home society and in the great adventure of the Irish people in America.

*See* Achievement of the Irish; Scots Irish; Emigration (5 entries); Labor Movement; Ireland: 1798–1998

William Forbes Adams, *Ireland and Irish Emigration to the New World* (New Haven, 1932).

Patrick J. Blessing, "The Irish," In *Harvard Encyclopedia of American Ethnic Groups*, ed., Stephan Thernstrom (Cambridge, 1980).

———, *The Irish in America: A Guide to the Literature and the Manuscript Collections* (Washington, D.C., 1992).

K. H. Connell, *The Population of Ireland, 1750–1845* (Oxford, 1950).

Mary P. Corcoran, *Irish Illegals: Transients between Two Societies* (Westport, Conn., 1993).

Alexis de Tocqueville, *Democracy in America* (Unabridged). 2 vols., 1839 (Reprint, New York, 1990).

Jay P. Dolan, *The Immigrant Church* (Baltimore, 1975).

David M. Emmons, *The Butte Irish: Class and Ethnicity in an American Mining Town, 1875–1925* (Urbana, 1989).

T. W. Freeman, *Pre-Famine Ireland: A Study in Historical Geography* (Manchester, 1957).

Oscar Handlin, *Boston's Immigrants* (New York, 1951).

Maldwyn A. Jones, "Scotch Irish," in *Harvard Encyclopedia of American Ethnic Groups*, ed., Stephen Thernstrom (Cambridge, 1980).

Robert E. Kennedy, *The Irish: Emigration, Marriage, and Fertility* (Berkeley, 1973).

J. J. Lee, *Ireland 1912–1985* (New York, 1989).

Audrey Lockhart, *Some Aspects of Emigration from Ireland to the North American Colonies between 1660 and 1775* (New York, 1976).

Cormac Ó Gráda, *Ireland: A New Economic History, 1780–1939* (Oxford, 1994).

Arnold Schrier, *Ireland and the American Emigration, 1850–1900* (Minnesota, 1958).

Stephan Thernstrom, *Poverty and Progress* (Cambridge, 1964).

———, *The Other Bostonians* (Cambridge, 1973).

PATRICK J. BLESSING

## IRISH LANGUAGE IN THE U.S.

Irish belongs to the Celtic branch of the Indo-European language family. It is closely related to Manx and Scottish Gaelic and more distantly related to Welsh, Breton and Cornish. The earliest remains of Irish are the Ogham inscriptions dating from ca. 400–600 A.D. found on some 300 stones in Ireland. With the advent of Christianity at the time of St. Patrick (ca. 432) came Latin learning and, by the late sixth century, the Latin alphabet was being used to write Irish. Irish is thus the oldest written vernacular of Western Europe. During the Middle Ages Irish language and literature flourished. But centuries of foreign oppression reduced Irish to a language spoken only in the most remote parts of Ireland and generally by the poorer classes of the population. The low status Irish came to have in Ireland was to be carried over to this country and led to the language being largely ignored by Irish-American leaders in the Church and in academe.

Irish speakers have undoubtedly been coming to America since early colonial days, but references are scarce. One of the earliest citations of the use of Irish on this continent was in the case of Goody Glover, a poor Irish washerwoman in Boston who was accused of being a witch and put on trial in 1688. At the trial, we are told, "the court could have no answers from her, but in the Irish; which was her native language, although she understood English very well." This poor unfortunate Irish-speaking woman was found guilty and was hanged as a witch in Boston in 1688.

In the eighteenth century evidence for Irish speakers can be found among a small number of advertisements published for runaway servants such as this one from the *Virginia Gazette* May 16, 1771:

> RUN away from the Subscriber, in *Bedford* County on *Great Falling* River, an *Irish* Servant Man named MICHAEL KELLY, about five Feet five Inches high, with short black Hair, wears a cut brown Wig, a blue Broadcloth Coat, spotted Flannel Jacket, and a Pair of old patched Breeches. Also an *Irish* Servant Woman named MARGARET KELLY, Wife to the said *Michael*. She wore a blue Calimanco Gown and Petticoat. They both speak Irish, but neither of them are known to speak English. I will give FIVE POUNDS on their being delivered to me, and FIFTY SHILLINGS if they are secured in any Jail in this Colony, upon Information of the same given to WILLIAM HAYTH.

In the early days of the United States of America, there are several references to the Irish language, including the fact that it was in use among a considerable number of George Washington's troops. Speaking in the House of Commons on April 2, 1784, about the loss of the American colonies, Luke Gardiner, Lord Mountjoy said, "America was lost through the Irish emigrants. . . . I have been assured on the best authority that the Irish language was commonly spoken in the American ranks." He obtained this information from an army officer who had fought in Pennsylvania. There were also some Irish speakers on the British side in the American Revolution such as Admiral Moriarity of West Kerry who forsook his study for the priesthood in France, joined the British Navy, changed his religion, made his way up through the ranks and participated in the Battle of Quebec. A song of praise in Irish was composed welcoming him home to Ireland.

In the early days of the Republic references can be found to clergymen who spoke Irish. Thus Charles Whelan, the first Catholic pastor in New York City after the Revolution, is described as being more fluent in Gaelic and French than in English. Fr. Philip Lariscy, a Tipperary native, spent several years in

Newfoundland and Nova Scotia before traveling to Boston, where he preached in Irish in 1818. He later moved on to New York, Brooklyn and Philadelphia where he was in great demand for his ability to hear confessions in Irish. Irish laborers in Lowell, Massachusetts in the 1820s requested and received the services of Irish-speaking priests. Fr. Jeremiah O'Callaghan, upon his arrival in this country, preached in Irish in the Cathedral in Boston in July 1830 before proceeding to the Vermont Missions.

There were at least a few learned and literate Irish speakers, both among the clergy and the laity, here in the early nineteenth century. Dr. William MacNeven, who came to New York after 1798, is said to have translated Ossianic manuscripts from Gaelic while serving time in a Scottish prison for his connection with the United Irishmen. Matthias O'Conway was a Galway-born linguist and interpreter in Philadelphia who, starting in the first decades of the nineteenth century, worked for more than thirty years on an Irish dictionary which was unfinished at the time of his death in 1842 and was large enough to fill a trunk. It was held by the American Catholic Historical Society until 1977 when it was sent to the National Library of Ireland. The Cork native, Bishop John England of Charleston, South Carolina, is credited with supplying the Irish translation of the phrase that was inscribed on the monument erected to Thomas A. Emmet in St. Paul's Churchyard in lower Manhattan in 1830. The Irish inscription on the Emmet monument, now (1998) nearly illegible, is given by O'Donovan Rossa in his book *Rossa's Recollections:* "Do mhiannaig se ard-mhathas chum tir a bhreith; Do thug se clu, a's fuair se moladh a dtir a bhais" (He contemplated great good for the land of his birth / He shed lustre, and received commendation in the land of his decease).

The only pre-Famine Irish language writer of note in the United States was Patrick Condon (Pádraig Phiaris Cúndún), a monoglot but literate Irish speaker. Born near Ballymacoda, Co. Cork, in 1777, Condon emigrated with his family to the Utica, New York, area in 1826. After working extremely hard for seven years to pay completely for his farm, he started writing letters and poems home telling about life in the United States. Condon's first letter, written to Bartholomew Chapel in 1834, tells about his new home: "I have a fine farm free forever, no one can ask me for rent. Our family can eat their fill of bread, meat, butter and milk any day we want all year and so I think it is better here than to stay in Ireland without land, food or clothing. It is a pity that the foolish Irish stay in Ireland. Look at the English and Germans. They come here in droves every year . . . they buy land and live like lords . . .". Like many immigrants, Condon came to have mixed feelings about his new land and he constantly longed for Ireland. His longest poem "An Account of the Western Regions" (Aiste na n-Iarthar) details all the faults of the new land and its people but begrudgingly admits the prosperity to be found there:

> Dá mhéid do mholaim a gcothrom 's a gcóisir,
> A ndram is a ndeocha is a mborrathuirc feóla,
> B'fhearr liom agam i bhfearann tsliocht Bhreógain
> Prátaí is salann cé dealbh an lón iad.
>
> (As much as I praise their fairness and parties,
> their liquor, drinks and mammoth slabs of meat,
> I would prefer to have, poor fare though it be,
> potatoes and salt in the land of Ireland.)

Unlike Condon, most Irish speakers who landed on these shores were illiterate in their native language and thus have left nearly no trace of their linguistic presence here. This is especially true of the thousands of poor Irish speakers who arrived during and after the Famine. Many of them were met at the docks by dishonest Irish-speaking "runners" who would try to steer the naïve newcomers to lodgings where they would be charged exorbitant rates. An indication of official lack of recognition of the Irish language can be seen in the legislation enacted by New York State in 1848, at the height of the Famine, to protect new arrivals from unscrupulous boarding-house operators. This legislation stipulated that: "Every keeper of such boarding house shall under a penalty of fifty dollars cause to be kept conspicuously posted in the public rooms of such house in the English, German, Dutch, French and Welsh language a list of the rates of prices which will be charged immigrants per day and week for boarding and lodging and also the rates for separate meals." The Irish language is not even mentioned although ten times more Irish speakers than Welsh speakers were entering this country in those years. Ironically, the best evidence for the large number of Irish-speaking immigrants at this time comes from the reports of organizations, such as the American Protestant Society and the American and Foreign Christian Union, who hired Irish-speaking converts to Protestantism to bring the Gospel in Irish to their Catholic compatriots and who claimed that five-eighths of the Irish population of New York spoke Irish. The published reports of the AFCU relate that men like Patrick J. Leo, Michael Welsh, Thomas Jordan, Jeremiah Murray and George MacNamara (an ex-Catholic priest, ordained at Maynooth in 1837) traveled up and down the streets of New York and Brooklyn in the early 1850s preaching the Protestant version of the Gospel to Catholic Irish speakers. There seems to have been no official Catholic counteroffensive to this work and, indeed, the major study on the Catholic Church in New York City at this time, Jay P. Dolan's *The Immigrant Church: New York's Irish and German Catholics, 1815–1865* ignores the Irish language question altogether, although it does deal extensively with the position of the German language vis-à-vis the Church.

The Protestant proselytizers were not the only literate Irish speakers active here in the wake of the Famine. After the unsuccessful rising of 1848, a number of Young Irelanders, including many who were fluent in Irish, fled to exile in the United States. These included Michael Cavanagh, Michael Doheny, John O'Mahony and John T. Rowland. O'Mahony, who was later to be the founder of the Fenians in the U.S., arrived in Brooklyn in 1853 and soon began translating Geoffrey Keating's *History of Ireland* (Forus Feasa ar Éirinn) to English using manuscripts which he received on loan from other Irish immigrants. One of these manuscripts belonged to the widow of James O'Dwyer who may have been the same James O'Dwyer, who, along with his pub "The Daisy" on Duane Street, was praised in a brief poem in Irish printed in the New York *Irish-American* on June 21, 1851, quite possibly the first poem in Irish composed in the United States to find its way into print.

Six years later, on July 25, 1857, the New York *Irish-American* started a new feature "Our Gaelic Department." This was a major undertaking for it meant that the newspaper had to go to the expense and trouble of obtaining a Gaelic font which did not exist in the United States at that time. It should be pointed out that no weekly in Ireland in July 1857 had a Gaelic column. In fact, when the Dublin *Nation* commenced its own Irish column in March 1858, the *Irish-American* proudly noted: "It is a source of no little gratification to us to find that our example has already begun to produce good effects, and that we may now calculate with certainty on a combined, vigorous effort, on both sides of the Atlantic, to rescue from oblivion the venerable tongue of our beloved Fatherland . . ." (April 17, 1858). The first Gaelic editor was apparently John O'Mahony with the assistance of Michael Doheny and Patrick O'Dea. The *Irish-American* Gaelic column would continue, albeit with a few significant breaks, until the paper ceased publication in 1915. Over the course of those decades it produced approximately 1,500 Gaelic columns consisting mainly of Irish poetry taken from manuscripts and books, Gaelic lessons, translations into Irish, but also a significant amount of original writing in Irish, including poetry and letters, as well as a good deal of folklore.

Irish language events on one side of the Atlantic tended to act as catalysts for similar activity on the other side. Such was the case with Irish language societies. After the establishment of the Ossianic Society in Dublin in the early 1850s, a branch of that society was founded in New York in 1856. This group may have been the first to offer Irish classes in North America, although an Irish language society was established somewhat earlier in Wilkes-Barre, Pennsylvania. The teacher of the New York Ossianic society class was David O'Keeffe, who was also busily engaged writing an Irish manuscript at the time. But the activities of this New York society were brought to a close by the Civil War and subsequent deaths of several of its members. In the early 1870s, the New York *Irish World* reported that Irish was being taught at the University of Notre Dame by Brother John Fleming, a native of Gort, Co. Galway. In 1873 another Galwayman, Michael Logan, started an Irish class in Brooklyn. This was followed by the establishment, first in Boston, and then in Brooklyn of Philo-Celtic Societies. News of these organizations may well have encouraged the setting up in Dublin of the Society for the Preservation of the Irish language in 1876. The effects of this event, in turn, rebounded across the Atlantic and by 1878 Gaelic societies were being formed throughout the major cities of the eastern United States. Some fine Irish scholars were connected with these schools, including David O'Keeffe who by this time was known as "the Patriarch." A colleague of his, Daniel Magner, published large amounts of material in the *Irish-American* which he copied painstakingly from manuscripts. In Boston, Michael C. O'Shea and P. J. O'Daly spearheaded the Gaelic movement. One writer estimated that one thousand individuals were attending the various classes in the New York area at this time.

In 1881 Michael Logan founded in Brooklyn *The Gael* (An Gaodhal), a bilingual monthly dedicated to the promotion of the Irish language. No such publication existed in Ireland at the time but its appearance was soon noted in Dublin where in 1882 the Gaelic Union started its own bilingual publication *The Gaelic Journal* (Irisleabhar na Gaedhilge). Logan's *Gael* provided Irish writers in the United States with a forum, in addition to the *Irish-American*. Soon Gaelic columns could also be found in weekly newspapers like the Chicago *Citizen* and the San Francisco *Monitor* and in monthly periodicals such as *Donahoe's Magazine* (Boston) and the bilingual *Irish Echo* (Boston 1886–1894). One writer whose poems are found in many of these journals was Patrick O'Byrne, a native of Donegal, who, writing under the pen name "Pádraic," can be regarded, along with Douglas Hyde, as an originator of modern poetry in Irish. "Pádraic" is also credited with writing the Irish text of the libretto for the first Irish language opera "The Bard and the Knight" (An Bard agus an Fó), written by Paul MacSwiney, a native of Cork, and performed in

Steinway Hall in New York in November 1884. Plays in Irish written by Irish speakers living in New York were performed there in the early years of this century and as late as the 1960s there was an Irish language drama competition among the city's various Gaelic societies. In 1891 Douglas Hyde visited the New York Gaelic societies and was greatly impressed by what he saw. In 1893 in Dublin, Hyde became one of the founders of the Gaelic League, the most dynamic of all the language organizations and the one responsible for the increased recognition given to Irish in the early decades of the twentieth century.

The teaching of Irish on this side of the Atlantic was carried on for decades, and indeed still is, by Gaelic societies throughout the country and frequently these organizations were the only providers of such education. More formal instruction in Irish was offered at the Catholic University of America with the establishment of a Chair of Gaelic in the 1890s funded by the Ancient Order of Hibernians. Harvard also started offering its first Celtic courses in the 1890s under the initiative of Professor Fred Norris Robinson. Evening courses in Irish were available at a small number of institutions from the 1920s to the 1940s, such as Columbia University and Boston College. In more recent years Irish has been increasingly included as a part of Irish Studies programs.

As indicated above Irish speakers have been present in this country from its earliest days but it is extremely difficult to gauge how numerous they have been. Several scholars have estimated that ca. 28% of the Irish immigrants at the time of the Famine were Irish-speaking. In 1878 Thomas O'Neill Russell estimated that there were at least 40,000 Irish speakers in Boston and 1–1½ million Irish speakers in all of North America. So numerous were Irish speakers in the second half of the nineteenth century in places such as Manhattan, Brooklyn, Upper New York State, Pennsylvania and Beaver Island, Michigan, that children learned Irish in the home as their first language. Such was the case of the Honorable Patrick G. Moloney who was born in New York City in 1811 to Irish-speaking parents from County Clare and whose obituary in the *Irish-American* (October 14, 1895) states: "He spoke Irish fluently, and delighted to converse in the old tongue which he had learned from his parents." Archbishop John Neumann of Philadelphia, noted for his ability in languages, is said to have learned Irish in order to be able to hear the confessions of monoglot Irish speakers on his missions across the length and breadth of Pennsylvania. Some areas had particularly high percentages of Irish speakers such as Butte, Montana, where Irish speakers thronged to work in the mines. Portland, Maine's Irish-born population around the turn of the century may have been over 50% Irish-speaking and Irish was spoken by Connemara longshoremen on Portland's docks as late as the 1960s. In the 1890s U.S. Gaelic League reports estimated that there were 400,000 Irish speakers in this country. More recently, the 1970 U.S. census indicated that of the 251,000 Irish born in this country 45,000 or 17% claimed Irish as their mother tongue, a figure far higher than the 1–2% of native Irish speakers in the population of Ireland at that time. In 1980 the U.S. Census language question was changed to "Does this person speak a language other than English at home?" Of 177,000 Irish-born residents, 20,000 or 11.5% said they spoke Irish at home. The 1990 U.S. Census (CPH-L-133) lists 24,040 who claim they speak Irish at home (with no reference to country of birth available), including 72 people who are listed as not speaking English at all. This figure is nearly ten times the 2,743 who speak Welsh and more than ten times the 2,022 who speak Scottish Gaelic in this country. The largest concentration of Irish speakers is in the Northeast where there are 14,021, with 6,577 in New York, 3,600 in Massachusetts, 1,383 in New Jersey and 1,157 in Pennsylvania. Although these figures indicate more Irish speakers in New York, it is in the Boston area that one can still hear Irish being used as a living language by Connemara and Aran immigrants after Mass on Sunday, in a number of pubs and at a variety of social events, such as dances, Gaelic football and hurling matches and currach races.

Today Irish courses are being offered by an ever-increasing number of colleges and organizations in this country. Some groups, like Daltaí na Gaeilge of New Jersey, hold a number of "Gaeltacht" weekends where learners can practice using the language in a near-immersion situation. More and more Americans are also attending summer Irish language courses in Ireland, such as those offered by University College, Galway in Connemara and by Oideas Gael in Donegal. In this country, Harvard Summer School regularly has a course in beginning Irish. In 1995 a new academic organization, the North American Association of Celtic Language Teachers (NAACLT), was formed largely in response to the growth of interest in the teaching of Irish in this country. Interest in Irish has manifested itself outside classes as well. Fordham University in New York has sponsored a bilingual radio program, "Míle Fáilte" (A Thousand Welcomes) presented by Dr. Séamus Blake since the 1970s. The Irish Book Shop in Manhattan not only has an extensive inventory of Irish language books and tapes but actually sells as many books in Irish as it does books in English. A few Irish language books deal with the experience of immigrant life in the U.S. such as Micí MacGabhann's *Rotha Mór an tSaoil* (which appeared in translation as *The Hard Road to Klondike*), Micí Dainín Ó Sé's *A Thig Ná Tit Orm* and *Greenhorn*, and Muiris Ó Bric's recently published *Spotsholas*. The New York *Irish Echo* publishes an Irish article "Macallaí" every week edited by Barra Ó Donnabháin and the New York *Irish People* publishes a weekly Irish lesson. A bilingual quarterly *An Doras* (The Door) is published in Chicago. Irish language material is also found on the Internet and various Gaelic e-mail lists have a majority of American subscribers. Several websites located in this country provide a wealth of Irish language related material, including Gaelic fonts which today can be downloaded with a few keystrokes unlike the days of the nineteenth century when lack of Gaelic font was a major obstacle to printing in Irish. Thus, a language that was pronounced moribund by an older generation of American Irish scholars who were themselves ignorant of it, has been taken up with vigor by a younger generation of Americans who enthusiastically sing the songs of Enya, Clannad and Altan.

David N. Doyle, *Ireland, Irishmen and Revolutionary America, 1760–1820* (Dublin and Cork, 1981).

Thomas Ihde, *The Irish Language in the United States: A Historical, Sociolinguistic, and Applied Linguistic Survey* (Westport, 1994).

Kenneth E. Nilsen, "The Irish Language in Nineteenth Century New York City," in *The Multilingual Apple: Languages in New York City*, eds. Ofelia García and Joshua A. Fishman (New York, 1997): 52–69.

———, "The Irish Language in New York City 1850–1900," in *The New York Irish*, eds., T. Meagher and R. Bayor (Baltimore, 1995): 253–274, 634–638.

———, "Micheál Ó Broin agus Lámhscríbhinní Gaeilge Ollscoil Wisconsin," *Celtica* 22 (1991): 112–118.

———, "Thinking of Monday: The Irish Speakers of Portland, Maine," *Éire-Ireland*, 25 (1991): 6–19.

———, "Collecting Celtic Folklore in the United States," *Proceedings of the First North American Congress of Celtic Studies, 1986* (Ottawa, 1988): 55–74.

———, "Three Irish Manuscripts in Massachusetts," *Harvard Celtic Colloquium*, vol. 5 (1985): 1–21.

Stiofán Ó hAnnracháin, *Go Meiriceá Siar* (Baile Átha Cliath, 1979).

Fionnuala Uí Fhlannagáin, *Mícheál Ó Lócháin agus An Gaodhal* (Baile Átha Cliath, 1990).

KENNETH E. NILSEN

## IRISH SONG IN AMERICA

> Oh Paddy Dear and did you hear
> The news that's going round?
> The shamrock is by law forbid
> To grow on Irish ground.

So begins "The Wearing of the Green," one of the most popular Irish songs in America from the 1860s into the early years of the twentieth century. Yet, although the song certainly is rooted in Ireland and the Rising of '98, it was popularized (and probably largely rewritten) in New York City by the Irish-born playwright/actor Dion Boucicault for his play *Arrah na Pogue* in 1865 (Zimmermann, 167–70).

The song was so well known in nineteenth-century America that it was frequently used as a model for musical comments on specific, localized events, such as the following piece from the large Irish community in Butte, Montana.

> Oh Paddy dear, and did you hear,
> The news that's going round?
> They're firin' all the Corkies,
> That are workin' underground.

Dating from around the turn of the century, this song goes on to complain that "Corkies" (miners from County Cork) were being replaced in the mines by "Bohunks" from Austria (Hand, et al., 26).

Within a decade this parody of "The Wearing of the Green" acquired a chorus from an entirely different song.

> Molly, my Irish Molly,
> My sweet achushla dear,
> I'm nearly off me trolley,
> My Irish Molly, when you are near.

While Boucicault's "Wearing of the Green" has some connection to Ireland, "My Irish Molly O" (1907) by William Jerome and Gene Schwartz was a pure Tin-Pan-Alley confection, its tune more *klezmer* than *ceili* (Hand, et al., 27).

Obviously, the songs of Irish America came from a variety of sources: from the Irish folk and broadside traditions, from the Church, from the popular theater and from the commercial publishing houses on both sides of the Atlantic. The immigrants themselves, of course, made their own songs for the tightly-knit, working-class communities clustered around the canal and railway lines, the lumber camps, the steel mills and the mine patches. Some, such as the song form Butte, clearly showed their Irish antecedents. Others, like "When the Breaker Starts Up Full Time" from the Pennsylvania anthracite region, suggest little that is Irish in either tune or structure. Yet this song speaks eloquently, if somewhat satirically, about the plight of the Irish miner's wife who fantasizes about what she will do with her husband's wages when the mines reopen.

> I'll ne're put me hand in the wash tub,
>    The Chinee man he'll get me trade,
> I'll ne're pick a coal on the dirt bank,
>    I'll buy everything ready made,
> I'll dress all me children like fairies,
>    I'll build up the house neat and fine,
> And we'll move away from the Hungaries
>    When the breaker starts up full time.

The song was collected in 1946 by George Korson, who suggests that it might have been written in the 1880s. Although the song has all the earmarks of a vaudeville song from that period, it has not been found in sheet music or in songsters. It seems to have lived out its life in the coal patch, probably the product of a skilled local tunesmith (Korson, 384–85).

As Robert R. Grimes points out, the Irish parishes of the large industrial cities had their own songs about temperance, Repeal, and politics (139–49). However, in such environments the community-made entertainments of ethnic communities of workers had to compete with the mass of commercial songs pouring from the post-Civil War vaudeville stage and the music publishing houses. Unlike the "Hungaries" and most other European immigrant groups, the Irish, being English speakers, were immediately open to American popular culture, participating both as entertainers and as audience. Therefore, much of Irish-American song culture incorporated commercial music, which included parlor ballads written for the middle-class market on both sides of the Atlantic, pieces from the minstrel and vaudeville stages, and, toward the end of the nineteenth century, formulaic songs churned out by Tin Pan Alley. And while Irish songwriters and performers were very popular by the middle of the nineteenth century, in the area of commercial entertainment anyone, regardless of ethnic background, could write and sing an "Irish" song.

The business of song writing had been given a boost at the end of the eighteenth century when publishers began to issue sheet music to meet a demand created by the increased sales of various keyboard instruments to middle-class households. While the less vulgar types of comic pieces were popular, in a romantic age the vast preference within this growing middle-class market was for sentimental songs. A few Irish songs, largely drawn from the folk tradition, had appeared in sheet music form in America around 1800. However, it was Thomas Moore's *Irish Melodies,* published (and pirated in America) between 1808 and 1834, that created the genre of popular Irish songs.

Moore, a Dublin-born Catholic, was a typical nineteenth-century man of letters; his output included epic poems, novels, biographies and criticism. The fact that it is only his *Irish Melodies* that still retains some popularity suggests that his unique talent lay in song writing. Even today his romantic, late Georgian lyrics can still come alive when sung to the traditional Irish airs for which they were fashioned. Moore's *Melodies* were enormously popular in the United States. Moore's themes—love of Ireland, a powerful feeling of nostalgia, especially the strong sense of loss that permeates so many of his songs—helped to define the Irish parlor ballad for other songwriters who followed in his wake.

A few songwriters, like fellow-Irishman Samuel Lover, whose artistic range was even broader than Moore's, occasionally adapted traditional Irish airs to their lyrics. Lover was particularly successful with his comic songs, such as "Rory O'More," "The Low-Backed Car," and "The Widow Machree," invariably set to jig tunes. Most composers who turned out "Irish" songs, however, preferred to write their own melodies, the best of which only hint at the structure of traditional Irish airs. Some songs were produced by Irish writers: "Killarney" (1861) by Edmund Falconer (Edmund O'Rourke) and Michael William Balfe; "The Rose of Tralee" (1846) with lyrics by William Pembroke Mulchinock; and "The Irish Emigrant" (ca. 1845) with lyrics by Lady Dufferin. Most, however, came from the pens of English writers who produced such favorites as "Come Back to Erin" (1866) by "Claribel" (Charlotte Arlington Barnard), and "Kathleen Mavourneen" (1838) by Frederick N. Crouch. The best of the parlor ballads, including many of Moore's *Melodies,* became part of Irish-American song culture, their popularity lasting into the twentieth century, when singers such as John McCormack recorded many of them.

Scholars tend to grumble about the lack of "authenticity" in these commercial works, written for the Anglo-American bourgeois market, and touted, and accepted, as "Irish" songs. Certainly, compared to the traditional songs of Ireland, even to Irish-American industrial ballads, the highly romantic parlor ballads seem to have little to do with the lives of the Irish immigrants and their children. Yet the Irish in America generally embraced these songs. With their emphasis on loyalty to and nostalgia for Ireland and the recurring themes of leave taking and the death of the beloved, the parlor ballads apparently touched on enough of the Irish immigrant experience, if only superficially, to make them seem "Irish" to Yankee and immigrant alike.

Owning no pianos upon their arrival, most Irish immigrants encountered popular songs at minstrel shows, in variety saloons and in the vaudeville houses, which sprang up after the Civil War. On the popular stage, sentimental songs about Ireland had to compete with rough-and-ready comic pieces about Paddy. At first glance, most of the vaudeville songs, too, seem to lack authenticity, and many are redolent with the stereotype of the stage Irishman. Yet, the growing Irish-American working class accepted most of them.

A few vaudeville songs did speak directly, and in simple language, to feelings and experiences of the immigrants in the audience. In songs about emigration the shamrock became the emblem of faithfulness to Ireland and the family left behind. For example, in "The Three Leaves of Shamrock" (1889) a girl hands the herb to an emigrating neighbor, telling him, "Take them to my brother, for I have no other / And these are the shamrocks from his dear old mother's grave." Other songs addressed the Irish-American's sense of dual nationality. In "That Sweet Bunch of Shamrocks" (1890), the singer makes this comparison:

> The good son loves his mother, tho' devoted to his wife,
> And he will defend them, Even with his life;
> So, I, America darling, would as freely die for thee;
> Though cherishing still old Ireland, and my
>     mother o'er the sea.

A few songs, echoing Fenian rhetoric, promised that the singer would return some day to Ireland with an Irish-American army to set the country free.

Songs such as these, the products of a growing and very competitive popular music industry, had an obvious appeal to Irish-American audiences. However, songs that looked back to Ireland represent only a minority of the pieces written about the Irish in the last decades of the nineteenth century. The typical vaudeville songs of the period were set in the American industrial cities in which so many of the Irish had settled. Therein lay part of their appeal. Songs written before the Civil War had dealt largely with the Irish peasant in Ireland or the newly landed immigrant in America. After the War, most songs focused on the new Irish working class in the industrial cities.

Some songs, such as "No Irish Need Apply," called attention to the experiences of these urban Irish immigrants. The original version seems to have emigrated from the British music hall along with its singer, Kitty O'Neil, in the 1860s. The song was quickly adapted to the American environment and was sung in vaudeville houses, such as Tony Pastor's theater on 14th street in New York City.

> I'm a dacent boy just landed, from the town of Ballyfad,
> I needs a new position and I wants one very bad,
> I've seen employment advertised, "It's just the thing,"
>     says I,
> But the dirty spalpeen ended, with, "No Irish Need Apply."

Although the singer tracks down the man who has placed the advertisement and gives him "such a welting as he'd get at Donnybrook," the song ends with a hint of the promise of life in America.

> Sure, I've heard that in America it always is the plan
> That an Irishman is just as good as any other man.
> (Wright, 650–52, 525.)

Sheet music for "No Irish Need Apply," written and sung by Miss Kathleen O'Neil

Unfortunately, this was a sentiment that not all Americans were quite ready to embrace.

In cities with large Irish populations, any song championing their cause was bound to be popular. Most vaudeville songs, however, were less than solicitous about Irish sensibilities. The early vaudeville audiences consisted largely of working-class males who liked a style of rough-and-tumble comedy that had to appeal to a broad spectrum of patrons, not just the Irish. We find, therefore, that many comic songs appear Janus-faced: they seemingly make fun of the Irish but in ways that were generally acceptable to much of the Irish working class. Take for example, "Is That Mr. Reilly?" (1883). Composed and performed by Pat Rooney, a very successful immigrant song-and-dance man (whose son and grandson took up his name and his trade), the song presents a fantasy of what an Irishman might do if he became president.

> I'll have nothing but Irishmen on the police
>     Patrick's Day'd be Fourth of July;
> I'll get me a thousand infernal machines,
>     To teach the Chinese how to die,
> I'd defend workmen's cause, Manufacture the laws,
>     New York would be swimming in wine,
> A hundred a day will be very small pay,
>     When the White House and Capitol are mine.

Very much a product of the New York variety stage, the song, nevertheless, reflects something of the reality of working-class Irish-American life at the time. The unpleasant reference to the Chinese reflects the bitter competition for jobs between Irish and Chinese on both the east and west coasts. Even the strutting braggadocio and wild fantasies of the Paddy president would have appealed to Irish in the audience. Although comically absurd to Yankees, such sentiments also represented a comic nightmare—Pat's revenge on the Yankee order of things. Then there was the chorus with its suggestion of Irish success.

> Is that Mr. Reilly, They speak of so highly
> Well, upon my word, Reilly, you're doing
>     quite well.

Pat Rooney's Mr. Reilly was one of a long parade of rising "micks on the make" who trotted across the vaudeville stage between 1860 and 1900. The most famous was Edward Harrigan's "Muldoon, the Solid Man" (1874). In the song, Muldoon relates how he came to New York City "when small from Donegal" and settled in a tenement in the Fourteenth Ward. However, "by perseverance I elevated, and went to the front like a solid man." A successful politician, Muldoon knows how to take care of his friends:

> Go with me and I'll treat you decent
>     I'll set you down and I'll fill your can
> As I walk the street each friend I meet
>     Says: "There goes Muldoon, he's a solid man."

There is an element of satire in many of these songs of Irish pride. Certainly, there is no question but that many popular plays, vaudeville skits and early Tin-Pan-Alley songs adopted and Americanized the old stereotype of the comic stage Irishman, originally an English invention. Indeed, the American stage Irishman in his new guise as urban workingman was as prone to fighting and drinking as his Old-World predecessor, although he sometimes lacked the latter's charm. In "The Irish Spree" (ca.

1880) an Irish gang trashes a bar and then slaughters the police who arrive to stop the riot.

More often, Irish destructiveness was self-inflicted, as in Joseph Flynn's "Down Went McGinty" (1889), in which the hero bets his friend that he cannot carry him, McGinty, up a ladder. At the point at which he may lose the bet, McGinty lets go and falls: "And tho' he won his five, He was more dead than alive." The song is one example out of many of the grotesque and chaotic qualities that became associated with the Irish in nineteenth-century American popular culture.

One of the most popular types of comic songs written between 1870 and 1890 made fun of immigrant-Irish social pretensions. In these songs the hero, having arrived at the next rung on the socio-economic ladder, hosts a celebration that inevitably ends in disaster. "Miss Mulligan's Home Made Pie" (1885) features a tea party thrown by an over-achieving Irish family. The culinary centerpiece of the event causes a near-death experience among everyone present. The flat-warming party in "McFadden's Uptown Flat" (1890) gets so wild that the landlord tosses McFadden out after only one night in middle-class splendor. "McGettigan's Social Soiree" (1883) culminates in a full-scale donnybrook. "Mrs. McCarthy's Party," (1888) concludes in general riot and the defenestration of guests. In fact, any attempt by an Irishman in a song to put on airs was bound to cause trouble. In "There Goes McManus" (1889), the hero attends a ball in rented pants. When they split during the dance, he rushes out to beat up the Jewish tailor who supplied them. He is then hauled into court because "he tried to be a swell."

While many middle-class Irish-Americans no doubt objected to such songs, the Irish working class in the vaudeville houses seems to have taken them in stride, responding to what Mick Moloney calls "the trickster element" in the stage Irish characterizations (Moloney, 90). The evidence for the popularity of these songs within the Irish community lies in publications such as *Delaney's Irish Songsters,* cheap collections of song lyrics marketed to the working-class Irish. Cheek by jowl with traditional Irish folk songs, Thomas Moore's verses, emigrant ballads and patriotic, nationalist songs and recitations were scores of these comic songs about Pat's hapless exploits. The fact that the titles of most of these comic songs featured an Irish name suggests that within nineteenth-century American popular culture the mere appearance of a McSomeone on the cover of a song signified humor. Yet, for many in the immigrant working class, the opportunity to see even a crude stereotype of themselves up on the stage was a kind of epiphany, a recognition that, one way or another, they were indeed a part of urban American life.

Fortunately, by the 1880s some songwriters and vaudevillians were beginning to attach positive images to the Irish stereotype. This gradually made it easier for the Irish to claim their right to cultural, as well as political, citizenship. Edward Harrigan was a key figure in this process. Harrigan, third generation Irish, was born in Cork Row on New York's East Side. A prodigious writer of vaudeville sketches, musical plays and songs, Harrigan, along with his partner Tony Hart (Anthony Cannon), were among the most popular entertainers in New York in the 1870s and 1880s. Although Harrigan got a lot of mileage out of the older comic Irish stereotype characterized by drinking and fighting, he added something new. In "Babies On Our Block" (1879) he celebrated Irish working-class families and the fathers who supported them, men who were "Quite easy with the shovel, And so handy with the pen." The fact that the lunch bucket in "My Dad's

Dinner Pail" (1883) doubled as a "growler" after dinner did not detract from Harrigan's evocation of this "emblem of labor." The boys and girls who gathered at "Maggie Murphy's Home" (1890) enjoyed dancing without resorting to excessive drink or shindies. In his plays and songs Harrigan made room within the Irish stereotype for the solid American virtues of loyalty to family and friends, hard work and good clean fun.

While the Irish were the central figures in Harrigan's multi-ethnic musical plays, his real subject was the city. Harrigan, as much as any other figure, defined the Irish within an urban context. "Mulligan's Alley," the locale of many of his "Mulligan Guard" musicals, was modeled on Five Points in New York's Lower East Side. In songs such as "Going Home with Nelly After Five" (1883) and "Danny By My Side" (1891) Harrigan set his younger Irish-American characters against the great backdrop of the metropolis and the Brooklyn Bridge. By 1890, it was virtually impossible for anyone to write a song about the city, such as "The Side Walks of New York," without sprinkling it with Irish names. By then the most negative elements of the Irish stereotype were disappearing from Tin-Pan-Alley songs, as they would shortly depart from vaudeville itself, as a rapidly growing Irish middle class began to police the arts to make sure the image of the Irish was respected.

Perhaps it was this newly-evidenced touchiness about the representation of the Irish that led Tin Pan Alley after 1900 to shift the setting for their songs about the Irish from the American city to "the Emerald Isle"—a popular-culture fantasy about an idyllic Ireland, less real than Harrigan's Mulligan's Alley but much more pleasant to contemplate and claim as a homeland. In Tin Pan Alley's Ireland there was no rain, poverty, unemployment or political agitation, only handsome young men, blue-eyed colleens, and white-haired old mothers awaiting the return of the homesick emigrant. It was, as the title of J. K. Brennan and Ernie Ball's hit suggested, "A Little Bit of Heaven."

Brennan and Ball's song was written for *The Heart of Paddy Whack* in 1915, one of the last big musical successes for Chauncey Olcott, the Irish-American lyric tenor and actor for whom a dozen successful "Irish" musicals had been written since 1898. Among the hit songs associated with Olcott were "My Wild Irish Rose" (1897), "Mother Machree" (1910), "When Irish Eyes Are Smiling" (1912), and "Too-ra-loora-loora" (1912), the staples of any Irish-American St. Patrick's Day sing-along for most of the twentieth century.

After World War I commercial record companies targeted the Irish neighborhoods with recordings made especially for them. The "McGinty" type songs, so dominant in the 1870s and 1880s, were only meagerly represented in company catalogs. Even Harrigan's more positive evocations of the urban Irish were relatively rare. The new songs of the "Emerald Isle" eclipsed the old knockabout vaudeville songs, at least within those twentieth-century Irish-American households that could afford record players (see Spottswood, vol. 5, 2737–2869).

The fact that the "Emerald-Isle" songs were popular with Irish-Americans suggests that, even though they were the products of Tin Pan Alley's tune industry, they nonetheless filled some need or addressed some sentiments within the community. By the 1920s many Irish-Americans were of the second and third generations. They had never seen and probably never would see Ireland. Yet, while anxious to continue their move into the American mainstream, they still wanted some cultural identity that acknowledged their Irish roots. The "Emerald-Isle" songs

are examples of what Herbert Gans has called "symbolic ethnicity": cultural artifacts that allowed one to assert an Irish identity freed from the burdensome memory of poverty, famine, repression, and the complications of Irish nationalist politics. Broadway, Tin Pan Alley, and eventually Hollywood, offered the American-born Irish simple, trouble-free images of a beautiful, happy "homeland." Moreover, this make-believe rural Ireland fitted the pattern of general nostalgia for the farmlands and small towns so many Americans had given up for the industrial cities. Even Yankees appeared willing to embrace the Emerald Isle.

Richard Spottswood's discography of the recordings made for the Irish market in the 1920s and 1930s reveals the role which popular song played in Irish-American communities. Most of the songs represented were commercial pieces written in New York, London and Dublin. There were relatively few traditional songs. Yet, the majority of the recordings were of instrumental pieces, almost all of which were traditional dance tunes—jigs, reels and hornpipes. Dancing played a vital role within many Irish-American communities, and, since musicians were needed to play for the dances, there was also a lively interest in playing traditional music. Music in Irish-American life was, therefore, split: dance tunes and instrumental styles remained tied to tradition while songs were largely drawn from commercial popular culture. Thus, while instrumental music and dances were confined within the community, Irish-American songs were shared, to some extent, with the rest of the nation. This is one of the reasons why so much of Irish-American ethnic identity has been defined and communicated through, indeed, almost embedded in, the general popular culture.

With the tapering off of new popular songs about the Irish after the 1920s, Irish-American song culture remained pretty much unchanged, fixed within the Chauncey Olcott mold, until the 1960s when Irish groups like The Clancy Brothers became popular in America, singing songs generally unknown to Broadway, Tin Pan Alley or Democratic Party fund-raisers. As more Irish folk groups toured America, a minor cultural clash developed between the visitors and the Irish-American communities. The Chauncey Olcott/Tin-Pan-Alley songs that had satisfied so many Irish-Americans for so long were either unknown to Irish singers or were objects of ridicule. On the other hand, the "genuine" songs that the Irish folk singers offered the American Irish could sometimes seem peculiar, even alien.

However, as Irish folk singers became more acquainted with America, and as American folk artists became more involved in Irish music, a small, slowly growing body of new Irish-American song began to take shape. For instance, Cathy Ryan of the group Cherish The Ladies has written several songs about the problems facing recent Irish immigrants to the United States. Terence Winch, a founder of Celtic Thunder, looks back with affection and a sense of loss to the old Irish-American enclaves that once gave urban, industrial America so much of its character. Winch, whose *Irish Musicians/American Friends* won the American poetry prize for 1986, writes songs about the urban Irish America in which he was raised and which has virtually vanished during in his lifetime. His "When New York Was Irish," written a hundred years after Edward Harrigan songs about the urban Irish, evokes a time when

> We dug all the subways, we ran the saloons
> We built all the bridges, we played all the tunes,
> We put out the fires, we controlled city hall,
> We started with nothing, wound up with it all.

The Irish-American song tradition is thinner than it was in 1900, but it will carry over into the twenty-first century, where it will continue to evolve.

Mari Kathleen Fielder, "Chauncey Olcott: Irish-American Mother-Love, Romance, and Nationalism," *Éire-Ireland,* 22/2 (1987): 4–26.

Jon W. Finson, *The Voices That Are Gone: Themes in Nineteenth-Century American Popular Song* (New York, 1994).

James W. Flannery, *Dear Harp of My Country: The Irish Melodies of Thomas Moore.* With performances by James Flannery, Tenor and Janet Harbison, Irish Harp [Book with 2 CDs], (Nashville, Tenn., 1997).

Robert R. Grimes, *How Shall We Sing in a Foreign Land? Music of Irish-Catholic Immigrants in the Antebellum United States* (Notre Dame, Ind., 1996).

Charles Hamm, *Yesterdays: Popular Song in America* (New York, 1983).

Wayland D. Hand, Charles Cutts, Robert C Wylder, and Betty Wylder, "Songs of the Butte Miners," *Western Folklore,* 9/1 (January 1950): 1–49.

George Korson, ed., *Pennsylvania Songs and Legends* (Baltimore, Md., 1949).

Don Meade, "The Life and Times of 'Muldoon, the Solid Man,'" *New York Irish History,* 11 (1997): 6–11, 41–48.

Mick Moloney, "Irish Ethnic Recordings and the Irish-American Imagination," *Ethnic Recordings in America: A Neglected Heritage,* Studies in American Folklife, No 1, (Washington, D.C., 1982): 85–101.

Richard Moody and Ned Harrigan, *From Corlear's Hook to Herald Square* (Chicago, 1980).

Cathy Ryan, "The Back Door," *Cherish The Ladies: The Back Door,* Green Linnet CSIF 119 (1992); "The Missing Piece," *Cherish The Ladies: Out and About,* Green Linnet CSIF 1134 (1993).

Derek B. Scott, *The Singing Bourgeois: Songs of the Victorian Drawing Room and Parlour* (Philadelphia, 1989).

Richard K. Spottswood, *Ethnic Music on Records. A Discography of Ethnic Recordings in the United States, 1893–1942,* vol. 5 (Urbana, Ill., 1990): 2737–2869.

William H. A. Williams, "From Lost Land to Emerald Isle: Ireland and the Irish in American Sheet Music, 1800–1920," *Éire-Ireland,* 26/1 (1991): 19–45.

———, "Irish Traditional Music in the United States," *America and Ireland, 1776–1976: The American Identity and the Irish Connection.* The Proceedings of the United States Bicentennial Conference of Cumann Merriman, Ennis, August, 1976. David Noel David and Owen Dudley Edwards, eds. (Westport, Conn., 1980): 279–95.

———, *'Twas Only An Irishman's Dream: The Image of Ireland and the Irish in American Popular Song Lyrics, 1800–1920* (Urbana, Ill., 1996).

Terence Winch, "When New York Was Irish," *When New York Was Irish* (Green Linnet, 1987).

Robert L. Wright, ed., *Irish Emigrant Ballads and Songs* (Bowling Green, Ohio, 1975).

Georges-Denis Zimmermann, *Songs of Irish Rebellion: Political Street Ballads and Rebel Songs, 1780–1900* (Dublin, 1967).

WILLIAM H. A. WILLIAMS

## IRISH STUDIES IN THE U.S.

In June 1905, President Theodore Roosevelt addressed the men of Holy Cross College in Worcester, Massachusetts. An enthusiastic admirer of Lady Gregory's *Cuchulain of Muirthemne,* he spoke of his hopes that Irish literature would be studied at American colleges and universities. He prophesied a growing ". . . awakening to the wealth of beauty contained in the Celtic sagas, and I wish to see American institutions take the lead in that awakening." It took another fifty years for American scholars to realize that "awakening" with Irish Studies courses and programs.

Interest in Irish Studies in the United States and around the world has developed for a number of reasons. First, there is the Irish presence abroad. As early as the sixth century, Irish monks established their foundations across Europe; seventeenth-century exiles distinguished themselves in continental armies; eighteenth- and nineteenth-century Irish emigrated to the Americas while others sailed to Australia in the holds of convict ships. In the twentieth century, Irish missionaries and lay workers have served as educators and health care providers particularly to people in developing countries.

Second, Ireland is the first of the modern nations. While its policy as a postcolonial nation has been one of neutrality, Ireland has actively fostered international understanding and peace since it was admitted to the United Nations in 1955. Despite Ireland's commitment to peaceful settlement, thirty years of troubles in Northern Ireland kept Ireland in the news as one of the world's unresolved trouble spots until the Good Friday Agreement of 1998 brought a ceasefire and opened the way for a permanent peace settlement. Those troubles have produced a literature of conflict and of national identity: novels by Jennifer Johnston, Benedict Kiely, Bernard MacLaverty and Brian Moore, a memoir by Seamus Deane, drama by Brian Friel and Frank McGuiness and a generation of poets of whom Nobel Laureate Seamus Heaney is the best known. Historians and social scientists have examined the complex issues of identity and community over two generations, and new areas of inquiry such as gender studies and peace studies have emerged.

Finally, there is Ireland's preeminent place in contemporary arts: in literature, in drama, in film, in popular music and dance. This recogniton and the Celtic Tiger economy has further contributed to the buoyant confidence of the Irish at the end of the century.

All of this interest in Ireland has coincided with the development of Irish Studies as a special topic within the disciplines or as interdisciplinary programs. The case for Irish literature is easily made: a roster of writers that goes from Samuel Beckett through James Joyce, Sean O'Casey, George Bernard Shaw, Jonathan Swift, John Millington Synge, Oscar Wilde and W. B. Yeats. Texts, bibliographies and critical studies of these writers have fostered the teaching of Irish literature and the situating of that literature in an Irish cultural context.

The study of Irish historiography has been supported by the development of a coherent historiography, a valid and dependable model for the historiography of modern nations. Irish language study has been the beneficiary of the general improvement in methods and materials for teaching foreign languages, and modern translations of important sources now exist: Thomas Kinsella's translation of the *Táin* and Seán O'Tuama and Thomas Kinsella's edition of *An Duanaire,* a bilingual edition of Irish poetry 1600–1900.

Scholars and teachers with Irish research interests have been well served by an Irish Studies organization, the American Conference for Irish Studies (formerly the American Committee for Irish Studies) that not only supports their work but also brings together academicians and others interested in Irish Studies.

Plans for ACIS were formulated by Thomas Brown, Gilbert Cahill, Emmet Larkin, Lawrence J. McCaffrey, Helen Mulvey and Arnold Schrier, American historians with Irish research interests, who met during the 1958 meeting of the American Historical Association to discuss how best to facilitate Irish historical scholarship in the United States. Their discussion led to the founding of the American Committee for Irish Studies in 1960, an interdisciplinary organization whose purpose is to encourage research and writing in Irish Studies and to promote Irish Studies as a distinct course of study in American colleges and universities.

ACIS draws members from across the disciplines, from every part of the United States and from wider constituencies than college and university faculties: graduate students, schoolteachers and interested members of the community. Beginning in 1963, ACIS has held an annual spring conference. In 1976, ACIS began to sponsor fall regional conferences in New England, in the Middle Atlantic States, in the South, in the Midwest and in the West.

A number of ACIS publications and affiliated publications, *The ACIS Newsletter*, the Reprint Series, and the *Irish Literary Supplement*, further encouraged the development of Irish Studies by providing news, reviews, bibliographies and research reports and queries. In 1977, ACIS authorized a survey to determine the extent to which Irish Studies were taught in the United States. Edited by Maureen Murphy, *A Guide to Irish Studies in the United States* appeared in 1979; subsequent editions appeared in 1982, 1987 and 1994. The *Guide* now appears on the worldwide web at http://athena.english.vt.edu/ACIS/irishstudies/guide.html.

In 1982, the *Guide* identified 365 colleges and universities that offered courses and programs in Irish Studies; in 1987, the number increased to 454 or about 25% of all postsecondary institutions in the United States. In 1994, the numbers were just about the same (452) and the pattern of course distribution also remained consistent. Literature courses led the way with special studies available in Joyce and Yeats. History courses were offered less often; however, courses in the social sciences, in Northern Ireland and in immigration were generally history-based. Opportunities in the United States to study the Irish language dipped slightly, but students participating in an increaed number of study abroad programs have the opportunity to learn Irish in Ireland.

The numbers themselves mask some significant changes: two worrisome, two hopeful. While there are some high-profile, well-endowed Irish Studies programs at institutions, including Boston College, New York University and the University of Notre Dame, and while the numbers of courses and programs have remained stable, two trends anticipate retrenchment ahead. In many places Irish Studies courses have been associated with an individual faculty member and have not been institutionalized. When the faculty member leaves or retires, the course disappears. Also, Irish Studies courses have been reduced from semester or annual listings to alternate years or to occasional offerings as courses must compete at department level with other faculty interests.

Hopeful signs include the growth of Irish-immigration or Irish-American Studies courses that reflect the interest in Irish family history and in the role of the Irish in shaping the American experience. The pioneering work of scholars of Irish-America, Patrick Blessing, Thomas Brown, Hasia Dinar, Charles Fanning, Suellen Hoy, Lawrence J. McCaffrey, Kerby Miller, Janet Nolan and Ellen Skerrett, have provided resources for teaching and research and have identified new areas of study.

The other positive sign is the number of active Irish cultural and historical societies (forty in the 1994 *Guide*), many of which work closely with the local academic community, that serve both the specialist and those whose interests are more broadly based. The oldest of these organizations is the American Irish Historical Society established in 1896; Theodore Roosevelt, then New York City police commissioner, was a founding member. The Society's library and archives are open to researchers, and their series of lecturers and cultural events are open to the public. Their journal, *The Recorder,* is published twice a year.

The wide range of programs created by the Irish American Cultural Institute has developed an appreciation of Irish heritage among young and old. Founded in 1992, by Eoin McKiernan, Professor of English at the College of St. Thomas, St. Paul, Minnesota and supported by local philanthropist Patrick Butler, the IACI and its local branches sponsored the Irish Fortnight lecture series: lectures, readings and concerts from 1971–1982 in cities around the country. Their very successful Irish Way program has offered a summer program in Ireland for high school students since 1976. The program offers classes in all aspects of Irish culture and concludes with a home stay. The IACI has published the scholarly quarterly *Éire-Ireland* since 1965; their newsletter of Irish and Irish-American life, *Dúchas,* was added in 1971.

The IACI moved its headquarters from the College of St. Thomas in St. Paul to Morristown, New Jersey, in 1995. The College of St. Thomas created the Center for Irish Studies that provides academic, scholarly and cultural program on Irish topics. Their quarterly, *New Hibernia Review. Iris Éireannach Nua,* launched in 1997 publishes articles of Irish and Irish-American interest.

These organizations are a way for students who have pursued Irish Studies courses or programs to stay involved. (A conservative estimate, based on *Guide* numbers, is that some 65,000–75,000 students were enrolled in Irish Studies programs in the United States between 1982 and 1998.) Some institutions have active outreach programs to their graduates (Boston College's Friends of Irish Studies) and to the community ( New York University's Glucksmans' Ireland House); both have a special welcome for Irish Studies graduates.

Other Irish Studies graduates have maintained their Irish interests by founding, directing and participating in Irish-interest societies associated with their professional organizations. The Irish Teachers Associations in New York and in Chicago have developed curriculum and resources to teach Irish Studies in their schools. The New York American Irish Teachers Association was instrumental in the passage of the 1997 bill requiring the Famine to be taught as part of the human rights curriculum in New York State public schools. This is the first step in formalizing Irish Studies at elementary and secondary school levels. At the end of the twenthieth century, Irish Studies has realized Roosevelt's hope and that awakening has not only informed the growth of Irish Studies in the United States, but it also has been the model for Irish Studies in nations associated with the Irish disapora around the world.

*See* American Conference for Irish Studies; Center for Irish Studies; Irish American Culture Institute

Lawrence J. McCaffrey, *Textures of Irish America* (Syracuse, 1992).

Maureen Murphy, *A Guide to Irish Studies in the United States* (Selden, 1994).

"International Cooperation: an Irish Studies Model," in *English Literature and the University Curriculum*, ed. Wolfgang Zach (Frankfurt am Main, 1992): 131–134.

MAUREEN MURPHY

# J

Andrew Jackson

## JACKSON, ANDREW (1767–1845)

U.S. President, soldier. Andrew Jackson was born in the Irish settlement of Waxhaw, South Carolina, on the North Carolina border, in 1767. His parents and two older brothers had emigrated from Carrickfergus, Co. Antrim, two years before. They were part of the substantial Scotch-Irish emigration that took place in the decade leading up to the American Revolution. Given the population of his native district, it is not surprising that, it is said, when excited, Jackson spoke with an Ulster accent! Judge Alexander Porter, a native of Donegal whose father had been hanged after the 1798 rebellion, confirmed, after diligent research conducted during a visit to his native land in the 1830s, that Jackson was born in Ireland.

When the Revolution began, the Jackson boys fought the British with a vengeance. Hugh was killed in combat in 1779. Andrew and Robert fought in the battle of Hanging Rock and were captured. While in prison the boy troopers got smallpox; after their release, Robert died either from the disease or from neglected wounds.

After the British capture of Charleston in 1780, Charles Cornwallis, in attempting to consolidate control of the area, dispatched the Volunteers of Ireland, which had been recruited in New York and New Jersey from Irish deserters from the Patriot forces, to the Waxhaw settlement. It was his belief that "as it was an Irish corps it would be received with a better temper by the settlers of the district who were universally Irish and universally disaffected." As a result of this sortie, the unit lost more soldiers from desertion than it gained recruits. It was probably on this occasion that a British soldier inflicted a saber wound on the face of the thirteen-year-old Andrew Jackson.

David N. Doyle provides a vivid assessment of the man: "Andrew Jackson, with piercing blue eyes, face as long as a Lurgan spade, high shock of red hair, and lonely resolution, would embark on the career of frontier soldier, land speculator, professional English-hater, southern politician and national hero, that would lead him to the Presidency by 1828, and make of him a symbol of the political reconciliation of the older Ulster Irish stock in America and the incoming thousands of Catholic Irish."

As a result of his colorful career as an Indian fighter and his victory over a British force at the battle of New Orleans in January, 1815, he became a popular hero, not least to the growing Irish population. He also appealed to them as the self-made man; like almost all of them, he started with virtually nothing and rose to be a major political force. In what was popularly perceived as a political deal between John Quincy Adams and Henry Clay,

Jackson, who achieved a plurality of both popular and electoral votes, he was denied the Presidency in 1824.

His overwhelming victory four years later was seen by many Irish people as a victory of one of their own over the machinations of the established order. His supporters in Boston had staged a lively campaign on his behalf. One of his opponents observed, "Proclaiming Jackson as an Irishman, they planted their flag in the menage of Broad Street; and holding him up as the champion of the poor against the rich, they received with 'hugs fraternal' the tenants of poorhouses and penitentiaries." A lively Inauguration Day parade was staged in the city on March 4, 1829, about which the same observer commented, "All Broad Street was invited as the peculiar favorites of the *Irish* President." The procession reminded him of convicts condemned to the galleys: "Nothing was wanting but the handcuffs."

Jackson's actions as President, particularly his battle against the privileged Bank of the United States, won massive support from Irish voters and they were eager to honor him. When he visited Boston in June 1833 the Charitable Irish Society presented him with an address of welcome at the hall in Tremont House. He told the assemblage, "It is with great pleasure that I see so many of the countrymen of my father. . . . I have always been proud of my ancestry, and of being descended from that noble race, and rejoice that I am so nearly allied to a country which has so much to recommend it to the good wishes of the world." He was clearly cognizant of the political condition of Ireland: "Would to God, sir, that Irishmen on the other side of the great water enjoyed the comforts, happiness, contentment and liberty that we enjoy here! I am well aware, sir, that Irishmen have never been backward in giving their support to the cause of liberty. They have fought, sir, for this country valiantly, and, I have no doubt, would fight again were it necessary. . . ."

In parting, he told the society's president, "There are few circumstances that have given me more heart-felt satisfaction than this visit." Jackson made similar statements before Irish organizations in his visits to other cities. In 1842, however, he declined to support the movement to repeal the union between Ireland and Britain, arguing that the U.S. should not interfere in the affairs of other countries.

In Philadelphia the *Irish Republican Shield and Literary Observer* was a strong supporter of Jacksonian democracy. During the 1832 presidential campaign, however, a large gathering of Irishmen in Independence Hall opposed Jackson's re-election because of his opposition to federal government sponsorship of internal improvements—such as roads and canals—which were major sources of Irish employment. Despite this, in the eyes of one section of his supporters, Old Hickory was the first Irish President of the United States of America.

Dennis Clark, *The Irish in Philadelphia* (Philadelphia, 1973).

James B. Cullen, *The Story of the Irish in Boston* (Boston, 1889).

Arthur B. Darling, *Political Changes in Massachusetts, 1824–1848* (New Haven, CT, 1925).

*Dictionary of American Biography*, vol. v (1929 ed.): 526–534.

David N. Doyle, *Ireland, Irishmen and Revolutionary America, 1760–1820* (Cork, 1981): xvi–xvii.

Elmer D. Herd, Jr., *Andrew Jackson, South Carolinian; A Study of the Enigma of his Birth* (Lancaster County Historical Commission, SC, 1963).

Arthur Schlesinger, Jr., *The Age of Jackson* (Boston, 1953).

ARTHUR MITCHELL

## JAMES, JESSE WOODSON (1847–1882)

Outlaw. James was born into Irish ancestry in Clay County, Missouri, the son of Robert and Zerelda (Cole); his mother was Catholic and his father a Baptist minister. Jesse and his brother, Alexander Franklin, were raised on a farm and received little education. As they entered young adulthood, the brothers became Confederate guerrillas under the charge of William Clarke Quantrill during the Civil War.

It was after the war that the James brothers began to engage in troublesome activities. Jesse and "Frank" joined a group of brigands and Jesse eventually became the proposed leader; initially, the band focused on committing bank robberies. However, in 1873 the group began what would become a notorious sequence of train robberies that spanned ten years. In 1876 several of the members were killed and several captured: only Frank and Jesse escaped. The brothers abandoned the robbing activity for close to three years; however, in 1879 they robbed a train and in 1881 two more. In 1882, Jesse was wounded in the back of the head and his brother surrendered himself six months later. Frank was brought to trial on two different occasions but was acquitted.

While they lived out the rest of their days without further illegal involvement, the James brothers were remembered for their criminal activity. Both were known to justify their actions by making appeal to various persecutory happenings in which they felt their actions were necessitated. Jesse was married in 1874 to Zerelda Mimms and they had two children. Little is known of what became of Frank, other than that the rest of his life was peaceful and free of legal troubles. In 1868, Jesse joined the Baptist Church and lived out the rest of his days as a believer and participant in Christianity. He died on April 3, 1882.

George Huntington, *Robber and Hero, the Story of the Raid on the First National Bank of Northfield, Minnesota in 1876* (1895).

Jesse E. James, *Jesse James, My Father* (1899).

Robertus Love, *The Rise and Fall of Jesse James* (1926).

*Dictionary of American Biography*, 9.

JOY HARRELL

## JAMESTOWN, VIRGINIA

Founded in May 1607 by the Virginia Company of London, Jamestown was the site of England's first permanent settlement in the New World and the capital of its Virginia colony until 1699. From the beginning, the venture in Virginia had close associations with Ireland, where England was concurrently engaged in the Plantation of Ulster.

Leading members of the Virginia Company were influenced by personal experiences in Ireland, where more than forty of them held office, owned land, or had other business interests. Some members of the founding expedition were veterans of the Irish wars, and had among their subordinates Francis Magnel, an Irish-born sailor who lived at Jamestown until April 1608.

Dennis O'Connor, a tradesman of Irish birth or descent, reached Jamestown in October 1608. He probably died there during the 1609–1610 winter famine known as "the starving time."

The architecture of the Virginia settlement also had Irish precedents. The plan of James Fort, a triangular enclosure erected in 1607, bore striking similarities to a 1601 fort built by English forces on the River Blackwater in Co. Tyrone. In orientation and layout, the town that later spread out from the Fort resembled the fortified villages built by English planters in Ulster.

Since 1994, archaeologists excavating the rediscovered fort have unearthed copper pennies and a halfpenny minted for use in Ireland. The Irish coins, dated 1601 and 1602, satisfied the Virginia settlers' needs for small change and for copper objects to trade with the local Indians.

*See* Virginia

William M. Kelso, *Jamestown Rediscovery III* (Richmond, Va., 1997).

David B. Quinn, *Ireland and America: Their Early Associations, 1500–1640* (Liverpool, 1991).

John W. Reps, *Tidewater Towns* (Williamsburg, Va., 1972).

BRIAN McGINN

## JEFFERS, ROBINSON (1887–1962)

Poet. Jeffers was born in Pittsburgh, PA, the son of a Presbyterian minister of Irish lineage. Educated at the University of Western Pennsylvania and Occidental College (B.A., 1905), he also studied at several other universities. He married Una Call Kuster in 1913 and had four children. He was awarded the doctor of humane letters by Occidental College (1937) and by the University of Southern California (1939).

Jeffers is one of America's great lyric poets whose mature work is in long narrative poems which often depict rape, incest and murder; it is these poetic modes and themes which may explain his mixed critical reception. He draws from classical and biblical sources, but it is the California Carmel and Big Sur region and Tor House, Jeffers's home overlooking the Pacific, which are the setting for many of his poems or the source for much of his nature imagery. Influenced by Nietzsche's concepts of individualism, Jeffers celebrates the natural world as a visionary pantheist, a philosophical poet and humanist, who seeks life lived in a simple relation to nature. Jeffers's god has rejected humanity, yet, Brother Antoninus/William Everson (1988) insists that Jeffers is a mystic with a "sacred vision."

Jeffers's first two volumes offer strong, confident love lyrics imitative of the English Romantic poets in *Flagons and Apples*

(1912), and reflect the Big Sur country in *Californians* (1916). But Jeffers soon found his original voice and subject in such volumes as *Tamar and Other Poems* (1924), which uses free verse and the long line and deals with the Old Testament story of incest and murder. In "The Alpine Christ" (1974), the poet recognizes that God is dead and love gives meaning to human life. The title poem of *The Roan Stallion, Tamar and Other Poems* (1925) celebrates a central Jeffers theme: how man has overvalued his place as the center of the natural world and lost touch with the more elemental forces of life. This volume includes *The Tower Beyond Tragedy*, his verse-play version of Aeschylus's *Oresteia*. *The Women at Point Sur* (1927), a long narrative poem, deals with sexual themes and violence, focusing on a minister who goes mad, driven by conflicting desires. *Cawdor and Other Poems* (1928) adapts Euripides's *Hippolytus* to the Big Sur coast, and *Dear Judas and Other Poems* (1929) presents Jesus's passion as a Noh play—Judas as a decent, moral man, a liberal humanist, and a female Christ-figure in "The Loving Shepherdess," set on the Sur coast. By the 1930s, Jeffers was probably the most widely read and discussed American poet, and he was the first American poet to appear on the cover of *Time* (4 April 1932).

Jeffers's paternal grandfather emigrated in 1810 from County Monaghan in Ireland, and the Jeffers family visited Ireland several times. Their stay on the northeast Irish coast and travel through Ireland, Scotland, and England resulted in *Descent to the Dead* (1931), and *Visit to Ireland* (1954), which includes excerpts from Una Jeffers's diaries, edited by the poet and containing entries by him.

Later poems such as *Be Angry with the Sun* (1941) and *The Double Axe* (1948) were not well-received due, no doubt, to their strong responses to war and especially to World War II. An adaptation of *Medea* was performed in 1947 with Dame Judith Anderson, and *Hungerfield and Other Poems* (1954) reconciles Jeffers with his wife's death. His lyric epitaph for her concludes the poem:

> Here is the poem dearest; you will never
> read it nor hear it. You were more
> beautiful
> Than a hawk flying; you were faithful and
> a lion heart like this rough hero
> Hungerfield. But the ashes have fallen
> And the flame has gone up; nothing human
> remains. You are earth and air; you
> are in the beauty of the ocean
> And the great streaming triumphs of
> sundown; you are alive and well in the
> tender young grass rejoicing
> When soft rain falls at night, and little
> rosy-fleeced clouds float on the dawn.
> —I shall be with you presently.

Jeffers lived another eleven years, writing mostly short poems celebrating the physical and natural world.

*See* Poetry, Irish-American

Jeffers, Robinson, *Tamar and Other Poems* (N.Y., 1924).
———, *Roan Stallion, Tamar, and Other Poems* (N.Y., 1925).
———, *Medea* (N.Y., 1946).
———, *Beginning and the End and Other Poems* (N.Y., 1963).
———, *Selected Poems* (N.Y., 1965).
———, *Selected Letters of Robinson Jeffers, 1897–1962*, ed., Ann Ridgeway (Baltimore, 1968).
———, *Collected Poetry of Robinson Jeffers*, 4 vols., ed., Tim Hunt (Stanford, Calif., 1988).

ANDREW M. McLEAN

## JOHNSON, SIR WILLIAM (1715–1774)

Pioneer, soldier, superintendent of Indian affairs. William Johnson was born in Smithtown, County Meath, the son of Christopher and Anne (Warren) Johnson. His mother was of the gentry; his father, a Catholic tenant farmer who concluded that "the only people who could remain Catholic in the British Empire were peasants, priests and martyrs." Accordingly, he adopted the precepts of Anglicanism.

Johnson emigrated to America in 1737 to manage the estate of an uncle, Admiral Sir Peter Warren, in New York's Mohawk Valley, and soon became a major land owner himself around what is now Schenectady. He also developed a close friendship with Indians of the area, adopting their dress and learning the language of the Mohawks. This led in 1744 to his being named superintendent of the affairs of the Six Nations, the grouping of the Mohawk, Iroquois, Oneida, Onondaga, Cayuga and Seneca tribes. It was the first of several appointments relating to Indian interests that gave Johnson a prominent role in the conflict between France and England for control of North America. The allegiance of the Indians was crucial to its outcome, and Johnson's rapport with them was instrumental in keeping the tribes of the Six Nations from aligning with the French in King George's War (1744–1748).

In 1755 Johnson was commissioned a major general, and he led English forces in the expedition against Crown Point. Though he failed to capture Crown Point itself, he defeated the French at the battle of Lake George, thus blunting threats from Canada to the northern English colonies. For this Johnson received the thanks of Parliament and was named a baronet with the title of "Sir." He subsequently took part in the campaign against Ticonderoga and Fort Niagara, and in 1760 assisted in the capture of Montreal, a military action that helped lead to an end to French power in Canada.

As reward for his services, Johnson received a king's grant of one hundred thousand acres of land north of the Mohawk River. This, combined with earlier acquisitions, made him one of the largest landholders in the English colonies, and he lived a life of baronial splendor with numerous servants and slaves. After the death of Catherine Weisenberg, a German servant of a Dutch family who may or may not have formally been his wife, Johnson took first Caroline, then Molly Brant, Mohawk women, into his home and fathered several children by each.

Throughout his life, Johnson displayed genuine interest in the educating and missionizing of the Indians, coming to favor the Anglicans in the latter enterprise. Indians, for their part, regarded him as a blood brother and full-fledged member of the Mohawk nation.

Johnson's services to the crown were substantial, but he proved a misreader of history. He envisioned a kind of static colonization with firm and limited boundaries, failing to see that the hunger for land would impel white settlers ever westward. He also misgauged the aspirations of new settlers for independence.

His son John, a veteran also of the French and Indian campaigns, succeeded to the baronetcy on the father's death on July 11, 1774. When the Revolutionary War broke out the following year, the son organized a loyalist regiment. It was a serious miscalculation. The Johnson estates were confiscated in 1779 as Tory property.

John A. Barnes, *Irish-American Landmarks: A Traveler's Guide* (New York, 1995).

*Encyclopaedia Britannica*, Volume 13 (Chicago, 1955).

Wayne E. Stevens, "Johnson, Sir William," *Dictionary of American Biography* (New York, 1933).

JOHN DEEDY

## JONES, "Mother" MARY HARRIS (1837–1930)

Labor agitator, union organizer, strike leader, political activist. Mother Jones was a leading and unique force in the American labor movement from the 1890s until her death in 1930. Short and sturdy, grey-haired, blue-eyed, bespectacled, wearing long black dresses and hats of her own design, she traveled throughout North America seeking justice for underpaid and overworked men, women and children—many of whom were immigrants like herself.

"I come from the fighting race." Mary Harris was born in 1837 in Cork City, Ireland, although she always claimed she was born in 1830. According to church records, she was baptized August 1, 1837, in St. Mary Roman Catholic Church. Her parents, Richard Harris and Ellen Cotter, had five known children: Richard, Jr., Mary, Catherine, Ellen and William. Mary grew up in a large, crowded poor industrial section of "Rebel" Cork near Shandon Hill above the River Lee. She probably attended the Presentation Sisters' School for poor girls.

"I was born in revolution," she said, describing her girlhood in Cork, 1837–1850. She witnessed the political agitations of Daniel O'Connell, Fergus O'Connor and Father Theobald Matthew, crusader for temperance among the hard-drinking Irish. From 1845 to 1848, Mary suffered with the victims of famines, fevers and evictions. The Young Irish uprising in 1848 brought troops and martial law to Cork and forced Mary's father to flee to America. In 1850, Mary left Ireland to join him. After a hazardous ocean crossing, she arrived in Boston aboard the bark, *SS Adonis* in May, the only Harris listed on its manifest. Mary Harris entered the Toronto Normal School in 1857 with two months' experience as a third-class teacher. She enrolled again in 1858 but was not listed as a graduate, according to school records. She was hired as a lay teacher in St. Mary's convent school in Monroe, Michigan, in August 1859 but left in March 1860. Her account read, "Paid in full, $36.43."

Following a short stint as a dressmaker in Chicago, Mary accepted a teaching job in Memphis, Tennessee, where she met and married George Jones, a union iron molder in 1861. A yellow fever epidemic swept through the Memphis Irish section known as "Pinch" in 1867, killing Mary's husband and four children. Mary Jones returned to Chicago where she encountered two more tragedies. The Chicago Fire, October 1871, destroyed her dressmaking business and all her possessions. Her father, the only family member she identified by name, died in Toronto, December 1871. Working for the rich but living among the poor, Mary Jones became incensed at the contrast between the two

classes and economic policies that did nothing to change it. She began to attend political and labor protest meetings and, with the Knights of Labor expanding west, adopted the Knights and their slogan, "Agitate, educate and organize." Terence Powderly of the Knights of Labor recalled her as "an attractive young woman with a sharp mind and even sharper tongue." With a missionary's zeal, Mary Jones began her campaign for workers. "My address is like my shoes; it travels with me . . . I live wherever there is a fight for right against wrong." She became an "adopter of boys"—first Irish railroad workers and miners—then all labor. With her scattered family, Mary Jones had no permanent home and no interests but her work. She moved with Celtic restlessness across the country.

In 1877, she was in San Francisco where "sand lots" meetings by fellow Corkonian, Dennis Kearney, led to the formation of the Workingman's Party of California. In 1880, she was in Chicago where labor unrest was rampant. She backed the Greenback, Socialist Labor and Populist Party candidates. In 1894, she preceded "General" Charles Kelly's branch of the Coxey Army from Oakland, California, to Council Bluffs, Iowa, seeking food, shelter and funds. She arrived in Chicago to add her support to Eugene Debs' American Railway Union and Pullman strikes. For her help, men began addressing her as "Mother" out of affection, appreciation and respect. She moved into Kansas City where she helped J. A. Wayland launch his radical paper, "Appeal to Reason," in 1895. As a secret organizer, she appeared at Eugene Debs' ARU meetings in Georgia and Alabama in 1896, and worked in southern cotton mills, where the use and abuse of child labor enraged her even more. In 1897, she joined Debs' Social Democracy and the United Mine Workers of America National Bituminous Coal strike in Pittsburgh, Pennsylvania, August 1897.

For the next twenty-five years, Mother Jones was a ball of fire rolling across America, inflaming workers' hopes, igniting their strikes and searing the ears of capital, labor and government. In 1899, she was in Arnot, Pennsylvania, saving a miners' strike with her energy and enthusiasm. Under this "grey-haired general," the women marched with pots, pans, mops and brooms to scare off scabs and mules. In 1900, from Maryland to the Pennsylvania anthracite region, the "re-incarnated Molly Maguire" and her "maids of MacAdoo" outmaneuvered sheriffs and militia to win another victory for the miners. Near Scranton, Pennsylvania, in 1901, Jones oversaw another win for the striking silk mill girls.

Now called "Angel of the Miners" (whether an avenging or guardian), she was considered a devil by her foes, especially in West Virginia, where she went as a commissioned organizer of the United Mine Workers in 1901. She tramped miles of railroad ties, scaled 700-foot cliffs and waded creeks to hold her secret meetings up hills and hollows, ignoring weather, gun shots and snakes. She was served enough injunctions to "line my coffin and make a shroud." When the strike call came in June 1902, she and the boys held firm. She was arrested and tried in Parkersburg, West Virginia, where she was declared "the most dangerous woman in America" and advised to seek a more fitting vocation.

Instead, she followed her own advice—"Pray for the dead and fight like hell for the living." In February 1903, seven strikers died from gunshots in a pre-dawn raid by deputies and Baldwin-Felts "thugs" at Stanaford City, West Virginia, the first battle in the West Virginia mine wars. Two hundred men and a boy were arrested, effectively ending the strike.

In June 1903, Mother Jones answered the call of striking textile workers and led her Children's March from New Kensington, Pennsylvania, to Oyster Bay, Long Island, the summer home of President Theodore Roosevelt. He had complained of the "race suicide" of his class, and she wanted to show him what happened to the victims of child labor. He refused to meet them.

She went, via Michigan's copper mines, to Colorado where she walked into another mine field and strike, 1903–1904. Deported three times and slandered by Colorado newspapers, she broke with UMWA President John Mitchell over union policies but continued working for the miners. She spoke at meetings around the country—for the Colorado miners, the Western Federation of Miners, the Socialist party and for any union needing funds and support, including the first convention of the International Workers of the World in 1905. In 1913, she joined miners in West Virginia's Paint Creek strike and extended it to Cabin Creek to fight the Baldwin-Felts mine "thugs." After the third declaration of martial law, Mother Jones was arrested, court-martialed and held under house arrest for three months for "stealing a cannon," "inciting to riot, etc." A guard slipped her out for a beer, and she slipped a message to Congress. From the frying pan of West Virginia, she jumped into the fire in Colorado's strike where she was arrested and held prisoner twice. Shortly after her release in 1914, she was in Washington, D.C., asking President Woodrow Wilson for help when the militia shot and fired a strikers' tent colony in Ludlow, Colorado, killing eleven women and children. Mother Jones precipitated and testified at several congressional hearings for miners, Mexican political prisoners and industrial workers. Her last major strikes were among the steel workers—Pittsburgh, 1919, and the coal miners of West Virginia, 1921.

In the 1920s, Mother Jones saw the destruction of her union work in West Virginia and Colorado and the rise of John L. Lewis in the UMWA, yet was honored royally in Mexico by its former political prisoners. She was plagued by the IRS for income taxes and mourned the deaths of T. V. Powderly and her brother, Dean William Richard Harris, a Catholic priest whose ordination took place in Rome, Italy, in 1870. She wrote her autobiography in 1924, declaring "it was the hardest damn job I ever did."

On May 1, 1930, Mother Jones celebrated her 100th birthday at the farm of Walter and Lillian Burgess near Silver Spring, Maryland. From 7 a.m. until 11 p.m., hundreds of visitors, including Maryland's governor and Jeff Davis, "King of the Hoboes," came to honor her. Food, drink and a birthday cake with 100 candles and the union label fed them, while the Old Soldiers' Home Band provided music. Mother Jones made her debut before newsreel cameras, protesting the Prohibition Act "as a curse upon the nation," violating her right to have beer instead of water. Mother Jones died quietly November 30, 1930, at the Burgess farm. After a funeral Mass at St. Gabriel's Roman Catholic Church in Washington, Mother Jones took her final train ride to Mount Olive, Illinois. After two days of lying in state and a funeral Mass at the Catholic Church of the Ascension, Mary Harris Jones was buried—as she had requested—in Union Miners Cemetery at Mount Olive.

*See* Labor Movement

Dale Feathering, *Mother Jones, the Miners' Angel* (Carbondale, Ill., 1974).
Mary Jones, *The Autobiography of Mother Jones* (Chicago, 1925).
Kyle McCormick, *The New and Kanawha River and Mine Wars in W. Va.* (Charleston, W. Va., 1959).
Edward M. Steel, *Correspondence of Mother Jones* (Pittsburgh, 1985).
———, *Speeches & Writings of Mother Jones* (Pittsburgh, 1989).
Ken Sullivan, *Goldenseal Book of West Virginia Mine Wars* (Charleston, W. Va., 1991).
*United Mine Workers Journal,* 1890–1918.
*Miners' Magazine,* 1900–1918.

LOIS C. McLEAN

## JORDAN, KATE (1862–1926)

Novelist, playwright. Born in Dublin, Ireland, to Micheal James and Katherine Jordan, Jordan left Ireland with her family and moved to New York before she was a year old. At the young age of twelve, she published her first story and set her ambitions toward being a writer. One of her early popular works was "The Kiss of Gold" which was published in *Lippincott's Monthly Magazine* in October of 1892.

In 1897 Jordan married Frederic Vermilye and continued to write under her maiden name. She was an avid traveler and spent a great deal of time in England and France. While in London she became involved in many social clubs including the Pen and Brush Club, the Lyceum, and the Writers' Club. In the United States she was an active member of the Society of American Dramatists and the Author's League of America. Jordan's memorable works include *The Other House, A Circle in the Sand, Time the Comedian, The Creeping Tides, Against the Winds, The Next Corner,* and *Trouble-the-House.* Jordan also wrote several plays including *A Luncheon at Nick's, The Pompadour's Protégé, Mrs. Dakon* and *The Right Road.*

Jordan's writing is remembered as vivid and varied and her plays were acclaimed for their command of the contemporary scene of the time. Jordan fell ill and suffered from insomnia for several years. In 1926, while visiting a relative in Mountain Lakes, New Jersey, she committed suicide by ingesting poison. Her body was then cremated and buried at Sleepy Hollow Cemetery.

*See* Fiction, Irish-American

*Who's Who in America* (1922–23).
*Bookman* (June 1913).
*Publishers' Weekly* (June 1926).
*Dictionary of American Biography,* vol. 10.

JOY HARRELL

## JOURNALISM, IRISH-AMERICAN

Not surprisingly for a culture that has placed such value on language, Irish America has a long, varied and lively tradition in journalism. In fact, Irish-American journalism can be divided into two traditions: mainstream, where the audience is as vast and diverse as America itself, and ethnic, which speaks to Irish-Americans exclusively.

Mainstream newspapers, and now the electronic media, have long featured Irish-Americans in the ranks of reporters, commentators and management. And the ethnic media, while not nearly as numerous as in the late 19th century and early 20th century, continue to play a key role in chronicling and interpreting the Irish-American experience in cities as well as suburbs. The ethnic media started with the publication of the first Irish-American weekly newspapers, and it continues into the 21st century with a plethora of Irish-American television and radio shows, such as public television's "Out of Ireland" program, and a variety of Irish-American Web sites on the Internet.

There has been an Irish-American presence in the mainstream as well as the ethnic press since the early years of the American republic, and journalism remains one of Irish America's signature professions even today—Irish-American columnists won four Pulitzer Prizes for commentary from 1986 to 1997 (Jimmy Breslin of the *New York Daily News*, Anna Quindlen of the *New York Times,* Jim Dwyer of the now-defunct *New York Newsday* and Eileen McNamara of the *Boston Globe*). And Irish-American political commentators and journalists are ubiquitous on television, from Pat Buchanan (*CNN*) to Tim Russert (*NBC*), and on prominent editorial pages: Maureen Dowd (*New York Times*), Michael Kelly (*National Journal*) and William F. Buckley (*National Review*).

Journalism was a key step toward reaching coveted middle-class status for Irish-American reporters and editors. At a time when prejudice, discrimination and a lack of skills kept most white-collar professions beyond the grasp of many Irish immigrants and their children, the raucous world of urban newspapering was a natural link between the neighborhood and the office. The intensely competitive world of late 19th-century journalism placed a high priority on scoops requiring an intimate knowledge of the streets and the precincts. As the Irish came to dominate both, it was not surprising that the Irish also rose in journalism.

Ethnic newspapers provided Irish-Americans with an outlet to critique their new country on their own terms and through the prism of the Irish struggle on both sides of the Atlantic. Everything from petty personal feuds to great issues of the day were played out and argued over in the pages of Irish-American journals. And just as mainstream newspapers conducted their business as if at war with the competition, Irish-American newspapers and their editors often saved their most savage invective for each other. In the 1880s, John Devoy of the *Irish Nation* took delight in describing his onetime friend Jeremiah O'Donovan Rossa as a raving drunk after Rossa founded his own, short-lived newspaper, *United Irishman.* And Devoy's rivals at the *Irish World* printed front-page accusations suggesting that Devoy was pilfering funds raised to export revolution from America to Ireland.

Journalism allowed the Irish to air their views about the subjects nearest their heart, whether it was assimilation, workers' rights or the cause of Irish freedom. Their contentious style clearly had its origins in the argumentative and extremely literate tradition of Irish journalism at home. Many of the Irish-American journalists who crowded into mid-19th-century urban newsrooms were influenced by such outstanding journals as *The Nation,* which was the organ of the Young Ireland movement, and the *Irish People,* the Fenian newspaper of the mid-1860s.

Irish-Americans began setting up their own network of newspapers in the early years of the 19th century. Among the first Irish newspapers was *The Shamrock,* which began publication in 1810. *The Emerald* soon followed.

*The Shamrock*'s front page featured two logos: The harp of Ireland and the eagle of America. The two symbols spoke volumes about the attitudes of immigrants even in this early stage of Irish-American life. The Irish eagerly embraced the democratic and republican values of their adopted land, but they hadn't forgotten their heritage. And the newspaper's editors encouraged this bifurcated tradition. They encouraged their readers to become

upstanding American citizens, but they reminded them that they were Irish too. The paper's founders were Edward Gillespy and Thomas O'Connor. The editors made their mission clear: They intended, they wrote, to expose "those illiberal opinions early sown by Ireland's enemies" in America.

The early newspapers set the tone for an explosion of Irish-American journalism, mostly in the form of weekly newspapers, by the time of the Famine immigration of mid-19th century. These newspapers varied in mission and tone, depending on the views of their editors and publishers. *The Citizen,* published in New York, became the voice of the patriot-exile John Mitchel from 1854 until it ceased publication in 1872. *The Chicago Citizen,* founded by fiery nationalist and onetime Congressman John Finerty, advocated in no uncertain terms for Irish freedom.

Some of these papers, like the *Irish American* and the *Freeman's Journal* of New York, were designed to help along the assimilation process. It was respectful of authority, particularly of the Church (the *Freeman's Journal* bitterly attacked Mitchel's *Citizen* when the latter assailed Catholic clergymen), but was vigilant in its defense of the rights of Irish-Americans who were battling discrimination in America's cities.

*The Boston Pilot* had a similar mission. Founded in 1836 by Patrick Donahue, it was closely aligned with the Roman Catholic Archdiocese (in fact, the paper would later become the official archdiocesan organ) but it was a steadfast champion of Irish nationalism, a cause which high-ranking clergy did not always embrace. The *Pilot*'s long-time editor, the poet, philosopher and nationalist John Boyle O'Reilly, was a onetime Fenian who served hard time in Australia but managed to escape that prison colony. An ally of his fellow journalist John Devoy and other adamant Irish-American nationalists, O'Reilly was a beloved figure in Boston, respected for his intelligence, polish and his advocacy on behalf of blacks, Jews, Indians and all immigrants. Well aware that many Irish immigrants dreamed of an Ireland free from Britain, he advised his readers that the promise of America contained a promise for Ireland: "We can do more for Ireland with our Americanism than we can with our Irishness," he told the new immigrants, referring to the possibilities that American politics provided.

While some Irish-American newspapers played on the understandable resentments of Irish immigrants and their children as they tried to find a place in hostile 19th-century America, the *Pilot* expressed boundless optimism: "There is a large and honorable . . . number of Americans who welcome Irish-American citizens to an equal share in the prizes of business and political life, and who are proud to be associated with them upon the same social plane," the *Pilot* wrote as early as 1866, even before Boyle O'Reilly's arrival. Once the onetime Fenian prisoner took over the newspaper's editorship, circulation climbed to more than 100,000, making the *Pilot* the largest Irish-American newspaper of the late 19th century. It became an arbiter of Irish-American life in New England, a voice that promoted assimilation as both achievable and necessary.

Two New York-based newspapers in the late 19th century distinguished themselves for the leading role they took in lobbying and agitating on behalf of Irish independence and, in effect, becoming a rallying point for Irish immigrants who were determined to win freedom for the old country from the shores of America. *The Irish World* was founded in 1870 by Patrick Ford, an immigrant from Galway who learned the printer's trade in Boston while working for the abolitionist William Lloyd Garrison.

The *World* started in Boston, but quickly moved to New York, where it became a radical advocate for Irish freedom and for the burgeoning union movement. During a long and bitter recession that began in 1873, Ford changed the name of his paper to suit his evolving world view: He called it the *Irish World and Industrial Liberator*. He remained adamant on the subject of Irish freedom, but he pointed out to his readers that the cause of Ireland was the cause of working people in America too. Exploitation, whether in the fields of County Cork or in the factories of New York, was to be condemned and overthrown.

By contrast, the *Irish Nation*, founded in 1881, focused with single-minded passion on the cause of Irish independence and the ways in which Irish-Americans could, and should, help achieve that goal. John Devoy served as the paper's publisher, editor and agitator-in-chief, and he gave the newspaper its distinct and often defiant voice. "Our aim will be to create an Irish party in this country whose actions in American politics will have for its sole object the interests of Ireland," Devoy once wrote. Devoy had come to America a decade before the *Irish Nation*'s founding, one of several Fenians who were arrested in the mid-1860s, sent to prison and then given amnesty from British Prime Minister William Gladstone.

Devoy settled in New York and eventually found a job in journalism at the *New York Herald* at the height of the newspaper's fame. And while the paper's owner, James Gordon Bennet, would later condemn Charles Stewart Parnell's land crusade and Irish nationalism in general, Devoy was one of several famous Fenians who found employment at the *Herald*, including Jerome Collins, the paper's meteorologist who founded Clan na Gael in 1867, and Joseph I. C. Clarke, a reporter who fled Ireland ahead of the police in the 1860s. Devoy, a self-taught student of international politics, worked his way through the paper's ranks to become foreign editor. And he worked side by side with his boyhood friend and fellow Fenian James J. O'Kelly, the newspaper's drama critic who won a small bit of fame with his coverage of the Orange Day riot in New York in 1871.

Devoy tried to balance his activism on behalf of Irish freedom—he was a leader of the Clan na Gael—with his journalistic career. Eventually, he ran afoul of his *Herald* bosses and was fired, a circumstance that led to his founding of the *Irish Nation*, which became the official organ of the Clan na Gael. The paper folded after a short and controversial run in 1885 after Devoy once again tried to balance journalism and politics. He supported James Blaine, the Republican candidate for president in 1884, over Grover Cleveland, a Democrat, a move that ended in disaster when Blaine lost and Devoy was perceived to be a traitor to the heavily Irish Democrats.

Some fifteen years later, Devoy tried his hand at newspapers once again, this time founding the far more successful *Gaelic American*, which served as the voice of Irish-American nationalism through the tumultuous years leading to the creation of the Irish Free State. His crowded office on the fourth floor of a walkup on William Street near Manhattan's newspaper row functioned as something of an Irish Republic in exile, and was visited by many of the patriots who would later find fame (and an early death) during the Easter Rebellion of 1916 and the War of Independence.

The ethnic newspapers performed a critical role in speaking directly to this huge immigrant group, crowded into cities that must have overwhelmed them at first. They also were key components in building an Irish exile political movement in the United States. And because of the latter role, some of the newspapers made news, rather than simply reported news, when Ireland renewed its fight for freedom early in the 20th century. In feuds that mirrored tensions in the Irish community, Devoy's *Gaelic American*, the Ford family's *Irish World* and a Philadelphia-based newcomer called the *Irish Press* pilloried each other in the period leading up to the compromise that created the Irish Free State in the early 1920s. Here again, advocacy journalism played a key role in shaping Irish-American public opinion, as the *Gaelic American* argued with some reservations for acceptance of the Anglo-Irish treaty and the Free State, while the *Irish World* and particularly the *Irish Press*—which was founded by Joseph McGarrity, an important ally and friend of Eamon de Valera—opposed the treaty. Newspapers were considered so critical in shaping Irish-American opinion that McGarrity and de Valera, along with two other allies, founded the *Irish Press* to serve as a counterpoint to the *Gaelic American*. De Valera later paid tribute to the paper and to his friends when he founded his own organ in Dublin and borrowed the name *Irish Press*.

Assimilation, the winning of a measure of Irish freedom, the decline of newspapers and the eventual flight of the Irish to the suburbs led to a sad but inexorable decline in the number of Irish ethnic newspapers. One by one they closed; the *Gaelic American* went out of business in 1950, when it was bought by the Ford family and folded into the *Irish World*—the newspaper that delighted in tormenting the *Gaelic American*'s founder, Devoy. By the 1970s, Irish newspapers were an endangered species: *The Irish World* soon closed, as did the New York-based *Irish Advocate*. While some ethnic newspapers remained in various regions, by the mid-1980s, only the New York-based *Irish Echo* commanded a weekly nationwide audience.

In the meantime, however, the Irish presence in mainstream journalism became even more conspicuous during the golden age of print journalism in mid-20th century.

Irish-American journalists owe a huge debt to a pair of pioneers from the golden age of newspapering, Finley Peter Dunne of the *Chicago Evening Post* and Nellie Bly of the *New York World*. In his columns about life in Chicago's immigrant neighborhoods, Dunne created the semifictitious character of Mr. Dooley, a wise Irish saloonkeeper with an opinion on everything from local politics to foreign affairs. The columns were written in an Irish dialect—he had Mr. Dooley holding forth one holiday season with sentences like this: "I see in th' pa-aper where some wan says Chris'mas dinners has been provided f'r twenty-thousan' poor people." Through Mr. Dooley and the characters who gathered in his saloon, Dunne wrote a narrative of Irish-American urban life that remains, more than a century later, a classic snapshot of late 19th-century life.

Nellie Bly, whose given name was Elizabeth Cochrane, was the daughter of an Irish-American judge in Pennsylvania. She barged her way into the extremely masculine world of journalism by being fearless and by wearing her emotions on her sleeve. Her journalism was intensely personal, and her crusades were passionate. But she won her greatest fame by participating in gimmicks such as one memorable trip around the world in 72 days. She was among the first celebrity journalists, and was still at the height of her fame when she died in 1922.

It is not such a long line between the days of Dunne and Bly to more recent Irish-American journalist-stars. Jimmy Cannon, Pete Hamill, Jimmy Breslin, Anna Quindlen, Mary McGrory, Mike Barnicle, Maureen Dowd and countless others have contributed mightily to the Irish tradition in mainstream American newspapering.

And in a development few would have predicted, Irish ethnic journalism has undergone a renaissance since the mid-1980s. *Irish America* magazine debuted just as a new generation of Irish immigrants was on its way to America, and it showed newcomer and native-born alike a successful, glamorous side to the Irish-American experience. Not long afterwards, the magazine's publisher, Niall O'Dowd, launched a weekly newspaper called *Irish Voice,* and it immediately challenged the *Irish Echo* with its coverage of news and celebrities of interest to the young immigrants of the 1980s. The *Echo,* however, responded brilliantly, adding color, new and younger editors and writers. Under the leadership of publisher Claire Grimes and editor Tom Connelly, the *Echo* turned potential adversity into renewed prosperity, establishing itself firmly as the nation's leading Irish-American newspaper. The *Voice's* challenge to the *Echo* led to more aggressive coverage of the Irish-American community, and the emergence of younger journalists meant that the coverage took on a far more irreverent tone. Institutions from the St. Patrick's Day parade to the Catholic Church to the vast network of Irish cultural and business organizations were subjected to rigorous scrutiny. In the meantime, the *Irish People,* with a small but national circulation, covered events in Northern Ireland from a republican point of view.

Other newspapers, such as the monthly *Boston Irish Reporter,* the *Irish Edition* in Philadelphia, the San Francisco *Gael,* the *Desert Shamrock* of Arizona and the *Irish American Post* of Chicago all took full advantage of the late-century explosion of interest in all things Irish. Yet another new publication, the *World of Hibernia,* was launched in the mid-1990s. A quarterly published by Kevin Kelly, the magazine fairly drips of accomplishment and affluence, and its tony advertisements speak volumes about Irish America's rise to power and money.

Ethnic journalism made it to the national airwaves with the debut of "Out of Ireland" in the mid-1990s. Hosted by Patricia O'Reilly, the half-hour show appears weekly on public television stations across the country. And dozens of Irish radio programs in markets across the country perform the very functions the weekly newspapers of old did: They offer a forum for ideas and news of interest to the Irish-American community, and they keep the community informed about events in Ireland as well as in local neighborhoods.

*See* Devoy, John; McGrory, Mary; O'Reilly, John Boyle

Margaret A. Blanchard, *History of the Mass Media in the United States; An Encyclopedia* (Chicago, 1998).

Terry Golway, *Irish Rebel* (New York, 1998).

Robert Francis Hueston, *The Catholic Press and Nativism, 1840–1860* (New York, 1976).

William Leonard Joyce, *Editors and Ethnicity: A History of the Irish-American Press, 1848–1883* (New York, 1976).

Carl Wittke, *The Irish in America* (Baton Rouge, 1996).

Lubomyr Roman Wynar and Anna T. Wynar, *Encyclopedia Directory of Ethnic Newspapers and Periodicals in the United States,* 2d ed. (Littleton, Colo., 1976).

TERRY GOLWAY

## JOYCE'S *ULYSSES* ON TRIAL

The backdrop of World War I provides a quick measure of the distinctive consciousness of James Joyce in the years 1914–18.

James Joyce

While the men of Europe either fought in the immense bloodletting, or read, thought and talked of little else, Joyce remained cloistered in Trieste and Zurich with his inner eye riveted on a city on Europe's fringes—his native Dublin. He was crafting, phrase by phrase, a modern version of the wanderings of the legendary hero, Ulysses, with a writing technique that was a shaft to the inner life of the mind and considered no human behavior outside the boundaries of art. The conventional mind of the day accepted the violence of the battlefield as a necessary part of life and thought literature a vaguely uplifting entertainment—nice to dip into when you had a little time to rest from *real* life. To the average person of his day Joyce was writing a book his Aunt Josephine termed "not fit to read." Joyce's response to his beloved aunt: "If *Ulysses* isn't fit to read, then life isn't fit to live." [Richard Ellmann, *James Joyce* (New York, 1983), p.537]. Joyce's *Ulysses* was the most detailed epiphany of the lives of ordinary men and women the world had ever seen.

But before anyone could read it, he had to find a publisher, and a printer brave enough to print it. Joyce was no stranger to censorship. Before his first prose book *Dubliners* was published, twenty-two publishers and printers refused it, and then the whole first edition was privately burned. [James Joyce, *Ulysses* (New York, 1961), p. xiii.] It was an American editor (and her Serbo-Croatian printer) who agreed to take the risk with *Ulysses.* After reading the opening lines of only one episode, Margaret Anderson decided to print *Ulysses* in serial form in her *avant garde* literary periodical, *The Little Review.* What she read was the flow or "stream" of consciousness of a modern Irish version of Telemachus, the son of Ulysses. Young Stephen Dedalus, an aspiring artist and emotional exile in his home town, is on a deserted Dublin beach pondering life and death and change and reality and the sea in the rather inflated mode of thought of a young intellectual: "Ineluctable modality of the visible: at least that if no more, thought through my eyes. Signatures of all things I am here to read, seaspawn and seawrack, the nearing tide, that rusty boot."[James Joyce, *Ulysses* (New York, 1961.), p. 37].

"We'll print it," Margaret Anderson wrote Joyce, "if it's the last effort of our lives." [Margaret Anderson, *My Thirty Years War* (New York, 1969), p. 175]. In March of l918 as the German armies were gathering for their final offensive of the War, the first episode of Joyce's masterpiece, *Ulysses,* slipped quietly into print.

As publication proceeded, the sentries of public morality across the ocean became ever more vigilant. By January 1920 U.S. post office officials had seized three issues of *The Little Review* as obscene. [Ellmann, p. 502]. The third was based on Ulysses' encounter with The Cyclops, a barbarous one-eyed giant in a cave. Joyce's modern cyclops is a loud, arrogant, single-minded bigot who roars one-eyed opinions—the clichés of the Irish nationalist—to a captive audience in a Dublin bar. On hearing the news that the magazine had been seized and burned, Joyce wrote to his patron, Harriet Weaver, "This is the second time I have had the pleasure of being burned while on earth so that I hope I shall pass through the fires of purgatory as quickly as my patron S. Aloysius." [Quoted in Ellmann, p. 502].

### The 1921 Trial: Four Episodes of *Ulysses*

While the confiscation of his "Cyclops" episode was taking place, Joyce was finishing up the most subtle and sensitive episode so far, "Nausicaa." In the Homeric legend, a king's daughter, finding Ulysses shipwrecked and naked on a beach, cleans, clothes and comforts him. In the modern parallel Leopold Bloom, a kind-hearted and sensitive man of Jewish ancestry, has just been verbally crucified by the Dublin cyclops' cruel barbs and anti-Semitic fury. Bloom is Ulysses, a wanderer in his native Ireland. He is alone on a beach. An attractive young woman is a little way off. It is twilight.

With his signature "stream of consciousness" technique, Joyce takes the reader into "Nausicaa's" thoughts—in her own voice and from the perspective of a young woman nurtured on women's romantic magazines. The silent attention of the dark stranger on the beach is stirring fantasies within her limited, and sentimental, experience of life. Then, true to his method of viewing any scene from multiple points of view, Joyce takes us into the consciousness of Leopold Bloom. Finding comfort in the beauty of a young woman across the way, he drifts into sexual fantasies. As evening slowly descends to the faint hymns and litanies of Benediction at the nearby church of Our Lady, Star of the Sea, the young woman rises and limps away, for she is lame.

"Nausicaa" was too strong a draught for John S. Sumner of the New York Society for the Prevention of Vice. In February 1921 Margaret Anderson and her partner Jane Heap were brought to trial in the Court of Special Sessions for publishing obscenity. In another irony for the Irish writer, the basis for the prosecution was an English common law principle laid down in *Regina v. Hicklin* [L.R. 2 Q.B. 360 (1868) in David M. O'Brien, *Constitutional Law and Politics* (New York, 1995), p.419]. The *Hicklin* test was the common legal litmus test on charges of obscenity: "whether the tendency of the matter charged as obscenity is to deprive and corrupt those whose minds are open to such immoral influences and into whose hands a publication of this sort might fall." [O'Brien, p. 419]. A book was seized if an official felt it might corrupt the morals of the emotionally immature, that it might corrupt a child. To insure the maximum shock effect, individual words and passages were lifted out of context and read aloud in court.

The trial took place before three judges of the Court of Special Sessions and Joyce himself couldn't have sketched a sharper scene of mental paralysis. His character of the single-minded and opinionated "cyclops" was written as social commentary on the level of conversation in a bar in Dublin; it turned out to be a remarkably apt metaphor for the men conducting the trial. Obscuring the legal issue was a thick coating of cultural assumption: the gentlemanly obligation to shield the young and "the ladies" from reading, seeing or hearing explicit references to bodily functions or sexuality—outside of a textbook. One of the judges objected to the obscene passages being read aloud in court in the presence of a lady.

"But," said defense counsel John Quinn, "she is the publisher." To which the judge responded, "I am sure she didn't know the significance of what she was publishing." [Anderson, p. 221]. To no one's surprise, the editors of *The Little Review* were convicted and fined, and the publishing of *Ulysses* halted. The doors of legitimate publishing houses were closed and bolted. [Ellmann, p. 504].

Joyce was drained. "My book," he said to his friend Sylvia Beach in her little bookshop in Paris that served as a haven for him, "will never come out now." In another of those ironies on which events often turn—a favorite theme of Joyce's—the legal blocking of publication became the catalyst for a small cameo moment sacred to the disciples of literature. Miss Beach replied: "Would you let Shakespeare and Company have the honor of bringing out your *Ulysses?*" [Ellmann, p. 504].

Indeed, he would.

And shortly after 7:00 AM on February 2, 1922, his 40th birthday, Miss Beach arrived at his apartment door to place the first copy of *Ulysses,* bound in the Greek colors of white and blue, in Joyce's hands. [Ellman, p. 524].

### 1933: Southern District of New York v. One Book called "Ulysses"

As the *auto-da-fé* in the U.S. Customs houses burned throughout the twenties, pirated editions sprang up like bootleg whiskey. And though illegal, both whiskey and *Ulysses* were reaching people far and wide. By the decade's end James Joyce was no longer the "Irish writer of dirty books"; he was a deity for a generation of modern writers, including the young American literary genius William Faulkner whose *The Sound and the Fury,* written from four points of view, appeared in 1929. Artists studied Joyce's style, academics dissected his multilingual literary and historical references, and a growing list of supporters, including clergy, protested the bootleg editions of *Ulysses* that robbed the author of royalties. The climate had changed. The time was ripe for a new legal test. In March 1932, Bennett Cerf of Random House contracted with Joyce to publish *Ulysses* in the United States. Both Cerf and Joyce, who relished a legal fight, braced for the battle.

When Random House brought a single copy of *Ulysses* through Customs the book was seized, and the case of The United States District Court v. One Book called "Ulysses" came to a federal court on July 11, 1933. The grounds, under the Tariff Act of 1930: "that the book is obscene . . . subject to seizure, forfeiture and confiscation and destruction."[Woolsey, Decision on *Ulysses,* p. vii]. Although the legality of importing *Ulysses* occasioned the trial, the broader and deeper questions on trial were the encapsulating of outdated moral conventions into law and the changing nature of public mores. The literate world on both sides of the Atlantic trained its attention on the courtroom of a United States judge who would hear the case "on motion without trial": Judge John M. Woolsey.

The passages of Joyce's story banned in the 1921 trial had ended on a beach in Dublin, at twilight. But basic to Joyce's method was a shift in style to capture the state of mind of his characters, and that state of mind, and style, changed with the lengthening day. The story that entered Judge Woolsey's courtroom in 1933 stretched over a full 18 hours of a day in June 1904. The sections set in the late night hours contained more explicit sensual material than what had been banned in 1921. Following his characters where their day, and their minds, led, Joyce trailed the young philosophical Stephen Dedalus to Dublin's Nighttown, mixing fantasies of a mind distorted by drink with the external realities of a brothel—all in words and images replicating the scenes. Finally, in the early hours of the morning the book lurches to its climactic close inside the head of "Penelope," Molly Bloom. Lying in bed, Molly mentally replays her romantic relationships until she reaches that breathless moment of first making love with Leopold, "when he said I was a flower of the mountain," and when "his heart was going like mad and yes I said yes I will Yes." [Ellmann, p. 783].

Molly's thoughts, read out of context, would surely have doomed *Ulysses*. So attorney Morris Ernst set out to discredit the old tactic that had dominated censorship cases and defined Joyce's work as obscene in 1921: to shock those present in court by cutting the sedate air of the courtroom with words and passages commonly considered "dirty" or "obscene." Ernst's argument: the only fair method of judgment was to view the work as a whole. Considered as one integrated piece of art in which each part relates to the whole effect, *Ulysses* was "a classic." But the traditional legal definition of obscenity was raised in regard to the waterfall of memories, images, thoughts, associations cascading from the consciousness of Molly Bloom. Judge Woolsey put the question to Morris Ernst that cut to the heart of the public's fears: "Suppose that a girl of 18 or 20 read the soliloquy of Marion Bloom, wouldn't it be apt to corrupt her?"

"I don't think that is the standard we should go by," argued Ernst. "Adult literature," under the law, need not "be reduced to mush for infants." ["Court Undecided on 'Ulysses Ban,'" *New York Times*, Nov. 26, 16:3].

Before reaching his verdict, Judge John M. Woolsey did a remarkably simple, and brilliant, thing: he announced to the court that he intended to read the book—to read the *entire* book—for himself. So, during the summer of 1933 Judge Woolsey retired to read the nearly 800 pages of the concatenation of thoughts and feelings and memories of young Stephen Dedalus and some rowdy medical students joking while a woman is in labor and a girl on a beach and Molly Bloom and a priest out for a stroll and the citizens of Dublin arguing or singing old Irish songs in a bar. And throughout, Dublin's own "Ulysses"—a decent Jewish man named Bloom—wandering and seeking like the ancient hero to find his son, walks and shops and feeds birds and goes to a funeral and thinks about his wife and her lover and helps a young man named Stephen who has had too much to drink and daydreams through the hours of a very long day. And the press and the lawyers and the publisher and the author all settled in to wait.

## JUDGE WOOLSEY'S DECISION

The first week of December 1933 spawned both the repeal of Prohibition and Judge Woolsey's decision on *Ulysses*. *This* time the mind assessing the work of one of the century's literary giants was equal to the task.

In his rather lengthy decision, Judge Woolsey first addressed the author's intention. Did Joyce *intend* to write pornography,

that is, to exploit obscenity? The Judge concluded that he did not: ". . . in spite of its frankness, I do not detect anywhere the leer of the sensualist." *Ulysses* was not pornographic. [Woolsey, Decision on *Ulysses*, pp. viii–ix].

Still, despite intention, was it "obscene" in the legal sense: "tending to stir sex impulses or to lead to sexually impure and lustful thoughts?" To lay the foundation for a critical legal distinction, the Judge reshaped the question: stir lustful thoughts *in whom?* An adolescent? A grown person with an immature or twisted mind? A normal person?

"It is only," declared the judge, "with the normal person that the law is concerned." [Woolsey, Decision on *Ulysses*, p. xii].

How did the judge determine the impact of *Ulysses* on a "normal person?" First he raised the standard of judgment to a person *capable of reading and judging literature,* then tested out the book's effect not only on himself, but on two other men whose opinions on literature he respected. Each of the three readers concluded independently that *Ulysses* did not meet the legal definition of obscene, tending to excite sexual impulses or lustful thoughts, when read *"in its entirety."* The final three words are critical. *As a whole,* the impact was ". . . only that of a somewhat tragic and very powerful commentary on the inner lives of men and women." [Woolsey, Decision, p. xi].

Judge Woolsey might well have stopped there. But his landmark decision stepped beyond what observers had come to expect from an officer of a court of law. Testifying to his respect for the author as a true artist, the Judge delivered one of the finest *critiques* of *Ulysses* that had yet appeared. The book, he said, was "not unlike a multiple exposure on a cinema film which would give a clear foreground with a background visible but somewhat blurred and out of focus . . ." [Woolsey, Decision, p. ix]. The judge was holding up the *artistic integrity of the author* as a standard of judgment. Joyce was using a new technique to explore inner lives; had he not been "honest . . . the result would be psychologically misleading . . . and artistically inexcusable." [Woolsey, Decision, p. ix]. Judge Woolsey pushed the legal envelope beyond what had been conventionally understood as literature, pushed it to encompass the new inner territory, and method, of James Joyce. "For his attempt sincerely and honestly to realize his objective has required him incidentally to use certain words which are generally considered dirty words and has led at times to what many think is a too poignant preoccupation with sex in the thought of his characters." [Woolsey, Decision, p. x]. But: "I have not found anything that I consider to be dirt for dirt's sake. Each word of the book contributes like a bit of a mosaic to the detail of the picture which Joyce is seeking to construct for his readers . . ."[Woolsey, Decision, p. x]. ". . . it must be remembered," wrote the Judge in an indelible line, "that his locale was Celtic and his season Spring." [Woolsey, Decision, p. x].

The verdict: Each person is free to choose not to "associate with such folk as Joyce describes." That is an exercise of free choice. "But when such a real artist in words, as Joyce undoubtedly is, seeks to draw a true picture of the lower middle class in a European city, ought it to be impossible for the American public legally to see that picture?" [Woolsey, Decision, p. x].

"Ulysses may, therefore, be admitted to the United States." [Woolsey, Decision, p. xii].

In New York, Bennett Cerf got the news by telephone and within minutes the Random House typesetters were at work. [Ellmann, p. 667]. In Paris, Joyce received the news by cable.

Having wished for a long time that someone would *enjoy* his story, would see the *fun* in it, [Ellmann, p. 524], he delighted in the judge's opinion. His statement, released through a friend: "Mr. Joyce finds the judge to be not devoid of a sense of humor." [Ellmann, p. 667]. Commented attorney Morris Ernst: ". . . we may now imbibe freely of the contents of bottles and forthright books." [Ernst, "Forward,", p. vi]. A quarter century later, in *Roth v. United States* and *Alberts v. California* [354 U.S. 476, 77 S.Ct. 1304 (1957)] the standards of the impact of a work of art on "the average person" and judging a literary work *as a whole* were adopted by the Supreme Court of the United States. [O'Brien, pp. 419–20].

For Joyce, Judge Woolsey's decision represented more than a legal victory. One of the themes weaving in and out of *Ulysses* is the nature of true community. Joyce had epiphanized the absence of community as men and women move about their days passing each other emotionally and intellectually like so many "wandering rocks." Believing that true community grows from authentic encounters between two human beings, Joyce tried to jar people into placing their minds in touch with the concrete stuff of life that was all around them, instead of exchanging threadbare clichés and sentimentalized emotions, and to recognize—amidst the brutalized social relations of a modern city—a single tolerant, compassionate man. Judge Woolsey—a singularly tolerant mind in the American legal system—had grasped his meaning.

As for the Irish in America, though many were initially as shocked by Joyce as their cousins back in Ireland, he was the artist of their experience too. The immigrants' experience was bound by the limits of ghetto culture. They had left their Dublin, only to find it waiting for them in Boston, and Chicago, and Brooklyn. *Ulysses* had held the mirror up to the whole cultural patchwork quilt that kept people repeating old patterns of thought and feeling. But Joyce was no cold iconoclast: he had sent down a vertical shaft to the root meaning of Irish civilization, and the redemptive meaning of its religion, then placed his own mind in continuous touch with the broader intellectual traditions of Europe. This penetrating and broad ranging consciousness—through which one might view the twisted forms of life around us—was distilled into *Ulysses*.

And, true to his sense of community as built upon authentic human encounter, Joyce was affecting, one by one, the minds of a younger generation of artists who felt something akin to reverence for the nearly blind old master and his infamous *Ulysses*. Perhaps William Faulkner summed up the feeling best:

"You should approach Joyce's *Ulysses* as the illiterate Baptist Preacher approaches the Old Testament: with faith." [Jean Stein, "William Faulkner," in Malcolm Cowley. ed. *The Paris Review Interviews: Writers at Work* New York: Penguin Books, 1986, p. 135].

Margaret Anderson, *My Thirty Years' War* (New York, 1969).
Harry Blamires, *The New Bloomsday Book* (New York, 1990).

Mary and Padraic Colum, *Our Friend James Joyce* (Garden City, New York, 1958).
Frank Delaney, *James Joyce's Odyssey* (New York, 1981).
Richard Ellman, *James Joyce* (New York, 1983).
Morris L. Ernst, "Forward," in James Joyce, *Ulysses* (New York, 1961).
James Joyce, "A Letter from Mr. Joyce to the Publisher, Reprinted in 1934 Edition by Permission of the Author," in James Joyce, *Ulysses* (New York, 1961).
——, *Ulysses* (New York, 1961).
Hugh Kenner, *Dublin's Joyce* (New York, 1987).
*The New York Times* (June 24, 1933: 14:4; July 12, 1933: 15:1; November 26, 1933: 16:3).
David O'Brien, *Constitutional Law and Politics*. Second Edition, Vol. 2 (New York, 1995).
Jean Stein, "William Faulkner," in Malcolm Cowley, ed. *The Paris Review Interviews: Writers at Work* (New York, 1986).
John M. Woolsey, Decision in the United States District Court, Southern District of New York, United States of America, *Libelant*, v. One Book called "Ulysses" Random House, Inc., *Claimant*. Opinion A. 110–59. December 6, 1933. Reprinted in James Joyce, *Ulysses* (New York, 1961): vii–xii.

PATRICIA A. O'CONNOR

## JUDGE, WILLIAM QUAN (1851–1896)

Theosophist and lawyer. Born in Dublin, Ireland, as one of the seven children of Frederick and Alice (Quan) Judge, William Quan is said to have had a normal childhood until the age of seven when he began to exhibit an unusual interest in the study of magic and Rosicruciansim. After Judge's mother died, his father took the family to the U.S. where Judge eventually studied law and became a partner in the firm of Olcott, Gonzalez & Judge. Judge prospered in the legal business and developed a popular and respectful reputation especially for his precision and dedication in his work. In 1874, he married Ella Smith and the next year became a member of the Theosophical Society after having represented Madame H. P. Blavatsky in legal matters. In 1883, it was Judge who reorganized the Theosophical Society after it had dissipated, and the theosophic movement began to spread in the U.S. In 1886, Judge initiated and undertook the beginning of the publication of *The Path*, a theosophical newsletter that he edited until his death. In 1893, Judge resigned from his legal practice to devote all of his time to the society. Under his influence the society prospered and when Judge died on March 21, 1896, the membership was reported as close to 400,000.

Theosophical magazines and newsletters: *The Path, Theosophist,* and *Lucifer.*
An anonymous history entitled *The Theosophical Movement 1875–1925* (1925).
*Dictionary of American Biography,* 10.

JOY HARRELL

# K

## KANE, HELEN (1904–1966)

Singer and film actress. Born Helen Schroeder in New York City to Irish descendants Louis Schroeder and Ellen Dixon, she attended schools in the Bronx and displayed an early interest for school productions. By the age of thirteen she was working several jobs to help family finances while trying to establish an early acting career. Her first break came when she was noticed by Chico Marx and was asked to join the Four Marx Brothers in a production at the Fordham Theater. This production paved the way to other opportunities such as singing in a popular club and a small part in *A Night in Spain* in 1927.

Her success continued on Broadway in *Good Boy* (1928), personal and radio appearances, and movies such as: *Nothing But the Truth, Sweetie, Pointed Heels, Dangerous Nan McGrew, Heads Up, The Pharmacist* and *Counsel on the Fence*. Kane also appeared in vaudeville circuits and her popularity grew in accord with the famous line she inserted into one of her songs, "boop-boop-a-doop." However, her good fortune was eventually disrupted by two lawsuits. In one lawsuit she sued Paramount Pictures for taking her characterization and inserting it into "Betty Boop" cartoons. The lawsuit did not end in her favor and the rest of her life was mired by failed investments and struggles with creditors. Kane is remembered, nonetheless, for her baby voice which became a popular sound in the early 1930s. She died in New York City on September 25, 1966.

New York Public Library's Performing Arts Research Center at Lincoln Center; National Film Information Service.
Stanley Green, *Encyclopedia of Musical Theater* (1976).
*Dictionary of American Biography,* supplement 8.

JOY HARRELL

## KANE, MARY THERESA (1936–  )

Educator, religious leader, feminist. Margaret Joan Kane was born on September 24, 1936, in the Bronx, New York. She was the fourth of seven children. Her parents, Philip and Mary (Faherty) Kane, although both natives of County Galway, Ireland, met and married in the United States. As first generation Irish-Americans, Margaret and her siblings were steeped in the ambiance of East Coast Irish Catholicism.

Margaret's birthdate—the Feast of Our Lady of Mercy—augured a choice she was to make in her mid-teens. At that time, she entered the novitiate of the Sisters of Mercy of the Union at Tarrytown, New York. She pronounced her final vows September 16, 1960, taking the name Mary Theresa.

Theresa's considerable administrative and business talents were soon engaged in a variety of responsibilities: first, she was appointed to St. Francis Hospital in Port Jarvis, New York; then, within six years of her final profession, she was selected to a leadership role in her religious congregation. Four years later, in 1970, she became Provincial Administrator of the Sisters of Mercy of the Union, Province of New York. She was elected to national leadership for the Sisters of Mercy of the Union, serving in the role of Administrator General from 1977–1983.

While serving as Administrator General, Theresa Kane was elected to the presidency of the Leadership Conference of Women Religious, 1978–1980. As President of the Leadership Conference, Theresa was invited to offer a few words of welcome to John Paul II in the National Shrine of the Immaculate Conception in Washington, D.C., on October 7, 1979. Her simple, three-minute address garnered the attention of the Catholic world and catapulted herself, the Leadership Conference and the Sisters of Mercy of the Union into an often controversial spotlight.

The fifth paragraph of a six-paragraph welcome stated simply: "As women we have heard the powerful messages of our Church addressing the dignity and reverence of all persons. As women we have pondered upon these words. Our contemplation leads us to state that the Church in its struggle to be faithful to its call for reverence and dignity for all persons must respond by providing the possibility of women as persons being included in all ministries of our Church." Overnight Theresa Kane became a widely recognized name among Catholic women in the United States, a sought-after guest on talk shows, and a lecturer for public gatherings. Mary Gordon remarked in a 1992 article: "In her radical rejection of the glamor of image and the lure of image makers, her simple commitment to effective justice, her sense of satisfaction with the limits of human possibility and human life, she presents us with the difficult example of genuine leadership and genuine courage" (*Ms Magazine,* July/August 1992).

Theresa Kane was also thrust into the public eye during the early 80s in a series of events surrounding the question of religious men and women serving in public office. Elizabeth Morancy and Arlene Violet in Rhode Island and Agnes Mary Mansour in Michigan were elected or appointed to public office at a time when the Sacred Congregation for Religious had begun to reexamine the appropriateness of such service. In 1982, Arlene Violet sought a first term as attorney general of the state of Rhode Island; in 1983, Agnes Mary Mansour was appointed Director of the Michigan Department of Social Services; and, in 1984, Elizabeth Morancy sought a fourth term in the Rhode Island Assembly. Eventually, all were asked to resign and/or to withdraw from their efforts to serve in public office. As Administrator General of the congregation, Theresa Kane advocated for reconsideration and negotiation, but was unable to prevent the ultimate withdrawal of all three women from membership in the Sisters of Mercy.

Since the completion of her term of leadership in the Sisters of Mercy of the Union, Theresa has continued to lecture extensively on matters related to the achievement of women's full dignity in church and society. Her interest in women's issues prompted her appointment as a representative of the Sisters of Mercy of the Union to the United Nations International Women's Conferences in Nairobi and, again, in Beijing. She has served in an advisory capacity to the Women's Ordination Conference, on the Board of the Association for the Rights of Catholics in the Church (ARCC) and as a featured speaker at the Future of the American

Church Conferences. Currently she is administrator of Mount Mercy in Yonkers, NY, and teaches at Mercy College, Dobbs Ferry, NY.

Mary Gordon, "The Woman Who Spoke Back to the Pope," in *Ms Magazine* (July/August 1992).

Madonna Kolbenschlag, *Authority, Community, and Conflict* (Kansas City, KS, 1986).

———, *Between God and Caesar* (New York,1985).

HELEN MARIE BURNS, R.S.M.

## KANSAS: THE EARLY YEARS

The opening of the West brought thousands of Irish to Kansas in the mid-1800s. Starving not only from the physical hunger of Ireland's Great Famine of 1845–49, Irish Catholics were hungry for the freedom to find employment, to provide homes or small farms for their families and to practice their cherished faith; rights long denied them by English rule. The Irish wanted to raise their children in America, a land filled with hope. Finding the cities on the eastern seaboard miserably overcrowded, many answered the call to come to the newly opened Kansas Territory, to begin what they hoped would be a better life on the open plains.

### EARLY HISTORY

Spanish explorer Francisco Vasquez de Coronado, in search of fabled gold, had led the first white men into the area which was to become Kansas. Osage, Wichita and Kansa Indian tribes hunted buffalo and raised beans and corn in the well-watered, fertile eastern section. To the west, Arapaho and Cheyenne, Comanche and Kiowa Indians followed huge buffalo herds across the rolling, endless prairie.

President Thomas Jefferson's 1803 Louisiana Purchase included most of present-day Kansas. In 1804, the expedition led by Meriwether Lewis and William Clark in search of a water route between the Atlantic and Pacific oceans, stopped to rest where the Missouri and Kansas rivers meet, on the site of the future Wyandotte, or Kansas City, Kansas.

With the growing development of the eastern states, the federal government had taken Indians' land in the East and given them in return Kansas land, which "no white man would covet." The Wyandot territory became part of a Delaware Indian reservation. The Wyandots, an industrious tribe transplanted by the government from Ohio, purchased the land in 1843, laid out "Wyandot City," and built there the first free school in Kansas. In 1858, Bishop John Baptist Miege sent Father Theodore Heinman from Leavenworth to hold services at Wyandotte for the many Irish-Catholic settlers there. This was the beginning of St. Mary's Parish, in one of the first settlements of Irish in Kansas.

Dublin-born Father T. Ambrose Butler of Leavenworth, in his booklet, *The State of Kansas and Irish Immigration* (1871), encouraged oppressed people in Ireland to make new homes in Kansas. "Come to the great free country, where you may soon grow rich and independent as a farmer, with yellow corn waving upon the breasts of prairies, and cattle grazing upon the hills, and no master over you but the Great Lord of Heaven and Earth."

A late 1850s poster distributed in the East advertised steamboat travel on the Kansas River: "The Kansas River Navigable to Shippers, Emigrants & Others. Wyandotte, at the Mouth of the Kansas River, Landing Point for Interior Kansas. There is now a line of steamboats plying between Wyandotte and Fort Riley . . . A daily line of stages leave this point for all parts of the territory." And *New York Tribune* editor Horace Greeley strongly encouraged newcomers to "Go west, young man."

And so they came, on prairie schooners, river boats and barges, from St. Louis, along the Missouri River to Fort Leavenworth and other Kansas "ports of call." The federal government had established military forts to protect travelers and settlers in the newly opened territories, and they traveled from one fort to the next. Oftentimes, an Irish father or son went ahead to line up work and a place to live, then sent back money for the rest of the family to travel on. Families would "leap frog," working to earn money on the east coast to buy a small inland farm. The Irish built canals, railroads and bridges, worked as farm laborers and dug in mines. They competed with slaves and freed blacks for jobs. Women worked as chambermaids, laundresses, cooks, nurses and teachers. Horace Greeley stopped at Fort Leavenworth before he wrote in his book, *An Overland Journey from New York to San Francisco in the Summer of 1859,* that some proprietors "find it convenient to keep on their staff a broth of a boy from Tipperary, standing six feet two in his stockings and measuring a yard or more across the shoulders, who stands ready, with an illegant brogue, a twinkle in his eye, and a hickory sapling firmly grasped in his dexter fist, to respond to all choleric, peremptory customers. . . .'"

### SETTLING IN

The Irish immigrants were not colonizers, so they eventually spread out over most of the state of Kansas. The driving force was finding employment and building homes for their families. Wherever these needs could be met, there were literally thousands of Irish there to fill a void. One of their overriding concerns was the availability of Catholic priests and places to worship.

Mary Paul Fitzgerald in her book on the Osage Mission, *Beacon on the Plains,* wrote, "The story of the Mission challenges a certain ideology which has been a traditional theme in Kansas history; that is, that the state was peopled by anti-slavery crusaders. The state's claim to uniqueness lies not in the spirit motivating the majority of its settlers, but rather in the fact that its ministers of the Gospel and its educators preceded rather than followed settlement."

"In the spring of 1847," continued Mary Paul, "an ox-drawn wagon train headed westward over the Kansas prairies. In the train there were one wagon and a few lumbering carts carrying five Jesuit missionaries and their baggage." The travelers stopped on a slight eminence to the east of the Neosho River, the site of the future Osage Mission, later St. Paul, Kansas.

After they arrived, the Jesuits, who were to staff the mission, saw a great need to provide education for the Osage Indian youth of the area and for the children of the early settlers who were soon to follow. Father Shoenmakers sent one of his priests to Loretto, Kentucky, to seek help. The priest was successful in getting the services of four Sisters of Loretto, among them Bridget Hayden of County Kilkenny, Ireland, who was to lead the mission. It took the sisters a full month to travel to Osage Mission from Kentucky.

Mother Bridget was in charge of Osage Mission for over forty years. The St. Francis Institute for boys and St. Ann's Academy for girls at the mission were a vital force in educating Osage Indian children and the settlers' children in the area, a large per-

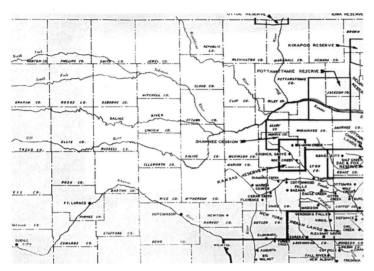

Missionary stations and churches in Kansas established by the Jesuit Fathers from the Osage Mission, 1859

centage of whom were Irish. The mission was closed in the 1890s, as the sisters moved on to new activities.

There hardly remains a doubt as to the part Osage Mission played in the early days of Catholicism in Kansas. Between 1847 and 1887, men from this mission established ninety-nine separate missionary stations and churches in southeast Kansas. Over 30% were created to serve primarily Irish immigrants, and while some lasted only a few years, several eventually became major Kansas cities.

The Jesuits had been sent to establish Indian missions in Kansas Territory in the early 1800s. Father John B. Miege, then a Jesuit priest, was made vicar-apostolic of the Kansas Territory. He built a log cabin cathedral at St. Mary's, Kansas, for the Pottowatomie Indians. It was the first center of Catholicism in Kansas and the Irish settlers soon found their way there. From Wyandotte, Leavenworth and other northeast Kansas settlements, some of the Irish moved south along the Missouri-Kansas border to a coal mining town named Scammon.

## THE 1854 KANSAS-NEBRASKA ACT

Under its provision for "popular sovereignty," the 1854 Kansas Nebraska Act allowed settlers to choose whether their state would enter the Union as a slave state or as a free state. It caused bloody conflict along the border between Kansas Territory and pro-slavery Missouri and was in direct opposition to the 1820 Missouri Compromise, which allowed only Missouri, of all the land in the Louisiana Purchase, to be a slave state. "No other territory in the nation underwent an experience comparable to that of Kansas between 1854 and 1859," wrote Kenneth S. Davis in *Kansas, A History*. "During those five years the unyielding determination of opposing groups to prevail in the debate over the extension of slavery gave rise to unprecedented violence and conflict." Runaway slaves were sheltered at Quindaro in Wyandotte County, and in 1856, abolitionist John Brown led his followers in a massacre at Pottawatomie Creek. At the time, land was being developed westward along the Kansas River and its tributaries, so countless Irish moved away from the then-nationally publicized "Bleeding Kansas" to find a more peaceful place to live.

They built dugouts or sod huts on the treeless prairie; later, small saw mills were set up along rivers, where trees were abundant. Others built mills where farmers could take wheat and corn to be ground into meal for food. Evangeline Thomas explained in *Footprints on the Frontier*: "At first, the newcomers were not looked upon with social favor, *unless they spoke English and were not Catholics*." The Irish were obliged to fight for recognition. But being quite willing to do that, they made their way.

In the summer of 1859, Bishop Miege asked Father Louis Dumortier, S.J., to search out and care for the Catholic pioneers north, south and west of St. Mary's Indian Mission, an area reaching halfway across the state of Kansas. Fr. Dumortier traveled on horseback, always sending his pony ahead to announce his arrival at the pioneers' log cabins, where he would say Mass for settlers who gathered to greet him. He organized some twenty-four Catholic congregations and was responsible for the building of five stone churches, one of which still stands at the predominately Irish settlement of Chapman, Kansas, and is listed on the National Register of Historic Places. Fr. Dumortier died of cholera at Fort Harker in the epidemic of 1867.

## THE CIVIL WAR

Kansas entered the Union as a free state on January 29, 1861, possibly triggering the Civil War, which began on April 12 of that year. The state of Kansas sent a greater percentage of its citizens to fight in the Civil War than any other state. A predominately Celtic unit, Co. B, 1st Regiment, Kansas Volunteer Infantry, served with "remarkable bravery" at Wilson's Creek near Springfield, Missouri, Loren Taylor wrote in "The Ethnic History of Wyandotte County." In 1863, William Quantrill's Confederate

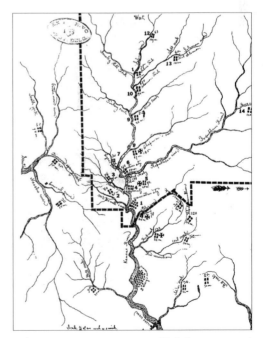

Father Louis Dumortier's 1866 map of Catholic stations cared for from St. Mary's Jesuit Mission

guerrillas burned Lawrence, Kansas, killing 150 people. During the last years of the war, the transcontinental railroad was being built across the state and Irish men cut the ties, laid the track, then settled there with their families. The war ended and Kansas was thriving.

## POST-WAR PROGRESS

"Kansas is free," exulted newly inaugurated Governor Samuel J. Crawford in his message to the legislature, January 10, 1865, "and now offers to the immigrant a home unsurpassed in beauty, richness, and fertility." Thus, Kenneth S. Davis explained in *Kansas, A History*, "did he announce the shift from political to economic developments as the main foci of the new state's attention, the main channel of its energies."

Kansas did not settle down to law and order after the Civil War. Writing to one of his priests in 1872, the bishop bewailed the moral conditions in cattle towns. There were thirty-six burials in Newton, Kansas, in 1872 and only one of them had died of natural causes. It was said that "there is no Sunday west of Junction City and no God west of Salina." Towns like Abilene, Ellsworth and Dodge City imported gun fighters to help calm the boisterous cowboys who rode the cattle trails from Texas to Kansas railheads. Lawmen like "Wild Bill" Hickok tried to maintain order, but peace did not come until the longhorn cattle left in the 1870s, with the closing of the trails.

## SOME IRISH PIONEERS

"Ad Astra per Aspera" is the Kansas State motto. Translated, "To the Stars through Difficulty" is indeed a fitting maxim with which to describe the difficult pioneer journey made by so many Irish, oppressed and famished in Ireland, in search of the opportunity for a better life in Kansas. They were willing to work hard for that chance, and many were successful in leading extraordinary lives under the those huge, starry, Kansas skies.

James McGee was the first white settler at Wyandotte, after the French traders. He owned 240 acres in 1828, three years before Rev. Isaac McCoy founded his Protestant mission at Kawsmouth, according to Loren Taylor in "The Ethnic History of Wyandotte County."

When Michael Malone moved to Wyandotte Town, it was still a trading point for the Indians and there were only four white families there. He graded the first street in the town and "reportedly had some of the largest contracts on works in that city."

Patrick McGonicle moved to Wyandotte County in 1855. The following year, he was approached by "Border Ruffians" and "Jayhawkers" who wanted him to join them in their fight over the slavery issue, but he refused. He later met and married Rose McGurgan, also a native of Ireland, and they had six children. The Union Pacific Railroad built tracks along his property, which grew in worth to over $500 per acre. He was active in the Democratic party and in the Roman Catholic Church.

The Abolitionist Emigrant Societies recruited many Irish before the Civil War, in the effort to bring Kansas into the Union as a Free State. They helped to swell the population of Irish in Wyandotte County, making the Irish its second largest ethnic group.

"The Wide-open Spaces of the prairies did not, on the whole, appeal to a convivial people whose rural landscape had been on a much more intimate scale," Stephen Small noted in *An Irish Century, 1845–1945: From the Famine to WWII*. But the presence of the church, with its clergy, did provide the familiar, more comfortable atmosphere they were used to, while supporting and bringing settlers together in good and bad times.

Young John Erwin and his family sailed for six weeks from their home in County Limerick, Ireland. "They landed in New Orleans, because they had heard the New England States were very cold," recalled Anna Erwin Thisler in *Pioneer Histories of Chapman plus the Sequel*. The mother died while they traveled up the Mississippi by boat and was buried somewhere on the bank of the river. The family proceeded to Illinois, and John went to Pennsylvania to work two years in a saw mill. Later, he worked with his brothers in Illinois building railroads; then, with a fine horse, five yoke of oxen and a 24-inch breaking plow, he came to Chapman Creek.

Many thrilling tales about the Erwins and the other pioneers linger in time. Facing down strapping big Kaw Indians with an ax on his shoulder, getting lost on the wide open prairie while on a buffalo hunt in a blinding snow storm, and firing his rifle to separate a thundering herd of thousands of buffalo heading straight for him are memories handed down through generations. The Erwins built a fine log cabin and their home soon became the area's center of pioneer hospitality and a station for the Overland Stage and Express. Missionary priests were made welcome with food and lodging in "the priest's room." When the Union Pacific Railroad came to Chapman in 1866, the people celebrated with a big dance at the the Erwin home, and settlers from as far away as Solomon and Junction City came to join the celebration.

James Patrick Grennan was born near Tullamore, Ireland, in 1828. While studying for the priesthood, he was stricken with a near-fatal fever and was advised to move to a more suitable climate. Grennan sailed for America in 1851. He settled on a farm on the Erie Canal near Syracuse, New York, where he met and married Hannah McDonnell. Hannah died in childbirth in 1861, leaving him with five children. In 1863, he traded his 40 acres in New York for 80 acres in Illinois, where he cleared the land with a two-edge ax, while the family lived on cornbread and fish. He married Honoria Phalen and moved to a homestead at Burlington, Kansas.

Grennan was a strong Catholic with a fervent desire to pass his faith on to his children and grandchildren. Eight generations and 174 direct descendants include three nuns, farmers, homemakers, lawyers, doctors, engineers and three priests, one of whom is Father James Patrick Grennan of Stockton, Kansas.

Determined to free himself from constant tyranny, Dennis Larkin, 17, left Dublin for New York in 1845. He labored in a brick factory for two years and earned enough money to bring his mother from Ireland. In 1850 they left for Cleveland, Ohio, but both were stricken by the dreaded cholera and his mother died. Dennis recovered and in 1858 walked and worked his way to Ft. Leavenworth, Kansas, where he earned enough money to buy a homestead at Skiddy, Kansas. Larkin, as required by law, returned to spend one night on his homestead every six months and then walked to Council Grove to pay his real estate tax and renew his claim. Despite horrendous trials of early pioneer life, his family grew and prospered on the homestead Larkin had provided.

Jack Nash, of Celtic origin and sporting memory, one of the first settlers of Dickinson County, had planted his domicile in the rich bottom of the Smoky Valley on the line of the Fort Riley and Santa Fe Stage route. With commanding enterprise, visions of aldermanic honors and swelling bank account, he proceeded at once to lay out the town of Newport. Nash had the distinguished honor of government appointment as postmaster for the new town, and to defeat the parsimony of the government in neglecting to erect a post office building, he supplied the deficiency by allotting a department in the upper story of his plug hat for post office purposes, free of rent.

The influence of the pioneer wife is told in a simple story of an Irish railroad construction laborer, as related to Father Colleton, a missionary priest.

> Three years ago I had only eleven dollars in my pocket and my spade on my shoulder. As my wife would have it, I came to Kansas, settled on a claim, and put up a tent for myself and my family. I said to my wife—she is a Tipperary woman, your Reverence—"Well, Mollie, what shall we do next? How shall we get bread for the young ones, now that we are settled as you wanted it?" "James," she says, "you have been working on a railroad for the last fifteen years; you drank all your money, and saved no more than eleven dollars. Here, at least, we have land enough to have a decent burial."

Some of the Irish were fairly affluent when they came to Kansas. Having prospered in the east, many discovered Kansas on their way to or from California and Colorado gold fields.

"Get me me pipe," old Mag used to command. The aging Margaret Callahan, prairie-weathered and tough, lived out her eighty years on the family farm near Abilene. She had come to Kansas as a middle-aged widow, with a large family and plenty of money. Their story began 125 years before, in County Wicklow, Ireland. Fifteen-year-old Patrick Callahan ran away from his County Wicklow home during the good times of 1787 and settled in Canada's Thousand Islands. His sons, lured by America's expansion, homesteaded in Illinois and sold their lands for profit. Patrick's son, Charles, sought California gold, but he and two of his sons were murdered by Indians on the overland trail. When Charles' wife, Margaret, arrived at Mud Creek with two ox-drawn Conestoga wagons, her gold pieces hidden safely in the water barrel, and her six surviving children, Margaret said, "This place looks good to me." The Callahans were the second family to settle in Abilene, which became the first and most notorious of the cow towns. They witnessed first-hand the wild and wicked days of Texas cowboys and longhorn steers, where the Union Pacific Railroad met the end of the Chisholm Trail. The first Mass of St. Andrew's Parish was held in Margaret's log cabin in 1859.

## ORPHAN TRAINS

The massive immigration to America in the mid-1800s created appalling, overcrowded conditions in New York; 30,000 children wandered the streets and unwanted babies were abandoned on doorsteps. Along with the Children's Aid Society, the Sisters of Charity, through the New York Foundling Hospital, cared for these children. When the problem grew too large, they devised a plan by which they could be sent "out West" on Orphan Trains, to be adopted by Catholic families living in more healthful conditions on the open prairie.

Parish priests in rural Kansas appealed to their parishioners, asking them to offer homes to the children. Connie DiPasquale, in *Orphan Trains of Kansas,* wrote that between 5,000 and 6,000 infants and youths were placed in Kansas homes between 1867 and 1930. Many of the children and adopting parents were Irish.

## THE CLERGY

In 1851, Bishop John Baptist Miege's jurisdiction covered the half-million square miles from the Missouri River to the Rocky Mountains and from the Canadian border to New Mexico. Serving the Indians in the beginning, then the French traders and, finally, the pioneer settlers and travelers, the church sent more and more priests and nuns into the Territory. They acted as "cultural and civilizing agents," directing settlement through religious and educational institutions, which they established. They stayed because both the Indians and the settlers, especially the Irish, wanted them to stay.

John S. Cunningham, bishop of Concordia, retained the flavor of his native Ireland to his death. He was "a typical Kansan," a westerner. He had the type of robust manhood that conquered the wilderness, fought and overcame nature in her wildest moods. When he came, there were twenty-two priests in the diocese. He brought many seminarians from Ireland to serve the church in Kansas, and when he left in 1890, there were over a hundred priests, ten parochial schools with 1,000 pupils and approximately 15,000 Catholics.

Father T. Ambrose Butler observed the plight of newly arrived Irish immigrants living in squalor in a poor section of St. Louis known as "The Kerry Patch." He helped to form the St. Louis Colonization Board of the Irish Catholic Benevolent Union, which formed a joint stock company to purchase Kansas land "in bulk" for the new settlers. The resulting St. Columbkille Parish in Blaine, Kansas, might well be described as the "most Irish Catholic parish in Kansas."

In 1845, Father Bernard Donnelly's Independence, Missouri, parish covered 14,000 square miles. Though young, he was a man of great vision and was instrumental in bringing several hundred Irishmen from the East to help build a town at the mouth of the Kaw River in Kansas Territory. Father Donnelly assured the men they would have satisfactory living quarters and adequate food. He insisted they attend Mass and that they not drink liquor. Many men attributed their success to the help they received from Fr. Donnelly, "The Apostle of Temperance."

Of the sixteen Sisters of Charity from Nashville, Tennessee, who came to help nurse and educate at Leavenworth in 1858, eleven had come from Ireland. In the next forty-five years, about 300 young women from Ireland joined them, some filling leadership roles as school supervisors and hospital administrators. Others worked with the downtrodden and those rejected by society, including many orphans.

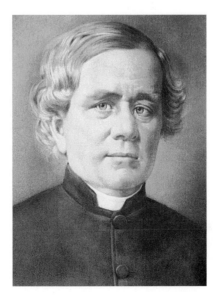

Father Bernard Donnelly

St. Bridget's Parish in Marshall County, established in 1857, was one of the earliest Catholic settlements in Kansas. As each new settler arrived, the homes of those who came before were thrown open to welcome the new immigrants. In 1862 the parish was officially organized under the direction of Father John Myers. He was the first priest to complete his theological studies at the newly founded St. Benedict's College at Atchison.

The Sisters of St. Joseph of Concordia and of Wichita worked selflessly with the early settlers. Mother Bernard Sheridan of Roscommon, Ireland, was the first superior at Wichita. She returned to Ireland many times to bring back to Kansas a total of 92 young Irish women who became Sisters of St. Joseph.

Although the Ursuline Sisters of Paola are originally of German stock, many Irish girls have joined the order and served to educate young girls in high schools and elementary schools in Kansas. Their motherhouse is at Paola, site of the early Osage Indian Mission.

It has been said that the Irish, in their hearts, never truly leave Ireland. It is also true, and in the same sweet way, that Kansans, though they may travel far, never really, in their souls, leave the golden mystery of the Great Plains of Kansas.

*See* Missouri

Thomas Ambrose Butler, *The State of Kansas and Irish Immigration* (Dublin, 1871).
Wm. J. Dalton, *The Life of Father Bernard Donnelly* (Kansas City, Kansas, 1921).
Kenneth S. Davis, *Kansas: A History* (New York and London, 1984).
Gilbert J. Garraghan, S.J., Ph.D., *The Jesuits in the Middle of the United States, Vol. III* (Loyola U. Press, 1984).
Mary Frances Lahey, *Harvest of Faith: History of the Diocese of Salina, Kansas* (Dallas: Taylor Publishing Company, 1987).

P. JOHN LAHEY AND
PATRICIA CALLAHAN WALKENHORST

## KAVANAGH, EDWARD (1795–1844)

Diplomat and governor. Edward Kavanagh was born in Damariscotta Mills, ME, on April 27, 1795, and died in Newcastle, ME, on January 22, 1844. The son of James and Sarah (Jackson) Kavanagh, Edward attended Georgetown College before graduating from St. Mary's College, Baltimore, in 1813. Then, before undertaking the study of law, he joined in his father's mercantile trade and traveled abroad.

### JACKSONIAN DEMOCRAT

With his legal knowledge, Kavanagh eventually moved into politics in the Age of Jackson. He was in the state legislature (1826–28) before he served in the United States Congress (1831–35). Defeated after two terms in Washington, Kavanagh became involved in American diplomacy as *chargé d'affairs* to Portugal (1835–41) and as a commissioner dealing with the disputed boundary between Maine and Canada which was eventually finalized in the Webster-Ashburton Treaty on August 9, 1842.

Returning to state politics, Kavanagh served in the state senate and was its president in 1843 when Maine's governor resigned his office. Thus, Edward Kavanagh became the first Catholic to serve as a governor in New England, entering office on March 7, 1843, and continuing until his own resignation on January 1, 1844.

### AN IRISH LEGACY

Kavanagh is buried in the village of Damariscotta Mills, Maine, in the cemetery of St. Patrick's Church, the oldest Catholic church in New England. While this church recalls the origins of an Irish community, including Edward's father going back to County Wexford in Ireland, the efforts of the governor in helping Bishop Benedict J. Fenwick of Boston to establish an Irish farming colony in what came to be Benedicta, ME, should not be forgotten in evaluating Kavanagh's legacy.

*See* Maine

Edward Kavanagh Collection, Special Collections, Georgetown University (Washington, D.C.).
Charles W. Collins, "Governor Edward Kavanagh," *United States Catholic Historical Society Records*, 5 (1909): 249–273.
William Leo Lucey, *Edward Kavanagh* (Francestown, N.H., 1947).

VINCENT A. LAPOMARDA, S.J.

## KEARNY, STEPHEN WATTS (1794–1848)

Soldier, conqueror of California. Kearny's paternal ancestors came from Ireland in 1720 and settled in New Jersey, where the future general was born in 1794. He joined the army in 1812 as a first lieutenant. By the end of the War of 1812, Kearny had been wounded, captured, and promoted to captain. Kearny spent the next three decades in a succession of western outposts, gradually advancing through the army ranks. With the outbreak of the Mexican War, Kearny was promoted to brigadier general and placed in command of the Army of the West. In May 1846, he led 1,660 men on march to Santa Fe, which he occupied in August. Kearny departed for the Pacific in September with a select command of 300 dragoons. Along the way, he joined with Commodore Robert Stockton and occupied San Diego by the end of 1846. The following January, Kearny's combined command of 600 men marched north and captured Los Angeles, meeting with little resistance. On January 13, 1847, Mexican authorities surrendered California to Lt. Col. John C. Fremont, the commander of civilian forces in the area. Kearny and Fremont soon became embroiled in a command dispute, ending with Kearny in overall command and Fremont returning east in disgrace. After occupying California, Kearny went to Mexico, briefly serving as civil governor of Vera Cruz and Mexico City. He contracted a tropical disease which forced his return to the United States. He died in St. Louis in 1848.

*See* California

*Dictionary of American Biography*, Vol. V, part 2: 272–74.
Thomas Kearny, *General Philip Kearny, Battle Soldier of Five Wars, Including the Conquest of the West by General Stephen Watts Kearny* (New York, 1937).
Dwight Lancelot Clarke, *Stephen Kearny, Soldier of the West* (Norman, OK, 1961).

TOM DOWNEY

## KEARNS, THOMAS (1862–1918)

Mining entrepreneur. The man whose mansion in Salt Lake City now serves as the official residence of the governor of Utah was born in Ontario, Canada, of Irish immigrant parents. While he was still a boy, the family moved to O'Neill, Nebraska. This was an experimental effort to establish an Irish "colony" in the far West and one of the few that could be considered reasonably successful.

But farming the windswept plains of Nebraska was not young Thomas' idea of how to make a living, and while still in his early teens he struck out for the gold mines of Deadwood, South Dakota. Unsuccessful, he returned home for a time before heading out west again.

He drove a team of horses in Tombstone, Arizona, for a time, but by 1893 was in Utah. He planned to save enough money to head for Butte, Montana, and work for Marcus Daly at the Anaconda Copper mine, but he elected to stay in Utah and try his luck on his own.

He spent seven years learning the business from the many canny miners in the area. Finally, he and some partners pooled their resources and the Silver King Mine came in. Thomas Kearns was a multimillionaire before he was 30.

Kearns spent the rest of his life as the leading "Gentile" (i.e., non-Mormon) citizen of Utah. Much against his desires, he allowed himself to be prevailed upon to serve a single term in the U.S. Senate after Utah finally achieved statehood in 1896. But the rest of his life was spent endowing good works, such as hospitals and orphanages. His mansion in Salt Lake City was donated to the state after his death and is now the home of Utah's governor.

John A. Barnes, *Irish-American Landmarks* (Detroit, 1995).

JOHN A. BARNES

## KEATON, BUSTER (1895–1966)

Actor, comedian, filmmaker. Of Irish lineage, Joseph Francis Keaton was born in 1895. Buster Keaton became one of the greatest comic actors and inventive filmmakers of the silent era. His show business parents, Joseph and Myron Keaton, were appearing in a tent show with Harry Houdini when six-month-old Joseph fell down the stairs. "What a little buster!" Houdini reportedly said, tagging the baby with a nickname that would stick.

Keaton is known as the "Great Stone Face," because of his deadpan, never-smiling face, usually topped by a saucer-rimmed, flat-topped hat. The mournful character he created always got into trouble, but he never felt sorry for himself or asked his audience to pity him. His strength was his ability to survive. He was a brilliant acrobat and never used a stunt man. His attention to detail was such that a whole house was calculated to collapse around him in *Steamboat Bill Jr.*

Keaton made his film debut with Fatty Arbuckle in 1917 in *The Butcher Boy,* but by the early 1920s he was producing, directing and starring in his own silent films. His twenty short films, filled with pratfalls and custard pies, were among his masterpieces, the best thought to be the 1922 *Cops.* His co-star was often a machine: a locomotive in *The General;* a movie projector in *Sherlock Jr;* a ship in *The Navigator.*

When the movies became talkies, his pantomime technique did not hold up. But the hapless character's ability to survive was as true in real life as on film. He went from great success in the early and mid-twenties to alcoholism, bankruptcy and marital troubles in the thirties. He enjoyed fresh fame in the fifties and sixties, even making some television appearances, and fi-

nally being recognized for the creative genius he was before his death in 1966.

*See* Cinema, Irish in

J. Concannon and Frank Cull, *Irish American Who's Who* (New York, 1984).

Joseph Curran, *Hibernian Green on the Silver Screen* (Westport, CT, 1990).

*Hollywood Album, Lives and Deaths of Hollywood Stars From the Pages of The New York Times* (New York, 1977).

EILEEN DANEY CARZO

## KELLEY, CLARENCE M. (1911–1997)

Director of the FBI. A former police chief, Clarence M. Kelley headed the Federal Bureau of Investigation from 1973 to 1978, a transitional period in the Bureau's history. Under Kelly's leadership, the FBI began new initiatives against white-collar and organized crime, and concentrated less on the campaign against communism that had long occupied Kelley's predecessor, J. Edgar Hoover.

Born October 24, 1911, in Kansas City, Missouri, Kelley was the only child of Minnie Brown and Clarence Bond Kelley. He graduated from the University of Kansas in 1936 with a bachelor of arts degree, and earned a law degree from the University of Kansas City Law School in 1940. He married Ruby Pickett in 1937; the couple had two children: Mary and Kent.

Kelley joined the FBI soon after graduating from law school. Apart from a short time in the United States Navy, he spent over twenty years with the Bureau before leaving to become police chief of Kansas City, Missouri. Known for his administrative capacities and law and order ethic, Kelley was named outstanding law enforcement officer in the United States in 1970 and was presented the J.Edgar Hoover Award by the Veterans of Foreign Wars.

In 1973, President Richard M. Nixon named Kelley Director of the FBI. In addition to its new focus on battling white-collar crime, Kelley is credited with updating the Bureau's crime-fighting techniques. His approach to running the FBI was perceived as modern and pragmatic and thought by some to provide a corrective balance to the Bureau after Hoover's death. A Christian, he was an elder in his church and a Sunday School teacher. Kelley died in Kansas City on August 6, 1997, at the age of 85.

Clarence M. Kelley and James Kirkpatrick Davis, *The Story of an FBI Director* (Missouri, 1987).

"Clarence M. Kelley," *The New York Times,* Section D, page 22 (August 6, 1997).

KATHLEEN N. McCARTHY

## KELLEY, FRANCIS CLEMENT (1870–1948)

Bishop. He was born in Summerville, Prince Edward Island, Canada, to John and Mary Ann (Murphy), who were Canadian-born descendants of Irish and Highland Scots immigrants. After high school, the young Frank began studies for the priesthood in Quebec. In 1892 he transferred to the Diocese of Detroit and was ordained on August 23, 1893. At the same time that he came to the United States, he changed the spelling of his name from

"Frank Kelly" to "Francis Kelley," a change which some regarded as a snobbish affectation.

While a pastor in Lapeer, Michigan, Kelley began giving lectures in small towns in order to supplement his income. This experience convinced him of the need for a national organization to assist the church in rural areas where Catholics were usually few and poor. Thus in 1905 he founded the Catholic Church Extension Society, and in the next year moved to Chicago to administer the society full-time. The main function of the Extension Society was to raise funds for the erection of Catholic institutions in rural areas. In 1906 Kelley inaugurated a magazine, *Extension*, as a fund-raising device, and in the 1950s the journal attained a circulation of over 500,000. The society was very successful in its early years, and by 1924, it was estimated that it helped finance half of the Catholic churches built in the United States between 1906 and 1924.

Kelley's second contribution to the domestic missions was his role in establishing and leading the American Board of Catholic Missions (ACBM), a national organization created in 1919 for coordinating all fund-raising activities in American dioceses for domestic and foreign missions. Despite strong opposition from the French-based Society for the Propagation of the Faith, the ACBM raised large sums of money, and by 1940 when Kelley stepped down as the organization's secretary, it had disbursed over $12,000,000 to the home missions.

In addition to his work for the home missions, Kelley tried his hand at international diplomacy. He went to the Versailles Peace Conference in 1919 on behalf of the Mexican bishops in order to secure a declaration on religious freedom in the final draft of the treaty. However, his endeavors on behalf of the Mexican church (which was languishing under anticlerical legislation brought on by the Revolution of 1910) came to nothing. He also became involved in Vatican-Italian affairs when he participated in an ill-fated attempt to settle the Roman Question. In 1920 he went to London and became embroiled in British foreign policy by his participation in the labyrinthine discussions over the expulsion of German Catholic missionaries from the British Empire after World War I. Upon his return to the United States, he convinced the American bishops not to issue a statement in support of Irish or Indian nationalism, which earned him the lasting distrust of many Irish-Americans.

In 1924 Kelley was appointed Bishop of Oklahoma, which was coterminous with the entire state and comprised 70,000 square miles. At that time, Catholics constituted only 3% of the population. Kelley earned a good bit of criticism while bishop there. He was not too successful in the fiscal administration of the diocese, and it was not until the boom years of World War II that the diocese was put on a sound financial basis. He was criticized for his frequent absences from his diocese which earned him a rebuke from the apostolic delegate. In 1928 he was nominated to become the president of the Catholic University of America, but Rome vetoed the appointment.

Throughout his later life, Kelley maintained his concern for the Catholic Church in Mexico, and in 1937 he helped found the Montezuma seminary in Las Vegas, New Mexico for the education of Mexican seminarians for service in their own country. Despite this solicitude, Kelley excluded Mexicans (as well as blacks and Native Americans) from the ranks of his own diocesan clergy.

As the prospects faded that Kelley would be promoted to a larger see, he turned increasingly to writing and speaking engagements. He authored 17 books, and his writing style even earned the praise of H. L. Mencken, a notoriously iconoclastic critic. Because of failing health, Kelley asked for a coadjutor to run the diocese although he stayed on as bishop. He died in Oklahoma City.

Thomas Brown, *Bible-Belt Catholicism: A History of the Roman Catholic Church in Oklahoma, 1905–1945* (New York, 1977).

James Gaffey, *Francis Clement Kelley and the American Dream* (Bensenville, IL, 1980).

Francis Clement Kelley, *The Bishop Jots It Down* (New York, 1939).

ANTHONY D. ANDREASSI

## KELLY, BRIGIT PEGEEN (1951– )

Poet. One of the more distinguished of contemporary young poets, Brigit Pegeen Kelly was born April 21, 1951, in Palo Alto, California. She was educated at the Ivy Technical Nursing School, where she received her L.P.N. in 1975. Three more degrees were to follow from the University of Oregon: a B.S. in fine arts, 1981; an M.F.A. in creative writing, 1983; and an M.S. in counseling, 1986. She taught at the University of Oregon from 1981 to 1983; since 1989 she has been on the faculty at University of Illinois at Urbana-Champaign where she currently teaches in the creative writing program. She is a member of the Academy of American Poets, Associated Writing Programs, and the Poetry Society of America. Her many honors and awards include two National Endowment for the Arts Creative Writing Fellowships (1985, 1995–1996); "Discovery"/*The Nation* Award (1986); the Theodore Roethke Poetry Prize (1988); a Bread Loaf Writers Conference Fellowship (1990); and the Cecil Hemley Award from the Poetry Society of America (1991). She received the Yale Series of Younger Poets Award for her first collection of poetry, *To the Place of Trumpets* (1987), and the Lamont Poetry Prize from the Academy of American Poets for her second book, *Song* (1994).

### POETRY

In his foreword to *To the Place of Trumpets*, James Merrill observes of Kelly's technique: "At the simplest level she retains the wild, transforming eye of childhood." Indeed it is the world of

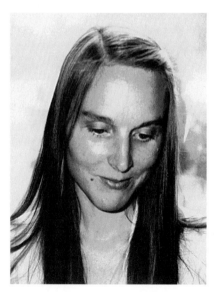

Brigit Pegeen Kelly

childhood (others, hers, her children) and childlike observance that pervades much of her work, though the adult's methods of transformation—not to mention the skill of retaining that eye—are many times quite complex. It is a world of Sundays and ice cream stores, of hot air balloons in a town full of people whose stories may themselves be full of hot air, where even "Joy can be made out of cloth and heated / with gas" ("Near the Race Track," *Trumpets*). It is also a world where cows with wings, "Maybe," do circles in a field when the moon comes up "The color of a body / Just stepping from a bath" ("Three Cows and the Moon," *Song*); where a dead deer is "for a moment no deer / at all / but two swans" ("Dead Doe," *Song*). Like Marianne Moore, Kelly relishes in the seeming mundane made marvelous by the glint of vision, in dissimilitude justified by imagination's rule. Like Moore, too, she is prone to the fabulous: a rebellious bull named Moses "all improbably" eats a burning bush; a goat's head sings sweetly from where it hangs on a tree to its body by the tracks, reminding the boys who killed it how "The heart dies of this sweetness" ("Song," *Song*).

Kelly's eye is none the less "wild, transforming" when it lights on the fabulous world of Christian tradition and her Catholic background. Like her forebear Emily Dickinson, Kelly seems determined (damned) to "Tell all the truth but tell it slant," though in this, in Merrill's words, "Kelly's imagination breeds heresies as innocent and plentiful as mayflies." One remarkable example occurs in "Imagining Their Own Hymns" (*Trumpets*) where the angels in stained glass, "sick of Jesus, / who never stops dying," bide time for the future when "One night they will get out of here":

> One night
> when the weather is turning cold and a few
> candles burn, they will leave St. Blase standing
> under his canopy of glass lettuce
> and together, as in a wedding march,
> their pockets full of money from the boxes
> for the sick poor, they will walk down the aisle,
> imagining their own hymns, past the pews
> and the water fonts in which small things float,
> down the streets of our narrow town, while
> the bells ring and the birds fly up in the fields
> beyond—and they will never come back.

Kelly's lines, like those rebellious man-made angels, fall into place and exult in the terms and transformations of their own "imagining."

*See* Poetry, Irish-American

Brigit Pegeen Kelly, *To the Place of Trumpets* (Yale University Press, 1988).
———, *Song* (BOA Editions Ltd., 1995).

TODD HEARON

## KELLY, EDWARD J. (1876–1950)

Civil engineer, politician, mayor of Chicago. The oldest child of nine, Edward Kelly was born in Chicago, Ill., on May 1, 1876. He was the son of an Irish immigrant father (Stephen Kelly) and a mother of German descent (Helen Lang Kelly), and at the age of nine sold newspapers to help support his family. He left school to work several jobs when he was twelve, which brought him into contact with the Colombian Exposition of 1893. The Exposition

inspired him to become an engineer. He took mathematics and engineering courses in the evenings and worked for the city's sewage and water systems during the day. By 1908 he was an assistant engineer in the sanitary district and chief engineer by 1920. This position launched him into involvement with some of the largest building projects of Chicago and close ties to an active local Democratic party. When an assassin's bullet intended to kill then president-elect Franklin D. Roosevelt struck and killed Chicago Mayor Anton J. Cermak, Patrick Nash, a local leader of the Democratic party, persuaded the city council to have Kelly finish out Cermak's term. The event was fortuitous. Kelly became an effective and popular mayor, restoring Chicago's financial health and winning three terms in 1935, 1939 and 1943. He supported public housing, improved the fire department, and persisted in establishing policies of nondiscrimination. Together with Patrick Nash, Kelly held a firm grip on more than 40,000 jobs in Chicago, which made the "the Kelly-Nash machine" a dominant force throughout the 1930s and vulnerable to accusations of corruption. Kelly was nevertheless persistent in silencing his critics until, in 1947, he was defeated by Martin H. Kennelly. Kelly retired from politics, but lived another three years to establish an engineering consulting firm and to raise $6 million for a new facility at Chicago's Mercy Hospital. Kelly died in Chicago at the age of seventy-four on October 20, 1950.

Ovid Demaris, *Captive City* (New York: L. Stuart, 1969).
Harold F. Gosnell, *Machine Politics: Chicago Model* (Chicago: The University of Chicago Press, 1937).
"The Kelly-Nash Machine," *Fortune* (August 1936).
*National Cyclopedia of American Biography* Current "B" (New York: James T. White & Co., 1927): 375.
Obituary, *New York Times* (October 21, 1950).

DANIEL J. KUNTZ

## KELLY, EMMETT L. (1898–1979)

Clown. Born in Sedan, Kansas, to a staunchly nationalistic Irish parentage, Kelly was named for the Irish patriot Robert Emmett. During his childhood, he lived on a farm and aspired to being a cartoonist. However, he soon discovered that a young country

Emmett L. Kelly

boy had little to offer to syndicate newspapers. Kelly made his first break by giving "chalk-talks" which were comic illustrations and caricatures. It was his job with Frisco Exposition Shows in Kansas City, doing illustrations and trapeze artistry, that led him to eventually take up circus life professionally.

He abandoned the cartoon job and joined Howe's Great London Circus in 1923, where he met his first wife Eva Moore. In the 1930s, he accepted a job as a general clown with the Hagenbeck-Wallace Circus where the inspiration for his renowned character was born. The character he created was a cartoon caricature of "Hobo Willie," who became the opposite of the traditional white-faced, bright clowns of the past. Hobo Willie resembled a real-life person, poor and destitute wearing tattered clothing and a face engulfed by a ragged beard and protruding nose. Given the times, the Depression era, it is remarkable how such a character managed to incite laughter; Willie's nature as a misfit seemed to evoke a common level of humor that was more than a performance but an embodiment of optimism.

In 1942, Kelly became a member of the Ringling Brothers Barnum and Bailey Circus where his career further blossomed and he became a regular feature. He entertained many notable figures such as Winston Churchill, the Queen of Spain, the Duke and Duchess of Gloucester, the Duke of Windsor and Emperor Haile Selassie. He made his first feature film appearance in Hollywood in 1950 in the *Fat Man* in which he took on the role of a villain. Kelly's career is remembered for the natural melancholic figure he created in Hobo Willie, the external portrayal of sadness being made possible by his own real-life serenity. Kelly died in 1979.

*Life* 23 (July 21, 1947): 45.
E. Kelly, *Clown* (1954).
*Christian Science Monitor* (June 1953): 13.
*CAB* (1954).

JOY HARRELL

## KELLY, GENE CURRAN (1913–1996)

Dancer, actor, choreographer, director. Born of Irish-American parentage on August 23, 1913, in Pittsburgh, Pennsylvania, Gene Kelly brought his good humor and athletic style of dancing to countless musical films from the 1940s through the 1960s.

During the Depression, Kelly joined with his two sisters and two brothers as the dance team, The Five Kellys, then opened his own dance studio in Pittsburgh. He began dancing on Broadway in the late 1930s; and, in the title role in *Pal Joey* in 1940, he was able to showcase his versatile dancing and effective singing talents.

Moving to Hollywood in 1941, Kelly concentrated on films for the next two decades. He introduced what he called cine-dancing, utilizing camera tricks for special effects: in *Anchors Aweigh* he created a dance with the cartoon mouse Jerry; and in *Cover Girl* he appeared to be dancing with himself. With exciting virile movements and athleticism, Kelly brought a synthesized ballet, tap and jazz style of dance to the American public in such popular films as *On the Town, An American in Paris* (for which he won a special Academy Award for choreography), *It's Always Fair Weather, Brigadoon,* and *Invitation to the Dance.* Kelly's most memorable role is that of the rain-soaked, love-struck character singing and dancing the title song in *Singin' In the Rain.* That scene alone puts the film at the top of the list of greatest musicals ever.

Gene Kelly

Kelly's directing credits include *Invitation to the Dance, Tunnel of Love, Gigot,* and *Hello Dolly,* as well as a number of television credits as choreographer, dancer, narrator, actor and program host. He won the Cecil B. DeMille Award in 1980, and was named Catholic Actor of the Year by the Catholic Actor's Guild in 1978.

*See* Cinema, Irish in; California

J. Concannon and Frank Cull, *Irish American Who's Who* (New York, 1984).
Joseph Curran, *Hibernian Green on the Silver Screen* (Westport, CT, 1990).

EILEEN DANEY CARZO

## KELLY, GEORGE ("Machine Gun") (1897–1954)

Bootlegger, kidnapper. Born in Memphis, George Kelly Barnes, Jr., spent most of his criminal career as a small-time bootlegger in the southwestern United States. Although physically imposing and possessing a growling voice, Kelly actually was something of a coward who shunned weapons and violence. His ca-

George "Machine Gun" Kelly

reer took a dramatic turn after meeting Kathryn Shannon, an ambitious and determined former prostitute and gun moll set on transforming George Kelly Barnes into a criminal she could be proud of. She bought him a machine gun, with which Kelly practiced diligently. In the meantime, Kathryn spent much of her time pumping up her husband's reputation with stories of daring bank robberies and crimes committed by "Machine Gun" Kelly. Kelly and his gang eventually became wanted in connection with a series of murders and bank robberies in the Southwest in the early 1930s, earning a nationwide reputation as fierce and desperate gangsters. Ever ambitious, Kathryn convinced Kelly to carry out a kidnapping scheme against Oklahoma oilman Charles F. Urschel. Kelly and a partner snatched Urschel on June 22, 1933, and collected a ransom of $200,000. Kelly and Kathryn fled north, while FBI agents quickly rounded up their accomplices in the kidnapping. The Kellys were captured in Memphis on September 26. Their trial marked the first test of a new nationwide kidnapping law recently enacted after the Lindbergh abduction and murder. Both defendants quickly received sentences of life imprisonment. "Machine Gun" Kelly died in Alcatraz in 1954.

*Dictionary of American Biography*, Supplement 5: 381–82.

Sandy Lesberg, ed., *A Picture History of Crime* (Indianapolis, 1976).

Jay Robert Nash, *Bloodletters and Badmen: A Narrative Encyclopedia of American Criminals from the Pilgrims to the Present* (New York, 1973): 301–305.

TOM DOWNEY

## KELLY, GRACE (1929–1982)

Actress. Born in Philadelphia to Margaret and John B. Kelly, an Olympic gold medalist for rowing and a wealthy contractor, on November 12, 1929, Grace Patricia Kelly first achieved fame as a Hollywood leading lady, appearing in eleven films before her marriage to Prince Rainier III of Monaco in 1956.

Kelly studied acting at the American Academy of Dramatic Art; and, while working as an actress and model in New York, became known for her promotional work for Old Gold cigarettes.

Grace Kelly

Having moved to Hollywood, Grace Kelly starred in highly acclaimed movies such as *High Noon* (1952), *High Society* (1956), and *The Country Girl* (1954) for which she won an Academy Award. Her cool reserve and regal bearing were best exploited in three Alfred Hitchcock thrillers: *Dial M for Murder* (1954), *Rear Window* (1954), and *To Catch a Thief* (1955).

Her acting career came to an end with her storybook engagement and marriage to Prince Rainier Grimaldi III of the principality of Monaco by which she became Her Serene Highness Princess Grace of Monaco. The couple had three children, Caroline, Albert, and Stephanie. Because she had become an international celebrity, Grace's death on September 14, 1982, shook the tiny principality of Monaco as well as the rest of the world. She was driving with her 17-year-old daughter Stephanie down a windy, most dangerous road from their family retreat in Southern France, not five miles from the Palace, when the car went out of control and crashed down the hillside. Stephanie recovered from her injuries, but Grace died the following day.

*See* Cinema, Irish in

*Life,* 32:142 (May 5, 1952; 36:117, August 26, 1954).

*Saturday Evening Post,* 227 (October 30, 1954): 28.

*Time,* 63: 102 (May 24, 1954; 65:46 June 31, 1955).

EILEEN DANEY CARZO

## KELLY, JOHN BRENDAN (1889–1958)

Building contractor, Olympian champion, Democratic Party leader. Kelly was born to Irish immigrants, John Henry Kelly and Mary Ann (Costello), the youngest of ten children. Kelly and siblings were urged toward success and more than half made noteworthy careers. Kelly's brother Walter became a popular actor and his brother George was a Pulitzer Prize-winning playwright.

In 1902 Kelly began working with his older brother Patrick at Patrick's construction firm; however, after conflicts ensued, he moved on to work in bricklaying. In 1909 he initiated a hobby that would eventually bring him much success: that of rowing for sporting clubs in a four-oar gig that eventually led him to single and double sculls competitions. By 1913 Kelly had won over nine races. His winning of the American Henley singles competition at Boston brought him recognition as a professional rower. Kelly's athleticism enhanced his budding career as a rower; he played football, basketball and boxing as well. Kelly took up boxing competitions overseas while serving with the American Expeditionary Force in World War I.

In 1919, Kelly obtained a loan from his brother Walter and with his brother Charles organized his own company titled John B. Kelly, Inc. Kelly's company focused on building construction and became a very profitable business. During this success, he began focusing once again on rowing and in 1919 and 1920 became the national single sculls champion. When he ventured to the 1920 Olympics he won the singles and doubles competition in the same day. Kelly's victory afforded him the opportunity to meet such persons as Jack Dempsey, Jim Thorpe and Babe Ruth and he became yet another star in the 1920s athletic showcase.

In 1924 at the Parisian Olympics, Kelly won the singles and doubles competitions once again. During the same year, he married Margaret Majer and they had four children who were successful as well; one daughter, Grace, became an Academy Award winner and gained fame as Princess Grace of Monaco and his son, John, Jr., won the Diamond Sculls at Henley twice and was a participant in four Olympic rowing competitions. Kelly and his family became socially prominent due to their sporting activities and their business success. Kelly engaged in several extra-curricular events such as track and field events, tennis and horse racing.

Kelly also became involved in politics. During the years 1934–1941, he filled the position of party chairman of the Democratic party in Philadelphia. Kelly ran for mayor in 1935, but he was defeated and plagued by attacks on his Irish-Catholic heritage. The following year he lost his bid for nomination to the U.S. Senate. Kelly, however, persevered and in 1940 introduced Franklin D. Roosevelt as the third-term presidential candidate at the Democratic National Convention. However, during the later stages of his life, Kelly grew in his conservatism and his eventual support of Senator Joseph McCarthy caused his democratic influence to wane.

In addition to his athletic and business career, Kelly established the John B. Kelly Award for the promotion of athletics. Kelly died in Philadelphia on November 25, 1958, leaving an extensive legacy and estate to his family and the public at large.

Foster Hirsch, *George Kelly* (1975).
Arthur H. Lewis, *Those Philadelphia Kellys* (1977).
Gwen Robyn, *Princess Grace* (1976).
*Dictionary of American Biography*, supplement 6.

JOY HARRELL

## KELLY, THOMAS (1833–1908)

Fenian. He was born in Galway and emigrated to America where he worked in New York, Tennessee and Ohio. A printer by trade, he also worked as a journalist in Memphis. In the Civil War he became a colonel in the 10th Ohio Regiment and at that time joined the Fenians. Kelly was a commanding and reserved figure who impressed on his fellow Fenians that he was more interested in actions than in words.

In 1865 he was sent to pressure James Stephens to fix a date for an Irish insurrection. He became Chief of Staff within the Irish Republican Brotherhood, the Irish Fenian movement, and

Thomas Kelly

he planned and participated in the rescue of Stephens from Richmond Jail on November 24, 1865. When Stephens was ousted from his office in the IRB, Kelly replaced him and returned to England from America, and with Richard O'Sullivan Burke, General Cluseret and Godfrey Massey, he planned an insurrection for February 11, 1867. The plans were disrupted, the rising was abandoned and Massey was arrested. On September 11, Kelly and Timothy Deasy were arrested in Manchester, and the following week a band of Fenians rescued them from a police van, but a policeman was shot in the shuffle. Kelly escaped to America, faded from Fenian circles and died in obscurity. Three Fenian laborers were hanged for the death of the policeman. And by a strange twist of fate, they are known to every Irish schoolchild as the Manchester Martyrs—William Allen, Michael Larkin and Michael O'Brien—while Colonel Thomas Kelly is just a minor footnote in Irish history.

*See* Fenians and Clan na Gael;
O'Donovan Rossa, Jeremiah

John Devoy, *Recollections of an Irish Rebel* (New York, 1929).
John O'Leary, *Recollections of Fenians and Fenianism* (London, 1896).
Jeremiah O'Donovan Rossa, *Recollections* (New York, 1898).

MICHAEL GLAZIER

## KELLY, WALTER ("Walt") (1913–1973)

Cartoonist, creator of the popular comic strip "Pogo." Kelly was born in Philadelphia and raised in Bridgeport, Connecticut, where he learned drawing from his father, a theater scenery painter. After high school, Kelly worked at a variety of editing, illustrating, and cartoonist jobs across the country. In 1948, his comic strip "Pogo" first appeared in print in the *New York Star*, and was syndicated the following year. The strip followed the adventures of a cast of animal characters residing in the Okeefenokee Swamp of Georgia, swapping a combination of puns and slapstick humor in thick Southern drawls. "Pogo" quickly became one of the most popular comic strips in America, with fans drawn not only to the strip's characters and humor, but to its often stinging satire and political edge. Kelly used the strip to comment on many of the leading issues of the day, particularly politics, in which guest characters bore an uncanny resemblance to such influential national politicians as Senator Joseph McCarthy and President Lyndon Johnson, as well as world leaders like Castro and Krushchev. More than any other cartoonist, Kelly pioneered in the use of comic strips as a means for political and social commentary. Although sometimes censored by local newspapers as too controversial, "Pogo's" nationwide popularity led to the publishing of 30 compilation books of Kelly's strip.

*Dictionary of American Biography*, Supplement 9: 452–53.
Kalman Goldstein, "Al Capp and Walt Kelly: Pioneers of Political and Social Satire in the Comics," *Journal of Popular Culture*, 25 (Spring 1992): 81–95.
Steve Thompson, *Walt Kelly and Pogo: Biographical Checklist*, 2nd. ed. (Richfield, MN, 1987).

TOM DOWNEY

## KENEDY, PATRICK JOHN (1843–1906)

Publisher, bookseller. Patrick John Kenedy's father, John, was born in Muckalee, County Kilkenny, in 1794, and was well educated despite the restrictive English penal laws. He came to America in 1815, eventually settling in Baltimore in 1826 with his wife Ellen (Timon), where he established a small book selling and publishing business near St. Mary's Seminary. His first published book was an abridgement of Alfonso Rodriguez' *The Practice of Christian Perfection* in 1834. His wife died in 1836 and he and his six children moved to New York City where there was a fast-growing concentration of Catholics, especially Irish immigrants. He came with the recommendation of the Archbishop of Baltimore, Samuel Eccleston. Kenedy identified himself as a Catholic publisher, and established his business near old St. Patrick's Cathedral on Mott Street in 1838. In 1842 the widower married Bridget (Smith), and their only child, Patrick John, was born September 4, 1843. Patrick, or "P. J.," studied at the Christian Brothers' School in Canal Street and was active in his father's business by 1860. Early bookseller-publishers more often bartered in books, trading for value not cash, and consequently widened their range of titles. The times called for publishing devotional works, catechisms, and aids in defense of the faith. The elder Kenedy also carried a variety of religious goods and articles, but it was a marginal business at his death on June 25, 1866. Patrick took over the firm at age twenty-three, and it remained in his control until 1904. He expanded the prayer books line, and sold books through door-to-door canvassers and at preaching missions which might last two weeks. The house moved to the Catholic publishing center in Barclay St. in 1873 near fashionable hotels, theaters and gambling establishments. Growth required a five-story building within twenty years, and at this location he sublet space to Patrick Ford who organized almost 2,500 U.S. branches of the Irish Land League, bringing in many visitors and potential books purchasers. He married Elizabeth Teresa Weiser also in 1873, and had four daughters and three sons. Kenedy published the first *Manual of the Children of Mary* (1868), and *A General Catechism of the Christian Doctrine* called for by the Third Plenary Council of Baltimore. He emphasized readable type, and issued Catholic novels, works of apologetics, Irish history, and parochial school textbooks sold at reasonable prices for a public that was far from wealthy, and contending with nativist sentiments. Kenedy expanded by acquiring legal rights, plates and stock from other financially strapped publishers including John J. Murphy of Baltimore, Peter F. Collier (Kenedy's first salesman), and D. and J. Sadlier. From Murphy Kenedy acquired Cardinal Gibbons' *Faith of Our Fathers,* a Bible line, and other important titles. P. J. Kenedy enjoyed being accessible to visitors in his office; he was a simple man with a strong faith who helped many. Pope Leo XIII conferred on him the title "Printer to the Holy See" in 1895 in recognition of his contributions to Catholic publishing, but his success was due as much to his astute real estate interests as to publishing. After Patrick's death the firm obtained the rights in 1911 to the *Catholic Directory* from a Milwaukee publisher, which various houses had issued since 1833; it continues annually as the *Official Catholic Directory,* a major church reference source. Patrick's sons Arthur and Louis continued the business after his death on January 4, 1906; he was buried in a chapel at St. Andrew's, Poughkeepsie, which he had built in honor of his son Eugene's entrance into the Society of Jesus.

*Dictionary of American Biography,* Vol. 10 (New York, 1933).

Robert C. Healey, *A Catholic Book Chronicle; The Story of P. J. Kenedy & Sons; 1826–1951* (New York, 1951).

John Tebbel, *A History of Book Publishing in the United States,* Vol. 2: *The Expansion of an Industry, 1865–1919* (New York, 1975).

ANNA M. DONNELLY

## KENNA, JOHN EDWARD (1848–1893)

U.S. Representative and Senator. John Kenna's father, Edward, was an Irish immigrant who practiced law in Cincinnati before marrying into a prominent Virginia family and settling in Kanawha County, Virginia (now West Virginia). His sudden death in 1856 left his family destitute. They moved to Missouri, where John grew up in near poverty. At sixteen, he joined the Confederate army. After the war, Kenna went back to West Virginia, where he studied law and was admitted to the bar in 1870. His law firm, Kenna & Watts, formed the nucleus of the "Kanawha Ring," a Democratic faction of young, ambitious Charleston lawyers interested in promoting the economic development of southern West Virginia. Kenna's election in 1872 to prosecuting attorney for Kanawha County marked the "Ring's" rise to political prominence. Kenna's war record, rural upbringing, and charisma made him popular with local voters. In 1876, Kenna was elected to the U.S. House of Representatives and won a Senate seat in 1883, where he worked to gain federal aid for transportation improvements in West Virginia. His efforts helped spark the "Kanawha Boom" of the 1870s and 1880s, opening the state's mining, timber, and other natural resources to development and exploitation. Members of the Kanawha Ring maintained close ties with outside capitalists, profiting financially from the boom and countering the agrarianism and anti-corporate agenda of its political opponents. Kenna died suddenly in 1893, at the age of forty-five.

*Dictionary of American Biography,* Vol. V, part II: 330–31.

George W. Atkinson and Alvaro F. Gibbens, *Prominent Men of West Virginia* (Wheeling, 1890).

John Alexander Williams, "The New Dominion and the Old: Antebellum and Statehood Politics as the Background of West Virginia's 'Bourbon Democracy,'" *West Virginia History,* 33 (1972): 317–407.

TOM DOWNEY

## KENNAN, GEORGE F. (1904–   )

Diplomat, author. George Frost Kennan was born February 4, 1904, at Milwaukee, Wisconsin. His great-great-great-great-grandfather, James MacKennan, emigrated to America from the north of Ireland (probably from County Antrim according to the family history) in the early 1700s.

Kennan was educated at Princeton University, B.A. 1925. In the following year he joined the Foreign Service and was stationed at various diplomatic posts in Europe. He was assigned to study Russian at the University of Berlin (1929–31) in anticipation of the need for a corps of trained experts on the Soviet Union. Kennan served in the American embassy in Moscow during World War II. From there he sent a series of brilliant dispatches back to the State Department, alerting Washington to Soviet designs for global expansion after the war. These dispatches were later published in *Foreign Affairs* in a famous article under the pseudonym "Mr. X." The article became the cornerstone of America's Cold War policy of containment over the next forty years.

After the war Kennan was made Chief of Policy Planning in the State Department. In this post he became a key architect of the Marshall Plan for reconstructing postwar Europe. His thinking was also instrumental in developing the Truman Doctrine and the North Atlantic Treaty Organization. Kennan's diplomatic career culminated in his appointment as United States Ambassador to the Soviet Union (1952–53) and to Yugoslavia (1961–63).

After his retirement from the Foreign Service, Kennan held faculty appointments at the University of Chicago, Harvard, Oxford, and Princeton. During this period he turned out a steady stream of twenty books on foreign policy topics. His *Russia Leaves the War* (1956) won the Pulitzer Prize in history, the National Book Award, the Bancroft Prize, and the Francis Parkman Prize. In 1967 his *Memoirs 1925–1950* was awarded a second Pulitzer Prize and another National Book Award. Kennan's brilliant career was also recognized by receipt of the Albert Einstein Peace Prize in 1981 and the Presidential Medal of Freedom in 1989. Kennan was elected president of the National Institute of Arts and Letters (1965–68) and the American Academy of Arts and Letters (1967–71). The Kennan Institute for Advanced Russian Studies in Washington is named in his honor. Kennan has received honorary degrees from Notre Dame, Harvard, Oxford, Yale, Wisconsin, Princeton, and Michigan among other universities.

Walter Isaacson and Evans Thomas, *The Wise Men: Six Friends and the World They Made* (New York, 1986).
George F. Kennan, *Memoirs 1925–1950* (Boston and Toronto, 1967).

THOMAS GILDEA CANNON

## KENNEDY, ANTHONY M. (1936–  )

Supreme Court Justice. Born in Sacramento, California, July 23, 1936, to Anthony J. and Gladys Kennedy, Anthony M. Kennedy joined the United States Supreme Court in 1988 as the appointee of President Ronald Reagan to fill the vacancy created by the resignation of Justice Lewis Powell. Kennedy's advancement was less than wholly auspicious, as he was actually Reagan's third choice for the post. The Senate rejected Reagan's first nominee (Robert Bork) for ideological reasons, and his second (Douglas Ginsberg) withdrew after revelations of marijuana smoking as a young man. Initial complications notwithstanding, Kennedy would prove a worthy addition to the highest court of the land.

Kennedy arrived at the Supreme Court after serving thirteen years as a federal appellate judge on the Ninth Circuit Court of Appeals in Sacramento. There he participated in some fourteen hundred decisions, wrote more than four hundred opinions, and acquired the reputation of being a pragmatic conservative. He was known for judicial restraint, respect for precedent, and a keen grasp of constitutional and tax law.

Many feared that Kennedy's appointment to the High Court would be decisive in locking the Court into a hard reactionary mold. Although Kennedy at first tended to position himself with conservative justices, he gravitated to a more centrist position, where in an ideologically divided Court he frequently holds the balance of power.

As a justice, Kennedy has produced several judicial surprises. In 1990, for instance, he joined in striking down the Flag Protection Act of 1989, which had made it a crime to burn or deface the American flag, the Court reasoning that the First Amendment's guarantee of free speech was being violated. The decision was strongly protested by patriotic groups. In 1996 Kennedy wrote the majority opinion in *Romer v. Evans,* which declared unconstitutional a Colorado state constitutional provision that nullified civil rights laws singling out homosexuals for protection. This ruling was hailed by homosexual groups as a major triumph in their struggle for equal rights.

An altar boy as a youth, and bookish rather than athletic, Kennedy attended McClatchy High School in Sacramento, then went on to Stanford University, where he completed his undergraduate degree requirements in three years. He was a Phi Beta Kappa scholar. Kennedy spent a year at the London School of Economics before obtaining a law degree, with honors, from Harvard in 1961. He served with the California Army National Guard, practiced law as a member of the firm of Evans, Jackson & Kennedy, and for more than twenty years was a professor of constitutional law at the McGeorge School of Law, University of the Pacific.

Kennedy came to national attention in the early 1970s, when he was enlisted by Ronald Reagan, then governor of California, to draft a tax-limitation measure that became known as Proposition 1. The bill was rejected by voters in a 1973 referendum, but it paved the way five years later for Proposition 13, which was credited with reducing property taxes in California by some fifty-seven percent. Impressed with Kennedy's skills, Reagan proposed his name to President Gerald R. Ford for the federal appellate judgeship that materialized in 1975.

Charles Moritz, ed., *Current Biography Yearbook, 1988* (New York, 1988).
*Collier's Year Book* (New York, 1988, 1990, 1996).
*Who's Who in America* (New Providence, N.J., 1998).

JOHN DEEDY

## KENNEDY, EDWARD MOORE (1932–  )

United States Senator. The youngest of Joseph P. and Rose (Fitzgerald) Kennedy's nine children, Edward Moore Kennedy was born in Boston on February 22, 1932. A 1956 Harvard graduate, he pursued postgraduate studies at the International Law School in The Hague, and on returning from Europe took a law degree in 1959 from the University of Virginia. In 1961 he was named an assistant district attorney for Suffolk County, Massachusetts, and in 1962 he entered the United States Senate, where he has served since.

His entry into the Senate was controversial, as he moved into a seat that seemingly had been "caretaker-ed" for him. There were four years remaining in the Senate term of his brother, John F. Kennedy, on the latter's elevation to the presidency in 1960. Edward Kennedy, 28 at the time, was two years shy of the constitutional age requirement for admission to the Senate. Benjamin A. Smith, a Harvard classmate and close friend of John Kennedy, was then named to the vacancy by Massachusetts Governor Foster Furcolo. Smith, in turn, resigned after two years, setting the stage for a special election won by Kennedy.

Kennedy won election to his first full term in 1964, although under harrowing circumstances. En route from Washington, D.C., to Springfield, Massachusetts, for the state's Democratic Party nominating convention on June 19, 1964, the small, private craft in which he was a passenger went down in a thunderstorm over the Connecticut River Valley. The crash claimed the lives of a political aide and the plane's pilot. Kennedy survived, although suffering a broken back. Initially there were worries of partial paralysis, but he recovered and with the support of a prosthetic brace was able to return to his Senate seat by January.

As senator, Kennedy is considered by many the most liberal of the three Kennedy brothers to occupy seats in the upper chamber. He is an articulate debater, an effective builder of political coalitions, and a consistent advocate on behalf of refugees, immigrants, the aged and minorities. He is also a strong proponent of tax reform and national health insurance. Typical of his legislative interests is a 1997 bill, co-sponsored with Senator Orrin G. Hatch of Utah, to expand children's health insurance coverage through higher cigarette taxes.

Kennedy's maiden speech in the Senate was an impassioned plea for the 1964 Civil Rights Bill, the origins of which were in his brother's administration. He stands for strict arms control, and maintains a close interest in foreign affairs, including those affecting Ireland. He once infuriated British nationalists and loyalists in Northern Ireland by telling Britain to get its troops out of Ulster lest the region become "another Vietnam."

On Kennedy's thirty-fifth year in public office, senatorial colleague Thomas A. Daschle of South Dakota praised him as one who inspired some and irritated others, then likened him to sand in an oyster. "Because of him," Daschle commented, "we produce pearls."

After the assassinations of his brothers—President John Kennedy in 1963 and Senator Robert Kennedy in 1968—many looked to Edward Kennedy to preserve the family's political mystique and perhaps one day achieve the White House himself. His name regularly cropped up as a presidential possibility, and in 1980 he at last made a bid for his party's nomination. It was unsuccessful. Analysts concluded his chances were fated from the start by an accident that occurred years before—the night of July 18, 1969—when a car he was driving plunged off a bridge on Chappaquiddick Island, off Martha's Vineyard, drowning a young female passenger, Mary Jo Kopechne, a campaign worker for his late brother Robert. The accident may have eroded his standing with the national electorate, but the voters of Massachusetts have remained constant, regularly reelecting him to office by comfortable margins.

Behavioral lapses have periodically troubled Edward Kennedy's life, and these led to an extraordinary appearance in 1991 at the Kennedy School at Harvard University, where he made a public apology to Massachusetts' voters for "the faults in the conduct of my private life."

Kennedy's life has been beset by tragedies. In addition to the assassinations of brothers John and Robert, another brother, Joseph, was lost in action in World War II and a sister, Kathleen, died in a plane crash in 1948. Unquestionably the deaths have impacted his public and private persona, but Kennedy for his part has admitted to no scarring. Author Garry Wills once asked Kennedy in narrow political context if he ever considered the family legacy as a burden, something that hampered more than it helped. Kennedy responded, "I can't think of my brothers that way. I'm just grateful for all the things they taught me, all the experiences we shared. For the rest, you just have to take that."

Kennedy's first marriage to Joan Bennett Kennedy ended in divorce. They had three children, one of whom, Patrick, serves in the Congress as a representative from the State of Rhode Island. There is another son, Edward Jr., and a daughter, Kara. In 1992 Kennedy married for a second time, to Victoria Anne Reggie. His office declared subsequently that the second marriage had been blessed by the Catholic Church, an indication that the first marriage had been annulled.

James MacGregor Burns, *Edward Kennedy and the Camelot Legacy* (New York, 1976).

James Carroll, "The Myths Have Died, but Ted Kennedy's Story Lives On," *Boston Globe* (November 1, 1994).

William H. Honan, *Ted Kennedy: Profile of a Survivor* (New York, 1972).

Garry Wills, *The Kennedy Imprisonment: A Meditation on Power* (Boston, 1982).

JOHN DEEDY

## KENNEDY, JOHN FITZGERALD (1917–1963)

Congressman, United States Senator, President of the United States. Second son of Joseph P. and Rose (Fitzgerald) Kennedy, John Fitzgerald Kennedy was born May 29, 1917 in Brookline, Massachusetts. He studied at Choate Preparatory School, then entered Harvard, graduating with honors in 1940 and producing a bachelor's thesis that became a best-selling book—*Why England Slept*. The book was an analysis of Britain's state of preparedness for World War II, and drew on observations Kennedy made as an aide to his father while the latter was Ambassador to the Court of St. James. Kennedy also studied briefly at Princeton, Stanford Business School and the London School of Economics. He enlisted in the U.S. Navy in 1941, and saw action in the Pacific Theater as commander of PT-109, a patrol boat rammed by a Japanese destroyer off Kolombangara in the Solomon Islands on August 2, 1943. Kennedy suffered severe back injuries in the engagement, but managed to save his crew of ten officers and men. He returned home a hero, his story becoming the subject of a Hollywood movie. War injuries would plague him, though, for the rest of his life.

Kennedy entered the political arena in 1946 at age twenty-nine, not as lofty idealist or progressive reformer (his political ideology as a young man was in fact amorphous), but rather, as historian William V. Shannon wrote, "in a typical Irish way: it was a profession in which a man could build a career." A Democrat, he stood for the United States House of Representatives from the Massachusetts Eleventh Congressional District, and

John F. Kennedy

was elected and served three unremarkable terms. (Critics alleged the only thing he was a leader in was absentees.) In 1952 he moved up to the Senate, unseating Republican incumbent Henry Cabot Lodge. In 1953 Kennedy married Jacqueline Bouvier in St. Mary's Church in Newport, Rhode Island. He suffered a flare-up of his war injuries in 1954–55, and underwent several delicate operations that involved the fusion of two spinal discs. During his hospitalization and convalescence he wrote *Profiles in Courage,* a book which was awarded the 1957 Pulitzer Prize for history and which projected him from anonymous freshman Senator to figure of national renown.

In the Senate Kennedy displayed a seriousness of purpose that was in marked contrast to his terms in the House. He battled for fair labor practices and against labor racketeering and, horizons broadened, initiated legislation to raise levels of foreign aid to India and Pakistan. His politics were liberal, although some held it suspect because of his cautious approach on delicate issues, including civil rights. It was a tactic supporters attributed to thoughtfulness and a propensity to question thoroughly before positing solutions. Kennedy's stature grew steadily within the party, such that in 1956, when Democratic presidential nominee Adlai Stevenson threw the choice of a running mate to open convention, there was strong sentiment for Kennedy. He lost in a hotly contested race to Tennessee Senator Estes Kefauver, but what seemed a political set-back at the time turned out to be a blessing. Kennedy's convention strength and his grace in conceding to Kefauver further enhanced his standing among Democrats. More important, he escaped the onus of occupying second place on a ticket that would be routed in the November elections and, of special note, he put a chink in the mythology, strengthened by Alfred E. Smith's defeat in 1928, that no Catholic could win national office in the United States.

That mythology of Catholic unacceptability on the national political level received its definitive testing in 1960 when Kennedy bid for a place on the national Democratic ticket—not as the vice-president, a modesty some urged upon him, but as the presidential nominee. He entered the race as no religious favorite son, for Kennedy was no Catholic conformist. He opposed many positions held by the American bishops, dissenting, for instance, on public financial aid to parochial schools and on aid to Eastern-bloc countries with large Catholic populations. He was against the appointment of an American ambassador to the Vatican, and though he held many cold-war positions, they were devoid of religious connotation. There was, for instance, no sense on his part of the West being locked in a holy war against atheistic communism. Nor, on the other hand, did Kennedy consider himself a moralist called to rid the country of political bigotry. He aspired to the presidency on the merits of one who felt he had the capabilities of the office and who only happened to be Catholic.

The religious issue did not factor in the early 1960 presidential primaries, but analysis of the voting in Wisconsin and West Virginia, later contests actually won by Kennedy, clued that it hovered just below the surface of events. Kennedy gained the Democratic Party's nomination on the first ballot at the national convention in Los Angeles, and with that the religious issue was joined. At a secret meeting in Switzerland, followed by a larger gathering in Washington, prominent Protestant religious leaders took aim at his candidacy, questioning whether a Catholic president could withstand "the determined efforts of the hierarchy of his Church" to impose its agenda on the land. Spokesman for the group was the Rev. Norman Vincent Peale, minister at Marble Collegiate Church in New York City, who proclaimed, "Our American culture is at stake. . . . I don't say it won't survive, but it won't be what it was."

Kennedy confronted his religious skeptics at a meeting of the Ministerial Association of Greater Houston (Texas) September 12, 1960. Father John Courtney Murray, S.J., Catholic authority on positions on church and state, was consulted on the contents of the address he would deliver, while James Wine of the National Council of Churches and John Cogley, a former *Commonweal* editor, coached him on questions to be expected from the floor. Careful preparation produced desired results. Kennedy put the religious question to rest with words that became for the country a religio-politico manifesto of sorts.

"I believe in an America where the separation of church and state is absolute," Kennedy said. "[W]here no Catholic prelate would tell the President (should he be Catholic) how to act and no Protestant minister would tell his parishioners for whom to vote—where no church or church school is granted any public funds or political preference—and where no man is denied public office merely because his religion differs from the President who might appoint him or the people who might elect him."

"I believe in an America that is officially neither Catholic, Protestant nor Jewish—where no public official either requests or accepts instructions on public policy from the Pope, the National Council of Churches, or any other ecclesiastical source—where no religious body seeks to impose its will directly or indirectly upon the general populace or the public acts of its officials—and where religious liberty is so indivisible that an act against one church is treated as an act against all."

Kennedy was elected the thirty-fifth President of the United States on November 9, 1960, edging Richard M. Nixon, vice-president under Dwight D. Eisenhower, in a very close race. Of nearly sixty-nine million ballots cast, fewer than 120,000 separated winner from loser. Historians have cited two factors as especially decisive in the Kennedy victory: success in television debates with Nixon, the first of their kind in history, and the Houston speech. At forty-three, he was the youngest president in U.S. history. His vice-president was Lyndon B. Johnson.

The Kennedy presidency began awkwardly with Kennedy consenting against his own better judgment to an operation inherited from the Eisenhower Administration for a U.S.-sponsored invasion of Cuba by Cubans refugees based in Guatemala. The invasion ended ignominiously after three days with the Bay of Pigs fiasco. Kennedy had been in office barely three months. He was embarrassed and angered, but he quickly steadied, and appealing to the pride and unselfishness of Americans challenged them to join in exploring what he called a New Frontier, identified as "uncharted areas of science and space, unsolved problems of peace and war, unconquered pockets of ignorance and prejudice, unanswered questions of poverty and surplus." The legislation that followed was characterized by such high ideals as to have people speaking of a modern Camelot.

Over objections it would become a refuge for beatniks and visionaries, Kennedy established the Peace Corps, an agency fashioned after religious missionary movements, most notably that of the Mormons. He initiated the Alliance for Progress, a ten-point program for social and economic betterment in Latin America. He energized the space program, pledging to land a man on the moon and return him safely to earth by 1970. He viewed racial equality as a moral issue and using his executive powers began expanding the presence of blacks in ambassadorships, judgeships and Federal posts, where their numbers had hitherto been sparse or nonexistent. In September, 1962, he used troops to enforce a court order for the integration of the University of Mississippi, and the following year federalized the Alabama National Guard to insure the peaceful integration of the University of Alabama. Meanwhile, he was drafting the most comprehensive civil-rights bill in the nation's history, one which he sent to the Congress in 1963. Kennedy would not live to steer the measure through the legislative process, but his bill would be the basis for the sweeping 1964 Civil Rights Act enacted during the Johnson Administration.

On the international front, Kennedy grappled with major crises involving the Soviet Republic, then under the leadership of Premier Nikita Khrushchev.

The first crisis came in 1961, when Khrushchev proposed formal recognition of East Germany, with Berlin becoming a "free city" under control of a "sovereign" German Democratic Republic. Such a move could have effectively isolated West Berlin, then an island of freedom within East Germany under protection of the West. Kennedy resisted. Khrushchev responded by instigating construction of a concrete divider, the Berlin Wall, sealing East from West Berlin. Kennedy in turn dispatched fifteen-hundred American troops in armored trucks across the *Autobahn,* through East German checkpoints to West Berlin, signaling by the action militant determination not to be squeezed out of the city. The crisis eased, though the Berlin Wall remained until the collapse of European Communism in 1989. Kennedy visited West Berlin in 1963 and from the steps of City Hall reiterated his commitment to the city and its citizens. "All free men, wherever they may live, are citizens of Berlin," Kennedy said. "And therefore, as a free man, I take pride in the words *'Ich bin ein Berliner.'"* The applause was thunderous.

More dramatic, because it brought the world to the brink of nuclear war, was the Cuban missile crisis of October, 1962. It began when American intelligence confirmed the construction of offensive missile sites on Cuba, some near-operational, and at the same time tracked a Soviet convoy en route to the island with a shipment of medium and intermediate range missiles, each with a payload estimated at twenty to thirty times the power of the Hiroshima bomb. Operational, the Soviet missiles would have a strike capability ranging on a arc from St. Louis to Washington, D.C. For Kennedy the presence of offensive missiles ninety miles from the American mainland was intolerable. Some advisors urged on Kennedy a direct military response to the situation, with the United States either invading the island or launching air strikes against the missile sites and other military targets. Kennedy opted instead for a naval blockade that would quarantine the island. It was a decision that then focused the crisis on the Soviet convoy headed for Cuba. Interference with it could be regarded as an act of war. The convoy kept coming and neither the United States nor the Soviet Union showed any sign of backing down. The world tensed. Finally, the Soviet convoy slowed on orders from Khrushchev, then circled and returned home. It was a moment of relief for the world—and one of triumph for Kennedy. But there was no exulting on his part, no claim of victory, not even an appearance on television. He limited public reaction to a short statement praising Khrushchev's "statesmanlike decision," terming it "an important and constructive contribution to peace."

Ten months later—July 25, 1963—Kennedy would conclude with Khrushchev a nuclear Test Ban Treaty outlawing all testing in the atmosphere, in outer space and under water, the first nuclear-controls agreement of any kind between East and West since the dawning of the nuclear age. There was strenuous opposition in some quarters to the treaty, but Kennedy viewed it as a necessary step towards cleaning up radioactive poisons in the atmosphere. (There had already been 336 nuclear explosions in the atmosphere by various countries.) He also saw the treaty as a curb on the arms race, and as a way of building mutual trust between nations. There are, he conceded to critics, "risks inherent in any treaty, [but] the far greater risks to our security are the risks of unrestricted testing."

Wary of military involvement in Southeast Asia, Kennedy nonetheless increased the presence of "military advisers" in South Vietnam from 685, when he took office, to 16,732 as of October, 1963. Though he acted with reluctance and kept his objectives limited—specifically, to help the South Vietnamese government rally its people, so it could fight its own war—the consequences proved fateful in the years to come.

In the Fall of 1963, Kennedy was a man confidently in control of his office. He fended off questions about running for re-election in 1964, but there was little doubt he would do so, particularly given his unfinished domestic legislative program. When he flew to Texas on November 21, therefore, it was, in Theodore Sorensen's words, a "barely disguised campaign trip." Kennedy hoped to harmonize fractious Texas Democrats, broaden his political base in the state, address right-wing attitudes and underscore the point that "ignorance . . . can handicap this country's security." On November 22, he arrived in Dallas from Fort Worth. After a reception at the airport, Kennedy headed in an open car for a luncheon at the Trade Mart. The streets were lined with friendly crowds. As the motorcade passed through Dealey Plaza, he was shot by a gunman, Lee Harvey Oswald, who took aim from a sixth floor window of the School Depository Building. It was 12:30 p.m. Kennedy was rushed to Parkland Hospital, where he was pronounced dead. His funeral Mass was offered by Richard Cardinal Cushing of Boston, a close family friend, in St. Matthew's Cathedral in Washington, with burial following in Arlington National Cemetery.

Many conspiracy theories cropped up in the wake of the assassination. However, the Warren Commission, a presidential investigative body headed by Chief Justice Earl Warren, concluded in a report issued September 24, 1964, that there was no evidence of a conspiracy and that the killing was the work of Oswald, acting alone. The report has been subjected to criticism, but no hard evidence has been turned up to contradict its essential conclusion.

The passing of years has also brought reassessments of Kennedy the person and Kennedy the president, but nothing has invalidated the words of *New York Times* columnist James Reston assessing his place in history soon after the assassination: "The tragedy of John Fitzgerald Kennedy was greater than the accomplishment, but in the end the tragedy enhances the accomplishment and revives the hope."

Ralph G. Martin, *A Hero for Our Time* (New York, 1983).
Albert J. Menendez, *John F. Kennedy: Catholic and Humanist* (Buffalo, 1978).
Kenneth P. O'Donnell and David F. Powers, *'Johnny We Hardly Knew Ye'* (Boston, 1972).
William V. Shannon, *The American Irish* (New York, 1963).
Theodore C. Sorensen, *Kennedy* (New York, 1965).

JOHN DEEDY

## KENNEDY, JOHN F., JR. (1960–1999)

Assistant District Attorney, publisher. Son of John Fitzgerald Kennedy and Jacqueline Bouvier Kennedy, John F. Kennedy, Jr., was born on Thanksgiving Day, November 25, 1960, three weeks after his father was elected President of the United States. He grew up very much in the nation's eye, with photographers catching him peeping gleefully from under the presidential desk in the Oval Office and soon after mournfully saluting the coffin of his assassinated father. Attention followed him through private schools, Brown University, from which he was graduated in 1983, through New York University Law School, and into a job as a prosecutor in the Manhattan District Attorney's Office. Four years later, expressing disenchantment with the practice of law, he resigned to found *George,* a glossy, para-political magazine. He was thirty-four at the time, but few believed that he had yet settled on his role in life. Many speculated that he would eventually enter politics and stand for public office. He deflected the idea, but never completely closed the door on the possibility.

On September 21, 1996, John Kennedy (he forewent middle initial and the junior) married Carolyn Bessette, a fashion publicist, in a small chapel on a barrier island off the coast of Georgia, a site chosen for its privacy. They took up residence in a loft of a converted business structure in lower Manhattan, where he still did not fade from the public's eye. He was a man of enormous celebrity, but he bore the fame of heritage with great dignity and grace, and quietly gave his time to a number of humanitarian causes.

Kennedy obtained a pilot's license on April 22, 1998. On the night of July 16, 1999, he was at the controls of a small plane when it disappeared off the Massachusetts coast. Also on board were his wife and sister-in-law, Lauren G. Bessette. They were en route to Kennedy's cousin Rory's wedding on Cape Cod, with a planned stop on the island of Martha's Vineyard to drop off Lauren. A massive search operation was launched and the wreckage with the bodies inside was found five days later. All three were buried at sea, the Navy providing the destroyer USS *Briscoe* for the ceremony. A private memorial Mass for John Kennedy and his wife was held the following morning at St. Thomas More Church in New York City with President and Mrs. Clinton among those in attendance.

JOHN DEEDY

John F. Kennedy, Jr., salutes his father during services for the slain president, 1963.

## KENNEDY, JOSEPH PATRICK (1888–1969)

Financier, ambassador. Born in Boston, September 6, 1888, the son of Patrick J. and Mary (Hickey) Kennedy, Joseph P. Kennedy achieved wealth as a financier and fame as a political operative and diplomat. His diplomatic career dissolved in ignominy in mid-life, but he enjoyed a redemption of sorts in advanced years as mentor to a large and politically influential family—three sons (John F., Robert F. and Edward M.) serving in the U.S. Senate, with one of them (John F.) moving on to the White House as President. After his death, a daughter (Jean Kennedy Smith) became United States Ambassador to Ireland.

The Kennedy forebears came to the United States in 1848, emigrating from Dunganstown in County Wexford in the wake of the great Irish potato famine. Joseph Kennedy's father, Patrick, a first-generation Irish-American, was a saloon keeper and state office holder, who made it a point to send his son to "proper Bostonian" schools. The son, accordingly, attended Boston Latin School and Harvard College, graduating in 1908 and 1912, respectively. Launched educationally and socially into the broader American society, Kennedy nonetheless stayed firmly rooted in Catholic culture and the Catholic community. In 1914 he married Rose Fitzgerald, daughter of Boston's mayor, John F. (Honey Fitz) Fitzgerald, the first American-born son of Irish ancestry to hold that office. The couple had four sons and five daughters.

Kennedy began his career as a bank examiner, and by age 26 was himself president of a bank, the Columbia Trust Company. During World War I he was assistant general manager of the Fore River (Massachusetts) plant of the Bethlehem Shipbuilding Corporation, afterwards turning to investment brokering and to Hollywood, where he integrated the Keith-Albee-Orpheum movie-house chain and reorganized major film companies, including Paramount Pictures. At the height of the Depression in 1934, he was said to be a millionaire several times over. His fortune would continue to grow.

Kennedy was a fund-raiser and adviser to President Franklin D. Roosevelt during the 1932 campaign, and in 1934 Roosevelt designated him chairman of the Securities and Exchange Commission, the agency newly formed to regulate stock exchanges. Success there led to chairmanship of the U.S. Maritime Commission, then assignment to England in 1937 as Ambassador to the Court of St. James's. He was the first Catholic and first Irish-American to hold the position.

Kennedy arrived in England full family in tow, and with his charming and informal ways quickly became the darling of the British media. The relationship was to sour. As the clouds of World War II gathered, Kennedy emerged first as an accommodator to totalitarian threats, then after the outbreak of hostilities as a defeatist in terms of England's prospects for survival. His gloomy views and increasingly isolationist sentiments put him at odds with Washington, and talk was rampant of a break between him and Roosevelt. When he left England for the United States in October, 1940, it was generally presumed Kennedy was returning to resign. This he did November 6, but with an understanding—one requested by the Administration—that the news not be made public until a replacement had been chosen.

A few days later Kennedy met in a Boston hotel room with a small group of reporters and in an expansive and reckless mood bared his political soul. "Democracy is finished in England," he said, and if the United States gets into the war "it may be here," too. Not stopping there, he disparaged Mrs. Eleanor Roosevelt, calling her a bother who was "always sending me a note to have some little Susie Glotz to tea at the Embassy." The *Boston Globe* published his remarks with predictable reactions on both sides of the Atlantic. The English were bitter and an embarrassed Washington expedited Kennedy's resignation as Ambassador. There was no letter of thanks from the President, *pro forma* or otherwise, and no bid to stay associated with the Administration. Kennedy maintained in his own defense that his was a background briefing to reporters and was thus off the record. But the damage was irreparable. At 52, he was a man without a portfolio, without a job, and without standing with the American public. He too was bitter. When Roosevelt ran for a fourth term in 1944, he extended no public endorsement.

In 1945 Kennedy founded the Joseph P. Kennedy, Jr. Foundation memorializing his oldest son, who died in World War II. He also received senatorial (as distinct from presidential) appointments to the Hoover Commission for the study of policy and organization of government. Mostly, however, his time was spent on dead-end projects, among them abortive attempts to capture control of the Democratic Party. The entrance of son John into national politics energized his later years, and as John climbed the political ladder a measure of celebrity returned. His influence on John's political career, and that of sons Robert and Edward, was significant, though for the sons it came with a certain amount of ideological baggage because of their father's reactionary past. The sons, in contrast to the father, were social and political liberals.

On December 19, 1961, Kennedy suffered a coronary thrombosis that left him an invalid, confined largely to the family compound at Hyannis, Massachusetts. He died in Hyannis on November 18, 1969.

Doris Kearns Goodwin, *The Fitzgeralds and the Kennedys: An American Saga* (New York, 1988).

Richard J. Whalen, *The Founding Father: The Story of Joseph P. Kennedy* (New York, 1964).

JOHN DEEDY

## KENNEDY, JOSEPH PATRICK II (1952–   )

Political figure, business executive. Eldest son of Senator Robert F. and Ethel (Skakel) Kennedy, Joseph P. Kennedy II was born in Brighton, Massachusetts, September 24, 1952. He was graduated from University of Massachusetts-Boston in 1976, afterwards founding and serving as chairman of the Citizens' Energy Corporation, a non-profit operation providing low-cost heating oil for low-income families and households of the elderly. He developed the operation into seven separate companies with annual revenues in excess of $1.5-billion.

Kennedy entered the United States Congress in 1986 as representative from the Eighth Massachusetts District. He served as a member of the House Banking and Finances Services Committee, and its subcommittee on Housing and Community Opportunity with focuses on affordable housing and credit availability for working people to buy homes and open businesses. He was also a member of the Committee on Veterans Affairs, where he has worked for a stronger and more effective veterans' health-care system.

Kennedy's legislative concerns had a strong social orientation, concerned with such issues as low-cost health coverage for the uninsured and protection of the elderly. As co-chairman of the Older Americans Caucus, he fought budget cuts in senior health-care programs and worked to keep nursing home care safe and affordable. Among other things, he advocated a national background check-system for nursing aides and a registry to identify workers with a history of abuse.

Kennedy supported legislation addressing the problem of stalking and domestic violence, and authored legislation on youth crime, with considerations both of prevention and effective prosecution. A commitment to human rights took him to Northern Ireland, Haiti, Germany and Armenia to speak against oppression.

Eyeing higher office, Kennedy signaled intention in 1997 to run for Governor of Massachusetts, and was widely favored to capture his party's nomination. However, a series of contretemps eroded popularity margins, prompting him to step aside in August before a formal announcement of candidacy was made. A complicating factor, though not the decisive one, was a book written by his first wife, Sheila Rauch Kennedy, challenging the Catholic Church's granting of an annulment of their marriage.

In March, 1998, Kennedy announced he was retiring after twelve years in Congress to devote more time to his family and the Citizens Energy Corporation, whose leadership he had reassumed after his brother Michael, then heading the corporation, died in a skiing accident on New Year's Eve, 1997. The year of family tumult and tragedy that was 1997 had brought, he said, "a new recognition of our own vulnerability and the vagaries of life." However, Kennedy did not rule out a return to political life, and he announced he was keeping his campaign fund account in place for that possibility.

Since 1993 Kennedy has been married to Beth Kelly Kennedy. He has twin sons by his first marriage, Joseph P. III and Matthew.

Sheila Rauch Kennedy, *Shattered Faith* (New York, 1997).

JOHN DEEDY

## KENNEDY, PATRICK J. (1967–   )

Congressman. The youngest of three children of Senator Edward M. and Joan Bennett Kennedy, Kennedy was born July 14, 1967 in Brighton, Massachusetts. He entered political life while an undergraduate at Providence College, standing in 1988 as a Democrat for the Rhode Island House of Representatives and winning election handily. He was 21 at the time, and anxious in his words "to continue his family's tradition of public service." He won reelection in 1990 and 1992, meanwhile receiving a bachelor's degree in 1991 from Providence College.

Kennedy ran for the United States Congress in 1994 and was elected as the representative from Rhode Island's First District, receiving seventy percent of the vote and carrying all twenty cities and towns of the district. On election he was the youngest member of the House of Representatives. He still serves in the Congress.

As a legislator, Kennedy is a political progressive. He is an advocate for the elderly, working families and minorities, as well as proponent of expanded educational opportunities, protection for the environment and quality health care. He opposes cuts in Medicare and Medicaid, and co-sponsored legislation to establish a commission to ensure the long-term solvency of the program.

He also introduced the Student Loan Affordability Act, which allows a tax deduction for the payment of interest on student loans. The bill was adopted by the Democratic leadership as part of its Families First Agenda in 1997.

Kennedy is a staunch supporter of gun control and attracted wide attention in March, 1996, with a floor speech opposing efforts to repeal the ban on assault weapons.

JOHN DEEDY

## KENNEDY, ROBERT FRANCIS (1925–1968)

United States Attorney General, United States Senator. In his brief lifetime, Robert F. Kennedy was a Cabinet member, Senator from the State of New York and, before being cut down by an assassin's bullet, contender for the Democratic nomination for President of the United States.

He was born in Brookline, Massachusetts, November 20, 1925, the seventh of nine children of Joseph P. and Rose (Fitzgerald) Kennedy. Less physically prepossessing than his older brothers, he was by way of compensation fiercely competitive, and early feelings of inadequacy dissipated as his personality toughened and he escaped the shadows of elders. He attended Milton Academy and Harvard College, where he distinguished himself more in sports than studies, then moved on to Virginia Law School, graduating in 1951, fifty-sixth in a class of 124. But academic grades proved an inaccurate measure of the man. Robert Kennedy had an acute intelligence that broadened as he matured.

Kennedy entered public life as a criminal investigator in the Department of Justice's Brooklyn office, leaving after brief service to manage his brother John's successful run for a Senate seat from Massachusetts in 1952. The following year he went to Washington as assistant counsel of the Senate's Permanent Investigations Subcommittee, then under the chairmanship of Senator Joseph McCarthy, Republican of Wisconsin, a family friend. It was an appointment his father promoted but one that his brother John advised against, fearing Robert would be tarred by the McCarthy association. He accepted the post, nonetheless, challenged by the thought of exposing corruption and communist conspiracies. He resigned after several months, disillusioned by McCarthy's hit-and-run tactics, but returned to the subcommittee in 1954 as counsel to the Democratic minority. In that capacity he wrote the minority report condemning McCarthy's investigation of the Department of the Army. When the mid-term election of 1954 restored control of the Senate to the Democrats, Kennedy moved up to chief counsel. Prosecutorial focus then shifted to graft and corruption in government, with one investigation resulting in the resignation of a Secretary of the Air Force.

Kennedy built a reputation as a relentless, even ruthless prosecutor, notably after taking over in 1957 as chief counsel to the Senate Select Committee on Improper Activities in the Labor or Management Field. He targeted union racketeering, moving most directly against the Teamsters on allegations of extortion, beatings, fund tampering and collusion with trucking associations. His prosecutions brought him into head-to-head conflict with successive Teamster presidents, Dave Beck and Jimmy Hoffa, both of whom ended up behind bars—Beck for larceny and income tax evasion; Hoffa for jury tampering and the diverting of Teamster pension funds. The Labor Reform Act of 1959 is traced to the Kennedy investigations.

Kennedy was enlisted by his brother, John F. Kennedy, to manage his 1960 campaign for the presidency, and afterwards he

Robert Kennedy

was offered the post of Attorney General. Doubts about age and experience gave Robert Kennedy pause, as well as concern that the appointment would be viewed as nepotism. Still he accepted, and in office proved a remarkably efficient Attorney General. He assembled a brilliant staff, launched drives against organized crime and political wrong-doing, and energetically pressed the Administration's civil rights program. There were anomalies, though. Kennedy, for example, dispatched Federal troops into the South to enforce integration laws, and in common conversation startled individuals, Catholic bishops not excepted, by inquiring what, if anything, they had done lately for Negroes. Yet, Kennedy also acceded to FBI Director J. Edgar Hoover's request to wiretap the telephones of civil-rights leader Dr. Martin Luther King, Jr.

During the Cuban missile crisis of 1962, Kennedy strenuously countered arguments within the National Security Council for a preemptive military strike, voicing moral anguish over the deaths that would result and contending that American principles and values would deem "a sneak military attack" repugnant. It was a viewpoint that ultimately prevailed, the option being for a naval blockade.

After the assassination of President Kennedy in Dallas in 1963, Kennedy continued as Attorney General in the Cabinet of President Lyndon B. Johnson. Theirs was not a congenial relationship. Their styles were markedly different and there were differences on points of policy, notably the war in Vietnam. When Johnson made clear that he would not choose Kennedy as his vice-presidential running mate in 1964, a post Kennedy dearly wanted, he resigned, established residency in New York and ran for United States Senator against Republican incumbent Kenneth Keating. Victorious, he returned to Washington, eyes firmly set on the White House.

Kennedy made his presidential bid in 1968, albeit reluctantly as he did not consider the timing felicitous. Prompting his change of mind was Minnesota Senator Eugene McCarthy's surprising showing against President Johnson in the New Hampshire primary and Johnson's subsequent withdrawal from the race. Kennedy's late entry into the field provoked angry charges of opportunism from McCarthy supporters, but Kennedy persisted, and activated his late brother John's seasoned political campaigners in pursuit of the Democratic nomination.

The contest developed into a three-way fight between himself, McCarthy and Vice President Hubert H. Humphrey, the Administration's candidate. Humphrey was favored to win the nomination, but Kennedy and McCarthy emerged as key players in the contest as the state primaries moved westward. Kennedy won over McCarthy in the Indiana and Nebraska primaries, but then lost to McCarthy in Oregon. That left the June 4 California primary as decisive for the chances of both of them. After a tumultuous campaign, Kennedy emerged victorious, and he seemed now within striking distance of Humphrey and his party's nomination.

In a victory speech in the ballroom of Los Angeles' Ambassador Hotel, Kennedy noted that he had also triumphed that same day in the South Dakota primary. "The most urban" of states and the "most rural"—he had won them both, he observed, adding "I think that we can end the divisions within the United States." Kennedy's supporters were buoyed, but joy turned suddenly to grief. Kennedy stepped down from the podium and headed from the hotel by way of the kitchen. It was shortly after midnight. As he passed through the kitchen area he was shot by Sirhan B. Sirhan, a Jordanian Arab embittered by Kennedy's pro-Israeli sympathies. He was mortally wounded, and died the next day, May 6, in Good Samaritan Hospital. His body was returned to New York for a funeral Mass in St. Patrick's Cathedral. Burial followed in Arlington National Cemetery. Kennedy was survived by his wife, the former Ethel Skakel, and eleven children, the last being born after his death.

Arthur M. Schlesinger, Jr., *Robert Kennedy and His Times* (Boston, 1978).
William V. Shannon, *The Heir Apparent: Robert Kennedy and the Struggle for Power* (New York, 1967).

JOHN DEEDY

## KENNEDY, ROBERT FOSTER (1884–1952)

Neurologist. Robert Foster Kennedy was born in Belfast, Ireland, to William Archer Kennedy, a Protestant physician, and Hessie Foster Kennedy. Shortly after his birth, the family moved to Czestochowa, Poland, where his father had accepted a managerial position at a linen factory.

Kennedy's mother, who was the daughter of Robert Foster Dill, a professor of obstetrics at Queen's College, Belfast, died at the age of thirty-four. Kennedy's father sent the five children back to Ireland to live with relatives. Kennedy, still an infant, lived with Dill and was cared for by his two unmarried aunts.

In 1894 Kennedy attended the Royal School in Dungannon, County Tyrone. From there he went on to study medicine at Queens College. After qualifying in 1906, he moved to London and became house physician to Sir William Gowers at the National Hospital, Queen Square.

His first three scientific papers were written with Gordon Holmes, a fellow countryman, on syringomyelia. During his tenure as resident medical officer at Queen Square, Kennedy took an interest in patients with brain tumors. Despite support from prominent physicians, he was unable to obtain a position in Dublin, Belfast, or any major center in Scotland and England.

Kennedy accepted an offer in 1910 to be chief of clinic at the newly founded Neurological Institute in New York. He remained active there as a consulting neurologist until 1934. Shortly after his arrival at the institute, he was appointed an instructor in neurology at Cornell University.

Kennedy's reputation rests on a paper he wrote soon after arriving in the United States: "Retrobullar neuritis as an exact diagnostic sign of certain tumors and abscesses in the frontal lobes." The paper was published in the 1911 fall issue of the *American Journal of Medical Science.* The syndrome about which he wrote, the loss of vision in an eye as the result of the compression of a tumor on the optic nerve, bears his name.

Kennedy determined that a swelling of the brain was the result of both a viral and allergic encephalitis. His ideas decades later led to the linkage of allergy with multiple sclerosis. Also, he was among the first to use electric shock to treat severe depression.

In 1912 Kennedy was elected a fellow of the Royal Society of Edinburgh. The following year he married Isabel McCann of Belfast in New Hampshire.

When war was declared in 1914, Kennedy volunteered to serve six months overseas. While in France, he helped an Englishman convert a building in the village of Ris-Orangis near Paris into a military hospital for French soldiers. Kennedy's wife joined him and worked in the kitchen. At the end of six months, they returned to New York.

In the summer of 1916, Kennedy returned to France for the duration of the war, attaining the rank of major. His assignment was as general casualty surgeon with a field ambulance unit in Flanders. After ten months with the unit, he joined the Harvard surgical unit at Boulogne. At the end of the war, he was made a Chevalier of the Legion of Honor.

In a 1918 issue of *War Medicine,* Kennedy wrote an analysis of shell shock. He argued that the phenomenon occurred as the result of a conflict between the emotion of loyalty to do one's duty, even to the point of self-sacrifice, and the natural instinct for self-preservation in the midst of violence.

After the war, Kennedy returned to New York and to Cornell University where he was appointed professor of neurology in 1919. He also accepted the position of head of the neurological service at Bellevue Hospital and carried on a successful private practice. At Bellevue, the first public hospital in the United States, Kennedy often gave financial assistance to poor patients.

Robert Foster
Kennedy

Among Kennedy's most famous patients were Winston Churchill and Franklin D. Roosevelt while he was president. Kennedy examined Churchill in December 1931 after an accident in which he was knocked down by a car. Churchill had no neurological damage, and the two men became friends. In 1941 Churchill even consulted Kennedy about the strength of the Isolationist Movement in the United States.

During the New York Stock Exchange "crash" of 1929, Kennedy lost almost half of his savings. His marriage ended in divorce in 1938; he and his wife had two daughters. Shortly after that, he suffered a massive hemorrhage from a nasal artery and never fully recovered his full strength.

In 1940 he married Katherine Caragol y San Abria, a young medical student. With her he had a third daughter who was born in 1943.

Kennedy joined the Charaha Club, a group of doctors who were concerned with history, literature, and art in medicine. He was president of the American Neurological Society and received many honors, including an honorary doctor of science degree from Queen's University, Belfast.

During his last days, while suffering from polyarteritis nodosa, Kennedy requested that he be taken to his own ward in Bellevue Hospital. He died there on January 7, 1952, shortly after admission to the ward.

J. K. Butterfield, *The Making of a Neurologist* (London, 1981).

Davis Coakley, *Irish Masters of Medicine* (Dublin, 1992).

John A. Garraty, ed., *Dictionary of American Biography* supp. 5 (New York, 1977).

J. L. Pool, *The Neurological Institite of New York, 1901–1974* (New York, 1975).

L. D. Stevenson, "R. Foster Kennedy, M.D., 1884–1952," *Neurology* (1952).

MARIANNA McLOUGHLIN

## KENNEDY, ROSE FITZGERALD (1890–1995)

Political matriarch. Mother of President John F. Kennedy and two United States senators, and wife of a wealthy businessman/ambassador, Rose Fitzgerald Kennedy was the presiding matriarch of a politically prominent American Irish family, renowned for its public triumphs and tragedies.

Born on July 22, 1890, in Boston, Massachusetts, Rose Fitzgerald was the eldest of the six children of Josephine Hannon and John (Honey Fitz) Fitzgerald, both descendants of Irish immigrants. Raised in privilege, Fitzgerald was introduced early to political life by her father, a Boston mayor and Massachusetts congressman who often took his daughter to public events. She graduated from Dorchester High School in Massachusetts, and attended Blumenthal Academy, a finishing school in the Netherlands, and Manhattanville College in Purchase, New York, both institutions run by the Sisters of the Sacred Heart.

On October 7, 1914, Rose Fitzgerald married Joseph Kennedy, a political lieutenant of her father. An astute businessman, Joseph Kennedy would amass a fortune estimated at $500 million, and was posted to the Court of Saint James as ambassador to Great Britain from 1938–1941, despite some controversy about his wealth and isolationist views. The couple had nine children: Joseph, John, Rosemary, Kathleen, Eunice, Patricia, Robert, Jean, and Edward. While her husband concentrated on his business holdings, which grew to include interests in banking, real estate, liquor, film and Wall Street, Rose Kennedy devoted herself to the

Rose Kennedy
with Joseph, Jr.

upbringing of their children. She derived much satisfaction from this devotion, querying in her 1974 autobiography, *Times to Remember,* "What greater aspiration and challenge are there for a mother than the hope of raising a great son or daughter?"

Kennedy's attentions turned again to things political when her children entered public life. She was active in Kennedy family political campaigns, including those of her three sons: President John F. Kennedy (dec.), Senator Robert F. Kennedy (D. NY) (dec.), and Senator Edward M. Kennedy (D. MA). The inauguration of her son John as the 38th president of the United States on January 20, 1961, was the apex of the family's political efforts, and served as a catalyst for the subsequent accession of other family members into public office.

The Kennedy family captured the imagination of the public, and consequently was the subject of intense media attention. Rose Kennedy was admired for her grace in triumph, and for her stoicism in the face of many personal tragedies, especially the early loss of four of her children. President Kennedy was assassinated in Dallas, Texas, in 1963, and Senator Robert Kennedy was assassinated in California during the 1968 presidential campaign. Her oldest son, Joseph, a navy pilot, was killed when his plane exploded over the English channel in World War II. A daughter, Kathleen, died in a plane crash in 1948. Another daughter, Rosemary, is mentally retarded. Mrs. Kennedy's husband suffered a stroke in 1961, and died in 1969.

A devout Roman Catholic, Kennedy relied on her religious faith for strength and consolation into her old age. After suffering the first of a series of debilitating strokes in 1984, she died at the age of 105 of complications of pneumonia in Hyannis Port, Massachusetts, on January 22, 1995.

Gail Cameron, *Rose: A Biography of Rose Fitzgerald Kennedy* (New York, 1971).

Barbara Gibson (with Caroline Latham), *Life with Rose Kennedy* (New York, 1986).

Doris Kearns Goodwin, *The Fitzgeralds and the Kennedys* (New York, 1987).

Rose Kennedy, *Times to Remember* (New York, 1994).

Laurence Leamer, *The Kennedy Women: Saga of an American Family* (New York, 1994).

KATHLEEN N. McCARTHY

## KENNEDY, WILLIAM (1928–   )

Novelist. William Kennedy took the American literary world by storm in 1984 when he won the Pulitzer Prize for his novel *Ironweed.* The prize was not awarded to a neophyte. Having already published three novels before *Ironweed,* Kennedy had been honing his craft for twenty years. Since the Pulitzer, he has continued to be a vital presence in American literature.

To date, Kennedy has written seven novels, two works of nonfiction, one stage play, a few screen plays, and numerous essays, reviews, and interviews. His writing style is characterized by both a clean journalistic objectivity and a lyrical virtuosity which can approach the surreal. As in the proletariat and political traditions of James T. Farrell and Edwin O'Connnor, Kennedy's subjects are grounded in urban American working class Irish neighborhoods and political machinery. His characters are outsiders who rebel against or learn to understand their communities. And although his writing is masculine, with women primarily in supporting and symbolic roles, his men strike a universal note in enacting the tension between the individual and society.

### BACKGROUND

William Joseph Kennedy was born in Albany, New York, on January 16, 1928, to Mary Elizabeth McDonald and William Joseph Kennedy, Sr.: "a Catholic working class family," Kennedy once said in an interview, "Irish on all sides" (McCaffery and Gregory). Specifically, he was born in North Albany, one of the city's Irish neighborhoods where his ancestors settled five generations before and which has emerged as the emotional center of all his fiction.

His mother worked as an accountant all her adult life, and his father found his way from barber, foundry worker, and pie salesman to politically connected Albany County deputy sheriff. The senior Kennedy was also a bit gambler and ward heeler for the Albany Democratic machine controlled for most of its fifty years by a party boss named Dan O'Connell. These biographical details are transformed into Kennedy's fiction. In his youth, Kennedy served as an altar boy and attended the Christian Brothers Academy, and he also frequented pool halls and accompanied his father on his rounds of political clubs and gaming rooms to collect party "contributions." He freely acknowledges the three powerful influences on his artistic vision: his Democratic father, Irish North Albany roots, and the Catholic Church.

Kennedy graduated from Siena College in Loudonville, New York, in 1949 and went to work as a sports writer for the Glens Falls [NY] *Post Star* until he was drafted into the Army during the Korean War. He was assigned as sports writer to the Fourth Division in Europe and continued in journalism upon his return to the United States in 1952 as a general assignment reporter for the Albany *Times Union.* In 1956 he accepted an offer to be assistant managing editor of a new English language newspaper in San Juan, the *Puerto Rico World Journal,* because for him Albany had become "an old man's town—moribund, no action." When the *World* folded, Kennedy worked briefly for the *Miami Herald,* and then settled for a few years in San Juan where he co-founded and acted as managing editor of the *San Juan Star.*

It was during this time that Kennedy started writing fiction, encouraged by Saul Bellow in a writing course at the University of Puerto Rico. Kennedy's first fictional attempts were set in Puerto Rico, but he soon found himself writing about Albany.

When in 1961, he returned to his home town to care for his sick father, by then a widower, the author didn't think he'd stay long; the Albany environs, however, have been his home ever since. In an interview with the *Washington Post* in 1983, he said, "I didn't think I'd stay long, but I was interested in my family's history, my neighborhood's history . . . [and] by inchworm's accumulation of imaginative progress, it became . . . as abundant in mythical qualities as it was in political ambition, remarkably consequential greed, and genuine fear of the Lord" (Dec. 28).

From his return home until 1970, Kennedy worked part-time ("lest [he] never write fiction again") at the *Albany Times Union* as a features writer. He wrote local color stories about Albany's history, neighborhoods, people, politicians, ethnic groups, bookies, barkeeps, and derelicts—the very people who would later populate his novels. In 1965, he was nominated for a Pulitzer Prize for a series he wrote on Albany's slums.

### EARLY WRITING

Kennedy published his first novel, *The Ink Truck* (Dial Press), in 1969, inspired by a 1964 newspaper strike at the *Times Union.* The narrator is a columnist and an anarchist named Bailey, who conspires against his paper during a strike. A review at the time said Bailey was "a loser of heroic dimensions" and Kennedy a man with "a keen sense of the absurd." The novel exaggerates the real strike and is probably more informed by the Civil Rights movement in the United States in the sixties, presenting a fictional world out of control in surreal and fantastic prose. Bailey, more a caricature than a character, represents the rebellious energies of an America oppressed by a capitalistic system. Bailey's city, while based on Albany, is unnamed and, except for one reference to the assassination of John Kennedy, is set merely in modern times, a sharp contrast to the rest of his corpus where time and place are as important as character.

Shortly after leaving the *Times Union,* Kennedy accepted an adjunct professorship at the State University of New York at Albany, writing in both artistic obscurity and financial straits the three novels which came to be known as his "Albany Cycle": *Legs, Billy Phelan's Greatest Game,* and the novel that put both Kennedy and Albany on the literary map, *Ironweed. Legs,* published by Coward Press in 1975, initiated Kennedy's fiction into a real place at a definite time in history: Prohibition Albany. The novel is a fictionalized account of the last year and a half of gangster Jack "Legs" Diamond, who made his final gambit at bootlegging alcohol in Albany and was shot to death in his underwear in a downtown rooming house in 1931. (Kennedy bought the row house in 1984 and now uses it as an office.) The author was drawn to Legs Diamond as a subject because he was at once a presence in the capital city and a personification of the "moral ambiguity" of the American dream of success. We meet characters in *Legs* who later appear in other novels, Kennedy already beginning at this early date to build a world which will grow into the worlds of his later fiction. All his fiction, in turn, emerges as a progressive view of Albany, New York: the author's American microcosm.

*Billy Phelan's Greatest Game* followed quickly on the heels of *Legs.* Published by Viking in 1978, this novel too is rooted in real Albany history. It is based on the unsuccessful kidnapping attempt in 1933 of John O'Connell, nephew of Democratic leader Dan O'Connell. Kennedy changes the time to 1938 and renames the O'Connells the McCalls. The novel is narrated by newspaper columnist Martin Daugherty, who also figures in the action peripherally when the McCalls ask him to keep the story out of the paper. The real story however is Billy Phelan's: a young sartorial pool shark and barfly from North Albany, who, like most of Kennedy's twentieth-century characters, in some way owes the political machine. Billy overhears information vital to Charlie Boy McCall's discovery, and faces either being a reluctant informer or incurring the wrath of the McCalls. His victory is in appeasing the bosses while not becoming a stool pigeon. The novel ends with Billy's celebratory stroll down Albany's Broadway, at once enthralled by his city yet independent of it.

Like *Legs* and *The Ink Truck*, *Billy Phelan* was ignored by the *New York Times*. Doris Grumbach, however, hailed the obscure American talent in the *Saturday Review:* "The cast of *Billy Phelan* is quite simply a wonder—a magical bunch of thugs, lovers, game players. No one writing in America today . . . has Kennedy's rich and fertile gift of gab; his pure verbal energy; his love of people" (*Saturday Review,* 2 May 1978).

### IRONWEED

After making a brief appearance in *Billy Phelan,* Billy's father Francis emerges as Kennedy's next protagonist in *Ironweed* (Viking, 1983). Kennedy moves us back a generation in Albany and introduces us to Francis Phelan as a young minor league baseball player who runs away from his hometown after inadvertently killing a trolley scab during a strike. He returns to marry and settle down in his own North Albany, only to run away again, this time for 22 years, when he fatally drops and kills his 13-day-old son Gerald. Driven by guilt, shame, and the drink, his exiled life spirals downward into the homeless life of a bum. The novel opens with his visit to Albany in 1938 to make some money by voting for the Democratic machine candidates (another detail gleaned from real life): Francis votes twenty-one times at $5.00 a vote. It is during this return that *Ironweed* intersects with *Billy Phelan,* when father and son reunite. The opening scene finds the protagonist doing day work at the cemetery where his parents and baby are buried, initiating the reentry of Francis to the family, community, and roots he had abandoned. Through memories, ghostly visitations, and walks through his old neighborhood, Francis reconnects with his past, and thus himself, and the novel ends with his tentative impulse to remain at home.

Viking rejected Kennedy's manuscript at first, as did thirteen other publishers. It was Saul Bellow who intervened on Kennedy's behalf by writing a letter to Viking saying that the author of *Billy Phelan* should not have a manuscript floating around without a publisher. As a result, Viking not only published *Ironweed,* it also reissued *Legs* and *Billy Phelan* as Penguin paperbacks, marketing all three novels as the "Albany Trilogy."

In his *Newsweek* review of *Ironweed,* Peter Prescott praised Kennedy as deserving a place "among the best of our current American novelists" (31 Jan. 1983). 100,000 copies of the novel sold in two years. In 1983, Kennedy won the Pulitzer Prize for fiction, the National Book Critics Circle Award, and the MacArthur Foundation Grant. By 1984, the author received the New York State Governor's Award; the State University of New York at Albany granted him tenure and sponsored a four-day "William Kennedy's Albany" celebration with walking tours, a museum exhibit, and lecture by the man himself; and Kennedy established the Writers' Institute at the State University. The same year, he wrote the screenplay for Francis Ford Coppola's *Cotton Club;* and he published his first nonfiction book, *O Albany,* a collection of his newspaper articles, essays, and memoirs about his home town, with a subtitle right out of his fiction: *Improbable City of Political Wizards, Fearless Ethnics, Spectacular Aristocrats, Splendid Nobodies, and Underrated Scoundrels.* Clearly, the literary star of William Kennedy was rising.

### LATER WRITING

Kennedy's next three novels explore the conditions which have shaped the lives of his characters in his first three Albany novels. By *Ironweed,* his readers have met not only the Phelans, but their neighbors, the Daughertys, and their in-laws, the Quinns. Kennedy devotes a novel to each of these families. *Quinn's Book* appeared in 1988, a picaresque tale of Albany in the mid-nineteenth century, chronicling the mass arrival of famine Irish immigrants, Albany's Civil War experience, and the decline of the Dutch power base. Amid these sweeping social changes, the story follows the rags to riches saga of Daniel Quinn, the ancestor of Billy Phelan's brother-in-law.

The next novel, *Very Old Bones* (Viking, 1992), moves back to the Phelan family, focusing on Peter Phelan, brother of Francis, an artist who, like Francis, has his own reasons for fleeing the North Albany nest. Narrated by Peter's illegitimate son, Orson, on a single day in 1958, the novel delves into the Phelan past as far back as 1887 to shed light on family secrets which shaped the dynamics of five generations of Phelans. Orson, not only illegitimate, but alcoholic, unable to sustain his marriage, and two-time sufferer of nervous breakdowns, appears to embody the sum total of the sins of his forbearers. Peter's painting and sculpting act as a metaphor for Kennedy's process of demonstrating how a family is molded into a certain shape, in this case a form misshapen and scarred by the past. To use another metaphor, by digging up those proverbial bones (and as it turns out, there's a real set buried in the basement), Kennedy also enacts the healing process for his contemporary batch of Phelans.

In 1996, *Flaming Corsage* (Viking) completed Kennedy's examination of his third Albany family, the Daugherty's. We met journalist Martin as a narrator in *Billy Phelan's Greatest Game,* and learned of a brief affair between the adolescent Francis Phelan and Martin's exotically beautiful mother, Katrina, in *Ironweed.* This affair is examined again by a sister of Francis, Sarah, in *Very Old Bones.* With *Flaming Corsage,* the Daugherty family takes center stage. Narrated periodically by Katrina and her playwright husband, Edward, the novel jumps back and forth from their courtship in 1885 to Katrina's death in Edward's arms in 1912. The intervening thirty years, all recalled in short out-of-sequence dramatic scenes, chronicle the rise and fall of the Daugherty marriage. Once again, the aim is to shine light on more old bones to explain the reasons behind the shape of this third North Albany family. Katrina's own narrative is sparse, but her diary, rescued from a house fire, is locked in a safety deposit box, waiting perhaps for a future novel.

Amid the prolific fiction writing, Kennedy wrote the screenplay for the movie version of *Ironweed.* Filmed in Albany, the movie starred Jack Nicholson and Meryl Streep and was directed by Hector Babenco. The world premier in December 1987 was also in Albany. Kennedy published a second book of nonfiction, *Riding the Yellow Trolley Car,* in 1994. A small selection from his hundreds of book reviews, interviews with writers, and essays on films, this book gives Kennedy's readers insight into the author's own artistic theories via his choice of subjects. During this time, he and his son Brendan published two books for children, *Charlie Malarkey and the Belly Button Machine* and *Charlie*

*Malarkey and the Singing Moose.* And in 1996, he staged his first play, *Grand View,* with the Capital Repertory Co. in Albany. The play enacts a story from the life of Patsy McCall, Kennedy's fictional version of party boss, Dan O'Connell.

William Kennedy lives just outside Albany in a nineteenth-century farmhouse in Averill Park, New York, with his wife, Dana Segara. The Kennedys have three children—Dana, Katherine, and Brendan—and one grandchild.

*See* Fiction, Irish-American

W. D. Adamson, "Very Old Themes: The Legacy of William Kennedy's Humanism," *Classical and Modern Literature: A Quarterly* 15/1 (Fall, 1994): 67–75.

Michael Gorra, "Once Upon a Time in Albany," Rev. of *Flaming Corsage, New York Times Book Review* (19 May 1996): 7.

"William Kennedy," *Current Biography Yearbook,* 1985.

Larry McCaffery and Sindra Gregory, "An Interview with William Kennedy." *Alive and Writing* (Urbana: University of Illinois Press, 1987).

Robert Rhodes, "Kennedy's Fact-Fiction Nexus," Rev. of *Riding the Yellow Trolley Car, Irish Literary Supplement* 13 (Fall, 1994): 7.

Tramble T. Turner, "*Quinn's Book:* Reconstructing Irish American History," *MELUS* 18/1 (Spring, 1993): 31–45.

Kenneth Van Doran, *Understanding William Kennedy* (Columbia, S.C., 1991).

MARGARET LASCH MAHONEY

## KENNY, ELIZABETH (1886–1952)

Nurse, medical pioneer. Born September 20, 1886, in Warrialda, New South Wales, Australia, daughter of Michael and Mary (Moore) Kenny, Elizabeth Kenny gained international fame in the treatment of poliomyelitis, known more commonly then as infantile paralysis (though the disease of course also struck adults). Her accomplishments are the more remarkable, for she had limited education and medical training. She studied at St. Ursula's College, but nonetheless her nursing credentials were so much in question that professional nurses in Australia once challenged her standing and doctors denied her access to hospital wards.

Kenny became interested in muscle disorders as a child of fourteen, while tending to a frail younger brother and drilling him in the muscle-building exercises of the Great Sandow, a strongman and physical-fitness guru of the times. She worked as a nurse in the Australian bush country from 1911–1914, and when World War I broke out joined the Australian Army's nursing corps. She saw service at the front in France, but most of her time was spent tending to the wounded on hospital ships. She made a dozen round-trip ocean crossings through submarine infested waters, and won the sobriquet "sister," a title accorded chief female caregivers in the British nursing tradition. The honorific was joined to her surname and she became known to millions around the world as Sister Kenny.

Kenny began caring for poliomyelitis patients about 1911, and sensed that many of the usual practices in treating the disease—most particularly the immobilizing of polio-damaged limbs with splints and casts—were wrongheaded. Instead, she contended, affected muscles should be stimulated, as with the help of hot compressors and blankets, and limbs reeducated through gentle movement.

Her "heat and motion" theories received a major testing in 1933 after a poliomyelitis epidemic hit Townsville, Australia.

Kenny set to work in a backyard under a make-shift awning covering an earthen floor, her treating of the ill meeting with amazing success. This led to the establishment of a clinic in Townsville based on her theories, with similar facilities following in other Australian communities. They were known as "Kenny Clinics." Though Kenny was responsible for many cures, her real feat was a dramatic lessening of the physical infirmities resulting from the disease.

In 1937 Kenny took her theories to England, and then in 1940 to the United States, where she lectured widely, often to skeptical audiences. However, she won the support of the *Journal of the American Medical Association,* and in 1941 of Basil O'Connor, head of the National Foundation for Infantile Paralysis. Orthopedic surgeons at the University of Minnesota College of Medicine endorsed her methods, and in 1943 an Elizabeth Kenny Institute was established in Minneapolis for the training of nurses and physiotherapists in the "Kenny Treatment." Its methods remained standard until the disease was virtually eradicated by the development of polio vaccines by Dr. Jonas Salk and Dr. Albert Sabin in the late 1950s.

Kenny also traveled to South America and continental Europe promoting her program of care. She wrote a number of books on poliomyelitis and its treatment, as well as an autobiography, *And They Shall Walk.*

Kenny died in Australia, November 30, 1952, and is buried at Toowoomba, Queensland. She never married.

Sister Elizabeth Kenny, with Martha Ostenso, *And They Shall Walk: The Life Story of Sister Kenny* (New York, 1943, 1980).

Robin McKown, *Heroic Nurses* (New York, 1966).

"Kenny, Elizabeth," *Collier's Encyclopedia,* vol. 14 (New York, 1996).

JOHN DEEDY

## KENNY, JOHN VINCENT (1893–1975)

Politician. Longtime political boss of Jersey City, New Jersey, John V. Kenny, known as the "little guy," was born in that city on April 6, 1893, to Edward Kenny and Katherine (Ward), one of six children. He attended Catholic schools and the New Jersey Law School for one year. He became a bookkeeper for the Erie Railroad and married Margaret Smith in 1918. They had one daughter. Kenny entered politics as a protégé of Frank Hague, who controlled the Jersey City Democratic Party, becoming a party committeeman in place of his brother who was murdered in 1916. Hague placed him in a railroad car cleaning business, and Kenny directed business to Hague. The young Kenny was Hague's political lieutenant in the second ward, known as the "Horseshoe" section of downtown Jersey City where his father owned a tavern and where John lived in a brownstone house for over forty years. He was accustomed to frequent the local neighborhood near St. Francis Hospital, directly assisting people seeking employment or party favors. His political power grew in the thirties and forties, particularly along the Jersey City waterfront, which was partially within the second ward. He became boss of the ward in 1931 and held a number of municipal and county jobs through his mentor Hague. When the latter retired in 1947, Kenny's ambitions seemed thwarted by the succession of Hague's nephew, Frank Hague Eggers, to head the political machine which Kenny's actions then began to irritate. Kenny was removed from the organization in 1948. Thereupon he assembled for the 1949 mayoral election an anti-Hague, ethnically mixed slate of city commission candidates to oppose the machine's customary all-Irish slate. Kenny and his associates defeated the Hague forces, ending a thirty-two year reign, and he became mayor in 1949. He held power in Hudson County for the next two decades, even without holding elective office, largely by spoils and patronage and brokering disputes; Kenny would pit political opponents against one another, and then convince them of an alliance with him. The fifties saw allegations of his involvement with waterfront crime and racketeering, as well as questionable city financial dealings. Yet his political strength allowed him to play an important part in selecting candidates for state government offices, including that of governor (Robert B. Meyner in 1953 and 1957, and Richard Hughes in 1961 and 1965). Known as the "pope of Jersey City," Kenny resigned as mayor in December 1953, but retained major political power. Despite escaping untouched from various investigations over the years, he was finally indicted in November 1970, along with eleven of his associates, for income tax evasion and extortion. He made court appearances in a wheelchair and the trial was severed because of his ill health. After a year of hospitalization he pled guilty and was sentenced in May 1972 to 18 years in prison and fined $30,000. John V. Kenny was paroled after 18 months however, time spent mostly in a prison hospital. His county political organization was broken, and he lived the remainder of his life in the Dell Ridge Nursing Home in Paramus, New Jersey, where he died of heart disease on June 2, 1975.

*See* New Jersey

---

*Dictionary of American Biography,* Supplement 9, 1971–1975 (New York, 1994).

William Lemmey, "Bossism in Jersey City: The Kenny Years, 1949–1972" (Ph.D. diss., City University of New York, 1978).

*New York Times,* obituary ( June 3, 1975): 37, col. 1.

ANNA M. DONNELLY

## KENRICK, FRANCIS PATRICK (1797–1863)

Archbishop of Baltimore. Francis Patrick was born December 3, 1797 to Thomas and Jane Kenrick in Dublin, Ireland. His uncle, Father Richard Kenrick, saw in Francis a judicious intelligence which he hoped to cultivate by sending him to a good classical school. He showed remarkable talent for academic work and pursued a course toward priesthood. He was selected to study at Rome at age eighteen where he soon became familiar with patristic and biblical writings. After his ordination, Kenrick was sent to the United States where he was appointed chair of theology at Bardstown Seminary in Kentucky where he served for the next nine years.

In 1829, Kenrick was appointed secretary to the assembly at the 1829 Provincial Council in Baltimore and served as Bishop Flaget's theological advisor. Kenrick's name had already been submitted to Rome for a bishopric, so that by 1830 when the aged Bishop Conwell went blind and frail, Kenrick replaced him as bishop of Philadelphia. At just 34 years of age, Kenrick was head of a diocese engulfed in divisions over an excommunicated priest and the status of Church funds managed by lay trustees. Kenrick brought stability on both fronts, and turned to establishing a seminary that later became St. Charles Borromeo at Overbrook.

Kenrick's concerns soon extended throughout all of Philadelphia. When a severe outbreak of cholera erupted in the city,

Kenrick mobilized the Sisters of Charity to comfort the growing numbers of sick and converted the parochial residence of St. Augustine's into a hospital. When the epidemic subsided, Kenrick and the Sisters of Charity were honored with a public thanks from the mayor as well as the city councils.

In the midst of anti-Catholic Nativist violence in 1844, St. Augustine's was burned down and two other parishes were attacked. The Catholic district further suffered the loss of several houses as well as the deaths of a number of members of their community before the Army could disperse the crowd. Kenrick ordered all church doors closed, the cessation of worship, clergymen to go about in civilian dress and the sacred vessels and vestments hidden with families for safety. The crisis subsided, and Kenrick remained in Philadelphia until 1851 with the death of Archbishop Eccleston at Baltimore. Kenrick became the new Archbishop of Baltimore and was honored with an appointment as Apostolic delegate. In this capacity, Kenrick convened the First Plenary Council of Baltimore of 1852.

In the following year, the Pope asked Kenrick to survey the American bishops regarding their opinion of the doctrine of the Immaculate Conception. In 1854, Kenrick traveled to Rome where he participated in the proclamation of the dogma, but returned to a new wave of anti-Catholic violence in the United States. Though the violence ended in the burning of many churches and convents as well as the loss of life, it did not reach Baltimore. However, on July 7, 1863, the slaughter at the battle of Gettysburg, so close to the Archbishop's home, weighed heavily on Kenrick who died the following day.

*See* Catholicism, Irish-American; Baltimore

---

Clarke, *Lives of Deceased Prelates* (New York, 1872).

Thomas R. Greene, "Kenrick, Francis Patrick," *The Encyclopedia of American Catholic History.* Michael Glazier and Thomas J. Shelley, eds. (Collegeville, 1997).

Francis Patrick Kenrick, *M.S. Diary and Itinerary* in Philadelphia Archives.

————, *Correspondence* in Archives of Baltimore.

John Gilmary Shea, *Catholic Church in the United States* (New York, 1892).

M. O'Connor, *Archbishop Kenrick and His Work* (Philadelphia, 1867).

John O'Shea, "Kenrick, Francis Patrick and Peter Richard," *Catholic Encyclopedia* (New York, 1913).

Spalding, *Sketches* (Baltimore, 1800).

DANIEL J. KUNTZ

## KENRICK, PETER RICHARD (1806–1896)

Archbishop of St. Louis, Missouri. Peter Richard Kenrick was born in Dublin, Ireland on August 17, 1806 to Thomas and Jane Kenrick. A pious young man, Peter was encouraged to study for the priesthood by his uncle who was a priest from Dublin. Kenrick attended Maynooth College at the age of 21 and was ordained to the priesthood by Archbishop Murray of Dublin. He quickly became involved in local missionary work until he joined his older brother, Francis Patrick, already in the United States and Bishop of Philadelphia in the1830s. Here he served as president of the seminary, rector of the Cathedral and vicar-general of the diocese. In 1840, he traveled to Rome where he had hoped to become a Jesuit, but was discouraged there by the superior. This was fortuitous, because during his stay in Rome, Kenrick made the acquaintance of Bishop Rosati of St. Louis, who was immediately impressed with the Irish-American priest. Rosati asked the Holy See to make Kenrick his coadjutor bishop and when the request was approved, Kenrick returned to the United States with Rosati who consecrated him at Philadelphia where his brother Francis assisted.

A short time later, Bishop Rosati died, leaving Kenrick with a large debt on the Cathedral and a general financial crisis that led him to the unusual approach of entering the real estate business. Kenrick was remarkably successful and caught the attention of a local businessman who helped Kenrick relieve the diocesan debt with a $300,000 donation to the Church. Kenrick's investments earned good returns for the diocese until the Civil War drove real estate prices downward.

It was during the Civil War that Missouri passed the "Drake Constitution," a law that required all ministers to take a test oath. Kenrick immediately ordered his priests to refuse it because of its insulting terms to the Catholic faith. As a result, a number of priests were arrested, which prompted Kenrick, by this time an Archbishop, to take the case from court to court where the law was declared unconstitutional.

Kenrick was also one of a minority who opposed the definition of Papal Infallibility at the First Vatican Council in 1869. The Archbishop accepted the dogma as authoritative, however, when it was proclaimed in 1870. In the succeeding years, Kenrick's accomplishments were numerous, including the large task of creating sixteen new dioceses from the single sprawling Diocese of St. Louis that stretched as far west as Denver, Colorado. Kenrick also produced several works including *Validity of Anglican Ordinations Examined* and *History of the Holy House of Loretto*. After several years of declining health, Kenrick died on March 4, 1896.

*See* Missouri; Catholicism, Irish-American

Executive Committee of Clergymen, *Life of Most Reverend Peter Richard Kenrick, D.D., Archbishop of St. Louis* (St. Louis, 1891).

John J. O'Shea, "Kenrick, Francis Patrick and Peter Richard," *Catholic Encyclopedia* (New York, 1913).

———, *The Two Kenricks: Most Rev. Francis Patrick, Archbishop of Baltimore. Most Rev. Peter Richard, Archbishop of St. Louis* (Philadelphia, 1904).

John Gilmary Shea, *Catholic Church in the United States* (New York, 1879).

Martin G. Towey, "Kenrick, Peter Richard," *The Encyclopedia of American Catholic History.* Michael Glazier and Thomas J. Shelley, eds. (Collegeville, 1997).

DANIEL J. KUNTZ

## KENTUCKY

The Irish in Kentucky got off to an early start. In his book *The Discovery, Purchase and Settlement of Kentucke* (1784), John Filson says ". . . The first white man that we have certain accounts of who discovered the province, was one James McBride, who, in company with some others, in the year 1754, passing down the Ohio in canoes, landed at the mouth of Kentucky river, and there marked a tree with the first letters of his name, and the date, which remain to this day."

There are two James McBrides mentioned in early Kentucky history. One held the rank of major and the other that of Captain of Kentucky Volunteers in the War of the Revolution. Major James McBride is mentioned as one of the settlers at Harrod's Fort in 1775. A James McBride is also listed among the first lotholders when the town of Lexington was formed in 1781. Also

included in this list were Stephen Collins and his two sons; James and Caleb Masterson; Samuel Kelly; John, Hugh, Samuel and William Martin; Alexander, James, Francis and William McConnell; Francis McDermid; James McGinty; Samuel Mc-Mullins; and Francis, Henry, Hugh, James, John and William McDonald.

Kentucky, an Indian name meaning "Dark and Bloody Ground," was formed in 1776 from Virginia. The three original counties, Fayette, Jefferson and Lincoln, encompassed the whole state. Kentucky was officially named a state in 1792 and is currently comprised of 122 counties. The total population is 3,685,296, of which 696,000 people are of Irish descent, according to the 1990 census.

### THE SCOTCH-IRISH

During the fifty years before the American Revolution, more than a quarter of a million Scotch-Irish came to America. Many of these immigrants headed for the Virginia frontier where land was cheap, and from which renowned explorers and surveyors John Finley and Daniel Boone had brought back glowing reports of the territory beyond. As a result of their brave explorations into this Indian-frequented frontier, two avenues of entry to Kentucky became evident, the Ohio River and the Cumberland Gap. It was through the latter that Boone led a group of settlers and established Fort Boonesboro on the banks of the Kentucky River in 1775. When Boonesboro was established as a town, by an Act of the Virginia Legislature in October 1779, trustees were appointed, among whom are mentioned Edward Bradley, John and Thomas Kennedy, and William Irvine.

"The active part which the Scotch-Irish took in the American Revolution was a continuation of popular resistance to British Policy that began in Ulster. If we were not so ignorant of the history of the Mountain People, it would not surprise us that they took such leadership in the movement for American Independence. The declaration and constitution of the Watanga Association in 1772; the declaration of Abingdon, Virginia, in January, 1775, and the raising of the flag of a new and independent nation called Transylvania at Boonesboro, Kentucky, May 23, 1775; the Mecklenburg Resolutions in North Carolina, May 31, 1775; all these declarations by Mountain men made possible the more widespread Continental Declaration of Independence at Philadelphia, July 4, 1776.

"The large population of Scotch-Irish scattered throughout all the colonies had not yet been absorbed by the older population and settled into conventional compliance. When Independence was being agitated, they naturally followed the fearless lead of their frontier brethren and thus gave unity to the whole movement" (*The Land of Saddle-Bags* by James Watt Raine).

### THE CATHOLIC IRISH

Captain James Harrod, a friend of Daniel Boone, established Harrod's Fort in 1774. Several Irish Catholic families were among the first settlers at the fort. They included the William Coomes family and Dr. George Hart, a Dublin-born-and-educated physician; Major Hugh McGarry and his wife and children; Richard Hogan and Thomas Denton and their families; and John Lynch. A year later, in 1775, of the 54 families living at Fort Harrod, 25 bore Irish names.

Mrs. Coomes had a schoolhouse built in the fort where she taught her own children and those of other settlers. This is believed to have been the first elementary school in Kentucky. In

1783, the Coomes family moved to the Pottinger's Creek area, near Bardstown in Nelson County, and purchased several tracts of land, one of which, a farm of 104 acres, they gave to the Catholic Church in 1804. Dr. Hart also moved to the Bardstown area. Later, he was involved in the foundation of the city of Louisville which was built on land owned by two Irishmen, John Connolly and John Campbell.

In the year 1785, a group of 25 Catholic families was formed in Maryland to journey to Pottinger's Creek. It was here that Holy Cross Church was built in 1792. This was the first structure for Catholic worship erected in the state. Between 1824 and 1825, Holy Cross Church was served by Fathers Butler and O'Bryan. In 1825, Fr. Robert Byrne took over as pastor. He was the son of Ignatius Byrne, an Irish-born settler who had moved to the area from Maryland. Fr. Byrne, who was locally ordained, retained the position of pastor until 1846, when Fr. Daniel Kelly succeeded him.

"The first priest to minister to the Catholic settlers in Kentucky was Father Charles Maurice Whelan, an Irish Franciscan. It is believed that he accompanied the group of immigrants led by Edward Howard, and that the party arrived in Kentucky in the spring of 1787" (*The Catholic Church on the Kentucky Frontier 1785–1812* by Mary Ramona Mattingly). However, Father Whelan didn't stay long. The priest most associated with the early church in Kentucky was Stephen Theodore Badin who served in the state for 50 years. Mattingly continues in her book, "Father Badin was ordained on May 25, 1793, by Bishop John Carroll, newly appointed Prefect Apostolic. He was the first priest ordained in what was formerly the English Colonies in America. In later years, he took great delight in signing himself 'Proto-Priest of the United States.' In a letter to Bishop Carroll which was written on May 25, 1807, he reminds the Bishop that this was the anniversary of his ordination when 'the first Bishop ordained the first Priest.' He later became known as the Apostle of Kentucky . . . traveling over one hundred thousand miles on horseback, over a period of fifty years, to visit his people throughout the state."

In 1811, Benedict Joseph Flaget, a 40-year-old Frenchman, became the first bishop of Kentucky. His see included Kentucky and Tennessee. Seven years later, St. Joseph's Cathedral was completed in Bardstown. This was the first diocese established west of the Allegheny Mountains.

In addition to Bardstown and Pottinger's Creek, Catholic settlements included Hardin's Creek, Cartright's Creek, Scott County, Rolling Fork, Cox's Creek and Breckinridge County. Among the families that came from Maryland to establish these settlements were the O'Daniels, Mattinglys, Montgomerys, O'Briens, Bradys and O'Bryans to name a few.

The Hardin's Creek settlement was founded in 1786, and in this and nearby settlements, Catholic churches were soon built, that of St. Charles being erected in 1806 by the noted missionary Charles Nerinckx. He later bought a farm of 311 acres to establish a school for boys and named it Mt. Mary's. Early in 1819, fire destroyed the principal building on the farm. To obtain financial assistance after this calamity to finish his project, Father Nerinckx set out on an almost fruitless voyage to Europe. When he returned in 1821, he founded St. Mary's College, then called St. Mary's Seminary, already established on Mt. Mary farm in Marion County, and operating successfully under the management of Father William Byrne, who was born in Wicklow, Ireland, and ordained in Bardstown Cathedral in 1819.

In the spring of 1821, Father Byrne founded St. Mary's College on the proverbial shoestring—his wealth was reported to have consisted of ten dollars and an old horse. An abandoned distillery on the premises was remodeled and became an institute of learning, with the storage rooms serving as classrooms and with the empty kegs and barrels serving as chairs and desks. Suitable buildings soon replaced the improvised distillery building. During the dozen years that followed when Father Byrne was in charge, more than one thousand youths were trained at St. Mary's, among whom were John Spalding, second bishop of Louisville and later archbishop of Baltimore, and Josue M. Young, bishop of Erie, Pa. In 1833, Father Byrne died of cholera and the Jesuits took over St. Mary's.

Jesuits from the province of Missouri also responded to Bishop Flaget's request for assistance with regard to St. Joseph's Church and St. Joseph's College in Bardstown. In June 1848, the retiring president, Father Edward McMahon, announced the Jesuit takeover at the annual commencement and introduced his successor, Father Peter J. Verhaegen, S.J. In 1822, nine local women volunteered to establish the first Dominican convent in America, St. Magdalen's. The first superior was Judith McMahon, a married lady. She and her husband, John, were childless and had agreed to separate and pursue religious vocations—she to be a nun, and he to be a priest. They came from County Cork, Ireland. John became a priest and served briefly in the St. Louis Diocese until he became a victim of cholera. The name of the Dominican convent was later changed to St. Catharine of Siena. It is quite a coincidence that St. Catharine's first school, like Father William Byrne's, was a converted distillery.

In 1848, the Trappist Monastery, Abbey of Gethsemani, was established in Nelson County on land donated by the Sisters of Loretto. Of the 176 monks entering the monastery during its first hundred years (1848–1948), 32 were born in Ireland and 18 were of Irish descent.

"Somewhat larger numbers of Catholic Irish, fleeing the Potato Famine during the 1840s moved into Kentucky and other southern states. The Irish were able to find jobs as day laborers on farms, as workers on road and railroad crews and as stonemasons. In the Kentucky Bluegrass Region, for example, farmers hired Irish stonemasons to erect rock fences to enclose fields and farmsteads. Stonemasons from Scotland, England and Ulster also contributed to the construction of Bluegrass rock fences and other stone structures. Their knowledge of traditional Irish and British construction techniques was passed to slaves, and freedmen later dominated the early twentieth-century rock fence construction trade" (*Atlas of Kentucky*).

## SPORT OF KINGS

It is said that when Daniel Boone first saw central Kentucky, the grass was in seed. The seed has a bluish tinge, so when he referred to it as "blue grass," the term has been extended to describe the area generally. Be that as it may, this part of the state has proved to be ideal for the breeding, raising and racing of thoroughbred horses.

Volumes have been written about the Sport of Kings in the Blue Grass. Suffice it to say that many Irish and Scotch-Irish have been involved since the beginning of the horse business in Kentucky. Some of them include: Samuel Riddle, the Scotch-Irish owner of Man O'War, considered to be the greatest racehorse ever, and sire of War Admiral, the triple crown winner in 1937; Irishman Price McGrath, who won the first Kentucky Derby with Aristides in 1875; and John Edward Madden, the son of Irish immigrant parents, noted as one of the outstanding breeders and trainers in the industry. Also, James Ben Ali Haggin, born of an Irish father and a Turko-Grecian mother, a copper baron who began his interest in horses on his Rancho del Paso 44,000-acre spread in California, bought the 544-acre Elmendorf farm in the Lexington area and soon increased his holdings to 10,000 acres in the Blue Grass. He was a great horse owner and breeder in the early 1900s. Matt J. Winn, son of Patrick and Julia Flaherty Winn, almost single-handedly built Churchill Downs, home of the Kentucky Derby. He also pioneered the use of pari-mutuel machines in America. Today, more than three hundred young Irish men and women are studying horse farm management on Blue Grass thoroughbred farms.

MOUNTAIN MUSIC

There is no doubt that current Kentucky mountain music has its roots in Ireland and Scotland. The toe-tapping, knee-slapping tunes are directly related to the reels, jigs, and hornpipes of those countries. Even the clogging (mountain dancing) is done to the same tempo as an Irish hornpipe.

In many cases, the instruments (fiddles and dulcimers) are made by mountain men either for themselves or for other musicians. Thomas D. Clark wrote in his book, *The Rampaging Frontier* (1939), "Irishmen, with traditional Irish recklessness and abandon, gave sufficient reason to justify the building of jails. Surely it was the Irish influence that Mann Butler had in mind when he said that in 1806 he found the western young men equipped with fiddles, packs of cards and pistols."

*See* Irish Heritage of the South; Scots Irish

Thomas D. Clark, *The Rampaging Frontier* (New York, 1939).
John Filson, *The Discovery, Purchase and Settlement of Kentucke 1784* (Published 1784; reprinted New York, 1962).
Sister Mary Ramona Mattingly, *The Catholic Church on the Kentucky Frontier 1785–1812* (Washington, D.C., 1936).
James Watt Raine, *The Land of Saddle-bags* (New York, 1924).
Richard Ulack, *Atlas of Kentucky* (Louisville, Ky., 1998).
Hon. Ben J. Webb, *The Centenary Catholicity in Kentucky* (Louisville, Ky., 1884).

RAYMOND P. McLAUGHLIN

## KERENS, RICHARD C. (1842–1916)

Railroad builder and politician. Born in Kilberry, County Meath, Ireland, Kerens was an infant when his parents, Thomas and Elizabeth (Gugerty) Kerens emigrated to the United States. The family settled in Iowa, where he attended public schools.

At the age of nineteen, Kerens joined the U.S. Army and became chief mule driver for the Army of the Potomac. In 1863 he was named chief of transportation for the Army of the Frontier in the Arkansas and Indian Territory.

Following the Civil War, he became proprietor of a livery stable at Fort Smith, a frontier Indian trading post. He contracted with the Pony Express system for carrying the Southern overland mail.

In 1867 he married Frances Jane Jones. They moved to San Diego, Calif., in 1874 where Kerens continued in the mail business. Two years later he realized that railroad construction would be a profitable venture, so he moved to St. Louis in order to take advantage of the booming business that would eventually crisscross the continent.

He played a prominent role in construction of the Cotton Belt & Northern Railway, the West Virginia Central & Pittsburgh, the St. Louis & North Arkansas, the San Pedro, Los Angeles & Salt Lake, and the St. Louis, Iron Mountain & Southern. Not only did he build the railway systems, but also he became a stockholder and director of several of those systems.

He then joined with Henry Gassaway Davis and Senator Stephen Benton Elkins to develop lumber and mining industries in West Virginia, ventures that substantially increased his financial fortune.

Kerens played a prominent role in Missouri politics for about forty years. He donated generously to Republican campaign funds and served as that party's national committeeman for three consecutive terms (1884–1900). During that time, he saw that the state received substantial federal patronage. However, Kerens' bid to become a U.S. senator was lost in 1905 when a deadlock occurred in the state legislature between him and Thomas K. Niedringhaus, the caucus nominee.

In 1891, he was appointed to the Continental Railway Commission by President Benjamin Harrison, one of three members from the United States. He served 10 years on the board and helped to complete a railway survey through fifteen South American countries.

For his liberal financial contributions and faithful service, Kerens was offered ambassadorships by Presidents Harrison and William McKinley. He declined the honors until 1909 when President William Howard Taft urged him to accept the post at Vienna, Austria-Hungary, a position he held for four years.

Kerens was a devout Catholic and was awarded the Laetare Medal from the University of Notre Dame in 1904.

He died September 4, 1916, in Merion, Pa.

J. W. Leonard, ed., *The Book of St. Louisans* (1906).
*Kansas City Star* (Sept. 4, 1916).
*St. Louis Globe-Democrat* (Feb. 13, March 19, 1905, Sept. 5, 1916).
*St. Louis Republic* (Dec. 21, 1909, Sept. 5, 1916).
*Who's Who in America* (1916–17).

MARIANNA McLOUGHLIN

## KERR, JEAN (Collins) (1923–  )

Writer. Considered one of the funniest women writers of her time, Bridget Jean (Collins) Kerr was born July 10, 1923, to Thomas J. Collins, a contractor, and Kitty (O'Neill), a second cousin to dramatist Eugene O'Neill, in Scranton, Pa. At Marywood College in Scranton she met Walter Francis Kerr (1913–1996), then drama professor at the Catholic University of America in Washington, D.C., who was attending a college production of *Romeo and Juliet* for which Jean was stage manager. In 1943 she graduated from Marywood and, having spent three summer semesters studying at CUA, married Kerr. In 1945 she earned a master's degree from Catholic U. The Kerrs collaborated on CUA productions, attracting critical attention. A 1947 CUA comedy by Jean, *Jenny Kissed Me,* opened on Broadway in 1948 and ran for only 20 performances. But a CUA musical revue for which the Kerrs wrote lyrics opened on Broadway as *Touch and Go,* and was a well-praised sellout. Also in 1949 the Kerrs moved to New York and Walter became drama critic for *Commonweal,* a Catholic weekly (1949–1951); he was later drama critic for the *New York*

Jean Kerr

*Herald Tribune* (1951–1966) and for the *New York Times* (1966–1983). Jean Kerr collaborated with Eleanor Brooke on *King of Hearts,* a 1954 comedy directed by Walter. Another of the Kerr's collaborations was the musical *Goldilocks* (1958) with music by Leroy Anderson, lyrics by Joan Ford, and choreography by Agnes de Mille. Her hugely successful Broadway play *Mary, Mary* (1961) was also made into a film; *Poor Richard* ran 1964–65; *Finishing Touches* was a 1973 situation comedy, and *Lunch Hour* (1980) a romantic comedy. Some of her song lyrics include "This Had Better Be Love," "I Never Know When to Say When," "Save a Kiss," and "Be a Mess." The Kerrs had six children, including twins. The inevitable tribulations of family life were the subject of Jean's 1957 best-selling humorous book *Please Don't Eat the Daisies*, originally a series of popular magazine articles, which was later filmed and serialized on television. Other essay collections written by Jean Kerr include *The Snake Has All the Lines* (1960), *Penny Candy* (1970), and *How I Got to Be Perfect* (1978). Her writing style is sharply witty, gentle and informal as she deals with the absurdity of the familiar. She has said, "The most important thing about me is that I am a Catholic." With her husband she received the Campion Award and Laetare Medal in 1971, and has been granted honorary degrees from Northwestern and Fordham Universities.

*Contemporary Authors*, New Revision Series, Vol. 7 (Detroit, 1982).
*Current Biography, 1958* (New York, 1958).
*Encyclopedia of American Humorists*, ed. Steven H. Gale (New York, 1988).
Virginia L. Grattan, *American Women Songwriters: A Biographical Dictionary* (New York, 1993).

ANNA M. DONNELLY

### KERRIGAN, JOHN E. (1907–1987)

*See* Boston, Twelve Irish-American Mayors of

### KIERAN, JOHN FRANCIS (1892–1981)

Sportswriter, naturalist, author. A native of the Bronx in New York City, John Kieran was born August 2, 1892, son of James M. and Kate (Donahue) Kieran. He studied at City College of New York from 1908–1911, then transferred to Fordham University and graduated cum laude in 1912. He worked as a teacher, in poultry farming and apple growing, and as a handyman on a sewer project before joining the *New York Times'* sports department in 1915. In the early 1920s he left for the *New York Tribune,* then the *New York American*—"a step up financially," in his words, though with "less prestige" than he enjoyed at the *Times*. In 1926 he was back with the *Times,* and the following year inaugurated "Sports of the Times," the first bylined column in the history of the paper. The column became an institution and continues to this day under succeeding authorships.

An extraordinarily literate person, Kieran would flavor his writings with mock verses in the meter of Quintus Horatius Flaccus or John Masefield, and spice assessments of an athlete's style with quotations from Keats, Browning or Virgil. He "rambled scandalously," touching on topics that rarely made their way onto sports pages. The range of knowledge was vast—his *Times* obituary said he could pronounce on virtually anything, "from the sex life of the aardvark to the process of zymosis"—and led to his becoming a panelist on "Information Please," a popular radio show where guests sought to stump experts. He was a panelist on the program from 1938–1948, becoming a national celebrity in the meantime.

Kieran was a keen naturalist, and wrote a number of books on sundry topics of nature, the most notable of which was *A Natural History of New York City,* published in 1960. The book opened eyes to a wonderland of nature in the forms of trees, shrubs, butterflies, migratory waterfowl, amphibians, reptiles and other wildlife flourishing in the metropolis of concrete and steel. It was a local study, but with broad appeal, and critics likened it to Gilbert White's *The Natural History of Selborn,* a classical study of nature in a small English village. Kieran's book won him the Burroughs Medal, highest honor of the John Burroughs Memorial Association.

From 1941–1944 Kieran was a columnist for the *New York Sun,* and afterwards an independent writer. He retired to Rockport, Massachusetts, in 1952, and there produced his memoir, *Not Under Oath: Recollections and Reflections.* He died in Rockport, December 10, 1981.

Kieran was a veteran of World War I, serving in France as a corporal with the Eleventh Engineers, American Expeditionary Force. He was married twice—in 1919 to Alma Boldtmann, who died in 1944, and in 1947 to Margaret Ford, a Boston editor and writer. There were three children by the first marriage.

Daniel Jones and John D. Jorgensen, eds., *Contemporary Authors: New Revision Series,* Vol. 62 (Detroit, 1998).
John Kieran, *Not Under Oath: Recollections and Reflections* (Boston, 1964).
*New York Times*, December 11, 1981.

JOHN DEEDY

### KILGALLEN, DOROTHY MAE (1913–1965)

Newspaperwoman, television and radio personality. Born in Chicago to James Lawrence and Mary Jane ("Mae")(Ahern), Kilgallen was raised by very protective Irish-Catholic parents in Laramie, Wyoming, and Indianapolis, Indiana. It was during her college years that she found part-time work at the New York *Evening Journal* and earned her own byline by the time she was twenty. Her penchant for detail and her own personal naivete made her speciality coverage of murders a fascination for her readers. She became a popular personality in her many pursuits and became well-known in many social circles.

In 1940 she married an actor, Richard Tompkins Kollmar, and they began the radio program "Breakfast with Dorothy and Dick" in which they commented on various glamour-related issues. Their program was popular for its right-wing politics and lavish advocacy of monetary sponsors. By 1950, Kilgallen was quite successful and respected for both her journalistic and broadcasting talent. She was chosen by the Columbia Broadcasting System for the television program "What's My Line?" in which contestants guessed the occupation of varying guests. Kilgallen helped the show to become very successful in the ratings and by 1965 it had captured ten million viewers.

Kilgallen was known for her outgoing personality but she always prized being a reporter more than anything. She made acquaintance with many eccentric people, many of whom were Irish, policemen, court officials, etc., who were loyal sources of information for her stories. She died tragically in her home in 1965 from a combination of drugs and alcohol, though her death was classified as accidental.

Personal scrapbooks stored at the Billy Rose Theatre Collection; newspaper pieces collected in her *Girl Around the World* (1936) and *Murder One* (1967).

*Dictionary of American Biography,* supplement 7.

JOY HARRELL

## KNIGHTS OF COLUMBUS, THE

A unique blend of faith and fraternalism, the Knights of Columbus is the largest organization of Catholic laity in the world. Over a 116-year history it has responded to the myriad needs of the local churches in the United States, Canada, Mexico, Puerto Rico, and the Philippines. This article traces the origins of Columbianism as a force in the church and society with particular focus on its character as a Catholic anti-defamation society. Since the anti-Catholic animus often expressed itself in caricatures depicting the Irish as either inebriated and slovenly immigrants or as fomenters of revolution, the K of C struggled against such egregious bias in popular culture.

Michael J. McGivney, the New Haven priest who founded the Knights of Columbus in February of 1882, implicitly fostered an American Catholic apologetic, one which was analogous to Daniel O'Connell's ("the Irish Liberator") Catholic Association as it extolled the harmony between religious liberty and Catholicism. Father McGivney's gifts were many and various. He was an unassuming pious priest who easily elicited the trust of the laity. Concerned with the strong appeal of the prohibited secret societies among Catholic youth and with the plight of the widows and children who suffered the loss of the breadwinner, he was eager to form a fraternal insurance society imbued with deep loyalties to Catholicism and to the American experience.

In early February 1882 McGivney and his associates placed their fledgling fraternal order under the patronage of Christopher Columbus. According to the few surviving documents, the Columbian motif represented several facets of the group's Catholic consciousness. Columbus was the symbol *par excellence* of the Catholic contribution to American culture. By portraying the navigator's landing at San Salvador as the Catholic baptism of the nation, the Knights were asserting religious legitimacy. Just as the heirs of the Pilgrims invoked the *Mayflower* as the Protestant symbol of their identity as early Americans, so the Irish-American Knights invoked the *Santa Maria* as the symbol of their self-understanding as Catholic citizens.

One of the charter members of the Order underscored the cause of Catholic civil liberty when he asserted that the Order's patron signified that, as Catholic descendants of Columbus "[We] were entitled to all rights and privileges due to such a discovery by one of our faith." The first-generation Knights were conscious of responding to the Irish need for a fraternal society based upon "unity, charity and brotherly love" which were the very "limitations of Irish Americans," stated the editor of *The Connecticut Catholic,* an independent weekly in the service to the archdiocese of Hartford. This editor and members of the Order noted that "personal antagonism in place of brotherly love has characterized Irishmen's relations with one another in this country." The *Hartford Telegram,* a secular newspaper, commented on a K of C parade within the contexts of class and ethnicity:

> There are some narrow minded people living in New England yet who imagine that the Irish race are idle, slovenly and often vicious. They judge the whole stock by the few unfortunates they meet. It is a fact, however, that the Irish will compare favorably with every other nationality in all that goes to make up good citizenship. The second generation in this country are intensely American in their instincts, and they are forging ahead to prominent positions in commerce, trade, and in the professions.

The quadricentennial of Columbus's landfall, the rise of another wave of anti-Catholicism in the form of the American Protective Association and the expansionist policies of the leadership engendered the development of Columbianism. The general spirit of patriotism, culminating in the Spanish American War, also animated the Order's character. Shortly after the institution of Boston's Bunker Hill Council (1892), Thomas H. Cummings of Boston became the Order's first national organizer hired to promote new-council development. From New England the Order expanded throughout the nation. By 1905 the Knights were in every state in the union, five provinces of Canada, Mexico, the Philippines and were poised to enter Cuba and Puerto Rico. The causation for this enormously successful period of expansion is primarily due to the way in which the Knights conveyed through the ceremonials their strong sense of American Catholic identity.

The initiation ceremonies were dramatic renditions of the heroic faith of Columbus, of the Catholic baptism of the American continent and of the nobility of religious liberty and American democracy. In a sense the ceremonials provided the candidates for knighthood with a rite of passage from old-world ties to loyalty to the new republic. Basic to their ethos was the prevailing notion of manliness: gender constriction manifested in fraternal sentiments and muscular Christianity was also evident in many Irish-American groups.

Columbianism was expressed in persistently optimistic and idealistic terms but, given the K of C consciousness of the ever-present threat from the forces of anti-Catholicism, Columbianism was also, of necessity, a rallying ground for the defense of the faith. The optimism of the Progressive era was countered by those groups which feared that the increased emigration from southern and eastern Europe (which totaled nearly seven million between 1897 and 1914) would ultimately result in the breakdown of "American" folkways. Anglo-Saxon nativism included anti-Semitism, widespread antagonism to Italian and Slavic peoples, a resurgence of racism in the South and North, and the growth of anti-Oriental sentiment in the West and Northwest, symbolized by the canard of the "Yellow Peril." This type of nativism was on the ascendant by 1907, when the new immigration reached its peak and was expressed in secular, even scientific, terms. Primarily aimed at immigrant restriction, it was popular among urban middle and upper classes. It did not spill out as overt anti-Catholicism because by this time these classes had developed a secular perspective through which to filter their anti-foreigner animus. Nativism was spread by the competition for jobs between "the natives and the swelling ranks of Irish Catholics."

In accord with the Order's anti-defamation character, it instituted in 1914 the Knights of Columbus Commission on Religious Prejudices. The latter was mandated "to study the causes, investigate conditions and suggest remedies for the religious prejudice that has been manifest through the press and rostrum." Under the chairmanship of Patrick Henry Callahan, then K of C state deputy of Kentucky and a wealthy industrialist known for his capital-labor profit sharing plan, the commission followed its mandate to the letter.

Columbian lay activism manifested itself in a new field of work in 1916 when U.S. troops were stationed along the Mexican border. After learning of the needs for recreational and religious centers, the Order established 16 buildings from the Gulf of Mexico to the Gulf of California for the needs of all soldiers and for the religious needs of Catholics.

As a result of this experience, the Knights offered such services to the U.S. government when it entered World War I in April 1917. American and Canadian K of C "Huts" with signs saying, "Everyone Welcome, Everything Free," were established in the training camps and eventually in Europe and Asia, even to the remote area of Siberia. The Order raised $1 million during the first year. As a result of a joint drive with the Y.M.C.A., the Jewish Welfare Board, the Salvation Army and others, the Order received over $30 million for its War Camp Fund. With a play on words the soldiers identified the Knights as Caseys (K of Cs) revealing their notion of the Irish-American character of the Order.

After the war the Knights established employment bureaus throughout the country to find jobs for veterans. They also provided college scholarships for returning servicemen and set up evening schools for veterans and all others interested in intellectual and vocational advancement. In January 1924 there were 69 evening schools with an enrollment of more than 30,000 students. The Knights received numerous commendations for war and reconstruction work, but the greatest tribute was demonstrated by the more than 400,000 men who joined the Order between 1917 and 1923.

During the 1920s Columbianism expressed itself in a variety of new programs. In response to those historians who stressed an economic interpretation of American history, who disparaged the idealism of the revolutionary period and who ignored the contributions of the various non-Anglo-Saxon immigrant groups, the Order established the K of C Historical Commission. The commission was charged with the responsibility "to investigate the facts of history, to correct historical errors and omissions, to amplify and preserve our national history to exalt and perpetuate American ideals and to combat anti-American propaganda by means of pamphlets . . . and by other proper means and methods as shall be approved by the supreme Assembly." Under

the direction of Edward McSweeney, a former trade unionist and immigration officer on Ellis Island, the commission awarded prizes for the best historical monographs. Works of such scholars who later earned national reputations as Samuel Flagg Bemis and Allan Nevins were published by Macmillan in the Knights of Columbus Historical Series.

In the autumn of 1922, McSweeney designed a unique set of historical studies entitled "The Knights of Columbus Racial Contribution Series." Three monographs were published in this ambitious series: *The Gift of Black Folk* by W. E. B. DuBois, *The Jews in the Making of America* by George Cohen, and *The Germans in the Making of America* by Frederick Franklin Schrader. In his introduction to each of these books, McSweeney summarized the history of immigration to America, the waves of nativism, anti-Catholicism, anti-Semitism and the persistence of racial prejudice in the life of the nation.

In 1921 Pope Benedict XV called upon Columbianism's Catholic anti-defamation character to respond to religious prejudice in Rome. The occasion was a Knights' pilgrimage to Europe, which included the unveiling of an equestrian statue of Lafayette, a K of C gift to the city of Metz, and which culminated in a private audience with the pope. In his address to the 200 Knights, Pope Benedict elaborated on how anti-Catholic propaganda was a strong factor in the Protestant evangelization of Rome and the degree to which it threatened to break down Roman youth's loyalties to the church.

Within a year after this historic audience, the Order had appointed a commission for the Order's Roman project, had established a $1 million Italian Welfare Fund through a per capita tax on the membership, had received permission to construct recreation centers from Benedict's successor, Pope Pius XI, and had contracted the services of a Roman engineer and architect, Enrico Galeazzi. Between 1924 and 1927 the Order opened five recreation centers, the most significant of which was St. Peter's Oratory. In the 1930s this program was absorbed into the Catholic Action movement.

During the Great Depression the Knights revived their anti-socialism, a crusade that included a social-justice component. At the Supreme Council meeting in August 1937, held in San Antonio, the crusade was unanimously endorsed by the delegates. Supreme Knight Martin Carmody reported that the *Daily Worker*, the official voice of the American Communist Party, had frequently vented "its wrath against the Knights of Columbus." Shortly after the convention, the Supreme Board of Directors approved Carmody's proposal to hire an anti-Communist lecturer, George Hermann Derry. Though he was a fervent anti-Communist, he was also anti-Fascist.

The administration of Luke E. Hart (1953–1964), John K. McDevitt (1964–77) and Virgil C. Dechant are identified with the modernization of the Order within the context of its traditional loyalty to Church and Country. Hart laid the basis for the modern insurance program that was later greatly refined by Virgil Dechant. Hart's conservatism on racial and labor issues alienated many members of the Order and the hierarchy. McDevitt led a movement to reform the policy governing admissions to local councils, thereby engendering racial integration. By this policy and by co-sponsoring a Human Rights Congress at Yale and fostering other programs related to social justice, McDevitt restored the confidence of the hierarchy in the Order's direction. In general John McDevitt's administration represents a synthesis of modern fraternalism and traditional faith.

Though Virgil Dechant was German-American, his rise from State Deputy of Kansas to Supreme Knight was promoted by Luke Hart and John McDevitt. Recognized for his command of the insurance program, his modernization of the structures of the Supreme office, and the many programs in support of the Vatican's restoration of St. Peter's Basilica and of Pope John Paul II's charities, Virgil Dechant has been well-known for his deep devotion to Father Michael J. McGivney. Not only has he transferred his remains to St. Mary's church, the birthplace of the Order, and sponsored many programs in his honor, but he has also initiated measures leading toward historical and theological investigation of the cause for beatification of the Irish-American founder of the Knights of Columbus.

Virgil Dechant, Supreme Knight since January of 1977, has established an administration that has led to phenomenal growth: in 1998 there were over 1.7 million Knights located in more than 11,000 councils. With over $25 billion of insurance in force and with the widespread programs of the Order, entailing contributions of over $100 million by Supreme, state and local councils in 1998 and over 25 million man-hours given to community service during that year, the Knights of Columbus still experience the vitality of their original mission to respond to the needs of the church and to witness to the unique character of the Catholic experience in America.

*See* Catholicism, Irish-American

The papers of the Order are located in the Archives in New Haven.

Christopher J. Kauffman, *Faith and Fraternalism: The History of the Knights of Columbus*, revised ed. (New York, 1992).

———, *Columbianism and the Knights of Columbus* (New York, 1992).

CHRISTOPHER J. KAUFFMAN

## KNOX, SAMUEL (1756–1832)

Presbyterian minister and educator. Born at Armagh, Ireland, in 1756, Samuel Knox was a descendant of the great Scottish reformer John Knox. Knox's early life is obscure, but it is certain that he studied at the University of Glasgow in Scotland where he received his M.A. in 1792. By 1795, Knox had emigrated to America where he served as pastor of a Bladensburg, Virginia, church until 1797. A powerful preacher and writer of theological tracts, Knox was also a remarkable teacher. His 1799 *Essay on the Best System of Liberal Education, Adapted to the Genius of the Government of the United States* won an award from the American Philosophical Society and laid the foundation for much of his future work. From 1797 to 1803, he was principal at Frederick Academy and head of a private academy that merged with Baltimore College in 1808. There he served as principal until 1820, and then in 1823 returned to Frederick Academy as its principal until 1827. Knox believed that the blending of the various groups and cultures that came to America could be effectively accomplished through education. It was for this reason that he advocated a nation-wide system of education that standardized textbooks and streamlined training and pay for teachers. Religious education was to be carried out by the various denominations, not by the government, and he called for the establishment of a college in every state. Knox's thinking was well received and respected by prominent figures of the day, including Thomas Jefferson, who was very likely influenced by Knox's *Essay* for the establishment of the University of Virginia before Knox's death in 1832.

*See* Scots Irish

*Daily National Intelligencer* (September 4, 1832).

*Maryland Historical Magazine* (September 1907, September 1909).

Frederick Rudolph, *Essays on education in the early Republic; Benjamin Rush, Noah Webster, Robert Coram, Simeon Doggett, Samuel Harrison Smith, Amable-Louis-Rose de Lafitte du Courteil, Samuel Knox* (Cambridge, 1965).

Bernard C. Steiner, *History of Education in Maryland* (Washington, D.C., 1894).

U.S. Bureau of Education, *Report of the Commissioner of Education for the Year 1898–1899*, vol. I. (1900).

DANIEL J. KUNTZ

## KU KLUX KLAN

### INTRODUCTION: THE MID-NINETEENTH-CENTURY ORIGINS

By the mid-1860s, the political status of newly freed blacks had developed into a controversial national issue. The Emancipation Proclamation of 1863 generated a hostile reaction among Southerners to the incorporation of African-Americans into mainstream American culture. Much of this reaction took the form of organized terrorism against blacks. The most famous anti-black organization was the Ku Klux Klan. Founded in Pulaski, Tennessee, in 1865, the hierarchical Invisible Empire established a platform denying political freedoms to newly emancipated blacks. By 1867, a Klan constitution had been drafted, and General Bedford Forrest was elected as the first Grand Wizard. White males in Tennessee and surrounding states flocked to the Klan in 1866 and 1867, to the point where it commanded an extensive regional membership.

Proclaiming itself "an institution of Chivalry, Humanity, Mercy and Patriotism," the Ku Klux Klan's platform purported to defend the weak and innocent in society, and protect American freedom and liberty ("The Ku Klux Klan: Organization and Principles, 1868," in Henry Steele Commager, ed., *Documents of American History*, New Jersey, 1973, p. 500).

In 1866 and 1867, Upper and Lower South states were divided on a chivalric model into Realms, Dominions, and Provinces. Prospective members were male, white, and invariably Christian, and were interrogated on their associations with Radical Republicanism, the United States Army, and black equality and suffrage. Members protected their identities with robes and hoods while engaging in terrorist activities such as whippings, beatings and burnings.

### THE KU KLUX KLAN DISBANDS IN 1869

Although still operating into the 1870s, the Ku Klux Klan officially demobilized in 1869, as the lawlessness and violence of its members weakened the organization. Ritualistic intimidation and scare tactics failed to dismantle black rights, and former Klan members turned to open violence against blacks, Republicans, Democrats, and Catholics, and even against the Southern education system.

While falling short of articulating a distinct anti-Irish platform, the Klan conducted campaigns against Irish individuals involved in politics or education. In Mississippi in 1871, Irish immigrant Cornelius McBride had taught black children in three

his reporting of Ireland's rural struggles for Patrick Ford's influential journal, *The Irish World and American Industrial Liberator*. George's book *Progress and Poverty* (1879) taught that the free market produced conflict and want only because the rent that owners of land extracted from the produce of industrious society ensnared workers and employers in needless conflict with each other for what remained of their own output. Private ownership of land thus inhibited new building to meet urban needs and plunged the entire economy into periodic crises. If every cent of that "unearned increment," the rent paid for unimproved land, were commandeered by the society whose exertions made the land valuable, George argued, the money could be used to build a healthy and creative environment for urban families and generate prosperity for workers and their bosses to share, while all other taxes be abolished. Here was a critique of acquisitive individualism attractive to trade unionists and many businessmen alike.

"The key note that will reach the American heart," wrote Powderly in 1883, was the attack on "the alien landlord, who first drives his victims from Irish soil and heads them off in this land by buying (stealing) up the land and compels his slave to go up in an eight-story tenement in a large city and live on a crust of bread or pay an exorbitant price for land which God made for all honest men instead of thieves."

Political mobilization around this theme was precipitated by the wave of strikes and boycotts that gripped urban America in 1886. More than 100 members of labor organizations in New York City were then indicted for conspiracy, coercion, and extortion, among them five officials of the Central Labor Union, who were sentenced to years of imprisonment in early July. In response, the unions, Knights, socialists, and land reformers of the city formed a new political party and offered its nomination for mayor to Henry George. The platform denounced "the crowding of so many of our people into narrow tenements at enormous rents" and proposed that "the enormous value which the presence of a million and a half people gives to the land of this city" be "taken in taxation and applied to the improvement and beautification of the city."

The subsequent campaign carried political debate into every working-class neighborhood. The 68,000 votes garnered by George could not match the 90,000 given Tammany's candidate, but the campaign itself excited more public interest than any other event of that tumultuous year, except Chicago's Haymarket Affair.

For the Irish, however, election day proved hardly the end of the excitement. Reverend Edward McGlynn, long known as a champion of the Land Leagues, had supported labor's campaign and then formed the Anti-Poverty Society to promote George's teachings, in defiance of Archbishop Michael A. Corrigan. McGlynn was stripped of his parish, then excommunicated. A furious storm of protest shook the city's Irish community. Large trade union contingents marched in support of the defrocked priest, among them Chairman John McMackin of the Central Labor Union, who reminded his listeners that "our Church has always been carried through by the poor," but added that Americans owed no more political allegiance to the pope than to the king of Spain.

Irish-American women were conspicuous among the supporters of George and McGlynn and also among the members of the Knights of Labor and the Land League. From their role in gathering voters' signatures for George through the innumerable parades in support of McGlynn, women participated actively in ways not previously seen in New York.

If most of those women had been married and aroused by the movement's promise of improved home environments and steadier employment for their menfolk, so too did the ranks of unmarried immigrants (who were more numerous among Irish than any other nationality) and daughters of immigrants provide the lion's share of women members of the Knights of Labor. Moreover, between the decline of the ten-hour movement among Yankee mill operatives after 1850 and the great awakening of Jewish garment workers in 1909, virtually all the best known women labor activists were Irish-Americans (except among shoe workers). Leonora Barry, who came from a Knights of Labor assembly in Amsterdam, New York, to head the order's Department of Women's Work, had been born in Ireland, as had Elizabeth Rogers, Master Workman of the 50,000-member District Assembly 24 in Chicago and a major ally of Powderly in his opposition to anarchists. Mary Elizabeth Lease, the Populist leader, began her career as a Knights lecturer. Alzina Stevens and Leonora O'Reilly, who later helped direct the Women's Trade Union League (WTUL), had their first experience in the Knights. Their younger WTUL colleague, Agnes Nestor, came from the AFL's glove makers. Dora Sullivan emerged from Troy's collar laundries (where the union heritage dated back to Kate Mullaney's initiative of the 1860s) to serve briefly as the AFL's special organizer for women, and was followed in that post by the Chicago bindery worker Mary Kenney.

As mention of the Women's Trade Union League (1903–1955) suggests, Irish lineage has continued to provide leading women of the labor movement throughout the twentieth century. While the already senior Mary Harris ("Mother") Jones began to rally striking coal miners and their families, Elizabeth Gurley Flynn became the "rebel girl" of the Industrial Workers of the World, and Julia O'Connor brought Boston's telephone operators into the electricians' union. Chicago's indomitable Margaret A. Haley not only organized the first teacher's union, but she also became the guiding spirit of President John Fitpatrick's efforts to link the Chicago Federation of Labor to the cause of political reform. By that time, however, San Francisco could claim the first rank for women's trade union involvement. Women in steam laundries,

Mary Harris
"Mother" Jones

binderies, tobacco factories, garment shops, cracker factories, shoe works, and restaurants provided numerous recruits to the city's unions, and most of them were Irish-Americans. When California granted women's suffrage in 1911, women unionists formed the Humane Legislation League to register women voters and campaign for welfare legislation.

## CONSTRUCTING AMERICA'S BUILDINGS

The support women provided for the teachings of Henry George and Father McGlynn was seconded by Irish leaders in the building trades. Irish-Americans have played a highly visible role in construction, both as trade unionists and as employers, from the 1870s to the 1990s. Before World War I, the single tax doctrine offered them a path to social reform and a critique of individualism, which promised to keep business in private hands while encouraging harmonious relations between organized workers and their employers, by freeing both from the incubus of private land ownership and rent.

There are three reasons for the importance of construction in urban Irish-American life. First, the complex network of subcontracting and low capital requirements that characterized this steadily expanding sector of the economy provided an ideal setting for the ambitious man, who was determined to get ahead in the world. Second, the decisive role of building permits, government inspection, and public contracts in this industry forced contractors to involve themselves in local politics, preferably those of the locally dominant party. The rise of James P. "Sunny Jim" McNichol to the top of Philadelphia's construction business and of the Republican Party machine personified this link. Third, Irish-American contractors preferred Irish-American employees. A disproportionate number of brick masons, stonecutters, plumbers, steamfitters, and boiler makers were of Irish extraction, and in newer trades like electricians, elevator riggers, and structural iron workers their preponderance was even more marked.

During the first decade of the twentieth century building tradesmen and coal miners together comprised half of all union members in the country. Construction also produced more strikes than any other industry, though the average strike involved fewer than 100 workers. The fact that it also held the records for lockouts and for sympathetic strikes suggests the endemic nature of conflict in this industry. Union practices in construction were determined by two basic facts of life: several employers were involved in the erection of any one building, and few workers could expect more than a few weeks' tenure on any one job. Union wage scales and work rules could be enforced only by the persistent solidarity of the workers themselves: by the ostracism of the scab.

Thus the building trades provided a case study of two interrelated phenomena. One is the celebrated rise of some immigrants from rags to riches. The other is the more covert forging of a working-class ethical code, which exalted mutuality and group welfare over acquisitive individualism. Every building trades union had some rule designed to prevent the subcontracting and sweating practices, which everyone knew provided the first rung on the success ladder, and which also, where they prevailed, made of life a Darwinian jungle. And all of them fought to restrict access to the trades through union-regulated apprenticeship. When the AFL chose a member union to lead off renewed struggle for the eight-hour day in 1890, it was the Peter J. McGuire's United Brotherhood of Carpenters and Joiners that accepted the challenge.

A decade later the conflict had become even more fierce. Nationwide contracting firms organized employers' associations that locked out tens of thousands of workers in Chicago in 1900 and New York in 1903, demanding dissolution of building trades' councils, an end to sympathetic strikes, abolition of restrictive practices, and separate negotiations by each craft with corresponding employers' associations. The militant employers (led in Chicago by Billy O'Brien, former head of the bricklayers' union) unleashed injunctions and strong-arm crews not to destroy unions (as "open shop" employers in manufacturing then attempted), but rather to police union practices. Building trades unions, in their turn, demonstrated remarkable resilience in the face of this onslaught. They not only survived, but erected the citadel of craft unionism for the remainder of this century.

The stormiest battlefront in construction, however, was held by the Bridge and Structural Iron Workers. Union solidarity was such that no workers would go up to their jobs without union approval, while the United States Steel Corporation refused to sell structural steel to builders who recognized the union. Although union standards were discreetly, even covertly, observed in most cities, contractors in Los Angeles held out for the open shop, urged on by editorial denunciations of organized labor in the *Los Angeles Times*. A dynamite explosion in the offices of the *Times* in 1910 was blamed on union officials John and James McNamara and Ortie McManigal, who were soon also indicted for numerous other bombings throughout the land. While the nation's press revived the specter of the Molly Maguires, the AFL threw all available resources behind the defense of the accused trade unionists. At a dramatic point in the trial, however, defense attorney Clarence Darrow abruptly switched his plea to "guilty," claiming no other course would save his clients' lives.

During the ensuing half-century the building trades remained bulwarks of established AFL practice. Although the industry suffered so severely during the Great Depression that employment became increasingly dependent on government projects and financing, more than 87% of its workers held union cards by 1947 (a density which declined steadily after that). Leaders like Hugh Frayne of the sheet metal workers, Peter Brennan of the painters, Richard Gray of the bricklayers, and "Mr. Asbestos," Joseph A. Mullaney sat in council with other officials of various ethnicities, all opposed to the new Congress of Industrial Organizations (CIO). Together they shaped a new relationship with state and federal governments, which was overseen by the Bronx plumber George Meany. President of the AFL after 1952, Meany guided the federation into a merger with the CIO, then governed the AFL-CIO with a firm hand from 1955 to 1979, while enjoying the apogee of his own influence in Washington during the administration of President Lyndon B. Johnson.

## SHAPING THE GOALS OF THE TWENTIETH-CENTURY LABOR MOVEMENT

Controversies over the purposes and strategies of the labor movement were especially vigorous and explicit during the first quarter of the century. Irish-Americans could be found among those taking every known position.

The National Civic Federation (NCF) drew together notable figures from the business world, trade unions, and the public in the pursuit of industrial peace from 1900 until the 1930s. It encouraged the negotiation of trade agreements between employers' associations and national unions, lent its offices to the mediation of disputes, and promoted workplace safety and health. President James O'Connell of the International Association of Machinists quickly joined the effort, as did Gompers' trusted adviser from the typographical union, James W. Sullivan, who had edited Henry George's campaign paper in 1886. The AFL's most ardent enthusiast for the NCF was John Mitchell, who had been born to Protestant parents from Ireland but converted to Catholicism as an adult. From 1899 to 1908 he was president of the largest union in the AFL, the United Mine Workers of America, which boasted a trade agreement covering virtually all midwestern bituminous production. Such was his charisma that, even though he openly enriched himself through business investments during his presidency, even miners who opposed Mitchell's policies did so with discretion.

Opposition to the NCF was articulated most vehemently by the Socialist Party of America, which sought to arouse workers to eliminate capitalism, not to collaborate with it. Even before the party had been founded, there were Irish voices promoting the socialist cause. Among them were John Tobin and James Carey of the shoe workers, whose union helped install America's first socialist municipal administrations in Brockton and Haverhill, Massachusetts, and such leaders of the Western Federation of Miners as Edward Boyce, Charles Moyer, and John O'Neill. Although Irish membership in the Socialist Party remained small, it included important AFL officials, such as the very popular P. J. Conlon of the machinists, who helped bring about O'Connell's removal from his union's presidency in 1911.

When the Industrial Workers of the World (IWW) embraced the gospel of "direct action," repudiating all political action in its quest for collective ownership of the means of production, it chose Vincent St. John (of Irish-Dutch parentage) as its chief national officer. Despite the eloquence of Elizabeth Gurley Flynn, however, the IWW generally met with a hostile reception from Irish workers in Eastern textile towns. Nevertheless, the influence of the IWW recrossed the Atlantic to Ireland itself, through the efforts of James Connolly and James Larkin, who infused the struggles of Belfast, Dublin, and Cork transport workers with the spirit of the general strike. The transatlantic connection also played its part in the founding of the Communist Labor Party in 1919. Most members of that so-called "American" party (as distinct from the "immigrant" Communist Party founded the same year) were Irish, among them Larkin. After the two parties merged in 1922, their ranks were joined by such major figures of the interwar Communist and Trotskyist movements as William Z. Foster, James Cannon, and Vincent Dunne.

The aftermath of World War I also produced the Farmer-Labor Party, which came to dominate Minnesota politics, with the St. Paul labor editor William Mahoney among its perennial stalwarts. A much less successful attempt at a national Farmer-Labor Party was supported by Chicago's John Fitzpatrick. Simultaneously, Pennsylvania's John Brophy emerged as the leading voice in the UMWA for independent politics and nationalization of coal mines.

Despite their diversity of views, Irish-American activists unanimously rejected the alternative of confessional unions. Catholic union movements arose in western Europe and in Quebec in the aftermath of Pope Leo XIII's encyclical *Rerum Novarum.* When the 1912 encyclical of Pope Pius X, *Singulari Quadam Cartiate,* clearly expressed a preference for purely Catholic unions, the idea won some favor in seminaries, but none whatever among

Catholic trade unionists. Reverend Peter Dietz did gather trade union executives into the Militia of Christ for Social Service between 1910 and 1914 to oppose the growing strength of socialism, but the organization took the form of a caucus within the AFL, not a rival labor federation. All of its members agreed that trade unions in the United States had to be "neutral" in orientation and open to all nationalities. Moreover, Hugh Frayne, James O'Connell, and many other Irish Catholics who supported the Militia of Christ simultaneously joined Protestant clergy on platforms of the Labor and Religion Forward movement, in hopes of recruiting more Protestant workers into their unions. During the 1930s and 1940s, the Association of Catholic Trade Unionists similarly sought to provide Catholic guidance within unions that defined their membership by occupation, not by religion, race, or nationality.

John Brophy returned to the national arena in 1936, when John L. Lewis summoned him to become Director of Organization of the newly formed Committee for Industrial Organization (CIO). His was but one of many Irish names found among leaders of the militant industrial unions, which brought millions of workers in basic industry into the union fold, but were ultimately expelled from the AFL and formed the Congress of Industrial Organizations in 1938. Among them were Harry Bridges of the Pacific Coast longshoremen (and mortal foe of Joseph Ryan, who controlled the East coast docks), Joseph Curran of the maritime union, Michael Quill of New York's Transport Workers (whose members adopted that illustrious Irish name for their union), James Carey and Albert Fitzgerald of the electrical workers, and Joseph P. Molony and Vincent Sweeney of the steel workers, not to mention Philip Murray, who became president of the CIO in 1940.

The Cold War purge, which culminated in the expulsion of nine constituent unions from the CIO on charges of "communist domination," found Irish-Americans once again on both sides of the ideological barricades. Far more of them, however, were to be found among supporters of the domestic and foreign policies of Harry S. Truman than among those who favored the Progressive Party of Henry Wallace. Although the 1955 merger of the AFL and the CIO ushered in decades of conformity within the labor movement, when renewal of social engagement brought about the first contested election for the office of president in

Philip Murray (seated at left), President of the CIO, opens a meeting of the Executive Board of the U.S. Steel Workers Union.

1995, both contenders, Thomas R. Donahue and John J. Sweeney, bore Irish names.

*See* Steel Industry; Coal Miners; Canals

Henry C. Browne, *The Catholic Church and the Knights of Labor* (Washington, D.C., 1949).

David Brundage, *The Making of Western Labor Radicalism: Denver's Organized Workers, 1878–1905* (Urbana, 1994).

David N. Doyle, "The Irish and American Labor, 1880–1920," *Saothar: Journal of the Irish Labour History Society*, 1 (May, 1975): 42–53.

David M. Emmons, *The Butte Irish: Class and Ethnicity in an American Mining Town, 1875–1925* (Urbana, 1989).

Gary M. Fink, ed., *Biographical Dictionary of American Labor* (Westport, CT, 1974).

Joshua Freeman, *In Transit: The Transport Workers Union in New York City, 1933–1966* (New York, 1989).

Bruce Laurie, *Working People of Philadelphia, 1800–1850* (Philadelphia, 1980).

David Montgomery, *The Fall of the House of Labor: The Workplace, the State, and American Labor Activism, 1865–1925* (New York, 1987).

———, "The Irish and the American Labor Movement," in *America and Ireland, 1776–1976: The American Identity and the Irish Connection*, eds., David Noel Doyle and Owen Dudley Edwards (Westport, CT, 1980): 205–218.

Theodore W. Moody, *Davitt and Irish Revolution, 1846–1882* (Oxford, 1981).

DAVID MONTGOMERY

## LALOR, ALICE (Mother Teresa) (1766–1846)

Foundress of the Visitation Order in the United States. Born in Ireland, she spent her childhood in Kilkenny. Early on, the young Lalor attracted the attention of her bishop and he worked with her in founding a community of Presentation nuns in the diocese. She accompanied one of her sisters to the United States and on her journey she befriended two women, both widows, who were eager to become nuns. Lalor and her companions landed in Philadelphia in 1795 and soon met the Rev. Leonard Neale, who became archbishop of Baltimore. Under his tutelage, the three women rented a house and began efforts to set up their own community.

When Fr. Neale moved to Georgetown College in Washington, D.C., the three women followed and lived with some Poor Clares while continuing their efforts to gain their own idenity and official recognition. Fr. Neale assisted them and managed to win approval of Rome; on December 28, 1816, the sisters took their solemn vows and became Visitation nuns. Lalor took the name Mother Teresa and lived with the community for twenty-seven years during which time she founded other houses in Mobile, Alabama (1832), St. Louis, Missouri (1833) and Baltimore, Maryland (1837). She died in 1846 and was buried near Archbishop Neale in the crypt of the convent.

J. B. Code, *Great American Foundresses* (1929).

*Dictionary of American Biography*, 18.

G. P. and Rose Hawthorne Lathrop, *A Story of Courage; Annals of the Georgetown Convent of the Visitation of the Blessed Virgin Mary* (1895).

JOY HARRELL

## LARKIN, EMMET (1927–   )

Historian. Emmet Larkin, Professor of Modern Irish and British history at the University of Chicago, was born in New York City on May 19, 1927. His father (Emmet, senior), a Chicago resident, was raised in the east Galway village of Kiltormer. His mother, Annabelle Ryder Larkin, came from the same area. His father fought in the Irish Republican Army in both the Anglo-Irish and Civil Wars. His IRA loyalties, opposition to the 1921 Anglo-Irish Treaty and the resulting Free State government forced him to leave Ireland and settle in Manhattan.

Emmet Larkin attended New York's public elementary and secondary schools. After military service in the army, he earned a B.A (1950) in history from New York University and an M.A. (1951) and Ph.D. (1957) in the same subject from Columbia University. During the 1955–56 academic year, he was a Fulbright scholar at the London School of Economics. Before joining the faculty at the University of Chicago in 1966, he taught history at Brooklyn College and humanities at the Massachusetts Institute of Technology. The same year that he came to Chicago, he married Dianne Willey. They have two daughters, Heather and Siobhan.

In 1965, the MIT and Routledge & Kegan Paul, Ltd. presses jointly published *James Larkin, Irish Labour Leader, 1876–1947*, a study based upon Emmet's Ph.D. dissertation. Pluto Press issued a paperback of this highly acclaimed biography in 1989. By the time the Larkin book appeared, Emmet already had started researching and writing on nineteenth-century Irish Catholicism, Ireland's most significant cultural as well as religious force, the essence of its national identity, but a topic lacking sufficient scholarly attention. He has now published numerous articles and seven of a series of nine projected books on the nineteenth-century Irish church.

In another book, *The Historical Dimensions of Irish Catholicism* (Washington, D.C., 1976, 1984, 1997), he reprinted an essay, "The Devotional Revolution in Ireland, 1850–1875," that first appeared in *The American Historical Review* (June 1972). It has stimulated more debate and inspired more research than any publication by an American working in Irish history. In "The Devotional Revolution" essay, Emmet makes a sharp distinction between pre- and post-Famine Catholicism, describing the former as afflicted with a poorly educated clergy; a quarreling bench of bishops; priest and chapel shortages; and a laity often ignorant of and indifferent to Catholic doctrine and practices. He designates the Famine as the beginning of reform. Through death and exile, hunger and disease, the rural population decreased. Many of its superstitions then disappeared, and the ratio between the number of clergy and the laity has reduced. Famine population pruning set the stage for Paul Cullen, rector of the Irish College in Rome, who became Archbishop of Armagh and Primate in 1849, and three years later succeeded Daniel Murray as archbishop of Dublin. Until his death in 1878, Cardinal Cullen dominated Irish Catholicism, increasing vocations; improving clerical conduct, discipline and education; imposing a public face of harmony on the hierarchy; building churches and schools; promoting a variety of religious devotions; emphasizing loyalty to Rome; and influencing the Irish at home and among the Diaspora to become the most devout, Romanized Catholics in the world.

Larkin's editing and translation of and "Introduction" to *Alexis de Tocqueville's Journey in Ireland, July–August, 1835* (1990) has also shed much light on pre-Famine Ireland, especially the Catholic Church and its bishops and priests.

In 1960 Larkin co-founded the American Conference for Irish Studies, an interdisciplinary organization that now has around 1,500 members, and he has always been a very active member. Emmet Larkin's scholarly achievements have won him many awards. He has done more than most to foster the study of Irish history and culture—and has inspired a generation of students to follow in his path.

*See* American Conference for Irish Studies

LAWRENCE J. McCAFFREY

## LAUGHLIN, JAMES [IV] (1914–1997)

Publisher, poet, editor, essayist, non-fiction writer, and translator. Born the son of a wealthy steel magnate in Pittsburgh, Laughlin used family money to found the influential New Directions Publishing Corporation in 1936 at the suggestion of Ezra Pound. Besides publishing some of the century's most significant authors, Laughlin became a respected writer. His poems reflect the influence of both the classics and moderns, especially of William Carlos Williams and Ezra Pound.

### BIOGRAPHY

Laughlin's family (pronounced Loch-lin) is descended from Scots-Irish Presbyterians. In 1824, his great-grandfather, James, sold his farm in Northern Ireland, purchased crockery, and sold it out of a wagon in Pennsylvania. He settled in Pittsburgh, where he founded a bank and a store. Later, he invested in what became the fourth largest steel company in America, the Jones and Laughlin Steel Co.

Laughlin grew up in a wealthy section of Pittsburgh and at the home of his aunt, Leila Laughlin Carlisle, in Norfolk, CT (where he eventually settled). He attended several boarding schools in the U.S. and Switzerland, graduating from Choate in 1932 (Wallingford, CT). There, under Dudley Fitts, Laughlin read the poetry of Pound, Eliot, Stein, and Cummings. He also published his first essay—in the *Atlantic*. He enrolled in Harvard in 1932. Dissatisfied with the English department's disapproval of modernist literature, he majored in Latin and Italian. During his sophomore year, Laughlin took a leave of absence and went, with letters of introduction, to Gertrude Stein's home in France (where he worked as her chauffeur) and then to Pound's "Ezuversity" in Rapallo, Italy.

He stayed with Pound for six months, studying Italian, writing poetry, and discussing literature and political economy. Pound eventually told him that he would "never make a writer." Instead, he suggested that Laughlin go back to the U.S. and "do something useful," namely, publish books. With a gift of $100,000 from his parents, and with Pound's recommendations, Laughlin returned to Harvard and began his career as one of the century's boldest publishers.

New Directions later moved its offices to New York, but Laughlin continued to spend most of his time in Norfolk, Connecticut. He also spent considerable time skiing (and writing on it) and developing the Alta ski resort in Utah. He traveled frequently to Europe (especially Italy, Switzerland and Ireland) and Asia (especially India). He married three times and had three children from his first two marriages.

James Laughlin

Laughlin also lectured at dozens of colleges and universities and worked as a "cultural scout" in Asia for the Ford Foundation (1952–54). In addition to his A.B. from Harvard in 1939, he received four honorary doctorates—from Hamilton, 1970; Colgate, 1973; Duquesne, 1981; and Yale, 1982—and earned an American Academy of Arts and Letters Award, 1977, and a National Book Foundation Medal for Distinguished Contribution to American Letters, 1992.

### NEW DIRECTIONS

New Directions, for most of its existence, has been nearly synonymous with James Laughlin. ND published many of the most significant writers of the century, its focus being on new and experimental literature. Usually it was the first U.S. publisher of its authors. A list of some of its writers illustrates Laughlin's contribution to literature in America: Apollinaire, Djuna Barnes, Borges, Paul Bowles, Brecht, Camus, Cocteau, Corso, Creeley, Durrell, Ferlinghetti, García Lorca, H. D., Hesse, Isherwood, Joyce, Kafka, Levertov, Merton, McClure, McDiarmid, Henry Miller, Nabokov, Neruda, Olson, Orwell, Pasternak, Paz, Pound, Raja Rao, Rexroth, Rilke, Rimbaud, Sartre, Snyder, Dylan Thomas, Valéry, Tennessee Williams, and William Carlos Williams.

Laughlin compiled his first book, *New Directions in Prose & Poetry,* in 1936. This first collection included contributions from Bishop, Cummings, Miller, Marianne Moore, Stein, Pound, Stevens, and W.C. Williams. As Eliot Weinberger noted in *The Nation,* "Laughlin was more than the greatest American publisher of the twentieth century: His press *was* the twentieth century" (December 15, 1997).

But ND did not become profitable for decades and survived because of Laughlin's inheritance, which enabled them to publish books for literary reasons. As Laughlin stated in 1992 (qtd. in *The New York Times, Obituaries,* November 14, 1997): "Of course, none of this would have been possible without the industry of my ancestors, the canny Irishmen who immigrated in 1824 from County Down to Pittsburgh. . . . I bless them with every breath."

### POETRY

Despite Pound's prediction, Laughlin continued writing poetry, encouraged and influenced by Williams. Laughlin's poems are known, in part, for their "natural" and colloquial diction. Laughlin was also concerned with the look of the words on the page, "where the eye meets the ear." In his innovative "typewriter line" poems, line lengths vary no more than two spaces in either direction from the previous line, the first line being somewhat random. We see Pound's influence in Laughlin's reliance on classical models, his uses of other languages within a poem, and his witty social commentary.

In his first collection, *Some Natural Things* (privately printed, 1945), "Technical Notes" laid the framework for his poetic project. The speaker declares Catullus his master, but he proposes "to build with plain brown bricks/the common talk American talk" because "a poem/is finally just/a natural thing." He also claims that "love/is my subject," and it continued to be a focus throughout his career. Hayden Carruth has noted that Laughlin's love poetry emerges from a European tradition, and notes the singularity of Laughlin's achievement as an American love poet ("Introduction," *Collected Poems of JL,* 1994). Later poems such as "In Another Country" (1978) continue these themes, poignantly illustrating innocent love and the experience of a young American in Europe.

In Laughlin's poetry, we find a gratifying play with language; a wit that is ironic, comic, and erotic; and a lyrical, colloquial voice contemplating both social issues and perennial issues of existence. He bridges the gap between American culture and the traditions of ancient cultures—French, Italian, Indian, Irish. His later volumes contain poems concerning Ireland and his Irish-American heritage as well as some moving, ironic meditations on old age.

*See* Poetry, Irish-American

James Laughlin, *The River* (a story, New Directions, 1938).
——, *Selected Poems, 1935–1985* (City Lights, 1986).
——, *The Master of Those Who Know: Pound the Teacher* (City Lights, 1986).
——, *The Owl of Minerva* (poems, Copper Canyon, 1987).
——, *Pound as Wuz* (criticism, New Directions, 1987).
——, *The Bird of Endless Time* (poems, Copper Canyon, 1989).
——, *This Is My Blood* (stories, Yolla Bolly, 1989).
——, *Random Essays; Recollections of a Publisher* (Moyer Bell, 1989).
——, *Random Stories* (Moyer Bell, 1990).
——, *Angelica* (a novella, Grenfell, 1992).
——, *The Man in the Wall* (poems, New Directions, 1993).
——, *Collected Poems, 1938–1992* (Moyer Bell, 1994).
——, *Heart Island* (poems, Turkey Press, 1994).
——, *Remembering William Carlos Williams* (New Directions, 1995).
——, *The Country Road* (poems, Zoland, 1995).
——, *Phantoms* (poems, Aperture, 1995).
——, *The Love Poems* (New Directions, 1997).
——, *The Secret Room* (poems, New Directions, 1997).
——, *The Lost Fragments* (poems, Dedalus, Dublin, 1997).
Norton has published Laughlin's correspondences with William Carlos Williams (1989), Kenneth Rexroth (1991), Delmore Schwartz (1993), Ezra Pound (1994), Henry Miller (1996), and Thomas Merton (1997). Also, *Conjunctions* (Winter 1981–82) did a double-issue festschrift in honor of James Laughlin.

JOSEPH LENNON

## LAWRENCE, DAVID LEO (1889–1966)

Mayor of Pittsburgh, Governor of Pennsylvania. David Lawrence was born in Pittsburgh, Pennsylvania, June 18, 1889, to Charles B. Lawrence and Catherine Conwell. Lawrence was educated at St. Mary's parochial school, and instead of high school, took a two-year course in commercial training. At fourteen, Lawrence went to work in 1903 as an office boy for William J. Brennan, the Democratic chairman of Allegheny County.

Lawrence spent the next ten years working for Brennan and served as a page at the 1912 Democratic National Convention in Baltimore. There Lawrence was inspired by Woodrow Wilson and his political vision and two years later took a job with the Judge Advocate General in Washington, D.C. Lawrence spent the First World War in the nation's capital, but returned to Pittsburgh in 1918 where he sold insurance and was later elected Allegheny County Democratic Chairman after Brennan's death in 1920.

After the 1932 Presidential election, Roosevelt appointed Lawrence collector for the Internal Revenue Service in western Pennsylvania. He held this position for a year, but resigned it in 1933 to become chairman of the Democratic State Committee. Lawrence served in this position for ten of the next twelve years and also as Secretary of the Commonwealth under governor George H. Earl. Earl's frequent indiscretions led to the perception that Lawrence was the "real ruler" behind the Pennsylvania governorship.

In 1939, Lawrence returned to the insurance industry and continued to cultivate his political career. He became a Democratic national committeeman the following year, and in this position later helped to secure Harry S Truman's nomination for president. In 1945, Lawrence was elected mayor of Pittsburgh and went on to become the only mayor in the city's history to serve four consecutive terms.

During his tenure, Lawrence earned the reputation for building a "better Pittsburgh." With Richard K. Mellon of Mellon National Bank, Gulf Oil, and Alcoa, and several other top executives in Pittsburgh, Lawrence worked to rebuild the city. Skyscrapers went up while Lawrence lobbied for, and enforced, anti-pollution measures that gave Pittsburgh its reputation for clean air and parks. By 1958, *Fortune* magazine ranked Pittsburgh among the best-run cities in America.

Lawrence was nominated for governor in the same year. Though he feared that his Catholic faith would handicap his campaign, Lawrence won a narrow victory over Republican Arthur T. McGonigle. Interestingly, over the next several years, Lawrence supported Adlai Stevenson over John F. Kennedy because he was sure Kennedy's Catholicism would diminish his chances for election. But when Stevenson pulled out of the race, Lawrence threw his considerable support behind the young Catholic Kennedy. The *New York Times,* in fact, reported that Lawrence's support was decisive in securing a Kennedy nomination on the first ballot.

Kennedy appointed Lawrence chairman of the President's Committee on Equal Opportunity for Housing when Lawrence's term as governor ended in 1962. Here Lawrence continued to campaign vigorously for issues in which he strongly believed right up to his death. It was while campaigning for a candidate that Lawrence suffered a heart attack and died seventeen days later in Pittsburgh, November 21, 1966.

*See* Pennsylvania

*Christian Science Monitor* (September 5, 1958).
*Life* (November 28, 1955).

David Lawrence, *The Editorials of David Lawrence* (Washington, 1970).
———, *The True Story of Woodrow Wilson* (New York, 1924).
*New York Herald Tribune* ( June 5, 1958; October 14, 1960).
*New York Post* (September 2, 1960).
*New York Times* (November 5, 1962; August 24, 1964).
*New York Times,* obituary (November 22, 1966).
*Saturday Evening Post* (March 14, 1959).
*Time* ( June 1, 1942; November 15, 1954; June 18, 1956; November 4, 1967; December 2, 1957; April 21, 1958; November 1, 1959; November 30, 1959; July 25, 1960; October 19, 1962).

DANIEL J. KUNTZ

## LEAHY, WILLIAM D. (1875–1959)

Admiral, governor, ambassador, White House chief of staff. William Daniel Leahy was born May 6, 1875, at Hampton, Iowa. He was the son of Michael A. Leahy and Rose Hamilton, both natives of Wisconsin. William's paternal grandparents, Daniel Leahy and Mary Egan, had emigrated from County Galway, Ireland, to America in 1836. The family settled in Wisconsin in 1849.

William Leahy grew up in Wausau and Ashland, Wisconsin. Influenced by his father's Civil War service in the 35th Wisconsin Infantry, William decided on a military career. Appointment to the U.S. Military Academy at West Point had already been filled so Leahy sought and obtained an appointment to the U.S. Naval Academy. He graduated from Annapolis in 1897. He served in the Spanish-American War (1898), the Philippine Insurrection (1899–1901), and the Boxer Rebellion in China (1900). Leahy was assigned to the Navy Department in Washington during 1913–1915 where he met Franklin D. Roosevelt, Assistant Secretary of the Navy. Their friendship would later play a key role in achieving victory in World War II. During World War I, Leahy commanded a Navy troop transport ship.

Leahy's organizational abilities were recognized as he worked his way up the Navy's command structure. He was appointed to the rank of Rear Admiral when he was named Chief of the Bureau of Ordnance, 1927–1931. He later served as Chief of the Bureau of Navigation, 1933–1935. Leahy was appointed to the Navy's top command position, Chief of Naval Operations, 1937–1939. In the latter year he reached the Navy's mandatory retirement age and was forced to leave the service. However, President Roosevelt appointed him governor of Puerto Rico in an effort to keep Leahy in public service as the clouds of war began to darken.

After the Nazis invaded France, Roosevelt appointed Leahy to serve in the key diplomatic post of ambassador to Vichy France, 1940–1942. When America entered the war, Roosevelt decided he needed the advice and counsel of Leahy on a daily basis. A new position of White House Chief of Staff was created expressly for the purpose of placing Leahy in direct contact with the president to manage the war on two fronts. As Chief of Staff, Leahy was one of the principal architects of the Allied victory in World War II. In 1944 Congress voted to promote him to five star rank as Fleet Admiral. Leahy continued as Chief of Staff under President Truman, finally retiring from government service in 1949. In the following year, he published his memoirs of World War II.

Admiral Leahy died on July 20, 1959, at Bethesda, Maryland. He was buried in Arlington National Cemetery. He left his papers to the State Historical Society of Wisconsin. Cape Leahy, Antarctica, was named in his honor in recognition of more than half a century of distinguished public service. Leahy's son, William Harrington Leahy, continued the family's martial tradition by also serving as an admiral in the Navy.

Henry H. Adams, *Witness Power: The Life of Fleet Admiral William D. Leahy* (Annapolis, 1985).
William D. Leahy, *I Was There: The Personal Story of the Chief of Staff to Presidents Roosevelt and Truman* (New York, 1950).

THOMAS GILDEA CANNON

## LEARY, ANNIE (1830–1919)

Philanthropist, settlement worker. Annie Leary was a wealthy Catholic laywoman who contributed financially and personally to a number of projects designed to aid Catholics. She was especially interested in Italian immigrants and helped support the work of Frances Cabrini's Missionary Sisters of the Sacred Heart of Jesus. Leary was a major benefactor of Our Lady of Pompei on Bleeker Street in Greenwich Village during the late nineteenth century. From about 1895 to 1905, she assumed all of the debts and supported the work of the parish. Her support enabled the parish to decorate and repair the church and maintain a "work school" for Italian children. During the first decade of the twentieth century, Leary clashed with the pastor of the church, Rev. Antonio Demo, C.S. She was not willing to consult the priest every time she chose to raise money for her charitable projects, including Our Lady of Pompei; and apparently broke with the parish completely. Her will did not disburse any of her $2,000,000 estate to Our Lady of Pompei. She founded and supported the Pius X Art Institute, also located in Greenwich Village. In recognition of her work for and with the American Catholic Church, particularly the Archdiocese of New York, Leary was given the title papal countess. She is buried beneath Saint Patrick's Cathedral in New York City.

Mary Elizabeth Brown, *From Italian Villages to Greenwich Village: Our Lady of Pompei 1892–1992* (New York, 1992).

MARGARET M. McGUINNESS

## LEGION OF MARY, THE

The lay association was founded in Dublin in September 1921 by Frank Duff and a small group of friends. Duff was a thirty-one-year-old government official with wide intellectual interests and deep religious and ecumenical commitments. The new organization got a very cold reception from the archbishop of Dublin who, like all the Irish hierarchy, believed that any religious organization should be in the control of the clergy.

Frank Duff felt that the world was entering a new epoch with the end of the Great War (1914–18) and with Ireland on the verge of some form of independence. The Legion of Mary broke with tradition. Run by layfolk, it attracted a dedicated following of men and women from all walks of life. They founded hostels for the homeless, unmarried mothers, and prostitutes seeking to turn their lives around. Their evangelization efforts were low-key and courteous; and they sought dialog with members of other religious affiliations.

In 1931 Father Joseph Donovan of St. Louis visited Dublin and was impresssed by the work and agenda of the Legion. On his return he established the first branch (praesidium) in St. Louis. From there it spread quietly all over America. Periodically, the Legion headquarters sent envoys to the United States, and their task was not only to establish new praesidia but also to keep the Legionaries true to their charitable, spiritual and ecumenical ideals. One of these dedicated envoys was Mary Duffy, who spent twelve years (1934–46) moving around America.

The Legion was welcomed by the hierarchies in 160 countries, and had exceptional acceptance in Asia. Consequently, Catholic Korean and Vietnamese immigrants in America were attracted to the Legion of Mary, with which many were acquainted in their homelands. The American activities of the Legion are recorded in the association's magazine *Maria Legionis*. In 1956 Frank Duff made his only visit to America; but until his death in 1980 he kept in constant contact with the praesidia in various dioceses. His vast correspondence over five decades gives a very perceptive view of American Catholicism.

*See* Ireland: 1798–1998

Frank Duff, *Miracles on Tap* (Bay Shore, New York, 1962).
Cecily Hallack, *The Legion of Mary* (London, 1950).
L. J. Cardinal Suenens, *Theology of the Apostolate* (Westminster, Md., 1976).

MICHAEL O'CARROLL, C.S.Sp.

## LEIGH, JANET (1927– )

Actress. Born Jeanette Helen Morrison on July 6, 1927, in Merced, California, she was married to film star Tony Curtis in 1951. The couple had two children, Kelly and Jamie Lee (a current star of film and television).

During her acting career, Leigh worked mainly for the MGM Studios. She played in such films as *Hills of Home* (1947); *That Forsythe Woman* (1949); *The Red Danube* (1949); *Scaramouche* (1952); *Houdini* (1953); *Prince Valiant* (1954); *Pete Kelly's Blues* (1955); and *Jet Pilot* (1957). But her most famous role was in the 1960 notorious Alfred Hitchcock thriller, *Psycho,* with Anthony Perkins as the peculiar Norman Bates. Leigh's shower scene in *Psycho* is one of the most powerful—and most parodied—scenes in film history.

J. Concannon and Frank Cull, *Irish American Who's Who* (New York, 1984).
Joseph Curran, *Hibernian Green on the Silver Screen* (Westport, CT, 1990).

EILEEN DANEY CARZO

## LIDDY, JAMES (1934– )

Poet, critic, editor and fiction writer. Liddy was born in Dublin, raised in County Clare, and educated at Glenstal Abbey, National University of Ireland (B.A., 1956; M.A., 1959) and the King's Inns, Dublin (Barrister-at-Law, 1961). He practiced law in Ireland (1961–66) and was coeditor of *Arena* (1963–65). For the next ten years he devoted himself to writing poetry and held various academic positions in America and Ireland until becoming a full-time academic teacher and scholar at the University of Wisconsin-Milwaukee where he is professor of English and coordinator of Irish Studies.

Liddy is a member of Aosdana, Irish Academy of Arts and Letters and received the Council of Wisconsin Writers Prize for Poetry (1995). Coeditor of *Poetry Ireland* (1962–67) and *The Corey Detail* (1977–83), Liddy has published over twenty monographs; numerous poems, essays and reviews have appeared in periodicals and newspapers.

If, as Liddy says, he gained "a sense of the aesthetic qualities of ritual, and of language" from the monks of Glenstal, and a childhood consciousness of "a Catholic conservative nationalism," it was from his mentor Patrick Kavanagh, "in the chapel of McDaid's" pub, that he learned "the technique of breathing in what it is to be a poet" (Arkins interview). This included an irreverent poetic dislike of the routine, hostility to traditional bourgeois values, and a delight in spontaneity and friendships, or, as he says in an early poem, "conversation, unusual people, and a casual life." In his later poetry, Liddy openly celebrates his homosexual sensibility as he does in his novella, *Young Men Go Walking* (1986). "Being queer, like being Irish and being Catholic," he comments, "has charted my imagination."

Liddy's Muse, equally at home in Ireland or America, draws upon the literary traditions of both countries, especially their emphasis on place and locality. So much of his work seems to arise spontaneously to celebrate an occasion ("Epithalamion I–IV"), a person ("Clare, the Butterflies," "To the Memory of Sylvia Plath, A Personal Note"), or a place (*In the Slovak Bowling Alley*). Liddy's verse is informed by Irish myth, Catholicism, and local color. The poems in *Corca Bascinn*, for example, capture externally the bleak landscape of this west Clare region, but they also divulge the poet's inward spiritual vision of the countryside. (Liddy's maternal grandparents were from County Clare, but they met in New York where his mother was born; she returned to Ireland where Liddy was born.) Other poems pay homage to older Irish writers (Yeats, O'Casey, Joyce), but also to its younger ones ("A Letter to Eamonn Wall").

Yet, Liddy's voice is also American; it reflects the wide range of Whitman's free verse and celebration of love, as in "Delphine and Hippolyta": "I wish to be destroyed in your body/And find in your forest freshness of the grave." Liddy has also been influenced by the contemporary poetics of Jack Spicer ("A Munster Song of Love and War"), and the Beat Generation ("Kerouac's Ronsard Dance"). His work is imbued with a modern sensibility influenced by the French Symbolists' "dissociation of language," Baudelaire's sexual energy (*Baudelaire's Bar Flowers*), and other contemporary voices. It is, perhaps, within the context of this dual literary tradition that John Ashbery's comment that Liddy is "the most original among living Irish poets" rings true.

This "merry/Dabbler" acknowledges that the nucleus of much good poetry "is spontaneity, the sudden moment." He "can't salute/The discovery of the ordinary poem"; instead, his poems are bold, often debunking traditional Irish pieties while restoring humor and sarcasm to Irish poetry. "Epitaphery," for example, is one of ninety-one wistful aphorisms in *Art Is Not for Grown-Ups* (1990):

> Alcohol I loved, and next to alcohol youth —
> I flirted with all, for all were worth
> my time; the pulse of hand and loins
> does not die down—and I am not ready to go.

This aphorism captures the language of heightened conversation characteristic of Liddy's mature work, and it is suggestive of how he combines the sensual and the intellect to enhance the poem's ability to capture the spontaneous moment.

*See* Poetry, Irish-American

James Liddy, *Esau My Kingdom for a Drink: Homage to James Joyce on His LXXX Birthday* (N.Y., 1962).

———, *In a Blue Smoke* (Dublin and N.Y., 1964).
———, *Blue Mountain* (Dublin and N.Y., 1968).
———, *A Life of Stephen Dedalus* (San Francisco, 1968).
———, *Baudelaire's Bar Flowers* (Santa Barbara, 1975).
———, *Corca Bascinn* (Dublin, 1977).
———, *At the Grave of Fr. Sweetman* (Dublin, 1984).
———, *Young Men Go Walking* in *Triad: Modern Irish Fiction* (Dublin, 1986).
———, *A White Thought in a White Shade: New and Selected Poems* (Dublin, 1987).
———, *In the Slovak Bowling Alley* (Milwaukee and Dublin, 1990).
———, *Collected Poems* (Omaha, Neb., 1994).
———, *Epitaphery* (San Francisco, 1997).

ANDREW M. McLEAN

## LINN, JOHN JOSEPH (1798–1885)

Texas patriot and merchant. John J. (Joseph) Linn was born in County Antrim, Ireland, on 19 June 1798. His father, John, was a college professor and active member of a movement known as the United Irishmen. The senior Linn eventually wearied over the strife in his homeland. Therefore, in 1798, having angered the British government through his participation in the recent anti-English Wexford Rebellion, John Linn, with his wife and new-born son, left Ireland for America, their ultimate destination being New York City.

At Poughkeepsie, New York, John Linn attained a teaching position. As time passed, the Linns resided not only in New York City, but for several years in Dutchess County, and then back in New York City once again. In 1816, the father apprenticed his son, John J., to a merchant in New York City, allowing the younger Linn to learn bookkeeping. In 1822, John J. Linn, only twenty-four years old and likely accompanied by some—if not all—of his family, moved to New Orleans. There he found employment in a mercantile house, but then entered into the trade and merchant business for himself.

His economic pursuits attracted John J. Linn to Texas, where he eventually settled in 1829. Building his home at Victoria, a few miles inland from the Gulf of Mexico, he established a warehouse at the small Lavaca Bay locale that came to be known first as Linn's Landing and then later as Linnville.

In 1833, at New Orleans, he married Margaret C. Daniels. The two became parents ultimately of fourteen children. At the same time, the Irishman brought all of his family to reside in or near Victoria. During the 1835–1836 Texan drive for independence from Mexico, he actively supported the Texans militarily, economically, and politically. He became quartermaster of the Texas army, *alcalde* of Victoria (1836), and later mayor of that city (1839). John J. Linn also represented Victoria at the Texas Consultation of 1835, a meeting held to support the federal concept of government entrenched in the Mexican Constitution of 1824. Elected as Victoria's representative to the convention that wrote Texas' 2 March 1836 Declaration of Independence from Mexico, Linn was unable to attend.

Of considerable importance, Linn became over the years a prominent Roman Catholic. Much of his perception of Texas history from the 1830s to the 1880s is recorded in his memoirs, *Reminiscences of Fifty Years in Texas,* which his friend and historian, Victor Marion Rose, ghost-wrote. John J. Linn died at his home in Victoria on 27 October 1885, mourned as one of Texas' most respected citizens.

*See* Texas

John Brendan Flannery, *The Irish Texans* (San Antonio, 1980).
Patrick Foley, "The Shamrock and the Altar in Early Nineteenth-Century Texas: Irish Catholics and Their Faith," *The Irish in the West* (Manhattan, Kansas, 1993).
John J. Linn, *Reminiscences of Fifty Years in Texas* (Austin, Facsimile Reproduction, 1986; originally published in 1883).
James Talmadge Moore, *Through Fire and Flood: The Catholic Church in Frontier Texas 1836–1900* (College Station, 1992).
Craig H. Roell, "Linn, John Joseph," *The New Handbook of Texas* (Austin, 1996).

PATRICK FOLEY

## LOGAN, JAMES (1674–1751)

Colonial statesman, scholar and founder. Born the son of Patrick Logan and Isabel (Hume) in Lurgarn, County Armagh, Ireland, Logan showed academic interest at an early age and was encouraged by his father, who was a schoolmaster. After having gained fluency in Greek, Latin and Hebrew, Logan made the acquaintance of William Penn, who commissioned him to be his personal secretary in 1699. In September of 1699, Logan and Penn boarded the *Canterbury* for Pennsylvania and upon arrival Penn appointed Logan secretary of the province and clerk of the Provincial Council in Pennsylvania. Logan held office during the "Border War" between Maryland and Pennsylvania and was eventually elected mayor of Philadelphia in 1722. In politics, Logan represented the Proprietary Party, which consisted of wealthy Philadelphia Quakers and supporters of the Penn family. Logan began a judicial career in 1726 after having been nominated by Governor Gordon. In 1731, Logan was appointed Chief Justice of the Supreme Court and filled this position until 1739.

Logan's private life was also successful; he found land investments and trade with the Indians to be a lucrative pursuit. After retirement in 1747, Logan further pursued his academic interests and contributed many scientific articles; of particular interest was his "Experiments Concerning the Impregnation of the Seeds of Plants." Logan died on October 31, 1751.

Edward Armstrong. ed., "Correspondence between William Penn and James Logan," in *Memoirs of the Historical Society of Pennsylvania,* vols. IX, X (1870–1872).
Logan Papers (45 volumes).
*Dictionary of American Biography,* 11.

JOY HARRELL

## LOGUE, MARY TRINITA (1895–1970)

Missionary. Kathleen Veronica Logue, was born in New York City on January 25, 1895, of Irish parentage. Logue worked for twelve years as a supervisor and chief operator in the New York Telephone Company after which she entered the Maryknoll Sisters in April of 1924. She received the name Sister Mary Trinita. In 1927 Trinita was assigned to the Philippines where she established St. Mary's Hall, a hostel for young women students from the University of the Philippines. In 1929 Trinita was named regional superior of the Maryknoll Sisters in the Philippines.

In December of 1941, Baguio Bay was bombed by Japanese troops. By January they entered Manila. Citizens of all countries at war with Japan were rounded up. Forty-six Maryknoll Sisters were interned at Assumption College in Manila. Trinita figured they might remain there about three weeks. Three weeks turned into three years. Trinita organized the gathering of and the passing on of medicines, clothing and food to men in prison, on the run, or in the hills, a network of activity about which very little was spoken, nothing written and names were well guarded.

On April 11, 1944, three Japanese men came to speak with Trinita. They were military police from Fort Santiago, a place of holding, interrogation, and torture for those suspected of activities against the occupation. One man read a letter addressed to Trinita from Baguio demanding that she give them other coded letters. Trinita denied having received any such letters. They then searched her, her desk, bed and workbench, finding nothing suspicious. Dissatisfied with her answers, they took her with them to Fort Santiago. where she was interrogated by a man with an interpreter, along with his two assistants. At 2 A.M. a three-hour interrogation began regarding a code letter brought to her from Baguio and Manila. The letter contained innocuous statements about the daily life of the sisters in Baguio, the garden, the animals, etc. Anywhere else this discussion would have been comical, but not at that time nor in that place. At 5 A.M. she was taken to another cell occupied by twenty-four women. All had to sit upright on the floor during the day. They could lie down on the dirt floor at dusk but were forbidden to speak. They became geniuses in communication, comforting one another, praying together, doing what they could to retain some sense of decency in spite of the indignities to which they were subjected. For the next two weeks Trinita was taken two or three times daily for further interrogation. The guard would slam the door and shout, "Church! Church! Church!" She was beaten, struck with clenched fists and bamboo rods, thrown down and kicked. The frustrated guards decided that the water torture might make her talk. Stretched on her back with wrists, knees and ankles tied with heavy electrical cord, a strong jet of water was forced directly into her eyes, ears, nose and mouth. Questions were asked. No answers. More water. . . .

After June 29, Trinita was no longer interrogated or tortured. She had lost over 80 pounds. Her erect posture and easy manner, her quiet self-confidence were gone, but she came back with a heart at ease in the knowledge that she had revealed nothing that could be used to hurt anyone.

On February 23, 1945, Trinita was among the 2,200 internees rescued by American paratroopers and Filipino guerillas. She saw many of her sisters in great need of rest, rehabilitation and medical care. She arranged for the most needy to return to the U.S. Trinita was urged to go herself but she chose to stay on to discover how her students, nurses and friends were faring and what might be salvageable of the schools and convents that had been bombed, eager to have a hand, however minor, in the restoration of the country she loved.

Trinita returned to the U.S. in 1946 to spend twenty-four more productive years in responsible posts in her homeland before her death in 1970, a witness to great faith, integrity and courage in suffering.

Jeanne Marie Lyons, "A Woman Called Church," *Maryknoll Magazine* (New York, 1968).
Maryknoll Sisters' Archives.

HELEN PHILLIPS, M.M.

## LOMASNEY, MARTIN M. (1859–1933)

Political leader. Martin M. Lomasney was born in the West End of Boston on December 3, 1859, and died in his native city on August 12, 1933. The son of Irish Catholic immigrants, Maurice Lomasney from Fermoy, County Cork, and Mary (Murray) Lomasney from Lismore, County Waterford, Martin received his political education by listening to the politics of the common council as a youth. Thus, he was able to argue both sides of an issue and followed this axiom: "Don't write when you can talk; don't talk when you can nod your head."

### FOUNDER OF THE HENDRICK'S CLUB

An exceptional political boss, Lomasney ruled Ward Eight in the West End, especially through the Hendricks Club, an organization which he had founded on December 20, 1885, to provide his Irish constituents with assistance in the form of food, housing, and jobs. Named in honor of President Grover Cleveland's Vice President, Thomas A. Hendricks, who cared much for Irish immigrants, it set an example for other leaders like James Michael Curley with his Tammany Club and John F. Fitzgerald with his Jefferson Club.

Known as "the Mahatma," Lomasney had integrity that manifested itself in a number of ways. He welcomed Jews from Poland into his section of the city, he proposed a resolution for Irish freedom at the 1916 Democratic National Convention, and he supported Irish-American candidates for public office, including stalwarts like James Michael Curley, John F. Fitzgerald, and David I. Walsh. So upright was his course of action that he brought about the defeat of Joseph C. Pelletier, a prominent Knight of Columbus, as District Attorney of Suffolk County after the latter had been disbarred by the Supreme Judicial Court. Lomasney was buried in Holy Cross Cemetery in Malden, and Boston honored him by naming Lomasney Way for him.

*See* Boston

Leslie G. Ainley, *The Boston Mahatma* (Boston, 1949).
Joseph F. Dinneen, *Ward Eight* (Boston, 1947).
Matthew T. Rafferty, "The Disappearance of Martin Lomasney" (B.A. Thesis, Williams College, 1994).

VINCENT A. LAPOMARDA, S.J.

## LOS ANGELES

"The only place in Ireland where a man can make a fortune is America," an Irish slogan asserts. In pursuit of that expectation as well as the lure of gold, Irishmen ventured to the promised land as part of the rush to California in 1849. Soon they were seeking the rich placer deposits and working the growing number of quartz mines. The majority were young, single, male and grateful to have escaped the famine at home. They were greeted by sympathetic neighbors who shared the sentiments expressed in the *Alta California* in April 1849, which urged commiseration and sympathy for the hungry of Ireland.

Irishmen had been welcomed to California even before the advent of the young argonauts of 1849. In 1795 a ship under the command of Irishman Joseph O'Cain visited Santa Barbara during a sea otter expedition. O'Cain returned later that year aboard a British craft after a typhoon had destroyed his vessel in the Pacific. Although denied residency by the Spanish governor, the undaunted O'Cain returned in 1813 sailing his own ship, the *O'Cain,* which plied the California waters for the next three years.

In 1814 the Irish sailor John Milligan, or Mulligan, having contracted scurvy, was forced to leave his ship, the *Todd,* at Monterey. Along with fellow crew member, John Gilroy, a Scotsman, he was allowed by the colonial authorities to become a permanent resident of California. A weaver by trade, Milligan, for whom Mulligan's Head in the Salinas Valley is named, soon became proficient in Spanish and served as occasional interpreter.

In 1843 surveyor Jasper O'Farrell arrived from County Wexford, Ireland. Noted for accuracy of his surveys, O'Farrell was appointed official land surveyor by Governor Manual Micheltorena. In payment he was granted a ranch in Marin County. In the ensuing years he surveyed 21 Mexican land grants including the 133,440-acre Rancho Margarita y las Flores for Governor Pio Pico in 1845 and Rancho San Jose in 1846, as well as executing the official survey of the bustling town of San Francisco.

In 1844, in an effort to stimulate greater Irish settlement, Vice-consul James A. Forbes secured from Californio leaders the endorsement of a plan of settlement headed by a young Irish priest, Eugene MacNamara, to bring 10,000 Irish immigrants to the San Joaquin Valley. The consequent doubling of the non-Indian population, it was felt, would serve to strengthen Roman Catholic institutions, which would act as buffers against the usurping Americans. The provincial assembly in session at Los Angeles approved the request on July 6, 1846. The grant of 3,000 square leagues extending across the eastern half of the San Joaquin Valley was approved within the week by Governor Pio Pico. But the project died aborning, for on July 7, American forces hoisted their flag over Californios' capitol at Monterey. The invading Americans secured claim to all of Alta California as a result of the United States' victory over Mexico, credit for which was shared by General Stephen Watts Kearney, head of the First United States Dragoons.

During the war with Mexico, Irishman William Shannon, a San Diego resident, became commandant of that strategic port. With the conclusion of hostilities, he became a delegate to the California constitutional convention. It was Shannon who introduced the resolution outlawing slavery in California.

Another Irish participant in the war was Richard M. Den, M.D., a native of County Kilkenny who served as the chief physician and surgeon for the Mexican forces. Although he had difficulty receiving reimbursement from either faction, he treated both Californios and the American prisoners, including Benjamin D. Wilson and his party captured at the Chino Ranch near Los Angeles in 1846.

In 1836 Richard Den had followed his brother Nicholas, also a doctor, to California via India, Australia, Peru and Mexico. While both Den brothers were medical men, Nicholas' practice had been put aside in favor of administration of the 70,000-acre Rancho Dos Pueblos and service as alcalde of Santa Barbara. He also devoted himself to preserving the local mission and establishing a Catholic seminary in Santa Barbara. In later years Nicholas Den was one of the seven organizers of the Society of California Pioneers.

While the recently arrived Richard Den was still a guest at his brother's ranch, he was summoned by the townsfolk of Los Angeles. There he successfully performed several operations. This resulted in the citizens' earnest entreaties that he become the permanent physician of the town. With the exception of a brief

sojourn in the gold fields and a decade's absence to administer Rancho San Marcos, until 1895 Richard Den served as the "Nestor of the medical fraternity of Los Angeles," leading the local citizens to adopt the motto, "After God, Dr. Richard." Although viewed with affectionate esteem, Dr. Den also aroused a certain awe in his later days as he made his rounds astride a black charger, dressed in black and wearing a black felt hat atop "a clustered mass of wavy hair as white as snow."

The Los Angeles Census of 1836 lists Daniel Ferguson as the sole Irish resident. But twenty-seven Irishmen, including a dozen soldiers, are listed in the first United States Census of Los Angeles in 1850. An analysis of that enumeration and those of 1860 and 1870 reveals that, as they accumulated capital, local Irish settlers shifted from service and semiskilled occupations to agriculture. More than one-third owned farms by 1870. However, as early as 1857 Irishman Matthew Keller held title to 13,316 acres of Rancho Topanga Malibu Sequit.

Irishmen were featured prominently in the various county histories published in the 1880s and 1890s. Foremost among these new elite was Judge H.K.S.O'Melveny who arrived with his family in November 1869, was elected county judge in 1872 and was appointed to the Superior Court in 1887. Another was public servant Andrew Boyle who in the 1860s built the first brick home on the bluffs east of the town later known as Boyle Heights.

Marching in the city's centennial parade in 1881 were representatives of the Ancient Order of Hibernians organized by the Irish of Los Angeles six years earlier. The group succeeded the earlier St. Patrick's Benevolent Society organized in 1870. The fate of Irish political prisoners was of particular concern to another local Irish group, the 80-member Irish Literary and Social Club. Other residents joined the Irish Temperance Society headed by Patrick Connelly. Members of these organizations were the Irish grocers, vineyardists, and orchardists who by the 1880s had become part of the community of Los Angeles.

In 1870 at least 222 of the 476 Irish-born residents were listed in the *Great Register of Voters,* which reveals that many of them had also become public servants. Former mountain merchant Edward F. Spence served in the California Legislature and even earlier as treasurer of Nevada. In subsequent years, Irishman Henry King, beginning in 1879, served two terms as Los Angeles police chief. Richard A. Ryan was tax assessor and William B. Lawlor held the post of justice of the peace.

Most notable among them was John G. Downey, born in County Roscommon in 1827. He arrived in the California gold fields in 1850, after attending Latin school in Baltimore, serving an apprenticeship in Washington, D.C., and working as a druggist in Cincinnati. A brief interlude in the Mother Lode was followed by a move to Los Angeles where Downey, in partnership with Dr. James P. McFarland, opened the town's first drugstore. The success of the operation permitted the ambitious young newcomer to acquire land including the Santa Gertrudis Ranch where he engaged in cattle and sheep ranching.

Having served several local offices, including collector of the port, superintendent of lighthouses and the local disbursing agent for the U.S. Treasury Department, Downey was elected to the state assembly in 1856 and lieutenant governor three years later. Four days after Downey's victory, Governor Milton S. Latham, who had been elected to the U.S. Senate, resigned, making Downey at 32, California's youngest governor. His leadership in that office was a critical force in keeping California in the Union ranks, although the majority of Downey's fellow Democrats were secessionists. Firm in his political convictions, he delivered six volunteer regiments to the Union cause.

Governor Downey garnered admiration across the state for his integrity and the sound management of his administration. He countered legislative cabals with a firm veto and, in the process, assured the future of private commerce along the city front of San Francisco. As a correspondent for a New York newspaper wrote: "By his firmness, he has saved the state millions of dollars . . . and discomfitted the whole hungry crew of schemers, plunderers and hounds."

Downey's career after serving as governor was equally successful. He profitably subdivided his lands into residential properties and created the city of Downey. He was a key organizer of the Los Angeles City Water Company and his two-block-long Downey Block at Main and Temple streets became the city's shopping center. His many philanthropies included the gift of a tract of land as the site of the University of Southern California.

Three other Irishmen were important in transforming Los Angeles from a town into a city. In 1896, U.S. Senator Stephen White successfully checkmated Collis P. Huntington of the Southern Pacific Railroad. The powerful member of the Big Four who had constructed the western link of the transcontinental railroad, wanted the federal government to construct a deep water port at Santa Monica, to which the Southern Pacific would have exclusive access. Senator White, the son of Irish immigrants, represented his fellow citizens of Los Angeles in seeking construction of a harbor at San Pedro free of the Southern Pacific's control. As the battle raged for more than six years, White's keen intelligence, knowledge of the law and masterful strategy proved equal to Huntington's wealth and political influence. In the final phase of the struggle, a committee of engineers, created as a result of legislation proposed by White, unanimously favored the San Pedro site. Senator White turned aside Huntington's last-ditch effort to foil the construction of the harbor at San Pedro and construction began in 1899.

Oil was another critical element in the economic development of Los Angeles as Edward L. Doheny demonstrated. Born in Wisconsin of Irish parents, Doheny arrived in Los Angeles in 1892 having ventured westward first as a government surveyor and later as a miner at the various mineral strikes which dotted the West. In Los Angeles he soon noticed the ubiquitous *brea* or tar, especially near Westlake Park. With Charles H. Canfield he leased a nearby section and, using makeshift tools, began to dig, hitting lethal natural gas at 50 feet and an impressive gusher at 600 feet.

Inspired by Doheny's triumph, Angelenos began drilling for oil in their backyards and in empty lots. As a result, by 1897 two thousand wells dotted the landscape in a half-mile swath reaching from Doheny's oil derrick to Elysian Park. His uncanny talent for finding oil led Doheny across California and into Mexico. The result was an enviable prosperity marred by political controversy over the leasing of the federal government's oil reserves at Elk Hills and personal tragedy before his death in 1935. His many philanthropies benefitting higher education and the Roman Catholic archdiocese permanently enriched Los Angeles.

A burst of urban growth was generated by another Irishman who understood the need for water in the West. William Mulholland, born in Dublin in 1855, arrived in Los Angeles in 1876 after sailing the seas and treking across a continent as far south as Panama City. The citrus groves and vineyards of the small town captured his imagination. Mulholland determined to settle down and was soon employed as a ditch tender. By 1878 he was in the employ of the Los Angeles City Water Company where the strapping, self-educated Mulholland was soon made foreman. When the city assumed operation of the water company, Mulholland was named chief and undertook the construction of the first long-distance, gravity flow aqueduct in the United States, which he completed ahead of schedule and under budget. Angelenos eagerly responded to his laconic invitation uttered upon the arrival of Owens Valley water in 1913: "There it is. Take it." Although the collapse of the St. Francis Dam, causing the death of 385 in 1928, for which "the Chief" unjustifiably assumed full responsibility, clouded his later years, Mulholland is remembered for his accomplishments, his keen Irish wit and his wideranging knowledge on a variety of subjects.

In June 1897 Joseph Scott alighted from the train at the Los Angeles station. Within ten months he was admitted to practice at the Los Angeles Bar. Scott later headed the Chamber of Commerce and served on the board of education. Through his mother, a native of County Wexford, Scott inherited an abiding interest in Ireland, staunchly supporting the cause of Irish nationalism. With the Rev. Peter Yorke of San Francisco, he organized statewide support for the Friends of Irish Freedom. Along with John Byrne, a native of County Wicklow, he helped shelter exiles and kept Irish nationalism alive despite press opposition. The *Times* described the independence movement as a "tragiccomedy." When Irish President Eamon de Valera visited Los Angeles, he and Scott were rebuffed by the mayor, and the Shrine Auditoreum was closed to them. Scott remained undaunted.

During sixty years of service as an attorney, Scott also forged uncommon links between the secular power structure and the local Irish hierarchy of the Catholic Church. The leadership of the local church by first- and second-generation Irishmen began in 1917 with the administration of Archbishop Joseph Cantwell and continued with Francis Cardinal McIntyre, Timothy Cardinal Manning and Roger Cardinal Mahoney. Over the decades Irish priests have continued to represent a significant portion of the secular clergy. There are also a number of Irish-based religious orders. The activities of Irish-based orders in Los Angeles range from teaching to social work in hospitals and prisons, and administration of charitable institutions. Among them are the Columban Fathers formed in County Clare, the Sisters of Charity of Ireland, the Presentation Order and the Sisters of St. Louis.

Between the turn of the century and World War I, increasing numbers of immigrants crossed the seas and ventured across a continent to share in the orange blossom dream of Southern California. Arrivals from Ireland worked in a variety of endeavors, including the emerging film industry. Among the cinema luminaries Irish by birth or descent are Pat O'Brien, Barry Fitzgerald, Irene Dunne and James Cagney. Others are Spencer Tracy, Maureen O'Sullivan, Dan Daily, Fred MacMurray, and Tyne Daly. More stars are Sean Penn, Aiden Quinn and Mel Gibson. They represent a significant portion of an industry which has significantly contributed to the prosperity of California since the 1920s.

On the threshold of the Great Depression, the census of 1930 listed 39,792 Irish residents of Los Angeles County. Despite the economic gloom of the 1930s and of the war years which followed, on festive occasions the local Irish congregated at such watering holes as Tom Bergin's or O'Shaugnessey's, or gathered for corned beef at Dinty Moore's, a downtown landmark since 1906, when it opened as a private club for baseball enthusiasts.

Today the Irish community numbers more than 20,000 Irish-born residents among the millions who claim some ties to Ireland. The newcomers have come to Los Angeles, which some describe as the quintessential post-modern city, in pursuit of employment opportunities in emerging biotech, media and cyber-based industries, among others. These have been identified by such private employment clearinghouses as the Industrial Development Agency of Ireland located in Santa Monica, one of several agencies lending cohesiveness to the local Irish community.

Although no Irish newspaper is currently published in Los Angeles, *The Irishman* published in San Francisco, along with several Irish radio programs, covers events throughout the state, including such events as the Rose of Tralee Pageant where a local representative is chosen to attend the pageant's finals in Ireland. St. Patrick's Day news traditionally reports the southland's several parades—in Los Angeles, Pasadena and Beverly Hills, along with the traditional Gaelic Mass celebrated at Holy Trinity Church at San Pedro.

The *Irish Cultural Directory* lists the many musical groups playing individually or for contra and ceili dances. Classes devoted to the music, song, folklore and literature of Ireland are available at various centers and departments, particularly at UCLA and California State University Fullerton, as well as from private organizations including The Gaelic Society and the Tara School of Irish Dance. Other Los Angeles groups include the American Irish Foundation, the Irish-American Cultural and Historical Association, the Shamrock Club, the Society of the Friendly Sons of St. Patrick, several branches of the Ancient Order of Hibernians and the Irish American Bar Association, among many others. More specialized groups include the Irish Northern Aid Committee, the Irish Forum and the Ulster-American Heritage Foundation.

Ireland's Own Social and Athletic Club is but one of many sports clubs and activities which constitute one of the most active manifestations of Irish culture to be found throughout the area and give public expression to an ethnic constituency which is deeply rooted in the history of the Los Angeles community.

*See* California; Cinema, Irish in

Geoffrey P. Mawn, "*Agrimensor y Arquitecto:* Jasper O'Farrell's Surveying in Mexican California," *Southern California Quarterly* LVI (Spring 1974): 1–12.

Robert Moes, "The Brothers Den," *Southern California Quarterly* LXXII (Summer 1990): 83–118.

Harris Newmark, *Sixty Years in Southern California, 1853–1913* (Los Angeles, 1990).

Timothy J. Scarborough, "American Recognition and Eamon De Valera: The Heyday of Irish Republicanism in California, 1920–1922," *Southern California Quarterly* LXIX (Summer 1987): 133–50.

Thompson and West, *The History of Los Angeles County, California* (Berkeley, California, 1959).

GLORIA RICCI LOTHROP

# LOUISIANA

## COLONIAL LOUISIANA

In 1759, sixty years after the French established a fort at Old Biloxi on the hostile northern shore of the Gulf of Mexico, the victory of the British at Quebec terminated French imperial presence on the North American continent. In New Orleans and in Louisiana west of the Mississippi, the Spanish succeeded the French and the Catholic Church continued as an established religion. Thus when Charles III sent the Irish-born General Alexander O'Reilly to restore Spanish rule and prestige after the Creole revolt of 1768, this governor would also be much concerned about church matters. His agenda, formulated with the help of Capuchin Superior Father Dagobert, called for the establishment of eleven new parishes and their effective staffing with eighteen priests throughout the colony. Clearly, O'Reilly was a religious reformer who was convinced that only a Louisiana with a strong Catholic presence would be an effective Spanish colony. Although O'Reilly did not remain in Louisiana to implement the religious, political, and economic reforms he initiated, Spanish governors established eleven parishes within the boundaries of the present state of Louisiana.

Although O'Reilly's stint in Louisiana was brief, the reforms he initiated helped to create a climate attractive to Irish adventurers who were denied opportunity in oppressed Ireland. Two of these came to colonial Louisiana by way of Philadelphia. Oliver Pollock (1737–1823), merchant and shipmaster, had come to New Orleans before O'Reilly and had married Margaret O'Brien in St. Louis Church in 1768, signed a contract with O'Reilly to supply the Spanish garrison with flour. Later during the American Revolution, he was with Governor Bernardo Galvez in the Gulf Coast engagements against the British at Baton Rouge, Mobile, and Pensacola, and as the American congressional agent at New Orleans, he supplied George Rogers Clark in the Old Northwest. His efforts for the American cause occasioned bankruptcy but brought him posthumous recognition as an Unknown Patriot. The other mercantile adventurer, Daniel Clark (1766–1813), was notorious rather than unknown. His uncle of the same name had preceded him, and Daniel Clark the Younger joined his uncle's firm in 1786, became a partner a year later and thus embarked on a remarkable career during which he accumulated an enormous fortune through speculation in real estate after the New Orleans fire of 1788. Politically, he served both the Spanish colonial government as consul and that of the Territory of Orleans as elected delegate to the ninth and tenth Congress. His reputation was tainted by rumors of involvement in the mysterious Burr Conspiracy and a duel with Governor W. C. C. Claiborne. Posthumous fame came when General Andrew Jackson used his home as his New Orleans residence when he arrived to defend the city late in 1814; and posthumous notoriety when his daughter Myra Clark Gaines, whom he never acknowledged, and her descendants claimed, in endless court suits, to be his legitimate heirs. The succession was not settled until 1890.

## ANTEBELLUM LOUISIANA

Bishop Luis Penalver y Cardenas was appointed to the See of Louisiana and the Floridas in 1793 but departed for Guatemala in 1801. Because of the endless Napoleonic wars, the infant diocese remained without a bishop until 1815. The result was administative chaos. This in the midst of a population explosion: refugees from Santo Domingo, Americans from the Old Southwest, and, increasingly, immigrants from Ireland. At the same time clerical numbers decreased; even the Irish missionaries, whose financial support had depended on the Spanish court, departed. Only three were active in Louisiana when Jackson defeated the British at New Orleans, and the Coalition's defeat of Napoleon at Waterloo brought peace. In Rome the Congregatio de Propaganda Fide appointed Louis William DuBourg bishop of Louisiana who, in turn, recruited Italian missionaries for his vast diocese.

## POLITICS

Given later identity of the Irish with the Democratic party, it is ironic to note that the recognized early leader of the Irish in Louisiana politics was Judge Alexander Porter, an aristocratic Whig sugar planter. His biographer has commented that "his political opponents made capital of the fact that 'Paddy' Porter did not possess all the attributes of a paddy" (Stephenson, *Alexander Porter*, 134). Porter came to America after his father was executed for suspicion of involvement in the 1798 United Irishmen Rebellion. When the young Alexander was studying law in Nashville, General Andrew Jackson urged him to seize the opportunity available in the Louisiana Territory. Much later he would tell an audience of successful Nashville gentry how he bid adieu to his friends, threw himself on a flat boat, and descended the river to make his fortune. Financially successful both as a lawyer and as a sugar planter in the southern bayou country (the site of his plantation on Bayou Teche is still called Irish Bend), Porter played a role in writing the state constitution of Louisiana in 1812, served as United States senator and, in general, enjoyed the role of a kingmaker in the state Whig party. He mentored another Irish lawyer-cum-sugar planter, Edward Douglass White, a United States congressman both prior to and after his term as Whig governor of Louisiana (1835–1839). He was father of a namesake who would become Chief Justice of the Supreme Court.

In Ireland, nationalists sought recogniton for Ireland as a sovereign state. The Irish in Louisiana echoed this determination very early. In 1809 at the first St. Patrick's Day celebration, among the distinguished guests were the political leaders of the Orleans Territory, including Governor W. C. C. Claiborne. The traditional seventeen toasts were offered to the honor of Ireland, America, George Washington, Louisiana, the Harp of Ireland, etc. A volunteer toast by Thomas Bolling Robertson, the Virginia-born friend of President Thomas Jefferson who had appointed him secretary of the Territory expressed a sentiment dear to Irish-American nationalists: "The people of Ireland: May they be as successful in establishing their own independence as they were conspicuous in aiding the accomplishment of the independence of the United States."

The participants were so pleased with this initial celebration that they formed a St. Patrick's Day Club. After the War of 1812 the Hibernian Society absorbed the St. Patrick's Day group and organized the celebrations (*Louisiana Gazette,* March 21, 1809. Quoted in Niehaus, *Irish in New Orleans,* 12).

Judge James Workman, a native of Cavan, Ireland, came to Louisiana in 1804 and became the most outstanding of the pre-1830 local Irish, largely because of his association with the Hibernian Society. He was the driving force behind the society and served as its president from the first meeting in 1817 until his death in 1832. Although the benevolent dimension of this institution was never obscured, the nationalistic and social components were also always equally visible. The presence of Governor Jacques Villere, United States Senator James Brown, and state officials at the 1819 anniversary banquet suggests the prestige of the organization.

Among the early Irish, who arrived in Louisiana with nothing except their wits and a determination to make the best of economic opportunities on a frontier, Maunsel White was remarkably successful. A native of Tipperary, White came to New Or-

leans from the Falls of the Ohio on a flatboat two years before the Louisiana Purchase. Starting as a clerk at the age of seventeen, he quickly mastered the commission business and had his own firm by 1808. A competent captain of a volunteer regiment at the Battle of New Orleans, he attracted the attention of Jackson and functioned as his cotton agent until the general's death in 1845. Identifying with the upstream American section, he was a leading promoter in the 1830s of the New Basin Canal, a link to Lake Pontchartrain dug through the swamps by Irish immigrants and accepted as the antebellum infrasructure having the greatest impact on local transportation prior to the 1850s railroad boom. Wealthy as a result of commission business, banking, and land speculation, White joined the caste of classical southern aristocrats by purchasing and managing four sugar plantations. It was as successful sugar planter that Colonel White was praised as an inspiration for later immigrants and, at the same time, portrayed as representative of the mind of the Old South. He died in 1863 at the age of eighty, on the eve of the collapse of the slave civilization with which he identified. The majority of the New Irish, those after 1820, were Roman Catholics and increasingly came from Liverpool on cotton ships. And because of the steamboat, the cotton gin, and new techniques for refining sugar, those who took advantage of the Liverpool-New Orleans connection came to a Gulf and western state which was booming. In 1810 the census recorded a state population of 76,556; the 1830 census, 215,739. In 1840, with a population of 102,193, New Orleans was the third largest American city, just a tad smaller than Baltimore.

Louisiana church historians agree that Bishop Antoine Blanc's appointment in 1835 was a turning point. For twenty-five years Blanc dealt effectively with the many problems at hand, in particular the need for parishes and clerical and religious personnel. His response to the needs of the Irish is our concern.

An exceptional Irish initiative was the founding of St. Patrick's on Camp Street in the heart of the American district. As it dates from 1833, it is recognized as the second Catholic parish in New Orleans. St. Patrick's would have been special simply because of its foundation date and its location. Its anecdotal history is associated with James Ignatius Mullon, its pastor from 1835 until his death in 1866. It was Father Mullon who built the imposing church building which proudly served as a pro-cathedral while St. Louis Cathedral was being rebuilt. It was Father Mullon who built a school, a hall, and supported an orphanage. He was the defender of the Irish in the crises of the 1850s. He was the kind of churchman the Irish Catholic community in antebellum New Orleans needed.

The Irish brick-and-mortar priests in the immigrant districts had a more difficult task than Mullon, for St. Patrick's was not a parish of well-to-do refugees. Bishop Blanc, in 1848, asked Father Cornelius Moynihan to build a church for Irish immigrants in the Third District (strictly speaking, the Third Municipality—until 1852 when the three municipalities were reincorporated and the contiguous city of Lafayette annexed). Sts. Peter and Paul underwent the customary construction pattern of a temporary wooden church, replaced in time by an imposing, indeed, monumental structure. Its Hibernian complexion was guaranteed by a succession of Irish pastors. The founding pastor was succeeded by J. D. Flanagan; when Flanagan died, Joseph Hanrahan succeeded.

In the upstream riverfront section of the city of Lafayette, the Fourth District after annexation, the Irish St. Alphonsus was not only the counterweight to the German St. Mary's Assumption, it was, to the amazement of twentieth-century students of either ethnicity or urban development, built directly across the street. Excellent studies of the ministry of Irish Redemptorists recount their heroic efforts during the l850s: the decade of the 1853 yellow fever scourge when one out of five Irish in this southern port died, the time of Know-Nothing intimidation, and the years when rumors circulated that the immigrant neighborhoods were conspiratorial hotbeds of abolitionism. Among the Irish, Redemptorist Father John B. Duffy became the priest hero. Like his confreres, he paid his dues during the epidemic. His reputation allowed him to be the force behind the construction of a new St. Alphonsus and a new school.

Pre-1855 Irish workers settled in another area. Archbishop Blanc commissioned Jeremiah Moynihan to establish St. John the Baptist parish in the back-of-town section near the city terminal of the New Basin Canal, a flood-prone area. In New Orleans the latest poor were living at the edge of the natural levee. Father Jeremiah Moynihan experienced achievements and setbacks. At first, successes: he replaced his small wooden church with a larger but still temporary structure, he recruited Irish Dominican Sisters who came to St. John the Baptist on the eve of the Civil War. The setbacks came during Reconstruction, specifically after the Panic of 1873. Because he persisted in plans for a monumental church, the parish was burdened with a debt that Moynihan could not finance, and he resigned.

Among religious superiors in Ireland (and other countries) New Orleans had a reputation as the most unhealthy city in the United States. There was a reluctance to send personnel to southern Louisiana "to die of yellow fever." By the same token there was a desperate need for organized charity, especially among the newly arrived immigrants. Sisters of Charity from Emmitsburg, Maryland arrived in 1830 to staff an orphanage. They were aided by the city's most famous philanthropist, Margaret Gaffney Haughery. This Irish-born widow who came to New Orleans in 1835 contributed her profits from a dairy and and pre-Civil War bakery to underwrite the following and similar institutions: St. Theresa Asylum, St. Elizabeth Asylum, and St. Vincent's Infant Asylum.

### THE IRISH VOTE

Although the Irish vote was a political factor in Louisiana and New Orleans during the Adams-Jackson campaign of 1828, the gubernatorial election of 1834 between Whig Edward Douglass White and Democrat John B. Dawson is remembered as a landmark in the political history of Louisiana. The press engaged in personal vilification, White being denounced as the creature of the "Irish foreigner" Porter, and after winning the election by a vote of 6,065 to 4,149, White was accused of delivering the state to the domination of foreigners. This angry frustration led to the formation of the Louisiana Native American Association with the Nativist William Christy as first president and leading organizer. A historian of Jacksonian Democracy in Louisiana refers to "its heritage of years of divisiveness and violence" as a cause of the division of New Orleans into three municipalites in 1836, and as poisoning all ethnic relationships (Joseph R. Tregle, "Edward Douglass White," 13–118, in Joseph G. Dawson, ed., *The Louisiana Governors From Iberville to Edwards,* Baton Rouge, 1990).

As the number of Irish voters increased, they were increasingly courted by Democratic leaders, especially John Slidell.

After the violent intimidation in the 1850s by Know-Nothing thugs, the Democratic party became the unqualified home of the Irish voters. Although he was a sugar planter and thus economically linked with the Whigs, Colonel Maunsel White remained a Democrat, being courted and lauded by Democratic editors until his death in 1863.

During the antebellum Louisiana years, Irish-American nationalism focused on three aspects of Ireland's history: Daniel O'Connell and his struggle for Catholic Emancipation, the Great Famine, and the Young Ireland movement of 1848. Louisiana enthusiasm for O'Connell's Catholic Association was channeled into a New Orleans chapter of the Friends of Ireland. James Workman was president and he succeeded in obtaining subscriptions in late 1828 and early 1829 from such diverse non-Irish notables as Bernard Marigny, the Creole leader, and James Caldwell, the theater manager and businessman associated with the American Second Municipality. During the early 1840s the most active group was a chapter of the Irish Repeal Association.

At the news of the revolutions of 1848, Irish nationalism peaked. Louisiana Irish leaders organized the American League for the Redemption of Ireland. Collected funds were forwarded to New York to be "promptly transmitted to the proper agents in England or Ireland." The Emmet Club forwarded a remittance of $1,000 to William Smith O'Brien, the Young Ireland leader in Dublin. Despite the failure of Young Ireland, the exiles of 1848 became revered heroes, and the visits of Thomas Francis Meagher and John Mitchel were occasions of public receptions. There is no doubt that the attitude of the Louisiana Irish towards Ireland was romantic and, at times, unrealistic; however, it was generous and survived bitter disappointments.

Response to the Great Famine took many forms. The Irish Relief Committee solicited fifty thousand dollars. Although passage by remittance was not unheard of prior to the famine, extensive passage by remittance was a famine-inspired phenomenon. An attempt was made to form an Irish Union Immigrant Society; its failure broke the heart of the most persistent and articulate friend of the local Irish, J. C. Prendergast, the editor of the *Orleanian.* The Irish orphans became the concern of private philanthropy, including the two Catholic institutions, New Orleans Female Orphan Asylum and St. Mary's Orphan Boys Asylum. Margaret Haughery was depicted as the orphan's mother, protectress, friend, and benefactress. Sister Regis, a Charity nun, was similarly described.

### 1860

When the census enumerator visited the homes of New Orleans' 25,000 Irish during the summer of 1860, his questions could have stimulated many to reminisce and some to appraise. As an ethnic group they had for a generation witnessed the port as a wide-open backdoor to the American West: 10,000 immigrants poured through in the 1820s, 50,000 in the 1830s, 161,657 in the 1840s, and 250,000 from 1850–1855. Colonel Maunsel White, who perhaps had sold lots in the Third District to the socially mobile among them, could have explained the role of cotton in making Liverpool as the chief port of embarkation. They had heard about the mortality rate of the navvies who in the 1830s had dug the New Basin Canal. They had personally experienced the 1853 Yellow Fever epidemic, when deaths amounted to over 10,000, and the Know-Nothing thugs who had turned elections into days of terror. They knew that in the job market they had won the fight, Paddy and Bridget replacing blacks on the docks and as domestics. This labor factor had changed the demography of the port city.

## THE CIVIL WAR

Only the most politically sensitive could have perceived how the nominating conventions of 1860, the most fateful in American history, would impact their lives. In the subsequent election, the Irish voted for Douglas and against secession; John Slidell wrote to President James Buchanan after the election that "seven-eights at least of the votes for Douglas were cast by Irish and German who are at heart abolitionists" (cited in Niehaus, *Irish In New Orleans,* 157).

After Lincoln's election, sentiment changed quickly in New Orleans. Public support for secession became overwhelming. When Governor Thomas Moore called for volunteers to defend the decision for secession, the foreign-born German and Irish rushed to arms. Now the situation of the South was compared to Ireland. Three of the best known Irish priests, Fathers Mullon, Duffy, and Richard Kane blessed the flags of Irish companies, declaring that it was "right and proper for those about to go forth to battle for their country, its rights and independence, for civil and religious liberty" to carry a consecrated flag. When the Redemptorist provincial asked for volunteers to act as chaplains for the Confederate Army, the Irish-born Father James Sheeran, missioned at St. Alphonsus, leaped at the opportunity and was assigned to the Army of Northern Virginia. In 1862 he was arguing with northern prisoners of war that the North had no right to force the South to remain in the Union as England had no right to force Ireland to remain in a union with her.

When the cruel reality of the carnage of war deflated the patriotic enthusiasm, local Irish leaders began to suspect that the number of Irish sent to the front was disproportionate. The Irish-born editor of the *True Delta* accused the governor of assigning his friends to safe positions at home while he dispatched the Irish "with readiness" to fight the country's battles. With the occupation of the port on April 26, 1862, an era ended for New Orleans and for New Orleans' Irish. The war dragged on for three years for Irish companies in Virginia and elsewhere including northwest Louisiana.

## RECONSTRUCTION

The economic factor affecting the Louisiana Irish community was the rapid decline of New Orleans as a port of entry, a change which began even before the Civil War. In the first half of the 1850s, 60,000 Irish immigrants used New Orleans; during the second half, only 4,000. Undoubtedly the major cause was a transporation revolution—the dominant rail lines were from eastern ports to the Midwest, St. Louis becoming a terminal in 1857. New Orleans was no longer America's western capital and its upriver rival claimed to be the gateway to the West. The United States census recorded the consequence: in 1860 the number of Irish born in New Orleans was 24,398; in 1870, 14,398; in 1880, 11,709. The cumulative effect of the yellow fever epidemic of 1853, the northern railroads, the destruction of cotton plantations during the war and the consequent loss of jobs for dock workers, and the panic of 1873 were to make the survival of the Irish ethnic community problematic.

The deaths of Irish clerical leaders—St. Patrick's pastor Father James Mullon in 1866, the brilliant journalist Father Kane in 1873, Irish Channel priest Father Duffy in 1874, and Moynihan brothers Cornelius in 1879 and Jeremiah in 1884—obviously weakened the Irish role in the local church. Fortunately, these losses were more than offset by the arrival of two groups of Irish nuns who established vibrant institutions. In 1860, Father Jeremiah Moynihan recruited Irish Dominican nuns for his school at St. John the Baptist. These sisters soon established a select school or academy which at the end of the war moved to the suburban village of Greenville. At this location Dominican Academy flourished, even evolving into a Normal School. It was the preferred educational institution for the daughters of socially mobile second-generation uptown Irish.

The Mercy nuns began their association with the New Orleans Irish at the end of the 1860s. The Redemptorist complex, which already had the School Sisters of Notre Dame for their German school, was eager to obtain Mercy nuns from their motherhouse in St. Louis for the French and Irish schools. On Easter Sunday, March 28, 1869, six nuns arrived after ten days on the *Mollie Able.* One of the six was the talented Mother Austin Carroll who for the next generation was, in many ways, the voice of the Irish, especially of the most needy. She used her journalistic and financial skills to establish and finance the institutions needed: schools, orphanages, residences. Just as she had supported Sister Regis and the Daughters of Charity in the Reconstructions years, Margaret Haughery helped Carroll and the Mercy nuns with their charitable operations. Because of their independent enterprises and the associated fund-raising, the Irish Mercy nuns experienced conflict with the German priests in the Redemptorist complex and the French-born Archbishop Francis Xavier Leray and the Dutch-born Archbishop Francis Janssens. Typically, these antagonisms were explained as rooted in ethnicity and this did not improve matters.

Mercy nuns staffed schools in St. Michael's, the last Irish parish established in New Orleans. It was erected by Archbishop Odin in 1869 and wedged between St. Theresa downstream and the Redemptorist complex upstream. Thomas Heslin, the Irish seminarian, who had returned with Odin on the *Sainte-Genevieve,* the French ship which Odin had chartered to bring fifty priests, brothers, seminarians, and religious to New Orleans in 1863, became pastor of this parish two years after it was established. He remained at St. Michael's until his appointment as bishop of Natchez in 1889.

Serious studies of Louisiana's Reconstruction politics have been published recently, but the nonspecialist remains leery of what a specialist has called its byzantine complexities. As for Irish involvement, it can be asserted that they played a significant role in the first stage of Free State Louisiana; however, a prominent leader of the Irish Republican Club resigned in 1870 because he thought that the club was too radical. Black leaders thought that, unlike the Germans, the Irish "have for the most part sided with the Democratic party against us" (Ted Tunnell, *Crucible of Reconstruction: War, Radicalism, and Race in Louisiana, 1862–1877,* 163).

## THE GILDED AGE

What is notable about the Irish and the church in Louisiana is what did not happen. There was no greening of the church, no hibernization of the clergy or the hierarchy. The 1840s was a terrible decade for Ireland: the million victims of the Great Famine, the death of Daniel O'Connell, the failure of Young Ireland in 1848. For the overseas Irish some events were positive. The Irish bishops, in 1842, established All Hallows as a missionary seminary, a seedbed which provided over fourteen hundred priests

paternal grandparents had emigrated from County Cork in Ireland and after a brief stopover in Canada, settled in Boston. After attending St. Vincent's College in Los Angeles, he began studies for the priesthood at St. Patrick's Seminary in Menlo Park (near San Francisco) and concluded his theological training at the North American College in Rome. Lucey was ordained on May 14, 1916 in Rome.

He began his priestly ministry at St. Vibiana's Cathedral in Los Angeles, and while serving here and in other urban parishes, Lucey became involved in campus ministry work at the Newman Club at U.C.L.A. In 1921 Lucey was named the diocesan director of Catholic Charities, and while in this position, Lucey began his life-long commitment to the advancement of the Catholic Church's teachings on social justice. Also at this time, he began working to introduce the Confraternity of Christian Doctrine (religious education courses for Catholic children in public schools) into the diocese. In 1929, he was named a pastor in Long Beach, California and began hosting a radio program, "The Saint Anthony Hour" on which he popularized the church's social teaching in light of Pope Pius XI's recent social encyclical, *Quadragesimo Anno.*

### BISHOP IN TEXAS

On February 10, 1934 Pope Pius XI named Lucey ordinary of Amarillo, Texas, and on May 1 of that year Archbishop Amleto Giovanni Cicognani, apostolic delegate to the United States, ordained him a bishop at the cathedral in Los Angeles. Amarillo proved to be a stepping stone for Lucey, for in 1941 he was transferred and named the second archbishop of San Antonio. Continuing in his commitment to social justice, Lucey worked to secure rights for Mexican-American migrant workers living in southwest Texas and advocated stronger child labor laws. He was a strong supporter of labor unions and made sure that the archdiocese only employed unionized workers. He was a vocal defender of the economic initiatives of President Franklin D. Roosevelt and argued that the New Deal embodied the principles of the Church's social teaching. Lucey also worked for improvement in race relations and began integration of Catholic schools in the archdiocese well before the landmark Supreme Court decision in 1954 that outlawed segregation in public schools.

Archbishop Lucey was a close friend of President Lyndon Johnson and delivered the invocation at his inauguration in 1965. Lucey came out in full support of Johnson's war on poverty and served on the National Advisory Council at the request of the President. In contrast to his progressive views on economics and race relations, Lucey was a strong supporter of America's involvement in Vietnam and incurred sharp criticism from more liberal Catholics.

Although initially Lucey supported the spirit and work of the Second Vatican Council (1962–1965), he soon grew defensive and angry when his priests began demanding a share in the governance of the archdiocese in light of the council's teachings on collegiality. Tensions mounted between him and some younger clergy, and in September 1968 a group of priests petitioned the apostolic delegate for Lucey's removal. Although Rome did not remove him, an apostolic visitor was named to investigate the troubled situation in San Antonio. In order to avoid further controversy, Archbishop Lucey acted on a new church rule which called for bishops to retire at the age of 75 and resigned from office in June 1968. In retirement he took up again work in support of catechesis, but in 1972 a serious illness precluded further active pastoral ministry.

Like some other leading churchmen of this time, Archbishop Lucey was a strong supporter of the rights of the poor and disenfranchised but became frightened when lower clergy and laity tried to apply these same principles to ecclesiastical structures. He died in San Antonio on August 2, 1977.

*See* Texas

Saul Broner, *Social Justice and Church Authority: The Public Life of Archbishop Robert E. Lucey* (Philadelphia, 1982).

Stephen A. Privett, S.J. *The Catholic Church and its Hispanic Members: The Pastoral Vision of Robert E. Lucey* (San Antonio, 1988).

ANTHONY D. ANDREASSI

## LYNCH, PATRICK NEISON (1817–1882)

Third bishop of Charleston (South Carolina), Confederate emissary to the Holy See.

Patrick N. Lynch was born in Clones, Co. Monaghan, in 1817, the eldest son of Conlaw Peter Lynch and Eleanor MacMahon Neison Lynch. In 1819 the family emigrated to the United States and settled in Cheraw, South Carolina, where Conlaw prospered as a builder and businessman. Devout and close-knit, the Lynches were socially prominent and Cheraw's leading Catholic family. Manifesting intellectual brilliance and a priestly vocation at an early age, Lynch became a protégé of John England, Charleston's first bishop, and was educated in England's academy and seminary in Charleston. In 1834 Bishop England sent him to Rome to complete his education at the Urban College of the Propaganda Fide along with the younger Charleston-born James Andrew Corcoran, future theologian and Lynch's life-long friend. England placed both boys under the protection and guidance of Dr. Paul Cullen, rector of the Irish College and later cardinal-archbishop of Dublin. Lynch formed a lasting friendship with Cullen.

In 1840 Patrick Lynch was ordained, took a doctor of divinity degree and returned to Charleston. He served as an assistant in the cathedral and England's secretary until the bishop's death (1842). Under England's successor, Ignatius A. Reynolds, Lynch was rector of the cathedral and of the academy and seminary, editor of the *United States Catholic Miscellany* and supervisor of the building of the stately stone Cathedral of St. John and St. Finbar, designed by Patrick Charles Keely. During the Famine Lynch helped to raise some $20,000 for relief donated by South Carolina Catholics. After Reynolds' death, Lynch was consecrated bishop in 1858.

Proud of his Celtic heritage, Bishop Lynch was a vocal proponent of Irish Home Rule, and was active in Charleston's benevolent Hibernian Society. Solicitous of the needs of his immigrant faithful, many of them Irish, the bishop often served as their communications link with loved ones in the old country, and he founded the St. John's Savings Association, a sort of bank for immigrants' savings. A vigorous defender of Catholicism, he occasionally engaged in polemical debates in the press with leading Protestant clergymen like the Lutheran John Bachman and the Presbyterian James Henley Thornwell.

When the American Civil War came, Lynch, like all Southern bishops, supported the Confederacy. In 1861 he defended the Southern cause in a newspaper debate with his old friend, Irish-born Archbishop John Hughes of New York. He had a *Te Deum* sung in his cathedral when Fort Sumter fell to the Confederacy. During the conflict, Lynch, his clergy and religious—notably the Sisters of Charity of Our Lady of Mercy, founded by England—

worked tirelessly, tending to hospitalized servicemen, assisting impoverished families and comforting Northern prisoners of war irrespective of race or creed. In December 1861 an accidental fire destroyed his cathedral and residence, Catholic homes and institutions, all the immigrants' savings and much of Charleston. Further damage resulted from bombardment during the long siege of Charleston (1863–1865), and later, when the City of Columbia burned during General William T. Sherman's invasion of the state (1865).

In 1864 Lynch accepted appointment by President Jefferson Davis as Confederate commissioner to the States of the Church. His instructions were to try to win the Vatican's diplomatic recognition of the Confederacy and to influence European opinion in the South's favor. En route to Rome he sojourned in Ireland where he met with Catholic bishops, encouraging their opposition to the recruitment of immigrant Irishmen by the Union armies. In this he supported the efforts of Father John Bannon, Confederate agent in Ireland, and took Bannon to Rome as his chaplain. Although he had friendly conversations with Pope Pius IX and Papal Secretary of State Giacomo Cardinal Antonelli, the Holy See refused to grant diplomatic recognition, and Lynch was received only as a bishop making an *ad limina* visit. Pius did not wish to give support to the institution of slavery, nor to antagonize the United States, with which the Vatican maintained cordial diplomatic relations.

While in Rome he wrote a lengthy pamphlet on slavery in the Confederate States, condemning the international slave trade, while defending "domestic slavery" on grounds that were practical and social, not theological or scriptural. This tract was published anonymously in Italian, German and French editions, but not in English. Bishop Lynch had been brought up in a slaveholding family and regarded slavery as part of the normal social order. He owned about 95 slaves, acquired mainly in order to protect black Catholic families, and it is unclear whether they were personal or diocesan property. Lynch was a benign master, as these things went. The pamphlet came too late to have any significant impact on the war.

The Confederacy's collapse left Lynch stranded in Europe, and he had to obtain a pardon from President Andrew Johnson before he could return to Charleston at the end of 1865. He believed that no American diocese had suffered greater material losses than Charleston (over $316,000), and for the rest of his life he labored to raise money for rebuilding. He wrote and lectured for fees and traveled constantly to beg donations. The bishop sought to encourage postwar Irish emigration to his diocese, and wrote an open letter extolling South Carolina's attractions, for publication in *The Irish in America* (1868), by his friend John Francis Maguire, mayor of Cork and member of Parliament. Lynch also tried to provide for needs of black Catholics by founding churches and a school for them and bringing in the Mill Hill Fathers (Josephites) to work especially among African Americans. He believed that segregated institutions were advisable so as to avoid racial antagonisms.

Bishop Lynch attended the First Vatican Council, which he described in a series of articles in *The Catholic World*—in collaboration with Bishop (later Cardinal) James Gibbons. After the Church, Lynch's greatest love was science. He often wrote and lectured on scientific topics, made contributions in the emerging field of geology and was an early member of the American Association for the Advancement of Science. He played a prominent role in the life of the Catholic Church, Charleston and South Carolina. He died in Charleston in 1882 and is buried in the cathedral crypt.

*See* Civil War

---

Lynch Papers, Archives of the Diocese of Charleston; Richard C. Madden, *Catholics in South Carolina; A Record* (Lanham, Md.: University Press of America, 1985).

David C. R. Heisser, "Bishop Lynch's Pamphlet on Slavery: A Contribution to the Confederate Cause," *Catholic Historical Review,* LXXXIV/4 (1998).

DAVID C. R. HEISSER

met," was the comment of England's future King Edward VII upon meeting him.) There was a spectacular attempt to assassinate him in San Francisco in 1895 by a speculator who held Mackay responsible for his misfortunes, but he died peacefully in 1902.

---

John A. Barnes, *Irish-American Landmarks* (Detroit, 1995).

JOHN A. BARNES

## MAHER, MARGARET (1841–1924)

Domestic servant. Margaret Maher, a servant employed in the household of Emily Dickinson, is believed to have played a role in preserving the written works of one of America's greatest poets. Dickinson stored handmade books of her poems in Maher's trunk and Dickinson's niece reports that the poet asked her maid to burn these poems upon her death—which Maher did not do. The only adult image of Dickinson, a daguerreotype disliked and discarded by the family, was saved by Maher and made available when the first volume of poems went posthumously to press. Dickinson's mention of Maher—"Maggie is with us still, warm and wild and mighty"—evinces a strong affection for a woman with whom she spent many kitchen hours while the maid cooked and the poet baked. In addition to domestic work, Maher was a skilled nurse who tended to the health needs of the extended Dickinson family.

Margaret Maher emigrated by the mid-1850s and was part of the first large wave of Irish immigrants who settled in Amherst, Massachusetts, during construction of the local railroad, a project pioneered by the poet's father. Irish immigration altered the servant recruitment patterns in the U.S. Through much of the nineteenth century, especially in cities of the Eastern seaboard, it appeared as if every servant was Irish. Women found it easier than men to secure employment, and more young, single women were included in the Irish migrations than from any other European country. Live-in service created a cash surplus that allowed them to send money home to pay rents or finance the emigration of family members.

Maher emigrated with her siblings Michael, Mary, and possibly Thomas, from Killusty, on the western slopes of Sliabh Na mBan, in South Tipperary. It is believed, by Dickinson scholar Jay Leyda, that Margaret Maher returned to Ireland to accompany her aged parents when they emigrated. The Maher family joined forces with another Tipperary immigrant, Thomas Kelley, upon his 1855 marriage to sister Mary. The families set up housekeeping in property Kelley purchased from the Dickinson family, which would come to be known as Kelley Square. (Thomas Kelley worked for the Dickinsons and was the poet's chief pallbearer.) According to Maher's letters—preserved by her first employers, the Boltwood family—she and her brother Thomas planned to move to California in 1868, probably to join their gold mining brother, Michael. Family tragedies and illness disrupted Maher's intended departure and led her to take what she claimed was a temporary job in the Dickinson household, which became a tenure of thirty years (1869–1899). Maher also ran a boarding house with her sister and brother-in-law. She never married and is buried with her brother Thomas and their parents in St. Mary's Cemetery, Northampton, Massachusetts.

---

Jay Leyda, "Miss Emily's Maggie," *New World Writing* (New York: New American Library, 1953): 255–67.

Aife Murray, "Kitchen Table Poetics: Maid Margaret Maher and Her Poet Emily Dickinson" (*The Emily Dickinson Journal,* Fall 1996, Vol. 5, No. 2): 285–296.
Aife Murray, "Emily Dickinson's Irish Wake" (*Journal of Women in Culture and Society*), forthcoming.

Additional sources on nineteenth-century Irish domestic servants:
Hasia Diner, *Erin's Daughters in America* (Baltimore, 1983).
Faye Dudden, *Serving Women: Household Service in Nineteenth-Century America* (Middletown, 1983).

AÍFE MURRAY

## MAHER, TERESA (1824–1877)

Educator, administrator, religious leader. Teresa Maher was born in Carlow, Ireland, in 1824. Hers was a prominent Catholic family distinguished by several ecclesiastical leaders: Cardinals Paul Cullen and P. J. Moran, Father James Maher, and Teresa herself. She entered the Sisters of Mercy at Kinsale in 1845, becoming superior of the community nine years later. When the convent at Kinsale determined to respond to a request for Sisters of Mercy from Archbishop Purcell of Cincinnati, Teresa Maher led the band destined for the United States. They arrived in Cincinnati on August 18, 1858, and immediately began visitation of the sick and instruction of the ignorant. Soon the sisters had developed a day school, a night school, shelter for destitute women, and soup kitchens for the unemployed. Teresa herself led a group of sisters to nurse casualties of the Civil War at Pittsburgh Landing. Both there and, later, in Cincinnati, the sisters dealt with epidemics of small pox and cholera, respectively. In an unusual episode, Teresa Maher and the Sisters of Mercy in Cincinnati undertook fund-raising for the building of a "free church." The cornerstone for the Church of the Atonement was laid in September 1871, but within two years the sisters found it necessary to deed the church and property over to the Archbishop. According to early accounts, Teresa Maher was an accomplished organist, possessed of uncommon intellectual gifts, large-hearted, generous and trusting. One biographer states simply that "she combined the simplicity of a child with mature wisdom" (Carroll, Vol. 4, p. 309).

*See* Sisters of Mercy

---

Austin Carroll, R.S.M., *Leaves from the Annals of the Sisters of Mercy* (New York, 1895).
Kathleen Healy, R.S.M., *Frances Warde: American Founder of the Sisters of Mercy* (New York, 1973).

HELEN MARIE BURNS, R.S.M.

## MAINE

The first governor of Maine of Irish descent, Edward Kavanagh, the son of Irish immigrants from Wexford, served in 1843. The second, Joseph Brennan, whose parents were also Irish immigrants, was elected in 1978. In the one hundred and thirty-four years between those two events, the Irish in Maine experienced notable ups and downs. Their influence on a state bound in Yankee culture sometimes seemed negligible, sometimes substantial, sometimes quite threatening. The culture the immigrants brought with them shaped their impact and their own experiences. Roman Catholics and Protestants had different experiences; so did Gaelic speakers and English speakers. All were influenced by the environment in which they found themselves—a state that was largely rural, largely Yankee and Protestant, and, after the Civil war, predominantly Republican.

Mostly poor, and mostly Catholic, many Irish settled in urban areas and eventually joined the Democratic Party, putting themselves in a distinct minority. They were greeted by cycles of welcome and hostility. Immigrant Irish and later generations had to respond to the changing economic fortunes of the state—its development from trade and fishing and lumbering to industrialization and tourism to deindustrialization. They struggled for a balance between maintaining their own cultural traditions and adapting to new ones. Eventually, along with other immigrant groups, they began to change the face of Maine.

Individuals of Irish descent are the third largest group in Maine, following only the English and Acadians and French-Canadians. According to the 1990 United States census, about 18% of people in Maine claim Irish ancestry. In some areas such as the cities of Portland and Bangor, the percentage is substantially higher and the cultural presence is still striking. Nonetheless, in contrast to the case in nearby Massachusetts, the Irish in Maine have never constituted such a large bloc as to develop major political or cultural power. On the other hand, they have never been a small enough group to lose their cultural identity or to pass unobserved.

## MIGRATION PATTERNS

Maine's geographic position has been crucial in shaping the Irish experience. On the north and eastern edge of the United States it is bordered by the Canadian provinces of Quebec and New Brunswick and is close to Nova Scotia. In the eighteenth century individual Irish men and women came directly to Maine's many active small ports on the Atlantic coast. These included Scots-Irish Protestants as well as some Catholics. The Scots-Irish tended to settle individually in rural areas and to intermarry with the English settlers. In the nineteenth century waves of primarily Catholic Irish migrants came south from Canada and north from Boston. Although some of them became farmers and assimilated, in general they maintained a group identity.

From settlement to the present, Portland, Maine's largest city, situated on the southern coast, has served as a major entry point. However, because travel to British ports was cheaper than passage to the United States, especially before 1850, many Irish immigrants arrived at Halifax, Nova Scotia, or St. John, New Brunswick. Some of the Irish then migrated west or south to rural areas in Northern Maine and towns like Houlton or "downeast" to the area around Eastport or inland to the lumber town of Bangor. Consequently a large part of Irish immigration before 1835 settled more in rural areas and smaller cities.

One area of early Irish settlement was Lincoln county in the central coastal area of Maine. James Kavanagh (father of the future governor) and Matthew Cottrill migrated from Wexford in 1781. They went first to Boston and then, ten years later, to Maine (then part of Massachusetts).They established a sawmill and then a shipbuilding business and took the lead in developing a Catholic community in the area of the towns of Newcastle and Whitefield. St. Patrick's Church, now the oldest Catholic church in Maine, was built in North Whitefield in 1808. By 1830 Irish Catholics were about a quarter of Whitefield's population of about 2,000. By general accounts, their presence there was uncontroversial. Cottrill and Kavanagh were respected leaders in the state. Kavanagh's son Edward was elected to Congress in

1831. A supporter of Andrew Jackson, he later served as envoy to Portugal, then returned to Maine. He was elected to the state senate and later, as president of the Senate, succeeded to the governorship when the incumbent resigned. Winifred Kavanagh, his sister, shared his sense of service. In 1877 she gave $25,000 for the building of a Catholic school for girls in Portland.

In the 1830s an agrarian community was deliberately established in northern Maine as an effort to divert Irish immigrants from urban settlement to a rural life. Benedicta, which still maintains much of its original identity, was the brainchild of Bishop Benedict Fenwick of the Boston Diocese (which then included Maine). The Diocese purchased land in Aroostook County, one of the northernmost counties of Maine, and Irish families from Boston headed north. In the 1830s and 1840s it became a relatively successful farming community and a center for Irish Catholic life in the area.

By the late 1830s, however, a new wave of Irish were coming to Maine. Their settlement was directed by the economic imperatives of industrialization and urbanization. Construction projects in cities like Augusta, the capital, and the building of railroads and canals, like the Cumberland and Oxford between Portland and Sebago and Long Lake, were made possible by the recruitment of Irish labor. Portland and Lewiston gained Irish immigrants as a result of these projects and their location. At the same time Bangor, on the Penobscot River, and about half way between New Brunswick and Boston, attracted Irish labor, including river drivers, and became the center of the largest Irish population in the state. While Irish men worked primarily as laborers, single Irish women took jobs as domestics for middle-class Yankee families.

## THE FAMINE YEARS

The famine years of 1847–50 had a further dramatic impact. Both in terms of numbers and location, the desperate migrants of that period created new communities and new cultural dynamics. Although many continued to land in St. John, Halifax, and Quebec, and move downward, an increasing percentage came directly to the United States. Steamships from Liverpool to Boston or Portland brought greater numbers to southern Maine. Portland began to replace Bangor as the major site of Irish settlement. In Portland, Maine's largest city, the new immigrants found an established community which had opened its first Catholic church, St. Dominic's, in 1828. They created two Irish neighborhoods—Munjoy Hill which also had a small African-American community, and Gorham's Corner near the waterfront. There the Irish were the largest single group of immigrants in the mid- and late nineteenth century. The men found work in construction and as longshoreman. Women worked as maids in private homes and as laundresses. Some also made liquor, a practice that did not sit well with Maine's powerful advocates of "temperance." Faced with overcrowding, lack of sanitation, disease and poverty, the Irish found themselves increasingly the targets of anti-Catholic attacks.

The 1850s saw the growth of power of the Know-Nothing party and a spurt of violence directed against the Catholic church and Irish communities. Bangor had already experienced an anti-Irish riot in 1833. In Bath, a midcoast town, the old South Meetinghouse that had been rented for use as a Catholic Church was burned to the ground in 1854. In the north, in Ellsworth a mob tarred and feathered a Swiss-born Jesuit priest, Father John Bapst, for protesting the compulsory reading of the Protestant version of the Bible in public schools. Although this hostility focused on religion, it was directed against Irish immigrants and included cultural and class antagonism.

The Irish responded by rallying around the Church. Part of Portland local lore is a story of how a group of longshoreman spent a night in the basement of St. Dominic's church as it underwent reconstruction and they waited with bats in hand to ward off an attack (that never came). The Irish middle class and successful businessmen began to contribute to institutions such as schools, churches, and relief associations. They also went into politics and government to secure their position in local society. The Maine Irish also fought their way into American society. The Civil War saw large scale participation by Irish men. Bangor's all Irish militia unit became part of Company I of Maine's Fifteenth Infantry. A historian of the town of Houlton in northern Maine noted that Irish-Americans in that area played an outstanding part in the Civil War.

During the war, immigration continued. One incident, in 1864, speaks to the continued dangers of the voyage across the Atlantic. In February of that year the steamship *Bohemia,* sailing from Liverpool to Portland ran onto Alden's Rock, off Cape Elizabeth, Maine, and sank. Of the 218 passengers, 42, mostly Irish immigrants in steerage, drowned. The bodies of twelve were unclaimed and were buried in an unmarked grave in the Catholic cemetery in South Portland.

## Late Nineteenth-Century Patterns

Irish immigration continued throughout the nineteenth century and into the twentieth century. After the Civil War, mill towns like Westbrook and Rumford saw increased Irish populations. In Portland, the Irish were concentrated in two neighborhoods that had become predominantly Irish before the Civil War—Munjoy Hill and Gorham's corner. The latter was the center of the immigrant community and maintained a strong Irish identity. Many of the Irish who came to Portland were from Galway and were Gaelic speakers. As late as the 1920s, that language was still common in that neighborhood. As other Irish dispersed and took different jobs or found better housing, new immigrants filled the buildings on Center, Danforth and Pleasant streets. St. Dominic's church and school and the neighborhood public school provided centers for the community. Similar neighborhoods developed in other cities and towns. In Lewiston the original Irish housing was in the area near the gas works and in small wooden cottages in areas called "patches" including "Shingle Patch," an area hit hard by cholera in 1854.

In this period many Irish immigrant and working class neighborhoods suffered from high rates of illiteracy, violence, lack of municipal services including sanitation, and disease, including death in childbirth and infant mortality. In 1900 in a predominantly Irish ward in Portland, for example, first- or second-generation Irish women with children had borne an average of 5.3 per mother. Of these children, a quarter had died by 1900. One Irish born woman, fifty years old and widowed, had given birth to twelve children of whom only one survived. In response to these problems, the Irish themselves and urban reformers began to look for solutions. Three areas to which the Maine Irish turned for solutions and which they, to varying degrees remade, were religion, labor unions, and politics and government.

## The Catholic Church

Some Irish immigrants came as Protestants or joined Protestant churches, especially Congregationalist, after they arrived. Some of the Scots-Irish maintained their identity through Orange lodges, such as the Loyal Orange Order in Portland. Others found religion oppressive or irrelevant. For the majority of Irish immigrants and children of immigrants, however, the Roman Catholic church played a major role. The Irish, or to be precise, the Irish hierarchy, essentially controlled the Catholic Church in Maine for a hundred years. From the creation of the Maine Diocese in 1855 and the building of the cathedral in Portland, a series of Irish-American bishops provided strong, and generally conservative, leadership. The Irish dominance lead to serious conflict with the other Catholic groups, notably the French in cities like Lewiston and Biddeford. The conflict became most bitter between 1906 and 1913 when Bishop Louis Walsh engaged in a series of battles with French and Slavic Catholic communities in Maine. In addition to appointing Irish priests as pastors of predominantly French parishes, Walsh took a strong assimilationist position that the French feared would contribute to the loss of their language and culture. The conflict between the Irish and the French took place in other arenas as well—in economic rivalry and sometimes in the streets. This conflict left both groups vulnerable. It would take the rise of a mutual enemy in the 1920s—the Ku Klux Klan—to ease some of the animosity.

The bishops also tended to take conservative positions in terms of labor and women's rights. Bishop James Healy was a major opponent of the Knights of Labor in Maine in the 1880s. He threatened Catholic workers with excommunication if they joined what he saw as a secret society. In other ways, however, Healy presented a model of reconciliation. Born in Georgia, Healy was the son of a slave named Mary Eliza Clark and an Irish born plantation owner, Michael Healy, who sent him north to school. Eventually he went into the priesthood. Healy became Bishop of Maine in 1875 and served there until his death in 1900. William O'Connell then spent a brief period as bishop of Maine before moving on to Boston. He was succeeded by Walsh, who worked hard to build up the Catholic educational system in Maine. In 1946, Dennis Feeney became the first Maine-born bishop. He was the product of St. Dominic's parish in Portland. What the Bishops had in common, besides their ethnicity, was that they all combined to defend the Church from external threats with an interest in making the Church and the Irish more accepted as a part of the American and local communities.

Besides providing a bulwark against external enemies and serving spiritual needs, the church provided two important services to the Irish (and others). Many men and women in poor or working-class Irish communities, like Gorham's Corner in Portland, found in the priesthood and in religious orders opportunities for education and meaningful employment they could not receive elsewhere. On the local level, particularly before the government programs of the New Deal, and later in the 1960s, the parish and religious orders provided the major social service network for people in need.

Women's religious orders in particular played a major role in creating social welfare, health and educational institutions. In Portland, for example, the Quebec-based Sisters of Notre Dame initially staffed the Catholic schools. When they left in 1873, the Sisters of Mercy, an order founded in Ireland, took over the schools. Under the leadership of the Irish-born Sister Stanislaus Finn, they brought the Catholic orphanage back to Portland from the town of Whitefield. They also ran academies for girls. In 1915 with the leadership of Sister Mary Xaviera Toohey, a second generation, Maine-born Irish-American, they received a charter from the state which made St. Joseph's College in Portland for many years the only Catholic women's college in the state and the only one still existing today, now coeducational. The Sisters of Mercy also opened the first Catholic schools in Bangor, including St. John's school in 1865. Many of the Sisters of Mercy, and of other orders, were Irish immigrants. Others were from Irish families in Maine or other New England states. Nuns played a major role in health care throughout Maine. The Sisters of Mercy opened Queen's Hospital in Portland in 1918 and Mercy Hospital in 1942. Other orders that included Irish women were active elsewhere.

## Work and Unions

During the nineteenth century some Irish prospered, like the Kavanaghs and like James Cunningham in Portland, an immigrant who made his fortune in construction. However, most of the first- and second-generation Irish remained in jobs at the bottom end of the employment scale. Except for small numbers in farming, men were primarily employed as laborers or in some industries like paper or iron molding. In cities like Portland and Bangor they became the dominant group of longshore workers. In the post famine migration to Maine, single woman were a slight majority of immigrants. They were frequently employed as domestics and laundresses. Reflecting changes in Maine's economy, many were employed as chambermaids in hotels and in summer resorts along the coast in the state's increasing tourist industry. Women and men worked in canning factories from Machias to Portland. At the lowest end of the scale Irish women were the majority of rag pickers and sorters.

After 1900 new jobs opened up. Some American-born Irish women were employed as clerks, stenographers and telephone operators. In some of these jobs they faced discrimination: some department stores had signs in their windows saying "No Irish Need Apply." Educational institutions, Catholic, public and private, offered access to other jobs. While some Irishmen became doctors and lawyers, Irish women increasingly went into teaching and nursing. There too they met resistance. No Irish woman or man had been hired as a teacher in the Portland public schools until Daniel O'Connell O'Donoughue, a Civil War veteran and engineer, was elected to the school board in 1869. The presence of Irish and Catholic members on school boards clearly affected the number of Irish and Catholic teachers hired by the public schools. In some school districts in Maine, discrimination, aimed at French-Canadians as well as Irish, lasted into the 1950s. This led to the creation of Catholic institutions for teacher training and the creation of the Catholic colleges in Portland and Van Buren. Similarly in nursing, the creation of Catholic hospitals and nursing schools in Portland and elsewhere provided jobs for Irish nurses and doctors as well as health care for their communities.

Another avenue of economic improvement for the Irish and for other workers in Maine was the creation of unions. Although unions were not as successful in Maine as in some other states, some industries were actively organized beginning in the 1850s and 1870s and again in movements at the turn of the century and in the 1930s. Beginning before the Civil War and continuing throughout the twentieth century, the Irish provided leadership and membership for unions such as the Typographical Union (Maine's first), the Paper workers union, and some CIO unions in the 1930s. Irish dockworkers in effect were the Portland Longshoreman's Benevolent Society, a union formed in 1880. The first head of the Maine State Federation of Labor was Henry M. Donnelly of the Iron Moulders Union. The president of the Council in the 1990s was Charles O'Leary.

Despite the Bishops' injunctions, some of Maine's Irish were attracted to more radical unions including the Knights of Labor. Elizabeth Gurley Flynn's father, Thomas Flynn, migrated from Canada through Machias and worked in the quarries in Maine and participated in the ten-hour-day movement before heading on to New Hampshire and New York. Cora Smith was one of the Irish-American women leaders of the telephone workers who engaged in a successful strike, with other telephone workers in New England, in 1919. In later years second and third generation Irish played notable roles in the teacher's unions and in state employees unions.

The employment in the public sector fit in with the increasing Irish role in politics in Maine. Unlike the experience of the Irish in Massachusetts, in Maine they never became a dominant force or were able to construct powerful political machines. Their success came in some smaller cities where they were the majority or in cities like Lewiston when they were able to form alliances with the French. After the Civil War, the two most prominent figures were Peter Keegan, elected to the state legislature from Van Buren, and Daniel J. McGillicuddy, a mayor of Lewiston who, in 1910, was the second Irish Catholic in Maine elected to the U.S. Congress, (the first since Kavanagh in 1831) and the last until Joseph Brennan was elected in 1986.

## The 1920s

In Portland Irish political success was cut short by an alliance of "good government" reformers and the Ku Klux Klan. In 1923 both groups supported a successful referendum to change Portland's government from a mayor and council elected by districts to a city manager and at-large council. At the same time the school board was changed from election by districts to at-large election. The effect was to eliminate Irish and Jewish representation from both groups. The *Boston Herald* of September 7, 1923 reported the views of Eugene Farnsworth, the head of the Klan in Maine: "Public schools are being dominated by representatives of the Catholic church. . . . We will not permit Catholics on the school board anymore and . . . we will not permit teachers who are Catholics to hold those positions until they become Americans." In the subsequent at-large election both the Catholic and Jewish candidates for the school board were defeated. In 1924, Ralph Brewster, the Klan-supported Republican candidate for governor, was elected. However, the Democratic candidate received fifty percent more votes than any previous Democrat had received and he carried most of the major cities, except Portland.

The hostility may have reflected the influence the Irish and other non-Yankee groups had been gaining as well as the role in some cities of the Knights of Columbus, a group the Irish dominated. In addition to getting positions in government (the first Irish police chief in Portland was appointed in 1914) they also were helping reshape the government to meet the needs of poor and working people. Daniel McGillicuddy's proudest accomplishment in Congress was his introduction of a Workman's Compensation bill. On the local scene, the Irish joined with middle class Protestant women social workers and doctors to improve public education and public health. During the progressive era, Lillian O'Donahue ran Portland's milk station for children. Katharine L. Quinn was the first public health nurse in Portland and she became the supervisor of the department.

In 1936 Maine had the distinction with Vermont of being one of two states that voted against the reelection of Franklin D. Roosevelt as president. The support of the Irish Mainers for the

Democratic party and the New Deal highlights the position they and other minorities like Maine's French and Italian population had in a predominantly Yankee and Republican state. Maine's Irish found recognition in other ways. John Ford, the son of Irish born John Feeney and Barbara Curran Feeney, was baptized at St. Dominic's in Portland and grew up in an Irish neighborhood. The films he made in Hollywood, from *Stagecoach, Young Mr. Lincoln,* and *Grapes of Wrath* in the 1930s to *The Last Hurrah* in 1958 changed American film. Ireland and the Irish in America became integral parts of American culture. The Works Project Administration also added to the visibility of the history of the Irish experience in the United States and in Maine. The sinking of the *Bohemian* in 1864 was the subject of a mural painted by Alzira Pierce for a South Portland post office.

## 1940s–1990s

The Second World War and its aftermath saw cultural and demographic changes that reached Maine. Even as the Irish moved out of some of the ethnically defined neighborhoods (and sometimes out of state), Maine became more open to diversity. Joseph Brennan's political career was one sign. George Mitchell's was another. Change came faster in some areas than others. The first Irish Catholic president of a state college or university was not appointed until the 1980s, after the University of Maine system was created and had Patrick McCarthy as its chancellor from 1975–86. His grandfather, also Patrick McCarthy, had graduated from the University of Maine in 1909.

Joseph Brennan, who grew up on Munjoy Hill in Portland, was the most clearly identified and successful Irish-American political figure in recent Maine history. Senator George Mitchell's experience presents a different story. Mitchell was raised in Waterville by a mother who was a Lebanese immigrant and a father who was the orphan of Irish immigrants and adopted by a Lebanese family in Waterville. Mitchell was elected to the U.S. Senate in 1982 and reelected in 1988, where he served as majority leader. As chair of the Northern Ireland Peace talks he played a key role in the agreement reached in the spring of 1998. It was a fitting role—representing the hopes of creating a society where people of different religions and cultures can live together.

At the same time as cultural identities became more complex, the Irish in Maine began to rediscover their past and to bring it into the narrative of Maine's history. In 1980, Bartley Conley, a postal worker in South Portland, discovered the story behind the mural of the sinking of the *Bohemian.* A local Irish group raised funds to mark the collective grave with a Celtic cross with the names of the dead. In the 1990s the threatened closing of St. Dominic's church has brought increased urgency to the need for the recording and interpretation of the history of the Irish and other immigrant groups in Maine.

James Paul Allen, *Catholics in Maine: A Social Geography* (Syracuse University, Ph.D. diss., 1970).

Rita Mae Breton, "Red Scare: A Study in Maine Nativism, 1919–1925" (M.A. thesis, University of Maine, 1972).

Margaret J. Buker, "The Irish in Lewiston, Maine: A Search for Security on the Urban Frontier, 1850–1880," *Maine Historical Society Quarterly,* 13 (1973): 3–25.

Michael Coleman Connolly, "The Irish Longshoreman in Portland, Maine 1880–1923" (Ph.D. diss., Boston College, 1988).

Connolly and Grimes, "The Migration Link between Cois Fharraife and Portland, Maine 1880s to 1920s," *Irish Geography,* 22 (1992): 22–30.

Eileen Eagan and Patricia Finn, "From Galway to Gorham's Corner: Irish Women in Portland, Maine," in Polly Kaufman, ed., *Striving Beyond Expectations: Women in Maine 1850–1960* (University of Maine Press, 1999).

Edward Thomas McCarron, "The World of Kavanagh and Cottrill: A Portrait of Irish Emigration, Entrepreneurship, and Ethnic Diversity in Mid-Maine, 1760–1820" (Ph.D. diss., University of New Hampshire, 1992).

James Mundy, *Hard Times, Hard Men: Maine and the Irish 1830–1860* (Scarborough, Maine, 1990).

EILEEN EAGAN

## MAKEMIE, FRANCIS (1658–1707/08)

Colonial Presbyterian leader. Francis Makemie was probably born in 1658 in County Donegal, Ireland. He graduated from the University of Glasgow in 1682 and was ordained by the Laggan Presbytery as an American missionary. In 1683, Makemie sailed to America where he preached throughout Virginia, Maryland, and North and South Carolina, hoping to unite the nonconformist Protestant churches against their suppression by the Church of England. Lacking organization or support for his cause, Makemie turned to the mercantile business and land trade in which he was very successful. Makemie was married to the daughter of a rich merchant and inherited from his father-in-law a large estate at Accomac County, Va. There, Makemie and his wife settled on the Eastern Shore of Virginia where he was able to obtain a license to preach in two of his houses. The first nonconformist minister to be licensed under the Toleration Act of 1689, Makemie joined with six other Presbyterian ministers to form the first American presbytery at Accomack, Va. in 1706. In 1707 Makemie was charged with the crime of preaching on Long Island without a license, but defended himself admirably in court. With the help of William Nicoll, James Reignere, and David Jamison, Makemie was acquitted of the charges, but still forced to pay the court costs of both the defense and the prosecution. Makemie nevertheless continued to make the case for his cause by printing the sermon that led to his arrest and publishing a book that described his prison trials. Having gained a moral victory in the colonies, the dissenting churches continued to claim further freedoms under England's Toleration Act. Makemie died within a year after his prison ordeal, and continues to be regarded as a leading founder of the Presbyterian Church in America.

*See* Emigration: 17th and 18th Centuries; Scots Irish

L. P. Bowen, *The Days of Makemie* (1885).

———, *Makemieland Memorials* (1910).

C. A. Briggs, *American Presbyterianism* (1885).

Francis Makemie, *A Narrative of a New and Unusual American Imprisonment of Two Presbyterian Ministers: and Prosecution of Mr. Francis Makemie, One of Them, for Preaching One Sermon at the City of New-York/ by a Learner of Law, and Lover of Liberty* (Boston, 1707).

DANIEL J. KUNTZ

## MALONE, DOROTHY (1925– )

Actress. Born Dorothy Maloney on January 30, 1925, in Chicago, Illinois, of Chicago Irish parents. She married Jacques Bergerac in 1959; the couple had two children, Mimi and Diane.

During her acting career, Malone starred in such hit films as *The Big Sleep* (1946); *South of St. Louis* (1949); *Mrs. O'Malley and*

Dorothy Malone

*Mr. Malone* (1950); *Torpedo Alley* (1953); *Young at Heart* (1954); *Five Guns West* (1955); *Battle Cry* (1955); *Artists and Models* (1955); *Man of a Thousand Faces* (1957); and *The Last Voyage* (1960). In the 60s Malone gained the attention of a new generation with her starring role in the provocative and innovative television series, *Peyton Place,* and again in 1976 with the series, *Rich Man, Poor Man.*

J. Concannon and Frank Cull, *Irish American Who's Who* (New York, 1984).

Joseph Curran, *Hibernian Green on the Silver Screen* (Westport, CT, 1990).

EILEEN DANEY CARZO

## MALONE, SYLVESTER L. (1821–1899)

Pastor. Born in Trim, County Meath, Ireland on May 8, 1821, to Laurence and Marcella (Martin), Sylvester Malone came to America at age seventeen on the invitation of Rev. Andrew Byrne, pastor of St. James Church in New York City, who visited Ireland to recruit candidates for the priesthood around 1838. Byrne was later made first bishop of Little Rock, Arkansas. Malone arrived in Philadelphia in 1839 and began his studies at St. Joseph's Seminary, LaFargeville, Jefferson County, New York, for a year, continuing at Fordham when the seminary was transferred there. He was ordained Aug. 15, 1844 and assigned by Bishop John Hughes to a little church, St. Mary's, built in 1840 in Williamsburg, Brooklyn, to accommodate 500 congregants, in the town of about 5,000. Fr. Malone would continue to minister as pastor, until his death, throughout this parish of fifteen square miles, which extended from Brooklyn's Myrtle Avenue on the south, west to the East River, north to Astoria and east to Middle Village in present-day Queens County. In three years he paid off St. Mary's debt, had the parish well organized, and in 1847 began building the Church of St. Peter and Paul, Brooklyn, the first gothic church of the diocese, to accommodate the growing congregation. Malone chose as architect P. C. Keeley, who had never designed a church before, but went on to plan some six hundred churches in the United States. In the course of caring for the many immigrants of the time Malone contracted smallpox and

then cholera in 1848–49, and a fire cost him his house and possessions. But he went on to build a new residence, a parochial school, the Academy of St. Joseph where the Sisters of St. Joseph taught, established a church library and literary association, and invited prominent persons to lecture regularly.

Malone was appointed theologian to Bishop Reynolds of Charleston, South Carolina, at the first Council of Baltimore in 1852. He enjoyed the friendship of Bishops John Hughes and John Loughlin, was often called upon to speak at important events, and his ecumenism gained him the high regard of persons of other faiths. His pulpit addresses, which he could remember verbatim years later, were wholly extemporaneous. In 1854 he attended the proclamation of the dogma of the Immaculate Conception in Rome. Progressive on social, political, and educational questions, he strongly supported the Union cause when the Civil War broke out and flew the American flag on the steeple of his church until the end of the conflict. After attending the Second Plenary Council of Baltimore in 1866, he toured the South in 1868, returning to urge Catholic involvement in its reconstruction and publicly demanding equal rights for all people. He was active in the Irish Land League movement, and steadfastly and publicly supported, even as far as the papacy, the Rev. Edward McGlynn, a social reformer and advocate of the poor, who came into conflict with Archbishop Corrigan over economic issues; McGlynn was excommunicated, but reinstated by Rome in 1892. In Malone's jubilee year of 1894 he was elected to the New York State Board of Regents. Among his published writings are: *Chapters Toward a Life of St. Patrick* (1892), *The Birthplace of St. Patrick* (1900), *Dr. Edward McGlynn* (1918, 1978 reprint), and various formal sermons. During his tenure the city of Brooklyn grew from a few thousand to over a million people. Rev. Sylvester Malone died December 29, 1899.

*Dictionary of American Biography*, Vol. 12 (New York, 1933).
*Memorial of the Golden Jubilee of the Rev. Sylvester Malone* (Brooklyn, 1895).
Denis R. O'Brien, "The Centenary of Rev. Sylvester Malone, Great Catholic and Great Citizen," *Journal of the American Irish Historical Society* 20 (1921): 178–192.

ANNA M. DONNELLY

## MANOGUE, PATRICK (1831–1895)

Miner, priest, bishop of Sacramento, California. Patrick Manogue was born March 15, 1831 in Desart, County Kilkenny, Ireland, the youngest of seven children born to Patrick and Catherine Costigan Manogue. Although Patrick's parents both died when he was three, the family managed to remain together, with Patrick receiving elementary education in the schools of Callan. However, the lure of economic opportunity attracted his elder brother Michael who immigrated to America, beginning a chain of migration that brought over the entire Manogue family.

At age seventeen Patrick joined Michael in Hartford, Connecticut where he found work in the textile mills. After earning enough money Manogue left Hartford in 1850 and realized a long-deferred dream when he began his studies for the priesthood in Chicago's University of St. Mary of the Lake. He was forced to terminate his course work in 1854 in order to assist his still financially dependent family and to recuperate from a brush with cholera that had afflicted him in Chicago. To regain his health and improve his own financial situation, Manogue and his brother James headed for the mining frontier of Northern California, settling for a time in Nevada City, California. There they joined their sister and brother-in-law and set to work as placer miners at a digging in Moore's Flat, about eighteen miles north of Nevada City. His years as a miner acquainted him with particular needs of the Catholic church in the rapidly growing and sometimes chaotic situation in the mining communities of the West. Despite the hard-drinking and wild-living atmosphere of the region, Manogue held fast to his intention to study for the priesthood.

In 1858 he acquired sufficient funds and presented himself to Archbishop Joseph Sadoc Alemany of San Francisco who sent him to the seminary of St. Sulpice in Paris. During his seminary years abroad, Manogue acquired the requisite theological knowledge for ordination to the priesthood and the formation of a personal and priestly spirituality shaped by the "French School" to which his Sulpician directors were devoted. He also observed the tremendous transformation of the city of Paris under Napoleon III and his favored urban planner, Baron Georges Eugene Haussmann.

Upon his ordination in Paris on December 21, 1861, he returned to the United States and was assigned to the parish and mission stations around Virginia City, Nevada. There he remained until his consecration as a bishop in 1881. His list of accomplishments were typical of the brick and mortar era of Catholic life on the Western frontier. He built up the parish of St. Mary of the Mountains, and helped to established an orphanage and a hospital run by the Daughters of Charity. Manogue was a popular figure in the thriving Comstock community and befriended any number of miners who later struck it rich. His closest friend and most loyal benefactor was John W. Mackay, who together with James Fair, James Flood and William O'Brien, hit the fabled "Big Bonanza" in 1873. Manogue proved to be such a skillful pastor and administrator that by a wide consensus of his clerical peers he was nominated as coadjutor bishop of Grass Valley in 1880 and consecrated in San Francisco by Archbishop Alemany on January 16, 1881. He succeeded O'Connell as Bishop of Grass Valley in 1884.

Witnessing the steady decline of the mining communities of the Sierras and Nevada, Manogue laid plans to move the diocesan headquarters from Grass Valley to the California state capital of Sacramento. By 1886, he was in the new location and had secured land to build a monumental cathedral a block north of the state capitol buildings. Paid for in large part by generous donations from the silver fortunes of John Mackay and Theresa Fair, the Cathedral of the Blessed Sacrament became one of the architectural gems of the city of Sacramento.

Since Manogue's diocese encompassed a vast territory of Northern California to the Oregon border and virtually half of the State of Nevada, he traveled extensively to make the required visitations and administer the Sacraments. Like many clerics of those pioneering days, Manogue proved to be a flexible and irenic leader, especially in dealing with persons of other denominations. This continued in Sacramento where he received substantial support from Protestants and Jews in the building of the Cathedral. In turn, he enthusiastically supported the efforts of development-minded Sacramentans who were eager to remake the somewhat sleepy capital into a major economic and social force in the Sacramento Valley. The completion of the cathedral in 1889 was Manogue's crowning work and in 1890 he departed for Europe for an extended vacation. While abroad, the first signs of the diabetes that would eventually take his life made their appearance and he returned to Sacramento in 1891 and steadily declined in health. He died on February 27, 1895, in his residence in Sacramento.

William Breault, S.J., *The Miner Was A Bishop: The Pioneer Years of Patrick Manogue, 1854–1895* (Rancho Cordova, 1988).

Clarence Roy Kline, "Patrick Manogue: Miner, Priest, Pastor, Bishop, 1831–1895" (M. A. Thesis, University of California, 1960).

John Bernard McGloin, S.J., "Patrick Manogue, Gold Miner and Bishop and His 'Cathedral on the Comstock,'" *Nevada Historical Society Quarterly*, 14 (1971): 24–31.

STEVEN M. AVELLA

## MANSFIELD, FREDERICK W. (1877–1958)

*See* Boston, Twelve Irish-American Mayors of

## MANSFIELD, MICHAEL J. (1903–    )

Congressman, senator, ambassador. Michael J. (Mike) Mansfield was born in New York City, March 16, 1903, son of Patrick and Josephine (O'Brien) Mansfield. His mother died when he was three years old, and he was sent to live with relatives in Montana. He did hitches in the Navy, Army and Marines between 1918 and 1922 (lying about his age to get into the Navy), worked as a miner in the copper mines of Butte, and at age thirty received a bachelor's degree from Montana State University. In 1934 he received his master's, whereupon he joined the faculty as a professor of political science and in Latin American and Far East history.

A Democrat, Mansfield won the seat from Montana's First Congressional District in 1942, and was assigned a place on the Foreign Relations Committee. He visited China in 1944 at President Roosevelt's behest, and returned many times thereafter on the invitation of Chinese leaders, becoming in the process a strong advocate of economic, political and cultural ties between the two countries. During the Truman administration he served on the United States delegation to the 1951–1952 session of the United Nations General Assembly.

Michael Mansfield

Mansfield entered the Senate in 1952, and in 1957 was chosen as majority whip by Senate Majority Leader Lyndon B. Johnson, who reportedly wanted someone who would present no challenge to his legislative leadership and style. Indeed, Mansfield was from an entirely different mold from Johnson, being scholarly, low-key and non-manipulative. The Senate, he philosophized, operated best "by accommodation, by respect for one another, by mutual restraint," and it was the way he guided the body when he succeeded Johnson as majority leader on the latter's election as Vice President. He dispersed the powers of the office, allowed senators to floor-manage their own bills, and worked closely with the Republican leadership. His conciliatory tactics came under fire from some fellow Democrats, and led to charges of indecisiveness and ineffectuality. The allegations dissipated over time in the face of steady, strong legislative accomplishment. Mansfield served as majority leader for sixteen years, longer than anyone in history.

Mansfield took a keen interest in foreign affairs, especially those involving the Far East. He initially backed Johnson's war policy in Vietnam, but a 1966 visit to the region persuaded him that a military victory was impossible, and he went public in opposition to the war, although only after failing to persuade Johnson on his point of view. Mansfield supported the Cooper-Church and McGovern-Hatfield amendments to end the war, then introduced one of his own in 1970. It called for an end to military operations as soon as possible and withdrawal of American military personnel, "subject to the release of all American prisoners of war." His amendment passed the Senate, but failed in the House.

Mansfield maintained courteous relationships with the Nixon and Ford administrations, though he frequently opposed their social policies. During the Watergate crisis he scorned Nixon's lack of honesty with the American people, but his criticism was measured—characteristically so—in comparison to that of other Democrats.

He retired from the Senate in 1977, and that same year was appointed ambassador to Japan by President Jimmy Carter. Republican President Ronald Reagan reappointed him in 1981 and he served until 1989, a total of twelve years. After returning to private life, he became a senior adviser on East Asian affairs at Goldman, Sachs & Company, and in his mid-nineties was still going each day to the office.

Nelson Lichtenstein, Eleanora W. Schoenebaum, *et al.*, eds., *Political Profiles,* the Kennedy and the Nixon/Ford Years, two volumes (New York, 1976, 1979).

Martin F. Nolan, "The Greatest Living Democrat," *Boston Globe* (March 4, 1998).

David E. Rosenbaum, "A Senator's Old Speech Holds Truth Today," *The New York Times,* national edition (March 22, 1998).

JOHN DEEDY

## MARTIN, HENRY NEWELL (1848–1896)

Physiologist and pioneer in cardiac research. Henry Newell Martin was born July 1, 1848, in Newry, County Down, Ireland. His father was a Congregational minister and later a teacher. Therefore, Martin received most of his early education at home.

When he was fifteen, Martin went to University College London to begin studies at the university's Medical School. At that time, he also became an apprentice to James McDonagh, an Irish doctor at Hampstead Road, dispensing medicine in return for room and board. At college he became a demonstrator for Michael Foster, an English physiologist.

In 1870 Martin received a scholarship to Christ College Cambridge and continued to assist Foster, who had moved to Trinity College. Martin received a bachelor's degree at Cambridge and a master's degree in London. He was the first to receive a doctor of science in physiology at Cambridge.

In 1874 Martin was made a fellow of Trinity College at Cambridge. While at the university, he continued to carry on biological instruction and research.

Martin worked with Thomas Henry Huxley at the Royal College of Science in London. The two co-authored the book *Practical Biology,* which was published in 1876. That same year, Martin accepted the honor of becoming the first chair in the biology and physiology department at the newly founded Johns Hopkins University in Baltimore, Maryland. The position was offered to Martin on the advice of Foster and Huxley.

Martin was among the first six professors who were carefully selected to serve on the university's faculty. He also became involved in the planning and building of Johns Hopkins Hospital, which took twelve years to complete, opening its doors in 1889.

In 1879 Martin married Hetty Cary, the widow of General Pegram, a Confederate officer. She helped him during the writing of his popular textbook, *The Human Body* (1881), which aroused wide interest in physiology.

During his seventeen years at Johns Hopkins, Martin used his position at the university to lay the foundation for instruction and research in the biological sciences, especially use of the experimental method. His work in that area brought distinction to the university and influenced other institutions.

Martin made several contributions to physiology, especially in his belief that physiology should be studied apart from its application to medicine. He was most successful in the study of a heart-lung preparation that would allow isolation of the mammalian heart. In *A Medical Bibliography,* L. T. Morton described Martin's achievement as "one of the greatest, single contributions ever to come from an American physiological laboratory."

Martin not only successfully isolated the heart but also studied the effect that temperature had on the heart beat, which the Royal Society of London used as the basis for its 1883 Croonian. That same year, he was elected a fellow of the society.

Martin also devised a method for measuring blood pressure and pulse wave, and did original research on the respiratory system. He also founded and edited the five volumes of *Johns Hopkins University Studies from the Biological Laboratory* (1877–93). The papers containing his researches were republished in 1895 by his friends and pupils as a memorial entitled *Physiological Papers.*

His health declined, possibly due to alcoholism, following his wife's death in 1892. Martin resigned his post at the university in 1893, the year that the new medical school he helped to establish and organize opened, and returned to England. He died of a hemorrhage in Yorkshire, England, on October 27, 1896.

Davis Coakley, *Irish Masters of Medicine* (Dublin, 1992).

W. B. Fye, "H. Newell Martin: A remarkable career destroyed by neurasthemia and alcoholism," *Journal of the History of Medicine,* 40 (1985): 133–66.

Dumas Malone, ed., *Dictionary of American Biography,* vol. VI (New York, 1933).

Henry Sewall, "Henry Newell Martin, professor of biology in Johns Hopkins University 1876–1893," *Johns Hopkins Bulletin,* 22 (1911): 327–33.

MARIANNA McLOUGHLIN

## MARYLAND

George Calvert (1582–1632) was given the Barony of Baltimore (Ireland) near the end of his royal service under King James I. As Lord Baltimore he planned his colony in the Upper Chesapeake as both a mercantile project and a haven of religious liberty. The colony's name, Maryland, was given in honor of Queen Henrietta Maria, consort of Charles I. The Catholic minority has always interpreted the name as something of a pious "double-entendre" honoring the Virgin Mary.

There were some Anglo-Irish among the original colonists on the *Ark* and the *Dove* on the 1633–1634 voyage but most of the early Irish in the colony were indentured servants.

The Maryland Assembly passed the famed "Act Concerning Religion" in 1649 articulating the toleration understood since Calvert's founding of the colony. Its provisions prohibited the reproachful calling of anyone an Anabaptist, Calvinist, Idolater, Jesuited Papist, Presbyterian, Puritan, Roundhead, or Separatist. This certainly invited migration from the varied religious persuasions of Ireland.

By 1657 Presbyterians were active in southern Maryland. Rev. Francis Makemie (1658–1708) led the Scots-Irish Presbyterians in the southern counties of the Eastern Shore. In fact, this Ulsterman is credited with organizing the first Presbyterian churches in the country. By the middle of the 18th century, West Nottingham Academy in Cecil County was established, a proud achievement of the Scots-Irish Presbyterians there. The founder, Samuel Finley (1715–1766), from County Armagh, went on to become the president of Princeton. There were Irish Quakers in Cecil County as well, centered around the Nottingham Meeting. A generous land grant, New Munster, was given Edwin O'Dwire and other Irish settlers in 1683, where Cecil County borders Pennsylvania.

The pioneer Methodist lay preacher in Maryland was Robert Strawbridge (1732–1781) who had emigrated from County Leitrim. From his base in what is now Carroll County, Strawbridge rode circuit throughout the colony, always remembered as an impassioned preacher. One of the great Irish-born missionaries of the Eastern Shore was Fr. Edward Henchy (1833–1895). He served nearly three decades tending the scattered Catholics of Caroline, Dorchester, Queen Anne, and Talbot counties.

Certainly the most notable Irish family of colonial Maryland into the Federal Period was the large Carroll family. Daniel Carroll II (1730–1796) signed the Constitution of the United States. His brother, John Carroll (1735–1815) served as the first Roman Catholic bishop in the nation and founded Georgetown University. Their cousin, Charles Carroll of Carrollton (1737–1832), arguably the richest man in the country, lived to be the last surviving signer of the Declaration of Independence. He had begun his public career in an acrimonious dispute with an Eton-educated landowner, Daniel Dulany, whose father had come from Ireland and belonged to the Anglican Church. Often the Carrolls gave Irish names to their estates: Doughoregan Manor, Litterluna, Clynmalira.

The early transportation industry was the magnet for many Irish immigrants from canal workers on the Upper Eastern Shore to longshoremen in Locust Point, to railway "gandy dancers" in Cumberland. Farming drew the Irish to the Long Green Valley and quarrying to Little Texas, both in Baltimore County. Numerous Irish workers were drawn to settlements from Rockville, Montgomery County to Little Orleans, Allegany County during the construction of the Chesapeake and Ohio Canal.

James McSherry (1819–1869) of Frederick authored a prominent *History of Maryland.* Prior to the Civil War, McSherry was both a historian and a lawyer at the Frederick Bar. His family, with roots in Courtmacsherry, County Cork, also produced a provincial superior of the Jesuits, William McSherry, S.J. (1799–1839). In 1837, John McElroy, S.J. (1782–1877), born in Enniskillen, built the monumental St. John the Evangelist Church in Frederick where he served for decades. He went on to found Boston College.

The Battle of Antietam, south of Hagerstown, was the bloodiest one-day battle of the Civil War. In the 1862 battle the Irish Brigade and the New York 69th Regiment took a most notable part and suffered many casualties.

During the Battle of Gettysburg in July 1863, the Daughters of Charity from Emmitsburg, Maryland, were called to nurse the wounded. Mother Ann Simeon Norris sent a dozen Sisters to Gettysburg including many who were Irish. One of these, Sr. Matilda Coskery, wrote a graphic account of the carnage. Though perhaps some 10,000 Irish fell at Gettysburg, the Sisters tended the wounded without distinction of religion or ethnicity.

The only Sister who died nursing the sick in Civil War service was a Daughter of Charity, Sr. Maria Conlan at Point Lookout, St. Mary's County, a Union equivalent of Andersonville.

The "Poet Priest of the South," Abram Ryan (1838–1886) was born at Hagerstown, Washington County. Within a decade his family migrated to Missouri. Father Ryan is remembered for authoring *The Conquered Banner* and *The Sword of Robert E. Lee.*

John McCaffrey (1805–1881), president of Mt. St. Mary's, Emmitsburg, was a strong supporter of the Confederacy. He often went through his friend "Dagger John" Hughes (1797–1864), Archbishop of New York (born in County Tyrone), to intervene with President Abraham Lincoln on behalf of captured alumni.

John Lee Carroll (1830–1911) continued the tradition of public service established by his great grandfathers, Charles Carroll and Thomas Sim Lee. Carroll served as governor of Maryland from 1876–1880. The memorable Baltimore and Ohio Railroad strike overshadowed the other events of Carroll's term. Beginning in heavily Irish Cumberland, the strike spread rapidly to Baltimore in the summer of 1877. Governor Carroll took "unflinching action in quelling the disorder."

The great strike of 1882 involved coal miners in the George's Creek area of western Maryland. It was not successful and led to the importation of new ethnic groups as strike-breakers replacing the Irish as well as the more established Welsh and Scots. Terrence V. Powderly (1819–1924) cut his teeth as grand master workman of the Knights of Labor with this strike.

An excellent chronicle of the Irish in the central and western reaches of the state was *A Century of Growth or The Catholic Church in Western Maryland.* Father Thomas J. Stanton (1864–1941) collected poetry, lore and history for this two volume work in the first decade of the twentieth century. He was born in Oakland, Garrett County, of Irish immigrant parents.

James Edward Walsh (1891–1981) was the most famous Irish-American of western Maryland. Born of a politically influential Cumberland family, he was educated at Emmitsburg and became a devoted Maryknoll Missionary to China. There he was imprisoned by the communist Chinese from 1958 to 1970.

Though Edward Cardinal Mooney (1882–1958), Archbishop of Detroit, was born at Mt. Savage, Allegany County, he and his family soon moved to Ohio. P. Francis Murphy (1933– ) was born in Cumberland. After serving in Rome and Baltimore he was named auxiliary bishop to Lawrence Cardinal Shehan (1898–1984).

Well into this century the Irish were largely centered in the Baltimore area. Indicative of their much broader distribution today is the presence of many Irish-American heritage and fraternal groups in Annapolis, Ocean City, Carroll and Harford Counties.

*See* Baltimore; Scots Irish; Carrolls of Maryland

---

Virginia Walcott Beauchamp, "The Sisters and the Soldiers," *Maryland Historical Magazine,* 81 (1986): 117–133.

Katherine A. Harvey, *The Best Dressed Miners, Life and Labor in the Maryland Coal Region: 1835–1910* (Ithaca, New York, 1969).

Edna Agatha Kanely, *Directory of Ministers and the Maryland Churches They Served, 1634–1990,* 2 Vols. (Westminster, Maryland, 1991).

James G. Leyburn, *The Scotch-Irish, A Social History* (Chapel Hill, North Carolina, 1962).

James McSherry, *History of Maryland From Its First Settlement in 1634 to the year 1848* (Baltimore, Maryland, 1849).

Thomas W. Spalding, *The Premier See: A History of the Archdiocese of Baltimore 1789–1989* (Baltimore, Maryland, 1989).

Thomas J. Stanton, *A Century of Growth, or the History of the Catholic Church in Western Maryland,* 2 Vols. (Baltimore, Maryland, 1900).

Frank F. White, *The Governors of Maryland, 1777–1970* (Annapolis, Maryland, 1970).

MICHAEL ROACH

## MASSACHUSETTS

In 1980, federal census takers found a larger percentage of sons and daughters of Erin in Massachusetts than in any other state of the Union. Although more populous states held larger numbers of Irish and Irish-Americans in that year, only in the Bay State did more than one in four inhabitants (27%) lay claim to Irish birth or ancestry. A decade later, using open-ended sampling techniques and different methods of calculating multiple ethnic origins, the Census Bureau reached similar results, concluding that 26% of Massachusetts residents in 1990 were of at least partial Irish descent.

Such numbers, combined with the impact of contemporary events—especially the election of John F. Kennedy to the presidency in 1960, and the media prominence of the celebrated Kennedy dynasty since the young president's assassination— have contributed to a public perception that "Massachusetts" and "Irish" are almost synonymous. It has not always been so.

### IRISH IN COLONIAL MASSACHUSETTS

Irish settlers were met with almost universal hostility in colonial New England. As the eighteenth century began, Cotton Mather denounced proposals to bring Irish of any denomination into Puritan Massachusetts Bay as "formidable attempts of Satan and his sons to unsettle us," and Governor Belcher assured London from Boston in 1736 that "there are but few Irish . . . and indeed the people of this country seem to have an aversion to them, so they find little encouragement." Encouraged or not, Protestant and Catholic Irish emigrated to colonial New England, though not in as large numbers as to the middle and southern colonies.

A few hundred Irish came involuntarily, prisoners and troublemakers expelled from their homeland during the turmoil of the seventeenth century, but larger numbers from the southern counties of Ireland were products of a modest indentured servant trade which engaged merchants of southern New England and their counterparts in Cork, Dublin, and Limerick in the eighteenth century. In Massachusetts, Newburyport, Salem, and Boston all counted a few Irish merchants who had begun to conduct their business from the New World prior to the Revolution. Some Irish arrived indirectly, including summer sojourners from Waterford to Newfoundland who tired of their transatlantic commute and instead moved south for the winter. Young John Riley's parents came north from Connecticut in about 1650, and their son later took up land along a brook which still bears the family name. The settlement of "Ireland Parish" which grew up around Riley's home place is now a portion of the city of Holyoke.

Belcher had scarcely reported "but few Irish" in Boston (*q.v.*) when the city witnessed its first St. Patrick's Day celebration in 1737, and the gathering of some forty self-defined "gentlemen, merchants, and others, of the Irish nation," to found the Boston Charitable Irish Society, the oldest continuous Irish ethnic organization in the United States. In the previous two decades, hundreds of Ulster Presbyterians had arrived at the port of Boston, where they found a grudging reception at best. When the first Ulster families landed in 1718, Boston's Puritan Fathers encouraged them to settle elsewhere, and most soon did so, though a few remained on the city's fringes at Concord and Milton. Some went north, where they established the soon flourishing settlement of Londonderry in New Hampshire, while others ventured fifty miles westward to Worcester. Finding Worcester no more hospitable than Boston, most of the Ulstermen and women moved on into the sparsely populated remote hills of western Massachusetts where, in a Franklin County community which they called Colrain, they could govern themselves and worship as they chose.

### THE PIONEER CATHOLIC IRISH

At the dawn of the Republic, by best estimates, there were some fifteen thousand people of Irish origin in Massachusetts, including Boston's James Flinn and other ex-soldiers who had distinguished themselves in the service of the recent Revolution. Flinn was one of the few who were Irish Catholics, since priests and "papists" had been proscribed by a Massachusetts version of Ireland's Penal Laws which remained in effect until 1780. The French Consul-General reported from Boston in 1789 that the Catholic congregation there consisted of but "one American, three or four French folk, and a score of poor Irish." When Bishop John Carroll of Baltimore visited the city two years later, he found only one hundred and twenty faithful to greet him, among them a handful of Catholic gentlemen and merchants.

Few Irish emigrants arrived in Massachusetts until the end of the Napoleonic Wars in 1815. Almost immediately thereafter, there began a steady flow of Irish to North America, prompted by long pent up emigration dreams, economic crisis in Ireland, demand for labor in the expanding United States, and limited government-sponsored emigration to Canada. Massachusetts, which had once shunned the Irish, now welcomed their cheap labor, a necessary ingredient of the shift from commercial to industrial capitalism which was occurring throughout the economy of southern New England.

By the end of the 1820s more than 10,000 Irish were annually sailing directly to United States ports, while thousands of others made the cheaper and shorter passage to Quebec or the Maritime Provinces of Canada. Many of the latter continued on foot or aboard vessels of the coastal trade bound for the United States, some immediately, others after a sojourn of months or years. Looking back from the vantage point of 1929, historian Marcus Hansen described this phenomenon as the "second colonization of New England." Throughout the nineteenth century, despite the unchanged aversion to all things Irish in Massachusetts, that state would receive the lion's share of the new colonists to the region. As Hansen wrote, "There was labor to be done—heavy dirty work that no New Englander would perform for the pittance offered: canals to be dug, foundations to be laid, dams to be constructed. And so the Irishman came."

The several score Irish of Boston in 1790 had become 8,000 by 1830 and perhaps twice that number were elsewhere in the Commonwealth. New Bedford in the southeast, Lowell thirty miles northeast of Boston, Worcester in the central part of the state, and Northampton in the west all counted settlements of Irish Catholics large enough to command regular visits from the handful of available priests. Lowell, assigned a resident pastor in 1827, four years later constructed a church dedicated to St. Patrick. Violence briefly flared against the church building effort, and in 1834 a mob torched the Ursuline convent in Charlestown, but the Irish were undeterred. Still they came.

Laborers from Ireland were the human fuel stoking the transportation and industrial revolutions then underway in Massachusetts, and they were indispensable to progress, as even the Yankee census taker who in 1840 described them as an "extraneous population" probably recognized. Before the mid-century Great Famine which ravaged their homeland, tens of thousands of Irish were hard at work as factory operatives in the cotton mills of Lowell and Chicopee, brass and iron-founders in Cambridge and Canton, glass-blowers in Sandwich, weavers of woolens in Oxford and Ware, and as artisans, day laborers, and domestics in every corner of the state. Every county of the Emerald Isle had a son or daughter living in Massachusetts before 1825, and every county of the state had received some new Irish inhabitants. Ulster natives, both Protestant and Catholic, were prominent among those who headed for developing textile centers in Bristol and Middlesex counties, but as emigration from Ireland's north slowed, and that from Munster soared in the 1830s, "Irish Massachusetts" gradually became virtually synonymous with "Catholic Massachusetts." Immigrants from Ireland's west joined the emigrant stream in significant numbers in the early 1840s.

### Facing Adversity: Famine, Nativism, and Civil War

The failure of Ireland's potato crop year after year in the late 1840s is too well known to need recounting, but nowhere were the effects of that calamity more dramatic than in Massachusetts. Neither state nor church officials could cope with the numbers who sought refuge in New England, and the Irish settlements already established were hard-pressed to succor the new arrivals. As David Doyle has recently written in *A New History of Ireland,* those areas of Ireland which had experienced significant emigration before the Famine were those best "equipped with their own bridges out of disaster." The very diversity of the Irish who had come to Massachusetts since 1815, and the substantial financial assistance they provided their homeland during the Famine (*see below*), helped to make the state the receiving end of one of those bridges.

By 1855 Boston teemed with 50,000 Irish, who had increased more than sixfold since 1830. The Irish were now almost one-third of the city's population, and about half of their number had arrived within the decade since the start of the Great Famine. On Boston's south shore, the quarries and boot shops of Quincy had drawn Irish settlers, 761 of them by 1850. Five years later, the state census enumerator found a 60% increase among the Irish living in that hometown of two presidents. In central Massachusetts, the influx was in many ways even more dramatic. Several small clusters of Irish settlers in Worcester numbered but 600 in 1845, but the city housed 3,300 Irish a mere five years later. Farming communities in surrounding Worcester County which knew no Irish before 1850 now filed census reports listing Ireland as the birthplace of ten to fifteen percent of their inhabitants.

The Famine-induced flood of newcomers produced tensions within established Irish ethnic communities. Immigrants of twenty years' standing who had become property owners and small businessmen felt their hard-won but scarcely secure respectability endangered by an influx of Irish cottiers, while day laborers feared the glut of new competitors for jobs. Lowell and Worcester were wracked by strife among the Irish in the late 1840s as middle class and working class, clergy and laity, Corkonians and Connaughtmen struggled with one another as they attempted to redefine the immigrant world in which they lived. In Worcester, the breakdown of law and order was so complete as to paralyze the Hibernian community, and Whiteboy-style attacks on the property of the middle class were so effective as to force most of the earlier Irish settlers from the city.

While the Worcester experience was extreme and its effect mainly local, the huge Famine immigration impacted Irish and Yankee alike, forcing each group to reassess the other. Tensions between Irish Catholics and descendants of Puritan settlers of English stock, never far below the surface, were brought to a boil in the early 1850s. The number of naturalized citizens in the Commonwealth had more than doubled within a few years, and the American Party, popularly known as Know-Nothings, demanded curbs on citizenship access and limits on the suffrage of those who were not native born. The party gained a wide following throughout Massachusetts by 1854, and state elections in that year took on strident anti-Catholic and anti-immigrant overtones. The Irish, object of most of the nativist invective, were then three out of four of the state's foreign born. American Party candidates captured control of the governorship and state legislature and proceeded to enact some of the suffrage restrictions for which they had argued—a waiting period of two years before a naturalized citizen could vote, and a literacy test—but more extreme measures failed passage.

The nativist tide receded in the late 1850s as slavery and abolition took center stage as the primary issues of public debate. While the American Party faded quickly as a national phenomenon, its brief supremacy in Massachusetts haunted future relations between Puritan and Celt. Old wounds would be reopened, and memories of Charlestown and of the Know-Nothings evoked when the state was swept anew by waves of anti-immigrant and anti-Catholic populism, in the 1890s fanned by the American Protective Association, and by the Ku Klux Klan in the 1920s.

Of more immediate concern in 1860, however, was slavery. On that matter native and Irish were again at opposite poles, the abolitionist position articulately defended by leading members of Yankee society while spokespersons for the staunchly Democratic Irish often passionately argued the inequality of Africans and the legitimacy of slavery. Nevertheless, once war between the states broke out, the Irish in Massachusetts flocked to the defense of the Union. Ironically, the division of the nation and the Civil War proved healing to the strained relations between the Massachusetts majority and the Irish who lived among them.

Thomas O'Connor's comment about Boston was true of the entire state: "Tensions between Yankee and the Celt moved into a sort of holding pattern, as the problem of controlling the immigrant became secondary to saving the Union and emancipating the slaves" (*Bibles, Brahmins, and Bosses* 1984:116). Early in 1861 Thomas Cass gathered members of the Columbian Artillery (a state militia unit of Irishmen forced to disband when the Know-Nothings dominated state government) and organized the Ninth Massachusetts Volunteer Infantry, known as "Boston's Irish." Later in the year more Irish volunteers responded statewide to the call for the *Faugh-a-Ballagh* ("Massachusetts Irish" Twenty-eighth Volunteer Infantry), which contained two companies assembled from among the boot and shoemakers of Lynn and Milford. Irish joined many other units as well, convinced that soldiering demonstrated loyalty in an even more tangible way than the citizenship oath which the Know-Nothings had so recently sought to deny them.

## Irish Organizations

The Boston Charitable Irish Society, founded in colonial days by middle-class Ulstermen for the relief of their "poor, indigent countrymen," welcomed middle-class Irish Catholics into its midst early in the nineteenth century. Meetings regularly toasted the glories of Republican government, praised the virtues of hard work and respectable conduct, and celebrated the economic promise which the New World offered. Dr. Thomas J. O'Flaherty, a Maynooth-trained priest and physician born in Tralee and the United States District Attorney for Boston, Ulster-American Andrew Dunlap, a native of Salem, both served as presidents of the organization during the 1830s. Counterpart organizations, such as the Hibernian Moralizing and Relief Society formed at Lowell in 1833 under the leadership of Charles M. Short, formed in other cities during the next three decades.

With a like-sounding name but different purpose, the Hibernian Relief Society of 1827 was Boston's initial O'Connellite organization. Transformed into the "Association of Friends of Ireland," it championed O'Connell's drive to repeal the Act of Union of 1800 for more than a dozen years. Issuing proclamations of support and collecting funds at eighty-five fund-raising Repeal Association meetings held in thirty Massachusetts cities and factory towns between 1842 and early 1845, its success was remarkable. Repeal, notes Brian Mitchell, was "an Irish movement which tied 'Mickey' to his immigrant father and, as a result appealed to a broad range of Irishmen." Thousands of Massachusetts Irish contributed to the campaign before the cause faltered, just as the Great Famine broke.

Fund-raising efforts for Ireland from Massachusetts turned from political causes to famine relief. Lowell's Famine Committee quickly raised more than $1,900 from a cross section of the community, and Worcester collected $1,000. Funds collected during a two-year effort by two complementary relief organizations, one organized by Bishop John Bernard Fitzpatrick of Boston, the other by Mayor Josiah Quincy, exceeded $300,000. About half the total had flowed almost spontaneously from Catholics in Massachusetts and the northern New England states early in 1847. Later phases of the humanitarian effort gathered donations from Protestant congregations, businesses, and individuals nationwide, though the majority of them came from within the Commonwealth.

After the Civil War, the relationship of Massachusetts Irish to Ireland and to the Irish national movement became increasingly complex, and no issue would unite them as Repeal had done. Fenian groups multiplied rapidly, briefly promoted by Patrick A. Collins, who organized seventy-five units in the eastern part of the state. Lawrence, Holyoke, and Pittsfield each sent off small bands to invade Canada. All returned ingloriously when interdicted by federal troops in Vermont. Every corner of Massachusetts was on the speaking circuit for a succession of Irish-American and Irish political figures, who included Senator James Shields, John Mitchel, Charles Stewart Parnell, and Michael Davitt. Dollars flowed to their causes. Land Leaguers successfully established local branches in a number of cities. In Holyoke a brief but sharp competition between rival Parnell and Davitt Leagues was evidence that factionalism, philosophical differences, and class antagonisms existed within more than one immigrant Irish community.

The temperance movement amongst the Irish began in the early 1840s, and spread rapidly following the visit of Father Theobald Mathew to Boston and nine other Massachusetts cities in 1849. As the century progressed, nearly every Catholic parish organized a temperance or total abstinence society, and many such societies became focal points for a wide range of social, educational, and recreational activities. In Fall River a Clan na Gael Hall served a similar purpose, but with a strong dose of Irish nationalism thrown in. Not to be outdone, either by other cities or by other ethnic groups within Lawrence, the Irish there developed a Hibernian Clubhouse, a Sheridan Dramatic Society, an Emmet Literary Society, and a Gaelic Athletic Association. Even small rural settlements of Irish had at least one or two such organizations.

Divisions of the Ancient Order of Hibernians sprang up throughout the Commonwealth wherever a few dozen Irish men and women could gather to parade their Irish and American colors. Their appearance was as obligatory on the Fourth of July as on St. Patrick's Day. At their peak, Boston's many AOH divisions counted 8,000 members. Forty-five divisions were active in the western portion of the state, where Pittsfield, with 275 members, long claimed the distinction as the largest single division.

## Arts and Letters

In Irish-American journalism of the nineteenth century, the Boston *Pilot* knew no peer. Begun as *The Jesuit* in 1829, in its pages the worlds of Catholicism, of the Irish in America, and of Irish nationalism merged, as did those of journalism, ethics, and literature. Under the guidance of Patrick Donahoe, the paper's publisher for some forty years, the *Pilot* contained news of current Irish events, but at the same time prompted its readers to American citizenship and patriotism. During the Repeal campaign of the 1840s (*see above*), the *Pilot*, then edited by Thomas D'Arcy McGee, proved its ability to influence and mobilize all of Irish New England. Its voice for defense of the Union in

1860, then that of Donahoe himself, resounded among the Irish nationwide.

During the 1850s Massachusetts was home to several accomplished Irish writers whose works appeared in its pages, among them Boston-born John Roddan, young priest-editor of the paper before his early death in 1858, and his contemporary "Paul Peppergrass," Donegal native John Boyce, who for years combined an exhaustive schedule of pastoral visits to scattered rural settlements of Catholics in Worcester County with a continuing output of popular novels set in both Ireland and the United States. Edited in the post–Civil War era by John Boyle O'Reilly, an accomplished poet of no mean talent, the *Pilot*'s subscriber list surpassed 100,000. When O'Reilly died in 1890, *Harper's Weekly* paid fitting tribute to the passing of "the most distinguished Irishman in America."

Two women born of Irish parents in Massachusetts, noteworthy for their contributions to the world of letters, are poet Louise Imogen Guiney, daughter of a celebrated hero of Boston's Irish Ninth, and Irish prose writer Mary Lavin, born in East Walpole shortly before the First World War. Guiney, encouraged by O'Reilly and mentored by Oliver Wendell Holmes, infused her poems and essays with the spirit of American Celticism after her grand tour of Ireland. Though she was widely published in leading American periodicals of the 1890s, the rewards were meager, and even her postal and library jobs failed to bring her financial security. Lavin's mother returned to Ireland with her nine-year-old daughter in 1921, resettling shortly thereafter in Dublin. Schooled there, Mary Lavin became one of Ireland's most talented short story writers by the mid-twentieth century, though she too struggled to make a living from her craft.

Two Irish-American men of Boston made their most noted contributions to the world of visual arts in other cities, but both began their careers in Massachusetts. From colonial Boston came John Singleton Copley, born shortly after his parents arrived there from County Clare in the late 1730s. An accomplished artist and noted portrait painter in his native city as a young man, Copley's best known works are of British historical subjects, produced after he moved to London in 1774. Born to an Irish father and Swiss mother in Boston in 1856, Louis Henri Sullivan developed the full range of his extraordinary talents as an architectural designer in the burgeoning city of Chicago late in the century. A pioneer of some of the nation's first skyscraper architecture, like Guiney in literature, Sullivan incorporated Celtic elements into the decorative features of many of his structures.

## The Many Faces of Irish Massachusetts

The Irish who came to the United States were a diverse group before they departed Ireland and they were no less so in New England, as the life of Louis Sullivan illustrates. As immigrants, the economic conditions they faced and the degree of social acceptance accorded them differed greatly from place to place and from time to time, even within the relatively small confines of Massachusetts. Irish perceptions of self and of ethnicity were often affected by such local circumstances, and immigration historians have turned repeatedly to local studies as keys to understanding larger group phenomena.

Oscar Handlin's pioneering study of the Boston Irish depicted a city crowded with involuntary immigrants, naive peasants without marketable skills who had fled the frying pan of famine only to be thrown into the fire of commercial capitalist Yankee Boston. The newcomers, Handlin contended, were "a massive lump in the community, undigested and undigestible," eking out an existence as casual day laborers and too poor to escape the port city. Handlin's characterization was only partially correct, even of Boston, and its focus on that city slighted the many Irish elsewhere in the state. Later scholarship on Boston and on other Irish communities, both within the Commonwealth and elsewhere, has helped to redress the balance. The wider picture suggests that the experience of immigrants and the growing number of Irish-Americans among them in the state of Massachusetts, even in the suburbs surrounding Boston, was both more varied and less bleak than that painted by Handlin.

Stephan Thernstrom's study of Newburyport, a Yankee city become one-quarter Catholic by 1880, found that wages for unskilled factory work remained virtually static for a full generation (thirty years) after the Famine. Though upward economic and social mobility was exceedingly rare among the ethnic Irish working class in Newburyport, they had achieved a surprisingly high rate of property ownership. Thernstrom was critical of the Irish passion to acquire real property, which he felt to be the product of Irish culture and a value structure fostered by their Catholic leaders. It had required so much sacrifice "as almost to blur the distinction between 'property' and 'poverty,'" he concluded.

While some of the Newburyport pattern has been shown to be replicated elsewhere in the state, Timothy Meagher's analysis of Worcester suggests an important corrective. The Irish of central Massachusetts began a pattern of upward economic mobility in the closing two decades of the nineteenth century, a period just after that studied by Thernstrom. Meagher found that the percentage of Irish who were white-collar workers nearly doubled between 1880 and 1900, and that of blue-collar workers rose by 31%. The Irish may have been only part way up the social ladder, and more Irish-Americans had moved upward than had first-generation immigrants, but "a substantial portion had escaped its bottom rungs."

Newburyport Irish were a commingling of Irish immigrants, Irish-Americans, and immigrants born in England or Canada to Irish parents. That profile was also part of many communities in the Commonwealth. Boston received a steady stream of Irish from the Maritime Provinces throughout the nineteenth century. Canadian Irish settled not only in seaboard Massachusetts, but in many communities of the interior, sometimes rejoining family from whom they had become separated during emigration. And like Newburyport, every textile-manufacturing center of Massachusetts drew workers from English cities, and those known as "Lancashire Irish" were a sizeable contingent of the labor force in such cities as Fall River and Lawrence.

To an extent that he had not expected, Thernstrom found the workforce of Newburyport constantly shifting. "Many workmen were transients," he wrote, "drifting from city to city according to the dictates of the labor market." Here was remarkable geographical mobility, and evidence that large numbers of Massachusetts Irish were not stuck in place, either in Boston or elsewhere in the post-Famine era. Within the Irish and English labor markets they had become industrial era spalpeens and many continued in that role in New England. Recent studies conclude that the Irish were not "drifting from place to place," but moving in very deliberate ways in search of better working conditions or wages. David Fitzpatrick's general study of Irish emigration notes that, regardless of destination, emigrants from Ireland during the nineteenth century gravitated to regions of expanding employment. Often willing to take low paying jobs at least initially, the Irish, writes Fitzpatrick, "in effect occupied the worst seats in the best theatres" (*Irish Emigration 1801–1921*, Dublin 1984: 34).

New England was well known as one of the better theatres of the time. Stephen Byrne's *Irish Emigration to the United States* (1873), specifically addressed to prospective Irish emigrants, appended wage scales which documented that in all categories of farm and common labor, as well as in domestic service, New England employers paid higher wages than did those of any other area except the remote Pacific coast states. There were then 216,000 natives of Ireland living in Massachusetts. Handlin and Thernstrom aside, most of them were neither stuck in the port at which they had arrived, nor migrating from job to job. Three out of four of them had moved beyond Boston, some only a few miles, numerous others to farms and factories in the interior of the state. Many had acquired property, their dollars invested in the land of the new state in which they had settled.

Many subtle forces were at work in the closing decades of the nineteenth century in Irish Massachusetts. The old pre-Famine emigration and that of the mid-nineteenth century had gradually blended, intermarried, and produced large families which were themselves maturing as the century ended. By 1910 Irish-Americans outnumbered those born in Ireland in every county of the state, in some areas by as much as two to one, and the two groups did not always see eye to eye. In Worcester, as Meagher has shown, newer immigrants made the Ancient Order of Hibernians their own, while the second generation flocked to the more American and multiethnic Knights of Columbus. Despite generational differences between Irish-American and Irish immigrant, there was every reason for Irish Massachusetts to celebrate its coming of age as children born to Irish parents in Massachusetts rose to leadership in both church and civil society early in the twentieth century. Examples often cited are those of Boston-born John F. Fitzgerald, who became mayor of the city in 1905, and Lowell-born William Henry O'Connell, elevated to Archbishop of Boston in 1907, and one of two Irish-Americans named cardinal in 1911.

These were but two very visible signs of a process which had been going on throughout the state, beginning in less prestigious offices, for thirty or more years past. As in Boston, where immigrants had paved the way into public office in the 1870s by practicing the "politics of accommodation" with elements of the Yankee establishment, so too elsewhere. In Lawrence, Tipperary native John Breen combined support from other ethnic groups with the votes of fellow Irishmen to win election in 1881 as the first Irish Catholic mayor of a major Massachusetts city. Lowell followed suit in the same year when it chose Irish-American banker John J. Donovan, and Holyoke in 1883, when James E. Delaney moved from city clerk to mayor. Worcester and Springfield, which could trace Irish settlement from the 1820s, would not see similar power in Irish-American hands until the early twentieth century.

Owen Coogan, immigrant owner of a successful tannery in Pittsfield, was sent by voters of Berkshire County to represent them on Beacon Hill in 1872. He was the first Irish Catholic member of the state legislature from that westernmost county. In that decade Irish throughout the state were beginning to assume seats on various local government boards, but few yet made it to the legislature. David Ignatius Walsh, born to Irish parents in northern Worcester County two years after Coogan's election, was also destined for state office. Young Walsh, who entered Democratic Party county politics soon after obtaining a law degree in 1897, was four years later elected state representative from his traditionally Republican Worcester County district. Though not the first Irish-American to be elected governor of Massachusetts (an honor claimed by James Sullivan in 1807), when he became the state's chief executive in 1914, David I. Walsh was the first Roman Catholic and the first offspring of Irish "second colonizers" to sit in the governor's chair of the once Puritan Commonwealth.

## IRISH MASSACHUSETTS IN THE TWENTIETH CENTURY

Immigration to Massachusetts from Ireland reached its peak in the 1890s, when nearly 260,000 residents of the Bay State were enumerated as having been born in Ireland. The rate of emigration from Ireland to the United States slowed during that last nineteenth-century decade, and fewer of the emigrants now chose Massachusetts as their intended destination. In each succeeding federal census, those of Irish nativity in Massachusetts became smaller, their numbers diminished both by the death of the pioneer immigrants of the nineteenth century and by shifting economic forces which made newer and more dynamic areas of America more attractive than the aging industrial cities of New England. The economic "best theatres" were now elsewhere.

As the Commonwealth's population became infused with southern and eastern Europeans in the four decades before immigration was restricted in 1921, and with a continuous influx of migrants from within the Americas, the almost century-long Irish dominance among the state's new inhabitants ended. Natives of Ireland, one in seven of all inhabitants of Massachusetts and 55% of the state's foreign born in 1875, were by 1910 only one in fifteen within the state, and but 21.2% of those who had been born abroad. By 1980, although more than 1,500,000 claimed Irish ancestry in Massachusetts, only 56,276 of them had been born in Ireland. The persistence of Irish ethnicity into the third, fourth, and fifth generations in Massachusetts, as illustrated in the disparity of those two figures, is testimony to the success of the "second colonizing of New England."

That success helps to make Massachusetts one of several preferred destinations in the United States of contemporary Irish emigrants. A new generation of young Irish—the "illegals" who defied American quota laws of the 1970s and '80s, legal immigrants under the enhanced quota system of the last decade, and professional-class transatlantic sojourners—has recently peopled the metropolitan Boston area. Employing modern media skills and technology, they communicate with their countrymen much as Thomas D'Arcy McGee and Patrick Donahoe once did through the pages of the Boston *Pilot*. The informal networking, newspaper notices, and immigrant guidebooks of yesteryear have given way to a small Irish Networking Society of modern support groups offering advice and counsel about housing, job opportunities, obtaining credit, American citizenship law, and more. "The Green Scene," a periodical newsletter electronically published on the Society's Web page, spreads the word. Several newspapers, radio programs, and Irish language courses at more than a dozen locations in Middlesex and Norfolk counties, as well as in Boston, evince the vitality of Irish life in the region today.

The city of Boston, which during the Famine reeled under the impact of those whom Handlin later called "undigested and undigestible," in 1993 dedicated a Great Hunger Memorial near Faneuil Hall to their memory. In early 1998 the Commonwealth

Museum sponsored a temporary exhibit from the State Archives devoted to the "Children of Erin" in Massachusetts, and an annual Stonehill Irish Festival raises funds for the Irish Cultural Centre and a permanent complex in Canton to preserve and celebrate Irish culture. The long and continuing history of the children of Erin in Massachusetts gives much to celebrate.

*See* Boston; Irish in America; Nativism

Richard D. Brown, *Massachusetts: A Bicentennial History* (New York, 1978).

Dennis Clark, "Yoked to Yankees—New England," *Hibernia America: The Irish and Regional Cultures* (Westport, Conn., 1986).

Donald B. Cole, *Immigrant City: Lawrence, Massachusetts, 1845–1921* (Chapel Hill, 1963).

Oscar Handlin, *Boston's Immigrants 1790–1865: A Study in Acculturation* (Cambridge, Mass., 1941; Revised and enlarged ed. 1959).

Marcus Lee Hansen, "The Second Colonization of New England," *New England Quarterly* (October, 1929): 539–560. Reprinted in *The Immigrant in American History* (Cambridge, 1942).

William F. Hartford, *Working People of Holyoke: Class and Ethnicity in a Massachusetts Mill Town, 1850–1960* (New Brunswick, N.J., 1990).

Robert H. Lord, John E. Sexton, and Edward T. Harrington, *History of the Archdiocese of Boston,* 3 vols. (New York, 1944).

Timothy J. Meagher, ed., *From Paddy to Studs: Irish-American Communities in the Turn of the Century Era* (Westport, Conn., 1986). Chapters on Lowell and Worcester.

Brian C. Mitchell, *The Paddy Camps: The Irish of Lowell, 1821–1861* (Urbana, 1988).

Katherine F. Mullaney, *Catholic Pittsfield and Berkshire* (Pittsfield, Mass., 1897).

Thomas H. O'Connor, "The Irish in New England," *The New England Historic and Genealogical Register,* 139 (July 1985): 187–195.

Vincent Powers, *Invisible Immigrants: The Pre-Famine Irish Community in Worcester, Massachusetts, from 1826 to 1860* (New York, 1989).

Stephan Thernstrom, *Poverty and Progress: Social Mobility in a Nineteenth-Century City* (Cambridge, Mass., 1964).

EDWARD J. O'DAY

## McAULEY, THOMAS (1778–1862)

Presbyterian clergyman and educator. In 1778, McAuley was born to Thomas A. and Eliza J. (Warden) McAuley in Coleraine, Ireland. Records of McAuley's early years are scarce other than reports of missionary work before he began college. McAuley graduated from Union Schenectady, N.Y., in 1804 and remained there as tutor and professor of mathematics and natural philosophy. In 1819, he was ordained and became a pastor at Rutgers Street Church, New York.

McAuley's personality melded well with his career as a clergyman and he became active in the theological development of the Presbyterian General Assembly in 1837. McAuley supported new theological factions which proposed new doctrinal points of clarification over and against the position of the so-called "old school." It was the turmoil caused by such doctrinal disputes that led to an eventual split in the governing presbyters of the Presbyterian Church as a whole.

McAuley continued his interest in education and was granted the LL.D. degree by Dublin University. In 1827 he was chosen as president of Transylvania University in Kentucky but declined the position. Instead, he took a significant part in the founding of Union Theological Seminary where he became the institution's first president. Similarly, he taught pastoral theology and church

polity until he resigned in 1840. McAuley's legacy remains both in his educational work and his support of the "Auburn Declaration," which called for greater clarity of doctrinal matters in the Presbyterian Church. He died on May 11, 1862.

E. F. Hatfield, *The Early Annals of Union Theological Seminary* (1876). *Dictionary of American Biography,* 12.

JOY HARRELL

## McCAFFREY, LAWRENCE J. (1925–   )

Historian. In a career spanning nearly fifty years, Lawrence J. McCaffrey has written scores of books and articles and taught Irish and Irish-American history to thousands of students in the United States and Ireland, as well as contributing depth and substance to television documentaries about the Irish experience.

Born on Aug. 10, 1925, McCaffrey grew up in Riverdale, a working-class suburb of Chicago. His father, John Thomas McCaffrey, had emigrated from County Cavan, Ireland, in 1912, quickly becoming "a staunch Democrat, a dedicated union member, and a baseball fan." Undaunted after losing his job during the 1916 New York transit strike, he moved to Chicago and worked his way up from the packinghouses on the city's South Side to a foreman's job at Acme steel in Riverdale and finally to a "lever man on the railroad."

Growing up in the predominantly German parish of St. Mary's, McCaffrey never took for granted his Irish identity: at an early age he could recite Robert Emmet's famous 1803 "Speech from the Dock." His years at St. Leo High School in Chicago's heavily Irish Auburn Park neighborhood also left their mark. McCaffrey remembers conductors on the Halsted Street line reciting Irish ballads and patriotic speeches, lessons reinforced by the Irish Christian Brothers who taught Irish history with texts used in the national schools of Ireland.

Thanks in large measure to the solid preparation he received at Leo, McCaffrey was able to take advantage of the G.I. Bill of Rights following his World War II tour of duty with the Coast Guard. He graduated from St. Ambrose College in Davenport, Iowa, in 1949 (during which time he met his wife, Joan McNa-

Lawrence J. McCaffrey

mara, a graduate of Mount Mercy College in Cedar Rapids, Iowa). After receiving a master's degree from Indiana University in Bloomington, Indiana, in 1950, McCaffrey was awarded a Ph.D. in history from the University of Iowa in Iowa City in 1954.

In 1960, with Emmet Larkin of the University of Chicago and the late Gilbert Cahill of the State University of New York at Cortland, McCaffrey founded the American Committee for Irish Studies (ACIS). Now known as the American Conference for Irish Studies, it has become the nation's foremost interdisciplinary organization promoting the study of Irish and Irish-American literature, history, language, anthropology, political science, culture, and the fine arts.

After a series of appointments, mostly at Midwestern universities and colleges, McCaffrey was named professor of history at Loyola University, Chicago in 1970. During his twenty-one-year tenure, he continued to write and publish widely. Advisory editor of *The Irish Americans,* a forty-two volume series published by Arno Press in 1976, McCaffrey also served on the editorial boards of such journals as *Ethnicity; The New History of Ireland; The Recorder;* the University of Illinois Press's *Chicago Ethnic Series; The New Hibernian Review;* and the *Multi-Cultural Review.*

Over the years, McCaffrey has become a well-known lecturer in Ireland at the summer sessions of the School of Irish Studies in Dublin and Cork. He was one of five historians—and the only American—to appear on Thames TV's production of *The Troubles,* a six-part documentary on Northern Ireland that first aired in 1981. Perhaps the most telling mark of the man is that he has not been reluctant to revise his own scholarship. In 1997, he changed the title of his seminal work on the American Irish to *The Irish Catholic Diaspora* and acknowledged that he had become "considerably more optimistic about the preservation of an Irish-American identity."

*See* American Conference for Irish Studies

Books by Lawrence J. McCaffrey:
*The Irish Catholic Diaspora in America* (Washington, D.C., 1997).
*The Irish Question: Two Centuries of Conflict* (Lexington, Kentucky, 1995).
*Textures of Irish America* (Syracuse, New York, 1992).
Editor, *The Irish in Chicago* (Urbana, Illinois, 1987).
*Ireland: From Colony to Nation State* (Englewood Cliffs, New Jersey, 1979).
*Daniel O'Connell and the Repeal Year* (Lexington, Kentucky, 1966).

ELLEN SKERRETT

## McCAREY, LEO (1898–1969)

Film director. Leo McCarey, son of Thomas J. ("Uncle Tom") McCarey, was born October 3, 1898, in Los Angeles, California, where his Irish parents encouraged him to study law rather than following his father who was a boxing trainer. His parents prevailed, and Leo enrolled at the University of Southern California Law School where he finished his studies but suffered a fall into an elevator shaft. McCarey collected $5,000 in damages from the University and with the money invested in the copper industry where he also secured work as a lawyer.

McCarey's copper ventures failed, however, and believing himself unsuited to the field of law, he made a failed attempt at song-writing. He next turned to Universal Studios where he secured a job as a "script girl" and then made his way up, with his considerable education, into directing.

In 1923, McCarey moved to the Hal Roach Studios where he made 300 short films, including the Charley Chase and Joe College series. The idea of a fat and lean comedy team came to him there which led to the remarkably successful Laurel and Hardy team. In 1926, McCarey became vice president of Hal Roach and served in that position until 1928 when he moved to RKO. There he directed *The Sophomore* which was a great success, but his next film, *Red Hot Rhythm,* proved to be a failure. When McCarey moved to Fox Studios in 1930, he directed *Roadhouse* and *The Kid from Spain,* which were both box-office hits, and *The Awful Truth,* for which he won an Academy Award in 1937.

A serious auto accident in 1940 slowed him down, but McCarey was able to finish making *Love Affair* which he remade in 1957 as *An Affair to Remember.* McCarey is perhaps remembered best for his direction of *Going My Way,* the Academy Award-winning film starring Bing Crosby and Barry Fitzgerald as two Catholic priests faced with a rapidly changing world. McCarey died of emphysema at St. John's Hospital July 5, 1969.

*See* Cinema, Irish in; California

Ephraim Katz, ed., "Leo McCarey," *The Film Encyclopedia* (New York, 1994).
*New York Times,* obituary (July 6, 1969).
Richard Schickel, *The Men Who Made the Movies* (New York, 1975).
Robin Wood, "McCarey, Leo," *International Dictionary of Films and Filmmakers—2 Directors* Laurie Collier Hillstrom, ed. (New York, 1997).

DANIEL J. KUNTZ

## McCARRAN, PATRICK ANTHONY (1876–1954)

Lawyer, U.S. Senator. Pat McCarran was the only child of Irish immigrants, Patrick and Margaret (Shea). His father fought with the U.S. Cavalry in Nevada, and settled as a homesteader and sheep rancher in that state where his son was born August 8, 1876. Pat attended the University of Nevada, quitting in his senior year to help his injured father and studying law part-time while sheep-herding. He married Martha Harriet Weeks in 1903 with whom he would have five children and was admitted to the bar in 1905. He first practiced law in Nevada mining towns, served as county district attorney, was elected to the state supreme court, serving 1913–1918, and became chief justice the last two years. He made landmark decisions on fingerprinting and property rights, but gained wider press in 1920 as the attorney who won a Nevada divorce for film actress Mary Pickford. Running unsuccessfully for U.S. senator in 1916 and 1926, he was elected in 1932 with Roosevelt and the Democratic sweep, but remained independent of party politics, opposing many programs of FDR and Truman. His bipartisan philosophy gained him re-elections until his death. McCarran fought Roosevelt's plan to enlarge the U.S. Supreme Court to reduce conservative influence, and acted to curb both federal bureaucracy and limit presidential treaty-making powers. A strong and influential senator, he chaired the Judiciary Committee, headed the important Appropriations Subcommittee, and continued to promote his state's mining, livestock, and irrigation interests. Military and commercial aviation received his legislative backing, and he favored the remonetization of silver. His support of Sen. Joseph McCarthy of Wisconsin in anti-communist and anti-subversive activities followed his sponsorship of the McCarran-Wood Act of 1950 requiring registration and government exclusion of communists. The McCarran-Walter Act (Immigration and Nationality Act) of 1952 restricted immigration and naturalization in the United States to 1965. Conservative, controversial and Catholic, Pat McCarran was a powerful and respected dissenter during the New Deal and early Iron Curtain eras. He died in Hawthorne, Nevada, on Sept. 28, 1954.

*Dictionary of American Biography*, Supplement 5, 1951–1955 (New York, 1977).

Jerome E. Edwards, *Pat McCarran, Political Boss of Nevada* (Reno, NV, 1982).

ANNA M. DONNELLY

## McCARTHY, CATHERINE (1875–1972)

Immigrant, housewife, seamstress. Catherine McCarthy was one of the thousands of anonymous Irish immigrants who walked through Ellis Island around the turn of the twentieth century to find a new home and establish a new family. She was a typical, ordinary immigrant.

Catherine McCarthy was born at 66 Jameston Road in Ferrybank across the river from Waterford. When asked about her birthday, she routinely replied, "the year Mary Toppin left for America." When a cousin visited the Ferrybank Church in 1966, and obtained a copy of her baptismal certificate indicating a few more years than she had admitted, Catherine curtly replied that the Irish didn't bother about such things.

Catherine McCarthy was born on September 1, 1875, the first of six children of Charles McCarthy and Mary O'Toole, both natives of Limerick. Her father had earlier immigrated to the United States, worked there for a decade as a stone mason, became a U.S. citizen in New York City on October 9, 1868 (Catherine became the family archivist and historian), and returned to Ireland where he married Mary O'Toole. According to family tradition, the McCarthy's had done stone work on several Irish churches.

Catherine loved to tell the story of her departure for the United States. She was semi-engaged to a local farmer. During one visit to the family, her suitor's mother wondered out loud if a city girl (she was then twenty-five) like Catherine was strong enough to do all the farm chores. Catherine then and there realized her beau wanted a milk maid rather than a wife. Then and there she decided to leave Ireland.

Catherine immigrated to Chicago in 1901 or 1902. Aboard ship, she became both seasick and homesick. Late one night, alone on the deck, she gazed at the vast ocean ahead and longed to go home. "I realized," she would later tell her grandchildren, "that I could not turn the ship around and go back to Ireland." And then she would add, "And besides, I was a bit curious to see what was on the other side." She never lost her sense of adventure. Catherine made her way to Chicago where she first stayed with relatives, the LaPlante and Keyes families. She was most at home, however, with a second cousin of her own age, Mae Nolan.

She found work as a maid with a doctor's family. When the doctor entered the room where she was sleeping with the baby one night, her sense of propriety was so offended that she quit the next day. She then became a chambermaid for the wealthy Eccles family, responsible for two of the mansion's thirty-five rooms. One Sunday, she had to watch the Eccles baby and missed Mass. She promptly quit, telling Mr. Eccles that Sunday

Catherine McCarthy

was for church, not for work. Mr. Eccles promised never to infringe again on her Sunday obligations; Catherine remained. She later told her grandchildren how strange and different she found Chicago from her home in Ireland. "The only thing that was the same was the Mass," she recalled.

Catherine worked for two years in Chicago, returned to Ireland for a visit, helped her sister, Mary, return with her to Chicago. She borrowed money from Mr. Eccles to pay her sister's passage, "paying back every cent," she later said with pride. All her brothers and sisters eventually followed her to Chicago, forming a close-knit, extended Irish family for more than half a century.

Mae Nolan had a twin brother, John. Catherine's first impression of him was that he was a ruffian. He, however, was smitten with her and courted her. She had doubts about the marriage, since the two were second cousins. The Irish relatives did not help, conjuring up stories of webbed feet and other abnormalities. On her return visit to Ireland, Catherine asked her parish priest's advice. "Do you love him?" the priest asked. When Catherine answered affirmatively, the priest told her to forget the Irish fables and marry him.

John Edward Nolan and Catherine McCarthy were married on November 30, 1905. The couple had three children, Charles (1906), John (1908), and Mary Elizabeth (1912). John had gone to work immediately after grammar school to help his twin sister attend high school. He worked in a variety of places—Illinois Central Railroad, U.S. Steel, several auto shops—before his gregarious nature found its natural outlet as a mail carrier; he worked for the postal service until he retired at seventy.

The family lived in a series of apartments until they bought half of an old duplex home in the Hyde Park area; they remained there for almost thirty-five years.

Catherine was an accomplished seamstress; she supplemented the family income by making dresses for the city's wealthy. She made capes for the local sisters and Mass vestments for parish priests. During World War II, she volunteered regularly at the Red Cross where she sewed clothing for European refugees.

A sense of extended family permeated the Nolan home. John and Catherine took in Catherine's Aunt Julia, whom she first accompanied to the United States, and later her brother Billy, whose fondness for alcohol meant he was usually unemployed and broke. Mae Nolan took in her mother. The Nolan household was regularly visited by grandmothers, aunts, uncle, and cousins, all very Irish. Catherine had an extraordinary family pride and kept track throughout her life of all her aunts, uncles, cousins, cousins-twice-removed, and other sundry family members.

John and Catherine's only daughter, Mary Elizabeth, died of diabetes at the age of fifteen. Their two sons attended Catholic grammar and high schools, working a variety of jobs to help with expenses. Charles and John had to give up their scholarships to St. Ignatius High School because the family could not afford the trolley fare; the boys walked several miles daily to Mt. Carmel, where Charles was in the first graduating class of 1925; John in the second. Both boys went to work for the Illinois Central Railroad immediately after high school and worked there until retirement.

John Nolan died in 1967. Catherine gave up the small apartment where they had spent their last years together. During her remaining five years, she moved back and forth from the homes of her two sons and daughters-in-law. She was a quiet, soothing presence, watching television, praying her rosary in her room, enjoying an afternoon glass of wine, and talking often of her wonderful family, past and present.

Catherine lived to see the first two of her eight great-grandchildren, Catherine Ann Nolan and Michael Scott Nolan. By now, three grandchildren's families were living outside Chicago in Georgia, Michigan, and Louisiana. The family's appreciation for education was passed down to this new generation, although their college interests varied from general engineering, electrical engineering, economics, and mathematics to art, communicative disorders, French, and journalism. Their occupations were just as varied: navy pilot; communications electrical technician; professional artist; college recruiter; and theater manager. This fourth generation also reflected America's varied cultural heritage with Polish, Swiss, German, English, Canadian, and Scotch ancestry mixed with the Irish.

Catherine McCarthy Nolan died on February 20, 1972, and was buried in Holy Sepulcher Cemetery next to her husband; daughter; sister-in-law, Mae; mother-in-law; and sister, Mary whom she had helped come to America.

CHARLES E. NOLAN AND
MARY CATHERINE NOLAN, O.P.

## McCARTHY, CHARLES LOUIS ("Clem") (1882–1962)

Sports broadcaster, journalist. Growing up the son of an Irish-born horse dealer and auctioneer, "Clem" McCarthy spent his childhood collecting a vast knowledge about horses and horse racing. At first he harbored dreams of being a jockey, but his large stature forced him to focus on a career as a handicapper and race reporter. In 1927, Arlington Park in Chicago hired McCarthy to be the voice of their public address system. The following year he broadcast the Kentucky Derby for the first time over radio. Hired by the National Broadcasting Company in 1929, McCarthy's voice announced some of the era's greatest moments in sports. His extensive knowledge of event participants combined with a rapid-fire delivery to make him a great favorite of sports fans nationwide. He regularly covered events such as the Kentucky Derby and Preakness, as well as a number of boxing title matches, including the legendary rematch between Joe Louis and Max Schmeling in 1938. McCarthy was also a fre-

quent contributor to local and national dailies and turf publications. He later did movie newsreels as well. Ironically, in spite of his horse racing knowledge, one of McCarthy's most famous broadcasts came in 1947 when he called the wrong winner in the Preakness Stakes. He switched to CBS that same year and made his last Kentucky Derby call in 1950. In 1957, he suffered injuries in a serious car accident, which left him in debt. He died in a nursing home in 1962.

*Dictionary of American Biography,* Supplement 7: 494–95.
Bud Greenspan, "The Man Who Blew a Derby," *Sports Illustrated* (May 17, 1971): 40–47.
*New York Times* (August 13, 1961).

TOM DOWNEY

## McCARTHY, COLMAN (1938–   )

Writer, peace activist. Born in Old Brookville, New York, March 24, 1938, Colman McCarthy has been described as "a pacifist, a bit of an anarchist, a Catholic, an animal-rights advocate, an ardent bicyclist, a stalwart opponent of injustice, a teacher of nonviolence, a friend of the homeless, a foe of the death penalty, a leftwing pro-lifer, and a fine writer."

He was graduated from Spring Hill College in Mobile, Alabama, in 1960, and entered a Trappist monastery for what he expected to be a few weeks. He stayed five years "making friends with cows . . . in his charge," and came to regard those years as the most important of his life. "It's therapeutic to have a period in your life of contemplation, of strenuous physical exercise and of opening your soul to spiritual concerns," he has remarked. "It has been a wonderful resource for me and helped me to love my family tremendously."

McCarthy started with *The Washington Post* in 1968 as a member of its editorial-page staff, and was soon writing a column that went to national syndication in 1978, appearing in fifty newspapers around the country. *The Washingtonian* described him as the "liberal conscience of the *Post,"* and when the column was terminated in 1997, there was an organized protest by readers outside the *Post* building. McCarthy for his part was sanguine, remarking that he felt "blessed" for having been given the space to write two thousand words a week, one hundred thousand a year for nearly three decades.

In 1987 McCarthy, a life-long pacifist, founded the Center for Teaching Peace, a nonprofit organization to teach children nonviolent methods of resolving conflicts, and as a volunteer he teaches peace education in two Washington-area high schools. He is also an adjunct professor at Georgetown University Law Center and the University of Maryland, conducting fourteen-week courses on "Law, Conscience and Nonviolence." He likewise lectures nationally on the subject of peace and nonviolence. The skills of nonviolence, McCarthy contends, should be taught with the same diligence that history, mathematics, science and languages are taught. "Otherwise," he comments, "how else do we break the cycle of violence?"

McCarthy holds five honorary degrees, and is author of a number of books, some incorporating his columns and essays. He is married to Mavourneen (Deegan) McCarthy, and they have three sons. A registered nurse and writer, Mrs. McCarthy assists in running the Center for Teaching Peace.

Bettijane Levine, "America's Professor of Peace," *Los Angeles Times* (February 14, 1994).

Colman McCarthy, "So Long, With Thanks," *The Washington Post* (January 7, 1997).
Matthew Rothschild, "Editor's Note," *The Progressive* (March 1997).

JOHN DEEDY

## McCARTHY, EUGENE J. (1916– )

Politician, poet. Hubert Humphrey, a fellow-Minnesotan Democrat, once described his fellow-presidential hopeful, Eugene J. McCarthy, as "the son of a Minnesotan farmer, handsome, witty, teacher, poet, Irish mystic, and a clever politician, cleverer for denying it." Born in Watkins, Minnesota, in Easter week 1916 (March 29), he received his B.A. at St. John's University, Minnesota, in 1935, followed in 1939 by an M.A. from the University of Minnesota. He taught high school for a time, and between 1940 and 1943, economics and education at St. John's. From 1945 he taught in the sociology department at the College of St. Thomas, Minnesota, eventually chairing it. Married to Abigail Quigley, they had four children, Ellen, Mary (whom he immortalized in the poem *Bicycle Rider*), Michael, and Margaret

In 1948 he entered the House of Representatives and in 1958, the Senate. He came to international prominence in 1968 when he challenged the incumbent president, Lyndon Johnson, for the presidential nomination on the question of continuing U.S. involvement in the war in Vietnam. McCarthy has carefully documented that campaign in his *The Year of the People* (1969).

After the ill-starred Chicago Democratic convention in August, he returned to the Senate. It became clear to everybody, except himself, that the fire had gone out of the belly, and he announced that he would not seek reelection in 1970. Unfortunately, he continued to "run" for president, and even once endorsed Ronald Reagan for president on Canadian broadcasting.

Robert Lowell wrote what amounted to his political obituary notice on July 6, 1968:

> I love you so . . . Gone? Who will swear
> you wouldn't have done good to the
> country, that fulfillment wouldn't have
> done good to you—

He made at least one noteworthy return to Capitol Hill when he appeared before the Senate Foreign Relations Committee hearings on the 1985 Supplementary Extradition Treaty between the U.S. and U.K., a cozy deal aimed totally at IRA "terrorists," worked out between an Anglophile State Department and "special relation" U.K. The scene is well described in Jack Holland's *The American Connection* (1987), which lists McCarthy "a venerable figure with his grey hair and slightly stooping gait—the very image of a Yankee statesman—as one of the most impressive of the thoughtful and authoritative figures, political, legal and academic, to advance objections to ratification." With gentle, chiding humor, he treated the committee—on which he had sat—to a history lesson that began with a quotation from Tacitus. That lesson suggested strongly that the new treaty should not be ratified. McCarthy would never return an IRA fugitive to either Northern Ireland or the Irish republic under any circumstances.

McCarthy may yet be best remembered as a political essayist and poet, as in *The Limits of Power America's Role in the World* (New York, 1967), in which he nostalgically notes—leapfrogging in reverse the Kennedy and Lyndon Johnson years—that the world he envisages might well have come into being in an Adlai Stevenson presidency. In one of the great speeches of

Eugene J. McCarthy

this century, he had nominated Stevenson for the presidency at the Los Angeles Convention, July 13, 1960. (The text is included as an appendix in *The Year of the People*.)

A more recent work is *A Colony of the World: The United States Today,* with its almost apocalyptic sub-title, *America's senior statesman warns his countrymen* (1992). As he sees it (p. 3), the most disturbing mark of the colonialism, or neocolonialism, of the United States is our loss of control over our foreign and military policy. Among his rather gloomy reflections, his view of modern Ireland puts a question mark on the Celtic Tiger image: "The Germans, especially, seem to have stopped off in Ireland to the chagrin of the Irish, who see a disposition to turn Ireland into a kind of retirement and recreational facilities for wealthy Europeans, with the Irish serving as maids and housekeepers and nurses, as horse trainers, grooms and jockeys, as butlers and waiters, and chauffeurs, and doormen, and as entertainers and musicians." Actually, the Irish have become almost as good as their former colonists at enlisting Third World help to replace them in their menial roles.

As a poet he often shows a lyrical tenderness, notably in the near-perfect, *The Heron,* while his satire is seen to best effect in *The Death of the Old Plymouth Rock Hen.*

> Decapitated, she did not act
> Like a chicken with its head cut off
> no pirouettes, no somersaults
> no last indignity.
> Like an English queen she died.

He could turn his verse powerfully toward political ends, as in his *Vietnam Message:*

> We will take our napalm and flame throwers
> out of the land that scarcely knows
> the use of matches.

Or in *My Lai Conversation:*

> American politician has said,
> "It is better to kill you as a boy in the elephant grass
> of Vietnam
> Than to have to kill you as a man in the rye grass
> in the USA."

*Complexities and Contraries* is a book of essays covering the Carter presidency, and McCarthy's self-description there complements that by Humphrey: "ironic rather than satirical; skeptical, not cynical; and optimistic, rather than pessimistic."

His most recent volume, *Selected Poems,* presumably includes his own favorites from several volumes of poetry, including *Other Things and the Aardvark.*

He is a poet in the Homeric, bardic tradition, a main feature of which is phenomenal powers of memorization, a gift brought to perfection by McCarthy in his long stopovers in airports on his speech circuits. Over recent years he has acquired a spellbinding, almost Ancient Mariner *persona:* "Just slightly shorter than the *Iliad,*" one heckler interjected at a Washington dinner-party when McCarthy announced that he would recite his most recently memorized poem, *The Wanderings of Oisin* by W. B. Yeats. In many ways he *is* Oisin, one of the *Scotti vagantes,* hell-bent on saving civilization, as pacific as Columcille, but as querulous as Columbanus.

When last sighted (on C-Span, June 29, 1998, on a panel on *The Election of 1968 and the Media*), he looked physically frail (a result of a protracted recent illness) but with the old clarity of thought and expression unimpeded, and still showing flashes of his mordant wit, the Socratic gadfly still picking holes in the appropriated infallibility of the *New York Times.*

Jack Holland, *The American Connection* (New York, 1987).

Eugene J. McCarthy, *Other Things and the Aardvark* (Garden City, New York, 1968).

———, *Complexities and Contraries: Essays of Mild Discontent* (New York, 1982).

———, *The Year of the People* (Garden City, New York, 1969).

———, *A Colony of the World: The United States Today, America's senior statesman warns his countrymen* (New York, 1992).

———, *Selected Poems* (Rochester, Minn., 1997).

THOMAS HALTON

## McCARTHY, JOSEPH R. (1908–1957)

U.S. Senator. Joseph Raymond McCarthy was born November 15, 1908, on his parents' farm in the town of Grand Chute, Outagamie County, Wisconsin. The McCarthy farm was located in a rural neighborhood known as "The Irish Settlement." He was the son of Timothy McCarthy (1866–1946) and Bridget Tierney (1870–1941). Three of Joe's grandparents were born in Ireland. His paternal grandfather, Stephen Patrick McCarthy (1821–1901), was a native of County Tipperary.

Young Joe McCarthy was educated in a one-room schoolhouse a mile south of his parents' farm. Following in the footsteps of his older siblings, McCarthy did not go on to high school in nearby Appleton. Instead, he worked on his parents' and uncles' farms, started a chicken business, and eventually managed a grocery store in nearby Manawa. In the fall of 1929, as his twenty-first birthday approached, McCarthy decided to enroll at Little Wolf High School. By studying sixteen hours a day, seven days a week, he completed the four-year curriculum in nine months. McCarthy was then admitted to Marquette University where he joined the boxing team. By the following year, McCarthy was coach of the team. He received his LL.B. degree in 1935.

McCarthy practiced law in Waupaca and Shawano, Wisconsin. In 1936 he won the Democratic nomination for District Attorney of Shawano County, but lost the general election to the Progressive incumbent. Three years later, McCarthy was elected circuit court judge by defeating a long-time incumbent. His hard work, engaging sense of humor, ebullient personality, and uncanny gift for creating a political issue had carried him to victory.

Taking office in January 1940 as the youngest circuit judge in Wisconsin's history, McCarthy proved to be a hardworking, but eccentric, judge who became known for granting "quickie" divorces. He was on the bench less than two years when America was pulled into World War II. Without resigning his judicial office, McCarthy enlisted in the Marines. He was assigned to a rear-echelon desk job as an intelligence officer. He volunteered for a few combat missions and accounts of these experiences were later exaggerated to portray McCarthy as a war hero. In one instance, McCarthy forged the name of a superior officer on a citation praising his exploits. McCarthy promoted a succession of stories sent back to Wisconsin newspapers describing him as "Tail Gunner Joe." On the strength of these stories, McCarthy announced his candidacy for the Republican nomination for U.S. Senate in 1944.

McCarthy's candidacy was an apparent violation of military law banning members of the armed forces from campaigning for partisan political office. It also violated the code of judicial ethics that prohibited judges from running for political office. McCarthy would later be censured by the Wisconsin Supreme Court for running for the Senate. In any event, he was defeated by the Republican incumbent, Alexander P. Wiley. However, two years later McCarthy defeated another incumbent, Robert M. LaFollette, in the Republican primary. He went on to win the general election. McCarthy, the ultimate political outsider, had won admission to the world's most exclusive political club at the age of thirty-seven.

McCarthy's first three years in the Senate were lackluster at best. However, in November 1949, he latched on to an issue that would make him (in)famous throughout the world. He leveled a charge of communism against the city editor of the Madison *Capital Times,* a long-time political nemesis. McCarthy found documentary evidence to support his charge. The result was massive and overwhelmingly favorable publicity in Wisconsin newspapers gave McCarthy's floundering political career a vital boost.

Three months later McCarthy delivered a speech in Wheeling, West Virginia, claiming (with no factual or documentary sup-

Joseph R. McCarthy

port) that 205 State Department employees (the number would fluctuate in later speeches) were communists who were formulating American foreign policy. The speech generated enormous publicity and McCarthy soon became a household name. McCarthy expanded his original claim to allege that four thousand federal employees were homosexual. He accused the Truman administration of being "puppets of the Politburo." In 1951 he went so far as to claim that General George C. Marshall has participated in "a conspiracy so immense and an infamy so black as to dwarf any previous venture in the history of man." The implication of treason against one of America's most distinguished citizens offended many, but did not appear to slow the McCarthy avalanche.

McCarthy seemed to have tapped into a deep reservoir of xenophobia and paranoia lurking on the underside of American society. He generated a large and vocal following in almost every state. In the fall elections of 1950, several key Democratic senatorial opponents of McCarthy were defeated. Wisconsin's junior senator was given credit in the press for his opponents' demise. Two years later the Democrats lost their twenty-year control of the White House. Again, McCarthy was identified as a key factor in the national Republican resurgence. Meanwhile, back in Wisconsin McCarthy was reelected to the Senate, but his victory margin of 140,000 votes was substantially less than his 1946 margin. In fact, he ran dead last on the Republican ticket in the state that year. McCarthy's national strength was such that many considered him the most powerful politician in the country—stronger than either Truman or Eisenhower. Both presidents assiduously avoided a head-on confrontation with the Wisconsin senator. Later, historians would refer to the decade of the 1950s as the McCarthy Era in recognition of his dominance of the period's political discourse.

McCarthy's reckless disregard for the truth, his failure to identify a single communist in government, and ultimately the fear that he was causing serious damage to important American institutions led to his downfall. The Democrats resented his wrecking the Truman-Acheson State Department and his questioning the Democrats' patriotism, but when McCarthy attacked Eisenhower's administration as well, he lost the necessary political backing to survive. The end came in 1954 when the Senate voted overwhelmingly to censure McCarthy for abuse of congressional power. Dispirited and broken by the censure, McCarthy's final years in the Senate were marked by political oblivion. He died in Washington on May 2, 1957, at the age of 48. Accompanied by an honor guard of U.S. Marines and 25,000 mourners, McCarthy was buried beside his parents in St. Mary's Catholic Cemetery in Appleton. A dark chapter in American political history ended with the crash of McCarthy's meteoric career.

Michael O'Brien, *McCarthy and McCarthyism in Wisconsin* (Columbia, MO, and London, 1980).
Thomas C. Reeves, *The Life and Times of Joe McCarthy* (New York, 1982).

THOMAS GILDEA CANNON

## McCARTHY, JOSEPH VINCENT ("Joe") (1887–1978)

Baseball player, manager. Born to Irish parents in 1887, Joseph McCarthy began his career as a talented minor league baseball player. A high school knee injury, however, kept him from the major leagues. In 1919, therefore, McCarthy used his skills as a player-manager for the American Association team in Louisville,

Ky. Two years later, McCarthy moved to full-time management of the team when he married Elizabeth ("Babe") McCave. His disciplined management style and effective teaching ability earned him a winning reputation. The Chicago Cubs of the National League hired him in 1926. McCarthy took the team from last place to the league pennant by 1929. Public opinion, however, turned against him when the Cubs lost their World Series match to Philadelphia, which led, in turn, to his resignation. The New York Yankees quickly picked him up, however, and by 1932 McCarthy brought the Yankees to the World Series where he defeated his old team, the Chicago Cubs. A string of World Series victories followed from 1936–1939, which led to the distinction of American all-star manager seven times from 1936 to 1946, and manager of the year in 1936, 1938 and 1943. World War II sent many of his experienced players into the battlefield, but McCarthy brought the most inexperienced rookies to the league pennant by 1942 and 1943. In 1946, McCarthy's health began to fail, forcing his retirement for three years. He returned in 1948 as manager of the Boston Red Sox, but retired permanently two years later. Elected to the Baseball Hall of Fame in 1957, McCarthy died on a farm near Buffalo, New York, at the age of 91 in 1978.

*See* Baseball

Joe McCarthy memorabilia, Baseball Hall of Fame at Cooperstown, N.Y.
Obituary, *New York Times* (Jan. 14, 1978).

DANIEL J. KUNTZ

## McCARTHY, MARY (1912–1989)

Mary McCarthy was an eminent writer and public figure whose novels, stories, essays, and reviews captured and satirized modern American life. She was born in Seattle, Washington, into a privileged American family of Irish Catholic, New England Protestant, and Jewish descent. But when she was six years old an idyllic childhood ended: her parents, ill with the Spanish flu, died on a train ride move to Minneapolis.

For the next five years Mary and her three younger brothers lived with their Great Aunt Margaret and her new husband Myers Shiner. These elderly guardians were incredibly stern, even denying the children pillows and taping their mouths shut at night, so they would not sleep with them open. When Mary won a statewide essay contest for an essay "The Irish in America," Myers kept the $25 prize money and beat her with a razor strop, lest she be "stuck up." But as she later wrote in *Memories of a Catholic Girlhood* (1957), "the injustices my brothers and I suffered in my childhood made me a rebel against authority, but they also prepared me to fall in love with justice, the first time I encountered it."

She was rescued from her aunt and uncle by her grandfather Harold Preston, a civic-minded lawyer from Seattle. From 1923–29 the Prestons cared for Mary and saw that she received a quality education, which included sending her to Annie Wright Seminary. McCarthy then attended Vassar from 1929–33, graduating as a Phi Beta Kappa, majoring in English. Her academic and social experience at Vassar influenced her greatly, and she later depicted this world in her novel *The Group,* a huge bestseller in the 1960s.

In 1933 she married Harold Johnsrud, an actor, and began to review novels for *The Nation* and *The New Republic.* By 1936 she divorced Johnsrud and moved to Greenwich Village.

Mary McCarthy

In 1937 she was living with Philip Rahv, and they joined Dwight McDonald, Fred Dupee, and William Phillips in reviving *Partisan Review,* with McCarthy as drama critic. She also worked for the leftist publisher Covici Friede.

She married prominent critic and novelist Edmund Wilson in 1938. He urged her to write fiction. They had a son Ruel, born on Christmas Day 1938. Soon McCarthy's stories appeared in *Harper's Bazaar, Partisan Review,* and other publications.

From 1945–46 McCarthy taught at Bard College. In 1946 she divorced Wilson and married Bowden Broadwater, who worked at the *New Yorker,* then at *Partisan Review,* and later as a prep school administrator. They traveled to Europe together and remained married until 1960, throughout McCarthy's most productive period. She published *The Oasis* (1949), *Cast a Cold Eye* and *The Groves of Academe* (1952), *A Charmed Life* (1954), and *Memories of a Catholic Girlhood* (1957). During these years she also taught briefly at Sarah Lawrence College and won two Guggenheim Awards (1949 & 1959). Oddly, Broadwater and McCarthy were not especially happy, and friends described them as extremely caustic to each other.

McCarthy met her fourth husband, James Raymond, in Warsaw, where she was invited to give a talk by the State Department. Raymond was a public affairs officer for the American Embassy in Warsaw. They each obtained a divorce and married each other in 1962. They lived mostly in Paris and maintained a vacation home in Castine, Maine.

In 1968 McCarthy went to Hanoi to write about the war in Vietnam for the *New York Review of Books.* She became an outspoken opponent of the war and in the 1970s also wrote sharply about Watergate. She published *Cannibals and Christians,* her last novel, in 1979. That same year she appeared on The Dick Cavett Show and accused Lillian Hellman of lying in her autobiography, claiming "every word she writes is a lie, including 'and' and 'the.'" Hellman launched a huge lawsuit, but died before it could come to trial. McCarthy spent a great deal of money defending herself, but critical examination of Hellman's work has confirmed the general truth of McCarthy's remarks.

Mary McCarthy's career spanned six decades and touched on many of the most important movements of the 20th century—communism, socialism, feminism, the Red Scare, the Vietnam War. Her work was overtly political, even her fiction, where she espoused her views at great length through representative characters. She was essentially a satirical writer who made unapologetic use of her own life, the lives of her husbands or friends, and the schools she taught at or attended. The people closest to her in life were some of the great intellectuals of the times, like Philip Rahv and Hannah Arendt, and the characters in her fiction are highly literate and cultured. However, Mary McCarthy told her brother Kevin McCarthy, the actor, in an interview, that her audience tended to be "quite a few simple people, not illiterate but very ordinary. I'm not an author that's greatly loved by an elite" (*Conversations with Mary McCarthy*).

Two books, in particular, illustrate McCarthy's skills as a satirist. *The Groves of Academe,* set in rural Pennsylvania at a college much like Bard, exposed the evils of McCarthyism and academic politics. *The Group,* while not focusing on intellectuals, highlighted the lives of college women who found emancipation less than ideal. It appeared in the 1960s and reflected new concerns that educated women had made little progress, especially in their personal lives.

Mary McCarthy is generally remembered as an outspoken and talented writer, whose personal life epitomized a new era when intellectual women would find a voice in public affairs and in the leading journals of the day. She spoke out about marriage, sexual expression, and women's roles in contemporary America. Her fiction and non-fiction illustrate her lifelong crusade for integrity and justice. She died in New York City on October 25, 1989, and was buried in Castine, Maine. Her other major works are: *The Company She Keeps* (1942); *The Hounds of Summer and Other Stories* (1981); *Birds of America* (1981); *Ideas and the Novel* (1980); *Occasional Prose* (1985); and *Between Friends: The Correspondence of Hannah Arendt and Mary McCarthy, 1949–75,* (1994).

Carol Brightman, *Writing Dangerously: Mary McCarthy and Her World* (New York, 1992).

Carol Gelderman, ed., *Conversations with Mary McCarthy* (Jackson, 1991).

———, *Mary McCarthy: A Life* (New York, 1988).

Doris Grumbach, *The Company She Kept* (New York, 1967).

KATHLEEN OCHSHORN

## McCARTHY, PATRICK HENRY (1860–1933)

Labor leader, politician. Killougheen, a townland near New Castle West in County Limerick was the birthplace of Patrick Henry McCarthy. Born on March 17, 1860, he was the fourth son and second youngest of five boys and four girls born to Patrick McCarthy and Ellen Hough McCarthy. Their father was a dairy farmer. The family lived on eighteen acres in the rich dairying country known as the "Golden Vale." Patrick Henry was educated in the national school less than fifty yards from his home. In his ninth year, both parents died, leaving him in care of an older brother and a local priest.

### Apprenticeship

Impressed with his schoolwork, his guardians planned to prepare him for a career in law. He, however, dissented vigorously and insisted he would be a carpenter. Finally, they arranged his apprenticeship to James McCormick of nearby Knockaderry, a man for whom the lad developed great admiration.

Assigned to construction of a new Catholic church in Ballingarry, McCarthy came in conflict with its parish priest, Timothy

Shanahan. The man insisted on nighttime work for all hands to complete the building on time. McCarthy disagreed and, although a mere apprentice, persuaded all the men to stop work, calling for hiring more workers to avoid night work. James McCormick arrived, agreed with his apprentice, and additional construction workers were hired. The incident foreshadowed a future in trade unionism for McCarthy.

## EMIGRATION

Nearing completion of his four-year apprenticeship, McCarthy obtained permission from (his) master McCormack to leave a few days early to join friends emigrating to America. An ambitious young journeyman, he had chosen the United States as most promising for his future in the building trade. Financed by his brother William, the voyage from Queenstown (now Cobh) took him to New York in late April. He proceeded to Chicago, arriving on May 2, 1880, where a married sister lived and provided lodging for him.

In Chicago he found work constructing a building on Halsted Street. The job lasted exactly one day. The contractor fired him for discussing union organization at lunch with fellow carpenters. In the fall of 1880 McCarthy moved to St. Louis and became associated with Peter J. McGuire, master organizer and founder of the national union of carpenters. Although McCarthy was unable to attend the founding convention in 1881 due to illness, he learned much from his contact with McGuire.

## SAN FRANCISCO

In 1886 McCarthy and two friends sojourned through the west, stopping for some time in San Francisco. Still single and reluctant to return to a torrid summer in the Midwest, the young journeyman decided to settle in the city by the bay. He joined Local 22, oldest of the carpenter unions in the city, became active and was elected president of it, holding the position for six terms. His leadership revitalized carpenters' organizations in the city. Understanding of relations between craftsmen of different ethnic backgrounds was one of his strengths. Local 304 conducted its affairs in German exclusively. The other two were mixtures of Scandinavians, Irish, Scotch, Italians and small numbers of other ethnics. To be effective, frictions had to be minimized and cohesion fostered—so that welfare for all was advanced equally.

## LORD OF BUILDING TRADES

P. H. McCarthy is best known for his dominance of the Building Trades Council (BTC) of San Francisco. A federation of local unions in all construction crafts in the city, it was created by McCarthy and others in 1896. Elected to its presidency in 1898, McCarthy continued to lead it through 1922. The most dramatic example of his ability was illustrated in the millmen's dispute of 1900. The AFL's campaign for an eight-hour day in that year had been won for all the building crafts in San Francisco through McCarthy's effective negotiations. However, operators of planing mills, which produce finished wood products for the industry, refused to go along and threatened a lockout of all union millmen rather than comply. Recognizing that the construction industry would come to a halt unless millwork was forthcoming, McCarthy, using funds raised from union sources, built a large planing mill in the city which operated at full capacity within six months. He then warned operators that, after mid-August of 1900, only millwork produced under eight-hour conditions would be used in San Francisco. Construction continued without interruption. Beaten by superior strategy, mill operators accepted an arbitration award establishing an eight-hour day in their shops.

The BTC was a body consisting of delegates from affiliated locals of craftsmen with representation based on size. "McCarthy's machine" was formed by cultivating delegates from the larger locals and by attracting those from various ethnic groups based upon their numbers in the workforce of the building industry. As a result, all agreements were handled by McCarthy himself rather than local affiliates, who normally negotiate them. This substantial power was exercised with considerable discretion. He discouraged ill-timed and badly conceived strikes and unrealistic demands. In fact, contractors gradually recognized that he kept matters within bounds of what economic conditions could bear. He also did much to minimize jurisdictional disputes, the bugaboo of the building industry.

McCarthy, a life-long Catholic, married Maude Saunders (late of Cork City), in 1893. She died eight years later without issue. However, in 1905 he married her sister, Jainette, who bore him eight children.

Flush with victory in the millmen's dispute, McCarthy broke with the San Francisco Labor Council (SFLC)—a federation of all local unions in the city, including those in construction—over a boycott the SFLC refused to support. He ordered all building craft locals to withdraw from SFLC. Next he established a state building trades council and became president of it as well. It gave him statewide influence.

## POLITICAL CAREER

The split lasted until 1910 when his order to disaffiliate from SFLC was lifted. Increasing cooperation over several years had preceded the move. This change of heart was inspired by McCarthy's decision to enter politics in 1907, when Eugene Schmitz, thrice-elected mayor on the Union party ticket, was undone by a graft scandal. The party was a creation of the trade unions, and McCarthy, a Democrat, had originally opposed it, but now recognized it as a potential vehicle for his becoming mayor if labor unity was restored in the city. Winning the nomination, he lost the election in 1907, but a second run in 1909 on a platform heralding San Francisco as the "Paris of America" won him a two-year term. Reelection in 1911 failed when voters lost faith in the Union party.

## DEMISE

McCarthy, nevertheless, retained his mastery of the construction industry as chief of both the city and state building trades councils until 1922. At that point he was unseated by turmoil resulting from the postwar recession which upset wage structures in the building industry and by an "American Plan" campaign mounted by employers to destroy construction union power. He had lost the confidence of his membership which had tolerated his autocratic leadership and finally resigned. McCarthy spent the remaining eleven years of his life as a building contractor and dabbling in real estate investment. Patrick McCarthy died July 1, 1933.

*See* Labor Movement

Robert E. L. Knight, *Industrial Relations in the San Francisco Bay Area* (Berkeley, 1960).

Patrick H. McCarthy, unpublished memoirs.

Frederick L. Ryan, *Industrial Relations in the San Francisco Building Industry* (Norman, Oklahoma, 1935).

L. A. O'DONNELL

## McCLENACHAN, BLAIR (?–1812)

Merchant, creditor, congressman. Born in Ireland, Blair McClenachan immigrated to Philadelphia at an early age. He became a merchant and pursued banking and shipping, eventually becoming the largest importer in Philadelphia after Robert Morris.

During the Revolution, McClenachan outfitted several privateers at great personal profit, and he served with the First Troop of Philadelphia Cavalry during the New Jersey campaign in 1776–77. In 1780, financier Robert Morris founded the Bank of Pennsylvania to help provision American forces. McClenachan subscribed 10,000 pounds to the bank, a sum equaled only by Morris himself. McClenachan also supplied money and credit to the Continental Congress.

Toward the end of the Revolution, McClenachan entered into the political scene, participating on several local committees. He chaired the Anti-Federal Convention which convened in Harrisburg in September 1788, and later expressed bitter opposition to the Jay Treaty, ending one harangue with the call to "Kick this damned treaty to hell." (Elkins and McKitrick, 432). A member of Pennsylvania's House of Representatives from 1790–95, he served a term in the Federal Congress from 1797–99.

Despite his political rank and lifestyle in the palatial mansion of Cliveden, the rough McClenachan never fully fit in with Philadelphia's refined elite. After the Revolution, McClenachan engaged in several unsuccessful financial pursuits which led him to debtor's prison. President Thomas Jefferson appointed him Commissioner of Loans, however, and McClenachan supported himself in that position until his death on May 8, 1812. Satirist William Cobbett once deemed him, "Blair, the Great, the Irish guardian of the state."

*See* American Revolution; Philadephia

*Biographical Directory of the American Congress* (Washington, D.C., 1971).

John H. Campbell, *History of the Friendly Sons of St. Patrick and of the Hibernian Society for the Relief of Emigrants from Ireland* (Philadelphia, 1892).

Stanley Elkins and Eric McKitrick, *The Age of Federalism* (New York, 1993).

Ellis P. Oberholtzer, *Philadelphia: A History of the City and its People*, 4 vols. (Philadelphia, 1912).

CHRISTIAN G. SAMITO

## McCLOSKEY, JOHN (1810–1885)

Archbishop, first American cardinal. John McCloskey was born in Brooklyn, New York, on March 10, 1810, the son of Patrick and Elizabeth Harron McCloskey, who had emigrated from County Derry, Ireland, two years earlier. In 1817 his family moved to New York City, where he attended Thomas Brady's classical school and St. Patrick's Church. On the death of his father in 1820 Cornelius Heeney, a well-to-do merchant, became his guardian. In 1821 at the tender age of 11 he was sent to Mt. St. Mary's College, Emmitsburg, Maryland, graduating in 1828 after completing both preparatory schooling and college. Returning as a seminarian to Mt. Mary's after a year at home, he was ordained at St. Pat-

John McCloskey

rick's in 1834, the first native New Yorker to be ordained a diocesan priest.

After a short time as assistant at the cathedral and chaplain at Bellevue Hospital, he was appointed to the faculty of the new seminary at Nyack, New York. This assignment, too, was short-lived, when the old farm house in which it was located was destroyed by fire. The end result was that he was given permission to go to Rome for three years' study at the Gregorian University, 1835–37. In Europe he made influential friends and traveled extensively, while deepening his understanding of the mind of the church.

On his return home in 1837 he was made pastor of St. Joseph's Church in Greenwich Village, where the lay trustees of the parish had been quarreling with Bishop Dubois. With prudence and forbearance he won the trustees over after they had threatened to close the doors on him. In 1841 he was named the first president of St. John's College (later Fordham University) by Bishop John Hughes, but remained in that post only a year, while continuing to serve as pastor of St. Joseph's. Hughes, whose style was confrontational in contrast to McCloskey's peacemaking ways, nevertheless selected him as his coadjutor with right of succession. McCloskey had been a priest only ten years when he was consecrated a bishop on March 10, 1844 at the age of 34.

While still pastor at St. Joseph's, he spent much of his time in visitations of parishes trying to work out difficulties and cooling down the anti-Hughes opposition among certain pastors. At the same time, Hughes depended upon his wise counsel in the nativist troubles and school controversy of that era.

The rapid growth of the New York Diocese, encompassing the whole state, led in 1847 to the creation of the dioceses of Albany and Buffalo. On May 27, 1847, he was named the first bishop of the Albany Diocese where he served for seventeen years. During that time the Catholic population almost quintupled and the number of churches increased from 47 to 120.

When he succeeded John Hughes as second archbishop of New York following his predecessor's death in 1864, many surmised that he had made good use of influential friends in Rome. Not until long after his death was it learned that he had written to Cardinal Reisach to try to head off his appointment on the grounds of frail health. One of his first projects was the resumption of construction of the new St. Patrick's Cathedral, suspended during the Civil War and dedicated by McCloskey in 1879. In concert with the Second Plenary Council of Baltimore in 1866, he silenced the Fenians with a letter of admonition against wild schemes of freeing Ireland and invading Canada, which was read from all pulpits in the diocese. At the First Vatican Council in 1870 he considered the declaration of papal infallibility inexpedient, but on the final ballot he voted in the affirmative.

Despite this hesitancy his influence rose in Rome, and in 1875 he was named the first American cardinal by Pius IX. When Pius IX died, McCloskey arrived too late for the conclave electing Pope Leo XIII in 1878, but received the cardinal's red hat from him on March 28 of that year. When he died on October 10, 1885, there were approximately 1,000,000 Catholics, 139 parishes, 279 priests and 2,136 women religious in the archdiocese.

*See* New York City

Florence D. Cohalan, *A Popular History of the Archdiocese of New York* (Yonkers, 1983).
John Cardinal Farley, *The Life of John Cardinal McCloskey* (New York, 1918).

JAMES J. HALEY

### McCLURE, GEORGE (1770–1851)

Soldier. Born near Londonderry, Ireland, McClure emigrated to America at the age of twenty. He eventually settled at Bath in western New York. There, McClure established himself as a leading merchant and entrepreneur, with his prominence earning him election to brigadier general in the local militia. His brigade was called into action at the outbreak of the War of 1812 to protect the Niagara frontier. Establishing his headquarters at Fort George on the Canadian side of the Niagara River, McClure sat largely inactive during the first year of the war. However, in late 1813, the British turned their attention to Fort George. By this time, McClure's force had dwindled to only one hundred men, as most of the militia returned home at the end of their enlistments. Outnumbered almost five to one, McClure abandoned Fort George in December, burning the neighboring village of Newark, Ontario, as he retreated. While claiming his intention was to deprive the British of winter quarters, McClure's action outraged both British and Americans. Newark's wanton destruction led to immediate calls for reprisals. On December 30, British troops set fire to Buffalo and Black Rock, New York, in retaliation, actions which Americans blamed McClure for instigating. He received a chilly welcome upon his return to New York and his conduct was publicly disavowed by his superiors. McClure retired from the military after the war and returned to his business ventures. He moved west to Elgin, Illinois, around 1834, where he died in 1851.

*Dictionary of American Biography*, Vol. VI, part 1: 594–95.
Louis L. Babcock, *The War of 1812 on the Niagara Frontier* (Buffalo, 1927).
Earnest A. Cruikshank, ed., *The Documentary History of the Campaign on the Niagara Frontier in 1814,* 9 Vols. (Welland, Ont., 1896–1908).

TOM DOWNEY

### McCLURE, SAMUEL SIDNEY (1857–1949)

Editor, social reformer. Born Feb. 17, 1857, the oldest of four sons, to Thomas McClure and Elizabeth (Gaston) on a small farm in County Antrim, Ireland, Samuel descended from Scotch-Irish Protestants on his father's side and French Huguenots on his mother's. When he was eight, his carpenter father was killed in a shipyard fall. This led his mother to bring her family to America and Valparaiso, Indiana, where two brothers and two sisters had already settled. The widow married an Irishman, Thomas Simpson, in 1867 and raised four more children on his hundred acre farm near town. In 1871, urged by his mother, Samuel, possessing only one dollar, entered the newly opened high school in Valparaiso, and in 1874 went on to Knox College in Galesburg, Illinois, having supported himself with odd jobs, and returning for a time to the family farm after his stepfather's death. In imitation of his classmates, he had added a middle initial, "S," which stood at first for Sherman, and later Sidney. In college he edited the *Knox Student*, started the Western College Press Association of which he was president, and produced an intercollegiate news bulletin for commercial sale. McClure also published a *History of Western College Journalism*. He hoped to marry a Knox professor's daughter, Harriet Hurd, despite the objections of both families; his mother took him to Ireland intending him to remain there, but he worked his way back to America and continued a seven-year on-and-off courtship. Graduating in 1882, he took a job with a Boston bicycle manufacturer which led to his editing and publishing the *Wheelman*, a periodical aimed at the current cycling fad. With his career launched, he finally married Harriet in 1883; they had three daughters and two sons, one adopted.

Leaving Boston, McClure joined the DeVinne publishing company in New York City, and later became a junior editor at the Century Company where he proposed syndicating material for sale to newspapers. For this suggestion he was let go and told he should start his own business. He did just that, forming McClure's Syndicate in October 1884 which bought serialized novels and stories from popular writers and sold them to newspapers nationwide. Energetic and persuasive, McClure traveled across the country and to Europe numerous times for the next six years and sought out such notable writers as Robert Louis Stevenson, Samuel Clemens, William S. Porter, Jack London, W. D. Howells, as well as Tennyson, Kipling, Hardy and many others. A fellow student from Knox College, John S. Phillips, ran the New York office by 1887, while McClure went about soliciting contributors. Despite debt, and with about 2,000 manuscripts on hand, he launched his monthly, *McClure's Magazine* during the panic year of 1893, aiming at a mass readership. He undercut competitors by selling issues at fifteen cents, instead of twenty- or thirty-five cents, and was supported at this critical financial time by Arthur Conan Doyle. Ida Tarbell's serialized biographies of Napoleon and Lincoln increased circulation, which reached 400,000 by 1900, as the magazine contained the largest amount of advertising in the nation. Lasting impact on the country came with the January 1903 issue containing articles on city political corruption by Lincoln Steffans, Ida Tarbell's disclosures on Standard Oil, and Ray Stannard Baker's article on the right to work. Theodore Roosevelt pejoratively called these exposés "muckraking," but they were followed by more in a similar vein, imitated by other periodicals, and became a major influence on general awareness of serious social issues, American public opinion, and on journalism itself. His autobiography was ghost written by Willa Cather, one of the magazine's contributors. McClure's temperament and success brought a desire for a major facilities expansion, but these led to the resignations of Phillips, Tarbell,

Baker, and Steffans, who felt the plans were unrealistic. The magazine declined, was revived several times, and finally ceased by 1930. S. S. McClure was attracted temporarily by Henry Ford's Peace Ship in 1915, and then by Mussolini and fascism. He spent his last years living at the Murray Hill Hotel in New York, and working with his papers at the Union League Club. He was awarded the Order of Merit by the National Institute of Arts and Letters in 1944 for his contributions to journalism. McClure died on March 21, 1949, of a heart attack at St. Barnabas Hospital in the Bronx and was buried in Galesburg, Illinois.

*See* Scots Irish

*American Magazine Journalists, 1900–1960.* First series/edited by Sam G. Riley (Detroit, 1990).
Willa Cather, *The Autobiography of S. S. McClure* (Lincoln, NE, 1997 [1914]).
Peter Lyon, *Success Story, the Life and Times of S. S. McClure* (N.Y., 1963, 1967).
Harold S. Wilson, *McClure's Magazine and the Muckrakers* (Princeton, N.J., 1970).

ANNA M. DONNELLY

## McCORMACK, JOHN (1884–1945)

Tenor. He is remembered as one of the most talented and popular singers of his time. Born in Athlone, he studied in Dublin and Milan where he was tutored by Vincenzo Sabatini. Under the name Giovanni Foli, he made his debut in *L'Amico Fritz* in Savona, moved on to Covent Garden and sang in Mozart's *Don Giovanni*. Shortly thereafter, he made his celebrated recording of "Il Mio Tesero." His operatic career reached its zenith in America where he sang with Patti, Melba and Tetrazzini.

McCormack was a singer of great versatility and his recitals all over the United States made him a household name. He catered to all musical tastes and made "The Fairy Tree," "The Rose of Tralee," and "The Old House" known to millions by his gramophone records which maintained their popularity for decades. He made several films, including *Song O' My Heart*.

In 1929 he sang in Ireland for the centenary of Catholic Emancipation, and his performance at the Eucharistic Conference

John McCormack

(1932) in Dublin was memorable. McCormack and his wife gave generously to charities, and he was honored by being made a hereditary papal count in 1929.

John McCormack retired to Ireland and died in Dublin in 1945. He left many admirers, and in 1949 Father James McDonald (d. 1961) founded the John McCormack Society and bequeathed the complete collection of McCormack's records to St. Charles Seminary in Philadelphia.

John McCormack, *I Hear You Calling* (Dublin, 1939).

JOAN GLAZIER

## McCORMACK, JOHN W. (1891–1981)

Congressman. Born in Boston, Massachusetts, December 21, 1891, John William McCormack was one of twelve children of Joseph H. and Mary E. (O'Brien) McCormack, an Irish-American couple of modest means. McCormack's father died when he was thirteen and in the eighth grade of public school. The death marked the end of McCormack's formal education, although not of learning. Forced to seek work to help support the family, he took a $4-a-week job as an office boy in a law firm, and there read law and prepped for the legal profession. He was admitted to the Massachusetts bar in 1913. He would subsequently receive a dozen honorary degrees.

In 1917 McCormack entered politics as a member of the Massachusetts House of Representatives. He advanced to the State Senate in 1920 and, after one failed attempt, won election in 1928 to the United States House of Representatives, serving from the Twelfth and later the Ninth Massachusetts Districts.

A progressive Democrat and during the Roosevelt administrations a staunch New Dealer, McCormack was named chairman of the House Committee Investigating Un-American Activities in 1934, and later became first chairman of the House Scientific and Astronauts Committee. In 1958 he sponsored legislation creating the National Aeronautics and Space Administration (NASA). McCormack served three terms as Majority Leader and then at age seventy became Speaker of the House. He was the first Catholic to hold that post. He sat forty-three years in Congress, nine as Speaker, and championed such legislation as the Marshall Plan, the lowering of the voting age to eighteen, civil rights and aid-to-education bills. In August 1970, he took a position in favor of an Equal Rights Amendment.

During the Nixon administration, McCormack was a strenuous critic, charging it with "playing on people's fears" and possessing "a callous disregard for the social needs" of the disadvantaged.

McCormack was a stern anticommunist and supporter of the war in Vietnam. His positions on the war, as well as his long-standing political friendship with conservative Southern politicians, triggered liberal challenges to his leadership as Speaker in 1969 and 1970. He survived both, although at political cost.

In 1969, his office was touched by scandal when his administrative assistant, a man McCormack described as a "devoted aide," was charged with influence-peddling and subsequently convicted of perjury. Attempts were made to implicate McCormack in the wrongdoing, but evidence was lacking. At worst, McCormack seems to have been guilty of sloppiness in the management of his office. "My life—personal and private—is an open book," he exclaimed, and seemingly it was. He was generally regarded as a man of rectitude and probity. In referring to him, colleagues commonly used the sobriquets "The Archbishop" and "Rabbi John."

In May 1970, McCormack announced he would retire from office at the conclusion of his current term. The decision came partly under political pressure, but also because of age and the declining health of his wife of fifty years, Harriet (Joyce) McCormack. He died November 22, 1981, in Dedham, Massachusetts.

*See* Massachusetts

JOHN DEEDY

## McCORMICK, ANNE ELIZABETH O'HARE (1882–1954)

Journalist. Anne Elizabeth O'Hare McCormick set a precedent for women in journalism. She was the first woman member of the *New York Times* editorial board and the first woman to win a Pulitzer prize in journalism.

Born May 16, 1882, in Wakefield, Yorkshire, England, McCormick was brought to the United States as an infant by her American parents, Thomas and Teresa Beatrice O'Hare. She grew up in Columbus, Ohio, attended private schools, graduated from St. Mary of the Springs Academy in 1898, and earned a bachelor of arts degree from the College of St. Mary of the Springs.

Around 1916 she married Francis J. McCormick, an engineer and importer who often traveled to Europe. She took a job as associate editor of the *Catholic Universe Bulletin,* a national Catholic weekly based in Cleveland. In a sense, she followed in her mother's footsteps, who had been a columnist and women's page editor for the *Bulletin.*

McCormick also wrote poetry for magazines, such as *Smart Set,* and had entries included in *Braithwaite's Anthology of Magazine Verse.*

During this time, she also began writing features on a freelance basis. Her articles were published in the *New York Times Magazine* and *Atlantic Monthly,* as well as several other publications.

While traveling abroad with her husband in 1920, McCormick began a series of articles for the *Times,* dealing with the rise of fascism in Italy. She was a lone voice among journalists of the time in noting that Benito Mussolini was "the master voice" in Italy.

In 1922, McCormick became a regular correspondent for the *Times,* and three years later, she was hired to write exclusively for the paper. However, she also wrote a series during 1933 and 1934 for the *Ladies' Home Journal.*

Her first interview with Mussolini was in 1926, and she conducted several more interviews with him over the following years. Interviews with other political leaders included Adolph Hitler, Joseph Stalin, Winston Churchill, Franklin Delano Roosevelt, Dwight Eisenhower, Harry Truman, Eamon de Valera and Leon Blum. Her interviews focused on the personality of the subject rather than their political views.

In 1939 she visited thirteen countries, writing features and news stories. Her experience abroad resulted in the writing of a thrice weekly column, first called "In Europe" and later "Abroad," for the *Times.*

McCormick was named to the *Times* editorial board in June 1936, the first woman to hold such a position. Besides her column, she began writing two unsigned editorials a week for the paper. In 1937 another distinction was awarded McCormick when she won the Pulitzer prize in journalism, again the first woman to be so honored.

Anne Elizabeth
O'Hare McCormick

McCormick covered events in Europe, Asia and the United States, having an "uncanny knack of being where the news was breaking," as noted by her colleagues. She wrote not only about national political conventions but also local stories of national significance. Her writing was characterized by its informality and impartiality.

She refused for years to be included in *Who's Who.* However, in 1939 she was named Woman of the Year, and throughout her career, McCormick received a number of other awards, including the University of Notre Dame's (Ind.) Laetare Medal in 1944 and the New York *Evening Post's* medal for distinguished foreign reporting.

Smith College, Northampton, Mass., Columbia and Fordham universities, New York, and eleven other institutions of higher learning in the United States honored her with honorary degrees. She also was a delegate to the United Nations Educational, Scientific and Cultural Organization conferences in 1946 and 1948.

McCormick's one book, *Hammer and the Scythe: Communist Russia Enters the Second Decade* (1928), garnered excellent reviews. Two collections of her *New York Times* articles were published, *The World at Home* (1956) and *Vatican Journal, 1921–1954* (1957), following her death on May 29, 1954, in New York City. She was eulogized by President Dwight Eisenhower as a "truly great reporter, respected at home and abroad for her keen analysis and impartial presentation of the news developments of our day."

*Current Biography* (1940).
Matthew Heon, ed., *Catholic Authors* (1948).
*Newsweek* (June 20, 1936).
*New York Times* (May 4, 1937, Feb. 25, 1940, and May 30, 1954).
*Time* (March 22, 1948).
H. W. Wilson, *Twentieth-Century Authors: A Biographical Dictionary of Modern Literature* (1942, 1st supp 1955).

MARIANNA McLOUGHLIN

## McCORMICK, RICHARD A. (1922–  )

Theologian, educator. Father Richard A. McCormick, S.J., was born in Toledo, Ohio, in 1922, to the distinguished physician

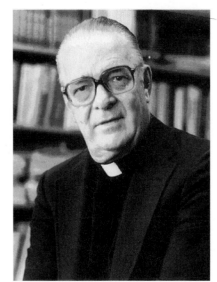

Richard A.
McCormick

Edward J. McCormick, M.D., who served in 1953–54 as president of the American Medical Association, whence perhaps his son's long-standing interest in medical ethics. He entered the Society of Jesus in 1940 and in 1957 began his career as a professor of moral theology. More than forty years later he is still teaching. After a dozen years at Georgetown University's Kennedy Institute of Ethics, he is now the John A. O'Brien Professor of Christian Ethics Emeritus at the University of Notre Dame.

Teaching has been the hallmark of McCormick's contribution to church and academy, whether from the lectern or in his pellucidly written and widely circulated articles on new directions in moral theology. For the scholarly quarterly *Theological Studies,* he contributed for twenty years an annual survey of the most important developments in the field. Pastors as well as professors eagerly awaited this survey, knowing that it would be as helpful in counseling troubled parishioners as in straightening out tangled ethical problems. He has also written regularly for *America* and other journals of opinion. There his own pastoral sense has illuminated for a wider audience such troubling issues as birth control, abortion, homosexuality, care of the terminally ill, and the limits of biological experimentation.

Neither courting controversy nor shy of it, McCormick has strongly defended the right and duty of theologians to explore fully the great Christian moral tradition in order to protect the freedom of believers. As a proponent of "proportionalism," he has argued against a narrow biological determinism in medical and sexual ethics. Rather, he has placed the meaning of the moral act within the context of fundamental human choices as they determine our stance toward God, the world and our fellow humans. Thus he challenged the view that human life should be maintained at all costs even in situations where the quality of that life, as in the case of persons in a persistent vegetative state, has declined to a subhuman level.

Similarly, he has come to the defense of colleagues like Fr. Charles Curran when they have been under attack from conservative Catholics and/or officials within the Roman Catholic Church. While acknowledging the right of the institutional Church to define doctrine and teach with full authority in matters of faith and morals, McCormick has persuasively argued for the necessity of theological debate and discussion as an integral part of the Church's learning and teaching. If doctrine truly de-

velops, as Cardinal Newman argued, the Church must make room for free and open discussion of controverted issues. Moral theologians then become a part of the process, rather than an institutional irritant. By his integrity as a scholar and his loyalty as a son of the Church, Fr. Richard McCormick has enriched the Catholic Christian community with a wealth of insights into the ever more perplexing issues of biomedical ethics.

Richard A. McCormick, *Notes on Moral Theology: 1965 through 1980* (Lanham, Maryland, 1980).
——, *How Brave a New World?* (New York, 1981).
——, *The Critical Calling: Moral Dilemmas Since Vatican II* (Washington, D.C., 1989).

JOHN BRESLIN, S.J.

## McCOURT, FRANK (1930– )

Author. Born in Brooklyn to Irish immigrant parents from Counties Limerick and Belfast, and raised in his mother's native Limerick, Frank McCourt spurred a whole new trend in memoir-writing following the incredible success of his first book, *Angela's Ashes*. Published in 1996, McCourt's tale of a poverty-ridden childhood in the back lanes of Limerick city soared to the top of the *New York Times* bestseller list within a matter of months, and won its author a coveted Pulitzer Prize in 1997.

Telling, as he put it, the story of a "miserable Irish Catholic childhood," McCourt's book caused controversy in Limerick, where many locals claimed his recollection was faulty, things had never been that bad. Others sided with the author, saying McCourt hadn't been harsh enough.

After watching three of his siblings die as children, and seeing his alcoholic father desert the family in the early 1940s, McCourt finally decided that he had had enough of Limerick, and returned to New York, the city of his birth, in 1949.

The draft, he often acknowledges, was to prove the making of young Frank McCourt. After spending two years in Germany during the Korean War, McCourt returned to study at New York University and qualified as a teacher.

As many young immigrants before him had done, McCourt saved enough money to be able to pay for his younger brother Malachy to join him in the U.S. Malachy did so in 1952, and

Frank McCourt

quickly became a fixture on New York's social scene, with Frank accompanying him to various functions. The two became known for their repertoire of stories, which they eventually consolidated into a two-man show called *A Couple of Blaguards*.

In 1995, after marrying New York publicist Ellen Frey, his third wife (he has a daughter, Maggie, from his first marriage, and two grandchildren), McCourt finally started work on the book that would become *Angela's Ashes*. "I suppose I could have done it earlier," he told *Irish America* magazine in 1997. "I should've cut back on the teaching, should've gotten it down, but I don't know if I could have. I wasn't ready, I think. Or maybe I was."

The success of the book surprised even its taciturn author. For over two years it was on the *New York Times* bestseller list. Movie rights were snapped up by Paramount Pictures and director Alan Parker (*The Commitments*) signed on to the project. Malachy's son Conor filmed a documentary about the four surviving Mc-Court brothers—Frank, Malachy, Alphie and Michael—which was well received by TV audiences both in Ireland and the States.

Ever the teacher, Frank McCourt speaks passionately about education, and the need for more tax dollars to be pumped into the school system, every opportunity he gets.

Frank McCourt, *Angela's Ashes* (New York, 1996).
*Irish America* Magazine, vol. xiii/4 (Jul./Aug. 1997); vol. xiv/2 (Mar./Apr. 1998).

DARINA MOLLOY

## McCREERY, MAUD LEONARD (1883–1938)

Suffragette, labor organizer, socialist, journalist. Maria Maud Leonard was born February 24, 1883, at Cedarburg, Wisconsin. She was the daughter of Sylvester S. Leonard, a veterinary surgeon, and Anna Reilly. All four of her grandparents were born in Ireland. Maud Leonard was married to Rex I. McCreery (1902–1918) and to James J. Walker (1923–1931). Both marriages ended in divorce, but Maud was always known by her first married name.

Maud Leonard McCreery began her public career by campaigning on street corners for women's suffrage throughout the nation between 1912–1917. On the eve of World War I she spoke all over the country on behalf of the League to Enforce Peace, an anti-war group. After the war she worked in Chicago for the Federated Press news service. From 1930 to 1936 she served as an editor for the *Milwaukee Leader,* a socialist newspaper published by Victor L. Berger. She traveled across Wisconsin doing organizational work on behalf of the American Federation of Labor during the 1930s. She also served as editor of the Sheboygan *New Deal,* 1936–1937. When her health began to fail, she accepted a faculty appointment in the University of Wisconsin School for Workers.

McCreery was a dynamic public speaker who raised many thousands of dollars for progressive social causes. She was revered as a champion of the underdog, a fighter who devoted her life to peace and justice issues. McCreery died in Milwaukee on April 10, 1938.

*Dictionary of Wisconsin Biography* (Madison, 1960).
Frederick I. Olson, "Maria Maud Leonard McCreery." *Notable American Women 1607–1950,* 3 vols, ed. by Edward T. James, *et al.* (Cambridge, MA, 1971) vol. 2:457–58.

THOMAS GILDEA CANNON

## McDERMOTT, ALICE (1953–   )

Novelist. Alice McDermott emerged on the American fiction scene in the early 1980s. Her four novels, written in fifteen years, all comment on the quality of life in the American suburbs, in particular those bedroom communities which grew up on Long Island after World War II. Increasingly, her fiction has come to deal with the Irish-American experience, with immigrants settling in the teaming boroughs of New York City and subsequent generations opting for the space and fragile security of Long Island.

### BACKGROUND

McDermott was born in Brooklyn, New York, on June 27, 1953, the daughter of Mildred Lynch and William McDermott. Both her parents were the children of Irish emigrants who moved to the United States at the end of the nineteenth century and settled in the burgeoning borough neighborhoods surrounding Manhattan. The family moved to Elmont, a Long Island suburb, where McDermott attended Catholic schools. In 1975, she graduated from the State University of New York at Oswego, and took a job with a vanity press in New York City, a setting that reappears in her first novel, *A Bigamist's Daughter*. Earning her MFA from the University of New Hampshire in 1978, she began having short stories published in popular magazines such as *Redbook, Madamoiselle,* and *Seventeen*. She stayed on at UNH to teach for a year, and then spent another year as a fiction reader for *Esquire* and *Redbook*.

It was during her year as fiction reader that McDermott submitted fifty pages of an unfinished novel to literary agent Harriet Wasserman. Wasserman soon asked to read everything she had written and set her up with editor Jonathan Galassi at Random House. Galassi was instrumental in getting her first novel published. In 1980, the young author was invited to teach for a year at the Univerity of California at San Diego. She now teaches at The Amerian University in Washington, D.C., and lives in Bethesda, Md., with her husband David Armstrong and two sons, Willie and Eames.

### NOVELS

In 1982, McDermott's first novel, *A Bigamist's Daughter,* was published by Random House and critically received by the American

Alice McDermott

literary world. The story concerns a young vanity press editor (from Long Island) without a man or a family, who begins a relationship with a fledgling Southern novelist. Developing love finds a corresponding search into her past which, in turn, finds a possible parallel in the Southern writer's own quest for an ending about his story of a bigamist. All three strands of the novel converge with a similar fate, and McDermott's use of bigamy grows as a controlling conceit for the fear to commit. Jean Strouse wrote in the review in *Newsweek*, "On the unlikely hook of bigamy, Alice McDermott has hung a wise, sad, witty novel about men and women, God, hope, love, illusion, and fiction itself."

Five years later, in 1987, Farrar, Straus & Giroux published McDermott's second novel, *That Night*, for which she was nominated for the National Book Award and received one of the ten annual Whiting Writers' Awards. Also set on Long Island, this novel concerns one night in a quiet neighborhood when a high school girl's enraged boyfriend tears up the family's front lawn with his gang, and the fight that ensues when the neighborhood fathers confront them with suburban weapons of rakes and bats and tennis rackets. Narrated from the point of view of a ten-year-old girl who witnesses the event, this novel both reviews and previews the lives of several of the involved characters to suggest causes and effects of that night of violence.

A third novel, *At Weddings and Wakes*, also published by Farrar, Straus & Giroux, followed in 1992, justly earning enthusiastic critical acclaim. Once again the setting is a Long Island suburb in the early 1960s. Narrated primarily by three children, the novel also takes us almost mystically into the consciousness of the adult characters as if on some level the children intuit these adults. The story follows the regular journeys of the children's mother back to the Brooklyn apartment in which she grew up. This apartment, with the children's grandmother and three unmarried aunts, is the heart and soul of the story, and McDermott uses it to reveal more to her readers than the children understand: the stories behind the family dynamics of love and hostility.

In early 1998, Farrar, Straus & Giroux released a fourth novel, *Charming Billy*. The story concerns the life and death of Billy Lynch, a sensitive and disappointed alcoholic, and the wide circle of friends and family who follow in his orbit. The novel is very much about these other characters as well, however, and paints Billy as much in their orbits as they are in his, thereby revealing the complicated interdependencies within families and the power, the glory, and abuse of love. *Charming Billy* won the National Book Critics' Circle Award for fiction.

## THEMES

McDermott's novels sort through reasons why individuals develop as they do. Through multiple points of view, compelling plots, and lush lyrical prose, the author evokes vivid settings and creates fully realized characters. She brings her readers with graceful ease effortlessly back and forth in time, revealing fleeting, yet significant, memories that have colored the present. At the same time she moves us back and forth in place, from the Long Island midsection and its windswept tip to Brooklyn and Queens from whence her characters at some generational point were spawned, as earlier seeds spread from Ireland.

The author once said in an interview with the *Washington Post* that hers was very much an American childhood, with ethnicity not emphasized in her home, yet her novels are filled with Connellys and Lynches and Daleys. And the similarity between her

use of place and of memory with that of Irish writers is striking. McDermott uses Long Island the way Irish writers use the United States: as a place characters move to for freedom, for space, for independence. McDermott's characters are thus immigrants, but immigrants who have left Brooklyn, the Bronx, or Staten Island, and in some cases the transition is as traumatic as it was for those who left Ireland the generation before.

Long Island does not always sustain McDermott's characters, as we see with Elizabeth in *A Bigamist's Daughter*, and we see it being abandoned even before the mortgages are paid off in *That Night*. In *At Weddings and Wakes*, we follow the young narrators on buses and subways from Long Island on near-mythic journeys back to Brooklyn because it is that place that forms the fabric of their mother's imagination. She has an almost uncontrollable need to return, and appears unable to truly free herself to be happy with her kind, playful husband and green lawn. Charming Billy never leaves Queens, refusing to return to Montauk even for a visit, until his life is nearly over.

While her central characters reflect various angles on the conflict between rootless individual freedom and grounded collective enclosure, McDermott's narrators, all young women or children, are the ones who learn from the stories told. By *Charming Billy*, the narrator has learned to accomodate herself without leaving the family—and for human happiness, that makes all the difference.

*See* Fiction, Irish-American

"Alice McDermott," *Current Biography Yearbook*, 1992.

Michiko Kakutani, "The Ties That Bind and the Regrets That Strangle," Review of *Charming Billy, The New York Times* (13 Jan.1998): C15.

Verlyn Klinkenborg, "Grief That Lasts Forever," Review of *At Weddings and Wakes, The New York Times Book Review* (12 April 1992): 3.

David Leavitt, "Fathers, Daughters, and Hoodlums," Review of *That Night, New York Times Book Review* (19 April 1987): 1.

Wendy Smith, "Alice McDermott," *Publisher's Weekly* (20 Mar. 1992): 85–86.

Jean Strouse, Review of *A Bigamist's Daughter, Newsweek* (22 Mar. 1982): 76.

Anne Tyler, "Novels by Three Emerging Writers," Review of *A Bigamist's Daughter, New York Times Book Review* (21 Feb. 1982): 1.

MARGARET LASCH MAHONEY

## McDONALD, RICHARD ("Dick") (1909–1998)

Fast-food pioneer. Born February 16, 1909, to Irish immigrants Patrick and Margaret McDonald, the young McDonald graduated from Manchester High School West in New Hampshire in 1928. He then moved to be with his brother Maurice ("Mac") in Hollywood, California.

After having spent close to seven years managing a movie theater, McDonald joined his brother in 1940 to open a barbecue drive-in restaurant in San Bernadino. It was after World War II that the brothers decided to amend their business to accommodate increasing demands for quick service. Therefore, the McDonald brothers eliminated the barbecue menu and the car hops, focusing instead on a fixed menu consisting of hamburgers and French fries wrapped in paper and sold at a window. The phenomenon of fast food was initiated and became a popular and lucrative venture for the two brothers.

It was the low cost and convenience of the McDonald store that brought them to a quick and steady success. The brothers began with fifteen-cent burgers, twenty-cent milk shakes and fries and Coke for a dime. The restaurant design centered on bright red and white tile with a sign out front that kept a running tabulation of the number of burgers sold. In addition to these trademarks, the business needed a symbol and Richard provided just that: the golden arches. Originally, the golden arches were meant to architecturally enhance the small building but they became a symbol of the fast-growing American economy and the changing times.

By 1954 the McDonald brothers had sold twenty-one franchises and opened nine outlets. Ray Kroc, a former milk shake machine salesman, traveled to San Bernadino to seek employment as a franchise agent. In 1955 Kroc founded the Franchise Realty Corporation and opened his first McDonald's in Des Plaines, Illinois. In 1960 Kroc changed the name to the McDonald's Corporation and one year later he bought the business for 2.7 million dollars.

Mac McDonald died in 1971. Later in the 1970s there arose a controversy concerning the publication of Kroc's biography, *Grinding It Out: The Making of McDonalds.* In the biography Kroc dates the origins of McDonalds to his first franchise in Des Plaines. However, Richard and Kroc later came to a clarifying agreement that gave credit to the McDonald brothers as pioneers of McDonald's and founders of the fast-food industry, with Kroc taking the credit for fostering one of the largest international industry franchises.

In 1992 the McDonald family rededicated the original site in San Bernadino and placed a plaque there to commemorate the origins. Richard died of complications from pneumonia in July of 1998, leaving a proud legacy and an undeniable stake in American culture.

Manchester, New Hampshire *The Union Leader* (July 1998).
*New York Times* (July 1998).

JOY HARRELL

## McDONNELL, JOSEPH PATRICK (1847–1906)

Fenian, journalist, labor reformer. Joseph P. McDonnell was born in Dublin March 27, 1847, to a prosperous middle-class Catholic family. He was educated in the national school on Marlborough Street, Dublin and in the recently established Catholic University of Dublin. While enrolled at the University he joined the Brotherhood of St. Patrick, a club dedicated to Irish independence. There he blossomed as a precocious orator offering words of passionate nationalism—not appreciated by faculty or administrators.

### FENIAN ACTIVIST

Expelled finally for conspiring with others to interrupt a welcoming celebration for the visiting Prince of Wales and his bride, he became deeply engaged in the Irish Republican Brotherhood (Fenians), which he had joined during the same period. He contributed to the Fenian organ, *Irish People,* and learned editing at the fiercely nationalist *United Irishman.*

In September of 1865 *Irish People* staff members were arrested after a government spy penetrated its ranks. Only two months later McDonnell, who had risen in Fenian hierarchy, was sent to Mountjoy Prison for ten months and then released without trial.

### LONDON MOVE

Moving to London in 1868 he resumed his journalistic career with two of that city's daily newspapers to earn a living, but much of his time was spent organizing and addressing monster rallies, usually before the "Reformers' Tree" in Hyde Park, to secure amnesty for Fenian prisoners. His effectiveness won the admiration of Karl Marx and Friedrich Engels then living in London. They recruited him for the International Workingmen's Association (IWA) as corresponding secretary for Ireland, assigned to establishing IWA sections among Irishmen in London and in Ireland. McDonnell became adept at orchestrating massive demonstrations. As the delegate representing Ireland he attended the last IWA Congress held at the Hague in 1872. Later, in Amsterdam, before thousands he denounced British jailing of Irish political prisoners and demanded their release "in the name of the working people of the world."

In March of 1871 McDonnell wed Mary McEvatt (daughter of his Fenian mentor), in the Franciscan church of Peckham, London.

### MOVE TO AMERICA

With his wife he sailed steerage class to America in December of 1872, arriving just in time for the severe recession of 1873. As corresponding secretary for the New York council of the IWA, McDonnell met Peter J. McGuire, Samuel Gompers and others engaged in debating the proper course of labor struggles. He argued that economic organization of workers was essential before attempting anything further. Pursuing this conviction McDonnell and a like-minded few (not including McGuire) founded the United Workers of America to organize among the Irish in New York. Affiliated with the IWA, the new union survived only briefly after the IWA died in 1876. McDonnell and his comrades obtained control of a radical paper, changed its name to the *New York Labor Standard* and made J. P. McDonnell its editor. McDonnell and three allies set out to organize employees in textile manufacturing and established the International Labor Union (ILU) for that purpose. The ILU was one of the first industrial unions. In pursuing that objective McDonnell came to Paterson, New Jersey in 1878 to unionize employees on strike at the R. H. Adams textile mill. He resided in Paterson and published the *Paterson Labor Standard* for the rest of his life.

### NEW JERSEY CAREER

As his passion for socialism abated, McDonnell instigated formation of important labor institutions. Early on (1879), the annual New Jersey Labor Congress had become a reality, meeting in the state capitol in Trenton to promote labor reform laws. Next, in 1883 the New Jersey Federation of Organized and Labor Unions materialized at his urging and he became chairman of its legislative committee. In that position he mobilized voting strength in industrial communities to elect candidates who pledged to support reform legislation after canvassing their position on the issues. There followed lobbying during sessions of the legislature to see that the specific bills were introduced and legislators who had agreed to vote for them actually did so. According to labor historian Herbert Gutman, McDonnell spent fifteen winters in Trenton lobbying in this manner. The fruit of his effort was reform laws: those restricting child labor, requiring safety standards in industry, limiting the workweek in manufacturing to fifty-five hours and those restricting the use of convict labor. In 1887 New Jersey became the first state to make Labor Day a legal holiday thanks to McDonnell.

In 1884 McDonnell organized the Paterson Trades Assembly (composed of local unions in the town). He established the

Paterson Typographical Union in 1886 and maintained membership for life. He was a general organizer of the American Federation of Labor from 1902 on. He was chosen chairman of the national Labor Press Association at its founding in the same period. Samuel Gompers, then president of the AFL, referred to him as "the Nestor of labor journalists" and further recalled that McDonnell "was to take a leading part in the development of the American trade union movement." (Gompers, *Seventy Years of Life and Labor,* New York, 1925, 103, 128). Joseph P. McDonnell died on January 20, 1906.

*See* Fenians and Clan na Gael

John W. Boyle, "Ireland and the First International," *Journal of British Studies* (May 1972): 44–62.

Herbert Gutman, *Work, Culture and Society in Industrializing America* (New York, 1976).

McDonnell Papers, State Historical Society of Wisconsin, Madison.

L. A. O'DONNELL

## McELROY, JOHN (1782–1877)

Priest, educator. McElroy was born in Enniskillen, County Fermanagh, Ireland. He came to the United States in 1803. Settling in Georgetown, D.C., McElroy experienced a religious calling and entered the Society of Jesus as a lay brother in 1806. Ordained in 1817, he became pastor at Frederick, Maryland, five years later. He soon played a leading role in expanding the Catholic faith in the area, building new churches at Liberty and Frederick, establishing an orphanage under the auspices of the Sisters of Charity in 1824, and also beginning the region's first local free school. In 1829, he founded St. John's Literary Institute, which for a time rivaled nearby Georgetown as the leading Catholic institution of higher learning in America. He further expanded church influence by leading a series of religious retreats in Virginia, Maryland, and Pennsylvania. During the Mexican War, McElroy served as a chaplain in the army of General Zachary Taylor. Returning from the war, McElroy was assigned to St. Mary's Church in Boston, becoming the first Jesuit pastor in that city's history. His tireless work for the church continued, establishing the Church of the Immaculate Conception in 1859 and playing a leading role in the creation of Boston College in 1860. His longevity became almost as well known as his work, becoming the nation's oldest Jesuit, both in age and years of service. He eventually returned to Frederick, where he retired from active service and remained until his death in 1877.

*Dictionary of American Biography*, Vol. VI, part 2: 36–37.

David R. Dunigan, *A History of Boston College* (Milwaukee, 1947).

Pierre D. Lambert, "Jesuit Education and Educators: Some Biographical Notes," *Vitae Scholasticae,* 7 (1988): 275–302.

TOM DOWNEY

## McENROE, JOHN PATRICK, JR. (1959–  )

Tennis player. Born into Irish-Catholic ancestry, McEnroe was born in West Germany to John and Kay McEnroe. His childhood is witness to his exceptional athletic talent: he took his first tennis lessons while a student at the Buckley Country Day School and by age eight made it to the semifinals of a club's tournament.

McEnroe steadily practiced and improved his game and in 1970 enrolled in the Port Washington Tennis Academy in New York; he moved up in the national ranking and won several national junior doubles titles and the clay court singles title for sixteen-and-unders in 1975. In 1977 he was officially listed as an amateur participant in the junior event at Wimbledon but risked play in the men's division and marked his stature in the professional world of tennis. He was the youngest player to advance to the men's semifinals in Wimbledon's one hundred year history. McEnroe's tennis career continued to flourish and he achieved ranking among the top players noted by the Association of American Tennis Professionals, being known for his tenacity and feisty personality. By June of 1979 he had won twenty-six tournaments and collected more than $800,000 in winnings, along with being ranked third in the world behind Bjorn Borg and Jimmy Connors.

*Sports Illustrated* 49 (1979): 34.

S. H. Burchard, *John McEnroe: Sports Star* (1979).

*CAB* (1980).

JOY HARRELL

## McGARRITY, JOSEPH (1874–1940)

Revolutionary. He was born in Carrickmore, County Tyrone on March 28, 1874. In his youth McGarrity was greatly influenced by Master Marshall, a teacher with a republican philosophy. In January of 1892, McGarrity emigrated to the United States. He settled in Philadelphia where he eventually made his mark in the wine and spirits trade. He joined the Clan Na Gael in 1893. On January 17, 1904 Joe was elected district officer for the Clan na Gael in Philadelphia and by 1918 he was a member of its national executive committee.

During his years in the Clan na Gael he had contact with most of the major figures in the Irish freedom struggle. He was responsible for financing the Howth gun importation prior to Easter Week and provided $1,000 of his personal money for the Easter Rising. It is estimated that he helped raise eight and a half million dollars for the Irish struggle.

Joe McGarrity had little interest in any solutions that did not establish a thirty-two county republic. This stance caused him to break first with John Devoy and later his good friend Eamon de Valera over the treaty that partitioned Ireland. In the 1930s he supported and helped plan a failed IRA bombing campaign in England.

McGarrity collected a library of over 10,000 volumes on Irish and Irish-American topics that he donated to Villanova University. His volume of poetry, *Celtic Moods and Memories* gives us an insight into his personal feelings for his native land. McGarrity was a big, tough man with a passion for his country's freedom without equal. He spent more than $100,000 of his personal money on the cause.

On June 11, 1911, McGarrity married Kathryn Hynes and they raised eight children. However, his work for Irish freedom often took him away from home. On his last trip to Carrickmore in 1939, he was served with an expulsion order. When he died on August 5, 1940, the *Irish Press* in Dublin announced on its front page, "Fighter for Irish Freedom Dead."

Séan Cronin, ed., *The McGarrity Papers: Revelations of the Irish Revolutionary Movement in Ireland and America* (Tralee, 1972).

SEAMUS METRESS

## McGEE, THOMAS D'ARCY (1822–1868)

Revolutionary, journalist, politician. Thomas D'Arcy McGee was born in Carlingford, Co. Louth, on April 3, 1825, and from the age of eight lived in Wexford town, where his father served in the coast guard. His mother was the daughter of a member of the United Irishmen. After a few years of schooling, in 1842, at the early age of sixteen, he sailed with his sister on a ship to America to stay with an aunt in Providence, Rhode Island.

The next year, having moved to Boston, he delivered an impressive Fourth of July oration outside Fanuel Hall. As a result of this, the "little curly-headed Paddy" was hired by Patrick Donahoe of *The Pilot* as a correspondent and traveling agent. Two years later he became junior editor of the paper and over the next year he vigorously examined a wide range of issues confronting the status of his people. He attacked the Yankee Puritan heritage in all its aspects, denouncing the "grotesque theology" and "narrowness of soul" of the "pioneer fanatics." He condemned the Whig Party as the oracle of nativism. A mighty verbal match ensued with *The Reporter,* another but moderate Irish paper in the city.

In the aftermath of this controversy, in 1845 McGee returned to Ireland where he became parliamentary correspondent for the *Freeman's Journal* and then a writer for Charles Gavan Duffy's newspaper, *The Nation.* A prolific writer, he produced two books in 1847—a biography of Art MacMurrough and a study of Irish writers in the seventeenth century. He lived through the great Famine and was a leading member of the Young Ireland movement. Also in 1847 he became secretary of the committee of the Irish Confederation. In 1848, the year of aborted rebellion, he went on a secret mission to Scotland to foment revolt among the Irish population of Glasgow and then attempted to do the same in Sligo.

Fleeing arrest, he returned to the United States later that year, this time to New York, where he promptly began his own newspaper, also called *The Nation.* Using this forum, he criticized the Catholic Church for its authoritarianism and hostility to republicanism. He soon was in conflict with Archbishop John Hughes. As part of his campaign for self-improvement for Irish immigrants, he was involved in the establishment of night schools in Boston, New Haven and Philadelphia. Church opposition to *The Nation* resulted in its closure in the Spring of 1850.

Thomas D'Arcy
McGee

Undeterred by this setback, he returned to Boston, where, in August 1850, he began the *American Celt.* Due to the apparent influence of Bishop John Fitzpatrick and the impact of the Know-Nothing movement, McGee now became an advocate of tradition—in religion, politics and nationality. Based on a series of lectures in 1850–51, he produced his *History of the Irish Settlers in North America* which took a generous and imaginative view of the accomplishments of natives of Ireland of any hue. Although not based on lengthy research, it was the first book to treat this subject and became a long-lasting source of pride to many Irish people. In 1855 he produced another work, *The Catholic History of North America,* which, among other things, celebrated the contribution that Irishmen had made to building the infrastructure of the nation. The same year he became a powerful advocate of Irish migration out of the eastern cities to the western open country. In 1856, having shifted his base once again, this time to Buffalo, he organized an Irish Immigrant Aid Convention which met in that city, but most delegates did not support the idea of western migration.

Surrounded by controversy, much of it self-generated, and beset by financial problems, but also restless and impetuous, the next year McGee left the United States for Canada, where he settled in Montreal. As always, he started a newspaper, this time called the *New Era,* in which, among other things, he opposed the influence of the Orange Order as an extension of sectarianism in the New World. He quickly plunged into politics and was elected to the Lower Canadian legislature in 1858. No longer merely a spokesman for the Irish, he saw his role to be that of a bridge between groups in the process of forming a nation. He hoped that Canada could avoid the serious ethnic divisions of the United States. He viewed allegiance to the British Crown as an effective brake on revolutionary republicanism and unfettered democracy.

He rose rapidly in Canadian politics, serving as president of the legislative council in 1862 and 1864, as well as minister of agriculture and emigration beginning in 1865. He also wrote a *Popular History of Ireland,* which appeared in 1862. A volume of his collected poems, edited by the Irish-American novelist Mrs. M. A. Sadleir, was published in 1869.

At the end of the U.S. Civil War he traveled to Ireland, where, in denouncing the bigotry and exploitation that Irish people faced in the New England states, he urged Irish people to stay at home. He also warned of the threat of the Fenian movement. During the American conflict Confederate agents had used Canada to stage three sorties across the border. After 1865 the Fenians in the U.S. prepared to reverse the process. Following the 1866 Fenian raids on Canada, he urged rigorous prosecution of the Fenian captives. As a result, he was expelled from the Montreal St. Patrick's Society and replaced as a minister in the Canadian cabinet. His principal achievement was as one of the leaders in the creation of the Canadian Confederation, which was formed in 1867. He was elected to the first Dominion parliament that year.

Both his abandonment of the United States and his pronounced opposition to Fenianism was met with hatred by many Irish-Americans. He was murdered by a Fenian supporter in 1868. A turbulent but creative life came to a premature end at the age of forty-three.

*See* Emigration: 1801–1921

Robin B. Burns, "D'Arcy McGee and the Fenians," in *Fenians and Fenianism,* ed., M. Harmon (Seattle, 1970): 77–92.

Martin, Chester., *The Foundation of Canadian Nationhood* (Toronto, 1955).
*Dictionary of National Biography*, vol. xii, pp. 529–530.
*Dictionary of Canadian Biography*, vol. ix, pp. 489–494.
Josephine Phelan, *The Ardent Exile: The Life and Times of Thomas D'Arcy Magee* (Toronto, 1951).
Isabel Skelton, *The Life of Thomas D'Arcy McGee* (Gardendale, Canada, 1925).

ARTHUR MITCHELL

## McGEEHAN, WILLIAM O'CONNELL (1879–1933)

Journalist. One of six children born to Irish descendants Hugh and Theresa (O'Connell), McGeehan grew up in San Francisco, California, and began a journalism career at age twenty-one. He covered sports at the *Call,* the *San Francisco Chronicle,* the *Bulletin* and the *San Francisco Examiner.* McGeehan eventually became city editor of the *Evening Post.* In 1914, he moved to New York and gained employment at the *New York Evening Journal* and then one year later joined the staff of the *New York Tribune* where he covered sporting events as well.

McGeehan served during World War I as a captain with the infantry. When he returned to the United States, he went to New York again and assumed his duties as sports editor at the *New York Tribune.* He then moved over to the *New York Herald* where he made a considerable impact on the sporting industry both in his columns and own personal promotion of various athletics. He contributed to several magazines and was known to write of historical and cultural interest topics as well. His writing style was enjoyed by many and was remembered for its moments of satire and drama.

One of the more memorable stories he covered was that of the Scopes trial in Dayton, Tennessee, in 1925. He published one book, *Trouble in the Balkans,* that was distributed in 1931. McGeehan died November 29, 1933, leaving his wife, Sophie Treadwell, journalist and playwright.

*Who's Who in America* (1932–1933).
*Who's Who in New York* (1929).
Clippings in the New York Public Library in the scrapbook entitled, "William O'Connell McGeehan, 1879–1933."
*Dictionary of American Biography*, supplement 1.

JOY HARRELL

## McGINLEY, PHYLLIS LOUISE (1905–1978)

Poet and prose writer. Born in Oregon, McGinley moved to a remote ranch in Colorado with her family in 1908. When McGinley was twelve years old her father died, so the family moved to Utah to live with relatives. She attended the University of Southern California and later studied at the University of Utah, where she was graduated in 1927. McGinley worked as a school teacher in Ogden, Utah, and eventually moved to New Rochelle, New York, to pursue writing while teaching high school (Johnson).

Having crafted a unique writing style, McGinley began to publish regularly, particularly in the *New Yorker.* She also worked as an advertising copywriter and poetry editor for *Town and Country* magazine (Glazier). Eventually she quit teaching, moved to New York City, and began to write full time. Her first published book of verse, *On the Contrary,* appeared in 1934. By the time she married Charles Hayden in 1937, McGinley had published *One More Manhattan;* like her first text, this work focused on urban themes, including acerbic social-satire poetry focusing on the

Phyllis McGinley

economic misery and pervasive militarism of the era (Quartermain). *A Pocketful of Wry* (1940), McGinley's third book of poems, followed the birth of her first daughter.

By 1940 she and her husband had moved to Larchmont, a suburb of New York City, which influenced McGinley's development as a writer. Establishing herself in Larchmont, which the poet described as "an adorable town full of old Victorian houses" (ibid), McGinley used her writing to celebrate the life and times of the small-town folk she grew to know and love, as well as their community, which provided a sense of belonging that she had lacked as a child. McGinley published seventeen children's books from 1944 to 1966 while continuing to write about the trials and tribulations of suburban life. In 1941 McGinley published a comic satire, *Husbands Are Difficult* (1941), followed by *Stones from a Glass House* (1946) and *A Short Walk from the Station* (1951).

With the publication of *Love Letters* in 1954, McGinley had attained a substantial readership; the text sold 80,000 copies, making her one of America's most widely read poets. McGinley's collection, asserted one critic, demonstrated her "growing ability to handle sophisticated themes and techniques without losing her light touch" (ibid), which had become her hallmark. She then published *Times Three* (1960), a collection of 200 previously released poems and 70 new works arranged chronologically. *Times Three*, which featured a preface by W. H. Auden, sold more than 50,000 copies and won McGinley a 1961 Pulitzer Prize, the first awarded for light verse.

After *Times Three* McGinley began to write prose. *The Province of the Heart* (1959) was followed by *Sixpence in Her Shoe* (1964). In *A Wreath of Christmas Legends* (1967) and *Saint Watching* (1969), McGinley invoked her spirituality and Catholic convictions thematically. McGinley was elected to the National Academy of Arts and Letters in 1955 and won a host of awards from Catholic groups—the most famous of which, the Christopher Medal, she received in 1955.

*See* Poetry, Irish-American

Michael Glazier and Thomas J. Shelley, *The Encyclopedia of American Catholic History* (Collegeville, MN, 1997).
Allen Johnson and Dumas Malone, eds., *Dictionary of American Biography,* Supplement 10 (1931). CD-ROM (New York, 1997).

Lina Mainiero, ed., *American Women Writers,* Vol. III (New York, 1981).

Peter Quartermain, ed., *Dictionary of Literary Biography,* Vol. 48: American Poets, 1880–1945, Second ser. (Detroit, 1986).

JAMES P. LEONARD

## McGIVNEY, MICHAEL J. (1852–1890)

Catholic priest and founder of the Knights of Columbus. Michael J. McGivney was the eldest of thirteen children of Irish-born Patrick and Mary Lynch McGivney of Waterbury, Connecticut, on August 12, 1852.

The Knights of Columbus originated as a result of the interaction between this young priest and a small group of Irish-American laymen at St. Mary's Church, New Haven, Connecticut. Father McGivney's ministry to youth was expressed in his chaplaincy of the St. Joseph's Young Men's Total Abstinence Society of the parish, which represented a strong strand of Irish-American parish life. It also sharpened his awareness of the rising popularity of fraternalism. The lodge was considered a refuge from the harshly competitive and atomistic character of industrial society. The economic depression of the early 1870s entailed the bankruptcy of many commercial insurance companies. Fraternal insurance societies replaced them with a cooperative rather than a competitive system of sick and death benefits. Father McGivney realized the value of insurance protection from the early death of his own father and from his ministry to those families suffering from the loss of the breadwinner. In contrast to the Irish folk belief that to enroll in an insurance society was to tempt Mr. Death, McGivney represents the ascendancy of Irish-Americans into the middle classes, remote from the folk life of Ireland.

Prior to entering the seminary McGivney worked in a spoon factory to help support the family. After completing theology at St. Mary's Seminary in Baltimore, he was ordained in December 1877 and immediately assigned to St. Mary's parish. On October 2, 1881, he chaired the first meeting in the church basement of what officially became the Knights of Columbus on March 29, 1882, the date of the order's incorporation in Connecticut.

In accord with second-generation Irish-American leadership, McGivney extolled the compatibility of Catholicism and American fraternalism. No doubt the priest was motivated by the wish to keep young Catholics from entering the ranks of condemned secret societies and by the need to protect families during sickness and death. He was equally persistent in his aim to establish a Catholic fraternal society imbued with zealous pride in the American Catholic heritage. Indeed, the Order's Columbian motif invoked pride in the Catholic origins of the nation. To assert Catholic legitimacy against nativism and anti-Catholicism, the *Santa Maria* was promoted as a Catholic counter symbol to the Puritan *Mayflower.* Of course, the struggle against Protestant hegemony was congenial with centuries of the Catholic experience in Ireland.

Prior to the decision to establish an independent fraternal society, McGivney visited with the leaders of the Massachusetts Catholic Order of Foresters, also composed of Irish-Americans, with the intention of exploring the foundation of a Connecticut branch of that order. Had the New Haven society affiliated with Foresters, their fraternal character would have represented Robin Hood and his merry men rather than Columbus with its distinctive American-Catholic symbolism.

In contrast to the Ancient Order of Hibernians, who extolled the pantheon of Irish heroes, the Knights of Columbus paraded American Catholic heroes before the public. Though there is no evidence of Knights among the Hibernians during the lifetime of Father McGivney, several members belonged to the New Haven Knights of St. Patrick organized principally to celebrate the feast-day of the great Irish saint.

As the first Financial Secretary, Michael McGivney was entrusted with daily management of the infant Order, a position in accord with his role as founder, organizer, and ambassador. The first council, San Salvador, was founded in New Haven in May 1882, but it was not until April 23, 1883, that Silver City Council No. 2 was instituted in Meriden. After the founder had written a long letter to the editor of the *Connecticut Catholic* in August 1883, in which he outlined the benefits of the Order, new councils were instituted during the following six months, in Middletown, a second in Meriden, and in Wallingford.

With expansion of the order assured, McGivney announced at the Supreme Council meeting of June 15, 1884, that he would not be a candidate for Supreme Secretary. However, he was elected Supreme Chaplain, an office that removed him from daily business concerns and was more compatible with his other priestly duties. The following November, Bishop Lawrence McMahon of Hartford, who had become chaplain of a Knights of Columbus council in Hartford, appointed him pastor of St. Thomas Church, Thomaston, Connecticut.

The priest-founder vigorously promoted the expansion of the Order. He personally was involved in the formation of Atlantic Council in Thomaston and he represented the Order in negotiating plans for new-council development with the bishop of Providence, Rhode Island. Since then Supreme Chaplains have frequently represented the Order in its relationship with bishops in the various dioceses and in the Vatican.

Never a man of robust health, McGivney was afflicted with pneumonia in January 1890. After traveling south on two occasions, the thirty-eight-year-old priest died on August 14.

Although the various funeral eulogies went unrecorded, there has been a considerable groundswell of devotion to the founder over the years. He was extolled as a priest of the people, a kind, approachable person who evoked confidence and trust. He certainly manifested a strong sense of determination in establishing the Knights of Columbus dedicated to charity, unity and fraternity. He forged a synthesis between Catholicity and American fraternalism. The forms of unity were designed according to the motif of a Columbian brotherhood. Fifteen years after McGivney died, the Order was in every state and territory, the five provinces of Canada, Mexico, the Philippines and was poised to enter Cuba and Puerto Rico. The success of this fraternal society was due to its insurance feature but, most significantly, Columbian fraternal ceremonies appealed to all Catholics, particularly to Irish-Americans, eager to participate in the initiation ceremonies—Catholic life "rites of passage" for first and second-generation immigrants into American society. Today there are 1.6 million Knights.

*See* Knights of Columbus

Christopher J. Kauffman, *Faith and Fraternalism: The History of the Knights of Columbus,* revised ed. (New York, 1992).

———, *Columbianism and the Knights of Columbus* (New York, 1992).

CHRISTOPHER J. KAUFFMAN

## McGLYNN, EDWARD (1837–1900)

Social activist, priest. Edward McGlynn was born in New York City on September 27, 1837, of parents who came from Donegal, Ireland, in 1824. He was baptized at Old St. Patrick's Cathedral, attended public schools in New York and went to Rome in 1851 at the age of thirteen to study for the priesthood at the Urban College of the Propagation of the Faith (*Propaganda Fide*). Ordained on March 24, 1860, Edward returned to New York that fall. His first assignment was to St. Joseph's, Greenwich Village, where the pastor, Thomas Farrell, gave McGlynn an abiding interest in social issues. Including St. Joseph's, McGlynn was stationed in four parishes in a two year period (1860–1862). He was appointed the chaplain during the Civil War (1862–1865) for the military hospital in New York's Central Park.

At the conclusion of his military service, Edward McGlynn was appointed assistant to Jeremiah Cummings, the founding pastor of St. Stephen's which also was McGlynn's home parish. Cummings died in January 1866 and McGlynn succeeded him. Appalled by the poverty and the exploitation of his parishioners, McGlynn became anti-capitalistic and anti-monopolistic. He desired the Church to be in the forefront of the battle for the people and to be confrontational.

When McGlynn spoke out against state support of religious schools (1870), a copy of his remarks was sent to Rome, and New York's Vicar General, Thomas Preston, forwarded to Archbishop McCloskey in Rome a protest against McGlynn's position composed by New York priests. No disciplinary action came from the incident. McGlynn was active in Midwest colonization schemes for Irish immigrants (1879–1882).

During this same period, McGlynn was active in the Irish Land League because he considered this the most important Irish question, since he believed Home Rule would be an illusion if the land question was not settled. Henry George, whose disciple McGlynn would become, went to Ireland (1881–1882) on assignment for Patrick Ford of the *Irish World*. George met Bishop Thomas Nulty of Meath and exchanged views on land. Nulty issued a pastoral condemning landlordism and proposing that land rent be used for the cost of government and social services. Both McGlynn and George read this pastoral and were influenced by it.

When the land reformer Michael Davitt gave the first speech of his United States 1882 tour on July 11 at Cooper Union, McGlynn spoke to the assemblage and urged the pure and rigid application of Davitt's doctrine. He then went a step further and called for the removal of all private ownership of property without a penny of compensation. This was reported to Rome.

In August 1882, McGlynn spoke at a picnic of the Land League in Cleveland, Ohio. The organization had been excommunicated by the local bishop, Richard Gilmour. This incident was reported to Rome by three bishops who called for the disciplining of McGlynn. As in the Davitt instance, no action was taken against McGlynn beyond being told by Rome to keep out of political issues.

The report of a McGlynn 1883 fund raising speech for Irish charities was sent to Rome. This time he was told not to attend Land League meetings and to retract certain material in this speech. McGlynn did have a retraction published but neither his archbishop, Michael Corrigan, nor Rome considered it a retraction.

All the troubles of McGlynn narrated thus far came from addressing Irish groups. They were an apt audience for McGlynn because they were exploited as workers and persecuted as Irish. When he spoke at the formal nomination of Henry George on October 1, 1886 for the mayoralty of New York after being warned by Archbishop Corrigan not to do so, McGlynn was suspended from priestly functions for two weeks. Though McGlynn did not actively participate in the George campaign, his endorsement was known by many, especially the Irish, and he did parade around the city in an open carriage on election day with Henry George and Terence Powderly, the head of the Knights of Labor. After the election, which George did not win but made a good showing in, Corrigan issued a pastoral upholding the right of private property. McGlynn was silent on this but did give an interview to the New York *Tribune* which was printed as one paragraph in a long article on the rights of women workers. McGlynn condemned "temporary measures for the relief of social distress" and recommended the reading of George's *Progress and Poverty*. Corrigan suspended him that very day until the end of 1886.

Edward McGlynn was called to Rome on December 4, 1886, but replied that he could not go. January 1887 he was removed from St. Stephen's. On March 26, he organized in the offices of George's newspaper, *The Standard,* the Anti Poverty Society which formalized the social thought of George and himself. Three days later he delivered for the first time his best known speech, "The Cross of a New Crusade." On May 4, McGlynn was given forty days to report to Rome or face excommunication. The deadline was July 3 but he received the notice on July 8.

Edward McGlynn spent his excommunicated period promoting the Anti Poverty Society, membership in which Corrigan made a reserved sin in January 1889. The works of Henry George were condemned in 1891 but this fact was not to be published. Though some friends tried to bring about the reconciliation of McGlynn, he was not cooperative. Archbishop John Ireland and Bishop John Moore should be credited for their efforts at reconciliation but it was only when Archbishop Francesco Satolli came in November 1892 to the United States as a papal delegate, apparently under instructions from Rome, that concrete efforts were made. Satolli met with Richard Burtsell, McGlynn's best friend. The conditions they set for the reconciliation of McGlynn were: a written exposition of his teachings, the acceptance of *Rerum Novarum* and a promise to see the Holy Father in Rome. These terms were met and Satolli reconciled McGlynn to the Church at Catholic University on December 23, 1892.

Archbishop Corrigan was upset that he had no part in McGlynn's return, and the Holy Office in Rome had ignored pending moral charges laid against McGlynn by Corrigan. For almost two years, Corrigan ignored his returned priest but finally did meet with him on December 21, 1894 and assigned him as pastor of St. Mary's, Newburgh, New York.

When Henry George died in 1897, Edward McGlynn preached at his funeral that October 31 at Grand Central Palace in New York. "There was a man sent from God. His name was Henry George," is the oft repeated line from the eulogy. McGlynn himself died on January 7, 1900 in Newburgh.

*See* New York City; Corrigan, Michael Augustine

Stephen Bell, *Rebel, Priest and Prophet: A Biography of Dr. Edward McGlynn* (New York, 1937).

Robert Emmet Curran, *Michael Augustine Corrigan and the Shaping of Conservative Catholicism in America, 1878–1902* (New York, 1978).

Gerald P. Fogarty, *The Vatican and the American Hierarchy from 1870 to 1965* (Wilmington, Del., 1985).

Alfred Isacsson, *The Determined Doctor: The Story of Edward McGlynn* (Tarrytown, 1996).

Dominic Scibilia, "Edward McGlynn: American Social Catholic," *Records of the American Catholic Historical Society of Philadelphia* 101 (Fall 1990): 1–16.

Manuel Scott "Jeff" Shanaberger, "A Missionary Priest and His Social Gospel," *U.S. Catholic Historian* 13 (Summer 1995): 23–47.

ALFRED ISACSSON, O. CARM.

## McGONIGLE, THOMAS (1944–  )

Novelist, critic, and editor. Thomas McGonigle was born in Brooklyn and raised in Patchogue, Long Island. He was educated at St. Francis de Sales Catholic Elementary School and at Patchogue H.S. McGonigle received degrees from Beloit College and Hollins College, though the part of his education that was the most important was his time spent as a student at University College, Dublin, which brought him into contact with the Irish literary scene, and served to develop and extend his knowledge of Irish writing, something which has been a central influence on his work.

### Novels

McGonigle is the author of two novels, *The Corpse Dream of N. Petkov* and *Going to Patchogue. Petkov* is set in Bulgaria and is an imaginative reconstruction of the final minutes in the life of Nikola Petkov, the last significant opposition leader to the Communist takeover. McGonigle, by mixing history, biography, the imagination, and elements from his own life, creates a complex and compelling mosaic. *Going to Patchogue* is a lyrical, stream of consciousness exploration of the disjunction between past and present. The novel's narrator, Tom McGonigle, leaves his apartment on the Lower East Side of New York to travel to Patchogue, Long Island, where he grew up. There, he hopes to recover some glimpses of his past, and to enter into dialogues with the ghosts of his dead parents, and with Melinda, his old girlfriend. However, because he left after completing high school, McGonigle is seen as an outsider and cannot penetrate the new Patchogue, which has replaced that place where he was raised. He is berated by a local man who reminds him that "I stayed here and you left. You don't know how decent people behave, living all those years away from this country and then living in the City. How do you expect to know how decent people live if all you do is associate with foreigners and City People?" (99) In the end, the narrator concludes that Patchogue, for all the years he spent there and for all that it has played on his mind over time, is just one more location where he has spent time and is no more or less important than Dublin, Sofia, Istanbul or other cities where he has lived. McGonigle's vision of Patchogue, like Joyce's of Dublin, is a deeply personal one, and one which is carried forward by a wounded and fractured, but deeply moral and hypnotic, narrative voice. It is clear from how McGonigle eliminates plot, provides multiple perspectives, and blends autobiography with fiction that he owes much to both modernist and postmodernist fictional techniques. In their manner of composition, McGonigle's novels belong more in the company of the works of Samuel Beckett, Thomas Bernhard, and Carole Maso than beside the works of other contemporary Irish-American writers such as William Kennedy and Mary Gordon. Thematically, McGonigle takes many risks in *Going to Patchogue*, particularly in his exposure of racism in suburbia where, in Patchogue at least, many of the local people are fearful that their oasis will become as multicultural as the New York City they fled. *Going to Patchogue* is both a magnificent achievement in itself and a coming-of-age work for Irish-American fiction as McGonigle is the first Irish-American novelist to successfully weave together the local world of Irish America and international, avant-garde literary techniques. McGonigle's innovative approach breathes fresh life into the Irish-American novel.

### Critic and Editor

McGonigle is a frequent contributor, as an essayist and reviewer, to *The Washington Post, The Chicago Tribune, The Los Angeles Times, Newsday,* and to *The Guardian* (Manchester, England). His focus is generally on innovative fiction from Europe, on which he is an expert. In a section entitled "Book Reviewing and the Literary Scene," which appears in the 1997 *Dictionary of Literary Biography,* McGonigle is cited for outstanding book reviews. In the 1970s and 1980s, McGonigle served as the editor of *Adrift,* an influential Irish and Irish-American literary magazine.

*See* Fiction, Irish-American

Thomas McGonigle, *The Corpse Dream of N. Petkov* (Elmwood Park, Ill., 1987).

———, *Going to Patchogue* (Elmwood Park, Ill., 1992).

———, *In Patchogue: The Beginning of an Epic* (New York, 1984).

EAMONN WALL

## McGRATH, JAMES HOWARD (1903–1966)

United States government official and educator. McGrath was born the son of John and Martha Carolyn (Schottin) into an Irish lineage taking root in Antrim, Ireland. McGrath grew up in Buffalo, New York, and went to college at the University of Buffalo to attain a liberal arts degree in languages, primarily German. In 1928, he was awarded the Bachelor of Arts degree and then continued his studies by pursuing a Master's degree in psychology. In 1930, he finished his Master's degree and continued lecturing in psychology for five years.

During his time lecturing at the University of Buffalo, he worked in various positions: as assistant to the chancellor and dean of administration and as a fellow at the University of Chicago where he eventually began work on a Ph.D degree in education and completed it in 1936. After completing his studies he moved to Washington, D.C., and was employed as a specialist in higher education for the American Council on Education. From February of 1942 to May of that same year, McGrath worked as special education advisor to the Chief of the Naval Personnel of the Department of the Navy in Washington and later became educational consultant of the National Roster of Scientific Personnel. It was later, in October of 1942, that McGrath held the position which would advance his career to new heights: he became lieutenant commander in the Navy, being the officer in charge of the education of over 300,000 students.

McGrath served the Navy until November 1944; the same year he married Dorothy Ann Leemon. He moved in 1945 to acting dean of the liberal arts program at the University of Iowa.

McGrath also began teaching again at the University of Chicago until his nomination and appointment as United States Commissioner of Higher Education in February of 1949. McGrath wrote several articles in academic journals including: *Journal of General Education, Educational Record, Journal of Higher Education* and the *Annals of American Academy.* He died in 1966, leaving an extensive legacy in the field of academics and education.

*New York Times* (February 1949): 2.
*Leaders in Education* (1948).
*Who's Who in America* (1948–1949).
*CAB* (1949).

JOY HARRELL

## McGRAW, ERIN (1957– )

Fiction writer, critic, essayist. Youngest daughter of C. Thomas and Eva Marie (Begovich) McGraw, Erin McGraw was born in Los Angeles, California, December 20, 1957. She received her A.B. in English/Writing from the University of California at Davis in 1979.

From 1985 through 1990, McGraw taught English and creative writing at DePauw University in Indiana. Since 1991, she has been a professor of writing and contemporary fiction at the University of Cincinnati. In 1992, she married the poet Andrew Hudgins whom she met at a writer's colony in 1988. She has also served on the faculty of several summer writing workshops in the Midwest.

Since her first publication in 1984, McGraw's fiction and nonfiction have appeared in numerous literary journals, including: *Ascent, Atlantic Monthly, The Georgia Review, Gettysburg Review, The Kenyon Review, The Laurel Review, The North American Review,* and *The Southern Review,* among others. McGraw is a regular book reviewer for *The Georgia Review* and has written numerous reviews and articles for *The North American Review.* Her first collection of short stories, *Bodies at Sea,* was published by the University of Illinois Press in 1989 as part of the Illinois Short Fiction series. Her second collection of short stories, *Lies of the Saints,* was published by Chronicle Books in 1996.

McGraw's fiction has earned numerous awards, including the 1987 General Electric Award for Younger Writers and a 1997 Pushcart Prize for her short story, "Daily Affirmations," which also appeared in *Cabbage and Bones,* an anthology of Irish-American women's fiction. Her story collection *Lies of the Saints* was a *New York Times* Notable Book for 1996, part of the 1996 Barnes & Noble "Discovery" series, and winner of the 1997 Ohioana Book Award. McGraw has received numerous fellowships and grants, including a 1988 fellowship at Yaddo, a 1988–1990 Wallace Stegner fellowship at Stanford University, a 1994 Individual Artist's Grant from the Ohio Arts Council, and a 1997 MacDowell fellowship.

McGraw's stories are noted for their dark, poignant, and quirky humor; their honesty, compassion, and rich understanding; and their casts of bizarre, but masterfully rendered, characters. Her writing has been praised for its penetrating dialogue, detailed precision, and subtle shifts from simple to lyrical prose. As she wrote for *The Georgia Review* in 1997, "the best stories look not so much for answers as for exploration of human dilemmas," a standard to which her own fiction always rises. In McGraw's stories—as in the short fiction about which she wrote the following—"human possibility is sometimes salvation and sometimes a pathetic, distant shadow, where we are invited, variously, to feel sympathy, regret, disdain and plain joy for the characters whose stories we hear" (*North American Review,* 1988).

KAREN HOLLENBECK

## McGRAW, JOHN JOSEPH (1873–1934)

Baseball player and manager. The first of nine children, John McGraw was born to Irish parents in Truxton, New York, where he found his first job as a newsboy on the local trains. It was in the vacant lots of New York City, however, where McGraw discovered his talents as a ball player and became an outstanding pitcher for the "Truxton Grays." At the age of seventeen, McGraw was offered two dollars a game for pitching for the East Homer team, but his success there was marginal. He left the East Homer team to finish out the season with another ball club where he began to hone his skills as an infielder. McGraw next drifted to Cuba and then to Florida where his excellent infielding skills were picked up by the Cedar Rapids club of the Illinois-Iowa League in 1891. There McGraw earned $125 a month as shortstop and established for himself a reputation that led to a contract with the Baltimore team of the American Association. With only two years between his parking lot days and this major league job, McGraw dazzled his fans as a third baseman. By the time he was twenty-six, McGraw was managing the Baltimore team part-time until he was sold to the St. Louis club in 1899. In 1902, Andrew Freedman offered McGraw management of the struggling New York Giants of the National League which McGraw brought to second place in the first year. In 1905 McGraw took the Giants to the World Series against Philadelphia for a five-game shut-out victory. Earning the title "the Little Napoleon of Baseball," McGraw brought the Giants to second place for the next three years in a row. By 1924 McGraw had won ten National League pennants, four of them in succession, from 1921 to 1924. Three world series victories in 1905, 1921 and 1922 made McGraw one of the "winningest" coaches of the time. Only Connie Mack rivaled McGraw's impressive record. McGraw retired in June of 1932 to New Rochelle, N.Y. where he died, childless, two years later, on February 25, 1934, leaving his wife, Blanche Sindall, behind.

*See* Baseball

Charles C. Alexander, *John McGraw* (New York: Viking, 1988).
Bozeman Bugler, "Genius of the Game," *Saturday Evening Post* (May 28, June 25, July 9, 1932).
John McGraw, *My Thirty Years in Baseball* (New York: Boni and Liveright, 1923).
Obituary, *Newsweek* (March 3, 1934).

DANIEL J. KUNTZ

## McGROARTY, SUSAN (Sister Julia) (1827–1901)

Educator. Susan McGroarty was born February 13, 1827, on a farm in Inver, County Donegal, Ireland, to Neil and Catherine (Bonner) McGroarty, the third of ten children. Brought to the United States at age four, she grew up in Ohio. Her father died in 1838, leaving her mother to raise the family aided by Susan's uncle, a Cincinnati physician. At thirteen, she began studies at the Cincinnati convent school of the Sisters of Notre Dame de Namur, a Belgian community, and entered that sisterhood in 1846, later taking the name of Sister Julia after the foundress,

Julie Billiart. Sr. Julia taught in the community's infant school, day school, and became mistress of boarders at the Academy of Notre Dame in Roxbury, Mass., in 1854. In 1860 she was the first American superior in her congregation while at its Philadelphia academy, there starting a night school for immigrant girls and a free school for black children (1870). In 1887 she became provincial superior of 1,500 sisters in twenty-six houses. Sr. Julia focused on improving the congregation's schools academically, standardizing the curriculum, and introducing other administrative innovations. She founded a large novitiate in Waltham, Mass., a California orphanage, and fourteen new schools.

Being a warm and inspirational leader and innovator, Sr. Julia was urged by Catholic educators as early as 1893 to establish a national Catholic college for women, particularly since the Catholic University of America admitted only men at the time. Facing strong conservative opposition, but with the support of administrators of Catholic University and Baltimore archbishop James Cardinal Gibbons, she gained papal approval for the founding of Trinity College, Washington, D.C., in the fall of 1897. Ground was broken in June 1899, and the first class of twenty-two students entered in October 1900. Despite her death the following year, her charism left a lasting stamp on Trinity College. Sister Julia died of apoplexy in Peabody, Mass., on November 12, 1901, at age seventy, and was buried in Cincinnati in the chapel of The Summit, one of the schools she had founded.

*Biographical Dictionary of American Educators* (Westport, CT, 1978).
Sister Helen Louise, *Sister Julia (Susan McGroarty) Sister of Notre Dame de Namur* (New York, 1928).
*Notable American Women, 1607–1950; A Biographical Dictionary,* Vol. 2 (Cambridge, MA, 1971).

ANNA M. DONNELLY

## McGRORY, MARY (1918–   )

Journalist, columnist. Mary McGrory was born in Boston, August 22, 1918, daughter of Edward Patrick and Mary (Jacobs) McGrory. She attended Girls' Latin School, and in 1939 received a bachelor of arts degree from Emmanuel College. She entered journalism in 1942 as a reporter for the *Boston Herald Traveler,* then joined the *Washington Star* in 1947 as a book reviewer. She was doing feature writing, when she was surprisingly assigned in 1954 to cover the Army-McCarthy hearings, the biggest news story of the day. It proved her "great breakthrough." Reader reaction was instant to her reporting. "All of a sudden," she remarked, "people wanted to adopt me, marry me, poison me, run me out of town."

McGrory has been doing news journalism and commentary since, and has won numerous awards, including the George Polk Memorial Award for national reporting in 1963 and the Pulitzer Prize for commentary in 1975. The Pulitzer award cited her "for trenchant commentary spread over more than twenty years as a reporter and a columnist in the nation's capital."

Her column has been syndicated nationally since 1960, her flagship newspaper currently being the *Washington Post,* an organization she joined after the *Washington Star* dissolved in 1981. In her eightieth year, she was still producing two columns a week (down from four at one time) and traveling widely to gather impressions first-hand for her writings. She went to Ireland, for instance, to observe the 1998 peace referendums. "Ireland hasn't had many happy endings," she wrote afterwards, but she expected "this [happy ending] is the real thing."

Mary McGrory

One of McGrory's trademarks is incisive assessment spiced with colorful illustration. As an example, when Richard Nixon was vice president in the 1950s, she alluded to him as one who "still stalks the light touch with all the grimness that the butterfly collectors bring to pursuit of a rare species." The disdain was hardly one-sided. With a colorfulness to match her own, Nixon suggested at his "farewell" press conference in 1962 that McGrory "was like a kamikaze pilot who keeps apologizing for the attack." McGrory continued as a Nixon hair shirt after his return to Washington as president, and this landed her in twentieth place on that administration's so-called enemies list. She esteemed the designation as the "nicest thing that ever happened" to her.

Assessing the news profession in 1997 and her role in it, McGrory said the "wonder of reporting" was the privilege of being "one of a select few in a ringside seat at great events." She commented, "There was never anything else I wanted to do. . . . It's fun masquerading as work."

Frances C. Locher, ed., *Contemporary Authors,* vol. 106 (Detroit, 1982).
Mary McGrory, Address to the Washington Independent Writers Group, Washington Press Club (November 21, 1997).

JOHN DEEDY

## McGUFFEY, WILLIAM HOLMES (1800–1873)

Educator, author. William Holmes McGuffey was born of Scotch-Irish ancestry in Washington County, western Pennsylvania, to Alexander McGuffey and Anna (Holmes). The family moved to Trumbull County, Ohio, near Youngstown when William was two years old. He received schooling from his mother, occasionally attended a rural school, taught his younger brothers and sisters, and studied with Rev. Dr. Wick in Youngstown. At eighteen he attended Old Stone (Greersburg) Academy directed by the Rev. Thomas Hughes in Darlington, PA.; he lived there with the college president, Andrew Wylie, who later became head of Indiana University, and graduated with honors in 1826. While in college he spent some time teaching in Ohio and Kentucky, and taught in a rural school at the age of fourteen. It was in Kentucky that he met Robert Hamilton Bishop, president of Miami University of Oxford, Ohio who offered him a teaching position at Miami. In his graduation year he became professor of languages (Greek, Latin, Hebrew) in Miami where he taught for ten years. In 1827 he married Harriet Spinning of Dayton; they raised five children.

McGuffey had been regarded as a prodigy by virtue of a powerful memory which enabled him to recall whole books of the Bible. Although never ordained to the ministry, he was licensed to preach in the Presbyterian church at Darrtown, Ohio, near Miami in 1829. He was accustomed to preach weekly and became a popular lecturer on the Bible, ethics and moral subjects. In 1832 he was head of Miami's department of mental philosophy, philology and general criticism, and in 1836 he was elected president of Cincinnati College. McGuffey organized, with Ohio state senator Samuel Lewis, an association to promote education interests, and aided Lewis in securing passage of the state law establishing the common or free school system in Ohio. By 1839 McGuffey was chosen president of Ohio University at Athens, and remained there until 1843 when the institution closed for five years in a dispute with the state legislature which refused land rent revaluation for university income. McGuffey taught from 1843 to 1845 at Woodward College, a Cincinnati secondary school, and then became professor of moral philosophy at the University of Virginia, Charlottesville. He was a highly regarded member of the faculty, and taught there until a few weeks before his death. His wife Harriet had died in 1853, and in 1857 he married Laura Howard, daughter of the university's dean, Henry Howard. Their only child, a daughter, died at the age of four. During the difficult Civil War and Reconstruction years, McGuffey was known for his undiscriminating generosity and aid to those who suffered from the conflict.

The noted educator had not been satisfied with the children's textbooks of his time, and he tried new methods of teaching local children. When a friend, Catherine Beecher, was asked by Cincinnati publisher Truman and Smith to write textbooks, she declined, and in 1833 recommended McGuffey instead. So were launched the spectacularly successful series of *Eclectic Readers* for grammar schools, beginning in 1836 with the First and Second Readers, followed by the Third and Fourth in 1837. The Speller was issued in 1838, the Fifth Reader in 1844, and the Sixth in 1857. They were produced with the assistance of McGuffey's younger brother, Alexander Hamilton McGuffey—the latter likely compiled the Speller and the fifth Reader alone. Many editions and revisions ensued to 1920 as over an estimated 122 million copies were sold and used in both public and private schools. They were used in translation in France and Japan as well. The McGuffey Readers became a household name, bringing selections and lessons from great English literature to the humblest pupils, opening the way to effective vocabularies, inculcating traditional moral values of honesty, kindness and truthfulness, and setting forth a common cultural heritage. McGuffey, through these readers, had an enormous educational and ethical influence on a vast number of Americans well into the twentieth century. A McGuffey Museum, his restored home, is a National Historic Landmark at Miami University in Oxford, Ohio. William Holmes McGuffey died May 4, 1873, in Charlottesville, Virginia.

*See* Scots Irish

*American Authors: 1600–1900* (New York, 1966).

Richard David Mosier, *Making the American Mind; Social and Moral Ideas in the McGuffey Readers* (New York, 1965 [c. 1947]).

Harvey C. Minnich, *William Holmes McGuffey and His Readers* (New York, 1975).

Dolores P. Sullivan, *William Holmes McGuffey: Schoolmaster to the Nation* (Rutherford, N.J., 1994).

ANNA M. DONNELLY

## McGUIRE, CHARLES BONAVENTURE (1768–1833)

Priest. Born in Dungannon Country, Tyrone, Ireland, Charles McGuire spent his early school years at a "hedge school" under a "refugee master." He was later driven to France and Belgium by the Penal Laws in Ireland for further study at Louvain. There he became a Franciscan priest and served a parish in France until the anticlerical Reign of Terror (1793–1794) swept him into an execution line. Spirited away by a barrelmaker, McGuire escaped, but the mob immediately cut McGuire's liberator to pieces. McGuire next moved to Rome until Napoleon again made McGuire's escape necessary. After conducting "confidential" work for the Franciscan order, McGuire aided the wounded at Waterloo and collected battle souvenirs for his benefactor, the Bohemian king. Desiring further adventure, McGuire set sail for America in 1817 where he served at the Latrobe mission in Pennsylvania. He next served as pastor of St. Patrick's Church in Pittsburgh where the increasing numbers of German and Irish workers prompted McGuire to build a large church with the help of a wealthy industrialist friend. By 1829 McGuire had the foundation laid at St. Paul's Church on Grant Hill which became one of the largest churches in America. McGuire never had episcopal ambitions, though he was recommended by Bishop Fenwick of Cincinnati for the new bishopric at Indiana in 1823. McGuire, nevertheless, remained a pastor at Pittsburgh until his death in 1833. He is buried at St. Mary's cemetery.

*See* Priests from Ireland

John Coughlin, "Maguire, Charles Bonaventure," *The Encyclopedia of American Catholic History,* Michael Glazier and Thomas J. Shelley, eds. (Collegeville: The Liturgical Press, 1997): 833–834.

A. A. Lambing, *History of the Catholic Church in the Dioceses of Pittsburgh and Allegheny From Its Establishment to the Present Time* (New York: Benziger, 1880).

*Records of the American Catholic Historical Society,* vol. III (1881).

*The American Catholic Historical Researches* (October 1894).

*N.Y. Weekly Register* (April 19, 1834).

*The Jesuit* (August 10, 1833).

DANIEL J. KUNTZ

## McGUIRE, PETER JAMES (1852–1906)

Labor organizer, founder of United Brotherhood of Carpenters and Joiners. Peter J. McGuire was born in New York City July 6, 1852, son of John J. McGuire and Catharine Hand (O'Riley) McGuire. Both parents fled the Irish potato famine in 1847. They married in New York in 1850. Catharine O'Riley had survived the loss of her first husband, Matthew O'Riley, and six of their eight children in Ireland. Peter J. was the oldest of five children (two boys, three girls) born to the second marriage of Catharine Hand. Their father supported his family as a porter in Lord & Taylor department store. They lived in a ghetto on the lower east side of Manhattan.

### TENEMENT DWELLERS

In 1885 P. J. McGuire gave a vivid description of the seventeenth ward—where the family lived—in testimony before a congres-

# McHENRY, JAMES (1753–1816)

Physician, soldier, Secretary of War. James McHenry was born in Ballymena, County Antrim, Ireland, and emigrated to America in 1771. While his father and brother established a successful business in Baltimore, James went to Philadelphia and studied medicine under Benjamin Rush. During the Revolutionary War, McHenry served with distinction as a physician with the Continental army. In May 1778, he became secretary to George Washington and later served on the staff of Lafayette. McHenry left the army in 1781 to serve in the Maryland senate and later sat in Congress from 1783 to 1786. He attended the Constitutional Convention in 1787, with his private journal becoming a valuable record of the proceedings. A staunch Federalist, McHenry favored ratification. His party loyalty led to appointment as Secretary of War in 1796, where his personal relationship with Washington made him an influential cabinet adviser and distributor of federal patronage. He continued his position into the administration of John Adams, but fell out of favor with the new president and resigned his cabinet post in 1800. His tenure in the War Department was loudly criticized by Republicans, but no formal investigation of his actions was undertaken. McHenry retired to his estate outside of Baltimore. He continued to support Federalist policy and strongly opposed the War of 1812, though his son volunteered in the defense of Baltimore and Fort McHenry, the bastion in the city's harbor named for his father and which became the inspiration for the *Star Spangled Banner*.

*Dictionary of American Biography*, Vol. VI, part 2: 62–63.

Frederick J. Brown, "A Sketch of the Life of Dr. James McHenry," *Maryland Historical Society Fund-Publications*, 10 (1877): 1–44.

Bernard Christian Steiner, *The Life and Correspondence of James McHenry, Secretary of War under Washington and Adams* (Cleveland, 1907).

TOM DOWNEY

# McINTYRE, JAMES FRANCIS (1886–1979)

Cardinal. He was born in New York City on June 25, 1886, to James F., a mounted policeman, and Margaret (Pelley), a dressmaker, a native of Galway, Ireland. After a fall from a police horse made his father an invalid (and his mother having died three years earlier), at 13 young Frank had to leave school to support his family. He landed a job on Wall Street as a runner and eventually began to attend Columbia University at night where he studied accounting and equities management. Study and hard work paid off, and at the age of 29, he was offered a partnership in the firm where he had started work as a boy. He declined this advancement in order to pursue his life-long dream of becoming a priest.

## A PRIEST IN NEW YORK

In 1915 he began his studies at Cathedral College in Manhattan and completed his training at St. Joseph's Seminary, Dunwoodie, in Yonkers, N.Y. He was ordained a priest of the Archdiocese of New York by Archbishop Patrick J. Hayes on May 21, 1921. After a brief assignment as a parish priest, McIntyre began his meteoric climb in the church with a job in the diocesan chancery office. In 1934 he was named chancellor of the archdiocese and in that year also was named a monsignor. With the coming of Francis J. Spellman to New York in 1939, McIntyre, using skills he had learned years earlier on Wall Street, distinguished himself

with his expert reorganization of the finances of the archdiocese. In 1941 he was ordained an auxiliary bishop of New York. After being named coadjutor archbishop of New York in 1946 (without right of succession), McIntyre's power and prominence grew significantly causing one priest to comment that while Cardinal Spellman ran the world, McIntyre ran New York. Showing another side, McIntyre maintained a cordial and supportive relationship with Dorothy Day at a time when many of her fellow Catholics accused her of being a Communist because of her radical sense of poverty and her support of pacifism. In 1946 Day wrote McIntyre thanking him for his courtesy and remarked that he had done more for her than he would ever know.

Because of his competence and genuine abilities in administration, McIntyre was not long for his auxiliary position in New York. In 1948 his career took another step forward when he was named the second archbishop of Los Angeles.

## A CARDINAL IN LOS ANGELES

McIntyre's tenure in Los Angles was coterminous with the unbridled expansion of southern California, and McIntyre made sure his archdiocese and its institutions kept pace. The Catholic population grew greatly during the postwar period, and for a time about 55,000 Catholics moved into the archdiocese each year. In order to meet their needs, McIntyre oversaw the creation of 97 additional parishes, the construction of 192 Catholic schools and the establishment of two new diocesan seminaries. During his first 15 years in Los Angeles, McIntyre set a new record in institutional expansion in American Catholicism by opening a new parochial school every 26 days! In 1952 he was created a cardinal by Pope Pius XII, an appointment which made him the first member of the sacred college to live west of the Mississippi River.

During his 22 years of leadership in Los Angeles, McIntyre worked to improve the lives of the poor and immigrants. He set up diocesan job agencies to help the thousands of people who were streaming to California looking for work, and he founded 22 schools in inner-city neighborhoods to educate the children of Mexican-American immigrants. In addition to his concern for the underprivileged, Cardinal McIntyre also developed a reputation for his unbending conservatism in both secular and religious affairs. He favored the use of atomic weapons in Korea and threw his support behind the conservative anti-communist investigation of Senator Joseph McCarthy. While a chancery official in New York, he accused the progressive Father George Barry Ford of *communicatio in sacris* for sending flowers to Riverside Church for an anniversary. At the Second Vatican Council (1962–1965), McIntyre argued for the retention of Latin in the liturgy saying that the active participation of the laity in the Mass would be a distraction ("*participatio actuosa insuper frequenter est distractio*").

## FINAL YEARS

The years after the Vatican Council were stormy in Los Angeles. McIntyre tried his utmost to hold back what he considered to be excesses in church reforms. When a group of Immaculate Heart of Mary sisters in his archdiocese sought to update their rule as other religious in the United States were doing, McIntyre angrily refused to allow changes. McIntyre did try to negotiate with the order's leaders, but in the heady days immediately after the Council, the order's leaders were intent on their plans and were unwilling to temper some of their more radical reforms. Subsequently a large number of sisters left the community, and the archdiocese and its institutions suffered in the long run by the intransigence of both McIntyre and the sisters. McIntyre stepped down as archbishop on January 21, 1970. Though his health declined, he spent many of his remaining years in a downtown Los Angeles parish doing the work of a simple parish priest which earned him the grudging respect of some of his critics. He died on July 16, 1979.

*See* Los Angeles

Thomas A. Lynch, "Dorothy Day and Cardinal McIntyre: Not Poles Apart," *Church,* VIII (Summer 1992): 10–15.
Thomas J. Shelley, *Dunwoodie: The History of St. Joseph's Seminary, Yonkers, New York* (Westminster, Maryland, 1993).
Francis J. Weber, *His Eminence of Los Angeles* (Santa Barbara, CA: 1997).

ANTHONY D. ANDREASSI

## McKEAN, THOMAS (1734–1817)

Statesman, legislator, lawyer, Revolutionary patriot. Of Irish lineage he was born in New London Township, Pennsylvania. McKean spent seven years at Reverend Francis Allison's nearby academy before studying law in New Castle, Delaware. Admitted to the bar at twenty, he cultivated a successful practice while engaged in various local government posts. In 1762 he commenced seventeen years in the Delaware Assembly and later served as a radical delegate to the Stamp Act Congress.

With tensions brewing between England and her colonies, McKean led Delaware's movement for a colonial congress and, except for a year long gap, represented it in the Continental Congress until 1783. In late summer, 1776, McKean took an active part in framing Delaware's first constitution although tradition erroneously ascribes authorship to him. Upon failing to win reelection to the Congress, he became speaker of the Delaware Assembly and in that capacity served as the state's acting president from September 22 to November 17, 1777. On July 28, 1777, McKean also began a twenty-two year tenure as chief justice of Pennsylvania, and between 1777–83, he held positions from both states.

As a congressman, he supported the Articles of Confederation and served as the body's president from July 10 to November 5, 1781. A Federalist, he helped secure Pennsylvania's ratification of the Constitution in 1787, and participated in that state's constitutional convention from 1789–90.

In 1792, McKean's Francophile sentiments compelled him to split with the Federalists and join the Jeffersonians. Selected as their gubernatorial candidate for the 1799 election, he won and soon established a spoils system in Pennsylvania.

McKean won reelection in 1802 with a large plurality, but an internal partisan schism led radicals to nominate another for the position in 1805. Moderate Republicans and Federalists united to return McKean to the governorship. Once there he sacked his Republican enemies in favor of supportive Federalists. The feisty, able McKean concluded his term and retired, frequently seen about Philadelphia until his death on June 24, 1817.

*See* Pennsylvania

Many of McKean's papers are located in the Historical Society of Pennsylvania.
Edmund C. Burnett, *Letters of Members of the Continental Congress,* 8 vols. (Washington, D.C., 1921–36).
"Governor McKean's Papers," *Pennsylvania Archives,* ser. 4 vol. 4 (Harrisburg, 1900).
*Journals of the Continental Congress 1774–1789, 34 vols.* (Washington, D.C. 1904–37).
Thomas McKean and Edmund Physick, *A Calm Appeal to the People of the State of Delaware* (Philadelphia, 1793).
*Proceedings of the Convention of the Delaware State . . . August, 1776* (Wilmington, 1776).

CHRISTIAN G. SAMITO

## McKENNA, CHARLES HYACINTH, O. P. (1835–1917)

Dominican friar, preacher. Born in the village of Fallalea, County Derry, Ireland, on May 8, 1834, Charles McKenna was the eighth of ten children of Francis and Anna (Gillespie-McDonald). The death of Francis from typhus and the ensuing Irish famine led Anna to bring five of the children (three died in infancy) with her to her brother in Lancaster, Pennsylvania, in 1851, where Charles attended public school and worked as a stonecutter. He later joined the family near Dubuque, Iowa, and was strengthened in resolve to study for the priesthood by the zealous Dominican missonary of the midwest, Samuel Mazzuchelli. McKenna attended nearby Dominican College of Sinsinawa Mound, Wisconsin. He made religious profession as Brother Hyacinth at St. Joseph's, Perry County, Ohio, in 1863, and although studies were disrupted by the Civil War, was ordained a Dominican friar for St. Rose's Priory, Kentucky, in Cincinnati on Oct. 13, 1867, serving first as assistant novice master, and later, sub-prior and pastor at St. Rose. In 1870 he came to St. Vincent Ferrer's Church, New York City, the order's mission band headquarters. He was prior at St. Louis Bertrand, Louisville, Kentucky (1878–1881), but in 1881 returned to New York which remained his home, even while assigned elsewhere, so that he could continue the mission apostolate. Catholic missions stirred the zeal of the faithful, and consisted of days or weeks of devotional exercises, sermons, and the sacraments. The friars could spend ten hours a day hearing confessions during missions, so many attended. Fr. McKenna's eloquent oratory throughout the country attracted thousands and brought him national acclaim. Ever supportive of church societies, he became director of the Rosary Confraternity and the Holy Name Society and wrote a variety of religious manuals. He was made Preacher General in 1881, a high honor in the order. In Kentucky, newly freed slaves formed half the devout Catholic congregation in Louisville, which prompted a sympathetic McKenna to take measures to establish a church especially to serve African Americans in New York, a plan he abandoned as being divisive long-term. He also established for a short time a community of Dominican sisters to care for the poor of the city. He lectured and preached in cathedrals, colleges and convents, and urged pastors to provide spiritual exercises especially designed for children. His humble preaching appealed to all classes. In ill health, he retired in 1914 to the Dominican House of Studies, Washington, D. C. Fr. McKenna died Feb. 21, 1917 in Jacksonville, Florida where he had been sent for his health and was buried in Calvary Cemetary, Long Island City, New York.

Charles Hyacinth McKenna, O.P., *How to Make the Mission,* New Rev. ed. (Boston, 1897).
*Dictionary of American Biography,* Vol. 12 (New York, 1933).

Victor Francis O'Daniel, O.P., *Very Rev. Charles Hyacinth McKenna, O.P., P.G., Missionary and Apostle of the Holy Name Society* (New York, 1917).

ANNA M. DONNELLY

## McKENNA, JOSEPH (1843–1926)

Associate Justice of the U.S. Supreme Court. He was born to Irish parents in Philadelphia on August 10, 1843. At an early age he decided to study for the priesthood and entered St. Joseph's Seminary, but quit to study law. He began practising in California where his family moved in 1854. In 1869 he married Amanda Francis Bornemann, and they had four children. He entered politics as a state assemblyman but failed in 1876, 1878, and 1880 to win a congressional seat, but he was elected in 1884 and served three terms. In Congress, McKenna supported railroads and high tariffs, and California issues, such as anti-Chinese legislation, free silver, and veteran's pensions. He voted against the establishment of the Interstate Commerce Commission in 1887. McKenna resigned in 1892 to become U.S. circuit judge for the ninth circuit. In 1897 President McKinley appointed him U.S. Attorney General and eight months later he was appointed to the Supreme Court. McKenna did not speak often for the court, but his few decisions were marked by a practical vision of political and social situations. He died in Washington, D.C., on November 21, 1926.

Matthew McDevitt, *Joseph McKenna: Associate Justice of the United States* (New York, 1974).
John T. Noonan, Jr., "The Catholic Justices of the United States Supreme Court," *Catholic Historical Review,* 67/3 (1981): 369-85.

KATHLEEN N. McCARTHY

## McKENNEY, RUTH (1911–1972)

Journalist, writer. Born in Indiana, McKenney was raised in Ohio by a schoolteacher mother who was an "ardent Irish nationalist" and a father who encouraged his daughter to take a night job at a printing shop at age fourteen (Block). McKenney attended Ohio State University but reportedly did not finish. In 1933 McKenney and her sister, Eileen, left Ohio for Greenwich Village in New York. From 1934 to 1937 McKenney worked as a reporter for the *New York Post* and the *Beacon Journal* in Akron and published semiautobiographical articles in the *New Yorker, Publisher's Weekly,* and various journals. McKenney married Richard Bransten in 1937. During the early 1940s, she and her husband worked as editors for the *New Masses,* in which McKenney published some of her own articles as well as a regular column, "Strictly Personal." In 1946 she and Richard were expelled from the Communist Party for deviating from party doctrine (Mainiero).

McKenney's 1938 *My Sister Eileen,* a compilation of previously published short stories, became a Broadway play, a motion picture, and eventually a musical, entitled *Wonderful Town.* McKenney also published *The McKenneys Carry On* (1940); an unsuccessful political novel, *Jake Home* (1943); *The Loud Red Patrick* (1947), which, like *My Sister Eileen,* became a Broadway play; *Love Story* (1950); *Here's England* (1950); *All About Eileen* (1952); *Far Far From Home* (1954); and *Mirage* (1956) (*Who Was Who in America*).

Of those works, McKenney is best known for *My Sister Eileen,* in which she writes of the "sometimes funny, sometimes poig-

nant experiences" shared while growing up with her sister. One critic notes that McKenney's popularity stemmed from her ability to recount life's comic misadventures "with a grace that is rare in extracting from the commonplace the dramatic and from the habitual the humorous" (Block). But McKenney could also write with a serious bent. Her nonfictional *Industrial Valley* (1939), written in journalistic form and incorporating actual newsclippings and names, focuses on Depression-era workers struggling to form a union in Akron. Thematically the work deals with political corruption, big business, and social manipulation (Mainiero). Her 1940 *Browder and Ford: For Peace, Jobs, Socialism* deals with similar subjects. *Industrial Valley* won McKenney the Best Fiction Book award at the Writer's Congress in 1938 and 1939 (Locher).

Moreover, McKenney wrote on less politically charged subjects as well, particularly in *Here's England: A Highly Informal Guide,* which she coauthored with her husband. Their 1950 text highlights various historical sites and tourist attractions in Great Britain. McKenney's 1956 *Mirage* traces the life of an imprisoned chemist during the French Revolution.

Overall, notes one biographer, "for the reading public . . . there are actually two Ruth McKenneys. Those who are *New Yorker* fans know her as [the] humorist author of the hilarious sketches which have appeared in book form as the best sellers" . . . and those who know her as "a radical, a serious student of social and economic conditions" (Block). But, given that McKenney's mother died when the author was eight years old and that McKenney self-mockingly described herself as a "moral leper, an outcast" who learned about the adult world as a teenager working in a print shop that failed during the Depression, the existence of "two Ruth McKenneys" testifies to the complex nature of an individual who suffered a great deal but frequently met rejection and pain with laughter.

*See* Fiction, Irish-American

Maxine Block, *Current Biography: Who's News and Why* (New York, 1942).
Frances Locher, ed., *Contemporary Authors: A Bio-Bibliographical Guide* (Detroit, 1980).
Lina Mainiero, ed., *American Women Writers,* Vol. III (New York, 1981).
*Who Was Who in America,* Vol. V: 1969–1973 (Chicago, n.d.).

JAMES P. LEONARD

## McKIERNAN, EOIN (1916–   )

Scholar. During folklorist Seamus Delargy's visit to the U.S. in 1939 (Delargy was preparing the way for a visit later that year by Eamon de Valera—a visit which did not, in the end, take place), he met Eoin McKiernan, then 24 years old, and employed by the Irish Industries Depot on Lexington Avenue in New York. In his diary Delargy noted: "McKiernan is a presentable young man, speaks Irish fairly well, has a good education, and is one of the very best Irishmen I met in America."

McKiernan was born of Irish parents (from Clare and Cavan) in Manhattan. He obtained his undergraduate degree in literature and classical languages from St. Joseph's College in New York, his master's degree in psychology and education from the University of New Hampshire, and a Ph.D. in English literature from Pennsylvania State University. He was professor of English and chairman of the Department of English for 11 years at the University of St. Thomas in St. Paul, Minnesota, and before that

Eoin McKiernan

held the same positions for 10 years at the State University of New York at Geneseo.

His first visit to Ireland was at the age of 15, when he won a scholarship to study Irish in Rosmuc. Since then he has been back over 300 times, including a year's stay in Dublin with his wife and nine children.

Jeanette (O'Callaghan) McKiernan, whom he met when he was 16, used to say that Eoin was pushing for an Irish-American Cultural Institute since the day she met him. In his mid-40s, in 1964, he and Jeanette and local philanthropists Patrick Butler and Lawrence O'Shaughnessy founded such an entity (still alive today, though McKiernan retired from its leadership in 1986).

The institute's membership grew initially from viewers of a 53-episode national public television series McKiernan wrote and broadcast during 1962–64. Over the years, the IACI has awarded over $400,000 to the arts in Ireland; published the scholarly journal of Irish studies *Éire-Ireland* continuously since 1964 (published quarterly, edited by McKiernan from 1964–85); established a program for American secondary school students to study in Ireland; pioneered a tree-planting effort for reforestation in Ireland, and much more. Honors have been conferred on McKiernan on both sides of the Atlantic.

Among numerous honors conferred upon McKiernan are an honorary doctorate from the National University of Ireland, Dublin; the John F. Kennedy Gold Medal from the Ancient Order of Hibernians; a lifetime honorary membership in the Royal Dublin Society; the Éire Society (Boston) Gold Medal Award, and an honorary doctorate in 1996 from the University of St. Thomas in St. Paul.

When asked to characterize the man inside the frame, it would be fair to say that few in 20th-century America have done as much for Ireland as McKiernan has. He possesses a remarkable vision, which is matched by a rare intelligence, generosity of spirit, dedication and hard work. Long before it was fashionable to take an interest in Ireland—before Riverdance, say, or the advent of the "Celtic Tiger"—McKiernan worked tirelessly to educate Irish-Americans about their heritage. A letter he received thirty-five years ago from Boston after the success of his television show, "Irish Diary," typifies those whom McKiernan hoped to reach with his life work: "You've done so much for my soul.

I was a domestic servant with more culture than the people I worked for. To them I was only Irish. The series was balm to my heart."

Here is a poem, by his poet daughter Ethna, written to celebrate his 80th birthday:

### DEORA DÉ

We walked through a tunnel of fuschia
and he called the bushes *Deora Dé.*
"From the Irish," he said, *Tears of God.*
How like him it was to pull his other language
from the air like that,

Threading the red blaze of color
and its teardrop song to the sorrow spent
by one creating it, petal by detailed petal
added to a burden of immense particulars
in a world still daily being made.

My father—his thin shoulders angling
through the patched tweed jacket,
our hands linked by the old stories,
fused history cast in common bone.
And the wild fuschia light
on the West Cork mountains
that October afternoon.

## McLOUGHLIN, JOHN (1784–1857)

Frontier businessman. John McLoughlin was born on October 19, 1784, in Quebec, Canada, the son of John McLoughlin, a native of Ireland, and Angelique Fraser. After his father's death, he was raised by his mother's family as a Protestant. He was sent to Scotland to study medicine but soon after his return became a trader for the Northwest Fur Company. By 1821 when the company merged with the Hudson's Bay Company, he had been made a partner and helped negotiate the union. As a chief factor of the Hudson's Bay Company, he was put in charge of the Columbia District, which included not only the Columbia River area but after 1825 all of British Columbia. In the absence of civil government, he also had civil and criminal jurisdiction over this vast region. He remained in control until 1846 as historical events unfolded in the settlement of the area known as the Oregon country.

### OREGON COUNTRY

When McLoughlin arrived in 1824 there were relatively few Americans in the territory, even though the treaty of 1818 had allowed for joint occupation of the Pacific Northwest. As chief factor his duty was to maximize company profits by keeping peace among the Native American tribes and monopolizing the fur trade with them, while preventing the influx of agricultural settlements. It was a duty at times difficult to fulfill and often hard to reconcile with his conscience. In general, however, he was successful in keeping the tribes at peace and in driving out the competition from American fur traders by his astute, and sometimes ruthless, business tactics, but he could not stop the relentless flow of settlers westward along the Oregon Trail.

When missionaries and settlers began arriving in the 1830s, McLoughlin did not hesitate to give them the credit and provisions they needed to survive, in spite of company policy. At the same time he counseled Americans against settling north of the Columbia River, believing it would be the boundary between Canada and the United States. When it became apparent that the boundary would be at the 49th parallel, he made preparations to move company headquarters to Fort Victoria on Vancouver Island. Then in 1846, the year the boundary treaty was signed, he retired and settled in Oregon City, Oregon, where he became an American citizen. In 1847 McLoughlin was made a Knight of St. Gregory. He died on September 3, 1857, "The Father of Oregon" as he came to be known.

Alberta B. Fogdall, *Royal Family of the Columbia* (Fairfield, Wash., 1978). Richard G. Montgomery, *The White Headed Eagle* (New York, 1934).

JAMES J. HALEY

### McMAHON, BERNARD (d. Sept. 18, 1816)

Horticulturist. Driven from Ireland for political reasons, Bernard McMahon became an "Exile of Erin" and came to America in 1796. He settled in Philadelphia where he constructed greenhouses, nurseries, and experimental gardens. Collecting rare flowers and successfully breeding some of the most exotic plants of the day, McMahon set up a seed and nursery shop on the east side of Philadelphia with his wife. The shop quickly became a center for prominent horticulturists and botanists to exchange scientific information. Active in these discussions, McMahon's opinion was so well respected that Thomas Nuttall, an English botanist, named an evergreen barberry after him.

In 1804, McMahon published a catalogue that listed about a thousand species of seeds in America, and in 1806, published America's first important horticultural work, the *American Gardener's Calendar,* which went through eleven printings over the next fifty years. McMahon was also instrumental in preserving and distributing throughout America the seeds that Lewis and Clark brought back from their long expedition. He also tried, but failed, to grow the coveted European wine grape (*Vitis vinifera*) in the eastern United States. McMahon died in 1816, but his wife carried on his business until she passed it on to other horticulturists.

Liberty Hyde Bailey, *The Standard Cyclopedia of Horticulture* vol. III (New York: Macmillan, 1915, 1947). *Dictionary of American Biography,* vol. XII, Dumas Malone, ed. (New York: Scribner's Sons, 1933): 137. Preface, *American Gardener's Calendar* (1857).

DANIEL J. KUNTZ

### McMAHON, BRIEN (1903–1952)

U.S. Senator, lawyer and politician. He was born in Connecticut into Irish heritage to William and Eugenie J. (O'Brien) McMahon and had a very fortunate childhood. McMahon attended Fordham University and received a B.A. degree in 1924 and then Yale University where he obtained an LL.B degree in 1927. After graduation, he shortened his name from James O'Brien McMahon and launched his own career in law in his hometown of Norwalk.

He served as city judge for a short interval and then found an alliance with Connecticut Democrat Homer S. Cummings and traveled to Washington with him. In the political atmosphere he moved from working as an assistant to Cummings to acting assistant attorney general in the criminal division where he focused on tax and criminal cases. He left government work for five years

beginning in 1939, returning to private law practice. In 1944 he won nomination to the United States Senate and gained the support of several influential Democrats. McMahon won his bid for a position in the Senate and became an ardent supporter of the following: civil rights legislation; price, wage and rent controls; public housing; increase for minimum wage; American membership in the United Nations and the Marshall Plan.

McMahon also capitalized on the opportunity to harvest research on atomic energy and sponsored a bill in the fall of 1945 to establish the Special Committee on Atomic Energy and subsequently became chairman of the committee. He kept a keen eye on Russian atomic progress and advocated accelerated production of weapons for defense. In 1950 he also worked for peace proposals and for arms reduction worldwide to be managed by the United Nations. McMahon's popularity increased and his political influence as well. He considered running for vice president but was prohibited in the long run by the discovery that he had cancer. He died in Washington on July 28, 1952.

Harold P. Green and Alan Rosenthal, *Government of the Atom: The Integration of Powers* (1963). Richard G. Hewlett, Oscar E. Anderson and Francis Duncan, *A History of the United States Atomic Energy Commission,* 2 vols. (1962, 1969). *Dictionary of American Biography,* supplement 5.

JOY HARRELL

### McMANUS, TERRENCE BELLEW (1823–1860)

Revolutionary. He was born in Temo, County Fermanagh in 1823. After spending time in England he joined the Young Ireland Movement in 1843. He participated in the July 1848 rising at Ballingarry, Tipperary. Later he was arrested while attempting to flee to the United States. The crown sentenced him to death for treason which was later changed to transportation for life to Van Dieman's Land (Tasmania) in 1849. In 1852 he escaped and settled down in San Francisco. He died there in poverty in December of 1860.

The Fenians decided to send his body back to Ireland for burial. It was carried across the United States by train while stops were made for viewing in areas where Irish-American populations requested it. McManus' remains did not leave for Ireland until September 1861. In Ireland Cardinal Cullen refused to bury him from a Catholic church.

The Irish Republic Brotherhood arranged to wake him at Mechanics Institute in Dublin. On November 10, 1861, up to 100,000 people followed the coffin to Glasnevin cemetery. The funeral cortege paused at every spot in Dublin sacred to republicanism—such as the house where Robert Emmet was hung, the house where Wolfe Tone's body was kept before burial and the house where Lord Edward Fitzgerald was wounded in 1798. Patrick Lavelle, a Mayo priest, buried him against the wishes of Cardinal Cullen.

R. F. Foster, *Modern Ireland 1600–1972* (London and New York, 1988). Desmond Ryan, *The Fenian Chief: A Biography of James Stephens* (Dublin, 1967).

SEAMUS METRESS

### McNEILL, HECTOR (1728–1785)

Revolutionary naval officer. Hector McNeill was born October 10, 1728, in County Antrim, Ireland. His parents, Malcom and Mary (Stuart) McNeill, emigrated to Boston in 1737 where Hector was educated, learned the sea trade, and became master of a vessel by the age of twenty-two. By 1750 he had become engaged in the French and Indian War, but was captured in 1755 by the Indians and made a prisoner in Quebec. On his release, he became involved in coastal trade from Quebec and served on the St. Lawrence River for the Colonies. By the summer of 1776, McNeill was in Boston with an appointment as captain in the Continental navy. In October of that year, he was ranked third on the captains list and commanded the new, twenty-four-gun frigate, *Boston*. In 1777, with Captain John Manley, commander of the *Hancock*, McNeill participated in a number of skirmishes, capturing the British frigate *Fox* in June. But in the following month, the American captains faced three British ships, forty-four-gun ship *Rainbow*, a frigate and a brig. Manley and McNeill were separated and the *Hancock* was captured. McNeill escaped with the *Boston* and sailed back to Boston where he was court-martialed for failing to rescue the *Hancock*. Trial records have not been preserved, but McNeill lost his commission in 1778. The real failure appears to have been poor communication and lack of cooperation between the two captains. For the remainder of his life, McNeill continued to command private merchant ships until in 1785, on Christmas night, McNeill's ship was lost at sea.

Gardner Weld Allen, *A Naval History of the American Revolution* (Boston and New York: Houghton Mifflin Company, 1913).

"Massachusetts Privateers of the Revolution," *Massachusetts Historical Society Collections*, vol. LXXVII (1927).

*Dictionary of American Biography*, vol. XII, Dumas Malone, ed. (New York: Scribner's Sons, 1933): 151.

DANIEL J. KUNTZ

## MacNEVEN, WILLIAM JAMES (1763–1841)

Physician, Irish patriot. William MacNeven was born on March 21, 1763, in County Galway, Ireland. He came from a family whose ancestors had been driven south a century before by Cromwell's army. He was raised in the wilds of Galway until at the age of ten or twelve, he traveled to Austria where he joined his uncle who had become a physician and baron of the Empress Maria Theresa. There MacNeven studied at Vienna where he received a Catholic education and a medical degree in 1784. He returned immediately to Dublin where he began a promising career as a physician.

MacNeven soon became a determined patriot and a member of the United Irishmen. His political activities, however, landed him in the Limainham prison and then to Scotland at the Fort George prison where he met Thomas Addis Emmet. His confinement there allowed him to study intensely and to prepare for further activity. On the condition of banishment, MacNeven was released and went to Switzerland, about which he wrote his first book in 1802. In the following year, he traveled to France where he tried to persuade Napoleon to invade Ireland, but without success. Hoping to further the cause of Ireland, he served in the Irish Brigade of the French army until 1805 when it became clear that his efforts to win European support for Ireland were without effect. He thus traveled to America and arrived in New York City on July 4, 1805. MacNeven soon established a medical practice and by 1808 had become professor of obstetrics in the College of Physicians and Surgeons at New York City. In 1813, Mac-Neven was given the chair of chemistry and six years later, he published his *Chemical Examination of the Mineral Waters of*

*Schooley's Mountains* and an *Exposition of Atomic Theory of Chemistry*. He became co-editor of the *New York Medical and Philosophical Journal and Review* and was elected a member of the American Philosophical Society.

All of these activities, however, did not shake the Irish cause from MacNeven's devotion. He published *Pieces of Irish History* in 1807, established an employment agency for Irish immigrants, and was the founder and president of the Friends of Ireland. After suffering a long attack of gout in 1838, MacNeven moved into the country where he lived with his son-in-law until his death on July 12, 1841. Bishop John Hughes of New York administered last rights to MacNeven, a devout Catholic.

*See* United Irishmen and America

*The Catholic Encyclopedia*, Vol. IX (1910).

*Dictionary of American Biography*, Vol. XII, Dumas Malone, ed. (New York: Scribner's Sons, 1933): 153–154.

S. D. Gross, *Lives of Eminent American Physicians and Surgeons* (1861).

Richard Robert Madden, *The United Irishmen, Their Lives and Times* (Philadelphia: Lea and Blanchard, 1842).

James Thacher, *American Medical Biography: or, Memoirs of Eminent Physicians Who Have Flourished in America* (Boston: Richardson & Lord, 1828).

DANIEL J. KUNTZ

## McNICHOLAS, JOHN TIMOTHY (1877–1950)

Dominican, archbishop. He was born on December 15, 1877, in County Mayo, Ireland, to Patrick and Mary Mullaney Mc-Nicholas. In 1881 his family emigrated to the United States and settled in Chester, Pennsylvania. After his high school education at St. Joseph's College in Philadelphia, at seventeen he entered the Dominican Order at St. Rose Priory in Springfield, Kentucky, taking John for his name in religion. Philosophical and theological studies were taken at St. Joseph Priory in Somerset, Ohio, and he was ordained on October 10, 1901, by Bishop Henry Moeller. Three years of study followed at the Minerva University in Rome where he obtained a lectorate in sacred theology in 1904.

In 1909 McNicholas was named national director of the Holy Name Society, with membership exceeding a million and a half. He established its headquarters in New York City, where he served as pastor of St. Catherine of Siena parish from 1913 to 1916. Recalled to Rome in 1916 to serve in the central administration of the Dominican Order as the English-speaking socius or counselor, he renewed or developed influential contacts which led to his appointment as bishop of the Duluth, Minnesota, Diocese on July 18, 1918 by Pope Benedict XV. In May 1925 he was first nominated bishop of Indianapolis, Indiana, but before he could take possession of his see, he was appointed archbishop of Cincinnati on July 8 of the same year.

As archbishop he continued the efforts of his predecessors by dramatically expanding the educational facilities of the diocese on every level. He gave public voice to his passion for social justice for all and strongly supported the rights of labor and of parents to state support, regardless of race or religion. On the national scene he also played an important role in the work of the American bishops. From 1930 to 1935 he chaired the department of education of the National Catholic Welfare Conference (NCWC) and again from 1942 to 1945. During much of that time he was also chairman of the episcopal committee on motion pictures and was instrumental in founding the National Legion of Decency. As a member of the episcopal committee for the Confraternity of Christian Doctorine (1934–45 and 1947–50) he played a part in the revision of both the New Testament and the Baltimore Catechism. For the last five years of his episcopacy he was also president general of the National Catholic Education Association. His intellectual gifts and zealous spirit found expression in the annual statements of the Catholic bishops and often as a Catholic spokesman on issues of national or world importance. He vigorously opposed totalitarianism, whether of the fascist or communist variety, and championed the cause of minority groups. He died of a heart attack on April 22, 1950.

*See* Ohio; Education, Parochial

Steven M. Avella, "John T. McNicholas in the Age of Practical Thomism" (Philadelphia, 1986).
John T. McNicholas, *Mosaic of a Bishop* (Paterson, New Jersey, 1957).

JAMES J. HALEY

## McNULTY, JOHN AUGUSTINE (1885–1956)

Writer, journalist. John McNulty was born in Lawrence, Massachusetts, on November 1, 1885. His father, a bricklayer, fell from a scaffold to his death when John was a child; and his mother ran a small candy store to support them. McNulty was born with the gift of gentle laughter and lived in a world bordering on Oz and wonderland; and that became apparent in his happy childhood years.

He dropped out of Colby College and Columbia University and joined the Associated Press in New York. He moved on to Columbus, Ohio, where he enjoyed a decade of journalism. When he returned to New York, he worked for the *Mirror,* the *News,* and the *Herald Tribune.* In 1937 he joined the *New Yorker* and found his literary home, where quality took precedence over deadlines. The streets and alleys of New York became the world for his unflagging comic spirit. For McNulty there were no people, only individual men and women in whose ordinary lives and worlds he saw transforming humor, sparkles of the wonderful and the extraordinary.

Cab drivers, men at the bar, bartenders, horse-players, mailmen, a legion of down-and-outs knew McNulty as their pal. And

John McNulty

though they never read a word he wrote, he immortalized them with affectionate and humorous sensitivity. He was a regular at Tim and Joe Costello's Saloon on Third Avenue, and friends who met him there knew that the happy spirit of McNulty evaded words in cold type but were incarnated in his daily anecdotes and comments when, with a gift for word and phrase, he coaxed them to see the wonders of the commonplace.

He had a love affair with Ireland and the Irish "Catlicks" he met on the streets of New York. He once remarked that "two thirds of Irish blood is grease paint." John McNulty died on his farm in Wakefield, Rhode Island, on July 29, 1956.

In his Appreciation in *The World of John McNulty* (1957), James Thurber wrote: "The angel that writes names in a book of gold must long ago have put McNulty down as one who delighted in his fellow men. . . . McNulty's love of humanity was not expressed at a distance, from a platform, but in pieces that have the last pulse of life in every sentence. Nothing, however commonplace, that he touched with words remained commonplace."

*See* New York City

John McNulty, *Third Avenue, New York* (New York, 1946).
———, *A Man Gets Around* (New York, 1951).
———, *My Son Jonnie* (New York, 1955).
———, *The World of John McNulty,* with an Appreciation by James Thurber (New York, 1957).

MICHAEL GLAZIER

## McNUTT, ALEXANDER (1725–1811)

Territorial land promoter. Probably born in the Londonderry area of Ireland, Alexander McNutt was born to Alexander and Jane McNutt *c.*1725. By his 28th year, McNutt sailed to America where he settled in Staunton, Virginia. There he served in the local militia under Major Andrew Lewis in the Shawnee expedition of 1756. McNutt soon rose to the rank of captain and was charged with raising replacements for the Massachusetts militia. For the next three years, McNutt represented Apthorp and Hancock of Boston as a land promoter for Nova Scotia. After successfully resettling a number of New Englanders there, he turned his attentions to the direct settlement of Irish Protestants in Nova Scotia. McNutt sought approval in England in 1761, but was later denied permission by the British government. McNutt nevertheless acquired the rights to 1,745,000 acres of Nova Scotian land, which went back to the British government between 1770 and 1788 as tensions mounted with the Revolutionary War. By 1778 McNutt worked to convince Congress that Nova Scotia ought to be included in the colonial struggle. Though his efforts failed, McNutt received a grant of $15,000 to build a road from the Penobscot River to St. John for the strategic use of the colonies. In 1780, McNutt proclaimed a "New Ireland" in Nova Scotia, publishing his *The Constitution . . . of the Free and Independent State . . . of New Ireland* in 1780. McNutt's dreams were never realized, but his enthusiasm for land speculation characterizes the spirit of the frontier era. McNutt finally settled near Lexington, Virginia, where he died *c.* 1811 without ever marrying.

*See* Emigration: 17th and 18th Centuries

A. W. H. Eaton, "Alexander McNutt," *Americana* (December 1913).
*Proceedings and Transcriptions of the Royal Society of Canada,* 3 ser., vols. V, VI (1912–13).

Beamish Murdoch, *A History of Nova Scotia*, vol. II (Halifax, N.S.: J. Barnes, 1866).

George Patterson, *A History of the County of Pictou, Nova Scotia* (1916).

H. H. McCormick, *Genealogies and Reminiscences* (rev. ed., 1897): 57–64.

DANIEL J. KUNTZ

## McQUAID, BERNARD JOSEPH JOHN (1823–1909)

Bishop and educator. Bernard Joseph John McQuaid was born in New York, NY, on December 15, 1823, and died in Rochester, NY, on January 18, 1909. The son of Bernard and Mary (Maguire) McQuaid, immigrants from County Tyrone, Ireland, young Bernard lost both parents shortly before he was ten years of age. He ended up in St. Patrick's Orphan Asylum in New York City where he was blessed to meet Elizabeth Boyle, a caring Sister of Charity, who helped him decide on a career in the priesthood.

After attending Chambly College, a seminary not too far from Montreal, and St. Joseph's College, the diocesan seminary once located at Fordham, McQuaid was ordained a priest by Bishop John Hughes of New York City on January 16, 1848, in the old St. Patrick's Cathedral. Assigned to St. Vincent's Church in Madison, NJ, as its pastor early in his career, McQuaid became interested in building churches and schools.

During the five years before he moved to Newark in 1853, McQuaid was working on three churches and two parochial schools. The first parochial school in New Jersey was his own parish school in which McQuaid taught for a half year. Subsequently, McQuaid became the rector of St. Patrick's Cathedral in Newark in 1853. While there he was active in the founding of Seton Hall College in 1856. Thus, he became its first president, holding this position for ten years (1856–57, 1859–68).

### THE BISHOP

McQuaid served as a chaplain in the Civil War in 1864. Appointed Vicar General of the Diocese of Newark in 1867, he was designated by Pope Pius IX first Bishop of Rochester, NY, on March 3, 1868. Archbishop John McCloskey of New York, assisted by Bishop James Roosevelt Bayley of Newark, NJ, and Bishop Louis de Goesbriand of Burlington, VT, consecrated him a bishop at St. Patrick's Cathedral on Mott Street on July 12, 1868. Hardly one to accept a position without thinking it out, McQuaid was among seven of the bishops from North America who initially voted with the minority in opposing the definition of papal infallibility at the First Vatican Council in 1870. Bishop McQuaid was later a participant in the Third Plenary Council of Baltimore in 1884.

Yet, throughout his many years as an American bishop, McQuaid was aligned to the conservative branch of the hierarchy rather than the liberal side. The latter, which emphasized the American rather than the European character of Catholicism, which McQuaid upheld, was led by James Cardinal Gibbons of Baltimore, Archbishop John Ireland of St. Paul, and Bishop John J. Keane of Catholic University.

McQuaid was known nationally for his support of a Catholic education from an early age through college. While other members of the hierarchy, including Ireland and Keane, strongly disagreed with him, the Bishop of Rochester regarded public school education as pernicious to Catholicism. So intense was the rivalry among the bishops that McQuaid prevented Keane from coming into his diocese and delivering a lecture at Cornell University in 1890.

But that was not the end of the matter. Later, when the Democrats nominated McQuaid to fill the seat on the New York State Board of Regents to replace a Catholic who had died, the Republicans nominated Sylvester Malone, a priest who had the support of both Archbishop Ireland and Bishop Keane. After Malone won the election, Bishop McQuaid took an unusual step on November 25, 1894, and mounted the pulpit of his cathedral in full regalia to rebuke Archbishop Ireland for coming into New York to campaign for Malone. Even though McQuaid was a strong advocate of Catholic education, the Vatican rebuked the indignant Bishop of Rochester for his stand against the Archbishop of St. Paul.

In the Diocese of Rochester, McQuaid did not hesitate to establish a Catholic school system and set up a minor (1870) and major seminary (1893) for the education of future priests. Though he was a staunch Europeanizer in the American Church and truly reflective of conservative ideas in his defense of Catholic education, McQuaid's contribution to seminary formation was somewhat liberal in his attempt to introduce an American way of seminary training rather than to adhere to the European style. Even though McQuaid favored what he regarded as the conservatism of the Jesuits and opposed the liberalism of Sulpicians as seminary teachers, his thinking had an element of the Americanizer. Later, the Bishop of Rochester was, of course, delighted with the apparent condemnation of the liberals by Pope Leo XIII's *Testem Benevolentiae* in 1899.

That the Jesuits chose to name their high school in his see city for Bishop McQuaid was an appropriate way to commemorate this exceptional American prelate who was supportive of their way of thinking about issues involving religion and society. Following his death, Bishop McQuaid was buried in Rochester's Holy Sepulchre Cemetery.

*See* New York State; Catholicism, Irish-American

Archives of the Diocese of Newark, Diocese of Rochester, and Seton Hall University.

Robert D. Cross, *The Emergence of Liberal Catholicism in America* (Cambridge, 1958).

Joseph L. Hogan, *A Historical Study of Bishop McQuaid's Outstanding Contributions Toward Catholic Education in the Diocese of Rochester* (Buffalo, 1949).

Norlene M. Kunkel, *Bishop Bernard J. McQuaid and Catholic Education* (New York, 1988).

Robert F. McNamara, *The Diocese of Rochester, 1868–1969* (Rochester, 1968).

Frederick J. Zwierlein, *The Life and Letters of Bishop McQuaid*, 3 vols. (Rochester, 1925–27).

VINCENT A. LAPOMARDA, S.J.

## McSORLEY, EDWARD (1902–1966)

Author, newspaperman. Edward McSorley was born July 6, 1902, in Providence, Rhode Island, the son of William and Ellen (McDermott). He married Lina Allegrini in 1928 and had three children, including twins. His early writing was for obscure publications, but he later became a newspaper writer for the *Providence Journal,* the *Worcester Telegram,* the *Bronx Home News,* the *New York World,* and the *New York Graphic,* among others. McSorley also did publicity work for Tammany Hall, the film industry, vaudeville, and in civil rights areas.

He published short stories, articles and reviews for magazines and newspapers. The protagonist of his first well-received novel, *Our Own Kind* (1946), which some feel has not been surpassed, provided a view of the working-class Irish of Providence in the early twentieth century, and uniquely presented Irish-Americans in a multi-dimensional way. *The Young McDermott* (1949) tells of a young reporter's career, and his last novel, *Kitty, I Hardly Knew You* (1956), concerns two Irish immigrants in America. The National Academy of Arts and Letters gave him the M. Peabody Waite Award in 1961. He died Dec. 22, 1966, of emphysema and heart problems in Tarrytown, N.Y.

*See* Fiction, Irish-American

*New York Times,* obituary (Dec. 23, 1966): 25.
Harry R. Warfel, *American Novelists of Today* (New York, 1951).

ANNA M. DONNELLY

## MacSPARRAN, JAMES (1693–1757)

Anglican missionary to colonial America and author of the first Irish emigrant's guide. MacSparran was born in Dungiven parish, Co. Derry. Descended from late 17th-century Scottish settlers in Ulster, MacSparran was raised by his uncle, a Presbyterian minister, and educated in Derry city and at the University of Glasgow (M.A., 1709). Licensed as a Presbyterian minister, in 1718 MacSparran immigrated to Boston and became pastor of the Congregational Church of Bristol (then in Massachusetts, now Rhode Island). However, facing charges of fraud and immorality, in 1719 MacSparran returned to Ireland, joined the Church of Ireland, and in 1720 was ordained an Anglican priest and licensed by the Society for the Propagation of the Gospel in Foreign Parts (S.P.G.) as missionary to St. Paul's parish in Rhode Island's Narragansett County. From 1721 until his death, MacSparran served St. Paul's congregation, dominated by wealthy planters and slaveowners. Reputedly one of the S.P.G.'s most able missionaries, MacSparran moved in the colony's highest circles, married the daughter of his wealthiest parishioner, and founded new churches in Bristol, New London, and elsewhere in New England. In 1729 he hosted the Anglo-Irish bishop and philosopher, George Berkeley, during the latter's American sojourn; in 1737 Oxford University awarded him a Doctorate in Sacred Theology; and later generations would memorialize him as the "Apostle of Narragansett." However, MacSparran despised colonial American society as barbaric, heretical, and democratic, and his relationships with New England's Puritans were acrimonious and litigious. In 1753 he published in Dublin a pamphlet, *America Dissected, Being a Full and True Account of all the American Colonies,* as "a Caution to Unsteady People who may be tempted to leave their Native County." Disappointed by his failure to return permanently to Ireland or to be appointed America's first Anglican bishop, MacSparran died at his home in South Kingston, R.I., and was buried under St. Paul's communion table.

*Dictionary of American Biography.*
*Dictionary of National Biography.*
Rev. D. Goodwin, ed., *A Letter Book and Abstract of Out Services Written during the Years 1743–1751 by the Rev. James MacSparran* (Boston, 1899).
W. Updike, *A History of the Episcopal Church in Narragansett, Rhode Island,* 2nd ed. (Boston, 1907).

KERBY MILLER

## McSWIGGAN, MARY THOMAS (1818–1877)

Religious sister and orphanage administrator. Sister Mary Thomas McSwiggan was born in County Tyrone, Ireland, on November 21, 1818. She entered the Daughters of Charity in Emmitsburg, Maryland, on November 21, 1838, served first in Emmitsburg and St. Louis, and was assigned to the Catholic orphanage in Natchez, Mississippi, about 1857.

During the Civil War, McSwiggan traveled to New Orleans and successfully persuaded General Benjamin Butler, so despised by Louisianians, not only to provide a monthly allowance and boat load of supplies for Natchez's needy orphans, but also to grant permission for two Daughters of Charity to bring medicine and food to the sick and wounded outside the Federal lines. She visited Bishop William Henry Elder of Natchez in Vidalia during his brief exile for refusing to order prayers for Federal officials in the Natchez Cathedral.

During the impoverished times that followed the war, McSwiggan self-sacrificingly sought help to maintain the orphans in her charge. She often visited on foot, by wagon, or by boat the levees to beg for her orphans from the construction laborers, many of whom were her fellow countrymen.

McSwiggan spent time with prisoners, assisted the sick daily during a yellow fever epidemic in the city, and served as a mother and counselor to many, both young and old, in addition to her responsibilities at the orphanage.

During McSwiggan's final illness, the local rabbi and Protestant ministers in Natchez publicly asked their congregations to pray for her recovery, an extraordinary event in the late nineteenth-century Protestant South. She died peacefully on September 22, 1877, and was buried in the Natchez cemetery.

"Remarks on Our Dear Sister Mary Thomas McSwiggan," in *Lives of the Sisters* (1877), including a copy of Elder's letter.
Charles E. Nolan, *St. Mary's of Natchez: the History of a Southern Catholic Congregation, 1716–1988* (Natchez, 1992).

CHARLES E. NOLAN

## McWHINEY, GRADY (1928–   )

Historian, educator. He was born July 15, 1928, in Shreveport, Louisiana. Following his discharge from the Marine Corps, he earned a B.A. from his hometown Centenary College in 1950. He then entered Louisiana State University to pursue graduate studies, but after taking an M.A. under Francis Butler Simpkins, McWhiney, like so many Southerners over the years, went north to complete his education. Civil War scholar and Abraham Lincoln authority David H. Donald became his mentor at Columbia University, where McWhiney completed a doctorate in 1960.

By then, he had also gained valuable experience as a teacher, thanks to a series of temporary faculty positions at Troy State University (1952–54), Millsaps College (1958–59), and the University of California, Berkeley (1959–60). McWhiney received his first permanent academic appointment at Northwestern University (1960–65), but that became only one of several stops in a distinguished teaching career that took him to the University of British Columbia (1965–70), Wayne State University (1970–75), University of Alabama (1975–84), Texas Christian University (1984–96), and McMurry University, where he is currently a Distinguished Scholar in Residence. McWhiney also enjoyed visiting professorships at Berkeley, Tulane University, University of Michigan, and University of Southern Mississippi, and he has

Grady McWhiney

been an immensely popular speaker—delivering over 200 talks during the past forty years—at historical symposia, academic conferences, and Civil War round tables.

Yet McWhiney's most enduring legacy rests on his published work. His 14 books and 85 articles and shorter pieces may well strike casual observers as an odd combination of military and social history, but the practiced eye quickly spots a consistent, over-arching theme: the American South. His enormous contribution to Civil War scholarship aside, no other portion of McWhiney's work underscores this emphasis more forcefully than his pioneering research on the Celtic roots of Southern culture. Building on Frank L. Owsley's classic *Plain Folk of the Old South* (1949), which showed that the contours of pre–Civil War Southern society had been defined more by middle-class farmers and herders than by wealthy planters, McWhiney explained the ethnic origins of that society.

From early in the colonial period, he suggested a flood of immigrants from Ireland, Scotland, and Wales had transported their habits, customs, values, folkways, and traditions to the South. By 1860, those Celts far outnumbered all other white inhabitants of the southern United States, and their diet, music, architecture, love of leisure, sensual pleasures, exaggerated sense of personal honor, and pastoral way of life—characterized by herding rather than farming—dominated the region. Equally important, he noted, those Celtic traits stood in stark contrast to the culture and values of the North's largely English and Germanic population.

McWhiney's work on the South's Celtic heritage, much of it done in collaboration with Professor Forrest McDonald, has had a profound intellectual impact, and while some scholars have challenged bits and pieces of his interpretation, McWhiney has forever altered our view of Southern culture and broadened our understanding of the region's ethnic underpinnings.

*See* Irish Heritage of the South

Grady McWhiney, *Cracker Culture: Celtic Ways in the Old South* (1988).
———, *Attack and Die: Civil War Military Tactics and the Southern Heritage,* with Perry D. Jamieson (1982).
———, "The Celtic Origins of Southern Herding Practices," *Journal of Southern History,* 51 (1985), with Forrest McDonald.
———, "The South from Self-Sufficiency to Peonage: An Interpretation," *American Historical Review,* 85 (1980), with Forrest McDonald.
———, "The Antebellum Southern Herdsman: A Reinterpretation," *Journal of Southern History,* 41 (1975), with Forrest McDonald.

DANIEL E. SUTHERLAND

## MEAGHER, THOMAS FRANCIS (1823–1867)

Editor, military officer, politician. Thomas Francis Meagher is best known for two things: his bombastic rhetoric championing the cause of Irish Independence and his limitless courage as a Union officer in the American Civil War. He was a brash yet charismatic young Irish immigrant who quickly rose to a position of leadership in the Irish-American community in New York in the 1850s, but his life was cut short in a mysterious steamboat accident in Montana in 1867.

Meagher was born in Waterford, Ireland on August 23, 1823, the son of a wealthy merchant. Educated at Catholic schools in both Ireland and England, he joined the Irish independence movement in 1845. Meagher was a popular speaker for the cause but his incendiary remarks against the English government led to his arrest for sedition. He was convicted of treason in 1848 and banished from Ireland the following year. After spending three years in a Tasmanian penal colony, Meagher escaped to the United States in 1852.

He quickly found success as a public speaker, lawyer, and newspaper editor within New York City's growing Irish-American community in the 1850s. Although he was a Democrat and sympathetic to the rights of southern states, Meagher rallied to the union cause when war was declared in 1861.

Meagher quickly organized a company of soldiers who became part of the 69th New York State Militia. After service at the first Battle of Bull Run and other minor skirmishes, Meagher returned to New York late in 1861 to enlist fresh troops under the banner of "the Irish Brigade." His success as a recruiter won Meagher a rank of brevet brigadier general early in 1862.

Over the next fifteen months, Meagher and his brigade fought in some of the bloodiest campaigns of the war. The "Sons of Erin," as the brigade was sometimes called, served at the Battles of Fair Oaks, Malvern Hill, and Antietam where it suffered devastating losses. Worse casualties came in December of 1862 when Meagher and the brigade charged Marye's Heights at Fredericksburg. At the end of the battle, the Irish Brigade had been reduced to less than 250 men. A final campaign at Chancellorsville in May of 1863 was followed by a return trip to New York where a disillusioned Meagher resigned his commission. He was feted at a grand banquet on June 25, 1863.

But Meagher found no peace in civilian life. In fact, he spent the next several months lobbying the federal government for a new military command. In January of 1864 Meagher was given back his rank and in the fall he was assigned the task of molding a provisional division out of stragglers, convalescents, and garrison troops. In January of 1865 Meagher and his motley division were sent to New Bern, North Carolina, in a holding operation. Meagher was relieved of duty for excessive drunkenness at the end of February and returned to New York. He resigned his commission a second time on May 15, 1865.

With the assistance of an increasingly vocal Irish community in New York, Meagher won a presidential appointment as secretary of the Montana Territory in the summer of 1865. Upon arriving in the territory, Meagher found that he was also "acting governor," a position he would hold for the next two years. Always controversial, he seemed to alienate both Democrats and Republicans in the territorial legislature. Meagher died in a mysterious accident when he fell from a steamboat into the Missouri River at Fort Benton. The cause of death was never determined because his body was never found.

*See* Civil War

Robert G. Ahearn, *Thomas Francis Meagher: An Irish Revolutionary in America* (Boulder, CO, 1949).
John Paul Jones, *The Irish Brigade* (New York, 1969).

TIMOTHY WALCH

## MEANY, GEORGE (1894–1980)

Labor leader. George Meany was the second son of Michael Joseph Meany and Anne Cullen Meany's ten children. His Meany grandparents emigrated from County Westmeath in 1853. His grandfather Cullen came from County Longford in the same year. George Meany was born August 16, 1894, and christened William George (but never used William) at 125th and Madison Avenue in lower Harlem—then a mostly Irish area. George and his older brother John and six younger children survived infancy. The family moved to the, then semi-rural, Bronx in 1899 where Meany was educated in public schools until dropping out at fourteen. As a youth he played semi-pro baseball and held a job as an errand boy for an advertising agency.

Michael Meany was himself a plumber and president of Local Two of the union in that craft, but opposed his sons entering the trade. Nevertheless, his second son sought apprenticeship in the trade and, after five years, became a journeyman and member of Local Two in 1917. His father's death and brother's enlistment in the army in 1917 required Meany to become the family bread-winner. On November 26, 1919, he wed Eugenie McMahon after a courtship of several years due to the financial strain.

### CAREER UNIONIST

From a less-than-active member of Local Two, Meany rose to become president of the American Federation of Labor (AFL) in

George Meany

1952 and, three years later, to head the AFL-CIO. His rise owed much to the force of his personality, his impressive analytical ability and unquestionable honesty—and, it must be said, his ambition. His memory was remarkable. He was articulate within the limits of his Bronx-accented vernacular. It began in 1920 with his election to the executive board of his local—attributed by him to being the son of Michael Meany. Two years later he ran for business agent of the local and won. Proving to be competent and fair, he became secretary of the New York City Building Trades Council organized to replace the existing one due to scandal caused by convicted extortionist Robert P. Brindell—its leader. The city-wide council for all AFL local unions in New York elected him to its executive board in 1932, and from there Meany won a seat on the board of the New York State Federation of Labor (NYSFL) in the same year. Seeing an opportunity to head the NYSFL, he campaigned for president of it twice and won it in 1934 on the second try—due to an adroitly organized campaign Meany himself put together.

### AMERICAN FEDERATION OF LABOR

There followed a period of five years as lobbyist for NYSFL in which he demonstrated outstanding political acumen in promoting some seventy-two pieces of legislation beneficial to labor, including a pioneer unemployment insurance law.

Recognized for his five years of effective work in Albany and elected Secretary-Treasurer of the AFL by acclamation in 1939, Meany concentrated on international relations. Meany was proposed by Teamster president Daniel Tobin to succeed Frank Morrison, Secretary-Treasurer of the AFL—then seventy-nine.

With ex-communist Jay Lovestone as his advisor, he campaigned against communist penetration of labor movements in Europe, Asia and Latin America—particularly in the postwar period—when the Soviet Union was expanding its hegemony. He kept the AFL out of the World Federation of Trade Unions (WFTU) because of its communist orientation.

An enthusiastic advocate of the Marshall Plan, he and James Carey (of the United Electrical Workers) proposed a plan to give technical assistance to European unions using American trade union operatives. The plan was adopted and met with success. In 1949 he participated in formation of the International Confederation of Free Trade Unions (ICFTU) to rally non-communist unions around the world. Hopeful in the beginning, he became disenchanted with its operation and leadership—then withdrew support.

### HEADING THE AFL-CIO

Elected president of the AFL after William Green's death in November of 1952, Meany actively sought merger with the Congress of Industrial Organizations (CIO). Once it was achieved in 1955, he was chosen president of the AFL-CIO and remained its head until retiring in November of 1979.

At the helm of the AFL-CIO, Meany had the ear of Presidents Eisenhower, Kennedy, Johnson and Carter. Under Meany the organization customarily endorsed the Democratic candidate for president—with the exception of George McGovern (in 1972), whose brand of liberalism Meany could not abide. He defended American intervention in Vietnam well beyond the time it became unpopular—but eventually recognized it as a mistake.

Meany had evolved from his original narrow craft union outlook to a moderate progressive one in domestic affairs. He championed the Civil Rights Act of 1964 (especially its fair employment provisions), Medicare in 1965, the Occupational Safety and Health Act of 1970 and other important social legislation. He presided over expulsion of the Teamsters union and several others found to be guilty of corrupt practices. His death on January 9, 1980, came little more than a month after his retirement.

*See* Labor Movement

George Meany Memorial Archives, Silver Spring, Maryland.
Joseph C. Goulden, *Meany* (New York, 1972).
Archie Robinson, *George Meany and His Times* (New York, 1981).
*New York Times,* obituary ( January 10, 1980).

L. A. O'DONNELL

## MELLON, ANDREW WILLIAM (1855–1937)

Financier, government official. Andrew Mellon's father Thomas came to Pittsburgh at the age of five with his parents from County Tyrone, Ireland in 1818. Both his father and mother, Sarah Jane (Negley) of Pennsylvania, were Presbyterians who reared their eight children to appreciate culture. Thomas, a lawyer and entrepreneur, became a judge of Allegheny County for ten years, and established a private banking firm which dealt mostly in real estate, T. Mellon and Sons, in 1896. Andrew, born March 24, 1855, attended Western University of Pennsylvania as had his father, leaving after four years in 1872 to run his father's lumber and building business. Thomas, seeing Andrew's special gifts for business and finance, transferred ownership of T. Mellon and Sons to Andrew in 1882. The firm thrived by identifying and investing in companies with growth potential at a time of technological advances. Andrew guided his banking house to becoming in the 1890s principal stock holder and developer of such companies as the Aluminum Company of America (Alcoa), the Carborundum Company, Gulf Oil, United States Steel, Standard Steel Car Company, and the New York Shipbuilding Company. In partnership Andrew Mellon contributed to the building of the Panama Canal, the George Washington Bridge and the Waldorf-Astoria Hotel in New York. He became an officer in over sixty corporations and accepted control of all his father's property for the family in 1890. By 1902 T. Mellon and Sons incorporated as the Mellon National Bank; Andrew was president, and shared control with his younger brother Richard and his friend, industrialist Henry Clay Frick. Criticism of the firm's monopolistic tendencies was raised, but little was known publicly of the socially reticent Andrew as late as 1921, although he had become a ranking officer of several important Pittsburgh institutions. On a transatlantic liner in 1898 he met twenty-year-old Nora May McMullen of a British brewing family in Hertfordshire, England; they married in 1900 and the couple had two children, Paul and Ailsa, but divorced in 1912.

Mellon became financially involved in conservative Republican Pennsylvania politics, opposing Woodrow Wilson and the League of Nations. Warren G. Harding, elected president in 1920, asked a reluctant Andrew Mellon to become Secretary of the Treasury, a post he held from 1921 to 1932 into the Coolidge and Hoover administrations. He met the challenges of reducing national debt, drastic tax reform, international financial settlements, and the economic shifts from prosperity to depression with skill, and was considered the greatest Treasury secretary since Alexander Hamilton. But his principle of benefiting the wealthy as the way ultimately to improve the lot of the rest of the

people drew hostility as class discrimination, in particular his opposition to sending surplus goods to the starving of other countries. Veterans and farmers opposed his fiscal policies, while middle and upper income groups applauded them. Mellon proposed controversial tax programs in 1921 and 1924. He did control federal spending and reduced income tax rates. As chair of the War Debt Commission in 1925 he promoted European countries' "ability to pay", but illogically disconnected this from war reparations owed to those nations. He enforced prohibition, reorganized the federal farm loan system, improved paper currency, and helped beautify the nation's capital. Mellon's Revenue Tax Act of 1928 drew great criticism for his benevolence toward big business. The Great Depression, though in part a result of World War I, led President Hoover to replace Mellon with Ogden L. Mills in 1932, and Mellon was appointed ambassador to Great Britain (1932–1933) where he assisted in implementing the war debt moratorium and advised on international finance. He was accused of underpaying taxes in 1931, but after legal proceedings, was vindicated in the mid-thirties. Mellon had acquired a major private art collection over the years, and gifted his classic paintings and sculptures in 1937 to the federal government to establish the National Gallery of Art in Washington, D.C. The collection was valued at over thirty-five million dollars. Mellon did not wish the institution to bear his name, and hoped it would prompt others' gifts, which has occurred. He never saw its completion in 1941. Andrew Mellon played a major role in the development of industry, in balancing the national economy, and in providing ongoing philanthropic institutions. He died of bronchial pneumonia on August 26, 1937 at the home of his daughter in Southhampton, Long Island, and is buried at Homewood Cemetery in Pittsburgh.

David T. Beito, "Andrew Mellon," in *Encyclopedia of American Business History and Biography: Banking and Finance, 1913–1989* (New York, 1990).
Philip H. Love, *Andrew W. Mellon, the Man and His Work* (Baltimore, 1929).
Thomas Mellon, *Thomas Mellon and His Times,* 2nd ed. (Pittsburgh, 1994).
Allan Nevins, "Mellon, Andrew William," in *Dictionary of American Biography,* Vol. 22, Supplement 2 (New York, 1958).
Harvey O'Connor, *Mellon's Millions, the Biography of a Fortune: The Life and Times of Andrew W. Mellon* (New York, 1933).

ANNA M. DONNELLY

## MEMPHIS RIOTS (1866)

On 1 May 1866, Memphis, Tennessee, erupted in riot following an altercation between officers of the city's Irish-dominated police force and discharged Black soldiers from nearby Fort Pickering. Within hours, violence engulfed South Memphis. When Federal troops restored order three days later, the grim statistics revealed a human toll of forty-eight dead, five rapes, and seventy-five injured. The extensive destruction of property included ninety-one homes, four Black churches, and twelve Freedman schools. Later consensus among Federal troops on the scene and members of a Congressional hearing placed blame on the Irish-dominated city government and police force, while local opinion blamed Blacks.

The Memphis riot was one of several in the Reconstruction South following the Civil War and spotlighted dramatic urban demographic changes and the resulting shift from ethnic to racial-based politics and policies. In addition, the riot in President Andrew Johnson's home state provided political ammunition for his opponents.

After receiving their final pay on May Day, 1866, discharged Black soldiers entered South Memphis for a day of celebration. In later testimony, five conflicting versions of the initial "incident" agreed only that the efforts of two Irish police to arrest Black veterans during the afternoon erupted into fistfights and gunfire. The police retreated, only to return around 5:30 p.m. with a "posse" of enraged white citizens.

Again repelled by battle-tested Black soldiers, white citizens (mostly immigrants from South Memphis) and police returned around 10 p.m. and commenced a third, more violent attack. The eventual arrival of Federal troops slowed, but failed to halt, the violence for two more days.

During the summer of 1866, the 39th Congress conducted an investigation into the "Memphis Riots and Massacres" and issued their findings in a document, *The Washburne Report.* Testimony before Congress spotlighted conflicting versions of events as well as "blame" for the riots.

For example, U.S. Major General Stoneman's complaints about lack of support from Memphis police in stemming the tide of violence was countered by praise by the local press and many citizens for the "gallant conduct of police."

Likewise, conflicting testimony addressed the actions of city officials and pointed out a dramatic powershift in city government that occurred largely as a result of the war and the defeat of the South. The decade prior to the outbreak of the Civil War marked a rapid rise in immigration to the Bluff City, with Irish, Italians, and Germans comprising an astonishing 49% of the free working population. With the disfranchisement of the traditional local leaders—former Confederates who refused to take the oath of allegiance—large numbers of Irish immigrants rushed to fill the power vacuum.

By 1866, the police and fire departments were bastions of Irish power with percentages of ninety and eighty-six percent respectively. The Irish likewise controlled city hall, filling the office of mayor, nine of sixteen alderman seats, and 67% of all city elected offices.

Meanwhile, Irish workers who had long dominated jobs along the docks and railroads faced increased competition for jobs from an influx of freedmen following the war. Freedman Bureau population estimates for Blacks at the time of the riots claim 16,509 of the city's 27,703 residents. The clash of cultures, competition for work, and, according to the Washburne Report, the inexperience of the city government in dealing with a myriad of new problems, resulted in Tennessee's worst riot.

C. G. Belissary, "Tennessee and Immigration, 1865–1880," *Tennessee Historical Quarterly,* Vol. VII/3 (September 1948).

Kathleen Berkeley, "Ethnicity and Its Implications for Southern Urban History: The Saga of Memphis, Tennessee," *Tennessee Historical Quarterly,* L/4 (Winter 1991).

*Daily Memphis Avalanche* (1 May 1866, 2 May 1866, 10 May 1866, and 18 May 1866).

Jack Holmes, "The Underlying Causes of the Memphis Race Riot of 1866," *Tennessee Historical Quarterly,* L/4 (1991).

DeeGee Lester, "The Memphis Riots of 1866," *Éire-Ireland* (1996).

Bobby L. Lovett, "Memphis Riots: White Reaction to Blacks in Memphis, May 1865–July 1866," *Tennessee Historical Quarterly,* XXXVIII/1 (Spring 1979).

U.S. Congress: *Memphis Riots and Massacres,*" House Report 101, 39th Congress, 1st session (Washington, D.C., 1866).

DEEGEE LESTER

## MICHIGAN

The history of the Irish in Michigan is both varied and complex. Immigrants fleeing every Irish cataclysm from the executions and deportations in Cromwellian times to the present political dispute in northeast Ireland have selected locations within the Peninsular State as a suitable alternative to their native land. Michigan's geographic location, with its short growing season, distance from the National Road and other key transportation routes, and reputation as an unhealthy climate, limited the absolute number of Irish-born who resided in the state to 43,313 in 1880. This was the apogee of Irish settlement in Michigan; after 1880 enumerators counted fewer Irish expatriates in each state and federal decennial census. The fact that the majority of Michigan's general population was derived from New England regions with a strong Puritan influence may have contributed to the high proportion of Michigan's Irish who adhered to Protestant rather than Catholic faith. Transmigration through Canada across the narrow waterways that separate the United States from the British Dominion is also a likely explanation for this phenomenon.

The dispersion of Irish immigrants across Michigan's landscape defies stereotype, as does their occupational history. A large number of Irish worked small farms in the state's hinterlands where they patronized their countrymen who had established themselves as shopkeepers and skilled tradesmen. Occupational mobility played an important role among Michigan's Irish settlers and was most probably aided by wide-scale participation in the Civil War. The areas outside of Detroit and Grand Rapids witnessed varying densities of Irish settlement ranging from solitary farm families in the agricultural districts to tightly clustered ethnic communities in mining and manufacturing towns. The low numbers of Irish in the state, combined with the conservative perspectives held by the general population, prompted swift acculturation and assimilation in all but a few enclaves. This, along with the rapid decline in the number of Irish during the twentieth century limited the preservation of Irish culture and language in Michigan.

The first Irish to set foot on Michigan soil arrived during the seventeenth century when the peninsulas were part of the vast tract of wilderness known as New France. Aside from the infrequent notation of an obviously Irish name in the *Jesuit Relations,* there are no remaining records concerning the lives of the Irishmen who served under the fleur-de-lis at Fort de Bouade near the Straits of Mackinac, or those hardy souls who explored the uncharted forests in search of beaver pelts for the European market. After the treaty of 1701 brought the promise of peace between the French and the Great Lakes tribes, a few Irish women joined their countrymen at the remote outposts. By the second quarter of the eighteenth century there were a small number of Irish families in Michigan. Galwayman John Farly and his wife, Mary Cary, raised their family near Fort Michilimackinac at the northern tip of the Lower Peninsula (Lareau 1970:19). During the French and Indian War another Irishman, John MacNamara, led a militia out of the fort (Thwaites 1966:185).

Irishmen were among Captain Donald Campbell's detachment of green-uniformed Royal Americans who replaced French soldiers in Michigan garrisons after Marquis de Vaudreuil ceded control of New France to the British in 1760. Sir William Johnson, a native of County Meath, is the best known of these men. Johnson emigrated to America in 1737 and settled in New York's Mohawk Valley where he established a prosperous farm and trading post. The honest character of his dealings with the Native Americans led to his marriage to a Mohawk woman and his adoption by that tribe. In 1756 the British government appointed Johnson, who had mastered the Mohawk language, Superintendent of Indian Affairs. While in Michigan he continued to exercise his diplomatic skills, persuading the Iroquois to remain neutral in the Pontiac War and negotiating agreements with tribes in the western Great Lakes. Sir William's death in 1774 ended a thirty-year career as the most important Indian Agent in British North America (Dunbar 1970:116, 124, 133–36).

The number of Irish in Michigan began to increase after the American Revolution but most of these immigrants settled in Detroit before the United States affirmed its hegemony over the Northwest Territory during the War of 1812. Irish began trickling into the River Raisin and Huron River valleys in the 1820s, forming small communities in Monroe, Lenawee and Washtenaw counties. By the late 1830s these settlements had distinctly Irish names, New Dublin in Monroe, Kerrytown in Ann Arbor, and the Irish Hills in western Lenawee County. Irish immigrants from Tipperary began farming near White Lake in Oakland County during the same decade, and small groups of Irish established farms near Michigan's territorial roads which radiated north and west of Detroit. By the 1840s there were distinct clusters of Irish immigrants scattered throughout the southern third of the state (Paré 1983:471, 479–80, 499).

The character of these ethnic communities was influenced by the origins and experiences of their inhabitants. An examination of the naturalization records for Irish immigrants who settled in Berrien County, in the extreme southwest corner of the state, indicates that most of the men were born in the Province of Ulster. A number of these Irishmen who swore allegiance to the United States between 1840 and 1860 mentioned the fact that they were of Protestant faith in their handwritten petitions for citizenship, an astute response to the rising anti-immigrant, anti-Catholic attitudes of the period (Berrien County 1840–1860).

Irish Protestants were not uncommon in nineteenth-century Michigan. In some counties less than half of the Irish immigrants can be identified as Catholic. Jackson County serves as an example of this phenomenon. The county seat, named in honor of Andrew Jackson, was an early urban center. The city was also a bastion of conservative values, a fact which led to its selection as the site where Whigs, Free-Soilers and Know-Nothings established the Republican Party as a viable political entity in 1854. The fundamentalist character of the community is further emphasized by the fact that Jackson's first Catholic church was not erected until 1856, nearly thirty years after the settlement was founded. These factors created a social environment that was more receptive to Protestant, rather than Catholic immigrants. Census enumerators counted more than one hundred Irish-born residing in Jackson in 1850; by 1870 there were eight hundred Irish natives in the city. Correlating the names in census manuscripts with membership rolls of Jackson's Protestant churches reveals that among the city's Irish population, Catholic immigrants were the minority group until the 1870s. In addition, family names recorded in the federal censuses of 1850, 1860 and 1870 suggest that a large number of these Protestant Irish had ancestral links to Ireland's English and Scottish settlements (Dun-

Built and dedicated in 1858, the Omena Presbyterian Church originates from the Reverend Peter Dougherty's 1839 mission, which was the first Protestant mission in the Grand Traverse area. A number of Michigan's nineteenth-century Irish were Protestant.

bar 1970:418–20; Paré 1983:578–79; U.S. Bureau of the Census 1850–1870; DeLand 1903; Interstate 1881). In contrast, Irish settlers downstream from Jackson in the Grand River Valley were most often Catholics who settled in close proximity to each other in several dozen rural and urban communities (U.S. Bureau of the Census, 1850–1880; McGee 1950:399–423).

Grand Rapids, situated at the head of navigation on the Grand River, expanded from a hamlet in 1835 to Michigan's second largest city in 1870. At the same time, Grand Rapids experienced a similar growth in the number of Irish in the city. There were less than one hundred persons living in the settlement when a contractor imported a group of Irish laborers to dig a mill race in 1835. Upon completing the project many of the immigrant workers settled in the area and sent for family members. These early arrivals formed the nucleus of the Irish community in the Grand River Valley. In the late 1830s Canada's Patriot Rebellion provided the impetus for a small number of Irish to make their homes near St. Andrew's Church in Grand Rapids. Irish Catholics who settled in the rural townships east of the city founded St. Patrick's Church near the farming communities of Ada, Grattan and Parnell during the 1840s. The Great Starvation, economic opportunities associated with rapid urban expansion, and an abundance of inexpensive land suitable for farming attracted more than five thousand Irish immigrants to the Grand River Valley during the late nineteenth century. An investigation of census manuscripts reveals that more than two-thirds of the Irish settled in small towns or agricultural townships within the drainage basin, indicating a preference for rural rather than urban lifeways (Vander Hill 1970:35–44; Everett 1878:8, 25).

The Saginaw Valley in Southeast Michigan witnessed similar settlement patterns among its Irish immigrants. Labor gangs, hired to dig the Saginaw and Grand Canal in the late 1830s, found themselves out of work when the Panic of 1837 forced Michigan to scale back internal improvement projects. A shortage of hard currency prompted contractors to pay off their employees in scrip redeemable for state-owned land adjacent to the proposed canal route. Thus, Irish laborers were propelled back to their agricultural origins by the instability of the nascent American economic system. Encouraged by the large crops produced in the fertile soils, a number of Irish promoted further settlement in the region with letters back to Ireland detailing their success. The communications, often accompanied by a few dollars to subsidize transportation costs to America, arrived on the eve of the Great Starvation, beginning a series of chain migrations that helped finance emigration for thousands who might have otherwise perished from starvation or disease. The majority of Irish immigrants continued to arrive in the region's agricultural townships until after the American Civil War, when industrial employment in the Saginaw-Bay City metropolitan area began to attract the greater proportion of new arrivals. Prior to the shift toward manufacturing jobs, farming was one of the most common occupations among Michigan's Irish immigrants during the nineteenth century (Gross 1962:38–40; Dunbar 1970:341; U.S. Bureau of the Census, 1850–1880). At the 1890 federal census one-half of the Irish-born men in the state claimed "farming" as their primary occupation. Most of these individuals resided in the southernmost five tiers of counties but a few Irish farms could be found as far north as the Keweenaw Peninsula, which juts into Lake Superior toward Isle Royale, the northernmost portion of the state (U.S. Bureau of the Census, 1860–1900).

Isle Royale experienced a brief boom in copper mining during the 1880s and 1890s, but the majority of extractive operations took place in Houghton, Keweenaw and Ontonagon counties in the century between 1850 and 1950. An 1843 expedition which shipped a huge boulder of nearly pure copper touched off a thirty-year wave of prospecting that discovered exploitable deposits of copper, silver and gold in five Upper Peninsula counties (Hybels 1950:97–119; Thurner 1974). Mining and smelting conglomerates bought up the most promising claims and turned Michigan into the nation's leading producer of copper in the late nineteenth century. High wages and aggressive labor recruiters attracted thousands of Irish immigrants to Michigan's Copper Country where many men found employment in the mines or as unskilled laborers in surface operations. By the 1860s Houghton, Hancock, Calumet, Ontonagon, Silver City and Rockland had substantial Irish neighborhoods (Thurner 1974:15; U.S. Bureau of the Census, 1860).

During the Civil War copper prices peaked at an unprecedented fifty-five cents a pound as the Union Army mobilized for a protracted fight against a stubborn Confederacy. Irish miners throughout the Copper Country demanded and received pay increases until wages soared to one hundred dollars per month. Mine owners, in an attempt to solve the labor shortage, transported four hundred Scandinavian immigrants to Houghton County for use as strikebreakers. Miners responded to management's anti-labor offensive by raising a bounty of three hundred dollars as payment to each man who volunteered for the Union Army. When the Scandinavians reached Portage Lake, a few miles east of Houghton, they were met by a committee representing the miners. The new arrivals accepted the bounty and marched off to war, leaving the Irish as victors in one of the first labor disputes in Michigan. Decades later, in the years preceding World War I, the Irish joined with Swedes, Norwegians, Finns, Italians, Croats and Poles under the aegis of the Western Federation of Miners when mine bosses and workers fought a series of bitter battles. In the end, the strikes mattered little. Copper mining in the region had passed its zenith and the large companies were shifting their resources toward more profitable deposits in Montana and Arizona.

The course of Irish-American history in Michigan's iron mining districts roughly parallels that of the Copper Country. The 1844 discovery of iron ore near Teal Lake in Marquette County created a similar demand for labor at the onset of the Great Starvation. Newly arrived refugees in port cities along the Atlantic Seaboard provided a ready, if somewhat distant, source of unskilled workers, well-suited for the tasks of shoveling and carting ore out of the pits. Irish-born Michael Cleary built the first house in Negaunee, the town adjacent to the mine. By 1870 more than three hundred Irish natives were counted among Negaunee's 2,569 residents. In the same census, enumerators recorded 526 Irish in the county seat, Marquette, and nearly thirteen hundred more in other areas of the county. The number of Irish in the Marquette iron range began falling in the 1870s, but many had moved southward to the Menominee Range, where owners eager to develop the high-grade deposits promised good wages for experienced miners. In the 1890s the Irish shifted again toward the Gogebic-Penokee Range where new mines were opening up in the western tip of the Upper Peninsula (Brotherton 1944:199–213; Lewis 1895:534).

Despite a persistent demand for miners, fewer than half of the Irish males who settled in the Upper Peninsula's mining districts worked at extracting ore during the late nineteenth century. Some worked as woodcutters or colliers in the subsidiary industry that supplied charcoal to the copper smelters and iron forges. A significant number of Irishmen were self-employed as blacksmiths, machinists, shoemakers, or at another skilled trade. Others toiled as section hands on regional railroads, as teamsters and draymen, or as day laborers in cities and towns. A few labored in the mines or nearby refining operations for years before going into business as a shopkeeper or establishing one of the many small farms that produced meat, milk and vegetables for consumption in nearby towns. Irish women who reported employment outside the home were most frequently servants or washerwomen, but some immigrant women owned boarding houses, restaurants and other business enterprises. Margaret McGrath, aided by her apprentice, Ellen Brennan, operated a millinery in Marquette. At the other end of the spectrum were Irish mine owners and managers who exercised a paternalistic control over company towns, limiting but never quite obliterating the rowdiness that tends to erupt in the first decade of many frontier settlement's existence (Thurner 1974:15; U.S. Bureau of the Census, 1850–1880).

Michigan's Irish immigrants adapted their skills to local environmental conditions, adopting new occupations whenever necessary. Although Ireland's underdeveloped fishing industry sent few emigrants to the Great Lakes region during the nineteenth century, Irish fishermen were instrumental in establishing and expanding fisheries on the upper lakes. Irish and French fishermen netted whitefish and perch in Lake Erie's Brest Bay, salting their catch and delivering it to Detroit markets in the 1820s and 1830s. The demand for salted fish rose in proportion to the number of European immigrants settling in Michigan cities. As a consequence, fishing operations moved northward into Lake Huron. By the late 1840s the Irish, who were beginning to dominate the fishing industry, were spreading their nets in Lake Michigan and trotlines in Lake Superior. Most of the Lake Superior catch was taken by widely dispersed anglers in the shallow bays along the South Shore. Marquette, Eagle Harbor and Portage Lake provided convenient markets for the small enterprises (Van Oosten 1938:107–120).

The majority of Irish fishermen centered their operations around the Straits of Mackinac and Beaver Island. Mackinac Island was an important fishing port in the mid-nineteenth century. The island, which had a long history of Irish settlement, also served as a transfer point for people and freight traveling on the upper lakes. The Mackinaw boat, a double-ended fishing craft superbly suited for sailing in all types of weather and easily maneuvered in bays and harbors, originated in the Straits area. These watercraft were an industry standard until steam- and diesel-powered vessels gained popularity around the turn of the century. Mackinac Island fishermen frequently ranged as far west as the Wisconsin shore and eastward to the inlets of Canada's Georgian Bay. The Mackinac Irish, like their countrymen sailing out of Alpena and a dozen other ports along Michigan's Lake Huron coastline, generally worked in small, family-based groups, delivering their salted catch to local markets or to Mackinac Island for shipment to Chicago or Detroit.

Beaver Island, situated in northern Lake Michigan at the center of the richest freshwater fishing grounds in the world, was settled by Irish immigrants. The majority of the Irish arrived on the island between 1840 and 1880 in what could be cited as a first-class example of chain migration. By 1900 the population of the Beaver Archipelago had surpassed one thousand persons. The vast majority of these individuals were either Irish immigrants or their descendants, and most of them depended on some aspect of the fishing industry for their livelihood. A few Irish built fishing boats, others manufactured the boxes and barrels necessary for shipping the catch to distant cities. Most of the remainder netted, sorted, cleaned and salted a wide variety of freshwater fish. The colony prospered until the 1920s when the effects of overfishing and pollution began to reduce the size of the annual catch. Young men and women left Beaver Island for job opportunities on the mainland, especially after World War II when the sea lamprey devastated the schools of whitefish and trout that had been a mainstay of the island's economy for nearly a century. By 1960 there were less than two hundred residents on the island. The remaining descendants of the Irish immigrants reacted to the decline by introducing a tourist industry that centers upon their unique ethnic experience (Cashman 1976:69–87; Collar 1976:27–50).

The lumber boom attracted Irish to Michigan's heavily wooded northern counties during the late nineteenth century. Post-war industrial growth, a population surge in the eastern cities, and settlement of the Great Plains created a growing demand for sawed lumber after the Civil War. Michigan was ideally suited to supply a substantial portion of the nation's requirement for softwood and hardwood products. The state had an established forest products industry with hundreds of sawmills and an experienced workforce of lumberjacks. Many of these lumberjacks were Irish immigrants who had left their homeland during the Great Starvation and worked their way across Canada as timber cutters or mill hands before crossing the narrow waterways that separated Ontario from Michigan. After arriving in the state they made their way to lumber camps in Michigan's White Pines Region or settled in districts that specialized in hardwood products harvested from deciduous forests dominated by extensive stands of beech, maple, oak and cherry trees (Catton 1976:155–56).

Another important but underdocumented element of Michigan's timber industry was composed of lumberman-farmers who raised crops on limited acreage during the state's short growing season, then migrated northward in winter seeking work as lumberjacks, teamsters or camp cadre in logging operations (King 1982). Census records and local archives support the lumberman-farmer thesis with a wealth of data illustrating the seasonal infusion of cash that enabled many Irish immigrants with marginal farms to feed their families and earn enough currency to purchase consumer products, pay the taxes, and support the church of their choice. At various times in Michigan's history, up to one-sixth of Irish families received some part of their annual income from forest products. The scope of involvement ranged from Francis Boyle, an immigrant who chopped cordwood for sale to lake steamers, to Jim Demsey, a famine refugee who worked his way up from axe man to proprietor of one of Michigan's largest lumber companies (Craker 1983:69; Russell and Baer 1954:27).

An impressive number of Michigan's Irish immigrants served in the state's regiments during the Civil War. Among the best-known of the Irish regiments was the Fifteenth Michigan Infantry, composed of men recruited in the southern portion of the state. Commanded by John McDermott, who served with Colonel Mulligan's Illinois Volunteers in 1861, the regiment left Monroe in the spring of 1862. After joining General Grant's Army in Tennessee the Fifteenth Infantry compiled an impressive war record and a long casualty list. Ninety-seven men fell during the Fifteenth's baptism of fire at Pittsburgh Landing. Following that engagement, the regiment participated in many of the bitter battles waged for control of the Mississippi Valley before reassignment to General Sherman's command. In the Atlanta Campaign, McDermott's men earned the nickname "Fighting Fifteenth." After General Johnston surrendered his Confederate forces at Greensboro in April 1865, the regiment was ordered to Washington where its Irish companies marched up Pennsylvania Avenue as part of the triumphant Grand Army of the Republic Parade on May 23, 1865 (Burton 1930:1083). The Irish regiment's valor demonstrated its members' allegiance to their adopted country and helped diminish but not fully obliterate the bigotry and discrimination directed toward their countrymen and the increasing swell of refugees fleeing the Eurasian landmass in the late nineteenth century.

Michigan's Irish population began a long decline in numbers after 1880. By 1910 there were 20,436 Irish immigrants residing in the state, less than half the 1880 total of 43,313. A drop in out-migration from Ireland contributed to the reduced number of Irish in the state; high mortality rates among the aging immigrant population account for another, more substantial portion of Michigan's Irish-born. The Ancient Order of Hibernians and other ethnic organizations ceased to flourish and by the 1930s most Irish cultural associations had succumbed as a result of falling membership levels. Many divisions and lodges might have collapsed sooner, but were sustained by a migration of Irish farmers who moved into the cities in the first three decades of the twentieth century. The surviving organizations were sustained by a trickle of Irish immigration that continued to flow into Michigan in the years after Ireland's War of Independence. A renewed interest in ethnic origins provided the impetus for reviving Irish language and culture in Michigan, but this movement which began in the 1970s is still emerging at a slow rate. The recent political strife in northeast Ireland has inspired a portion of this cultural revival, sending immigrants and speakers to Michigan's remaining Irish communities in Ann Arbor, Grand Rapids, Houghton, Marquette, Detroit and other cities. Irish Studies programs at the University of Michigan, Michigan State, Calvin College and Oakland University are also instrumental in renewing interest in Irish-American history as are programs offered by the Gaelic League and the Irish Heritage Society of Western Michigan. These gatherings, however, tend to be small focused groups of individuals unlike St. Patrick's Day celebrations where Michigan residents turn out in large numbers to celebrate their heritage in dozens of cities and towns.

*See* Detroit

Ray A. Brotherton, "The Discovery of Iron Ore: Negaunee Centennial (1844–1944)," *Michigan History* 28 (1944):199–213.

Clarence M. Burton, *The City of Detroit, Michigan, 1701–1922*, Vol. II (Detroit, 1930).

William Cashman, "The Rise and Fall of the Fishing Industry," *Journal of Beaver Island History* 1 (1976): 69–87.

Bruce Catton, *Michigan: A Bicentennial History* (New York, 1976).

Helen Collar, "Irish Migration to Beaver Island," *Journal of Beaver Island History* 1 (1976): 27–50.

Kathy Nickerson Craker, *They Came to South Fox Island* (Chelsea, MI, 1983).

Charles V. DeLand, *History of Jackson County* (Indianapolis, 1903).

Willis Frederick Dunbar, *Michigan: A History of the Wolverine State* (Grand Rapids, 1970).

Franklin Everett, *Memorials of the Grand River Valley* (Chicago, 1878).

Stuart D. Gross, *Indians, Jacks and Pines: A History of Saginaw* (Saginaw, 1962).

Robert James Hybels, "Lake Superior Copper Fever, 1841–47," *Michigan History* 34 (June 1950): 97–119.

Interstate Publishing, *History of Jackson County, Michigan,* Vol. 1 (Chicago, 1881).

Joseph A. King, *The Irish Lumberman-Farmer* (Lafayette, CA, 1982).

Paul J. Lareau, *Genealogical Notes on the Early Settlers of Michilimackinac* (Unpublished manuscript, dated "1970," held in the collection of the Toledo-Lucas County Public Library).

Lewis Publishing Company, *Memorial Record of the Northern Peninsula of Michigan* (Chicago, 1885).

John W. McGee, *The Catholic Church in the Grand River Valley, 1833–1950* (Grand Rapids, 1950).

Naturalization records for Irish immigrants who attained U.S. citizenship in Berrien County, Michigan, 1840 to 1860. Original copies are stored in the archives of the Berrien County Historical Society, Berrien Springs, Michigan.

George Paré, *The Catholic Church in Detroit, 1701–1888* (Detroit, 1983).

Curran N. Russell and Donna Degen Baer, *The Lumberman's Legacy* (Manistee, MI, 1954).

Seventh through Twelfth Censuses of the United States, 1850–1900.

Arthur W. Thurner, *Calumet Copper and People: History of a Michigan Mining Community, 1864–1970* (Chicago, 1974).

Reuben Gold Thwaites, *Early Western Travels, 1748–1846,* Vol. 2 (New York, 1966).

C. Warren Vander Hill, *Settling the Great Lakes Frontier: Immigration to Michigan, 1837–1924* (Lansing, 1970).

John Van Oosten, "Michigan's Commercial Fisheries of the Great Lakes," *Michigan History* 22 (1938): 107–143.

RICHARD A. RAJNER

## MILITARY SOCIETIES (1870–1890)

Compared to Irish railroad workers and miners in the West, Irish soldiers were a numerical minority. However, members of these laboring groups often expressed their Irish martial spirit especially during slack times or when unemployed. During the 1870s and 1880s dozens of semi-private military organizations formed in Western cities and mining towns. Irish in Virginia City, Nevada, Butte, Montana, and Denver, Colorado, assembled military societies whose membership was proudly expressed by the company's name. For example, Butte had the *Meagher Guards* and Denver had its *Mitchell Guards* and *Hibernian Guards.* These organizations existed as men's clubs generally attracting the numerous Irish bachelors residing in western towns.

They met several times each month and practiced close order drills and marches. John Nankivell explains that "competitive drills between the various organizations were quite a feature of National Guard activities in the Eighties, and excited much friendly rivalry and almost as much attention as a good local football game does today." Denver's *Mitchell Guards* were so accomplished at precision drills that they traveled to Texas in 1888 for a national contest. On special occasions like St. Patrick's Day or Independence Day, company members would don their uniforms and perform in the parades and associated festivities. However, in times of crises these companies were called into service by the state or federal government. The Colorado National Guard mustered in several Irish military companies after the Army clashed with Utes at Milk River Colorado in 1879. The *Emerald Rifles* of Georgetown were joined by Leadville's *Wolf Tone Guard* and the *Emmett Guards* of Central City, the latter described as "mountain miners and mechanics, all Irish and Irish Americans." Although these particular Irish companies never entered battle, they nevertheless fulfilled an important role in western military history and helped to strengthen the bond between Irish immigrants and the American West.

John Henry Nankivell, *History of the Military Organizations of the State of Colorado, 1860–1935* (Denver, 1935).

KEVIN STANTON

## MILLER, KERBY (1944– )

Historian. He was born December 30th, 1944, in Phoenix, Arizona, attended Pomona College in Claremont, California, and received his M.A. in 1967 and Ph.D. in 1976 at the University of California, Berkeley.

Miller's *Emigrants and Exiles* received a number of awards for distinction, including the Merle Curti Award for the best book in U.S. Social History (1984–85); the Theodore Saloutos Award for best book in U.S. Immigration & Ethnic History (1986); the Distinguished Scholarly Book Award, Missouri Conference on History (1987). It was also among the finalists in the 1986 Pulitzer Prize in History.

This work quickly established itself as the most important study of Irish emigration to North America until this time. It is an analytical narration on the emigrant experience based on a large quantity and variety of original sources, especially including a vast number of letters written by emigrants over more than one hundred years, located and collected by the author. It was the first significant study of Irish emigrants to fully integrate the social and cultural origins of the emigrants with their experience in America. *Emigrants and Exiles* thus established the once-neglected dimension of cultural origins as one of the standards of modern scholarship on the subject of Irish America. The book examines the patterns and culture of emigration from Ireland from the time of the early plantations to the founding of the Irish Free State. The "Exiles" of the title suggests the underlying theme uniting the broad chronological scope of Miller's *magnum opus,* interweaving an original analysis of the "Gaelic-Catholic" tradi-

Kerby Miller

tion with the "myth of exile" that eventually became the mental premise of the American-Irish nationalist movement in the generations of emigrants during and following the Great Famine. All subsequent scholarship on the subject of American-Irish nationalism has had to deal with this thesis.

Since *Emigrants and Exiles* (1985), Kerby Miller has published numerous scholarly articles and essays that greatly deepened our understanding of the Irish experience in America, making him the leading scholar of the subject. The 1995 TV documentary, *Out of Ireland,* whose script he wrote based on his own research, was seen by millions in Ireland and North America. Soon to be published, *To Ye Land of Canaan: Letters and Memoirs by Irish Immigrants of the Colonial and Revolutionary Eras, 1675–1814,* is a unique collection of immigrant letters with historical commentary by Miller, David Doyle, Arnold Schrier, and Bruce Boling, which will soon become a major new resource for scholars and students of the Irish in America from colonial times to the 20th century.

Kerby Miller, *Emigrants and Exiles: Ireland and the Irish Exodus to North America* (New York, 1985).
———, *Out of Ireland: The Story of Irish Emigration to America* (Washington, D.C., 1994).
———, *Irish Popular Culture, 1650–1850* (Dublin, [co-edited with James S. Donnelly, Jr.] 1997).

ROBERT SCALLY

## MILMOE, alias MILMORE, MARTIN (1844–1883)

Sculptor. One of the most distinguished and sought after portraitists in marble of his day. Martin Milmoe was born on a farm in Kilmorgan, County Sligo, on 14 September 1844 to Sarah Harte, shortly before the death of his father who bore the same name. In 1850, his mother and eldest brother emigrated to America, followed by Martin and his two remaining brothers in 1853. One of these, Joseph Milmoe (1842–1886), was also an exceptional sculptor whose achievements deserve due recognition here. They were second cousins of General Corcoran of New York whose ancestry traces to Patrick Sarsfield. Among his other cousins is the celebrated Mexican financier Don Patricio Milmo.

Having settled in Boston, Martin entered the Brimmer School and continued his studies for a brief period at Boston Latin. While at Brimmer his artistic gift was fostered by a Miss Duncan who nurtured his drawing skills and continued to assist him after leaving Brimmer by finding buyers for his first castings in plaster.

### EARLY INFLUENCES

Given his background, there is little surprise in his development as all his brothers were exceptionally gifted in working with their hands, the fruits of which were witnessed by Martin as they produced their creations and practised their crafts in their Boston home. Charles was a skilled cabinet maker and both Patrick and Joseph were woodcarvers. Having served a full apprenticeship Joseph turned his carving skill to marble, having first worked as a marble cutter. He had developed a reputation as the most skilled worker of marble in Boston. Another brother, James, followed the same trade. And so it could be said that marble dust ran through the veins of Martin Milmoe before he gained his first employment in an Ornamental Ironworks. But he had developed a passion for carving. Through sheer perseverance, he secured an unpaid position as assistant to the sculptor Thomas Ball who was, at the time, carving the *Washington* monument for Boston Public Garden. In the meantime, Martin secretly carved a bust of Ball which he presented to his master as a Christmas gift. Ball was so impressed he promoted Milmoe and his career was launched on a firm footing.

Although he had already come to the attention of the Boston art patrons, he did not receive public acclaim until 1862 when he exhibited a bust of *Devotion* at the Sanitary Fair in Boston. His first major public commission was for the Boston Horticultural Hall which he adorned with large carvings of *Flora, Ceres* and *Pomona.*

### BEST KNOWN WORKS

However, it was as a portraitist that Martin Milmoe's exceptional skill will be remembered. Amongst these sculptures are busts of *Ralf Waldo Emerson, Wendell Phillips, Charles Sumner, George Ticknor* and *Thomas Woodrow Wilson.* He is also notable for a number of military monuments, the best known of which is the *Soldiers and Sailors* monument on Boston Common. Others worth mention are those at Charlestown, Forest Hill, New Brookfield, Waterville and his carving of *America* at Fitchburg. Many of these works were produced in partnership with Joseph, some of which were in granite, the *Sphinx* in Mount Auburn Cemetery being one of the best examples of these.

Martin Milmoe's genius was not to develop to full maturity. As a young man of thirty-nine years, he died on 21 July 1883, in his Boston home on Hammond Street and lies in Forest Hills Cemetery beneath Daniel French's monument *Death and Young Sculptor.*

*Martin Milmore: Sketch of the Distinguished Irish American Sculptor* (Sligo Champion, April 27th, 1878).
John C. McTernan, *Worthies of Sligo: Profiles of Eminent Sligonians of Other Days* (Sligo, 1994).

DOMINIC MILMO-PENNY

## MILWAUKEE

The history of Milwaukee's Irish community is actually two stories: A tale of struggle, hardship, and tragedy in the nineteenth century, and a record of assimilation, dispersal, and upward socioeconomic mobility in the twentieth century.

The city of Milwaukee, formed by the merger of three competing villages on January 31, 1846, and originally part of the Michigan Territory, entered the union of the states with the admission of Wisconsin on May 29, 1848.

The 1850 federal census—the first to include data on place of birth—indicated that 2,800 (14 percent) of the city's 20,061 residents were born in Ireland. The 1860 federal census recorded the population of the city as 45,246, of which 3,161 were born in Ireland (7 percent). Irish migration to Milwaukee peaked in the pre–Civil War era. In the 1900 federal census, Milwaukee's Irish-born residents constituted .93 percent of the city's population, lagging considerably behind the more recently arrived Polish-born.

### Irish Neighborhoods

Studies of Milwaukee's Irish community have focused almost exclusively on the city's Third Ward (the "bloody Third") Irish, who clustered in the nineteenth century in what was then the southeastern corner of the city. Two Irish farming communities, at least one of which predates the Third Ward Irish, have been largely ignored.

Shortly after Wisconsin was opened for settlement by the federal government in 1835, Irish immigrants settled in what is now the suburb of Greenfield. This farming community was composed of Irish who, while not wealthy, had considerably more financial resources than their fellow countrymen of a decade or so later, many of whom were forced to struggle for a meager existence in the urban setting of Milwaukee's Third Ward. Surely the most famous son of the Greenfield Irish was Jeremiah Curtin, world-renowned ethnologist and linguist, who is said to have mastered seventy-two languages and who is best known for having translated Henry Sienkiewicz's *Quo Vadis* from Polish to English. Most of the Greenfield Irish came from the northern and western counties of Ireland.

Even less attention has been devoted to a small settlement of Irish that took hold on the city's northwest side in the 1840s and 1850s in what was then the town of Granville. Like the Greenfield Irish, the Irish who settled in this area were farmers. The 1850 federal census recorded seventy-six Irish families in Granville, while the 1860 census listed 118 Irish families.

The "Famine Irish" who drifted into the city's Third Ward in the 1840s and 1850s were, with few exceptions, poor. While the city-dwelling Irish were from the southern and western counties of Ireland and were overwhelmingly Roman Catholic, they did have certain characteristics in common with the Greenfield and Granville Irish. Most of the Milwaukee area's Irish were products of "staged immigration," well over half of them having lived for a time elsewhere in the United States or Canada before finally settling in Milwaukee. Many of the Third Ward Irish came to Milwaukee from upper New York state, the Fall River region of Massachusetts, Connecticut, or from other cities in the upper Midwest. As products of "staged immigration," the Milwaukee Irish had a familiarity with American customs, mores, and traditions that was lacking in the city's considerably larger German community.

The Irish came to Milwaukee in search of jobs and improved economic opportunities. For the city's Third Ward Irish, this meant heavy, unskilled labor. Like other cities in early stages of development, Milwaukee had an abundance of this kind of work to offer—trees, hills, and bluffs to be cleared for townsite development, swamps to be filled and streets to be graded. The construction of plank roads and canals, along with harbor improvements drew the Irish to Milwaukee in the 1840s and 1850s. Railroad construction in the 1850s continued the demand for Irish brawn.

### Politics and Tragedy

As in other expanding American cities of the era, the Irish in Milwaukee played a political role out of all proportion to their actual numbers. Despite the very real socioeconomic and educational disadvantages of an immigrant ghetto, the Irish always managed to turn out the vote. Evidence of their success was the election of two Irish aldermen (Richard Murphy and Leonard Carty) and a constable to Milwaukee's first city government in 1846. Two of Milwaukee's seven delegates to the state's first constitutional convention were Irish-born, and the city elected its first Irish-born mayor, Hans Crocker from Dublin, in 1852. In fact, the marked success of the Irish in local politics often aroused the ire and fear of Milwaukee's "Yankee" and German communities, as letters from representatives of both groups to Wisconsin Senator William F. Vilas (U.S. Senator, 1891–97) attest. Nativist, anti-Irish sentiment was evident in Milwaukee as elsewhere in the country in this era, and local civic leaders spent much time agonizing over the political influence of the city's small Irish community.

Political success did not, however, insulate the Third Ward Irish from the poverty, illiteracy, alcoholism, and periodic acute unemployment that plagued many ethnic enclaves in the urban America of the late nineteenth century. In an effort to improve wages, working conditions, and job security, many Irish were active in the city's labor movement. As elsewhere, the labor movement in Milwaukee faced strong opposition from paternalistic industrial leaders who were often fiercely anti-union. One of the most effective union busters in the Milwaukee area was Patrick Cudahy, a son of Erin, who took delight in recording in his memoirs the tactics he used in crushing the Amalgamated Meat Cutters and Butchers of North America local in his meat packing plant in 1906.

Two great tragedies befell Milwaukee's Irish community in the nineteenth century. The first was the *Lady Elgin* disaster of September 7–8, 1860, in which 366 Third Ward Irish—among them a number of prominent political leaders—perished in Lake Michigan when the passenger liner was rammed by the lumber schooner *Augusta* in a dense fog. It was estimated that one out of every three homes in the Third Ward lost a relative on the *Lady Elgin*.

The second disaster occurred on October 28, 1892, when the city's worst fire leveled almost sixteen blocks of the Third Ward, destroying nearly 300 buildings and leaving approximately 2,500 people homeless. The fire accelerated the exodus of the Irish from the Third Ward and their dispersal westward and northward throughout the city and its emerging suburbs. Succeeding the Irish as the dominant ethnic group in the Third Ward were the Italians, a fact which led local wags to observe that whereas ancient Ireland refused to be absorbed by imperial Rome, modern Italy had conquered the Third Ward.

### Outward and Upward

Dispersal and the consequent loss of ethnic cohesion pose serious challenges to scholarly analysis of Milwaukee's twentieth-century Irish community. Furthermore, the kind of statistical research that would either support or refute Andrew Greeley's thesis (see Andrew Greeley, *The Irish Americans: The Rise to Money and Power,* New York, 1981) of Irish-American success as applied to Milwaukee has simply not been done. However, one source, cited by Greeley, namely JoEllen Vinyard's 1972 doctoral dissertation, *The Irish on the Urban Frontier* (University of Michigan), which focuses on U.S. Census Bureau statistics for ethnicity and occupations, argues that the Irish were considerably more successful in Midwestern cities than they were in the large cities of the Northeast.

Scattered evidence suggests that the Greeley/Vinyard thesis of Irish-American success applies to Milwaukee. Irish involvement in the formation of various Catholic churches in Milwaukee indicates that both before, and especially after, the Third Ward fire, the Irish were moving out of the old ethnic enclave northward and westward into the more affluent and socially mobile neighborhoods in Milwaukee and its suburbs. The Irish, for example, appear in very large numbers in parish registers of Catholic churches in two of the city's more affluent western (Wauwatosa) and northern (Shorewood) suburbs in the early twentieth century. And though anti-assimilationists may bemoan the loss of ethnic cohesiveness that dispersal and assimilation entail, few would question that then, as now, a move "outward" was a move "upward."

The first directory for the aforementioned Village of Wauwatosa, published in 1926, lists three clearly Irish surnames among the village's eight physicians. In the same directory, the Irish account for between one quarter and one third of the village's business proprietors. Of the 1,497 "dependent families" listed in the 1908 Annual *Report of the Department of Outdoor Relief for the County Poor Farm and Almshouse for Milwaukee County,* a total of thirteen Irish families were listed as having received aid. In striking contrast, the same report listed 366 Polish families and 496 German families on its relief rolls. Irish surnames are liberally sprinkled throughout almost all the city's neighborhoods in the street and address directories from 1921 on. And the Irish are well represented in the ranks of the professions and businesses in all of the Milwaukee city directories from the start of the twentieth century.

While such disparate evidence is not conclusive proof of mainstream acceptance or status for Milwaukee's twentieth century Irish-Americans, the evidence at least points in that direction. In broad outline, the story of the Irish in Milwaukee reflects the history of most white ethnic groups in nineteenth and twentieth century urban America. In this context, the larger question of whether American society is willing or able to afford the same opportunities for movement "outward" and "upward" to its racial minorities is writ particularly large in Milwaukee, one of the nation's most racially segregated cities.

*See* Wisconsin

Harry H. Anderson, "Jeremiah Curtin's Boyhood in Milwaukee County," *Historical Messenger* of the Milwaukee County Historical Society, 27 (June 1971): 30–50.

Robert G. Carroon, "John Gregory and Irish Immigration to Milwaukee," *Historical Messenger* of the Milwaukee County Historical Society, 27 (June 1971): 51–64.

Patrick Cudahy, *His Life* (Milwaukee, Wisconsin, 1912).

Margorie R. Fallows, *Irish Americans: Identity and Assimilation* (Englewood Cliffs, N.J., 1979).

Andrew M. Greeley, *The Irish Americans: The Rise to Money and Power* (New York, N.Y., 1981).

Lawrence McCaffrey, *The Irish Diaspora in America* (Bloomington, Indiana, 1976).

JoEllen McNergney Vinyard, "The Irish on the Urban Frontier: Detroit, 1850–1880" (University of Michigan, 1972).

CHARLES W. COONEY

## MINNESOTA (outside the Twin Cities)

The story of the Irish in so-called "greater Minnesota," outside the metropolitan Twin Cities, differs from the history of the group in the rest of the United States in two significant ways. The first, as Ann Regan notes in her valuable survey in *They Chose Minnesota,* is the uncharacteristically high number of Irish in Minnesota who pursued farming as a career. And within the atypical history of the agrarian Irish-Americans, those in Minnesota have a second distinction; the state was home to a series of planned agricultural communities, the most well-known of which were founded under the leadership of Archbishop John Ireland.

The story of the Irish in the state begins with such a planned colony. The first Irish to enter what is present-day Minnesota arrived hundreds of miles from the lands opened by riverboat and rail in the mid-nineteenth century. Instead, they entered Minnesota in the state's northwest corner. These Irish, most of them from Sligo, had been lured along with a greater number of Scottish Highlanders to Manitoba in 1812 to take part in the colonization efforts of the Earl of Selkirk, a Scottish nobleman who controlled 100,000 square miles in the Red River Valley. The colonizer himself had never traveled west of Montreal. Unsuccessful as farmers and exploited in the rivalry between fur companies, the Selkirk colonists abandoned the project within a few years. An early history of Catholicism in North Dakota notes that, in August of 1818, a straggling group of Selkirk's colonists—some Irish among them—worked their way down to Pembina rather than face the famine that would surely follow the ravages of the grasshoppers that summer.

Other early Irish in Minnesota arrived with the military forces on the American frontier. Of the 263 Irish-born persons found in the Minnesota Territory in the 1850 census, more than a third were soldiers at Forts Snelling and Gaines, the former at the confluence of the Minnesota and Mississippi, the latter a northern outpost that was later renamed Fort Ripley. These were transient visitors and their impact on the state's early history is largely forgotten—though in 1977, a group of Irish-American activists protested the defamatory portrayal of the Irish soldiers offered in the historical reenactments at Fort Snelling.

Logging was Minnesota's first major industry, and other early Irish immigrants were among those who worked in the timber harvest. Regan notes that most were "lumberjacks who arrived by way of the Canadian Maritime Provinces and Maine." This was precisely the pattern followed by the family of Walter O'Meara, the Cloquet native whose memoir *We Made it Through the Winter* chronicles the latter days of the lumber camp culture. Among the incidents that O'Meara records is a 1903 St. Patrick's Day melee in which a lumberjack named Big Jake distinguished himself by "vaulting onto the bar of McCarthy's saloon and waltzing down its length kicking off the customer's glasses and bellowing 'The Protestant Boys.'"

When the lands of southeastern Minnesota were opened for settlement through advances in river travel and, later, the railroad, Irish arrivals proved conspicuous. A concentration of Irish settlements emerged in southeastern Minnesota, especially the counties along the Mississippi and Minnesota Rivers.

Jessenland Township in Sibley County appears to have been the first Irish farming community in the state, dating back to 1852. The nearby settlements of Green Isle, Washington Lake and Faxon also gave an Irish character to the lower Minnesota River Valley, as did the townships of Glendale, Eagle Creek, Cedar Lake, New Market and Credit River in Scott County, San Francisco and Hollywood in Carver County, and Derrynane and Tyrone in Le Sueur County. Regan found that the townships of Dakota County bordering the Minnesota gave that county the greatest number of rural Irish in 1860. The Irish antecedents—and indeed, the agricultural origins—of the communities are obscured today. With the exception of the Sibley County communities, all of these areas now lie within the Twin Cities metropolitan region.

Farther from Minneapolis and St. Paul, in the Mississippi Valley, Irish farmers clustered near such settlements as Brownsville and Caledonia in Houston County, Chatfield in Fillmore County, and along the valleys of the Root and Zumbro Rivers and Winnebago Creek. An area near Lanesboro, for instance, was called "Irish Ridge" for the seventeen Irish Catholic families there who occupied adjoining farms. River towns such as Winona, Lake City and Hastings were home to many Irish laborers and craftsmen; in the last-named town the 1850 census disclosed that one-fifth of the male labor force was Irish.

By 1870, 65% of the state's Irish-born population was found outside the Twin Cities in southeastern Minnesota. Some 58% of the Minnesota Irish was engaged in farming, a proportion that was matched only by Wisconsin and Iowa.

Irish settlements that grew out of sponsored colonization schemes have played an unusually visible part in the group's history in the state. Shieldsville, in Rice County, became the first organized Irish settlement in Minnesota in 1855. The community was but one of the innumerable projects of General James Shields, a talented but restless Irish-born attorney, politician and entrepreneur who made Minnesota his home in the 1850s. A native of Kilkenny, Shields was named one of Minnesota's first senators when statehood was declared. A statue of Shields stands in the rotunda of Minnesota capitol—a rather more permanent honor than his brief tenure in the state may warrant. After the general laid out the townsite of Shieldsville and nearby Erin township, seven Irish St. Paulites took up the first farms in his new community. By vigorously promoting the project in the Catholic press in the eastern U.S., Shields attracted hundreds of Irish to his settlements and to adjacent areas, including the county seat of Faribault. By the end of the decade Shields and his colonists had become embroiled in an acrimonious fight over a surcharge on their deeds, and the opportunistic founder moved on to California. The Irish presence in Rice and Le Sueur counties remained conspicuous for another half-century, but ultimately waned.

Bishop Thomas Grace made an abortive attempt to involve the Catholic church in assisted settlements in 1864, but little came of his efforts. The work of the Catholic Colonization Bureau, undertaken in 1876 by his successor Bishop John Ireland—with considerable assistance from his friend and colleague Dillon O'Brien, then editor of the diocesan newspaper—proved more successful.

The new bishop was a man of relentless optimism, perfectly suited to the expansionist tenor of his century. He saw opportunities everywhere. Ireland rejected the wariness of his ecclesial colleagues; he welcomed Catholic participation in civic life, and asserted that in the United States, Catholicism could flourish as never before. Conservative eastern bishops, notably John Hughes of New York, had distrusted the earlier colonizing efforts of D'Arcy McGee and others who sought to move the Irish out of the eastern cities where they had found refuge, believing that they were better served by remaining among their own people and ministered to by familiar priests. In contrast, Ireland saw in the unsettled lands of western Minnesota a means of rescuing the Catholic population from the evils of urban life. He and his associates insisted that temperance be vigorously promoted in the new settlements. An 1879 pamphlet promoting the Bureau waxed that in the church-sponsored colonies, one could find neither "rowdies nor the saloons that vomit them forth . . . [sober rural life] . . . is the anchor of family unity and love and the harbinger of prosperity."

The Catholic Colonization Bureau avoided the financial problems of earlier settlement schemes by working in tandem with the St. Paul and Pacific Railroad. The Bureau served as an agent for the railroad; thus, it bought no land. In a span of only three years, the Bureau contracted for 369,000 acres in southern and western Minnesota, centering its efforts in the communities of DeGraff and Clontarf in Swift County, Adrian in Nobles County, Avoca, Iona, and Fulda in Murray County, Graceville in Big Stone County, and Ghent in Lyon County. German and Belgian Catholics actually outnumbered the Irish in these projects. Still, census analyses show that the numbers of foreign-born Irish increased until the turn of the century. The story of the colonies is carefully examined in James P. Shannon's 1957 *Catholic Colonization on the Western Frontier.* Shannon fairly characterizes Ireland and O'Brien's efforts as "the largest and most successful Catholic colonization program ever undertaken in the United States."

Though the Bureau's efforts do, in fact, surpass any comparable attempts, in the larger story of Irish immigration the numbers are unimpressive. Shannon estimates that a total of 4,000 families of all nationalities found homes, if only for a time, in the colonies. Far more Irish settled in rural Minnesota via the normal processes of homesteading and land speculation than ever arrived through formal schemes. In the vast majority of cases, individuals and families arrived in a pattern of staged migration, which, as Regan tracks them, "included arrival in New York or Canada and one or two subsequent moves over a period of years to Pennsylvania, Ohio, Indiana, Illinois, Wisconsin and Iowa and then on to Minnesota."

Efforts to move immigrants directly to the land from Ireland inevitably failed. One was undertaken by John Sweetman, a prosperous Catholic land owner in County Meath, who had grown disenchanted with Michael Davitt's efforts to achieve land reform and had grown convinced that assisted emigration would be the only solution to Ireland's economic woes. He funded a colony near Currie, in Murray County, in 1881, only to see it fail for lack of preparation and commitment on the part of his impoverished settlers.

Moreover, the organized colonies never addressed the clergy's goal of rescuing the poorest immigrants from the slums, for the simple reason that participation in John Ireland's projects required a substantial stake. Only those Irish who were already upwardly mobile could afford the minimum of $400 to $500 that the organizers themselves estimated was needed to make it through the first season on a farm.

The unfeasibility of placing indigent immigrants directly on the land was emphatically demonstrated in Graceville, almost on the South Dakota border, in 1880. At the urging of James Nugent, an Irish priest stationed in Liverpool, Bishop Ireland agreed to take responsibility for 309 destitute residents of Connemara, the remote Irish-speaking section of west Galway. (Bishop O'Connor of Omaha had already refused to accept such unprepared emigrants in his Nebraska settlements.) Nugent hoped to begin a chain migration that would in time alleviate suffering in the poorest "congested districts" of Connemara. The unfortunate events that followed have become by far the most well-publicized chapter in the history of Irish settlement in Minnesota.

As soon as he met the arriving immigrants in Boston, Ireland's assistant Dillon O'Brien warned against pursuing the scheme. He wrote to Bishop Ireland that Nugent had sent "not the industrious but the shiftless, a group of mendicants who knew nothing of farming, and were entirely unfit for the life upon the American prairie." Still, the trainload of "Connemaras" headed west to take up the homes and farms that had been procured for them.

The story played out with disastrous consequences for the twenty-four families involved. As historian Gerard Moran notes, "While the Irish Catholic Colonization Society had made clear to those settlers who came from the east the difficulties to be overcome . . . nobody thought fit to make those points known to the Connemara settlers." Everything worked against them. They arrived late in the year, were lonely and isolated, and, when offered the opportunity to earn wages at day labor, had fresh and bitter memories of exploitation at such work back in Ireland. Even Moran's sympathetic essay recognizes that a "dependency culture" had taken hold in the Connemara immigrants, a culture sure to offend their new neighbors and the bishop. After enduring a particularly brutal winter (when reports of their hardships were reported as far afield as the front page of the *New York Times*) all but a handful of the Connemara families were relocated to St. Paul.

The organizers had failed to recognize the realities of the Connemara historical experience and—in this episode at least—naively trusted in the salubrious effects of life on the prairie. Though only a small number of immigrants were involved, the incident would dampen confidence, nationally and internationally, in future colonization projects. The Connemara experiment has continued to draw examination, inspiring a book-length study by Bridget Connelly, as well as a documentary aired on the Irish-language television service, Telefís na Gaeilge, in 1996.

Most writers have explained the failure of even the well-prepared Minnesota Irish to persist on the land by citing the group's lack of capital and farming experience, as well as a temperamental disinclination for farm life. Such explanations are probably facile. Historian Malcolm Campbell's study of the 19th-century Irish settlements in Minnesota and in New South Wales challenges the idea that the Irish suffered an inherent ill-preparedness for rural life. The failures of the colonization plans, he writes, "should be explained in terms of their conceptualization, operation and timing." Campbell found that the unsuc-

cessful immigration schemes tended to site Irish colonies in locations that earlier Irish settlers had avoided; to attract the under-capitalized; and coincided with a larger urban drift. "[T]he very point that such numbers of Irish did in fact settle in rural locations . . . is sufficient to rebut the commonly made assertion that the Irish found frontier life uncongenial."

Sociologist Kieran Flanagan's 1969 study of Irish immigration to Minnesota argues that the experience of the Irish immigrant in America tended, in comparison to other groups, to have more of an "exile" consciousness; a concern with the homeland gave rise to an Irish-American subculture that impeded full participation in American life. The Minnesota Irish deviated from this pattern, Flanagan suggested, because the Irish who were interested in advancement moved west at least in part to escape this "backward-looking" system.

Still, there are scattered examples of explicitly "Irish" activity in non-urban Minnesota as well as in the cities. One of the more flamboyant was an abortive 1871 Fenian invasion of Manitoba by an army of thirty-five men led by the Rosemount schoolteacher William B. O'Donoghue. Constitutional nationalist Charles Stewart Parnell—for whom Irish settlers named townships in both Polk and Traverse counties—addressed enthusiastic crowds in Winona and Lake City on his 1880 trip to Minnesota, as well as in Minneapolis and St. Paul. Chapters of the Irish National Land League were formed in many Irish communities in the 1870s; an 1881 letter from Ireland, now in the possession of the Daly family of Minneapolis, defends the family in Ireland defending themselves against their Minnesota relatives' charges that they lacked zeal for land reform. Nonetheless, assimilationist pressures were almost certainly stronger for the Irish in Minnesota than for their eastern counterparts. The speeches and writings of Irish leaders like Archbishop Ireland and the Dakota County entrepreneur and politician Ignatius Donnelly overflow with exhortations to join into American life.

There were, of course, occupations unrelated to farming in which the Irish found employment—as domestics, laundresses, teamsters, laborers and many other trades. A popular belief that the Irish played a large role in railroad construction work is not borne out by the facts. A significant number of Irish did work in Minnesota's rail industry, but chiefly in the shops and in managerial positions. Despite the often-repeated legend that James J. Hill employed great numbers of Irish to build the railroad, the railroads in Minnesota were built chiefly with Swedish labor. Similarly, the Irish largely missed the iron mining boom in Northern Minnesota. Those who did work in this new industry in the early twentieth century drew attention because the more recently arrived immigrants from eastern Europe frequently elected their Irish, English-speaking, colleagues as political leaders. This power-brokering role was a familiar one for the Irish throughout the United States, as was the prominent part that Irish labor leaders played in organizing the state's mining labor force. The Jesuit priest Daniel Berrigan, who with his brother Philip gained a national reputation in the Vietnam era for radicalism, was born in the iron mining community of Virginia, Minnesota. The Berrigans have traced their concern for social justice to having grown up as the sons of a labor activist on Minnesota's Iron Range.

The diminished presence of the Irish-born and their descendants in Minnesota's farms and small towns is well documented. The trend is confirmed by anecdotal evidence. Green Isle—named by the immigrant Christopher Dolan in 1854—

abandoned its community celebration of St. Patrick's Day around World War II, but began celebrating an Oktoberfest in 1972. In recent years, there have been glimmers of Irish activity in regions outside the Twin Cities—informal gatherings of the Irish professionals at Rochester's Mayo Clinic; the mounting of an Irish lecture series in Owatonna in the 1980s; the 1978 chartering of a new chapter of the Ancient Order of Hibernians in Belle Plaine, the state's first new chapter in more than forty years; and the continued popularity of a St. Patrick's Day parade in Waseca. These scattered incidents do not bespeak any deep community connection with Ireland. The Irish presence in non-urban Minnesota has been in decline for at least the last century; and the establishment of Irish communities in greater Minnesota was anomalous in the group's history, even when the Irish character of those few villages and farming regions was at its peak.

*See* St. Paul and Minneapolis

Malcolm Campbell, "Immigrants on the Land: Irish Settlement in Minnesota and New South Wales, 1830–1890," *New Hibernia Review*, 2/1 (Spring 1998).

Kieran Flanagan, "Emigration, Assimilation and Occupational Categories of Irish Americans in Minnesota" (MA thesis, University of Minnesota, 1969).

Gerard Moran, "'In Search of the Promised Land': The Connemara Colonization Scheme to Minnesota, 1880," *Éire-Ireland*, XXXI/3 & 4 (Fall/Winter 1996).

Ann Regan, "The Irish" in *They Chose Minnesota. A Survey of the State's Ethnic Groups,* ed., June D. Holmquist (St. Paul, 1981).

James P. Shannon, *Catholic Colonization on the Western Frontier* (New Haven, 1957).

JAMES SILAS ROGERS

## MISSIONARIES IN SPANISH FLORIDA AND LOUISIANA

In the late eighteenth and early nineteenth centuries, the Spanish Empire included much of the future lower Southeastern United States plus the vast Louisiana Territory that stretched northward along one or both banks of the Mississippi River. As Protestant English-speakers poured into this area in increasing numbers, the Spanish faced a dilemma: expulsion or toleration of an often industrious Protestant population in a colony where all by law must be loyal not only to the king, but also to the pope. Since neither solution was politically expedient, Spanish officials both at home and in the colony devised an ingenious third way to avoid the dilemma: recruit, train, and commission a cadre of young Irish priests to establish parishes and win over by persuasion the Protestant colonists. Thus began the Irish mission to Spanish Louisiana and the Floridas.

Most recruits came from the Irish colleges and universities in Spain where Irish clerics were being trained to return home; most attended the University of Salamanca. They volunteered to set sail for America to win over the Protestants to the customs, allegiance, and religion of Spain.

On December 16, 1778, the first two young priests, Thomas Hassett and Michael O'Reilly, were commissioned to assist the impoverished Minorcan colony in Florida. The sea blockades during the American colonies' struggle for independence, however, prevented an immediate Florida landing. Not until 1784 did Hassett and O'Reilly arrive at St. Augustine where they worked among the colonists in general rather than just the Minorcans.

The challenge to the Spanish government became particularly acute in West Florida where a strong English-speaking population was growing at Natchez, nearby Cole's Creek, and the small military post at Nogales (Vicksburg). More Irish priests were recruited to establish parishes there. Louisiana Governor Estevan Miró's proposal that all children, regardless of their parent's religion, must be baptized as Catholics and attend Catholic schools was modified by Spanish officials at home. Protestants could remain in the Floridas if they took an oath of political allegiance and fidelity and agreed not to leave their present districts without the governor's permission. The Irish priests would win converts by gentle persuasion rather than force or law.

Miró drew up the master plan for the new missionary endeavor in West Florida. The centerpiece was two new parishes for the rapidly-growing Natchez District: one parish near St. Catherine Creek; another at Cole's Creek. A third parish was planned along the Tensas River forty-five miles above Mobile (Tombigbee). Miró felt that the clustering of families around these new church sites would be good for politics, economics, education, and religion. A fourth parish at Nogales never materialized.

The Bishop of Salamanca recruited the new Irish missionaries. Father William Savage, vice rector of the Royal Irish College at the University of Salamanca, was the first to volunteer. Three other volunteers joined Savage: Gregory White and Constantine McKenna from the *Casa de Venerables* in Seville and Michael Lamport from Cadiz. The four missionaries arrived in New Orleans via Havana in August 1787.

Lamport was sent to Mobile pending the establishment of the parish at Tensas. The other three priests left New Orleans for Natchez in mid-1788. Savage was appointed as the first pastor of the new parish of San Salvador del Mundo; McKenna and White were his assistants, the latter for the Cole's Creek community. The priests were to administer the sacraments, preach, and conduct a school that included classes in reading and writing Spanish. The school was never opened.

The Catholic parish of San Salvador del Mundo at Natchez flourished for only ten years under the leadership of William Savage (1788–1793), Gregory White (1793–1794), and Francis Lennan (1794–1798). The Spanish-supported clergy departed in 1798 when the district became an American territory.

A third group of priests, Michael Crosby, Constantine McCaffrey, O. Carm., and Michael Wallis, O.P., arrived at St. Augustine in 1791. A fourth group, Patrick Mangan, Patrick Walsh, Francis Lennan, James Coleman, George Murphy, and Charles Burke set sail for the Louisiana colony in 1792; all except Mangan were newly-ordained. Coleman served as pastor of St. Michael's Parish in Pensacola from 1794 until 1822; he was also appointed Vicar General for West Florida in 1806.

Two additional priests, Juan Brady, O. Carm., and James Maxwell, a former French naval chaplain, were commissioned for Louisiana in 1795. James Maxwell was sent immediately to St. Genevieve in upper Louisiana. He remained after the Spanish departure, was chosen by President James Madison as one of the nine people to form a governing council for the new territory of Missouri in 1812, and died at his post in 1814 after a fall from a horse. John Brady also remained after the Spanish departure, serving for almost twenty years in the Baton Rouge–Pointe Coupee areas before leaving Louisiana around 1826. Three additional priests, John Maguire (1797), Francis Bodkin (1787?), and Patrick Lonergan, O.F.M. (1804?), served in the Spanish colony.

The Spanish lost their Louisiana and Florida colonies to the rapidly expanding United States: the Natchez District in 1798; the Louisiana Territory effectively in 1803; West Florida in 1810; East Florida in 1821.

The Irish priests did not succeed in their primary and unrealistic mission—the widespread conversion of Protestants. The poor moral example of many colonial Catholics, the small number of Irish clergy, the ineffectiveness of several Irish missionaries, the Protestant attachment to their culture and religion as well as their dislike for Spanish rule, the failure of the Spanish government to provide the means to establish schools, the presence of Protestant missionaries—all thwarted the missions' main objective.

These twenty priests, however, made a major contribution to the preservation of the Catholic religion in a mission greatly understaffed by clergy. The priests served at St. Augustine and Pensacola in Florida; Mobile and Tombigbee in Alabama; Natchez, Cole's Creek, and Nogales in Mississippi; New Orleans, Baton Rouge, Bayou Sara, Attakapas (St. Martinville), Iberville (St. Gabriel), LaFourche (Donaldsonville), Pointe Coupee, Avoyelles (Mansura), Rapides (Alexandria) in Louisiana; and St. Genevieve in Missouri.

Three priests died at their mission posts during the Spanish period. Michael Lamport died at Mobile (1789); William Savage, at Natchez (1793); Constantine McKenna, the pastor of Bayou Sara (Louisiana), at New Orleans (1802). Five who remained in the United States territories died there; Thomas Hassett at New Orleans (1804); Patrick Lonergan, pastor of Avoyelles and Rapides, at New Orleans (1804); Patrick Walsh, at New Orleans (1806); James Maxwell, pastor of St. Genevieve at Cahokia (1814); and Michael Crosby at St. Augustine (1822).

Michael O'Reilly, Michael Wallis, Constantine McCaffrey, Charles Burke, James Coleman, John Maguire, Patrick Mangan, George Murphy, and Gregory White returned to Europe; Patrick Mangan left for Mexico. Francis Bodkin left in 1803; suspected of "peculiar ideas," he was forbidden to return to Florida in 1806. Juan Brady left Louisiana around 1826.

*See* Florida; Louisiana

Michael J. Curley, *Church and State in the Spanish Floridas, 1783–1822* (Washington, D.C., 1940).

Gilbert C. Din, "The Irish Mission to West Florida," *Louisiana History*, 12 (Fall 1971): 315–334.

Charles E. Nolan, *St. Mary's of Natchez: The History of a Southern Catholic Congregation, 1716–1988* (Natchez, 1992).

Charles Edwards O'Neill, "'A Quarter Marked by Sundry Peculiarities': New Orleans, Lay Trustees, and Père Antoine," *The Catholic Historical Review*, 76 (April 1990): 235–277.

CHARLES E. NOLAN

# MISSISSIPPI

The Irish presence in Mississippi was circumscribed by five major demographic, political, social, and economic factors. The first was the state's large African-American population, initially as slaves and, after emancipation, as poor laborers in a society that defined its boundaries by race. Mississippi's African-American population outnumbered whites until the 1940s. The large African-American population discouraged foreign immigration.

The second factor was the early white settlement of the state largely by transplanted easterners whose European ancestors came to America two, three, four, and even five generations earlier. These Mississippi pioneers were often of mixed European ancestry including Irish and Ulster- or Scotch-Irish. When they were active religiously, they generally belonged to one of the state's three major Protestant denominations—Baptist, Methodist, and Presbyterian.

The third factor was the presence of a small, but cohesive Catholic population. During the nineteenth century, many Catholic communities included a small, sometimes transient group of first-generation Irish. The Irish Catholic presence in Mississippi, however, was diluted by the concentration of about half the state's Catholics on the Gulf Coast whose culture, language, and religious practices more closely reflected French-speaking New Orleans and Mobile than English-speaking Vicksburg, McComb, and Jackson. In a 1905 report, only 571 natives of Ireland were listed among the state's more than 22,000 Catholics. Almost half of these were concentrated in three cities: Vicksburg (124), Meridian (110), and Natchez (46). Seven other cities (Water Valley, Lexington, Columbus, Hattiesburg, Bay St. Louis, Biloxi, and Jackson) had between sixteen and twenty-six native-born Irish. No other city or town had more than thirteen native-born Irish Catholics. The figures reflect the small, widespread presence of Irish Catholics in Mississippi.

The fourth factor was the state's predominantly agricultural, rural economy. There were few large cities in Mississippi to provide work for and attract newly-arriving immigrant populations as did the rapidly-growing eastern and midwestern cities. By 1910, when the great period of Irish immigration had already ended, Mississippi's five largest cities were Meridian (23,285), Vicksburg (20,814), Natchez (11,791), Hattiesburg (11,733), and Greenville (9,610). Jackson, the state capital, numbered only 7,816 residents. A large percentage of all these cities' residents were of African descent.

The fifth factor was the recurring outbreak of epidemics such as yellow fever, the last of which occurred in 1905. Newly-arriving immigrants were particularly vulnerable to the epidemics. Of the 158 people who died in Yazoo City and the surrounding area during the decimating yellow fever epidemic of 1853, twenty-six were natives of Ireland, a third of the native Irish residing in the county only three years earlier.

Because of these factors, Mississippi became the home of only a small portion of the vast nineteenth-century Irish immigration to America. While the 1880 U.S. census listed 4,529,523 Americans with Irish-born fathers and 4,448,421 with Irish-born mothers, the comparable figures for Mississippi were a minuscule 7,804 and 6,426. Mississippi's total foreign-born population in that census was only 9,209 (.0082%).

Mississippi's European origins are found in French and Spanish Louisiana and Spanish and British Florida rather than the eastern colonies. Except for the Gulf Coast and Natchez, there were few significant European settlements in the state prior to statehood in 1812. Native Americans continued to occupy most of the land until the Treaty of Dancing Rabbit Creek in 1822; the treaty opened vast new lands to European settlement and began the forced migration of Native Americans west of the Mississippi River. The new residents of European background used the newly-acquired land for farming and particularly for raising cotton with African and African-American slaves and later, sharecroppers, as their main laborers.

## Irish Immigrants and their Descendants

Despite these limiting factors, there has been an Irish presence in Mississippi since colonial times. Irish immigrants moved to Natchez District during the English and Spanish colonial periods. The funeral registers of San Salvador del Mondo, the Catholic parish at Natchez, included the Hispanized names of more than a dozen natives of Ireland between 1793 and 1798: Father Guillermo Savage; Juan Ferr; Juan Spenza; Jacobo Morsy; Andres McCormic "who renounced the errors of the Calvinist Sect"; Martin Gill; Juan Neuton; Juan Fowler; Santiago Maor; Juan Carol; Miguel Dohaldy; Pedro Debein; Jorge Schviene; Timoteo Macarty; and Juan MegDonnell. Other natives of Ireland, women as well as men, are found in the settlement's colonial baptismal and marriage records.

Throughout the nineteenth century, Irish and Irish descendants continued to settle in Mississippi, but in small numbers compared to the east and midwest. Irish Catholics contributed to the growth of Catholic congregations in Natchez, Vicksburg, Jackson, and Yazoo City. At Paulding in east-central Mississippi, Father Ghislain Boheme, a Belgian, gathered a small community of Irish Catholics around the Church he built in 1843. James J. Shannan edited there the *Eastern Clarion,* Mississippi's largest newspaper before the Civil War. A handful of Irish-Catholic families built the first Catholic chapels in Attala County in 1859 and in Neshoba County in 1860.

Michael O'Rourke (1818–1904), a former Irish seminarian, migrated first to New Orleans, and finally settled in Wilkesburg near Bassfield where he remained until his death. O'Rourke became an active Mason, lost interest in his childhood religion, and became a teacher in nearby Columbia. His wife, Sarah Tines, became Catholic and persuaded O'Rourke to reconcile himself to the church. O'Rourke became one of Mississippi's early ardent Catholic lay leaders. He purchased quantities of Catholic literature, especially *The Faith of Our Fathers,* which he distributed to his neighbors. At his small store, O'Rourke led long "crackerbarrel" discussions on religious matters. He and his wife broke down much local prejudice and helped convert several people to the Catholic faith, including Mr. & Mrs. James Clark and James Cavanaugh. The three men—O'Rourke, Clark, and Cavanaugh—built a small church on property donated by Clark; Bishop Thomas Heslin blessed the chapel in 1890. Additional Irish immigrants and transplanted Irish settlers from Paulding, including the Daley, Kerley, Fagan, and Hanegan families, increased the small community. Descendants of the three pioneer families made up much of the Catholic community when Bassfield became an independent parish in 1915.

At the same time, a steady stream of settlers with more distant Irish and Scotch-Irish roots moved west or south to Mississippi, often from the original Southern colonies, Tennessee, and Kentucky. These Irish descendants tended to blend with the predominately Protestant culture. In the monumental *History of Mississippi: The Heart of the South,* published in the 1920s, Volumes III and IV provide biographical sketches of more than a thousand leading white male citizens. Where ancestry is indicated, about half of these men had at least one Irish or Scotch-Irish immigrant ancestor. Most were third-, fourth-, and fifth-generation Americans who came to Mississippi via Georgia, Tennessee, the Carolinas and other early states. Many were lawyers, doctors, newspaper editors, businessmen; almost all were Protestants. They were often natives and/or leading citizens of such small, unfa-

miliar Mississippi towns or settlements as Cotton Gin Port, Langley, Tiplersville, Daisy, Guntown, Toomsuba, and Pittsboro.

Robert Uriah Galloway, born in Kosciusko in 1864, became a newspaper editor in Durant. His paternal grandfather was Scotch and moved to Mississippi from Kentucky; his maternal grandfather was Irish and moved to Mississippi from Alabama. His parents were natives of Mississippi; his father, a physician. He was active in the Methodist Episcopal Church.

Wallace B. Rogers, born in Clinton, Iowa, in 1870, was a Laurel businessman and banker of Irish, Scotch, and English ancestry. He established Laurel's First National Bank and was instrumental in building the city's first Opera House and office building. His parents were natives of Ohio.

J. L. Power was born in Tipperary in 1834. After moving to Mississippi, he became a prominent newspaper man—the owner of the Jackson *Clarion* and part owner of the Jackson *Clarion-Ledger.* He served as secretary to Mississippi's secession convention and secretary of state from 1895 until his death in 1901. For thirty-three years he was grand secretary of the Masonic Grand Lodge of Mississippi, one of several masonic organizations in which he was active.

Samuel C. Cook (1855–1924) was born in Oxford. His parents, natives of North Carolina, were of Scotch-Irish ancestry. Cook was an attorney and member of the state's House of Representatives before serving on the Mississippi Supreme Court from 1912 to 1921. Cook was active in the Methodist Church.

Frank J. Duffy (1867–1950) was born in St. Louis, Missouri, and moved to Natchez around the turn of the century. He became a bank president, hotel owner, active Catholic civic leader, and successful planter in nearby Concordia Civil Parish in Louisiana. Following the 1929 failure of Duffy's local Bank of Commerce, he repaid each depositor "dollar for dollar" from his personal fortune over the next years—a unique page in American banking history.

John Sidney Eason, M.D., was born near Wall Hill in 1884; his ancestors were from Germany, France, and Ireland. Judge Charles L. Crum was born in Hickory Flat in 1867 of Dutch, Irish, French, and Welsh ancestry. His parents were natives of Tennessee and Indiana. Judge Crum served in Mississippi's House of Representatives and was active in the Christian Church. James Alexander Terral was born in 1860 in Quitman of Scotch, Welsh, Irish, and German descent. He was an insurance executive and a member of the Methodist church.

A large influx of transient Irish laborers came to the state to work on the levee system that was rapidly expanding in the 1850s and, to a lesser degree, on the newly-emerging rail system. These shadowy, often anonymous Irishmen not only provided part of the brawn to create or expand Mississippi's transportation infrastructure, but were often generous contributors to the Catholic Church. Many joined the Confederate army when the outbreak of war halted levee and railroad construction. Irish laborers and workers again figured prominently in the rapid railroad expansion of the late nineteenth century.

With the brief exception of Paulding, the Irish in Mississippi were not concentrated enough to form their own rural enclaves or city neighborhoods. They tended to blend into the general population more quickly than in other parts of the country.

## Local Presence: Yazoo County

Much of the Irish presence in Mississippi is found only in local records and histories. In Yazoo County to the northwest of Vicksburg, many of the original land grantees were of Irish or Anglo-Saxon ancestry. James H. O'Neal was one of Yazoo County's earliest white immigrants, arriving in 1822; his property became known as O'Neal's Creek. His daughter, Mary, was the first white child born in the county; she married Walter Leake Johnston, grandson of Mississippi's territorial governor. Dr. J. W. Morough, a graduate of the University of Dublin, was among the early physicians in Benton in the 1830s.

Richardson Bowman (1779–1834) participated in the 1798 Irish revolt, fled to the United States where he married Nancy Rilley of South Carolina, fought in the Creek War, and finally settled on a plantation outside Benton in 1828. A house on his property served as the county's first school and interdenominational place of worship. Bowman became a school teacher, clerk, planter, and the father of ten children.

In 1850, Yazoo County numbered 4,069 free whites and 10,349 slaves. Seventy-five of the 151 foreign-born were Irish. Daniel Byrnes, a native of Limerick, came to Yazoo City in the 1840s via New Orleans. His great-grandson, also born in Yazoo City, was Rev. George Owen Twellmeyer, S.J. John Clunan, a native of Galway, settled on a farm in Yazoo County in 1856. "The Clunans were Roman Catholic, but they enjoyed the esteem of their largely Protestant neighbors." James G. Barbour (1827–1891) immigrated to Memphis before the Civil War, served as a lieutenant in the Confederate army, and moved to Yazoo City in 1880.

Dr. Peter James McCormick (1830–1905), a native of Frenchpark, County Roscommon, immigrated to the United States at the age of sixteen with his family. He taught school in Savannah, Georgia, attended the University of New York where he received his medical degree in 1857, practiced medicine briefly in New Jersey, and, in 1858, settled at Silver Creek in Yazoo County. He served as a surgeon in the 46th Mississippi Regiment during the Civil War, rising from private to major. He married Belle Lambeth of Mississippi in 1866; the couple had six children. The family moved to Yazoo City where McCormick established his medical practice. He served as chairman of the county democratic executive committee (1875–1879) and president of the state medical association (1876–1877).

Patrick Riley (1837–1906) immigrated to the United States with his family at the age of nine. The family lived first in New York and moved to Yazoo County before 1860. Patrick married Irish-born Margaret Keyes, managed a plantation, and then purchased his own place in the county where the family settled permanently. The Rileys donated the land for Yazoo City's Catholic cemetery across the road from Concord Baptist Church.

## Clergy and Religious

Many of Mississippi's clergy were Irish or of Irish or Scotch-Irish ancestry. Protestant ministers belonged to the latter group; Catholic priests to the former.

Alexander Newton, born in Summit in 1859 of Scotch and Irish ancestry, became a Presbyterian minister and school superintendent in Covington County. His parents were natives of Tennessee and North Carolina. James Carl Watson, born in Puckett in 1886 of Scotch and Irish ancestry, became the Presbyterian pastor of Louisville in 1919. Rufus Garrison Moore was born in Holly Springs in 1892 of Irish and English ancestry; he served as Methodist Episcopal pastor in Duck Hill and Hesterville before spending four years (1918–1922) as a missionary and professor of geology and history at Soochow University

in China. Upon his return to Mississippi, he became the pastor in Coldwater.

Robert Lee Breland was born in Neshoba County in 1870 of English, Irish, and Scotch ancestry. His grandparents migrated from South Carolina to Pike County in 1809. Breland became a teacher and was ordained a Baptist minister in 1907 in Philadelphia where he assumed his pastorate. His father, three brothers, and four nephews were also Baptist ministers.

Irish clergy and religious have formed an integral, important part of Mississippi Catholicism from the Spanish colonial period to the present. Early efforts by the Spanish crown to convert the growing Protestant population at British West Florida were implemented by a unique cadre of Irish priests trained in Spain and sent to the colony with limited resources to build churches and schools, but with unrealistic hopes of mass conversion. The early Natchez sacramental books bear such unlikely signatures as Fathers Guillermo Savage, Gregorio White, Constantino McKenna, Francisco Lennan, and Juan Brady. The priests served the small communities at Natchez, at nearby Cole's Creek, and at the post at Nogales (later Vicksburg) before the area was incorporated into the United States in 1798.

Large numbers of Irish-Catholic priests have followed these colonial missionaries to Mississippi. About twenty percent of the priests who served in the state between the Civil War and World War I were Irish-born. A steady influx of new Irish priests bolstered the Mississippi Catholic clergy after World War I until the 1960s. In 1998, the chancellors of both Catholic dioceses in Mississippi were natives of Ireland: Father Andrew Murray in Biloxi and Father Michael Flannery in Jackson.

Two Irish-born Catholic bishops served in Mississippi. Thomas Heslin (1845–1911) was born in Killoe, County Longford, ordained in New Orleans in 1869, ministered for twenty years in Louisiana parishes, and served as Bishop of Natchez from 1889 until 1911. He fostered the growth of Catholicism among African-Americans by establishing the first five parishes for them.

John Edward Gunn (1863–1924) was born in Fivemiletown, Country Tyrone, was educated in Ireland, England, France, and Italy, was professed in the Marist Order in 1884, and was ordained to the priesthood in 1890. He taught in Ireland and Washington D.C. and did pastoral work in Georgia prior to his appointment to Natchez in 1911. Gunn was an outspoken Irish and American patriot and one of Mississippi's most ardent supporters of American participation in World War I. Gunn became "the bishop of poor churches and especially of the colored, the Indians and the abandoned white Catholics of the distant parts of Mississippi."

Catholic Sisters from Ireland played leading roles in the church's educational programs and services to the needy. Sister Mary Thomas McSwiggan was born in County Tyrone in 1818, entered the Daughters of Charity in Emmitsburg, Maryland, in 1839, and served in Emmitsburg and St. Louis before arriving in Natchez about 1857. She became "an untiring friend of the needy, the most devoted and affectionate mother of the orphans." She died in Natchez in 1877. During her final illness, the local Jewish rabbi and Protestant ministers asked their congregations to pray for her recovery—a remarkable story in the Protestant bible belt where anti-Catholic bigotry is often presupposed. Another Irish-born Daughter of Charity, Lydia McGowan (1874–1953) became Natchez's "ministering angel of mercy," working with the orphans and daily visiting patients of all denominations at the local Charity Hospital for more than forty years.

CONCLUSION

A small but important Irish presence can be traced from the late colonial period throughout the nineteenth and twentieth centuries. Most were third-, fourth-, and fifth-generation immigrants of mixed European ancestry. Most were Protestants. Their presence was spread throughout the many small towns that sprang up in the state in the nineteenth-century. During the twentieth-century, their Irish origins were further diluted by intermarriage. The vast migrations of United States citizens after World War II also brought many northerners of Irish background to Mississippi.

In the nineteenth century, Irish Catholics tended more often to be first- and second-generation immigrants. Many were transient laborers on the levees and railroads; many others settled in the state's small towns and rural villages. Irish clergy and religious formed an integral part of Mississippi Catholicism down to the present. Protestant Mississippians tended to be third-, fourth-, and fifth-generation Americans of mixed European ancestry; many held positions of prominence in their local communities.

Much of Irish Mississippi history is found in small towns like Durant, Winona, Gloster, and Walthall as much as the larger cities such as Natchez, Vicksburg, and Meridian. The story of the Irish in Mississippi is very much the story of men and women whose ordinary lives were remembered mainly in their local communities. The Irish played important roles in establishing and expanding Mississippi's religious denominations, both Protestant and Catholic.

Harriet DeCell and JoAnne Prichard, *Yazoo: Its Legends and Legacies* (Yazoo City, 1976).

*History of Mississippi: The Heart of the South,* vols. III & IV (Chicago, 1925).

Richard Aubrey McLemore, ed., *A History of Mississippi,* 2 vols. (Hattiesburg, 1973).

Charles E. Nolan, *St. Mary's of Natchez: The History of a Southern Catholic Congregation, 1716–1988* (Natchez, 1992).

Nolan-Pillar research notes and draft for *The Catholic Church in Mississippi, 1865–1910* (in preparation by Charles E. Nolan).

James J. Pillar, *The Catholic Church in Mississippi, 1837–1865* (New Orleans, 1965).

John Ray Skates, *Mississippi: A Bicentennial History* (Nashville, 1979).

CHARLES E. NOLAN

## MISSOURI (outside St. Louis)

Few Irish immigrants ventured as far west as the Missouri Territory before 1770. Though rich in natural resources and ripe with promise, the sparsely settled wilderness lay at what was then the distant edge of American civilization. As one lonesome early Irish settler wrote: "(At home) I could spend the winter's nights in a neighbor's house cracking jokes by the turf fire. If I had there but a sore head, I could have a neighbor within every hundred yards of me that would run to see me. But here (in Missouri Territory) everyone can get so much land . . . that they calls them neighbors that live two or three miles off."

The first Irish-born adventurers arrived in the Missouri territory in and around what is now St. Louis on the banks of the Mississippi River, in the 1760s. Ulster Presbyterians for the most part, they came as estate managers, traders and merchants and professional soldiers loyal to the Spanish government. Missouri, then, was but a small piece of the Louisiana Territory,

managed for the Spaniards by Count Alexander O'Reilly, a native of County Meath.

An Irish-born, Spanish-educated priest, Father James Maxwell, established a Catholic mission at Ste. Genevieve, south of St. Louis around 1790 and ministered to Missouri's first acknowledged Irish settlement, a rough and tumble encampment on the Mississippi River called the Boise Brule Bottom. His pastoral charges included Irish, French and Spanish Catholics for 100 miles around, in fledgling towns like Potosi, Old Mines, Perryville and New Madrid. Father Maxwell reportedly served as one of the first territorial representatives to President Thomas Jefferson when the lands of Missouri became part of the United States in 1803. Four years later Joseph Charles from Westmeath founded *The Louisville Gazette* (later *The Missouri Gazette*), the first paper west of the Mississippi. He had been a United Irishman who fled to America in 1798.

By the time Missouri became a state in August of 1821, Irish immigrants were thick in and around St. Louis, and beginning to settle in increasing numbers in villages and camptowns along Missouri's eastern rivers. Andrew McNair of County Donegal was Missouri's first governor. His wife, Margaret O'Rheilly, a Catholic, organized charitable works to benefit immigrants to the new state, as more and more Irish traveled upriver from the port of New Orleans. In the coming years, many Irish continued heading west via the muddy Missouri River, to the far-flung settlements of St. Joseph and Chouteau's Landing (later the Town of Kansas and, later still, the city of Kansas City).

By the late 1840s many deck- and dock-hands on the Mississippi and trans-Missouri steamboat lines were uneducated Irish working their way toward free or inexpensive land out west. Additional Irish and Scots-Irish came with a small migration of southern farmers to tame the tobacco-friendly hills of western Missouri, near Weston and St. Joseph. A few even brought slaves with them.

Irish-born Indian agents claimed property along the Missouri River on the far western edge of the state, near the fur trading post of St. Joseph, as early as 1837. As the French founders of the settlement moved on, newly arrived Irish took over. John Corby, a native of Limerick, established a local Hibernian Benevolent Society and helped a countryman, Father Tom Scanlan, form the first Catholic parish in St. Joseph in 1845. Across the Missouri River from the state capitol of Jefferson City, Irish immigrant laborers and stone masons established a settlement while they built a new capitol building in 1844. Hibernia Street is all that remains of the settlement today.

As a newly ordained Catholic priest in 1845, Bernard Donnelly from County Cavan found himself standing ankle-deep in the mud of a riverboat landing of the far western edge of Missouri, surrounded by oddly dressed Indians, hardened French traders, laboring Blacks and half-breeds. At the time, he couldn't even fathom just how big his new parish was. He'd only been told that the Town of Kansas was at the center of a mission "equal in extent to a European kingdom." Father Donnelly over the years explored virtually all of that kingdom on horseback, preaching in French, English and Osage by day, spending nights under wagons and stars. Only rarely in those early years did Father Donnelly hear the welcome sound of a brogue. Missouri, beyond the great trading center of St. Louis, was still an isolated place then, hilly and heavily timbered, roamed by bandits and rattlesnakes. In spite of the hard travel and crude conditions, Donnelly frequently wrote letters exhorting his friends and family back in County Cavan to come join him. "Fate," he wrote, "is as relentlessly cruel to Ireland as its brutish oppressor. Don't go to heaven as a martyr—come to America, and when you die, go to God as a saint!" Donnelly was personally responsible for prompting hundreds of his countrymen to make the journey to America, specifically to the farms and fledgling cities of a still-raw and bountiful Missouri.

## THE SEARCH FOR FORTUNE AND PEACE

With the discovery of gold in California, throngs of '49ers filled the streets and fields of Independence, Liberty, St. Joseph, Westport, the Town of Kansas and other "jumping off" places to the Oregon and Santa Fe trails. Greenhorn emigrants were among the crowds who camped out while ox teams were purchased and wagons assembled and outfitted. "Murphy Wagons" built at the St. Louis factory of County Louthman Joseph Murphy surrounded Missouri's western settlements and later created traffic jams on the Great Plains. The name "Murphy" became synonymous with "covered wagon." More than 200,000 Murphy wagons were built for private and military use in the 1840s and '50s.

As happy as he was to see a few more Irish in western Missouri, Father Donnelly blamed California-bound fortune seekers for ruining what he called "the golden age of Missouri." Indeed, the fifty thousand adventurers who bunched up in the area while being outfitted for the long trip to the gold fields brought with them cholera, fevers, whiskey and disreputable women.

Behind the '49ers came the track builders. St. Louis-area businessmen John O'Fallon and Edward Walsh from County Tipperary were among the original incorporators of the Pacific Railroad. Hundreds of Irish laborers and crew bosses were involved in the grading and laying of track as the critical link progressed west to Kansas City.

## IRISH WILDERNESS

Prejudice seethed in St. Louis as more and more unskilled and uneducated Irish arrived, filling and creating ghettos and tinkering with the local politics. Riots broke out in the mid-1850s, prompting many young Irish to pack up and move on. Those who chose to stay seemed destined to be servant girls or roving railroad hands. Father John J. Hogan, a 29-year-old native of Limerick, in 1858 led a band of 58 young men and women to the forests of southeast Missouri, in search of property and clean living. The "Irish Wilderness," spread in and around what are now Wayne, Madison, Reynolds and Iron counties, flourished briefly before harsh conditions and outlaws wiped out the tiny farming commune. Founder Hogan went on to become the first bishop of the St. Joseph and Kansas City dioceses. His Irish Wilderness settlements are today part of the scenic Mark Twain National Forest.

Celtic names like Kelly, Duley and Burnes are among the original settlers of Columbia (now home to the University of Missouri) in Boone County. Irish immigrants were instrumental in building dozens of towns and cities in Missouri, including Cameron, Pierce City, Carthage, Webb City, Maryville and Lexington, and loaned their names to entire counties, including Sullivan, Shannon, Carroll, Barry, and McDonald.

Having saved enough money for a small house or farm, Irish laborers and craftsmen left the railroad gangs and carved new communities out of the hills of central and northwest Missouri. In communities like Conception, first known as Irish Settlement in Nodaway County, life was often much harsher than the hopeful immigrant had anticipated. William Brady, who helped found the twenty-thousand-acre settlement with Waterford-born Father James Power in 1856, wryly noted that, if St. Peter promised his wife an express train to redemption to stay in Conception one more day, "still she would prefer living elsewhere and run the risk of paddling her own canoe to heaven."

The census of 1850 recorded 14,734 Irish-born in Missouri, and Buchanan County boasted one of the highest concentrations in the state. In St. Joseph, the Curtain brothers helped carve paved streets into and across the river bluffs. R. Boyle became mayor and James O'Keefe wharfmaster. A Clare man, John Kelly, became a respected member of the county court. J. W. Hartigan helped found and organize what became a major stockyards operation. Teamster Michael Pendergast and his wife, Mary, both from Tipperary, set up housekeeping in 1857 and began raising a couple of politically savvy boys who would one day organize the Irish vote in Kansas City and gain national notoriety with their dominant political machine.

## IRISH COULD APPLY

In 1857, the steamboat landing in the newly christened "Kansas City" was constantly congested. Every flat spot and hollow along the river was filled with shanties, tents, slapped-together businesses and warehouses. Some 60 boats were running regular schedules between Kansas City and St. Louis. Crews of men struggled to break through the 120-foot high limestone bluffs with narrow, canyon-like streets. Father Donnelly placed appeals in the *Boston Pilot* and the *Freemans Journal* (N.Y.), calling for immigrant laborers. Healthy men were offered steamboat passage to Kansas City, and promised above-average wages. Father Donnelly's advertisement coincided with editorials in the popular Irish-American paper, *The Citizen*, which regularly urged immigrants to escape the seaboard cities and proceed at once "to the Western country, where a virgin soil, teeming with plenty, invites them to its bosom." More than 300 Irishmen responded, creating an ethnic majority in Kansas City that would shape the city for the next 150 years.

## 'A DEADLY LABORATORY' FOR CIVIL WAR

It can be argued that the Civil War began, not at Fort Sumter, but in the western counties of Missouri, in and south of Kansas City, where pro-slavery guerrillas and the abolitionist Kansas Jayhawkers traded terror and death for years prior to the official outbreak of war in 1861. Farmers, among them Irish immigrants, were constantly terrorized, if not burned out or murdered in conflicts between non-uniformed "irregular" armies before and during the war. Reported to be among the guerrillas was one Jesse James, whose mother was of Irish descent.

Loyalties in Missouri were mixed and strained. Many of the state's Irish settlers had first lived in the South after arriving on immigrant ships at New Orleans. Others jumped at a chance to serve the Union—and to do battle with the British-backed Confederates. Freshly discharged from the Indian Wars in New Mexico, Kerry-born Michael O'Doherty arrived in Westport, Mo., in August 1861, when conscription efforts were at a fever pitch, and men of experience were being recruited for local volunteer units—both Confederate and Yankee. "I sold my pony," he wrote, "as there was no show in the world (worth) going south (for) without joining the southern army . . . Myself being registered with my full rank of quartermaster seargent, they were not slow to offer me the rank of captain. I respectfully declined . . . as I had sworn allegiance to the stars and stripes and no consideration could make me betray my obligation as an Irishman and a federal soldier . . ."

Many of Kansas City's prominent business and civic leaders went south early on in the war, leaving shuttered businesses, empty homes and broken rungs in the social ladder. Irish immigrants found themselves in charge of things. In 1861, Cavan-born Pat Shannon was elected to the city council, Ed O. Flaherty became the city engineer and E. O. O'Flaherty the city assessor. Cross-country railroad construction—proceeding at a frantic pace in previous years—came to a halt when war was declared. The big rail push stopped just outside of Kansas City, leaving hordes of Irish laborers and crew bosses looking for some place to sign up for service, or a safe place to ride out the war.

The harp insignia flew over many a home militia unit in Missouri, including Irish Company B in Kansas City, led by Capt. William Miller, 1st Lt. Daniel Cahill and 2nd Lt. David O'Neil. In St. Louis, many Irish, including students from St. Louis University, followed Irish-born priest Father John Bannon, an army chaplain, to the side of the Confederacy. A middle-class group of Irish from around Market Street formed the First Missouri Confederate Brigade in 1861. Led by Patrick Cannif and Joseph Kelly, the unit was one of many Missouri outfits calling itself "the Fighting Irish Company."

Missourian and Union Colonel James Mulligan commanded a regiment of Irish under the harp and shamrock at the Battle of Lexington. General Phil Sheridan, who emigrated from Cavan at age two, spent the first year of the war leaving "scorched earth" across Missouri in an unsuccessful campaign to eradicate confederate guerrillas. General James Shields, who was born in Tyrone and retired in Carrolton, Mo., played prominent roles in both the Mexican War and the Civil War, and became the only man in history to serve in the U.S. Senate from three different states. During it all, Irish-born Sisters of Mercy from Missouri tended the dying and wounded.

## FENIAN FERVOR

Fueled by the rhetoric of the Fenians, many an Irish Civil War veteran refused to shed his uniform after Robert E. Lee and the South finally surrendered in 1865. The New Fenian Brotherhood, although condemned from the Catholic pulpit, captured the imagination—and wallets—of Irish-Americans with grand visions of 200,000 battle-hardened Civil War vets marching on British-controlled Canada.

"The circle in Kansas City worked hard," Michael O'Doherty wrote. "We subscribed the very little money we wanted for our families to the general funds. We bought Fenian bonds that wasn't worth the paper they were printed on . . . . These bonds were furnished to agents, supposed to be good patriotic Irishmen, for sale and they were bought up by poor hardworking men and women all over the country. Bought one myself for the last few dollars I had to spare and so did others in Kansas City."

O'Doherty was chosen as Missouri's delegate to the Fenian Convention in Troy, New York, in September 1866, and he gave a rousing speech, pledging the support of his fellow Irish from the Show-Me state. But pomp, ceremony, political infighting and disorganization proved to be the hallmarks of the Fenian Brotherhood leadership, and when the first actual "attack" was launched at the border near Buffalo, New York, in 1866—with 800 men—the results were disastrous and embarrassing. After

several more ineffectual raids on Canada, many disheartened Fenian men from Missouri joined comrades from across the country at the O'Neill Colony in Northeast Nebraska, where a Fenian general had established a utopian Irish community.

## FLEXING IRISH MUSCLES

After the war, rail construction resumed, and Missouri's economy boomed. Patrick Shannon was elected mayor of Kansas City in 1865. By 1870, 55,000 Irish-born men and women called Missouri home. Fully nine percent of Kansas City's population talked with a brogue. Greenhorns were in competition with migrating "Exodusters" (former slaves) and uneducated whites who were pouring into Missouri cities from war-torn farmsteads throughout the lower Midwest.

The Irish were aggressive and, sometimes, disruptive. As a writer for the *Kansas City Journal* recalled: "Pioneers were pioneering along the railroad and Kansas City was their headquarters. The Irish laid the rails across the continent and they were a hard drinking as well as hard working set." From 1873 to 1891, Kansas City's exploding Irish-Catholic population flexed first its ethnic pride and later its civic muscle with a series of mile-long parades that highlighted daylong celebrations that included Catholic Mass, big lunches, nationalist songs, suds, whiskey and temperance meetings. The fire department, three-quarters of its members Irish, marched in costume, as did the eleven local chapters of the AOH.

Brothers and sisters sent money home for trans-Atlantic fares for their siblings. Communities throughout Missouri received record numbers of immigrants in the 1870s. Louisiana, Missouri, in the northeast part of the state saw an influx of Irish-speaking men and women from the Gaeltacht of western Ireland. The Irish there helped build an important bridge over the Mississippi and established a Catholic parish in 1874.

As the Irish provided the labor for Missouri's burgeoning foundries, railroad centers, farm implement, stockyard and packing house operations, labor unions found a foothold. In 1886, Irishman Terence Powderly of the Knights of Labor led a successful rally at Kansas City's levee to bring attention to local railroad strikes. In 1890, Kansas Citian William D. Ryan helped found the United Mine Workers of America, and Missouri labor lawyer Frank P. Walsh honed the skills he would later use to serve as Eamon De Valera's representative at the Versailles Peace Conference in 1919, and as chairman of the American Commission for Irish Independence.

Political aggressiveness led to a backlash against Missouri's working-class Irish. Prejudice festered in the 1880s and 1890s, culminating with a bloody confrontation between the American Protective Association (A.P.A.) and Irish ward workers in Kansas City during the spring elections of 1894. A city inspector, Mike Callahan, was one of seven Irishmen killed or wounded when poll workers and "nativists" fought over vote control on the predominantly Irish west side.

About the same time, "Big Jim" Pendergast emerged as the strongest Democratic vote-getter in Kansas City, beginning a 50-year period in which Irish Democrats ruled Missouri politics. Glib-gifted Irish politicians and railroad-trained Irish contractors delivered patronage contracts and jobs, and the "Irish vote" rolled in strong and dependable from the neighborhoods of St. Louis, Kansas City, St. Joseph, Columbia, Maryville and Sedalia. In the new century, Missouri's political scepter was handed to Big Jim's younger brother, T. J. "Boss Tom" Pendergast, who was unparalleled in his ability to control City Hall, the statehouse and, through Independence resident Harry S. Truman, had influence in the White House.

## LOYAL TO TWO LANDS

By the turn of the century, the western cities of Missouri were in full-tilt production, supplying newer cities farther west with building supplies and, in turn, receiving, processing and trading crops and cattle from Kansas, Nebraska and Iowa. The stockyards of Kansas City and St. Joseph employed more than 7,000 workers. Jobs were plentiful, lace curtains attainable, and "Turas," or pilgrimages, back home to Ireland affordable, for some. Postmasters like Meath-born Philip Donnelly in Lebanon, Mo., regularly received letters from lonely, aging parents in Erin who had not laid eyes on their adult children since their loved ones departed for America. Patrick Sullivan, a Kansas City quarryman, received many a letter like this one from his mother in Listowel:

> My Dear Son Patrick,
>     I want to know from you is it in a quarry you are working or not. Tell me in your next letter is there any employment near you, if any of your children be able to work. I thought I would never again get a letter from you. . . . I do always be expecting a letter from you when any person goes to post around the place. It gives me I think longer life to hear from you good boy
> I am your truly mother untill death
>
> > Johanna Sullivan
> > rite soon dont delay XXXXXX

In the years before the Easter Uprising and World War I, Missouri's established Irish, educated by strong Catholic schools and elevated into jobs of status and responsibility by politicians and wealthy Irishmen like Kansas City streetcar magnate, Bernard Corrigan, began to spread out of the railroad areas and into middle-class neighborhoods. Admiring a crowd of 4,000 at Kansas City's 1916 Irish-American picnic, the *Catholic Register* noted: "The fact that the Irish are receiving their share of success in the commercial world was evidenced by the great number of them who came in automobiles. Fully 400 machines were in the park during the day."

Irish Republican speeches and fund-raisers kept the ethnic flame alive in Missouri until the establishment of the Free State in 1922. Parochial and statewide politics dominated Irish interest in the mid-1920s and '30s. In Kansas City, "Rabbit" Boss Joe Shannon and the Pendergast "Goat" faction fought over control of City Hall, the Jackson County Courthouse and the state capitol at Jefferson City. Missouri, and especially Kansas City, became nationally infamous for governmental corruption and vote fraud. After benefiting from the economic safety net of Pendergast-controlled jobs in the Depression years, Missouri's Irish-Americans gradually disowned the boss system, and downplayed their immigrant roots.

Small waves of immigrants after World War II helped rekindle ethnic pride, and re-energized Hibernian chapters and other social, political and benevolent societies. Parades and freedom dinners enjoyed a resurgence. A shrine to the patron saint was built at St. Patrick in Lark County, above the Mississippi north of Hannibal, and another in the Ozarks country at Laurie, not far from the old Irish Wilderness settlements. At the turn of the 21st century, Kansas City's St. Patrick's Day Parade is one of the largest in the United States, and an annual Gaelic Mass packs one of the city's largest churches with green-clad worshipers.

Since 1770, Missouri has received and sheltered a dozen generations of Irish-Americans. Today, 1.1 million Missourians—nearly twenty-two percent of the total population—point proudly to at least a wee bit of Irish heritage. And yet another wave of immigrants, many from Dublin, is spawning youthful and spirited groups like The Celtic Fringe, helping expose Missouri's proud Irish population to contemporary music, dance and film from the old country.

*See* St. Louis; Kansas

A. Theodore Brown, *Frontier Community, Kansas City to 1870* (Columbia, Mo., 1963).

A. Theodore Brown and Lyle W. Dorsett, *K.C. The History of Kansas City, Missouri* (Boulder, Co., 1978).

William J. Dalton, *Pioneer Priest, The Life of Father Bernard Donnelly* (Kansas City, Mo.,1921).

Charles Deatherage, *Early History of Greater Kansas City* (Kansas City, Mo., 1928).

William B. Faherty, S.J., *The Fourth Career of John B. Bonnan* (Portland, Oregon, 1994).

Russel L. Gerlach, *Immigrants in the Ozarks*, a study in ethnic geography (Columbia, Mo., 1976).

Donald L. Kinzer, *An Episode in Anti-Catholicism: The American Protective Association.* (Seattle, 1965).

Michael O'Laughlin, *Irish Settlers on the American Frontier* (Kansas City, Mo., 1984).

William V. Shannon, *The American Irish* (New York, 1963).

Carrie Whitney, *Kansas City Missouri—Its History & Its People*, vol. 1 (Chicago, 1908).

PATRICK O'NEILL

## MITCHEL, JOHN (1815–1875)

Militant. Famed Irish leader, and outspoken journalist, editor, and orator, John Mitchel maintains a special place in the roll call of Irish nationalism.

### EARLY LIFE

Mitchel was born on 3 November 1815 in Camnish, Co. Derry, to a Unitarian minister, Rev. John Mitchel and Mary (Haslett) Mitchel. Raised in a family of Protestant Dissenters in Presbyterian-dominated northern Ireland, young Mitchel learned early in life to take strong stands and to speak out amid opposition.

After receiving a B.A. from Dublin's Trinity College (1834), Mitchel worked in the Haslett family bank in Derry. While studying law, Mitchel strengthened two crucial relationships—with pro-Repeal publisher Charles Gavan Duffy and with 14-year-old Jane "Jenny" Verner, Mitchel's future bride. The young couple eloped to England with Jenny's father in hot pursuit. Mitchel was arrested and charged with abduction, jailed, and later transferred to Armagh. The month in jail embittered the unrepentant Mitchel. The couple successfully reunited two months after Mitchel's release and married in Co. Down in January 1837. Sworn in as a barrister on 3 June 1839, and envisioning the charmed life of a farmer, Mitchel moved to Banbridge with his growing family that soon included four children: Johnnie, James, Henrietta, and William.

Caught in the excitement of Daniel O'Connell's Repeal movement, and amid the (October 1842) publication of *The Nation* by his Young Ireland friends, Gavan Duffy and Thomas Davis,

John Mitchel

Mitchel added his own distinctive voice to the nationalist fervor. In 1845, Mitchel moved his family to Dublin and catapulted to the position of chief editorial writer for *The Nation,* following the death of Davis. Mitchel's prominent role and militant writings emphasized the growing chasm between the "controlled threat" of violence of O'Connell's followers and the blatant promise of violence by the most vocal of the Young Irelanders, led by Mitchel.

O'Connell's retreat in the face of British opposition to a planned monster meeting in Clontarf outraged Mitchel and his followers and spotlighted a serious split within the Young Ireland organization. Duffy increasingly rejected Mitchel's editorials. In response, an angry Mitchel resigned and began editing his own rival publication, *The United Irishmen,* in 1847.

### ARREST AND EXILE

By 1848, Mitchel was arrested on charges of felony treason and imprisoned at Newgate until his trial. The jury delivered a guilty verdict and sentenced Mitchel to transportation to a penal colony for fourteen years.

He and three hundred other prisoners boarded *The Neptune* for a tortuous five-month voyage to Van Diemen's Land in Australia, where he was joined by Jenny and the children (now numbering six). He later described in detail the years in prison and exile in his successful book, *Jail Journal.*

One by one, the Irish exiles—MacManus, Meagher, Mitchel—escaped from Australia to the United States. Arriving in San Francisco, Mitchel continued east with his family, arriving in New York City in 1853. By 1854, he was again the editor of a prominent Irish newspaper, *The Citizen.* However, his hero status in New York soon diminished amid a public row with Archbishop Hughes over the temporal power of the pope.

### THE REBEL

During a June 1854 visit to Virginia, Mitchel heard about the beauty of East Tennessee and, sight unseen, immediately began making plans to move his family there. In October 1857, Mitchel and Knoxville Mayor William Swan founded a pro-slavery newspaper, *The Southern Citizen,* in the heart of anti-slavery East Tennessee. (See separate entry on *The Southern Citizen*). Throughout his brief stay in Tennessee, Mitchel kept up a ferocious public

speaking schedule with speeches in cities such as Nashville, New Orleans, and St. Louis. A popular, fiery orator, Mitchel focused his speeches on British treatment of people in Ireland and India. In October 1858, James Stephens, leader of the Irish Revolutionary Brotherhood, traveled to Knoxville to solicit Mitchel's support for the Fenian cause.

Meanwhile, a lack of support for *The Southern Citizen* forced Mitchel and Swan to move the newspaper from Knoxville to Washington, D.C., where, in 1859, Mitchel and his family took up brief residence during the paper's short six-month existence. Later that year, the potential for war between Britain and France sent Mitchel rushing to Paris in hopes of stirring fires for Irish freedom. The conflict never materialized, but in the U.S., the approaching Civil War lured Mitchel back to Virginia as editorial writer for the *Richmond Enquirer* (sic) before switching to the *Richmond Examiner* in 1864. Mitchel's three sons—John, James, and William—served in the Confederate army, with only James surviving. (James' son, John Purroy Mitchel, later became mayor of New York City.)

Following the war, Mitchel moved to New York as editor of *The Daily News.* There, his continued anti-government rantings brought another prison term—this one as a fellow inmate of Confederate President Jefferson Davis at Fortress Monroe. As Mitchel's health failed, a powerful Irish-American lobby secured his release. In 1865–66, Mitchel served in Paris, France, as financial agent for the Fenian cause, but he returned to New York City as editor of the *Irish Citizen* and continued his vocal opposition to the federal government.

Militant opponent of the British to the end, Mitchel returned to Ireland and in 1875 was elected to Parliament. Disraeli declared Mitchel ineligible, but a second election returned Mitchel's seat by a greater margin. Before validation of that election, Mitchel died.

*See* Ethnic Relations: The African-Americans and the Irish

William Dillon, *The Life of John Mitchel,* Vols. I & II (London, 1883).

DeeGee Lester, "John Mitchel's Wilderness Years in Tennessee," *Éire-Ireland* (Summer 1990): 7–13.

William O'Brian and Desmond Ryan, eds., *Devoy's Post Bag,* Vol. I (Dublin, 1948).

Rebecca O'Connor, *Jenny Mitchel, Young Irelander* (Tucson, AZ, 1988).

*The Southern Citizen* (Knoxville, TN, 1858).

Samuel C. Williams, "John Mitchel, The Irish Patriot, Resident of Tennessee," *East Tennessee Historical Society Journal,* 10 (1938).

DEEGEE LESTER

## MITCHELL, GEORGE J. (1933– )

Judge, United States senator, diplomat. George J. Mitchell was born in Waterville, Maine, August 20, 1933, the descendant of Irish grandparents on his father's side. He is the son of George J. and Mary (Saad) Mitchell, and a 1954 graduate of Bowdoin College. He served in the army from 1954–1956, afterwards graduating from Georgetown University Law School. From 1960–1962 he was a trial attorney in the anti-trust division of the U.S. Department of Justice, and from 1962–1965 was executive assistant to Senator Edmund Muskie of Maine. He practiced law in Maine from 1965–1977, then became United States Attorney in Maine and subsequently a United States District Judge.

In 1980 Mitchell, a Democrat, was elected to the United States Senate from Maine, and served on the environment and public

George Mitchell

works, veterans affairs and finance committees. He was also a member of the national ocean policy study group and the arms control observer group, and *ex officio* member of the intelligence committee. He gained a reputation for even-handedness and steady leadership, and in 1988 was elected Senate Majority Leader, a post he held until he stepped down from the Senate in 1995. Six times he was voted the body's "most respected member."

On retiring from the Senate, Mitchell planned to devote himself to private law practice in Washington. Instead, he found himself plunged into the maelstrom of the politics of Northern Ireland.

The involvement began when President Bill Clinton asked him to act as his economic adviser on Ireland and in that capacity to organize a trade conference in Washington to encourage American investment in Ireland. The assignment was to last only a period of months, and end when Clinton visited Northern Ireland in December 1995. Just a few days before that visit, however, the British and Irish governments, eager to employ his judicial and legislative skills, and tangentially the good offices of the United States, asked Mitchell to chair a commission to address the knotty issue of the paramilitary weapons in the hands of the contending Nationalist (largely Catholic) and Loyalist (largely Protestant) forces in Northern Ireland, weapons which in recent years had contributed to the deaths of more than 3,300 persons. His work on that commission led, in turn, to his being appointed in 1996 as independent chairman of the Northern Ireland all-party peace talks.

Initially, Unionists were cautious about Mitchell, fearing that as a Catholic he might be biased in favor of Nationalists. The Rev. Ian Paisley, fundamentalist Protestant churchman, for one, thundered that Mitchell was "from the Kennedy stable of the Boston lobby of republicanism," a reference to Senator Edward M. Kennedy of Massachusetts and his political sympathies. Mitchell, however, proved a fair and effective negotiator, and is credited as one of those most responsible for the peace agreement brokered in Belfast April 10, 1998. As a negotiator in Ireland, Mitchell logged more than one hundred transatlantic flights over a three-year period. In the midst of those travels, the Eire Society of Boston awarded Mitchell its 1997 Gold Medal, expressing "deep admiration for his leadership, diplomacy, statesmanship, fair-mindedness, courage and commitment to peace."

*See* Republicanism, Irish-American

*Boston Sunday Globe*, "The Long, Bloody Path to Irish Peace" (April 19, 1998).
*Irish America*, "Top 100 Irish Americans of 1998" (March–April 1998).

JOHN DEEDY

### MITCHEL, JOHN PURROY (1879–1918)

*See* New York: Irish-American Mayors

### MOLLY MAGUIRES, THE

Twenty Irishmen were hanged in the anthracite region of Pennsylvania in the late 1870s, convicted of a series of assassinations stretching back to the Civil War. The convicted men were members of a secret society called the Molly Maguires, thought to have been imported from the Irish countryside, where a society of the same name was active in the 1840s. Like many similar societies, the Molly Maguires in Ireland were so-named because their members (invariably young men) disguised themselves in women's clothing, used powder or burnt cork on their faces, and pledged their allegiance to a mythical woman who symbolized their struggle against injustice. The clothing and makeup were more than a disguise; they also served to invest the "Molly" with the authority of the symbolic figure on whose behalf he was fighting. In Pennsylvania the Molly Maguires were also linked to a fraternal ethnic organization called the Ancient Order of Hibernians (AOH), founded in New York City in 1836 as a peaceful, benevolent society. The AOH was clearly used for violent as well as fraternal purposes in the anthracite region, and most of the convicted Molly Maguires were members.

There were two distinct waves of Molly Maguire activity in Pennsylvania, one in the 1860s and the other in the 1870s. The first wave, which included six assassinations, occurred during and directly after the Civil War. Nobody was convicted of these crimes at the time, though a mysterious group called the Molly Maguires was widely believed to be responsible. Only during the famous trials of the 1870s were the killings of the previous decade retrospectively traced to individual members of the Ancient Order of Hibernians. At the heart of the violence in the

A meeting of the Molly Maguires

1860s was a combination of resistance to the military draft with some form of rudimentary labor organizing by a shadowy group known variously as the "Committee," the "Buckshots," and the "Molly Maguires." In the context of the wartime emergency, labor organizing and draft resistance were seen by the mine owners and their political allies as tantamount to treason. The second wave of violence did not occur until 1875, in part because of the introduction of a more efficient policing and judicial system, but mainly because of the emergence of a powerful new trade union, the Workingmen's Benevolent Association (WBA), which united Irish, British, and American workers across the lines of ethnicity and skill.

The labor movement of the anthracite region now took two distinct but overlapping forms. A powerful trade union movement, open to all workers, united the labor force. Half the leaders of the union were Irish-born. But there was also a second, shadowy organization, the Molly Maguires, composed only of Irishmen and favoring tactics of violence that the union always condemned as self-destructive. To gather information against both groups, but especially the Mollys, Franklin B. Gowen of the Reading Railroad hired America's foremost private detective, Allan Pinkerton. Pinkerton sent one of his best men, the Irish-born James McParlan, to work in the anthracite region undercover. It was largely on his evidence that the Molly Maguires were executed.

The defeat and collapse of the WBA during the "Long Strike" of 1875 led directly to the second wave of Molly Maguire assassinations. Temporarily assuming the unofficial leadership of the labor movement, or at least of its radical violent wing, the Mollys assassinated a policeman, a Justice of the Peace, a miner, two mine foremen, and a mine superintendent in the summer of 1875. In 1876 and 1877 more than fifty men, women, and children were indicted for Molly Maguire crimes. The trials, conducted in the midst of enormously hostile publicity, bordered on a travesty of justice. The defendants were arrested by private policemen and convicted on the evidence of an undercover detective who was accused of being an *agent provocateur,* along with a series of informers who turned state's evidence to save their necks. Irish Catholics were excluded from the juries as a matter of course. Most of the prosecuting attorneys worked for railroads and mining companies. The star prosecutor at the great showcase trials in Pottsville was none other than Franklin B. Gowen. Twenty Molly Maguires were sent to prison and twenty more were hanged, ten of them on a single day, June 21, 1877, known to the people of the anthracite region as Black Thursday.

Wayne G. Broehl, Jr., *The Molly Maguires* (Cambridge, Mass., 1964).
J. Walter Coleman, *The Molly Maguire Riots: Industrial Conflict in the Pennsylvania Coal Region* (Baltimore, 1936).
Kevin Kenny, *Making Sense of the Molly Maguires* (New York, 1997).

KEVIN KENNY

## MONTAGUE, JOHN [Patrick] (1929– )

Poet, critic, story writer, professor.

### EDUCATION

John Montague was born in Brooklyn, New York, the son of a republican father, James Montague, and Mary ("Molly") Carney, both of County Tyrone. In 1933 Montague was sent back to Ireland to live with his father's sisters in Garvaghey. He was schooled there and in Glencull and went on scholarship to St. Patrick's College, Armagh (1941–46), where he won a scholarship to University College, Dublin, studying with Roger McHugh and receiving a B.A. and M.A. (1946–51). Montague returned to the United States (1953–56) to study at Yale University, Indiana University, and at Paul Engle's Iowa Writers Workshop—including an excursion to Mexico.

### CAREER

After working at Bord Fáilte in Dublin, and later for *The Irish Times* in Paris, Montague returned to the United States to teach at the University of California, Berkeley (1964, 1965), and then taught Yeats and modern Irish poetry for Roger McHugh at University College, Dublin (1967–71) and the experimental Université de Vincennes, Paris. In 1972 he settled in Cork to raise a family and teach at University College, Cork (1972–88), taking temporary posts at the State University of New York (1974), University of Toronto (1975), the University of Vermont (1977), the Sorbonne (1982), Berkeley and the State University of New York (1987), which awarded him a D. Litt. in 1987. During this period Montague travelled three times to India, represented Ireland at cultural festivals in Britain and on the continent, and received the literary award of the Irish American Cultural Institute (1976) and a Guggenheim Fellowship (1980).

### WRITINGS

Excepting Padraic Colum of the generation before him, and perhaps Eamonn Wall or Paul Muldoon of the generation after him, John Montague may be counted as the most American of Irish poets, as his "circling failure to return" for good to his birthplace suggests. Montague's attention to his father's stymied republican politics informs his masterpiece *The Rough Field* (1972), and that epic sequence has its origins not only in the "Troubles" in Northern Ireland, but also in the motives for Irish diaspora, as shown in "The Cage" or "The Country Fiddler." Likewise, Montague's exposition of his "fosterage" and its familial griefs in *The Dead Kingdom* (1984) has roots in the wounds dealt by the very same diaspora. Montague's writing—from criticism to memoir, from story to poem—engages the often overlooked, intricate destiny of being Irish-American, as David Lampe's selections in *Born in Brooklyn: John Montague's America* (1991) suggest.

From *Forms of Exile* (1958) through *Time in Armagh* (1993), each of Montague's collections contains elements distilled from his engagement with the emotional and geological American landscape, with the experience of the Irish in America in the transition through the Kennedy years into the activist 1960s. Montague made his way through the established New Critical poetic into the "Beat" poetic that emerged—thanks to William Carlos Williams, Allen Ginsberg, Gary Snyder, and Kenneth Rexroth—after McCarthyism and the Korean War. He witnessed the first public reading of Ginsberg's *Howl*, for example, as well as the start of the Free Speech movement a decade later, before les Événements de Mai in Paris and incitement of the Ulster crisis, with its ambushes, sieges, and hunger strikes.

Perhaps the most clearly American in poetic tone and device of Montague's collections is *A Chosen Light* (1967), which, along with *Tides* (1971), was republished by Chicago's Swallow Press. In those poems, and in *All Legendary Obstacles* (1966), from Liam Miller's Dolmen Press, Montague tempers the American confessional style as he portrays the unravelling of his fifteeen-year marriage to Madeleine de Brauer, whom he met in the United States.

The aesthetic of *A Chosen Light* provides a key both to Montague's striving for exactitude and to his later confessional turns in *Tides*. In both collections Montague masters not only the contrasting rhetorics and the variable metric of American poetry, but also the aesthetic of "saying something/Luminously as possible"—no matter what the cost of such clarity. Montague's *The Love Poems* (1992) or *About Love* (1993), published in Toronto and New York respectively, and especially *The Great Cloak* (1978) depict both darkly and brightly his twenty-year marriage to Evelyn Robson, whom he married in Gloucester, Massachusetts, in 1972. That aesthetic receives its best prose statement in Montague's modest "Note on Rhythm" (1972).

Montague's engagement with American scenes and motifs, popular culture and poetics, shows strongly in the essays collected in *The Figure in the Cave* (1989) beginning with "Fellow Travelling with America" (1951) and "American Pegasus" (1959) and culminating in "The Impact of International Modern Poetry on Irish Writing" (1973) and "The Unpartitioned Intellect" (1985). Other uncollected essays and reviews give examples of Montague's insistent importation into Irish writing of American poetic means and literary methods. Likewise, his nurturing of the younger poets of Cork—among them Seán Dunne, Nuala Ní Dhomhnaill, and Thomas McCarthy—entailed passing on to them American modes and models. Conversely, early on Montague introduced such Dolmen poets as Austin Clarke and Thomas Kinsella to American readers in Henry Rago's *Poetry* (1959). Not collected are Montague's 1950s film reviews for the Dublin *Standard* that reflect his attention to the Hollywood renderings of the American Frontier and his affection for Zane Grey and the cowboy "flicks" of World War II in Northern Ireland. These Western motifs appear in the fiction of *Death of a Chieftain* (1965) and *A Love Present* (1997).

*See* Poetry, Irish-American

Works: *About Love: Poems* (Riverdale on Hudson, N.Y., 1993); *Born in Brooklyn: John Montague's America*, ed. David Lampe (Fredonia, N.Y., 1991); *Collected Poems* (Winston Salem, N.C.; Oldcastle, Co. Meath, 1995); *The Faber Book of Irish Verse*, ed. John Montague (London, 1974); *The Figure in the Cave*, ed. Antoinette Quinn (Syracuse, N.Y., 1989); *New Selected Poems* (Oldcastle, Co. Meath; Newcastle-upon-Tyne, 1989); *The Rough Field*, 5th ed. (Winston-Salem, N.C.; Oldcastle, Co. Meath; Newcastle upon Tyne, 1989).
Criticism: Robert F. Garratt, *Modern Irish Poetry: Tradition and Continuity from Yeats to Heaney* (Berkeley, 1986); Dillon Johnston, *Irish Poetry After Joyce* (Notre Dame, IN; Mountrath, 1985); John Montague Issue, ed. Christopher Murray, *Irish University Review*, 19: 1 (Spring 1989); *Hill Field: Poems and Memoirs for John Montague*, ed. Thomas Dillon Redshaw (Minneapolis; Oldcastle, Co. Meath, 1989); M. L. Rosenthal, *The New Poets: American and British Since World II* (New York, 1967).

THOMAS DILLON REDSHAW

# MONTANA

Let me begin with a discussion of myth. With the possible exception of Wyoming, Americans generally perceive Montana as the most quintessentially "western" of the states—"Marlboro Country," as it was once called; vast and splendid; rural; agricultural or pastoral; and peopled, where it is peopled at all, by men and women descended from a narrow band of European national and ethnic "stock." Ignoring for the moment the racialist presumptions of the terms, that stock would have been identified as "Anglo-Saxon," "Aryan," or "Nordic." By whatever name, however, these westering people were a Protestant people. Indeed, their Protestantism was central to who and what they were. (See, e.g., Madison Grant, *The Conquest of a Continent, Or the Expansion of Races in America* [New York, 1933]; Josiah Strong, *Our Country* [orig. pub. 1886; Cambridge, Mass., 1963]; G. Edward White, *The Eastern Establishment and the Western Experience: The West of Frederic Remington, Theodore Roosevelt, and Owen Wister* [orig. pub. 1968; Austin, 1989]).

This aspect of the Western myth was both limited and limiting. It was also artificially contrived and imposed externally. (David M. Emmons, "Constructed Province: History and the Making of the Last American West," *Western Historical Quarterly*, XXV (Winter 1994), 437–488). But whatever its origins, it became the standard image of Montana and the last West. The Western hero, the character played by, say, John Wayne, did not go to Catholic Mass. The two images could not be juxtaposed without doing violence to the first. Americans could imagine Walter Brennan's character or Andy Devine's attending Mass, but even with them, there could be no public display of it. By definition, the nameless Mexican asleep under the tree attended Catholic services. But Walter Brennan and Andy Devine played "sidekicks"; they fetched and carried. The Mexican was even more clearly subordinate—in large measure because he did attend Mass. The heroes of the Western meta-narrative were nominal Protestants.

From the 1880s forward, they and their pioneering grit were contrasted sharply with the "new immigrants," mostly Catholics who were moving by the millions into the cities of the East. Discussions on this point of contrast were seldom civil and never without a powerful streak of nativist prejudice. From Josiah Strong and Frederick Remington to Owen Wister and Madison Grant, the West had become non-East, a place where "true" American values, Protestantism conspicuous among them, survived and flourished. Montana was and remains at the center of this West (Grant, *Conquest;* Strong, *Our Country;* White, *Eastern Establishment*).

Thus did Eastern image-makers invent a Montana of wide-open spaces, big mountains, and bigger skies, peopled by hardy pioneers. Hardy pioneer, however, resonated with Protestant, not so much for ecclesiastical or theological reasons—though there were some of those, too—but because the Catholic peoples of Europe were thought deficient in the requisite pioneering skills—tenacity, for example, manly courage, resiliency, and the ability to "go it alone." The Montana paladin was, by definition, a Protestant paladin, a descendant of the conquering races.

In 1971 the National Council of the Churches of Christ conducted a national census of church membership. The results for Montana, though unpublicized then or since, were wildly divergent from the state's image as the home of the staunchly individualistic sons and daughters of "old stock" Protestants. The council defined religious preference on the basis of forty percent of a county's population identifying themselves as belonging to a certain congregation, faith community, or denominational sect. The unchurched appear not to have been counted, but of those who professed a religious affiliation, Catholicism dominated in Montana to a quite remarkable extent.

Montana's fifty-six counties divided themselves into only three denominational categories: Lutheran, Catholic, and mixed Protestant. Eight of those fifty-six counties were Lutheran; eighteen were mixed Protestant; thirty were Catholic. If the populations of those counties are taken into account, the majority Catholic component of Montana's population is equally obvious. In 1970 the combined population of the thirty Catholic counties was over 391,000 or almost fifty-seven percent of the state's total population. These figures came as a surprise to scores of experts in Montana history who were asked to fill in the blanks in the denominational map of the state. No one of them even came close to an accurate accounting; indeed, no one of them assumed there were more than six Catholic counties! Old myths die hard. (Figures and map cited in Ellis Waldron and Paul Wilson, *Atlas of Montana Elections, 1889–1976* [Missoula, 1978], p. 153).

There are three possible explanations for these figures: huge numbers of Catholics moved into the state between, say, 1950 and 1970; thousands of Protestant pioneers converted to Catholicism; or Catholics were the dominant group from the beginnings of the territory until the 1971 survey. Only the last is possible. Montana is a Catholic state because the people who settled it and who still live in it were disproportionately Catholic.

But this is an essay on Irish not Catholics and the importance of the survey by the Church of Christ must be interpreted in terms of ethnicity not doctrine. Who were these Catholic people? Where did they come from? First of all, let it be noted with emphasis that there were many counties in eastern Montana whose Catholicism is explained by the immigration of large numbers of ethnic Germans from the Ukraine; there are many counties in western Montana with large French Canadian populations. Let it also be noted that all the counties with Indian reservations were Catholic. (There's an important story there, too, but not for present purposes.) But let it also be stated that the dominant ethnic group in the state and the most fruitful source of all of those Catholics was the Irish. They came early; they came in great numbers; and their descendants still call Montana home. Catholicism in the West generally may have been more an Irish than a Mexican institution, may have owed more to the Devotional Revolution in Ireland than to the folk Catholicism of Mexico, but it was surely such in Montana.

The origins of this Irish presence need to be explored. Like all the mountain West, Montana was a mining region. The first gold discoveries of the 1860s gave way to silver mining and milling in the '70s and finally to a long and prosperous copper mining and processing era lasting until the late 1970s. Add to the mines, mills, smelters, and refineries the railroads necessary to haul the ore and the finished products, and the image of Montana as one vast uninterrupted expanse of rangeland needs further revision (Michael Malone, Richard Roeder, and William Lang, *Montana, A History of Two Centuries* [Seattle, 1988]; David M. Emmons, "Social Myth and Social Reality," *Montana the Magazine of Western History,* 39 [Autumn, 1989], 2–9). But the important point here is that Irish Catholics participated fully in all of this industrial and commercial activity—and in the Indian removal and "pacification" that made it possible. The casualty lists from the Little Big Horn, for example, read like a gathering of the clans. Patricia Limerick's well-publicized contention that the white settlement of the West was more nearly a bloody conquest may be significantly overdrawn, but to the extent that conquest does define the westering experience, the Irish were the blunt instruments of that conquest (*The Legacy of Conquest: The Unbroken Past of the American West* [New York, 1987]). They were a conspicuous part of the frontier army; they helped build the railroads, haul the freight, mine and smelt the ores.

As those thirty Catholic counties would indicate, the Montana Irish were fairly well scattered about. Their headquarters, however, were clearly in the mining town of Butte, home of the giant Anaconda Copper Mining Company (ACM), at one time the producer of 40 percent of the world's copper. It would be easy to dismiss this most densely urban and intensely industrial place as a Western anomaly, the industrial exception that proves the agricultural rule. The problem with that is that Butte and ACM were so large and so economically dominant in Montana that the agricultural sections of the state become the anomalies and Butte the state's industrial norm. For most of the years between 1890 and 1960, fully one in every four Montanans lived in Butte; one in every three lived in Butte or the copper smelting and refining cities of Anaconda and Great Falls; one-half of the wage earners in the state worked for ACM with its corporate offices in the Hennessey Building in Butte. (See Michael Malone, *The Battle for Butte: Mining and Politics on the Northern Frontier, 1864–1906* [Seattle, 1981] and U.S Bureau of the Census, Population: Montana [Census years 1890–1940].)

But Butte was not just the home of ACM and its copper mines. It was also the most Irish town in America with a higher percentage of Irish per capita than Boston, New York, Philadelphia, Chicago, or San Francisco. Montana became one of the nation's most Irish Catholic states in large measure because Butte was so Irish and Catholic a town (David M. Emmons, *The Butte Irish: Class and Ethnicity in an American Mining Town, 1875–1925* [Urbana and Chicago, 1989]; James Paul Allen and Eugene James Turner, *We The People: An Atlas of America's Ethnic Diversity* [New York, 1988, 49–50]). The Irishness of the place was reflected in both the management of the Anaconda Company and the huge mine workforce the company assembled. To simplify the corporate genealogy of the company, the first four CEOs of ACM from 1876 until 1956 were Marcus Daly, William Scallon, John D. Ryan, and Cornelius Kelley. Each was Irish, Catholic and a member of one or both of Butte's major Irish associations, the Ancient Order of Hibernians, with three divisions; or the Robert Emmet Literary Society, Butte's chapter of the revolutionary Clan-na-Gael and the second largest chapter behind Chicago's in the United States. But the entire Anaconda boardroom, not just the head of the table, was disproportionately Irish. Managers of mines, smelters, lumber yards and timber lands, lawyers, metallurgists, foremen and shift bosses and other hiring officers—the whole management team of this fourth largest corporation in America—was dominated by associational Irish Catholics. Little wonder that waste rock from the Butte mines was known as "Protestant ore" (Emmons, *Butte Irish*).

Suggested by this is that Butte's Irish had more freedom to prosper than, say, Boston's; that the farther west an immigrant went, the better his or her prospects. There is some truth to this immigrant upraised thesis as applied to Montana's Irish, but there is a misleading aspect to it as well. There seems little doubt that the Irish who got to Montana early—in the 1870s or 1880s—did experience less overt prejudice, less, in fact, of any social presence at all, than those Irish who stayed in Eastern port cities or moved only to Midwestern industrial ones. Later Irish arrivals, however, encountered a built society, not one in the process of becoming, and the only advantages they had were those provided in the name of ethnic solidarity by the early arriving and prosperous Irish.

Ethnic solidarity, however, was not always enough to raise all the immigrants. A long running immigration tends to fragment an ethnic community on the basis of social class—early arrivals do well; later arrivals must break into the social system built by those who preceded them. For the Irish, this relationship, for all its b'hoy good fellowship, was essentially dependent and often filled with tension. Shared Irish ethnicity and religion—and a shared hatred of Britain—calmed some of those tensions but, as Montana's intra-Irish feuds would attest, not all of them.

As with every other aspect of Irish life in Montana, the best place to witness this complex interplay of Irish solidarity and Irish fragmentation was Butte. The ACM was Irish run, but so were the mine and smelter workforce and the unions that represented their interests. There can be no doubt that, for an Irishman, working for another Irishman in Butte was better than fighting through the "no Irish need apply" signs and working for a vestigial Know-Nothing in Boston. Certainly, the Irishmen understood this and their unions worked hard to protect the privileged position Irish miners held in Butte.

The largest and most influential of those Irish-run organizations was the Butte Miners Union, formed in 1878, destroyed by internal dissent in 1914, resurrected in 1934. From its 19th-century beginnings to its decline, fall, and rebirth, the BMU was led by Irishmen for a predominantly Irish workforce. But the labor movement of the entire state took its cues from the BMU. And there were times when Irish officers of the BMU, as well as the Montana State Trades and Labor Assemblies, joined Irish capitalists and employers in public displays of Irish nationalism, condemning British perfidy with a fine disregard for the social distance between them. There were also times when Irish employers clearly favored Irish job applicants, prompting the Montana branch of the nativist American Protective Association to bleat that "NO ENGLISH NEED APPLY" signs were posted on ACM mines.

But those times must be balanced against those perhaps more common times when Irish labor leaders condemned Irish capitalists as gombeen men and shoneens—exploiters and small-scale apers of British ways; too much can be made of interclass Irish harmony. There were wealthy and successful Montana Irish. Marcus Daly, born in County Cavan in 1841 and the founding father of ACM, may stand for all of them. There were also angry and rebellious Montana Irish who condemned Daly, his company, and the tendency of both to play on Irish themes in the interest of ACM profits. Ed Boyce, born in County Donegal in 1863 and an officer of both the Butte Miners Union and president of the potentially radical Western Federation of Miners, may stand for them.

These tensions were a part of the Montana Irish story—rather like faction fights in medieval Ireland. But despite them, the combination of Irish-owned mines and Irish-dominated miners that was unique to Butte was a powerful attraction to westering Irish. There can be no doubt that Marcus Daly and all of those Irish-hiring officers who worked for his Anaconda Company were primarily responsible for the Irish presence in Butte and, though less directly, the entire state. As the Irish-born Father Patrick Brosnan wrote to his father in 1918: "Marcus Daly was the man that made Butte an Irish town. . . . He did not care for any man but an Irishman and . . . did not give a job to anyone else." For job-hungry Irish in the late 19th century that was all the allure Montana needed. (The preceding paragraphs were drawn from *ibid.*)

But Daly and high-paying jobs in his mines were not the state's only appeal to the Irish. Others were drawn by the agricultural possibilities of the region and here the name of Thomas Francis Meagher must be added to that of Daly. Meagher was governor of the Montana Territory from 1863 until 1867. By the time of his governorship, Meagher, a Waterford native, had been convicted of treason for his involvement in the Irish Rising of 1848, transported to the penal colony of Van Damien's Land, escaped and gone to New York. There he edited a newspaper, organized an Irish battalion and led it at Fredericksburg in the Civil War, and was appointed secretary to the governor of the newly created Montana Territory. When the governor left unexpectedly, Meagher took over executive responsibilities. In 1867 he drowned in the Missouri River outside Fort Benton, Montana, likely the victim of Irish, Catholic, and Democratic hating vigilantes. It had been a busy life (Robert G. Athearn, *Thomas Francis Meagher: An Irish Revolutionary in America* [orig. pub. 1949; New York, 1976]).

Even prior to his arrival in Montana, Meagher had proposed that the territory be used as a place to colonize the often desperately poor Irish of the Eastern cities. He had told Bishop Thomas Grace of St. Paul that he intended to settle Montana's agricultural and pastoral lands with as many dispossessed Irish as he could persuade to come. This proposal, when it became known in the Territory, may have been his undoing, but before he died he managed to bring Montana to the attention of countless thousands of Irish. If Butte's Irish are a result of Daly's efforts, then the Irish agricultural settlements of Shonkin, Charlo, and outside Plentywood, among others, may perhaps be the indirect results of Meagher's (*Ibid.,* 143–44).

Whether found in mines, boardrooms, or farms, Montana's Irish gave frequent and often segregant expression to their Irishness, most often by forming Irish-American fraternal associations. Butte's Irish were without question the most active, and not only in Montana; the Robert Emmet Literary Association, the Butte camp of the Clan-na-Gael was the most generous in America in its support of Irish republicanism and direct action to achieve it. But Clan-na-Gael camps in Anaconda, Great Falls, and Helena were almost as committed to the liberation of the homeland. And Irish throughout the state formed Ancient Order of Hibernian divisions that were only slightly less advanced in their nationalism than the Clan (Emmons, *Butte Irish*).

Both Clan and AOH, however, were more (and less) than nationalist organizations. They were self-help fraternities that attempted to socialize the uncertainties of Montana life, getting newly arrived Irish jobs—or trying to; paying out sick and death benefits; holding wakes; and paying off mortgages. It was also they who raised the money for the equestrian statue of Meagher that still stands before the state capitol in Helena; Marcus Daly, appropriately, was the chairman of the fund-raising committee. They also sponsored parades and fetes of various kinds, commemorating everything from St. Patrick's Day and the anniversary of the Manchester Martyrs to Miners Union Day, the Fourth of July and, in Butte, New Year's Eve with a gala ball hosted for more than seventy years by the Robert Emmets (*Ibid;* Emmons, "The Socialization of Uncertainty: The Ancient Order of Hibernians in Butte, Montana, 1880–1925." *Eire-Ireland,* XXIX [Fall, 1994], 74–92).

All of this would suggest that the Irish compelled the state to adjust to them as surely as they adjusted to it. Irish organizations, for example, were entirely segregant in the sense of being intraclass and inter-ethnic. Only Irish needed apply, but all Irish were encouraged to. Butte was a special case, but the entire state took a variety of social and cultural cues from that most Irish of cities. There was a striking correlation between the "Catholic" or liturgical counties and a permissive attitude toward such issues as liquor, gambling, and prize fighting, a correlation even more striking when the Catholicism of a county was the result of its Irish population. Conversely, those counties with mixed Protestant or Lutheran majorities were far more "pietistic" or restrictive in their attitudes toward those same issues. Culture wars are not simply recent phenomena in Montana or elsewhere, and Irish Catholics were culture warriors long before the 1970s (Waldron and Wilson, *Atlas*, 153).

But the Irish Catholic influence may also have been felt indirectly, and unwittingly. Other Catholic ethnic groups, for example, may have been more willing to settle in Montana because the Church was in place, both at the diocesan and parish levels; they may also have been more self-conscious as a result of Irish assertiveness. Similarly, the Irish concept of *muintir*—of community carefully crafted and tenaciously sustained—may have become a part of the cultural values of any number of non-Irish. Related to the liturgical-pietistic split noted above, Butte's well-deserved reputation for toughness and rowdiness, shorn of its Irishness, was easily transferred to the entire state. It was a Butte Irishman, Neil Lynch, who once observed that without Butte, no one would be able to tell the difference between Montana and North Dakota. He was only half kidding.

The numerical dominance of the Catholic Church in Montana has already been noted; the powerful role of Irish-run labor unions has been hinted at. But as enduring a legacy—and related directly to Irish ethnicity, Catholicism, and unions—may be the state's strong and, until very recently, lasting commitment to the Democratic Party. Irish-American allegiance to the Democrats has been much chronicled. Irish Montana was no exception to the national rule. Distrustful of Republicanism for its open dalliance with nativism in the 1850s, 1890s, and 1920s, Montana's Irish of every social class—millionaire capitalists included—gave unwavering support to the Democratic Party. There was an occasional backlash from the non-Catholic counties, but, though the dominance of the Democrats in Montana can be attributed to a variety of forces, one of them must be the solidly Democratic returns from Butte, Anaconda, Great Falls, Phillipsburg, and Missoula—the Irish heartland. Montana's Irish Catholic Democrats, including Senators James Murray and Mike Mansfield and Congressman Pat Williams, to mention only three, looked and often acted more like Eastern or Midwestern pols than like any fictive and stereotypical Western politician—another aspect of the western myth that needs more attention and correction (Waldron and Wilson, *Atlas*, passim).

Implied, then, by Neil Lynch's remark is that Butte not only distinguished Montana from North Dakota—or any place else he might have imagined—it made Montana Montana. It provided the state with its character and, it must be added, a disproportionate share of its characters. There were always some who were unhappy with Butte's dominance; Joseph Kinsey Howard, for example, called the city Montana's "black heart." He got it half right (*Montana: High, Wide, and Handsome* [New Haven, 1943], 85). But like it or not, Montana does not fit the image that has been assigned it, largely because Irish Butte fits no known Western image at all. In important ways, Montana was Butte writ large. Which recalls another analogy that is often used to describe the state: With its huge expanse and sparse population, Montana has been likened to a medium-sized city with very long streets. It's

not a bad description. But add to it another reality: There are Irish on every corner.

*See* Labor Movement

Robert Athearn, *Thomas Francis Meagher: An Irish Revolutionary in America* (Orig. pub. 1949; New York, 1976).

David M. Emmons, *The Butte Irish: Class and Ethnicity in an American Mining Town, 1875–1925* (Urbana and Chicago, 1989).

———, "Constructed Province: History and the Making of the Last American West," *Western Historical Quarterly*. (Winter, 1994) 437–459.

———, "Social Myth and Social Reality," *Montana the Magazine of Western History* (Autumn, 1989): 2–9.

———, "The Socialization of Uncertainty: The Ancient Order of Hibernians in Butte, Montana, 1880–1925." *Eire-Ireland* (Fall, 1994): 74–92.

Joseph Kinsey Howard, *Montana: High, Wide, and Handsome* (New Haven, 1943).

Patricia Nelson Limerick, *The Legacy of Conquest: The Unbroken Past of the American West* (New York, 1987).

Michael Malone, Richard Roeder, and William Lang, *Montana, A History of Two Centuries* (Seattle, 1988).

Michael Malone, *The Battle for Butte: Mining and Politics on the Northern Frontier, 1864–1906* (Seattle, 1981).

Ellis Waldron and Paul Wilson, *Atlas of Montana Elections, 1889–1976* (Missoula, 1978).

G. Edward White, *The Eastern Establishment and the Western Experience: The West of Frederic Remington, Theodore Roosevelt, and Owen Wister* (Orig. pub. 1968; Austin, 1989).

DAVID M. EMMONS

## MOONEY, THOMAS JOSEPH (1882–1942)

Labor radical. Born the eldest of three children to Bernard and Mary (Hefferon, or Heffernan). His father was an Irish immigrant who worked as a coal miner in Indiana. Mooney attended parochial and public schools before being forced to work in a factory at the age of fourteen. It was in the factory that the young Mooney learned the skill of iron molding, and he eventually joined the trade union.

Mooney traveled to Europe in 1907 and converted to Socialism. When he returned to the United States, he became a proponent of Socialism and campaigned for the cause in the 1908 presidential campaign. Mooney became involved in various radical and labor groups, some of which included the San Francisco Socialists and the Industrial Workers of the World. In 1913, Mooney joined a long and often violent strike of electrical workers against Pacific and Electric Company. Mooney's involvement soon caused him trouble; he was charged with being involved in a bombing incident during the San Francisco Preparedness Day parade in July of 1916. Mooney was convicted of first-degree murder and efforts at retrial were not granted. He was sentenced to death by hanging.

Mooney's case gained much international interest and he was able to gather petitioners for his cause. Some of Mooney's supporters protested his conviction by marching on the American embassy in Petrograd in 1917, and President Wilson then urged California's governor to retry Mooney's case. Mooney's sentence was commuted to life imprisonment in 1918 and, while the interest in his case waned, he still retained several steadfast supporters. Upton Sinclair, while campaigning for governor, promised to free Mooney if elected; similarly, efforts at appeal were made to the Supreme Court on the grounds that his conviction depended upon a perjured witness.

Mooney was finally pardoned by Culbert Olson, Democratic governor, on January 7, 1939. After his pardon, Mooney suffered from financial debt and died in California in 1942.

*See* Labor Movement

Richard H. Frost, *The Mooney Case* (1968).
Ernest J. Hopkins, *What Happened in the Mooney Case* (1932).
*Dictionary of American Biography,* supplement 3.

JOY HARRELL

## MOORE, BRIAN (1921–1999)

Author. Brian Moore, whose publishing career spanned five decades, was born August 25, 1921, and grew up in Belfast, Northern Ireland. Despite his Catholic upbringing, his paternal heritage was Protestant, gesturing towards a cultural ambivalence strengthened by subsequent travels as a journalist. He immigrated to Canada in 1948, taking citizenship, but spent much time abroad, particularly in California. Claimed as their own by Irish, Canadian, and American alike, Moore styled himself as a nomad, in exile permanently from Ireland. This simultaneous rejection of and desire for origins are mirrored in the spiritual restlessness of his novels' protagonists.

*The Lonely Passion of Judith Hearne* (1955) was his first novel of serious acclaim. Grimly realistic, it depicts the spiritual and imaginative poverty of a culture, Protestant and Catholic alike, shackled to joyless religion and social conformity. Moore's Belfast makes an apt comparison with James Joyce's *Dubliners* as the center of a paralysis evident also in *The Feast of Lupercal* (1957) and *The Emperor of Ice-Cream* (1965). With *Fergus* (1970) and *Catholics* (1972), but particularly with *The Great Victorian Collection* (1975), we note a new direction in his fiction away from the realism for which he had become acclaimed to an exploration of the frankly miraculous. In Moore's hands, Catholicism renders blind superstition and pure miracle dangerously akin, and never more so than in its central sacrament, the Eucharist, where mundane matter mystically transforms into sacred reality. In *GVC*, the nonreligious Tony Maloney dreams in Carmel, California, of a collection of victoriana only to discover, upon waking, that a "secular miracle" has occurred and the dream has become a tangible fact. *Cold Heaven* (1983) also renders Carmel as the scene of miracle, with Marie, unbelieving and adulterous, chosen to witness a vision of the Virgin. Apparently in retribution for her resistance to the vision, her husband is killed, only to return from the dead in order that she may believe. Our willing suspension of disbelief is pressed to extremity as Moore affronts credulity and challenges the boundary between faith and reason, miracle and coincidence. He himself noted the analogy between his protagonists and himself as novelist, saying of *GVC* that the book chose him. The character who glimpses the possibility of miracle is inevitably the least likely: unremarkable, skeptical, these prosaic failures are, nonetheless, elected by some cosmic power ("God" seems too benign a term) to be the instrument of mystery. The trial of faith is bound up with the trial, triumph, and failure of individual identity. *Black Robe* (1985) depicts the sad and sometimes comical clash between the beliefs and value systems of the local tribes of Champlain's "New France" and the besieged faith of a young Jesuit priest. Despite the untranslatability of the cultures—Father Laforgue can find no way to explain baptism, which the Huron see as water sorcery for the plague—he eventually rediscovers some inner peace and wonder in belief.

"Mystery," for Moore, was a palpable phenomenon and one that thrived, ironically, on realism. The "mystery" thriller, with its semiotics of intrigue, seems a natural form for his narratives. *The Statement* (1995), featuring a pro-Nazi French collaborator on the run from a mysterious Jewish commando unit, explores the spiritual and moral interior of that which is as unthinkable to ethics as miracles are to reason. His thrillers, published in succession, unfold in highly charged contemporary political scenes: *Color of Blood* (1987), *Lies of Silence* (1990), set in terrorist Belfast, and *No Other Life* (1993). In this last, the political and spiritual conflate by representing the president, Jeannot Cantave (note his initials), as a Christ-figure. Here faith, in its broadest dimension, emerges as a political as much as doctrinal possibility.

Alongside these themes, which, bodied thus, might risk collapsing the distinctness of each novel, one notes the painstaking detail of his remarkably diverse settings. This "nomad" writer wanders through centuries, continents, and arcane knowledges, writing about each new world as if it were the first and only. His carefully individuated landscapes transform into an existential place in which the protagonists encounter the darker consequences of self, belief, and destiny. In this respect, his fiction compares with that of Graham Greene, whose extrovert imagination is also powered by the eyes of a journalist. Moore wrote nonfiction that, although considered separate by him from his serious work, often blurs boundaries between genres, and does so especially in *The Revolution Script* (1971), a docu-novel about the kidnapping of James Cross in 1970 by the Front de Libération du Québec. In the 1950s, Moore wrote pulp fiction for income, distancing it from his "serious" work by the use of pseudonyms, "Bernard Mara" and "Michael Bryan." This distance between his "escape" and his "serious" fiction, although commonly accepted, should not be made into too much of a dogma, for the sheer craft of storytelling is one of Moore's great strengths and cuts across any such divide. Evident throughout his work, but perhaps most so in his later novels up to his most recent, *The Magician's Wife* (1997), where prestidigitation transfigures into political alchemy and then miracle itself, Moore's own "magic" of fiction-making offers us his ultimate and most artful effecting of the transmutation of reality.

Other novels by Brian Moore: *The Luck of Ginger Coffey* (1960); *An Answer from Limbo* (1962); *I Am Mary Dunne* (1968); *The Doctor's Wife* (1976); *The Mangan Inheritance* (1979); *The Temptation of Eileen Hughes* (1981).

The major research resource is the archives of Brian Moore's work held in the Special Collections Division of the University of Calgary.
Hallvard Dahlie, *Brian Moore* (Boston: Twayne, 1981).
Jo O'Donoghue, *Brian Moore: A Critical Study* (Dublin: Gill and Macmillan, 1990).
Robert Sullivan, *A Matter of Faith: The Fiction of Brian Moore* (Westport, CT: Greenwood, 1996).

VALERIE ALLEN

## MOORE, JOHN (1834–1901)

Roman Catholic bishop. Born in Rosmead, County Westmeath, Ireland, Moore left Ireland after his elementary schooling and went to Charleston, South Carolina, in 1848 where he attended the Collegiate Institute and the Seminary of St. John the Baptist. Later, Moore went to Urban College in Rome and was ordained in April of 1860. He then returned to Charleston and worked in St. Finbar's Cathedral under Bishop P. N. Lynch.

Like his bishop, Moore was a staunch Confederate and his Southern sympathies led him to refuse an oath of allegiance to the Union, causing him trouble and eventually postal censure by the government. However, he persisted in his ministry, acting as a confessor and nurse during the Civil War for both sides. Moore was appointed and consecrated second bishop of St. Augustine in May of 1877 and proved to be an effective administrator during his ministry. When the cathedral burned the same year, Moore organized efforts for reconstruction. In 1888, at the outbreak of the yellow fever epidemic, he worked tirelessly as an aid to those suffering.

Bishop Moore is remembered for his advocacy of immigration and his openness to relations with other ministers of differing denominations. In 1884 he was appointed as a member of the Third Plenary Council of Baltimore and helped carry its decrees to Rome. He died on July 30, 1901.

J. G. Shea, *The Hierarchy of the Catholic Church in the U.S.* (1886).
F. J. Zwierlein, *The Life and Letters of Bishop McQuaid,* 3 vols. (1925–1927).
*Dictionary of American Biography,* 13.

JOY HARRELL

## MOORE, MARIANNE (1887–1972)

Poet, essayist, translator. Marianne Moore was born November 15, 1887, in St. Louis, Missouri. Her father, John Milton Moore, left the family when Moore was an infant; she grew up, with her mother, Mary Warner Moore, in the home of her grandfather, John R. Warner, a Presbyterian minister. In 1894 the family moved to Carlisle, Pennsylvania. Moore received her education there, at the Metzger Institute, and then at Bryn Mawr. Following graduation, in 1909, she entered Carlisle Commercial College where she taught stenography until 1915 in the commercial department of the United States Indian School. In 1918 she moved to New York, working for a time as a tutor and secretary before, in 1921, becoming an assistant at the Hudson Park branch of the New York Public Library, a position she held until 1925.

While in New York, Moore attended meetings in Greenwich Village where she established relationships with other young poets, Wallace Stevens and William Carlos Williams among them. Her verse began to appear in journals, first in *The Egoist* and *Poetry,* and in Alfred Kreymborg's anthology, *Others* (1915). In 1921, her first book, *Poems,* was published without her knowledge by friends at the Egoist Press. Her second volume, *Marriage,* appeared in 1923; of it T. S. Eliot was to write: "I can only think of five contemporary poets—English, Irish, French and German— whose works excite me as much or more than Miss Moore's."

By 1920 Moore had begun to publish in the *Dial,* and in 1925 she received the review's award for "distinguished service to American letters" for *Observations* (1924). In that year, she became acting editor of the journal and remained with it until its demise in 1929. *Selected Poems* appeared in 1935, bearing high tribute again from Eliot in his introduction: "Miss Moore's poems form part of the small body of durable poetry written in our

Marianne Moore

time"; he furthermore ranked her as "one of those few who have done the language some service in my lifetime."

In 1947, Moore became a member of the National Institute of Arts and Letters. In 1951, her *Collected Poems* received the Bollingen and Pulitzer prizes and the National Book Award. Her translations of La Fontaine's *Fables* appeared in 1954, followed by *Predilections*, a collection of reviews and essays, in the following year. She was elected to the American Academy in 1955. In her later life, Moore enjoyed a certain celebrity, admired by readers and critics for her wit, for her undeviating standards, and for a modest eccentricity. She died in New York on February 5, 1972.

### POETRY

In a postscript to her *Selected Poems*, Moore writes: "In my immediate family there is one 'who thinks in a particular way'; and I should like to add that where there is an effect of thought or pith in these pages, the thinking and often the actual phrases are hers." Moore is speaking of her mother, but the phrase, thinking "in a particular way," is an apt description of the poet's own style. With its emphasis on the detail and the concrete commonplace, her art relishes in the particulars of life, creating "imaginary gardens with real toads in them" ("Poetry"). One "particular way" Moore has thought about poetry is as "the lion's leap" (from her essay "Feeling and Precision," *Predilections*, 1955), the deadly grace of which would be "mitigated almost to harmlessness if the lion were clawless, so precision is both impact and exactitude, as with surgery." Furthermore, "you can't be exact by being restrained." That said, a technique of restraint with exactitude as its aim informed her verse from its beginning. Detectable, too, is the mixture of strong feeling and precision—of passion without pretension, precision in abnegation. She distrusts the showy; "high-sounding interpretations" she "dislike[s]" ("Poetry"). Eschewing both the lavish and the florid, in her "gardens" she prefers "models of exactness," advising that "there is a great amount of poetry in unconscious / fastidiousness" ("Critics and Connoisseurs"). An avid lover of animals and athletes (she was as frequently to be seen at the Bronx Zoo as at Ebbets Field watching her favorite baseball team, the Brooklyn Dodgers), Moore's poems read at times like bestiaries, at others like quiet paeans to mastery discovered in unexpected places, and still at others like miscellanies of obscure lore drawn from obscurer sources. Her talent was a yoking, with graceful vigor, the virtues of poetry and prose; lyricism measured in plain-spoken syllables; what Patrick Kavanagh called "the passionate transitory" dealt out with the cool regularity of scientific method. Her "predilection" for the factual nugget is evidence of her passion; she "detects" new worlds of "marvelous specifics," of "what had been seen before but seen without feeling." And as Jean Garrigue has observed, "This is to say it had not been seen before" (*Marianne Moore*, University of Minnesota Press, 1965). Highly influential in her own generation—one that included such literary giants as Pound, Eliot, Williams, and Stevens—she exerted as profound an influence on the talented generation that followed. Writers as diverse as Robert Lowell, Ted Hughes, Elizabeth Bishop, Donald Hall, Howard Nemerov, and John Crowe Ransom have acknowledged a debt to her unerring vision in their works.

Marianne Moore, *Poems* (London, 1921).
———, *Observations* (New Yorkl, 1924).
———, *What Are Years* (New York, 1941).
———, *The Fables of La Fontaine* (New York, 1954).
———, *A Marianne Moore Reader* (New York, 1961).
———, *Complete Poems* (New York, 1967).
———, *The Selected Letters of Marianne Moore*, ed. Bonnie Costello (New York, 1997).
Craig S. Abbot, *Marianne Moore: A Descriptive Bibliography* (University of Pittsburgh, 1977).

TODD HEARON

## MORAN, MARY CONCILIA (1930–1990)

Administrator, lecturer, religious leader. Anne Amelia (Mary Concilia) Moran was born August 7, 1930, in Altoona, Pennsylvania. She and a twin brother joined two other siblings. Her parents, Elmer and Velma (Ivory) Moran, were first generation Irish-Americans. Anne received an elementary and secondary education in schools staffed by the Sisters of Mercy of the Union—Scranton Province. She entered this Roman Catholic religious congregation in the fall of 1948.

A woman of much energy and considerable talent, Concilia Moran taught elementary students in schools in the Harrisburg Diocese; served as Director of the Mercy Hospital School of Nursing in Johnstown, PA; and then as administrator of that hospital. In 1970, she was elected Provincial Administrator of the 800-member Scranton Province. One year later she was elected the youngest Administrator General of the six-thousand member congregation of the Sisters of Mercy of the Union. During her six-year term she addressed national and international challenges which the post–Vatican II Roman Catholic Church posed for religious women.

Concilia Moran challenged both institutions and religious congregations to reevaluate the role of religious sponsorship and the fundamental purpose of Catholic health care. "It is not easy," she said, "to question the effectiveness of our ministry when to question at all opens the possibility that we are not what we claim to be; but question we must."

Concilia Moran died on January 7, 1990, after a long and courageous struggle against cancer. The eulogy delivered by Helen Amos, President of the Sisters of Mercy of the Union, described Concilia as one "unafraid to walk where there was no path."

*See* Sisters of Mercy

Mary Regina Werntz, *Our Beloved Union* (Westminster, Maryland, 1989).
———, *Union Scope* (1971–1977).

HELEN MARIE BURNS, R.S.M.

## MORRIS, CHARLES RICHARD (1939–   )

Author, journalist, lawyer, businessman, public servant. Born on October 23, 1939, in Oakland, California. Raised in Philadelphia, he attended grammar school and high school in that city. After graduating from the University of Pennsylvania in 1961, Morris worked in New Jersey as Director of the State Office of Economic Opportunity, Director of the State Drug Addiction Programs and Director of the Community Action Agency in Trenton.

In 1969, he went to work in New York City. He served in a variety of positions in city government. For the next four years he served as Director of the city's welfare, Medicaid and food programs. In addition Morris was Acting Director of City Social Service Programs and Assistant Budget Director for the City of New York. While commuting between New York and Philadelphia, Morris received his law degree from the University of Pennsylvania, and was admitted to the bar in New York and Washington.

Between 1973 and 1976, Morris served as Director of Social and Health Services for the state of Washington. While there he was in charge of the state prison and juvenile correction systems, as well as state institutions for the mentally ill, developmentally disabled and aged veterans. In addition he directed Washington's welfare, Medicaid and social service programs.

In 1976, Morris became an on-loan civil servant to the British Home Office. For the next two years, he, his wife and three children lived in London, where he was Director of the London Vera Institute of Justice. In this capacity he coordinated relations between the Home Office and the Metropolitan Police. In addition, he helped to modify pretrial processing and detention procedures.

Upon returning to America, Morris joined Chase Manhattan Bank as vice president. From 1979 to 1983 he worked at Chase in corporate banking. He also worked in the field of international banking and trade. It was during this period that he wrote *The Cost of Good Intentions*, which was chosen by the *New York Times Book Review* as one of the "Best Books of 1980." This book is used in colleges and universities throughout the United States.

In 1983, Morris moved to the health care industry, where he was vice president of Sanus Corp. Health Systems. He managed the startup of the first for-profit, private-practice HMO's in Dallas and Houston. This business was later sold to New York Life in 1984. That same year Harper and Row published his second book, *A Time of Passion: America, 1960–1980*. An overview of the past two decades, the *New York Times* reviewer wrote that Morris "has a remarkable facility for elucidating such potentially murky subjects as economics and sociology." In 1987, his third book *Iron Destinies, Lost Opportunities* dealt with the Cold War and the arms race, and was praised in *Foreign Affairs* as "vividly told and richly documented."

Between 1985 and 1994, Morris was the Managing Partner for Devonshire Partners, Inc. Devonshire dealt with business valuation, market research services and consulting, primarily serving the banking community. Clients included Merrill Lynch, Equitable Capital Management and the Blackstone Group. He also developed technology-oriented market research and strategic consulting practice for clients such as Xerox, Apple and Texas Instruments. In addition, he performed consulting work for the pharmaceutical and biotechnology industries.

Increasingly, Morris has given more time to his first great love, writing. Since 1990 he has written four books, with one more forthcoming in 1999. *The Coming Global Boom* (1990) addressed international economics, and was chosen by the *New York Times Book Review* as one of the "Notable Books" of 1990. *Computer Wars* was co-authored with Charles H. Ferguson in 1993. The book, which focused on the fall of IBM, was selected by *Business Week* as "one of the Ten Best Business Books of 1993." 1996 saw the publication of his *The AARP: America's Most Powerful Lobby and the Coming Clash of Generations*, which was called "an invaluable case study" on the front-page of the *New York Times Book Review.*

For several years, Morris, born and raised a Catholic, had contemplated writing a book on American Catholicism. At a cocktail party, Morris says, "I fell into one of those intense Catholic conversations with a woman I was introduced to, and as we talked, an aide to Mario Cuomo came over. He listened for a few minutes, then asked: 'How do you pick each other out in a room like that?' It was a good question, and it got me to thinking about Catholics as a special kind of tribe."

After several years of research and interviews with leading American Catholic spokespersons, Morris wrote *American Catholic: The Saints and Sinners Who Built America's Most Powerful Church*. Morris' book was immediately hailed in both popular and academic circles as one of the best single-volume histories of American Catholicism ever written. What made the book so popular was Morris' own engaging writing style, as well as his use of a variety of disciplines and sources, among them oral history, sociology, theology and history. The *New York Times* and the *Washington Post* enthusiastically endorsed *American Catholic*. One historian hailed it as "an important book," while *America* described it as "something truly exceptional." The book has become required reading in religious studies programs throughout the country.

In addition to his books, Morris has written regularly for a variety of journals, including the *Los Angeles Times*, the *Wall Street Journal*, the *Atlantic Monthly* and the *New York Times*. He has also appeared on television and radio shows such as NPR, CNN, and NBC's Today Show.

Charles R. Morris, *The Cost of Good Intentions: New York City and the Liberal Experiment, 1960–1975* (New York, 1980).

————, *A Time of Passion: America, 1960–1980* (New York, 1984).

————, *Iron Destinies, Lost Opportunities: The Arms Race Between the United States and the Soviet Union, 1945–1987* (New York, 1988).

————, *The Coming Global Boom* (New York, 1990).

———— (with Charles H. Ferguson), *Computer Wars: The Fall of IBM and the Future of Global Technology* (New York, 1993).

————, *The AARP: America's Most Powerful Lobby and the Coming Clash of Generations* (New York, 1996).

————, *American Catholic: The Saints and Sinners Who Built America's Most Powerful Church* (New York, 1997).

————, *Money, Greed, and Risk* (New York, 1999).

PATRICK J. McNAMARA

## MOYLAN, STEPHEN (1737–1811)

Revolutionary War soldier. The son of a successful merchant, Stephen Moylan was born in Cork, Ireland, in 1737. Completing his Catholic education at Paris because of England's penal laws, Moylan traveled to Lisbon where he spent three years in the shipping industry. He was remarkably successful and turned to the American colonies in 1768 where his wealth and social prestige allowed him to move freely among Philadelphia's elite. In 1771, Moylan was elected the first President of the Friendly Sons of St. Patrick.

Moylan became a zealous patriot four years later when the Revolutionary War broke out. He was muster-master general under General George Washington and fitted out a number of privateers who were to sabotage British shipping in the early years of the war. In March of 1776, Moylan became General Washington's secretary, and by June, Congress had selected him to succeed Thomas Mifflin as quarter-master general. In this position, Moylan worked to reorganize the army, but was frustrated by opposition from Congress. In protest, he resigned, and drafted a long letter to Washington explaining his reasons. He continued to serve as a volunteer, however, and with special distinction served at the battle of Princeton.

In 1776 Washington turned again to Moylan to organize and lead a regiment to join the American cavalry under the Polish General Casimir Pulaski. Pulaski and Moylan often quarreled over strategy, however, which led to Moylan's trial by court martial in 1877. The Irish privateer was acquitted, and when General Pulaski resigned in the spring of 1778, Washington asked Moylan to be his replacement. Troop numbers were low and the equipment was rough, but Moylan turned his men into an effective fighting force. They joined Lafayette in Virginia in 1781 until Cornwallis surrendered to Washington at Yorktown on October 18. Congress made Moylan a brigadier-general after the war and in his retirement served again as President of the Friendly Sons of St. Patrick. Moylan died in 1811, leaving behind his wife, Mary Ricketts Van Horn of Phil's Hill, N.J.

*See* American Revolution

Marquis de Chastellux, *Travels in North America* (Chapel Hill, [1787] 1963).

Martin I. J. Griffin, *Stephen Moylan* (Philadelphia, 1909).

Frank Monaghan, "Stephen Moylan in the American Revolution," in *Studies: an Irish Quarterly Review* (Dublin, September 1930).

*Poulson's American Daily Advertiser* (April 16, 1811).

DANIEL J. KUNTZ

## MOYNIHAN, DANIEL PATRICK (1927–  )

Educator, ambassador, senator. Daniel Patrick (Pat) Moynihan overcame a difficult childhood to become a notable figure in academia, high-profile diplomat and member of the United States Senate. He was born in Tulsa, Oklahoma, March 16, 1927, son of John H. and Margaret A. (Phillips) Moynihan, and grew up in straightened circumstances in New York City. His father, a former Tulsa newspaperman, deserted the family when Moynihan was an infant, leaving his wife to raise the family on income from a tavern she owned and managed. Young Moynihan did his bit, shining shoes on Broadway and hawking newspapers in bars. He graduated first in his class from Benjamin Franklin High School in Harlem, worked as a longshoreman, briefly attended

Daniel Patrick
Moynihan

City College of New York, then enlisted in the Navy in 1944. After military service he studied at Tufts University, receiving a bachelor's degree in 1948, and a master's degree in 1949 from its Fletcher School of Law and Diplomacy. A doctoral degree would follow in 1961. Moynihan also studied as a Fulbright Fellow at the London School of Economics in 1950–1951.

In the 1950s Moynihan worked in secretarial positions to Governor W. Averell Harriman of New York, and in the 1960s he wrote several papers on urban affairs for the presidential campaign of Senator John F. Kennedy. Once president, Kennedy named him special assistant to Secretary of Labor Arthur Goldberg. Moynihan advanced subsequently to the position of assistant secretary of labor, and with Sargent Shriver, James Sundquist and Adam Yarmolinski, he helped draft the legislation that later under President Johnson became the Equal Opportunity Act.

Meanwhile, Moynihan attracted wide public attention for a 1963 book, *Beyond the Melting Pot,* written with Nathan Grazer, that dealt with ethnic group dynamics and the failure of some groups to be assimilated into the American mainstream, and two years later for a Labor Department study that, among other things, contended that black children were hindered educationally by the absence of a father figure in the home. The latter study—formally titled "The Negro Family: The Case for National Action," but commonly known as the Moynihan Report—was severely criticized by African-American leaders for what was interpreted as negative inferences on the black way of life. Moynihan countered that a broad phenomenon was at work, and that the country (and other parts of the world as well) was experiencing a "momentous" change in social behavior, one still not yet fully grasped. One evidence of this change, in Moynihan's logic, was the rising number of nonmarital births, which by some estimates could reach 50 percent in the United States by the year 2004. Moynihan's concerns about the American family, once "denounced, rejected, and seen as refuted," are now taken with great seriousness, including on the presidential level.

In 1966 Moynihan was named director of the Joint Center for Urban Affairs at Massachusetts Institute of Technology and Harvard, and subsequently became a professor of government at the Kennedy School of Government at Harvard. He left Harvard in 1969 to join the Nixon administration as Counsellor to the President for Urban Affairs—a surprising move given his background as a liberal Democrat and that just months before he was associated with the presidential campaigns of Robert F. Kennedy and Eugene J. McCarthy.

In the Nixon White House, Moynihan once again became a lightning rod of controversy, this time with a 1970 memorandum to the president suggesting that the issues of race in the country could benefit from a period of "benign neglect." The memorandum was leaked to the press and there was an outcry from the black community, who felt it demonstrated administration indifference to racial problems. Moynihan declared that the intent had been misunderstood, and that his message was meant for those administration officials whose comments on race were inciting rabid responses at both ends of the political spectrum.

Moynihan resigned his White House post in 1971 and returned to Harvard as a sociology professor, but in 1973 was back in public service as ambassador to India, serving in the post until 1975. Once again he returned to Harvard, but he was not to stay for long, being named that same year as the United States' Permanent Representative to the United Nations, with the rank and status of Ambassador Extraordinary and Plenipotentiary. President Ford made the appointment shortly after Moynihan published an article in *Commentary* magazine which criticized American diplomacy at the U.N. and contended it was time "that the American spokesman came to be feared in international forums for the truths he might tell." His bluntness continued at the U.N. with Moynihan complaining on one occasion that the General Assembly was "becoming a theater of the absurd" by adopting reports "riddled with untruths."

Moynihan resigned his U.N. post in February 1976, returned to Harvard, then announced he was running for United States Senator from the state of New York. It would be his second try at elective office, having lost in a bid for the Democratic nomination for president of the New York City Council in 1965. He was elected to the Senate in November 1976, defeating Republican incumbent James L. Buckley, and he has served there since.

Predictably, Moynihan's strength and influence in the Senate are in areas of domestic policy. His is an authoritative voice on issues such as social security solvency, deficit reduction, welfare reform, universal health care, tuition tax credits and the war on drugs. He is also a figure in the debate over income inequality and the implications of the sweeping changes in the composition of households.

As he closes his political career, the scholarly Daniel Patrick Moynihan is regarded as one of the great senators of the century and the country shares Michael Barone's judgment that Moynihan is "the nation's best thinker among politicians since Lincoln and the best politician among thinkers since Jefferson."

*Collier's Year Book* (New York, 1976).

Daniel Patrick Moynihan, *Miles to Go: A Personal History of Social Policy* (Cambridge, 1996).

Nelson Lichtenstein, Eleanora W. Schoenebaum, *et al.,* eds., *Political Profiles,* The Johnson and Nixon/Ford Years, two volumes (New York, 1976, 1979).

JOHN DEEDY

## MULHOLLAND, ST. CLAIR AUGUSTIN (1839–1910)

Soldier. Born on April 1, 1839, in Lisburn, County Antrim in Ireland, Mulholland immigrated to America with his parents as a boy. Settling in Philadelphia, Mulholland received his education there and, as a young man, joined the local militia.

As Civil War wracked the nation, Mulholland helped organize the One Hundred Sixteenth Pennsylvania Infantry to serve in the Federal army, and attained the rank of lieutenant colonel on June 26, 1862. The regiment was assigned to the Irish Brigade and during that unit's gallant charge up Marye's Heights on December 13, 1862, Mulholland received his first wound. Due to heavy casualties, the One Hundred Sixteenth was consolidated into a battalion with Mulholland recommissioned as its major. At Chancellorsville the following May, Mulholland recaptured a Union battery and later commanded the picket line which covered the withdrawal of the Army of the Potomac across the Rappahannock River. Major General Winfield Scott Hancock noted Mulholland's superb service during the battle and decades later, on March 26, 1895, Mulholland received the Congressional Medal of Honor for his bravery.

Mulholland became colonel of the reorganized One Hundred Sixteenth Pennsylvania, suffering his second wound at the Wilderness on May 5, 1864, and yet another on May 10. After recovering, the Irish colonel returned to his unit only to receive a severe wound at Totopotomy Creek on May 31. In mid-October, 1864, Mulholland assumed command of a Second Corps' brigade and commanded it through the Petersburg campaign. On October 27, 1864, Mulholland led his men in the capture of Confederate fortifications at the Boydton Plank Road, and for his gallantry in this action, he received a brevet promotion to brigadier general on March 13, 1865.

On June 3, 1865, Mulholland mustered out of service and returned to Philadelphia, where he served as the city's police chief from 1868–71. President Cleveland appointed Mulholland a pension agent in Philadelphia, a post he held for twelve years. Mulholland also expressed himself through art and devoted much energy to writing and speaking about the Civil War. He died on February 17, 1910.

*See* Civil War

David Power Conyngham, *The Irish Brigade and its Campaigns* (New York, 1867).

William Corby, *Memoirs of Chaplain Life* (Notre Dame, 1894).

St. Clair Augustin Mulholland, *The Story of the 116th Pennsylvania Volunteers in the War of the Rebellion* (Philadelphia, 1903).

*The War of the Rebellion: A Compilation of the Official Records of the Union and Confederate Armies,* 128 vols. (Washington, D.C., 1880–1901).

CHRISTIAN G. SAMITO

## MULVANY, JOHN (c. 1839–1906)

Painter. Born to a poor, landless family in pre-Famine Co. Westmeath, Mulvany emigrated to the U.S. at twelve years of age. He obtained an education in art somewhat informally at the National Academy of Design. From 1861 he worked in Chicago as a free-lance artist for Irish newspapers. He allegedly joined, or was associated with, the Union Army at the outbreak of the Civil War where he continued his art, sketching in the field. In this capacity, according to Tuite, he knew Custer, Logan and Sheridan. At the end of the war, he went to study in Dusseldorf, Munich and Antwerp. In Munich he studied under Piloty, the history painter and dramatic exponent of battle scenes; in Antwerp he studied with the Flemish battle painter de Keyser. On his return to the U.S. he resided at St. Louis, Chicago (where he lost the contents of his studio in the Great Fire) and Cincinnati, before moving to the Iowa-Nebraska border where he began his western paintings. *The Preliminary Trial of a Horse Thief—Scene in a Western Justice's Court* was exhibited at the National Academy of Design in 1876 and sold for an impressive $5,250.

Mulvany then moved to Kansas City where he spent two years working on *Custer's Last Rally,* commemorating the decisive defeat of General Custer by Native Americans on June 26, 1876, at Little Big Horn. (The existence of the original is unsure, or at least its location is unknown, but an artist's copy in poor condition may still be extant.) Mulvany sought maximum authenticity by making preliminary portrait studies of Custer and the officers, researching the costumes and artillery, visiting the battlefield and the Sioux reservation. Dated 1881, measuring 11 by 22 feet, it depicted Custer at the center of the vivid, crowded canvas, holding a revolver fully extended in one hand and a shining saber by his side in the other. His face registers both despair and courage. He stands erect, undaunted and sublime as he meets his foe. The painting then began its extensive peregrinations, and at its first stop in Boston, Mulvany was induced to make some modifications, following which it was commended for its realism, its fidelity to detail and its knowledge of contemporary American warfare. In New York it was seen by Walt Whitman, who eulogised its qualities at length in the *New York Tribune.* In Louisville the *Courier-Journal* described Mulvany as nothing less than a genius. And the painting continued on to Chicago where it was lithographed and exhibited with a number of other works by Mulvany, including *The Scouts of the Yellowstone.* Some seventeen years later the painting was still on the move. Other Western subject pictures include *Lynch Law, Back to the Wigwam, Perils of the Pony Express*, and *Sheridan's Ride from Winchester.* In addition, Mulvany was an accomplished and prolific portrait painter, painting portraits of Brigham Young, Robert Emmet and Sitting Bull, amongst others. But it was from *Custer's Last Rally* (which was ultimately purchased by H. J. Heinz of Pittsburgh in 1898 who subsequently commissioned Mulvany to make the duplicate) that Mulvany apparently made a fortune. Other of his paintings include, *Love's Mirror, The Old Professor, A Discussion of the Tariff Question, Sunrise, On the Rocky Mountains* and *The Striker.*

His Irish political pictures, such as *The Battle of Aughrim* and *The Anarchists,* continued his exploration of the heroic at key political moments in history. Strong nationalist views were inculcated during his early schooling in Ireland and were strengthened by his association with exiled Irish Fenians such as John Devoy and with Clan na Gael. *The Battle of Aughrim* was probably commissioned by the Irish American Club of Chicago in 1883.

Notwithstanding, or perhaps indeed because of his choice of controversial subject matter and his politically charged connections, Mulvany's work underwent a significant deterioration. However, in 1901 Mulvany embarked upon *The Anarchists,* which depicts six men cutting cards to select the murderer of Fenian Dr. Cronin in Chicago. Ann Weber-Scobie speculated that his painting may actually have portrayed the participants and that murder, rather than suicide, was the cause of Mulvany's death in 1906.

Robert Taft, *Artists and Illustrators of the Old West 1850–1900* (New York, 1953).

Thomas P. Tuite, "John Mulvany, Great Irish Painter," in *Gaelic American* (March 6, April 3 and 10, 1909).

NIAMH O'SULLIVAN

Audie Murphy

## MURPHY, AUDIE LEON (1924–1971)

Soldier, actor. Murphy was America's most decorated soldier of the Second World War. He grew up in poverty, one of twelve children born to a Texas sharecropper. Murphy acquired little formal education and worked at a number of jobs until America's entry into the war. Rejected by the Marines because of his small size, Murphy joined the army in June 1942. During training, he quickly demonstrated himself as an exemplary soldier. He first saw combat in Sicily in 1943, followed by considerable action at Anzio and Rome. He earned his first decoration in February 1943, a Bronze Star, after destroying a German tank during a night patrol. In August 1944, Murphy was part of the allied invasion of southern France, where he received the majority of his decorations. On January 26, 1945, Murphy earned the nation's highest military honor, the Congressional Medal of Honor, after single-handedly fending off a series of German attacks using only a .50 caliber machine-gun from a burning allied tank. At war's end, Murphy had received a total of thirty-three medals and decorations and had been wounded three times. He wrote of his war exploits in his book *To Hell and Back*. The war-hero turned actor after the war, making a number of films and acquiring a moderately successful reputation as a film star. However, celebrity and success failed to bring Murphy happiness. He suffered a series of emotional problems, including nightmares and compulsive gambling, and died in a plane crash in 1971.

*Dictionary of American Biography*, Supplement 9: 574–76.
Don Graham, *No Name on the Bullet* (New York, 1989).
Audie Murphy, *To Hell and Back* (New York, 1949).

TOM DOWNEY

## MURPHY, FRANCIS (1836–1907)

Temperance reformer. Born in Tagoat, County Wexford, Ireland, Murphy's father died shortly before his birth and he spent his childhood helping to support his widowed mother. At age sixteen he emigrated to the United States and went to New York where he drifted from job to job before settling on an upstate farm. While working on the farm, the outbreak of the Civil War led him to enlist and he served a three-year term until 1865.

After his career in the army, Murphy borrowed money from his older brother James and used it to become proprietor of the Bradley Hotel in Portland, Maine. However, Murphy's penchant for drinking began to consume his life and he succumbed to the wiles of his habit. In 1870 he was sent to jail for an assault he instigated in a local tavern. While serving his sentence he met Cyrus Sturdevant, a religious sea captain who visited and converted Murphy to a life of temperance. Murphy signed an abstinence pledge in 1870 and upon release from jail became the president of a state reform club. Murphy began an evangelistic outreach and he devised his own pledge which became known as "the Murphy pledge." He obtained over 12 million signatures to his pledge and became a popular social figure in his many addresses and work for sobriety.

Murphy's outgoing personality made his social gospel a success. He did not support or join the drive for legislative prohibition, instead emphasizing the personal aspect of the pledge to sobriety. He died on June 30, 1907, in Los Angeles, after having suffered a long period of illness.

Francis Murphy, *Talks by Francis Murphy* (1907).
E. H. Cherrington, *Standard Encyclopedia of the Alcohol Problem*, vol. IV (1928).
A. F. Fehlandt, *A Century of Drink Reform in the U.S.* (1904).
*Dictionary of American Biography*, 13.

JOY HARRELL

## MURPHY, FRANK (1890–1949)

Associate Justice of the U.S. Supreme Court. Frank Murphy was born in Harbor Beach, Michigan, on April 13, 1890. He was educated in local public schools and at the University of Michigan, where he earned a law degree in 1914. He taught at Detroit college of Law before serving in World War I. While in Europe, Murphy studied law at Lincoln's Inn, London, and at Trinity College, Dublin. In 1919 he became assistant U.S. attorney, taught law at the University of Detroit, and was elected judge of the Recorders' Court for two terms. In 1930 he was elected mayor of Detroit. He was a strong supporter of President Roosevelt's New Deal. In 1932 Roosevelt appointed him governor-general of the Philippine Islands; when the islands became autonomous in 1935, he was made high commissioner.

Murphy was elected governor of Michigan in 1936 and served three years. His settlement of the automobile workers' sit-down strike in Flint, Michigan, in 1937, in which he refused to enforce a court order compelling the strikers to return to work, brought Murphy national recognition, but he was defeated for reelection in 1938, and was named U.S. Attorney General by Roosevelt.

Murphy was an activist attorney general whose accomplishments included setting up a civil rights division in the Department of Justice. In 1940 he was nominated by Roosevelt to the Supreme Court where he served nine years and voted most often with the court's liberal bloc. Never married, Murphy died in Detroit on July 19, 1949.

Sidney Fine, *Frank Murphy*, Vol. 1, *The Detroit Years,* Vol. 2, *The New Deal Years,* Vol. 3, *The Washington Years* (Ann Arbor, 1975–84).
Richard D. Lunt, *The High Ministry of Government: The Political Career of Frank Murphy* (Detroit, 1965).

KATHLEEN N. McCARTHY

## MURPHY, GEORGE (1902–1992)

Actor, singer, dancer, politician. Born George Lloyd Murphy on July 4, 1902, in New Haven, Connecticut, Murphy married Julie Johnson in 1926 and had two children, Dennis and Melissa. Murphy was an entertainer through most of his life and played in some forty-five film comedies, musicals, and non-musical dramas, mostly for MGM and RKO in the thirties and forties. Some of his hits included *Jealousy* (1934); *Top of the Town* (1937); *Broadway Melody* (1938); *Little Nellie Kelly* (1940); *The Mayor of 44th Street* (1942); *Bataan* (1943); *Tenth Avenue Angel* (1948); *Battleground* (1949); and *Walk East on Beacon* (1952).

Some time after his retirement from the movies, Murphy became involved in community work and politics. He served two terms as president of the Screen Actors Guild beginning in 1944. A self-described "Eisenhower Republican," he was elected to the United States Senate from California in 1965 and served until 1971, and he was known to be one of the more conservative men in Washington at the time.

*See* Cinema, Irish in

J. Concannon and Frank Cull, *Irish American Who's Who* (New York, 1984).

Joseph Curran, *Hibernian Green on the Silver Screen* (Westport, CT, 1990).

EILEEN DANEY CARZO

## MURPHY, JOHN (1812–1880)

Publisher, printer. Known as a publisher of high standards and integrity, John Murphy was born to Bernard and Mary (McCullough) in Omagh, Tyrone, Ireland, on March 12, 1882. The family came to New Castle, Delaware, in 1822, and later John went to Philadelphia to learn the printing business. Around 1835 he became entrepreneur of a printing and stationery house in Baltimore, adding a book publishing line not long after. Marrying Margaret E. O'Donnoghue in 1852, they had six children, including son Frank K. Murphy who would become his successor. His house, Murphy & Company, published general materials, but specialized in Catholic books, with spiritual and devotional works being the largest component of his output. Murphy gained the high regard of Catholic prelates for issuing theological works which had a limited market, and meeting losses from the profits of commercial publications. He published at low cost bibles, hymnals, prayerbooks (some non-English) and religious guides. His periodical publications included *The Religious Cabinet,* begun in 1842, which became *United States Catholic Magazine* a year later, *The Metropolitan* (1853–59), and the *Catholic Youth's Magazine* (1857–61). His *Metropolitan Catholic Almanac and Laity's Directory* (1833) was a forerunner of the present *Official Catholic Directory.* Book publications included the best-selling *Faith of Our Fathers* by Cardinal Gibbons, the five-volume *Works* of John England, Butler's *Lives of the Saints,* the works of Cardinal Wiseman, and translations of foreign Catholic writings, such as Châteaubriand's *Genius of Christianity.* Publishing *Definition of the Dogma of the Immaculate Conception* gained him a papal gold medal in 1855; and for issuing the *Acta et Decreta* of the Second Plenary Council of Baltimore he acquired the title of "Typographer of the Holy See" in 1866. His house also published congressmen's speeches, including those of Jefferson Davis and Stephen Douglas, and quality historical and legal ma-

terials for the State of Maryland. His firm was not dissolved until 1943 when the New York publishing house of P. J. Kenedy assumed its assets. John Murphy died suddenly from paralysis on May 27, 1880, and was buried from the Catholic cathedral of Baltimore.

*Dictionary of American Biography,* Vol. 13 (New York, 1934).
*New Catholic Encyclopedia,* Vol. 10 (New York, 1967).

ANNA M. DONNELLY

## MURPHY, JOHN BENJAMIN (1857–1916)

Surgeon. John Benjamin Murphy was born Dec. 21, 1857, to Irish parents, Michael and Ann (Grimes) Murphy, in Appleton, Wis. He grew up on a farm and attended public schools.

After preliminary medical studies with a local doctor, he entered Rush Medical College, Chicago, and graduated in 1879. Upon completion of his internship at Cook County Hospital, Murphy spent two years in graduate study in Vienna, Austria.

When he returned to Chicago, he went into practice with Dr. Edward W. Lee. In 1884 he began lecturing in surgery at Rush Medical College. Other teaching positions followed: professor of clinical surgery at the College of Physicians and Surgeons, Chicago (1892–1901); professor of surgery, Northwestern University Medical School (1901–05 and 1908–16); professor of surgery, Rush Medical College (1905–08). He became the preeminent teacher of clinical surgery, characterized by Dr. William J. Mayo as "without a peer" in that field.

On Nov. 15, 1885, he married Jeannette C. Plamondon of Chicago. They had five children, one son and four daughters.

In 1895 he was appointed chief of the surgical staff at Mercy Hospital, a position he held until his death. Throughout his career he was an attending surgeon at Cook County Hospital.

Murphy was best known, however, for the Murphy button, a mechanical device he produced in 1892 that simplified the mending of intestines more quickly and accurately. The device made gastrointestinal surgery safer and brought about life-saving operations that would not have been considered before its invention.

He was interested in all aspects of the abdomen, and investigated the cause and treatment of peritonitis following appendicitis. In 1889 he performed an appendectomy that greatly improved the operation's technique. His interest also extended in later years to surgery of the lungs, nervous system, bones and joints. He had a special interest in deformities that resulted from infections. Among his other interests was the use of antiseptic methods in surgery, taking precautions to ensure the exclusion of bacteria during operations.

Murphy received many honorary degrees from both American and foreign universities. In 1902 the University of Notre Dame bestowed upon him the Laetare Medal. Pope Benedict XV made him a Knight-Commander of the Order of St. Gregory the Great in 1916.

Throughout his career, Murphy held membership in the main American and European surgical societies. He was president of the American Medical Association, 1910–11, and the Clinical Congress of Surgeons, 1914–15.

He wrote the article "Surgery of the Appendix Vermiformis" for *Surgery, Its Principles and Practice* (1908) by W. W. Keen. In 1911 he published *General Surgery* and from 1912–16 he produced five volumes on *The Surgical Clinics of John B. Murphy, M.D., at Mercy Hospital.*

For several months before his death, on Aug. 11, 1916, at Mackinac Island, Mich., Murphy suffered from attacks of angina pectoris, brought on probably by the stress of his work. In his honor, Murphy Hospital on Belmont Avenue in Chicago was opened in 1921. The American College of Surgeons began the John B. Murphy Memorial in Chicago in 1926 to house the headquarters of the college.

L. E. Davis, *J. B. Murphy: Stormy Petrel of Surgery* (New York, 1938).
H. A. Kelly and W. L. Burrage, *American Medical Biographies* (1920).

MARIANNA McLOUGHLIN

## MURPHY, MAUREEN O'ROURKE (1940–   )

Academic. Maureen Murphy was educated at S.U.N.Y. Cortland; she received her M.A. and her Ph.D. from the Folklore Institute, Indiana University. She was a Fulbright Fellow at University College, Dublin, in 1965–66. She joined the English Department at Hofstra University; from 1980 until 1993, Murphy served as Dean of Students and University Advisement but continued to teach Irish literature, history and the Irish language.

Murphy has edited a variety of books of Irish interest. Her current projects include a book about Irish domestic servants in the United States and a biography of Asenath Nicholson. She is a senior editor of the *Dictionary of Irish Biography.*

Murphy was president of the American Conference for Irish Studies from 1987 till 1989; she has been a member of the board of the International Association for the Study of Irish Literatures since 1979 and served as chair of that organization from 1991–1994. She has been a member of the board of the American Irish Historical Society since 1985 and has served as its historiographer.

Murphy has written and lectured widely on Irish and Irish-American topics, primarily in the United States and Ireland.

In 1998, Murphy directed the grant awarded to Hofstra University by the New York State Education Department to produce the Famine curriculum for fourth- through twelfth-graders. The project involved developing and field-testing lesson plans and producing a teacher's resource guide, a web site and a CD ROM.

*See* Irish Studies in the U. S.

## MURPHY, ROBERT DANIEL (1894–1978)

Diplomat and business executive. Robert Daniel Murphy was born Oct. 28, 1894, in Milwaukee to Francis Patrick and Catherine Louise (Schmitz) Murphy. His father was a saloon owner and a railroad worker. As a youngster, Murphy realized his family couldn't finance higher education for him.

However, he was an excellent student at Gesu Parochial School and earned a four-year scholarship to Marquette Academy. Following graduation from high school, he attended Marquette University, but left in 1916 to take a clerical position in Washington, D.C., with the United States Post Office. In the evenings, he attended George Washington University Law School and received a law degree in 1920.

In 1917 Murphy joined the State Department and was assigned to the American legation in Bern, Switzerland, as a code clerk. In 1921 he joined the foreign service and served as a vice consul at Zurich, Switzerland, but almost immediately went on to Munich, Germany, where he served from 1921–25.

During his tour in Munich, Murphy witnessed firsthand the consequences that resulted from extreme economic and political instability in Germany. He also served in Paris from 1930 to 1940 as consul and then counselor of the embassy. That experience led the State Department to place him in the position of chargé d'affaires to the Vichy government, following the German conquest of France in 1940.

At the request of President Franklin D. Roosevelt, Murphy went to French North Africa in 1941 to negotiate an economic agreement with Gen. Maxime Weygand, commander of the 150,000 French troops stationed in Africa. American aid was promised to the French colony in Algeria and the French protectorates in Tunisia and Morocco in order to undermine the Vichy government.

After the United States entered the war and Roosevelt selected North Africa for the first American amphibious landing in mid-1942, Murphy was ordered to secure the support, or neutrality, of French forces. Murphy was successful in persuading Admiral Jean Darlan, Weygand's successor, to sever ties with the Vichy government just as United States troops landed on North African beaches Nov. 7–8, 1942.

As a result of that deal, Roosevelt named Murphy his personal representative in North Africa with the rank of minister. However, Murphy became a controversial public figure who was criticized for the alliance with Darlan, who was anti-Semitic and anti-British.

Following his success in North Africa, Murphy was attached to Gen. Dwight D. Eisenhower's command, serving as the general's political attache during the North African fighting and the invasion of Italy. He helped negotiate the Italian armistice and, in 1944, he served as Eisenhower's political adviser on German affairs, attending the Potsdam Conference in July 1945. He remained in Germany as chief diplomatic adviser to the United States High Commission.

Murphy then returned to the United States to direct the State Department's Office of German and Austrian Affairs. In 1949 President Harry S. Truman appointed Murphy ambassador to Belgium. Three years later he was transferred to Tokyo, being honored as the first postwar United States ambassador to Japan.

With Eisenhower's election to the United States presidency, Murphy was appointed in 1953 assistant secretary of state for United Nations affairs. Later that year, Eisenhower promoted him to deputy under secretary of state.

Murphy's diplomatic skills were tapped by Eisenhower when he sent Murphy to London and Paris in 1956 to help avert a military confrontation in the Middle East when Egypt seized the Suez Canal. Even though the confrontation occurred, Murphy was recognized as playing a vital role in establishing the United States' opposition to the Anglo-French use of force. Murphy was called on again in 1958 when Eisenhower wanted to pave the way for sending 14,000 American troops to Lebanon.

After 42 years of a diplomatic career, he retired in 1959. That same year, he was awarded the Laetare Medal by the University of Notre Dame. Although retired, he maintained an active lifestyle, serving as chairman of Corning Glass International and as a director of Corning Glass Works. In 1969 he assisted President Richard M. Nixon in selecting major diplomatic appointees, and he served on the Foreign Intelligence Advisory Board under President Gerald B. Ford in 1976.

On March 3, 1921, Murphy had married Mildred Claire Taylor, with whom he had two children. In November 1977 he became incapacitated by a stroke. He died Jan. 9, 1978, in New York City.

H. W. Brands, *Cold Warriors: Eisenhower's Generation and American Foreign Policy* (1988).
William L. Langer, *Our Vichy Gamble* (1947).

MARIANNA McLOUGHLIN

## MURPHY, ROLAND E. (1917–   )

Old Testament scholar. Roland E. Murphy was born in Chicago on July 19, 1917. He entered the Carmelites and was professed on August 15, 1935. After theological studies at Catholic University, he was ordained on May 23, 1942. Continuing his studies, he obtained degrees in Semitic languages and philosophy as well as a doctorate in theology from Catholic University. He was a professor there in Semitic languages (1949–55) and of Old Testament in the School of Theology (1956–70). In 1958 he received the licentiate in Scripture from the Pontifical Biblical Institute. Besides being a visiting professor at Pittsburgh Theological Seminary, Yale University Divinity School, Princeton Theological Seminary and the University of Notre Dame, he became the George Washington Ivy Professor of Biblical Studies at Duke University (1971).

As editor-in-chief of the *Catholic Biblical Quarterly* (1959–65) he was in the midst of many attempts to defend and promote American Catholic biblical scholarship. He was part of the attempt to have Cardinal Meyer place more representative Americans on the Pontifical Biblical Commission. In the controversy in Rome over Myles Bourke's article on Matthew 1 and 2, Murphy tried to protect the Biblical Institute and then wrote a clarifying note on the controversy for the *Catholic Biblical Quarterly*. In the conflict that pitted the *American Ecclesiastical Review* and its editor, Joseph Fenton, against biblical scholars, Murphy withstood the Apostolic Delegate, Archbishop Egidio Vagnozzi. Only when Archbishop Patrick O'Boyle of Washington threatened to withhold his imprimatur from the *Catholic Biblical Quarterly* did Murphy agree to modify the resolution passed by the Catholic Biblical Association in defense of attacks by Fenton and others.

Murphy is the author of many articles and books, but perhaps his most noted work is the co-editorship of the popular *Jerome Biblical Commentary*.

Gerald P. Fogarty, *American Catholic Biblical Scholarship: A History from the Early Republic to the Vatican II* (San Francisco, 1989).

ALFRED ISACSSON, O. CARM.

## MURPHY, WILLIAM P. (1892–1987)

Physician, Nobel Laureate. William Parry Murphy was born February 6, 1892, at Stoughton, Wisconsin. He was the son of Thomas Francis Murphy and Rose Anna Parry. Murphy attended public schools in Wisconsin and Oregon. He graduated from the University of Oregon (B.A. 1914) and Harvard University Medical School (M.D. 1920). Murphy married Pearl H. Adams in 1919; the couple had two children, Priscilla and William, Jr.

Murphy served an internship at Rhode Island Hospital in Providence and a residency at Peter Bent Brigham Hospital in Boston. In 1924 he joined the faculty of Harvard Medical School.

Murphy collaborated with George H. Whipple and George R. Minot in 1925–1926 to work on finding a cure for anemia. The three men discovered that pernicious anemia patients could make a full recovery from near death by ingesting up to half a pound of liver per day. Further study refined the treatment to a low cost injection of liver extract. Eventually, vitamin B-12 was identified as the key agent in the cure of anemia. At first fellow physicians refused to accept liver therapy, but later studies confirmed the results obtained by Murphy, Whipple, and Minot. In 1934 the three physicians were awarded the Nobel Prize in medicine. Murphy continued to practice medicine in Boston for the next half-century. He died in Brookline, Massachusetts, on October 9, 1987.

Steven C. Martin, "William Parry Murphy, 1934," *Nobel Laureates in Medicine or Physiology: A Biographical Dictionary*, ed. by Daniel M. Fox, et al. (New York & London: Garland Publishing, Inc., 1990).
David Patechuk, "William P. Murphy, 1892–1987: American physician and pathologist," *Notable Twentieth-Century Scientists*, 4 vols., ed. by Emily J. McMurray et al. (Detroit, 1995).

THOMAS GILDEA CANNON

## MURRAY, JOHN COURTNEY (1904–1967)

Theologian. Born on September 12, 1904, in Manhattan, New York City, John Courtney Murray was the son of an Irish mother (née Margaret Courtney). His father (Michael John) was of Scottish descent. Ordained a priest on June 25, 1933, he received his doctorate from the Gregorian University, Rome, in 1937. Returning to Woodstock, Maryland, he spent the remaining thirty years of his life as a professor of systematic theology. From 1941 until 1967 he was editor of *Theological Studies* and was associate editor of *America* from 1945 until 1946. From 1951 until 1952 he was visiting professor of medieval philosophy and culture at Yale University. He wrote extensively on the issues of church-state relations and religious freedom. He also contributed to public debates in the United States on funding for private schools, the Communist threat, and the problem of conscientious objectors. He was featured on the cover of *Time* magazine on December 12, 1960 after the publication of his book, *We Hold These Truths: Catholic Reflections on the American Proposition*. This work was highly important in the run-up to the election of John F. Kennedy as the first Catholic president of the United States, as it cleared up many popular misconceptions at the time regarding the candidacy of a Catholic for president. In 1963 Murray was appointed by Francis Cardinal Spellman as a theological advisor to the American bishops at the Second Vatican Council and he helped to draft the Declaration on Religious Freedom (*Dignitatis Humanae*).

As a result of questions raised about his work on church and state, Murray was obliged in 1955 to submit further work in this area for censorship to Rome. He had argued that the establishment of Catholicism as the state religion was not part of Church doctrine. Thus, it appeared to his opponents, among them Cardinal Ottaviani, that he was promoting separation of church and state, something which had been condemned by successive popes from Pius IX to Pius XII. Murray had argued, however,

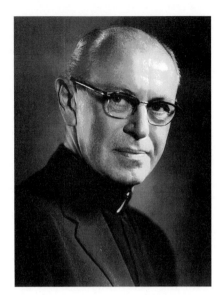

John Courtney
Murray

particularly in his examination of the writings of Leo XIII, that his position on separation, which corresponded to that of the First Amendment of the American Constitution, was very different to that which was condemned by the popes. His position did not correspond to Continental Liberalism which tended to absolutize the power of the state. Rather, he upheld the principle of separation, first elaborated by Pope Gelasius I in 494, which recognized the legitimate autonomy of both the secular and sacred powers.

Murray furthermore argued that the American system of separation was compatible with Catholicism. His work involved a study of the Anglo-Saxon tradition of democracy and an examination of the consensus on which the American Constitution is based. He held that the natural law was the basis for this consensus and, if America was to move beyond the rhetoric of anti-Communism as the sole binding force for its unity, it would be necessary to restore again the natural law tradition. Murray believed that Catholics, since they never lost sight of the natural law, were eminently placed to revitalize the American consensus which was coming increasingly under threat from secularism.

At the Second Vatican Council, Murray worked strenuously to ensure that the Declaration on Religious Freedom would be approved by the Council Fathers. Instead of basing the right to religious freedom on the principle of freedom of conscience, which proved to be inadequate in obliging governments to respect religious freedom, since an erroneous conscience does not bind others to grant liberty to its free exercise, agreement was reached whereby the right to religious freedom was based on the principle of the dignity of the human person. Effectively, the Declaration vindicated Murray's position on the church-state issue although it did not endorse his political argument of the limited state as the best argument in support of the right to religious freedom.

Murray, nevertheless, showed the possibility of remaining within the Catholic tradition while at the same time being open to historical developments, thus allowing new understandings of doctrine to emerge and greater cooperation between church and state to be achieved. The principles he worked out for achieving a unity in plurality in church-state relations and the right to

religious freedom based on the dignity of the human person continue to have an impact on public debate today. Just as the framers of the American Constitution, who sought a practical solution to the problem of creating a unity in a nation of diverse beliefs, built "better than they knew" (*We Hold These Truths,* p.66), so, too, the work of John Courtney Murray has significance for both church and state beyond the limits of the discourses in which he engaged.

*See* Catholicism, Irish-American

John Courtney Murray, *We Hold These Truths: Catholic Reflections on the American Proposition* (New York, 1960; reprinted 1988 with an introduction by Walter Burghardt).
———, *The Problem of God, Yesterday and Today* (New Haven, 1964).
J. Leon Hooper, S.J., ed., *John Courtney Murray, Religious Liberty: Catholic Struggles with Pluralism* (Louisville, KY, 1993).
———, *Bridging the Sacred and the Secular: Selected Writings of John Courtney Murray, S.J.* (Washington, D.C., 1994).

DAVID STRATTON

## MURRAY, PHILIP (1886–1952)

Miner, labor leader. Philip Murray was the son of Roseanne (Layden) Murray and William Murray. He was born May 25, 1886 in Bothwell, Scotland. Both parents were children of fathers who fled Ireland for participating in the Young Ireland Rising of 1848.

### MINING BACKGROUND

William Murray, a coal miner age twenty-three, married Roseanne Layden, nineteen, in St. Joseph's Catholic Church in Blantyre. Both Blantyre and Bothwell were mining communities in Lanarkshire located across the River Clyde from each other. Philip was the second child of the couple—his sister, Mary, was born in 1884. In 1887 William Murray's first wife died leaving him with two small children. However, Murray continued working in the coal pits and remarried in 1889. His second wife, Elizabeth Buchanan, widow of a miner, brought one child to the marriage, a daughter, Jane Dingsdale.

Philip Murray's education began in 1892 in the parish school at St. Joseph's Catholic Church. In spring of 1896 he became his father's helper in a Bothwell mine. Two years earlier he had (after school hours) helped collect food for the miners' soup kitchen during a strike. His father, a leader of a miners' local union instructed his son about the necessity for trade unions.

When coal prices fell sharply in 1901, William Murray decided future prospects in Lanarkshire were dim. His brother Philip had already settled in a coal town in Westmoreland County, Pennsylvania. William visited there to appraise the possibilities. Philip and his father emigrated to the United States in 1902 and were joined in the town of Madison, Pennsylvania by the rest of the family in 1903. Madison is located in the rich bituminous coal region of western Pennsylvania. An experienced and confident coal miner by 1910, Philip Murray married Elizabeth Lavery on September 7 of that year. The couple raised one child, Joseph, whom they adopted.

### UNION CAREER

Philip Murray's union career began in 1904 while working in a mine in Herminie, Pennsylvania. He disagreed with the weighmaster on the amount of coal he had dug that day. A fight ensued and he was fired. A walkout in support of Murray was to no avail. Sheriff's deputies put him on a train for Pittsburgh and warned him not to return. Meanwhile, he had been elected president of the local miners' union in the town.

In 1912 Murray was elected to the executive board of the United Mine Workers (UMW), helped by his association with Francis Feehan, president of District 5 of the UMW. Earlier, Feehan's campaign to organize non-union mines in the District had led to a long strike which was opposed by some members, but with support from Murray and others, Feehan was reelected District 5 leader in 1912, with Murray winning a seat on the UMW executive board at that time. Philip Murray was elected president of District 5 in 1916 in a special convention presided over by John L. Lewis.

### Association with John L. Lewis

A close association between Lewis and Murray grew over a period of thirty-four years as Lewis became UMW president in 1920 and Murray was elected vice president regularly—beginning in that same year. Murray was his faithful lieutenant and able mediator in disputes between and within local unions. He also attended to the details of contract terms after Lewis had made a (usually dramatic) industry-wide settlement. Appointed a member of the National Bituminous Coal Production Committee during World War I, Murray also participated on a regional panel of the War Labor Board for Pennsylvania at that time. He had supported Franklin Roosevelt's run for governor of New York in 1928. After Roosevelt's election as President, Murray was appointed to the Labor and Industrial Advisory Board of the National Recovery Administration.

### Organizing Steel

The UMW had suffered serious crises during the 1920s, but had recovered vigorously in the early thirties under the New Deal. Both Lewis and Murray championed Roosevelt's reelection campaign in 1936 and helped it financially thanks to a newly replenished UMW treasury. In the same year Lewis appointed Murray chairman of the Steelworkers Organizing Committee. By 1942, after a successful organizing effort, it evolved into the United Steelworkers of America (USW), with Murray as its elected president.

The Committee for Industrial Organizations founded by Lewis in 1935 became the Congress of Industrial Organizations (CIO) in 1938, with Lewis as its president. In the interim, Lewis had turned against Roosevelt. In the aftermath of the 1940 presidential election, Lewis kept his vow to resign as CIO president if Roosevelt won. He effectively promoted Philip Murray as his successor. Under strain, Murray spent some months in the hospital in the summer of 1941. Friendship between the two men did not survive thereafter. Lewis withdrew the UMW from the CIO and, vindictively, severed all Murray's offices, membership and pension rights in the mineworkers' union. Murray, however, recovered and remained president of both the CIO and the USW until his death.

### Leftwing Opposition

Leaders of some CIO unions following the Communist party line caused problems for Murray. After the Russo-German non-aggression pact, they opposed Roosevelt's defense mobilization policy. When Germany invaded Poland they labeled it an "imperialist war" and some defense plants faced strikes. However, when Germany invaded Russia, all-out production was the goal in the war to "save democracy." Hard won gains in negotiations were to be sacrificed in favor of speed-ups. The postwar party line called for opposition to the Truman Doctrine, the Marshall Plan and support for Henry Wallace in 1948 rather than President Truman whom the CIO had endorsed. In 1949 unions continuing to follow the party line were expelled from the CIO, weakening it moderately, but not fatally.

### Industrial Council Plan

Before, during and after World War II Murray regularly proposed a system of industrial democracy to foster cooperation and productivity. It was modeled on the tripartite industry council plan suggested by Pope Pius XI in an encyclical circulated in 1931. As a devout Catholic, Murray enthusiastically embraced it. Although there was substantial labor-management cooperation during the war, a wave of strikes followed in 1946, leading to the Taft-Hartley Act of 1947, which imposed restrictions on unions and which neither the labor movement nor President Truman's veto could derail. Murray led strikes in the steel industry in 1946, 1949 and 1952.

In addition to his union career and political activism Murray was an executive board member of the National Association for the Advancement of Colored People, a longtime member of the Ancient Order of Hibernians, and, from 1919 to 1943, remained on the Board of Education of the City of Pittsburgh.

He died in San Francisco on his way to a national convention of the CIO. His funeral in Pittsburgh was said to be the largest in that city up to that time.

*See* Labor Movement; Coal Miners

P. F. Clark, P. Gottlieb and D. Kennedy, eds., *Forging a Union in Steel* (Ithaca, 1987).
Melvyn Dubofsky and Warren Van Tine, *John L. Lewis* (New York, 1977).
Philip Murray Papers, Catholic University of America, Washington, D.C.

L. A. O'DONNELL

## MURRAY, THOMAS EDWARD, JR. (1891–1961)

Engineer and industrialist. Son of a noted industrialist scientist and inventor, Thomas E. Murray Jr. was born in Albany, New York, June 20, 1891, and raised in Brooklyn. He attended Xavier High School and Yale University, graduating in 1911 with a degree in mechanical engineering and entering the field of electric and gas power, where his father had made his fortune. The senior Murray (1860–1929) held more than eleven hundred U.S. patents, second only to those of Thomas Alva Edison, and his son added another two hundred to the family's total. Among the son's inventions was an electric welding process that made possible the mass production of mortar shells during World War I.

Murray emerged as a leader in the business world in 1929 when he succeeded his father as president of the Metropolitan Engineering and the Murray Manufacturing companies. In 1932 a public career opened up when he was named federal receiver of New York City's bankrupt Interborough Rapid Transit Company and of the Manhattan Railway Company, firms he would successfully merge into a single metropolitan transportation system.

In 1943 Murray received a War Department citation and the personal thanks of President Franklin D. Roosevelt for contributions to the nation's World War II programs. Among other things, he arbitrated several war-time labor disputes, eliciting from John L. Lewis, head of the United Mine Workers of America, the accolade of being "the country's greatest industrial statesman."

In 1950 President Harry Truman named Murray to the newly constituted U.S. Atomic Energy Commission, where he pushed for development of the hydrogen bomb and wide application of nuclear power in the nation's land, sea and air military forces. In time he came to worry about the threat nuclear weapons posed to civilization, but he remained a firm believer in its civilian possibilities, likening nuclear power's potential to that of coal and the steam engine. Nuclear energy, he said, was "a thrilling manifestation of the power, the beauty and the providence of God." Murray was a contentious presence on the AEC, and President Dwight D. Eisenhower declined to reappoint him when his term came up for renewal in 1957. In 1958 he sought the Democratic Party's nomination for U.S. Senate, but failed.

Murray and his wife, the former Marie Brady, had eleven children, two of whom became Jesuits. The family lived on New York City's Park Avenue, where Mass was celebrated daily in the chapel of their home. He died in New York on May 26, 1961.

Francis P. O'Hara, "Vast Scientific, Industrial Progress Credited to Tom Murrays Sr. and Jr.," *The Catholic Free Press* (Worcester, Massachusetts, March 7, 1952).

Richard G. Hewlett, *Dictionary of American Biography,* Supplement VII (New York, 1981).

JOHN DEEDY

## MUSIC OF THE EARLY EXILES

The most concise description of the relationship between the Irish people and American culture may be music historian Charles Hamm's assertion: "The Irish came early and often to America" (Hamm: 42). The musical repertory of the Irish-American community before the Civil War was a complex web of interconnected strands of traditional Irish, Scottish and British music, emerging forms of American popular music, and a variety of other musical influences including European-art and African-American music. It is as possible that an Irishman learned an American minstrel song in Dublin as that he first heard a Thomas Moore song in Boston. And just as the musical culture of Ireland was changing radically in the eighteenth and early nineteenth centuries, so too was the musical culture of the Irish-American community.

### Music in Ireland around 1800

All of Irish culture was under extreme strain in the eighteenth century. The incursions of English culture, the loss of traditional social structures, and the waning use of the Irish tongue all contributed to the rapid loss of a centuries-old musical heritage. The bards of Ireland's royal courts became roving minstrels, and by the second half of the eighteenth century the Irish were painfully aware that the art music of Ireland—the music of the harpers—was dying out. The last of the great performers and composers on the Irish harp, Carolan, died in 1738. The gradual loss of a na-

tive aristocracy and government, which began under Elizabeth I and continued for centuries, spelled the doom of the instrument which was the very symbol of the Irish nation. In 1786 Joseph Walker published his *Historical Memoirs of the Irish Bards* noting that, as English customs were adopted, the entire bardic tradition of Ireland was being lost, although "a number of their airs have come into the hands of foreign musicians, who have attempted to fashion them according to the model of modern music" (Walker: 157). Walker's statement is almost prophetic; at the Belfast Harp meeting of 1792—a last attempt to preserve some of the great musical tradition of Ireland—Edward Bunting transcribed the music of the aging harpers. From these transcriptions John Stevenson and Thomas Moore would produce the Anglicized recension of the harper repertory; these new melodic versions of Ireland's "high art" would survive in a popular medium and travel to America before many of the Irish themselves. To Moore's credit, he recognized that musical notation could not fully capture the genius of the traditional tunes of Irish art music; he admitted that the songs' "peculiarity of character," which he saw as their chief attribute when he performed them, was lost when they were transferred to the printed page.

The harpers were not the only musicians of Ireland. The ballad singers, fiddlers, and pipers of the country constituted what might be called the "folk music" of the island. Their tradition was a fluid one, characterized by oral transmission and a great deal of local variation. Many of their melodies survived in American folk traditions, both country and urban, and also in George Petrie's transcriptions of ballad singers of mid-nineteenth-century Ireland. Petrie recognized the fluidity of this tradition, especially in the large number of versions he collected of the same songs. These two strands, the middle-brow recension of ancient harp melodies and the on-going folk tradition of ballads and dances, would be the two lines of music which both preceded and followed the Irish emigrant to America. The first, already frozen in a literate form, would remain relatively stable down to the present day. The second would continue to evolve and interact with other musical influences encountered in the new world.

The Irish brought ballads and dance music to America, as is shown in this Currier and Ives print.

## IRISH MUSIC IN AMERICA

The first Irish music to come to the new world was brought by the so-called Scotch-Irish in the seventeenth and eighteenth centuries. English-speaking Protestants from the north of Ireland, they brought a repertory of ballad songs and dance music (including the jig, reel, and hornpipe) that shared traits—and even some melodies—with the folk arts of England and Scotland. In rural America, the folk music of Ireland, England, and Scotland solidified into a repertory that endured into the twentieth century in the folk traditions of Appalachia. These traditions also constituted important sources for the distinctively "American" musical styles called country and western.

To both Americans and British in the 1800s, the epitome of Irish music was the work of Thomas Moore. Moore's lyrics were usually coupled with the melodies of Bunting's transcriptions, arranged and harmonized by John Stevenson. The first set of songs was published in England in 1807 and subsequently appeared in many editions on both sides of the Atlantic. Moore's songs—such as "The Harp That Once Through Tara's Halls"—were ubiquitous, sung by professionals and amateurs, sung in the church, theater, and home, by Irish and non-Irish alike.

The arrival of large numbers of Irish Catholics in America did not begin until the end of the Napoleonic Wars. The United States Government began keeping record of the number of immigrants in 1820; almost every year for the next thirty the Irish represented the single largest ethnic group among the new arrivals. While many of these Irish moved inland as laborers on America's canals and railroads, an even greater number remained in the eastern cities. At the beginning of the twentieth century, Francis O'Neill of Chicago recalled that his mother taught her children the traditional music of Ireland "naturally . . . by her lilting and singing to her children, inheriting a keen ear, a retentive memory, and an intense love of the haunting melodies of their race" (O'Neill: 12). Urban neighborhoods became the locus of Irish music: the *Boston Pilot* (7/4/1846) referred to "places of low resort, where the fiddle or the bag-pipes can be heard until 11 or 12 o'clock" in Irish neighborhoods; Charles Dickens, in his *American Notes,* reported on a saloon in New York's heavily Irish Five Points neighborhood where "the fiddler grins, and goes at it tooth and nail, [and] there is new energy in the tambourine; new laughter in the dancers." It was in such urban settings that Irish, African, and other musical influences could ferment into new styles of song and dance such as those that were to emerge on the American stage. The oral transmission of Irish music allowed it both to survive within the ethnic community and interact with other musical cultures to produce new forms of "popular" music.

The Catholic Church did not encourage the retention of either the Irish tongue or traditional folk rituals in America. While the traditional tunes were played and sung, new English lyrics were constantly being composed to address the changing situation of the Irish in America. In keeping with the Irish tradition of "street ballads," the Irish-American press frequently published new lyrics for traditional tunes. For example, for St. Patrick's Day of 1833, the lyrics "Hail glorious apostle, selected by God," written by one of the nuns of the ill-fated Ursuline convent of Charlestown, were coupled with the traditional tune "St. Patrick's Day." The new "hymn" was sung in Boston's cathedral and other churches, printed as a broadside, performed at choral concerts, and published as sheet music with surprising frequency over the next thirty years. Lyrics, wedded to traditional Irish tunes, and advocating temperance, the repeal of the Act of Union of Great Britain and Northern Ireland, and the election of political candidates were created and printed in newspapers and as broadsides throughout the United States.

The Irish *caione* (anglicized "Keen"), the traditional Irish lamentation for the dead, rarely survived in America. Its form was tied to the Irish language, its practice was discouraged by the Catholic Church, and its nature disturbed both English and American witnesses, including the diarist George Templeton Strong, who was horrified at hearing the "unearthly . . . uncanny sound" of "keening" at the site of a construction accident in 1850s New York City. The keen may also have evoked unpleasant memories for the immigrants; keening was often performed at the so-called "American wakes," held the night before emigrants left their home for America. Yet despite strong opposition from both within and without the Irish community, the practice discreetly survived in a very few locations into the twentieth century.

Sheet music—inexpensive editions of music published mainly for the use of amateurs—was printed in the United States as early as the 1780s, and from the very beginning Irish tunes and songs were popular with both publishers and consumers. As the music industry grew in the 1820s, so too did the number of "Irish" titles. Songs and dances directed towards the Irish community continued to be published, but anti-Irish and anti-immigrant songs also found a strong market. Irish-like tunes now accompanied lyrics such as: "Did you ever go into an Irishman's shanty?/ Ah! there boys you'll find the whiskey so plenty/ With a pipe in his mouth there it's Paddy so free/ No king in his palace is prouder than he."

On the minstrel stage the Irish stereotype was far worse. A simian-like, drunken, violent fool, the stage Irishman of the minstrel show was an object of scorn and ridicule. The 1844 anti-Irish riots in Philadelphia inspired lyrics such as these on the minstrel stage: "But de Irish shoot white natives down/ An' spill dar blood around de town;/ Our rulers while dese wounds were sore,/ Allowed dem guns to shoot down more." The irony of the anti-Irish sentiments of the minstrel stage is that, in the years leading up to the Civil War, Irish-American performers would more and more become the favored performers in American popular music.

The Civil War was a turning point for many American Irish. Fighting on both sides of the war, the immigrant recognized himself more and more as an American. Both North and South marched to Irish tunes: the North to Patrick Gilmore's "When Johnny Comes Marching Home," the South to "The Bonny Blue Flag." Perhaps the most telling story of Irish music in the Civil War was the recollection of a Yankee soldier: encamped one evening on the north shore of the Rappahannock River in Virginia, the Union army began to sing "Deep in Canadian Woods We Met," a classic Irish immigrant song; in the distance they could hear the voices of the Confederate Army, camped across the river, join with them in the song (*The Contemporary Review* 43 (1883): 751).

After the Civil War, the Irish moved into the mainstream of American popular music. Ned Harrigan in the late 1800s and George M. Cohan in the early 1900s were among the most popular entertainers of their times. A new genre of "Irish" music, e.g., "When Irish Eyes are Smiling," developed out of Tin Pan Alley and had no connection to the music of Ireland. The Irish were less "ethnic" than the newly arriving immigrants from eastern and southern Europe; the Irish had became so much a part of American popular music that they no longer seemed Irish. Yet the final decade of the nineteenth century also saw the beginnings of a "folk revival" of Irish music and culture in the new world, led by the publications of Chicago's Francis O'Neill.

*See* Irish Song in America

Robert R. Grimes, *How Shall We Sing in a Foreign Land?: Music of Irish Catholic Immigrants in the Antebellum United States* (Notre Dame, 1996).

Charles Hamm, *Yesterdays: Popular Songs in America* (New York, 1979).

Lawrence McCullough, "An historical sketch of traditional Irish music in the U.S.," *Folklore Forum,* 7 ( July 1974): 177–91.

Michael Moloney, "Irish Music in America: Continuity and Change" (Ph.D. diss., University of Pennsylvania, 1992).

Captain Francis O'Neill, *Irish Folk Music: A Fascinating Hobby* (Chicago, 1910).

Society for the Preservation and Publication of the Melodies of Ireland, *Ancient Music of Ireland, the Petrie Collection* (1853–55).

Joseph C. Walker, *Historical Memoirs of the Irish Bards* (Dublin, 1786 [Garland, 1971]).

Robert L. Wright, *Irish Emigrant Ballads and Songs* (Bowling Green, 1975).

ROBERT R. GRIMES, S.J.

employed as strike-breaking scabs, for unskilled jobs, and frightened that emancipated slaves would flood the labor market, they told the founding father of modern Irish nationalism to mind his own business and not to interfere in things American.

### FENIANISM

In the wake of their unsuccessful, almost comic opera 1848 rebellion that concluded in Widow McCormack's Tipperary cabbage patch, Young Irelanders replaced O'Connell on Irish-America's heroic stage. In 1858, two of them, John O'Mahoney and Michael Doheny, established the first significant voice of Irish-American nationalism, the Fenian Brotherhood, dedicated to the establishment of a democratic Irish republic through revolutionary means. O'Mahoney, a Gaelic scholar, named the organization after the Fianna of ancient Irish mythology. He persuaded his friend and fellow veteran of '48, James Stephens, to launch the Irish Republican Brotherhood (IRB) in Britain and Ireland. According to Fenian strategy, the IRB would muster an Irish army of liberation; Irish America would prepare it for battle.

Fenianism, the popular designation for physical force republicanism on both sides of the water, had about 50,000 enlistees in each place and collected a considerable amount of money in the United States, almost $500,000 in 1866. Like later nationalist movements, Fenianism had recreational as well as political appeal. Class distinctions and puritanical Catholicism restricted social activities in Ireland. IRB cells filled a vacuum by offering picnics, hiking, and athletic competition. Starting with the Fenians, Irish-American nationalists also sponsored fun and games events. In the late nineteenth century, Finley Peter Dunne's fictional Chicago saloon keeper, Martin Dooley, remarked: "if Ireland cud be freed be a picnic, it'd not on'y be free today, but an impire begorra."

Physical force republicanism drew vehement opposition from Paul Cardinal Cullen and the Irish hierarchy. Bishop David Moriarty of Kerry described Fenians as "swindlers" and "criminals," saying that for them "eternity is not long enough, nor hell hot enough." Prelates frowned on the secret society nature of the IRB, its advocacy of violence, and its embrace of American egalitarianism and lack of deference to religious and secular authority. They also worried that radical Fenian rhetoric and revolutionary

# NATIONALISM, IRISH-AMERICAN (1800–1921)

Irish-American nationalism was almost the exclusive preserve of Catholic immigrants and their descendants whose religion functioned as the essence and symbol of ethnicity, a psychological and spiritual comfort station, a social as well as a religious focal point of parish neighborhoods, and a bridge of continuity between rural Ireland and urban America. Politics has meant power and through power a path to economic security. Expressions of Irish-American nationalism have indicated the changing status of the community. At first, it expressed alienation and rage, the resentments of poverty-stricken casualties of American nativism. Many of the Irish held Britain responsible for their emigration to the United States where they again became victims of prejudice. Famine refugees of the 1840s and early 1850s were particularly bitter, more so than their relatives back home. They did not hesitate to accuse Britain of genocide. Although anger continued to play a role in nationalist motivations, in time it was joined, frequently surpassed, by a search for respectability. For some, nationalism degenerated into a narrow-minded chauvinism; for others it was an idealism that guided protests against injustices on both sides of the Atlantic.

Irish-American passion and dollars inspired and fueled constitutional and physical force efforts to liberate Ireland from British control. Various nationalist organizations attempted to influence American foreign policy in anti-British directions. While the Anglo-Protestant establishment usually frustrated such efforts, occasionally Irish-American political pressure did influence Washington's view of Anglo-American relations, especially in regard to recent troubles in Northern Ireland.

### O'CONNELL, CATHOLIC EMANCIPATION, AND REPEAL

In the 1820s Daniel O'Connell's agitation for Catholic emancipation attracted considerable Irish support throughout the United States, from Protestants as well as Catholics. But when anti-Catholic American nativism began to focus on the Irish as its leading target, Protestants, claiming Scotch Irishness, ceased to seek common ground with Catholics, who then became the almost exclusive constituency for Irish-American nationalism. In 1843, they organized Repeal clubs in many places that sent money to the Loyal National Repeal Association in Dublin. O'Connell boasted that American dollars would help him revoke the 1800 Act of Union fettering Ireland to Britain. But when he condemned American slavery as contrary to the liberal values and objectives of Irish nationalism and censured supporters of such a vile institution, a number of Irish-Americans repudiated his leadership. Notorious for racial bigotry, competing with blacks, sometimes

James Stephens

potential would discourage Prime Minister William Ewart Gladstone and his liberal government from making concessions to Irish-Catholic grievances. Reacting to the denunciations of the hierarchy, Charles Kickham, the novelist, and others on the staff of the IRB newspaper, *The Irish People,* instructed readers to heed bishops and priests when they preached religion but to ignore them when they talked politics.

In the United States, physical force republicans substituted a pledge for an oath of secrecy, but some American bishops still condemned the organization. Others, however, were either indifferent or sympathetic. New York's Archbishop John Hughes was prominent in the latter category. In 1861, he demonstrated his Fenian predilections by presiding at a funeral Mass for Terence Bellew McManus in St. Patrick's cathedral.

After the failed 1848 rising, British authorities transported McManus to Van Dieman's land. After escaping, he settled in San Francisco until his death. Fenian leaders decided to honor the deceased Young Irelander and to promote their cause by shipping his body back to Ireland for burial. The long journey home by sea and rail was punctuated by requiem Masses along the way, including one in the cathedral in Queenstown (Cobh). But Cullen made it clear that he would not tolerate any public religious displays in Dub-lin that could be construed as a tribute to physical force republicanism. Therefore, Fenians waked McManus in the Mechanics Hall (later the Abbey theatre) and hundreds of thousands crowded sidewalks as the funeral procession made its way to Glasnevin cemetery.

In Ireland, nationalists anxious to sever the Union with Britain sympathized with the American South's desire to separate from the American Union. They also resented so many of their sons and brothers dying to defend the Stars and Stripes. Most Irish-American Catholics had little or no sympathy for abolitionism, but a significant number fought against the Stars and Bars to demonstrate their love for the United States. Fenians had another motive. They wanted to preserve the Union so that American military power might some day defeat Britain and free Ireland. A considerable number of young men joined both the Union and Confederate armies to obtain military expertise for a future engagement with Britain. Many delegates to Fenian conventions wore blue uniforms.

Those who thought that post–Civil War Fenianism would concentrate on the Irish struggle were disappointed when the Brotherhood erupted in personality and strategy conflicts. Its Senate, led by Colonel William R. Roberts, protested O'Mahoney's leadership and his focus on revolution in Ireland. Instead, they advocated an attack on Canada, believing that it would lead to a war between Britain and the United States that would result in an Irish republic.

In February 1866, Fenians failed to capture Campo Bello, a small island off the New Brunswick coast. Three months later, six hundred Fenians, armed with surplus Civil War guns and ammunition, invaded Ontario. After routing a Canadian militia company, they retreated before British soldiers. For a while, the United States government ignored or sometimes encouraged Fenian activities. Secretary of State William Seward hoped that the Irish republican threat to Canada might persuade Britain to compensate the United States for damages that an English-built Confederate blockade runner, the *Alabama,* had inflicted on Union shipping. He also wanted Westminster to recognize the American naturalization of former British citizens. Once Britain diplomatically surrendered to Washington's demands, President

Grant turned on the Fenians, making clear that his administration would no longer tolerate an anti-British government-in-exile to operate in the United States.

Because American Fenians were so distracted by the O'Mahoney-Roberts imbroglio and preoccupied with the Canadian strategy, they failed to adequately supply the IRB. Rather than reenact the 1848 farce, Stephens postponed revolution in Ireland. Meanwhile, British spies infiltrated the IRB, leading to the 1865 arrest of Stephens and other leaders. At the same time, Fenians had penetrated British security. Contacts in the ranks of the constabulary and in the prison system enabled John Devoy to arrange Stephens' escape. He went to Paris and then New York in an effort to end the quarrel between O'Mahoney and Roberts. But by the time he landed in New York, the Fenian Senate had already deposed President O'Mahoney, and Stephens' acerbic personality caused more dissension than harmony. Accusing him of cowardice for canceling rebellion in Ireland, American republicans deposed Stephens as IRB head centre. Except for a brief, unsuccessful 1879 attempt to rally Americans around his leadership, the IRB founder lived in Paris until he returned to Ireland in 1886, a virtually forgotten man.

In the late winter of 1867, frustrated by delayed orders to fight and the Irish-American failure to equip them, and angered by the arrest of some of their leaders, small Fenian bands in Clare, Cork, Dublin, Kerry, and Limerick rose in rebellion. British soldiers and members of the Royal Irish Constabulary easily defeated, often captured them. In September of that year, the IRB, while freeing two Irish-American Fenians, Colonel Thomas Kelly and Captain Timothy Deasy, from a police van in Manchester, accidentally killed a police sergeant. Although there was no convincing evidence that any of them had fired the fatal bullet, judge and jury, representing an enraged British public opinion, convicted and sentenced to death W. P. Allen, Michael Larkin, Michael O'Brien, and Edward Condon. Just before the scheduled execution, the government reprieved Condon because he was a citizen of the United States. O'Brien made the same claim, but he had previously used it to avoid a stiff sentence for republican activities. The government had no intention of repeating such leniency.

The deaths of the "Manchester Martyrs" provoked waves of anger and sympathy in Ireland. Prayers for the repose of their

Manchester Martyrs

souls rose from Catholic pews and altars. Bishops and priests joined with business executives and professional people in an Amnesty Association urging paroles for jailed rebels. Respectable people, clerical and lay, felt free to honor Fenian courage and patriotism when it no longer threatened law and order. Irish nationalism, in the form of Home Rule, had returned to the constitutional mainstream.

### HOME RULE, THE CLAN NA GAEL, AND THE NEW DEPARTURE

In 1870, Isaac Butt, a Protestant barrister who had served as a Conservative MP and had defended Young Irelanders and IRB members in 1848 and 1867, and was president of the Amnesty Association, founded the small Home Government Association. Three years later it expanded into the more public Home Rule League. Home Rule argued for local legislatures in Ireland, Scotland, Wales, and England subordinate to the Imperial Parliament at Westminster. Butt believed that the popularity of federalism following the North's victory in the American Civil War, exhibited in the 1867 British North American Act that created the Dominion of Canada, would persuade British opinion that Home Rule was a conservative solution to the long-standing Irish Question. He also concluded that it could convince Protestants that they had more to gain than to lose in cooperating with Catholics in a self-governing Ireland.

The Grant administration's enmity, the failure of the Canadian strategy, and unsuccessful insurrections in Ireland undermined American Fenianism. Although it survived into the 1880s, by that time the Clan na Gael spoke for physical force republicanism in the United States. Jerome J. Collins founded the Clan in 1867 but, following his release from a British prison in 1871, John Devoy came to New York and became its leading personality. Six years later, the Clan formed an alliance with the IRB. They established a joint Revolutionary Directory to plan the liberation of Ireland. As the more powerful partner and the source of most of physical force nationalism's financial resources, the Clan was able to dictate policy to the IRB. When Kickham and the IRB adopted a neutral stance to Home Rule, permitting some of its members to participate in parliamentary politics, the Clan rejected such a policy and forced a change.

More disciplined and secretive than the Fenians, the Clan enlisted notable Irish-Americans. For example, Terence V. Powderly, grand master workman of the Knights of Labor and former mayor of Scranton, Pennsylvania; S. B. Conover, United States Senator from Florida; John W. Goff, who became a New York State Supreme Court justice; and many local government politicians and journalists were members. The number of successful Clansmen signified that Irish-American Catholics were seeking acceptability in the United States as much as revenge against Britain. By the close of the nineteenth century, they had climbed from the unskilled to the skilled working class with considerable penetration of the lower-middle class, but still attracted scorn. Many believed that other Americans rejected them because their mother country existed in servitude. Therefore, to liberate Ireland was to advance Irish America. In 1880, Michael Davitt articulated this position when he told Irish-Americans that if they wanted respect they must "aid us in Ireland to remove the stain of degradation from your birth . . ."

During diplomatic tensions between Britain and Russia, Clan emissaries encouraged the latter's belligerence. And they attempted to persuade Spain that a war with Britain might end in the return of Gibraltar. The Clan also made an unintentional contribution to American naval strength when they financed John Holland's early attempts to build a functioning submarine. Despite its various projects designed to emancipate Ireland from British colonialism, for a long time the Clan failed to gather mass support. Like the Fenians and IRB, it suffered from narrow vision. Failure to address the economic and social problems faced by Irish peasants and Irish-American workers irritated Patrick Ford, publisher of the New York based *Irish World*, the largest circulating Irish-American newspaper with a considerable reading audience in Ireland as well. Like so many American populists, Ford, a Galway native, was tainted with anti-Semitism. But he was far more perceptive about Irish America than Devoy, who always remained a brooding exile, emotionally and psychologically dwelling in Ireland, never the United States. Ford, a foe of agrarian capitalism in Ireland and industrial capitalism in the United States, criticized the limited focus of Clan leaders. He suggested that they should initiate a war on landlordism to mobilize the Irish people behind their revolutionary agenda.

Events in Ireland reinforced Ford's demand for a "New Departure" in Irish nationalism. In 1876, Charles Stewart Parnell, a Wicklow Protestant landlord and a member of the Home Rule Irish parliamentary party, began to challenge its chair, Isaac Butt. He criticized the apathy and lack of discipline of Home Rule MPs, and the party's refusal to express and remedy the economic and social grievances of its constituency. Since members of the British Parliament paid their own election expenses and served without salaries, quite often those who represented Irish nationalism at Westminster were opportunists, lukewarm in their enthusiasm for the cause. Butt was a kindly, highly intelligent Irish patriot, but he lacked the fire and was too preoccupied with financial burdens to concentrate on his duties as party chair. Most nationalist newspapers in Ireland supported Parnell in his dispute with Butt and, like Ford, complained that constitutional as well as physical force nationalism lacked an economic and social purpose.

While the Irish party and the Home Rule League were caught up in a controversy over Irish party strategy, in the late 1870s agrarian Ireland went into a deep economic recession. This disaster resulted from years of bad weather and the impact of North American grain imports on a free trade United Kingdom market. With poor harvests and declining prices, many tenant farmers found it difficult to pay rents. As a result, eviction and emigration, especially in Connacht, reached their highest level since the late 1840s and early 1850s.

Responding to the crises in Ireland and Ford's appeal for a more comprehensive national platform, the Clan decided to initiate an attack on landlordism, demanding secure tenures at fair rents and the farmer's right to sell his interest in the land on leaving. Tenant rights were intended as a prelude to peasant proprietorship. The agrarian dimension of the Clan's projected New Departure was designed to capture the rural populace for a revolutionary future. Although Devoy and his colleagues abhorred parliamentary politics as a corrupting compromise with British colonialism, they decided that Parnell could be trusted. When the time was right, hopefully 1882, the centenary of Grattan's Parliament, they wanted him to demand immediate Home Rule. When the British denied it, as they most certainly would, Parnell and his allies in the Irish party were to leave Westminster and establish an Irish parliament in Dublin. He could depend on the Irish people, with the aid of Irish America, to defend its sovereignty.

The Clan selected Michael Davitt to launch the land war in Ireland. As a child, Davitt moved with his family from Mayo to Lancashire, where at age eleven he lost an arm in a cotton mill accident. His injury did not prevent him from becoming a member of the IRB. Fenian activities cost him seven years in Dartmoor prison. On his 1877 release, the Clan sponsored a lecture tour so that Davitt could visit his mother in the United States. While in New York, he became a disciple of the New Departure, and in 1878 returned to Ireland and organized the Land League of Mayo that quickly became the National Land League.

Parnell responded cautiously to Devoy's alliance terms. In his effort to reconstruct the Home Rule movement, he needed Irish America, particularly its financial resources. But he was reluctant to surrender his independence to the manipulations of the Clan na Gael, and he realized that too close an affiliation with physical force republicanism would antagonize the Irish-Catholic hierarchy. The bishop's blessing was at least as important as Irish-American goodwill. Making it clear to Clan envoys that he welcomed a working relationship, Parnell stopped short of endorsing the New Departure in totality. He did, however, embrace its war on landlordism.

At a Land League meeting in Ennis, County Clare, Parnell told listeners "to keep a firm grip on their homesteads," and to shun all those who cooperated with the landlord system. League members applied his advice to a County Mayo estate managed by a Captain Charles Cunningham Boycott with so much success that "boycotting" became a key Land League tactic and a new word in the English language. Emigrant veterans of the land war introduced it as a weapon in the conflict between American labor and capital.

Observing Parnell's popularity, unselfish Davitt persuaded the Home Ruler to take his place as Land League president. In that capacity, Parnell toured the United States, met the leaders of Irish America, addressed a joint session of Congress, and successfully solicited funds for the land war. In the midst of his tour he had to return to Ireland for the general election of 1880. He contested and won three seats, decided to sit for Cork, and became Irish party chair.

Through the Irish National and Industrial League of the United States, a Clan na Gael front, and other Irish-American organizations, such as the Ancient Order of Hibernians, Americans financed the land war in Ireland, enabling tenant farmers to hold out against eviction threats. Davitt referred to Irish America as "the avenging wolfhound of Irish nationalism." Land League posters lauded the United States as the foe of British tyranny.

Despite League efforts to avoid violence, at times the land agitation bordered on revolution. Finally, turbulence in Ireland persuaded Gladstone's Liberal government to enact an 1881 Land Act conceding tenant rights. Davitt, a disciple of Henry George, a single-tax American socialist, wanted land nationalization, but most Irish farmers were satisfied with their victory. In fact, the Land Act established a dual ownership of the land, initiating a process that by the early twentieth century culminated in peasant proprietorship and the end of landlordism.

Once the land issue was on the road to final settlement, Parnell redirected his energies and Irish-American funds to Home Rule politics. In recreating the Irish party, he recruited talented young candidates, frequently journalists, paid their election expenses, and provided them with stipends so that they could concentrate on their duties. Tightly disciplined, strongly led, with a highly organized constituency base, the Irish party became a model of parliamentary politics copied by the Conservative, Liberal, and later Labour parties. By 1885, electoral changes in the United Kingdom—the 1872 secret ballot and the 1884 Reform Bill—returned eighty-six Home Rule MPs to Westminster. With this much strength, Parnell switched party tactics from obstruction to balance of power. His ability to determine whether Liberals or Conservatives would form a government was instrumental in committing Gladstone to Irish Home Rule.

This Irish-Liberal alliance produced Home Rule Bills in 1886, 1893, and 1912. A split in the Liberal party defeated the first, a House of Lords veto killed the second, and the threat of armed resistance by Ulster unionists delayed application of the third. In August 1914, Britain was on the verge of civil war. The House of Commons had passed Home Rule three times and, according to the 1911 Parliament Act, the House of Lords had exhausted its veto power. But Ulster Protestants made it clear that they considered Home Rule to be Rome Rule and a menace to their industrial economy, and, if necessary, they would resist it by force. To prove their sincerity, they mustered and armed an Ulster Volunteer force. Refusing to be intimidated, nationalists in the South created the Irish Volunteers to defend Home Rule. A revived and energized IRB played an important role in this nationalist army. While British Conservative politicians, newspapers, and people high on the social register were championing "brave little Ulster," Liberals were suggesting partition as a compromise solution. And the government could not rely on army officers with their conservative and Protestant biases to enforce Home Rule against Ulster defiance. For many Britains their country's entry into World War I seemed a lesser calamity than the prospect of civil conflict. As soon as Britain joined the fray, the government put Home Rule on the statute books but postponed its application until after the war when it could address the Ulster dilemma. After the Irish party won the parliamentary game, British politicians changed the rules. They did not realize that they triggered a growing disillusionment in Ireland with constitutional nationalism, setting the stage for the 1916 Easter Week rebellion and the 1919–21 Anglo-Irish War.

In the late 1870s the Clan na Gael had tried to employ Parnell as a stalking horse for physical force nationalism, but by the 1880s he had captured Irish America for Home Rule. The Irish National League of America endorsed the policies of and contributed funds to the Irish National League of Ireland. Theoretically, the Clan na Gael and the Irish National League of America were separate organizations, but both had the same leadership cadre. In the 1880s, Alexander M. Sullivan and his followers gained control of both organizations. Sullivan, a crafty, unscrupulous Chicago politician, had not abandoned physical force methods. In 1884, without IRB approval, he used an old skirmishing fund to finance a dynamite campaign in London. Instead of intimidating Britain into conceding Irish independence, dynamiters gave physical force nationalism a thuggish reputation, provoking John O'Leary, William Butler Yeats' Fenian hero, to remark that "There are some things that a man cannot do for his country."

## CULTURAL NATIONALISM

Although Irish-Ireland cultural nationalism had much less of an impact on Irish America than it did on Ireland, beginning in the 1870s there were a number of Irish language societies in urban America. In 1898, they joined in the Gaelic League of America. For the most part, Irish-Americans preferred to compete in sports that originated in the United States rather than in Ireland. In the late nineteenth and early twentieth centuries, they excelled in baseball and boxing and were on the verge of making an impact on football. But some, usually immigrants, played hurling, Gaelic football, and camogie (a Hibernian version of women's field hockey). During the 1890s, hurling and Gaelic football clubs in New York, representing Irish county associations, began to compete on Sunday afternoons. In 1904 they formed the Irish Counties Athletic Union. It was replaced in 1907 by the United Irish Counties Association of New York which became the New York Gaelic Athletic Association in 1914 with close ties to the GAA in Ireland. During the 1890s, Chicago had fifteen Gaelic Athletic Clubs with two thousand members. They played against each other and clubs from other areas. Frequently champion teams from Ireland crossed the Atlantic to challenge those from New York and later Chicago.

Cultural nationalism with a Gaelic twist did help instill some self-esteem in a people coping with an Anglo-Saxon racism popular in academia, politics, and journalism. Unfortunately, it also propelled many Irish-Americans into an escapist, romanticized Irish past, unconnected to the realities of their present. In Ireland, the cultural revival inspired a body of excellent poetry, prose, and theatre. In the United States it discouraged an honest, perceptive literary analysis of Irish-American urban life. Finley Peter Dunne's Mr. Dooley essays in the *Chicago Evening Post* were an exception, creating the first genuine ethnic neighborhood in American writing. Cultural nationalism's defensiveness tended to narrow intellectual and aesthetic perspectives in both Ireland and the United States. In 1911, the Abbey Theatre's New York presentation of John Millington Synge's *The Playboy of the Western World* received the same hostile reception as it had in Dublin four years earlier. The thin-skinned, Irish audience in both cities could not tolerate what they considered the playwright's negative view of the Irish peasant, the ideal Gael.

### DIVISIONS IN IRISH-AMERICAN NATIONALISM

Irish-American nationalism experienced troubling times in the 1880s and 1890s. Strategic and personality differences between followers of Devoy and Sullivan split the Clan na Gael and Irish National League. In 1889, Sullivanites killed a popular Chicago physician, Patrick Cronin, a staunch Devoy supporter. His murder, largely attended wake and funeral, and the court trials of the indicted assassins blemished the character of Irish-American nationalism, giving it a Mafia-like image.

Politics also splintered and sullied Irish-American nationalism. Prosperous Irish-Americans and some members of the Catholic clergy criticized Patrick Ford's attacks on industrial capitalism. During the 1886 New York mayoral campaign, he enthusiastically endorsed the candidacy of Henry George, whose pro-Land League record won the admiration of Irish-American workers. But the middle class and the bishops, reacting to his radical economic and social theories, supported the regular Tammany candidate. Contemptuous of pragmatic Irish-American politicians and their slavish loyalty to the Democratic party, John Devoy insisted that the Irish vote should go to the highest bidder, the party that was prepared to do the most to advance Irish freedom. Therefore, in 1884 and 1888 he and his followers worked to elect Republican presidential candidates. They discovered that Irish-Americans were more interested in the bread and butter issues of their existence than the liberation of Ireland, and that nationalists could not compete with politicians for their vote.

Their efforts to do so often contradicted the idealism of their cause.

No doubt the biggest blow to nationalism in the United States as well as in Ireland was the fallout from the 1890–1891 Parnell divorce scandal. In both countries Parnellites and anti-Parnellites were at each other's throats. Parnell died in 1891 but the dispute lingered until 1900 when the Irish party reunited under Parnellite John Redmond. Once more Irish-American money, collected by the United Irish League of America, went to the party's constituency organization, the United Irish League in Ireland. But with the failure to achieve Home Rule in 1914, the United Irish League of America, like the Irish party and the United Irish League in Ireland, declined into apathy.

### IRISH AMERICA AND REVOLUTION IN IRELAND

In March 1916, the Friends of Irish Freedom (FOIF), the public face of the small, secret Clan na Gael, became the leading voice of Irish-American nationalism. The FOIF attracted many prominent people. Victor Herbert, the composer, served as the organizations first president. Clansmen used the large FOIF membership, 270,000 at its peak, to muster popular support for the Easter Week martyrs and later the Irish Republican Army (IRA). Devoy and associates participated in planning the 1916 Rising and urged Germany to supply Patrick Pearse, James Connolly, and their IRB and Citizen Army comrades. From August 1914 to April 1917, Clan-instructed Irish-Americans joined with German Americans in efforts to keep the United States neutral. But once it entered World War I, they exchanged anti-British isolationism for enthusiastic American patriotism so well expressed in the songs of George M. Cohan. At the conclusion of hostilities in Europe, the Clan and its FOIF puppet strongly advocated the Sinn Fein cause during the Anglo-Irish War and supplied cash and weapons to the IRA. At the Versailles Peace Conference, their emissaries urged President Woodrow Wilson to apply his self-determination principles to Ireland. When he failed to do so, they turned against him and his League of Nations and, for the first time, many of the American Irish deserted the Democrats in the 1920 presidential election.

In 1921, the Clan and the FOIF, like Sinn Fein in Ireland, split over the merits of the Anglo-Irish Treaty. Devoy, Judge Daniel Cohalan, and some other Clan leaders agreed with Michael Collins that it provided Ireland with more independence than O'Connell's Repeal or Parnell's Home Rule and, if the Irish people so desired, could lead to an even greater degree of sovereignty. Others, such as Joseph McGarrity of Philadelphia, shared the opinion of Eamon de Valera, president of the Irish Dail (parliament), that Dominion status, with its oath of allegiance to the British monarch, betrayed the Irish Republic established on Easter Monday, 1916. Much of the Cohalan and Devoy Treaty support stemmed from their dislike of de Valera, who, during his 1919–1920 tour of the United States, made it clear that he and the Dail, and not Irish-Americans, would decide Ireland's domestic and foreign policies.

### DIMINISHING IRISH-AMERICAN NATIONALISM

While Irish-American Catholics continued to have an impact on events in Ireland, after 1921 nationalism had a decreasing importance in their lives. They lamented partition and the mistreatment of coreligionists in Northern Ireland, but they were generally satisfied with the Free State. They considered the debate over the oath of allegiance to the British monarch more theological than political in tone, and were repelled by the fratricidal Civil War that it generated. Few of the Irish in English-speaking America had much enthusiasm for the exclusive, introverted Gaelic nationalism that the Free State and later Irish Republic governments promoted. But for the most part, it was American rather than Irish events and situations that widened the gap between the Irish at home and the American Diaspora.

See Irish in America; O'Connell, Daniel, and America; United Irishmen and America

Donald H. Akenson, *The United States and Ireland* (Cambridge, Mass., 1993).

Thomas N. Brown, *Irish-American Nationalism* (Philadelphia, 1976).

Francis M. Carroll, *American Opinion and the Irish Question, 1910–1923* (New York, 1978).

R. V. Comerford, *The Fenians in Context: Irish Politics and Society, 1848–1882* (Atlantic Highlands, N.J., 1985).

Sean Cronin, *Washington's Irish Policy, 1916–1986, Independence, Partition, and Neutrality* (Dublin, 1986).

Joseph Edward Cuddy, *Irish-America and National Isolationism, 1914–1920* (New York, 1976).

William D'Arcy, *The Fenian Movement in the United States, 1858–1886* (New York, 1971).

Charles Fanning, *The Irish Voice in America: Irish-American Fiction from the 1760s to the 1980s* (Lexington, Ky., 1990).

Michael F. Funchion, *Chicago's Irish Nationalists, 1881–1890* (New York, 1976).

———, ed., *Irish American Voluntary Organizations* (Westport, Conn., 1983).

Terry Golway, *Irish Rebel: John Devoy and America's Fight for Irish Freedom* (New York, 1998).

Brian Jenkins, *Fenians and Anglo-American Relations During Reconstruction* (Ithaca, N.Y., 1969).

Lawrence J. McCaffrey, ed., *Irish Nationalism and the American Contribution* (New York, 1976).

Kerby Miller, *Emigrants and Exiles: Ireland and the Irish Exodus to North America* (New York, 1985).

Joseph Patrick O'Grady, *Irish-Americans and Anglo-American Relations, 1880–1888* (New York, 1976).

C. C. Tansill, *America and the Fight for Irish Freedom, 1886–1922* (New York, 1957).

Marie Veronica Tarpley, *The Role of Joseph McGarrity in the Struggle for Irish Independence* (New York, 1976).

Alan J. Ward, *Ireland and Anglo-American Relations, 1886–1922* (London, 1969).

Andrew J. Wilson, *Irish America and the Ulster Conflict, 1968–1995* (Washington, D.C., 1995).

LAWRENCE J. McCAFFREY

## NATIONALISM, IRISH-AMERICAN (1921–1998)

In the nineteenth century, Irish-Americans played a vital role in providing political and material support for both constitutional and physical force nationalist movements in Ireland. Later, they also made a significant contribution to the Easter Rising and to the War of Independence, 1919–21. Yet, despite its long history and importance, Irish-American nationalism suffered a steady decline after the establishment of the Irish Free State. Most Irish-Americans accepted the Anglo-Irish Treaty as a first step toward independence. The partition of Ireland was not the same burning issue as British subjugation of the whole island. Consequently, membership of Irish-American nationalist groups plummeted and their influence was greatly reduced. This pro-

cess was further accelerated by continuous internecine feuds and splits within the most prominent organizations.

Only a small minority of Irish-Americans rejected the Treaty and clung to militant irredentism. In the 1920s and 1930s, their activities were sustained by IRA exiles who fled to America after the Civil War. These men left Ireland with an intense bitterness toward the Irish Free State and kept Irish republicanism alive in America despite all the odds. Many of them later provided leadership for the groups that formed in response to the outbreak of violence in Northern Ireland in the late 1960s.

Joseph McGarrity emerged as the leading figure within Irish-American republicanism in the 1920s. Originally from County Tyrone, he made a fortune through his business ventures in Philadelphia. During the War of Independence, McGarrity sent large amounts of cash and supplies of modern weapons to the IRA. He supported the irregulars during the Civil War but later split with Eamon de Valera over Fianna Fáil's entry into constitutional politics.

In the 1930s, McGarrity strongly opposed socialist elements in the IRA and supported the launching of a violent campaign against Britain. He eventually helped finance and plan a succession of bombing attacks in England, some of which killed and maimed innocent civilians. Public opinion on both sides of the Atlantic reacted strongly against the IRA, and the Irish government began interning republican leaders.

Despite the abject failure of the bombing campaign in England, Irish-Americans did play an important part in helping preserve Ireland's neutrality at the beginning of World War II. British Prime Minister Winston Churchill sharply condemned de Valera's decision not to join the war and was particularly concerned that Britain regain control of naval bases they had returned to Ireland in 1938. At one stage, Churchill suggested that partition could be ended if de Valera opened the Irish ports to the Royal Navy. When this proposal collapsed, the British government considered a military invasion to seize the ports.

De Valera looked to Irish America for support and encouraged formation of the American Friends of Irish Neutrality in November 1940. The AFIN began a campaign of political lobbying to ensure that President Roosevelt would pressure the British not to invade. The State Department eventually warned Churchill that hostile actions against Ireland could undermine American efforts to assist Britain's war effort. The possibility of sustained Irish-American political agitation undercut British consideration of military options and helped preserve Irish neutrality in a period when it was seriously threatened.

Ireland's neutrality throughout World War II accelerated the decline of Irish-American nationalism. For over a century, Irish immigrants had maintained that an independent Ireland would be a strong ally of the United States. Yet, while thousands of American troops were dying fighting the Nazis, de Valera made formal complaints about the presence of G.I.s in Northern Ireland. David Grey, U.S. minister in Ireland, was strongly critical of de Valera, particularly when the Dublin government sent an official message of condolence to the German ambassador after Hitler's death.

The damage done to Irish-American nationalism by de Valera's neutrality was compounded by social changes in the post-war era. Socio-economic success emptied old Irish neighborhoods and eroded ethnic solidarity. As Irish-Americans became increasingly concerned with improving their position in the United States, their support for nationalism continued to decline. In the 1950s, the American League for an Undivided Ireland failed to generate public outrage against partition. The development of the Cold War, in which the Anglo-American "special relationship" became central to Western defense, produced particularly unfavorable conditions for anti-British agitation. Similarly, the IRA's Border Campaign between 1956 and 1962 received virtually no assistance from the diaspora, save for a few isolated gunrunning schemes.

## IRISH AMERICA AND THE ULSTER CONFLICT, 1968–92

By the mid-1960s, it seemed that the long history of Irish-American involvement in the political destiny of their homeland had finally ended. Yet the outbreak of the "troubles" in Northern Ireland produced a revival of interest among a small, but significant, number of Irish-Americans. Most sympathized with the goal of Irish unification but were repelled by the violent tactics of the IRA. Their moderate nationalist views were represented by Senators Edward Kennedy and Daniel Moynihan, Speaker of the House Thomas "Tip" O'Neill, and Governor Hugh Carey of New York, the "Four Horsemen" of Irish-American politics.

During the first years of the Northern Ireland crisis, these leading politicians flirted with militant nationalism. But following representations from John Hume, leader of the Social Democratic and Labour Party (SDLP), and senior Irish government officials, the Four Horsemen were transformed into an important source of support for constitutional nationalism on Capitol Hill.

On St. Patrick's Day, 1977, the Four Horsemen issued a groundbreaking joint statement condemning Americans who supported the IRA. Edward Kennedy and Tip O'Neill also played a leading role in persuading President Jimmy Carter to endorse their position and promise U.S. financial assistance in the event of a political settlement in Ulster. These initiatives eventually contributed to a general decline in Irish-American republicanism during the late 1970s. The Four Horsemen also successfully marginalized the influence of congressman Mario Biaggi's Ad Hoc Committee on Irish Affairs, a Washington lobbying group with a more militant agenda.

In March 1981, the Four Horsemen consolidated their position on Capitol Hill by forming the Friends of Ireland. This congressional group, containing some of the most influential politicians in America, continued to support the initiatives of constitutional nationalism in Ireland. Their efforts achieved greatest success with the signing of the Anglo-Irish Agreement in 1985, which gave the Dublin government its first formal role in Northern Ireland affairs.

The contribution of the Friends of Ireland to the Agreement was most significant after a tense summit between Margaret Thatcher and Taoiseach Garrett FitzGerald in November 1984. The British prime minister's blunt rejection of Dublin's proposals seemed to signal a deterioration in Anglo-Irish relations. Faced with this possibility, the FitzGerald administration appealed to the Friends for assistance. The Irish-American politicians, through contacts with Secretary of the Interior William Clark, helped persuade Ronald Reagan to discuss Anglo-Irish affairs during a December 1984 meeting with Thatcher.

This American pressure, combined with domestic influences, brought a more conciliatory approach from Margaret Thatcher. She presented the Irish government with a comprehensive political proposal in January 1985. When Thatcher came to the United States in February to address a joint session of Congress, Tip

O'Neill emphasized his group's desire to see political progress in Northern Ireland. In her speech, the British prime minister lavished great praise on Garrett FitzGerald and promised renewed Anglo-Irish cooperation in solving the Ulster conflict.

As the pace of Anglo-Irish discussions intensified, leaders of the Friends traveled to Dublin and gave assurances of U.S. financial support for a political settlement. They also helped block a potentially serious challenge to the Agreement from Irish opposition leader Charles Haughey. When the accord was finally signed at Hillsborough Castle on November 15, 1985, it represented not only a major achievement for the FitzGerald administration and the SDLP but also for the Friends of Ireland. Kennedy, O'Neill and company later consolidated their achievement by ensuring U.S. financial backing for the Agreement through the International Fund for Ireland.

## IRISH-AMERICAN REPUBLICANS AND THE IRA

While concerned Irish-Americans have generally tended to support constitutional nationalism, a number of activist organizations adopted a more militant agenda. Groups such as the Irish National Caucus, Irish American Unity Conference, and American Irish Political Education Committee, while not officially endorsing IRA militarism, recognized its right to "resist oppression." These Irish-American organizations concentrated their resources on publicizing alleged human rights abuses by the security forces in Ulster and working for a British withdrawal.

Despite the efforts of Mario Biaggi's Ad Hoc Committee, militant Irish-America nationalist groups had only limited influence in Washington. Their activities have been more effective at the state and municipal levels, where local politicians are much more susceptible to organized Irish-American lobbying. The MacBride Principles campaign, aimed at securing equitable employment practices by American companies in Northern Ireland, stands as their greatest success. It won support from a wide spectrum of political organizations and played a major part in pushing the British government to introduce a new fair employment act in 1989.

Since its establishment in 1970, the Irish Northern Aid Committee (Noraid) has been the most prominent and controversial militant nationalist group in America. It has firmly endorsed the IRA's "armed struggle," provided important financial aid to the republican movement, and orchestrated continuous anti-British publicity campaigns.

Official reports to the Justice Department show Noraid sent nearly $3 million to republican agencies in Ireland from 1971–1990. The group continually claimed these funds went to the families of imprisoned republicans for welfare purposes.

British, Irish, and American authorities dismissed this "charitable facade" and alleged that most donations were used by the IRA to buy weapons. The Justice Department further claimed that the group's official financial reports were significantly understated and that large amounts of cash were secretly sent to the Provos. While a substantial body of circumstantial evidence supports these claims, law enforcement agents never uncovered a direct link between Noraid funds and arms procurement.

The dispute over the use of Noraid funds is mostly academic. The group's financial contribution helped the IRA because it freed other cash which could then be used to buy arms. Even if all Noraid funds went to republican families, it still performed an important role in sustaining morale through the support of dependents. As Noraid founder Michael Flannery once commented, "An I.R.A. soldier freed from financial worries for his family is a much better fighter!"

The most direct way in which Irish-American republicans have helped the IRA is through trans-Atlantic gunrunning. In the early 1970s, veteran New York activist George Harrison shipped the first consignments of American rifles to Belfast. Later, the Provos sent their own emissaries to the U.S. to coordinate the gunrunning network. They eventually acquired batches of Armalite rifles through a group of Irish-American republicans in Philadelphia. These weapons modernized the Provo's firepower and were ideal for its military operations. By 1977, the British government claimed that 80% of the IRA's weapons were coming from America.

From the late 1970s, IRA weapons procurement focused less on the United States and increasingly turned to Eastern Europe, the Middle East, and Libya. Despite this trend, Irish-American gunrunners continued to make an important contribution to the Provo arsenal. They focused on supplying weapons, such as the M-60 machinegun and Barrett .50-caliber rifle, which were more difficult to acquire from other sources. A number of individuals also provided sophisticated components for remote control bombs.

In the 1980s, one of the IRA's primary objectives was to acquire weapons to bring down British helicopters. The Irish-American republican network again played a key role in this strategy. Some conspirators worked on the development of more effective rockets which would explode close to the target, without requiring a direct hit. Others tried to obtain the Stinger missile, highly valued because of its capacity to penetrate the electronic defenses on British helicopters.

Anti-British publicity campaigns have perhaps been the most influential contribution of Irish-American republicans. While these efforts constantly suffered from the negative public reaction to IRA atrocities, a number of important breakthroughs were achieved by Noraid. In 1972, the group became a catalyst for popular revulsion at the Bloody Sunday killings of fourteen Catholic demonstrators in Derry by the British Parachute Regiment. During the hunger strikes of 1980–81, in which ten republican prisoners starved themselves to death, Noraid organized large public demonstrations and helped convince many politicians and newspapers that Margaret Thatcher was largely responsible for the prison crisis. The group's fund-raising reached unprecedented heights, and its membership increased nationwide.

Noraid's success during the hunger strikes convinced its leaders to organize annual tours of Northern Ireland. Beginning in 1983, militant activists traveled to the province to experience life under "British oppression." These tours became valuable publicity events for the republican movement in Ireland and helped create the impression of widespread Irish-American support for the IRA. Many of those who participated in the tours returned to America with a renewed dedication to work for the republican cause.

United States government agencies continually worked against this Irish-American republican network. The Justice Department tried to undermine Noraid fund-raising while the FBI broke numerous gunrunning conspiracies. The Immigration Service launched deportation and extradition proceedings against a succession of IRA fugitives who were given cover by sympathetic Irish-Americans.

In addition to pressure on them from federal authorities, Irish-American republicans were plagued by internal divisions and hostility from the U.S. media. Despite all these forces working against them, militant Irish-American nationalist organizations continued to function and even made valuable contributions to the republican movement in Ireland.

### THE CLINTON ADMINISTRATION AND ULSTER PEACE PROCESS

The development of the Northern Ireland peace process in the early 1990s has led to the formation of new dynamic Irish-American groups. There has also been a considerable realignment among the traditional organizations. Some of the antagonisms between constitutional nationalists and republicans have been diluted as both joined to secure common goals created by the political changes in Ulster.

During the 1992 presidential primaries, a loose coalition of politicians, lawyers, trade union activists, and business leaders formed Americans for a New Irish Agenda which aimed at encouraging candidates to address Irish issues. ANIA's most prominent members included former congressman Bruce Morrison; Niall O'Dowd, publisher of the *Irish America* magazine; and William Flynn and Charles Feeney, both wealthy businessmen with a deep interest in Ireland. The group gave strong support to Bill Clinton, and then worked to ensure he remained committed to his Irish campaign pledges while in the White House.

As the peace process blossomed throughout 1993, ANIA leaders were convinced that Irish republicans could be persuaded to eschew violence and enter political negotiations on the future of Ireland. O'Dowd and his associates believed that a major American concession to Gerry Adams, president of Sinn Fein, could help him convince republican militants that a cease-fire would reap significant dividends. Acting on this assessment, ANIA began working to secure a visa for Adams to visit New York in January 1994.

One of the most important achievements in the Adams visa campaign was winning support from Edward Kennedy. Despite his longstanding opposition to Irish republicanism, the senator was persuaded to use his influence for the Sinn Fein leader. Kennedy's chairmanship of the Senate Labor Committee, vital to the White House's efforts to reform welfare and health care, gave him considerable clout with President Bill Clinton.

The "Kennedy Factor" also played an important role in ANIA communications with the White House. In 1993, with the Clinton administration officially adhering to a no-contact policy with Sinn Fein, O'Dowd and his group established a subterranean line of communication between Irish republicans and Trina Vargo, Edward Kennedy's foreign policy adviser. Vargo, in turn, relayed information to Nancy Soderberg, then chiefly responsible for Irish issues at the National Security Council, and also a former Kennedy foreign policy aide.

The information which Nancy Soderberg received through the ANIA pipeline helped bring her and National Security Advisor Anthony Lake into the pro-visa lobby. Their influence, despite fierce opposition from the State Department and British government, eventually played a key role in Clinton's decision to allow Gerry Adams to address a foreign policy forum in New York.

The Adams visa helped precipitate debate within the IRA over the merits of a cessation of violence. ANIA leaders tried to influence the decision by proposing that Irish-American dollars could enable Sinn Fein to build the best political machine in Ireland and that republicans would have the opportunity to use the United States as a springboard for getting their views heard across the world. In addition, the Clinton administration implied that it would use its influence to ensure parity for Sinn Fein objectives in any negotiated settlement. These assumptions eventually became a major component in the IRA's decision to declare a cease-fire on August 31, 1994.

The White House responded to the cease-fire by making incremental concessions to republicans. With the encouragement of senior Irish-American legislators, led by Ted Kennedy and Chris Dodd, Bill Clinton met with Gerry Adams in Washington on St. Patrick's Day, 1995. Adams was permitted to raise millions of dollars in the U.S., through a new support group called the Friends of Sinn Fein, and establish a lobbying office in Washington. Later that year, Clinton became the first incumbent American president to visit Northern Ireland. The rapturous reception he received from crowds in Belfast encouraged him to believe aides who were convinced that the U.S. role in Ulster had saved hundreds of lives and that the peace process was unstoppable.

The February 1996 IRA bombing of Canary Warf in London, which killed two people, shattered the Clinton administration's sense of euphoria over its Northern Ireland policy. Yet, despite considerable pressure to sever all links with the republican movement, White House staff maintained lines of communication with Sinn Fein, hoping that dialogue rather than exclusion had the best chance of restoring the cease-fire.

The initial hope for a speedy return to peace was quashed by the IRA's continued attacks in England. Despite continuous appeals from President Clinton and Irish-American political leaders for an end to violence, the IRA also resumed its campaign in Northern Ireland, detonating two car bombs at British Army headquarters on October 7, 1996. As the White House's anger and frustration grew, Gerry Adams was advised not to apply for a visa to attend the 1997 St. Patrick's Day festivities in the United States.

When political developments produced a renewed IRA cease-fire in July 1997, Irish-Americans again played an influential role. Bruce Morrison relayed assurances to Irish republicans that the Clinton administration would react positively to a second cease-fire. In the weeks following the end of violence, Gerry Adams was permitted to resume fund-raising in America. As the cease-fire held, the Justice Department suspended deportation proceedings against seven former IRA men who had illegally entered the United States. In addition, the State Department excluded the IRA from a list of terrorist organizations, thus exempting the organization from a series of severe legal restrictions.

The second IRA cease-fire eventually laid the basis for the convening of multi-party talks in October 1997. Former Senator George Mitchell, as chairman of these talks, played a pivotal role, both in winning respect as an impartial arbiter and by imposing a deadline for agreement. In the final hours of negotiations Bill Clinton telephoned all the key participants, using his powers of persuasion to help overcome their misgivings about elements of the deal. When the Good Friday Agreement was eventually signed, it was not only an important breakthrough for Ulster's political parties, but also a major success for the American role in the peace process.

The Clinton administration continued to use its influence to ensure the success of the Good Friday Agreement. Bill Clinton strongly encouraged voters to support it in referenda in both

parts of Ireland. He also used his influence to help bridge some of the most difficult issues. In the days before his second visit to Northern Ireland in September 1998, he helped persuade Gerry Adams to issue a statement disassociating Sinn Fein from violence and accepting his party's cooperation with efforts to decommission IRA weapons. These announcements opened the way for the first face-to-face meeting between Adams and David Trimble, the new first minister of Northern Ireland and leader of the Ulster Unionist Party.

The Irish-American interventions may be the most significant in the diaspora's long history of involvement in Irish political affairs.

Trevor Birney and Julian O'Neill, *When the President Calls* (Derry, 1997).
Sean Cronin, *The McGarrity Papers: Revelations of the Irish Revolutionary Movement in Ireland and America 1900–1940* (Tralee, 1972).
T. Ryle Dwyer, *Irish Neutrality and the USA, 1939–47* (Dublin, 1977).
Jack Holland, *The American Connection: U.S. Guns, Money and Influence in Northern Ireland* (N.Y., 1987).
Conor O'Clery, *Daring Diplomacy: Clinton's Secret Search for Peace in Ireland* (Boulder, 1997).
Ray O'Hanlon, *The New Irish Americans* (Colorado, 1997).
Andrew J. Wilson, *Irish America and the Ulster Conflict, 1968–95* (Washington, 1995).

ANDREW WILSON

## NATIONALISM AND WORLD WAR I

The enmity that had existed for centuries between Ireland and England played a significant factor during World War I in how Irish-Americans responded to whether the United States should side with the British in 1914 when war broke out in Europe. During the war's early years, the Irish-American press and many prominent Irish-Americans pushed for the United States to support Germany. It wasn't a love for Germany or interest in Germany's objectives that prompted such groups to urge support for the Central Powers, but rather it was the prevalent dislike for all things English.

Even though England had approved home rule for Ireland by 1914, the problem of unification with Ulster remained unresolved. American Irish, however, demanded independence for their native land and hoped that this could be accomplished if Germany was victorious or if the United States applied pressure on England. It must be noted that after the United States joined with the Allies and declared war in 1917, President Woodrow Wilson requested the American ambassador in London to explore with the British government the question of self-rule for Ireland.

Disagreement about what was best for Ireland was noticeable among the various Irish publications. In 1892 *The Irish World* had denounced Irish nationalists and in 1914 supported John Redmond, Irish party leader in Parliament, for home rule and parliamentary procedures. The *Gaelic-American* was positive that England would never voluntarily relinquish control of Ireland. Complete independence for Ireland was favored by the Ancient Order of Hibernians, and John Redmond was denounced by the Clan-na-Gael for offering assistance to England during the war.

### ETHNIC GROUPS PROTEST ALLIANCE

A secret Anglo-American alliance was feared by many national groups in the United States. Both the Irish National Alliance, which was organized in 1895, and the National German-American Alliance, formed in 1899, declared that America should be first. They opposed union with foreign nations unless it helped their native land. Irish-Americans demonstrated throughout the United States, and Irish societies sent letters of protest to Washington, D.C., against an Anglo-American alliance. German-Americans and Irish-Americans signed each others' petitions.

However, the majority of Irish-Americans didn't necessarily agree with these positions and didn't belong to an organization that had a political agenda. Some Irish-Americans even believed that their countrymen were spreading propaganda for the Germans. Many Irish-American financiers and industrialists were pro-Ally. When Mayor James Curley of Boston supported England during the war, *The Gaelic-American* had no kind words for him and went so far as to label him a traitor to his parents' native land.

Even the Irish Volunteers considered England as the real instigator of the war, and Irishmen complained about how the American press was reporting the war. A committee of the Clan-na-Gael met with the German ambassador in New York and may have discussed ways to incite a revolution in Ireland. Prominent Irish-Americans were suddenly popular speakers at German-American gatherings, and vice versa. The German and Austro-Hungarian bazaars, which helped to raise funds for the wounded and orphaned, always had an Irish Night. A demonstration in Madison Square Garden in 1915 resulted in the formation of a German-Irish group known as The Friends of Peace.

## PUBLICATIONS LAUNCH ATTACK

Both Irish- and German-American newspapers purported that Germany was fighting a defensive war for freedom of the seas and that the pro-British press of the United States was misrepresenting the war. *The Gaelic-American* even reported that the Kaiser carried a four-leaf shamrock as a good luck charm, and in 1916 published an article citing that nearly two-thirds of the German Empire was Catholic.

The British finally saw a need to counteract some of the Irish-American propaganda. John Redmond, Horace Plunkett and other Irishmen were sent to the United States to give interviews and write articles in support of Great Britain. The book, *The Irish at the Front,* with an introduction by Redmond, was distributed following the Easter Rebellion in 1916.

Irish-Americans were skeptical that Wilson would maintain America's neutrality. They accused Wilson of attempting to make the United States a "vassal state" of England, and questioned the shipment of war materials to the Allies by American manufacturers and the sale of British and French war bonds to American investors. Wilson also alienated many Americans who weren't of English or Scotch ancestry by viewing them as "hyphenates" and labeled their ties of sentiment with the old country as "divided loyalty."

The Irish-American press even justified the sinking of the *Lusitania* in 1915 by a German submarine, resulting in the loss of many American lives, by asserting that the British passenger ship was carrying munitions. In March 1916, nearly 2,300 Irish met at a convention in New York to assert self-rule for Ireland and to demand that the United States remain neutral. Prominent Irish-Americans didn't escape criticism. Irish tenor John McCormack was condemned for sending cigarettes to English soldiers, and Cardinal James Gibbons of Baltimore was criticized for

being a friend of Redmond and participating in international movements.

A rash of newspapers sprang up during the war to further Irish national needs: *The Irish Voice* in Chicago, *The Irish Review* in Los Angeles, *The Irish Press* in Philadelphia, and *Bull,* a satirical weekly.

Theatre also played a role in furthering Irish sentiments about the war and reenforcing Irish nationalism. Produced during these pre-war years were the novel *Ireland a Nation;* a two-act propaganda play, *John Bull on Trial;* and the play *Ireland's Easter,* by two Philadelphia priests about the 1916 Easter Rebellion. Lecturers from Ireland addressed audiences across the country and Irish music was revived.

England unknowingly aided the Irish-American cause by its "butchery of Irish patriots" following the Easter Rebellion. In the United States, funds were raised to relieve those in jail; Masses were celebrated for the Irish martyrs; and Boston held a public meeting to honor Ireland's "holy dead." Media in the United States and politicians condemned the executions, and Cardinals Gibbons, John Farley of New York, and William O'Connell of Boston appealed for relief to aid the victims of the Easter Rebellion.

During the 1916 presidential campaign, controversies over American neutrality continued, and Irish-Americans viewed Wilson's remarks about those who need "hyphens" in their names as slurs against their loyalty. Although the Democratic party lost many votes in the eastern cities, where there were large groups of Irish, Wilson was reelected. The Democratic slogan, "He Kept Us Out of War," may have influenced the majority of voters.

## IRISH PROVE PATRIOTISM

When Germany resumed submarine warfare in 1917, Wilson broke diplomatic relations with Germany and requested Congress to declare war. German and Irish organizations continued to the last minute to petition against war. When war was declared, however, their loyalty to America was never questioned. They purchased war bonds and their men served in the military.

One of the first American units to go to the European front was the Sixty-ninth New York, commanded by "Wild Bill" Donovan, and the Catholic Church sent chaplains. The Irish served as responsibly as they had done in earlier wars.

Some Irish, particularly members of the American Truth Society and the Friends of Irish Freedom, continued their tirade against the British, preaching from soap boxes on New York street corners. *The Gaelic-American* continued to attack the British throughout 1917. Attacks in Irish media against the Allied powers became so abusive that *The Gaelic-American, The Irish World* and *The Freeman's Journal* lost their mailing privilege or were held in the post offices so that the newspapers' contents could be investigated. All the newspapers throughout the country that were founded to support Irish-American beliefs and self-rule for Ireland finally went out of business by the end of 1918.

When the war ended in November 1918, Irish-Americans were concerned about what good might come out of the peace conference for Ireland. They hoped that Wilson would endorse negotiations between Great Britian and Ireland that would lead to self-rule for Ireland. He did nothing. Irish dissatisfaction with Wilson's record on Ireland probably brought about the defeat of the Democratic presidential ticket in 1920. Warren Harding, the

Republican candidate, carried the large eastern cities, which had strong Irish populations, by a strong majority.

John Devoy, *Recollections of an Irish Rebel* (New York, 1929).
Harold Evans, *The American Century* (New York, 1998).
William V. Shannon, *The American Irish* (New York, 1966).
Carl Wittke, *The Irish in America* (Baton Rouge, La., 1956).

MARIANNA McLOUGHLIN

# NATIVISM

## INTRODUCTION

From earliest settlement in America, the phenomenon of nativism has been associated with the Irish immigrant experience. Generally defined as the favoring of native-born American interests over those of immigrant groups, nativist opinion targeted Irish immigrants since the seventeenth century. Anti-Irish sentiment appeared in the annals of popular culture: in balladry, street theater, and pamphlet literature and verse throughout the colonies. By the 1820s and 1830s, anti-Irish humor took on a virulent tone and developed into a direct attack on Irish settlement, Irish culture, and Irish prospects in America. Isolated incidents of anti-Irish prejudice in the seventeenth and eighteenth centuries depicted Irish immigrants as backward and uncivilized. These incidents were superseded by a new kind of organized hostility in the nineteenth century, publicly expressed by a succession of nativist organizations. These groupings may be viewed as the backbone of both the nativist movement and of anti-Irish feeling in America. As such, they constitute the primary focus of this section.

## THE ORIGINS OF NATIVISM DIRECTED AGAINST IRISH IMMIGRANTS

Where did this prejudice originate? Why were Irish immigrants to America targeted by specific elements within the American population? The answers lie in colonial settlement patterns. From the seventeenth century on, English settlers transported an anti-Catholic agenda to the American colonies. Rooted in the Protestant doctrinal ideology that developed out of the sixteenth-century Reformation in Europe, anti-Catholic sentiment permeated the colonies. Protestant English settlers cultivated the attitude that Catholicism posed a serious threat to their unique work ethic, to the institutions they founded and, ultimately, to the very cornerstone of the American Republic.

As the American Revolution ushered in the First Party System, the ideal of a pure democracy unsullied by alien Latin rituals and superstitions gained a firm foothold among native-born white Americans of Anglo-Saxon stock. While still a minority—albeit a dominant one—in the early years of the Union, English settlers dreamed of creating a new order in the new republic, free from Catholic or "Romish" control over liberty-loving Americans. To English Protestant settlers, the hierarchical values of Catholicism conflicted directly with the principles of life and liberty underpinning the foundations of the United States as a nation and a democracy. In sum, to English Protestant settlers and their descendants, Catholicism represented an un-American agenda which would always be at odds with American republican values.

## ANTI-IRISH SENTIMENT IN POPULAR CULTURE

For native-born Americans of English stock, the long tradition of discord between Britain and Ireland was instrumental in the de-

velopment of nativism. During the seventeenth century, anti-Irish sentiment was often couched in humor, especially in the form of short sketches involving stereotypical Irish characters. Anecdotes, tall tales and crude verse appeared frequently in the contemporary pamphlet and almanac literature. For example, in 1797, *The Farmer's Diary* quoted the following: "On the banks of a rivulet in the north of Ireland," it ran, "is a stone with the following inscription . . . Take notice, that when this stone is out of sight, it is not safe to ford the river" [*Poor Richard Revived: Being the Farmer's Diary . . . for . . . 1797*, 31099 in *Early American Imprints*. Robert K. Dodge, *Early American Almanac Humor* (Bowling Green: Bowling Green, 1987, p. 55)].

This type of satirical humor took on a more strident tone in the early decades of the nineteenth century, however, as Irish immigration increased to a steady stream. Considerable attention was paid to this swelling tide by Protestant evangelical revivalists of the Second Great Awakening, a movement which enjoyed tremendous support in the early 1800s. Protestant fears of the moral depravity of the papacy intensified, together with increased apprehension over the dangers posed by Irish "papist" immigrants to American liberty. The British government's grant of legislative freedoms to Catholics in Ireland under the Catholic Emancipation Act of 1828 further galvanized American-Protestant opinion to the idea of protecting American institutions from Irish-Catholic corruption.

## NATIVIST VIOLENCE AND LABOR DISCRIMINATION

The rise in hostile incidents perpetrated against Irish Catholics in the early nineteenth century played a vital part in the development of the American nativist agenda. During the 1820s and the 1830s, numerous incidents of mob violence against Irish churches, homes and individuals characterized the Irish assimilation process. Violent episodes occurred most commonly in northern cities containing the combination of a dominant minority of English Protestant stock, a sizable working-class sector, and a large Irish immigrant population, such as Boston, New York, and Philadelphia. Anti-Catholic riots in Philadelphia in April 1822, the stoning of Irish-Catholic homes in Boston for three days in 1829, the robbing and burning of St. Mary's Roman Catholic Church in New York in 1831, and the burning of an Ursuline convent in Charlestown, Massachusetts by a mob of rioters in 1834 stand as evidence of the intensification of nativist feeling against Irish Catholics. In September 1836, nativist mobs in Boston took pot-shots at a statue of Bishop Benedict Fenwick and at a papal effigy conveyed in mock procession through the streets. Further westward, three years later, ten men were killed by militia on the occasion of a riot between German-Protestant and Irish-Catholic workers on the Chesapeake and Ohio Canal.

By the 1840s, incidents of anti-Irish mob violence were on the increase. As one Philadelphia report from May 1844 documented, "at least one person is killed and more than fifty injured as nativist mobs riot against Catholics. A second mob gathers in the evening to threaten a Catholic school, but disperses after armed guards kill two rioters and wound several more. Violence continues on May 8, with a Catholic church and school burned, together with a row of Irish homes. Troops arrive to scatter the mob before it can demolish two more churches" (Michael Newton and Judy Ann Newton, *Racial & Religious Violence in America: A Chronology*, New York and London: Garland Publishing, 1991, p. 116).

## PROTESTANT NATIVIST ORGANIZATIONS IN THE ANTEBELLUM ERA

Even as Irish immigrants struggled against localized, socio-economic victimization, a more powerful threat appeared on the horizon. Organizations promoting a more rigorous nativist agenda mushroomed in the early 1800s, attracting huge memberships across the United States and exerting a direct influence on the nation's politics. Deriving largely from Protestant evangelical roots, these organizations directly affected Irish assimilation, and have recently been accorded new significance in shaping the broad course of American history.

Nativist organizations promoting an anti-Irish agenda amalgamated critiques of Irish impoverishment and drinking stereotypes with the notion that as a race, the Irish were unassimilable. Closely associated with the Second Great Awakening, such organizations as the American Bible Society, the American Tract Society, and the American Home Mission Society grew out of local bible societies and Christian literature promotions in the 1800s and 1810s. Founded in New York in 1816 and 1825 respectively, the American Bible Society and the American Tract Society promoted Christian values and " the interests of vital godliness and sound morality," according to a promotional pamphlet (*American Tract Society Statement of Purpose,* 1825). Utilizing a system whereby members distributed Christian literature to immigrants, these organizations pursued a distinctly anti-Catholic and anti-Irish agenda, promoting Protestant religious and moral values over the tide of superstition and corruption they characterized as distinctly Irish Catholic.

The Great Famine emigration of 1845–49 drove over a million Roman Catholics to the United States from Ireland. Perceived by Protestant nativists as an alien, priest-ridden culture, Irish settlers were castigated as extremely harmful to American society. Confronted with these arrivals, bible societies labeled Irish Catholics as unfit for civilized American society, and wholly undesirable as settlers. As historian David Bennett remarked, "the missionary zeal that characterized the American Bible Society and the American Tract Society, inspiring the creation of a series of religious newspapers and the founding of the New York Protestant Association and similar groups, was thoroughly nativist in both form and content" (*The Party of Fear: The American Far Right From Nativism to the Militia Movement,* New York, 1995, p. 36).

Similar in structure and agenda to the Bible and Tract societies, the American Foreign and Christian Union expanded rapidly in New York and through the northeast United States in the 1840s and 1850s. During the early 1850s, in the aftermath of the Famine arrivals, the Union clashed with Bishop John Hughes of New York on the issue of nativist attacks on Irish settlers. An Irish immigrant himself, Hughes was instrumental in publicly confronting specific nativist attacks, and in circumventing general nativist aggression in the city.

Conflicts between the large working-class Irish immigrant populations of east-coast cities and nativist groups flared up in 1853 and 1854. During these years, Italian Archbishop Cajetan Bedini paid a visit to the United States to report to the papacy on the state of American Catholicism. During his tour, the American Foreign and Christian Union instigated outbreaks of violence against pro-Bedini Irish Catholics, incurring the wrath of Hughes and prominent Irish clerics in the U.S.

One of the most powerful of the religious-based nativist societies was the American Protestant Association, founded in Philadelphia in 1842. Building on earlier collectives such as the New York Protestant Association and the Protestant Reformation Society—active in New York and Pennsylvania during the 1830s—the Association marketed its anti-Catholic platform to the more prosperous American Protestants. The Association toned down the hostile rhetoric of the past in favor of a more moderate approach.

That the Association counted large numbers of Protestant Irish as members did nothing to dispel tensions between this organization and Irish Catholics. Rather, Irish Protestant—or Scotch-Irish—settlers' long-standing antipathy toward Catholics guaranteed the opposite effect. The Scotch-Irish transplantation of the Loyal Orange Order to the United States in the eighteenth century organized Irish Presbyterians and Methodists in a fraternal organization that perpetuated Irish Protestant-Catholic hostilities on American soil. Similar in structure to Freemasonry and the eighteenth-century European organizations of the Illuminati—both identified with anti-Catholic platforms—the Orange Order perpetuated the sharp divisions between Irish Protestants and Catholics. The Order's anti-Catholic rhetoric survived in semi-secrecy within its lodge system, igniting occasionally into outbreaks of violence in New York and Philadelphia later on in the 1870s and 1880s.

## PATRIOTIC ORGANIZATIONS IN THE ANTEBELLUM PERIOD

Between 1800 and 1860, the intensification of competition for work generated increased anti-Irish feeling across the larger industrializing centers of America. Undercutting pre-existing wage-levels with their willingness to work for lower pay than native-born Americans, Irish settlers struggled against hostility and discrimination in the area of employment. "No Irish Need Apply" signs frequently appeared in stores and businesses, as a public reminder of anti-Irish feeling. In short, by the 1830s, socio-economic nativist forces exerted considerable negative influence over the Irish acculturation process in America.

While commercial and industrialist interests in the larger urban centers demonstrated the foundations of a nativist agenda by the mid-nineteenth century, Irish male and female workers were automatically restricted to the lowest-paying manual labor. During the same mid-century decades, while nativist Protestant organizations cultivated a similar anti-Irish-Catholic agenda, another type of organization was combining antipathy to immigrants with a new and strident American nationalism. During the Jacksonian Age and into the 1840s, an outpouring of American patriotic fervor emanated from organizations promoting a general anti-immigrant platform. The larger northeastern cities played host to a number of small-scale organizations touting nativist manifestos. For example, one such group styling itself the American Brotherhood expanded and subsequently divided into three separate organizations in New York City in the 1840s: the Order of United Americans, the Organization of United Americans, and the Order of United American Mechanics. These groups enjoyed considerable support, appealing particularly to working men's collectives in the larger East Coast urban centers. Nativist pride in the workplace and in a distinctly American identity increased working-class suspicion of the intrusion of foreigners into America. Irish miners and construction workers constituted clear targets. Intensifying the pressure of economic nativism, the United Sons of America in Philadelphia adopted a particularly vigilant platform against the incursion of Irish laborers working for lower wages than native-born Americans.

## Political Nativism: Know-Nothingism in the 1850s

As the forces of sectionalism paved the road to civil war in the 1850s, the dramatic rise of the American Party, more commonly identified as the Know-Nothings, constituted a high point in anti-Irish activism. A political movement in form and structure, the Know-Nothings attracted Americans who believed that the Whig and Democratic parties had failed to recognize Irish Catholics and other foreigners as a menace to democracy. Members of localized nativist organizations such as the Order of United Americans, the Native American party, and the Independent Reform Party in New York and Pennsylvania sought a larger political forum through which to campaign against the Catholic threat to American liberty. By the same token, the organizations hoped to rid the country of Whigs and Democrats who failed to address the dangers being posed to Americans.

North and South, the Know-Nothings expanded rapidly on a platform designed to appeal to Americans seeking moral stewardship on the issue of immigrant status in America. In language reminiscent of Great Awakening rhetoric, Know-Nothingism was officially launched in 1849 in New York as the secret Order of the Star Spangled Banner. Building on the Whig legacy of patriotism and anti-sectionalism, the Know-Nothings harnessed an anti-Catholic, anti-Irish and anti-foreign platform to a political campaign against the Democrats in 1854 and 1855. Targeting Irish immigrants as the most serious threat to the *security* of American democracy, the spectacular expansion of Know-Nothingism throughout eastern and midwest America was built on the platform of its secret manifesto of immigration restriction and the exclusion of non-citizens from public or political office. By the mid-1850s Know-Nothingism succeeded in attracting large enough numbers of dissatisfied Whigs and Democrats to generate a new national political movement and create a new political party.

The most public and most political demonstration of anti-Irish feeling in the United States to date, the *Principles of the American Party* articulated clearly that Americans were prepared to settle for nothing less than "the radical reform of abuses, and the preservation of our institutions and our liberties, under the name of the American party." Further, the *Principles* intoned that "as Americans, we cannot consent to give our political suffrages to any other than those born on our soil and nurtured among our institutions" (*Principles of the American Party,* New York, 1849, p. 1).

However, the rapid rise of Know-Nothingism as America's first coherent anti-Irish political platform was matched by its equally dramatic decline. Although anti-Irish sentiment remained strong throughout the 1850s, the Know-Nothings failed to find common ground on the issue of slavery. Coupled with the birth of the Republican Party in the mid-1850s, divisions over the slave question destroyed Know-Nothingism in a few short years. By 1860, the party had crumbled, and had almost entirely disappeared before the outbreak of the Civil War.

If political nativism in the shape of Know-Nothingism disappeared by the 1860s, organized nativism persisted. Even as Irish settlers in America made important strides in the settlement process, especially in politics and education, nativist organizations continued to attract considerable support. Groups such as the National League for the Protection of American Institutions, the Order of the American Union, the Patriotic Order of the Sons of America, and the United Order of Pilgrim Fathers continued the nativist agenda of Know-Nothingism in a localized fashion.

Primarily East Coast collectives in the 1870s and 1880s—particularly in New York, Massachusetts, Pennsylvania, Ohio and New Jersey—these groupings represented the beginnings of a shift away from the intense anti-Irish feeling of earlier organizations. At this point, not only were Irish settlers successfully assimilating into mainstream American society, but Irish immigration declined dramatically from mid-century levels. Precipitated by the factors of improved economic conditions and a steadily declining population in Ireland, by the early twentieth century Irish immigration had virtually ground to a halt. As Eastern and Southern European immigration increased spectacularly between 1870 and 1900, nativist attention gradually shifted away from Irish Catholics and onto these other immigrant groups.

## Women's Patriotic Organizations

Two women's groups attracted considerable attention in this period, the Daughters of the American Revolution and the Patriotic Daughters of America. Both played a meaningful role in the "Americanization" movement of the 1880s and 1890s, but are not usually associated with a specific anti-Irish platform. The establishment of the Patriotic Daughters of America in 1885—a sister-organization of the American Patriotic League—and the DAR in 1890 as patriotic orders for women descended from participants in the American Revolution brought members into contact with the nativist agenda of the 1890s. However, in the context of anti-Irish nativism, the PDA and the DAR were less focused on the removal of immigrants than their successful assimilation into American society. As such, the PDA and the DAR may be viewed as exemplifying the deceleration of nativism targeting Irish immigrants in the turn of the century era.

## Decline of Anti-Irish Nativism

As the twentieth century approached, American interest in nativism persisted, but lessened considerably toward Irish settlers. The activities of the Red, White and Blue Organization in the 1880s generated anti-Catholic attitudes, but did not focus exclusively on Irish immigrants. The organization itself was short-lived, compared with a similar, but more successful body founded in Iowa in 1887. The American Protective Association ignited a much more widespread explosion of nativist feeling in the 1890s, claiming upwards of two million members. Advocating the protection of American liberties against corruptive foreign influence, not the least of which was Catholicism, the APA agenda echoed that of the Know-Nothings some decades earlier. However, the intensity of its anti-Irish platform never matched that of pre–Civil War organizations. The organization declined rapidly in the early 1900s with the improvement in economic conditions throughout the Midwest.

A gradual shift away from anti-Irish nativism may be identified from the 1890s on. For example, the Immigration Restriction League's 1894 campaign to limit foreign settlement in America was concerned less with Irish arrivals than Southern and Eastern European Catholics. Likewise, the American Defense Society and the American Protective League in the 1910s and the 1920s were much more concerned with anti-German feeling than with anti-Irish antagonism.

From the 1920s on, nativism and nativist activities altered in form and focus, with organizations concentrating primarily on an anti-radical, rather than an anti-Catholic agenda. For the most part, the end of the nineteenth century witnessed the decline and disappearance of anti-Irish organizations and activities. In the

1910s and the 1920s, bodies such as the Joint Legislative Committee Against Seditious Activities, under State Senator Clinton R. Lusk of New York, concentrated specifically on the issue of radicalism in American society. The Ku Klux Klan (see separate entry) maintained a rigorous anti-Catholic platform, but even this was dwarfed by racial prejudice against African-Americans. Anti-Irish feeling persisting into the twentieth century was stabilized to some degree by the election of John F. Kennedy to the presidency in 1960, by which point the success of Irish assimilation must be seen as significant in the disappearance of nativist groups organized specifically to prevent that same assimilation process.

Tyler Anbinder, *Nativism and Slavery: The Northern Know-Nothings & the Politics of the 1850s* (New York, 1992).

David H. Bennett, *The Party of Fear: The American Far Right From Nativism to the Militia Movement* (New York, 1995).

Ray Allen Billington, *The Protestant Crusade, 1800–1860: A Study of the Origins of American Nativism* (New York, 1938).

Robert K. Dodge, *Early American Almanac Humor* (Bowling Green, 1987).

Henry O. Dwight, *The Centennial History of the American Bible Society* (New York, 1916).

John Higham, *Strangers in the Land: Patterns of American Nativism 1860–1925* (New York, 1970).

———, "Another Look at Nativism," *Catholic Historical Review,* 46 (July 1958): 147–158.

Michael F. Holt, "The Politics of Impatience: The Origins of Know-Nothingism," *Journal of American History,* 60 (1973): 309–331.

Noel Ignatiev, *How the Irish Became White* (New York, 1995).

Mary C. Kelly, "Forty Shades of Green: Conflict Over Community Among the New York Irish, 1860–1920" (unpubl. Ph.D. diss., Syracuse University, 1997).

Dale T. Knobel, *America for the Americans: The Nativist Movement in the United States* (New York, 1996).

Thomas H. O'Connor, *The Boston Irish: A Political History* (Boston, 1995).

MARY C. KELLY

## NEBRASKA

Nebraska doesn't come readily to mind as an Irish enclave, but the first white child born there was of Irish descent. The Fenians found adherents within its borders, and myriad place names attest to Celtic influence—Avoca, O'Neill, Milligan, Kelly, Carroll, Lynch, Irish Flats, Mullen, Parnell, Belfast, Sheridan and other towns that echo Ireland.

Short of discovering some itinerant Gael attached to the retinues of Spanish and French adventurers, we must wait until the nineteenth century for evidences of an Irish presence.

In 1804, armed with a commission from President Jefferson and sparingly funded by Congress, Captain Meriwether Lewis and Lieutenant William Clark launched their exploration of the newly-acquired Louisiana Purchase expanse. On August 3rd of that year they met with the Otoe and Missouri at a site a few miles north of the future city of Omaha. Nearly a third of their military escort had names suggesting Irish or Scotch-Irish lineage—Collins, Colter, Shields, Floyd and others, right down to the youngest member of the expedition, 17-year-old George Shannon.

Fifteen years later, Major Stephen Long explored the South Platte Valley, deeming it "unfit for cultivation," and fur traders followed, including Thomas Fitzpatrick, and map makers like John C. Fremont, aided by Kit Carson. Trails were carved out, trading posts established, and hordes of travelers crossed these plains in the first half of the 19th century. Some were after gold; some, like the Mormons, sought a safe haven for their families; missionaries of all faiths came to convert the tribes; and thousands of settlers trekked west to the promise of Oregon. Inevitable conflict between these newcomers and the resident Native Americans created a growing military population.

"The army on the Plains comprised men from many different walks of life," wrote historian Ray Mattison. "From the point of national origin, the United States ranked first, Ireland second . . ." Although Mattison was measuring enlistments somewhat later in the century, the Irish were soldiers early on, drawn by the relative financial security and excitement of the vocation.

Some of these Irish recruits were with David Mitchell and Thomas Fitzpatrick in 1851 at Horse Creek in western Nebraska as they forged a treaty during the largest assembly of Indians ever held in this country. A scant three years later a rash young lieutenant named John Grattan attacked a Sioux camp, provoking decades of hostilities. The subsequent massacre of his command was avenged at Ash Hollow by General William Harney. General George Crook's later campaigns were catalogued by Lt. John G. Bourke. In those names we hear Tipperary, Roscommon, Galway and several Ulster locales. At Fort Robinson, the post surgeon was named McGillycuddy, and Indian agents in the region were O'Fallon and O'Dougherty. Even the "Irish washerwoman," usually the wife of an enlisted man, figures into the mix as a post laundress.

During the Civil War, the First Nebraska Regiment boasted a Major William McCord from Plattsmouth, a pair of captains named Kennedy and McConihe, plus a large contingent of soldiers with names like Spellman and McClelland. The brogues often heard in the John Ford/John Wayne westerns were no Hollywood invention.

In 1854, President Pierce signed the bill creating the Nebraska Territory, which ran from the Kansas border north to Canada, and from the Missouri to the Rockies. A decade later, after further subdivision, the state assumed its present shape. While a number of small communities, notably Bellevue, existed prior to Omaha's settlement (1854), that city grew rapidly, fueled by supply needs of Colorado-bound gold seekers and abetted by Irish businessmen. In 1855 we find a dry goods store operated by James Megeath and, a year later, William Kennedy's jewelry store. Vincent Burkley's Morning Star Clothing Store opened and, still later, the Sheeley Brothers advertised their butcher shop.

### THE CREIGHTON LEGACY

The most influential Irishman of that era was undoubtedly Edward Creighton, son of County Monaghan immigrants. In 1857, Edward, his brother John, and some cousins, settled in Omaha, having first visited the town a year earlier while constructing telegraph lines across Missouri. By 1861, the Creightons and their crew completed the major part of the "Western Union" line, linking both coasts, starting from Omaha and terminating in Salt Lake City. Ed Creighton proved the feasibility of this route by first travelling it alone—in winter.

This "singing wire" supplanted the short-lived Pony Express whose riders bore names like Irish Tom, Carrigan, Donovan, Egan, Hogan, Whelan, Kelly and the famed "Buffalo Bill" Cody, whose ancestors came from Kilkenny. Cody later created his

Edward Creighton

"Wild West Show," and his Scout's Rest Ranch near North Platte remains a tourist attraction.

Creighton, made wealthy by his telegraph enterprise, branched out into the freighting business, founded the First National Bank, and is often given credit for accidentally establishing Nebraska as a ranching center when oxen he had abandoned during his line-building years were discovered after a winter in the sandhills, not only still alive, but fatter. A similar story is told of another Irishman, John F. Coad.

Creighton's greatest legacy was the "free school for poor Irish Catholic boys" funded according to his wishes by his widow, Mary Lucretia. No longer free, nor exclusively Irish or Catholic, Creighton University continues to exercise considerable impact, both regionally and nationally.

Regardless of who is given credit for discovering Nebraska's kinship with cattle, that industry flourished. Longhorns made it to Ogallala in 1867 when Texas drovers might have slept in Rooney's Hotel. If they got as far as Broken Bow, their horses might have been shod by blacksmith John Delane.

As a natural follow-up to cattle raising, Omaha eventually became the meat-packing center of the world, surpassing Chicago. This began when Edward and Michael Cudahy, associates of Armour, came to Omaha in 1887 to augment the stockyards. The Cudahys (a name found in Kilkenny and Cork) helped develop some farmland into a South Omaha community of twenty-six thousand, peopled largely by Irish packinghouse workers initially, followed by an influx of eastern European immigrants.

Speaking in 1937 to Omaha's Irish American Club about the state's Irish pioneers, Ralph Coad cited the Creightons and Cudahys, the McShanes ( John McShane, president of the Union Stockyards, was also elected to Congress), the Haydens, Frank and Andrew Murphy, James Boyd (two-term Omaha mayor, later governor, and owner of Boyd's Opera House, where Oscar Wilde performed in 1882), Ben Gallagher (former post trader who created a coffee empire), Richard Cushing, John Rush, Major Furey and his own father and uncle:

> It will be noted that none of the Irish Pioneers in this State went to school beyond the grades. Not one of them went to high school, yet they were able to compete in business and debate with the graduates of Michigan, Wisconsin, Ohio, Harvard and Yale. These men studied after leaving school. They had determination, vision, ambition, good constitution and grit.

While these men were building a city, other pioneers spread across the territory. A Captain W. T. Donovan moved to Lincoln, futilely hoping to make his fortune from the salt flats there. In Cedar County, an R. T. O'Gara was among the first to homestead and settle permanently in northeast Nebraska. More Irish were on the way.

On the eastern seaboard discrimination against the post-Famine Irish was rampant, evidenced by the "NO IRISH NEED APPLY" signs, the rantings of the Know-Nothing zealots, and, more subtly, by re-introduction of the term, Scotch-Irish, to distinguish Ulster Protestants from the later arrivals. Aware of these conditions, Midwestern bishops wrote to eastern cities, encouraging migration west.

In February of 1856, an Irish Emigrant Aid Convention was held in Buffalo, N.Y., to facilitate an exodus to the prairie states. Irish journalist Thomas D'Arcy McGee, a friend of Daniel O'Connell, addressed the ninety-five clerical and lay delegates. One delegate, Father Jeremiah Trecy, born in Drogheda, began recruiting for proposed colonies in Nebraska. Some of the eastern hierarchy disapproved of these schemes, contending they would further ghettoize the Irish.

Nonetheless, Trecy did manage to lure settlers to Nebraska, creating the village of St. John's, which lasted less than four years, with the remaining citizens shifting to nearby Jackson. This didn't discourage other projects.

One venture involved the efforts of the eccentric General John O'Neill, a Civil War veteran who joined the Fenian movement and led a couple of quixotic forays into Canada, essaying to capture that country and trade it for Ireland's freedom. His escapades led to a jail term in Vermont where he conceived the notion of transplanting east coast miners to farmland in the Middle West. After extensive travel in 1872–73, O'Neill settled on Nebraska as the best site for his colonies and started proselytizing for volunteers. By 1874, he had founded a community bearing his name in what is now Holt County, and established similar settlements later in Atkinson and, to the south, in Greeley County. It was tough going in those early years, struggling against everything from resistant sod to grasshoppers, but O'Neill's dream survived, and those two counties remain stridently Irish to this day. Among other things, O'Neill was home to Frank Leahy, the Notre Dame coach whose record matched Rockne's. Around that part of the state, Leahy is spoken of in the same hushed tones reserved for Nebraska University's legendary football mentor, Bob Devaney, whom sportswriters tritely dubbed "the genial Irishman."

Bishop James P. O'Connor of Omaha purchased twenty-five thousand railroad acres for settlement in Greeley County. Like O'Neill and others, he was somewhat disappointed that his invitation to migrate drew fewer east coast laborers than farmers from Pennsylvania, Ohio and Indiana. Several of these towns suffered when bypassed by the railroads.

## RAILROADS AID IMMIGRATION

"Swarms of ould Ireland's sons," according to one anonymous account, helped build the transcontinental railroads, especially Union Pacific. Track-laying crews were characterized as "mostly Irish and discharged soldiers." Railroad agents set up offices in

Dublin and Belfast to attract both workers and settlers, offering transportation, work, and even a savings plan for Irish relatives. After the Irish laid the rails, many also laid home foundations. They became part of the landscape.

And they brought their religion with them. From the outset, Irish clergy dominated, although German priests and prelates contributed heavily to the spiritual and educational progress of prairie Catholics. Bishops O'Gorman and O'Connor were pioneer members of the Nebraska hierarchy, and their successors to the present day have a strong Celtic strain. The first residential pastor in Omaha was Father Francis Cannon, a Benedictine from Waterford, and the parishioners listed as builders of the first church, St. Mary's (1856) are all Irish. That church was dedicated by a Father Thomas Scanlan. When Omaha's first cathedral was planned, a Father Patrick Egan was the primary fund raiser. He solicited contributions not only from eastern cities and Nebraska's more urban areas, but also walked the railroad tracks, accepting donations from Irish laborers. Bishop O'Gorman's list of cathedral donors is almost exclusively Irish.

Perhaps Nebraska's most famous priest was Roscommon-born Father Edward Flanagan who, discouraged by the penal system's failure to reform criminal adults, founded Boys Town to head off problems earlier. This institution, managed well by Father Flanagan's non-Irish successors, changed the lives of thousands of boys and, in recent years, girls. The founder's vision spread nationally and internationally, with Boys Town as the model, creating satellite homes and other youth services.

Also worth noting for its Irish connections are the Colomban Fathers, a missionary society founded in Ireland in 1920 as the Maynooth Mission to China. This group, with worldwide outreach (especially in the Far East) was invited to make its American headquarters in Nebraska and did so, locating on a Bellevue hilltop, south of Omaha.

Some have accused the Irish of treating politics like a religion and, in Nebraska, as in New York and Massachusetts, they've taken naturally to this challenge. In the very first contest for a territorial delegate to Washington, Sam Daily won the seat, retiring unbeaten after three terms. We hear of an 1858 state senator, Michael Murphy, engaged in a brawl over the location of the territorial capital. John McShane and W. J. Connell served in Congress and Howard Kennedy was the first superintendent of schools, while Thomas O'Connor served a stint as sheriff and later as the first register of deeds. County Commissioners Thomas Davis and James McArdle prevailed in the 1856 election, and contemporaries Patrick Ford from Sligo and Michael Lee from Limerick were elected to the Omaha City Council. Benson, now part of Omaha, had a succession of Irish mayors—McCoy, McGuire and Tracy. Arthur Mullen, a south Omaha attorney, nominated William Jennings Bryan for president and later, at the 1932 Democratic Convention, served as Franklin Roosevelt's floor leader. This century's Omaha mayors included a Butler, Cunningham, Leahy and Boyle, and one of the state's incumbent congressmen is Bill Barrett.

But the most colorful Irish politician of this century has to be Tom Dennison, son of a couple that emigrated from Limerick and Tyrone as part of Father Trecy's colonists. For the first three decades of this century, "Boss" Dennison virtually controlled Omaha, making appointments, punishing enemies, influencing elections. He died in 1934.

Allied to their penchant for campaigning, the Irish were also attracted to law enforcement. As far back as 1867, Omaha's po-

Tom Dennison

lice force included a John Logan, John Morrissey, Patrick Swift and Thomas Welch. Three hundred and thirty miles west, Barney Gillan was sheriff of Ogallala. A glance at the 1920 Omaha police roster reveals a third to be Irish, including several first generation members, like Detective Thomas Keane and Matron Ella Gibbons.

A similar ethnic prominence is evident in the Omaha Fire Department and a 1924 commemorative brochure, edited by attorney Charles B. Morearty, names John Casey and T. E. Heafey as directors of the Fireman's Relief Association.

To be fair, Nebraska also had its Irish on the other side of the law—men like Joel Collins, who ran with Sam Bass, and James Riley, alias "Doc Middleton," a Robin Hood-like outlaw. Other errant Gaels were Quinn Bonanan, Jim Berry, Barney Doran and scores of similar miscreants. Although less obvious in his criminal behavior, Tom Dennison deserves to be part of this tally.

By the turn of the century, Irish in Nebraska constituted nearly five percent of the state's population, ranking behind the Germans and Swedes. In urban areas the Irish impact was heaviest and their involvement in labor issues more pronounced. Omaha's Edward "Paddy" Walsh was elected first president of the Bricklayer's Local Number One, while Frank Roney and John Kerrigan held similar posts with the Iron Moulders and Carpenters. A butcher named Michael Donnelly organized South Omaha packinghouse workers in 1903 and went on to perform this task nationally. Labor historian William Pratt calls Donnelly "perhaps the most important union leader to come out of the Omaha labor movement." Continuing this tradition today is President Terry Moore of the Omaha Federation of Labor, AFL-CIO, who can trace his heritage back to "the seven septs of Laois."

## ROADS NOT TRAVELLED

So many untold stories remain: the scandal-provoking cache of Fenian arms in Lincoln's capitol building; the sister of Irish novelist and dedicated Fenian, Charles Kickham, dying in childbirth at Superior; the Fathers Manning, missionaries from Dingle, interred at Alliance, their High Cross markers inscribed in Irish; actress Dorothy McGuire launching her career at the Omaha Playhouse; the Fitzgeralds, son and grandson of immigrants, growing the Commercial Federal Bank chain, and Leo A. Daly presiding over one of the world's largest architectural firms. The Irish have been visible in every aspect of Nebraska's history and in every corner of its geography.

Nebraskans of Irish heritage make up seventeen percent of today's state population, with half of them resident in urban areas, primarily Omaha and Lincoln. Some hundred thousand Irish-Americans live in adjacent suburbs or scattered small towns, while only five percent of the total are classified as farmers.

Tavern names in Omaha reflect the Celtic reputation for drink and hospitality as well as a vocational choice—Clancy's, Gilligan's, Sullivan's, Ratigan's, Kelly's, Muldoon's, O'Flaherty's, O'Bannion's, Paddy Murphy's, Barley Corn, Duffy's Tavern and The Dubliner. Many of them showcase Irish music, by either travelling bands or local aggregations like Donnybrook and The Turfmen.

There are, of course, those March 17 exuberances that take the form of parades, shamrock-painted roadways, the inexplicable green beer, and related excesses, but Nebraska's Irish have moved beyond such annual pursuits. Hibernian societies operate in various communities and a statewide chapter of the Irish-American Cultural Institute provides lessons in Irish dancing and the Irish language, along with monthly programs featuring Irish and Irish-American lecturers and entertainers. A more recent group, headquartered in Lincoln, is NISIA (Nebraskans of Irish and Scotch-Irish Ancestry), which sponsors genealogy workshops and publishes a family roots newsletter. One of Omaha's fourteen theatrical companies, Brigit St. Brigit, makes a specialty of Irish plays.

Halfway between Omaha and Lincoln, above the Platte River, sits Mahoney State Park, a 500-acre, multi-faceted recreation area. One collection of cabins here is called Cork Row, with each cottage christened for a Cork village. A directional signpost reproduces the shape and lettering of Irish road markers, with the black and white words in English and Irish—CORK ROAD and BÓTHAR CORCAIGH.

Nebraska's New-World Irish have come full circle.

Henry W. Casper, S.J., *History of the Catholic Church in Nebraska,* vol. 1 (Milwaukee, 1960).

Ralph C. Coad, *Irish Pioneers of Nebraska* (Speech) (Omaha, 1937).

Dorothy Devereux Dustin, *Omaha and Douglas County: A Panoramic History* (Woodland Hills, 1980).

Donald R. Hickey, *Nebraska Moments* (Lincoln, 1992).

Lawrence H. Larsen and Barbara J. Cottrell, *The Gate City; History of Omaha* (Lincoln, 1997).

Ray H. Mattison, *The Army Post on the Northern Plains, 1865–1885* (Lincoln, 1954).

James C. Olson, *History of Nebraska* (Lincoln, 1955).

James P. Shannon, *Catholic Colonization of the Western Frontier* (New Haven, 1957).

Nellie Snyder Yost, *Before Today: A History of Holt County, Nebraska* (O'Neill, 1976).

ROBERT T. REILLY

## NEESON, LIAM (1952– )

Actor. Born William John Neeson on June 7, 1952, in Ballymena, County Antrim, Northern Ireland, he was the third of four children of Barney and Kathy Neeson. As a boy, he took up boxing at a local boys' club and won the Irish youth heavyweight championship. He attended Queen's College in Belfast for one year and then attended St. Mary's in Newcastle-upon-Tyne in England.

Neeson entered the world of theatre with the Lyric Players Theatre in Belfast and with the Abbey Theatre in Dublin. It was while playing the part of Lennie in *Of Mice and Men* that he was noticed by British filmmaker John Boorman who cast him as the knight Gawain in the 1981 film *Excalibur.*

Neeson moved to Los Angeles in 1987, where he gave strong, thoughtful and sensuous performances in more than 20 films, including *Suspect, The Good Mother, Crossing the Line, Ethan Frome,* and *Shining Through.* But it was his riveting performance in *Schindler's List* as the German Catholic businessman, Oskar Schindler, who used his cunning and bluff—and his fortune—to save over one thousand Jews from extermination in Nazi Germany, which brought him wide acclaim, as well as the 1993 Oscar nomination for Best Actor.

Taking a break from Hollywood in 1993, Neeson made his Broadway debut in the revival of Eugene O'Neill's 1921 drama, *Anna Christie.* His tremendous talent and his strong on-stage presence in the popular play earned him rave reviews and a nomination for the Tony Award.

Neeson and actress Natasha Richardson were married in 1994.

*See* Cinema, Irish in

Ingrid Miller, *Biography of Liam Neeson* (1998).

Aine O'Connor, *Hollywood Irish: In Their Own Words* (1997).

Ingrid Miller, *Liam Neeson: The First Biography* (1996).

EILEEN DANEY CARZO

## NEVADA

### THE COMSTOCK: THE BEGINNING FOR A STATE AND THE IRISH

The Irish played a prominent role in each of the chapters of Nevada history including that of the state's very beginning. Peter O'Riley and Patrick McLaughlin discovered a gold and silver ore body in June 1859 that inspired the famed Rush to Washoe, the founding of Virginia City, and the creation of the Nevada Territory in 1861. Although they profited only slightly from their find and faded from history soon after, O'Riley and McLaughlin set a precedence for Irish involvement in the region.

The 1860 census, taken thirteen months after the gold and silver strike, documents approximately three hundred Irish immigrants in the mining district. At roughly 10 percent of the total population, this early Irish presence only hinted at its subsequent importance. With a booming population, the Nevada Territory became a state in 1864. As more people arrived from throughout the world to profit from opportunity, Nevada could boast one of the highest percentages of foreign born in the nation. The Irish were leaders in these statistics throughout the nineteenth century.

While the Irish became a dominant ethnic group on the Comstock and in Nevada, they needed to deal with the diversity of their new environment. Unlike eastern states, however, Nevada was a newborn, lacking an established native Protestant hierarchy to inhibit Irish success. This was a western state with more freedom and access to opportunity.

The Irish, hearing of Nevada's amazing riches, came from eastern states and from places such as Australia. Within a few years of the Comstock strike, Nevada was also attracting direct immigration from Ireland. These later arrivals often came from County Cork, one of the few places where the Irish could obtain mining experience.

The vast majority of the people who came to Nevada first settled within the Comstock Mining District, and the Irish were no exception to this. There was a tendency for the Irish to prefer Virginia City among the communities. In contrast, the Cornish, for example, often found homes in neighboring Gold Hill, but there were hundreds of exceptions to these generalizations. St. Patrick's Catholic Church stood in Gold Hill as testimony to the Irish presence there, and the most important Comstock Methodist Church, home to Cornish faith, was in Virginia City. Nonetheless—and in spite of the thousands of Chinese, Germans, English, North Americans, and others who lived there—Virginia City came to be known as something of an Irish town. At the height of the Comstock success in the mid-1870s, approximately one-third of the roughly 18,000 people who lived there were Irish or Irish-American.

Numerical importance, fresh opportunity, and opulent wealth combined to give the Irish of Nevada a unique chance to accomplish a great deal and to help shape a territory and young state. Indeed, Irish involvement in Nevada politics began early. In 1863, Comstock workers formed the first miner's union in the west. Mine owners thwarted the initial attempt with the help of Territorial Governor James Nye, teaching the labor force that to organize effectively, a union would need to control as many elected positions as possible. Subsequent efforts at unionization in the 1860s included the election of union men to local and state positions, ensuring that the might of government would not assist the mine owners when conflict arose. The Irish were extremely important in these early labor movements. Many sons of Erin subsequently found themselves as elected officials and guardians of their fellow workers' rights.

At the same time, Irish immigrants formed the most important military organizations in the state. Answering a call from local newspapers to become a presence in the 4th of July parade of 1864, the Virginia City Irish formed the Emmet Guard. The unit became the core of the Nevada National Guard, but it began as the military wing of the local circle of the Irish Republican Brotherhood. Other Nevada circles soon followed this lead. The Comstock Irish also formed the Sarsfield, Sweeney, and Montgomery Guards. The Irish of Hamilton, in the eastern part of the state, founded the Wolfe Tone Guards. These military organizations were prize attractions in parades, crack shots in competitions, and the focus of Irish nationalism as immigrants expressed their frustration at being thousands of miles from an island they missed deeply and profoundly wished to help.

During the Fenian excitement of the mid 1860s, Nevada newspapers carried extensive coverage of events as they unfolded in the United Kingdom, in the eastern states, and in Canada. The Irish formed new circles of the Irish Republican Brotherhood throughout Nevada, met in statewide conventions, and participated in fund raisers. During one week, for example, the Gold Hill Fenian Circle raised $1,600 to send to New York to assist in the cause. The organization managed this even though it was not as large as its Virginia City counterpart. The example illustrates not only the fervent nationalism of exiles 6,000 miles from home, but also the opulent free-flowing wealth of Nevada's mines. The Irish, as a group, enjoyed a degree of success that would be difficult to match anywhere else in the world.

Because so many Irish immigrants lived in the Comstock area, then the center of population for Nevada, they attracted the attention of the Irish at home. Nationalists Thomas C. Luby, Thomas F. Burke, and Jeremiah O'Donovan Rossa each visited the Comstock. Later, in the 1880s, Michael Davitt came to help found a local chapter of the Irish Land League.

## SUCCESS IN THE MIDST OF BONANZA

While most of the Irish who came to Nevada prospered, there were a few who did remarkably well. William Woodburn, for example, was born in County Wicklow in 1838 and was associated with the early Comstock unions. A lawyer who built a successful business in the legally contentious environment of mining, he found his most remarkable success as an elected official. He served in Congress from 1875 to 1877 and then again from 1885 to 1889. Woodburn became the State Attorney General in 1901 and remained in office until 1903. He died in 1915.

In 1869, Peter Cavanaugh was a builder who won the contract to construct the Nevada State Capitol in Carson City. Employing fellow countrymen as well as a gang of Scottish stone cutters, Cavanaugh built a lasting monument to the Irish contribution to the Silver State.

The most impressive Irish success story on the Comstock involved the rise of what became known as the Bonanza firm. Two Irish immigrants, John Mackay and James Fair, arrived, like thousands of others, in the early 1860s looking for success. Independently, they both showed an aptitude for mining and rose to supervisory positions. Through shrewd investments and hard work, their fortunes elevated them above the rank and file of miners. In the early 1870s the two men began to collaborate. Mackay and Fair recognized a unique opportunity in one of the Comstock properties and quietly sought the financial assistance of two Irish immigrants from California, James Flood and William O'Brien. These men had struck it rich as saloon keepers during the California Gold Rush.

Like Mackay and Fair, they were Irish, Catholic, and Freemasons, making them unusual in the largely Protestant and rarely Irish fraternal organization. The four men obtained stocks and seized control of a mine that appeared worthless, but instinct told Mackay and Fair that there was potential in the property. Subsequent exploration uncovered an ore body that became known as the Big Bonanza, yielding wealth of fabulous proportions that captured international headlines for years. Mackay, holding two-fifths of the Bonanza firm's interest, was soon one of

John Mackay

James Fair

the wealthiest men in the nation. Fair used his riches to secure a seat in the U.S. Senate.

Father Patrick Manogue was yet another Irish immigrant turned California gold miner who came to Nevada for greater fame. After working the gold fields in the 1850s, Manogue went to France where he studied to become a priest. He was given the new parish of Virginia City and became the spiritual leader of the state for the next several decades.

### THE DECLINE OF MINING: 1880–1900

One of the more noteworthy successes of the Nevada Irish was far subtler than wealth and fame. It is a well-noted aspect of Irish immigration that men and women tended to arrive in North America in nearly equal numbers. It is also a stereotype that more men came west than women and this was certainly true of Nevada where there was an extreme gender imbalance in the general population throughout the nineteenth century. In the case of the Irish, however, statistics demonstrate that there were almost as many Irish women as Irish men in nineteenth-century Nevada. This, combined with their overwhelming numbers during the 1860s and 1870s, enabled the Irish to establish communities of families, complete with ethnic neighborhoods, a rarity in the complex diversity of early Nevada. The Irish were more successful at building communities than many of the ethnic groups who came to Nevada.

It is an inevitability in the mining industry that the glory days of bonanza are followed by decline. Those who lived on the international mining frontier understood this and were usually prepared to leave for the next big strike. The Irish, however, struggled against the consequences of economic downturn. Although many left when mining declined in Nevada during the 1880s, statistics show that Irish families lingered longer than most, both during the good times and the bad. It appears that having built a community, the Irish were more reluctant than others to abandon roots, no matter how recently established. In contrast, the Cornish miners, for example, were often bachelors who were quick to leave. Evidence of this survives today. On the Comstock, Gallaghers, Donovans, McCarthys, and Flanagans remain, descendants of nineteenth-century immigrants who came to the mining district. The original Cornish immigrants now

have few representatives, and these invariably descend from a Cornish man who married an Irish woman.

Although the Irish were tenacious to a degree unknown by many other immigrant groups, many left with the others. Still, there is evidence that they traveled as much as possible with one another. John Cronin, for example, was a shoemaker who could have secured employment anywhere in the West, but when the mines of Virginia City failed, he left for other mining districts, following his community. Members of the McCarthy family traveled between Virginia City and Butte, as well as other mining districts of the West, seeking employment, but always maintaining contacts between relatives and fellow immigrants from County Cork.

In the midst of depression, there was still room for success, and the economic pendulum would swing back, rewarding those with the tenacity to remain in the state. Patrick McCarran, born in Derry in 1834, invested in agriculture near Reno and found it easier to stay than those who clung to the mining frontier. His son, Patrick Anthony McCarran, established a career that rose to national importance. As a newly established lawyer at the turn of the century, he was in a perfect position to prosper with the ensuing turn of events in central Nevada.

### THE GOLDFIELD-TONOPAH RUSH

In 1903, prospectors discovered a fabulous gold deposit in central Nevada, launching one of the last gold rushes of the West. The population of Nevada again swelled, this time coming to the emerging cities of Tonopah and Goldfield, the capitals of the new excitement. As before, the riches of Nevada's mines won international attention. The lure of wealth attracted immigrants from throughout the world, but native North Americans dominated this rush, and the Irish would not claim the numerical preeminence that they secured during the flush times of the 1860s and 1870s. Even so, historian Sally Zanjani points out that half of those who signed a document organizing the Goldfield Mining District were of Irish ancestry.

One young Irish immigrant serves as an example of those who arrived. Matthew Murphy of County Cork was born in 1883 and immigrated to Montana at age 10 with his brothers. In 1906, he came to Goldfield where he worked in the mines. When the gold ran out a few years later, he used a political network that promoted Irish interests, giving immigrants the ability to stay and prosper. Murphy became the Reno City Superintendent of Parks in 1926. In 1934, he was elected as State Mine Inspector, retiring in 1947.

Perhaps the most important contribution of the sons and daughters of Erin at this time came from the children of the original immigrants. Irish tenacity afforded the second generation the opportunity to succeed in Nevada of the early twentieth century. Emmet Derby Boyle, for example, was born to Irish parents in Gold Hill in 1879. He served as Governor from 1915 to 1922.

Young Patrick Anthony McCarran was also part of this emerging second generation. He served as district attorney in Tonopah from 1906 to 1909. He then became a Nevada Supreme Court Justice from 1912 to 1918. McCarran's most important contribution came when he was elected to the U.S. Senate, where he served from 1932 to 1954. In his growing position of power, McCarran was responsible for the strict immigration law that dominated policy for the remainder of the century. The airport in Las Vegas and numerous streets and structures throughout

Emmet Derby Boyle

Patrick Anthony
McCarran

Nevada bear McCarran's name, testimony to the success and importance of an Irish immigrant's son.

THE MINES FAIL AGAIN; NEVADA FINDS A NEW BONANZA

As before, the mining boom gave way to depression. The prosperity of Goldfield and Tonopah dwindled with the passing of the first decade of the twentieth century. Population declined, and again, the Irish were some of the more tenacious residents of the state. Flush times would not begin to return until the rest of the nation sank into the Great Depression. In the early 1930s, Nevada legalized gambling, creating a basis for subsequent economic growth. With this mid-twentieth-century boom and with the growing importance of national migration to the West, Nevada's population began again to grow. In the process, however, it would lose the status it once had as having one of the highest percentages of foreign-born. People from throughout the world continued to come to the Silver State, but the foreign-born, including the Irish, were of less numerical significance. Although new Irish immigrants came to Nevada, they were more isolated

than they had been in the 1860s and 1870s. They found companionship, however, with the thousands of Nevadans who celebrated Irish ancestry.

In 1966, the Irish of southern Nevada formed the Las Vegas Sons of Erin, eventually followed by the formation of the Las Vegas Daughters of Erin. In 1969, a group of Irish-Americans in Reno founded the Sons of Erin, later renamed the Sons and Daughters of Erin. These organizations reasserted an Irish presence that once dominated the state, politically and culturally. Gone were the days when the Irish could claim the numbers they once enjoyed. Still, the Irish-American clubs serve as reminders that the Irish played an important role in the development of the state and that they remain as a part of Nevada's diversity.

Ronald M. James, "Erin's Daughters on the Comstock: Building Community," from *Comstock Women: The Making of a Mining Community*, Ronald M. James and C. Elizabeth Raymond, eds. (Reno, 1998).
———, "Timothy Francis McCarthy: An Irish Immigrant Life on the Comstock," *Nevada Historical Society Quarterly*, 39/4 (Winter 1996): 300–308.
———, *The Roar and the Silence: A History of Virginia City and the Comstock Lode* (Reno, 1998).
Wilbur S. Shepperson, *Restless Strangers: Nevada's Immigrants and Their Interpreters* (Reno, 1970).
Sally S. Zanjani, *Goldfield: The Last Gold Rush on the Western Frontier* (Athens, Ohio, 1992).

RONALD M. JAMES

## NEW HAMPSHIRE

In June 1642, John Winthrop recorded in his *Journal* that "one Darby Field, an Irishman, living about Pascataquack, being accompanied by two Indians, went to the top of the white hill." Winthrop's journal entry is the first written account of an ascent of New Hampshire's Mount Washington, the highest peak in the northeastern United States. It is also the first record of an Irish settler in provincial New Hampshire. Field lived in Exeter and later the town of Dover, both located in New Hampshire's Great Bay estuary, a part of the Piscataqua River watershed.

Throughout the seventeenth century, the European population of New Hampshire was small and predominantly English in origin. Occasional Scottish and Irish settlers found their way into the seacoast region of the province, but they were few in number. Until the year 1719, New Hampshire was an "English" province, generally divided socially and politically between settlers who favored close ties to "Puritan" Massachusetts and those—particularly Anglicans and Quakers—who favored direct ties to England over domination by their Puritan neighbors to the south.

All of this began to change in 1718 with the arrival in Boston of hundreds of emigrants from Ulster. They generally migrated as families or even as neighborhood groups from the same parish. The vast majority of these settlers were Presbyterians of Scottish ancestry—some were even natives of Scotland, although most were natives of Ireland whose families had lived in Ulster for one or more generations. The largest and best organized group of Ulster immigrants left Boston and after a miserable winter in Maine decided to seek a more promising haven by sailing up the Merrimack River. They were told that an area known locally as "Nutfield" was awaiting settlement, and the group quickly took up residence in the future town of Londonderry, New Hampshire.

The Nutfield, or Londonderry, settlers were mostly from Aghadowey parish, in the Bann River Valley. In time, they were joined by other Presbyterians from the Bann Valley—from Coleraine, Ballymoney, Ballywatick, Balleywillan, Kilrea, and Mocasquin. The "patriarch" of the Aghadowey parishioners was fifty-eight-year-old David Cargill, whose son-in-law, the reverend James MacGregor—later styled the "Moses of the New England Scotch-Irish," was parish minister to the group on both sides of the Atlantic. Cargill's son David, and his sons-in-law James Gregg and James McKean were among the early lay leaders of the community.

Upon arriving at Nutfield, and believing they had settled within the boundaries of Massachusetts, the Ulster settlers petitioned Boston authorities for incorporation as a Massachusetts town. They were turned down. Officials in Boston would have preferred that the group had remained in Maine. Furthermore, Nutfield was poorly defined geographically. Portions of Nutfield clearly fell within the province of New Hampshire, and portions were located on lands in the Merrimack Valley claimed by both Massachusetts and New Hampshire. To further confuse the issue, portions of Nutfield included land located within the Massachusetts town of Haverhill, as defined by Haverhill's 1667 grant.

Having failed to get satisfaction in Massachusetts, the Nutfield settlers petitioned for incorporation in New Hampshire. Officials in the capital of Portsmouth were receptive. They befriended the settlers, noting in their official records that the emigrants from Ireland were families of "credit and reputation." Portsmouth authorities finally incorporated the Nutfield settlers as the New Hampshire town of Londonderry in 1722. The decision to recognize the area as a part of New Hampshire angered officials in Boston, and it touched off a serious boundary controversy between the two provinces that was not resolved until 1740.

Having found a haven in friendly New Hampshire, the Londonderry immigrants actively encouraged others in Ulster to join them. The actual number of immigrants who came to New Hampshire from Ireland in the eighteenth century has never been determined. Most of the Ulster Presbyterians had Scottish and English names, and by the time of the American Revolution, if not sooner in many cases, they were intermarrying with their English neighbors. Hence, the first federal census of 1790 is a very unsatisfactory means of estimating "Irish" presence in New Hampshire.

It appears that approximately 10% of New Hampshire's population was Irish during the later provincial period. In 1731, Jonathan Belcher, who served as governor of both New Hampshire and Massachusetts, estimated that there were one thousand Irish residents in New Hampshire, out of a total population of roughly ten thousand. During the 1730s, at a time when emigrants from Ulster were generally avoiding Boston in preference for New York and Philadelphia, Londonderry was sending agents to Ulster in search of new settlers. Most who accepted the challenge emigrated as families or free individuals. Very few came to New Hampshire as indentured servants. By 1742, it had become necessary to divide Londonderry into three parishes.

Although there are no recorded "waves" of Ulster emigration to New Hampshire after the beginning of hostilities associated with King George's War in 1744, migration from Ulster to provincial New Hampshire never ceased completely. There is evidence to suggest that a number of Ulster weavers, for instance, arrived in New Hampshire shortly before the beginning of Revolutionary hostilities in 1775. By the first provincial census of 1767, Londonderry had become New Hampshire's second largest town. Yet families and "transients" from Ulster poured across the borders of Londonderry as well. They settled in towns, townships, and unclaimed lands along the Merrimack River and beyond. Others came to New Hampshire indirectly. Many of the early settlers of Peterborough, New Hampshire, for instance, had initially settled in Massachusetts before moving north. In time, roughly twenty-five provincial New Hampshire towns in the southern and central part of the province contained either a majority or a considerable minority of Ulster Presbyterians.

During the Massachusetts/New Hampshire boundary controversy, Boston officials were alarmed by the aggressive Ulster immigrants who were settling, or "squatting," on lands claimed in part by Massachusetts—and they were doing so as agents of New Hampshire. Boston authorities countered by granting townships throughout the disputed territory. To their chagrin, many of these "paper townships" were then quickly overrun by the Irish. In many cases, Ulster settlers were harassed by Massachusetts men, and some were fined and imprisoned for "encroaching" upon land claimed by the Bay Colony. The Irish responded in kind. Some Massachusetts men living in the disputed territory were arrested. Others were subjected to acts of vandalism and violence. In derision, Massachusetts authorities labeled their frontier foes "Irish," "Romans," and even "Papists." James MacGregor, in a now-famous letter, protested these charges, writing, "We are surprised to hear ourselves termed Irish people, when we so frequently ventured our all for the British crown and liberties against the Irish papists. . . ." However, if the Londonderry settlers did not like being called "Irish," they were unsuccessful at coming up with a better label of their own. In their petitions and other official correspondence, they styled themselves in clumsy fashion, such as settlers "originally from north Britain but Last from Ireland," or "people lately arrived from Ireland," or "inhabitants of the Kingdom of Ireland . . . being Protestants."

When the Privy Council in London finally resolved the boundary question in 1740, most Ulster immigrants in the area became official New Hampshire residents. The English population of New Hampshire discerned some ethnic traits associated with their Ulster neighbors. The latter's Presbyterianism frequently led to disputes over the choice of a town minister. The Ulster immigrants planted fields of flax, introduced an "improved" spinning wheel to the province, and began manufacturing linen cloth on a commercial basis. They also brought potatoes and planted the first potatoes grown by Europeans in New England. Of course, the Ulster farmers were equally puzzled at first when observing the fields and gardens of their English neighbors, only to see maize, squash, and pumpkins. In time, both groups began to grow the same crops, although the settlers of Londonderry seem to have maintained their superiority in linen manufacturing throughout the colonial period. Finally, the Ulster immigrants gained a reputation for being aggressive and skilled frontier fighters. Their experiences in Ireland may have contributed to this trait, although, more than likely, their frontier skills resulted from the simple fact that they lived on the New Hampshire frontier. Towns with Ulster-born populations were attacked frequently during King George's War, and they were threatened repeatedly during the French and Indian War. It was during the latter conflict that Robert Rogers, of the little "Scotch-Irish" town of Dunbarton, New Hampshire, gained fame as the leader of "Rogers' Rangers," ably assisted by, among others, two brothers from the same town, John and William Stark.

Emigrants from Ulster continued to find their way to New Hampshire in the years after the American Revolution, but their numbers were small. The number of Irish Catholics coming to New Hampshire was even smaller. Catholicism was a rarity in Protestant New Hampshire. No Irish Roman Catholic parishes were formed in New Hampshire, and the state's 1784 constitution specifically limited public office holding to Protestants. Even for Londonderry Protestants, Ireland was a forgotten episode. In 1819, as Londonderry geared up for the centennial of its original settlement, town historians went to great lengths to revive memories in residents of the transatlantic migration from Ireland made by their ancestors. Historians in other towns with Ulster origins followed suit.

In the process of retelling the story of the immigration of Ulster settlers to southern New Hampshire, local historians made adjustments to appeal to the sensibilities of Protestant Americans in the third and fourth decades of the nineteenth century. For one thing, the centennial celebrations of Londonderry and neighboring towns came at a time when Scotland's reputation was at its height in America. As a result, historians of New Hampshire's southern towns chose to gloss over the Irish "interlude" of their ancestors, highlighting instead their Scottish ancestry. Mid-nineteenth century New Hampshire town histories were seasoned with the poetry of Burns and tales of Wallace and Bruce. To further make the connection with Scotland, local historians began referring to the first settlers as "Scotch-Irish."

New Hampshire authors were quick to claim that the term "Scotch-Irish" did not imply ethnic blending. Quite the opposite. Local historians maintained that their Scottish ancestors had always been antagonistic to the native or Catholic Irish. Their accounts generally extolled the virtues of the Scottish covenanters in Ulster, while simultaneously condemning Catholic "atrocities" in 1641 and 1689. And yet they portrayed their ancestors as individuals shaped in part by their travels. In 1839, the Peterborough town historian defined the Scotch-Irish character as "the sternness of the Scottish covenanter softened by a century's residence abroad amid persecutions and trial, wedded there to the comic humor and pathos of the Irish, and then grown wild in the woods among these our New England mountains."

Until roughly 1850, the term "Scotch-Irish" was accepted but not widely used in New Hampshire. Nor did the term make any sense at all to the growing number of more recent immigrants from Ireland. Irish-American historian Thomas D'Arcy McGee dismissed the term Scotch-Irish in 1852 in a footnote, citing the "inaccuracy of certain New Hampshire orators and others, in inventing a mixed race, whom they call 'Scotch-Irish.'" Yet the appearance of increasing numbers of Irish immigrants in New Hampshire near mid-century enhanced the popularity of the term "Scotch-Irish."

By 1850, if not a little earlier, New Hampshire began suffering a serious labor shortage. Since the 1820s, New Hampshire's growing textile mills had relied upon youths from nearby farms to operate their machinery. As labor conditions deteriorated in the 1840s, however, the local labor force proved inadequate and undependable. Another source of labor was needed. The incorporation of railroads at the same time simply compounded the need for labor. When a political compromise ended New Hampshire's "railroad war" in 1844, over a dozen chartered state railroads began surveying rights-of-way through New Hampshire's

rugged terrain. Hence by 1850, New Hampshire textile mills were searching for male and female operatives to run machinery, while New Hampshire railroads were looking for men to perform the back-breaking work needed to build railroads by hand. Irish immigrants, then pouring into nearby Boston, proved to be the obvious answer.

A few Irish laborers had worked their way into New Hampshire before the famine in Ireland. Irish names appear infrequently in the records of the Amoskeag Manufacturing Company of Manchester as early as 1840. By 1850, however, the Irish were becoming more numerous in the Granite State. There were 14,000 foreign-born in New Hampshire, mostly Irish or German. Some were working on the state's railroads, like the seventy-six railroad construction workers listed in the 1850 census returns of the otherwise "Yankee" hill town of Wentworth. By 1860, the number of foreign-born in New Hampshire was about twenty thousand. Roughly 60% were Irish. City directories for the manufacturing towns of Dover, Nashua, Somersworth, and Manchester list increasing numbers of Irish names, as well as the names of Catholic churches. In 1850, 9.5% of Manchester's work force was Irish. Nashua was slower to turn to Irish labor. In 1855, there were only about four hundred Irish workers in Nashua—the year when Father John O'Donnell arrived in town and began holding Mass in the opera house. Yet over the next two years, the numbers of Irish in Nashua swelled; in 1857, there were two thousand communicants in Father O'Donnell's church, about one-fifth of Nashua's population.

While mill owners and railroad executives welcomed the Irish as a labor force, there was little love among New Hampshire's "Yankee" population for the Irish as people. The Protestant hill farmers of New Hampshire disliked the recent Irish immigrants for a variety of reasons—their poverty, their willingness to work for low wages, their adherence to the Roman Catholic Church, among others. In addition, Irish poverty was almost always linked in the popular mind with alcoholism. The Irish arrived in New Hampshire when the temperance movement was peaking. Reformers of English and Scottish ancestry were not only quick to point out the social evils of "King Alcohol," but the apparent affinity for liquor held by those not born in this country.

The Irish arriving in New Hampshire after mid-century also found themselves in political trouble. During the 1830s and 1840s, New Hampshire was one of the most solidly Democratic states in the Union. Yet the state's powerful Democratic Party, ably led by Franklin Pierce, found itself split over the slavery issue in 1846. From this point on, Pierce and the Democrats were opposed by a coalition of Independent Democrats, Whigs, and Free Soilers—most of whom were not only opposed to slavery, but active proponents of a number of other social reforms, including temperance. Yet the coalition members opposing the Democrats were not only advocates of social reform, they were also tainted with nativism. Many Whigs, Independent Democrats, and social reformers in general longed for a state and nation that echoed the simpler, purer society of their fathers, one that was perceived to be Anglo-Saxon in character. Some of the more extreme nativists in New Hampshire had become members of the American, or Know-Nothing, Party by 1850. Hence, Irish and German immigrants coming to New Hampshire in the 1850s had little incentive to join with these groups; nor were they welcomed. In addition, Irish workers were told by Democratic Party organizers that freed slaves would leave the South and take their jobs in the North. Hence, New Hampshire's Irish gravitated toward the Democratic Party, not realizing that New Hampshire's once-powerful Democrats were headed for almost permanent minority status after 1855.

Tension between Irish immigrants and nativists erupted into violence at least once in New Hampshire in the years before the Civil War. Problems began when a Protestant in Manchester was accused of killing a young Irish worker in the summer of 1854. The accused was arraigned on July 3. Irish youths, incensed by the death of their friend and perhaps further driven by the one hundred degree heat, gathered that night along Elm Street, Manchester's main street, and began lighting bonfires, all the while hurling insults and objects at passing Protestants. The next day, a mob of roughly five hundred Protestants retaliated by raiding and demolishing Irish tenements along Elm Street. Riots continued throughout the week, attracting national attention and outside agitators. Ten days after the riots began, Edward Z. C. Judson, better known by his pen name Ned Buntline, came to town. He not only decried the evils of the foreign Catholic influence in America, but tried to convince his audience that the annexation of Texas, the Fugitive Slave Law, and the Kansas-Nebraska Act were all part of a Jesuit plot to take over the United States.

The Manchester riot died down, but hatred of Irish immigrants did not. In September, the Know-Nothing Party opened up a party newspaper in Manchester. Their *Stars and Stripes* proclaimed on its masthead, "Our Own Countrymen first, and the rest of mankind afterwards." The New Hampshire Know-Nothings then formed a coalition with former Whigs, Independent Democrats, and Free Soilers, and managed to defeat the Democrats in the state elections of 1855. Not only was a Know-Nothing elected governor, but the coalition controlled the state legislature that elected two U.S. Senators that year. Governor Ralph Metcalf ran on a platform that publicly denounced Catholicism and advocated residency in the United States for twenty-one years before becoming eligible to vote.

After 1855, the various parties and factions opposed to the New Hampshire Democratic Party came together to form a new Republican Party, which has dominated most state elections to the present. New Hampshire's Irish workers maintained their affiliation with the minority Democratic Party; Catholics were not even allowed to hold public office in New Hampshire until 1878. By that time, Irish immigration to New Hampshire had fallen off dramatically. Whereas Irish immigrants had been the vanguard of the Catholic Church in New Hampshire in the 1840s, by 1875, most Roman Catholics in New Hampshire were French-speaking laborers from Quebec, whom factory owners in New Hampshire had turned to for their labor needs in the years after the Civil War.

Near the turn of the twentieth century, the Irish community in New Hampshire was divided along religious lines. Descendants of the eighteenth-century Ulster migration continued to embellish the Scotch-Irish myth, adding accounts of Scotch-Irish patriotism during the American Revolution and highlighting the accomplishments of a few notable Scotch-Irish heroes in America. Irish Catholics, on the other hand, actively challenged the Scotch-Irish myth in New Hampshire. Two of the more famous "debunkers" were Penacook's John C. Linehan and Peterborough's James F. Brennan. Linehan argued that the Irish and Scots were one and the same people, even if it was necessary to go back to Roman times to make the connection. Brennan simply argued that the Ulster immigrants, by virtue of the fact that they had lived in Ireland for a few generations, were "Irish," just as people who had lived in America for a few generations were

"Americans." Both men had their work published by the American Irish Historical Society, for among other reasons, to bolster the understanding in the United States that there was one Ireland and one Irish people.

Throughout the twentieth century, an Irish presence has remained in New Hampshire. For example, there are generally several Catholic churches in New Hampshire's small cities, one of which is always known locally as the "Irish Church," as opposed to those dominated by Franco-Americans, Italians, Poles, and others. Yet the number of Irish-born in New Hampshire has remained small. In 1930, only 8.6% of New Hampshire's foreign born population came from Ireland. Today, most of those of Irish ancestry in New Hampshire have come to the Granite State from other states of the Union. During the decade of the 1970s and 1980s, New Hampshire was the fastest growing state in New England, with the second highest rate of growth of any state east of the Mississippi River. By 1990, less than half of New Hampshire's population was native to the state. The rest are more recent arrivals, representing a blend of undetermined ethnic origins.

*See* Scotch-Irish and American Politics; Nativism

Charles Knowles Bolton, *Scotch Irish Pioneers in Ulster and America* (Boston, 1910).

Peter Haebler, "Nativist Riots in Manchester: An Episode of Know-Nothingism in New Hampshire," *Historical New Hampshire,* 39 (Fall/Winter 1984): 121–138.

Edward L. Parker, *The History of Londonderry, N.H.* (Boston, 1851).

R. Stuart Wallace, *The Scotch-Irish of Provincial New Hampshire* (Ph.D. Diss. University of New Hampshire, 1984).

R. STUART WALLACE

# NEW JERSEY

## I. New Jersey, Ireland and "Crises of Identity"

New Jersey is a curious place with a curious history to match. Wedged between New York and Pennsylvania, its southernmost tip is below the Mason-Dixon line and it seems too geographically indeterminate to enjoy political unity. When Benjamin Franklin allegedly called it a "barrel tapped at both ends," its contents draining towards New York or Philadelphia, he expressed a sense that it had no identity of its own. He was not the first to think so. Even as early promoters praised its ideal situation "betwixt the South parts of Carolina, which is over hot, and the North parts of Pemaquitte, which are coldest" (Wacker 39), they failed to mention that it was politically dislocated. Between 1682 and 1703 there were two New Jerseys, East and West. The division ended with the appointment of the first royal governor, Francis Cornbury, who replaced government by proprietors with the supposedly firmer grip of Queen Anne herself. Yet formal unity was more easily achieved than a sense of oneness, as the egregious Cornbury himself demonstrated. He may have been a hermaphrodite: the perfect personification of a colony that was neither one thing nor the other. Long after he left ambiguity remained. During the revolution, New Jersey was divided, the southern counties less directly involved in the struggle than those to the north, where patriotism and toryism were both more intense. Division was also apparent after the revolution. In the years before the Civil War, New Jersey, on slender evidence, was persistently characterised by outsiders as a northern state with southern sympathies (Gillette 1). In the 20th century any crisis of identity seems altogether more prosaic. New Jersey, now not so much the Garden as the Suburb state, is neither town nor country but both in one. Yet geography still shapes the attitudes of those who live there. New Jerseyans, a defensive breed, loudly protest their distinctiveness from New Yorkers. (Unsurprisingly, New Yorkers agree.) "Few states," writes Thomas Fleming, "have equalled the multiplicity and duration of New Jersey's internal quarrels" (Lurie 2). It seems an odd fate for a place described in 1670 as "capable of entertaining so great a number of inhabitants, where they may with God's blessing and their own industry live as happily as any people in the world" (Wacker 33).

It may be little comfort for New Jerseyans that their identity crisis lacks the protracted intensity of that of Ireland. Because it is an island, Ireland has been thought to be home to a unitary Irish "nation." In fact, different settlements over time—Celt, Viking, Anglo-Norman, Scottish—have produced varieties of Irishness; separate strands sometimes blending, sometimes not. The result is confusion. To speak of the "Irish problem" is thus itself problematic because it assumes one Irishness and one problem. It is precisely that Irishness is in dispute. Think of Arthur Wellesley, Duke of Wellington. Asked if he was Irish, he replied indignantly that a man born in a stable does not thereby become a horse. Here, for all of Wellington's famous obscurantism, was a more subtle understanding of national identity than that of many contemporaries.

New Jersey and Ireland are similar not because each suffers an identity crisis but because in part they suffer the *same* crisis. From the beginning, New Jersey was a medley of peoples. Only half the European settlers in New Netherland in 1664 came from the Dutch Netherlands. By 1693 among Swedes living along the Delaware River, "many Hollanders were also intermingled [and] many others afterwards added themselves. . . . English, Scotch, Irish and German families, all using the Swedish language" (Purvis 19). So wrote Israel Acrelius, New Sweden's first historian. These Scotch and Irish were not separable along national lines. Ulster people came from Ireland, for instance, but were they *Irish?* In 1757 Edmund Burke wrote of those "who in America are generally called Scotch-Irish." In 1760 Lord Adam Gordon travelling in Virginia encountered "a spurious race of mortals known by the appellation of 'Scotch-Irish.'" The term was in use in New Jersey by 1766 when men described as "Scotch-Irish" murdered two Indian women in Burlington County. Indeed it has a longer pedigree. When Donegal-born Francis Makemie enrolled in the University of Glasgow in 1676, he registered as "Franciscus Makemus Scoto-Hyburnus." Makemie, founder of American Presbyterianism, played a part in New Jersey history. He served a prison sentence for unlicensed preaching in Newark in 1705 (Mahony, "Irish in Newark," 133).

Problems such as these are not merely of ethnographic interest. Often they have ideological consequences. When Gordon saw the Scots-Irish as "spurious" he thought it strange that a mongrel should claim pride of parentage. Some Irish-American historians take a similar line. Consider W. H. Mahony, an early 20th-century historian of the New Jersey Irish. Mahony dismissed the Scotch-Irish as an "ethnical hermaphrodite" unknown before 1835, a characterization that sits oddly with his own list of "Irish," which included many who understood themselves to be ethnically distinct from their countrymen. To disparage the very notion of Scots-Irishness, claiming that centuries of settlement "transformed the Scottish element in Ulster into Irishmen" is to offer politics in the guise of history. This is itself significant: Irish-American historiography sometimes seems a continuation by other means of the ancient enmities of Ireland.

There is a connection, in short, between problems of identity and those of identification. In the first place, to identify national groups tends to assume that such a classification had meaning for the groups themselves. But early settlers grouped themselves along religious and linguistic as well as national lines. Nationality was only one (not always the most important) demographic identifier in early New Jersey. Language was another, so also was religion. And there is another problem. Identification by surname, a standard device, has hidden hazards. It is not always possible to distinguish between Scots and Irish immigrants; or to recognize Irish settlers with English surnames; or to tell the difference between an Irish-born father and an American-born son. The above-mentioned Mahony, attempting to assess the number of Irish in colonial New Jersey, made a mess of it on these grounds alone. Perhaps two-thirds of New Jerseyans with Scottish names in the 18th century were Scots-Irish, the remainder Scots (Purvis 18, 27). Exactitude beyond this is impossible.

## II. THE 17TH CENTURY: PIETY AND PRACTICALITY

The Irish element in New Jersey may be traced to the earliest days. Almost as soon as the curtain arose on the Duke of York's proprietary colony in 1664, people from Ireland were on stage: individuals mainly, sometimes entire communities, attracted to the economic possibilities of a place largely empty save for Indians. Seventeenth-century settlement was patchy, with little in the way of systematic plantation. Nor is much known of the settlers, who appear to us as names, little more. Still, they were not negligible. Consider Richard Bryan from Armagh, who settled in Milford, Connecticut in 1639 and prospered as a merchant. He was among forty-one founders of Newark in 1666. Consider also Patrick Falconer, preacher and merchant, who died in Newark in 1692. Falconer was devout—"a Real Saint who suffered much for Christ"—but worldly enough to leave a solid legacy (Mahony "Irish in Newark," 132). The fluidity of early America helped men such as Dennis Lynch, who acquired 300 acres in Cape May County from the West Jersey Company in 1696; John de Byrne, who received a deed for "120 acres in Essex County" in 1694; William Steele of Cork, who acquired 500 acres in Gloucester County in 1685; John White of Carlow, who acquired 2,000 acres, also in 1685. These early entrepreneurs moved freely along the seaboard and inland, buying land in Pennsylvania, New York, and New Jersey. Mostly they had some skill or trade, as mariners, merchants, weavers, and maltsters. But even a laborer, Francis Buckley, could acquire 200 acres in Salem County in 1686 and another 100 ten years later. Of course, we know of such men precisely because they succeeded, but that bias notwithstanding their social ambition is striking (Mahony, "Seventeenth-Century Irish," 243–254).

Entire communities also came to New Jersey, mainly for spiritual reasons. The earliest English speakers in West Jersey, now Camden County, were Quakers from Ireland. Their agent, Robert Lane of Dublin, arrived in 1677 to arrange passage for more than 100 in 1681. Establishing themselves in the land between the Pennsauken and Timber Creeks, they dominated an area that was soon designated the "Irish Tenth." (Years later the road between Gloucester and Salem was still "the Irish Road.") They faced the usual difficulties—small numbers, a hard first winter, many Indians who "put a dread upon our spirits, considering they were a savage people." But according to Thomas Sharp, the first conveyancer and surveyor of Gloucester County, they achieved "prosperous success and eminent preservation." The land along Newton Creek and Gloucester, a "wilderness . . .

planted with good seed," became a harvest both for God and man (*Journal of the American Irish Historical Society*, 1908–9, 207). The seed may have been more English than Irish, but that hardly mattered to West Jersey officials who considered the area an Ireland away from Ireland.

One contribution of the "Irish Tenth" to West Jersey was currency. Mark Newby, a Quaker who arrived on the Delaware in 1680 and in Gloucester County in 1681, brought a substantial quantity of halfpence coins that had been declared illegal in Ireland by the English government. Known as "Newby's Irish halfpence" or "St. Patrick's halfpence" (the saint was depicted on the reverse side with shamrock and crozier), the coins were for a time the only effective currency in New Jersey. An act of 1682 "for the more convenient payment of small sums" recognized them as legal tender and made Newby *de facto* banker of the Province (Mahony, "Irish Footsteps," 162).

Quakers were not the only spiritual community in West Jersey. Cohansey in Salem County was established in 1683 by Baptists from Tipperary under the leadership of the Reverend Elias Keach. For years the congregation remained "sound in the faith, respectable in size, and in a flourishing condition" (Hoffman 355). Later they were joined by Presbyterians, who seem to have become the predominant group. Certainly the area was a magnet for settlers of all sorts. Fenwick's *Historical Account of the First Settlement of Salem, in West Jersey* reported that "emigrants were flocking into Cohansey from New England, Long Island, Wales and Ireland" by 1700 (O'Brien, "Some Early Irish Settlers," 123). Other evidence confirms the Irish presence. Legal documents, especially wills, reveal Fitzgeralds, Murphys, O'Neills, and Reillys in Cohansey in the early 18th century. (The first Murphy in New Jersey marriage records dates to 1729, the first Fitzgerald to a will of 1703, the first Sullivan to a will as far back as 1696.) (O'Brien, "Probate Records," 77, 81, 92, 93).

### Seventeenth-Century Catholics

These glimpses of seventeenth-century migration reveal a settlement that was not exclusively of Scots-Irish from Ulster. We know of immigrants from Dublin, Carlow, Wexford, Waterford and Clonmell, the last two commemorated in settlements of the same name in Gloucester and Burlington Counties. Nor should Catholicism be overlooked. The Concessions and Agreement of 1665, drawn up by New Jersey's first proprietors Berkeley and Carteret, was an exceptionally generous instrument of government. Full freedom of conscience was guaranteed to prospective settlers, "they behaving themselves quietly and not using this liberty to licentiousness" (McCormick 25). This proved important after the failure of Jacobitism in Ireland, when some Catholics sought refuge in New Jersey. We know of one William Golden, an officer at the Battle of the Boyne, who acquired over 1,000 acres at Egg Harbor in Cape May County in 1691 (O'Brien, "Probate Records" 124). Escape from Williamite Ireland was no guarantee of freedom. When New Jersey became a royal colony in 1702, religious toleration was extended to all except Catholics, the better to avoid "dangers which may happen from papish recusants." The command indicated that Irish Catholics were coming to the colony in greater numbers than before.

### III. THE 18TH CENTURY: TEACHERS, PREACHERS, AND FIGHTERS

### Ulster-Scots

By the early 18th century, then, there were both Irish Catholics and Protestants in New Jersey. The latter predominated: mainly Presbyterians from the North with their familiar qualities of hardihood, independence, and fear of God. These characteristics, polished now to the point of caricature, have entered historical literature as a myth almost as resilient as the Ulster-Scots themselves. The settlers of Morris, Hunterdon and Sussex counties—cold, remote, unpromising terrain—certainly had need of frontier virtues. They established settlements that still bear their names: Hackettstown in Morris County, founded by Samuel Hackett of Tyrone in the 1720s; Flemington in Hunterdon County, founded by Thomas Fleming of Tyrone in 1746 (O'Brien, "Probate Records," 125). To some extent the hardihood was a necessity of their own making. Compared to German settlers, for example, they worked on poorly laid out farms and lived in poorly constructed houses. Worse, they had the vices of their virtues. Self-reliant and devout, the Scots-Irish were also belligerently intolerant, to the despair of those charged with their governance. Squatting on another's land, for example, was second nature to them. In 1720 James Logan, Armagh-born Provincial Secretary of Pennsylvania, praised his "brave fellow-countrymen" as "a leading example to others." Ten years later he wanted to be rid of these "troublesome settlers to the government and hard neighbors to the Indians." Logan feared that "if they continue to come they will make themselves proprietors of the province." True to his wish, many Pennsylvania Irish left for New Jersey between 1718 and 1730, bringing to their new home Calvinism and cantankerousness in equal measure.

The majority of these internal migrants stayed in central New Jersey, hugging the Millstone, Raritan and Passaic rivers. Many lived in Camden County, close to Philadelphia. They were middling folk for the most part: preachers, teachers, farmers, lawyers, merchants, and politicians. The first wave comprised indentured servants, weavers and small farmers. By the middle of the century the Scots-Irish had moved up a rung. Some remained poor, of course, but modest mobility seems to have been the rule. "New Jersey," said Governor Belcher in 1748, was "the best country I have seen for middling fortunes and for people who live by the sweat of their brows" (Lurie 6). He might have been speaking of the influx from Ulster.

### Teachers

Consider teachers. Teaching attracted substantial numbers of Irish people in eighteenth-century New Jersey, often because it provided a means of performing indentured service, less frequently because it represented an avenue to greater prestige. "Many of our school teachers were Irishmen," claimed the historian of early Dutch settlement in Monmouth County. "Smart, passably educated young Irishmen" did some of the schooling of Middlesex County. The teachers of Somerset County were "generally immigrants from Ireland, England or Scotland." It was not high-powered work. In most cases literacy, presentability, and sobriety sufficed for qualification. Some names have survived: John McCarter and William Crosby of Sussex County; Hugh Knox and Francis Barber of Elizabethtown; Robert Taylor of Kingwood; Timothy Murphy and Charles Kelly of Raritan. Their efforts did not end at the schoolhouse. McCarter and Crosby fought in the Revolutionary War, Taylor (who became an ironmaster) supplied weaponry, Barber organized the third New Jersey Battalion, and Knox had the distinction of teaching Alexander Hamilton (O'Brien, "Schoolmasters," 125–129). If intelligence combined with lowly status can make men radical, the patriot cause was the beneficiary in New Jersey.

The College of New Jersey (Princeton University) was higher in the social scale. It was established as a "New Light" Presbyterian seminary in 1746, growing out of the "Log College" of Neshaminy, Pennsylvania, which was founded in 1727 by William Tennent of Armagh and his sons Gilbert, William and John. Rev. Samuel Finley, president in 1761, and John Blair, first professor of theology, were both Irish-born. Samuel Smith, son of a Derry immigrant, became college president in 1795. Princeton's student body also had solid numbers of Scots-Irish in the college's early decades.

*Catholics*

Catholicism was hard to see in New Jersey before the mid-eighteenth century but it was not invisible. In 1740 an Anglican rector reported that up to eighty Irish Catholics had moved into his parish at Alloway's Creek, Salem County (Kelly 5). Local lore claimed they had been shipwrecked. They found work in the Wistar glassworks (where Mass was first celebrated in South Jersey in 1743), then in the iron foundries of Atsion, Batsto and Pleasant Mills: desolate, gloomy places. Years later, in 1879, Bishop Michael Corrigan of Newark visited Egg Harbor and Pleasant Mills. He was shown a baptismal register for the 1830s containing "about 100 names, chiefly Irish." Thoughts of "the few Catholics lost in this wilderness of sand" moved him deeply (Mahoney and Wosh 181). The Irish stuck it out until the mills closed in the 1860s: a lonely exile for a scattered flock.

There were Irish Catholics elsewhere. From 1765 until his death in 1787, a German missionary, Fr. Ferdinand Farmer, worked in the scattered villages and homesteads of northwestern New Jersey. His ministry was primarily to Germans but ninety-nine of his flock had Irish or English names, among them ironworkers employed by the Ringwood Company, thirty-six miles north of Newark. The company provided a livelihood for nearly 600 men, many of them Irish. Indeed the area directly behind the foundry was called "Irishtown." Fr. Farmer, as much anthropologist as pastor, noticed how national style manifested itself in religious practice. The Germans baptized their children immediately, with or without a priest; the Irish preferred to wait, sometimes bringing whole families to be baptized at once. Perhaps German caution was more sensible than Irish confidence. The mission was a precarious affair, never guaranteed to survive from year to year. Farmer himself carried in his baptismal register, as a kind of *memento mori*, the official notice of Governor Bernard that Catholics were specifically excluded from religious liberty. The sheer remoteness of the homesteads, Irish or German, did the work of decatholicizing New Jersey better than any formal prohibition.

Farmer's mission was exceptional. Mostly the scattered Catholics of New Jersey went without priests, thereby losing any faith inherited from parents or distant memories of Ireland. At the end of the revolution there may have been as few as 200 of them (John Rutherford's estimate in "Notes on the State of New Jersey" in 1786) or as many as 900 (the guess of Barbe de Marbois, French Agent-General in New York) (Kupke 24). However calculated, the numbers were small. New Jersey was not natural territory for papists, who although granted religious freedom were barred from public office (and probably from voting) by the state constitution of 1776 and kept in that position until a new constitution was adopted in 1844. Nevertheless, Irish Catholics (practicing or otherwise) were to be found in many parts of the colony and state. In the last third of the century there were Donnellys in Burlington, Duffs in New Brunswick, Dwyers in Trenton, McDonoghs in Newark, McGlones in Salem, and Kellys and Murphys in Trenton, Gloucester, Princeton, Elizabethtown, Bound Brook and Sussex. As with Ulster-Scot settlers earlier in the century, they fell squarely into the category of middling folk: merchants, farmers, carpenters, innkeepers, ironworkers, and servants. In Morris County the Hibernia Furnace had a mainly Irish and Dutch workforce. (To keep them sober a law of 1767 prevented the keeping of a tavern within four miles of the place.) Else-where the Irish worked for themselves. Terence Reilly taught "book-keeping, merchant's accounts and mathematicks . . . in the best and most approved methods." Michael Kearney imported horses. Alexander McCormick was "a noted player on the Irish pipes." Garret Meade advertised "choice Irish beef" (Mahony, "Irish Footsteps," 250–254). Thomas Kane ran a bar, the Fox Chase Tavern, where Trenton's first Mass was celebrated in 1782 or 1783, mainly for Irish immigrants. Here, in these latter instances, not only was Irishness preserved but marketed. Assimilation was quite compatible with the desire to maintain a potentially profitable ethnic identity.

*The Irish at Large*

Irishness was not always willingly embraced. Some tried to disavow it, generally in an effort to escape the law. Scattered throughout 18th-century newspapers were advertisements for runaway servants, mostly Irish. In 1742 Jacob Ford of Morris County sought the whereabouts of "Richard White, an Irishman, with somewhat of the brogue on his tongue . . . [and] very impertinent in his talk" who had absconded with "Michael Collins, an Irishman." Both men, incidentally, were Catholic. In 1751 a reward was offered for Nicholas McDoniel "lately arrived from Ireland, said to have gone to his uncle in Amboy." In 1766 William Gilliland sought "James Ramsay, who came from County Armagh, [and is] known to be in New Jersey." Denial and disguise were the only options. In 1768, an absconded servant called O'Bryan styled himself "Bryan." Another claimed that "he was born in England but has the brogue on his tongue." Such comic efforts at concealment were manifestly unsuccessful. For conspicuousness, however, there were probably few to match in 1754 "an Irish servant man named James Murphey . . . kept in the station of a schoolmaster" who "sometimes ties his hair behind with a string, [is] a very proud fellow, loves drink and when drunk is very imprudent and talkative, pretends much and knows little, was in the French service and can talk French" (Thayer 107).

Eccentricity aside, these runaways make an important point: Irishness was common enough in 18th-century New Jersey that Irish people could be recognized as such. But how common was it and how does New Jersey compare with the rest of colonial America? In 1790, when the first census was taken, New Jersey's population was 184,139. The white population was primarily English (50.6%) and Dutch (20.1%). Only 11% were Irish or Scots-Irish—less than 7% from Ulster, 4% from the rest of Ireland. Total population, in short, was surprisingly small and the Irish component of it even more modest. Moreover, "New Jersey's proportions of English, Scots, Scots-Irish and Irish were approximately half those of Pennsylvania" (Purvis 22). Throughout the century Pennsylvania and Southern Appalachia had always been much greater magnets, especially for Ulster Presbyterians. Yet this should not minimize the Irish contribution to 18th-century New Jersey: rather the opposite. It is precisely the modesty of the numbers that suggests a disproportionate importance. As founders of towns, colleges, and businesses, people from Ireland left a mark that belied their lack of demographic strength. Nowhere was this more apparent than in the revolution itself.

## IV. Revolutionary New Jersey

If the Scots-Irish of eighteenth-century New Jersey were notable for fortitude and independence, they nevertheless offer to us a paradox: when they were most themselves they were at their most American. On the eve of the Revolution, and during it, this convergence had political consequences, as they began to speak an American language of rights of which they were partial progenitors. "Call this war by whatever name you may, only call it not [American]," wrote a British officer in 1778. "It is nothing more than a Scots-Irish Presbyterian rebellion." This was an intelligent intuition. In New Jersey patriotism was strongest where New Englanders and the Scots-Irish were strong, in Morris County and lower Cumberland. Religion and the frontier had imbued them with a democratic imagination, a rude egalitarianism that translated easily into revolutionary zeal. They may have seemed unprepossessing—"the errantest rustics you ever beheld," the wife of a Continental officer described them in 1777, "you'd laugh to hear them talk" (Thayer 87)—but their bravery was second to none.

The history of ethnic groups in the Revolution is generally written as a parade of notables. This is understandable: most of the Irish farmers, schoolmasters, and tradesmen who fought in Washington's army are unknown to us, as are the foundry workers in the Hibernia forge who supplied its weaponry. The New Jersey notables include William Paterson—delegate to the Constitutional Convention, later Senator, Governor, and Supreme Court Justice—who was born in County Antrim; John Neilson—member of the Continental Congress—whose father was a Belfast man; Reverend James Caldwell, the "rebel high priest," who was born in Virginia of Irish parents. To be sure, there were also Irish Tories. A Hugh Quigg arrived from Ireland twelve years before the Revolution and with his two sons joined the British in Morris County. One Michael Kearney became a captain of the navy (Thayer 194). The Irish were certainly not patriots to a man. In this they reflected New Jersey as a whole.

From a military perspective New Jersey was, of course, the cockpit of the revolution. Washington wintered his troops there on three occasions: in 1777 in Morristown, in 1778–79 in Bound Brook, in 1779–80 in Morristown again. The last of these encampments was especially difficult due to severe weather, poor food, and chronic boredom. By March 1780 Washington was sufficiently alarmed by "mortifying proofs of inattention and relaxation of discipline" that thoughts of a mutiny crossed his mind. To raise morale he gave permission for a St. Patrick's Day Ball, hoping that "the celebration of the day will not be attended with the least rioting or disorder." The hope was vindicated. A loyalist newspaper reported that festivities began "with music and the hoisting of colors, exhibiting the thirteen stripes, the favorite Harp, and an inscription declaring in capitals, The Independence of Ireland. . . . The simple-minded Teagues were charmed with the sight of the harp, forgot their sufferings, dropped their complaints, and seemed perfectly happy for the moment, though not a drop of whiskey or taffie was to be seen in the camp" (Thayer 244).

Washington's ostensible reason for the celebration was mutual affection between Ireland and America. Both countries loved freedom, he said, because each had suffered Britain's "heavy and tyrannical oppression." This was a standard theme of Irish politics in the 1770s when, as one Belfast Presbyterian minister put

it, there was "scarcely a Protestant family of the middle classes who does not reckon kindred with the inhabitants of that extensive continent." Twenty years later, as Ireland itself experienced revolution, the connection bore unusual fruit. In 1795 Wolfe Tone, leader of the Society of United Irishmen, fled to America. He went first to Philadelphia, then to Princeton. He liked the latter—it had "a college and some good society"—and he found New Jerseyans "lively and disengaged." Unfortunately, the Irish he met turned out to be as "boorish and ignorant as the Germans, as uncivil and uncouth as the Quakers, [with] ten times more animal spirits than both" (Elliott 267, 274). Thus despising at close quarters what he romanticized at a distance, he returned to Europe and revolutionary politics in January 1796. Had New Jersey offered greater charms, the history of Ireland might have been substantially different.

## V. The 19th Century

In 1799 William Griffith, a lawyer who advocated reform of New Jersey's constitution, complained that "our polls swarm with the very refuse of the English, Irish, Dutch and French emigrations, people whom convenience, inclination, intrigue or crimes induce to take a footing in the State" (Pole 50). He could not have known then that the swarm was only beginning. Between 1820 and 1850, New Jersey was overwhelmed with newcomers. The crucial decade was the 1840s, when the population increased by 31% to 489,555, of whom 56,000 were immigrants, 31,000 of them Irish. By 1870 New Jersey's population was 906,096, of whom 188,943 were foreign-born. Of this latter group, 86,784 were from Ireland, 54,001 from Germany. Irish immigration remained high at the end of the century—in 1900, 94,848 residents of New Jersey had been born in Ireland—but an influx of Germans, Italians, Austrians, Hungarians and Poles balanced it. By 1900 most foreigners living in the state were from southern and eastern rather than northern and western Europe (Hinrichsen 421).

The reasons for the exodus are, of course, well known: the "Big Wind" of 1839, the Famine of 1845–50, agricultural distress in the 1870s, the "Big Blizzard" of 1883. To add to the trauma, the new Irish were rural, poor and Catholic in an increasingly urban, industrial, Protestant state. Why New Jersey? To the extent that it appealed to them at all it was because of proximity to New York, where many of them had landed, because Irish people were there already, and because there was work. Men took what jobs they could find: as tanners and shoemakers in Newark, textile workers in Paterson, carpenters and joiners in Camden, laborers in Jersey City. They built the Morris Canal in the 1820s, the Delaware and Raritan Canal in the 1830s, and the Morris and Essex Railroad in the 1840s and '50s. They opened shops, served in bars, became firemen and policemen, and—respectability finally beckoning—produced a goodly number of priests and politicians. Women were employed in domestic service. They all lived in various little Irelands: the Ironbound in Newark, the Fourth Ward in Trenton ("Irishtown" in the 1850s), the "Dublin" section of Paterson, the Horseshoe in Jersey City. "New Jersey is rapidly becoming a great manufacturing state . . . a place of resort for emigrants seeking work," wrote Bishop James Bayley of Newark in December 1853. "The emigration is again flowing in upon us," he wrote to the Rector of All Hallows in Dublin in 1860. "I was never more in want of good zealous priests."

At first the Irish had little to offer except muscle. They came to New Jersey just as the national craze for canal building was getting under way and as a result almost every waterway built between 1825 and 1850 was largely their work. Their part in building the Morris Canal is well known. Less familiar is their contribution to Delaware and Raritan Canal, begun in 1830 and completed fours years later, which linked Trenton and New Brunswick. Using shovels and sometimes their bare hands, they created a waterway which became, in the 1860s and 1870s, one of the busiest in the nation. Largely forgotten now is that its construction was marked by tragedy. In 1832 an epidemic of Asiatic cholera swept the area around Princeton, killing hundreds and causing local panic. Many of the victims were Irish canal men who, it seems, were buried where they fell. Little commemorates them except the canal itself, now defunct, and a verse of contemporary doggerel. "Ten thousand Micks / They swing their picks / To build the new canal / But the choleray / Was stronger than they / And twice it killed them all."

### A Pattern of Integration: The Paterson Experience

The canal men had muscle but some other Irish immigrants had skill. Consider those who came to Paterson in the early years of the 19th century. Much has been made of the fact that impoverished peasants, rural, pre-modern and Catholic, arrived in an urban, industrial and Protestant state, as if that alone were responsible for the social pathologies that made their existences wretched. Drink, ghetto life, chronic nostalgia for home: these are typically taken to be the Irishman's lot. But those who came to Paterson tell a different story. They found themselves at home almost immediately. Paterson was a magnet for weavers from all parts of Ireland, especially Ulster, and they brought to the town an artisan radicalism that shaped its politics in the years before mechanization rendered their skills redundant. Ironically they came to a textile town just as it was changing, and if their resistance to mechanization was inevitably doomed, they learned nonetheless that there was strength in concerted industrial action. That lesson served them well in politics, where the Democratic Party, and in particular Andrew Jackson, gained their first allegiance.

For a group supposedly untutored in the ways of democracy, the Irish showed practical skill and conceptual sophistication. The skill manifested itself in an ability to win elections. In 1831, for instance, Irishmen held ten of thirty-eight elected positions in local government. The conceptual sophistication lay in their willingness to speak the language of rights in a republic founded on civic virtue. Consider for example a curiously Irish-American political iconography, an early blending of two distinct traditions. At a dinner to celebrate Andrew Jackson's election to the presidency toasts were drunk to the "sprig of the shellaleh and the root of the hickory" and "the Eagle to watch and the Harp to tune the Nation till the tree of liberty be planted throughout the world." Here was a kind of transatlantic republicanism that united both countries in freedom's cause. In the same manner, the Friends of Ireland—eighty-five strong in Paterson in 1828—supported Catholic Emancipation as an effort to change "that system of laws by which the majority of the people of Ireland . . . have been so long oppressed" (Harris 581–585). The Friends also called for the abolition of slavery in the District of Columbia in 1828. There was hardly a progressive cause, in other words, that did not receive Irish endorsement.

Many resented this prominence. In the summer of 1835 two thousand textile workers went on strike in a stoppage widely attributed to Irish militancy. The strike was exceptionally bitter, producing nativist bile that had clearly been developing over several years. The Paterson *Intelligencer,* organ of the mill-owners, was typical. The strike, it argued, was the fault of workers easily stirred by "wonderful display[s] of cabbage oratory." As slurs go, this was suggestive. Even as the Irish turned proletarian, as it seemed to imply, they remained peasants at heart. In truth, the Paterson experience implied quite the opposite. Nativists, however, were never quick to see the obvious.

### Urbanism, Catholicism and Nativism

Paterson was typical of the transformed social geography of New Jersey. In the first half of the century that transformation gathered pace and produced two related phenomena: a growth in the number of Catholics and a rise in nativist resentment of the newcomers. Consider Newark. The city's Irish population grew substantially in the 1790s and by 1826 a Catholic parish was created to cater for it. From 1833 to 1866, the pastor was Patrick Moran of Loughrea, County Tipperary, an indefatigable organizer of libraries, Sunday schools, temperance societies, and literary groups. Or consider Paterson. In 1833 a church was opened to cope with the overflow of Irishmen working on the Morris Canal. Likewise in Jersey City: in 1856 Father John Kelly preached a mission for 200 Irish laborers building the Erie Railroad tunnel through Bergen Hill, and a parish was formed as a result. Southern New Jersey tells the same story. In 1849 an Irish parish was formed in Gloucester, and for 20 years its priests were Fathers Waldron, Donoghue, Finnegan, Hannigan and Daly.

New Jersey's growth as a state and Catholicism's growth within the state were thus parallel processes. The number of foreign-born residents in New Jersey doubled between 1850 and 1860, from 60,000 (12% of the total population) to 123,000 (18% of the total). Many were Irish. In 1855, there were 40,000 Catholics and 35 priests, 17 of them from Ireland. By 1872 there were 170,000 Catholics, 113 churches, 62 priests, and a seminary, Seton Hall College. This was prodigious growth by any standards.

One sign the Irish had come to stay was that many wished them to go. Nativism in the middle years of the century was New Jersey's besetting sin. Consider again Newark. In 1834 the city held its first St. Patrick's Day Parade: it was jeered from the sidewalks. In 1853 Protestant heckling marred the installation of James Roosevelt Bayley as the city's first Roman Catholic Bishop. The worst excess occurred in September 1854 when a procession of the American Protestant Association in Newark led to a riot in which two Irishmen died. Nativists brandishing illegally held revolvers entered the immigrant quarter and a group of Irishmen was forced inside a German Catholic Church for safety. The mob eventually seized the building, destroyed its fittings, and would have torched edifice and occupants had not the police arrived to stop them. "False statements were immediately published throwing the whole blame on the Irish Catholics," wrote Bishop Bayley in his diary (Sullivan 22). Manifestly, fault lay in the opposite direction, as even a rather biased coroner's jury later found. The event, editorialized *The New York Tribune,* brought "great discredit on Newark and belligerent Protestantism." For all that, the Irish gave as good as they got, firing some rounds from the Church before help arrived. Whatever the calculus of innocence or guilt, the episode was a reminder of ugly social forces not simply in mid-century New Jersey but in urban America as a whole.

A variant of nativism held that if the Irish were not fighting their neighbors, they were fighting each other. In February 1857 Bayley recorded in his diary "a terrible riot between the Irish factions engaged in making the [Jersey City] tunnel" in which 1,200 men were said to have participated (Sullivan 50). The riot was essentially a Saturday night brawl, although with 200 participants and forty-seven arrests an unusually nasty one. Gangs from Munster and Connacht fought each other, apparently because Corkonians had trespassed on shanties occupied by the Connachtmen. Whiskey also played a part, thus confirming the suspicions of nativists for whom boozy factionalism made a better story than social deprivation. This nativist understanding was intellectually lazy. The problem with Know-Nothingism was that it knew everything, offering an explanation—the same explanation—for all ills regardless of social or political context. The Irish—poor, plentiful and papist—made easy targets. Almost any story could be told of them in the 1850s and believed.

### Temperance

Yet caricatures only work when they contain an element of truth. For all its crudity, the nativist notion of the Irish as drink-soaked was partially accurate. The lives of the urban poor—nasty, brutish and occasionally short—were sweetened by the saloon. Often, of course, those same lives were destroyed by it. Bars were street theaters, job-markets and means of escape rolled into one. The clergy knew how seductive they could be and made strenuous efforts to keep parishioners away from them, perhaps as much to assert their own authority as to curb an objective social evil. Throughout the century New Jersey's temperance campaigns were led by Irish priests: Patrick Moran in Newark in the 1820s, James McKay in Orange in the 1860s, Thomas Killeen in Newark in the 1870s. These men were larger than life. Killeen indeed was legendary. On Saturday nights, a clerical contemporary wrote, "he was worth a score of policemen" as he single-handedly cleared every bar in his parish before midnight (Hinrichsen 189). New Jersey's bishops were aware of the problem, too. Michael Corrigan, who succeeded Bayley in 1873, visited Colt's Neck in 1877. "A committee came to see me about getting an Irish priest," he recorded. "They were drinking men and careless Catholics, members of the AOH" (Mahoney and Wosh 136). In 1884 Winand Wigger, Corrigan's successor, ordered that the last rites of the Church be denied to those who sold drink to minors or drunkards. Wigger was of German extraction, as were most of Newark's brewers. The saloonkeepers were Irish. On this slender evidence—and because he was a tough disciplinarian when Irish priests themselves fell off the wagon—he was charged with anti-Irishness. (Germans themselves were hardly abstainers: their Sabbath beer drinking was a perpetual political issue between 1870 and 1910.) The truth, obvious to Wigger and many others, was simpler: the Irish in drink were their own worst enemies.

### A Pattern of Integration: The Jersey City Experience

The Irish did not have far to go if they were looking for enemies. As we have seen, they were in copious supply in Paterson and Newark, where Irish assertion and nativist backlash were both in evidence in the early century. The same was true in Jersey City in mid-century, where the Irish found work in substantial numbers as laborers and artisans in the 1850s. The census of 1860 revealed their strength and weakness. Compared with British and German immigrants, for example, they were plentiful. Their strength, in other words, lay in numbers. That was also their weakness. The fact that there were too many of them prompted the usual local anxieties. Besides, they were also poor and un-skilled, deficiencies that compounded native distaste for them. Over forty percent of American-born citizens in Jersey City in 1860 were nonmanual workers; the comparable figure for the Irish was less than seven percent (Shaw 87).

In local eyes Irish poverty was explained by Irish popery. Sectarianism was an ugly feature of Jersey City in mid-century. Proselytism was class warfare by other means, and it was waged in Hudson County with vigor. In 1853 Irish prisoners and inmates in Jersey City almshouses were required to attend Protestant services. In the 1860s members of missionary organizations dominated school boards. In the 1870s the Tract Society delivered monthly literature to every home.

But the Irish had resources of their own. By 1861 they had begun to realize that politics offered a means of resistance, and, as with their countrymen in Newark and Paterson, they gave strong support to the Democratic Party. In 1861 they mobilized to defeat the city recorder, Thomas Tilden, whose record as a prosecutor for public order offenses had revealed nativist tendencies. In 1862 they forced the Democrats to nominate an Irishman for police chief, then carried the day for him in the election. The curiosity was that the Democratic leadership of Jersey City was dominated by former Know-Nothings, making it seem odd that such a party could win Irish support. Republicans suspected that the trick was to cultivate pliant candidates, taking care "to exclude Irishmen of character and intelligence" from office (Shaw 89). Perhaps so, but there were less sinister explanations. Democrats were generous patrons. Irish laborers and policemen depended for their jobs on Democrat control of city hall and at election time they did not forget it. Besides, towards the end of the 1860s nativist rhetoric faded as it became counter-productive. The Irish by then had acquired sufficient self-confidence that they were able to turn political sectarianism on its head. As the *Evening Journal* reported in November 1868, the "old Know Nothing Democrats had once been smart enough to honeyfugle the Irish into doing all the heavy voting and yelling while they took all the fat offices themselves." Now "Pat has worked up to a conscious sense of his power, and demands the offices himself" (Shaw 89–90).

As a result Jersey City elected nine Irish-born aldermen out of a total of twenty in 1870, entirely changing the coloration of local politics. But the victory was short-lived. Unable to resist Irish advances in electoral politics, nativists blunted their effect by emasculating local government itself. In 1871 Republicans and some Democrats at state level adopted a new city charter that transferred most powers to the New Jersey legislature. The old Know-Nothing strain was thus not quite dead in Democrat politics. It took nearly a generation for the Irish to regain political hegemony in Jersey City.

### Civil War . . .

Newark, Paterson and Jersey City were thus typical of Civil War New Jersey in that Republicans and Democrats throughout the state were eager for Irish support but conscious that it carried political dangers. Democrats were usually better placed to play the ethnic card. In the election of 1860, Newark, Trenton, Jersey City and Camden, all with solid Irish populations, supported Douglas; only Paterson supported Lincoln. In 1864 New Jersey was one of only three states to vote Democrat, in part because of strong Irish-Catholic support for McClellan (Gillette 294). The Democrat case was unashamedly racial: why should Irish workers fight to free blacks who would then take their jobs? This appeal fell on receptive ground. In June 1863, when draft officers visited Irish sections of Newark, local women stoned them. New Jersey was spared draft riots but ethnic tension was sharp nonetheless. One resident of Elizabeth, for instance, deplored the "fiendish unreasoning cruelty" of the Irish "towards the un-offending blacks" (Gillette 242). Yet this was extravagant. If Irish fears were crude, they were also understandable. Nor were they the only group to express class anxiety in racial terms. Moreover, many of them, for whatever reason, fought and died for the Union cause. For all that, antagonism between Irish and Blacks was a reality and Democrats knew how to exploit it.

Republicans played ethnic politics, too, and benefited from anti-Irishness whenever their opponents overreached. The Democrat nomination of an Irishman to be Essex County sheriff in 1862 was a case in point. Here was racial politics taken too far, and Republicans exploited the backlash to secure an unexpected victory. Similarly in the state assembly election in 1864, the *Woodbury Constitution* praised the Republican candidate in Gloucester, South Jersey as "not an Irishman: he is a Jerseyman." Yet Republicans were not beyond an appeal for Irish votes themselves. In the election of 1864 they claimed to be the party of Irish independence. This effort to garner Irish votes without pain was rejected for the sham that it was.

Between Democrat tokenism and Republican nativism there was perhaps little to choose. If both were unsubtle, at least each acknowledged that the Irish presence, especially in cities, could not be ignored. The standard Republican charge—that the Irish marched unthinkingly behind a Democratic banner—was one part truth to two parts jealousy. It was certainly suspicious that in the election of 1864 Irish voters, Democrats to a man, registered at the last possible moment in Newark, Orange, and Jersey City (Gillette 288). But even as Republicans charged Democratic corruption, privately they may have admired the efficiency. In another sense, however, their fears were overdone. New Jersey rejected Lincoln in 1864 but compared to 1860 that election actually marked an underlying shift towards the Republican Party (Gillette 294). The strength of the Democrats lay in their Irish base; that was also their weakness.

### . . . And After

In post-war New Jersey, Irish politics took the form of support for nationalism in Ireland and social amelioration in America. With a large anti-British population, New Jersey was fertile soil for the Fenian Brotherhood, Irish-America's distinctive contribution to the cause of freedom in Ireland. Fenianism alarmed church authorities on both sides of the Atlantic, who rightly saw its anti-clericalism as part of a wider subversiveness. "Lectured at Orange on St. Patrick and the mission of the Irish people," wrote Bishop Bayley in 1866. "Gave a good strong rap at Fenianism." Some years later, Bishop Corrigan had similar problems with the Ancient Order of Hibernians. Secretive and quasi-Masonic, they were close to troublemakers such as the Molly Maguires and may indeed have had overlapping membership. But the AOH was popular and Catholic. "I am much [afraid] of encouraging the Ancient Order of Hibernians by a spirit of opposition on the one hand," Corrigan wrote in 1874, "and alienating [it] from the Church on the other." He reluctantly decided that members "should not be debarred from receiving the sacraments for the mere fact of their belonging to that society." This lawyerly solution, saving face as well as souls, satisfied the delicate sensibilities of both parties.

Corrigan, the child of immigrants, was otherwise friendly towards Irish causes. In 1880 he organized a collection throughout the Newark diocese for the relief of famine distress in Ireland. Twenty thousand dollars were raised—a tribute to the size of the Irish community and to its compassion.

### Fin de siecle

Towards the end of the century, concern for the plight of Ireland was less pressing than the need to consolidate the Irish position in New Jersey itself. Assimilation took priority over romantic attachment to long distance nationalism. As a result, Irish-Americans, long the outsiders, began to constitute the dominant culture against which other groups pitted themselves. Tensions with Germans, for example, were an increasing feature of New Jersey's ethnic politics in the 1880s and 1890s. Consider Irish leadership of the temperance movement. When Germans insisted on music, dancing and beer on Sundays, they offended an improbable alliance of native puritans and Irish priests. The rhetoric of the dispute now appears comically extravagant. "Newark," thundered the Reverend James Brady in 1891, following a great German song festival, "supplied herself abundantly with her most odoriferous and gummy fluid; tricked in her most variegated finery, and flounting in her red, white, and blue bunting presented herself to dance obedience to the Sabbath befouling sackbuts of the Sabbath defiling Teuton" (Popper 129). Beer was clearly wasted on Brady: words alone could intoxicate him. More significantly, the hyperbole suggested one who intuited that his cause was ultimately doomed. In 1906 temperance won a victory when the New Jersey legislature passed the "Bishop's Law" raising the fee on liquor licenses. But public reaction was hostile and elections in 1908 saw those associated with the conservative cause—Republicans mostly—receive a drubbing. This outcome may not have been unwelcome to some of the Irish themselves.

If temperance offered one proof of respectability, leadership in the church provided another. The Irish were well entrenched in the Catholic establishment and here, too, newer immigrants occasionally resented their power. The sharpest religious dispute of the 1890s centered on "Cahenslyism," a movement that promoted German-speaking parishes, German practices, and German bishops within the church. New Jersey's Irish priests would have none of it. For Fr. Patrick Corrigan of Newark, Cahenslyism was a conspiracy to "Germanize the country by means of the Church." For Fr. Thomas Killeen of Bayonne, Germans had "no right to a church of their nationality any more than [have] the Irish or any other race" (Sullivan 226, 253). Here was a telling acknowledgement of assimilation. "We are all Americans," Killeen pointed out, the remark partly directed at his own bishop, the supposedly German-favoring Winand Wigger. Whatever of that, the dispute surely suggests an irony. Nativists had long complained that Catholicism was un-American. Killeen and others were able to use Cahenslyism to assert that Catholics in general, the Irish in particular, were as American as the next man.

The ethnic element in New Jersey Catholicism remained strong, of course, but total ghettoism was avoided. To that extent the failure of Cahenslyism anticipated a double phenomenon of the 20th-century: the capacity of Catholicism to assimilate to itself the practices of multiple ethnicities; and the related ability of the church to assimilate those ethnicities to a wider American community.

## VI. The 20th Century

### The Church, The Union, The Ballot Box

The story of the Irish in twentieth-century New Jersey is thus one of increasing assimilation. By 1900, as Italians, Poles, Blacks and East European Jews poured into the state, the Irish seemed suddenly respectable. They were not yet white, of course, but they had become noticeably paler since 1850. They had paid their dues and intended to enjoy the acceptance that came from a debt fulfilled.

Catholicism played an important role in this integration. Even as the Church asserted its institutional distinctiveness, it represented a potent force for Americanization. Priests "served the familiar Irish role as middlemen between the new immigrants and Anglo-Saxon culture" (Kelly 16), inculcating civic virtues as well as Christian ones. If this meant that Irish-Americans became "less and less Irish and more and more Catholic" (Kelly 16), the political authorities could hardly complain. To be sure, anti-Catholicism remained an ugly strain in New Jersey life, with cross-burning in Camden and Gloucester in the 1920s, a Ku Klux Klan riot in Perth Amboy in 1923 to cleanse it of the "pollution" of Romanism (Ellis 5), and strong opposition to Al Smith's presidential bid in 1928. But by mid-century sectarianism began to dissipate, not least because Irish-Americans, so far from being alien, seemed almost extravagantly patriotic. They had fought in the First World War, even making common cause with Britain as proof of their loyalty to America. After the Second World War, their Catholic anti-communism matched the mood of the day. If Irish-Americans were sometimes intemperate in their enthusiasms—figures such as Charles Coughlin and Joseph McCarthy come to mind—their Americanism was never in doubt.

Politics and trade unionism also offered important avenues of integration and social mobility. Irish workers were active in labor causes, taking part in the Paterson silk strike of 1913, the Gloucester City trolley strike in 1919, and the Camden shipyard strike of 1934. In quieter times they made their way up the ranks of union leadership. Arthur Quinn from Perth Amboy was president of the Brotherhood of Carpenters (Buenker 83); Joseph McComb and John Farrell of Camden were vice-presidents of the local AFL and CIO (Kelly 15).

But struggles against bosses were only partly to their taste. The Irish much preferred, in a political sense, to be bosses themselves. In early and mid-century their genius for political organization became apparent in the "Boss System." Men such as "Little Bob" Davis of Jersey City, "Big Jim" Smith of Newark, Thomas McCran of Paterson, and—*capo di tutti capi*—Frank Hague of Jersey City, controlled machines that dominated urban politics for decades. "Bossism" has had a generally bad press, often because the squeamishness of a later age finds its coercive methods indelicate. Of course, many contemporaries deplored bossism, too. Dayton David McKean complained in 1940 that the Hague organization, "alone among American city machines, . . . systematically utilized . . . terrorism, infiltration of groups, suppression of criticism, and the hierarchical principle of leadership [characteristic of] fascist regimes in Europe" (McKean xv). But political machines should be understood for what they were—channels of welfare and group protection, and occasionally progressive instruments of urban reform. Besides, the Irish dominated them for perfectly honorable reasons. Unlike more recent immigrants, they spoke English; had had political experience in Ireland; had been in New Jersey for a couple of generations; had stayed longer

in the wage-earning class (Buenker 81). Moreover, the notion of machines as menacing—which certainly contains an element of truth—needs to be set against their sometimes enlightened politics. In the progressive era, "a considerable number of machine politicians in the New Jersey General Assembly lent their names to a surprising array of political reforms" (Buenker 98), often fracturing the unity of the machine itself. Bossism was not all good; it was not all bad either.

### A Pattern of Integration: Jersey City Again

Nowhere was this more evident than in Jersey City. In the 1860s the Irish struggled against the established order: two generations later they constituted it. One man in particular dominated Jersey City politics for thirty years. From 1917 to 1947, Mayor Frank Hague turned Hudson County into a personal fiefdom, dispensing favors and delivering votes with the self-confidence of a boss who was courted by Presidents and parish priests alike. Born in 1876 in the "horseshoe," a gerrymandered downtown district where Republicans had hoped to squeeze as many Irish Democrats as possible, Hague inched his way through saloon politics to a job in City Hall in 1908 and eventually the mayoralty in 1917. Hague's Irishness was never in doubt—he played up his lowly birth and choppy grammar when necessary—but he was never a gladhander in the mold of, say, James Michael Curley of Boston. In looks and manner he was more Patrician Puritan than Paddy. Non-smoking, non-drinking, personally devout, he resembled the Boston Brahmins whom Curley despised. There was severity in his politics, too. "I know the people want a clean city and I give it to them. I do not allow any nightclubs or dance halls where liquor is served. That recommends me to every respectable home in the city" (Connors 73). Hague and the Irish were well matched: he gave them respectability because he wanted it himself. He was also good for City Hall: efficiency, not charm, was the key to his municipal success. Hague was a master at cajoling money from Trenton and Washington, supplying votes to the benefactor in return. The system worked to mutual satisfaction until after the Second World War. "You'll notice I'm still here," he remarked in a 1936 interview. "And why? Organization and good government. I've played square with the organization and the customers. That's why" (Connors 57).

Hague's machine was Irish to the core. His slate for the city commission, elected quadrennially, never varied: four Catholics, one Protestant, all Irish. He was adept at the politics of gesture: forcing the Board of Education to remove "pro-British" textbooks from city schools, for instance, or endorsing the presidential ambitions of Al Smith. Ethnic prejudice also played a part. Republicans were always "black Protestant Republicans" in Hague's lexicon, supporters of a party (despite Lincolnian roots) hostile to strangers and minorities. Above all, Hague was a master of patronage, especially what may be termed second-generation jobbery. "He paid particular attention to the Irish lawyers," suggests his biographer. "The old immigrant patronage posts (policemen, firemen, and sanitation workers) were of little value [to the creation of a machine] so the Boss turned to . . . 'bourgeoisie' patronage"—judgeships, receiverships and the like. "Patronage provided the political glue to hold them in the organization . . . even after they moved . . . out of their downtown flats onto the heights" (Connors 94).

Those who live by ethnic politics may die by them. Hague's power declined in the 1940s when the "great Trenton job drought" (as the *Newark Sunday Call* termed it in 1946) began to take its toll. "Six years without . . . the thousands of little [state] jobs which keep a political machine functioning," wrote the paper's political reporter, "have hurt Hague . . . deeply" (Connors 160). Hague might have survived had he played the ethnic card more delicately. He resigned in 1947 but handed power to his nephew, Frank Hague Eggers, an act of baronial arrogance which offended Italians, Poles, and Slavs who thought that the Irish day had come and gone. In 1949 the anti-Hague Freedom ticket of John Kenny defeated Eggers. "Here Lies the Remains of the Hague Machine," read one sign on election night. "36 Years of Age."

Hague's mistake was not so much to outstay his welcome as to misunderstand its nature. Irishness alone was a shaky platform on which to build political appeal. It smacked of blarney when, by 1947, Jersey City might have preferred baloney. (All the same, Irish Bossism did not end with Hague: John Kenny's machine ruled the city until Kenny was jailed for income tax evasion in 1972). To the irony of a potentate without potency may be added another. An exodus of WASPS allowed the Irish to dominate urban politics in the years before the Second World War, so that, in effect, the first flight to suburbia left the cities in Irish hands. The second flight was of the Irish themselves. The cities were left to others and the assimilation cycle began anew.

### Richard Hughes

This complex coming of age may be seen in the history of one family. Consider Richard P. Hughes, whose story is emblematic of many. Hughes arrived in Baltimore from County Clare in 1856. In 1862 he enlisted on the Union side in the Civil War, anxious for pay more than glory. After the war he married an Irish-born New Jersey widow, Alice Lynch Duffy, and, consummating a union of another sort, became an American citizen in 1876. (His citizenship papers contain no signature; merely his mark). Hughes became a father the year he became a citizen. His son Richard went on to typify the upward movement of the Irish of the second generation. Involving himself in Democratic Party politics he was at various times warden of Trenton State Prison, a state civil commissioner and Mayor of Burlington.

The mobility reached an apogee in his own son, also Richard. That child, born in 1909, graduated from New Jersey Law School, served as Mercer County Democratic Chairman, ran unsuccessfully for Congress in 1938, was appointed to the Appellate Division of the Superior Court in 1957, and was elected Governor of New Jersey in 1961. Hughes was triumphantly reelected in 1965 and left office in 1970. A remarkable career was not yet over. His successor William Cahill—another Irish Catholic, although a Republican—appointed Hughes Chief Justice of New Jersey's Supreme Court in 1974.

### Journey's End

The journey that brought Richard P. Hughes's grandson to a governor's mansion was rich in irony and historical echo. No one was more alive to those echoes than Hughes himself. Shortly after leaving office he spoke to a Saint Patrick's Day dinner in Massachusetts:

In New Jersey, Governors live in an executive mansion called Morven, . . . built in 1701 by the grandfather of Richard Stockton, one of the signers of the Declaration of Independence. [A history of Morven recalls that] "in November, 1830, work began on a stretch of canal between Rocky Hill and Trenton. Gangs of Irish laborers made the nights hideous with their drunken brawls." Still another history recalls that it was some-

times necessary for one of the Stocktons . . . to discipline the Irish with a whip. The next time there is any record of anything Irish happening in Morven was St. Patrick's Day, 1962, when the Hughes clan moved in. And now, another Governor of Irish lineage is in residence. How does one say "touché" in Gaelic?

The question was well taken. Assimilation is the story of history—raw and elemental—becoming agreeable, unthreatening "heritage." For Irish-Americans that transformation reached its culmination with John Kennedy's election as president in 1960. Hughes's election marked the parallel point in New Jersey's history. Irishness had become safe enough to be celebrated. Assorted Friendly Sons of Saint Patrick donned their annual green and everyone was Irish for a day. Yet if that was the point of assimilation, it was also its paradox. Cars, homes and backyard barbecues proclaimed that the Irish had come into their inheritance. They proclaimed, in short, that they were hardly Irish at all.

John D. Buenker, "Urban, New-Stock Liberalism and Progressive Reform in New Jersey," in *New Jersey History*, Vol. 87 (1969).

David Cohen, *America, The Dream of My Life* (New Brunswick, 1990).

Richard P. Connors, *A Cycle of Power* (Metuchen, N.J., 1971).

Barbara Cunningham, "The Irish-Americans of New Jersey," in Barbara Cunningham, ed., *The New Jersey Ethnic Experience* (Union City, N.J., 1977).

Marianne Elliott, *Wolfe Tone: Prophet of Irish Independence* (New Haven, 1989).

Larry Gerlach, *Prologue to Independence: New Jersey in the Coming of the American Revolution* (New Brunswick, N.J., 1976).

William Gillette, *Jersey Blue: Civil War Politics in New Jersey 1854–1865* (New Brunswick, N.J., 1994).

Howard Harris, "The Eagle to Watch and the Harp to Tune the Nation: Irish Immigrants, Politics and Early Industrialization in Paterson, New Jersey 1824–1838," in *Journal of Social History* (Spring 1990).

George Hills, *The Ku Klux Klan of the Present Day* (New York, 1923).

Carl D. Hinrichsen, *The History of the Diocese of Newark 1873–1901* (Washington, D.C., 1962).

Milton J. Hoffman, "Religion in Colonial New Jersey," in *Irving Kull, New Jersey: A History*, Vol. 1 (New York, 1930).

Joseph J. Kelly, *The Irish in Camden County* (Camden, 1984).

Raymond Kupke, *Living Stones: A History of the Catholic Church in the Diocese of Paterson* (Clifton, N.J., 1987).

Maxine Lurie, ed., *New Jersey: An Anthology* (Newark, N.J., 1994).

Joseph Mahoney and Peter Wosh, eds., *The Diocesan Journal of Michael Augustine Corrigan, Bishop of Newark, 1872–1880* (Newark, N.J., 1987).

W. H. Mahony, "Irish Footsteps in New Jersey Sands," in *Journal of the American Irish Historical Society* (New York, 1927).

———, "The Irish Element in Newark, N.J." in *Journal of the American Irish Historical Society* (New York, 1922).

———, "Irish Settlers in Union County, N.J.," in *Journal of the American Irish Historical Society* (New York, 1929–30).

———, "The Irish in Princeton, N.J.," in *Journal of the American Irish Historical Society* (New York, 1928).

———, "The Melting Pot—Irish Footsteps in New Jersey," in *Journal of the American Irish Historical Society* (New York, 1926).

———, "Some Seventeenth-Century Irish Colonists in New Jersey," in *Journal of the American Irish Historical Society* (New York, 1927).

Richard P. McCormick, *New Jersey from Colony to State* (Princeton, N.J., 1964).

Dayton David McKean, *The Boss* (Cambridge, MA, 1940).

Michael O'Brien, "Some Early Irish Settlers and Schoolmasters in New Jersey," in *Journal of the American Irish Historical Society* (New York, 1911–12).

Michael O'Brien, "The Irish in the New Jersey Probate Records," in *Journal of the American Irish Historical Society* (New York, 1928).

J. R. Pole, "Suffrage in New Jersey 1790–1807," in *Proceedings of the New Jersey Historical Society,* Vol. 71 (1953).

DERMOT QUINN

## NEW MEXICO

Irish contact with and influence in New Mexico is almost as old as the state itself, dating back to its early Spanish Colonial period. Interestingly, that contact comes through Irish military men and priests from Spain to Mexico and into New Mexico. One of those early men, Fray Juan Agustin de Morfi, was centered in Mexico City and traveled throughout the northern frontier of Mexico that included New Mexico. Another was Hugo O'Conor, who was appointed in 1772 inspector in chief of all military forces on the far-reaching northern frontier of New Spain.

Both men were but two of the many "Wild Geese" who, as Irishmen, "either themselves or their forebears had left Ireland to escape the dominance of an English rule" (Sean Galvin, p. vii), or, as another historian has put it, "thousands of young Irishmen began to flee their homeland to escape the persecution from the Protestant English who occupied the Emerald Isle" (Marc Simmons, p. 25).

"Scattering themselves throughout Europe they had little difficulty in procuring employment, for as fighters they were without equal, as was appreciated by such countries as Austria, Italy and France, all of which had regiments of Irish soldiers. Yet of all the European countries it was in Spain that they achieved the most recognition" (Sean Galvin, p. vii).

The next statement by Sean Galvin clearly states the reason these "Wild Geese" found themselves in the Spanish New World. ". . . Not only did they find themselves Catholics in a Catholic country; their situation stemmed from the very correct belief that Ireland had been settled by people of Iberian culture about three thousand years before Christ. Thus the 'Wild Geese,' as they were called, settled themselves in Spain as Spaniards and were treated as such" (Sean Galvin, p. vii).

In fact, Spain provided funds for the education of the sons of these "Wild Geese" at Douai, France, Louvain, and Antwerp and in Salamanca the university had a special college just for them. Clearly, as Maurice Hennessy has shown in his *The Wild Geese: The Irish Soldier in Exile,* Spain was more than accommodating of its new Irish immigrants as cited in a letter by Philip III:

> To the Rector, Master of the Schools and Cloister of the University of Salamanca:
>
> As the Irish people who have been living a kind of community in this city have resolved to avoid themselves of the opportunities it affords for advancement in letters and languages, a house being prepared for them, in which they intend to live under the direction of the Fathers of the Society of Jesus, besides allowing them this letter to charge you, as I do, to regard them as highly recommended, so as not to allow them to be maltreated in any way but to favour and aid them as far as you can: that as they have left their own country and all they possessed in it, in the service of God our Lord, and for the preservation of the Catholic Faith, and make profession of returning to preach and suffer martyrdom in it, if necessary, they may get in that University the reception they are hoping for."

The letter signed by Philip III, on August 2, 1592, goes on to stress that the Irish students "may be able to pursue their studies with content and freedom, and thereby attain the end they have in view" (Maurice Hennessey, p. 187).

With this type of not only acceptance but also sovereign mandate, it was not unusual that Irishmen as Spaniards would find their way to the New World and the far reaches of Spain's most northern colony, New Mexico.

So who were our two noted Spanish Colonial Irishmen? As mentioned earlier they were Franciscan Missionary Fray Juan Agustin de Morfi (Murphy?) and Hugo O'Conor. In 1770, Morfi wrote an account of disorders in New Mexico. And although some scholars have questioned whether Morfi actually traveled throughout New Mexico's colonial settlements and missions, his keen eye recorded details too real to be imagined.

The other early Irishman who had an impact on Spanish Colonial New Mexico was Hugo O'Conor. In 1772, O'Conor was appointed Commandant Inspector of the Interior Province of New Spain. O'Conor's duties were demanding, as hostile Comanches and Apaches made both Spaniards and friendly Pueblo Indian peoples' lives precarious at best. Throughout colonial settlements he reorganized troops and instilled and established better regulations and a tougher discipline. In Santa Fe he observed that the presidio had only 80 soldiers, but he believed that if he could mobilize a citizens' militia of Spaniards and friendly Indians, the settlers could readily defend themselves. Few Irishmen, much less Americans in general, realize the vital role that both the Irish priest and the Irish soldier, Father Juan Agustin de Morfi and Commandant Inspector Hugo O'Conor, played in the settlement of the early Spanish Colonial frontier, particularly New Mexico. New Mexico's checkered history of contact with Irishmen does not end with the end of Spanish rule but continued into its Mexican period, the opening of the Santa Fe Trail and into its colorful yet violent period of regional wars such as the infamous Lincoln County War and Billy the Kid himself.

Early Irish-American entrepreneurs also took part in trading over the Santa Fe Trail. While many writers describe only the romance, adventure and hardships of trading over the Trail, inflated prices paid by buyers at the end of the Trail made many a merchant rich and prosperous.

A sampling of the 1860s and 1870s New Mexico censuses provides details as to who these Irish merchants were, their worth, age and their place of business. They all gave their nation of origin as Ireland (Susan Calafate Boyle, pp. 180–190).

| Name | Age | Worth | Residence |
|---|---|---|---|
| (1860) Robert H. Stapleton | 30 | $ 26,000.00 | Socorro, NM |
| (1860) Henry O'Niel | 33 | $ 18,000.00 | Santa Fe, NM |
| (1870) Joseph Reynolds | 45 | $ 30,500.00 | Mesilla, NM |
| (1870) Lawrence Murphy | 35 | $ 12,500.00 | Lincoln, NM |
| (1870) James Dougherty | 26 | $ 3,025.00 | Mora, NM |
| (1870) Therese Fortune | 45 | $ 600.00 | Socorro, NM |

It is important that we remember Mr. Lawrence Murphy of Lincoln County, NM, for he would be as colorful and memorable a character as Billy the Kid in that regional confrontation known as the Lincoln County War. Most adults are familiar with the names of Billy the Kid, Sheriff Pat Garrett and Lew Wallace, but few Americans realize the part that others with Irish names like Murphy, Dolan and Riley played in that violent and most infamous of frontier conflicts. The romance and myth of the six-shooter and cowboy shoot-outs at high noon quickly end when the lawlessness, bloodletting, revenge and violence of the Lincoln County War become evident. The best analysis for the cause of the war is given by John P. Wilson in his book, *Merchants, Guns and Money: The Story of Lincoln County and Its Wars.* He writes,

> The Lincoln County War of 1878–1879 was not a cattle or a range war, nor even a feud. Essentially it grew out of a struggle for economic power in a land where hard cash was scarce and federal contracts for the supply of provisions, especially beef, for the military posts and Indian reservations were the grand prizes. The competition for these contracts became bitter and frequently ruthless. ( John P. Wilson, p. 27)

The details of these contracts and of the lives of all these Irishmen involved in this conflict are described in Wilson's excellent book.

As New Mexico was slowly and painfully maturing into statehood, other Irishmen would leave their mark on New Mexico history. James O'Brien served as Chief Justice to the Territorial Supreme Court from 1890–1893. Named by President Benjamin Harrison, O'Brien found himself a full docket upon his arrival to New Mexico. During his time spent in New Mexico, he wrote some 20 opinions and presided as judge of the fourth judicial district headquartered in Las Vegas, New Mexico. He returned to Minnesota to practice law there in 1894. Upon his death in 1909, the Minnesota State Bar Association said of him: "Judge O'Brien's many friends bear witness that as a teacher he was thorough and energetic; as a writer, fluent and forcible; as a speaker, pleasing beyond the majority of even good speakers and as a lawyer and judge, he was able and painstaking, honorable and upright" (Arie W. Poldervaart, p. 154). Las Vegas in the 1890s was still a town that was trying to recover from its image as one of the wildest towns in the West. While western lore is full of stories of Tombstone and Dodge City, one can only surmise Judge O'Brien's experience there as judge of the fourth judicial district headquartered in Las Vegas.

In more recent times, Irish-Americans have served in numerous prominent capacities throughout New Mexico. Santa Fe, for example, established in 1607 by the Spanish, had a very popular Irish-American mayor, Leo Murphy, who served three terms from 1956–1962.

In New Mexico, the Irish have played an important role in its history since the Spanish arrived in the New World. Coming full circle, it is not surprising that Celts and Spanish people have something in common. Both Celtic and Spanish history tells us that Celts inhabited parts of Spain in the third century B.C. and eventually spread over the entire peninsula. And many words that Spanish-speaking New Mexicans consider Spanish are in reality of Celtic origin or base. For example, gancho (hook), corcovada (hump), and camisa (undershirt) are only a few. In an article in the *Irish Times,* July 1995, entitled "Celtic and Hispanic," Douglas Carter gave a brief history of this Celtic-Spanish connection, particularly the linguistic part of that connection (Douglas Carter, p. 1, pp. 5–6).

In an overview essay such as this, it is impossible to list every Irish man and woman who has contributed to New Mexico's his-

torical, artistic and cultural life. The Irish in New Mexico today are not only alive and well but also are reminders of what Douglas Carter himself has so adeptly described about Celtic life in New Mexico. "Celticity is not a matter of race but of culture and culture is acquired" (Douglas Carter, p. 1, pp. 5–6).

Susan Calafate Boyle, *Comerciantes, Arrieros y Peones: The Hispano and the Santa Fe Trade.* Santa Fe, New Mexico: Southwest Regional Office, National Park Service, Department of the Interior, Division of History, Professional Papers #54, 1994.

Douglas Carter, "Celtic and Hispanic," *Irish Times,* No. 7–95 (Irish American Society of New Mexico: Albuquerque, New Mexico, July 1995).

Sean Galvin, ed., and trans., *A Description of the Kingdom of New Spain* by Senor Don Pedro Alonso O'Crouley, 1774 (San Francisco, 1972).

Maurice Hennessy, *The Wild Geese: The Irish Soldier in Exile* (Greenwich, 1973).

Arie W. Poldervaart, *Black-Robed Justice: A History of Justice in New Mexico from the American Occupation in 1846 until Statehood in 1912,* Vol. 13 (Historical Society of New Mexico Publications in History: Santa Fe, 1948).

Marc Simmons, "Spain's Wild Geese," in his column, "Trail Dust," *The Santa Fe Reporter* (April 26, 1995).

Marc Simmons, ed., and trans., *Father Juan Agustin de Morfi's Account of Disorders in New Mexico, 1778* (Albuquerque, 1977).

John P. Wilson, *Merchants, Guns and Money: The Story of Lincoln County and Its Wars* (Santa Fe, 1987).

ORLANDO ROMERO

## NEW ORLEANS, IRISH DOMINICANS IN

The Congregation of St. Mary's in New Orleans had its origins in a cloister in Cabra near Dublin, a community that had begun in Galway in 1644. But the penal laws, turmoil, wars, plagues and famine that ravaged seventeenth- and eighteenth-century Ireland had their repercussions on the nuns of the Dominican convent in Galway. They suffered exile in Spain, persecution at home, and loss of outward identity as women religious. Repressive measures necessitated loss of cloister routine, use of their legal names and wearing of contemporary garb. Leadership in the early years was borne by Sisters Julian Nolan and Mary Lynch. They survived exile to reestablish the monastery in Galway, but others took over as the cloister moved to Channel Row, to Clontarf and finally to Cabra in Dublin. At each new location and with all the hardships, these nuns managed to preserve the spirit, if not the appearance, of the cloister, still maintaining their status as cloistered contemplative women.

During their apostolic period that began in 1860, the nuns of Cabra opened a number of daughter houses. They went in November 1860 to New Orleans where Father Jeremiah Moynihan, a parish priest, had begged for teachers for St. John the Baptist School. The seven women who answered his call were Mary John Flanagan, founding prioress, Mary Magdalen O'Farrell, subprioress, Mary Hyacinth McQuillen, Mary Xavier Gaynor, Mary Ursula O'Reilly and two lay sisters, Osanna Cahill and Bridget Smith. These Irish pioneers first served in the parish school, an unusual practice in the United States at that time, because most communities of women religious began by operating an academy of their own. However, in the following year, the New Orleans Dominican nuns opened their own St. Mary's Academy for girls.

When they volunteered, these pioneer women expected trials and adversities but not a Civil War. They endured many hardships along with the citizens of the city. The food and house furnishings were of the barest. The nation was in turmoil, and the blockade of the Confederacy threatened dire consequences for the Crescent City. Despite these conditions, the nuns refused the offer from Cabra to return to Ireland. The Dominicans determined not to close their schools, but to expand. In 1863, their academy accepted boarders, and the following year, Mother Mary John Flanagan procured a larger property in Greenville. It was there that mothers of many girls sought safety with their daughters from St. Mary's.

The year 1865 brought a cessation of hostilities but not an end to adversity. The nuns, like the people at large, could tolerate their poverty better than the yellow fever epidemics that struck in 1867 and again in 1878. The epidemics resulted in the deaths of friends and benefactors of the monastery. Financial reverses caused untold misery. Conditions were so bad that the nuns had to beg from door to door.

The troublesome problems through the years did not deter these stalwart women from opening new schools, a general hospital, and St. Mary's College, the first Catholic college for women in Louisiana. In recent years, like many apostolic groups, the members of St. Mary's Congregation have diversified their ministries to meet the needs of a new era.

*See* Women Religious from Ireland

---

*Cabra Dominican Annals.*
"Weavings: Celebrating Dominican Women," unpublished ms. (Dublin, 1988).
Margaret Smith, "The Great Schism of the West," unpublished ms. (1990).

LORETTA PETIT, O.P.

## NEW YORK CITY

The Hudson River is named after the English explorer, Henry Hudson, who on September 3, 1609, discovered Manhattan. His patrons, the Dutch West India Company, saw the commercial possibilities of its splendid harbor and rich backland, and in 1629 Peter Minuet purchased from the Indians what is now New York City, Long Island, Connecticut and New Jersey for 60 guilders worth of gewgaws (about $670). In 1653 it was named New Amsterdam and had a population of about 800. The British captured it in 1664 but the Dutch retook it in 1673. In 1674 the Treaty of Westminster between the Dutch and the English ceded it to England, and henceforth it was known as New York and the colony received a royal charter in 1686.

### THE COLONIAL PERIOD

New York as a port city attracted travelers and immigrants from Ireland from its foundation as a Dutch colony. Their numbers were very few in the early years, but their presence is attested by the occasional reference in the records of old New Amsterdam. The French Jesuit missionary, Father Isaac Jogues (later martyred in 1646), mentioned in a letter that he met two Catholics, one Irish (whose confession he heard) and a Portuguese woman, when passing through in 1643. But Irish names appear more frequently after the English administration took over permanently from the Dutch in 1674.

In 1683 an Irish Catholic, Thomas Dongan, was appointed governor of the colony by the Duke of York (later James II). Dongan, a native of Co. Kildare, became a notable exception in the long line of autocratic governors by introducing progressive legislation. In his five-year administration, Dongan was considered to have been one of New York's constructive governors. Dongan sponsored a Charter of Liberties and Privileges which guaranteed freedom of religion to all denominations and protected basic civil rights. He invited five English Jesuits—Henry Harrison, Charles Gage, Thomas Harvey and two lay brothers—to open a small school (which they did on the site of the current Trinity Church in Lower Manhattan), and the first public Mass in New York was celebrated on October 30, 1683. He also had plans to bring in colonists from Ireland but that hope died when his tenure ended. After the defeat of his patron, King James II, by William of Orange at the Battle of the Boyne in 1690, the era of religious tolerance ebbed away and English penal laws were again periodically enforced.

Vessels sailing from England to America often stopped along their route to get supplies and not uncommonly to take on crews and some passengers, especially in ports in the south of Ireland. The trickle of Irish immigrants began to increase greatly in the early eighteenth century, and they were soon represented in many facets of the commercial life of the city. The historian Michael J. O'Brien chronicled the Irish presence in colonial New York in several books and articles. O'Brien's painstaking culling of rather mundane records of civil and religious life of the seventeenth and eighteenth centuries revealed the presence of individuals of Irish origin in numbers beyond what had been previously suspected. His *In Old New York* compiled excerpts from many of the records of the Anglican (Episcopal) Church, particularly from Trinity Church and St. Paul's Chapel, whose entries alone contained literally hundreds of names of early Irish residents.

Other religious denominations had their share of Irish as well. A group of Palatine immigrants from Ireland founded the first Methodist church in 1766, a congregation which survives to this day as the John Street Methodist Church. A large number of immigrants coming to America from the north of Ireland in the eighteenth century were instrumental in establishing the city's first Presbyterian congregations, and in the 1820s a distinct Irish Presbyterian congregation was organized near Canal Street in Lower Manhattan. The first Roman Catholic congregation, St. Peter's on Barclay Street, which was heavily Irish in composition, was established in 1785 following the close of the American Revolution and grew rapidly.

Some Irish merchants, with surnames like Gaine, Duane, Waddell, Carroll, and Pilson, prospered in the small city. (In 1698 it had only 10,000 inhabitants.) There was always a touch of raffishness about New York City business. Some merchants worked with pirates periodically when it was economically feasible—just as the business community in the seventeenth century worked with the notorious Captain Kidd who was a respected New Yorker and a founding patron of Trinity Church. The Irish in the city before the Revolution represented a cross section of the community. There were many merchants, several of whom engaged in the import trade, and skilled tradesmen, from wig makers to chocolate makers, but the majority of the Irish were of the laboring class and lived quiet lives largely unnoticed in a city full of immigrants from many European countries.

The Irish became somewhat more visible in the 1760s when the festive celebrations of St. Patrick's Day began to receive notice in the press. In the 1760s a parade composed of a unit of Irishmen serving in the British Army and local civilians turned out to honor Ireland's patron saint on the morning of the seventeenth of March. It was a humble beginning for an event that would go on to become the largest annual parade in the United States. Slowly over the years St. Patrick's Day, with its attendant festivities, became a special day when the Irish in all parts of America celebrated their identity.

## AN AMERICAN CITY

A pattern of Irish settlement in Manhattan can already be traced in the years after the close of the American Revolution. Based on the distribution of Irish-surnamed inhabitants which appear in city directories of the 1790s, the Irish had already begun to settle in their own distinctive neighborhoods not just in the vicinity of the first Roman Catholic church (St. Peter's on Barclay Street), but along the waterfront, especially in the area from where the Brooklyn Bridge stands today to the streets of the present City Hall. The early development of the Catholic Church in the city during the nineteenth century serves as a good geographic measure of the growth and distribution of the Irish neighborhoods, which moved steadily northward on the island of Manhattan. Except for some French and German Catholics, there were relatively few non-Irish Catholics in New York until the American Civil War, and, consequently, the Catholic Church and the Irish community were virtually synonymous for decades.

In 1808 the Holy See appointed an Irish Dominican, Richard Luke Concanen, to be the first bishop of New York, but he died in Naples awaiting passage to America. Unable to appoint a new bishop to New York quickly due to his imprisonment by Napoleon, in 1814 Pope Pius VII appointed another Irish Dominican, John Connolly, bishop and he arrived in New York the next year to rule a diocese comprising all of New York State and northern New Jersey, with a Catholic population of about 15,000. He had seven priests to assist him (most of whom left) and one school. In ten years his flock had swelled to 100,000, composed mostly of poor Irish laborers, some of whom remained in the city while most found work upstate constructing the Erie Canal.

Significantly, the second church edifice to be built in New York was named St. Patrick's and was dedicated in 1815. The neighborhood around this church became part of a city which would take on a strong Irish flavor. Nearby, along Prince Street, could be found meeting halls where the city's numerous Irish societies held their entertainment and gathered to begin many of their ethnic parades and celebrations.

In 1777 John Jay was the principal architect for the new state constitution for New York. Resenting the increased number of Catholics in the city and state, Jay inserted anti-Catholic clauses, one of which forbade the naturalization of Catholics until they renounced allegiance to the pope. But bigotry was not rampant in New York and was offset by Protestants of tolerance and vision such as James, George and DeWitt Clinton.

James Clinton was born in Ulster in 1733 and his younger brother, George, was born in New York in 1739. Beginning in 1777 George began his six terms as governor and in 1808 became vice president of the United States under James Madison. In 1784 Governor Clinton appointed James Duane, the son of an Irish-born merchant, mayor of New York. He was the first Irish-American to hold this office in 119 years. DeWitt Clinton, son of James, was one of the most talented and illustrious men of his era and served as mayor of New York from 1803–1815 (with the exception of two annual terms during 1807–1808 and 1810–1811). The Clintons welcomed Irish immigrants and the exiles of

DeWitt Clinton

the 1798 and 1803 insurrections. During DeWitt Clinton's mayoralty, the anti-Catholic laws were struck down by the courts in 1806.

The outlook, politically and culturally, of the Irish community in the city was influenced at an early period by events in Ireland. The failure of the 1798 Rising and the consequent emigration of Irish political exiles to America caused many of them to seek a home in New York, despite the fact that some of the most notable American politicians of the Federalist stripe had opposed their influx into the United States, and they especially opposed supporters of the United Irishmen. Nevertheless, several of the most prominent Irish leaders established themselves successfully in the city, including the brother of the executed revolutionary Robert Emmet, Thomas Addis Emmet, a gifted lawyer and influential New York political leader who served frequently as the defender of the embattled immigrants. Fellow exiles William MacNeven, a native of Co. Galway and a physician, sometimes called the "Father of American Chemistry" for his work in scientific experimentation, and William Sampson, who also had a successful legal career in New York, became visible symbols of the rise of the Irish to prominence in New York life. The 1798 men established a political base in New York civic life as well. By the first decade of the nineteenth century their influence enabled a number of candidates more in sympathy with Ireland and the plight of the Irish to defeat some of their old anti-immigrant Federalist enemies at the ballot box.

The Irish cause soon found its way into print through the efforts of the 1798 exiles. The first weekly Irish paper in the city, *The Shamrock,* or *Hibernian Chronicle,* was founded in 1810 by Edward Glimpse and featured as coeditor Thomas O'Conor, a member of the Irish noble family of Co. Roscommon which had produced the last kings of Connaught. This newspaper and dozens of similar ones, which would soon appear in the years to follow, cemented the Irish community together and reinforced the bitter memories of colonial exploitation in the old country. The appearance of the Irish-American weekly newspaper in the city marked the beginning of a long history of agitation for the cause of Irish freedom and kept the exiles in America informed of nationalist activities in Ireland. New York in the nineteenth century developed into a center for the publication of not only Irish-American weekly newspapers but also of books on Irish literature and history.

New York developed into a bigger and more important city as the 1800s rolled on and as Irish immigrants spread out from Manhattan. By mid-century, Vinegar Hill, an area of undeveloped farmland directly across the East River from Manhattan near the old navy yard, which took its name from the last stand of the ill-fated forces in 1798 in Co. Wexford, developed into one of the most heavily Irish communities in America ("Irishtown"). The need for large numbers of laborers brought thousands of Irish to and through the city as roads, railroads and new housing expanded out from the city's center. On the fringes of this burgeoning metropolis could be found colonies of these Irish engaged in construction work of all types. Other communities of Irish were involved in agricultural work in the then independent villages within the confines of what is now the Greater City of New York. Many Irish among them began their labor as simple farm hands and soon elevated themselves to the status of tenant farmers before finally buying land to take their place alongside the descendants of earlier waves of immigrants of Dutch or English ancestry.

Increased numbers of Irish immigrants came to the city in the period following the economic recession in Europe after the end of the Napoleonic wars and the Congress of Vienna in 1815. These numbers reflected a shift in emigration from Ulster and Leinster to the rest of Ireland. The new immigration was also more Catholic in composition, and this fact was soon noticed, not always favorably, by the predominantly Protestant population. From the first decade of the nineteenth century there had been some periodic manifestations of anti-Irish feeling with the appearance of effigies of St. Patrick hung from lampposts before the saint's feast day, but events became more serious as the Irish community grew. Disturbances occurred outside St. Peter's Church as early as 1807, only a year after Catholics were first permitted to hold elective office in the state, and in 1831 St. Mary's on Grand Street on the Lower East Side was destroyed by arsonists. On July 12, 1824, Orangeman's Day, a serious clash occurred in the largely Irish enclave of Greenwich Village when Orangemen marched into the neighborhood with bands playing their sectarian tunes. Sporadic anti-Catholic and anti-Irish violence continued into the 1840s through the 1870s as a result of a more organized xenophobic political movement known as the Know-Nothings. (See *Orange Riots.*) In 1844 and again in 1854 mobs threatened to destroy Old St. Patrick's Cathedral, but on at least one of those occasions they were dissuaded from taking any action by armed Irishmen hiding behind the tombstones in the adjoining churchyard.

## Two Leaders

After the failure of the 1798 Insurrection, followed by the abolition of the Irish parliament (1801) and the unorganized revolt of Robert Emmet (1803), there was a leadership vacuum in Ireland. Thus Daniel O'Connell (1775–1867), a highly educated and competent Kerry lawyer, formed the Catholic Association in 1823. He asked the Irish to forego revolutions and to put their hope in political organization and agitation. He led Ireland to Catholic Emancipation (1829) and organized, on a local level, a massive drive for Home Rule. Irish men and women who came to America in the post-1830 era brought with them the political experience and organizational techniques devised by O'Connell.

In New York John Hughes, an immigrant from Co. Tyrone, was appointed bishop of New York in 1842 and became its first

Archbishop
John Hughes

archbishop in 1850. Like O'Connell, he was a no-nonsense realist who had worked as a laborer and realized that, despite their poverty, the New York Irish were the most literate immigrant group in the city. For over two decades he was their Moses, leading a downcast people into the promised land of American life. He showed them that education, communal solidarity, political participation and self-respect were the exits from the ghettos of Five Points and New York's other degrading slums. He excoriated the anti-Catholic school system which was run by a Nativist board of clergy and politicians. He told the Irish to organize and vote, and for the first time they used their political clout at the ballot box. As a result, New York got its nondenominational public school system. It was a step forward, but Hughes moved on to establish a separate Catholic network of parochial schools, staffed mostly by Irish nuns and teachers. In 1844, when a wave of Protestant bigotry threatened church burnings, Hughes stood his ground and threats ceased. It is told that Hughes supposedly thundered, "If a single Catholic church is burned, the city will become a second Moscow."

In 1858, ignoring the sneers and derision of the elite, Hughes broke ground for a new St. Patrick's Cathedral in an unclassy area of the city and vowed that it would be built with the offerings of the poor and one day would rival the cathedrals of Europe. He organized the Emigrants Savings Bank, and he started a new religious congregation of women with his sister, Agnes, as superior. He invited the Jesuits to take over St. John's College (later Fordham University) and allowed them to found a school and parish in Manhattan (the former College of St. Francis Xavier). He invited the Christian Brothers to start Manhattan College and encouraged women's higher education by sponsoring the Academy of the Sacred Heart and the College of Mt. St. Vincent. He believed that education would eliminate the slums and open a better future. He befriended the nondenominational Friendly Sons of St. Patrick (f. 1836) and backed the founding of orphanages and relief organizations to help meet the needs of the new exiles from the Great Famine. He advised the Irish to become involved in the political process; Tammany Hall (f. 1789) welcomed them and the Irish vote made New York City a Democratic stronghold.

When the Civil War broke out, Hughes—who only favored gradual emancipation of the slaves—sided with the Union and toured Europe to drum up support for the North. He tried to calm Irish mobs during the Draft Riots of July 1863. The people trusted Hughes and followed his counsel to alleviate their grievances by voting, not rioting. John Hughes gave the New York Irish leadership in the crucial era of their history.

## THE FAMINE IMMIGRANTS

The Great Famine, which swept Ireland in 1845–49, sent thousands of additional Irish to the city, many of whom had to endure the effects of a long voyage and horrible conditions aboard ship before they reached New York. (See entry on *Emigration: 1801–1921.*) The Quarantine Station on Staten Island or the hospital and asylum complex at Blackwell's Island were unfortunately the stopping places for thousands of sick immigrants who hoped for a recovery from typhoid and cholera which frequently followed in the wake of starvation and privation. Thousands of Irish died from direct and indirect causes related to the Great Famine in the period from 1847 to 1853, but thousands more found homes in their new city. The immigrants of the Great Famine were spared some of the horrible privations of immigration, such as those experienced at the British North America depot at Grosse Isle in Quebec, because of the presence of a large well-established Irish community in New York who were close enough to render assistance and pressure officialdom to take some steps to aid the suffering of their fellow countrymen.

While the Irish continued to be underrepresented in many professions and skilled occupations in the city until well after the middle of the century, New York with all its poverty was nonetheless a small improvement over life in rural Ireland. The rise of an Irish middle class can be traced in the pages of the weekly Irish newspapers. By then immigrants could read accounts of elaborate activities of the various Irish societies of the city and scan through the advertisements for goods and services. There were doctors, lawyers, teachers, grocers, hotel keepers, real estate developers, retail merchants, saloon keepers and dozens of tradesmen offering their wares and services in the pages of the *Irish American* and similar newspapers. The destitute immigrants found hope in New York.

Hibernian Hall and Montgomery Hall on Prince Street echoed the sounds of political meetings and social events as New York saw an emerging leadership role for the Irish-American in the city. It was from these Irish meeting halls on Prince Street that the Irish fraternal society, the Ancient Order of Hibernians (founded at St. James parish in 1836), reached out for the first time to organize the Irish in the scattered communities from coast to coast. It was also in these halls that the independent military companies like the Sarsfied Guards and Mitchel Guards drilled. The independent military companies had the twofold purpose of offering physical and military training while at the same time creating a force which might one day be used to free Ireland by military force. The independent companies would see action sooner than most thought when a majority of their members were recruited into state military units like the 69th Regiment, the premier Irish military unit in the city.

## THE CIVIL WAR AND AFTERWARD

By 1860 on the eve of the Civil War, the New York Irish comprised about one-quarter of the city's population and harbored mixed feelings over the impending crisis. But after shots were fired at Fort Sumter in April 1861, the Irish rallied to preserve the Union. Over 51,000 Irish volunteered from New York state and many of those were from Manhattan and Brooklyn. In 1860

Col. Michael Corcoran, who was dismissed from his command of the 69th Regiment of the militia for his refusal to parade during the visit of the Prince of Wales, returned the following year to resume command. His regiment was decimated at the First Battle of Bull Run. In the fall of that year, his replenished regiment was merged with two others to form an Irish Brigade under the command of Thomas Francis Meagher, a hero of the aborted 1848 Irish revolt but a reckless officer.

The slaughter at Gettysburg in the first week of July 1863 defeated the army of Major General George Gordon Meade and the Irish regiments suffered great losses. The government decided to resort to national conscription and the Irish, the Germans and other groups disapproved, especially after the Emancipation Proclamation of January 1, 1863. They felt that the war had assumed a double purpose—to preserve the Union and to free the slaves of the South. There was strong anti-Black sentiment among Irish laborers who were earning less than 14 cents an hour. This was exacerbated when Black workers were used to break a dock strike in the spring of 1863.

The Irish also felt that it was becoming a rich man's war as anyone who would pay a fee of $300 was exempted from the draft. (Folks like John Pierpont Morgan, Andrew Carnegie, and two future presidents—Benjamin Harrison and Grover Cleveland—bought themselves exemptions.) On Friday, July 10, 1863 the first list of draftees was published and it became obvious that the Irish wards had higher quotas than others. Over the weekend resentment festered and on Monday, July 17, Irish laborers skipped work and gathered at West 59th Street. Led by a volunteer fire unit, they approached the recruiting station and ignored the warnings of the police (many of them Irish), and skirmishing led to rioting. The protesters were joined by family and friends, and bands of looting marauders roamed the streets. The Colored Orphan Asylum was burned; Blacks were beaten and several were lynched. The Chinese were also attacked, and the homes of the wealthy and newspaper offices were invaded. The pleadings of civic leaders were ignored; Thomas Meagher was spurned; and the city fell into chaos and terror as the week passed. Eventually the city voted $2.5 million to buy exemptions for those drafted. Calm was restored only after Union troops were hurried back from Gettysburg. Archbishop Hughes urged the crowds to fight by using their votes in the upcoming election, and to forego rioting. This was Hughes' last public appearance before his death early in January 1864. When peace and order returned, rumors exaggerated the scope of damage and inflated the number of casualties. The best estimates attest that about 107 died and roughly 1,500 were injured. Only 67 rioters were charged and received light sentences.

As the Civil War progressed, the Irish fought and died in every major battle; they provided nuns and nurses to care for the wounded; and 38 Union regiments had "Irish" in their names. In some respects, the American Civil War established the Irish community in New York. In time of need, the Irish helped save the Union and it gave them a sense of belonging. The respect won by the Irish on the battlefield took the edge out of the anti-Irish feelings which had been so prevalent before the war.

Hostility to the Irish and Catholics was still to occur again and again, particularly in the movement led by the American Protective Association (APA) in the 1890s and the slow-to-die habit of caricaturing the Irish as ignorant half-wits continued in print and on the stage. New York humor magazines, like *Puck* and *Judge,* would linger into the next century perpetuating negative stereotypes, but the post–Civil War period is remembered for

The Irish responded heartily to posters such as this one. Over 51,000 Irish from New York State, particularly Manhattan and Brooklyn, volunteered for the Union Army. ©Collection of The New-York Historical Society

the great economic advances made by immigrants and their children.

Ireland was never far from the minds of the New York Irish. The collapse of the 1848 Rising in Ireland had resulted in the exile to New York of eloquent Irish nationalist leaders like Michael Doheny, Michael Corcoran, John Mitchel, John O'Mahony and Thomas Francis Meagher. A secret society known as the Fenian Brotherhood was organized in New York in 1859 for the avowed purpose of bringing about a rebellion against British rule in Ireland in conjunction with the Irish Republican Brotherhood there. Funds, arms and men were sent to Ireland in the next few years, but one faction of the movement believed something could be done for the cause in North America. The New York Irish supplied many volunteers for the Fenian plan to invade Canada to win concessions for Ireland. Many New York Irish participated in several mini-invasions of Canada beginning in 1866, and continued support with diminishing enthusiasm over the next few years. The collapse of another rebellion in Ireland in 1867 resulted in the imprisonment of many nationalists in the old country, and some of them were released to emigrate to America. Two militant nationalist immigrants, Jeremiah O'Donovan Rossa and John Devoy, set much of the pace for the revolutionary activity in Ireland.

The advocates of physical force as a solution to Ireland's national question were never far out of the picture in the New York Irish community. The secret society Clan na Gael, founded in the city in 1867, replaced the failed Fenian movement by the 1870s as the coordinator of the militant nationalist sympathizers in America. Much of its strength and money came from its dozens of branches in New York and Brooklyn. Its influence was felt in all the Irish organizations of the city, in the Ancient Order of Hibernians, in the Irish county societies, and sports and athletic clubs.

During the Civil War Irish nationalists hoped that after the conflict disbanded, Irish soldiers would form a Fenian force and liberate Ireland. There was an anti-English sympathy for the Fe-

nians in Irish-American communities across the country. New York was the capital of Irish nationalism which was a cohesive force which kept the old country in the hearts and minds of the exiled Irish. But the Fenians had more able talkers than practical planners, and the organization was splintered by internal feuds and the lack of an able leader and lost its influence. It was not until John Devoy (1842–1928) came on the scene and dominated nationalist politics that Irish-Americans had a competent leader. He was born in Kildare, joined the Fenians, and sought military experience by joining the French Foreign Legion (1861–62). Devoy was arrested and jailed in 1866 and in 1871 came to New York and was one of the founding members of Clan na Gael, of which he soon became the unquestioned leader. He tolerated no opposition and had an acute sense of political realism which separated him from extreme militarists and utopian idealists. He founded two newspapers, the *Irish Nation* (1882) and the *Gaelic American* (1903–28). Like Archbishop Hughes in earlier decades, Devoy knew the political dreams and hopes of Irish-Americans. He was their Parnell, and he influenced Irish affairs from the 1870s down to the foundation of the Irish Free State (which he supported).

## FACTORS FOR CHANGE

It is difficult for an Irish-American today to envision the appalling conditions of immigrant life in pre–Civil War New York City. Prior to the Great Famine, Irish Catholics came to America with a sense of persecution and discrimination, in part engendered by educational deprivation and religious bigotry as a result of the penal laws ("popery laws") which were enforced intermittently from 1695 to 1829. But the Famine immigrants had a bigger burden to bear. The wonder is how they retained some semblance of and commitment to a Catholic tradition. The squalid poverty was too much for many. One out of every three children died in infancy. By 1850 over 85 percent of mental patients in Bellevue Hospital were Irish-born, and over 700 prostitutes examined in 1858 in the Penitentiary Hospital were Irish. But things began to improve after the Civil War with the great growth of industry and the building of the city.

Two main factors which helped in the economic emancipation of the slums were the influence of the Catholic Church and Democratic politics. The rise of the Irish-American clergy, the sons of poor immigrants, was paramount. From personal experience they knew the spiritual and economic poverty of the people. They encouraged their parishioners to go to school as well as to go to church and advised them to get involved in the social and political life of the parish and the ward. Priests in poor parishes had a tough task, as did the unnumbered and forgotten nuns who staffed overcrowded schools, hospitals and orphanages decade after decade. The laboring class built the Catholic Church in America at the time it was deserting it in Europe.

While the church was primarily interested in building schools and churches to cater to the educational and spiritual needs of the people, some priests felt that this was not enough and that the clergy should speak out against social injustices and fight for the fair treatment of workers. The most famous of these "socialist" priests was Edward McGlynn (1837–1900), the son of a wealthy builder. Father McGlynn was an ardent nationalist and an advocate of fair wages. He allied himself with Henry George, the apostle of the single tax and other radical economic reforms. In the era of the robber barons and industrial expansion, the status quo was sacred, and the economic demands of workers

Rev. Edward
McGlynn

were dubbed "socialism." For McGlynn, fighting for a fair deal for working men and women was more than an economic challenge—it was a Christian duty. McGlynn clashed with two conservative archbishops, John McCloskey (d. 1885 and who was the first American cardinal) and Michael Augustine Corrigan who succeeded him and who in 1887 excommunicated McGlynn (who was later reconciled and given a pastorate). By the time Edward McGlynn died in 1900, he had put social justice on the agenda of the church and the politics of New York City.

The Irish immigrants had learned the political techniques of organizing and standing together from the crusades of Daniel O'Connell. They found a political home in the Democratic party which opened its Tammany Hall doors to them. (See separate entry on *Tammany Hall.*) The evil that some Tammany leaders perpetuated is well remembered, but the tremendous help it gave to Irish—and later Italian and Jewish—immigrants is often forgotten. Its shady reputation is traced to a few infamous men such as William Meagher "Boss" Tweed (1823–78), a nonpracticing Presbyterian of Scots-Irish descent whose name is synonymous with political corruption and who died in jail. Toward the end of the century, Richard "Boss" Croker (1841–1922), a Dublin immigrant, made graft a fine art, and in 1901 he fled to Ireland. (When he died, he was buried in Glasnevin cemetery, with his mistress on one side and his favorite racehorse on the other.) In 1872 "Honest" John Kelly took command of Tammany and was the first of ten Irish leaders who, with the exception of Croker, served the city well and helped the Irish eventually to move from shanty to lace curtain, from slums to suburbia.

IRISH INVOLVEMENT

Influential New York papers like the *Irish American,* the *Irish World* as well as other short-lived weeklies were read not only in America, but also back in Ireland where they provided the spark for militant nationalists. The *Irish World,* published by Patrick Ford, a native of Co. Galway, was a crusader in many Irish causes from temperance to the rights of the workingman from the newspaper's foundation in 1870. The *Irish World* was extremely instrumental in aiding the Irish Land League movement in the early 1880s, a movement which would eventually succeed in securing ownership of property for landless tenant farmers. The American counterpart of the Land League organization was boosted by the many visits of Michael Davitt, the organization's leader, and by the agitation of the frequently New York-based Fanny and Anna Parnell, sisters of Charles Stewart Parnell, the Irish Protestant parliamentary leader in Westminster. The organization raised thousands of dollars which were used to keep the agitation alive against the tiny but powerful Irish landlord class and its influential allies. The success of tactics such as withholding rent and boycott offered the hope that perhaps nonviolent methods could be used in Ireland to bring about a thorough reform of conditions. With the visit of Charles Stewart Parnell to New York in 1880, support for a limited form of self-government known as the Home Rule movement gained the support of many New Yorkers. A steady number of Irish members of Parliament followed in his wake, visited with sympathizers, and appeared at huge rallies at New York forums such as Madison Square Garden and Cooper Union. The Irish Parliamentary Fund was established in New York in 1883 to collect funds for the Irish representatives in the British Parliament.

Although several New York mayors claimed Irish origins, it was not until the election of Mayor William R. Grace in 1880 that the city elected its first Irish Catholic mayor. Grace was the successful importer/exporter and shipping magnate who built a trade largely based in South America into a financial empire. He was not a militant Irish nationalist, but he was an active backer of the Land League and the Irish parliamentarians. His tenure as mayor, in which he served two nonconsecutive terms, made little real difference to the Irish community. He happened to be a mayor who was born in Ireland (Queenstown, Co. Cork), but he acted in office much the same as any other mayor of the city had in the past. Whether a mayor was sympathetic or not to the Irish and their causes, they had no great effect on the day-to-day running of the city.

The office of mayor, however, could be used to preserve significant symbolic traditions. Grace's fellow Democrat and successor to the office of mayor, Abraham Hewitt, was the choice of virtually the same people who had put Grace in office. Hewitt came to power with a party that was dominated by Irish politicians. However, Hewitt proceeded to offend the Irish community by making a series of anti-Irish and anti-immigrant statements after

Richard "Boss"
Croker

winning office. Mayor Hewitt brought things to a head just before St. Patrick's Day in 1888. For more than forty years it had been the annual practice to fly the Irish flag above city hall and for the mayor to review the city's largest civic parade from its steps. Hewitt scrapped these customs, forgetting that his political life rested in the hands of Irish politicians who controlled Tammany Hall and Democratic politics. He was not reelected.

In the last four decades of the nineteenth century, the more educated Irish in the poor sections of New York began moving into the crafts and trades. A small number entered the professions and became doctors, engineers, and lawyers. But most moved out of tenements by becoming bricklayers, masons, painters, transport workers, printers, police and firemen. Some became shop assistants and others set up small businesses. No doubt, some became wealthy, but they were the exception.

Single Irish-American women increasingly found jobs as domestic servants, maids and nannies, and a minority became nurses and teachers. Those who married inevitably quit their jobs and became homemakers. But economic progress was slow for men and women alike. By 1900 only ten percent of Irish New Yorkers held white-collar positions. With the merging of Brooklyn, Staten Island, Queens and the Bronx with Manhattan in 1898, the New York Irish had a bigger city and brighter hopes.

As the Irish settled in various parts of the city, the names of some of the Roman Catholic parishes oftentimes became the strongest demographic indicators of neighborhoods rather than the names of the neighborhoods themselves. In many cases Irish-born pastors of long tenure helped solidify the concept of parish and ethnicity. The domain of the pastor extended beyond spiritual matters and encompassed the temporal welfare of his parishioners as well. At the turn of the century, priests such as Msgr. Henry Brann at St. Agnes on East 43rd Street, Father Charles McCready at Holy Cross on West 42nd Street and Msgr. James McGean at St. Peter's on Barclay Street were instantly recognizable to most members of New York's Irish community as clergymen who were notable not just for their ecclesiastical roles but also for their influence in social, cultural and political issues affecting the Irish community.

## CULTURE AND SPORT

For many Irish immigrants, life in New York was an endeavor largely spent in trying to duplicate the social conditions left back in the old country. Leaving Ireland had been for most of them the inevitable consequence of marginal farms unable to support a family. In the nineteenth century and for much of the twentieth, emigration had been a one-way journey with little chance to see friends and family ever again. The church provided for spiritual worship in almost identical fashion to the old country, but the immigrant had to provide a social life for himself. The dances, picnics, and excursions run by the Irish societies like the local branches of the Ancient Order of Hibernians (AOH), the Gaelic League or individual Irish clubs and organizations, did much to keep alive the music, dance and literature of Ireland. The Irish language societies like the Gaelic League and the Philo-Celtic Societies provided additional places for speakers to meet and converse with one another.

Several religious orders came from Ireland in the middle of the nineteenth century to New York and Brooklyn. They staffed several primary and secondary schools and a college. Because of a steady infusion of new sisters and brothers from Ireland, these institutions were able to maintain a very Irish educational program for their students which included lessons in Irish history, music and literature. Some religious congregations, such as the Irish Christian Brothers and the Carmelites, were instrumental in promoting the Irish language and culture in addition to their spiritual duties. Many pastors of predominantly Irish parishes in the city were anxious to have an Irish religious order at work in their parish as a means to attract newcomers to their church and to build it up spiritually and financially.

In addition to the average Irish organizations were the local and county societies. These groups brought together immigrants from specific places in the old land. Sometimes it was an organization composed of people from the same town or parish, but most often it was a county organization. The attraction of meeting people from the same county was enough to draw people to annual picnics or excursions in large numbers in the years prior to World War I. No other city in America had the number or variety of local and county organizations as New York.

Gaelic sports had long been a pastime of Irish New Yorkers; the first hurling games were played before the Revolutionary War. In the 1850s the Elysian Fields in Hoboken was the frequent Sunday destination of sportsmen anxious to use their hurleys. Most of the early teams were independent clubs. An "invasion" of top hurling and Gaelic football teams from Ireland in 1888 sparked the formation of an American branch of the Gaelic Athletic Association in 1891, but it lasted only a few years. The teams survived independently as they played on Sundays at parks in Brooklyn, Long Island City and Astoria while their names (the Emmets, the Sarsfields, the Irish-Americans, the Thomas Meaghers, etc.) continued to remind players and spectators of their Irish heritage.

In 1897 a number of private investors purchased a park not far from Calvary Cemetery in Queens and christened it Celtic Park. It featured a combination of Olympic type sports (running and jumping contests) as well as the traditional games of the Gael. It became an instant success and made a good profit for its investors when the property was sold as a site for apartments in the late 1920s. After the turn of the century, the old names of the Gaelic teams were changed to the names of individual counties and the number of teams increased. Various other parks were used for the games. Gaelic teams became bigger and better, and on the eve of World War I, the Gaelic Athletic Association (GAA) was finally successfully organized in the city. The GAA put Gaelic games on the same standard as those played in Ireland.

Both the professional and amateur theater groups were heavily involved in Irish-related entertainment up to the Great War. Playwrights like Dion Boucicault, John Brougham, Harrigan and Hart, Chauncey Olcott and many others produced a steady stream of entertainment with strong appeal to Irish-Americans. New York and Brooklyn legitimate theaters regularly featured Irish plays which often toured the rest of the country after a successful run in Gotham. Under the influence of Victor Herbert, the Dublin-born composer whose light operas became very popular early in this century, classical forms of Irish music were popularized as well. Herbert's early days in New York had resulted in his collaboration in several excellent musical programs of the New York Gaelic League.

In the opening decades of the twentieth century, the stage Irishman was completely out of vogue. Comics such as Gallagher and Sheean had become household names and George M. Cohan was the song and dance idol of the era. Cohan—whose father had changed his name from Keohane—captivated audiences with his romantic comedies, light musicals and popular "all-American" songs. This versatile playwright, songwriter, actor, dancer and producer blended Irishness and patriotism and wrote, among other great songs, *Over There* which was the most popular song of World War I. But Cohan's art was not the end of the journey. At that time the leading playwrights in the English-speaking world were Irish—William Butler Yeats, George Bernard Shaw, John Millington Synge, and Sean O'Casey. But they were shunned by the New York Irish whose rioting closed Synge's *Playboy of the Western World.* The Ancient Order of Hibernians called Synge, Yeats and others "so-called Irish dramatists." So when Eugene O'Neill, born in New York in 1888, came on stage, he clashed with Cohan who rejected O'Neill's stark realism and lack of sentimentality. The Irish nationalists of New York spurned the work of O'Neill who was no prophet to his own people. But he was and is America's greatest playwright who won four Pulitzer Prizes and the Nobel Prize for literature (1935).

## War, Irish Freedom and its Aftermath

Events in Europe began to dominate the news more and more as the first decade of the century ended. People in Ireland looked for the long-awaited Home Rule Bill. Elsewhere in Europe the major parties continued to arm themselves in preparation for what many observers conceded was inevitable war. The Irish in New York had a long military tradition behind them. The 69th Regiment of New York was one of the best known military units in the nation and the pride of the local community. In addition to the formal military, there was an equally long tradition of independent military companies which combined the old American tradition of target shooting with a formal military training. The Irish Volunteers, founded in New York in 1871, was the largest of these independent bodies and was organized in several companies in New York and Brooklyn and the surrounding area. The First World War drew most of the Volunteers into the ranks of the regular army, many of them into the Irish 69th Regiment.

In 1916 a great meeting of Irish-Americans gathered at the old Astor hotel on lower Broadway to lay the groundwork for a new organization, the Friends of Irish Freedom, to gather American support for Irish independence. (See entry *Voluntary Organizations.*) Some of the leaders, such as the old Fenian John Devoy, knew that an insurrection was planned a few weeks later in Ireland and the meeting was just a part of a worldwide effort to win support for Irish self-determination. The rebellion failed, but in its failure it sowed the seeds for future success. Although a majority of the leaders were captured and executed, a New York-born mathematics professor, Eamon de Valera, was spared the death penalty. After his escape from British imprisonment, in 1919 he was spirited out of the country to New York where he resided for the next two years, organizing and speaking on behalf of the fledgling Irish Republic. De Valera's New York birth went a long way in building up support for the Irish independence movement in the United States and in the founding of the Friends of Irish Freedom and later the American Association for the Recognition of the Irish Republic.

The establishment of the Irish Free State in 1922 ended the hostilities against the British but left Ireland divided over the acceptance of the division of Ireland into two parts, north and south. The civil war in the south over the creation of the Irish Free State was duplicated in America (at least on the political level) with both sides, Free State and Republicans, battling for the minds and hearts of the Irish-American community. A certain demorali-

zation affected the Irish community and membership dropped off in many societies, and for a time even the size of the St. Patrick's Day parade was greatly reduced. Although immigration from Ireland picked up after the war, it all but ceased after the early 1930s when economic depression hit the country. A whole generation of Irish immigrants went elsewhere until after World War II, and then immigration to New York City was only a fraction of what it had been in earlier years. (See entry *Emigration: 1922–1998.*)

The highlight of the 1920s was Al Smith's run for the presidency of the United States in 1928. He was the first Roman Catholic to attempt this. He had been "adopted" by the Irish as one of their own and he chose to be Irish. (His father's parents were Italian/German; his mother's were Irish/English.) Al Smith lost in a landslide, but he had opened a new horizon, even though anti-Catholicism was one of the leading factors in his losing most states including New York.

Another event of Irish literary concern was the founding of the *New Yorker* by Harold Ross. Since its inception, it has had an Irish connection. Its name was coined by John Peter Toohey, who also started the famous Round Table at the Algonquin Hotel, where the wittiest and best of New York's literary elite met. Down the years Irish-American writers—from John McNulty to Brendan Gill, from Maeve Brennan to Elizabeth Cullinan—have made the *New Yorker* their forum. The 1920s went out with a new Irish newspaper, *The Irish Echo* (1928); the great financial crash of 1929; and with Jimmy Walker, the playboy mayor, who gave sparkle to the city and took bribes gracefully.

The Great Depression, which finally ended with the coming of World War II, was New York's dark night. The war turned the economy around and changed the life of the city. New York women entered the job market while young Irish-Americans from all quarters fought and died in every theater of conflict. When peace came, the G.I. Bill opened college gates to the returning servicemen. This was the beginning of a new epoch which saw Irish-Americans enter the professions in large numbers, and the sun set on the days of Irish women domestics.

Although by the end of World War II, the Irish-born population of the city had been greatly reduced, a revival took place in the 1940s and 1950s as a result of new immigration from Ireland. A lively Irish social scene was revived with large dance halls in midtown providing a mecca for the young Irish and Irish-Americans as well. An interesting recognition of the contributions of the American Irish occurred in 1948 when Irish Gaelic football authorities voted to allow the All Ireland football final between Kerry and Cavan teams to be played at the Polo grounds. It was an extraordinary event akin to holding the world series in Dublin.

New York became the headquarters of the effort to roll back the partition of Ireland in the late 1940s and 1950s. For almost two hundred years Irish political refugees had made their way to America and thousands of former participants in the War for Irish Independence still lived in the New York area. Rallies and demonstrations were held frequently to promote the cause which was then being actively promoted in Irish communities worldwide by the government of Ireland.

The election of William O'Dwyer, a native of Bohola, Co. Mayo, in 1945 was in a sense a last "hurrah" for Irish politicians in the city. O'Dwyer had worked his way up to the office of mayor by taking advantage of the opportunities for education and he became a popular lawyer and later the district attorney of Brooklyn. He was very well known in the Irish community since he had served as president of more than a dozen Irish societies and numbered literally thousands of the members of these organizations as his friends. Although he enjoyed wide support among many ethnic, civic and political associations, no one worked harder for his election than the Irish community which knew him best. But accusations of corruption darkened his last years as mayor, and President Harry S. Truman extricated him by naming him American ambassador to Mexico. His younger brother, Paul O'Dwyer, while mainly unsuccessful in winning elective office, was the leading Irish-American nationalist and defender of liberal causes. (See entry *O'Dwyer, Paul.*)

The immigrants from Ireland who arrived in the 1950s and after were increasingly more upwardly mobile than their predecessors. The new immigrants included larger numbers of skilled workers and professionals who tended to eventually settle outside of the city in the more accommodating suburbs. Vast changes came to the Irish makeup of the city as one Irish neighborhood after another vanished between the 1950s and the 1990s. Not surprisingly, many of the cultural and social events which had defined the New York Irish community for over a century shifted to the suburbs or faded away.

The John F. Kennedy presidency was glory days for New York's Irish. The assassinations of John and Robert Kennedy were more than a tragedy. However, their achievements gave the Irish pride, and a sense of assurance that they had indeed arrived. In the subsequent decades, the Irish presence was taken for granted in the top echelons of the professions and in the business world.

The closing decades of the century were a literary spring for Irish-American writers in the city. Authors such as Brendan Gill, Maureen Howard, Mary Gordon, Jimmy Breslin, Maureen Brady, Pete Hamill, Frank O'Hara and scores of others showed the city and the nation the Irish gift of language. In addition, Irish-Americans have moved easily into the faculties of all the colleges and universities in Greater New York, and several of these institutions have inaugurated Irish studies programs, responding to the desire of many to learn more about Irish history and culture. As the twentieth century comes to a close, so does the extraordinary career of Senator Daniel Patrick Moynihan, one of the most brilliant legislators that Washington has seen for many generations.

Emigration from Ireland has slowed to a trickle as the country has become one of the most economically progressive in Europe. Now the emigrants will not come to New York, but Irish-Americans will visit the land of their forebears to celebrate their heritage and keep their memories green.

*See* Irish in America; Scots Irish; Ireland: 1798–1998; New York State; Emigration (5 entries); Draft Riots

Ronald H. Bayor and Timothy J. Meagher, eds., *The New York Irish: Essays Towards a History* (Baltimore, 1995).

Edwin G. Burrows and Mike Wallace, *Gotham: A History of New York City to 1898* (New York, 1998).

Florence D. Cohalan, *A Popular History of the Archdiocese of New York* (Yonkers, 1983).

S. J. Connolly, ed., *The Oxford Companion to Irish History* (New York, 1998).

Jay P. Dolan, *The Immigrant Church: New York's Irish and German Catholics, 1818–1865* (Baltimore, 1975).

Robert Ernst, *Immigrant Life in New York City, 1825–1863* (New York, 1949; 1979).

Michael Glazier and Thomas J. Shelley, *The Encyclopedia of American Catholic History* (Collegeville, 1997).

William O'Brien and Desmond Ryan, eds., *Devoy's Post Bag, 1871–1928* (Dublin, 1948).

William V. Shannon, *The American Irish* (New York, 1966).

JOHN RIDGE

## NEW YORK CITY: IRISH-AMERICAN MAYORS

### JAMES DUANE (1733–1797)

Mayor of New York 1784–89. (See separate entry on Duane.)

### DEWITT CLINTON (1769–1828)

Clinton was of Irish Protestant heritage, and he is best known for his role in promoting and building the Erie Canal while serving as governor of New York. His father, James Clinton, was a general in the American Revolutionary Army; his uncle, George Clinton, preceded him as governor of New York. DeWitt Clinton served as a secretary to his uncle, the Governor, shortly after American independence. It was the beginning of a long and storied career in New York politics. He won appointment to the U.S. Senate in 1802, then was appointed mayor of New York City in 1803. Save for two yearlong interruptions, he served as mayor until 1815.

During that time, he presided over the creation of such institutions as the New-York Historical Society and the city's Orphan Asylum. The city expanded under his administration, although it remained of secondary importance to cities such as Boston and Philadelphia. Once he became governor in 1817, New York City's role as the dominant commercial center of the United States was established. The Erie Canal, which he opened in 1825, turned New York into the preeminent port city and the young nation's commercial center. Before becoming governor, however, Clinton became one of the first in a long line of New York mayors to display national ambitions. He ran for president in 1812 against James Madison, and like so many other mayors of New York since, his ambitions were thwarted.

### WILLIAM RUSSELL GRACE (1831–1904)

Grace was born in County Cork. He rose to the top of American business and New York City politics. He emigrated to Peru in 1851 and went into the nitrate fertilizer business, quickly becoming a partner in the Bryce Brothers firm. In 1866, a year after the American Civil War ended, Grace moved to New York City and established his own company, W. R. Grace, on Wall Street. Taking advantage of his years in South America, he founded his business on trade with nations south of the border. The company would grow to become one of the powerhouses of New York commerce. His fortune firmly established, Grace soon became involved in Democratic Party politics, and in 1880, he was elected as the first Irish-Catholic mayor of New York, running with the support of Tammany Hall. He was reelected in 1884 (after losing in 1882). The company he founded, W. R. Grace, continued to be one of New York's most important businesses nearly 100 years after his death, and his descendants are important civil and business leaders in the city he once ruled.

### HUGH JOHN GRANT (1852–1910)

Grant was a well-educated and mediocre mayor, born to New York Irish immigrant parents. His father prospered with a chain of West Side saloons, patronized by politicians and an Irish clientele; and he was determined to give his son the best education that money could buy. After high school, young Grant moved to Berlin, where he mastered German which was an asset with German New Yorkers in his future political career.

After getting his law degree at Columbia University, Grant enmeshed himself in Irish affairs, frequenting county gatherings. He became a prominent figure in Tammany Hall, especially after the 1882 scandal when many politicians were caught taking bribes in exchange for street car licenses. He became sheriff of New York County in 1885, and in 1888 he ran for mayor and easily defeated Abram S. Hewitt who courted the anti-immigrant vote. As mayor, Grant favored giving generous municipal help to city services and to developing areas. He was reelected in 1890 and refused to run in 1892. He tried and failed to regain the mayoralty in 1894, losing to William L. Strong. Meantime, Richard Croker wrested control of Tammany Hall from Grant, who quit politics in disappointment and thereafter devoted his time to his business affairs.

## William J. Gaynor (1848–1913)

Gaynor was born in Oriskany, New York. After a successful career in the judiciary, William Gaynor was elected mayor of New York City in 1909. He won with the support of the newly installed leader of Tammany Hall, Charles Francis Murphy, whose progressive views and determination to make Irish-American politics respectable coincided with Gaynor's reform agenda. Upon winning office, Gaynor made a series of appointments of like-minded commissioners with no connection to Tammany. He immediately established his reputation as one of New York's most independent chief executives. Gaynor was born in upstate New York to a farming family of Anglo-Irish ancestry; he was educated in Catholic schools before moving to Brooklyn as a young man. He found work as a journalist, but soon found himself more comfortable as a player rather than an observer. He was not a gregarious man; indeed, he was quite the opposite. He wore top hats to baseball games at the Polo Grounds and Ebbets Field, and he seldom smiled. With a fine, white beard and an austere bearing, Gaynor was a serious man who saw himself engaged in the serious business of reforming New York politics after the corrupt reign of Richard Croker, one of Tammany's most infamous bosses. Although known for his patience, he also was given to high-decibel outbursts when developments did not go his way. He was in the process of rooting out abuses of the public payroll when, in the fall of 1910, he was shot by a would-be assassin while waiting to board a ship that would take him to Europe for a holiday. Dramatic pictures taken of the shooting show a stricken Gaynor in a suit and a derby, being helped from the scene, with blood pouring from his mouth. Though he survived, his health was never quite the same. He spent the rest of his term fighting for such causes as city ownership of New York's fledgling subway lines, an idea he advocated well ahead of its time. Tammany eventually abandoned him, but he was determined to win reelection on a reform platform in 1913. But he did not get the chance. He died on a ship bound for Europe before he could face voters. His funeral procession up Broadway drew tens of thousands of mourners.

## John Purroy Mitchel (1879–1918)

He was the youngest person ever elected mayor of New York. He won election to that office in 1915 on a reform-minded fusion ticket. In contrast to the Tammany Hall crowd whom he openly disdained, Mitchel was educated and polished, but—and here

again the contrast with his political enemies—he was brusque and disdainful of street-level politics. He attended Columbia University and immediately became involved in efforts to root out municipal corruption. He won election to the city's Board of Alderman (now the City Council) and gained a reputation as a strong-minded reformer. Woodrow Wilson appointed him to a federal post as Collector of the Port of New York—a job widely considered a choice patronage position—and from there was elected mayor in 1915. He prevailed over Tammany and its boss, Charles Francis Murphy. He won praise from reformers for his appointments, but the city's various ethnic and neighborhood constituencies found him to be aloof from their problems. Irish-Americans who wanted the U.S. to remain neutral during World War I so that they could foment a rebellion in Dublin despised him for his pro-British positions. Irish nationalists in New York, including John Devoy and Judge Daniel Cohalan, soon became vociferous enemies; ironically, Mitchel was the grandson of one of the nationalists' great heroes, the journalist and agitator John Mitchel. Eventually, Mitchel's opponents lined up behind Judge John Hylan, who defeated Mitchel in a bitter election in 1917. The defeated mayor immediately signed up for the U.S. Air Corps, but was killed in a training mission.

## John Francis Hylan (1868–1936)

Hylan was an up-from-the-streets, Irish-American success story. His father was an immigrant from County Cavan who served in the Union army during the Civil War, and his mother was, in Hylan's own words, an "upstate Yankee" whose great-grandfather fought with Lafayette during the American Revolution. Hylan eventually came to New York, got a job as a motorman and wound up being elected mayor of New York in 1917. He was born on a farm in the Catskills, and he spent an idyllic childhood in the Hudson Valley. The Hylan family frequently spent Sundays in the countryside, eating picnic lunches and picking blueberries. He spent his formative years performing the arduous work of a farmboy, rising at 5 A.M. to help his father with the chores. As a young man, he put the agrarian life behind him for the chaotic life of New York. He put himself though law school at night while working as a motorman on one of the city's many elevated rail lines, and eventually he became friendly with local Democratic Party leaders. Those contacts helped him land a judgeship in Brooklyn in 1906. In 1917, Tammany Hall nominated him over incumbent Mayor John Purroy Mitchel, and, in a bitter campaign that split the Irish-American vote, Hylan prevailed by nearly 150,000 votes. He won reelection four years later, but was defeated by Jimmy Walker in a Democratic primary in 1925. He returned to the judiciary, becoming a judge in Children's Court. Despite his loss to Walker, he remained popular with New Yorkers. Hylan Boulevard, one of the busiest roads on Staten Island, is named in his honor.

## James J. Walker (1881–1946)

Known to his adoring public as "Jimmy" and to history as a charismatic but flawed public official, Walker served as mayor of New York from 1926 to 1932. Walker's first love was show business, and, in fact, he wrote a song that became a popular standard: "Will You Love Me in September As You Did in June." But paternal pressure forced him to give up entertainment for the more prosaic business of law. Eventually, the law led him to politics, where he had a chance to display his flair for showmanship. He was elected to the state Assembly in 1909 and to the state Senate in 1914. Contrary to his later image as an inattentive playboy, Walker was a key lawmaker in the state legislature. He was an important ally of Governor Alfred E. Smith, and helped smooth passage of Smith's landmark social legislation that later became the foundation for Franklin Roosevelt's New Deal. With a nod from the governor, Walker ran for mayor in 1925, taking on the incumbent (and fellow Irish-American) John Hylan. Walker won the primary and the general election, and took over City Hall at the height of the Jazz Age. The era and the man were a perfect match; Walker was the personification of pre-Depression New York, He loved the city's nightlife and frenetic energy, and the people loved him for his glamour and charisma. His first term was a huge success—and among his achievements was the preservation of the 5-cent subway fare. He swamped his Republican challenger, Fiorello LaGuardia, in the election of 1929, but soon his administration, along with the economy, collapsed. Even as the Depression settled in on New York, ending the Jazz Age, Walker found himself fending off charges of corruption. Governor Franklin Roosevelt, Smith's successor, ordered an investigation, and Walker soon understood that his time was over. He resigned in 1932, sailed to Europe with his mistress (whom he eventually married) and so ended his public life. He remained popular, a symbol of his age, and he eventually returned to New York, where he died in 1946.

### William O'Dwyer (1890–1964)

O'Dwyer occupies an important place in New York political history. He was the last Irish immigrant in the 20th century to win election to New York's highest elective office, and, given current trends in immigration and sociology, he may well be the last Irish native to hold the post. He started out his working life in New York as a police officer, was awarded a law degree and went on to become Brooklyn district attorney just before World War II. As a prosecutor, O'Dwyer gained fame for his crusade against organized crime and the infamous Murder Inc. His work as a prosecutor made him an instant candidate for higher office, but his first bid for mayor ended in defeat when O'Dwyer failed to dislodge popular incumbent Fiorello LaGuardia in 1941. Four years later, with LaGuardia out of the race, O'Dwyer succeeded, and took the oath of office as mayor in January 1946. He was a popular mayor, and won reelection in 1949, but during his tenure the press reported allegations of corruption at the highest levels of the administration. With his support fading, O'Dwyer accepted Harry Truman's offer to be ambassador to Mexico. He resigned the mayoralty in 1950. His brother, Paul O'Dwyer, went on to become a leading civil rights lawyer and a voice for justice in Northern Ireland.

### Robert F. Wagner (1910–1991)

Of mixed ethnic heritage (his ancestors were Irish and German), Wagner was the son of Robert F. Wagner Sr., a German immigrant who was one of New York's greatest U.S. Senators. The younger Wagner was elected mayor in 1953 and went on to serve three successful terms. Wagner was born into public service, attending Yale Law and Harvard Business School and becoming a state Assemblyman in 1938, at the age of 28. He served in World War II and came back to join the administration of William O'Dwyer. He was elected Manhattan borough president in 1950, a post he used as a platform for his first campaign for mayor. As the city's chief executive, Wagner was a builder, adding thousands of units to the city's public housing stock. And as the son of a pro-labor New Deal senator, Wagner presided over a huge expansion of public employee unions. After two terms, Wagner lost the support of the remnants of Tammany Hall, represented by the organization's leader, Carmine de Sapio. He retained, however, the respect and affection of many of the city's civic leaders, and he ran for a third term by denouncing the very bosses who supported him during his first two terms. The tactic worked, and Wagner defeated strong challenges from fellow Democrat Arthur Levitt and, in the general election, from Republican Louis Lefkowitz. Wagner declined to run for a fourth term in 1965. He did try to revive his career in 1969, but he failed to win the Democratic Party nomination. Wagner then went into private law practice for the powerhouse New York firm of Shea, Gould. His son, Robert, also embarked on a career in public service, winning a seat in the New York City Council and serving as an advisor to Mayor Ed Koch.

*See* New York City

*Dictionary of National Biography,* 5th ed. (New York, 1997).

Irene S. Fishbane, *The History of the Mayoralty of New York City 1800–1883* (Ph.D. thesis: University of New York, 1949).

Melvin G. Holli, *The American Mayor: The Best and the Worst Big-City Leaders* (University Park, Pa., 1999).

Melvin G. Holli and Peter d'A. Jones, eds., *Biographical Dictionary of American Mayors 1820–1980* (Westport, Conn., 1981).

Kenneth T. Jackson, ed., *Encyclopedia of New York City* (New Haven, Conn., 1995).

Chris McNickle, *To Be Mayor of New York: Ethnic Politics in the City* (New York, 1993).

TERRY GOLWAY

## NEW YORK STATE

The Irish in New York State have a long and rich history, beginning in colonial days and continuing into the present time. Contrary to popular belief, significant emigration from Ireland was not limited to the period surrounding the Great Famine of the late 1840s. While it is true that the steady flow of Irish immigrants spiked in the late 1840s and continued with some abatement until the American Civil War (1861–1865), Irish emigration was an ongoing phenomenon throughout the history of New York State.

Most of the Irish emigration to New York State can be characterized as relocation due to problems in Ireland brought about by economic, political, and religious issues, thus necessitating a push toward leaving for foreign lands. The equally attractive pull of opportunities, such as better jobs, the abundance of food and land, and religious and political freedom also provoked a desire to relocate among the Irish. New York State proved to be a prime destination for hundreds of thousands of Irish immigrants because of its opportunities for employment, first due to international trade, and later because of major state-sponsored projects such as the canals, and then a plethora of municipal occupations in its cities during the 19th century.

### The Pre-Colonial Period

Before the 18th century, Irish immigration into colonial New York was very slow. It has been reported that the first Irishman to be buried in New York was John Colman, a shipmate of famed explorer Henry Hudson (who sailed under a Dutch flag). Colman was killed by Indians and buried in 1609 on the banks of the Hudson River.

In 1643 Father Isaac Jogues, a Jesuit priest who later became a saint, reported a rare visit from an Irishman in New Amsterdam (later New York City). Prior to the capture of the Dutch territories of Beverwyck (now Albany) and New Amsterdam by the English, few non-Dutch settlers mixed with the predominantly Flemish population in the territory now known as New York State, which was at the time limited to sparse trading outposts and farms along the Hudson River, between what are now the cities of Albany and New York. In the 1640s, however, one Irishman, recorded as John Anderson (d. 1664), ventured to Beverwyck to live among the Dutch traders and fur trappers. He is recorded as "Jan Andriessen de Iersman van Dublingh" and appears to have been the first Irishman in upstate New York.

An ironic note to the slow immigration into colonial New York was that, from 1682 until 1688, the governor of New York was Thomas Dongan (1634–1715) of County Kildare, Ireland. Dongan served as the only Irish Roman Catholic governor of New York until the 20th century. Dongan was followed by many English and Dutch settlers when the English established the colony of New York and absorbed the Dutch outposts. Notable in this Dutch to English transformation was the appointment of several Irishmen to local posts, such as William Hogan as surveyor of customs and later the sheriff of Albany County. These early Irish settlers who came to the newly incorporated cities of Albany and New York (chartered by Governor Dongan in 1686) were mostly Protestants who became absorbed into the Dutch Reformed Church, oftentimes having their names transformed into loose Dutch (e.g., Hogan is often recorded as Hoogen).

Overall, relatively few Irishmen, whether Protestant or Catholic, chose New York as their destination until after 1700. Those who settled in New York prior to 1700 were engulfed by the Dutch and English culture of the period and were limited to the few settlements open to European transplants (i.e., the Hudson Valley and, to a lesser degree, the French settlements in what is now northern New York State near the Canadian border). The total number of Irishmen in New York State at the time of English overthrow of the Dutch, judging by surnames, can be estimated at only a few dozen.

### The Colonial Period and Revolution

During the 1700s the greatest periods of immigration were during the late 1710s and early 1720s, the late 1720s and early 1730s, and during the 1770s. Many of these immigrants were from Ulster. During the eighteenth century, the Irish who emigrated to New York included Irish soldiers enlisted in the British army, indentured servants, and merchants drawn by the commerce between Ireland and New York.

Most of these merchants and tradesmen were Protestant, middle class, and skilled, who blended well with the Dutch and English colonists of New York who composed most of the population. These Irish Protestants were either Anglo-Irish Episcopalians or Scotch-Irish Presbyterians from northern Ireland who engaged in trade, most notably that of flaxseed.

Irish Catholic immigrants into New York were rare and many who immigrated to New York left the Catholic Church due to the lack of priests and churches. Overall, Irish Catholic emigration remained low in New York even though about one-quarter of all immigrants into the American colonies were Irish Catholics fleeing Ireland due to persecution, failed revolution, and poverty during the late 18th century.

In New York State, the laws restricting the Catholic Church were very stiff. As a result, most Irish Catholic immigrants settled in Maryland and Pennsylvania where religious freedom was practiced, although often reluctantly. The records of the early and mid-1700s reflect a growing population of Irish in the existing counties of New York State. Most of the records merely list the names and occupations, but a careful reading can detect the presence of numerous Irishmen due to their surnames (i.e., Sullivan, Ryan, Connor, to name a few). New York City and Albany had the largest Irish populations; however, the counties of Suffolk, Dutchess, and Schoharie seemed to have dozens of freeholders with Irish surnames.

The growing number of Irish in New York during the mid 1700s may have resulted in strong anti-Irish and anti-Catholic feelings among the colonists. In 1741 the "negro plot" was uncovered by New Yorkers, which alleged that several blacks and "papists" (Catholics) were guilty of arson in the city of New York. It resulted in numerous executions of blacks, several Catholics, and one Irish individual who was charged with being a Catholic priest. The resultant anti-Catholic feeling continued to persist for decades.

Later 18th-century records show an increase in the number of Irish and in their intermarriage with Dutch and English colonists. By the time of the Revolutionary War with England, the Irish population was slightly less than ten percent of the total population of the colony of New York. Many Irish were introduced to upstate New York and the areas that now comprise the counties of Yates, Oswego, Saratoga, and Washington during the French and Indian War (1754–1763). Sir William Johnson (1715–1774), himself a Protestant of Irish lineage, commanded many of his fellow Irishmen during the war. Johnson is best known for his dealings with the Indians in New York on behalf of the British prior to the Revolutionary War. During the French and Indian War, many Irish conscripts in the British army deserted once they arrived in the wilds of upstate New York. Also of note is that the French also employed a number of Irishmen in their unsuccessful war with the English in the province of New York. Many of the men of the "Irish Brigade," in service to France during this war, settled in northern New York and Canada after the hostilities.

A large number of these New York Irish served in the Continental Army during the war and supported the cause for independence. Among these was James Duane (1733–1797), the first mayor of the City of New York after the Revolution. General John Sullivan, although an Irishman who resided in New Hampshire, was active in freeing New York from loyalist forces. Sharpshooter Timothy Murphy (1750–1818) single-handedly turned the tide at the Battle of Saratoga by picking off two British commanders. Also of aid to the American forces during the Revolution was Irish-born tailor Hercules Mulligan who served as General Washington's spy in British-held New York City. Anglo-Irishman James Clinton (1733–1812) served as a brigadier general in the war and his brother, George Clinton (1739–1812) served as governor of New York during and after the war (1777–1795, 1801–1804) and later became vice president of the United States (1805–1812).

During the Revolution, American forces did not total more than approximately 25,000 men; however, about 4,000 claimed to be of Irish ancestry. In New York City about two-thirds of the nearly 25,000 inhabitants were believed to be loyalists, a minority of those were Irish.

Despite the appearance of being outside the mainstream religions of New York, many Irish Catholics served side-by-side with their Protestant countrymen in the fight for independence from the English during the Revolution. Until the large waves of immigration in the 1840s, there was not a clearly delineated split between the Protestant Irish and the Catholic Irish that would later cause many problems. Even after the establishment of the United States government under the Constitution and the Bill of Rights, which guaranteed freedom of religion, the safety of the fledgling Catholic Church in New York State, numbering less than 2,000 adherents, was still unsure. This fact would not change significantly until the later part of the 19th century when sheer numbers helped establish an alternative Irish Catholic culture in many of New York State's larger communities.

Bigotry, both racial and religious, plagued the Irish Catholics both before and after the American Revolution. Fear of their allegiance to the pope and to the Catholic world powers (i.e., Spain and France) made the majority Dutch and English Protestant population uneasy. While an overwhelming number of Irish fought on the side of the Revolution, the Catholicism of some Irish was still seen by the Protestant mainstream as troubling.

The Act of Quebec, passed by the British Parliament in 1774, seems to have made matters worse for the early American revolutionaries, as well as the Irish Catholics living in the colonies. This act allowed the Catholics in Canada freedom of worship and allowed them to forgo the usual oath of loyalty to the Crown by his subjects. This enraged American colonists who sought to encourage Canadian participation in the fight for freedom. It also led the Protestant majority to look warily upon the Catholics in the American colonies who had seen the Catholics of Canada elevated to British collaborationists. After the winning of the Revolution, the first Catholic diocese in the United States, which governed all of New York State, was established in Baltimore in 1790. New York followed with its own Catholic bishopric in 1808.

### Early Nineteenth-Century Irish Immigration

The destination of poorer Irish Catholics stayed the same (primarily Pennsylvania or the South) until the state of New York undertook a massive turnpike-building campaign in the 1810s, which required thousands of laborers. This project was the first of several major transportation initiatives that drew Irish immigrants, many of whom were Catholic, to the United States and, for the first time into heavily Protestant New York State. It was the beginning of a branching outward of the small communities of the state and the establishment of a string of cities along the Erie Canal. Expansion was slow, however, due to a number of problems including the presence of the powerful Iroquois Confederacy in the western part of the state, the pristine nature of upstate New York's unmapped forests and mountains, and a lack of reliable forms of communication.

Emigration by the Irish into New York State was aided considerably by the digging of the Erie Canal in 1817 to 1825, carried out under Governor DeWitt Clinton (1769–1828), himself of Anglo-Irish origins. By 1818, a year after the Erie Canal was started, there were more than 3,000 Irishmen working on its expansion. The subsequent development of railroads increased the need for more Irish laborers who sent for their families and opened small businesses along the routes of the turnpikes, canals, and railroads.

With the digging of the canal came a massive distrust of the laboring Catholic Irish. Since the Irish were used to low wages, they often worked for much less than what was required by many experienced native New Yorkers and rival ethnic canal diggers (i.e., Welsh, German, Black, etc.). The legendary rowdiness of the Irish Catholics who spent a large portion of their wages on alcohol at local saloons, known as "grog houses," also did much to alienate them from the mainstream in the developing cities in western and central New York State.

A numerically small but significant influx of Irish occurred in 1837, following the "Patriots' War" in Canada, which sent a number of Irish Revolutionaries, including famed state historian Edmund B. O'Callaghan (1797–1880), into New York State. This small war between Canadians seeking independence from England and those seeking to stay allied to the Crown involved many Irish-American New Yorkers. The great majority of these Irishmen were from Buffalo where in December 1837 a brief attempt was made by these "patriots" to establish a small independent government on Navy Island just north of Niagara Falls. The establishment was a failure and most of the participants (both Canadians and American sympathizers) fled to New York State permanently. The strained relations between the United States and Britain (and by extension British Canada) did not slow Irish emigration from Ireland via the St. Lawrence River.

Contrary to the American stereotype of immigrants all coming through New York harbor, a great number of 19th-century Irish took advantage of low cost, substandard British shipping to emigrate to Canada, often at landlord expense, and then migrated south to their future homes in the Empire State. The majority of Irish immigration to North America in the 1820s came from Ulster to Canada. Most of these immigrants landed in St. John or Quebec. During the late 1830s, the port of embarkation shifted to Liverpool. It was not until the 1840s that the overwhelming majority of Irish immigration shifted to the United States rather than Canada. The lion's share of this immigration was to New York City.

The Great Famine in Ireland during the late 1840s and early 1850s increased the number of Irish entering New York through New York City. It was during this era of immigration that tens of thousands of Irish-born immigrants entered New York State, with a great number of them forsaking farm life for an urban life.

Traditionally a culture that centered on farming and raising livestock in Ireland, the New York Irish immigrants opted for urban dwelling and city life. The routes of their immigration throughout New York State followed the canals, railroads, and turnpikes. The cities in which they settled were quickly populated by their fellow countrymen who gathered together in certain parts of each city. These areas became overwhelmed by the Irish who kept to themselves, forsaking the larger American society for closeness with their own.

The cities of Buffalo and Rochester in the west, Syracuse and Utica in the center, Albany, Schenectady and Troy in the northeast, and New York City in the south all had significant Irish and Irish-born populations by the Civil War. The immigration came both from the north through Canada and from the south through New York City. An interesting side note to this immigration is that it seems to have come directly from Ireland to these regions. Immigration of one generation of Irish to the state and the subsequent migration of these Irish families to another region of the state was not the norm.

## CULTURE AND RELIGION

The perceived differences among the Catholic Irish and the Protestant Irish, of which there were both Scotch-Irish and Anglo-Irish, widened between the American Revolution and the century that followed. The Scotch-Irish were mostly Presbyterian, middle-class who had been in America for several generations. These Scotch-Irish maintained strong ties to their Scottish religion (Presbyterianism) and their separate identity as culturally distinct from both the Irish and the English. The Anglo-Irish were mostly Episcopalian or Church of Ireland Irishmen who shared a common history with the Catholic Irish. Many were originally Catholic who changed their religion in the New World.

The Catholic Irish were foreigners brought to New York State as poor laborers prior to the 1840s or who came to escape hunger and persecution during the Great Famine. The increase in foreign-born Catholic Irish during the period of turnpike and canal building combined with mass emigration of poor Irish during the Great Famine struck fear into the English and Dutch New Yorkers who composed the largest percentage of the population.

By the 1850s an anti-immigrant, anti-Irish and anti-Catholic feeling spread across New York State. New Irish immigrants came to New York with little or no money, few skills, and little education. Their arrival by the thousands unnerved the Yankee ruling class, which feared a marginalization of their power and numbers in light of this mass immigration. To the Protestant mainstream in New York, who resented the strong Catholicism of these new Irish immigrants, this was their first contact with Catholics and immigrants in large numbers.

The earlier generations of Irish who settled in New York prior to the Revolution were either Protestant or lost their Catholic identity. Many were assimilated into the English and Dutch cultures since they found themselves without ties to the Catholic Church and found it easier to become mainstream. As the Irish immigration increased in the 1840s, the mainstream Yankee Protestant New Yorkers, especially those who claimed Scotch-Irish or Anglo-Irish ancestry, distanced themselves from the immigrant Irish Catholics. Many native Irish of the 1840s and 1850s found it far more palatable to claim distant relations to the Irish or merely claim to be Anglo-Irish or Scotch-Irish than to be associated with the new Irish immigrants who practiced Catholicism and lived in severe poverty.

An ironic note to the split between the Protestant and Catholic Irish is that the freedom of religion that was fought for by the minority Catholic Irish was championed by two Protestant Irishmen in the early 1800s. Thomas Addis Emmet (1764–1827) and William Sampson, both Irish Protestants who fought in the failed Irish rebellion in 1798–1799, successfully fought for the rights of Catholics to practice freely without government intervention. Their famed case, *People vs. Philips*, argued on behalf of the Catholic Irish, is still cited today in religious freedom cases. Sampson and Emmet were only a few of the exiled Irish (many of whom were Protestant) who fought the English for self-rule and eventually settled in New York State.

After the periods of great emigration brought about by the canals and the famine, the line between the Protestant Irish and the Catholics was greatly highlighted. Until that time it was not uncommon to see both Protestant and Catholic Irish as part of the same struggle for freedom in Ireland and common culture in the United States. For example, the first New York City St. Patrick's Day Parade in 1779 was not sponsored by Catholic Irish but by Protestants from a loyalist regiment. After the delineation developed between the Catholic Irish and the Protestants, social organizations were developed by each that usually excluded the other. Eventually, the St. Patrick's Day Parade became a mostly Catholic event that was used to inspire respect for, and pride in, the Catholic Irish. Some institutions that had previously been Irish in nature without regard to religion were changed and adapted to either Catholicism or Protestantism. Overall, many institutions sprang to life in the 19th century, such as the newspapers *The New York Packet and American Advertiser* in 1776, *The Shamrock* in 1810, the *Irish-World* in 1870, and, later, *The Gaelic American* in 1903. Dozens of immigrant welfare groups also were founded between the beginning of the 19th century and the Civil War.

An aspect that seems to separate the Irish from many of the other ethnic groups that emigrated during the 19th century is that the Irish had about an equal number of men and women immigrants. The Irish women who immigrated seem to have had longer life spans than Irish men and also broke into the professions faster than did their male counterparts. This is evidenced by the presence of Irish women school teachers in the late 19th century and the relegation of Irish men to jobs mostly in the field of labor or municipal work. The Irish, unlike many other immigrants, had a very low rate of return to their home country once they arrived in New York State. The Irish also had the advantage of knowing the English language.

A growing unrest with increased Irish immigration spurred such movements as the nativist Know-Nothings, who formed the American Party and tried to fight the Irish immigrant tide by establishing restrictive laws on the Irish and their Catholic faith. It polarized Yankee public opinion during the 1830s against immigration, more specifically the Irish and German Catholic immigrants. It lasted until the late 1850s when its adherents were absorbed into other political parties. Few officials were sustained in elected office as members of the Know-Nothing or American Party. However, a candidate for president of the United States ran unsuccessfully on that ticket in 1856—former president and New York State native, Millard Fillmore. The advent of the Civil War proved to be the demise of the American Party.

The savior of Catholic identity among the Irish of New York in the 19th century was the combination of religion and politics. This was partly instilled in them by a series of New York City bishops of Irish descent, especially Archbishop John Hughes, who sought to preserve the faith of the Catholics of New York, especially the Irish, who were discriminated against much more so than many other foreigners. The establishment of Catholic dioceses and colleges in upstate New York had a similar effect on the Irish upstate. This was accomplished through the building of schools, parishes, social halls, and the strengthening of the ties between the Irish and Catholicism.

The establishment of Roman Catholic dioceses in New York State reveals a strong Irish presence. Since the creation of many of these dioceses closely mirrored the establishment or enlargement of New York's upstate cities, it exhibited the growing Irish and Catholic population of New York State. New York City, which was created as a diocese in 1808, had a series of Irishmen as bishops starting with Hughes and including John Cardinal McCloskey (the first American cardinal), Michael Corrigan, and John M. Farley. The other dioceses around the state experienced the same patterns. The first series of bishops in New York State during the 19th and early 20th centuries in Buffalo (Timon, Ryan, Quigley), Albany (McCloskey, Conroy, McNeirny, Burke), Syracuse (Ludden), Rochester (McQuaid, Hickey), and Brooklyn (Loughlin, McDonnell) were *all* Irishmen.

Barred from most of the fields controlled by the Yankee establishment, the Irish created their own niche as members of municipal departments, most notably those of fire and police. A pride in their own schools and social clubs was coupled with the attainment of political power by electing Irish to public office and the domination of various trades or city departments. For example, by 1855 one-third of the voters in New York City and about 300 of its 1,100 police officers were Irish immigrants.

## The Civil War and After

Respectability was achieved after the Civil War with the return of thousands of decorated veterans who fought bravely for the Union in Irish regiments. This was compromised, however, by the draft riots in New York City when the city was placed under martial law in order to quell rioters who protested the draft, many of whom were Irish. Ironically, many of the police used to quell the rioters were also Irish. Nonetheless, Irish regiments, such as Corcoran's "Fighting 69th" catapulted many New York Irish into elected politics and respectability. Dozens of soldiers from New York were proclaimed heroes of the war and aided the Irish in their search for respectability. Prominent among those were the famed general Philip Sheridan, who was supposedly born in Albany, and Patrick Henry O'Rourke (1836–1863) of Rochester, who graduated first in his class from West Point and was killed in battle.

The fervor over the war briefly led to another attempt to annex or free Canada by a group of pro-democracy Civil War veterans. As was the case in the Patriots War in 1837–1838, the Fenian Raids in 1866 were launched from the Niagara frontier by Irish-Americans, notably Irish Catholic John O'Neill (1834–1878). The underlying cause of this brief conflagration was the hostile attitude toward Britain during the Civil War. During the war, many New York State newspapers, especially those in Buffalo, Utica, and New York City, mentioned the possibility of creating a northern United States by annexing Canada.

After the war, thousands of Irish-Americans, many of them veterans, organized under the name of the Fenian Brotherhood and proposed a raid into Canada to free the country and rid it of British rule. The Fenians hoped that they would be able to capture part of southern Canada, be aided by thankful Canadians who would help establish a free republic, and then gain recognition by the United States. On June 1, 1866, after weeks of preparation, the Fenians attacked Canada. The Fenians were soon vanquished and fled back to New York State, but not until the United States issued a proclamation of neutrality. Most of the Fenians were arrested and later released, thus ending the Irish hope of freeing Canada and establishing an anti-British government that would prove helpful to their countrymen back in Ireland, who had recently failed in revolution against the English. The Irish involved were absorbed by the Irish populations in Buffalo and western New York.

By 1870 many of the cities in New York State had significant Irish populations. In New York City, 202,000 out of 942,292 residents were Irish-born and 73,986 of Brooklyn's 376,099 residents were born in Ireland. In the upstate cities of New York State, a similar pattern of Irish-born immigration was found: Albany had 13,276 Irish-born out of 69,422; Buffalo, 11,264 out of 117,714; and Rochester, 6,078 out of a total population of 62,386. Because of these large populations, contingents of Irish assemblymen, state senators, and congressmen were elected from urban areas, such as Albany, Buffalo, and New York City both before and after the Civil War.

In New York City, the notorious Democratic Tammany Hall, once a haven of anti-Irish sentiment, was swayed toward the Irish due to the large number of Irish voters and politicians. The attainment of local offices by the Irish, including that of mayors Michael Nolan in Albany and William Russell Grace (1832–1904) in New York began a long line of Irish Catholic involvement in the Democratic Party on both the local and state levels. Tammany Hall was eventually overtaken by the Irish and subsequently made famous by its corruption. Its leaders were eventually prosecuted by an Irish Catholic, Charles O'Conor (1804–1884), in 1872. However, Tammany Hall, as well as Irish Catholic Democratic machines, built during the years after the Civil War, lasted until the late 20th century. In Albany, the Irish under Daniel P. O'Connell captured control of the city and county governments and ruled the capital district from 1921 until his death in 1976. He is often regarded as the longest tenured political boss in recent history, having reigned for 55 years.

## The Twentieth Century

An increase in anti-Irish public opinion occurred in the 1910s and lasted until the 1930s. It was sparked in part by another large wave of Catholic immigrants, most notably those from the Mediterranean basin. The wave of nativism it sparked engulfed Irish Catholics and was exacerbated by the coming of World War I and its effect on American public opinion. The strong anti-English sentiment of Irish Catholic New Yorkers was perceived by the Anglo-Saxon Americans as pro-German and, far worse, as unpatriotic. New York City served as a lightning rod for this debate between those favoring Irish independence and those seeking to support the English in the war with Germany.

After America declared war on the Axis powers in 1917, the Irish Catholics, whose hatred for the British had been strengthened by the failure of the 1916 Irish revolution and the subsequent execution of its leaders by the British, were caught in a difficult situation. They reluctantly supported the war in order to further self-determination (as was espoused by President Woodrow Wilson) and fend off allegations that they were not patriotic. However, strong anti-English sentiment was felt by a majority of the Irish Catholics in New York State both during and after the war when Irish independence was not realized and the English Empire was preserved. When Sinn Fein leader Eamon de Valera visited New York in 1919 and Terence MacSwiney (the Lord Mayor of Cork) died on a hunger strike protesting the English in 1920, the New York Catholic Irish were once again at odds with the Protestant majority who chose to champion Americanism over what was perceived as allegiance to foreign powers (i.e., Ireland and the Vatican) instead of the United States. Great rallies in New York City greeted de Valera and huge funeral Masses were held in Catholic churches throughout the state for MacSwiney. In New York City, the Mass at St. Patrick Cathedral for MacSwiney turned into a riot when Irish Catholics sacked the pro-English Union Club of New York after leaving.

The anti-Catholic feelings among New Yorkers did not keep Alfred E. Smith (1873–1944), who was elected governor in 1918 and ran unsuccessfully for president in 1928, from breaking the back of bigotry and attaining national prominence as the first in a series of Irish Catholic Americans who sought high public office. Since Governor Smith, dozens of Irish Roman Catholics have held high elective and appointive offices in New York State, including Senators Robert F. Kennedy, James Buckley, Daniel Patrick Moynihan, Governor Hugh Carey, and Postmaster General James A. Farley (under President Franklin Roosevelt). The same can be said of the professions in New York State today, which count many Irish amongst their ranks. In a similar vein, many avenues that were previously closed to them have been opened, including all the fields of education, law, medicine, and big business.

The respectability once yearned for by the immigrant Irish of the late 1840s was eventually realized through a long struggle. Immigration was greatly reduced during World War I and World War II and continued to dwindle until the 1980s when immigration from Ireland to New York City, much of it illegal, increased noticeably. Thereafter, time has "Americanized" the millions who claim to be descendants of the 19th- and early 20th-century Irish immigrants. Today, there is very little Irish immigration into New York State compared to the hundreds of thousands in the late 1840s. Time and the aging of New York State's cities have also greatly reduced the size and population of the Irish urban neighborhoods, although many Irish communities, including pockets in New York City, remain close knit.

The great majority of those who claim Irish ancestry do so by links with relatives who immigrated decades ago. The separation of the Irish from mainstream society has mostly disappeared. In fact, the stereotypical career route of the Catholic Irish—politics, municipal work, or the Church—or the Scotch-Irish involvement in mostly upper crust business careers is not as recognizable today. The perceived differences between the New York Irish are not as defined by careers or economic station in life today, and it is just as common to see corporate executives or elected officials from diverse backgrounds.

*See* New York City; American Revolution; Emigration (5 entries)

Ronald H. Bayor and Timothy J. Meagher, *The New York Irish* (Baltimore, 1996).

Edward Cuddy, "The Irish Question and the Revival of Anti-Catholicism in the 1920s," *The Catholic Historical Review*, Vol. LXVII/2 (April 1981): 236–255.

Richard D. Doyle, *The Pre-Revolutionary Irish in New York* (Ph.D. diss., Saint Louis University, 1932).

Leroy V. Eid, "Irish, Scotch and Scotch-Irish, A Reconsideration," *American Presbyterians*, Vol. 64/4 (1986): 211–225.

William D. Griffin, ed., *The Irish in America, 1550–1972* (Dobbs Ferry, N.Y., 1973).

David G. Hackett, "The Social Origins of Nationalism: Albany, New York 1754–1835," *Journal of Social History*, Vol. 21/4 (1988): 659–681.

Lawrence Mannion and Richard Murphy, *The History of the Friendly Sons of Saint Patrick in the City of New York 1784 to 1955* (New York, 1962).

Kenneth Moss, "St. Patrick's Day Celebrations and the Formation of Irish-American Identity, 1845–1875," *Journal of Social History*, Vol. 29/1 (Fall 1995): 125–148.

JOHN T. EVERS

## NOLAN, JANET ANN (1946– )

Historian, author, and professor. Janet Nolan was born in San Francisco. After living in Seattle, Jacksonville, and Massachusetts, she entered the first grade in Winston-Salem, NC, and graduated from high school in Lynn, MA, twelve years later. She received a bachelor's degree in history from the University of Massachusetts in Amherst where she was a member of Kappa Kappa Gamma sorority and a recipient of that sorority's national scholarship award.

After nine years of teaching in two states, Nolan earned a master's degree in modern European history at the University of Rhode Island in Kingston, where she received the "Outstanding Achievement in European History" award. She went on to complete a Ph.D. in History at the University of Connecticut where she was elected to Phi Beta Kappa. She maintained a perfect 4.0 grade point average at both URI and UCT. Her dissertation, *Ourselves Alone: Women's Emigration from Ireland, 1885–1920,* was published by the University Press of Kentucky in 1989.

Hired as an assistant professor of history at Loyola University Chicago in 1987, Nolan received tenure and a promotion to the rank of associate professor at that university in 1993. She teaches a wide variety of courses in several fields at Loyola, including graduate courses in Irish and Irish-American studies.

Nolan's scholarship has earned her wide recognition. Her work has led to invitations to speak throughout the United States as well as in Switzerland, Northern Ireland, the Republic of Ireland, and England. She has been interviewed by Irish, British, and American television about Irish women and their migration patterns, and she has published extensively on the subjects of women in Irish and Irish-American history. She is currently working on a manuscript, *St. Patrick's Daughters: Education and Women's Mobility in Ireland and Irish America, 1880–1920.*

Nolan's many professional activities include serving as the president of the American Conference for Irish Studies (ACIS) Midwest Region. She has also been a member of the ACIS executive board and its nominations and book prize committees. She is a member of the Irish American Cultural Institute, Phi Beta Kappa, and the American Historical Society. She is an advisory editor for *The New Hibernia Review*, *The Oral History Review*, and *Mid-America: An Historical Review*.

Janet Nolan

Janet Nolan's study of Irish women is a step forward in that neglected area; and her widespread research and meticulous scholarship opens up a new chapter in the appreciation of the contribution of Irish women in education and other fields.

*See* Education: Irish-American Teachers in Public Schools

Janet Nolan, "Education and Women's Mobility in Ireland and Irish America, 1880–1920: A Preliminary Look," *New Hibernia Review* 2:3 (Autumn 1998): 78–88.

———, "The Great Famine and Women's Emigration from Ireland," in *The Hungry Stream: Essays on Famine and Emigration*, ed. by E. Margaret Crawford, 67–75. (Belfast, 1997).

———, "The National Schools and Irish Women's Mobility in the Late Nineteenth and Early Twentieth Centuries," *Irish Studies Review* 18 (Spring 1997): 23–28.

———, "Patrick Henry in the Classroom: Margaret Haley and Chicago Teachers' Federation," *Éire-Ireland*, XXX/2 (Summer 1995): 104–117.

———, "L'extraordinaire aventure de l'emigration des femmes irlandaises 1885–1920," in *Vers un ailleurs prometteur . . . l'emigration, une reponse universelle a une situation de crise?,* ed. by Claudine Sauvain-Dugerdil and Yvonne Preiswerk, 129–138 (Paris and Geneva, 1993).

———, Guest Editor and Introduction, Special Issue. "The Catholic Woman in Urban America," *Mid-America: An Historical Review* 74/3 (October 1992).

———, "Irish-American Teachers and the Struggle Over American Urban Education, 1890–1920: A Preliminary Look," *Records of the American Catholic Historical Society of Philadelphia* 103/3–4 (Winter 1992): 13–22.

———, *Ourselves Alone: Women's Emigration from Ireland, 1885–1920* (Lexington, 1989).

———, *Connecticut Workers and a Half Century of Technological Change, 1930–1980: The Catalogue of Interviews,* with Michelle Palmer and Brian O'Connor. (Storrs, 1983).

MICHAEL PATRICK GILLESPIE

## NOONAN, JAMES PATRICK (1878–1929)

Labor leader. Born in St. Louis to Irish immigrant parents, Noonan left school at age thirteen and worked at a variety of jobs. He saw service briefly in the Spanish-American War. After his discharge from the army, Noonan took a job as an electric lineman in St. Louis and soon became involved in local labor activities. In 1901, he joined the International Brotherhood of Electrical Workers. He advanced quickly within the union, rising from local president to a position as vice president in the national union by 1904. In 1919, Noonan became president of the IBEW following the retirement of Frank Joseph McNulty. Large and heavy set, Noonan combined a tough determination with a reputation for honesty and common sense to become one of the most prominent labor leaders of the 1920s. By 1924, Noonan was named to the executive council of the American Federation of Labor. He was also a widely recognized expert of the effects on labor by electric power, which earned him appointments to a number of state and national power commissions. In 1924, Noonan was the only labor delegate to attend the World Power Conference in London. He died in 1929 from burns suffered from a fire started after he fell asleep smoking in the bed of his Washington, D.C., apartment.

*Dictionary of American Biography*, Vol. VII, part 1: 544–45.

Gary M. Fink, ed., *Biographical Directory of American Labor* (Westport, CT, 1984): 437.

Michael A. Mulcaire, *The International Brotherhood of Electrical Workers: A Study in Trade Union Structure and Functions* (Washington, D.C., 1923).

TOM DOWNEY

## NOONAN, JOHN T. (1926– )

Federal judge, legal educator, author. John Thomas Noonan, Jr., was born in Boston, Massachusetts, October 24, 1926, son of John T. and Marie (Shea) Noonan. He studied at Harvard University, the Catholic University of America and Cambridge University, receiving a total of four degrees, two of them doctorates, and developing skills as a moralist, historian and lawyer. He also became proficient in the reading of seven languages.

Noonan worked in 1954–1955 with the National Security Council in Washington, then as an attorney in Boston from 1955–1961, whereupon he became a professor of law at the University of Notre Dame. In 1967 he joined the law faculty at the University of California, Berkeley, serving until 1985 when he was named a judge of the U.S. Court of Appeals, 9th District, in San Francisco.

Over the years Noonan has received numerous honors. He was the Oliver Wendell Holmes, Jr., Lecturer at Harvard University Law School in 1972, the Cardinal Bellarmine Lecturer at St. Louis University Divinity School in 1973, and in 1984 was recipient of the University of Notre Dame's Laetare Medal. In 1991 he was appointed an Overseer of Harvard.

A scholar of the first rank, Noonan is noted for a series of books, strongly Catholic in orientation, on usury, human sexuality, annulments and abortion. His *The Scholastic Analysis of Usury* (1957) was cited by University of California economics Professor John Letiche as a book without precedent and needing no successor, "a classic." Another book, *Contraception: A History of Its Treatment by the Catholic Theologians and Canonists,* won the John Gilmary Shea Prize of the American Catholic Historical Association as the most original and distinguished contribution to historical knowledge in 1965.

That same year Noonan was invited to serve as a consultant to the Commission on the Family, Population and Natality, named by Pope Paul VI to study the question of artificial birth control.

John T. Noonan

The thesis advanced in Noonan's book—namely, that change in the church's teaching on contraception was possible—prevailed among the majority of the commission. However, its recommendation favoring change was rejected by Paul VI and traditional church teaching was restated in the 1968 encyclical *Humanae Vitae.*

A 1979 Noonan book on abortion—*A Private Choice: Abortion in America in the Seventies*—challenged the legality and morality of the Supreme Court's 1973 decision making the procedure a fundamental right of women.

In addition to books exploring legal, historical and moral issues, Noonan has translated *The Decretals,* Book IV, by Pope Gregorius IX (1967). His most recent book, *The Lustre of Our Country* (1998), probes the American experience of religious freedom.

Noonan served as editor of *Natural Law Forum* from 1961–1970, and of the American Journal of Jurisprudence in 1970. He is married to the former Mary Lee Bennett. They have three children.

Linda Metzger, ed., *Contemporary Authors: New Revision Series,* vol. 13 (Detroit, 1984).

Kenneth Woodward, "Noonan's Life of the Law," *Newsweek* (April 1, 1985).

JOHN DEEDY

## NOONAN, PEGGY (1950– )

Speechwriter, author. Peggy Noonan was born in Brooklyn, New York, September 7, 1950, daughter of James and Mary Jane (Byrne) Noonan. She is second-generation Irish, the third of seven children, and Roman Catholic. ("I'm just your basic bad Catholic," she has written, "utterly believing and yet full of the flaws that make for real interesting confessions.") At age five, her family moved to Massapequa in suburban Long Island, then to Rutherford, New Jersey. After graduating from Fairleigh Dickinson University in 1974, she joined CBS radio station WEEI in Boston as a news and editorial writer. In 1977 she moved to CBS network headquarters in New York as a writer, producer and sometimes drafter of commentary for TV anchorman Dan Rather.

Republican and conservative (she shed Democratic-liberal proclivities while in college), Noonan served from 1984–1986 as special assistant to President Ronald Reagan and worked on some of his memorable addresses, including that marking the fortieth anniversary of D-day and those for the Geneva summit meeting with Soviet premier Mikhail Gorbachev. She also wrote his moving response to the *Challenger* space-shuttle explosion of January 28, 1986, that claimed the lives of seven crew members, including that of Christa McAuliffe, the New Hampshire civilian school teacher.

During Reagan's second term, Noonan sparked controversy by publicly acknowledging which presidential speeches were hers, prompting one critic to exclaim that "a speechwriter is supposed to have a passion for anonymity."

In 1988–1989 Noonan was chief speechwriter to Vice President and subsequently President-elect George Bush, and drafted the Republican nomination acceptance speech that resonated with such phrases as "a kinder, gentler society" ("gentler" was Bush's insert), "read my lips—no new taxes," and "a thousand points of light." The last phrase, intended as shorthand for the network of helping organizations that existed across the country,

Peggy Noonan

struck a particularly strong chord with the electorate. Noonan termed it her "favorite phrase," for its power in describing "an expanse of separate yet connected entities sprinkled across a broad and peaceful sky, which is America, the stretched continent."

Noonan's facility with language once prompted a Reagan administration official to characterize her as "the girl who does the poetry." Her political texts were laced with literary and patriotic allusions, and spiced with wit as well as the occasionally charged reference—as, for example, Reagan's terming the Nicaraguan contras "the moral equal of our Founding Fathers."

Noonan lives in New York City, where she is an independent writer and frequent television commentator. She was married in 1985 to Richard Rahn. They divorced in 1990. There was one son, Will.

Peggy Noonan, *What I Saw at the Revolution: A Political Life in the Reagan Era* (New York, 1990).

———, *Life, Liberty and the Pursuit of Happiness* (New York, 1994).

Susan M. Trosky, ed., *Contemporary Authors,* vol. 132 (Detroit, 1991).

JOHN DEEDY

## NORRIS, KATHLEEN THOMPSON (1880–1966)

Author. Kathleen Thompson Norris, author of more than 80 novels and 1,500 newspaper and magazine articles, enjoyed long-lasting literary success. Born into an Irish-Catholic family in California, Norris was forced to support herself and her siblings after both her parents died within a month of each other when she was nineteen. Thus, before beginning her writing career, she was eclectically employed, at various times, as a bookkeeper, sales associate, teacher, and journalist for two San Francisco papers. In 1909, she became part of an American writing family when she married Charles Gilman Norris, brother of Frank Norris. In addition to her novels, which earned her the appellation "grandmother of the American sentimental novel," Norris was a widely read short story writer and essayist, in such publications as *Colliers, Atlantic Monthly, Woman's Home Companion, McClure's* and *Munsey's.* She covered the Bruno Hauptmann trial for the *New York Times,* cementing a friendship with the bereaved father Charles Lindbergh. Other disparate admirers of her work included Theodore Roosevelt, Noel Coward, and Harpo Marx. A brief bibliography includes her first novel, *Mother* (1911), *Certain People of Importance* (1922) and *The American Flaggs* (1936), two of her more critically acclaimed novels, and the essays "My San Francisco" (1932) and "My California" (1933), both tributes to her beloved home state. Norris's prolific pen allowed her to enjoy considerable financial success; at her death, her writing fortune exceeded several million dollars.

In her *New York Times* obituary, Norris is described as a feminist, a pacifist, a supporter of Prohibition, and an opponent of the death penalty. Her strong political views belie the family-centered plots of much of her writing. Designated a sentimentalist, Norris is dismissed by some critics for the domestic focus of her fiction. Typically, there is a sense of impatience on the part of those critics who take note of her proclivity for happy endings and her "relentlessly wholesome" themes.

However, she is also praised for the lucidity and candor of her writing and the skillfulness with which she draws her characters. Norris's Irish-Catholic legacy is evident in her population of wise and jolly immigrant Irish women who dispense practical advice along with steaming mugs of tea in their cramped kitchens, and in her plots featuring a matter-of-fact material Catholicism of novenas and nuns, rosaries and redemption. Norris's Catholic conservatism on social issues is very easy to find in her plots, but her traditional Catholic positions on family life may be more complicated than they first appear. For instance, her apparent "orthodoxy" is belied by the centrality of powerful women and the marginalization of men in her work. Also, while her themes are infused with Catholic values, her interpretation of the enactment of those values reveals her individual conscience as well as the collective conscience of her church. A story focusing on the plight of an unwed mother may portray the community's moral disapproval but also features its practical concern: arranging a job for the mother-to-be, deciding how to procure child support from the father, and finally arranging a marriage between the two parents. Norris's interest in portraying how spiritual values are etched upon the surface of everyday life is clearly an ongoing focus.

Kathleen Norris's writing is many-voiced, and while she is quoted as affirming the centrality of women's roles as wives and mothers, Norris indicates that in this female role there is true power: domestic society, as a microcosm of the broader community, allows women to shape the universe beyond their family circle. For Norris, therefore, the personal is universal. Norris's long career is indicative of her inventiveness, and that inventiveness is particularly noteworthy in her literary attempts at fusing traditional Catholic positions with innovative interpretations of their significance. Kathleen Norris died in 1966.

MARIE REGINA O'BRIEN

## NORTH CAROLINA

The present site of North Carolina lies amidst the part of the New World that was first explored and in time settled by people from the British Isles. As such it was the earliest place in America to which the Irish came. Walter Raleigh (1552?–1618), soon to be knighted for his efforts to discover, explore, and colonize a portion of the New World, became involved with affairs in Ireland in 1580. Under a grant from Queen Elizabeth I for a large portion of what became the United States but was called Virginia between 1584 and 1590, Raleigh planned and financed three expeditions to Roanoke Island on the Atlantic coast of North America. The purpose of his grant was to unite newly discovered lands in America "in more perfecte league and amitye" with "our Realmes of England and Ireland."

### THE FIRST IRISH IN AMERICA?

In 1584 Raleigh sent a small reconnaisance expedition to identify a site for a colony. In 1585, to direct that first colony, Raleigh selected Ralph Lane, the sheriff of County Kerry in Ireland, to be governor. Serving under Lane's military leadership were John White, a skilled artist, and Thomas Harriot, an experienced scientist. They explored and described large areas of American territory, collaborated in gathering information, making maps, and painting very clear and detailed watercolor pictures of the native people, their houses and boats, and wildlife.

Failing to receive timely supplies from home, after eleven months Lane returned to Britain with his men in 1586. In 1589 he was named muster-master general and clerk of the check in Ireland. Knighted in 1593, he was badly wounded in an Irish rebellion in 1594 but continued to serve in Ireland until his death in 1603. Among the men who remained nearly a year with Lane's colony were several Irishmen: Darby Glande (Glaney or Glavin, as it also appears in the records) and Edward Nugen or Nugent, identified as Lane's servant and who had probably been in Kerry earlier with Lane. Others among this first British colony in America, who most likely were Irish, were John Costigan and Edward Kelly.

In 1587, in the final phase of his plan to colonize America, Sir Walter Raleigh, who had now been knighted, chose John White to be governor. This undertaking came to be known as "The Lost Colony." Among the 117 colonists this time there were 17 women and 9 boys, including at least one nursing baby. Clearly intending to lay the foundation of a permanent settlement, Raleigh enlisted people with varied abilities, occupations, and nationalities.

Among White's colonists was Glande, crossing the Atlantic a second time, and Elizabeth Glande, who may have been his wife. Elizabeth, however, arrived at Roanoke Island alone as Darby deserted in Puerto Rico. Yet Elizabeth may not have lacked for companionship in the New World as Irishmen Denice Carrell, Thomas Butler, and James Lasie were also aboard.

Although this was a short-lived colony, it is distinguished in American history because Governor White's 19-year-old daughter, Eleanor, wife of colonist Ananias Dare, was among the settlers. On August 18, 1587, she gave birth to Virginia, the first British child born in America. Just as in the case of the Lane colony, supplies did not arrive when expected and Governor White returned home to try to expedite their shipment. Difficulties at home delayed his return to Roanoke Island, the colonists disappeared, and later efforts to locate them were fruitless. White retired to one of Sir Walter Raleigh's estates in Ireland and spent the remainder of his life at Newtown in the Great Wood of Kilmore, County Cork.

In 1866 the British Museum acquired a portfolio of John White's watercolor drawings in Ireland after it had been in the possession of the earls of Charlemont for nearly a century. In the late 20th century the ruins were discovered of the house believed to have been occupied by White. David B. Quinn, a native of Ireland and a late 20th-century historian, in compiling *The Roanoke Colonies* (2 vols., London, 1955), examined documents trying to learn the origin of John White, but he was unable to determine whether he was Irish or English.

From his residence in Ireland in 1593, White sadly wrote that he still hoped his colony might be found. In 1607, fourteen years later, newly inspired settlers began to arrive in America from the British Isles. From the tiny seed of a very uncertain settlement named Jamestown, a colony eventually emerged. There were hardships to overcome, but fertile land began to be occupied farther away from Jamestown.

## Permanent Settlement

The first permanent settlers reached the Carolina region by about 1650. It was over a hundred miles from Jamestown but only a bit more than 30 from the birthplace of Virginia Dare. In Ireland, a rebellion in 1641–42 resulted in land being forfeited to England, and soon much of the northeastern part of Ireland was settled by Protestants—Scots, Welsh, and English. During the English Civil War (1642–51) and for a number of years afterwards North Carolina was still regarded as "Ould Virginia," retaining its name from Raleigh's time. While bold venturers from Jamestown occasionally appeared in the Carolina area and an occasional ship from New England or the Caribbean stopped by, many years passed before settlers arrived in significant numbers.

With the restoration of the monarchy following the Civil War, there was renewed interest in the vast region. In 1663 King Charles II granted to eight of his supporters a broad belt of land south of Virginia which extended from the Atlantic Ocean to the Pacific. From a Latin form of Charles, it was named Carolina in honor of him. A scheme for colonial government was prepared and plans made to encourage settlement. Royal policy for many years was to encourage Scottish migration to Ireland, and it took little imagination to make America a destination as well. Scots were regarded as docile and amenable to English ways. The Irish, on the other hand, were seen as less industrious and were regarded as "wild" and unruly. The English reasoned that the movement of Scots to the northern counties of Ireland, only 20 miles across the North Channel, would displace some whom they regarded as troublemakers; the more industrious Scots, they felt, would make the area more profitable to England. The Scots newly settled in the northeast of Ireland succeeded too well and in time contributed to overpopulation and proved to be serious competitors with the English in the production of linen and woollen cloth. Following the defeat of the Scots at the Battle of Culloden Moor in 1746, even Scottish-held land was assigned to victorious English army officers, and the struggle to get to America became frantic.

## Pioneer Irish Colonist

One of the earliest Carolinians to be clearly identified as Irish was Dr. John Brickell, a physician who was practicing in Edenton in 1729. Among his patients was the family of Governor Sir Richard Everard, but he is best recognized today as the compiler of the *Natural History of North-Carolina,* gleaned from the writings of his contemporaries, the fellow naturalists John Lawson and John Clayton. This work, printed in Dublin in 1737, was based on folk practices and remedies. Among the subscribers were medical men, apothecaries, and surgeons. Many Irish family names long found in North Carolina are represented among those who subscribed for Brickell's book: Connor, Carson, Delany, Dobbin, Durham, Fergus, Gordon, Hill, Mitchell, Pierson, and Richardson. Their early association with this work

suggests that it may have drawn their attention to the colony. The first known Catholic priest in the colony was Patrick Cleary, a native of Ireland who arrived in 1784 to settle the estate of his deceased brother. He remained until his own death in 1790 when, for want of a Catholic church, he was buried on the lawn in front of Christ Episcopal Church.

James Garzia, an Anglican missionary in North Carolina, in 1741 reported that there were an even dozen Roman Catholics in the colony. The Rev. James Reed in 1760 from New Bern wrote, "As for papists, I cannot learn there are above 9 or 10 in the whole County." Five years later royal Governor William Tryon reaffirmed that belief: "Every sect of religion abounds here except the Roman Catholic. . . ."

After people of Scottish descent appeared in large numbers in Ulster, as the northern counties of Ireland were called, the descriptive term Scotch-Irish or Scots Irish came into use. More often than not the Irish were of the Roman Catholic faith while the Scots were Presbyterian. Many Scottish families, however, were of the Anglican faith. In the course of events people of these backgrounds intermarried until now only rarely are there families entirely of one or the other, yet people may be found who will proclaim that they are "pure Irish." Occasionally someone may have been described in the records as "meer" Irish, which often bears a derogatory connotation. The more recent term "lace-curtain Irish" was not heard in North Carolina because none are known to have created neighborhoods, occupational bonds, or religious fraternities to which the term was applied. If any chose to come or were sent to the state during the potato famine in Ireland, they were few in number and melded into existing communities. Nevertheless before 1835 much of North Carolina was economically depressed and was sometimes referred to as "the Ireland of America."

The Irish, however, often were as proud of their descent as if they had been members of the peerage. Books bearing armorial bookplates of Irish families from eighteenth-century North Carolina families survive in the North Carolina Collection in the University library in Chapel Hill. The *Colonial Records of North Carolina* (14:676–80) contains a letter of December 2, 1769, from Edanus [Aedanus] Burke of Stafford, England, to his relative, Dr. Thomas Burke, in North Carolina, expressing deep gratitude for their Irish heritage. Referring to themselves as "Native Irish," the writer reported having recently read Geoffrey Keating's history of Ireland which inspired in him a sense of pride. The Irish, he noted, were of "the old Milesian race," descendants of people taken there by descendants of the sons of a Spanish king, Milesius, around 1300 B.C. In 1782 Dr. Burke received another letter in the same spirit. Archibald Maclaine, a North Carolina legislator, apparently had been described as a Scotsman and he was correcting that impression. He was only "half a Scotchman" as his mother had been Irish.

## In North Carolina

Large tracts of land in North Carolina were granted on very generous terms to newcomers as well as to groups of interested investors. New products began to be exported, and by 1735 it was reported that flax had been grown in the colony. A few years later flax seed was sent from North Carolina to Pennsylvania where port faciliites were better for shipment abroad. Several royal governors and other officials of Scotch-Irish origin encouraged settlement of the colony to increase productivity and a larger tax revenue to the advantage of their political record. Some newcomers acquired thousands of acres of land in their own name while others formed land companies in hope of promoting settlement at a profit. Henry McCulloh received two grants—one for 60,000 acres and another for 72,000—on which he promised to settle 6,000 Protestants who would produce raw materials for British manufacturers. Such activity brought in thousands of new Scotch-Irish settlers and soon the assembly created new counties: Johnston and Granville (1746), Anson (1750), Orange (1752), and Rowan (1753).

By the second half of the nineteenth century it was customary for writers to denigrate the Irish while at the same time often lauding the Scotch-Irish as wholly Scottish. Their hyphenated name, it was said, merely indicated that they had once lived in Ireland. North Carolina historians R. D. W. Connor, Chalmers Davidson, Archibald Henderson, and Hugh T. Lefler were among those who followed national writers Theodore Roosevelt, Frederick Jackson Turner, Thomas J. Wertenbaker, and others in heaping high praise on the Scots and showing disdain for the Irish. In the late twentieth century, however, this practice was generally abandoned in favor of regarding the Scotch-Irish as one people—an amalgamation of the two.

James G. Leyburn, a history professor at Washington and Lee University, undertook a fresh look at the Scotch-Irish and in 1962 the University of North Carolina Press in Chapel Hill published his *The Scotch-Irish: A Social History* (377 pp). This work demonstrates how many popularly recognized traits of the Scotch-Irish have also long been cited as qualities of the American population in general: deep religious convictions, belief in democracy, and support of education.

Leyburn compared the older Scotch-Irish to the second- or third-generation of immigrants to America from Poland, Greece, or Germany who had only a vague tradition of their origin which he called a "folk memory." The Scotch-Irish or Ulster Scots, he pointed out, were a "people of a new nationality with its own traditions and culture and points of reference." Before the American Revolution, colonial officials often referred to these people as Irish because they had come to America from Ireland. They were not offended by this except when they were confused with the Roman Catholic Irish—they were Protestant, largely Presbyterian, and that was what was important to them.

Writers, educators, and politicians frequently mention how much the United States owes to the experience and contributions of the Scotch-Irish for the nation's success. In a speech before the United States Senate in 1910, Henry Cabot Lodge praised those forbears as intellectual, not emotional, people who were penetrating and logical in their thinking, and who delighted in abstractions.

TRAITS OF SCOTCH-IRISH

Because as individuals they are so diverse, the Scotch-Irish have not been easy for American historians either to characterize as a body or to classify as individuals. R. D. W. Connor, highly respected North Carolina historian, first archivist of the United States, and Scotch-Irishman himself, concluded that "there is perhaps no virtue in the whole catalogue of human virtues which has not been ascribed to them; no great principle of human liberty in our political and social system which has not been placed to their credit; no great event in our history which they are not said to have caused. . . . [T]he Scotch-Irishman was domestic in his habits and loved his home and family; but we know also that he was an unemotional being, seldom giving expression to his

affections and accordingly presenting to the world the appearance of great reserve, coldness, and austerity. He was loyal to his own kith and kin, but stern and unrelenting with his enemies. He was deeply and earnestly religious, but the very depth and earnestness of his convictions tended to make him narrow-minded and biggotted. He was law-abiding so long as the laws were to his liking, but when they ceased to be he disregarded them, quietly if possible, forcibly if necessary. Independent and self-reliant, he was somewhat opinionated and inclined to lord it over any who would submit to his aggressions. He was brave, and he loved the stir of battle. . . . His whole history shows that he would fight, he would die, but he could never be subdued. In short, in both his admirable and his unadmirable traits, he possessed just the qualities which were needed on the Carolina frontier in the middle of the eighteenth century. . . ." It was they who cleared the land, made it productive, and were in the vanguard of those who expanded the American frontier to the Pacific Ocean.

An unscientific examination of selected entries in the *Dictionary of North Carolina Biography,* published in six volumes by the University of North Carolina Press (1979–96), reveals that subjects bearing known Irish or apparent Irish or Scotch-Irish names predominate. Included are people who were prominent or noteworthy from the early colonial period until late in the twentieth century. In addition to those who made notable contributions to North Carolina as well as the nation, there are scoundrels, thieves, murderers, and other unsavory characters among them.

Of those whose biographies confirm that they are of Irish descent there will be found: 1 actor; 1 Catholic priest; 1 chart or map maker; 1 compiler of a stud book; 2 botanists; 2 geologists; 2 machinists; 3 merchants; 3 musicians; 3 presidents of the United States and a vice-president; 3 state officials; 4 Indian traders; 4 writers/authors and five poets; 6 Confederate officers; 6 journalists; 6 planters; 7 governors of North Carolina; 8 federal officials; 10 physicians; 11 judges; 12 military persons; 12 Revolutionary soldiers and one heroine; 18 attorneys and 18 clergyman. In addition to the mere handful selected for reference here, there were hundreds more whose presence was important in the creation of the state and the nation. It has often been noted that it was the people of Scotch-Irish descent who made North Carolina the successful state that it became. They arrived early and in larger numbers than the eighteenth-century Germans who trailed them from Pennsylvania. The small Welsh group that arrived during the years 1730–1734 were confined to a small region and left little mark on the colony.

*See* America's First Irish Visitor; Roanoke Island;
Scots Irish; Irish Heritage of the South

R. D. W. Connor, *Race Elements in the White Population of North Carolina* (Raleigh, 1920).

Hugh T. Lefler and William S. Powell, *Colonial North Carolina, A History* (New York, 1973).

James G. Leyburn, *The Scotch-Irish: A Social History* (Chapel Hill, 1962).

William S. Powell, ed., *Dictionary of North Carolina Biography*, 6 vols. (Chapel Hill, 1979–1996).

William S. Powell, *North Carolina through Four Centuries* (Chapel Hill, 1989).

Stephen C. Worsley, "Catholicism in Antebellum North Carolina," *North Carolina Historical Review,* 60 (October 1983).

WILLIAM S. POWELL

# NORTH DAKOTA

The Irish came to North Dakota under several different labels: Protestant Irish, Catholic Irish and, to confuse things, Scotch-Irish. The Catholic Irish were the only ones who displayed a sense of special identity. The Protestant Irish came mingled with a variety of other British Isles people and were generally regarded as "Yankees." They attended Old American churches, joined their organizations and behaved like their counterparts from New England. The term "Irish," therefore, in North Dakota meant, and still means, Catholic. And Catholic Irish were anything but invisible. They have left their mark on much of the state's history.

Seen in a larger perspective, North Dakota Catholics of every ethnic background, except during the first territorial years, have always been a minority. The state today is predominantly Protestant, made up chiefly of people from Scandinavian and Germanic backgrounds. Yet, though they have seldom numbered more than twenty-five percent of the population, Catholics in the state have never suffered from a sense of inferiority. This has been due to two circumstances. The first was the presence of the French Catholics who, coming as explorers and fur traders, intermarried with the native peoples and established the first permanent European-style villages with churches and schools a generation before other white settlers arrived.

The second reason for Catholic confidence was the Irish who came at the same time as the Yankees and, with them, are still remembered as the state's genuine pioneers. One-fourth, even one-half, of the enlisted men at every military post were Irish-Catholic. Their officers for the most part were of Anglo background, yet Captain Myles Keogh of Custer's Fort Lincoln command was an Irish adventurer who, after a stint in the Vatican's Papal Guards and in the American Civil War, died wearing the Pope's medal, *Pro Petri Sede,* at the Little Big Horn battle.

## SOLDIERS AND PIONEERS

Some of these Irish soldiers of fortune liked the wide open spaces and took root. One of the first squatters in Emmons County was ex-soldier John Manning (the winter of 1875). Likewise, Dennis Hallahan and Bailey Murphy became early settlers in Sioux County. Some married Indian maidens. Barney Lannigan, a soldier from Fort Yates, had a Sioux wife, as did Joshua Murphy, who was formerly of the Fort Rice garrison.

Footloose, with a certain affinity toward bachelorhood, enjoying the sense of adventure and relishing the comradeship of friends, the Irishmen were at home not only in barracks, but also in the tent camps of the railroad construction gangs. They came to build Dakota's railroads—the Northern Pacific in the seventies and the Great Northern in the eighties. Indeed, some dropped off at sidings and became permanent residents. One of the early shanty parts of Bismarck, an Irish section, is still remembered under the name "Kerry Patch."

They were cowboys too. Here again was mobility and the carefree life. They were everywhere—on the O-X and the Three Sevens spreads in what are now Slope and Bowman Counties, the D-Z ranch of Sioux County, the H-T and Roosevelt operations of Little Missouri River fame.

Some acquired their own cattle ventures. Pat McCoy, an ex-soldier from Fort Yates, set up a horse ranch in Sioux County. Once a year, on St. Patrick's Day, he sponsored a wild and woolly dance at his little log house on Cedar Creek. Jack McCravy, who campaigned with Sibley in 1862, ran one thousand head of cattle and three hundred horses in the early years of Emmons County.

The first ranchers in Mercer County were known as the "Knife River Irish"—the Keoghs and the Crowleys. Further west in Billings County were the Connellys, O'Briens, Brennans and Reillys. Lanky and independent, they welcomed on horseback the first missionary priests, and their descendants drive pick-up trucks to catechism at the local parishes today. The Irish, like other British Isles groups, liked ranching. They still reside in the Badlands, the breaks and the sandhills of the state.

The Irish came in the greatest numbers, though, as homesteaders, following the line of settlement, coursing out ahead of it in an almost reckless fashion. Unlike off-the-boat immigrants who clustered in settlements, they had no need to huddle in groups. In 1869, ex-soldier Anthony Nolan was the first man to farm in what became a predominantly Norwegian area, the lower Sheyenne River Valley. The first farmer in the Turtle River region was ex-railroad surveyor Mike Ferry. He settled near modern-day Manvel in 1869. Bob McGahan was the first to file a homestead in Mercer County. (He became the county's first sheriff.) Michael Cuskelly homesteaded just north of Dickinson. (He became the city's first postmaster.)

## SMALL-SCALE SPECULATORS

In spite of their numbers, Irish tended to leave the land, at least the plow and furrow kind of land. They were what history calls the "boomers," speculators on a small scale. Their presence is evident in the land records and baptism ledgers of every North Dakota township, but their grandsons and granddaughters are seldom there today. (Dublin Township in Williams County hasn't a single present-day Irish resident.) The German and the Slavic Catholics clasped their fields as dearly as life itself, but not the Irish. For them, the farm was not a way of life, it was a way to acquire a bit of ready cash.

Local history books are filled with instances where self-confident Irishmen, with their land sale money or railroad wages, moved into the newly established town sites. They had seen the same promising moments occur in previous decades in eastern frontier states; now their gregarious and political instincts came into full play on Dakota's agricultural frontier. They became the tavern keepers, the hotel owners, and the draymen. Jack Flynn and Jerry Hart, ex-soldiers, started a saloon in early Winona; they called it Temperance Hall. Two gentlemen named Mullen and O'Neill had a dance hall in Bismarck in 1873. Mullen was killed in a shoot-out during a row with Custer's troops. Charles and Elizabeth Dolan set up the first hotel in Mandan. Across the river in Bismarck was Jack McGowan's Dacotah Hotel.

In doing this, they seldom rivaled the financially and socially advantaged gentry, the merchants, the owners and the politicians who were the "boomers" on a grand scale. In fact, the Irish were often the junior partners of these knowledgeable "first citizens" whose roots went back to colonial times and whose contacts in the nation's "Eastern Interests" allowed them to buy and sell in a big way in the developing prairie environment.

By rights, the Irish opportunists should have opposed the Yankees. Their ancestors had suffered under their domination: "No Irish need apply." They were Democrats by instinct in a Republican territory; they had been drinking folks in a prohibition culture; they had been Catholic in a Protestant world of nativist and Know-Nothing sentiments. Apparently the antagonism of the earlier generations had diminished. In Dakota they became allies, or at least a loyal opposition to the Anglo-American power figures.

## Guardians of Culture

North Dakota received another group of Irish settlers, Irish men and women who were never part of the American military, cowboy or railroad life, but whose experience in the New World had felt the same cold touch of British disdain. These were the transplants from Ontario. When the attention of the Canadian public after 1870 was turned toward settlement in the prairie provinces, many Irish, both Protestant and Catholic, took the hint and traveled along American railways to the Red River Valley. Some ignored the niceties of citizenship and stayed in Dakota. In fact, it is probably true that three-fourths of the Irish who took land in the northeastern part of North Dakota were really of Ontario background.

Perhaps the frontier engendered a feeling of equality. Maybe a sense of democracy did arise when the rigidities of New England culture were transplanted a thousand miles westward into the more primitive setting of the Great Plains. Most likely, however, the origins of the apparently amicable relations that existed between the Calvinists and the Irish arose because of the simple fact that both groups found themselves surrounded by a tidal wave of off-the-boat immigrants. In Dakota, both the Britons and the Irish were islands in a world that was increasingly foreign. The Irish tended to see themselves as "real Americans," and the Yankees begrudgingly admitted that they were at least partially correct.

It was Irish girls, and often Irish men, who paradoxically became guardians of Anglo-Saxon culture in Dakota. Hundreds, perhaps thousands, took jobs as the first teachers in country and village schools. They spoke the nation's language, knew its history, and could teach its phonetics, its etiquette, its literature, and political ways.

As the villages developed into cities, their wit and easy manner propelled the Irish, as in previous decades, into political jobs. Very often they are remembered as the town's first constable, the head of its fire department, its sheriff. Tom Campbell, for example, was Minot's chief of police in the 1880s, and Pat Hennessey was his counterpart in Grand Forks. Almost from the beginning, sons of Erin occupied posts in the lower and middle levels of city halls and court houses. T. F. McHugh was Grafton's mayor in 1890; in that same year Ed O'Connor was superintendent of Grand Forks' water works. The postmaster in Bismarck was named Slattery; in Mandan his name was Flynn. Judge Sullivan presided in Fargo, Judge Conmy in Pembina.

Before long even the larger cities, Bismarck, Fargo and Dickinson, had Irish mayors. In Grand Forks, the second mayor was Michael McCormack; a town founder and patron of the university was Thomas Walsh.

## Church Influence

The self-confidence of the Irish layman was enhanced by the type of clergy that increasingly staffed the parishes of the state. From 1890 to 1909, Bishop John Shanley brought to Dakota more than one hundred Irish-born or Irish-American priests. These were not immigrants who stumbled through their sermons in heavy foreign accents. On the contrary, they were men who spoke in polished phrases, who punctuated their comments with quotes from the greats of English literature. The best of Anglo-America's cultural past was featured very often at Sunday morning Mass.

Nor were the Irish clergy shy. Whether newly arrived "instant Americans" or lifetime Americans, they, too, felt at home in a Protestant world. They knew the social graces of that world and could dress "properly" and sup their soup with the appropriate culinary utensils. Indeed, they seldom took a back seat to their Yankee counterparts. Parish houses in North Dakota were often as elegant as the dwellings of the nearby lawyers and merchants. They might have lived on a frontier, but the Irish clergyman believed that a priest should live as a proper gentleman.

The Irish in Dakota were reinforced, even more, by the presence of nuns of Irish background. The Presentation Sisters, for example, arrived in Fargo at an unbelievably early date, 1882 (less than a decade after the town's founding), and established Sacred Heart Academy. Seventy-five miles north of Fargo, Mother Stanislaus Rafter and her staff of Irish-oriented nuns set up a prestigious high school and an embryonic college at Grand Forks in 1883. Both schools became hubs of Catholic life. The influx of nuns from Ireland to Fargo's Presentation motherhouse and its various institutions throughout eastern North Dakota continued until the 1950s.

The bishops of the Fargo Diocese, John Shanley and his successors, could be proud of the heritage of their faithful lay men and women, and also of their clergy. The church in Dakota would never have a sense of inferiority. Its outlines would never be foreign; its activities were part and parcel of the Great Plains landscape.

## Foreign Newcomers

However, the church of the early Dakota generations was not without its problems. Immigrants from northern and eastern Europe were arriving in massive numbers, engulfing the English-speaking first arrivals.

The Irish tended to look down on the foreign newcomers, which inevitably caused resentment. When North Dakota became a state, the Norwegians, the most numerous of all new groups, began demanding their rightful place in the political limelight. Everyone in politics—Yankee, German, Irish—began to feel the heat of their expanding presence. Norwegians and others joined the Ku Klux Klan in surprisingly large numbers in the 1920s. Their targets, in most cases, were Catholics. Crosses were burned in large cities but also in rural enclaves.

One group of immigrants, however, regarded the Irish as friends—North Dakota's Jewish settlers. Everywhere in the state, in town and countryside, there existed a certain comradeship and cooperation. Jewish men were often "honorary members" of the local Knights of Columbus. Catholic hospitals, almost inevitably, had Jewish members on their advisory boards.

Of greater significance, however, was the Irish relationship to their fellow Catholics of non-English speaking backgrounds. Those new arrivals were in no mood to abandon their cultural heritages. If becoming American meant becoming a Yankee, they would balk at it; if becoming an American Catholic meant becoming an Irish kind of Catholic, they would be equally obstinate.

Accordingly, Bishop John Shanley and his successor, James O'Reilly, were forced to compromise in a dozen different ways. Shanley complains in his memoirs that "in a few places [the people] were informed by the pastor that the Irish bishop had no use for Germans and French."

Reluctantly, no doubt, the bishops allowed the growth of national parishes. Bohemians set up a Bohemian church, St. Wenceslaus, across town from Dickinson's St. Patrick's Church. Poles in Minot established Sacred Heart Church a few blocks from St. Patrick's Church.

The Irish hegemony was challenged increasingly in the middle and the western part of North Dakota with the arrival of the twentieth century. The early Irish clergy and settlers were swept aside by a veritable avalanche of late-arriving Germans from Russia, resolute people from Black Sea colonies. The first itinerant Irish clergy set up a framework of parish life and retreated, thereafter, to more amenable circumstances. A historical account of Dickinson said, "The first Catholics were a few Irishmen who stayed on after the railroad was built in the early 1880s. . . . Toward the end of the century, more and more German-speaking immigrants came to Stark County. They could not understand the English sermons at St. Patrick's, so they wanted their own parish." St. Joseph's Church in Mandan was a place where St. Patrick's Day was observed with the same solemnity as a holy day of obligation. The situation in Mandan changed rapidly; the parish became a bastion of German community life.

A troubled Bishop Shanley says in his memoirs, "Any attempt to introduce law met with determined and violent opposition. The so-called Cahensly Movement (advocates of a German national diocese) was the question of the day."

In a celebrated burst of anger, Shanley used his newspaper, *The Bulletin,* to strike out at the behavior of "ruffians" in several German-Russian parishes. In one, he said, they fired a shot into the priest's house; in another they ran the priest out of the parish by refusing to pay his salary. The bishop complained, "One cause of trouble is the title to the property of the church, another is the organist, another the schoolteacher."

One area of contention between Irish John Shanley and his German faithful was the matter of liquor. Bishop Shanley regularly fulminated against evils associated with the deadly drink. One can only imagine what such vehemence meant in the minds of the newly arrived Germans, a people for whom beer was considered a staple of life.

The tensions between Irish and German Catholics seem to have surfaced, to a certain extent, in the division between the Knights of Columbus and the Catholic Order of Foresters. The Knights of Columbus, of Connecticut origin, retained a New England Irish flavor as it moved westward. By the turn of the century it became a primary outlet for the social energies of North Dakota Catholic laymen. Bishop Shanley's newspaper, *The Bulletin,* featured items about its affairs in every issue.

The Catholic Order of Foresters, on the other hand, was founded not in Irish New England, but in Chicago. Though it included members of all national origins, it was especially appealing to men of midwestern German background. It took root in North Dakota's almost solidly German areas, the middle and western parts of the state. Rarely, if ever, were its affairs mentioned in Bishop Shanley's *Bulletin.* In one issue of his paper, Shanley complains that the *Volksfreund* (to use his word) held a dance and were drinking beer in the parish school at St. Anthony in Morton County. The bishop wrote, "We do not know who in this state is at the head of the society known as the Catholic Order of Foresters. Whoever he is will please note that societies calling themselves Catholic are expected to observe the laws of the church and the state. Dancing under Catholic auspices and selling beer or other intoxicants at church society gatherings are against church law in this Diocese. . . ."

It is likely that Bishop Shanley in 1909, tired and of ill health, privately encouraged authorities such as Archbishop John Ireland to divide the state into two ecclesiastical regions, not just because of logistic difficulties, but because of the more basic problem, ethnic differences. Even though he died before a division took place, he probably would have welcomed it with a sigh of relief.

The new diocese, the western half of the state, was placed in the hands of a man whom Shanley trusted and one who truly "understood" the German: Vincent Wehrle, a Swiss-born missionary-monk, abbot of the Benedictine Monastery at Richardton. Wehrle was named the first bishop of Bismarck on March 21, 1910, nine months after Shanley's death. (Ten of the twelve clerics who had a key role in the installation ceremony were of German extraction.)

The Germans could hold sway in the western diocese, but Catholic life, with an Irish emphasis, continued in the east, the Fargo diocese. In fact, it is hard to avoid the impression that the Irish clergy in that diocese constituted a kind of privileged class. The hands of John Shanley and of James O'Reilly held sway for a long time, from 1890 to 1934. One should almost expect to find some preferential treatment, for the two prelates naturally understood their fellow countrymen. They could, therefore, cooperate or fight with their Irish clergy according to rules that were mutually recognized and accepted. Clergy assignment lists in 1920 and 1930 show that parishes throughout the more prosperous Red River Valley and, in fact, in most of the prominent towns in the Fargo diocese, were in the hands of Irish clerics. It is clear that the German, the French and the Slavic priests were stationed in what might be called the hinterlands.

John Shanley and James O'Reilly were succeeded by two bishops of resoundingly German background, Aloysius Muench from the German part of Milwaukee, and Leo Dworschak of Eastern European roots. Perhaps it was a sign of the times. The state was no longer being run by the Anglo-Americans or the Irish. A Sudetan-German was in the Capitol building, the immensely popular former member of Casselton's St. Leo parish, William Langer.

## BROADER HORIZONS

The Irish, for the most part, left the farms, the small towns and eventually the larger cities of North Dakota. Why? Maybe it was because they were fluent in English; they did not have to stay in the state when droughts and depressions set in. Maybe it was the confinement of the countryside and the villages; it was too limited, too isolated. Perhaps the reason was even more basic; the Irishmen never possessed an affection for the large scale, big-sky Dakota kind of rural setting, a far cry from the "green hills of Erin."

The process by which the Irish left is known. Some women married local non-Irish boys; most single males and females drifted to the larger cities. The men often took new jobs in the West—railroad building, timber cutting in the Rockies, and mining in Idaho.

Whether men or women, they went to "college," college as it was known in those days: business schools, nursing schools, certification courses at teacher colleges. Some, however, opted for multiyear degrees. The first classes at the University of North Dakota contained an abundance of Irish names. Diplomas in hand, the majority left the state for better opportunities elsewhere.

If they stayed, the Irish moved *up* in the state. With the passing of the decades, they built homes in the town's better class areas. They appeared at an early date in the legal and medical professions.

In retrospect, no one would ever be able to accuse Irish Catholics of being unpatriotic. They did not wait to be drafted; they enlisted in large numbers in World War I and World War II. Their motivations were mixed; war was adventure and a test of manhood, just like the thrill of following the trail herds or railroad crews at an earlier age. A list of North Dakota's American Legion commanders shows that, until 1958, twenty-five had Irish names.

Today a full-blooded Irish resident in North Dakota is hard to find—half Irish, yes; one-fourth Irish, yes; but seldom one hundred percent. The "Kerry Patch" no longer exists; Donnybrook in Burke County is a German village. The state's clergy are seldom of Irish ancestry. The Knights of Columbus members are of mixed origins. Yet the Irish-Catholic traditions can be seen everywhere: devotions, parish structures, clergy styles, institutional outlines. The Irish Catholic's main legacy today is more subtle. Catholics can say, "We were pioneers, we built much of North Dakota. We belong here."

William C. Sherman, "The Irish and Assorted Others," *Scattered Steeples, The Fargo Diocese,* eds., Jerome D. Lamb, Jerry Ruff and William C. Sherman (Fargo, 1988): 64–71.
Robert P. Wilkins, "People of the British Isles," *Plains Folk: North Dakota's Ethnic History,* eds., William C. Sherman and Playford Thorson (Fargo, 1986): 51–60.

WILLIAM SHERMAN

## NORTON, MARY TERESA HOPKINS (1875–1959)

Congresswoman. Born in Jersey City, New Jersey, of Irish immigrants, Norton attended public and parochial schools and, in 1896, was graduated from Packard Business College in New York. She married Robert Francis Norton in 1909. Having lost her only child in infancy, Norton worked publicly to promote child care. In 1916, she became president of the Day Nurseries Association of Jersey City, which provided care for children of working mothers (Garraty).

Two factors influenced Norton's move into politics: the support of Frank Hague, mayor of Jersey City, and ratification in 1920 of the Nineteenth Amendment, legalizing the right to vote for women. Norton subsequently won the vice chair and chair of the Democratic State Committee in 1921 and 1932, respectively. In 1924 she became the first woman Democrat to hold a seat in the House of Representatives. By 1932, overcoming a cool reception in Washington, Norton headed the House Committee of the District of Columbia. In the same year, she became the director of the New Jersey Democratic National Committee.

Known for her lifelong work on behalf of labor and as a loyal supporter of New Deal legislation, Norton pushed through FDR's Wages and Hours Bill in 1938 (ibid). After Republicans won the majority in Congress in 1946, Norton resigned her position on the Labor Committee. However, she returned to Congress in 1949 to head the House Administration Committee. Having served in Washington for twenty-six years, Norton retired in 1951, retaining her reputation as a defender of the urban, working-class Catholic constituency from which she came.

John Garraty, ed., *Dictionary of American Biography,* Supplement Six: 1956–1960 (New York, 1980).
*The National Cyclopaedia of American Biography,* Vol. XLVI (n.p., 1963).
*Who Was Who in America,* Vol. 3 (Chicago, 1960).

JAMES P. LEONARD

## NOTRE DAME AND THE IRISH

The University of Notre Dame du Lac at Notre Dame, Indiana, was founded in 1842 by members of a French religious community, the Congregation of Holy Cross. Six Brothers and a priest had been sent to the United States in 1841 to work in the diocese of Vincennes, Indiana, where they proposed to start a college near Montgomery in Daviess County in southern Indiana. When this proved unfeasible, Bishop Hailandiere of Vincennes offered the community land that he owned in the northern part of the state on condition that they start a school there in four years. In November 1842, Rev. Edward Sorin and "seven of the most industrious of the Brothers" arrived in South Bend, took possession of the land and announced the opening of Notre Dame du Lac College.

Although all the Holy Cross missionaries who had come to the United States the previous year were French, they had immediately begun to recruit new members to their community from among the Catholic population of the United States. Among these were several Irish immigrants and when the contingent was sent out to found the college near South Bend, four of the seven Brothers in the party were Irish: Brothers Patrick (Michael Connelly), Basil (Timothy O'Neil), William (John O'Sullivan) and Peter (James Tully). In succeeding years, a number of Irish, men and women, immigrants and the descendants of immigrants, would make their contribution to what became the University of Notre Dame.

Despite the sizeable component of Irish among his collaborators in the founding of the university, Sorin did not initially have a high regard for them. He remarked in his *Chronicles of Notre Dame du Lac* that "the [Irish] are by nature full of faith, respect, religious inclinations, and sensible and devoted; but a great defect often paralyzes in them all their other good qualities: the lack of stability. They change more readily than any other nation" (p. 16). Sorin held an even lower opinion of "genuine Americans" as fit subjects for religious life.

But like them or not, the Irish kept coming. In 1843, four Holy Cross Sisters arrived from France to work at Notre Dame. When they began to recruit local women to their ranks, the first to be accepted was Bridget Coffey, 20, born in Ireland. The list of victims in a cholera epidemic at Notre Dame in 1846 includes two Brothers and a Sister who had been born in Ireland and had joined the Congregation of Holy Cross at Notre Dame: John the Baptist (William Rodgers), Anthony (Thomas Dowling) and Mary of Mount Carmel (Marie Dougherty). The student body contained its share of Irish names as well in Notre Dame's early years. The first graduating class in 1849 had two members, Neal Gillespie, an Irish-American, and Richard Shortis, born in County Cork. Both became priests in the Congregation of Holy Cross. Other Irish-born graduates in these years were Rev. Edmund Kilroy ('52), Rev. E.M. O'Callaghan ('56), John Collins ('60), Timothy E. Howard ('62), Rev. Daniel J. Spillard, C.S.C., ('64) and Rev. John Flynn ('65). When Gillespie's sister, Eliza, joined the Holy Cross Sisters at Notre Dame in 1853 as Sr. Mary of St. Angela, she became Sorin's vicar for the governance of the Sisters.

### IRISH PRESIDENTS AND FACULTY

During the Civil War, Sorin sent seven Holy Cross priests from Notre Dame to serve as chaplains to the Catholic soldiers, most of them Irish, in the Union Army. Three of these priests, Peter P. Cooney, James Dillon and Paul Gillen, were Irish-born. A fourth,

William Corby

Edward Malloy

William Corby, was the son of an Irish immigrant father. In 1865, the last year of the war, Sorin relinquished the presidency of the university to Patrick Dillon, born in Galway, who was elected to the general council of the Congregation of Holy Cross the following year. Sorin appointed William Corby as Dillon's successor. From Dillon's accession to the presidency of the university in 1865 down to Edward Malloy in 1998, all the Holy Cross priests who have served as Notre Dame presidents save one, Sorin's nephew, Auguste Lemonnier (1872–1874), have been either Irish-born or the son of at least one Irish or Irish-American parent: Patrick Dillon (1865–1866), William Corby (1866–1872 and 1877–1881), Patrick Colovin (1875–1877), Thomas Walsh (1881–1893), Andrew Morrissey (1893–1905), John W. Cavanaugh (1905–1919), James A. Burns (1919–1922), Matthew J. Walsh (1922–1928), Charles L. O'Donnell (1928–1934), John F. O'Hara (1934–1940), J. Hugh O'Donnell (1940–1946), John J. Cavanaugh (1946–1952), Theodore M. Hesburgh (1952–1987) and Edward A. Malloy (1987–    ).

Among the Holy Cross Brothers who literally built Notre Dame was Charles Borromeo (Patrick Harding), born in Carrick on Suir, County Waterford, in 1838. When the present Sacred Heart Basilica, the university church, was being planned, Brother Charles, a self-taught architect, builder and construction manager and the immigrant son of a carpenter, oversaw the raising of the building between 1868 and 1875. When the Main Building at Notre Dame burned down in 1879, he supervised the construction of a new building according to the design of another architect. He was both architect and construction manager of several other buildings erected on the campus between 1868 and 1911, most notably Corby Hall, St. Edward's Hall and Carroll Hall.

Brother Florian (James Flynn), a native of County Mayo, was the longtime refectorian and guest master at Notre Dame in the late nineteenth and early twentieth centuries. As the porter at the Main Building, he welcomed all guests. Brother Bonaventure (Patrick Casey) from County Cork was long remembered as the prefect of the study halls and the friend of student athletes. Brother Edward (John Fitzpatrick), born in Liverpool of Irish immigrant parents, served as the treasurer of the University for over twenty years before his death in 1901. Brother Alexander (Charles Smith), a legendary teacher at Notre Dame for more

than forty years, 1873–1907, was born in Wisconsin of parents who had emigrated to America from Ireland.

Although members of the Congregation of Holy Cross constituted the bulk of the faculty and staff at Notre Dame until the second decade of the twentieth century, there were several outstanding Irish-born laymen on the faculty in the nineteenth century who would be long remembered and honored by the university. Timothy E. Howard, BA 1862, MA '64, LLB '73, was Professor of Rhetoric and English Literature, but he also taught mathematics, science, engineering and law. He joined the law faculty at Notre Dame in 1876 and continued as a member until 1916, while serving in the Indiana legislature and from 1893 to 1899 on the Indiana State Supreme Court, where he was chief justice at the end of his term. He wrote the fifty-year history of the university in 1892, received Notre Dame's highest award, the Laetare Medal in 1898, and had a residence hall named after him in 1924.

"Colonel" William J. Hoynes, born in Kilkenny, Ireland, in 1846, became dean of the Notre Dame Law School in 1883 and held that post until 1919. From 1889 until his death in 1933, Hoynes was one of the bachelor dons who lived in rooms in the student residence halls, a tradition at Notre Dame until well past the middle of the twentieth century. When the law school moved into its own building on the campus in 1919, it was named the Hoynes College of Law.

According to Arthur Hope in *Notre Dame, One Hundred Years,* most of the students at Notre Dame by 1877 were the sons of parents who were either Irish or Irish-American and the festivities of St. Patrick's Day had become a regular feature in the university's calendar, unique in that no other ethnic group had a comparable celebration. The objection that such a celebration interfered with studies and discipline was met with an announcement from the administration that "according to a custom of long standing, . . . entertainments . . . are always given the evening before, and as the day following is a holiday, the extra sleep . . . in no way interferes with their studies" (pp. 177–178).

## THE TWENTIETH CENTURY

While members of the Notre Dame community in the twentieth century with Irish names tended to be American-born of Irish descent rather than Irish-born, the new century opened with a native Irishman as president of the university, Rev. Andrew Morrissey, C.S.C. (1893–1905). Brother Ephrem, C.S.C., (Dennis O'Dwyer) of County Tipperary served as treasurer of the university during the Depression (1931–1933) and Rev. Patrick J. Carroll, C.S.C., born in County Limerick in 1876, served as the vice-president of Notre Dame (1926–1928) and then for eighteen years (1934–1952) as editor of *Ave Maria,* the weekly Catholic magazine published at Notre Dame. Brother Conan (Eugene Moran), a native of County Leitrim, managed the Notre Dame bookstore for fifty years, 1939–1989.

Notre Dame's athletic teams had played under a variety of names in the late nineteenth and early twentieth centuries, among them "the Irish" and "the Horrible Hibernians." In 1927, President Matthew Walsh, C.S.C., whose father had emigrated to the United States from County Cork, approved "The Fighting Irish" as the official name for the university's teams. However, Presidents James A. Burns, C.S.C., and Walsh were sympathetic with other fighting Irish and supported home rule and autonomy for the land of their ancestors. When Eamon de Valera, president of the Dail Eireann, which proclaimed itself the parliament of Ireland, visited the United States in 1919 to secure U.S. and League of Nations recognition of an independent Republic of Ireland, one of his stops was at Notre Dame. President Burns received him and accompanied him as he laid a wreath at the campus statue of Father William Corby blessing the troops of the Irish Brigade at the Battle of Gettysburg. De Valera then addressed the student body to explain Ireland's cause, independence from Britain, at the end of which he received a thunderous ovation.

As the twentieth century wore on, the presence of Irish-born faculty, staff and students at Notre Dame diminished almost to the vanishing point, although the number of Irish names on the university's rosters was as prominent as ever. In the decades after World War II, as many Irish-American males married women of other nationalities, an Irish name no longer signified Irish descent on both sides of the family tree. The admission of women undergraduates in 1972 only compounded the ethnic mix among the student body at Notre Dame, which in fact reflected the overall situation among people of Irish descent in the United States in this period.

### The Notre Dame Center in Ireland

As the twentieth century drew to a close, the University maintained its Irish connection in symbolic ways. The nickname for its athletic teams, "The Fighting Irish," the "An Tostal" spring festival, which became an annual event in the 1970s, and the uproarious celebration of St. Patrick's Day, although no longer a university holiday, all bear witness to the influence that the Irish and Irish-Americans have had on Notre Dame since its founding. In the 1990s, the University began to support Irish Studies, building on the magnificent Hibernian Collection, a gift of some fifteen hundred volumes of Irish literature and history that had been received in 1931. In 1993 a year of studies abroad in Ireland was begun with Notre Dame students going to Trinity College and University College in Dublin and in 1998 the University established the Notre Dame Center at Newman House on St. Steven's Green in the Irish capital.

Instrumental in the founding of Notre Dame, prominent in its development and conspicuous in its leadership, generations of Irish and Irish-Americans have played a key role in making the University what it is today. As the twenty-first century opens, the University of Notre Dame is poised to send students back to Ireland to study the culture of the land whose sons and daughters have served the University so well.

*See* Education, Higher; Notre Dame Football

Arthur J. Hope, *Notre Dame, One Hundred Years* (Notre Dame, 1943).

Philip S. Moore, *A Century of Law at Notre Dame* (Notre Dame, 1969).

Thomas J. Schlereth, *A Dome of Learning: The University of Notre Dame's Main Building* (Notre Dame, 1991).

———, *A Spire of Faith: The University of Notre Dame's Sacred Heart Church* (Notre Dame, 1991).

———, *The University of Notre Dame: A Portrait of Its History and Campus* (Notre Dame, 1976).

Edward Sorin, *The Chronicles of Notre Dame du Lac* (Notre Dame, 1992).

JAMES T. CONNELLY, C.S.C.

## NOTRE DAME FOOTBALL— "THE FIGHTING IRISH"

### The Origin of the Fighting Irish Nickname

"O'Reilly, why doesn't Notre Dame have a mascot?"

"Just never got around to it . . ."

"Well—Yale has a bulldog, Princeton a tiger, we [University of Southern California] have a horse—why don't you try a pig? I should think Paddy's Pig would be a good symbol for the Irish. Then there's the old rhyme:

'They kept the pig in the parlor,

And that was Irish too.'"

—From *O'Reilly of Notre Dame*
by Francis Wallace, 1931.

This exchange in a novel about college sports in the first decades of the twentieth century catches the prejudices that many Americans held toward their fellow citizens of Irish descent. But unlike other immigrant groups who tried to submerge their ethnicity into the American melting pot and considered all nicknames as insults, the Irish gloried in many of theirs, particularly the one given to the University of Notre Dame football team, the Fighting Irish. (The school also embraced Irish mascots: from the mid-1930s until the mid-1960s, Irish Terriers named "Clashmore Mike" and, subsequently, the Leprechaun figure.)

The origins of the Fighting Irish nickname are both obvious and obscure. The many Irish-American boxers and champions in the popular nineteenth-century sport of prizefighting; the valor of Irish-American "Fighting Regiments" in the Civil War; the stereotype of Irishmen as bellicose and brawling; all of these cultural images combined with the University of Notre Dame's preponderance of students, faculty, and administrators of Irish-Catholic descent to produce the Fighting Irish nickname. But the original application of the term to a Notre Dame athletic team has never been established and probably cannot be, despite many dubious anecdotes that purport to describe its first utterance.

An early printed reference to the term occurred in a 1904 Notre Dame student newspaper account of the football team in action: "The fight of our boys won the applause of the crowd, who rooted for the 'game Irishmen' all during" the contest. Other newspapers in this decade occasionally lauded the "eleven fighting Irishmen" from Notre Dame. However, the sporting press usually called the team the "Catholics," or, if anti-Notre Dame, "Papists," "Horrible Hibernians," "Dumb Micks," and "Dirty Irish"—fans of opposing squads often yelled these insults during games.

For many years, the priests who ran Notre Dame disapproved of all the nicknames, even when "Catholic" and "Irish" were employed positively. However, after World War I, ND students started using the Fighting Irish phrase in campus slang and in their publications; then, in the early 1920s, Notre Dame's head football coach, Knute Rockne, sometimes used the expression in interviews, and the Chicago and New York press began to adopt it. Yet, the ND administrators refused to sanction it until 1927 when, in hopes of short-circuiting all of the pejorative nicknames, school president Father Matthew Walsh officially approved "the name 'Fighting Irish' as applied to our athletic teams . . . It seems to embody the kind of spirit that we like to see carried into effect by the various organizations that represent us on the athletic field. I sincerely hope that we may always be worthy of the ideals embodied in the term 'Fighting Irish.'"

Notre Dame students and athletes of non-Irish descent also approved of the nickname. A 1920s player of German ancestry, Harry Stuhldreher, wrote that the phrase represented the team's "fighting, competitive spirit," and he quoted Rockne's frequent retort to reporters who listed all the non-Irish players on the ND roster—"'They're all Irish to me. They have the Irish spirit and that's all that counts.'" Rockne himself was Norwegian Lutheran (he converted to Catholicism), and many of his players were Catholics of Italian and other heritages, and some were Protestants and Jews. Nevertheless, during Rockne's coaching years and the following decades, approximately half of all ND varsity football players had Irish family names, and an Irish contingent remains on the Notre Dame roster to this day.

### KNUTE ROCKNE'S FIGHTING IRISH

Notre Dame began playing intercollegiate football in 1887, forty-five years after the school's founding. Because of its athletic culture—until the 1920s, ND was a boarding school for boys of all ages, including many primary and secondary students—Notre Dame teams participated in many sports, particularly baseball, track, boxing, and football. The school's intercollegiate football program became increasingly important during the first decades of the twentieth century and achieved a number of notable victories, e.g., over the University of Michigan in 1909, and Army in 1913. Yet, as late as 1919, the Fighting Irish played a nine-game schedule that included such small colleges as Kalamazoo (Michigan), Mount Union (Ohio), Morningside (Iowa), and Western Michigan; moreover, total attendance for that season was 56,500.

At this juncture in the history of Notre Dame football, the brilliant young head coach, Knute Rockne—captain of the 1913 ND team—began to construct a national powerhouse and to take his squad to major cities to play the best teams in the country. With such superb athletes as George Gipp, Notre Dame won the national championship in 1920 and started to build a national following. Aiding Rockne's strategy was the economic boom of the 1920s and the public's increasing appetite for spectator sports, fed by an expanding sporting press that glorified such Fighting Irish players as Gipp and, a few years later, the backfield known as "The Four Horsemen."

Rockne had a talent for manipulating and massaging press egos, but equally adept was Notre Dame's Prefect of Religion of the time, Father John O'Hara (later a Cardinal). O'Hara traveled with the team and promoted the Fighting Irish with evangelical fervor, frequently stating that "Notre Dame football is a spiritual service because it is played for the honor and glory of God and of his Blessed Mother." O'Hara believed that the purpose of ND "victories [was] to acquaint the public with the ideals that dominate" the Catholic school; however, gridiron wins were not an end in themselves, they must aid and never tarnish Notre Dame's religious reputation. If the school adhered to this mandate, increasing numbers of Catholic families would support it, many would send their boys to study at ND, some to play for the Fighting Irish, and the University of Notre Dame would achieve athletic, academic, and spiritual success.

As a result of the efforts of O'Hara and Rockne, and the latter's ability to construct winning teams, the Fighting Irish became a national phenomenon, attracting fans in every part of the country (all other college teams, except the military academies, had only local or regional followings). Aiding the fame of Rockne's teams was the move, in 1923, of the yearly Notre Dame-Army game from a small field at West Point to a major stadium in New York City, the media capital of the United States. ND president Walsh prevailed upon the Army authorities to make the move, and it resulted in enormous press attention and huge paydays for both schools; it also transformed the Notre Dame-Army game into one of America's premier annual sporting events, ranking with the World Series and the Kentucky Derby, and dominating the football season (college and professional) for the following two decades.

The on-field victories of Rockne's teams excited many Americans, particularly working-class ethnics, who previously had no interest in college sports or higher education, but now rooted fervently for the University of Notre Dame's Fighting Irish. The press nicknamed this group of fans in New York City, the "Subway Alumni." Similar groups of Fighting Irish rooters sprung up in other areas—the "Coalfield Alumni" in western Pennsylvania, the "Parish Alumni" of Chicago, the "Butchertown Alumni" of San Francisco, *et cetera*. A crucial event for the new and old Fighting Irish fans occurred in 1924 when Notre Dame played Princeton for the first time (Ivy League schools had founded big-time college football and still dominated it in the 1920s). The game allowed the Fighting Irish to symbolically battle their most entrenched antagonists, the Protestant Yankees, embodied by Presbyterian Princeton. Protestant contempt for the "Papists" was as old as the first immigration from Ireland and, even in the 1920s, "NINA" signs—"No Irish Need Apply"—still appeared in shop windows and want ads. The Princeton Tigers were not prepared for what swept over them on October 20, 1923, as Rockne's quick and superbly trained squad routed the Ivy power, 25-2, in Princeton's stadium. A large part of Notre Dame's football fame, and the reason why huge numbers of poor and middle-class ethnics came to support the Fighting Irish, resulted from these clashes with—and triumphs over—opponents claiming superiority in class and wealth.

Capping the undefeated 1924 season was Notre Dame's victory in the Rose Bowl over Stanford. Even more than the game itself, the slow train trip to and from California—constantly interrupted by parades in cities along the route—placed the Fighting Irish in the national consciousness and consolidated their new fan base. Knute Rockne was quick to capitalize on this situation; not only an exceptional football coach but also a great promoter, he envisioned the Fighting Irish as "a national team" and he expanded the regular schedule to include games in all parts of the country. He began the series with the University of Southern California in 1926; played Big Ten teams in Soldier Field in Chicago (a stadium able to hold 120,000 at the time); went east for annual contests against Army and Navy; and south for matches against Georgia Tech in the heart of Ku Klux Klan territory. The long victory marches of the Fighting Irish became a source of pride and group esteem for millions of Irish-Americans and members of other ethnic groups. Winning was the key and to this day, Rockne possesses the best won-loss record of any big-time college football coach. By 1929, attendance at Fighting Irish games had increased to 551,112, almost ten times the number of a decade before, and the revenue from football helped the school weather the coming Depression.

One indication of Rockne's shrewdness was his policy of refusing to schedule Catholic opponents, including the excellent Boston College and Fordham teams of his era. He did not want Notre Dame to share football fame, fortune, and fans with other Catholic institutions, and spark unnecessary rivalries. Mainly because of his dictum, Notre Dame never played a fellow Catholic school from 1928 to 1975 (except for one contest: in 1951, ND visited the University of Detroit as a special favor to the latter's longtime coach, Gus Dorais, Rockne's college roommate at Notre Dame).

In the late 1920s, Rockne and the priests in the Golden Dome (the school's administration building) also embraced the new medium of radio. In order to reach as many Fighting Irish fans around the country as possible, Notre Dame allowed radio stations and networks to broadcast its games free-of-charge. As the Fighting Irish broadcasts grew in popularity during the 1930s, each of the national networks tried to convince ND to accept payment in exchange for exclusive broadcasting rights, but the school's administrators refused to change the open-door policy. In the late 1930s, Father O'Hara, now ND president, estimated that the ongoing refusal had cost Notre Dame millions of dollars, but the policy provided the Fighting Irish with the largest radio audience of any college football team in America and, as significantly, it helped enlarge the ND fan base in a number of key demographic areas, especially among non-Irish and Protestants.

Also enhancing the fame of the Fighting Irish was the 1940 Warner Brothers film, *Knute Rockne—All-American,* starring Pat O'Brien as the coach and Ronald Reagan as George Gipp. This popular movie contributed many important elements to the ideology of big-time college sports, particularly the student-athlete metaphor and the coach-as-culture-hero. The movie also gave Ronald Reagan his most famous part and speech, his deathbed "Win one for the Gipper" request, subsequently serving as his political motto during successful gubernatorial and presidential campaigns. That *Knute Rockne—All-American* was mainly Hollywood fiction, with neither the cinematic coach or the Gipper remotely resembling their historical reality, was irrelevant to the central role that the movie occupies in the mythos of college sports and Ronald Reagan's political career. In addition, as one of the first Hollywood films to depict a Catholic institution and the priests running it in highly positive terms, the film helped change Protestant America's attitudes about Catholics, particularly those of Irish descent. When coupled with other popular movies like *Going My Way* (1944), the Rockne biopic and the entire Fighting Irish phenomenon formed part of the bridge from the anti-Catholic prejudices of the past, exemplified by the

Frank Leahy

overwhelming defeat of Al Smith in the 1928 presidential election, to John F. Kennedy's success in 1960.

## LEAHY'S LADS

In 1941, Notre Dame hired Frank Leahy, one of Rockne's former players and a man with a pure Fighting Irish pedigree, as its new head football coach and athletic director (Leahy always used the Irish term "lads" when referring to his players). The priests in charge of the school insisted that Leahy sign a memorandum pledging absolute adherence to the school's "Constitution for Intercollegiate Athletics," including the clause that "victories or winning teams are to be sought only in accordance with the Constitution, policies, practices, and the principles of true sportsmanship." In addition, the memorandum stated that when the Notre Dame football program stayed within the prescribed rules, it performed "an apostolate for the working of incalculable good." However, if coaches ever deviated because of a desire to win at all costs, they would bring immeasurable harm upon "Our Lady's School."

Father O'Hara had rewritten the Constitution in the 1930s, and Notre Dame alumni and Fighting Irish fans, at first skeptical about its insistence on total purity in all aspects of intercollegiate athletics, came to take great pride in it—for Catholic America, the school's clean *and* winning athletic program represented a religious and social triumph. Then the film *Knute Rockne—All-American* set the policy in stone: Notre Dame players had to be athlete-heroes and excellent students, and ND coaches had to be innovative, inspirational, and win within the rules like the cinematic Rockne (the real coach had been far less scrupulous but the film buried the man under a ton of hagiography).

Frank Leahy was an exceptional and obsessed coach, devoting all of his time and energy to maintaining Notre Dame's winning tradition. He succeeded brilliantly, ending with a total record topped only by Rockne. He also surpassed his mentor in many areas, including constructing the Fighting Irish's longest undefeated streak, from September 1946 to October 1950. In the postwar period, Notre Dame came to symbolize the best in football in the same way that the New York Yankees epitomized it in baseball, and Citation in horse racing. This greatly pleased the millions of ND supporters, the aura of excellence enveloping them. Furthermore, for ND rooters as well as most other college sports fans, Notre Dame not only meant "Number One" on the field but, as a scandal-free program, the Fighting Irish also represented the traditional ideals during one of the most corrupt periods in intercollegiate athletics.

During this period Notre Dame began to attract increasing numbers of supporters for non-religious and non-ethnic reasons. A famous sportswriter (Francis Wallace) explained "why the American public, and not just the Irish and Catholics, like it [ND] and root for it." Using Hollywood war movies as his reference, he discussed one of the school's greatest heroes, Jack Chevigny. As a player, Chevigny starred in the "Win One for the Gipper" game, the film *Knute Rockne—All-American* highlighting his deeds. Then, in WWII, although over age, he joined the Marine Corps and died on Iwo Jima. Wallace maintained that Chevigny's "Notre Dame credo"—"My *team,* my *school,* my *family,* my *friends,* my *faith,* my *country*"—was simply the basic "American credo," and that the public had come to see Notre Dame as a quintessentially American phenomenon, not merely a Catholic and Irish one.

Frank Leahy resigned after the 1953 season, his workaholicism having impaired his health. The young president of Notre Dame, Father Theodore Hesburgh, asked his former pupil and ND star halfback, the twenty-five year old Terry Brennan, to assume the most difficult head coaching job in college sports. Brennan, with bona fide Fighting Irish credentials, began with winning seasons but slipped to 2-8 in 1956, encountering the wrath of many Notre Dame fans, particularly the "Subway Alumni." He never restored confidence in his coaching ability and left after two more seasons. His successor, Joe Kuharich, also a former ND football player, flopped worse than Brennan, and his failure prompted the ND authorities to hire the first non-Notre Dame alumnus in a half-century to coach the Fighting Irish, Ara Parseghian.

Despite being Protestant and with no Irish forebearers, Parseghian pleased the Fighting Irish faithful by consistently accomplishing one task—his teams won most of their games and ascended to the top of the national polls, obtaining national championships during his regime. But, like Frank Leahy, Ara Parseghian ended his ND career as a winning coach and mentally and physically exhausted. Coaching the Fighting Irish, because of their multitude of demanding fans, their imposing history and cultural importance, had become the tiger ride of college sports— there was no way to dismount gracefully. The "Era of Ara" concluded in 1974.

### At the End of the Twentieth Century

The post-Parseghian period of Notre Dame football appears as a drama written long ago, with actors playing totally scripted parts. The head Notre Dame football coach must have the public persona, including the humility, of the hero of *Knute Rockne— All-American;* in addition, he must win consistently like the real Rockne, Leahy, and Parseghian; and he must handle the immense pressure of the job with grace and dignity. Parseghian's successor, Dan Devine, won many games and a national championship but lacked the required personality traits. Gerry Faust, "Mr. Personality," could not consistently win football games during his five years at the helm. Lou Holtz followed him, immediately capturing a national championship but, as he won more

Terry Brennan (*left*)

games, he became rather egotistical and flinty and lost some of the fans' adulation. The verdict is still out on his successor, Bob Davies. Meanwhile Fighting Irish fans are as demanding as ever, and the media spotlight never dims.

Upon the huge base of Catholic and ethnic supporters, Notre Dame long ago added millions of secular rooters, enabling the school to have its own network TV contract (no other university possesses one), and to sell more sweatshirts and other items with its logo upon them than any other educational institution in America. By the end of the twentieth century, Notre Dame football had moved to the absolute center of the American mainstream but, in so doing, had lost some of its distinctive Irishness. Perhaps that transition was inevitable, paralleling the similar migration of Irish-Americans into the cultural and economic mainstream, ironically speeded up by the general population's acceptance of the ND Fighting Irish.

Finally, the on-and-off-the-field accomplishments of the University of Notre Dame's football team have been remarkable, far exceeding those of any other college athletic team. Probably the Notre Dame Fighting Irish will never again make as important a mark on American life as they did during the twentieth century, particularly from the 1920s through the 1940s. Much of the story of the Fighting Irish is one of mission accomplished.

Jim Beach and Daniel Moore, *Army vs. Notre Dame: The Big Game 1913– 1947* (New York, 1948).

Michael Oriard, *The End of Autumn: Reflections on My Life in Football* (Garden City, N.Y., 1982).

Thomas Schlereth, *The University of Notre Dame: A Portrait of Its History and Campus* (Notre Dame, 1976).

Murray Sperber, *Onward to Victory: The Crises That Shaped College Sports* (New York, 1998).

———, *Shake Down the Thunder: The Creation of Notre Dame Football* (New York, 1993).

Francis Wallace, *Notre Dame: From Rockne to Parseghian* (New York, 1966).

———, *The Notre Dame Story* (New York, 1949).

MURRAY SPERBER

*The New Encyclopaedia Britannica,* volume 8.
Frederick M. Thrasher, *The Gang: A Study of 1,313 Gangs in Chicago* (Chicago, 1927).

JOHN DEEDY

## O'BRIAN, JOHN LORD (1874–1973)

Constitutional lawyer and public official. Born into Irish heritage to John and Elizabeth (Lord) O'Brian, he attended public schools in Buffalo, New York, and then attended Harvard University and graduated in 1896. In 1902 he married Alma E. White and they had five daughters.

O'Brian opened his own law office and in 1907 was elected to the New York State Assembly. In 1909 President Roosevelt appointed him U.S. Attorney for the Western District of New York and he was later nominated again by Presidents William Howard Taft and Woodrow Wilson. In 1917 he was appointed head of the War Emergency Division of the Department of Justice and after World War I he returned to his private practice in New York. However, in 1929 he was called to Washington to serve as head of the Anti-Trust Division of the Department of Justice. O'Brian worked tirelessly for many causes in Washington and became renowned for his superb legal tenacity and analytical ability.

O'Brian also had a sterling private life in which he was involved in several civic causes, primarily education. He served as trustee for the University of Buffalo, regent for the University of the State of New York, overseer for Harvard University and chairman for the Endowment Fund of Harvard Divinity School. He received numerous awards, some military and some from his many civic engagements. He also was awarded several honorary degrees from Hobart College, Syracuse University, Brooklyn Polytechnic Institute, Brown University, Harvard University, Yale University Law School and Harvard Divinity School. O'Brian had a long and successful career and was still active at his D.C. office at the age of ninety-eight. He died on April 10, 1973, and was buried in the Washington National Cathedral as a tribute to his life of service and devotion.

State University of New York at Buffalo, Faculty of Law and Jurisprudence.
The Columbia University Oral History Research Office for audio tapes.
*Buffalo Law Review,* Twentieth Anniversary Issue (1971).
*Dictionary of American Biography,* supplement 9.

JOY HARRELL

## O'BRIEN, FITZ-JAMES (1828–1862)

Journalist, poet and author. Born in County Limerick, Ireland, O'Brien was the son of James and Eliza (O'Driscoll) O'Brien. The early years of his upbringing are vague, but accounts give witness to an early penchant for writing by O'Brien. Early on, he decided on a literary career and before arriving in America is said to have produced close to twenty-seven poems, one story and twelve articles in Irish and English journals. In the U.S., O'Brien quickly gained popularity in New York's literary circles. He submitted selections of his work to such publications as *American Whig Review, Putnam's Magazine, Harper's Weekly, Vanity Fair,* and the *Atlantic Monthly.* Similarly, O'Brien's most valuable exposure was in *Harper's Magazine* and the *Evening Post* and *New York Times.* O'Brien also wrote several plays, one of which gained notoriety, *A Gentleman from Ireland,* which he produced in 1895.

## O'BANION, (Charles) DION (1892–1924)

Gangster, bootlegger. In the 1920s, when Chicago was a virtual hostage to its criminal elements, the gang of Dion "Deanie" O'Banion was as notorious as any in town, including those of gangland overlords Johnny Torrio and Al Capone. O'Banion was born of Irish heritage in 1892 in Aurora, Illinois, and grew up in the North Side neighborhood of Chicago known as Little Hell. He was a social anomaly to say the least. A former altar boy, delightful Irish tenor and lover of flowers, he was also a safe-cracker, burglar and worse. When he was gunned down at the age of 32, Chicago's police chief congratulated the citizenry on the death of "an arch-criminal, who was responsible for at least twenty-five murders." A psychiatrist classified him as a man of "sunny brutality."

It was a combination of Prohibition and O'Banion's gifts as a ward heeler that brought him to prominence—the former nudging him into bootlegging; the latter producing political connections for his operations. O'Banion came to control the best distilleries and breweries on Chicago's North Side, and he serviced the fashionable clubs and restaurants of Chicago's fabled Gold Coast. He became enormously rich. Meanwhile, indulging his passion for flowers, he acquired half-interest in a florist shop across the street from Holy Name Cathedral. That was ill-advised, for it was there that O'Banion met his fate. On the morning of November 10, 1924, three men entered the shop ostensibly to pick up the floral arrangements for the funeral of the president of the Unione Siciliana. While one of the men clasped O'Banion's hand in greeting (thus preventing him from reaching for one of three guns he was known to pack), the other two pumped bullets into him. It was a classic gangland slaying.

O'Banion took his leave in style. The chiefs of Chicago's gangs turned out to pay their respects, including Torrio and Capone. They were among a throng of fifteen thousand "mourners." Scalpers hawked prime viewing locations, and twenty-six trucks were needed to move the flowers of sympathy to the grave site in Mount Carmel Cemetery. O'Banion was lowered into the ground in a sterling casket valued at ten thousand dollars. A soaring obelisk marks the spot. All told, the funeral cost an estimated one hundred thousand dollars.

O'Banion's gang limped along after his death, the remnants going to their deaths in the St. Valentine's Day massacre of February 14, 1929.

The character "Sweet Rolls" Sullivan in Andrew Greeley's novel *Irish Whiskey* is said to be modeled on "Deanie" O'Banion.

*See* Chicago, Aspects of

Jack Kelly, "Gangster City," *American Heritage* (April 1995).
Joe Kraus, "The Jewish Gangster," *American Scholar* (Winter 1995).

O'Brien's achievements were marred only by his own squanderous personality. While circulating in the New York literary circles, O'Brien was known for his late night socializing and orgiastic behavior which eventually lead to his financial downfall. Beginning in 1858, O'Brien encountered hardship and was reduced to an impoverished existence. Thus, at the onset of the Civil War, O'Brien joined the National Guard where he cultivated a campaign for gathering recruits. However, on February 16, 1862, he received a shoulder injury and due to inadequate treatment died of tetanus on April 6.

William Winter, *Poems and Stories of Fitz-James O'Brien* (Boston, 1881). *Dictionary of American Biography,* 12.

JOY HARRELL

## O'BRIEN, HUGH (1818–1895)

*See* Boston, Twelve Irish-American Mayors of

## O'BRIEN, LAWRENCE F. (1917–1990)

Presidential assistant, Postmaster General, basketball commissioner. A native of Springfield, Massachusetts, Lawrence F. (Larry) O'Brien virtually cut his teeth on Democratic politics. He was born July 7, 1917, son of Lawrence F. and Myra T. (Sweeney) O'Brien, immigrants out of County Cork, and at age eleven was canvassing with his father, a local Democratic leader, on behalf of Alfred E. Smith in the 1928 presidential race. He proudly recalled having shook Smith's hand, and that of Franklin D. Roosevelt four years later.

After service in World War II, O'Brien directed the 1946, 1948 and 1950 congressional campaigns of his friend, Foster Furcolo, and when Furcolo won the Second Massachusetts District seat in 1948 he accompanied him to Washington as his administrative assistant. O'Brien returned to Massachusetts in 1950 to the family's real estate and public relations business, but was quickly back in politics as director of organization for John F. Kennedy's 1952 senatorial bid against Republican incumbent Henry Cabot Lodge. His innovative campaign tactics were a major factor in Kennedy's upset victory, and his expertise was called upon again when Kennedy stood for reelection in 1958. O'Brien's efforts helped Kennedy roll up the 874,608-vote margin that projected him nationally as a presidential prospect. Soon after, he was traveling the country laying the foundations for that presidential bid.

Once president, Kennedy named O'Brien his Special Assistant for Congressional Relations and Personnel, and O'Brien steered many of the administration's liberal domestic measures through the congressional maze, among them a hike in the minimum wage, an omnibus housing bill and a constitutional amendment barring the poll tax.

After Kennedy's assassination, O'Brien stayed on as President Lyndon Johnson's Special Assistant for Congressional Relations, successfully lobbying Medicare and the Voting Rights Act through Congress. He became Postmaster General in 1965, and proposed the organizational reforms that led to the department's being removed in the next administration from Cabinet status and established as a quasi-public, professionally managed corporation. O'Brien stepped down as Postmaster General in 1968 to work in the presidential campaign of Robert F. Kennedy and, after Kennedy's death, he aligned himself with Hubert H. Humphrey. O'Brien served as chairmanship of the Democratic National Committee from 1968 to 1972, except for a seven-month interval in 1969 when he was engaged in management consulting and investment banking in New York City.

Lawrence F. O'Brien

It was during the second phase of O'Brien's tenure as Democratic National Committee chairman that Republican intelligence operatives with links to the Nixon White House and the Committee for the Re-election of the President broke into DNC headquarters in the Watergate apartment complex in Washington, D.C., and burglarized and bugged the office. O'Brien regarded the act as "espionage" and was irked that many in Congress and the media were initially inclined to dismiss it as a "caper" or "third-rate" burglary. He was also annoyed when a number of Washington attorneys, some old friends, declined to handle the civil damage suit he initiated as a result of the break-in, lest their law practices suffer.

There were many theories surrounding the Watergate affair, but in his political memoir O'Brien reduced them to one. The political reality, he said, was that the break-in was staged "to secure all possible information that would help destroy the Democratic Party and its chairman. It's as simple as that." He charged further that a "program of harassment" had been directed at him for years by Nixon Republicans, and he conceded that it had taken its toll. "Make no mistake about it," O'Brien declared, "the government can grind you down. The Nixon administration harassment never silenced me, but I would be dishonest if I didn't admit that it hurt me financially, sapped my energies, and often left me deeply depressed."

That O'Brien was a special target of the Nixon administration seemed no delusion. A private White House investigator was assigned to probe his business and financial affairs, and the Internal Revenue Service audited and reaudited his tax returns for the year 1969. But it was Jeb Stuart Magruder, once a White House aide and, at the time of the break-in, deputy director of the Committee for the Re-election of the President, who confirmed all suspicions. The committee was out to "discredit" O'Brien, Magruder said on national television, adding "there was general concern that if he was allowed to continue as Democratic National Chairman, because he was certainly . . . their most professional political operator, that he could be very difficult in the coming campaign. So we had hoped that information [from the break-in] might discredit him."

In 1973 O'Brien left political life, his integrity intact, and returned to management consulting as head of O'Brien Associates, a firm he founded. Two years later he became commissioner of the National Basketball Association, serving until 1984. The association's world championship trophy is named for him.

*See* Kennedy, John Fitzgerald

Lawrence F. O'Brien, *No Final Victories: A Life in Politics from John F. Kennedy to Watergate* (New York, 1974)

Nelson Lichtenstein, Eleanora W. Schoenebaum, et al., eds., *Political Profiles,* the Kennedy, Johnson and Nixon/Ford Years, three volumes (New York, 1976, 1979).

JOHN DEEDY

## O'BRIEN, MARGARET (1937–   )

Actress. Born Angela Maxine O'Brien on January 15, 1937 in Los Angeles, California, of Irish parents, Margaret O'Brien was a major motion picture star of the 1940s.

O'Brien did some modeling when she was only three years old, and she won a small part in *Babes on Broadway* (1941) when she was only four. She was cast in a major part in *Journey for Margaret* (1942) and was immediately thrown into the limelight as a star. MGM signed her to a long-term contract, and she made numerous films, both dramas and musicals, for that studio throughout the 1940s, including *Madame Curie* (1943), *Meet Me in St. Louis* (1944), *Our Vines Have Tender Grapes* (1945), *Tenth Avenue Angel* (1947) and *Little Women* (1949). In 1944 she received a special Academy Award for the "Outstanding Child Actress" of her day.

O'Brien retired from the screen in the 1950s, although she has accepted occasional parts and appearances throughout the years.

J. Concannon and Frank Cull, *Irish American Who's Who* (New York, 1984).

Joseph Curran, *Hibernian Green on the Silver Screen* (Westport, CT, 1990).

EILEEN DANEY CARZO

## O'BRIEN, PAT (1899–1983)

Actor. Born William Joseph O'Brien, Jr., in Milwaukee, Wisconsin, on November 11, 1899, he was well-known and loved for the Irish-American characters he played so well—rugged Irish cops, priests, tough army sergeants, reporters and inspirational coaches.

O'Brien's four grandparents were Irish: the McGoverns settled in Wisconsin from County Galway, and the O'Briens came from County Cork to Manhattan—all around the middle of the nineteenth century. Pat (he took the name in honor of his paternal grandfather) attended Marquette Academy, a Catholic secondary school on a scholarship; and it was there that he met another student named Spencer Tracy. The two became fast friends at Marquette, sharing their love of the theatre, and then enlisted in the Navy together in 1918.

After World War I, O'Brien attended law school at Marquette University, but he was becoming drawn to the theatre, particularly after his starring debut in a campus production of *Charley's Aunt.* He pursued his dream of a stage career, going to New York and attending Sargent's School of Drama with Spencer Tracy. He

got his break on Broadway with the part of Charlie Groff in *A Man's Man* in 1925. This six-month run was followed by a series of stage successes, including *Henry Behave, Gertie, Broadway, The Up and Up,* and *Overture.*

Although he had made his film debut in *Fury of the Wild* and *The Freckled Rascal* (both 1929), O'Brien rose to stardom on the big screen in the part of Hildy Johnson in Howard Hughes' enormous hit *The Front Page* (1930). After that, one movie followed another, and he was teamed with some of Hollywood's biggest stars, including Jimmy Cagney in action-packed films such as *Here Comes the Navy* (1934) and *Angels With Dirty Faces* (1938).

O'Brien's favorite and best-known part was his title role in *Knute Rockne—All American* (1940), a film about the legendary Notre Dame football coach (with actor Ronald Reagan as George Gipp). His inspirational speech to the players in the locker room is one of the most memorable scenes in film history.

He is best remembered today for a series of biographical films he made in the '40s and '50s, including *The Fighting 69th* (1940), *The Iron Man* (1943), *Fighting Father Dunne* (1948), and *The Last Hurrah* (1958) with his friend Spencer Tracy.

In the 1950s he developed a nightclub act, reciting poetry and parts from his movie roles, telling jokes and Irish stories, and singing songs; and his congenial, warm and comfortable presence delighted the audiences. He returned to the theatre in a broad range of parts; and his wife, the retired actress Eloise Taylor, whom he married in 1931, joined him on stage in 1958. He reappeared on Broadway in 1957 in *Miss Lonelyhearts* to favorable reviews, but the play closed after a brief run. He dipped into television acting, starring for one season in a series about a father/son lawyer team in *Harrigan and Son*

O'Brien was awarded the coveted John F. Kennedy Medal by The Ancient Order of Hibernians, and he was honored by the United Irish Societies of Southern California at a testimonial dinner in 1983. He and his wife Eloise had four children, Mavourneen, Brigid, Patrick Sean, and Terence Kevin, and six grandchildren. He was a sentimental Irishman, an intensely dedicated family man with deep religious faith.

Joseph Curran, *Hibernian Green on the Silver Screen* (Westport, CT, 1990).

EILEEN DANEY CARZO

## O'BRIEN, WILLIAM S. (1825–1878)

Entrepreneur. Neither a miner nor a financial genius, unlike his three partners in the so-called "Irish Four"—John W. Mackay, James C. Flood and James G. Fair—O'Brien brought to the partnership what would today be called a flair for public relations.

A native of Co. Laois and a famine immigrant, O'Brien arrived in San Francisco virtually penniless, working for his passage aboard the ship as a deckhand. When he stepped ashore, he must have presented a pathetic site, for the first stranger who saw him immediately bought the young Irishman a new pair of shoes. Later, when he was a wealthy millionaire, O'Brien sought to identify the good Samaritan so he could thank him properly, but in vain.

O'Brien met his future business partner James C. Flood in the city and they decided to go into business together as bar owners. Their clientele consisted heavily of stock brokers and traders on the nearby stock exchange. Flood would work the bar while O'Brien worked the street, using his Irish brogue and easy manner to sweep customers inside. Together they learned the ways in which easy riches could be had on the stock market.

Eventually, they went in the brokerage business themselves and came into partnership with the miners Mackay and Fair. Together, they brought in the Virginia Consolidated mine, from which they took over $100 million in silver.

O'Brien, whom the press nicknamed "the jolly millionaire," probably enjoyed his wealth more than the others. He never married and lived in a house with his widowed sister and her three children. His one form of relaxation was poker, which he enjoyed playing in saloons with old cronies. His one concession to his wealth was the stack of silver dollars he habitually kept at his elbow, so that a player whose luck was against him would not have to quit the table for lack of funds.

O'Brien's quiet diplomacy often kept the partnership together when things were sometimes at the breaking point. He also managed to keep public resentment toward the suddenly rich partners to a minimum. "He has more friends in all walks of life, and fewer enemies, than . . . most rich men," wrote a local newspaper.

John A. Barnes, *Irish-American Landmarks* (Detroit, 1995).

JOHN A. BARNES

## O'BOYLE, PATRICK CARDINAL (1896–1987)

Cardinal Archbishop of Washington, D.C. The only child of working-class Irish immigrants, Patrick O'Boyle was born in Scranton, Pennsylvania, on July 18, 1896. His father Michael had come from County Sligo to work in Scranton's steel mills where he witnessed firsthand the struggle against brutal conditions and unjust wages. It is not known if Michael O'Boyle was actively involved in the labor disputes, but his finances were sufficiently secure to support a modest home in St. Paul's parish where he and his wife from County Mayo, Mary Muldoon O'Boyle, sheltered a steady stream of immigrant relatives. Their son later counted some fourteen newcomers to America who at different times lived with the family until his father was able to secure employment for the men in the mines and mills and the women in domestic service.

All this changed when Michael died in 1906, forcing his widow to support herself and their son, who eventually dropped out of school to help. Later, Mary O'Boyle became housekeeper for two local priest-professors, a position which included lodging for the O'Boyles and a chance for Patrick to return to school. A conscientious student, he went on to St. Thomas College (now the University of Scranton) where he graduated at the head of his class in 1916. Sure of a vocation to the priesthood, he was turned down by the local bishop, whose seminary enjoyed a surplus of candidates. He matriculated instead at St. Joseph's, Dunwoodie, in the Archdiocese of New York where he was ordained in 1921.

### A NEW YORK APPRENTICESHIP

The period of O'Boyle's early priesthood was important in the development of modern attitudes toward such issues as immigration, race relations, and the government's obligation to the socially disadvantaged. The future cardinal's experiences helped form his progressive social philosophy. His first assignment was to St. Columba's parish on Manhattan's lower West Side. Here generations of hard-working Irish and German immigrants had started life in America, many eventually making their way up the economic ladder and moving on. Those left behind formed an urban underclass whose lives were haunted by poverty, disease, and crime, conditions that instilled in the immigrant's son an abiding concern for problems facing America's ethnic minorities and working poor. His concern led to increasing involvement in citywide welfare projects and eventually to matriculation in the graduate program at the New York School of Social Work.

Between 1932 and 1936 the young priest taught social work at Fordham University before graduating to varied and responsible positions in New York's Catholic Charities. In 1941, now a monsignor, O'Boyle assumed the post of director of Catholic War Relief Services, with responsibility for collecting vast sums of money and distributing 60,000 tons of food and supplies in forty-eight nations. After the war he became head of Catholic Charities, but served only six months before Pope Pius XII appointed him to lead the newly independent Archdiocese of Washington, a post he assumed on January 21, 1948.

### ARCHBISHOP OF WASHINGTON

O'Boyle transformed the Church in the postwar capital. He established forty-six new parishes and constructed more than 300 buildings, many at bargain prices, but all, this son of a Scranton steelworker insisted, constructed with union labor. His motto, "Steadfast in the Faith" accurately underscored the man's uncompromising sense of loyalty—not only his own fidelity to the Holy See and the social class from which he had sprung, but, no less exacting, the fidelity he expected from his subordinates. This sense of loyalty helped explain the seeming contradictions in an episcopal career that combined the outlook of a serious social crusader, especially in the area of race relations and social justice, with an uncompromising defender of the magisterium.

O'Boyle's profound sense of loyalty was especially manifest in the two defining events of his career as archbishop, his championship of racial justice and civil rights, and his support of Pope Paul VI in the controversy over artificial contraception. In his first years in Washington he integrated the diocese's churches and schools, before the Supreme Court ruled on the matter and despite considerable opposition among some local Catholics. He chaired the city's influential Interracial Committee on Race Relations and joined with Martin Luther King, Jr., in the historic 1963 March on Washington. Religious around the country used his approval for Washington's priests to participate in demonstrations for racial justice, such as the march in Selma, Alabama, in 1965, as license for their own participation. In 1967 he organized the Urban Rehabilitation Corporation for funneling diocesan money into urban renewal projects in minority neighborhoods. He saw his elevation to the College of Cardinals in 1967 as papal recognition for the ecumenical battle waged by Washingtonians for social justice.

On the other hand, O'Boyle's uncompromising defense of *Humanae Vitae,* the encyclical that upheld the Church's traditional teachings on birth control, also touched on his sense of loyalty and led, after strenuous efforts at reconciliation, to his depriving thirty-nine priests of various faculties. Although the cardinal never faltered in his resolve during the long fight over birth control, his sorrow over the loss of so many of his priests overshadowed his final years which were spent quietly in Washington until his death on August 10, 1987.

MORRIS MacGREGOR

## O'CALLAGHAN, JEREMIAH (1780–1861)

Priest. One of fourteen children born of Jeremiah and Mary (Twohig) O'Callaghan in County Cork, Ireland, Jeremiah O'Callaghan was ordained to the priesthood in 1805 by the bishop of Cloyne. Early in his career, O'Callaghan became a zealous opponent of the practice of usury. His preaching caused such a stir with bankers and profiteers that his bishop removed him from his parish and transferred him to another one in 1818. O'Callaghan preached the same message with the same intensity there until the bishop had to censor him. The priest drifted until he opened a classical school at Ross Carberry in 1820, but three years later emigrated to New York. Bishop Connolly, knowing of O'Callaghan's anticapitalist views, refused to place him in a parish, nor would Baltimore or Quebec take him. O'Callaghan therefore set to writing *Usury, or Interest, Proved to be Repugnant to the Divine and Ecclesiastical Laws, and Destructive to Civil Society* in 1824. The book sold immediately and was republished in 1825, 1828, 1834 and 1856. After making another attempt to secure a parish back in London, England, O'Callaghan traveled to Boston where a close friend of his recommended O'Callaghan to Bishop Fenwick. Fenwick sent him to Vermont where the priest's good works and passionate pastoral zeal won him the appellation "the apostle of Vermont." Building the first Catholic Church in Vermont at Burlington, O'Callaghan also organized a Catholic school and continued publishing polemical works on Protestantism, the banking industry, and Catholic doctrine. By 1854, O'Callaghan was moved to Holyoke, Massachusetts, where he built St. Jerome's Church and served as pastor there for seven years. After his death on February 23, 1861, O'Callaghan was memorialized by his parishioners with a monument that still stands in his memory.

*Catholic Encyclopedia*, vol. XV (New York: The Encyclopedia Press, Inc., 1913).

Jeremiah O'Callaghan, *Memoir* in *Usury, or Interest, Proved to be Repugnant to the Divine and Ecclesiastical Laws, and Destructive to Civil Society* (New York: [s.n.] 1856).

William Byrne, *History of the Catholic Church in the New England States*, 2 vols. (Boston: The Hurd & Everts Co., 1899).

DANIEL J. KUNTZ

## O'CALLAHAN, JOSEPH T. (1905–1964)

Priest and hero. Joseph T. O'Callahan was born in Somerville, MA, on May 14, 1905, the son of Cornelius J. and Alice (Casey) O'Callahan, and died in Worcester, MA, on March 18, 1964. Shortly after he graduated from Boston College High School, he entered the Society of Jesus on July 30, 1922, and was ordained a priest by Bishop Thomas A. Emmet in Weston, MA, on June 20, 1934.

A professor of mathematics and physics at the College of the Holy Cross, Father O'Callahan enlisted in the United States Navy as a chaplain in World War II. Serving on the U.S.S. *Franklin* when it was attacked by Japanese aircraft on March 19, 1945, O'Callahan exhibited extraordinary heroism. In recognition of this, he was awarded the Congressional Medal of Honor by President Harry S Truman on January 23, 1946.

As the first chaplain ever to win that honor, Father O'Callahan returned to his teaching career at the College of the Holy Cross where today his remains rest in the Jesuit Cemetery. But his memory was perpetuated by the Navy when, on October 21, 1965, Sister Rose Marie, his sister, christened the U.S.S. *O'Callahan* in his honor, and a special memorial was dedicated in the Medal of Honor Grove of Freedoms Foundation in Valley Forge, PA, on October 6, 1979. His memory is also honored at the College of the Holy Cross which named its science library for him.

Archives, College of the Holy Cross.

M. C. Blackman, "The Bravest Man I Ever Knew," *New York Herald Tribune* (March 20, 1964).

Donald F. Crosby, *Battlefield Chaplains* (Lawrence, KS, 1994).

Joseph T. O'Callahan, *I Was Chaplain on the Franklin* (New York, 1956).

VINCENT A. LAPOMARDA, S.J.

## O'CONNELL, DANIEL, AND AMERICA

Historians remember Daniel O'Connell (1775–1847) in different ways. He was "the Counsellor" whose courtroom victories became the stuff of legend. He was "the Liberator" who successfully led the campaign for Catholic Emancipation in 1829. His attempts to repeal the act of union with Great Britain failed but he effectively invented constitutional nationalism in Ireland as well as a more modern and popular type of political organization and style. As Sean O' Faolain remarked in 1938, O'Connell "taught simple men to have pride, and he taught them how to fight."

O'Connell's radicalism was influenced by the ideas and events of contemporary Europe. Catholic Ireland had long looked to the Irish colleges and brigades of France, Spain and Austria as a world free from the Penal Laws. It did not regard the New World to the west as the promised land which America's Ulster-Scots immigrants extolled in their letters to Ireland. O'Connell's poor understanding of America partly reflected these "old world" attitudes of his community. His formal campaign to seat Catholics in Parliament (1823–29) was also rooted in the eighteenth century. The original Catholic Association had been founded in 1759 to reach an accommodation with George III and exorcise the ghost of the Stuarts. The association's last chapter opened in 1823. It was funded by the "Catholic rent" of £1 a year. However, its associate membership of a penny a month greatly broadened its base and brought many lower-class Catholics to identify with the association's aims and organization. Especially at local level,

Daniel O'Connell

it also looked to the Catholic clergy for support. As such, instinctively and in fact, O'Connell's program of reform became unequivocally associated with Catholicism.

America's Irish immigrants welcomed the drive towards Catholic Emancipation. However, they stressed the morality and justice of O'Connell's cause rather than the confessional trappings which it developed in Ireland. In doing so, they reflected the influence of the more interdenominational United Irish *emigrés* over the (especially urban) Irish communities of the early-nineteenth century. In New York, for example, the Protestant United Irishman, William Sampson, supported Emancipation as a cause of the "oppressed" and "virtuous." The city's Friends of Ireland was founded in 1825 to support this altruism and raised money and whatever other public support it could. After Emancipation had been granted, the $1,000 that was left in the Friends' coffers was used to erect a monument to the memory of another Protestant United Irish leader, Thomas Addis Emmet, who had died in 1827.

Even allowing for the influence of Emmet and Sampson, New York's Irish organizations were not as coherent as might first appear. There are at least three reasons why this was so. First, despite their almost heroic status, the "older" leaders of the city's Irish community were being challenged by "newer" types who were more ethnically introspective than those of Emmet's generation or background. Second, Catholics were beginning to immigrate in growing numbers into the cities of the eastern United States and provided a new source of support for an increasingly assertive church. Third, Catholicism became as *bona fide* an expression of Irish ethnicity as nationalism and Irish immigrants could look to Catholic as well as nationalist opinion-formers to articulate their sense of identity in the United States. Catholic newspapers such as the (New York) *Truth Teller* and the *Boston Pilot* foreshadowed an Irish-America that was different from that of the generation of the United Irishmen.

Against this background, some objected to the Catholic "tone" of the Friends of Ireland. On the rolls of New York's Friendly Sons of St. Patrick where, by tradition, the presidency alternated between a Protestant and Catholic, there was no formal mention of O'Connell until he opened the second phase of his career in the 1830s. In Philadelphia, some Protestants of Irish background refused to donate funds or attend meetings. Most Catholics did not unduly worry about this, thus repeating the point that the composition and leadership of the city's Irish community were changing and that such domestic factors, over and above the policy issues that were identified by the campaign in Ireland, also determined the reactions of Irish-Americans to events in the Old Country. In Augusta and Charleston, where the leading Irish societies attracted Protestant and Catholic, fund-raising was a poor second to moral support. In New Orleans, "various nationalities and religious persuasions" raised $1,518.50 for O'Connell. However, the New Orleans Friends took a broad and non-confessional view of the Catholic Association. In its view, no other organization was more dedicated "for the melioration of man, more liberal in its views, more useful in its designs, or more moderate and cautious in its proceedings." In other words, support from New Orleans was also limited by its own liberal American interpretation of O'Connell's campaign.

When Emancipation was granted in 1829, it was celebrated by over 30 support groups across the country: on the Erie Canal and in St. Louis, New Orleans, Boston, New York, Baltimore and Augusta, among other American cities. In Philadelphia, a grand dinner was held in Independence Hall and the Liberty Bell pealed. However, the bell cracked and has not been rung since. 1829 was as much a watershed for Irish-America as it was for Ireland.

In Boston, the Hibernian Relief Society regarded the achievement of Catholic Emancipation as a vindication of its own efforts. It had energetically collected and sent "rent" to Ireland. However, it had taken its lead from the Catholic Association in Dublin rather than from the local Irish "establishment." On the Erie Canal, the remittances that were made from there had also not been made in the name of either participating in or mobilizing the "Irish-American community" per se in support of O'Connell. The workers wanted to return something to their struggling kith and kin whom they had left in Ireland. Both the Erie and Boston groups were driven by recently arrived and less-established immigrants. In New York, however, the Friends of Ireland were led by Sampson and MacNeven who couched their support of O'Connell in terms of their United Irish background. In 1825, MacNeven urged O'Connell to adopt a wider program of reform as well as home rule for Ireland. O'Connell preferred to concentrate on Emancipation and rejected this advice. The rebuff is important because it underlines what was to become an enduring theme in the relationship between movements in Ireland and their American supporters: America may pay the piper but Ireland had to call the tune. For the moment, MacNeven took the point and concentrated on raising money. However, the link between the two sides of the Atlantic was not easy and would be challenged again during the 1830s and 1840s.

O'Connell's drive to repeal the act of union was not formally launched until 1840. In America, the groups that had previously supported Emancipation were reconstituted to promote repeal. In cities such as Boston, the carryover between the two organizations is striking, as is the fact that many of the leaders were of humble background. In Philadelphia, some $2,000 was collected within one week, "proof that the Repealers of this country are hand and heart with their friends abroad." These associations established a national directory to coordinate their activities and in 1842 they held a national convention in Philadelphia which was attended by representatives of 27 different groups. The Repealers thought that a national forum would make their campaign more effective. However, it also attracted criticisms that they should not be interfering in "the legislation of a foreign country." That they were doing so was "a direct infringement of the laws and constitution of the United States." Such comments suggested that Irish immigrants also had "divided loyalties." This issue would become more contentious during the following decades and as Oscar Handin has suggested, it would eventually have to be "justified in terms acceptable to all Americans." It also provided part of the backdrop to the maturing of the notion of the "hyphenated American" and the nativist attacks that this inspired.

Many Irish-Americans saw repeal as picking up where the United Irishmen had left off. O'Connell did not see it that way and in 1841, he stated that the United Irishmen had been "weak and wicked men who considered force and sanguinary violence as part of their resources for ameliorating our institutions." In New York, Emmet's son took umbrage at the attack on the "men of '98" and resigned as president of the repeal organization. By 1845, the more militant view of the Young Ireland movement was more popular in America, especially after Thomas D'Arcy McGee took over as editor of the *Boston Pilot* in 1844.

O'Connell's denunciation of slavery also did not help his relationship with Irish-Americans. Outside of Boston, Irish immigrants were not known for their support of the abolitionist movement. Some feared competition for jobs from free Blacks while others criticised the Protestant leaders of abolitionism for not expressing support for the poor and downtrodden in Ireland. O'Connell did not accept any of this. "It was not in Ireland you learned this cruelty," O'Connell suggested. "How can your souls have become stained with a darkness blacker than the Negro's skin?" He also wrote that if Irishmen "dare countenance the system of slavery . . . we will recognize you as Irishmen no longer." The *Boston Pilot* suggested that he should tone down his attacks and instead "make the freedom of Ireland sure before we turn our strength to the liberation of any other race." O'Connell did not take this advice and roundly denounced apologies for slavery that he received from a number of places in the United States. He denounced even Andrew Jackson as a slave-owner, despite Jackson's status as hero to most Irish-Americans. As a result, the repeal movement in America became irretrievably undermined. In 1845, financial contributions were half those of 1843. The repeal organizations in Charleston, Natchez and New Orleans folded in 1843 and those in Cincinnati, Philadelphia and New York during 1844 and 1845.

In any event, Irish-American support of repeal had not been offered to O'Connell as an uncrowned king of Irish-America. Many took offense when O'Connell used Irish immigrants as a pawn in his negotiations with Britain during the dispute on the Oregon Territory. At that time, he suggested that Irish-Americans would fight *against* America and *for* Britain if O'Connell's demands were met. Irish immigrants regarded his comments on slavery in a somewhat similar light: a presumption. They constituted an unacceptable meddling in the affairs of their new homeland and an intrusion into their backyard. The *Boston Pilot* bluntly suggested that O'Connell and "his associates" had been "misled" by abolitionists and warned against the "painful influence" of being "betrayed into any violent attack upon the American people." As a result, the repeal movement in America, regardless of how it had developed and was perceived, ultimately underlined the "Americanism" of Irish immigrants. For a brief period before the Famine, Irish immigrants had become more Irish-American than American-Irish.

*See* Irish in America; Emigration: 1801–1921

---

Owen Dudley Edwards, "The American Image of Ireland: A Study of Its Early Phases," *Perspectives in American History*, IV (1970).

Thomas F. Moriarty, "The Irish American Response to Catholic Emancipation," *Catholic Historical Review*, LXVI (1980).

Gilbert Osofsky, "Abolitionists, Irish Immigrants, and the Dilemmas of Romantic Nationalism," *American Historical Review* (October 1975).

Douglas Riaich, "Daniel O'Connell and American Anti-Slavery," *Irish Historical Studies* (March 1976).

MAURICE J. BRIC

## O'CONNELL, WILLIAM HENRY CARDINAL (1859–1944)

Cardinal archbishop. William Henry O'Connell was born in Lowell, MA, on December 8, 1859, and died in Brighton, MA, on April 22, 1944. The son of Irish immigrants, John O'Connell, from County Meath, and Bridget (Farley) O'Connell, from County Cavan, William was the last of eleven children. Educated in the public schools of Lowell, O'Connell endured the prejudices against the Irish and the Catholics in Yankee New England.

After beginning his studies at St. Charles College in Baltimore, O'Connell completed them at Boston College in 1881. Then Archbishop John J. Williams of Boston sent him to the North American College in Rome to study for the priesthood. Ordained in Rome's St. John Lateran by Raphael Cardinal Monaco on June 8, 1884, Father O'Connell returned to Boston and was assigned first to St. Joseph's in Medford and, later, to St. Joseph's in Boston. Yet his heart remained in Rome and, not surprisingly, on November 21, 1895, O'Connell's career took a sudden turn upward when he was appointed Rector of the North American College. At the time, the Roman Catholic Church in the United States was divided between Americanizers who opted for a Catholicism that was integrated into American society and Europeanizers who favored separatism.

In Rome, as the head of the seminary, O'Connell improved the institution by increasing its enrollment and solving its financial problems. Elevated, on June 9, 1897, by the Pope to the rank of Monsignor, O'Connell clearly was making a good impression, especially among the churchmen in the Vatican where he was proving himself to be a staunch Europeanizer as compared to his immediate predecessor, Denis O'Connell, an Americanizer.

O'Connell's career advanced when, on February 8, 1901, Pope Leo XIII appointed him third bishop of Portland, ME. On May 19, 1901, O'Connell was consecrated bishop in the Corsini Chapel of the Basilica of St. John Lateran by Francesco Cardinal Satolli who was assisted by two titular archbishops, Rafael Merry del Val and Edmond Stoner.

In Portland, Bishop O'Connell cared for a diocese of Catholics with diverse ethnic backgrounds and reached out to people of other faiths. However, he was frequently absent from his diocese and this was notably clear when he was sent on a papal mission to Japan by Pope Pius X. Subsequently, the latter appointed him, on February 21, 1906, Coadjutor to the Archbishop of Boston.

### CARDINAL ARCHBISHOP

O'Connell succeeded John J. Williams on August 30, 1907, and his advancement was due, in part, to Rafael Cardinal Merry del Val, the Vatican Secretary of State, whom the new archbishop had befriended in his Roman years. As Archbishop of Boston, O'Connell became the first occupant of that see elevated to the College of Cardinals on November 27, 1911. In this capacity, he presided over the sixth diocesan synod in April of 1919; conducted a pilgrimage to the Holy Land in 1924; led 800 pilgrims to the International Eucharistic Congress in Dublin, Ireland, in 1932; celebrated his golden jubilee as a priest in June of 1934; received an honorary degree from Harvard on June 24, 1937; and ordained his successor, Richard J. Cushing, as auxiliary bishop on June 29, 1939. And, throughout these years, he increased the number of the churches, schools, and the social and charitable network of the Church within his large archdiocese.

Initially, earlier historians had regarded the Cardinal as a magisterial and powerful churchman, but later historians have moved away from that view of O'Connell. Today the Cardinal is regarded more critically as an administrator whose authoritarian style made him very much feared or disliked by his priests and not very much liked by his contemporaries in the hierarchy. Actually, O'Connell left something to be desired in dealing fairly and honestly not only with his own priests, but even with his peers among the bishops and, above all, with higher authorities in Rome. Specifically, O'Connell was capable of overlooking his own administrative shortcomings.

Yet, at the same time, Cardinal O'Connell was a very lonely churchman whose positive achievements cannot be overlooked. He had effectively reorganized the administration and the finances of what had been a rather extensive archdiocese which had operated haphazardly before he came to Boston. And the Cardinal brought dignity to the Catholics of his archdiocese by helping to break down the barriers which had excluded them from full participation in the social, political, and economic life of American society.

Occasionally, O'Connell did not hesitate to let the power circles of Boston know what he ("Number One") thought when a certain moral or religious issue was involved. At the same time, he safeguarded the religious liberty of his flock, advanced the integration of Catholic immigrants into American society, provided for the expansion of the Church's social programs, and developed the Catholic educational system on every level.

By the end of his episcopacy, O'Connell had nudged his extensive flock, made up mainly of Irish, in claiming its rightful role in a society whose establishment was dominated by people of another faith. Although Bishop Bernard J. Fitzpatrick had been honored by Harvard University with an honorary degree on May 25, 1861, the same honor for O'Connell symbolized a benchmark in the improved relations between the Irish and the Yankee in the social life of Boston and Massachusetts, even though he had fostered a separate Catholic culture that was out of harmony with the vision of the Americanizers of the last century.

However, Cardinal O'Connell was one who had the courage to denounce early the anti-Semitism of the Nazis and their crimes against the Jews. He was a man of some faults and more virtues. Such is the legacy of the controversial Cardinal O'Connell, whose remains rest in the mausoleum constructed for him on the grounds of St. John's Seminary in Brighton.

*See* Boston; Catholicism, Irish-American

Archives of Archdiocese of Boston, Diocese of Portland (ME), North American College.
Paula M. Kane, *Separatism and Subculture* (Chapel Hill, 1994).
William Henry O'Connell, *Recollections of Seventy Years* (Boston, 1934).
Thomas H. O'Connor, *The Boston Irish* (Boston, 1994).
James M. O'Toole, *Militant and Triumphant* (Notre Dame, 1992).
Dorothy G. Wayman, *Cardinal O'Connell of Boston* (New York, 1955).

VINCENT A. LAPOMARDA, S.J.

## O'CONNOR, CARROLL (1924– )

Actor. Born in New York City on August 2, 1924, O'Connor was an established, well-respected character actor on stage, in the movies, and on television before rising to stardom for his award-winning portrayal of Archie Bunker, the working-class bigot, in Norman Lear's ground-breaking television series, *All in the Family.*

O'Connor grew up in a home vastly different from the Bunkers'. His family was an educated one: his father, Edward Joseph O'Connor, was a lawyer, and his mother, Elise (O'Connor) O'Connor, was a teacher. His paternal grandfather was born in Ballinasloe, County Galway, and he was named for his paternal grandmother whose maiden name was Carroll; his maternal grandmother, Anne McGrath O'Connor, was born in Mulli-

Carroll O'Connor and *All in the Family* cast members

nahone, County Tipperary. His maternal grandfather, John C. O'Connor, born in Brosna, County Kerry, founded the Irish American weekly newspaper *The Irish Advocate* in New York City in 1893.

After a stint in the Merchant Marines during World War II, he enrolled at the University of Montana where he studied English and journalism and began to develop an interest in the theatre. It was there that he met his future wife, Nancy Fields, while performing in an amateur production of *Life With Father.* O'Connor continued his studies at the National University of Ireland; Nancy Fields joined him there, and they were married in 1951.

O'Connor began his professional acting career with a variety of roles at the Dublin Gate Theatre, then in various productions throughout Ireland, London, Paris and Edinburgh. Returning to the United States with high hopes for Broadway, he found himself to be another out-of-work actor. He returned to the University of Montana, earned his M.A. degree in 1956, and worked in Manhattan for two years as a high school English teacher.

He finally became established in the theatre in the late 1950s. He played Buck Mulligan in *Ulysses in Nighttown,* Padraic Colum's stage adaptation of James Joyce's *Ulysses;* and he got rave reviews for his portrayal of the blackmailing producer in *The Big Knife* (1959), directed by Peter Bogdanovich

In the 1960s, O'Connor played in twenty-seven films for the major movie studios, and he became known as one of the most versatile character actors in Hollywood. Some of his films included: *Fever in the Blood* (1961), *Lonely Are the Brave* (1962), *Cleopatra* (1963), *Waterhole No. 3* (1967), *Not With My Wife, You Don't* (1966), *Marlowe* (1969), and *Death of a Gunfighter* (1969). He wrote and co-directed a three-act comedy, *The Ladies of Hanover Tower,* in 1964.

Despite his prolific work, O'Connor was still a relatively unknown actor to the public when Norman Lear offered him the leading role in the new sitcom, *All in the Family.* With O'Connor as the bullying racist Archie, Jean Stapleton as his long-suffering wife, Sally Struthers as their daughter, and Rob Reiner as the long-haired liberal son-in-law, the show dealt frankly and humorously with bigotry and sexual issues in a way that had heretofore been taboo on television. The series was phenomenally successful and ran from 1971 through 1979. In 1972 O'Connor received the Emmy Award for Best Actor and again in 1973, 1977, 1978 and 1979. Subsequent popular television series were *Archie Bunker's Place* and the drama *In the Heat of the Night.*

*See* California; Cinema, Irish in

J. Concannon and Frank Cull, *Irish American Who's Who* (New York, 1984).
Joseph Curran, *Hibernian Green on the Silver Screen* (Westport, CT, 1990).

EILEEN DANEY CARZO

## O'CONNOR, EDWIN (1918–1968)

Novelist. Edwin O'Connor wrote four "Irish" books, which collectively attempt to portray the generational changes undergone by the Irish in the New World.

Born in Providence, Rhode Island, and raised in a suburban neighborhood of Woonsocket, O'Connor was the first child of Dr. John V. and Mary Greene O'Connor. Both his parents were the children of Irish immigrants. Dr. O'Connor was a respected specialist in Internal Medicine, and the novelist's mother taught school before her marriage. O'Connor attended public grade school and a Catholic secondary school. His childhood was typical of the middle class Irish-American community of his era; several generations removed from Ireland, the Irish had begun to enter the professions, and sent their children to college in the expectation of full assimilation into American life. In 1935, O'Connor entered Notre Dame. He changed his major from journalism to English after taking a class from Frank O'Malley, the influential professor well known for his courses on faith and literature. O'Connor remained close to O'Malley for the rest of his life and dedicated *The Edge of Sadness* to his inspirational teacher.

Even before graduating from college, O'Connor had decided to become a writer. He doggedly worked at his craft despite such career detours as a short attempt at graduate school, work as a radio announcer in cities from New England to Florida, and service in the Coast Guard from 1942–45. After the war, O'Connor returned to radio work briefly before becoming a full time freelance writer in 1946. Many of his early short stories and essays appeared in *The Atlantic,* a publication with which O'Connor would be closely linked throughout his career. *Atlantic* editor Edward Weeks also introduced O'Connor to comedian Fred Allen, for whom he edited a collection of radio scripts and ghostwrote an autobiography.

Several of O'Connor's early stories feature the vibrant Irish-American ambiance upon which he would later earn his reputation, but as a young writer he failed to recognize the literary potential of this material. He began and abandoned two non-Irish novels before successfully completing his first book, *The Oracle* (1951). A satirical story about a smug and amoral radio announcer, the story contains no identifiably Irish content. Arthur Schlesinger said of the book that "The novel evidently tried to achieve English urbanity rather than Irish extravagance." *The Oracle* sold poorly and received scant critical attention.

There is a moment in *The Edge of Sadness* when the narrator recalls how, as children, he and his friends played a game in which they imagined a buried treasure and faked a treasure map on a page torn from an old book, "*Traits and Stories of the Irish Peasantry*—a clue perhaps, to its remaining unread." The message is clear: while later generations pursue imaginary riches, they fail to recognize the genuine, if vanishing, treasure that is right at hand in the colorful, story-rich Irish experience.

Such a realization must have come over O'Connor in 1952, when he began work on the unabashedly Irish *The Last Hurrah,* published in 1956. One of the most successful political novels ever written (despite the author's personal indifference to electoral politics), it recounts a mayoral campaign in an unnamed eastern city. The leading candidate is career politician Frank Skeffington, a man distinguished for political hardball, humorous oratory, and an abiding memory of having being an outsider in the Yankee power establishment. The Skeffington character inevitably drew comparisons to the real-life career of Boston's James Michael Curley, which O'Connor emphatically denied; Curley himself relished the notoriety.

The story is framed around Skeffington's wish to show his nephew, Adam Caulfield, the inner workings of a campaign. Extended scenes in wakes, rallies and political confrontations open a window on the vanishing world of the old-time Irish boss. Speaking to Adam, Skeffington explains his relationship to the Irish community: ". . . I'm not just an elected official of the city; I'm a tribal chieftain as well. It's a necessary kind of dual officeholding, you might say; without the second I wouldn't be the first."

Skeffington's opponents field a singularly bland unknown, Kevin McCluskey, to run against him. Unlike Skeffington's camp, McCluskey's handlers understand political packaging and the new media of television. On election night, Skeffington suffers the worst defeat of his lifetime. Later, Adam asks a politically astute friend how the colorless McCluskey could have won such a stunning upset. The friend explains that the old style boss was destroyed by the shift of power to impersonal social agencies in Washington, a process that began with FDR. "Then you think, really, that under these circumstances almost anybody could have beaten my uncle?" asks Adam; to which his friend answers, "Almost anybody did."

*The Last Hurrah* was a huge bestseller, bringing immediate celebrity and wealth to its author. O'Connor's next project was a forgettable children's story, *Benjy* (1957). He then returned to serious fiction by writing *The Edge of Sadness,* which won the Pulitzer Prize for Fiction in 1962.

*The Edge of Sadness* is narrated by Hugh Kennedy, a middle-aged priest assigned—or perhaps exiled—to Old St. Paul's, a seedy downtown parish, after a long stay at a desert alcohol recovery center. Kennedy's inertia is broken when he is drawn back into the lives of his closest boyhood friends, the Carmody family, and their miserly father Charlie, whom Kennedy's own father once called "As fine a man as ever robbed the helpless."

One of those friends, John Carmody, is in fact pastor in the old neighborhood. Kennedy spends an increasing amount of time with the Carmodys and the now-elderly Irish men and women with whom he grew up. O'Connor skillfully plays off Hugh's fond memories of his father and the intimate geniality of his Irish-American origins against John's contempt for his family and the suffocating atmosphere of the parish he serves. Underneath its ruminative tone, *The Edge of Sadness* presents a scathing indictment of Irish Catholic complacency. In a climactic scene, John savagely describes Hugh's multicultural parish at Old St. Paul's: "That's not a real parish at all, is it? We all know what a real parish is. A real parish is an old-time parish. One with a fine, big, old-fashioned, well-kept church with—and here's the important thing—lots of Irish to put inside it! People like our-selves, Hugh."

*The Edge of Sadness* ends on a note of redemption, with Ken-nedy choosing to commit himself to his pastorate at Old St. Paul's. He turns down an opportunity to retreat into the comfort of the familiar, parochial Irish world of his past, and reflects, "The new was something of another kind, something I had never known before. And at this moment, here in the rectory hallway, I stood aching with excitement. . . ." Almost universally recog-nized as his best book, the seriousness, character development, and nuanced storytelling of *The Edge of Sadness* are unequaled anywhere in O'Connor's fiction.

Fr. Kennedy's understated tone did not carry into O'Con-nor's next book, *I Was Dancing* (1964), which tells of an aged vaudevillian, Waltzing Daniel Considine. O'Connor—a talented amateur magician who enjoyed performing—saw vaudeville as another symbol of a colorful past giving way to homogeneity. After years of neglecting his family, Waltzing Daniel returns to his son Tom's home with the expectation that he will live out his days being looked after by a grateful child. His eccentric friends parade through Tom's home before the inevitable conflict erupts. Originally written as a play, and performed briefly on Broadway, *I Was Dancing* contains familiar O'Connor elements—a forceful male central figure, uproarious talk and anecdotage, a flawed father-son relationship, and a plot that resolves by sudden col-lapse. But, though entertaining, the story is simply too slim and the characters too broadly drawn to sustain lasting interest.

O'Connor's last finished work, *All in the Family* (1966) chron-icles a New England Irish Catholic family named Kinsella, whose patriarchal father pushes his sons into politics with a dream of someday winning the White House. Though it is a work of con-siderable narrative and psychological subtlety, the novel's liter-ary merits have been overshadowed by the judgment that it is merely a *roman à clef* about the Kennedys. Readers who focus on the Kennedy parallels miss the much richer story of the narrator, Jack Kinsella (a cousin of the political family), which weaves in and out of the family's electoral wrangling. This quieter narra-tive tracks Jack's warm childhood memories that end with his mother's apparent suicide, indirectly follows the processes of his marital estrangement and reconciliation, and concludes with the happy discovery that his wife is pregnant.

*All in the Family* is a novel of Irish America after the assimila-tion process. The overblown Irish characters who brought their eccentric energies to O'Connor's previous novels have vanished; the dominant ethnic theme in *All in the Family* is the family as the irreducible core of Irish life. The Irish in America may have "arrived" both politically and economically but their deepest experiences are lived out between parents and children, and among siblings. O'Connor's presentation of the Irish family is deliberately ambiguous. Though Jack's uncle effectively destroys the lives of his own children, Jack's own reconciliation and his impending parenthood remind us that families also bring heal-ing and a sense of purpose.

After *All in the Family,* O'Connor began work on "The Car-dinal," a novel about a dying Catholic prelate; this work-in-progress was included in the posthumous *The Best and Last of Edwin O'Connor* (1970). O'Connor also envisioned a novel about the first generation of Irish immigrants to New England, sug-gesting that he had come to think of his work as a larger project of rendering the full Irish-American experience.

O'Connor died on March 23, 1968, following a massive cere-bral hemorrhage. He is buried in Holyhood Cemetery in Brook-line, Massachusetts.

*See* Fiction, Irish-American

Richard A. Betts. "The 'Blackness of Life': The Function of Edwin O'Con-nor's Comedy" MELUS: The Journal of the Society for the Study of Multi-Ethnic Literature (Spring 1981).

David Dillon, "Priests and Politicians: The Fiction of Edwin O'Connor," in *Irish-American Fiction: Essays in Criticism,* ed., Daniel Casey and Robert Rhodes (New York, 1979).

John V. Kelleher, "Edwin O'Connor and the Irish-American Process," *Atlantic* (July 1968).

William Keough, "X-Rays of Irish America: Edwin O'Connor, Mary Gordon and William Kennedy," in *Memory, Narrative, and Identity: New Essays in Ethnic American Literature,* ed., Amritjit Singh, Joseph Skerrett, and Robert Hogan (Boston, 1994).

Edwin O'Connor, *The Oracle* (New York, 1951).

———, *The Last Hurrah* (Boston, 1956).

———, *The Edge of Sadness* (Boston, 1961).

———, *I Was Dancing* (Boston, 1964).

———, *All in the Family* (Boston,1966).

———, *The Best and Last of Edwin O'Connor* (Boston, 1970).

Hugh Rank, *Edwin O'Connor,* Twayne's United States Authors, No. 242, (New York, 1974).

JAMES SILAS ROGERS

## O'CONNOR, JOHN JOSEPH CARDINAL (1920– )

Cardinal Archbishop. John Joseph O'Connor's paternal grand-parents migrated from County Cork and County Roscommon in Ireland; his mother's ancestry was German. He was born in Phila-delphia, Pennsylvania, on January 15, 1920, and baptized at Saint Clement's Church. Developing his vocation under the guidance of the Christian Brothers at West Catholic High School, O'Con-nor received his priestly training at Saint Charles Borromeo Semi-nary in Overbrook and was ordained December 15, 1945.

Fr. O'Connor's ministry took a new direction when in 1950 he volunteered as a chaplain in the Korean conflict. He spent his career in the Navy, becoming Navy chief of chaplains in 1975 and retiring with the rank of Rear Admiral in 1979. During this pe-riod he developed communication methods that served him well later in life. He wrote his first book, *A Chaplain Looks at Vietnam* (1969), and developed a system for using closed-circuit tele-vision to provide devotional opportunities and education for naval personnel on duty aboard ships.

On May 27, 1979, in Rome, Pope John Paul II consecrated him a bishop and named him auxiliary in charge of military chaplains to Terence Cardinal Cooke, O'Connor's first official link with the Archdiocese of New York. In this position, O'Connor worked with Elie Wiesel to produce *In Defense of Life* (1981). O'Connor served on a five-member National Conference of Catholic Bish-ops committee to draft the 1983 pastoral letter *The Challenge of Peace: God's Promise and Our Response.* He became Bishop of Scranton May 10, 1983, archbishop of New York January 31, 1984, and cardinal May 25, 1985. In 1995, O'Connor notified Pope John Paul II that he had reached 75, the age at which the pope requested bishops offer to retire.

Until O'Connor's episcopate, New York prelates had distin-guished themselves as builders and as public leaders. O'Connor could not follow his predecessors' in construction records. O'Connor became archbishop during a difficult economic period. The New York stock markets, the engine for both city and national economies, suffered a serious drop in 1987 and did not fully recover until 1993. Demographics prevented what success the stock market did enjoy from reaching the archdiocese. White ethnics who had filled urban parishes since the early nineteenth century continued to leave. In some cases, they were replaced by Catholic immigrants who could not contribute to the same degree as their predecessors; in other cases, non-Catholics moved in where Catholics had been. O'Connor's initiatives consisted mostly of finding new uses for parish buildings; in 1986 he opened a portion of Saint Veronica's parish plant on Christopher Street in Greenwich Village as a hospice for AIDS patients, and the offices of the National Pastoral Life Center opened at 299 Elizabeth Street, in a building that had once been the parochial school for the Sicilian-American parish of Our Lady of Loreto and then a Holy Name shelter for men on the Bowery.

The Cardinal did continue the tradition of Archbishop Hughes and Cardinal Spellman in being a very public leader of the faithful. He took steps to prevent forces outside Catholicism from influencing the practice of the faith in his archdiocese. In 1984 he participated in a coalition that pressed, successfully, for the courts to overturn a municipal directive prohibiting sexual discrimination in employment, thus permitting the archdiocese to continue its policies regarding the employment of homosexuals. In 1986, he forbade parishes to sponsor Catholic speakers whose presentations conflicted with Catholic doctrine. He also turned the tables, and instead of protecting Catholicism from outside forces sought to change those outside forces. The Catholic League for Religious and Civil Rights, founded in 1973 to monitor anti-Catholicism in the media, the workplace, and educational institutions, moved to space in archdiocesan headquarters at 1011 First Avenue during O'Connor's tenure.

O'Connor made Catholic teaching more newsworthy by tying his expressions of it to public figures. In 1989, he co-authored a book with then-Mayor Edward I. Koch, *His Eminence and Hizzonor,* allowing him to reach a larger audience for his reflections on current events. In 1990, he warned Catholic politicians who favored abortion rights that they risked excommunication; he had public comments on two such politicians in particular: Governor Mario M. Cuomo and Representative Geraldine Ferraro, the latter in 1984, when she ran for vice-president on the Democratic ticket. He also protested the University of Notre Dame's plan to award its Laetare Medal to Senator Daniel Patrick Moynihan. By the 1990s, he had become so well known that he could attach his own name to an issue and thus make it well known. In 1998, he protested the major league baseball schedule, which scheduled games for Good Friday, and the local Little League baseball schedule, which scheduled games for Sunday morning. Others also used O'Connor to attract attention to their causes: in 1990 the activist group ACT-UP made him and Saint Patrick's Cathedral targets of a protest against what it perceived as the Church's lack of support for efforts to prevent AIDS by encouraging condom use.

The Cardinal's interest in Irish and Irish-American affairs provides examples of pastoral care via the media. In 1984, O'Connor was part of a four-prelate fact-finding mission to Northern Ireland that expressed concern over reported human rights violations in Northern Ireland and suggested the Americans press the British for a political solution to Ireland's troubles. The next year,

the Ancient Order of Hibernians named as grand marshal of the Saint Patrick's Day Parade Peter King, an Irish Republican Army supporter. The Cardinal's public acceptance of King, and his verbal support of those who "legitimately struggle for justice" upset others who feared that struggle might turn violent. (The 1985 grand marshal choice was further complicated by the candidacy of Dorothy Hayden Cuddahy, who would have been the first female grand marshal had not the AOH ruled that only male AOH members were eligible for the honor.) In 1988, O'Connor happened to be visiting Ireland with Koch when an IRA bomb killed (mistakenly, the IRA later announced) a Protestant family; O'Connor expressed his shock and asked for prayer. From 1987 to 1992, O'Connor opposed extraditing Joseph Patrick Doherty, a fugitive IRA member convicted in absentia of killing a British police officer.

The most persistent issue involved participation in the Saint Patrick's Day Parade of units marching under banners identifying them as Irish and Irish-American homosexuals and lesbians. In 1991, O'Connor broke with tradition by not greeting parade dignitaries, including Mayor David Dinkins, who was marching with an Irish homosexual group. In 1993, New York City also broke with tradition, awarding the parade permit not to the AOH but to the Saint Patrick's Day Parade Committee, an ad hoc group which planned to include homosexual and lesbian marching units. O'Connor claimed New York's decision encroached upon the separation of church and state, many long-time participants threatened to boycott, and the ad hoc committee ceded the permit to the AOH. In 1994, the AOH named Cardinal O'Connor honorary grand marshal of the 1995 parade. The parade became more of a media event than ever, used by some to rally around one set of values and by others as an occasion to challenge those values.

*See* Catholicism, Irish-American

Nat Hentoff, *John Cardinal O'Connor: At the Storm Center of a Changing American Catholic Church* (New York, 1988).

MARY ELIZABETH BROWN

## O'CONNOR, MARY AGNES (1815–1859)

Administrator, religious leader. Mary O'Connor was the youngest of ten children born to Patrick and Mary O'Connor of Kilkenny, Ireland. She was a vivacious, intelligent, and beautiful child who maintained both her spirit and fine intellect into maturity. Her physical beauty was marred, however, by dropsy, a disease which eventually took her life. Mary determined in her early twenties that she would forego offers of marriage and, instead, enter a religious congregation. She visited several convents in Dublin, finally presenting herself at the door of the Sisters of Mercy, Baggot Street, in 1838. Her preparation for reception and profession were conducted by Catherine McAuley, the foundress of the Sisters of Mercy.

At the age of twenty-nine, Mary Agnes O'Connor was sent to London to establish the fifth house of the Sisters of Mercy in England. While she was serving in that setting, Bishop John Hughes arrived at the St. Catherine's Convent in Dublin seeking Sisters of Mercy for his expanding New York diocese. Agnes O'Connor was called back from London and she and seven companions set sail for New York from Ireland on Easter Monday, April 13, 1846, arriving a month later. Under her gentle leadership, the spiritual and corporal works of mercy multiplied; a circulating library, a home for working women and a teacher training school were established. Her death on December 20, 1859, at the age of forty-five, was preceded by several years of gradual debilitation.

*See* Sisters of Mercy

M. Austin Carroll, *Leaves from the Annals of the Sisters of Mercy*, 4 vols. (New York, 1881, 1883, 1888, 1895).

HELEN MARIE BURNS, R.S.M.

## O'CONNOR, (Mary) FLANNERY (1925–1964)

Short-story writer, novelist, and essayist. Though decades have passed since Flannery O'Connor's death at 39, her uniquely crafted stories continue to startle and impress modern readers and critics alike. Considered to be one of America's most influential Southern writers, O'Connor displays a sharp ear for Southern dialect as she utilizes grotesque imagery, shocking characterization, violence, and bizarre, paradoxical irony, to focus upon themes of the action of grace upon man, redemption, original sin, and the resurrection of Christ.

Among O'Connor's most memorable "Christ-haunted" characters, are: Hulga, a one-legged intellectual who holds a Ph.D. in philosophy, who loses her artificial leg to a traveling Bible salesman in a hayloft; The Misfit, a former gospel singer who murders a grandmother for enjoyment because he is unable to believe in the resurrection of Christ; Hazel Motes, an Army veteran who returns home to immerse himself in sin until undergoing an agonizing transformation amid a world of complacent Christians; and Mr. Guizac, a hard-working, efficient, "displaced" farm-worker from Poland, whose murder by passive negligence demonstrates how evil moves into hearts in which there is an absence of love.

### CHILDHOOD AND IRISH CATHOLIC ROOTS

Mary Flannery O'Connor, the only child of Regina L. Cline and Edward F. O'Connor, Jr., was born into a devout Roman Catholic family in Savannah, Georgia, on March 25, 1925, where she attended St. Vincent's Grammar School and Sacred Heart Parochial School in Savannah.

Flannery O'Connor

She received notoriety at an early age when she was filmed by a Pathé News crew with a pet chicken that walked backwards. The news clip of five-year-old Mary Flannery with her pet chicken was shown in theaters across the country, and was undoubtedly instrumental in establishing her lifelong love of peacocks, ducks, and other fowl as pets.

Biographer Sally Fitzgerald traces O'Connor's roots to some of the first Irish Catholic settlers of Georgia. Her maternal great-grandfather, Hugh Donnelly Treanor, participated in the first Catholic Mass in Milledgeville in his hotel apartment in the 1840s, and his widow, Johannah Harty Treanor, donated the land for the city's Catholic church. O'Connor's grandfather, Peter James Cline, not only was a successful merchant and farmer, but served as Milledgeville's mayor for many years.

On Flannery O'Connor's paternal side, her great-grandfather, Patrick O'Connor, came from Ireland in the mid-1830s and established a wagon manufacturing company in Savannah. Her grandfather, Edward F. O'Connor, Sr., became a wealthy banker and investor and her father, Edward F. O'Connor, Jr., distinguished himself as an Army officer in France during World War I. He also served as Commander of the American Legion for Georgia in 1936, but—due to the poor business conditions of the Depression—he was never very successful in his real estate and construction businesses.

In March 1938, when Flannery O'Connor was 12, her father accepted a position with the Federal Housing Administration in Atlanta. The family moved to Atlanta, but within a few months, Flannery and her mother returned to the family home in Milledgeville. The home, with its tall white columns, had served for a short time as the Governor's mansion when Milledgeville was Georgia's capital and had been purchased in 1886 by Flannery O'Connor's grandfather.

Flannery O'Connor's father remained in Atlanta until 1940, when he became gravely ill and joined his wife and daughter in Milledgeville to recuperate. Only a few weeks before Flannery's sixteenth birthday, however, he died from complications arising from disseminated lupus erythematosus.

### YEARS AT GSCW AND IOWA

Upon graduation from Peabody High School in 1941, O'Connor chose to attend Georgia State College for Women (GSCW), located only a block from her home. She served as art editor for the campus newspaper *The Colonnade,* which often included her block print cartoons, and edited the literary magazine *The Corinthian* during her senior year. She graduated with an A.B. in Social Science in 1945.

That same year, she shortened her name from "Mary Flannery O'Connor" to "Flannery O'Connor" and applied for admission to the University of Iowa's graduate journalism program. She was accepted and began taking classes in the fall of 1945. Once there, O'Connor met with Paul Engle, director of the University's Writer's Workshop. Initially Engle was taken aback by O'Connor's almost unintelligible Georgia accent, but upon being shown some of her work, he immediately recognized her as a talented writer and encouraged her to transfer into his M.F.A. program.

While participating in the Iowa Writer's Workshop, O'Connor kept a very low profile. She rarely spoke in class and usually deferred the reading of her own work to others. However, her drive and talent were encouraged by Engle and visiting faculty. In 1946, she sold her first story "The Geranium" to *Accent* and in the following year, won the Rinehart-Iowa Fiction Award, which brought her a $750 honorarium and gave Rinehart the option to purchase her first novel. Using those and other funds, O'Connor remained at Iowa another year to complete her master's thesis, *The Geranium: A Collection of Short Stories.* She left Iowa in mid-1947 with her M.F.A. and excellent contacts that were to prove helpful throughout her career.

## NEW YORK AND CONNECTICUT AND LUPUS

A few months after leaving Iowa, O'Connor was invited in early 1948 to Yaddo, a prominent artists' colony in Saratoga Springs, New York. There she worked on her first novel *Wise Blood*, which she had begun at Iowa under Engle's direction, and met poet Robert Lowell, who introduced O'Connor to her future editor, Robert Giroux, and to the noted translator Robert Fitzgerald and his wife Sally.

O'Connor completed several draft chapters of *Wise Blood* at Yaddo, but was disappointed with the approach taken by her Rinehart editor, John Selby. As a result, she asked to be released from her contract and began working with Harcourt Brace.

O'Connor left Yaddo in March 1949 after she, Lowell and others became embroiled in a dispute in which Lowell had accused Yaddo Center Director Elizabeth Ames of being a Communist sympathizer. The Board rallied to Ames' cause and several writers left, including O'Connor, who moved into an apartment in New York City. A few months later, she accepted an offer from her friends, Robert and Sally Fitzgerald, to move into their garage apartment near Ridgefield, Connecticut.

During the first years after she left Iowa, O'Connor was hard at work: she saw three of her short stories published, and compiled drafts of several other stories that were to become chapters in her first novel, *Wise Blood.* Though O'Connor found living so near the Fitzgeralds to be pleasant and productive, in the fall of 1950, she complained of feeling a heaviness in her arms while typing. A local doctor suggested that she might have early signs of arthritis and he urged her to undergo a thorough medical examination during her next visit home.

In December 1950, during a train trip to Milledgeville to visit her mother, 25-year-old O'Connor became critically ill. A specialist diagnosed her as having disseminated lupus erythematosus, the same disease that had killed her father ten years earlier. O'Connor spent much of the following year receiving blood transfusions and shots of the experimental drug ACTH in the Emory University Hospital in Atlanta. She was finally released to the care of her mother during the summer of 1951.

O'Connor and her mother moved to a dairy farm a few miles north of Milledgeville that Mrs. O'Connor had inherited in 1947. That farm, "Andalusia," with its two-story white farmhouse, land, and various out-buildings, was to be her home for the rest of her life.

## AT ANDALUSIA

Once she regained the strength to do so, Flannery O'Connor devoted her mornings to writing while her mother ran the farm. The two then typically ate a midday meal, often at the Sanford House in Milledgeville, and returned home so O'Connor could rest, tend her peacocks and other fowl, and read or paint.

Though largely home-bound, O'Connor was certainly not a recluse. She corresponded with many friends and writers and she enjoyed entertaining visitors, from groups of school children, who came on school field trips to see the peacocks, burros,

cows and other farm animals, to aspiring and well-known writers, reporters, members of the clergy and friends. All were graciously greeted and welcomed as company.

Because of her frail health and her reliance upon crutches after 1953, travel for O'Connor was difficult. Still, she managed to make a trip to the shrine of Lourdes, gained an audience with Pope Pius XII in Rome in May 1958, and accepted opportunities to lecture at more than a dozen colleges and universities. Drafts of those lectures, which she usually read word-for-word, are carefully scrutinized by readers to discern the true intentions for her fiction.

Flannery O'Connor's writings, her meditative life on the farm, and the devoted attention and care she received from her mother served as the focal points for her life at Andalusia until her death. She died at 39, in Milledgeville, Georgia, August 3, 1964, from complications of her recently reactivated lupus. She lies buried next to her father and mother in Memory Hill Cemetery in Milledgeville.

## WRITINGS

During her years at Andalusia, O'Connor finished *Wise Blood* (Harcourt, Brace, 1952); her short story collection, *A Good Man Is Hard to Find and Other Stories* (Harcourt, Brace, 1955); *The Violent Bear It Away* (Farrar, Straus and Cudahy, 1960); the Introduction to *A Memoir of Mary Ann* (Farrar, Straus and Cudahy, 1962), and spent her last days working on stories for her posthumously published collection, *Everything That Rises Must Converge* (Farrar, Straus and Giroux, 1965).

After O'Connor's death, Robert and Sally Fitzgerald compiled and edited O'Connor's essays for *Mystery and Manners: Occasional Prose* (Farrar, Straus and Giroux, 1969). Two years later, Farrar, Straus and Giroux published *The Complete Stories*, with an introduction by Robert Giroux. Sally Fitzgerald's edited collection of O'Connor's letters, *The Habit of Being: Letters of Flannery O'Connor* (Farrar, Straus and Giroux), followed in 1979.

Other important compilations of O'Connor's work include her book reviews, compiled by Leo Zuber and edited by Carter Martin, *The Presence of Grace and Other Book Reviews by Flannery O'Connor* (U of Georgia Press, 1983); the O'Connor-Cheney correspondence in the Vanderbilt University Library, edited by C. Ralph Stephens, *The Correspondence of Flannery O'Connor and the Brainard Cheneys* (UP of Mississippi, 1986); and, Rosemary M. Magee's collection of O'Connor interviews, *Conversations with Flannery O'Connor* (UP of Mississippi, 1987).

## THE FLANNERY O'CONNOR COLLECTION

The *Flannery O'Connor Collection* at Georgia College & State University (GC&SU) serves as the principal repository for O'Connor's manuscripts and letters. That collection, most of which was given by her mother, Regina Cline O'Connor in 1971, includes a variety of materials of interest to scholars. The catalog of manuscripts in the collection is described by Stephen G. Driggers, Robert J. Dunn, and Sarah Gordon in *The Manuscripts of Flannery O'Connor at Georgia College* (U of Georgia Press, 1989).

The *Flannery O'Connor Memorial Room*, dedicated in 1974, contains many items donated by the family, including Victorian period furnishings from Andalusia and the several hundred books that comprised O'Connor's library at her death. Those books are cited and described in Arthur F. Kinney's, *Flannery O'Connor's Library: Resources of Being* (U of Georgia Press, 1985).

### AWARDS AND HONORS

O'Connor received many awards and honors for her writing, including: two *Kenyon Review* Fellowships (1953, 1954); a National Institute of Arts and Letters Grant (1957); a Ford Foundation Fellowship (1959); O. Henry First Prize awards for "Greenleaf" (1957), "Everything That Rises Must Converge" (1963), and "Revelation" (1964); a Henry H. Bellaman Foundation award in 1964; and, honorary degrees from St. Mary's College, Notre Dame (1962) and Smith College (1963). Most significantly, her posthumously published *Complete Stories* (1971) won the National Book Award for Fiction in 1972.

### TELEVISION, FILM, AND DRAMATIC PRODUCTIONS

Two of O'Connor's stories were produced for television: "The Life You Save May Be Your Own" starring Gene Kelly (1957), and Horton Foote's adaptation of "The Displaced Person," as part of the *American Short Story Series* in 1976.

John Huston's noteworthy film version of *Wise Blood*, produced by Michael and Kathy Fitzgerald and based upon Benedict Fitzgerald's screenplay, was distributed by New Line Cinema in 1980.

Cecil Dawkins' dramatic adaptation of selections from five O'Connor short stories, titled *The Displaced Person*, was produced in New York's American Place Theater in 1966 and again by the Theatrical Outfit of Atlanta in 1998.

### BIBLIOGRAPHIES AND CRITICISM

Two principal bibliographies relate to O'Connor's work: (1) David Farmer's *Flannery O'Connor: A Descriptive Bibliography* (Garland, 1981) which cites and describes various editions and translations of her writings; and, (2) Robert F. Golden and Mary C. Sullivan's, *Flannery O'Connor and Caroline Gordon: A Reference Guide* (G.K. Hall, 1977), the first half of which describes books and articles about O'Connor's life and work. While Martha E. Cook's bibliographical essay on O'Connor in *American Women Writers: Bibliographical Essays* (Greenwood Press, 1983, pp. 269-96), serves as a helpful starting point for beginning scholars, *The Flannery O'Connor Bulletin*, published since 1972, is the principal scholarly journal focusing on O'Connor's life and work.

### SIGNIFICANCE OF O'CONNOR'S WORK

By drawing upon the strengths of such writers as Sophocles, Dante, Henry James, Nathaniel Hawthorne, Edgar Allan Poe, William Butler Yeats, James Joyce and William Faulkner, O'Connor has—in turn—exerted considerable influence upon the styles and approaches of such contemporary writers as Walker Percy, Alice Walker, Alice Munro, Joyce Carol Oates, and Harry Crews.

Adding to her reputation is the fact that the list of articles, books, dissertations and theses that explore the nature of her life and work now numbers in the thousands and that her stories are represented in virtually every introductory literature anthology used in American colleges and universities.

While more than a few Southern writers have focused upon religious themes, none has done so in quite the manner as O'Connor. Her interest in the effect of God's grace upon the complacent Christian and her pursuit of this theme deep into the hearts and minds of her readers has one very specific goal: to turn her reader toward Christ for guidance and redemption.

Stating, "for the hard of hearing you shout, and for the almost-blind you draw large and startling figures," O'Connor used cutting satire to support acts of violence in her work. That use, though intentional, is by no means gratuitous. Instead, it is used to shock readers into the realization that their own intellectual abilities are far too limited to provide a clear understanding of the nature of the universe and to urge them to carefully consider Christ's offer of redemption.

The genius of O'Connor's writing lies in how she uses straightforward, simple prose to lure her readers into the inner world of her characters. Then, once there, she hopes they will recognize—in these characters' evil and sinful ways—their own flawed character and look to Christ for redemption and deliverance.

Despite the unusual nature of her themes, she has an established reputation as one of America's most important Southern fiction writers.

Frederick Asals, *Flannery O'Connor: The Imagination of Extremity* (Athens, 1982).

Jill P. Baumgaertner, *Flannery O'Connor: A Proper Scaring* (Wheaton, Ill., 1988).

Harold Bloom, ed. and intro., *Flannery O'Connor* (New York, 1986).

Robert H. Brinkmeyer, Jr., *The Art and Vision of Flannery O'Connor* (Baton Rouge, 1989).

John F. Desmond, *Risen Sons: Flannery O'Connor's Vision of History* (Athens, 1987).

Kathleen Feeley, *Flannery O'Connor: Voice of the Peacock* (New Brunswick, N.J., 1972).

Sally Fitzgerald, "Root and Branch," *Georgia Historical Quarterly* 64/4 (1980): 377–87.

*The Flannery O'Connor Bulletin* (1972– ).

Melvin J. Friedman and Beverly Lyon Clark, eds., *Critical Essays on Flannery O'Connor* (Boston, 1985).

Marshall Bruce Gentry, *Flannery O'Connor's Religion of the Grotesque* (Jackson, 1986).

Richard Giannone, *Flannery O'Connor and the Mystery of Love* (Urbana, 1989).

James A. Grimshaw, Jr., *The Flannery O'Connor Companion* (Westport, Conn., 1981).

Suzanne Morrow Paulson, *Flannery O'Connor: A Study of the Short Fiction* (Boston, 1988).

Brian Abel Ragen, *A Wreck on the Road to Damascus: Innocence, Guilt, and Conversion in Flannery O'Connor* (Chicago, 1989).

Sura Rath and Mary Neff Shaw, eds., *Flannery O'Connor: New Perspectives* (Athens, 1996).

Carol Shloss, *Flannery O'Connor's Dark Comedies: The Limits of Inference* (Baton Rouge, 1980).

Ted R. Spivey, *Flannery O'Connor: The Woman, the Thinker, the Visionary* (Macon, Ga., 1995).

Martha Stephens, *The Question of Flannery O'Connor* (Baton Rouge, 1973).

R. NEIL SCOTT & MARIE F. HARPER

## O'CONNOR, MICHAEL (1810–1872)

First Bishop of Pittsburgh (1843) and first Bishop of Erie (1853). Michael O'Connor was born at Cobh in County Cork, Ireland, on September 27, 1810, and died in Woodstock, Maryland, on October 18, 1872. The son of Charles and Ellen (Kirk) O'Connor, and the brother of James (1823–90), first Bishop of Omaha, he came from one of eight families (Bolands, Carrolls, Foleys, Hurleys, Kenricks, Lenihans, O'Connors, and Shanahans) with brother bishops of Irish descent in the United States. Educated at the College of Propaganda in Rome, he was ordained a priest on June 1, 1833, and received his doctoral degree in theology on March 31, 1834.

## TWICE A FIRST BISHOP

Less than ten years later, on August 15, 1843, Michael was consecrated bishop in St. Agatha's Chapel at the Irish College in Rome by Giacomo Filippo Cardinal Frasconi. Though interested in entering the Society of Jesus, Michael had obeyed Pope Gregory XVI and became Bishop of Pittsburgh before pursuing his preference to become a Jesuit. While O'Connor's role in Erie was short-lived (1853–54), he achieved prominence as the Bishop of Pittsburgh. During his tenure there for slightly more than fifteen years (1843–53, 1854–60), O'Connor set up parishes, built churches, including his own cathedral, encouraged schools and colleges, founded a diocesan weekly and a seminary, and welcomed religious groups, especially the Sisters of Mercy under the leadership of Mother Frances Xavier Warde in 1843.

## A PIONEERING JESUIT

He finally fulfilled his ambition to become a Jesuit on December 22, 1860, when he entered the novitiate of the Society of Jesus at Gorheim, in Sigmaringen, Germany. He became a pioneer in race relations in the American hierarchy when, as a bishop, he had opened the Chapel of the Nativity for black Catholics at Pittsburgh, on June 30, 1844. O'Connor continued this work when he returned to the United States as a Jesuit by obtaining funds to establish Baltimore's St. Francis Xavier Church in 1863. This church, the first opened exclusively for black Catholics in the United States, became the house of worship for a black Catholic community which can today trace its origins back to 1793.

*See* Pittsburgh

Charles N. Branson, Jr., *Ordinations of U. S. Catholic Bishops, 1790–1989* (Washington, 1990).
"Father Michael O'Connor," *Woodstock Letters*, 2 (1873): 59–69.
Andrew A. Lambing, *A History of the Catholic Church in the Diocese of Pittsburgh and Allegheny* (New York, 1880).
Henry A. Szarnicki, *Michael O'Connor, First Catholic Bishop of Pittsburgh, 1843–1860* (Pittsburgh, 1975).

VINCENT A. LAPOMARDA, S.J.

## O'CONOR, HUGO (1734–1779)

Soldier, administrator, governor. O'Conor was the first Irish soldier to enter and see action in the American West. This native of Dublin was exiled from Ireland after an unsuccessful "rising" in 1848. As a member of the "Wild Geese," O'Conor eventually journeyed to Spain and joined their military, rising quickly through the ranks to become a colonel. Most of his enlistment was served in the New World and between 1765 and 1776 O'Conor was stationed in the American Southwest serving in what today is Texas and Arizona. He led several successful military expeditions against both Apaches and Comanches whose skills and resolve would necessitate the services of other Irish soldiers nearly one hundred years later. One of O'Conor's last acts in the West came during his tenure as Commandant Inspector of the Interior Provinces when he established a *presidio* or fort in what soon became Tucson, Arizona. Although this post was not named for its founder, other forts established in the next century

did bear Irish names and honor Irish and Irish-American soldiers. These include Fort Connor, Fort Keogh, Fort Meagher, and Fort Kearny.

Robert W. Frazer, *Forts of the West* (Norman, Ok., 1965).
Mary Lu Moore and Delmar L. Beene, "The Interior Provinces of New Spain: The Report of Hugo O'Conor, January 30, 1776," *Arizona and the West*, 13 (Fall 1971): 265–75.
David M. Vigness, "Don Hugo O'Conor and New Spain's Northeastern Frontier, 1764–1776," *Journal of the West*, 6 ( January 1967): 27–40.

KEVIN STANTON

## O'DOHERTY, BRIAN (1935–  )

Artist, writer, film producer, art administrator. Brian O'Doherty was born in Ballaghderrin, Co. Roscommon, in 1935. He trained as a medical doctor in University College Dublin, followed by post-graduate studies in experimental psychology at Cambridge University in England. From his early student days, he began to attract attention as a painter and at seventeen years of age was included in the 1951 Irish Exhibition of Living Art. With the assistance of the artist Jack B. Yeats he secured a scholarship to Harvard in 1957 where he graduated with a master's in science. In 1960 he married the art historian Barbara Novak.

It was in America that his career as an artist gathered momentum. From that time, too, he began to establish a reputation as an influential and perceptive art critic. By the mid-1960s Brian O'Doherty's own art began to emerge in a number of highly individual conceptual idioms which today as then continue to expand the parameters of artistic enquiry. In 1969 he was appointed director of the Visual Arts Programme for the National Endowment for the Arts (NEA) in Washington, D.C. In this influential capacity he affected a whole decade of artistic development by financially supporting "uncommerical" experimental art practice. From 1977 to 1996 he was director of the Media Arts Programme (NEA) and encouraged similar creativity in film and video. His own innovative film on Edward Hopper, *Hopper's Silence*, gained him the Grand Prix at the 1981 Montreal International Festival of Films on Art. He was adjunct professor, Barnard College, Columbia University, from 1970 to 1997 and was later professor of Fine Art & Media, Southampton College, Long Island University.

## ARTIST

As an artist in the late 1960s Brian O'Doherty was a central figure in the conceptual experiment among a group that included Sol Le Witt, Eva Hesse, Dorothea Rockburne, Robert Smithson, Dan Graham and composer Morton Feldman. However, in the context of the last thirty years, he has carved out his own distinct place within the sphere of postminimalist conceptual art. Of signal importance in the history of conceptual art is O'Doherty's "Portrait of Marcel Duchamp" (1966), whose heartbeat he recorded on a cardiograph machine and which was the inspiration for an eighteen-part series of drawings and motorized box sculpture where the heartbeat appears as a dot of light. These works were shown at the Corcoran Gallery of Art in Washington, D.C., to coincide with the major Duchamp retrospective at MOMA in 1974.

In 1967, O'Doherty curated "Aspen 5+6," a conceptual exhibition in the form of a multimedia magazine of writings, recordings and visual art pieces which explored conceptual principles and which included contributions he commissioned from such heroes of the younger generation as Marcel Duchamp, Naum Gabo, Susan Sontag, Roland Barthes, Michell Butor, Sol Le Witt and a recording of excerpts from Beckett texts read by Irish actor Jack McGowran. It also included one of Brian O'Doherty's own "structural plays" and an introduction written by one of his pseudonyms, Sigmund Bode. This portable museum, according to art critic Dorothy Walker, presented "one of the key works of the conceptual movement in the United States."

In 1972 Brian O'Doherty changed his artistic name to Patrick Ireland as a response to the events which took place on Bloody Sunday that year in Derry, Northern Ireland, when British paratroopers killed thirteen civil rights marchers. As an artist for whom a central line of inquiry has been the question of identity, his renouncement of his own name was a profound protest aimed at drawing international attention to the event. The artist vowed that all his art would from then on appear under the name Patrick Ireland until such time "as the British military presence is withdrawn from Northern Ireland and all the citizens are granted their civil rights."

An exhibition in Derry (1998) further revealed that in addition to the artistic Patrick Ireland pseudonym, Brian O'Doherty the writer, also conducted his life through a number of other identities. Each of the five are separate, distinct and hitherto were largely undisclosed to the public. There are four men and one woman: Brian O'Doherty (b.1934), Sigmund Bode (b.1949), Patrick Ireland (b.1972), William Maginn (1793–1842) and Mary Josephson (b.1950), "all telling the same truth and lie."

Throughout his career, O'Doherty/Ireland's work has been informed by a fascination with linear configurations, grids, systems, the use of codes, the ancient Irish Ogham alphabet and the motif of the labyrinth. Since 1973, in further extension of such investigations, the artist has evolved the "Rope Drawings" which explore the linear mapping of space and the intrinsic role of the spectator's vantage point.

ART CRITIC AND WRITER

As an art critic, Brian O'Doherty launched into the national scene in the U.S. in the late 1950s with a pioneering series of television programmes, in conjunction with the Museum of Fine Arts, Boston and later with the NBC "Today" show. He was art critic for *The New York Times* and *Newsweek* during the 1960s and 1970s, editor of *Art in America* from 1970–74 and contributed to *Arts Magazine*, *Art International* and many other publications. Throughout the 1960s O'Doherty's writing both plumbed and charted the maelstrom of American art development of the period from Abstract Expressionism through Pop, Op, Kinetic, Object, Minimal, Funk, Land, Body, Performance and Conceptual art. In 1967 he published *Object and Idea*, an anthology of criticism that established him as one of the foremost critics of the period, at a time when New York was the crucible of much questioning and debate about the direction art was taking. O'Doherty's *Inside the White Cube: Ideology of the Gallery Space* is an analysis of the sociological, economic and aesthetic context within which we experience art. This series of essays, later printed as a book, exerted enormous influence on curators and artists of the day and prompted the writer Barbara Rose to observe: "These essays mark a turning point in artistic perception." In 1988 the artist published *American Masters: The Voice and the Myth*, on the lives and work of eight giants of American art, including Hopper, Rothko, de Kooning and Pollock.

As a recent novelist, O'Doherty won the British Society of Authors Award in 1992 for his novel *The Strange Case of Mademoiselle P.*

Patrick Ireland, *Patrick Ireland: Gestures Instead of an Autobiography* (Youngstown, Ohio, 1994).

Liam Kelly, *Thinking Long: Contemporary Art in the North of Ireland* (Kinsale, Co. Cork, 1996).

Lucy Lippard (essayist), *Patrick Ireland: Drawings, 1965–85* (National Museum of American Art, 1986).

Victoria Newhouse, *Towards a New Museum* (London, 1998).

Jan Van Der Marck (essayist), *Patrick Ireland: Labyrinths, Language, Pyramids and Related Acts* (Madison, 1993).

Dorothy Walker, *Modern Art in Ireland* (Dublin, 1997).

CHRISTINA KENNEDY

## O'DONNELL, EMMETT, JR. ("Rosy") (1906–1971)

Air Force general. Emmett O'Donnell was born in 1906 to a Brooklyn, N.Y., high school English schoolteacher, Emmett O'Donnell, Sr., and Veronica Tobin. O'Donnell attended Manual Training High School in Brooklyn and when he graduated in 1924, he was accepted into the United States Military Academy at West Point. There he earned the nickname "Rosy" because of his often flushed and reddish face. An excellent athlete, he graduated in 1928 and was commissioned a second lieutenant in the infantry. O'Donnell then decided to enter pilot training for the Army Air Corps and by 1930 joined the First Pursuit Group. In the following December, O'Donnell married Lorraine Muller with whom he had three children.

After his first two assignments, O'Donnell attended Air Corps Tactical School at Maxwell Field in Alabama (1940) and was assigned to the Eleventh Bombardment Group at Hickam Field, Hawaii. In the following September, O'Donnell led a squadron of nine B-17 bombers across the western Pacific to the Philippines, thus demonstrating the reach of the B-17 in the South Pacific. O'Donnell was instantly a part of the action when the Japanese attacked Pearl Harbor. Just three days after the catastrophe, O'Donnell had already won the Distinguished Flying Cross by leading a B-17 raid against the Japanese in Northern Luzon. In the following year, O'Donnell was transferred to operations in the Far East, where he was soon evacuated as the Japanese closed in on Java. In India, O'Donnell was operations officer for the Tenth Air Force which flew supply missions over the Himalayas into China. His next assignment took him to the advisory council of General Henry "Hap" Arnold, commander of the Army Air Forces, but he soon requested a return to action. He was therefore assigned command of the Seventy-Third Bombardment Wing as a brigadier general. O'Donnell led his 111 B-29s in the first raid against Tokyo for the Twenty-first Bomber Command.

After the war, O'Donnell was promoted to major general in 1948. He served in various capacities in the United States until in August he became commander of the Fifteenth Air Force. By June of 1950 the Korean War brought O'Donnell to Japan where his Far East Bomber Command conducted so many B-29 bombing missions over North Korea that there were few strategic targets left to demolish. His brief for the Senate claimed that "everything is destroyed. There is nothing standing worthy of the name." After a series of disagreements with his superiors over strategy, O'Donnell was rotated back to the United States early in 1951. By May of 1953 O'Donnell was deputy chief of staff for personnel as a lieutenant general and then promoted to full general and commander in chief of the Pacific Air Forces in May of 1959. After advocating support for South Vietnam's war against the Viet Cong, O'Donnell retired in July of 1963 and died eight years later in McLean, Va., in 1971.

W. F. Craven and J. L. Cate, *The Army Air Forces in World War II,* vols. I and V (Chicago: University of Chicago Press, 1948 and 1953).

82d Congress, 1st session, *Hearings on the Military Situation in the Far East* (1951).

Robert F. Futrell, *The United States Air Force in Korea 1950–1953* (New York: Duell, Sloan and Pearce, 1961).

Obituary, *New York Times* and *Washington Post* (December 27, 1971).

DANIEL J. KUNTZ

## O'DONNELL, KENNETH P. (1924–1977)

White House Special Assistant. Kenneth P. (Kenny) O'Donnell was born in Worcester, Massachusetts, March 4, 1924, son of Cleo and Alice M.(Guerin) O'Donnell. He served during World War II as an Army Air Force bombardier, flying thirty missions over Europe. He studied at Harvard under the G.I. Bill, captained the 1948 football team, and was graduated in 1949 with a degree in politics and government. At Harvard, O'Donnell developed a close friendship with Robert F. Kennedy, and campaigned for his brother, John F. Kennedy, when the latter entered politics in 1946 as a candidate for Congress. O'Donnell remained close to the Kennedys and assisted in other Kennedy campaigns. In time he became a central figure in the network of Kennedy intimates that the media dubbed the "Irish Mafia."

O'Donnell first went to Washington in 1957 as a special assistant to the Senate committee investigating racketeering in labor and management, being brought there by Robert Kennedy, who had taken over as chief consul. O'Donnell was in business at the time in Boston.

President Kennedy brought him into the White House in 1960 as his "appointments secretary." Despite his modest title, O'Donnell exercised a wide range of responsibilities, acting as liaison to the FBI and Secret Service, handling the logistics of Kennedy's travels, and controlling access to the Oval Office. Kennedy press secretary Pierre Salinger termed him the most powerful member of the White House staff, and writer Joe McCarthy described him as "the President's political right hand, troubleshooter, expediter and devil's advocate."

O'Donnell was in charge of the political arrangements for President Kennedy's fateful trip to Texas in November 1963, and was in the car behind Kennedy when he was shot in Dallas. It was O'Donnell who, circumventing local authorities, demanded that the body be returned immediately to Washington aboard Air Force One.

Though O'Donnell had opposed the choice of Lyndon B. Johnson as Kennedy's running mate, he remained as a member of the Johnson administration, acting as a link to Democratic leaders in the Northeast and Midwest. He resigned January 16, 1965, the last of the Kennedy team to depart the Johnson administration, and launched his own public-relations and management firm.

O'Donnell strongly supported the idea of Robert Kennedy's challenging the incumbent Johnson for the presidency in 1968, contending, as one Kennedy biographer records, that Johnson was a bully and a coward who would run away from a fight.

Johnson indeed did withdraw, and Kennedy did run. O'Donnell managed the campaign that ended with Kennedy's assassination in Los Angeles.

In 1966 O'Donnell stood for governor of Massachusetts, but was defeated by some 100,000 votes in the Democratic primary by Edward McCormack, nephew of John W. McCormack, Speaker of the House. A factor in the race was the neutrality of Senator Edward M. Kennedy, who was anxious not to alienate the Speaker. A second gubernatorial effort in 1970 was also unsuccessful.

O'Donnell died at 54 in Boston's Beth Israel Hospital, September 9, 1977.

*See* Kennedy, John Fitzgerald

*The Boston Globe* (September 10, 1977).

Nelson Lichtenstein, et al., eds., *Political Profiles, The Kennedy and the Johnson Years* (New York, 1976).

Kenneth P. O'Donnell and David F. Powers, *Johnny, We Hardly Knew Ye* (New York, 1970).

Arthur M. Schlesinger Jr., *Robert Kennedy and His Times* (Boston, 1978).

JOHN DEEDY

## O'DONOVAN ROSSA, JEREMIAH (1831–1915)

Fenian. He was born in County Cork and at an early age left the farm and opened a grocery business in Skibbereen. In the small town he was known for his sharp intelligence and patriotic political interests. In 1856 he founded the Phoenix Literary and Debating Society, which became his political forum, and two years later he joined the Irish Republican Brotherhood. In 1859 he was arrested and jailed for sedition. After his release he became widely respected in Fenian circles, and in 1862 he won a by-election in Tipperary but was denied his parliamentary seat as he was a convicted felon. Also in this year, James Stephen, the founder-leader of the I.R.B., appointed him business manager of the Fenian paper, the *Irish People*.

He was arrested again in 1865 and spent six years in prison where he and other Fenians were brutally treated. Upon his release in 1871, he emigrated to America where he edited the *United Irishmen* and wrote the first volume of his memoirs, *O'Donovan*

Jeremiah
O'Donovan Rossa

*Rossa's Prison Life* (1878). He was very active in Fenian and Clan na Gael politics and organized the Skirmishing Fund (1875) to finance American Fenianism and militant activities. Strong-willed and argumentative, he alienated himself from most of the leaders of Irish nationalism and split with Clan na Gael in 1880. In 1884 his name appeared on a novel, *Edward O'Donnell, A Story of Ireland* (but it was actually written by his friend Edward Moran), and *Rossa's Recollections 1838–1896* appeared in 1898. By then he was politically a spent force with few friends, little influence and a drinking problem.

But his name was fresh and green in Ireland, and when he died in June 1915, his body was returned to his homeland for burial. In Glasnevan Cemetery, Padraic Pearse made his famous oration at the grave of O'Donovan Rossa: "The fools, the fools, they have given us our Fenian dead, and while Ireland holds these graves, Ireland unfree will never be at rest." And Jeremiah O'Donovan Rossa became the symbol of Irish nationalism, remembered wherever Pearse's words are invoked.

*See* Fenians and Clan na Gael; Devoy, John

R. F. Foster, *Modern Ireland: 1600–1972* (London and New York, 1988).
Louis McRedmond, ed., *Modern Irish Lives* (Dublin, 1996).
Desmond Ryan, *The Fenian Chief: A Biography of James Stephen* (Dublin, 1967).

MICHAEL GLAZIER

## O'DOWD NIALL (1953– )

Publisher. Niall O'Dowd is founding publisher of *Irish America* magazine and the *Irish Voice* newspaper, the two largest and most prominent Irish-American publications. He was also the founder of the Irish-American peace delegation which helped bring about the August 1994 IRA ceasefire.

On his role, the London *Observer* newspaper, in an article on March 26, 1995, stated that he was "at the hub of Clinton's secret diplomacy between the various factions in Irish America, between the White House and the government in Dublin and Sinn Fein in Belfast."

He is currently an analyst on Northern Ireland affairs for CNN, *The Irish Times* and *Ireland on Sunday* newspaper. He has also appeared on all the major networks discussing the Northern Ireland peace process and has written on Irish affairs for *The New York Times.*

O'Dowd is a native of Co. Tipperary and a graduate of University College Dublin. After a spell as a high school teacher he emigrated to the United States and founded an Irish-American newspaper in San Francisco in 1979.

In 1985 he moved to New York and founded *Irish America,* the first ever successful Irish-American magazine. *The New York Times* described it as "a sleek success story, indicative of the newfound confidence among the American Irish."

Among the successful features that he founded in the magazine were the "Top 100 Irish-Americans" and the "Business 100," both of which lists identified Irish-Americans of diverse backgrounds and accomplishments who had contributed much both to the U.S. and to their ancestral land. President Bill Clinton personally accepted the "Irish American of the Year" award from *Irish America* in 1996.

In 1987 he founded the weekly *Irish Voice,* the first new Irish weekly in over sixty years. A key focus of the new newspaper was the drive to legalize tens of thousands of young Irish living in undocumented status in the United States. The situation was redressed with the Donnelly and Morrison visa programs, and the *Irish Voice* played a prominent role in ensuring their passage.

Long believing that the U.S. could play a key role in bringing peace to Northern Ireland, in 1992 O'Dowd founded "Irish-Americans for Clinton/Gore" after meeting with the candidates. Later that year, he led a group of four Irish-Americans to Northern Ireland, including two leading Irish-American businessmen, and brokered a 10-day IRA ceasefire which was used as a direct signal to the U.S. government that the IRA were interested in coming in from the cold.

Through the lead-up to the ceasefire he was the key conduit for Sinn Fein leader Gerry Adams to the White House and leading politicians such as Senator Edward Kennedy. In addition, he helped establish contacts for leading American politicians and businessmen with major figures on the Loyalist paramilitary side and among the mainstream Unionist parties.

Later, he and businessman Bill Flynn put together the strategy to have Sinn Fein leader Gerry Adams come to the United States to address a conference hosted by Flynn's group, the National Committee on American Foreign Policy. Following the granting of the visa, Adams later told the media that the visa had "moved the Irish peace process forward by one year."

*See* Journalism, Irish-American

## O'DWYER, PAUL (1907–1998)

Lawyer and politician. Paul O'Dwyer was born June 29, 1907, the eleventh and last child of Bridget McNicholas and Patrick O'Dwyer, both school teachers, in Lismirrane, Parish of Bohala, County Mayo, Ireland. From there, the future lawyer and New York City Council President brought memories of hard work in bogs, a deep love of family and Ireland, and an acute sense of wrongs suffered by the oppressed. All these were in baggage that Paul O'Dwyer carried to New York when he arrived on April 21, 1925. He enrolled the following year in St. John's Law School. Following the execution of the anarchist-pacifists Nicola Sacco and Bartelomeo Vanzetti, he wrote "There is no one to protest

Paul O'Dwyer

against the legal lynching of two defenseless immigrants, made martyrs, in our America," but O'Dwyer *would* protest. Sympathy with and relationship to the less privileged and the less acceptable became a hallmark of his career. He usually ran against the current.

O'Dwyer graduated from St. John's in 1931, in the midst of the Depression. His legal career began by defending pickets against injunctions, alien agitators against deportation, and the rights of unionists to organize. In 1932, Paul O'Dwyer joined what would become the still-existing firm of O'Dwyer and Bernstien. The firm became a classroom. Here came John L. Lewis, president of the United Mine Workers of America, and actors like Barry Fitzgerald fresh from the Abbey Theatre, Dublin. He was active in the Mayo Men's Patriotic and Benevolent Association and was elected president at the age of twenty-five.

The real test of O'Dwyer's legal capabilities and his support for unpopular causes came during the Cold War and heated attacks against Communists and supposed allies. O'Dwyer, often being attacked for "red-sympathies," replied by becoming more active in the National Lawyers Guild, and its president in 1947, and on the national board of directors from 1948 to 1951. He fought to rescind President Harry Truman's Executive Loyalty Order, part of a "national witch-hunt," and a threat to "civil liberties in America." He was attacked by Edward Q. Curran, president of the International Catholic Truth Society, and editors of the Catholic newspaper, *The Tablet*, as well as T.V. personality Ed Sullivan.

In 1949, he defended members of the Guild before the House Un-American Activities Committee (H.U.A.C.). He represented playwright Lillian Hellman and actor Paul Robeson, when they were accused or physically attacked by, as O'Dwyer wrote, "hooligans."

In 1948, he was asked to run for Congress from the Washington Heights-Inwood district. He received American Labor Party and Democratic Party support, but this was a flawed alliance. The American Labor Party supported Henry Wallace as Progressive Party candidate for president and Democrats backed incumbent Harry Truman. Charges that O'Dwyer was a Communist eroded Irish support. His denial of such accusations were of little use, as were his often stated support of the Constitution. He was not elected.

In 1960, he again attempted to gain the Democratic nomination for Congress, but failed this time, partly because he was William O'Dwyer's brother, the former Mayor of New York City who was accused of association with organized crime, and partly for his long history of left-wing, radical affiliations.

When John Kennedy received the Democratic presidential nomination in 1962, O'Dwyer was co-chairman of his New York state campaign, having been chosen by Robert Kennedy. In that year, reform Democrats asked O'Dwyer to run for United States Senator, opposing incumbent Jacob Javits. Despite a spirited primary campaign, O'Dwyer did not succeed. The following year O'Dwyer was asked to run for councilman-at-large for Manhattan, one of two newly created posts on the City Council. He managed to gain Democratic support and was elected to the Council. Here he gained new success and was able to enact, with strong union pressure, a minimum-wage law. He left the Council at the end of his two-year term.

In 1963, members of the National Association for the Advancement of Colored People (N.A.A.C.P.) conducting a civil rights struggle asked O'Dwyer to assist in defending Lois Chaffee, a college teacher accused of inciting riot. In Jackson, Mississippi,

he argued that her arrest violated civil rights. Eventually, with a reduced charge and a fine, Chaffee was freed.

O'Dwyer also supported and worked for extending the franchise to all and participated in the work of the Mississippi Freedom Democratic Party (hereinafter "F.D.P."). As a delegate to the 1964 Democratic Presidential Convention, he led a bitter fight to seat F.D.P. members. A compromise to allow such delegates to be admitted as guests was supported by Lyndon Johnson and Martin Luther King, but was rejected by O'Dwyer and other F.D.P. members. "These delegates did not come to Atlantic City," retorted O'Dwyer, "to ride in the back of the bus." Although unsuccessful in 1964, by 1968 convention rules were changed to allow full representation. He also found himself in opposition to American involvement in the Vietnamese War and in 1972 threw his support to Eugene McCarthy as Democratic nominee for president. O'Dwyer received the Democratic nomination for United States Senate. Disarray in the party which chose Hubert Humphrey helped his defeat in November, as well as Paul O'Dwyer's. Trying again for political office, he lost the contest for Democratic nominee for state senate in 1970, but as in 1968 carried New York City. Then he was called upon to defend a number of Catholic priests and nuns, "the Harrisburg Seven," accused of anti-war conspiracy. After a bitter fight, most charges were dropped.

In 1973, O'Dwyer sought the City Council President's office. This time with support from reform Democrats, trade unions as well as that of Irish weeklies and minority papers, he was successful despite the opposition from *The New York Times* and regular members of the party.

He became involved in the endless private and public battles centered around state allocations of funds to "short falls" in the budget. After months of negotiations, a Municipal Assistance Corporation "Big Mac" was established, which created long-term bonds. O'Dwyer opposed the plan since banks were not committed to purchase any bonds, but could set social policy.

His love of city history was critical in creating a new archival management department, that of Records and Information Services (D.O.R.I.S.). The often horrendous condition of city archives had caused loss of valuable records. Noticing the date 1664 on the city seal and flag, which marked the time of surrender of New Netherland to the British, O'Dwyer successfully introduced a bill in the City Council changing the date to 1625, a year which saw the founding of New Amsterdam and the future New York City. This, he argued, was not "twisting the lion's tail," but celebrating the early creation of the city.

With his term as Council President ended, O'Dwyer thought again of a run in 1976 for United States Senate, but found his way blocked by the growing popularity of Daniel P. Moynihan. He attempted to retain his council seat, but was defeated in the Democratic primary by State Senator Carol Bellamy. Being defeated by a woman, he thought, was some solace for this champion of women's rights.

Throughout his career, he always returned to his law practice and to promoting Irish cultural and political causes. From 1948 to 1956, plans were formed for an Irish Cultural Institute as a center for Irish activities in the United States and Ireland. John F. Kennedy spoke before the group in 1956. O'Dwyer was the first president of the Institute which also raised money for victims of troubles in Northern Ireland.

In 1984, he helped found the Irish Roundtable and Irish Institute. He was appointed Manhattan Borough Historian in 1986, and was the moving force behind publication of *The New York Irish* in 1996. In 1990 he was appointed New York City Commissioner to the United Nations and had the Brehan Law Society admitted to that body as a nongovernmental organization.

O'Dwyer was an early and staunch ally of the State of Israel and in 1948 helped persuade President Truman to recognize that nation's independence.

The immigrant from Ireland, poor in wealth, but rich in spirit, created a legend of courage and service to society—a defense counsel in the cause of civil rights and justice. The great progressive died at his home in Goshen, New York, on June 12, 1998.

*See* New York City

"Biographical Resource File," Municipal Reference & Research Center, 31 Chambers Street, New York.

Paul O'Dwyer, *Counsel for the Defense, the Autobiography of Paul O'Dwyer* (New York, 1979).

LEO HERSHKOWITZ

## O'DWYER, WILLIAM (1890–1964)

*See* New York City: Irish-American Mayors

## O'FALLON, JOHN (1791–1865)

Soldier, merchant, philanthropist. John O'Fallon was the son of James O'Fallon, an ambitious and adventuresome native of Ireland, and Frances Eleanor Clark, sister of George Rogers Clark and William Clark. O'Fallon's father died in 1794, leaving the education of his sons in the hands of their Uncle William Clark. After an extensive education in Kentucky, O'Fallon joined the army and participated in General William Henry Harrison's Indian campaign, receiving a serious wound at the Battle of Tippecanoe in 1811. During the War of 1812, O'Fallon rose to the rank of captain and served as Harrison's secretary and aide-de-camp. He left the army in 1818 with a determination to make a fortune in business. Arriving in St. Louis, he soon established a successful mercantile operation, making a fortune as an Indian trader and army contractor. He further enhanced his wealth with a number of highly profitable real estate speculations, helping make O'Fallon one of Missouri's wealthiest citizens. His business activities also included service as president of the St. Louis branch of the Bank of the United States and as president of two railroads as well. He was generous with his fortune, however, making liberal contributions to O'Fallon Polytechnic Institute, St. Louis University, and Washington University. Indeed, it seemed there was hardly a church, library, fire company, or any other beneficent organization which did not receive a measure of support from O'Fallon's seemingly limitless purse. Twice married, O'Fallon died in St. Louis in 1865 and was survived by four sons and a daughter.

*Dictionary of American Biography*, Vol. VII, part 1: 632–33.

Mary Ellen Rowe, "A Respectable Independence: The Early Career of John O'Fallon," *Missouri Historical Quarterly*, 90 (1996): 393–409.

J. Thomas Scharf, *History of Saint Louis City and County*, 2 vols. (1883): I: 344–54.

TOM DOWNEY

## O'GORMAN, RICHARD (1821–1895)

Politician. A classic example of the idealistic Irish political exile turned machine politician in America, O'Gorman was born in Dublin, the son of a Catholic merchant, educated at Trinity College, and trained in London to become a barrister. In 1844 he joined Daniel O'Connell's Repeal Association and became a secondary leader of the rebellious Young Ireland faction. After the abortive 1848 revolution, O'Gorman fled to Europe and on June 1, 1849, embarked for the United States, where he settled first in St. Louis, but from 1850 on, lived in New York City, where he joined the New York bar and the élite Society of the Friendly Sons of St. Patrick, and formed a successful law partnership with John Blake Dillon. O'Gorman eschewed the radical Irish-American nationalism of other Young Ireland exiles in New York—taking "little part in Irish affairs . . . save in what may be called the ornamental, oratorical [St.] Patrick's day line"—and instead amassed a fortune in corrupt alliance with Democratic Party "Boss" William M. Tweed of Tammany Hall. In 1865 O'Gorman was elected Corporation Counsel and, as the city's chief law officer, became a pivotal figure in the infamous "Tweed Ring" which looted the city's finances until Tweed lost power in 1871. O'Gorman survived these scandals, by 1876 had re-emerged as a spokesman for political reform, and in 1882 was elected to a Superior Court judgeship, which he held until 1890. When he died on March 1, 1893, his funeral at fashionable St. Francis Xavier Church was attended by a cross-section of New York City's native and Irish-American political, social, and religious leaders.

A. B. Callow, *The Tweed Ring* (New York, 1965).

Richard Davis, *The Young Ireland Movement* (Dublin, 1987).

D. McAdam, et al., *History of the Bench and Bar of New York*, I (New York, 1897).

*New York Times*, obituary (March 2, 1895).

KERBY MILLER

## O'HARA, FRANK (1926–1966)

Poet, playwright, art critic. Francis Russell (Frank) O'Hara was born in Baltimore, Maryland, on June 27, 1926, the eldest child of Russell and Katherine O'Hara. Of his conventional, middle-class upbringing he was later to be quite harsh: "I had rather summarily deduced that my whole family were liars and, since our 'community' consisted of a by and large very mixed national descendency it couldn't be that they were Irish liars, they must be Catholic liars" ("Autobiographical Fragments"). It was a milieu he was ultimately to reject, along with all things rural and "confusing." He spent his childhood in Grafton, Massachusetts, and later attended parochial schools in Worcester where he studied piano with the dream of becoming a composer. Following a brief term in the Navy during the Second World War, O'Hara entered Harvard where he was to major in music before turning to English literature. While there, he helped to found the Poet's Theatre; he read widely, wrote and published in the *Advocate*, and began to develop his personae as poet and critic. He took his A.B. in 1950 and left for graduate study at the University of Michigan where he completed his M.A. in comparative literature in 1951. That year he moved back east and settled in New York.

### NEW YORK

Frank O'Hara was urban at heart, a poet of the city. "[W]here does the evil of the year go," he asks, "when September takes New York / and turns it into ozone stalagmites / deposits of light." As Alan Feldman has observed, O'Hara was "the first American writer to see the city not only as a lovable melting-pot or a den of sin, but as a work of art" (*Frank O'Hara*, Twayne, 1979). And indeed it was the art and the artists of New York that became O'Hara's pastime, preoccupation, and vocation. Upon arriving, he found work at the information desk of the Museum of Modern Art, a position from which he eventually rose to the prestigious title of Associate Curator of painting and sculpture, well on his way to a full curatorship when he died. He became an editor at *Art News* where he wrote reviews and occasional articles.

## ART

O'Hara was deeply intrigued with the intersection of poetry and painting, though his interests expanded to include music, film, and popular culture. Anti-establishment when the term was not an alternative ("I don't believe in god, so I don't have to make elaborately sounded structures," he declared in "Personism: A Manifesto"), O'Hara was one of the first to champion the *avant-garde* work of the Abstract Expressionists, many of whom were his friends. He worked on the first international exhibition devoted exclusively to their work and at the same time revised an exhibition of Jackson Pollock for showing abroad. An astute observer of art, he valued what he saw as the living elements of a painting or an exhibition, finding the numinous in an art of the everyday.

## POETRY

Frank O'Hara's poetry is perhaps best characterized by a juxtaposition of extremes—the lyrical and the chatty, pop culture and high art, the durability of concrete beneath the play of light. His technique aims to encompass the totality of a given experience. Against "effete" abstraction in poetry, O'Hara asserts a fullness of person, not so much the involvement of "personality" as the self involved with another: "[Personism] puts the poem squarely between the poet and the person . . . the poem is at last between two persons instead of two pages." The poem for him stands as both a burst and a record of self-assertion—similar to an electric current or a phone call—the spontaneity of which guarantees the poet's presence in the poem, a presence by nature ephemeral but in being particularized, paradoxically permanent.

Many of O'Hara's books were products of collaboration and a crossing of artistic disciplines. His first volume, *A City Winter and Other Poems* (1952), contained drawings by Larry Rivers; it was followed by *Oranges* (1953) bearing a hand-painted cover by Grace Hartigan. In 1957, *Meditations in an Emergency* appeared, his first book with a commercial press, though it had an initial run of only one thousand copies. In 1960, however, O'Hara's work came to national attention by its inclusion in Donald Allen's pivotal *The New American Poetry 1945–1960*, an anthology which included not only some of his best published work to date, but introduced the public to previously unpublished poems. *Odes* emerged in 1960, bearing serigraphs by Mike Goldberg. In 1964 City Lights published *Lunch Poems,* and in that year another book-length manuscript appeared as an edition of *Audit / Poetry. Love Poems (Tentative Title)* followed in the next year. At his death in 1966, only a fraction of his poetry had been published. Much, though not all, of the remainder has been gathered by Donald Allen in the volumes *Early Writing* and *Poems Retrieved. Selected Plays* appeared posthumously, as well as collections of his art criticism. A controversial figure, but one loved by fellow artists, O'Hara remains a subject of tribute. His short life ended on July 24, 1966, when he was struck by a dune buggy on Fire Island. He died that evening in Mastic Beach, Long Island.

*See* Poetry, Irish-American

Frank O'Hara, *The Collected Poems of Frank O'Hara* (New York, 1971).
———, *The Selected Poems of Frank O'Hara* (New York, 1974).
———, *Art Chronicles 1954–66* (New York, 1975).
———, *Standing Still and Walking in New* York (Bolinas, Calif., 1975).
———, *Early Writing* and *Poems Retrieved* (Bolinas, Calif., 1977).
———, *Selected Plays* (New York, 1978).
Bill Berkson and Joe Le Sueur, eds., *A Homage to Frank O'Hara* (Bolinas, Calif., 1978).
Alan Feldman, *Frank O'Hara* (Boston, 1979).
Marjorie G. Perloff, *Frank O'Hara: Poet among Painters* (New York, 1977).

TODD HEARON

## O'HARA, JOHN H. (1905–1970)

Novelist, short story writer, journalist. In his own words, "the hardest working author in the U.S.," John O'Hara published over thirty novels and collections of short stories in a career that spanned thirty-five years. Among his most popular books, with critics and the reading public, are: *Appointment in Samarra* (New York, 1935), *Butterfield 8* (New York, 1935), *Pal Joey* (New York, 1940), *Ten North Frederick* (New York, 1955), and *From the Terrace* (New York, 1958). Several films have been adapted from his fiction including *Pal Joey* (Columbia, 1957) with Frank Sinatra as the charismatic rogue, Joey, and *Butterfield 8* (MGM, 1960) with Elizabeth Taylor as the tragic party girl, Gloria Wandrous.

### BIOGRAPHY

Born in Pottsville, a small city in northeastern Pennsylvania, on January 31, 1905, to Dr. Patrick H. and Katherine Delaney O'Hara, John was, by all accounts, an aggressive, cantankerous youth who had a chip on his shoulder for much of his time in Pottsville. Although the son of a prosperous, highly esteemed physician and a well-respected mother, he felt rejected by the local aristocracy, his social life at the mercy of old antagonisms and prejudices that marked many small towns in America in the early part of the twentieth century and later. An Irish Catholic, no matter if a member of the *nouveau riche* or of a prominent family, had to face a WASP establishment of "old" families. That John O'Hara had a taste for alcohol (he didn't stop drinking until an ulcer hemorrhaged in 1953) did not help him to receive the party invitations, to escort the women he admired, or to socialize with the country club set. Indeed, even as his career progressed and his reputation grew, many Pottsvillians took the position

John O'Hara

that O'Hara was "getting even" by airing their dirty laundry in public, an attitude that had more to do with Pottsville's decline as an important center of the coal industry, and its concomitant sense of insecurity and inferiority in changing socioeconomic times, than with O'Hara's fiction.

Pottsville, the county seat of Schuylkill County, once prided itself on being the gateway to the rich anthracite coal fields of Pennsylvania, and, in fact, coal was king, and helped to fuel the industrial revolution in the United States. The Schuylkill Canal System and, in time, the railroads, supported the coal fields close to Philadelphia. Wealth, in the hands of a minority, grew, and with it a quite rigid class system. Miners, and not only the Irish, who populated many areas in what is locally known as "the Region" had to depend on the company for housing (in "patches"), medicine, education, nourishment, and entertainment. Labor unrest tore the area apart, and led to a revival of the Molly Maguires, many of whom were executed in Pottsville for murder and terrorism. Mine bosses, usually Welsh and English, were attacked; some were murdered.

The antagonisms between the haves and the have-nots, the Catholics and the Protestants, the Irish and the English, continued into O'Hara's day. Then, just after World War I, the pandemic influenza visited the "Region." Dr. O'Hara went to various patches to help the sick and the dying. (cf. O'Hara's great story "The Doctor's Son" for his perspective on the ravages of the flu.)

It was out of this milieu that O'Hara's artistic vision emerged, and although he paid scant attention to the plight of the poor, Schuylkill County's history helped shape his fiction. His experiences as a journalist, both in "the Region" and in New York City, sharpened his always acute ear for the way people spoke, and focused his ever-attentive eye on what they wore, where they went to school, what automobiles they drove, and how they went about living and dying.

O'Hara's formal education was erratic. His ambitions were Ivy League; his ability to conform to the role of a student was less than resolute. He was dismissed from Fordham Preparatory School in 1921, and from Keystone State Normal School (now Kutztown University) in 1922. In 1924, after being chosen class valedictorian at Niagara Preparatory School, he was not allowed to graduate. His true education resulted from his days as a journalist, and from a novelist's attention to details.

In 1931, O'Hara married Helen Ritchie Petit ("Pet") but the marriage ended in divorce in 1933. In 1937, he married Belle Wylie, a union that produced his only child, Wylie. Belle O'Hara died in 1954, and John, in 1955, married Katharine Barnes Bryan ("Sister") with whom he remained until his death in 1970.

John O'Hara lived a full life. He traveled in the best social and literary circles, worked in Hollywood with F. Scott Fitzgerald, grew rich and famous. However, it was "the Region," which he left in 1928, that remained a major center of his imagination. O'Hara returned to his hometown only periodically, but after one of his last trips to his "Gibbsville" he wrote that it "was nice to know that 130 miles away [from Princeton where he lived and died] I have roots some of which were planted two centuries ago."

To say that O'Hara's short fiction is what he will be remembered for is not to lessen the achievement of some of his novels. However, it is his short stories, most first appearing in the *New Yorker,* that reveal his extraordinary ability to capture people and events realistically. The terseness of the form, the constriction of plot, theme and characterization forced him away from the broader scope of the novel. Not mere slices of life, his best stories, such as, "The Doctor's Son" (1935), "Imaging Kissing Pete"

(1960), or "Winter Dance" (1962), force the reader to watch an event unfold, take on significance, and conclude in a satisfactory way. His short fiction did much to influence writers as different as John Cheever, John Updike, Raymond Carver, and Richard Ford, just as O'Hara himself was influenced by F. Scott Fitzgerald and Ring Lardner.

The best of O'Hara's novels explored ways to delineate character, treat unpopular subjects (lesbianism, adultery, alcoholism, etc.), and utilize plot to extend our knowledge of how we live and act. On the other hand, unlike *Appointment in Samarra,* his first and still considered by many his best novel, many of his later novels seem formulaic, overwritten, unwieldy. Indeed, many of his novels seem written with the best seller lists on which he often appeared in mind.

## GIBBSVILLE

Most of O'Hara's best fiction, whether short stories or novels, are set in Gibbsville (Pottsville) and in Lantenengo County (Schuylkill County), an imaginary geographical area he created to situate his fiction. Like William Faulkner's Yoknapatawpha County (Lafayette County, Mississippi), Gibbsville will remain one of the most completely realized fictional places in literature. In over fifty short stories and a handful of novels set in what he called "my Pennsylvania protectorate," O'Hara gave life and voice to styles of life and manners. Matthew J. Bruccoli, the doyen of O'Hara studies, observes that his Gibbsville stories and novels "might be called the *locale à clef,* that is, the development of a fictionalized but recognizable setting in a series of stories and novels" (*Gibbsville,* 17). Just as one can follow Leopold Bloom's journey on June 16, 1904, in the Dublin of James Joyce's *Ulysses,* so, too, can one visit sites associated with O'Hara's Gibbsville and environs.

## REPUTATION

Certainly, John O'Hara's national and international reputation rests, for the most part, on his Gibbsville fiction. Whenever critics and reviewers discuss his work, they usually comment on his superb eye for details, his wonderful ear for dialect and dialogue, and his unwavering faith in his own talent and skills. However, he has not been granted entrance to the pantheon occupied by the likes of Hemingway, Faulkner, and Fitzgerald. Instead, O'Hara is seen as a major minor author, one just outside the hallowed ground, banging his head on the door. He did little to advance the novel's form; he failed to offer remedies for social ills; he was politically incorrect; and he was too eager to cater to a lowbrow readership. Or so claim his detractors.

Perhaps O'Hara does not rank with the crowned heads of literature, but his admirers, and there are many, point to a renewal of interest in his work. The best of his books are back in print, three biographies have appeared, and a study of his short fiction is in the works. Even Pottsville seems to have forgiven their most famous son. In 1978, the *John O'Hara Journal* was founded, and although it only lasted for ten issues, it provided an early forum for scholars and critics. In addition, Pottsville hosted two O'Hara conferences complete with panel discussions, lectures, and bus and walking tours of his Gibbsville. John O'Hara has become a tourist attraction.

After his death on April 11, 1970, his wife had placed the following inscription on his stone: "Better than anyone else/He told the truth/about his time He/was a professional He wrote/honestly and well."

Charles W. Bassett, "John O'Hara: Irishman and American," *John O'Hara Journal,* 1, 2 (Summer 1979): 3–81.

Matthew J. Bruccoli, *Gibbsville, PA* (New York, 1992).
———, *The O'Hara Concern: A Biography* (New York, 1975).
Finis Farr, *O'Hara* (Boston, 1973).
Steven Goldleaf, *John O'Hara: A Study of the Short Fiction* (New York, 1999).
Frank MacShane, *The Life of John O'Hara* (New York, 1980).

VINCENT D. BALITAS

## O'HARA, MAUREEN (1921–  )

Actress. Born Maureen FitzSimmons on August 17, 1921, at Milwall, near Dublin, this popular, auburn-haired beauty began acting at an early age and has played in over 55 motion pictures throughout her career. Her mother, Marguerite Lilburn FitzSimmons, was an actress and singer and performed on the Dublin stage. Her father, Charles FitzSimmons, was in the retail clothing business and, owing to his passion for soccer, was a founding member and vice-president of Dublin's Shamrock Rovers.

After earning her first money with an appearance on a radio program at the age of twelve, O'Hara was enrolled in the Abbey Theatre School and won numerous awards. She attended Trinity College and, at fifteen, was the youngest student to complete the Guildhall School of Music's drama course. At the age of seventeen she won the All-Ireland Cup for her portrayal of Portia in *The Merchant of Venice*.

While performing with the Abbey Players, O'Hara was discovered by Charles Laughton, who chose her for the leading female role in his movie, *Jamaica Inn* (1939). He then brought her to Hollywood to star opposite him in *The Hunchback of Notre Dame* (1939). An instant success, O'Hara starred in one film after another and was generally considered one of the best actresses of her day.

Some of her favorite films were directed by John Ford: *How Green Was My Valley* (1941); *Rio Grande* (1950); and *The Quiet Man* (1951), filmed on location in Cong, County Mayo, and including an almost all-Irish cast including her brothers James and Charles. Among other notable Hollywood films she appeared in are: *A Bill of Divorcement* and *Dance* (both 1940); *To the Shores of Tripoli, Ten Gentlemen from West Point,* and *The Black Swan* (all 1942); *This Land Is Mine* (1943); *Buffalo Bill* (1944); *The Spanish*

Maureen O'Hara

*Main* (1945); *Miracle on 34th Street* (1946); *Sinbad the Sailor* (1947); and *A Woman's Secret* (1949). She also played in the 1973 television movie, John Steinbeck's *The Red Pony*.

June Parker Beck, *A Biography of Maureen O'Hara* (1996).
*American Movie Classics Magazine* (October, 1989).

EILEEN DANEY CARZO

## OHIO

Before the Europeans arrived in Ohio, Paleo-Indians, hunters and gatherers lived in the area as long as 15,000 years ago. It was about 1000 B.C. when Indian tribes known as the Mound Builders, a farming and hunting society, arrived and built the enormous ceremonial and burial structures that are still in evidence today. Early white settlers, unable to believe that they had been constructed by Indians, had various theories, including that the great Serpent Mound was the biblical Garden of Eden.

By the mid-18th century when the first Irish came to Ohio, the Mound Builders had disappeared, but there were about 15,000 Indians in the area. Small numbers of Irish had been coming to the colonies throughout the 17th century, but in the 18th century, the immigration that had been a trickle became a flood. From 1718 until just before the American Revolution 300,000 Irish emigrated to America from the Ulster seaports of Londonderry, Portrush, Larne, Belfast and Newry, where a network of agents representing shipping interests lured immigrants to America from throughout the province. Letters from relatives in the colonies urged them to come, and beguiling newspaper advertisements about the promised land never mentioned the risks of the arduous passage to the far distant shore.

### PIONEERS IN COLONIAL AMERICA

The Irish left Ulster because the mercantile laws that so angered colonial Americans had also damaged the Irish woolen and linen trade and upset the economic structure on which the province depended. The increased cost of living and the higher rentals of their tenant farms pressed them to emigrate. Another major irritant to the Presbyterian Irish, later known as Scotch-Irish, was the requirement that they pay tithes to the Church of England. These problems, combined with the attractiveness of cheap land and a freer political atmosphere in America, propelled them to the New World.

The large proportion of primarily literate Scotch-Irish (300,000) in a total population of about three million colonists at the time of the Revolution helps to explain the enormous impact that they exerted on the social, religious, political and economic institutions of the United States. When the Irish first arrived, some became indentured servants, but others were skilled workers who prospered in developing urban centers. One of this number was James Gamble, a soap maker, who formed a company in Cincinnati with William Proctor, a candlemaker from England, to produce candles in Cincinnati and later the famous Ivory soap.

Yet the Irish were not always welcome. In Massachusetts, Puritan leaders regarded them as unruly and religiously incorrect. Other colonies refused to recognize Presbyterian marriage rites and required that tithes be paid to the Church of England. In the Quaker colony of Pennsylvania, however, they were gladly received and encouraged to settle in its western parts.

The Scotch-Irish settlers soon became the "cutting edge of the frontier." They moved down the Shenandoah River into Virginia, Tennessee and Kentucky, and later into the Carolinas and the Ohio country. Unfortunately, the Indians became pawns in the struggle between the British and the French over possession of the land and rights to the valuable hunting grounds. Among the leaders of the British forces in the pre-Revolutionary period were Irishmen from Ulster, experienced frontiersmen who knew the local Indians and persuaded some of them to become allies of the British.

The Scotch-Irish frontiersmen were inept farmers but skilled Indian fighters and, later, excellent soldiers in Washington's armies. Some, like Daniel Boone, became a part of American mythology in tales of winning the West. Others, though, were ruffians, lawless hooligans who behaved ruthlessly toward the Indians.

When the Ohio country was finally opened for settlement after the Treaties of Greenville (1795) and Fort Industry (1805), many of the Scotch-Irish left Pennsylvania, Virginia and Kentucky to migrate to Ohio, which became a state in 1803. Cincinnati, which had been founded in 1788, attracted many of these Scotch-Irish.

Cleveland, founded in the northeastern corner of the state in 1796, was developed at about the same time that the state of Connecticut sold its western lands to the Connecticut Land Company of the Western Reserve, which in turn sold acreage to residents of New England and New York. Although some Scotch-Irish arrived during this migration, the Irish did not arrive in Cleveland in large numbers until the building of the Erie Canal.

In Ohio the first Irish worked the land, built Presbyterian churches and named their towns and hamlets after places in their native Ulster—two Belfasts, two Londonderries, and others such as Colerain, Antrim and Tyrone. Other towns were named after men prominent in their communities, such as Crawford and Campbell's Town. Altogether there are about three dozen place names of Irish origin in Ohio.

These Scotch-Irish valued education and supported both public schools and the building of colleges, especially with the education of clergy in mind. Case Western Reserve University and The College of Wooster are two of the several colleges in Ohio whose creation was strongly supported by the Presbyterians.

Dissenting Presbyterian clergymen, Thomas Campbell and his son Alexander, who urged all Christians to give up the singular doctrines that divided their churches, eventually joined with other Christians to form a new church simply called the Disciples of Christ. Having attracted many converts from the Methodists, Presbyterians and Baptists, the Disciples claimed ninety churches in Ohio by mid-century and created Hiram College in 1850. The Disciples of Christ was one of the largest of the indigenous American religious movements that were pervasive during the 19th century.

Many of the Scotch-Irish clergy and leading citizens were active in the anti-slavery movements that culminated in the formation of the Republican Party in 1855. However, not all Ohioans favored the Civil War. While Republicans from the northeastern part of the state supported Lincoln, the anti-war Democrats or Copperheads found a champion in Congressman Clement L. Vallandigham, a leading Democrat who was a Presbyterian of Scotch-Irish ancestry.

A thorn in Lincoln's side, Vallandigham was a brilliant man, self-righteous and stubborn, and an excellent orator who supported states' rights. After the war began, he was found guilty by a military court of advocating secession and was banished to the Confederacy. He managed to run for governor of Ohio, but the tides of war were against him, and his candidacy was rejected.

By the end of the 19th century, most of the Scotch-Irish in Ohio had been integrated into the mainstream of American life. Those who farmed the hardscrabble lands of southeastern Ohio, however, were often defeated by the harsh environment of poor soil and rugged hills. Although the land was well endowed with woods and mineral wealth, its resources were exploited by absentee landowners who left behind isolated communities of Scotch-Irish "Appalachians." Many of these families came for work to the cities of Ohio between 1910 and 1920 and after World War II.

On the other end of the social scale were the Scotch-Irish Ohioans who became presidents of the United States. Ohio has been called the "Mother of Presidents," eight in all, including one who came to Cincinnati as a soldier, married an Ohio woman, and settled in the state. Three of these presidents had roots in Ulster—Ulysses S. Grant, B. H. Harrison and William McKinley. All had been prominent as officers in the Civil War and were considered virtuous middle-class Protestants. They came from the third most populous state, whose people were representative of the diversity of the nation.

BUILDERS OF A NATION

While Catholic Irish were present in Colonial America, it was not until the 1820s that they arrived in large numbers, spurred by depressed economic conditions at home and attracted by booming times in the United States. To the Irish, America was the "promised land" where the "sun always shines," and where there is "bread and work for all." Their sad exile from the green fields of Ireland was lamented in song and verse, although they seldom returned. But these poor, working-class people sent thousands of dollars home to stave off starvation and bring family members to join them in the New World. It was their money that financed the struggle for Irish freedom.

This new wave of Irish found jobs in the emerging cities and in the construction of the canals in New York State and Ohio and, later, on the roads and railroads that began to span the nation. Many had learned stone cutting while working on roads and canals in the British Isles.

When the first spade of earth was turned for the Ohio Canal on July 4, 1825, Ohio was still a thinly populated state. By the time the expansive network of Ohio canals was completed in 1845, Cincinnati had grown from 9,642 (in 1820) to 46,338. In the same period, Cleveland grew from 600 to 6,071 and Dayton went from 1,000 to 6,607. All of these cities had significant Irish populations.

The completion of the Ohio Canal in 1833 opened up northeast Ohio to the farmers and merchants of the region and became the foundation of mercantile and industrial development in Cleveland. With coal brought by canal from the Mahoning Valley, iron ore shipped from Lake Superior, and barrels of oil transported from Pennsylvania, Cleveland became the nexus of the iron and oil industries and a host of related enterprises. From the Ohio River through Chillicothe, Columbus and Akron, the canal, a network of roads and the railroads stimulated the economies of the towns they served. Similar development occurred in the west of the state after the Miami Canal was completed from Toledo on Lake Erie to Cincinnati on the Ohio River in 1845.

The shanty towns of the Irish laborers who built these canals and railroads became the Irish ghettos that survived into the 20th century. In all the seven Ohio cities spawned by the transportation network in the state, the Irish were the pioneer workforce of this newly emerging urban America. Like their fellow countrymen from Ulster, they left Irish place names and surnames along the paths of their settlement—Dublin, Limerick, Sligo, and Murphy and Riley, as well as religious derivations such as St. Patrick's, and Chapelhill.

In the land from which the Irish had come, the failure of the potato crop in the 1840s brought disaster. In the west of Ireland, where people were entirely dependent on the potato, the fungus that destroyed the crop also destroyed the life of the peasants—from Cork in the south to Donegal in the north. By 1852 half of the country's population of eight million had either died of starvation and disease or were forced to emigrate to the British mainland or to Canada and America. In the year called "Black '47" 20,000 of the 110,000 peasants who fled to Canada died in the "coffin ships" or at their destination.

Two million Irish emigrated to the United States between 1819 and 1860, with more than 714,000 arriving in the last decade of that period. The famine Irish who managed to emigrate between 1847 and 1852 were the poorest of the poor, most of them Gaelic-speaking Catholic peasants. Many of these refugees were attracted to railroad construction projects and to Ohio's booming cities, where they worked long hours for low pay.

Many Americans, both white and black, could not or would not compete with the strong backs and desperation for work of the immigrant Irish. On the canals the men worked knee-deep in water. When it rained they received no pay but were still charged for room and board. Their shelter consisted of make-do shanties, and they were reported to be dirty and poorly clothed. Death from cholera, malaria, dysentery and accidents was all too common.

Like other immigrant groups, these canal workers were exploited by contractors, including their own countrymen. They fought back by forming secret societies that were incipient trade unions, but the influx of more Irish workers inhibited their organizational efforts. Brawls among the Irish from different counties in Ireland were common and earned the Irish "canalers" a reputation for drunkenness. These were mainly single men, removed from the support and restraints of church and family.

Although much has been recorded about the young Irish men who built the canals, young Irish women were unrecognized in the written records of the time. It is known that they found work in the homes of the growing upper and middle classes and in the hotels and boarding houses of urban centers. Some of them worked in the numerous factories that had sprung up in Cincinnati. Those who were married tended to settle in the new cities and raise the large families that were common in the 19th century. Their exposure to the Victorian mores of their employers hastened the American socialization of their families, and their strong commitment to the Catholic Church actually supported the process.

As the Irish population expanded, it was the women who sent their daughters, as well as their sons, to the schools organized by religious orders, whose discipline was strict and where physical punishment was frequent. The American Catholic Church also provided sanctuary and hope for poor, bewildered Irish immigrants. The only words of encouragement in their new world came from their priests and nuns who were regarded with awe.

## FACING DISCRIMINATION

Ironically, while the Catholic Church was a support for the Irish in an alien land, their religion was also the basis for much of the discrimination they faced in a state dominated by a Protestant ethos hostile to "Romanism." As Catholic immigrants swarmed to the shores of America, the country's Anglo-Saxon founders feared they were under siege from a priest-ridden populace whose churches and religious schools would undermine their hard-won democracy and its bulwark, the public schools. Furthermore, both Irish and German Catholics opposed the puritanical blue laws that closed down social activities on the Sabbath.

Discrimination against the Irish was also economic and racist in nature. Workers feared that the massive influx of Irish laborers would lower their wages and lengthen the working day. Riots against Catholics broke out in Cincinnati, as well as in the larger eastern cities of Boston, New York and Philadelphia. The Irish bore the brunt of these attacks. The riots of the 1830s and 1840s were a response to the heavy immigration of those years. The Know-Nothing party focused the anti-Catholic bigotry that was to last well into the 20th century. The anti-Irish assertions of the English press and cartoons in the magazine *Punch,* which depicted them as ape-like in appearance, were widely reprinted in American newspapers.

*The Cleveland Leader,* edited by Edwin Cowles, was one of the Ohio newspapers that fanned the flames of bigotry. Cowles was eager to do battle with Bishop Richard Gilmore (1847–1891) over his plans to build schools in every parish of his sprawling diocese. Cowles was convinced that the pope was determined to undermine democracy, and he took every opportunity to label the Irish immigrants as "absurdly foolish and gullible," and dangerous "dynamite fiends." The *Leader*'s cartoons, modeled on the attitudes of the English journalists, also depicted primitive, ape-like Irish.

As Ohio became more urbanized, the Irish workforce moved to the docks and riverside warehouses of the state's cities, and later to jobs in construction or in the iron and steel mills of Cleveland. Most were strong laborers, and some possessed a knowledge of horses that was acquired in Ireland and proved useful in the rapidly expanding drayage and stevedore jobs, making them skilled teamsters. Hugh O'Neill of Cleveland, an 1885 immigrant from County Derry, started out as a stable boy for J. B. Perkins, a wealthy Clevelander. His expertise in training and caring for horses opened up opportunities for him among the city's elite, and within a few years, he became a horse trader of note. By 1905 he started a cartage company that laid the foundation for Leaseway Transportation Corporation, today a *Fortune* 500 company.

In the crowded tenements of Cincinnati neighborhoods, the newly arrived Irish shared foul living space with migrants from Kentucky and Virginia and with freed slaves. All jostled with each other for the unskilled jobs on the wharves and in the slaughter houses of that city. One investigator found that even as late as 1912 "poverty was the common denominator among the people [who] held the meanest, poorest paying, and most irregular jobs." The streets were filled with horses and wagons, peddlers selling food, clothing and rags, and people who seemed to live on the streets to escape their wretched, over-crowded housing. The conditions in Cincinnati were similar to those in Irish ghettoes in every Ohio city.

## CLIMBING THE LADDER OF SUCCESS

Gradually, the Catholic Irish began to emerge from the poverty of the ghetto. They became owners of saloons, funeral homes, and other small businesses. During the Civil War, many were recognized for the bravery with which they fought in the Union armies. Nevertheless they saw themselves as being in economic competition with blacks and many never favored abolition. When the war came, a Union doctor noted that most of the Celtic recruits he examined were in excellent physical condition and could read and write. During the rapid urban expansion of the post–Civil War period, the Irish readily found jobs, building streets, sewers, and water and utility lines in the cities.

While the proportion of Irish in the United States gradually declined in relation to the numbers of new immigrants from eastern and southern Europe, economic distress in western Ireland and letters from the States prompted another million to emigrate between 1871 and 1890. Thanks to the Education Act that the English had passed for Ireland in 1834, many Irish immigrants had an elementary education and could speak and write English. Ironically, this act of cultural "colonial imperialism" gave them a headstart over other immigrants.

Being naturally sociable and able at last to make their voices heard, the Catholic Irish enjoyed the excitement and drama of politics. Often deprived of the vote in Ireland, they flocked to the polls in America where their active participation in the political process was nurtured by Irish ward bosses, who harnessed the clannishness of the Irish to induce them to vote in effective blocs for the Democrats.

Their allegiance was to the Democratic Party of President Andrew Jackson, an American of Scotch-Irish descent who had wrested power from the political establishment of the 1830s—eastern bankers and New England conservatives. In subsequent years, the Democratic Party stood against the anti-Catholicism and anti-immigration policies of the Know-Nothing Party. When the Republican Party was formed in 1855 in Ohio, its abolition platform and the anti-Catholic, anti-Irish attitudes of Republican newspapers throughout Ohio repelled Irish voters.

It was a time of machine politics when the spoils were supposed to go to the victors, but in 1879 one dissatisfied Cincinnati Irishman questioned why the Irish should "be hewers of wood or drawers of water for the Democratic Party" when they could sometimes get a favor from a Republican, while a Democrat would more likely refer them to someone else who would forget it. The Irish might have been happier in Cleveland at the turn of the century when the mayor was an Irish Democrat named John Farley, or in Cincinnati a couple of years later when Edward Dempsey was a Democratic reform mayor (1906 to 1907). The real problem may have been that the Democrats were very seldom in power in Cincinnati.

One of the first Irish Catholics to win statewide office in Ohio was the son of famine Irish immigrants, Timothy S. Hogan, who was born in Jackson County, Ohio, in 1864. As a schoolteacher in a small Ohio town he had come under attack from the anti-Catholic American Protective Association, an organization that flourished in Ohio in the latter part of the 19th century. Despite, or perhaps because of this experience, Hogan became a lawyer who would earn a reputation as a crusader for the rights of women and dissenters.

In 1910 he was elected to the office of attorney general of Ohio, where he made many political enemies fighting election fraud.

Four years later he lost the race for United States Senator to Warren G. Harding, the future president. Walls throughout Ohio were plastered with this anti-Catholic campaign ditty: "Read *The Menace* and get the dope, go to the polls and beat the Pope."

Increasingly, the Irish were able to climb the economic ladder of success despite the frequent posting of "No Irish Need Apply" signs. The simple facts that they were English-speakers and the first foreign immigrants to arrive in large numbers during a period when industrial growth and municipal employment were expanding gave the Irish unique opportunities in the numerous Ohio cities. As their political influence and educational level grew, Irish-Americans were able to move into positions in the police and fire departments. Young Irish women who had received excellent courses in office skills in school were well trained for employment in municipal offices. They also apprenticed as nurses and took more traditional jobs as nannies, housekeepers and household help.

Irish men were active in trade unions, but for many years only the craft workers, such as the carpenters and bricklayers, were able to organize. The American Federation of Labor, which was formed in 1886 in Columbus, excluded unskilled workers and women. The iron and steel industries in Cleveland, Youngstown and other Ohio cities were difficult to organize because owners were able to use a succession of more recently arrived immigrants to break the strikes. The blacklisting of committed trade unionists kept them out of the mills. A series of attempts to organize the steel industry, culminating in the great steel strike of 1919, ended in failure. The 1920s were marked by the aggressive anti-union activity of many Ohio employers who labeled unions "un-American." Union leaders, many of whom were Irish, would not succeed until the reforms of the Roosevelt years in the 1930s.

The Great Depression curtailed the upward mobility of the Catholic Irish, but made them completely committed to President Franklin D. Roosevelt. These years of economic disaster witnessed the rise of militant trade unionism throughout Ohio. Union organizers used the National Industrial Recovery Act, Section 7A, to obtain union recognition in every industry in the state. The popularity of FDR surpassed even that of Father Coughlin, an anti-Semitic populist whose radio talks were admired among the Irish.

There is no doubt that America's entrance into World War II brought an end to the Depression. When the Japanese attacked Pearl Harbor in 1941, a united nation sent men and women off to war or to work in the industries that supported it. There was no reluctance on the part of Irish-Americans to participate, despite the Irish history of antagonism towards the English. Irish-American patriotism and sorrow found expression in the naming of a U.S. Navy ship in honor of the five Sullivan brothers who died together when their American ship was torpedoed.

Not only did Americans of Irish ancestry fight the battles of the war, but also they went to work on the home front. Ohio women found employment replacing the men who were in service. From Irish neighborhoods, married women, traditionally limited to homemaking roles, joined unmarried ones in the defense industries.

In 1944, as the war drew to a close, Congress passed the GI Bill of Rights in preparation for the return of the nation's servicemen. This landmark legislation provided a stipend for financial support for those who enrolled in tradeschools or colleges and universities, as well as weekly unemployment checks for veterans for up to 52 weeks until they found jobs in the post-war economy. The state of Ohio supplemented these transition supports with a stipend of up to $400, depending on length of military service. These measures not only protected the economy of the nation but also were of inestimable value in helping integrate Irish and other ethnic groups into American society.

Other federal legislation had a similar impact. Low-interest GI loans were made available for the purchase of houses, and the federal Interstate Highway Act of 1956 paved the way out of ethnic ghettoes into new suburban neighborhoods. In Ohio and elsewhere, the upward mobility of Irish-Americans received a significant boost.

### POLITICAL ACHIEVEMENTS

Their achievements in law and politics during the post-war period are illustrative of their success in a wide range of business and professional occupations. By the 1960s the children and grandchildren of Irish immigrants were being elected to many public offices—school boards, city councils, county commissions, Congress, and municipal, county and state judgeships. The lengthy Ohio ballot, commonly called the bed sheet ballot, was full of Irish names. In Cleveland, a city that had attracted thousands of immigrants from the rocky coast of Ireland's County Mayo, the roster of judges echoed the names on tombstones in the old Achill Island cemetery where so many of their ancestors lay buried.

By the next decade, large numbers of women, as well as men, had graduated from law schools and were beginning to achieve success as lawyers, judges and leaders in the Bar. Patrick F. McCartan, the son of a Youngstown, Ohio, policeman, is now the managing partner of Jones, Day, Reavis and Pogue, one of the most prestigious law firms in North America. Kathleen Burke, another Irish-American, became the first woman president of the Ohio Bar Association in the 1990s.

Nowhere was the success of Ohio's Irish-Americans more evident than in the career of Governor John J. Gilligan. Jack Gilligan's family operated a successful funeral home in Cincinnati. He attended Xavier University and became a professor of literature at his alma mater. Like many young Irish-Americans, his idealism was given new direction by the clarion call of President John F. Kennedy: "Ask not what your country can do for you. Ask what you can do for your country."

Gilligan, a Democrat, ran for elective office, holding positions in the Cincinnati City Council and the United States Congress before becoming governor of Ohio in 1971. He was an attractive, intelligent candidate who, contrary to the Irish stereotype, possessed a wry wit and diffident manner that was often mistaken for intellectual arrogance. In an act of political courage, he ran on a reform platform proposing that Ohio pass a state income tax to overcome its dismal lack of support for education and public services. Despite heavy opposition from a Republican legislature, he managed to secure passage of the income tax, the first major new tax source in Ohio since the 1935 sales tax. He was able to fight off an immediate attempt to repeal the income tax but did not survive his bid for a second term.

As the 20th century draws to a close, nearly twenty percent of Ohio's 10.8 million residents are of Irish descent. Their story is the story of Irish-Americans across the country. While they did not exactly receive the Gaelic "hundred thousand welcomes" when they arrived, America was to become their land and the Irish eventually emerged as "preferred ethnics." Irish-Americans' contributions to many walks of life continue to bear out the prophecy of Orestes Brownson, writing in the *Boston Globe* in 1854: "Out of these narrow lanes, blind courts, dirty streets, damp cellars and suffocating garrets will come forth some of the noblest sons [and daughters] of our country, whom she will delight to own and honor."

Jonathan Bardon, *A History of Ulster* (Belfast, 1992).

Nelson J. Callahan and William F. Hickey, *Irish Americans and Their Communities of Cleveland* (Cleveland, 1978).

R. J. Dickson, *Ulster Emigration to Colonial America, 1718–1775* (Belfast, 1966).

Leonard Dinnerstein, Roger L. Nichols, and David M. Reimers, *Natives and Strangers* (New York, 1979).

Walter Havighurst, *Ohio, A Bicentennial History* (New York, 1976).

Melvin G. Holli and Peter d'A. Jones, eds., *Biographical Dictionary of American Mayors, 1820–1980* (Westport, Conn., 1981).

Christine Kinealy, *This Great Calamity, The Irish Famine 1845–52* (Boulder, Colo., 1995).

George W. Knepper, *Ohio and Its People* (Kent, Ohio, 1989).

Lawrence J. McCaffrey, *The Irish Diaspora in America* (Bloomington, 1976).

Kirby A. Miller, *Emigrants and Exiles, Ireland and the Irish Exodus to North America* (New York, 1985).

Zane L. Miller, *Boss Cox's Cincinnati, Urban Politics in the Progressive Era* (New York, 1968).

Ohio Writers' Project, *The Ohio Guide* (New York, 1940).

Harry N. Scheiber, *Ohio Canal Era: A Case Study of Government and the Economy, 1820–1861* (Athens, Ohio, 1969).

Thomas H. Smith, *An Ohio Reader, Reconstruction to the Present* (Grand Rapids, Mich., 1975).

Thomas H. Smith, *An Ohio Reader, 1750 to the Civil War* (Grand Rapids, Mich., 1975).

David D. Van Tassel and John J. Grabowski, eds., *The Encyclopedia of Cleveland History* (Bloomington, 1996).

Carl Wittke, ed., *The History of the State of Ohio, Volumes I–VI* (Columbus, Ohio, 1941–44).

Carl Wittke, *The Irish in America* (Baton Rouge, Louisiana, 1956).

THOMAS F. CAMPBELL

## O'KEEFFE, GEORGIA (1887–1986)

Artist. Georgia Totto O'Keeffe was born November 15, 1887, on her parents' farm in Sun Prairie, Wisconsin. She was the daughter of Francis Calixtus O'Keeffe (1853–1918) and Ida Ten Eyck Totto (1864–1916). O'Keeffe's paternal grandparents were born in Ireland: Pierce O'Keeffe (1809–1869) was a native of County Cork while Catherine Mary Shortall (1813–1897) was born in County Kilkenny. The O'Keeffe family emigrated to Wisconsin in 1848.

Georgia O'Keeffe's first formal instruction in art was received at the Sacred Heart Academy, a Dominican convent boarding school outside Madison. O'Keeffe won the gold prize from her first art teacher, Sister Mary Angelique, O.P. O'Keeffe claimed in later life that the Dominican school was the only educational institution in which she ever learned any new ideas. O'Keeffe continued her education at the Art Institute of Chicago, the Art Students League in New York, and Columbia University. She found work as a commercial artist and held a number of teaching positions in various parts of the country between 1908 and 1918. In the latter year she moved to New York City. Six years later she married the famous photographer, Alfred Steiglitz (1864–1946). She proved to be Steiglitz's favorite photographic model.

Georgia O'Keeffe

Frank Lloyd Wright, another native of rural Wisconsin, tried to persuade O'Keeffe to join him in starting his Taliesin artists' colony in Spring Green, Wisconsin. O'Keeffe declined because by then she had become enchanted with the austere environment of the American Southwest. In 1929 she began a series of annual visits to New Mexico. In 1949, three years after her husband's death, O'Keeffe moved to New Mexico for good. She divided her time between homes in Abiquiu (winter and spring) and Ghost Ranch (summer and autumn).

O'Keeffe is considered America's preeminent modern painter. Her flowers, barns, landscapes, and skyscapes all reveal the love of nature she first developed on her parents' Wisconsin farm. O'Keeffe spoke of herself as emerging from the earth of the American heartland like the colorful flowers she painted on canvas. Her focus on nature resulted in a total exclusion of human presence from her paintings. Her confident, strong-willed, independent personality and passion for art made her into a cultural icon. She was regarded as a popular symbol of the emerging feminism of the 1970s although she had little patience with women's groups. She avoided people generally, was uncomfortable with cities, and was little influenced by other artists or their schools. She was famous for her lifelong habit of wearing black clothing, a trait she picked up from her widowed Irish grandmother.

O'Keeffe died March 6, 1986, in Santa Fe, New Mexico. Her ashes were scattered over her beloved Ghost Ranch.

Jan Garden Castro, *The Art & Life of Georgia O'Keeffe* (New York, 1985). Roxana Robinson, *Georgia O'Keeffe: A Life* (New York, 1989).

THOMAS GILDEA CANNON

## O'KELLY, ALOYSIUS C. (1853–c. 1941)

Painter and illustrator. Aloysius Kelly was born in Dublin and emigrated to London at the age of eight where he adopted the Irish prefix "O." He was one of the most enigmatic Irish artists of his time. He belonged to a highly political family, the Kellys of Roscommon and Dublin, who were deeply involved in the Fenian and Home Rule nationalist movements. The most distinguished political member of the family was James J. O'Kelly, described by his contemporaries as Parnell's closest confidante.

Aloysius O'Kelly was James J.'s younger brother. Another brother, Stephen, was a sculptor who executed a number of large commissions for the New York State Monuments Commission in the 1890s, commemorating, for example, the Battle of Gettysburg in a number of separate monuments.

Aloysius O'Kelly's paintings—influenced by his studies at the prestigious Ecole des Beaux-Arts where he enrolled in 1874 with the illustrious Jean-Léon Gérôme and later with Léon Bonnat—although highly accomplished, are eclectic in style. His early figure paintings reveal his debt to Gérôme while his portraits, influenced by Bonnat, are outstanding studies in realism. He was one of the first Irish artists to go to Brittany and in Pont-Aven he met with the American colony of artists, including William Lamb Picknell, who were paternalistically presided over by the American painter Robert Wylie until his premature death in 1877. O'Kelly's association with the American contingent was obviously a factor in his decision to emigrate to New York in 1895. Although he also painted in Paris and Fontainbleau, he was drawn to Brittany where he painted in Pont-Aven in the 1870s, and later in Concarneau to which he returned regularly through the early decades of the twentieth century. In Brittany his work oscillates between a Bastien-Lepage type rural realism and the plein-airism of the Impressionists.

Aloysius O'Kelly was one of the first artists to paint in the West of Ireland, where in the new realist mode of the time he painted *Mass in a Connemara Cabin,* first exhibited in the Paris Salon in 1884. In the early 1880s he was appointed to the highly coveted position of Special Artist to the *Illustrated London News.* For this pictorial newspaper he vividly illustrated activities of the Land League, formed in 1879 to combat recurring land problems and famine; and he depicted with accuracy the political events in which his brother played such a seminal role in bringing together the revolutionary and constitutional factions of Irish nationalism in the formation of the New Departure. His illustrations in the *Illustrated London News* encapsulated many of the critical issues that led to the overthrow of landlordism, a first step toward national self-determination in Ireland.

Although North Africa was a common destination for many European artists, it was unusual for an Irish artist to spend such a considerable period of time painting there, especially around Cairo. There is no other Irish artist of this period whose nationalism took on such an international dimension as O'Kelly's. He went to the Sudan in 1884, and his illustrations for the *Pictorial World* show that his sympathies lay with the Mahdi, the self-proclaimed prophet intent on expelling all imperial forces from his country.

O'Kelly emigrated to the U.S. in 1895, sailing against the artistic tide, at a time when American artists traveled in the opposite direction, from the U.S. to Europe. Immediately upon his arrival he applied for American citizenship, but contravened the residency requirements by returning repeatedly to Europe. On one occasion in 1897 he actually proposed himself for election on the death of Luke Hayden, the Parnellite M.P. for Roscommon. In 1895 he took the extraordinary step of changing his name; and thereafter submitted work to the Paris Salon and the Art Institute of Chicago under the name of Arthur Oakley, an act for which there is no clear explanation.

In 1899 the Irish-American periodical *The Gael* welcomed the "famous and gifted" Irish artist, Aloysius O'Kelly, to New York. He was previously described in the House of Commons by T. P. O'Connor as a young painter of genius and admired by

Vincent van Gogh, but it is extraordinary that O'Kelly remained such a shadowy figure who seems to have systematically effaced his much-traveled footsteps. His life in New York is equally difficult to establish but he seems to have traveled extensively in the U.S. He executed a number of portraits of prominent politicians with Irish interests or connections, such as John Purroy Mitchel, mayor of New York City. His last dated work is 1924 shortly after which there is no further mention of O'Kelly. But some hold that he returned to France, living in Paris until he died during the war.

His work is mainly in private collections in Ireland, France, England, the U.S. and North Africa. He first exhibited at the Royal Academy in London in 1876, giving his address as 233 Stanhope Street, the address of his uncle, John Lawlor, the renowned sculptor of the *Albert Memorial*. In addition to the Royal Academy, he exhibited at the Paris Salon, the Royal Society of British Artists, the Royal Institute of Painters in Watercolours and the Institute of Painters in Oil Colours in London, the Walker Gallery in Liverpool, the Manchester City Art Gallery, the Royal Hibernian Academy in Dublin, the National Academy of Design, the New York Water Color Club (of which he was a member), the American Water Color Society and the Society of American Artists in New York, the Art Institute of Chicago, the Corcoran Gallery in Washington, and the Boston Art Club.

*Irish Impressionists: Irish Artists in France and Belgium, 1850–1914* (Dublin, 1984).

Niamh O'Sullivan, "Through Irish Eyes: The Work of Aloysius O'Kelly in the *Illustrated London News*," in *History Ireland* (Autumn 1995).

Homan Potterton, "Aloysius O'Kelly in America," in *Irish Arts Review Yearbook* (1996).

NIAMH O'SULLIVAN

## O'KELLY, JAMES (c. 1735–1826)

Methodist minister. Most of O'Kelly's early life is uncertain, born either in Ireland or Virginia. He saw service in the Revolution as an ardent supporter of the patriot cause and became a Methodist around this time, preaching wherever he found an audience. After the war, O'Kelly quickly established himself as an influential leader of the Methodist church in Virginia. At the Baltimore "Christmas Conference" of 1784, O'Kelly became an elder in the newly organized Methodist Episcopal Church. While a zealous defender of Methodist doctrine, O'Kelly also displayed a fierce independence against the authority of church hierarchy. He strongly opposed the first Council plan of Bishop Asbury, criticizing his power and opposition to a General Conference. Asbury eventually assented to a General Conference in November 1792, where O'Kelly sought unsuccessfully to dilute the power of bishops over Methodist clergy. Rebuffed, O'Kelly and his supporters left the Conference and established the Republican Methodist Church. The new church favored congregational governance and developed a strong anti-slavery stance. The Scriptures were to be the only creed and rule of faith. The established church lost eight thousand members in the schism, with O'Kelly's new faction gaining a large following in Virginia and North Carolina, which soon called themselves simply "Christians." While some accused O'Kelly of heresy, in actuality he protested governance and policy, not doctrine. He published several pamphlets

on his actions and viewpoints, continuing these efforts until his death in North Carolina in 1826.

*Dictionary of American Biography*, Vol. VII, part 1: 7–8.

Edward J. Drinkhouse, *History of Methodist Reform*, 2 Vols. (Baltimore, 1899).

James E. Kirby, Russell E. Richey, and Kenneth E. Rowe, eds., *The Methodists* (Westport, CT, 1996): 333–34.

TOM DOWNEY

## O'KELLY, JAMES J. (1845–1916)

Fenian, journalist, republican and member of parliament (Irish Parliamentary Party). Born in Dublin, James J. O'Kelly emigrated to London to study sculpture with his uncle, John Lawlor, sculptor of the *Albert Memorial,* London. He returned briefly to Ireland to his father's blacksmithing business where he and John Devoy assuaged their fledgling nationalism making pikes. He joined the Irish Republican Brotherhood in 1860, and following a period of study in the Sorbonne in Paris, he enlisted in the French Foreign Legion in 1863 and fought in Algeria and Mexico. He deserted when John Devoy told him that an insurrection was imminent. He was captured and sentenced to death, but escaped and arrived in London in time to caution against the rising, on the basis that the people were inadequately trained or armed for such an endeavour. He became a member of the Supreme Council, afterward playing a leading role in building up the Irish Republican Brotherhood in both Britain and Ireland, masterminding the development of a nationalist arsenal. He rejoined the Foreign Legion, and according to the Colonial Office, he was made a colonel and authorised to organise an Irish Brigade for service in France, a scheme which was abandoned upon the surrender of France at the end of the Franco-Prussian War.

O'Kelly fled Britain after an arrest which he evaded on a technicality, and arrived in New York in 1871 where he secured a position on the *New York Herald,* rising steadily through its ranks to become special correspondent. In 1873 he was sent to Cuba where he risked death by penetrating insurgent lines to report on, and give advice to, the guerrilla fighters led by Cespedes, president of the Cuban Republic. Upon re-entering Spanish territory he was arrested, courtmartialed and sentenced to death. Following diplomatic representation, he was transported to prison in Santander, Spain, from which he finally escaped. His remarkable account of his role in bringing the Cuban war of independence to an international audience is told in his book *The Mambi-Land or Adventures of a Herald Correspondent in Cuba* (1874). He also wrote a play based on his experiences there. O'Kelly was with the United States army while it was engaged in the campaign against the Sioux, remaining until Sitting Bull was driven to take refuge in Canada.

In 1875 he married twice. He married first, in an irregular arrangement, a young girl whom he had made pregnant and whom he exported to Paris to live under the care of his brother, the painter and illustrator Aloysius O'Kelly. Some months later he married Harriet Clarke, sister of J. I. C. Clarke, the Fenian, journalist and poet who also worked on the *New York Herald.* Upon the discovery of his duplicity, Harriet divorced him, creating one of the most salaciously reported divorces of its time. O'Kelly left New York and returned to Ireland where he attempted to reorganise the IRB and where subsequently, against the advice of

Parnell, he put himself up for election in 1880 in Roscommon, defeating the O'Connor Don. His fund-raising tour of the U.S. in 1879 was said, by his supporters, to have netted £800,000 and, by his detractors, to have financed his personal political campaign in Roscommon.

It was James J. O'Kelly who first recognised Parnell's potential and who proposed the New Departure which he and Devoy conceptualised, thus bringing the political and physical force factions of Irish nationalism together for the first time. He had first met Parnell in 1877 in Paris. He was a highly astute strategist who was extensively involved in the Land War, and was imprisoned under the Coercion Act with Parnell in Kilmainham, where all the important Land Leaguers were sketched for the *Illustrated London News* by O'Kelly's brother, Aloysius.

His later years were marred by ill-health. The temporary loss of his parliamentary seat in 1892 to an anti-Parnellite was exacerbated by the lurid exposure of details of his personal affairs and by chronic financial difficulties. He died in 1916.

John Devoy, *Recollections of an Irish Rebel* (Dublin, 1929).

Desmond Ryan, *The Fenian Chief: A Biography of James Stephens* (Dublin, 1967).

NIAMH O'SULLIVAN

## OKLAHOMA

Oklahoma is one of but five states to enter the Union in the twentieth century, having been admitted on November 16, 1907. Hence it should surprise no one that its pattern of white settlement, and of Irish settlement, should date no earlier than the latter half of the nineteenth century.

A number of distinct stages of population development can be traced in the region that is today Oklahoma. The earliest known settlers were the Osage Indians, a branch of the great Siouan family of tribes, who made their home in a four-state area that included Oklahoma sometime around 1750, having journeyed through the Ohio Valley from their original home near Chesapeake Bay. They were afterward joined in the Oklahoma region by the Kiowas and Comanches, who migrated north from Texas before the advancing Spanish.

Beginning in 1808, the Osages were gradually dispossessed by the American government, whose policy of Indian removal called for placing certain tribes from the Carolinas, Georgia, Florida, Alabama, Mississippi, and Tennessee into this part of the Louisiana Purchase west of the great river, so as to accommodate the demands of plantation owners. The tribes so relocated were the Cherokees, Creeks, Choctaws, Chickasaws, and Seminoles, known collectively as the Five Civilized Tribes because of their long history of contacts with the British and Americans, which had heavily influenced their political and educational structures. By 1840 the forced marches of these tribes, known as the Trail of Tears, was over. The reservations thus created were supposed to be, and largely were, off-limits to Anglo-Americans, but an enterprising white man could marry into the tribe and conduct business on the reservation under the legal shelter of tribal membership. In addition, the government licensed agents and traders for the various tribes.

In 1834 Congress created the Indian Territory, defined as all the land between the Mississippi River and the Rocky Mountains that was not already a state or territory. With the Compromise of 1850 and the Kansas-Nebraska Act of 1854, the Indian Territory became identified with the present state of Oklahoma, minus its Panhandle.

The next stage of development came after the Civil War, as veterans found they could not go home again and sought to follow Horace Greeley's famous advice to go west. The railroads were also crossing the plains, especially through Kansas. A prime source of freight income was the great herds of Texas longhorns, which were becoming increasingly popular as beef replaced pork as a staple of the American diet. The resulting cattle trails with their legendary cowboys flourished until 1890, when further rail links made them obsolete.

Also during the 1870s and 1880s, the Federal armies were taking on the aroused tribes of the Great Plains, who had lost patience with broken promises and the ever-shrinking herds of buffalo that were the basis of native sustenance and culture. The lands originally granted to the Civilized Tribes were divided and redistributed to the defeated Cheyennes, Arapahoes, and Apaches, as well as to less numerous tribes. Most of these new reservations involved some reimbursement to the Cherokees, some of whose members were active cooperators with the government in making such deals. One such reservation was that of the Osages, who returned to Oklahoma in 1872 after bloodless negotiations prompted by the insistence of Kansas settlers.

In setting up the new reservations, mapmakers worked from the edges of the Indian Territory inward, with the result that about two million square acres in the center were left unallocated to any tribe. These Unassigned Lands became the focus of a heated lobbying effort throughout the 1880s. Heavily publicized civil disobedience was the lever that worked this machinery, as organized bands of settlers boldly and repeatedly entered the forbidden region, set up camp, and waited for the army officers to escort them back out again. Finally, in March 1889, a rider was attached to the Indian Appropriations Bill that opened the Unassigned Lands to white settlement. The new president, Benjamin Harrison, set noon on the day after Easter, April 22, as the official opening. It is estimated that at least 50,000 persons from all over America and Europe were ready at the boundaries as the guns went off, far more than could be accommodated by the number of 160-acre plots available for claim. In the years that followed, arrangements were made that allowed further land runs, until by 1906 all the reservations had been dissolved as legal entities, and Oklahoma could apply for admission as the forty-sixth state.

### EARLY IRISH

The first white men to enter what is today Oklahoma were Spanish explorers and French fur trappers. In the early nineteenth century a few Irish names, such as Benjamin Murphy's, appear in the records of these journeys. Two Irishmen, Nolan and Myers, attached to the poorly-organized expedition of Major Stephen H. Long in 1820, distinguished themselves by deserting. The Irish were the largest immigrant group to serve in the United States Army throughout the 1800s; thus they frequently staffed such posts as those set up across Oklahoma to deal with matters involving Native Americans, beginning with Fort Gibson in 1824.

### RAILROAD WORKERS

A further Irish presence in the Indian Territory began in June 1870, when the first spike for an extension of the Missouri,

Kansas, and Texas Railway—MKT or Katy, for short—was pounded in just south of Chetopa, Kansas. The Katy was in a race with two other rail companies; whichever one could run its tracks to the Territory's boundary first would get the lucrative franchise to build into Texas. The Katy won this race and thus was awarded the right to construct the first railroad through the Territory.

Although the owners and managers of the line were of English or Scots ancestry, the greater part of the tracklayers—the section gang workers—were first-generation Irish, as was the construction foreman, John Scullin, who is generally credited with pushing through the obstacles and actually getting the line built. The first train crossed the Red River on Christmas Eve of 1872. Other Irish workers included section foreman Patrick Shanahan, who married a Cherokee woman and settled in the new town of Vinita.

Because no priests were resident in the Territory until 1875, the pastoral care of the Indian Territory was in the hands of the Bishop of Little Rock, who delegated Irish priests at Fort Smith as occasional missionaries to the region. One of these was Father Michael Smyth, born in County Cavan, whose brother, Father Laurence Smyth, was pastor in the Arkansas town. (One of Laurence Smyth's duties was to accompany condemned prisoners to the gallows outside the courthouse of the famous Hanging Judge, Isaac Parker.)

Both Smyth brothers ministered to the railroad workers, but it was Father Michael who persuaded them to build the first Catholic church in the Indian Territory. This was a small frame building, built on land donated by the railroad, at what was then the head of construction, the village of Atoka in the Choctaw Nation. In October 1875 a pair of émigré French Benedictines arrived at Atoka to establish a prefecture apostolic in the Indian Territory. (Among the first to join them was Killkenny-born Brother John Laracy, who would later teach a class of ex-slaves near the monastery, Sacred Heart Mission.) With jurisdictional lines redrawn, the priests from Fort Smith largely withdrew from the Indian Territory, and years passed before an Irish priest said Mass there again.

## MINING

The greatest influence on early Irish emigration into the Territory, however, was the emergence of a coal mining industry in the Choctaw Indian Nation, which comprises roughly the southeast quarter of the present state. This centered on the town of McAlester, where the Scots entrepreneur James J. McAlester, already armed with Army ordnance maps showing coal deposits in the area, set up a mining company in partnership with the Choctaws. When the Choctaws decided that the actual labor of coal mining was not for them, McAlester traveled to Pennsylvania where he recruited miners from among the English, Scots, Welsh, and Irish. (A few years later, Italian, Polish, and Lithuanian miners would arrive on the scene and remain there, so that today few remember that the early complexion of the mining community was much different than it would be later.)

The example of Patrick Shanahan and McAlester reflects a widespread practice whereby whites became citizens of Indian tribes through intermarriage, thus gaining access to tribal lands and resources such as coal and oil. By the last quarter of the nineteenth century, all the major tribes in Oklahoma included intermarried whites, many with British or Irish names, whose wealth and power was based on their access to Indian land.

## LAND RUN

In the mad scramble that followed the April 1889 land run, 756 men or women with British or Irish names were among the thousands who staked out claims. (The available tracts had been surveyed previously, their corners marked by a blaze on a tree or a splash of paint on a stone. To establish a claim to residency, one was required to make a minimum improvement on the desired property, such as pounding a wooden stake into the ground. Then the claim was registered at a government office. There were many competing claims, suits and countersuits, and confusion that lasted in some cases for many months.) In 1890 Congress created the Oklahoma Territory, lying to the west of the original Indian Territory, and this region would be the focus of white settlement and political development until statehood.

Most of the English-speaking newcomers tried to establish farms, though many headed for the new cities such as Guthrie or Oklahoma City. By 1900 the number of these newcomers had expanded to 4,290, with the English leading, followed by the Irish, the Scots, and the Welsh. On the other hand, the American-born population with British or Irish parentage numbered over 10,000 at the start of the twentieth century, the largest group of any foreign background in the territories that became the state of Oklahoma.

The rural experience was hard and lonely. The lack of useable lumber on the prairie meant that homesteads were often constructed of rough bricks made by cutting blocks of sod. The "soddies" were liable to melt under the force of a Great Plains thunderstorm, and they frequently contained such treasures as live reptiles emerging from the walls and ceilings.

Few newcomers from Ireland traveled directly to the Twin Territories. On the average, British and Irish settlers arrived in Oklahoma after a remarkable average of thirty years' residence in the United States. Most had lived in at least three other states before coming to the Twin Territories. Most were married, but only one out of four Irish had married non-Irish spouses. Eighty percent of the Irish had already gone through the naturalization process before arriving in Oklahoma, well ahead of the other English-speaking groups.

## POLITICAL FIGURES

Surprisingly for a region where Catholics were an insignificant percentage of the population, first- and second-generation Irish in America were important to the early political development of Oklahoma. Irish-born General Philip Sheridan was a hero of the Civil War and was noted, if not distinguished, for his conduct of the Army's program to round up and resettle Plains tribes that were in the way of white expansion westward. It was Sheridan who sent George Custer to the 1869 attack on Cheyenne chief Black Kettle's village, setting the stage for the flamboyant Custer's later defeat at the Little Big Horn River seven years later.

Republican Dennis Flynn served as the Congressional delegate from the Indian Territory from 1890 until statehood in 1907, when the newly-enfranchised voters went overwhelmingly Democratic. Matthew Kane, born in Pennsylvania of Irish parents, was elected a justice of the first Oklahoma Supreme Court, and later served as chief justice. As the court's only Catholic, Kane felt obliged to recuse himself in a 1918 case involving the state's right to forbid importation of sacramental wine. (The remaining justices voted unanimously to override the legislative act, thus providing the precedent for a exemption to the Prohibition amendment of the following year.) Another prominent Irish-American, Thomas H. Doyle, was chosen to serve on the first state Court of Appeals.

Perhaps, though, the most spectacularly successful Irish politician of the early statehood period was Kate Barnard. Possessed of a strong social conscience and appalled by the conditions that Territory prisoners had to endure in the Kansas penitentiary, she campaigned in the 1907 elections for the office of Commissioner of Charities and Corrections, a post that was likely created for her by her mentor and fellow Catholic, Peter Hanraty. "Our Kate" won the election handily, even though as a woman she was not permitted to vote. She built the state prison at McAlester, regarded in its day as the one of the most enlightened facilities in the United States, and she concerned herself vigorously with the rights of laborers and the poor. She served but one term in office, however; disgusted by the venality of those who had come into elected office with her, she refused to compromise her principles or to run again.

These early Irish successes in Oklahoma politics were not destined to last. In 1920, Tulsa oilman and banker James J. McGraw ran for the office of Republican National Committeeman—then a far more critical position in American politics than it is today—and was solidly defeated. By then the Ku Klux Klan had come to influence state voters, and McGraw's religion weighed heavily against him.

Patrick J. Hurley, on the other hand, rose from poverty in Lehigh, Coal County, to high non-elective office, serving as Secretary of War in the Hoover administration and then as Franklin Roosevelt's special envoy to Mao Tse Tung following the Long March to Yenan, in western China. Yet another political activist was Tulsa lawyer Patrick Malloy, who also was appointed to the Roosevelt administration in 1932, but died suddenly before taking office as assistant attorney general.

Oklahoma has had three Catholic governors, beginning with Dewey Bartlett, later a U.S. Senator, elected in 1966. In 1994, the largely fundamentalist state was treated to the spectacle of two Catholic candidates battling for its highest office—the incumbent, Governor David Walters, and his challenger, Frank Keating, former U.S. Assistant Attorney General for Alcohol, Tobacco, and Firearms. Keating, a member of a prominent Tulsa political dynasty, is the first man of Irish ancestry to hold the Oklahoma governorship.

## Oil

In the industry most closely identified with Oklahoma, that of oil exploration and production, the Irish have been somewhat less prominent than they have been in politics. William G. Skelly, founder of the oil company that bears his name, was born in Belfast and made his fortune first in Pennsylvania and then in Oklahoma, becoming a major benefactor to the city of Tulsa. William J. Connelly was born in Cleveland of Irish parents and began his career in the oil fields of Pennsylvania in the 1880s. He became an aide to Harry Sinclair and rose to succeed his former boss as chairman of the board of the Sinclair Oil and Gas Company, headquartered in Tulsa. Other important Irish or Irish-American magnates of the early days of the Oklahoma oil industry included David F. Connelly, Thomas Walsh, William Sherry, and Peter McMahon.

Outside the executive board room, however, Irish workers were well represented among the oilfield derrick workers—often called roughnecks, because their erratic schedules did not allow

for getting haircuts—surveyors, geologists, and accountants that were critical to the success of the complex industry. A monument to these workers is in the town of Shamrock. Today the place is literally a shell of its former glory, with a population of less than two hundred, but one can still see the street signs that indicate Tipperary Road, and the streets named for Cork, Dublin, Ireland, Saint Patrick, and Killarney. The town was active between 1915 and 1932, with a population of 10,000; it had two newspapers, *The Brogue* and *The Blarney.*

Although nearly all the Irish were Catholic when they arrived in this country, subsequent defections among Irish laity were not uncommon, especially as the migration moved inland from the coastal regions. The first cause was the opportunity for advancing in employment and social status. The Irish were the sole immigrant group that was chiefly Catholic and also in command of the English language. This was a huge advantage in situations like those of the southeastern Oklahoma coal mines, where most of the miners were at the mercy of the owners because they did not speak English. Many of the Irish discovered they were in demand as foremen. If they were willing to turn a blind eye to the owners' injustices, they might become managers and get out of the wretched and dangerous coal pits altogether; and if they renounced their religion and moderated their brogue, all of the American dream could be theirs.

In the first twenty years after the original Land Run, religious tolerance was generally the rule in Oklahoma. The drain on human resources needed to establish a new society did not allow too much for petty squabbles over religious differences. Concomitant to World War I, however, there was a revival of the Ku Klux Klan. At first, the purpose of resurrecting this relic of the Civil War era was to restore a sense of law and order among a people whose values had been shaken by exposure to European decadence and rivalries. It soon became basic to Kluxer thought, however, that the real problem was not the values that Americans had imbibed from Europe; rather, the difficulty lay with foreigners in America, including Catholics, Jews, and, of course, blacks (no matter where they might have been born). The Klan's heyday was brief—most of its depredations were over by 1925—but its influence in the minds of Oklahomans was lasting. There are numerous stories of Catholics losing their jobs, or never getting hired in the first place, when their religious adherence was discovered. For some Catholics, it was simply easier to trade their religious tradition for the security of a job and the acceptance of the majority culture.

Much has been written about the difficulties priests faced in reaching remote parts of their mission territories, but less has been recorded about the problems of Catholics families living in almost priestless areas. In Oklahoma, for instance, there were only five hundred miles of paved roads as late as 1925. This meant that a drive of only a few miles in a horse and wagon could often be impossible for families on farms or small settlements outside the towns. Combined with the fact that most of the priests had heavy French or Belgian accents and shared in the overall attitude of Europeans that Americans were not people of culture, they relied heavily on Latin prayers and rubrics to console and inspire, and it is easy to see that much slippage could and did occur, especially among those whose language skills made it possible for them to find other venues for their religious feelings.

One result of this phenomenon in Oklahoma is the prevalence of unusual spellings of Irish surnames—Murfee, Magbee, and Odneal are examples—which infer an abandonment of cultural baggage, including religion.

## CLERGY

By 1998 eight Catholic bishops had headed the dioceses of Oklahoma. Of these, five were of Irish heritage, although none was native either to Ireland or to Oklahoma. The first was Francis Clement Kelley, who was born in the Canadian province of Prince Edward Island in 1870. He was ordained for the Detroit diocese in 1893, founded the Catholic Church Extension Society in 1905, and became Oklahoma's second bishop from 1924 until retiring three years before his death in 1948. He was followed by Eugene J. McGuinness (born in Pennsylvania in 1889) who was the third bishop from 1945 to 1957, and then by Victor Reed, who was the nearest to being a native of the state. He was born in Indiana in 1905, and when he was five his parents came west as part of the oil boom. He was ordained the fourth bishop in 1958 and died in Oklahoma City in 1971.

Reed's successor was Bishop John R. Quinn, auxiliary of San Diego and a California native. He was born in 1929, ordained bishop in 1967, installed in Oklahoma City and in Tulsa in 1972, appointed first archbishop of Oklahoma City the following year, and promoted to San Francisco in 1977. He resigned in 1995.

The final Oklahoma bishop of Irish extraction is the present bishop of Tulsa, Bishop Edward J. Slattery. He was born in Chicago in 1940 and was ordained for the Archdiocese of Chicago in 1966. In 1971 he began a career as vice-president of the Catholic Church Extension Society, and soon after succeeded to the presidency of the organization. He was appointed to Tulsa in November 1993, and was ordained by Pope John Paul II in St. Peter's Basilica on January 6, 1994.

Irishmen were counted among the Oklahoma priests almost from the Church's beginnings there in the 1870s, but they were few in comparison with French monks and Belgian seculars. Beginning with the arrival of Bishop Kelley in 1924, however, other priests like himself, born in Prince Edward Island of Irish heritage, began making their way to Oklahoma. Prominent among these were Msgr. James Rooney (arrived 1925), who devoted himself to establishing a parish for African-Americans in Tulsa and later served in other Tulsa-area parishes, and Msgr. Gavan Monaghan (arrived 1941), who was for eighteen years, until his death in 1959, the diocesan superintendent of schools. He is still regarded as one of the most talented priests ever to serve in Oklahoma, and he was responsible for recruiting a second generation of Prince Edward Island men in the late 1940s. During Kelley's tenure, another Canadian priest, Father A. O. Murphy, came to Oklahoma. Fr. Joseph Duffy, born in England of Irish and English parents, arrived in 1944.

Early in his career, Bishop Kelley persuaded two groups of religious based in Ireland, the Holy Ghost Fathers and the Sisters of the Holy Ghost, to take charge of parishes and schools he was establishing for blacks throughout the diocese. Outstanding among these was Father Daniel P. Bradley, C.S.Sp., who was pastor at a ghetto parish in Tulsa from 1935 to 1967.

As soon as the end of World War II permitted the resumption of transatlantic travel, Bishop McGuinness, in concert with other American bishops, headed for Europe to recruit priests and seminarians. He stopped in London, where he interviewed Polish displaced priests, including an entire community of Capuchins, but his main destination was Ireland, where as a result of his visits a large number signed up for service in the former Indian Territory. In later years, graduates of the national seminary at Maynooth or St. John's, Wexford, would simply be allocated to certain U.S. dioceses, including Oklahoma. In addition, Pennsylvania natives who had an interest in the priesthood were occasionally referred to Bishop McGuinness by his old friends among the Philadelphia clergy.

Among those who came from Ireland at this time were Fathers Gerald O'Nolan, Patrick H. Reid and his brother, Martin Reid, John O'Brien, Philip Donohoe, Denis and Michael Hanrahan, Michael Hughes, Michael Keatinge, Daniel Keohane, Patrick Murtaugh, Anthony Spain, and Fintan McMahon. Among the native Pennsylvanians was Father James McGlinchey, who for fourteen years managed the Tulsa office of Catholic Charities.

Of all of them, however, the best remembered Irish priest in Oklahoma is Father James McNamee. Born in County Longford in 1902, he came to the Sooner State at the suggestion of his uncle, who was the pastor of a parish in southwestern Missouri. In 1925 he was one of the first two priests ordained by Bishop Kelley. Quickly he began working with Father James Rooney in the apostolate to blacks in Tulsa. A man of prophetic vision, he was an advocate of Church reforms that did not come to pass until decades after he first enunciated them. He was an outspoken adversary of positions taken by the editors of Oklahoma newspapers, especially in the cause of social justice. Named founding pastor of a Tulsa parish in 1947, he was responsible for erecting a church that won the approval of the state chapter of the American Institute of Architects. His was the first Catholic parish to affiliate with the National Conference of Christians and Jews. He was a brother of Father Michael McNamee, and an uncle of Father John McNamee, both of whom also served in Oklahoma.

Patrick J. Blessing, *The British and Irish in Oklahoma* (Tulsa, 1980).

Don Lohbeck, *Patrick J. Hurley* (Chicago, 1956).

John McNamee, ed., *Breaking the Crust of Custom* (Tulsa: privately printed, 1975).

David F. Monahan, *One Family, One Century: A Photographic History of the Catholic Church in Oklahoma, 1875–1975* (Oklahoma City, 1975).

James D. White, *The Souls of the Just: A Necrology of the Catholic Church in Oklahoma* (Tulsa, 1983).

James D. White, ed., *Diary of a Frontier Bishop: The Journals of Theophile Meerschaert* (Tulsa, 1994).

JAMES D. WHITE

## O'MAHONEY, JOHN (1816–1877)

Fenian. He was born at Kilbenehy, County Limerick in 1816. His father and uncle had fought in the Rebellion of 1798. He eventually joined the Young Ireland Movement and participated in the Ballingarry Rising in Tipperary in 1848. O'Mahoney fled to France and later joined his comrade John Mitchel in New York. He immediately became active in Irish exile groups devoted to promoting Irish freedom. In 1855 he helped organize with Micheal Doheny the Emmet Monument Association which became the Fenian Brotherhood in 1858. O'Mahoney provided the money which enabled James Stephens to establish the Irish Republican Brotherhood in 1858.

With the advent of the American Civil War, O'Mahoney joined the Union Army and rose to the rank of Colonel. He was responsible for recruiting the 99th regiment, an Irish unit, with the New York Brigade. It was hoped that the war experience would produce seasoned soldiers who would eventually fight for Irish freedom. When the American Fenians split into two factions after the war, O'Mahoney and John Devoy headed the wing that wanted to send money, arms and men to Ireland rather than invade Canada as proposed by the Roberts wing. He was involved in an ill-fated attempt to capture Campo Bello Island, New Brunswick, Canada, in April 1866, that cost him his credibility.

After the failed Fenian Rising of 1867 in Ireland O'Mahoney continued to live in New York where he died on February 7, 1877. He was buried in Ireland at Glasnevin Cemetery.

O'Mahoney was educated at Trinity College and was a classical and Irish scholar of some repute. In 1857 he published an English translation of Geoffrey Keatings' early 17th-century manuscript *Foras Feasa Ar` Eirinn.*

*See* Fenians and Clan na Gael

R. V. Comerford, *The Fenians in Context: Irish Politics and Society 1848–82* (Dublin, 1985).

Desmond Ryan, *The Fenian Chief: A Biography of James Stephens* (Dublin, 1967).

SEAMUS METRESS

## O'MAHONEY, JOSEPH CHRISTOPHER (1884–1962)

Journalist and U.S. Senator. Born to Irish immigrants Denis and Elizabeth (Sheehan) O'Mahoney, he attended Cambridge Latin School and then Columbia University in 1905. In 1907, O'Mahoney began working as a newspaper reporter and editor and then settled in Colorado in 1908. In 1913 he married Agnes O'Leary.

In 1917, he began studying law and received his degree from Georgetown University. He then moved to Cheyenne, Wyoming, and began his own law practice. He also became active in politics and served Democratic Governor John B. Kendrick's campaign for re-election. O'Mahoney played a significant role in the drafting of the 1932 Democratic platform and he was appointed first Assistant Postmaster General of the United States in 1933. O'Mahoney took Kendrick's place when he died and was elected to the Senate in 1934 and again in 1940 and 1946 by his own initiative.

His greatest impact was as an antimonopolist and he crusaded for the resolution that established the Temporary National Economic Committee; as chairman of the TNEC he oversaw investigations into monopolies of wealth and the subsequent effects on technology and economic conditions in general. He gained a reputation for being a New Deal reformer; his independent personality led him to severe critiques of bureaucratic power; and he opposed several of President Roosevelt's proposals. O'Mahoney worked towards gaining support for the admission of Alaska and Hawaii as states and also as the chairman of the Defense Appropriations Subcommittee for American financing during the Korean War. He suffered a stroke in 1959, retired in 1961, and died on December 1 of the following year.

Frank Alan Combs, "Joseph Christopher O'Mahoney: The New Deal Years" (Ph.D. diss., University of Illinois, 1968).

Gene M. Gressley, "Joseph C. O'Mahoney, FDR, and the Supreme Court," *Pacific Historical Review* (May 1971).

*Dictionary of American Biography,* supplement 7.

JOY HARRELL

## O'MALLEY, FRANK WARD (1875–1932)

Journalist and theatrical writer. Born in Pittston, Pennsylvania, he was the son of William and Catherine (Ward) O'Malley. Early ambitions of O'Malley gravitated toward architecture or artistry and with time the latter proved more fruitful. O'Malley attended the Arts Student League in Washington, D.C., the University of Notre Dame and the Pennsylvania Academy of Fine Arts in Philadelphia. Upon arrival in New York in 1902, he became a writer for the *Morning Telegraph* where his articles stirred the interest of the managers of the *Sun,* where he was eventually employed as a reporter in 1906. O'Malley's flavorful articles were concerned primarily with the circumstances of those involved in the "white light" district in New York during the Prohibition days. After resigning from the *Sun,* O'Malley sought different writing options in his employment at the *Saturday Evening Post* and focused often on the theme of virtue and weakness among the Irish in America. He published two books, *The War-Whirl in Washington* (1918) and *The Swiss Family O'Malley* (1928). In conjunction with E. W. Townsend, O'Malley wrote two plays, *The Head of the House* (1909) and *A Certain Party* (1910).

O'Malley's predominant success came in his journalism career and he was remembered as frank and congenial except in the matter of Prohibition where he became bitter and oppositional.

Later in his life, O'Malley developed diabetes and died in Tours, France, on October 19, 1932.

F. M. O'Brien, *The Story of the Sun* (1918).

*Dictionary of American Biography,* 14.

JOY HARRELL

## O'MALLEY, WALTER FRANCIS (1903–1979)

Major league baseball team owner. Born in the Bronx to Irish descendants Edwin J. and Alma (Feltner) O'Malley, he did well in school in his youth and then went to the University of Pennsylvania and obtained an engineering degree in 1926. From there O'Malley attended Fordham University Law School until his father went bankrupt; he then worked three part-time jobs and earned his law degree in 1930. In 1931 he married Kay Hanson and became the father of two children.

O'Malley's career blossomed during the Great Depression and he specialized in bankruptcy cases. In addition to his practice, he also was involved in the management of several banks and put his financial talent into investments which eventually made him a multimillionaire. His involvement in baseball began when he was asked to be the attorney for the Dodgers' baseball club. By 1950 O'Malley had become the team's owner and eventually he took over the team as his own financially. He also became an influential persona in the major league baseball establishment and served on key committees, including the powerful executive council. He became a chief proponent of expansion in the major leagues, especially when he announced that he was moving the Dodgers from Brooklyn to Los Angeles.

In 1962 O'Malley opened the new Dodger Stadium which he built for $20 million and which hosted close to 2.7 million spectators. Following this expansion, his team went on to win six National League championships and two World Series. In 1970, when he turned the business over to his son Peter, its net value was close to $50 million. O'Malley remained very active in the management of the team and in 1975 was awarded the first

Busch Award for his service in the industry of baseball. He died of heart disease on August 9, 1979.

*See* Baseball

The National Baseball Library in Cooperstown, New York.
The Los Angeles Dodgers baseball club.
Roger Kahn, *The Boys of Summer* (1972).
Harold Parrot, *The Lords of Baseball* (1976).
*Dictionary of American Biography*, supplement 10.

JOY HARRELL

## ONAHAN, WILLIAM JAMES (1836–1919)

Businessman, civic leader. On Nov. 24, 1836, William James Onahan was born to John and Johanna Onahan in Leighlin Bridge, County Carlow, Ireland. He lived in Liverpool, England, before immigrating to the United States in 1851 and lived for a time in New York. Three years later, Onahan joined his family in Chicago, where he found work as an office boy and shipping clerk in a flour commission brokerage.

Through hard work and perseverance to improve his status in life, Onahan became a prominent figure in the business world and achieved clout in Chicago's political circles. He was among the active supporters in Stephen A. Douglas's presidential campaign.

In 1860 Onahan married Margaret Duffy. When an Irish brigade was recruited for the Union Army during the Civil War, Onahan volunteered as secretary for the unit. His experience during the war influenced Onahan's support for the peace movement and involvement in Democratic ward politics.

Religion was a primary influence throughout Onahan's life. He used his business acumen in debates at the Catholic Institute and Catholic Lyceum. Among those he assisted were Bishop James Duggan of Chicago and religious orders, including the Jesuits and numerous women's congregations.

Notable among his achievements for the church was his role as director of the Catholic Asylum and Reformatory and the organization of St. Patrick's Society. He joined Archbishop John Ireland in that prelate's promotion of Irish Catholic colonization projects in Minnesota and Nebraska.

In 1863 Onahan was appointed a member of the Chicago Board of Education. He was instrumental in reforming the position of city collector and served in that position for six terms. Other civic activities included service as city comptroller, jury commissioner, and president of the public library and the Home Savings Bank. Onahan also was involved in strike arbitrations, temperance campaigns, and formation of tactics against immigration restrictions.

For these civic and religious achievements, Onahan received the prestigious Laetare Medal from the University of Notre Dame in 1890 and was named honorary private chamberlain by Pope Leo XIII in 1895.

Besides his business and civic activities, Onahan was Chicago correspondent for the New York *Freeman's Journal* and contributor of articles in several periodicals, including *American Catholic Historical Researches, Illinois Catholic Historical Review,* and *Catholic World.* Other published writings included *Our Rights and Duties as Catholics and Citizens, Our Faith and Our Flag,* and *The Influence of the Catholic Layman,* as well as several lectures he had given on the Jesuits.

During his career, he was a corresponding member of the Chicago Historical Society for four decades. He also served as president of the Illinois Catholic Historical Society and honorary vice president of the Illinois State Historical Society.

Onahan's stature among church and civic leaders in the late 19th century led to his selection as chief architect of the Catholic Lay Congress in Baltimore in 1889. When the World's Fair was held in Chicago, he was influential in proposing an international lay congress to be held there at the same time. In 1893 he served as organizing chairman of the Columbian Catholic Congress, which met with the Parliament of Religions.

Onahan was recognized as the outstanding layman of the late 19th century. He died Jan. 12, 1919, in Chicago, the city that reaped untold benefits from his religious and civic achievements.

*See* Chicago, Aspects of

*New Catholic Encyclopedia* (New York, 1967).
M. S. Pahorezki, *The Social and Political Activities of William James Onahan* (Washington, 1942).

MARIANNA McLOUGHLIN

## O'NEALE, MARGARET (1796–1879)

Wife of John H. Eaton, secretary of war under Andrew Jackson. O'Neale was born into Irish heritage to William and Rhoda (Howell) O'Neale; her father owned a popular tavern in Washington, D.C., and she was spoiled in her youth amongst the guests visiting the tavern. She attended Mrs. Hayward's Seminary and Madame Day's School in New York. She married John B. Timberlake at an early age and they had two children.

Andrew Jackson was a famous friend of the family and O'Neale (Mrs. Timberlake) entertained him with her piano skills on several visits. In 1828 her husband died, and Senator John Eaton, with whom she had socialized previously and been criticized for impropriety, proposed to her and they were married in 1829. Their marriage did not stop the rumors and ill will their union stirred; thus, when Jackson set out to select his cabinet and included Eaton for the secretaryship of war there were several protests, primarily because of Eaton's new wife and the ensuing uproar. However, President Jackson did not allow such ill will to alter his choice, but it was Eaton who resigned and was then appointed governor of Florida in 1834.

Shortly after, Eaton and O'Neale (Mrs. Eaton) traveled to Madrid and lived there for four years where they enjoyed the nonjudgmental society. After having returned to the United States, Eaton died in 1856 and his wife became a wealthy widow who devoted her time to her grandchildren. She remarried once again and was deceived by her new husband who robbed her of property and respect. She died on November 8, 1879, after a turbulent life.

*The Autobiography of Peggy Eaton* (1932).
Meade Minnigerode, *Some American Ladies* (1926).
Queena Pollack, *Peggy Eaton, Democracy's Mistress* (1931).
*Dictionary of American Biography,* 14.

JOY HARRELL

## O'NEILL, EUGENE GLADSTONE (1888–1953)

Dramatist. "One thing that explains more than anything about me is the fact that I'm Irish." Thus did Eugene O'Neill acknowl-

Eugene O'Neill

edge the high importance of his Celtic heritage. Another crucial given in his background was Catholicism. Even after a bitter and permanent break with the Church, he would later concede, "Once a Catholic, always a Catholic." It seems quite clear, then, that O'Neill's ethnic and religious inheritance deeply affected his world view and his artistic vision.

Eugene's father, James O'Neill (1849–1920), who became an American matinée idol, had been driven with parents and siblings from his native Kilkenny in the mid-century famine exodus. He had suffered a deforming fear of poverty, very likely an effect of his childhood uprooting and penury. The shadow of that trauma would later darken the lives of his wife and sons. This history is relived in Eugene's searing family tragedy, *Long Day's Journey into Night* (1956).

O'Neill's mother, Ella (Quinlan [1857–1922]), was born in New Haven to immigrants from Tipperary. She enjoyed a privileged convent education at St. Mary's Academy in South Bend, Indiana. But, like James, she confronted a personal nemesis: Ella O'Neill fell victim to morphine addiction, the drug prescribed to relieve her pain after Eugene's birth. That event took place in the Barrett House, a hotel at 43rd and Broadway, on October 16, 1888.

"I was nursed in the wings," O'Neill said of the years when he accompanied his parents on tour. Among the most formative influences on the playwright-to-be was surely his father's numbing enslavement (nearly 6,000 performances) to an immensely popular recycling of the Dumas novel, *The Count of Monte Cristo,* a warhorse melodrama that earned James O'Neill a fortune. But the endless repetition of one role precluded his developing an undeniable acting talent. Eugene came to regard his father's theater as false and shallow, but he also gained from his "house" privileges an astonishing knowledge of stagecraft and theater business.

As Ella had been, her sons were boarded at the best Catholic schools: James, Jr. ( Jamie [1878–1923]), at Notre Dame minim and prep departments, Georgetown, and Fordham; Eugene at Mount St. Vincent in the Bronx and De La Salle Academy in Manhattan. Contented and obedient in their early years, each boy in his turn was devastated when he learned of his mother's drug addiction. To Eugene ". . . it made everything in life seem

rotten!" Thus, at fifteen, he lost all belief in a compassionate and personal God. Reluctantly, James entered the young apostate in Betts Academy in Connecticut, and later in Princeton. But, if he had gotten his way, Eugene remained forever haunted by his Catholic sensibility. Again and again his plays offer variations on the themes of sin, guilt, and the search for redemption.

Goaded by Jamie, his "creator," Eugene had spun out of control even before leaving college. Near the end of his first year (1907), failing academically, O'Neill was dropped from the Princeton rolls. Yet, as he always had, he continued to read omnivorously: in addition to fiction and poetry, Emma Goldman's anarchist magazine, *Mother Earth,* Shaw's *Quintessence of Ibsenism,* and selected works of Nietzsche. In 1909 Eugene entered into an ill-advised marriage with Kathleen Jenkins of New York, who bore a son, Eugene, Jr. In 1912 Kathleen would divorce the unprotesting father, who had made no effort to see the boy. O'Neill had been making little headway. On a gold-prospecting expedition to Honduras (1909), he had discovered only malaria. Over the next two years he sailed as an ordinary seaman on several voyages: to British, African and South American ports of call. These travels were interrupted by periods of panhandling and dereliction. Whatever good came from these rough adventures was more accidental than planned: an earned certificate as able seaman and, somewhat in the manner of Melville, an appreciation for the sea and ships that would provide material for his art.

By 1911 O'Neill was nearly exhausted by the psychological and physical damage he had inflicted upon himself. For a time he lived the meanest waterfront existence, staying in a flophouse-bar called "Jimmy-the-Priest's." Here he fell into an even more desperate state of personal degradation and once attempted suicide. He would recall this period in *Anna Christie* (1921) and *The Iceman Cometh* (1946). Somehow he managed a rally and moved into his family's New London headquarters in the summer of 1912. He began working as a reporter on the *New London Telegraph.* Still, the dissipation had taken a toll. Diagnosed in November to have a mild case of tuberculosis, Eugene entered the Gaylord Farm Sanatorium, where he remained for five months.

This period of enforced withdrawal offered an opportunity for reflection and profitable reading. Earlier, knocking about with Jamie and others, O'Neill had taken advantage of his access to Broadway houses (via James's *carte blanche*). He had seen a great deal of the new drama: Ibsen (*Hedda Gabler*), Shaw (*Mrs. Warren's Profession*) but especially the works of Abbey Theatre playwrights: Synge, Yeats, and Lady Gregory. "It was in seeing the Irish Players [on a first American tour in 1911–1912] that gave me a glimpse of my opportunity. I went to see everything they did. . . ." At Gaylord O'Neill began to read these new playwrights in earnest.

### EARLY RELATIONSHIPS, PERSONAL AND PROFESSIONAL

The decade 1914–1924 reveals a period of astonishing self-reclamation in O'Neill's life. These years mark his development from theater tyro to world dramatist. By 1922 he had already won Pulitzer Prizes for *Beyond the Horizon* (1920) and *Anna Christie.* His path of ascendancy was not without dips but it was generally steady. Indeed, James was so impressed by Eugene's efforts that he financed the publication of his son's first book, *Thirst and Other One Act Plays,* and paid his tuition as a special student at Harvard in George Pierce Baker's advanced "English 47," a workshop in playwriting.

In the summer of 1916, in Provincetown, Massachusetts, O'Neill met George Cram "Jig" Cook, specialist in Greek drama, and his playwright wife, Susan Glaspell. Their group included poets, political writers, and idealists of all varieties—in general a crowd sympathetic to the socialist philosophy espoused by Emma Goldman and Alexander Berkman: Max Eastman and Michael Gold, Edna St. Vincent Millay and Louise Bryant, Hutchins Hapgood and John Silas Reed, et al. Some of them had heard about and asked to read O'Neill's plays. They read *Bound East for Cardiff* (1916): "Then we knew what we were for," said Glaspell. With O'Neill the Provincetown Players vowed to produce new American plays "of artistic, literary and dramatic—as opposed to Broadway—merit."

By 1918 O'Neill had found his path. In April he married Agnes Boulton (1893–1968), a modestly talented fiction writer. Like O'Neill, she had been married and had one child. But, because each had personal ambitions to fulfill, their relations were never entirely compatible. Shane Rudraighe was born in Provincetown in 1919. A daughter, Oona (later Mrs. Charles Chaplin), was born in Bermuda in 1925. Clearly, O'Neill had not severed his Irish roots.

The Provincetown Players established a regular-season playhouse on Macdougal St. in Greenwich Village. O'Neill, drawing further on his sailing experiences, included three other one-act pieces with *Cardiff* and named the quartet the *S. S. Glencairn* cycle. In November 1920, the Provincetown offered *The Emperor Jones*, a radically experimental play, starring the gifted black actor, Charles Gilpin, as Brutus Jones. So successful was the production that on December 27 it was moved uptown and began a Broadway run of 204 consecutive performances.

But *The Emperor's* very success foredoomed the Provincetown's claim on O'Neill. Soon he developed close working relations with two other theater geniuses, critic-director Kenneth Macgowan and designer-producer Robert Edmond Jones (the "triumvirate"). These three organized the Experimental Theatre, Inc., official successor to the Provincetown. They produced an impressive list of O'Neill plays: *Welded*, an adaptation of *The Ancient Mariner, All God's Chillun Got Wings,* and *Desire Under the Elms* (all in 1924); *The Fountain* (1925) and *The Great God Brown* (1926). A little later O'Neill sought the services of the Theatre Guild (a spinoff of the Washington Square Players), with its greater financial resources and professionalism. The Guild staged *Marco Millions* and *Strange Interlude* (in 1928), *Dynamo* (1929); and, with Robert Jones, *Mourning Becomes Electra* (1931), *Ah,Wilderness!* (1933) *Days Without End* (1934), *The Iceman Cometh,* and *A Moon for the Misbegotten* (1947).

## BOLD EXPERIMENTS, DARK THEMES, AND A FAILED SEARCH FOR GOD

In 1926, his marriage to Agnes unravelling, O'Neill began a relationship with the actress-beauty, Carlotta Monterey (1888–1970). After their marriage in July 1929, Carlotta devoted her life to O'Neill, a devotion so fierce that she often alienated his friends and children. Guarding his reclusion (1938–1943), Carlotta acted as gatekeeper of Tao House, their retreat near Danville, California. Here O'Neill wrote his final and greatest plays, including *The Iceman Cometh* and *Long Day's Journey into Night.* Although their relations were often stormy, Eugene and Carlotta remained married. They are buried side by side in Forest Hills, Boston.

Theater historians credit O'Neill with single-handedly bringing a serious American drama into being and with setting new directions in world drama. He is regarded as a bold experimenter, especially in the 1920s, as a playwright who sought to revive the grand tragedy, and as an artist who wrestled with the question of meaning in modern life. For, out of his own experience and as a disciple of Nietzsche, O'Neill concluded that God was dead.

Between 1920–1929, some eighteen original O'Neill plays were mounted in the New York art theaters and on Broadway, an output that virtually guaranteed a certain number of failures. He combined the techniques of expressionism with the themes of naturalism. The arrogant "emperor" Jones rules his West Indies "subjects" until they rebel. As he runs for his life through the moonlit forest, all outer signs of his power shredding with his uniform, the action is intensified by a frantically accelerating beat of tom-toms. In his last moments Jones is found a quivering mass, victim of his own fears. *Jones* is both allegory and psychological realism.

Another triumph of expressionism is *The Hairy Ape* (1922). A modern Neanderthal, Yank Smith, delights in his brute strength, confident that his power "makes de woild move." By accident he discovers that capital, not brute force, controls society; he is merely a replaceable part in the mechanistic order of things. The play examines modern man's dawning recognition that, having lost his harmony with Nature, he has lost his place in the natural order.

*Desire Under the Elms,* as Joseph Wood Krutch observed, treated "the eternal tragedy of man and his passions." In this, and its theme about the wages of sin, the play is typically O'Neill. Men and women covet what others have: land, gold, sexual partners. To get them, they commit vile and violent acts: theft, adultery, infanticide. American in setting, *Desire Under the Elms* was called a return to high tragedy—Greek in theme, Shakespearean in vision.

Perhaps O'Neill's boldest experiment was to "reinvent" the mask of classical Greek drama. *The Great God Brown,* brilliant but confusing, finally baffles the audience: the actors' repeated masking and unmasking only defeats the viewer's attempts to follow the play's logic. Still, he had bravely accepted the challenge to dramatize Jung's archetypes, the *persona* and *anima.* O'Neill was searching for "god-substitutes" which science, he said, had failed to provide. And the idea of God-equivalents was what he hoped to advance in *Lazarus Laughed* (1927), *Strange Interlude,* and *Dynamo. Lazarus,* virtually unproducible with its 420 roles, espouses Nietzsche's doctrine of Eternal Recurrence. The hero transcends his fear of death when he comprehends his participation in the cycle of Nature. *Strange Interlude,* a Broadway smash (426 performances) and a best-seller, was a nine-act marathon. In it O'Neill reclaimed the use of asides, a device that permitted characters to speak their inner thoughts as their opposites "freeze," unaware. *Dynamo,* with Lee Simonson's futuristic set and special effects, offered the idea of electricity as a force to be worshipped.

O'Neill produced only three new plays in the 1930s, two that have become classics, the other a bitter failure. *Mourning Becomes Electra* retells the House of Atreus myth, here set in New England but with a Civil War background. In this trilogy the author outdid his *Interlude* demands in a bold presentation of thirteen acts. The evening began at 5:30, was interrupted for dinner, and finished near midnight.

Unlike all of O'Neill's other plays, *Ah, Wilderness!* is all-American in its small town, home-and-hearth charm and its Fourth of July setting and remains a summer stock favorite. It is a picture of the youth and family life the author might have preferred. Richard Miller, a generous but hot-headed adolescent, represents young O'Neill. In the play's 1933 Broadway première (285 performances), the father was played by perennial song-and-dance man, George M. Cohan, whose own father, with James O'Neill, had helped to found the Catholic Actors' Guild. The following year (1934) O'Neill seemed to signal a wish to reclaim his lost faith. In *Days Without End* two actors play antithetical extremes within a single character (John Loving), one part cynical and sneering, the other searching for his childhood beliefs. The unregenerate self wears a mask and can be heard by the hero (and the audience) but not by the other characters. The play failed, as did O'Neill's search for faith.

## LONELY JOURNEY TO OLYMPUS

Although he was named the 1936 Nobel laureate in literature, O'Neill's reputation was, ironically, in decline. Between 1934–1946, he would have no Broadway premières. Yet the period 1935–1943 may have been his most fruitful. For five years he was occupied with plans for a massive family saga that would cover 150 years. Called *A Tale of Possessors, Self-dispossessed,* it would trace the corruption of the American soul by greed. But ill health and a sense that he had lost focus caused O'Neill to shelve the project in late 1939. Of eleven projected plays, only two manuscripts have survived: *A Touch of the Poet* and *More Stately Mansions.* The late Travis Bogard, eminent O'Neillian, observed, "[The *Tale*] was a work of astonishing scope and scale. . . . Nothing in the drama, except Shakespeare's two cycles on British history, could have been set beside it."

At Tao House, forgotten but left in welcome seclusion, O'Neill mined the tragedy of his own past and found universal themes in his personal experiences. Now, with a full understanding of the sorrows of his parents and brother, he came to fathom the fate of everyman: to be caught in the nets of time. In these straits he located his family, his colleagues and friends, himself. Two, perhaps three of his final works, have entered the world's canon of great drama. *Long Day's Journey into Night* gives us four characters (the O'Neills, here named Tyrone) who torture each other in a kind of internecine warfare. In this towering tragedy we can see the dilemma of the human family: One is denied love and therefore withholds love. In this profitless enterprise, one is always self-defeated.

"*The Iceman* is a denial of any other experience of faith in my plays." The pessimism of the play is terrible, for it confirms that God is dead. Comfort is found only in the self-deception that one's life has a purpose. In Harry Hope's Raines-Law flophouse, the "hell hole" where O'Neill himself attempted suicide, one survived only by regarding the life of his fellows as hallowed. O'Neill had never regained faith, but he found at Hope's, not the debris of the cosmos, but the "best friends I ever had." The Irish-Catholic O'Neill had not lost his identity; he saw life as a vale of tears. The dynamics of these last plays is the confessional. In *A Moon for the Misbegotten,* Jim Tyrone (Jamie) confesses his heartless binge in response to the death of his mother. In *Hughie* a second-rate Broadway sport, in a momentary casting aside of pathetic bravado, accepts his need for human connection.

O'Neill's final decade was his own hell. He had long suffered a degenerative palsy (akin to Parkinson's) that increasingly robbed him of his capacity to write. Losing that, he had lost his *raison d'être.* Her role as protector of the artist's privacy thus cancelled, Carlotta had now become supernumerary. In these grey years they often fell to quarreling, but she remained with him until his death (in another hotel room). The 1946 production of *The Iceman Cometh,* ballyhooed for the playwright's return to Broadway, received only a mediocre reception. The next year *A Moon for the Misbegotten* stumbled in its Columbus tryout and closed in St. Louis.

An O'Neill revival began in 1956 and has hardly abated. That year *Long Day's Journey* was given its world première by the Royal Dramatic Theatre in Stockholm. *A Touch of the Poet* (1957) and *More Stately Mansions* (1962) also premièred there. O'Neill's reception in Sweden had been a genuine phenomenon since the 1923 Scandinavian première of *Anna Christie.* (See Tom J. A. Olsson in Floyd, bibliography.) In May 1956, a revival of *The Iceman Cometh* (565 performances at Circle in the Square Theatre, directed by José Quintero and starring Jason Robards, Jr.) received rave reviews. In November *Long Day's Journey* was given its American debut at the Helen Hayes Theatre (390 performances).

O'Neill stands as a giant in the modern theater, even if he has seldom won unqualified support from the critics. To the literati his faults have been grievous: grandiloquence (dialogue), forced seriousness of situation (bathos), and adventures in philosophy (issues beyond his depth). O'Neill himself had wished for the grace of language: he recognized that he seldom attained literary heights. Yet he has drawn the approval of audiences worldwide throughout the century. Actors vie for parts in O'Neill and credit him with an uncanny sense of theatricality and a genius of character motivation. All have praised his uncompromising integrity in the face of demands to cut his plays to win easy popularity. No other playwright has documented so profoundly as O'Neill did the arch theme of modern drama: the individual's anguish as he clings desperately to old answers in the face of a ubiquitous challenge to faith.

Asked in 1946 if he had returned to the faith of his boyhood, O'Neill replied, "Unfortunately, no." He had spoken with finality and honesty. Yet a kind of religious sensibility had apparently remained a part of his nature. Something serious in the theater was reborn with Eugene O'Neill, who saw the playhouse as modern man's last temple.

Normand Berlin, *O'Neill's Shakespeare* (Ann Arbor, 1993).

Travis Bogard, *Contour in Time: The Plays of Eugene O'Neill.* Rev. ed. (New York, 1988).

Eugene O'Neill, *Collected Plays of Eugene O'Neill,* 3 vols. Travis Bogard, ed. (New York, 1988).

———, *Selected Letters of Eugene O'Neill.* Travis Bogard and Jackson R. Bryer, eds. (New Haven, 1988).

Virginia Floyd, ed., *Eugene O'Neill: A World View* (New York, 1979).

Arthur and Barbara Gelb, *O'Neill.* Rev. ed. (New York, 1973).

Michael Manheim, ed., *The Cambridge Companion to Eugene O'Neill* (Cambridge, 1998).

Margaret Loftus Ranald, *The Eugene O'Neill Companion* (Westport, Conn., 1984).

Edward L. Shaughnessy, *Eugene O'Neill in Ireland: The Critical Reception* (Westport, Conn., 1988).

Louis Sheaffer, *O'Neill: Son and Playwright* (Boston, 1968).

———, *O'Neill: Son and Artist* (Boston, 1973).

EDWARD L. SHAUGHNESSY

## O'NEILL, JAMES (1849–1920)

Actor. Born in Kilkenny, Ireland on November 15, 1849, O'Neill's parents brought him to America at the age of five. His first experience on the stage occurred in Cincinnati in 1867, and proved less than successful. Yet, O'Neill continued to act and improve in companies in Baltimore, Cleveland, Chicago, and other cities. In 1875, he married Ellen Quinlan; their son was Eugene O'Neill, the American dramatist.

On October 2, 1876, O'Neill became a member of New York's Union Square Theatre Company, debuting in a moving role as the cripple Pierre in *The Two Orphans*. He soon became known for his handsome appearance, graceful manner and intellectual ability, and played in many impressive roles. In 1877, O'Neill went to San Francisco for three years. There he performed the role of Christ in Salmi Morse's *Passion Play* at the Grand Opera House, a controversial work that was subject to such opposition that it was withdrawn under legal pressure and the members of the company were arrested and fined.

In 1882, O'Neill played the character for which he would be thereafter remembered—Edmond Dantes in *Monte Cristo*. For years he played this role in various cities and, although he tried to perform in other plays, it was his Count of Monte Cristo that the public wished to see. It was a part he would play over six thousand times.

In later life, O'Neill helped make a motion picture of *Monte Cristo*. For two years prior to his death, the actor was in failing health due to an automobile accident. He died on August 10, 1920, at New London, Connecticut, which he had made his home for some time.

*See* Theater, Irish in

Thomas A. Brown, *A History of the New York Stage,* 3 vols. (New York, 1903).

H. G. Fiske, "James O'Neill," in Frederic E. McKay and Charles E. L. Wingate, eds., *Famous American Actors of Today* (New York, 1896).

Arthur Hornblow, *A History of the Theatre in America,* 2 vols. (Philadelphia, 1919).

Arthur H. Quinn, *A History of the American Drama from the Civil War to the Present Day,* 2 vols. (New York, 1927).

CHRISTIAN G. SAMITO

## O'NEILL, JOHN (1834–1878)

Fenian, soldier. Born on March 8, 1834 in Drumgallon, County Monaghan, Ireland, O'Neill's father died before his birth. In 1848, the youth emigrated to America, joining his mother and older siblings in Elizabeth, New Jersey, where they had settled a few years earlier. O'Neill attended school for a year, adding to the rudimentary education he received while in Ireland, then worked as a shop clerk, book agent, and ran a Catholic bookstore in Richmond.

In 1857, O'Neill joined the Second United States Dragoons during the so-called Mormon War, but deserted while in Utah and went to California. He joined the First Cavalry there, attaining the rank of sergeant by the time the Civil War erupted. O'Neill accompanied the regiment east, where it fought with the Federal army on the Peninsula in 1862. In December, 1862, O'Neill was promoted to second lieutenant in the Fifth Indiana Cavalry, and became first lieutenant the following April. A daring officer, O'Neill performed admirably in several engagements, and received a severe wound at Walker's Ford on December 2, 1863.

Feeling he was not being promoted as rapidly as he should, O'Neill resigned in the spring of 1864 and accepted a captaincy in the Seventeenth United States Colored Infantry. He resigned that commission in December of the same year.

O'Neill then settled in Tennessee, where he found work as a claims agent. He became involved with the Fenian Brotherhood and in May 1866, led a contingent from Nashville to participate in a planned invasion of Canada. The design was to win Ireland's freedom by attacking the British territory. On June 1, 1866, O'Neill commanded a detachment of six hundred men across the Niagara to occupy the Canadian village of Fort Erie, and he defeated a Canadian force near Ridgeway the next day. As British troops moved against him, O'Neill and his Fenians escaped by boat, only to be arrested by a United States warship and released after a few days.

Several months later, O'Neill assumed the position of inspector-general of the Irish Republican Army and by 1867 became president of his branch of the Fenian Brotherhood. He organized another assault on Canada and raided Eccles Hill on the Vermont border on May 25, 1870, but his soldiers fled before a Canadian attack. A United States Marshal captured O'Neill and the Irish activist was sentenced to two years imprisonment, although he was released by presidential pardon three months later.

Under the influence of W. B. O'Donoghue, O'Neill decided to again invade Canada, setting Manitoba as his target despite the Fenian council's adopting a less than enthusiastic stance. O'Neill led a small band to seize a post on the Hudson Bay at Pembina on October 5, 1871, but United States forces swiftly captured him. Again, O'Neill avoided lengthy punishment and he ended his days working to settle Irish in Nebraska. He died in Omaha on January 7, 1878.

*See* Fenians and Clan na Gael

George T. Denison, *History of the Fenian Raid on Fort Erie* (Buffalo, 1866).

G. McMicken, *The Abortive Fenian Raid on Manitoba* (1888).

New York *Irish American* (September 28, 1867; January 19, February 2, 1878).

Wilfried Neidhardt, *Fenianism in North America* (University Park, Pennsylvania, 1975).

Hereward Senior, *The Last Invasion of Canada: the Fenian Raids, 1866–1870* (Toronto, 1991).

CHRISTIAN G. SAMITO

## O'NEILL, ROSE CECIL (1874–1944)

Creator of the Kewpie doll. O'Neill was born in Pennsylvania, but moved west when she was four. A natural artist, she began to sell illustrations to local publications at an early age. At age seventeen, she moved to New York to develop her talents further, but moved back to her family farm in Missouri, "Bonniebrook," two years later. Her most famous creation, the Kewpies (a shortened version of Cupid), first appeared in the *Ladies Home Journal* in 1909. The androgynous, cherub-like characters soon developed into full-page adventures, gaining an immediate popular following in a number of women's journals. The Kewpies became a national craze, with the diminutive creations found on everything from radiator caps to Jell-O advertisements. In 1913, O'Neill patented the Kewpie doll, from which she would garner at least one million dollars in royalties. Generous to a fault, O'Neill spent her money lavishly in New York and on a Connecticut mansion, "Carabus Castle," where she used her fortune to support a number of struggling artists, poets, and musicians. She also developed as a more serious artist and exhibits of her later artwork were held in New York and Paris. The Depression and the decline of the Kewpie phenomenon caused the demise of O'Neill's fortune. She retired to her family farm, "Bonnie-brook," in the Missouri Ozarks where she resided until her death by a stroke in 1944.

*Dictionary of American Biography*, Supplement 3: 573–74.

Shelley Armitage, *Kewpies and Beyond: The World of Rose O'Neill* (Jackson, MS, 1994).

Miriam Formanek-Brunell, ed., *The Story of Rose O'Neill: An Autobiography* (Columbia, MO, 1997).

TOM DOWNEY

## O'NEILL, THOMAS P. ("Tip"), JR. (1912–1994)

Congressman. Thomas P. O'Neill Jr., called "Tip," a nickname of baseball derivation, was born in North Cambridge, Massachusetts, an area known as Old Dublin. His parents, Thomas P. and Rose Anne (Tolan) O'Neill, were of County Cork lineage, their forebears emigrating at the time of the Irish potato famine. O'Neill's father was a bricklayer, who at the moment of his son's birth—December 9, 1912—was marching in a picket line protesting Harvard University's hiring of nonunion masons. It was a circumstance full of symbolism in the context of Tip O'Neill's political career and social outlook.

O'Neill has been encapsulated as "a sentimental, God-loving, old-fashioned gentleman and patriot, a devout Democrat and thorough-going extrovert." As politician, he was a self-described "bread-and-butter liberal." Solidly rooted in traditional Democratic Party values, he considered loyalty the most defining of political virtues, and believed that the essential challenges of electoral life were securing help for the needy, jobs for the unemployed, and health care for the ill. It was a social philosophy that underpinned more than a half-century of public service, and which propelled him from state representative and school committeeman to Speaker of the United States House of Representatives.

O'Neill attended parochial schools, then Boston College, graduating in 1936 with a bachelor of arts degree, afterwards entering the insurance business. His collegiate record was undistinguished, yet over the years O'Neill would receive another thirty-five degrees, all honorary, including one from his alma

Thomas "Tip" O'Neill

mater and another from Harvard University. The University of Notre Dame awarded him its Laetare Medal in 1980, and in 1991 he was decorated with the Presidential Medal of Freedom.

Politics coursed through O'Neill's veins from his earliest years. As a youth he involved himself in the campaigns of others, then at age 22 and while still a student at Boston College he stood for the Cambridge City Council. That was in 1934. O'Neill lost the race but learned what he said was the great political lesson of his life: "All politics is local." He lost, he discovered, because he had not worked hard enough in his own neighborhood. Two years later he campaigned again, this time for the Massachusetts State Legislature, winning handily. He never lost another election.

The Massachusetts House was a Republican bastion when O'Neill entered it in 1936. It turned Democratic after World War II for the first time in more than 100 years, and O'Neill was elected its Speaker, serving in the position from 1948–1952. One of his proudest political achievements, he reflected later, was the expansion and improvement during his tenure of the Massachusetts mental-health care program.

Meanwhile, in the mid-1940s O'Neill became a member of the Cambridge School Committee under pressure from his local monsignor, who felt Irish-Catholic presence on the committee needed strengthening. He importuned O'Neill and a fellow parishioner as candidates. It was a Hobson's-choice situation. Either one of them ran or both would be "read" from the altar. They flipped a coin and, as O'Neill recounted, "I lost." He stood for the seat, won—and chalked up the experience to paying one's political dues.

O'Neill went to Congress in 1953, filling the seat from the Eleventh District that became vacant upon John F. Kennedy's move to the Senate. He moved steadily ahead, serving as Majority Whip from 1971–1973, Majority Leader from 1973–1977, and Speaker from 1977–1987. He was one of the first and most visible of establishment politicians to break with President Lyndon B. Johnson on the war in Vietnam, and he pressed for the impeachment of President Richard M. Nixon after the Watergate scandal, saying he had "desecrated the office of the presidency." In 1979 he comprised with Senators Edward M. Kennedy and Daniel P. Moynihan and New York Governor Hugh Carey the so-called "gang of four" that sought to exert pressure on Britain for a peace settlement in Northern Ireland.

Critics referred to O'Neill as the "last of the big spenders," a derogation he regarded as a compliment. "I've always believed in our responsibility as a nation to pay for the health and welfare of the American people," he said. "Yes, I've supported higher taxes, but it's those taxes that made possible the tremendous progress we've seen. Over the years, I've witnessed some miraculous improvements in this country."

O'Neill resigned from Congress in 1987. "Most people don't leave public life too happy," he reflected. "Sometimes the voters have to tell them. Sometimes their families and friends have to tell them and they don't like it. One of the things I got right was to get out when I did. I left before I got pushed." O'Neill returned to Massachusetts. He died in Boston, age 81, January 5, 1994. He was married to Mildred Anne Miller, and they were the parents of five children.

*See* Boston

Paul Clancy and Shirley Elder, *Tip: A Biography of Thomas P. O'Neill, Speaker of the House* (New York, 1980).

Thomas P. O'Neill (with William Novak), *Man of the House: The Life and Political Memoirs of Speaker Tip O'Neill* (New York, 1987).

Tip O'Neill (with Gary Hymel), *All Politics Is Local: And Other Rules of the Game* (New York, 1994).

JOHN DEEDY

## ORANGE ORDER
### (Loyal Orange Institution in the U.S.A.)

The Loyal Orange Institution in the United States of America is an autonomous Protestant organization loosely affiliated with the Grand Orange Lodge of Ireland. Besides Ireland and the United States, Orange lodges are found in Scotland, England, Australia, New Zealand, Canada, and West Africa. Affiliates of the American lodge exist in California, Connecticut, Delaware, Florida, Illinois, Massachusetts, Michigan, New Jersey, New York, and Pennsylvania. Candidates for membership must be Protestant, should promote "temperance, charity, and honesty," and must support "the laudable objects of the Orange Institutions" around the world. Orange orders are named after Prince William of Orange who defeated Catholic King James II at the Battle of the Boyne in 1690. According to Ireland's Grand Lodge, the name "Orange" honors Prince William "because his victory over despotic power laid the foundation for the evolution of Constitutional Democracy in the British Isles."

The Orange Order evolved from the bitter conflict between Catholics and Protestants in late eighteenth-century Ireland. Secret urban and rural Protestant groups like the Peep O' Day Boys, Oakboys, and Steelboys formed to oppose militant armed Catholics like the United Irishmen and to preserve Protestant Ascendancy. Many of these groups seemed to have merged into the Loyal Orange Institution, formed in 1795 after a brief skirmish on September 21 in which Peep O' Day Boys were said to have killed forty-eight Defenders at the Battle of the Diamond, a crossroads in County Armagh. Orangemen claim that after the battle Protestants joined hands in a circle and pledged their loyalty "to the Crown, the Country, and the Reformed Religion." Formally organized on July 12, 1796, the Orange Grand Lodge included rural peasants and urban workers but was controlled by the Irish gentry. Maintaining that it supported "civil and religious liberty for all," the first grand lodge banned Irish Catholics from membership and required all followers to swear allegiance "to his majesty George II and his successors so long as he and they support the Protestant Ascendancy."

The Orange Order spread quickly and paraded some ninety lodges in the first Boyne Day demonstrations in Lurgan in 1796. Clashes on Boyne Day occurred so regularly thereafter that Britain finally banned the Order in 1825 and 1836, only to allow its revival in the 1860s in response to Fenian efforts to liberate Ireland.

Ulster immigrants launched an Orange chapter in New York in the 1820s. Many other Orangemen migrated to Canada, finding Canadians far more congenial than Americans like those in Jeffersonian Baltimore who mobbed and murdered Orangemen during the Anglo-American War of 1812–1815. Still, the American Orangemen remained undaunted and clashed frequently with Irish Catholics. In 1824, the two groups battled during a Boyne Day celebration in Greenwich Village. In 1831, hundreds of Irish Catholics stoned Orangemen in Philadelphia, although in that city's nativist riots of 1844, Orange weavers may have joined Irish Catholic weavers in fighting nativists. Such alliances

were rare. From the 1830s on, many Orangemen paraded their colors but also joined such nativist groups as the American Protestant Association and the Order of United American Mechanics, which began sponsoring annual celebrations on Washington's birthday in the 1850s in New York and elsewhere.

Little is known about Orange lodges outside New York City, where distinct chapters appeared in the Orange revival of 1867 and held Boyne Day festivities the following two years. Officially chartered by the Irish Grand Lodge in 1870, the Loyal Orange Institution of the United States claimed 43 lodges by 1872, and 120 with ten thousand members by 1875. By 1897, there were Orange affiliates in 21 states. Throughout the late nineteenth century, lodge members met regularly to discuss Orange history and Protestant values, tried to counter Irish-Catholic political power, and alerted Americans about Papal efforts to undermine American schools and other institutions. By the 1890s, Orangemen and others protested against the increasing immigration from southern and eastern Europe.

The Orangemen were relatively obscure throughout the nation's history, but they received widespread attention in 1870 and 1871 when their parades sparked bloody riots in New York City. The Boyne Day celebrations in both years left scores dead and injured. Reformers used the 1871 riot to drive William Marcy "Boss" Tweed and his Irish Catholic constituents from power and to replace them with native-born Protestant elites. The events altered New York politics for years, although the Orangemen did not parade again until 1890.

After 1900, the Orangemen seem gradually to have shifted their activities to ceremonial and philanthropic functions. They occasionally welcomed visiting Orangemen from abroad, hosted world Orange councils, and down to the 1990s stayed abreast of the continuing controversy surrounding Orange parades in Ireland. In 1901, the Loyal Orange Institution opened an orphanage in Hatboro, Pennsylvania, which became a retirement home in 1948. Disputes within the order apparently were rare, although a major split erupted in 1926 when dissidents left the American Order to form the International Orange Association. The two factions merged in 1930.

*See* Nativism; Ku Klux Klan

Hereward Senior, *Orangeism in Ireland and Britain 1795–1836* (London, 1966).

Samuel E. Long, *A Brief History of the Loyal Orange Institution in the United States of America* (Orange Institution, 1979).

MICHAEL A. GORDON

## ORANGE RIOTS OF 1870 AND 1871

Feuds rooted deep in Irish history reemerged explosively in New York City in 1870 and 1871. On July 12 in both years, Irish Catholic workers tried to prevent members of the Loyal Orange Institution and their supporters from parading through city streets to celebrate the victory of Prince William of Orange over King James II at the Battle of the Boyne in 1690. The resulting riot in 1870 left eight dead, fifteen reported injured, and six arrested. In 1871, at least sixty-two died, one hundred were hurt, and 105 were arrested.

The Orangemen had only recently revived their annual celebrations. Formed in Ireland in 1795, the Orange Order helped to sustain Protestant Ascendancy against efforts by Irish-Catholic nationalist groups and secret agrarian organizations to drive out British rule. Ulster immigrants formed an American branch of the Orange Order in New York in the 1820s. In following decades, American Orangemen occasionally taunted Irish Catholics during July 12 celebrations and often joined with members of the American Protestant Association (APA) and other nativist groups to celebrate Washington's birthday. New York branches of the renamed Loyal Orange Institution of the United States reorganized after the Civil War and sponsored small July 12 events in 1868 and 1869.

The following year, over two thousand Orangemen and APA members paraded from lower Manhattan to Elm Park at Ninety-second Street and Ninth Avenue, where they planned to join their families for an afternoon Boyne Day picnic. En route, the boisterous group and its bands taunted Irish-Catholic construction workers with insulting banners and the strains of "Protestant Boys," "Croppies, Lie Down," and "Boyne Water." One Orangeman reportedly fired a pistol at a Catholic church. Incensed by these events, hundreds of Irish-Catholic workers left their construction jobs and trudged to the park with pistols and makeshift weapons. Many Orangemen were also armed, and the police arrived too late to prevent a melee. Workers broke down the park gates, scaled fences, and attacked those inside. Fighting spilled onto nearby streets, then eastward into Central Park, then down to Eighty-second Street, and finally onto Eighth and Ninth Avenue streetcars as Orangemen and APA members tried to hurry their families to safety. Battles on the Eighth Avenue cars raged for thirty blocks before a sudden cloudburst squelched the rioting.

Both sides suffered heavy casualties. Six workers, one of them a teenaged tool carrier, died from the effects of Orange pistols and clubs. John Gardiner, found unconscious with an Orange badge pinned to his chest, died on July 14. And Francis Wood, a member of the APA's No Surrender Lodge, died on July 13 from a smashed head he received on a streetcar.

Many New York Protestants and anti-Catholic newspapers blamed the 1870 violence on Irish-Catholic ruffians who they claimed undermined traditional American values and supported corrupt city Democratic officials led by the Tammany Hall leader, William Marcy "Boss" Tweed. On July 13, for example, the *New York Daily Tribune* claimed the riot added proof that Tweed's Irish supporters threatened the city "with free murder, free drunkenness, and free rioting." Irish Catholics viewed things differently. Many believed that Orangemen and their Protestant supporters sought to limit Irish-Catholic rights and opportunities in America, just as they had done in Ireland. Claiming that Orangemen supported oppressive landlords in rural Ireland and an oppressive home government, the *Irish-American* asserted that "the entire of our northern frontier, today, is settled by the descendants of Irish Catholics, driven from their original homes by the persecution to which they were subjected, not on *religious* but on *political* grounds."

The 1870 riot and the tensions it sparked helped set the stage for a more dramatic showdown the following year that would reveal how deeply the city was divided by ethnicity and class. During the early summer, city newspapers rumored that Orangemen were planning another Boyne Day parade and that Irish-American nationalist organizations and fraternal groups were secretly preparing a coordinated armed response. Worries about another major riot were intensified by a July 1 letter to the press from Orange grand master John J. Bond, who announced that his order planned to march downtown on July 12 from Orange headquarters at Twenty-ninth Street and Eighth Avenue, to Cooper Union on the Lower East Side. Bond said that the police had promised to protect the Orangemen because he had received many violent threats, "written in fearful language," if the parade took place. Still, Bond worried that the police could not safeguard his members *or* American values. He asked that Protestants and "the better portion of our community" demand adequate protection to demonstrate that the nation could "guarantee freedom in peace, law and order to her Protestant citizens. . . ."

Bond tossed a calculated political chip into the parade's context, but an even more powerful one surfaced on July 8 when the *New York Times* launched its massive exposure of government fraud under Tweed's regime and urged reformers to oust the boss and his cronies. The impending parade and the *Times*'s disclosures threw city Democratic leaders into a crisis. Groups like the Ancient Order of Hibernians (AOH) and the Knights of St. Patrick demanded that city authorities ban the parade. Wealthy Protestants demanded that the city resist "mob rule" and support "equal rights." Mayor A. Oakey Hall was worried about the potential loss of his constituents if the parade occurred, but also about how a riot would add fuel to reformers' demands. Hall sought to escape this dilemma on July 11 by ordering police superintendent James J. Kelso to ban the parade, but that night Democratic governor John T. Hoffman overruled Hall and called up National Guard regiments to protect Orangemen.

Hoffman's order made headlines in the next morning's newspapers and sent rumors of an impending riot throughout the city. Shopkeepers along the parade route closed their doors early in the morning. For several hours, police and guard units raced on stages and streetcars to stop fights involving Irish longshoremen, street laborers, and quarrymen. Meanwhile, AOH members assembled for military drills at Hibernian Hall and the Fenian Brotherhood armory in Prince Street. Shortly before noon, a large police force clubbed its way inside Hibernian Hall and broke up a meeting, while nearby, other policemen chased after some two hundred longshoremen who were being led uptown by a man waving a sword.

By early afternoon, several thousand people had crowded onto the sidewalks and into nearby streets along Eighth Avenue from Twenty-ninth to Twenty-third streets. Near Orange headquarters, police were showered by bricks and stones as they clubbed back tough knots of men and broke up fights. Shortly after 2:30 PM, some one hundred Orangemen, carrying banners and led by Twyford's twelve-piece band, stepped onto Eighth Avenue to begin their parade. Parts of five national guard regiments and scores of police surrounded the Orangemen as they made their way down the street. At once, crowds of angry observers began hurling objects and screaming at the parade from sidewalks, windows, and rooftops. For the next thirty minutes, people along the avenue rushed at the procession from side streets, tossed bottles, refuse, boots, kettles, stones, and other missiles, and occasionally fired pistols at the Orangemen and their protectors. Rattled guardsmen occasionally fired at people on rooftops and in alleyways, but they launched a full-scale response after some of them saw a man shoot in the head a woman who had waved an orange handkerchief, and as lead guard units themselves were fired on near Twenty-third Street. As pistol shots and broken crockery rained down on them, a bloodied Orangeman urged troops to "fire on the murderous scoundrels," and, without warning, panicked Eighty-fourth Regiment soldiers opened fire on the sidewalk crowds and buildings on the northeast corner of Twenty-fourth Street. Members of other regiments joined the assault, and for the next several minutes scores were killed and wounded as terrified spectators tried to escape the carnage. Suddenly, the shooting stopped, and the procession reformed and wound its way downtown.

New Yorkers differed sharply in reacting to the violence. City officials worried because their Irish-Catholic supporters blamed them for allowing a celebration that led to so many Irish deaths. After all, military fire had taken the greatest toll on Irish protesters. Guard fire accounted for 55 of the 62 deaths, and for 60 of the 100 injuries. Most of the casualties were Irish immigrants. Three soldiers and two policemen—but no Orangemen—died. Yet Boss Tweed and Mayor Hall also had to contend with charges by Protestant reformers that they were not only corrupt but incompetent as well. Trying to put the affair behind them as quickly as possible, civil and military authorities alike dismissed pleas for a full investigation, punished suspected policemen and soldiers, publicly honored "heroic" policemen and troops, and released nearly all Irish Catholics who had been arrested for rioting.

The Orangemen did not parade after 1871, but their outings in 1870 and 1871 affected city politics for years. As in 1870, Protestants again accused Tweed's legions of pandering to a "dangerous class" that took orders from Rome. But this time, such sentiments coalesced into a nativist political reform movement that toppled Tweed from power. Led by the Committee of Seventy, wealthy Protestant merchants and lawyers helped prosecute corrupt city officials, obtained a new city charter, elected Republicans to city offices, campaigned against public aid to parochial schools, and in other ways tried to suppress Irish-Catholic influence in city life. Other reformers helped to reform the Democratic party and even merged with Tweed's old Tammany Hall Democrats in the mid-1880s.

Irish-Catholic workers did not abandon the Democrats, but increasingly throughout the 1870s and 1880s they responded to what they perceived were the threats posed by Orangeism and Protestant rule in New York by channeling their concerns into union activity, independent political efforts, and especially Irish-American nationalism. By the mid-1880s, as Democrats of all stripes rallied around Abram Hewitt for mayor, many Irish-Catholic workers took their demands for land and labor reform into the Knights of Labor, and especially into Henry George's powerful but unsuccessful bid to become the city's mayor.

*See* Nativism; Ku Klux Klan; New York City

---

Michael A. Gordon, *Orange Riots: Irish Political Violence in New York City 1870, 1871* (Ithaca, 1993).

MICHAEL A. GORDON

## OREGON

Oregon, admitted to the Union in 1859, had a significant Irish presence from the earliest days of white settlement. The self-consciously Irish population increased through the nineteenth century, and reached a peak in community awareness and unity in the years just before World War I. Conflicting allegiances during World War I, and during the campaign for the recognition of Irish independence, brought disunity to the Oregon Irish, especially in Portland. After about 1920, the bulk of the Irish-American population found its primary identifications outside the ethnic framework.

### THE FATHER OF OREGON

Dr. John McLoughlin (1784–1857), the most prominent of the Oregon Country pioneers, was born in La Riviere du Loup, Quebec. His paternal grandfather had emigrated to Quebec from Ireland. Although both his parents were Catholics, McLoughlin was raised in the Protestant home of his maternal grandfather. McLoughlin became a physician, then joined the Northwest Company, which later merged with the Hudson's Bay Company. He traveled overland to Fort George (Astoria), became chief factor of the company at Fort Vancouver (in Washington today), where he moved the headquarters in 1825. He refused to sell alcohol to the Indians, and maintained good relations with them throughout his tenure. He built the first sawmill in the Northwest in 1827; the first permanent settlement in Oregon came in 1829 when McLoughlin permitted French Canadians from his company to settle at St. Paul in the Willamette Valley. Against the wishes of his employer, McLoughlin did much to aid the American settlers, and so eventually had to resign. He converted to Catholicism in 1842, and retired in 1846 to Oregon City, where he died. In 1957 the legislature bestowed on McLoughlin the title "Father of Oregon."

### SETTLEMENT PATTERNS

Until the 1880s the Irish were the largest foreign-born group in Portland, and behind only the Chinese in the state as a whole. By 1910, the Irish foreign-born in the state ranked behind the Germans, Canadians, British, Chinese, Swedes, Norwegians, Italians, and Russians. In 1910, of the 4,995 Irish-born in the state, 2,267 lived in the city of Portland.

A notable rural pocket of Irish emigration arose in Lake County in south central Oregon. The first Irishman, Michael McShane, came from County Armagh in 1869. Sheepherders from County Cork helped to establish a lasting Irish colony. Dr. Bernard Daly (1858–1920), born in County Mayo and educated in the United States, came to Lake County in 1887. He ran the only hospital in the county seat, established a bank, served as a judge for 12 years, and was elected to both branches of the state legislature. The bulk of his estate went to the Bernard Daly Educational Trust, which has provided for the education of more than one thousand Lake County students with college scholarships. Ralph Friedman, historian of rural Oregon, notes: "No one during their lifetime stamped their character more indelibly upon any part of Oregon than Dr. Bernard Daly did upon Lake County."

Another rural pocket of Irish settlers, also largely sheepherders in the early settlement, arose in Morrow County in eastern Oregon. Judge John Kilkenny, historian of this county, lists 168 Irish family names in the county, which had a total population of only 7,625 in 1990.

### IRISH-AMERICAN INSTITUTIONS

By 1910 the Irish in Portland had established a network of organizations. The diocesan newspaper, the *Catholic Sentinel,* as its historian Rev. Wilfred Schoenberg, S.J., reports, at this time devoted far more attention to the campaign for Irish independence than to events in all the rest of Europe. Among the leaders of the clergy were Irish-Americans Rev. Edwin Vincent O'Hara (later a bishop), Rev. William Daly, Rev. George Thompson, and the bishop himself, Alexander Christie.

Portland had a chapter of the Ancient Order of Hibernians as early as 1877. Rev. Hugh Gallagher, a Holy Cross priest and native Irish speaker himself, who had studied Irish history and Celtic languages at graduate school at the Catholic University of America, served as a chaplain for the Hibernians in Portland.

The Ancient Order of Hibernians promoted Irish-American pride in their ancestry and fought against anti-Irish bigotry and discrimination. The Hibernians held their national convention in Portland in 1910; the local chapter built its own meeting hall in Portland in 1914. The Ancient Order of Hibernians reached its maximum membership in Portland, 490 members, in 1916.

The more militant and secret organization, Clan na Gael, also known as the United Brotherhood, used "Robert Emmet Literary Society" as its cover in Portland. This group, whose local leader was Irish-born attorney Thomas Mannix, advocated violent overthrow of British rule in Ireland. In Oregon it concentrated on raising money to assist the Irish campaign for independence, and on raising awareness about the Irish struggle.

The Irish Catholic community in Portland was certainly not as dominant or visible as those in San Francisco or Butte, Montana (the principal Irish centers in the West), but it was by 1916 a proud and self-aware group with its own distinctive institutions.

## Labor Unrest in the Northwest

Perhaps the most notorious labor radical of the early century in Oregon was Dr. Marie Equi (1872–1952), who came from an Italian-Irish family in New Bedford, Massachusetts. Equi attracted attention by her campaign for the eight-hour day, her arrest along with Margaret Sanger for distributing birth control information, her arrest for threatening policemen during the cannery strike of 1913, and her frequent leadership of anti-war demonstrations. The U.S. District Attorney in Portland described her as "the most dangerous woman in the West."

## World War I and Irish-American Disunity

World War I brought fragmentation to the Irish in Oregon, as it did to Irish communities throughout the country. In Portland, when an Irish fund-raiser and propagandist teamed up with Dr. Equi, this liaison split the local Irish community, who became torn between allegiance to Ireland and allegiance to the United States. Some local Irish-Americans also felt their social respectability under threat from this agitation and the great amount of public attention it received in the newspapers, as demonstrated in the conflict between the leading physician and one of the most active lawyers.

Among the most prominent Irish-Americans in the city was Dr. Andrew C. Smith (1856–1943), both of whose parents were Irish-born. Smith's family came to Oregon from Wisconsin when he was eight years old. After studying medicine in California, he served with the army in Indian campaigns. Following eight years in private practice in California, he studied in Vienna, and observed at hospitals in Berlin, Glasgow, and London, then returned to Portland to set up practice.

Dr. Smith, a pioneer in the use of X-ray equipment, became county physician in 1891, and was elected first president of the Oregon State Board of Health. Twice elected as a state senator and once as a state representative, Smith was by 1916 a respectable Irish-American, a member of the local establishment. He was also one of the wealthiest people in the state, with extensive business interests in Oregon and Alaska.

Thomas Mannix was born in Ireland and raised in Massachusetts, where he earned a law degree. Although a prominent attorney in Portland, he was on the periphery of polite Irish Catholic society because of his divorce. The local leader of Clan na Gael,

he became the leader of the more public local chapter of the Friends of Irish Freedom during World War I. The more militant local Irish often had their meetings in his law offices. Mannix, although deeply committed to the Irish nationalist cause, was also mindful that his position as a prosperous local lawyer necessitated his staying within the law.

During World War I, Clan na Gael leaders on the East Coast sponsored Irish activists coming to the United States to raise money for the revolution and to create support for an independent Ireland. Dr. Gertrude Kelly (1862–1934), head of the Irish Women's Council in New York City, recruited Irish women, often relatives of the slain leaders in Ireland. Women were particularly effective during the war, because males of military age often had difficulty travelling.

## Kathleen O'Brennan and Marie Equi

Dr. Kelly arranged for Kathleen O'Brennan to visit Portland on a propaganda and fund-raising tour of the United States. O'Brennan's brother-in-law, Eamonn Ceannt, one of the leaders of the Easter Rebellion in 1916, had died before a British firing squad. Kathleen O'Brennan, who traveled throughout the United States from 1914 to 1922, wrote a pamphlet which included Ceannt's letters from prison, written the night before his execution.

O'Brennan came to Portland for what she intended to be a short fund-raising and propaganda visit in July 1918. Frightened by the constant surveillance by both the U.S. Army Intelligence and the Bureau of Investigation, and feeling ill, she sought help from the radical Dr. Equi, whose sympathies for Irish freedom were well known. Equi confronted the agents at gunpoint and tore the listening device out of O'Brennan's hotel room. Equi also persuaded O'Brennan to make her talks more radical. O'Brennan then attracted big crowds in Portland and Seattle, and the government agents noted that she was the most successful of the Irish agitators in Portland.

O'Brennan moved into Equi's hotel room and stayed in Portland for six months, through Equi's trial and through the armistice. Despite warnings from local Irish-American leader Mannix about Equi's notoriety, O'Brennan compromised her Irish mission by siding so publicly with Equi when it was clear that this would alienate the middle-class Irish-Americans. O'Brennan became an honorary member of the Industrial Workers of the World, penned resolutions on behalf of Equi from organized labor, and even assisted Equi with a jury-tampering scheme and a plot to avoid trial by faking an attack of influenza (when that disease was at epidemic levels).

Mannix, with his courthouse and police connections, knew that the federal agents were gossiping about a romantic relationship between Equi and O'Brennan, and he knew about the jury-tampering scheme. The Bureau of Investigation infiltrated an Irish-American volunteer agent into Equi and O'Brennan's company, and she reported daily on their activities. Even the archbishop of Portland, Alexander Christie, had come under surveillance by the Bureau of Investigation as a result of indiscreet remarks made by O'Brennan. Mannix also knew of Equi's reputation as a lesbian and an abortionist. Mannix wanted a break from O'Brennan, for fear of public scandal.

Dr. Smith, not understanding the potential for public scandal, insisted on support for O'Brennan, whom he saw as a crusader for Ireland. He believed O'Brennan when she said that Mannix was lazy and simply did not want to do what was necessary to support Ireland. Mannix could not, or would not, reveal to Smith the real nature of his reservations about O'Brennan and

Equi. One tense meeting ended in a shouting match with Mannix denouncing Smith as a "millionaire dabbler."

Equi went to a widely publicized trial just as the war was ending. At the end of the trial, Equi fought with the local head of the Bureau of Investigation in the courthouse; he knocked her to the floor, an event covered by all the local papers. The labor unions, stirred up by O'Brennan, demonstrated loudly and sent petitions asking for Equi's release. Kathleen O'Brennan, much to the dismay of the polite Irish Catholic community, was constantly at Equi's side.

Equi went to San Quentin Prison, and O'Brennan had to use her California political connections to avoid deportation. The wide publicity given to the trial, the frequent references to socialism at a time of the growing Red Scare, and the public involvement of O'Brennan in the proceedings severely compromised O'Brennan's Irish mission and divided the Portland Irish community.

When released from prison after serving ten months of her three-year sentence, Dr. Equi returned to Portland, but never again achieved the notoriety of the war years. Irish-American radical labor agitator Elizabeth Gurley Flynn (1890–1964), a leader in the I.W.W. and later in the Communist Party, lived during 1926–1936 in Portland with Equi. O'Brennan returned to Ireland in 1922, where she maintained her republican sympathies, but without the strong socially radical flavor of her Equi-influenced Portland adventure.

## DE VALERA'S VISIT

Eamon de Valera, who described himself as the president of republican Ireland (when he was president of the Dail), visited Portland in November 1919, during his tour of the United States to raise money for the revolution and to try to win the support of the American government for Irish freedom.

De Valera's visit coincided with the "Centralia Massacre" (November 11, 1919) in which members of the Industrial Workers of the World killed four Legionnaires after the American Legion staged a parade in front of the Industrial Workers of the World headquarters in Centralia, Washington. Centralia, about ninety miles from Portland, was a coal-mining center where the miners had been on strike. An American Legion parade turned into a gun battle with four Legionnaires dying, including a decorated Army colonel who had been a University of Washington football star. The mob lynched one radical. On de Valera's arrival in Portland, he received an unfriendly reception from members of the American Legion, who tore the Irish flag from his automobile and demonstrated against him. Partially because of O'Brennan's previous connections with Equi, the American Legion, angry about Centralia, associated de Valera and the Irish nationalists with anti-American radicalism.

At Columbia University (renamed the University of Portland in 1935), de Valera received a warm reception. He came accompanied by Archbishop Christie, the millionaire Catholic physician Dr. Andrew Smith, and Thomas Mannix, who was then the president of the local chapter of the Friends of Irish Freedom. Rev. Hugh Gallagher, C.S.C., then vice president of Columbia University, greeted de Valera in Irish. This event marked the height of local solidarity among the Irish-Americans.

## REV. DOMINIC O'CONNOR

When Terence MacSwiney, the Lord Mayor of Cork, starved himself to death in 1920 as a protest against British counterrevolutionary reprisals, he received last rites from Capuchin priest Dominic O'Connor. O'Connor found himself exiled to Oregon, where he served with distinction in the rural Baker diocese. In 1930 he published the first history of that sparsely populated diocese, which is twice the size of Ireland. In 1958, he and another Capuchin exile were returned for burial in Rochestown, Ireland, with church and state honors.

## KU KLUX KLAN AND THE CATHOLIC SCHOOLS

In the November election of 1922, the compulsory public school initiative, supported by the Ku Klux Klan and clearly directed against the Catholic schools, passed 106,910 to 92,530. The United States Supreme Court unanimously declared this measure unconstitutional on June 1, 1925.

John P. Kavanaugh, a circuit court judge whose father was born in Dublin, received the DeSmet Medal from Gonzaga University for his legal work in the Oregon School Bill Case. Kavanaugh helped to persuade the Knights of Columbus to finance the successful appeal. The Oregon School Bill Case mobilized the Catholics of Oregon, but the Irish Catholics fought this battle against nativism as Catholics rather than as Irishmen.

Another influential Irish-American politician of this era, also noteworthy for his fight against local bigotry, was Frank Lonergan, speaker of the state House of Representatives 1931–33, who became co-chairman of the National Conference of Christians and Jews, and later a judge of the Multnomah County Circuit Court.

## DISPERSAL AND ASSIMILATION OF THE IRISH-AMERICANS

After World War I the Irish in Oregon increasingly dispersed from the specifically Irish neighborhoods and towns. Membership in the Ancient Order of Hibernians fell in the 1930s to only one chapter with 30 members; the Order died out entirely in the state during World War II. The *Catholic Sentinel* no longer ran so many articles on events in Ireland, and its pieces reflected the disillusionment many Irish-Americans felt at the Civil War in Ireland. The Hibernia Commercial and Savings Bank failed in December 1931, after its deposits declined precipitously.

## IRISH IN OREGON TODAY

The All-Ireland Cultural Society (founded in 1938 in Portland as the All-Ireland Social Club) is a nonprofit organization that sponsors social opportunities, Irish entertainment, and cultural education. Efforts are currently underway to revive the Ancient Order of Hibernians in Oregon. As an example of the current interest in Irish-American history, more than four hundred people attended the Irish Heritage and Potato Famine Commemoration Day events, held at what had been the Hibernian Hall in the former Irish neighborhood in Portland on June 1, 1997.

Timothy Michael Dolan, *"Some Seed Fell on Good Ground": The Life of Edwin V. O'Hara* (Washington, D.C., 1992).

Ralph Friedman, *The Other Side of Oregon* (Caldwell, ID, 1993).

Paul G. Merriam, "The 'Other Portland': A Statistical Note on Foreign-Born, 1860–1910," *Oregon Historical Quarterly* 80 (Fall 1979): 258–268.

Edwin V. O'Hara, *Catholic History of Oregon* (Portland, OR, 1916).

Dominic O'Connor, *A Brief History of the Diocese of Baker* (St. Benedict, OR, 1930).

Lawrence J. Saalfeld, *Forces of Prejudice in Oregon, 1920–1925* (Portland, OR, 1984).

Wilfred P. Schoenberg, *Defender of the Faith: The History of the* Catholic Sentinel, *1870–1990* (Portland, OR, 1993).

Wilfred P. Schoenberg, *A History of the Catholic Church in the Pacific Northwest, 1743–1983* (Washington, D.C., 1987).

Oliver Snoddy, "A Clan na Gael Constitution and Ritual from Portland, 1916," *Irish Sword* 9 (1969–70): 216–239.

Mary Jane Sorber, ed., "The Irish in Early Oregon History" (Portland, OR, 1993).

William S. Stone, *The Cross in the Middle of Nowhere: The History of the Catholic Church in Eastern Oregon* (Bend, OR, 1993).

Joseph A. Schiwek, "Some Prominent Oregon Lay Catholics Over the Years," *Oregon Catholic Historical Society Newsletter* 9 (Summer, 1997): 5–6.

ARTHUR WHEELER, C.S.C.

## O'REILLY, JOHN BOYLE (1844–1890) and MARY (Murphy) O'REILLY (1850–1897)

Fenian, poet, journalist, orator, and civil libertarian. Born in Dowth, Co. Meath, to William David and Eliza (Boyle) O'Reilly, one of eight children. The family lived at Dowth Castle where William ran a national (grade) school. Due to family financial problems, O'Reilly began his work life at age eleven as a printer's apprentice with the Drogheda *Argus.* When he was fifteen, the *Argus* closed down, and O'Reilly moved to Preston, Lancashire, where he lived with an aunt and worked as a cub reporter for the Preston *Guardian.* His three-plus years in Preston, which included part-time service in the Eleventh Lancashire Rifle Volunteers, he described as among the happiest in his life.

### O'REILLY AND THE FENIAN PLOT OF 1865

In 1863, at his father's request, O'Reilly returned to Ireland. Having enjoyed his first taste of soldiering, he enlisted as a full-time cavalryman in the elite Tenth Hussars in Dublin. In 1865, recruited by John Devoy, he joined the revolutionary Fenian movement, while continuing his service with the Hussars. In that year, a raid by the authorities on the Fenian newspaper office in Dublin led to the discovery of plans for a rebellion against British rule and to the revealing of the identity of many Fenians, including O'Reilly. He was court-martialled, found

John Boyle O'Reilly

guilty of failing to inform his superiors of "an intended mutiny" and sentenced to death. The death sentence was immediately commuted to twenty years' penal servitude, the first year of which, beginning in September 1866, he spent in brutal conditions in English prisons, the worst of which was Dartmoor. He made three unsuccessful escape attempts, once remaining at large for two days.

### O'REILLY AND AUSTRALIA

More to his relief than trepidation, in October 1867 O'Reilly was placed on board the convict ship *Hougoumont,* along with sixty-two other Fenians and over two hundred "regular" criminals, for transportation to a convict settlement in Western Australia. (This was the last convict transportation to Australia.) Despite O'Reilly's grim portrayal of life on a convict ship in his novel *Moondyne,* the Fenians in general had quarters separate from the criminals and were well treated. For the last seven weeks of the eighty-nine day voyage, they produced, with consummate skill and with O'Reilly as co-editor, their own weekly paper *The Wild Goose,* which even the ship's officers and captain enjoyed. The *Hougoumont* docked at Freemantle on January 10, 1868.

Although the forced labor conditions, which involved cutting roads through virgin forest in the searing heat, were harsh, O'Reilly was moved and mystified by the exotic beauty of the Australian scenery, and this is reflected in several of his Australian poems. As A. G. Evans put it, O'Reilly's poetry shows "a rare understanding, sensitivity and warm regard for the strange environment which he inhabited for a short time." O'Reilly's model behavior as a prisoner quickly led to his promotion to trainee assistant constable, a position which gave him considerable freedom of movement as he was regularly used as a messenger by his work-gang boss, Warder Henry Woodman.

From the moment he arrived in Australia, O'Reilly had contemplated escape. He shared his thoughts with the local Catholic priest, Fr. Patrick Mc.Cabe who arranged a secret passage for him on an American whaler. With plans for the escape well under way, O'Reilly faced a painful dilemma. During the course of his several trips from the bush to Warder Goodman's home on the latter's business, O'Reilly and Goodman's daughter Jessie had fallen in love and entered a passionate sexual relationship.

As his escape attempt loomed nearer, something drove O'Reilly to despair. Either Jessie broke off her clearly doomed relationship with O'Reilly, or he felt hopelessly torn between his love for Jessie and his desire to escape to America. In any case, on December 27, 1868, O'Reilly walked into the bush and slashed the veins in his left arm. Only the fact that he was discovered by a fellow-prisoner saved his life.

About six weeks later, O'Reilly proceeded with the escape plan developed by Fr. Mc.Cabe. At an agreed time O'Reilly slipped into the bush where he was met by a friend of the priest's, James Maguire, and some of the latter's friends. After an agonizing miscue with the whaler *Vigilant,* and after several anxious days in the bush, O'Reilly and his companions rowed out to sea. He was taken aboard the New Bedford whaler, *Gazelle,* captained by David Gifford, with whom Fr. Mc.Cabe had made a new arrangement after the *Vigilant* failure.

On board, O'Reilly and the young second-mate, Henry C. Hathaway, developed a friendship that was to last a lifetime. Twice on the voyage Hathaway saved the adventurous O'Reilly's life—once when the latter was injured during a whale hunt, and the second time when Hathaway helped conceal O'Reilly from the authorities who searched the *Gazelle* at the British port of Roderique. Later O'Reilly transferred for safety to the American whaler *Sapphire* which took him to Liverpool, where he was hidden for a few days. His final transfer was to the *Bombay* which landed him in Philadelphia on November 23, 1869. O'Reilly promptly took out U.S. citizenship papers.

### JOURNALIST, ORATOR, CIVIL LIBERTARIAN

From Philadelphia O'Reilly quickly went to New York to a tumultuous Fenian reception. The New York Fenians recommended that he move on to Boston, where he would have more scope for his talents as a writer. With the help of some introductions from New York, he soon signed on as a reporter for the weekly *Pilot,* the largest Irish Catholic paper in the U.S.

One of O'Reilly's first assignments was to cover a Fenian raid from St. Alban's, VT, into Canada. The raid was one of a brief series that began in 1866, with the idea of seizing a piece of Canada and using it as a bargaining chip to negotiate with the British for Irish independence. O'Reilly initially approved of the St. Alban's raid but its dismal failure helped move him in the direction of the non-violent Irish Home Rule Party, whose cause he came to advocate with eloquence. He was always, however, prepared to countenance the use of violence in the Irish cause as a last resort.

O'Reilly used the columns of the *Pilot,* of which he became editor in 1873 and co-owner with the Archbishop of Boston in 1876, to plead the cause of Irish Home Rule and the cause of the Irish in the U.S. He also recommended in the *Pilot* that all Irish immigrants, Orange and Green, declare their loyalty to the U.S., a move O'Reilly saw as the best way the immigrants could help both themselves and Ireland. He championed the rights not only of the Irish, but of all minorities in America, except for the Chinese who could never, he felt, integrate into American society. He also championed the cause of the Democratic Party from a strongly Jeffersonian viewpoint. He published the works of promising young writers, including W. B. Yeats and Oscar Wilde. Under his editorship, the *Pilot* reached a circulation of 1.5 million.

His journalism, his poetry, his progressive views (though he did not believe in female suffrage) and his appealing personality (Michael Davitt wrote, "No man or woman could resist the magnetic charms of O'Reilly's personality" and Justin McCarthy M.P. said "It was one of the curious privileges of John Boyle O'Reilly to be universally liked") quickly made O'Reilly one of the most popular men in Boston. He was an active member of several clubs, notably The Papyrus, of which he was a founder. The Papyrus was a club for men of letters which also honored prominent women writers. Among his friends he numbered Patrick Collins, Robert Dwyer Joyce, Oliver Wendell Holmes, Henry W. Longfellow, Thomas Manning, the abolitionist Wendell Phillips, John Greenleaf Whittier, and several other eminent Bostonians. He did much to allay the Yankee fear of the Catholic Irish influx to Boston. In August, 1872, he married Mary Murphy (q.v.) of Charlestown, which borders Boston. The couple lived in Charlestown and had four daughters.

O'Reilly was a man of tremendous energy. In addition to his journalistic output, he was much in demand as a speaker, nationwide, on topics ranging from the role of the Irish in America to Home Rule and Civil Rights. He gave addresses of welcome to Parnell, Smith O'Brien, and other members of the Irish Parliamentary Party on their visits to Boston. He enjoyed boxing, rowing, fishing and shooting. His was the genius behind the extraordinary rescue from Australia, in 1876, of six remaining Fenian prisoners by the New Bedford whaler, *Catalpa.*

### LITERARY OUTPUT

O'Reilly began writing poetry as a boy. By the time he arrived in the U.S., his reputation as a poet was already established. In addition to his journalistic writings, he produced four volumes of poetry, some fiction and one non-fiction work. *POETRY: Songs of the Southern Seas* (1873); *Songs, Legends and Ballads* (1878); *The Statues in the Block* (1881); and *In Bohemia* (1886). *FICTION:* A novel based on his Australian prison experience, *Moondyne,* appeared in 1879. He cooperated with Robert Grant, Frederic J. Stimson and John T. Wheelwright on a futuristic novel *The King's Men* (1884). His *Ethics of Boxing and Manly Sport* appeared in 1888.

His poetry is seldom read today, but was highly popular in its time, not only with the public (*Songs, Legends, and Ballads* went into an eighth edition), but with established poets like Longfellow, Whittier, and James Whitcomb Reilly. O'Reilly was the official poet for the O'Connell centenary celebration in Boston in 1875, for the dedication of the Pilgrim Monument at Plymouth in 1889, and for the dedication of Catholic University, also in 1889. He received an honorary LL.D. from Notre Dame in the last week of June 1881 and was made an honorary member of Phi Beta Kappa at Dartmouth College that same week, his poetry being cited in both instances. Horace Greeley was so impressed by "The Amber Whale," a poem inspired by O'Reilly's time on the whaler *Gazelle,* that he attempted (unsuccessfully) to get O'Reilly to join the staff of the New York Tribune.

O'Reilly frequently used a ballad measure and declamatory style that was popular with the Young Ireland poets but this style does not read comfortably in the late twentieth century. Further, as his friend James Jeffrey Roche pointed out, O'Reilly was more concerned with content than style. Yet the poetry deserves much more attention that it receives today and A. G. Evans has recently called for an edition of O'Reilly's best poems. Such an edition would certainly contain many of his fine poems on Australia, which are free of Irish-American and Young Ireland influence, and would include the well-wrought lyric, "A White Rose":

> The red rose whispers of passion
>    And the white rose breathes of love;
> Oh, the red rose is a falcon,
>    And the white rose is a dove.
>
> But I send you a cream-white rosebud
>    With a flush on its petal tips;
> For the love that is purest and sweetest
>    Has a kiss of desire on the lips.

### O'REILLY'S DEATH

An element of mystery surrounds the premature death of John Boyle O'Reilly at the age of forty-six. He was a chronic insomniac and had been badly overworked in the year leading up to his death. Mary O'Reilly was also an insomniac and chronic invalid. The received story for generations has been that O'Reilly accidentally took an overdose of her sleeping medicine and died as a result.

There has however, always been some suspicion that the death was a suicide and the recent book (see Bibliography) by A. G. Evans lends some credence to that idea, citing recently discovered early unpublished poems which suggest, on O'Reilly's part, a tendency toward severe depression. Evans also cites O'Reilly's Australian suicide attempt, which he (Evans) amply documents. Further, the fact that O'Reilly's wife was a chronic invalid and one of his daughters, Blanid, a semi-invalid must have taken a toll on him. It is quite conceivable that, in those early hours of August 10, 1890, at his summer home in Hull, MA, the exhausted O'Reilly simply decided to end it all.

O'Reilly's untimely death led to a massive outpouring of grief on an international level. Letters of condolence from several parts of the world poured into Boston, including one from President Benjamin Harrison. An impressive memorial service, addressed by some of Boston's most distinguished citizens (white and black), was held at the Tremont Temple. O'Reilly is buried in Holyrood Cemetery, Brookline, beside Boston. An excerpt from the introduction to Schofield's fictionalized biography (see bibliography) could well have served as O'Reilly's epitaph: "He brought new strength to the fight against bigotry and oppression, new force and integrity to American journalism, new enthusiasm to American democracy. It was our good fortune to have had him with us, though briefly; it was Ireland's misfortune to have lost him."

## MARY (MURPHY) O'REILLY (1850–1897)

Born in Charlestown, MA, her parents were John Murphy from Co. Fermanagh, (b. 1823) and Jane Smiley from Co. Donegal (b. 1830). Mary met O'Reilly in the year of his arrival in Boston. He had enjoyed a short story written under the *nom de plume* "Agnes Smiley" in the Boston Catholic youth magazine "The Young Crusader." He inquired as to the writer's identity, discovered that her real name was Mary Murphy, and he obtained an introduction.

It appears that the young couple fell rapidly in love, but waited to marry until O'Reilly's financial position was secure. The following announcement appeared in the *Pilot* of August 24, 1872: "Married, on Thursday August 15, the Feast of the Assumption, in St. Mary's Church, Charlestown, by Rev. George A. Hamilton, Mr. John Boyle O'Reilly, of Boston, to Miss Mary Murphy, of Charlestown. The couple spent their honeymoon in New Hampshire and Maine and then moved into what was to be their permanent home at 34 Winthrop St., Charlestown." Mary bore O'Reilly four daughters: Mollie (b. 1873); Eliza Boyle (b. 1874); Agnes Smiley (b. 1877) and Blanid (b. 1880). The marriage appears to have been a happy one, and O'Reilly liked to refer to Mary by the pet-name "Mamsey." He regularly turned over all of his salary to Mary, whom he described as a "wonderful manager." It was she who made the plans for the reconstruction of the summer house that the couple bought in the seaside town of Hull in 1879.

Some years into the marriage, Mary became a chronic invalid and insomniac. (This situation could not have been helped by the fact that the youngest child, Blanid, was a semi-invalid). Nonetheless, Mary was able to accompany O'Reilly on a long trip in late 1889, which included the dedication of Catholic University and a trip to the Metropolitan Museum in New York, where she was fascinated by Barye's animal sculptures and deeply moved by Millet's "L'Angelus."

It was Mary, waking from her sleep, at four a.m., who discovered the dying and by then inarticulate O'Reilly in the tower-room of their Hull home on August 10, 1890. She summoned the family doctor, who arrived promptly, but her husband died within the hour. So prostrate was Mary with grief that she was unable to attend the funeral Mass three days later at St. Mary's, Charlestown, where she and O'Reilly had married.

It was Mary who edited her husband's *Complete Poems and Speeches* as part of James Jeffrey Roche's 1891 biography of O'Reilly. She died in 1897, at age 47, and is buried near O'Reilly in Holyrood Cemetery. Of her daughters, only Agnes married. Agnes's son, retired Professor Richard Boyle O'Reilly Hocking resides in New Hampshire, and the Boyle O'Reilly name will live on in the U.S. through his children and grandchildren.

*See* Boston; Nationalism, Irish-American (1800–1921)

John Amos, *The Fenians in Australia, 1865–1880* (Kensington, 1988).
A. G. Evans, *Fanatic Heart: A Life of John Boyle O'Reilly* (Nedlands, 1997).
James Jeffrey Roche, *John Boyle O'Reilly: His Life, Poems and Speeches* (New York, 1891).
William G. Schofield, *Seek for a Hero: The Story of John Boyle O'Reilly* (New York, 1956).
——, *A Memorial of John Boyle O'Reilly from The City of Boston*, 2d ed. (Printed by order of the Common Council: Rockwell and Churchill Press, Boston 1891).

CONOR JOHNSTON

## O'SHAUGHNESSY, IGNATIUS ALOYSIUS (1885–1973)

Oil company executive. Ignatius Aloysius O'Shaughnessy was born July 31, 1885, in Stillwater, Minn., to John and Mary (Milan) O'Shaughnessy. His grandfather, John O'Shaughnessy, had emigrated from Ireland in 1835 and settled in Milford, Mass.

He was educated at St. Thomas Military Academy, St. Paul, Minn., and received a bachelor's degree from the College of St. Thomas in 1907. While pursuing his studies, O'Shaughnessy was secretary of the college from 1905–07.

In 1908 he married Lillian Gertrude Smith of St. Paul. They had five children.

From 1907–1917 he worked in the insurance business and banking. In 1917 he organized the Globe Oil & Refining Co. in Blackwell, Okla. While president of that company, he also served as president of the Lario Oil & Gas Co., beginning in 1927, and the Globe Pipeline Co. in 1934, both of which were affiliated with his original company.

O'Shaughnessy also served as a director of the First National Bank and the First Bank Stock Corp. of St. Paul. He belonged to several civic organizations, including the St. Paul Association of Commerce; St. Paul Institute of General and Applied Science; the Minnesota, Somerset, Town and Country, and Athletic clubs of St. Paul; the Chicago Yacht Club; the Wichita (Kan.) Club; Indian Creek Golf Club, Miami, Fla.; and the Elks. He was a 25-year member of the Petroleum Society, and a member and director of the American Petroleum Institute.

He was a prominent Roman Catholic and served as a director of his alma mater, the College of St. Thomas, and a trustee of the University of Notre Dame and St. Paul Seminary. He was a member of the Knights of Columbus, a Papal Chamberlain of the Sword and Cape, Knight of the Holy Sepulchre, Knight of Malta, and Knight Commander of St. Gregory. In 1967 he was named a papal count.

Georgetown University, Washington, D.C., honored him with its Ignatian award, and the University of Minnesota, its regent's medal. He also received the Pax Christi medal and the St. George medal from the Boy Scouts of America. He was granted an honorary doctorate of letters from the University of Notre Dame in 1946 and also received honorary degrees from Loyola University and De Paul University, Chicago.

In 1943 he contributed $200,000 toward strengthening the University of Notre Dame college of arts and letters; the university acknowledged his donation by establishing the O'Shaughnessy Fine Arts Foundation. He also donated $500,000 to the College of St. Thomas for a physical education building and $100,000 to St. Louis (Mo.) University for a library, both of which were named in his honor.

For his many charitable works for several Catholic charities and academic institutions, the University of Notre Dame bestowed its Laetare Medal on O'Shaughnessy in 1953.

*National Cyclopedia of American Biography* (New York, 1946).
*Who's Who in America* (1972–1973).

MARIANNA McLOUGHLIN

## O'SHAUGHNESSY, MICHAEL MAURICE (1864–1934)

Hydraulic engineer. Born in Limerick, Ireland, to Patrick and Margaret (O'Donnell), O'Shaughnessy attended Queen's College, Cork, and Queen's College, Galway, before entering Royal University, Dublin, where he was graduated with honors in the field of engineering. In 1885 he emigrated to California and began work with the Sierra Valley & Mohawk Railroad before moving to the Southern Pacific Railroad in San Francisco in 1887.

O'Shaughnessy preferred working with private corporations and focused on his specialty of hydraulic engineering. He worked on several notable projects including: constructing a water supply for twenty sugar plantations in Hawaii; he was chief consultant for the Southern California Mountain Water Company at San Diego; worked on the Salmas River for Shreelo Sugar Company; a masonry dam on the Merced River; a water works at Port Costa, California; and finally a position as chief engineer in San Francisco where he designed many public works such as the extension of streets and sewers, new boulevards, tunnels, bridges, and hydroelectric projects. In addition, he added to the city of San Francisco the municipal railway system, the main sewer under the Golden Gate Park, the Stockton Street and Twin Peaks tunnels, and he constructed an auxiliary high-pressure fire system.

O'Shaughnessy's greatest feat was that of the construction of the Hetch Hetchy water supply system, a project he worked on for over twenty years. This project afforded him the honor of naming one of the many consitituents the O'Shaughnessy Dam in the Hetch Hetchy Valley, a 344-foot-high dam. However, in 1934 near the end of this consuming project O'Shaughnessy suffered a heart attack and died shortly before a celebration that was to honor him for his contributions. He is remembered for his engineering brilliance and dedication to the city of San Francisco.

*Engineering News-Record* (October 18, 1934).
*Who's Who in America* (1934–1935).
*Dictionary of American Biography*, supplement 1.

JOY HARRELL

## O'SULLIVAN, MARY KENNEY (1864–1943)

Union organizer, feminist. Mary Kenney O'Sullivan was born in Hannibal, Missouri, January 5, 1864, the daughter of Michael and Mary (Kelly) Kenney, Irish immigrants of the early 1850s. The parents were married in New Hampshire and moved west with a railroad construction crew—he as a foreman and mechanic; she as a cook for the "gandy dancers," or railroad workers. The family settled in Hannibal when the father took a permanent job with the Burlington Railroad. Mary attended convent school, but was transferred out after questioning its disciplinary code and promotion practices. She never completed grammar school, going to work first as a dressmaker's apprentice, then as a bookbinder. A protracted strike at the Burlington Railroad in 1888 made her a strong partisan of trade unionism. It was a cause that would motivate her the rest of her life.

After the death of her father, Mary Kenney worked as a bookbinder in Iowa and Illinois. In Chicago she organized a women's bindery union, which led to appointment to the city's Trades and Labor Assembly. She also lobbied for Illinois' first factory laws, and worked briefly in the state's factory inspection department. Her endeavors drew the attention of Samuel Gompers, president of the American Federation of Labor, and in 1892 he appointed her the AFL's first national female organizer. In that role she worked to organize garment workers in New York, as well as printers, binders, carpet weavers and shoe workers in Massachusetts.

In 1894 Kenney married John F. O'Sullivan, another AFL organizer, as well as a labor writer for the *Boston Globe*. The wedding took place in Manhattan with Gompers as the official witness. The couple settled in Boston, where Mary had four children before being widowed in 1902. She married a second time as a Tierney, but subsequently she resumed her first husband's surname.

In 1903, with the support of the Women's Educational and Industrial Union, O'Sullivan co-founded the National Women's Trade Union League to promote trade unionism among women. Among other things, she campaigned for shorter hours, increased wages and improved on-site conditions. She taught English and housekeeping to immigrants, and helped run a summer camp in Winthrop for a social welfare organization. O'Sullivan was also involved in the peace movement (she vigorously opposed World War I), housing for the poor, prohibition, and progressive politics. Her activities made her one of the most visible feminists of her time.

The Lawrence (Massachusetts) textile strike of 1912 found O'Sullivan on the side of the strikers, and when the Massachusetts legislature two years later created a Division of Industrial Safety (partly in response to the strike), she was named a factory inspector. She served in that capacity for twenty-three years, retiring in 1937. O'Sullivan died in Medford, Massachusetts, January 18, 1943, and was buried in St. Joseph's Cemetery, West Roxbury.

In 1995 the Massachusetts legislature appropriated funds for a portrait of O'Sullivan to hang in the State House, the first Irish-American woman to be so honored.

*See* Labor Movement

George E. Ryan, "Mary Kenney O'Sullivan: Labor Reformer 'Elected' to State House," *Eire Society Bulletin* (Boston, February 1998).

Charles Shively, "Mary Kenney O'Sullivan," *Dictionary of American Biography,* Supplement 3 (New York, 1973).
*Massachusetts Humanities* (Spring 1998).

JOHN DEEDY

## O'SULLIVAN, MAUREEN (1911–1998)

Actress. Maureen Paula O'Sullivan was born in County Roscommon, Ireland, on May 17, 1911, to Maj. Charles Joseph O'Sullivan and the former Mary Lovatt Fraser. She was educated in convents of the Sacred Heart in London, Dublin and Paris. Interested in acting from an early age, she concentrated her education on writing and music. At eighteen, she had a chance meeting with the American director Frank Borzage, who gave her a screen test and a part in the film *Song of My Heart,* starring the celebrated tenor John McCormack.

Although she appeared in over 60 movies throughout her career in Hollywood, O'Sullivan will always be remembered as "Jane," the wife of the jungle man, Tarzan. She played Jane opposite John Weissmuller's *Tarzan* in six movies in the series throughout the thirties and forties.

In addition to the Tarzan films, some of O'Sullivan's hits include *A Connecticut Yankee* (1931), *Big Shot* (1932), *Cohens and Kellys in Trouble* (1933), *The Thin Man* (1934), *David Copperfield* (1935), *Pride and Prejudice* (1940), and *Never Too Late* (1965).

In 1980, O'Sullivan was honored by the Roman Catholic Interracial Council as "a distinguished Catholic who has worked to combat racial and religious bigotry and discrimination in our society."

In 1936, O'Sullivan married John Farrow with whom she had seven children, including Maria (Mia), a movie star in her own right. She was widowed in 1963 and married James Cushing in 1983. When she died in Arizona in 1998 she was the matriarch of a large family—with thirty-two grandchildren and thirteen great-grandchildren.

*See* Cinema, Irish in; California; Farrow, Mia

Maureen O'Sullivan

J. Concannon and Frank Cull, *Irish American Who's Who* (New York, 1984).
Joseph Curran, *Hibernian Green on the Silver Screen* (Westport, CT, 1990).

EILEEN DANEY CARZO

# P

## PALATINES FROM IRELAND

America was the intended destination of many of those who partook of the great Rhineland exodus of 1709, including one Michael Switzer, whose passport still uniquely survives. That Switzer should have come to Ireland instead is one of the quirks of history, which yields a fascinating story in its own right (O'Connor, 1996).

From initial roots struck between 1709 and 1720, a distinctive Irish Palatine community emerged based upon the primary hearths of the Southwell estate about Rathkeale in Co. Limerick and the Ram estate at Gorey and Old Ross in Co. Wexford. The Rathkeale settlement was by far the larger and from it a number of secondary colonization drives were sponsored between c. 1740 and c. 1776. Such drives occurred to the Pallaskenry, Kilfinane and Adare areas of Co. Limerick, the Tarbert and Ballymacelligott areas of north Co. Kerry, and to the Barker estate at Kilcooly on the Tipperary-Kilkenny borderland. Along with the distinctive endogamous communities of the parent colonies, all the secondary colonies figure prominently in the story of Palatine migration to America.

Emigration, once initiated, proves all too often to be a self-sustaining process. So it transpired in the case of the Irish Palatines. With them the seeds had been sown as early as 1756 when a small group of Co. Limerick Palatines sailed for America (Lapp, 1977, 71). This was to be decisively eclipsed four years later when a much larger group, containing some of the most vital and energetic members of the Palatine community, set out on the long Atlantic voyage to New York.

Arrival on the far side was duly noted. On August 18, 1760 the New York *Mercury* reported that "the ship Pery . . . arrived here on Monday in nine weeks from Limerick . . . with a number of Germans, the fathers of many having settled there in the year 1710; but not having sufficient scope in that country, chose to try their fortune in America."

The cohesion displayed by the Palatines in Ireland readily transferred on to American soil. There were Cookes, Dulmages, Emburys, Hecks, Hoffmans, Laurences, Lowers, Poffs, Shimmels, Shires, Sparlings and Ruttles, and their spousal interconnections. The bulk remained in New York where, in accordance with the principles of chain migration, they were joined by another Irish Palatine party in 1765.

All of these people had heard the message of Methodism and some had embraced it, but none had promulgated it in their newly found, raw and worldly environment. This was a matter which caused deep concern to one of their number, Barbara Ruttle Heck. She, it is agreed, was the force in persuading her double first cousin, Philip Embury, to commence preaching in his own house to his own community (O'Connor, 1996, 72). From such beginnings in 1766, the cradle of American Methodism translated two years later to a little church on John Street, New York, the very first of the Methodist churches of America.

Having made their pioneering contribution, the close-knit Palatine community found the call of rural living too strong an impulse to resist any longer. Accordingly, in 1770 they moved to a tract of land in Camden Valley within the province of New York. Adding to their strength, a trickle of immigrants continued to filter in from the homeland, but sadly and prematurely, Philip Embury died in 1773. Still the benefit of his inspiration lived on in a colony that, by 1777, had attained the numerical strength of at least one hundred adults (Lapp, 1977, 163–4).

By then, however, the spectre of the American War of Independence had darkened over the valley, and for a people who kept their allegiance to the Crown, this inevitably spelled disruption and eventual displacement. From 1778 onward the members of the Palatine colony at Camden Valley swelled the ranks of the Empire Loyalists as these proceeded northward to the loyal world of Canada.

Again in the northern land, once the dust had settled, it is possible to pick out cells of former Camden Valley colonists. Moreover the drift of the Palatines continued from their Irish homeland, punctuated by spurts in hard times and marked by the process of chain migration (Elliott, 1988, 251–3). The province of Upper Canada, or Ontario (as it became), proved to be the great cellular gathering ground (Heald, 1994), so much so that for many the American dream came as a belated experience. For example, all the known U.S.A. Teskeys of Palatine descent came south from Canada or alternatively like the Millers from around Rathkeale (O'Connor, 1993, 32–40) emigrated directly to the United States at a late date, i.e. post 1850.

Today families of Irish Palatine descent range all across North America, and the initial letters of their family names fill the entire spectrum of the alphabet (Jones, 1990).

*See* Emigration: 17th and 18th Centuries

Bruce S. Elliott, *Irish Migrants in the Canadas: A New Approach* (Belfast, 1988).

Carolyn A. Heald, *The Irish Palatines in Ontario: Religion, Ethnicity, and Rural Migration* (Gananoque, 1994).

Henry Z. Jones, *The Palatine Families of Ireland* (Camden, 1990).

Eula C. Lapp, *To Their Heirs Forever* (Belleville, 1977).

Patrick J. O'Connor, *All Worlds Possible: The Domain of the Millers of Coolybrown* (Newcastle West, 1993).

———, *People Make Places: The Story of the Irish Palatines* (Newcastle West, 1996).

PATRICK J. O'CONNOR

## PARIS PEACE CONFERENCE (1919), IRISH-AMERICANS AT

The First World War created an international situation that revolutionary Irish nationalists recognized as an opportunity to replace moderate home rule within the United Kingdom with complete independence under a republican form of government. Revolutionary nationalists in both Ireland and the United States sought that objective in the 1916 Rebellion, but their hopes were not crushed with the suppression of the Rebellion. The war aims of the Allies, to defend small nations, was augmented in 1917 and

Woodrow Wilson

1918 by President Woodrow Wilson's appeal for self-determination for all nations. These ideals offered an opportunity for Irish independence through the peace settlement. To promote these and other objectives, the Clan na Gael organized a large Irish Race Convention in Philadelphia in February 1919. By that time politicians in the United States had already begun to urge Irish self-determination at the Peace Conference. Meanwhile, in Ireland the December 1918 general elections had returned 73 Sinn Fein members of parliament, of which 27 met in Dublin on 21 January and declared Irish independence, proclaimed a republic, and later proposed sending Eamon de Valera, Arthur Griffith, and Count George Noble Plunkett to the Peace Conference.

The Race Convention sent a delegation to New York on 3 March to meet with President Wilson, who had returned briefly from the Peace Conference to close the session of Congress. Wilson was reluctant to meet the Irish-Americans, and they disagreed over what the President could do for Ireland. Although Wilson said he was sympathetic with Irish aspirations, he argued that he was not at liberty to bring up the domestic issues of the Allied powers. Wilson sailed back to Paris angry over the confrontation. This exchange did not satisfy the Irish-American delegation either, with the result that three members of the Convention were appointed to go to France to work for Irish independence at the Peace Conference. This group was called the American Commission on Irish Independence.

The chairman of the Commission was Frank P. Walsh, a Missouri labor lawyer, newspaper editor, and progressive democrat with strong connections in the Democratic Party. Walsh had advised Wilson on labor matters in 1912 and Wilson had appointed Walsh chairman of the Industrial Relations Commission in 1913 and later co-chairman (together with former President William Howard Taft) of the National War Labor Board. Thus, Walsh enjoyed the prestige of successful national public service and a working relationship with Wilson. The second commissioner was Edward F. Dunne, a successful Chicago lawyer who had served as circuit court judge, as mayor of Chicago, and from 1912 to 1917 as reform Governor of Illinois. Dunne was one of the leading Irish-American politicians in the United States. The third member of the Commission was Michael J. Ryan, a longtime city solicitor for Philadelphia and more recently the public

service commissioner. Ryan had national stature as the former president of the United Irish League of America, the organization that had been the major support for the home rule movement in the United States. He had broken with the Irish Parliamentary Party over the question of Irish support for Britain in the war.

The American Commission on Irish Independence arrived in Paris on 11 April 1919, to be met by the Dail Eireann envoys, Sean T. O'Kelly and George Gavan Duffy. They began holding meetings with both American journalists and members of the American Peace Commission, including Colonel Edward M. House, Wilson's trusted advisor. The Irish-Americans were urged to write to Wilson stating their objectives, which were to seek Wilson's assistance in persuading the British to grant de Valera, Griffith, and Plunkett safe conduct to travel to Paris to present the Irish case to the Peace Conference. Wilson met with the Commission on 17 April, said that he understood the importance of the Irish question, and promised that he would speak privately to the British Prime Minister about it. The Commissioners were also told by Colonel House that the British Prime Minister would talk to them, but as days passed it was suggested that the Commission go to Ireland to see conditions there. The Irish-Americans were delighted by the opportunity.

The Commission was greeted in Dublin by de Valera on 3 May and taken to the Mansion House; they were introduced to the prominent figures in the Dail; and they traveled across the country, from Belfast to Cork. On the 9th of May they addressed a session of the Dail Eireann. Throughout these travels the Commissioners spoke strongly in favor of Irish independence and in support of the Dail government, to the delight of their audiences. The trip to Ireland was a triumphal procession. However, their speeches were widely covered in the press and their strong nationalist sentiments provoked protests in England and among Unionists in Ireland. The British government was criticized for allowing the Commission to go to Ireland at all. The Commission left for France on 16 May for a much less cordial reception. Both the British Prime Minister and Colonel House had been embarrassed by the words of the Commissioners, and the proposed meeting with Lloyd George was canceled. New correspondence by the Commission was met with polite but cool responses from the American and British diplomats. President Wilson did talk to them one more time, and in response to their appeal to the principle of self-determination Wilson uttered the famous remark, "You have touched on the great metaphysical tragedy of today." Wilson also warned the Commission not to make trouble for him about the Irish question; he said that the diplomats had just about been successful in bringing the Irish delegation to Paris, but "it was you gentlemen who kicked over the applecart."

It is difficult to measure the American Commission on Irish Independence in terms of success or failure. Whether Lloyd George would have allowed de Valera, Griffith, and Plunkett to come to Paris, any more than he would have agreed to allow the Commissioners to speak to him on behalf of Ireland, seems questionable (he also refused to allow the Egyptian nationalists to come to Paris). Nevertheless, the Commission was successful in obtaining publicity for the Irish cause in the international arena. The Dail envoys in Paris felt they had done excellent work, and Sinn Fein supporters in Ireland were much encouraged by their strong speeches. When the Commission returned to the United States they joined ranks with the opponents of the League of Nations and the Versailles Treaty. The Commissioners spoke at the

Senate Foreign Relations Committee hearings, where they were among the most effective critics of Wilson and the Peace Conference. In that respect they were able to successfully shift onto President Wilson the blame for the failure of the Conference to deal with the Irish question. Although its mission to Paris was over, the Commission was given one further task. In 1920, with the Irish-American nationalist organizations split, de Valera turned to the Commission, and particularly Frank P. Walsh, to direct his campaign to raise money in the United States through the sale of Bond Certificates. Although the Dail sent out a number of people to help, and many Irish-American organizations assisted, the American Commission on Irish Independence provided the leadership that enabled the Dail to raise over $5,500,000 in 1920 and 1921.

*See* U.S. Foreign Policy and Irish Affairs

Francis M. Carroll, "The American Commission on Irish Independence and the Paris Peace Conference of 1919," *Irish Studies in International Affairs,* Vol. II, No. 1 (1985).

F. M. Carroll, ed., *The American Commission on Irish Independence, 1919: The Diary, Correspondence and Report* (Dublin: Irish Manuscripts Commission, 1985).

F. M. Carroll, *American Opinion and the Irish Question, 1910–1923* (New York, 1978).

Alan J. Ward, *Ireland and Anglo-American Relations, 1899–1921* (London, 1969).

FRANCIS M. CARROLL

## PECK, GREGORY (1916–  )

Actor. Born Eldred Gregory Peck, of Irish lineage, on April 5, 1916. He became one of the most prominent and respected actors in Hollywood in the post–World War II era. Tall, handsome and dignified, with a distinctive sonorous voice, he was the archetypal "good guy," both personally and in the roles he played.

As a premed student at the University of California at Berkeley, Peck was recruited by the director of the University of California's Little Theatre because he was looking for a "tall" actor. After appearing in five plays there, Peck changed his major to

Gregory Peck

English literature and graduated with an interest in making acting a career.

Peck moved to New York and studied acting at Sanford Meisner's Neighborhood Playhouse School of Theatre. After appearing in four Broadway plays, he was signed on in 1943 to star in *Days of Glory,* a wartime film which gained notoriety as the picture that launched Peck's career. A bidding war for him broke out among the studio heads; and, in an era where actors were virtually the property of the major studios, he was able to maintain his independence and choose his own roles.

Peck fast became a matinee idol and dominated the American movie scene until the mid-1960s. He is most celebrated for his brilliant portrayal of Atticus Finch, the virtuous southern father and lawyer defending a black man accused of rape in *To Kill a Mockingbird,* for which he won an Oscar for best actor. He was nominated for his performances as Father Chisholm in *The Keys of the Kingdom* (1945), as the father in *The Yearling* (1946), and as a writer discovering the realities of religious bigotry in *Gentleman's Agreement* (1947). He appeared in such diverse films as *Yellow Sky* (1948); *12 O'Clock High* (1949); *The Gunfighter* (1950); *The Snows of Kilimanjaro* (1952); *Pork Chop Hill* (1959); *Beloved Infidel* (1959); and *Arabesque* (1966). In *Roman Holiday* (1953), one of his most successful films, Peck proved his ability to play light comedy roles.

Although the availability of good parts waned in the 1970s, Peck starred in a few box office successes, among them the horror thriller, *The Omen* (1976); *MacArthur* (1977); and as the Nazi Josef Mengele in *The Boys From Brazil* (1978).

A lifetime liberal, the popular and respected Peck was often urged by Democratic party officials to run for public office—to become the Ronald Reagan of the left. He declined, although his ties to the party and to liberal politics remained strong throughout his life. He was named by President Lyndon Johnson to the National Council on the Arts as a founding member in 1965, and he served as chairman of its Film Advisory Council. He has been the recipient of numerous awards including the Medal of Freedom (1969) and Life Achievement Awards from both the American Film Institute (1989) and the Lincoln Center Film Society (1992).

*See* Cinema, Irish in; California

*New York Herald Tribune,* IV (April 29, 1945).
*Time,* 45 (January 1, 1945): 40.
*International Motion Picture Almanac* (1946–47).

EILEEN DANEY CARZO

## PENDERGAST, THOMAS JOSEPH (1872–1945)

Political boss. Tom Pendergast was the fourth of nine children born to devout Irish-Catholic parents residing in St. Joseph, Missouri. He received his introduction to politics from his older brother, James. The elder Pendergast was a saloon owner who organized powerful Democratic clubs in Kansas City's working-class wards. Under the tutelage of his brother, Tom Pendergast was groomed to become the successor as Democratic boss of Kansas City. Tom earned a series of patronage-rife city offices and served on the city council from 1910–1914, which would be the last elected office he ever held. Inheriting his brother's political machine, Pendergast soon worked to spread its influence beyond the working-class wards. Through diligent use of bribes,

Tom Pendergast and his nephew James

patronage, city contracts, vote fraud and occasional intimidation, Pendergast's influence eventually reached white-collar areas of Kansas City and into rural Jackson County. For much of the 1920s and 1930s, Pendergast was one of the most powerful urban political bosses in the nation. His control of the Kansas City vote influenced statewide elections as well, best illustrated by the election of Pendergast protégé Harry Truman to the United States Senate in 1934. He reached the peak of his power in the 1930s through his manipulation of New Deal-funded patronage. His power was finally cracked in 1939 with a conviction for federal income tax evasion. Pendergast served fifteen months in Leavenworth, Kansas, and his Kansas City machine collapsed without his leadership. He died in 1945.

*See* Kansas

---

*Dictionary of American Biography*, Supplement 3: 596–97.

Lawrence H. Larsen and Nancy J. Hulston, *Pendergast!* (Columbia, MO, 1997).

William M. Reddig, *Tom's Town: Kansas City and the Pendergast Legend* (Philadelphia, 1947).

TOM DOWNEY

## PENNSYLVANIA

Pennsylvania is almost unique in being linked to Ireland from its beginnings as an English colony. Over the past three hundred years, immigrants of different ethnic backgrounds have come from Ireland and helped shape Pennsylvania's major contributions to the world—its experiment in religious toleration, begun in the seventeenth century; its fostering of American independence and republican government; its powering of industrialization through the nineteenth century; and its cultural pluralism, which grew from colonial times to become a pattern for the United States in the twentieth century.

### WILLIAM PENN'S "HOLY EXPERIMENT": THE QUAKER PATH FROM IRELAND

William Penn, the English Quaker who founded the Pennsylvania colony in 1681, began the connection with Ireland. Penn's mother Margaret was part of the English and Dutch colony at Kilrush, County Clare. His father, Admiral William Penn, served Cromwell in Munster, at one time besieging Bunratty Castle, that popular destination of tourists today. Born in 1644 in London,

Penn underwent his religious conversion in Cork in 1667 and was shaped by his family's colonial experience in Ireland. That experience, rooted in the Cromwellian conquest, was an important influence on the foundation of the colony. Paradoxically, it led to ideals of pacifism and religious toleration, and it began an immigrant path from Ireland that continues through the 1990s. At the end of the seventeenth century, a world was being thoroughly destroyed in Ireland and a new world created three thousand miles away. In the birth of Pennsylvania, there is a direct link between the axes cutting down Irish forests— the symbolic end of the Gaelic order—and the axes ringing in Penn's woods.

Penn's missionary work for the Quakers involved him in plans for American colonies. Penn became a shareholder in the West Jersey settlement in the 1670s, which developed from the Duke of York's gift to Lord Berkeley, Lord Lieutenant of Ireland in 1670–71. Seventeen of the 120 shareholders in the West Jersey colony were from Ireland, and these were concentrated in the area directly across the Delaware River from the future site of Philadelphia. When Penn received his royal charter for Pennsylvania, he brought with him more colonists from Ireland—some ten percent of the settlers—to play leadership roles in the province. His greatest aide, James Logan, the most eminent Pennsylvanian between Penn and Benjamin Franklin, was a Quaker from Lurgan whose Scots father had emigrated to Ulster. Whereas Quakers had not held office in England, they *had* in Ireland; thus, some of these settlers had experience in colonial government to bring with them to West Jersey and Pennsylvania. Two early governors of Pennsylvania were from Penn's Cork estate at Shanagarry: his cousin William Markham and Captain Charles Gookin. Another governor, Captain John Blackwell, was formerly Cromwell's Treasurer at War and a friend from Dublin. The streets of Philadelphia were laid out by Captain Thomas Holme from Waterford, one of Admiral Penn's naval veterans. As Surveyor-General of Pennsylvania, Holme helped choose the site for Philadelphia and laid out the city in its grid pattern.

Penn's Irish experience also shaped the ideals of the new colony to which his people were going. Penn's first experience of religious persecution occurred in Ireland, where he was jailed shortly after his conversion. The fratricidal history of Ireland in the seventeenth century, along with his experience with the established church, undoubtedly contributed to the religious toleration expressed in both the West Jersey and Pennsylvania constitutions. The ideal was to be "A Holy Experiment" in religious diversity and toleration.

Penn's experience in Ireland not only shaped his belief in religious toleration, but also his benign, if paternalistic, attitude toward the native peoples of Pennsylvania. The grievances of the Irish Catholics were over land more than religion, and Penn was determined not to create grievances among the natives about their land. (Comparisons between the Indians and the Irish were commonplace since Elizabethan times.) The Lenni Lenape and the Susquehannock were to be treated better, if only for prudential reasons, than those dispossessed by the Penns in Cork: the McCarthys of Macroom, and the Powers, Fitzgeralds, O'Heas, and O'Donovans around Shanagarry.

### THE 1700S AND THE COMING OF THE "SCOTCH-IRISH"

Jonathan Swift's "A Modest Proposal" (1729) savagely documents Irish misery in the early 1700s—misery that was leading to extensive emigration. On three occasions, in 1727, 1740, and 1770, Ireland suffered from major crop failures that led to famine. (One estimate of deaths in the famine of 1740–41 is 400,000.) Coinciding with particularly hard times, peak periods of immigration occurred in 1717–18, 1725–29, 1740–41, and 1771–75.

One estimate is that between 250,000 and 400,000 immigrants made their way from Ireland to the English colonies during the period 1700-1776, mostly as families seeking economic betterment. Approximately one-fifth of the immigrants were Catholic, and one-fifth of them Church of Ireland. Three-fifths, by far the predominant group, were Presbyterians from Ulster. By the early 1700s this group had already achieved an ethnic identity distinct from the two other ethnic groups in Ulster—the Gaelic-speaking native Irish, and the English—and from lowlands Scotland, from which they had emigrated in successive waves during the course of the seventeenth century. Their distinctiveness emerged from their shared experience as beseiged settlers surrounded by hostile "natives," attachments to Ireland that developed from residence there for as many as four and five generations, their acceptance of English legal and political arrangements for the governance of Ulster, and the increasing "Ulsterization" of the Presbyterian clergy in Ulster. Whereas other European immigrant groups shaped a distinctive ethnic identity only after emigration to the colonies, Ulster Presbyterians had already "become ethnic" in Ulster.

Ulster Presbyterians made large settlements in the Shenandoah Valley of Virginia and the Piedmont area of the Carolinas and Georgia. But Pennsylvania has been called the cradle of the "Scotch-Irish" culture in America. The main immigrant destination was Pennsylvania. The immigrants settled in a broad area surrounding Philadelphia and stretching across the colony. Cumberland County was the gateway for further migration to the southwestern region. As the century went on, the Scotch-Irish made significant contributions to Pennsylvania: to its transformation from a colony to a state in an independent nation, and a state in relationship to a new federal government. They provided new leaders in religion, education, business, and politics. Also, although nearly half of the immigrants settled in Philadelphia or the southeastern counties, they created a "back-country" culture, particularly strong in central and western Pennsylvania, that drew upon their experience in Ulster. The differences between that culture and the English Quaker and Anglican culture of Philadelphia account, in part, for the east/west cultural division that persists in Pennsylvania, and the animus against Philadelphia frequently expressed throughout the state. Pennsylvania's "Bible Belt"—the large expanse of rural population between Greater Philadelphia and Greater Pittsburgh—was shaped in part by the militant Christianity of the early settlers from Ulster. James Logan, who was instrumental in bringing fellow Ulstermen to Pennsylvania, consciously intended these non-pacifists to serve as a buffer population between the Quakers and the native peoples and French to the west. Logan made the connection between Ulster and Pennsylvania explicit in 1718: "We were under some apprehension from ye norther Indians. . . . I therefore thought it might be prudent to plant a settlement of such men as those who had so bravely defended Derry and Inniskillen, as a frontier in case of disturbance. Accordingly ye Township of Donegal [Lancaster County] was settled." The main force in the Pennsylvania militia that helped capture Fort Duquesne for the British Army in 1758 were Scotch-Irish. Groups of Scotch-Irish frontiersmen could be volatile: in 1763, "the Paxton Boys"

killed twenty innocent Susquehannock Indians at Conestoga, and then marched on Philadelphia, threatening the Quaker city because they believed that peace with the Indians threatened their freedom.

The principal institutional bond among the Scotch-Irish was the Presbyterian Church. Francis Makemie, of the Laggan presbytery in County Donegal, led the foundation, in Philadelphia, of the first presbytery in the English colonies in 1706. As the number of congregations grew across Pennsylvania, William Tennent, a cousin of James Logan from Antrim, established, in 1727, an academy for educating ministers and lay leaders at Neshaminy, Bucks County. Known as the "Log College," it was the first such academy in America, and provided the foundation of what became, in 1746, the College of New Jersey in Princeton (later, Princeton University). Graduates of the Log College went on to start academies of their own and became influential teachers. One, Francis Allison from Donegal, taught in his Chester County school the morality of resisting established authority to such students as Thomas McKean, Joseph Reed, and Charles Thomson, all Scotch-Irishmen later prominent in the American Revolution. Allison, who later became professor of moral philosophy at the College of Philadelphia and pastor of the First Presbyterian Church, taught the writings of Irishmen William Molyneux and Francis Hutcheson.

The Scotch-Irish in Pennsylvania played a crucial leadership role during the American Revolution. With grievances against England for misgovernance at home, renewed periodically by continual emigration, they arrived in large numbers in the years before the crisis of the mid-1770s, making Anglophobia prevail in Pennsylvania over Anglophile tradition. The first regiment authorized by the Continental Congress was Colonel William Thompson's Pennsylvania regiment, made up of nine companies, seven almost entirely Scotch-Irish. Thus the American army has its origins in the "Pennsylvania line," which Colonel Harry Lee of Virginia dubbed "the line of Ireland."

Charles Thomson, from Maghera, County Derry, called "the Sam Adams of Pennsylvania" by John Adams, was secretary of the Continental Congress. Two of Pennsylvania's nine signers of the Declaration of Independence were born in Ireland: James Smith from York, and George Taylor, an Anglican from Easton. The first printing of the Declaration was in the *Pennsylvania Packet,* published by John Dunlap of County Tyrone. The radicalism of the Scotch-Irish also shaped the framing of Pennsylvania's new state constitution of 1776, the most democratic in the thirteen colonies, organizing government by a unicameral legislature. Political leaderhip was provided by George Bryan, a Dubliner, who was a Philadelphia merchant and an important lay leader in the Presbyterian Church, and he later led that Church's call for the abolition of slavery in 1787. The 1776 constitution represented a shifting of political power in Pennsylvania away from Quaker and Anglican leaders, who generally opposed Independence, to Presbyterians, who favored it.

## Irish Catholics in the 1700s

Although the Scotch-Irish were the predominant immigrant group in the eighteenth century, Irish Catholics were a presence in Pennsylvania, the most liberal colony on religion. In small numbers, Catholics had been present since William Penn's times: Quakers from Ireland were known for bringing Irish servants with them. Beginning in 1704, Catholics were visited by German and English Jesuits operating from Bohemia Manor in Cecil

County, Maryland. In 1733, the Jesuits established St. Joseph's Church in Philadelphia, which became the only church where Mass could legally be held in the English-speaking world. It is now a national shrine for religious toleration. Across the state, Irish and other immigrants continued to be reached by missionaries. In 1741, for example, German priests lodged with Thomas Doyle in Lancaster.

St. Joseph's survived one episode of anti-Catholicism in 1755. When news of Braddock's defeat by the French reached Philadelphia, a mob tried to destroy the church, but were restrained by Quakers. In the revolutionary period, St. Joseph's place as the principal parish in the city was taken by St. Mary's, founded a short distance away in the 1760s, largely by Irish contributors.

By the revolutionary period, Pennsylvania had achieved something rare in the English colonies: it had permitted a few Irish Catholics to achieve power and prestige. Philadelphia's thriving mercantile economy had attracted such individuals as Stephen Moylan and Thomas Fitzsimons, members of active Irish and Franco-Irish mercantile families. Fitzsimons cofounded, with Robert Morris, the Bank of North America. Other prominent individuals were George Meade, Fitzsimons' brother-in-law and partner, and John Mease. Old connections between Ireland and France since the days of the "The Wild Geese" were being newly forged as American ties in Pennsylvania. Years later, during the 1788 celebration of the ratification of the Constitution, Fitzsimons rode in a procession representing the French Alliance, riding on the white horse of Rochambeau, the French hero of Yorktown. In that battle, Irishmen in American units had fought along with France's "Irish Brigade."

In 1771, the Irish in Pennsylvania created a unique ecumenical organization: the Friendly Sons of Saint Patrick for Relief of Emigrants from Ireland in Philadelphia. Stephen Moylan, whose brother was Bishop of Cork, became the first President; John M. Nesbitt, an Ulster Presbyterian, became the second President. Since that time, the presidency has alternated between Catholic and Protestant members for over two hundred years. This remarkable organization from its earliest days has had honorary members, such as George Washington, who welcomed association with such Irishmen.

Irish Catholics in Pennsylvania played key roles in the American Revolution. Many served in the front lines with their Scotch-Irish brethren. Stephen Moylan became Washington's Quartermaster, achieving the rank of Brevet Brigadier General, the highest rank attained by a Catholic. In 1776, the first British ship captured by a commissioned American ship fell to Commodore John Barry, commanding the *Lexington*. The Wexford-born Barry went on to perform outstanding service throughout the war.

THE IRISH IN THE FEDERAL PERIOD:
WHEN PHILADELPHIA WAS THE NATION'S CAPITAL

When Philadelphia was capital of the new nation, from 1790 to 1800, it possessed a diversity of population unparalleled in the colonies. Scotch-Irish and Irish Catholics made their way through a city that contained, besides people from England, Scotland, and Wales, Germans (forty percent of Pennsylvania's population), other Europeans, and many African-Americans, both freemen and slaves. Such diversity, rare in its time, was in fact exemplary of the nation that the United States would become.

The Irish had contributed to that diversity. They were also major players in that special time for Pennsylvania when local,

state, and national politics were each being shaped simultaneously. Individuals' self-interest, political ideals, and the varying weights of religious and ethnic loyalties naturally made for ambivalence and complexity. Yet, one certainty is that, in Pennsylvania, as in few other states, Irish people were at center stage in shaping the new nation. For example, while Pennsylvanians overwhelmingly supported the new United States Constitution in 1787, many Scotch-Irish voiced opposition, casting anti-federalist votes from fear that the Constitution represented the return to state power of Anglican and Quaker elites. At the same time, Thomas McKean, prominent among the Scotch-Irish and President of the Hibernian Society, was a conspicuous leader for ratification. Further, allied with McKean as a Federalist was Thomas Fitzsimons. In the first election of the new government, Fitzsimons became a U.S. Representative from Pennsylvania, and led the lobbying that made Philadelphia the national capital in 1790.

The first major challenge to the authority of the new federal government arose in southwestern Pennsylvania in 1794, when opposition to an excise tax on whiskey, led by Scotch-Irish on the frontier, resulted in "The Whiskey Rebellion." This revolt, which involved the burning of the house of John Neville, President Washington's tax collector, and attacks on government agents, ended only through the personal intervention of the President, who arrived with 13,000 militiamen.

During the era of the French Revolution, fears of Irish radicalism grew as immigration greatly increased in the late 1790s. Some 30,000 Irish people arrived in Philadelphia in the 1790s; Irish immigrants accounted for fifty-five percent of all naturalized citizens from 1789 through 1800. Radical leaders associated with the United Irishmen in Ireland, and favoring Thomas Jefferson's Democratic Republican party, included Mathew and James Carey, John Daly Burke, William Duane, Dr. James Reynolds, Samuel Parke, and Daniel Clark. (Wolfe Tone himself, during a brief exile, spent some time in Philadelphia in 1796.) The Alien and Sedition Acts (1798), the federal government's first enactment of xenophobic legislation, expressed the concerns of President Adams and other Federalists about such Pennsylvania Irishmen, notorious for extreme democratic views.

As the century ended, Irishmen were embattled. However, McKean, running on the Republican ticket, won the Governorship in 1799. In Pennsylvania, if not in Ireland, the ideal of "United Irishmen" had achieved some success, in a land where more liberty and more equality held more promise of fraternity.

MATHEW CAREY

The Irish contribution to Pennsylvania during the American Enlightenment is epitomized by the publisher and writer Mathew Carey (1760-1839), whose career spans the Revolutionary and Federalist eras and ends shortly before the Famine. Carey, a Catholic from Dublin, came to Philadelphia in 1784 after writing for the most radical patriot newspapers and issuing two inflammatory pamphlets. During a brief exile in France, Carey met Benjamin Franklin and Lafayette, and went to work for Franklin at his press in Passy. That connection ultimately led him to Philadelphia, where he became the most influential publisher of his time. In politics, Carey expressed an "Irish" Federalism that valued the new nation as a unique creation, in the vanguard of the international struggle for human rights, and thus he fostered national and nationalistic perspectives over regional and ethnic ones. He championed internal improvements through roads and canals, tariffs to protect American industry, scientific agriculture, a strong navy, and a national bank. His *American Museum,* published from 1787 to 1792, was self-consciously designed to be the first national magazine. It began by supporting the ratification of the Constitution and encouraged literary nationalism by featuring the best samples of American writing. Like other Irishmen, Carey drifted away from the Federalists as they moved away from supporting revolutionary France to supporting England. He broke with them after the Jay Treaty in 1794, and he worked hard for Jefferson's victory in 1801. In 1798–1799, he engaged in a controversy with William Cobbett after Cobbett had charged him and his brother James with engaging in a United Irishmen conspiracy.

Carey changed book publishing from a regional enterprise to a national one, making use of a network of booksellers as far west as the Mississippi. He contributed to the making of the American pantheon of heroes through the bestselling biography of Washington, written by his most famous bookseller, Mason Weems. His 1814 pamphlet *The Olive Branch: or Faults on Both Sides, Federal and Democratic,* a plea for national unity after the War of 1812, was the most widely read pamphlet since *Common Sense.* In 1819 Carey opposed conventional American views about Ireland in *Vindiciae Hibernicae,* which refuted the idea that Irish massacres had justified the Cromwellian conquest. Later in life, his *Essays on the Public Charities of Philadelphia* (1828) and *Address to the Wealthy of the Land* (1831) defended the poor against charges of idleness and argued the case for public charities. His *Case of the Seamstresses* (1833) and *The Wages of Female Labour* (1829) showed his special concern for poor working women. Such publications, and Carey's personal philanthropy, explain why his 1839 funeral was one of the largest that Philadelphia had ever seen.

### PRE-FAMINE IMMIGRATION TO PENNSYLVANIA

As he promoted internal improvements and American industry through the 1830s, Mathew Carey had no way of knowing just how much of the required labor would come from his native land. And yet, in the history of the Irish in Pennsylvania in the nineteenth century, this is the dominant fact.

The Irish had already made up a good percentage of the work force in late eighteenth-century Pennsylvania. As the new century began, they provided labor to transport the state's rich produce and timber over its arduous terrain. They dug canals such as the great Pennsylvania Canal from Philadelphia to Pittsburgh (1834), the Union Canal above Reading, the West Branch Canal from Sunbury to Lock Haven, and the Delaware and Hudson Canal from Carbondale to New Jersey. For the Pennsylvania Canal, John Dougherty designed canal boats that could be disassembled, passed over the Alleghenies, and reassembled on the other side. For decades after the work, canal locks and stations bore such names as Foley's, Jack McCarthy's, Joe McKane's, and Pat Gannon's. In Harrisburg, Irish canal workers in the 1820s made up the parishioners of St. Patrick's Church, which grew from a Jesuit mission established near Harris's Ferry in the 1780s.

As early as 1805, John Gormley was running a foundry that began the great iron and steel industry of Pittsburgh that drew so many Irish immigrants there throughout the century. In Berks County, Daniel Buckley hired Irish laborers, Protestants and Catholics, as he operated the iron furnace at Hopewell from 1800 to 1828.

The chief energy source for the industrial revolution in Pennsylvania and the wide world was coal. Three-fourths of the earth's hard coal deposits were in Pennsylvania. As more desperate waves of Irish immigrants arrived in the 1830s, they were drawn to hazardous work in the mines of the anthracite region, which became, after Philadelphia and Pittsburgh, the major area of Irish population in the state. During the period of 1830 to 1880, Schuylkill County's population rose from 11,000 to 116,000. In 1840, the first Catholic Mass was said in Scranton; by 1868, the Diocese of Scranton had been established, with a network of seventy-three mission outposts.

As the Irish filled Pennsylvania's factories and mills, they very quickly became engaged in labor agitation. In an extraordinary instance of unskilled workers leading the way for skilled ones, the general strike in Philadelphia in 1835 began when unskilled Irish dock workers, coal heavers on the Schuylkill River, walked off the job demanding a ten-hour work day instead of the customary fourteen. They won that fight, but lost in 1836 when they demanded an increase in wages over the customary one-dollar-a-day with twelve-and-a-half cents for overtime. In the 1840s, Irish immigrant John Campbell, a radical socialist, rose to prominence as a writer/publisher speaking for labor. In a letter to the *New York Tribune* in 1850, he complained that the problem with Philadelphia workingmen was that they "showed too much caution."

While Irishmen like Campbell frequently cooperated with native-born workers, they were often enmeshed in conflict with them. In the anthracite region, the Irish also competed with Welsh and English immigrants who had preceded them. In Philadelphia, competition was particularly fierce with African-Americans for jobs at the bottom of the scale. Violent clashes between Irish and Blacks occurred throughout the 1830s and 1840s. With white native-born Americans, conflict was fostered by a revival of Protestant evangelicalism that was vehemently anti-Catholic. Scotch-Irish Pennsylvanians were part of this revival, and they were joined by new generations of immigrants, who continued to come to Pennsylvania even after most Ulster emigrants began to prefer Canada. In 1831, a riot erupted in Philadelphia during an Orange march. Toleration of Catholics in Pennsylvania was eroding in the face of far greater numbers than ever before, and Irishmen of far lower social standing than the generation of the founding period. In the nadir of this conflict, a dispute over Irish Catholics' refusal to read from the King James Bible in school became a pretext for mob action in the Kensington section of Philadelphia in May 1844, followed by a second flare-up in July. Before order was restored, two Catholic churches in the city had been burned down and a third set fire to. About eighteen people died, and scores were injured. One year before the Great Famine, the Irish people in Pennsylvania had suffered a trauma. Famine immigrants would come to a state where the Irish were both indispensable and unwelcome.

### POST-FAMINE IMMIGRATION TO PENNSYLVANIA

With the Famine, countless thousands of lives begun in counties like Roscommon, Mayo, and Cavan were to unfold in cities whose names still ring with the sound of loud machinery: Pittsburgh, Erie, Altoona, Reading, Allentown, Bethlehem, Easton, Wilkes-Barre. In 1846, the chartering of the Pennsylvania Railroad provided the Irish jobs as diggers, trainmen, engineers, and brakemen, and served to disperse the immigrants across the state. The industries that grew up with the railroad—coal mining, iron, steel, and construction—provided employment in all corners of Pennsylvania. In Erie County, naturalization records for the 1850s and 1860s show scores of Irish people applying for citizenship—to the displeasure of many local residents. In 1859, when oil was first discovered at Drake's Well in Titusville, also in northwestern Pennsylvania, thousands of Irish rushed to fill the sudden employment available there.

By 1860 there were 10,000 Irish-born people in Pittsburgh, and 100,000 in Philadelphia. In the years before the Civil War, these recent immigrants feared Blacks as competitors for their jobs, and indulged in the all-too-human habit of one oppressed group asserting superiority over another. Politically, the Irish were Democrats in a state with many economic ties to the South and a tepid abolitionist movement. However, when war came, many served in the Union army; some, as conscription began, received bounties and served as substitutes for wealthier Pennsylvanians. (Miners in Schuylkill County rioted against conscription in 1862, yet the 48th Pennsylvania Regiment from that county became one of the finest units in the army.) New immigrants and Irish-Americans served with distinction, including on those dramatic days when the union was saved in Pennsylvania, at Gettysburg, in July 1863. Providing a link to earlier generations of immigrants to Pennsylvania was the leader on the battlefield at Gettysburg: General George Gordon Meade, a descendant of the Franco-Irish merchant John Meade of the revolutionary era. The heavily Irish 116th Pennsylvania Regiment was led by General St. Clair Mulholland. Today, a tall Celtic cross marks the Regiment's 200 casualties at Little Round Top. At the center of Meade's lines on July 3, directly facing Pickett's Charge, was the 69th Pennsylvania infantry, led by Colonel Dennis O'Kane, who was killed that day along with 150 others, in a unit of 258 men.

In the decades after the war, the story of the Irish in Pennsylvania frequently seems like the history of another civil war—between labor and management. In the great railroad strike of 1877, Pennsylvania's rail workers, largely Irish, protested reductions in the crews providing service between Pittburgh and Altoona. After National Guard troops killed twenty people in a crowd of protesters in Pittsburgh, rioters burned the Union Depot, and then engaged in gunfire with troops that left another twenty people dead. Beginning that same year, twenty men, all Irish Catholics, were hanged in the anthracite towns of Pottsville and Mauch Chunk, executed for crimes, including murder, committed as "Molly Maguires." The story of the Molly Maguires is still controversial. The Mollies brought to Pennsylvania a tradition of Irish agrarian violence against landlords and their agents that they applied to miners' conflicts with owners and bosses. However, historians still debate the factors that led to the executions, in which the public prosecutor was an interested party: Franklin B. Gowen, the President of the Philadelphia and Reading Railroad. Some historians emphasize the pervasive anti-Irish bigotry across the state, and the fear of a secret Catholic terrorist organization within the Ancient Order of Hibernians. (After the Civil War, Scotch-Irish anti-Catholicism was at its peak, with the formation of lodges of the Loyal Orange Institution in Philadelphia and Pittsburgh.) Other historians stress the desire of mine owners to crush all attempts at labor organization. Others see the events as the clash between two criminal conspiracies, one represented by the owners of the mines and railroads, who had their own private force, "the coal and iron police," and the other represented by desperate miners led by the Mollies. Still others point to the ruthless "frontier" environment of the mining districts, in which hundreds lost their lives annually in mining accidents, in violent feuds, and in confrontations with police. Concerns about the irregularities of the Mollies' trials,

perceived by Irish miners as judicial murders, have persisted over the years. In 1978, the family of Jack Kehoe obtained a reversal of conviction signed by Governor Milton Shapp.

In the last decade of the century, the Amalgamated Association of Iron and Steel Workers, led by Hugh O'Donnell, struck against the Carnegie Steel Company. The Homestead Strike of 1892 degenerated into a pitched gun battle along the Monongahela between workers and 300 Pinkertons. Seven workers and three Pinkertons were killed. The Homestead disaster seriously weakened unionism in the steel industry until the 1930s.

Pennsylvania's labor strife produced some outstanding individual leaders. Born in Ireland, the son of a tenant farmer evicted by his landlord, John Siney of St. Clair organized the Miners National Association in 1873—the origins of the United Mine Workers union. In 1869, Siney gave a memorable speech on workers' rights to safety after the Avondale mine explosion, which killed 110 men—the worst coal mine disaster until that time. Siney's legacy was the idea of a large industrial union, solidarity among workers across ethnic divisions, and union discipline. Under Terence Powderly, born in Carbondale to Irish parents, the Knights of Labor became the largest union in the nation in the 1880s, with nearly three quarters of a million members. First by political agitation, education, and workers' cooperatives, and, then, after 1885, by strikes, the Knights fought for such goals as the end of child labor and the eight-hour work day. Through negotiations with Cardinal Gibbons, Powderly mollified the Catholic Church's concerns about unions' secret oaths, and thus helped pave the way to Pope Leo XIII's encyclical "De Rerum Novarum," which explicitly approved the right of workers to organize unions. Powderly also served three terms as Mayor of Scranton and, linking Pennsylvania to Ireland, organized chapters of Michael Davitt's Land League, and served as Finance Chairman of Clan na Gael.

As Powderly's career suggests, some Pennsylvania Irish, in an era when Americans fought a Civil War for a cause, joined a movement that was to have reverberations across the Atlantic: Fenianism. The first national convention of the Fenian movement took place in Philadelphia in 1863. Prominent Pennsylvania Fenians were printer James Gibbons and Dr. William Carroll, a Presbyterian from Donegal, a leader in Clan na Gael. Carroll tried to persuade Parnell, who visited Pennsylvania in 1876 and 1880, to support complete Irish independence. In 1888, the British spy Le Caron reported that Philadelphia was the center of Irish revolutionary activity in the United States. Prominent in a Clan na Gael bombing campaign in England in the 1890s was Luke Dillon, who lived long enough to take the Republican anti-Treaty side in the 1920s. The epitome of the tradition in this century was Joseph McGarrity (1874–1940), an immigrant from County Tyrone, who devoted his life and business fortune to arming and financing Irish nationalists. McGarrity played a major role during the Easter Rising and mobilized American support for Eamon de Valera and Irish independence.

As many Irish Pennsylvanians struggled for a living, and some engaged in turbulent labor and nationalistic movements, a minority achieved middle-class status. By the 1890s, Scranton, for example, had a recognizable Irish middle class active in business, law, and education. Across the state, the Catholic middle class was instrumental in beginning institutions of higher learning such as Villanova College (1842), St. Francis College (1847), St. Joseph's College (1851), LaSalle College (1868), Duquesne College (1878), and Scranton College (1892). The total influence of Irish people on Pennsylvania's colleges and universities can be seen by adding to this list the colleges begun as Presbyterian institutions by the Scotch-Irish: Dickinson College, Washington and Jefferson College, Lafayette College, Allegheny College, Grove City College, Wilson College, Beaver College, Westminster College, Waynesburg College, and the University of Western Pennsylvania, now the University of Pittsburgh. The schoolmaster of the nation was William Holmes McGuffey, born of Scotch-Irish parentage near Claysville in western Pennsylvania. *McGuffey's Eclectic Readers,* published between 1836 and 1857, with an estimated sale of 122 million, shaped the moral imagination of mid-century America.

## Twentieth-Century Assimilation and Ethnic Revival

In the twentieth century, Irish Catholics in Pennsylvania made a slow, steady climb to economic stability and social respectability, and largely assimilated into mainstream American life. At the same time, the Irish in Pennsylvania continually expressed the vitality of a hyphenated Irish-American identity. They exemplified a cultural pluralism, characteristic of Pennsylvania, that has become a pattern for the nation, which faces increasing diversity in population. William Penn's "Holy Experiment" in diversity led to Pennsylvania's becoming the "motley middle" in the eighteenth century, far more heterogeneous than Massachusetts or Virginia; industrialization in the nineteenth century then opened the gates to more peoples from around the world. Today, Pennsylvania is, in terms of ethnic origins, a microcosm of the nation, with the Irish, Italian, African-American, and Jewish populations virtually identical to the national average, and German and East European populations above the average. Not segregated but spread out across the state and within the cities, the Irish in Pennsylvania have had long practice in living as a people among other peoples. This is a fundamental component of the Irish-American identity in Pennsylvania. Another component is the strong tradition of the Scotch-Irish, which, though now attenuated, adds an element of diversity within the Irish-American identity that is missing in many other states.

Remarkably, the rise of Irish Catholics to respectability in Pennsylvania was accomplished without exceptional political leadership at the state or city level by mid-century. One major factor in this was a Republican machine that dominated Pennsylvania politics from the Civil War until after World War II. Also, the Irish adapted to an environment where political leadership by charismatic individuals was not highly valued. Traditionally, strong ideological leaders have not been prized in Pennsylvania, where politics begins with the ruling economic interests, frank acknowledgement of the state's diverse population and competing voting blocs, and non-ideological bargaining. Henry Adams noted the difference between Massachussetts and Pennsylvania, and E. Digby Baltzell has described the prevailing private, rather than public, ethos of the state in his *Puritan Boston and Quaker Philadelphia.* The Irish adapted to this pragmatic arrangement. More than elsewhere, they became Republican in the long decades when the Democrats seemed doomed to be forever out of office. By the time urban Democrats in Philadelphia and Pittsburgh finally came into power at mid-century, the immigrant experience was largely a memory. David Lawrence was elected Mayor of Pittsburgh in 1945 and led the "Pittsburgh Renaissance" during his four terms. Elected as the first Catholic Governor in 1959, he, along with newly elected President Kennedy, symbolized Irish achievement and assimilation. In Philadelphia, Democrats did not come into power until 1951, when reform can-

didate Joseph Clark's election as Mayor was engineered by such Irish-Americans as U.S. Congressman William Green, contractors John B. Kelly and Matthew McCloskey, and political operative James Finnegan. The first Irish-Catholic Mayor, James H. J. Tate, was not elected until 1962.

With anti-Irish bigotry abating in the first half of the twentieth century—with exceptions like the Klan revival during the Al Smith campaign of 1928—the Irish found a home in the Quaker state, where prejudice had never isolated them into segregated enclaves. Generally, they were able to own their homes, usually with Protestant working-class people of various backgrounds working close by, and with descendants of immigrants from Germany, Italy, Poland, Russia, and other nations. The principal institution in making Pennsylvania home for the Irish was the Catholic Church, which transformed Irish immigrants into American Catholics. A message of strict morals and respectability was delivered by Pennsylvania's conservative clergy, represented by such a figure as Dennis Cardinal Dougherty, who led the Archdiocese of Philadelphia from 1918 to 1951.

The result was assimilation into a culturally conservative state, where German Lutheranism was also strong, and where Quaker liberal political opinions coincide with conservative social habits. It is entirely characteristic that the Philadelphia St. Patrick's Day parade in the 1950s, under Cardinal O'Hara, was an expressly devotional parade, with controversy surrounding the use of advertisements or anything distracting from the commemoration of the saint.

By the 1950s, Irish assimilation was epitomized by two Kellys, one from Philadelphia and one from Pittsburgh, who became two of the most popular American film stars. Grace Kelly, the daughter of contractor and champion sculler John B. Kelly, had an outstanding acting career, and then, through marriage, become Princess of Monaco. Gene Kelly, from Pittsburgh, became recognized as one of the world's great dancers and performers. Their success represented, to the Irish in Pennsylvania, the larger society's appreciation of the talent, beauty, and athleticism of Irish-American people of working-class origins.

The outstanding Irish-American novelist of the time was John O'Hara, from Pottsville, author of *Appointment in Samarra* and *Ten North Frederick.* Like the two Kellys, O'Hara was not notably "ethnic"—although his personal obsession with social climbing and his fierce resentment of criticism betrayed an anxiety characteristic of successful Irish-Americans at mid-century. As a writer, O'Hara's accomplishment in portraying "Gibbsville" (Pottsville and environs), an area known today as "O'Hara Country," marks an important moment: an Irish-American had re-created his Pennsylvania home, and his times, in fiction of high literary merit.

The frailties of Pennsylvania's Irish Catholics at mid-century were satirized in the novels of Scranton's Tom McHale, and dramatized by Scranton's Jason Miller, whose play *That Championship Season* won the Pulitzer Prize for the best play in the 1971–72 season. *That Championship Season* is a classic presentation of white ethnics in Pennsylvania and the tragic divide between them and African-Americans.

In Pennsylvania, as throughout the nation, recent decades have seen a white ethnic revival that is asserting Irish-American identity in terms fairly independent of the Catholic Church. By the late 1960s, in the aftermath of Vatican II and white flight to the suburbs, Irish Catholic Pennsylvanians had lost their familiar parish culture. For some, the conflict in Northern Ireland has meant a renewal of Pennsylvania's strong traditions of Irish nationalism. For most, however, the search for a new Irish cultural identity has been stimulated by the revival of Irish traditional music and dance, and the achievements of Irish literature, which give expression to their longing for history and community after the breakdown of traditional communities. Building upon Pennsylvania's strong heritage of Irish music, today's festivals, radio programs, events on college campuses, and the *Irish Edition* newspaper keep cultural traditions alive, especially in the ethnic strongholds of Philadelphia, Pittsburgh, and the anthracite region. Fusion events such as the Chieftains' *Another Country,* where the music of Ireland meets the music of Nashville, have strong resonance in Pennsylvania, hearkened to by citizens whose traditions embrace both the besieged and the besiegers of Derry.

*See* Pittsburgh and Western Pennsylvania; Quakers

E. Digby Baltzell, *Puritan Boston and Quaker Philadelphia* (New York, 1979).

Wayne G. Broehl, Jr., *The Molly Maguires,* 1964 (Cambridge, 1965).

Dennis Clark, *The Irish in Pennsylvania: A People Share a Commonwealth* (University Park, Pennsylvania Historical Association, 1991).

David Noel Doyle, *Ireland, Irishmen and Revolutionary America, 1760–1820* (Dublin and Cork, 1981).

David Hackett Fischer, *Albion's Seed: Four British Folkways in America* (New York, 1989).

James N. Green, *Mathew Carey: Publisher and Patriot* (Philadelphia, 1985).

Owen Ireland, *Religion, Ethnicity, and Politics: Ratifying the Constitution in Pennsylvania* (University Park, 1995).

Donald L. Miller and Richard E. Sharpless, *The Kingdom of Coal: Work, Enterprise, and Ethnic Communities in the Mine Fields* (Philadelphia, 1985).

Kerby A. Miller, *Emigrants and Exiles: Ireland and the Irish Exodus to North America* (New York, 1985).

Billy G. Smith, *The "Lower Sort": Philadelphia's Laboring People, 1750–1800* (Ithaca, 1990).

James H. Smylie, *Scotch-Irish Presence in Pennsylvania* (University Park, 1990).

Anthony F. C. Wallace, *St. Clair: A Nineteenth-Century Coal Town's Experience with a Disaster-Prone Industry,* 1981 (New York, 1987).

JOSEPH J. KELLY

## PEYTON, PATRICK (1909–1992)

Holy Cross priest, evangelist. He was born in Carracastle, County Mayo, on January 9, 1909, to John and Mary Gillard Peyton. Patrick felt the call to be a missionary early in life, but his poor school record caused him to be turned down for seminary training. Eventually he dropped out of school altogether and dreamed of going to America. With some persuasion his father agreed and he and his brother Thomas immigrated to America in 1927.

Tom and he both entered Holy Cross seminary at Notre Dame in 1929, professed their vows in the Congregation of Holy Cross in 1933, and were ordained in 1941. During his second year of theology he was struck down by tuberculosis and with the help of a priest summoned the faith to be healed of the disease through the intercession of the Blessed Mother. Despite the time lost from his studies, he received a special dispensation from Rome to be ordained with his classmates, and promised to dedicate his life to restoring family prayer, especially the rosary, in America.

In May 1945 he gained a national radio audience for the family rosary with a special program over the Mutual Broadcasting System on Mother's Day. Two years later he launched the Family Theater radio series which aired nationally for over twenty years. In 1950 Family Theater began producing television programs and films as well, and was aided by Helen Hayes, Irene Dunne and other prominent actors in stage and screen.

Beginning in 1947 he conducted Family Rosary Crusades throughout the United States and Canada, using the slogan: "The family that prays together stays together." Over the next four decades the crusades reached every continent, some drawing more than a million people. At the same time he built an organization that specialized in adult catechesis and formation. He died on June 3, 1992.

Jeanne Gosselin Arnold, *A Man of Faith* (Colonie, New York, 1983).

Patrick Peyton, *The Ear of God* (London, 1954).

———, *All for Her* (Garden City, New York, 1967).

JAMES J. HALEY

## PHELAN, JAMES (1821?–1892)

Entrepreneur. James Phelan knew he was born in Queen's Co. (Laois or Leix) around 1821, but he never made an issue of trying to establish the exact date. Starting points were unimportant, he frequently said. It was destinations that mattered. He certainly was in a position to know. Phelan's final destination was that of a very rich man.

Arriving in the United States at age five or six, young Phelan's father started a business, but it eventually failed. James, the middle of three brothers, had to quit school to find work. But as a $5-a-week grocery clerk, he quickly absorbed the ways of the business world and discovered he had a knack for it. By 1846, he was running his own very profitable dry goods business in Cincinnati.

When word arrived of gold in California, Phelan sensed opportunity. His canniness became apparent, however, in that he did not intend to pan for gold himself. Instead, he would sell goods to the others who came to pan for gold. Selling his business and buying as much nails, tacks, cooking utensils, tar paper and anything else that would conceivably be of use in the gold fields, he shipped the entire consignment to San Francisco in three different ships. (A good precaution: one sank en route.) Upon arrival, he quickly sold out his entire stock.

He reinvested the profits in the city's booming real estate, banking and insurance sectors. By 1883, he was sufficiently established to construct the huge Phelan Building, which still stands at the intersection of O'Farrell and Market streets in San Francisco.

Phelan was one of the early proponents of the Panama Canal and in 1882 formed a partnership with several others to build a huge mechanical digger that Phelan thought could get the job done. The digger proved impractical, however, and the idea was abandoned.

*See* California

John A. Barnes, *Irish-American Landmarks* (Detroit, 1995).

JOHN A. BARNES

## PHELAN, JAMES DUVAL (1861–1930)

Politician, philanthropist. The only son of James Phelan, James Duval Phelan was a worldly, sophisticated youth who appreciated art and culture, very much unlike his no-nonsense father. He carried on honorably his father's name and legacy for four decades after the patriarch's death; however the son's contribution would be in the field of philanthropy and public service rather than in business.

Phelan won the first of three terms as mayor of San Francisco in 1897. He was a major exponent of the "city beautiful" movement popular at the turn of the century, and the wide boulevards, splashing fountains, and public parks that mark San Francisco today are largely his legacy. He also served a single term in the U.S. Senate from 1914 to 1920.

His main legacy is the Villa Montalvo, in nearby Saratoga, California, which was willed to the state after his death. Housing his magnificent art collection (Phelan never married), it also hosts concerts and plays.

*See* California

John A. Barnes, *Irish-American Landmarks* (Detroit, 1995).

JOHN A. BARNES

## PHELAN, JAMES JOSEPH (1871–1934)

Financier. James Joseph Phelan was born Oct. 14, 1871, in Toronto, Ontario, Canada, to James W. and Catherine (Colbert) Phelan. In 1878 his parents moved to the Boston area, where James attended public schools.

In 1888 Phelan began working for the banking firm of Hornblower & Weeks, one of the foremost banking houses in the country dealing in bonds and security issues. He became a partner in 1900 and continued working throughout most of his life in executive positions for several corporations, banks and stockbrokerages.

On June 19, 1899, he married Mary Meade, and they had three children before her death in 1907. He then married Mabel J. McGaffee April 23, 1913, with whom he also had three children.

While working for Hornblower, Phelan also was director and chairman of the Massachusetts Bonding and Insurance Company and director of Union Mills, Inc. He served on the executive committee of Bangor & Aroostook Railroad and N.E. Power

James Joseph Phelan

Association; as a trustee of Massachusetts Utilities Associates, Boston Wharf Company, U.S. Smelting, Refining & Mining Company, and Suffolk Savings Bank for Seamen.

He served with the Massachusetts Naval Brigade from 1893–96. Before the United States became involved in World War I, Phelan had organized the Northeast Sawmill Unit, which was recognized as a major contributor toward helping America win the war.

During the war he was assistant food administrator for Massachusetts, working full-time at the statehouse for 22 months. He assisted in the Liberty Loan campaigns and in raising more than $100,000 for members of the 101st U.S. Infantry and their families, while the regiment was serving in France. His efforts during the war also included helping to raise more than $200 million for the United War Campaign.

During a coal strike from 1922–23, Phelan took the reins as fuel administrator of Massachusetts for a seven-month period.

Phelan was involved with several charitable institutions around the Boston area. He was a member of the boards of managers for Children's Hospital, Boston Community Health Association, Travelers' Aid Society, and the Franklin Foundation, for which he was vice president.

He was chairman of the Massachusetts committee to procure relief for Ireland. Under his leadership, the Massachusetts nonsectarian group raised $800,000 out of the $5 million that the national committee sent to women and children in Ireland.

His benevolence extended to raising $1 million for relief following the San Francisco earthquake in 1906. He served also on relief committees helping after the Ohio floods, Chelsea fire, Salem fire and Messina earthquake. For these charitable works, the University of Notre Dame honored him with its Laetare Medal in 1931. He had served as a trustee of the university since 1927.

During the first two decades of the 1900s, Phelan was one of the most prominent Roman Catholic laymen in the country. He was appointed chairman of the reception committee for the visit of Cardinal Mercier of Belgium to Boston in 1920. Boston College honored him with an honorary doctorate in 1925.

In 1927 Phelan was honored by Pope Pius XI by being named the first Knight of Malta in the United States. He also was appointed Knight Commander of the Order of Pope Pius IX in 1926; received the Grand Cross of the Sovereign Military Order of Malta in 1928; and was named master of the American Chapter of the Knights of Malta.

He died Oct. 16, 1934, at his home in Brookline, Mass.

*National Cyclopedia of American Biography* (New York, 1930).
*Who's Who in America: 1897–1942* (1962).

MARIANNA McLOUGHLIN

## PHILADELPHIA

*Philadelphia, Here I Come!*, Brian Friel's 1964 play, alludes to a city that has been an immigrant destination for more than three centuries. "I'm Off to Philadelphia in the Morning," sung by John McCormack, has been heard on radio in countless homes along the banks of the Shannon, and then heard again in new homes along the banks of the Schuylkill. Epitomizing the history of an entire state, the Irish experience in Philadelphia reveals the vitality of a cultural identity that can persist through many changes over a long period of time.

## THE CITY OF BROTHERLY LOVE

Five of the six original counties of Pennsylvania were named after English counties or towns: Bucks, Chester, Kent, Sussex, and New Castle. Philadelphia's un-English name expresses a desire to transcend history—a history which included the unbrotherly traumas of England and Ireland in the seventeenth century. The Cromwellian conquest of Ireland was the background for William Penn's "Holy Experiment" in religious diversity and toleration. The son of a Cromwellian admiral with estates in Ireland, Penn was part of a Quaker movement that flourished among the English soldiers and adventurers there. Some sixty meetings were established between 1654 and the end of the century, with centers at Lurgan and Dublin as well as Cork, where Penn was converted in 1667. In founding Philadelphia in 1681, with ten percent of the early settlers coming from Ireland, Penn began the Ireland-Philadelphia connection with an idealistic dream. For later immigrants from Ireland, that dream has meant that the bonds between Ireland and Philadelphia would be extremely close, that all varieties of people from Ireland would come to Philadelphia, that Irish immigrants from the earliest times would mingle with people from all over the world, and that the city had established an ideal of love to oppose the hatred that marred Christendom during the wars of religion. Of course, mixed motives, present from the beginning of Pennsylvania, put in doubt whether the colony was to be a "holy experiment" or a proprietary grant to Penn, or an extension of royal control. There truly was no chance that Philadelphia would become *utopia*.

Helping Penn choose the site for Philadelphia was Captain Thomas Holme from Waterford, who had served Admiral Penn under Cromwell. The Surveyor-General of Pennsylvania, Holme modified Penn's first city plan ("a greene Country Towne") and drafted a rectangular grid of 1200 acres between the Delaware and Schuylkill Rivers, containing four squares, similar to garrison towns such as Londonderry that England was planting across Ireland. Importantly for later generations of immigrants, the plan provided larger city limits than any other early American town, thus allowing for many years of orderly expansion to accommodate increased population.

Penn's Ireland-Philadelphia connection was fortified by Quakers from Ireland who became prominent Philadelphia merchants. Robert Turner, a Dubliner, was a founding subscriber to the Free Society of Traders in Pennsylvania, the joint-stock company incorporated by Penn in 1682. Early Mayors from Ireland include Thomas Griffiths, from Cork (1729–30 and 1733), and Dubliner Robert Strettell (1751).

## PRESBYTERIANS AND CATHOLICS IN COLONIAL PHILADELPHIA

While Quakers from Ireland remained a presence in the city, the main group of immigrants in the eighteenth century were Presbyterians. Pennsylvania was the main immigrant destination from Ulster and the cradle of "Scotch-Irish" culture in America. The back-country culture of the "Scotch-Irish" became particularly strong in central and western Pennsylvania. Less well known is that nearly half of the immigrants settled in Philadelphia and the southeastern counties. They provided the city with new leadership in religion, education, business, and politics. As early as 1706, Francis Makemie, of the Laggan presbytery in Donegal, founded in Philadelphia the first presbytery in the English colonies. Francis Allison, also from Donegal, became professor of moral philosophy at the College of Philadelphia. During the American Revolution, Philadelphia was led by such Scotch-Irishmen as Thomas McKean, Joseph Reed, and Charles Thomson. They were part of the "Presbyterian Party" in the city that triumphed over Quaker and Anglican loyalism. George Bryan, from Dublin, an important merchant and lay leader in the Presbyterian Church led the framing of Pennsylvania's new state constitution of 1776, the most democratic in the thirteen colonies. The successes of these individuals established a strong tradition of Protestant emigration to Philadelphia—including members of the Church of Ireland and other faiths—that persisted through the twentieth century. This meant that Irish Catholics in later generations found that theirs was not the only tradition active in the city. More diversity than was common in other areas of Irish America was evident in Philadelphia.

Irish Catholics began coming to Philadelphia as servants to the early Quakers and continued to do so throughout the eighteenth century, mainly from Ulster and Leinster. In 1733, Quaker toleration of Catholicism was tested when Jesuits established St. Joseph's Church in Willings Alley, serving English, German, and Irish immigrants. While other colonies were enforcing the Penal Laws, Philadelphians permitted St. Joseph's to become the only church in the English-speaking world where Mass could be said legally. As the Catholic population grew, the principal Irish parish became St. Mary's, a short distance away on Fourth Street.

Much of the city's workforce came from the ranks of Irish immigrants. Yet an extraordinary number of its leaders during the revolutionary and federal eras did so too. Almost unique among cities in the English colonies, Philadelphia had Irish Catholics in the elite of its mercantile economy. Prominent were individuals whose families had strong traditions as merchants between Ireland and France: Thomas Fitzsimons, Stephen Moylan, and George Meade. These individuals represented an Irish identity that flourished during the American Enlightenment.

As part of this Enlightenment, bonds between Catholic and Protestant Irishmen in Philadelphia were fostered by the Friendly Sons of Saint Patrick, founded in 1771, and still thriving today. Those ties were strengthened during the Revolution. Seven of the nine companies in Colonel William Thompson's Pennsylvania regiment were almost entirely Scotch-Irish. Catholics also served in the front lines, and prominent individuals such as Stephen Moylan and Commodore John Barry played major roles: Moylan, as Washington's Quartermaster, and Barry in naval combat. After the war, during the struggle to ratify the Constitution in 1787–88, war veterans Thomas Fitzsimons and Thomas McKean worked together to ensure Pennsylvania's support for the new government, despite the suspicions of federalism expressed by the Scotch-Irish in the western part of the state. In the memory of the Philadelphia Irish, this era seems golden: a period when America's and Ireland's interests were perceived as intertwined, and Irish Protestants and Catholics pursued those interests together.

In the 1790s, as the new national government began, some leading Catholics, such as Mathew and James Carey, and Protestants, such as William Duane and James Reynolds, worked to support the United Irishmen in Ireland. (Wolfe Tone visited Philadelphia in 1796.) These individuals represented a strain of Irish nationalism and republicanism that was to play a large part in Philadelphia's history for the next two centuries. But they lost ground as Federalist fears of French and Irish radicalism grew with news of revolutionary atrocities in France. As Philadelphia, the new national capital, witnessed the arrival of 30,000 immigrants from Ireland during the 1790s, Congressman Harrison Gray Otis feared "hordes of wild Irishmen." Uriah Tracy of Connecticut called the United Irishmen he met in Pennsylvania "the most God-provoking democrats this side of hell." Such fears resulted, in 1798, in the Alien and Sedition Acts, which restricted the naturalization, and hence the voting rights, of immigrants. Within the Irish community in Philadelphia, internal divisions were expressed in 1799 at St. Mary's Church, where an attempt by United Irishmen to protest the Acts while Catholics were attending Mass led to a fracas. Better news in 1799 was the election of Republican candidate and Jeffersonian ally Thomas McKean as Governor of Pennsylvania.

## A NEW IRISH CATHOLIC IDENTITY: THE "DEVOTIONAL REVOLUTION" IN PHILADELPHIA

As the new century began, Philadelphia's Irish Catholic community had an educated elite, led by publisher-author Mathew Carey (1760–1839). Carey remains a cultural hero among the Philadelphia Irish for his combination of personal success, American patriotism fused with devotion to Ireland, and public-spirited concern for laboring people and the poor—the subjects of his last works. In the next generation, American-born Robert Walsh (1784–1859), son of Baron Shannon, wrote *Letter on the Genius and Dispositions of the French Government* (1810), an attack on Napoleon, and founded the Federalist *American Review of History and Politics* (1811–12). Pro-English against France, Walsh nevertheless also wrote *An Appeal from the Judgments of Great Britain Respecting the United States of America* (1819), which earned the praise of Jefferson and John Quincy Adams. Walsh edited the *National Gazette* (1820–35), served as professor of English and trustee of the University of Pennsylvania, and later represented the United States as consul in Paris.

Philadelphia uniquely allowed for "Enlightened Catholics" to enter the leadership of the new republic. However, during the 1820s and 1830s, a conflict within the Irish Catholic community changed the relationship between the Irish and the city. Philadelphia became the center of a conflict between "Enlightened Catholics" and clergy leading a religious counterrevolution against the Enlightenment in the aftermath of the French Revolution. The result was a reform of the Catholic church in Philadelphia in the 1830s that anticipated the "devotional revolution" in Ireland led by Archbishop Paul Cullen after the Famine. That reform was to have an enormous influence on the Irish community in Philadelphia for well over a century, from the 1830s through the 1950s.

The conflict began in 1820 with the appointment, by the trustees of St. Mary's Church, of William Hogan, from Limerick, as assistant pastor. An erratic personality, Hogan saw himself as an enlightened priest well suited to the Catholicism of the new republic. He and his followers described unenlightened clergy as despotic; they declared that Ireland had been ruined not only by the English, but by such clergy. They described bishops as "un-American" in language virtually identical to nativist diatribes against the Irish. At the time, the new Bishop of Philadelphia was the elderly Henry Conwell, the former Vicar General of Armagh. After Conwell excommunicated Hogan in 1821, the trustees of St. Mary's petitioned the state legislature to declare that only American-born trustees—laymen, not clergy—had the right to select pastors. They stated that to allow bishops to appoint pastors was to succumb to a foreign influence. New Irish immigrants to the city were on both sides of the controversy. Some

proponents of the Bishop characterized the trustees' position as "Protestant" and blatantly appealed to traditional prejudice. After much public scandal, including Hogan's conversion to Protestantism and marriage, and the bishopites' burning of Washington Hall, the headquarters of the dissenting trustees, the "Hogan Schism" ended in 1829 when the Baltimore Council asserted bishops' control over the churches. A new era began in 1830 with the arrival of Bishop Francis Patrick Kenrick, a Dubliner, a friend of Paul Cullen, and an extremely gifted administrator. Kenrick was educated for the priesthood at the College of Propaganda in Rome, and was the first graduate of the College sent to the United States. Under Bishop Kenrick, Philadelphia became a pioneer in the Romanization of the Catholic Church: the creation of a church very different from the church the immigrants had known at home. Irish immigrants arriving in Philadelphia under Kenrick found a Counter-Reformation Church reasserting itself. In 1832, Kenrick founded a diocesan seminary and named it for St. Charles Borromeo, the guiding spirit of the Council of Trent. Under Kenrick, from 1830 to 1851, Catholic parishes grew in number from four to nineteen, and construction began on the Cathedral of Saints Peter and Paul. Proselytizing by Redemptorists, Jesuits, and Augustinians was encouraged. Priests began to insist on being called "father," and laymen were discouraged from joining with Protestants in temperance societies and other enterprises. Long-standing tendencies of the Catholic middle class toward assimilation were challenged as the Catholic Church in Philadelphia asserted new imperatives as an institution.

## PRE-FAMINE IMMIGRATION

The strongly conservative Catholicism characteristic of Philadelphia's Irish community through Vatican II was shaped in the early decades of the nineteenth century. At the same time, so was the community's sense of Irishness as deeply rooted in a working-class identity. In the early 1800s, refugees from the United Irishmen movement came to the city and allied with the Jeffersonians to extend democratic rights. Arriving in 1805 was John Binns, a United Irishman and also a member of the London Corresponding Society, who had worked to ally Irish interests with the interests of English labor. Editor of the *Republican Argus* while he lived in Northumberland County, Binns began the *Democratic Press* in 1807. A Protestant, Binns voiced the interests of the Irish working classes as a city alderman through the 1840s.

During the War of 1812, as the city feared a possible British attack, Irish labor mobilized: more than two thousand workers volunteered to build fortifications across the Schuylkill without pay. As the canal system began, Philadelphia's Irish labor was transported to work sites for the Schuylkill Navigation Company, the Delaware and Raritan Canal, and the Lehigh Navigation Canal. In 1835, the Philadelphia Irish led one of the first recorded attempts by unskilled labor to organize. Some 300 coal heavers along the Schuylkill River, seeking a ten-hour day, started the first general strike in an American city. As more unskilled Irish emigrated to Philadelphia and competed for menial jobs, they frequently clashed in ugly race riots with African-Americans, who had long held those jobs. Conflict was exacerbated as political debate roiled over the issue of abolition.

In the 1840s, the Irish community in Philadelphia was divided over slavery. Strongly abolitionist opinion had been expressed in Robert Walsh's *National Gazette* and in the essays and poems of Thomas Brannagan. Others, however, feeling politically insecure as newcomers in America, did not want the Irish identified with the vehement criticism of American immorality and hypocrisy that came with the abolitionist position. Local leaders also knew that the majority of their countrymen feared African-American competition for jobs. Strong statements from Daniel O'Connell, urging, and then demanding, that the Irish in America join the abolitionists caused a split in the local chapter of the Repeal Association. (John B. Colahan was the outstanding opponent of slavery within the Association.) After the political disaster for O'Connell and Repeal at Clontarf (October 1843), the Liberator increasingly lost moral authority as he made more statements professing loyalty to Britain and criticized the slave-owning nation of the United States.

## THE RIOTS OF 1844

In 1844, a number of forces came together to produce a trauma to the Irish Catholics of Philadelphia that has been preserved as a memory of victimization, intimately tying the community to past centuries of persecution in Ireland. Irish homes, the seminary of the Sisters of Charity, and two churches, St. Michael's and St. Augustine's, were burned to the ground in May 1844 during a riot between the Irish and nativists that began in Kensington and proceeded to center city. A third church, St. Philip Neri, in Southwark, was attacked in a second riot in July, where nativists confronted militia trying to protect the building. In all, about eighteen people were killed—most of them nativists shot by the Irish in May and the militia in July. Scores were injured. The precipitating event was a campaign to "Save the Bible" in the schools, reacting to Bishop Kenrick's opposition to Catholic students in public schools being forced to read from the King James Bible. A public meeting called on May 3 to set up a branch of the American Party in the Irish section of Kensington was disrupted—predictably—by the Irish. Nativists returned in a few days, and the burning and shooting began. A force behind the riot was the rise of the American Protestant Association, asserting the authority of the evangelical clergy against a newly militant Catholic Church. Also, a new wave of nativism had arisen as increased immigration caused competition for jobs. Philadelphians had also developed a habit of resorting to violence in all manner of conflicts during this era. In the same Kensington neighborhood in 1842–43, the handloom weavers had engaged in a violent strike against employers. The conflict also was internecine: Irish Protestants from Ulster were prominently involved. (Earlier, in 1831, a riot had occurred during an Orange parade.)

The riots of 1844 were a watershed event for Philadelphia. In their wake, civil authorities, determined to end decades of urban violence, consolidated the various local police forces between 1844 and 1850, and consolidated the government of the city and county in 1854. This prepared city bureaucracy for the vast and rapid expansion of industry through the Civil War era. The immediate effect of the riots was a short-lived ascendancy of the "Know-Nothings": the first mayor in the consolidated city represented the American Party, and the first police were recruited from the ranks of the nativists. The riots also strengthened the Catholic Church's resolve to build its own, separate school system.

## POST-FAMINE IMMIGRATION

Famine immigrants to Philadelphia found two opportunities much harder to find in New York and Boston. First, they found the chance to work in a variety of occupations as the city became the premier industrial city in the nation. Second, they found the

chance to live in their own home as the city's ample land area and rowhouses created neighborhoods of home owners. Although it often took decades, families' poverty and despair gave way to hope. The misery of the Famine generation can be epitomized by one statistic from Philadelphia's state hospital in 1856: two-thirds of the insane were Irish-born.

Much larger than Boston, Philadelphia had, by 1850, 72,000 Irish-born residents in a total population of 340,000, as compared to Boston's 35,000 in a population of 113,000. By 1860 the Irish-born population grew to 95,000. The Irish would remain the largest foreign-born group in the city until 1910.

In 1850, perhaps a third of the city's Irish population were unskilled laborers. Skilled or not, the Irish were welcomed by the city's business leadership, who oversaw a boom in the Civil War era that increased manufacturing enterprises from 6,467 in 1860 to 8,262 in 1870. World famous for machine-tool fabrication, Philadelphia invited the Irish into the metalworking that was at the heart of the industrial enterprise. The Irish also worked in the fifty brickyards, located in both South and North Philadelphia, that were expanding the "red brick town" with houses. They worked in the new booming textile factories and on the Schuylkill and Delaware docks. A railroad hub, the city offered employment on the seven railroads feeding into it. Irish women, by the thousands, were working in the textile factories during the 1880s. Others found work as servants and boardinghouse operators. In the 1890s, women started to move into such occupations as nursing, teaching, and sales.

The Irish quickly came to dominate the building trades and produced contractor bosses who were vital in the economic and political life of the community and city. Railroad contractors included such individuals as Thomas Costigan, Patrick McManus, and James B. Reilly. Contractor John Ryan brought over stonemasons from Kilkenny to build the Reading Railroad Terminal Building.

While originally concentrated in a few sections of South Philadelphia and Kensington, the Irish were able to move rather quickly into a variety of neighborhoods in the industrial city. The spread of factories across the city, coupled with the rise of streetcars allowing easy travel to work, encouraged the population to disperse. The growth of building and loan associations fostered homeownership in rowhouse neighborhoods. As a result, by 1880, while the Philadelphia Irish developed their separate institutions, they were not ghettoized in particular locations: many "Irish neighborhoods" developed, but the Irish lived amid a variety of other groups within the city.

In Philadelphia, occupational mobility allowed some Irish to enter into business and thrive. Thomas Cahill, a coal shipper, went on to endow Roman Catholic High School (1890), the first free Catholic secondary school in America. Thomas Fitzgerald grew wealthy as the publisher of the *Philadelphia Item,* the newspaper most read by the immigrants from 1847 through the 1890s.

The outstanding Irish civic leader in the Civil War era was lawyer Daniel Dougherty, renowned for his oratory and learning. A Democrat, Dougherty nevertheless supported Lincoln and was a founder of the Union League. His speeches at the outbreak of war rallied a reluctant Irish population to the cause. At Gettysburg, the heavily Irish 116th Pennsylvania Regiment was led by General St. Clair Mulholland, a Catholic immigrant from Lisburn.

In 1863, in the middle of the war, the first national convention of the Fenian movement took place in Philadelphia. The local Fenian leader was a printer from Donegal, James Gibbons, who inherited the city's strong republican tradition from the era of the United Irishmen. Fenianism caused consternation among the hierarchy. Bishop Wood condemned the movement in a pastoral letter, and started a new diocesan newspaper, the *Catholic Standard,* because he distrusted the Fenian sympathies of the *Catholic Herald* editor, James Spellissy. (One clerical friend of the Fenians was the pastor of St. Augustine's, Patrick Moriarty, the foremost preacher of the time.) In 1866, Philadelphia Fenians were linked to the ill-advised raid on Canada: Gibbons and associates had purchased 4,200 arms from the Bridesburg Arsenal. Joining Gibbons as an ally in 1867 was Dr. William Carroll, a Presbyterian from Donegal and a Civil War veteran. Carroll later represented Clan na Gael in talks with Parnell when he visited the city in 1876 and 1880. Carroll also became president of the Celtic Society, promoting the study of the Irish language. The growth of Irish nationalism in the city during the decades after the Famine was summarized by British intelligence in 1888, which described Philadelphia as the center of revolutionary activity in America. In the 1890s, as part of Clan na Gael's campaign, Luke Dillon bombed the House of Commons.

While the Fenians were a militant presence, Irish nationalism found an eloquent, moderate voice in Martin Griffin. Griffin established the Irish Catholic Benevolent Union to unify the older emigrant aid societies throughout the United States; allied with Davitt and Parnell to establish more branches of the Land League than any other individual; and strove for Home Rule. A leader in the temperance movement and the founder of the American Catholic Historical Society, the tireless Griffin embodied the virtues of Victorian Philadelphia's Catholic leadership.

Griffin was closely allied to the principal institution in the community: the Church, which forged a Roman Catholic identity along the lines envisioned by Bishop Kenrick in a rapid and steady growth of parish schools. In 1850, there were five parish schools; in 1870, twenty-six; in 1884, fifty-eight. Stimulated by the Third Plenary Council in Baltimore (1884), the number grew to 103 by 1903. At the dawn of a new century, under Archbishop Ryan, the Archdiocese was an effective institution for assimilating Irish working-class people to the industrial city by providing education and inculcating habits of respectability. In 1912, Hallahan became the first diocesan high school for girls in the United States. Under Cardinal Dougherty (1918–1951), Philadelphia uniquely offered free tuition for both elementary and high school students, paid for by the parishes with no additional cost to parents.

After the Civil War, the temperance movement, dormant since the 1840s, revived with the foundation of the Catholic Total Abstinence Union in 1866. The seat of the national headquarters, Philadelphia had more local societies than any other city. In every parish, societies organized immigration bureaus and libraries, and built halls for "dry" celebrations. The temperance halls served to replace other institutions, less respectable, that had been important in neighborhood life in the city: volunteer fire companies, often indistinguishable from gangs and taverns— a business the Irish had run in Philadelphia as early as the 1750s. The low repute of the fire companies and related gangs such as "The Killers" and "The Schuylkill Rangers" had earned the Irish a reputation for violence in the city. (The fire companies were replaced by professional firefighters in 1871.) The reputation of taverns, long associated with drunkenness and prostitution, gradually ameliorated. In the neighborhoods, taverns remained centers for ward politics and social life; by the 1880s, they were also a presence in center city, with a clientele of politicians and journalists enjoying Irish hospitality.

The Irish regularly took part in labor agitation during the 1850s, and assumed second-tier positions in labor organizations by the late 1860s. In the era of the Molly Maguires, the Philadelphia Irish found ethnic identity in militant labor unions. The Knights of Labor, begun in Philadelphia in 1869 by Uriah Stephens, became, in the 1880s, the nation's largest union under the leadership of Terence Powderly of Scranton.

By the end of the century the Irish in Philadelphia were powerful enough to provoke a new wave of animosity. The Irish at the bottom of the social order, who sometimes engaged in the thuggery endemic to ward politics, were satirized in *Solid for Mulhooly* (1881), reprinted in 1889 with such Thomas Nast cartoons as "His Paddy-gree" and "His First School." A notorious figure was William "Bull" McMullen, a former "Killer" from the Moyamensing Hose fire company, who was the Democratic leader in South Philadelphia. At the same time, the institutions that were "civilizing" the Irish, particularly the separate Catholic school system, were so strong that nativist anxiety produced the American Protective Association. Pennsylvania's A.P.A. membership was third in the nation.

## TWENTIETH-CENTURY ASSIMILATION AND ETHNIC REVIVAL

As the twentieth century began, bloody clashes on Broad Street regularly took place during the Orange parades each July 12. Also, Irish life in the city still had a large share of chronic unemployment, alcoholism, disease, and mental illness. In America's "most English city," forty percent of all female servants were Irish. In 1910, about twenty percent of the Irish in the Schuylkill neighborhood were reported as unable to read or write. Eventually, however, atavistic conflict and poverty gave way to assimilation and success.

The Philadelphia Irish did not produce and rally around strong political leaders—as they did in other cities. They adjusted to the politics of "the private city," where individualistic concerns dominated over public concerns. This was the city that Lincoln Steffens characterized as "corrupt and contented" and the worst governed in the nation. The abandonment of politics by the city's patricians to middle-class Protestants, accelerating after 1870, opened the way for the Irish to enter into pragmatic arrangements with native-born Americans with whom they regularly came into contact. Patrician withdrawal from public life also set an example that, in Philadelphia, unlike Boston, political leadership, in itself, was not something prestigious that bright immigrants need aspire to. Furthermore, with a Republican machine firmly in place, lasting into the 1950s, Irish loyalties to the Democratic Party locked them out of city leadership. At the same time, individuals in Philadelphia, more than elsewhere, joined the Republican Party in order not to wander in a political wilderness. Personal opportunities and acquiescence to the status quo, rather than a burning desire for ethnic control, characterized the Irish in local politics. The first Irish Catholic Mayor, James H. J. Tate, did not take office until 1962.

A Philadelphia alternative to the political boss was the contractor boss: individuals with economic and political clout whose companies made an enduring mark on the city. "Sunny Jim" McNichol, the first Irish Catholic prominent in the Republican Party (in the 1890s), completed the subway from City Hall to South Philadelphia, constructed the Torresdale water filtration plant, and built the Benjamin Franklin Parkway and the Roosevelt

Boulevard. Matthew McCloskey built more schools than any other contractor in the city, and he built Convention Hall and Penn Center. National finance chairman of the Democratic Party from 1955 to 1962, McCloskey was appointed Ambassador to Ireland by President Kennedy. John McShain built the Board of Education building, the Municipal Court building, Veterans Hospital, and the Naval Hospital; he also was responsible for an extraordinary number of projects in Washington under government contracts. McShain kept close ties to Ireland, where he owned an 8500-acre estate in Killarney. John B. Kelly, Olympic oarsman, father of actress Grace Kelly, was known for the ubiquitous "Kelly for Brickwork" sign across the city. Kelly ran, unsuccessfully, as the New Deal candidate for Mayor in 1935.

During Ireland's national struggle, two men represented the two streams of nationalism in Philadelphia. The physical force tradition was embodied by Joseph McGarrity from Tyrone (1874–1940), who had become a successful distiller and real estate agent. McGarrity was the chief American financier and propagandist for the Easter Uprising. He brought Roger Casement and James Larkin to the city to speak prior to the rising. In 1919, he dominated the Irish Race Convention, held in Philadelphia, wresting control from New York's John Devoy and Daniel Colahan, who wanted to use the Irish Victory Fund to defeat President Wilson and the League of Nations. McGarrity insisted that the Fund be used to rally support for Eamon de Valera, the sole surviving leader of the 1916 rebellion. In this way he prevented a split in the early days of the Republic and mobilized American support for Irish independence. Michael J. Ryan (1862–1943), a lawyer from Gesu Parish, the "lace curtain" parish in North Philadelphia, worked tirelessly for Home Rule from the Parnell era on. He brought William A. O'Brien and John Dillon to the city for fund raising, and later he was elected President of the United Irish League. In 1919, Ryan was part of the delegation to Paris that presented Ireland's case for nationhood—only to be frustrated by President Wilson. Locally, he was President of the Friendly Sons of St. Patrick and twice a political candidate: for the Democratic nomination for Governor (1914), and for the office of Mayor (1915).

From the 1920s through the 1950s, assimilation gained in momentum across Greater Philadelphia. Cardinal Dougherty, "God's Bricklayer," built churches and schools rapidly during the 1920s, but increasingly he was building them in the suburbs, removed from older neighborhood ties that sustained Irish identity. Also, the Cardinal's extreme insistence that all Catholics attend Catholic school, his elevation of obedience as the foremost virtue, his disdain for collaborating with non-Catholics, his fulminations against popular culture, especially movies, were less an expression of shared community values than a sign of strong social forces moving the other way. Nevertheless, the Philadelphia Irish were still largely in the city, in communities they identified by parish name, and comfortable with "obedience" as an instinct for loyalty inherited from Irish parentage and now being transferred to such "Irish" institutions as Catholic League sports teams, Notre Dame football, and the United States Marine Corps.

One individual who helped the community retain older Irish ties was radio broadcaster Pat Stanton, whose program "The Irish Hour" began in the Sesquicentennial celebration of 1926 and continued into the 1970s—the longest running ethnic radio program ever under one person's guidance. Because it is likely that there were more radios in Greater Philadelphia than in Ireland during the 1920s, Stanton is said to have been the first radio

voice of the Irish. "The Irish Hour" showcased traditional musicians such as fiddler and composer Ed Reavy, from the "Corktown" section of West Philadelphia. Stanton's loyalty to the New Deal, and aversion to anti-Semitism, led him to refuse to broadcast Father Coughlin in the late 1930s, despite some bitter protests by clergy and others. After he began his own station, WJMJ, he welcomed other ethnic groups: he aired programs in Yiddish, Polish, Italian, and Greek. In later years, Stanton's listeners were the immigrants and first-generation Americans who belonged to the county societies—Donegal, Tryone, and Mayo having the largest membership. Such individuals organized much of the community's social life during this era. In 1958 the creation of the Irish Center in Germantown gave that social life a central location, where it remained strong through the 1970s. Generational changes and a variety of new venues for Irish music and entertainment have decentralized social life in Philadelphia since then.

The death of Cardinal O'Hara in August 1960, just as plans were beginning for Vatican II, marked the end of an era. He was the last in a sequence of Irish archbishops—Ryan, Dougherty, O'Hara—who put a conservative stamp on Philadelphia Catholicism in the twentieth century. Soon, Catholics were radically changing their attitudes toward the Church and society. At the same time, second- and third-generation Irish were leaving old neighborhoods in accelerating white flight. An individual's desire to hold on to an Irish identity without the familiar moorings of church and neighborhood seemed futile.

An ethnic revival along cultural lines occurred during the 1970s, fostered by Dennis Clark, whose series of books, beginning with *The Irish in Philadelphia* (1973), gave the community a history, a tradition it could claim. A sociologist, social activist, and philanthropist, Clark revived the cultural ideal of Mathew Carey: an enlightened lay leader, devoted to his people but ecumenical, at home with all segments of the city, and passionately concerned with justice and help for the poor in body and spirit. During the bicentennial era, as the nation turned back to its founding period for guidance, Clark, along with other Irish-American academics at local colleges, restored a secular intellectual tradition.

*Daily News* columnist Jack McKinney added a strong journalistic voice, expressing, incisively, the city's tradition of Irish nationalism in his coverage of Northern Ireland. In his personal style, McKinney also was a Philadelphia cultural hero, an erudite but street-smart man who could hold his own with anyone—a man equally adept at discussing Ireland, U.S. policy in Latin America, Italian opera, boxing, or Eagles' football.

Mick Moloney, a well-known musician from Limerick who came to study folklore at the University of Pennsylvania, stimulated the revival of the city's Irish musical heritage. Moloney's comprehensive scholarship on Irish music in America was strongly rooted in Philadelphia, which has strong traditions from such regions as the Sligo/Mayo border and Donegal.

By 1981 the Philadelphia community had its own monthly newspaper, the *Irish Edition*. Some 300 lawyers of Irish descent were members of the Brehon Society. At the same time, prophetic voices were challenging ethnic complacency: Father John McNamee of St. Malachy's Parish, and Father Michael Doyle of Sacred Heart in nearby Camden, New Jersey, drew suburban parishioners back to inner-city parishes long associated with the Irish and now associated with the worst contemporary misery. In the 1990s, the Irish/African-American encounter—which is also an Irish self-encounter—was still unfinished business in Philadelphia.

The distinctive quality of the Irish in Philadelphia is the persistence of a local patriotism, or *duchas,* at all social levels in the community. It encompasses loyalty to the home sports teams, despite (or because of) their history of heartbreaking losses, and a passionate devotion to place lore, to tales of "old neighborhoods" such as Swampoodle, parishes such as Our Lady of Mercy, and Philadelphia's industrial history more generally. At times merely nostalgic, this patriotism often achieves true connections between individuals and forges community bonds by relying upon the power of personal stories—not upon a presumption of ethnic bonds. The future of the city's Irish identity lies in the continuity of family life, the source of memories passed on from generation to generation, supported by community leaders who value such narratives. Doubts about continuity fade when set against the frequent contacts between Ireland and Philadelphia today, and the readiness and willingness of a changed Philadelphia community to retain contacts with the Irish people, who themselves have changed considerably since the 1950s.

*See* Pennsylvania; Emigration: 17th and 18th Centuries; Emigration: 1801–1921

E. Digby Baltzell, *Puritan Boston and Quaker Philadelphia* (New York, 1979).

Dennis Clark, *Erin's Heirs: Irish Bonds of Community* (Lexington, 1991).

———, *Hibernia America: The Irish and Regional Cultures* (Westport, 1986).

———, *The Irish in Philadelphia: Ten Generations of Urban Experience* (Philadelphia, 1973).

———, *The Irish Relations: Trials of an Immigrant Tradition* (Rutherford, 1982).

James F. Connelly, ed., *The History of the Archdiocese of Philadelphia* (Philadelphia, 1976).

Michael Feldberg, *The Philadelphia Riots of 1844: A Study of Ethnic Conflict* (Westport, 1975).

Noel Ignatiev, *How the Irish Became White* (New York, 1995).

Bruce Kuklick, *To Everything a Season: Shibe Park and Urban Philadelphia, 1909–1976* (Princeton, 1991).

Dale Light, *Rome and the New Republic: Conflict and Community in Philadelphia Catholicism between the Revolution and the Civil War* (Notre Dame, 1996).

John T. McGreevy, *Parish Boundaries: The Catholic Encounter with Race in the Twentieth-Century Urban North* (Chicago, 1996).

Harry C. Silcox, *Philadelphia's Politics from the Bottom Up: The Life of Irishman William McMullen, 1824–1901* (Philadelphia, 1989).

Russell F. Weigley, ed., *Philadelphia: A 300-Year History* (New York, 1982).

JOSEPH J. KELLY

## PHILADELPHIA RIOTS

In 1844, violent incidents of nativism erupted in Philadelphia. Anti-Catholic sentiment in the city had been growing for some time following the request of Bishop Francis Patrick Kenrick that Catholic children attending public schools be allowed to read from the Catholic version of the Bible. The trouble began on May 3, 1844, when the Native American Party met in the Kensington section (largely populated by Irish) of the city. That meeting did not end in violence, but on May 6, the party held another gathering; this time a number of members arrived carrying weapons. An Irish citizen and a member of the party began to fight,

and a Native American was killed and an Irish person was wounded. Later that night, nativists returned to the area and began to loot private homes. During the evening, a Sister of Charity was hit with a brick and knocked unconscious. The next day, the nativists began to demolish the building belonging to the Hibernian Hose Company. The military was sent to restore order, and St. Michael's Church was placed under armed guard. The following day, May 8, the mob returned and succeeded in torching St. Michael's Church. Later that night, St. Augustine's Church was burned, along with its library and monastery. During the days that followed, mobs attempted to burn down St. Mary's, St. John's, and St. Philip's, but were unsuccessful.

On July 4, 1844, the nativists held a large demonstration. The pastor of St. Philip Neri had received information that the nativists planned to destroy the church and asked the civil authorities for protection. He was given permission for armed guards to be placed around the church. The result was prolonged rioting between nativists and Catholics; thirteen were killed and fifty wounded. Although a shaky peace was restored, it was not until the end of the month that the troops were withdrawn from the city.

*See* Philadelphia; Nativism

James F. Connelly, ed., *The History of the Archdiocese of Philadelphia* (Philadelphia, 1976).

MARGARET M. McGUINNESS

## PITTSBURGH AND WESTERN PENNSYLVANIA

In the quarter-millennium from mid-eighteenth century to the curtain drop of the twentieth century, Irish men and women by the tens of thousands, and in corporate anonymity, have made the truest and most pervasive contribution to life in western Pennsylvania.

Irish immigrants and their increasingly influential descendants have permeated every field of endeavor. From the lone pioneers and traders of the Ohio Valley to the multitudes who became farmers, tradesmen and professionals, the communal Irish presence has been significant. The Irish made their presence known not only in the industrial growth of western Pennsylvania but also in its schools and churches.

For reasons doubtless geographical and economic, not many Irishmen chose western Pennsylvania for home and fortune as the eighteenth century reached the midway point and receded past the American Revolution. One who did was George Croghan, who came out from Ireland's midland. He set up a trading post at Logstown, below the forks of the Ohio River in the 1740s. From there he expanded through the lands of the Delawares, Shawnees, and Wyandots. In due course, Croghan became "King of the Traders" as England successfully challenged France for the territory beyond the mountains.

Croghan was contemporary to William Johnson, another Irish midlander who cast his lot with the Iroquois nations to the north. With his half-Indian son, who was knighted Sir William, Johnson helped stabilize Britain's stance in Canada.

The Croghan trading empire extended westward virtually to the Mississippi. Joined by family members, Croghan is said to have made, lost, and regained several fortunes over a long and influential career. He acquired vast areas of land in present-day Pittsburgh and elsewhere.

A part of these passed down in the nineteenth century to a collateral descendant, Mary Croghan Schenley, who deeded 400 acres to Pittsburgh to become Schenley Park, crown jewel of the city's magnificent public park system. Also on these lands were built Carnegie Library and Music Hall, the world-famous Phipps Conservatory, a portion of Carnegie Mellon University, the city golf course, and the erstwhile Schenley Oval Harness Racing Track, which has since been developed into a sports recreation area, including a football field, an ice-skating rink, and the city's largest battery of tennis courts.

The Irish have achieved distinction in many western Pennsylvania fields: government, religion, education, labor, industry, finance, and their own social and cultural organizations. To attempt to do justice by name and achievements to all who have contributed notably in all or any of these civic areas would be impossible in a major volume, let alone a brief resume.

## CHURCH GROWTH

Churches in western Pennsylvania have succeeded long after modest beginnings. In 1758 when the Catholic French yielded Fort Duquesne to the Protestant British, Presbyterian Reverend Charles Beatty preached a thanksgiving sermon. Was he an Irishman from Ulster? Two centuries later, the Reverend Dr. Charles P. Robshaw embarked on a twenty-five year pastorate of Pittsburgh's magnificent East Liberty Presbyterian Church. Since he was Dublin born and president of the Gaelic Arts Society of Pittsburgh, there was no question of his Irishness. Over those two centuries, Irish Presbyterians had achieved greatly in every phase of western Pennsylvania life, along with gifted adherents of many other Protestant denominations.

Irish Catholics, however, soon made up for the departed French. A scattering of pioneer priests ministered to small but increasing Irish flocks of the post-Revolutionary days of westward expansion. In due course a small church was built, thanks in substantial part to the generosity of James O'Hara, who had come out from Ireland prior to the Revolution and prospered in business in Philadelphia. During the war, he served as quartermaster of the Continental Army. Afterward he journeyed west to Pittsburgh, where he prospered still further, running a retail store, brewery, sawmill, tannery, and gristmill. In partnership with Isaac Craig, O'Hara set up a window glass and bottle factory. He was also involved in shipbuilding and had vast interests in real estate. Not unjustly, he was acclaimed father of Pittsburgh commerce and industry.

Meanwhile, an irregular sequence of Irish priests looked to the spiritual needs of their countrymen in far-flung exile. Among these were Fathers Patrick Lonergan, Lawrence Phelan, Charles Ferry, Patrick O'Neill, William F. X. O'Brien, and, most famous of all, Charles Bonaventure Maguire, a Franciscan from Dungannon, County Tyrone, the home also of Thomas Mellon, founder of Pittsburgh's most famous banking and financial family.

Father Maguire, a brilliant scholar and linguist, came to America after a spectacular European experience that included graduation from Louvain, a harrowing escape from the French Reign of Terror, a teaching term in Rome, and ministering to the wounded on the field of Waterloo. He was pastor in 1820 of Pittsburgh's first parish, St. Patrick's. He taught languages for eight years at the Western University of Pennsylvania, now the University of Pittsburgh. When Father Maguire died in 1833, he was succeeded by Father John O'Reilly, also an able administrator and builder.

## CREATION OF A DIOCESE

When St. Paul Parish at Fifth Avenue and Grant Street was founded, Father Michael J. O'Connor from County Cork was named its first pastor on June 17, 1841. On August 8, 1843, the Diocese of Pittsburgh was created with Michael O'Connor its first bishop and St. Paul Parish as his cathedral. Of Pittsburgh's eleven bishops, eight have been of Irish birth or ancestry: Michael O'Connor, 1843–1860; John Tuigg, 1876–1889; Richard Phelan, 1889–1904; John Francis Regis Canevin, 1904–1920; Hugh C. Boyle, 1920–1950; John F. Dearden, 1950–1959; John J. Wright, 1959–1969; and Vincent M. Leonard, 1969–1983.

Pittsburgh's Irish bishops served with dedication and distinction. All faced problems inevitable to diocesan administration, but O'Connor and Tuigg struggled and suffered through decades of financial stringencies and sometimes virulent opposition, not only from without but also from within their own flocks. Each prevailed in the end, though in seriously impaired health. O'Connor recovered to achieve a lifelong ambition, after resigning his bishopric, to enter the Society of Jesus. Two of the Irish bishops, Dearden and Wright, became cardinals of the church—Dearden as archbishop of Detroit and Wright in Rome in a Vatican post of high responsibility. Both filled active and effective roles in Vatican Council II.

Among Bishop O'Connor's many fruitful achievements was his persuasion of the authorities of the then newly organized Irish Sisters of Mercy in County Carlow to send to Pittsburgh a band of seven volunteer nuns under the leadership of Sister Francis Xavier Warde, a woman of tremendous zeal, energy, and vision. From its first small convent at the edge of downtown Pittsburgh, the tiny delegation spread nationwide in America. Within a few years, Sisters of Mercy staffed many of the parish schools of the diocese. At their convent they taught music and art. They opened an academy for young ladies and the motherhouse of their Congregation, high over Fifth Avenue, the city's eastward artery. This venture became Mount Mercy, the eventual site of the presently distinguished and expanding Carlow College.

In 1846, three years after establishment of the diocese, the Sisters opened Pittsburgh's first hospital, now the famed and vast Mercy Hospital System. In a far different and unique departure into current-day activity, Mercy Sister Michele O'Leary is a respected leader of The Irish Institute, perhaps the most successful stateside promoter of Irish-American economic and interpersonal relations, based in Pittsburgh.

## EDUCATIONAL ACHIEVEMENTS

From earliest times, Irish talent, both Protestant and Catholic, has enlivened educational development. Irish educators, lay and clerical, have been prominent in public, private, and parochial schools as founders, administrators, and teachers. The parochial systems of the Dioceses of Pittsburgh and Erie, and later Greensburg and Altoona, have been almost totally dependent upon religious orders—Mercy, Charity, Franciscan, and Divine Providence—all of them significantly Irish by birth or ancestry. Also, Irish Christian and Marist Brothers have manned the leading Catholic high schools of the district for more than half a century.

Duquesne University, by far the largest Catholic institution of higher learning in western Pennsylvania, as well as one of the most acclaimed in the nation, is an unmistakable Irish achievement almost from its inception. In 1878 Bishop Tuigg invited a small coterie of Holy Ghost Fathers, expatriates from the Prussian regime of Bismarck, to found a modest Catholic school for boys in the rooms above a shop in Pittsburgh's uptown Hill District. The German fathers, with their energetic leader, Father Joseph Strub, were very soon afterward given another assignment elsewhere by their superiors. The Pittsburgh College of the Holy Ghost then became the charge of the Irish Province of the Congregation, with Father John Murphy its president.

The college bought land on Bluff Street high above the Monongahela River and less than a mile from its old home on the Hill. Construction began there of the five-story red brick structure known today as the Old Main Building. It housed classrooms for college and high school students, rooms for the Holy Ghost Fathers and Brothers of the faculty and staff, administrative offices, and a refectory.

Growth of the college was steady under eight presidents: Fathers Murphy, Martin A. Hehir, Jeremiah J. Callahan, Raymond Kirk, Francis P. Smith, Vernon F. Gallagher, Henry J. McAnulty, and Edward L. Murray—all Irish. Holy Ghost College became Duquesne University of the Holy Ghost in 1911 during Father Hehir's long watch. The various professional schools followed as the campus expanded and the student body grew to its present total of nearly 10,000 from all the states of the Union and scores of countries around the globe.

Dr. John E. Murray, Duquesne's first lay president, has led the university in the past decade to a well-merited place among the academic elite. Dr. Murray, of course, is also Irish, as is a sizable quota of Holy Ghost Fathers from the Old Country who are among his top aides.

Duquesne by no means stands alone in its field. Irish men and women have held and are holding positions on the faculty and in administration at Pittsburgh's Carlow and La Roche Colleges, Erie's Mercyhurst and Gannon Colleges, and St. Francis College of Loretto—all Catholic schools. A notably visible Gaelic strain is found at the University of Pittsburgh, Carnegie Mellon University, and the many Protestant sectarian colleges of the region.

## POLITICAL INROADS

In western Pennsylvania's government, many-faceted as it has always been, Irish representation has been early and constant. Pittsburgh's first mayor, elected in 1816, was banker-merchant Ebenezer Denny. His successors have included Bernard McKenna, William A. Magee, William N. McNair, Cornelius D. Scully, David L. Lawrence, Joseph M. Barr, Peter Flaherty, Thomas Murphy, and others of less obvious Celtic background.

A list of Allegheny County stalwarts of recent years shows the Revered John J. Kane, of county parks and county hospitals fame, Charles McGovern, Peter McArdle, Peter and Thomas Flaherty, Dr. William McClelland, and, in a special way, James W. Knox, who has added to a distinguished public service years of devoted activity on behalf of the noted Irish Room in Pitt's Cathedral of Learning and in the cultural affairs of the Gaelic Arts Society.

Of them all, David Lawrence stands preeminent. Dave Lawrence was the prototypical Democratic leader—not "Boss," a term he rejected and despised. The son of Charles and Catherine Conwell Lawrence, Catholic immigrants from Ireland's north, Lawrence was born in 1889 at the Point, the very heart of Pittsburgh. His own heart never left the neighborhood of his birth and St. Mary's, "The Point Church," parish of his baptism and, ultimately, his funeral.

Higher education for Lawrence meant two years of business instruction at St. Mary's after local public school. He found political education in his neighborhood—in small jobs as he grew up, and as clerk-stenographer for two decades in the law office of William J. Brennan, leader of a county Democratic party that subsisted modestly in the shadow of, and in subservience to, the wealthy, entrenched Republican machine.

Lawrence thoroughly learned the rules of the game. By the time of the 1932 Roosevelt landslide, Lawrence was ready to create the local Democratic juggernaut that still functions with Irish collaboration, although somewhat diminished, as the twentieth century draws to a close. Lawrence led with a skill, zeal, and influence that was felt not only statewide within the party but also on a national basis. His seal was on a multitude of officeholders, elective and appointive, but he was notoriously reluctant to seek public office for himself, partly in apprehension of bigoted opposition to an Irish Catholic political leader.

Eventually, however, after a major role in the successful 1934 Pennsylvania campaign of George Earle for governor and Joseph Guffey for the United States Senate, it became a logical necessity for Lawrence to accept appointment as Secretary of the Commonwealth in the Earle cabinet. While in that office, Lawrence spent four years guiding the politically inexperienced governor and achieving his own hands-on education in the intricacies of government as practiced in the state capital.

In the Spring of 1945, support of Mayor Scully for a third term in Pittsburgh had waned and Democratic leaders were at a serious loss for a candidate to accept the party's nomination. Lawrence, over his vigorous and sustained reluctance, agreed to seek the mayoralty nomination and election, both of which he won very decisively.

Lawrence served three full terms of four years each as mayor—the longest and most effective administration of the twentieth century. His leadership extended to all phases of municipal government. Lawrence's tenure was highlighted by his joining with Republican Richard King Mellon in producing the nationally famous Pittsburgh Renaissance, which virtually made over a depressed, out-moded pre–World War II city into a sparkling metropolitan community-keyed downtown in the mayor's old neighborhood at the Point.

Lawrence could have continued indefinitely as mayor, but in 1958 during his fourth term, another Democratic candidacy crisis erupted. This time the governorship of Pennsylvania was on the line as George Leader's single-term limit wound down. Again, a violently reluctant Lawrence was coerced to rescue the party, and in January 1959 he was sworn in as the first Catholic governor of Pennsylvania.

During four years in Harrisburg, Lawrence captained a tight ship and led the Commonwealth, with hard-won bipartisan support, through an inherited fiscal stringency to a high level of stability.

Even in 1963, at the age of 73 as his term as governor ended, Lawrence was not ready to retire. He accepted an urgent invitation from President John Kennedy to chair the new Committee on Equal Opportunity in Housing as a special assistant to the president. He also held that distinguished national post in the Lyndon Johnson administration. While introducing gubernatorial candidate Milton Shapp at a Democratic rally in Pittsburgh, he suffered a stroke from which he never regained consciousness. Lawrence died November 21, 1966, ending probably the greatest political career in the annals of Pennsylvania.

## BUSINESS AND INDUSTRIAL LEADERS

In the realms of finance, industry, business, entertainment, and sports, western Pennsylvania Irish representation has been so extensive that brief individual mentions, plus regretful acknowledgement of a galaxy of worthy absentees, must be a space-imposed resort.

Thomas Mellon, progenitor of Pittsburgh's most eminent business, finance, and industrial dynasty, seems an appropriate lead-off figure. He migrated from County Tyrone as a boy in 1823 and crossed the Atlantic, then the Alleghenies, to come upon a Pittsburgh just about ready to welcome and reward a uniquely endowed young entrepreneur-to-be. Willing to work and eager to succeed, Mellon prospered moderately in real estate and allied ventures. He married a daughter of the locally esteemed Negley family and she bore him three sons: Andrew W., Richard B., and William L., who joined him in the Mellon Bank and the creation of the financial, business, and industrial empire, as well as the philanthropies that the bank ultimately engendered.

Andrew, a quiet but eminently effective man, served ably as Secretary of the Treasury in the Harding-Coolidge-Hoover era and later, for three years, as ambassador to Britain's Court of St. James. Most notably, he founded, endowed, and stocked from his own magnificent collection of paintings the National Gallery of Art, undoubtedly the cultural epitome of America's capital.

The Mellons held heavy interests in such industrial giants as Gulf Oil, Pittsburgh Coal, Koppers, and Aluminum Company of America, to name a representative few. Richard B. was Alcoa's first president and president of the bank from 1920 until his death in 1933. His son, Richard K., as noted, co-engineered the Pittsburgh Renaissance.

Today, Mellon Bank's dominance is challenged by PNC Bank, led by Thomas H. O'Brien, president and chief executive officer, who has seized advantage of liberalized banking laws to expand PNC significantly into the East and Midwest.

Prominent, too, in Pittsburgh's fiscal field is Federal Investors, Inc., founded in 1955 by John F. Donahue and his Central Catholic High schoolmate, Richard B. Fisher. It has since grown to rank with the largest money managers in the country. Donahue is the scion of an Irish immigrant family who settled in Pittsburgh in 1823 and has been active in community affairs far into a second century.

Irish leadership in organized labor in western Pennsylvania has included the widely recognized figure, John J. Kane, who gained fame as organizer-head of the mammoth Pressmen's Union before his dominant entry into the political mainstream of Allegheny County. Other leaders included Patrick Fagan, who was dominant in the sometimes turbulent Coal Miners' Union; the immortal Philip Murray, who fought and broke with John L. Lewis and the United Mine Workers, became first president of the United Steel Workers of America, and co-founded with Pittsburgher David McDonald and other leaders the mighty Congress of Industrial Organizations to solidify the forces of unskilled labor. Among these leaders must be numbered the great labor priests, Fathers James R. Cox and Charles Owen Rice.

The earliest western Pennsylvania ventures in industry rallied the Irish. In 1859 banker-merchant James Laughlin incorporated Laughlin and Company. He built two Eliza blast furnaces together with coke ovens on the south bank of the Monongahela. On that site grew the mighty Jones & Laughlin corporation, the backbone of a steel industry that would supply the sinews of every American war from the Civil War through World War II and give Pittsburgh its "Steel City" sobriquet.

Allied to industry has been district transportation with J. Dawson Callery developing the Pittsburgh Railways Company and David I. McCahill heading the interurban Butler Short Line.

## ENTERTAINERS AND ATHLETES

The Irish have contributed a great deal to the arts and writing. Stephen Collins Foster, of Irish stock, serenaded the nineteenth century with "My Old Kentucky Home," "Oh, Susannah," "Old Black Joe," "Old Folks at Home," and many other beloved melodies. Victor Herbert was second director of the Pittsburgh Symphony. David McCullough produced the splendid, definitive biography of President Harry Truman, as well as other scholarly works.

In journalism, the old "Sun-Telegraph" was noted for such Irishmen as James J. Long, Charles J. "Chillie" Doyle, and Davis Walsh, while "The Pittsburgh Catholic," the oldest American Catholic weekly in continuous publication, achieved acclaim for the sustained excellence of editor-essayist John Collins.

In the sphere of entertainment, John P. Harris established history's first nickelodeon in downtown Pittsburgh during the dawn of the moving picture era. He subsequently developed a local theater chain that included "The Harris," a popular vaudeville house on Diamond Street, and several cinema theaters around the community. Later, John H. Harris, of the family's second entertainment generation, took over the old ex-trolleycar-barn Duquesne Garden ice-skating rink and entered the Pittsburgh Hornets in the American Hockey League. Soon afterward, the ambitious younger Harris created the brilliant Ice Capades, which quickly attained the top echelon of nationally renowned skating troupes.

In the broader field of sports, men of Irish origin or ancestry merit listing for an assortment of distinctions. Arthur Rooney of the North Side, after a personal career of note in football, boxing, and baseball, joined with partner John McGinley in the early 1930s to launch a Pittsburgh entry into the burgeoning National Professional Football League. Now celebrated as the Steelers and run by Rooney's son Dan, the Steelers have attained several Super Bowl championships.

The historic Pittsburgh Pirates of National League fame in baseball offer an Irish connection in their late president, Bill Benswanger, whose mother was born in the west of Ireland. In the highly individualized game of tennis, the three O'Loughlin brothers, Dr. Dave, Dr. John, and Billy, dominated western Pennsylvania for a long generation from the 1920s to the 1950s. Dave was national boys champion with brother John and Jim O'Connor his most formidable local challengers. Chuck Garland of Edgewood won the first national junior championship and later, at Yale, added the national intercollegiate title. Meanwhile, but by no means incidentally, his uncle, Congressman Robert Garland, gave the world Daylight Saving Time as a World War I innovation that has survived almost universally.

On stage and screen, another pair of Pittsburgh Irish brothers, Fred and Gene Kelly, established enduring marks. Fred created the title role of "Pal Joey," toured until tired of the life of the stage, and became a young retiree with a solid reputation. Gene invaded Hollywood to become cinema's immortal song and dance man. His "Singin' in the Rain" sequence from *An American in Paris* has become enshrined as an all-time highlight of the screen.

ETHNIC SOCIETIES

Finally, western Pennsylvania has been socially, culturally, and spiritually enriched by its varied Irish societies. From the very beginning of Irish settlement in western Pennsylvania, the Ancient Order of Hibernians, with its splendid Ladies' Auxiliary and the Knights and their Ladies of Equity have established and loyally sustained the traditional features—parades, dinners, dances, entertainments, and the like—of St. Patrick's Day and other occasions of significance.

In current times, two culturally and socially dedicated organizations, the Gaelic Arts Society and the Irish Centre of Pittsburgh, have enhanced and enlivened the local Irish scene. The Gaelic Arts Society, founded in 1955 by Brother Dominic Reardon, C.S.Sp., of Duquesne University, is a nonsectarian and nonpolitical group that delivers a varied program of educational, literary, historical, musical, and social events through an extensive annual ten-month season.

The Irish Centre, fruit of the plans of Irish-born Father Patrick McCarthy, provides Pittsburgh with a family meeting place for sports, recreation, theatricals, dancing classes, and all manner of cultural and spiritual pursuits. The four-acre landscaped site is virtually surrounded by the wooded hillsides of Frick Park. The elegant Centre structure includes a ballroom to accommodate several hundred persons, a commodious stage, a modern kitchen facility, a large outdoor swimming pool, two auxiliary accommodations to house smaller gatherings and a caretaker family, and ample parking areas. For several decades, the Centre has encouraged Gaelic football, curragh rowing on Pittsburgh's historic waterways and an annual fair. Dancing instruction at the Centre has produced an International Rose of Tralee champion, Elizabeth Shovlin, daughter of Peter Shovlin, a gifted Irish violinist.

This modest resume of the Irish in western Pennsylvania ends as it began, with tribute to the grand unsung body of the Irish populace whose corporate contribution to the greatness of the community far exceeds the sum of the herein celebrated achievements.

*See* Pennsylvania; Lawrence, David

Francis A. Glenn, *Shepherds of the Faith, A Brief History of the Bishops of the Diocese of Pittsburgh* (1992).
Stefan Lorant, *Pittsburgh, The Story of a City* (1988).
Henry A. Szarnicki, *Michael O'Connor, First Catholic Bishop of Pittsburgh* (1975).
Dale Van Every, *Forth to the Wilderness, the First American Frontier* (1961).
Michael Weber, *Don't Call Me Boss, David L. Lawrence, Pittsburgh's Renaissance Mayor* (1988).

PAUL G. SULLIVAN

## PLUNKETT, CHRISTOPHER ALEXANDER (1649–1697)

Martyr, Capuchin priest, missionary in the Colony of Virginia. Alexander Plunkett was born in 1649 in Donsaghly, and entered the novitiate of the Order of Capuchin Friars Minor in Charlesville, France, on April 18,1669. He was given the name Christopher. Plunkett came to the Colony of Virginia in 1680 to minister to the Catholics on the plantation of a kinsman, John Plunkett. The Capuchins had been present in the Colony of Virginia since 1629 and charged with its care in 1630 when the Prefecture of New England, which included Virginia, was established and entrusted to them by the Sacred Congregation of Propaganda. At the time of Plunkett's arrival, most of those Capuchins ministering in Virginia had been driven out by the English colonial government that, in 1646, attempted to do away with all Catholics. During his nine years of ministry, Plunkett's missionary zeal, as well as that of four other Capuchins, John Baptist Dowdall, Fiacre Tobin, and two others, Edmond and Raymond, whose surnames have been lost, prompted Protestant authorities to hunt for him in order to prevent his efforts. He was eventually imprisoned in the winter of 1689–90 and exiled to one of the islands of Barbados where he was continually tortured and died in 1697. He is considered one of the first martyrs of the United States and with his death Capuchin missionary activity in the Virginia colony came to an end.

Melchior a Pobladura, Historia generalis O.F.M. Cap. II, 379. *Lettere Antiche*, Volume 260, fol. 378 (373?), Archives of the Congregation for the Propagation of the Faith.
Theodore Roemer, *The Catholic Church in the United States* (St. Louis, 1950).

REGIS J. ARMSTRONG, O.F.M. CAP.

## POETRY, IRISH-AMERICAN

What does it mean to be an Irish-American poet? The question is not merely rhetorical, for it raises to consciousness the issue of a certain kind of imaginative identity that has rarely, if ever, been adequately explored. Indeed, the question is so fundamental that we might want to rephrase it in such a way that something of what is at stake behind the question enters into its form. Hence: Does the experience of being Irish-American predispose the Irish-American poet to embrace any characteristic themes, subjects, or styles? Is there in such poetry something that might be identified as a uniquely Irish-American sensibility, in the same way one might identify Jewish-American poetry or African-American poetry? And, if not, is it worth even using the appellation "Irish-American poetry," as though such a thing existed in any artistically commendable form? Such questions construe Irish-American poetry as a problem to be wrestled with, and possibly constructed (to use a term that has gained currency), rather than as an established tradition to celebrate alongside Irish-American forays into politics or the entertainment industry. Charles Fanning, for one, in his magisterial study *The Irish Voice in America* (Lexington, Ky. 1990), remarks that while Irish-American fiction and drama constitute a distinctive and complex literary heritage, Irish-American poetry has been afflicted by a "simplicity" that verges on the stage Irish: "Over the years many Irish Americans have published poems, and by the 1880s critic E. C. Steadman was referring to an 'Irish-American School' of poets. This poetry has often been popular, and the legions of green-covered volumes of verse stretching back to the 1810s and the 1820s have had their effect on the Irish-American literary self-consciousness. And yet, there have been few memorable Irish-American poems, especially before recent times. The problem has been an endemic blight of programmatic melancholy or bravado that emerged from the experience and perception of forced exile. The stock-in-trade of Irish-American poetry has been the immigrant's lament for a lost, idealized homeland and the patriot's plea for Irish freedom from British oppression. Such materials make good songs but bad verse that exhibits simplistic strains of nostalgia and righteous indignation" (*The Irish Voice in America*, p. 4).

Unless one is willing to elide any distinction between "popular" poetry and the poetry of considered literary achievement, it is fruitless to contradict Fanning's judgment. Moreover, if we assume as Fanning does that an Irish-American literature must by definition involve distinctively Irish-American "subjects, themes, styles, plot-lines and character types" (*Ibid.*, p. 3), then what perhaps ought to be a dominant theme in Irish-American poetry—the immigrant experience—is almost virtually absent from the work of those Irish-American poets who have assumed, in some notable cases, highly prominent positions within the pantheon of American poetry.

In his poem, "To Robinson Jeffers," Nobel laureate Czeslaw Milosz chides the preeminent American poet of nature's majesty for proclaiming "an inhuman thing." Yet, as Milosz's poem suggests, the source of what he sees as Jeffers' embrace of human diminishment before brute nature lies, initially at least, in a deep-seated cultural identification. "If you have not read the Slavic poets so much the better," Milosz's poem begins, "there's nothing there for a Scotch-Irish wanderer to seek." For Milosz, Jeffers is not so much an American as someone whose Scotch-Irish ancestry and Ulster heritage—and in particular his father's Calvinist theology—shapes his imaginative identity. Unquestionably there is a stark transcendence and austere virility to Robinson Jeffers' vision, and while we might want to hesitate before endorsing Milosz's cultural rebuke, his insight nevertheless raises the question of whether there is something in Jeffers' poetry that is distinctly Irish-American, or a variation of being Irish-American: a restlessness born, perhaps, of historical circumstance, as well as a preoccupation with nature and the metaphysical. Thus we may ask whether there is more than merely a generic thematic connection between Yeats' "rook-delighting heaven," or Heaney's victims of tribal violence and Jeffers' own disturbing version of the sublime among California's brooding headlands.

In contrast, Marianne Moore is a poet whose imaginative proclivities and evocations of people and places, and particularly animals, incline toward the fabulous. Her whole sensibility stands in stark contrast to that of Jeffers. Not surprisingly, the difference is perhaps most evident in both poets' use of line. Moore's formal interest in the precision of syllabic verse appears utterly alien to Jeffers' vigorous free-verse. And if, to risk being fanciful, Robinson Jeffers braces himself like a hermit on Skellig Michael before the violent majesty of nature, then we can likewise picture Marianne Moore similar to a monk bent over an illuminated manuscript obsessively working over one of her fantastic creatures. Nevertheless, in the last line of her poem "Spenser's Ireland" she writes, "I am troubled, I'm dissatisfied, I'm Irish," a declaration that resonates with the more turbulent stirrings of Jeffers' efforts to "befriend the furies." Indeed, "Spenser's Ireland" is a noteworthy poem by an American modernist whose influence and achievement ranks her, with Jeffers, among the most important twentieth-century American poets. Moreover, it is a highly anthologized poem that not only admits but examines the poet's Irish ancestry. From yet another standpoint, however, one might object to the poem's declaration that Spenser's Ireland "has not altered;—/ a place as kind as it is green," the "greenest place" the poet has never seen, for in so doing the poem effectively disavows history even as it obscures the fact that Spenser's Ireland was anything but kind, especially considering the great English poet's own administrative role in a mechanism of conquest. As such, while Marianne Moore's "Spenser's Ireland" stands as an artistically achieved moment of consciousness on the part of

Irish-American poetry, it also defines the limits of that consciousness within the poet's sense of identity.

Both Jeffers and Moore were born in the latter years of the nineteenth century and, taken together, their work comprises a significant Irish-American contribution to American modernism. In turn, Louise Bogan, who was born near the turn of the century and whose paternal grandfather emigrated from Londonderry, stands as one of this century's most important early exemplars of what Adrienne Rich has called "the female sensibility" in poetry. While the question of being Irish-American does not enter into Bogan's poetry, her terse visionary, and at times incantatory, poems are laudable for their willingness to engage often unconscious, irrational processes as fit subject matter for poetry. Her work crosses the Romantic tradition with depth psychology, even as she breaks new imaginative ground for poetry written by women. A similar spirit of directness and radicality inheres in the poems of Thomas McGrath. Born in 1916, McGrath was a lifelong communist and campaigner for social justice who refused to testify before the McCarthy House Subcommittee on Un-American Activities, and whose poems range formally from a Whitmanesque expansiveness to the illuminating concision of haiku. While, certainly, his political beliefs have curtailed a general appreciation of his achievement (though his work has been lauded with numerous fellowships and prizes), there is no diminishing his poems' passionate intensity even as they eschew political cant; and, though like Bogan the question of being Irish-American never really informs the poetry, his concern with political exile and with social and metaphysical justice could place him prominently within a tradition of poets of dissent, of which the Irish are not excluded.

Few American poets, of any ethnicity, have been as troubled or disaffected as John Berryman and fewer still with the exception of Lowell and Sexton have dramatized their own psychomachia with as much vigilance and artistic strength. Born in 1914, of the same stellar generation of poets that produced Elizabeth Bishop, Robert Lowell, Randall Jarrell, and Delmore Schwartz (among others), Berryman's Irish connection may be traced through his grandmother, Mary Kanar, whose family emigrated from County Cork (see John Haffenden, *The Life of John Berryman*, Boston, 1982). Of particular significance to seeing Berryman's work through the prism of "Irish-American poetry" is the final section of his masterwork, *The Dream Songs*. There, Berryman makes a pilgrimage to Ireland which comprises nothing less than an imaginative confrontation, if not with his ancestral roots, then with one of the most significant "hiding places" of his own artistic powers. "I have moved to Dublin to have it out with you / majestic Shade, you whom I read so well / so many years ago," so he writes in "Dream Song 312." The Shade is obviously William Butler Yeats, and the urgency with which Berryman seeks to "have it out" with him is testimony to the Irish poet's influence of his American disciple. Moreover, given the fact that Berryman's eastern passage is a journey through which he leaves "behind the country of the dead," we can understand the poet's self-imposed exile from America as a kind of return from Tir Na nOg, an imagined reversal of the nineteenth-century immigrant's journey.

A lesser instance of an American poet's engagement with compelling Irish shades are John Logan's "At Drumcliffe Churchyard, County Sligo" and "Dublin Suite: Homage to James Joyce." Logan's work, though not of the same monumental power as Berryman's, likewise reveals a considerable autobiographical impulse, as well as a fascination with the theme of the poet's peripatetic physical and metaphysical wandering, and has won him many awards. The like is true of the poetry of Alan Dugan who has won both a Pulitzer Prize and a National Book Award, and whose work is fueled by an acerbic wit which, in the poem "Mockery Against the Irish Censorship," he turns against a country that "was better in its dream" because it has sought to curtail the imaginations of its poets. In marked distinction to Dugan's poetry, the richly celebrated and highly influential work of Frank O'Hara engages the world with little, if any, dissatisfaction. His own wanderings through the streets of his beloved New York are occasions for discerning wonder within the quotidian and recording those spots of urban time with painterly precision. Still more explicitly visionary is the work of Galway Kinnell whose ecstatic religious sensibility places him equally at home in portraying nature's awe-inspiring presence ("Flower Herding on Mount Monadnock") or in evoking the vivid street-life of a modern immigrant ghetto ("The Avenue Bearing the Initial of Christ into the New World"), or in embarking on a kind of metaphysical dream quest (*The Book of Nightmares*). Less prominent, the poetry of Ned O'Gorman likewise evinces a strong religious and particularly Catholic sensitivity. Born to this same generation of poets, X. J. Kennedy's work exhibits a wryly satirical intelligence. In contrast, and despite the influence of the "epic" Projectivist, Charles Olson, the poetry of Robert Creeley embraces a minimalist aesthetic. Creeley's poems are almost always short and focus on the moment, though with none of O'Hara's penchant for lush, seemingly off-hand description. Instead Creeley's work operates through a pared-down clarity of perception, and so the poems assume an almost etched quality. In turn, though not nearly as influential as Creeley's work, Robert Kelly's poems record an Irish-American presence likewise influenced by the work of the Projectivists and of the Black Mountain School of American poetry. Finally, yet another Irish-American who has had a profound influence on the history of American poetry is James Laughlin. A devotee of Ezra Pound, Laughlin not only wrote his own poems, but also at the master's suggestion began New Directions, one of the most important avant-garde houses in American publishing history.

Nevertheless, despite all of these achievements, with the exception of certain individual poems, no single poet from among this diverse group places his/her work consistently within an Irish or Irish-American context. If there are common themes—social or psychic dissatisfaction, the relationship to family and the natural world, varying brands of religious sensibility—they rarely if ever refer to anything that might be identified as a specifically Irish-American ethnic milieu. The same could not be said for most, if not all, important African-American or Jewish-American poets. One obvious reason for this circumstance is that, for significant social reasons examined by Noel Ignatiev in his study *How the Irish Became White* (New York, 1995), the Irish, like peoples of European lineage, were able to assimilate more fully into American society than either of these groups, despite their having been largely vilified as a minority whose religion and cultural practices were deemed anti-American. Hence, the achievement of Irish-American poets—great as it is through such figures as Jeffers, Moore, Bogan, Berryman, O'Hara, and Kinnell—reveals something of a collective cultural amnesia. Thus, while the Irish-American poetry of the nineteenth century remains largely "programmatic" (to use Fanning's term) in its treatment of Irish-America, the very substantial work of those that followed largely neglects to treat imaginatively the historical and social circumstances from which it arose.

This has not been the case among those Irish poets who have spent substantial periods of time in the United States and whose presence here has greatly influenced their work. Padraic Colum's presence in America warranted that his work be included in at least one American anthology of poetry. The like is true of Oliver St. John Gogarty. Brian Coffey's "Missouri Sequence" was born of his time as visiting professor at the University of St. Louis during the late forties and early fifties. Similarly, Thomas Kinsella's poem "The Good Fight," inscribed to John F. Kennedy on the tenth anniversary of his death, and Eavan Boland's poem "The Irish Emigrants" demonstrate these Irish poets' success at giving voice to what should be considered Irish-American subjects. To a more sustained degree, James Liddy—who has spent over thirty years teaching and writing in the United States—has composed a hybrid body of work that may be understood as a marriage between the Whitman tradition, as embodied in American Beat poetics, and Kavanagh's parish. Younger poets like Eamonn Grennan, Eamonn Wall, Gerard O'Donovan, Greg Delanty and Sara Berkeley continue a tradition of poets who adhere to a hyphenated sensibility more strongly and readily than most Irish-American poets whose work has been incorporated into anthologies of American verse. One Irish-American poet, whose work is rarely seen as Irish-American and who begrudges that fact, is John Montague. Montague's *oeuvre*, of not only Irish but international renown, is in large part the product of what he has called his "double birth"—his having been born in America to Irish immigrant parents at the beginning of the Great Depression and then repatriated back to County Tyrone in his early childhood—as well as his almost mythopoeic connection to his ancestral home. If any poet has succeeded in portraying the complex world of Irish-America in light of his own autobiography it is John Montague.

In many ways John Montague is a pivotal figure, for in his work the idea of being an Irish-American poet enters into and becomes to a great extent the subject of the poetry. In this regard his work at once overtly manifests an imaginative identity that has remained unexamined in most Irish-American poetry until recent years, and establishes a bridge to the old world without recourse to nostalgia, at the same time as it anticipates those newer Irish-American poets who seem determined to include at least some of their own historically charged ethnic identity into their poems. Brendan Galvin is one such poet who understands his work as emerging from a specifically Irish-American milieu. In addition to being obsessed with landscape and seascape in and around his native Massachusetts, in his *Saints in Their Ox-Hide Boat* (Baton Rouge, 1992), Galvin establishes a metaphorical connection between his own identity as a poet and that of the Irish saint who, in legend at least, "discovered America" centuries before Columbus or the first Norse settlements in Newfoundland. Likewise, Tess Gallagher's poems move with ease between both Irish and American subjects, enjoining each with a lyricism that borders on the visionary. Still other poets, like Maura Stanton, Ethna McKiernan, Nuala Archer, Thomas Lynch, Wesley McNair, Gibbons Ruark, Michael Heffernan, Maureen Seaton, and Terence Winch, continue to write compelling poems that emerge from a sensibility that is uniquely Irish-American. Others, like Michael Ryan, Mary Swander, Richard Kenney, Kay Ryan, Mekeel McBride, Diana O'Hehir, Susan Howe, Alice Fulton, Campbell McGrath, James McManus, and Brigit Pegeen Kelly, while not expressly writing on Irish-American themes, collectively have produced a range of work that speaks to the vitality of the Irish-American presence in the wide and varied world of American poetry. As such, "Irish-American poetry" remains a vigorous presence within the heritage of American poetry, a presence that is by now well-nigh indispensable.

*See* Fiction, Irish-American

Charles Fanning, *The Irish Voice in America* (Lexington, Ky., 1990).
John Haffenden, *The Life of John Berryman* (Boston, 1982).
Noel Ignatiev, *How the Irish Became White* (New York, 1995).

DANIEL TOBIN

## POETS, CONTEMPORARY IRISH-AMERICAN WOMEN

That there is no established canon nor poetic genealogy of Irish-American women poets derives, in great part, from lack of critical attention to their work. Without such attention—being reviewed, accepted as texts in classes, discussed in dissertations and articles—even works of genius will fade from view. In mid-century, Phyllis McGinley was one of America's most widely published and acclaimed poets, yet her work is virtually unavailable thirty years later. Whether a woman poet of the next generation wishes to emulate McGinley's caustic and irreverent style, or to object to it, is irrelevant; the invisible give rise to no crisis of influence. Where all effort goes into building a foundation, the number of stories will inevitably be limited.

Late 20th-century Irish-American women writers, then, are not typically aware of such forebears as Alice and Phoebe Cary, Anna Charlotte Lynch Botta, Katherine Eleanor Conway, or Mary Elizabeth McGrath Blake, each of whom was a widely regarded poet in her day. This break in the chain of succession means that each generation of Irish-American women poets has essentially re-invented itself—an individual rather than a group effort for, where a tradition is uncharted, a poet is unlikely to seek to locate herself within it.

The latter part of the 20th century, however, has seen many poets writing with greater self-consciousness of their ethnic heritage, whether Irish or other. Significant anthologies emphasize the racial and national backgrounds of writers as part of an effort toward acknowledging America's multicultural society. Irish-American writers are one part of this "salad" (an image which has replaced the earlier "melting pot") and, as a direct result, Irish-American women are exposed, more than in earlier generations, to anthologies and other publications which make ethnic connections. Recent collections of Irish-American work include a significant number of women, permitting newer writers to forge and respond to connections unseen to earlier generations.

Despite the newness of this tradition, certain shared themes and images are readily charted. Primary among these is the return, either literally or figuratively, to what Irish poet Eavan Boland has named "The Lost Land." Often reared in homes where Ireland was held up as a kind of Tir na nOg, an enchanted island, poets like Ethna McKiernan and Julie O'Callaghan reverse the path of their grandmothers, seeking to solidify an identity which becomes all the more tenuous once the holy ground is reached. Susan Donnelly goes even further back, looking to Eden itself for ways to reinvent the feminine.

Irish history, too, finds its way into Irish-American women's poems. Most provocatively, poets employ the image of the Famine as a powerful metaphor for the female spirit's yearning and hunger for freedoms and power society denies. Margaret Blanchard writes compelling dramatic monologues about women

struggling with both physical and spiritual hunger, while O'Callaghan makes the poetic quest itself a kind of foraging for "edible anecdotes."

Two powerful archetypal figures, both with roots in Ireland, appear in Irish-American women's work. These are the grandmother and the rebel-lover. The first represents, for most contemporary Irish-American writers, the last Irish-born generation; even when not herself Irish-born, she stands two generations closer to Ireland than does the poet, forging a link between the lost land and the new one. She is thus a liminal figure: the immigrant, no longer at home in Ireland but never fully American. The fact of immigration remains close to Irish-American poetic consciousness, providing a primary image of the search for new ground. The grandmother thus amply represents the complexity of creation. She is the ancestor, and she is an adventurer; similarly, her granddaughter poets innovate within traditions.

McKiernan's "Going Back" recounts the poet's standing at the very place from which her grandmother departed for America, where she finds that she too "cannot make my roots take hold" in Ireland, despite feeling similarly rootless in America. For McKiernan, the grandmother is the part of the psyche that remains an immigrant, forever homeless, forever seeking shelter, forever abandoning that shelter. She is a powerful image of the woman poet who enters new territories of language and the spirit.

For Mary Swander, the grandmother is the primary link in the family chain, the woman who both holds one back and holds one up. So important is the grandmother image to Swander that she has written an entire series focusing on it. Where McKiernan sees in the grandmother a rootlessness which mirrors her own, Swander sees a strength which inspires her.

For Renny Golden, "Grammudder" is the link between the poet and the rebels and revolutionaries who appear in much of her work, for it is at grandmother's table that Irish history is recited and songs of protest are learned. Golden's poems addressed to the rebel are deeply erotic; the rebel embodies passion, which "has no coals, only this flaming." However passionate, Golden's rebels are ascetic ones, fervently in love with their ideals. The rebel in Golden's work is always a rebel with a cause—one that gives self-sacrifice meaning. But the erotic undertone never diminishes.

The same idea appears in McKiernan, where the rebel appears as the adulterous lover who, rebelling against marital promises, puts the poet in a morally ambiguous situation. Like a political rebel who must believe sufficiently in a cause to accept the innocent suffering it creates, the "other woman" of McKiernan's poems is aware of the pain she causes the lover's wife. McKiernan's rebel, while eroticized, is also a demonized vision of the disruptive power of sexual knowledge.

In the works of Tess Gallagher, we find several incarnations of the rebel. He appears as "the kidnapper" who draws the woman to himself with innocent questions before abducting her. He is also more typically a political rebel, both menacing and enticing. Most profoundly, the rebel appears as "the double," a part of the poet who can "say all the last words and the first" and who will transcend the world of "the country-club poets" to embark upon "a dangerous mission. You/could die there. You/could live forever." Acknowledged as part of the poet herself, this divisive yet dynamic rebel powers the woman into a new relationship with language itself.

Two contradictory trends seem likely to influence the future of Irish-American women's poetry. On the one hand, the greater awareness of ethnic identity as a rich source of imagery has already created a climate in which poets regularly mine that material; in addition, the influx of New Irish in the latter decades of the twentieth century has occurred simultaneously with an increased public acceptance of Celtic heritage. On the other hand, greater economic wealth is eroding Ireland's distinctive characteristics which were based in poverty, with the quaint thatched cottage often replaced by a substantial bungalow; increased communications and access to entertainment media mean that Ireland is both influenced by and influencing American culture directly. Grandmothers will no longer be the only artery to the heart of Ireland, nor will rebels hold the same emotional power as the peace process progresses. In the next century, Irish-American women poets will create in a new cultural setting—with awareness, perhaps, of their poetic foremothers.

Barbara Adams, *Double Solitaire* (Geryon Press, 1982).
Jody Aliesan, *States of Grace* (Seattle, 1993).
Nuala Archer, *The Hour of Pan/Ama* (Galway, 1992).
———, *Whale on the Line* (Dublin, 1981).
Margaret Blanchard, *At the Listening Place: Languages of Intuition* (Maine, 1993).
Kathy Callaway, *Heart of the Garfish* (Pittsburgh, 1982).
Susan Donnelly, *Eve Names the Animals* (Boston, 1985).
Finvola Drury, *Burning the Snow* (Landers and Francis, 1990).
Susan Firer, *The Underground Communion Rail* (West End Press, 1992).
Tess Gallagher, *Moon Crossing Bridge* (St. Paul, Minn., 1992).
Ethna McKiernan, *Caravan* (Minneapolis, Minn., 1989).
Patricia Monaghan, *Seasons of the Witch* (Chicago, 1994).
———, *The Next Parish Over: A Collection of Irish-American Writing* (Minneapolis, Minn., 1994).
———, *Unlacing: Ten Irish-American Women Poets* (Fairbanks, AK, 1987).
Julie O'Callaghan, *Edible Anecdotes* (Dublin, 1983).
Mary Sander, *Succession* (Athens, Ga., 1979).
Maureen Stanton, *Cries of Swimmers* (Pittsburgh, 1991).
———, *Tales of the Supernatural* (New York, 1988).
Mary Swander, *Driving the Body Back* (New York, 1986).

PATRICIA MONAGHAN

## POWDERLY, TERENCE VINCENT (1849–1924)

Labor leader, politician, government official. Terence Vincent Powderly was born on January 22, 1849 in Carbondale, Pennsylvania. He was the eleventh of twelve children (eight boys and four girls) born to Terence Powderly (Senior) and Margery (Walsh) Powderly. Both parents were immigrants from Ireland and Roman Catholics. Three of their children did not survive beyond infancy.

### ANTECEDENTS

According to Powderly's posthumously published autobiography, *The Path I Trod* (New York, 1940), his ancestors came from France. They were Huguenots by the name of Pouderle. Hugo Pouderle left France in 1685 after Louis XIV revoked the Edict of Nantes promulgated in 1598 by Henry IV to protect the rights of Protestants. Hugo Pouderle proceeded to England and then to Ireland. At some point the spelling of the name was altered slightly.

Terence Powderly's parents married in Ireland in 1826. They left it one year later seeking relief from effects of the Penal Laws, which, though most had been repealed by then, had left their legacy of shame.

According to his second youngest child, the elder Powderly had run afoul of the law in County Meath by carrying a gun and killing a rabbit on the estate of Lord Cunningham. For this crime he had paid the price of three weeks in jail at Trim. Well before this time all desirable land in the island had been transferred to the ownership of British landlords. The couple sailed for eight weeks on the Royal George, arriving at Montreal on July 27, 1827 and transferred to a smaller vessel for a trip to Ogdenburgh, New York on the St. Lawrence River. Just prior to calling at Ogdenburgh a baby girl was born to the couple.

Their funds all but depleted, the small family settled in the village of Ogdenburgh for two years while the father earned a living as a farm hand. Tall and vigorous, he was able to provide sufficiently, even to save something for a further move 260 miles south to a frontier community ultimately known as Carbondale in the anthracite region of Pennsylvania. Located on the Lackawanna River, it was fifteen miles northeast of Scranton.

Living on a small farm with a house sufficient to accommodate a large family, the Powderlys were not impoverished as were most Irish immigrants in the coastal cities. Indeed, the father was an enterprising individual who participated in the early stages of the anthracite industry as a miner and eventually opened a small mine of his own. However, the enterprise failed in 1858 and the father obtained work with the Delaware and Hudson Canal Company, a firm engaged in transporting coal for the New York market.

Setbacks did not deter Powderly's father. He became a respected figure in Carbondale, ran successfully for membership on the town's first council and had a thoroughfare named after him. He capably provided for his large family, saw to their education and helped them secure jobs.

### ENTERING WORKFORCE

Terence Powderly began work at age thirteen as a switch tender for the Delaware and Hudson Railway Company, successor to the D&H Canal Company. After three years he was apprenticed to master mechanic James Dickson in the D&H Railway shops. One of his first tasks was to disassemble the Stourbridge Lion—first locomotive to operate on a commercial line in the United States. The young apprentice respected his master mechanic and became absorbed in the trade. He proved to be a competent craftsman, completing his apprenticeship on August 1, 1869.

At age twenty-three Powderly married a hometown girl, Hannah Dever. The marriage in September of 1872 produced but one child, Margery, who, unfortunately, died in infancy.

### UNION CAREER

As a young man Powderly had multiple ambitions. Not only interested in advancing as a craftsman, he also endeavored to develop skill in writing and public speaking. In November of 1871 he joined the Machinists' and Blacksmiths' Union (M&B Union). In less than two years he was elected president of the union's local branch in Scranton. Shortly thereafter he took on the duties of corresponding secretary of the same local branch—in the interest of furthering his writing skills. He soon came to the attention of national leaders of the union. Shortly thereafter they appointed him organizer of the union in western Pennsylvania.

While young Powderly rose rapidly in ranks of the union, he soon learned of attendant difficulties. At the time of the recession of 1873 he was employed by the Delaware, Lackawanna and Western Railroad. Due to his union offices he was discharged early and blacklisted in Scranton by Walter Dawson, superintendent of the railroad. Searching for work in western Pennsylvania and Ohio, he discovered the blacklist followed him. Finally, returning to Scranton, he obtained work where Dawson's effort to get him fired was thwarted by W. W. Scranton, son of the family who pioneered railroad and iron firms in the area. Scranton was then general manager of the Lackawanna Iron and Coal Company. These experiences served to reinforce Terence Powderly's commitment to trade unionism.

In 1876 he was initiated into the Noble Order of the Knights of Labor (the Order), a secret labor organization founded in 1869. Powderly brought the M&B Union with him into the Knights of Labor. He became master workman of the Scranton assembly of the Order in the following year and, in 1879 was chosen to succeed Uriah Stephens, the original head of the Order—the title of the position was Grand Master Workman (later changed to General Master Workman).

One year before his rise to leader of the Order, Powderly had successfully run for Mayor of Scranton on the Greenback-Labor ticket. He was twenty-nine at the time and was reelected twice more, serving for a total of six years. During that period his reputation for honest government, tax reform and improvements in sewage disposal and public health was impressive. He demonstrated an ability to handle the duties of mayor and leader of the union at the same time.

Certain ideals characterized Powderly's thinking. He found that many of them were embodied in the principles of the Knights organization. First of all, it welcomed all members of the "producing classes." Only bankers, brokers, lawyers, doctors and gamblers—and those in the liquor business—were to be excluded. Black workers and women were welcomed. As a youth Powderly had joined the Father Mathew Total Abstinence Society. He practiced and preached total abstinence thereafter. The slogan of the Order "an injury to one is the concern of all" was, according to Powderly, adopted at his suggestion. The organization advocated a "cooperative commonwealth," in which producers' cooperative enterprises would compete favorably with corporations and in which family farms and small businesses would prosper. Leaders of the Order endorsed an end to the "wage system" which had lowered the status of the citizen craftsman, they said, to that of a common day laborer. Ideally, strikes were to be replaced by conciliation, mediation and arbitration.

## POWDERLY AND GIBBONS

Most significant of Powderly's contributions to American labor was his handling of the religious issue. Founders of the Order gave it a definite spiritual flavor (though definitely not a Catholic one). This was reflected in its initiation ceremony and other rituals which used passages from the Bible and had Masonic overtones. Its first leader, Uriah Stephens, was himself trained for the Baptist ministry at one time. Its secrecy stemmed from these sources and also the widespread use of blacklists by employers.

The quasi-Protestant mode and Masonic tone of the Order as well as the secrecy disturbed Catholic members and especially the Catholic clergy, who were particularly mindful of the Molly Maguire episode of recent memory. Numbers of them became dyspeptic at the thought of any and all secret societies.

Powderly was well aware of this problem from his early associations with the Order. He estimated that as many as two-thirds of its members were Catholics. He recognized it as a serious dilemma and began to advocate eliminating the secrecy and the quasi-religious rituals. On becoming Grand Master Workman he was criticized for slavishly following the wishes of the Catholic clergy. On the other hand, for many priests he was not doing enough to eliminate objectionable features. Alexandre Taschereau, Archbishop of Quebec, was violently opposed and applied to the Vatican for condemnation of the Order. At length, too impatient to wait for a response, he denounced the organization and excommunicated anyone who remained a member.

By 1882 Powderly, as head of the Knights of Labor, had succeeded in persuading the organization to abolish the secrecy and most of the objectionable rituals. In 1886 he contacted James Cardinal Gibbons of Baltimore, the leading Catholic churchman in the United States, to resolve the issue once and for all. Gibbons, also the son of Irish immigrants, proved to be a sympathetic listener when Powderly explained that secrecy and sectarian rituals had been eliminated several years earlier. A second conference initiated by the Cardinal eleven months later completed the successful diplomatic efforts to solve the problem. Gibbons had no wish to alienate Catholics who were members of labor organizations. His view was accepted by other members of the American hierarchy. Only four years later Pope Leo XIII issued the encyclical *Rerum Novarum*, the first statement from the Vatican which explicitly endorsed the right of workers to organize unions for their economic protection and betterment.

## IRISH NATIONALISM

As a seventeen-year-old apprentice Powderly invested in a five-dollar bond of the Irish Republic after hearing Civil War veteran Colonel John O'Neill speak about the Fenians and their plan to liberate Ireland. He regularly read Patrick Ford's *Irish World* which informed him about the land question. A friend explained how Michael Davitt had founded the Land League. He met Davitt in Boston in the company of John Boyle O'Reilly the journalist. When Charles Stewart Parnell visited America in 1880 to raise funds for the Land League, at one point he came to Scranton. Mayor Powderly introduced him to an interested audience which contributed $3,500 to the cause. A branch of the Land League formed in Scranton and elected Powderly its president.

The *Irish World* published nationwide figures on funds raised for the Land League and identified Pennsylvania as the leading contributor. Within the state, more came from the anthracite region than any other. In part this was due to Terence Powderly's travels to nearby communities on behalf of the League. He also used these occasions to organize for the Knights of Labor of which he was General Master Workman.

## RAILROADS

The life of Terence Powderly was linked closely to the railroads. They had extended to the Mississippi River only a few years after he was born. His first job, his apprenticeship and much of his other work involved railroad firms. He was blacklisted by a railroad official. His ideas about land, influenced by Henry George, led him to oppose the vast land grants made to railroads, especially those made to the transcontinental railroads. Important railroad strikes determined the fortunes of the Knights of Labor when he was leader of the organization—although he consistently opposed strikes.

By the 1880s a number of railroads had become the first giant corporations, employing thousands of workers and commanding capital in the millions. One of Wall Street's barons, Jay Gould, controlled three important railroads. A strike over wage cuts on his Southwest System occurred in 1885. The strike succeeded in restoring the wages, but after its termination these firms began laying off employees who had joined the Knights of Labor. A wave of strikes broke out in protest and Powderly was forced to come to their support. He negotiated with Gould and operating executives. Employees were rehired. This show of strength in dealing with a powerful rail magnate was so impressive that thousands of workers rushed to join the Order. The membership swelled to 700,000, largest of any union up to that time.

During the following year a second strike by employees on a Gould-owned line was broken by bringing in replacements for strikers. Once again Powderly attempted to restore strikers to their jobs, but met with adamant refusal. The great avalanche of new members now began to leave. Thereafter, the Order declined steadily while the American Federation of Labor grew. By 1893 the Order could claim only 75,000 members—and in that year Powderly was ousted as General Master Workman in a palace revolt.

GOVERNMENT OFFICIAL

Terence Powderly did not find work as a machinist after leaving the Order, but took up the study of law. He was admitted to the Pennsylvania Bar in 1894. Earlier, in Cleveland, he had become acquainted with William McKinley, and in 1896 campaigned effectively for him. He was rewarded with an appointment as Commissioner General of Immigration. He continued as a government official (interrupted only briefly due to a misunderstanding with President Theodore Roosevelt) until his retirement in 1921. He lived in Washington, D.C. with his second wife, Emma Fickenscher, whom he married in 1919, eight years after his first wife died. Terence Powderly died on June 24, 1924.

*See* Labor Movement

Vincent Falzone, *Terence Powderly: Middle Class Reformer* (Washington, D.C., 1978).
Terence Powderly, *The Path I Trod* (New York, 1940).
Samuel Walker, "Terence Powderly Machinist: 1866–1877," *Labor History* (Spring 1978): 165–84.

L. A. O'DONNELL

## POWER, FREDERICK TYRONE (1869–1931)

Actor. Born in London, England, to a famous Irish lineage, including his father Harold and mother Ethel Laveneu and his grandfather Tyrone Power, the well-known actor. Power moved to the United States at an early age, having been sent to Florida to learn to grow citrus fruit. However, by the age of seventeen the young Power had won a small role in Madame Janauschek's company of actors and he toured with them for three seasons. He then moved on to Augustin Daly's company and remained with them for almost ten years. In 1894, with the Daly company, he made his first major appearance in London.

In New York, 1899, he appeared as Lord Steyne in Mrs. Fiske's production of *Becky Sharpe* which attracted quite a bit of attention to the young actor. He found a budding succession of well-received performances such as his role as Judas in *Mary of Magdala* (1902), his role of the Drain Man in Rann Kennedy's play *The Servant in the House* (1908) and his role as Brutus in *Julius Cesar* (1912). He became noted for his strength and his ability to play heroic and poetic personas with finesse. His other performances included: *Adrea,* a romantic tragedy, and *Ulysses.*

However, it was the onset of World War I that lessened Power's opportunities and the interest that he had stirred. He went to Hollywood in 1927 and sought employment in the "talking pictures" but died soon after on December 30, 1931.

Power is remembered for continuing his family's acting legacy and most notably for his performances in *Becky Sharp, Mary of Magdala* and *The Servant in the House.* His was a large figure with dark eyes and a very noble gait. He was married several times and was survived by a divorced wife, Mrs. Patia Power.

*Dictionary of American Biography,* 15.
*New York Times* and *New York Herald* (December 31, 1931).
John Parker, *Who's Who in the Theatre* (1925).
William Winter, *The Wallet of Time*, 2 vols. (1913).

JOY HARRELL

## POWER, TYRONE (1914–1958)

Actor. Born in Cincinnati, Ohio, to Frederick Tyrone and Helen Emma (Reaume), the young Power grew up surrounded by the proud theatrical performers of his family including his great grandfather who was a famous Irish actor during the early nineteeth century and his father and mother, noted Shakespearean actors. He spent his childhood in New York and California before his family moved to Cincinnati in 1923. Power attended Purcell High School and became active in the drama department. After graduation he played several small roles in a Shakespearean repertory company at the Chicago Civic auditorium and his first professional production was that of *The Merchant of Venice.*

After his father's death in 1931 he visited various motion picture casting offices where he met Arthur Caesar, a screenwriter who helped the young actor's career. Power lived with Caesar until he left for New York, taking a permanent side-stop in Chicago where he found employment with Circuit Theatre productions and on several radio programs. He then found a role in the play *Romance* being staged at the Blackstone Theatre. After the eight-week showing of *Romance,* Power returned to New York and found roles in two plays, *Romeo and Juliet* (1935) and *Saint Joan* (1936). Soon after, Power signed a contract with Twentieth Century Fox and began a successful series of major

Tyrone Power

motion pictures including: *In Old Chicago, Alexander's Ragtime Band, Suez, Marie Antoinette, Jesse James, The Rains Came, Yank in the RAF,* and *Crash Dive.*

During World War II Power served in the Marine Corps where he earned the rank of first lieutenant. After the war he returned to Fox Studios and signed another contract in 1946, beginning with his performance in a screen adaptation of Somerset Maugham's *The Razor's Edge.* His performance was one of his most memorable and he earned many rave reviews. He also acted in *Nightmare Alley, Captain From Castile, Prince of Foxes, The Black Rose, Mister Roberts, John Brown's Body, The Dark is Light Enough, Rawhide, The Mississippi Gambler, The Long Gray Line, The Eddy Duchin Story, The Sun Also Rises* and *Witness for the Prosecution,* his last film. It was in his last performance that he offered one of his finest. He died of a heart attack on November 15, 1958, in Madrid while working on the set of *Solomon and Sheba.* Power was buried with military honors at the Hollywood Memorial Park Cemetery.

Fred L. Guiles, *Tyrone Power: The Last Idol* (1979).
David Niven, *Bring on the Empty Horses* (1975).
*Dictionary of American Biography,* supplement 6.

JOY HARRELL

## POWERS, DAVID F. (1912–1998)

Presidential aide. David F. (Dave) Powers was the most colorful of the so-called "Irish Mafia" who surrounded President John F. Kennedy. In the White House he held the title of special assistant, but he was neither political adviser nor strategist. Rather, he was ally, chum and wit, someone Kennedy enjoyed having around as much as possible. He was Boston to his fingertips.

He and Kennedy came together one evening in 1946 while Powers was baby-sitting his widowed sister's children on the top floor of a three-decker house in Charlestown, a thoroughly Irish-Catholic community abutting downtown Boston. He answered a knock at the door and encountered "this tall, thin, handsome fellow" canvasing for votes in his first bid for elective office. "My name is Jack Kennedy," said the knocker. "I am a candidate for Congress. Will you help me?" Powers immediately signed on. "I look back on it now," Powers reflected years later, "and shudder at the thought that if the President had gotten tired on the second floor of my three-decker I probably would still be selling newspapers." (Powers' father died when he was ten and as a lad he sold newspapers to help support the family.) Powers remained close to Kennedy for the next seventeen years. He worked in all his campaigns and was in the car behind the presidential limousine when Kennedy was shot in Dallas.

Powers was born in Charlestown on April 25, 1912, son of John and Kate (Green) Powers, immigrants from Castletown, County Cork, Ireland. He served in World War II and worked for city and state housing boards before going to Washington. As presidential aide he frequently functioned as greeter and escort, sometimes with a startling informality. He remarked to the Shah of Iran on one occasion, "I want you to know you're my kind of Shah," and after shepherding the archbishop of Canterbury into the Oval Office, he cautioned the president that "this would get him no votes in Charlestown."

After Kennedy's assassination, Powers often went at Jacqueline Kennedy's request to her residence in Georgetown to read stories and have lunch with John F. Kennedy, Jr. To young Kennedy, Powers was "Uncle Dave."

Powers remained for a year as a special assistant in the Johnson administration, then became curator and so-called "keeper of the flame" at the John F. Kennedy Library in Boston. He was a veritable walking encyclopedia on Kennedy history. He retired in 1994 and died March 27, 1998. Burial was from Charlestown's St. Catherine of Siena Church, where he once ushered at five Masses every Sunday. Senator Edward M. Kennedy delivered the eulogy, saying, "All of us loved Dave like a brother."

*See* Kennedy, John Fitzgerald

*The Boston Globe,* March 29, 31, April 2, 1998.
*The New York Times,* March 28, 1998.
Kenneth P. O'Donnell and David F. Powers, *"Johnny, We Hardly Knew Ye"* (Boston, 1970, 1972).

JOHN DEEDY

## POWERS, J. F. (1917–1999)

Novelist, short story writer, educator. James Farl Powers, like Jane Austen, chose to play out his exceptional literary and satirical gifts within a very limited arena; his "little bit (two-inches wide) of ivory" was Midwestern Catholic clerical life from the late 1940s to the early 1970s—if anything, a world even more restricted than hers. But like her, too, Powers showed that working with "so fine a brush" on so small a surface can produce remarkable literary results.

He was born (1917) and raised in Jacksonville, Illinois and was to score his greatest success with the idioms of his native turf. His mother was a writer (like John Updike's) and his father a dairy-and-poultry manager. After high school and in the midst of the Depression he moved to Chicago, taking courses at Northwestern University and keeping himself alive with odd jobs. For moral and political reasons he chose to become a conscientious objector during World War II and paid the price of more than a year in jail. He married Elizabeth Alice Wahl, also a writer, in 1946 and had five children. He taught at St. John's University, Collegeville, MN (1947, 1976–93); and as a visiting professor at Marquette University, Milwaukee, WI; University of Michigan, Ann Arbor, MI; and Smith College, Northampton, MA.

### THE PRINCE OF DARKNESS

Powers won his first literary award in 1947 at the age of 30: an O. Henry Award for "The Valiant Woman," and in the same year had his first collection of stories published by Doubleday with the title *Prince of Darkness,* the title itself a pastor's sardonic (and much circulated) pun on his curate's photographic hobby. The play of sacred and secular there and the satiric wit were to be the signature of Powers' sparse publications for the next four decades.

The eternal battle of age and youth, in a system that gives most of the weapons to the former, takes on a further hue from a setting demanding religious fervor but more often exhibiting only its pale shadow. The satirist's favorite target is hypocrisy and there are few areas of life in which vice pays more shadow tribute to virtue than professional religion. But though wily bishops and pastors often get Powers' best lines, he had a sneaking admiration for their more fervent assistants, especially when that fervor extended to the needs of the poor.

His preferred target was the clerical *l' homme moyen sensuel* who also lacks subtlety, like Father Burner, titular hero of *Prince of Darkness* and foil for a cat narrator in two later stories (in *The*

*Presence of Grace,* 1956). But in the end, Powers holds out hope for him as well. Deprived of his last chance of advancement by the sudden recovery of his aging pastor, Father Burner manages with some grace to welcome the tyrant back and wins for his pains the grudging approval of his natural foe, Fritz, the rectory cat.

## Morte D'Urban

In 1962 Powers published the novel that was to win him the National Book Award: *Morte D'Urban,* a title with two self-conscious literary puns in as many words. This first attempt at sustained fiction allowed him a much broader field for his inquiry into American religion of the Midwestern Catholic variety. Father Urban, whose motto is "Be a Winner" and who "travels out of Chicago," firmly believes in the good life and sees no contradiction between riding the Limited and living the Gospel. Indeed, it might be taken to be his job as the Order of St. Clement's principal preacher and fund-raiser. The central paradox of Powers' fiction is thus announced in the novel's opening pages.

But Urban soon learns to his dismay how different the rich are from you and me, and not just because they have more cash, either. In his picaresque journey of self-discovery, he encounters all the vexations of the flesh and many of the spirit before he learns the hard lessons of his sudden dismissal to a decaying Clementine house in rural Minnesota. His first instinct is to show up the new provincial superior who clearly undervalues his star player. Urban will turn a dilapidated monastery into a first-class lay retreat center complete with golf course. And with the help of his chief benefactor, Billy Cosgrove, and several others, he succeeds magnificently, but at a cost. First of all, he accidentally gets beaned on the course by the bishop's golf ball which initially works in his favor, shaming the prelate into supporting Urban's efforts. But the comical injury has serious long-term repercussions on his health.

Then he begins to reap the even more bitter fruit of his fundraising success. Billy, and later, the wealthy Mrs. Thwaites and her daughter Sally reveal to Urban just what Jesus meant when he referred to benefactors as "lording it over" their recipients.

In a disgruntled mood because Urban's worm of conscience finally turns on him, Billy sends him toppling into one lake, and Sally leaves him stranded in the middle of another when he declines her invitation for a seductive midnight swim. A sopping wet and disillusioned Fr. Urban begins to reconsider his priorities.

And it is precisely then, of course, when he has surrendered all his grand schemes, that he wins the long-coveted prize of election as Father Provincial. To everyone's surprise, he takes no revenge on his enemies nor does he strike out boldly in new directions. He sees himself now not as Churchill but Atlee, destined to preside over the decline of the Clementine "empire," modest as it was to begin with. The go-getter has become a caretaker, in several senses. His intermittent headaches become fiercer and more frequent. His efforts to disguise them from visitors by swivelling around in his chair and grasping his breviary earn him an increasing reputation for piety which, ironically, is "not entirely unwarranted now."

## Wheat that Springeth Green

The critical and commercial success of *Morte D'Urban* put Powers in an entirely new literary league. Reviewers and reviews that had ignored his short story collections now took him up. But he still kept to his deliberate pace, not publishing another book until 1975 when a slim collection of stories appeared as *Look How the Fish Live.* Some of these short pieces were in fact early drafts of a novel that would not appear until 1988 as *Wheat that Springeth Green.*

Both the characters and the venue are by now quite familiar: Catholic priests in Minnesota, but the time is now the late 1960s and both church and nation have undergone radical changes. Father Joseph Hackett, whom we meet first as a baby, then as a young altar boy in disgrace, and still later as a randy teenager and an ascetic seminarian, has certain convictions from which he will not swerve. Inevitably, they get him into trouble with his contemporaries and superiors in the Church where "getting along" and "going along" are no less linked than in the Congress.

He's close to 40 when he gets his first parish, after five years as a curate (for a real mystic) and seven at the chancery. But Joe soon finds himself beset by all manner of fools and frauds, representing both God and Caesar (it is 1968, after all). But unlike the young conscientious objector he encourages to flee to Canada, Joe faces no clear and present danger to his comfortable life in suburbia. Indeed, it is middle-class life and its detritus (shopping malls and their cheerleader squads, ecclesiastical fund-raisers, kneejerk patriots) that threaten what's left of a once robust, if somewhat flashy, spiritual life that Joe practiced during his seminary days.

For Joe the battle lines are clear: "the separation of Church and Dreck . . . a matter of life and death for the world" is being steadily undermined by the apparatchiks at the chancery. His only consolation comes in the unlikely form of his bejeaned young curate whose surprise arrival provides one of Powers' great comic set pieces as Joe desperately attempts to discover his name without having to admit he doesn't know it. Father Bill is still playing his guitar at the end, but in the meantime he and Joe have become a team (they even play "father-son" catch in the driveway). They have also established in the tentative ways possible across a cultural and ecclesial generation gap a genuine "priestly fellowship" that includes late-night discussions of theology, politics and baseball as well as a ritual signoff: "G'night, Bill." "G'night, Joe."

By novel's end, Joe has visited his young draft-resister friend at his Catholic Worker house in Montreal, helping out for eleven days. As Joe leaves, Greg urges him to "keep it up," without further specification. The meaning only becomes clear in the brief final chapter. The last word we hear from Joe in the novel comes as he responds to a question while driving off to his new assignment from a suburban farewell barbecue: "'Where is it you're stationed now—Holy . . . Faith?' Joe shook his head and kept going, calling back 'Cross.'"

Powers certainly hoped the reader would remember references to the slum parish Bill once yearned for. (He's staying in the suburbs.) But those emphatic italics whose first function is to suggest Joe's typically laconic corrective tone surely serve another purpose for the novel's final word. Without elaboration, as usual, Powers sends his hero off—as he sent off Fr. Urban—to work out his salvation under the preeminent sign of the Paschal Mystery whose other image of seed and sheaf was set in the novel's title.

*See* Fiction, Irish-American

J. F. Powers, *Prince of Darkness and Other Stories* (New York, 1947).
———, *The Presence of Grace* (New York, 1956).

———, *Morte D'Urban* (New York, 1962).
———, *Look How the Fish Live* (New York, 1975).
———, *Wheat that Springeth Green* (New York, 1988).
John V. Hagopian, *J. F. Powers* (New York, 1968).
Alfred Kazin, *Contemporaries* (Boston, 1962).
Gene Kellog, *The Vital Tradition: The Catholic Novel in a Period of Convergence* (Chicago, 1970).

JOHN BRESLIN, S.J.

## POWERS, JESSICA (1905–1988)

Nun, poet. Born Agnes Jessica Powers on February 7, 1905, to John Powers II and Delia Veronica Trainer, she was raised in Juneau County, Wisconsin, where she began writing poetry as a child. (While still young she switched her first and middle names to Jessica Agnes). Her grandparents had emigrated from Ireland and Scotland in the nineteenth century to this rural farming community which was largely Irish and Catholic in composition. Jessica Powers attended a local public school until the age of eleven when she began attending a Catholic school in the larger town of Mauston, requiring her to board with other children, though she returned home on weekends.

In 1922 Jessica Powers began attending Marquette University in Milwaukee but had to withdraw after only one semester for lack of funds. She moved to Chicago where she found work as a secretary, continued reading and writing, and began attending an informal literary salon at a Dominican friary in River Forest (near Chicago). Also at this time she began corresponding with Jessie Pegis, a writer and wife of the philosopher Anton Pegis. A bout of tuberculosis forced Jessica to return home in 1927. While there, her mother died suddenly, forcing her to stay in Wisconsin and care for her two unmarried brothers. She maintained the family farm during the Great Depression while continuing to publish her verse and began reading the profound writings of the sixteenth-century Spanish mystic, St. John of the Cross. After both brothers eventually married, Jessica moved to New York, lived with Anton and Jessie Pegis, and joined the Catholic Poetry Society.

In 1941, just as her literary genius was attracting serious attention, Jessica Powers decided to enter a Carmelite monastery in

Jessica Powers

Milwaukee and took the name Sister Miriam of the Holy Spirit. She continued writing poetry as a cloistered nun and published her work in several popular Catholic journals. Eventually five volumes of her verse were published, including one anthology for children. Taken as a whole, Jessica Powers' work reflects her struggles with loss, Irish-Catholic background, appreciation of nature and longing for the divine. She died on August 18, 1988.

Here is one of her poems:

> Obscurity Obscurity becomes the final peace.
> The hidden then are the elect, the free.
> They leave our garish noon and find release
> in the evening's gift of anonymity.
>
> Lost not in loneness but in multitude
> they serve unseen, without the noise of name.
> Should you disdain them, ponder for your good:
> it was in this way that the angels came.

*See* Poetry, Irish-American

M. Kappes, *Track of the Mystic: Carmelite Influence on the American Poet Jessica Powers* (Kansas City, 1994).
D. R. Leckey, *Winter Music: A Life of Jessica Powers Poet, Nun, Woman of the 20th Century* (Kansas City, 1992).
R. Morneau, *Mantras from a Poet* (Kansas City, 1991).
J. Powers, *Mountain Sparrow* (Reno, 1972).
———, *Journey to Bethlehem* (Pewaukee, WI, 1980).
———, *The House at Rest* (Pewaukee, WI, 1984).
———, *Selected Poetry of Jessica Powers* (Kansas City, 1989).

ANTHONY D. ANDREASSI

## PRESENTATION SISTERS FROM IRELAND

The Sisters of the Presentation of the Blessed Virgin Mary were founded in Cork, Ireland, by Nano (Honora) Nagle, a rich Catholic woman who was concerned about the condition of the Irish poor, especially the ignorant poor children. In 1775–1776, she founded the Sisters of Charitable Instruction of the Sacred Heart with three companions to serve the poor. They taught school, which was then illegal under the Penal Laws, visited the sick in their homes and public hospitals and ran a home for aged women. There were still only about four sisters when Nano Nagle died on April 26, 1784. The sisters took the title of the Presentation in the 1790s and in 1805 become an order with solemn vows and enclosure, against the will of Bishop Francis Moylan, a close associate of Nano Nagle. They then devoted themselves to education.

The order spread to many places in Ireland, especially after Catholic Emancipation in 1829. Their first foreign foundation was in Newfoundland (1833), followed by Manchester, England (1836), and India (1844). In 1854 an agent of Archbishop Joseph Sadoc Alemany, O.P., of San Francisco, Father Hugh P. Gallagher, came to Ireland to recruit priests and sisters for his remote diocese. At the Presentation Convent, Midleton, County Cork, five sisters volunteered under the leadership of Mother M. Joseph Cronin. The others were Sisters Mary Augustine Keane, Xavier Daly, Clare Duggan and Ignatius Lanigan. The latter became ill and was replaced by Sister Mary Teresa Comerford of the Kilkenny Convent.

When the sisters arrived in San Francisco, there was no one to meet them. They were destined for Sacramento to found a school

Sisters on the move

there, but it was decided that Sacramento was too wild a place for cloistered nuns, and they began to teach in a school in San Francisco. They expected to teach in publicly funded schools as they had in Ireland, but this support only lasted to 1856. In October 1855, a postulant, Margaret Cassian joined them, but Mothers Joseph and Augustine had to return to Ireland. Sister Clare eventually returned there also. Archbishop Alemany appointed Mother Teresa Comerford to be the new superior. In December 1855, they moved into their new convent on Powell Street, aided by donations from rich Irish men. Other sisters came from Ireland and women in San Francisco joined. In 1869 Mother Teresa founded another house in the city and, in 1878, a house in Berkeley. In 1879, with the aid of her cousin who was the pastor there, she founded the first recruiting novitiate in Ireland at Kilcock. She died in 1881 in San Francisco.

A new archbishop, Parrick W. Riordan, severed their connection with Kilcock and amalgamated the houses in the archdiocese under Mother Josephine Hagarty. They were allowed to charge tuition and teach in parochial schools. In 1890, Mother M. Ignatius McDermott left San Francisco. In 1895 she founded the Presentation Convent at Rawalpindi, now Pakistan. Another sister went to Mexico for twelve years but did not succeed in making a go of her mission. She was Sister M. Loyola Higgins and she left the religious life in 1902. After 1912 most of the houses were owned by parishes. They took in a foundation from Fitchburg, MA, at Gilroy, CA, and expanded to Los Angeles in 1919. After the 1960s they began many works of a social nature.

### New York and Massachusetts

The next American foundation from Ireland was at St. Michael's Convent, New York City in 1874. Eight sisters and four postulants from Terenure, Clondalkin and Tuam came under the leadership of Mother Joseph Hickey. The sisters opened the parochial school on September 29, 1874 with more than 600 poor immigrant children. They also instructed over a thousand adults. In 1884 they founded a home for destitute children from St. Michael's on Staten Island, and, in 1886, Mother Magdalen Keating led a group of sisters to Fitchburg, MA. According to the Presentation rule, each of these convents remained autonomous. In 1890 Mother Agnes Barry left Fitchburg to take over a school in Gilroy, CA. The Fitchburg sisters were in education and eventually spread to Connecticut, Rhode Island, and New Hampshire. In 1997 the sisters who had originated at St. Michael's with headquarters at Newburgh, N.Y., joined with the Fitchburg sisters to

form a new entity, Sisters of the Presentation of the Blessed Virgin Mary with headquarters at New Windsor, N.Y. The Staten Island sisters did not join.

### Watervliet

In 1881 five sisters under the leadership of Mother Paul Cahill came from Fermoy, County Cork to found an orphanage at Watervliet for siblings, so that families would not be separated. Their first institution was St. Colman's, Watervliet. They later founded schools, programs for alcoholic children, autistic children and others in need.

### Iowa

Bishop John Hennessy of Dubuque, IA, requested sisters from the Presentation Convent, Mooncoin, near Kilkenny. Mother Vincent Hennessy set out with Alice Howley, Kate Reed and Ellen Ahearne, prospective postulants. They arrived in Dubuque on November 13, 1874. After several months they took a school in the town of Key West, IA. The three young women were received and professed on September 8, 1876. Sister Agnes Burke and three more postulants came also, and the sisters opened a boarding and day school at Ackley, IA. In 1879 Mother Vincent Hennessy established St. Vincent's Academy at Dubuque. She died two months later. The bishop asked them to make their headquarters in Dubuque. They spread to other towns in Iowa and other midwestern states, in the field of education. In 1908 Archbishop John Keane of Dubuque proposed the amalgamation of the Presentation Convents in the U.S., but nothing came of his proposal.

### The Dakotas

On March 7, 1880, Mother M. John Hughes of George's Hill Convent, Dublin, her sister, Mother M. Agnes Hughes of Doneraile, County Cork, and Sister Teresa Challoner of the Manchester, England, convent, with two choir postulants and a servant aspiring to be a laysister, set out from Ireland for the far-off Dakota Territory. Bishop Martin Marty, O.S.B., had invited them to come and teach Indian children. Their first school was at St. Ann's, Charles Mix County, in what is now South Dakota. In the spring the building became unsafe and the sisters went to Deadwood, now South Dakota, but their observance of the vow of enclosure put them on the road again. They finally made a foundation in Fargo, now North Dakota, in July 1882. The Sisters begged for money in mining towns and other places to build a new school. Mother John requested help from California and four sisters came to give assistance until they could get new recruits from Ireland. In 1886 the sisters began a new foundation in Aberdeen, now South Dakota. Mother John Hughes, Sister M. Aloysius Chriswell and Ellen Butler, later Mother M. Joseph, began classes in October 1886. In 1892 Bishop Marty appointed Mother Aloysius Chriswell superior at Aberdeen and Mother John Hughes, two other sisters and a postulant went back to Fargo. No one knows exactly what caused the separation, but Archbishop John Ireland arbitrated a property problem between the two groups. In 1889 the Dakotas became two states ruled over by two bishops. It was not an easy life in the Dakotas; the sisters were poor and the rule was strict. The Fargo sisters founded an orphanage and free school and an academy in 1897, the year Mother John Hughes died. The sisters in Fargo founded new schools under the leadership of Mother Baptista Bowen (1910–1919) and Mother Joseph Cregan (1920–1937). In the late thirties, Bishop Aloysius Muench urged the Fargo sisters to undertake health care as it

Mother M.
Joseph Butler

would afford greater financial security. Two sisters were trained and opened the first of several hospitals in 1939.

In the meantime the Aberdeen sisters entered health care after a black diphtheria epidemic struck the area. They nursed the sick in their homes and in the school. In 1901 they built the first of several hospitals and clinics. Later they founded a junior college at Aberdeen.

### New Irish Wave

Just ninety-eight years after the Presentation Sisters came to San Francisco, a new wave of Irish Presentations began to arrive. In 1953 three Presentation sisters from Bandon, County Cork, came to teach at San Antonio, TX, at the invitation of Archbishop Lucey. Led by Sister Magdalen Lyne, the three sisters began teaching with American sisters for two years and then began teaching in their own school. They became an autonomous motherhouse. In the 1950s, 1960s and early 1970s, Presentation sisters from various dioceses in Ireland responded to invitations primarily in the southwestern and southeastern parts of the United States—part of the great growth of Catholic schools after World War II. About twenty Irish sisters who had been working in Pakistan came to southern California and opened a novitiate in 1967. Twenty-five convents were established by this new Irish wave. In 1976 most of the Presentation motherhouses in Ireland formed the Union of the Sisters of the Presentation of the Blessed Virgin Mary. This union included sisters in Pakistan, India, the Philippines, and Africa as well as the British Isles and U.S. In 1989 the sisters from Irish motherhouses in the United States formed a new province. In the 1980s the International Presentation Association, involving the Union, the Australian Society and most of the North American sisters, came into being.

After Vatican II most of the groups founded missions in Latin America and widened their scope from education and healthcare to pastoral work and many types of social work, in some cases going back to work done by the early sisters before the enclosure, as a result of the search for the charism.

*See* Women Religious from Ireland; Sisters of Mercy

Archives of the Archdiocese of San Francisco.
Presentation Archives, Aberdeen, Dubuque, Fargo, New Windsor, Phoenix and San Francisco.

M. Raphael Consedine, *Listening Journey* (Victoria, Australia, 1983).
Ann Curry, *Mother Teresa Comerford* (San Francisco, 1980).
Mary Margaret Mooney, *Doing What Needed to Be Done* (Fargo, N.D., 1997).
Susan Carol Peterson and Courtney Ann Vaughn-Roberson, *Women with Vision: The Presentation Sisters of South Dakota, 1880–1985* (Urbana, 1988).
T. J. Walsh, *Nano Nagle and the Presentation Sisters* (Dublin, 1959).

ANN CURRY, P.B.V.M.

## PRIESTS FROM IRELAND

### Introduction

This essay is about the Irish-born and Irish-seminary educated Roman Catholic priests who have lived and worked in the United States. Their numbers are steadily declining due to death and the lack of new recruits. While Ireland remains the most priest-rich nation in the world, countries like the United States, who have benefitted from Ireland's largesse, scramble to find substitutes to fill the positions once occupied by these priests (Hoge 1987).

American Catholicism's roots are in nineteenth-century Ireland and the Irish diaspora which followed made American Catholicism as much a culture as a religion (Morris 1997). American Catholicism was influenced by the pietism and puritanism of the Irish Church (McCaffrey 1976). Irish Catholicism has always contained elements from its peasant culture, but Anglo-Protestant and Roman cultural forces have strongly influenced Irish Catholicism. Irish bishops in America practiced an authoritarian management style, similar to that of the bishops in Ireland, and they contributed to the bureaucratization of the emerging Church in America. According to Will Herberg (1983:138), "The Irish Americanized and 'plebeianized' the Catholic Church in America, and so set it on the path it was to follow thereafter." Irish priests have left an indelible mark on the soul and the structure of American Catholicism. During the latter part of the nineteenth century and up through the middle of the twentieth century, the majority of priests and bishops were of Irish descent, whether native Irish or Irish-American.

The declining number of Irish priests is occurring at a most crucial time for the Catholic Church in the USA. The average diocese (there are 33 archdioceses and 148 dioceses) lost 20 percent of its active priests during 1966–1984. It is projected that by 2005, that figure will increase to 40 percent. American seminaries are producing 59 new priests for every 100 who leave the active ministry (Schoenherr and Young 1993). As of 1996, there were 32,834 diocesan and 16,717 religious order priests in the USA and in 1996 there were 505 seminarians ordained to the priesthood. While fewer men seek ordination to the priesthood, the Catholic population continues to increase. Andrew Greeley (1991) estimates that there are approximately 60 million Catholics in the USA and Richard Schoenherr and Lawrence Young (1993) predict that by 2005 the Catholic population will increase to 74 million, making Roman Catholics the largest religious group in the USA.

Irish seminaries, once the source of a multitude of newly ordained priests, have all but eliminated the sending of clergy abroad. The Irish are also experiencing a vocations crisis as are other western European countries. There were 150 ordinations for Irish dioceses and dioceses abroad in 1970. By 1995, that number had decreased to 59. In 1995, there were 3,659 diocesan clergy in Ireland, 285 fewer than in 1970. The decline among religious order priests has been much more precipitous than among diocesan priests. In 1995, there were 4,564 religious order priests in Ireland, a decline of 3,382 from 1970. These changes have stemmed the flow of Irish priests to the USA to, at best, 15–20 a year (Hoge 1987). Realistically, the number is probably more like 6 or 7 a year. As of 1996, there were only 13 Irish seminarians studying for American dioceses.

Up through the 1960s, due to large surpluses of clergy and religious, Ireland became a major exporter of priests and nuns. Roger Finke and Rodney Stark (1992:137) state, "Without these Irish 'imports' it is hard to imagine how churches could have met their staffing needs." More than a third of the priests in the Archdiocese of San Francisco, in 1963, were born and ordained in Ireland. Eighty percent of the clergy in the Archdiocese of Los Angeles, in the 1940s and 1950s, were Irish-born (Unsworth 1991). As Tim Unsworth (1991:35) states, "Most fell in love with their new country, becoming more American than the Americans themselves." Of all the foreign-born priests in the USA, the Irish have considered themselves to be the most American (McAvoy 1964). They always have been more aware of their identity than other priests (Edwards 1987), and due to their tradition, they have been more conservative and purist religiously (McAvoy 1964). McAvoy (1964:37) states, "The special contribution of the Irish clergy to American Catholicism has been a hope for freedom basically political and economic but eventually social and cultural."

Irish priests, although fewer in number, play an important role primarily in the Western and Southern parts of the USA. As of 1996, there were between 1,000–1,150 Irish-born and Irish-seminary educated priests residing in the USA. This figure is based on data provided by Irish seminaries and an estimate of the number of priests who came from St. Kieran's College, Kilkenny, and St. Patrick's College, Maynooth. These seminaries were unable to provide data. Based on information from five key seminaries, a total of 3,365 Irish priests have served in the USA.

## A Brief History

Foreign clergy, especially priests from European dioceses, played a very significant role in the development of the early Church in America. Large numbers of Irish-born priests began immigrating to the USA in the late 1780s and by the early 1800s they dominated the clergy which consisted of French-born, English-born, German-born, and a small number of native-born citizens. Irish Catholic immigration grew tremendously in the 1840s and 1850s and in response, more Irish priests were elevated to the episcopacy. These bishops recruited priests from Irish seminaries to serve in their dioceses (Ellis 1971; Miller 1990). Irish immigrants requested Irish-born priests for their parishes (Edwards 1989; McCaffrey 1976). By the mid-1800s, 59 percent of the priests in the Diocese of New York were Irish-born and by 1900, 62 percent of the bishops were Irish, more than half of them Irish-born (Dolan 1975; Dolan 1985).

Ireland experienced a "Devotional Revolution" during the first half of the nineteenth century (Larkin 1984). This revolution in Irish Catholicism brought about a large increase in the number of religious vocations. As vocations increased, the population of Ireland decreased as a result of involuntary and voluntary emigration. Four million Irish left for the USA from 1845–1900, many fleeing starvation as a result of the potato famine. While prior to the "Devotional Revolution" there was actually a shortage of religious in Ireland, during and after this incident, there

was a surplus of religious, many of whom found a home in the USA, Australia, and Great Britain. Ireland's religious bounty was a blessing to countries that were receiving large numbers of Irish immigrants.

Those Irish priests who settled in the USA prior to the "Devotional Revolution" were not as educated as the French, British, and American-born clergy (McCaffrey 1976). The Irish who emigrated prior to the "Devotional Revolution" were less devout than those who came in the mid-1800s (Greeley 1988). Frenchmen, like the Archbishop of Baltimore, Ambrose Marechal, did not like the presence of and the growing dependence on Irish priests in the American Church. He believed these priests were unreliable, undisciplined, and sources of scandal (McCaffrey 1976). Some of them had been in trouble with their bishops in Ireland (Ellis 1969). Even Irish-born John England, the Bishop of Charleston, South Carolina, questioned the motives and character of Irish-born priests seeking appointments in his diocese (Miller 1983). The non-Irish clergy in America were fearful of the growing power and influence of the Irish within the Church and they believed this was a liability because Anglo-Americans did not consider the Irish as their equals (McAvoy 1964). There was also tension between Irish-born priests and American-born Irish priests. The Irish-born (also known as "FBIs": foreign-born Irish) believed that the American-born Irish disliked them and therefore were prejudiced toward them (Funchion 1995; Edwards 1989). The common belief in Ireland and the USA, during this time and continuing into the twentieth century, was that the Irish priests recruited for service abroad were second rate in comparison to those who remained in Ireland. While rumor and innuendo followed Irish priests wherever they went, many credit them as being "unsung heroes" because they worked hard for their parishioners (McAvoy 1964).

## The Role of Irish Seminaries

Six seminaries in the Irish Republic have educated the vast majority of Irish priests in the USA: All Hallows College, Dublin; St. John's College, Waterford; St. Peter's College, Wexford; St. Patrick's College, Carlow; St. Patrick's College, Thurles; and St. Kieran's College, Kilkenny (the seminary at St. Kieran's College is now closed). There are no Catholic seminaries in Northern Ireland. St. Patrick's College, Maynooth, is the National Seminary and it has not sent many priests to the USA. Since its founding in 1795, St. Patrick's College has educated seminarians affiliated with Irish dioceses who intended to stay in Ireland. St. Patrick's College, Maynooth, has always been viewed as the premier Irish seminary which has produced many of Ireland's hierarchy.

All Hallows College is the only non-diocesan seminary among the six listed above. All Hallows was founded specifically to educate priests who would follow their countrymen to destinations around the world. These priests knew they would leave Ireland and serve the foreign missions, while those who attended local diocesan seminaries would either be selected to stay and serve the local home missions or would volunteer or be recruited by bishops from foreign dioceses such as bishops from American dioceses. Since local Irish bishops could place only a small number of future priests in their own dioceses, they gladly encouraged American bishops to recruit other seminarians. Many of these seminarians did not want to stay in Ireland and they looked forward to their service abroad. An Irish priest now serving in the Diocese of Tucson summed up this feeling quite well, "I had a desire to be a priest since high school, but not necessarily for the home missions. My sense was that there was a glut of priests in Ireland; we were overstocked. The diocese often sent the newly ordained out to England or some other place for four to five years until an opening came up at home" (Unsworth 1991:37). As one priest states who participated in the pilot study (Smith 1998) to be discussed shortly, "Being a priest in Ireland never appealed to me. At that time, to get into Maynooth was for the top of the class. Those of us who were average were left out and were advised to look elsewhere." Once a seminarian was committed to an American diocese, that diocese assumed financial responsibility for his seminary education. Revenues obtained from American bishops helped to keep Irish seminaries afloat.

The number of Irish priests recruited to serve in America is listed by their respective seminaries in Table One. The number of Irish priests residing in America in 1996/97 is listed in Table Two. All Hallows College, Dublin, sent 1404 priests to the United States. The largest cohort of priests, from All Hallows College, arrived in the USA between 1949–1965, while the second largest cohort arrived half a century earlier between 1891–1911. The most recent cohort (1966–1991) included 144 members. The major destination for All Hallows graduates has been California, especially the Dioceses of Los Angeles, Sacramento, San Francisco, Monterey, and Fresno. Large numbers of All Hallows graduates have served in the Midwest and the South, especially in Georgia and Florida.

Table 1. The Number of Irish Priests Sent to America by Seminary

| | |
|---|---|
| All Hallows College, Dublin | 1404 |
| St. Patrick's College, Carlow | 1043 |
| St. Patrick's College, Thurles | 511 |
| St. John's College, Waterford | 244 |
| St. Peter's College, Wexford | 163 |
| Total | 3365 |

Table 2. The Number of Irish Priests in America during 1996/97 by Seminary

| | |
|---|---|
| All Hallows College, Dublin | 292 |
| St. Patrick's College, Carlow | 254 |
| St. Patrick's College, Thurles | 176 |
| St. John's College, Waterford | 182 |
| St. Peter's College, Wexford | 94 |
| Total | 998 |

St. Patrick's College, Carlow, has produced the second largest contingent of Irish priests for the USA. By 1993, 1,043 had served in the USA. Dioceses receiving large numbers of graduates include Los Angeles, San Francisco, Natchez, St. Louis, and Mobile. As of 1997, St. Patrick's College alumni resided in 24 states with the largest concentrations in Mississippi, California, Florida, New Jersey, Texas, Alabama, Louisiana, and Georgia.

St. Patrick's College, Thurles, ordained 511 priests for service in the USA. The dioceses of San Francisco, Los Angeles, Sacramento, Dubuque, Seattle, Great Falls, and Miami have received the largest share of St. Patrick's alumni. Overall, graduates of St. Patrick's have resided primarily in California, Florida, and Montana. As of 1997, a little more than half of all active alumni in the USA reside in California and Florida. They are affiliated with 48 dioceses.

Between 1894–1996, 244 priests were ordained for dioceses in the USA at St. John's College, Waterford. The largest group came between 1961–1970. The second largest cohort preceded them between 1916–1930, while the smallest group came between 1986–1996. The Archdiocese of Los Angeles has been home to the largest number of St. John's graduates. The majority of graduates have joined Southern and Western dioceses. As of 1996, 182 active priests were found in 26 states with the largest concentrations in California, Florida, Texas, New Jersey, Georgia, and New York.

St. Peter's College, Wexford, sent 163 priests to the USA between 1919–1995. The dioceses of Camden, Los Angeles, Mobile, Birmingham, and San Diego received the largest number of alumni from St. Peter's College. As of 1996, 94 alumni resided in 18 states with the largest concentrations in California, Florida, and Texas.

Prior to 1948, it was not unusual for seminarians to begin their studies in Irish seminaries and then complete them in American seminaries. Those priests were not included in the above-mentioned figures. This practice ended after 1948 because Irish bishops did not want their seminaries, especially the smaller ones, to become juniorates (seminaries that required the last 2–3 years of education to be completed elsewhere).

Pilot Study Findings

This section summarizes the findings from a pilot study I conducted in the Fall of 1996 (Smith 1998). Alumni of St. Peter's College residing in the USA were surveyed regarding a variety of issues related to their priesthood and the Church. Alumni from All Hallows College, St. Patrick's College, Carlow, St. Patrick's College, Thurles, and St. John's College residing in the USA were surveyed in 1997.

The average age of those priests who participated in the pilot study was 65, whereas the average of diocesan priests is 55. This finding is not surprising since fewer Irish priests have been recruited in the last three decades, thus inflating their average age in comparison to diocesan priests. Most of the priests from St. Peter's College were in their fifties, sixties, and seventies. The majority were in their sixties. Most relocated to this country soon after ordination. More than one half of them were ordained in the 1950s. The average number of years spent in the USA is 37 and all but two were recruited or volunteered for service here.

The profile created from data gathered in the pilot study paints a picture of an aging, but still vigorous, committed, and dedicated group of priests who reside primarily in the South, West, and Southwest. They will most likely be the last of a long continuous line of priests to serve in the USA. They are overwhelmingly satisfied with their priesthood, yet concerned with the future of the Church. They are almost evenly split regarding whether Vatican II went far enough or not far enough in modernizing Catholicism and a slight majority still identify themselves as more Irish than Irish-American. They admit that American culture has influenced their philosophy and theology of life. They have assimilated well into American society. Loneliness, overwork, and wondering if they make a difference in people's lives are cited most frequently as problems. The most pressing ecclesiological and theological issue identified is the regulations regarding priestly ordination. The majority of these priests were found to be neither highly conservative nor highly liberal in their faith and morals. They were ill-prepared for dealing with American culture. Most of them lamented the anxiety, stress, and misunderstanding which accompanied their initiation into American culture. While they experienced culture shock, they were in agreement that for the most part, their seminary education was adequate.

Hoge, Shields, and Griffin (1995) found that priests are not experiencing a decline in morale and happiness. Actually, priests have reported higher levels of morale and happiness in both 1985 and 1993 than they did in 1970. It appears from the data gathered in the pilot study that Irish priests likewise are happy and have a fairly high level of morale. Overwork and loneliness were also reported by diocesan priests as important problems, but they identified coping with authority and the rising expectations of the laity as even more problematic, while the Irish priests did not. Younger and older diocesan priests are more traditional in their support of celibacy requirements, while the Irish priests who are supportive of optional celibacy and the ordination of married men and women are mostly in their sixties.

### Conclusion

Irish priests in the USA are a dying breed and it is very unlikely that we will see a shift in the demographic patterns. Irish society is becoming more modern and secular in its values. While religion and the Roman Catholic Church are still powerful social forces in Ireland, their impact has weakened. If countries like the USA cannot produce enough native vocations, they must look to other nations such as India, Africa, Poland, and areas of Southeast Asia where vocations are abundant. American bishops are recruiting priests of Mexican background to serve in areas once populated by Irish priests. Times are changing, but let us not forget the contribution made by Irish priests to the Roman Catholic Church in the USA. It is amazing how many religious (priests, nuns, brothers, and monks) the tiny country of Ireland has produced and dispersed to countries around the world.

*See* Women Religious from Ireland

Jay P. Dolan, *The Immigrant Church* (Baltimore, 1975).

———, *The American Catholic Experience* (New York, 1985).

Owen Dudley Edwards, "The Irish Priest in North America," in *The Churches, Ireland, and the Irish*, ed., W. J. Sheils and Diana Wood (Oxford, 1989): 311–352.

John Tracy Ellis, *American Catholicism* (Chicago, 1969).

———, *The Catholic Priest in the United States: Historical Investigations* (Collegeville, 1971).

Roger Finke and Rodney Stark, *The Churching of America, 1776–1990* (New Brunswick, 1992).

Andrew Greeley, "The Success and Assimilation of Irish Protestants and Irish Catholics in the United States," *Sociology and Social Research*, 72 (1988): 229–236.

———, "The Demography of American Catholics: 1965–1990," in *Religion and the Social Order: Vatican II and U.S. Catholicism*, Vol. 2, ed., Helen Rose Ebaugh (Greenwich, 1991): 37–56.

Will Herberg, *Protestant-Catholic-Jew: An Essay in American Religious Sociology* (Chicago, 1983).

Dean R. Hoge, *The Future of Catholic Leadership* (Kansas City, 1987).

Emmet Larkin, *The Historical Dimensions of Irish Catholicism* (Washington, D.C., 1984).

Thomas T. McAvoy, "The Irish Clergyman in the United States," *Records of the American Catholic Historical Society of Philadelphia*, Vol. LXXV (1964): 6–38.

Lawrence J. McCaffrey, *The Irish Diaspora in America* (Bloomington, 1976).

Kerby A. Miller, *Emigrants and Exiles: Ireland and the Irish Exodus to North America* (New York, 1985).

———, "Class, Culture, and Immigrant Group Identity in the United States: The Case of Irish-American Ethnicity," in *Immigration Reconsidered*, ed., Virginia Yans-McLaughlin (New York, 1990): 96–129.

Charles R. Morris, *American Catholic: The Saints and Sinners Who Built America's Most Powerful Church* (New York, 1997).

Richard A. Schoenherr and Lawrence A. Young, *Full Pews and Empty Altars: Demographics of the Priest Shortage in United States Catholic Dioceses* (Madison, 1993).

William L. Smith, "Irish Priests and American Catholicism: A Match Made in Heaven," in *Research in the Social Scientific Study of Religion*, Vol. 9, ed., Joanne Greer and David Moberg (Stamford, 1998).

Tim Unsworth, *The Last Priests in America* (New York, 1991).

WILLIAM L. SMITH

## PURCELL, JOHN BAPTIST (1783–1883)

Archbishop. He was born in Mallow, County Cork, on February 26, 1783 to Edward and Johanna (Keefe). Since Catholics were unable to attend college in Ireland, at 18 the young Purcell came to the United States. He started out working as a tutor in Baltimore and then in 1820 enrolled at Mt. St. Mary's College in Emmitsburg, Maryland. After spending three years there, he went to Paris to study at the Seminary of St. Sulpice and was ordained a priest on May 27, 1827. He returned to the United States and began teaching at Emmitsburg and in 1829 was named president of the college.

### Life as a Bishop

In 1833 Purcell was named the second bishop of Cincinnati and spent the next 50 years leading the church there while overseeing a rapid expansion of the diocese. During his tenure the Catholic population rose from 7,000 to 500,000, the clergy grew from 14 to 480 and the number of churches increased from 16 to 500. Hoping to avoid tensions with German Catholics, in 1834 Purcell founded the first German national parish west of the Alleghenies, and in 1837 helped establish the periodical *Der Wahrheitsfreund*. In 1840 he invited the Jesuits to take over a diocesan college (which they renamed in honor of St. Francis Xavier), and in 1851 he opened Mt. St. Mary's Seminary of the West (which is still open today). In 1850 the see was elevated to an archdiocese, and as an archbishop, Purcell presided over three provincial councils (1855, 1858 and 1861).

A man of strong convictions, Purcell was a vocal supporter of the Total Abstinence Society and abolitionism, and he used his newspaper, the *Catholic Telegraph*, to call for universal manumission five months before the Emancipation Proclamation. He often engaged in public and rancorous debates with Protestants, and this, in addition to the many missions he sponsored, brought about a large number of conversions in his diocese in the late 1830s. In 1853 he calmed an anti-Catholic mob intent on burning the cathedral because of the presence of Archbishop Gaetano Bedini, the papal nuncio to Brazil, who had stopped to visit with Purcell on his way to South America.

At the First Vatican Council Purcell believed the definition of papal infallibility to be inopportune and thus left Rome before the final vote. Upon his return to Cincinnati, he spoke about an address he had prepared for the Council (but never delivered) in which he praised the American system as the "best form of human government" and argued for the separation of church and state and for freedom of religion. Opinions such as these ran contrary to the pronouncements of Pope Pius IX, and it was not until the Second Vatican Council (1962) that the church came to accept the more liberal positions of Purcell and others like him.

## FINAL YEARS

Purcell's later years as archbishop were marred by a financial crisis brought on by the failure of a church-sponsored bank set up by his brother Edward (who was also a priest of Purcell's archdiocese and the editor of the *Catholic Telegraph*), and in 1879 the diocesan seminary was forced to close for eight years because of these fiscal problems. Embarrassed by these events, in 1880 Purcell accepted William Elder as his coadjutor and retired soon thereafter. Archbishop Purcell died on July 4, 1883 and was buried in the cemetery of the Ursuline sisters in St. Martin, Ohio.

*See* Ohio

Gilbert J. Garraghan, *The Jesuits of the Middle United States* (New York, 1938).

James Hennesey, *American Catholics: A History of the Roman Catholic Community in the United States* (Oxford and New York, 1981).

M. E. Hussey, "The Financial Failure of Archbishop Purcell," *The Cincinnati Historical Society Bulletin*, 36 (1978).

Robert Trisco, *The Holy See and the Nascent Church in the Middle Western United States, 1826–1850* (Rome, 1962).

ANTHONY D. ANDREASSI

## QUAKERS FROM IRELAND

In his classic monograph, *Immigration of the Irish Quakers into Pennsylvania* (1902), Albert Cook Myers estimated that 1,500–2,000 Irish Friends entered Pennsylvania between 1682 and 1750. Approximate figures are not available for other areas. However, most of the immigration of Irish Quakers to America occurred before the Revolutionary War.

### THE SOCIETY OF FRIENDS IN IRELAND

In 1654, the first Quaker meeting in Ireland was held at the home of William Edmondson in Lurgan, County Ulster. Edmondson was typical of early converts to the Society of Friends: a conservative who was attracted to Quakerism as a radical extension of Puritanism. He had served in Cromwell's army from 1645 to 1652, and emigrated to Ireland in 1654. Many other Irish Quakers were also with Cromwell, having received grants of land in areas from which the native Irish had been expelled. Although George Fox's Society of Friends attracted primarily Protestant believers from all classes of society, it particularly appealed to craftsmen, farmers, and other working-class people. Most Quaker converts in Ireland were from the middle classes of English birth or descent; little success was seen among the Presbyterians of Scottish background or the native Roman Catholics.

Traveling Quaker ministers from England arrived in Ireland in 1654, holding meetings and preaching wherever they could. Edmondson himself had been convinced—a Quaker term for conversion—in 1653 when he visited Westmorland and met James Nayler. The former traveled with John Tiffin and went to Londonderry on a religious visit with Richard Clayton. William Edmondson was jailed in Armagh when he established a meeting at Grange. After his release, he was even more active, encouraging Irish Friends in the nonpayment of tithes. In the summer of 1655, Francis Howgill and Edward Burrough landed in Dublin and began to preach. They attracted many Irish converts. Howgill and Burrough were arrested and finally banished from Ireland. After the Restoration in 1660 in England, a law was passed forbidding Quakers to meet in public worship. Until the Act of Toleration was passed in 1689, Friends suffered imprisonment for failure to pay tithes, refusing to take an oath, and other nonconformities.

### EARLY PERIOD, 1682–1719

In Ireland, as elsewhere, Quakers endured persecution. However, excepting the matter of tithes, harassment of Quakers in Ireland was less severe than in England after the Restoration. In fact,

Irish Quakers benefited from a measure of political toleration in the late 1600s. By the early eighteenth century, however, the English Parliament passed legislation restricting competition from Irish-based industries. Only the linen industry escaped the restrictive regulations. A smaller economic base left the country vulnerable to bad harvests and recessions. In her article, "Quakers and Emigration from Ireland," Audrey Lockhart cites continuing resentment over tithes, the effect of the Test Act, oppressive landlordism, poor industrial prospects, recurrent economic recessions, and periods of famine, as some of the negative conditions that contributed to an increase in emigration after 1700.

It was the responsibility of the local monthly meeting to issue certificates of removal, the letters of recommendation for members who intended to transfer their membership to another meeting. Only two books of certificates survive from Ireland in the seventeenth century, one for Dublin, and one for Carlow. The Dublin volume dates from 1682, a year after the National Meeting had agreed that meetings should issue such documents, including a statement of the meeting's approval of the move and the member's marital status and/or clearness in relation to marriage. The dates of issue suggest that large groups of immigrants to America often traveled together. In Dublin in 1729, for instance, thirteen certificates are recorded to Pennsylvania alone, some individual certificates including entire families.

By some accounts, Irish Quaker meetings discouraged emigration simply to escape religious persecution, preferring Friends to endure imprisonment and other penalties for the sake of their Quaker beliefs. In 1682, Friends who signed Nicholas Newlin's certificate of removal from Mountmellick to Concord Monthly Meeting (Chester County, Pennsylvania), expressed outright dissatisfaction with his motives for the move. They cited: "godly jealousy . . . that his chief ground is fearfulness of suffering here for the testimony of Jesus."

Quaker merchants and ship owners who remained in Ireland profited from the surge in emigration by Quakers and non-Quakers alike. In fact, the testimony of integrity in all things, including business, brought the Quakers recognition and trust. Much of the early emigration of all groups from Ireland to America was directly promoted and facilitated by members of the Society of Friends.

William Penn distributed pamphlets, including *Some Account of the Province of Pennsylvania, etc.* (1681), throughout Ireland citing the natural resources, improvements, and other incentives to emigration. Early Irish settlers wrote back to their native land lauding the numerous advantages of the countryside.

Robert Turner, Samuel Clarridge and some other prominent Irish Friends were members of the Free Society of Traders; this group made a purchase of twenty thousand acres in Pennsylvania. In 1682, a shipload of Friends from Dublin sailed for America on the vessel of Quaker captain Thomas Lurting. They settled in the Irish Tenth in New Jersey and established a meeting at Newton, first held at the house of Mark Newby.

James Logan (1674–1751) was born in Lurgan, the son of a Scottish school teacher who became a Quaker. Logan became William Penn's secretary in 1699, and sailed with him to Pennsylvania the same year. Penn appointed him secretary of the province and clerk of the provincial council, a post in which he served until 1717. When the proprietor returned to England, Logan remained and served as Penn's land agent, representing the Penn family interests in the colony.

## MIDDLE PERIOD, 1719–1750

Most early Irish Quaker immigration was to the Middle Atlantic colonies. Myers found that ninety percent of Irish Quakers presented their certificates of removal to Philadelphia Monthly Meeting and to the monthly meetings of Chester County (including today's Delaware County). Quaker immigration reached its peak in 1729. Although it has been argued that the relationship between Quakers and Irish Catholics in Ireland deteriorated after 1719, the primary reason for emigration continued to be economic. On January 13, 1730, the *Pennsylvania Gazette* reported that a total of 1,150 Irish immigrants had landed in the province in the previous year. Of these, 925 were paying passengers and 220 indentured servants. This was, by far, the largest national group represented in the published figures. Previous reports in the same newspaper had described severe economic conditions in Ireland in 1729, forcing emigrants to endure the hazards of passage.

Emigrants had the choice of paying their own fares or of obtaining passage by entering indentured service, usually for four years. Some paid a part of their own fare, lessening their obligation. Quakers in England and Ireland sometimes helped prospective immigrants, usually heads of families, with gifts or loans of money. Emigration and growing trade expanded transatlantic Quaker family and business ties.

With expansion of the colonial frontier, many Irish Quakers joined the south and westward migrations. Some of these settlers moved into the Shenandoah Valley and established a monthly meeting at Opequan (Hopewell) in 1735. Others moved into North Carolina and founded Cane Creek and New Garden meetings.

## DECLINE, 1750 AND BEYOND

After 1750, the pattern of immigration began to change. Areas in Nova Scotia, New England, and the Carolinas opened up. Until the second half of the eighteenth century, for instance, the only Quaker meeting in South Carolina was located in Charleston. In 1751, a group of Irish Quaker immigrants from Timahoe in County Kildare, intending to settle in North Carolina on the land of Arthur Dobbs, mistakenly landed in South Carolina. Members of the Milhouse, Wyly, Tomlinson, Kelly, and Russell families had received certificates of removal from Dublin and Edenderry Monthly Meetings. Richard Milhous Nixon, the American president, was a maternal descendant of Thomas Milhous. The latter, son of John Milhous and Sarah Mickle, married Sarah Miller in 1721 at the meeting house in Timahoe. Thomas, Sarah, five children, and Sarah's parents were granted a certificate of removal from Dublin. They established a Quaker community at Wateree (Camden), about 130 miles from Charleston. The first few years in South Carolina were very difficult and there were a number of deaths. The new arrivals also suffered for their observance of the Quaker peace testimony. In 1762 Fredericksburg Monthly Meeting reported that two of its members had been taken into custody temporarily for refusing to bear arms, and that two others had goods seized and then restored to them. The migration of Quakers from northern colonies to the newly opened land in the West resulted in the establishment of a separate monthly meeting at Bush River in 1770. Some of the original Irish Quaker families at Wateree moved north to Virginia and North Carolina, and others, like Furnas, Kelly, and Milhouse, set-tled within the boundaries of Bush River. In 1783, Fredericksburg Monthly Meeting ceased to exist.

After the Revolution, increasing prosperity in their native country gave Quakers who had remained in Ireland little incentive to move to the new United States. But other Irish immigrants continued to arrive. Some embraced the religion of their Quaker employers. Daniel Kent was born a Methodist in Limerick, the son of William and Anne Kent whose families had settled in Ireland several generations earlier. In 1785, he traveled to Cork and Waterford looking for work as a cutler. Being unsuccessful, he indentured himself to a ship's captain and took passage to Philadelphia. Upon arrival, Kent was bound to Joseph Hawley, a Quaker farmer in Chester County. He completed his term in three years and later joined Bradford Monthly Meeting. In 1788, Kent wrote: "I like this Country Better than I did at my first Settlement here So I think I could spend my Lifetime here And Though I have to work Harder here than at home my Wages being proportional I Choose this Country before my Native Country."

## CONCLUSION

Although Irish Friends made no attempt to live apart from the larger community of English Quakers, unlike the Welsh or Germans, some scholars have argued that they did distinguish themselves from their English counterparts in some ways. Gerelyn Hollingsworth, in an article, "Irish Quakers in Colonial Pennsylvania," contends that although a minority in the Province, Irish Friends held proportionately more public offices. In general, they arrived with more capital; many were able to get an earlier start in commerce. Also, their anti-Proprietary sentiments and activities were more pronounced than those of the English settlers. They sided with the Calverts in the boundary dispute between Penn and Lord Baltimore, opposed Penn's quitrents, and exhibited other antiproprietary behavior in the provincial assembly. Other researchers, including Albert Cook Myers, have hypothesized that the Irish Quakers, more inured to privation and hardship, were more able than English or Welsh Friends to cope with the difficulties of settling a new country.

But new Irish Quaker arrivals were absorbed quickly into the much larger English Quaker communities. This was primarily due to the fact that most members of the Society of Friends in Ireland came from families who had been resident in Ireland for only one or two generations. They had English surnames, and were already well connected to the trans-Atlantic Quaker community. It is clear that the Irish Friends did not attempt to maintain physically separate communities from the English and other Quakers. They were quickly assimilated. Intermarriage and migration make it almost impossible to separate the groups, limiting the ability of the scholar to ascribe unique characteristics to descendants of Irish Quakers in America beyond the first generation.

*See* Emigration: 17th and 18th Centuries

Kenneth L. Carroll, "The Irish Quaker Community at Camden," *The South Carolina Historical Magazine* (1976).

Olive C. Goodbody, *Guide to Irish Quaker Records, 1654–1860* (Dublin, 1967).

Gerelyn Hollingsworth, "Irish Quakers in Colonial Pennsylvania: A Forgotten Segment of Society," in *Journal of the Lancaster County Historical Society* (1975).

Audrey Lockhart, "The Quakers and Immigration from Ireland to the North American Colonies," in *Quaker History* (1988).

Albert Cook Myers, *Immigration of the Irish Quakers into Pennsylvania, 1682–1750, with Their Early History in Ireland* (Swarthmore, 1902).

Maurice J. Wigham, *The Irish Quakers: A Short History of the Religious Society of Friends in Ireland* (Dublin, 1992).

PATRICIA C. O'DONNELL

## QUILL, MICHAEL JOSEPH ("Mike") (1905–1966)

Labor leader, politician. Michael Quill was born in Kilgarvan, County Kerry, September 18, 1905, second youngest of eight children (three girls, five boys), of John Daniel Quill and the former Margaret Lynch of Ballygourney, County Cork. Gortloughera, the family farm, was three miles from the village of Kilgarvan. Michael was educated in the Kilgarvan national school. Quill's father was a dedicated Irish nationalist and village historian, who instructed his children in the lore of the Land League and the Fenians. The father joined the South Kerry volunteers of the Irish Republican Army after the Easter Rising of 1916. The farm became a hotbed of IRA activity. Harassed by the "Black and Tans" after World War I, the family thereafter opposed the treaty with Britain which divided Ireland. Several sons joined antitreaty forces in the civil war which followed. Having chosen the losing side, they opted to leave for America when it ended.

### COMING TO AMERICA

Michael sailed from Cobh in March of 1926, two years after his brother John departed. Without urban skills Quill pursued a living in a series of menial jobs—doorman, elevator operator, sandhog (digging subway tunnels), door to door salesman and so forth. At length he settled for a job as ticket agent in the New York subway system. Shortly, the Great Depression closed in. The job yielded pay in the thirty to forty cents per-hour range—with twelve-hour days and seven-day work weeks. For an Irish rebel this was not satisfactory.

### ORGANIZING TRANSPORT UNION

New York transit firms hired numerous Irish immigrants in semiskilled jobs involving contact with passengers for two reasons: they were willing to work for low pay and they spoke English. In prosperous times turnover was heavy. In the depression, however, alternative jobs were non-existent. Efforts to unionize normally failed because subway companies had developed effective anti-union methods including company unions, labor spies and using Pinkerton agents to infiltrate fledgling organizations to provoke premature strikes which failed—followed by use of imported strike breakers.

Mike Quill's generation, however, proved equal to overcoming these obstacles. Men in their late twenties or early thirties with experience in the IRA, they understood the importance of secrecy and discipline. They could communicate in Gaelic to confound spies and had proven courage. Furthermore, they received financial aid and advice from Irish Workers Clubs established by the Communist party under William Z. Foster. In addition, Clan na Gael associations, Irish nationalist in orientation, welcomed veterans of the civil war in the old country. At Clan na Gael social gatherings in Tara Hall on west Sixty-sixth Street, Mike Quill met Austin Hogan, Gerald O'Reilly, Thomas O'Shea and eight or nine other IRA veterans who provided a nucleus for founding the Transport Workers Union (TWU) in 1934. Mike Quill was elected president in 1935.

In structure the TWU was industrial rather than craft-based, having been influenced by ideas of James Connolly, Irish socialist and nationalist hero executed for his role in the Easter Rising. As such TWU had an affinity with the Committee for Industrial Organization (CIO)—from which it received a charter in 1937 signed by CIO president John L. Lewis. Quill became a member of the national executive board of the Congress of Industrial Organizations, successor to the Committee for Industrial Organizations in 1938.

Quill and other leaders of TWU followed the Communist party line. For example, in 1937 Quill was elected to the New York City Council on the American Labor party (ALP) ticket. The ALP was established by (non-Communist) union officials in the needle trades. He remained for one term, but then repudiated ALP for its condemnation of the Russian-German treaty of 1939—a treaty given fulsome praise in Communist publications. As an independent, Quill ran twice more for the same office, succeeding in the second try. Again in 1945, Quill, often referred to as "Red Mike" in the daily press, won a city council seat—this time accepting ALP support. For complex pragmatic reasons ALP had endorsed him though he still hewed to the party line. During this same period he was an officer of the New York Area Council of the CIO, winning its presidency in 1947. At that time delegates from Communist-dominated unions enjoyed substantial power in the Area CIO Council.

### BREAK WITH COMMUNISM

In early 1948 Quill's support for the party line began to fall apart. For one thing the party's insistence on holding subway fares to five cents precluded any wage increase for TWU members in Quill's opinion. The other matter was party line endorsement of Henry Wallace for president in 1948, while the national CIO backed Harry Truman. Quill refused to alienate Philip Murray, president of the CIO and, with Murray's financial aid, ousted party liners from leadership positions in the TWU at the Chicago national convention of the union in December of 1948. *Daily Worker* columns now referred to him as Mike "Judas" Quill. Quill was a delegate from the CIO to conventions of the International Confederation of Free Trade Unions—founded by opponents of the Communist-dominated World Federation of Trade Unions. He attended ICFTU conventions in 1949 and 1950.

On December 26, 1937 Quill married Mary Theresa "Mollie" O'Neill from Cahirciveen, County Kerry, whom he had met in New York years earlier. They had one child, John Daniel. His first wife died of cancer in 1959. He married Shirley Uzin in 1961.

### LEADERSHIP

Mike Quill enjoyed talents which enabled him to become an effective, charismatic leader. Early on, he became well known at social gatherings of Irish immigrants for his gregarious, witty personality. As someone with an Irish Republican background he could identify with former IRA militants, and they with him. Chosen to replace Thomas O'Shea, first head of TWU, after that individual, known as "pope roaster" for his anti-clericalism, advocated using dynamite as an organizing device, Quill proved more sensitive to the largely Catholic workforce in New York transit. Though accepting aid and instruction from Communist sources, he regularly appeared at Sunday Mass in Irish neighborhoods to blunt their objections. He welcomed support from these neighborhoods later when he broke with the Communist party.

His County Kerry brogue and outrageous humor were well suited to union convention and public oratory. He was pragmatic enough to recognize that the future of the TWU required change when Communist connections became more of a liability than a help. His orchestration of the 1948 TWU convention provides ample evidence of his capacity to give direction to the union.

### Last Hurrah

In one of his final television appearances he was seen tearing up an injunction against the TWU strike of 1966 and shouting: "That judge can drop dead in his black robes" (*New York Times,* December 31, 1965, 1, 3). Subsequently he was jailed for contempt, hospitalized and later released after a satisfactory settlement with the New York Transit Authority. He died of heart failure January 28, 1966.

At his funeral mass in St. Patrick's Cathedral, celebrant Monsignor Charles Owen Rice said of him: "He ran a good union with complete honesty and had no care for personal wealth or luxury" (*Pittsburgh Catholic,* February 3, 1966, 4).

*See* Labor Movement

Joshua Freeman, *In Transit* (New York, 1989).
Shirley Uzin Quill, *Mike Quill-Himself* (New York, 1984).
L. H. Whittemore, *The Man Who Ran the Subways* (New York, 1968).

L. A. O'DONNELL

## QUINDLEN, ANNA (1953– )

Journalist. novelist. Anna Quindlen is one of the finest contemporary American writers. She was born in Philadelphia, Pennsylvania, on July 8, 1953 to an Irish-American father and an Italian-American mother. Married with three children, she makes her home in New Jersey.

Quindlen attended Barnard College and after graduating started her professional career as a reporter for the *New York Post,*

Anna Quindlen

where she had worked as a student. In 1977, she began writing for the *New York Times* as a general assignment reporter and rose to write the "About New York" column, becoming the youngest person to whom it had ever been assigned. She held various positions at the *Times,* including deputy metropolitan editor, and wrote its "Life in the Thirties" and "Public and Private" columns. Her work earned her the Pulitzer Prize for commentary in 1992. Fiction, however, has always been Quindlen's passion, and in 1991 she published her first novel, *Object Lessons,* which was followed by *One True Thing* in 1994. Her book *Black and Blue* (1998) was on the *New York Times Bestseller List* and was chosen by Oprah Winfrey for her book club. Quindlen's fiction is deeply intimate and focuses on women's lives and the choices they face. Whether it is Ellen in *One True Thing* telling the story of witnessing her mother's battle with cancer or Frannie who leaves her abusive husband in *Black and Blue,* both narrators tell stories of women and family and how they survive from day to day. One of Quindlen's gifts is her ability to develop authentic voices for her characters so their stories feel like those of a confidant or friend. While her fiction isn't explicitly Irish-American, the family in *Object Lessons,* like herself, is half Irish and Italian and Frannie in *Black and Blue* comes from an Irish-American family. Themes of motherhood and sacrifice resonate in her work.

Although Quindlen's full-time job is writing fiction, her columns offer a glimpse into who she is and how her craft as a writer developed. In addition to her novels, her work from the *Times* has been collected. Her nonfiction books, *Living Out Loud,* and *Thinking Out Loud: Reflections on the Personal, the Political, the Public and the Private,* were published in 1988 and 1993 respectively.

In the introduction to *Living Out Loud,* Quindlen writes how the death of her mother when she was nineteen changed her life: "It was not until the aftermath of my mother's death that I began to realize that I would have to fashion a life for myself—and that is what I have been trying to do, in a workmanlike way, ever since." Quindlen is a craftsperson who has made writing her trade. Using her life as a starting point, she has been praised for her candor about her experience as a woman, wife and mother. She has channeled that same type of introspection into her characters so readers of her fiction are rewarded with a profound sense of discovery. Quindlen has examined the lives of her fictional characters with the same grace with which she has "fashioned" her own.

*See* Fiction, Irish-American

*Contemporary Authors,* volume 138.
Vineta Colby, ed., *World Authors 1985–1990* (Wilson, H. W. 1995).
Anna Quindlen, *Living Out Loud* (Random House, 1988).

CALEDONIA KEARNS

## QUINN, ARTHUR HOBSON (1875–1960)

Educator, literary historian and biographer. Quinn was born in Philadelphia, Pennsylvania, to Irish descendants Michael A. and Mary (MacDonough) Quinn. He attended the University of Pennsylvania in 1894 and received a B.S. He promptly became a mathematics professor and later an English instructor. Following this time, he went to the University of Munich and studied modern philology and then returned to the University of Pennsylvania for his Ph.D. in 1899.

Quinn's interest led him to write some fiction and to begin teaching courses in literature. In 1905 he taught a course on American literature and in 1918 the first course on American drama. He then produced several works, including: *Representative American Plays* (1917); *Contemporary American Plays* (1923); *The Literature of America* (1929); *The Early Plays of James A. Herne* (1940) and *The Complete Poems and Tales of Edgar Allan Poe* (1946). Among the most influential of his works are his contributions to the studies of Edgar Allan Poe, of which he was able to retrieve and expose new data as was produced in his work *Edgar Allan Poe* in 1941.

In 1950 Quinn also edited *A Treasury of Edith Wharton* and capitalized on his interest in national literature by becoming general editor of *Literature of the American People* in 1951. For his outstanding contributions he was named the John Welsh centennial professor of history and English literature in 1939. Quinn's contributions continued to benefit the generations after him. He became an emeritus professor, special lecturer and continued his work until his death on October 16, 1960.

*New York Times,* obituary (October 17, 1960).
Jay B. Hubbell, ed., *Eight American Authors* (1956).
*Dictionary of American Biography,* supplement 6.

JOY HARRELL

## QUINN, JOHN (1870–1924)

Lawyer, patron of the arts. Known by virtually every major modern western artist and writer of the early twentieth century, and personal friends with many of them, John Quinn was born in Tiffin, Ohio on April 24, 1870 to James William Quinn of County Limerick, Ireland and Mary (Quinlan) of County Cork. He grew up in nearby Fostoria, Ohio with six brothers and sisters (two others died in infancy). He began to collect books even as a youngster, and after matriculating for a year at the University

John Quinn

of Michigan, went to Washington, D.C., as private secretary to a friend of his mother, Governor Charles Foster, who had become Secretary of the Treasury to President Benjamin Harrison. Quinn had campaigned for Foster for Congress. While in Washington, Quinn earned a law degree at Georgetown University in 1893, and took another law degree at Harvard in 1895. He moved to New York City, working in the law offices of General Benjamin F. Tracy, and later joining the firm of Alexander and Colby there in 1900. His political experience, combined with knowledge of corporation and financial law drew him into Democratic Tammany contacts. His mother and two sisters died in 1902, affecting him profoundly. But that same year, Quinn went abroad to England and Ireland, the first of many trips to Europe, where he became acquainted with the Yeats family from whom he bought paintings, and entered the literary circles of the Yeats, Douglas Hyde, George Moore, and Lady Gregory among others, whose continued friendships would bring Quinn substantial volumes of correspondence. His legal assistance to writers bought him many manuscripts, proof copies, and limited editions, and gained him contacts with such prominent writers as Ezra Pound, Joseph Conrad and James Joyce.

Back in New York, he supported Irish Home Rule and a branch of the Irish Literary Society. By 1906 Quinn headed his own law office. His interest in tax law led to a successful campaign to remove duty on modern works of art brought into the U.S., and protected the rights of living artists. Quinn developed an interest in the works of modern French, British and American artists, and he gradually amassed a personal art collection of works by such notables as Picasso, Matisse, Gauguin, Brancusi, Cézanne, Augustus and Gwen John, and Walt Kuhn. He was heavily involved in organizing the controversial 1913 International Exhibition of Modern Art, known as the Armory Show, held in New York, one of the greatest displays of contemporary art ever held to that date. Quinn also tried (1920) and won in the Supreme Court the case that settled the constitutionality of the Trading with the Enemy Act of 1918 which upheld the validity of seizing alien-owned property in the U.S.

John Quinn had collected a library of 18,000 items, two-thirds of which were sold in 1923. These included all of Joseph Conrad's manuscripts and the manuscript of James Joyce's *Ulysses,* which were bought by the Philadelphia dealer A. S. W. Rosenbach. After Quinn's death, 2,800 of his art works were offered for sale in Paris in 1926, and the rest, 500 pictures and 300 sculptures, were sold in New York in 1927. Tall and energetic, cosmopolitan John Quinn combined law, literature and art as a major patron and benefactor of the arts in the twentieth century. Though a nominal Catholic for most of his life, he accepted the last rites of the church before his death on July 28, 1924; he was buried with his family beneath a Celtic cross in Fostoria, Ohio.

Benjamin Lawrence Reid, *The Man from New York; John Quinn and His Friends* (New York, 1968).
Aline B. Saarinen, *The Proud Possessors* (New York, 1958).
Judith Zilczer, *"The Noble Buyer": John Quinn Patron of the Avant-Garde* (Washington, D.C., 1978).

ANNA M. DONNELLY

# R

## REAGAN, RONALD WILSON (1911–   )

Actor, governor, President of the United States. Ronald Reagan's paternal roots are in Doolis, West Tipperary, his forebears arriving in the United States in 1856 by way of England and Canada, and settling in rural Illinois. The family name underwent changes in the process—going from O'Regan to Regan to Reagan. The family's religion was Roman Catholic, and when Ronald Reagan's parents—John Edward and Nelle (Wilson) Reagan—married, it was in a Catholic ceremony. The vows were exchanged in a rectory as Nelle was not Catholic. In 1910 Nelle, a conscientious reader and quoter of the Bible, joined the Christian Church, an offshoot of Presbyterianism, and she raised the two children of her marriage in that church—John, who was baptized a Catholic according to the marital pledge; Ronald, who was not. John would return to Catholicism; Ronald, baptized in 1922 into the Christian Church, remains a Protestant. The brothers were born in Tampico, Illinois, Ronald on February 6, 1911.

Ronald Reagan has described his childhood as "a Huck Finn idyll," but it hardly could have been. His father was an alcoholic, and the family was forced to move often as he lost job after job. Most of Reagan's growing-up was in Dixon, Illinois, and it was in that small town that he went to high school, then headed off to Eureka College, about one hundred miles' distant, on a partial athletic scholarship. Reagan received his degree in 1932, and went to work as a radio sportscaster. In 1937 he accompanied the Chicago Cubs baseball team to their California spring-training

Ronald Reagan

camp and used the occasion to obtain a screen test. This led to a career in motion pictures and later television that spanned almost three decades. His acting was generally regarded as competent, but short of stardom quality. His credits include no classic films.

Reagan's first foray into politics was with a speech in 1945 at Hollywood Legion Stadium sponsored by a committee of Hollywood artists and other professionals who had originally banded together in support of Franklin Delano Roosevelt and the New Deal. A Democrat at the time, Reagan described himself as a "hemophiliac liberal" and there was talk of his standing for Congress. Several years' service as president and board member of the Screen Actors Guild raised his political profile and quickened his liberal image. In fact, Reagan was in ideological transition. A lifelong hatred for fascism had worked its way to the fore in a special dislike of Communism, and before the 1940s were over Reagan was enlisted by the FBI as an informant on alleged Communist sympathizers within the Screen Actors Guild. Thereafter, a strong anti-Communism was to color his perspectives, personal and political.

Reagan, by now a conservative Republican, arrived on the national political scene in 1964 as a campaigner for Senator Barry Goldwater, delivering in the final days of the campaign a nationwide speech that electrified a network audience. The speech did not save the election for Goldwater, but it caught the attention of Republican leaders and helped seed the idea of a Reagan presidency. The day after the election, conservatives in Owosso, Michigan, for instance, formed a "Republicans for Ronald Reagan" club.

The road to the presidency would lead through Sacramento, where Ronald Reagan sat two terms as Governor of California—from 1967–1974. Leaving office, he employed his time as a businessman, rancher and commentator on public policy. After testing the presidential waters in 1976, he gained the 1980 Republican nomination for President, and went on to oust Democratic presidential incumbent Jimmy Carter by a landslide vote. He won a second four-year term with a similarly convincing victory in 1984 over Democratic challenger Walter Mondale.

Reagan proved a surprisingly successful, thoroughly conservative President. He worked effectively with Congress, pushing through large-scale tax cuts, tax reform and cutbacks in government programs he deemed bloated. He signed a bill designed to protect the solvency of Social Security, but at the same time he worked strenuously to build up further the nation's military machine. In 1982 he sent the military as a peacekeeping force to Lebanon, and in 1983 he ordered troops into Grenada to restore democratic rule after a Marxist government had been installed there. His opposition to international terrorism prompted him to order air strikes against Libya. He supported anti-Communist governments in Central America, but was open enough to hold four summits with Soviet leader Mikhail Gorbachev. The 1987 summit led to the elimination of short- and medium-sized missiles from Europe. Domestically, the economy prospered under Reagan's leadership, though there were high budget deficits throughout his eight years in office.

Reagan survived an assassination attempt in 1981. Later in life he came down with Alzheimer's disease. He made the news known in 1994 in a moving handwritten letter to the American people.

John A. Barnes, *Irish-American Landmarks: A Traveler's Guide* (New York, 1995).

Lou Cannon, *Reagan* (New York, 1982).
Anne Edwards, *Early Reagan: The Rise to Power* (New York, 1987).

JOHN DEEDY

## REDICK, DAVID (c. 1750–1805)

Surveyor, lawyer, land speculator, and political leader of western Pennsylvania's Irish in the late eighteenth century. Redick was born c.1750 into a Presbyterian family in north County Down, and immigrated to Pennsylvania shortly before the American Revolution, first settling in Lancaster County. Still landless in 1779, at some point Redick married Ann Hoge, whose father and uncles, also from Ulster, owned several thousand acres in southwestern Pennsylvania. In 1781, when Washington County was created, Redick surveyed that portion of the Hoge estate that became Washington town, the county seat, where he and his family settled and, during the next decade, acquired title to at least 1,000 acres. Admitted to the bar in 1782, Redick associated with George Bryan, William Findley, and John Smilie in defense of Pennsylvania's 1776 constitution and in opposition to the Federal Constitution of 1787. In 1786 Washington County elected Redick to the state's Supreme Executive Council; in October 1788 he served for a few weeks as Pennsylvania's Vice-President, following the incumbent's early resignation; and in 1790 he was a delegate to the state constitutional convention. His statewide political ambitions thwarted by Federalist opposition, Redick retired to Washington County, where in 1791–92 he became prothonotary and clerk of the county courts and an early leader of the Jeffersonian Republican Party. Chastened by Federalist accusations that he had abetted "treason" and "anarchy" in the Whiskey Rebellion (1794), Redick quickly became "prominent in defense of law, order, and the constitution," resigned from Washington town's Democratic-Republican Society, and joined William Findley in vain efforts to quell the agitation and persuade President Washington that federal military intervention was unnecessary. After 1794 Redick abandoned politics for lucrative land speculation and development in western Pennsylvania and the Ohio country, often in association with moderate, Ulster-born Federalists such as William Irvine.

B. Crumrine, *History of Washington County . . .* (Philadelphia, 1882).
R. J. Ferguson, *Early Western Pennsylvania Politics* (Pittsburgh, 1938).

KERBY MILLER

## REDSHAW, THOMAS DILLON (1944– )

Scholar and editor. Thomas Dillon Redshaw (born August 14, 1944) has played a central role in scholarly publishing in Irish Studies in the United States.

Born in Salem, Massachusetts, Redshaw's middle name recognizes what he calls his "remote Ulster antecedents," his maternal grandfather Thomas Stevenson Dillon. He attended Mount Hermon school before earning an undergraduate degree in English from Tufts in 1966.

Redshaw's interest in Irish literature began with a summer seminar at Columbia University in 1965 taught by Kevin Sullivan. "It was great stuff," he would tell an interviewer years later, "Passion, sex, puns, rhetoric. I thought, 'That's what I want to study, not history or philosophy.'"

Redshaw attended University College, Dublin in 1966–67, where he earned an M.A. in Anglo-Irish Literature, studying with Roger McHugh. He was a lively participant in the literary life of Dublin during his student years, attending and organizing readings and frequently contributing poems to student and literary magazines. His first two collections of poetry were both published in Dublin: *Such a Heart Dances Out* (New Writers' Press, 1971), and *Heimaey* (Dolmen Press, 1974). Two further collections of his poetry were issued by small presses in Minnesota in the 1970s.

Redshaw attended New York University from 1967–70, where he wrote his dissertation on the poetry of John Montague, under the direction of M. L. Rosenthal. He joined the English faculty of the University (then College) of St. Thomas in Minnesota in 1971, where he has taught since. In 1974, Redshaw began his association with the quarterly journal *Éire-Ireland*. He served as associate and assistant editor of *Éire-Ireland* until 1986; after a three year hiatus in service for that journal—during which period Redshaw spent one year as a Senior Fellow in Irish Studies at The Queen's University, Belfast—he returned as editor in 1989. During his editorship he expanded the journal's editorial board, introduced a section devoted to new poetry by Irish writers, and reinvigorated its art covers.

After resigning from *Éire-Ireland* in 1995, Redshaw and many of his editorial colleagues launched *New Hibernia Review/Iris Éireannach Nua,* published by the St. Thomas's Center for Irish Studies. The first issue appeared in March, 1997, and it has provided a regular quarterly record of Irish Studies since that time. Besides editing *New Hibernia Review,* Redshaw also serves as academic director of the center.

Redshaw's own research and publication history has focused on mid-century and contemporary Irish poetry, notably Austin Clarke, George Reavey, Thomas McCarthy and John Montague. In 1988, he compiled and edited *Hill Field: Poems and Memoirs for John Montague,* in observance of the poet's sixtieth birthday. His articles and reviews have appeared in such places as *Irish University Review, Irish Literary Supplement, Tracks, Linen Hall Review, Studies,* and *Études Irlandaises.*

*See Éire-Ireland*

JAMES SILAS ROGERS

## REHAN, ADA (1860–1916)

Actress. Born at Limerick, Ireland, to Thomas and Harriet Crehan, Rehan immigrated with her family to Brooklyn, New York, and began her acting career in Newark, New Jersey. It was due to a printing error that Rehan was billed as Ada Rehan rather than Crehan, her family name. Following her successful debut performance, a co-worker convinced her to retain the name Rehan.

Rehan worked for many stock companies and theater troupes and was a favored Shakesperean actress. In her role as Bianca in *The Taming of the Shrew,* she was discovered by Augustin Daly and invited to join his New York theater company. In 1879 Daly opened his own theater and Rehan appeared as Nelly Beers in *Love's Young Dream.* She remained with Daly until the theater's close twenty years later; during her time with Daly, Rehan became the leading woman of the company and dominated the stage with her many performances. She played a variety of roles and especially excelled at comedic performances. Among her more memorable performances are her roles in *Twelfth Night, The School for Scandal, Cyrano de Bergerac, The Great Ruby, The Taming of the Shrew* and *Divorce.*

Rehan gave her last performance at a benefit given at the Metropolitan Opera House in New York in 1905. She then retired in New York and died at Roosevelt Hospital in 1916 from an arterial illness.

William Winter, *The Wallet of Time,* vol. 2 (1913).
———, *Ada Rehan* (1898).
L. C. Strang, *Famous Actresses of the Day in America* (1899).
*Dictionary of American Biography,* vol. 15.

JOY HARRELL

## REILLY, ROBERT T. (1914–   )

Businessman, writer. Born into an Irish-American family in Lowell, Mass., Robert Reilly joined the 78th Division in World War II, served with distinction and was decorated after his release from a POW camp.

After graduate school, he was an advertising executive; and later, after moving to Nebraska, became a partner in the advertising firm of Holland, Dreves and Reilly. He joined the University of Nebraska and occupied the Keyser Chair, teaching business writing, advanced writing and Irish literature.

Ever active in Irish affairs, he wrote hundreds of magazine and newspaper features and television scripts and has published 13 books, including *Red Hugh, Prince of Donegal* (later a Walt Disney film and miniseries); *Come Along to Ireland; Facets of Diamond* (poetry); and *The Omaha Experience.*

JOAN GLAZIER

## REPUBLICANISM, IRISH-AMERICAN

Organizations dedicated to Irish freedom were founded wherever the Irish settled in the United States. Just as in Ireland, these organizations favored two principal approaches: constitutional nationalism, which sought greater autonomy for Ireland within the British Empire through gradual, peaceful change; and physical force republicanism, which insisted on outright independence by whatever means necessary. Especially between 1798 and 1921, the movement for Irish freedom took on a vital transatlantic dimension, with the American Irish generally, and those of New York City in particular, playing a critical role in winning independence for Ireland. Thereafter, Irish-Americans have played a diminished but still significant part in Irish nationalist affairs.

### From the United Irishmen to the Young Irelanders

The tradition of republicanism on both sides of the Atlantic can be traced to the United Irishmen of the 1790s. Ireland at that time had its own parliament, with autonomy over local affairs. But the United Irishmen, led by Theobald Wolfe Tone (1763–98), wanted a fully independent republic and were willing to fight in order to get it. Irish republican clubs, including the American Society of United Irishmen, were formed in the U.S. in the 1790s, combining strong Irish support for Thomas Jefferson and his Republican faction with an equally strong antipathy toward the then-dominant Federalist party. After the crushing defeat of a major insurrection in Ireland in 1798, many prominent Irish republicans came to the United States as political exiles, among them Thomas Addis Emmet (1764–1827), William MacNeven (1763–1841), and William Sampson (1764–1836).

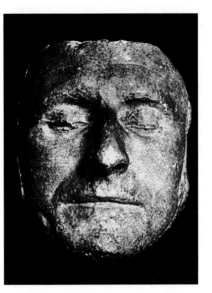

Theobald Wolfe Tone's death mask

The movement for Irish freedom in the first half of the nineteenth century was dominated by the towering figure of Daniel O'Connell (1775–1847), one of the chief architects of Irish constitutional nationalism. After winning Catholic emancipation in 1829, O'Connell devoted the remainder of his life to a campaign to repeal the Act of Union of 1800, which had abolished the Dublin parliament and placed Ireland under direct rule from London. O'Connell initially gained massive support in the United States, only to lose it when his principled stand against slavery alienated most Irish-Americans. Impatient with O'Connell's peaceful strategy and moderate goals, a group of younger nationalists broke away to form the Young Ireland movement in the early 1840s, launching an abortive rebellion in 1848. Many Young Irelanders subsequently settled in the United States, temporarily or permanently, including Thomas D'Arcy McGee (1825–68), John Blake Dillon (1816–66), Thomas Francis Meagher (1823–67), and John Mitchel (1815–75).

### The Fenians, Clan na Gael, and the New Departure

It was another veteran of 1848, John O'Mahony (1816–77), who founded the Fenian Brotherhood in New York City in 1858. A sister organization to the Irish Revolutionary Brotherhood, organized in Dublin by James Stephens (1825–1901) in the same year, its aim was to rid Ireland of English rule by providing American money and manpower to encourage insurrection. By 1865 it had attracted 250,000 followers, many of them Civil War veterans, and an Irish Republican government on the American model had been set up at Philadelphia. By 1870, however, Fenianism lay in ruins on both sides of the Atlantic, following an abortive uprising in Ireland and three failed invasions of Canada, designed to provoke war between the United States and England. The Irish political exile, Jeremiah O'Donovan Rossa (1831–1915), assumed the Fenian leadership in New York City in the 1870s, but the dynamite campaign he launched against British cities thereafter was unpopular among Irish-Americans, not to mention Americans generally. By the 1870s, the Fenians had been overshadowed by a new republican organization, Clan na Gael, which had close links to the Irish Republican Brotherhood in Dublin. Its leader, John Devoy (1842–1928), who had arrived in New York City in 1871 on the same ship as O'Donovan Rossa, was the chief ideologue of Irish republicanism on either side of the Atlantic in the late nineteenth century. For most of the forty-year period before the insurrection of 1916, however, militant republicanism of the type espoused by Devoy was a distinctly minority pursuit in both Ireland and America, paling by comparison with the movement for Home Rule.

The Home Rule movement, which demanded autonomy for Ireland along the lines of the Dublin parliament of the late eighteenth century, reached its peaks under the leadership of Charles Stewart Parnell (1846–91) in the 1880s and John Redmond (1856–1918) in the decade before World War I. While the goal of Home Rule was ultimately antithetical to that of hard-line republicanism, temporary coalitions between the two nationalist traditions were possible, the most powerful of them being the New Departure of the early 1880s which brought together Parnell, Devoy, and the nationalist land reformer Michael Davitt (1846–1906) in a potentially very powerful alliance. Predictably, the alliance soon divided over goals and strategy, but not before Irish nationalism had assumed a powerful new American dimension. Parnell and his followers repeatedly visited America in the 1880s, as did Davitt, who gained the vocal support of the Irish-American radical Patrick Ford (1837–1913). And the New Departure confirmed the status of New York City-based John Devoy as the preeminent exponent of the physical force tradition of Irish nationalism.

### FROM HOME RULE TO THE FREE STATE

Irish-American republicanism retained its role as a crucial auxiliary to hard-line Irish nationalism in the early twentieth century, playing a central role in the planning of the Easter 1916 rebellion and in subsequent fund-raising and political agitation on behalf of an Irish republic. After the enactment of Home Rule in 1914 was followed by its postponement for the duration of World War I, Irish republicans on both sides of the Atlantic acted on their long-standing adage that "England's difficulty is Ireland's opportunity" by launching an insurrection in the midst of the war. Irish-American republicans John Devoy and Daniel P. Cohalan, the new leader of Clan na Gael, sought alliances with Germany, financed the visit of Roger Casement to that country in search of military support, and lent substantial financial and military support to the insurrection of 1916. Among the leaders of the rebellion were several men who had spent time in the United States, the most prominent being James Connolly (1868–1916) and Thomas Clarke (1857–1916). The Irish declaration of independence issued in 1916 acknowledged the substantial debt owed to Irish republicans in the United States when it stated that Ireland's uprising was "supported by her exiled children in America."

The brutal executions that followed the insurrection provoked a remarkable shift in public opinion away from constitutional nationalism and in favor of physical force and independence on both sides of the Atlantic. With a de facto republic in place after 1916, Sinn Fein rapidly replaced the Irish Parliamentary party as the embodiment of nationalism in Ireland, while the replacement of the constitutionalist United Irish League of America (UILA) by the Irish Race Conference and Daniel Cohalan's Friends of Irish Freedom (FOIF) marked the same transition in the United States. These latter organizations exerted considerable pressure on President Woodrow Wilson to press the case for Irish independence, especially at the postwar peace conference at Versailles, but to no avail. Thereafter, Cohalan and his followers increasingly shifted their attention from the cause of Irish indepen-

dence to a campaign against Wilson's League of Nations. When the president of the de facto Irish Republic, Eamon de Valera (1882–1975), toured the United States in 1920 he grew increasingly frustrated with the immersion of FOIF in purely American politics. De Valera established his own rival organization, the American Association for the Recognition of the Irish Republic (AARIR), so that the almost six million dollars he had raised in republican bonds could be sent directly back to Ireland. So bitter was the dispute between de Valera and the Irish-American republican leaders that Devoy and Cohalan supported the Free State against de Valera during the Irish civil war in 1922, even though de Valera's stand on republican principle in that conflict more closely resembled their own intransigent position over the previous decades.

### IRISH-AMERICAN REPUBLICANISM SINCE 1921

While hard-line Irish republicans fought a civil war because the new Free State government fell short of the goal of full republican independence, the differences between the two sides were negligible from the vantage point of the United States. Irish-Americans gave the republican rebels little support or sympathy. But many embittered republicans made their way to the United States after the Irish civil war, keeping alive the hard-line tradition in a manner analogous to the IRA in Ireland, which was outlawed and went underground. This hard-line tradition has reemerged with renewed vigor since the late 1960s, with the resumption of "the Troubles" in Northern Ireland.

The current "Troubles" began as a movement for civil and political rights for Ulster Catholics, inspired to some extent by developments in the American South. Among the American Irish, however, this early movement met with little support. Indeed, when the outspoken nationalist leader Bernadette Devlin toured the United States in the late 1960s and linked the plight of Catholics in Northern Ireland with that of African-Americans in the South, she was bitterly denounced by many Irish-Americans. But when the breakaway Provisional IRA assumed leadership of the struggle in the early 1970s, emphasizing a united Irish republic rather than social justice, the American Irish were considerably more receptive. Despite the efforts of some prominent Irish-Americans (including Senators Edward Kennedy and Daniel Patrick Moynihan, Representative Tip O'Neill, Governor Hugh Carey, and businessman Tony O'Reilly) to pursue peaceful avenues of economic and legal change, the primary contribution of Irish-American nationalists over the last generation has been to provide money and munitions to the republican movement.

The most powerful of the contemporary Irish-American republican organizations was the Irish Northern Aid Committee. Popularly known by its acronym, NORAID, it was founded in 1970 by Michael Flannery, a veteran of the Irish war of independence and civil war, in close cooperation with the other American-based republican veterans and leaders of the Provisional IRA in Ireland. Although NORAID claimed that its fund-raising is strictly for "humanitarian" purposes, few people doubted that the bulk of the money it raised in America was used to finance the purchase of arms. Arms and munitions were also shipped directly from the United States to Ireland, leading to a series of sensational court cases, such as those of George Harrison and his associates in 1982, or the "Boston Three" in 1990. And Irish- and American-born republicans like Peter Gabriel McMullan, Dessie Macken, William Quinn, and Joseph Doherty were at the center of celebrated trials which tested the limits of treaties on extradition and political asylum (the first two winning their right to stay in the U.S. but the other two being extradited or deported).

In the late 1990s, Irish-American republicans have had to grapple with the same issues as their counterparts in Ireland, especially the questions of whether to widen their political agenda and how to respond to the possibility of a peace settlement. Strikingly similar debates and divisions have occurred on both sides of the Atlantic. In Ireland in the 1980s, Sinn Fein leader Gerry Adams inaugurated a new policy of "politicization," restoring questions of civil rights and social justice to the republican platform without reneging on violence, a strategy encapsulated in the slogan "a ballot box in one hand and an armalite rifle in the other." The logical outcome of this progression was the decision by the Provisional IRA and Sinn Fein to declare a cease-fire and to join the all-party peace talks that began in 1997. But the price has been to alienate hard-liners within the republican movement, who have formed splinter groups to continue the armed struggle. It is only against this background that recent schisms in Irish-American republican circles make sense. Pursuing much the same course as Adams, Martin Galvin assumed the leadership of NORAID, while its founder, Michael Flannery, left to form the hard-line Cumman na Saoirse, still dedicated to bringing about a united Ireland through armed struggle. Gerry Adams, now being granted visas to enter the United States on a regular basis, has increased his popularity in nationalist circles on both sides of the Atlantic, even as he inches ever further away from extremism and closer to championing constitutional reform and social justice. Quite what will become of the alternative tradition of physical force republicanism remains to be seen. But the Good Friday Agreement of 1998 augurs well for peace and the end of violence.

*See* Nationalism, Irish-American (2 entries)

Thomas N. Brown, *Irish-American Nationalism, 1870–1890* (Philadelphia, 1966).

Alan J. Ward, *Ireland and Anglo-American Relations, 1899–1921* (Toronto, 1969).

Andrew J. Wilson, *Irish America and the Ulster Conflict, 1968–1995* (Belfast, 1995).

KEVIN KENNY

## REYNOLDS, DEBBIE (1932–  )

Actress. Born of Irish decent as Marie Frances Reynolds in El Paso, Texas, on April 1, 1932, Debbie Reynolds is best known for her roles in the movies as the All-American girl-next-door.

Growing up in Burbank, California, she was outgoing and active in music and sports. It was her claim to the title "Miss Burbank of 1948" which drew the attention of a talent scout for Warner Brothers and led to a minor role in the 1950 film *The Daughter of Rosie O'Grady*. (It was Jack Warner who re-named her Debbie.) Shortly thereafter, Reynolds was put under a long-term contract with MGM, began to seriously study drama and dance, and landed supporting roles in *Two Weeks with Love; Mr. Imperium;* and in *Singin' in the Rain,* starring Gene Kelly and Donald O'Connor. Reynolds was recognized as a hard-working, skillful comedienne, singer and dancer; and her vivaciousness, girlish innocence and sweetness brought a freshness to the musical comedies she starred in over the next two decades: *I Love Melvin, The Tender Trap, The Affairs of Dobie Gillis,* and *Tammy and the Bachelor,* just to name a few. Perhaps the highlight of her career

was in the title role in *The Unsinkable Molly Brown,* released in 1963, for which she received wide critical acclaim.

Debbie Reynolds was married to popular singer Eddie Fisher in 1955, and the couple had two children, Carrie and Todd. Their marriage ended as a result of Fisher's highly publicized affair with Elizabeth Taylor. Debbie married Harry Karl, a wealthy businessman, in 1960.

*See* Cinema, Irish in

Joseph Curran, *Hibernian Green on the Silver Screen* (Westport, CT, 1990). *Who's Who of American Women* (1945–65).

EILEEN DANEY CARZO

## RHODE ISLAND

### The Protestant Pioneers

The Irish presence in Rhode Island dates from the mid-seventeenth century. Our knowledge of this Irish vanguard stems from the research of several Irish-American genealogists and apologists, such as Rhode Island's Thomas Hamilton Murray, who scoured the records of the American colonies to establish a long Irish-American lineage and thus overcome the charge of "foreignness" hurled at the nineteenth-century Irish and their Catholic Church. Ironically, most of these early Irish Rhode Islanders were Protestants—mainly Baptists, Quakers, Presbyterians, or Anglicans—and those few with Catholic antecedents soon lost their religious affiliation for lack of Catholic clergy within the colony. Among the handful of seventeenth-century Irish Rhode Islanders were Charles McCarthy, an original proprietor of (East) Greenwich in 1677, and Edward Larkin of Newport and Westerly, who served briefly in the colonial legislature.

In the early eighteenth century the colony's most notable Irishmen served as clergymen or schoolmasters. Among the former was Derry-born Reverend James MacSparran (1693–1757), for thirty-seven years the distinguished rector of St. Paul's Church (Wickford), which served the spiritual needs of South County Anglicans. MacSparran, who tutored President Thomas Clap of Yale, gained renown by publishing *America Dissected* (Dublin, 1753), a collection of his letters to friends in Ireland, which proved for its British audience a valuable source of information on the American colonies. Another even more illustrious Irish scholar and clergyman was George Berkeley, the Anglican essayist and philosopher, who stayed at Whitehall Farm in present-day Middletown during his eventful sojourn in America from 1729 to 1731. After the failure of his cherished but impractical project of establishing an Anglican college in Bermuda, Berkeley returned to Ireland, where he was rewarded with the bishopric of Cloyne.

Notable Irish tutors (of whom there were a good number in relation to the small Irish population) included Stephen Jackson (1700–1765), who left Kilkenny and settled in Providence. This teacher and prosperous farmer had a son, Richard, who became president of the Providence-Washington Insurance Company (1800–1838) and a four-term congressman, and a grandson, Charles, a prominent industrialist who served as governor in 1845–46. Other Irish schoolmasters were John Dorrance (1747–1813), a Providence civic leader, and the Reverend James "Paddy" Wilson of Limerick, first a teacher and then the colorful pastor of Providence's Beneficent ("Roundtop") Congregational Church. James Manning, first president of the College of Rhode Island (now Brown University) and the son of a New Jersey farmer, was probably of Irish descent. Though a Baptist in religion, Manning graduated from the College of New Jersey (Princeton), then a citadel of Irish Presbyterianism. Despite the fact that Manning's Celtic origins are in doubt, it is certain that Protestants in Ireland financed much of the initial endowment for his College of Rhode Island.

Colonial Rhode Island's most famous Irish craftsman was Kingston silversmith Samuel Casey, and its most renowned business family (Irish or otherwise) were the Brown brothers of Providence—James, Nicholas, Joseph, John, and Moses. The Browns' mother, Hope Power, was the daughter of Nicholas Power (1673–1734), a native of Ireland who served in the Rhode Island General Assembly and as a colonel in the state militia. Colonel Power's oldest daughter, Mary, was the mother of Nicholas Cooke, the state's Revolutionary War governor (1775–1778). In view of the sparseness of their numbers (one genealogist counted only 166 Irish surnames in the pre-1776 colonial records), the impact of the Irish on the English colony of Rhode Island was considerable.

During the American Revolution nearly three hundred Irish names appeared on Rhode Island's military and naval rolls, and the American commander in New England's largest military engagement, the inconclusive Battle of Rhode Island, was General John Sullivan of New Hampshire, whose parents had emigrated from Ireland in the 1720s. When Rochambeau's French army came to Newport as allies of the American cause in 1780, many of its soldiers were Irish nationals, particularly those men from Colonel Arthur Dillon's regiment who served in Lauzun's Legion.

A strong journalistic supporter of the Revolutionary cause was John Carter (1745–1814), the son of an Irish naval officer killed in the service of the Crown. Carter came to Providence as a journeyman printer from Philadelphia, where he had been apprenticed to Benjamin Franklin. From 1767 until 1814 he molded public opinion in Providence as the editor of the *Providence Gazette*. A major supporter of the ratification of the federal Constitution, Carter also served as Providence postmaster from 1772 to 1792. His daughter Ann (1769–1798) married Nicholas Brown, Jr. (son of the famous Providence merchant), the great benefactor of Brown University. The present-day Brown family is descended from their only child, John Carter Brown.

Whereas John Carter was the child of an Irish naval officer, two notable Rhode Island commodores of the early national period were sons of an Irish immigrant mother. Newport's Oliver Hazard Perry (1785–1819), hero of the decisive Battle of Lake Erie (1813), and Matthew Calbraith Perry (1794–1858), who opened Japan to Western trade and influence, were the children of Sarah Wallace (Alexander) Perry, a native of Newry in County Down, and mariner Christopher Perry of South Kingstown, who met Sarah when he was confined to a British internment camp in Kinsale, Ireland, as a Revolutionary War prisoner. After the conflict, Perry sailed back to Ireland to bring Sarah to America.

## 1815–1922

The first significant migration of Catholic Irish to North America began in the aftermath of the War of 1812, and Rhode Island partook of this influx. During the three decades between 1815 and 1845, a million Irish, most of whom were Roman Catholics, came to North America. Perhaps five thousand settled in Rhode Island.

The overwhelming majority of Irish migrants to Rhode Island became urban dwellers despite their rural background. They entered this unfamiliar milieu because they needed immediate employment, which Rhode Island's burgeoning economy provided,

and because they lacked the funds to continue onward to frontier areas. The federal census of 1850, the first national survey to record the nativity of the population, revealed that Rhode Island had 23,111 foreign-born out of a total population of 147,545. At this point the natives of Ireland totaled 15,944, or 69 percent of the foreign-born. By the time of the first state census in 1865, the foreign-born population had climbed to 39,703; of this figure the Irish-born accounted for 27,030, or 68 percent. By the federal count of 1870, there were 31,534 of Irish birth, and Providence ranked sixth among the cities of the nation in its number of Irish-born residents.

By 1875—sixty years after the onset of their immigration—the Catholic Irish had established settlements and churches in all the urban and industrial areas of the state, including Newport (especially the lower Thames Street neighborhood), Providence (mainly in Fox Point, the North End, Smith Hill, Olneyville, Manton, Wanskuck, and South Providence), Pawtucket, Woonsocket, the mill villages of Lincoln and Cumberland (including Central Falls, Valley Falls, Lonsdale, and Ashton), Harrisville, Pascoag, Greenville, Georgiaville, Cranston (especially Arlington and the Print Works district), the Pawtuxet Valley (particularly the villages of Crompton, Riverpoint, and Phenix), East Greenwich, Wakefield, Westerly, Warren, and Bristol. Aside from the English, no other Rhode Island ethnic group dispersed so widely.

Of the thousands of Irish who flocked to the state in the middle decades of the nineteenth century, many found their circumstances bleak. Depressed to the status of paupers by the conditions of their flight from Ireland, driven into debilitating slums or drab mill villages by their position as unskilled laborers, and isolated intellectually by their cultural background and physical segregation, these Irish saw insuperable social, economic, and religious barriers between themselves and the so-called "Yankees."

During the nineteenth century, Irish immigration and the growth of the Catholic Church were closely intertwined. The first tiny Irish Catholic communities were at the Portsmouth coal mines and in the Fox Point section of Providence near that town's bustling harbor. French priests from Boston began to visit both areas during the second decade of the century. The Providence Irish secured the use of a building on Sheldon Street as the state's first Catholic church in 1813, but the structure was destroyed by the Great Gale of 1815.

A more significant influx of Irish occurred in the mid-1820s, prompting Bishop Benedict Fenwick of Boston to dispatch Father Robert Woodley to Newport in 1828 as Rhode Island's first resident priest. There, in April 1828, the young cleric founded St. Mary's, the state's oldest parish. In 1829 the busy Woodley—whose mission territory included the states of Rhode Island and Connecticut in their entirety, plus southeastern Massachusetts—built the state's first Catholic church specifically constructed for that purpose at St. Mary's, Pawtucket.

When Woodley came to Rhode Island to establish a Catholic presence, Rhode Island's Roman Catholics numbered about 600 out of a total state population of 97,000, a mere six-tenths of 1 percent. The 600 faithful served by Woodley in 1828 were concentrated in Newport, where they worked as laborers on Fort Adams; in Portsmouth, where they were employed as miners at the coal pits; and in Providence, Cranston, Pawtucket, and Woonsocket, where they served the needs of the growing factory system or were employed in such public works projects as the construction of the Blackstone Canal. Nearly all of them were Irish.

In the 1830s, as the railroad came to Rhode Island, this Irish migration continued, and in the 1840s and 1850s, in the wake of Ireland's disastrous Famine, it reached impressive proportions. By 1865 three out of every eight Rhode Islanders were of Irish stock, the state's Irish Catholic community numbered nearly 50,000, and pioneer missionary priests like the Reverend James Fitton had established twenty widely scattered parishes. The energetic and seemingly ubiquitous Fitton, a founder of Holy Cross College (1843), was a driving force in the development of Rhode Island Catholicism, serving in every major area of Irish settlement.

The decade of the 1840s saw several important developments affecting the Irish Catholic community. One was the famous Dorr Rebellion, which occurred between 1841 and 1843 over an attempt to broaden democracy in Rhode Island and replace the antiquated royal charter of 1663 with a written state constitution. The opponents of political reformer Thomas Dorr were partly motivated by anti-Catholic prejudice and political nativism, themes that have often been ignored in discussions of this colorful episode. Over the objections of Dorr, Rhode Island's state constitution of 1843 established a real estate requirement for foreign-born voters that was designed to discriminate against Irish Catholic immigrants.

Another event of importance was the John Gordon murder trial—the Sacco-Vanzetti case of the nineteenth century. This 1844 travesty of justice, which on the basis of circumstantial evidence resulted in the hanging of a young Irish Catholic immigrant for the killing of a prominent industrialist, Amasa Sprague, caused such misgiving that it contributed to the abolition of the death penalty in Rhode Island eight years later.

In 1850 William Tyler was succeeded as bishop of Hartford by Irish-born Bernard O'Reilly, called "Paddy the Priest" by some native Rhode Islanders. In 1851 this bold and strong-willed bishop brought Mother Xavier Warde and the predominantly Irish Sisters of Mercy to Providence, where they immediately founded a school for girls, St. Xavier's Academy, the first Catholic secondary school in the state. Four years later, during the height of the Know-Nothing movement, O'Reilly personally defended the Mercy nuns from an anti-Catholic mob that had congregated at St. Xavier's Convent to "free" a young girl who had allegedly been confined therein.

The last bishop of Hartford to preside over Rhode Island was Francis Patrick McFarland, whose episcopacy coincided with the Civil War and Reconstruction years. This gentle and scholarly prelate's tenure was marked by the emergence of a Catholic presence in the social and political affairs of Rhode Island. McFarland's energy and learning built the first bridges to the non-Catholic community of the state, resulting in a lessening of the ethno-cultural antagonisms that had dominated the 1840s and 1850s.

The Civil War was a testing ground that also helped to mollify native fears of Irish Catholics. Animated by a desire to preserve the Union and thereby prove their Americanism, Irish immigrants and their sons fought side by side with Yankee boys. Two members of the local Irish community—John Corcoran and James Welsh—were recipients of the newly created Congressional Medal of Honor for their wartime heroism.

The other salient fact of this period was the role of the lowly Irish immigrants in building the Diocese of Providence. During the years prior to 1872, almost the only influences upon Rhode Island Catholicism were those distinctive Irish traits that gave the local Catholic community a unified religious outlook and produced what was in reality an Irish national church. The creation of the Diocese of Providence (with Irish-born Thomas F. Hendricken its first bishop) was the Irish immigrants' first notable achievement in Rhode Island.

During the last third of the nineteenth century, the era of America's Industrial Revolution, the Irish of Rhode Island made a slow yet significant climb up the socioeconomic ladder as new immigrants from French Canada, eastern Europe, and the Mediterranean took their place on the bottom rungs. Political advancement also became less difficult as more native-born Irish reached voting age. Whereas the 1865 state census revealed that "only one in twelve or thirteen of the foreign-born of adult age was a voter," economic advancement for the Irish immigrant and native birth for his male children combined by the 1880s to make the real estate requirement for voting and officeholding much less restrictive.

According to the census of 1885, the state had 92,700 citizens with at least one parent of Irish birth, but for the first time more than half of these (50,313) were native-born. When these foreign-stock Irish (immigrants or their children) were added to second- and third-generation Irish-Americans, the total number must have easily exceeded 100,000 in a general Rhode Island population of 304,000. This one-to-three ratio was the relative high point of Irish numerical presence in the state.

Numbers plus native birth equaled political clout. Leading the Irish political advance was Charles E. Gorman (1844–1917), Boston-born of an Irish father and a Yankee mother. An outspoken advocate of equal rights and suffrage reform, Democrat Gorman successively became the first Irish Catholic member of the bar (1865), state legislator (1870), Providence city councilman (1875), speaker of the House (1887), and U.S. attorney (1893). His younger colleague, attorney Edwin Daniel McGuinness (1856–1901), became the first Irish Catholic general officer, winning election as secretary of state in 1887. In 1896 Democrat McGuinness also became Providence's first Irish Catholic mayor, but the city's most notable chief executive of this or any era was Thomas Doyle, of Irish Protestant stock, whose eighteen years of service between 1864 and 1886 constituted an unparalleled era for Providence's growth and development. A contemporary of Doyle's, Dublin-born Thomas Davis, was a prominent businessman who served one term (1853–1855) in the Congress of the United States. Although Davis was a Protestant, he was an outspoken foe of nativism.

Attorney James H. Higgins, who had succeeded the colorful and dynamic John J. Fitzgerald as mayor of Pawtucket in 1903, won election in 1906 and again in 1907 as Rhode Island's first Irish Catholic governor. Galway-born Democrat George O'Shaunessy (1868–1934) became another local Irish Catholic pathbreaker, securing election four times to the U.S. House of Representatives (1911–1919). He was followed to Washington two years later by five-term Irish Republican congressman Ambrose Kennedy of Woonsocket. In 1913, after the victory of Joseph Gainer, the Irish began their unbroken sixty-two-year grip on the Providence mayoralty, and by that time they were firmly in control of the organizational structure of the Democratic Party.

The Irish economic rise, though less spectacular, had some "rags to riches" scenarios. The most notable climb was made by Joseph Banigan (1839–1898), Rhode Island's first Irish Catholic millionaire. The Irish-born son of parents who migrated to Rhode Island from Scotland in 1849, Banigan got in on the ground floor of the emerging rubber goods industry and improved

Charles Goodyear's process for the vulcanization of rubber. By 1889 he opened the Alice Mill in Woonsocket, then the largest rubber-shoe factory in the world. Three years later, Banigan helped form the massive U.S. Rubber Company and became its president (1893–1896). In 1898 he financed the construction of Providence's first "skyscraper," the ten-story Banigan Building.

By the end of the century Irish-born William and Thomas Gilbane had directed their firm (established 1873) to the forefront among local building contractors, and James Hanley (1841–1912), another Irish immigrant, had become the region's most prominent brewer. Though such Horatio Alger stories were not common, Irish-American small businessmen, lawyers, and physicians were becoming increasingly so in the early years of this century. Especially notable was Dr. John William Keefe, a founder of St. Joseph Hospital, a World War I surgeon, president of the Rhode Island Medical Society (1913–1914), president of the American Association of Obstetricians, Gynecologists, and Abdominal Surgeons (1916–1917), and founder of a surgical center in Providence.

In the blue-collar field, Irish-Americans made great strides in the building trades, acquiring skills as masons, carpenters, plumbers, steamfitters, painters, plasterers, electricians, and ironworkers. Railroad, streetcar, and public utility employment, professional police work, and fire fighting also had strong appeal.

As Irish-American labor leaders affiliated with the Knights of Labor or the AF of L led the fight for the eight-hour day, Americans used their newly acquired leisure to partake of such popular spectator sports as professional baseball. The new national pastime produced a number of local Irish-American luminaries, including "Orator Jim" O'Rourke, batting star of the national champion Providence Grays, and Hugh Duffy of Cranston, whose 1894 batting average of .438 with Boston of the National League is still the unapproachable major league record. Both O'Rourke and Duffy are enshrined in the Baseball Hall of Fame.

A more genteel spectator activity of great popularity was vaudeville. Here also the Rhode Island Irish community produced performers of national stature, the most magnetic of whom was George M. Cohan. Born in the Fox Point section of Providence on July 3, 1878, to variety performers Jerry and Nellie (Costigan) Cohan, George joined his sister Josie and their parents on stage well before he reached his teens. The four Cohans left the local circuit for Broadway during the 1890s. Cohan eventually became America's most successful theatrical producer, and during his fifty-five years in show business, he composed more than five hundred songs, including such patriotic airs as "Over There," "You're a Grand Old Flag," and "Yankee Doodle Boy."

In 1917, Bishop Matthew J. Harkins (the fourth and most productive in a line of seven Irish Catholic bishops of Providence spanning the years from 1850 to 1971) joined with a group of Irish professionals and businessmen and the Dominican Fathers of the Province of St. Joseph to found Providence College. By the time Providence College was founded, Rhode Island Irishmen had already achieved distinction for their cultural and literary attainments. In 1884 Alfred Thayer Mahan, descendant of an eighteenth-century Irish immigrant, began a productive tour of duty at Newport's newly created Naval War College, where he served both as professor and president. In 1890 Mahan (1840–1914) published *The Influence of Seapower upon History*, the most famous and influential of his numerous historical volumes advocating American expansion on strategic grounds.

In the late 1880s and early 1890s, the local Irish were given an advance look at the literary efforts of several promising young Irish authors by a most unlikely source—the *Providence Journal*. For forty-five years (1839–1884), while the paper had been under the malign influence of nativist and machine Republican Henry B. Anthony, Irish Catholics and Democratic politicians had been its twin nemeses. This changed (at least temporarily) when Alfred M. Williams (1840–1896) began his seven-year tenure as *Journal* editor in 1884. The most notable aspect of Williams's career became his study and promotion of Irish literature. He wrote several works on the topic and published in the newly created *Sunday Journal* the early efforts of several then-obscure Irish authors, including William Butler Yeats, Douglas Hyde, Katherine Tynan, and Mary Banim. Professor Horace Reynolds, in his booklet, *A Providence Episode in the Irish Literary Renaissance,* calls these works "a record in miniature of the beginnings of a movement that is today recognized as one of the most distinctive in the stream of English letters."

By 1922, the year the Irish Free State was created, Rhode Island's Irish had made major advances in all walks of life. No major political office, except for U.S. senator, had eluded their grasp, and they dominated the hierarchy of the state's Democratic Party, though that party was still the minority.

## 1922–1998

In the three generations from the early 1920s to the present, Rhode Island's Irish-Americans achieved distinction and success commensurate with their rapidly increasing numbers. With two of every nine Rhode Islanders claiming Irish ancestry by the 1990 federal census, an essay of this limited scope can scarcely do justice to its subject.

During the two decades between world wars, the state experienced a turbulent political transformation from traditional Republican Party dominance to rule by the Democrats. The Irish were the architects of that upheaval. By finally mastering the game of ethnic politics (much later than their counterparts elsewhere) and by taking advantage of economic shifts, social changes, and cultural trends on both the state and national levels, Irish Democratic politicians weaned Franco-Americans, Italians, Jews, Poles, and Blacks from their traditional Republican allegiance and ushered them into an Irish-led Democratic fold that dominated state government from 1940 through the elections of 1982.

The spearheads of this Irish political advance were a handful of young legislators who entered the General Assembly in the years following the outbreak of World War I. Foremost among them were William S. Flynn of South Providence, Holy Cross, and Georgetown Law School; Robert Emmet Quinn, a Brown- and Harvard-educated attorney from West Warwick and the nephew of Colonel Patrick Quinn, who had carved that mill town from Warwick's western sector in 1913; Francis B. Condon, a Georgetown Law School graduate from Central Falls; and Thomas Patrick McCoy, a Pawtucket streetcar conductor.

Of all Irish political leaders of the World War I era, Robert Emmet Quinn was the most durable. Quinn rose from the state Senate (1923–1925 and 1929–1933), where he led the famous 1924 filibuster, to the lieutenant governorship (1933–1937), where he presided over the Bloodless Revolution, to the governorship (1937–1939), where he battled with Narragansett Park director Walter O'Hara in the ludicrous and nationally scandalous "Race Track War" of 1937. Although that episode and a national recession cost "Battling Bob" re-election, he was later appointed to the Rhode Island Superior Court (1941–1951) and then to the newly established U.S. Court of Military Appeals (1951–1975), where he served as chief judge.

One Rhode Island Celt who sought from the start to carve out his political career on the national level was Thomas Gardiner ("Tommy the Cork") Corcoran (1900–1981), a leading draftsman and lobbyist for much of the legislation now labeled Franklin D. Roosevelt's New Deal. Recommended by his Harvard Law School professor Felix Frankfurter, Corcoran joined the New Deal "Brain Trust" and drafted such landmark laws as those creating the Securities and Exchange Commission, the Federal Housing Administration, the Tennessee Valley Authority, and the Fair Labor Standards Board. Corcoran, a Pawtucket-born son of an Irish immigrant, often entertained Roosevelt with Irish ballads and drafted some of the president's political speeches. Another local Irishman lured to the Potomac was John Fanning, a twenty-five-year member of the National Labor Relations Board who chaired that body from 1977 to 1981.

During the decades following 1935, when the Irish-led Democratic Party solidified its hold on state government, a new wave of home-grown Irish-American political leaders emerged. Most notable of these Roosevelt-era luminaries were J. Howard McGrath, John E. Fogarty, Dennis J. Roberts, William E. Powers, and Harry F. Curvin.

William E. Powers of Central Falls overcame the handicap of blindness, the result of a childhood accident, to rank at the top of his Boston University Law School class. After five terms in the House (1939–1949), Powers served nine years as attorney general before his elevation in January 1958 to the state Supreme Court. In 1973, having stepped down after fifteen distinguished years on the high-court bench, he re-emerged to chair that year's highly successful state constitutional convention.

Dennis J. Roberts, a noted high school athlete at LaSalle Academy, was, perhaps, the most powerful figure in state government during the decade following World War II. From 1941 to 1951 he served as mayor of Providence under that city's first strong-mayor charter, and he presided as governor from 1951 to 1959.

John E. Fogarty was even more durable. This bricklayer-turned-politician went to Washington as congressman from Rhode Island's Second District in January 1941. There he remained until his sudden death twenty-six years later. Fogarty's many achievements in the area of health care legislation won him the national title of "Mr. Public Health," but the man with the green bow tie was equally renowned as an unrelenting supporter of Irish unification.

Woonsocket-born J. Howard McGrath was undoubtedly the state's most versatile politician. After spending the war years as Rhode Island's governor, he was appointed U.S. solicitor general by his close political ally Harry S. Truman. In 1946 McGrath was elected to the U.S. Senate, the first Rhode Island Irish Catholic ever elected to that office. The following year Truman named him Democratic national chairman, and McGrath quickly proved his worth in the 1948 elections by overseeing Truman's surprising upset of presidential hopeful Thomas E. Dewey. In the following year, the ambitious Rhode Islander gave up his Senate seat to become U.S. attorney general. Others who deserve to be remembered are United States Senator Jack Reed; U.S. Congressmen Jeremiah O'Connell, James M. Connell, Bob Tiernan, Eddie Beard, and Patrick Kennedy (of the famous Kennedy clan); Supreme Court chief justices Thomas Roberts (brother of Governor Roberts) and Thomas Fay; Lieutenant Governor, acting Governor, and Superior Court justice John S. McKiernan; interim U.S. senator and federal District Court judge Edward L. Leahey; and four-term governor J. Joseph Garrahy.

In the annals of Irish achievement, the past two decades have been notable for the rise of women to the top of the political ladder. One such achiever worthy of special mention is Florence Kerins Murray of Newport, who became, successively, the first woman associate justice of the Superior Court (1956), that court's first female presiding justice (1978), and the first woman to sit on the Rhode Island Supreme Court (1979).

From the 1920s until 1971, Irish-Americans continued their dominance in the local hierarchy of the Catholic Church. William Hickey became coadjutor bishop of Providence in 1919 when Matthew Harkins was in declining health, and ascended to the See of Providence in his own right when Harkins died in 1921 and presided until 1933. Hickey's successor, Francis P. Keough (1934–1947), was a popular bishop who made some important innovations. After the departure of Keough to the archbishopric of the primal See of Baltimore in 1947, Russell J. McVinney (1948–1971) assumed spiritual direction of the diocese—the only Rhode Island native to hold that post. During his episcopacy the Church made impressive material gains that attest to McVinney's administrative expertise. His tenure was a period in which Rhode Island Catholicism expanded its social role.

Many other able Irish clerics served as administrators in the Providence diocese or were raised here and then departed to assume positions of church leadership elsewhere. John Cardinal Dearden, archbishop of Detroit, was born and spent his boyhood in the Blackstone Valley, and Daniel P. Reilly of South Providence, a former diocesan chancellor, became bishop of Norwich, Connecticut, and then of Worcester, Massachusetts.

In the field of letters, Rhode Island's Irish-American community produced two noteworthy novelists of Irish-American life. In 1946 Edward McSorley, who lived for a time on Providence's South Side, published *Our Own Kind.* This widely circulated Book-of-the-Month Club selection poignantly depicts the travails of the McDermotts, an Irish working-class family in St. Malachi's (St. Michael's) Parish. Its sequel, *Young McDermott,* appeared three years later. Even more famous and widely read than McSorley was Woonsocket's Edwin O'Connor (1918–1968). This product of the LaSalle Academy had among his credits such Irish-American literary classics as *The Last Hurrah* (1956), the Pulitzer Prize-winning *The Edge of Sadness* (1961), and *All in the Family* (1966).

In Irish-American nonfiction, George W. Potter, an editor at the *Providence Journal,* penned one of the best general histories of the early nineteenth-century Irish migration—his popularly written and posthumously published *To the Golden Door: The Story of the Irish in Ireland and America* (1960). Potter, following the example of *Journal* editor Alfred Williams, also bequeathed his Irish books to the collections of the Providence Public Library.

Thomas N. Brown, who taught for six years at Portsmouth Priory, was the author of *Irish-American Nationalism, 1870–1890* (1966), the standard account of Irish-American reaction to the home rule movement led by Charles Stewart Parnell. More recently, Professors Robert W. Hayman, Matthew J. Smith, and Patrick T. Conley of Providence College have published books on nineteenth-century Rhode Island Catholicism emphasizing the impact of the Irish on Church growth, while Professor William G. McLoughlin of Brown University established himself as one of the foremost authorities on the history of American Protestantism. Another Brown historian, David Herlihy, was a leading scholar in the field of medieval history and immediate past president of the American Historical Association at the time of his death in 1991.

In the modern period, the Rhode Island Irish community produced several nationally prominent entertainers, most notably Eddie Dowling of Woonsocket (1889–1976), a Pulitzer Prize-winning playwright, Broadway composer, and producer; jazz trumpeter Robert L. "Bobby" Hackett (1915–1976) from Providence; Woonsocket's famed soprano Eileen Farrell; and Warwick's James Woods, a noted Hollywood actor.

But it was in baseball that Rhode Island's Irish-Americans made their greatest impact. O'Rourke and Duffy of an earlier era were succeeded in the Hall of Fame by Woonsocket-born Charles "Gabby" Hartnett. The oldest of fourteen children, Hartnett made his major league debut with the Chicago Cubs in 1922 and played with them for a nineteen-year span that included four World Series. Joe McCarthy, the great Yankee manager, labeled Hartnett "the best catcher of all time."

Also making their mark in the big leagues were the Cooney family of Cranston. James John Cooney, born in Cranston in 1865, was the patriarch of the clan. He had four ballplaying sons, and they in turn produced six grandsons in the same mold. Jimmy Cooney, Sr., played for three years as a shortstop with Cap Anson's Cubs in the early 1890s. He then passed on the fundamentals of the game to his sons, two of whom—Jimmy, Jr., known as "Scoops," and John—also went on to the major leagues. Scoops Cooney won acclaim as one of the classiest-fielding shortstops of his era. In May 1927 he accomplished that extreme rarity in baseball, an unassisted triple play. Johnny Cooney played for twenty seasons in the major leagues with Boston and the Brooklyn Dodgers. An excellent outfielder, he led the National League twice in fielding and made only thirty-four errors during a career consisting of 1,172 games.

Although it is now more than three centuries since the first Irish pioneers settled in Rhode Island, the Irish community remains a distinct and vigorous presence in Rhode Island: local Irish traditions are much in evidence, interest in the ancestral homeland continues strong, and the tendency of Irish-Americans to identify themselves as such is pronounced and decisive. The Irish have exerted a significant impact on Rhode Island in every walk of life. In few other American states, if any, has the Irish community been so prominent in relative numbers and achievements.

Patrick T. Conley, *The Irish in Rhode Island* (Providence, 1986).

Patrick T. Conley and Matthew J. Smith, *Catholicism in Rhode Island: The Formative Era* (Providence, 1976).

Robert W. Hayman, *Catholicism in Rhode Island and the Diocese of Providence, 1780–1921,* 2 vols. (Providence, 1982, 1995).

PATRICK T. CONLEY

## RICE, CHARLES OWEN (1908–   )

Priest and social activist. Born in New York City, November 21, 1908, Charles Owen Rice was the second of three children of Michael and Anna (O'Donnell) Rice, Irish immigrants. The mother, a convert from Protestantism, and her youngest child, a daughter, died within a month of one another in 1913. Charles was thereupon sent to Dundalk, County Louth, along with older brother Patrick, to be reared by relatives. In 1920 the brothers rejoined their father, now working in Pittsburgh. After studies at St. Vincent Seminary in Latrobe, they became priests of the Diocese of Pittsburgh, Charles going on to achieve wide fame as social activist, supporter of organized labor and champion of unpopular causes.

Charles Owen Rice

Charles Owen Rice was ordained in 1934 at the height of the Great Depression. He was strongly influenced by Pius XI's labor encyclical of 1931, *Quadragesimo anno,* and as a young priest plunged into issues involving the poor and the working class, initially through the Catholic Radical Alliance, a local action group, and subsequently as founder of a Pittsburgh unit of the Association of Catholic Trade Unionists [ACTU] and of St. Joseph's House of Hospitality, a Catholic-Worker type home, where he was resident priest from 1940–1950. Dorothy Day was a role model, though Rice did not embrace her pacifism during World War II, nor, conversely, was he as temperate as she during the Cold War period. Rice energetically supported the war effort (he was the Office of Price Administration's area rent director for ten western Pennsylvania counties), but came to second thoughts about the militancy with which he fought leftists in trade unionism after the war, notably in the United Electrical, Radio and Machine Workers of America [UE].

Rice was a regular presence on labor's picket lines, becoming in the process a confidant of CIO president Philip Murray and a darling of the rank and file. Public impact grew further through a provocative weekly radio program and a column in the *Pittsburgh Catholic,* though his high standing with many old allies dipped when he attacked the pervasiveness of racism in American society, including trade unions. Rice marched with Dr. Martin Luther King, Jr. during the civil rights assertions, and he was a strident opponent of the Vietnam war, marching elbow to elbow in protest demonstrations with such figures as poet Robert Lowell and Dr. Benjamin Spock, including at the Pentagon itself. Antiwar sentiments expressed in his newspaper column were quoted by Radio Hanoi.

In the 1950s Rice's activites were curbed by Bishop John Dearden, then head of the Pittsburgh diocese, but he was rehabilitated by Dearden's successor, Bishop John Wright, and in his late 80s was still living a life full of activity and honors.

John Deedy, "Crusader for Social Justice," *Ave Maria,* October 5, 1963.

P. Mark Fackler and Charles H. Lippy, eds., *Popular Religious Magazines of the United States,* "Pittsburgh Catholic" (Westport, Conn., 1995).

Patrick J. McGeever, *Charles Owen Rice: Apostle of Contradiction* (Pittsburgh, Pa., 1989).

JOHN DEEDY

## RIORDAN, PATRICK WILLIAM (1841–1914)

Second Archbishop of San Francisco. Riordan was born in Chatham, New Brunswick to Matthew Riordan, a ship carpenter, and Mary Dunne. His parents had emigrated from Ireland in the 1830s, Matthew from Stradbelly, County Leix, and Mary from Kinsale, County Cork. They met and married in Canada. In 1848, the Riordans moved to Chicago, where Patrick attended school. In 1856, he began studies at the University of Notre Dame, where he decided to become a priest for the Archdiocese of Chicago. In 1858, he was sent to study in Rome at the Urban College of the Congregation for the Propagation of Faith. He became one of the first students at the newly created American College, but poor health forced him to withdraw after less than a year. He studied briefly in Paris before he enrolled at the American College at Louvain, Belgium in October 1861. He was ordained to the priesthood in Mechlin, Belgium on June 10, 1865 by Cardinal Englebert Sterckx.

In 1866, Riordan returned to Chicago and was appointed to teach at St. Mary's of the Lake Seminary. In 1871, he became pastor of St. James parish in Chicago, where he distinguished himself as an excellent administrator, builder and fundraiser. These qualities led to his appointment in 1883 as coadjutor archbishop of San Francisco with the right of succession. He was consecrated bishop by Archbishop Patrick Feehan on September 16, 1883 in Chicago, and succeeded Joseph Alemany as Archbishop of San Francisco on December 28, 1884.

Riordan took over an archdiocese that was still relatively young. Riordan's most significant building project was the completion of a new Cathedral, St. Mary's of the Assumption, which was dedicated on January 11, 1891. The old Cathedral, also named St. Mary's, was located on the edge of Chinatown in the midst of an increasingly dissolute part of town, no longer thought to be appropriate for the Cathedral. Riordan turned the old Cathedral, now known as Old St. Mary's, over to the Paulist Fathers.

Riordan also sought to provide a native clergy for the Archdiocese. Riordan obtained the services of the renowned seminary teachers, the Sulpicians, to staff a seminary and so St. Patrick's Seminary in Menlo Park was opened in 1898, the only such seminary on the West Coast until the 1930s. For years to come a large number of seminarians had Irish surnames, though most were second- or third-generation Irish-Americans.

Riordan also succeeded in resolving the Pious Fund case with the government of Mexico. In 1843, the Mexican government had confiscated a trust fund established to support the missions in California. After close to a half century of litigation, Riordan brought the case before the Permanent Court of Arbitration at the recently established Hague Tribunal. In 1902, the Tribunal decided in favor of the archdiocese and a payment schedule established, though payments were disrupted by the Mexican Revolution in 1910.

In 1906, Riordan saw much of his work destroyed in the devastating earthquake and fire that struck San Francisco. More than 12 churches and numerous other buildings were damaged, most notably Riordan's beloved St. Patrick's Seminary. Undeterred, Riordan rallied the city in a speech in which he proclaimed in the words of St. Paul, "I am a citizen of no mean city, although it is in ashes," and he promised, "We shall rebuild." Most of the last decade of Riordan's life was spent supporting the rebuilding of the archdiocese.

Riordan's thirty-year episcopate had been one of enormous growth for the Archdiocese: parishes increased from 50 to 120, the clergy increased from 100 to 350, and numerous charitable and educational facilities had been established.

James Gaffey, *Citizen of No Mean City: Archbishop Patrick Riordan of San Francisco* (Consortium, 1976).

JEFFREY M. BURNS

## ROANOKE ISLAND

Sheltered behind the Outer Banks of present-day North Carolina, Roanoke Island was the site of Sir Walter Raleigh's attempts to establish the first English colony within the boundaries of the modern United States. Among the sailors, soldiers, and servants in Raleigh's expeditions were five documented Irishmen, and several others whose surnames suggest Irish origins.

Richard Butler, a Tipperary-born sailor in Raleigh's service, was a member of the reconnaissance expedition that discovered and explored Roanoke Island in 1584. Three others—Darby Glavin, Edward Nugent and an unnamed Irish servant—reached Roanoke in 1585 as members of a 108-man colony. During nine months on the island, they were under the command of Captain Ralph Lane, an English officer who had previously served as Sheriff of Kerry.

English demands soon alienated the local Indians. When Lane attacked an Indian village on the mainland in 1586, his Irish servant shot the Indian chief Wingina in the buttocks with a cavalry pistol. Nugent, an Irish soldier under Lane, pursued and beheaded the wounded chief.

Along with Glavin, an Irish sailor pressed into Raleigh's service, Nugent and the anonymous servant returned to England in 1586. Raleigh's second attempt to plant a settlement ended with the disappearance of all 117 men, women and children who landed on Roanoke in 1587. Two Irishmen narrowly avoided becoming part of this legendary Lost Colony. Dennis Carroll and his shipmate Darby Glavin, the 1585 veteran, deserted the ill-fated expedition in the West Indies. Carroll's later history is not recorded. Glavin reappeared in 1595 as a soldier in Spanish Florida.

*See* America's First Irish Visitor

Karen Ordahl Kupperman, *Roanoke: The Abandoned Colony* (Totowa, New Jersey, 1984).

David Beers Quinn, ed., *The Roanoke Voyages: 1584–1590*, 2 vols. (London, 1955).

BRIAN McGINN

## ROBERTS, WILLIAM RANDALL (1830–1897)

Politician, Fenian leader, congressman. Born in Mitchelstown, County Cork, Ireland, on February 6, 1830, William Roberts was the son of Randall and Mary (Bishop) Roberts. William intermittently attended schools until he left Ireland for New York City at the age of 19 in 1849. There he worked as a dry-goods clerk for eight years and established a business of his own only to come to ruin in the economic downturn of 1857. Roberts bounced back in the following year, however, and established another store that was so successful that by 1869, Roberts could retire as a millionaire.

It was during the Civil War that Roberts began to take leadership roles in the Irish societies around New York City. He became president of the Knights of St. Patrick by the end of 1865 and president of the Fenian Brotherhood's senate. In the same year, Roberts began putting together plans for an invasion of Canada against England and by June 1866 had several thousand men poised along the Canadian border. The effort was a complete failure, and the U.S. government, until now unopposed to the Fenian leader's plans, was sufficiently embarrassed to issue a proclamation calling for the arrest of Roberts and many of his followers for a breech of neutrality laws. Roberts was released quickly, however, and by June 1867, had traveled to Paris where he joined with other members of the Brotherhood to organize collaborative efforts between American- and British-based Irish organizations. Efforts toward cooperation were expressed, but little was accomplished. At the end of the year, Roberts resigned from the presidency.

All of this, however, prepared Roberts for a career in New York City politics. He was elected to the House of Representatives as a Democrat in 1870 and served until 1874. His activity was filled with a Fenian agenda. He fought for the protection of American Fenian prisoners in Canada and opposed repressive measures against them in the South. He was particularly opposed to policies that favored British over Irish causes and violently attacked British policy more than once. In 1874 he left the House and by the end of the decade was president and then member of the board of alderman in New York and ran for sheriff on the Tammany ticket, but lost. Roberts supported Grover Cleveland in both state and national campaigns, and when Cleveland was elected president of the United States, Roberts was appointed minister to Chile from 1885 to 1889. These relatively peaceful and uneventful years ended for Roberts when he suffered a paralyzing stroke and lived a further eight years without recovery. Roberts returned to the United States and died August 9, 1897, at Bellevue Hospital in New York, separated from his wife and nearly forgotten at his death.

*See* Fenians and Clan na Gael

Matthew Patrick Breen, *Thirty Years of New York Politics* (New York: The Author, 1899).

*Dictionary of American Biography*, vol. VIII (New York: Charles Scribner's Sons): 19.

John Rutherford, *The Secret History of the Fenian Conspiracy*, 2 vols. (1877).

C. P. Stacey, "Fenianism and the Rise of National Feeling in Canada," *Canadian Historical Review* (September 1931).

DANIEL J. KUNTZ

## ROGERS, MARY JOSEPHINE (1882–1955)

Foundress. Mary Josephine Rogers was born in Boston in 1882, of Irish ancestry during a period of great cultural transition and profound social change affecting American Catholicism. In 1901 she became a student at Smith College where mission activity among the Protestant students was vibrant. She was deeply moved in seeing young women signing the Student Volunteer Pledge, offering their lives for the mission fields.

Returning to Smith in 1906 on a fellowship , she was asked by the Faculty Advisor of the *College Association for Christian Work* to organize some kind of religious activity for the Catholic students. She formed a mission study class and wrote to Fr. James A. Walsh, Director of the Society for the Propagation of the Faith in Boston asking for mission materials saying, "The particular motive of these classes is to inspire girls to do actual mission work when they leave college." She closed her letter with a prophetic line, "Who knows but that the little we do here may be the beginning of greater efforts in later life."

Mary Josephine associated herself closely from 1908 to 1911, with the work of Father Walsh, a leader in the emerging missionary movement, using the mission magazine, *The Field Afar*, as a means of propagating this idea. At this time no American religious order existed for young women who wanted to become foreign missioners. There was a real urgency to establish such a group.

Other women offered their services to Father Walsh to help the American Church in its new mission movement. They accompanied the co-founders, Walsh and Price to Hawthorne, New York, in January 1912. The women became known as "Teresians," with St. Teresa of Avila as their patron and model. Mary Josephine's cooperation with Fr. Walsh involved and committed her to a response which was the foundation of the Maryknoll Sisters. On February 14, 1920, they received official recognition as the Foreign Mission Sisters of St. Dominic-Maryknoll Sisters—a milestone in the religious history of American Catholicism.

In February of 1921, she and twenty-two Sisters professed their first vows. In November of that same year, the first group of six Sisters left for Hong Kong. Wanting to experience the mission life of her Sisters, Mother Mary Joseph made her first visitation in September of 1923 as she accompanied seven more Sisters to China. Mother Mary Joseph's mission spirituality blended the contemplative and apostolic. This was clearly demonstrated by the establishment, in 1932, of the Cloistered branch of the Congregation.

By 1940 Maryknoll Sisters were in China, Japan, Korea, Manchuria, the Philippines, Hawaii, and on the West Coast of the U.S. In March of 1943, they began their work in Latin America with a mission in Bolivia, then the following year in Nicaragua and Panama. They now are a multicultural community of over seven hundred Sisters from twenty-two countries of origin who minister in various ways in 31 nations throughout the world. Mother Mary Joseph died in New York on October 9, 1955.

Sr. Jeanne Marie Lyons, M.M., *Maryknoll's First Lady* (Maryknoll, N.Y., 1964).

Camilla Kennedy, M.M., *To the Uttermost Parts of the Earth* (Maryknoll, New York, 1987).

HELEN PHILLIPS, M.M.

## RONEY, FRANK (1841–1925)

Fenian, iron molder, labor organizer. Born in Belfast on August 13, 1841, Frank Roney was the eldest of eight children of a skilled carpenter married to the daughter of a Presbyterian family who converted to Catholicism just prior to their wedding. Her father, Gordon Augustus Thomson, from an old, propertied, Presbyterian line, was a world traveler and adventurer who died in Australia. Roney's father was the secretary of the first carpenter union in Belfast, who later became a contractor prosperous enough to provide for his large family.

### EDUCATION AND APPRENTICESHIP

Frank Roney attended a national school for two years, then studied at the Ellis Academey, a private school—as well as a government school of design where he learned to cast sculptures. Finding craftsmanship appealing, he chose apprenticeship in the molders' trade (against his mother's wishes). In 1855 he ventured forth to reform the world, becoming a runaway apprentice in Dublin until restored to Combs Foundry by his father at considerable expense, to complete his apprenticeship.

## FENIAN ACTIVIST

John Nolan, a Fenian recruiter, persuaded him to join the organization—after listening to Roney's first speech. Assigned to military preparations, he met Fenian leader James Stephens, who, impressed with his work, made him Centre (Colonel) of the Ulster Province. Roney was in and out of Dublin meeting Jeremiah O'Donovan Rossa, "Pagan" O'Leary and other Fenian agents. Traveling to London and back to smuggle arms to Ireland and recruiting new members and so forth, he encountered plentiful clerical denunciation. A pastoral from Cardinal Cullen prohibited Fenians from receiving the sacraments. Jailed twice for his Fenian activities, Roney was never tried, and, in 1867, finally released on condition he emigrate to America—by virtue of his father's influence.

## EMIGRATION

Arriving in New York, he gradually abandoned his Irish nationalism as he worked his way west to Chicago, St. Louis and Omaha plying the foundryman's craft. In 1868 he settled in Omaha, headquarters for building the Union Pacific Railroad. He joined and became active in the molders' union there, becoming secretary and later president of Local 190. The National Labor Reform party was the political arm of the National Labor Union (NLU). Both were dominated by William Sylvis, president of the Iron Molders International Union. Roney corresponded with Sylvis and later toured Nebraska with Sylvis's successor (Richard Trevellick), speaking in behalf of the National Labor Reform Party—and reporting on it for the *Omaha Herald*. Roney claimed these efforts fostered progressive politics in the state. While in Omaha, several investment opportunities which proved highly profitable were urged upon Roney by friends. He rejected them and later regretted it.

## CALIFORNIA CAREER

In 1875 Roney arrived in San Francisco with a woman he married in Omaha and their two children with another on the way. They faced severe poverty for lack of employment due to the 1873 recession, which had finally impacted San Francisco. Until conditions improved, they survived by selling their furniture, borrowing from friends and from his Odd Fellows Lodge—and moving frequently. Desperate, Roney took any kind of work, but found little.

Once back on his feet with a job at the Union Iron Works, he resumed participation in labor affairs. He was briefly associated with the Workingmen's Party of California until he broke with Denis Kearney, its founder, whom he disliked for his brutal vilification of Chinese character. Roney recognized immigration from China depressed wages and working conditions, but remembering how unwelcome Irish immigrants were treated, he held no prejudice toward Orientals.

Roney was an innovator in regard to union structure. As early as 1869 he conceived ideas for improving organizational structure. He called for local craft unions in a specific industry to be joined together in a council in each locality—such as a metal trades council, a building trades council and so on. Each local union was to be affiliated with the appropriate national union, and national craft unions were to be affiliated in councils mir-

roring those at the local level. Putting his ideas into practice, he formed the Federated Iron Trades Council of San Francisco, and was leader or founder of other organizations—namely the Seamans' Protective Association, the San Francisco Trades Assembly and the Vallejo Labor Council. In 1885 he convened a gathering which established the Federated Trades of the Pacific Coast. This evolved into the central council for all local unions in the city. During these activities he was fired from the Union Iron Works no less than four times. Professor Cross noted that Roney "dominated the labor movement in San Francisco during 1881–1886" (Roney, x).

Although he defended the character of Chinese immigrants, for economic reasons Roney formed an organization to press for limiting immigration from China. It lasted until the Chinese Exclusion Act became law in 1882. Roney's first wife died in 1904. He married twice more. His second wife died in 1912. Thereafter, he moved to Southern California living in Watts, Los Angeles and Long Beach where he died leaving his third wife a widow on January 24, 1925.

Roney is buried in San Gabriel, California.

*See* Labor Movement

Frank Roney, *Frank Roney, Irish Rebel and California Labor Leader, An Autobiography,* ed., Ira B. Cross (Berkeley, 1931).
Alexander Saxton, *The Indispensable Enemy* (Berkeley, 1971).
Neil Shumsky, "Frank Roney's San Francisco—His Diary: April 1875–March 1876," *Labor History* (Spring 1976): 244–64.

L. A. O'DONNELL

## ROONEY, PAT (1880–1962)

Songwriter, actor, dancer, and vaudeville entertainer. Pat Rooney was born to the singer Patrick James Rooney and the actress Josie Granger in New York City in 1880. After his father's death twelve years later, Rooney and his sister Mattie took to the stage as variety stage actors. In 1897 and 1898 Rooney's career flourished with *In Atlantic City,* a musical comedy that toured throughout the East. Between 1901 and 1907 Rooney sang, danced and directed many Rogers Brothers productions. In an English pantomime called *Mother Goose* Rooney met Marion Bent, whom he married on April 10, 1904, and had a son. Together they formed an impressive dance team. In 1925 they starred in *The Daughter of Rosie O'Grady* with a waltz clog that Rooney had made famous. Four years later, Rooney danced in one of the first sound films ever made, *Night Club.* Though his wife retired in 1932, Rooney continued his career with Herman Timberg. Together they made an Irish-Jewish team that charmed audiences at the Palace Theater. In 1940 Rooney's wife, Marion, died. Over the next two years Rooney declared bankruptcy and then married Helen Rubon Rooney, his son's divorced wife. After her sudden death in 1943, Rooney married Carmen Schaffer in 1944. In 1948 Rooney appeared in the movie *Variety Time,* and created the role of Arvide Abernathy in 1950 for the stage production of *Guys and Dolls.* Rooney continued to perform on television and for nightclubs and banquets right up until his death in New York City on September 9, 1962.

*See* Cinema, Irish in

Abe Burrows, "The Making of *Guys and Dolls,*" *Atlantic Monthly* (January 1980).
Extensive materials documenting Rooney's career are available at the Theater Collection of the New York Public Library.

John B. Kennedy, "We've Forgotten How to Fight," *Collier's* (May 11, 1929).

Gilbert Millstein, "Clean-living Rooney Marches On," *New York Times* (June 29, 1952): II:1.

Obituary, *New York Times* (September 11, 1962).

Alexander Woollcott, "The Play," *New York Times* (March 16, 1921).

DANIEL J. KUNTZ

## ROWAN, STEPHEN CLEGG (1808–1890)

Naval officer. Born near Dublin, Ireland of Protestant parents, Rowan and his family eventually settled in Piqua, Ohio. He began his naval career as a midshipman in 1826. He spent the next two decades on a wide variety of assignments from the West Indies to the Mediterranean to the Pacific. During the Mexican War, Rowan assisted General Stephen Kearny in the capture of San Diego and Los Angeles. After the war, Rowan continued to serve in posts on both land and sea. At the start of the Civil War, Rowan and the steam-sloop *Pawnee* saw some of the first naval action of the war, assisting in the defense of Washington and unsuccessful attempts to relieve Fort Sumter and capture the Norfolk Navy Yard. In February 1862, Rowan assembled a flotilla in the North Carolina sounds, destroying a gunboat and cooperating with General Ambrose Burnside in capturing Roanoke Island on February 8. The next day, Rowan's flotilla routed a Confederate squadron and captured Elizabeth City and Edenton, North Carolina. His success along the North Carolina coast continued through the spring and into the summer. In July, Rowan was promoted to captain and commodore on the same day. His next command, the *New Ironsides,* joined the South Atlantic Blockading Squadron and saw considerable action at Charleston Harbor from July to September, 1863. Rowan remained in the navy after the war, attaining the rank of vice admiral by the time of his retirement in 1889.

*Dictionary of American Biography*, Vol. VIII, part II: 196–97.

S. C. Ayres, *Sketch of the Life and Services of Vice Admiral S. C. Rowan* (1910).

William B. Cogar, *Dictionary of Admirals of the U.S. Navy*, 2 Vols. (Annapolis, 1989): I: 153–54.

TOM DOWNEY

## RUARK, GIBBONS (1941–  )

Poet. An American poet of Irish ancestry, Ruark stresses the importance of quiet reflection, memory, friendship, and sense of place. He is known for his use of traditional poetic forms, and his work is marked by its calm, contemplative tone.

Ruark, the son of a Methodist minister, was born in Raleigh, North Carolina and grew up in parsonages in several North Carolina towns. He received his A.B. from the University of North Carolina and an M.A. in English from the University of Massachusetts. He began teaching in 1965 and has been a professor at the University of Delaware since 1968. Married since 1963, he has two daughters.

Ruark's first publication came in the *Massachusetts Review* in 1965. *A Program for Survival*, his first book and a National Arts Council selection, appeared in 1971. Other awards have included the 1984 Saxifrage Prize for *Keeping Company* and multiple fellowships from the National Endowment for the Arts.

Frequent use of loose meter, off-rhyme, and a deft control of diction allow Ruark to maintain a natural, contemporary voice while using traditional poetic techniques and forms, especially the sonnet. His work is marked by a subdued, meditative mood appropriate to his subject matter. He values moments of silence and reflection, both while alone and while interacting with family or friends. The poetry conveys a sense of the poet's moods and inner life, but the primary focus is on his connection to other people, whether it is his wife and children, literary friends such as Seamus Heaney and James Wright, or unnamed companions in a pub. Thoughts of distant loved ones and the memory of Ruark's dead father haunt a number of poems.

In one poem Ruark describes "one man lifting his thoughtful head / To late September, in the early evening. / He moves so slowly you know he means to last. / He moves alone but his lamp may yet light / Faces of friends before the stars come clear." This description of Robert Francis, Ruark's friend and fellow poet, could easily be a portrait of Ruark himself. The unhurried, thoughtful man who quietly recalls absent friends while attending to the cycle of days and seasons is a figure frequently reappearing in Ruark's work.

Whether it is a childhood home in North Carolina or the cities and villages of Italy and Ireland, a strong sense of place always permeates Ruark's poetry. He quickly evokes a setting through brief narratives filled with local names and details, as in "Last Day At Newbliss: Remembering Richard Hugo," where he describes "wet roads going nowhere / But Cootehill, the way to Lourdes through Castleblayney," and "Miss Annie McGinn of Newbliss [who] delivers / A dark pint slow and silent as the island rain."

Ruark's appreciation of his Irish ancestry has increased over the years. This is particularly apparent in *Rescue the Perishing*, which is full of references to Irish locales and to authors such as Heaney, Yeats, and Swift. Among vignettes of Irish people and places is an occasional reference to the political situation in Northern Ireland. "North Towards Armagh" recounts an angry encounter between two women, one Irish and one English. But Ruark, never a political poet, mutes the conflict and ends the poem with calm images of "Windowlights, eyeglasses, slick pints of stout, the shine / Of a moment's stillness, permitting reflection."

Throughout his work, Ruark celebrates what he values most: peaceful contemplation and quiet companionship. Even when discussing conflict or grief, his response is to turn back to that which will provide comfort: friendly conversation, the sharing of a drink, and the ability to appreciate silence, stillness, and thoughtfulness.

*See* Poetry, Irish-American

Gibbons Ruark, *A Program for Survival* (Charlottesville, 1971).

———, *Reeds* (Lubbock, 1978).

———, *Keeping Company* (Baltimore, 1983).

———, *Rescue the Perishing* (Baton Rouge, 1991).

———, *Passing Through Customs: New and Selected Poems* (Baton Rouge, 1999).

CHRISTOPHER ANDERSON

## RUSSELL, MARY BAPTIST (1829–1898)

Social worker, administrator, religious leader. Katherine Russell, California's pioneer Sister of Mercy, was born in Newry, Ireland, in 1829. She was a child of the emancipation. Her parents Arthur and Margaret Russell provided their children with an education that was a unique blend of the academic, spiritual, social and pragmatic. This education served to form not only three Mercy superiors but also Lord Charles Russell, the first Catholic Chief Justice of England since the Reformation.

Katherine Russell, known as Mother Mary Baptist, touched the fiber of life in San Francisco on multiple levels. She established the first Catholic hospital on the West Coast, built a House of Mercy for working girls, missioned her sisters for service in elementary education, organized adult education classes and an employment service for women, established a Magdalen Asylum for women drawn into lives of prostitution, opened a home for the elderly and personally engaged in ministry to the prisoners of San Quentin. These vast works of mercy not only contributed to the quality of life in San Francisco but extended to the Northern California area.

In 1857 Mary Baptist Russell and her assistant Mary DeSales Redden traveled up the Sacramento River to the gold country. Sacramento was greatly in need of education for its emerging community. Here, in this gateway to the gold mines, life was raw and services minimal. Flooding, a constant threat, was first encountered by the sisters in the devastating floods of 1861. Parts of the city remained mired in water months after the initial floods. While her sisters ministered to the needy in boats, Mary Baptist opened the doors of St. Mary's Hospital in San Francisco to flood victims providing shelter, food and hope. The hospital became a social service center as well as haven for the sick. In 1868 Mary Baptist once more extended her services to the heart of the gold mining area by opening a school and orphanage in Grass Valley, California.

The accomplishments of Mary Baptist Russell are all the more remarkable due to the climate of her times. San Francisco in the mid-1850s was rife with anti-Catholic sentiment. Mary Baptist and her sisters were attacked in the press as exploiting the sick, being negligent in caring for the most infirm and using the commission from the county for care of the sick for their own benefit. This attack was met with a combination of silence and an invitation from Mary Baptist to the Grand Jury to investigate the institution which was under the direction of the sisters. The Grand Jury not only vindicated the sisters but cited them as one of the city's three services of distinction.

In addition to prejudice the sisters had to deal with vigilantism and major public health crises. Mary Baptist consistently offered the nursing services of the sisters during these major disasters. Whether it was the cholera epidemic of '55, the typhoid outbreak in Sacramento or the small pox epidemic of 1868, their presence was constant. A writer of the time said: "Those devoted Sisters of Mercy willingly presented themselves and entered on a mission of charity from which all others shrink in dismay and affright. . . . Their fearless, self-sacrificing love is an honor to their church and to their order" (Carroll, Vol. 4, p. 51).

Katherine Russell was intelligent, practical, compassionate and committed to the service of the poor. Her early training provided her with a clear understanding of the importance of human relationships. She was careful never to embarrass or shame those who benefited from her charity. Whether visiting a condemned killer such as San Quentin's "Tipperary Bill" or bringing food and linen to an impoverished family, she recognized their intrinsic value as human persons. This woman of mercy died on August 6, 1898. In a letter summing up her life, Father R. E. Kenna, S.J.,

said of San Francisco's Mother of the Poor: "Gentle as a little child, she was brave and resolute as a Crusader. Prudence itself, yet she was fearless in doing good to the needy, and in advancing the interests of religion. All who met her were forced to admire; and those who knew her best loved her most" (McArdle, p. 183).

*See* Sisters of Mercy

Mother Mary Austin Carroll, *Leaves from the Annals of the Sisters of Mercy*, Vol. 3 and 4 (New York, 1895).

Katherine Doyle, R.S.M., "*Mary Baptist Russell of California*," in MAST, Vol. 5/1 (Fall 1994): 40–46.

Sister Mary Aurelia McArdle, *California's Pioneer Sister of Mercy, Mother Mary Baptist Russell* (Fresno, CA., 1954).

Rev. Matthew Russell, *The Life of Mother Mary Baptist Russell, Sister of Mercy* (New York, 1901).

KATHERINE DOYLE, R.S.M.

## RYAN, ABRAM JOSEPH (1838–1886)

Roman Catholic priest, poet, journalist and editor. He was born on February 5, 1838, at Hagerstown, Maryland. He was the son of Irish parents, Matthew and Mary (Coughlan) Ryan, from County Tipperary, Ireland, who previously had immigrated to the United States from the Emerald Isle. In America, when Abram was still a young boy, the Ryan family moved west from Maryland to Missouri, settling ultimately in St. Louis. Baptized Matthew Abram Ryan, at his Confirmation the teen-age Irishman received the name Joseph. He then later discontinued using "Matthew" (Nolan, 1224).

Undertaking his early formal education at the Christian Brothers' School in St. Louis, Ryan afterwards attended the Vincentian-run St. Mary's of the Barrens Seminary at Perryville, Missouri, an institution situated eighty miles south of St. Louis. Subsequently, in 1854, he joined the Vincentians (Congregation of the Mission), taking his final vows on November 1, 1856. Following studies at Our Lady of Angels Seminary in Niagra Falls, New York, Ryan was ordained a priest on September 20, 1860, in St. Louis.

Moving between New York, Missouri and Illinois for the initial two years of his priesthood, in September 1862, Father Ryan was assigned to St. Mary's Church in Peoria, Illinois. It was about that time that he requested to be released from his vows as a Vincentian. In the meantime, the American Civil War having erupted, Father Ryan had begun to show strong pro-Confederate sympathies: ones which were to influence considerably his writing of poetry and prose. For the remainder of his life, Father Ryan was troubled over the destruction that came with that struggle. And the battlefield death of his younger brother, David, only served to exacerbate the priest's southern loyalties. He carried that sadness throughout the remainder of his life. As a result, much of Father Ryan's poetry, employing Roman Catholic themes, memorialized the cause of the South.

For a while Father Ryan served as an uncommissioned chaplain for the Catholic soldiers in the Confederate Army. But after the peace at Appomattox, he blossomed as a poet and editor. From 1864 to 1870, he served in first the Diocese of Nashville and then the Diocese of Savannah. In the latter diocese, he became editor of the *Banner of the South*. On June 8, 1870, Father Ryan moved to the Diocese of Mobile, being assigned to the cathedral staff there and serving for a short time as secretary to Bishop John Quinlan, himself an Irishman from Cloyne, Ireland. In 1877 Father Ryan was named pastor of St. Mary's Church in Mobile.

From 1872–1875, from Mobile, Father Ryan served as an editor of Archbishop of New Orleans Jean-Marie Odin's newly established newspaper the *Morning Star and Catholic Messenger* (Baudier, 422). In 1881, the Irish priest retired to Biloxi, Mississippi. Father Ryan died on April 22, 1886, while making a retreat with the Franciscans in Louisville, Kentucky. Roger Baudier called him "the famous poet-priest of the South" (Baudier, 422). Among his best-known works are *Father Ryan's Poems* (Mobile, 1879); *Poems: Patriotic, Religious, Miscellaneous* (Baltimore, 1880); and *A Crown for Our Queen* (Baltimore, 1882).

*See* Civil War

"Father Abram Ryan," address by Roger Baudier, Confederate Memorial Hall, New Orleans, 21 October 1950, Baudier Historical Collection, Archives of the Archdiocese of New Orleans.

Roger Baudier, *The Catholic Church in Louisiana* (New Orleans, 1939, reprinted 1972).

I. Dillard, "Father Ryan, Poet-Priest of the Confederacy," *Mississippi Historical Review,* 36 (October 1941).

E. A. Egan, "Ryan, Abram Joseph," *New Catholic Encyclopedia,* vol. XIV (Washington, D.C., 1967).

Thomas Kennedy, *Father Ryan: The Irish-American Poet-Priest of the Southern States* (Dublin, n.d.).

Charles Nolan, "Ryan, Abram Joseph (1838–86)," *The Encyclopedia of American Catholic History* (Collegeville, 1997).

PATRICK FOLEY

## RYAN, CORNELIUS JOHN ("Connie") (1920–1974)

Journalist and author. Ryan was born in Dublin, Ireland, the son of John Joseph and Amelia Clohisey. He graduated from the Irish Christian Brothers Academy and then went to study at the Irish Academy of Music where he focused on developing his talent for playing the violin. However, with the advent of World War II, Ryan left his musical pursuits in Ireland when offered the position of secretary under Garfield Weston, a member of parliament in Great Britain.

Ryan's first reporting job was in 1941 with the London office of Reuters News Agency and he covered such stories as the London Blitz of 1940–1943, the training of American troops in England during the Normandy invasion and eventually he followed General George S. Patton's Third Army on its victorious march across Europe. By 1945, he was asked by the *Daily Telegraph* to open its Tokyo office and there he covered the emergence of atomic bombs and the postwar aftermath. During this time he was inspired to write two books: the *Star-Spangled Mikado,* coauthored with Frank Kelly (1948), and *MacArthur* (1950). In 1947 Ryan returned to New York City and soon married writer Kathryn Ann Morgan, who worked for *House and Home* and *Architectural Forum* publications.

In 1950, Ryan was invited to work for *Collier's* as an associate editor and he continued there until it closed in 1956. During these years he worked on another book entitled *The Longest Day* which he believed to be his most important work. The close of business at *Collier's* brought serious financial strain to Ryan due to the debt he had incurred while researching for his book. However, he soon found employment with *Reader's Digest* and within three years he became an editor and retained this position until his death. This job allowed him the time and resources to continue writing and he produced several subsequent works.

Ryan's most significant works include: *The Longest Day* (1959), *The Last Battle* (1966), and *A Bridge Too Far* (1974). His style was hailed as being both suspenseful and accurate and reflected overall his talent in reporting and covering stories. His book *The Longest Day* was very successful as a war history and Ryan further developed it into a screenplay version for a movie in 1962. It was his writing success that eventually covered the financial loss he had suffered earlier. Ryan's task as he described it was to bring war-time stories to the level of human spirit, to write about ordinary people and to expose the heroic acts shrouded in the ordinary courage and compassion of those he wrote about. Ryan invested his own money, to the sum of $60,000, to research appropriately the stories he wanted to tell. He took ten years to write *The Longest Day,* six years for *The Last Battle* and seven more for *A Bridge Too Far.* In his book *A Bridge Too Far* he interviewed Otto Gunshie, who was the last living associate of Adolf Hitler. He was also able to access Soviet archives and thus became among the few Americans ever permitted to view Soviet records.

Ryan's books took popular placement on the *New York Times'* best-seller list and have been translated into twenty languages. Ryan died on November 23, 1974.

*New York Herald Tribune* (March 16, 1966).
*Publisher's Weekly* (December 2, 1974).
*Time* (December 9, 1974).
*Dictionary of American Biography,* supplement 9.

JOY HARRELL

## RYAN, JOHN AUGUSTINE (1865–1945)

Social theorist. He was the foremost thinker and advocate on social issues for the Catholic Church in the United States during the period 1906–1945. He was born in Vermillion, Minnesota, the eldest of eleven children born to William and Mary Ryan. The Ryans had immigrated to the United States from Ireland in the early 1850s as a result of the potato famine. In 1887, John decided to become a priest for his home diocese of St. Paul. He studied at St. Thomas Seminary in St. Paul and was ordained to the priesthood on June 4, 1898. The same year, he was sent for advanced study in moral theology at the Catholic University of America (CUA) in Washington, D.C. In 1915, Ryan returned to CUA as a professor in the school of sacred theology, where he remained until 1940 (though he spent his last three years as a professor in the school of social sciences). He also taught at Trinity College for women and later at the National Catholic School of Social Service.

Ryan was influenced at an early age by the populist thinking of Ignatius Donnelly and that of Patrick Ford, editor of the *Irish World,* as well as by the forthright stands of his archbishop, John Ireland. At St. Thomas Seminary he was exposed to Leo XIII's social encyclical, *Rerum novarum.* Ryan spent the rest of his life exploring the practical implications of the encyclical and applying them to the American scene. While at CUA, he studied under the great Catholic "scientific" social reformers, Thomas Bouquillon and William Kerby, who insisted that questions of social morality had to be grounded in precise observations of social reality and not just considered in abstract terms. They provided the tools by which Ryan analyzed and applied *Rerum novarum.*

In 1906, Ryan completed and published his doctoral dissertation, *A Living Wage: Its Ethical and Economic Aspects.* Ryan argued that each worker had a natural right to a wage that allowed the worker to live in accord with his or her dignity as a human being. This was a minimum of justice. The so-called "iron law of wages," which sought to pay the worker as little as possible was not only bad economics, it was also immoral. The worker had a *right* to a wage that enabled him to ensure the basic rights for himself and his family—food, shelter, clothing, and insurance against sickness, disability, and old age. The living wage was a fundamental right; while acknowledging the right to private property and the right to a profitable return on an investment, Ryan denied that these were absolute rights. Both rights were subordinate to the worker's right to a living wage, which was grounded in a more fundamental right—the right to life.

Ryan endorsed unions and collective bargaining as a means of securing the living wage, but when these failed, he argued, it was the duty of the state to step in and secure that right. Critics objected that Ryan's program violated the right of "free contract" between employer and employee, but Ryan exposed the lie of free contract which he saw as neither a right nor a reality. No worker freely consented to less than a living wage unless forced to do so by a superior economic force. "The name free contract is a misnomer. There can be no freedom of contract [for] laborers who must work or starve" (Ryan, p. 68). The worker's right to a living wage superseded all other economic rights, and served as the keystone to Ryan's economic thought.

Ryan's second major scholarly work, *Distributive Justice: The Right and Wrong of Our Present Distribution of Wealth,* was published in 1916. He considered this his "most important work" (Ryan, p. 136). Adopting the economic theory of John A. Hobson that depressions resulted from underconsumption and over-saving, Ryan argued that the central economic problem was one of distribution, not production. The United States was able to produce enough to supply all of its people with an adequate standard of living. Depressions resulted when supply exceeded demand, but the lack of demand was the result of a lack of purchasing power created by a maldistribution of wealth, or as Ryan observed, "speaking generally we may say that capital receives too much purchasing power and labor too little" (Ryan, p. 68).

Ryan was not content to argue abstractly over economic theory. He also proposed detailed plans of social legislation and worked to see his agenda enacted into law. The ultimate test of any economic theory for Ryan was its social utility. Did it contribute to "human welfare" (Curran, p. 32) or in other words, the common good? Ryan believed in gradual, not radical reform. While upholding the ideal as the ultimate goal, he worked for short-term gains.

In 1909 he clearly articulated his short-term goals in an article in the *Catholic World* entitled, "A Program of Social Reform by Legislation." His proposal included a call for a legal minimum wage, an eight-hour workday, protective legislation for women and children, the right to boycott and picket, unemployment insurance, employment bureaus, social security against sickness, accidents, and poverty in old age, public housing, public ownership of utilities, of mines, and of forests, control of monopolies, land taxes, and prohibition of speculation in the stock market (Broderick, pp. 58–59). These proposals became the basis of his life's work.

In 1919, Ryan's proposals received an enormous boost when, at the urging of Father John O'Grady, he reworked a speech he had intended to deliver to the Knights of Columbus of Louisville into a program of social reconstruction for the post–World War I world. Included in his program were such perennial Ryan concerns as minimum wage legislation, social security insurance, and public housing. Ryan's program was adopted with few revisions and published by the Administrative Board of the National Catholic Welfare Conference as the Bishops' Program of Social Reconstruction in 1920. The Program was the first major episcopal statement by the U.S. Bishops on the economy, and represented a bold step by the American hierarchy. The progressive tone of the program was met by many with a good deal of surprise, and was referred to by socialist Upton Sinclair as the "Catholic miracle" (Broderick, p. 107). Several U.S. bishops were not quite so enthused and distanced themselves from the program.

In 1919, Ryan was appointed director of the newly created Social Action Department (SAD) of the NCWC. With the able assistance of Father Raymond McGowan, Ryan served as director until 1944. The SAD served as a platform from which Ryan could publicize his notions of social reform, and through which the general public could be educated as to the basic tenets of Catholic social teaching. To further this end Ryan initiated the Catholic Conference on Industrial Problems in 1923 as a forum to discuss and disseminate information.

During the 1920s Ryan became an advocate of international peace through disarmament. In 1927, he assisted in the creation of the Catholic Association for International Peace. The association avoided pacifism, opting to propagate the Catholic theory of the just war. Ryan also belonged to the National Council for the Prevention of War but resigned when the orientation of the Council became too pacifist, and because the Council sided with the antichurch forces during the Mexican disputes of the 1920s and '30s.

During the first years of the Depression, Ryan was outspoken in his criticism of the Hoover administration. Ryan argued, as he had earlier, that the Depression was brought on by underconsumption, which was created by a maldistribution of wealth. Real purchasing power had to be returned to the public if the Depression was to be reversed. Ryan, eschewing American Catholic fears of government power, urged federal and state governments to become more active, advocating minimum-wage laws, and public works programs.

In 1931, Pope Pius XI promulgated his important social encyclical *Quadragesimo anno,* "On Reconstructing the Social Order," forty years after *Rerum novarum.* Many heralded it in the United States as an endorsement of John Ryan's social agenda. CUA rector Fr. Thomas Shahan reportedly observed, "Well, this is a great vindication of John Ryan" (Broderick, p. 196).

Following *QA,* Ryan adopted Pius XI's call for a "vocational group system," similar to the medieval guild system in which labor and management worked together cooperatively directing their industry. The vocational group system intended to give the worker greater control over the industrial process but to maintain the right of individuals to private property.

While this remained a long term goal, Ryan insisted on the right of the state to ensure immediate economic justice and order by guaranteeing the natural rights of the worker. The state was to provide for the common good by protecting the weak (the laborer) from the strong (the rich capitalist). He was fond of quoting the following passage from *Rerum novarum,* "Whenever the general interest or any particular class suffers, or is threatened with evils which can in no other way be met, the public authority must step in to meet them" (Ryan, p. 44). Whenever Ryan was accused of being too socialistic because of his heavy reliance on the state, he referred people to this passage from *RN.*

Though initially lukewarm to Franklin Delano Roosevelt, Ryan became an ardent supporter of the New Deal, which he regarded as the closest approximation to Catholic social teaching. The New Deal, Ryan believed, provided a middle road between socialism and individualism. Ryan served on government panels, most notably the Industrial Appeals Board of the National Recovery Administration. In 1936, in response to the increasingly bitter attacks on FDR by the radio priest, Father Charles Coughlin, Ryan defended FDR and the New Deal in a nationally broadcast radio speech. Coughlin sarcastically called Ryan "Right Reverend New Dealer," and the title stuck. In 1937, Ryan became the first Catholic priest to provide benediction at a presidential inauguration. For the remainder of his life, Ryan supported FDR, even supporting his infamous court-packing plan.

In 1940, Ryan retired from CUA but continued as director of SAD until 1944. He died on September 16, 1945.

### CONCLUSION

In an era in which Catholics were hesitant to address public policy issues that did not directly affect Church concerns, Ryan clearly enunciated Catholic social teaching. In an era in which American-Catholic social thought was primarily negative, antisocialist, hesitant, and isolated, he presented a positive, practical agenda for social reform. Most importantly, he did so in a way that was understandable to non-Catholic Americans and reformers. Henceforth, the Catholic Church in the United States would be involved in the debate over public policy issues and on the economy.

F. Broderick, *Right Reverend New Dealer: John A. Ryan* (New York, 1963).
C. Curran, *American Catholic Social Ethics: Twentieth-Century Approaches* (Notre Dame, 1982).
J. McShane, *"Sufficiently Radical": Catholicism, Progressivism, and the Bishops' Program of 1919* (Washington, 1986).
D. O'Brien, *American Catholics and Social Reform: The New Deal Years* (New York, 1968).
J. Ryan, *Social Doctrine in Action: A Personal History* (New York, 1941).

JEFFREY M. BURNS

## RYAN, THOMAS FORTUNE (1851–1928)

Entrepreneur. Born to a Southern Irish family in Lovingston, Virginia, Ryan grew up on a farm, but was orphaned at fourteen without money. He made his way to Baltimore where he found a job as an errand boy at a dry-goods store and when he was twenty-one, Ryan moved to New York. He found a job as a messenger in a Wall Street brokerage firm and, in the next year, married Ida M. Barry, the daughter of the dry-goods owner in Baltimore. With his father-in-law's help, Ryan became a partner in the Lee, Ryan and Warren firm and later bought a seat on the New York Stock Exchange. Over the next ten years he quietly, but successfully built a small fortune and contributed to the Tammany Hall general committee. It was the emerging street-railway franchises in New York City, however, that catapulted Ryan into big business. He became integral to the financing of New York's subway system and then in consolidating competing subway systems into one. With a partner, Ryan later gained control of the State Trust Company, and though never convicted, was investigated for using funds from the Trust to bankroll his subway operations in New York. Ryan survived the crisis and went on to merge several other banking institutions and to organizing the National Bank of Commerce in 1903. The financier gained international attention when King Leopold of Belgium asked him to lead a delegation into the Belgian Congo to develop diamond, gold and copper. By 1905 Ryan had amassed a fortune of more than fifty million dollars with considerable power over banking, public utilities, and other industrial enterprises. He was never completely trusted and was accused of buying political influence by William Jennings Bryan. Ryan retired in 1910 to a large home on Fifth Avenue where his wife died October 17, 1917, leaving twenty million dollars to the Catholic Church. Ryan remarried on October 29, 1917 and died eleven years later on November 23, 1928 worth over two hundred million dollars.

Harry James Carman, *The Street Surface Railway Franchises of N.Y. City* (New York: AMS Press, 1969, 1919).
Burton Jesse Hendrick, *The Age of Big Business,* Chapter V (New Haven: Yale University Press, 1921).
——, "Great American Fortunes and Their Making. Street-Railway Financiers," *McClure's Magazine* (November, December 1907, January 1908).
Obituary, *N.Y. Times* and *Baltimore Sun* (November 24, 1928).
Thomas F. Ryan, "Why I Bought the Equitable," *North American Review* (August 1913).

DANIEL J. KUNTZ

S

## SADLIER, MARY ANNE MADDEN (1820–1903)

Novelist. Born in Cootehill, County Cavan, Ireland on 31 December 1820. Died 5 April 1903 in Montreal, Quebec Canada. Her father, Francis Madden, a successful merchant, provided an education for his daughter at home. Both parents instilled in the child an appreciation of literature, although her mother died when Mary Anne was relatively young. Evidence of her writing talents emerged early. The eighteen year old succeeded in publishing some verse in an English literary periodical, *La Belle Assemblee.*

Financial setbacks in the 1840s plagued her father and evidently contributed to his death in 1844. Later in that same year, the twenty-four-year-old Madden immigrated to Montreal. As a poor, single Irish woman with some proven literary talent, she wrote to support herself financially. Her first publication, *Tales of the Olden Time: A Collection of European Traditions,* appeared in serial form in 1845.

That same year, she met James Sadlier, a leading Catholic publisher who, with his brother Denis, owned D. & J. Sadlier. They married in 1846 and remained in Montreal until 1860. During those fourteen years, Mary Anne gave birth to six children, three sons and three daughters. Only one son survived his mother.

In 1860, the Sadliers moved to New York City where James could oversee Sadlier's publications. Mary Anne's literary fame garnered her the friendship of such prominent Catholics as Archbishop John Hughes, Orestes Brownson, Isaac Hecker, and Thomas D'Arcy McGee. She also became a Catholic philanthropist, sponsoring a Foundling Asylum, a Home for the Aged, and a Home for Friendless Girls. All were alternatives to the Protestant charitable societies, which sought the conversion of their Catholic dependents.

Nine years after moving to New York City, James died, and Mary Anne helped Denis Sadlier manage the publishing company until his death in 1885. In that same year, Mrs. Sadlier went back to Montreal to join some of her then grown children. From Canada, Mrs. Sadlier continued to oversee the company for the next ten years, until P. J. Kenedy and Sons gained control of the publishing operation, including the copyrights to her writings. From 1895 until her death in 1903, Mary Anne Madden Sadlier faced financial difficulties and survived through funds raised by her Montreal friends. During this same period, she achieved formal recognition of her contributions to the Catholic community. In 1895, Notre Dame awarded her the Laetare Medal.

### LITERARY CAREER

Over her lifetime, Mary Anne Madden Sadlier published nearly sixty works. Prominent among these were texts promoting the Catholic faith. In response to the death of her own son, Francis Xavier, a Jesuit, Sadlier composed *Purgatory: Doctrinal, Historical and Poetical* (1886).

Besides catechetical and devotional publications, Sadlier produced edited collections, plays, and essays. She edited a collection of the poems of her friend, Thomas D'Arcy McGee as well as a collection entitled *A Young Ladies Reader* (1875). Her interest in reaching Catholic youth also found expression in play writing, like *The Babbler, a Drama for Boys in One Act* (1863). Her articles appeared in such popular periodicals as *Literary Garland, True Witness,* the Boston *Pilot,* James McMaster's *Freeman's Journal,* and *American Celt.*

The most noted works, however, are her novels. Many first appeared as serials in the Sadlier publication, the *Tablet.* Sadlier's husband, James, provided advice on the growing market of immigrant readers. The majority of her novels feature the Irish enduring the hardships encountered either on the island of their birth or in their new homes as poor, struggling immigrants. She also recounts heroic tales of Ireland's past.

During their fourteen years in Montreal, Mary Anne produced six novels including *The Blakes and the Flanagans: A Tale Illustrative of Irish Life in the United States.* The story contrasts the deleterious effects of a public school education on immigrants' faith and familial loyalty with the positive results of a Catholic education. Another, published after the move to New York, is *Bessy Conway; or, the Irish Girl in America.* It recounts an Irish domestic's triumph through her unwavering faith and virtue despite threats and temptations and her return to Ireland in time to save her village. Both of these, like the 1864 *Confessions of an Apostate,* portray the harsher aspects of immigration including virulent anti-Catholicism, the immigrants' precarious economic situation, especially Irish women's vulnerability, and the many temptations to abandon one's Irish cultural and religious identity.

### SIGNIFICANCE

Most twentieth-century literary critics have dismissed Sadlier's novels as too sentimental or lacking sophisticated prose. In recent feminist literary analysis, however, Sadlier's works have received new consideration because of their depiction of Irish-Catholic women's struggles both in Ireland and in North America. Within cultural studies, her novels are recognized as sociologically and ethnographically important sources given their depictions of Irish Catholic immigrant culture and perceptions of Irish Catholic identity both here and in the motherland.

Mary Anne Madden Sadlier's accomplishments as a successful Irish Catholic author demonstrate how an Irish immigrant woman could use her ethnic and religious identity as a means to accommodate her new social and cultural setting. Her literary talent and publishing connections allowed her to take advantage of the popularity of female-authored fiction at the end of the nineteenth century. Her personal history as well as her novels illustrate the concern generated by the sizable migration of single Irish women to the United States and Canada in the second half of the nineteenth century and the precarious financial state of the single woman, whether she was unmarried or a widow. Mary Anne Madden Sadlier also epitomized the resourcefulness of many Irish Catholic women faced with the challenges of survival.

Mary Anne Sadlier, *The Red Hand of Ulster* (Boston, 1850).
———, *The Blakes and the Flanagans* (Dublin, 1855).
———, *Old and New; or Taste Versus Fashion* (New York, 1862).
———, *Bessy Conway; or The Irish Girl in America* (New York, 1861).

————, *Confessions of an Apostate* (New York, 1864).

————, *The Old House by the Boyne* (New York, 1865).

————, *Aunt Honor's Keepsake* (New York, 1866).

————, *Maureen Dhu, The Admiral's Daughter* (New York, 1870).

————, *The Invisible Hand: A Drama in Two Acts* (New York, 1873).

————, *O'Byrne; or the Expatriated* (New York, 1898).

*Dictionary of Irish Literature* (1979) s.v. "Sadlier, Mary Anne."

E. C. Donnelly, *Round Table of Representative American Catholic Novelists* (New York, 1897).

*Essays on Canadian Writing*, 29 (Summer 1984): 96–116.

*The Feminist Companion* to Literature in English (1990) s.v. "Sadlier, Mary Anne (Madden)."

Michele Lacombe, "Frying Pans and Deadlier Weapons: The Immigrant Novels of Mary Anne Sadlier."

Liz Szabo, "The Mary Anne Sadlier Archive," available from http://avery.med.virginia.edu/~eas5e/Sadlier.

SANDRA YOCUM MIZE

## ST. AUGUSTINE, FLORIDA

Founded by Spain in 1565, St. Augustine is the oldest European town in North America. Two Irishmen in the service of Spain reached this remote outpost on Florida's Atlantic coast during the final decade of the sixteenth century. Fr. Richard Arthur from Limerick was appointed parish priest in 1597, and had as one of his parishioners an Irish-born soldier named Darby Glavin.

Fr. Arthur was well prepared for life in the garrison town. Before entering the priesthood, he had served as a Spanish soldier in Flanders, Italy and Malta. St. Augustine's parochial registers, which date back to 1594, list the baptisms and marriages he performed there from 1597 to 1604, when age and infirmity overtook him. In 1606, the Bishop of Cuba reported that Fr. Arthur had died in Florida. He was the first Irish-born priest to minister in what is now the United States.

In 1585 and 1587, Darby Glavin participated in Sir Walter Raleigh's attempts to plant English colonies in the area then known as Virginia. He deserted from the second in Spanish-ruled Puerto Rico when the English fleet stopped for fresh water. The suspicious Spaniards first sentenced Glavin to a term as a galley slave in Cuba, and in 1595 sent him as a soldier to St. Augustine.

In 1600, Glavin gave St. Augustine's Spanish governor a colorful account of his 1585 experiences with the English on Roanoke Island. The Irish soldier was still unaware that the 1587 colony had disappeared. But Glavin's reference to brickmaking on Roanoke Island has proved invaluable to modern archaeologists investigating the site of Raleigh's 1585 colony.

Maynard Geiger, *The Franciscan Conquest of Florida, 1573–1618* (Washington, D.C., 1937).

Ivor Noel Hume, *The Virginia Adventure: Roanoke to James Towne* (New York, 1994).

David Beers Quinn, ed., *The Roanoke Voyages, 1584–1590*, 2 vols. (London, 1955).

BRIAN McGINN

## ST. LOUIS

When the Louisiana Territory became part of the United States in 1804, the congenial French residents of St. Louis welcomed Irish immigrants, Catholic and Protestant, with a warmth unmatched on the eastern seaboard. As a result, many Irishmen adapted quickly to the frontier town.

Jeremiah Connor arrived in 1805, purchased considerable property, and was chosen sheriff. Joseph Charless came from Ireland in 1808 and published a weekly paper, the *Missouri Gazette*. Father James Maxwell, who had served the region since Spanish days as pastor of Ste. Genevieve, Missouri, sixty miles south of St. Louis, was elected president of the Territorial Council at its inaugural meeting in St. Louis in 1812. Unfortunately, he died accidentally within a year.

By the close of the War of 1812, St. Louis numbered many Irish businessmen: bilingual John Mullanphy, a wealthy cotton broker who had lived a short time in France; John O'Fallon, a nephew of Territorial Governor William Clark; Thomas Brady and the McKnights—known as the "Irish Crowd"; Ulsterman Robert Campbell; and the Timon, Rankin, and Finney brothers. Many of these joined Jeremiah Connor when he started the Erin Benevolent Association to work for Irish freedom.

In 1818, the bishop of Louisiana Territory, Louis W. V. Du Bourg, planned a brick cathedral in St. Louis. French, Irish, and Anglo-Americans contributed. Jeremiah Connor and Thomas McGuyre made large personal donations and set out to collect the pledges. Thirty Celtic names appear in the list of donors. About twenty other names of Anglo-American background had Irish connections. By the time of the incorporation of the city in 1822, one out of seven St. Louis men was Irish.

The Catholic Irish profited from their identity of faith with the colonial French and from their identity of language with the Anglo-Americans. They readily intermarried with both long-established Creole families and new-coming Anglo-Americans. A short-lived dispute about language in the cathedral ended in a compromise.

When Vincentian Superior Father Joseph Rosati became first bishop of St. Louis in 1827, he invited Belgian Jesuits, who had staffed a combined Indian school and Jesuit seminary in nearby Florissant, to man St. Louis College, previously conducted by diocesan priests and lay associates. A few Irish enrolled among the greater numbers of French, Mexican, and Anglo-American students. The school won a university charter in 1832.

John Mullanphy helped to bring the Religious of the Sacred Heart, under St. Philippine Duchesne, from Florissant, Missouri, to start an academy for young girls, and gave a subsidy to the Daughters of Charity from Maryland to open a hospital. Both congregations recruited Irish members. By 1830 St. Louis had 5,852 inhabitants.

The St. Louis Irish celebrated St. Patrick's Day with banquets, usually on a steamboat. They toasted Irishmen from Brian Boru to Daniel O'Connell.

When Bishop Rosati planned a cathedral of federal style in the early 1830s, five Irish and three French served on the organizing committee.

After the dedication of the cathedral, Bishop Rosati sought as his auxiliary a fellow Vincentian, Irish-American John Timon, who had grown up in St. Louis. Father Timon turned down the pope's appointment since he was committed to a new Vincentian mission in the recently established Republic of Texas.

By 1840, when Pope Gregory XVI sent Bishop Rosati on a special mission to Haiti, St. Louis had grown to 16,469. Father Peter Richard Kenrick, the brother of the bishop of Philadelphia, became auxiliary bishop. A native of Dublin and a graduate of Maynooth, Kenrick became second bishop of St. Louis in 1843 at Rosati's death, and in 1847 first archbishop.

While Rosati had been a pastoral prelate, Kenrick was a scholarly theologian. Though aloof by nature, he handled the day-today business of the People's Bank—a forerunner of the modern-day credit union—when its founder, young Father Ambrose Heim, died prematurely.

In the mid-1840s, three new parishes grew up: St. Vincent's, French and Irish, and St. Patrick's and St. Francis Xavier's, predominantly Irish. Father Timon, now Vincentian superior, challenged the men of St. Louis to form the first unit of a new organization, the St. Vincent de Paul Society. Many Irish-Americans, among them Mayor Bryan Mullanphy, Judge Joseph O'Neill, and an architect, Robert Mitchell, were active members.

Bryan Mullanphy, a lawyer, left much of the fortune he inherited from his father, John Mullanphy, to set up a fund to aid Irish immigrants arriving penniless in St. Louis; it eventually coalesced into "Travelers Aid."

In that decade, too, the Sisters of St. Joseph of Carondelet, just beyond the southern limits of St. Louis, and the Lorettines in Florissant began academies for French, Anglo-American, and Irish girls.

By 1850, refugees of the Irish famine and of the abortive German unification effort brought the population to 77,860. Many destitute Irish squatted beyond the city limits in an area dubbed "Kerry Patch." Nativists stirred up violence against the newcomers during the election years 1852 and 1854. The agitation lasted only a short time and touched only certain neighborhoods, but it had two lasting effects. First, it split Irish Protestants and Catholics. Many Protestants began to coalesce with their fellow Protestant Anglo-Americans. Secondly, the medical faculty separated from Saint Louis University. To mention one specific result of this split, John O'Fallon, a Methodist, who had earlier given two buildings to the Saint Louis University School of Medicine, soon helped the newly forming Eliot Seminary, later Washington University.

The Irish Catholics continued to move forward socially and economically. They opened four new parishes in the West End shortly after 1850. Father John B. Bannon, the Dublin-born pastor of one of these, St. John the Evangelist, was chaplain of the Temperance Society and local units of the state militia. When these militia units joined the Confederate forces in 1861, Father Bannon followed to serve them.

Immigration from Ireland dropped dramatically during the war years, and never regained its pre-war high. But second-generation Irish moved to new areas and built churches with interest-free loans as a result of a bequest of a little-known businessman, John Thornton. He left several thousand dollars to Irish-American nephews and nieces and $500,000 to the archdiocese. Half of this went to specific charitable institutions; the other half formed a revolving fund for parish expansion. Archbishop Kenrick set no restrictions on these loans to new parishes. Each parish paid back the money if and when it could.

The Irish Catholics looked to their parishes rather than to any citywide manifestation of Irish pride, except for the St. Patrick's Day parade on the near north side. The Irish formed and joined many organizations: the Catholic Total Abstinence Society, the United Sons of Erin, and the Ancient Order of Hibernians. The Catholic Knights of America welcomed Irish and other nationalities and spread to thirty-four branches with 2,819 members. The one Irish effort that failed to win Archbishop Kenrick's approval, the Fenian Movement, had a good goal—Irish freedom—but flawed means.

At the Vatican Council in 1870, Archbishop Kenrick opposed the definition of papal infallibility as lacking scriptural and traditional foundation, but accepted the decision of the council.

During the following years, the veteran archbishop left the routine administration of the St. Louis church to his close friend and coadjutor Patrick Ryan. When the latter became archbishop of Philadelphia in 1884, Kenrick took control again.

Over the years the Christian Brothers began a college, two academies, and grade schools at seven predominantly Irish parishes. Many priests of the archdiocese were to begin their study of Latin under the tutelage of the Christian Brothers.

The Sisters of St. Joseph and other congregations opened schools for girls in many Irish parishes. The Sacred Heart Convent and the Visitation Academy enrolled a growing number of pupils of Irish background, as did Saint Louis University's academic department after it closed its boarding facilities in 1880.

One of the first issues Archbishop Kenrick had to face, once he resumed control, dealt with the Church's approval of America's first great labor union. To the surprise and dismay of many in St. Louis and elsewhere, Archbishop Kenrick opposed the Knights of Labor. In this, he ran into opposition with one of his most vocal priests, Father Cornelius O'Leary, and all but one of his fellow archbishops. Cardinal Gibbons of Baltimore defended the Knights and prevented a Roman condemnation of the union. Master General of the Knights of Labor, Terence Powderly, praised Father O'Leary as the only *priest* who spoke in favor of the working man, before *Rerum Novarum*, Pope Leo's great encyclical on the condition of labor.

Archbishop Kenrick wanted a zealous, young priest of limited experience, Brady by name, as his coadjutor. The St. Louis pastors preferred Bishop John J. Kain of Wheeling, West Virginia, who came in 1893. Archbishop Kenrick ignored him. Two tense years ensued. Finally, in 1895, the new archbishop gained full authority. He favored men who had not asked for him and turned against those who supported him, such as the skillful editor of the *Western Watchman,* Father David Phelan. When Phelan wielded a pen with devastating humor, the archbishop pulled back his condemnation of the *Watchman.*

On the positive side, Archbishop Kain gave full status to the pastors of national churches and supported the Christian Brothers whose European superiors failed to see American realities. The Knights of Columbus made great headway at that time. Simultaneously, three authors of the Irish community won national recognition: short story teller Kate O'Flaherty Chopin; critic and editor Marion Reedy; and juvenile novelist Father Francis Finn.

At their college and at parishes where they taught, the Christian Brothers started soccer teams that helped to galvanize parish loyalties and gave a great push to the image of St. Louis as a "soccer center."

In the spring of 1903, Bishop John J. Glennon, auxiliary of Kansas City, became coadjutor to Archbishop Kain. The tall, handsome, eloquent native of Westmeath found the city religiously rudderless but culturally alive, as it prepared for the coming celebration of the Louisiana Purchase centennial. Shortly after the highly successful World's Fair, the new archbishop planned a great cathedral. With that underway, Archbishop Glennon laid plans for Kenrick Seminary in suburban St. Louis. During these years, at almost every major occasion of the Church, such as the centenary of the diocese of New York in 1908 and the funeral service of Cardinal Gibbons, Archbishop Glennon gave the sermon or eulogy.

Basically conservative, Archbishop Glennon opposed women's suffrage, dancing at parish festivals, and the Prohibition movement. He reflected the Republicanism of President William Howard Taft, not the Democratic leanings of his people.

Congressman William P. Igoe, representing a heavily Irish district in north St. Louis, voted against America's declaration of war in 1917. With the conflict still raging, he was re-elected the following year. Father Tim Dempsey, who was gaining local renown by providing homes for homeless men and women, spoke out against England for its treatment of the Irish and strongly opposed America's entrance into the war.

In the mid-1920s, Daniel A. Lord, S.J., of English-Irish ancestry, took charge of the Sodality of Our Lady at its headquarters in St. Louis and expanded it greatly, especially on the high school level. Father Lord wrote 40 books and 224 religious tracts that won wide distribution. The first Senatus of the Legion of Mary also developed in St. Louis.

The archdiocese opened McBride High for boys under Marianist direction and Rosati-Kain High for girls with a combined staff of Sisters of St. Joseph and School Sisters of Notre Dame. Dominican Sisters, Sisters of the Incarnate Word, and BVMs taught at elementary schools and opened academies with a largely Irish-American clientele.

The Great Depression of 1929 hit all classes, but especially the unskilled laborers. Fortunately, most Irish working men belonged to craft unions. Archbishop Glennon had little specific guidance for the growing labor union movement in the late 1930s. Likewise, he gave little attention to the long-standing black Catholics, as well as to the growing number of Protestant Blacks who came to St. Louis for work in war industries during both wars. Nonetheless, Pope Pius XII named him a cardinal of the church in the consistory of 1946. The new cardinal died at the presidential palace in Dublin on his return home.

World War II had demanded a national unity of purpose. Particular ethnic issues declined among various nationalities, including the Irish. Returning GIs sought homes away from the parishes of their birth in new suburban areas that lacked ethnic identification. Many took advantage of the GI Bill to enroll at Saint Louis University, a school that was moving into a significant era in its history. Its president, Patrick Holloran, was of Irish background, as were many of its distinguished faculty members, among them Professors Thomas Neill, James Collins, John F. Bannon, and Bernard Dempsey.

Sports remained popular among the Irish. The Saint Louis University basketball team, led by All-American "Easy Ed" Macauley, gained national prominence in 1948. The baseball Cardinals, managed by Eddie Dyer in 1946 and by Johnny Keane in 1964, won the world championship. Harry Keough, captain of America's best World Cup team of 1951, coached Saint Louis University's soccer teams to five NCAA championships with many players of Irish ancestry.

Seventeen priests of Irish background of the St. Louis Archdiocese became bishops over the years. Among these, five became archbishops and one, John Cody, a cardinal. John Cardinal Carberry, a native of Brooklyn of Irish ancestry, headed the St. Louis Archdiocese from 1968 to 1980. In the political world, Thomas Eagleton served two terms in the U.S. Senate; John Cochran, John B. Sullivan, and his wife Lenore, in the House; and Raymond Tucker in the mayor's office. Irish scholars, Sister Isadore Lennon, R.S.M., Sister Dolorita Dougherty, C.S.J., Sister Dan Hannefin, D. of C., and Mother Louis Callen, R.S.C.J., wrote histories of their religious congregations. Many other Irish Catholics wrote and published books. Among men of science, James Macelwane, S.J., of Ulster ancestry, pioneered in seismology.

In recent years, Irish St. Louisans chose Galway as their sister city. They sponsor a civic parade in the heart of the city on the Saturday before St. Patrick's Day, with a guest of honor from Galway presiding.

The many active units of the Ancient Order of Hibernians plan its neighborhood parade on St. Patrick's Day itself in the city's one heavily Irish-American, working-class neighborhood. St. Louisan George Clough served as president of the Order from 1990 to 1994.

The Saint Louis University Law School began a concentration in Irish legal lore, and the University of Missouri-St. Louis, under the chancellorship of Blanche Touhill, is developing an Irish studies program.

In the 20th century, St. Louis did not rate as high in the constellation of Irish-American cities as it did in the 19th century. Many cities of the eastern seaboard that had reluctantly accepted Irish immigrants during the 19th century, came to welcome later generations, and gradually overshadowed St. Louis as an Irish center. The St. Louis Irish occupy a less conspicuous position, but remain a confident, creative community.

*See* Missouri

Ellen Meara Dolan, *The Saint Louis Irish* (St. Louis, 1967).

W. B. Faherty, S.J., *Dream by the River: Two Centuries of St. Louis Catholicism 1765–1997,* Third Edition (St. Louis, 1967).

W. B. Faherty, S.J., and NiNi Harris, *St. Louis: A Concise History* (St. Louis, 1994).

Paul C. Schulte, *The Catholic Heritage of St. Louis* (St. Louis, 1934).

WM. BARNABY FAHERTY, S.J.

## SAINT PATRICK'S CATHEDRAL

Two churches, both named Saint Patrick's, have served as New York's (arch)diocesan cathedral. The earliest, situated between Mott and Mulberry, Prince and Houston Streets, opened in 1815. It was partially destroyed by fire in 1866, and rebuilt with the idea that it would in the future be a regular parish church. The diocese purchased the site for the new cathedral, located between Fifth and Madison Avenues, 50th and 51st Streets, in 1810. When New York was elevated to an archdiocese in 1850,

St. Patrick's Cathedral, located between Fifth and Madison Avenues, 50th and 51st Streets

Archbishop John Joseph Hughes suggested a new cathedral. Hughes laid the cornerstone August 15, 1858, and secured the services of architect James Renwick, who designed a Gothic structure. John Cardinal McCloskey formally opened the building May 25, 1879, but some of the building's noted features were added later: the spires in 1888, the Lady Chapel in 1906, the organ (still in use) in 1930, the main altar (still in use) in 1942, and the bronze doors in 1949. Saint Patrick's was named for the patron saint of Ireland and contains many reminders of the Irish presence in New York: two windows in the south transept honor Saint Patrick; there is a statue of Saint Patrick in front of the cathedral throne; a side altar with Celtic motifs honors Saint Brigid (and Saint Bernard); above this altar is a window honoring Saint Columbanus; and on Saint Patrick's day, there is a parade-reviewing stand in front of the cathedral. The cathedral is also an integral part of the archdiocese, being the parish church for the area between Third and Seventh Avenues, 44th and 59th Streets.

Margaret Carty, *St. Patrick's Cathedral* (Wilmington, DE, 1983).

C.-B. Costecalde, *A Short Tour of Saint Patrick's Cathedral* (Strasbourg, 1997).

*Saint Patrick's Cathedral* (Charlotte, n.d.).

MARY ELIZABETH BROWN

## ST. PATRICK'S DAY PARADE

In his *Confessio,* which he wrote to defend his missionary work in Ireland, Patrick relates that he was born in Roman Britain in the first decade of the fifth century. His grandfather was a priest, and his father, Calpurnius, was a deacon. At the age of sixteen he was kidnapped by Irish marauders and enslaved as a shepherd for six years on the bleak hills of Antrim. He escaped but was haunted by an inner call to return and spread the gospel among the Irish. After studying in Gaul, he was ordained priest and bishop and returned to Ireland in 432 with a group of companions.

Patrick did not introduce Christianity to Ireland as there is ample proof that it already had roots there. For instance, the irascible St. Jerome relates that in 416 an Irish theologian argued a doctrinal point with him and he dismissed him as "an ignorant calumniator . . . full of Irish porridge." And there is a record that in 431 Rome had appointed a bishop to tend to the needs of Irish Christians. Yet Patrick, a British immigrant, has for over fifteen centuries been regarded as the patron saint of the Irish, a symbol of all they hold dear. And Ireland is also bound to Patrick as his

St. Patrick's Day Parade 1969, New York City

writings are the earliest extant documents written in Ireland. Over the centuries Patrick assumed a special and pivotal role in the cultural and spiritual life of the country; and the people expressed their devotion to him in song, poetry, prose, prayer and pilgrimage.

But it was in colonial America that the Irish first paraded to express their identity and solidarity to let others know that they were proud of being Irish. Ironically those who marched in the first St. Patrick's Day parade were Irishmen in British uniform, soldiers stationed in New York to preserve the grip of the crown on a restless colony. Until 1774 parading military units were a distinctive feature in the St. Patrick's Day celebrations in New York. After 1783 Irish-American soldiers participated in the parade until 1812 when some societies—such as the Friendly Sons of St. Patrick and the Shamrock Friendly Association—cooperated to run the parade, which consisted of small groups marching from the headquarters of their organizations to the first St. Patrick's Cathedral and other local churches. Since 1776 Boston also had its own parade.

After 1820 the increased flow of Irish immigrants brought St. Patrick's Day parades to wherever they settled in large numbers. All through the nineteenth century, Irish workers manned the mines, built the canals and laid the railroads, and March 17 became their special day when the wearing of the green symbolized their identity as they paraded their Irish pride.

John Concannon, the Archivist of the Ancient Order of Hibernians and coauthor with Frank Cull of the historically valuable

Celebrating St. Patrick's Day in Kansas City, Missouri, 1880s

Maureen O'Hara, Grand Marshall, marching up Fifth Avenue in New York City, St. Patrick's Day Parade 1999

*The Irish Who's Who* (New York, 1984), has become the collector and custodian of data and lore connected with St. Patrick's Day parades across America. His research has traced their history over two centuries, and has provided interesting insights into the life of the immigrants.

Pride, nostalgia and loneliness blended when parades came to such cities as Savannah (1812), Carbondale, PA (1833), New Haven, CT (1842), Chicago (1843), San Francisco (1852), Scranton (1853), Atlanta (1858), and Cleveland (1867). Concannon makes an annual survey of St. Patrick's Day parades, and for 1998 he reported that there were 235 in 44 states. But every town in America dons green on March 17 to celebrate what America has done for the Irish and what the Irish have done for America.

*See* Achievement of the Irish in America;
New York City; Irish in America

John J. Ridge, *St. Patrick's Day Parade in New York* (New York, 1988).

MICHAEL GLAZIER

## ST. PAUL AND MINNEAPOLIS

The history of the Irish in the Twin Cities of Minneapolis and St. Paul, Minnesota, differs from the group's story in seaboard ports of entry. For the most part, the Irish who arrived in the Twin Cities were not impoverished immigrants; direct arrivals from Ireland have been exceptions. Most arrived having already acquired considerable experience with American life, and in the Twin Cities, neither they nor their children needed to claw their way past a power elite that had been entrenched for generations.

Generalizations about the Irish presence in Minneapolis and St. Paul communities are misleading. Minneapolis has a reputation as a Scandinavian center, and with good cause; still, there has been a significant Irish presence in Minneapolis since the 1880s. Indeed, one of the defining memoirs of American Irish parochial life, Mary McCarthy's *Memories of a Catholic Girlhood*, describes the author's 1920s childhood in the solidly Irish enclave of St. Stephen's parish in south Minneapolis. A more paradoxical situation exists in the capital city. St. Paul has been stamped with an unmistakably Irish reputation even though, as Ann Regan notes in her examination of Twin Cities' Irish history in *They Chose Minnesota*, the Germans have outnumbered the Irish in St. Paul since earliest days. Regan suggests several sources for the Irish image, including the recent promotion of St. Patrick's Day festivities by area businessmen; the fact that St. Paul is the seat of a prominent Catholic diocese for many years headed by an Irish-dominated hierarchy; and most importantly, the high profile of Irish names in the city's political history.

White settlement in St. Paul began earlier than in its neighboring city across the river. As early as 1821, settlers were attracted to the regions around Fort Snelling, the military post overlooking the confluence of the Minnesota and Mississippi rivers. Some miles downstream, the city that would become St. Paul was establishing its origins. A classic muddy frontier village with the memorable name of Pigs Eye's Landing, scattered numbers of Irish were found among the mostly French-Canadian first settlers of the city. In 1852 a seminarian wrote that "My mission is among the dirty little ragged Canadian and Irish boys . . . To take charge of these impudent and insulting children of unthankful parents was the greatest mortification I ever underwent." One infamous early resident of St. Paul was Irish-born Edward Phelan, who in

September 1839 was arrested for the murder of his claim partner John Hays, also Irish. Released for insufficient evidence, the accused murderer took up a new claim on the east side of St. Paul, where a popular lake and adjoining city park bear his name.

As elsewhere, a strain of Protestant civic leaders with Irish names can be observed in early Twin Cities history. For example, the pharmacist and territorial office holder Robert Ormsby Sweeny designed the great seal of the state on its admission to the Union in 1858. This tradition, however, is usually considered as a subset of the Yankee, or Old Stock American, experience, which also has deep roots in the Twin Cities. Historically, the power elite in Minneapolis had an unusually strong association with New England Congregationalist history.

The *Minnesota Pioneer* reported the first sermon in the Irish language in Minnesota on November 21, 1854—an extraordinary incident, given the low stature of the language in the years just after the Great Famine. The building of Catholic churches demonstrated the growing Irish presence in St. Paul. In 1867, the Church of St. Mary opened in the Lowertown area. For the next seventy years it was an Irish stronghold. St. Michael's parish, across the river, opened in 1868, established in part because the poorer Irish did not wish to pay the toll to cross the bridge. When the Church of St. Mark opened in the city's westernmost neighborhood in 1889, it was not identified as an Irish "nationality parish," though in fact its earliest members were almost entirely Irish-born railroad workers in the nearby train yards.

In Minneapolis, the Irish also concentrated near the city's center. Regan notes that in 1880, two-thirds of the community's Irish population could be found within a six-block radius of three Catholic parishes, Immaculate Conception, St. Anthony, and Holy Rosary. Minneapolis's Irish pockets were more mobile than in the capital, shifting first to the city's north side and later to south Minneapolis.

Kathleen O'Brien's study of occupational status in the Minneapolis Irish shows a steady and dramatic rise toward white-collar employment as the Irish entered the middle classes. In 1880, 36.8% of persons living in Irish households worked as laborers. Over the next twenty-five years that percentage dropped to exactly half, 18.4% in 1905. Simultaneously, while only 7.5% of the Irish employed in the city in 1880 were clerical workers and civil servants, that percentage had more than tripled by the later date. In St. Paul, Irish occupational choice showed another familiar pattern by gravitating to the police and fire departments. Irish-born citizens accounted for one-fifth of St. Paul's turn-of-the-century public safety employees.

In 1884, Christopher O'Brien, a son of Archbishop John Ireland's personal secretary Dillon O'Brien, was elected mayor of St. Paul, one of the earliest Irish names in what would become a litany of such names in that office. Other St. Paul politicians of the era lived out the role of the "Boss." Patrick H. Kelly, who was born in County Mayo in 1831, arrived in Minnesota by way of Canada in 1857. Over the next several decades, Kelly—a wholesale grocer by profession—along with his associate Michael Doran and the quiet support of rail magnate James J. Hill, presided over an efficient political machine. In 1884 Kelly served as a national committeeman for the Democratic Party and was instrumental in securing the presidential nomination for Grover Cleveland.

In the temperance movement of the nineteenth century, the religious leaders of the Irish in the Twin Cities worked vigorously to disprove one of the stereotypes that had been attached to their group. Not surprisingly, Irish Twin Citians were extensively involved in the liquor trade, particularly before 1880. The legitimacy of their business was at least challenged—though far from overthrown—by an Irish-led temperance campaign. Joan Bland's history of the movement, *Hibernian Crusade,* chronicles the large role that Minnesotans played in the national Catholic Total Abstinence Union, which was founded in 1872. Led by John Ireland, a group of young priests gained prominence in this effort, among them future bishops Cotter of Winona, Shanley of Fargo, O'Gorman of Sioux Falls, and McGolrick of Duluth.

Irish ties to their ancestral home were sustained by patriotic groups, such as the Friends of Ireland, organized in St. Paul in 1877. Community response to visits by such nationalist leaders as land reformer Michael Davitt and constitutional nationalist Charles Stewart Parnell was reported to be "wildly enthusiastic." However excited the response to visiting Irish leaders may have been, the more frequent activities of the Irish community were based on social activities. Dramatic productions, literary societies, and parish festivals provided opportunities for Irish Twin Citians to meet with one another and share in group pride and achievement. The fraternal Ancient Order of Hibernians (AOH) and its Ladies Auxiliary thrived in Minnesota in the decades following its organization in 1879; by 1912, there were eighty-two AOH divisions statewide, most of them in the Twin Cities. Myriad social activities are recorded in the pages of the *Irish Standard,* a St. Paul-based newspaper associated with the AOH from 1885 to 1920. The diocesan paper, the *Northwestern Chronicle,* likewise reveals an Irish tilt in its coverage of news and social activities.

An unusual history attaches to St. Paul's most public expression of Irish identity, the St. Patrick's Day parade. As in most American cities, March 17 was the occasion of public celebrations by the Irish from the 1850s forward, capped by a parade which often called on the governor and usually ended at the cathedral, where the bishop gave a celebratory address. In Minnesota, the event often took on a further role as a joyous proclamation of winter's end. For unknown reasons, public celebrations of St. Patrick's Day were abruptly discontinued after 1901; the most frequently given explanation is that Archbishop John Ireland felt that rowdiness was bringing discredit to the saint's day, though no proof of this has ever been found. The St. Paul parade stayed dormant until 1967, when it was revitalized by a group of downtown restaurateurs and boosters. The popular new parade maintains an informal, even frivolous, character. Most participants march under banners bearing their family names. Minneapolis launched its parade in 1969.

If John Ireland's concern for maintaining public decorum was indeed the reason for the parade's sudden departure, his concern for a respectable image for the Irish would have been consistent with the group's dramatic ascent into the middle class and the professions. By 1900, Irish-Americans in the Twin Cities were confidently "arrived" citizens. In that year, the College of St. Thomas that the bishop had founded in 1885 graduated 162 young men—of whom eighty-six, or 53%, bore Irish surnames. The ethnic origins of the women who in 1905 entered the new College of St. Catherine in St. Paul followed a similar pattern. It was out of this milieu of new-found status that St. Paul produced its most famous Irish-American author, F. Scott Fitzgerald. Born into a prosperous St. Paul family in 1896, the young novelist's early life was dominated by his mother and grandmother McQuillan—both women whose social ambitions exceeded their financial means. In William V. Shannon's words, "this exile from the lace curtain parlors of St. Paul . . . became the poet of our mocking affluence."

Two areas in which Irish-Americans have distinguished themselves in twentieth-century Minnesota have been in the political life of the capital city and in the leadership of organized labor. In the forty years following 1932, nine out of ten St. Paul mayors, from both parties, had Irish surnames. Some historians have argued that the coalition between labor, Farmer-Laborites, and regular Democrats that formed around John J. McDonough's 1940 mayoral campaign served as the groundwork for the resurgence of the Democratic Party in statewide politics. One beneficiary of that resurgence was St. Thomas economics professor Eugene McCarthy, who began his national career when elected congressman from St. Paul in 1948.

In common with their counterparts throughout the United States, Irish-Americans in the Twin Cities have been conspicuous in organized labor. In the Depression era, among the most prominent area leaders were the Dunne brothers, who played a role in the violent 1934 Minneapolis Teamster's strike. Vincent Dunne was an avowed Trotskyite; he was frequently criticized in print by his brother Bill, who edited a communist paper. A somewhat more moderate labor leader in the same decade was William Mahoney of St. Paul, a president of the Machinist Union, editor of the *Union Advocate* newspaper, and a founder of the Farmer-Labor Party. Mahoney served one term as mayor of St. Paul in 1934, but was unable to effect the municipal ownership of all public services promised in his platform.

One legacy of Bishop Ireland's political activism in the nineteenth century has been the succession of progressive Catholic churchmen in the Twin Cities. Diocesan priest John A. Ryan gained national prominence by providing a Catholic response to the demagoguery of Fr. Charles Coughlin. His endorsement of the New Deal was recognized in 1936 when Ryan became the first Catholic priest to take part in a presidential inauguration. Francis Gilligan, a native of Massachusetts and long-time instructor at the St. Paul Seminary, also gained national recognition for his writings on issues of race and integration in his book *The Morality of the Color Line.* James P. Shannon, auxilary bishop of St. Paul, offered outspoken opposition to the Vietnam War as early as 1966, when much of the American Catholic hierarchy was decidedly hawkish.

Though Irish have been prominent in St. Paul, by mid-century its reputation as an Irish town was more entrenched than the facts support. A survey of the 1955 city directory shows no Irish prevalence in the city's professions. In that year, 19.8% of the attorneys, less than fourteen percent of the physicians, and only 8.7% of accountants bore recognizably Irish surnames. In the same year, Mayor Joseph Dillon presided over a nine-member city council on which only three members were Irish. It may well be that the long-standing rivalry between the two cities contributed to the persistence of St. Paul's Irish image. The smaller city seized on its Irishness as a badge of civic distinction that would contrast it with its larger neighbor across the river, which boasted of being home to more Swedish-born persons than Stockholm.

The American Irish were early participants in the exodus to suburbia in the years following World War II. In Minnesota, such first-ring suburbs as West St. Paul and Roseville saw a dramatic influx of Irish-American families in the 1950s. An anecdote told of a priest in Edina, west of Minneapolis, tells of how he openly joked about his flock of "Roman Cadillacs," suggesting that the church might be renamed "Our Lady of the Minks." By the early 1960s, the much-chronicled blandness of suburban life, coupled with the waning of Irish immigration, threatened to obliterate Irish self-consciousness in urban Minnesota and elsewhere.

However, Irish identity in the Twin Cities has enjoyed a steady resurgence. In the 1960s and '70s, St. Paul and Minneapolis proved supportive of the efforts of Dr. Eoin McKiernan, whose campaign to bring sophisticated Irish cultural programming to America struck a new note in the group's history. McKiernan himself has often cited the open-mindedess of his Twin Cities base—as opposed to the entrenched and highly politicized environment with which East-coast Irish projects must contend—as one of the reasons for the success of his Irish American Cultural Institute, which was based in St. Paul for its first 34 years. The Center for Irish Studies, established in 1996 after a major gift from St. Paul philanthropist Lawrence O'Shaughnessy to the University of St. Thomas, continues the academic portion of McKiernan's work.

Minneapolis is home to Irish Books and Media, the first exclusive distributor for the work of Irish publishers in the United States. The worldwide appreciation of traditional Irish music that began in the mid-1970s took early root in St. Paul. Several prominent musicians—notably Paddy O'Brien, Daithi Sproule, and Sean O'Driscoll—chose to settle in the Twin Cities, attracted in part by an impressive cadre of American-born musicians. The Irish Music and Dance Association of Minnesota was established in 1977, providing a busy schedule of performances, instruction, and publicity for the folk art ever since. Other voluntary cultural efforts in the Twin Cities include Gaeltacht Minnesota, a small but persistent coterie of enthusiasts for the Irish language who have met regularly since 1981; several amateur theatre groups such as the Na Fianna Company that are devoted to presenting Irish plays; and the Minnesota-based Irish Genealogical Society, whose more than 2,000 members throughout the nation have built an outstanding research library for family historians.

Seamus Heaney noted in a 1996 *New York Times* article that Ireland has become "chic." Many Twin Citians who currently flock to Irish events have, perhaps, only a superficial understanding of their Irish heritage. Yet both Minneapolis and St. Paul enjoy a well-developed Irish cultural infrastructure surpassing that of many larger cities. The depth of Irish community support in the Twin Cities suggests that the group's identity will be well maintained in the years ahead, even after a faddish popularity has passed.

*See* Minnesota

Joan Bland, *Hibernian Crusade: The Story of the Catholic Total Abstinence Union of America* (Washington, D.C., 1951).

Virginia Kunz, *St. Paul: Saga of an American City* (Woodland Hills, Calif., 1977).

Kathleen O'Brien, "The Irish in Minneapolis: 1880–1905" (seminar paper, University of Minnnesota, 1973).

Ann Regan, "The Irish," in *They Chose Minnesota. A Survey of the State's Ethnic Groups,* ed. June D. Holmquist (St. Paul, 1981).

James Rogers, "1982 Minnesota Irish History Calendar" (St. Paul, 1981).

Mary Lethert Wingerd, "City Limits: Politics, Faith and the Power of Place in Urban America: St. Paul, Minnesota, 1838–1934" (Ph.D. diss., Duke University, 1998).

JAMES SILAS ROGERS

## SAINT-GAUDENS, AUGUSTUS (1848–1907)

Sculptor. Augustus Saint-Gaudens was born on March 1 at 35 Charlemont Street in Dublin. His father, Bernard Paul Ernst Saint-Gaudens, was originally from the village of Aspet, eight miles from St. Gaudens, France, and had come to Dublin via London as a journeyman cobbler. During his seven years in Ireland, he met his future wife, Mary McGuinness, from Ballymahon, Co. Longford, at his Dublin workshop where she was employed as a stitcher. They married in the Pro Cathedral in Dublin in 1841. Augustus was their third son, the first two children having died in infancy. Six months after his birth, the family emigrated to the United States, first to Boston and shortly afterwards to New York. Though not directly affected by the potato famine, they joined the thousands of Irish families who sought new hope and lives in the New World.

### EARLY CAREER

Regarded today as one of America's finest sculptors, Augustus began his career by being apprenticed from the age of thirteen to a French stone cameo cutter, Louis Avet, and three years later with Jules Le Brethon, a shell cameo cutter. At nighttime he studied first at the Cooper Union Institute and from 1865 at the National Academy of Design. At nineteen years of age he decided to pursue a career as a sculptor and headed for Paris, one of the first American artists to do so. There he studied at the Ecole des Beaux-Arts and worked in the atelier of the sculptor François Jouffroy. On the outbreak of the Franco-Prussian War in 1870 he moved to Rome where he remained until 1875. There he studied classical art and architecture and carried out some commissions for travelling Americans. It was there, too, that he met his future wife, an American art student, Augusta Homer, whom he married in 1877. On his return to America in 1875, Saint-Gaudens worked for a brief spell as a mural painter under John La Farge, who was decorating Trinity Church, Boston.

### SCULPTOR OF THE AMERICAN RENAISSANCE

His rise to fame began in 1876 when he received his first major commission: a monument to Civil War Adm. David Glasgow Farragut. It was unveiled in Madison Square Park, New York in 1881. Its dramatic harmony of allegory, movement and realism set it apart from previous American sculpture. It was a watershed in the young sculptor's career. Further commissions followed, in-

Augustus Saint-Gaudens

cluding what is perhaps Saint-Gaudens' greatest achievement of the period, The *Robert Gould Shaw Memorial* (1897) on Boston Common which depicts a scene from the Civil War and took fourteen years to complete; the *Standing Lincoln* in Chicago; the *Adams Memorial* (1891), dedicated to Mrs. Henry Adams, in Rock Creek Cemetery, Washington; the *Peter Cooper Monument;* and the *Gen. John A. Logan Monument. Diana* (1892), designed originally for Stanford White's Madison Square Garden, is now at the Philadelphia Museum of Art. As a member of the McMillian Commission, he was a central figure in the scheme to preserve the architectural and artistic heritage of the nation's capital and participated in the renewal of the L'Enfant plan for Washington. His collaboration with architects and landscape designers to integrate his public sculpture within their settings was a new departure in city planning. Based in Paris from 1897 to 1900, he won the Grand Prix and gold medal at the Exposition Universelle in 1900 for four sculptures including the *William T. Sherman Monument* and the *Shaw Memorial*. He was further honoured by being made an officer of the Legion d'Honneur by the French Government in 1901. At the request of President Roosevelt he created a new United States gold coinage, which resulted in the ten and twenty dollar gold pieces of 1907.

## PORTRAIT RELIEFS

In addition to his public sculpture, Saint-Gaudens' portrait reliefs single him out as an artist of superlative achievement. Technically very difficult, bas relief sculpture relies on the manipulation of light to create nuance and perspective. Whether working in bronze, wood, marble or plaster, Saint-Gaudens succeeded in capturing the essence of the sitter's character with great subtlety of expression. He produced more than one hundred portrait reliefs including Robert Louis Stevenson, Cornelius Vanderbilt and Samuel Gray Ward.

## INFLUENCE ON AMERICAN ART DEVELOPMENT

Such was the demand for his work that from an early stage Saint-Gaudens had to take on several young sculptors as assistants. In the twenty-six years that followed he exerted enormous influence over a whole generation of artists. He taught at the Art Students League and was artistic advisor to the Columbian Exposition of 1893 in Chicago. He played a significant role in founding the American Academy in Rome. His studio, and from 1900 full-time home in Cornish, New Hampshire, gave rise to the renowned artists' colony of the same name. Twelve years after the artist's death in 1907, Saint-Gaudens' widow and son established the Saint-Gaudens Memorial, dedicated to preserving the site as a monument to the artist. In 1965 the trustees of the Memorial donated the property to the National Park Service.

## DUBLIN MONUMENT TO CHARLES STEWART PARNELL

Despite being diagnosed with cancer in 1900, Saint-Gaudens continued to work tirelessly. One of his last major commissions was the monument to Charles Stewart Parnell for Dublin. Despite his ill health the sculptor went to great lengths to ensure that the monument would succeed. He built a scale-model of the streets and buildings bordering the site in O'Connell Street in order to determine the scale and the placement of the monument. He had erected in a field near his studio a full-scale wooden replica of the monument with a plaster-cast of the figure placed in front of it. He even obtained from a firm of Dublin tailors replicas of the clothes that they had last made for Parnell. In 1904 a

fire in the sculptor's studio destroyed correspondence, sketchbooks and several works in progress, including Parnell, considerably setting back the schedule. The monument arrived in Dublin in 1907, shortly after the sculptor's death.

Forthcoming: *Augustus Saint-Gaudens* (working title), 200 page catalogue, nine contributors, to accompany major retrospective exhibition, opening at the Musee Des Augustins, Toulouse, France, and Royal Hibernian Academy, Dublin, 1999.

Wilkinson Burke, *Uncommon Clay: The Life and Works of Augustus Saint-Gaudens* (San Diego, 1985).

Royal Cortissoz, *Augustus Saint-Gaudens* (Boston, 1907).

John H. Dryfhout, *The Work of Augustus Saint-Gaudens*, Catalogue Raisonne (Hanover, New Hampshire, 1982).

Kathryn Greenthal, *Augustus Saint-Gaudens Master Sculptor* (Exhibition catalogue, The Metropolitan Museum of Art, 1985).

Homer Saint-Gaudens, ed., *The Reminiscences of Augustus Saint-Gaudens*, 2 Vols. (New York City, 1913).

Gregory C. Schwarz, Brigid Sullivan, and Ludwig Lauerhass, *The Shaw Memorial: A Celebration of an American Masterpiece* (New Haven, Cornish, 1997).

Louise Hall Tharp, *Saint-Gaudens and the Gilded Era* (Boston, 1969).

CHRISTINA KENNEDY

## SAMPSON, WILLIAM (1764–1836)

Lawyer, author, Irish patriot. Born in Londonderry in January 1764, Sampson studied law at Lincoln's Inn, London. After gaining admittance to the Irish bar, he became involved in the reform movement, penning articles for nationalist periodicals, defending prisoners and, in December, 1796, presiding over a Belfast meeting later deemed treasonable.

When revolution erupted, Sampson's documentation of government troops' wrongdoings, coupled with a false rumor that he held a major generalcy in the French army, led to his imprisonment without trial. He accepted an offer of release conditioned on his exile to a country then at peace with England but the Adams's administration prevented admission to the United States. He went to Portugal in 1799 before proceeding to France

William Sampson

for six years and spending nearly a year in Hamburg. Arriving in London in 1806, with a passport from a British minister, Sampson was immediately arrested and sent to New York, where his family joined him four years later.

Admitted to the bar shortly after his arrival, Sampson became known for his eloquence, defense of personal rights, and publication of over a dozen transcripts of newsworthy cases. In 1813, he successfully intervened to prevent a Catholic priest from being compelled to report matters disclosed in confession and, though a Protestant, he aided the prosecution of Orangemen who had attacked Catholic Irish in Greenwich Village, New York, in 1824. Between 1825–30, he lived in Georgetown, D.C., and appeared before the Supreme Court several times.

Sampson was an early supporter of codifying the common law, corresponding with jurists and leaders on this point and influencing the next generation of legal scholars. Among his writings was the 1807 *Memoirs of William Sampson,* which vehemently attacked British policy toward Ireland. He died in New York City on December 28, 1836, survived by a wife and a daughter.

*See* United Irishmen and America

Charles C. Beale, *William Sampson, Lawyer and Stenographer* (Boston, 1907).
E. J. McGuire, "William Sampson," *Journal of the American Irish Historical Society* (October 1916).
Lilla B. Sampson, *The Sampson Family* (Baltimore, 1914).
William Sampson, *Memoirs of William Sampson* (New York, 1807).
———, *The Catholic Question in America: Whether a Roman Catholic Clergyman be in Any Case Compellable to Disclose the Secrets of Auricular Confession Decided at the Court of General Session in the City of New York* (New York, 1813).
New York *American*, December 29, 1836.

CHRISTIAN G. SAMITO

## SAN FRANCISCO, ASPECTS OF

San Francisco is at the end of the western world, and in many ways it is an Irish city. First settled by Europeans in 1776, when the Spanish built a mission and a presidio on the peninsula long inhabited by several Native American villages, the city of today had its roots in a small trading village called Yerba Buena on the bay side of the peninsula where the present financial district is located. In 1846 the area was conquered by the United States and became a part of the United States at the Treaty of Guadalupe Hidalgo in 1848. Also in 1846, a group of Mormons headed by Irish Sam Brannan sought to escape the United States. They were unsuccessful but doubled the population of the little settlement whose name was changed to San Francisco in 1847. The next year, 1848, gold was discovered in the foothills of the Sierras and San Francisco soon became the entry port to the gold country. In the Gold Rush of 1849 people came from all over the world to find their fortune and San Francisco became an instant city. By the census of 1852, 32,000 people lived in the erstwhile village of perhaps a thousand. By 1865, the population was estimated at 150,000. San Francisco had become and would remain one of the leading cities of the United States. It is now the center of the fourth largest metropolitan area of the country and also a leading world city.

The first growth of the city coincided with the Irish Diaspora due to the Great Famine of the 1840s. Irishmen came from Ireland, Australia, South America and the eastern United States. Those who survived the Famine were not friendly to Anglo-Protestant values and did not try to assimilate the behavior which would make them agreeable to Anglo-American ladies and gentlemen. This was one of the causes of the revolt known as the Vigilantes. (I say Irishmen because very few women made the dangerous trip to California.) The Irish, along with the Germans and Chinese, were the largest foreign groups in the city in the nineteenth century. The city has always had one of the largest foreign-born populations in the United States. In the census of 1980, when people gave their ethnic preferences, the Irish accounted for about four percent of the population. This count is probably short because there are many undocumented Irish in San Francisco. In the 1990 census, 73,457 said they were Irish or part Irish out of a population of 723,911. Irish influence in the city is larger than these numbers show. The district attorney is Terence Hallinan, the sheriff is Michael Hennessey and one of the two members of the State Assembly from the city is Kevin Shelley. During the recent mayoralty of fifth Irish mayor, Frank Jordan, several of the supervisors of the city were Irish. (San Francisco is a combined city and county and has a board of supervisors rather than a city council.)

Looking back to the period before the American conquest, a few Irish people had reached this outpost of empire, among them Don Timoteo Murphy (1828), and the Miller and Lucas families of Marin County to the north of the city. The large Bernard Murphy family (1844) lived to the south and east of the city on ranches. Patrick Breen and John Sullivan were early San Francisco landowners. Sullivan donated land for the Catholic orphanage, Old St. Mary's Cathedral and Calvary Cemetery, as well as money to several Catholic charities. Many Irish immigrants profited by selling supplies to the 49ers, rather than from mining gold themselves. The Tobin brothers, of a still influential family, helped found the Hibernia Bank, similar to the Emigrants Bank, which enabled immigrants to own their own homes. It became the largest savings bank.

C. D. O'Sullivan, Patrick Fenton, Peter, James and Michael Donahue, James Phelan, Joseph A. Donohoe and later Abby Meighan Parrott, Daniel T. Murphy and D. J. Oliver were generous donors to Catholic causes, as were other rich Irish families. William Chapman Ralston, probably the greatest city builder of all, attended Calvary Presbyterian Church. He entered banking with Joseph A. Donohoe and Eugene Kelly, but left to found the Bank of California. Ralston built the Palace Hotel, woolen mills, a furniture factory, a blanket factory and others. He cut through New Montgomery Street, a move that was about one hundred years ahead of his time. He also financed other city builders like Peter Donahue. The latter built a foundry, gas company, street railway, railroad, a monitor for the U.S. Navy and locomotive engines, among other things, before he began building railroads to the north of the city with shops at Tiburon in Marin County.

As the city took shape, it followed the plans of Irish engineer Jasper O'Farrell. It was he who drew the streets straight up the hills and surveyed diagonal Market Street, dividing the town in two, with large industrial blocks to the south of Market and smaller commercial and residential blocks north of Market. The O'Farrells remained prominent for many years. A later Irish engineer designed the Municipal Railway (1912) and the water system bringing water from the Sierra Nevadas to the city. He was Michael M. O'Shaughnessy. The engineer who designed the great

Los Angeles water supply bringing water from the Owens River Valley was William Mulholland, another Irishman.

What about the ordinary Irish San Franciscan? According to Robert Burchell, author of the *San Francisco Irish 1850–1880,* the Irish did well for themselves in early San Francisco, though not as well as the native-born or English immigrants. The name for an early model steam shovel, the steam paddy, shows what type of work many of them did, digging through the sand dunes that covered most of the city. While many Irish people of that time were illiterate and/or did not speak English, there were about twenty percent who could be deemed modern or educated. These became the teachers, sisters, priests, doctors, clerks and so on. The Irish also experienced upward mobility—fewer of the second generation were unskilled laborers or domestics. In general they did better for themselves than in eastern cities where Anglo Protestant elites governed. They were not a marginalized group as portrayed in a recent motion picture, "Good Will Hunting," about the Irish in a Boston suburb.

## Early Politics

The Irish in the United States are said to excel in politics and getting government jobs. Frank McCoppin became the first Irish Catholic mayor in 1867, before either New York or Boston had Irish Catholic mayors. Curiously in a city where Irish politicians are legendary, there have only been five Irish mayors. Some say the Irish had other opportunities, but it is curious, nonetheless. The Irish mayors were Frank McCoppin (1867); James Duval Phelan (later U.S. Senator), the son of early capitalist James Phelan (1896); P. H. McCarthy, influential labor leader (1910–12); John Shelley, also a labor leader (1964–68); and Frank Jordan, former police chief (1992–96). Of twenty police chiefs from 1878 to 1972, eleven were Irish. Of 229 supervisors from 1909 to 1971, thirty-eight percent were Irish.

The police and fire departments were virtually Irish clubs until recently when they were integrated by court order. Legend has it that an Irishman had but to apply to city hall to get a job. Studies are being made to investigate this hypothesis.

In the School Department, there has been only one Irish superintendent since 1856. For much of this time, superintendents were elected as were the many Irish police and fire chiefs. By 1910 Irish teachers were twenty-five percent of the teaching force. One of the most famous teachers was Kate Kennedy (1829–90), a native of Ireland, who with the help of Irish-born State Senator Philip A. Roach had two bills pass the California State Legislature in 1874. One gave women teachers equal pay for doing the same work as men and the other gave voteless women the right to run for education-related political office. The former is thought to be the first equal pay law in the whole world. (The San Francisco department got around this by giving men jobs with different titles from those given women.) Kate Kennedy left the Catholic Church at the time of the Famine when she heard priests counselling their dying flocks that their sufferings were the will of God. Kate Kennedy thought the sufferings were the will of the English government. Kate Kennedy's sister, Ann Cushing, had to do with setting up structures for juvenile justice. Her niece, Katherine Delmar Burke, founded a famous private school, Miss Burke's, later Katherine Delmar Burke School. Her nephew, James K. Moffitt, was the head of the Crocker Bank and a regent of the University of California where a library is named after him. Another nephew, Herbert C. Moffitt, M.D., has a hospital at the University of Cali-

fornia, San Francisco, named after him. There was much strife between Protestants and Catholics in the School Department. Deputy Superintendent Joseph O'Connor lost his position in 1886 because of his Catholic religion.

Early Irish politicians included several United States senators, beginning with David C. Broderick (1856–59), who died in a duel with Justice David A. Terry. Broderick was the leader of the anti-slavery Democrats. His "machine" was the target of the Vigilance Committee of 1856. This group was dominated by the merchant class who were worried about the bond ratings of the city. Many of them made arrangements so they would not have to serve on juries themselves, but felt that juries were too lenient. They thought that the Irish voted early and often, but did not prove it. As mentioned above, many of the Irish seemed to have been boorish toward the Anglo financial elite. The committee killed four men and exiled twenty-eight Irishmen. Additionally, the fighter Yankee Sullivan died in their custody, supposedly a suicide. The crime rate remained the same after the Vigilantes dispersed after several months of mob rule, but the bond ratings went up.

Until 1867 the Peoples Party ruled San Francisco after its inception by the Vigilantes. But in general there was less anti-Irishness in San Francisco than in Eastern and Midwestern cities, but there definitely was some prejudice. In the late 1870s, the Irish workingmen, many of whom were unemployed, joined the Workingmen's Party of California, while the Sandlot orator Denis Kearney announced his slogan, "The Chinese must go." After the completion of the transcontinental railroad, many of the Chinese and Irish workers went to San Francisco where they vied with each other for ill-paying jobs. This rivalry was a continual process. Kate Douglas Wiggin, well-known writer and kindergarten teacher, expressed her opinion of these matters in a little book called *The Story of Patsy.* The men with unpronounceable names were "the largest . . . army of do nothings that the sun ever shone upon." She seems not to have noticed that it was a time of high unemployment. Their females were worthy of them, adding "copiously to the world's population" when "for the country's good" they should have had few children or none at all.

Other Irish senators were John Conness, Broderick's successor. Conness favored public schools over Catholic ones. Eugene Casserly was in the senate from 1869 to 1873. Silver millionaire James G. Fair, who moved to San Francisco after making a fortune on the Comstock Lode, was a senator from 1881 to 1887.

In the 1870s the so-called Silver Kings, who dominated the Virginia City silver mines, moved to San Francisco. They were John W. Mackay, James G. Fair, James C. Flood and William S. O'Brien. While Kate Douglas Wiggin was writing her little criticism of the Irish, John Mackay, a resident of San Francisco, was considered the richest man in the world. The Silver Kings founded the Nevada Bank (now part of Wells Fargo) in competition with Ralston's Bank of California. Mackay later sold out his interests in San Francisco and went East where he began Postal Telegraph. Fair's daughters built the Fairmont Hotel. Its neighbor on Nob Hill, the Pacific Union Club, was formerly James Flood's brownstone mansion.

## Banking

The pioneer James Phelan founded the First National Gold Bank, now part of Wells Fargo. When William C. Ralston left his partnership with Joseph A. Donohoe, the bank became the

Donohoe-Kelly Banking Company. Eugene Kelly was the bank's agent in New York, as mentioned. This bank was taken over by the Bank of America, which also took over the Hibernia Bank from the successors to the Tobins. The Tobins are now prominent in the Chronicle Publishing Company, TV Stations, also owning land, buildings and so forth. They remain players in high society, as do the descendants of the Donohoes, Abby Parrott, and others. The Barbara Phelan Sullivan Foundation is still active as are other trusts and foundations founded by the old Irish families.

When Italian A. P. Giannini founded the Bank of Italy (1904), now the Bank of America, Irish William Fagan bought several of the original shares. The Bank of America was at one time the largest bank in the world. James K. Moffitt, Kate Kennedy's nephew, was head of the Crocker Bank, now part of Wells Fargo. These are a few of the Irish prominent in banking and finance.

## Architects

The Irish were significant architects and builders. Even today Irish companies are leading members of the building trades. An early architect, Thomas England, nephew of Archbishop England of Charleston, S.C., designed Old St. Mary's Cathedral on Nob Hill, St. Francis Church on Vallejo Street and the two Presentation schools demolished by the earthquake and fire of 1906. The prominent yellow brick Sacred Heart Church on Hayes Street Hill was designed by architect Thomas J. Welsh as was St. Peter's, a wooden church still extant in the Mission District. This church, especially under Father Peter C. Yorke, was long the capital of Irish activity. St. Patrick's Church was rebuilt after the fire as a monument to the Irish church, with stained glass windows of saints from every county in Ireland, as well as Irish heroes. St. Patrick's is now a Filipino parish, but they join in the celebration of the patronal feast day which precedes the St. Patrick's Day Parade which began in the 1850s. Perhaps the most prominent church in the cityscape is St. Ignatius, the Jesuit church, near Lone Mountain. It was designed by Charles Devlin, who also designed Star of the Sea and St. Charles churches, the Presentation Convent on Masonic and Turk, the Religious of the Sacred Heart School in Menlo Park, as well as the original St. Patrick's Seminary. Frank T. Shea designed Mission Dolores Basilica, and St. Monica's and St. James Churches, the Knights of the Red Branch Hall and the mausoleum at Holy Cross Cemetery. Going up Market St., one passes the Mechanics Monument dedicated to Peter Donahue, the site of the original Palace Hotel built by Ralston, now a Beaux Arts edifice built after the fire. On the left facing east is the large terra-cotta Phelan Building. Up a block is the Abby Meighan Parrott Building, formerly the Emporium Department Store and opposite the Flood Building, built by James L. Flood, the Silver King's son. These two buildings were designed by Albert Pissis, a Mexican architect, who also designed the Hibernia Bank at Jones St. and Market. Archbishop Joseph T. McGucken built St. Mary of the Assumption Cathedral atop Cathedral Hill. It is in the shape of a hyperbolic paraboloid and was designed by Italian architects Pier Luigi Nervi and Pietro Belluschi. These are but a few of the Irish-designed or Irish-built buildings in the city. Church buildings bring us to the Catholic Church, an organization long dominated by the Irish.

## The Catholic Church

The organization in which the Irish were most prominent was the Catholic Church. Many Irish were probably Presbyterians or Episcopalians—there were two Orange Lodges in town. The Archdiocese of San Francisco was erected in 1853, with Archbishop Joseph Sadoc Alemany, O.P., at its head. There has never been an Irish-born archbishop in San Francisco, but five of Alemany's successors were Irish and the sixth is Irish and Portuguese—William J. Levada. There were few priests in California in the early 1850s, and Alemany sent Father Hugh P. Gallagher to Ireland in 1854 to recruit priests and sisters. Gallagher returned with some priests and two orders of sisters. At that time sisters in Catholic schools were paid by the State. This situation ended in 1856. The two groups of sisters were the Sisters of Mercy from Kinsale, headed by Mother M. Baptist Russell, and five sisters of the Presentation from Midleton, Co. Cork and Kilkenny headed by Mother M. Joseph Cronin, and later by Mother M. Teresa Comerford. They joined the Sisters of Charity (Emmitsburg) under Sister M. Francis McEnnis who worked at the Roman Catholic Orphan Asylum at St. Patrick Parish. The Presentations began their free school in December 1854. The Mercies taught briefly in 1855 and began to nurse in the public hospital. Hugh P. Gallagher founded St. Joseph Parish in San Francisco. He also promoted the beginning of the Golden Gate Park and assisted the Mercy Sisters' Magdalen Asylum financially.

Another prominent Irish priest was James Croke, brother of Archbishop Croke of the Gaelic Athletic Association. He had come to Oregon to evangelize the Indians but came to California around the time of the Gold Rush. Croke also went often to the mines to collect for Catholic institutions in the city. Eugene O'Connell came in the fifties to teach in the seminary and returned later as vicar apostolic of Marysville and first bishop of Grass Valley. John J. Prendergast was vicar general and helped found the Sisters of the Holy Family, the only existing order founded in San Francisco.

The second archbishop, Patrick William Riordan, ruled from 1884–1914. Born in Chatham, New Brunswick, Canada, he spent part of his childhood in Ireland, but grew up in Chicago. He attended Notre Dame, Rome and the American College of Louvain. He was a great builder. He found many wooden buildings, but because of his memory of the Chicago Fire tried to rebuild in masonry. This was not always advisable in earthquake country, and many structures had to be rebuilt. He asked for a coadjutor and requested Edward J. Hanna, a priest of the Diocese of Rochester, a protege of Riordan's friend Bishop Bernard McQuaid, but instead got Denis O'Connell, one of the leaders of the Americanist faction as auxiliary. Hanna was suspect because he had written a Modernist article in the *New York Review,* as well as several articles in the *Catholic Encyclopedia.* Hanna was of Scotch-Irish and Irish background, and finally became Riordan's auxiliary in 1912 and archbishop in 1915. He was very beloved by the Catholic people. He also was active in labor arbitration and the Catholic School Case in Oregon. He headed the NCCB for a number of years and acted as arbitrator at the General Strike of 1934. John J. Mitty, bishop of Salt Lake City and a New Yorker became his coadjutor in 1932 and archbishop at Hanna's resignation in 1935. Mitty again was a great builder.

Mitty was very concerned to have an excellent well-educated corps of priests. Morale was high. He tried to have priests trained in many areas, so there would be a priest expert in almost every field. He built many churches and schools and was considered a fine businessman, though very strict. Mitty had attended St. Joseph Seminary, Dunwoodie, at the time of the Modernist crisis there. He put on spendid liturgical spectacles. The Catholic Church was important in the life of the city. Archbishop Mitty died in 1961 shortly after the end of the Rosary Crusade preached by Father Patrick Peyton, C.S.C. The crusade ended with an assembly in Golden Gate Park of hundreds of thousands of people, the largest religious gathering ever held in Northern California. The Archdiocese was then divided, with Oakland, Santa Rosa and Stockton becoming new dioceses, with some territory from the Diocese of Sacramento exchanged. San Francisco Irish priests Mark Hurley and Merlin J. Guilfoyle became bishops of Santa Rosa and Stockton respectively.

Joseph T. McGucken, American-born bishop of Sacramento, who spent part of his childhood in Ireland, became a priest in Los Angeles and Archbishop in 1962. He was to have a hard row to hoe as the winds of change generated by Vatican II swept through the land. After Riordan-built St. Mary's Cathedral burnt down, a drive was held for a new cathedral and a facility for the elderly. The latter did not materialize, but the former, as noted above, became one of the most modern cathedrals in the world. Since it was built in the 1960s there were many protests. Later the high school teachers went on strike. The old patterns were simply not working. Social activist Father Eugene Boyle was pastor of Sacred Heart Church in the African American Fillmore neighborhood. He allowed the Black Panthers to serve breakfast in the church basement, but damaging materials were planted to falsely implicate him. There were problems at St. Patrick Seminary. Priests and sisters were leaving in large numbers. It was a very confusing time but McGucken survived until 1977 when Archbishop John Raphael Quinn of Oklahoma City was appointed. Quinn served on important committees such as the evaluation of women religious in the U.S. after serving as president of the National Council of Catholic Bishops. He resigned in 1995 and William J. Levada took over. Patrick J. McGrath was one of the auxiliary bishops and in 1998 was appointed coadjutor bishop of San Jose. Other priests of Irish surname were prominent in the archdiocese, although Archbishop Mitty would not accept Irish-born priests, so there are not many of them in the archdiocese compared to neighboring dioceses.

## IRISH RELIGIOUS

As mentioned above, the first sisters in the city were the Sisters of Charity headed by Irish-born Sister Francis McEnnis, who remained Sister Servant for many years after her arrival. They took over the orphanage from Father John Maginnis, pastor of St. Patrick's. Irish-born Father Maginnis had spent many years in the eastern U.S. before coming to San Francisco and founding the orphanage in 1851, with the help of a Gentleman's Society with many Irish members. The Sisters of Charity taught at St. Patrick School and founded a clinic and a foundling hospital. The Sisters of the Presentation (1854) founded two large free schools in the city and two in the suburbs. After 1906, they began to teach in parochial schools. The Sisters of Mercy from Ireland under Mother Baptist Russell set up institutions as noted above and also taught in free schools. In the 1860s several Franciscan Brothers of Brooklyn under their founder, Brother John McMahon from Galway, taught at the Cathedral School. At Archbishop Alemany's request, in 1868 the Christian Brothers came under the leadership of Brother Justin McMahon to take over St. Mary's College, founded by diocesan priests. In 1874 Brother Justin founded Sacred Heart College High School which included the first three years of college. It was the first diocesan high school for boys in the country. It was also the first whose teams were called "The Fighting Irish," predating Notre Dame. Two Irish students of St.

Ignatius and Sacred Heart got the idea for the first high school football game in San Francisco. The Christian Brothers also taught at St. Peter School in the Mission District. Brother Justin was a leader of the Christian Brothers in America who thought Latin should be taught in their schools and was backed in this by Archbishop Patrick W. Riordan, among other American bishops. The brothers also set up a recruitment center in Ireland, possibly patterned after the Presentation one at Kilcock. Italian Jesuits from the Province of Turin founded St. Ignatius Academy and Church in 1855. They were soon recruiting Californians named O'Sullivan, Kenna and so on. Rich Irish benefactors helped most of the orders.

In 1862 the Dominican Sisters, now of San Rafael, founded by Archbishop Alemany and Belgian Sister Mary Goemare, began St. Rose Academy in the south of Market District. Two of the original members were from St. Mary of the Springs, Ohio—one English and one Irish, Louisa O'Neil, who headed the order for a time. Later they were headed for many years by Irish Mother Mary Thomas Golden and Louis O'Donnell, Irish recruits who entered in California. They also taught at Sacred Heart Elementary School in San Francisco and founded Dominican College in San Rafael with the help of Peter Donahue and other benefactors. Even the German Dominicans, now of Mission San Jose, who came to teach in German schools were soon infiltrated by Irish recruits. The Sisters of Notre Dame de Namur from San Jose sent Irish recruits to teach in their Notre Dame College of San Francisco founded in 1866. They were an international order with members from Belgium, England and other countries. The only order in existence founded in San Francisco, the Sisters of the Holy Family, was founded by Australian-born Elizabeth Armer, with the help of Mary Ann Regan Tobin, her mentor, and Irish Father John Prendergast. Tobin was born in Chile of partly Irish descent. These sisters founded day care centers and kindergartens and taught Christian doctrine to public school children. They also nursed the sick in their homes.

The Religious of the Sacred Heart came at the invitation of Archbishop Riordan in 1888. Their first superiors were Mary Keating and Mary O'Meara, though their personnel was international. When the Salesian Fathers came to San Francisco in 1898, they soon brought their first Irish member, Bernard G. Redahan. The Sisters of Charity of the Blessed Virgin Mary (BVMs) also came at Riordan's invitation and founded schools at St. Brigid and later at St. Paul, St. Philip and Most Holy Redeemer parishes. Their headquarters were in Dubuque, Iowa, but their founders were from Ireland and they had many Irish members.

After World War II other Irish orders came here to teach such as Sisters of Mercy from County Galway, but they have since returned.

## SPORTS

Many Irish people were active in sports. A few were Benicia Boy Heenan, unofficial champion in the 1850s, and "Gentleman Jim" Corbett, World Heavyweight Champion from 1892, when he defeated John L. Sullivan, until 1897. He appeared on the stage with John L. also during the 1890s. A clerk for the Nevada Bank before his fighting career, he was a member of the Olympic Club, the first athletic club in America. It was founded in the 1850s by the (non-Irish) Nahl brothers, but built up over a period of thirteen years by Donegal man William Greer Harrison. The club fielded teams in many sports, often playing college teams. Many of the members were Irish.

Many Irish excelled in handball, a more plebeian sport. Another well-known athlete usually thought of as Irish was German-French-Irish Frank J. (Lefty) O'Doul, major league ball player and manager of the local, the Seals, as well as other coast teams. Many members of St. Mary's College baseball teams became professional in the early twentieth century. Edward J. "Slip" Madigan was their famous football coach in the 1930s.

## WRITERS

Many Irish people are talented writers and journalists. There is only room for a few examples. J. Ross Browne came here about the time of the Gold Rush, and Daniel O'Connell, nephew of the Liberator, came in the late 1860s. He founded a short-lived paper called the *Evening Post*. Later he edited the *Chronicle*, the *Bulletin* and the *Wasp*. O'Connell was also a founder of the Bohemian Club, a men's club for people interested in the arts, which still exists and has a campout during the summer attended by very prominent men at the Bohemian Grove near the Russian River. Around the turn of the century, Frank Norris wrote *The Octopus,* an exposé of the activities of the Southern Pacific Railroad, and *The Pit* about the commodities exchange in Chicago. *McTeague* was the saga of a San Francisco dentist. Norris died before he could fulfill his promise. His sister-in-law, Kathleen Norris, was a well-known women's author. The novelist Jack London, author of *The Call of the Wild* and other adventure novels, found to his disappointment, that his father was Irish.

Well-known historians include John Patrick Diggins, James J. Sheehan, David Herlihy, Robert I. Burns, S.J., and Kevin Starr. Pat Dowling has chronicled the Irish of California in *California: The Irish Dream*. He also founded the Irish library at the Irish Cultural Center. John McGloin, S.J., was another chronicler of San Francisco and taught a number of the above authors at the University of San Francisco as well as James Walsh, author of *The Irish of San Francisco.*

Agnes Tobin of the pioneer family was a poet and translated Petrarch. She was a friend of William Butler Yeats. Alfred M. Bender, an Irish Jew, was a prominent patron of the arts as were James D. Phelan and his nephew, Noel Sullivan.

## ORGANIZATIONS

Since 1857, San Francisco has held a St. Patrick's Day Parade sponsored by the United Irish Societies. Participants range from the St. Mary's Chinese School Drum Corps to owners of Irish wolfhounds. The Ancient Order of Hibernians, a mutual benefit society, is one of the larger groups. Others are the Rebel Cork, Knights of the Red Branch, the Fenians, the Knights of St. Patrick, the Emerald Guard, Mayo Men's Association, and Sons of the Emerald Isle. Irish people founded the Young Men's Institute and the Young Ladies Institute. (Y.M.I. and Y.L.I.). The Siena Club and the Reverent Observance of Good Friday Movement were other Irish-founded organizations, as well as the Kate Kennedy Schoolwomen's Club, a teachers union founded by Margaret Mahoney, a primary school teacher.

## LABOR

The Irish have always been prominent in the labor movement. Unfortunately this enabled them to exclude African Americans from many trades. As mentioned they were prominent in the Workingman's Party of California headed by Denis Kearney in the 1870s. Frank Roney dominated the labor picture in the 1880s, emphasizing organizing unions on trade lines and forming federations, rather than opposing Chinese labor. He also created the Seaman's Protective Association to guard the rights of sailors against shanghaiing and captains. Michael Casey, leader of the Teamsters in the strike of 1901, with the aid of Father Yorke was able to establish some rights for laboring men. This strike established San Francisco as a labor town. P. H. McCarthy began the Building Trades Council in 1898 which dominated the building trades for many years. McCarthy was mayor after the Graft Trials, 1909–1911. By 1947, three-fourths of San Francisco's employees were union members. In 1998 the AFL-CIO is headed by John Henning.

## MORE POLITICS

The Irish presence in politics in San Francisco is legendary, although they are not as powerful as legend would have it. The Blind Boss, Christopher Buckley, ruled the city during most of the 1880s. He sponsored the first Jewish members of the Board of Education. The graft trials after the earthquake involved Irish people on both sides. Former mayor James D. Phelan was one of the prominent rich men who financed the trials and the prosecutor was John J. Heney. The target was Jewish Abe Ruef and his minion, German-Irish Eugene Schmitz. Father Yorke's brother was a contractor mixed up in the scandal, so he joined with many Jews on the side of Ruef.

Tom Mooney was a radical accused of a bombing in the Preparedness Parade of 1916. He was pardoned in 1939. Mayor James J. Rolph, mayor from 1911 to 1930 was not Irish but appointed many Irish people to political jobs. He appointed Agnes Regan as a member of the Board of Education. She later went to Washington, D.C., and founded the National Catholic School of Social Service, now part of Catholic University. In the thirties and forties, William Malone was chair of the Democratic Central Committee. He was influential in picking Truman. He backed future mayor John Shelley and future Governor Edmund G. "Pat" Brown. Brown's son, Edmund G. "Jerry" Brown, also became governor (1975–1983) and was elected mayor of Oakland in 1998. Tom Maloney, long-time member of the state legislature, wrote some of the most important laws on workman's compensation, benefits for the aged and blind, housing for veterans and payment for the sick and disabled. The German-Irish Burton brothers, Phillip and John, broke the power of the old Irish machines. Phillip went to Congress, where he stayed until his death in 1983, after having sponsored many measures to benefit the poor. John Burton is a member of the state legislature, reelected in 1998. Other prominent Irish politicians were Leo J. Ryan, Eugene McAteer, Leo McCarthy and John Foran.

Indeed the city by the bay shows the influence of its Irish citizens in many areas, not all of which can be touched on here. Though now a minority, they have left and are still leaving their mark on San Francisco.

*See* California; Sisters of Mercy;
**Presentation Sisters**

Gunther Barth, *Instant Cities* (New York, 1975).
R. A. Burchell, *The San Francisco Irish, 1848–1880* (Berkeley, 1980).
Miriam Allen DeFord, *They Were San Franciscans* (Caldwell, ID, 1941).
Richard Edward de Leon, *Left Coast City* (Lawrence, KS, 1982).
Patrick Dowling, *California: The Irish Dream* (San Francisco, 1988).
James Gaffey, *Citizen of No Mean City* (Wilmington, DE, 1976).
John Jacobs, *A Rage for Justice: The Passion and Politics of Phillip Burton* (Berkeley, 1995).

David Lavender, *Nothing Seemed Impossible: William C. Ralston and Early San Francisco* (Palo Alto, 1975).

John Bernard McGloin, S.J., *San Francisco* (San Rafael, 1978).

Paul E. Peterson, *The Politics of School Reform* (Chicago, 1985).

Thomas F. Prendergast, *Forgotten Pioneers* (San Francisco, 1942).

Hugh Quigley, *The Irish Race in California and on the Pacific Coast* (San Francisco, 1878).

James P. Walsh, ed., *The San Francisco Irish, 1850–1976* (San Francisco, 1978).

Frederick M. Wirt, *Power in the City* (Berkeley, 1974).

ANN CURRY, P.B.V.M.

## SAN FRANCISCO SISTERS AND SOCIAL SERVICE

The usual picture of an Irish politician or social activist is a man sitting in a smoke-filled room behind a saloon or Denis Kearney in a sandlot shouting, "The Chinese must go!"—not a nun in her convent or school. In a time when government did not take responsibility for welfare, sisters were political and social activists in many ways. San Francisco had many examples of this, as well as sisters showing other women and girls what they could do.

There were no religious orders for women in California before the American conquest in 1846. The first sisters came in the 1850s. In the city the first arrivals were the Sisters of Charity from Emmitsburg led by Irish born Sister Francis McEnnis. There were few women in San Francisco in the early fifties as the trip was considered too dangerous for women. Indeed, two of the Sisters of Charity died on the way. They came to take over the Roman Catholic Orphanage founded by Father John Maginnis in 1851 at St. Patrick Church. They were followed in 1854 by the Sisters of the Presentation and the Sisters of Mercy from Ireland. Social conditions in the new city were not good. There had been a cholera epidemic leaving a number of ophans; many criminals and even insane people had come to town; there was a depression in 1853 and 1854. Many of the buildings were ramshackle shacks. To many San Francisco was merely a waypoint to riches, not a place to be built up. The sisters found plenty to be done.

The orphanage was in a brick building on Market Street near what is now New Montgomery Street, next to the wooden St. Patrick Church. The sisters took care of the orphans and taught school for them and other children in schools called St. Patrick and St. Vincent. The district south of Market was designed as an industrial section, but housed many poor people also in small wooden houses. In 1854 Sister Francis built a wooden building in Marin County near San Rafael on land donated by Don Timoteo Murphy, but it was decided to make this into the boys orphanage and the sisters returned to San Francisco. As the sisters expanded their work, they moved the infants and smaller children to a country-like setting near the southeastern city limits in 1861, where they also maintained a foundling home and infants' shelter. The rest of the girl orphans moved out to the new area in the 1870s. The sisters taught in the school until the 1960s when the school moved to the Visitation Parish.

In 1874, with the aid of the new Men's and Ladies' St. Vincent de Paul organizations, the sisters set up an infirmary in the parish. Later the sisters founded Mary's Help Hospital for the diocese in 1899, only to see the incomplete building destroyed in the earthquake and fire of 1906. Kate Johnson had endowed the hospital to be free for women and children, but the endowment was taken up by having to rebuild so the hospital was finally opened in 1912 as a charitable hospital. They also had a home for unwed mothers called St. Elizabeth's, still in existence. The orphans received a state subsidy until they were fourteen. The sisters founded St. Francis Technical School to shelter these girls until they were old enough to make it on their own. They taught them domestic work and fine sewing to help them earn their living. The sisters, now called Daughters of Charity, continue many of these good works until this day.

The other two orders to arrive in the 1850s, the Sisters of the Presentation and the Sisters of Mercy, were also founded to help the poor, the former in Cork in 1775–1776 by Nano Nagle and the latter by Catherine McAuley in Dublin in 1831. The Presentation had become an order in 1805, giving up some of their original works of visiting the sick, and confined themselves mostly to teaching. Under Mother Joseph Cronin, the five sisters arrived on November 13, 1854, and began teaching in a school in St. Francis Parish in December. Their schools were free, but they had thought that they would be paid by the state as they were in Ireland. Due to political disputes as the Know-Nothing anti-Catholic party took power, they lost the state subsidy and carried on their schools as free schools until the 1890s when they charged for a select school within one of their large schools. They did this at the expense of their own life-style, as well as teaching music, foreign languages, china painting and so on. Mother Joseph Cronin was forced to return to Ireland, leaving Mother Teresa Comerford and Mother Xavier Daly with a postulant, Margaret Cassian, who had joined in October 1855.

Mother Teresa believed passionately in free education for the poor. The nuns' friends, pitying them for their hand-to-mouth existence, advised them to charge tuition for those able to pay. Mother Teresa thought that in the egalitarian atmosphere of the United States, parents would be too proud to ask for charity and just send their children to what she termed the "godless" public schools. The sisters founded two convents, the Presentation Convent which got its own handsome building in 1856 and the Sacred Heart Presentation Convent in 1869. In the 1870s the Presentation Sisters in their two schools taught 1,500 of the 5,000 children in Catholic schools in San Francisco. They also taught poor women in the evening and maintained a large free library. They had promised not to change their customs when they left Ireland, and much to Mother Teresa's dismay they had to maintain cloister and could not visit the children in their homes. Archbishop Patrick W. Riordan had some of their rules changed when he amalgamated the houses in the Archdiocese of San Francisco in 1888 so that they could charge tuition, teach in parochial schools and teach catechism in outlying parishes. After the fire and earthquake destroyed their two city convents they were not able to maintain their free schools which they had kept up for fifty years. In a time when there was a great deal of prejudice against African Americans, the sisters had school for African American girls in a small building behind their regular school. It was the only Catholic school for African Americans in the state in the 1860s. However about 1867 it had to be discontinued because the white parents who were sending their children to the free school refused to send their children unless the black school ended. In 1874 African Americans were admitted to the public schools. In 1905 the sisters were teaching black girls again, but it's not known when they came back to the Presentation Convent on Powell Street.

The second group to arrive in 1854, the Mercies set up a veritable privately funded welfare system. Their superior was twenty-four-year-old Mother Baptist (Kate) Russell, a woman of great dynamism. She had become interested in the poor helping her mother during the terrible days of the Famine and joined the Mercy Convent Kinsale under Mother Francis Bridgeman, who maintained a remarkable outreach to the poor. Mother Bridgeman had given the eight sisters their dowries when they left, so they were able to buy the building which contained the public hospital they ran from 1856–1857. However, the city would not pay rent or cover the expenses in a timely way, so they withdrew and founded their own St. Mary's Hospital, which was the center of their charitable endeavors. Archbishop Joseph S. Alemany credited the Mercies with restoring harmony after the Know-Nothings had sowed discord. Because of uncertain revenue, they charged some patients and supported other works such as St. Peter School (1878). In 1856 a prostitute asked for shelter and the sisters started the Magdalen Asylum. The register at the Mercy Archives, Burlingame, CA shows that they admitted African American and Chinese women as well as Caucasians. This was partially state-funded until 1879. The sisters also maintained the city Industrial School for Girls, a kind of reform school, in the Magdalen Asylum building near the outskirts of the city.

The Mercies also ran shelters for young girls and women who were just out of the hospital, as well as an employment agency. They nursed patients in epidemics when no one else would; they visited the sick poor in their homes and prisoners in the city jail and the penitentiary. They began an old age home, now Mercy Center in Oakland. Mother Francis Bridgeman advised Mother Baptist not to charge tuition in their schools as this would bring about invidious comparisons with the Presentation free schools. Besides St. Peter's, they had a school near the hospital at St. Brendan's and one in Oakland. Mother Baptist also founded a school in Sacramento. This is only part of the remarkable ministry of the Mercy Sisters in San Francisco.

The first religious to reach California was Belgian Mother Mary Goemare of the Dominicans now headquartered in San Rafael. She was joined by several sisters including two from Ohio, one of whom, Louisa O'Neil was Irish born and later directed the community for some time. These sisters founded St. Rose Academy in St. Rose Parish, south of Market. Sister Thomas Golden was principal there for many years. Of Irish background, she was a new woman in every sense of the word. She instilled in the girls the idea that a woman's mind was equal to that of a man. It would please her when a priest would say that the girls did better in any study than the boys. The girls at St. Rose learned telegraphy, shorthand, mental arithmetic and rhetoric. When girls in public schools were not able to take part in debate, the girls at St. Rose had their debate club, the Rosinas and the Presentation girls had the Nano Nagle Debating Circle. Girls in Catholic schools saw women adminstrators at the higher levels, while public high schools were administered by men. According to *The Monitor* of June 10, 1880, the Dominican sisters "are not unmindful that *eloquence* may be obtained in a *high degree* by *woman* as by *man*."

Founded by Elizabeth Armer, an Australian woman who attended the Presentation Convent and was brought up in the Tobin family, the only order still extant founded in the city is the Sisters of the Holy Family. They maintained day care centers, nursed the sick poor in their homes and instructed public school children in religion. Armer, now Mother Dolores, had as second in command Sister Teresa O'Connor. Several of the early members were of Irish ancestry. Father John Prendergast, of Irish birth, was one of Mother Dolores' sponsors, as was partly Irish Mrs. Mary Ann Regan Tobin.

This is only a sample of the social activities of nineteenth-century Irish sisters in San Francisco. They certainly do not fit the steretype of Victorian ladies. Perhaps many Victorian women were not what we think of as "Victorian." Again these are only the achievements of Irish sisters in one city. It was repeated again and again in many parts of the U.S. in areas where Irish women are not thought of as social activists. More research will uncover many more interesting adventures of Irish sisters in the nineteenth-century United States.

*See* California; Sisters of Mercy; Presentation Sisters

Most of the research for this paper was in archives: Archives of the Archdiocese of San Francisco; Daughters of Charity Archives, Los Altos; Dominican Archives, San Rafael; Holy Family Archives, Fremont; Mercy Archives, Burlingame; Presentation Archives, San Francisco.
Sister Ann Curry, *Mother Teresa Comerford* (San Francisco, 1980).
Sister Aurelia McArdle, *California's Pioneer Sister of Mercy* (Fresno, 1954).

ANN CURRY, P.B.V.M.

## SAN PATRICIO BATTALION

In September, 1847, near the end of the war between the U.S. and Mexico, the U.S. Army hanged a group of fifty deserters at three locations near Mexico City. The final hangings on Sept. 13 were the stuff of high drama. The presiding officer waited several hours until the conquering U.S. flag flew atop the nearby Chapultepec Castle before giving the signal, thus completing the largest execution of deserters in U.S. history.

### A FOREIGN LEGION

The condemned were members of the St. Patrick's Battalion, a foreign legion within the Mexican army composed chiefly of U.S. army defectors. The Mexicans called them the *San Patricios*. Besides the fifty who were hanged, fifteen others received lesser sentences—fifty lashes and brandings on the face or hip with the letter "D" for deserter. Thirty-four deserters were Irish-born immigrants. The rest were Americans, Germans, Scots, French and Polish. The leaders were Irish, including Captain John Riley of County Galway, Ireland. A former private in Company K, U.S. Infantry, Riley was one of the first to desert by swimming across the Rio Grande to the village of Matamoros, Mexico in the early stages of the war. He then led his men against the U.S. forces in all the major battles of the two-year conflict. After his capture at the battle of Churubusco, Riley was spared capital punishment since he had deserted before the U.S. had officially declared war with Mexico.

### MOTIVATIONS

Some U.S. historians have dismissed the San Patricios as adventurers, misfits and opportunists. Historian Richard Blaine McCornack called them "bewildered and ignorant" and wrote that the principal motivation for the defections was drunkenness. Historian Kerby Miller disagrees, pointing out that drink may have movitated some desertions, but it would not have led the San Patricios to don the enemy's uniform and fight to the death against their former comrades. Instead, Miller and other scholars believe that the immigrant soldiers, with fresh memories of starvation and evictions in Ireland, were reacting to brutal treatment from nativist officers. They were also convinced, Miller says, that the U.S. was fighting an unjust war of conquest against a Catholic country.

Plaque, located at the Plaza San Jacinto in Mexico City, commemorating the San Patricio Battalion

## THE GREAT HUNGER

Many historians writing about the San Patricio Battalion make only passing references to the Great Famine in Ireland, the nativist movement in the U.S. and the doctrine of Manifest Destiny. Yet these historical realities strongly influenced the attitudes and habits of immigrant soldiers.

In recent years Christine Kinealy and other Famine scholars have shown that the potato blight was only partially responsible for more than a million Irish deaths. They explain that the British government restricted aid to the victims, claiming that the Irish were indolent and lacked ambition. These laissez-faire policies led to the unnecessary deaths of hundreds of thousands of Irish peasants and forced the emigration of two million more in the space of ten years. The immigrants' bitter memories of the famine were hardly alleviated when they arrived in America and found that Anglo-Americans also rejected them, hanging out signs that read: "No Irish Need Apply."

In the mid-1840s, nativist publications justified ill treatment of Irish immigrants and Mexicans by relying on racial stereotypes to denigrate both groups. Historian Michael Hogan has shown that the Irish were portrayed in cartoons as indolent, drunken and violent, while the Mexicans were described as uncivilized and "in no way deserving to be called white."

## "BUCKING AND GAGGING"

Historians Robert Ryal Miller and Peter Stevens have documented the nativist attitudes permeating the U.S. officer corps during the invasion of Mexico in 1846. One of their sources is George Ballentine, who wrote in his diary that for the same offenses Irish and German Catholic soldiers received harsher punishments than native-born U.S. soldiers. "Bucking and gagging," hanging a soldier by his wrists with a gag in his mouth for hours, was typical. Ballentine wrote: "Such a poor state of feeling existed between men and officers that I was not surprised that it led to numerous desertions."

## MANIFEST DESTINY

Such nativist attitudes coincided with the doctrine of Manifest Destiny formulated, ironically, by John O'Sullivan, editor of the

*Democratic Review.* Sullivan wrote: "It is our manifest destiny to overspread the continent allotted by Providence of our yearly multiplying millions." U.S. Gen. William Worth phrased the teaching more succinctly vis-à-vis the war with Mexico: "What does Mexico matter? Have not our Anglo Saxon race been land stealers from time immemorial? And why shouldn't they? When their gaze is fixed on other lands, the best way is to make out the deeds."

Despite protests from Abraham Lincoln, John Quincy Adams and Henry David Thoreau, Congress supported the invasion and conquest of Mexico in 1846. Two years later, after heavy human losses on both sides, U.S. and Mexican diplomats signed the Treaty of Guadalupe Hidalgo. Mexico was forced to sign away nearly half its territory for the sum of $15 million.

## SPARSE DOCUMENTATION

Other than a few letters from John Riley and the unreliable court martial testimony of his companions, the San Patricios left only sparse documentation on their views of the war and why they deserted. Riley's writings, however, clearly show his intentions to defend the cause of Mexico. In a letter to a former employer in Michigan he wrote: "Be not deceived by a nation that is at war with Mexico. For a kindly and more hospitable people than the Mexicans there exist not on the face of the earth."

For decades after the war, nativists used the desertions and executions of the San Patricios as a badge of shame against Irish immigrants. It is no wonder, therefore, that Irish Catholics would seek to distance themselves from the battalion and that historians would trivialize them as misfits. But new insights into the war, the Irish Famine period and the background of these men offer us different perspectives. Now the question can legitimately be asked: were these men traitors or heroes?

Michael Hogan, *The Irish Soldiers of Mexico* (Guadalajara: Fondo Editorial Universitario, 1997).

Christine Kinealy, *This Great Calamity: The Irish Famine, 1845–52* (Boulder, Colo., 1995).

Richard Blaine McCornack, "The San Patricio Deserters in the Mexican War," *The Americas,* VIII (1951): 131–42.

Kerby Miller, Videotaped interview, Columbia, Mo., March 14, 1994.

Robert Ryal Miller, *Shamrock and Sword* (Norman, Oka., 1989).

Peter Stevens, *The Rogue's March: John Riley and the San Patricios* (Washington, D.C., 1998).

Dennis J. Wynn, *The San Patricio Soldiers: Mexico's Foreign Legion* (Southwestern Studies; Monograph 74, El Paso, 1984).

MARK R. DAY

## SANGER, MARGARET HIGGINS (1879–1966)

Birth control advocate. Margaret Sanger, the leader of the American birth control movement, was born Margaret Louise Higgins on September 4, 1879 in Corning, New York. The sixth of eleven children of Irish-American Anne Purcell and Michael Hennessey Higgins, a stone mason from Canada, Sanger was influenced more by her atheist father than by her Roman Catholic mother. After attending Clarevack College, a private preparatory school in the Catskills, New York, Sanger trained as a nurse at White Plains Hospital. She married architect William Sanger in 1902; the couple had three children before divorcing in 1920. In 1922, Sanger married millionaire manufacturer J. Noah Slee.

Sanger moved to New York City in 1912 with her family and became active there in the women's labor movement and the

Margaret Higgins
Sanger

Socialist Party. While working as a nurse on New York's Lower East Side, Sanger began to construct connections between the poverty, disease and premature death she was seeing, and what she deemed unchecked childbirth. She came to believe that informed control over childbearing was the key to female emancipation, and that sexual reform was the paramount issue for women.

In support of her beliefs, Sanger wrote newspaper articles on feminine hygiene and sexuality, published a militant radical journal, *Women Rebel* (later *Birth Control Review*), and a pamphlet, *Family Limitations* (1914), in which she coined the term "birth control," and called for the legalization of contraception. Upon publication of *Family Limitations,* Sanger was indicted for violating the Comstock Law of 1873 which prohibited obscene material being sent throught the U.S. mail, and moved to Europe. The case against Sanger was later dismissed, and she returned to the U.S. and her writing. Among her books were: *What Every Woman Should Know* (1917); *Woman and the New Race* (1920); *My Fight for Birth Control* (1931).

Sanger served 30 days in prison for opening a birth control clinic with her sister in Brooklyn, New York, in 1916. With the support of her wealthy second husband, Sanger founded an advocacy group, American Birth Control League in 1921, and the Birth Control Research Bureau in 1923, a medical clinic which became the model for some 300 others around the country. The two organizations merged in 1942 to become Planned Parenthood, a group known today for its advocacy of birth control and legal abortion. Sanger founded a lobbying group in 1929 that successfully sued to allow the mailing of contraceptive materials within the United States. In the 1950s, she induced philanthropist Katharine Dexter McCormick to help fund development of a birth control pill and helped found the International Planned Parenthood Foundation.

Sanger's radical sexual ideology, which at base separated sex from procreation, was controversial and was thought by many to be outside the American mainstream. While they have come to exercise great influence, Sanger's beliefs have also been criticized as immoral. Indeed, scrutiny of Sanger's writings reveals an interest in eugenics: she advocated birth control partly as a means to maintain the dominant position of the white race over others.

Sanger died on September 6, 1966, in Tucson Arizona, at the age of 87.

Ellen Chesler, *Women of Valor: Margaret Sanger and the Birth Control Movement in America* (New York, 1992).

Emily Taft Douglas, *Margaret Sanger: Pioneer of the Future* (New York, 1970).

Madeleine Gray, *Margaret Sanger: A Biography of the Champion of Birth Control* (New York, 1979).

Harold Hersey, *Margaret Sanger: The Biography of the Birth Control Pioneer* (New York, 1938).

David Kennedy, *Birth Control in America: The Career of Margaret Sanger* (New Haven, Conn., 1970).

Lawrence Lader, *The Margaret Sanger Story and the Fight for Birth Control* (New York, 1955).

Margaret Sanger, *An Autobiography* (New York, 1938).

KATHLEEN N. McCARTHY

## SAVANNAH

When James Oglethorpe founded the town of Savannah, Georgia, in 1733, there were no Irish settlers among the pioneer group which accompanied him to the new colony. Potential settlers in general were deterred from coming to the fledgling settlement because of its limitation on landholding and its ban on the increasingly lucrative slavery. When the charter expired in 1752, Georgia became a royal colony. Many settlers, including numbers of Irish Protestants, used Savannah as a staging point for their journey into the fertile back countries of Georgia and South Carolina.

A few of these earliest Irish settlers stayed in Georgia's first capital. By the 1790s some may have been Catholics. In 1791 Savannah's city council accepted an application from the city's Catholics to purchase a lot for a Catholic Church. In the early 1800s priests visiting from Charleston remarked that the city's small Catholic population was made up of Irish immigrants and some refugees from Santo Domingo. Thus, the majority of Savannah's Irish residents were still Protestant. Eminent members of this community founded Savannah's Hibernian Society in 1812, using the local Independent Presbyterian Church for their first St. Patrick's Day celebrations.

In addition to serving as an outlet for social activities, the society also collected funds from its members to aid the increasing numbers of poorer immigrants arriving in the city. On a number of occasions in the 1820s and 1830s the Society came to the rescue of unemployed Irish canal and railroad workers. The Society also began to take a keen interest in Irish politics. At their annual St. Patrick's Day celebrations during these same decades they praised Daniel O'Connell and his efforts as well as welcoming Bishop John England of Charleston as their keynote speaker in 1824, 1827, and 1832. England, a native of County Cork, was an eloquent defender of Irish Catholics and made a great impression on the Hibernians. At the 1824 meeting, they made him an honorary member of the Society and began their celebrations at the Catholic Church of St. John the Baptist.

The Hibernians' growing recognition of an Irish Catholic presence in their society paralleled the increasing influx of new immigrants into the city. Attracted by job opportunities on the docks and on the Central of Georgia Railroad (which commenced construction in 1836), Irish immigration to the city increased. The Great Famine caused an explosion in Irish migration to Savannah. Many Irish came South after first arriving in New York

City, Philadelphia, or Charleston but large numbers during this time period also came directly to Savannah. In particular, a number of ships arrived in Savannah from Wexford, bringing with them what would become some of Irish Savannah's most prominent families. By 1850 Savannah's Irish population stood at 1,555, making up 10.2 percent of the total population and 18.5 percent of the white population. Ten years later it reached its peak at 3,145, making up 14.1 percent of the total population and 22.7 percent of the white population. In 1860, the Irish in Savannah accounted for just under half of the total Irish population in Georgia.

Most of the famine Irish who came to Savannah followed their predecessors into the sections of town with the poorest housing. East and west of the original city the Irish lived in the "Old Fort" and "Yamacraw" neighborhoods. Crowded into these low lying and unsanitary areas which contained numerous taverns, brothels, and boarding houses, Savannah's Irish gained a reputation for alcoholism, crime, and violence. Many Irish suffered injury and occasionally death at the hands of fellow countrymen, while others succumbed to disease due to poor sanitation. The yellow fever outbreak of 1854 was particularly devastating to the Irish of Savannah. Most worked menial jobs in construction, the railroad, or the docks. Their livelihoods were in the city, and they could not afford to leave the city during an epidemic.

The Irish, however, exploited their niche at the lower end of the urban labor market. They were very mobile, moving on numerous occasions to find the work with the best pay. They also had a reputation for labor unrest. Irish workers, while maintaining a reputation as trouble-makers, were able to continue working because urban employers depended upon them for tasks once reserved for slaves. Planter demand for slaves had increased in the 1850s as cotton prices grew higher throughout the decade. In Savannah the urban slave populations declined rapidly, and thus, slaves became much more expensive to buy or hire. At the right wages, the Irish were glad to fill this vacuum in the southern labor market.

Not every Irish person in Savannah worked as a laborer. Large numbers found livings as skilled artisans. Irish bricklayers, carpenters and plasterers were also a vital element of Savannah's workforce. Some artisans such as wheelwrights, saddlers and harnessmakers managed to become self-employed and purchase property. A few prospered enough to purchase slaves. Savannah's Irish women, on the other hand, usually worked as domestics, although a few did operate small stores.

The Savannah Irish did more than just play an important role in the city's economic life, they also celebrated their ethnic and religious heritage. The Hibernian society elected its first Catholic president in 1856. The Irish who could not join the exclusive Hibernians instead joined such organizations as temperance societies, an Irish militia unit (the Jasper Greens), the Workingmen's Benevolent Association, and various Irish political clubs. After the Civil War the Irish continued their interest in Irish affairs by supporting the Fenian Brotherhood, the Irish Land League, and the Ancient Order of Hibernians. These organizations gave the Irish a social outlet. Visitors to nineteenth-century Savannah were as likely to see Irishmen at meetings, drills, or parades as to see them unloading a ship at the waterfront.

The ethnic character of these various organizations gave the Irish more than just occasions to socialize. They also gave them a chance to celebrate their Irishness and to remain aware of events in Ireland. Savannah's Repeal Association kept in constant touch with Daniel O'Connell's Loyal National Repeal Association, even after O'Connell endorsed the American abolitionist movement. Recognizing a market for news from Ireland, local newspapers kept Irish Savannahians aware of the Famine, Young Ireland and Fenian rebellions, and the land agitation of the 1870s and '80s. Savannah's Irish societies were quick to respond with meetings and money for Irish causes.

Savannah's Irish also generously supported the Catholic Church in the city. Initially, however, most were too poor to do so. The pioneering Father Jeremiah O'Neill, originally from County Kerry, faced enormous pressures catering to his rapidly increasing post-Famine population. He and other priests worried that the new Irish arriving would quickly lose their Catholic faith. In 1845 he brought nuns to Savannah from the Charleston mother house of The Sisters of Our Lady of Mercy. These predominantly Irish sisters educated large numbers of new immigrants and also, when the need arose, ventured outside the walls to help the indigent poor and the victims of yellow fever epidemics. In 1850, the Vatican acknowledged the need for a separate diocese for Georgia (since 1820 the state had been under the jurisdiction of the diocese of Charleston), and established the see at Savannah. The first two bishops of Savannah, Francis X. Gartland and John Barry, were natives of Ireland.

Bishops, priests, and nuns laid a solid foundation for Catholicism in Savannah, but it was the Irish laity who made it flourish. In the early 1870s, the Irish were generous subscribers to the construction of the Cathedral of Saint John the Baptist, and its reconstruction after a fire that destroyed it in 1898. The Irish in Yamacraw had paid for their own church, St. Patrick's, on the west side of town in 1863. Other prominent Irish people on their deaths provided large and small sums of money to the diocese in their wills.

Intense Irish interest in Ireland and the Catholic Church could have isolated the Irish in Savannah from the southern mainstream. On the contrary, it gave them the confidence to move beyond their own immigrant community and take a more active role in Savannah's civic life. Heavily influenced by the writings of John England, church authorities in Savannah emphasized the compatibility of Roman Catholicism and American republicanism. Thus, the Irish felt no compunction about participating in local politics. Most were Democrats and turned out *en masse* to support the party's candidates. Some natives complained that the Irish campaigned too vigorously, and violence between Irish Democrats and their opponents was common on election day. The Know-Nothing challenge of the 1850s increased tensions, but Savannah's nativism never possessed the virility it had in Boston, Baltimore, or New Orleans. The Know-Nothings never gained control of Savannah, due in some part to the Irish vote for the Democrats. The Irish received city jobs as a reward for their loyalty to the party of Andrew Jackson. More prominent Irish businessmen gained lucrative federal positions and places on the party slate for local elections. These activities on behalf of the majority party in the South helped move the Irish into the southern mainstream.

Another crucial element in the gradual assimilation of the Irish in Savannah was their acceptance of the "peculiar institution." Although not rabid supporters of slavery, Irish Savannahians did not object to its existence, and when they could afford to, did not hesitate in buying human chattel. Many natives, however, feared that contact between the poor Irish and poor blacks would threaten the laws regulating slavery in the city. There was some justification for these fears. The Irish neighborhoods contained the largest numbers of slaves and free blacks, and thus, the Irish were the most likely to be charged with such offenses as selling liquor to slaves. Circumvention of city ordinances, however, did not grow into abolitionism. The Irish knew that freed slaves would compete for their jobs. Irish Savannahians did not actively push for an end to slavery, because they associated abolition activity with "Yankee" nativists and English evangelicals who had preached that Ireland's Great Famine had been the benign will of God.

After Abraham Lincoln's election to the presidency in 1860, the Irish in Savannah proved loyal to Georgia and its institutions. Only ten years before, the Irish had stood up for the Union, but now they were prepared to support secession. Father Jeremiah O'Neill, the spiritual leader of the Savannah Irish, spoke at meetings calling for the break-up of the United States. After secession, Irish Savannahians volunteered in droves to fight for their new home. The Jasper Greens provided two companies, while other Irishmen filled units such as the Montgomery Guards. Given a hero's send-off by families, friends, and clergy, Savannah's Irish served from Georgia to Virginia. Many never came back, and those who did faced the reality of a defeated people and devastated Georgia.

Savannah, however, had escaped the worst effects of the Union invasion, and there were still some opportunities for the former Confederates. Numbers of Irish Confederates used their new status as defeated heroes to improve their economic situation. The Irish had proved their loyalty during the Civil War. The soldiers' efforts, along with the Sisters of Mercy who had nursed wounded soldiers throughout the state, opened new doors for the Irish. For example, Tipperary native John Flannery was a clerk when he enlisted in Confederate service in 1862. After the war he got involved in the postwar cotton boom. He became very wealthy and by 1910, the year of his death, he was or had been an organizer, director and president of a bank, vice-president of one railroad and on the board of numerous others, and a director of a cotton press company, lumber firm, and hotel company. The latter part of the nineteenth century was indeed a golden era for the Savannah Irish and in particular for their American-born children. Their economic situation improved as freed blacks now took the menial jobs. As loyal Democrats, many of Savannah's Irish were elected to city and state office. The Sisters of Mercy operated St. Joseph's hospital, dominating health care in the city. The Irish had become so assimilated that they were able to hammer out a compromise with other Savannahians to allow for the public support of Catholic schools.

The price of this success was a dilution of ethnic identity. After the Civil War, Irish immigration to Savannah virtually ended. The "New South" of sharecropping and Jim Crow did not have much to offer to new migrants. Therefore, Irish Savannahians became members of the "Solid South." Apart from occasions such as the 1894 longshoremen strike when Irish, Irish-American, and African-American workers picketed and marched together to protest against their conditions, Irish Savannahians did not publicly challenge the negative racial attitudes which gripped the nation. On a personal level, many of the Irish in Savannah and their descendants continued to have good relations with their now free black neighbors, but as the Irish gained affluence and moved out of the neighborhoods, those relationships began to dissipate.

Irish assimilation into the Georgia power structure was not, however, total. As Catholics in the deep South and as urbanites in a rural state, they were still different from the majority of Georgians. Rather than shying away from expressing their continuing distinctness, they embraced it. The Knights of Columbus (Council 631 of Savannah, founded in 1902, is Georgia's mother council), the Ancient Order of Hibernians, the Hibernian Society, the Jasper Greens, and the Total Abstinence societies remained very active and continued to instill confidence in the "Irish" community. Therefore, they vigorously opposed the racist rants of Tom Watson and the Ku Klux Klan and attempted to thwart the introduction of prohibition. When the dominant "crackers" were defeated by the Irish at state level, the Irish turned Savannah and its county into the "free state of Chatham." Until 1960, Savannah had its own Irish political machine which could be justifiably compared to any other machine in the country.

Irish-Americans are not as influential in Savannah politics as they once were. They still, however, leave a large imprint on the city. There are over a dozen Irish-American organizations in the city and the Knights of Columbus still have sizeable "Irish" contingents. Every St. Patrick's Day they take over the city and run one of the largest parades in the United States (uninterrupted since 1922, although the first parade dates back to 1824). Festivities preceding parade day include an Irish festival and a *feis*. Savannah's Irish-Americans also pay tribute to their ancestors at the Celtic Cross in (Robert) Emmet Park, an appropriate commemoration for their forebears, who left a legacy much greater than their small numbers could ever have indicated.

*See* Georgia

Brian Edward Crowson, "Southern Port City Politics and the Know-Nothing Party in the 1850s" (Ph.D. diss., University of Tennessee, 1994).

David Thomas Gleeson, "The Irish in the South, 1815–1877" (Ph.D. diss., Mississippi State University, 1997).

J. J. O'Connell, *Catholicity in the Carolinas and Georgia: Leaves of Its History* (Spartanburg, S.C., 1972).

Edward M. Shoemaker, "Strangers and Citizens: The Irish Immigrant Community in Savannah, 1837–1861" (Ph.D. diss., Emory University, 1990).

Thomas Paul Thigpen, "Aristocracy of the Heart: Catholic Lay Leadership in Savannah, 1820–1870" (Ph.D. diss., Emory University, 1995).

Herbert Weaver, "Foreigners in Ante-Bellum Savannah," *Georgia Historical Quarterly,* 37 (March 1953): 1–17.

DAVID GLEESON

## SAYERS, VALERIE (1953–  )

Novelist and teacher. *Due East,* Valerie Sayers' literary ground zero, in real life is Beaufort, South Carolina, where she was one of seven children of Irish-American parents. Her mother's family came to America early in the 19th century, her father's in the 20th, from Killorglin, Co. Kerry. She describes "a very sentimental longing" for Ireland and a rose-tinted nostalgia on the part of both parents, but Sayers' own work does not belong to that soppy school.

At seventeen she moved north to Fordham University. She insists her novels are not autobiographical, yet her fiction follows an eccentric band of characters from places she has been and down roads she has traveled.

Valerie Sayers

*Due East* is the title of her first novel, published in 1986 (her five novels have been published by Doubleday). It is the story of Mary Faith Rapple, fifteen, who is in trouble from page one. Her mother is dead. She's pregnant and keeps waiting for her father to notice, which he never does, until eventually she imagines that "somehow I'd get through nine months and a delivery, and one night he'd say, 'How did that baby get to the supper table?'"

Eventually she tells him. It will be a virgin birth, she explains. Her father is skeptical. He suggests an abortion, but Mary Faith won't hear of it. Her father drives off into the night, leaving her disconsolate. Yet she is imbued with a rich imaginative life. Though a Baptist herself, if only nominally, and "even if I didn't believe in God, I was always fond of Mary, and I always thought the idea of a virgin birth was something fine. Fine and wicked, too, the way it made it seem as if Jesus Christ was too good for the love of a man and a woman."

Many of Sayers' preoccupations are evident here. There is a religious aspect, with emphasis on earthy sin and unorthodox redemption. There is a misfortune aspect—"I'm interested in pursuing people in trouble," she has said. There is relentless candor. If the love is lusty, she says so. Her people's stomachs sometimes growl. "My view of fiction has always been a moral view," she sums up.

After Fordham she returned briefly to teach at Beaufort, then taught in New York. The writing, she has said, gradually grew on her. She married Christian Jara, a filmmaker, and they have two sons, Christian and Raul. Like many artists, she manages to make her own life sound much more ordinary than her many characters whose journeys often parallel her own.

It is Franny Starkey, the school slut, for example, who, in her fourth novel, *The Distance Between Us,* goes north to the fictional Jesuit University of America where Michael Burke lies in wait, and he with a devilish halo of red hair, a really loud Irish lad from Brooklyn whom no mother in her right mind would want her daughter messing with.

But messing is precisely what Franny is soon doing with Burke, amid amazing ropes of talk and unpredictable goings-on.

"Michael came out of the Safeway looking like a circus clown, a dozen cans of tuna fish in his pockets and a sirloin steak tucked in the back of his jeans, the scarlet blood running down the backs of his legs." He's just "liberating stuff," he tells Franny. For practice. For the upcoming revolution. Half a block away, he donates the purloined groceries to a startled old woman. Michael Burke's option for the poor. Son of Playboy of the Western World, "the sheer variety of drugs he consumed was appalling, even to her. You couldn't possibly ingest as many drugs as he did and be celibate as long as he claimed."

Sayers' second novel, *How I Got Him Back,* is still set in *Due East,* four and a half years after Mary Faith's baby is born. The erosion of old dreams is condensed by one character: "That night, when we collapsed in our hotel rooms, I found my rosary beads in my makeup bag. I couldn't make out why they were there—I stopped saying rosaries the day I signed my mother into the state hospital—but there they were, black beads covered with a fine mist of lavender eye shadow. So I said the sorrowful mysteries."

Nearly every character is haunted by religion. In her third novel, *Who Do You Love,* Dolores Rooney is described as a Mary not a Martha, and before long her husband Bill is trying to confess sins of impurity while the hip priest insists he hasn't committed a sin worth confessing. Then, in her fifth novel, *Brain Fever,* Tim, a divorced failure but a holy fool of sorts, is in love with the still-single Mary Faith—the bizarre and the divine elbowing one another from *Due East* up north.

Sayers became director of the creative writing program at the University of Notre Dame in 1993. Her sensibility, not surprisingly, is more Irish-American than Irish. She visited Ireland with her husband in the early 1970s and again in the early 1990s. The Ireland of her imagination was so ill-formed, she says, so cobbled together from family sentimentality and personal reading, "I don't have a firm enough grasp of what Ireland is to have it wrenched away from me." Yet she experiences Ireland as "sand in the sheets" and in 1998, as she worked on her next novel, *Cab Ride to Dixie,* was still longing to go back, as if to finish unfinished business.

But this work in progress, centering on an "African-Irish-American young man," exploring "the question of race in the South and how that connects with ethnic identity," hints that Sayers, like so many others of Irish ancestry, has come home to America.

*See* Fiction, Irish-American

Valerie Sayers, *Due East* (New York, 1987).
———, *How I Got Him Back or Under the Moon's Shine* (New York, 1989).
———, *Who Do You Love* (New York, 1991).
———, *The Distance Between Us* (New York, 1994).
———, *Brain Fever* (New York, 1996).

MICHAEL FARRELL

## SCANLAN, PATRICK FRANCIS (1894–1983)

Newspaper editor. Born in New York City on October 7, 1894, one of seven children born to Michael and Maria O'Keefe Scanlan. His father emigrated to America from County Cork, opening a chain of grocery stores in New York and Philadelphia. The family moved to Philadelphia in 1901, where Scanlan attended St. Elizabeth's parochial school. He later attended the Jesuit-run St. Joseph's High School and St. Joseph's College in Philadelphia, receiving a bachelor's degree in 1914.

After graduation, Scanlan studied at Dunwoodie for two years, leaving due to illness. He then taught at St. Peter's High School for Boys, recently established on Staten Island. In 1917 he was hired as temporary managing editor for the *Tablet*, the official newspaper of the Diocese of Brooklyn, where he had recently taken up residence. He took the place of Joseph Cummings, who had been drafted into the army during World War I. After Cummings died, Scanlan received a permanent position at the *Tablet*. He remained there for a total of 51 years.

One of Scanlan's major concerns during the 1920s was the growth of anti-Catholicism, especially that directed against Irish-American Catholics. He urged Catholics to band together in defense against the Ku Klux Klan, a rapidly growing organization during that decade. During the 1928 presidential campaign, popular anti-Catholic sentiment helped in the defeat of Democratic candidate Alfred E. Smith. The prejudice displayed served to confirm Scanlan's belief that Catholics were still outsiders in America.

The rise of domestic Communism was a major concern of Scanlan's during the 1930s. Over nearly four decades, he warned readers on a weekly basis about Communists in labor, education, government and politics. By the mid-1930s, Scanlan was the foremost supporter of Father Charles E. Coughlin, the "radio priest," in the American Catholic press. He continued to support Coughlin even after the latter's turn to an overt anti-Semitism in late 1938.

As American entry into World War II became increasingly imminent, Scanlan espoused a strongly isolationist (and anti-British) stance. After the bombing of Pearl Harbor, however, he urged Catholics to fulfill their patriotic duties and support the war effort. At the same time he continued to criticize America's alliance with Soviet Russia, an understandable approach, given his ardent anti-Communism. For Scanlan, Communism was a greater threat to the Church than Fascism.

He supported Senator Joseph R. McCarthy's campaign against domestic "radicalism." He took a more ambivalent approach to the Korean conflict. He supported the effort to halt Communist expansion, but he felt that the war could have been avoided if FDR had taken a tougher stance at Yalta in 1945.

Scanlan publicly supported Vatican II (1962–1965), but privately he had many misgivings about taking on a new understanding of the Church after so many years. He was wary of the new ecumenism, liturgical changes, and a more general openness toward the modern world. He found himself unable to deal with changes in the American church as clergy and laity joined the various popular movements of the 1960s. Scanlan retired from the *Tablet* in June 1968 at age 74, spending his retirement in Long Island. In 1974, he was moved to a nursing home where he died at age 88 on March 27, 1983.

Patrick J. McNamara, "A Study of the Editorial Policy of the Brooklyn *Tablet* under Patrick F. Scanlan, 1917–1968" (M.A. Thesis, St. John's University, 1994).

———, "Patrick F. Scanlan, The Brooklyn *Tablet*, and the New Deal," *New York Irish History*, 8 (1994): 8–12.

PATRICK J. McNAMARA

## SCIENTISTS, IRISH-AMERICAN

Very little notice has been taken, even in Ireland, of those Irish-Americans in the 18th and 19th centuries who contributed vast knowledge to the fields of science and technology. However, the contributions of at least twenty such men place them among the prominent figures in a relatively backward America of that period.

Some of the men left Ireland while still children, while others did so after being involved in conspiracies against British rule and spending time in prison. The list of those who attained scientific prominence in America can be divided into medical practitioners, scholars, and innovators.

### MEDICAL PRACTITIONERS

Foremost among those who paved the way for modern chemistry was William James MacNeven (1763–1841), who was born in County Galway, Ireland. MacNeven studied medicine at the universities of Prague and Vienna, and returned to practice in Dublin.

In 1805 he emigrated to New York and established a practice. He was elected professor of obstetrics in the College of Physicians and Surgeons at New York Hospital in 1808. Three years later he became chairman of the chemistry department and began the first chemical laboratory in New York. MacNeven has been acknowledged as the founding figure of American chemistry.

Edward Hudson (1772–1833), born in County Wexford, Ireland, of English-Quaker parents, was a pioneer American dentist. He practiced in Philadelphia after emigrating to America in 1802. Hudson was one of the first to remove dental pulp and fill the root of the tooth with gold foil.

A supposed institutional cure for alcoholism brought notoriety to Leslie E. Keeley (1832–1900), who was born in St. Lawrence County, New York. He began his treatment of alcoholism and drug addiction in 1879, and the following year published a small pamphlet on the opium habit and its treatment. Keeley's treatment for alcoholism consisted of hypodermic injections of chloride gold, given to patients at one of the many clinics he had established around the country.

Although in 1895 Keeley claimed a total of 250,000 cures, the medical profession was skeptical, ascribing the good results more to suggestion, and the sudden dislike of liquor to injections of apomorphin and strychnine.

### SCHOLARS

One of the earliest Irish-American academics on record was James Logan (1674–1751) from Lurgan, County Armagh, Ireland, a contemporary of Sir Isaac Newton and Robert Boyle. In 1699 Logan became William Penn's secretary and sailed with him to Pennsylvania.

Logan was elected mayor of Philadelphia in 1722. After retiring from political office in 1747, he returned to his major interest, the study of natural science, and published several articles on botany, optics and astronomy. When he died, his large collection of books and papers were willed to the city, thus forming the nucleus of Philadelphia's Public Library.

Irish-born mathematician Robert Patterson (1743–1824) was from near Hillsborough in the north of Ireland. He emigrated to America in 1768 and landed in Philadelphia, where he eventually was appointed professor of mathematics at the University of Pennsylvania in 1779. He served there until 1814 and was succeeded by his son, Robert M. Patterson. Several of his lectures were published, as well as a small book, *Newtonian System of Philosophy*. In 1805 President Thomas Jefferson appointed Patterson director of the mint.

Thomas Freeman (d. 1821), a civil engineer, astronomer and explorer, emigrated to America in 1784. He was appointed one of the surveyors for the new capital of the United States in 1794 and mapped the entire northern portion of Washington, D.C. He was the first to map the lower Red River and the boundary line between Tennessee and Alabama. He also was commissioned surveyor of public lands of the United States south of Tennessee.

Matthew Carey (1760–1839), born in Dublin, Ireland, had edited both the *Freeman's Journal* and *Volunteer Journal* before he was twenty-four. During an "enforced" stay in Paris, Carey worked on the printing press established by Benjamin Franklin.

In 1785, a year after his arrival in America, Carey started the *Philadelphia Herald,* with financial assistance from the Marquis de Lafayette, whom he had met in Paris. He also formed the Hibernian Society for the relief of Irish immigrants.

Because the flood of English goods into America following the Revolutionary War was undermining manufacturing efforts, Carey promoted a protective policy for the country. He was an early advocate of soil conservation and various advances of agricultural technology. He and his son, Henry, did more than anyone else, except Alexander Hamilton, to establish the American nationalist school of economic thought.

Robert Adrain (1775–1843) was the most outstanding mathematician in America in his time. Born in Carrickfergus, Ireland, of Huguenot stock, Adrain emigrated to America and taught at several schools in New Jersey and Pennsylvania, including the University of Pennsylvania. His greatest contribution, however, occurred in 1808 when he set forth the exponential law of error, which the German mathematician Karl Gauss demonstrated a year later.

Adrain also calculated an improved figure for the ellipticity of the Earth, moving it a step closer to today's value. Through his calculations and writings, Adrain came to be ranked as one of the first two creative mathematicians in America.

Johns Hopkins University, Baltimore, and the advance of physiology in America owes much to the scholarship of Henry Newell Martin (1848–1896). Born in Newry, County Down, Ireland, he attended the Medical School of University College in London, then went to Cambridge on a scholarship where he studied under Aldous Huxley and became the first to earn a doctor of science degree in physiology.

During his seventeen years at Johns Hopkins University, beginning as chair of biology in 1876, Martin established guidelines for instruction and research in the biological sciences. His greatest contribution was the discovery of a method to study the isolated heart of mammals and to observe the effect of temperature on the heart. His studies led the way to later research by others on the functions of the heart and introduced modern physiology to America.

### INNOVATORS

Throughout the 19th century, Ireland sent many inventors and innovators to America. From County Armagh came John Stephenson (1809–1893), who designed and built the first omnibus made in New York. He also designed and built the first car for the first street railway in the world, the New York and Harlem Railroad. Stephenson also devised the idea of an entrance at both ends of the car that allowed the line to operate more efficiently. His company became the largest streetcar builder in the world.

Two other Irish inventors totaled more than two hundred patents between them. Patrick Bernard Delany (1845–1924) from Killavilla, Kings County, Ireland, was an excellent telegraph operator by the time he was sixteen years old. Among his notable inventions were the anti-Page relay; anti-induction cables; a synchronous, multiplex telegraph by which six messages could be sent simultaneously over a single wire; the Vox Humana talking machine; and telegraphic keyboard apparatus, as well as devices for submarine detection. John Forrest Kelly (1859–1922) from Carrick-on-Suir specialized in transmitting electricity at very high voltages over long distances and was the first to form a stable iron electromagnet core.

Kinsale-born James J. Woods (1856–1928) had about 240 patents to his name. While working at a lock company, he designed a horizontal steam engine before he was seventeen. Ten years later, he was manufacturing oil engines. His floodlighting system was used to illuminate the Statue of Liberty.

Woods' oil engines provided power for the invention of a compatriot, John Philip Holland (1840–1914) of Liscannor, County Clare, Ireland. In 1898 Holland launched the first submarine equipped with a gasoline engine for surface propulsion and electric storage batteries and motor for submerged cruising. In 1904, he devised a respirator for escape from disabled submarines, which was similar to a device adopted by the United States Navy twenty-five years later. During his final years, Holland experimented in aeronautics.

*Dictionary of American Biography* (New York, 1930–1936).

Sean O'Donnell, "Early American Science: The Irish Contribution," *Éire-Ireland,* 18/1 (Spring 1983).

———, "Irish-American Scientists," *Éire-Ireland,* 14/2 (Summer 1979).

MARIANNA McLOUGHLIN

## SCOTCH-IRISH AND AMERICAN POLITICS

Particularly in the revolutionary era and its immediate aftermath, a large number of immigrants from Ireland and their immediate descendents made their American mark as important political figures in both Pennsylvania (including New Jersey and Delaware) and the piedmont areas of Virginia and the Carolinas. Only their noteworthy martial expertise in the American Revolution overshadows their parallel political achievement. The political experience of these immigrants with a brogue makes clear how complex was the society where the "people" declared in 1776 for freedom. The oft-antagonistic groups that formed the Scotch-Irish displayed an uncharacteristic unity in their opposition in the 1770s to what they viewed as tyranny and a bit less unity in their reaction to Federalist persecution in the late 1790s. Their strong-willed approach to later controversial American issues guaranteed that they would generally be in leadership roles on both sides of a political divide. In what follows, "Ulster Scot" will refer to those clearly identified as Presbyterians of Scottish descent who were living in Ireland before emigrating to America, "Anglo-Irish" will refer to Irish Anglican emigrants, and "Scotch-Irish" will be the ambiguous label describing Irish Protestants and their descendents without any reference to denomination or racial background. Four items will now be discussed: Scotch-Irish presidents; eighteenth-century Scotch-Irish areas; their important political role in the American revolutionary and antebellum eras.

### AMERICAN PRESIDENTS

With good reason, every writer on the Scotch-Irish emphasizes the large number who have become U.S. presidents. For over fifty years between the inauguration of Andrew Jackson and the termination of Woodrow Wilson's eight years in office, the White House was occupied by men of direct Ulster descent, three of them [Jackson, Buchanan, Arthur] being the only first-generation American presidents. William Clinton, Jimmy Carter, and Richard Nixon trace their Irish roots to Southern Ireland Protestant settlers, a category that in the colonial period would generally have been listed under the Irish category that in time became known as the Scotch-Irish. One could also include losing candidates such as Samuel Houston, Stephen A. Douglas, DeWitt Clinton, Horace Greeley, John Bell, James G. Blaine. Jefferson Davis, of course, is in a special category. Notable early Scotch-Irish vice presidents would include George Clinton and John C. Calhoun.

James K. Polk, James Buchanan, and Woodrow Wilson's ancestries illustrate exactly the Ulster Scot version of Scotch-Irish. Polk's family is first noticed in Lowland Scotland before their intense Covenanter version of Presbyterianism caused them to seek greater religious freedom in Coleraine in Northern Ireland. Then the family moved to Cumberland, Pennsylvania, a county bearing one of the key place-names among Presbyterians seeking greater religious freedom in America. The future president was born in Mecklenburg County, North Carolina. President James Buchanan was Ulster Scot Presbyterian on both sides of his family. His paternal ancestors similarly resided in Scotland, in his family's case along the southeast shore of Loch Lomand until they moved to Ramelton, Co. Donegal, on Laugh Swilly in Northern Ireland. In America, they made Pennsylvania their home in the midst of a large Ulster-Scot region. Part of Woodrow Wilson's ancestry followed the McKinley pattern as his grandfather emigrated from Strabane, Co. Down, and died five decades later in eastern Ohio. His strongly Presbyterian upbringing, many Scottish ancestral ties, a Shenandoah upbringing, and his later intense opposition to Ireland's self-determination unmistakably marked President Wilson as an Ulster Scot type of Irishman. President William McKinley's religious affiliation was also Presbyterian and his family emigrated from Dervock an area of Co. Antrim near the Giant's Causeway. In America they moved into Pennsylvania before finally settling in eastern Ohio. His background only lacks the documented family land in Scotland to be prime Ulster Scot.

Presidents Jackson, Polk, and Andrew Johnson's presidential administrations form an interesting Southern contrast to those of Buchanan, Grant, and McKinley. While a common core of Presbyterian Ulster Scot values may infuse the value systems of all six presidents, they are nevertheless distinguishable by the more general cultures from which they drew their voting constituency. Successful politicians in the Upland South (with borrowings from the Virginia lifestyle) evinced a tougher, more aggressive, more willful approach to life. Both Jackson and Polk's pugnacious presidential administrations are American re-enactments of the old Scot border customs recently outlined by D. H. Fischer in *Albion's Seed*. In contrast, the Buchanan-Grant-McKinley American Midland Culture more generally emphasized conciliatory interaction as essential for its individualist marketplace form of politics.

President Chester Arthur exemplifies a common Scotch-Irish variation from the Ulster Scot model since his Northeast Ireland background showed in his father's accent, but the Arthurs were Anglican and Baptist, not Presbyterian. Grover Cleveland's grandfather was from a patriotic Irish Protestant family, but his presidential style may reflect his northern Puritan-derived culture. In more recent times President Richard Nixon's strong Irish descent shows another variation, since his family started in Scotland but moved to County Wexford in the south of Ireland before moving on to the Pennsylvania-Ohio region. Bill Clinton and Jimmy Carter have multiple Protestant Irish strains on their family trees. President Reagan with his Catholic County Tipperary ancestry is not generally considered of Scotch-Irish descent but his lost connection to Catholicism and his mother's Scots-English background would most likely have gotten the Reagans classified in early American history as Scotch-Irish. While Abraham Lincoln's family was partially from Donegal in Northern Ireland and was certainly Protestant, his main paternal line came to Massachusetts in the early seventeenth century. Hence, Honest Abe is not normally considered Scotch-Irish. The only president of Irish lineage who was not Scotch-Irish was John F. Kennedy. His strong association with the Catholic-Irish tradition precludes any Scotch-Irish label. However, many a Catholic from Ireland, swept along in the great mass of eighteenth-century colonial movement, would convert (as did a number of wealthy Philadelphia merchants) or more generally would slide in time into the Scotch-Irish pot as their Catholicism failed to survive the priest-free frontier. Bishop John England, for example, in 1839 agreed with some European thinkers that three million Catholic Irish had ceased being Catholics in America.

### SCOTCH-IRISH STRANDS

Few Scots from Ulster rubbed shoulders with the one hundred thousand or so mostly Catholic seventeenth-century immigrants from Ireland, although many of the Irish Catholics became Protestant and were thus easily confused with the eighteenth-century Ulster Scot dominated movement. In any case, few of these poor seventeenth-century immigrants have any notable political history.

The quarter of a million or so emigrants from Ireland in the eighteenth-century reveal a dominant Presbyterian Ulster Scot flow, itself breaking down unequally into the rather differing characteristics of Ulster and Dublin Presbyterianism. The latter's importance can be seen, for example, in the career of George Bryan, the radical Pennsylvania revolutionary and slavery abolitionist. Ulster Presbyterian political expertise also varied when

James Buchanan

it was practiced in the Shenandoah Valley (south) or in the Philadelphia area (west). Ulster Protestants coming over after the Revolutionary War era and settling along the Philadelphia-Pittsburgh axis generally became rather more successful in nonpolitical leadership roles, particularly financial and entrepreneurial ones. In contrast, after the Civil War the numerous members of the Southern backcountry arm of the eighteenth-century Scotch-Irish movement found themselves with diminished economic and political power. In addition, and in uncertain numbers, two variant streams parallel the dominant Presbyterian ones; namely, an English-descended Anglo-Irish element and a Celtic portion not strongly identified at that time with Catholicism.

As the turn-of-the-century Proceedings of the Scotch-Irish Society document, even a notable number of successful politicans appeared in areas such as New England not usually associated with Scotch-Irish colonizing activity. The settlement of Londonderry, New Hampshire, in 1718 represents stereotypically the Ulster Scot segment of the Scotch-Irish world. The dozen or so communities in four states that sprung from it, with an estimated aggregate population of 100,000 by the 1850s, produced half of the governors of that New England state in the first fifty years of its existence. Matthew Thornton, the Irish-born signer of the Declaration of Independence, was associated with the original settlement while Horace Greeley, the newspaper editor who ran for the presidency in 1872, was from one of the daughter foundations. Organized, thrifty, and educated congregations of deeply religious people, as in Londonderry, produced political leaders. And the gradation of higher and lower religious courts as well as the lay administration of the Presbyterian parish (particularly as it evolved in a more democratic fashion in America) encouraged political leadership.

### THE SCOTCH-IRISH AND THE AMERICAN REVOLUTION

By the early 1760s, the Scotch-Irish suffered again from the same kind of oppression seen earlier in Ireland where Anglican religious authority had combined with political authoritarianism and class privilege. The Presbyterian communities in a notable collaboration began to counterattack. Most Presbyterian ministers in America had a common education, had shared an oppressive regime in Ireland, and had their synods in union exercise a centralized authority. When aroused by what they saw as the repetition of the experience in Scotland and Ireland, the ministers worked through an unofficial Presbyterian Committee of Correspondence and argued their case. A number of widespread Presbyterian communities sponsored the publication of texts proclaiming liberty. Mecklenburg, North Carolina, was an example. Finally, signers of the Declaration of Independence include the Scotch-Irish Matthew Thornton, James Smith, George Taylor, Thomas McKean, and George Read.

The Regulator Movements in the two Carolinas saw the first exercise of Scotch-Irish political muscle if not exactly power. Prudent patriarchal political control saved the Virginia Shenandoah Valley from this turmoil. Around the same time, and in union with German Calvinists, Pennsylvania Presbyterians moved to lead the often unruly frontier Scotch-Irish, and were supported by the more prosperous Scotch-Irish with connections in the Philadelphia area. This Presbyterian coalition swept the Quakers and their Pennsylvania allies out of political power. As David Noel Doyle has pointed out in his *Ireland, Irishmen and Revolutionary America,* Quakers and others in the Middle Colonies were lukewarm toward independence partially because they under-

stood what Massachusetts and some Virginia revolutionaries did not: An independent America would be a diverse multicultural society that would reflect neither the southeast Anglia culture of New England nor the southwest English culture embodied in the Virginia way of life.

The middle colonies' revolutionary movements were, however, disinctly Scotch-Irish only in the most inclusive usage of that protean label. For example, some Anglo-Irish such as Thomas Lynch, Pierce Butler, and the Rutledges ably championed American independence in the Carolinas. Anthony Wayne of Ulster descent not only served his country well in the military but as an Anglican he resisted Presbyterian political power in Pennsylvania. Although of Presbyterian and Scottish background, both Dr. Benjamin Rush and James Wilson also identified in Pennsylvania politics with Anglicans in their political struggles against the Presbyterian Irish. The Anglo-Irish New Yorker George Clinton personified the revolutionary movement as New Yorkers elected him both governor and lieutenant governor at the same time while simultaneously making him both a general in the Continental Army and the New York militia.

### SCOTCH-IRISH POLITICS IN THE NEW NATION

With the end of the revolutionary era, the Scotch-Irish label stood increasingly for little in the Early American political realm. It's true that the Virginian Ulster Scots universally supported Jefferson's disestablishment of the Anglican Church in Virginia, that large bodies of rural Scotch-Irish opposed or were apathetic towards the new 1787 constitutions, that the nonurban Pennsylvania Scotch-Irish opposed the Whiskey Tax, and that subsequently both rural and urban Scotch-Irish became followers of Thomas Jefferson and targets of the Alien and Sedition Acts of 1798; but more generally the Scotch-Irish had by the beginning of the nineteenth century simply become "American," as James Leyburn has emphasized in his *The Scotch Irish.*

While the contention of many authors that the Scotch-Irish were peculiarly adverse to changing opinions may be true for individuals, the Scotch-Irish areas regularly split politically on candidates and issues. At the turn of the century, William McKinley was a Republican while Grover Cleveland a Democrat. Closer to the historical dynamics of Ireland, Northern Ulster Scots generally opposed Polk's slavery agenda, and he won the White House on the strength of the rural Scotch-Irish in the north and the native Celtic Irish in the major cities. The Civil War issue, in particular, exemplifies widespread Scotch-Irish tenacity and division in a context of a fundamental split on a prickly issue that was economic, political, and ethical. As the stormy Civil War career of the Ohio Copperhead Clement L. Vallandigham shows, the Scotch-Irish split among themselves in those Northern states with significant numbers of "Butternuts" of Southern origin. While Vallandigham, the symbol of the Democratic opposition to the Civil War, found strong supporters among the native urban Irish, he ran very well in the rural areas of his constituency where the 1990 census showed more [Scotch-Irish] people claiming Irish descent than in Boston, Massachusetts. Besides this Scotch-Irish support in the North for a pro-union but anti-abolition position, the large number of Southern Upland whites (with Andrew Johnson their presidential spokesperson) who remained loyal to the Union also exemplified the original immigrant Scotch-Irish overwhelming commitment to the states united.

Many of those identified with the entrepreneurial and militant Protestant part of the Scotch-Irish tradition began deserting the rapidly changing Democratic Party in the 1830s and became Whigs, a move based on perceived economic interest and dislike for the Catholic Irish increasingly associated with the Democratic Party. By the Civil War, most self-conscious Protestant Irish registered as Republicans. In some of their areas they continued the tradition of the Orange parades on July 12 which, as in 1824 New York City, led to Catholic counterattacks and bloodshed. An increasingly smaller segment of this anti-Catholic Irish group (sometimes through the lodges of the Orange Order) helped fuel the nativistic Know-Nothing movement of the 1850s, and the American Protective Association of the 1890s.

The firmly Scotch-Irish, even often Presbyterian Ulster Scot, rural Ohio county of Harrison illustrates the importance of their contributions to America's political life. Its now defunct Franklin College (but then the fountainhead of the Eastern Ohio Abolition movement) gave three alumni to the U.S. Senate and three Ohio representatives to the U.S. House of Representatives—all Scotch-Irish in some way. Another example, John A. Bingham became the father of the Fourteenth Amendment, and presided over the trial of Lincoln's killers and the impeachment proceedings against President Johnson. Another Harrison county politician, Edward Stanton, performed brilliantly as Abraham Lincoln's Secretary of War. Even the relatively small number of alumni (but who were at least seventy-five percent Scotch-Irish) of Washington and Jefferson College in neighboring Pennsylvania included by 1921—according to an authoritative count—eleven senators, ten governors, ninety-one congressmen, and four cabinet members.

In short, Scotch-Irish politicians (particularly of the Ulster Scot variety) won many elective offices throughout American history because, while flexible and many-sided in nonessentials, they were generally firm when principles were concerned.

David Noel Doyle, *Ireland, Irishmen and Revolutionary America* (Dublin, 1980).

Charles A. Hanna, *The Scotch-Irish*, 2 vols. (New York, 1902).

Owen S. Ireland, *Religion, Ethnicity, and Politics* (University Park, Penn., 1995).

Carlton Jackson, *A Social History of the Scotch-Irish* (New York, 1993).

Maldwyn A. Jones, "Scotch-Irish," *Harvard Encyclopedia of American Ethnic Groups*, ed., Stephen Thernstrom (Cambridge, Mass., 1980): 895–908.

James G. Leyburn, *The Scotch-Irish: A Social History* (Chapel Hill, 1962).

Michael J. O'Brien, *Irish Settlers in America*, 2 vols. (Baltimore, 1979).

LEROY V. EID

# SCOTS IRISH or SCOTCH-IRISH

## PART I

From 1700 to 1820, between a quarter of a million and half a million immigrants came from Ireland to America. They accounted for 30 percent of all European immigrants in that period (and 50 percent between 1776–1820). They constituted the largest single nationality group from Europe, and the largest up to 1800 from any single political jurisdiction anywhere, the Kingdom of Ireland.

Irish immigrants were themselves ethnically and radically subdivided. The largest element between the mid-1740s and mid-1790s consisted of Protestants from the north of Ireland, or Ulster. These were themselves ethnically and religiously subdivided, with most of them being of Scottish origin and Presbyterian in

faith. This emigration was unrepresentative of the population of the region as a whole, which was only a third Presbyterian and roughly 45 percent native Irish and Catholic in 1715, with the balance (a fifth) being English and Anglican (Episcopalian) with some Baptists and Quakers. In the period 1720–1835, disproportionate Presbyterian migration altered that ratio to one-quarter Presbyterian and over one-half Catholic, with a larger change in west Ulster. Migration from Ulster to America always included Anglican, Catholic and Quaker elements. Perhaps from the mid-1790s, certainly after 1812, Presbyterians no longer were the majority, if a plurality, until the mid-1830s, and a very sizable element thereafter.

### TERMS AND USAGES

Thus in strict usage, Scots Irish or Scotch-Irish refers only to this Ulster Presbyterian *plurality* of the overall *Irish* migration, 1700–1820, and to the *majority* element within overall *Ulster* migration in the same years. Ulster today consists of Northern Ireland together with the surrounding counties of the Irish Republic: Cavan, Monaghan and Donegal; there was also some Presbyterian settlement (later depleted) in contiguous counties of Louth, Leitrim and Sligo. In educated American usage between 1870–1925, however, the term was also used to refer to any Protestants in or from this area (and their descendants), regardless of ethnic origin. Confusion resulted when many later were described as Scotch-Irish, even southern Irish Presbyterians (such as Dublin-born George Bryan, the anti-slavery governor of revolutionary Pennsylvania).

Although the term Scotch-Irish wasn't unknown, it was rarely used in the 18th century itself, either in Ireland or colonial America, but the reality of Ulster Presbyterians and their subculture was then well recognised in both countries. Indeed, the majority of the descendants of the migration, especially in the southern United States today, refer to themselves as of Irish descent for this reason. "Scotch-Irish" became a more common term from the 1850s as the Know-Nothing party and other prejudices caused Protestants of Irish origin to set themselves apart from an Irish-America redefined as Catholic. That was the consensus of most Americans according to the demographics and character of emigration from Ireland since the 1820s, and by the post-Famine remaking of Irish society in America's cities and mining and industrial areas. The old claim of Irish nationalists and others (such as Woodrow Wilson and Theodore Roosevelt, both historians) that the term refers to a "mixed race" has no meaning. Nor has the claim that the Scots Irish were basically part of one pan-Gaelic people any force, even if a quarter of first-wave settlement, those from west Galloway, Argyll and elsewhere, spoke Scots Gaelic and, in turn, recruited Irish speakers to their first congregations.

This was not an age of cultural nationalism. Evidence suggests that isolated groups of Irish were absorbed where early Scots settlement was dominant, as in north Down (as one might expect on a frontier). Intermarriage was not uncommon, following the earliest migration, which was largely male. And the reverse happened among isolated Scots settlers. Later there were some conversions, notably where a few Irish-speaking ministers were active. More usually as religious antagonism and land rivalry sharpened from the 1630s, and as further migration and population growth made it fully feasible, endogamy within the Scots community became the norm, except where there was marked overlap with English settlement. It was monitored in the oversight of relationships by kirk sessions and kinship group; and it expressed the solidity of subcultural preference, at least into the early 19th century.

In Europe today, these Irish Presbyterians of largely Scottish origin live almost wholly in Northern Ireland. This polity now allows all its citizens a dual identity, British and Irish. In the 18th century, the Scots Irish at home had in effect a triple identity: Scottish in religion, local dialect and specific culture; Irish by birth, polity and local associations; and British by ultimate political allegiance and aspects of their wider culture (educated speech, legal and commercial procedures, etc.). Their national and ethnic identities were scarcely fixed, and they themselves were divided about these, as was politically evident between 1775–83 in America, and between 1775 and 1815 in Ireland itself. Their sense of affinity with Scotland was as strong as their sense of descent from it was weak: in Ulster, genealogies in the mid-18th century were invariably traced since settlement in Ireland. This was an age of localities. Terms of wider identification are not common in the letters and papers of the time, and self-description as Scots Irish was very rare. Yet their collective behaviour requires some such term. Similar problems are well understood by scholars of most of Europe's national and subcultural populations before about 1850.

Noncontemporary literary and political overemphasis on the variable British dimension of this people came much later in the 1850s. It has had four consequences for scholarship. It displaced mixed Irish elements by combined British ones (English, Welsh, Scottish and Scots Irish) as the preponderant fact of all in-migration in the formative 18th century. (Irish and Scots Irish persons had been together only about 2.5 percent to less than 5 percent of all immigrants in the first formative century, 1609–1699). This reinforced now outmoded and restrictive characterizations of American nationality (as preferentially white, Protestant and of pre-Revolutionary and British origins). Second, it was used to differentiate later immigrants from Ireland, about 1825–1932, on a similar basis, to give advantage to those of presumed greater affinity with such a national norm. As a stereotype, it thus screened out the modernizing aspect of most Irish immigrants (literacy, small commercial skills, market experience, English language, social discipline) by downplaying these in all but northern Protestant newcomers. Third, and ironically, the Scots Irish tradition became part of the sustaining ideology of Northern Ireland within the United Kingdom between 1922 and 1985, as a polity preferentially British, Protestant and of colonial origin. The irony stems from the complex nature of past Scots Irish culture, its long erosion and its homogenization toward an Ulster standard between 1780 and 1900, and its always being a minority strain even within Ulster. (Ulster's leading Unionist historian, J. C. Beckett, always opposed use of the term and tradition as inaccurate and noninclusive.)

Further, Irish nationalists, largely Catholic, in effect denied *any* Scots Irish identity, as a fourth result of exclusive Scots Irish/ British linkages. Seeking recognition and advancement in America, they reacted against the restrictive implication of the term, as a buttress to white Protestant definitions of the society, and they perhaps resented the supposed ease with which new Irish Protestant immigrants (as well as older stock) could rank within it. (The actual and comparative performance of Presbyterian and Catholic immigrants in industrial America from the 1830s remains unstudied.) Predictably enough, nationalists in Ireland, seeking national autonomy or independence, feared any recognition of Irish Protestant subcultures as an obstacle to their goals.

Very few of them in Ireland, outside Ulster and Dublin, had any direct knowledge of Ulster Presbyterians. In the diaspora, experience in cities like Philadelphia, Toronto and even New York did not always redress this ignorance, but sometimes added a prejudicial edge to it. The result was a general failure to grasp the real character of Ulster Presbyterian society, and of its own Scots Irish diaspora. The simple view that these were ordinary Irish led to false claims about the Ulster Presbyterians' patriotic traditions, both American (1775–83) and Irish (1798). This led to exaggerations of the Irish nationalism of Ulster Scots and its force within Ulster itself.

Simple identification also led to false expectations of familiarity with a largely evangelical America in the years about 1820–1880s, as T. C. Grattan recognised in the 1840s. Since the Scots Irish were apparently accepted, the mass of the Irish claimed the same on arrival. The failure to grant the distinctiveness of the Scots Irish thus helped lead many Irish to a false understanding of the otherness of America in those years. This complicated problems of assimilation, even though it sharpened eventual realism about their self-dependence. (This was by contrast with Canada, where a gingerly Irish Catholic respect for the dominant position of Anglicans and Presbyterians in their own nationality group had different results.)

With the acceptance from 1985 of the complex and mutual character of Northern Ireland, agreed by its peoples in 1998, these prejudices should give way to a wider appreciation of the distinctive Scots Irish past, just as the fuller democratization of American culture in our century (anticipated between 1795 and 1835) has long led the United States Irish of different traditions to cooperate politically and socially.

## BACKGROUND: SETTLEMENT, RELIGION AND ECONOMY, 1605–1715

The Scots Irish originated in a sequence of colonization projects from Britain to Ireland, designed to ensure the island's political dependence on England. In southern Ireland (Munster and Leinster) these built on a medieval pattern of English immigration, descendants of which, the Old English, were distanced from the Tudor and Stuart monarchies by their retention of Catholicism. Hence, new projects were begun to create a Protestant and politically reliable colonization. The last major barrier to English authority, the Gaelic lordships of Ulster, were overthrown between 1595 and 1603. Within a month of the submission of Hugh O'Neill, Earl of Tyrone, and his allies, Elizabeth I died and was succeeded by her Stuart cousin, James VI of Scotland, who also became James I of England.

Long at odds, different in culture and languages, and differentially developed, England and Scotland now had a single monarch, whilst retaining distinct laws, parliaments, politics, administrations, church life and schools. The Reformation was dominant and Calvinist in both countries by 1603, but in Scotland, the reform had tended to Presbyterianism and the denial of bishoprics. The Stuarts sought to retain bishops there, and were successful even before 1637, and sought much less successfully to modify Calvinist theology. (Most Protestants in Ireland upheld this theology, as in 1615, creating common ground between Scots and English settlers. Isolated groups of Scots, as in Fermanagh, were well integrated into the Church of Ireland before Presbyterian structures spread from the 1640s.)

James I at first accepted the conditions of the native Ulster surrender. Yet he was obliged to foster the interests of English and

Scottish factions and administrators, and to help the Crown's many officers and veterans ("servitors") in Ireland. There was also the legal problem of how to transform loose native lordships into English-style landownership without increasing the real power of the defeated. Pressures on the Ulster nobility and their lands mounted. Their leaders fled to the continent in 1607 and their lands were declared forfeit. The future of most of Ulster lay now in the hands of a Scottish king with English power, in a sense, the first British king. The result was a state blueprint for the "plantation" of six of Ulster's nine counties. (Antrim and Down were already partly planted with Lowland Scots, at the edge since the 1570s, more fully since 1605; Monaghan was omitted.) Scotland is visible from the east Ulster coast only several hours away by sea.

Thus, the settlement of Scots Lowlanders in Ireland was subordinate to renewed English colonization. A Scots king in England favoured such joint colonization, which would give flesh to the juncture of his two kingships. He realized that the "ruder" Scots might prove better intermediaries with Irish culture. There was a problem: the Lowlanders were strongly Protestant but estranged from non-Calvinist culture and post-Calvinist change in England. Implanted in a newly conquered region without major "Old English" tradition, they were less inclined to temporize politically with Irish-born Catholics (notably the English-speaking ones of eastern Irish towns and manors, whom London found often useful to conciliate). These Scots came chiefly from the modern Strathclyde and Galloway, directly opposite east Ulster, then from Ayrshire, Renfrew, Wigtonshire, Bute and parts of Agyll. Economically this was a rural and partly commercial society, less developed than that of England. They came to a land not radically dissimilar to their own, so that practically the Scots settlers had greater affinities with the lifestyles of the Ulster Irish than did many English there or elsewhere. This made them suitable colonists in the area, and they gradually displaced their English fellow settlers in areas such as rural Londonderry and towns like Coleraine. There was even a precedent, in the Gaelic-speaking older Highland Scots settlements of north Antrim, which had merged with the Lordship of the Isles (the Scottish Hebrides) by Randall MacDonnell. Symptomatically, these Catholic Scots were called Irish after the plantation began, and later joined forces militarily with the Stuart cause in Scotland (led by Montrose) to oppose their Presbyterian rivals there in 1645 as they did in Ulster itself.

Under the plantation schemes, six counties were divided into tracts and estates called precincts, usually of 1,000 acres. These were granted to Scots and English "undertakers" to settle with at least ten British families as key tenants, and to do so around a central settlement (with church and fortified dwelling). Much of Colerain County (renamed Londonderry) was given to London companies on similar terms. In turn, the undertakers' or companies' chief tenants would settle further British families of small holders and craftsmen. Limited Irish settlement was later accepted from 1628.

Church lands, up to one-sixth of all Ulster, some skeletally settled from the 1570s by ex-soldiers, were given to the Episcopalian bishops (or purchased from them) for less restrictive settlement, as were tracts granted to "servitors" (equivalent to the veterans' land grants of 18th-century America). Native Irish remained on both of these with (or in place of) newcomers, under newly domiciled gentry (not always the owner). Between 1609–1641, some estates were regranted to select native gentry, most of whom were later dispossessed. On much of all these lands, Scots were settled in varied numbers. The post-1605 settlement of south Antrim and north Down also filled out rapidly (notably into the "route" of northwest Antrim). Further colonization spread with formal plantation.

The core Scots area took shape by 1630, more clearly by 1659: a coastal and riverbank crescent from 15 to 30 miles deep, stretching from northeast Donegal through County Londonderry to the first settlements in southeast Antrim and northeast Down [Robinson, maps 7 and 8, pp. 94, 98]. This zone remained accessible to Scottish ports. It was the most viable *en bloc* colonization in modern Ireland. After the initial waves of plantation, 1605–1620, further less formal immigration and internal migration (from Antrim and Down) strengthened it, notably between 1630–41 and again in the 1680s and the 1690s–c. 1710. There were also inland enclaves, in mid-Cavan, mid-Armagh, and south Tyrone, more subject to native Irish and to English acculturation and erosion over time.

By contrast, the second-wave English settlement came between 1654 and the 1670s, and was thereafter minimal. Even from the 1620s, the English settlers remigrated and concentrated where fellow settlers, market access, good land, security, more wooded landscapes, and favourable leases encouraged them: within the inland mid-Ulster belt, from the Lagan valley across the rich soils south and west of Lough Neagh, thence to the Lough Erne area. Thus, a broad regional segregation set Scots and English apart, despite heavy initial overlap. Landlords excepted, surprisingly little is known about this English zone, which has led American historians in the past to take its emigrants as Scots Irish, but this was not so. Even the two dialects did not begin to influence one another much until the 19th century.

Despite its repute as the most stringent of the many varieties of 17th-century Calvinist puritanism in the British empire, Scots Presbyterianism took shape slowly and with mixed characteristics. The rigors of clergy and elders did not always affect folkways in either the Lowlands or in Ulster. Unlike in England, there was no real persecution of Catholics as such in Scotland before the crisis of the 1640s, although in Ireland the Scots were on the defensive, and attitudes were sharper from the start. Stuart pressures for adoption of the (Episcopalian) Book of Common Prayer resulted in the National Covenant in Scotland in reaction (1637), and two short "bishops' wars" against the Crown. Ulster Scots were divided between those who would also adopt this covenant and those who would let things be.

Two events dramatically changed these positions. The Dublin administration attempted to force compliance with the King's religious control by enforcing oaths of acceptance. Then the native Irish rose in revolt in October 1641, and the Ulster Scots now believed the security of their religious culture and of their new farms and towns were inextricably linked, a view strengthened by the arrival of a Scottish Army in 1642, many of its soldiers veterans of the wars for the covenant. With encouragement from the Ulster Scots, presbyteries were first formally organised, although long hampered by insufficient ministers and few churches (kirks). The role of lay conveners and elders was thus often stronger than in Scotland, and worship more communal and informal. Fragmentation of authority in Ireland ensued as England's Civil Wars followed and deepened this Irish revolt. Royalist, Scots Presbyterian, pro-Parliamentary and Irish Confederate forces played their distinct Irish interests, but also acted as auxiliaries to the main parties in both England and Scotland.

That the Irish Confederation was explicitly Catholic, and that the revolt opened with some atrocities (although Scots settlers were less commonly the victims than English) gave a sharp edge to the convergence of Presbyterian recommitment and fear for homes, farms and estates. For another century or more, the Ulster Scots were torn between the demands of Presbyterian distinctiveness, in a state officially Episcopalian, and the need for security against Irish Catholics by reliance upon that same state. They could never unanimously support a single policy line, but they were now much more consciously an Irish Presbyterian people. Their initial harassment at the hands of victorious Parliamentarians, and even more by the restored Charles II, confirmed this identity. But the succession of the Catholic Stuart, James II, whose Irish forces briefly controlled the island, before his defeat at Londonderry and the Boyne (1689–90), likewise confirmed their dependence on a British-run Irish polity.

On the other side, despite contemporary allegations, administrators in Dublin could never systematically persecute, much less dispossess, this bulwark people of the state's Protestant establishment, rooted as they were in the province of strongest native resentments. But the state did discourage attempted Ulster Scots settlement beyond their traditional zones (e.g., southward to Drogheda, Belturbet and Longford), and disliked attempts by the Synod of Ulster to provide ministers to southern towns. Times of real state pressure were rare: in 1637–41, 1648–53, 1661–63, 1704–14, and usually during wartime insecurity. By contrast, Charles II inaugurated a grant to Presbyterian ministers in 1672, sustained even when his forces were harrying their more radical co-religionists in Scotland.

Full toleration was effectively accorded mainline Presbyterians by 1690, to match the recognition of the same faith as the official Church of Scotland in their fatherland. The church then established the Synod of Ulster, which presided over ten presbyteries, including Down, Antrim, Route (north Antrim), Belfast, Laggan (east Donegal) and Tyrone. The ten later accredited many ministers to America. The presbyteries also tried to exert ministerial guidance over early lay initiative, sent future ministers to Scotland for training, and attempted the fuller Christianization of their often uncatechised and undisciplined people. This history means that growth and distribution of mainline Presbyterian churches offers only a broad outline of the Scots Irish increase in Ulster to 1690, and is deceptive thereafter: from thirteen congregations between 1611 and 1640 to seventy by 1660, and to one hundred and four by 1690, with only forty-four additions thereafter to 1720 and only six more by 1740. Thus, too, "there is no absolute identification between settlement and culture" [Gailey].

Progress for Presbyterians was hampered by their exclusion from higher civic, state and military office after 1704. As with Catholics, virtual exclusion from the landowning class by the 1720s was perhaps more demeaning, and would of itself have ensured much of this civic incapacity in an age when most such offices went to the gentry and nobility. But as with Catholics also, an exaggerated account of such things became itself part of the survival, cohesion and group memory of the Scots Irish. Protestants pledged to native Catholic exclusion, their relationship with the ruling Anglo-Irish was one of convenience and irritation, not one of affection *nor* of radical estrangement. All of this has much to due with the psychodynamics of Scots Irish migration to America, and the traditions brought over with it. Little is known of the actual relations of the Scots Irish and ordinary English settlers in Ulster. The full Union of Scotland and England in 1707 made a socially composite Presbyterianism part of the legal establishment across the Irish Sea. By contrast, socially, politically and legally, the Scots Irish now became the largest bloc of Protestant

dissent in the British Isles, a whole community (unlike the varied social fragments elsewhere). This explains the élan and ease with which they would later fit into the American drive for republican polities and religious disestablishment in a broadly Calvinist framework.

Contrary to later self-praise by Victorian businessmen in Belfast or Pittsburgh, the original Scots Irish were initially no models of the Weber thesis as to the mutual support of Calvinism and industrious innovation. Contrary to their critics, neither were they, as such, progenitors of the indolent backwoods subsistence of the Ozarks and remoter Appalachian valleys of the years before the automobile. Contrary also to quasiofficial ideology in Northern Ireland from the 1870s–1950s, they had not been the sudden source of modernization in Ulster after 1610, or its sole stem after 1720. Nor had they represented a sharp break with supposedly rudimentary native Irish lifestyles. They themselves changed markedly over time. Their development in Ulster, was shaped by varied Scots backgrounds (regional and social), by the patterns, locations and density of their settlement, and by preexistent Gaelic Irish economic activity. Local Irish and British market and communications networks, technical innovations and their diffusion, immigrant English example, commercial legislation in London and Dublin, and, perhaps above all, the local structure of landownership all prompted Scots changes within Ulster. Adaptability and borrowing capacity went together.

Ulster was markedly underpopulated in 1605. Immigration itself was a key to growth. This was well understood at the time. Early population figures are incomplete (indeed this remains true of Irish surveys as late as 1821). That so many counts were made, if often only of heads of households, showed that officials were zealous not merely for plantation and taxes but also for development. The slow, phased subordination and concentration of the native Irish within Ulster's tenancies owed as much to economic situations as to political calculation. Productivity required population, and settlers themselves came slowly and preferred to come to fruitful fields and pastures. The myth that the Scots Irish were thus natural frontiersmen, used to pioneering wilderness from scratch, is nonsense. Migrants returning to America, and even their adult offspring, expressed shock at what total wilderness entailed. It is not known how many persons of Irish, Scotch, and English stock there were at any time, since English and Scots were usually aggregated. Religious statistics (as in 1732 or 1766) offer only a rough retrospect and guide, and the poor generally, and native Irish particularly, were undercounted. By the 1630s, there were over 14,000 British adult males in Ulster, perhaps two-thirds Scottish, and 20,000 by 1659. Native Irish were probably twice those figures. A total Ulster population of less than 250,000 in 1659 was 15 percent of Ireland's apparent total. By 1706, Ulster population had doubled, and was then 25 percent of Ireland's. Thereafter it stagnated at around 600,000 for the next forty years. The years to about 1706 were also years of net in-migration; those from the later 1720s of probably net out-migration. Later again, after 1753, Ulster would enter a period of sustained economic and population growth. Before that, however, there was no neat relationship between the two, yet apart from war years (1641–53 and 1689–91) the rise in Ulster's population did indicate real growth to about 1705.

Most Scots came from a countryside undergoing improvement, at least from the 1630s. Famines and even dearths, common before, were almost unknown after the 1650s, although a major one between 1695–1699 prompted further flight to Ireland. In the better Lowlands, tenants (even lesser ones) were borrowing against rising assets of stock and better housing. Gentry were often indebted to them. Larger landowners encouraged the efficient, fostered farm consolidation, and patronised the rise of crafts and skills both among those displaced to villages, towns and estates, and among those settled as cottars in the vicinity of farms, and unlike Irish cottiers, these supplied service skills and functions to tenant farmers. As in Ireland, if less markedly so, this pattern was modified by considerations of wider family. Tenants with favourable long leases and larger holdings, tacksmen, were often kin of the granting gentry (lairds), if not of the lord and landowner. On the other hand, labourers had lower wages and higher food costs than counterparts in Ireland. But such changes were far from universal, and less marked in the secondary areas of settler recruitment to Ulster (the borders and uplands above England) than in the sea-fronting counties which were its primary origin. Indeed, some less innovative tenants, labourers and smallholders may have fled to Ulster (as later their grandsons fled to the American backcountry) to escape commercial pressures rather than to exploit them. Others indeed would have come with working knowledge of such changes. Native Ulster, by contrast, had affinities with the more traditional, but not noncommercial, parts of Scotland. Kin-rights were much stronger to favourable lands. Ulster, too, had a partially monetary economy, based largely upon cattle raising, and on cultivation of oats, rye and barley, pursuits common in Scotland. There was also native, if small-scale, linen and woolen output, first imitated and then improved by newcomers. The old, open fields system of tillage in the Lowlands, jointly ploughed and periodically redistributed, paralleled that of native Ulster. It was called "run-rig" in Scotland and "rundale" in Ireland. The attested readiness of native Ulstermen to pay double rents and to add additional dues of produce "in kind," in order to stay on farmlands newly owned by British undertakers and servitors, shows the resilience of native economy. By contrast, a similar poverty was endured by lesser ranks in both societies, including one-room thatched cabins, without chimneys, shared with calves (and a cow or two during storms or frosts).

Scots and English in the six forfeited counties settled according to the existent patterns of the old society. Estates were divided or sectioned into *ballyboes* or townlands. These were various-sized units of productivity geared to the cattle-grazing capacity required by two or more families of some status, i.e., acreage for twenty cows or more, with some tillage land for oats. As the Scots increased, they tenanted the better land within the ballyboes, adding to the overall numbers of tenants (for the Irish often remained). They then slowly squeezed the Irish onto marginal lands. Both used the same markets, mills and towns; the plantation towns all developed both Scotch and Irish streets and quarters. Thus, a pattern of ethnic mini-segregation accompanied by the 1660s the wider map of regional segregation. Despite politicoreligious rivalry, this pattern actually testified to the wealth of the province, rising at a pace probably stimulated by mutual competition. Yet this was a stumbling growth. Hundreds of markets and villages established in the first years of plantation (1610–30), failed to flourish (a sequence later common to new settlements in America). This was especially true of inland centres. As the Scots became dominant in the English ports of Londonderry, Coleraine and Carrickfergus and partly turned their trade toward Scotland, and as the port of Belfast emerged to connect largely English mid-Ulster with Liverpool, Chester and London, the economy of the entire province quickened. The restrictive English Navigation and Cattle Acts reshaped Irish commerce as a whole from the 1660s. The former before 1707 did not include trade with Scotland, but rather gave a new impetus to it, although the Scots did bar Irish live cattle from 1672. How far the more varied and finished businesses, skills and farm techniques of the English settlers transformed those of the Scots (as was the hope of the Crown) awaits proper study of these English.

The landlord structure was a key element in first encouraging Scottish emigration, and then (in quick succession) shutting it off and directing discontented Scots Irish to America beginning about 1717. For a century before that Scots lords normally imposed short leases to tie their tenants to prompt efficient production, while the less able were forced off, and subdivision of land, especially subletting, was strongly discouraged. In contrast, Ulster tenures were designed to attract and retain rural population, not discriminate between types of producers. Scots landlordism was "hands-on" and closely involved with discipline, innovation and output. Until after 1700 in Ulster, the undertakers and servitors owed a basic Crown rent and were usually of a different faith and ethnicity (English or at least Scots Episcopalian), and usually lived away from their estates. To pay their own dues, and earn the costs of their status, they used tenants and nonfarming stewards and bailiffs to get it from them. These found that only life tenures, or even three lives, could entice Scots to come, farm and stay. Even native Irish were granted similar tenures although at higher rents. Only with political security after 1690, and a base settler population achieved, could Ulster landlords begin to move, albeit slowly, toward a Scottish or mainline English pattern of landlordism. By then, however, tenant customs were very strongly entrenched, including patterns of subletting that brought profits to intermediate farmers and others. Subletting also underpinned ethnic mini-segregation (even between Scots and English, as on the Rawdon estates in Down). It also facilitated social bonding amongst layers of the Scots Irish. This bonding grew with the rising stress on customary and kin duties amongst them, and with their efforts to avoid, negotiate and curb the costs of the interplay of Irish boundary systems and customs. It was also aided by remembered Scots rights and laws and by English efforts to recast landholding and obligation through their own law systems (directly or as modified in Dublin). Because the top layers of tenants in Ulster were in effect "tacksmen," they could sublet safely. Because the economy was less developed, the cottier subtenants needed parcels of farmland; they could not rely on sale of their skills, unlike cottars in Scotland. Futile top-down attempts to change all this with the threat or possibility of hard times prompted the first real emigration to America, not of the capable and innovative, but rather of tenants used to perhaps the most relaxed landlord regimen in the British Isles, and fearing its loss. Indeed, Scots Irish tenants threatened emigration as a lever against "modernising" owners through the 18th century. (See special bibliography for Part I.)

## PART II

### 18TH-CENTURY ULSTER AND ITS EMIGRATION

Economy and culture quickened from about 1695, and "took off" from the 1740s, if unevenly, and variously, by district. Where an emigrant came from, and at what date, tells most about the outlook and skills he brought, not the mere fact of his being Scots Irish. Francis Makemie's early injunction to the first settlers in America to promote towns and trade was understood by contemporaries. Thus while inheriting the formative experiences and folk memories of the years 1610–1700, most Scots Irish emigrants came from a changing Ireland, that of the 18th century. Even their religious culture reflected this as many congregations recruited "New Light" ministers, influenced by the "Common Sense" fusion of theology and rationality taught in Glasgow; these did not subscribe to the benchmark of their ancestors, the Westminster Confession. This was a century of social and economic acceleration, most marked after 1745. From 1700–1775, Irish exports increased in value almost five times, with cattle and their products among these tripling in worth. Hemp, flax and linen multiplied almost thirty times in value, until they accounted for 52 percent of the earnings of all Irish exports. Most of the production of linen was now north of a line from Drogheda to Sligo, and largely in east and mid-Ulster.

Since Ulster's population roughly doubled in these years, on paper it enjoyed an impressive rise in per capita income. It was protected from the worst ravages of the famine of 1740–41, which elsewhere caused proportionately more deaths than did the great 19th-century Famine of 1845–51. There were marked gains in living standards, and dwellings and holdings were improved. Numbers of taxable homes increased faster than population, suggesting a shift from untaxed impoverished cabins by some. Business in Ulster's ports expanded, and Londonderry, Belfast, Coleraine and Newry traded regularly with Philadelphia and other North American towns, which offered markets for finished linens, while sending back the flax seed most preferable to Ulster's smallholders. These links offered the base for an organized emigrant trade. Ironically, because ships' captains could make enough from the flax and linen trade, they were not pressured (as were captains sailing from Dublin, Cork or Rotterdam) to fill up outgoing vessels with indentured servants. Instead, independent passengers, often families realizing the market value of their "interest" in their farms (the land of which was owned by landlords), went out as free, paying passengers. These were recruited both in the ports and in the inland market towns of the linen districts. Yet the main migration from Ireland from the 1680s to 1717 was from southern ports. Only after 1717 did Ulster surpass an established Leinster/Munster outflow, which it never fully displaced. The main movement of Irish emigrants to America apparently came in waves: in 1717/18–1720, 1725–29, 1740–41, 1754–55, 1766–67 and 1770–75. These movements were related to crises of living costs. Probably (as later with 19th-century Irish patterns generally) contemporaries noticed only such periodic bulges, exaggerated these, and missed a continuous low-level flow. The flow was also mixed. Half of the servants from west Ulster indentured in Philadelphia in 1745–46 were neither of Scottish nor English stock. Among free migrants, Scots Irish predominated.

Numbers are irrecoverable, despite heroic efforts by scholars such as R. J. Dickson, M. Wokeck, and G. Kirkham. Even for later emigrations, Robert Swierenga, Cormac O Gráda and others have shown the unreliability of most figures (by nationality and volume) for emigrants to the United States as late as the 1860s, forty years after mandatory reportage of arrivals there. By contrast, very few 18th-century port records survive listing arrivals. The method of multiplying the tonnage of incoming vessels by a passenger-per-ton vessels multiplier (usually 1 or 1.5 per ton) begs many questions, not least of which is the great difference between pack-them-in ships with indentured servants and cargo vessels with a few cabin and deck passengers. Ship tonnages were routinely exaggerated in Ireland to attract business. Moreover, wherever scholars drill new holes into uncharted areas of surviving 18th-century documentation (customs records, advertisements for sailings, lists of incoming arrivals) new patterns emerge (as for 1700–1725 and 1783–1800). Arrivals to minor ports such as Kittery (now in Maine), Savannah or Annapolis, even early New York, often, if not usually, went unrecorded, as did sailings from lesser Ulster ports, such as Ramelton, Portrush, Kilkeel and even Newry. Remigration from Portpatrick, Glasgow, Dublin and elsewhere is unstudied. Unlike Belfast, Londonderry, the main port sending out emigrants, lacked a newspaper advertising sailings for much of the 18th century. Indeed, the hunt for specificity in these matters may still have something of the ring of the ethnic point scoring of the decades 1905–1930, when a quasi-racist ranking of population groups in 1790 was used as a basis for entitlements to 20th-century immigration quotas. In short, quasiracism fueled the search for quasinumbers.

As to proportional rankings between the ethnic groups leaving Ulster in those years, uncertain evidence provides almost little guide. Literary evidence, Irish reports indicating areas of recruitment, return letters, American genealogical and church records from colonial times, and (more reliably, though still contestable) census tract nomenclature studies, all point to the Scots Irish and Presbyterian character of the emigrant majority from the province. But actual numbers remain elusive. One can only report that this knowledge is not broadly inconsistent with traditional and recent estimates. These range from a careful estimate of 108,600 Irish immigrants altogether (1700–1775) [Fogelman], of whom probably two-thirds sailed from northern ports, if the pattern of the Delaware ports holds generally true [Wokeck]. They rise to "probably 200,000" [Leyburn] or "at least 250,000" (1680s–1775) Ulster Scots alone [Doyle]. These are now discounted. From 1776–1809, a further 149,500 Irish immigrants are estimated [Fogelman]. Claims that "perhaps 100,000" of these were from Ulster [M. A. Jones] do not match other evidence that an increasing portion were from southern Ireland, or from among the non-Scottish, Catholic and Anglican populations of Ulster [Bric].

Overall, then, a reliable minimum of 150,000 Scots Irish came to America between the 1680s and 1810, possibly more, arguably many more. The Scots Irish were from 6 percent to 15 percent of the white heads of household in 1790, with 10.5 percent the best estimate [Purvis]. They provided most of the [only] 15,000 full membership of the main Presbyterian church in 1800. These indications suggest that the lower emigration figures are more likely. But much depends on how many with Scottish surnames in 1790 are assessed as properly Scots Irish. This may not be relevant if (as in east Ulster the previous century) there was a trend for the Scots Irish to absorb other Scottish, north of England, and Irish elements. Demographic reconstitution from parish and kirk records in Ulster may eventually give more certainty in all this.

As Ulster was improving, why did they go? Land values and hence rents rose even more dramatically than overall output. Thus, both rising and thwarted, expectations played joint parts. Tithes, county and parish taxes, market charges and a host of legal and professional dues, even semifeudal payments in kind, depreciated the gains of effort and belittled civic pride. Unstable linen prices cheated the calculations of honest debtors. Although religiously and ethnically fragmented in the later 17th century, Ulster had then offered Presbyterians security in their "column" of society. In the 18th century, they were subject to the rigours of market pressures as to the interplay of earnings, rents and other costs. Catholics and plebeian Anglicans bid higher rents as leases fell due. While outlets in trade and artisanship in the rising towns existed, the upper ranks of rural society were largely closed to non-Anglicans, as were those of government by the Test Act of 1704, left unchanged by the Toleration Act of 1719. Even fairly prosperous farmers faced the problem of providing for their numerous offspring. They encouraged the migration of all but two or three family members, or sometimes anticipated this loss by choosing to migrate themselves when with young families. The alternative was to see the probable downward mobility of at least some of one's offspring.

Reports from relatives and neighbours who had gone to America were almost wholly laudatory about land quality and availability, livelihood, living costs, status, and general contentment. Only the familiarity, kin and sociability of a more crowded Ulster were missed. Men harassed by debt and worry were less inclined to cherish such things than those looking back to them. If modern economic historians celebrate Ulster's textile-driven prosperity, social and cultural historians are less sure. The new changes were labour intensive. Women worked in the fields, kitchen gardens and hen-runs and over the spinning wheel, as well as doing the household tasks of cottage and family. Therefore, women were often keen to go. Men of an older rural culture given to easier rhythms (the transition was regional not chronological in Ulster), and used to much visiting, drinking, hunting, and "cayleying" [in evening gatherings], found attractive the backcountry style in the colonies. Later 18th-century emigrants were often more commercially minded, sometimes even avoiding their kin in the Appalachian valleys and Carolinas' piedmont district who embodied an earlier 18th-century outlook, now marginalised in Ulster. In short, some went to avoid the burdens of change; others to apply the lessons of change to broader opportunities; still others because they simply wished wider fields. Almost all, however, went to reestablish the Ulster priorities of family, kin and community in more secure circumstance, not to cut loose as frontier individualists. Some even took servants with them, or later purchased the time of imported indentured ones, whether Scots Irish or native Ulster Catholics. Perhaps they believed that the Ulster way of life was more fully portable than later proved the case.

## Toward an Ulster America, 1720–1790

Late colonial America was proportionately more Irish than the United States in 1850 or 1900, if the Irish-born and their American offspring are any measure. Because these people were usually rural and often aggregated, they inclined to that partial retention of culture over generations that is usually associated with Pennsylvania's colonial Germans. Yet from the start, what they had was a mutating lifestyle, mediated through inherited patterns of kin, kirk, spoken language and song, as well as some farm practices, that had not been fixed in Ulster either. Thus, the new way of life in America accentuated a preexistent adaptability. Partial isolation had the same effect that only strong concentrations could attain in the late 19th century, that of a viable collective inheritance. It also meant that such transmission was quite compatible with wide-ranging practical alterations in semi-frontier and post-frontier conditions. While some aspects of material culture were imported, others were adopted from colonial neighbours, and others newly prompted by fresh exigencies. Borrowings included the V-notched log cabin of the Swedes and Finns of the Delaware valley, and winter foddering techniques and wagon styles from the Germans of Pennsylvania. Such acculturation varied by region. Valid re-creations of the experience exist at Staunton, Virginia, and in the Ulster American Folk Park at Omagh in Northern Ireland.

The newcomers to America did *not* choose the wilderness as such. The Scots Irish reputation as frontiersmen came with the behaviour of their post-Revolutionary descendants. The immigrants largely sought and settled available lands proximate to inhabited and developed areas. This is evident in their first settlements in Delaware and eastern Maryland (from 1683), northern New England (from 1718), in the Jerseys (from the 1690s), and the lower Hudson valley. More numerous were those going to southeastern Pennsylvania (from 1717/18), which then enjoyed a century-long inflow. The counties along the lower Delaware became the hub of a diffusion northward in its valley (1728–30) and that of the lower Susquehanna (1710–1731), and thence north and west to the Cumberland valley (1725–55). Another flow turned south between the Blue Ridge/Catoctin and Appalachian mountains into western Maryland (1727) and the Shenandoah valley (1730–41). The preemption of coastal and tidewater lands in the South, and the direction of this intermountain valley system southwestward directed the flow into western Virginia, then beyond it southward into the rolling piedmont country of the inland Carolinas (1740/45), where it met a direct colonization from Ulster coming in from the coast (since 1736).

By the 1750s the eddies of the migration reached a similar direct inflow into backcountry Georgia via Savannah. Entrepreneurial encouragement and official sponsorship was active in many of these movements (e.g., James Logan, William Gooch, William Beverley, Benjamin Borden, James Patton, Arthur Dobbs and Matthew Rea). The now 700-mile crescent was linked back to Philadelphia by the Great Wagon road, which had spread with the colonists. If some backcountry settlers regressed socially and culturally, those in the main, road-served, valleys were market-dependent, varying from multiple-market initiatives (Pennsylvania) to mixing farm production for home use with commodity-led enterprise (Virginia Valley). In North Carolina, butter casks were produced, as flax and potatoes were in Pennsylvania, to lend Ulster notes to the output of livestock and grain. A partly commercialised farming/trade nexus thus promoted reconstruction of familial and kin networks, and prompted the rise of families of the "better sort." These often remained Presbyterian, and were the backbone of that faith's spread in the South; whereas, less prosperous and the simply more isolated groupings later became Baptist or Methodist. Probably the reunificatioon of Presbyterianism in 1758 had left many desirous of a simpler, more accessible and enthusiastic Calvinism for which the New Side already had set a precedent. The hostile evidence of Charles Woodmason, prejudiced by his Anglo-Irish and pro-episcopal outlook, is debatable (and belied by his own work on behalf of the Regulators in 1767–71), if accounts of later Ulster newcomers to the backcountry confirm some of his strictures.

A trading class, with associated teachers and lawyers, serviced this population from York and Lancaster in Pennsylvania down through Staunton and Rockbridge in Virginia and on to towns like Camden in the Carolinas. Its members often came from families similarly engaged in Ulster, where crafts, merchandising and the professions ran in families, and among the sons of farmers apprenticed to them. Ulster Quakers (if rarely of Scots backround) joined this flow. The so-called backcountry was thus developed by greater or lesser levels of activity, depending on the nearness of such a service grid, which was extended even by newcomers well beyond 1800 (as at Asheville, North Carolina). The entire region wanted sound, just, representative and orderly government, ethnically and socially (but not racially) inclusive, if stronger farmers and traders sought to be its preferred personnel. The distinct Regulator movements of North Carolina (1768–71) and South Carolina (1767–69), the Paxton uprising (1763) and even the later Whisky Insurrection (1794) have to be understood in that context, as does the drive for greater western representation in those colonies before the Revolution. The relative political peace in the Virginia valley confirms this, since government and administration there had such early characteristics. Far from seeking to escape from relations with the seaboard elites, the Scots Irish sought an interaction of mutual advantage. Likewise, their relations with German Protestant and Anglo-American stock seem to have been proper and friendly, if distant. With Indians, of course, it was a much more negative relation. Slavery characterised but few families, was often thought un-Christian, and spread widely in the upcountry only after 1815, although some prominent Shenandoah and Carolinas low-country Scots Irish were slaveholders even in the settler generation.

## PART III

### During and After the American Revolution

In this era, 1763–1800, the Scots Irish properly hold a place in "world history" as a key component in the first of the great modern revolutions. Whether one emphasizes the strictly Scots Irish inheritance prompting this role, or stresses that Amercan circumstances and ambitions fueled and defined it, their place in the Revolutionary era is secure. Filiopietistic celebration of their anti-imperial patriotism, and post-F. J. Turner beliefs that their frontier activism was formative of democratic habits have now passed. Modern studies of 18th-century political cultures and ideas have sustained a close and appropriate relation between these middle-brow, enterprising and rights-seeking localists of strong, if secularising, Calvinist bent, and the mind-sets and politics of the revolutionary mainstream everywhere (except in the seaboard plantation areas, with their distinctive cultures and motivations). In the middle colonies, especially in Pennsylvania, New Jersey and Delaware, they furnished committed blocs to pre-independence agitation, to the War of Independence, and to the radical and moderate politics of revolutionary change. In Maryland, Virginia and the Carolinas, most (not all) supported both the war and associated political change, if slower of original commitment. Only in New York was there less decision and more confusion (as also among that colony's Presbyterians generally). This was partly a response to long-term British occupation, to economic interests in empire and to the inchoate nature of politics in the Hudson valley, recently seigneurial, as also to Calvinist fragmentation.

Pennsylvania was central. The key link on the north-south axis of the colonies, it was at least one-fifth of Scots Irish derivation. Yet Philadelphia, home to the two Continental Congresses and first capital of the Confederacy, and then the United States, had only a smallish Scots Irish element before the Revolution (skeletal to judge by church mortality records but more from indications from among the town's "lower sort"). By the end of the century, it had become their major centre in America. This change epitomises the story. During the Revolutionary era, the Scots Irish came from the colony's political margins to the centre of state events. Before the 1760s, they were powerless, and their settlements (then largely mid-Pennsylvanian) were very underrepresented in government. Even liberal newcomers like Benjamin Franklin had felt more at home with the secular, Quaker and interdenominational cultures of the long-settled southeastern counties. Ulster's immigrants were also badly fractured by the split between New Side and Old Side Presbyterianism (1745–58). Although there were Ulster-born leaders on both sides, most incoming clergy from Ulster, whether New Light or Old Light, stuck with the Old Side in America (which emphasized an educated ministry and ordered worship) against the experiments, revivals and subjectivism of the New Side. Reunion in 1758 created the largest mid-colonial denomination, and a vital link to New England Congregationalism when London pressed for an Anglican episcopate for the colonies in 1763.

Meantime, plainer frontier farmers had become aware of Quaker disdain for their security: The Paxton boys murdered Christian Indians and marched on Philadelphia to make their point, just as the Quakers became aware of their own isolation from influence in London. Convergent attempts at imperial regulation as the Seven Years War ended, with new taxation, currency and settlement policies, enabled the Ulster Presbyterians to fuse frontier, religious and American interests together against both Quakers locally and the British imperially, buttressed by a strong connection to New England (1763–68). Thus, a nationalist "Presbyterian Party" emerged. Yet since most nonimportation and other agitations took place in port cities, not until the 1770s did the inland Scots Irish move to the forefront of events.

They did this by joining with radical seaport elements. Encouraged by the Continental Congress, they displaced the Quaker assembly, and through a network of committees, established first a constitutional convention and then a radical constitution with a unicameral assembly, general male suffrage, and a unique "council of censors" to guard the experiment. Wartime had brought a sense of crisis. A Calvinist coalition, including German, Dutch and other elements, as well as urban radicals of English descent, sought to impose tests of loyalty (to the new nation and the state's constitution) by oaths which thereby restricted the political community, and deprived Quakers and Anglicans of civic and political rights. When the British invaded and occupied Philadelphia and its environs (Sept. 1777–June 1778), the Scots Irish sought to defend the state militarily, both by local militias and through the Continental Army. George Washington himself seems to have avoided tilting to any one party among Irish Pennsylvanians, despite the preponderance of the Scots Irish, whose localism he probably mistrusted. Realism, ambition and the needs of the nation as a whole caused more conservatve and educated Scots Irish, such as Thomas McKean, George Read, Joseph Reed and Charles Thompson, to lead and moderate the state's revolutionary coalition. McKean, Read, John McKinly and William Paterson were also instrumental in securing the allegiance of both nearby Delaware and New Jersey to the American cause by adopting more cautious courses than were used in Pennsylvania. Despite massive documentation on specific services (by scholars from 1880–1940), the Scots Irish military contribution in the mid-colonial campaigns has not been proportionately quantified, nor properly assessed. If visibly greater in western campaigns (under John Armstrong, James Potter and others), probably the greater numbers fought at Brandywine, Germantown and their environs, mixed with all the then-ethnicities of a rising nationality. That one of them, James McHenry, later became Secretary of War under John Adams was a sign of the Scots Irish contemporary recognition, even though his political career was later made in Maryland. The Pennsylvania Line of the Continental Army, called by some "the Line of Ireland," was preponderantly Scots Irish, though not wholly so (nor indeed wholly Irish). The bugbear of American Tories and British officers, it was credited by members of the Continental Congress with saving it on occasion, and thus America's independence, as reported in the circle of the Marquis de Chastellux.

In Virginia, political enfranchisement and representation of the Scots Irish of the Shenandoah and its environs, and the acceptance of kirk sessions to fill the local functions of Anglican vestries elsewhere, inclined the Presbyterians to support the tidewater patriot planters wholeheartedly. They were also linked by remigration, trade and culture with their patriot kin in Pennsylvania. In the Carolinas, matters were more complex. The Scots Irish on the uplands were remote from the seaboard. Deprived of representation, governance and law adequate to their social order, yet periodically exploited by outsider circuit justices, they had fought "Regulations" (in South Carolina against their own frontier lawless men; in North Carolina against coastal injustices). Mostly second and third generation, they included some more recent immigrants from Ireland (via Charleston). Then largely without slaves (which changed in the 1820s), they had little in common with the propertied and patrician bias of seaboard patriot politics. While this meant a certain hesitancy as to wartime solidarity, any doubts disintegrated with the British invasion of the backcountry by Gen. Charles Cornwallis, who miscalculated their temper. If, as in Pennsylvania in 1777, some Scots Irish joined Loyalist militias, in the Carolinas, too, the active majority fought as American forces: notably in the battles of the Waxhaws, Camden, King's Mountain, Cowpens and Guildford Couthouse (May 1780–March 1781). They thus helped secure British exhaustion and withdrawal.

The Revolutionary War precipitated the Scots Irish to full civic participation and political action everywhere except New England. Residual prejudice against them disappeared. Their goal was to enter the American mainstream, and falling barriers now ensured this. Their experience that minority rights were jeopardised by ethnic majorities, power concentrations or religious establishments, whether based in London, Dublin, Philadelphia or Charleston, placed most of them on the radical-to-moderate side. Their special fear of any convergence of such forces biased them strongly in favour of states rights and even more of local administrations as the best bulwark of their freedom. Doctrines thus later linked to slaveholders were for them independently rooted. The foundations were there for their later association with the party of Jefferson, and later of Jackson. Their belief in minority rights and states rights found outlet in the planter champions of regional autonomy, slavery and the common man. Their stance on democracy itself was ambiguous before the 1800s. Their belief in open access to skills, property and hence to office holding had not yet eliminated the notion (taught by Francis Alison to a generation of their leaders) that there was a natural order in society and polity, duly weighted to men of probity and substance. This antiegalitarianism, when taken with their localism, helps account for the shifts and divisions of their positions between 1776–1790.

Thus, in the middle states, the strains between backcountrymen and those elevated by America's independence were considerable. Many of the latter were also absorbed into the Masonic networks that were then fashionable. Yet immigrant United Irishmen of the 1790s, committed to a doctrinal (though not practical) egalitarianism and to a centralist (not localist) idea of revolutionary authority, found the Americanised Scots Irish of every sort difficult to fathom: wedded to a practical, but not doctrinal, equality of opportunity and to an anticentralist view of power. Moreover, the Scots Irish majority remained broadly Christian (with their deist minority respecting this) unlike many newcomers who were often assertively secular. There was some political excitement in Philadelphia and New York among newcomers and poorer urban Scots Irish in the 1790s. The Federalists disliked all the Irish (and did not distinguish among them), and the nascent Jeffersonian opposition sought to harvest any Irish support. This story is much retold to create an early American pedigree for both Irish-American nationalism, and for later Irish participation in popular and reform politics within America. Most immigrants of the 1780s–90s, however, were apolitical, politics having failed them in Ireland. The Scots Irish, so recently established but out of power from 1790–1800, preferred this, so as not to disturb their own status gains. They were happy to see any malcontent Scots Irish (whether among newcomers, United Irishmen or once-Whiskey insurrectionists) made politically safe within the Jeffersonian coalition that triumphed in 1800. In the next year, the "Plan of Union" between Presbyterian and Congregational churches confirmed this advancing assimilation, while in Kentucky and Tennessee the revival meetings of James McGready and others confirmed the drift of second- and third-generation Ulster Americans in the South toward the revivalist churches.

The social rise in the middle and south Atlantic states was matched by another result of the postrevolutionary era. The Scots Irish, by *now* frontiersmen proper, flooded westward from the 1770s in three major movements. Streams of Scots Irish crossed the Alleghenies into western (and northern) Pennsylvania. From there groups entered the Ohio country (as the Indians were cleared), often initially as land grantees under bounty laws for military service. Others entered Kentucky and Tennessee via the Cumberland Gap, while yet others filled up the far western intermountain portions of North Carolina and western and southwestern Virginia. Movements into Alabama and Mississippi came after 1800, as did a full dispersal into the Great Lakes basin. If American-born Scots Irish were largely involved, all these movements drew settlers (often cousins) direct from Ulster. Otherwise, how *Scots Irish* a story it was will be long debated, probably at least as authentically as the main *Irish-American* story is Irish in the years 1880–1920. Acculturation in the older rural distribution or source areas had been limited by partial isolation and by much endogamy or intramarriage (often to cousins) within the older communties.

The study of the cultural continuity, fresh immigration, and, from the 1830s, final total assimilation of the Scots Irish (and hence of their differentiation from a newer Irish America) has not been subject to the same scrutiny as the story before 1800. Until it has, it would be foolhardy to attempt a synthesis in the absence of even a rudimentary literature. There are sufficient indications to suggest that it may finally prove as substantive a subject as that of the colonial era. Indeed, it raises key questions about the fate of ethnicity in American life. Between 1775 and 1820, the Scots Irish (with others) pioneered the parameters, rights, laws, politics and institutions of cultural diversity in the

United States, on which the incoming Irish would now rely. Simultaneously, these Ulster Americans were also pioneering the abandonment of such enclaves for a full assimilation and (except in unconscious retentions) a full acculturation. Both modes of being *e pluribus unum* became central to the history of the country thereafter.

*See* Emigration: 17th and 18th Centuries;
Irish in America; Scotch-Irish and American Politics

*Bibliography for Part I:* Jean Agnew, *Belfast Merchant Families in the Seventeenth Century* (Dublin, 1996); Roger Blaney, *Presbyterians and the Irish Language* (Belfast, 1996); T. M. Devine and David Dickson, eds., *Ireland and Scotland, 1600–1850* (Edinburgh, 1983); Brendan Fitzpatrick, *Seventeenth Century Ireland: The War of Religions* (Dublin 1988); R. L. Greaves, *God's Other Children: Protestant Nonconformists . . . 1660–1700* (Stanford, 1997); E. M. Johnston-Liik, "The Development of the Ulster-Scottish Connection," John Erskine and Gordon Lucy, eds., *Cultural Traditions in Northern Ireland: Varieties of Scottishness* (Belfast, 1997): 27–44; Rosalind Mitchison and Peter Roebuck, eds., *Economy and Society in Scotland and Ireland, 1500–1939* (Edinburgh, 1988); T. W. Moody, F. X. Martin, and F. J. Byrne, eds., *A New History of Ireland,* III, *Early Modern Ireland, 1534–1691* (Oxford, 1976); Philip Robinson, *The Plantation of Ulster,* 2nd ed. (Belfast, 1994); Peter Roebuck, ed., *Plantation to Partition* (Belfast 1981): 14–63; John Stevenson, *Two Centuries of Life in Down* (Belfast, 1920, 1990); Alvin Gailey, "The Scots Element in North Irish Popular Culture," *Ethnologia Europaea,* 8:1 (1975): 2–22; Raymond Gillespie, *Colonial Ulster: The Settlement of East Ulster, 1600–1641* (Cork, 1985); idem., "The Transformation of the Borderlands, 1600–1700," R. Gillespie and H. O' Sullivan, *The Borderlands* (Belfast, 1989): 75–92; R. Gillespie, ed., *Cavan: The History of an Irish County* (Dublin, 1995): 73–114; Linde Lunney, "Ulster Attitudes to Scottishness," Ian S. Wood, ed., *Scotland and Ulster* (Edinburgh, 1994): 56–70.

*Background:* W. H. Crawford and Brian Trainor, *Aspects of Irish Social History* (Belfast, 1969); David Dickson, *New Foundations: Ireland, 1660–1800* (Dublin, 1987): esp. 96–127; Martin Dowling, *Tenant Right and Agrarian Society in Ulster, 1600–1870* (Dublin, 1999); Kevin Herlihy, ed., *The Politics of Irish Dissent, 1650–1800* (Dublin, 1997); T. W. Moody and William Vaughan, eds., *A New Hisory of Ireland,* IV, *Eighteenth Century Ireland* (Oxford, 1986); A. T. Q. Stewart, *The Summer Soldiers: The 1798 Rebellion in Antrim and Down* (Belfast, 1995).

*Migration and Settlement:* H. Tyler Blethen and C. W. Wood, Jr., eds., *Ulster and North America: Transatlantic Perspectives on the Scotch-Irish* (Tuscaloosa and London, 1997); R. J. Dickson, *Ulster Emigration to Colonial America, 1718–1775* (London, 1966, 2nd ed., Belfast, 1988); David N. Doyle, *Ireland, Irishmen and Revolutionary America, 1760–1820* (Cork and Dublin, 1981); David H. Fischer, *Albion's Seed: Four British Folkways in America* (New York, 1989); Maldwyn A. Jones, "The Scotch-Irish in British America," B. Bailyn and P. D. Morgan, eds., *Strangers within the Realm* (Chapel Hill, 1991); Guy S. Klett, *Presbyterians in Colonial Pennsylvania* (Philadelphia, 1937); James G. Leyburn, *The Scotch-Irish: A Social History* (Chapel Hill, 1962); Sharon Salinger, *'To Serve Well and Faithfully': Labor and Indentured Servants in Pennsylvania, 1682–1800* (Cambridge, 1987); T. P. Slaughter, *The Whiskey Rebellion* (New York, 1988); E. T. Thomson, *Presbyterians in the South, 1607–1861* (Richmond, 1963); Charles Woodmason, *The Carolina Backcountry on the Eve of the Revolution,* ed. R. J. Hooker (Chapel Hill, 1953); Maurice J. Bric, "The American Society of United Irishmen," *Irish Journal of American Studies,* vii (1997): 163–77; D. N. Doyle and K. M. Miller, "Ulster Migrants in an Age of Rebellion," *Irish Economic and Social History,* 22 (1995): 77–87; Russell E. Hall, "American Presbyterian Churches—A Genealogy, 1706–1982," *Journal of Presbyterian History,* 60 (1982): 95–128; T. L. Purvis "The European Ancestry of the United States Population, 1790," ibid., 41 (1984):

85–101; Albert H. Tillson, Jr., "The Southern Backcountry: A Survey of Current Research," *The Virginia Magazine of History and Biography,* 98 (1990): 387–422.

DAVID N. DOYLE

## SCULLION, MARY (1953– )

Community organizer, social worker, advocate for homeless persons. Mary Scullion was born June 6, 1953, to Joseph and Sheila (Garvin) Scullion. Her parents, born in Ireland, had moved to Philadelphia by the time of Mary's birth. She entered the Sisters of Mercy, Merion Station, Pennsylvania, in September 1972 and made profession of vows on August 2, 1975. The 1976 Eucharistic Congress in Philadelphia proved a turning point in her experience. Speakers such as Mother Teresa, Dorothy Day and Rev. Pedro Arrupe challenged participants to address critical human needs worldwide. Mary combined her work as an elementary teacher with more and more work among the homeless of Philadelphia. Then, in 1978, she began full-time work at Mercy Hospice, a shelter for homeless women and children in Center City (Philadelphia). She opened Women of Hope in 1985, a shelter for women and, in 1988, gained notoriety when she and other homeless advocates turned the basement of the Municipal Services Building in Philadelphia into a temporary shelter. In 1989 Mary and Joan Dawson-McConnon co-founded Project H.O.M.E. (Housing, Opportunities, Medical Care, Education), an organization that combats homelessness through a layered program of advocacy, shelter, education, and job placement. Controversy and appreciation have made her name known by street people of Philadelphia, government officials, neighborhood groups, and concerned persons throughout the United States. She has, as one magazine writer observed, "been described as relentless, as a fighter, and even as a terrorist, but . . . could never be called . . . selfish and unforgiving" (Wasowski, p. 52).

Project H.O.M.E. Annual Reports.
Sara Rimer, "First Steps to Reclaim Streets Are Precise, Joyful, Loud," in the *New York Times* (January 12, 1998): A–14.
Matt Wasowski, "Though she is ever so humble, there is no place like H.O.M.E.," in *The Player* (February 1998): 52–53.
Ginny Wiegand, "This Woman Is No Saint," in *The Inquirer,* The Washington Inquirer Magazine (November 22, 1992): 12+.

HELEN MARIE BURNS, R.S.M.

## SCULLY, SEAN (1945–   )

### EARLY YEARS

Artist. Sean Scully was born in Dublin in 1945. Reduced circumstances necessitated his family's move to London where the artist grew up in a tough, working-class environment. Though possessed of innate artistic talent from a young age, he describes himself as "intellectually bankrupt" until that critical day when he wandered into the Tate Gallery where he saw Vincent Van Gogh's *Chair,* the powerful effect of which confirmed in him his ambition to become an artist. In an interview with Irving Sandler in 1995, Scully recalls his teenage years and his decision to become an artist: "Something about painting has always profoundly moved me and I think it must have its roots in this kind of poetic Irish sensibility I grew up in . . . this love of things other . . . outside normality."

## EDUCATION AND CAREER

Scully attended Croydon's College of Art by night from 1965 to 1968, followed by further study and teaching at the University of Northumbria in Newcastle-Upon-Tyne from 1968–72. A Frank Knox fellowship enabled him to go to Harvard University in 1972. From 1975 Scully based himself in the USA and became an American citizen in 1983. From 1977 until 1983 he taught part-time at Princeton University, New Jersey. In 1982 Scully spent a residency at the famed playwright Edward Albee's artists' colony in Montauk, Long Island. In 1983 he won a Guggenheim Foundation Fellowship, followed the next year by the prestigious National Endowment for the Arts Artist's Fellowship for painting. He had solo exhibitions at some of the most prestigious art centers in America and Europe.

## ARTISTIC DEVELOPMENT AND STYLE

Sean Scully is one of the leading Abstractionist painters of the late 20th century. His early career began in figuration, inspired by the rythmic, stylised elements of the paintings of Van Gogh and the Post-Impressionists and during a period of art in England which was lionised by Bacon and Freud. His passion for colour and regard for Matisse were enhanced by a trip to Morocco in 1969 where the intensity of the light and dramatic visual patterns left a lasting impression. A visit to a Rothko exhibition in London and a growing knowledge of Mondrian awakened him to the possibilities of abstraction. Another early influence was the geometric paintings of the British painter Bridget Riley.

In summary, Sean Scully's mature work is characterised by a distinctive, deliberately restricted vocabulary of forms which he has forged. His compositional elements are verticals, horizontals, chequerboard squares, rectangles and stripes. From about 1970 his work moved away from figuration and became more conceptual and rigorous. He began in particular to investigate the grid as a form. Tightly controlled, linear and painted in subdued hues, though these grid paintings of the 1970s and early 1980s suggest some affinity with Minimalism, Scully eschews such a label on the grounds of his disinterest in the Minimalist "puritanical" desire to take "all the smoke and dirt out of art" (Hugh Lane Memorial Lecture, Dublin 1994). From about 1980 Scully began to embolden his grid forms, widening and developing the "stripe" element into a motif in its own right. Experimenting with the physicality of the paint and the restricted, classical simplicity of the form, he began to invoke, through overpainting and the creation of rich strata of hues and colour juxtapositions, a sensual and intrinsically emotional content which is quite unique in abstract painting. His paintings are at once ascetic and yet extremely romantic.

Arthur C. Danto, Mario-Andreas von Luttichau, and Michael Semff, ed., *Sean Scully: Works on Paper, 1975–1996* (Staatliche Graphische Sammlung Munchen, 1996).

Danilo Eccher and David Carrier, *Sean Scully, Villa della Rosa* (Charta, Milan, 1996).

Mark Glazebrook and Irving Sandler (interview), *Sean Scully: Paintings* (Manchester City Art Galleries, 1997).

Hans-Michael Herzog, *Sean Scully: The Catherine Paintings* (Germany: Kunsthalle Bielefeld, 1995).

Maurice Poirier, *Sean Scully* (New York, 1990).

Ned Rifkin, Victoria Combalia, Lynne Cooke, and Armin Zweite, *Sean Scully: Twenty Years, 1976–1995* (Atlanta, 1995).

CHRISTINA KENNEDY

## SHANNON, WILLIAM V. (1927–1988)

Journalist, educator, author, ambassador. William V. Shannon was born August 24, 1927, in Worcester, Massachusetts, son of Patrick J. and Nora A. (McNamara) Shannon. His father was a carpenter. Shannon received his bachelor's degree from Clark University in 1947, and a master's degree from Harvard University in 1948, whereupon he became a free-lance writer in Washington, D.C. He joined the *New York Post* in 1951, working in Washington as the newspaper's capitol correspondent and bureau chief until 1957. From 1957 to 1964 he was a columnist for the *Post* and other newspapers, at which point he became a member of the editorial board of the *New York Times.* He also wrote a column on national affairs for *Commonweal* that continued until 1968.

As a journalist, Shannon won a number of awards, including in 1951 the Page One Award of the New York Newspaper Guild for coverage of national affairs, and while at the *Times* two Edward J. Meeman Awards from the Scripps-Howard Foundation for conservation writings.

In 1977 Shannon was named ambassador to Ireland by President Jimmy Carter and served four years in the post with great distinction. In fact, the conservative *National Review,* though distancing itself from some of Shannon's essentially liberal positions, rated the appointment "perhaps Jimmy Carter's best." Helping commend Shannon to Carter's attention was Shannon's 1963 book, *The American Irish: A Political and Social Portrait.* The *New Republic* lauded the book as "a detailed and sensitive brief for the liberal cause within the Roman Catholic church as exemplified by the American Irish."

Shannon wrote several other books, among them *The Heir Apparent: Robert Kennedy and the Struggle for Power* (1967) and *They Could Not Trust the King: Nixon, Watergate and the American People* (1974). The American Irish Historical Society presented him its gold medal in 1979, and there were honorary degrees from several universities.

On his return from Ireland in 1981, Shannon taught courses in journalism and the American presidency at Boston University and wrote a column for the *Boston Globe.* He died of lymphoma September 27, 1988. Among those offering tributes at his funeral was Senator Edward M. Kennedy, who ventured that a principal reason for President John F. Kennedy's triumphal reception on his state visit to Ireland in 1963 was that many of his comments had been written by Shannon.

Shannon was married to the former Elizabeth McNelly. They had three sons: Liam, Christopher and David.

*See* Historians of Irish America

Ann Evory, et al., eds. *Contemporary Authors, New Revision Series,* vol. 6 (Detroit, 1982).

James Finn, "The Ambassador Goes Home," *Commonweal* (October 21, 1988).

*The National Review,* "William V. Shannon, RIP" (October 28, 1988).

William V. Shannon, "Au Revoir," *Commonweal* (May 24, 1968).

JOHN DEEDY

## SHAUGHNESSY, THOMAS G. (1853–1923)

Railroad baron. Thomas George Shaughnessy was born October 6, 1853, at his parents' home in Milwaukee, Wisconsin. He was the son of two Irish immigrants: Thomas Shaughnessy

(1818–1903), a native of Ashford, County Limerick, and Mary Kennedy (1826–1906), who was born in Killarney, County Kerry. The younger Shaughnessy grew up in Milwaukee's Third Ward, home to the city's largest Irish neighborhood. He was educated by the Jesuits at St. Aloysius Academy.

Shaughnessy became active in community organizations. He was appointed adjutant of the First Regiment of the Wisconsin Militia and served as president of the Curran Literary Society. In 1875 he won a special election as alderman of the Third Ward. He was reelected to three terms on the city's Common Council in 1876, 1879, and 1882. In the latter year he was elected president of the Common Council, the second most powerful position in city government. Throughout his public career, Shaughnessy worked for the Milwaukee Road (Chicago, Milwaukee & St. Paul Railway Co.).

In 1882 Shaughnessy abruptly resigned from the Common Council to follow his former Milwaukee Road boss, William C. Van Horne, who had become general manager of the Canadian Pacific Railway. Shaughnessy's personal ability showed itself quickly in Montreal. In 1899, at age 46, he became president of the Canadian Pacific. Shaughnessy built the railroad into the world's largest transportation system. Under his leadership, the Canadian Pacific also became one of the largest landowners and one of the largest shipowners in the world at the time.

Shaughnessy was knighted by Queen Victoria in 1901. He was created a Knight Commander of the Victorian Order in 1907 by King Edward VII. As a result of his service to Great Britain during World War I, Shaughnessy was made a baron by King George V in 1916. His formal title was Thomas George, First Baron Shaughnessy of Montreal and Ashford. The hereditary peerage enabled him and his heirs to sit in the House of Lords. In 1912 Shaughnessy was offered the post of Lord Lieutenant of Ireland, the highest office in his parents' homeland. Shaughnessy declined the offer and, instead, served as chairman of the Canadian Pacific board of directors until his death in Montreal on December 10, 1923.

Thomas Gildea Cannon, "Thomas G. Shaughnessy—Railroad Baron," *Irish Genealogical Quarterly,* 2/2 (1993): 14–18.
John A. Eagle, "Baron Thomas Shaughnessy: The Peer That Made Milwaukee Famous," *Milwaukee History* 6/1 (1983): 28–40.

THOMAS GILDEA CANNON

## SHEA, JOHN GILMARY (1824–1892)

Historian. The foremost American Catholic historian of the nineteenth century, John Dawson [Gilmary] Shea was born in 1824 New York City. His father was James Shea, an Irish immigrant who taught English at Columbia University and served as a leader in Irish Catholic affairs in New York. His mother was Mary Ann Flannigan, a homemaker who traced her roots to Ireland through her eighteenth-century ancestors. A devout Catholic all his life, John Shea wrote extensively on the Church in the United States, but had little to say about its Irish heritage.

Shea was a gifted student who was educated at a parochial school run by the Sisters of Charity. He showed particular skills as a writer and by the age of 14 he was writing for the *Catholic Children's Magazine.* After grammar school, Shea explored careers in finance and law, but quickly lost interest in those professions. He entered the Society of Jesus in 1848 and studied at what is now Fordham University and St. Mary's College in Montreal

John Gilmary Shea

for the next four years. It was at the time of his entry into the Jesuit order that Shea adopted Gilmary as his middle name. Shea abandoned his religious vocation in 1852 and returned to research and writing as his career. His first major work was *Discovery and Exploration of the Mississippi Valley* (1852), a book that won him favor with the historians of his day.

Following his marriage to Sophie Savage in 1854, Shea established himself as a prolific author and translator and several of his historical textbooks were widely used in Catholic parochial schools. Among the books he wrote during those years were *A General History of Modern Europe* (1854) and *The Catholic Church in the United States: A Sketch of Its Ecclesiastical History* (1856). In 1857, he translated Tachet De Barneval's *The Saints of Erin* from the French, one of Shea's few works related to Ireland. Over the next 35 years, Shea turned out a wide range of historical narratives, dictionaries, encyclopedias, collections of documents and church chronicles. Many of these works ran to multiple volumes.

Following the Third Plenary Council of Baltimore in 1884, Shea began to research and write his magnum opus, *History of the Catholic Church in the United States,* a four-volume work that was published between 1886 and 1892. Shea received financial assistance from the U.S. Catholic bishops in this effort. This work was monumental yet impartial and remained useful well into this century. In 1887, Shea joined with Archbishop John Ireland and others to found the U.S. Catholic Historical Society and served as president of that organization in 1890.

In spite of his productivity as a historian and a writer, Shea found it difficult to earn enough money to support his family. He begged small writing assignments and administrative jobs from his friends in the Catholic hierarchy. Finally in 1889, near the end of his life, he became an editor of *The Catholic News,* the archdiocesan newspaper in New York. He died at his home in Elizabeth, New Jersey, in 1892, largely unappreciated for all that he had done to preserve and interpret American Catholic history.

*See* Historians of Irish America

Peter Guilday, *John Gilmary Shea* (New York, 1926).
John Gilmary Shea, *A Child's History of the United States,* 3 vols. (New York, 1872).

———, *History of the Catholic Church within the Limits of the United States,* 4 vols. (New York, 1886–1892).

TIMOTHY WALCH

## SHEEHAN, LUKE FRANCIS (1873–1937)

Capuchin missionary, pioneer of the Church in Oregon. Luke Sheehan was born Francis Bernard Sheehan in Cork City, Ireland, on February 28, 1873. After his ordination in 1896 and teaching philosophy for six years in the Capuchin House of Formation in Kilkenny, Sheehan embarked upon the first phase of his missionary life by volunteering to work in Aden, the British colony on the Southwestern coast of the Arabian peninsula. Shortly after his arrival, Sheehan was appointed Pro-Vicar Apostolic and, from 1902 to 1908, traveled to Somalia, to the remote islands of Aden, and to Bombay, India, to preach retreats and missions. Forced to leave Aden because of illness, Sheehan returned to Ireland. When he learned that his replacement had died of the same illness, Sheehan immediately returned and remained until he was too weak to continue his work. He returned again to Ireland where he remained until 1910, when Bishop Joseph O'Reilly of the Diocese of Baker City, Oregon, asked the Irish Capuchins to come to the United States.

In 1910 Luke Sheehan, together with Thomas Dowling, arrived in Hermiston, Oregon. Within four months his companion returned to Ireland, leaving Sheehan to explore the possibilities of developing the Church of Eastern Oregon. When his Irish confreres sent Casimir Butler to help, Sheehan left him to care for Hermiston and moved to reconnoiter Crook County, Oregon, and the barely developed town of Bend, where there were only one hundred and fifty Catholics scattered over an area of eight thousand square miles. After taking up residence in a small room over a wooden dance hall, the Irish Capuchin walked or rode on horseback thousands of miles, intent on solidifying the Church's presence. When the railroad came to Bend in 1916, Sheehan began building a new church and, shortly thereafter, St. Charles hospital. Twenty years later he succeeded in opening a parish school.

In addition to suffering innumerable physical hardships, he endured the bigotry of many of Crook County's residents, especially members of the Ku Klux Klan. Barriers were continually placed in the way of his attempts at purchasing property for the church; once built, the windows of the new church were repeatedly broken; and Sheehan himself was often denounced and maligned. The Capuchin, however, never relented in his efforts and in 1935 he courageously challenged the Klan at one of their meetings and was instrumental in their decline in Oregon.

Luke Sheehan died at Hood River, Oregon, on February 11, 1937, twenty-seven years after his arrival in Bend. His sole possession was a breviary. His Capuchin confreres praised him as "the greatest missionary of them all, whose life bore great fruit, for he was a man of single purpose."

Conrad Donovan, "The Irish Capuchins in the United States of America," *Capuchin Annual* (1973): 249–289.

REGIS J. ARMSTRONG, O.F.M. CAP.

## SHEEN, FULTON JOHN (1895–1979)

Educator, author, apologist, preacher, radio and television personality and archbishop. Fulton Sheen was born Peter Sheen on

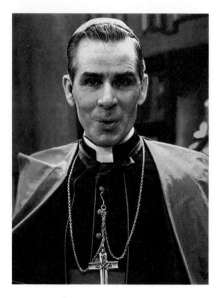

Fulton Sheen

May 8, 1895 in El Paso, Illinois, the son of Irish-American farmer, Newton Morris Sheen and Delia Fulton. His maternal grandparents were natives of County Roscommon and his paternal grandfather was also an Irish national. He later took the name "John" when he was confirmed and his mother's maiden name "Fulton" when he entered high school. He began his schooling at St. Mary's Cathedral School in Peoria, Illinois (1901–1909) and his high school at Spalding Institute (1909–1913) operated by the Brothers of Mary. Sheen attended St. Viator's College and Seminary in Bourbannais, Illinois where he completed undergraduate and graduate work in 1917. He continued his studies for the priesthood at St. Paul's Seminary in St. Paul, Minnesota and was ordained a priest for the Diocese of Peoria by Bishop Edward M. Dunne on September 20, 1919. Sheen's academic ability compelled Bishop Dunne to send him for advanced work in theology and canon law at the Catholic University of America where he earned the S. T. L. and J. C. B. in 1920. The following year Sheen was sent to the Catholic University of Louvain, Belgium, where he received his doctorate in 1923. There, Sheen was steeped in the essentials of the neo-Thomistic revival spearheaded in Belgium by Cardinal Desire Mercier. The philosophical and theological framework of neo-Thomism would define the intellectual parameters of Sheen's teaching and preaching for the remainder of his life. His dissertation, *God and Intelligence in Modern Philosophy: A Critical Study in the Light of the Philosophy of St. Thomas* rigorously scrutinized a spectrum of contemporary philosophical belief and exposed his debilities while upholding the superiority of the method and content of St. Thomas Aquinas.

In 1926 his dissertation was published as *God and Intelligence* and made him the first American to win the coveted Cardinal Mercier Prize for International Philosophy. Sheen pursued additional studies after Louvain at the Sorbonne and the Angelicum in Rome, where he received his S. T. D. in 1924. He taught briefly at St. Edmund's College, Ware, England where he became acquainted with G. K. Chesterton, who wrote a warm and admiring introduction to *God and Intelligence*.

In 1926 Bishop Dunne compelled Sheen to turn down a lectureship at Oxford as well as an offer to start a program in scholastic philosophy at Columbia University and insisted that he come home and serve as a curate at St. Patrick's Church in

Peoria. His parochial service was of brief duration as Dunne was satisfied with Sheen's obedience and allowed him to join the faculty of The Catholic University of America. He joined the School of Theology in 1926, but was later transferred to the Department of Philosophy and the chair of Apologetics where he remained until 1952. Sheen's reception among his fellow faculty members at the University was always mixed. His heavy public speaking schedule precluded the kind of intense research that might have advanced his career.

## Sheen and the Media

In 1930, he was catapulted to national fame when he became the host of the NBC Radio Network's "Catholic Hour Broadcasts" sponsored by the National Council of Catholic Men. *The Catholic Hour* was one of several nationally broadcast religious programs that included evangelist Billy Sunday's *The Back Home Hour* (1929–1931), *The CBS Church of the Air* (1930–1947) and ABC's *The Old Fashioned Revival Hour* (1930–1950). Sheen appeared on the show from 1930 until 1952 and at his height reached a listening audience of some 4,000,000. With the popularity of his radio program, Sheen definitively switched his publishing efforts to more popular works, churning out more than sixty titles that were distillations of his radio addresses and including the highly popular *Peace of Soul* (1949) which reached number six on the *New York Times* best-seller list. A popular *Life of Christ* was issued in 1958, adorned with a dust-jacket image of Salvador Dali's "St. John of the Cross."

Sheen's media recognition brought him into regular contact with some of the high and mighty of the American Catholic elite and also made him the natural point of inquiry for a number of prominent figures who converted to Catholicism under his direction. These included politician Clare Boothe Luce, automaker Henry Ford II, musician Fritz Kreisler and communist journalist Louis Budenz. In 1951, Sheen was consecrated auxiliary bishop of New York and took up permanent residence in the city.

Although short of stature, Sheen's photos portrayed a strikingly handsome man of dominant proportions with piercing hawk-like eyes. Sheen stood quite distinct from the average American Catholic preacher of his day who often read from prepared notes or from standard preaching guides. Gifted with a flair for the dramatic, he knew when to raise and lower his voice, to speak sternly or to lapse into tender sentimentality as he recited the saccharine "Lovely Lady Dressed in Blue." His messages were rarely polemical, except when he was exposing some modern philosophical error or assailing the evils of communism.

## Sheen and the Religious Revival of the Fifties

Sheen has been acknowledged by historians as one of the representative figures of the religious revival of the fifties. Not only did his radio and television messages reflect the kind of religious amalgam reflected in Will Herberg's classic *Protestant, Catholic, Jew* (1960), but he also was an icon for many of the major trends in American life of the post-war era. He especially exemplified concerns about the Cold War, the rise of television and the surging upward social mobility of American Catholics in this epoch.

Sheen's ideological antipathy to communism was reflective of the larger difficulties the Catholic church had with the system even before the war and which had been roundly condemned by Pius XI's *Divini Redemptoris* (1937). Better than most, Sheen brought to expression the anger and loathing many Catholic Americans felt as they witnessed the post-war Soviet domination of Eastern Europe and the systematic persecution of the Church behind the Iron Curtain. To allay the fears of his listeners that communism's hydra-headed evils would come to the United States, Sheen urged an intensification of Marian devotion and urged his listeners to pray the rosary for world peace. At this time he became a particularly warm admirer of the cult of Our Lady of Fatima, the apparition of Mary that took place in Cova da Iria, Portugal between 1915–1917. Mary's messages to the children included strong injunctions to pray for the conversion of Russia. Sheen was a staunch American-Catholic cold warrior and most elements of his anti-communist message resonated widely with similar feelings in American society.

Sheen delivered many of these salvos against the evils of communism through the medium of television. As radio had proliferated in the twenties and thirties, so the post-war era saw a tremendous burst of technological innovation that made television more accessible to Americans. As the fifties unfolded Americans in increasing numbers were purchasing television sets and tuning into sporting events, situation comedies such as *I Love Lucy* and musical variety shows hosted by Frank Sinatra and Ed Sullivan. Into this new medium stepped the handsome and telegenic Sheen who began his popular *Life is Worth Living* series in 1955 sponsored by the Admiral Corporation and first shown on the short-lived Dumont network (1952–1955) and then on ABC (1955–1957). His performances were delivered in episcopal regalia, with wide sweeping gestures reminiscent of Pope Pius XII and with an animated angel that erased his prop blackboard. When he accepted an Emmy Award in 1952, he thanked his writers "Matthew, Mark, Luke and John."

Sheen was also able to tap into the increasing wealth and upward mobility of American Catholics in the fifties through his fundraising efforts for the Society of the Propagation of the Faith. Sheen had been awakened to the needs of the missions after a Pacific tour with Cardinal Francis Spellman in 1948. Appointed national director of the Propagation in 1950, Sheen tirelessly educated American Catholics regarding the needs and opportunities that the missions presented. He wrote two nationally syndicated newspaper columns that appeared in diocesan newspapers and edited the two periodicals of the Society, *World Mission* and *Mission* which touted the needs of the organization. He also used his television broadcasts to do likewise. He personally raised millions of dollars for the increasing number of missionary endeavors being sponsored by American religious communities and dioceses. Over the course of time he raised over $100 million to support 300,000 missionaries, 150,000 schools, 26,000 hospitals, 5,000 orphanages and 400 leper colonies. Sheen himself contributed handsomely to the coffers of the Propagation, devoting a considerable part of his six figure salary from *Life is Worth Living* as well as book royalties to the organization.

Sheen's headship of the Propagation was accompanied by episcopal consecration in 1951 which made him a subordinate to Cardinal Francis Spellman of New York. Rumors of feuding between the two very strong-willed men circulated for a long time and were no doubt exaggerated by the re-telling. Nonetheless, the two did quarrel over Spellman's efforts to "sell" government-donated milk to the Propagation of the Faith and required papal intervention. Sheen was upheld by the pontiff but Spellman retaliated by withdrawing Sheen's permission to appear on television. Spellman also chose to serve as a sounding board for members of religious communities who felt short-changed in Sheen's apportionment of the centrally collected mission funds.

## BISHOP OF ROCHESTER AND END OF CAREER

Sheen's transfer to the Diocese of Rochester in 1966 came just after the end of Vatican Council II. He had been an enthusiastic participant at the Council and a member of the Committee on Missions. Imbued with the spirit of the Council, and alert to the growing turbulence of American domestic politics in the late sixties, Sheen came to Rochester determined to act boldly and forcefully. Internally he signaled a more collegial approach to diocesan administration by creating a priests' senate and polling his clergy for the names of those who would best serve in the diocesan bureaucracy. He sought to broaden and expand the training of Rochester's seminarians by bringing the diocesan St. Bernard's Seminary into a working relationship with nearby Protestant seminaries. In the areas of social justice and politics he was equally bold. He made a host of new clerical appointments that highlighted his concerns for the deteriorating inner city in Rochester. Drawing on his well-honed skills for the dramatic, he made headlines in July 1967 when he called on President Lyndon Johnson to withdraw all American troops from Vietnam. The same type of dynamic attended his 1968 decision to turn over the inner city church of St. Bridget to the U.S. Department of Housing and Urban Development with the proviso that the land be used to build housing for the poor. This action set off a firestorm of opposition from the pastor and parishioners who had not been consulted as well as from some of his priests. The sharp backlash eventually compelled him to rescind the offer. The St. Bridget embarrassment demoralized and depressed Sheen and brought an end to his innovations and public visibility. In 1969, one year short of the mandatory retirement age of 75, Sheen unexpectedly resigned.

The remaining ten years of his life were spent back in New York. He took to the road again preaching parish missions, giving retreats to priests and making a series of highly popular tapes of his talks. He retained his considerable public speaking talents to the end, but the subject of his sermons often contained jabs at the life-styles of younger priests and some elements of Vatican II-inspired renewal. He died on December 9, 1979 and is buried in St. Patrick's Cathedral, New York.

John Tracy Ellis, *Catholic Bishops: A Memoir* (Wilmington, Del., 1984).

Kathleen Riley Fields, *Bishop Fulton J. Sheen: An American Catholic Response to the Twentieth-Century* (Ph.D. diss., University of Notre Dame, 1988).

Thomas J. McSweeney, *The Rhetorical Fulton J. Sheen, 'Life is Worth Living,' 1952–1957* (Ph.D diss., University of Maryland, College Park, 1996).

STEVEN M. AVELLA

## SHEIL, BERNARD JAMES (1886–1969)

Auxiliary bishop of Chicago, Illinois. He was born February 18, 1886 in Chicago, the only son of James and Rosella Barclay Sheil, both descendants of Irish immigrants. Bernard grew to maturity at St. Columbkille's Parish, a rapidly changing Irish parish on Chicago's near north side. He attended St. Viator's College in Bourbannais, Illinois and flirted with the idea of becoming a professional baseball player. He decided instead to enter the seminary at St. Viator's and was ordained to the priesthood on May 21, 1910 by Archbishop James Quigley of Chicago. He served for a time as curate at St. Mel's Church on Chicago's West side and performed chaplaincy services at the Great Lakes Naval Training Station during 1918–1919. In the twenties he became a chaplain at the Cook County jail and his work with juvenile offenders convinced him that he had to do something to prevent youth from choosing a life of crime. Taking a page from the books of such successful organizations as the YMCA and Wesley Baden-Powell's Boy Scout movement, Sheil made his mark as an organizer of one of the most successful Catholic Youth organizations in America.

## AUXILIARY BISHOP AND HEAD OF THE CYO

Articulate and affable, Sheil won the attention of Archbishop George Mundelein who used his services to help organize the Eucharistic Congress held in Chicago in 1925. Sheil was later elevated to the rank of vice-chancellor and later chancellor of the archdiocese and on May 1, 1928, Mundelein consecrated him an auxiliary bishop of Chicago. In 1933 he was appointed pastor of St. Andrew's parish on the near north side of Chicago where he built himself a palatial suite of rooms by adding a third floor to the existing rectory.

With a broad grant of authority from Mundelein, Sheil began in 1930 to consolidate a variety of existing youth programs and put them together with archdiocesan fund-raising and social welfare operations already in place to form the Catholic Youth Organization (CYO). Under his leadership the Chicago CYO became one of the most visible and successful youth operations in American Catholic history. Under its aegis Sheil ran camps, educational programs and summer schools. However, the main thrust of the program was an extensive athletic program that welcomed Chicago youth of any creed or color. Local boxing competitions were especially popular. These contests annually climaxed at a city-wide bout that was attended by thousands of Chicagoans. When criticized for promoting these morally dubious pugilistic events, Sheil stoutly defended them as a successful means of preventing urban youths from turning to gangs or urban crime. Sheil's success in Chicago inspired CYO copies around the nation.

Sheil shared his patron Mundelein's interest in politics and was an indirect beneficiary of the cardinal's close association with Franklin Delano Roosevelt. With the assistance of his personal lawyer and later Federal judge William Campbell, Sheil cultivated his contacts with Roosevelt insiders such as Thomas G. (Tommy the Cork) Corcoran and State Department official G. Howland Shaw. He endeared himself to FDR's inner circle by publicly attacking Father Charles Coughlin, and when Mundelein died unexpectedly in October 1939, Sheil went on the air to speak favorably of the president's interventionist foreign policy. Sheil also cemented a close relationship with organized labor when he appeared in 1937 at a huge CIO sponsored rally in behalf of Chicago's meat-packers.

When Mundelein died, Sheil entertained hopes that he would be the cardinal's successor and grateful officials of the Roosevelt administration made some efforts on his behalf. When the appointment went to Milwaukee archbishop Samuel A. Stritch, Sheil struck out on his own to convince higher officials in Rome that he was worthy of a major diocese of his own. In 1940 he reorganized the Catholic Youth Organization moving it away from its heavy emphasis on athletics and attempted to give it a more intellectual bent. He made sure that his ideas got the widest public exposure through his own public relations department and the "Sheil School of Social Studies," which began in CYO headquarters in 1943. The Sheil School, referred to in its heyday as a

"Catholic Times Square" offered a host of adult-education programs and provided for thousands of Chicagoans their first exposure to any number of new trends in Catholic intellectual life from scripture to liturgy. However, these very public efforts to curry favor and win respect as a leading intellectual and socially minded prelate did not win Sheil the much desired status of archbishop or bishop in his own right. Indeed Sheil's activities won only a half-hearted toleration from his superior, Cardinal Stritch, whom he rarely consulted and out-right antagonism from such episcopal heavy-weights as Cardinal Spellman of New York whose jurisdiction he occasionally entered without the requisite courtesy call of one prelate to another.

### DECLINE

As his hopes for episcopal preferment went by the board, the CYO also began to experience a decline. Sheil continued to add programs to the already over-burdened organization's financial structure and frequent personnel shake-ups created serious morale problems among the organization. In an ironic twist, although he himself had been an ardent proponent of unionization, he refused to permit it among his own employees. All this came to a head in April, 1954, when Sheil leveled a verbal blast against the tactics of Senator Joseph McCarthy of Wisconsin. In September of that year, Sheil dramatically resigned from the leadership of the expanded CYO and returned to full-time parochial work. The intersection of the two events led many to believe that Sheil was removed for criticizing the senator. In fact, Sheil's financial woes were the real reason for the abrupt departure as it meant an escape from the burden of debt. Cardinal Stritch dismantled the once vast CYO "empire" and graciously retired the outstanding liabilities with archdiocesan funds.

After his resignation, Sheil withdrew from public view, occasionally re-emerging to lend his name or influence to some pet cause. Using his own contacts in Rome, he secured for himself the title of "Honorary Archbishop," a title that eluded him in his active career. After an appointment to a high level preparatory commission of Vatican II, he failed to attend the meetings and never made a single session of the Council. In 1967, Cardinal John Cody demanded his resignation from St. Andrew's and Sheil moved to retirement in Arizona, where he died on September 13, 1969.

Steven M. Avella, *This Confident Church: Catholic Leadership and Life in Chicago, 1940–1965* (Notre Dame, 1992).

Edward Kantowicz, *Corporation Sole: Cardinal Mundelein and Chicago Catholicism* (Notre Dame, 1983).

Roger Treat, *Bishop Sheil and the CYO* (New York, 1951).

STEVEN M. AVELLA

## SHERIDAN, PHILIP HENRY (1831–1888)

Union general. Sheridan's parents immigrated to America from County Cavan, Ireland about 1830. They settled briefly in Albany and, although the location remains uncertain, Sheridan was probably born near that city on March 6, 1831. The elder Sheridan brought his family to Somerset, Ohio while he sought work on the roads and canals being built in the area. There, young Philip received a basic education, interrupted when he became a clerk in a local store at the age of fourteen. Though disappointed at being too young to enlist for the Mexican War, the youth en-

Philip Henry
Sheridan

tered West Point on July 1, 1848, where he had a tempestuous career. During a disagreement with a cadet-officer, Sheridan fixed his bayonet on his superior, for which he was suspended from the Academy for a year. Sheridan succeeded in graduating from West Point in 1853, however, ranking thirty-fourth in a class of forty-nine.

The new officer first served a year by the Rio Grande, then confronted Indians in the Northwest. At the beginning of the Civil War, Captain Sheridan was quartermaster and commissary of Union troops in southwest Missouri. He found administrative duty unsatisfying, however, and was happy with his appointment as colonel of the Second Michigan Cavalry on May 25, 1862. While commanding a brigade at Boonesville, Missouri, Sheridan defeated a much larger Confederate force and won his first star. He led a division at Perryville, and put up a staunch defense during Stones River. He received promotion to major general on December 31, 1862.

The following year, Sheridan led his division at Chickamauga and Chattanooga, where he captured the eye of Ulysses S. Grant, along with the heights of Missionary Ridge. Upon Grant's promotion to lieutenant general, he appointed Sheridan commander of the Army of the Potomac's cavalry corps.

Sheridan energetically set himself to reorganizing the corps and led several effective raids against Confederate communication lines. In August, 1864, Sheridan assumed command of the Army of the Shenandoah, which confronted a southern force deployed in that fertile valley under Jubal Early. After defeating Early at Winchester and Fisher Hill in mid-September, Sheridan pillaged the Shenandoah Valley and took pride in the efficiency and totality of the destruction he wrought.

Early counterattacked and surprised Sheridan's men at Cedar Creek on October 19, 1864. Although Sheridan was at Winchester, twenty miles away, the general rode to the field of battle to rally his routing troops and turned the day to his favor. From February 27 to March 24, 1865, Sheridan continued his raiding operations, destroying railroads, canals, and depots before winning the decisive battle at Five Forks on April 1, 1865. With the Confederate position at Petersburg rendered untenable, Robert E. Lee's tattered army began what would be its final campaign. Sheridan pursued the Southerners and won another victory at Sayler's Creek. Surrounded, Lee surrendered at Appomatox Court House on April 9, 1865.

After the war, Sheridan was ordered to administer the military division of the Gulf, an uneasy spot due to tensions along the Mexican border. With the Reconstruction Act of 1867, Sheridan was appointed military governor of the Fifth Military District, comprised of Louisiana and Texas with headquarters in New Orleans. Sheridan's hard-handed measures led President Andrew Johnson to reassign him to Missouri, where the general pursued and vanquished hostile Indians.

On March 4, 1869, President Grant appointed Sheridan lieutenant general with command of the division of the Missouri. In 1870–71, Sheridan traveled abroad to observe the Franco-Prussian War, where he met Otto von Bismarck and witnessed the Battle of Sedan. Returning to resume his command, Sheridan was put in charge of the western and southwestern military divisions in 1878. In 1884, Sheridan succeeded William T. Sherman as commander-in-chief of the army and on June 1, 1888, became a full general.

In the twilight of his life, Sheridan wrote his *Personal Memoirs*, signing the preface only three days before his death at Nonquitt, Massachusetts on August 5, 1888. His funeral was held in Washington, D.C., with military and civil honors, and he was buried at the National Cemetery at Arlington.

*See* Civil War

Roy Morris, Jr., *Sheridan: The Life and Wars of General Phil Sheridan* (New York, 1992).

Horace Porter, *Campaigning with Grant* (New York, 1897).

Philip H. Sheridan, *Personal Memoirs of P. H. Sheridan, General, United States Army*, 2 vols. (New York, 1888).

*The War of the Rebellion: A Compilation of the Official Records of the Union and Confederate Armies*, 128 vols. (Washington, D.C., 1880–1901).

CHRISTIAN G. SAMITO

## SHIELDS, JAMES (1806–1879)

Soldier and senator. Born in Altmore, County Tyrone, Ireland, to Charles and Katherine (McDonnell) Shields, Shields was educated in the classical tradition and enjoyed sword play in his spare time. It is reported that he left Ireland in 1822 and sailed by way of Liverpool for Quebec; however, the ship wrecked somewhere along the Scottish coast. Shields remained then in Scotland and took up the profession of tutoring.

In 1826 he left for the United States and arrived in New York; he then went on to settle in Illinois. In Kaskaskia, Illinois, he taught French and studied law. In 1836 he was elected as a member of the legislature. By 1843 he was elected to the Supreme Court by Governor Thomas Ford and re-elected in 1845. His political and legal work gained him a reputation as a diligent and common sense legal mastermind. However, he left these duties at the outbreak of the Mexican War and was then commissioned as a brigadier-general of the Illinois volunteers in 1846. He was seriously wounded while serving at Cerro Gordo and after recovery he led the charge of New York Irish and South Carolina volunteers. In 1848 Shields returned to Kaskaskia and resumed his law practice.

Shields is remembered for his work as a senator; he was a significant proponent in the stimulation of an Irish movement in his region and he organized townships such as Shieldsville, Erin, Kilkenny, Montgomery, Lesueur and Rice counties along with the town of Faribault. In 1859 he was elected to the federal Senate by the electorate of Minnesota. From his work in the Senate he moved to San Francisco where he met and married Mary Ann Carr, originally of Armagh, Ireland. In 1863 he began lecturing for religious, Irish and other charitable causes; in 1879 he was elected to the Senate again but had to decline due to failing health. He retired and soon after died while on a lecturing tour. In his honor a colossal statue was built and later placed in the Capitol in Statuary Hall at the request of the Grand Army of the Republic.

W. H. Condon, *Life of Major-General James Shields* (1900).

H. A. Castle, "General James Shields" *Minnesota Historical Society Colls.*, vol. XV (1915).

*Dictionary of American Biography*, 17.

JOY HARRELL

## SHRIVER, EUNICE MARY KENNEDY (1921–  )

Social activist. Born July 10, 1921, in Brookline, Massachusetts, Shriver was the fifth child of Rose Fitzgerald Kennedy and wealthy businessman Joseph P. Kennedy, later the American Ambassador to Great Britain from 1938–1941. Educated in private schools by the Roman Catholic Society of the Sacred Heart, Shriver earned a B.S. degree in 1943 from Stanford University. In 1953, she married Robert Sargent Shriver, Jr., the first Director of the Peace Corps, and the Democratic candidate for vice president in 1972. The couple has five children: Robert Sargent III, Maria, Timothy, Mark, and Anthony.

Concerned with social issues, Shriver was associated with the Special War Problems Division of the State Department from 1943–1945, and with the National Conference on the Prevention and Control of Juvenile Delinquency from 1947–1948. She served as a social worker with the Federal Penitentiary for Women in Alderson, West Virginia, with the House of Good Shephard and with the Juvenile Court, both in Chicago, Illinois.

Shriver is perhaps best known for her pioneering work with the mentally handicapped. Inspired by the example of her disabled sister, Rosemary, Shriver has led efforts to change the way developmental disabilities are understood and treated. A consul-

Eunice Kennedy Shriver

tant to the Presidential Panel on Mental Retardation in 1961, she wrote an influential article, "Hope for Retarded Children" for the *Saturday Evening Post* in 1962. In 1968, Shriver founded Special Olympics International, a program that involves the disabled in sports training and competition.

Shriver has also helped her prominent family realize its political ambitions by assisting in several Kennedy campaigns for public office, including those of her three brothers: President John F. Kennedy; Senator Robert F. Kennedy (D. NY); and Senator Edward M. Kennedy (D. Mass.). A committed Roman Catholic, Shriver is an outspoken opponent of legalized abortion.

An executive vice president of the Joseph P. Kennedy, Jr. Foundation and trustee of the John F. Kennedy Library Foundation, Shriver has received numerous honorary degrees and awards, including the Presidential Medal of Freedom in 1984.

---

Doris Kearns Goodwin, *The Fitzgeralds and the Kennedys* (New York, 1971).

Lawrence Leamer, *The Kennedy Women: The Saga of an American Family* (New York, 1994).

KATHLEEN N. McCARTHY

## SISTERS OF CHARITY OF THE BLESSED VIRGIN MARY (B.V. M.)

Forty-eight hundred women have joined the Sisters of Charity of the Blessed Virgin Mary since its foundation in Philadelphia, PA, in 1833. Of these, 246 were born in Ireland, another thousand have a parent from Ireland and many others claim Irish ancestors.

When the original members Mary Frances Clarke and her four friends, Margaret Mann, Eliza Kelly, Catherine Byrne and Rose O'Toole set sail from Ireland for the United States, they intended to continue their work in education. As a group of laywomen they had established a little school, Miss Clarke's Seminary, for the poor girls in Dublin who could not afford to attend the convent schools of the day. A missionary from the United States convalescing in Ireland convinced the young women to become educators of the poor children of the Irish immigrants working in the textile mills of Philadelphia. When the group arrived at Old St. Joseph Church, Philadelphia, on September 7, 1833, a local parishioner introduced them to the former pastor, Rev. Terence J. Donaghoe. He was a native of County Tyrone, Ireland, and he offered to assist the women in establishing a school for poor girls.

### ORIGINS OF THE CONGREGATION

Acting on the suggestion of Donaghoe, the five women formed a pious organization called the Sisters of the Blessed Virgin Mary and made acts of consecration on November 1, 1833. This date is claimed as the foundation of the congregation later known as the Sisters of Charity of the Blessed Virgin Mary (BVMs). The women chose Mary Frances Clarke as "Mother" of the community, and Donaghoe declared himself the "Superior." The new congregation attracted new members.

### MOVEMENT TO THE AMERICAN FRONTIER

Bishop Mathias Loras invited the sisters to the Diocese of Dubuque in 1843 to educate the children of Native Americans, miners and pioneer farmers along the American frontier. The Dubuque Diocese encompassed the territories of Iowa, Minnesota, the Dakotas, and parts of Wisconsin and Illinois. The bishop had heard of the sisters from John Norman, a teacher in Dubuque, whom Donaghoe had trained as a catechist in Philadelphia. Five sisters traveled with Loras to the Mississippi River town in the Iowa Territory, arriving on June 23, 1843. They began teaching in a log cabin, St. Mary's Academy, located near the primitive cathedral of the diocese.

Because of ecclesiastical politics in Philadelphia and because of the Nativists rioting against the Irish immigrants, Donaghoe and the other members of the community accepted Loras' invitation to move to the Iowa Territory. On September 8, 1843, fourteen sisters and Donaghoe settled in the river town. Loras provided the little community with the canonical status it needed to become an official women's religious congregation. He requested that the sisters wear a religious habit and he added the word "Charity" to their title. The congregation built its first motherhouse on the Iowa prairie ten miles outside Dubuque.

### GROWTH OF CATHOLIC SCHOOLS

While serving as Loras' vicar general, Donaghoe encouraged local pastors to establish parish schools which he staffed with BVMs. He purchased land to build boarding academies for girls and young women which the sisters operated. In 1867 he sent sisters to open schools within Holy Family parish, Chicago, IL. After his death, January 5, 1869, Mary Frances Clarke assumed the roles of both "mother" and "superior." Clarke incorporated the congregation as a not-for-profit corporation in 1869, obtained papal approbation in 1877, and continued to send the sisters to teach in newly opened parish schools and academies. From graduates of their early schools, the BVMs attracted other women with the pioneer spirit needed to follow the frontier westward along the railroad lines and the rivers. BVMs arrived in San Francisco in 1887 to begin St. Bridget's parish school. It was the last school to which Mary Frances Clarke sent sisters before her death December 4, 1887.

### EXPANSION AND RENEWAL

The BVMs elected Mary Gertrude Regan, who had been a student at the sisters' first Philadelphia school, to succeed Clarke as the mother superior. She moved the motherhouse and the novitiate from the prairie to its present site at Mt. Carmel, located on the Mississippi River bluffs in Dubuque. The sisters continued expanding education for young women and in 1902 the girls' boarding academy, Mt. St. Joseph, Dubuque, received a college charter from the state of Iowa. The college was renamed Clarke in 1928 after its founder. Today it accepts both women and men into its student body. A second college, Mundelein, was established for young women in Chicago in 1929. This college merged with Loyola University of Chicago in 1991. In 1964, to accommodate the great number of women entering the congregation, the sisters built Guadalupe College in Los Gatos, CA. Following Vatican II and the changes affecting religious life this college was closed. To obtain the advanced professional degrees necessary to staff colleges the sisters began attending Catholic University, Washington, D.C., in 1911. Later they attended both private and public universities.

Six other mother superiors followed Gertrude Regan in governing the congregation until 1968. Following the renewal of religious life prescribed by Vatican II, the governance has been directed by an elected president and two vice presidents. The BVMs continue educational ministries within the academic structures.

Also they continue the works of education informally by serving as hospital and hospice chaplains, parish associates, literacy teachers of prisoners and immigrants, family therapists, counselors, wherever they see a need. Presently there are 938 sisters ministering throughout the United States, South and Central America and Africa.

Jane Coogan, B.V.M., *The Price of Our Heritage* (Dubuque, IA, 1975).

Lambertina Doran, B.V.M., *In The Early Days* (St. Louis, 1911).

Kathryn Lawlor, B.V.M., ed., *Terence J. Donaghoe: Co-Founder of the Sisters of Charity, B.V.M.* (Dubuque, IA, 1995).

Laura Smith-Noggle, ed., *My Dear Sister, Correspondence and Notes of Mary Frances Clarke* (Dubuque, IA, 1987).

KATHRYN LAWLOR, B.V.M.

## SISTERS OF MERCY

An active religious congregation of women founded in Dublin, Ireland, in 1831 by Catherine Elizabeth McAuley to respond to the needs of poor persons in the environs of Dublin, especially young working women. The Institute of the Sisters of Mercy of the Americas is the official title of a 1991 restructuring of seventeen independent congregations of Sisters of Mercy with motherhouses in the United States. In 1997, the Institute of the Sisters of Mercy of the Americas numbered 6,049 women serving primarily in the United States, Central America, Latin America, Belize, Guyana, Jamaica, Guam, and the Philippines.

### BEGINNINGS OF THE SISTERS OF MERCY IN IRELAND

Catherine McAuley was born on September 29, 1778, at Stormanstown House to the north of Dublin. She was the eldest of three children born to James and Elinor (Conway) McAuley. A series of financial reversals and the early death of their parents left Catherine and her siblings destitute and virtually homeless by the time Catherine was twenty years old. Eventually she obtained employment as caretaker and estate manager for William and Catherine Callaghan, a wealthy couple living outside of Dublin. As the sole beneficiary of the Callaghan estate, Catherine found herself, in her mid-forties, a wealthy spinster. Her determination to use her wealth, as a contemporary recalls, "to secure the lasting relief of the suffering and the instruction of the ig-

Catherine McAuley

norant" (Sullivan, p. 151) led her to construct a House of Mercy on Baggot Street in Dublin. Here a variety of social services were made available to poor persons in the surrounding neighborhoods, especially young working women.

From its beginning, the House of Mercy was supported and encouraged by Dublin's Archbishop Daniel Murray. Murray was one of several Irish episcopal leaders who offered leadership to nineteenth-century efforts to revitalize Catholic identity and self-esteem. His particular focus sought to renew the sacramental life of the people, to address the basic needs of impoverished faithful, and to increase the number of clergy, churches and schools in his diocese. Support of Catherine's work fit quite naturally into this larger schema.

Ultimately it was Archbishop Murray who persuaded Catherine and her sisters to seek approbation as a religious congregation. A letter to her spiritual advisor, Rev. Francis L'Estrange, O.D.C., makes clear that Catherine's original intention was not to establish a religious congregation but rather to create a setting in which "ladies who prefer a conventual life, and are prevented embracing it from the nature of property or connections, may retire" (Bolster, *Correspondence*, p. 2). Eventually, however, the works and women multiplied to such an extent that Catherine found herself confronted with a choice: to disband in the face of harsh criticism or to seek approbation as a religious congregation. Catherine began the process for approbation in 1833. In July 1841 formal approbation was given to the *Rule and Constitutions*. By this time, Catherine was visibly failing from the ravages of tuberculosis. On November 11, 1841, she died in the House of Mercy, leaving a legacy of community and service. Already the Baggot Street House had dispersed women to eleven additional sites in Ireland and two locations in England and requests had been received from Newfoundland and the United States.

### BEGINNINGS OF THE SISTERS OF MERCY IN THE UNITED STATES

The nineteenth century was a time of high unemployment in Ireland and of migration to urban areas of the country. Uneven educational opportunities, neighborhood decay, urban and rural tensions, and the threat of poor houses and work houses awaited most migrants to the cities. As a result, men, women, and children sought relief in emigration to other countries. Requests for assistance with the immigrant population came to various convents of Mercy in Ireland from around the world.

The first band set foot on the North American continent within six months of Catherine's death. Bishop Anthony Fleming of St. John's, Newfoundland, sent Frances Creedon to Ireland to be formed as a Sister of Mercy. When she returned to St. John's, Newfoundland, in June 1842, Mary Ursula Frayne and Rose Lynch accompanied her. They came after several earnest requests from Bishop Fleming who depicted his territory as "a country . . . whose institutions are in their infancy, without a single charitable asylum from one end to the other of an island larger than Ireland, possessing a rapidly increasing population, among whom honesty and sobriety prevail" (Annals, Vol. III, p. 18).

Between 1843 and 1890, an additional sixty-two women in nine different groups left from various Mercy convents in Ireland and in England to found Mercy communities in the Americas. Six of these "colonies," as they were termed by their contemporaries, were destined for the United States. One colony departed for Buenos Aires, Argentina; while two journeyed to the Caribbean region—Jamaica and British Guyana. The stories of these early women come to us through the simple tools of women's history: diaries, letters, house chronicles, and occasional newspaper clippings. Frances Warde and six companions came from Carlow to Pittsburgh (1843). Dublin's Baggot Street Convent sent Agnes O'Connor and seven companions to New York City (1846). Teresa Farrell and three companions from Naas traveled to Little Rock (1851) with three hundred farmers and their families. The Mercy Convent in Kinsale sent Baptist Russell and seven companions to San Francisco (1854) and, four years later, sent Teresa Maher and eight companions to Cincinnati (1858). Agnes Healy and Mary Teresa Perry, sent from Ennis, divided their eleven member colony into two groups to found the congregation in Meridan and Middletown, Connecticut (1872).

Most of these first women of Mercy in the United States were under the age of thirty. Many were recently professed. Some were only novices or postulants. Mary Baptist Russell was twenty-five years old, three years professed, when she set sail as superior of the band headed for San Francisco. Frances Warde, Teresa Maher, and Agnes O'Connor were all in their early thirties. The seven Sisters of Mercy who journeyed to Pittsburgh represent the mixed profile of most of the early colonies. Frances Warde, Josephine Cullen and Elizabeth Strange were all professed and, in the case of Frances and Josephine, experienced administrators in their early thirties. Aloysia Strange, a novice, would become the first Sister of Mercy to make her vows in the United States. Philomena Reid, also a novice, would die within two years. Margaret (Mary Agatha) O'Brien, a twenty-one-year-old postulant, would profess her vows in May 1846, and in September of the same year would become leader of the new community of Sisters of Mercy in Chicago. Veronica McDarby, the only one who had not volunteered for service in America, served as portress for the convent in Pittsburgh for forty years. Her death was mourned by the poor of the city among whom she had become a beloved figure of compassion and concern.

When the first Sisters of Mercy arrived in Pittsburgh in 1843, the vast mission territory of the United States consisted of only twenty-three dioceses, the newest of these—Chicago, Hartford, Little Rock, Milwaukee, Pittsburgh, and Portland (Oregon)— having been formed that same year. Within days of their arrival, whatever their destination and whatever the circumstances into which they walked, the Sisters began visitation of the sick, comfort of the distressed, and Christian education programs for adults and children. Various educational, health care and social service institutions often followed in each location.

There were also events which called forth courage, resourcefulness and compassion to an extraordinary degree. The typhoid epidemic of 1848 in Pittsburgh claimed the lives of four sisters in one month, including Xavier Tiernan, the first woman in the United States to become a Sister of Mercy. Six years later in Chicago cholera claimed the lives of four sisters in a single weekend. When derogatory newspaper articles greeted the arrival of the Sisters of Mercy in San Francisco, their honor was defended by the captain of the ship that carried them into port. Likewise, when several hundred members of the Know-Nothing Party in Providence, Rhode Island, in 1855 threatened the Mercy Convent of Frances Warde and her sisters, local citizenry came to their rescue. The Civil War called forth still another outpouring of practical energy and gentle concern. Pittsburgh, New York City, Chicago, Vicksburg, Cincinnati, and Baltimore sisters either opened their own facilities to care for the wounded or traveled wherever they were needed.

A period of expansion followed the Civil War for the country and for the Sisters of Mercy. Catherine McAuley, in accounting

for the beginnings of the Sisters of Mercy, recalled that "it commenced with two, Sister Doyle and I" (Neumann, p. 154). She would have been astounded at the growth and institutionalization of the Sisters of Mercy and their works throughout the nineteenth and early twentieth century. By 1929 membership in the Sisters of Mercy in the United States numbered 9,308 women in sixty independent mother houses (Sabourin, pp. 296–297).

## CONTINUATION OF THE SISTERS OF MERCY OF THE AMERICAS INTO THE TWENTY-FIRST CENTURY

The Institute of the Sisters of Mercy of the Americas is one of eight such Mercy organizations that have been formed throughout the world since 1841. Others are located in Ireland, Australia, Great Britain, New Zealand, Newfoundland, and the Philippines. Worldwide, Sisters of Mercy number nearly thirteen thousand. In the United States, these women are joined in their efforts by 1,458 Mercy Associates, men and women who make a formal commitment to share in various aspects of Mercy life and ministry. Since 1978, thirty-some men and women of all ages and backgrounds have been commissioned annually to Mercy Corps, a volunteer lay ministry program whose participants spend one or two years in service in ministry sites sponsored or staffed by Sisters of Mercy. The Institute Office for the Sisters of Mercy of the Americas is located in Silver Spring, Maryland. Twenty-five regional community offices are located in Albany, Brooklyn, Buffalo, Dobbs Ferry, and Rochester, NY; Auburn and Burlingame, CA; Baltimore, MD; Cedar Rapids, IA; Chicago, IL; Cincinnati, OH; West Hartford, CT; Dallas, Erie, Merion Station, and Pittsburgh, PA; Farmington Hills, MI; Windham, NH; Watchung, NJ; Belmont, NC; Omaha, NE; Portland, ME; Cumberland, RI; St. Louis, MO; and Burlington, VT.

M. Angela Bolster, *Catherine McAuley: Venerable for Mercy* (Dublin, 1990).

Carmel Bourke, *A Woman Sings of Mercy* (Sydney, 1987).

Helen Marie Burns and Sheila Carney, *Praying with Catherine McAuley* (Winona, MN, 1996).

M. Austin Carroll, *Leaves from the Annals of the Sisters of Mercy*, 4 vols. (New York, 1881, 1883, 1888, 1895).

Catherine Darcy, *The Institute of the Sisters of Mercy of the Americas* (New York, 1993).

M. Bertrand Degnan, *Mercy Unto Thousands* (Westminster, MD, 1957).

M. Ignatia Neumann, *Letters of Catherine McAuley* (Baltimore, 1969).

M. Justine Sabourin, *The Amalgamation* (St. Meinrad, IN, 1976).

Mary Sullivan, *Catherine McAuley and the Tradition of Mercy* (Notre Dame, 1995).

HELEN MARIE BURNS, R.S.M.

## SMILIE, JOHN (1742–1813)

Politician. A leader of western Pennsylvania's predominantly Irish political radicals during and after the American Revolution, Smilie was born in or near Greyabbey, Co. Down, into a Presbyterian family of middling circumstances. In 1762, aged nineteen, he sailed from Belfast to Philadelphia, in a horrific voyage during which sixty-four passengers died of starvation. In 1771 Smilie owned and farmed merely eighty acres in Dromore Township, Lancaster (now Dauphin) County, but the American Revolution precipitated his rapid rise to wealth and influence. In 1775 he was a member of Lancaster County's revolutionary committee, and in 1776 he was chosen a militia sergeant and a member of the provincial congress. In 1778 and 1779 Lancaster's voters elected Smilie to the Pennsylvania General Assembly, but in 1781 he moved his family west of the Alleghenies and settled in Tyrone Township in what was then Westmoreland (from 1784 Fayette) County. By 1783 he owned three hundred acres, later purchased at least six hundred more, and became part of western Pennsylvania's frontier élite. His political career also flourished: between 1783 and his death, Smilie won election to the state's Council of Censors (1783), the General Assembly (1784–89 and 1795–98), the Supreme Executive Council (1786–89), the state convention that ratified the Federal Constitution (1787), the state constitutional convention (1789–90), the state Senate (1790), and the U.S. House of Representatives (1793–95 and 1798–1813). Despite his new affluence, Smilie represented the Scots-Irish radicalism that generally prevailed in Pennsylvania's backcountry. An ally of George Bryan and William Findley, Smilie defended Pennsylvania's ultra-democratic 1776 constitution, supported the state's abolition of slavery (1780), and became a violent Anti-Federalist in 1787–88, a Jeffersonian Republican in the 1790s, and, his Federalist enemies alleged, an instigator of the Whiskey Rebellion in 1794.

*See* Scots Irish

---

E. Everett, "John Smilie, Forgotten Champion of Early Western Pennsylvania," *Western Pennsylvania Historical Magazine,* 33 (1950): 77–89.

R. C. Henderson, "John Smilie, Antifederalism, and the 'Dissent of the Minority,' 1787–1788," *idem.,* 77 (1988): 235–61.

On Smilie's voyage, see his letter in the *Belfast News-Letter* (May 13, 1763).

KERBY MILLER

## SMITH, ALFRED EMANUEL (1873–1944)

Governor of New York and presidential candidate. Smith was born on December 30, 1873, on the Lower East Side of Manhattan where immigrants took racial diversity and poverty as normal. He was named Alfred Emanuel Smith after his father, who was of Italian and German parentage (and there is no record of when he assumed the name Smith). His mother, Catherine Mulvihill, was born of an Irish father and an English mother. So young Alfred, known as Al, personified the ethnicity of the land of immigrants—part German, Italian, Irish and English. He grew up surrounded by Irish neighbors, opted to be Irish, and was accepted as such forevermore.

He attended the local Catholic school, where he was an average student, and became an altar boy at St. James Church. In 1884 he won a citywide oratory contest for an oration on Robespierre. The following year his father, a trucker by trade, died and left his wife and two children in poor financial shape. Shortly thereafter, Al quit school and took odd jobs. He worked for two years at the Fulton Fish market and later went to work for a boiler company; but realized that politics was his exit ticket from dead-end jobs.

Local saloons were community meeting houses, and their owners, especially when they had political connections, were men of standing and influence. Tom Foley, whose bar was a Democratic forum, showed Al Smith the ropes of Tammany politics. In 1894 Foley successfully opposed Richard Croker's and Tammany Hall's selection of the Fourth District's congressional seat, and Smith's diligence won the confidence of Foley, who used patronage with finesse. The following year Smith was appointed process server for the commissioner of jurors with a salary of $800 a year, a good salary for a young man at the time. Tom Foley mended his fences with Tammany Hall, the Democratic nerve

Alfred E. Smith

center in New York, and in 1903 he had Smith selected as a Democratic candidate for the state assemby of New York. His winning was due to the political muscle of Tammany Hall.

Tammany Hall was originally a social club whose early members included Aaron Burr and Andrew Jackson. When Jackson was elected president in 1828, Tammany became a powerful political machine in New York City. Over the decades its significant social contributions were overshadowed by the corruption of some of its leaders, especially William Marcy "Boss" Tweed, whose graft and fraud landed him in jail where he died in 1878. Again, during the leadership of Richard "Boss" Croker from 1896 to 1902, corruption became so blatant that New Yorkers elected Seth Law as a reform mayor in 1901. Regardless of the probity of most of its leaders, Tammany Hall was a tarnished name in the public mind.

Smith became an expert in assembly procedures and the structures of state government. In this he was aided by Robert Wagner, a future governor and U.S. Senator. He became Wagner's roommate and both sided with the interests of working families. Gradually, Smith became one of the best-informed advocates of labor legislation and insurance reform. In 1911 he became the leader of the Democratic majority and chairman of the Ways and Means committee, and two years later he was chosen as Speaker of the Assembly. He became closely associated with humanitarian issues such as workmen's compensation, rent control, and decent working conditions for women and children. He became the ardent advocate of home rule for New York City and for a state conservation department. Al Smith was a pragmatist and rose above ideological and partisan bickering. He was not beholden to Tammany Hall but he kept his connections and conferred regularly with its leader, Charles F. Murphy, and the men who dispensed favors and patronage. Reformers were drawn by Smith's commitment to social reform and decent government, and gradually he became the political friend of progressives and earned the support of the reformist Citizen's Union. This was a good base for an ambitious young politician.

A tragic fire brought Smith into wider prominence. In 1911, a fire at the Triangle Shirtwaist Company in Manhattan took 146 lives, most underpaid women and children. America was appalled at the dreadful working conditions in too many factories in cities. Smith sponsored legislation for an investigating commission to examine working conditions in factories in New York State. Robert Wagner was chosen as chairman, and Smith as vice chairman. The commission brought together the brightest and the best among social activists and reformers. The inquiry's findings in 1915 shocked the nation and gave Smith the opening to launch sweeping legislation on health, sanitation and fire laws, on workmen's compensation, and on the working conditions for women and children. Smith's reputation grew and his outlook broadened. He became a convert to women's suffrage. At the constitutional convention, Smith led the way for government reforms and advanced the fight for home rule for New York City. His mastery of procedure and of the intricacies of state government won him the plaudits of republican stalwarts, such as Henry Simpson and Elihu Root.

He sought and fought for political advancement, and in the autumn of 1915 he was elected sheriff of New York City. He needed the position as it offered an income of $60,000 a year, and financial security, something he had never known. He had married Catherine Dunn, an Irish woman from the Bronx, and they had five children: Alfred Emanuel, Emily, Catherine, Arthur, and Walter. His new position gave him an opportunity to enjoy family life and some leisure.

## Legendary Governor

Friends urged him to run for mayor in 1917. But Tammany's leader, Charles F. Murphy, had other plans, and he picked John F. Hylan of Brooklyn, who won easily, while Smith was elected president of the board of aldermen. But in the following year he was chosen over William Randolph Hearst to be the Democratic candidate for the governorship of New York. He selected talented helpers, as he usually did, such as Frances Perkins, Joseph Proskauer, Belle Moskowitz, and many other able and versatile men and women flocked to Alfred E. Smith. It was a Republican year, but in the GOP sweep, Smith beat Governor Charles S. Whitman by 15,000 votes.

Smith's constructive agenda for the first of his four terms as governor of New York set his course and hopes. Despite unrelenting Republican and business opposition, he sponsored low-cost housing, the temporary extension of rent controls, control on milk prices, and the reorganization of state government. He opposed anti-sedition legislation, which sought to curtail the civil liberties of socialists and other groups that disagreed with the rightist positions of the proponents. He ran into unexpected grassroots opposition when he successfully sought to outlaw the Ku Klux Klan.

He lost reelection to Republican Nathan L. Miller. Two years later he overwhelmed Miller; in 1924 he easily defeated Theodore Roosevelt, Jr.; and in 1926 he swamped Ogden Mills for his fourth term. Will Rogers wrote of him: "The man you ran against ain't a candidate, he is a victim." Smith is regarded as one of the great governors of New York. In the face of opposition from many quarters, his persistence reduced 152 unwieldy state agencies to a handful of cabinet posts. He stood fast for social equality, conservation, safety regulations, bond issues for parks and recreation facilities, the extension of state education, and civil liberties.

## National Politics

In 1920 Al Smith's name was mentioned as a possible Democratic candidate, and his name became known and accepted nationwide. James M. Cox was selected, with Franklin D. Roosevelt as his running mate. Warren G. Harding won a landslide victory for the GOP, and Al Smith decided to seek the nomination in 1924.

The Ku Klux Klan was revived in Georgia in 1915 and spread rapidly in Southern and Western states. By 1924 it was a political factor with its anti-Catholic, anti-Jewish, anti-immigration agenda; and it became the divisive issue in the Democratic convention in New York. The delegates failed to endorse a resolution to condemn the Klan, whose members were prominent in many Southern and Western delegations. Smith realized he had underestimated the undercurrent of bigotry in American life.

The leading candidate, William McAdoo of California, refused to take a stand on the issue, and Smith felt his neutrality was a tacit endorsement of the Klan. McAdoo had wide Southern and Western support and sought the backing of fundamentalist stalwarts such as William Jennings Bryan. Smith disliked McAdoo, whose supporters felt that as the son-in-law of Woodrow Wilson and as a former secretary of the treasury he should win the nomination. Smith was nominated by Franklin D. Roosevelt, whose speech is one of the memorable episodes of the tumultuous convention. Roosevelt closed with the famous Wordsworth couplet: "This is the happy warrior: this is he/Whom everyman in arms should wish to be." In the long run, the speech benefited Roosevelt more than Smith. The balloting began on June 30 and McAdoo led Smith all the way but hadn't the votes needed for nomination. Day after day, in sultry heat, the balloting dragged on, Smith held firm, and on July 9 McAdoo knew that he had lost in a deadlocked convention after 109 ballots. The weary delegates turned to John W. Davis of West Virginia and chose Charles Bryan, William Jennings' brother, for vice president.

It was a weak ticket and in the presidential election, Calvin Coolidge had an overwhelming victory, polling over fifteen million votes to Davis's eight million. Robert LaFollette ran impressively as a Progressive Socialist and drew almost five million votes. The Republicans won both houses of Congress. But in New York Smith won his fourth term as governor by a comfortable margin of over a million votes, and prepared for the presidential election of 1928.

## Candidate Smith

To humor the South, Houston was chosen as the site of the Democratic convention of 1928. Four years of planning and publicity made Smith the unbeatable candidate. Again he was nominated by Franklin D. Roosevelt, but his nomination was never unanimous. Four Southern states refused to vote for him, and the platform supported prohibition while Smith opposed it. His selection gave hope that a Democrat would occupy the White House for the third time since the Civil War and a Catholic would be elected president of the United States. He chose Joseph T. Robinson—a dry and a Southern Protestant—as his running mate.

The candidate usually selected the head of the Democratic National Committee, and against the advice of seasoned politicians, he selected John J. Raskob, a rich industrialist, a Catholic, and a Republican. While Harry Byrd of Virginia, Scott Ferrio of Oklahoma, Nellie Taylor Ross of Wyoming, and other national and state Democrats joined the Smith camp, the real power was vested in a select executive committee consisting of James Hoey, Franklin D. Roosevelt, George Van Namee, Herbert Lehman, Belle Moskowitz, and Peter Gerry (the only non-New Yorker).

The GOP selected Herbert C. Hoover, Secretary of Commerce, a solid, experienced and conservative Republican, who felt that

America with a booming economy would not elect a Catholic with a Tammany background. He was right. The campaign brought out the worst in American life. Prohibition, which Hoover called "the noble experiment," was a grassroots issue with support much wider than its fundamentalist base. Will Rogers got it right: "The voting strength of this country is dry."

The Catholic question was the big issue for vocal bigots, but it also created discussion and reservations in academic and professional quarters. *The Atlantic Monthly* published an article by an eminent Episcopalian lawyer, Charles C. Marshall, in April 1927 which questioned Smith's ability as a Catholic to be president. Smith retorted that he wasn't a theologian and "never heard of these bulls and encyclicals and books." Reluctantly, he responded and Joseph Proskauer drafted a reply and had it vetted by Fr. Francis P. Duffy, Irving Lehman, and others. When Smith's rebuttal was published, it created some discussion, but it influenced few in prosperous America. And the business community, basking in a booming economy and projecting increasing prosperity, backed Hoover as a trustworthy guardian of free enterprise. In agricultural quarters, Smith was the Tammany urbanite politician who knew little of rural America's problems and values. The farmers didn't like him.

When the votes were counted, Herbert Hoover was swept to the White House with some twenty-one million votes while Alfred E. Smith trailed with fifteen million. Hoover won 444 electoral college votes to Smith's 81. The loss of the election was a disappointment, but his rejection by the voters of his own state was the most painful episode of the campaign.

### Bitter Verdict, Bitter Loser

After the election, Smith was a disillusioned man; his political career had come to an end, and power and influence ebbed away. Franklin Roosevelt had bucked the Republican sweep and won the governorship of New York. He quickly disengaged himself as neatly as possible from Smith, whose disappointment festered and grew into resentment. After the stock market collapsed in 1929 and the economy floundered, Roosevelt dubbed Hoover the architect of economic disaster and set his course to oust Hoover in 1932. Smith was moved by economic devastation and was appalled by the inaction of the government. But he resented Roosevelt and viewed his professed concern for "the forgotten man at the bottom of the economic pyramid" as political opportunism. He launched a futile attempt to deprive Roosevelt of the 1932 Democratic nomination and felt that he, not Roosevelt, should oust Hoover from the White House.

Smith became a celebrity and was the welcome guest at the leading social and socialite events. He took up residence in an exclusive Fifth Avenue apartment and moved in the best business circles. He became president of the Empire State Building Corporation (with the help of John J. Raskob, one of its powerful directors) with a salary of $50,000. He joined corporation boards and became a prominent speaker for executive gatherings. As chairman of a trust company, he attacked the New Deal; and in a monthly column in the *New Outlook* he excoriated its policies. He joined the Liberty League, founded in 1934 for industrialists, corporation lawyers, and conservatives of both major parties, and the League actively opposed such measures as the Wagner-Connery Labor Relations Bill and the Wealth Tax Bill. In 1936 he voted for Republican Alfred Landon and canvassed for Wendell Willkie in 1940. Many of his old friends and supporters felt betrayed. He died in October 1944, and it is per-

plexing that a major biography of Alfred Emanuel Smith has yet to be written.

*See* New York City; New York State; Tammany Hall

Oscar Handlin, *Al Smith and His America* (Boston, 1958).

Matthew and Hannah Josephson, *Al Smith: Hero of the City* (New York, 1969).

E. A. Moore, *A Catholic Runs for President: The Campaign of 1928* (New York, 1956).

Moskowitz, Haogood and Henry, *Up from the Streets: Alfred Smith* (New York, 1927).

Elizabeth Israels Perry, *Belle Moskowitz* (New York, 1987).

Alfred E. Smith, *Up to Now: An Autobiography* (New York, 1929).

———, *Public Papers,* 8 vols. (Albany, 1919–38).

MICHAEL GLAZIER

## SMITH, JEAN KENNEDY (1928–  )

Ambassador. Smith was born February 20, 1928, in Brookline, Massachusetts, the eighth child of Rose Fitzgerald Kennedy and Joseph P. Kennedy, a wealthy businessman who also served as American ambassador to Great Britain from 1938–1941. Educated in private schools by the Roman Catholic Society of the Sacred Heart, Smith earned a BA degree from Manhattanville College in 1949. She married businessman Stephen E. Smith (dec.) in 1956; the couple had four children, including two by adoption: Stephen, William, Amanda, and Kym.

Interested in the arts, Smith was an assistant to Father James Keller, M.M, the founder of the Catholic group, The Christophers, and worked on The Christopher Hour, a weekly television program. In 1974, Smith founded Very Special Arts, an international arts program for young disabled people, and serves as its director and chair. In 1993, she authored (with George Plimpton) *Chronicles of Courage,* a book about the program and its participants.

Since 1956, Smith has helped her prominent family realize its political ambitions by assisting in several Kennedy campaigns for public office, including those of her three brothers: President John F. Kennedy; Senator Robert F. Kennedy (D. N.Y.); and Senator Edward M. Kennedy (D. Mass.).

Smith was appointed American ambassador to Ireland in 1993 by President William Clinton. She served for five years, before resigning in 1998. During Smith's tenure, the American government involved itself more directly in efforts to end conflict in Northern Ireland, in particular by granting entry visas to the United States to members of the Irish Republican Army (IRA) and its political wing, Sinn Fein. Some see this involvement as having contributed to the IRA ceasefire and subsequent peace process in the region, which led to the Good Friday Agreement of April 1998.

Smith is a trustee of the Joseph P. Kennedy, Jr., Foundation, the John F. Kennedy Center for the Performing Arts, and the recipient of several civic and humanitarian awards.

Doris Kearns Goodwin, *The Fitzgeralds and the Kennedys* (New York, 1987).

Lawrence Leamer, *The Kennedy Women: The Saga of an American Family* (New York, 1994).

KATHLEEN N. McCARTHY

## SOUTH CAROLINA

Irish emigration to South Carolina was concentrated in the period 1730–1775. It was the major site of settlement of Irish in the southern colonies. A majority of these, called Scotch-Irish, were from the northern province of Ulster, but there was also a substantial number of immigrants of the older Irish stock from all parts of Ireland. That more of the Catholic Irish group did not come in this period was due, in part, to the general hostility to Roman Catholicism in the colonies. In the early years of the eighteenth century, the South Carolina Assembly attempted to block immigration of Catholic Irish, but the legislation was vetoed by the colony's proprietors who viewed it as an encroachment on their rights. In his pioneering *History of South Carolina,* David Ramsay declared, "Of all countries none has furnished the province with so many inhabitants, as Ireland."

Captain Florence O'Sullivan, from Kinsale, County Cork, for whom Sullivan's Island is named, was one of the original settlers in the Carolina colonly. Land owner, legislator, Indian fighter and first surveyor-general, he was an energetic and controversial figure. Local legend has it that when O'Sullivan came ashore in 1760 at Bull's Island, north of Charleston, he was greeted by a native Irishman, a "Mr. Oppossum." O'Sullivan obviously was not Scotch-Irish. Neither was this true of John Barnwell, a native of Dublin for whom Barnwell County is named, who was part of the Protestant Irish group that began to arrive in the late eighteenth century.

The South Carolina proprietors sought Irish emigrants through a variety of means. Two pamphlets extolling the virtues of the colony were printed in Dublin during the 1680s. The earliest organized venture of emigration from Ireland took place in 1716 when five hundred Irish Protestants, encouraged by generous land offers, settled the Yemassee lands. Three years later the proprietors decided to abandon their efforts to settle this area, with the consequence that the Irish settlers "lost the title to their land and they could not even recover the money they had paid for the land."

South Carolina had two Irish-born governors in the early colonial period. Thinking that a governor from abroad would be more devoted to their interests, the proprietors appointed Richard Kyrle of Cork, a knight and timber merchant, to this position in 1684, but he died shortly after his arrival from Ireland. The other Irish-born governor was James Moore, a descendant of Roger Moore, a leader in the 1641 rebellion in Ireland. "The blood of his rebellious ancestors seemed to evidence itself in Moore's own activities, for he soon identified himself with the discontented elements and was active in movements of protest" (*Dictionary of American Biography,* vol. vii). He was elected governor by the colonial council in 1700 and served until 1703. His son, General James Moore, led the effort that ended the proprietors' control in 1719 and was governor until 1721.

The pressing need to increase the population was addressed by Governor Robert Johnson when he put forward in 1730 a land settlement plan for several European groups. A settlement for Irish Protestants at Williamsburg (named for William of Orange) was begun with an area of twenty square miles. A Dublin newspaper announced in 1733 the impending departure of the *Charming Sally,* which would arrive "within twenty miles of the Irish settlement."

In 1751 a small group of Irish Quakers, from Timahoe, County Kildare, established a community at Mulberry on the Wateree River. A Friends Monthly Meeting was maintained until the early 1780s, by which time some Irish Quakers had moved to North Carolina and Virginia.

The colony launched several bounty schemes directed at the Protestant Irish in the 1760s. These included money payments for each immigrant and land grants to heads of families. The bounty of 1767 included free passage. These attractions undoubtedly were largely responsible for the increased emigration from Ireland in the period leading up to the Revolution.

After 1760 Irish immigration shifted from the low country to the western hill area, as the Scotch-Irish moved down the Appalachians. According to D. D. Wallace, this group "fairly swarmed into the up country." The townships of Belfast, Londonderry and Boonesborough were designated for Irish Protestants and thousands of Irish settlers moved down to the backcountry from Pennsylvania through the Great Valley of Virginia. Speaking of this influx into the colony in the 1760s, Wallace comments: "This was mainly the Scotch-Irish era, as the 1730s and 40s were mainly the German era." In the late 1760s the Irish-born Anglican clergyman Charles Woodmason was not impressed with one community he encountered: "They are very poor owing to their Indolence. They delight in their present low, lazy, sluttish, heathenish, hellish life, and seem not desirous of changing it."

In his history of South Carolina and Georgia published in 1779, Alexander Hewatt noted the migration of English and Scots in this period, then commented: "But of all other countries none has furnished the province with so many inhabitants as Ireland. In the northern counties of that kingdom the spirit of emigration seized the people to such a degree it threatened almost a total depopulation. . . ." Further, shipping agents, finding the bounty equivalent to the expenses of the passage, "persuaded the people to embark for Carolina, and often crammed such numbers of them into their ships that they were landed in such a starved condition that numbers of them died before they left Charleston." He went on the account for this exodus:

> Many causes may be assigned for this spirit of emigration that prevailed so much in Ireland: some, no doubt, emigrated from a natural restlessness of temper, and a desire of roving abroad without any fixed object in view. Others were enticed over by flattering promises from their friends and relations, who had gone before them. But of all other causes of emigration oppression at home was the most powerful and prevalent. . . . Hence it happened that many poor people forsook their native land, and preferred the burning sky and unwholesome climate of Carolina to the Temperate and mild air of their mother country.

In the few years before the outbreak of the Revolution there was heavy Irish immigration to the ports of the colonies and Charleston was no exception. The *South Carolina Gazette* noted the arrival of several shiploads of Irish people in 1772. A Dublin newspaper estimated that in the period 1772–75 about one thousand Irish arrived at Charleston or Charles Town, as it was then named. In 1773 a Mr. Hunt advertised in a Dublin newspaper that he had chartered the brig *Hope* for a voyage to South Carolina and was prepared to take passengers, including "young married couples," to settle his lands in South Carolina and Georgia.

Most of the Irish arrived as indentured servants. Henry Laurens of Charleston denounced the cruel treatment, that "would make your humanity shudder," meted out to a group of Irish who arrived in 1768. Another view of the situation is provided by a letter written in Charleston in 1773: "The Irish are considered as welcome Guests as they are generally industrious, and in this low and marshy Country have a Value in being what others deride them for—Bog Trotters."

## THE REVOLUTION IN SOUTH CAROLINA

Irishmen were prominant in the Revolution in South Carolina. These included the Rutledges, Lynchs, O'Neales and Burkes. Two of the four South Carolina signatories of the Declaration of Independence were of Irish stock. Edward Rutledge's father, John, emigrated from Ireland in 1735. Thomas Lynch, Senior, was the grandson of an immigrant from Connaught. Edward Rutledge's brother, John, was one of the four state signers of the Constitution of 1789, as was Pierce Butler, a native of County Carlow, and later the first U.S. senator from South Carolina.

Notable figures in the revolutionary Carolinas were two Burkes—Thomas and Aedanus, both natives of Ireland and probably related. They are representative of a substantial group of educated Irishmen who were part of the radical and revolutionary movement that spanned the Atlantic in the late eighteenth century. Dr. Thomas Burke, born in Galway in 1747, emigrated to Virgnia in 1759 or 1760. Moving to North Carolina in 1771, he quickly rose to be a member of Congress and then governor of his adopted state, where he rallied opposition to the British invasion of 1781.

Aedanus Burke was born in 1743, also in Galway, and arrived in America some time before 1769. In South Carolina he served as an officer in the militia, judge, delegate to state conventions, congressman and chancellor of the state court of equity. It has been said of him that "neither principle nor policy obscured his courage, his Irish wit or his irascible temper."

Saint Patrick's Day was regularly observed in the Continental Army (and in the British Army!) and this included units from South Carolina. On March 16, 1778 the order was issued to the First Regiment of the South Carolina Line that "tomorow being St. Patrick's Day such Non-Commissioned officers and soldiers as are Natives to the kingdom of Ireland are to be Excused Duty and the paymaster will pay them tomorrow the pay due to them."

Almost all military historians agree that the battle of King's Mountain was a turning point of the war in the South. Here too there was an Irish dimension. In October 1780 a British force headed west along the Carolina border hoping to join forces with loyalist Scottish Highlanders. A formation composed largely of Scotch-Irish, drawn from what were later named Burke County, North Carolina, and Sullivan County, Tennessee, and other places, defeated this force.

Henry Clinton, the British Commander-in-Chief, viewed the Irish as "our most serious antagonists." In order to divert opposition from this source, in 1778 he formed the Volunteers of Ireland, a regiment composed of Irish deserters from the Continental Army. Having risen to a strength of three hundred, the regiment was shipped from New York to South Carolina in 1780. Charles Cornwallis, whose army had just occupied Charleston, dispatched this unit to Waxhaw, on the North Carolina border, in the belief that "as it was an Irish corps it would be received with a better temper by the settlers of that district who were universally Irish and universally disaffected." Instead of gaining recruits, its commander found he was losing soldiers by desertion. It was probably at this time and place that a British officer inflicted a saber wound on the face of young Andrew Jackson, both of whose parents were born in Ireland; Jackson did not forget either matter.

After the war what remained of the Volunteers was shipped to Ireland and the unit was disbanded in 1784.

One of the areas of greatest Patriot support in South Carolina, the Chester district, also had a large Irish population. The leading rebel in the area was General Edward Lacey. His biographer, Maurice A. Moore, states, "Lacey organized companies and battalions as the fortunes of war demanded and after the manner of partisan leaders, with which he annoyed the Tories greatly, taking many of them prisoners. Of these there were a few in his neighborhood, but not among the Irish. To their eternal honor let it be spoken, none of these York or Chester Irish were Tories, and but few of them took British protection." One of Lacey's officers was Captain John McClure, a hero of the battle of Rocky Mount in 1780. Benson Lossing says that "he was one of the master spirits of South Carolina . . . and his men were known as the Chester Rock Creek Irish."

Dr. David Ramsay, a South Carolina historian, whose two-volume history of the war published in 1793 is considered to be the best initial chronicle of the conflict, saw the Irish as a key factor in the outcome: "The Irish in America, with few exceptions, were attached to independence. They had fled from oppression in their native country, and could not brook the idea that it should follow them. Their national prepossessions in favor of liberty were strengthened by their religious opinions. They were Presbyterians, and people of that denomination . . . were mostly Whigs."

Another South Carolinian, Alexander Garden, who also had direct experience of the Revolution, declared: "In the ranks of our armies there were many of the sons of Erin, who felt the injuries heaped upon us, as injuries to themselves, and fought for America as they would have fought for Ireland." William Gilmore Simms has asserted that, alone among the foreign-born groups in Charleston, the Irish opposed continued British rule. According to Bishop John England of Charleston, the involvement of the Irish in the Patriot cause was largely responsible for the removal of religious disabilities imposed on Catholics following the Revolution.

One of the Irishmen who remained loyal to the Crown was Robert Cunningham (1739–1813), who arrived from Ireland in 1769 and settled in the Ninety-Six district. As a result of his opposition to the Revolution, he was imprisoned in Charleston but was released when the British occupied the city in 1780. He served as a brigadier general in the loyalist militia and after the war went into exile in Nassau. Another Irishman was James O'Fallon (1749–1794), who, after medical training in Edinburgh, served as a surgeon in the Continental Army. Following the war he was a member of the Charleston Marine Anti-Britannic Society. In 1790 he was appointed general agent of the South Carolina Yazoo Company and became involved in a plan to create a separate political entity along the Mississipi. President George Washington squelched the plot with a public proclamation.

After the war Aedanus Burke took the lead in the process of reconciliation in South Carolina. David Ramsay paid tribute to this "Irish gentleman, who, with the gallantry characteristic of his nation, . . . generously undertook to advocate the cause of those who, in the hour of danger, had by a change of allegiance sought protection from the present conqueror" (*History of South Carolina*, v. 2, 273–74).

## IRISH ORGANIZATIONS

The first Irish organization to emerge in South Carolina was the Irish Society of Charleston, formed in 1749. Following its first St.

Patrick's Day gathering, a poem by Joseph Dumbleton appeared in the *South Carolina Gazette*:

> The Muse an Ode select prepares,
> With splendid Bowls the Board in crown'd
> Thine Harp awakes in solemn Airs
> O Saint! while thy great Name goes round,
> As Victims on thy festal Day,
> Our choicest Firstlings we resign,
> And for glad Libation, pay
> Our finest Wheat and purest Wine.

This group was probably the forerunner to the Friendly Sons of St. Patrick, which was organized in 1773, with Edward Rutledge as its secretary-treasurer. After the war, in 1786 the Friendly Brothers of Ireland was formed, with Pierce Butler as its president. The 1798 rebellion in Ireland inspired the establishment of the Hibernian Society of Charleston the next year. It is the oldest organization of ethnic origin with its own premises in the country. Its principal purpose was "to contribute towards the fund to relieve distressed emigrants." The society proceeded to build an imposing Greek-style meeting hall and its membership was composed of the leading political, professional and business people of Charleston. Although Irish immigration to the state was small, the society provided financial assistance to just about every Irish person who applied up to the Civil War. In 1830 when James Kenny asked for help towards purchasing a horse, thirty dollars were provided.

Two other long-established Irish organizations were the Irish Volunteers Company of Charleston, founded in 1798, and the St. Patrick's Benevolent Society, formed in 1817, whose long-time president was John Magrath, a 1798 refugee and father of a South Carolina governor. At a joint St. Patrick's Day dinner of the three groups in 1841, the guest of honor was John C. Calhoun.

## CAROLINA LIFE

A leading figure in the intellectual world of Charleston was the Irish-born priest Dr. Simon Gallagher (1756–1825). He not only was the pastor of the first Catholic parish in the state, St. Mary's, but, beginning in the early 1790s, he was a faculty member in the College of Charleston, teaching courses in logic, mathematics, natural philosophy and astronomy. In 1811 he became the first chairman of the Charleston Board of School Commissioners. Another Irish-born priest, James Wallace, educated in Maynooth seminary in Ireland and Georgetown University, played an important role in the intellectual development of South Carolina College in the early years of the nineteeth century. Michael Tuomey (1805–1857) wrote valuable studies on South Carolina geology (1848) and pleistocene fossils (1857).

John England was an important figure both in South Carolina and the Catholic Church in the early nineteenth century. Born in Cork city in 1786, he was appointed bishop of Charleston in 1820 for a diocese that covered both Carolinas and Georgia. While expanding the structure and membership of his church, England established both a non-sectarian classical academy and a Catholic seminary. Although Charleston was not to be an important center of Irish emigration, and the Catholic Church thus only grew to modest proportions, England was prolific as a spokesman for his religion and Irish concerns. Established in 1822, his *United States Catholic Miscellary* was the first long-lasting Catholic newspaper in the country and a major forum for a wide variety of public affairs. The matter of slavery reared its head in 1842. In a sweeping condemnation of the slave system, Daniel O'Con-

nell declared, "Over the broad Atlantic I pour forth my voice, saying, come out of such a land, you Irishmen; or if you remain and dare to counternance the system of slavery that is supported there, we will recognize you as Irishmen no longer."

England, who was a friend of O'Connell, made the principal reply. He charged that O'Connell had assumed the Irish in this country were heartless wretches because "we cannot at once do all that your imagination conceive to be perfection, and which we who have the experimental knowledge have irrefragable evidence to be destructive folly." He concluded by hoping "that you may succeed in raising the ruined population of Ireland to the level of the comfort of the Carolina slave." But he returned to the matter of slavery in his final literary effort, *Letters on Domestic Slavery*. He had often been asked if "I am friendly to the existence or continuation of slavery. I am not—but I also see the impossibility of now abolishing it here. When it can and ought to be abolished is a question for the legislature and not for me."

John C. Calhoun was representative of the Scotch-Irish. Born in the western hill country, he was a son of the Irish-born Patrick Calhoun, from Donegal, who at the age of five emigrated with much of his extended family in 1733. Patrick's mother, a brother and several cousins were killed in an Indian attack on the Irish colony at Long Cane in Abbeville County in 1760. Nine years later Patrick led an armed band one hundred forty miles to the nearest polling place to secure representation in the legislature for the backcountry. Upon joining the Irish Emigrant Society of New York in 1844, John C. Calhoun declared, "I have ever taken pride in my Irish descent. . . . As the son of an emigrant, I cheerfully join your Society. Its object does honor to its founders."

During the nullification crisis of 1832 Calhoun squared off with another South Carolinian of Irish stock—President Andrew Jackson. The Irish Volunteers of Charleston militia company held a meeting to confront the issue. Despite the plea of Bishop England to remain faithful to the Union, the company voted to support nullification.

By this period Charleston had a sizeable Irish population. In his study of antebellum South Carolina, Rosser H. Taylor declares, "Among the non-English elements in Charleston, the Irish were the most turbulent and pugnacious. There were a great many Irishmen in Charleston who, true to Irish form, drank whiskey freely and fought with or without provocation." Jacob Schirmir mentions several disturbances created by the Irish, of which the following is somewhat typical: "Fight this afternoon as the boat was leaving the Island. A row took place near the boat between some young men and the Irish when Scott and Carter were considerably cut up" (*Ante-Bellum South Carolina*, p. 38). Neither Scott nor Carter are Irish names.

In the 1820s a small Irish community grew in Columbia, the state capital, with the influx of laborers, stone cutters and masons to work on the new capital building, designed by James Hoban of Dublin, and the Columbia Canal. They were responsible for the establishment of St. Peter's Catholic Church. Although the numbers were small, in midcentury the Irish were the largest foreign-born group in the city. During court week and other public days there was much riot and revelry. Rosser Taylor comments, "The 'fighting Irish,' a small but vocal element in Columbia, doubtless accentuated the tumult and shouting customarily in evidence on public days" (*Ante-bellum South Carolina,* p. 32).

As they did elsewhere, the Irish provided labor to build the railroads and canals. Canals were needed to transport cotton to the coast. As was the case in other parts of the South, slave owners refused to use their slaves for this demanding task. The labor force was Irish, many of whom had their passages paid by promoters who contracted with canal-building companies. Stories about the Irish diggers are still recalled at Landsford Canal State Park in Chester, S.C. In all, Irish labor built eight canals in the state.

Anne Riggs Osborne related that "These Roman Catholic laborers brought their religion with them, and for the first time, Catholic churches were built in South Carolina. Strong, hard-working and adaptable, the Shanty Irish soon became Lace Curtain, with influence in the politics of every town where they settled" (*The South Carolina Story,* p. 71). Some Irishmen were brought in to work on plantations. One plantation mistress asked Bishop England if he could provide a priest for her Irish work force.

### FAMINE TIME

The tragedy of the Irish Famine of the late 1840s met with a generous response in South Carolina. The Hibernian Society led the relief effort. One of its members, Major Alexander Black, implored the membership to action: "At a period when the cry of wailing, lamentation and woe resounds throughout the land of our forefathers, when the birth place of the fathers and founders of this benevolent institution is doomed to famine, pestilence, starvation and death, while Ireland is suffering under this national calamity, it ill befits the impulses and sympathies of the heart that we should indulge in feasting and rejoicing." The annual St. Patrick's Day banquet was cancelled and a relief committee, headed by Henry Connor, raised $15,000 as well as contributions of rice, flour, cornmeal and other articles of food. The St. Patrick's Benevolent Society was also active in this effort. The South Carolina Railroad shipped the produce without charge.

According to Augustine Smythe, the members of the Hibernian Society "stood with open hands welcoming to our shores those poor and distressed emigrants who fled from starvation and ruin." Although the great majority of famine immigrants went to northern states, there was a steady flow of Irish people into Charleston and other southern ports. One effect of this was vigorous competition between free blacks and Irishmen in various trades and service occupations.

The nativist or Know-Nothing movement of the early 1850s met with a muted response in South Carolina. Only a small number of politicians attempted to make capital of the perceived influence of foreigners and Catholics in American politics. Despite a general Southern resentment about the massive wave of immigrants that was strengthening the position of the North, the dominant S.C. Democratic Party did not take the bait of nativism, which it believed would divide white people.

### WAR IN SOUTH CAROLINA

With secession and the outbreak of civil war, the Irish in South Carolina rallied to the cause of the Confederacy. The Irish Volunteer company of Charleston joined the new army. Another Irish unit in the city, the Meagher Guards, quickly changed its name after Thomas Francis Meagher, a leader in the 1848 rebellion in Ireland, shifted his position and decided to support the Union side. Columbia also had an Irish unit. Bishop Patrick Lynch of Charleston, a native of Clones, County Monaghan, and a slave owner, became an official Confederate representative in Europe and wrote a lengthy pamphlet defending slavery. Andrew G. Magrath, whose father was a 1798 refugee, had the distinction of being the last (and only Catholic) governor before General Sherman's army roared into the state at the beginning of 1865.

In the aftermath of defeat and destruction South Carolina entered a period of racial upheaval and political controversy. The Hibernian Society, struggling to survive, ceased to provide assistance to needy Irish immigrants, very few of whom arrived in any case. This was despite the claim of Bishop Lynch in 1867 that "nowhere has there been a more earnest sympathy for the struggles of Irishmen at home, nowhere will the Irish immigrant be received with greater welcome, or be more generously supported in all his rights" than in South Carolina. One of the bright spots was the emergence of Michael Patrick O'Connor. Son of an emigrant from Charville, County Cork, O'Connor was a political moderate, prolific orator and noted lawyer. Elected to Congress as a Democrat in 1878, he conducted a national speaking tour in support of the Irish land agitation following in the wake of the address to the House of Representatives by Charles Stewart Parnell. A promising political career was cut short by his death in 1881.

### TWENTIETH CENTURY

During the Progressive era Richard I. Manning was governor from 1911 to 1915. The great-grandson of an immigrant from Ireland and the third member of his family to serve as governor, Manning supported expanded educational opportunities, electoral reform and welfare legislation. During this period the Irish urban political style found representation in John P. Grace, who served as reform mayor of Charleston from 1911 to 1915 and from 1919 to 1923. No detail was overlooked when Grace presided at the official welcome provided to Eamon de Valera when the President of the rebel Irish Republic visited the city in April 1920. That progressive spirit was renewed by Joseph P. Riley, who has served as mayor for over twenty years, being first elected in 1975.

Outside of Charleston there has not been an overtly Irish presence in politics. Born to Irish parents in Charleston, James Francis Byrnes, former altar boy at St. Patrick's Church, served as Congressman, Senator, Governor and Secretary of State under Harry Truman, but established his political base in the midlands. Two other political figures of Irish origins are Richard W. Riley, Governor from 1979 to 1987 and Secretary of Education in the Clinton Administration, and Attorney General Charles Condon of Charleston.

The Ancient Order of Hibernians, which dates to 1836, has branches in Charleston, Columbia and Myrtle Beach. There are courses in Irish history and literature at the University of South Carolina. Dr. Jack Weaver was instrumental in organizing two Scotch-Irish heritage festivals at Winthrop University in Rock Hill in 1980 and 1983. The papers presented at the conferences provide important insights into the involvement of Irish people in the history of the Carolinas. Southern regional meetings of the American Conference for Irish Studies were held at the College of Charleston in 1995 and the University of South Carolina in 1998. Beginning in 1982 a semi-Irish St. Patrick's Day fest has been held in Columbia. Since 1984 an Irish Children's Summer Program, initiated by Mary Ellen O'Leary, has brought about a hundred young people annually from both communities in Belfast to Columbia, Greenville, Spartanburg, Anderson and Laurens County. According to a sampling of national origins in the 1980 Census, in South Carolina people of Irish extraction represent fourteen percent of the population, with German being fifteen and English twelve percent.

---

Pat Berman, "From Potatoes to Politics, S.C. Irish Roots Run Deep," *The State* (Columbia, S.C., 17 March 1995).

Doyle Willard Boggs, Jr., *John Patrick Grace and the Politics of Reform in South Carolina, 1900–1931* (Ph.D. diss., 1977, University of South Carolina).

Robert M. Calhoon, "Aedanus Burke and Thomas Burke: Revolutionary Conservatism in the Carolinas," in D. Chestnutt and C. Wilson, eds., *The Meaning of South Carolina History: Essays in Honor of George C. Rogers, Jr.* (Columbia, S.C., 1991): 50–66.

Dennis Clark, "The South's Irish Catholics: A Case of Cultural Confinement," in R. Miller and J. Wakelyn, eds., *Catholics in the Old South* (Macon, Georgia, 1983): 195–209.

David N. Doyle, *Ireland, Irishmen and Revolutionary America, 1760–1820* (Dublin and Cork, Ireland, 1981): 133–35.

John J. Duffy, *Charleston Politics in the Progressive Era* (Ph.D. diss., 1963, University of South Carolina).

David Heisser, "Bishop Lynch's Pamphlet on Slavery: A Contribution to the Confederate Cause," *Catholic Historical Review* (1999).

John C. Meleney, *The Public Life of Aedanus Burke: Revolutionary Republican in Post-Revolutionary South Carolina* (Columbia, S.C., 1989).

Patrick Melvin, "Captain Florence O'Sullivan and the Origins of Carolina," *South Carolina Historical Magazine,* vol. 76 (1975): 235–49.

———, "John Barnwell and Colonial South Carolina," *The Irish Sword; the Journal of the Military History Society of Ireland,* vol. xi, no. 42, pp. 5–20; no. 43, pp. 129–141.

Arthur Mitchell, *The History of the Hibernian Society of Charleston, South Carolina, 1799–1981* (Charleston, 1982).

Joseph L. O'Brien, *John England, Bishop of Charleston, the Apostle of Democracy* (New York, 1934).

Michael J. O'Brien, "The Irish in Charleston, South Carolina," *Journal of the American Irish Historical Society*, vol. xxv (1926): 134–136.

Christopher Silver, "A New Look at Old South Urbanization: the Irish Worker in Charleston, South Carolina, 1840–1860," *South Atlantic Urban Studies,* vol. 3, pp. 141–172.

Jack Weaver, ed., *Selected Proceeding of the Scotch-Irish Heritage Festival at Winthrop College, 1980* (Rock Hill, 1981).

———, *Selected Proceedings of the Scotch-Irish Heritage Festival at Winthrop College, II, 1983* (Baton Rouge, 1984).

ARTHUR MITCHELL

## SOUTH DAKOTA

South Dakota consists of three regions. East River, the area east of the Missouri River, where the bulk of the state's population lives, is made up of farms, towns and a few cities and is part of the Upper Midwest. West River, west of the Missouri, contains two additional regions: the Great Plains, a vast and sparsely settled area with a European American population scattered on large ranches and in small hamlets and an American Indian population located mainly on several reservations; and the Black Hills, a far more densely populated region, adjacent to the Wyoming border, with a tradition of gold mining and tourism. The Irish have played a visible role in the history of all three regions in the state. The Irish experience in South Dakota has had much in common with the Irish experience in more populated areas of the United States, but it also diverges in certain respects owing mainly to the rural nature and ethnic composition of the state.

### ARRIVAL

Some of the first Irish to live in what later would become South Dakota were soldiers who came to frontier army posts during the mid-1850s. Within a few years, at least one of these, John Stanage, a County Cavan Protestant, began farming along the James River. Soldiers turned settlers, however, were not the norm. The vast majority of Irish coming to South Dakota came as part of the general stepwise westward migration of European Americans.

There were a handful of Irish among the small number of settlers who moved into the extreme southeastern part of the Dakota Territory in the late 1850s and early 1860s. For various reasons—the Civil War, fear of Indians, and concern about the quality of the land for farming—migration into this region stood at a standstill for most of the 1860s. Then, from 1868 to 1873, the population of this area swelled with the arrival of several thousand European Americans, including a number of Irish.

Around this time certain American Irish leaders, both lay and clerical, attempted to promote the movement of some of the vast numbers of Irish living in poverty-stricken neighborhoods in the large Eastern cities to the free or cheap lands still available on the western end of the prairies; they claimed the move would improve both the financial and moral condition of the people. Two of these settlement proposals involved South Dakota, but both failed. In 1869, Charles Collins, editor of the Sioux City *Times*, tried to enlist the support of his Fenian colleagues in establishing an Irish colony in Brule County along the Missouri River, but after they saw his proposed site, they decided against the project, and although Collins later managed to attract a few settlers to the area, his dream of an Irish colony never materialized. Another attempt to bring Irish to the region was the Vermillion Convention, held in 1872 in the southeastern Dakota town of Vermillion. Delegates at this gathering adopted resolutions expressing concern about the plight of the Irish in Eastern cities, and urging them as well as other Irish to move west. The Vermillion resolutions, however, failed to spur any immediate settlement. For one thing their timing was bad: during the next five years white migration into the eastern part of the territory diminished to a mere trickle because of a combination of natural disasters (droughts and grasshopper plagues) and the Panic of 1873, which delayed railroad expansion into the territory. In any event, it seems unlikely the Vermillion Convention's hope of enticing the Irish in the urban East to move to Dakota would have worked in the best of times, as relatively few Irish in the urban East came west at this time. Most Irish who homesteaded in Dakota came not from the urban East but from the rural Midwest.

If natural and economic disasters brought to a virtual halt white settlement in eastern Dakota during the mid-1870s, the discovery of gold in the Black Hills in 1874 triggered the opposite phenomenon in the Black Hills at the western edge of the territory. In 1874 an army expedition discovered gold and in the following year a gold rush began. The Irish were involved from the beginning. Charles Collins, the Sioux City newspaper editor, sponsored one of the first civilian (and illegal) expeditions into the Black Hills in 1874, and John Brennan helped establish Rapid City, which lay in the foothills of the Black Hills and became the major city in the area. Less well known than people like Collins and Brennan but also important were the numbers of ordinary Irish who settled and made their living as miners, merchants, and the like.

As the Black Hills attracted newcomers, movement into the eastern part of the territory resumed with the start of the Great Dakota Boom in 1878. During the years of the Boom (1878–1887), as a result of good natural conditions and railroad expansion, about a quarter million settlers, seeking free and/or cheap land and other economic opportunities, moved into the eastern half of what would become South Dakota. The Germans (including the Germans from Russia) were the most numerous, followed by the Norwegians and then the Irish. The Irish settled mainly in the southern three-quarters of East River. Except for Brown County with the city of Aberdeen, fewer Irish settled in the northern counties near the North Dakota border. An examination of federal census manuscripts, as well as the many family histories in county history books and the like, reveals that the overwhelming majority of these Irish newcomers came from agricultural areas of the Upper Midwest, particularly southeastern Minnesota, northeastern Iowa, southern Wisconsin and northern Illinois. Relatively few came directly from the East or from Ireland. Furthermore, none of the Irish came as part of organized colonies, although it may be that groups like the Irish Catholic Colonization Association, which established a few Irish colonies elsewhere, helped to publicize opportunities in the Dakota Territory and thus drew some settlers. While some came to work on railroads and in other non-agricultural jobs, most Irish came to till the land. Though some of these later abandoned farm for town life, according to the U.S. Census for 1900, a clear majority (59 percent) of men of Irish birth or parentage were working as farmers or in other agricultural jobs at the turn of the century.

The Great Dakota Boom ended in 1887. Several years of droughts in the late 1880s and early 1890s followed by a national economic depression during the mid 1890s slowed expansion. A few years later, however, South Dakota had another growth spurt when during the first decade of the twentieth century thousands of settlers moved into the hitherto sparsely populated plains region west of the Missouri River. The population of the state increased by nearly 50 percent from 401,570 in 1900 to 583,888 in 1910. A combination of factors triggered settlement: the extension of railroads into the region, the opening of additional Indian lands to white settlement and a series of years with unusually high amounts of rainfall, which offered hope that farming was possible. As in the previous three movements into the state, the Irish were among the newcomers to West River.

The return of dry conditions in 1910 and 1911 ended the West River boom and led to an exodus of thousands who gave up the hope that farming was possible in the region. As it turned out the West River boom was the last major influx of settlers into the state. The population of the state rose modestly in the two decades after 1910 reaching 692,849 in 1930, before spiralling downward during the Great Depression. Growth stagnated thereafter. Not until 1990 did the state's population surpass—and then, only slightly—what it had been in 1930.

POPULATION TRENDS

The Irish along with other European Americans thus moved into South Dakota in a series of migrations between the late 1860s and 1910. The overwhelming majority of these migrants were of northwestern European origin, and of these the Germans (including the Germans from Russia) were by far the largest. The Norwegians followed and the Irish came in a somewhat distant third. In the 1890 census, taken one year after South Dakota entered the Union, German immigrants and their children (including the Germans from Russia) made up 18.3 percent (63,633) of the state's population, while the comparable figures for the Norwegians and Irish stood respectively at 11.2 percent (38,897) and 5.1 percent (17,858). The percentage of Irish foreign stock (persons of foreign birth or parentage) dropped thereafter, falling to 4 percent (16,056) in 1900 and 2.9 percent (17,399) in 1910.

The Irish portion of the state's population actually remained more even from 1890 to 1910 than the foreign stock percentages would indicate due to the increasing number of third-generation Irish who do not appear as Irish in the federal census. Accurate figures for the total Irish component are impossible to obtain, but

based on my own comparison of the 1900 printed U.S. census with the census manuscripts for certain townships in eastern South Dakota, it is estimated that around six percent of the state's population was Irish in 1900, instead of the four percent, if one considers only foreign stock.

From 1910 up until 1980, when it reported the ethnic origins of the American people, the federal census becomes increasingly meaningless for determining the Irish portion of the state's population, as the ratio of Irish immigrants and their children dropped continuously as the number of immigrants and their children decreased. The South Dakota State Census, however, fills this gap to a large extent because in 1915, 1925 and 1935, it recorded the ancestry of persons. Clearly a valuable source (South Dakota may have been the only American state to have taken such a count), the census has problems, one of which is that it failed to record the ancestry of a sizeable minority of the population, reporting them as "American," "others," or "not reported." Whatever their shortcomings, these censuses do indicate that the Irish portion of the state's population remained fairly constant. In 1915 the Irish made up 7.5 percent (26,543) of those persons reporting an ancestry other than "American," while in 1935 they made up 8.1 percent (30,486) of this group. In 1915 the Irish ranked as the fourth largest ancestry group behind the Germans, Norwegians and English, while in 1935 they were in third place, ahead of the English but still behind the Germans and Norwegians.

After the South Dakota census of 1935, the next attempt to determine the ethnic background of South Dakotans came in 1980, when for the first time the federal census reported on the ancestry of the American people. According to the 1980 U.S. Census, 3.2 percent (21,874) of South Dakotans claimed only Irish ancestry, while another 10.4 percent (72,048) listed themselves as partly Irish, giving a total Irish component of 13.6 percent (93,922). The 1990 census also reported ancestry, though unlike the 1980 census, it listed the Irish and Scotch-Irish separately. The results of the 1990 census are remarkably similar to those of the 1980 census. In 1990, 2.7 percent (18,721) of South Dakotans claimed only Irish ancestry, while another 9.9 percent (68,944) reported themselves as Irish and of one other ancestry, giving a total of 12.6 percent (87,665) Irish. If one adds to these the 1.4 percent (9,980) of the population claiming full or partial Scotch-Irish ancestry, the total Irish component for 1990 was 14 percent (97,645) of the population. Since the state censuses listed persons only under one ancestry, while the federal censuses listed persons with mixed ancestry under more than one ethnic group (the 1990 census limited this to two groups), and since there has been considerable ethnic intermarriage since 1935, precise comparisons between the 1935 census and the two most recent U.S. censuses are impossible to make. Nonetheless, one can say that a comparison of the data suggests that the Irish portion of South Dakota's population has remained fairly stable in the years since 1935, with the 1935 percentage figure of 8.1 percent for the Irish roughly lying in the middle between the percentages for "full" and "part" Irish in the 1980 and 1990 censuses. As in the 1935 census, both the 1980 census and 1990 census show the Irish as the third largest ethnic group in the state far behind the Germans but considerably closer to the Norwegians.

Thus during more than a century of statehood, the percentage of the population with Irish origins appears to have remained fairly constant, as indeed has the general ethnic makeup of the state. During the entire history of the state, the vast majority of white South Dakotans have been of northwestern European background, and thus unlike the Irish in many American cities, few Irish in South Dakota came into contact with new immigrant groups from southern and eastern Europe. (Those in the mining town of Lead were one of the exceptions.) When it came to contact with non-European Americans, the Irish experience in South Dakota also differed from that in much of the rest of Irish America. Unlike many Irish-Americans in the twentieth century, few South Dakota Irish regularly have encountered African Americans, Hispanics, and Asians, while at the same time the Irish in the West River country have had contact with American Indians, a group most Irish-Americans never have encountered.

## IRISH COMMUNITIES

Unlike certain other ethnic groups who located in a few highly concentrated settlements, the Irish were widely dispersed throughout the state, except for most of the northern quarter of East River (save for Brown County) where their numbers were lower than elsewhere. In 1910, for example, in the fifty-nine predominantly white counties in the state, the percentage of Irish (in this case the Irish-born and the American-born with two Irish-born parents) fell within a narrow band from a low of 0.3 percent in Campbell County in the north to a high of 3.5 percent in Union County in the southeast. While the Irish were widely dispersed on a state-wide level, however, it would be wrong to assume that most settled without any pattern. If one examines the population of some of the towns and rural townships, varying degrees of clustering appear in a number of places. For example, an examination of the U.S. census manuscripts for Mc-Cook County in 1900 shows that the Irish (immigrants, children and grandchildren) made up 37 percent of the population in one rural township, 27 percent in a second, and 21 percent in a third, while in six others they accounted for less than five percent of the population. Thus, while some lived in places with few fellow Irish, many Irish (probably a majority) arrived in groups and tended to cluster to some extent in certain areas. Though they did not seem to require the type of dense concentrated settlements typical of certain non-English speaking groups, these Irish wanted to live among a certain number of their own kind.

In discussing Irish settlements one needs to make a clear distinction between Irish Catholics and Irish Protestants who basically constituted two separate ethnic groups. It is difficult to determine exactly the religious makeup of the Irish who migrated to South Dakota. If the results of recent research on the religious composition of the Irish in over fifty townships in eastern South Dakota who are listed in the U.S. Census manuscripts for 1900 are correct, then about 15 percent of the Irish-born were Protestants. Irish Protestants came to South Dakota in smaller groups than did Catholics and seemed to blend in with Anglo-American Protestants, freely intermarrying with them and joining Presbyterian, Methodist and Episcopal churches. Except for those in a few places, Irish Protestants had lost their distinctiveness.

Irish Catholics were quite different, remaining a distinctive people well into the twentieth century, mainly because of their religion. In several areas of Irish-Catholic settlement there were at first few other Catholics nearby, and in these places the Irish established parishes that were predominantly Irish. Most of these parishes were located in towns. There were some parishes like St. Mary's at Garryowen in Union County where the church was located in the countryside, but these never became the norm, since the Irish generally did not settle in high-density levels in rural townships and a good portion of them lived in the towns.

Besides those areas where the Irish accounted for most of the Catholic population, there were several other localities where they lived near significant numbers of other Catholics, and in such cases they joined with them in forming ethnically mixed parishes. In most cases, the Irish found themselves sharing parishes with Germans, the largest Catholic group in the state, but there were a few places where this was not so. In St. Ann's Parish in Badus Township in Lake County, for example, the Irish worshiped alongside Romansch-speaking Swiss.

The Church played an extremely important role in the lives of Irish Catholics. Although the first wave of Irish settlers in a particular locality would arrive before the church, establishment of a Catholic parish was one of the settlers' first priorities. At first they had to settle for the occasional services of travelling priests, but within a few years' time the larger communities had churches with resident pastors, while the smaller ones had churches served on a regular basis by non-resident priests. In time, some Irish parishes like Our Lady of Good Counsel in Elkton in Brookings County established parochial schools, often staffed by Sisters of Irish birth or descent, most notably the Presentation Sisters, who first came to South Dakota from Ireland during territorial days. Whether it had a school or not, the local parish was an essential institution to the Irish. It served their spiritual needs, as well as meeting some of their social ones.

The early Irish-Catholic communities were clearly Irish as well as Catholic. In some communities in the early days, for example, Irish settlers went around to their neighbors collecting money for Irish causes such as the Land League and forwarded it (usually with a letter denouncing the British) to the *Irish World* in New York City. St. Patrick's Day festivities of one kind or another were common, of course. Because of the relatively small numbers of people, there were few regular Irish organizations; Elkton in Brookings County and Flandreau in Moody County, both close to the Minnesota border, had divisions of the Ancient Order of Hibernians, while Lead in the Black Hills had a camp of the Clan na Gael.

Since their numbers were small, the Irish in South Dakota appear by necessity to have interacted more frequently with non-Irish than did their urban cousins. For example, in American cities the Catholic Church allowed non-English speaking Catholic ethnic groups to have their own separate national parishes, which meant that for many decades the Irish usually had the regular (called "territorial") parishes all to themselves. In contrast, national parishes were never an option in the small towns of South Dakota (the only national parish created in South Dakota was in Aberdeen where the Germans from Russia had exerted pressure for one), so that the Irish, whether in predominantly Irish parishes or in ethnically mixed ones, worked with non-Irish in forming and maintaining Catholic parishes. Ethnic tension existed in some parishes, but cooperation rather than controversy generally prevailed.

Besides cooperating with their fellow Catholics in religious matters, Irish Catholics interacted with them as well as with their Protestant neighbors in several other ways. In the countryside Irish-Americans attended one-room schools alongside non-Irish children, while in towns Irish businessmen dealt with a variety of customers. The Irish also encountered non-Irish at social events like community dances and picnics and as members of certain social and fraternal groups. In politics, whether state or local, the Irish operated in a multi-ethnic milieu. Yet a degree of suspicion existed between certain Catholics and Protestants. In the 1920s, for example, the Ku Klux Klan received support in certain areas of South Dakota in its campaign against Catholics. On the whole, when it came to non-Catholics, the early Irish seemed to have had more social contact with Anglo-American Protestants than with non-English speaking ones like German and Norwegian Lutherans, as the latter differed from the Irish not only in religion but also in language. The last two volumes of Ole Rolvaag's trilogy on the Norwegians in South Dakota (the first volume, *Giants in the Earth,* is better known) give a good glimpse into the often tenuous relations between Irish Catholics and Norwegian Lutherans at the end of the nineteenth century.

As the twentieth century progressed, the South Dakota Irish communities gradually became less Irish. Although the rate and process of transformation differed from place to place, depending on such variables as the number of Irish and the ethnic and religious composition of the surrounding population, certain factors such as the dwindling number of those with close ties to Ireland (few Irish immigrants came to South Dakota after 1900) as well as ethnic intermarriage worked to weaken the Irish character of these communities. Yet, that which the early settlers would consider to be their most important legacy—the Catholic parish—continues to flourish (because of rural de-population some of the smaller parishes have been amalgamated with larger ones), although many of the parishioners with Irish ancestors have German, Scandinavian and other non-Irish surnames. Beyond the religious heritage, for some descendants of the Irish pioneers there still survives some sense of Irish identity. For example, several places have St. Patrick's Day festivities, and a few have parades. Sioux Falls, the largest city in the state, and a twin city of Strabane, County Tyrone, has a fairly active Irish group which sponsors several events. Thus, there is still an Irish presence in the state.

Sister M. Claudia Duratschek, O.S.B., *Builders of God's Kingdom: The History of the Catholic Church in South Dakota* (Yankton, S.D., 1985).

Robert F. Karolevitz, *With Faith, Hope and Tenacity: The First One Hundred Years of the Catholic Diocese of Sioux Falls, 1889–1989* (Mission Hill, S.D., 1989).

David Kemp, *The Irish in Dakota* (Sioux Falls, S.D., 1992).

William J. McDonald, *The Nunda Irish: A Story of Irish Immigrants: The Joys and Sorrows of Their Life in America and Dakota* (Stillwater, Minn., 1990).

*Our Lady of Good Counsel, 1879–1979, Elkton, South Dakota* (Elkton, S.D., 1981).

Susan Carol Peterson and Courtney Ann Vaughn-Roberson, *Women with Vision: The Presentation Sisters of South Dakota, 1880–1985* (Urbana, 1988).

MICHAEL F. FUNCHION

## SOUTHERN CITIZEN, THE

Co-founded in 1857 by Knoxville, Tennessee, mayor William G. Swan and fiery Irish nationalist John Mitchel, *The Southern Citizen* had a brief, controversial existence as a pro-slavery newspaper in the midst of anti-slavery East Tennessee and, later, in Washington, D.C.

Readers were confused and astonished by the paper's stretch in equating Southern state's rights with the plight of Ireland and embracing the enslavement of Blacks in the United States, while simultaneously condemning British racism and enslavement of citizens in Ireland and India. Abolitionists denounced the edi-

torial policy of *The Southern Citizen,* while local Know-Nothings bristled at the notion of the immigrant Mitchel as editor of a local newspaper.

Mitchel studied law, but achieved fame as a journalist, orator, and militant spokesman for "Young Ireland" in the 1840s. (See separate entry on Mitchel.) His radical views and promotion of armed resistance against the British government in articles for *The Nation* and as editor of *The United Irishmen* resulted in his arrest and forced transportation to Bermuda and then to Tasmania. Mitchel escaped to New York where he edited *The Citizen,* an Irish-American newspaper. But Irish enthusiasm for the hero of '48 cooled following Mitchel's disagreements with Archbishop Hughes. Mitchel moved his family to Tennessee in 1855 and, following a brief stint as a farmer in the Smoky Mountains, established a new home and newspaper in Knoxville.

Mitchel's opinions and personality immediately riled local editors. The bitterness between Mitchel and John Fleming of the *Knoxville Register* erupted into a fistfight on the city streets. Meanwhile, William G. "Parson" Brownlow, editor of *Brownlow's Knoxville Whig* (and future Reconstruction governor of Tennessee) kept up a steady barrage against the views of "insolent Irishmen and foreign convicts."

Expressed editorially, those views centered on two major themes: (1) states' rights and the perpetuation of slavery; and (2) attacks on British policies in Ireland and India. Mitchel eagerly supplied readers with the "facts" of British actions and constantly warned of British treachery.

With regard to his claims of British treachery toward the United States in general and the southern states in particular, Mitchel cited Britain's interruption of American shipping as a plot to "hem us in," the encouragement of abolition as a maneuver to divide the nation, and Britain's emancipation of Jamaican slaves as "disaster" for the South.

Mitchel's barrage of warnings within the pages of *The Southern Citizen* were augmented by speeches throughout the region in cities such as Nashville, Memphis, Mobile, New Orleans, and Kansas City.

However, articles were not limited to issues of slavery and British imperialism. Other topics included current legislation, cotton prices, concerns about Mormonism, and other issues. Throughout its brief history, the focus of *The Southern Citizen* remained national or international rather than local.

In 1858, Mitchel moved his family and *The Southern Citizen* to Washington, D.C. Within six months, the newspaper folded. However, his journalistic talents continued to find outlets, first as a correspondent in Paris, France, and, in 1864, for papers in Richmond, Virginia.

Today, historians may view five 1858 microfilmed issues of *The Southern Citizen* at the Tennessee State Library and Archives in Nashville, Tennessee. The issues include January 21, February 4, March 11, March 18, and June 3.

*See* Mitchel, John

*The Southern Citizen* (Knoxville, TN, 1858).

*Brownlow's Knoxville Whig* (Knoxville, TN, 1858).

*The Knoxville Register* (Knoxville, TN, 1858).

DeeGee Lester, "John Mitchel's Wilderness Years in Tennessee," *Éire-Ireland,* XXV/2 (Summer 1990): 7–13.

Rebecca O'Connor, *Jenny Mitchel, Young Irelander* (Tucson, AZ, 1988).

DEEGEE LESTER

# SPANISH FLORIDA: IRISH CONNECTIONS

One of the lesser known aspects of Irish immigration to the new world is the presence of Irishmen in the Spanish colonies, particularly in Florida prior to the American Revolution. In general, they served as clergy or military personnel, often as officers in service to the Spanish crown with unquestionable loyalty. One reason for that service is that Roman Catholicism constituted a common bond between the Irish and the Spanish. Another reason, of course, is the mutual antagonism the two groups shared towards England. For the Irish, that feeling intensified after the Elizabethan conquest of Ireland which destroyed the old Gaelic order, religiously, politically and economically.

Father Ricardo Artur, born in Ireland, was the first parish priest in America and worked in St. Augustine about 1598–1605, not long after the foundation of St. Augustine by Pedro Menendez in 1565 and the Elizabethan Act of Uniformity which mandated that all Catholic priests must leave Ireland by 1605 ( Jane Brooke Evans, *Journal of the American Irish Historical Society*, Vol. XXXII, 1941).

Other Irish priests, trained at the Irish College at Salamanca, served in Florida. Prominent among them were Father Thomas Hassett, Vicar and Ecclesiastical Judge of East Florida, who was brought to St. Augustine from Philadelphia, and Father Miguel O'Reilly, Chaplain of the Hibernian Regiment in Cuba, who also was assigned to St. Augustine. Both men arrived in 1784, at the beginning of the Second Spanish Period which ended in 1821 when all of Florida was then annexed by the United States.

Father Hassett's greatest accomplishment was the establishment of the first free American school in St. Augustine in 1787; he became Vicar General of New Orleans where he died in 1804. Father O'Reilly, born in Longford in 1752, was the son of John O'Reilly and Catherine Sheridan. He carried on the educational work, in addition to the building of the Cathedral, dedicated in 1797. O'Reilly died in 1812 and is buried in St. Augustine's Tolomato Cemetery under a fitting monument attesting his accomplishments.

Father Miquel Crosby, a Dubliner also trained in Salamanca, administered the last rites to O'Reilly and recorded his death in the official records for Governor Kindelan [Letter of Crosby to Kindelan, September 13, 1812 (Folio 26, St. Augustine Historical Research Library)]. Crosby endured the painful annexation of the city to the United States under Governor Coppinger, fearing the American confiscation of the cathedral and church property, and died in St. Augustine in 1822. Constantine McCaffrey, O.Carm., and Michael Wallis, O.P., both arrived in St. Augustine in 1791, as did Father Crosby, Fathers Francis Lennan and James Coleman, who arrived in 1792 and worked in Pensacola. Father Francis Bodkin arrived about 1797 for Pensacola service [Michael J. Curley, C.S.S.R., *Church and State in the Spanish Floridas (1783–1822)* (Washington, D.C., 1940)].

During the Second Spanish Period in East Florida, 1784–1821, three governors were of Irish descent: Enrique White, 1796–1811, Sebastian Kindelan, 1812–1815, and Jose Coppinger, 1816–1821. They lived in the Government House still extant in St. Augustine and served for twenty-three years. It alternated between war and peace with the British, Indian, and American marauders along the Georgia border continually disturbing the peace.

Governor White's administration has been the topic of an M.A. thesis by Rogers C. Harlan, *A Military History of East Flo-rida During the Governorship of Enrique White: 1796–1811* (Florida State University, Tallahassee, 1971). It is a saga of military history and civilian subjection to commanders who assumed political leadership. White, born in Dublin, 1741, governed during the decline of the Spanish colonial system, as Harlan writes, a history of loyal men hopelessly dedicated to the preservation of a dying system upon which they themselves depended (p. 208).

White, a bachelor, prospered under the system, acquiring wealth and position in the colony. His collection of seventy-five books, mostly in English, included the New Testament, Book of Prayers, and Meditations for the Mass. He left over 300 pounds sterling, 11,000 pesos, and three slaves who were freed on White's death. Father O'Reilly distributed some of the wealth to White's cousins in Ireland; the remainder was willed to Carlos Howard and Pedro O'Daley of the Hibernian Regiment, Joseph Noriega of the Pensacola garrison, and Guillermo O'Cavanagh, formerly of the Hibernian Regiment, retired in Galicia, Spain ( James Gregory Cusick, *Ethnic Groups and Class in an Emerging Market Economy: Spaniards and Minoreans in Late Colonial St. Augustine* [University of Florida Ph.D. Thesis, Gainesville, 1993], and *Library of Congress, East Florida Papers Reel 142, Proceeding on death of Enrique White, 1811*).

Father Crosby officiated at the High Requiem Mass, followed by a ceremonial march to the Tolomato cemetery. A monument was ordered which was inscribed with a coat of arms and noted his service to the king of Spain for almost 47 years, from a cadet to the Brigadier of the Royal Armies and Governor of East Florida. However, the monument has never been found, nor has the burial site, unlike O'Reilly's site and that of another famous Irishman of the period, Wexford-born John Barry, Father of the American Navy, buried in St. Mary's Cemetery in Philadelphia, 1803 [Albert J. Nevins, M.M., *Our American Catholic Heritage* (Huntington, Ind., 1972)].

Governor Kindelan y Oregon (O'Regan) was born in 1763 at Ceuta, a North African Spanish barracks town, to Don Vicente Kindelan, born in Ireland and a Colonel in the Infantry of the Irish Regiment, and Maria Francisca O'Regan y Mac Manus, born in Barcelona. His sister, Maria, married Philippe O'Sullivan, Conde de Berehaven, not a well-known fact. Kindelan was buried in Cuba, 1826 [Francisco Xavier de Santa Cruz y Mallen, *Historia de Familias Cubanas,* Vol. 1 (Havana, 1940)].

Kindelan's governorship was a nightmare. In 1812, President James Madison and Secretary of State James Monroe were clandestinely supporting the American "Patriots" who had captured *Fernandina* and sailed to St. Augustine. Assisted by U.S. soldiers, they encamped outside the fort until Governor Kindelan's firm and diplomatic response ended the stalemate. He wrote to the American Commander, reminding him that their nations were at peace, while secretly using the Seminoles and free Blacks to harass the Americans, offering $1,000 for the scalp of the "Patriot" leader, Commander McIntosh and $10 for any other scalp. The strategy worked. The Americans left Florida in August, 1813. The rest of Kindelan's tenure was peaceful, but unstable, for he had to remain neutral during the War of 1812 between England and the American states. Happily, Kindelan returned to Cuba, being replaced by Governor Jose Coppinger [Jean Parker Waterbury, *"The Oldest House," Its Site and Its Occupants, El Escribano* (St. Augustine, FL, 1984)].

Coppinger, the son of Cornelio Coppinger O'Brien, a native of Cork City, and a Spanish mother, was born in Cuba, 1771. Jose, at the early age of ten years, became a cadet, and as a first lieutenant he fought in the Regiment of Ireland against France in North Africa, Rosellon, and Catalonia (1793–1795). Coppinger was the Governor of Trinidad, Cuba when he was appointed Governor of East Florida, with Kindelan's recommendation. Leaving his Spanish wife and their three children in Cuba, Coppinger began a very difficult task, unaware that he would be the last governor [ J. Isern, *Gobernadores Cubanos de la Florida* (Miami, 1974); L. David Norris, *Jose Coppinger in East Florida, 1816–1821: A Man, A Province, and A Spanish Colonial Failure* (Ph. D. Thesis, University of Illinois, Carbondale, 1981)].

From beginning to end, chaos ruled the province. The Seminole Chief, Bowlegs, appealed for help against the Americans who were invading his territory, which was under Spanish jurisdiction. He told the governor that the Spanish inhabitants were supporting the Americans and Coppinger was powerless. He was also unsuccessful in getting compensation from the British for the rich planters' escaped slaves used against the Americans during the War of 1812. Poor morale and no salary caused seventy military personnel to try desertion. Heavily in debt, Spain finally agreed to cede East and West Florida to the United States. This occasion was Coppinger's finest hour. With pomp and circumstance, and flags flying, on July 10, 1821, he handed Spain's 1565 province, excluding the 1763–1783 British occupation, to an infant nation. Then, he sailed home to Cuba, replaced by Andrew Jackson [John H. Matthews, *Law Enforcement in Spanish East Florida, 1783–1821* (Catholic University of America, Washington, D.C., 1987)].

In West Florida, Arturo O'Neill (1781–1793) and Enrique White (1793–1795) were the only Irish governors. O'Neill, a Lieutenant Colonel in the Hibernian Regiment, served Bernardo de Galvez at the battle of Pensacola, 1781. This decisive British defeat led to the Yorktown surrender five months later and O'Neill's immediate governorship. He was born in County Tyrone (1728) and died in his eighty-seventh year, fighting in all the European and American wars of his lifetime [*The Dublin Evening Post* (February 4, 1815); Thomas J. Mullen, Jr., *The Hibernia Regiment of the Spanish Army, Irish Sword* (Dublin, Summer, 1968)].

The Hibernian Regiment played an important role in this period when Spain regained her territory lost to Britain in 1763. These were more light-hearted days. The regiment, quartered in Havana, was assigned the duty of reclaiming Florida. In 1784, the new Governor, Don Vizente Manuel de Zespedes, selected Capt. Carlos Howard of the Hibernians for his secretary. His most recent service was at the battle of Pensacola, in 1781, and friendship with O'Neill was a valuable asset. Howard was sent earlier to make way for Zespedes, who arrived escorted by Colonel Guillermo O'Kelly and Captain Eduardo Nugent, both seasoned veterans of the Hibernian Regiment. Two members, Juan O'Donovan and Guillermo Delaney, left indelible marks in St. Augustine [Helen Hornbeck Tanner, *Zespedes in East Florida. 1784–1790* (Jacksonville, 1989)].

Lieutenant O'Donovan duped Father Miquel O'Reilly to clandestinely perform a marriage ceremony between Dominga Zespedes and himself. The Governor was enraged, jailed O'Donovan, and sent him to Havana for final judgment. Eventually, the lovers were properly remarried in St. Augustine in 1785. She was widowed and remarried in 1797; her government pension was transferred to their only child, nine-year-old Juan Vicente, born and baptized in St. Augustine.

No happy ending was in store for Delaney. On November 20, 1785, he was severely beaten and stabbed several times by unknown attackers. He managed to reach his destination, the home of Catalina Morain, an Anglo-American seamstress with whom he was having an affair, enjoying sexual pleasure at his own risk. She was also having affairs with other men, and jealous rage was suspected. Captain Nugent and Colonel Kelly started an extensive investigation with no verdict reached. Lieutenant Delaney died on January 4, 1786.

The Irish clergy in Spanish Florida left no such record of misconduct. They worked tirelessly, caring for people, converting some of the British who remained after the British withdrawal and maintaining an aura of respectability in a frontier community. Fathers Hassett and O'Reilly are two worthy graduates of the Irish College at Salamanca. Their accomplishments are proud standards of the Irish zeal and dedication to the Catholic religion.

The Irish military who served in Florida were extraordinary men. Governors O'Neill, White, Kindelan, and Coppinger, against overwhelming odds, kept Florida Spanish beyond anyone's expectation. Carlos Howard, whose skills kept the Americans at bay during the Spanish recovery of its Florida province, was a remarkable man. Historians, past and present, are amazed by the stamina and service to Spain of all these men. As often noted, why were they not serving Ireland?

*See* Florida

EILEEN A. SULLIVAN

## SPELLMAN, FRANCIS JOSEPH (1889–1967)

Archbishop of New York, Cardinal. Spellman was born on May 4, 1889, in Whitman, MA, the first of five children of William and Ellen (Conway) Spellman, both of whom were born in Massachusetts of Irish immigrant parents. William owned a grocery store that he inherited from his father. Francis made a point of his parents' American birth and once corrected his official biographer, Robert I. Gannon, S.J., for referring to him as an Irishman rather than an American. After graduating from Fordham College in New York, he entered the seminary at the North American College in Rome, where he studied at the Urban College of Propaganda. Study at the college could be a stepping stone for ecclesiastical preferment, for the professors were predominantly Italian diocesan priests destined for service in the Curia. Spellman cultivated his professors, notably Francesco Borgongini-Duca. From the turn of the century, the American hierarchy had become increasingly Romanized, as bishops depended more on a Roman patron than on American peers for their promotion. Spellman symbolized the zenith of this trend.

### THE BOSTON AND ROMAN YEARS

Spellman was ordained in Rome on May 14, 1916, for the Archdiocese of Boston. After two years in parish work, he was named vice chancellor by Cardinal William O'Connell, with whom he had a falling out. He was then assigned to several menial tasks, including diocesan archivist and proofreading for the Boston *Pilot*. In 1925, he accompanied a group of Boston pilgrims to Rome, where he renewed his acquaintance with Borgongini-Duca and formed friendships with Enrico Galeazzi, an engineer and Roman agent for the Knights of Columbus, and with Nicholas and Genevieve Brady, American-Catholic millionaires with a residence in Rome. He procured a position in the Vatican Secretariat of State, but was supported by his official job as the superintendent of the Knights of Columbus playgrounds for poor children in Rome. For the next seven years, he remained in Rome and sprinkled his diary with references to new-found friends who were ascending in prominence, especially Eugenio Pacelli, who became Cardinal Secretary of State in 1929. By 1931, the Fascist government had shut down the church presses, so Spellman was entrusted with the task of smuggling the encyclical condemning Fascism, *non abbiamo bisogno,* out of Italy to be published in Paris by the Associated Press and United Press International.

### AUXILIARY BISHOP OF BOSTON

In 1932, Spellman was named auxiliary bishop of Boston. He was consecrated on September 8 in St. Peter's Basilica by Cardinal Pacelli, assisted by Archbishops Borgongini-Duca and Giuseppe Pizzardo. Pius XI himself had given him his motto, "Sequere Deum." Borgongini-Duca had designed his coat of arms that included Columbus's ship, the *Santa Maria,* crossing the ocean. At his consecration, Spellman wore the vestments Pacelli had worn when he was consecrated by Benedict XV. Romanization and Americanization had been wed.

Spellman's appointment was ironic. Cardinal O'Connell had been named coadjutor Archbishop of Boston in 1905, although he had not been placed on the official list of nominees then in use in the American Church. He owed his rise to his friendship with Cardinal Raffaele Merry del Val, the Secretary of State. But in 1932, he had not requested an auxiliary bishop, much less Spellman. Spellman's Roman patron, Pacelli, was also Secretary of State, but would rise still higher. Spellman's initial reception in Boston was far from cordial. Upon his arrival, he was simply told by the cardinal's secretary to take an empty room in the seminary. A full month went by before he was granted an audience with O'Connell, who lived in a residence on the same grounds as the seminary. For the next seven years, Spellman's relations with the cardinal were at best strained, a situation well known among the other bishops. In 1933, he received word that he would be named coadjutor of Boston only to learn that the appointment was blocked in Rome. In the meantime, he asked to be named pastor of Sacred Heart Church in Roslindale, a prestigious parish, but instead received a letter from the cardinal, "couched," as he recorded in his diary, "in peremptory tones." It appointed him "Removable Parish Priest" of Sacred Heart Church in Newton Center. Spellman and O'Connell disagreed on other matters. While the cardinal made no secret of his antipathy for Governor James Michael Curley, Spellman maintained close relations with the governor. As he had in Rome, he cultivated high-ranking people. He also maintained his Roman contacts. In 1936, Cardinal Pacelli visited the United States, ostensibly as the personal guest of Genevieve Brady. But he also wanted to meet President Franklin D. Roosevelt to discuss relations between the Vatican and the United States as war in Europe was becoming inevitable. Spellman arranged through Joseph Kennedy for the cardinal and president to meet at Hyde Park, the residence of Roosevelt's mother. He then accompanied the cardinal on a tour of the United States. Pacelli's visit enhanced Spellman's reputation, but it cost him his friendship with Mrs. Brady who then omitted him from her will. But Spellman's star was on the rise.

### ARCHBISHOP OF NEW YORK

In 1938, Cardinal Patrick Hayes of New York died. The favored candidate to succeed him was Archbishop John T. McNicholas of Cincinnati. But, in February, 1939, Pius XI died before confirming the appointment. The conclave to elect his successor chose Pacelli, who took the name Pius XII. Spellman's patron now held the highest position in the Church.

On April 15, 1939, Spellman was named Archbishop of New York, much to the surprise of other American bishops. Yet, even then he could not escape the specter of O'Connell. Out of deference, Spellman had asked the cardinal to impose the *pallium,* the sign of metropolitan authority, on him, at a ceremony on March 12, 1940. At the last moment, however, O'Connell claimed a sore throat made it impossible for him to attend, so Spellman turned to Cardinal Dennis Dougherty of Philadelphia, who had earlier declined an invitation to be present. While he made an inauspicious beginning, Spellman was an indefatigable administrator. When he first took office, he was given ten problems, some of long standing, to be solved. Within two years, he reported to Pius XII that he had completed all those tasks. One issue was arranging some type of diplomatic relations between Washington and the Vatican.

### WORLD WAR II

In addition to being Archbishop of New York, Spellman was military ordinary, or bishop over the armed forces. This brought him into frequent contact with Roosevelt and his successors. By Christmas of 1940, he succeeded in having Roosevelt name Myron C. Taylor as his personal representative to Pius XII, a substitute for diplomatic relations that would need Senate approval. Early in 1943, he undertook an extended tour of military forces abroad. Before leaving he met with Roosevelt and received the president's request to military authorities to show him every courtesy. In Spain, he saw Generalissimo Franco and explained that the American alliance with the Soviet Union did not mean any sympathy for Communism. From North Africa, he then departed for Rome, where the pope had asked his presence. Although he confided neither to his diary nor to Gannon the nature of his conversations with the pope, other evidence indicates they discussed, among other issues, the British incarceration of Italian missionaries. As Spellman continued his journey, he visited London, a trip he described in *Action This Day.* He met Winston Churchill and brought up the situation of Italian missionaries. The bombing of Rome in July, 1943, however, caused Spellman to curtail his plans to visit the Far East and return to New York. Although Spellman would meet with Roosevelt at least three more times, the bombing of Rome put a strain on their relationship, which became yet more strained by the bombing of the papal villa at Castel Gandolfo early in 1944. On February 22, Spellman strongly protested this in a sermon before the Knights of Columbus in St. Patrick's Cathedral. After that, he never seemed to enjoy his previous warm relationship with the president.

After Allied troops entered Rome on June 4, 1944, the bombing of the city had ceased to be an issue. During the late summer and early fall, Spellman returned to Europe to visit American forces—he began penning *No Greater Love* while living with the troops in Germany. But he interspersed his visits to the military with three trips to Rome. In September, the pope asked him to become Secretary of State, and, for the next year, U.S. State Department officials reported the possibility of his appointment, but apparently Spellman rejected it. Another issue that Spellman and the pope discussed during those summer audiences, however, was the succession to O'Connell, who had recently died. He seems to have recommended that Pius XII appoint Richard J. Cushing, then auxiliary bishop, as the new Archbishop of Boston.

Back in the United States, Roosevelt died in April, 1945, and Spellman never seemed to enjoy the same friendship with President Harry S Truman. He was, however, present in the White

House on August 11, when Truman read to him the acceptance of the Japanese surrender. For Spellman, the war was a chance for Catholics to prove their American patriotism, a theme that he would continue to espouse in the postwar years. His poem, "The Risen Soldier," virtually equated the war effort with Christian redemption.

### Postwar Years

In 1946, Spellman, Edward Mooney of Detroit, Samuel Stritch of Chicago, and John Glennon of St. Louis were named cardinals by Pius XII in his first consistory, delayed because of the war. In the eyes of the American public, Spellman now became the principal spokesman for American Catholicism on the domestic and foreign fronts. But he never quite dominated the American hierarchy. Mooney, Stritch, and Archbishop McNicholas of Cincinnati, formed what they called the "Hindenburg Line" to prevent him from extending his influence into the Midwest. On the east coast, Spellman was influential in the appointment of key archbishops, notably Patrick J. O'Boyle to Washington in 1947 and John O'Hara to Philadelphia in 1950. But outside that region, he succeeded in gaining only the appointment of James Francis McIntyre, his coadjutor, as the second Archbishop of Los Angeles in 1947.

In the postwar years, Spellman emerged as a strong opponent of Communism. In 1949, he publicly accused the union leaders of grave diggers in Catholic cemeteries of being influenced by Communists because they were affiliated with the CIO. After the grave diggers went on strike, he replaced them with seminarians. The union was forced to break from the CIO and join the AFL. His anti-communism also led him to embrace the controversial Senator Joseph McCarthy. On the political front, he never had the same access to Truman that he had to Roosevelt. Truman had retained Taylor as his personal representative to Pius XII and, after the latter's resignation in 1950, he nominated General Mark Clark as ambassador to the Vatican in 1951. But, after Clark withdrew his name, he made no further nomination. In 1953, Spellman reported to Pius XII that Senate opposition was so intense that confirmation of any ambassador would be impossible. This led G. B. Montini, then the pope's substitute secretary of state and later Pope Paul VI, to charge that American Catholics had not sufficiently defended the Holy See in the controversy over diplomatic relations and against Paul Blanshard's strong criticism of the Church. Spellman replied with a sharp letter recounting the activities of the American Church in defending Catholic rights at home and abroad, even in nations like Italy.

Spellman was frequently involved in public controversy. In 1949, Eleanor Roosevelt, the president's widow, devoted her regular newspaper column to support a bill, then pending in Congress, prohibiting aid to parochial schools. Spellman issued a statement accusing her of anti-Catholicism and of "discrimination unworthy of an American mother." The press reported the controversy, which ended only when Spellman paid Mrs. Roosevelt a conciliatory visit at Hyde Park. He also strongly protested decreasing censorship of American films. In a rare address from his cathedral, he struck out against the release of *Baby Doll* late in 1956. Although his protests may, in fact, have increased the popularity of such films, he continued to have influence on the motion picture industry.

### Vatican II and Beyond

Spellman's theology, like that of most other American bishops, was conservative, but on some issues he was progressive. Prior to Vatican II, he resisted efforts of the apostolic delegate, Archbishop Egidio Vagnozzi, to stifle biblical scholarship. Once the council was underway, he gained the appointment as an expert on John Courtney Murray, S.J., the theologian then held suspect for his teaching on Church-State relations and religious liberty. When he learned that religious liberty might be removed from the conciliar agenda, he summoned the American hierarchy to sign a petition in its favor and personally presented it to Pope Paul VI. He thus played a key role in having the council adopt the "Declaration on Religious Liberty." Yet, he also resisted the concept of episcopal collegiality as diminishing papal authority.

After the council, Spellman is better remembered for his support of the American effort in Vietnam, which he saw as part of the fight against Communism. After visiting the troops in Vietnam during Christmas, 1965, he paraphrased the patriotic phrase of Stephen Decatur, "Right or Wrong, My Country," which evoked strong criticism from the increasing anti-war movement.

Spellman had presided over New York during a period of transition. During World War II and the Cold War, he was intent on showing the patriotism of American Catholics, a stance that led to his unpopularity in the 1960s. In addition to the patriotic works he wrote during the war, he also published *Prayers and Poems* (1946), *Heavenly Father of Children* (1947), *The Foundling* (1951), *Cardinal Spellman's Prayer Book* (1952), and *What America Means to Me and Other Poems and Prayers* (1953). Although he was frequently branded a conservative, he was also known for defending his priests and for allowing experimentation, especially in accommodating the Puerto Ricans who were migrating to his diocese. He died in New York on December 2, 1967.

*See* Catholicism, Irish-American

John Cooney, *The American Pope: The Life and Times of Francis Cardinal Spellman* (New York, 1984).
Gerald P. Fogarty, S.J., *The Vatican and the American Hierarchy from 1817 to 1965* (Stuttgart, 1982; Collegeville, 1985).
Robert I. Gannon, S.J., *The Cardinal Spellman Story* (Garden City, 1962).

GERALD P. FOGARTY, S.J.

## STEEL INDUSTRY AND IRISH WORKERS

### From Iron to Steel

Historically, the Irish in the American steel industry composed a relatively small but influential group. Their heavy involvement in the building of the railroads put them in touch with job opportunities in the mines and mills that grew up in close symbiosis with rail. Their entry as laborers into the American iron industry at the time of its rapid expansion afforded many of them an opportunity to rise into the ranks of the skilled and semi-skilled crafts at the very moment when technological change ushered in the age of steel. They would play an important role in the evolution of the American steel industry, primarily as union organizers and leaders.

By and large the Irish influence exercised itself through the organization and leadership of both craft and industrial unions. Their presence as a rising force in the highly unionized iron industry of the 1870s and 1880s positioned them for leadership on the side of labor in the titanic struggle that would engage capital and labor with the coming of the age of steel. The fact that the top leadership of the American steel industry was mostly Protestants from Scotland, England and Northern Ireland certainly did not dampen the Irish union activists' ardor for labor struggle. With their command of the English language, a long history of clandestine political organization and their Catholicism, they often became spokespersons for the masses of Eastern and Southern European immigrants who at the turn of the century became grist for America's dark, satanic mills.

There is an important exception to this picture of the Irish as leaders of labor rather than of industry. William Kelly, whose father John had left Ireland as a rebel after the 1798 rising, was born in 1811 in Pittsburgh where he developed an interest in iron making. In the late 1840s he began experimenting with a pneumatic or "air boiling" process for making steel in Eddyville, Kentucky. While traditional steel making needed enormous amounts of fuel and time to produce small amounts of steel, Kelly proved that a blast of cold air blown through the molten iron rather than on the fuel did not cool the metal but actually ignited the latent carbon in the metal, converting the iron to steel. Henry Bessemer patented this same idea in England later in 1856 leading to a bitter patent fight in the United States. Andrew Carnegie's man, Alexander Holley, who had worked with Bessemer, helped insure the triumph of the Bessemer name by his perfecting of the process (Boucher 47–51, Wall 263–4).

The Irish provided a significant measure of leadership in worker organizations such as the Sons of Vulcan (Hugh McLaughlin), the Knights of Labor (Terence Powderly) and the Amalgamated Association of Iron and Steel Workers. While the Irish dominated no particular industry as Germans did brewing, Italians the stone and cement trades, or Jews the needle trades, in the words of labor historian David Montgomery, "they were everywhere and into everything." Based in stable communities in urban areas, conditioned by history to be resisters, they dominated the leadership of organized labor by the early 20th century (Montgomery 205).

## THE HOMESTEAD WATERSHED

The Irish were rising to leadership in the iron industry at the dawn of the age of steel. Individual craft unions in iron (puddlers, heaters, rollers etc.) were united into the Amalgamated Association of Iron and Steel Workers in 1876 in Pittsburgh. "The bright young men of the craft" were dominant at the 1892 convention of the Amalgamated Association held in Pittsburgh just three weeks before the famous Homestead battle. The strike, more properly a lockout, began at the end of June and came quickly to a head on July 6, 1892 at a battle that is the most famous in American labor history. Seven workers and three Pinkerton agents died in the shootout. The Pennsylvania militia occupied the town and the strike was broken. Labor's defeat would mean the virtual exclusion of unionism from the steel industry for 45 years (Demarest 33, 181–4).

John McLuckie, steelworker and upright Burgess of Homestead during the famous Homestead steel lockout and battle, joined with fellow unionist Hugh O'Donnell as the primary public spokespersons for the union forces during the strike. O'Donnell was the leader of the union Advisory Committee that imposed a cease-fire and accepted the surrender of the three hundred armed Pinkertons at the end of the day-long gun battle. The Advisory Committee at Homestead included as members David Shannon, David Lynch, John Coyle, Jack Clifford, William McConeghy, John Durkin, Patrick Fagan, Reid Kennedy, John Murray and Martin Murray. After the occupation of Homestead by the well-organized Pennsylvania state militia, O'Donnell became an advocate for a quick settlement on almost any terms. The

union committee rejected his advice and the strike was broken (Burgoyne 38).

Following the defeat, the Amalgamated Association of Iron and Steelworkers rapidly declined from its pre-strike position as the country's most powerful craft union. Many Irish moved into local politics as pro-labor democrats. In 1901, W. J. O'Donnell, mayor of McKeesport, supported an abortive attempt at union organization. P. J. McArdle, President of the Amalgamated Association of Iron and Steel workers in 1910 and eventually a well-known Pittsburgh Republican Councilman, was associated with the Militia of Christ movement of Fr. Peter Dietz and became its founding president in 1912. The militia was an early attempt by Catholics to inject Christian principles into the labor movement. The conservatism of the Amalgamated Association in its latter days came to be symbolized by Michael Tighe, president of the union from the 1919 steel strike into the depression years, who steadfastly resisted efforts to organize steel on an industrial rather than a craft basis.

### THE 1919 STEEL STRIKE

While some Irish moved into conventional Democratic or Republican politics, others, embittered by the suppression of workers' rights in basic industry, became some of the leading radicals of the day. Four of them became major figures in the great 1919 steel strike despite the fact that none of them had ever worked in steel.

Fannie (Mooney) Sellins was a garment worker in St. Louis who became an organizer and one of the few female leaders of the United Garment Workers of America in 1910. In 1913, she began to work as an organizer for the United Mine Workers and was jailed for three months. Her jailing came in response to a speech in which she defied a court injunction and said: "I am free and have a right to walk or talk any place in this country as long as I obey the law. I have done nothing wrong. The only wrong that they say I have done is to take shoes to the little children . . . and when I think of their little bare feet, blue with the cruel blasts of winter, it makes me determined that if it be wrong to put shoes upon those little feet, then I will do wrong as long as I have hands and feet to crawl. . . ." Sellins was brutally beaten and shot by sheriff's deputies near the gates of Allegheny Steel in Brackenridge PA. Her mutilated face was on a flyer that hung in nearly every union hall or office during the 1919 steel strike under the headline: "Shall Fiendish Cruelty Rule America?" (Cassidy 34–46).

The 1919 steel strike mobilized workers against an industry whose brutal twelve-hour days, six- or seven-day weeks, and horrendous health and safety conditions provided ample incentive for rebellion. Three radicals of Irish descent were prominent strike leaders of an unskilled and semi-skilled workforce that by the time of the walkout was mostly Eastern European: William Z. Foster, John Fitzpatrick and Mary Harris "Mother" Jones.

William Z. Foster was an organizer who moved from radical syndicalism to Communism after an early life of adventure and work in numerous occupations. He teamed up with fellow Irishman John Fitzpatrick, President of the Chicago Federation of Labor, first to organize the meat packing industry and then to take on the power of steel. Fitzpatrick's diplomatic skills maintained the uneasy alliance of AFL craft unions that succeeded in calling what was then the largest strike in U.S. history. The strike, initially successful in Gary and Johnstown, was broken in Pittsburgh's Monongahela Valley where Slavic workers went solidly out on strike, but the bulk of English-speaking second- and third-generation workers stayed on the job. Black workers from the South, driven from the land by the boll weevil infestation, were massively and cynically employed as strike breakers. Indeed, before her death, Fannie Sellins made heroic efforts to reach out to Black workers out of sympathy for their plight. These internal divisions in conjunction with the wealth and power of the steel companies and its political allies spelled defeat for the strikers and the National Committee to Organize Iron and Steel Workers (O'Donnell 122–36; Brody 112–78).

Mother Jones, with an imposing reputation as the "miner's angel," made forays into the Pittsburgh district to rally the steel strikers. In one famous incident she confronted U.S. Steel's political stranglehold on the Monongahela Valley by defying prohibitions against any public labor gathering. As recounted in her autobiography, when she addressed a large rally on the main street of Homestead, PA, she was arrested and taken to a magistrate. "A cranky old judge asked me if I had a permit to speak on the streets. 'Yes, sir,' said I. 'I had a permit.' 'Who issued it?' he growled. 'Patrick Henry; Thomas Jefferson; John Adams!' said I. The mention of those patriots who gave us our charter of liberties made the old steel judge sore. He fined us all heavily" (Jones 213).

## PHIL MURRAY AND THE UNITED STEEL WORKERS OF AMERICA

Following the 1919 strike, unions were smashed in steel, but when they rose up again out of the depths of the Depression, Irish leaders again played an important role. No one was more influential than Philip Murray. Born in Scotland of Irish (Donegal) roots, the eldest of thirteen children, Murray came to the United States on Christmas day in 1902 as a young boy of sixteen. He was already a coal miner and union member when he arrived in Western Pennsylvania and he rose rapidly in the ranks of the United Mine Workers of America. In 1916, at the age of 30, he became President of District Five in the heart of Western Pennsylvania's bituminous fields. His experience during World War I on the National Bituminous Coal Production Committee and Pennsylvania Regional War Labor Board made him disposed to viewing tripartite Labor-Government-Business boards and government intervention in general as being useful to the interests of labor (David Brody in Clark 13–39).

Murray became the most trusted lieutenant of the autocratic John L. Lewis, president of the United Mine Workers of America. They were such a contrast that historian Melvyn Dubofsky termed them "Labor's Odd Couple." While Lewis was colorful, extravagant of lifestyle and autocratic, Murray was self-effacing, deeply religious and accessible to common workers. When Lewis advanced the banner of industrial unionism as president of the Congress of Industrial Organizations, he placed Murray at the head of the Steel Workers Organizing Committee (SWOC) in 1936. Vin Sweeney became the first editor of *Steel Labor,* the official paper of SWOC and later the United Steelworkers of America (Melvyn Dubofsky in Clark 30–44; Bernstein 441–7).

SWOC had spectacular success in capturing the company unions that U.S. Steel had formed through Employee Representation Plans. A leader in this effort was Elmer Maloy, who was elected to head the company union at the corporation's Duquesne works and in 1937 was elected mayor of Duquesne. The SWOC forces, riding the momentum of Roosevelt's 1936 victory, managed to get the company unions to adopt SWOC's wage and hour demands. As the company union representatives turned to the CIO, so did the rank and file. On July 5, 1936, steelworker

organizers, led by Pat Fagan and Emmet Patrick Cush, sons of 1892 strikers, opened the CIO organizing drive in steel with a meeting at the graves of the 1892 union dead. This organizing momentum inside the steel corporation's plants would be dramatically slowed by the sudden and unexpected negotiated union recognition agreement engineered by Lewis and U.S. Steel's Myron Taylor (Serrin 189–214; Fink 231).

Murray would be the beneficiary of Lewis' preemptive agreement with U.S. Steel in 1937, but would experience bitter defeat in the Little Steel strike that ended in blood in the Memorial Day massacre at Republic Steel's gates in south Chicago. Murray and Lewis had a terrible falling out over election support for Roosevelt in 1940. Murray succeeded Lewis as president of the CIO and became the first President of the United Steelworkers of America. He served on numerous government boards during the war. The 1946 strike wave in steel, auto and electrical led to post-war economic prosperity and a rising standard of living for workers. In 1949, Murray's steelworkers gained one of the first pension plans for industrial workers (Bernstein 432–98).

After the war Murray was gradually forced to deal with the issue of Communism in the CIO as the iron curtain descended and the cold war began. His Irish friend and confidant, Pittsburgh labor priest Father Charles Owen Rice, pushed him hard on the issue. By 1948, the Berlin blockade and the Communist Party's support for the Progressive Party that threatened to throw the presidential election to the Republicans prompted action. He supported Rice and anti-Communist union activist John Duffy in an all-out fight to break the party's power in the union movement. The effort led to the split of the United Electrical Workers (UE), the expulsion of the left-led unions from the CIO, and the removal of some officials from the steelworkers union. Murray died in 1952 on the campaign trail for Adlai Stevenson (McCollester 109–17).

## MANAGING THE UNION

David J. McDonald succeeded Phil Murray as president of the USWA. Where Murray had always lived modestly and enjoyed the company of miners and steelworkers, McDonald became the archetype of the limousine-chauffeured labor leader. McDonald loved the high life and cultivated an aura of equality with corporate bigwigs in Pittsburgh. His regime sparked several revolts in the union. Notable among these revolts was the "dues rebels" movement in 1956 led by Donald Rarick and an Irishman from McDonald's own Hazelwood neighborhood of Pittsburgh, Frank O'Brien. The rebellion was crushed in a heavy-handed fashion, but O'Brien went on to become a state legislator and first chairman of the Steel Valley Authority, a grassroots effort to stop the collapse of the steel industry in the 1980s. An internal revolt and hard-fought election campaign led by I.W. Abel in 1965 toppled McDonald. Jim Griffin, who went on to chair the U.S. Steel negotiating committee in 1968 and in 1971, managed McDonald's campaign. Another Irishman, Joseph Patrick Moloney, who had been an organizer for SWOC and a union district director in Buffalo, managed Abel's successful challenge. Moloney, as Vice President of the USWA, went on to lead a nine-month copper strike in 1967–8 (Serrin 258–315; Fink 253).

In the 1970s, Msgr. Charles Owen Rice supported a number of rank-and-file insurgencies inside the steel union during the Abel and McBride regimes. None of these was ultimately successful, but Rice became a vocal defender of community and union activists during the industrial collapse of the 1980s that devastated

Pittsburgh's manufacturing base. Rice, who spent part of his childhood in Ireland where he witnessed the aftermath of the Easter Rebellion, mixed his union and civil rights commitments with active support for Irish republicanism. He became reconciled with the leadership of the USWA under Lynn Williams and good relations continued under George Becker (McCollester 183–200).

Lloyd McBride, who served as president of the steel union from 1977 until his death in 1983, was confronted with a deepening crisis in the steel industry and felt compelled to accept concession bargaining as a means to preserve union jobs. McBride was a decent man who was dealt a terrible hand by fate. The rank-and-file insurgency against concessions and plant closings in the Monongahela Valley was led by the Homestead USWA local 1397's Ron Weisen and Michelle McMills. Russ Gibbons, communications director of the USWA under McBride and Williams, became as president the leader of efforts in the 1990s to commemorate the history of the steelworkers.

Irish in the American steel industry were important well beyond their numbers. As leaders of steel unionism they ranged in political belief from Communist and anarchist to Catholic and conservative. It was their ability to understand and express the aspirations of workers in one of the nation's most important industries that gave them their opportunity. The combination of their political aptitude and the evolution of the steel industry determined the form and measure of their contribution.

*See* Labor Movement

Irving Bernstein, *Turbulent Years: A History of the American Worker, 1933–1941* (Boston, 1969).

John Newton Boucher, *William Kelly: A True History of the So-Called Bessemer Process* (Greensburg, PA, 1924).

David Brody, *Labor in Crisis: The Steel Strike of 1919* (Urbana and Chicago, 1987).

Arthur G. Burgoyne, *The Homestead Strike of 1892* (Pittsburgh, 1979).

James Cassidy, "A Bond of Sympathy: The Life and Tragic Death of Fannie Sellins," *Labor's Heritage*, vol. 4/4 (Winter 1992).

Paul F. Clark, Peter Gottlieb, and Donald Kennedy, eds., *Forging a Union of Steel: Philip Murray SWOC, and the United Steelworkers* (Cornell, 1987).

David Demarest, et al., *"The River Ran Red": Homestead 1892* (Pittsburgh, 1992).

John Hoerr, *And the Wolf Finally Came* (Pittsburgh, 1988).

Mary Harris Jones, *The Autobiography of Mother Jones* (Chicago, 1977).

Charles McCollester, ed., *Fighter With a Heart: Writings of Charles Owen Rice, Pittsburgh Labor Priest* (Pittsburgh, 1996).

David Montgomery, "The Irish and the American Labor Movement," in Doyle and Edwards, ed., *America and Ireland, 1776–1976* (Westport, 1980).

L. A. O'Donnell, *Irish Voice and Organized Labor in America: A Biographical Study* (Westport, 1997).

William Serrin, *Homestead: The Glory and Tragedy of an American Steel Town* (New York, 1992).

CHARLES J. McCOLLESTER

## STEINFELS, MARGARET O'BRIEN (1941– )

Editor, author. Born in Chicago, July 28, 1941, Margaret O'Brien Steinfels is the daughter of John and Mercedes (Steinbach) O'Brien. She received her bachelor's degree from Loyola University of Chicago in 1963, and a master of arts from New York University in 1971. She also studied as a nondegree student at Columbia University and at the Sorbonne in Paris.

Margaret O'Brien Steinfels

O'Brien Steinfels is author of *Who's Minding the Children: The History and Politics of Day Care in America* (New York, 1974), and she writes regularly for leading periodicals of the country, her articles focusing on such issues as day care, family concerns, bioethics, religion, and national and international politics. She has served in a number of publishing positions, being editor of the *Hastings Center Report* from 1974–1980; social science editor at Basic Books, 1980–1981; business manager and later executive editor of *Christianity & Crisis,* 1981–1984; director of publications at the National Pastoral Life Center in New York City, 1984–1987, and founding editor of its quarterly magazine *Church.*

In 1988 she succeeded her husband, Peter Steinfels, as editor of *Commonweal,* a biweekly journal of opinion edited by Catholic lay people—her appointment coming after her husband had moved to the *New York Times* as senior religion correspondent. *Commonweal* had had several women on its editorial staff since its founding in 1924, but O'Brien Steinfels was the first woman to become editor. Among her many awards are honorary degrees from the University of Notre Dame and Fordham University.

JOHN DEEDY

## STEPHENS, MICHAEL (1946– )

Novelist, essayist, poet, and dramatist. Michael Stephens was born in Washington D.C. He was raised in Brooklyn and on Long Island, both of which are central locations in his work. Stephens received his early education at Catholic schools on Long Island and went on to receive BA and MA degrees from City College in New York, and an MFA from the Yale University School of Drama. Stephens has taught at Fordham University and the University of Hawaii, and is currently on the faculty of Emerson College in Boston. In addition to writing and teaching, Stephens was for a short time a semi-professional boxer, fighting as a middleweight in "smokers" in Upstate New York.

### FICTION

Michael Stephens is best known as the author of two remarkable novels, *Season at Coole* and *The Brooklyn Book of the Dead.* Both novels feature the Cooles, a large Irish-American family transplanted from the "holy ground" of Brooklyn to Long Island in pursuit of some measure of gentility. In both novels, Stephens presents devastating portrayals of an Irish-American family that sought respectability in the decades after World War II, but whose dreams were unrealized. Stephens' vision owes much to Eugene O'Neill and James T. Farrell, though his representations, as they take into account a different time and artistic consciousness, are, if anything, more searing. A central theme in *Season at Coole* is dislocation. By moving away from the tightly-knit world of East New York, the Cooles have abandoned the domain which gives them a sense of belonging to place. On Long Island, without the busy apartment life and the loves and hatreds of the ghetto, they are lost. Unable to blend in with homogenous suburban life, their home falls into disrepair, and they become a blight on the new neighborhood. It is as if the Cooles seek to duplicate the ghetto in suburbia. As a result of the move away from the city, and as a consequence of various addictions to alcohol and drugs, the family is in a state of collapse. In *The Brooklyn Book of the Dead,* the Cooles have returned to East New York to wake their father, as stipulated in his will. Although the sixteen grown-up sons and daughters have been brought together for the wake in the old neighborhood, the occasion offers further evidence of the degree to which they have lost their way, individually and collectively. For all the grim material, these are very funny novels in which Stephens shows a brilliant ability to forge humor from catastrophe, in the manner of Flann O'Brien and Samuel Beckett. Also, Stephens explores with great insight, honesty, and linguistic verve, the world populated by those Irish who did not rise with the tide of success which Irish-Americans forged for themselves in the decades after World War II and which reached its highest point with the election of John F. Kennedy as president. The Irish-Americans of these two remarkable, ground-breaking, and deeply lyrical novels are part of the contingent of the race who did not make it in America, and Stephens is their witness and voice.

### ESSAYS, PLAYS, POETRY

In addition to fiction, Stephens has published volumes of essays and poetry, and a play. *Green Dreams: Essays Under the Influence of the Irish* is focused on Stephens' youthful years in Brooklyn and his early interest in literature in a world where books were few. In a section devoted to writers, Stephens reveals his debts to Irish writers and to Joyce, Beckett, and Flann O'Brien in particular. Other literary essays focus on Italo Calvino and Thomas Bernhard (both of whom also serve as important influences on his work) and highlight Stephens' gifts as a critic. In fact, although Stephens' focus in his writing is generally on Irish America, the writers who have influenced him the most are from Europe, something which contributes in no small way to Stephens' unique artistic sensibility, which is at once local and cosmopolitan. *Our Father,* Stephens' play which ran on weekends for five years in New York, is, like *The Brooklyn Book of the Dead,* an exploration of the death of the father and how this event has affected his family. In his poetry, as in all his work, Stephens displays an extraordinary facility with language and form.

*See* Fiction, Irish-American

Michael Stephens, *Alcohol Poems* (Binghamton, N.Y., 1973).

———, *After Asia: Poems* (New York, 1993).

———, *The Brooklyn Book of the Dead* (Normal, Illinois, 1994).

———, *Circles End* (New York, 1981).

———, *Green Dreams: Essays Under the Influence of the Irish* (Athens, Ga., 1994).

———, *Jigs & Reels* (Brooklyn, N.Y., 1992).

———, *Lost in Seoul and Other Discoveries on the Korean Peninsula* (New York, 1980).

———, *Our Father* (New York, 1997).

———, *Paragraphs* (New York & Northampton, Mass., 1974).

———, *Season at Coole* (New York, 1972).

———, *Shipping Out: A Novel* (Cambridge, Mass., 1979).

———, *Still Life* (New York, 1978).

EAMONN WALL

## STERLING, JAMES (1701?–1763)

Clergyman, author, colonial official. Born in Dowrass, Kings County (Laois), Ireland, Sterling was the son of a British army officer. In 1720, he was graduated from Trinity College in Dublin and in 1733, obtained his master's degree from that university.

Sterling initially tried his hand as a playwright, his first work coming in 1722 with the *Rival Generals.* His *Parricide* ran briefly in 1736 but neither play brought him the success which he had hoped. Sterling is also reported to have written some political pieces for the opposition party at the time.

About 1733, Sterling took Holy Orders and became a regimental chaplain. Just prior to this, he had lost his first wife, a Dublin actress. After several years, Sterling traveled to Maryland to serve in several parishes. Inducted at St. Paul's in Kent County on August 26, 1740, he remained its rector until his death on November 10, 1763.

Sterling also entered public debate, believing that Britain's future strength lay with the development of her colonies. He authored an imperialistic poem of sixteen hundred lines entitled *An Epistle to the Hon. Arthur Dobbs,* published in London and Dublin when he visited there in 1752. In 1755, Sterling also penned a sermon criticizing French encroachments in America.

Sterling obtained appointment as customs collector of Chester, a post created at his own suggestion for the development of Maryland's trade. Governor Sharpe, Maryland customs officials, and several London merchants with trading interests in the colony opposed the appointment, but Sterling's connections and influence at the treasury maintained him in the position until his death.

*Archives of Maryland,* vol. VI (Baltimore, 1888); vol. XI (1890); vol. XLVI (1929).

George D. Burtchaell and Thomas U. Sadleir, eds., *Alumni Dublinenses* (London, 1924).

L. C. Wroth, "James Sterling," *American Antiquarian Society Proceedings* (April 1931).

CHRISTIAN G. SAMITO

## STEWART, ALEXANDER TURNEY (1803–1869)

Merchant. Born in Lisburn, County Antrim, Ireland, the son of Alexander and Margaret (Turney), he grew up under the comfortable protection of his Scotch-Irish Protestant mother and grandfather. Stewart's grandfather desired a clerical life for his grandson and therefore sent him to an academy in Belfast where he was to receive ministerial training. However, after his grandfather died Stewart abandoned the clerical lifestyle and emigrated to New York. While in New York Stewart taught at a private school for a short time and then staked a claim on his inheritance and began investing in trade products, particularly Irish lace.

In 1823 he opened a small shop and invested in three thousand dollars' worth of Irish lace. His investment brought him a nice return and he was able to gradually move to a larger shop. During the depression of 1837, Stewart bought stocks of failed businesses and made large profits on them. By 1846 he was able to build his own retail dry goods business, which gained for him a large trade among wealthy and popular people. Stewart's enterprises prospered and he extended his business deals to include Army and Navy contracts as well as an invested share in many mills in New England, New York and New Jersey. Stewart's most memorable purchase was that of the Hempstead Plains on Long Island, where he built his own town called Garden City. After the Civil War, he also built a mansion on Fifth Avenue. His mansion became a symbol of his prosperity and ingenuity in investing and marketing. Stewart died in 1869, and in 1878 a scandal arose when the coffin containing his remains was stolen from St. Mark's churchyard and held ransom. The ransom was paid and the remains were taken to Garden City.

*New York Times* (March 1869).
*Harper's Weekly* (April 1876).
C. H. Haswell, *Reminiscences of an Octogenarian of the City of New York* (1896).
*Dictionary of American Biography,* vol. 18.

JOY HARRELL

## STEWART, CHARLES (1778–1869)

Naval officer. The son of a Belfast seaman, Stewart was commissioned a lieutenant in the U.S. Navy in 1798, and in 1800 was in command of the schooner *Experiment* which captured two armed French ships. He married Delia Tudor of Boston and had a daughter also called Delia.

He was made captain for his distinguished service with the Barbary States 1802–1806. In the War of 1812 he commanded the *Constitution* from December 1813 to the end of the war. He was regarded as an outstanding officer and had a varied career. In 1859 he was made senior flag officer, and in 1862 was made a rear admiral on the retired list.

His daughter, Delia, married John Henry Parnell of Wicklow—and they were the parents of one of Ireland's greatest leaders, Charles Stewart Parnell

*Dictionary of American Biography,* 5th ed. (New York, 1997).
R. F. Foster, *Charles Stewart Parnell: The Man and His Family* (Hassocks, 1976).

MICHAEL GLAZIER

## STRITCH, SAMUEL ALPHONSUS (1887–1958)

Cardinal archbishop of Chicago. He was born August 17, 1887, the fifth son of Garrett Stritch, a native of Ballyheigue in County Kerry and American-born Katherine Malley. Garrett Stritch was part of the post-Famine migration to America. His career included a stint as a schoolmaster in Limerick and association with the Fenian movement. He arrived in the United States in 1870 and settled near relatives in Louisville, Kentucky. There he met and married Katherine Agnes Malley. Securing work with railroad construction, he moved his growing family to Nashville, Tennessee. Garrett died in 1896 when Samuel Alphonsus was nine years of age. A precocious and bookish lad, by the age of fourteen he had completed high school work and entered St. Gregory's

Seminary in Cincinnati. In 1904 he was dispatched to Rome to complete his final studies for the priesthood at the Urban College of the Propaganda in Rome. He was ordained in 1910 at the Lateran Basilica and returned to Nashville the next year.

### EPISCOPAL CAREER

In 1921 he was named the second bishop of Toledo, Ohio and was consecrated by Archbishop Henry Moeller of Cincinnati on November 30, 1921. In his years in Toledo (1921–1930) he devoted much attention to the consolidation of educational enterprises, enhancing the quality of teacher preparation and building an expensive and elaborate new cathedral which was in part a replica of the one in Toledo, Spain.

In 1930 he succeeded Archbishop Sebastian Messmer as the archbishop of Milwaukee. During his Milwaukee incumbency, he was continually beset by the serious economic dislocations of the Great Depression. To forestall serious shortfalls in the operations of Catholic social welfare agencies he launched a successful charity drive. His program of financial austerity prevented several parishes from falling into bankruptcy and his reluctance to spend "extravagantly" even prevented him from repairing the archdiocesan cathedral, which was badly damaged by a fire in 1935. As in Toledo, he turned a great deal of attention to education, insisting that the sisterhoods begin teacher certification equivalency programs in their motherhouses, professionalizing the administiration of the archdiocesan school office, and consolidating Catholic Action programs under central diocesan direction.

In 1940 he was chosen to succeed Cardinal George Mundelein as Archbishop of Chicago. Building on the strong administrative legacy of his predecessor, Stritch left the *minutiae* of administration to his two trusted lieutenants, Monsignors George Casey and Edward Burke. He himself became a visible public figure, living in the city rather than the distant seminary, appearing regularly at public events and priests' funerals, and continuing his work with the National Catholic Welfare Conference. His eighteen years as head of the Chicago archdiocese were pivotal years of growth and expansion especially after World War II. As Catholics moved from the city to the ring of suburbs surrounding Chicago, Stritch attempted to keep up by a massive program of parish and school building. Yet as the city's population emptied into the suburbs, Stritch was also confronted with a corresponding weakening of the urban parishes and institutions that had for so long been the bulwark of Catholic life in the city. He also had to deal with the increasingly vexatious problem of race relations, as an expanding African-American population began to move into white neighborhoods and apply for admission to Catholic schools. In efforts to stabilize neighborhoods and preserve a Catholic presence in the rapidly-changing urban environment, Stritch assigned full-time priests to be his liaisons for urban affairs with both public and private sectors. The Archdiocese of Chicago worked closely with urban developers to carve a place for Catholic parishes, schools, and social welfare institutions in the plans for the renovation of urban space. At Stritch's direction, the Archdiocese also entered into alliances with community organizers such as Saul D. Alinsky to mobilize grassroots support for neighborhood preservation. In dealing with race relations, Stritch was more tentative. His southern background and abhorrence of public controversy made him wary of "race-mixing" and integration in general. Nonetheless when pressed by circumstances and key advisors, he insisted that African-American Catholics be admitted to parishes and schools without opposition. His primary gesture toward the growing African-American community in Chicago was to send them priests and religious who would work with them.

Stritch attained some national prominence by his compilation of the papal utterances on the subject of international peace, an effort of the Catholic bishops to affect the direction of post-war peace settlements based on the principles of natural law and just order. He also maintained close contacts with Federal officials such as assistant postmaster general Gael Sullivan and former F.B.I. agent and later federal judge Edward A. Tamm, who represented his interests in higher circles. In Chicago, he maintained close ties with the Edward Kelly and Martin Keneally administrations, but did not often speak out on urban issues.

With his priests Stritch had the reputation of being an easygoing administrator, but he disliked both liturgical innovation and any sort of communication with Protestants. In 1954 he forbade Catholic participation in the World Council of Churches meeting at Evanston. His relations with his auxiliary Bernard Sheil were strained due in large measure to Sheil's "go-it-alone" style of episcopal ministry.

In 1958, at the age of seventy-one, he was appointed to be Pro-Prefect of the Congregation for the Propagation of the Faith in Rome, in order to assist the failing Cardinal Pietro-Fumasoni-Biondi. But on May 27, 1958, he suffered a serious heart attack and died. His body was shipped back to the United States and was buried in Chicago's Mount Carmel Cemetery.

*See* Chicago, Aspects of

Steven M. Avella, *This Confident Church: Catholic Leadership and Life in Chicago, 1940–1960* (Notre Dame, 1992).
———, "Samuel A. Stritch: The Milwaukee Years," *Milwaukee History*, 13 (Autumn 1990): 70–91.
Marie Cecilie Buehrle, *The Cardinal Stritch Story* (Milwaukee, 1959).
Lawrence Mossing, *Young Shepherd of the Diocese of Toledo* (Toledo, 1989).
Thomas J. Stritch, *The Catholic Church in Tennessee: The Sesquicentennial Story* (Nashville, 1987).

STEVEN M. AVELLA

## SULLIVAN BROTHERS, THE (d. Nov. 12, 1942)

Naval casualties. They came from Waterloo, Iowa; their father, Thomas Sullivan, was a freight conductor on the Illinois Central Railroad. Their names were George (29), Frank (26), Joseph (23), Madison (22) and Albert (20). They all joined the U.S. Navy early in World War II and were assigned to the *Juneau,* a light cruiser. In the Battle of the Solomon Islands, the Japanese torpedoed their ship and the five brothers died together.

This family tragedy touched the heart and the soul of the nation, and President Franklin D. Roosevelt spoke for all Americans when he described it as "one of the most extraordinary tragedies which has ever been met by any family in the U.S.A." Their grieving mother, Alleta Abel Sullivan, drew on her deep faith and said, "Christ had five wounds too." The nation remembered the Sullivans, and a popular movie, "The Fighting Sullivans," depicted their brief lives. Later the U.S. Navy named a ship in honor of them and decreed that brothers should never again serve on the same warship.

MICHAEL GLAZIER

## SULLIVAN, EDWARD (Ed) (1901–1979)

Newspaper columnist and television personality. Born in Manhattan one of seven children to Irish descendants Peter Arthur and Elizabeth (Smith) Sullivan, Sullivan spent his childhood in Port Chester, New York, and attended St. Mary's Parochial School. He then went to Port Chester High School where he discovered his talent for writing. After graduation Sullivan became a reporter for the Port Chester *Daily Item* and in this position he covered several stories ranging from weddings and deaths to social and athletic events. In 1919 he left this position and began work for the New York *Evening Mail;* in 1920 he found his first major reporting event to be that of the Westminster Kennel Club Show at Madison Square Garden. His coverage of this event brought him recognition and acclaim in the journalism world.

After a series of jobs with various newspapers, Sullivan joined the New York *Daily News* in 1932 where his column appeared under the title *Little Old New York* and eventually went into syndication with twenty-seven other newspapers. In 1932, he was part of the broadcast crew of Columbia Station WABC and his first radio show led him to introduce popular personae such as Jack Benny, Jack Pearl, Irving Berlin and George Cohan. In addition to these pursuits, he conducted his own vaudeville units and contributed to Broadway musicals and various acting positions in major motion pictures. He wrote the original story for the comedy film *There Goes My Heart* and the screenplay for *Big Town Czar.* Sullivan also became a popular figure during World War II when he hosted several benefit shows and made appearances in hospitals and camps. In 1942 his show *Ed Sullivan Entertains* became a feature on CBS and his daily newspaper column continued during the war. In 1950 he received the *Look* magazine award as television's best master of ceremonies and in 1951 Sullivan's contract with CBS was renewed for five years. In 1951–1952 he hosted *Toast of the Town,* a biographical feature show of celebrated personas. He died in 1979 after a long and rich career in radio, news, and television.

*Collier's,* 129 (June 21, 1952): 47.
*Dictionary of American Biography,* 1952.
*International Motion Picture Almanac* (1950).
*Time,* 57 (June 25, 1951): 49.
*World Biography* (1948).

JOY HARRELL

## SULLIVAN, JOHN L. (1856–1918)

Pugilist, entertainer. John Lawrence Sullivan was this nation's first great sports celebrity. "The Great John L.," as he came to be known, was born in Boston in 1856, the son of Michael Sullivan and Catherine Kelly. From his father, John inherited a fiery temper and fearless disposition and from his mother came his great size and strength.

Young John was a mediocre student and his efforts to learn several skilled trades went for naught. His real passion was sports and as a teenager he discovered that he could earn as much as twenty-five dollars a game playing baseball in the Boston area.

But baseball faded into the background as Sullivan grew in size. Combined with his fearless disposition and temper, his physical prowess made him a natural contestant for the emerging sport of professional boxing. Sullivan fought his first exhibition match in 1878 and won, but he spent the following year attending other matches to study boxing techniques. Finally, on March 14, 1879, Sullivan returned to the ring to defeat John "Cockey" Woods, a victory that was recorded in the *Boston Globe*.

With the aid of promoter William Muldoon, Sullivan quickly set his sights on fighting Paddy Ryan, a boxer generally regarded as the American champion. After three years of exhibition fights Sullivan got his chance. On February 7, 1882, Sullivan met Ryan in a ring in Mississippi City, Mississippi. The "Boston Strong Boy" knocked out Ryan in the ninth round and became the American champion.

For the next decade, Sullivan fought a wide range of opponents, and showed a particular interest in taking on "foreign fighters." His greatest challenge during those years came from an English champion named Charlie Mitchell, who actually knocked Sullivan down on one occasion. With little in the way of real competition, Sullivan became flabby and careless by the end of the decade. His last bare-knuckle fight was a draw against Jake Kilrain on July 8, 1889.

Sullivan's greatest fight would be his last. On September 7, 1892, Sullivan entered the ring for a gloved fight against James J. Corbett. It was a contest that captivated the nation and pushed the upcoming presidential election from the front pages of newspapers. Sullivan was fierce in his determination to win, but he proved no match for the younger, more agile Corbett. After Corbett defeated him in the twenty-first round, Sullivan remarked: "I'm glad it was an American who beat me."

Sullivan found little success outside the ring. He turned to acting in plays both in this country and abroad and later appeared on the vaudeville circuit. He opened saloons in New York and Boston, but found himself in almost constant debt. He did find a measure of happiness with his second wife, Kate Harkins, whom he married in 1908. Together they acquired a farm in West Arlington, Massachusetts in 1912. But he was devastated by Kate's death in 1917 and the "Great John L." died of a broken heart on February 2, 1918.

*See* Boxing

John Barr Chidsey, *John the Great: The Life and Times of a Remarkable American, John L. Sullivan* (Garden City, NY, 1942).
Michael T. Isenberg, *John L. Sullivan and his America* (Urbana, IL, 1988).
Gilbert Odd, *I Can Lick Any S.O.B. in the House* (London, 1980).

TIMOTHY WALCH

## SULLIVAN, KATHLEEN M. (1956– )

Legal scholar. Kathleen Sullivan is professionally regarded as one of the leading constitutional lawyers in America. She was born on Long Island, New York, into a family with deep Irish-American roots. In 1999 she was chosen as Dean of Stanford Law School and was the first woman in Stanford's 106-year history to hold that prestigious post.

She received a B.A. from Cornell University in 1976 and in 1978 received a second B.A. from Oxford University, which she attended as a Marshall Scholar. Three years later she received a J.D. from Harvard Law School, where she won the moot court competition. She practiced constitutional and criminal law before joining Harvard Law School (1984–1993); and was the first recipient of the Albert M. Sacks–Paul A. Freund Award for Teaching Excellence.

In 1993 she joined the faculty at Stanford Law School as the Stanley Morrison Professor of Law. In 1996 she was elected to the

Kathleen M. Sullivan

American Academy of Arts and Sciences. An expert in constitutional law, she was co-author, with Gerald Gunter, of the 13th edition of the classic casebook *Constitutional Law*, and also co-authored *New Federalist Papers: Essays in Defense of the Constitution*. At Stanford she received the John Bingham Hurlbut Award for Excellence in Teaching.

Sullivan became more widely known with her perceptive articles in such outlets as *The New York Times*, *The Washington Post* and *The New Republic* and for her lucid exposition of debated constitutional issues on several television programs. After her first argument before the United States Supreme Court some years ago, *The American Lawyer* forecast her brilliant career when it wrote that she "appears to be on a fast tract to forensic stardom."

JOY HARRELL

## SUPREME COURT JUSTICES

*See* Brennan, William J.; Butler, Pierce; Kennedy, Anthony M.; McKenna, Joseph; Murphy, Frank.

## SWAN, HAROLD J. C. (1922– )

Physiologist and pioneer in cardiac research. Harold James Charles (Jeremy) Swan was born June 1, 1922, in Sligo, Ireland. Both his parents were doctors; his father had a thriving practice in Sligo and his mother, Marcella Kelly, practiced medicine in England for about thirty years.

Between 1939 and 1945, Swan studied medicine at St. Thomas Hospital, London. During his student years, he was stricken by meningococcaemia and survived due to his mother's quick diagnosis and treatment. He served as casualty officer and house physician at St. Thomas Hospital.

After becoming a member of the Royal College of Physicians of London in 1946, Swan entered the Royal Air Force medical service and served at a hospital in Iraq. Following World War II, he became an assistant to Henry Barcroft, a physiologist at St. Thomas Hospital.

Swan published the first paper on the effects of noradrenalin on blood flow in human muscle and skin. Also, he co-authored

Harold J. C. Swan

with Barcroft the treatise *Sympathetic Control of Human Blood Vessels,* published in 1953 by the Physiological Society.

Swan received his doctorate in 1951 and began working in the physiology department at Mayo Clinic, Rochester, Minnesota. He took a year (1954–55) to study physical chemistry, electrical measurements and biostatistics at the University of Minnesota. He made rapid strides at the Mayo Clinic, being appointed consultant physician to the clinic in 1955, assistant professor of physiology a year later, and director of the cardiology laboratory in 1959. After taking some time to learn about cardiac angiography in Stockholm, Sweden, Swan set up a diagnostic catheterization and angiographic unit at the Mayo Clinic.

Swan's work at the Mayo Clinic led to his appointment as professor of medicine at the University of California in Los Angeles in 1965. He also became director of cardiology at Cedars/Sinai Medical Centre. It was during this time that Swan made a breakthrough in using catheterization in the treatment of acute myocardial infarction.

He conceived the idea of putting a flotation balloon on the end of a flexible catheter to ease the catheter's passage to the pulmonary artery. Swan worked with Edwards Laboratories to develop the device. When it was completed, Swan and William Ganz, a graduate of Charles University, Prague, experimented with the device on an animal.

The catheter was such a success that Swan and Ganz introduced it to the coronary care unit. Use of the Swan-Ganz catheter became widespread, even among the staff of other departments, who found it helpful in making clinical decisions for noncardiac patients. The result of Swan's work was published in the *New England Journal of Medicine* in 1970.

Swan's work led to a change in how physicians diagnose and treat patients whose blood flow is deficient, as well as treatment for disturbances in other cardiopulmonary functions.

Although advancing technology was important to Swan, he never lost sight of the importance of treating the patient. In a 1988 article in *Clinical Cardiology,* J. W. Hurst praised Swan as "the perfect blend of scientific cardiologist and compassionate physician." In 1985 Swan received the prestigious honor of being named a master in the American College of Physicians.

He was named a Fellow of the Royal College of Physicians and is a member of American and British physiology societies, as well as the American College of Cardiologists of which he was president. Swan's research on dynamics of the diseased heart and congenital cardiac malformations of infants and children has been published.

He has maintained ties with Ireland and delivered the Stokes Lecture to the Irish Cardiac Society in 1990. He also has received several awards, including the Walter Dixon Memorial, awarded by the British Medical Association in 1950, and the James B. Herrick Award of the American Heart Association in 1985.

Davis Coakley, *Irish Masters of Medicine* (Dublin, 1992).
J. W. Hurst, "H. J. C. Swan," in *Clinical Cardiology,* 11:727–28 (1988).

MARIANNA McLOUGHLIN

## SWEENEY, JOHN J. (1934–  )

Labor union official. John J. Sweeney was born May 5, 1934, in the Bronx, New York, the son of Irish immigrants. His mother worked as a domestic, and his father was a city bus driver. The father was active in the Transportation Workers Union, then headed by the colorful Michael J. Quill, a Sweeney household idol. Sweeney attended St. Barnabas School and Cardinal Hayes High, then went on to Iona College in New Rochelle. He worked as a gravedigger and building porter to help pay his college tuition fees. Sweeney graduated with a degree in economics, and went to work in 1956 for IBM, the computer giant. Soon afterwards, he left IBM for a job as a researcher with the International Ladies Garment Workers Union at one-third the pay.

In 1960 Sweeney was recruited by the Building Service Employees International Union, where in twenty years' time he rose from contract director to president. The union, renamed the Service Employees International Union (SEIU), grew under his leadership into the third-largest labor organization in the United States, its membership strength deriving largely from the unionization of janitors, building-service employees and health-care workers. While leading SEIU, Sweeney became a vice-president of the AFL-CIO, the umbrella federation of autonomous unions that began as the then-separate American Federation of Labor and Congress of Industrial Organizations. Sweeney was active on many AFL-CIO committees, including those dealing with civil rights, Social Security and an Equal Rights Amendment.

In 1995 Sweeney, then in his fourth term as head of the SEIU, stood for the AFL-CIO presidency, and was elected by a 7.3 million to 5.7 million vote. With his new leadership team, he moved quickly to increase the number of women and minorities in the federation's leadership positions, and to establish a multimillion dollar organizing fund, targeting particularly workers in southern and sun-belt states. He also signaled his intention to defend medicare and medicaid, and to fight for medical reform.

Sweeney's style counters certain popular stereotypes concerning labor leaders. Calm and soft-spoken, he shuns fiery rhetoric, preferring instead what has been described as a "heart-to-heart" approach. He has collaborated on several books, the latest *America Needs a Raise: Fighting for Economic Security and Social Justice,* written with David Kusnet (1996). His wife, Maureen (Power) Sweeney, was once a schoolteacher in New York City. They have a son John and daughter Patricia.

*See* Labor Movement

Judith Graham, ed., *Current Biography Yearbook 1996* (New York, 1996).

JOHN DEEDY

## SWEENEY, JOSEPH A. (1895–1966)

Missionary among lepers. Joseph A. Sweeney was born September 4, 1895, in New Britain, Connecticut. He attended St. Thomas Preparatory Seminary in Hartford and St. Mary's Seminary, Baltimore, Maryland. He completed his philosophy and theology studies at Maryknoll Seminary, Maryknoll, New York, and was ordained a priest February 8, 1920. In 1921 he was assigned to the Orient. After serving in Korea and northern China, he was summoned in 1932 to the Maryknoll mission of Kongmoon in southern China to establish a facility for the care of the many lepers of the area. He prepared for this challenge by investigating leprosaria in Louisiana and the Hawaiian islands as well as colonies in China. With the help of a young lay physician, Harry Blaber of Brooklyn, New York, the latter's nurse wife Constance White, and later Dr. Artemio Bagalawis of the Philippines, and other Maryknoll missioners, he organized a simple leprosarium at Sunwui. At a session of the Academy of Tropical Medicine in St. Louis, the quality of Sweeney's work was highly praised by the President of the American Leprosy Foundation, who had personally inspected the site. In 1938 the leprosarium was transferred to more extensive property at nearby Ngaimoon. From 1941, however, the buildings became the target of Japanese shelling. Fear, along with shortages of food and medicine, caused the population to drop to 81. In 1944 Sweeney was himself obliged to go to the United States for medical care, but returned in 1945 to rebuild the facility for 500 lepers. In 1950 Chinese authorities took charge of the institution; Sweeney was forcibly deported in 1953. In 1955 he was assigned to Korea, where, with the assistance of Dr. Bagalawis, he continued to devote himself to care of lepers until his death in Seoul on November 27, 1966.

James Keller and Meyer Berger, *Men of Maryknoll* (N.Y., 1943).
Jean-Paul Wiest, *Maryknoll in China* (rev. ed., Maryknoll, N.Y., 1997).

WILLIAM D. McCARTHY, M.M.

gional director of the Middle Atlantic states of the Jesuit Insitute of Social Order; he then moved to Washington, D.C., to work at the Jesuit national headquarters at Georgetown University. Talbot became a trustee of the United States Catholic Historical Society and then founded several organizations, including the Catholic Book Club (1928), the Spiritual Book Associates (1932) and the Pro Parvulis Society (1934). From 1947–1950 he served as president of Loyola College in Baltimore, Maryland, and he was assistant archivist at Georgetown. He also helped in founding two academic journals, *Thought* and *Theological Studies*.

Talbot's own publications include: *Richard Henry Tierney* (1930), a biography of one of his colleagues at *America; Shining in Darkness* (1932), on the dramas of the the nativity and resurrection; *Saint Among Savages* (1935), a study of French missionary Isaac Jogues; and *Saint Among the Hurons* (1949), a study of the missionary activity of Jean de Brebeuf. He helped to edit several books including: *The Eternal Babe, The America Book of Verse,* and *Fiction by Its Makers.* Talbot also contributed many articles to the *Encyclopedia Britannica* regarding Roman Catholicism. He died in Washington, D.C., on December 3, 1953.

John La Farge, "Father Talbot, S.J., 1889–1953" *America* (December 19, 1953).
"Father Francis Xavier Talbot, S.J.," *Woodstock Letters* (1956).
*Dictionary of American Biography,* supplement, 5.

JOY HARRELL

## TALLCHIEF, MARIA (1925– )

Prima ballerina of the New York City Ballet. Elizabeth Marie (Betty Marie) Tall Chief was born in Fairfax, Oklahoma, on the Osage Indian Reservation on January 24, 1925. Her real estate executive father, Alexander Tall Chief, was a descendant of Chief Peter Big Hear, an influential late 19th-century Osage leader. Her mother, Ruth Porter Tall Chief, came from pioneer Scots-Irish stock. In 1933, the Tall Chiefs moved to Beverly Hills, California, where young Betty Marie took extensive training in dance with David Lichine and Bronislava Nijinska, sister of the legendary Russian dancer, Vaslav Nijinsky.

In 1942, she made her professional debut with the New York-based Ballet Russe de Monte Carlo, and soon Europeanized her name to Maria Tallchief. During her five-year stint with Ballet Russe, Tallchief caught the eye of its brilliant choreographer, George Balanchine, who made her his protégé, and in 1946, his wife. Their professional partnership would leave an indelible mark on the American ballet theater.

From 1947 to 1965, Tallchief was the prima ballerina of Balanchine's new company, the New York City Ballet (NYCB). During that time she created roles for most of Balanchine's repertoire, establishing the NYCB as a critical and financial success. Tallchief will forever be identified with two of those roles: the mythical bird-woman in Igor Stravinsky's *The Firebird* (1949), and the Sugar Plum Fairy in Peter Ilich Tchaikovsky's Christmas classic, *The Nutcracker* (1954). Her strength and agility, as well as her technical proficiency, electrified audiences and critics alike. "She is so sure, so strong, and brilliant," wrote *Newsweek* in 1949, "that it is doubtful if her superior as a technician exists anywhere today."

During the 1950s and early 1960s, Tallchief toured Europe and Asia with the NYCB, gaining international fame as the first American-born, American-trained ballet superstar. She also per-

## TAGGART, THOMAS (1856–1929)

Politician, hotel proprietor, and banker. Born the son of Thomas and Martha (Kingsbury) in County Monaghan, Ireland, Taggart emigrated to the U.S. in 1861 where he spent his childhood battling poverty. At the age of twelve, he began working in a restaurant and in accord with his efficiency was transferred to another restaurant in Indiana, where he later became active in politics. Taggart eventually gained the position of auditor in Marion County and chairman of the Democratic county committee. In 1895, he became the mayor of Indianapolis and served until 1901.

Taggart's continued efforts on behalf of the Democratic party enabled the nomination of John Worth Kern for vice-president, the placement of Samuel M. Ralston into the office of governor, and an influential support of the nomination of Woodrow Wilson. Taggart exercised his influence in Indiana politics and became a prized consultant of the governor and Democratic officials. In 1916, he was appointed senator and served in this position for less than a year before being replaced in the following elections. Taggart then continued his successful management of such business ventures as the operation of the Grand and Denison Hotels in Indianapolis, interests in the mining and banking fields, and presidency of the Fletcher-American Company. He also served as chairman of the board of directors at Fletcher-American National Bank. Taggart died on March 6, 1929, and was remembered as a keen businessman of congenial personality, husband to Eva D. Bryant and father of five.

B. Stoll, *History of the Indiana Democracy, 1816–1916* (1917).
*Dictionary of American Biography,* 18.

JOY HARRELL

## TALBOT, FRANCIS XAVIER (1889–1953)

Roman Catholic priest and writer. Born in Philadelphia into Irish heritage to Patrick Francis and Bridget Peyton, Talbot attended St. Joseph's Preparatory School in Philadelphia. He entered the Society of Jesus at St. Andrew-on-the-Hudson in New York in 1906 and after two years made his vows as a member of the Jesuit order. He then spent two years studying classics at St. Andrew and then philosophical studies at Woodstock College in Maryland.

Talbot taught English at Loyola School in New York City and religion at Boston College during the years from 1913 to 1918. He was ordained a Roman Catholic priest at Woodstock on June 29, 1921, and soon after became the literary editor of the Jesuit weekly publication *America.* Eventually, Talbot became the editor-in-chief of *America* and *Catholic Mind.* He also was named reformed on popular television programs, such as *Omnibus*, *Hallmark Hall of Fame*, and *The Ed Sullivan Show*, and in 1953 played the famous Russian ballerina Anna Pavlova in the film *Million Dollar Mermaid*. She made guest appearances with most of the prestigious ballet companies of the day, and twice won the coveted annual Dance Award.

Tallchief's marriage to Balanchine (but not their professional association) ended in annulment in 1952. A brief second marriage to Elmourza Natirboff ended in divorce. In 1956 she married Chicago construction company executive, Henry D. Pashen, by whom she bore her only child, Elise Maria, in 1959. She retired from the stage in 1966 and settled permanently in Chicago. There she formed the Ballet School of the Chicago Lyric Opera in 1974, and trained a whole new generation of dancers in the Balanchine tradition. From 1980 to 1988 she and her sister Marjorie (also retired from a highly successful dance career in Europe) directed the Chicago City Ballet.

John Gruen, "Tallchief and the Chicago City Ballet," *Dance Magazine,* 58 (December 1984): HC25–HC27.

Francis Mason, *I Remember Balanchine: Recollections of the Ballet Master by Those Who Knew Him* (New York, 1991).

Elizabeth Myers, *Maria Tallchief: America's Prima Ballerina* (New York, 1966).

CONSTANCE B. RYNDER

## TAMMANY HALL AND THE NEW YORK IRISH

Evidence of the participation in New York City political life by the Irish exists a full century before the creation of Tammany Hall. Thomas Dongan (1634–1715), a Catholic from Kildare, was named governor of New York by James II. He served from 1682–1688 and is remembered for approving a "Charter of Liberties," which greatly expanded civil and religious freedom in the colony. James Duane, son of Irish immigrant Anthony Duane, became the city's first post-revolutionary mayor in 1784.

Tammany Hall originated in 1788 as a fraternal society, the Society of Saint Tammany or Columbian Order, as an egalitarian alternative to the many aristocratic gentlemen's clubs founded at the time. Comprised mainly of artisans and small merchants, the organization chose as their "patron saint" the Delaware Indian chief Tamanend (nicknamed Tammany) and employed Indian terms such as "sachem" for council member, "brave" for a rank-and-file member, and "wigwam" for their meeting hall. The latter accounted for the organization's popular name, Tammany Hall.

Initially Tammany was a social and charitable agency not connected with politics. Tammany also had no original connection with the Irish and espoused an enthusiastic Americanism that took a dim view of foreigners. Most Irish New Yorkers in the early republic supported Jefferson, as his party was identified with opposition to the Alien and Sedition Acts and support for France (by definition an anti-British posture). However, Aaron Burr and later Martin Van Buren transformed the society into their personal political organization and promoted an agenda that appealed to the growing number of poor Irish entering the city: universal manhood suffrage, abolition of imprisonment for debt, and tolerance of ethnic and religious minorities.

Three trends coincided in the 1830s to account for Tammany Hall's rise as a political force strongly identified with the Irish. First, universal white manhood suffrage (adopted in 1827) inau-

Tammany Hall

gurated an era of mass popular politics. Second, the city entered a period of rapid expansion in size, population, business, and government, creating unprecedented opportunities to establish a successful political organization which rewarded supporters with cash, jobs, favors, and contracts. Third, due to the first sustained wave of Irish immigration (200,000 entered the port of New York in the 1830s), a recognizable Irish community arose comprised of many poor immigrants eager for the opportunities and services offered by Tammany officials.

Irish immigrants possessed a number of qualities which ensured their early success in municipal politics. While some arrived speaking only Irish, the great majority spoke English—a decided advantage over their German counterparts. Large numbers of Irish immigrants were also familiar with democratic politics, having participated in Daniel O'Connell's grassroots movement for Catholic Emancipation. In addition, strong cultural traditions of loyalty to village and clan were easily adapted to neighborhood and party.

Mass politics as it emerged in the 1830s was decidedly rough and tumble with its close connections to male urban culture of saloons, brawling, and volunteer fire companies. The latter often served as a means by which an ambitious man earned a reputation in his district. Six New York City mayors and countless aldermen and lesser officials got their start in public life via volunteer fire companies.

Successful politics also relied as much on physical force as it did on rhetoric or skillful organization. Voting was open (the secret ballot would not be adopted until 1897) and "shoulder hitters" patrolled polling stations to "assist" wavering voters in their decision. Those who strayed might find themselves out of a job or cut off from charity during the next recession. Riots frequently broke out between supporters of rival candidates. When physical force proved ineffective, Tammany employed election fraud in the form of stolen ballots, repeat voting, or premature naturalization of foreigners.

By the 1840s Tammany's style of so-called "ward politics" was firmly established, as was its relationship with the Irish, whose numbers surged in the decade following the Famine. By 1855 the city counted more than 175,000 Irish-born residents and tens of thousands of American-born Irish, the vast majority of whom supported the Democratic party. As one writer observed in 1864, "By a kind of instinct, the Irish have attached themselves almost universally to the Democratic party. They got the idea that it was the party of popular rights, the anti-aristocratic party, the liberal party." A strong indication of this alliance is revealed by the fact that twenty-five percent of the city's police force—jobs awarded by alderman—was Irish-born by 1855.

One of the most important elements in Tammany's appeal was the cultural defense it offered its immigrant constituents. Nativism, or anti-immigrant sentiment, rose concurrently with the increased arrival of immigrants, especially the Irish. Nativists despised the Irish for their poverty, their enjoyment of drink (a serious liability in the era of temperance crusades), and most especially for their Catholicism. Frequently, nativist politics erupted over Irish opposition to what they deemed an anti-Catholic public school curriculum. Publisher James Harper was elected mayor in 1844 as the candidate of the nativist American Party with pledges to clean the city streets, lower taxes, and drive the Irish out through restrictive naturalization laws and a ban on public employment. Harper's political career was short-lived and Tammany officials like former nativist Mayor Fernando Wood cultivated the image of the party of tolerance. Of course, the national version of this policy—anti-abolitionism and support for southern states rights—tinged their politics with an overt hostility toward African Americans, a fact illustrated by the anti-abolitionist riots which occurred in the Irish Sixth Ward in the 1830s and the Draft Riot of 1863.

The one official who embodied all these trends was William Tweed. Although not Irish himself (his background was Scots Presbyterian), Tweed gained notoriety in the 1840s as the brawling foreman of his volunteer fire company Americus No. 6 (whose Tiger logo eventually came to symbolize Tammany). Assiduously cultivating the Irish vote in the Seventh Ward, he rose quickly through the ranks of the Tammany apparatus, becoming head of the Tammany General Committee in 1863. Known thereafter as "Boss" Tweed, he soon began making huge sums of money from printing firms he owned that had fat contracts with the city. By 1870 Tweed had assembled a loyal cadre of city officials, among them the Head of the Department of Public Works Peter B. Sweeney and Comptroller Richard B. Connolly. Known as the Ring, they conspired to bilk the city of millions of dollars through an elaborate series of kickbacks. The most notorious of these was the new New York County Courthouse (known to this day as the Tweed Courthouse), a project intended to cost $250,000 which eventually cost $13 million—a stunning 5,200 percent cost overrun. Tweed's undoing came at the hands of a disgruntled office seeker named James O'Brien who handed over damning records to the *New York Times,* which began its exposé in July 1871.

When Tweed and the Ring were driven from office and into jail, Republicans and reformers rejoiced that Tammany and its Irish base were finished as a political power. The *New York Times* led the charge when it announced that "[t]he ignorant, unthinking, bigoted hordes which Tammany brought up to its support year after year are hopelessly scattered" and that New York City would no longer be "tyrannized over by our esteemed friends from the Emerald Isle."

The *Times* and those whose views it represented erred on two counts. Despite his size and bravado, Tweed was never as powerful as he appeared. Indeed it was his lack of authority that necessitated his distributing more than $500,000 in bribes in the State Legislature to gain the passage of a new city charter in 1870. Moreover, Tammany was not dead. Under the leadership of "Honest" John Kelly—the first of ten consecutive Irish Catholic bosses—Tammany emerged from the wreckage of the Tweed scandals a stronger and more influential force.

The key to Kelly's success was his respectable image and low-key style (in contrast to Tweed) and thorough restructuring of the Tammany organization. One contemporary remarked at Kelly's death that he had found Tammany a horde and left it an army. He created a tightly organized hierarchy (modeled, many mused, on the Catholic Church), of Assembly District leaders, election captains, and ward heelers. Cementing this new system was Kelly's complete control of patronage and nominations. It was during his tenure that people began to characterize Tammany as a "machine."

The return of Irish political power under Kelly alarmed nativists, reformers, and Republicans alike, so much so that the latter proposed in the mid-1870s to re-establish property requirements for voting—a thinly disguised attempt to disenfranchise the bulk of the poor Irish vote. This and other attempts to block the resurgence of Tammany failed in the face of Kelly's adept leadership and the machine's consistent ability to defend their immigrant constituents from nativist politics (e.g., Sunday saloon closings) and deliver jobs, favors, and contracts. The prominence of the latter both reflected and promoted the emergence of an Irish middle class. Some even became rich, as in the case of William Kingsley, John D. Crimmins, and John B. McDonald, who won contracts to build the Brooklyn Bridge, a new water tunnel, and the subway system, respectively. Another wealthy Irishman, shipping magnate William R. Grace, was elected the city's first Irish Catholic mayor in 1880.

Behind the veneer of respectability exhibited by Kelly, Grace, and others, Tammany continued to benefit from its traditional practices of election fraud and voter intimidation. Equally important was the enormous amount of money Tammany garnered by selling patronage jobs, demanding kickbacks from city contractors, and levying protection fees from a vast economy of vice the Tammany-controlled police allowed to flourish. It was a system reformers railed against, but consistently failed to defeat.

Another aspect of Tammany rankled many of its working-class constituents. All Tammany officials portrayed themselves as champions of the "honest working man." However, their ties to the Catholic Church (staunchly anti-radical and leery of labor unions) and business interests meant that Tammany stymied working-class politics, especially occasional attempts to establish an independent labor party. In 1886, for example, when thousands of Irish workers supported United Labor Party mayoral candidate Henry George, Tammany officials pulled out all the stops to ensure his defeat. In the process Boss Richard Croker (who took over for Kelly in 1886) and his lieutenants learned a valuable lesson: working-class voters demanded more than platitudes; they wanted government intervention on their behalf for better wages, hours, and conditions.

The late-nineteenth century also witnessed the rise of bosses and machines in places not yet incorporated into New York City. In Brooklyn Hugh McLoughlin, "The Sage of Willoughby Street," created a tightly run machine in what at the time was the nation's third largest city. In Long Island City (part of the future borough of Queens), Patrick J. "Battle Ax" Gleason ruled with an iron fist, or more precisely, an ax, which he frequently used to attack the property of business interests which crossed him.

In the mid-1890s merchants, real estate interests, and good government reformers began to push for "consolidation"—that is, the merger of forty local governments into Greater New York. Gleason supported the idea, largely because he believed he would be the first mayor of the enlarged city. McLoughlin opposed it to the bitter end, fearing the loss of his organization's power and influence to Manhattan-based Tammany Hall. Many reformers promoted consolidation for the opposite reason. They envisioned Brooklyn's large base of Republican voters diluting Tammany's growing power. Theirs proved to be a serious miscalculation, for consolidation (which took effect January 1, 1898) simply made Tammany stronger.

Charles Francis Murphy led Tammany into a new era when he took over for Croker in 1902. His quiet and respectable aura proved invaluable (as it had been for Kelly) in enabling Tammany to overcome a decade of corruption and vice scandals which erupted under Croker. He also skillfully avoided conflict with the Brooklyn machine by placating it with a sizeable share of patronage and offices, including the mayoralty (William J. Gaynor, 1909–1913 and John F. Hylan, 1917–1921). Most importantly, Murphy presided over the transformation of Tammany into a force for progressive change. This resulted as much from liberal idealism as practical politics: the flood of new immigrants from southern and eastern Europe meant that Irish political power could no longer rely on Irish demographic superiority and appeals to ethnicity. To gain and hold the loyalty of the newly arrived Jewish and Italian voters, Irish politicians supported legislation on factory safety, child labor, tenement reform, and women's suffrage, and opposed immigration restriction and Prohibition. Under Murphy's tutelage Alfred E. Smith earned a reputation in the State Assembly as a reformer and became the first Irish Catholic governor (1918–1920, 1922–1928). Between 1903 and 1933 every mayor was Irish-American, including anti-Tammany reformer John Purroy Mitchel, grandson of the famed Fenian John Mitchel, who served between 1913 and 1917.

Tammany and the Irish political power it represented reached its apex in the 1920s. Although Murphy died in 1924 he was succeeded by George W. Olvany, the organization's first college-educated boss. Al Smith occupied the governor's mansion and was considered the likely Democratic party nominee for president in 1928. The flamboyant and witty James "Jimmy" Walker, the personification of the jazz era, was elected mayor in 1925 and re-elected in 1929. In that same year Tammany opened a new hall on East 17th Street, a spacious edifice that suggested Tammany might rule the city forever.

But the fortunes of Tammany, and with it the long run of Irish dominance in city politics, collapsed with the onset of the Great Depression. Indeed the start of Tammany's demise might more accurately be pegged to Al Smith's landslide loss at the hands of Herbert Hoover in 1928. Jimmy Walker's turn came in 1932 through his own doing. An investigation charging him with accepting large sums of cash from city contractors forced him to resign on September 1, 1932. Any hopes of a comeback in 1933 were dashed when Tammany, under pressure from Catholic Church officials scandalized by Walker's flagrant affair with actress Betty Compton, dropped him from the ticket.

Fiorello LaGuardia's victory in 1933 on an explicitly anti-Tammany platform marked the end of Tammany's run. Although his twelve years in office did not kill Tammany, they dealt it a blow from which it would never recover. LaGuardia formed a new coalition of Jewish, Italian, African American and reform-minded Democrats that cut deeply into Tammany's traditional base. At the same time, LaGuardia garnered millions of dollars in federal New Deal funding, a mountain of patronage that Tammany officials could only peer at from outside the circles of power. The organization's diminution was symbolized vividly in the forced sale of the new Tammany Hall building in 1943 due to its inability to meet mortgage payments.

Two years later, the election of William O'Dwyer as mayor seemed to suggest another comeback for Tammany and Irish political influence. But it was short-lived. In 1949 Carmine DeSapio became the first non-Irish boss of Tammany since the demise of Tweed in 1872 and although O'Dwyer won re-election in that year, he resigned in 1950 over allegations linking him to organized crime. Robert Wagner, Jr., was elected the city's last Irish mayor (his mother was Irish) in 1953 with the help of Tammany, but turned against the organization in his bid for a third term in 1961, the same year DeSapio was ousted as boss. Ironically, Irish dominance in New York City politics effectively ended the year John F. Kennedy took the oath of office as the nation's first Irish-Catholic President.

Since the 1960s New York City has continued to have numerous politicians of Irish heritage. But upward mobility into the middle class and outward mobility to the suburbs, coupled with assimilation and little new immigration from Ireland, have eliminated any semblance of the city's Irish residents as a voting bloc.

*See* New York City; Smith, Alfred Emmanuel

Oliver Allen, *The Tiger: The Rise and Fall of Tammany Hall* (New York, 1993).

Stephen Erie, *Rainbow's End: Irish-Americans and the Dilemmas of Urban Machine Politics, 1840–1985* (California, 1988).

Jerome Mushkat, *Tammany: The Evolution of a Political Machine, 1789–1865* (Syracuse, 1971).

Gustavus Meyers, *History of Tammany Hall* (New York: Dover, 1971; orig. publ. 1917).

M. R. Werner, *Tammany Hall* (Garden City, N.Y., 1928).

EDWARD T. O'DONNELL

## TEMPERANCE CRUSADE OF FATHER MATHEW

Father Theobald Mathew's temperance crusade was the most remarkable mass mobilization of men and women for any cause in Ireland in the 19th century. The Capuchin friar's missionary career as a preacher of charity sermons and administrator of "the pledge" led him to visit most of Ireland as well as the Irish diaspora communities in Scotland, England, and America. Beginning in 1838, his "Cork Total Abstinence Society" (CTAS) enrolled somewhere between three and four million Irish men, women, and children, or approximately half the population, each of whom renounced the use of alcohol for life. Hundreds of enthusiastic local societies established reading rooms, erected

Father Mathew

"temperance halls," and sponsored teetotaler bands, parades, dances and banquets. Between 1838 and 1843, official whiskey production declined by nearly sixty percent. Other measures of alcohol production and consumption—beer production, liquor licences issued to spirit-grocers and publicans, and even the detection of illegal stills—showed similar patterns of decline.

### The Growth of the Movement

In April 1838, Father Mathew agreed to aid several Cork Protestant temperance activists in promoting the anti-alcohol movement. From modest beginnings (some fifty people attended the first meeting), thousands soon traveled to Cork to enroll in his membership book. Mathew's decision in November 1839 to visit Limerick to dispense the pledge transformed his movement from a local to a regional cause. In the six months that followed, he conducted nearly fifty missions in the area north of Cork and south of Dublin. Towns such as Limerick and Waterford became, with Cork, centers of temperance organization and activity. CTAS membership was measured in the millions by mid-1840. Visits to Dublin, Connaught, and Ulster soon made the movement national. After 1841, although his society continued to grow, Mathew's missions were primarily confined to Ireland south and west of Dublin. The incredible size and enthusiasm of the crowds (often in the tens of thousands) that gathered wherever the "Great Apostle of Temperance" held his meetings attest not only to the charisma of Mathew, but also to the compelling appeal of his message. Taking the camp-meeting enthusiasm and the gospel of self-improvement that were already hallmarks of temperance efforts, Mathew and his supporters crafted a distinctly Irish crusade, laden with pietistic and patriotic features. Although Mathew's movement was non-sectarian, the CTAS was most successful among the Catholic poor and lower middle class, and very few Protestants appear to have joined.

### The Decline of the Movement

The sudden and spectacular growth of the temperance movement was matched by its equally rapid decline after 1842–43. The causes of this collapse were complex. Mathew's relationship with his own church was often troubled, and most Irish priests did not support the temperance reformation. The CTAS encoun-

tered additional opposition from key members of the Catholic hierarchy. This opposition was devastating to the temperance cause in the long run because it prevented the great gains that had been made from being consolidated.

A second problem arose out of the successful recruitment of many temperance societies and temperate individuals, despite Mathew's disapproval, into Daniel O'Connell's mass movement for repeal of the Act of Union that peaked in 1843. Mathew's fear of offending British authorities during the tense months of 1843 paralyzed the CTAS, halting missionary activity in Ireland for the better part of a year. It is also likely that the demoralizing collapse of the repeal cause had a very unfortunate effect on the vitality of the temperance movement.

A third but ultimately associated factor in the movement's decline were the financial difficulties of Mathew himself. By 1842, his debts, brought on by his laudable but imprudent generosity, restricted his ability to travel. Mathew's image was damaged after his bankruptcy became public knowledge the following year. Despite public appeals to relieve his distress, Mathew's finances never fully recovered.

### In America

The Great Famine broke the back of the temperance movement, even as it broke the health and spirit of Mathew, who organized relief efforts in Cork despite suffering a stroke in 1848. In part to escape his creditors, Mathew left Ireland in 1849 and spent over two years touring America among the many emigrant branches of his society and other Irish organizations. While his efforts were a popular success, his finances and his health both deteriorated. Mathew returned to Cork in 1851 and died at Rathcloheen, Co. Cork, in 1856. Even before Mathew's death, per capita consumption of alcohol in Ireland approximated the levels of the mid-1830s, although some of his temperance societies in Ireland and the United States remained strong for many years.

*See* Catholicism, Irish-American

Father Augustine, OFM Cap., *Footprints of Father Mathew, OFM Cap., Apostle of Temperance* (Dublin, 1947).

Colm Kerrigan, *Father Mathew and the Irish Temperance Movement, 1838–1849* (Cork, 1992).

Elizabeth Malcolm, *Ireland Sober, Ireland Free: Drink and Temperance in 19th Century Ireland* (Dublin, 1986).

John Quinn, "Father Mathew's Disciples: American Catholic Support for Temperance," *Church History*, Vol. 65/4 (December 1996).

PAUL A. TOWNEND

## TENNENT, GILBERT (1703–1764)

Presbyterian clergyman. The eldest son of William Tennent, Gilbert Tennent was born in County Armagh, Ireland, on February 5, 1703. At about age fourteen, he joined his family in immigrating to America.

Educated well by his father, Tennent studied medicine for a year before presenting himself to the Philadelphia Presbytery in May, 1725. Admitted to the ministry, he went to New Brunswick, New Jersey, in the fall of 1726, with the mission of preaching to the area's English-speaking population. Tennent was supported by the local Dutch, themselves aroused by the evangelism of Theodorus Frelinghuysen. Frelinghuysen allowed Tennent to use his buildings and, occasionally, the two addressed the same congregation, each in his native language.

Following an illness, Tennent's religious zeal increased and he became a major catalyst in the "Great Awakening." George Whitefield deemed Tennent one of the "burning and shining Lights of this Part of America," and Tennent journeyed to New York with the eminent preacher. An intense, passionate orator, Tennent made an evangelical tour of southern New Jersey and portions of Maryland in the fall of 1739, and in November 1740, he traveled to Boston and preached in over twenty towns in Massachusetts and Connecticut.

Tennent returned before the Philadelphia Synod convened in May 1741. His disdain toward and disagreement with the more conservative elements in the Church led some ministers to protest Tennent at the convocation. Among other charges, they accused him of disregarding the Synod's authority. Tennent and his supporters in the Presbytery of New Brunswick countered by withdrawing, creating a schism which lasted seventeen years.

In 1743, Tennent moved to Philadelphia to lead a newly established Presbyterian Church composed of Whitefield adherents, remaining there until his death. In time, he strove for reunion with the Presbyterian Church and became an active trustee of the College of New Jersey. Dying on July 23, 1764, Tennent was among the salient leaders of the "Great Awakening."

*See* Scots Irish

Archibald Alexander, *Biographical Sketches of the Founder and Principal Alumni of the Log College* (Princeton, 1845).

Milton J. Coalter, *Gilbert Tennent Son of Thunder* (New York, 1986).

Charles Hodge, *The Constitutional History of the Presbyterian Church in the United States of America,* 2 vols. (Philadelphia, 1839–40).

Charles H. Maxson, *The Great Awakening in the Middle Colonies* (Chicago, 1920).

*The General Assembly's Missionary Magazine* (May 1805).

See also *The Journal of the Presbyterian Historical Society.*

Richard Webster, *A History of the Presbyterian Church in America from its Origin Until the Year 1760* (Philadelphia, 1857).

CHRISTIAN G. SAMITO

## TENNENT, WILLIAM (1695–1746)

Presbyterian clergyman, educator. Born in Ireland, William Tennent graduated from the University of Edinburgh on July 11, 1695. He was ordained a deacon on July 1, 1704, and became a priest in the Church of Ireland on September 22, 1706. Sometime during 1716–18, he, his wife, four sons and a daughter immigrated to Philadelphia and on September 17, 1718, the Synod of Philadelphia admitted Tennent to the Presbyterian ministry. He lived in East Chester, New York, from November 1718 to May 1720, then served in a church in Bedford until August 1726. In the fall of 1726, Tennent became Pastor at Neshaminy, Pennsylvania, a post he held until his death.

A pious and educated evangelist, Tennent also trained others for leadership in the ministry. Although he had been teaching before, he purchased one hundred acres of land on the road between Philadelphia and New York in 1735 and erected Log College for the education of ministers the following year. Tennent's three younger sons trained there along with other future Presbyterian leaders. Tensions with the Philadelphia Synod over Tennent's evangelism, teaching methods, and his welcoming of George Whitefield helped precipitate the 1741 schism within the Presbyterian Church.

Tennent continued instructing until his death on May 6, 1746, at which time Log College ceased to function. Its supporters joined others to establish the College of New Jersey later that year.

*See* Scots Irish

Archibald Alexander, *Biographical Sketches of the Founder and Principal Alumni of the Log College* (Princeton, 1845).

Elias Boudinot, *Memoirs of the Life of Rev. William Tennent* (Morristown, 1807).

Ezra H. Gillett, *History of the Presbyterian Church in the United States of America,* 2 vols. (Philadelphia, 1864).

*The Journal of the Presbyterian Historical Society* (June 1902; June 1904; June, September, 1912; September, December, 1913; September 1914; September, 1915; September, 1919; October, 1927).

Charles H. Maxson, *The Great Awakening in the Middle Colonies* (Chicago, 1920).

Thomas Murphy, *The Presbytery of the Log College* (Philadelphia, 1889).

Richard Webster, *A History of the Presbyterian Church in America from its Origin Until the Year 1760* (Philadelphia, 1857).

CHRISTIAN G. SAMITO

## TENNESSEE

Tennessee history, society, and culture strongly reflect the influence of early settlement of the Scots-Irish and the mid-nineteenth-century migrations of Irish Catholics.

Statistically, one in five Tennesseans claimed Scots-Irish ancestry in the 1990 census. Geographically, the Irish impact is reflected in the founding of cities such as Knoxville and Nashville, as well as towns such as Rogersville, Erin, and McEwen. Glimpses of Irish impact on the vernacular, or built environment, may be seen in the stonework of buildings, bridges and rock walls which dot the rural landscape, as well as the routes of railroads and highways originally laid by Irish workers.

The Irish historical and political impact includes contributions of three U.S. presidents, a distinguished war record that gave Tennessee its nickname as the "Volunteer State," a powerful influence on state and local politics, a major contribution to Texas independence, and a little-known, but impressive role in Irish nationalism.

### Early Settlement (to 1840)

Originally the southwest region of North Carolina, the frontier settlements that became the state of Tennessee were characterized by war and crude organizational efforts. Frustrated by differences with North Carolina's eastern establishment and attracted by opportunities for land and better lives, the first trickle of Scots-Irish migrated over the mountains in the late 1760s and early '70s. The first permanent settler on the Watauga River was Scots-Irish Capt. William Bean (1768). Hearty folk, largely subsistence farmers, followed, fueling Indian wars with the Cherokee that continued until 1776.

Meanwhile, settlers (mostly Scots-Irish) in need of some form of frontier government to deal with daily legal and judicial matters formed the Watauga Association (1772). Following the signing of the Treaty of Transylvania, Wataugans purchased 2,000 square miles from the Cherokees, extending lands for settlement westward to the fertile Cumberland Valley.

Removed geographically from the colonial war for independence, Watauga and Holston Valley settlers responded to British threats to cease aid to the revolutionaries by joining other frontiersmen and marching to King's Mountain, S.C. Utilizing guerrilla-style battle tactics learned from the Cherokees, the frontiersmen defeated British forces in the decisive battle in the south.

Although warfare and farming dominated their attention, the Scots-Irish also focused on the building of the frontier, and were instrumental in the forming of towns and laying the foundations for statehood, which was granted to Tennessee in 1796.

James White co-founded and laid out the streets of Knoxville. Samuel Carrick established that city's Presbyterian Church and founded a school that became Blount College and later, the University of Tennessee.

In middle Tennessee, James Robertson and John Donelson founded Fort Nashborough on the banks of the Cumberland on Christmas Day, 1779. The settlement around the fort became Nashville. Donelson's daughter, Rachel, later married Andrew Jackson, destined to become the hero of the War of 1812 and the first of Tennessee's three U.S. presidents (including Ulster descendants James K. Polk and Andrew Johnson). Other Tennessee Scots-Irish descendants destined for folk-hero status in Texas' war for independence were Davy Crockett and Sam Houston.

Although Ulster Protestants dominated Tennessee's Irish population, by the 1820s–'30s there was evidence of a growing Irish Catholic presence. In Nashville, Irish workers employed to build a bridge across the Cumberland River constructed the state's first Catholic church (Holy Rosary) on the northeast side of present-day Capitol Hill.

In Memphis (founded 1819), Irish immigrant Eugene Magavney pioneered public school education in the south, establishing the Memphis public school system, while the predominately Irish St. Peter's Church served a growing urban Irish population comprised of navy yard and waterfront workers, according to Thomas Stritch (*The Catholic Church in Tennessee: The Sesquicentennial Story,* 1987).

## Immigrant Waves (1840–1860)

Memphis was indicative of the changing dynamics of Tennessee life. By the late 1840s, the Scots-Irish had achieved status among Tennessee's "old families," and Irish Catholics dominated a new, largely urban, wave of famine immigrants.

While drawn to the availability of dock work in the state's four major river cities, migrations of Irish Catholics also followed the east to west routes associated with the construction of railways and roads. Irish populations in Knoxville. Nashville, and Memphis increased four-fold. Irish railroad workers dominated towns such as Erin and nearby McEwen, an area known as "little Ireland." Based on the growth of its Irish population, Tennessee ranked first in the south and tied seventh nationally between 1850 and 1860, according to a study by Morton Winsberg (*Éire-Ireland,* 1985).

A number of these urban immigrants rose quickly to middle-class status. Nashville's Michael Burns, Robert Orr, and George Cowan ranked among those regarded as "gentlemen" through their contributions to the city's economic development, local charities, and participation in state and local politics. Burns, a saddler from County Sligo, rose to directorship of two railroads and two banks, and served in the Tennessee legislature.

The success of men such as Burns lay in stark contrast to the lives of most Irish immigrants. Unskilled and semiskilled workers crowded into urban shacks and tenements near potential employers such as docks and railways. Located in odorous gulches,

plagued by poverty and crime, and victim to frequent flooding and disease, these areas acquired such horrible names as "The Jungle," "Hell's Half Acre," and "Black Bottom" in Nashville, and "The Pinch" in Memphis.

Angered by the influx of immigrant (largely Catholic) poor, and spurred by the rise of anti-Catholic "Know-Nothing" political rhetoric and the writings appearing in the Nashville *Christian Advocate* and books such as *Americanism versus Romanism,* a public backlash developed against immigrants. Tame in comparison to many places, it nonetheless contributed to fearful events such as the mob scene outside the Catholic Cathedral on Christmas Eve 1855.

The courting of ethnic votes by political parties and inroads to local politics and patronage as a result of Irish domination of certain wards (such as Nashville's sixth), drove the nativist backlash that led to Know-Nothing victories around the state, including Memphis, in the 1850s.

Irish reaction was the development of a solidarity that found expression in organizations, ward politics, religion, and a shot of Irish nationalism.

The first dramatic infusion of Irish pride occurred in 1855 with the arrival in East Tennessee of Ireland's exiled hero of '48, John Mitchel. Settling first in the Tuckaleechee Cove, Mitchel moved his family to Knoxville where he edited *The Southern Citizen,* a pro-slavery newspaper. His impact on Tennessee's Irish morale, however, resulted from a series of popular speeches across the state. His famous meeting with IRB leader James Stephens took place in Knoxville (1858), shortly before Mitchel moved from the state.

Tennessee again brushed Irish republican history when a *future* leader in "the cause of Ireland" moved to Nashville in 1857; Thomas J. Kelly took residence in an Irish ward and worked as a printer's foreman at the Southwest Baptist Publishing House (1857–60). Later IRB chroniclers claimed Kelly founded a newspaper in Nashville, although no known copies remain in existence. With the outbreak of the Civil War, Kelly enlisted in the Tenth Ohio, U.S. Army, as Tennessee and his fellow immigrants struggled with the matter of secession.

## Rebels and Politicos (1860–1870)

Nativists blamed the "foreign vote" for the defeat of Tennessee's first vote on secession in February 1861. Like other border states (Kentucky, Maryland, Delaware), Tennessee voters wrestled with secession, but following the fall of Fort Sumter, voted overwhelmingly to join the Confederacy.

Historians such as Kathleen Berkeley have noted the pressures exerted on Irish and other immigrants to prove their loyalty or risk home and job. Irish units formed, including The Kelly Troopers, McCowan Guards, The Burns Light Artillery, and three famous regiments—the Second Tennessee Volunteer Infantry (nicknamed the "Irish Regiment"), Nathan Bedford Forrest's notorious Third Cavalry (dominated by Irish soldiers), and the Tenth Tennessee, known as "The Sons of Erin," which fought the River Fort Campaign and in battles including Chickamauga, Missionary Ridge, Atlanta, Franklin, Murfreesboro, and Nashville. In 1997, a special exhibit at the Tennessee State Museum featured the tattered battle flag of the "Sons of Erin."

Throughout the war, Fenians, the American wing of the IRB, openly recruited in both Union and Confederate camps. When the state fell to Federal forces in 1863, Tennessee was the only southern state that sent delegates to the first Fenian convention in Chicago. The small Nashville circle, led by D. L. Mundy, attended all subsequent conventions, maintaining a senate seat and providing the national organization with one of its three authorized agents for the sale of Fenian bonds. In 1865, the Fenian Council, meeting in Cincinnati, tapped former Nashvillian Thomas J. Kelly as military representative to Ireland, where he replaced Stephens (1866) as head of the IRB.

The pride and unity instilled by Irish regiments during the war spilled over into local organizations. Fenian donations supported efforts by Nashville Catholics to build an orphanage in 1863. A weekly newspaper, *The Catholic Herald,* united the Irish community and mobilized political efforts. By 1868, the Nashville Irish community organized a branch of the Ancient Order of Hibernians, followed later by the Hibernian Benevolent Society, the Parnell Branch of the Irish National League, and other organizations. In 1866, the activities of Nashville's Irish community and its Fenian Circle attracted new residents, Col. John O'Neill and a British spy, Thomas Billis Beach (a.k.a. Henri LeCaron).

In the spring of 1866, as Fenians planned the invasion of Canada, local newspapers reported a flurry of activity, fund-raising, speeches, drilling, and preparations by the Nashville Circle. By late May, trainloads of Tennessee Fenians gathered in Memphis and moved north, where they were placed under the leadership of O'Neill.

The Fenian invasion of Canada failed. O'Neill's regiment, including the thirteenth Tennessee, provided the only successful moments in the doomed effort—the seizure of Fort Erie and a brief skirmish known as the Battle of Ridgeway. O'Neill's hopes for an "Alamo-style" defense of Fort Erie were dashed by day three of the invasion and by demands to return to U.S. soil by his disgruntled troops.

During that evacuation, O'Neill and his men were arrested by U.S. forces on orders from President Andrew Johnson (a Tennessean and, until then, considered a friend to the Fenian cause). Within days, the tiny Nashville circle managed to raise $10,000 toward the Fenian bail. O'Neill's notoriety soon catapulted him to national prominence in the Fenian organization. By 1868, he had risen to the post of Head Center of the Fenian Brotherhood in the U.S. Two former Nashvillians—O'Neill and Kelly—now controlled Irish nationalist efforts.

The Irish in Tennessee were not entirely focused on Irish nationalism. The end of the war and slavery placed free Blacks in competition with the Irish for low-level jobs. Hostilities erupted in Memphis in 1866, resulting in a three-day riot that left forty-eight dead and the destruction of one hundred buildings. A Congressional investigation uncovered the level of Irish control over the city's police (ninety percent), fire department (eighty-six percent), as well as the office of mayor, nine of sixteen alderman seats, and sixty-five percent of elected or appointed city offices.

### ASSIMILATION (AFTER 1870)

The slow erosion of the Irish as a distinct force in Tennessee resulted from a number of factors. The competition from free Blacks for jobs pushed many Irish farther west. The tragic yellow fever epidemics in Memphis (1870s) devastated poor Irish neighborhoods. The return to political power of the disfranchised white elite, the reformist backlash against Irish political and police power in Memphis and Nashville, and the eventual breakup of ethnic ward concentrations as more Irish dispersed into middle-class suburbs, effectively removed their power base of solidarity.

However, a resurgence of interest in preservation and local history is reintroducing Tennesseans to Irish contributions and continuing traditions, such as the annual pilgrimage to Nashville's St. Patrick's Church by Tennessee's still-existent band of Irish "travelers" (or "tinkers"). Nashville's new arena sits on the nineteenth-century site of "Black Bottom," and in 1995, Nashville and Belfast entered a sister-city relationship. Perhaps most significantly, the sounds of the fiddle and steel guitar daily remind Tennesseans of their cultural hearthstone.

C. G. Belissary, "Tennessee & Immigration, 1865–1880," *Tennessee Historical Quarterly,* VII (March–December 1948): 229–48.

Robert E. Corlew, *Tennessee: A Short History,* 2nd ed. (Knoxville, 1981).

F. Garvin Davinport, *Cultural Life in Nashville on the Eve of the Civil War* (Chapel Hill, 1941).

Don Doyle, *Nashville In The New South, 1880–1930* (Knoxville, 1905).

James Joseph Flanagan, "The Irish Element in Nashville, 1810–1890: An Introductory Survey" (M.A. thesis, Vanderbilt University, 1951).

Ed Gleeson, *Rebel Sons of Erin* (Indianapolis, 1993).

Billy Kennedy, *The Scots-Irish in the Hills of Tennessee* (Londonderry, 1995).

DeeGee Lester, "John Mitchel's Wilderness Years In Tennessee," *Éire-Ireland* XXV/2 (Summer 1990): 7–13.

———, "The Memphis Riots of 1866," *Éire-Ireland* XXX/2 (Fall 1995): 59–66.

———, "Tennessee's Bold Fenian Men," *Tennessee Historical Quarterly* (1998).

Thomas Stritch, *The Catholic Church in Tennessee: The Sesquicentennial Story* (Nashville, 1987).

James Summerville, "The City & The Slum: 'Black Bottom' in the Development of South Nashville," *Tennessee Historical Quarterly* XL/2 (Summer 1981): 182–92.

DEEGEE LESTER

## TENNESSEE: FIFTH CONFEDERATE INFANTRY REGIMENT

The Fifth Confederate Infantry Regiment was made up of nearly all Irishmen from Memphis, Tennessee and was called the 'Irish Regiment.' The regiment was organized on May 11, 1861 as the Second (Walker) Tennessee Infantry Regiment (*Tennesseans in the Civil War,* 174). The Second Tennessee was mustered in at the Ancient Order of the Druid Hall in Memphis, and a flag was presented to the company called the Emerald Guards (*Memphis Avalanche Newspaper,* May 17, 1861). Father Daly tended to the spiritual needs of the men (Daniels, 18). They were mustered into Confederate service and ordered to Fort Pillow in August 1861 (*Tennesseans in the Civil War,* 174).

They were ordered to Kentucky and ferried across the Mississippi River in the Battle of Belmont, Missouri on November 7, 1861 (*Tennesseans in the Civil War,* 174). Captain C. W. Frazer remarked on the conduct of the men: "I well remember their dash and courage on that occasion, . . . they bore themselves as veterans . . . my observation being that Irishmen take to this as readily as ducks to water" (Lindsley, 146).

The regiment was ordered to Mississippi and fought at Shiloh. Colonel James Smith would later write that "nine-tenths of the rank and file of the regiment were 'wild Irishmen,' but better soldiers did not fight in the 'lost cause' . . . . Whenever the command 'forward' was given it was replied with a yell" (Lindsley, 173–174).

On July 21, 1862 the Second Tennessee was consolidated with the Twenty-First Infantry to form the Fifth Confederate. Most of the companies of the Twenty-First were also Irishmen from Memphis (*Tennesseans in the Civil War,* 174).

The regiment participated in the Kentucky Campaign of 1862 and were transferred to Patrick Cleburne's command. They had a great deal of love, respect, and admiration for Cleburne (Lindsley, 152).

The unit was engaged in heavy fighting at Murfreesboro, Chickamauga and Chattanooga. Cleburne's Division defeated Sherman at Missionary Ridge and saved the army at Ringgold Gap (Buck, 180–185). The Fifth fought in the Atlanta Campaign and killed General James B. McPherson. McPherson was one of only two United States Army commanders to die in combat (Lindsley, 151). The Army of Tennessee withdrew from Atlanta and in the fall started the 1864 Tennessee Campaign. At Franklin, Tennessee, Cleburne's Division attacked the center of the Federal position. Frazer stated that [Cleburne] "sought out our regiment, charged in and died with it. He could have selected no better place . . ." (Lindsley, 151–152).

The Fifth fought at Nashville and retreated to Tupelo, Mississippi. Their last battle was in North Carolina in March of 1865. On the 26th of April of 1865, the last of the Fifth Confederate surrendered with ten men. Frazer said of the gallant Irishmen that their friends across the Atlantic are assured that the name and fame are upheld by the Fifth Confederate (Lindsley, 151–152).

Irving A. Buck, *Cleburne and His Command* (New York, 1908).

Larry J. Daniels, *Soldiering in the Army of Tennessee: A Portrait of Life in the Confederate Army* (Chapel Hill, 1991).

John Berrien Lindsley, *Lindsley's Military Annuals of Tennessee Confederate* (Nashville, Tennessee, 1886).

*Memphis Avalanche Newspaper* (May 17, 1861).

Howell and Elizabeth Purdue, *Pat Cleburne: Confederate General* (Hillsboro, Texas, 1973).

*Tennesseans in the Civil War: Part One* (Nashville, Tennessee, 1964).

THOMAS Y. CARTWRIGHT

## TENNESSEE: TENTH INFANTRY REGIMENT

In April 1861, Randall McGavock formed Company D for the state militia. The company was called the Sons of Erin (Gleeson, 11–12). The company flag had the national colors, while the other side was green satin, bearing a golden harp and the inscription: *Sons of Erin, go where glory waits you* (Fisk). The Tenth Tennessee was also called the Irish Regiment (Daniels, 18).

On May 25, the regiment was ordered to help in the building of Forts Donelson and Henry. They joined other Irishmen under Colonel Adolpus Heiman, who was building the forts. On May 29, Heiman formed the Tenth Tennessee, keeping the title Sons of Erin and the flag. McGavock was elected Lieutenant Colonel. Of the ten companies for the unit, seven were from Nashville, and the other three were from Clarksville, McEwen, and Pulaski (Gleeson, 15–20).

The unit escaped capture at Fort Henry and fought with gallantry at Fort Donelson; however, the fort surrendered on February 16, 1862. Most of the Tenth were sent to Camp Douglas, Illinois and were paroled at Vicksburg in September 1862. McGavock succeeded Heiman as Colonel (Gleeson, 99–100).

Colonel McGavock was killed in the Vicksburg Campaign (Griffin, 555). The Tenth fought at Chickamauga where they assisted in the capture of nine cannons (*Tennesseans in the Civil War,*

195). They were the last to leave their position when the Federals broke the center at Missionary Ridge (Gleeson, 268).

On August 31, 1864, the chaplain for the Tenth, Father Bliemel, was killed by an artillery shell in the Atlanta Campaign. Bleimel was the only Catholic chaplain to die in the war (Gleeson, 304–305).

The Tenth was engaged in all of the battles in the 1864 Tennessee Campaign. At Murfreesboro they again held their ground when other units retreated. Brigadier General T. B. Smith praised the unit for their gallantry. They lost most of their regiment at Nashville. One man was left to surrender in North Carolina on May 1, 1865 (Gleeson, 304–323).

*See* Civil War

Larry J. Daniels, *Soldiering in the Army of Tennessee: A Portrait of Life in the Confederate Army* (Chapel Hill, 1991).

Mary Elizabeth Fisk, "The Confederate Irishman," *Historical Papers and Reminiscences* (United Daughters of the Confederacy, Tennessee Division). The article was read by Miss Fisk on October 2, 1908 at the Historical Meeting of the Nashville Chapter No. 1, U.D.C.

Ed Gleeson, *Rebel Sons of Erin* (Indianapolis, Indiana, 1993).

Pat Griffin, *Confederate Veterans Magazine,* vol. 13, no. 12.

Randall W. McGavock, *Pen and Sword* (Jackson, Tennessee, 1960).

*Tennesseans in the Civil War: Part One* (Nashville, Tennessee, 1964).

THOMAS Y. CARTWRIGHT

## TEXAS

### AN EARLY IRISH PRESENCE: NEW SPAIN AND MEXICO

The Irish influence on Texas' historical formation matured more prominently in history than is commonly realized. Reaching back into the eighteenth-century decades of Spanish rule over the lands on New Spain's far northern frontier from which the province of Texas was carved out, and continuing on into the nineteenth century, Irish personages emerged visible in—among other aspects of society—Texas' political and religious life, military affairs, farming and ranching transformation, and economic development.

By a certain point in time, however, the Irish impact on the growth of Texas had assumed a permanent form. That influence mirrored the establishment of an Irish presence in Texas that could brag of a true Irish heritage leaving its mark on the state's history.

With the Texas story advancing through the decades of the late 1800s into the 1900s, this Irish permeation continued to germinate. In so doing, it broadened its reach to expand beyond the areas already mentioned: touching the arts, journalism, the sciences, sports, and other segments of Texas life and society.

No name stands more prominent among the Irish who served the monarchy of Spain, as it colonized the province of Texas, than that of Hugo Oconór: an Irishman whose Gaelic appendage was Hugh O'Connor. He was born in Dublin, Ireland, in 1734. Having come into conflict with the English, O'Connor fled to Spain. There he entered the service of the Volunteer Regiment of Aragon. Subsequently O'Connor was stationed first in Cuba and then in Mexico. In the course of all that, he rose steadily in the ranks of the Spanish military. At the same time the Spanish began to refer to him as Hugo Oconór. And, because of his red hair, he became known also in Spanish circles as "Capitán Colorado."

In 1767 the Dubliner was sent to Texas as governor of that province, a position which he held into 1770. He then was appointed, in 1772, "Comandante Inspector," responsible to the Viceroy of New Spain for establishing order and security along the northern frontier of the Spanish colonial territories from Texas to California. In that capacity, the colonel from Dublin re-organized and re-formed much of the Spanish military structure throughout the vast region: inaugurating new norms for dress, setting uniform standards for salary and rank, and more. Earn-ing well-deserved credit for bringing peace to the area, but ex-hausted and broken in health from his efforts, O'Connor was transferred to the Yucatán as governor. There he died in 1779, having lived only into his forty-fifth year.

Beyond the legacy of O'Connor, surnames such as Morfi, Obre-gón, Barragan, and O'Donojú loom significant in the annals of Spanish and Mexican suzerainty over Texas. But those Span-ish-Mexican appellations were simply "translations" of the Irish family names Murphy, O'Brien, Berrigan, and O'Donoghue. One of Texas history's most respected early historians was Father Juan Agustín Morfi. (Murphy). His *History of Texas, 1673–1779* re-mains today a highly respected study of the missions, presi-dios, villages, and life of the indigenous peoples in Texas during those decades (see Donald E. Chipman, *Spanish Texas, 1519–1821*, 245–46).

Ignacio Obregón was a large landowner in Mexico. Joaquín Obregón served as head of the Finance and Commerce Commit-tee in the Mexican government of Emperor Augustín de Iturbide that emerged from the Mexican revolution against Spain final-ized in 1821, retaining authority over Texas.

General Miguel Barragan acted as interim President of Mexico for a time under Antonio López de Santa Anna. Another Barra-gan, Captain Marcos, was with Santa Anna at the Battle of San Ja-cinto on 21 April 1836, the decisive victory of the Texans over the Mexicans that cemented Texas' independence. Almost ironically, it was Captain Marcos who—having escaped the clutches of the Texans at San Jacinto—carried the news of Santa Anna's defeat to the other major Mexican army commander maneuvering in the field against the Texans, General José Urrea.

Perhaps the best known of all the Irishmen whose legacy grew in association with Spanish colonialism in the Americas was Don Juan O'Donojú (Sean O'Donoghue), recorded in history as the last Viceroy of New Spain. He represented the Spanish royal government in its formal accession to Mexican independence in 1821, signing with Iturbide the *Tratados de Córdoba*. It was O'Donoghue who early on came into contact with a Roman Ca-tholic priest of Spanish and Irish lineage who came to play a vis-ible role in the Catholic saga of Texas, but remains to this day a most elusive figure, Father Miguel (Michael) Muldoon.

Muldoon was born in Spain of a Spanish mother and an Irish father, the latter of whom had earlier fled Ireland for Spain. In that Iberian nation the senior Muldoon met his future bride and the two soon were married. Their son, young Michael, completed his studies in Spanish seminaries and was ordained a priest in that land of *Los Reyes Católicos* not long before the Mexican revo-lution against Spain was culminated in 1821. Being of an adven-turous spirit, the Spanish-Irish cleric asked to be sent to a mis-sion field in New Spain. Arriving in Mexico in that final year of the Mexican revolution, 1821, he served for a brief time as chap-lain to Viceroy O'Donoghue.

A decade after his arrival in Mexico, in 1831, Father Muldoon appeared at Stephen Fuller Austin's Texas colony of San Felipe, assuming the position of resident priest. He acted in that capacity through much of 1832, being one of only four Catholic clergy-

Historical marker near La Grange, Texas, honoring Father Michael Muldoon

men laboring in Texas at the time. Father Muldoon endeared him-self to the settlers of Austin's colony, adapting well to the primitive living conditions of the Texas frontier while exhibiting a "friendly and jovial disposition" (Flannery, *The Irish Texans*, 23).

Some scholars have judged him harshly for what they saw in him as a tendency toward being unnecessarily lax in Catholic Church discipline. David Weber in his *The Mexican Frontier, 1821–1846: The American Southwest under Mexico* referred to Mul-doon as a "liberal and highly pro-American priest" (80). The late Carlos Eduardo Castañeda, Catholic Texas' most pre-eminent historian, questioned Muldoon's sincerity (*Our Catholic Heritage in Texas*, vol. 6, 348). Perhaps the most accurate assessment of Father Muldoon, however, is that of Father James Talmadge Moore, who in his fine study *Through Fire and Flood: The Catholic Church in Frontier Texas, 1836–1900* wrote that "Muldoon was an enigmatic figure, loved by some, hated by others. He was called lax in religious practice by some in Austin's colony—the same ones, it is easy to suspect, who would have complained loudest if he had been strict. He was called immoral, yet all that is really known is that he drank wine and brandy just as most colonists did. The fact that he was a Catholic priest, of course, made him persona non grata with some" (27).

## THE IRISH IMMIGRANTS

At virtually the same time that Muldoon had ventured to the San Felipe colony, Texas had begun to experience a major demo-graphic metamorphosis. In a major sense, Texas stood at the far northern borderland of an Hispanic Catholic world that had come into being with its roots set deep in the mother country of Spain and its other identity, that of the indigenous, molded as part of its centuries-long pilgrimage through the Valley of Mexico and northward. At the same time Texas was becoming an at-tractive final destination point for Americans and Europeans— of Protestant and Catholic backgrounds—who formed one as-pect of the vanguard of a westward movement from the eastern United States entering the area. Just as they were in the growth of immigrant America, the Irish were conspicuous in that migration of new peoples into Texas.

John Brendan Flannery emphasizes that one of the earliest locales in Texas bragging of a definite Irish influence was the 1806

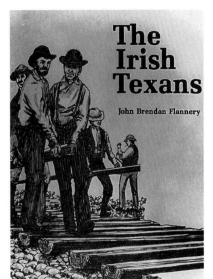

A recent popular
narrative of the
Irish in Texas

settlement of Villa de Santísima Trinidad de Salcedo, situated in northeastern Texas west of Nacogdoches on the Trinity River. Established first by Louisianans and then, in January 1807, reinforced by citizens from San Antonio de Béxar, it counted a number of Irishmen and their families among its earliest residents. Within a few years of its origin, surnames such as Quinn, Magee, Sheridan, Lunn, Coyle, Fear, Mulroney, Fitzgerald, and Barrett were on the roll of the colony's population.

Yet, the main Irish influx into Texas began to make its appearance farther south in the 1820s and 1830s. Refugio and San Patricio de Hibernia both were important colonies, which, from those decades of the twenties and thirties to the outbreak of the American Civil War, were seen as the centers of Irish settlement in Texas. As such, they reflected a more distinct Gaelic identity than any other sites in that vast land.

But again, Flannery argues that "the Irish in Texas are generally thought of in terms of the so-called 'Irish colonists' of San Patricio and Refugio. They were the most noticeable Texas Irish. However, there were Irish who had come from the United States to the Austin, De León, Peters, DeWitt and Robertson colonies and to the eastern part of the state near the Louisiana border. Most of them came to the province of Texas because of the availability of inexpensive land" (*The Irish Texans*, 27).

Austin's colony included among its population a number of Irish, with such surnames as Allen, McCormick, Jackson, Callaghan, Clark, Cummings, Fitzgerald, Hughes, Kennedy, Kelly, Lynch and Moore (*The Irish Texans*, 27). And Martin de León from Mexico invited a number of Irish into his colony, including a personage who was to become one of Texas' most prominent Irish citizens, John J. Linn. More will be said of Linn later.

In the meantime, the early 1830s witnessed the establishment of a contingent of Irish families at Staggers Point northwest of present-day Houston. And a few years later the northern reaches of Texas—centered on the present-day Dallas–Fort Worth region north to Oklahoma—saw many Irish settle in what was known as Peters Colony. At this time, however, attention must be directed to the empresario colonies of Refugio and San Patricio de Hibernia.

The founders of those two settlements, James Power and Dr. James Hewetson, connected with Refugio, as well as John Mc-

Mullen and James McGloin of San Patricio de Hibernia, were native Irishmen. Power was born in 1788 in County Wexford, Ireland. Shortly after his twenty-first birthday he emigrated from the Emerald Isle to the United States. Power resided first in Philadelphia and later at New Orleans, before finally settling in Saltillo, Mexico, capital of the state of Coahuila. There he became a Mexican citizen and married a Mexican woman from Matamoros by the name of Dolores Portilla. Likely given inspiration by his father-in-law, Don Felipe Roque de la Portilla, in Saltillo Power organized a colonial effort for Texas in partnership with Dr. Hewetson.

Hewetson was eight years younger than Power, born in County Kilkenny, Ireland, in 1796. He too emigrated from his homeland to Philadelphia and he studied to be a physician. The young Irish doctor followed Stephen Fuller Austin to Texas in 1821, but, learning of the success of the Mexican revolution against Spain in that same year, he decided to continue on in his travels to Monclova, Mexico, and then ultimately to Saltillo (it should be noted that a large assemblage of Irish resided in Saltillo at that time). In the latter city he ventured into business and married Josefa Guajardo, a well-to-do property owner.

Power and Hewetson's original empresario grant to bring Irish colonists to Texas was issued in June 1828; and, like all other such agreements, it carried a time limit of six years. In 1833, with the grant soon to expire and Dr. Hewetson having opted to remain in Saltillo with his family, Power made a voyage back to Ireland to recruit colonists. Returning to Texas in 1834, after a very difficult voyage, he brought with him enough Irish to lay a solid foundation for the colony of Refugio.

John McMullen and James McGloin also emerged as notable Irish immigrants in Texas during the early to middle decades of

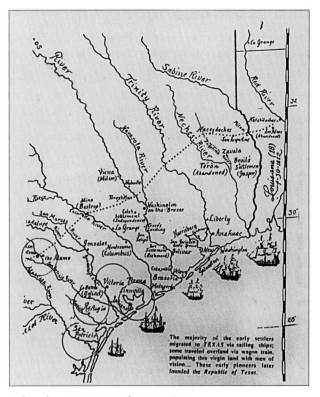

Early settlements in nineteenth-century Texas

the nineteenth century. In assuming prominence as leaders in the Irish populating of Texas, they must be seen also as players in the rejuvenation of a Roman Catholic presence in that land from the 1830s through the 1850s. John McMullen was born in 1785, possibly in eastern Donegal County, Ireland. James McGloin first saw the world fourteen years later in County Sligo, Ireland. McMullen emigrated from his mother country to Baltimore, Maryland—the center of Catholic settlement in English colonial America—and then ventured on to Savannah, Georgia, and ultimately to Matamoros, Mexico. While in Savannah in 1810, McMullen married Esther Cummings. In the meantime, McGloin surfaced at Matamoros also—almost by chance it seems, since he initially planned to migrate to Australia but missed his ship at Liverpool, England, and instead ventured to the American continent, with Mexico as his destination. At Matamoros he met the McMullens, married Esther's daughter by a first marriage, and entered into partnership with John to found an Irish colony in Texas.

In 1827 the two immigrants filed a joint grant application with the Mexican government to establish their settlement. Failing to receive approval for that request, McMullen and McGloin filed a second time on 14 August 1828. After some delay, that latter action resulted in Mexico's granting them permission to lead colonists to the Nueces River in Texas. There McMullen and McGloin established the colony of San Patricio de Hibernia.

Perhaps no Irishman stands greater in the annals of Texas history than John J. Linn. Though himself not an empresario, he did enter Texas as an immigrant in 1829, seeking to develop a merchant enterprise there. Marrying and planting his entire family in Texas, Linn went on to become a leading merchant, public figure, Catholic layman, Texas patriot, and even an historian. He was born on 19 June 1798, in County Antrim, Ireland. His father, John Linn, was a college professor who allied with the patriotic movement and acted as a member of the United Irishmen.

Fleeing the wrath of the English for his support of the 1798 Wexford Uprising, John Linn "with his wife and one child, the author of these reminiscences, took passage on a ship bound for New York" (*Reminiscences of Fifty Years in Texas,* 9). The Linns spent several years in New York before John J. Linn moved on to New Orleans in 1822, seeking opportunities in the merchant trade business. Pursuing further economic ventures, in 1829 John J. Linn was attracted to Texas.

In Texas the Irishman constructed a home in the town of Victoria, not far inland from the Gulf of Mexico, and erected a warehouse on the banks of Lavaca Bay at a locale that was first called Linn's Landing, and later Linnville. He was to live for more than a half-century in that very same house at Victoria, until his death on 27 October 1885. In 1833, he married Margaret C. Daniels in the city of New Orleans. The two were to become the parents of fourteen children. In the meantime, John J. Linn's mother and father, as well as his three brothers, Edward, Henry, and Charles, all settled in Texas with or near John J. and Margaret. Each proved to be a contributor to the building of Texas society.

During the course of his fifty-six years as a resident of Texas, John J. Linn proved a significant figure in the history of that land in many ways. He visibly supported the Texans in their revolt against Mexican rule. Then he served as "alcalde" of Victoria (elected in 1836); and when that title was discarded, Linn became that city's first mayor (1839). He also represented the Victoria district as a member of the House of Representatives in the second and third congresses of the Republic of Texas. Ultimately

John J. Linn

holding several other positions of service to Texas, he at the same time emerged as an influential merchant. In 1883, two years before his death, he published his famous *Reminiscences of Fifty Years in Texas.*

## THE CATHOLIC FAITH OF THE IRISH TEXANS

While Protestantism—especially Presbyterianism—was visible as the religion of some of the Irish immigrants to Texas in the nineteenth century, Roman Catholicism was the religion of most. Thus, Catholicism in its historical maturation in Texas, from the 1820s on, carried with it a strong Gaelic character. That Irish influence can be seen as a continuing one. For example, prominent names among late nineteenth-century and early twentieth-century Catholic bishops in Texas include Nicholas Gallagher (Galveston), Christopher E. Byrne (Galveston), Edward Joseph Dunne (Dallas), and Joseph Patrick Lynch (Dallas).

As previously suggested, the Catholic presence in Texas had declined since reaching its apex with the work of Spanish Franciscan missionaries in the eighteenth century. Secularization of the missions, from 1794 through 1830, combined with a lessening focus of the Spanish royal government on its vast far northern frontier and then the ultimate revolution of the Mexican people against the mother country, Spain, in 1821, followed by the Texas war for independence from Mexico in 1835–1836, contributed to the growth of an unfriendly environment for the Catholic Church in Texas.

Added to these situations, the appearance in Texas of the previously discussed vanguard of European and American immigrants as the mid-decades of the nineteenth century approached presented the Catholic Church with new challenges in that terrain. How was it to nurture the religious life of the Mexicans and Catholicized indigenous peoples long resident on the land, while at the same time seeing to the spiritual needs of the incoming migrants? In that enterprise the Catholic Irish of Texas assumed a leading role.

In 1840, the Catholic Church commenced a revival of its presence in Texas by sending a French missionary, Vincentian Father Jean-Marie Odin, C.M., into the region to head up the new effort as vice prefect apostolic. John J. Linn hosted Father Odin at his home in Victoria many times, advised the French priest on the issue of reclaiming church properties from the Texas republic, headed the effort to build a new church at Victoria, and remained a staunch supporter of the Church until his own death in 1885.

Discussion of the nineteenth-century Irish in Texas and their Catholic faith cannot possibly highlight even a fair number of the Irish who were prominently associated with the Church in Texas, but a few others must be mentioned. Among them would be, once again, James McGloin; an Irish-American Vincentian priest named John Timon; and Mother Margaret Mary Healy-Murphy.

Possessing a similar spirit to that which John J. Linn mirrored in his life, James McGloin stood out as a man of a simple but dignified character. In her study, *The Forgotten Colony: San Patricio de Hibernia: The History, the People, and the Legends of the Irish Colony of McMullen-McGloin,* Rachel Bluntzer Hébert gave her readers an insight into McGloin's faith. Describing the interior of the Irishman's residence at Round Lake near San Patricio in 1853, on his return home after the 21 January 1853 murder of his stepfather-in-law, business partner, and long-time friend John McMullen at San Antonio, Bluntzer Hérbert wrote:

> He opened the gate and strode toward the cabin, entered and absent-mindedly barred the door. Bright flames leapt up the chimney and lit up a room that was neat and well arranged. The furniture was hand-made and consisted only of bare necessities. The roughly plastered walls were a background for a crucifix which hung above the beds and a holy water fountain near the front door. Two pictures flanked the chimney—one of the Virgin and another of Saint Patrick (3).

Father John Timon, C.M., has long been remembered in the annals of Texas Catholic history. Though never a permanent resident of Texas himself, he was the priest who sent Father Odin to the Lone Star Republic to rebuild the faith there. Timon gave his confrère steadfast support until his own consecration as the first Bishop of Buffalo, New York, in 1847.

Margaret Mary Healy, born in County Kerry, Ireland, in 1834, emigrated to the United States with her physician father, two brothers, and aunts and uncles in 1845. Within a few months the entire family struck out for Texas. En route Margaret Mary's father died at New Orleans. The clan then ultimately settled in Matamoros, Mexico. There Margaret Mary met and, on 4 May 1849, married John B. Murphy, a soldier from County Cork, Ireland, in General Zachary Taylor's army that had invaded Mexico in 1846.

The deprivation of her own Irish people at the hands of the English, which she witnessed as a child back in County Kerry, and the extremes of poverty and injustice that she saw in her native land as well as in the United States and Mexico, made a lifelong impression on Margaret Mary Healy-Murphy. The result was that she then devoted her life to helping the oppressed. Settling finally with her husband in Corpus Christi, Texas—where he lived for many years as a successful lawyer, judge, and politician, until his death in 1884—Margaret Mary Healy-Murphy became especially concerned with helping the African Americans of the Corpus Christi–San Antonio vicinities. She is perhaps best known for founding a religious community of nuns known as the Sisters of the Holy Ghost, a sisterhood that today remains overwhelmingly Irish in its make-up. Mother Margaret Mary Healy-Murphy, as she became known, died on 25 August 1907.

TEXAS INDEPENDENCE AND AFTER

It is unnecessary to offer any historical judgments regarding the moral positions that the opposing sides in both the Texas war for independence from Mexico during 1835–1836, and the American Civil War from 1861–1865, assumed. But it is important to point out that Irish personages—some Irish-born, others first, second, or third generation descendants—played much more visible roles in those struggles than often is realized.

A most interesting statistic of the Texas revolution against Mexico is that a dozen Irish-born Texans died at the Alamo on 6 March 1836. Others of Irish heritage, including Davey Crockett—who it is reported was the son of an Ulsterman—also gave their lives at the Alamo. And even Sam Houston, who was not present at the Alamo but certainly was a major player in the Texas revolution, claimed lineage back to Ireland (County Tyrone). Numerous Irish-born, or early generation Irish descendants, served in such battles as Coleto Creek, Goliad, and San Jacinto, many of them dying in those engagements.

The story of Peggy McCormick, who emigrated from Ireland to Texas with her husband in 1822 (her spouse later drowned in the San Jacinto River) and settled on a tract of land near Houston, is noteworthy. The incident of her riding up to a wounded Sam Houston—who was sitting on the ground propped up against a tree on her property after the Battle of San Jacinto—and rudely ordering him to remove the dead Mexicans from her land, cannot be forgotten. Dr. Alexander Ewing, a native of County Derry, Ireland, acted as chief surgeon for Houston's army in that battle.

The American Civil War counted many Irish Texans who supported the Confederacy, as well as others who served the Union. While a good number of Texas Irish opposed secession of the Lone Star State from the United States, a contingent of eighteen of them actually signed the 1861 ordinance of secession. Any number of Irish names appear on the rolls of men who fought for the blue and the grey. None among them emerged better known in Texas history than three who heroically participated in the 1 January 1863 Confederate recapture of Galveston from occupying Union forces. They were Michael McCormick, son of Peggy McCormick of the Battle of San Jacinto fame; Peter Fagan of Refugio; and Dick Dowling, from County Galway, Ireland, who commanded the Company F Texas heavy artillery unit, "better known as the Davis Guards or the 'Fighting Irishmen'" (Flannery, *The Irish Texans,* 101).

As with much of the United States, the immigrant period of settlement and formation in Texas waned as the nineteenth century gave way to the twentieth. But the immigrants profoundly left their mark as the twentieth century unfolded. John Brendan Flannery writes that

> Irish are still coming to Texas. According to the 1970 Federal census there were then 12,134 Irish-born residing in the state. The number of Texas descendants of Irish-born antecedents is probably incalculable. They are scattered throughout the state (*sic*) and Irish surnames are prominent in its business, industrial, political, educational, religious and civic life (141).

William Foley, a late nineteenth- and early twentieth-century dry goods merchant who became an important businessman and civic leader, is a prime example of Flannery's reference. Foley's department stores today can be found throughout the state, but are no longer owned by the original Irish Foley family. Bobby Bragan and Nolan Ryan are Texas sports legends in the world of baseball. In the spectrum of journalism, no one at the present time reflects more that Irish legacy than Tommy Denton, a senior editor of the *Fort Worth Star Telegram,* a major newspaper in Texas.

Of the many Irish scholars treating Texas, the late Sister M. Loyola Hegarty, C.C.V.I., a native of Cork, Ireland, holds a special place for her outstanding study *Serving With Gladness: The Origin and History of the Congregation of the Sisters of Charity of the Incarnate Word, Houston, Texas.* And an Irish-ancestry Texas governor, John Connally, was with the President of the United States, John Fitzgerald Kennedy, when the latter was assassinated in Dallas, Texas, on 22 November 1963.

The Irish dramatically influenced the history of their adopted Texas from the eighteenth century onward, and in so doing the Irish Texans were significant in helping to lay the base for today's Lone Star State. The uniqueness of their Gaelic heritage will always be seen as an essential element in any assessment of the evolution of Texas history.

*See* Linn, John Joseph; Timon, John

John Brendan Flannery, *The Irish Texans* (San Antonio, 1980).

Patrick Foley, "The Shamrock and the Altar in Early Nineteenth-Century Texas: Irish Catholics and Their Faith," *The Irish in the West* (Manhattan, Kansas, 1993).

Rachel Bluntzer Hérbert, *The Forgotten Colony: San Patricio de Hibernia, the History, the People and the Legends of the Irish Colony of McMullen-McGloin* (Burnet, Texas, 1981).

John J. Linn, *Reminiscences of Fifty Years in Texas* (Austin, Texas, Facsimile Reproduction, 1986, originally published in 1883).

Lawrence J. McCaffrey, "Irish Catholics in America," *The Encyclopedia of American Catholic History,* eds., Michael Glazier and Thomas J. Shelley (Collegeville, Minnesota, 1997).

James Talmadge Moore, *Through Fire and Flood: The Catholic Church in Frontier Texas, l836–1900* (College Station, Texas, 1992).

Craig H. Roell, "Linn, John Joseph," *The New Handbook of Texas* (Austin, Texas, 1996).

PATRICK FOLEY

# THEATER, IRISH IN

The Irishman was a familiar type in American theater as early as the colonial period, and consequently the Stage Irishman has been said to be as old as American theater. The involvment of the Irish in American theater, however, proceeded through quite distinct phases with different artistic and political dynamics. Colonial immigrants to America from Ireland found a caricature of themselves already on the American stage; later immigrants and second-generation Irish-Americans appropriated this image, along with a great proportion of theatrical commerce in America, and revised it; they exploited what proved to be a key agent of assimilation so successfully and they integrated themselves into American theatrical culture so completely as to become both ubiquitous and invisible. The Irish as a distinct dimension of American theater, then, is a drama with both a beginning and an end.

America was a likely scene for Irish theatrical endeavors. Irish immigrants to colonial America included large numbers of artisans and professionals who found an English culture favorable for their commercial interests. They also understood English theater, which was already influenced by Irish figures such as Richard Brinsley Sheridan and Oliver Goldsmith. Later Irish immigrants, in flight from famine Ireland, were lower in economic class, rural in origin, and often Irish-speakers. They brought with them a different theatrical heritage of a highly developed culture of storytelling, music, and dance. In the period before the American Civil War, the Irish began to dominate American theater at the same time that Irish immigrants were mostly urban, impov-erished, and encountered barriers to acceptance in American society. After the Civil War, the Irish in American theater confronted stereotypes by putting images of themselves onstage, frequently in humorous fashion, and so helped neutralize nativist hostility to their presence. By the twentieth century, Irish men and women followed the American entertainment preference for film and became exurbanites—and both factors conspired against theater.

## COLONIAL PERIOD

The Irish were on the American stage as early as *The Disappointment* in 1767, which featured a singing, dancing, drinking, comic stereotype. *The Battle of Brooklyn* of 1776 is an early example of both specifically Irish-American experience onstage and the use of stage dramas to communicate a message to largely illiterate audiences. These and others from the period and after, such as *The Irish Widow* (1773) and *The True-born Irishman* (1787), were English in authorship, production, and performance. The first Irish playwrights to arrive in American became American dramatists. John Daly Burk, who left Dublin for Boston, produced historical spectacles on American themes, such as *Bunker Hill or, The Death of General Warren* (1797). In these and other political dramas, Irish interest in hostile portrayals of English characters and cultures took the form of American patriotism rather than Irish nationalism.

## PRE–CIVIL WAR AMERICA

In the early 19th century, Irish immigrants began to assume leadership roles in the business dimensions of theater. One of the first was William Niblo, who in 1828 successfully combined beer garden settings with light vaudeville entertainment at Niblo's Garden and Theatre on Broadway in New York City. Unique in New York for single-price admissions, Niblo's Garden, as it was known, was also an important venue for early Italian opera productions in America.

The beginnings of a movement for Irish portrayals of the Irish were inspired by the American tours of the Irish actor Tyrone Power beginning in 1833. The first of a theatrical family dynasty, Power was a playwright as well as an actor. After his death in the sinking of the *S.S.President* in 1841, two Irishmen were ejected for hissing at a revival of his play *O'Flannigan and the Fairies,* which gave prominence to Irish whiskey and superstition, thus giving early warning that portrayals of the Irish onstage, even by the Irish, could be controversial.

In 1842 the first of the major figures of Irish-American drama arrived in New York in the person of John Brougham, a graduate of Trinity College who had worked in London in the 1830s in association with the leading theatrical management team of Madame Vestris and Charles Mathews. He made his American debut at the Park Theatre in *His Last Legs* and soon after began to make long tours through the American south and to the west coast. Prolific and associated with more than 100 scripts, Brougham, lacking a precedent for recognizably Irish drama, concentrated on solo performances of historical figures, including some Irish ones such as the temperance advocate Father Mathew and Daniel O'Connell. Like John Daly Burk, Brougham also developed stage spectacles on themes from American history, such as *The Declaration of Independence* (1844). He was a major contributor to the rise of American burlesque in its earliest form of musical travesty and satire, notably in *Pocahontas; or, The Gentle Savage* (1855), which was performed throughout army camps during the Civil War and remained popular for another thirty years. On Irish topics, Brougham's work included *The Game of Love* (1855), a comedy about a Murphy family of social climbers. Brougham was celebrated more as a performer than a playwright, and his impact on American theater was limited by his consistently bad business decisions. However, as early as 1846 he was praised in the *New York Herald* for efforts "to elevate the Irish character, and to dispel the prejudice which exists against our fellow citizens of Irish birth."

One year after Brougham made his American debut, another kind of Irish-American theatrical enterprise made its debut in New York. In 1843 the Virginia Minstrels, founded by Dan Emmett and others, opened at the Bowery Amphitheatre, creating the blackface genre that thrived until supplanted by vaudeville and musial comedy late in the century. Irish and Irish-Americans, such as Emmett, Richard Hooley and Dan Bryant, were always central to the minstrel stage. Among the many factors underlying Irish-American impersonation of African-Americans on the stage were theatrical policies against black performers and Irish familiarity with black culture from integrated urban districts. Integration and common grievances of Irish- and African-Americans in antebellum New York were epitomized by several dancing contests in the 1840s between Master Jack Diamond and William Henry Lane, known as Juba. In addition to a conspicuous racial dynamic, minstrel shows also contributed to American theater popular songs, such as Emmett's "Dixie," and the sketch-driven folk comedy that was quite distinct from plot-driven society dramas imported from the continent.

Another kind of ethnic theater made its debut in New York in 1848 with the opening of Benjamin Baker's *A Glance at New York,* with Mose the Bowery B'hoy as an immigrant ne'er-do-well and heroic fireman. This was a dramatic type that became popular when immigrant Irish men and women were streaming from famine to urban America. One immigrant, Barney Williams, born in Cork, became one of the most popular stage performers of this type of hard-drinking, irrascible and lovable Irish stereotype. His wife, Maria Pray, performed a compatible female stereotype of loyalty and dignity under adverse conditions. Such character types also provided opportunities for the Irish comedian and singer John Collins

Barney Williams and Maria Pray, seeking vehicles for their reliable Irish character types, engaged James Pilgrim, who, though English, became one of the most prolific mid-century writers of Irish plays. The first work commissioned by the Williamses was *Paddy the Piper* (1850), which was followed by *Ireland and America* (1851), *Robert Emmet* (1853), and *Irish Assurance and Yankee Modesty* (1853). His many other plays attracted broad American audiences at a time when American cities were flooded with unskilled Irish laborers who crowded slums and the ranks of the unemployed. The conjunction of English authorship and native American audiences encouraged paternalistic morality plays in scenes of gross disease and impoverishment. In this context, the Irish type on stage became more needy than charming and the stereotype more demeaning than comical.

## DION BOUCICAULT

In 1853, a decade after John Brougham, another Irish theatrical journeyman arrived in New York through London: Dion Boucicault. Like Brougham, Boucicault had learned about professional theater from Madame Vestris and Charles Mathews. He enjoyed a sudden rise to celebrity with their 1841 production of his play *London Assurance,* to which Brougham claimed part au-

thorship. A society comedy comparable to *School for Scandal,* it became one of the most popular nineteenth-century plays in America and England. Its first production introduced the box set for the illusion of realism, and Boucicault subsequently was always involved in set designs, usually more for spectacular effects, and he introduced set safety precautions such as fire proofing.

Much like Brougham, Boucicault spent his first years on the American stage experimenting with different vehicles for his acting talents. Many were original in that they took as subject topical news rather than historical materials. Examples of these are *The Poor of New York* (1857), about slum life; *Jessie Brown; or, The Relief of Lucknow* (1858), about the Sepoy Rebellion while it was in progress; and *The Octoroon* (1859), about American slavery. These alone, along with his acting renown, would make Boucicault a major figure in nineteenth-century American drama.

His greater contribution, however, emerged in 1860, when he wrote a drama, *The Colleen Bawn,* based on Gerald Griffin's novel *The Collegians.* It was an enormous success, in part because of a spectacular pool scene and in part because of his own charisma in the Irish rogue role of Myles-na-Coppaleen. Boucicault claimed "When I wrote *The Colleen Bawn,* I invented Irish drama. It was original in form, in material, in treatment, and in dialogue." Though noted for exaggerations and prevarications, Boucicault can be allowed the originality of putting western, rural Ireland on stage in New York before it was onstage in London or even in Dublin. His romantic imagery of ruined abbeys and round towers was a corrective to the prevailing slum-dwelling stage image of the Irish in America. Though he was from Dublin and educated in London, he could also claim the credibility of his Irish birth as proof against non-Irish opportunists such as James Pilgrim. Later in his career he would state this assertively: "let me disclaim any pretension as an actor to excel others in the delineation of the Irish character. It is the Irish character as misrepresented by the English dramatists that I convict as a libel."

Boucicault had continuing success with other kinds of plays, notably *Rip Van Winkle* (1866), but he would remain best known in America and abroad for his Irish plays, which were extremely popular in Ireland. After *The Colleen Bawn,* he wrote and performed in *Arrah-na-Pogue* (1864), a melodrama about the 1798

Dion Boucicault (Courtesy of Billy Rose Theatre Collection, The New York Public Library for the Performing Arts, Astor, Lenox and Tilden Foundations)

rising in Ireland. Unlike his other plays, it opened in Dublin rather than in New York. It included a version of the song "The Wearing of the Green" with edited lyrics so incendiary that the song was banned in the British commonwealth. As always, it included a comic role for himself, this time as Shaun the Post. Such work, with romantic heroes and faithful heroines, when performed in America, as *Arrah-na-Pogue* was in 1865, provided an image of the Irish alternative to the depictions of the draft riots in New York two years before.

In 1874 Boucicault opened at Wallack's Theatre in New York in the title role of *The Shaughraun,* his greatest success. Frequently derided for its melodramatic revelations about escaped Fenian revolutionaries returning to saintly maidens plagued by lacivious land agents, his decision to put Fenian causes on stage in a noble light was both risky and partisan in the 1870s. In the Irish-English context, that became apparent when subsequent touring productions visited London and Boucicault published an open letter to Prime Minister Benjamin Disraeli seeking a general pardon for all Fenian prisoners. But the political edge was even sharper in New York, where in the 1870s there had been major riots at Orange Day parades which celebrated William of Orange's victory at the Battle of the Boyne. In addition, the image of the Irish as noble rather than needy continued to offset one-sided portrayals of the growing Irish immigrant population. When Henry James reviewed *The Shaughraun* in *The Nation,* he deplored the familiar "Irish types" of the domestic maid variety and thus so welcomed Boucicault's construction of "love, devotion, self-sacrifice, humble but heroic bravery, and brimming Irish *bonhomie* and irony."

## POST-CIVIL WAR

One of the first to parody Boucicault's romanticism was Edward "Ned" Harrigan, a New Yorker of Irish descent who learned stagecraft in minstrel companies. In 1873, he opened a pastiche called *Arrah-na-Brogue,* and in 1875 he appeared with his partner, Tony Hart (born Anthony J. Cannon), in a parody of *The Shaughraun* ("the rascal") called *The Skibbeah* ("the hangman"). These were libelous offenses, and the second production was the subject of a successful lawsuit by Boucicault. They were also theatrical departures from Boucicault's notion of a dignified Irish play that would rebound to Irish-America's benefit. In reaction to Orange Day parade riots and resurgent American nativism, Harrigan and Hart instead chose comedy, farce, and the vaudeville sketch as a means to humanize the image of the Irish in America.

Harrigan met Hart in Chicago in 1871, and they quickly became one of the most successful partnerships on the national circuit of vaudeville halls. Harrigan wrote the short sketches, often placing Irish stereotypes in comic contrast to African Americans, German Americans, Italian Americans, and Chinese Americans, all participants in what he called "the pageant of American immigration." He also wrote lyrics to many sentimental songs that were set to music by his father-in-law, David Braham. Songs that had enormous popularity quite apart from theater included "I Never Drink Behind the Bar," "Why Paddy's Always Poor," "The Last of the Hogans," and "The Gallant 69th." One, "Danny By My Side," was a favorite of both Mayor of New York City Jimmy Walker and Governor of New York Al Smith.

In sketches Harrigan began to play the character Dan Mulligan, an Irishman with the usual weaknesses of drink, gambling, and naive ambitions but who is ultimately revealed to be loyal and generous. Against Harrigan's tall, baritone Mulligan, Tony

Harrigan and Hart

Hart played short, vulnerable, tenor roles, often in blackface or drag. The sketches evolved into a popular series about the Mulligan Guard, or a ragged and undisciplined company of volunteer militia. In *The Mulligan Guard Ball* (1879) the sketch material first appeared in full dramatic setting with the plot of love attraction between young Tom Mulligan and Katrina Lochmuller. The series was quickly extended through new plays such as *The Mulligan Guard Christmas* (1879), *The Mulligan Guard Surprise* (1880), and *The Mulligan's Silver Wedding* (1880). One of the later and more respected by contemporary standards was *Cordelia's Aspirations* (1883) about the Mulligan family's thwarted plans for respectability, with commentary by Tony Hart as the black maid Rebecca.

The Harrigan and Hart partnership ended in 1885, and neither prospered after it. In 1886 William Dean Howells wrote in *Harper's Magazine* that "we recognize in Mr. Harrigan's work the spring of a true American comedy, the beginnings of things which may be great things." Harrigan and Hart 's work certainly was the beginning of a new Irish-American comedy that lampooned its own pretensions to respectability and assimilation. In this it was quite different, and more direct, than Boucicault's romanticization of Ireland. After Harrigan and Hart, Irish-Americans gained respectability by degrees and sometimes objected to comic versions of their social upward mobility.

Nor in this period was "low" culture Irish-America's only culture. One of the distinguished Irish-American theatrical families was the Drews at the Arch Street Theatre in Philadelphia. John Drew, born in Dublin, came as a child to New York, where his father worked in Niblo's Garden. After a brief return to Ireland, he built a stage career in America on the Irish roles found in Restoration comedies and on new society plays such as *The Irish Tutor.* Mrs. Drew, born Louisa Lane in London, had from 1827 built her career on a series of Shakespearian roles. In 1853 they became co-managers of the Arch Theatre, and from 1861 she alone created one of the most distinguished American companies staging a repertory of classics. She was also grandmother to Lionel, Ethel, and John Barrymore.

In the 1870s two products of the Arch were brought to New York by Augustin Daly, one of the great theatrical producers in

American history. The first was the Drews' son John Drew, who made his New York debut in Daly's *The Big Bonanza* in 1875 and continued playing a variety of English and American roles through the 1920s. The second was Ada Rehan, who was born Ada Crehan in Limerick and later adopted a misspelling as her stage name. In 1879 she appeared in Daly's *Pique* and *L'Assommoir,* both, like most of Daly's shows, adaptations of noteworthy novels. With the younger John Drew, she was a regular performer in Daly productions and combined classic, tragic roles with contemporary comedies. Daly, from Virginia, had produced his first play in New York in 1863 and become the most important theater owner as well as producer of his time. He leased, restored, or built the Fifth Avenue Theatre, the Grand Opera House, and, of course, Daly's, and booked them with dramas and comedies that, in comparison with Harrigan and Hart, were distinctly "high" culture.

Two of the most important Irish-American playwrights of the time worked on American rather than Irish material. James A. Herne, who shortened his proper name, Aherne, was born in upstate New York and learned stagecraft by joining a traveling troupe and writing skits to be performed by trained dogs. Later, he was best-known for *Hearts of Oak* (1880) and *Margaret Fleming* (1891), both psychological dramas and the second one of the earliest works in America to show the influence of Henrik Ibsen. In the same decades Bartley Campbell, having helped convert Hooley's in Chicago from minstrel shows, settled in San Francisco and wrote a series of plays including *The Vigilantes* (1877) that used the American West rather than Ireland as a setting.

Two forms of drama did prolong earlier directions to the end of the nineteenth century, when the continuing news of general interest from Ireland concerned Home Rule and Land League organization. The first was historical melodramas, a form equally popular in Dublin, which added life to the romanticized image of Ireland associated with Boucicault. In America, as in Ireland, Robert Emmet was a favorite subject. Robert Emmet plays were written and staged in St. Louis by P. T. Cunningham; in Ohio by B. M. Boylan; and in New York by Brandon Tynan, whose 1902 production had a cast of 150.

The second was an extension of the Harrigan and Hart rendition in humorous manner of the Irish immigrant experience in

George M. Cohan

America. Musically, the most important performer was Chauncey Olcott, another graduate of minstrel shows, who starred in a long series of musicals such as *Mavourneen* (1892) through *Macushla* (1912) and introduced songs such as "When Irish Eyes Are Smiling" and "My Wild Irish Rose." In the late nineteenth century, as Irish-American influence over political organization grew, the comic dramas took politics as a subject. Edgar Selden's *McKenna's Flirtation* (1889), Gratton Donnelly's *A Tammany Tiger* (1896), and E. W. Townsend's *McFadden's Row of Flats* (1904) were examples of theater that maintained the comic portrayal of Irish-America, complete with vaudeville stagings, despite the gravity of the topics of housing and graft. Only the second of those three playwrights was Irish-American, and increasingly Irish-Americans again began to protest their portrayal by others on stage. *McFadden's Row of Flats,* for example, was subject to protests and demonstrations organized by the *Gaelic-American.*

One of the remarkable links in American theater history is that a young actor who made his debut in Boucicault's *The Colleen Bawn* would be the father of Eugene O'Neill, thus being associated with one of the most important playwrights in America of the nineteenth and the twentieth centuries. James O'Neill was born in Kilkenny and brought to America as a child. In 1883, after twenty years of very varied theatrical experience, he took the lead of Edward Dantes in the popular melodrama *The Count of Monte Cristo,* a role to which he remained yoked for nearly forty years. The character of a senior, celebrated actor of a premodern style of theater, with his banality and his frustration, is the center of son Eugene O'Neill's chief work, *Long Day's Journey Into Night.*

## TWENTIETH CENTURY

Twentieth century drama is quite different from nineteenth century drama in numerous ways, both aesthetic and sociological. In America, three factors altered the practice of theater of specific interest to the Irish. First, commercial interest attracted others to the production of Irish plays and often the results were banal. Second, after the Irish Literary Revival, Irish drama emanated from Dublin rather than New York, where Boucicault had invented the Irish play. Third, as in other dimensions of the Irish immigrant experience, successful assimilation processes opened broader opportunities and less specific identities for actors and playwrights.

Immediately after the turn of the century, both romanticized versions of Ireland and political drama of Irish New York began to proliferate. In 1902, a play written by Arthur Sullivan, in collaboration with someone other than William Schwenck Gilbert, opened to great acclaim in New York with the title *Emerald Isle: or, The Caves of Carrig-Cleena.* Though built on the kinds of characters familiar from Boucicault, it reduced them to banality, and it certainly lacked the knowledge of Ireland that Boucicault thought necessary to prevent libels of it. The more realistic political play suffered the same fate as *The Man of the Hour* (1906), a drama based on the Irish-American New York Mayor George McClellan that was written by the English-American playwright George Broadhurst. In Edward Sheldon's *The Boss* (1911) and James Barcus's *The Governor's Boss* (1914) the pattern of others portraying Irish-Americans continued. Perhaps the most famous later examples of this trend were *Abbie's Irish Rose* (1922) by Anne Nichols and *Finian's Rainbow* (1947) by Yip Harburg and Fred Saidy. The first was an exercise in American stereotypes, Irish and Jewish, without the Harrigan and Hart wit, and the second, for all its musical sophistication, reduced Irishness to friendship with leprechauns.

Two important exceptions to that pattern were James Gleason and George M. Cohan. Gleason was the child of a theater family who used that experience to fashion the comedy *The Shannons of Broadway* (1927), one of several successful plays he wrote in the 1920s. Also from a theatrical family, George M. Cohan began an unusually prolific career of popular successes with *Little Johnny Jones* in 1904. It included his songs "Give My Regards to Broadway" and "The Yankee Doodle Dandy." In the 1920s Cohan opened a number of Irish-American shows, such as *Little Nellie Kelly* (1922), *The Rise of Rosie O'Reilly* (1923), and *The Merry Malones* (1927). Though his contribution helped move vaudeville toward drama, Cohan is generally credited more with popular than with artistic success.

Playwrights from Ireland began to seize the opportunity opened by local productions. Bernard Shaw found an Irish-American disciple in Arnold Daly, who was not related to Augustin Daly. Arnold Daly began producing Shaw plays in America with *Candida* in 1903 and achieved his greatest notoriety when *Mrs. Warren's Profession* (1905) was closed by the police after a single performance. One agent of censorship was William McAdoo, one-time President of the American Irish Historical Society, who would be linked to other American censorship cases including James Joyce's *Ulysses* and Avery Hopwood and Al Woods's *The Demi-Virgin*.

Touring companies from the Abbey Theatre in Dublin began to visit America in 1911. On their first visit, the Irish Players, as the company was named, met fierce opposition from Irish-American demonstrators against its production of J. M. Synge's *The Playboy of the Western World* in Boston, New York, and Philadelphia, where the company was arrested. Like opponents of the play in Ireland, the demonstrators objected to the portrayal of Irish characters as prevaricators and gullible fools, but the sensitivity in America had the added urgency that this image of the Irish was being presented to a general audience of other immigrants and xenophobic American nativists. Abbey companies began to tour America regularly in the 1930s. Their traveling repertory was less ambitious than their productions at home, with the result that American experience of Irish drama was limited to a small and unvaried group of plays.

The first tour, however, had great influence among young American theater playwrights and designers such as Susan Glaspell and Robert Edmond Jones. In the period when "art" theater evolved in intellectual and bohemian society, new theater groups, such as Washington Square Players or The Neighborhood Playhouse, often looked to Irish playwrights for exciting new work and the Abbey Theatre as a model company. In the 1920s Lord Dunsany visited New York to see acclaimed local productions of his work, and James Joyce's play *Exiles* had its first English-language production in New York in 1925.

## EUGENE O'NEILL

One who credited the Irish Players with "opening my eyes to the existence of real theatre" was Eugene O'Neill, who dominates any history of American drama as much as any history of Irish-American drama. In that sentiment O'Neill was attempting to distinguish his interests from those of his father James O'Neill, whose theater the son found "unreal, artificial, and irrelevant." In keeping with his time, O'Neill's work is both intellectually and aesthetically ambitious. His characters, who are drifting socially and emotionally, explore conscious and subconscious limitations in relentless examination that onstage often take the form of long, poetic speeches. In it Ireland and the Irish imagination are less often an explicit kind of material for the stage than an implicit frame for action, and in this O'Neill's work demonstrates a kind of assimilation of Irish-American drama into American drama.

Born in New York City and sometimes on tour with his father's *The Count of Monte Cristo,* O'Neill dropped out of Princeton for manual jobs and then shipped out on cargo ships as an able seaman. His theatrical training included both the practical experience of acting in versions of his father's play and the intellectual experience of Professor George Peirce Baker's seminar in drama at Harvard University. His first two produced plays were staged by the Provincetown Players in summer season at Cape Cod in 1916, and *Bound East for Cardiff* and *Thirst* were so successful that the company relocated to Greenwich Village. The company and O'Neill were influenced by the Abbey, and J. M. Synge in particular; and they staged work as one-act plays in the spirit of *Riders to the Sea.*

In the 1920s O'Neill's work was the most important on the American stage. His first full-length play, *Beyond the Horizon,* earned a Pulitzer Prize in 1920. It was followed by works that included *The Emperor Jones* (1920), *Anna Christie* (1921), *The Hairy Ape* (1922), *All God's Chillun Got Wings* (1924), *Desire Under the Elms* (1924), *The Great God Brown* (1926), and *Strange Interlude* (1928). The last, a nine-act Freudian anatomy of marriage, was called by Alexander Wolcott "*Abie's Irish Rose* for the intelligentsia."

O'Neill's 1931 play *Mourning Becomes Electra* was an American version of the Greek *Oresteia* staged as a trilogy that took five hours in a single evening. Though he received the Nobel Prize in 1936, O'Neill withdrew from public life because of illness and also disgust with contemporary drama and the critical reception of his own plays. *The Iceman Cometh* opened on Broadway in 1946, but it was a production of that play in 1956, three years after O'Neill's death, that led to a general reassessment and revival of his work. Part of that revival was the American premiere in 1956 of *Long Day's Journey Into Night,* O'Neill's scathing portrayal of the elderly Irish actor father, the lace-curtain Irish mother declining into drug addiction, and aimless sons. They were specifically Irish-American characters, as are the characters in *A Touch of the Poet* and *A Moon for the Misbegotten,* both of which were produced posthumously in 1957. Because they are all unflattering images of the Irish, they would have attracted protests and demonstrations earlier in the century. Their acceptance is testament to both the artistic accomplishment of O'Neill's work and to the greater security of an Irish-America that had by mid-century successfully assimilated itself into American culture.

Two playwrights contemporary to O'Neill help illustrate the process of assimilation that, by its success, largely extinguished a distinctively Irish-American drama. Philip Barry was a second-generation Irish-American who graduated from Yale and, like O'Neill, from Professor Baker's drama seminar at Harvard. His work focused almost entirely on American high society, for example *Holiday* (1928) and *The Philadelphia Story* (1939). George Kelly was a Philadelphian connected to both high society, in the person of his Olympian champion brother John B. Kelly (father of Grace Kelly), and to vaudeville theater, in the person of his other brother, Walter C. Kelly, who had a popular act as an Irish laborer. His first plays were comedies on theatrical themes, such as *The Torch-Bearers* (1922) and *The Show-Off* (1924). Later, though, his work concentrated on unflattering examinations of society figures, especially women, as in *Craig's Wife* (1925) and *Reflected Glory* (1936).

CONTEMPORARY PERIOD

In recent years, Irish drama continues to originate in Ireland and the Irish-American theater has been absorbed into American theater as much as Irish-Americans have into American society. There are exceptions that seek specifically Irish-American subjects. Frank Gilroy's *The Subject Was Roses* (1964) was about an Irish-American family's trauma over the return of a son from military service. William Alfred's *Hogan's Goat* (1965) returned to the subject of Brooklyn party-machine politics, which had to be set in the 1890s to be convincingly Irish. But the many contemporary playwrights with Irish-American names are no longer limited to or evidently interested in exploration of specifically Irish-American subjects. Song revues and dance programs continue to be popular, but dramatic depictions of the Irish-American experience have found better presentation in film and television than in theater.

> *See* Cohan, George; Boucicault, Dion; O'Neill, Eugene; Cinema, Irish in

Gerald Bordman, *The Oxford Companion to American Theatre,* 2nd ed. (New York, 1992).

Harry Cronin, *Eugene O'Neill: Irish and American* (New York, 1976).

Arthur Gelb and Barbara Gelb, *O'Neill* (New York, 1962).

John P. Harrington, *The Irish Play on the New York Stage* (Lexington, KY, 1997).

Richard Moody, *Ned Harrigan: From Corlear's Hook to Herald Square* (Chicago, 1980).

Montrose J. Moses, *The American Dramatist* (Boston, 1925).

George C. D. Odell, *Annals of the New York Stage* (New York, 1937).

Arthur Hobson Quinn, *A History of the American Drama: From the Beginning to the Civil War* (New York, 1923).

———, *A History of the American Drama: From the Civil War to the Present Day* (New York, 1943).

Kenneth R. Rossman, *The Irish in American Drama in the Nineteenth Century* (New York, 1939).

Maxine Schwartz Seller, ed., *Ethnic Theatre in the United States* (Westport, CT, 1983).

Townsend Walsh, *The Career of Dion Boucicault* (New York, 1915).

Carl Wittke, *The Irish in America* (Baton Rouge, LA, 1956).

JOHN P. HARRINGTON

## THOMSON, CHARLES (1729–1824)

Educator, legislator, merchant, secretary of the Continental Congress. Born in County Derry, Ireland, Thomson was one of six orphaned children who came to New Castle, Delaware, his mother having died in Ireland and his father on shipboard. Thomson attended Dr. Francis Allison's academy at New London, Pennsylvania, before he himself began conducting a private school. In 1750, he received an appointment as tutor in the Philadelphia Academy through Benjamin Franklin's help, and from 1757–60 was master of the Latin school which later became the William Penn Charter School. In 1760, Thomson also began a prosperous career as a merchant.

Enjoying an honorable reputation, Indians selected Thomson to keep their record of the proceedings leading to the treaty of Easton in 1757, and the next year, the Delaware tribe adopted him with a name meaning "man who tells the truth."

During the period preceding the Revolution, Thomson actively participated in public affairs and was prominent for his critical stance toward Great Britain. Joseph Galloway and other Pennsylvania conservatives blocked his selection as delegate to the Continental Congress but Thomson impressed John Adams as "the Sam Adams of Philadelphia, the life of the cause of liberty," and he was chosen by Congress to be its secretary. (C. F. Adams, ed., *The Works of John Adams* 2: 358)

When the Continental Congress reassembled in May 1775, Thomson was again selected its secretary, and for the next fourteen years he recorded its debates and discussions, chronicling the birth of the nation. Thomson notified George Washington of the general's election as president, but on July 23, 1789, resigned from his post. He retired to his estate of Harriton, near Philadelphia, where he spent the next two decades translating the Septuagint and New Testament for publication in 1808 as *The Holy Bible, Containing the Old and New Covenant, Commonly Called the Old and New Testament*. He died August 16, 1824.

> *See* Scots Irish

The Library of Congress has Thomson's official and private papers and a segment of his translation of the New Testament while the Historical Society of Pennsylvania holds Thomson's 1784 letter book and several other manuscripts.

James E. Hendricks, *Charles Thomson and the Making of a New Nation, 1729–1824* (Rutherford, 1979).

*Pennsylvania Magazine of History and Biography*, October, 1891, 327–35; January, 1892, 499; July, 1909, 336–39.

Boyd S. Schlenther, *Charles Thomson: A Patriot's Pursuit* (Newark, 1990).

Arthur M. Schlesinger, *The Colonial Merchants and the American Revolution, 1763–1776* (New York, 1918).

John F. Watson, *Annals of Philadephia* (Philadelphia, 1830).

CHRISTIAN G. SAMITO

## THORNTON, MATTHEW (1714–1803)

Signer of the Declaration of Independence. Born in Ireland, Thornton and his parents immigrated to Maine in 1718 before settling near Worcester, Massachusetts. Thornton received an education in medicine, completing his studies at the Worcester Academy in 1740 and practicing in the Scotch-Irish community of Londonderry, New Hampshire. He resided there until 1779, taking part in public affairs and raising his family of five children.

In 1745, Thornton participated in the Louisbourg expedition in the capacity of "under-surgeon" of the New Hampshire contingent and later held a colonelcy in the militia under the royal government. In 1758, Thornton represented Londonderry in the legislature, beginning his prominent career in colonial and state government and in 1768, he was granted the township that bears his name today. He voiced outspoken protests against the Stamp Act and stood as a member of the growing revolutionary movement. When the colonies broke from England, Thornton won election as president of New Hampshire's provincial congress of 1775 and chaired the Committee of Safety which organized resistance and stood as the general government during the early Revolution.

In the tumultuous Revolutionary period, Thornton held various posts such as speaker of the house, member of the council and chair of the state's constitutional committee. In 1776, he was selected as an associate justice of the superior court, sitting on the bench until 1782 despite his lack of formal legal training. In

1776–77, Thornton also served in the Continental Congress and was among the signers of the Declaration of Independence before returning to state government. In 1780, he moved to Merrimack County and represented it in New Hampshire's Senate from 1784–86 before retiring to his farm as a revered elder leader. He died on June 24, 1803, while visiting his daughter in Newburyport, Massachusetts, and was buried near his home in Merrimack.

*See* Declaration of Independence; New Hampshire

Thornton's papers and a manuscript biography by contemporary William Plumer are held at the archives of the New Hampshire Historical Society at Concord, New Hampshire.

Charles T. Adams, *Matthew Thornton of New Hampshire: A Patriot of the American Revolution* (Philadelphia, 1903).

W. H. Bailey, "Matthew Thornton," *Granite Monthly* (March 1892).

John Sanderson, *Biographies of the Signers to the Declaration of Independence*, 9 vols. (Philadelphia, 1823–27).

C. H. Woodbury, "Matthew Thornton," *Proceedings of the New Hampshire Historical Society,* vol. 3 (1902).

CHRISTIAN G. SAMITO

## TIERNAN, FRANCES CHRISTINE (1846–1920)

Author. Frances Christine Fisher was born July 5, 1846, in Salisbury, N.C., to an Episcopalian father and a Roman Catholic mother, Col. Charles Frederick and Elizabeth (Caldwell) Fisher. Frances was reared a Catholic and was confirmed by the Rt. Rev. James Gibbons, who was vicar apostolic of North Carolina at the time.

Her father, a Confederate officer, was killed in 1861 at the battle of Manassas. A maiden aunt became her companion in the family home. She was devoted to her religion and had a church dedicated to the Sacred Heart built on the family land.

Although not a recluse, she ventured from the family estate only for visits to Asheville, N.C., and avoided social occasions. Writing became the mainstay of her life in that small, western North Carolina mountain town.

In 1870 her first novel, *Valerie Aylmer,* was published under the pseudonym Christian Reid. That was the beginning of a prolific career, during which she produced nearly fifty novels and hundreds of short stories, poems and travelogues.

A sampling of the early period of her writing included *Morton House* (1871); *A Daughter of Bohemia* (1874); *A Question of Honor* (1875); *The Land of the Sky* (1876), set in western North Carolina; *Bonny Kate* (1878); and *Hearts of Steel* (1883).

On Dec. 29, 1887, she married James Marquis Tiernan of Maryland and moved with him to Mexico, where he was employed in developing mines. While the couple lived there, she made use of her experience and included Mexican settings, characters, history and legends in her writings.

Among her novels of that period were *A Cast for Fortune* (1890); *Carmela* (1891); *A Comedy of Elopement* and *A Little Maid of Arcady* (1893); *The Land of the Sun* (1894); *The Picture of Las Cruces* (1896); and *The Man of the Family* and *Fairy Gold* (1897).

After her husband's death in January 1898, Tiernan returned to Salisbury and continued her writing. She was a loyal member of the United Daughters of the Confederacy. *Under the Southern Cross* (1900), a drama in which Tiernan showed her devotion to the Confederacy and her belief in the right of secession, became nationally famous as a presentation of the Confederate's cause.

Tiernan's later writings included *A Daughter of the Sierra* (1903); *Princess Nadine* (1908); *The Light of the Vision* (1911); *The Wargrave Trust* (1912); and *A Far-Away Princess* (1914).

In 1909 Tiernan was awarded the Laetare Medal by the University of Notre Dame. She died March 24, 1920, in Salisbury.

*See* Fiction, Irish-American

E. A. Alderman and C. A. Smith, *Library of Southern Literature* (Atlanta, 1929).

S. A. Allibone, *A Critical Dictionary of English Literature* (Philadelphia, 1863–1971).

W. J. Burke and W. D. Howe, *American Authors and Books* (New York, 1943).

Eleanor C. Donnelly, *et al., A Round Table of the Representative American Catholic Novelists* (1887).

R. Johnson, ed., *Biographical Dictionary of America* (Boston, 1906).

*The Guide to Catholic Literature,* 2 vols (Detroit, 1940–44).

MARIANNA McLOUGHLIN

## TIMON, JOHN (1797–1867)

First Bishop of Buffalo, New York (1847–1867). John Timon was born to Irish immigrant parents at Conswego Settlement near York, Pennsylvania, on 12 February 1797. His father and mother, James and Eleanor Leddy Timon, had emigrated from County Cavan, Ireland, to Pennsylvania shortly before John's birth. Three years after John came into the world, in 1800, the Timon family moved to Baltimore. With the passage of time, James Timon prospered as a merchant in that Chesapeake Bay city.

In 1818, the Timon family moved west. Stopping over first at Pittsburgh, then Louisville, the Timons ventured on to St. Louis, where they settled permanently in 1819. In that frontier city just across the Mississippi River, John Timon worked with his father to establish a merchandise business venture, "Timon & Son." However, the weak economic environment from the East had already reached the Mississippi River region, forcing the Timons, in 1820, to abandon "Timon and Son."

In St. Louis he came to know Father Felix De Andreis, C.M., one of the co-founders in the United States—along with Father Joseph Rosati, C.M.—of the Congregation of the Mission, the Vincentians. At the same time, Bishop Louis William DuBourg, ordinary of the Diocese of Louisiana and the Floridas, took Timon into his newly-established college in St. Louis (the future St. Louis University).

On 19 July 1822, Timon matriculated to the Vincentian seminary at Perryville, Missouri, later to be called St. Mary of the Barrens. He was ordained to the priesthood on 23 September 1826. Meanwhile, Timon also joined the Vincentians. It was then that he met and labored with the priest who was to mature as his best friend and closest confrère, Jean-Marie Odin, C.M., the future first Bishop of Galveston, Texas, and second Archbishop of New Orleans.

During the next two decades John Timon, C.M., developed as one of the American frontier's best-loved missionaries. In the course of that growth he was named first Visitor of the American Vincentians (1835) and then Prefect Apostolic of Texas (1839). Sought by many for the Catholic episcopate of the United States—an appointment he regularly sought not—Timon, on 23 April 1847, was named first Bishop of Buffalo, New York. His consecration at the hands of Bishop John Hughes of New York, assisted by Bishops William Walsh of Halifax and John McClosky of Albany, took place at St. Patrick's Cathedral in New York City on

17 October 1847. Serving for twenty years as a dedicated church-man, vocal opponent of slavery, and ecumenically-oriented prelate, Bishop John Timon died at Buffalo on 16 April 1867.

*See* New York State

Ralph Bayard, C.M., *The Lone-Star Vanguard: The Catholic Re-Occupation of Texas, 1838–1848* (Saint Louis, 1945).

James Talmadge Moore, *Through Fire and Flood: The Catholic Church in Frontier Texas, 1836–1900* (College Station, 1992).

Leonard B. Riforgiato, "John Timon and the Succession to the See of Baltimore in 1851," *Vincentian Heritage* (Spring 1987): 38–49.

John E. Rybolt, C.M., ed., *The American Vincentians: A Popular History of the Congregation of the Mission in the United States, 1815–1987* (Brooklyn, 1988).

PATRICK FOLEY

## TITANIC AND IRISH PASSENGERS

The *Titanic* was built by Harland and Wolff of Belfast, one of the world's great shipbuilders, which was founded in 1862. Its highly skilled workers were proud of being both Harland and Wolff men and Orangemen besides. Over the decades a token number of Catholics were employed; but in 1912—a year of religious strife and industrial bigotry—all Catholics were ousted.

The story of the *Titanic* began in 1908 when the White Star Line resolved to replace the Cunard Line as the leading carrier on the lucrative North Atlantic routes, and it assigned Harland and Wolff to build three super liners, the *Olympia*, the *Titanic* and the *Gigantic* (renamed the *Britannic,* which was torpedoed in 1916). Working a 49-hour week, the skilled workers at Harland and Wolff built the *Olympia* in less than two years; and on February 16, 1912, the work on the *Titanic* was completed.

### MAIDEN VOYAGE

The *Titanic* was the most luxurious liner afloat—882.5 feet long, 60,250 tonnes and capable of carrying 3,000 passengers at a top speed of 24 to 25 knots. It was, in the last analysis, owned by John Pierpoint Morgan, who personally controlled the International Mercantile Marine Company (IMM) which owned the White Star Line.

While there were some disputes about some engineering matters, there was a firm and unanimous conviction, in all quarters, that the *HMS Titanic* was unsinkable. Many professionals, including some naval inspectors, thought that fitting the liner with sixteen life boats and four inflatable craft (which would carry only 1,178 passengers) was an unnecessary safety gesture for a ship that would never sink.

Amid wild celebrations and adulation, the *Titanic* sailed out of Belfast on April 10, 1912, and headed for Southampton (where there was a dock strike) to begin its maiden voyage. After taking on passengers and supplies, it headed for Cherbourg where it took on European passengers, a batch of rich Americans and mail; and after a stop of ninety minutes sailed for Queenstown (Cobh). There 113 steerage passengers, including five children, boarded together with seven Irish-American second-class passengers. Interestingly, the *Titanic* took on 1,385 bags of mail, much of it intended for Irish exiles scattered across America. The local immigration officer, E. J. Sharpe, checked the sailing lists and reported that there were 2,208 people aboard, including a crew of 892. (Several authors have taken issue with Sharpe's figures, but the differences are not significant.)

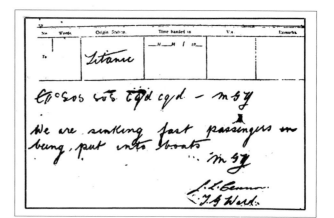

A last message from the *Titanic*

Two young men disembarked at Queenstown. One was crewman James Coffey, a local resident, who decided to jump ship; and the other was Francis Brown (1880–1960), a Jesuit scholastic and an avid photographer who had boarded at Southampton. He sailed first class (a gift from his uncle, the bishop of Cloyne) and his camera was rarely out of his hand; he photographed every accessible part of the liner and anyone who would pause on the deck. His photographs (discovered in 1985 by E.E. O'Donnell, S.J., in the Jesuit archives in Dublin) form the only comprehensive collection of *Titanic* pictures. Brown was a classmate of James Joyce at the Royal University, where he topped Joyce in English and Joyce outclassed him in Latin. He appears as "Mr. Brown, the Jesuit" in *Ulysses*.

After two hours in Queenstown, the *Titanic* set course for New York. The American social register was at sea—Astors, Benjamin Guggenheim and his mistress, Thayers, Wideners and scores of the social elite toasted with their British counterparts. The 495 steerage passengers, including the 113 Irish who boarded at Queenstown, listened to emigrant Patrick Daly, clad in kilts, play the mournful "Erin's Lament" on his bagpipes as the great ship left Ireland behind.

### DISASTER

On April 14, as evening came and darkness fell, passengers walked the decks, stared at the endless calm sea, ate and drank, played cards, listened to music, chatted and relaxed, and some retired early. But the sense of safety and serenity was short-lived. From early evening at least seven messages warning the *Titanic* of ice fields ahead were received or intercepted but they got cursory attention. When it was too late to alter course, a huge iceberg was seen in the path of the *Titanic*, and at 11:40 P.M. it ripped the side of the great ship. Within minutes disbelief gave way to anxiety, but by 12:25 panic and pandemonium swept the passengers, and Captain Smith gave orders to abandon ship and ordered the lowering of the life boats. The unsinkable ship was sinking; and within two hours the *Titanic* broke in two and was swallowed up by the cold waters of the North Atlantic. Of the 2,208 passengers only 651 survived.

### DISCRIMINATION?

Movies and myths have given distorted pictures of the living conditions of steerage passengers. The planned menu shows that the food was good, wholesome and varied. Dinner was served at noon rather than in the evening when the upper decks dined. But men and women were segregated, men's sleeping quarters were forward and women and children were near the stern in the lowest deck of the *Titanic*. It was a new ship on its first voyage and conditions were clean and sanitary.

Controversy surrounds every aspect of the *Titanic* disaster. Journalists embellished the stories of survivors and moviemakers obfuscated the historical facts with dramatic and inaccurate details (such as swarms of rats in the steerage quarters and locked gates preventing third-class passengers from reaching the top deck). But still the statistics are chilling: 64 percent of first-class passengers were saved; 31 percent of second-class; 29 percent of third-class; and 20 percent of the crew. The 495 steerage passengers were at a great disadvantage as they were housed in the bowels of the ship and confusion was compounded by the fact that most of them did not speak English. Of the 113 Irish who boarded at Queenstown 39 were saved.

At the Senate Investigation, chaired by Senator William Alden Smith, sworn testimony of several steerage survivors contradicts some prevailing myths and charges of discrimination. For instance: Irishman Daniel Buckley testified: "I think the passengers in the third class had as much a chance as passengers in the first and second class." Berk Pickard, a Jewish resident of London, swore: "The steerage passengers, so far as I could see, were not prevented from getting to the upper decks by anyone, or by closed doors, or by anything else."

After two world wars and massive catastrophes at sea, the *Titanic* disaster, more than all others, has captivated the imagination and curiosity of generations. The tragedy of the Irish-built liner has been placed on the shoulders of many, including the designers, the owners and the crew. But in the final analysis the root of the tragedy was the misplaced confidence and the firm belief that the *Titanic* was unsinkable and was a match for the cruel waters and icebergs of the North Atlantic.

Daniel Allen Butler, *The Full Story of HMS Titanic* (Mechanicsburg, Pa., 1998).

Tom Kuntz, ed., *The Titanic Disaster Hearings: The Official Transcripts of the 1912 Senate Investigation* (New York, 1998).

Walter Lord, *A Night to Remember* (New York, 1956).

Edward E. O'Donnell, *Father Brown's Titanic Album* (Dublin, 1997).

———, *The Last Days of the Titanic* (Chicago, 1997).

Public Record Office, *Titanic: 14th–15th April, 1912. The Official Story* (London, 1997).

MICHAEL GLAZIER

## TOBIN, MAURICE J. (1901–1953)

*See* Boston, Twelve Irish-American Mayors of

## TOOLE, JOHN KENNEDY (1937–1969)

Novelist. John Kennedy Toole was a bitter, lonely, obscure man when he committed suicide in Biloxi, Mississippi, on March 26, 1969. Twelve years later he was an internationally famous bestselling author. In this respect, his story is perhaps unparalleled in literary history.

### TOOLE'S LIFE

Toole was born in New Orleans, Louisiana, in 1937, into a half-Irish family. His father, John Toole, was a car salesman. An only child, he was raised by his domineering mother, Thelma Ducoing Toole, a music and elocution teacher.

Toole went to public schools and entered Tulane University in New Orleans at sixteen where he majored in English and received his B.A. in 1958 (Phi Beta Kappa). Then he went to Columbia University on a Woodrow Wilson scholarship (M.A., 1959) and taught for a year at Manhattan's Hunter College. In 1960, he returned to Louisiana and taught at the University of Southwest Louisiana in Lafayette. He started a doctorate at Tulane but never completed it.

In 1961, Toole was drafted and served in the U.S. Army from 1962–63 in Puerto Rico where he worked in a typing pool and also taught English as a second language to Spanish-speaking recruits. It was there that Toole wrote the first draft of the novel that would later be an international bestseller, *A Confederacy of Dunces*.

After completing his military service, Toole returned to New Orleans where he lived with his aging parents and taught at St. Mary's Dominican College.

During this period, Toole was trying to get his novel published. Initially, he was encouraged by Robert Gottlieb at Simon & Schuster and Toole thought that it would be published after a reasonable number of revisions. In 1966, however, Gottlieb rejected it for reasons that are not clear. Toole was shattered and sank into a deep depression. Some friends felt he was clinically paranoid.

In January 1969, he abruptly resigned from Dominican, got into his car and drove around the U.S. for nearly two months. On March 26, only a few hours away from New Orleans, he stopped near Biloxi, Mississippi, rigged a hose from his exhaust to his car, and asphyxiated himself.

### A CONFEDERACY OF DUNCES

After two years passed, Mrs. Toole started submitting the manuscript to other publishers. At least eight rejected it. In 1976 she took the manuscript to novelist Walker Percy, who was teaching at Loyola University. Percy agreed, reluctantly, to read it, and he perused the opening pages of the smudged carbon copy, "first with the sinking feeling that it was not bad enough to quit, then with a prickle of interest, then a growing excitement, and finally an incredulity: surely it was not possible it was so good."

Percy arranged for sections of the novel to be published in Loyola's *New Orleans Review* and recommended the manuscript to his agent, who tried to place it with New York publishers. They were, however, reluctant to publish the first novel of a dead author. Finally, Percy convinced Louisiana State University Press to publish it. LSU did so, but somewhat hesitantly. They limited the initial printing to 1,500 copies. People, particularly in New Orleans, started talking enthusiastically about the book and LSU Press printed another 2,500 copies, which were all sold within a few weeks. It soon was clear from the initial reviews and the response of readers that *A Confederacy of Dunces* would be a runaway bestseller.

### PLOT SUMMARY

*A Confederacy of Dunces* is the story of Ignatius J. Reilly, who is in Walker Percy's words, "a slob extraordinaire, a mad Oliver Hardy, a fat Don Quixote, a perverse Thomas Aquinas, rolled into one." Ignatius is devoted to medieval philosophy and spends much of his time in bed alternately masturbating and writing indictments of the modern world and its trespasses against "theology and geometry." His outrage is directed at diverse targets, including Greyhound Scenicruisers, Doris Day, fashion, ambition and sex. His mother thinks he should get a job, his girlfriend thinks he just needs sex, and several people think he should be locked up in a jail or an asylum. Ignatius, however, considers himself a genius and aspires to be a reformer: when he does go to work in a pants factory he organizes the black workers in a "Crusade for Moorish Dignity." When the crusade and the job end in chaos, he becomes a hot dog vendor in the French Quarter, selling few hot dogs but sowing a good deal of confusion, particularly when he tries to organize homosexuals as "Sodomites for Peace." Finally he is caught up in the exposure of a pornography ring that operates out of the Night of Joy nightclub, and he flees New Orleans in the back seat of a car to escape his mother's plan to commit him to a mental hospital.

*A Confederacy of Dunces* won the 1981 Pulitzer in fiction and a Faulkner Award nomination from P.E.N. It was selected by the Book-of-the-Month Club, Grove Press bought the paperback rights, and Twentieth Century-Fox bought the movie rights. It has been translated numerous times and there are now even editions in Greek, Turkish, Swedish and Catalan. World sales of *A Confederacy of Dunces* have probably passed one million copies.

In 1989, Grove published *Neon Bible*, a short novel which Toole had written at the age of sixteen.

*See* Fiction, Irish-American

John Kennedy Toole, *A Confederacy of Dunces* (Baton Rouge, Louisiana, 1980).
———, *Neon Bible* (New York, 1989).
Kenneth Holditch, *Genius Among the Dunces: A Biography of JKT* (forthcoming).
Barbara McIntosh, *Mama's Boy: The Life and Death of John Kennedy Toole* (forthcoming).
Toole's papers: http://www.tulane.edu/~lmiller/TooleFamily.html

MARCUS SMITH

## TOWNSEND, KATHLEEN KENNEDY (1951– )

Lieutenant Governor of Maryland. Born July 4, 1951, into the politically prominent Kennedy family of Massachusetts, Townsend was the first of the eleven children of Senator Robert F. Kennedy (D. N.Y.) and Ethel Skakel Kennedy. Educated in private preparatory schools in Maryland and Vermont, Townsend graduated from Radcliffe College and the University of New Mexico Law School. In 1973, she married academic David Townsend; the couple has four daughters: Meghan, Maeve, Rose Katherine, and Kerry.

After managing the senatorial reelection campaign of her uncle, Senator Edward M. Kennedy (D. Mass.) in 1982, Townsend worked for Massachusetts Governor Michael Dukakis as a policy analyst in the Office of Human Resources. Moving with her family to her husband's home state of Maryland in 1984, Townsend soon became the first Kennedy woman to run for political office, albeit ultimately failing in her 1986 bid to represent Maryland's second congressional district in the House of Representatives. Following her defeat, Townsend headed the Student Service Alliance of Maryland's Department of Education, successfully leading efforts to make community service programs mandatory for high school students across the state.

In 1993, Townsend was appointed a deputy assistant attorney general in the Department of Justice under President William J.

Kathleen Kennedy
Townsend, 1970s

Clinton. A Democrat, she was elected lieutenant governor of Maryland in 1994 and won reelection to this office in 1998.

Sixteen when her father was assassinated during his presidential campaign in 1968, Townsend helped create the Robert F. Kennedy Human Rights Award, given annually to further his memory. She has also written magazine essays on the themes of voluntarism and service.

Jay David Andrew, *Young Kennedys: The New Generation* (New York, 1998).
Lawrence Leamer, *The Kennedy Women: The Saga of an American Family* (New York, 1994).
Harrison Rainie and John Quinn, *Growing Up Kennedy: The Third Wave Comes of Age* (New York, 1983).
Jonathan Slevin and Maureen Spagnolo, *Kennedys: The Next Generation* (Maryland, 1990).

KATHLEEN N. McCARTHY

## TRACY, SPENCER (1900–1967)

Actor. Spencer Bonaventure Tracy was born April 5, 1900, in his parents' home in Milwaukee, Wisconsin. He was the son of John E. Tracy (1873–1928) and Carrie Brown (1874–1942). Tracy's paternal grandparents were born in Ireland: John D. Tracy (1828–1901) was a native of Tynagh parish, County Galway, and Mary Guhin Tracy (1848–1918) was born into an Irish-speaking family in Ballyferriter, County Kerry.

Tracy was educated at a number of parochial and public schools in Milwaukee. He graduated from St. Rose grade school and attended Marquette Academy, the Jesuit preparatory school in the city. It was there he met Pat O'Brien. Tracy and O'Brien enlisted in the Navy during World War I. After the war, Tracy finished high school and entered Ripon College where he began acting in school productions. In 1922–1923 Tracy and O'Brien enrolled in the American Academy of Dramatic Arts in New York. After graduation Tracy appeared in various stock companies throughout the country. In 1926 he caught the eye of George M. Cohan, then Broadway's biggest producer. Cohan mentored the young Tracy to stardom on the stage. In 1930 Tracy signed with the Fox Studio to act in his first movie, *Up the River.*

Spencer Tracy

Over the next thirty-seven years, Tracy starred in seventy-four movies. His consecutive Oscar awards for "Best Actor" in *Captains Courageous* (1937) and *Boys Town* (1938) was a record unequaled for nearly sixty years. Tracy was also nominated seven more times (also a record) for "Best Actor": as Father Tim Mullin in *San Francisco* (1936), as Stanley Bonds in *Father of the Bride* (1950), as Macreedy in *Bad Day at Black Rock* (1955), as the old man in *The Old Man and the Sea* (1958), as Henry Drummond in *Inherit the Wind* (1960), as Judge Hayward in *Judgment at Nuremburg* (1961), and finally as publisher Matt Drayton in *Guess Who's Coming to Dinner* (1967).

Tracy's extraordinary acting ability transcended ethnicity. Nevertheless, some of his most memorable roles found him playing Irish-American authority figures (priest, cop, politician). Tracy called Father Edward Flanagan (his character in *Boys Town*) the "greatest man I ever met." His highly acclaimed performance in *The Last Hurrah* (1958) as Mayor Frank Skeffington (a character modeled on the legendary James Michael Curley of Boston) was so realistic that Curley sued Columbia Pictures for invasion of privacy. In a 1950 poll of 250 veteran Hollywood movie professionals Tracy was rated the number one actor in sound picture history. Tracy's career made an important contribution to advancing the assimilation and social acceptance of the Irish in America.

*See* Cinema, Irish in; California

Thomas Gildea Cannon, "Spencer Tracy—Actor," *Irish Genealogical Quarterly* 6/2 (1997): 3–8.
Seldin West, Forthcoming biography of Spencer Tracy to be published by Alfred A. Knopf (New York, 1999).

THOMAS GILDEA CANNON

## TRAVELERS, IRISH: A UNIQUE COMMUNITY

North Augusta, South Carolina, is now home to what must be a unique community of people called the Irish Travelers. These people are little known and less understood by the average American citizen. Nor is this surprising because they have kept to themselves and lived apart for generations. As Irish immigrants and tinkers by trade they arrived in this country in the second half of the nineteenth century. They lived in tents and traded mules throughout the length and breadth of Georgia and the neighbouring states.

Bonded together by heredity, religion, lifestyle and language, they have shown neither interest nor inclination toward integration into mainstream American society. They have their own set of values, strong religious beliefs and customs, and are remarkably independent and unconventional. They shun publicity and are happy to be left to their own pursuits. However, this self-chosen exclusion and privacy has a downside. The uncomprehending outsiders or "country people" perceive them to be mysterious, highly secretive, superstitious and devious.

At present there are approximately five hundred families living in a settlement called "Murphy Village," so called in recognition of the Catholic priest, Father Joseph J. Murphy, who in the early 1960s initiated and facilitated the process of transfer from nomadism to a more settled way of life. Pete Sherlock, a Traveler, referred to this momentous change as a "quantum leap" in the life of his people, "for whom it was the shortest trip, but the longest journey," he said. There is an estimated total population of two thousand persons in Murphy Village, and due to marriage and intermarriage almost exclusively within the group, the majority of these families are now kin to each other, to a greater or lesser degree. For the same reason there are only seven or eight surnames, the most predominant being Sherlock, Carroll, Riley, O'Hara, Gorman, Costello, Mack (formerly McNamara) and McNally. This is the biggest single group of Irish Travelers in the United States and they are generally referred to as the "Georgia" Travelers, from the time they made Atlanta their headquarters for the mule trade. They form a separate parish with their own church and resident pastor.

Forming a smaller settlement, approximately one hundred families have made Memphis in Tennessee their home base. Besides these, small seminomadic groups are scattered throughout the South. Interaction between the various groups is now more by accident than design, whereas prior to the widespread motorization, annual reunions were prearranged. It is difficult, if not impossible to say with any degree of certainty what the total numbers are, though in 1941 Grace Stephens could write: ". . . they make up a vast family of ten thousand. More remarkable, it is a family with not one member out of a job, not one on government-made work, not one on relief" (*Catholic Church Extension*, p. 10). We are not told how this figure was arrived at. The aim and accepted norm for the Irish Traveler is to be self-employed. From the time of their arrival in the United States, they have shown a remarkable independence and self-reliance and always earned their own living.

### OCCUPATIONS

Mechanization and the widespread use of tractors in the mid-1950s saw the demise of the mule trade which had been their speciality. It was then that the menfolk turned to selling linoleum floor covering, shop tools and equipment and to spray-painting farm buildings. Some work locally, but the majority are away from home for prolonged periods and travel vast distances. The women, who remain at home, are responsible for all the usual household duties and deal with outside agencies such as schools, hospitals and business personnel. There is an all-absorbing concern for the welfare of children among the entire extended family, a concern which borders on indulgence. Even a casual visitor to Murphy Village will become aware of the priority given to the sick and elderly.

## EDUCATION

School-age children attend the local schools and those who attend state schools receive their religious education in their own parish at Murphy Village. On education, Mary Elizabeth Andereck states, "The values towards formal education have not been incorporated into Traveler culture although there has been an increase in school years completed over generations." *(Irish Travellers in a Catholic Elementary School, a thesis for Texas A & M University,* 1988, p. 163). Present indications give rise to some optimism in this area. A number of young adults, albeit mostly women, have returned to study and achieved success in public examinations. Others have taken up more advanced computer and administrative studies, while a few are pursuing medical and nursing professional studies.

## EARLY DAYS IN THE UNITED STATES

These families are the direct descendants of a group of Irish Tinkers who emigrated from Ireland some time after the Great Famine of the mid-1840s. The dearth of documentation for this period leave writers and researchers largely dependent on the folk-memory of these people. Some of the Sherlocks claim an earlier arrival, others believe they came about 1850. An informative article written in 1935 by Fr. M. F. Kearney, former pastor of St Patrick's, Nashville gives 1865 as the correct date *(The Register,* Nashville, Tennessee, May 1941). This date is also favoured by Fr. J. Murphy, who had contact with the last living member of the original group, a certain Bridget Carroll.

Every Traveler will tell you that "Old Man" Tom Carroll was the first to arrive and there is absolutely no disagreement on this point. He was from all accounts an intrepid pioneer, who led his people into a new land and remained an inspiration for them. In Westview Cemetery, Atlanta, where he is buried, a simple inscription on his tombstone reads:

> Tom Carroll,
> December 22, 1830
> September 26, 1910
> Born in Ireland.

He died in the little town of Saundersville, Georgia. His funeral on April 28, 1911, was attended by Travelers from all parts of the Southern states and beyond. The *Atlanta Constitution* reported that ". . . today's funeral will be the largest of its kind ever held in this city. Every carriage in Atlanta has now been hired and many will be compelled to go to the cemeteries on the street cars." Soon after his arrival Tom Carroll sent for his family amongst whom were his brothers Pete, Jimmy and Brian. These were later joined by his friends, Patrick O'Hara and his wife Sabina O'Donnell, Peter Sherlock and some of the MacNamaras—Tinkers all of them, who obviously were already known to each other in Ireland. They came from such places as Dublin, Sligo, Roscommon, Cork, Mayo and Belfast.

Like the vast majority of Irish immigrants, they were too poor and lacking in resources to travel beyond the large urban centres of New York, Boston, Buffalo and Philadelphia. They also were the objects of the widespread anti-Irish, anti-Catholic prejudice of the time. As Edward J. O'Hara, alias "Big Shot" relates, "When my people came to this country they had two strikes against them. One strike you was Irish and two strikes you was Catholic. You couldn't get a job if you was Irish and Catholic" (taped interview with writer). We are told that Patrick O'Hara set up a tin shop on Irish Row in Washington, while others operated livery stables, worked in the steel mills in Pittsburgh and as haulers in New York, where they found themselves in competition with the Jews.

## SOUTHBOUND

Sometime in the 1870s "Old Man" Tom Carroll and Patrick O'Hara embarked on the more lucrative horsetrading business. Followed by the entire group, they gradually moved south toward such places as Nashville, Memphis and Atlanta, where some of the largest stockyards in the United States were located. Some indication for the timing of this move can be derived from the Catholic Church sacramental records in Atlanta. Among the names recorded are Carroll, Sherlock, Riley and MacNamara. Some of the accompanying marginal notes are interesting, and indicate a concern to identify these unusual sojourners. These include entries such as "Irish Tinkers," "Gypsies," "Irish Horse Traders," "Born in the Gypsy Camp," "Vagabondi," "Vagi," and "Born in the Horse Traders Camp." Similar records exist in numerous churches throughout the South and can be a good source for data as to their journeyings.

Atlanta, which was the nerve centre for the flourishing mule trade at that time, became a kind of mecca for the Irish Travelers. For many years it remained a place to rendezvous, where they bought their stock and from where they fanned out to every corner of Georgia, South Carolina and its neighbouring states. The mild southern climate was more suited to their nomadic lifestyle. According to the Irish Travelers it was they who developed the mule trade to the huge proportions it attained. The extensive cotton plantations of the South and large farms offered profitable outlets where they sold healthy mules and took back weak and sickly animals with money to boot.

The women contributed to the domestic economy by peddling supposedly "Irish" lace from door to door. The main supplier was Sweeney and Johnston, Cincinnati, Ohio, who also acted as a channel of communication between the widely scattered groups. A note or letter would be placed with an order and forwarded with later consignments to various campsites and thus news was disseminated. Tents were pitched in the pine groves or on a farmer's land at a minimal cost. The large inner section served as sleeping quarters, with each bed curtained off for privacy. The outer section served as kitchen cum dining cum general purpose room.

## BURIAL CUSTOMS: JOY AND SORROW MINGLE

The annual group burials on April 28 in Atlanta and May 1 in Nashville created quite a stir and never failed to amaze onlookers. This unique practice began when groups were scattered over the South and without means of communication. The above dates were fixed and, as they approached, every Irish Traveler knew it was time to gravitate toward Immaculate Conception Church in Atlanta and then to St. Patrick's Church in Nashville, and set up camp.

When a member died during the year the body was brought to a funeral home in Atlanta, embalmed and kept until the appropriate dates. There could be as many as six burials on these occasions. We are told that great demonstrations of grief and loud keening accompanied the solemn ceremonies (Stephens, *A Family of 10,000*). These gatherings were also social events where marriages were solemnized, baptisms perfomed and matches made for the following year. A Traveler woman recalled an occasion when a young girl attended her father's funeral at St. Patrick's Church in the morning, returned to the same church to be married in the afternoon, followed by a lavish celebration in the evening. Since the advent of motorization and settlement, the Travelers bury their dead in the local cemetery as death occurs.

## LANGUAGE

The Irish Travelers still possess a remnant of what is referred to as Cant, which is derived from the Shelta spoken by the Travelers in Ireland and which in turn is based on carefully disguised Irish Gaelic. The techniques employed for this are described and demonstrated by Jared V. Harper (see *The Irish Travellers of Georgia,* 1977). This Cant is not to be confused with the Romany language of the Gypsies.

Extensive research has been done on the origins, formation and use of Shelta, beginning with Charles G. Leland in 1886. Other contributors include such eminent scholars as Kuno Meyer and John Sampson in the early part of this century and later R. A. Stewart Macalister in his truly comprehensive work (*The Secret Languages of Ireland*). We are also indebted to Pádraig MacGréine and Micháel MacÉnri for their fieldwork with the Travelers in Ireland in the 1920s and 1930s.

Of special significance here is the work of the American scholar Jared V. Harper, who in the 1970s conducted his doctoral research with the Travelers in Murphy Village. He noted that while Macalister had collected a list of 900 Shelta words, the Travelers in Murphy Village knew only about 150 Cant words, a loss which he attributes to ignorance of the Irish content and pronunciation. It was particularly useful in trade and business transactions in the presence of outsiders. Its main purpose was to conceal certain information from non-Travelers and is still employed for that purpose. For this reason it was also known as a Secret Language. Macalister states that "Shelta is a language concocted for the purpose of secrecy by a community living parasitically in the midst of Irish speakers" (*The Secret Languages of Ireland,* p. 164). A venerable Traveler from Murphy Village remembers when it was almost a crime to reveal any of the Cant to outsiders. ". . . they would be flogged. Nobody know'd that language except the Travelers, nobody" (taped interview, 1991).

## CHURCH, CHANGE, SETTLEMENT

There was never any doubt about the Catholic identity of the Irish Travelers. A perusal of Church documents and registers testify to their fidelity. "Many a priest would have gone hungry only for the Irish Travelers," recalls Monsignor Daniel Bourke of Savannah. "They went in search of the priest," says Fr. J. Murphy, "and knew every little town that had a Church and which ones did not. They were tremendous people for Mass. All of a sudden on Sunday morning the Church would be crowded and everyone knew the Travelers were in town" (taped interview with author, 1990).

Fr. Joseph Murphy, a native of Charleston, South Carolina, first met the Irish Travelers when he became pastor of Our Lady of Peace Church, North Augusta, in 1948. He helped them to acquire property and they built a village and later erected a church in 1964. As described earlier, it was called Murphy Village and grew to contain five hundred families.

Frederick S. Arnold, "Our Old Poets and Tinkers," *Journal of American Folklore,* Vol. X 1/X LII ( July–September 1998): 210–220.

George Gmelch, *Urbanization of an Itinerant People* (Cummings Pub. Co. Calif., 1977).

Jared V. Harper, *Unpublished Ph.D.* (University of Georgia, Athens, 1977).

———, "Irish Traveller Cant in its Social Setting," *Folklore Quarterly,* 37 (1973).

Charles G. Leland, *The Gypsies* (Houghton Mifflin and Co. 1882).

———, "Shelta," *Journal of Gypsy Lore Society,* 1 (1907–08): 73–82.

Stewart Macalister, R.A., *The Secret Languages of Ireland* (Cambridge University Press, London, 1937).

Pádraig MacGréine, "Irish Tinkers or Travellers: Some Notes on their Customs and Manners and their Secret Language or Cant," *Béaloideas, The Journal of the Folklore of Ireland Society,* 3 (1931–32): 170–186.

———, "Further Notes on Tinkers Cant," *Béaloideas, Journal of the Folklore of Ireland Society,* 3 (1931–32): 290–303.

Marguerite Riordan, "The Irish Mule Traders," *American Cattle Producer* (October 1950): 9–10, 25–28.

Grace Stephens, "A Family of 10,000," *Catholic Extension Society* (February 1941): 10–11, 37–39.

RITA KINCH

## TUKE'S ASSISTED EMIGRATION SCHEMES

The English philanthropist James Hack Tuke visited the West of Ireland at the height of the subsistence crisis in late 1880. He concluded that assisted emigration from the congested districts of Connacht was the only solution to the perennial destitution and overpopulation. A group of prominent Englishmen formed an emigration committee in March 1882 to foster the emigration of whole families from the poorer areas of Ireland to North America and raised £8,000 through private subscriptions. The Tuke Committee concentrated its early efforts on Clifden in Connemara but quickly concluded that the dimension of the problem was so vast that it was outside the scope of any private committee to bring about fundamental change through limited assisted emigration.

In 1883 and 1884 the British government gave a total of £150,000 for assisted emigration purposes, and this sum was administered by the Tuke Committee and individual poor law guardians. The Tuke Committee oversaw the scheme in the poorer unions of Clifden, Oughterard, Newport, Belmullet and Swineford. Between 1882 and 1884, 24,700 left Ireland, of whom 9,500 were assisted by Tuke. Those most likely to succeed were to be helped. The committee looked after the emigrants from the time of their departure to their arrival in North America. They received new clothes for the journey and transport was provided to bring them from their homes to Galway, where overnight accommodation was arranged. On landing in North America the emigrants were looked after by agents employed by the committee who ensured that they got safely to their destinations. Tuke wanted to ensure that the emigrants knew where they would settle before they departed and what types of employment opportunities were available in the host country. It was hoped that, once established in the New World, the emigrants would remit money and that their letters would encourage more privately funded departures.

While the schemes generated much excitement and enthusiasm, the emigrants encountered many difficulties in North America. Tuke hoped the emigrants would settle in either Canada or in the midwestern region of the United States, as these destinations were under-populated and had rich agricultural lands. He favored Canada because the Canadian authorities were prepared to look after those emigrants who were sent to their jurisdiction and because they placed less restrictions on the type of emigrant that they would accept. However, though most emigrants wanted to settle in the United States, they were only aided if their friends and relations there would support them.

Most were happy with their new lives in North America, for they were away from the incessant poverty and destitution that they had encountered in Ireland. Their letters to Ireland encouraged friends and relations to seek assistance from Tuke in 1883 and 1884. Those who settled in the midwestern states encountered problems, especially those who worked on the railways, for they had to survive on seven months' wages over a twelve-month period. They also had never experienced the severe weather conditions of the region.

Some American states were worried about the influx of such poor emigrants, especially when it was reported that Irish poor law unions were assisting workhouse paupers. They feared that they would be left with large numbers of people who would become a burden on the American system. Many poor law unions did send out pauper inmates and this factor had a negative effect on the Tuke schemes. Also, Irish-American groups were opposed because of the involvement of the British government and they called them "Mr Tuke's Transatlantic Fool's Paradise." Reports from New York, Boston, Cleveland and Toronto showed that many emigrants were left in a poor state and were often destitute. As a result, the American and Canadian governments withdrew their support and brought the schemes to an end in March 1884.

*See* Emigration: 1801–1921

Gerard Moran, "Escape from Hunger: The Trials and Tribulations of the Irish State-Aided Emigrants in North America in the 1880s," *Studia Hibernica*, no. 29 (1995–7): 99–116.

———, "From Galway to North America: State-Aided Emigration from County Galway in the 1880," in Gerard Moran, ed., *Galway: History and Society* (Dublin, 1996): 487–520.

———, "James Hack Tuke and Assisted Emigration from Mayo and Galway in the 1880s," in Mary Clancy, ed., *The Emigrant Experience* (Galway, 1991).

———, "State-Aided Emigration from Ireland to Canada in the 1880s," *Canadian Journal of Irish Studies,* vol. 20, no. 2 (December 1994): 4–14.

GERARD MORAN

## TULLY, JIM (1888–1947)

Novelist, journalist, screenwriter, short story writer. Born one of six children to Irish immigrants, Jim Tully grew up in abject poverty outside rural St. Mary's, Ohio. Tully's youth was as lugubrious as a character's in Dickens. He would later recall that his first home was a log house built by his father, an alcoholic ditch digger who worked in the pestilential St. Mary's reservoir, and which burned to the ground in a fire that consumed everything but a clock and a cornhusk mattress. Tully's mother died while still in her middle-thirties; Tully's father, ill-equipped to handle the rigors of child-rearing alone, abandoned his family. Tully spent five years in an orphanage before being rescued at the age of eleven by his beloved sister, Virginia. She would later play a recurring role in his largely autobiographical fiction.

By the age of fourteen, Tully was, in his own words, "a road kid . . . the most vicious product of underworld America," tramping, riding the rails, and occasionally staying with his sister, who ran an ad-hoc boarding house for indigents out of her Chicago flat. His experience with tramps as "liars, ingrates, and

thieves" cost him his moralistic Marxian idealism, but it provided fodder for much of his best-known fiction. After failing as a newspaper reporter, a chain maker, a tree surgeon, and a boxer, Tully wrote his first novel, a 100,000-word single paragraph he recalled hammering out on a typewriter his sister purchased for him on an installment plan. The novel, *Emmet Lawler* (1922), a fictionalized account of his own life, generated enough enthusiasm to convince him that he could make a success as a writer.

Settling in California, Tully took work as a public-relations counselor, a studio screenwriter, and as a freelance journalist, specializing in amusing Hollywood profiles, for periodicals ranging from *Photoplay* and *True Confessions* to *Scribner's* and *Vanity Fair*. In 1928, H. L. Mencken's *American Mercury* published a condensed version of what would become Tully's masterpiece, *Shanty Irish*. This fictionalized autobiography of Tully's Ohio youth builds a compelling portrait of the Irish-American underclass at the turn of the century. It is composed of a series of painstakingly realized vignettes, among them: a "raid" by Tully's family on a Methodist revival meeting to rescue an Irish Catholic from conversion; a contest by Irish and German ditchdiggers to see who can toss dirt the farthest; and an Irish wake, at which maudlin mourners are terrified by a practical joke which causes the corpse to rise from the coffin. The story, which overflows with jokes, riddles, and songs, so impressed Mencken that he compared Tully favorably to Gorky.

During the balance of his life, Tully wrote more than twenty other books, mostly concerned with the lives of the underclass, and countless articles, stories, and screenplays. With earnings from highly lucrative movie fan-magazine profiles, he purchased a three-acre estate near Hollywood, and an eighty-acre ranch to which he imagined he could retreat when the inevitable revolution occurred. He counted among his friends Charlie Chaplin, Jack Dempsey, Langston Hughes, and Upton Sinclair. George Jean Nathan called him a great American realist, and Damon Runyan ranked him one of contemporary American literature's five greatest writers. Yet Tully never imagined himself a realist. Instead he believed that he was a romantic, descended from Irish balladeers, whose circumstances had warped him into composing grim treatments of hobo life. He regarded himself as an intellectual and spiritual agnostic, rejecting middle-class American values as hypocritical and socialistic alternatives as naive; but he owed his success to his understanding that while he had little aptitude for the formulation of social or political agendas, he was gifted with a rare talent for unsentimental observation. He died, of a heart ailment, in 1947.

*See* Fiction, Irish-American

Jim Tully, *Emmet Lawler* (New York, 1922).
———, *Beggars of Life* (New York, 1924).
———, *Shanty Irish* (New York, 1928).

RON EBEST

## TUMULTY, JOSEPH PATRICK (1879–1954)

Secretary to President Woodrow Wilson. He was born on May 5, 1879, in Jersey City, New Jersey. His father, an Irish Catholic by the name of Philip Tumulty, owned a grocery store in the Irish section of the city and supported his family well. As a young man, Joseph Patrick Tumulty in rapid succession graduated from St. Peter's College (1899), was admitted to the bar (1902), and married Mary Catherine Byrne (1903).

It was not long until Tumulty entered politics, joining the "progressive" wing of the Democratic Party. In 1906 he was elected to New Jersey's state assembly from Hudson County. When Woodrow Wilson, President of Princeton University, ran for Governor of New Jersey in 1910, Tumulty initially opposed him. But Wilson's alliance with the progressive Democrats broke down Tumulty's resistance and attracted his support.

Consequently, Tumulty served Governor Wilson as his secretary. When Wilson was elected President of the United States in 1912 and assumed office in 1913, he again named Tumulty his secretary, this time at the White House. In those days the presidential secretary served in a capacity similar to today's presidential Chief of Staff. As time passed and America's military and political involvement, first in Mexico and then later in World War I, increasingly came to dominate President Wilson's focus, while domestic issues also continued to loom prominent, Secretary Tumulty remained faithfully at Wilson's side.

By 1917, however, anti-Catholic prejudices among different factions close to Wilson, in combination with antagonism to Tumulty coming forth from Wilson's second wife, caused the two men to drift apart. In 1920, Wilson, suffering from the effects of an earlier stroke, misread a Tumulty speech delivered at the Democratic national convention, seeing it as favoring his opponent for the presidential nomination from the party, James Cox. Thus he broke with Tumulty. After Wilson left the White House Tumulty returned to private law practice in Washington, D.C., ever faithful to the Wilsonian ideals. Tumulty died on April 8, 1954, at Olney, Maryland.

John M. Blum, *Joe Tumulty and the Wilson Era* (Boston, 1951).

J. J. Huthmacher, "Tumulty, Joseph Patrick," *New Catholic Encyclopedia,* vol. XIV (Washington, D.C., 1967).

Raymond J. Kupke, "Tumulty, Joseph 1879–1954," *The Encyclopedia of American Catholic History* (Collegeville, 1997).

Joseph P. Tumulty, *Woodrow Wilson As I Knew Him* (Garden City, 1921)

PATRICK FOLEY

## TUNNEY, JAMES JOSEPH ("Gene") (1898–1978)

Boxer, world heavyweight champion, businessman. James Tunney was born in New York City in 1898 to Irish parents. As a youth, he worked as a clerk for the Ocean Steamship Company and between 1915 and 1917 began to box with a genuinely natural talent. In 1917, when the United States entered the First World War, Tunney joined the U.S. Marine Corps and won the light heavyweight championship of the American Expeditionary Force in Paris. The "Fighting Marine" returned home to a boxing career that took him to the U.S. light heavyweight championship in 1922. Tunney lost to Harry Greb—his only professional defeat—but took the title from Greb in the following year. After his decisive knockout of Georges Carpentier in 1924, Tunney fought as a heavyweight. Two years later, in September of 1926, Tunney challenged Jack Dempsey in Philadelphia. The favored winner, Dempsey lost to Tunney by decision after 10 rounds. The next year, Dempsey challenged Tunney in Chicago in a rematch that became one of the most hotly contested fights of the decade. The controversy over the "long count" began with the seventh round when Tunney was knocked to the floor. Dempsey failed to immediately return to a neutral corner which delayed the start of the count, thus giving Tunney several extra seconds to recover. On the ninth count, Tunney got up to defeat Dempsey in the 10-round fight by decision. Tunney defended the title again against Tom Heeney in 1928 and then announced his retirement after fifty-six career victories out of seventy-six matches. Tunney next turned to business where he was successful in banking, manufacturing, insurance and as a newspaper executive for the *Toronto Globe and Mail.* In 1932 Tunney was author of *A Man Must Fight* and his autobiographical work, *Arms for Living,* which appeared in 1941. Tunney had four children, one of whom—John V. Tunney—became a United States Senator from 1971–1977. Tunney died November 7, 1978, in Greenwich, Connecticut, at the age of 80.

### *See* Boxing

Bruce J. Evensen, *When Dempsey Fought Tunney: Heroes, Hokum, and Storytelling in the Jazz Age* (Knoxville: University of Tennessee Press, 1996).

David L. Porter, *Biographical Dictionary of American Sports: Basketball and Other Indoor Sports* (New York: Greenwood Press, 1989).

James Joseph Tunney, *Arms for Living* (1941).

DANIEL J. KUNTZ

## TUOHY, PATRICK J. (1894–1930)

Artist. Patrick Tuohy was born in North Frederick Street, Dublin, the son of a surgeon. Despite having been born without a left hand, from boyhood he showed great talent for drawing and as a mature artist proved himself to be one of the most gifted portrait painters of his day. Tragically, he died in New York at the early age of thirty-six years, apparently the result of suicide.

### EARLY YEARS IN DUBLIN

Tuohy was a young man during the advent of the Irish Free State and no doubt greatly affected by the violent political upheaval of the Easter Rising, War of Independence and the Civil War. His parents, who were ardent nationalists, sent him to Padraic Pearse's School, St. Enda's. There, he was encouraged to further his art studies by Pearse's brother, William, who was a sculptor and art master at the school. He attended the Dublin Metropolitan School of Art by night, where he was taught by William Orpen, who considered Tuohy one of his finest pupils. However, as a young man he was often despondent—always striving for perfection which he felt eluded him. Added to that, his evolution as an artist was not helped by his father's disapproval, financial difficulties and the conservative, lack-lustre Dublin art world. In 1915 he won the Taylor Art Memorial Scholarship which enabled him to travel to Spain to see in particular the masterworks of Velasquez and Zurbaran, whose use of restrained colour and tone confirmed his own technique. With the dawn of the New State, national identity was an obsession. On the issue of the establishment of a native school of painting, unlike artists such as Sean Keating, Tuohy was convinced that Irish artists should look to European painters for inspiration. From 1918 he began to teach at the Metropolitan School of Art and to exhibit at the Royal Hibernian Academy. In 1922 he was included in "L'Art Irlandais" a Paris exhibition of Irish art organised in celebration of the New State which Maud Gonne McBride had helped to arrange, held at the Galeries Barbazanges. In 1923 he went on a study tour of Italy in the company of Phyllis Moss, his fiancée and also a painter.

### TUOHY THE PORTRAITIST

Though he also painted still-lifes and some landscapes, Tuohy is best known for portraits of arresting frontality and intensity.

The number of portraits by him are limited, as he worked slowly and methodically. Among those who sat for him are James Joyce whom he painted in Paris, John Stanislaus Joyce (the writer's father), and James Stephens. James Joyce attached particular importance to those three paintings, for in 1927 he wrote in a letter: "It is rather singular that for the last three years I have been carrying three photographs of Tuohy's portraits in my pocket—those of my father, myself and James Stephens." Between 1922 and 1926 Tuohy carried out a series of compelling pencil sketches of Irish theatre personalities. The establishment of the Irish Free State provided Tuohy with his share of official portraits and he also carried out a number of church commissions. One of Tuohy's key works, for which he was awarded the Tailteann Silver Medal, is "The Baptism of Christ," a large canvas, 180 x 303 cms. It shows the influence of symbolist painter Puvis de Chavannes and brought the artist to the attention of a wider audience when it was exhibited in the Royal Academy, London, in 1925. It features fellow artists of the day, including Sean Keating, Sean O'Sullivan and Phyllis Moss.

## Tuohy in America

Despondent with his career in Ireland, which he felt would never provide him with enough of a living to get married, Tuohy emigrated to America in 1927. He first went to South Carolina and stayed at 907 Richland Street at the home of Dr. E. C. L. Adams, whom he had met in Paris and who was a friend of the Irish poet Padraic Colum. The doctor arranged a number of commissions for him, one of which was that of South Carolina Governor John G. Richards. From the outset Tuohy was dispirited. He argued with clients about Southern injustices toward negroes and sometimes failed to complete his commission. It was at this time that Tuohy was diagnosed as a manic depressive. All the while he kept up correspondence with Phyllis Moss in Paris and actress Ria Mooney in Dublin. Tuohy moved to New York where he was in regular contact with prominent Irish-Americans such as Padraic and Mrs. Colum, Mrs. Boyd Barrett, Jeremiah O'Leary, Eddie Carberry, Jerome Conor, L. F. Barry and many others. He was acquainted with the actor Dudley Digges and his wife, actress Maire Quinn, both of whom had emigrated and established a successful career in New York and Hollywood. The artist was one of the founders of the Irish University Club in New York. At some stage in 1928 he went to Los Angeles where he painted a portrait of Joseph Campbell. During his time in New York he kept in contact with Augustus John and William Orpen in England and Sylvia Beech in Paris. From 1929 he lived at 145 Riverside Drive.

## Public Acclaim

In autumn of that year he returned home to Ireland for a holiday and also to help gallery owner Helen Byrne Hackett gather works for her first American exhibition of Contemporary Irish Art. While back in Ireland he told Hilda Roberts that he planned to return in two years. Located at No. 9, East Fifty-Seventh Street, the Hackett Galleries exhibition was highly successful. Tuohy was singled out by Henry McBride, art critic of the *New York Sun* (30 March 1929), in a headline which ran: "Tuohy stands out as a Portrait painter." McBride declared that "(he) paints portraits better than any one we have at present in America." The same exhibition was later shown at the Grace Holmes Gallery in Trinity Court, Boston. Much in demand, Tuohy's portrait practice does not seem to have been greatly affected by the Wall Street disaster of 1929. He was feted by critics and collectors and delivered lectures on art which were published in leading American newspapers. In preparation for a second exhibition of Irish art at the Hackett Galleries, Tuohy planned to have his *Baptism of Christ* brought over from Dublin. Despite his successes during this period Tuohy suffered recurring bouts of depression. To cheer him up James Joyce sent him two inscribed copies of the first edition of *Ulysses*. Through Nora Corcoran, he received the commission to paint the film star Claudette Colbert. This was the portrait which was found, unfinished, on Tuohy's easel when the artist was discovered dead in his studio as a result of gassing. His body was embalmed and removed for Solemn Requiem Mass at the Church of St. Paul the Apostle. The funeral was attended by his many friends and a special representation of the Irish University Club. His body was taken to Dublin on the Scythia liner for burial in Glasnevin cemetery.

There are paintings by him in the Hugh Lane Municipal Gallery of Modern Art in Dublin, the National Gallery of Ireland and in various private collections.

Thomas Bodkin, *Memorial Exhibition Patrick Tuohy RHA* (Dublin, 1931).

Anne Crookshank and the Knight of Glin, *The Watercolours of Ireland* (London, 1994).

S. B. Kennedy, *Irish Art and Modernism, 1880-1950* (Belfast, 1991).

Rosemary Mulcahy, *Patrick J. Tuohy, 1894–1930* (Dublin, 1989).

Patrick J. Murphy, *Patrick Tuohy, 1894–1930* (Dublin, 2000).

John Turpin, *A School of Art in Dublin since the Eighteenth Century* (Gill & Macmillan, 1995).

CHRISTINA KENNEDY

# U

## U.S. FOREIGN POLICY AND IRISH AFFAIRS

Benjamin Franklin received a cordial welcome in Dublin on visits in 1769 and 1771. The Irish were "strongly in favor of the American cause," he wrote. [By "Irish" he meant the Anglo-Irish Ascendancy class.] He proposed an informal alliance between Ireland and the American colonies for their mutual benefit in their quarrels with the imperial government of England.

"I found them disposed to be friends of America, in which I endeavored to confirm them with the expectation that our growing weight might in turn be thrown into one scale, and, by joining our interests with theirs a more equitable treatment from England might be obtained for themselves as well as for us," Franklin wrote.

When the First Continental Congress assembled at Philadelphia on September 5, 1774, it issued this declaration to the people of Ireland: "Your Parliament has done us no wrong. You had ever been friendly to the rights of mankind; and we acknowledge with pleasure that your nation has produced patriots who have nobly distinguished themselves in the cause of humanity and America."

Franklin and his fellow delegates at the Continental Congress had in mind the Anglo-Irish Protestant Ascendancy and their parliament in College Green, Dublin, when they spoke of the "Irish." This parliament was subject to the veto of the English parliament. Franklin had no contact with the mass of the people of Ireland, the Catholic peasantry, who were subject to penal laws.

Before the delegates in Philadelphia adjourned in October they agreed to hold a second Continental Congress in May 1775. The Lexington clash on April 19, 1775, between redcoats and militiamen, began the American War of Independence with "the shot heard around the world." George III denounced the colonists as rebels and traitors. The Irish Protestant Ascendancy supported the crown. The Catholic bishops, who had no rights under the constitution, prayed for the success of the king's arms to win his approval, no doubt.

### CATHOLICS IN THE ARMY

Catholics were permitted to join the British army for the first time to fight in America. Reportedly, many deserted to Washington's militiamen. A Dublin radical, James Napper Tandy, condemned the use of "military force to enslave our fellow subjects in America."

The most zealous soldiers in Washington's army were Scotch-Irish Presbyterians whose forebears settled in Antrim and Down in the late sixteenth and early seventeenth centuries. They defended Derry against James II and fought at the Boyne for Wil-

liam of Orange. When their leases expired and their rents increased, they emigrated to New England. A Hessian captain paid them the compliment when denouncing the rebels that it was "a Scotch-Irish Presbyterian rebellion."

Belfast Presbyterians founded the United Irishmen in 1791 to win "an equal representation of the people in Parliament." Tom Paine's "Rights of Man" was "the bible of Belfast," according to Wolfe Tone, who wrote a pamphlet urging an alliance of Catholics and Presbyterians. Tone and his friend, Thomas Russell, an Irish officer in the British army, were among the founders of the United Irishmen.

The American revolution stimulated the drive for an independent Irish Parliament by seeking abolition of the English Declaratory Act of 1719, which empowered London to veto Irish bills.

### DUNGANNON CONVENTION

When General Burgoyne surrendered at Saratoga in October 1777, the British Empire experienced the shock of defeat. France and Spain openly supported the rebels. Ireland, denuded of troops, prepared for a French invasion. The Presbyterians of Belfast organized Volunteer companies to defend Ulster. On February 15, 1782, delegates from 143 Ulster Volunteer Corps held a convention at Dungannon to demand an independent Irish parliament, rejecting the claim of "any body of men, other than the King, Lords and Commons of Ireland, to make laws binding Ireland."

"We hold the right of private judgment in matters of religion to be equally sacred in others as in ourselves," they stated. "That as men, as Irishmen, as Christians and Protestants, we rejoice in the relaxation of the penal laws against our Roman Catholic fellow subjects. . . ."

In March 1782, Henry Grattan proposed in the Irish Parliament that "no power on earth but the King, Lords and Commons of Ireland is competent to bind Ireland." The motion was carried unanimously. A Renunciation Act in the British Parliament conceded Ireland's right to be bound by its own laws and courts exclusively. This was the famous so called "Revolution of 1782."

### THE UNITED IRISHMEN

Was it really a revolution? Theobald Wolfe Tone denied it. He saw little value in a revolution that left political power in the hands of the Ascendancy and denied Catholics a vote. He noted that Catholics and Protestants sat side by side in the French National Assembly and the American Congress. Why not in Ireland? The reason, he concluded, was that Ireland needed a real revolution like France and America. He was determined to organize one.

Tone sailed to Delaware in June 1795. In January 1796 he left the United States to seek French help for an Irish revolution. James Monroe, the U.S. minister in Paris and a future president of the United States, helped him with the French language and officials.

Tone's initiative resulted in an expedition of 15,000 French troops to Bantry Bay at Christmas 1796. Raging storms dispersed the fleet. The troops could not land and the enterprise was abandoned. A gloomy Tone returned to France to await another opportunity.

Among the 2,000 United Irishmen who found refuge in America after the rebellions of 1798 and 1803 were Thomas Addis Emmet, later attorney general of New York state, elder brother of Robert who was hanged in Dublin, and Dr. William James MacNeven, professor of chemistry at Columbia. A monument to these United Irishmen is in St. Paul churchyard, Broadway, New York City.

## YOUNG IRELAND AND FENIANISM

In July 1848, a committee in New York urged the Irish to support William Smith O'Brien's Young Ireland rebellion. Two Irishmen, one American born, were arrested in Dublin with arms. The United States demanded their release. The formidable British Foreign Secretary, Lord Palmerston, ruled that a man born in Ireland was a British subject. The U.S. minister in London rejected Palmerston's claim.

Public meetings "to dismember the British Empire, by separating Ireland from the dominion of the British Crown," were held in U.S. cities, Palmerston charged. Conspirators went to Ireland "to assist in the rebellion, which they had intended to organize (with) money, arms, ammunition and agents." The U.S. minister stood firm and the two Young Ireland revolutionaries returned to America.

Fenianism began in New York among the refugees of the rebellion of 1848 when the Catholic clergy in Tipperary ordered the local people to abandon Smith O'Brien, fearing a repeat of the Wexford bloodshed in 1798. The children of the famine generation in America fought in the U.S. Civil War and became Fenians. They were told they could free Ireland by invading Canada.

Anglo-American relations were cool because of British support for the Confederacy. Fenianism thrived. President Johnson was asked to release John Mitchel, the Young Ireland revolutionary journalist transported to Australia in 1848, who escaped to America in 1853. He blamed the priests for the failure of 1848 and was denounced by Archbishop John Hughes of New York. He moved to the South and lost two sons fighting for the Confederacy.

Whatever Mitchel's views on the U.S. Civil War, he would always be a hero to the Irish. He was imprisoned in Fort Monroe after the war, and a Fenian delegation went to the White House to seek his release. The president was polite, as *The Nation* reported [November 16, 1867]. President Johnson freed Mitchel.

## FENIAN INVASION OF CANADA

In *Jail Journal* Mitchel speculated that "the United States Government may really contemplate the policy of permitting, or at least conniving at any enterprise that the Irish-Americans may undertake." The enterprise was an invasion of Canada. The plan was drafted by a serving officer of the Union army, the experienced and capable Brigadier General T. W. Sweeny who had fought in the Mexican and the Civil War. In April 1864, he commanded the second division of Sherman's army at Atlanta and was cited in dispatches.

General John O'Neil, the Fenian field commander at the battle of Ridgeway, Ontario, rose through the ranks to command a battalion in the Civil War. He knew the president. Another "friend" was Henri Le Caron, whose real name was Thomas Miller Beach, a British spy.

Early on June 1, 1866, O'Neil led his Fenians across the Niagara River near Buffalo, NY, into southern Ontario. After seizing Fort Erie, they struck south to Ridgeway and clashed with Canadian militia and British regulars who arrived by train. A U.S. military journal gave O'Neil the victory.

When the promised reinforcements and provisions did not arrive, O'Neil withdrew to the frontier and was arrested. Le Caron continued in his role of secret agent for the British in Clan na Gael for a quarter century until he dropped his cover by testifying against Parnell for the London *Times*.

## O'NEIL AND THE PRESIDENT

Le Caron told of going to the White House with O'Neil in 1868. He quoted President Johnson as follows: "General, your people unfairly blame me a good deal for the part I took in stopping your first movement. Now I want you to understand that my sympathies are entirely with you, and anything which lies in my power I am willing to do to assist you.

"But you must remember that I gave you five full days before issuing any proclamation stopping you. What, in God's name, more did you want? If you did not get there in five days, by God you could never get there; and then, as President, I was compelled to enforce the Neutrality Laws or be denounced on every side." We do not know, of course, whether this is true or a Le Caron invention.

The former secretary-treasurer of the Land League and ex-member of the Supreme Council of the IRB, Patrick Egan, who was wanted by the British, supported Alexander Sullivan, the head of Clan na Gael's dynamite wing, rather than John Devoy, in America. He backed the Republican, James G. Blaine, in the 1884 election.

Blaine lost, but three years later as secretary of state he made Egan U.S. minister to Chile. The British were outraged. They tried to have the Extradition Treaty revised to include "fugitive criminals" like Egan deported and put on trial in Ireland, but failed.

## THE FIRST WORLD WAR

Clan na Gael supported the Boers in the South African War of 1899–1903. Irish and Irish-American volunteers fought for the Boers. The Fenian creed prescribed that an Irish rebel movement must seek the support of England's enemies in war, which is what Devoy did in August 1914 when he asked the German ambassador for arms for an Irish rebellion.

In 1914 Home Rule was inevitable, everyone agreed. When Britain declared war on Germany, John Redmond, Parnell's successor, told the House of Commons: "I say to the Government they may tomorrow withdraw every one of their troops from Ireland and the coast of Ireland will be defended from foreign invasion by her armed sons." Patrick Egan, Parnell's lieutenant, supported Britain's war.

Although Ireland's contribution to Britain's war effort was considerable, the British press rarely acknowledged it. The Irish death toll was 49,400. A message to Berlin from Clan na Gael in New York, supposedly sent by Judge Daniel F. Cohalan, Devoy's right-hand man, urged bombing raids on England during Easter week.

Cohalan, a member of Clan na Gael from 1904, was an adviser of Charles F. Murphy, the boss of Tammany Hall. In June 1912, when the Democratic National Convention met in Baltimore to choose a presidential candidate, Tammany opposed Woodrow Wilson. It took 46 ballots to nominate him. In September 1917, after the United States entered the war, Washington released the document Cohalan sent to Berlin from a German office in Wall Street on April 17, 1916. It read:

The revolution in Ireland can only be successful if supported from Germany, otherwise England will be able to suppress it even though it be only after hard struggle. Therefore help is necessary. This should consist, primarily, of aerial attacks in England and a diversion of the fleet simultaneously with Irish revolution. Then, if possible, a landing of troops, arms and ammunition in Ireland, and possibly some officers from Zeppelins. This would enable the Irish ports to be closed against England and the establishment of stations for submarines on the Irish coast and the cutting off of the supply of food for England. The services of the revolution may therefore decide the war.

The papers were seized in a Secret Service raid on the Wall Street office of a German agent. Cohalan said he never met or knew the German agent von Igel, "and never sent or requested the sending of the remarks which are attributed to me."

## Irish Neutrality

Ireland, partitioned in 1920, failed to win full independence in the 1921 treaty negotiations with Britain. Irish neutrality was not understood in the United States. Prominent Irish-Americans, like General "Wild Bill" Donovan, the head of OSS, were sent to Dublin to persuade Eamon de Valera to lease the ports to Britain.

When Frank Aiken, de Valera's closest cabinet colleague, flew to the United States in March 1941 to ask for arms to defend Ireland's neutrality, the request upset Franklin D. Roosevelt. He "grabbed the table cloth and pulled it and I suddenly saw knives and forks flying all over the room."

In June 1940, Churchill sent Malcolm MacDonald to Dublin "to induce Eire to abandon her neutrality," Anthony Eden wrote. If de Valera agreed, it would result in "some form of union between Eire and Northern Ireland." De Valera "could only contemplate a united Ireland on the basis of Ireland's as a whole being neutral in the war."

Talk of ending partition was not on, Eden wrote in December 1943, because of "the very strong views which are widely held on this question both in Great Britain and in Northern Ireland. . . ." He said, "it would be wiser for the U.S. Government to postpone for the present the approach to Mr. de Valera which they have had in mind."

David Gray, the U.S. minister in Dublin, who was related to the Roosevelts by marriage, drafted a note to the Irish government to take "appropriate steps for the recall of German and Japanese representatives in Ireland." He was told to present it on February 21, 1944. "Of course our answer will be no," de Valera told Gray. When Britain and Canada presented similar notes a few days later, de Valera suspected a plot "to exert pressure on a weak neutral."

## Gerry Adams in America

President Clinton permitted Gerry Adams, the president of Sinn Fein barred from America as a "terrorist," to visit the United States because he was an elected official: a member of Parliament for West Belfast. The issue was resolved in the Sheraton Hotel, Manhattan, during the presidential primaries in April 1992.

On December 15, 1993, Albert Reynolds and John Major, the Irish and British prime ministers, issued the Downing Street declaration calling for peace in Northern Ireland. In August 1994, Reynolds made a public appeal to the IRA "to end violence completely" as the price of Sinn Fein's admission to talks on the future of Northern Ireland. An IRA cease-fire followed in early September.

President Clinton held a White House Investment Conference in June 1995, which sought to improve the economic future of Ireland, North and South. George Mitchell, the former U.S. senator from Maine and senate majority leader, took charge of arrangements for a Northern Ireland peace settlement. This resulted in the Good Friday Agreement which provided a representative structure for Northern Ireland under the British Parliament. Clinton stayed in touch by telephone with the parties working on

a settlement until full agreement was reached. He masterminded the entire procedure from the Oval Office.

The final steps in the process were Assembly elections on a party basis in Northern Ireland with voter acceptance at stake. A constitutional referendum in the Republic of Ireland abandoned de Valera's claims in Articles 2 and 3 of the 1938 constitution that "the national territory consists of the whole island of Ireland." The country's laws apply only to the 26 counties of the former Irish Free State. Ironically, the six counties of Northern Ireland are now excluded from the state called "Ireland."

*See* Devoy, John; Paris Peace Conference;
de Valera, Eamon; Ireland: Partition

León Ó Broin, *Fenian Fever* (London, 1971).
Lord Bryce, *The American Commonwealth,* vols. I and II (London, 1897).
Seán Cronin, *Irish Nationalism: A History of Its Roots and Ideology* (Dublin, 1980).
————, *Washington's Irish Policy, 1916–1986* (Dublin, 1987).
George Dangerfield, *The Damnable Question* (Boston and Toronto, 1976).
John Devoy, *Recollections of an Irish Rebel* (New York, 1929).
Florence E. Gibson, *The Attitudes of New York Irish Towards State and National Affairs, 1842–92* (New York, 1951).
P. S. O'Hegarty, *The Victory of Sinn Fein* (Dublin, 1924).
Patrick Keating, *A Singular Stance, Irish Neutrality in the 1980s* (Dublin, 1984).
Lord Longford and T. P. O'Neill, *Eamon de Valera* (Boston, 1971).
Dorothy McArdle, *The Irish Republic* (London, 1937).
John Mitchel, *Jail Journal* (Dublin, 1913).
Conor O'Clery, *The Greening of the White House* (Dublin, 1997).

SEÁN CRONIN

## UNITED IRISHMEN AND AMERICA

The foundation of the United Irishmen in October 1791 opened the final chapter in the history of the eighteenth-century Irish reform movement. The society sought "a complete and radical reform of the representation of the people." However, its resolve to include "Irishmen of every religious persuasion" in its program marked it from its predecessors, as did its support of the more popular campaign against tithes. Links with like-minded republican societies abroad also suggested an international brotherhood of which the United Irishmen were a domestic expression.

Viewed from any of these levels, it was inevitable that the society would be proscribed in 1794. The immediate effect was twofold. First, it drove the organization underground, thereby enhancing its image as a conspiracy. Second, it obliged some of the society's leaders to emigrate to America. However, given that republicanism was seen as an international movement, such leaders were exiles rather than immigrants and they used their involvement with republican networks in America toward the "emancipation of Ireland." A toast that was offered in Philadelphia on 18 March 1799 underlined this point: "*The Emigrant Irish Republicans*—Soon and successful be their return" to Ireland.

As capital of the United States until 1800, Philadelphia was an obvious attraction for the United Irish *emigré*. By the end of 1795, Theobald Wolfe Tone, Napper Tandy, James Reynolds and Archibald Hamilton Rowan were all living in or near the city. As a group who had made "great sacrifices in the cause of Liberty," they were befriended by the circles of Thomas Jefferson and the French minister, Pierre Adet. As a result, when Tone left for Paris

Theobald Wolfe Tone

in January 1796, he did so with letters of introduction to members of the Committee of Public Safety, to James Monroe, then the U.S. minister in Paris, and to other influential figures in the French capital. Britain's secret service acknowledged that Philadelphia's United Irishmen facilitated contacts between France and Ireland. In 1797, one agent reported that the "first solicitation" to France from the United Irishmen in Ireland had been made through Philadelphia, while another observed that the plans for France's ill-fated expedition to Bantry Bay (1796) were known in America three months before it actually took place.

Tone's republican journey outside Ireland was international in literal as well as in ideological terms. Reynolds and Rowan confined themselves to the more local networks of Jeffersonian republicanism in Philadelphia. During 1795, Rowan's active opposition to Jay's Treaty with Great Britain reinforced his ties with his Jeffersonian friends. It also appealed to the many Irish immigrants who had streamed into Philadelphia since 1765. As a result, these immigrants became quickly and publicly associated with criticisms of the policies and direction of the presidency of John Adams. The American Society of United Irishmen was central to the attempts to create an alternative "party" ideology and structure to the Adams Federalists and, as such, it attracted considerable comment during the 1790s.

It is difficult to say when precisely the American society was founded. Although the earliest copy of its constitution was dated in August 1797, the society was toasted in Philadelphia on St. Patrick's Day 1795. Members dedicated themselves to "the attainment of liberty and equality to mankind," "a free form of government, and uncontrolled opinion of all subjects." They also swore that they would "never, from fear of punishment, or hope of reward, divulge any of its secrets." Ideally, each "section" was limited to forty and was financed by fines and monthly fees. Sections kept in touch with one another through a system of "delegates" who, in turn, interacted with state committees and an overall General Executive Committee which supposedly sat in Philadelphia. According to William Cobbett, Delaware, Maryland, South Carolina, New York and Pennsylvania each had its own state committee. Cobbett is not always a reliable witness but no membership rolls of the American society survive. In May 1798, one newspaper suggested that in the greater Philadelphia area alone there were 1,500 members.

In any event, the exact number of American United Irishmen is less important than the perception of the society as a loud and active critic of the Adams government. At their monthly meetings, sections discussed contemporary radical works, through which they highlighted the professed invidiousness of "the British system." As many felt that Adams' policies were becoming too pro-British, Americans were warned to "beware" and not to allow their "rights" to be "trampled on" in the same way as the British were supposedly doing in contemporary Ireland. In these circumstances, some came to see the society as a group who were not only "disaffected Irishmen" but also "disaffected with the government of the United States." The society's secretive culture intensified its "dark and desperate" image. Federalists also alleged that the United Irishmen were always ready to assist France against the United States. "Can any one be silly enough to suppose," Cobbett asked, "that the [United Irish] conspiracy had only Ireland in view?" As a result, the term "United Irishman" evolved in Federalist parlance as one that was meant to suggest disloyalty, disruption, conspiracy and violence.

As America and France moved closer to war during 1797 and 1798, Federalist officials in Philadelphia gave special attention to these supposed fifth-columnists who were "plotting Mischief." Every effort was made to minimize their influence on American politics. The growing electoral success of Philadelphia's Jeffersonian coalition was facilitated by the organization and votes of the city's sizable number of (especially recently arrived) Irish immigrants. In October 1797, one Israel Israel was elected as state senator for part of the Philadelphia area by "procuring hordes of United Irishmen" to vote for him. Israel's election was challenged and overturned in a second contest in February 1798. Nonetheless, the elections had highlighted the influence of the "Irish vote" and led the secretary of state, William Pickering, to review the existing immigration and naturalization laws.

Federalists used the issues that were raised during the elections to argue that American politics was under too much "foreign influence" and that, as a result, the very stability and security of the Union was under threat. Such views were as old as they were familiar, suggesting that all the partisan controversy that America had seen since 1783 had been spearheaded by immigrants. Congressman Fisher Ames suggested that the *salus republicae* "plainly requires the power of expelling or refusing admission of aliens" while Harrison Grey Otis stated that he did not wish to "invite hordes of wild Irishmen, nor the turbulent and disorderly of all parts of the world, to come here with a view to disturb our tranquillity." An act of 1798 increased the period of naturalization from five to fourteen years, while the alien acts of the same year obliged ship captains to file more detailed information on their passengers. They also enabled the president to deport any alien whom he deemed to be dangerous to the peace and safety of the Union or whom he suspected (with or without evidence) to be "in treasonable or secret machinations against the government."

In London, the American minister, Rufus King, blocked the emigration of nearly 100 United Irish leaders when they applied to go to America after the rebellion of 1798 failed. King argued that they would never become "useful citizens of ours" and that their "principles and habits" were "utterly inconsistent with any practicable or settled form of Government." In America, Pickering ordered that descriptive lists should be drawn up lest these "United Irish Desperadoes" immigrate indirectly into the United States. However, these actions did not stop everybody, although King's exertions ensured that important leaders, such as Thomas

William MacNeven

Addis Emmet, William Sampson, William MacNeven, Robert Adrian and Thomas O'Connor, did not land in America until after Jefferson's election in 1800.

After 1800, the United Irishmen in America settled under a republican regime and a president with whom they closely identified. In cities such as Baltimore and Charleston, they founded new organizations and social clubs, some of which last to the present day. In New York, Emmet was their acknowledged leader, although after 1801 most of them belonged to the city's Hibernian Provident Society. Their unequivocal support of De Witt Clinton established the Irish as a political power in New York that continued into the twentieth century. They used this influence to confront their old antagonist, Rufus King, when he ran for the assembly in 1807 and for governor in 1816. King's supporters defended the policies of 1799 and again questioned the integrity of foreign-born voters. However, Emmet's influence was enough to help defeat King in the two outings.

In Pennsylvania, the United Irish leaders of the 1790s, Reynolds and Mathew Carey, as well as post-1800 arrivals such as John Binns, wielded considerable political influence into the new century. Sampson became one of the leading lawyers of his generation and Adrian a distinguished mathematician. However, the days of the United Irishmen as a discreet organization belonged to the years before 1800. Thereafter, the Irish community, including those who had belonged to the United Irishmen, differed on how Jefferson and republican governors and legislatures should use their electoral successes. Tensions also arose between those who before 1800 had been united in deed as well as in word. Nationalism replaced internationalism and the "older" leaders who had invented the politics of the new republic gave way to those who would develop that legacy into the so-called second party system.

*See* Irish in America; New York City

Maurice J. Bric, *Ireland, Irishmen and the Broadening of the Late-Eighteenth-Century Philadelphia Polity* (Ph.D. diss., The Johns Hopkins University, 1990).

Michael Durey, *Transatlantic Radicals and the Early American Republic* (Kansas, 1997).

David A. Wilson, *United Irishmen, United States* (Dublin, 1998).

MAURICE J. BRIC

## URSULINE CONVENT (Charlestown) BURNING (1834)

It was 1826 when the Ursuline Sisters came to Massachusetts from Quebec. They located in Charlestown, a stronghold of Protestant orthodoxy adjacent to Boston, and opened a boarding school. Religious sisters were then a new and not especially welcome sight in Massachusetts, and the Ursulines had to cope with insinuation, denunciation and the slander of those worried about "popery" and a Roman Catholic takeover of America.

The summer of 1834 was a peaceful one, however, and the Ursulines—a community of ten, most of them Irish, with surnames such as O'Keefe, Quirk and O'Boyle—planned for the return of their forty-four resident pupils.

But serenity was not to be theirs for long. On July 28 a young nun, described as pious but unstable, "eloped" from the convent, sought refuge with friends, then just as suddenly returned. Had she fled alleged servitude and cruelties of the convent? Had she been lured back under specious promises? Those questions, posed from evangelical pulpits and in the press, inflamed the non-Catholic citizenry, and on the night of August 11, 1834, a mob of enraged vigilantes ransacked and burned the convent, along with its auxiliary buildings, among them a barn, stable and icehouse. The superior, Mother Mary Edmond St. George, a native Canadian, led the sisters over a rear fence to the safety of a nearby farmhouse, where, settled on a sofa, she expressed a wish for a clean handkerchief and a pinch of snuff.

But Mother St. George had left behind a threat. If any ill befell the convent, she had warned in the tense days leading up to the burning, the bishop had twenty thousand Irishmen at his command who would avenge its fate. Indeed, the day after the burning, Irish railroad workers in Lowell, Worcester and Providence started for Boston to right the wrongs that had been done to their nuns and their church. But cooler heads prevailed. Boston's Bishop Benedict J. Fenwick dispatched priests to head off the men and dissuade them from any violence, and he himself hurried into the pulpit of the cathedral to preach forgiveness and reconciliation. There were no acts of retaliation—but there was little retributive justice either. Nine men were brought to trial. Eight were acquitted. The one conviction was of a seventeen-year-old boy who had joined in the attack as a lark.

As for the Ursulines, they closed their school and returned to Canada. Ownership of their property was conveyed in 1844 to the Archdiocese of Boston, but the site, not far from Bunker Hill Monument commemorating the Revolutionary War battle of June 17, 1775, was left undeveloped, almost "as if to contrast the glory and the shame of Massachusetts." The site was sold in 1875 for civic development.

Historians classify the burning of the Ursuline convent as one of the most shameful incidents of the nativism spawned by the rising tide of Catholic immigration.

Daniel H. Lord, et al., eds., *The History of the Archdiocese of Boston* (Boston, 1945).

Albert Bushnell Hart, ed., *Commonwealth History of Massachusetts* (New York, 1930).

JOHN DEEDY

## UTAH

### AN OVERVIEW

Irish immigrants were among the first Europeans to explore and settle the mountainous region that today comprises the state of

Utah. They were instrumental in building the territory's railroads and opening Utah's mining industry. While patterns of Irish immigration and migration were similar in many ways to those of the surrounding mountain states, the story of Utah's Irish is uniquely tied to Utah's turbulent history. While a few Irish converts to the Church of Jesus Christ of Latter Day Saints arrived with the Mormon pioneers in 1847, the majority of Utah's early Irish came to the region with military forces sent to counter Mormon domination of the Utah Territory. Large numbers of Irish served in the ranks of Albert Sidney Johnson's "Utah Expeditionary Force" during the Utah War in 1857–58. They remained with the occupying army at Camp Floyd until the withdrawal of Johnson's Army at the start of the Civil War. More Irish arrived with Col. Patrick Edward Connor's California and Nevada volunteers in 1862 and remained through 1868. Many of these same Irish would stay to play crucial roles in the development of Utah's natural resources.

Because they were closely associated with hostile forces pitted against local authorities, the Irish were generally regarded as unwelcome outsiders by Utah's Mormon settlers. In addition, the Irish were often engaged in commercial and industrial enterprises that were off limits to the Mormons, including the hard rock mining industry, liquor distilling, brewing and the saloon trade. Since association with the Gentiles was discouraged, few Mormons had reason or opportunity to become acquainted with their Irish neighbors. Moreover, the Irish were not easily assimilated into the Mormon farming communities. Religious, ethnic and social factors contributed to the settlement of the Irish in population pockets associated with military, mining and railroad communities. Ethnic and cultural isolation were common in early Utah. Many minorities shared similar experiences. This isolation is in large measure responsible for the continued vitality of Utah's ethnic minority populations, and in particular that of Utah's Irish community.

### Irish Trappers, Explorers, Pioneers, 1824–1842

The Irish influence on Utah history began with the expansion of the western fur trade in the 1820s. Many Irish were employed by Canadian and American fur companies. The most prominent of these frontiersmen was Irishman Thomas Fitzpatrick, born in County Cavan, Ireland, in 1799. Fitzpatrick immigrated to the United States in 1817 and by 1822 was exploring the West. Known as "Broken Hand" by the western Indians, he was regarded by his contemporaries, Kit Carson and Jim Bridger, as King of the Mountain Men. In March of 1824 he discovered South Pass, the overland gateway to Utah, Oregon and California. Fitzpatrick guided the first two wagon trains over the Oregon Trail and acted as guide to John C. Fremont (*The Pathfinder*). He was among the first to explore Utah's Uintah Basin and work the Green River, Weber River, and Bear River drainages. Fitzpatrick blazed trails that would later be followed by army surveyors, Mormon Pioneers, California-bound Forty-Niners, and the Transcontinental Railroad.

### Irish Pioneers, 1842–1847

A number of Irish families passed through Utah before the arrival of the Mormon pioneers. Martin Murphy, a native of Wexford, Ireland, traversed the valley of the Great Salt Lake with a party of California-bound immigrants in 1844. Murphy had immigrated to Canada and started a family there in the 1820s. Murphy immigrated to "Irish Grove" in Holt County, Missouri, in the late 1830s before starting on the long trek west. This pattern of immigration to Canada, to the American Midwest, and finally to the far west would be repeated by many of Utah's most prominent Irish families including Ivers, Judge, Hogle and Gilmore.

### The Donner Party, 1846

Several Irish families were among the pioneers of the ill-fated Donner party, including Murphy, Dolan, Hallorahan, Reed and Breen. Patrick Breen's diary entries, written in the snows of the Sierra Nevada during the winter of 1846–47, recorded the climactic episodes of the greatest tragedy in the western migration. Historians agree that the two weeks the company spent hacking a wagon road through the rugged Wasatch Mountains and down into the Salt Lake Valley sealed their fate. The costly delay would result in the party's eventual disaster when early snows hit the Sierra Nevada. Irish immigrant Luke Hallorahan would not make it that far. He died on the shores of the Great Salt Lake on August 24, 1846. His resting place near Black Rock Beach was unquestionably one of the first European graves in the Salt Lake Valley. The Donner party left a permanent mark on the Utah landscape and its history. The trail they blazed through the wilderness was used by the Mormon Pioneers the following summer to cross the Wasatch Mountains and enter the Salt Lake Valley. It was a road built in large measure by Irish labor.

### Mormon Pioneers, 1847

A few Irish converts to the Latter Day Saints Church arrived in the Salt Lake Valley with the first Mormon colonists in July of 1847. Irish immigrants John and Catherine Campbell Steele arrived with a company of Mississippi Mormons on July 29, 1847. On August 9, Catherine gave birth to young Elizabeth Steele, the first European child born in the Salt Lake Valley.

### The Gold Rush, 1849–1854

The California Gold Rush sent more than 200,000 fortune seekers across the plains. Many of these were Irish who had fled the 1840s potato Famine in Ireland. The specter of thousands of rough California-bound prospectors passing through Salt Lake City convinced Mormon leader Brigham Young that his dreams for the "State of Deseret" could not be achieved if his people were drawn to the allure of the gold fields. The Mormons were directed to avoid prospecting for gold or engaging in the precious metals industry. As a result, the development of Utah's mineral resources would be undertaken by non-Mormons (the Gentiles) and these would be largely Irish.

### The Utah War, 1857–1858

Brigham Young's territorial claims for his State of Deseret stretched from the Colorado Rockies to the High Sierra and Southern California. These claims were rejected by Congress and smaller boundaries were mandated for the Utah Territory. The Mormon practice of polygamy and the refusal of Brigham Young to submit to federal authority brought the Mormons to open warfare with the U.S. government. On July 18, 1857, the 10th Infantry set out from Fort Leavenworth, Kansas. It was only the first detachment of the Utah Expeditionary Force. Before it was over more than 7,000 U.S. Army regulars would be involved in the campaign. Most of the enlisted soldiers were immigrants, and most of these were Irish.

Mormon raiders under Lot Smith conducted a guerilla war against the federal troops of General Albert Sidney Johnston by burning supply trains, destroying food stuffs, capturing and stampeding cattle and horses, and setting fire to rangeland and crops ahead of the advancing army. Without supplies or forage for their livestock, the U.S. Army's campaign ground to a halt. General Johnston recognized that his army would need to be re-supplied and strengthened before any advance could be made against Salt Lake City. Over the winter of 1857–58, a treaty was arranged between Brigham Young and the federal authorities. The Utah Territorial administration would be accepted, but Johnston's army would be required to quarter fifty miles south of the city at Camp Floyd in Cedar Valley. At its height, Camp Floyd (later re-named Fort Crittenden) consisted of nearly 400 buildings. At a time when Salt Lake City had only fifteen thousand inhabitants, the Gentile population of Cedar Valley had climbed overnight to nearly 7,000. When *New York Tribune* editor Horace Greeley visited the post in 1859, he described it for his paper as "the largest military force ever concentrated upon the soil of our country in time of peace." Most of the enlisted men stationed at Camp Floyd were Irish and German immigrants. The force also had a number of Irish-born officers including Captain Tracy of the 10th infantry and his company commanders Lieutenants Kearney and Kelly. The regimental surgeon was Irish-born Major John C. Moore. A lonely desert cemetery is now one of the only reminders of Camp Floyd and Fort Crittenden. Among the seventy-four graves are a scattering of German immigrants, but the vast majority are of Irish immigrant soldiers.

With the approach of the Civil War, the Utah Expeditionary force was withdrawn and returned to the East. But the federal government continued to be wary of Mormon intentions and, within a year, a force of 750 volunteers from California and Nevada was on its way to Utah under the command of Col. Patrick Edward Connor. Connor, a decorated hero of the Mexican American War, was born Patrick O'Connor on St. Patrick's Day, 1820, in County Kerry. At the outbreak of the Civil War, Governor Downey of California offered command of the Third California Infantry to fellow Irishman, Patrick E. Connor. Connor raised and organized much of the regiment himself, so it was little wonder that the unit was comprised primarily of Irishmen. The officers included: Major Patrick Gallagher, Major J. B. Moore, Major Nicolas O'Brian, Captains McKean and Matheson, and Lieutenants Clark, Quinn, Murray, and Egan. In 1862 the regiment was given the lead position in San Francisco's St. Patrick's Day Parade. Connor and the men of the Third California Volunteers entered Salt Lake City without opposition on October 20, 1862. Although there were no hostilities, his reception was cold. A correspondent of the *San Francisco Bulletin* who accompanied the troops wrote: "Every crossing was occupied by spectators and every window, door, and roof had their gazers. Not a cheer, not a jeer, greeted us. There were none of the manifestations of loyalty that any other city in a loyal territory would have made." The Mormon attitude toward the Civil War was ambiguous at best. For the most part, Mormon Utah was neutral during the Civil War.

Col. Connor's assignment was ostensibly to guard the central Overland Trail from Indian attack, but part of his job was to keep an eye on the Mormons. Connor's Fort Douglas was not built forty miles from the city as Camp Floyd had been, but on the high east bench overlooking the Mormon capitol. On this strategic position, later known as Federal Heights, Patrick Connor placed his artillery. This was how Col. Connor chose to defend the Overland Trail from Indian attack. Soon after his arrival, Connor had his troops scouring the Utah Territory prospecting for mineral deposits. He filed Utah's first mining claims, organized the first mining districts and founded Utah's first mining towns, Stockton and Ophir. In 1863 he was promoted to the rank of Brigadier General. In July of 1864 Connor outlined his policy in a letter to his superior, Adj. General R. C. Drum in San Francisco:

> My policy in this Territory has been to invite hither a large Gentile and loyal population, sufficient by peaceful means and through the ballot box to overwhelm the Mormons by mere force of numbers, and thus wrest from the church, disloyal and traitorous to the core, the absolute and tyrannical control of temporal and civil affairs, or at least a population numerous enough to put a check on Mormon authorities. . .With this view, I have bent every energy and means of which I was possessed both personal and official, toward the discovery and development of the mining resources of the Territory.

### THE FENIANS OF FORT DOUGLAS

James Stephen's Fenian Brotherhood was an Irish secret society whose not so secret purpose was the liberation of Ireland by military force. Stevens' revolutionary ideas found fertile ground among the exiled Irish serving the Union Army during the Civil War. The most ardent Fenians in the American West were to be found at Fort Douglas overlooking the valley of the Great Salt Lake. Three circles of the Fenian Brotherhood would operate out of Camp Douglas in the 1860s: The Robert Emmet Brigade, The Wolf Tone Brigade, and the Patrick Sarsfield Brigade. Beginning in 1864 and continuing through 1867, notices for various Fenian meetings were prominent in the camp's newspaper, *The Daily Union Vedette*. Irish and Fenian news were regular features in the paper and editorials frequently drummed for the cause of Irish liberation. St. Patrick's Day celebrations were held every year during General Connor's term of command at Fort Douglas. Balls, parades, parties, and commemorations were given by Connor's troopers at posts throughout the Utah Territory.

Many of Connor's original troopers were mustered out of the army in 1867. Connor himself would temporarily retire from military service in 1868. Connor started a steamship line on the Great Salt Lake to haul ore from distant mines to smelters. He also operated excursion steamboats on the lake for pleasure seekers. Connor established the town of Corrine (originally Connor City) on the Bear River, near the Bear River Bay on the Great Salt Lake as his Gentile headquarters. Corrine quickly grew into a freighting and shipping center. Connor hoped to eventually make the town Utah's capital. Salt Lake City's newspapers rejoiced at the reduction of the Fort Douglas garrison and the departure of General Connor from the city. On March 18, 1869, a Salt Lake newspaper mocked Connor's new enterprises and seemed to revel in the disappearance of the Irish:

> THE SEVENTEENTH OF IRELAND,
> or St. Patrick's Day, yesterday, was a very tame affair in this city. Not even a drunk was reported on the police docket. In former years when the bold sons of Erin commanded the "sojer boys" on the bench considerable to-do was generally kicked up on the 17th of March, bands were out and the military paraded through the streets of this city, preceded by a large green flag, the emblem of Old Ireland, which cast into the shade "entirely" the renowned grid-iron of Uncle Sam. But the "Jineral" has been extinguished, or at least subsided to flatboat "Cap'n", Othello like, his occupation in the military line gone, and his

bold compatriots now find more peaceful and useful occupation at their old trade working on the railroad. Hence there was no 17th of Ireland here yesterday.

Salt Lake City, Ut. Terr.
March 18th, 1869

## THE IRISH AND THE RAILROAD, 1866–1869

Patrick Connor continued to develop his mining properties and promoted Utah's mineral wealth to investors outside the territory. But there was insufficient Gentile labor in Utah to fully exploit the claims he had already located, and the Mormons had been directed not to participate in Connor's mining ventures. But in California an immense construction army of eleven thousand Chinese was pushing through the snows of the Sierra Nevada headed for Utah, and on the plains west of Omaha, Nebraska, over five thousand Irishmen were working on the same project, the transcontinental railroad. The road bed for the Union Pacific Railroad from Omaha, Nebraska, to Utah was prepared by a huge track gang made up almost exclusively of Irish laborers. The road bed for the Central Pacific Railroad was prepared by Chinese, but Irish blacksmiths, track layers, gandy dancers, and engineers worked with both railroad companies. It was a crack Irish track-laying crew of the Central Pacific that laid ten miles of track in one day, a record that has never been equaled. For one brief moment on May 10, 1869, the attention of the country was fixed on Promontory, Utah. When the Golden Spike was driven into the polished laurel rail, thousands of Chinese and Irish laborers were simultaneously fired. These men flooded into the infant mining camps of the Intermountain West, and the era of hard rock mining in Utah began with an Irish Brogue and a Chinese lilt.

## THE IRISH AND UTAH'S MINES, 1869–1900

Through the nineteenth century, General Connor and his fellow Irishmen continued to contribute substantially to building Utah's mining industry and the general economy. Connor and his men helped bring Utah from economic isolation to commercial and industrial union with the rest of the nation. It was a contribution that has been widely acknowledged by Mormon and Gentile alike. General Connor's role in Utah's history is secure and he is now honored with the title: "The Father of Utah Mining."

Irish prospectors and mining engineers were responsible for the discovery and development of some of the West's richest and most productive mining properties including Park City's Silver King, Ontario, Daly West, Daly Judge, Valejo, and Crescent mines. Many of the original claims in Bingham Canyon were made by Irishmen including the Quinn Group, and claims on a geologic feature called Parnell Ridge included the St. Patrick and Robert Emmet claims. Irishmen were also responsible for major discoveries at Ophir, Mercur, Eureka, Leeds, and Silver Reef.

Irishmen also played an important part in the commercial and industrial development of the region during Utah's territorial period (1847–1896). Many of Salt Lake City's principal commercial buildings, as well as many of the mansions on South Temple Street, were built by Irish immigrants or first-generation Irish-Americans who made their fortunes in Utah's mines. Thomas Kearns, born to Irish immigrant parents, walked into Park City, Utah, with ten cents in his pocket and ten years later was a multi-millionaire. Kearns would serve as one of Utah's first U.S. senators. His mansion on South Temple Street is now the official residence of Utah's governor. Irish immigrant miner and saloon keeper James Hogle (Gilmore) established a real estate and financial empire, and would help found the Salt Lake Chamber of Commerce. The name is preserved in Salt Lake City's Hogle Zoo. Like many of Park City's miners, first-generation American John Judge would die of silicosis from working beside the miners in his own mine. His fortune would go to the establishment of Judge Miners Hospital, later Salt Lake City's Judge Memorial Catholic High School. Many of the principal buildings in downtown Salt Lake City were built by Irish immigrants or their children, including the Kearns Building, the Judge Building, the Keith-O'Brien Building, and the Daly Block. For more than a century, Irish Catholics owned and operated Salt Lake City's principal daily newspaper, *The Salt Lake Tribune*. The Irish were also instrumental in the establishment and the building of Utah's Catholic Diocese of Salt Lake City.

## IRISH CATHOLICISM IN UTAH

While Irish missionary priests passing through Utah celebrated Mass at Camp Floyd, it was not until arrival of Col. Connor's California and Nevada Volunteers that any attempt was made to establish a permanent Catholic presence. Father Edward Kelly, who previously had held services at the old Mormon Tabernacle on Temple Square, acquired property from Brigham Young for Utah's first Catholic parish in 1866. Most of Utah's pioneer Catholic priests were Irish including Rev. Patrick Walsh, Rev. James Foley and Rev. Lawrence Scanlan. Scanlan would serve Utah's Catholics for 43 years and in 1891 became the first bishop of the Catholic Diocese of Salt Lake City. With the aid of Utah's Irish community, Bishop Scanlan would build the imposing Cathedral of the Madeline, one of Salt Lake City's principal landmarks. Bernice Maher Mooney's *Salt of the Earth: The History of the Catholic Diocese of Salt Lake City, 1776–1987* (Salt Lake City: 1992) documents the contributions of many hundreds of Irish clergy and religious who served in Utah from territorial times. Irish priests and nuns built and staffed schools, hospitals, and orphanages throughout the Utah Territory. Irish priests directly from Ireland continue to serve many of Utah's Catholic parishes to this day.

## IRISH REVOLUTIONARY SOCIETIES

Utah Irish were unusually active in Irish nationalist and revolutionary societies, and many of Ireland's most influential political leaders came to the state to enlist support for causes back home. James Steven's Fenian Brotherhood was immensely successful among the Irish of Fort Douglas in the 1860s. In the 1880s, Charles Stuart Parnell's Parliamentary Party raised money throughout Utah's mining towns as did his campaign for the Irish National Land League. In 1920 Eamon de Valera and Liam Mellows visited Salt Lake City twice to elicit support for the Sinn Fein movement and Irish Independence.

From 1864 through the end of the 19th century, there were annual St. Patrick's Day events in Utah. At least eight Irish organizations were active in the state. The activities of these groups were mostly restricted to hosting balls and hat passes for Irish causes back home. It was inevitable that the Irish of the Intermountain West would eventually draw the attention of the British government, their agents and the Pinkerton Detective Agency. On March 13, 1888, an unusual branch of the Knights of Robert Emmet was founded in Park City, Utah. The minutes of that organization are intact from that date until 1891. In addition to fundraising, the main activity of the Knights seems to have been the careful investigation of every Irishman who set foot in the town. The log book contains the name, age, physical description and occupation of each new arrival. Investigating committees were then appointed to find out if the man in question was indeed the person he claimed to be. Often this entailed sending members to distant cities.

## PATTERNS OF MIGRATION AND POPULATION STUDIES

The Irish came to Utah in several distinct waves and from several directions. Excluding those who arrived with the military or the railroad, many of Utah's early Irish came to the territory via Canada. Several histories document this migration. *The Hogles* (Salt Lake City: McMurrin-Henricksen Books, Western Epics Publishing, 1988) follows the migration of a group of Irish immigrants along a similar route to Quebec in the 1830s to Illinois in the 1840s to Pikes Peak and Colorado in 1859, to Virginia City and Helena, Montana in 1863–64 and then to Salt Lake City, Utah in the early 1870s. R. O'Dwyer, in his series *Who Are My Ancestors?* (Astoria, Illinois: K.K. Stevens Publishing Co.), has extensively documented the migration of many Irish from the copper regions on the Beara peninsula in Western County Cork to mining towns in Utah and Montana via Canada. Most of the Irish who worked in Utah mines were previously miners elsewhere in the intermountain west or California before arriving in Utah. The Irish tended to migrate to places where they had relatives or close friends. Irish miners working California's Comstock Lode migrated to Goldfield, Nevada and Park City, Utah, when the Comstock mines closed in the early 1880s. Many of the Irish miners who came to Silver Reef, Utah, in the 1880s had previously worked in Pioche, Nevada, before the mines there closed. There are also many examples of continuous migration between specific towns and states. Some of these migrations are unique to specific extended families. The Utah Irish in Park City had close connections with the Butte, Montana, Irish, and cross migration between the two mining towns was common. David M. Emmons, in *The Butte Irish: Class and Ethnicity in an American Mining Town, 1875–1925* (Urban and Chicago: University of Illinois Press, 1989), indicates that migration from Park City and Eureka, Utah, to Butte, Montana was particularly heavy in the first few decades of the twentieth century, as mines closed in Utah or mine owners imported non-union labor. Irish miners made up a large portion of the militant Western Federation of Miners (UFW) and other western mining unions. The activities of these unions lead directly to the importation of Italian, Greek and Slavic miners who began replacing earlier immigrant workers—including the Irish—by the turn of the century. Butte, Montana eventually collected most of the Irish miners in the West.

The largest concentrations of Irish in Utah during the nineteenth century were in and around Salt Lake City, in the Bingham and Cottonwood Mining Districts, Park City (Summit County), Ogden, (Weber County), and the Tintic Mining District including Eureka (Juab County). There were also many Irish at various times in other smaller mining settlements including Ophir, Mercur and Stockton (Tooele County), Frisco (Beaver County) and Silver Reef (Washington County).

The actual number of Irish-born residents of Utah varied greatly from year to year during the Territorial period. The 1870 census reported about 500 Irish-born residents. But these figures are extremely misleading. If the census had been taken in 1869 when the railroad was being built, the number of Irish in Utah would have been in the thousands. The figures do not include military personnel nor many of the transient mining and railroad workers who lived in Utah during non-census years. The 1890 census recorded a little over 2,000 Irish born residents. But the records of Utah's Irish nationalist organizations and the advertisements for their events reveal that many of the residents identified as being "Canadian" had an unusually keen interest in Irish politics. The Irish population of Utah declined sharply over the first three decades of the twentieth century. Residual pockets of Irish remained in Park City, Salt Lake City, Murray, Ogden, Eureka, and Tooele. In 1980 one in ten Utahans claimed Irish ancestry (137, 479).

With the founding of the Utah Hibernian Society in 1977, the Utah Ulster Project in 1984, and the Golden Spike Ulster Project in 1988, numerous Irish social, cultural and educational programs have been initiated or revived. Courses in Irish history and literature have been offered and Irish balls, concerts, siamsas, poetry readings, and plays are annually held. The LDS Church Genealogical Library is a center for Irish genealogical research, and the internationally respected journal *The Irish at Home and Abroad* is published out of Salt Lake City. The annual St. Patrick's Day Parade in downtown Salt Lake City (revived in 1978) has grown over the years into one of the premiere celebrations in the country. Monuments commemorating the Irish contributions to Utah are found at the National Golden Spike Monument Visitor Center at Promontory Point, Utah; The Irish Railroad Worker Monument at Union Station in Ogden, Utah; The Celtic Cross Monument at The International Peace Gardens in Salt Lake City; and General Connor Memorial at The Fort Douglas Military Museum. Other Utah localities with Irish connections include Salt Lake landmarks: The John W. Gallivan Plaza, The Kearns' Mansion, Hogle Zoo, and the Cathedral of the Madeleine.

Juanita Brooks, *The Mountain Meadows Massacre* (University of Oklahoma Press, 1950).

Robert Joseph Dwyer, *The Gentile Comes to Utah* (Catholic University, 1941).

Dean L. May, *Utah: A People's History* (Bonneville, 1987).

Gerald M. McDonough, *The Hogles* (McMurrin-Henriksen, Western Epics, 1988).

George R. Stewart, *Ordeal by Hunger: The Story of the Donner Party* (Houghton Mifflin, 1988).

James F. Varley, *Brigham and the Brigadier: General Patrick Connor and His California Volunteers in Utah and Along the Overland Trail* (Westernlore Press, 1989).

GERALD McDONOUGH

information would be understandable, but the contrary is the case. From the founding of the Green Mountain State in 1791, the Irish played an active part in its history.

### MATTHEW LYON

Irish names are scattered throughout Vermont's early history. A number of Irishmen, for example, worked in the saw mills established by Ethan and Ira Allen, the two men most responsible for settling northern Vermont in the 1770s and 1780s. In the Allen Family Papers at the University of Vermont, one reads of Irish workers Michael Fortune, James McManus and Denis Downing. In 1785 an Irishman named Patrick O'Brien was buried in Irasburg, a frontier town near the Canadian border owned by Ira Allen. But because they were common workers, we know little about these early Irish transplants.

The first Irishman to make a name for himself in Vermont was Matthew Lyon (1749–1822). Born in County Wicklow, Lyon sailed for Connecticut in 1764 as an indentured servant and later migrated to Vermont where he joined the Green Mountain Boys and participated in the capture of Fort Ticonderoga in 1775.

A member of the Allen-Chittenden clique which dominated Vermont politics in the state's early years, Lyon was twice elected to Congress—1796 and 1798—where he was an outspoken critic of Federalist policies. His views earned him a caning in Congress by Connecticut's hot-tempered Representative, Roger Griswold, and jail-time under the repressive Sedition Act.

In 1801 Lyon and his family left Vermont for the softer climate and more fertile soil of Kentucky. There he continued his political activism, representing his new state in Congress from 1803–1811. He died in 1822 in Arkansas while engaged in a commercial venture.

### THE CANADA CONNECTION

Despite the presence of a few Irishmen in Vermont in the 18th century, it was not until after the Napoleonic Wars (1799–1815) that significant numbers of Irish found their way to the Green Mountains. They did so because British policy, encouraging emigration to Canada over the United States, made it less expensive to travel from Ireland to Quebec City or Montreal than to New York or Boston. But many of these immigrants did not stay long in Quebec. Jobs were scarce and the French culture alien. Hundreds of immigrants who had just gotten off boats at the quays in Montreal traveled to the port town of St. Jean on the Richelieu River and caught steamboats to Lake Champlain and Vermont.

### THE BURLINGTON IRISH

As the busiest port on the lake, Burlington became an important stop for the Irish. Jobs were plentiful. The opening of the Champlain Canal in 1823 made Burlington a boom town. Strong backs were needed to load and unload the sloops, schooners and steamboats that plied the lake; nearby textile and sawmills employed hundreds; and there was constant work for carpenters, masons and teamsters.

According to research done by Brian Walsh, by 1830 Burlington's population of 3,526 was about 11% Irish. Other evidence supports Walsh's findings. On a trip to Burlington in 1835, Nathaniel Hawthorne noted the large numbers of Irish there. In an essay entitled "The Inland Port," he wrote that the Irish "swarm[ed] in huts and mean dwellings near the lake, lounge[d] about the wharves, and elbow[ed] the native citizens entirely out of competition in their own line." In Hawthorne's description the

---

## VAN SUSTEREN, GRETA (1954– )

Attorney, professor, television personality. Greta Van Susteren was born June 11, 1954, in Appleton, Wisconsin, daughter of Urban and Margery (Conway) Van Susteren. Her father was a Wisconsin judge, who managed the 1946 campaign of Joseph McCarthy that brought McCarthy to the United States Senate. Greta Van Susteren, spurning political definition, describes her political ideology as "fluid."

Van Susteren received a bachelor's degree in economics from the University of Wisconsin in 1976, and a law degree from Georgetown University in 1979, being admitted that same year to the bar of the District of Columbia. She was a Stiller Fellow at the Georgetown Law Center in 1980, and beginning in 1985 an adjunct professor of law at Georgetown. She has also been engaged in private legal practice, specializing in criminal and federal civil litigation. She won her first murder case when she was twenty-seven.

Van Susteren's wider fame results from her work on television as legal analyst and commentator for the CNN Network. That phase of her career began when CNN tapped her to do commentary on the 1991 William Kennedy Smith rape trial. She became the network's star legal commentator during the O. J. Simpson murder trial, when CNN's daily coverage was estimated to have reached fifteen million persons. Some viewers felt Van Susteren was pro-Simpson, but she countered her only interest was that the case be heard on its evidence. CNN subsequently signed Van Susteren as host of her own program, "Burden of Proof," which airs five days a week. On television she is known for her straightforwardness and a facility to render complex legal language in terms readily graspable by the average viewer.

Van Susteren is married to John Coale, a civil attorney.

Betsy Israel, "Making Sense of Simpson," *People Weekly* (March 13, 1995).

*Who's Who in American Law,* 6th edition (Chicago, 1990–1991).

JOHN DEEDY

---

## VERMONT

As a small agricultural state long depicted in the media as quintessentially Yankee in culture, the contributions of Irish men and women to Vermont's history have been largely overlooked. There is no book on the Vermont Irish and only a handful of articles in *Vermont History*—the journal of the Vermont Historical Society—deal with Vermont-Irish themes. If the Irish had played an inconsequential role in the development of the state this lack of

most characteristic trait about Burlington in the 1830s was its Irishness.

### Thomas Ryan

While most of the Irish coming to Vermont in the 1820s and 1830s settled in and around Burlington, a few moved to the countryside. Typical of this group was Thomas Ryan (1790?–1849), an emigrant from Tipperary. Ryan arrived in Burlington shortly after the conclusion of the War of 1812, stayed a few years working as a tailor, then moved to Fairfield, a small farming community forty miles northeast of Burlington. There he bought a farm and prospered. Writing back to Ireland he encouraged others to come join him, and through his efforts a strong Irish community composed of Denivers, O'Neills, Rooneys and Collins was established in Fairfield by 1830. This group was later augmented by a number of families escaping the Irish Famine of the 1840s—among them Branons, Howrigans and Branigans. Today, this small community founded by Thomas Ryan so long ago remains closely connected to its Irish roots.

### Rev. Jeremiah O'Callahan and Bishop John Henry Hopkins

The coming of so many Irish to northern Vermont—almost all of whom were Catholics—moved the Bishop of Boston, whose diocese then included the Green Mountain State, to assign a priest there. In 1830 the Bishop appointed the Rev. Jeremiah O'Callaghan (1780–1861), a native of Macroom, County Cork, the first resident English-speaking priest in the Green Mountain State.

O'Callaghan was an odd man, who at fifty years of age had already had a checkered career as a priest. Ordained in Cork in 1805 he soon found himself in trouble with his bishop, for early in his life O'Callaghan had developed a hatred of usury, which he defined as the giving out of money at *any* interest rate, even ones which fair-minded people considered reasonable. His verbal attacks on the banking community caused his bishop to dismiss him in 1819. For the next few years he traveled to France, to the United States and to Canada, looking for a diocese that would accept his services. Initially, none would have him.

On a return trip to the United States in 1829 he chanced to meet Bishop Benedict Fenwick of Boston. Now his luck turned. Aware of the growing Irish and French-Canadian Catholic population in northern Vermont, Fenwick had been casting about to find someone to station there; and here was O'Callaghan begging for an assignment. The deal was struck; O'Callaghan was off to Vermont.

O'Callaghan made Burlington his headquarters, building a church—St. Mary's—in 1833. For the next twenty-two years he ministered to the Catholics of northern Vermont, riding a circuit that brought him north to St. Albans, then east through the hill country of north central Vermont, and then back again to Burlington. To this day many northern Vermont towns note that O'Callaghan was the first priest ever to say Mass there.

But O'Callaghan continued to get himself into trouble, and, of course, it was over money-lending. When he roundly criticized the opening of the Burlington Savings Bank in 1834, the *Burlington Free Press* said, ". . . this Reverend Paddy, who according to his own showing, has thrice been spewed from the Church and his native country is a shatter[sic]-brained disorganizer." The more he railed against the banking community the more he was dismissed as a crackpot.

Another source of friction was his hostility towards the Episcopal Bishop of Vermont, John Henry Hopkins (1792–1868). The conflict was as much personal as theological, and may have had as much to do with their common Irish roots, for Hopkins had been born in Dublin and came to America with his parents in 1800. Hopkins was elected Episcopal Bishop of the newly created Diocese of Vermont in 1832. And, like O'Callaghan, his home base was Burlington. This was unfortunate.

They lived as neighbors, but these two Irishmen never got along. Both took their religions seriously and neither shrank from casting barbs at the other's beliefs. In 1834–35 Hopkins published two short books, *Primitive Church* and *Primitive Creed,* attacking Roman Catholicism. Fuming over Hopkins's criticisms, O'Callaghan immediately began work on his own treatises, warning those interested that "Facts and truths which you did not expect shall meet your eye, in their innate and natural features, stript naked of all party colouring." His works, *On Protestant Matrimony* and *The Vagaries and Heresies of John Henry Hopkins,* appeared in 1837 and denied the legitimacy of the Episcopal Church. The feud died down in the 1840s and each man served his church till the end of his days.

### Vermont and the Famine Irish

The flood of Irish emigration resulting from the Great Famine (1845–47) affected Vermont no less than the rest of New England. From all directions Irish poured into Vermont—from Canada to the north and from Boston and New York to the south. What attracted them was work, for Vermont in the 1840s was experiencing rapid industrialization: muscle was needed to build railroad lines connecting Burlington to Boston; and strong backs were required to work in the granite quarries of Barre, the slate works in Fair Haven, and the marble quarries in West Rutland and Proctor. In addition, there were plenty of positions available for eager workers in the hundreds of cotton and woolen mills which had opened in Vermont since the 1830s.

### Population Growth

As a result of this influx, the number of Irish in Vermont rose dramatically in the 1840s and 1850s. According to the 1860 Census, 4.3% of Vermont's population of 315,098 was born in Ireland, a higher percentage than in either Maine or New Hampshire at the time. But this figure tells only half the story, for it includes only Irish-born, not the thousands of children born in Canada and the United States to Irish parents or the descendants of earlier immigrants. Calculated this way the Irish-American population of Vermont was much higher, perhaps as high as 10–12% of the total. In the only detailed study of the Burlington Irish, for example, Brian Walsh looked at surnames rather than country of birth and concluded that in 1860 Irish-Americans constituted 37.9% of the city's population. In Northfield at the same time, Gene Sessions calculated that 17% of the population was either born in Ireland, or were the children of Irish parents.

These examples point to another reality of the Irish experience in Vermont: that while the Irish sometimes were found farming in the countryside they tended to concentrate in a few urban areas—areas where demand for unskilled labor was high. The railroad centers of Rutland, St. Albans, Bennington and Brattleboro had large numbers of Irish-Americans—perhaps as high as 30% by the 1860s. The same was true of Fair Haven and Proctor, towns noted for their stone quarries. In Betsy Beattie's study of ethnicity in Colchester—a town famous for its woolen mills in the 19th century—she concluded that 21.6% of the population was Irish-American in 1860. While the Irish could be found everywhere in Vermont by the middle of the nineteenth century, in a few places their presence was overwhelming.

## JOHN LONERGAN

For Irish Vermonters the Civil War was a watershed event in their assimilation into American society. Dorothy Canfield Fisher in her insightful work *Vermont Tradition* said of the years following the war, "The Irish soldiers, now G.A.R. men, were no longer immigrants; they were Vermont boys." Yankee Americans could not fight side-by-side with Irish-Americans through one of the bloodiest wars in history, and then keep their distance in peace time.

Not all Irish-Vermonters, however, supported the war. There were instances of army recruiters being assaulted by Irishmen. In one incident in West Rutland in 1863, Irish quarry workers pelted recruiters with marble chips. In the same year a squad of recruits passing through a heavily Irish section of Burlington was attacked and ridiculed. According to the newspaper account of the incident, the reason for the attack was that the Irishmen were hostile to any man who would consent to wearing a soldier's uniform.

This anti-military sentiment, however, was not widespread among the Vermont Irish. The career of John Lonergan (1841–1902) was more typical. Born in Tipperary, Lonergan emigrated with his family in 1845 to the United States where they came to reside in Burlington. Bright and ambitious, young Lonergan sometimes worked alongside his father as a cooper, and sometimes in the grocery business, but in his free time he drilled and trained with a local militia unit.

When the war broke out in 1861 Lonergan quickly enlisted, received a captaincy, and eventually formed his own company made up primarily of Irishmen from Burlington, Westford and Rutland. Throughout the war this unit, Company A, 13th Regiment Vermont Volunteers, was known as Emmett's Guards, and distinguished itself in the Battle of the Wilderness and Gettysburg. For his actions at Gettysburg Lonergan received the Congressional Medal of Honor. Back home proud Vermonters's noted that ". . . the Shamrock of Ireland and the Evergreen of Vermont were entwined around the staff of our victory flag."

## THE FENIAN RAIDS OF 1866 AND 1870

While the Civil War raged, Fenian activists from New York and Boston stumped Vermont, organizing secret clubs or "centers" in every Irish community. By war's end there were thirteen Fenian units spanning the state from Bennington in the south to St. Albans in the north. Many of the Vermont Fenians were, like John Lonergan, veterans of the Civil War.

In the Green Mountains Fenian activity channeled itself into organizing events which expressed a self-consciousness and pride in being Irish. On March 17, 1866 the Burlington Fenians held the first ever St. Patrick's Day parade in Vermont, and they would do so for another dozen years. Other towns copied them, and through the 1860s, 1870s and 1880s there were St. Patrick's Day festivities in all major Vermont towns.

Besides being entertaining social events the parades were also vehicles to drum up support for the Fenian goal of winning Irish independence through violence. And twice in the years immediately following the Civil War, the Vermont Irish found themselves at the center of Fenian plans. In 1866 and 1870 the national Fenian organization orchestrated invasions of Canada, and on each occasion the eastern flank of the assault was through Vermont.

Both attacks were embarrassing fiascos, but they did receive widespread support from the Vermont Irish, and from many Vermonters. Recently discharged veterans had not forgotten that Britain had tacitly supported the Confederacy during the war, and that a group of Confederates raiding out of Canada in 1864 had robbed a St. Albans bank, taking the life's savings of a number of local families.

Thus when Fenians from New York, Connecticut, New Jersey and Massachussetts disembarked from trains in St. Albans in 1866 and 1870, they were roundly welcomed. John Lonergan participated in both 1866 and 1870, while in the 1870 attempt the commanding officer of the 1st Fenian Cavalry was a Captain William Cronan of Burlington. Moreover, Vermont-Irish paid more than their share in support of the cause; in the 1870 attempt there were ten Irish casualties, and three were from Vermont. With the failure of these invasions Fenian activity in Vermont declined, as it did elsewhere in America.

## COLLAR AND ELBOW WRESTLING

In the second half of the 19th century Irish immigrants introduced country wrestling to the United States, where it became known as "Old Sod" or Collar and Elbow Wrestling—the latter because the grapplers initially stood facing one another, with one hand on the other's shoulder or collar, and the other on his elbow. The object was to first get the opponent down—"bring him to grass"—and then pin his shoulders to the ground.

Collar and Elbow Wrestling became intensely popular in the Irish communities of Vermont. One authority on the subject, Charles Morrow Wilson, estimated that between 1856 and 1896—the heyday of the sport—Vermont produced twenty-one accredited national champions, seventeen of whom were of Irish descent.

The greatest of these was John McMahon (1841–1912). Growing up on the family farm in Bakersfield, Vermont, he learned how to wrestle from his father and brothers, and by the time he was fifteen he was winning more matches than he lost. It was during the Civil War, however, that he established his reputation as a wrestler. As an enlistee with the 13th Regiment of Vermont Volunteers, he took on all challengers.

While he returned to help a brother on the family farm after the war, much of his time was spent pursuing a career as a professional wrestler. Possibly his most famous match took place in 1880 at Boston's Music Hall. There, in front of a crowd estimated as "the biggest and most enthusiastic in the sporting history of greater Boston," McMahon fought fellow Vermonter Henry Dunn to a draw. The match lasted six hours, with one ten-minute break so the *crowd* could take a rest. In 1884 McMahon traveled to England where he defeated John Tedford, "The Terrible Welshman," for the world championship in wrestling. In the next few years he traveled to Australia and Argentina where he captured national titles. For a time in the 1880s Franklin County, Vermont, was the wrestling capital of the world.

## VERMONT POLITICS

In Boston, New York City, Chicago, Kansas City and San Francisco, Irish-American politicians performed on the big-stage, but they were no less successful in achieving political power in the nation's smaller towns. Vermont is a case in point. By the turn of the l9th Century Irish politicians mobilized the ethnic voters of Burlington, Montpelier and Rutland—French-Canadians, Italians, Scots, Welsh and Jews—and wrested control from the Republican establishment.

Irish political clout first made itself felt in Rutland, where Irish railroad and quarry workers twice elected Limerick-born Dr. John Hanrahan (1844–1927) President of Rutland's Village Council. Hanrahan, a Civil War veteran and graduate of New York University's Medical School, welded Rutland's diverse ethnic community into a solid Democratic block. In the 1880s and early 1890s Hanrahan led the Democratic Party on the state level, but with less success.

In the state capital of Montpelier, the people elected a grocer, Frank McMahon Corry, mayor in 1903, and thereby started an Irish political dynasty. His son William served as mayor from 1939–1945, while another son, Frank C., represented Montpelier in the state senate from 1937–1941.

### JAMES EDMUND BURKE

In terms of longevity though, no Vermont mayor to this day can compete with the career of James Edmund Burke (1860–1940). Burke was born of Irish parents in Jericho, Vermont, but when still young his family moved to Burlington. After a few years of grammar school Burke took up the trade of blacksmith and went to work. His neighborhood, the Third Ward, was an ethnic enclave, made up primarily of Irish, French-Canadians, and a scattering of Jews and Italians.

In 1903 Burke felt strong enough to take on the Republican establishment. In a bitter mayoral contest the scrappy Irish blacksmith defeated the Republican candidate, giving a Democrat the mayor's office for the first time in the city's history.

Burke espoused the progressive thinking of the day, and supported laws and statutes which alleviated the hardships of poor people. This made him wildly popular with Burlington's working classes, and they elected him mayor four more times. In all, Burke served intermittently as Burlington's chief officer from 1903 to 1935. In the following thirty years the power base he built produced six more Irish-American mayors of Burlington.

Not until the 1950s, however, did the Vermont-Irish begin to make an impact on politics at the state level. In 1954, Frank Branon, a farmer from the old Irish enclave of Fairfield, ran for governor and came within a few percentage points of becoming the first Democratic governor of Vermont since the founding of the Republican Party. Branon's showing was followed in 1958 by Bernard Leddy, a Burlington attorney, who came within eight hundred ballots of becoming governor. Encouraged by these near misses the Democrats continued to put forth candidates and in 1962 captured the governor's office for the first time in over a century.

The first Irish-American governor of Vermont was Thomas Salmon (1932– ), a Rockingham lawyer and Boston College graduate, elected in 1972. Responding to fears that Vermont was being overrun by out-of-state developers, Salmon campaigned on an environmental platform which declared that "Vermont is not for sale." His popular stand on the environment and on property tax reform won him re-election in 1974. In 1991 in the midst of a financial and leadership crisis, the University of Vermont called Salmon out of private life to lead that institution as its president, which he did until retiring in 1997.

Patrick Leahy (1940– ) perhaps best exemplifies the story of the Vermont Irish. His grandfather came to Vermont in the late 19th century to work in Barre's granite industry. There he worked and raised a family, but after years of breathing in the fine stone dust of the quarries he died of black lung disease. His grandson, born in Montpelier just a few miles away from the granite pits, eventually went to St. Michael's College in Colchester, then on to Georgetown Law, and by the late 1960s was the State's Attorney for Chittenden County. In 1974 this descendant of an Irish quarry worker was elected U.S. Senator from Vermont, and achieved a double first; for besides being the first Irish-American senator from Vermont, he was also the first Democratic senator.

### BISHOP JOSEPH JOHN RICE AND LE PETIT EGLISE

Since the days of Jeremiah O'Callaghan the Irish had played a leading role in the history of the Catholic Church in Vermont, but they frequently found themselves at odds with their French-Canadian co-religionists. This rivalry extended from jobs—French-Canadians were often brought into Vermont in the late 19th century as strike breakers—to control of the local parish. If the parish priest was an Irishman—and often he was—and the sermon was given in English, French-speaking Canadians felt uncomfortable. Rejecting Irish control of the parish in Burlington in 1850, the French-Canadians of the city petitioned the Diocese of Boston to allow them to establish their own French language church. Thus, in 1850, St. Joseph's Church in Burlington became the first French National Church in New England. Within a few decades other French churches were founded, leading to a pattern whereby many Vermont towns had a "French" church and an "Irish" church.

This Irish/French rivalry reached a peak in Vermont in 1910 in a little publicized affair known as *Le Petit Eglise* or, the little church. The background was this: Vermont's first bishop, the Rev. Louis deGoesbriand (1820–1899), a Frenchman from Brittany, kept the peace between his French-Canadian and Irish flock by making sure he brought in as many French priests as Irish. It was deGoesbriand who supported the creation of French language churches. His successor, the Rev. John Michaud (1843–1908), who became bishop in 1899, appealed to both communities, as he had been born and raised in Burlington, with a French-Canadian father and Irish mother. When he died in 1908, however, there was intense interest over who would be the next bishop.

By 1908 many of the French-Canadian clergy in Vermont had become concerned that their people were losing their language and their customs; soon, they feared, they would also lose their religion. This reaction against assimilation they termed *survivance*. In their eyes one of the threats to *survivance* was the growing domination of the church in New England by the English-speaking Irish clergy of the archdiocesan center in Boston. Thus it was extremely important to their goal of cultural *survivance* that an individual friendly to French-Canadian culture be appointed bishop.

Thus as soon as Michaud passed away, a group of these priests began lobbying for a French-speaking bishop. They called themselves *Le Petit Eglise*. By various means they advanced the names of French-Canadian candidates; they pleaded their case with Boston, and even went over the Archbishop's head and petitioned Rome directly. When Boston seemed to turn a deaf ear to their requests, they changed tactics, and advanced the name of Rev. Daniel O'Sullivan (1853–1918) of St. Albans. O'Sullivan was a Vermont Irishman, but he had been trained at the Sulpician Seminary in Montreal, spoke French fluently, and was supportive of *survivance*. The hopes of *Le Petit Eglise* were dashed, however, when thirty-eight year old Joseph John Rice (1872–1938), a Massachussetts Irishman, was named bishop in 1910.

For the proponents of *survivance* Bishop Rice was their worst nightmare. First, he was an outsider; a Massachussetts man, born in Leicester of Irish parents. Secondly, though he had attended the Sulpician Seminary in Montreal he had never become comfortable with French. More importantly, though, he had gone on for advanced study at the American College in Rome where he had become a Romanist, a supporter of the idea that national distinctions within the Church should be suppressed. On the announcement of Rice's appointment as bishop, the *Burlington Free Press* said that Archbishop O'Connell of Boston, another Romanist, wanted to introduce "more of the customs of Rome into the ceremonies here and the years of study at Rome will enable Bishop Rice to meet this desire." Members of *Le Petit Eglise* looked apprehensively to the future.

Once in office Rice chose to ignore *Le Petit Eglise*, but dissent and rancor continued. Only when Rice threatened to terminate their faculties to minister in his diocese did *Le Petit Eglise* cease to resist.

Since the days of Bishop Rice, Catholic leadership in Vermont has been dominated by a succession of Irish-American bishops: Matthew Brady, 1938–1944; Edward Ryan, 1945–1956; Robert Joyce, 1956–1971; and John Marshall, 1972–1992. The old hostility between the French and the Irish gradually died away, partly because both groups were increasingly being assimilated into American society, but also because Bishop Brady initiated a policy whereby all priests in Vermont, of whatever ethnic background, had to speak French.

### SISTER STANISLAUS O'MALLEY

In 1872 Bishop deGoesbriand contacted the Sisters of Mercy at their convent in Manchester, New Hampshire about supplying nuns to teach in Vermont. The Sisters of Mercy—an Order founded in Ireland—responded favorably, and sent a small group of young Irish nuns to Burlington to begin their teaching mission. They were led by Galway-born Mother Stanislaus O'Malley (1846–1921), later recognized as the Foundress of the Order in Vermont.

Under the leadership of Mother O'Malley the Sisters of Mercy thrived in the Green Mountains. They established their first school, St. Patrick's Academy, in 1874 in Burlington. Quickly outgrowing that facility they opened a larger school, Mount St. Mary's Academy in 1886. In the years to come they founded and staffed schools across Vermont. To meet the educational needs of young Catholic women in the state, in 1925 they established Trinity College in Burlington which to this day serves the needs of Vermonters. No other teaching Order has had as much impact on the education of Vermont's Catholics as has the Sisters of Mercy.

John Joseph Cadden, "Father Jeremiah O'Callaghan, Economist and Pioneer Missionary" (M.A. Thesis, Catholic University, 1935).

James O'Beirne, "Some Early Irish in Vermont," *Vermont History,* 28/1 (1960).

Gene Sessions, "Years of Struggle: The Irish in the Village of Northfield, 1845–1900," *Vermont History* 55/2 (1987).

Brian Walsh, "The Burlington Irish" (M.A. Thesis, University of Vermont, 1993).

VINCENT FEENEY

# VIRGINIA

Virginia did not attract the large waves of Irish immigrants who flooded the shores of the Northeast. Its economy was based on plantations, which in turn relied on slavery. Religiously, it was a mixture of lukewarm Anglicans in the Tidewater region, Presbyterians especially in the Shenandoah Valley, and Baptists and Methodists sprinkled throughout mainly small farming communities. It was not a welcome place for Catholic immigrants.

In 1634, Lord Baltimore's expedition to Maryland encountered some Irish on the Caribbean island of Guadalupe, where they fled after being banned from Virginia. A decade later, St. Isaac Jogues reported that in New Amsterdam he heard the confession of an Irish refugee from Virginia, which he may have confused with Maryland. Penal laws in Virginia prohibited the exercise of Catholicism throughout the colonial period, although one family, the Brents, survived and prospered on the Northern Neck, between the Rappahannock and Potomac Rivers, from 1650 until American independence. In 1786, however, Virginia became the first state formally to disestablish a state church with its Statute of Religious Liberty. With legal restrictions removed, cultural prejudice remained.

### LAY TRUSTEEISM IN NORFOLK AND THE ESTABLISHMENT OF THE DIOCESE OF RICHMOND

In the years after the Revolution, Alexandria, technically part of the District of Columbia until 1846, Martinsburg, Richmond and Norfolk were the only places with Catholics. In Alexandria, Colonel John Fitzgerald, a native of Rothdowny, Ireland, and George Washington's aide de camp, led the movement in the 1790s to establish the first parish, St. Mary's, which was, however, principally composed of Catholics of English ancestry. Norfolk was the first city with a significant Irish presence. Members of an emerging Irish middle class, many of these early immigrants fled after the abortive French invasion of Ireland in 1798. In the port city, they engaged in commerce and soon entered into conflict with the French priest, originally assigned to them by Archbishop Leonard Neale of Baltimore. The French-Irish tension was exacerbated with the succession to Baltimore in 1817 of Archbishop Ambrose Marechal, a refugee from revolutionary France.

The trustees in Norfolk, principally Irish, but led by a Portuguese physician, began issuing a series of learned, but tedious disquisitions on their rights to nominate pastors and even bishops. They also plotted to have an Irish Dominican, Thomas Carbry, consecrated as bishop by the schismatic Bishop of Utrecht. In 1820, contrary to Marechal's explicit advice, the Holy See attempted to settle the dispute by establishing the new diocese of Richmond under an Irish bishop, Patrick Kelly from Waterford. The lay trustee schism ended, but Kelly returned to Ireland without ever having visited Richmond. Virginia was returned to the administration of Baltimore.

Only in 1841 did Richmond receive its second bishop, Richard Vincent Whelan, born in Baltimore of Irish ancestry. In 1846, he moved to Wheeling, then part of Virginia, which was experiencing growth because of the National Pike. In 1850, the Holy See divided the diocese of Richmond and established the new diocese of Wheeling with Whelan as bishop and named John McGill to Richmond. Born in Philadelphia of Irish ancestry, McGill was ordained for the Diocese of Bardstown (later Louisville).

## The Irish in Richmond and the Railroads

In the meantime, while Norfolk remained the principal Irish center for some years, the development of the Catholic community in Richmond was due to the work of an Irish priest, Timothy O'Brien. Born in Mayo and ordained for Baltimore, he arrived in Richmond in 1832, when the most prominent members of the community were French. Gradually, however, several Irish families immigrated to the city. Many came to work on the Kanawah Canal connecting Richmond to Lynchburg. For the female orphans of these poor workmen, O'Brien had the Sisters, later Daughters, of Charity open an asylum. Many of these sisters were themselves of Irish birth or ancestry. But some of the newcomers were not poor. In 1837, John Dooley and his wife moved to Richmond, where he became a successful hatter and furrier and established himself as a leader in Richmond society. He and his wife had nine children, several of whom would play major roles in the city. From Richmond, O'Brien also ministered to the growing Irish community in Lynchburg. By the 1850s, Richmond's Irish population necessitated a second parish, St. Patrick's, closer to the flour mills and tobacco warehouses, where many of the Irish worked. But work on the railroads, from Richmond to the Shenandoah Valley and around Martinsburg in the northern part of Virginia, became the greatest attraction to the Irish. In 1844, St. Francis of Assisi parish was established in Staunton in the Shenandoah Valley under an Irish-born priest, Daniel Downy, who settled a strike of railroad workers. Although a few German Catholics formed the original congregation, the parish remained almost exclusively Irish well into the twentieth century.

## Priests from All Hallows

To care for these new Irish settlers, Whelan and his successors needed priests. He had established a short-lived seminary in Richmond, but then became the first bishop in the South to rely on All Hallows College outside Dublin for recruits. Over the next 150 years, Virginia was second only to California in the number of All Hallows priests. The first five Irish recruits arrived in 1850, just as the diocese was split. McGill chose three of these for Richmond to care for the increasing number of Famine Irish who came to work on the railroads and who spoke no English. Urging potential Virginia missionaries to learn Irish before coming, one of the new recruits, Father Andrew Talty, stated the problem succinctly: "I prefer to be able to speak Irish than to be a second St. Thomas." He ministered to the Irish around Harpers Ferry and Martinsburg, where the B&O Railroad was beginning its trek westward. Although the charge is made that many Irish were lost to the Church for lack of priests, Talty's records, like those of other priests, indicate that he made every effort to take the Church to the people. He frequently said Mass in the homes of laborers and baptized children in the camps along the railroad line. One Sunday each month, he also said Mass in Winchester in the Shenandoah Valley, an old Catholic community that had become increasingly Irish. But it was arduous work; Talty was dead by 1862.

Railroads also drew Irish immigrants to the area of Virginia near Washington. Alexandria had been ceded back to Virginia in 1846, but it had declined as a port city, because it failed to develop rail connections. That changed in the 1850s, and Irish answered advertisements to work on the Orange and Alexandria Railroad. In 1858, the Jesuits at St. Mary's in Alexandria, the only parish in the region, founded a mission for these Irish laborers at Fairfax Station.

When McGill took office in 1850, all but one of his seven priests were Irish. No sooner had he arrived in Richmond, however, than O'Brien departed. O'Brien had expended a small fortune of his own wealth in building Richmond's only church and the orphanage. But McGill accused him of using his office to accumulate wealth. Although O'Brien was exonerated by a special committee of bishops at the First Plenary Council in 1852, he moved to St. Patrick's parish in Lowell, MA, where his brother, John, was pastor. John had also served briefly in Virginia and was, incidentally, the inventor of "Father John's Medicine," a popular cold remedy.

O'Brien was not the only Irish priest of independent wealth who came to Virginia. In 1852, Matthew O'Keefe took up residence in Norfolk. Born in Waterford, he was ordained for Baltimore from which he was on loan to Richmond for the next thirty-six years. Norfolk's Catholic population was by then predominantly Irish workers at the shipyard.

## Yellow Fever and Nativism

Not all of Norfolk's Irish, however, were poor. Walter Herron had amassed a small fortune in Norfolk. Since he and his wife, Ann Plum, had no children, he went to Ireland where he adopted his sister's daughter, Ann Behan, who took the complicated name Ann Behan Plum Herron. During the Yellow Fever epidemic, she turned her home into a hospital and herself fell victim to the disease. Her initial generosity, however, aided by her brother, James Behan, who had also emigrated from Ireland to Norfolk, led in 1856 to the establishment in Norfolk of St. Vincent's Hospital, staffed by the Daughters of Charity. The epidemic was an occasion for Catholic heroism. Many doctors and ministers joined the exodus from the city. But the Daughters of Charity, who staffed the orphanage in O'Keefe's parish, had nursed many of the victims. O'Keefe twice came down with the fever and entered a pact with a Protestant minister that, if either died, the other would celebrate the funeral. Both survived the fever, but O'Keefe later presided at his Protestant friend's funeral.

No sooner had the Yellow Fever abated, however, than Virginia Catholics faced a new threat in the Know-Nothing campaign for governor. Irish workers on the railroad between Richmond and the Shenandoah Valley were particular targets of anti-Catholicism. In Petersburg, Anthony Keiley, a New Jersey native of Irish ancestry and then an attorney and newspaper editor, used his paper to attack the Know-Nothings. In Norfolk, O'Keefe was the target of an assassination attempt, but he drew a pair of revolvers on his would-be killers and turned them over to the sheriff. Frederick Wise, the Democratic candidate, had sharply condemned the Know-Nothings' anti-Catholicism and ultimately won the election, but Virginia was now caught up in the debate over slavery.

## The Civil War

Some Irish, like the Dooleys in Richmond and Quinlans in Staunton, owned a few household servants, but none owned plantations. While most of Virginia's Irish were not slave owners, the Civil War tested their loyalty. In Richmond, the Irish had already formed the Montgomery Guards in 1850 under Captain Patrick Moore. In 1861, John Dooley was elected captain when Moore became colonel of the First Virginia Infantry Regiment. Bishop McGill blessed the pikes of the company in the cathedral as it prepared to march off resplendent in gray uniforms trimmed in green. Dooley's sons, James and John, Jr., also served in the unit as did Benjamin Keiley, Anthony's brother. Its chaplain was Father John Teeling, pastor of St. Patrick's Church and one of the All Hallows recruits. But loyalty to the Confederacy among Richmond's Irish depended on social class. The Irish laboring class formed a second company, the Emmett Guards. It served for only one year, when it disbanded, and some Irish claimed exemption from further military service because they were British subjects. Such appeal to British citizenship was not singulat. At Harpers Ferry, Father Michael Costelloe, an All Hallows priest, was reported to have hoisted the Union Jack over St. Peter's Church to preserve it from bombardment by either army. But the Irish in Norfolk, Lynchburg, and Petersburg generally flocked to the Stars and Bars, although they did not raise their own units. Father O'Keefe in Norfolk was named a brigade chaplain, a distinction he proudly proclaimed until his death. In Petersburg, Anthony Keiley joined the army. He was elected to the state legislature while serving at Gettysburg. Nursing in battlefield hospitals on both sides of the conflict were many Daughters of Charity, some of whom were Irish, such as Sister Aloysia Kane, whom one Catholic Confederate chaplain described as "a sweet and timid dove . . . who shows the boldness and the courage of a lioness as soon as there is a question of defending the Faith."

Despite the sacrifices of so many sons and daughters of Erin for the Confederacy, prejudice still persisted in Richmond. On Holy Thursday, March 5, 1863, 1,000 women rioted in Richmond in protest at the shortage of bread. A day later, the *Richmond Examiner* commented that the women were "prostitutes, professional, Irish and Yankee hags, gallows birds from all lands but our own." McGill cooperated with civil authorities in quelling any Irish- or German-Catholic looters, but contemporary research indicates that Catholics, native or foreign born, played at most a minor role in the fracas. Nativism was clearly alive even as Richmond's Irish Catholics were dying in the war. At war's end, however, the loyalty of Virginia's Irish to the lost cause more than offset any suspicions about their foreign birth.

### Reconstruction

Reconstruction brought to the fore several Irish leaders. Keiley moved from Petersburg to Richmond, where he published the *Examiner.* He also took over the management of the Norfolk *Virginian* for which he hired a young Irish immigrant and Confederate veteran, Michael Glennon. With financial backing from O'Keefe, Glennon later purchased the paper and remained its proprietor and editor until his death. Back in Richmond, Keiley was elected major in 1870, at the same time that James Dooley, who inherited his father's military rank of "Major," was elected to the legislature. Neither made a secret of their Catholic faith. Both took an active part in founding the St. Vincent de Paul Society at St. Peter's Church. In 1870, both joined in the public protest in Richmond at the loss of papal temporal power. Because of this, the Italian government later proclaimed Keiley *persona non grata* when he was nominated as U.S. ambassador—the Austro-Hungarian government likewise rejected him as ambassador because he was married to a Jew. Keiley was also active in national Catholic affairs and was president of the Irish Catholic Benevolent Union.

The Keiley and Dooley families moved in the highest of Richmond circles. Benjamin Keiley was ordained in Richmond for the Diocese of Wilmington and later became Bishop of Savannah. John Keiley, also a Confederate veteran, moved to New York to become an editor of the *Freeman's Journal.* Nora Keiley entered the Visitation Monastery in Richmond. John Dooley, Jr., entered

the Jesuits, but died before he was ordained. James later made a fortune in railroads and speculation in mineral rights. At his death in 1921, he left $3 million to build a new orphanage, St. Joseph's Villa. The Dooley women were equally prominent. Sarah entered the Visitation Monastery, and Mary, Josephine, Nora, and Alice were all active in the Equal Suffrage League.

But the prominence of Irish in Virginia social life was limited almost exclusively to Richmond and Norfolk. Railroads continued to draw Irish to Virginia in the postbellum years. In 1872, they were numerous enough in Falls Church outside of Washington to necessitate establishing a second mission for St. Mary's in Alexandria. By 1882, Roanoke in the Shenandoah Valley became an Irish haven for laborers on the Norfolk and Western Railroad. Within a decade, it was the principal city in the valley.

### Catholicism, Virginia Style

In the years after the Civil War, Virginia became a stepping stone to national prominence for some Irish or Irish-American clergy. In 1872, James Gibbons succeeded Bishop McGill. Born in Baltimore, he was raised for a while in Ireland. In 1877, he was named coadjutor Archbishop of Baltimore and succeeded to the nation's oldest see before departing from Richmond. In 1886, he became the nation's second cardinal. Richmond's new bishop was John J. Keane, a native of Ireland, who was raised in Baltimore. He would serve until being named the first rector of the Catholic University of America in 1887. Virginia's Catholics in general, and the Irish in particular, had developed a distinctive style. A mixture of workers and middle-class professionals, they had established a *modus vivendi* with their Protestant neighbors, losing no opportunity to cooperate in civic affairs to show publicly that they were Christian, but adamant in preserving their faith. Gibbons, for example, regularly used Protestant churches to hold confirmations in towns where there were no Catholic churches. Cooperation with Protestants was simply part of daily life, but so was concern for the working class. This Virginia tradition shaped Keane's positive response to Terence Powderly when the Knights of Labor held their convention in Richmond in October 1886, the largest assembly of organized labor up to that time. Keane and Gibbons would later be in the forefront of the move to gain the Vatican's toleration of the nation's first labor union. The same Virginia tradition might have contributed to the movement called Americanism, in which Gibbons, Keane, Archbishop John Ireland of St. Paul, and Denis J. O'Connell, a Richmond priest, were the leaders in the 1890s, for they each had firsthand experience of accomodating Catholicism to the prevailing Protestant culture without surrendering any essential Catholic doctrines.

With Keane's appointment to the Catholic University, Cardinal Gibbons tried unsuccessfully to have his protege, O'Connell, appointed as bishop. O'Connell had been born in Ireland, but raised first in South Carolina and then North Carolina—he claimed to come from an old South Carolina family since his grandfather had immigrated there before his parents. Ordained in 1877, he was named rector of the American College in Rome in 1885, a position that Leo XIII thought too important to be vacated for the sake of Richmond. In 1888, despite the opposition of Gibbons and Keane, Augustine van de Vyver, born in Holland, recruited by McGill at the American College in Louvain, and the vicar general of the diocese, became bishop. For a generation, he governed the church in Virginia whose priests came from Flanders or were of Irish birth or ancestry and whose people remained predominantly Irish-American. He remained aloof from the quarrels that divided the American hierarchy in the 1890s, quarrels in which his predecessors, Gibbons and Keane, played such major roles. In fact, he hardly corresponded with Gibbons, his metropolitan, for his entire episcopate. His episcopacy, however, did witness the generous benefaction of one of America's wealthiest men.

Thomas Fortune Ryan had been born in Virginia, but accumulated his wealth in New York, where he speculated in railroads, tobacco, and the insurance business. He and his wife were solely responsible for building the Cathedral of the Sacred Heart in 1905. He or his wife also contributed to other churches and schools around the state.

## THE TWENTIETH CENTURY

In 1911, van de Vyver died, and Gibbons finally maneuvered O'Connell's appointment as bishop. By this period, Virginia's Irish no longer held prominent elected office. One exception was John Purcell. The scion of an old Richmond Irish family, he was elected state treasurer for several terms, but his campaign for re-election in 1924 became the target for an anti-Catholic crusade from the Ku Klux Klan. In general, Virginia's Catholics relied on friendly Protestants in the legislature to prevent the passage of such anti-Catholic measures as convent inspection bills that had been enacted in other states. In the wake of Al Smith's defeat in 1928, Catholics became more defensive and anxious to prove their patriotism. The diocesan newspaper, *The Catholic Virginian,* published a series of articles on Catholic Confederate heroes, many of whom were Irish. While Catholics, Irish or otherwise, actively participated in Virginia's civic and patriotic affairs, elective office was in general barred to them. As late as 1941, only one Catholic, John A. K. Donovan from Falls Church, sat in the legislature.

Northern Virginia was only slowly developing into what would become the dominant region in the state. Its first Catholic growth in this century was due to Irish working menial jobs in Washington. By 1907, many Irish had settled in the area near the Potomac River across from Washington, but were too poor to pay the streetcar fare to the parish in Falls Church. As a result, a new parish was established for them in the village of Clarendon in what later became Arlington County. The area underwent another growth spurt during World War I, but then would have to wait until World War II and the postwar years to take its present shape. But in the first quarter of the twentieth century, Northern Virginia also had its wealthy Irish. Michael Ahern, the bachelor son of Irish immigrants, operated a tavern in Alexandria and bought houses for the poor. When he died in 1924, he left a small fortune to the diocese for the education of seminarians and other charities. But his was not the wealth of the Dooleys or the Ryans.

By the 1920s, most of Virginia's Irish had been assimilated. Unlike other regions of the nation, however, few entered the field of politics or the clergy—in the 1930s, the Vatican queried why Virginia had failed to produce native vocations. Yet, with the exception of van de Vyver, all of Richmond's bishops have been of Irish birth or descent. O'Connell was compelled to resign in 1926 for reasons of health. His successor, Andrew Brennan, was born in Scranton of Irish parents. After he suffered a stroke in 1934, Peter L. Ireton, a native of Baltimore of Irish descent, was named coadjutor in 1935 and bishop in 1945 when Brennan resigned. With Ireton's death in 1958, John J. Russell, Bishop of Charleston, also a Baltimore native of Irish ancestry, succeeded. At his retirement in 1974, Walter F. Sullivan of both Irish and Dutch ancestry became Bishop of Richmond, while Thomas J. Welsh became the first bishop of the new diocese of Arlington.

Virginia's Irish made up for their small numbers by contributing to an unusual public style of accommodation to a culture that was Christian though Protestant. Frequently bereft of Sunday Mass, they concentrated on Catholic practices such as Friday abstinence to preserve their identity. Overt patriotism became their avenue toward acceptance in what had been a hostile Protestant environment. Prominent families such as the Dooleys and Keileys in Richmond mirrored Irish families elsewhere—they were financially generous to the Church and their sons and daughters entered religious life. But Virginia has had to rely heavily on priestly recruits from other American dioceses and Europe, especially Ireland, to serve what still remains in part a missionary territory.

*See* Irish Heritage of the South

James H. Bailey, *A History of the Diocese of Richmond: The Formative Years* (Richmond, 1956).

GERALD P. FOGARTY, S.J.

## VOLUNTARY ORGANIZATIONS: A CHRONOLOGY

| Organizations | Date / Key Events |
|---|---|
| | *ca. 1715* |
| | Large-scale Scotch-Irish immigration to America begins. Approximately 250,000 Scotch-Irish immigrants arrive in America prior to the American Revolution. |
| | *1737* |
| Charitable Irish Society (Boston). | |
| | *1767* |
| Ancient and Most Benevolent Order of the Friendly Brothers of St. Patrick (New York). | |
| | *1771* |
| Society of the Friendly Sons of St. Patrick for the Relief of Emigrants from Ireland (Philadelphia). | |
| | *1775–1783* |
| | American Revolution. |
| | *1784* |
| Society of the Friendly Sons of St. Patrick in the City of New York. | |
| | *1798* |
| | United Irishmen Rebellion fails. A number of United Irishmen emigrate to the United States during the next few years. |

| Organizations | *Date*<br>Key Events | Organizations | *Date*<br>Key Events |
|---|---|---|---|
| | **1799** | | **1848** |
| Hibernian Society of Charleston, South Carolina. | | Hibernian Benevolent Emigrant Society (Chicago); Irish Emigrant Society (Detroit). | Young Ireland Rebellion fails. Several Young Irelanders emigrate to the United States in the next few years. |
| | **1801** | | |
| Hibernian Provident Society of New York. | Ireland becomes part of the United Kingdom. | | |
| | **1803** | | **1855** |
| Hibernian Society of Baltimore. | | Emmet Monument Association. | |
| | **1816** | | **1856** |
| Shamrock Friendly Association (New York). | | Irish Catholic Society for Promotion of Actual Settlements in North America. | |
| | **1823** | | **1858** |
| | Catholic Association under the leadership of Daniel O'Connell formed to fight for Catholic Emancipation. | Fenian Brotherhood. | Irish Republican Brotherhood established in Ireland. |
| | **1825** | | **1861–1865** |
| Friends of Ireland [for Catholic Emancipation] (first groups formed; others formed during next few years). | | | American Civil War. |
| | | | **1865** |
| | **1829** | | British moves against the Irish Republican Brotherhood severely hamper the revolutionary movement in Ireland. |
| | British government grants Catholic Emancipation. | | |
| | **ca. 1835** | | |
| | Beginning of large-scale Irish Catholic emigration to the United States. Growth in anti-Catholic nativism. | | **1866** |
| | | | Unsuccessful Fenian raids on Canada. |
| | **1836** | | **1867** |
| Ancient Order of Hibernians in America. | | Clan na Gael. | Unsuccessful uprisings in Ireland. |
| | **1840** | | **1869** |
| Repeal Associations (first groups formed; others formed during next few years). | Daniel O'Connell begins his campaign to repeal the union between Great Britain and Ireland. | Catholic Total Abstinence Union of America; Irish Catholic Benevolent Union. | |
| | | | **1870** |
| | **1841** | Loyal Orange Institution of the United States of America (some local lodges had been established previously). | |
| Irish Emigrant Society (New York). | | | |
| | **1843** | | **1871** |
| | Repeal campaign suffers major defeat. | Irish Confederation. | |
| | **1845–1849** | | **1874** |
| | Irish Famine; massive Irish emigration to the United States during the late 1840s and early 1850s. | | Irish Parliamentary party established under the leadership of Isaac Butt. |
| | **1847** | | **1876** |
| | Young Irelanders form the Irish Confederation as a rival to the Repeal Association. | Catholic Colonization Bureau of St. Paul (its predecessor, the Minnesota Irish Emigration Society established in 1864); United Irish Societies of Chicago. | |

| | Date | | | Date | |
|---|---|---|---|---|---|
| *Organizations* | | *Key Events* | *Organizations* | | *Key Events* |

| *Organizations* | *Key Events* | *Organizations* | *Key Events* |
|---|---|---|---|
| **1879** | | **1897** | |
| Irish Catholic Colonization Association. | Irish National Land League established in Ireland. | American Irish Historical Society. | |
| **1880** | | **1898** | |
| Irish National Land League of America; *Irish World* Land League; Ladies' Land League. | Charles S. Parnell takes over the leadership of the Irish Parliamentary party. | Gaelic League (national organization formed in 1898; first member organization formed in 1873). | |
| **1881** | | **1900** | |
| | Irish Land Act of 1881 passed by British Parliament. | | Irish Parliamentary party reunited with the United Irish League as its national organi- zation. |
| **1882** | | **1901** | |
| | Irish National League established in Ireland. | United Irish League of America. | |
| **1883** | | **1902** | |
| Irish National League of America; Mission of Our Lady of the Rosary for the Protection of Irish Immigrant Girls. | | Irish Fellowship Club (Chicago); Irish Music Club (Chicago). | |
| **1884** | | **1904** | |
| | Gaelic Athletic Associ- ation established in Ireland. | United Irish Counties Association of New York. | |
| **1885** | | **1912–1914** | |
| Irish Parliamentary Fund Association. | | | Irish Home Rule crisis; Home Rule Bill passes, but Ulster Protestant resistance prevents its implementation. |
| **1886** | | **1914** | |
| | First Irish Home Rule Bill defeated. | | World War I begins. |
| **1889** | | **1916** | |
| Scotch-Irish Society of America; Scotch-Irish Society of the United States of America. | | Friends of Irish Freedom. | Easter Rising in Dublin. |
| **1890** | | **1917** | |
| Gaelic Athletic Association (hurling and football clubs begin to mushroom in Irish-American communities; Chicago GAA established in 1890, New York GAA in 1914). | Irish Parliamentary party splits in the wake of the Parnell-O'Shea divorce scandal. | Irish Progressive League. | United States enters World War I. |
| **1891** | | **1918** | |
| Irish National Federation of America. | Irish National Feder- ation established by anti-Parnellites in Ireland. | | World War I ends; Sinn Féin victorious in the British general election of December 1918. |
| **1893** | | **1919** | |
| | Second Irish Home Rule bill defeated; Gaelic League estab- lished in Ireland. | American Commission on Irish Independence. | Dáil Éireann established in Dublin as the gov- ernment of the "Irish republic"; Anglo-Irish War begins; Paris Peace Conference. |
| **1895** | | **1920** | |
| Knights of Equity. | | American Association for the Recognition of the Irish Repub- lic; American Commission on Conditions in Ireland; Ameri- can Committee for Relief in Ireland. | Brutal Anglo-Irish War continues; Home Rule governments established for Northern Ireland and South- ern Ireland; Southern government inoperative due to Sinn Féin opposition. |

| Organizations | *Date*<br>Key Events | Organizations | *Date*<br>Key Events |
|---|---|---|---|
| | **1921** | | **1949** |
| | Anglo-Irish Truce in July; Anglo-Irish Treaty in December gives dominion status to twenty-six-county Irish Free State and allows the six counties of Northern Ireland to remain in the United Kingdom. | | Republic of Ireland declared; Ireland leaves Commonwealth. |
| | | | *ca.* **1950** |
| | **1922–1923** | Emerald Societies. | |
| | Irish Civil War between Free Staters and Republicans; Republicans defeated, and new Irish Free State survives. | | **1960** |
| | | American Committee for Irish Studies; Shamrock Club of Wisconsin. | |
| | **1927** | | **1962** |
| Ulster-Irish Society (New York). | | Irish American Cultural Institute. | |
| | **1929** | | **1963** |
| | Great Depression begins; tremendous drop in Irish immigration during the 1930s. | American Irish Foundation. | |
| | | | **1965** |
| | **1932–1937** | | New Immigration Act enacted. After it takes effect in 1968, Irish immigration, which had witnessed a modest revival during the post–World War II period, is cut to a mere trickle. |
| | Éamon de Valera's Fianna Fail government breaks all significant ties with Great Britain but remains in the Commonwealth; new constitution adopted in 1937; state now known as Ireland (Éire) instead of Irish Free State. | | |
| | | | **1966** |
| | | Irish Centre of Pittsburgh. | |
| | | | **1967** |
| | **1933** | American Irish Immigration Committee. | |
| Thomas Davis Irish Players (New York). | | | **1968** |
| | **1937** | | Civil rights marches in Northern Ireland result in violence; present troubles in Northern Ireland begin. |
| Éire Society of Boston. | | | |
| | **1939** | | **1969** |
| All-Ireland Cultural Society of Portland, Oregon. | World War II begins; Ireland remains neutral despite British pressure to enter the war. | | Violence in Northern Ireland escalates significantly; British troops sent into province; Provisional Irish Republican Army breaks with Official Irish Republican Army. |
| | **1940** | | |
| American Friends of Irish Neutrality. | | | **1970** |
| | | Irish Northern Aid Committee. | |
| | **1941** | | **1971** |
| | United States enters World War II. | American Committee for Ulster Justice; Irish Republican Clubs of North America; National Association for Irish Freedom (its predecessor, the National Association for Irish Justice, formed in 1968); United Irish Cultural Center of San Francisco (building not completed until 1975). | |
| | **1945** | | |
| | World War II ends. | | |
| | **1947** | | |
| American League for an Undivided Ireland. | | | |

| Organizations | Date / Key Events |
| --- | --- |
| | **1972** |
| Comhaltas Ceoltóirí Éireann. | Government of Northern Ireland suspended as Britain imposes direct rule from London pending the establishment of a provincial assembly acceptable to both Catholics and Protestants. |
| | **1973** |
| | New Northern Ireland "power-sharing" assembly meets. |
| | **1974** |
| Irish National Caucus. | New Northern Ireland executive made up of both Catholics and Protestants takes office on January 1; hard-line Protestant opposition forces the collapse of the assembly in May; the British reimpose direct rule from London, which continues to the present day. |

| Organizations | Date / Key Events |
| --- | --- |
| | **1975** |
| Greenwood Lake Gaelic Cultural Society (Greenwood Lake, New York); Ireland Fund. | |
| | **1977** |
| Ad Hoc Congressional Committee for Irish Affairs. | |
| | **1978** |
| Irish American Teachers Association (Chicago). | |
| | **1981** |
| Friends of Ireland. | |
| | **1998** |
| | Good Friday Agreement. |

Compiled by Michael F. Funchion and reprinted from *Irish American Voluntary Organizations* with the permission of Greenwood Press, Inc.

tary fame into a favorable marriage, extensive landholdings and mercantile interests, and a seat in the colonial North Carolina Assembly. In 1766, he was a leader in protesting the Stamp Act, but still maintained the confidence of Governor William Tryon, who made Waddell commander-in-chief of the state's military forces. In 1771, Waddell led a command against the Regulator uprising, but saw little action. He took ill shortly thereafter and died several months later.

*Dictionary of American Biography*, Vol. X, part I: 301–302.
*The Colonial Records of North Carolina*, 10 Vols. (Raleigh, 1886–1890).
*National Cyclopedia of American Biography*, IX: 472–73.

TOM DOWNEY

## WADDEL, JAMES (1739–1805)

Clergyman. Waddel was born in Newry, Ireland, the son of Thomas Waddel. Waddel's family emigrated to the U.S. in 1739 and settled in Pennsylvania. While preparing for the ministry Waddel tutored and taught at the academy of Robert Smith at Pequea in Lancaster County and at the liberal arts school of John Todd in Virginia. Waddel was licensed to preach in 1761 and was then ordained at the presbyterate convocation in Prince Edward County in 1762. Waddel held several positions in various congregations ranging from the Shenandoah Valley to Charlottesville. In 1768 he was married to Mary Gordon and became the father of ten children.

Waddel was known for his passionate preaching and his humble and gentle demeanor. He was a defender of Calvinist theology amidst Anglican critiques and he was strictly opposed to the philosophical deism that reigned in the South. His ministry also helped to establish friendly relations between the Virginia squirearchy and the Presbyterian Church. Waddel met misfortune in health when he lost his eyesight in 1787; however, during the eleven years that ensued he continued to preach and minister. He died at his home on September 17, 1805.

*See* Scots Irish

J. W. Alexander, *Memoir of the Reverend James Waddel* (1880).
W. B. Sprague, *Annals of the American Pulpit,* vol. III (1858).
*Dictionary of American Biography,* 19.

JOY HARRELL

## WADDELL, HUGH (c. 1734–1773)

Soldier. Hugh Waddell was born in Lisburn, County Down, Ireland. He spent his childhood in Boston, but moved to North Carolina after the death of his father. In 1754, Waddell joined the Virginia effort to expel the French from the Ohio valley. He saw no action, but his skill earned him a promotion to captain. In the winter of 1754–55, Waddell served as clerk of council to Governor Arthur Dobbs. Impressed with the young man's abilities, Dobbs placed Waddell in charge of defending the North Carolina frontier. Waddell built Fort Dobbs in Rowan County and commanded the garrison there until 1757. The previous year, Waddell assisted in negotiating a treaty with the Cherokee and Catawba. In 1758, Governor Dobbs promoted Waddell to major and gave him a command in the successful expedition against Fort Duquesne. The following year, Waddell again was placed in charge of defending North Carolina against Indian attacks, gaining fame for his defense of Fort Dobbs in 1760. Waddell parlayed his mili-

## WAGNER, ROBERT F. (1910–1991)

*See* New York City: Irish-American Mayors

## WALKER, FRANK C. (1886–1959)

Businessman, political advisor, postmaster general. Although he was best known as postmaster general during World War II, Frank C. Walker made his most important contributions as a confidant and advisor to President Franklin D. Roosevelt during the New Deal. Born in May 1886, Walker was raised in Butte, Montana, then a center of mining activities and Irish-American life in the west. He was educated in local parochial schools, attended Gonzaga University and eventually earned his bachelor's degree in law from the University of Notre Dame in 1909.

Walker began his professional career as an attorney and politician in Montana. But following military service in World War I, and a fitful return to Butte, Walker became the legal counsel for the New York-based Comerford Theater chain in 1925. He moved his family to New York City and never again lived in Montana.

Walker remained keenly interested in politics all of his life. Not surprisingly, he was attracted to the gubernatorial and presidential campaigns of New York governor Alfred E. Smith, the first Catholic to run for president on a major party ticket. Walker joined the group of men who were early supporters of Franklin Roosevelt's campaign for president, a group that later became known as the "Friends of Roosevelt Before Chicago." Walker was an extraordinary fund-raiser and personally contributed tens of thousands of dollars to the campaign. As a reward, Walker was made treasurer of the Democratic National Committee in 1932.

Following Roosevelt's inauguration, Walker served the president by coordinating relief activities with various cabinet agencies between 1933 and 1935. Although he did not work in the Roosevelt administration between 1936 and 1940, Walker remained active in national Democratic politics. He continued to advise the president and promote his candidacy during the 1936 and 1940 election campaigns.

Following the 1940 election, Roosevelt prevailed upon Walker to serve as postmaster general. In this new job, Walker was involved in both innovation and controversy. He introduced "V-Mail" to the American people. During World War II, V-Mail insured that the maximum amount of mail was shipped between the troops and their families at minimum cost and with all appropriate security. Walker also used his censorship powers to revoke the second-class mailing permit of *Social Justice*, the right-wing magazine published by the notorious political activist, Father Charles Coughlin.

In 1943, Walker also served as chairman of the Democratic National Committee and was active in Roosevelt's renomination and reelection campaign in 1944. The death of Franklin Roosevelt on April 12, 1945 was the beginning of the end of Walker's career in government. Without Roosevelt, Walker had no desire to stay on in government and he resigned as Postmaster General in July 1945.

Walker returned to his law practice and later served as chairman of the Notre Dame foundation and the president of the university's lay board of trustees. For this and related service, Walker received the university's 1948 Laetare Medal, given annually to an outstanding American Catholic lay person. Walker's health began to deteriorate in 1958 and he died in his New York apartment on September 13, 1959.

Bernard F. Donahoe, *Private Plans and Public Dangers* (Notre Dame, 1965).

Robert H. Ferrell, ed., *The Autobiography of Frank C. Walker* (Boulder, CO, 1995).

George Q. Flynn, *Roosevelt and Romanism: Catholics and American Diplomacy, 1937–1945* (Westport, CT, 1976).

TIMOTHY WALCH

## WALL, EAMONN (1955–   )

Poet. Wall was born in Enniscorthy, County Wexford, Ireland, the son of hoteliers. He was educated at University College, Dublin, University of Wisconsin-Milwaukee, and the City University of New York, from which he received a Ph.D. in 1992. He first published poems in the Gorey Arts Festival magazine; his first U.S. publication was *Fire Escape* (1988), which was followed by *The Tamed Goose* (1990), an imaginative looking-back at his Irish childhood from an American perspective. The title refers to the "Wild Geese," the Jacobite exiles from Ireland in the 17th and 18th centuries. Memory, the weapon of the diaspora Irish, is widely used here to reinvent the small city of his origin and the pieties of an Ireland both plain and pagan.

In recent years, Wall has become a more flamboyant artist. His concern now is to integrate his Irish and American Midwestern experience, and his poetry has increasingly been dualistic, the merging of the prairie and the rath, the reservation and burned mansions of his first habitat. The work that results is a cosmopolitan summation of trans-Atlantic literary sensibility, perhaps a mixture of Patrick Kavanagh and Sherwood Anderson. These recent books, from Salmon in Galway, are *Dyckman-200 Street* and *Iron Mountain Road*. One of the innovations he has adapted here, especially in the later volume, are long lines and prose poems.

The changes in Wall's poems have been significant. His earlier work touches on the very intimate Irish connections to the visible world and the villages of friends. Two events have forced him into a sterner and more complex subject matter: the keenness of his exile (sharper of course in Nebraska than in New York) and the burgeoning of his attention to his family.

In these poems he comes alive as a transplanted Irish writer and intellectual, and, by way of contrast, as a devoted family man who projects past, present, and future into his children. His themes could be seen as a combination of personal and family uprooting. What strikes the reader is the affability of Wall's exploration of a new landscape and culture, and the backward-looking power of his nostalgia, pitched to his childhood: he is an Odysseus of departure and return.

Wall is an excellent writer of critical prose and his interests, though focused on Ireland, are divergent. He has written reviews for *The Washington Post, The Chicago Tribune,* and *The Review of Contemporary Fiction.* His stories have appeared in *Ireland in Exile: Irish Writers Abroad* and *The Sunday Tribune.* He has been foremost in the "New Irish Writers" movement which sets up a more contemporary and realistic assessment of emigrant Irish writers in the U.S. He has published essays on this topic, notably in *Forkroads,* and he is an impressive critic of both Irish-American and Irish-in-America writing.

*See* Poetry, Irish-American

Emmon Wall, *The Celtic Twilight* (Gorey, 1974).

———, *Fire Escape* (New York, 1988).

———, *The Tamed Goose* (New York, 1990).

———, "Four Paintings by Danny Maloney," in *Ireland in Exile,* ed., Dermot Bolger (Dublin, 1993).

———, *Dyckman-200 Street* (Galway, 1994).

———, *Iron Mountain Road* (Co. Clare, 1997).

JAMES LIDDY

## WALKER, JAMES J. (1881–1946)

*See* New York City: Irish-American Mayors

## WALSH, DAVID I. (1872–1947)

Governor and senator. David Ignatius Walsh was born in Leominster, MA, on November 11, 1872, and died at St. Elizabeth's Hospital in Brighton, MA, on June 11, 1947. His parents were immigrants from Ireland, James Walsh from Mallow, Country Cork, and Bridget (Donnelly) Walsh from County Roscommon. Graduating from the College of the Holy Cross in 1893, Walsh earned a law degree from Boston University Law School in 1897 and passed the bar the same year.

Entering politics on the local level, Walsh chaired the Democratic Committee in Clinton, MA, before he was elected to the state legislature where he helped to shape laws protecting the rights of workers (1899–1903). Though initially unsuccessful in

Eamonn Wall

running for lieutenant governor in 1911, he was elected to this office in the following year and served for one year (1912–13) before he was elected Governor of Massachusetts for the next two years (1913–15). As the first Irish-American Catholic to hold that office, Walsh reconstructed the Democratic Party in his home state.

NATIONAL POLITICIAN

From governor of his native state, Walsh aimed for higher office. Although there were slight interruptions during his years in Washington (elected in 1918, defeated in 1924, re-elected in 1926 and continuing until 1947), Walsh served as a United States Senator from Massachusetts nearly continuously from 1919 to 1947. Consequently, Senator Walsh was involved in national politics throughout the critical years at the end of World War I, the Great Depression, and World War II.

If, during his twenty-five years in Washington, Walsh went on record against the League of Nations in 1920, he was in favor of the United Nations in 1945. While he opposed Franklin D. Roosevelt on his 1937 plan to pack the Supreme Court, the Massachusetts Senator spearheaded one of the President's favorite programs in the rebuilding of the nation's navy in 1938 as Chairman of the Naval Affairs Committee. At the same time, Senator Walsh was very protective of the rights of the working man and of the shoe and textile industries in New England.

A bachelor throughout his life, Walsh spent his retirement with his sisters, Julia and Mary, who survived him. Buried in St. John's Cemetery in Lancaster, MA, where a huge cross marks the site, Walsh is memorialized in a statue which was erected in 1950 on Boston's esplanade near the Charles River.

*See* Massachusetts

Archives of the College of the Holy Cross, David I. Walsh Papers.

Edward B. Hanify, *Memories of a Senator* (Boston, 1994).

J. Joseph Huthmacher, *Massachusetts People and Politics, 1919–1933* (Cambridge, 1959).

Dorothy G. Wayman, *David I. Walsh, Citizen-Patriot* (Milwaukee, 1952).

VINCENT A. LAPOMARDA, S.J.

## WALSH, EDMUND ALOYSIUS (1885–1956)

Priest, writer, historian, diplomat. Born in South Boston, Massachusetts, on October 10, 1885, Edmund A. Walsh was the last of six children born to John and Catherine Noonan Walsh, both of whose parents had emigrated from Ireland to Boston in the 1840s. John Walsh was one of the first Irish-American members of Boston's Police Department, serving for a total of 39 years. Young Edmund Walsh attended public grammar schools in Boston, earning a scholarship to the Jesuit-run Boston College High School, from which he graduated in 1902.

In August 1902, Walsh entered the Jesuit novitiate in Frederick, MD, and was ordained a Jesuit priest in 1916. During that time, he studied at Woodstock College in Maryland and taught in Georgetown University's high school department. Between 1912 and 1914, showing great promise, his superiors sent him for advanced classical studies at Dublin's National University and the University of London. This experience abroad helped hone his interest in international relations, and the need for American schools to focus on this topic.

From 1913 to 1914, Walsh studied theology at Innsbruck, Austria. When war broke out in the summer of 1914, he was sent back to America, where he resumed studies at Woodstock College. In 1918, he returned to Georgetown as Dean of Studies. In the fall of that year, he was called into service by the War Department as assistant educational director to the Student Army Training Corps.

This experience influenced Walsh in two important ways. First, it led him to realize that isolation was a thing of the past, and America that would have to take its place in international affairs. Second, he realized that there were no American schools specializing in diplomacy or international relations. When he returned to Georgetown in late 1918, he took steps to establish such a school. In early 1919, Georgetown University opened the School of Foreign Service, the first of its kind in America. Numbers rose steadily to the point that by 1941, it was estimated that Georgetown graduates composed the bulk of State Department personnel.

From early 1922 to December 1923, Walsh served in Russia as Director of the Pontifical Relief Mission, affiliated with Herbert Hoover's American Relief Administration. He directed relief work in Moscow and western Russia, feeding as many as 10,000 a day. Walsh was also an unofficial Vatican emissary to the Soviets, keeping in close contact with Pope Pius XI and Jesuit General Vladimir Ledochowski. His task was to negotiate for the freedom of imprisoned priests and bishops, as well as to keep the Catholic churches open in Russia.

Ultimately, this attempt failed. Walsh returned to America a committed anti-Communist. Over the next three decades he wrote four books and numerous articles on Soviet Russia, delivering 1,500 lectures on this topic. Walsh led opposition to American diplomatic recognition of Russia in 1933. During the 1930s he testified several times before congressional hearings on Communism in America. From the 1930s through the early 1950s Walsh lectured at the FBI training academy. While an internationalist, Walsh was an opponent of the New Deal and was particularly opposed to Franklin D. Roosevelt's 1937 court-packing plan, and tended to favor capital during the labor struggles of the period.

During World War II, Walsh served as a lecturer for the War Department and a consultant for the geopolitical Division of Military Intelligence. He became increasingly interested in the science of geopolitics during the 1920s and 1930s. In 1945, he was appointed civil consultant to Justice Robert H. Jackson, Chief of Counsel at the Nuremberg trials. Walsh was in charge of questioning General Karl Haushofer, Hitler's geopolitical advisor.

Walsh was not popular with the Roosevelt administration, but at the onset of the Cold War he acquired a new level of prestige. He was frequently consulted by government officials on questions of Soviet foreign policy and ideology. In 1948 he served as a consultant to the State Department's Policy Planning Staff on German affairs. He also served on the President's Commission on Universal Military Training in 1946–1947.

Walsh is most often remembered as the person who "started" McCarthyism. In 1950, Walsh and Senator Joseph R. McCarthy were at a dinner party. According to journalist Drew Pearson, Walsh advised McCarthy to undertake his anti-Communist crusade. Walsh refused to answer Pearson's accusations. He suffered a stroke in 1952 and died in 1956.

Donald F. Crosby, S.J., *God, Church and Flag: Senator Joseph R. McCarthy and the Catholic Church, 1950–1957* (Chapel Hill, N.C., 1978).

Louis J. Gallagher, S.J., *Edmund A. Walsh, S.J.: A Biography* (New York, 1962).

Peter McDonough, *Men Astutely Trained: A History of the Jesuits in the American Century* (New York, 1992).

Richard Gid Powers, *Not Without Honor: The History of American Anti-communism* (New York, 1995).

Edmund A. Walsh, S.J., Papers, Special Collections Division, The Lauinger Library, Georgetown University, Washington, D.C.

PATRICK J. McNAMARA

## WALSH, FRANCIS PATRICK (1864–1939)

Attorney, public official, progressive reformer. Frank Walsh came from the Midwest with the reputation of an astute lawyer with a zeal for the welfare of the poor. Unlike some reformers motivated by noblesse oblige or guilt, Walsh was influenced by the dire poverty he experienced when his father died leaving a widow and six children. The third eldest, Walsh was seven at the time.

### ORIGINS

Born in St. Louis July 20, 1864, he was the second son (third child) of James Walsh and Sarah Delany Walsh, both of whom were American-born Irish Catholics. His father ran a small business in grain and coal. In 1867, optimistic about the future, the family moved to the bustling rail center of Kansas City. However, in 1871, Walsh's father died leaving his family with the prospect of poverty. Furthermore, the devastating and prolonged recession of 1873 was in the offing. At age ten the boy was obliged to forego schooling and enter the world of work. Newspaper boy, telegram messenger and like jobs eventually led to clerical work in railroading. There he learned bookkeeping. For a railway clerk stenography was an asset and he studied it. From there, recognized for his intelligence and enthusiasm, he succeeded in becoming a court reporter. Acquainted with legal processes, he recognized law as a promising career—and one with potential for helping the poor.

In the 1880s he read law under attorney Gardiner Lathrop in Kansas City and was admitted to the bar in 1889. With growing confidence he opted to become a trial lawyer. He proved to be a vigorous, articulate, and highly successful advocate. An authentic progressive, Walsh entered local politics.

### POLITICS

A Democratic stronghold, Kansas City was dominated by the Pendergast machine. One faction within the party led by Joseph H. Shannon (known as the "Rabbits") occasionally challenged the Pendergast family (the "Goats"), and Walsh became allied with Shannon. Frank Walsh's reputation advanced as a result of his court contests with James A. Reed, who, backed by the "Goats," was first elected mayor of Kansas City and later to the U.S. Senate. From the less-than-saintly Shannon faction, Walsh began to attack the Pendergasts for their corrupt practices.

A comfortable income from law practice enabled Walsh to support his wife, Katherine (nee O'Flaherty), and their nine children. Appointments to a number of local boards and commissions came his way. He accepted those related to relieving poverty, such as the Tenement Commission. He was responsible for establishing the Board of Public Welfare in Kansas City. He carried his dedication to a higher level by promoting a Bureau of Social Service within the Democratic National Committee. His reputation as a reformer grew accordingly.

### INDUSTRIAL RELATIONS COMMISSION

Alarmed by a series of violent labor-management clashes—most dramatically in the *Los Angeles Times* bombing of 1910—Congress chartered the U.S. Industrial Relations Commission to investigate. A trial lawyer involved in a number of notable labor cases with a reputation as a Progressive, Walsh was chosen by President Wilson to chair the commission in 1913.

Armed with competent research directed by economist John K. Commons from the University of Wisconsin, Walsh conducted public hearings in various locations around the country. He was particularly forceful in revealing the hypocrisy of John D. Rockefeller, Jr., who pleaded ignorance of any knowledge about the Ludlow Massacre of 1914 where two wives and eleven children of miners were killed during a strike at the Colorado Fuel and Iron Company—owned by Rockefeller interests. Walsh produced subpoenaed correspondence demonstrating that on-site managers had kept the young millionaire well informed and that he fully supported their specific labor policies. Walsh incurred fierce criticism in business circles as a result. However, his standing was such that Wilson named him co-chairman (with ex-President Taft) of the War Labor Board early in 1918.

### IRISH NATIONALISM

Though several generations removed from his immigrant forebears, Walsh was a dedicated Irish nationalist. He chaired the Commission for Irish Independence and lobbied Versailles Treaty negotiators for that goal as a logical application of Wilson's principle of national self determination. Wilson refused to consider it. Becoming acquainted with Eamon de Valera, president of the newly declared Irish Republic, Walsh enthusiastically participated in marketing bonds to finance it, and strongly urged American recognition of it. Alienated by Wilson's position on the Irish issue, Walsh did not support James M. Cox, Democratic candidate for president in 1920. In 1924 he backed Progressive candidate Robert M. LaFollette. Four years later, however, he endorsed Al Smith for president as well as Franklin Roosevelt for Governor of New York. In 1932 he organized the National Progressive League for Franklin Roosevelt. He was chairman of the Catholic Citizens Committee for Ratification of the Federal Child Labor Amendment from 1936 to 1939. Until his death on May 2, 1939, Walsh was a vigorous advocate for Franklin Roosevelt's New Deal. He lived long enough to see many of the reforms for which he fought become reality during the period of the Great Depression—specifically, programs to relieve poverty, regulate child labor, assure employee rights to organize, and provide income for the unemployed and for aged members of the population.

Graham Adams, Jr., *Age of Industrial Violence* (New York, 1968).

Sr. M. Eucharia Meehan, "Frank Walsh and the American Labor Movement" (Ph.D. diss., New York University, 1962).

U.S. Commission on Industrial Relations, *Final Report* (Washington, D.C., 1915).

L. A. O'DONNELL

## WALSH, JAMES ANTHONY (1867–1936)

Bishop, missionary, co-founder of Maryknoll Society. James A. Walsh was born on February 24, 1867, in Cambridge, Massachusetts, the son of immigrants from Cork, James Walsh and Hanna Shea. He was ordained a priest of the archdiocese of Boston on May 20, 1892.

In 1911, Walsh, together with Fr. Thomas F. Price of North Carolina, received authorization from the archbishops of the United States and Pope Pius X to found a society of secular missionary priests and lay brothers, The Catholic Foreign Missionary Society of America. They established the society's permanent headquarters and major seminary near Ossining, New York, on a hilltop which they named Maryknoll in honor of Mary the mother of Jesus. Walsh served as the first General Superior of the Society, directing its development in the United States and overseas until his death. He likewise collaborated with Mary Josephine Rogers in the founding of the congregation of missionary women that came to be known as the Maryknoll Sisters. Price led the first group of four Maryknoll priests to China in 1918, dying there in 1919.

In recognition of Walsh's commitment to the missionary cause Pope Pius XI named him titular bishop of Siene in 1933. He died at Maryknoll April 14, 1936, leaving the Society with growing missions in China, Korea, Japan, the Philippines and Hawaii, and a strong commitment to mission education in the United States through its magazine (today *Maryknoll*) and other publications.

George C. Powers, *The Maryknoll Movement* (Maryknoll, N.Y., 1926).
Daniel Sargent, *All the Day Long: James A. Walsh, Cofounder of Maryknoll* (New York, 1941).
James A. Walsh, *Observations in the Orient* (Ossining, 1919).
Jean-Paul Wiest, *Maryknoll in China: A History, 1918–1955* (Armonk, N.Y., 1988; Maryknoll, N.Y., 1997).

WILLIAM D. McCARTHY, M.M.

## WALSH, JAMES EDWARD (1891–1981)

Missionary, bishop, Superior General of Maryknoll Society. James E. Walsh was born April 30, 1891, in Cumberland, Maryland, son of William Walsh and Mary Concannon. His grandfather, William Walsh, Sr., an immigrant from Ireland, had served two terms in Congress as a representative from Maryland. James Walsh completed his college studies at Mt. St. Mary's, Emmitsburg. Accepted in 1912 as a candidate for the recently founded Catholic Foreign Mission Society of America, popularly named Maryknoll, he was ordained a priest on Dec. 7, 1915. After serving 3 years as director of Maryknoll's minor seminary in Clark's Summit, Pennsylvania, he was named a member of the first group of the Society assigned to China. In 1919 he became superior of the group, and in 1927 was ordained the first bishop of the Vicariate of Kongmoon. From 1936 to 1946 he served as Superior General of Maryknoll, directing the Society during the critical years of World War II and initiating new missions in Latin America and East Africa. In 1948 he returned to China to serve the bishops as executive secretary of their national coordinating agency, the Catholic Central Bureau in Shanghai. After 1951 his activities were severely restricted by the Chinese government, and in 1958 he was falsely charged as a U.S. spy and sentenced to 20 years imprisonment. He was confined for 12 years, being released and deported from China in 1970. Pope Paul VI, on receiving him at the Vatican, stated, "You have been a witness, authentic and simple, in joy and in sorrow, then in suffering and humiliation, and finally in separation from the people you loved so much. For all this we thank you on behalf of the entire Church of Christ." In his final years he visited missioners in various parts of the world, affirming them in their apostolic commitment. He died at Maryknoll, New York, on July 29, 1981.

Raymond Kerrison, *Bishop Walsh of Maryknoll: A Biography* (New York, 1962).

Robert E. Sheridan, *Bishop James E. Walsh As I Knew Him* (Maryknoll, N.Y., 1981).
James E. Walsh, *Zeal for Your House*, ed., Robert E. Sheridan (Huntington, Ind., 1976).
———, *The Church's World Wide Mission* (New York, 1948).
Jean-Paul Wiest, *Maryknoll in China: A History, 1918–1955* (rev. ed., Maryknoll, N.Y., 1997).

WILLIAM D. McCARTHY, M.M.

## WALSH, JAMES P. (1937– )

Historian. His publishing focus has been on the Irish as an American ethnic minority, particularly in California and the West. Born in San Francisco, he received B.S. and M.A. degrees from the University of San Francisco, and a Ph.D. from the University of California, Berkeley. At San Jose State University he has been professor, chair, dean, and academic vice president. Walsh co-founded the American Conference for Irish Studies-West.

Walsh's early work focused on ethnic militancy in San Francisco at the end of the nineteenth century as evidenced in the career of Father Peter C. Yorke. As a regent of the University of California, Yorke interacted with Irish and other leaders within a larger, more diverse culture. This work and its early spin-offs earned Walsh the California History Prize (1972) for original scholarly interpretation. His conclusion is that the Irish experience in California differed significantly from the Irish experience elsewhere in the United States. The basic reasons sustaining this western interpretation are the California environment, the timing of Irish arrival, and self-selection of those who made it west.

Variations on the western theme guided Walsh's treatment of the central figures in two biographies, Vincent Hallinan and James Duval Phelan. Hallinan, a legendary San Francisco attorney, ran for president with an African-American woman for vice president. Both were Progressive Party members and had the support of the Communist Party. Hallinan sued the Catholic Church (to the shame of his sister, a nun), defended accused Communists and served time in federal prisons. He stood on the steps of San Francisco's City Hall encouraging California students disrupting the House Un-American Activities Committee and commencing the protest generation.

Quite differently, but well within the western theme, James Duval Phelan had presided over California's transformation from frontier culture to the regional one so distinct today. Phelan's domain was progressive reform, education, urban planning, civic adornment, beauty and art. These two diverse Irish-Americans owed their unique existence and expression to California's place, time, and selectivity.

Walsh considers this western theme historiographically awkward at best. It remains a lump within efforts to offer a comprehensive explanation of the American Irish. For the most part, American generalists persist in accepting the "uprooted" interpretation of nineteenth-century European immigrants. Irish-Americans, historians and non-historians, accept "victimization" as the key to interpreting Ireland's history. Extending that organizing idea to Irish-American history is, Walsh maintains, just a bit too simple. En route, its application erodes the texture of history and compels an incomplete, deformed vision of an America which rightly belongs to everyone.

Because frustration springs from an acceptance of uprootedness and victimization, Walsh has aimed instead at the California alternative—revenge. Out west the best revenge remains the good life.

*See* California

S. P. BREATNAC

## WALSH, MARY (1850–1922)

Foundress. One August morning in 1876, on a street in New York City, an immigrant woman from Limerick, Mary Walsh, was on her way to work when stopped by the call of a child. Death had come to the family in the tenement upstairs, to people who had no place to turn for help. Mary dropped her work to care for them, and immediately lost her job as a laundress for wealthy New Yorkers. That single call for help led to another and another, as Mary came upon the sick who lived in hopeless poverty. Knowing she had to do something, she begged God to help her decide what could be done for such destitute families.

Mary found a few women willing to join her in caring for the poor who were ill. Together they took in laundry a few days a week to support themselves. Other women came to help, but many found the poverty, the work and the sickness too difficult and did not stay. However, the reputation of the group spread, and young women responded to the urgent need for this new ministry to the poor, not in hospitals or other institutions, but in the places where they lived.

For twenty years Mary Walsh and her small corps of women struggled together to carry on their work. Their goal by now was to become a Dominican religious community. Two young priests, upon hearing of their struggles, came to their assistance in many ways. One priest was the Paulist, Peter J. O'Callaghan, who formed an auxiliary to raise funds for the work. The other was the Dominican John T. McNicholas, who began communicating with the Dominican Master General concerning the possibility of their becoming a new community of Dominican Sisters.

In 1904 the women were incorporated in New York to care for the destitute sick poor in their own homes. They were called Dominican Sisters of the Sick Poor. Finally, in August 1910, the little band of twelve women became a canonical congregation approved by the Church.

Mother Mary Walsh died November 6, 1922, at Hampton Bays, N.Y. Her worn-out heart stopped beating. The special work of caring for the sick poor in their homes continued for the next seventy years in New York, then Ohio and Michigan, Colorado, Minnesota and Virginia. In July 1995 the Dominican Sisters of the Sick Poor joined with two other Dominican congregations of women to become the Dominican Sisters of Hope.

MARIE ATKINSON, O.P.

## WARDE, FRANCES XAVIER (1810–1884)

Educator, administrator, religious leader. Frances Teresa Xavier Warde was the youngest of six children born to John and Mary (Maher) Warde. She was born at Bellbrook House in Abbeyleix, Ireland, in 1810. Her father was a prominent merchant. Her mother was a member of a well-known family of ecclesiastics and political leaders. Her mother died in the same year that Frances was born. Vestiges of Ireland's Penal Laws occasioned the loss of Bellbrook in 1819. Frances Warde and her sisters remained in the care of the Maher family, while her brothers accompanied their father to Dublin to start a new life in the city. By the time she was

fourteen years old she had also lost in death her father, a favorite brother, John, and a sister, Helen.

"Fanny," as she was called by family and friends, was educated privately in both the arts and sciences, although she much preferred the former. Biographers speak of Frances as "impatient and fiery by nature," "passionately fond of music," and "the ruling spirit wherever she happened to be" (Healy, p. 47; Carroll, Vol. 4, p. 282; Garety, p. 15). Her most recent biographer suggests further that "the early loss of her mother, followed by the extra-ordinary sorrows she experienced as a young girl, gave impetus to the development of initiative and individuality which was almost phenomenal in a teen-age Irish girl of the eighteen-twenties" (Healy, p. 18).

In 1827, Frances Warde was introduced to Catherine McAuley, soon-to-be foundress of the Sisters of Mercy. A much bereaved, although energetic and vivacious, seventeen-year-old Fanny seems to have been immediately attracted to the more mature woman. Theirs was a deep and lasting friendship sustained by a mutual desire to utilize their talents in service and in community. A Mercy annalist records that, forty-three years after their first separation, Frances Warde tearfully confessed: "I don't know how I ever survived the parting from Reverend Mother" (Carroll, Vol. 1, p. 175).

Survive she did, however, and much more. Her great reverence for the person and the vision of the foundress energized a long life in which she freely applied and interpreted that vision in the founding of one hundred institutions of Mercy in the United States and in the forming of hundreds of young women in the tradition of the Sisters of Mercy. Frances Warde undertook her first foundation at the direction of Catherine McAuley, who appointed her twenty-seven-year-old friend superior of St. Leo's Convent, Carlow, Ireland in 1837. Forty-six years later she established her last foundation in Dover, New Hampshire, at the age of seventy-three. The Dover community was one of the few that Frances Warde did not accompany in their first months of founding, but already her health and eyesight were failing her.

No request brought to her was too simple or too complex. The institutions she founded range in purpose and location: a parochial school (the first free Catholic school west of Chicago) and select school in Omaha, NE; orphanages in innumerable settings; a hospital in Pittsburgh, PA; a Home for Aged Women in Providence, RI. Likewise, her leadership fostered innovation in others. Frances Warde directed her sisters to teach in public schools in response to local need, to care for wounded soldiers of Union or Confederate uniform, and to teach reading and domestic science to Abnaki Indian women.

She was a woman of independent mind and spirit who often found herself in controversy within and without the congregation. Within the congregation she clashed with Mary Baptist Russell (San Francisco) in an early controversy regarding pension schools and tuition schools; and with Mary Austin Carroll, who seems to have regretted her abrasive personality. Both Bishops Frances Haly (Carlow, 1840s) and James Healy (Portland, 1870s) made no pretense about their wishes for a more docile Mother Superior. Yet, the jubilee greetings on the occasion of her fiftieth anniversary of vows (January 1883) attest to a wide and profound influence in the American Church: greetings came from Mercy sisters worldwide; from her close friend and benefactor, Emily Harper; from Fathers Isaac Hecker, Fidelis (Kent) Stone, and Abbot Boniface Wimmer. On August 2, 1883, in a unanimous tribute to her services, an ailing Frances Warde was elected superior once again of the Sisters of Mercy in Manchester, New Hampshire. In March 1884 she contracted pneumonia and, never fully recovering, died on September 17, 1884. Bishop James Healy's eulogy lamented the loss of "her experience, her kind advice, her wise government, the never wearying care, the love, the grand religious presence" (Healy, p. 466).

*See* Sisters of Mercy

M. Austin Carroll, *Leaves from the Annals of the Sisters of Mercy*, 4 vols. (New York, 1881, 1883, 1888, 1895).

Mary Benigna Doherty, *The First Hundred Years of the Manchester Sisters of Mercy* (Manchester, New Hampshire, 1968).

Mary Catherine Garety, *Rev. Mother M. Xavier Warde* (Boston, 1902).

Kathleen Healy, *Frances Warde: American Founder of the Sisters of Mercy* (New York, 1973).

HELEN MARIE BURNS, R.S.M.

St. Vincent's Orphan Asylum

# WASHINGTON, D.C., IRISH WOMEN AND CATHOLIC CHARITY, 1850–1900

Between 1850 and 1900, Irish women immigrated to Washington. An overwhelming number of them were Catholic. Thus, the Catholic churches of Washington, D.C., provided a familiar institution in an unfamiliar setting. This unfamiliar setting often proved hostile to Irish immigrants. The Catholic churches of Washington provided a mediating influence that served as a safety net for Irish women and their children. That safety net included charity in the form of money, food and coal for the winter months, respite care for indigent children and vocational and educational training for Irish women and their children. This charity network assisted Irish women and their children in their times of need.

### St. Vincent De Paul Society

The first St. Vincent de Paul Conference of Washington, D.C. (a parish branch of the parent Society) was founded in St. Matthew's Catholic Church in 1857. In the following forty years, fourteen Washington churches established Conferences to support parish communities through financial and material means. Irish businessmen, professionals and laborers contributed their time and money to the well-being of Irish women and children. The members of the parish Conferences aided and counseled Irish women about their finances, cared for deserted children and provided for their support in Catholic schools and asylums.

Irish women received subsidies of rent, food and coal. One such woman was Mary O'Neill whose husband, Cornelius, died in 1861 leaving the widow and mother of five without support. The St. Aloysius Conference of the St. Vincent de Paul Society provided that support by giving the O'Neill family forty cents each week, shoes for the children and extra coal during the harsh winter months. Unfortunately, Mary died about seven months after her husband. The St. Aloysius Conference members found Irish homes for Cornelius and Mary O'Neill's children. One of the members took two of the boys. Another boy found a home with an uncle and the oldest daughter and baby went to live with the Sisters of Charity at St. Vincent's Orphan Asylum and Day School.

By 1870, however, the number of Irish women helped by the St. Vincent de Paul Conferences dwindled. The women and children the Conferences assisted no longer needed the extra forty or fifty cents each week. Through the support of the Conferences, these families could now support themselves. Children, who were

apprenticed to local businessmen and craftsmen, now earned their own living. Irish women and children, who received vocational and educational training at the behest of the St. Vincent de Paul Society, found employment in the Irish community of Washington.

### Little Sisters of the Poor, Home for the Aged

Established in 1871, the Home for the Aged was a residential facility maintained by eleven Little Sisters of the Poor who ministered to their wards by cooking their meals, washing their clothes and caring for them through illness and infirmity. Irish women Ann Murphy, Kate Keaton and Mary Callahan lived at the home and were cared for by Sister Bridget O'Hara. This Home serviced an increasingly large number of Irish men and women throughout the last half of the nineteenth century. Although the Home was open to men and women of any ethnicity, in 1880 over half of the residents were Irish. These men and women found refuge with the Irish nuns that worked in the Home for the Aged.

### St. Ann's Infant Asylum

Founded in 1863, St. Ann's was established for the maintenance and support of foundlings, orphaned babies and children. The Asylum provided refuge and safety for pregnant women with no means of substantial support and a home for children of indigent parents. As the children grew, they received an elementary education including reading, writing and arithmetic. Irish Sisters of Charity Costello, Gwynn, Carroll, Ryan and Shea were granted the authority to bind out any of the children in their charge. As apprentices, St. Ann's charges learned housekeeping skills by working in the homes of Washington families. An integral part of the Catholic community and Washington society, St. Ann's became essential for the placement of orphan and indigent children throughout the city. Washington's chief of police publicly noted his indebtedness to St. Ann's for this useful service they provided in the Washington community.

### St. Joseph's Male Orphan Asylum

Through Reverend O'Toole of St. Patrick's Catholic Church, St. Joseph's Orphan Asylum was established in 1856. Run by the Sisters of the Holy Cross, St. Joseph's cared for young orphaned boys in the Washington community. In 1860 Irish Sisters Mary McDermott, Mary Duffe and Mary Delaney cared for the thirty-one boys in the Asylum. Over the next decade, the Asylum doubled in size, but the proportion of Irish boys housed with the sisters decreased. By 1870 only four out of seventy-four orphans were Irish. In the last decades of the nineteenth century, the Asylum continued to increase and the proportion of Irish boys who lived in the Asylum continued to decrease.

## St. Vincent's Orphan Asylum and Day School

St. Vincent's Orphan Asylum and Day School opened in 1825 under the charge of the Sisters of Charity at St. Patrick's Catholic Church. The sisters provided for the spiritual, physical and future well-being of their charges. At St. Vincent's, orphans from the town and surrounding area were clothed, fed and educated. The Sisters of Charity at St. Vincent's prepared Irish girls for their place within the community. Daily life consisted of cleaning and cooking for the maintenance of the community, tutoring in academic work, lessons in sewing and music and religious training.

As respite care, the Asylum offered temporary care for children of the poor. Parents placed their children with the Sisters of Charity at St. Vincent's and brought them back to their own homes several months or years later. These immigrant families were new to Washington and had a difficult time supporting their children. The Asylum offered immigrant parents an opportunity to establish themselves in the community. Irish girls were left with the Sisters of Charity as a temporary measure and stayed no longer than five or six years. Most often it was a shorter period of a few months. The lengthier stays were very young children who left St. Vincent's with a relative or found employment with a benefactor. Of the fourteen girls not released to family, one was adopted. The remaining thirteen left with a benefactress with the intended purpose of learning a trade or they left on their own to take a domestic position.

Throughout the last half of the nineteenth century, St. Vincent's cared for Irish children among many others. In the 1850s, the Sisters of Charity housed and educated a handful of Irish girls. By the 1860s a third of St. Vincent's children were Irish immigrants with another third second- and third-generation Irish immigrants. This trend culminated in 1870, when nine of the fourteen children who lived at St. Vincent's boasted Irish parents. However, as the last decades of the nineteenth century approached, few Irish children found refuge with the nuns of St. Vincent's.

## St. Rose's Industrial School for Girls

Primarily a school for the teaching of sewing, needlework and tailoring, St. Rose's began with three girls and one Sister of Charity in the attic of St. Vincent's in 1872. From this modest beginning came an institution that trained Irish women for occupations suited to domestic positions and provided a foundation for married life. Irish girls entered St. Rose's at the age of thirteen after finishing training at St. Vincent's. When they reached the age of twenty-one, they were on their own.

St. Rose's was the idea of Sister Blanche Rooney. She grew concerned with the treatment of girls after they took work outside of the Asylum. Several girls were returned or remanded back to the custody of the Sisters of Charity due to the ill treatment they received from their employers. Sister Rooney saw St. Rose's as the answer to the mistreatment her wards suffered at the hands of employers. Sister Rooney could house the girls until they were twenty-one but also train them in a suitable skill that would support the girls when they left the Industrial School. This two-fold objective of the institution, charity and education, assisted Irish girls in earning their support whether through skills taught or job placement. At St. Rose's, girls were given a broad education.

For those girls who displayed a given talent, the Sisters provided an academic education. However, for the majority of Irish girls at St. Rose's, an academic career was not in their future. These girls received training in bookkeeping, how to be a store clerk, sewing, needlework, millinery, housekeeping and laundry.

In 1880 three of the five Sisters of Charity that taught for St. Rose's were Irish immigrants and a fourth was born in Washington to Irish immigrant parents. Of the twenty-nine students who lived at St. Rose's in 1880, three were Irish immigrants and two were second-generation Irish born in Washington. Mary McClain and Bridget and Katie Lynch learned dressmaking skills at St. Rose's. They, along with second-generation immigrants Mary Sullivan and Mary Roach, found a home with the nuns of St. Rose's.

## St. Mary's House of Industry

Another vocational institution for girls was St. Mary's House of Industry. Organized in 1876 through the St. Aloysius' Relief Society and headed by Mrs. Ewing Sherman, this institution taught Irish girls the same academic subjects as other schools in the city, but concentrated their curriculum on skills of home maintenance and marriage. At the school, girls between the ages of fourteen and twenty were taught needlework and homemaking skills by the Sisters of Notre Dame. The girls frequently made clothing for the poor and used the skills they learned to assist others in need. At St. Mary's House of Industry, girls found work in families and elsewhere in Washington or earned a wage out of the proceeds of the custom department that was an independent self-supporting institution. The custom department was well known throughout Washington. Ladies from the city would come to St. Mary's, be fitted for clothing, and the girls of the school would design and make elaborate dresses, coats and other clothing items for them.

## Conclusion

Central to the upward mobility of Washington's Irish women and their children was the support they received from Catholic churches and institutions. The two-fold approach of charity and education gave Irish women and their children a foothold in the community and connected them to the larger community of Washington. The upward mobility of Irish women and their children was supported through this alliance of immigrant and church that created a network of resources. Financial support for the destitute and housing and training for the young provided a network of Irish Catholics to nourish Irish women's health and well-being. Moving up did not mean having to move out of the community when the church provided an institutional infrastructure to support those in need. Arriving in the District as the wife of an absent husband, the wife of an under-employed husband, a widow or indigent did not deter Irish women and their children's upward mobility, given the safety net the Catholic churches of Washington provided through charity and education for its own.

*See* Irish in America; Washington, D.C., to 1900

Jennifer Altenhofel, "Charity in Education for Irish Women in Nineteenth-Century Washington," *Catholic Historical Society Newsletter* (April–June, 1997).

Morris J. MacGregor, *A Parish for the Federal City, St. Patrick's in Washington, 1794–1994* (Washington, D.C., 1995).

Thomas W. Spalding, *The Premier See: A History of the Archdiocese of Baltimore, 1789–1989* (Baltimore, 1989).

JENNIFER ALTENHOFEL

## WASHINGTON, D.C., TO 1900

Industrialization and the growth of trade brought Irish laborers and their families to Washington. The Irish community in Washington, D.C., began as Irish communities did elsewhere in the United States: some came seeking jobs and others followed family members. Although a small number of Irish men and women specifically chose Washington as their new home, the majority were part of a chain of migration that continued throughout the nineteenth century. The proximity of Georgetown and the District of Columbia to the port of Baltimore assisted in the settling of Irish Catholics in the national capital. Irish Catholics, seeking the religious freedom Maryland offered, came to the region, settling in the Baltimore/Washington area. Later in the century, relatives and friends of relatives made their way to the District to join their extended families.

### IMMIGRATION

Although Irish immigrants arrived in Washington from its inception as the capital in 1791, the largest number of Irish immigrated to Washington following the Irish Potato Famine of the late 1840s and early 1850s. Throughout the late eighteenth century and the first decades of the nineteenth century, Irish men and women continued to immigrate to Washington so that by 1850, 2,197 Irish immigrants lived in Washington, Georgetown and the surrounding Washington County. In 1860 they increased to 6,610 and by 1870, 7,705. The peak of Irish immigration came in 1880 with 7,840 Irish immigrants living within the city and county. However, in 1890 that number declined to 7,224 and by 1900 to 6,220.

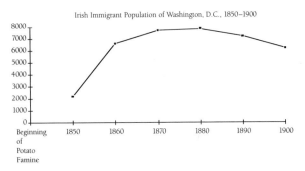

Irish Immigrant Population of Washington, D.C., 1850–1900

Until the turn of the century, the Irish comprised the largest immigrant group and the largest ethnic group after African-Americans. The Irish immigrant population of the District, although smaller than that of Boston, New York or San Francisco, doubled that of the Germans and all other populations as well. The proportion of Irish in the foreign-born population declined with the immigration of southern and eastern Europeans in the last decades of the nineteenth century. This disparity, however, tends to mask the sizable number of second- and third-generation Irish-Americans living in the District. Although there were fewer Irish immigrants arriving in Washington, the Irish community had created a strong ethnic network in the city. By 1900 there were nine divisions of the Ancient Order of Hibernians within the District alone. Parish records, newspaper accounts and Irish associations create a picture of this well-established ethnic community born from the initial immigrant community.

Throughout this period more Irish women immigrated to Washington than Irish men. In 1850 there were only thirty-seven more Irish men in Washington than Irish women. However, by

1860, Irish women outnumbered Irish men by 870 and by 1,107 in 1870. Similar to the northeastern urban centers that attracted so many Irish, Washington garnered its share of Irish women. The lure was the ready housing and employment available in the domestic industry of Washington's hotel, hospital and institutional work. With the rise of Washington as the seat of the nation's government, hotels and service industries sprang up overnight. At the close of the Civil War, Washington's hotel and service industry continued to increase. The ready jobs that came with this rise in service industries attracted Irish women to the cooking, laundry and domestic-service jobs multiplying in the city.

### OCCUPATIONAL STRUCTURES

The changes in the composition of Washington's Irish reflects the changing needs of the city. Throughout the last decade of the eighteenth century and throughout the first half of the nineteenth century, Irish men found ready employment in canal and road construction and the accompanying edifice-building projects in the growing capital. In the latter half of the nineteenth century, the needs of the city changed. With the primary infrastructure of the community and region established, Irish men emigrated to other parts of the United States seeking the laboring jobs no longer available in Washington.

In the first half of the nineteenth century Irish men and their families sought Washington as a place to establish a business or trade. The growing commercialism that Washington offered Irish artisans and skilled craftsmen proved lucrative for a lucky few. One such Irishman was Thomas Corcoran. While traveling to Richmond to settle there, Corcoran came through Georgetown. He was so pleased with Georgetown that he moved his family there and opened a dry goods store. His son, William W. Corcoran, partnered with George Riggs, of Riggs Bank in Washington, and made his fortune in banking and land speculation. Another celebrated Irishman in Washington is James Hoban, the architect and designer of the White House.

The Irish men who migrated to work on Hoban's projects and other construction works were primarily the young and hearty. Laboring jobs were plentiful throughout the first half of the nineteenth century. By 1850 most Irish men in Washington were between the ages of twenty and thirty; by 1860 the majority of Irish men were between the ages of thirty and forty; but, by 1870, the median age remained between thirty and forty. This speaks to the small settlement of Irish men within Washington. By 1870, those men who married and started families stayed in Washington. However, fewer and fewer Irish men stayed in Washington on a permanent basis. Irish men arrived in Washington in smaller numbers and stayed in Washington even less frequently in the last half of the nineteenth century.

For those Irish men and women who settled in Washington, manual labor, government work and business ownership provided the bulk of employment. Irish men who came to the District in the first decades of the nineteenth century worked as priests, artisans, craftsmen and professionals. A class division is evident between the earliest settlers from the last decades of the eighteenth century and the first decades of the nineteenth century and those immigrants who arrived after 1830. The Irish who immigrated to Washington after 1830 came primarily as laborers. Even as late as 1870, Irish men continued to work in manual labor. Although the percentage of Irish men as laborers began to decrease after the Civil War, the primary occupation of Irish immigrant men was that of laborer. However, for second- and third-generation Irish immigrants, business ownership and government work provided the bulk of steady employment. As the Washington government infrastructure grew, so did the availability of federal and District jobs for second- and third-generation Irish.

For Irish women, service work and laboring jobs provided for their immediate needs upon arriving in the District. Working as domestics, washing clothes and sheets, or cleaning rooms in the many Washington hotels, Irish women provided for themselves and their extended families. However, in the first decades of the nineteenth century, most of the Irish women who immigrated to the District were nuns who served at the Sisters of Charity orphanage or Georgetown Visitation Convent. Irish women who immigrated to Washington in their twenties settled in the city on a permanent basis. The largest age group of Irish women was approximately twenty to thirty in the first half of the nineteenth century, and by 1860 that age group still outnumbered all others in the city. By 1870 women between the ages of thirty and forty comprised twenty-eight percent of Irish women in Washington while women between the ages of twenty and thirty comprised twenty-seven percent of Irish women in the city. Of these Irish women employed after 1870, service work continued to provide steady employment.

Although service work was available, Irish women increasingly turned down these positions and opted for marriage instead. As the occupation of choice, keeping house (homemaking) comprised sixty-three percent of Irish women's employment by 1870. The lace curtain had arrived, and Irish women, married to men of foreign or American birth, shared middle-class respectability with their American neighbors. Instead of working as servants in the last decades of the nineteenth century, Irish women hired servants to work in the homes they shared with husbands and children. Of the Irish men and women who married while in Washington, half married each other while the other half married American, Italian, Hungarian, French and German men and women. Not included in those of American birth are Irish-Americans who married Irish immigrants throughout the latter half of the nineteenth century.

## HOUSEHOLD STRUCTURE

The structure of Irish households varied throughout the nineteenth century. Early in the century, larger households of a husband, wife, many children and a servant or two was the norm. After the new class of laborers arrived, Irish households shifted to include the large number of single men who boarded and the increasing number of single Irish women who worked as live-in servants, cooks and nurses. Throughout antebellum Washington, Irish servants working alongside slave and free African-American women in the same household was common. Also common were the increasing numbers of Irish women heading their own households. As Irish men searched for jobs outside of Washington, Irish women headed their own homes. As the century progressed, the number of single women living under one roof increased. Usually related to each other, these women shared shelter and raised one another's children.

## SETTLEMENT PATTERNS

These Irish initially settled in an area about a half mile north of the Capitol along the Tiber River known as Swampoodle, near and surrounding present-day Union Station. They flocked to this area for the ready-made housing, shanties and cheaply built structures. Squatters' rights prevailed in this part of Washington as the area was not yet developed. Another area of town around New Hampshire Avenue, between Twentieth and Twenty-First Streets and M and N Streets, northwest, was known colloquially as Paddy Mageetown. These Irish immigrants worked for the Washington Gas Company and lived in what is known today as Foggy Bottom. Another area of Washington that grew with Irish residents was the nineteenth-century Ward Seven. This included the Mall, bounded on the east side by the Smithsonian, up to and including the Tidal Basin. This also was bounded on the east by South Capitol Street all the way to the Potomac. The Irish here worked on the docks and for the Bureau of Engraving and Printing.

By the turn of the century, Irish neighborhoods took on a slightly different look from their original shanty-town appearance. Second-generation families and the wealthier class of recent immigrants moved into growing middle-class neighborhoods while Georgetown continued to attract Irish immigrants. Margaret Gormly's Georgetown row houses on Jefferson Street provided room and board for members of her extended Irish family. Moreover, Margaret Gormly's row houses reflected the growing affluence of established Irish residents. The ornate carvings and style of her home told all of the growing affluence of Irish residents. The last migration Irish residents made before leaving the city in the twentieth century was to Brookland, near the Catholic University of America. The up-and-coming professionals of second- and third-generation Irish families lived in this housing development. Brookland soon became synonymous with the middle-class life shared by second- and third-generation immigrants.

## THE CATHOLIC CHURCH

This community of Irish immigrants formed the foundation of church-community relations in Washington's Catholic churches. The relationship between the Irish community and Washington's Catholic churches was present from the beginning of the capital's history. Founding and prominent members of Washington's Catholic churches include many Irish immigrants. Father John McElroy, a young Irish priest, served at Holy Trinity in its earliest years and was responsible for much of its growth. Although initially a church of the elite, Georgetown's Holy Trinity soon filled with laboring immigrants and their families who came to work on the canal, street and edifice projects. These Irish remained the largest immigrant group in the Georgetown parish throughout the nineteenth century. Two prominent members, the Donoghue brothers, were well-known businessmen in Georgetown and Washington; Peter was a cloth merchant and Timothy owned a grocery. They and their extended families consistently filled Holy Trinity's pews.

The first Catholic church in the city of Washington, St. Patrick's, grew in response to the needs of Irish immigrants. As Irish men and their families immigrated to Washington for work, Father Anthony Caffry from Dublin ministered to them in the growing parish. Within the first four decades of the nineteenth century, two more Catholic churches were built to meet the needs of the growing Irish population. St. Peter's in southeast Washington and St. Matthew's on the corner of H and Fifteenth, northwest, provided services for Irish Catholics in their parishes. St. Matthew's brought the Irish residents of the neighborhood a church and priest to shepherd the flock that lived and worked in the White House area. St. Matthew's Irish priest, Father John P. Donelan, along with Irishmen Thomas Carberry, Ignatius Mudd and John Callan served on the building committee, while Irishmen Nicholas Callan, Jr., Ambrose Lynch and Gregory Ennis helped in other capacities. Along the outskirts of Swampoodle, the northeast area where Irish laborers and their families lived in the nineteenth century, was St. Aloysius. This church, if any in Washington, boasts of Irish origins. Throughout the nineteenth century, Irish immigrants and their families comprised two-thirds of this parish's residents with the original land donation for the church building given by Irishman Ambrose Lynch.

### Morbidity

Irish men and women died from a variety of causes throughout the nineteenth century. Diseases and illnesses of the respiratory system were the primary causes of death; however, women died of complications in childbirth and men died from work accidents. These accidents ranged from a bale of hay falling on an Irishman's head to an intemperate fellow who was run over while asleep on the train tracks. The elderly, both male and female, typically proved to be most vulnerable to illness and disease, dying at a higher rate than all other age groups.

### The End of the Century, 1900

Throughout the late eighteenth and the nineteenth centuries, Irish men and women immigrated to Washington. They came in response to needs in their homeland and abroad. They chose Washington as their place of permanent and temporary residence. As the city changed over the decades, so did the type of Irish immigrant who chose Washington. In the early years, families and skilled single men came to the city to be a part of building the national capital. As the century progressed, more women joined the Irish community in Washington to support the domestic infrastructure of jobs within the city's hotel and institutional industry. But, as the century neared its end, Irish men and women found themselves no longer the newcomer but part of the established community of Washington residents. It was they who became part of the host community other immigrants found upon arriving in their new nation's capital city.

Jennifer L. Altenhofel, "Keeping House: Irish and Irish Immigrant Women's Labor in Nineteenth-Century Washington, D.C.," and "Charity in Education for Irish Women in Nineteenth-Century Washington," *Catholic Historical Society Newsletter* (Washington, D.C., April–June 1997).

Morris J. MacGregor, *A Parish for the Federal City: St. Patrick's in Washington, 1794–1994* (Washington, D.C., 1994).

William W. Warner, *At Peace with All Their Neighbors: Catholics and Catholicism in the National Capital, 1787–1860* (Washington, D.C.: Georgetown University Press, 1994).

JENNIFER ALTENHOFEL

## WASHINGTON, D.C., 20th CENTURY

At the beginning of the 20th century, the Washington Irish were a significant presence in the federal city: 6,220 out of a total population of 278,000. Although few of them were prominent citizens, they were a readily recognizable ethnic population in every ward, but concentrated in a few neighborhoods. On one extreme was the Irish-born Tom Walsh, the "Colorado Croesus," who had struck gold and moved to Washington in 1898. The Walsh Mansion at 2020 Massachusetts Avenue NW, completed in 1903 at a cost of $835,000, had sixty rooms, including a gilded apartment on the third floor. Like many *nouveaux riches* who came to Washington for its mild winter, its parks and its social cachet, Walsh had no relationship with his countrymen. Next

on the social scale came the successful merchants of Irish extraction—the Nees, Haltigans and Morans—who lived on Columbia Road NW, and belonged to a chapter of the Ancient Order of Hibernians in that section of the city. A larger group was composed of the small Irish professional class, modestly successful entrepreneurs, and federal bureaucrats ("narrowbacks"), most of whom were second- or third-generation Washingtonians, descendants of early nineteenth-century mechanics and laborers. Then came the skilled and semiskilled tradesmen, numerically the largest class among the turn-of-the-century Irish; and lastly, a small and shrinking class of laborers, who were finding it increasingly difficult to survive in competition with African-Americans and southern Italians, who were then just beginning to appear in large numbers on the Washington construction sites.

A more graphic sense of this distribution may be inferred from the occupations of the 270 Murphys (surely a representative cross section of the Irish) listed in the 1908 city business directory. Among the entrepreneurs were a hotelier, the proprietress of a boarding-house, and E. J. Murphy, Inc. (Paints, Oils and Glass). In the professional class were three official reporters, two physicians, an architect, and a lawyer. The largest classes by which males were identified were: clerks (thirty-one), laborers (nine), Naval Yard workers (eight), barkeeps (eight), grocers (seven), bricklayers (six), trolley conductors (five), policemen (four), and plasterers (three). Female Murphys were: widows (seventeen), clerks (twelve), domestics (five), teachers (five), nurses (four), and seamstresses (three). Other occupations included firemen, coach painters, porters, watchmen, tinners, laundresses and plumbers. There was a lithographer, a fisherman, a farmer, a humane society agent, a map mounter, and an artificial limb maker. These listings show that the Irish were not confined to the stereotypical occupations, but were moving into jobs which required capital, education, or at least technical training. The Murphys' principal employers were the Navy Yard, the Bureau of Printing, and various governmental agencies. Indeed, the federal government in this company town was the biggest employer: 25,000 in 1903, to increase tenfold by 1940. Thus "clerking" (the term embraced many technical and administrative skills in the earlier decades) was the modest but secure way to success, drawing a salary that was 50% above that of the average industrial worker. As we see from the occupational sample, the local economy did not lack for other kinds of employment: manufacturing, service and tourist industries (2,295 firms; 350,000 visitors in 1900) provided about as many jobs as the federal government.

Most of the Irish were members of a "second migration": coming to Washington by way of other cities in the U.S. (most list New York as port of entry). Although the majority of the earlier arrivals originated in Cork, they also hailed from Roscommon, Galway, Dublin, Cavan, Wexford, and Waterford. There are clusters of names from West Limerick and North Kerry, which suggest that immigration chains were operative here as elsewhere in the U.S.

We find our 1908 Murphys with addresses in every ward of the city. There were seven divisions of the Ancient Order of Hibernians and more than two hundred Irish-run saloons similarly distributed. Nevertheless, the majority were to be found in a few of the poorer sections. The largest of these enclaves and the only one that could be accurately described as an Irish neighborhood was "Swampoodle," notorious for violence and overcrowding, its cows and goats, and its noxious Tiber Creek. This neighborhood fell between Pennsylvania and Florida Avenues, NW, and embraced the rise up North Capitol Street known as "Patterson's

Woods." In this warren of streets and alleys centered on St. Aloysius' clock tower, the poor Irish and their black neighbors coexisted in their narrow red brick row houses. They patronized O'Leary's and Daley's saloons, Kennealey's drugstore, and the Jesuit church of St. Aloysius. In the open field behind the future site of Union Station, or at Camp Meigs (next to the Florida Avenue Farmers' Market) young men with the names Kelly, Gannon, Walsh and Joyce played Gaelic football on Sunday afternoons. With the arrival of thousands of Italian laborers engaged in the construction of Union Station (1905–7), and the availability of more spacious row houses further up North Capitol Street, this neighborhood began to dissolve, so that by 1940 it was no more.

In the early years of the century, another Irish neighborhood could be found in Foggy Bottom on a street known as "Connaught Row." This was a swampy area south of Virginia Avenue and around the storage towers of the Washington Gas Light Company, the main employer. Members of St. Stephen the Martyr's parish, they formed the West End Hibernian Society, fielded a baseball team, the Emerald Athletic Club, and an American football team, the Irish Eleven.

A third Irish neighborhood could be found in St. Dominic's parish, in an area of the southwest known as "The Island." Originally made up of railroad workers and stone cutters, by 1910 it had an infrastructure of saloons, grocery stores and restaurants centered on 4 1/2 St., SW. Isolated from the rest of the city by the Mall, a creek and rail lines, this community shared its environs with Jews and African-Americans. There were smaller enclaves of Irish in St. Peter's and St. Joseph's parishes (Capitol Hill), and along the Georgetown waterfront, many of the latter by the 20th century third-generation Washingtonians, and owners of small businesses.

In the early decades of the century, these communities maintained many of their traditional customs: wakes, Saturday night "kitchen rackets," Lenten recitation of the "short rosary" in Irish, and continued support of the Irish nationalist cause. They maintained an informal family support system, "caring for but not about" one another, married later than other groups, had sizable families, and supported the Church, the St. Vincent de Paul Society and their parents in old age.

They sent their sons and daughters to Catholic schools, which prepared them to enter the federal work force or the professions, enabling them to move to more commodious housing further out of town. This dispersal began with the gradual extension of row houses contiguous to the main trolley lines radiating from downtown: via North Capitol Street and Michigan Avenue NE to Brookland; via 7th Street NW, Georgia Avenue, and on to Silver Spring and White Oak, Maryland; and later to Virginia via the Key and Memorial Bridges, constructed in the 1930s (D.C. had the highest ratio of automobiles per capita in the U.S. at this time). This exodus speeded up still more after 1940 with the further development of Petworth and Crestwood, and the planned communities of Greenbelt, Wheaton, and later developments in Arlington. The cumulative effect of these shifts, encouraged by the Alley Dwelling Authority, was to break up the old Irish neighborhoods in favor of the ease and conveniences of suburban living. These radical shifts saw the total population of the greater Washington area grow from one to four million between 1940 and 1990, whereas the numbers in D.C. fell from 750,000 to 600,000 in the same period.

Brookland, in the vicinity of Catholic University, was, in the 1920s and 1930s, the last neighborhood in D.C. with a significant Irish presence. Its independent houses, open fields and trees, and proximity to Catholic University and its satellite houses of religious study and the Franciscan Monastery, made it a paradise of ease after cacophonous Swampoodle. The Irish now belonged to multiethnic parishes such as St. Anthony's and St. Gabriel's, which they shared with Italians and Germans. In consequence, they began to think of themselves as American Catholics rather than as Irish-Americans.

The New Deal and World War II expanded the federal service dramatically (reaching 276,000 by 1942), and drawing service personnel from all over the United States. This brought a whole new wave of Irish-Americans in-migrating from other parts of the country, especially from cities with a strong Irish presence. These migrations moderated the weakening of the Irish identity of the out-migrating Washingtonians, especially in the new suburbs in Northern Virginia then expanding around the Pentagon and related military and industrial concentrations. The figures from the 1980 census dramatize the shift: of the 4 million residents of the greater Washington area, approximately 650,000 claim Irish ancestry, only 38,000 of whom lived in the District. The historically steady trickle of new immigrants to Washington surged in the late 1980s, so that the total number of Irish-born tripled to around three thousand during the ensuing decade. This influx embraces all social and intellectual classes: medical researchers at the National Institute of Health, economists to the World Bank, academics to area institutions, health professionals, hoteliers, diplomats and clerics, as well as small contractors, carpenters, bartenders, entertainers, cooks, and travel agents.

Between 1960 and 1980, the Irish-American subculture went through a small renaissance, so that today there are approximately 40 special-interest associations in the area. These include a half-dozen chapters of the AOH (all in the suburbs), three *céilí* clubs, an Irish-American Club (with mainly Irish-born members), several schools of Irish step-dancing which sponsor annual *feiseanna,* a branch of Comhaltas Ceoltóirí Eireann, Conradh na Gaeilge, the Washington Gaels GAA club, and a dozen Irish bars with their commercialized Irish entertainment, a few Irish import shops, a weekly radio show, two annual St. Patrick's Day parades, and one or two weekend outdoor festivals of Irish traditional music.

The Irish Embassy (established in 1924, and since 1949 located on Sheridan Circle) gives Ireland a real presence in the political life of the city. The Northern Ireland conflict has given birth to several lobbying groups with offices in Washington, notably the Irish National Caucus. Academic institutions offer courses in Irish history and literature, and Catholic University has had an endowment supporting Celtic/Irish Studies since the beginning of the century.

The material culture of Washington has a small Irish inventory: the archives of Catholic and Georgetown universities, as well as the Library of Congress, contain valuable collections of literary and historical books and manuscripts. There are public monuments to Irish and Irish-Americans, including Edmund Burke, Commodore John Barry, Cardinal Gibbons, Archbishop John Carroll, "The Nuns of the Battlefield," and Robert Emmet (the latter three by Jerome Connor). There is an Evie Hone window in the National Cathedral (Episcopal), and an altar dedicated to Our Lady of Knock at the Shrine of the Immaculate Conception.

Lecture courses on Irish culture sponsored by the National Geographic Association and the Smithsonian Institution are the most heavily subscribed of all "ethnic" series sponsored by these Washington establishments. So, the descendants of the denizens

Robert Emmet statue

of Connaught Row and Swampoodle still retain some links with the Irish past.

*Boyd's Directory of the District of Columbia* (Washington, 1908).

Tom Kelly, "I Knew My Parents Were Irish as Soon as I Knew Anything," *The Washingtonian* (March 1979).

Michael McDermott, interview. 144–50.

Frederick M. Miller and Howard Gillette, Jr., *Washington Seen: A Photographic History, 1875–1965* (Baltimore, 1995).

Susan Sherwood Unger, "Foggy Bottom: Blue-Collar Neighborhood in a White-Collar Town," in Katherine Schneider Smith, ed., *Washington at Home: An Illustrated History of Neighborhoods in the Nation's Capital* (Northridge, 1988).

COILIN OWENS

## WASHINGTON STATE

The Irish in Washington State represent a minority of Irish immigrants and their Irish-American descendants in the U.S. More than demographic fate, however, has led to the distinctive experience of the Irish in Washington being overlooked in most accounts of the Irish in America. Unlike their counterparts in the Northeast who encountered "a community with entrenched and dominant anti-Irish traditions of social discrimination and religious prejudice," most Irish in Washington found a shifting social order with no established elites, cheap land, and broad economic opportunity (Sarbaugh, *Journal of the West* [henceforth *JW*], 1992). They took advantage of these prospects to become farmers, bankers, mine owners, entrepreneurs, merchants, publishers, civic leaders, philanthropists and politicians. Some Irish in Washington State became extremely wealthy; most solidly middle-class. Most simply do not fit into the conventional categories for understanding the Irish experience in the U.S.—urban ghetto, church, and boss. For the vast majority of Irish in Washington, aspirations for achievement far more than "Irish" heritage—national, ethnic, or religious—shaped their self-identity.

### EARLIEST PRESENCE (TO 1846)

Irish have been present in what is now Washington State since the earliest European and American explorations. Irish and Scotch-Irish served as crew aboard Spanish, English, and U.S. vessels that explored the Washington Coast and Puget Sound during the second half of the eighteenth century. They participated in land-based explorations as well. Patrick Gass is the best-known Irish member of Lewis and Clark's 1804–1806 Corps of Exploration. Scotch-Irish and Irish trappers such as Ross Cox and John Reed had entered the Oregon Country with the Canadian North West Company and John Jacob Astor's Pacific Fur Company by 1810.

The Irish presence increased in the region after 1824 when the Hudson's Bay Company dispatched Dr. John McLaughlin to Fort Vancouver to take charge of the Columbia District. His group included a minority of Irish from Canada in a Company corps dominated by Scots, French-Canadian, and Metis. These Irish were single men, and many married Indian wives, some Irish/Spanish wives.

Catholic Church records from Vancouver and Stellamaris Mission give evidence of the Irish presence from the 1830s: Francis Heron, an Irish employee of the Hudson's Bay Company; his son, George, born at Fort Nisqually in 1834; and Marie McDermot, daughter of Andrew McDermot, wife of Richard Lane, a Hudson's Bay Company clerk, to name only three. The same records show Irish entering the Oregon Country from California: John Howard and William McCarty both came north with the Ewing Young party in 1834. The records also list Irish directly from Ireland (some by way of Australia), such as Patrick James McGowan who entered the fishery business at Chinook, and the farmer, William Ryan. During these early decades of European and Euro-American settlement, Irish came to the region that would become Washington State from the Canadian north, Californian south, and from the west as well as from the east. The Hudson's Bay Company presence made secure immigration to the Oregon Country possible. Irish and Irish-Americans were among the steady stream of immigrants to cross the Oregon Trail during the "Great Migration" of 1843 (White and Solberg, 1989).

In 1844 a small group of immigrants chose to settle north of the Columbia River. Among them was a Kentuckian of Irish descent, Michael T. Simmons, his wife and seven children. Simmons' family settled near present-day Olympia along with the family of George W. Bush, a Black man barred from owning land in the Willamette Valley. The Bush and Simmons families fostered the first U.S. settlement in what is now Washington State (White and Solberg, 1989; Bosanko, *JW*, 1992).

Simmons served as commissioner of Newmarket (later Tumwater), performed marriages, and acted as judge. His wife was the first schoolteacher. Simmons sold his claim in 1850 to the Irishman Clanrick Crosby, a sea captain (and ancestor of Washington's best known Irishman, Bing Crosby), and established himself as an influential leader in Olympia. He prospered as landlord of a building that served as the center of the city's life in its early days, providing space for residence and lodge rooms, the *Columbian*, a newspaper begun by McElroy and Wiley in 1852, and the court. Crosby was successful in Tumwater, distinguishing himself in economic and civic ventures. Eventually he was elected to serve in the State Legislature (Bosanko, *JW*, 1992).

Irish women who came to Washington from the earliest settlement until after the 1890s were more likely to be married than single and to have non-Irish spouses. This led to greater property ownership by Irish in Washington and in the West generally (Burchell, *JW*, 1992). Teresa Lappin Eldridge is illustrative. Teresa escaped the Irish Famine by seeking domestic work in the U.S. In 1851 she accompanied the family that employed her to

California. On the voyage she met Captain Edward Eldridge, who served as second mate. They married in 1852 and in the spring of 1853 arrived at Bellingham Bay. Her husband helped build and operate a sawmill in Bellingham. He worked in various other trades and professions, and eventually became a delegate at large to the territorial constitutional convention in 1878, and a member of the state constitutional convention in Olympia in 1889. Teresa, the first white woman to reside on Bellingham Bay, became known as the "Mother of Whatcom" (Bosanko, *JW*, 1992).

### FROM U.S. POSSESSION INTO THE SECOND WAVE OF IMMIGRATION (1846–1890)

Irish and Irish-Americans were among the increasing European and European-American population of Washington during the years 1846–1890. Several factors contributed to this growth: sole possession of the Oregon Country going to the U.S. in 1846; the California Gold Rush in 1848; subsequent gold, silver, lead and coal strikes in present-day Washington, Idaho, and British Columbia between the 1850s and 1880s; the Oregon Donation Land Law of 1850; the Civil War; and the Homestead Act of 1862.

In 1849 there were 304 registered whites in what would be Washington. One hundred eighty-nine were U.S. citizens, the remaining 115 were aliens, principally from Canada, Scotland, England, and Ireland. In 1850, the population tripled to 1,049. This increase was due to the continued arrival of foreign-born and latecomers from the midwestern and eastern United States who were being diverted from the Willamette Valley to the newly formed counties north of the Columbia River. In 1853 Washington Territory was established, partly as a result of the population increase in the Oregon Territory (from 8,000 in 1850 to nearly 30,000 in 1855) (White and Solberg, 1989).

Between 1853 and 1880 the Irish in Washington clustered in Clark, King, and Walla Walla Counties, sites of military posts and mining operations. By 1880, first-generation Irish were second only to Canadians as the largest European immigrant group with 2,243 Irish listed in the 1880 decennial census. In terms of overall population, however, the Irish lagged considerably behind the Chinese and Germans. By 1890 they would be outdone by Scandinavians as well (White and Solberg, 1989; Carlos Arnaldo Schwantes, *The Pacific Northwest: An Interpretive History*, revised edition [Lincoln: University of Nebraska Press, 1996]).

As was the case during the earliest period of settlement, from 1846 until the turn of the century, Irish were often the first and leading settlers in various regions of Washington State. Many of the sixty-nine naturalized Irish who served as enlisted men in the United States Army Cavalry at the Vancouver Barracks and Fort Nisqually (established in 1848) remained after their terms ended. Among them was William O'Leary from Cork County, Ireland, who settled on the south shore of Gray's Harbor in 1848. O'Leary, a bachelor, was followed by the family of Irishman William Medcalf and his English wife, Martha Ann. They were the first white family to settle near the lower Chehalis River. While O'Leary and Medcalf farmed, others turned to mining or businesses related to mining, lumber, or transportation (White and Solberg, 1989).

In 1853, the same year that Teresa and Edward Eldridge arrived at Bellingham Bay, Daniel Jefferson Harris also arrived. Harris, born to Irish immigrant parents in 1826 on Long Island, New York, took to the sea as a young teenager, and decided upon his arrival at Bellingham Bay to build a seaport. He spent thirty years as a subsistence farmer, fisherman, and smuggler, and earned a reputation as the town eccentric, "Dirty Dan Harris," before his dream of wealth became a reality in 1883. Harris platted the town of Fairhaven and built the Fairhaven Hotel. Though he achieved wealth, the personal tragedy of his wife's death prevented its enjoyment. Harris died in 1890 in Los Angeles (Bosanko, *JW*, 1992).

In 1867 the Irishman Samuel Benn, part of the wave of post–Civil War immigrants to Washington, bought seven hundred acres of government land along the north shore of the Chehalis River and both shores of the Wishkah, site of present day Aberdeen, Washington. A successful dairyman, Samuel and his wife Mary were at the center of the town's social life (Bosanko, *JW*, 1992).

The farming community of Farghar Lake, north of Vancouver, was settled in the late 1860s by a group of Scots and Irish. Early homesteaders included James Langon and James Daly, with a Mr. S.S. Campbell as schoolteacher (Bosanko, *JW*, 1992).

The Walla Walla Valley attracted many Irish after the Civil War as did the Dublin district of Clark County. Nicholas and Catherine Whealen, both Irish-born, arrived in eastern Washington in 1867 from northern California. They prospered raising cattle to feed the miners in Idaho (White and Solberg, 1989). During the late 1860s, the 1870s and 1880s some of eastern Washington's most prominent and successful pioneers came from Ireland.

The one hundred and eighty-five Irish in Spokane County in 1880—nearly one-half directly from Ireland and another one-fourth representing first-generation Irish with both parents coming from Ireland—comprised only four percent of a total county population of 4,267. Most of them lived in rural areas and farmed. Among the homesteaders was John Blakely. Born in Ireland in 1832 he immigrated with his mother to the U.S. in 1847. Blakely homesteaded in Spokane County in 1877, having worked his way west employed in lumber mills and on railroads. He farmed for the remainder of his life with the support of his wife, Sarah Bell, also from Ireland, and his six children. His death in 1909 was reported in the *Spokesman Review* as "Death Calls Old Pioneer." Other successful homesteaders and farmers included Edward Sheehy and Jerry Sullivan (Sarbaugh, *JW*, 1992).

Irish immigrants to eastern Washington also filled traditional occupations of unskilled workers such as domestic service and mining, but many achieved rapid financial and civic success. Successful Irish in Spokane engaged in business and finance included Notre Dame graduate Thomas Conlan, who arrived in Spokane in 1883 and in 1888 established the Spokane Hardware Company, recognized within a year as "one of the city's pre-eminent business establishments." Peter Costello, the child of Irish parents living in Canada, arrived in Spokane in 1887 where he organized a prosperous contracting business. The Costello brothers constructed the city's major streets and sewers. Peter Costello became one of the city's most generous philanthropists. Another businessman and millionaire, Patrick "Patsy" Clark, was a leading figure in Spokane's social and financial elite class. He was among the best known mine owners in the United States (Sarbaugh, *JW*, 1992).

Besides farming, business, and finance, Washington's Irish between 1846 and 1880 engaged in many other occupations including government service, political office, printing and publishing, and law. J. M. Murphy and E. T. Gun served respectively as Auditor and Treasurer of the Washington Territory in the 1870s. Henry McGill served as acting governor of the territory in 1860. Irish names appear among federal officials in the territory: McFadden, Kearney, McMeeken and Johnson to name four. In printing and publishing, J. M. Murphy of the *Washington Standard*;

M. J. Mooney and Brothers of the *Kalama Beacon;* A. J. Cain of the *Dayton News;* E. T. Green of the *Transcript;* James Power of the *Bellingham Bay Mail;* and David Higgins of the *Seattle Intelligencer* all were Irish (Quigley, 1878).

This sampling of Irish in Washington State illustrates how profoundly the mobility and opportunity of the frontier shaped the context for their lives and provided the chance for them to meet their hopes for economic improvement. Most Irish in Washington did not remain in the mines but moved among occupations and across geographic space seeking economic opportunities. The Washington Irish farmed and ranched successfully, countering the general claim that the Irish in the U.S. left farming whenever possible. Economic and transportation connections between Butte, Montana, and Spokane, and travel up and down the Pacific Coast between San Francisco and Puget Sound allowed immigration from what were western Irish population centers.

The mobility and opportunity of life on the frontier altered the way the Irish in Washington understood themselves. They shed their identification as Irish as they achieved prosperity in Washington. They "looked upon past traditions, wounds, and memories of the 'Old Sod' as irrelevant and, at best, as remote" (Sarbaugh, *JW,* 1992). Their mobility and transformation from Irish immigrants to Washingtonians also influenced their religious affiliation and identification. The frontier experience set these Irish apart from many of the Irish who would come after the railroads.

### Railroads and the Twentieth Century (1890–1945)

The railroad rapidly increased the Irish population of Washington and offered new yet limited employment opportunities in the region. As with the Irish cavalrymen forty years before, many Irish remained. Some of these laborers were illiterate and more strongly identified with their Irish and often Catholic heritage than did their Irish predecessors to the region. By the time they arrived, a nascent social elite existed in the state. Therefore, after 1880 some Irish in Washington experienced ethnic and religious prejudice in ways they had not previously (White and Solberg, 1989).

The railroads also changed the pattern of immigration. Most of the Irish who came to Washington before the railroad already had lived in other parts of the U.S. The railroad offered Irish and other Europeans a chance to settle in communities with an ethnic character. The railroad also brought more women to Washington and so undercut intermarriage among immigrants of different ethnic groups (White and Solberg, 1989).

From 1880–1910 Washington's foreign-born population rose from fourteen to twenty-one percent (241,197 of the total 1,141,990 people). They were widely dispersed throughout the state (White and Solberg, 1989). In 1900 Washington had a higher percentage of foreign-born residents than the U.S. as a whole (Schwantes). The Irish continued to be a minority of those present, less than two percent of the state's population in 1920 (Allen and Turner, 1988).

With the increase of population during this period a small concentration of Irish unskilled laborers became visible, especially in Tacoma and Seattle. They were involved in the anti-Chinese agitation and expulsion of 1885–1886 as a result of racism and anxiety over wages. As increased population diminished economic opportunity, some Irish who arrived during this period were less economically successful than those who had preceded them.

Beginning in the 1880s, Irish in Washington were involved in growing numbers in labor movements such as the Knights of Labor, the Western Labor Union, the Western Federation of Miners, and the United Mine Workers. They identified with these movements, however, more as laborers than as Irishmen.

While more laborers settled in Washington after 1880, the business, financial, and farming success of other Irish residents did not decline. Two notable Irishmen were William Pigott and John Joseph Donovan. William Pigott was born in New York City, June 27, 1860, the child of Irish immigrants. After learning iron and steel manufacturing in Ohio and Colorado, he came to Seattle in 1895. In 1904 he organized the Seattle Steel Company and then served as president of the Seattle Car Manufacturing Company. Wealthy and successful, Pigott contributed to local Seattle affairs including the Chamber of Commerce.

John Joseph Donovan was born to Irish immigrant parents on September 8, 1858, in New Hampshire. With degrees in education and engineering, Donovan went to work for the Northern Pacific Railroad, designing and constructing bridges and tunnels in Washington and Montana. In 1888 Donovan left the employ of the Northern Pacific and moved to Fairhaven on Bellingham Bay. He built a railroad there and was involved in other enterprises. Donovan was instrumental in establishing St. Joseph's Hospital in Bellingham. Both Catholics, Pigott and Donovan became key advisors to Edward O'Dea, Bishop of the Diocese of Seattle. They served the diocese in many capacities.

Irish organizations appeared in Washington after 1880. One of the largest was the Ancient Order of Hibernians, established in 1889. Irish nationalistic activities and the Irish Rebellion of 1917 increased interest in Irish social, nationalistic, and religious organizations among some of the Irish in Washington State. In 1917, the state president of the A.O.H., Rev. John E. O'Brien of Everett, sought to institute a course in Irish history in the parochial schools of the Diocese. A Celtic Cross Association was organized out of the Ancient Order of Hibernians to assist the Irish in Ireland with social relief in 1921.

Some tension existed between the Ancient Order of Hibernians and the bishops of Seattle. In 1924 Bishop O'Dea declined a Hibernian request that St. Patrick's Day celebrations be made their sole responsibility. O'Dea expressed the view that asking the pastors to forego their parish entertainment on St. Patrick's Day "would diminish, if not greatly endanger, the interest in the day we celebrate with so much pleasure and spiritual profit" (Archives of the Archdiocese of Seattle [henceforth AAS], 2/16/24). In 1939, the Hibernians and Bishop Shaughnessy discussed who would handle arrangements for the visit to Seattle of the Premier of Ireland, Mr. Eamon de Valera. Bishop Shaughnessy resisted Hibernian efforts to run anything that took place in parishes or on a diocesan level, including Irish nationalistic activities at the beginning of WWII (AAS).

The Irish in Washington who still identified themselves as Catholic in some way were affected during the early twentieth century by growing anti-Catholic sentiment. Anti-private school initiatives sponsored by the Ku Klux Klan in the 1920s spread across the country. The fight against Initiative 49 in Washington in 1924 included strategic planning and financial assistance from Irish businessmen William Pigott and J. J. Donovan. While the measure was defeated by nearly 60,000 votes, over 131,000 citizens in Washington had voted for it. This increased a sense of Catholic identity and at the same time, separateness, for many Irish and other Catholics in the state (Buerge and Rochester, 1988).

## 1940 TO THE PRESENT

World War II brought a massive population increase to the Pacific Northwest and especially Washington State, home to large army, air force, and navy bases. The war industry in the region, which included Boeing, Kaiser Aluminum, logging, and shipbuilding brought large numbers of people from the East and the Midwest, among them Irish-Americans. Many of these Irish-Americans carried a pronounced sense of Irish ethnic identity with them, while others saw the west as a place where they might break free of the past.

Irish social organizations continued to exist during the war and in the post-war years. The Society of Friendly Sons of St. Patrick was a "non-sectarian" organization that held an annual meeting and banquet on St. Patrick's Day. Three-quarters of the membership was Catholic (AAS). Another group, known as St. Patrick's Society, succeeded and failed in the space of four years; its primary purpose was to provide an annual program to honor St. Patrick. A new archbishop, Thomas A. Connolly, improved the relationship between the archdiocese and the Ancient Order of Hibernians. Connolly provided a chaplain to the Ladies Auxiliary of the A.O.H., assigning them the service work of assisting with the St. Peter Clavier Interracial Center (AAS). The order itself, however, was declining in membership.

In 1953 recent immigrants from Ireland formed the Gaelic American Club. The club's purpose was to support new emigrants from Ireland to Washington State. It took over the functions the A.O.H. and its Auxiliary had performed in earlier years. Bishop Shaughnessy named Fr. William Treacy as first moderator of the club. The forty-five immigrants were not sufficient to maintain a club and so it was opened to Irish-Americans as well. As the organization grew, the ordinaries became concerned that it would compete with other Catholic social organizations such as the Catholic Daughters of America, the Young Ladies Institute, the Knights of Columbus, the Foresters, and others. In 1956, Archbishop Connolly did not want the club to "isolate and cut [the Irish] off from the general current of life in the community" (AAS, 3/22/1956). By 1959 the club was being called the Irish-American Society. It continued to exist into the 1960s. Between 1948 and 1955 the *Irish Information Bulletin,* a politically motivated national publication calling for a unified Ireland, sought sponsorship for a Washington Chapter. Bishops Shaughnessy and Connolly were in favor of a unified Ireland, but did not want such a political organization in Washington. Washington's Irish did not appear to participate in Irish nationalistic activities in any institutionalized manner. Membership in Irish ethnic organizations declined by the end of the 1960s.

Very small numbers of emigrants from Ireland to Washington are reported from 1950 to the present. In 1980 all Washington counties contained between two and five percent of their population claiming Irish descent or nationality. Only five counties, all rural—Okanogan, Pend Oreille, Garfield, Asoton, and Whitman—claim between five and ten percent of their population as being of Irish descent or nationality. These figures are lower than for most other western states (Allen and Turner). Given settlement patterns in Washington from the southern border states, more of Washington's population may in fact be of Irish descent than the 1980 census data indicates, but its citizens no longer identify themselves as such. Neither Irishness nor religious affiliation are central to the identities of most Irish in Washington.

## RELIGION AND THE IRISH IN WASHINGTON

Washington is one of the least churched and most religiously diverse states in the union and has been since the earliest European settlement. In 1900 about seventeen percent of its population claimed church membership. By 1920 that figure had risen to about twenty percent. In 1990 it was slightly more than thirty percent (*Churches and Church Membership in the United States, 1990.* Atlanta, GA: Glenmary Research Center, 1992). Mobility and preoccupation with economic achievement leached institutional religious affiliation out of many Protestant and Irish Catholics in Washington State.

Scotch-Irish Presbyterians from Canada and Ireland evangelized in Washington during the late nineteenth and early twentieth centuries. By the mid-twentieth century, however, no significant sense of Irish identity was associated with Presbyterians in the state.

The Catholic Church in Washington played a role in promoting Catholic and Irish identity during the twentieth century. Four of the seven Ordinaries of the first continuous diocese in Washington have been Irish-American, beginning with the third bishop of Seattle, Edward John O'Dea, ordained bishop on September 8, 1896. O'Dea moved the See of the Diocese of Nesqually from Vancouver to Seattle in 1903, renamed the diocese Seattle in 1907, and served until his death in December 1932. His successor, Bishop Gerald Shaughnessy, who served from 1933 to 1950, and Archbishop Thomas A. Connolly, who served from 1950 to his retirement in 1975, were also Irish-American, as was the sixth Ordinary, Thomas J. Murphy, who served from 1991 until his death in 1997. Connolly came to the diocese from the Catholic Church in San Francisco, which traditionally had a strong Irish character.

The Archdiocese of Seattle has very few national parishes. Though Irish were associated with particular parishes in the diocese at various times—St. Michael's Parish in Olympia, Holy Rosary Parish in Seattle, St. Patrick's in Tacoma, St. Aloysius in Spokane—these associations had more to do with residential patterns and movements in these cities than with any organized goal toward the creation of national parishes.

The interactions of Irish organizations such as the Ancient Order of Hibernians, the Friends of St. Patrick, and the Gaelic-American Society with Bishops O'Dea and Shaughnessy and with Archbishop Connolly, reflect the delicate balance these ecclesiastical leaders maintained in their efforts to keep the Irish Catholic and at the same time foster their Americanization.

Men and women religious, from Ireland and from Irish ghetto communities in the Midwest and the East, served the Catholic Church in the Pacific Northwest in education, health care, and social services. These religious shared their "Irish" Catholicism with parochial school students and parishioners. In the 1950s and 1960s Catholic sisters, brothers, and priests were actively involved in the public celebration of St. Patrick's Day, appearing at parades and in parish and community celebrations. Sisters taught Irish dance and folklore to students in Catholic Schools.

Irish-born clergy became a significant presence in the Archdiocese of Seattle beginning in the 1920s until the late 1960s. There was a significant influx of Irish priests to Washington State after WWII. Archbishop Connolly reviewed various seminaries for potential candidates, and many were ordained specifically for the Seattle diocese. In 1966, sixty-two foreign-born Irish priests served the Archdiocese out of a total of four hundred seventy-eight. One of the best known of these Irish-born clergy was Fr. William Treacy who, among other services to the Archdiocese, participated in the pioneering ecumenical television program, *Challenge,* on KOMO TV in Seattle during the 1960s. Both the ecumenical anti-Klan strategies promoted by Catholic laymen J. J. Donovan, William Pigott, and others in the 1920s, and the *Challenge* program of the 1960s, illustrate the impact of Irish-Americans on the Church and the cooperative character of Catholicism in Washington from its earliest days.

CONCLUSION

Irish and Irish-Americans came to Washington with aspirations for a better life. The experience of mobility and opportunity on the western frontier transformed them. While ethnicity and religion remained important for many as personal markers of identity, in the social world of the frontier, individual character, economic achievement, and contribution to the common good mattered far more. One does not find many people in Washington with a distinctive Irish identity today precisely because most of the Irish who came to Washington found what they were looking for.

*See* Nativism; Ku Klux Klan

James Paul Allen and Eugene James Turner, *We the People; An Atlas of America's Ethnic Diversity* (New York, 1988).

AAS-Organizational Records, Bishops Correspondence, Archives of the Archdiocese of Seattle, Seattle, Washington.

Marilyn S. McCleary Bosanko, "Among Colored Hats and Other Gewgaws: The Early Irish in Washington State."

David M. Buerge and Junius Rochester, *Roots and Branches; The Religious Heritage of Washington State* (Seattle, 1988).

R. A. Burchell, "Irish Property-holding in the West in 1870."

*Catholic Church Records of the Pacific Northwest. Vancouver Volumes 1 and 2 and Stellamaris Mission.* Translated by Mikell de Lores Wormell Warner. Annotated by Harriet Duncan Munnick (St. Paul Oregon, 1972).

Hasia R. Diner, *Erin's Daughters in America: Irish Immigrant Women in the Nineteenth-Century* (Baltimore, 1983).

David Noel Doyle and Owen Dudley Edwards, eds., *America and Ireland, 1776–1976: The American Identity and the Irish Connection* (Westport, CT, 1980).

*Harvard Encyclopedia of American Ethnic Groups.* Ed. by Stephen Thernstrom (Cambridge, MA, 1980).

Timothy J. Sarbaugh, "Celts with the Midas Touch: The Farmers, Entrepreneurs, and Millionaires of Spokane's City and County Pioneer Community."

*Journal of the West,* 31, no. 2 (April 1992).

Hugh Quigley, *The Irish Race in California, and on the Pacific Coast* (San Francisco, 1878).

Sid White and S. E. Solberg, eds., *Peoples of Washington; Perspectives on Cultural Diversity* (Pullman, WA, 1989).

PATRICIA O'CONNELL KILLEN AND
CHRISTINE M. TAYLOR

## WAYNE, JOHN (1907–1979)

Actor. Marion Michael Morrison was born in Winterset, Iowa, on May 26, 1907 to Clyde L. Morrison, a druggist, and Mary Mar-

John Wayne

garet Brown Morrison, a native of County Cork, Ireland. He was nicknamed Duke as a child after his pet Airedale dog. Throughout a career that spanned almost fifty years, John Wayne developed the persona of a true American hero—in his film roles as well as in his personal life. A physically imposing 6 foot 4 inch man with a laconic but commanding voice, he played honest, tough, straight-shooting men in films which became symbolic of American morality and spirit.

Having moved with his family to southern California as a young boy, he was a good student and athlete, and won a football scholarship to the University of Southern California when an alternate appointment to Annapolis did not work out. He studied at USC from 1925 to 1927 before working as a prop man and doing bit acting parts at Fox Film Corporation in Hollywood. His first full acting assignment was in Raoul Walsh's western *The Big Trail* (1930). Walsh takes credit for giving him the name "John Wayne" shortly after the release of that picture. Over the next nine years he played in numerous B and C movies, mostly westerns, for various studios. His big break came from John Ford, who hired him for the part of Ringo Kid in the blockbuster *Stagecoach* (1939) which won three Oscars and catapulted Wayne into stardom.

One film followed another. Wayne did his best work under the directorships of John Ford (*The Long Voyage Home,* 1940; *Fort Apache,* 1948; *She Wore a Yellow Ribbon,* 1949; and *Rio Grande,* 1950) and Howard Hawks (*Red River,* 1948; *Rio Bravo,* 1959; and *Hatari,* 1962). He won wide acclaim for his title role in Ford's *The Quiet Man* (1952) about an American prizefighter who returns to his native Ireland and begins courting an Irish beauty played by Maureen O'Hara. His first Oscar nomination was for his performance in *The Sands of Iwo Jima* (1949).

After some 200 films, Wayne finally won the 1969 Oscar for best actor for his portrayal of the crusty, one-eyed U.S. marshal Rooster Cogburn—almost a parody of himself—in *True Grit.* After battling lung cancer for over ten years, Wayne gave a riveting performance in *The Shootist* (1976). He played a gunfighter dying of cancer, seeking to live out his last days in dignity.

The actor was an avid political arch-conservative and fierce anti-Communist. He actively supported Republican presidential candidates and spoke at the 1968 Republican Convention.

The public responded heartily to his straightforward illustration of the essence of the American spirit. He died in Los Angeles in 1979.

*See* California; Cinema, Irish in

*World Biography* (1948).
*Movie Life Yearbook* (1947).
*Life,* 2 (January 28, 1972): 42.
Mike Tomkies, *Duke* (1971).

EILEEN DANEY CARZO

## WEST VIRGINIA

### EARLY HISTORY

Between 1730 and 1750, families of Irish descent moved into what is now the Eastern Panhandle of West Virginia (Bond 12). They were among the first of countless thousands of Irish immigrants and their descendants who would leave their indelible marks on all aspects of West Virginia history as they settled throughout western Virginia and, after June 20, 1863, the new state of West Virginia. Settlements in the 1770s included Currence Fort, built by William Currence in Randolph County, and a community of indentured Irish servants on George Washington's land in Mason County (Bosworth 334; Bice 231). Wherever the Irish and Scots-Irish settled, they built communities, such as Murphytown, Ireland, Irish Corner, and Irish Mountain (McLean). They also left their imprints on the river cities of Wheeling, Parkersburg, Charleston, and Huntington.

### NINETEENTH-CENTURY SETTLEMENT

The Irish earned their way across western Virginia as laborers on the roads, canals, railroads, and rivers that opened the area for settlement. The National Road, from Cumberland to the Ohio River, reached Wheeling in 1818. The Irish helped build this road and the Chesapeake and Ohio Canal, which paralleled the Potomac River, coming near Harpers Ferry in 1833. John Madden (born 1815 in County Galway) and Morris Hanifan (born 1820 in County Cavan) were among the hundreds of Irish immigrants on this canal project, living in hastily constructed shantytowns (Lambert 1:143). Madden and Hanifan both settled in Randolph County (Roaring Creek) in 1847.

The Staunton-Parkersburg Turnpike, completed in 1847, stretched 209 miles across Pocahontas, Randolph, Upshur, Lewis, Gilmer, Ritchie, and Wood counties. Patrick Flanigan and Patrick O'Connor, two early settlers in Randolph County, both worked on the turnpike (Bosworth 276–78). The Irish also built the Baltimore and Ohio Railroad, which ran from Baltimore to Grafton, then north to Wheeling and, as the Northwestern Virginia Railroad, west to Parkerburg, a feat requiring construction of twenty-three tunnels and several major bridges. Immigration agents helped import Irish laborers for the project, and more than 2,500 arrived in Cumberland, Maryland, during the winter of 1850–51 to join the experienced Irish already on the job (Dilts 359).

Irish communities developed along these roads and railroads, in such places as Huttonsville, Beverly, and Middlefork (Randolph County), Weston (Lewis County), Wheeling (Ohio County), and Parkersburg (Wood County). Donal O'Donovan's account of the Irish confirms the importance of the turnpike for Irish settlement: "In Upshur County, Irish settlements were es-

tablished in Kingsville, McDermot Settlement, Burks, Vegan, and later at Roaring Creek (Coalton). Kingsville received its name from the King family who originated in the Clifden area of County Galway, Ireland" (O'Donovan 5).

Irish immigration patterns suggest that many from the same community in Ireland elected to sail together or followed one another to new communities in America. In Randolph County, families named O'Connor, Riley, Gilhooley, Durkin, Burke, Conley, Corley, Crickard, Cunningham, Currence, Ferguson, and Joyce came from the counties of Mayo, Roscommon, Longford, and Galway. Most came seeking land which, in western Virginia, could be had for as little as $1.25 per acre in the 1850s (Bosworth 280).

The number of Irish-born settlers increased in the wake of the potato famine in Ireland, 1845–1850. Census data for Virginia (including western Virginia) show an increase of Irish-born from 11,643 in 1850 to 16,501 in 1860 (Blessing 291). The 1870 census for West Virginia, the first after statehood, reported 6,832 of Irish birth. Of the 53 counties, 11 had more than 200 Irish. Ohio County had 1,594; Wood County, 600. By 1880, Ohio County had 1,694 Irish immigrants.

### THE CATHOLIC CHURCH

Most of the Irish who came into western Virginia were Roman Catholic. Bishop Richard Vincent Whelan, who would become the first bishop in Wheeling, presided over the Diocese of Richmond when he toured western Virginia in 1841. In a letter to All Hallows Missionary College, Drumcondra, Dublin, he described his diocese: "The Catholics are very few, and generally very scattered, requiring one priest sometimes to attend a circuit of one hundred miles in diameter. The Western part of the state is quite unimproved—more so, perhaps, than many portions of the remote west—exceedingly mountainous, with bad roads and a very uncultivated population" (quoted in O'Donovan 21).

Wheeling, with the largest concentration of Irish in the state, erected the first Catholic church in 1821. In 1850 Pope Pius IX established the Diocese of Wheeling, with Bishop Whelan as its first bishop. The 13,000 residents of Wheeling in 1850 included 500 Irish Catholics (O'Donovan 28). The three parishes in the diocese were St. James's in Wheeling (now St. Joseph's Cathedral), St. Patrick's (Weston) and St. Mary's (Wytheville, Virginia).

John Monahan of Wheeling, born in County Mayo, was twenty years old when his crew closed the tracks between Baltimore and Wheeling on December 24, 1852, at Roseby's Rock, Marshall County, West Virginia. Like many Irishmen in America, he worked for the railroad most of his life.

The first three bishops had Irish roots: Richard Vincent Whelan (1850–74), John J. Kain (1875–93), and Patrick James Donahue (1894–1922). Many Irish also served as diocesan priests and members of religious communities.

The courage of the Wheeling Irish was tested on January 4, 1854, when Apostolic Nuncio Gaetano Bedini accepted Bishop Whelan's invitation to visit the city. A crowd of people, aroused by Know-Nothings, planned to attack the cathedral during Archbishop Bedini's sermon. Bishop Whelan warned the rioters against trespassing on cathedral property, a warning that was heeded when Irish Catholics with rifles surrounded the cathedral (Connelley 114–18).

During the nineteenth century, Catholic churches were built in most of the larger railroad and river towns, with mission outreach to smaller communities. In 1845, Fathers Austin Grogan and Charles Farrell arrived in the Northwestern Virginia Mission (nine counties of approximately 1,500 square miles). After Fr. Farrell's death in 1847, Fr. Grogan was responsible for the entire area. He established St. Patrick's Parish and supervised the building of the first Catholic Church in Weston in 1847–48. Smaller mission churches (St. Bernard's, St. Bridget's, and St. Michael's) were established in Sand Ford, Goosepen, and Fleshers Run in the 1870s. Baptismal records from St. Patrick's confirm the presence of significant numbers from the same parishes in Ireland: "Most of the Irish who settled in the Loveberry-Cove Lick area and the Murray Settlement section of Lewis County came in great part from the parishes of Killgaffin in County Roscommon and Kilahan and Cloonfinlough in County Galway. . . . In the Knawl Creek area of Braxton County, we find only County Donegal people among the Irish settlers" (O'Donovan 3–4). Parishioners included the Carneys, Greens, Griffins, Mahoneys, McDonalds, Morans, and Sweeneys.

The diocese grew after 1850 as the famine drove Irish to western Virginia and as laborers from elsewhere in Europe sought jobs there. Historian Barbara Howe summarizes this growth: "There were 48 churches, 7 chapels, and over 40 stations attended by 29 clergymen in 1875. The number of Catholic institutions had also increased dramatically in 24 years, as there were 6 academies for girls, 4 convents, 1 hospital, 1 college, and 1 orphan asylum to serve the approximately 18,000 Catholics in the diocese in 1875" (Howe, Caruso, and Floyd, "Rural Life"). By 1896 there were 72 churches with 24,000 parishioners.

## Employment Opportunities and Unionization

In addition to building roads and railroads, the Irish helped develop the oil and gas fields in Lewis, Monongalia, Marion, Doddridge, Wood, and Ritchie counties and worked in the lumber and coal industries across the state. Wherever they labored, they also built communities. Murphy's Mill (Murphytown), for example, is situated just west of the Volcano gas field (Allen, "Route 50 Towns"). Coalburg, in Kanawha County, became home to many Irish when William Henry Edwards opened his first mine in 1853 with John Burke as manager. According to the 1880 census, fifty-two Irish families lived there. The Good Shepherd Catholic Mission Church, built in 1866, was the first Catholic church in the Kanawha Valley. Beside the church, William Seymour Edward erected a large Celtic cross to honor the contributions which Irish workers had made to his and his father's mining operations. It casts shadows on graves with names like O'Gara, Layden, Farry, Burke, Quinn, McGinley, Sullivan, and Malone (Harrah 8).

Census statistics of nativity and occupations provide only a small window on the total Irish population in the state but do confirm general impressions. The Occupations Report from the 1900 census, for example, lists 6,735 Irish males (born in Ireland or son of a parent born there) in significant numbers in the following lines of employment: mines and quarries (520), steam railroad employees (556), laborers, unspecified (628), iron and steel workers (297), merchants and dealers (208), and oil wells (199).

While men helped to build the transportation systems and major industries in West Virginia, Irish women also played their parts, in their own homes and in the homes and businesses of others. Historian Barbara Howe's continuing research on employment for women is beginning to fill in the missing pieces. In the larger towns between 1860 and 1900, domestic service was the principal employment for younger women, sometimes as young as eleven years of age. As women matured, they secured positions as seamstresses, washwomen, mantua makers, housekeepers, and cooks (Howe, "Irish Wage-Earning"). A few became teachers or nurses. Some women, such as Mary Carroll of Guyandotte (Cabell County) and Ellen McAndrews of Clarksburg (Harrison County), ran boarding houses. McAndrews opened the business after her husband, Michael (County Mayo), was killed in the mines in 1868. Later she made clothing and quilts for a living (McAndrew 56). The 1,210 Irish-born women listed in the 1900 census were agricultural workers (119), teachers or professors (114), dressmakers (147), and domestic and personal service workers (385, of which 27 were boardinghouse keepers).

Probably the best-known Irish woman in West Virginia was not a permanent resident, though she came several times. Mary Harris "Mother" Jones (born 1830 in County Cork) first came in 1902, as the United Mine Workers of America sought to unionize the coal fields of the state. She returned for the Paint Creek-Cabin Creek strikes of 1912–13. Following several strike-related deaths, Jones was convicted and sentenced to twenty years in prison. Public pressure forced Governor Henry Hatfield to release her after 85 days and later to suspend the sentence of the 84-year-old woman.

The Irish were involved in the labor movement from the beginning, as they fought for better working conditions and higher wages. The Ohio Valley Trades and Labor Assembly, organized in 1885 to represent trades in the Wheeling area, included William O'Neill, John W. Donahue, Michael Mahoney, and John J. Byrne among the officers for 1901 and 1902. During the early decades of the twentieth century, leaders, both radical and conservative, of UMW Districts 17 and 29 were Irish (Carnes, Craigo, Dwyer, Keeney, Mooney, Gatens).

## Political Life

The political contributions of the Irish and Scots-Irish began before statehood. Colonel Andrew Donnally (from Northern Ireland), an early salt manufacturer, was the first state representative from Kanawha County after its formation in 1789. Among the men participating in the development of West Virginia's constitution in 1863 were E. W. Ryan (Fayette County) and John Hall (Mason County). Between 1866 and 1979, five Irishmen (Michael J. Reilly, T. S. Riley, John T. McGraw, Robert Kelly, and R. P. McDonough) served as Democratic Executive Committee chairmen. McDonough is said to have persuaded John F. Kennedy to enter the West Virginia primary in May 1960. This primary victory helped Kennedy secure the Democratic nomination and, so many believe, the White House. The tradition of Irish political leadership in West Virginia continued in 1996, when Thomas Patrick Maroney, a Charleston attorney, was named co-chairman of the Democratic Party.

The Irish are found at all levels of government, from county courthouse to state capitol. Governors had Irish roots: William Stevenson (1869–71), William MacCorkle (1893–1897), and Henry Hatfield (1913–1917). Thomas S. Riley of Wheeling was attorney general of West Virginia (1892 to 1896). Thomas O'Brien (1830–1909), a veteran of the Civil War, served as state treasurer from 1880 to 1884. Judge James B. Riley (1896–1958) served on the West Virginia Supreme Court of Appeals from 1936–1958, one of the longest terms in the state's history. William Gilligan, grandson of Patrick J. Gilligan of Wheeling (born 1848 in County Sligo), served as State Senator from Sistersville (1971–1982). Among the latest Irish descendants to serve the state are Darrell McGraw (West Virginia Supreme Court and later State Attorney General), Alan Mollohan (U.S. Congress), and John McCuskey (West Virginia Supreme Court).

## IRISH BUSINESSES

Around the state, Irish men and women have built successful businesses and contributed to the civic life of their communities. Michael Kelly established Kelly's Foundry (Kelly & Co.) in 1847 in Parkersburg. This business managed to thrive even during the Great Depression of the 1930s (Allen, "Influence"). John P. Keeley (born 1867) headed Keeley Construction in Clarksburg, one of the largest construction and contracting firms in West Virginia. His son continued the business, numbering among his projects the airport at Wheeling in 1946.

In Kanawha County at the turn of the century were a number of successful businessmen of Irish birth or descent. Among them were David Egan, a building contractor, born in 1836 in County Cork, and David Brawley, whose great-grandparents came from County Cork. Brawley ran a prosperous hardware business in Kanawha County and also served as county judge and county commissioner (Laidley 495, 535). Peter Carroll, whose father was born in County Kildare, ran Carroll Hard Wood Lumber Company in Charleston and became a director of Kanawha Banking and Trust Company (Laidley 615). Michael J. Owens (1859–1923), born in Mason County, the son of immigrant parents from County Wexford, invented the glass-bottle-blowing machine, which he patented in 1899. The factory he and his partner Edward Libbey built near Fairmont in 1909 could produce 600,000 bottles a year. In 1916 the partners formed Libbey-Owens Sheet Glass Company in the Kanawha City area of Charleston. It became the world's largest producer of window glass (Barkey 36).

Multimillionaire Bernard P. McDonough (1903–1985) was one of West Virginia's most successful businessmen. From his corporate headquarters in Parkersburg, he managed construction, concrete, and transportation businesses until he sold the McDonough Company, a Fortune 500 company, in 1980. In 1962 he purchased Dromoland Castle, near Shannon Airport, and over the next decade converted it into a luxury hotel. McDonough also owned three additional hotels in that area of Ireland.

## CULTURAL LIFE AND THE ARTS

Social life for the Irish in West Virginia was often associated with the Ancient Order of Hibernians. The first chapter in West Virginia was established in Parkersburg in 1876. Twenty years later, chapters were also found in Berkeley, Mineral, Taylor, Marion, Wetzel, Marshall, Ohio, Harrison, and Kanawha counties (Allen, "Historic Green Home"). In Coalburg (Kanawha County), the Hibernian Hall was built next to the church. The main floor had a kitchen and dining room for dinners; the second floor had a dance floor (Harrah 4). Clearly, such centers helped to keep alive the Irish cultural heritage of storytelling, song, and dance. Elsewhere in rural West Virginia the Celtic heritage continued to thrive on its own, passing informally from generation to generation to the present.

Storytellers, poets, and artists of Celtic ancestry have contributed to the cultural life of the state. Anna Egan Smucker, who grew up in the steel-mill town of Weirton, captured her experiences for children in *No Star Nights* (1989). Louise McNeill Pease (1911–1993), teacher, scholar, and poet, was born in Pocahontas County on land that had been in her family since 1769. In 1979 she was named Poet Laureate of West Virginia, and in 1985 she was honored as an Outstanding West Virginian. Her poems, inspired by West Virginia's history, can be found in *Gauley Mountain* (1939), *Elderberry Flood* (1977), and *Hill Daughter* (1991).

Among the visual artists of Irish descent are John J. Owens (1887–1931), Patrick Sullivan (1894–1967), and Frances Benjamin Johnston (1864–1952). Owens, a portrait painter from Wheeling, completed the portrait of Governor Henry Hatfield, which hangs in the capitol. Sullivan was an outstanding American Primitive painter and two of his paintings hang in the Museum of Modern Art in Washington, D.C. Johnston, born in Grafton (Taylor County), was a principal photographer during the presidencies of Grover Cleveland, William McKinley, and Theodore Roosevelt. Among those who sat for her were Mrs. Frances Cleveland and suffrage leader Susan B. Anthony (Shannon).

The story of the Irish in West Virginia is far from complete. Many second- and third-generation Irish have yet to be recognized for their achievements, and a few Irish continue to immigrate to West Virginia. According to census records for 1920, the total of native Irish was 1,459. The 1980 census lists 35 from Northern Ireland and 175 from Eire (Blessing 291–295). One of these recent immigrants came in 1955. After serving aboard great ocean liners, Francis J. Gallagher (born in County Donegal) arrived in West Virginia that year to join the staff at The Greenbrier, one of the great spa resorts. In 1956, he served in Dwight D. Eisenhower's suite during the North American Summit Conference. According to Gallagher, that experience ranks second only to a day in June 1957, when he became an American citizen. His sentiments echo those of the thousands of Irishmen and women who found their way to West Virginia: "I remember the Ireland of my boyhood, and always will, but these other green hills are my home now" (Gallagher 58–59).

*See* Coal Miners; Labor Movement

Bernard Allen, "Historic Green Home Major Part of Irish Influence in Parkersburg," *Parkersburg News*, 6 August 1989.

———, "Influence o' the Irish Continues in West Virginia," *Parkersburg News*, 16 July 1989.

———, "Route 50 Towns Rich with Irishmen," *Parkersburg News*, 20 August 1989.

Fred Barkey, "Mike Owens's Glass Company," *Goldenseal* 22 (Spring 1996): 35–37.

David A. Bice, *A Panorama of West Virginia* (Marceline, Mo., 1991).

Donovan H. Bond, *The Scots-Irish in the Virginias and the Carolinas* (Bruceton Mills, W.Va., 1996).

Patrick J. Blessing, *The Irish in America: A Guide to the Literature and the Manuscript Collections* (Washington, D.C., 1992).

A. S. Bosworth, *History of Randolph County West Virginia* (WV, 1975).

James Callahan, *History of West Virginia* (Chicago: American Historical Society, 1923).

J. F. Connelley, *The Visit of Archbishop Bedini to the United States of America* (Rome-Piazza Della Piotha, 1960).

James D. Dilts, *The Great Road: The Building of the Baltimore and Ohio, the Nation's First Railroad, 1828–1853* (Stanford, 1993).

Francis J. Gallagher, "Migrating to the Mountain State: An Irishman Comes to The Greenbrier," *Goldenseal* 19 (Fall 1993): 55–59.

Joyce Harrah, "Tracing Irish History through Coalburg, West Virginia," Unpublished essay, 1997.

Barbara Howe, "Irish Wage-Earning Women in West Virginia, 1860–1900," Unpublished research, 1997.

Barbara J. Howe, Camille Caruso, and Robin Floyd, "Rural Life in Central West Virginia: The Bulltown Country," Report prepared for U.S. Army Corps of Engineers, Huntington District, 1981.

W. S. Laidley, *History of Charleston and Kanawha County, West Virginia, and Representative Citizens* (Chicago, 1911).

Oscar Lambert, *West Virginia: Its People and Its Progress*, 3 vols. (Charleston: Historical Records Assoc., 1958).

Mike McAndrew, "Four Generations: An Irish Family in West Virginia," *Goldenseal* 14 (Fall 1988): 55–60.

Lois C. McLean, "Irish Mountain: The Story of a West Virginia Immigrant Community," *Goldenseal* 17 (Spring 1991): 47–56.

Donal O'Donovan, *The Rock from Which You Were Hewn* (Parsons, W.Va., 1989.)

Anna Shannon, "Frances Benjamin Johnston (1864–1952)," *Missing Chapters: West Virginia Women in History*. Edited by K. Frazier. (Charleston: West Virginia Women's Commission, 1983): 19–37.

Edward C. Smith, *A History of Lewis County, West Virginia* (Weston, 1920).

JOYCE EAST AND MARGARET BRENNAN

## WHELAN, MAURICE CHARLES (1741–1806)

Capuchin, first resident priest of the Archdiocese of New York; pioneer missionary in Kentucky. Born in 1741 in Ballycommon, Charles Whelan entered the Order of Capuchin Friars Minor in 1770 at which time he received the name Maurice. After his ordination he was named Novice Master and Provincial Secretary and came to the United States in 1780 with at least one other Capuchin as chaplain to the French troops on board the *Jason,* one of the ships sent by King Louis XVI to help the American Revolution. Whelan was present at the British surrender at Yorktown, October 1781. When the French fleet proceeded to the West Indies to engage the English, he was imprisoned with 7,000 Frenchmen on the island of Jamaica and remained there for thirteen months.

In 1784 Whelan made his way to New York, the temporary seat of the Government of the United States, where he began ministering to the city's 200 Catholics. His request for faculties was refused by Ferdinand Farmer, Vicar-General to the newly appointed Prefect Apostolic, John Carroll, because Farmer considered him an intruder. Whelan had recourse to the Papal Nuncio, Joseph Doria Pamfili, in Versailles. He was not only granted faculties but, at the urging of the French Consul in New York, Hector St. John de Crevecouer, was appointed pastor of the Catholics of New York. By that time, New York's Catholics had incorporated themselves according to the laws of New York State,

purchased property on Barclay Street, and had begun building the church of St. Peter. The following year, the parish trustees, influenced by the Protestant emphasis on preaching and weary of Whelan's poor sermons, turned their loyalty to another Capuchin, Andrew Nugent, a flamboyant preacher, and prevailed upon Carroll to name him Whelan's successor.

In 1786 Whelan made his way to visit his brother in Johnstown, NY, and was then sent by Carroll to the territory of Kentucky, where he ministered as its first priest until 1790. In a letter of August 1, 1788, to the Irish Provincial seemingly intent on recalling Whelan to Ireland, John Carroll wrote of his activities in Kentucky. "Not only has he kept alive the spirit of religion among the Catholics," he wrote, "but in addition he has gained a great increase for the Church of Jesus Christ, by converting numbers of different sectaries." Another bad experience with trustees, this time with those of his Kentucky church who reneged on paying for his upkeep, forced him to leave Kentucky. He then returned to Johnstown, NY, where he ministered to the needs of the Oneida Indians for an unknown period of time. In 1799 Whelan worked in Wilmington, Delaware, and, in the following year, in Coffee Run, New Castle Co., Delaware. Four years later a letter to Carroll indicates that he was ministering in White Clay Creek, Delaware. He died on March 21, 1806, in Bohemia Manor or Old Bohemia, Cecil Co., Maryland, where he is buried.

Stanislaus, O.F.M. Cap., "Two Irish Capuchin Pioneers: (1) Maurice Charles Whelan, O.F.M. Cap.: An Apostle in New York, U.S.A.," *Capuchin Annual* (1959): 140–150.

John M. Lenhart, "Contributions to the Life of Charles Whelan, O.F.M. Cap.," *American Historical Society of Philadelphia Records,* Vol. 37 (1926).

REGIS J. ARMSTRONG, O.F.M. CAP.

## WHELTON, DANIEL A. (1872–1953)

*See* Boston, Twelve Irish-American Mayors of

## WHITE, KEVIN H. (1929–  )

*See* Boston, Twelve Irish-American Mayors of

## WILDE, RICHARD HENRY (1789–1847)

Poet, politician. Born in Dublin, Ireland, Richard Henry Wilde came to America as a young boy. His father established a store in Baltimore, but upon his death in 1802, the family moved to Augusta, Georgia. Wilde worked briefly as a clerk, but soon began to study law. Admitted to the bar in 1809, the talented lawyer soon became a prominent political figure. He represented Georgia in Congress from 1815 to 1817, returning again in 1827. However, dissatisfaction with politics led Wilde to retire in 1835 in order to focus on his first love: writing. Wilde wrote poetry earlier in his life, with his piece, "My Life Is Like a Summer Rose," earning high praise from his contemporaries. Wilde traveled to Europe in 1835, settling in Florence where he undertook extensive studies of Italian literature and art. He returned to Augusta at the start of 1841. The following year, his book, *Conjectures and Researches Concerning the Love, Madness, and Imprisonment of Torquato Tasso,* was published, his only full-length work to appear during his lifetime. Although his writing received much favor, Wilde returned to his legal career to support his family. In

1843, he set up practice in New Orleans and in 1847 was appointed professor of constitutional law at the University of Louisiana (now Tulane University). His work was cut short in 1847, when Wilde fell victim to a yellow fever outbreak. Many of his works were later published posthumously by his son and others.

*Dictionary of American Biography*, Vol X, part I: 206–207.

Joel Myerson, ed., "Antebellum Writers in New York and the South," *Dictionary of Literary Biography* (Detroit, 1979): III: 372–73.

Edward L. Tucker, *Richard Henry Wilde: His Life and Selected Poems* (Athens, Ga., 1966).

TOM DOWNEY

## WILLIAMS, EDWARD BENNETT (1920–1988)

Lawyer and philanthropist. Edward Bennett Williams was born in Hartford, CT, on May 31, 1920, and died at the Georgetown University Medical Center in Washington, D.C., on August 13, 1988. The son of a Welsh father, Joseph Barnard Williams, and an Irish mother, Mary Bennett, he regarded himself as an Irish Catholic, as his name indicated. A graduate of Bulkeley High in his native city in 1937, he entered the College of the Holy Cross, one of the most prestigious of American institutions for Irish Catholics, and graduated with distinction in 1941.

After serving in the Army Air Force for two years (1941–43), Williams earned a degree from Georgetown University Law School in 1945 in Washington, D.C., where the Irish were not handicapped by the prejudices that confronted them in Yankee New England. Williams, however, had such talent that he would have been a successful trial lawyer in any part of the nation.

Though his law career began with the Washington firm of Hogan and Hartson, Williams entered into partnership with Paul R. Connolly in a law firm that grew to more than a hundred lawyers by the time of his death. Despite his enemies, Williams emerged as one of the few exceptional lawyers in the United States because of his brilliant defense of the constitutional rights of such controversial figures as Polly Adler, Bobby Baker, Dave Beck, John B. Connally, Frank Costello, Bernard Goldfine, Jimmy Hoffa, Joseph R. McCarthy, Victor Posner, Adam Clayton Powell, and Robert Vesco.

### Influential American

Williams was also a national figure in sports and politics in addition to law. In professional sports, he was highly regarded as part owner of the Washington Redskins, the football team, and as owner of the Baltimore Orioles, the baseball team. Though his politics had shifted from Democratic to Republican in 1948, Williams had returned to the Democratic Party by 1964 and, in the words of one biographer, became "the man to see" in Washington. At the same time, he had access to every American President from John F. Kennedy to Ronald Reagan and accepted minor appointments from some and refused major ones from others.

Living a very active life, which brought him even into the lecture halls of prominent universities, Williams was at Mass daily whether he was at home or on the road. A leader of the Knights of Malta in the United States, he provided for such charities as the work of Mother Teresa of Calcutta. He was survived by his second wife, three daughters, and four sons. His funeral was at St. Matthew's Cathedral in Washington, D.C., and he was interred in St. Gabriel's Cemetery in Potomac, MD. The memory of Edward Bennett Williams lives on in the faculty fellowships at

Edward Bennett Williams

the College of the Holy Cross, in the law library named after him at Georgetown, and in many of his other good deeds.

Joseph A. Califano, Jr., et al., "IN MEMORIAM," *Georgetown Law Review*, 77 (October 1988): 1–17.

Colin Evans, *Super Lawyers* (Detroit, 1998).

Robert Pack, *Edward Bennett Williams for the Defense* (New York, 1983).

Evan Thomas, *The Man to See* (New York, 1991).

Edward Bennett Williams, *One Man's Freedom* (New York, 1962).

VINCENT A. LAPOMARDA, S.J.

## WINCH, TERENCE (1945– )

Poet, musician and Head of Publications, National Museum of the American Indian, Smithsonian Institution. Winch was born in New York; his mother was Bridie Flynn from Cahercrea, outside Loughrea in County Galway. Winch's father, Paddy Winch, was the son of a German father and an Irish mother, Margaret Guthrie from County Clare. His parents met in New York in the 1920s and married in 1930. His father played the tenor banjo and encouraged any interest by his children in Irish culture.

Terence Winch is a performer and composer with Celtic Thunder, a traditional Irish group. He has published three albums with this band. *The Light of Other Days* (1989) won the INDIE award for best Celtic album, and his most recent recording is *Hard New York Days* (1995). Winch has published many books of poetry of which perhaps the best known is *Irish Musicians/American Friends* (1986). *Irish Musicians* was separately published some years before and is a wonderful and realistic poetry miscellany of friends of his father who were bohemian musicians of the Irish sub-culture in New York before WWII. In poems like "The Irish Riviera" Winch explores with gusto and subtlety the epic quality of such obscure figures. The special quality in this volume is a profound if flip-seeming humor and irreverence, which is partly inherited. Winch's father and his friends were as important to his art as a similar milieu was to James Joyce. Winch's later poetry becomes more complex and contemporary. He adopts at times a version of surrealism for a major style, a language both enticing and chilly but which preserves a native zest and provocation. His work combines insights into ancestral Irish culture

Terence Winch

and the popular culture of the last 30 years. Important volumes are *The Great Indoors* (1995) and *Rooms* (1992). Winch's imaginative arrangements are diverse; he can write arresting prose poems like those in *Total Strangers* (1981) and gritty fiction like *Contenders* (1989). The breath of his achievement, inside and outside the Irish-American community, can be suggested by the anthologies in which his work has been published. In another context, his standing in American literary culture is emphasized by the list of magazines in which individual poems have appeared: *The Paris Review, The New Republic, The American Poetry Review, The Brooklyn Review* and others.

Winch has done considerable radio and television work, including interviews with front-ranking Irish poets, and has been on "All Things Considered," National Public Radio, for St. Patrick's Day 1986. He has received honors and awards, notably a Maryland State Arts Council grant in 1997 and NEA creative writing fellowship in 1992. His education was all in New York: an M.A. from Fordham University and a B.A. from Iona College.

Terence Winch, *Irish Musicians/American Friends* (Minneapolis 1986).
———, *Contenders* (Oregon, 1989).
———, *The Great Indoors* (Oregon, 1995).
———, *The Light of Other Days* (album with Green Linnet, 1989).

JAMES LIDDY

# WISCONSIN

## EARLY HISTORY

Ireland's ties to Wisconsin began in the early eighteenth century when three European powers sought to colonize the Great Lakes region. The first Irishman associated with what later became the state of Wisconsin was Sir William Johnson, a native of Ireland, prominent fur trader, and Indian agent for the British who was active in the area in 1715. Later a French settlement was established at Green Bay that, during the period 1763–74, contained such Irish surnames as O'Callaghan, Sullivan, Farley, Moran, Fitzpatrick, Riley, Boyle, Dunlavy, and Shields. In 1769 the governor of Louisiana, Don Alexander O'Reilly, asserted claims on behalf of Spain to the territory now encompassing Wisconsin. Some of these early colonial functionaries appear to have been

descendants of the famed "Wild Geese" who left Ireland after the Treaty of Limerick in 1691 (Scanlan 1914, 240–43). However, they represented a relatively isolated and sporadic presence in Wisconsin as the influence of the various European powers waxed and waned in the Upper Midwest. It was not until the following century that significant numbers of Irish immigrants began to settle permanently in Wisconsin.

## SETTLEMENT PATTERN

The first Irish ethnic settlements in the future state were established in the 1820s in the lead-mining region in the southwestern corner of Wisconsin (McDonald 1954, 40–48). Large-scale European settlement of Wisconsin became possible after the conclusion of the Black Hawk War in 1832 and the advent of public land sales by the federal government in 1834. A trickle of Irish immigrants began to enter Wisconsin Territory in the 1830s, and that trickle developed into a steady stream in the 1840s as a result of the Great Famine in Ireland (1845–50). The Irish were "stage" immigrants; rather than coming directly to Wisconsin from Ireland, they tended to work their way west in stages, spending an average of seven years in eastern states before arriving in Wisconsin (Ibid. 10–12). The highwater mark of Irish settlement in the state occurred in 1860 when the census enumerated 50,000 Irish-born residents in Wisconsin (Ibid. 8). The Irish constituted 6.4% of the state's population in that census and represented the second largest foreign-born ethnic group (after 124,000 Germans) in Wisconsin. Nonetheless, by 1860, the Irish were already in decline as a proportion of the state's overall population, having fallen from 6.9% of the total state population in the 1850 census. By 1900 the Irish-born percentage of Wisconsin's population had dropped to a meager 1%, but this figure did not include second- and third-generation Irish-Americans (Rippley 1985, 43). The most recent federal census measured ancestry rather than foreign birth. According to the 1990 census, 656,000 Wisconsinites or 13.4% of the total state population claimed Irish (including 43,000 or 0.9% Scotch-Irish) ancestry.

The settlement pattern of the Wisconsin Irish largely determined the character of their immigrant experience in the state. There was never a large cohesive Irish community in Wisconsin as there was in New York, Boston, and Chicago. Rather, the Wisconsin Irish clustered together in widely dispersed rural communities scattered throughout the state. Of the 50,000 Irish-born residents of Wisconsin in 1860, 81% resided in rural areas of the state and 58% of the Irish-born adult males listed their occupation as farmer or farm laborer (McDonald 1954, 121–22). The 1860 census enumerated Irish-born residents in every county in Wisconsin where they tended to assimilate (by marriage to non-Irish) into the American mainstream more rapidly than other ethnic groups in the state (Lewis 1978, 178). Since the Irish never constituted a major segment of the state's population, they lacked the numerical strength to monopolize the political machinery of the Democratic party or the ecclesiastical hierarchy of the Catholic Church as was the case in other states. Their geographical dispersion prevented even a regional dominance. Failing to control institutional structures or establish a regional power base, the Wisconsin Irish were nevertheless able to make valuable contributions to the development of the state and nation. These contributions, however, tended for the most part to be made on an individual basis rather than as the product of an organized ethnic bloc or transcending community ethos.

## TOPONYMY

Irish immigrants were in the vanguard of non-native settlers in mid-century Wisconsin. Consequently, they had a significant impact on the developing toponymy of the new state. Pioneer settlements began to spring up alongside ancient landforms bearing such Hibernian names as Druid Lake in the town of Erin (Washington County), Erin Corner and Erin Prairie (St. Croix County), Irish Creek (Dodge County), Irish Diggings (Lafayette County), Irish Hollow (Iowa County), Irish Ridge (Crawford, Grant, and Vernon counties), Irish Road (Calumet County), Irish Settlement (Outagamie County), Irish Valley (Buffalo and Monroe counties), and Mackville (Outagamie County). In a number of instances, Irish immigrants named their new communities after their native places in Ireland: Askeaton (Brown County), Ashford (Fond du Lac County), Avoca (Iowa County), Bangor (La Crosse County), Dublin (Iowa County) and New Dublin (Ozaukee County), Glenmore (Brown County), Kildare (Juneau County), Newport (Columbia County), Newry (Vernon County), Sligo (Sauk County), Tory Hill (Milwaukee County), Waterford (Racine County), and Westport (Dane County). Another group of toponyms included places named after patriotic or prominent Irishmen: Burke (Dane County), Emmett (Dodge and Marathon counties), Mitchell (Sheboygan County), O'Connellsville (Waukesha County), and St. Kilian (Fond du Lac County) (Robinson and Culver 1974).

Other communities were named after prominent Irish-Americans. Sheridan (Waupaca County) is derived from General Phillip H. Sheridan (1831–88), a Civil War hero and son of immigrants from Killinkere, County Cavan. Shields (Dodge County) was named in honor of General James Shields (1806–79), a native of Altmore, County Tyrone, who was elected to the United States Senate from three different states. The largest category of place-names influenced by the Irish settlement of Wisconsin involved places named after early Irish settlers who themselves became prominent in their new state. Representative of this category are Fitzgerald Station (Winnebago County), derived from William Fitzgerald (1792–1873), a pioneer Wisconsin settler who was born in Drinane, County Cork; and Jennings (Oneida County), named after Thomas Jennings (1839–1934), a son of immigrants from County Mayo, who built a successful lumber business in northern Wisconsin. Of course, most Irish immigrants clustered in rural communities that did not bear Irish names. Among the more homogeneous, high-density Irish settlements in Wisconsin were Poygan (Winnebago County), Clyman (Dodge County), Granville (Milwaukee County), and Maple Grove (Manitowoc County). Even today these places contain Roman Catholic cemeteries in which nearly every gravestone preserves an Irish surname.

## THE IRISH REGIMENT

One of the distinctive features of the American Civil War was the recruitment of ethnic regiments. Wisconsin designated the 17th Infantry as its Irish Regiment under the command of Colonel John L. Doran, a prominent Milwaukee lawyer, Democratic state legislator, and native of Ireland. Colonel Adam G. Malloy succeeded Doran in November 1862 with Lieutenant Colonel Thomas McMahon second in command. Recruited in part from pre-war Irish militia units in the state, the Irish Regiment included companies named the Mulligan Guards, Corcoran Guards, Emmett Guards, and Peep O'Day Boys (McDonald 1954, 141).

The regimental flag, restored in 1989 and currently displayed at the Wisconsin Veterans Museum in Madison, contains the Irish military motto, *Faug a Balac,* "Clear the Way!" The emerald green flag has a traditional gold harp in the center with a sunburst above and a wreath of shamrocks below. The reverse side of the flag is identical except that the motto is *Erin go Bragh,* "Ireland Forever." The regiment was cited for valor at the battle of Corinth (October 1862). The regiment's political proclivities were revealed by the fact that it was the only one of Wisconsin's fifty-two military regiments to vote Democratic in the wartime elections (Current 1976, 364). The Irish Regiment had a cultural impact beyond its military mission in that it "served to stimulate a group consciousness among the Irishmen of the state which was not existent prior to this time" (McDonald 1954, 142).

Of course, not all Wisconsin soldiers who served in the 17th Infantry were Irish, nor did all the Irish who served in the Civil War enlist in the 17th. Among other Wisconsin Irish soldiers who made a mark in the Civil War was James P. Sullivan, son of Irish immigrants and a sergeant in the 6th Infantry, who compiled an important first-hand memoir of Wisconsin's famed Iron Brigade (Beaudot and Herdegen 1993). Three Wisconsin Irishmen won the Congressional Medal of Honor, the nation's highest decoration for heroism, for their service in the Civil War: Dennis J. F. Murphy, native of Cork and color sergeant of the 14th Wisconsin Infantry; Albert O'Connor, sergeant in the 7th Wisconsin Infantry; and Thomas Toohey, sergeant in the 24th Wisconsin Infantry. The Civil War provided the Irish in Wisconsin and elsewhere an opportunity to overcome nativist prejudice by "proving" their American patriotism.

## POLITICS AND GOVERNMENT

Irish influence in Wisconsin politics was demonstrated early in territorial days when Charles Dunn (1799–1872) was appointed first Chief Justice (1836–48) of the Wisconsin Territorial Supreme Court by President Andrew Jackson. Chief Justice Dunn, after whom Dunn County is named, was the son of an Irish immigrant from Dublin. His brother, Francis J. Dunn, was Secretary of Wisconsin Territory in 1841. Irish and Irish-Americans also made a strong showing in the first territorial elections, those held to name delegates to the First Constitutional Convention (1846) and Second Constitutional Convention (1847–48). Eleven of the 175 delegates to these two assemblies were born in Ireland: Henry S. Baird (Dublin), John L. Doran, James Fagan (County Westmeath), Garrett M. Fitzgerald (Killarney, County Kerry), William H. Fox (County Westmeath), Wallace Graham (Crageycroy, County Antrim), David Harkin, Patrick Petroney (Dunover, County Meath), Patrick Rogan (Rossglass, County Down), Edward G. Ryan (Endfield, County Meath), and Patrick Toland (County Tyrone). Another dozen delegates were of Irish ancestry (Quaife 1919, 756–800; Quaife 1928, 900–33). Thomas M. McHugh of Mohill, County Leitrim, was elected secretary of the latter convention. In the following year, McHugh was elected Wisconsin's first Secretary of State.

The Wisconsin Irish seized the opportunity to demonstrate their political muscle in the 1852 state legislature, one of the few controlled by the Democrats, when they secured passage of a resolution expressing sympathy for imprisoned Irish patriots (John Mitchell, Smith O'Brien, and Thomas Francis Meagher) and urging the president to force Britain to release the prisoners so they could emigrate to America (Burton 1988, 20). The early political success of the Irish, however, was not without opposition from other ethnic groups and the Know-Nothing element. For example, the *Wisconsin Demokrat,* a German newspaper in Manitowoc, editorialized in 1854: "[W]e are for liberty, and against union with Irishmen who stand nearer barbarism and brutality than civilization and humanity. The Irish are our natural enemies, not because they are Irishmen, but because they are the truest guards of Popery" (Rippley 1978, 30).

Irish immigrants benefitted greatly by their ability to speak English, their experience of mass democratic political organization stemming from Daniel O'Connell's successful campaign for Catholic emancipation in Ireland in 1829, and their involvement in American politics prior to settlement in Wisconsin. Moreover, the Wisconsin Irish enhanced their political clout by voting as a solid bloc for the Democrats. In fact, it has been asserted by one modern historian that the Democratic party in Wisconsin was held hostage to the Irish vote in the state (Burton 1988, 20). Consequently, the Irish exercised a disproportionate influence because of their skillful exploitation of the political process. A case in point is the career of Edward O'Neill, a native of Burnchurch, County Kilkenny. O'Neill, a Democrat, was elected to four terms as mayor of Milwaukee in the 1860s, a time when the Irish comprised less than seven percent of the city's population.

Although the Irish declined proportionately as a factor in Wisconsin's electoral base throughout the late nineteenth and twentieth centuries, they nevertheless continued to play a prominent role in the state's politics—especially those of the Democratic party. For example, in 1932 half of the state's congressional delegation was Democratic and all of the latter were of Irish ancestry: Senator F. Ryan Duffy and Representatives Charles W. Henney, Raymond J. Cannon, Thomas D. P. O'Malley, Michael K. Reilly, and James F. Hughes. Another period of Irish dominance occurred after World War II when a group of Irish-Americans virtually took over the leadership of the state Democratic party. This group was led by Patrick J. Lucey and included Robert E. Tehan, John W. Reynolds, and James E. Doyle (Cannon 1992– ). Throughout the past century and a half individual Irish and Irish-Americans have achieved great success in Wisconsin politics.

Three men of Irish ancestry have been elected governor of Wisconsin. Francis E. McGovern, a Progressive, served two terms (1911–15). His administrations enacted the most far-reaching social legislation in the state's history. McGovern's father was a native of Newport, County Mayo; his mother was born in Tralee, County Kerry. McGovern worked closely with Charles McCarthy (1873–1921), the renowned reformer who developed the Wisconsin Idea and the Legislative Reference Bureau. John W. Reynolds, a Democrat, held the gubernatorial chair for a single term (1963–65) before moving on to become chief judge of the federal district court in Milwaukee. His grandfather, Thomas Reynolds, emigrated to Wisconsin from Killasona, County Longford. Patrick J. Lucey, another Democrat, was elected governor of Wisconsin for two terms (1970–77) before resigning to accept an appointment as United States Ambassador to Mexico. His great-grandfather, also Patrick Lucey, was a native of County Cork (Cannon 1992– ).

Three United States senators of Irish ancestry were Wisconsin natives. The first of these, Thomas J. Walsh, was born in Two Rivers, Manitowoc County, and graduated from the University of Wisconsin Law School. He later moved out west where he won election to four terms as a Progressive senator from Montana (1913–33) before being nominated as Attorney General of the

United States. Walsh's father was born in County Armagh; his mother was a native of County Mayo. F. Ryan Duffy, Democrat from Fond du Lac, was elected senator for one term (1933–39) and thereafter became chief judge of the United States Court of Appeals in Chicago. His father was a native of Castleblaney, County Monaghan. Joseph R. McCarthy of Grand Chute, Outagamie County, served two terms in the Senate (1947–57). He dominated, and in fact came to personify, the regressive politics of the 1950s to such an extent that he was deemed by many as more powerful than the president. McCarthy was censured by the Senate in 1954 for abuse of congressional power. His grandfather, Stephen McCarthy, was born in County Tipperary.

Perhaps the most distinguished government career belongs to Admiral William D. Leahy (1875–1959). The grandson of immigrants from Galway, Leahy grew up in Wausau and Ashland. He served as Chief of Naval Operations, governor of Puerto Rico, ambassador to France, and chief of staff to presidents Roosevelt and Truman. Another key diplomat during and after World War II was Robert D. Murphy (1894–1978) of Milwaukee. Murphy, grandson of an Irish immigrant, served as President Roosevelt's secret personal envoy in North Africa and Europe during the war. Thereafter, he was appointed by President Truman as ambassador to Belgium and to Japan. President Ford named Murphy chairman of the Foreign Intelligence Advisory Board in 1976. Leo T. Crowley (1889–1972) of Milton Junction served as an important New Deal administrator. President Roosevelt appointed him chairman of the Federal Deposit Insurance Corporation where he helped restore confidence in the nation's banking system during the depths of the Depression. During World War II Crowley served as head of the Office of Economic Warfare where, among other tasks, he ran the crucial lend-lease program. Crowley's father was born in County Clare and emigrated to Wisconsin as a child. Another important political figure was Maud Leonard McCreery (1883–1938), native of Cedarburg and granddaughter of Irish immigrants. McCreery was a prominent reformer and leader of the women's suffrage movement whose work helped secure the right to vote in 1920.

## The Church

Irish immigrants brought their Roman Catholicism with them to Wisconsin. Of the three hundred eighty-two Catholic parishes established in the state during the nineteenth century, one hundred thirteen (30% of the total) were of Irish origin (Rummel 1976, 125). The cult of Irish saints was an important part of the immigrants' religious heritage as shown by church dedications: St. Patrick (thirty-nine), St. Brigid (six), St. Kilian (six), St. Columba (two), and Saints Brendan, Finbar, Gall, Kevin, Lawrence O'Toole, Malachy, and Wendel (one each) (Heming 1896). St. Patrick's Church in Walker's Point on Milwaukee's south side contains one of the finest collections of stained-glass windows in the Midwest and is on the National Register of Historic Places. It was founded in 1876 by Father John Vahey, a native of County Mayo.

Father Patrick O'Kelley, a native of Birchfield, County Kilkenny, was the first resident pastor (1839–42) in Milwaukee. Despite this fact, the hierarchy of the Archdiocese of Milwaukee remained under the firm control of German prelates throughout the nineteenth century. The first four archbishops (Henni, Heiss, Katzer, Messmer) were German-speaking, European-born prelates. Their failure to promote Irish priests, and claims of anti-Irish bias at the archdiocesan seminary, were causes of ethnic tension in the Church (Blied 1955, 37–39). This conflict was ameliorated in the present century with the appointment of three Irish-Americans as archbishops of Milwaukee: Samuel A. Stritch (1930–39) whose father was born in Ireland; Moses E. Kiley (1940–53), grandson of immigrants from Waterford and Wexford; and William E. Cousins (1958–77). In addition, Alexander J. McGavick (1921–46), John Patrick Treacy (1946–64), and Raymond L. Burke (1995–  ) were named bishops of La Crosse; William Griffin served as auxiliary bishop of La Crosse (1935–44); William Patrick O'Connor (1945–67) and Cletus F. O'Donnell (1967–92) headed the diocese of Madison. O'Connor served previously as bishop of Superior (1942–45).

The Irish have also been prominent in other spheres of the Church in Wisconsin. Mother Emily Power (1844–1909) was born in Barrettstown, Tramore, County Waterford. She was the head of the Sinsinawa Dominican order, a predominantly Irish community, for more than forty years and established numerous schools and colleges throughout the country. Father Solanus Casey (1870–1957) was a Capuchin friar born in Prescott, Pierce County. In 1995 he was declared "Venerable" by Pope John Paul II, the first step on the road to canonization in the Church. His father was born in Castleblaney, County Monaghan; his mother came from Camlough, County Armagh. Humphrey J. Desmond (1858–1932) was a nationally recognized Catholic journalist, lawyer, and historian in Milwaukee. He was editor of the *Catholic Citizen* for more than fifty years. His grandfather was a native of Gurteen, Bandon, County Cork. Michael Denis Cullen is a prominent Catholic social activist, founder of Casa Maria House of Hospitality in Milwaukee, and member of the Milwaukee 14 who was deported to his native Ireland for destruction of military draft records during the Vietnam War. Cullen was born in Ashford, County Wicklow.

## LAW

The judicial branch of government in Wisconsin has been headed by several chief justices of Irish birth or ancestry. In addition to Chief Justice Dunn mentioned previously, Edward G. Ryan, a native of Endfield, County Meath, served as chief justice 1874–1880. His maternal grandfather was John Keogh (1740–1817), head of the Catholic Committee, the first civil rights organization in Ireland. Keogh was responsible for winning the Catholic Relief Act of 1793, the earliest relaxation of the penal laws. Chief Justice Ryan is considered by most legal scholars as the greatest jurist ever to sit on the Wisconsin Supreme Court. He was known nationally as a strong foe of corporations, railroads, and lumber barons during his tenure on the court. John E. Martin, a popular figure with voters, was elected to five terms as attorney general of Wisconsin before being elevated to the Supreme Court where he served as chief justice from 1957 to 1962. Martin was the grandson of Irish immigrants. Nathan S. Heffernan, chief justice 1983–1995, was a highly regarded and scholarly jurist whose great-grandfather, Maurice Heffernan, was born in County Tipperary. Two grandsons of Irish immigrants to Wisconsin, Richard D. Cudahy and John L. Coffey, currently sit as judges on the United States Court of Appeals. Raymond J. Cannon (1890–1951), Milwaukee lawyer and great-grandson of immigrants from Rosbeg, County Donegal, established a world record by winning one hundred consecutive jury trials between 1918 and 1920. Recognized as one of America's premier trial attorneys, Cannon was hailed as a champion of the poor throughout his legal and congressional career.

## EDUCATION

Toward the end of the nineteenth century there was a large exodus of the grandchildren of the early Irish immigrants off the farms and into the urban areas of Wisconsin (Lewis 1978, 178; Holmes 1944, 179–80). This transition was fueled in part by the availability of higher education at such institutions as the University of Wisconsin (founded 1848) and Marquette University (founded 1881). As a Catholic institution, Marquette held a particular appeal for Irish-Americans, enhanced no doubt by the fact that most of its Jesuit presidents were themselves of Irish ancestry: Fathers Thomas S. Fitzgerald (1884–87), James McCabe (1908–11), Herbert C. Noonan (1915–22), William M. Magee (1928–36), Raphael C. McCarthy (1936–44), Edward J. O'Donnell (1948–62), and William F. Kelley (1962–65). Robert M. O'Neil, the great-grandson of Irish immigrants, served as president of the University of Wisconsin (1980–85).

The state's two major universities were early leaders in the field of Irish studies. In 1937 the Wisconsin legislature established a chair of Gaelic and Irish History and Literature at the University of Wisconsin. Professor Myles Dillon of Dublin, noted Celtic scholar and scion of a prominent political family in Ireland, was appointed to the chair (1937–46). He assembled an important collection of Irish manuscripts and books for the university's library (Buttimer 1989, 1–15). Professor James S. Donnelly, Jr., a historian of popular culture in nineteenth-century Ireland, is currently on the faculty. Marquette University has had a number of notable Irish historians on its faculty, including Lawrence J. McCaffrey, an authority on the Irish in America, and Thomas E. Hachey, who has written widely on modern Irish politics. Professors Janet and Gareth Dunleavy, a pair of distinguished scholars, were long-time faculty members at the University of Wisconsin-Milwaukee. The Dunleavys edited the O'Conor Don family papers and wrote a biography of Douglas Hyde. Sister Grace McDonald, historian and later president of Viterbo College in La Crosse, wrote *History of the Irish in Wisconsin in the Nineteenth Century*, a seminal study of Irish settlement in rural America.

## ARTS, SCIENCE, AND LETTERS

The Wisconsin Irish have made important contributions to arts, science, and letters. Georgia O'Keeffe (1887–1996) of Sun Prairie was America's preeminent modern painter. Her landscapes, skyscapes, barns, and flowers exhibit a profound link to the nature she encountered growing up on her parents' Wisconsin farm. O'Keeffe's paternal grandparents were born in counties Cork and Kilkenny. Actor Spencer Tracy (1900–67) of Milwaukee was voted by Hollywood movie professionals as the number one actor in sound picture history. He won consecutive Oscar awards as best actor in 1937 and 1938. His grandfather was born in Tynagh parish, County Galway, and his grandmother was born into an Irish-speaking family from Ballyferriter, County Kerry. Tracy's Marquette Academy classmate, Pat O'Brien (1899–1983), was widely loved for his roles as Irish-American priest, policeman, and politician. O'Brien's grandparents were natives of counties Cork and Galway. Movies starring O'Brien and Tracy were influential in promoting the social acceptance of Irish Catholics in America. In 1981 Edward J. Ward, whose grandfather came from County Meath, founded Milwaukee's Irish Fest—the largest Irish music festival in the world. Irish Fest draws more than 100,000 people annually to what the Smithsonian Institution has rated as America's best ethnic celebration.

In the field of science, William P. Murphy (1892–1987), a native of Stoughton, Dane County, was awarded the Nobel Prize for medicine in 1934 in recognition of his discoveries concerning the treatment of anemia. Dr. John B. Murphy (1857–1916) of Appleton was a brilliant surgeon who won international acclaim for his pioneering treatment of appendicitis and pulmonary tuberculosis. His father was born in County Limerick; his mother came from County Clare. Jessica Powers (1905–1988), a Carmelite nun from Lemonweir, Juneau County, was one of the leading poets of the Catholic intellectual revival in the 1920s. Her grandparents emigrated to Wisconsin from Kill parish, County Waterford. Horace Gregory (1898–1982) of Milwaukee was another widely acclaimed poet who won the Bollingen Prize in 1965. His paternal grandfather was born in Listowel, County Kerry. Walter W. "Red" Smith (1905–82) of Green Bay was awarded a Pulitzer Prize in 1976 for distinguished commentary for his sports columns in the *New York Times*.

## BUSINESS

The Wisconsin Irish achieved great success in business, for the most part as the gradual result of education and assimilation. Thomas G. Shaughnessy (1853–1923) of Milwaukee became head of the world's largest transportation system as president of the Canadian Pacific Railroad and its shipping line. Shaughnessy was knighted by Queen Victoria and created a baron by King George V. Shaughnessy's parents came from Ashford, County Limerick, and Killarney, County Kerry. Patrick Cudahy (1849–1916), a native of Callan, County Kilkenny, amassed a fortune as the founder of Cudahy Brothers Company, a Milwaukee firm that pioneered the use of refrigerated storage to become one of the nation's largest meatpackers. His grandson, Michael J. Cudahy of Milwaukee, has built Marquette Electronics into one of the world's leading manufacturers of sophisticated medical technology. James F. Fitzgerald of Janesville was one of Wisconsin's best-known businessmen as president and owner of the Milwaukee Bucks franchise in the National Basketball Association, 1976–85. Northwestern Mutual Life Insurance Company, one of the nation's largest insurers, was headed by Michael J. Cleary (1876–1947), the son of immigrants from Coolaney, County Sligo, and from County Wicklow. His successor was Edmund Fitzgerald (1895–1986) of Milwaukee, scion of a family famous for its Great Lakes ship captains. Fitzgerald's name became known around the world in 1975 when his namesake, the *Edmund Fitzgerald*, a 730-foot freighter, sank suddenly in Lake Superior with all hands on board. Catherine B. Cleary, daughter of Michael, achieved prominence as president of First Wisconsin Trust Company. She was a pioneer woman in the boardrooms of corporate America, being the first woman to serve as a director of such business giants as General Motors, American Telephone & Telegraph, Kraft Foods, and as a trustee of the University of Notre Dame.

## SPORTS

Athletic contests have played an important role in the assimilation of Irish-Americans as sports evolved from recreational pastime into a major segment of the entertainment industry. The Irish in Wisconsin have produced many outstanding athletes and coaches including the following inductees in the Wisconsin Sports Hall of Fame in Milwaukee: Terry Brennan, star halfback of Notre Dame's national championship football teams (1946–47) and later head coach of the Fighting Irish; "Sleepy Jim" Crowley, All-American halfback in football's most famous backfield, the "Four Horsemen" of Notre Dame; Joseph "Red" Dunn, All-

American quarterback on Marquette University's undefeated football teams (1922–23) and star of the Green Bay Packers world championship teams (1929–30–31); Conrad M. Jennings, long-time athletic director and head track coach at Marquette University; George McBride, shortstop with the Washington Senators and later manager of the Pittsburgh Pirates and St. Louis Cardinals; Al McGuire, coach of Marquette University's national championship basketball team (1977) and popular sports commentator for NBC and CBS television; John "Blood" McNally, halfback for the Green Bay Packers world championship football teams and member of the Pro Football Hall of Fame; Frank Murray, successful head coach of Marquette University's "Golden Avalanche" football teams; Pat O'Dea, greatest kicker in the history of college football while a member of the University of Wisconsin team and holder of the college field goal record (62 yards); John "Big Train" Sisk, All-American halfback at Marquette University, world record holder in the 40- and 50-yard dashes, and halfback on the Chicago Bears world championship teams (1932–33); and William "Billy" Sullivan, standout catcher for the Chicago Cubs.

## WISCONSIN AND IRELAND

Despite a distance of four thousand miles, Wisconsin and Ireland have continued to maintain close ties. In addition to private family remittances, the Wisconsin Irish raised funds for a variety of causes, including Daniel O'Connell's Irish Repeal Association, famine relief projects, the Irish Land League, Friends of Irish Freedom, and more recently, such organizations as the American Ireland Fund and Irish Northern Aid. In return, many prominent Irish figures have visited Wisconsin: Thomas Francis Meagher in 1857, Jeremiah O'Donovan Rossa in 1875, Charles Stewart Parnell in 1880, Michael Davitt in 1880 and 1886, Douglas Hyde in 1906, and Eamon de Valera in 1919. Jeremiah Curtin (1835–1906) of Greenfield, a renowned linguist who spoke seventy languages, made several visits to Ireland to collect and publish four important volumes of Irish folklore. His father came from Bruree, County Limerick; his mother was born in Buttevant, County Cork. Thomas G. Shaughnessy was offered (but declined) the post of Lord Lieutenant of Ireland. The appointment of Shaughnessy would have made the Wisconsin-born peer the most powerful man in Ireland. John C. Cudahy (1887–1943) of Milwaukee served as United States Minister to Ireland (1937–39) in the critical years leading up to World War II. Cudahy's diplomatic appointment to his father's native land was of great symbolic importance in bringing the story of the Wisconsin Irish full circle.

William J. K. Beaudot and Lance J. Herdegen, *An Irishman in the Iron Brigade: The Civil War Memoirs of James P. Sullivan* (New York, 1993).

Benjamin J. Blied, *Three Archbishops of Milwaukee* (Milwaukee, 1955).

William L. Burton, *Melting Pot Soldiers: The Union's Ethnic Regiments* (Ames, Iowa, 1988).

Cornelius Buttimer, *Catalogue of Irish Manuscripts in the University of Wisconsin-Madison* (Dublin, 1989).

Thomas Gildea Cannon, 1992–, Series of articles on notable Wisconsin Irish in *Irish Genealogical Quarterly* 1, no. 4 and continuing.

Richard N. Current, *The History of Wisconsin. Volume II: The Civil War Era, 1848–1873* (Madison, 1976).

Margaret E. Fitzgerald and Joseph A. King, *The Uncounted Irish in Canada and the United States* (Ontario, 1990).

Harry H. Heming, *The Catholic Church in Wisconsin* (Milwaukee, 1896).

Fred L. Holmes, *Old World Wisconsin: Around Europe in the Badger State* (Eau Claire, 1944).

Herbert S. Lewis, "European Ethnicity in Wisconsin: An Exploratory Formulation," *Ethnicity* 5:174–88.

Grace McDonald, [Sr. M. Justille], *History of the Irish in Wisconsin in the Nineteenth Century* (Washington, D.C., 1954).

Milo M. Quaife, *The Attainment of Statehood* (Madison, 1928).

———, *The Convention of 1846* (Madison, 1919).

La Vern J. Rippley, *The Immigrant Experience in Wisconsin* (Boston, 1985).

Arthur H. Robinson and Jerry B. Culver, *The Atlas of Wisconsin* (Wisconsin, 1974).

Leo Rummel, *History of the Catholic Church in Wisconsin* (Wisconsin, 1976).

Charles M. Scanlan, "History of the Irish in Wisconsin," *Journal of the American Irish Historical Society* (1914): 13:237–60.

THOMAS GILDEA CANNON

## WOMEN, NINETEENTH-CENTURY

Among the European immigrant groups which sent substantial numbers of its daughters and sons to the United States in the nineteenth century, and the early part of the twentieth, the Irish may assert a number of claims for uniqueness. They were the first sizable group to come to the United States with a culture and religion that differed dramatically from that of the Protestant, American mainstream. They were the first to organize themselves politically to challenge the hegemony of the long-established native-born elite and it was their presence which gave birth to American xenophobia.

Among their many assertions of uniqueness none played as key a role in the shaping of Irish-American communities and culture as the fact that only among the Irish immigrants did women outnumber men. Most other groups either demonstrated the classic pattern of migration being a predominantly male experience, or over time, with the immigration of full families, men and women migrated in equal number. The Irish alone demonstrated the idiosyncratic characteristic of having women outnumber men. The demographic and cultural profile of Irish America bore witness to this particular phenomenon.

The Irish migration to America took place in three waves, and it was only in the third that the female-heavy migration took place. Yet the largest number of Irish immigrants came in that latter phase, and because of the sheer size of that influx, the process of building and sustaining community received its most substantial impetus. It was also in that final phase that Irish women as independent historical actors in America emerged and a distinctive Irish women's culture in America developed and flourished.

Irish immigrants, heavily Protestant from Ulster, had been opting for life in America from the colonial period onward. Many came to America as indentured servants attracted by the promise of land ownership upon the completion of their contract for work. In that migration men rather than women made up the bulk of the newcomers. Even among the earliest Catholic Irish immigrants, who began to predominate among those leaving Ireland in the 1820s, men still outnumbered women and a distinctive history for Irish women in America could not be said to have begun. Importantly though, among the Catholic Irish emigrants of the early Republican and Jacksonian periods, the gender gap started closing and women were showing up among the migrants more often than before.

The Great Famine of the 1840s constitutes a separate and discrete stage in the Irish migration to America. Described both at the time, and by subsequent historians, as a flight from hunger and death rather than a mass voluntary migration, the Famine-era flood saw women and men, adult and children, arrive without much in the way of systematic planning. Fundamentally poorer than those who migrated before, or those who would follow after them, the Irish emigrants of the Famine years proved to be exceptional rather than typical. At this stage the numbers of women and men tended to be the same, and children and parents as well as single people sought out America as a refuge from the devastation and landlords' evictions.

Beginning in the 1850s and continuing into the early twentieth century, the largest number of Irish Catholic women, and men, made their way to America. By this point the migration was predominantly female, and with each decade the female preponderance grew. Women, for example, made up about 53.8 percent of all Irish immigrants in 1900 as compared to 35 percent in the 1830s.

The Irish immigrant women who arrived in the United States and who so shaped Irish-American society and culture, shared several characteristics, which, along with their sex, influenced their migration and adaptation. Almost universally, these daughters of small farmers were single. They migrated to America with other, similarly-situated young women, and their migration grew out of their quest for a livelihood.

The reason for the feminization of the Irish migration to America in the middle of the nineteenth century helps explain the kinds of choices which these women made, both in Ireland and in America. One of the Famine's most enduring legacies involved a dramatic shift in patterns of both land-inheritance and marriage in rural Ireland. Before the Famine, parents tended to subdivide their holdings, almost always rented plots, upon the marriages of their sons. Holdings became smaller and smaller as the Irish diet came to be increasingly focused on the almost sole consumption of potatoes. The more substantial leaseholders or owners of modest, but workable, holdings did not do this, and they tended to pass on land intact to their sons.

With the devastation of the Famine, the latter behavior came to predominate, and indeed became universal in rural Ireland. Partly because the poor, the ones who had been the most notorious subdividers, suffered the most from the Famine in terms of constituting the bulk of the casualties and the masses of the refugees, those who were left tended to be the least prone to subdividing. Additionally, the poor who remained in Ireland were convinced of the errors of their past ways and shifted to the system of single, non-partible inheritance. Even more significant, the landowners consolidated their holdings and refused to allow the kind of practices which had been common previously.

Fathers and mothers held on to their control of the land until late in life and they transferred the title to only a single son. Only the son who was chosen by his parents for the inheritance married, and he married a woman who brought with her a dowry. That dowry went essentially to pay for the dowry of one of her groom's sisters so that she too might marry. Irish parents did not customarily pick the oldest, or youngest, son as the one chosen to get the land and the daughter selected to receive the dowry. Instead they chose on the basis of personal traits or other, less predictable factors. Children had, essentially, no way of knowing if they would or would not be selected for marriage.

These families therefore had large numbers of excess sons and daughters, men and women who could not marry and therefore remained in the rural Irish communities. Over the course of the last half of the nineteenth century the age at marriage among the Irish climbed higher and higher, and the Irish, despite their continued rural and agricultural lives, became Europe's latest marriers. Additionally, the rate of marriage plummeted, and a pattern of lifelong bachelorhood and spinsterhood became common in Ireland.

Unmarried men, usually referred to as "boys" throughout their lives, were more likely than unmarried women to stay put and work, often as hired hands, on their brothers' farms. Both single women and men, however, found themselves with a need to migrate, and that migration took them out of Ireland, because unlike most other European countries, Ireland experienced no growth of industrial, urban opportunities to absorb those young people with no place in the rural economy.

The centripetal nature of Irish rural life played itself out differently for women and for men. Men had more options to stay put, and the presence of a substantial population of bachelors in any small Irish community meant that men had a peer group with which to socialize. Men were more likely than women to migrate short distances, particularly to England for seasonal labor, so that they could return home for harvests and other critical moments in the agricultural year. Single women were needed neither throughout the year nor seasonally in rural Ireland, and that centripetal force pushed them further afield than it did their brothers.

If the rearrangement of landholding and marriage patterns in post-Famine Ireland served to push out the majority of women, the young and single, economic conditions in the United States served to pull them in. Irish women, those who were single, were attracted to America because of the availability of work. The nature of that work reveals much about the motives for the migration and the kinds of cultural patterns which informed their lives in America.

Domestic service provided the single most common job opportunity for young, single Irish immigrant women. Middle-class Americans, white, native-born, Protestants primarily, endured a constant "servant problem." American families felt a continuous need to employ women to help in the tasks of cooking, cleaning, mending, and tending their children, and they had few options to satisfy this need.

By and large, and with some regional exceptions such as Scandinavian women in the Upper Midwest and some Polish women, most women from most other immigrant communities refused to go into domestic work. Since they lived in ethnic enclaves which basically had too few women in their midst, women married relatively young, and universally. Among immigrants who came with full families, daughters lived with parents and other siblings, and when they went out to work, they tended to opt for mill and factory work or needle work within a family workshop, not domestic service, which in the nineteenth century generally was "live-in," with the servant sharing a domicile with her employer. Native-born, white American girls, even those who had left their parents' homes on farms and small towns, eschewed working in domestic service, considering it demeaning, beneath their dignity, and a violation of their American entitlement to independence.

Indeed in general, the only group with whom Irish women competed for domestic service jobs were African-American women, who also clustered in these positions. The competition was, however, not direct because Black women evinced very different employment and living patterns. They tended not to live-in, while Irish women did. This put Irish women at an advantage because employers preferred, through the end of the nineteenth century, domestic helpers who lived in their houses.

Domestic service was the most common job opportunity for young Irish immigrant women.

Domestic service functioned as America's most significant economic lure for Irish women. Irish women already in the United States working as servants used their contacts with employers to secure jobs for sisters, nieces, cousins, and female friends still in Ireland. American housewives often turned to their Irish servants when they sought additional help, and although Irish women were the focus of widespread and vicious ethnic stereotyping for their concentration in domestic service, and the reputed poor skills in cooking and in other chores, American women relied on their Irish domestics to help recruit other women to come and work.

As a job, domestic service shaped Irish women's encounter with America, at the same time that it reflected the nature of their migration and culture. It actually paid better than any other job available to unskilled women. As a job limited to single women it fit with the newly-fashioned, but already profound tendency of the Irish to marry relatively late in life, or to not marry at all. For a group of women who migrated without parents or spouses it provided them with a ready-made place to live, with food, usually more abundant and varied than they had ever tasted before, and with clothing, even if it had been cast off by the employer. Additionally, the presence of other Irish women domestic servants in the same, or in neighboring houses, meant that Irish women had close by a community of friends, often relatives.

A few other characteristics of domestic service help demonstrate its impact on the history of Irish women in America and on the Irish as a group. First, it was one of the few jobs available to nineteenth-century women workers where it was possible to save money. In numerous Irish-American community histories and in the records of Irish religious and charitable institutions in the United States, the substantial financial contributions of Irish women domestic servants indicates that they had some disposable income at their command.

Irish servant "girls" in America sent millions of dollars back to Ireland in the form of remittances, used there to facilitate the migration of additional family members to America, to allow the family to move out of the status of renter to that of landowner, to improve the family farm and the like. As long as Irish women remained in service and did not leave it for marriage, they could continue to fulfill their obligations to their families and communities in Ireland. Upon marriage they could no longer do so, and for the large—although relatively inestimable—number in America who never married, the ability to serve their families through remittances proved important in shaping their sense of self.

Irish women additionally used that money which they did not need for their own basic sustenance to save towards their dowries at such point in time when they could marry. This investment played a not insignificant role in the emergence of an Irish-American population of working-class homeowners.

Domestic servants, more than most Irish immigrants—women or men who labored in factories, on railroad crews, in construction, and in the other unskilled or semi-skilled jobs available to them—gained an exposure to American culture. Through the medium of their employers' families and homes, they learned how middle-class Americans lived. In their employers' homes they developed standards of American consumption, in terms of language, food, furnishings, dress, and gender roles. Irish women who labored as domestic servants in these middle-class homes and then married seem to have modeled their consumption patterns in part on that which they had seen on the job. The fact that so many second-generation Irish-American women, the daughters of the immigrants, became schoolteachers, may have attested to the impact of that exposure to the American middle class.

Finally, Irish women domestic servants, unlike Irish men who worked in unskilled and semi-skilled jobs and competed against many other men, had a near monopoly on their work. Since so few other women were willing or able to work in domestic service, Irish women could use their solo presence as a bargaining point with employers, and extract from them better pay, days off to attend church, to visit with family and friends, and other improvements in the conditions of work. They moved around a great deal, picking the best employers to work for, and leaving when they found better situations. This leverage which they had in setting some of the terms of employment was unmatched by any other group of women workers in the nineteenth century.

Not all Irish women could be domestic servants. In some communities, particularly industrial villages with a relatively small middle class, like Lowell, Massachusetts, or Troy, New York, few opportunities existed. These women constituted the other large segment of Irish women workers. In textile mills, garment factories, commercial laundries, and basically any industry that relied upon women workers, Irish women labored.

The story of their work in those factories conformed in large part to that of most women laborers: long hours, poor pay, unsafe conditions, and little chance for advancement. Yet in one important way, the history of Irish women in industrial employment took a different turn. Irish women, unlike most other women workers in industry (and in other sectors of the economy as well), were drawn to the labor movement. While nineteenth- and early twentieth-century labor organizers struggled over the problem of "the woman worker," and how to convince women to join trade unions, Irish women in a variety of fields flocked to the labor movement as both rank-and-file members and as leaders with both local and national reputations for their organizing abilities. In this they resembled Irish men, who also demonstrated a high commitment to unionization.

The roster of Irish women in high profile positions in the American labor movement reads like a roster of the key players in American labor history: Kate Mullaney, who successfully organized the collar laundresses in Troy, New York, in the 1860s, Leonara Barry, who became a full-time organizer for the Knights of Labor, Augusta Lewis, who helped organize women printers, Mary Kenney O'Sullivan, who began organizing women in the book-binding trades and ended up as the first woman organizer for the American Federation of Labor, Leonora O'Reilly, a founder of the Woman's Trade Union League, Agnes Nestor, an organizer of the glove makers, and Margaret Haley, Kate Kennedy, and Katherine Goggins, who organized schoolteachers. These names represent just a small sampling from the list of Irish women who deviated from the more common American pattern in which women did not belong to, or participate in, trade union activity.

The presence on this list of Irish-American women union activists of the names of Kate Kennedy, Margaret Haley, and Katherine Goggins, organizers of public schoolteachers, points to an important employment development for the second generation. Large numbers of Irish-American women, daughters of immigrants, entered the ranks of America's school teachers by as early as the 1870s. In that year already, only two decades after the Famine, 20 percent of New York City's teachers were Irish. From that decade onward, the percentage grew even larger, and was replicated in every city which had a substantial Irish presence.

Schoolteaching had connections to other parts of Irish-American culture and society and fit into the contours of Irish-American social history. Schoolteaching, like domestic service, required that women remain single as long as they were employed. Since Irish women entered adulthood and employment with models of unmarried women working and serving their communities, the non-marriage that went along with public schoolteaching was not a negative characteristic of the job.

Additionally, before the Progressive era, public schoolteaching was very much connected to the mechanisms of urban politics. In New York and Chicago and most other large cities, jobs as teachers were recognized basically as plums of political patronage. As Irish men had moved themselves into positions of considerable power in the municipal government of one city after another, Irish women used those political connections to secure for themselves their teaching positions. Even after the shift to less partisan control of school systems, Irish women well into the 1930s dominated this field of employment.

Because of the availability of these professional opportunities for Irish women, girls tended to stay in school longer and out-achieve their brothers educationally. Whereas even in the second and third generations, Irish-American men tended to replicate their fathers' occupational status, and they experienced economic mobility in a rather slow manner, Irish-American women far outstripped their mothers, often moving in one generation from domestic servant to schoolteacher.

They travelled along this trajectory in the field of nursing as well. Importantly these two fields, teaching and nursing, which provided professional employment and a space for personal development for Irish-American women, existed within the Catholic religious communal framework as well. Many Irish women in America in the post-Famine decades, like those who remained in Ireland, were drawn to the religious sisterhoods which experienced unprecedented growth in the latter half of the nineteenth century.

Under the aegis of many religious orders, Irish and Irish-American women played a crucial role in their communities by teaching, tending the sick, and dispensing charity. In orders like the Sisters of Mercy, the Sisters of Charity, the Sisters of the Good

Nursing provided professional employment for Irish-American women.

Shepherd, and others, Irish women, in more substantial numbers than women from other Catholic immigrant groups, found ways to combine religiosity and practical work. In the process they created a substantial communal infrastructure of service. They also provided a powerful role model for young girls of women who did not marry, who functioned as professionals, at the same time that they fulfilled deep acts of religious piety and obligation. It is noteworthy that Irish women worked as nurses and teachers both as nuns in the Catholic framework and as lay women in the public sector. In both sectors, however, singleness was the key.

The dominant themes in the social history of Irish women were played out community by community and family by family. Irish families tended to experience relatively slow levels of economic mobility from the poverty of the immigration period. Over the course of one or more generations, families and communities struggled with poverty, alcoholism, domestic violence, and male marital desertion. Irish women were viewed both at the time by the clergy and by social workers, and by subsequent historians, as the stabilizing influences within their homes and neighborhoods, at the same time that they tended to be the ones who bore much of the brunt of that social disorganization. Widowhood, for example, was a common and devastating experience for Irish women who then had to face the crisis of supporting their children.

Yet, individual Irish immigrant women, and more substantially their American-born daughters, entered into numerous fields of endeavor despite the vicissitudes they had faced. Political activists, novelists, poets, and essayists, journalists, and actors, as well as the labor leaders, contributed towards the creation of an Irish-American public culture. Likewise, on a local level Irish women, both lay and religious, made up the backbone of the Irish charitable world within their parishes and on a larger scale of orphanages, training schools, shelters, and other service institutions which helped ease the slow process by which the Irish immigrants faced with poverty and dislocation became Irish-Americans of the middle class.

*See* Emigration: 1801–1921; Domestics;
Labor Movement

Hasia Diner, *Erin's Daughters in America: Irish Immigrant Women in the Nineteenth Century* (Baltimore, 1984).
Robert E. Kennedy, *The Irish: Emigration, Marriage and Fertility* (Berkeley, 1973).
Kirby Miller, *Emigrants and Exiles: Ireland and the Irish Exodus to North America* (New York, 1985).
Janet Nolan, *Ourselves Alone: Female Emigration From Ireland, 1825–1920* (Lexington, 1989).
Arnold Schrier, *Ireland and the American Emigration, 1850–1900* (Minneapolis, 1958).

HASIA R. DINER

## WOMEN AUTHORS, NINETEENTH-CENTURY: A SELECTION

During the last quarter-century, literary scholars who focus on nineteenth-century American writing have begun to look more closely at the period's women authors. Much of their work had been virtually ignored by critics, or, when acknowledged, was frequently dismissed as sentimental trollop and relegated to the bookshelves of prepubescent girls, as was, for instance, Alcott's *Little Women,* or to high-school English classes as historical relic, as was, for instance, Stowe's *Uncle Tom's Cabin.* The general critical consensus was that works by women were conceived with worthy intentions but written with a decided lack of literary or artistic merit. With the critical reevaluation made possible by feminist scholars such as Julia Kristeva and Hélène Cixous, who identify and illuminate *l'écriture féminine,* literature generated by a separate and distinct female ethos, and Jane Tompkins, who cogently asserts that the supposed passivity of domestic fiction is superseded by its transformative power, the study of American women writers has undergone a renaissance.

There are still blank spots on the page, however. Much of the critical exegesis of women authors has served to present a monolithic impression of American culture and society, lacking cultural, ethnic, racial, religious, and socio-economic diversity (the voice of the lesbian is again more difficult to find). By and large, most of the writers newly given credence are middle-class, white Protestants of Anglo-Saxon descent. As representatives of the totality of female experience in the nineteenth-century United States, they are necessarily limited. Although there has been some effort to explore the heterogeneity of American womanhood, one group has still been largely overlooked: the Irish-American Catholic. Considering the dramatic numbers of these women whose presence transformed nineteenth-century America, the omission is startling.

In his seminal work, *The Irish Voice in America: Irish-American Fiction from the 1760s to the 1980s,* Charles Fanning provides a comprehensive overview of many of these neglected women and their work. As Fanning notes, much of their achievement derives from their ability to voice the concerns of a segment of American society that was simultaneously scorned and overlooked, even as the large numbers who immigrated to the United States in the wake of repeated occurrences of the potato blight and the ensuing Great Hunger in Ireland indelibly transformed the USA. These Irish-American writers wrestled with the difficulties of assimilation into a new culture without engulfment and loss of identity, as well as with the challenges of enacting their Roman Catholicism in a hostile environment. Later, as the initial identity crisis eased and the practice of Catholicism was under less attack, the work of Irish-American women became less inward-looking and more deeply evocative of the multiple textures of American society. A brief overview of some of the women authors will provide a sense of the depth and breadth of their ambitions and achievements.

## KATHERINE E. CONWAY (1853–1927)

She grew up in Rochester, New York, as the daughter of Irish immigrants, later becoming editor of the *Boston Pilot,* an Irish-American newspaper. A brief bibliography of her work, which comprises poems and non-fiction as well as novels, includes *On the Sunrise Slope* (1878), *A Dream of Lilies* (1893), *Making Friends and Keeping Them* (1895), *In the Footprints of the Good Shepherd* (1907) and *In the Harbor of Hope* (1907). Conway's fiction might most accurately be called transitional, a blend of the more formulaic sentimentalism and forceful defenses of Catholicism that characterize the fiction of the mid-century and the turn-of-the-century work that reflects the changing Irish-American experience as the new immigrants carved out a space of their own in American society, moved away from the Eastern seaboard cities, and discovered that their faith practices were no longer believed to pose an imminent danger to democracy in the United States.

Her 1901 novel, *The Way of the World,* tells the story of Esther Ward, a celebrated artist who is taken up by the society matrons of Boston's Irish-Catholic set. Conway's decision to center her novel around a female artist is significant, since part of the plot's tension arises from the unconscious suspicion with which Esther is viewed: "The fact that she had to work raised a nice question in our set. . . . Mrs. Ray did not really care to know people who worked for their living, but after a little talk with her husband, she told the ladies of the Whist Club that in her opinion neither painting pictures nor writing books was work" (7).

If Conway grapples with the evolving position of women and artists at the end of the Victorian era, she has another focus as well. One of the most notable thematic changes in Irish-American fiction by women in regards to its treatment of Catholicism is that a certain impassioned defensiveness has cooled. For one thing, this is a world in which Catholics and Protestants mix socially; the earlier "us versus them" mentality is absent. Also, earlier anti-Catholic vitriol, which frequently ended in rioting and violence, had dissipated, so writers portray the practice and practitioners of Catholicism in a less idealized way. For instance, Conway's Catholic socialites disdain Lent because it forces them to curtail their social activities. In addition to being seen as a somewhat unwelcome intrusion upon secular practices in *The*

Katherine Conway

*Way of the World,* Catholic ritual has also been metamorphosed into a cosmic talisman; one of the upper-class women journeying to Europe doesn't fear the ocean voyage because she has a convent full of nuns praying for the safety of her ship. Indeed, Catholics in Conway's novels sometimes sound suspiciously like Protestants: when one of Esther's sympathetic friends comes up with work for her under false pretenses, she asserts, "That's where I think it's right to lie. Of course I know Father Herman wouldn't agree with me, but one has to follow one's conscience" (187).

The priest in the novel is kindly but ineffectual and unable to alleviate Esther's emotional and spiritual suffering. Ironically, in the end, her cathartic confession to a woman friend brings about the resolution the Church could not. But, in a nod to sentimental convention, Conway does include a pathos-filled deathbed scene, a conversion effected by the sufferer, and a deathbed marriage. However, readers should note one crucial departure from sentimental tradition: Conway ultimately does not kill off her heroine, but rather, resurrects her, choosing to end the novel with the hint of a resumption of earthly pleasure rather than an assumption of heavenly reward. Conway comments about her protagonist, "So you see that Esther was not at all like the devout heroines of certain Sunday-school books, who are saints from the start; but a poor little *natural* woman, thirsting for a full draught of that earthly happiness of which she had barely tasted" (189; emphasis added).

Finally, Conway problematizes the purpose of her writing; clearly she doesn't intend a didactic tale. Esther is not a passive sufferer; she questions the trials that have come before her. Conway comments, "If I were inventing a little story whose prime purpose was edification, I would tell my readers here of Esther's prayerful resignation to the calamity which had befallen her. But *to be true to life* I must tell, rather . . . her prayer was: "O, my Father, let this chalice pass from me!" (188; emphasis added). Therefore, Conway apparently sees her role as to reflect reality rather than instruct, and the changing nature of fictional Catholicism is thus exemplified by her redefinition.

Conway expands upon these themes in another novel, *Lalor's Maples* (1901), in which she follows the fortunes of an assimilated Irish-American family. John Lalor sends one of his daughters to a convent school for several years, but she eventually leaves. When one of the nuns decries Mildred's lack of vocation, the Mother Superior replies, "Doesn't God want good women, bright minds, and noble characters in the world as well as in the cloister?" (72). This sensibility is absent from earlier writing. Katherine Conway's fiction, therefore, while noted for revisiting familiar themes, is notable instead for the revisioning of those themes.

## ANNA THERESA SADLIER (1854–1932)

Roughly a contemporary of Conway's, Anna Theresa Sadlier was the daughter of Mary Anne Madden Sadlier, one of the most celebrated and prolific immigrant women writers of the mid-century. Although not nearly as central to the Irish-American literary set as her mother had been in her day, Anna Theresa Sadlier did achieve recognition in her own right. Born in Montreal, she was a contributor to Canadian and English Catholic periodicals as well as American ones. The number of her books, which included historical romances and children's stories, is generally believed to be forty to fifty. She also wrote at least two hundred short stories and articles for periodicals. Additionally, as a gifted linguist, she translated many works from French, Italian, and German. Her prose works include *Ethel Hamilton; or, Lights and Shadows of the War of American Independence* (1877), *Seven Years and a Mair* (1878), *Women of Catholicity* (1885), *Wayward Winifred* (1905), and *Ethan Allen's Daughter* (1917). Sadlier's novels were very popular in Catholic schools, where they were often given to students as prizes.

*Gerald de Lacey's Daughter; An Historical Romance of Colonial Days* (1916) recreates New York at the turn of the eighteenth century. In it, Evelyn de Lacey, daughter of a former soldier, faces growing religious intolerance in the colony. The novel skillfully evokes old New York as it is transformed from Dutch to English and from colonial outpost to bustling metropolis; there are descriptions of Trinity Church in lower Manhattan, as well as Stadt Huys, the City Hall, and soldiers gaming upon the Bowling Green, all of which are familiar names to present-day New Yorkers.

The book also has as one of its themes the idea of the old world corrupting the new; dissipated Europe, as represented by the officials of the colonial English government, sneers down on the colonists, as represented by Evelyn. Tellingly, this New World Eve(lyn) is friendly with the local Indians and conversant in their language. Sadlier's narrative's emphasis on life's transience reveals the twentieth-century pessimism that erupted during the Great War, on the eve of the Russian revolution. Her focus on the brevity of earthly pleasures is apparent when she comments that the colonial governor, Lord Bellomont, who "arrived with so much pomp and majesty . . . could not have foreseen that he was never to leave those shores again; that, before many years had passed, his bones would lie beneath the Fort, and that the silver plate from his exhumed coffin, after a decade of two more had elapsed, would be stared at by the curious in a museum" (24)

Anna Theresa Sadlier's fictional fatalism thus differs from her mother's, which often takes the form of the Irish immigrant rejecting his/her new land. However, she shares the thematic interest in the persecution of Catholics. Indeed, the character of Evelyn assumes a martyr-like mien, for when Catholic persecution becomes more vicious, Evelyn declares, "It would be after all so fine a thing, father . . . if we should be called upon to suffer for the Faith" (142).

Sadlier's novel also explores the traditional role of women, with contradictory results. For instance, Evelyn's friend gets engaged, but her betrothal brings sadness both to her and to Evelyn. Says the bride-to-be, "And [my heart] is broken. . . . only I suppose I must marry someone." To which Evelyn replies: "Yes . . . you must marry someone. It's the common doom" (161). Despite this apparent rejection of matrimony, the novel concludes conventionally, with Evelyn's marriage to a dashing English officer, after she has convinced him to convert to her faith. Thus, *Gerald de Lacey's Daughter* continues the championship of Catholicism by Catholic writers. However, there are important distinctions between this work and earlier work. Anna Theresa Sadlier's tone is certainly not as didactic as was her mother's, for one. Also, significantly, Anna Theresa Sadlier depicts the history of her Catholic characters as inextricably bound with the history of the United States. Evelyn de Lacey is a proud Manhattanite/ American who doesn't suffer the cultural division that the immigrant protagonists of previous novels do.

## KATE McPHELIM CLEARY (1863–1905)

Not all writing by Catholic women seemed to exist independently of trends in contemporary American literature. In post–Civil War America, when men such as Stephen Crane, Theodore

Kate McPhelim
Cleary

Dreiser, and Frank Norris were reevaluating the American experience and women like Sarah Orne Jewett were becoming known as important local colorists, Kate McPhelim Cleary's work engaged the new literary trends. Cleary, born to Irish immigrants in Canada, lived in Co. Tipperary as a child after her father's death and later came to the U.S., living in such disparate places as Philadelphia, Chicago, and Nebraska. The Catholic version of sentimentalism as practiced by some of the earlier women writers evolves into the tradition of naturalism exemplified in Cleary's work as the nineteenth century becomes the twentieth.

For instance, some of her literary forebears mourned the rustic splendor that was lost to immigrants who had left behind the Irish countryside, and who, living in the slums of crowded Eastern cities, couldn't afford to migrate to the American prairies. In her 1897 novel *Like a Gallant Lady,* Cleary presents a rather different perspective on natural splendor: "The only people who associate solitude, romance, and all that sort of thing with the plains are those who write about them without having any personal experience" (267–268). She goes on to comment on the Nebraska landscape: "Such isolation! Such monotony! Such drudgery! And the hopelessness of ever escaping from these conditions accentuates the horror of them" (63).

When the elements weren't alienating because of their monotony, they were perilous, as this description of a blizzard indicates: "Was this bitter whiteness snow? She had always thought of snow as soft, gentle, tender. This that assailed her was icy, and so sharp that it stung like flying particles of metal where it struck her face" (212).

Besides revisioning the natural world as inimical to humans, Cleary's fiction, unlike the faith-centered plots of earlier writers, has other foci. For one thing, Kate Cleary does not equate religious and cultural identity. If Katherine Conway's writing reformulates the theological tropes, it seems that Cleary's world lacks any divine presence at all. In *Like a Gallant Lady,* when the town doctor, who is addicted to morphine, sees children being plagued by swarms of flies during a Nebraska drought, he thinks, "there [is] no God in heaven, no compassion nor supreme intelligence anywhere" (249–250).

The absence of the faith-centered narrative is not confined to Cleary's longer fiction. In her 1901 short story "The Stepmother," a dying woman's deathbed lacks all sentimental pathos, as well the presence of a doctor or a priest. Far from being an occasion to reveal the happiness of a soul returning to its maker, the dying woman instead ends her life by advising her stepson, "And [remember] that a woman isn't always well—or happy—just because she keeps on her—feet—and doesn't—complain" (239).

In the same story, Cleary hints at the lonely farm wife's sexual unfulfillment as disclosed by her decidedly non-maternal awareness of the physicality of her 23-year-old stepson: "She could see his great chest rising and falling, and the muscles of his arms working under the worn sleeves of his shirt" (235). The sexual dynamics revealed here are a far cry from earlier fiction in which, as Herbert Ross Brown acerbically comments in his early study of sentimentalism, although "largely devoted to recitals of attempts to violate the body of the heroine, there is practically no evidence to indicate that the heroine was aware that she possessed a body" (122).

Cleary's real-life domestic experiences—mother of several children and a talented cook who often contributed recipes to women's magazines—do not form the basis for her often spare, bleak fiction. Her contribution to the Irish-American canon is the demonstration that an accomplished writer may pursue her art for its own sake rather than devise it merely as a reflection of her politics.

## MYRA KELLY (1875–1910)

Like Cleary, Myra Kelly had her career cut short by her untimely death. Kelly was a Dublin native who emigrated as a child with her family to Manhattan's Lower East Side. After graduating from Columbia's Teachers College in 1899, she embarked on a career as a teacher, starting at PS 147, near the Bowery.

She became famous for her semi-autobiographical collected stories, which describe the experiences of a Lower East Side teacher. Both *Little Citizens; The Humours of School Life* (1904) and *Little Aliens* (1910) feature Miss Constance Bailey as the redoubtable schoolteacher, along with a cast of students who represent New York's cultural diversity, then as now dependent on continuing waves of immigration. Other works include *The Isle of Dreams* (1907), *New Faces* (1910), and *Her Little Young Ladyship* (1911). Her work attracted the attention of President Theodore Roosevelt, from whom Kelly received a letter of appreciation. Kelly began a correspondence with another fan, Allan Macnaughtan, whom she married in 1905. After losing her one child in infancy, Kelly's health failed steadily, and she died of tuberculosis at the age of thirty-five.

Critics have noted Kelly's emphasis on the sometimes comedic tensions of the process of Americanization. Stories from her *Little Aliens* collection embody these themes. The story "Games in Gardens" relates the struggles of Miss Bailey's first graders to understand and reenact the spectacle of athletic competition that one of their classmates had witnessed at Madison Square Garden. Humorous misunderstandings that need to be cleared up by the teacher abound: the children think that the javelin thrower is trying to hit someone; and they are shocked to hear that the competitors, garbed in white outfits, are running around in their "underclothes," for instance. Kelly successfully draws a connection between the misapprehensions that children have as they grow in experience and the bewilderment of the immigrant encountering the unknown custom.

She also manages to depict authentically the uneasy place of the immigrants, both in terms of how they represent the world around them and how they perceive each other. For example, Patrick Brennan, son of a policeman, offers up his yard as the site of the planned first grade olympiad: "We'll use my yard. . . . When me mother has company she always calls our yard a garden" (41). The irrepressible Patrick envisions himself as champion-to-be, and his incessant boasts prove too much for his classmate, Nathan Spiderwitz, who declares, "You ain't the only boy what can run und jump, you old-show-of-freshy Irisher" (43).

In another example of the sometimes explosive ethnic tensions that do not get left behind in the old country, one of the tales features a new Russian student whose dislike for the Jewish students is intense. This child tells a teacher, "he will not speak to Jews or to—and by this he means you [Miss Bailey]—a seeming Christian, who makes the Jew her friend, and allows Jewish babies to touch her hands" (79).

Despite the occasional friction, Kelly's Lower East Side is one in which the immigrants must co-exist, uneasily or not, for ultimately they are dependent on one another, as the neighborhood "fire-lighters" symbolize: "It was the Jewish Sabbatical Law which gave the derelicts an opportunity to earn a few pennies every Saturday, for no Orthodox Jew may kindle fire on the Sabbath" (86). Thus, literally and symbolically, neighbors bring light and warmth to one another. Still, Kelly has no illusions about the harshness of the downtown ghettos. In one story, a child must be brought to the hospital, and while awaiting the ambulance, a colleague reminds Miss Bailey to remove for safekeeping a gold locket the child is wearing since "I know that there would be precious little gold left on him by the time he reached the ward" (93).

Since many of Kelly's stories are set in the schoolroom, they are a literal demonstration of the transformative power of education to shape minds and transmit culture. However, she also recognizes that some of the children have immediate needs that cannot be met in a classroom. "A Brand from the Burning" recounts the efforts of school authorities to force a truant child to attend classes. These authorities do not realize that the street child needs food and shelter more urgently than reading and writing, but Miss Bailey's students understand. One of them explains the routine of the homeless child, "He lays in sleep by barrels; comes somebody, und he runs. He lays in sleep on sidewalks by bak'ry stores where heat and smell comes; comes somebody, und he runs. He lays in sleep by wagons, maybe, maybe by stables where horses is, und straw" (82). The difficulties of the teacher's task occasionally prove daunting to Miss Bailey, as in this scene, when she regards her lack of success in winning over the truant: "And so [she] sat on the floor and regarded the bitter fruit of her striving. A child—a little child, hunted, wounded, as far as she could see even unto death. And for the thousandth time she let despair roll over her. What was the use? What *was* the use?" (93). Her despair is a jarring glimpse of paralyzing frustration and failure; such emotions are rarely represented in earlier novels, which contain characters whose faith will never allow them to surrender hope completely.

The changing face of New York's immigrant population is apparent in Kelly's work, in which the Irish-American Miss Bailey represents the ascendant culture to her mostly Jewish and Eastern European students. These immigrants now face the same struggles the Irish had previously. For instance, "The Origin of Species" relates the confusion of young Esther Morowsky, whose widowed father, Jacob, symbolically re-"christens" himself John

Nolan, after an old Irishman who ran the Roman Catholic religious supply story at which Jacob Morowsky works. Upon the real Nolan's death, Jacob Morowsky inherits both the business and the name. Episodes like these demonstrate that Kelly's classroom fiction provides valuable insights into the cyclical process of immigration, alienation, and assimilation.

## ANNE O'HAGAN SHINN (1869–1933)

The maturation of Irish-American fiction that is revealed by its growing diversity of theme and technique parallels the increasing confidence with which the writers perceive their place in American society. Moreover, with the dawning of the twentieth century, that place was no longer as restrictive towards women. Anne O'Hagan Shinn was born in 1869 in Washington, D.C., and received a Bachelor's degree from Boston University. She was an Episcopalian. In 1908, she married Francis Shinn. Although Irish-American women had been noted for their lack of involvement in effecting political change, O'Hagan Shinn was a visible activist. A supporter of women's suffrage, she had a career that included a stint as a reporter for the *New York World and Journal* as well as a position in the editorial department of the literary journal *Munsey's*, to which she was a frequent contributor of short stories as well as feature articles. Some of the many O'Hagan titles that may be found in *Munsey's* include "The Robbery at Oldport; The Strange Meeting of Two Sentimental Pilgrims and Two Most Unsentimental Ones" (29:244–249), "The Great Northeastern and the Cow Girl; The Story of an Interesting Campaign Which Ended in a Double Surrender" (29:925–932), a feature article with photographs in March 1906 about the Fenway, the new and notable Boston museum (33.6:655–678), and in volume 35, a profile of the British aristocrat who was also a socialist, entitled "The Countess of Warwick" (569–573).

O'Hagan's stories vary greatly in both style and content. "A Christmas Incident at Santo Domingo; How an Outcast Sinner Came to His Own Again" contains some recognizable elements: the plot focuses on the role of mother, as well as on sin and forgiveness. The story relates the misadventures of Theodore Carey, who has driven the family company into bankruptcy through reckless speculation. His mother's reaction is one of complete rejection: "You have made me a reproach, my name a dishonor. . . . I wish that I might die before I have to face the world . . . I am glad that you are going away. . . . you are weak and wicked at the core, and dishonor will be your portion" (406). Mrs. Carey's diatribe certainly is a departure from the idealization of the maternal and thus from traditional depictions.

However, her bitterness is tempered by the Christian love and charity shown by Ted's deserted fiancée, Elizabeth. The two women seek the fugitive all over the Americas and end up in Santo Domingo on Christmas day, where they attend services at a Catholic church, which the narrator describes with a palpable lack of reverence as "tawdry" and "evil-smelling." However, as in earlier Catholic fiction, the Catholic church is the locus of salvation. By chance, Theodore Carey enters the church:

> What impulse led him to the adobe church with the cracked belfry he did not know. He had not been in such a place since last he had accompanied his mother to the family pew in the white-steepled Congregational church at Elmburg. . . . He rose and knelt awkwardly enough with the others. He listened to the simple Spanish sermon with a reverence he had not expected to feel. It was all of love and forgiveness and the tenderness of God made manifest in the tender Mother of the

Stable—and in all tender mothers, the kind old priest finished by saying. (411)

Not surprisingly, the reunion between Mother, Ted, and Elizabeth at the conclusion of the Mass is joyous, as the congregants have taken the sermon to heart; in this respect, the story embodies the familiar trope of redemption through (Catholic) faith.

Although immigration is not a major focus of O'Hagan's writing, she does present a wide variety of Irish immigrant characters, who enhance and diversify the fictional portrait of Irish-Catholics. "The Abdication of Mrs. Dougherty" is a case in point. The grandmother of the title is a forceful, independent woman. A fight between her family and the neighboring Dwyer clan over who will have the honor of inviting the priest to Sunday dinner leads to a showdown in which Grandmother Dougherty thinks the priest is favoring the Dwyers, so she vehemently declares that she will no longer attend Mass as long as Father Tom is in residence. In this story, the practice of faith has degenerated into an opportunity to show up the neighbors, and the priest is not exempt from the political jockeying: this fictional development would surely have shocked earlier writers, whose work was notable for its piety and devout characters. However, Mrs. Dougherty's refusal to countenance the priest's purported "meddling" allows for a delineation of character that far exceeds the rather one-dimensional folk of other fiction.

"The Waterloo of Mrs. McCormack Dunn; How Millicent Dunn, Alias Milly, Brought Ruin to her Mother's Highest Ambition" returns to the theme of strong-willed mother. Here, the plot complication involves the Irish mother's yearning for the social success of her children, a familiar preoccupation. As we have seen many times, the ties with the old nation and old ways that must be broken are often symbolized by the creation of a new identity: "Mrs. McCormack Dunn had married her husband in the days when he was Tim Dunn. The fact that thirty-five years later he was known, without debate, as McCormack Dunn epitomized the triumphs of the lady's career. The struggle from 'Tim' to 'McCormack' had been gradual and laborious; at times it had been grim, at times, grotesque, but it had been successful" (718).

Mrs. Dunn's hope that her youngest daughter will make a socially advantageous marriage is dashed when she marries a laborer. Of course, she tries to break up the match, but her husband will not allow it: "[I]t does my heart good to think there'll be one of the children's houses where I can sit in my slippers by the kitchen fire once in a while" (724–5). In this incident, O'Hagan reveals her understanding of the sacrifices that are made when immigrant parents better their children, including alienation from those very children.

O'Hagan Shinn's writing recognizes long-standing immigrant concerns, but it also explores previously unthinkable plots, such as that of "Margaret McDonough's Restaurant; The Story of the Beginning and Ending of a Business Career." The story presents a woman in business for herself, who is stalwart enough to face down an armed robber all alone. In the face of danger, she shows courage and resourcefulness. When he swears an oath, she tells him with dignity that he may rob her, but he may not blaspheme. Then she announces that the restaurant's takings are in her stocking, and orders the thief to turn around while she retrieves the money. Once he does, she tackles him.

Margaret is temporarily daunted when her errant husband returns and tries to reclaim the business. She is most upset when she relates what her husband has done to the restaurant's sign: "The sign! He's had my name painted out, an' his painted on"

(864). To avoid losing her business, Margaret appeals to her friend, Barney Nolan, an influential politician, and he arranges a divorce for her. The implication that women can seek freedom by ending their bad marriages is new in the fiction of Irish-American women, whose Catholic thematic emphasis had prevented such a notion. Interestingly, however, O'Hagan seems to revert to a more conventional plot twist when she has Margaret eventually get remarried—to Barney Nolan. After the marriage, Margaret no longer works at the restaurant.

Anne O'Hagan Shinn's fictional universe is populated with highly individual characters, whose marked difference from one another echoes the growing diversity of the Irish-American experience. That diversity of experience continues to shape the lives of Irish-Americans and to enrich their fiction. On the cusp of the twenty-first century, Irish-American women writers enjoy substantial critical and popular acclaim. Their work no longer is the exclusive province of an Irish-American audience. We should be grateful for the expanded range of their voices, but we should also be mindful of those earlier voices, many of whom have worthwhile stories to tell.

*See* Fiction, Irish-American

Nina Baym, *American Women Writers and the Work of History, 1790–1860* (New Brunswick, N.J., 1995).

Herbert Ross Brown, *The Sentimental Novel in America, 1789–1860* (New York, 1959).

Suzanne Clark, *Sentimental Modernism: Women Writers and the Revolution of the World* (Bloomington, 1991).

Kate McPhelim Cleary, "The Stepmother," 1901, *The Nebraska of Kate McPhelim Cleary.* Ed. James Mansfield Cleary (Lake Bluff, IL, 1958): 164–172.

———, *Like a Gallant Lady* (Chicago, 1897).

Katherine Conway, *The Way of the World* (Boston, 1900).

———, *Lalor's Maples* (Boston, 1901).

Hasia Diner, *Erin's Daughters in America: Irish Immigrant Women in the Nineteenth Century* (Baltimore, 1983).

Charles Fanning, *The Irish Voice in America: Irish-American Fiction from the 1760s to the 1980s* (Lexington, 1990).

Philip Fisher, *Hard Facts: Setting and Form in the American Novel* (New York, 1985).

Myra Kelly, *Little Aliens* (New York, 1910).

Janet A. Nolan, *Ourselves Alone: Women's Emigration from Ireland, 1885–1920* (Lexington, 1989).

Patrick O'Sullivan, ed., *Irish Women and Irish Migration* (London, 1995).

Anna Theresa Sadlier, *Gerald de Lacey's Daughter; An Historical Romance of Colonial Days* (New York, 1916).

Anne O'Hagan Shinn, "The Abdication of Mrs. Dougherty," *Munsey's,* 33 (May 1905): 249–252.

———, "A Christmas Incident at Santo Domingo; How an Outcast Sinner Came to His Own Again," *Munsey's,* 30 (1903): 405–411.

———, "Margaret McDonough's Restaurant; The Story of the Beginning and Ending of a Business Career," *Munsey's,* 31 (Sept. 1904): 861-864.

———, "The Waterloo of Mrs. McCormack Dunn; How Millicent Dunn, Alias Milly, Brought Ruin to her Mother's Highest Ambition," *Munsey's,* 31: 718–725.

MARIE REGINA O'BRIEN

## WOMEN RELIGIOUS FROM IRELAND (1812–1914)

### The Journey Out

By 1914, Irish women who journeyed out to the New World as women religious (professed sisters, novices, postulants, or aspi-

rants) had established a fairly routine pattern of migration. It began in 1812 when three Ursulines from Cork arrived in New York to open the first foundation of Irish women religious in the United States. Although they returned home after only three years, stating that promises made to them were not kept, they had forged a migration trail that would become familiar for more than a century. As a group, they also represented the first wave of Irish Catholic sisters to come to America at the invitation of bishops and priests, often Irish-born themselves.

The first wave would last into the 1880s and be overlapped by a second that started in the 1860s and continued well into the twentieth century. The second wave was made up of young women, usually not professed sisters or even novices, recruited by women religious already in the United States who launched, as Hasia Diner first noted in *Erin's Daughters in America* (Baltimore, 1983), "major drives in Ireland to gain new members" each year during the spring and summer. These trans-Atlantic efforts resulted in the emigration of thousands of women who left Ireland to join American religious communities and receive training for their life work.

For many, particularly those in the second wave, their greatest impact was in the classrooms in America's emerging parochial school system. In cities and towns from the East Coast to the West, these sister-teachers devoted themselves to their students' success, making it their prime ambition, as essayist Richard Rodriguez has noted in *Hunger of Memory* (New York, 1982). Without them, the needs of the Catholic Church as defined by the bishops in the 1880s would not have been met. However, their impressive network of schools came at a cost to the sisters, who gave of themselves for a long time with little compensation or recognition.

The never-ending demands of their schools also curtailed many of the pioneering ministries of the first wave—caring for orphans, housing working and unwed mothers, educating adult immigrants, and nursing the sick in their homes. Yet over time, both waves of women, united more by their resourcefulness and commitment to doing good than by their professional aspirations and achievements, grew into a unique body of American Catholic women.

Not all Irish women religious, of course, were recruited as adults in Ireland. Many came to the United States as children or were born in the United States, the daughters of Irish emigrants, and later entered religious life, influenced by teachers, relatives, or possibly those who staffed their favorite charities. Still other Irish women joined religious communities in Europe, often

Forty-five Irish women, recruited by the Sisters of St. Joseph of Carondelet, sailed from Cobh aboard the *Pennland* on February 24, 1898.

France, and subsequently found themselves missioned to an American convent. In 1900, there were about 40,000 women religious in the United States and, fifteen years later, between 60,000 and 70,000 (based on figures in Catholic directories and in George C. Stewart's *Marvels of Charity* [Huntington, IN, 1994]). Although it is impossible to know the exact number, as many as 10 percent of them may have emigrated as sisters from 1812 to the beginning of World War I in 1914. These women religious are the subject of this entry.

In the fifty years before the Great Famine of the late 1840s, nearly a million Irish came to North America. Many of them arrived first in Canada, through the ports of Montreal, Quebec, or Halifax, and then traveled to the United States, where they finally settled. During the 1830s, after passage of the 1829 Catholic Emancipation Act, the Irish Catholic Church focused its missionary activity on this diaspora. Irish clergy, followed by Irish nuns, left their homeland to bring the faith to America's new Catholic immigrants and their children.

## THE FIRST WAVE

Perhaps the best known of the first wave of Irish women religious to establish a foundation in the United States were the Sisters of Mercy. Sometimes called "walking nuns" because they were so often seen in Dublin streets, the Mercys sought out those in need. Their founder, Catherine McAuley, encouraged them to be fearless and to go wherever they might do good. In 1843, when the Cork-born Bishop of Pittsburgh, Michael O'Connor, invited the sisters at St. Leo's Convent in Carlow, all twenty-three volunteered. In less than a month, Frances Warde and six other sisters boarded the *Queen of the West* and headed for America. In April 1846, another group of seven Sisters of Mercy left St. Catherine's Convent in Dublin for New York City at the request of Bishop John Hughes, also Irish-born. Five months later, Frances Warde accompanied five Pittsburgh sisters, headed by the Carlow-born Agatha O'Brien, who had traveled to America in the original group of Mercys, to Chicago where they established themselves as the first Catholic sisters in the city (and the only ones for a decade). Their arrival barely preceded that of the surge of Irish emigrants fortunate enough to escape the Famine.

For those living in the west and south of Ireland, the Famine was definitely a watershed. Because of it, unusually large numbers of men and women and sometimes whole families left their farms, villages, and towns for American port cities (rather than Montreal, Quebec, or Halifax) where they stayed or continued on to the Midwest in search of jobs and housing. During the Mercy Sisters' first year (1846-1847) in New York City, they located positions for more than 1,000 women, young and old. The sisters also opened a House of Mercy for homeless immigrant women, hundreds of whom inundated them daily. The same held true in Chicago, where throngs of Irish newcomers everyday tested the mettle of the young and indefatigable Sisters of Mercy.

The heavy influx of Irish immigrants to the United States did not end with the Famine. Between 1851 and 1920, 3.3 million Irish settled in American locales. Among national groups, single women began to dominate the Irish emigration by the mid-1880s. For the most part, they, too, came from counties in Ireland's west and south. Many traveled alone and were met by relatives, who gave them lodging and helped them find jobs (frequently as domestic servants). During the 1880s, a smaller group of Irish women, who never traveled alone, ventured across the Atlantic to become religious sisters in an expanding immigrant

church. Most of them, however, were not personally invited by bishops and priests; instead, they were recruited by missionary sisters of the first wave.

First-wave women religious, especially their leaders, were self-confident, strong-willed women. They were also generally older (usually over twenty when they entered a religious community) than those in the second wave. These pioneers tended to have notable family connections, coming as they often did from Catholic families who were wealthy or securely middle-class. Thus, as daughters of substantial farmers, professionals, or shopkeepers, they could bring to their orders sizeable dowries, between £200 and £600 depending on time and place.

Teresa Comerford, who traveled to San Francisco in 1854 from the Presentation Convent in Midleton following a visit from Father Hugh P. Gallagher, is an example of first-wave leaders. When she left Ireland for the United States, she was thirty-three. The daughter of Nicholas Comerford and Margaret Hendrican, she was born into an old Norman family at Coolgraney, Gowran, County Kilkenny in 1821. She was educated at home by tutors and governesses and later attended Catholic academies in Kilkenny and Tullow. When she entered the Presentation Convent in Kilkenny, she did so on the personal recommendation of the bishop of Ossory.

Teresa Comerford and women like her chose religious life for a number of reasons. All of them believed they had a vocation, a calling from God to a life of service in the Catholic Church. But convent life, especially that of the new active religious orders founded in nineteenth-century Ireland, offered other attractions as well. It provided to educated and benevolent women a welcome alternative to the life choices available at the time: marriage and motherhood or spinsterhood. By entering a religious community, these women could develop their talents, use their education, and accomplish a great deal of good. Again and again, first-wave women religious became respected and powerful figures in American educational and charitable institutions.

Not all who journeyed out, even in the first wave, were so privileged. Each group of missionary sisters usually included one or two "lay" sisters. This category dated from the Middle Ages, when wealthy women entering the cloister brought maids with them. Since only the educated and well-to-do could read the Latin prayers of the Liturgical Office and contribute adequate dowries, only they could be admitted to the "choir." Their maids, left to do the community's life-sustaining chores, became lay sisters.

In nineteenth-century Irish convents, lay sisters were a kind of religious servant. Generally working-class girls, they could provide only a small dowry or none at all. Thus it was their responsibility to keep the teaching and nursing sisters, along with their charges, healthy and clean. Lay sisters ordinarily took simple vows, dressed differently from the choir sisters, and did not recite the Liturgical Office with them. Lay sisters were not necessarily illiterate, and they became better educated as the century progressed and as Ireland's national school system developed. Yet, the distinction between choir and lay sisters lingered into the twentieth century, largely because convents needed servants and were hesitant to hire outsiders.

Young women of Ireland's working-class families, who knew how hard life could be, were not put off by the idea of becoming lay sisters. In fact, many saw it as an opportunity to better themselves. They were attracted to a community of kind and educated women, who would provide for them each day and care for them in illness and old age. Like choir sisters, lay sisters also believed themselves called by God to a life of service. In the end, some may have been disappointed with their choice, but a large number lived productive and satisfying lives. One such woman was Agatha O'Brien, who entered as a lay sister but was chosen to become the Mercy Sisters' first superior in Chicago. According to Bishop Michael O'Connor, she was "capable of ruling a nation."

## THE SECOND WAVE

So were others in the second wave, those young recruits who came to the United States at the bidding of first-wave women religious like Teresa Comerford of the Presentations or the American-born Angela Gillespie of the Sisters of the Holy Cross. During the 1870s, the head of this French order, which Father Edward Sorin brought from LeMans to Notre Dame, Indiana, in 1843, went to Ireland in search of fitting candidates—devout and educated young women willing to aid her congregation "in saving souls in America." Mother Angela spent nearly three months in the spring and summer of 1873 visiting convents, schools, and sodalities in Dublin, Kildare, Cork, Limerick, Cashel, Thurles, Clonmel, and Waterford. At each gathering, she explained the pressing need, especially as a result of "the great Catholic emigration from Ireland," and assured candidates that the dowry was "of minor consideration—£50 being all that [was] strictly required."

Mother Teresa returned to Ireland from San Francisco on two occasions. During the second visit in 1879, she established a school and "Missionary Novitiate" at Kilcock, County Kildare, to train middle-class women as sister-teachers for San Francisco and Berkeley. By the following year, Kilcock had 150 girls in the school, and six postulants had become novices. However, with the death of Teresa Comerford in 1881 and without the support of San Francisco's new archbishop, the novitiate eventually closed. Before doing so, however, it sent fifteen sisters to the Presentation convents in California during the 1880s.

A more successful experiment was St. Brigid's Missionary School, begun in 1884 by the Sisters of Mercy in Callan, County Kilkenny. Modeled after Dublin's All Hallows Missionary College, which trained priests for the foreign missions, St. Brigid's remained open until 1958 and prepared more than 1,900 young women for convents in Australia, New Zealand and the United States. Despite its success in instructing missionaries, it did not receive any financial support from the Society for the Propagation of the Faith as did All Hallows.

The two women most responsible for the foundation and operation of St. Brigid's were Mothers Michael Maher and Joseph Rice. The former, superior of the Mercy Convent at Callan, was a member of a prominent Irish Catholic family. Her cousin was Bishop Patrick Moran of Sydney, Australia, formerly bishop of Ossory; and her father, Patrick Maher, was uncle to Ireland's first Cardinal, Paul Cullen. She, like her family, had an avid interest in the Catholic Church's revival in Ireland and its expansion abroad.

In 1881, when Mother Michael decided to establish a missionary school, she received the approval of the local bishop, her cousin and friend. Without his backing, she could not have begun this project. By the time St. Brigid's opened in 1884, Bishop Moran had departed for Australia; but the school was firmly founded. Mother Joseph then became "sister in charge" and remained so for almost thirty years.

Those who entered St. Brigid's (a majority from towns and farms in Ireland's south and west) became "aspirants" rather than postulants. St. Brigid's was a *preliminary* novitiate where vocations could be tested and educations enhanced. Aspirants studied languages (French, Italian, and Latin), music (piano, violin, and voice), painting, and drawing. They also learned how to teach. Those accepted at St. Brigid's had completed their primary education, were at least fourteen years old, and wanted to become sisters. Although they had not officially entered religious life, their daily routine resembled that followed in Mercy convents around the world.

Because of Bishop Moran's initial support and continued interest, Australia and New Zealand received the largest number (359) of Callan-trained sisters, according to an undated list of 1,204 aspirants. Another 250 young women accepted invitations to make their homes in the United States. Many became Sisters of Mercy, and nearly all became educators.

The number of American Catholics tripled between 1860 and 1890, and the demand for teaching sisters increased as well. No wonder that Sister Mary Eustace Eaton, moderator of the Child of Mary Sodality at Our Lady's Hospice, Harold's Cross, Dublin, insisted sharply that she was "training *Religious* not schoolmistresses," when she received an urgent appeal from Chicago for teachers, accompanied by "a liberal offer to pay all expenses."

## IMPORTANCE OF EDUCATION

By 1900 a significant change had occurred: education replaced dowry for women religious in the second wave. Advertisements in local Irish newspapers demonstrated this fact. In 1898 and 1899, for example, the Mercy Sisters in Hornellsville, New York, placed several ads stating explicitly that they would "receive as novices respectable young girls of good education who feel called to the religious state . . . no dowry will be required." As time went on, a monetary dowry was not even mentioned. The need for teaching sisters in American Catholic dioceses was simply too great to let the Old-World dowry requirement stand in the way.

In the 1880s and 1890s, American bishops and clergy made the parochial school "the centerpiece of Catholic strategy," according to Charles R. Morris in *American Catholic* (New York, 1997). It began in earnest when the Third Plenary Council of Baltimore met in 1884 and promulgated legislation on education. Decrees on the parochial school urged pastors to build them, parishoners to support them, and parents to enroll their children in them. Although schools were expensive ventures, a separate Catholic school system was created. A large part of its success can be credited to educated teaching sisters—many American-born, but others transplanted from abroad, particularly Ireland.

Not all who left Ireland for American religious communities taught. Some joined those that operated hospitals, orphanages, and homes for the aged. The Galveston Sisters of Charity of the Incarnate Word are a case in point. Known and respected in Tipperary County, the recruiting sisters there simply encouraged interested young women (often members of their own families) to apply. After 1882, when Bishop Nicholas Gallagher prohibited any non-English-speaking candidates from France in his diocese, almost all the Incarnate Word's recruits came from the west of Ireland. Remarkably, a succession of mothers general, beginning in 1894, had come of age in Tipperary town or county.

It was not by chance that these capable, steadfast women of faith left Ireland as sisters or to become sisters during the nineteenth and early twentieth centuries. They were invited or recruited, and they came with a purpose. Although those in the first and second waves differed in age and status, they shared a common mission and culture. Together they formed an important part of the chain and serial migration that was so prevalent among the millions who left Europe prior to 1914.

*See* Sisters of Mercy; Presentation Sisters; Priests from Ireland

Hasia Diner, *Erin's Daughters in America: Irish Immigrant Women in the Nineteenth Century* (Baltimore, 1983).

Suellen Hoy and Margaret MacCurtain, *From Dublin to New Orleans: The Journey of Nora and Alice* (Dublin, 1994).

———, "The Journey Out: The Recruitment and Emigration of Irish Religious Women to the United States, 1812–1914," *Journal of Women's History,* 6–7 (Winter/Spring 1995): 64–98.

Deirdre Mageean, "Making Sense and Providing Structure: Irish-American Women in the Parish Neighborhood," in Christiane Harzig, ed., *Peasant Maids—City Women: From the European Countryside to Urban America* (Ithaca, 1997): 223–60.

Janet A. Nolan, *Ourselves Alone: Women's Emigration from Ireland, 1885–1920* (Lexington, Ky., 1989).

Walter Nugent, *Crossings: The Great Transatlantic Migrations, 1870–1914* (Bloomington, Ind., 1992).

Ellen Skerrett, ed., *At the Crossroads: Old St. Patrick's and the Chicago Irish* (Chicago, 1997).

George C. Stewart, Jr., *Marvels of Charity: History of American Sisters and Nuns* (Huntington, Ind., 1994).

SUELLEN HOY

# WYOMING

Wyoming Territory was formed from sections of Dakota, Utah, and Idaho territories by act of Congress on July 25, 1868. The name "Wyoming" was taken from a Delaware Indian phrase, *mecheweami-ing,* meaning "at the big flats." At the time the territory was formed, fewer than ten thousand people lived there. Twenty-two years later when Wyoming was admitted to the Union as the forty-fourth state, more than sixty thousand people lived in Wyoming. Irish immigrants and their descendants were among the first white settlers in the area and included several prominent figures in the early history of the State.

## TRAILS, TEARS AND TRIALS

High mountains, low plains, unspoiled streams and abundant wildlife drew hosts of early trappers, traders and explorers to the nearly 100,000 square miles of land that would become the state of Wyoming in 1890. Names and faces from Ireland were among those who poked, pried, mapped and trapped this wild land from very early days. While going about their business, these men discovered and named many of the mountains, streams and peaks; built forts; followed Indian trails; and discovered the vital gateway to the Pacific coast, South Pass.

John Colter, once a member of the Lewis and Clark Expedition, led a fur-trapping expedition into the territory in 1807–1808. From that date until the mid-nineteenth century, fur trade dominated the economy in Wyoming. Trappers discovered and marked many of the trails that would become popular routes for westward expansion, including the Oregon Trail. These men of European descent lived as the Indians did, learned from them, traded with them, and fought with them. Many of these trappers also died at the hands of the Indians.

By the 1830s missionaries had followed the fur trappers to the area. The Reverend Samuel Parker and Dr. Marcus Whitman were among the first missionaries in Wyoming when they reached the Green River rendezvous on August 12, 1835. Whitman returned to the east coast to try to recruit missionaries to work among the Indian tribes; Parker continued to travel west. The following year, Whitman returned with the Reverend H. Spalding; both were accompanied by their wives. These women were the first of European descent to make the journey over this trail.

Although thousands of emigrants from the east passed through Wyoming, few settled in the area until the Mormons began arriving in 1847. Irish men and women were among the Mormons' First Pioneer Company of 1847. The company included Robert E. Baird from Londonderry, Howard Egan from County Kings, James Craig from County Clare, Nancy McClenahan from Tyron, and Fanny Parish from Wicklow, Ireland. Thousands of Mormons followed these first pioneers across Wyoming over what was to become known as the Mormon Trail.

A number of these travelers settled, for awhile at least, in western and southwestern Wyoming. Others continued on to the Valley of the Great Salt Lake in Utah. Members of the Willie and Martin Handcart Companies of 1856 endured especially harsh conditions. Many of their company died in a blizzard that overtook them on their journey. Survivors of the ordeal included two Irish families, those of Joseph McKay and James Laird from Antrim, Ireland.

The discovery of gold in California in 1848 brought an enormous increase of travelers along Wyoming's trails. Gold diggers followed the Oregon Trail across Wyoming's center and the Overland Trail through southern Wyoming. Later the Bozeman Trail, running north and south, would carry miners into the Montana gold fields.

Increased travelers exacerbated the need for some form of communication with the east coast. In 1851 John M. Hockaday and William Liggett established a semi-monthly stage line for mail and packages from St. Louis to Salt Lake City. By 1859 this service had become well established as the Central, Overland, California and Pikes Peak Express Company. In 1860 the company established the Pony Express along the Oregon Trail.

Stories of people making the journey across Wyoming's trails, living in "mobile towns," could be a study in itself. The diaries of women making this long journey reveal both their own reluctance to leave the comforts of the East and the tremendous challenges they faced in caring for their families as they traveled. Mary Ringo was the wife of Martin Ringo, a Kentuckian possibly of Irish background. After serving in the Mexican War, Martin Ringo married Mary Peters in Missouri, later settling in Indiana. Mary Ringo's diary began on Wednesday, May 18, 1854, when she and her family left their home to undertake the long trek to California.

Although she made no mention of it in her diary, Mary was pregnant with her sixth child at the time. Her journal contained regular descriptions of campsites, conditions of cattle and sightings of Indians. Her entry for Saturday, July 30, was of an entirely different kind. Martin Ringo had accidentally shot himself with his own shotgun. His grave is located near present day Glenrock, Wyoming, and has been identified and preserved by the Oregon-California Trail Association. Mary and Martin's oldest son, John, grew up to be the notorious cattle rustler, Johnny Ringo, whose exploits inspired a song and countless books and articles.

## THE MILITARY ON THE FRONTIER

Although forts had been established in Wyoming as early as the 1830s, the need for them and for added military personnel increased as the numbers of people traveling through Wyoming grew. Recruiting men for these posts was a formidable task. Military life at its best was unappealing; at its worst it was full of hardships and danger. Because personnel and other resources were low, soldiers were pressed to do all the chores of building and maintaining a fort as well as those of guarding it. A soldier often used a shovel or ax as much as a musket or saber. Patrick Keighan, a private assigned to Camp Walbach at the edge of Cheyenne Pass, scrawled in the post guard book: "Pat Keighan is My name and Ireland is My Nation. Cheyenne Pass is My Dwelling Place and Hell is my Expectation."

The climate, food and harsh regulations, along with long hours of labor, wrought havoc on these frontier soldiers. Reports to the U.S. Congress showed that each year a soldier required, on the average, three hospitalizations. One in thirty-three men died from various diseases each year. Causes of death recorded in the crude cemeteries at each post included not only skirmishes and battles with the Indians but also typhoid, cholera, peritonitis, pneumonia, small pox, consumption, and accidents of every nature imaginable.

These records also show the large number of Irish counted among the dead. Private Thomas Dolan of Company F, 4th U.S. Infantry, for example, was discharged from the army on May 2, 1877, after losing his right leg. He died of cancer twenty days later. Wives often followed their husbands to military posts in Wyoming. Some women were able to find work to supplement their husbands' low military wages. Census records show that many laundresses at the forts had come from Ireland.

Irish men who survived their stints at these frontier posts often found exceptional business opportunities that were not available to them in the East. John and Tim Mahoney, cousins from Gloun, Kilcohane, in County Cork, Ireland, were good examples. John Mahoney had been the first brother to emigrate from Ireland to the United States. His first stop was in Paterson, New Jersey, where he found a job that paid him well enough to send the fare for his cousin's passage to America from Ireland. He wrote to Tim: "Hurry and join me at the Irish boarding house where I'm staying. The food is good and there are good Irishmen to associate with."

Both John and Tim were employed until the Panic of 1873 struck. After a failed attempt to find honest work in New York City, they joined the army. Tim became a foot soldier at Fort Sill, and John was assigned to Fort Laramie in Wyoming. While serving under General Phil Sheridan, a fellow Irishman, John Mahoney, was shot in the leg. Against the doctors' advice, John refused to have his leg amputated. Somehow his leg healed, and he was discharged from the army with honors. He also had a considerable amount of pay he had been saving. In partnership with other investors, John Mahoney bought a band of sheep and ran them on a range near Rawlins, Wyoming.

After being discharged from the army, Tim Mahoney married and settled in Denver, Colorado. With his cousin's encouragement, he also invested in sheep in Wyoming. The Mahoneys' financial success in Wyoming drew a long list of pioneers from County Cork, Ireland, to central Wyoming. These pioneers included Pat Sullivan, who later became one of Casper's first mayors, a member of the state legislature, and a U.S. senator.

Irish men came west not only with the military but also with the "bull trains" delivering supplies to the numerous settlements and mining camps that had sprung up around the forts. Abe Majors, founder of the firm of Russell, Majors and Waddell, was one of the first to establish a freighting business. An experi-

enced ox driver himself, his firm at one point owned 6,250 wagons and 75,000 oxen. By 1860 nearly five hundred freight wagons crossed the Great Plains daily. Five years later the amount of freight hauled exceeded eleven thousand tons.

Personnel were needed to "drive" the oxen. Once again, the Irish saw this as an employment opportunity. The "bull trains" crossing the plains had many an Irishman walking beside them or cracking the whips above the heads of the slow beasts. Wherever men went in the pioneer period, whiskey went with them, or soon followed. The Irish were no exception. Those who worked driving the oxen of freighting companies soon found a way to wet their dry throats coated with trail dust. They used a corkscrew to bore a hole in one of the whiskey casks and then inserted a straw as needed along the trail. Buyers and sellers tolerated the shrinkage in their cargo as long as it was not overdone.

## BUILDING A RAILROAD AND A STATE

Before 1862 it would have been impossible to build a transcontinental railroad because of political and financial reasons. The Railway Act of 1862, however, provided ten sections of public land for each mile of track laid. It also arranged for first-mortgage loans in the form of government bonds to be paid to two subsidized corporations charged with building the railroad. The Union Pacific was to build west from Council Bluffs, Iowa, to the western boundary of Nevada. The Central Pacific was to build east from Sacramento, California.

A second Railway Act in 1864 doubled the land grant and included mineral rights. This provision had significant influence on the ultimate route of the railroad. In 1865 General Grenville M. Dodge discovered a pass across southern Wyoming as he was returning from a military expedition in the Power River country. This location was then chosen for the Union Pacific route not only because it was forty miles shorter than the Oregon Trail but also because it ran through coal districts.

In 1866 Congress passed a bill that allowed both companies to keep building until the connection was formed. Construction thus became a grand race as each company strove to build as far as possible in order to acquire greater shares of the promised government subsidies. Railroad workers engaged in various tasks were scattered over hundreds of miles. Completely accurate figures are not possible, but existing records suggest that as many as six thousand men were employed by Union Pacific Railroad during the summer of 1868. Laborers earned $3.00 a day. Many of these laborers were Irish, drawn from the East, from mining camps and border towns, by good wages and steady work. It can be said that the Union Pacific Railroad was built by the Irish.

The railroad spawned many towns; often these "towns" simply moved from spot to spot as the railroad progressed. Others, such as Cheyenne, Laramie, Benton and Green River, remained after the railroad passed through the site. In 1868 Congress created the territory of Wyoming, and in 1869 its first legislature granted suffrage to women.

## WYOMING GRASS: A NATURAL FEEDING GROUND FOR LIVESTOCK

The great open ranges of Wyoming provided natural feeding grounds for livestock. Construction of the transnational railroad had increased commerce in the state and had brought the necessary military protection from Indian attacks. These developments, along with provisions of the Homestead Acts, attracted immigrants to Wyoming. After making his "Declaration of Intent" to become a citizen of the United States, an immigrant could work his homestead claim for five years. At the end of that time, providing he met the necessary requirements, he obtained title to his homestead acres, up to 1,120 acres of land.

Some people built on their original claims to develop even larger farms and ranches. Others sold to adjoining ranchers. Cattlemen became quite adept at using provisions of the Homestead Act to acquire large tracts of land, as reflected in Wyoming's status as one of the leading states in amount of land homesteaded. The Wyoming Stock Growers Association became one of the most influential bodies in Wyoming and the most powerful organization of its kind in the nation.

Naturally, some of those coming to Wyoming to make their fortune in raising cattle included men and women from Ireland. Ellen Searson, granddaughter of Owen O'Sullivan from Tipperary in Ireland, came to the United States in 1883. She first settled in Kentucky, where her father was located. She soon discovered, however, that jobs with decent wages were hard to find in the East. Western mining towns, on the other hand, had plenty of opportunities for employment for women who were willing to work in laundries or in rooming and eating houses. Ellen and a friend flipped a coin to decide whether to travel to Central City, Colorado, or to the Dakota Territory. They arrived in Dakota in 1885. Five years later Ellen Searson married Sidney Thomas, a Welshman who gained his U.S. citizenship that same year. In 1894 Ellen and Sidney were granted a homestead patent for land just north of Beulah, Wyoming, in Crook County. The family farmed the land with irrigation rights from Sand Creek. Later their daughter, Edith, homesteaded the adjoining land. When Edith married John Crago, the ranch's grazing land for cattle was extended another 320 acres as Edith and John homesteaded nearby land. The Crago ranch existed for nearly one hundred years.

Tim Kinney was another Irishman to invest in Wyoming's ranges. Kinney left Ireland during the Great Famine. He first made his way to Wisconsin, where he worked as a laborer until he landed a job as a car repairman in the Union Pacific railway shops and moved to Rawlins, Wyoming. Kinney served the railway in various jobs until 1874, at which point he believed he had saved enough money to quit his job and enter the cattle-raising business. He established a ranch west of Rock Spring, Wyoming. The extremely harsh winter of 1889–1890 destroyed more than three-fourths of his herd.

Kinney decided to cut his losses by selling off the remaining cattle and investing in 17,000 head of sheep instead. Even though he had no experience with sheep, his operation flourished. During the Panic of 1893, Kinney held onto his herd, even selling his wool clip when it became necessary to keep the operation afloat. In 1899 Kinney made his first large sale—$62,350 worth of sheep and $72,000 for 500,000 pounds of wool.

Kinney established his sheep ranch in Uinta County near the Idaho line. He employed more than one hundred men to look after his flocks. Kinney became very active in the politics and business of the area. Over the years he held several prominent offices, including member of the Wyoming Board of Sheep Commissioners, president of the First National Bank of Rock Springs, and head of a large Rock Springs mercantile house. Although quite wealthy, Kinney led a simple life. He always carried his bedroll and cooking gear in his buckboard and often spent the night on the open prairie. He traveled from camp to camp in order to provide personal supervision of his various enterprises. As the *Wyoming Industrial Journal* reported in 1901, "Though a millionaire, he prefers the wild and uninhabited desert and the companionship of his thousands of sheep to the refinements of city life."

## COMMUNITIES AND CHURCHES

As the cattle and sheep industries were developing, Wyoming towns were also growing. Towns that survived the passing of the railroad crews replaced their tent-saloons with churches and schools. People from all ethnic backgrounds, including the Irish, worked with each other to make these communities thrive. Their accomplishments included forming the Laramie County Library Association in 1886 as the first county library system in the United States.

In 1870 nearly one-third of the foreign-born population of Wyoming was Irish. Their accents could be heard in churches, saloons, and town celebrations. Their lifestyles could be seen in the cities, on the range, or in the mines and oil fields across the state. This Irish presence was especially strong across southern Wyoming where the Union Pacific Railroad tracks had been laid.

Irish immigrants formed various clubs to celebrate their heritage and holidays. One of these groups was the Fenian Brotherhood, which held its first meeting in Cheyenne on March 4, 1868. This group invited their friends to join them in a Saint Patrick's Day parade and ball, which were grand successes.

Not all Wyoming residents were impressed with the Fenians. In 1880 Father Cummiskey of Laramie and other clergymen attacked several Irish political groups, particularly the Fenians, for being at variance with church teaching. After his public denunciation of them, a bitter dispute arose and the Fenians lost many members.

It was the men and women of Irish descent who brought the Catholic Church to Wyoming. By 1887 Catholic presence in the territory was strong enough that the Vatican established the Diocese of Cheyenne; previously, the territory had been incorporated in the Diocese of Omaha. The first four bishops of Cheyenne were Irish or Irish-American: Maurice F. Burke (1887–1893), Thomas M. Lenihan (1897–1901), James J. Keane (1902–1911) and Patrick McGovern (1912–1951).

When Bishop Burke arrived in Cheyenne from Chicago, he discovered that the diocese was three times the size of his native Ireland and with few priests and religious to minister to about seventy-five hundred people of various cultures. He used the railroad, stagecoach and backboard to reach the outer limits of the diocese. During one of his journeys in June 1888 to the northern areas of the state, Burke presided over the laying of the cornerstone for St. Stephen's Indian Mission.

Four years elapsed between Burke's assignment to the Diocese of St. Joseph and the appointment to Cheyenne of Thomas Mathias Lenihan, another native of Ireland. Lenihan traveled throughout the state visiting parishes and monitoring building programs. Following his death on December 15, 1901, he was succeeded by James John Keane of Joliet, Illinois.

One of Keane's first acts as bishop was to incorporate the Diocese of Cheyenne according to Wyoming state law. He also required pastors to do the same in their parishes. Keane was insistent that parishes and diocesan offices maintain accurate record-keeping and be accountable in financial matters. On his numerous preaching trips around the country, Keane recruited priests who were interested in the missionary work within his diocese.

Since the diocese did not have a cathedral, Keane purchased land near the state capitol for a cathedral and presided over the laying of its cornerstone on July 7, 1907. The cathedral was placed under the patronage of St. Mary. In 1911 Keane was transferred to the Archdiocese of Dubuque.

Bishop Patrick Aloysius McGovern was a priest in Nebraska when he was appointed fourth bishop of Cheyenne in 1912. Shortly after his arrival in the diocese, he called a synod to meet the priests and to formulate statutes for working with the clergy and the laity. In June 1948 he called a Second Diocesan Synod, which was held at St. Stephen's Indian Mission. Again, consultations with the priests resulted in guidelines for discipline and the strengthening of religion within the diocese. McGovern was bishop of Cheyenne until his death on November 8, 1951.

Irish laity were also instrumental in building the Church in Wyoming, even as they served the civil community. Moses Patrick Keefe, for example, born in Mitchellstown in Ireland, initiated construction of St. Mary Cathedral in Cheyenne in 1907. Keefe had also supervised construction of many of the buildings at Fort S. A. Russell and other government facilities across the United States and in foreign countries, as well as construction of the rock dam that provided Cheyenne's water supply. In addition, Keefe served as mayor of Cheyenne.

## WYOMING IN THE TWENTIETH CENTURY

Today, Wyoming is still called "the Cowboy State." This nickname has special meaning for the people of Wyoming. For them the cowboy represents a simple, direct, courteous, tough, independent and self-reliant type of individual. From its earliest days, people in Wyoming were judged not by where they came from or how they spoke but by how they conducted themselves and their affairs. Wyomingites love their mountains, plains and way of life. They cherish their informality and wide open spaces. The Irish, along with so many others from across the nation and the world, worked hard to form the legacy that Wyoming has today.

Tracing Irish activities past the turn of the century thus becomes a formidable task. As "the equality state," Wyoming has encouraged the Irish, and all other nationalities, to blend into the state's melting pot. People worked with other citizens as they became a part of their community, their county and their state. Irish names can be found in every occupation, organization and event in Wyoming. Most family trees of Wyoming residents include Irish names along with those of many other places and countries. The Irish who came to Wyoming did just what every other nationality did—they contributed their labor, gifts, insight and humor to making Wyoming what it is.

Ichabod S. Bartlett, ed., *History of Wyoming* (Chicago, 1918).

Susan Ward Easton, comp., *Members of the Willie and Martin Handcart Companies of 1856: A Sesquicentennial Remembrance* (Salt Lake City, n.d).

———, comp., *Pioneers of 1847: A Sesquicentennial Remembrance* (Salt Lake City, n.d.).

Sharon Lass Field, ed., *History of Cheyenne, Wyoming, Laramie, County*, vol. 2 (Cheyenne, Wyo., 1989).

———, *Fort Fetterman's Cemetery* (Cheyenne, Wyo., 1970).

Lewis L. Gould, *Wyoming: A Political History, 1868–1896* (New Haven, Conn., 1968).

Ellen Crago Mueller, Interview by Sharon Lass Field (Cheyenne, Wyo., 1997).

Robert Fryer, Personal Journal. Used with permission of Porter family.

Michael Glazier and Thomas J. Shelley, eds., *The Encyclopedia of American Catholic History* (Collegeville, Minn., 1997).

*Graves and Sites on the Oregon and California Trails: A Chapter in OCTA's Efforts to Preserve the Trails* (Independence, Mo., 1991).

Gordon Olaf Hendrickson, ed., *Peopling the High Plains: Wyoming's European Heritage* (Cheyenne, Wyo., 1977).

Kenneth L. Holmes, ed., *Covered Wagon Women: Diaries and Letters from the Western Trails*, vol. 8, *The 1864 Journal of Mary Ringo* (Glendale, Calif., 1989).

Taft Alfred Larson, *History of Wyoming* (Lincoln, Neb., 1965).

Velma Linford, *Wyoming Frontier State* (Denver, 1947).

Philip J. McAuley, "The Irish: Their Roots are Deep in Wyoming," *Casper Star Tribune*, 15 (March 1964): 5.

Robert A. Murray, *Military Posts of Wyoming* (Fort Collins, Colo., 1974).

Edwin L. Sabin, *Building the Pacific Railway* (Philadelphia and London, 1919).

Robert M. Utley, *Frontiersmen in Blue: The United States Army and the Indian, 1848–1865* (New York, 1967).

Joan Wheelan, "Irish Immigrant Was Sheep King," *Casper Star Tribune*, special edition, 31 (March 1974): 14A.

Writers' Program of the Works Projects Administration in the State of Wyoming, comp. *Wyoming: A Guide to Its History, Highways and People* (New York, 1941).

Wyoming State Archives and Historical Department. *Wyoming: Some Historical Facts* (Cheyenne, Wyo., 1978).

SHARON FIELD

# Y

## YEATS, JOHN BUTLER (1839–1922)

Artist, writer, conversationalist. John Butler Yeats was Ireland's finest portrait painter of the late nineteenth and early twentieth centuries. He painted and drew many leading figures of Irish cultural life, among whom were his famous sons and daughters, William, who won the Nobel prize for literature in 1923; Jack, one of the most significant expressionist painters of the twentieth century; Susan Mary, known as Lily, and Elizabeth Corbet, known as Lollie, immortalised in James Joyce's *Ulysses* as the "two designing sisters," who were actively involved in the arts and crafts movement in Ireland and who ran the Dun Emer Industries and later the Cuala Printing Press.

Born in Co. Down, Northern Ireland, John Yeats studied law at Trinity College, Dublin, and qualified for the Bar. While a student he visited his school friend George Pollexfen from Co. Sligo, of a family of shipowners, whose sister Susan he fell in love with and married. From their father, the Yeats children inherited magnanimity of spirit and love of conversation, from their mother's side industry and horse sense. Yeats's decision to leave law for art did not impress the Pollexfens. He attended the famous Heatherley Art School where he made a wide circle of friends with whom he formed a brotherhood devoted to Pre-Raphaelite ideals. Back in Ireland he began to work in earnest as a portrait painter. But from the very outset he was dogged by that trait which would impact on his career as a painter for the rest of his days: a pathological reluctance to "finish" a painting—always chasing the spontaneity of the sketch yet invariably losing the freshness of the initial effort by meddling with it. Yet when it worked, he succeeded in evoking the very essence of the sitter with incomparable sensitivity and originality of style.

On the other hand, his charcoal sketches imposed no such burden. He plunged into them with great brio, dispensed with all but the most essential elements and, as a result, created drawings full of vitality and personality. During the 1880s and 1890s he travelled back and forth between London and Dublin, bringing his family with him, until they were old enough to resist. He returned to Ireland in 1901, drawn to the burgeoning literary and artistic climate. In that year he showed forty-three works in a joint exhibition with landscape painter Nathaniel Hone, out of which he received a major commission by Hugh Lane to paint portraits of prominent Irishmen including writers John Synge, George Moore, Gaelic scholar and later first president of the Irish Republic Douglas Hyde, and revolutionary John O'Leary. Characteristically, he began the commission but later chafed under the obligation of it all and abandoned it, having finished only five of the portraits. The rest of the commission was completed by William Orpen.

### AMERICA

In 1907 fellow painter Sarah Purser and Hugh Lane, as a philanthropic gesture, raised monies to send the sixty-eight-year-old painter on a tour of Italy. True to character Yeats quietly resisted their well-intentioned plans and at the eleventh hour used the money instead to travel to New York with his daughter Lily. His plan was to capitalise on his Irish-American connections who, he was sure, would set up commissions for him, to take New York by storm and arrive home in Dublin a wealthy man. Despite the urgent protestations of his friend John Quinn, an eminent Irish-American lawyer and great patron of the arts, that it was the worst possible time because of the economic slump, Yeats arrived in New York full of optimism. Quickly enough it became apparent that he was highly sought after for his captivating conversation and after-dinner speeches rather than his painting. Added to that, he was hopelessly unbusiness-like as far as making money was concerned, being content to sketch people for nothing, much to the irritation of his benefactor Quinn. Indeed, Quinn and the artist's son William would periodically bail out the elder Yeats for the rest of his days. Quinn introduced him to many interesting and wealthy people at the Players and Vagabond Clubs and they dined regularly at Delmonicos. People thought of him as another Walt Whitman, full of amusement, he told his daughter Lollie in a letter. Yeats attended and sketched scenes at one of the most famous murder trials of the day, that of Harry K. Thaw for the murder of the renowned architect Stanford White. Unfortunately, the location of the sketches is unknown today.

### CENTRE OF ARTISTIC AND LITERARY CIRCLE

Yeats soon drifted from the clubs and great suburban homes and found his own society in the French Section, on Twenty-Ninth Street, between Eighth and Ninth Avenues, where there was a lively, young artistic scene. He took up lodgings at the Petitpas pension run by the Breton sisters and remained there for the rest of his days. His brilliant conversation drew young artists and writers to his table every night. Notable among the diners were John Sloan, Robert Henri, Arthur B. Davies and George Luks, who with their colleagues were known as "The Eight," central figures of what was later called the Ashcan School. Yeats exhibited with them in the Independent Exhibition of 1910, organised in opposition to the National Academy's spring exhibition, showing some of his paintings borrowed from John Quinn and a number of sketches. He is included in a painting by George Bellows called "Artists Evening," set at the Petitpas (Coll. Vassar College Art Gallery), and in 1917 Walt Kuhn painted his portrait. The acclaimed literary critic and historian Van Wyck Brooks greatly valued his friendship with Yeats as did poet Alan Seeger, writer Conrad Aiken and playwright R. W. Sneddon, who enshrined the artist under a disguised name in a short story, "The Orange Moth." In 1917 his published letters, entitled *Passages from the letters of John Butler Yeats* (edited by Ezra Pound and printed by the Cuala Press), the first of three books, established his name as a hot literary property, drawing admiring critiques from, among others, the young T. S. Eliot.

John Butler Yeats never returned to Ireland, despite his family's and John Quinn's best efforts to mastermind it. He loved New York and in 1922 died there at the age of eighty-three. He is buried in Rural Cemetery in Chestertown, New York, in the Adirondacks, not far from Lake George. Comprehensive collections of John Yeats's work are located in the National Gallery of Ireland, and the Hugh Lane Municipal Gallery of Modern Art, Dublin.

R. Gordon, *John Butler Yeats and John Sloan: The Records of a Friendship* (Dublin, 1978).

J. Hone, ed., *J. B. Yeats: Letters to His Son W. B. Yeats and Others, 1869–1922* (New York, 1946).

William Murphy, *Prodigal Father: The Life of John Butler Yeats (1839–1922)* (Ithaca and London, 1978).

William Murphy, *The Yeats Family and the Pollexfens of Sligo* (Dublin, 1971).

Hilary Pyle, *Yeats: Portrait of an Artistic Family* (London, 1997).

James White, *John Butler Yeats and the Irish Renaissance* (National Gallery of Ireland, 1972).

CHRISTINA KENNEDY

## YORKE, PETER C. (1864–1925)

Pastor, labor leader, reformer. Yorke was the most noted Irish priest of his generation in San Francisco; many contend he was the most significant priest in the history of the Archdiocese of San Francisco. Born in Galway, Ireland, the son of Gregory Yorke, a sea captain, and Bridget Kelly, Yorke decided at an early age to become a priest. He studied at St. Patrick's College in Maynooth from 1882 to 1886. In the latter year, he was adopted by the Archdiocese of San Francisco and sent to complete his studies at St. Mary's Seminary in Baltimore, where he was ordained by Cardinal James Gibbons on December 17, 1887. After a short stay in San Francisco, he was enrolled at the recently established Catholic University of America in Washington, D.C. In 1891, he completed a licentiate in theology.

In 1894, he was appointed Chancellor of the Archdiocese and Secretary to Archbishop Patrick W. Riordan. The same year he was appointed editor of the archdiocesan newspaper, *The Monitor.* As editor he gained fame and popularity within the Catholic community by openly attacking the anti-Catholic American Protective Association, which he "vanquished" in a series of public debates and exposés published in *The Monitor.* During the conflict Yorke developed his acerbic rhetorical style, castigating his opponents in most unflattering terms.

Yorke's experience in the APA controversy whetted his appetite for public debate, much to the dismay of Archbishop Riordan. Yorke soon lost favor with Riordan for becoming too overtly and belligerently political. Though Yorke's ecclesiastical star may have dimmed, his stature in the Irish-Catholic community did not. In 1901, Yorke dramatically supported labor in the famed Teamster Strike of 1901 in San Francisco, in which he emerged as the spiritual leader and chief publicist for the union. Yorke argued the workers' right to organize had been validated in Pope Leo XIII's encyclical *Rerum Novarum*. During the controversy, Yorke squared off against second-generation Irishman James Duval Phelan, Mayor of San Francisco. Yorke believed Phelan had been elected by Irish working-class votes, and that during the strike Phelan had turned his back on the Irish worker and allowed the police to brutalize the strikers. In a highly publicized encounter with Phelan, Yorke reported that Phelan had said, "If the workers do not want to get clubbed, let them go back to work." Phelan denied the comment but Yorke dubbed him "Clubber Phelan." The strike was ultimately won by the Teamsters, and Yorke was lionized by San Francisco labor for his role in the strike. To the present day Yorke continues to be considered a champion of San Francisco labor.

In 1902, Yorke established an Irish newspaper, *The Leader,* which provided him a platform on which to address local and national issues. He had left *The Monitor* several years earlier in a dispute with Riordan. Yorke also worked for the creation of an Irish republic, supporting the efforts of Eamon de Valera in particular. He actively participated in the Friends of Irish Freedom and the American Association for the Recognition of the Irish Republic. When de Valera visited San Francisco in 1919, Yorke ushered him about the town. Peter Yorke died in San Francisco on Palm Sunday, 1925.

Yorke was so beloved by the Irish working class and by San Francisco Labor that the anniversary of his death became a major labor and Irish celebration. Each year on Palm Sunday, a memorial mass is offered at St. Peter's in San Francisco, followed by a procession to Yorke's grave at Holy Cross Cemetery in Colma.

*See* California; San Francisco, Aspects of

Joseph Brusher, S.J., *Consecrated Thunderbolt: A Life of Father Peter C. Yorke of San Francisco* (Hawthorne, N.J., 1973).

Jeffrey M. Burns, "¿Qúe es esto? The Transformation of St. Peter's Parish in San Francisco," in James Wind and James Lewis, *American Congregations* (Chicago, 1994).

James P. Walsh, *Ethnic Militancy: An Irish Catholic Prototype* (San Francisco, 1972).

JEFFREY M. BURNS

# CONTRIBUTORS

Allen, Valerie, University of South Florida, Tampa, Florida

Altenhofel, Jennifer, Bakersfield, California

Anbinder, Tyler, Arlington, Virginia

Anderson, Christopher, Willington, Connecticut

Andreassi, Anthony D., Washington, D.C.

Appleby, R. Scott, University of Notre Dame, Notre Dame, Indiana

Armstrong, Regis J., O.F.M. Cap., Interlaken, New York

Atkinson, Marie, O.P., Newburgh, New York

Aurand, Harold W., Penn State University, University Park, Pennsylvania

Avella, Steven M., Marquette University, Milwaukee, Wisconsin

Balitas, Vincent D., Pottsville, Pennsylvania

Barnes, John A., Brooklyn, New York

Bayor, Ronald H., Georgia Institute of Technology, Atlanta, Georgia

Bieter, John, Boise, Idaho

Blalock, Kay J., Edinburg, Texas

Blessing, Patrick J., Bloomington, Indiana

Boyle, Charles J., Spring Hill College, Mobile, Alabama

Breatnac, S. P., San Jose, California

Brennan, Margaret, Wheeling, West Virginia

Breslin, John, S.J., LeMoyne College, Syracuse, New York

Bric, Maurice J., University College Dublin, Ireland

Brooks, Joan, Desert Hot Springs, California

Brown, Mary Elizabeth, Staten Island, New York

Brymer, Elizabeth, Southern Illinois University, Carbondale, Illinois

Burns, Helen Marie, R.S.M., Mio, Michigan

Burns, Jeffrey M., Alameda, California

Callahan, Nelson, Bay Village, Ohio

Callahan Walkenhorst, Patricia, Blue Springs, Missouri

Campbell, Thomas F., Cleveland, Ohio

Cannon, Thomas Gildea, Mequon, Wisconsin

Carey, Patrick W., Marquette University, Milwaukee

Carroll, Francis M., University of Manitoba, Winnipeg, Manitoba, Canada

Cartwright, Thomas Y., Franklin, Tennessee

Carzo, Eileen Daney, Wilmington, Delaware

Casey, Daniel J., Burlington College, Burlington, Vermont

Castelli, Jim, Burke, Virginia

Casway, Jerrold, Columbia, Maryland

Clarke, Brian, Emmanuel College, Toronto, Ontario, Canada

Cole, Terrence M., University of Alaska, Fairbanks, Alaska

Conley, Patrick T., East Providence, Rhode Island

Conley, Rory T., Leonardtown, Maryland

Connelly, James T., C.S.C., University of Portland, Portland, Oregon

Conrad, Agnes C., Honolulu, Hawaii

Coolahan, John, National University of Ireland, Maynooth, Co. Kildare, Ireland

Cooney, Charles W., Milwaukee, Wisconsin

Corbin, Frank, Pelham, New York

Corcoran, Mary P., Dublin, Ireland

Corry, Emmett, O.S.F., Brooklyn, New York

Crews, Clyde F., Bellarmine College, Louisville, Kentucky

Cronin, Seán, Washington, D.C.

Cull, Frank, Chestnut Ridge, New York

Curry, Ann, P.B.V.M., San Francisco, California

D'Arcy, Frank, Derry, Northern Ireland

Day, Mark R., Vista, California

Deedy, John, Rockport, Massachusetts

DeFerrari, Patricia, Washington, D.C.

Diner, Hasia R., Washington, D.C.

Doan, James E., Nova Southeast College, Fort Lauderdale, Florida

Donnelly, Anna M., St. John's University, Jamaica, New York

Downey, Tom, Aiken, South Carolina

Doyle, David Noel, University College Dublin, Ireland

Doyle, Katherine, R.S.M., Auburn, California

Dunn, Edmond J., St. Ambrose University, Davenport, Iowa

Dwyer, Claudette, Blue Island, Illinois

Eagan, Eileen, University of Southern Maine, Gorham, Maine

East, Joyce, Marshall University, S. Charleston, West Virginia

Ebest, Ron, Webster Groves, Missouri

Eid, Leroy V., University of Dayton, Dayton, Ohio

Emmons, David M., University of Montana, Missoula, Montana

Evers, John T., Albany, New York

Faherty, William Barnaby, S.J., St. Louis University, St. Louis, Missouri

Fanning, Charles, Southern Illinois University, Carbondale, Illinois

Farrell, Michael, *National Catholic Reporter,* Kansas City, Missouri

Feeney, Vincent, Burlington, Vermont

Ferro, Salvatore A., C.F.C., New Rochelle, New York

Field, Sharon, Cheyenne, Wyoming

Fitzpatrick, David, Trinity College, Dublin, Ireland

Fogarty, Gerald P., S.J., University of Virginia, Charlottesville, Virginia

Foley, Patrick, Azle, Texas

Funchion, Michael F., South Dakota State University, Brookings, South Dakota

Giffin, William W., Indiana State University, Terre Haute, Indiana

Gillespie, Michael Patrick, Chicago, Illinois

Gillespie, Raymond, National University of Ireland, Maynooth, Co. Kildare, Ireland

Glazier, Joan, Rehoboth, Delaware

Glazier, Michael, Rehoboth, Delaware

Gleason, Philip, University of Notre Dame, Notre Dame, Indiana

Gleeson, David, Armstrong Atlantic State University, Savannah, Georgia

Golway, Terry, Maplewood, New Jersey

Gordon, Michael A., Milwaukee, Wisconsin

Greeley, Andrew, University of Chicago, Chicago, Illinois

Green, Paul M., Governors State University, Union Park, Illinois

Grimes, Robert R., S.J., Fordham University, Bronx, New York

Haley, James J., Wilmington, Delaware

Halton, Thomas, Catholic University of America, Washington, D.C.

Hanna, Fergus, New York, New York

Harper, Marie F., Sante Fe, New Mexico

Harrell, Joy P., Hyattsville, Maryland

Harrington, Daniel J., S.J., Weston School of Theology, Cambridge, Massachusetts

Harrington, John P., Cooper Union, New York, New York

Hearon, Todd, Jamaica Plain, Massachusetts

Heisser, David C. R., The Citadel, Charleston, North Carolina

Hershkowitz, Leo, Freeport, New York

Hogan, Neil, Wallingford, Connecticut

Hogan, Peter E., S.S.J., Baltimore, Maryland

Hollenbeck, Karen, Fort Collins, Colorado

Hotten-Somers, Diane, Jamaica Plain, Massachusetts

Hoy, Suellen, Chesterton, Indiana

Isacsson, Alfred, O. Carm, Tarrytown, New York

James, Ronald M., Carson City, Nevada

Johnston, Conor, Roslindale, Massachusetts

Kauffman, Christopher J., Catholic University of America, Washington, D.C.

Kearns, Caledonia, Brooklyn, New York

Kelly, Joseph, College of Charleston, Charleston, South Carolina

Kelly, Joseph J., Haddonsfield, New Jersey

Kelly, Mary C., Rindge, New Hampshire

Kennedy, Christina, Hugh Lane Gallery, Dublin, Ireland

Kenny, Kevin, Boston College, Chestnut Hill, Massachusetts

Killen, Patricia O'Connell, Parkland, Washington

Kinch, Rita, Mount Merrion, Dublin, Ireland

Kinealy, Christine, Merseyside, England

Kuntz, Daniel J., Washington, D.C.

LaGumina, Salvatore J., Nassau Community College, Garden City, New York

Lahey, P. John, Solomon, Kansas

Lapomarda, Vincent A., S.J., College of the Holy Cross, Worcester, Massachusetts

Lawlor, Kathryn, B.V.M., Dubuque, Iowa

Lee, Joseph J., University College Cork, Ireland

Lennon, Joseph, Willimantic, Connecticut

Leonard, James P., Medfield, Massachusetts

Leonard, Stephen, Metropolitan State College, Denver, Colorado

Lester, DeeGee, Hendersonville, Tennessee

Liddy, James, University of Wisconsin, Milwaukee, Wisconsin

Lothrop, Gloria Ricci, Pasadena, California

MacGregor, Morris J., Arlington, Virginia

Mahoney, Margaret Lasch, Albany, New York

Marman, Edward D., Wayne, Michigan

McCaffrey, Lawrence J., Evanston, Illinois

McCarthy, Joseph F.X., Guilford, Connecticut

McCarthy, Kathleen N., Jackson Heights, New York

McCarthy, William D., M.M., Maryknoll, New York

McCollester, Charles J., Pittsburgh, Pennsylvania

McDonald, Forrest, University of Alabama, Birmingham, Alabama

McDonough, Gerald M., Salt Lake City, Utah

McGinn, Brian, Alexandria, Virginia

McGrath, Roger D., Thousand Oaks, California

McGuinness, Margaret M., Cabrini College, Randor, Pennsylvania

McIlroy, Brian, University of British Columbia, Vancouver, Canada

McLaughlin, Raymond P., Lexington, Kentucky

McLean, Andrew M., University of Wisconsin-Parkside, Kenosha, Wisconsin

McLean, Lois C., Beckley, West Virginia

McLoughlin, Marianna, Lady Lake, Florida

McMahon, Eileen M., Palos Park, Illinois

McNally, Michael J., St. Charles Seminary, Overbrook, Pennsylvania

McNamara, Patrick J., Silver Spring, Maryland

McWhiney, Grady, McMurry University, Abilene, Texas

Metress, Seamus, University of Toledo, Toledo, Ohio

Miller, Kerby, University of Missouri, Columbia, Missouri

Milmo-Penny, Dominic, Dublin, Ireland

Mitchell, Arthur, University of South Carolina, Allendale, South Carolina

Mize, Sandra Yocum, University of Dayton, Dayton, Ohio

Molloy, Darina, New York, New York

Monaghan, Patricia, Chicago, Illinois

Montgomery, David, Yale University, New Haven, Connecticut

Moran, Gerard, Wolfson College, Oxford University, Oxford, England

Mulrooney, Margaret M., Marymount University, Arlington, Virginia

Murphy, John A., University College Cork, Cork, Ireland

Murphy, Maureen, Sea Cliff, New York

Murray, Aife, San Francisco, California

Newland, Sam J., Carlisle Barracks, Pennsylvania

Niehaus, Earl, S.M., Xavier University, New Orleans, Louisiana

Nilsen, Kenneth E., St. Francis Xavier University, Antigonish, Nova Scotia, Canada

Nolan, Charles E., New Orleans, Louisiana

Nolan, Janet, Evanston, Illinois

Nolan, Mary Catherine, O.P., University of Notre Dame, Notre Dame, Indiana

Norris, Frank, Anchorage, Alaska

Oates, Mary J., C.S.J., Regis College, Weston, Massachusetts

O'Brien, Marie Regina, Elmhurst, New York

O'Carroll, Michael, C.S.Sp., Blackrock College, Blackrock, Dublin, Ireland

Ó Cathaoir, Brendan, Bray, Co. Wicklow, Ireland

Ochshorn, Kathleen, University of Tampa, Tampa, Florida

O'Connor, Patricia A., Springfield, Ohio

O'Connor, Patrick J., University of Limerick, Limerick, Ireland

O'Day, Edward J., Southern Illinois University, Carbondale, Illinois

O'Donnell, Edward T., Hunter College, New York, New York

O'Donnell, L. A., Malvern, Pennsylvania

O'Donnell, Patricia C., Swarthmore, Pennsylvania

O'Leary, Jennie L., Glendale, Arizona

O'Neill, Patrick, Kansas City, Missouri

O'Sullivan, Niamh, Dublin, Ireland

O'Toole, James M., Boston College, Chestnut Hill, Massachusetts

Owens, Coilin, Springfield, Virginia

Owens, Gary, Huron College, University of Western Ontario, London, Ontario

Parkhill, Trevor, Belfast, Northern Ireland

Patkus, Ronald D., Boston College, Chestnut Hill, Massachusetts

Patton, Edward J., Lake View, New York

Petit, Loretta, O.P., Chicago, Illinois

Phillips, Helen, M.M., Maryknoll, New York

Powell, William S., University of North Carolina, Chapel Hill, North Carolina

Pula, James S., Catholic University of America, Washington, D.C.

Quinn, Dermot, Seton Hall University, South Orange, New Jersey

Rajner, Richard A., Waterville, Ohio

Redshaw, Thomas Dillon, Center for Irish Studies, St. Paul, Minnesota

Reilly, Robert, Fordham Law School, New York, New York

Reilly, Robert T., Omaha, Nebraska

Ridge, John T., Brooklyn, New York

Roach, Michael, Manchester, Maryland

Rogers, James Silas, Center for Irish Studies, St. Paul, Minnesota

Romero, Orlando, Fray Angelico Chavez Historical Library, Sante Fe, New Mexico

Ruppert, Paul W., American Irish Historical Society, New York, New York

Ryan, George E., Scituate, Massachusetts

Rynder, Constance B., University of Tampa, Tampa, Florida

Samito, Christian G., Babylon, New York

Scally, Robert, New York University, New York, New York

Scott, R. Neil, Georgia College, Milledgeville, Georgia

Shafer, Ingrid, Chickasha, Oklahoma

Shaughnessy, Edward L., Indianapolis, Indiana

Shea, Peter G., Largo, Florida

Sherman, William C., Grand Forks, North Dakota

Shoemaker, Edward M., Decatur, Georgia

Simmons, Bridget, American Ireland Fund, Boston, Massachusetts

Skerrett, Ellen, Chicago, Illinois

Smith, Karen Sue, New York, New York

Smith, Marcus, Loyola University, New Orleans, Louisiana

Smith, William L., Georgia Southern University, Statesboro, Georgia

Spalding, Thomas W., Louisville, Kentucky

Sperber, Murray, Indiana University, Bloomington, Indiana

Stanton, Kevin, Boulder, Colorado

Stratton, David, Drogheda, Co. Louth, Ireland

Sullivan, C. W., III, East Carolina University, Greenville, North Carolina

Sullivan, Eileen A., Gainesville, Florida

Sullivan, Paul G., Pittsburgh, Pennsylvania

Sutherland, Daniel E., University of Arkansas, Fayetteville, Arkansas

Tate, Mary Jo, Ripley, Mississippi

Taylor, Christine M., Seattle, Washington

Tobin, Daniel, Carthage College, Kenosha, Wisconsin

Toomey, Elizabeth, American Irish Historical Society, New York, New York

Townend, Paul A., Chicago, Illinois

Unsworth, R. Timothy, Chicago, Illinois

Walch, Timothy, Iowa City, Iowa

Wall, Eamonn, Creighton University, Omaha, Nebraska

Wallace, R. Stuart, Plymouth, New Hampshire

Wheeler, Arthur, C.S.C., University of Portland, Portland, Oregon

White, James D., Tulsa, Oklahoma

Williams, William H. A., Union Institute, Cincinnati, Ohio

Wilson, Andrew, Oak Park, Illinois

Woods, James M., Georgia Southern University, Statesboro, Georgia

# PHOTO CREDITS

Page 564: Evanston Photographic Studio, Inc.

Page 566: Courtesy of Charles Nolan

Page 568: University of Notre Dame Archives

Page 569: Courtesy of the Boston Public Library, Print Department

Page 571: Courtesy of the Boston Public Library, Print Department

Page 573: *Currier and Ives: The Irish and America* by Kevin O'Rourke

Page 575: University of Notre Dame Archives

Page 576: University of Notre Dame Archives

Page 577, top: University of Notre Dame Archives

Page 577, bottom: James Higgins

Page 578: © Jane E. Levine, Courtesy Farrar, Straus & Giroux

Page 582: University of Notre Dame Archives

Page 583: University of Notre Dame Archives

Page 588: *The Washington Post*

Page 591: Courtesy of the St. Louis Cardinals

Page 595: James Higgins

Page 598: Doubleday

Page 601: Courtesy of Grady McWhiney

Page 602: The George Meany Memorial Archives

Page 605: Richard Rajner

Page 609: Courtesy of Kerby Miller

Page 623, top: *Irish Echo*

Page 623, bottom: *Harper's Weekly*, January 31, 1874

Page 630: Courtesy of the Boston Public Library, Print Department

Page 633: University of Notre Dame Archives

Page 635: Courtesy of the Boston Public Library, Print Department

Page 639: University of Notre Dame Archives

Page 641: *Currier and Ives: The Irish and America* by Kevin O'Rourke

Page 658: Nebraska State Historical Society

Page 659: Nebraska State Historical Society

Page 661: Nevada Historical Society

Page 662: Nevada Historical Society

Page 663, top: Nevada Historical Society

Page 663, bottom: Nevada Historical Society

Page 679: New York State Historical Association

Page 680: University of Notre Dame Archives

Page 682: © Collection of The New-York Historical Society

Page 683, top: University of Notre Dame Archives

Page 683, bottom: Courtesy of the Boston Public Library, Print Department

Page 693: Courtesy of Janet Nolan

Page 694: University of Notre Dame Archives

Page 695: © Kelly Campbell

Page 703, left: University of Notre Dame Archives

Page 703, right: University of Notre Dame Archives

Page 706: University of Notre Dame Archives

Page 707: University of Notre Dame Archives

Page 709: Courtesy of the Boston Public Library, Print Department

Page 712: University of Notre Dame Archives

Page 715: Courtesy of the Boston Public Library, Print Department

Page 719: Special Collections, Ina Dillard Russell Library, Georgia College

Page 725: Brooklyn Public Library—Brooklyn Collection

Page 728: Archive Photos

Page 730: Courtesy of the Boston Public Library, Print Department

Page 735: Fritz Kaeser, Courtesy of The Snite Museum of Art

Page 743: Courtesy of the Boston Public Library, Print Department

Page 747: John J. Burns Library, Boston College

Page 753: University of Notre Dame Archives

Page 757: Courtesy of the Boston Public Library, Print Department

Page 759: Courtesy of the Boston Public Library, Print Department

Page 760: Courtesy of the Boston Public Library, Print Department

Page 761: Patrick O'Neill

Page 768: University of Notre Dame Archives

Page 784: Courtesy of the Boston Public Library, Print Department

Page 787: From *Winter Music: A Life of Jessica Powers* by Dolores R. Leckey. Reprinted by permission of Sheed & Ward, an apostolate of the Priests of the Sacred Heart, 7373 South Lovers Lane Road, Franklin, Wisconsin 53132

Page 788: Courtesy of the Sisters of the Presentation of the Blessed Virgin Mary

Page 789: Presentation Heights Archives

Page 797: © Joyce Ravid, Courtesy Random House

Page 798: *The Man from New York* by B. L. Reid

Page 799: University of Notre Dame Archives

Page 808: Brooklyn Public Library—Brooklyn Collection

Page 820: *Currier and Ives: The Irish and America* by Kevin O'Rourke

Page 821, left: *Kansas City Star*

Page 821, top right: Archer Associates

Page 821, bottom right: Douglas Healey

Page 824: *The Reminiscences of Augustus Saint-Gaudens*, vol. 2, 1913

Page 825: Chicago Historical Society; ICHi-29925

Page 833: Robert Ryal Miller

Page 834: Courtesy of the Boston Public Library, Print Department

Page 837: Steve Moriarty

Page 840: Library of Congress

Page 853: University of Notre Dame Archives

Page 854: University of Notre Dame Archives

Page 857: *Biographical Sketches of Eminent American Patriots*, 1907

Page 858: University of Notre Dame Archives

Page 860: *Catherine McAuley and the Tradition of Mercy* by Mary C. Sullivan

Page 862: Courtesy of the Boston Public Library, Print Department

Page 879: Courtesy of Margaret Steinfels

Page 883: Courtesy of Kathleen M. Sullivan

Page 887: *Harper's Weekly*, 1868

Page 890: University of Notre Dame Archives

Page 895: Courtesy of the University of Texas, San Antonio, Institute of Texan Cultures

Page 896, left: Courtesy of the University of Texas, San Antonio, Institute of Texan Cultures

Page 897: Courtesy of the University of Texas, San Antonio, Institute of Texan Cultures

Page 900: Billy Rose Theatre Collection, The New York Public Library for the Performing Arts, Astor, Lenox and Tilden Foundations

Page 902: Chicago Historical Society; ICHi-17760; J & M Co.

Page 906: Archive Photos

Page 908: Frank Teti Collection

Page 909: Courtesy of the Boston Public Library, Print Department

Page 918: Courtesy of the National Library of Ireland

Page 919: *United Irishmen, Their Lives and Times*, 1842–1846

Page 937: Courtesy of Eamonn Wall

Page 942:  Courtesy of the Washingtoniana Division, District of
 Columbia Public Library

Page 948:  © *The Washington Post*, reprinted by permission of the
 District of Columbia Public Library

Page 952:  Courtesy of the Boston Public Library, Print Department

Page 953:  Brennan Family Collection

Page 957:  Courtesy of the Boston Public Library, Print Department

Page 958:  © Terence Winch

Page 964:  Alice Austen Collection, Staten Island Historical Society

Page 966:  The Photography Collection, Carpenter Center for the
 Visual Arts, Harvard University

Page 967:  University of Notre Dame Archives

Page 968:  *Poems* by Margaret Kelly McPhelim, Kate McPhelim Cleary
 and Edward Joseph McPhelim, 1922

Page 971:  Courtesy of Sisters of St. Joseph of Carondelet Archives,
 St. Louis Province